For

reference

Shakespeare's Language

Second Edition

A Glossary
of Unfamiliar Words
in His Plays and Poems

EUGENE F. SHEWMAKER

Facts On File
An imprint of Infobase Publishing

Shakespeare's Language, Second Edition

Copyright © 1996, 2008 Eugene F. Shewmaker

Facts On File, Inc.
An imprint of Infobase Publishing
132 West 31st Street
New York NY 10001

Library of Congress Cataloging-in-Publication Data
Shewmaker, Eugene F.
Shakespeare's language / Eugene F. Shewmaker.—2nd ed.
p.   cm.
Includes bibliographical references and index.
ISBN-13: 978-0-8160-7125-8 (acid-free paper)
1. Shakespeare, William, 1564–1616 —Language—Glossaries, etc.
2. English language—Early modern, 1500–1700—Dictionaries.
3. English language—Obsolete words—Dictionaries. I. Title.
PR2892.S447 2008
822.3'3—dc22   2007016138

Facts On File books are available at special discounts when purchased in bulk quantities for businesses, associations, institutions, or sales promotions. Please call our Special Sales Department in New York at (212) 967-8800 or (800) 322-8755.

You can find Facts On File on the World Wide Web at http://www.factsonfile.com

Text design by Kerry Casey

Printed in the United States of America

VB CGI 10 9 8 7 6 5 4 3 2 1

This book is printed on acid-free paper and contains 30% post-consumer recycled content.

Contents

Acknowledgments

I should like to express my gratitude for several sources that proved invaluable in preparing this glossary, chief among them the monumental *Oxford English Dictionary,* with its comprehensive coverage of Elizabethan words; the *Shakespeare Lexicon and Quotation Dictionary* by Alexander Schmidt, first printed 1874, reissued 1971; and *A Shakespeare Glossary* by C. T. Onions (rev. 1986 by R. D. Eagleson)

The text quotes (except for the sonnets, *King Edward III, Sir Thomas More,* and *The Two Noble Kinsmen*) are from *The Arden Shakespeare,* general editor Richard Proudfoot. For the sonnets, I have used *The Oxford Shakespeare,* edited by W. J. Craig (1966), A. L. Rowse's *Shakespeare's Sonnets,* Helen Vendler's admirable edition, *The Art of Shakespeare's Sonnets,* as well as Katherine Duncan-Jones's recent *Arden* edition. For *King Edward III* I have used the Cambridge University Press edition, edited by Giorgio Melchiori; for *Sir Thomas More,* the Kessinger Publishing edition; and for *The Two Noble Kinsmen,* the text in *The Riverside Shakespeare,* edited by G. Blakemore Evans. In addition to the *Riverside* and *Arden* editions, I made use of several other outstanding one-volume editions of the plays and poems: *Shakespeare, the Complete Works* (Harcourt, Brace: G. B. Harrison, ed.); *The Complete Plays and Poems of William Shakespeare* (Houghton Mifflin: William Allan Neilson and Charles Jarvis Hill, eds.); *The Yale Shakespeare* (Wilbur L. Cross and Tucker Brooke, eds.); and *The Complete Works of Shake-speare* (HarperCollins: David Bevington, ed.). Also of substantial help were *The Oxford Shakespeare* (Standard Authors Edition, 1966) and *The Works of Shakespeare* (Oxford, Head Press Edition, 1938).

Of considerable help, too, were Harley Granville-Barker's perceptive *Prefaces to Shakespeare;* Hardin Craig's *An Interpretation of Shakespeare;* George Freedley and John A. Reeves' *A History of the Theatre;* G. B. Harrison's *Elizabethan Plays & Players;* Gerald E. Bentley's *The Profession of Player in Shakespeare's Time;* Andrew Gurr's *The Shakespearean Stage, 1574–1642;* Frank Kermode's *The Age of Shakespeare;* and William B. Worthen's *The Idea of the Actor.*

Merriam-Webster's *Third International Dictionary* (1961) and *Eleventh New Collegiate Dictionary* (2003) proved inestimable sources of information on archaic words. Valuable sources of biographical and geographical information were, as always, Merriam-Webster's *Biographical Dictionary* and their *Geographical Dictionary.* My ever-present copy of *The Random House Dictionary* served faithfully to correct the spelling and syllabification of contemporary English.

Also consulted were Hinman's magnificent *The First Folio of Shakespeare* (Norton) and the facsimile edition published by Yale University Press as *Mr. William Shakespeares Comedies, Histories, & Tragedies.* Of immense interest were Russell Fraser's *Young Shakespeare* and its companion volume *Shakespeare: The Later Years,* as well as Robert Giroux's fascinating *The Book Known as Q: A Consideration of Shakespeare's Sonnets* and Robert M. Adams's *Shakespeare: The Four Romances.*

For many of the tips on the interpretation of the plays and poems I am greatly indebted to Mr. Barrie Ingham, longtime member of England's fabled Royal Shakespeare Company. His delightful and immensely informative seminars at The Shakespeare Society in New York City a few seasons back were packed with insights and humor that could come only from a lifelong devotion to the material.

E. F. S.

Preface to the Second Edition

Since the first edition of this book appeared 12 years ago, there has been an increased acceptance of three more plays into the Shakespeare canon: *The Two Noble Kinsmen, King Edward III,* and (with somewhat less enthusiasm) *Sir Thomas More.* Many of the newer editions of the complete works now include these three plays, and they have also been issued in separate editions under Shakespeare's name. *Kinsmen,* written around 1613, was probably Shakespeare's last play and was almost certainly done in collaboration, most likely with John Fletcher. *Edward* and *More,* both early plays, are thought to be the products of several collaborators, though some scholars are willing to give Shakespeare most (or even all) of the credit for *Edward.* The manuscript of *More* has miraculously survived and resides in the British Library. A portion of the play (some 147 lines) is believed by a number of scholars to be in Shakespeare's hand and is referred to as Hand D. For the most part the play is undistinguished, and there is no record of its ever being produced in Shakespeare's day (the subject matter was highly inflammatory), but if generally accepted this would be the only fragment of a Shakespeare manuscript known to exist. This would bring the present canon to 40 plays, including, of course, *Pericles,* not added to the first compilation of Shakespeare's works in 1623 (the First Folio) but added in the Third Folio of 1664. In this edition I have added words from these recent additions and trust that they will rest comfortably with the authenticated vocabulary. Some modern editors

believe they can identify with reasonable certainty the precise passages of these works that are in Shakespeare's hand, and it is from these that I have selected words for inclusion. Only time and future scholarship will decide if they deserve their place in Shakespeare's language.

As I stressed in the first edition, the main obstacle in assembling an adequate glossary/dictionary of Shakespeare's language is that no two editions of his works entirely agree. First, none of Shakespeare's manuscripts survive (though see above) to authenticate or corroborate the text of the plays that have come down to us. As the distinguished scholar and teacher Harold Jenkins has said, ". . . as far as we can tell [Shakespeare] didn't expect his plays to be read and never lifted a finger to assist their publication." We know them only through the printed editions of his day and the first collection of his works, familiar to us as the First Folio, published in 1623, seven years after his death. Since then, generations of editors have revised, emended, and theorized an endless number of editions into print, each with newfound confidence that this one corrects previous errors and misconceptions and presents Shakespeare as he would have had it.

The early printings (those printed for the most part during Shakespeare's lifetime) were known as "quartos" (printed on four-page forms) and were of varying quality. Several (perhaps a dozen) of the plays were brought out in "good quartos," meaning that they appear to have been printed from the author's manuscripts or, more likely, from prompt books owned by his theater company and used as the basis for stage productions. Six or seven of the plays were published in pirated editions, perhaps pieced together from actors' "sides" supplemented by the fallible memory of an actor or two. There is also reason to speculate that some were even surreptitiously taken down during performance in some sort of shorthand (possibly accounting for Hamlet's "too too solid [or 'sullied' or 'sallied'] flesh"). These became known as the "bad quartos." One or two of the other quartos were of marginal reliability. For instance, all 12 extant copies of the *Lear* quarto vary to some extent, which would appear to indicate that corrections were made on each form as the printing progressed. It is only fair to add that some editors believe that these "bad quartos" were actually earlier plays, earlier versions of some of the Folio plays, or shortened versions for taking "on the road." These are matters that can be cleared up only as additional evidence comes to light.

Many of these problems were set right with the publication of the First Folio, which brought together 36 of Shakespeare's plays, 18 of them appearing in print for the first time. The only play (of the traditional canon) not included was *Pericles,* perhaps because the only text available was the unauthorized and corrupt 1609 quarto or because the play was known to Shakespeare's colleagues as a collaboration, with Shakespeare most likely contributing Acts III, IV, and V. In any case, the play was included much later in the second edition of the Third Folio (1664) and thereafter was accepted as part of the complete works.

The importance of the First Folio's contribution to world literature can hardly be overestimated. Were it not for this compilation in 1623 we might well have lost half of Shakespeare's plays (including *The Tempest, Macbeth, Julius Caesar,* and *Antony and Cleopatra*) and would have only inferior versions of at least five others (including *Othello* and *King Lear*). Our main debt of gratitude is to John Heminges and Henry Condell, two of Shakespeare's colleagues in the King's Men Company (before 1603 called the Chamberlain's Men), which performed at the Theatre and later at the Globe and Blackfriars theaters. It was Heminges and Condell who, as a tribute to their good friend, collected Shakespeare's works, presented them to the printer in their best available form, and then stayed with the project another two years or so until bound books were produced.

That so much of Shakespeare's work survived is itself a major miracle. Despite the hunger of Elizabethan audiences for an endless supply of stage entertainments, the playwright, like the player, was regarded as little more than a vagabond entertainer. A "poet" was in most cases a university-trained gentleman who wrote lyric verse or composed elaborate poems around mythological or historical subjects, which he did primarily to display his accomplishments and amuse or impress his friends. The best-known group of these was the University Wits (Marlowe, Greene, and Kyd were among their number), who sometimes wrote for the stage, but always as a lark and with disdain, seldom with any thought of earning a living.

This effort to gain acceptance is no doubt the reason that Shakespeare early in his career published two long poems, *Venus and Adonis* and *The Rape of Lucrece,* and dedicated them to his highly placed patron, the Earl of Southampton. The sonnets, though lyric gems, were written over a period of several years and circulated privately, beginning in the early 1590s. They were not published in collected form until 1609, and then, it would appear, without Shakespeare's knowledge or sanction. So far as we know, Shakespeare never had anything to do with the publication of his plays, perhaps believing that such efforts were not the work of a poet but simply the hire and pay of a journeyman playmaker. More likely, though, he considered his chief vocation that of an actor.

That he fully succeeded in being accepted as a poet from the early years of his career is testified to in contemporary allusions to "honey-tongued

Shakespeare," one in direct poetic descent from Homer and Ovid. Southampton, a noble at the court of Elizabeth and immensely wealthy, appears to have tangibly expressed his gratitude for being made the dedicatee of *Venus* and *Lucrece,* with the result that a strong friendship developed between poet and nobleman. Many scholars are convinced that most of Shakespeare's early sonnets (most likely numbers 1 through 126) were addressed to Southampton.

Generally, when a playwright completed a manuscript, either he or a professional scribe would make a "fair copy," correcting errors in the process. This had to be submitted to the Master of the Revels, a city official of London, for approval and licensing. When licensed for performance, the fair copy became the official manuscript (prompt copy) for all performances of the play and was held in the custody of the company's prompter. The author was then paid for his work, and it became the property of the company, as did the original manuscript (the author's "foul papers"), which usually remained in the company's archives as insurance against loss of the prompt copy. Actors' sides were made from the fair copy, and the prompter added stage directions, indicated sound effects, and wrote in any other directions necessary for staging the play.

Approval by the Master of the Revels often was contingent upon the making of various changes, deletions, etc., in the manuscript, in which case the specified changes would have to be made before a prompt copy could be made ready and production of the play could proceed. The prompter's copy, either in rehearsal or performance, may have been amended (with or without the author's approval) and such changes incorporated in subsequent revivals of the play. Lines may have been simplified to oblige actors, cuts made, entrances changed, lines reassigned, and so forth. At this point, the promptbook was considerably less authoritative than the author's foul papers or a verbatim transcript of them. Over the years, of course, copies were made of copies, becom-

ing at each remove less reliable than the original manuscript. By the time materials were being assembled for the First Folio, many of Shakespeare's plays had been performed, retired, revived, and so on for a period of 20 to 30 years, picking up any number of changes along the way. And it appears that in several instances the author's manuscript was no longer available. However, many editors see evidence that foul papers were used in preparing at least some of the plays for the First Folio.

A printer wishing to publish a play (legitimately) bought it outright from the acting company and usually printed his quarto edition from the promptbook, thus perpetuating any deviations from the original manuscript. The printer then owned the play, and any subsequent printings of it could be done only with his permission or that of his designated heirs. Obtaining such permissions was one of the chief obstacles for Heminges and Condell in assembling the First Folio. *Troilus and Cressida* had begun to be printed immediately following *Romeo and Juliet* in the "Tragedies" section when negotiations apparently broke down with the printer-owner, and another play had to be printed in its place. *Troilus* was finally acquired and appears at the end of the "Histories" section, following *Henry the Eighth.*

In the Elizabethan Age, the spelling of English had not yet been standardized. "Fadom" was just as acceptable as "fathom," "extract" was often written as "extraught," "music" as "musicke," "sheriff" as "shrieve," etc. Add to this the fact that Shakespeare frequently worked under pressure and was not particularly concerned about spelling, indicating who was speaking, or being precise about exits and entrances, etc., secure in the knowledge that the other members of the company would know what he had in mind or that he would be there to answer their questions.

As a further complication, Shakespeare coined many words (expressure, dishabited, circummured, vastidity, etc.), which may have confused the copyists as well as subsequent typesetters. Typesetters, of varying degrees of competence and working under pressure, made errors in the printing of the plays and most likely "corrected" an occasional word or passage that appeared wrong to them. Later editors have reconstructed (or "improved upon") Shakespeare's original intentions in a variety of ways. That is why, in such a line as "But I will wear my heart upon my sleeve/ For daws to peck at . . ." [*Othello,* I, i, 64], another editor will make a plausible case for "doves" to replace "daws" and confidently set about making the change in the text.

Aside from the many Elizabethan words that have disappeared from the language, other words that have acquired fairly precise meanings in our own age (e.g., pregnant, still, deceive, presently) often meant something quite different to an Elizabethan. In certain passages, the wordplay can be murky, if not incomprehensible, for a modern audience, as in *Merry Wives,* I, i, 16–21, when "coat" is misunderstood by another character as "cod" and "luce" (pike) is subsequently misunderstood as "louse," with the confusion resulting in a considerable amount of cross-punning. Later in the same scene, "words" is misunderstood as "worts" (cabbages), causing even more confusion. Elizabethan audiences loved puns, and Shakespeare

happily obliged, often throwing in a bawdy sense as another possible interpretation (such as cod, understood as codpiece, understood as penis). The "Unfamiliar Words" of this book's subtitle, then, refers as well to familiar words used in unfamiliar ways.

An attempt to penetrate and re-create the immediacy of Shakespeare's language is the chief reason for assembling the present glossary/dictionary. In most passages, I have opted for the literal, or most obvious, interpretation and tried to indicate when puns and equivocations seem to be at work. When inescapable, I have not shied away from the bawdy, since it was a vital part of the Elizabethan's theatergoing experience and pleasure.

How to solve the dilemma of British and American spelling? I have been quite arbitrary and put the main entry words and the glosses and defining phrases in "American" (whenever a contradiction arose), since this present edition is aimed primarily at American readers. The text quotations, on the other hand, remain in British English, as originally cast by the editors. Should any confusion result, I apologize but assume it will be minimal.

Eugene F. Shewmaker

An Introduction to Shakespeare and His Language

Following Shakespeare's death in 1616, two of his former theatrical colleagues in the King's Men Company, John Heminges and Henry Condell, set about collecting his plays with the idea of publishing them in a single commemorative volume. Appearing seven years later in 1623, the book was entitled *Mr. William Shakespeares Comedies, Histories, & Tragedies* and contained 36 of his plays, 18 of them published for the first time. It became known as the First Folio and also included tributes from other friends and associates, among them playwright Ben Jonson, who wrote:

"He was not of an age, but for all time!"

William Shakespeare had been born 59 years earlier, in 1564, in Stratford-upon-Avon, a town some 100 miles northwest of London. The facts of his life are scanty. We know that he received a sound basic education in the Stratford grammar school that included Latin and Greek and at the age of 18 married a local woman several years his senior and fathered three children. The next several years remain a mystery. Whether he set off on his own to seek his fortune in London or joined one of the many theatrical troupes that came through Stratford, we have no records. Sometime in the late 1580s he apparently apprenticed himself to a London-based theatrical troupe as an actor and playwright. We do know that by the beginning of the next decade he was in London and gaining a reputation both as a performer and as a promising playwright.

At some point he joined one of the city's leading companies, The Lord Chamberlain's Men, later known under James I as The King's Men. There is a record of his playing a leading role in Ben Jonson's *Everyman in His Humour* with the company in 1598 and, the next year, the part of the old servant Adam in his own play *As You Like It,* most likely followed a year later by the ghost in *Hamlet.* As an interesting sidelight, most scholars agree that women's parts on the London stage were taken by prepubescent boys. One tradition, however, has Shakespeare in the role of the bumpkin William in *As You Like It,* being "spurned" by his 19-year-old brother Edmund in the role of the shepherdess Audrey. If true, this would seem to indicate that at least some female roles were acted by men, a subject that has yet to be fully investigated and documented. In any event, after collaborating with other members of the company on the reworking of older plays, Will became a prolific and successful playwright on his own and was soon elevated to the status of shareholding and profit-sharing member of the company. He continued writing plays until he was almost 50, then retired to his hometown of Stratford, probably around 1611. He briefly enjoyed a comfortable retirement, after buying one of the finest houses in Stratford, and died there five years later at the age of 52.

Shakespeare was born at a time of great events, but also a period of turbulent politics. Elizabeth, third child and second daughter of Henry VIII, had inherited the British throne six years before

Shakespeare's birth, in 1558. It was a difficult time, a time of plague, poor harvests, food riots, persecution of Catholics, a thwarted attempt by Mary of Scotland to gain the throne, and the attack and defeat of the Spanish Armada that had attempted an invasion of England in 1588 aimed at putting the country again under the religious authority of Rome. Despite all this, the Elizabethan Age has come down in history as a time of glorious achievement in the arts as well as the sciences.

This was a time when the English language was being enriched from all directions. The English had recently established colonies in the New World, and merchant ships regularly traded throughout Europe, the Middle East, and the Orient. Shakespeare absorbed quantities of new words and, when these were inadequate, invented many of his own. (These include *circumstantial, dauntless, disgraceful, immediacy, investment, lackluster, laughable, lonely, premeditated, swagger, unmitigated,* and *worthless,* among dozens of others.) He also increased the flexibility of the language, giving old words new shades of meaning and letting nouns serve as verbs, adjectives as nouns, and the like, as when a character says "I'll thither" or, more whimsically, "My often rumination wraps me in a most humorous sadness."

It is assumed that in the early years of his career Shakespeare learned his trade by working with other members of his company on the revision of old plays. In more recent times his name has been attached to a number of early Elizabethan plays, including *A Yorkshire Tragedy, Arden of Feversham,* and even as the author of some additions to Thomas Kyd's extremely popular *The Spanish Tragedy.* None of these early collaborations can be pointed to with any certainty, but there is some agreement that *Sir Thomas More, King Edward III,* and possibly the first of the three parts of *King Henry VI* survive as early examples of his work as a collaborator. It is for this reason that the importance of the First Folio can hardly be overemphasized. Without this monumental

achievement half of Shakespeare's plays would probably have been lost forever.

During Shakespeare's lifetime plays were not regarded as literature; at best they were tolerated by the authorities as popular entertainments. In the early years of his professional life, however, Shakespeare wrote two lengthy poems, *Venus and Adonis* (1593) and *The Rape of Lucrece* (1594), which were printed and circulated widely to considerable critical acclaim. The London theaters had been closed in August 1592 and remained closed for most of 1593, due to an outbreak of the plague. Quite possibly Shakespeare was in need of money, since these two poems are his only works that he published under his own supervision and was able to profit from directly. In any event these works solidified Shakespeare's reputation as a poet of considerable stature. They were also dedicated to a well-connected nobleman, the Earl of Southampton, who is thought to have rewarded Shakespeare handsomely in both instances.

The theater of Shakespeare's time was essentially a round, walled-in structure open to the sky (as well as the weather). The stage was an extended platform around which most of the audience, known as the "groundlings," stood on three sides on the bare ground. It was said that the Globe, where Shakespeare's company performed, could hold 3,000 spectators. Performances, always in daylight, began around 2 P.M. and lasted two or sometimes three hours without intermissions, depending entirely for their source of light on the open sky. Rows of gallery seats, protected from the weather, lined the walls and were available to those who could afford them. At the back of the stage platform was a door on each side for entrances and exits and near the front of the stage a trapdoor for special effects, as, for example, the appearance and disappearance of the ghost in *Hamlet.* There was little or no attempt to provide scenery, though some essential properties were used (a throne chair for King Lear) and costumes were often elaborate and of costly materials. As the audience is requested by the Chorus that opens *Henry V:*

And let us, ciphers to this great account,
On your imaginary forces work . . .
Piece out our imperfections with your
thoughts . . .

Approximately three-quarters of Shakespeare's dramatic writing is in verse and in a meter (or rhythm) called *iambic pentameter*. This form consists of a weak beat followed by a strong beat, with five pairs of such beats to the line. This meter supplies the framework, the underpinnings so to speak, of the verse, as in:

Not marble nor the gilded monuments
Of princes shall outlive this powerful
rhyme . . . (*Sonnet 55*)

This verse form did not originate with Shakespeare. Chaucer used it 200 years before him. Marlowe, Shakespeare's contemporary, used it and was known for his "mighty line"—"Was this the face that launch'd a thousand ships?" Indeed, the Greek philosopher Aristotle, writing more than 2,300 years ago, said: "Once dialogue had come in, Nature herself discovered the appropriate measure. For the *iambic* is, of all measures, the most colloquial: we see it in the fact that conversational speech runs into *iambic* lines more frequently than into any other kind of verse." (*Poetics*, IV)

This is as true today as it was 400 years ago, in Shakespeare's time, or 2,300 years ago, in Aristotle's. A simple conversational statement, such as "The sweater was a gift from Auntie Mae" or "I'll have the tuna and a chocolate shake," lends itself perfectly to iambic pentameter, so it all sounds much more complicated than it really is. The general (though by no means rigid) rule is that ordinary conversation between Shakespeare's characters is in prose, but with the introduction of heightened emotion shifts into verse. An example of this is in *As You Like It*, Act I, scene iii, where Rosalind and Celia are chatting happily in prose. Then the Duke enters and announces that Rosalind is being banished from the court. At this point the emotional level of the scene intensifies sharply, and the language shifts into verse, continuing in verse so between the two girls after the Duke's exit.

You will encounter a number of unfamiliar words as you read the plays, many of them interesting words no longer in use, but which add flavor and spice to the lines and to the characters who speak them. You will also come across words that look familiar, but which have unfamiliar senses. Here are a dozen or so to watch for: **clept,** called or named: ". . . mongrels, spaniels, curs . . . and demi-wolves are clept/ All by the name of dogs"; **addition,** reputation: ". . . with swinish phrase [they] soil our addition . . ."; **jump,** to agree or go along: "I will not jump with common spirits [people]"; **exchange,** disguise: "I am much asham'd of my exchange . . ."; **fancy-sick,** love-sick: "All fancy-sick she is, and pale [bereft] of cheer . . ."; **hugger-mugger,** secrecy: ". . . we have done but greenly [foolishly]/ In hugger-mugger to inter him . . ."; **boot,** to be of help to: "It boots thee not to be compassionate [self-pitying] . . ."; **office,** function or purpose: "Which serves it in the office of a wall."; **meacock,** timid; apathetic: "How tame . . . A meacock wretch can make the curstest [most disagreeable] shrew."; **popinjay,** parrot, hence a prattling, affected person: "To be so pester'd with a popinjay . . ."; **scope,** intellectual attainments: "Desiring this man's art [skill], and that man's scope . . ."; **counterfeit,** drawn or painted: "The counterfeit presentment [likeness] of two brothers"; and **stoup,** large pot: "Marian, I say! A stoup of wine!"

One thing that may cause confusion is the use of "you" and "thou" in Shakespeare's plays. In Elizabethan times "you" was regarded as the polite form of address, while "thou" was the familiar form. The general rule was that superiors were addressed as "you" while inferiors were addressed as "thou." An employer would address his or her servant as "thou" and the servant would address the employer as "you." The convention seemed to be that the socially superior person could show familiarity with the underling, but such familiarity or affection was not to be openly reciprocated. A good example of this is in *The Merchant of Venice*, where Portia, the lady of the house, addresses her waiting-woman, Nerissa, as "thou" ("I pray thee over-name them, and as thou namest/ them, I will describe them . . ."), while Nerissa addresses Portia as "you" ("How say you by the French lord, Monsieur Le Bon?") and a fellow servant, a little lower in the social order, as "thou" ("Quick, quick I pray thee, draw the curtain straight . . .").

To spell it out grammatically, "thou" is the subjective pronoun (Thou art the King's son); "thee" is the objective pronoun (We have spoken to thee); "thy" is the possessive adjective (I request thy permission); and "thine" is the possessive pronoun (This land is thine). Generally, "you" served as the plural, but occasionally you will encounter the much older form "ye," used especially by older characters or in declamatory statements (as in *The Tempest* when Prospero declaims "Ye elves of hills, brooks, standing lakes, and groves;/ And ye that on the sands with printless foot/ Do chase the ebbing Neptune . . .").

"Thou" was also used as an expression of affection among people of the same class. Juliet, on first meeting Romeo, says politely, "Good pilgrim, you do wrong your hand too much . . ." but later, alone on her balcony, she speaks longingly : "O Romeo, Romeo, wherefore [why] art thou Romeo?/ Deny thy father and refuse thy name." When Richard II says to his uncle: "Hast thou according to thy oath and bond/ Brought hither Henry Hereford, thy bold son . . ." he addresses him affectionately, not formally or with condescension. Such usage can also waver between the familiar and the polite, varying with the strength of the bond, as when Claudius speaks to Laertes in *Hamlet*: "You cannot speak of reason to the Dane/ And lose your voice. What wouldst thou beg, Laertes,/ That shall not be my offer, not thy asking?"

The use of "sir" and "sirrah" is not always obvious. "Sir" is clearly a term of respect, unless of course the context makes it clear that it is being used sarcastically or as an order or reprimand ("You, sir, what trade are you?"). "Sirrah," on the other hand, makes it clear that the speaker is addressing an inferior. In *The Merchant of Venice*, as Portia exits she speaks to her waiting-woman: "Come Nerissa" and to her serving-man: "Sirrah, go before." A particularly interesting use of the word "sirrah" occurs in *Henry IV, Part I,* when King Henry addresses Hotspur as "you" in recognition of his noble rank, but when it appears that Hotspur is resisting the king's order to bring him the Scottish prisoners, the King as a patient elder shifts to the more familiar "thou" ("Thou dost belie him, Percy . . . Art thou not ashamed?"), then makes it clear he will not be crossed and goes back to the polite "you" combined with a direct order ("But, sirrah, henceforth . . . Send me your prisoners with the speediest means,/ Or you shall hear in such a kind from me/ As will displease you.").

The best way to savor Shakespeare's language is to speak it aloud on your feet and, if possible, with others. The words were written to be spoken, and, as the great director and writer Harley Granville-Barker said, they demand to be heard, not just imagined. Shakespeare himself was an actor, and he knew better than anyone how to write effectively for other actors. In fact the best possible advice on acting the plays comes from Shakespeare himself in the guise of Hamlet (Act III, ii) when the young prince advises the players at length how he would like his lines spoken ("Speak the speech, I pray you, as I pronounced it to you, trippingly on the tongue . . ."). Probably no more useful advice has ever been offered to actors.

It may come as a surprise at first to hear your own voice reading Shakespeare, but the initial shock is soon gotten over. First of all, make an effort to discover the sense of the passage. Try to determine what the scene is *about*. Why have these particular characters come to this particular place? What do they hope to accomplish in this meeting? What aids them or what hinders them? What is the result of the meeting? If there are troublesome words, try to guess their meaning from the context. If that doesn't help, look them up. That's the purpose of this book, to give useful synonyms that can be substituted for the difficult words or phrases. If possible, determine how the unusual words are used in the passage. Do they function as nouns, verbs, or adjectives? Then try the scene or passage again and discover how much more meaningful it is. Try it one more time with the appropriate feeling. Put some anger into it, some humor, some resentment, or whatever seems to be called for. You'll begin to discover how much more sense it makes to you and how much easier it is to speak. You'll also begin to feel a part of the play and realize that you're beginning to connect with the other characters.

A note of caution: Beware of adopting a mellifluous voice you feel might be suitable for such fine writing and then slathering it over the words. Using what you feel is a cultured voice for this is every bit as inappropriate as trying to force an everyday conversational tone on the material. One is just as out of place as the other. Keep to the basics of the thought and the emotion, and keep it as honest and straightforward as you can. Learn to trust the language, and make sure you understand what's going on. As the renowned stage director John Barton tells his Royal Shakespeare Company actors: "Don't take a line faster than you can *think* it." A last warning: Don't break up the line; keep it going. The words are the character's thought. He or she needs those words to express that particular idea or emotion. Break up the line and you've chopped up the thought as well as the emotion. And don't let your voice run down at the end of the line; keep it up. Remember that the last word in the line is often the most important one.

In Shakespeare's *Twelfth Night*, Viola, the young heroine, survives a shipwreck and is washed up on the shore of Illyria. She disguises herself as a boy, calls herself Cesario, and is taken on as a

page in the household of Count Orsino. Orsino, who is wildly infatuated with the Countess Olivia, sends Cesario to woo her on his behalf. After an unsuccessful attempt at this, Cesario/Viola is returning to the Count when she is overtaken by Olivia's haughty steward, Malvolio, who throws a ring at her feet, saying his mistress wants none of it, and stalks away. Viola, completely dumbfounded, says:

> I left no ring with her: what means
>   this lady?
> Fortune forbid my outside have not
>   charm'd her!
> She made good view of me, indeed so
>   much,
> That sure methought her eyes had lost
>   her tongue,
> For she did speak in starts distract-
>   edly.
> She loves me, sure; the cunning of her
>   passion
> Invites me in this churlish messenger.
> None of my lord's ring? Why, he sent
>   her none.
> I am the man: if it be so, as 'tis,
> Poor lady, she were better love a
>   dream. (II, ii, 16–25ff.)

In the first line she is merely puzzled. Then, in the second line, the thought strikes her that Olivia might have been attracted to her, thinking she was a boy. She remembers that Olivia looked her over with great interest and had trouble speaking. Viola knows that the Count didn't send Olivia any ring, so that must be the answer. Then she's amused. If that's what was going on in Olivia's head, the lady is clearly in for a big disappointment.

Troublesome words? "Outside" is her boy's attire. "Invite" is to lure or entice her (by sending this messenger). "I am the man" means Viola realizes that Olivia has fallen in love with the "man" Cesario instead of Orsino.

Notice how quickly Viola's emotions change. In the first line, puzzlement; in the second, shock. As she carefully reconstructs the interview, it slowly dawns on her what was going on in Olivia's head. There was no ring, so her attraction to Cesario/Viola has to be the answer. But Viola is afraid her mission was a failure and Orsino will be angry with her because Olivia has rejected his suit. She realizes how difficult it's going to be to explain this to Orsino, and she wants very much to please him. (She's beginning to find him very attractive.) Then she laughs as she realizes what a ridiculous situation it all is:

> O time, thou must untangle this, not I,
> It is too hard a knot for me t'untie. (II, ii, 39–40)

There's more to the speech, which you will want to investigate. See also the delightful scene between Viola (as Cesario) and Olivia that precedes the above speech, in which Viola/Cesario does her best to woo Olivia, as she's been sent to do (I, v, 169–302). It's in an elegant and rhythmic prose that approaches the lyricism of verse.

In *Julius Caesar* we are back in ancient Rome. The conspirators, led by Brutus, have assassinated Caesar. Brutus has just addressed the assembled crowd and convinced them that it was necessary to kill Caesar because he was an ambitious tyrant and that he, Brutus, and his coconspirators have acted only for the good of the Roman people. Mark Antony, a close friend of Caesar's, is granted permission to say a few words on behalf of Caesar, and he begins with:

> Friends, Romans, countrymen, lend me your ears;
> I come to bury Caesar, not to praise him.
> The evil that men do lives after them,
> The good is oft interred with their bones;
> So let it be with Caesar. (III, ii, 75–79ff.)

The words sound appropriate enough, but don't forget that the crowd has sided with Brutus. They don't want to hear anything Antony has to say. It's possible that he has to shout his first words over the crowd noises and doesn't succeed in quieting them until "So let it be with Caesar." Then he resumes:

> The noble Brutus
> Hath told you Caesar was ambitious.
> If it were so, it was a grievous fault,
> And grievously hath Caesar answer'd it. (III, ii, 79–82)

More antagonism from the crowd when they hear the words "Caesar was ambitious," but he quiets them with "grievous fault." He then adds, pointedly, that Caesar has paid for his fault "grievously." He feels that they are beginning to pay attention, and he goes on:

> Here, under leave of Brutus and the rest,
> (For Brutus is an honourable man,
> So are they all, all honourable men)
> Come I to speak in Caesar's funeral. (III, ii, 83–86)

He is quite deferential to Brutus, at least for the moment. But note that the other conspirators are referred to as "the rest," not "the other gentlemen." Brutus is mentioned as "an honourable man." Pay particular attention to that word "honourable." It keeps reappearing in his speech, each time with more of an edge. It becomes apparent that the more he praises Caesar the more he's undermining Brutus's motive for the crime. He tells the crowd how much Caesar loved Brutus:

> For Brutus, as you know, was Caesar's angel.
> Judge, O you gods, how dearly Caesar lov'd him. (III, ii, 183–184)

He also tells the crowd how much Caesar loved them and even mentioned them in his will. But he reassures them that "I am no orator, as Brutus is,/ But (as you know me all) a plain blunt man . . ." He tells them he doesn't want to stir them up, because they might do heaven knows what. However, he does want to show them poor Caesar's body:

> Kind souls, what weep you when you
> but behold
> Our Caesar's vesture wounded? Look
> you here!
> Here is himself, marr'd, as you see,
> with traitors. (III, ii, 197–199)

Antony throws off the shroud covering Caesar's body, hammers home the word "traitors," and the crowd gasps. He has won over the crowd, and they are ready to turn on Brutus. How self-serving Antony's actions have been will be made clear later in the play, but Shakespeare gives us a masterful example of how easily an angry mob can be manipulated. It's a long speech, nearly 200 lines with crowd interruptions, but one of the great ones. It repays close study. See also the angry scene between Brutus and coconspirator Cassius, in which they accuse each other of wrongdoing. (IV, iii, 1–122)

Frank Kermode, in his splendidly illuminating book, *Shakespeare's Language,* reminds us that Elizabethan audiences loved high-flown, ornately embellished language, as well as strong, vivid, and purely bombastic language. Shakespeare's early plays (*Henry VI, Henry V, Titus Andronicus*) catered to this appetite and were full of bombast and grandiloquence, which gave the spectators torrents of richly beautiful language. Elizabethan audiences were good listeners, and they expected and relished these eloquent flights of oratory.

Early in his career Shakespeare began writing a series of sonnets, 14-line poems often with a love theme. They numbered 154 by the time they were published in 1609, and since they were apparently published without Shakespeare's permission and cooperation (and quite possibly without his knowledge), we don't know whether they related to his personal life or had been commissioned by a patron. In any case, one of the most beautiful and accessible is number 18:

> Shall I compare thee to a summer's
> day?
> Thou art more lovely and more temperate:
> Rough winds do shake the darling
> buds of May,
> And summer's lease hath all too short
> a date:

The question is asked and immediately brushed aside as inadequate. Summer, particularly a day in summer, is much too fleeting and is frequently disturbed by the whims of nature's ever-changing weather.

> Sometimes too hot the eye of heaven
> shines,
> And often is his gold complexion
> dimmed;
> And every fair from fair sometimes
> declines,
> By chance, or nature's changing
> course, untrimmed:

The sun glares or it's clouded over, and no beauty can ever retain the beauty of the early years. As a result of happenstance or the unpredictability of life one will eventually be robbed of physical beauty.

> But thy eternal summer shall not
> fade,
> Nor lose possession of that fair thou
> ow'st,
> Nor shall death brag thou wander'st in
> his shade
> When in eternal lines to time thou
> grow'st:

But you have a kind of beauty that will withstand these natural forces. Even death will be unable to claim you when you advance toward mortality down the inevitable paths of time. And he sums up:

> So long as men can breathe or eyes
>   can see,
> So long lives this, and this gives life to
>   thee.

Your immortality will be achieved by these lines that I have written, and your legendary beauty will be remembered throughout eternity by all who read them.

Troublesome words? "Temperate" means not given to extremes of behavior (like the weather). "Summer's lease" is the period that summer stays. "Date" is the amount of time. "Eye of heaven" is the sun. "Every fair from fair" means every beauty from beauty (inevitably declines). "Chance" is fate or fortune. "Untrimmed" is shorn of beauty. "Shade" is shadow (of death). "Lines to time" most likely refers to the pathways one follows from cradle to grave.

One of the most famous of all speeches in Shakespeare is Portia's lovely "Quality of mercy" speech in *The Merchant of Venice*. The merchant Antonio is on trial for failing to repay the moneylender Shylock the money he has borrowed on behalf of his friend Bassanio. Shylock insists on claiming his forfeit, which, according to Venetian law, is a pound of Antonio's flesh. Portia, disguised as a man and an attorney defending Antonio, admits that Shylock's claim is within the law, but she tells him he should be merciful, and she tells him why:

> The quality of mercy is not strain'd,
> It droppeth as the gentle rain from
>   heaven
> Upon the place beneath: it is twice
>   blest,
> It blesseth him that gives, and him
>   that takes,
> 'Tis mightiest in the mightiest, it be-
>   comes
> The throned monarch better than his
>   crown.

> His sceptre shows the force of tempo-
>   ral power,
> The attribute to awe and majesty,
> Wherein doth sit the dread and fear
>   of kings:
> But mercy is above this sceptred sway,
> It is enthroned in the hearts of kings,
> It is an attribute to God himself;
> And earthly power doth then show
>   likest God's
> When mercy seasons justice. (IV, i,
>   180–193ff.)

It's the ancient argument of justice versus mercy. Should mercy temper justice? If so, to what extent? Marjorie Garber, in her admirable book *Shakespeare After All,* says that Portia's speech is "a *humanist* as well as a 'Christian' argument." This view is set in sharp contrast to Shylock's Old Testament, eye-for-an-eye concept of justice and his insistence on his right to a strict, literal interpretation of Venetian law. Shakespeare doesn't let his characters off that easily, however, and it's clear throughout the play that Christians can sometimes be less than loving or merciful in their dealings with others.

Troublesome words? "Strained" means forced or imposed. "Twice blest" means giving a double blessing. "Mightiest in the mightiest" refers to mercy as one of the noblest characteristics of great persons. "Temporal" means earthly. "Attribute to" means a symbol of; four lines later it means a characteristic of. "Sceptred sway" is the power that a sceptre represents. "Earthly power" refers to the courts, which administer earthly justice. "Seasons" means to take into consideration, especially to lessen or alleviate (the severity of justice) as a result.

Near the end of the play, as the lovers are reunited, Lorenzo speaks to his beloved Jessica about the extraordinarily beautiful night:

> How sweet the moonlight sleeps upon
>   this bank!

Here will we sit, and let the sounds of
music
Creep in our ears—soft stillness and
the night
Become the touches of sweet harmony:
Sit Jessica,—look how the floor of
heaven
Is thick inlaid with patens of bright
gold. (V, i, 54–59ff.)

No problems with the words, except possibly
"patens," which are platelike disks. After this the
other lovers return, there is some serious talk, a
little bawdy humor exchanged, and all ends in
music and a joyous dance.

Often regarded as Shakespeare's supreme
achievement, *Hamlet* is the story of a young prince
caught between conflicting forces he is unable to
deal with. His father, King Hamlet, has recently
died and his mother has married again, not only
with unseemly haste but to Claudius, the brother
of her late husband, regarded by the young prince
as "no more like my father than I to Hercules."
Alone, Hamlet speaks his innermost thoughts.
Desperately unhappy, he even thinks of suicide:

O that this too too sullied flesh would
melt,
Thaw and resolve itself into a dew,
Or that the Everlasting had not fix'd
His canon 'gainst self-slaughter. O
God! God! (I, ii, 129–132ff.)

Here "sullied" means defiled or contaminated
(in some editions the word is "solid" or even "sallied"); "the Everlasting" is God; "canon" is church
law; and "self-slaughter" is, of course, suicide.

To make matters much worse, Hamlet is visited by the ghost of his father, who tells him not
only that he has been murdered but that "The
serpent that did sting thy father's life/ Now wears
his crown." Hamlet vows vengeance, but later he
wonders if the spirit he confronted could have

been the devil, tempting him to an act that would
damn his soul:

The spirit that I have seen
May be a devil, and the devil hath
power
T'assume a pleasing shape, yea, and
perhaps,
Out of my weakness and my melan-
choly,
As he is very potent with such spirits,
Abuses me to damn me. (II, ii, 594–
599ff.)

Hamlet decides to feign madness in order to
observe Claudius more easily and see what signs
of guilt he can detect. The stress, however, is so
overwhelming that at one point he again considers suicide as a possible and even desirable solution to his dilemma:

To be, or not to be, that is the question:
Whether 'tis nobler in the mind to
suffer
The slings and arrows of outrageous
fortune,
Or to take arms against a sea of troubles
And by opposing end them. (III, i,
56–60ff.)

But as he examines the possibility of suicide,
he concludes there would also be the likelihood
of ridding himself of known problems only to
encounter others far worse that he doesn't know
about:

Who would fardels bear,
To grunt and sweat under a weary
life,
But that the dread of something after
death,
The undiscover'd country, from whose
bourn

No traveller returns, puzzles the will,
And makes us rather bear those ills
    we have
Than fly to others that we know not
    of? (III, I, 76–82)

A couple of problem words: "fardels" are burdens; "bourn" is outer limits or confines.

At the end of the speech Ophelia enters. She is in great distress because of Hamlet's behavior, and she tells him she is returning his gifts since, "Rich gifts wax poor when givers prove unkind." The language suddenly veers into prose as Hamlet becomes increasingly abusive. Note that the prose also has a rhythmical beat much like the verse.

At the beginning of the play Hamlet is a self-dramatizing young rebel given to outbursts of temper and thoughts of suicide. At the end we see him as a fully matured Renaissance prince who can say to Laertes:

Sir, in this audience,
Let my disclaiming from a purpos'd
    evil
Free me so far in your most generous
    thoughts
That I have shot my arrow o'er the
    house
And hurt my brother. (V, ii, 236–
    240ff.)

The play brilliantly shows Shakespeare's use of *dramatic time.* A prime example of his manipulation of time is in the first scene of the play, which begins at midnight and ends at dawn, though the actual playing time of the scene is perhaps 20 or 25 minutes. The action of the entire play covers what seems to be a few months, though Hamlet's character progresses from adolescence to full maturity in the course of it. Near the end of the play the grave-digger asserts that Hamlet is 30 years old, though at the beginning the young prince is intent on returning to university. At a time when life expectancy was about 40, this would clearly have been ludicrous for a 30-year-old man. But Hamlet does seem young in the early scenes and mature toward the end, as a result of Shakespeare's ingenious use of dramatic time.

The above will, I hope, serve as the briefest of introductions to the glories of Shakespeare's writing. There are many additional examples that should be included, but space is necessarily limited and the subject is so vast. Do look, however, at *Romeo and Juliet*, particularly the rapturous first meeting of the lovers, when they share a sonnet as they dance: "If I profane with my unworthiest hand/ This holy shrine, the gentle sin is this . . ." (I, v, 92–93ff.), also the balcony scene that follows. In a lighter vein, investigate the rambunctious wooing scene between Petruchio and the shrew Katherina, as he attempts to tame her: "Good morrow, Kate, for that's your name, I hear." (II, i, 182ff.)

Othello is a tragedy of love destroyed by jealousy fed by malicious mischief. Read Othello's description of the love between himself and Desdemona: "She lov'd me for the dangers I had pass'd,/ And I lov'd her that she did pity them./ This only is the witchcraft I have us'd." (I, iii, 168–170ff.) Then turn to *As You Like It*, a story of love and courtship in the Forest of Arden, and read about the seven ages of man: "All the world's a stage,/ And all the men and women merely players." (II, vii, 139ff.) And, for sheer beauty, see the Roman soldier Enobarbus's description of Cleopatra on her barge: "The barge she sat in, like a burnished throne,/ Burned on the water; the poop was beaten gold;/ Purple the sails, and so perfumed that/ The winds were love-sick with them . . ." (II, ii, 201–204ff.)

And, as a final suggestion, savor the words of Prospero in *The Tempest* as the play draws to a conclusion. This, so far as we know, was the last play written entirely by Shakespeare's hand and incontestably one of his greatest. Some see a distinct parallel between Prospero's laying aside his magic powers and Shakespeare's laying down his pen:

Our revels now are ended. These our
   actors,
As I foretold you, were all spirits, and
Are melted into air, into thin air:
And, like the baseless fabric of this vi-
   sion,
The cloud-capp'd towers, the gorgeous
   palaces,
The solemn temples, the great globe
   itself,
Yea, all which it inherit, shall dissolve,
And, like this insubstantial pageant
   faded,

Leave not a rack behind. We are such
   stuff
As dreams are made on; and our little
   life
Is rounded with a sleep. (IV, i, 148–
   158ff.)

In the words of the great scholar and teacher G. B. Harrison, "There will doubtless come a time when this prophecy is fulfilled; but until the English language in its turn has perished, in *The Tempest* lies its greatest achievement."

E. F. S.

Abbreviations

abbrev.	abbreviation	Epil.	Epilogue
abridg.	abridgment	equiv.	equivalent
accomp.	accompanied	esp.	especially
addit.	additional	euphem.	euphemism
alt.	alteration	exclam.	exclamation
ambig.	ambiguous	exten.	extension; extended
appar.	apparent; apparently	fem.	feminine
approx.	approximate; approximately	ff.	[and the] following
attrib.	attributed; attributive	fig.	figurative; figuratively
back form.	back formation	fl.	flourished
bet.	between	fol.	followed [by]
cap.	capitalized	fr.	from
caps.	capital letters	Grk.	Greek
cent.	century	iden.	identified
Cf.	compare	i.e.	id est; that is [to say]
char.	characterized [by]	imit.	imitative
Chor.	Chorus	Induc.	Induction
class.	classical	interj.	interjection
colloq.	colloquial	interp.	interpret; interpreted
compar.	comparative	Ital.	Italian
contemp.	contemptuous; contemptuously	l.	line
d.	died	l.c.	lower case
derog.	derogatory	lit.	literal; literally
dial.	dialect; dialectal	mispron.	mispronunciation
dim.	diminutive	myth.	mythology; mythological
disting.	distinguished	N	north; northern
E	east; eastern	NE	northeast; northeastern
ed.	editor; edited	nr.	near
edit.	edition; editions	NW	northwest; northwestern
eds.	editors	occas.	occasional; occasionally
Eliz.	Elizabethan	opp.	opposite
ellip.	ellipsis	orig.	original; originally

past	past tense	S	south; southern
past part.	past participle	SD	stage direction
pejor.	pejorative	SE	southeast; southeastern
perh.	perhaps	sing.	singular
pers.	person	Sp.	Spanish [for]
pl.	plural	specif.	specifically
poss.	possible; possibly	suff.	suffix
pref.	prefix	superl.	superlative
pres. indic.	present indicative	SW	southwest; southwestern
pres. part.	present participle	syll.	syllable; syllables
Prol.	Prologue	syn.	synonym
prob.	probable; probably	synon.	synonymous
pron.	pronoun; pronounced; pronunciation	tradit.	traditional
		trans.	translated; translation
prov.	proverb; proverbial	typog.	typographical
ref.	reference; refers; referring	usu.	usually
refs.	references	var.	variant; various; variously
rev.	revised; revision	W	west; western

Shakespeare's Works

PLApYS

All's W	All's Well That Ends Well
Ant & Cleo	Antony and Cleopatra
As You	As You Like It
Errors	The Comedy of Errors
Cor	Coriolanus
Cymb	Cymbeline
Ham	Hamlet
J Caes	Julius Caesar
Edw 3	King Edward III
1 Hen 4	King Henry IV, Part 1
2 Hen 4	King Henry IV, Part 2
Hen 5	King Henry V
1 Hen 6	King Henry VI, Part 1
2 Hen 6	King Henry VI, Part 2
3 Hen 6	King Henry VI, Part 3
Hen 8	King Henry VIII
K John	King John
Lear	King Lear
Rich 2	King Richard II
Rich 3	King Richard III
Love's L	Love's Labour's Lost
Mac	Macbeth
Meas	Measure for Measure
Merch	The Merchant of Venice

Wives	The Merry Wives of Windsor
M N Dream	A Midsummer Night's Dream
M Ado	Much Ado About Nothing
Oth	Othello
Per	Pericles
Rom & Jul	Romeo and Juliet
More	Sir Thomas More
Shrew	The Taming of the Shrew
Temp	The Tempest
Timon	Timon of Athens
T Andr	Titus Andronicus
Tr & Cr	Troilus and Cressida
T Night	Twelfth Night
Two Gent	The Two Gentlemen of Verona
W Tale	The Winter's Tale
Kinsmen	The Two Noble Kinsmen

POEMS

Sonn	Sonnets
Luc	The Rape of Lucrece
Ven & Ad	Venus and Adonis
Lover's Comp	A Lover's Complaint
Pass Pil	The Passionate Pilgrim
Phoenix	The Phoenix and the Turtle

Note: Line breaks in quotations are indicated with a slash, but the reader should be advised that the line numberings (herein mostly from the Arden edition) are approximate and will vary from one edition of Shakespeare to the next.

A

a¹, *pron.* Also, **'a,** he: "A must then to the Inns o'Court short-ly . . ." *2 Hen 4,* III, ii, 12.

a², *prep.* **1** in: "But what a God's name doth become of this?" *Rich 2,* II, i, 251. **2** in the: "Why, what a devil's name, tailor, call'st thou this?" *Shrew,* IV, iii, 92. **3** on: "Wednesday is too soon./ A Thursday let it be, a Thursday, tell her . . ." *Rom & Jul,* III, iv, 19–20. **4** kind of a: "What a woman are you?" *Wives,* IV, ii, 38.

a³, *pref.* old past part. use, carried over to adjectival use: "Tom's a-cold. O! do de,/ do de, do de." *Lear,* III, iv, 58–59.

a⁴, *suff.* meaningless syllable appended to a word in a poem or song to fill out the meter: "Or lace for your cape,/ My dainty duck, my dear-a?" *W Tale,* IV, iv, 317–318.

a-, *pref.* used with gerunds to indicate "in the act of": "At game a-swearing, or about some act/ That has no relish of salvation in't . . ." *Ham,* III, iii, 91–92.

a', *prep.* **1** of: "With all the spots a' th' world tax'd and debosh'd . . ." *All's W,* V, iii, 205. **2** have: "If I could a' remem-bered a gilt counterfeit . . ." *Tr & Cr,* II, iii, 26. **3** he: "Yes, that a' did; and said they were devils/ incarnate." *Hen 5,* II, iii, 32–33.

abandon, *v.* to banish: ". . . the time seems thirty unto me,/ Being all this time abandon'd from your bed." *Shrew,* Ind., ii, 115–116.

abate, *prep.* **1** except for (a): "Abate throw at novum, and the whole world again/ Cannot pick out five such . . ." *Love's L,* V, ii, 538–539.
—*v.* **2** to shorten or cause to seem shorter: "O long and te-dious night,/ Abate thy hours!" *M N Dream,* III, ii, 431–432. **3** to blunt: "Abate the edge of traitors [traitors' swords], gra-cious Lord . . ." *Rich 3,* V, v, 35. **4** to deprive; take away from: "She hath abated me of half my train . . ." *Lear,* II, iv, 160. **5**

abate her nothing, not detract from her in the least: I would/ abate her nothing, though I profess myself her adorer, not her friend." *Cymb,* I, v, 64–66.

abated, *adj.* **1** diminished, as in force or quality: ". . . from his metal was his party steel'd,/ Which once in him abated, all the rest/ Turn'd on themselves . . ." *2 Hen 4,* I, i, 116–118. **2** humbled; humiliated: ". . . deliver you as most/ Abated cap-tives to some nation . . ." *Cor,* III, iii, 131–132.

abatement, *n.* **1** loss of quality or value: ". . . falls into abate-ment and low price,/ Even in a minute!" *T Night,* I, i, 13–14. **2** reduced amount: ". . . letting them thrive again/ On their abatement . . ." *Cymb,* V, iv, 20–21.

ABC, *n.* hornbook primer, used for learning the ABC's, Lord's Prayer, etc.: ". . . to sigh, like a schoolboy that had lost his/ ABC . . ." *Two Gent,* II, i, 21–22.

a-bed, *adv.* in [our] imagination: ". . . unto us it is/ A cell of ignorance, travelling a-bed . . ." *Cymb,* III, iii, 32–33.

abhominable, *adj.* old spelling (and pronunciation) of **abominable:** "This is abhominable,/ which he would call abominable . . ." *Love's L,* V, i, 23–24.

abhor, *v.* **abhor me,** fill me with abhorrence; disgust me: "I cannot say 'whore': It does abhor me now I speak the word . . ." *Oth,* IV, ii, 163–164.

abhorred ends, *n.* intended mischief: ". . . reveal/ themselves till they attain to their abhorr'd ends . . ." *All's W,* IV, iii, 21–22.

abide, *v.* **1** to remain; stay: "What say you boys? will you abide with him . . ." *T Andr,* V, ii, 137. **2** to wait for: "Abide me if thou dar'st, for well I wot/ Thou runn'st before me, shifting every place . . ." *M N Dream,* III, ii, 422–423. **3** to bear the consequences of: ". . . and let no man abide this deed/ But we the doers." *J Caes,* III, i, 94–95. **4 dear abide,** to pay for (some-

1

thing) dearly: ". . . 'tis certain he was not ambitious."/ "If it be found so, some will dear abide it." *J Caes*, III, ii, 115–116.

ability, *n.* [usually pl.] strong defenses: ". . . altogether lacks the abilities/ That Rhodes is dress'd in." *Oth*, I, iii, 25–26.

a-birding, *v.* hunt small birds; here, using a hawk to scare birds from the bush: ". . . to my house to breakfast; after, we'll a-birding/ together—" *Wives*, III, iii, 214–215.

abject, *adj.* **1** low; common: "The abject people gazing on thy face/ With envious looks . . ." *2 Hen 6*, II, iv, 11–12.
—*n.* **2** pun on "subject," with addit. meaning of "wretched, mean, or base": "We are the Queen's abjects, and must obey." *Rich 3*, I, i, 106.

abjectly, *adv.* contemptuously: "Let him that thinks of me so abjectly/ Know that this gold must coin a stratagem . . ." *T Andr*, II, ii, 4–5.

abjured, *adj.* rejected; sworn off: "As Ovid be an outcast quite abjur'd." *Shrew*, I, i, 33.

able, *adj.* **1** vigorous: "Would it not grieve an able man to leave/ So sweet a bedfellow?" *Hen 8*, II, ii, 141–142.
—*v.* **2** to vouch for: "None does offend, none, I say none; I'll able 'em . . ." *Lear*, IV, vi, 170.

abode, *v.* **1** to foretell; foreshadow or forebode: "The night-crow cried, aboding luckless time . . ." *3 Hen 6*, V, vi, 45.
—*n.* **2** act of staying or remaining; abiding: ". . . that of Cleopatra's,/ which wholly depends on your abode." *Ant & Cleo*, I, ii, 172–173. **3** delay: "Sweet friends, your patience for my long abode . . ." *Merch*, II, vi, 21.

abodement, *n.* [often pl.] forebodings: "Tush, man, abodements must not now affright us . . ." *3 Hen 6*, IV, vii, 13.

abominable, *adj.* inhuman or unnatural [fr. sense of old form *abhominable*]: "From their abominable and beastly touches/ I drink, I eat . . ." *Meas*, III, ii, 22–23.

aborn, *n.* auburn: "Not wanton white, but such a manly color/ Next to an aborn . . ." *Kinsmen*, IV, ii, 124–125.

abortive, *adj.* **1** unnatural; monstrous or freakish: ". . . and allay this thy abortive pride . . ." *2 Hen 6*, IV, i, 60.
—*n.* **2** [usually pl.] abnormalities, esp. freakish births: "Abortives, presages, and tongues of heaven,/ Plainly denouncing vengeance upon John." *K John*, III, iii, 158–159.

abound, *v.* to experience wealth and plenty: ". . . never/ They shall abound as formerly." *Hen 8*, I, i, 82–83.

abounding, *adj.* abundant; profuse: "Mark then abounding valour in our English . . ." *Hen 5*, IV, iii, 104.

about, *adv.* **1** here and there; in all quarters; here, with verb "go" understood: "I'll about/ And drive away the vulgar from the streets . . ." *J Caes*, I, i, 68–69. **2** the same used as a command or exhortation; go! get moving!: "Revenge! About! Seek! Burn! Fire! Kill!/ Slay! Let not a traitor live." *J Caes*, III, ii, 206–207.
—*prep.* **3** in; concerning: "Else shall you not have any hand at all/ About his funeral." *J Caes*, III, i, 248–249.

above, *prep.* **1** more than: ". . . men shall swear I have discontinued school/ Above a twelvemonth . . ." *Merch*, III, iv, 75–76. **2 above a number,** more than many [others]: ". . . (so much I am happy/ Above a number) . . ." *Hen 8*, III, i, 33–34. **3 above the rest,** above all; more than anything else: "Do as I bid thee, or rather do thy pleasure;/ Above the rest, be gone." *Lear*, IV, i, 47–48.

Abraham Cupid, *n.* prob. comparison of Cupid to the half-naked beggars of the day called "Abraham-men": "Young Abraham Cupid, he that shot so trim/ When King Cophetua lov'd the beggar maid." *Rom & Jul*, II, i, 13–14.

Abraham's bosom, *n.* heaven [Biblical ref.]: "The sons of Edward sleep in Abraham's bosom . . ." *Rich 3*, IV, iii, 38.

abram, *n.* colloq. var. of **auburn**; reddish-brown: ". . . our heads are some brown, some black, some/ abram, some bald . . ." *Cor*, II, iii, 19–20.

Abram, *n.* var. of **Abraham:** "This Jacob from our holy Abram was . . ." *Merch*, I, iii, 67.

abridged, *adj.* reduced or curtailed: "Nor do I now make moan to be abridg'd/ From such a noble rate . . ." *Merch*, I, i, 126–127.

abridgment or **abridgement,** *n.* **1** something, as an entertainment or diversion, to make the time pass quickly: "Say, what abridgement have you for this evening,/ What masque, what music?" *M Dream*, V, i, 39–40. **2** interruption or intrusion: ". . . for look where my abridgement comes." *Ham*, II, ii, 416.

abroach, *adj.* **1** tapped or opened, as a cask; also, unleashed: "Alack, what mischiefs might he set abroach/ In shadow of such greatness!" *2 Hen 4*, IV, ii, 14–15.
—*adv.* **2** in motion; afoot: "The secret mischiefs that I set abroach . . ." *Rich 3*, I, iii, 325.

abroad, *adv.* **1** up and about; nearby: "The trumpets sound, the king is now abroad." *Edw 3*, II, ii, 21. **2** in or from the outside world: "How now, fair lords! What fare? What news abroad?" *3 Hen 6,* II, i, 95. **3** other than myself: ". . . here have I few attendants,/ And subjects none abroad . . ." *Temp,* V, i, 166–167. **4** into public view: "Is he ready/ To come abroad?" *Hen 8,* III, ii, 82–83.

abrook, *v.* to endure: ". . . ill can thy noble mind abrook/ The abject people gazing on thy face . . ." *2 Hen 6,* II, iv, 10–11.

abruption, *n.* interruption: "What makes this/ pretty abruption?" *Tr & Cr,* III, ii, 63–64.

absence, *adj.* parson's misuse for "absent": "I will not be absence at the/ grace." *Wives,* I, i, 242–243.

Absey book, *n.* ABC book; a child's primer: ". . . that is Question now;/ And then comes Answer like an Absey book . . ." *K John,* I, i, 195–196.

absolute, *adj.* **1** blunt; uncompromising: ". . . and with an absolute 'sir, not I,'/ The cloudy messenger turns me his back . . ." *Mac,* III, vi, 40–41. **2** faultless; peerless: "This Philoten contends in skill/ With absolute Marina . . ." *Per,* IV, Cho., 30–31. **3** precise; strict: "How absolute the knave is. We must speak by the/ card . . ." *Ham,* V, i, 133–134. **4** certain; free of any doubt: "I am absolute/ 'Twas very Cloten." *Cymb,* IV, ii, 106–107.

abstract, *n.* **1** list: ". . . he hath an/ abstract for the remembrance of such places and/ goes to them by his note." *Wives,* IV, ii, 54–56. **2** epitome; here, budding qualities that characterized his father: "This little abstract doth contain that large/ Which died in Geoffrey . . ." *K John,* II, 1, 101–102. **3** perh. a barrier that, when removed, would free Antony to return to Cleopatra [in some edit. "obstruct"]: "Which soon he granted,/ Being an abstract 'tween his lust and him." *Ant & Cleo,* III, vi, 60–61. **4 abstract and brief chronicles,** summary; here, a ref. to the general practice of commenting on contemporary events in plays: ". . . let them be well used, for/ they are the abstract and brief chronicles of the time." *Ham,* II, ii, 519–520.

absurd, *adj.* insipid; without taste or savor: "No, let the candied tongue lick absurd pomp . . ." *Ham,* III, ii, 60.

Absyrtus, *n.* brother of Medea, whom she murdered; when escaping with Jason, she cut up her brother's body and threw the pieces overboard, forcing her father to delay his pursuit while gathering up the fragments: "Into as many gobbets will I cut it/ As wild Medea young Absyrtus did . . ." *2 Hen 6,* V, ii, 58–59.

abuse, *v.* **1** to deceive or wrong; take advantage of: ". . . my Lady Hero hath/ been falsely accused, the Prince and Clau-

dio/ mightily abused . . ." *M Ado,* V, ii, 89–91. **2** to delude: "Old fools are babes again, and must be us'd/ With checks as flatteries, when they are seen abus'd." *Lear,* I, iii, 20–21. **3** to misuse or misapply: "And their gross painting might be better used/ Where cheeks need blood; in thee it is abused." *Sonn 82,* 13–14. **4** to slander: "I'll have our Michael Cassio on the hip,/ Abuse him to the Moor . . ." *Oth,* II, i, 300–301.
—*n.* **5** deception: "Are all the rest come back?/ Or is it some abuse, and no such thing?" *Ham,* IV, vii, 47–48. **6** fault; offense; vice: ". . . that he might stick/ The smallest opinion, on my greatest abuse [that he might find fault with even my worst offense]?" *Oth,* IV, ii, 110–111. **7 use their abuses,** practice their vices: ". . . good people/ in a commonweal, that do nothing but use their/ abuses in common houses . . ." *Meas,* II, i, 41–43.

abused, *adj.* cheated; also, repelled: ". . . her delicate/ tenderness will find itself abus'd . . ." *Oth,* II, i, 230–231.

abusing times, *n.* period when the rightful succession was abused: ". . . to draw forth your noble ancestry/ From the corruption of abusing times . . ." *Rich 3,* III, vii, 197–198.

aby, *v.* to pay for: "Disparage not the faith thou dost not know,/ Lest to thy peril thou aby it dear [pay for it dearly]." *M N Dream,* III, ii, 174–175.

abysm, *n.* abyss: "What seest thou else/ In the dark backward and abysm of time?" *Temp,* I, ii, 49–50.

academe, *n.* academy, modeled after Plato's which gathered in ancient Athens: "Our court shall be a little academe . . ." *Love's L,* I, i, 13.

accent, *n.* **1** power of speech: "And 'midst the sentence so her accent breaks . . ." *Luc,* 566. **2** modulation of the voice in speaking: "Action and accent did they teach him there . . ." *Love's L,* V, ii, 99. **3** sound or expressiveness of the voice: "For why, the senseless brands will sympathize/ The heavy accent of thy moving tongue . . ." *Rich 2,* V, i, 46–47. **4** language; here, foreign languages: "How many ages hence/ Shall this our lofty scene be acted over,/ In states unborn, and accents yet unknown!" *J Caes,* III, i, 111–113.

accept, *v.* **1 accept of,** to receive: "Accept of him, or else you do me wrong." *Shrew,* II, i, 59.
—*adj.* **2** agreed-on: ". . . we will suddenly/ Pass our accept and peremptory answer." *Hen 5,* V, ii, 81–82.

acceptable, *adj.* welcome; pleasing: "I take my leave, and fairly will return/ Your acceptable greeting to my king." *Edw 3,* I, ii, 38–39.

access, *n.* admittance; here, to the company of Silvia: "Under the colour of commending him,/ I have access my own love to prefer." *Two Gent,* IV, ii, 3–4.

accessible, *adj.* being a possible way to go: "Accessible is none but Milford way [There is no other place to go but toward Milford]." *Cymb,* III, ii, 83.

accessory, *adj.* willing or yielding; here, conduct that would make her an accessory to the crime: "... that never was inclin'd/ To accessory yieldings, but still pure ..." *Luc,* 1657–1658.

accidence, *n.* Latin grammar: "I pray you, ask him some questions in his accidence." *Wives,* IV, i, 12–13.

accident, *n.* (often pl.) occasions; events: "All solemn things/ Should answer [correspond to] solemn accidents." *Cymb,* IV, ii, 191–192.

accidental, *adj.* fortuitous; hence, divine: "Of accidental judgments, casual slaughters ..." *Ham,* V, ii, 387.

accite, *v.* **1** to induce; excite: "And what accites your most worshipful/ thought to think so?" *2 Hen 4,* II, ii, 56–57. **2** to summon: "Our coronation done, we will accite/ ... all our state ..." *2 Hen 4,* V, ii, 141–142.

accommodate, *v.* to supply or equip: "Sir, pardon: a soldier is better accommodated than/ with a wife." *2 Hen 4,* III, ii, 65–66.

accommodated, *adj.* having or given an advantage: "Accommodated by the place ... With their own nobleness ..." *Cymb,* V, iii, 32–33.

accommodation, *n.* convenience; comfort: "... all th'accommodations that thou bear'st/ Are nurs'd by baseness." *Meas,* III, i, 14–15.

accomplements, *n.* full battle dress: "Some twenty naked starvelings ... Hath driven back a puissant host of men/ Arrayed and fenced in all accomplements." *Edw 3,* IV, vi, 38–39.

accomplice, *n.* ally; associate: "Success unto our valiant general,/ And happiness to his accomplices!" *1 Hen 6,* V, ii, 8–9.

accomplish, *v.* **1** to perform: "... honourable action,/ Such as he hath observ'd in noble ladies/ Unto their lords, by them accomplished." *Shrew,* Ind., i, 108–110. **2** to fit out; equip: "... from the tents/ The armourers, accomplishing the knights ..." *Hen 5,* IV, Chor., 11–12.

accomplished, *adj.* furnished: "... for even so look'd he,/ Accomplish'd with the number of thy hours [at the same age] ..." *Rich 2,* II, i, 176–177.

accompt, *n.* **1** var. of **account:** "What need/ we fear who knows it, when none can call our power/ to accompt?" *Mac,* V, i, 36–38. **2** heed; notice: "Takes no accompt/ How things go from him ..." *Timon,* II, i, 3–4. **3 accompts,** account books; records: "At many times I brought in my accompts,/ Laid them before you ..." *Timon,* II, ii, 137–138. **4** wordplay on "sum total" and "story": "And let us, ciphers to this great accompt,/ On your imaginary forces work." *Hen 5,* Prol., 17–18. **5** a sin that is recorded but is not part of one's spiritual reckoning: "... our compell'd sins/ Stand more for number than for accompt." *Meas,* II, iv, 57–58. **6 cast accompt,** to do [keep] accounts: "The clerk of Chartham: he can write and read and/ cast accompt." *2 Hen 6,* IV, ii, 81–82.

accord, *n.* **1** harmony; here, musical harmony: "*Gamut* I am, the ground of all accord—" *Shrew,* III, i, 71. **2** [usually pl] the will; another's wishes: "Then let your will attend on their accords." *Errors,* II, i, 25.
—*v.* **3** to agree: "... how apt our love was to accord/ To furnish him with all appertinents ..." *Hen 5,* II, ii, 86–87.

accordant, *adj.* being in accord; agreeable: "... if he found her accordant, he meant to ... instantly break with you of it." *M Ado,* I, ii, 13–14.

according, *adj.* agreeing; assenting: "And she agreed, within her scope of choice/ Lies my consent and fair [readily] according voice." *Rom & Jul,* I, ii, 18–19.

accordingly, *adv.* correspondingly: "... he is very great in knowledge,/ and accordingly valiant." *All's W,* II, v, 7–8.

accost, *v.* to introduce oneself to: "Accost, Sir Andrew, accost." *T Night,* I, iii, 48.

account, *n.* **1** number or amount: "... a beggarly account of empty boxes ..." *Rom & Jul,* V, i, 45. **2** reckoning or calculation: "... by which account ... some twelve days hence/ Our general forces at Bridgnorth shall meet." *1 Hen 4,* III, ii, 176–178. **3** estimation; worth: "No shape so true, no truth of such account ..." *Sonn 62,* 6. **4** accounting before God of one's earthly sins: "No reck'ning made, but sent to my account/ With all my imperfections on my head." *Ham,* I, v, 78–79. **5 in account,** by all accounts or reports: "When yet you were in place and in account/ Nothing so strong and fortunate as I." *1 Hen 4,* V, i, 37–38.
—*v.* **6** to think; consider or regard [as]: "If thou account'st it shame, lay it on me." *Shrew,* IV, iii, 178. **7 account of,** to appreciate; esteem: "How esteem'st thou me? I account of her beauty." *Two Gent,* II, i, 59.

accountant, *adj.* accountable; liable: "Accountant to the law upon that pain." *Meas*, II, iv, 86.

accoutrement, *n.* equipment: "... not only ... in the simple office of love, but in all/ the accoutrement, complement, and ceremony of it." *Wives*, IV, ii, 3–5.

accuse, *v.* **1** to impugn; reflect upon: "Let not my cold words here accuse my zeal [loyalty]." *Rich 2*, I, i, 47.
—*n.* **2** accusation: "And dogged York ... By false accuse doth level at my life." *2 Hen 6*, III, i, 158–160.

ace, *n.* lowest throw [one] using only one of a pair of dice [die]; also, wordplay on "ace" and "ass": "No die, but an ace for him; for he is but one." *M N Dream*, V, i, 296.

acerb, *adj.* sour; bitter: "... shall be to him shortly as acerb as the coloquintida." *Oth*, I, iii, 350.

Acheron, *n.* **1** river of Hades: "The starry welkin cover thou anon/ With drooping fog, as black as Acheron..." *M N Dream*, III, ii, 356–357. **2** prob. standing for Hades itself: "I'll dive into the burning lake below,/ And pull her out of Acheron by the heels." *T Andr*, IV, iii, 43–44.

aches, *n. pl.* pron. as two syllables, like "H's": "I'll rack thee with old cramps,/ Fill all thy bones with aches..." *Temp*, I, ii, 371–372.

achieve, *v.* **1** to capture; here, also, execute: "Bid them achieve me and then sell my bones." *Hen 5*, IV, iii, 91. **2** to gain; obtain: "... he hath achiev'd a maid/ That paragons description..." *Oth*, II, i, 61–62.

achievement, *n.* **1** sexual conquest: "'Achievement is command; ungain'd, beseech.'" *Tr & Cr*, I, ii, 298. **2 for achievement,** to conclude the matter; also, instead of victory: "He'll drop his heart into the sink of fear,/ And for achievement offer us his ransom." *Hen 5*, III, v, 59–60.

Achilles' horse, *n.* the great warrior's horse, here judged to be worth several of his master: "Let this be granted, and Achilles' horse/ Makes many Thetis' sons." *Tr & Cr*, I, iii, 211–212.

Achitophel, *n.* (in the Bible) adviser to Absalom, King David's rebellious son: "A whoreson Achitophel! A rascally/ yea-forsooth knave..." *2 Hen 4*, I, ii, 35–36.

acknowledge, *v.* **1** to greet (another) as friend or acquaintance: "I may not evermore [henceforth] acknowledge thee..." *Sonn 36*, 9. **2 acknowledge itself,** to become known; be disclosed: "If the encounter acknowledge itself hereafter..." *Meas*, III, i, 252.

aconitum, *n.* poisonous plant wolfsbane (or monkshood); also, poison extracted from this plant: "... it do work as strong/ As aconitum or rash gunpowder." *2 Hen 4*, IV, iv, 47–48.

acquaintance, *n.* **1** friend or friends: "Balk logic with acquaintance that you have..." *Shrew*, I, i, 34. **2 altogether's acquaintance,** is very well acquainted: "... it is a/ 'oman [woman] that altogether's acquaintance with Mistress/ Anne Page..." *Wives*, I, ii, 7–9. **3 desire (someone) of more acquaintance,** to desire to become better acquainted with (another): "I shall desire you of more acquaintance, good Master Cobweb..." *M N Dream*, III, i, 175. **4 how creeps acquaintance?,** how did you worm your way into his acquaintance?: "But how comes/ it he is to sojourn with you? how creeps acquaintance?" *Cymb*, I, v, 21–22. **5 will acquaintance strangle,** will end our relationship: "I will acquaintance strangle, and look strange [appear a stranger]..." *Sonn 89*, 8.

acquit, *v.* to release, as from a vow or obligation: "How... may I give him that/ Which I have given to you?"/ "I will acquit you." *T Night*, III, iv, 216–217.

acquittance, *n.* **1** discharge of a debt: "... your neck, sir,/ is pen, book, and counters; so the acquittance/ follows." *Cymb*, V, iv, 170–172. **2** receipt or other verifying document: "... acquittances/ For such a sum from special officers/ Of Charles his father." *Love's L*, II, i, 160–162. **3** acquittal; exoneration: "Now must your conscience my acquittance seal..." *Ham*, IV, vii, 1.
—*v.* **4** to acquit; clear: "Your mere enforcement shall acquittance me..." *Rich 3*, III, vii, 232.

acre, *n.* unplowed ridge in a field, sometimes used as a border: "Between the acres of the rye ... These pretty country-folks would lie..." *As You*, V, iii, 20–22.

across, *adj., adv.* (in tilting) not a direct hit; here, an awkward jest: "... so I had broke thy pate/ And ask'd thee mercy for't."/ "Good faith, across!" *All's W*, II, i, 65–66.

act, *n.* **1** scene in a play: "... when thou seest that act afoot,/ Even with the very comment of thy soul/ Observe my uncle." *Ham*, III, ii, 78–80. **2** achievement; accomplishment: "A lower place, note well,/ May make too great an act." *Ant & Cleo*, III, i, 12–13. **3 act and place,** [according to] the circumstances and one's rank: "As he in his particular act and place/ May give his saying deed..." *Ham*, I, iii, 26–27. **4 out of act, a.** into a state unfit for service: "... on us both did haggish age steal on,/ And wore us out of act." *All's W*, II, i, 29–30. **b.** into nothingness: "Like Patience gazing on kings' graves, and smiling/ Extremity out of act." *Per*, V, i, 138–139.

—*v.* **5** to enact: "Here is a hand to hold a sceptre up,/ And with the same to act controlling laws." *2 Hen 6,* V, i, 102–103.

Actaeon, *n.* **1** (in Greek myth.) hunter who was transformed into a stag and torn apart by his own hounds because he had witnessed Diana bathing: "Thy temples should be planted presently/ With horns, as was Actaeon's . . ." *T Andr,* II, iii, 62–63. **2** same, as symbol of cuckoldry because of the horns he wore as a stag: ". . . divulge Page himself for a secure and/ wilful Actaeon . . ." *Wives,* III, ii, 38–39.

acted, *past part.* consummated: "Think true love acted simple modesty." *Rom & Jul,* III, ii, 16.

action, *n.* **1** legal action, as for debt: ". . . the wearing/ out of six fashions, which is four terms, or two/ actions . . ." *2 Hen 4,* V, i, 76–78. **2** lawsuit; here, a case: "Whose action is no stronger than a flower?" *Sonn 65,* 4. **3** appropriate gestures: "Action and accent did they teach him there . . ." *Love's L,* V, ii, 99. **4 action is eloquence,** here, Volumnia acts out for her son how to make conciliatory gestures: ". . . for in such business/ Action is eloquence, and the eyes of th'ignorant/ More learned than the ears . . ." *Cor,* III, ii, 75–77. **5 enter an action,** to commence a lawsuit: "Master Fang, have you entered the action?" *2 Hen 4,* II, i, 1. **6 hope of action,** expectation of military action: "The Duke . . . Bore many gentlemen—myself being one—/ In hand, and hope of action . . ." *Meas,* I, iv, 50–52.

action's self, *n.* the event itself: ". . . lose some life/ Which action's self was tongue to [was less impressive than the actual event] . . ." *Hen 8,* I, i, 41–42.

action-taking, *adj.* settling matters at law rather than with a duel: ". . . action-taking, whoreson, glass-gazing, super-serviceable, finical rogue . . ." *Lear,* II, ii, 16–17.

Actium, *n.* promontory and ancient town in W Greece: ". . . from the head of Actium/ Beat the approaching Caesar." *Ant & Cleo,* III, vii, 51–52.

act of darkness, *n.* See **darkness** (def. 3).

actor, *n.* malefactor; wrongdoer: "Mine were the very cipher of a function/ To fine the faults . . . And let go by the actor." *Meas,* II, ii, 39–41.

acture, *n.* mere physical act; here, one of passion: "Love made them not: with acture they may be,/ Where neither party is nor true nor kind . . ." *Lover's Comp,* 185–186.

acutely, *adv.* wittily: "I am so full of businesses I cannot answer thee/ acutely." *All's W,* I, i, 202–203.

adage, *n.* **cat in the adage,** from the French, "The cat loves fish, but he doesn't want to get his feet wet": "Letting 'I dare not' wait upon 'I would,'/ Like the poor cat i' th' adage?" *Mac,* I, vii, 44–45.

Adam, *n.* **1** ref. to Adam as the first gardener: "Thou, old Adam's likeness set to dress this garden . . ." *Rich 2,* III, iv, 73. **2** the arresting sergeant likened to Adam, dressed in skins [leather] when he left the Garden of Eden: "Master . . . what, have you got the picture of old Adam new-apparelled?" *Errors,* IV, iii, 13–14. **3** syn. for original sin or innate depravity: "And whipp'd th' offending Adam out of him . . ." *Hen 5,* I, i, 29. **4 penalty of Adam,** ref. to harsh weather that replaced Eden's eternal summer after Adam's fall: "Here feel we not the penalty of Adam . . . the icy fang/ And churlish chiding of the winter's wind . . ." *As You,* II, I, 5–7.

adamant, *n.* hardest substance known, esp. the lodestone, a magnetic rock: "You draw me, you hard-hearted adamant—" *M N Dream,* II, i, 195.

adder, *n.* **ears more deaf than adders,** fr. Biblical injunction, "The wicked . . . are like the deaf adder that stoppeth her ear . . ." [Psalms 58]: ". . . pleasure and revenge/ Have ears more deaf than adders to the voice/ Of any true decision." *Tr & Cr,* II, ii, 172–174.

addition, *n.* **1** title, rank, etc., by which a person is addressed: "According to the phrase or the addition/ Of man and country." *Ham,* II, i, 48–49. **2** new title or honor: "He bade me . . . call thee Thane of Cawdor:/ In which addition, hail . . ." *Mac,* I, iii, 105–106. **3** exaggeration: "Truly to speak, and with no addition . . ." *Ham,* IV, iv, 17. **4** credit: ". . . think it no addition, nor my wish,/ To have him see me woman'd." *Oth,* III, iv, 192–193. **5** reputation: "They clepe us drunkards, and with swinish phrase/ Soil our addition . . ." *Ham,* I, iv, 19–20. **6 particular additions,** unique characteristics: "This man, lady, hath robbed many beasts of their/ particular additions." *Tr & Cr,* I, ii, 19–20.

addle, *adj.* addled; muddled or scrambled; (of an egg) rotten: ". . . thy head hath been beaten as addle/ as an egg for quarrelling." *Rom & Jul,* III, i, 23–24.

address, *v.* **1** to make ready; prepare oneself: "Let us address to tend on Hector's heels." *Tr & Cr,* IV, iv, 144. **2 address thee,** prepare thyself: "Address thee instantly." *2 Hen 6,* V, ii, 27. **3 address thy gait,** See **gait** (def. 3).

addressed or **addrest,** *adj.* prepared; ready: "Our navy is address'd, our power collected . . ." *2 Hen 4,* IV, iv, 5.

ad dunghill, misuse for Latin *ad unguem,* to a T [lit., to the fingernail]: "... thou has it *ad dunghill,* at the fingers' ends, as/ they say." *Love's L,* V, i, 70–71.

adhere, *v.* **1** to be friendly toward: "... two men there is not living/ To whom he more adheres." *Ham,* II, ii, 20–21. **2** to be suitable or auspicious: "Nor time, nor place,/ Did then adhere, and yet you would make both ..." *Mac,* I, vii, 51–52.

Ad Jovem, [Latin] to Jove [Jupiter]: "*Ad Jovem,* that's for you: here, *Ad Apollinem* [to Apollo]:/ *Ad Martem* [to Mars], that's for myself ..." *T Andr,* IV, iii, 53–54.

adjudge, *v.* to sentence or condemn (to): "... thou art adjudged to the death,/ And passed sentence may not be recall'd ..." *Errors,* I, i, 146–147.

adjunct, *adj.* **1** related: "And every humour hath his adjunct pleasure ..." *Sonn 91,* 5. **2** attendant; following as a consequence: "Though death be adjunct, there's no death supposed." *Luc,* 133.
—*n.* **3** aid to the memory; memento: "To keep an adjunct to remember thee ..." *Sonn 122,* 13.

Ad manes fratrum, [Latin] to the shades [spirits] of our brothers: "Give us the proudest prisoner of the Goths,/ That we may ... *Ad manes fratrum* sacrifice his flesh ..." *T Andr,* I, i, 96–98.

admiral, *n.* flagship of a fleet, which carried a signal light at the stern: "... thou art our admiral, thou bearest the lantern in the/ poop ..." *1 Hen 4,* III, iii, 24–25.

admiration, *n.* wonder; amazement or puzzlement: "What makes your admiration?" *Cymb,* I, vii, 38.

admire, *v.* to be astonished: "... these lords/ At this encounter do so much admire,/ That they devour their reason ..." *Temp,* V, i, 153–155.

admired, *adj.* **1** amazing; incredible: "You have displac'd the mirth, broke the good meeting/ With most admir'd disorder." *Mac,* III, iv, 108–109. **2** admirable; delightful: "... she dances/ As goddess-like to her admired lays." *Per,* V, Chor., 3–4. **3** admiring: "'Tis thou that ... Settlest admired reverence in a slave ..." *Timon,* V, i, 49–50.

admit, *v.* **1** to permit; allow: "... your honesty should/ admit no discourse to your beauty." *Ham,* III, i, 107–108. **2** to suppose: "Admit no other way to save his life ..." *Meas,* II, iv, 88.

admittance, *n.* **1** reception or welcome in the best social circles: "... a/ gentleman of excellent breeding, admirable discourse, of great admittance ..." *Wives,* II, ii, 217–219. **2**

acceptance: "... any tire [attire] of/ Venetian admittance." *Wives,* III, iii, 51–52.

ado, *n.* **1** fuss; to-do; here, a quarreling: "Would you had hit it too!/ Then should not we be tir'd with this ado." *T Andr,* II, i, 97–98. **2** difficulty: "... such a want-wit sadness makes of me,/ That I have much ado to know myself." *Merch,* I, i, 6–7.

Adonis, *n.* (in Greek & Roman myth.) a beautiful youth loved by Aphrodite [Venus]: "Describe Adonis, and the counterfeit/ Is poorly imitated after you ..." *Sonn 53,* 5–6.

Adonis' gardens, *n.* myth. gardens famed for their splendor; here, perh. alluding to their description in Spenser's *Faerie Queene:* "Thy promises are like Adonis' gardens,/ That one day bloom'd, and fruitful were the next." *1 Hen 6,* I, vi, 6–7.

adoption, *n.* acceptance or approval: "Those friends thou hast, and their adoption tried [tested] ..." *Ham,* I, iii, 62.

adoptious, *adj.* assumed; adopted: "... a world/ Of pretty, fond, adoptious christendoms [pet names] ..." *All's W,* I, i, 169–170.

adorning, *n.* something that enhances or complements the center of attention [here, the person of Cleopatra]: "Her gentlewomen ... tended her i' the eyes,/ And made their bends adornings." *Ant & Cleo,* II, ii, 206–208.

a-doting, *adv.* in love: "Till Nature, as she wrought thee, fell a-doting ..." *Sonn 20,* 10.

Adsum, [Latin] I am here: "Adsum." / "Asnath!/ By the eternal God, whose name and power/ Thou tremblest at ..." *2 Hen 6,* I, iv, 23–24.

a-ducking, *v.* go a-ducking, to take to the water [like ducks]; also, perh., risk drowning: "Let the Egyptians/ And the Phoenicians go a-ducking ..." *Ant & Cleo,* III, vii, 63–64.

adulterate, *adj.* adulterous: "Ay, that incestuous, that adulterate beast ..." *Ham,* I, v, 42.

adulterate eyes, *n.* eyes that see only wickedness: "For why should others' false adulterate eyes/ Give salutation to my sportive blood?" *Sonn 121,* 5–6.

adultery, *n.* poss. misuse for "assault and battery": "... we/ shall see wilful adultery and murder committed." *Hen 5,* II, i, 36–37.

advance, *v.* **1** to promote; here, enhance by wearing and displaying: "... honour me so much/ As to advance this jewel; accept it and wear it,/ Kind my lord." *Timon,* I, ii, 165–167. **2** to raise or lift: "... like unback'd colts, they prick'd their ears,/

Advanc'd their eyelids . . ." *Temp,* IV, i, 176–177. **3** to display: "Advance our waving colours on the walls . . ." *1 Hen 6,* I, vi, 1.

advanced, *adj.* **1** raised; outstretched: ". . . how he jets under his advanced/ plumes!" *T Night,* II, v, 31–32. **2** (of a flag) displayed or flown: "These flags of France, that are advanced here . . ." *K John,* II, 1, 207.

advancement, *n.* **1** dignity; honor: ". . . his own disorders/ Deserv'd much less advancement." *Lear,* II, iv, 201–202. **2** opportunity to advance in rank: "Sir, I lack advancement." *Ham,* III, ii, 331.

advantage, *n.* **1** chance or opportunity: "For where there is advantage to be gone,/ Both more and less have given him the revolt . . ." *Mac,* V, iv, 11–12. **2** means of achieving: "Either to be restored to my blood,/ Or make mine ill th' advantage of my good." *1 Hen 6,* 128–129. **3** suitable occasion or time: "What there is else/ keep close, we'll read it at more advantage." *1 Hen 4,* II, iv, 534–535. **4** interest: "The money shall be paid back again with/ advantage." *1 Hen 4,* II, iv, 540–541. **5** [often pl.] pardonable exaggerations: "But he'll remember with advantages/ What feats he did that day." *Hen 5,* IV, iii, 50–51. **6** advances; here, inroads: "When I have seen the hungry ocean gain/ Advantage on the kingdom of the shore . . ." *Sonn 64,* 5–6. **7 in advantage lingering,** able to hold out because of an advantageous [military] position: "Drops bloody sweat from his war-wearied limbs,/ And, in advantage lingering, looks for rescue . . ." *1 Hen 6,* IV, iv, 18–19. **8 in the best advantage,** at your first opportunity: "And bring her after in the best advantage . . ." *Oth,* I, iii, 297. **9 to the advantage,** luck being with me: ". . . she let it drop by negligence,/ And, to the advantage, I being here took 't up . . ." *Oth,* III, iii, 315–316. **10 upon advantage,** seizing an opportunity: ". . . the best part of my power,/ As I upon advantage did remove . . ." *K John,* V, vii, 61–62.
—*v.* **11** to benefit; take advantage of: "Whose hours [the king's] the peasant best advantages." *Hen 5,* IV, i, 290.

advantageable, *adj.* suitable or profitable: "Augment, or alter, as your wisdoms best/ Shall see advantageable for our dignity . . ." *Hen 5,* V, ii, 87–88.

advenged, *past part.* var. of **avenged:** "Be bold in us . . . And be adveng'd on cursed Tamora." *T Andr,* V, i, 13–16.

adventure, *n.* **1** luck; chance: "I have by hard adventure found mine own." *As You,* II, iv, 42. **2** hazard; risk: "To try the fair adventure of to-morrow." *K John,* V, v, 22. **3** hazardous undertaking: ". . . if you fall in/ the adventure, our crows shall fare the better for you . . ." *Cymb,* III, i, 81–82. **4 at all adventures go,** take whatever comes along: "I'll say as they say, and persever so,/ And in this mist at all adventures go." *Errors,* II, ii, 215–216.
—*v.* **5** to dare; take a chance: "I am almost afraid to stand alone/ Here in the churchyard. Yet I will adventure." *Rom & Jul,* V, iii, 10–11. **6** to risk: ". . . by adventuring both,/ I oft found both . . ." *Merch,* I, i, 143–144.

adventurous, *adj.* bold; courageous: "And from her bosom took the enemy's point,/ Sheathing the steel in my advent'rous body." *T Andr,* V, iii, 111–112.

adversary, *n.* **1** enemy; enemy forces: ". . . some band of strangers i' th'/ adversary's entertainment." *All's W,* IV, i, 14–15. **2** misunderstood by Caius as "spokesman" or "promoter": "I will be thy adversary toward Anne/ Page. Said I well?"/ "By gar [God], 'tis good; vell said." *Wives,* II, iii, 87–89.

adverse, *adj.* **1** unfriendly; hostile: "It hath in solemn synods been decreed,/ . . . To admit no traffic to our adverse towns . . ." *Errors,* I, i, 13–15. **2** opposing or opposite: "The twentieth part/ Of those that live are men enow to quail/ The feeble handful on the adverse part." *Edw 3,* IV, vi, 48–50.

advertise, *v.* **1** to inform or advise; also, warn: "Please it your Grace to be advertised/ The Duke of York is newly come from Ireland . . ." *2 Hen 6,* IV, ix, 23–24. **2** to be attentive: "Advertising and holy to your business . . ." *Meas,* V, i, 381.

advertisement, *n.* **1** advice or admonition: "My griefs cry louder than advertisement." *M Ado,* V, i, 32. **2** information: "For this advertisement is five days old." *1 Hen 4,* III, ii, 172.

advice, *n.* **1** consideration; reflection or deliberation: "My Lord Bassanio upon more advice,/ Hath sent you here this ring . . ." *Merch,* IV, ii, 6–7. **2** spiritual guidance or solace: "He wants [needs] advice."/ "He will hear none." *Meas,* IV, ii, 144–145. **3 on his more advice,** after his thinking better of it: "It was excess of wine that set him on;/ And on his more advice we pardon him." *Hen 5,* II, ii, 42–43.

advise, *v.* **1** to consider or reconsider; also, as a warning, be advised: "Thursday is near. Lay hand on heart. Advise./ And you be mine, I'll give you to my friend . . ." *Rom & Jul,* III, v, 190–191. **2** to take heed; be careful: "Advise you what you say: the minister is here." *T Night,* IV, ii, 97. **3 advise yourself,** think; consider: ". . . have you nothing said . . . 'gainst the Duke of Albany?/ Advise yourself." *Lear,* II, i, 26–28.

advised, *adj.* **1** aware; mindful: "You were advis'd his flesh was capable/ Of wounds and scars . . ." *2 Hen 4,* I, i, 172–173. **2** deliberate: ". . . never by advised purpose meet/ To plot . . . any ill . . ." *Rich 2,* I, iii, 188–189. **3** careful; watchful or attentive: "I shot his fellow . . . The self-same way, with more advised watch/ To find the other forth . . ." *Merch,* I, i, 141–143.

4 agreed: "Are ye advis'd? the east/ side of the grove." *2 Hen 6,* II, i, 49–50. **5** well-advised; prudent: ". . . yet I am advis'd to do it,/ He says, to veil full purpose." *Meas,* IV, vi, 3–4. **6 advised age,** wise old age: "The silver livery of advised age . . ." *2 Hen 6,* V, ii, 47. **7 advised by aught,** persuaded by any inducement: "Or whether since he is advis'd by aught/ To change the course . . ." *Lear,* V, i, 2–3. **8 advised doom,** deliberate judgment: "When they had sworn to this advised doom,/ They did conclude to bear dead Lucrece thence . . ." *Luc,* 1849–1850. **9 advised respects,** prudent considerations; here, prob. differences of birth and circumstances: "Called to that audit by advised respects . . ." *Sonn 49,* 4. **10 well advised, a.** extremely cautious: ". . . there be well advis'd/ How you do leave me to mine own protection." *Merch,* V, i, 234–235. **b.** behaving rationally: "Were not you here, but even now, disguis'd? . . . And were you well advis'd?" *Love's L,* V, ii, 433–434.

advisedly, *adv.* **1** deliberately: "My soul upon the forfeit, that your lord/ Will never more break faith advisedly." *Merch,* V, i, 252–253. **2** thoughtfully; with the mind made up: "And to the flame thus speaks advisedly . . ." *Luc,* 180.

advocate, *n.* (in a court of justice) person who pleads the cause of another; here, Autolycus means a bribe: "What advocate hast thou to him? . . . Advocate's the court-word for a pheasant . . ." *W Tale,* IV, iv, 741–743.

advocation, *n.* pleading on behalf of another: "My advocation is not now in tune . . ." *Oth,* III, iv, 120.

Aeacides, *n.* another name of Ajax, after his grandfather Aeacus: ". . . for, sure, Aeacides/ Was Ajax, call'd so from his grandfather." *Shrew,* III, i, 50–51.

aedile, *n.* officer under the authority of the tribunes: "The aediles, ho! [Enter an Aedile.]" *Cor,* III, i, 171.

Aegles, *n.* nymph for whom Theseus was said to have abandoned Ariadne: "Didst not thou lead him through the glimmering night . . . And make him with fair Aegles break his faith . . ." *M N Dream,* II, i, 77–79.

Aeneas, *n.* **1** hero of Virgil's *Aeneid;* here, ref. to Aeneas' account to Dido of the destruction of Troy: ". . . wherefore dost thou urge the name of hands,/ To bid Aeneas tell the tale twice o'er . . ." *T Andr,* III, ii, 26–27. **2** used as an example of man's falseness, because of his betrayal of Dido: "True honest men, being heard like false Aeneas,/ Were in his time thought false . . ." *Cymb,* III, iv, 59–60.

Aeolus, *n.* god of the winds, who had imprisoned them in a cave: "Yet Aeolus would not be a murderer,/ But left that hateful office unto thee . . ." *2 Hen 6,* III, ii, 91–92.

aery, *n.* aerie, the lofty nest of an eagle; also, an eagle's brood: "And like an eagle o'er his aery towers . . ." *K John,* V, ii, 149.

Aesculapius, *n.* (in myth.) the god of healing; son of Apollo: "Come, come;/ And Aesculapius guide us!" *Per,* III, ii, 113–114.

Aeson, *n.* father of Jason, restored to youth by Medea's magic: "In such a night/ Medea gathered the enchanted herbs/ That did renew old Aeson." *Merch,* V, i, 12–14.

afar off, *adv.* indirectly; here, by association: "He who shall speak for her is afar off guilty/ But that he speaks." *W Tale,* II, i, 104–105.

afeard, *adj.* afraid: "But tell me, Hal, art not/ thou horrible afeard?" *1 Hen 4,* II, iv, 361–362.

affair, *n.* topic of conversation; subject or matter: ". . . start not so wildly from my affair." *Ham,* III, ii, 301.

affairs, *n. pl.* **1** business; errand: "What's your affairs, I pray you?" *Tr & Cr,* I, iii, 246. **2 take and give back affairs,** to conduct business: "She could not sway her house, command her followers,/ Take and give back affairs and their dispatch . . ." *T Night,* IV, iii, 17–18.

affect, *v.* **1** to desire or enjoy: ". . . he does neither affect company/ Nor is he fit for't, indeed." *Timon,* I, ii, 31–32. **2** to love; feel affection toward: "Dost thou affect her, Claudio?" *M Ado,* I, i, 276. **3** to react to; like: "How doth your Grace affect their motion?" *1 Hen 6,* V, i, 7. **4** to strive toward; aim at: "'Tis policy and stratagem must do/ That you affect . . ." *T Andr,* II, i, 104–105. **5** to choose: "I go from hence/ Thy soldier, servant, making peace or war,/ As thou affects." *Ant & Cleo,* I, iii, 69–71. **6** to resemble: "The accent of his tongue affecteth him." *K John,* I, i, 86. **7** to practice for their own sake: "Would seem in me t'affect speech and discourse . . ." *Meas,* I, i, 4. **8** to regard favorably: "Not to affect many proposed matches . . ." *Oth,* III, iii, 233.
—*n.* **9** [pl.] affections: "As 'twere to banish their affects with him." *Rich 2,* I, iv, 30. **10** [often pl.] natural inclination; passion: "For every man with his affects is born . . ." *Love's L,* I, i, 150.

affected, *adj.* **1** in love: ". . . that which we lovers entitle affected." *Love's L,* II, i, 231. **2** regarded with affection; loved: ". . . to intrude where I am grac'd/ And may, for aught thou knowest, affected be." *T Andr,* II, i, 27–28. **3** disposed; inclined: "I am in all affected as yourself . . ." *Shrew,* I, i, 26. **4 ill affected,** badly disposed; disloyal: "No marvel then though he were ill affected . . ." *Lear,* II, i, 98.

affectedly, *adv.* lovingly: "With sleided silk feat and affect-edly/ Enswath'd, and seal'd to curious secrecy." *Lover's Comp,* 48–49.

affecting, *adj.* affected; fanciful: "The pox of such antic lisp-ing affecting phantasimes . . ." *Rom & Jul,* II, iv, 28.

affection, *n.* **1** desire; wish; natural inclination: "I weigh my friend's affection with mine own . . ." *Timon,* I, ii, 214. **2** disposition: ". . . there grows/ In my most ill-compos'd af-fection such/ A staunchless avarice . . ." *Mac,* IV, iii, 76–78. **3** instinctive feelings: ". . . affection/ (Master of passion) sways it to the mood/ Of what it likes or loathes . . ." *Merch,* IV, i, 50–52. **4** [usually pl.] emotions; passions: "And great affec-tions wrastling in thy bosom . . ." *K John,* V, ii, 41. **5** [often pl.] wild or debauched actions; lusts: "My father is gone wild into his grave,/ For in his tomb lie my affections . . ." *2 Hen 4,* V, ii, 123–124. **6** affectation: ". . . your reasons at dinner/ have been . . . witty without affection . . ." *Love's L,* V, i, 2–4.
—*v.* **7** to love; show affection for: "But can you affection the 'oman [woman]?" *Wives,* I, i, 208.

affectioned, *adj.* affected: ". . . an affectioned/ ass, that cons state without book, and utters it/ by great swarths . . ." *T Night,* II, iii, 147–149.

affeered, *adj.* confirmed; accepted or recognized: ". . . wear thou thy wrongs;/ The title is affeer'd!" *Mac,* IV, iii, 33–34.

affiance, *n.* trust or confidence: "Ah! what's more dangerous than this fond [foolish] affiance?" *2 Hen 6,* III, i, 74.

affianced, *adj.* betrothed: ". . . and truth in virtue,/ I am affianc'd this man's wife . . ." *Meas,* V, i, 225–226.

affied, *past part.* of **affy;** betrothed: "Where then do you know best/ We be affied . . ." *Shrew,* IV, iv, 48–49.

affined, *adj.* **1** bound by duty: ". . . be judge yourself,/ Wheth-er I . . . am affin'd/ To love the Moor." *Oth,* I, i, 38–40. **2** re-lated; joined together by a common cause: "The hard and soft, seem all affin'd and kin . . ." *Tr & Cr,* I, iii, 25.

affinity, *n.* **of great affinity,** having impressive family connec-tions: ". . . he you hurt is of great fame in Cyprus,/ And great affinity . . ." *Oth,* III, i, 46–47.

affliction, *n.* terror; horror: ". . . man's nature cannot carry/ Th' affliction nor the fear." *Lear,* III, ii, 48–49.

afford, *v.* **1** to give or offer: "What charitable men afford to beggars." *Timon,* III, ii, 77. **2** to achieve or accomplish: "Love, give me strength, and strength shall help afford." *Rom & Jul,* IV, i, 125. **3** to excuse or exonerate (someone): "We cannot af-ford you so [we can't let you off so easily]." *All's W,* IV, i, 48.

affray, *v.* to frighten: "O, now I would they had chang'd voices too,/ Since arm from arm that voice doth us affray . . ." *Rom & Jul,* III, v, 32–33.

affright, *v.* to terrify: "The one affrights you,/ The other makes you proud." *Cor,* I, i, 168–169.

affront, *v.* **1** to accost; encounter: "That he, as 'twere by ac-cident, may here/ Affront Ophelia." *Ham,* III, i, 30–31. **2** to confront; also, balance: "That my integrity . . . Might be af-fronted with the match and weight/ Of such a winnow'd pu-rity in love . . ." *Tr & Cr,* III, ii, 163–165.
—*n.* **3 gave the affront,** made the assault: "There was a fourth man . . . That gave th' affront with them." *Cymb,* V, iii, 86–87.

affy, *v.* **1** to trust: "Marcus Andronicus, so I do affy/ In thy uprightness and integrity . . ." *T Andr,* I, 1, 47–48. **2** to be-troth: "For daring to affy a mighty lord/ Unto the daughter of a worthless king . . ." *2 Hen 6,* IV, i, 79–80.

a-field or **afield,** *adv.* **1** in the pasture: ". . . when thou didst keep my lambs a-field,/ I wish some ravenous wolf had eaten thee." *1 Hen 6,* V, iv, 30–31. **2** on the battlefield: "Aeneas is afield,/ And I do stand engag'd to many Greeks . . ." *Tr & Cr,* V, iii, 67–68.

afoot, *adv.* **1** on foot: "How now, my noble lord! what! all afoot?" *2 Hen 6,* V, ii, 8. **2** in action: ". . . and, squire-like, pension beg/ To keep base life afoot [sustained]." *Lear,* II, iv, 216–217. **3** on the march: "Of Albany's and Cornwall's powers you heard not?"/ "'Tis so, they are afoot." *Lear,* IV, iii, 49–50. **4** **well afoot,** up and about; here, in good health: ". . . were our witty empress well afoot,/ She would applaud Andronicus' conceit . . ." *T Andr,* IV, ii, 29–30.

afore me, *interj.* upon my word; indeed [lit., "Before God," a mild oath]: "Afore me, it is so very late that we/ May call it early by and by. Good night." *Rom & Jul,* III, iv, 34–35.

Afric, *n.* **1** Africa, esp. the continent S of the Mediterranean coastal cities: "Methinks our garments are now as fresh as when/ we put them on first in Afric . . ." *Temp,* II, i, 66–67. **2** some vast desert: "I would they were in Afric both togeth-er . . ." *Cymb,* I, ii, 98.
—*adj.* **3** African: "And it were better parch in Afric sun . . ." *Tr & Cr,* I, iii, 370.

Africa, *n.* land thought to have incredible wealth: "I speak of Africa and golden joys." *2 Hen 4,* V, iii, 97.

afront, *adv.* abreast: "These four came all afront, and mainly thrust at/ me . . ." *1 Hen 4,* II, iv, 196–197.

after[1], *prep.* **1** according to: "What man/ didst thou ever know unthrift that was beloved after/ his means?" *Timon,* IV, iii, 311–313. **2** at; at the rate of: "I'll rent the fairest house in it/ after three pence a bay." *Meas,* II, i, 238–239. **3** for: ". . . my servant Travers whom I sent/ On Tuesday last to listen after news." *2 Hen 4* I, i, 28–29.

after[2], *adv.* **1** afterward: "I should knock you first,/ And then I know after who comes by the worst." *Shrew,* I, ii, 13–14.
—*adj.* **2** reserve or standby; also, following behind: "The Ottomites . . . Have there injointed with an after fleet—" *Oth,* I, iii, 33–35.

after-eye, *v.* to follow with one's eyes: "Thou shouldst have made him/ As little as a crow, or less, ere left/ To after-eye him." *Cymb,* I, iv, 14–16.

after-inquiry, *n.* Final Judgment: ". . . jump [risk] the after-inquiry on your own/ peril . . ." *Cymb,* V, iv, 184–185.

after-loss, *n.* later loss or grief: "And do not drop in for an after-loss." *Sonn 90,* 4.

after-meeting, *n.* later or subsequent meeting: "As the main point of this our after-meeting . . ." *Cor,* II, ii, 39.

after-supper, *n.* dessert course: "Come to me, Tyrrel, soon at after-supper . . ." *Rich 3,* IV, iii, 31.

against, *prep.* **1** by or beside: "Against the Capitol I met a lion,/ Who glaz'd upon me, and went surly by . . ." *J Caes,* I, iii, 20–21. **2** in anticipation of; in preparation for: "They'll talk of state, for everyone doth so/ Against a change . . ." *Rich 2,* III, iv, 27–28. **3** in time for: "I was promised them against the feast . . ." *W Tale,* IV, iv, 237. **4** anticipating the time when: "Against my love shall be, as I am now . . ." *Sonn 63,* 1. **5** despite the contrary declaration of: "I do believe it/ Against an oracle." *Temp,* IV, i, 11–12. **6** competing with: "An Antony were nature's piece [masterpiece], 'gainst fancy . . ." *Ant & Cleo,* V, ii, 99. **7** opposite; here, "aimed at": "To intercept this inconvenience,/ A piece of ordnance 'gainst it I have plac'd . . ." *1 Hen 6,* I, iv, 14–15. **8** before; in front of: "Mine enemy's dog . . . should have stood that night/ Against my fire." *Lear,* IV, vii, 36–38. **9** defying: ". . . set up the bloody flag against all patience . . ." *Cor,* II, i, 75. **10 against rain,** when rain threatens: ". . . more clamorous than a parrot against/ rain . . ." *As You,* IV, i, 143–144.

Agamemnon, *n.* leader of Greek forces in the Trojan War: "Thou art as valorous as Hector of Troy,/ worth five of Agamemnon . . ." *2 Hen 4,* II, iv, 216–217.

agate, *n.* **1** ring of agate, usually with an incised design: "His heart, like an agate, with your print impress'd . . ." *Love's L,*

II, i, 235. **2** dwarf: ". . . manned with [served by] an agate." *2 Hen 4,* I, ii, 19. **3** figure, often in the shape of a dwarf, cut in agate for a seal ring: "If low, an agate very vilely cut . . ." *M Ado,* III, i, 65.

agazed, *adj.* **agazed on,** astonished at: "All the whole army stood agaz'd on him." *1 Hen 6,* I, i, 126.

age, *n.* **1** seniority: ". . . let my father's honours live in me,/ Nor wrong mine age with this indignity." *T Andr,* I, i, 7–8. **2** life; lifetime: "My age was never tainted with such shame." *1 Hen 6,* IV, v, 46. **3 age is in,** Dogberry's confusion of "age" with "ale" in a popular saying: ". . . as they/ say, 'When the age [ale] is in, the wit is out' . . ." *M Ado,* III, v, 32–33. **4 age is unnecessary,** old people are useless: "Age is unnecessary: on my knees I beg/ That you'll vouchsafe me raiment, bed, and food." *Lear,* II, iv, 156–157. **5 in our ages,** in our lifetimes: ". . . we shall hardly in our ages see/ Their banners wave again." *Cor,* III, i, 7–8.

aged, *adj.* **1** brought on by age: "Aged contusions and all brush of time . . ." *2 Hen 6,* V, iii, 3. **2** experienced: ". . . An ag'd interpreter, though young in days." *Timon,* V, iii, 8. **3** settled or constant: ". . . as dangerous to be aged in/ any kind of course as it is virtuous to be constant . . ." *Meas,* III, ii, 218–219. **4 oppression of aged tyranny,** being oppressed by a tyrannical old father: ". . . an idle and fond bondage in the oppression of aged/ tyranny . . ." *Lear,* I, ii, 50–51.

Agenor, *n.* King of Sidon; his daughter Europa was wooed by Zeus, who assumed the form of a bull to carry her off: "O yes, I saw sweet beauty in her face,/ Such as the daughter of Agenor had . . ." *Shrew,* I, i, 167–168.

agent, *n.* **1** doer: ". . . derive a liberty/ From heartiness . . . And well become the agent . . ." *W Tale,* I, ii, 112–114. **2** [pl.] senses; also, organs: ". . . when his glutton eye so full hath fed,/ His other agents aim at like delight?" *Ven & Ad,* 399–400.

aggravate, *v.* **1** to emphasize: "Once more, the more to aggravate the note,/ With a foul traitor's name stuff I thy throat . . ." *Rich 2,* I, i, 43–44. **2** prob. misuse for "abate": "I beseek you now, aggravate your choler." *2 Hen 4,* II, iv, 159. **3** prob. misuse for "moderate" or "modulate" but perh. also with subconscious sense of "add weight to": "But I will aggravate my voice/ so, that I will roar you as gently as any suck-ing/ dove . . ." *M N Dream,* I, ii, 76–77. **4 aggravate his style,** to expand his achievements [to include cuckold]: ". . . I will aggravate his style; thou, Master Brook,/ shalt know him for knave and cuckold." *Wives,* II, ii, 273–274. **5 aggravate thy store,** increase your strength [or resources]: ". . . live thou upon thy servant's loss,/ And let that pine to aggravate thy store . . ." *Sonn 146,* 9–10.

aggriefed, *adj.* Fluellen's pron. of "aggrieved": ". . . the man that has but two legs that shall/ find himself aggriefed at this glove . . ." *Hen 5,* IV, vii, 166–167.

Agincourt, *n.* town near the N coast of France; site of English victory over French 1415: "Where, O for pity! we shall much disgrace . . . The name of Agincourt." *Hen 5,* IV, Chor., 49–52.

agitation, *n.* **1** physical movement or activity: "In this slumbery agitation, besides her walking and/ other actual performances . . ." *Mac,* V, i, 11–12. **2** misuse for "cogitation": "I was always plain with you, and so now/ I speak my agitation of the matter . . ." *Merch,* III, v, 3–4.

aglet-baby, *n.* poss. a doll or a prostitute bedecked with spangles: ". . . marry him to a/ puppet or an aglet-baby, or an old trot . . ." *Shrew,* I, ii, 77–78.

agnize, *v.* to acknowledge: "I do agnize/ A natural and prompt alacrity . . ." *Oth,* I, iii, 231–232.

agone, *adv.* ago: "For long agone I have forgot to court . . ." *Two Gent,* III, i, 85.

agood, *adv.* aplenty: "And at that time I made her weep agood . . ." *Two Gent,* IV, iv, 163.

agreement, *n.* **upon agreement from us,** when we agree to his terms: "Upon agreement from us to his liking,/ Will undertake to woo . . ." *Shrew,* I, ii, 181–182.

ague, *n.* severe fever, esp. malarial: "A lunatic lean-witted fool,/ Presuming on an ague's privilege . . ." *Rich 2,* II, i, 115–116.

agued, *adj.* trembling, as if with malaria: ". . . and faces pale/ With flight and agued fear!" *Cor,* I, iv, 37–38.

ague's fit, *n.* attack of chills and high fever: "And he will look as hollow as a ghost,/ As dim and meagre as an ague's fit . . ." *K John,* III, iii, 84–85.

a-height, *adv.* on high: "Look up a-height; the shrill-gorg'd lark so far/ Cannot be seen or heard . . ." *Lear,* IV, vi, 58–59.

a-high, *adv.* aloft: "One heav'd a-high, to be hurl'd down below . . ." *Rich 3,* IV, iv, 86.

a-hold, *adv.* same as "a-hull," nautical term for "stopped in the water": "Lay her a-hold, a-hold! set her two courses [sails] . . ." *Temp,* I, i, 49.

a-hungry, *adj.* very hungry [emphatic form]: "I am not a-hungry, I thank you, forsooth." *Wives,* I, i, 247.

aid, *n.* **upon his aid,** on his [Macduff's] behalf: "Thither Macduff/ Is gone to pray the holy King, upon his aid/ To wake Northumberland . . ." *Mac,* III, vi, 29–31.

aidance, *n.* aid or support: "Attracts the same for aidance 'gainst the enemy . . ." *2 Hen 6,* III, ii, 164.

aidant, *adj.* helpful: ". . . be aidant and remediate/ In the good man's distress!" *Lear,* IV, iv, 17–18.

aim, *n.* **1** target; here, a mark or butt for blows: "Thou wouldst have chang'd thy office for an aim, or thy name for an ass." *Errors,* III, i, 47. **2** point at which something is aimed: ". . . when the cross blue lightning seem'd to open/ The breast of heaven, I did present myself/ Even in the aim and very flash of it." *J Caes,* I, 3, 50–52. **3** guess; conjecture: "What you would work me to, I have some aim . . ." *J Caes,* I, ii, 161. **4 cry aim,** applaud or shout their approval: ". . . and to these violent proceedings all/ my neighbours shall cry aim." *Wives,* III, ii, 39–40. **5 gave aim to,** was the object of: "Behold her that gave aim to all thy oaths . . ." *Two Gent,* V, iv, 100. **6 give me aim,** bear with me: "But, gentle people, give me aim awhile,/ For nature puts me to a heavy task." *T Andr,* V, iii, 149–150.
—*v.* **7** to guess: "They aim at it,/ And botch the words up fit to their own thoughts . . ." *Ham,* IV, v, 9–10. **8 aim at,** to intend; mean: "My mind will never grant what I perceive/ Your Highness aims at, if I aim [guess] aright." *3 Hen 6,* III, ii, 67–68. **9 aim reports,** make reports based on conjectures: "As in these cases, where they aim reports . . ." *Oth,* I, iii, 6.

aimed, *adj.* guessed; understood: "Well aim'd of [for] such a young one." *Shrew,* II, i, 231.

Aio te, Aeacida, [Latin] the ambiguous message Pyrrhus received from the oracle when he asked about conquering Rome: "*Aio te, Aeacida,/ Romanos vincere posse* [I say that you, the son of Aeacus, the Romans can vanquish]." *2 Hen 6,* I, iv, 60–61.

air¹, *n.* **1** air as representing insubstantiality; vapor: "If I should speak,/ She would mock me into air . . ." *M Ado,* III, i, 74–75. **2 air on't,** look of it: "I have belied a lady . . . and the air on't/ Revengingly enfeebles me . . ." *Cymb,* V, ii, 2–4. **3 out o' the air,** away from the fresh air [considered harmful to wounds]: "O, bear him out o' the air." *Oth,* V, i, 103. **4 take air,** become known [lit., become exposed to the air]: "Nay, pursue him now, lest the device take air,/ and taint [spoil]." *T Night,* III, iv, 132–133.

air², *n.* tune: ". . . your tongue's sweet air/ More tuneable than lark to shepherd's ear . . ." *M N Dream,* I, i, 183–184.

air-braving, *adj.* heaven-defying; lofty: "Shall lay your stately and air-braving towers,/ If you forsake the offer of their love." *1 Hen 6,* IV, ii, 13–14.

air-drawn, *adj.* moving through the air; also, imaginary: "This is the air-drawn dagger, which, you said,/ Led you to Duncan." *Mac,* III, iv, 61–62.

Aire, *n.* **Joan of Aire,** another name for Joan of Arc, prob. misreading of "Jone Are" in Holinshed; in cast of characters called "Joan la Pucelle": "I muse we met not with the Dauphin's Grace,/ His new-come champion, virtuous Joan of Aire . . ." *1 Hen 6,* II, ii, 19–20.

aired, *past part.* **be aired abroad,** live abroad; breathe foreign air: ". . . though I/ have . . . been aired abroad, I desire/ to lay my bones there." *W Tale,* IV, ii, 4–6.

airy, *adj.* insignificant; trifling: "Three civil brawls bred of an airy word . . ." *Rom & Jul,* I, i, 87.

airy devil, *n.* (in demonology) the devil responsible for thunderstorms: "Some airy devil hovers in the sky,/ And pours [is about to pour] down mischief." *K John,* III, ii, 2–3.

Ajax, *n.* **1** Greek hero of the Trojan War, maddened when he was not awarded the armor of the slain Achilles. He slew a flock of sheep, thinking them the enemy: "By the Lord,/ this love is as mad as Ajax: it kills sheep, it kills me . . ." *Love's L,* IV, iii, 5–6. **2** pun on "jakes," privy: ". . . your lion, that holds his poll-axe sitting on a close-stool, will be given to Ajax . . ." *Love's L,* V, ii, 571–572. **3 Ajax is their fool,** Ajax is regarded as a fool [by such knaves]: "None of these rogues and cowards/ But Ajax is their fool." *Lear,* II, ii, 125–126.

Ajax Telamonius, *n.* hero of the Trojan War [above], here identified as the son of Telamon: "And now, like Ajax Telamonius,/ On sheep or oxen could I spend my fury." *2 Hen 6,* V, i, 26–27.

alablaster, *v.* var. of *alabaster*: "Why should a man whose blood is warm within,/ Sit like his grandsire, cut in alablaster?" *Merch,* I, i, 83–84.

alack, *interj.* an exclamation of despair: "Alack, my fellows, what should I say to you?" *Timon,* IV, i, 3.

alarm, *n.* disturbance, esp. a call to arms; here, a trial by combat: "Marshal, command our officers-at-arms/ Be ready to direct these home alarms." *Rich 2,* I, i, 204–205.

alarum, *n.* [pron. as three syll.] **1** call to arms, usually sounded by trumpet and often with drum: "Sound, sound alarum; we will rush on them." *1 Hen 6,* I, ii, 18.

—*v.* **2** to summon to action or combat: ". . . and wither'd Murther,/ Alarum'd by his sentinel, the wolf,/ Whose howl's his watch [watchword] . . . Moves like a ghost." *Mac,* II, i, 53–56.

alarums and excursions, stage direction for a call to arms, warning of an imminent attack, followed by the movement of troops across the stage: "Alarums. Excursions. Enter Queen Margaret, the Prince, and Exeter." [SD] *3 Hen 6,* II, v, 125.

Albion, *n.* Latin name for England: "And this the royalty of Albion's king?" *2 Hen 6,* I, iii, 45.

Alcides, *n.* **1** earlier name of Hercules, meaning "grandson of Alcaeus": ". . . not Enceladus . . . Nor great Alcides . . . Shall seize this prey out of his father's hands." *T Andr,* IV, ii, 93–96. **2 Alcides' shoes upon an ass,** ref. to Hercules wearing the skin of the Nemean lion he had slain; also, to the fable of the ass clothed in a lion's skin: "It lies as sightly on the back of him/ As great Alcides' shoes upon an ass . . ." *K John,* II, i, 143–144. **3 Alcides' twelve,** ref. to the 12 labors of Hercules: "Yea, leave that labour to great Hercules,/ And let it be more than Alcides' twelve." *Shrew,* I, ii, 255–256.

alderliefest, *adj.* dearest [an obsolescent form]: "With you mine alderliefest sovereign,/ Makes me the bolder to salute my king . . ." *2 Hen 6,* I, 1, 28–29.

ale, *n.* **1** alehouse; also, church festival at which ale was featured, hence the "Jew" and "Christian" jibes: ". . . thou hast not so much charity in thee as to/ go to the ale with a Christian." *Two Gent,* II, v, 49–50. **2 in his ales,** intoxicated: ". . . did, in his ales . . . kill his best/ friend, Cleitus." *Hen 5,* IV, vii, 39–41.

Alecto, *n.* one of the Furies, believed to have hair filled with writhing snakes: "Rouse up Revenge from ebon den with fell Alecto's/ snake . . ." *2 Hen 4,* V, v, 37–38.

alehouse guest, *n.* contrast between nobility of Richard (a "beauteous inn") and vulgarity of Bolingbroke and his victory: "Why should hard-favour'd grief be lodg'd in thee,/ When triumph is become an alehouse guest?" *Rich 2,* V, i, 14–15.

alehouse painted signs, crude semblances of real men: ". . . ye sanguine, shallow-hearted boys!/ Ye white-lim'd walls! ye alehouse painted signs!" *T Andr,* IV, ii, 97–98.

aleven, *adj.* var. of **eleven:** ". . . aleven widows and nine maids is a/ simple coming-in for one man . . ." *Merch,* II, ii, 154–155.

ale-wife, *n.* woman who keeps an alehouse: "Ask Marian Hacket, the fat/ ale-wife of Wincot . . ." *Shrew,* Ind., ii, 21–22.

Alexander, *n.* Alexander the Great, king of Macedon [d. 323 B.C.]: "He presents Hector of Troy; the swain, Pompey the/ Great; the parish curate, Alexander . . ." *Love's L,* V, ii, 529–530.

Alexandrian feast, *n.* type of riotous feast with which Cleopatra had entertained Antony: "This is not yet an Alexandrian feast." *Ant & Cleo,* II, vii, 95.

alight, *v.* to get off or leave (the victim): "Bid her alight,/ And her troth plight . . ." *Lear,* III, iv, 125–126.

alive, *adj.* **1** of immediate concern: "Well, to our work alive. What do you think/ Of marching to Philippi presently?" *J Caes,* IV, iii, 195–196. **2** being in existence; available: ". . . the bricks are alive at this day to testify . . ." *2 Hen 6,* IV, ii, 142.

all, *adj.* **1** any; any kind of: "Things without all remedy/ Should be without regard . . ." *Mac,* III, ii, 11–12.
—*adv.* **2** merely; just: ". . . my desire . . . did spur me forth:/ And not all love to see you . . ." *T Night,* III, iii, 4–6. **3** completely; altogether: ". . . choose/ Mine heir from forth the beggars of the world,/ And dispossess her all." *Timon,* I, i, 140–142. **4** at the same time; together: "'Tis wonder that thy life and wits at once/ Had not concluded all." *Lear,* IV, vii, 41–42. **5** only; nothing but: "The Jew shall have all justice . . ." *Merch,* IV, i, 316. **6 all along,** at full length; stretched flat: "Under yond yew trees lay thee all along/ Holding thy ear close to the hollow ground . . ." *Rom & Jul,* V, iii, 3–4. **7 all so,** just as: "But all so soon as the all-cheering sun/ Should . . . begin to draw/ The shady curtains from Aurora's bed . . ." *Rom & Jul,* I, i, 132–134.
—*pron.* **8** everything that has been said: ". . . every word by all my wit being scann'd,/ Wants wit in all one word to understand." *Errors,* II, ii, 150–151. **9 all away,** deprived of food: "Thus do I pine and surfeit day by day,/ Or [either] gluttoning on all, or all away." *Sonn 75,* 13–14. **10 all of all,** sum of [it] all: "The very all/ of all is . . . that/ the king would have me present the princess . . . with some . . . show . . ." *Love's L,* V, i, 100–103. **11 for all,** once and for all: "This is for all./ I would not, in plain terms, from this time forth . . ." *Ham,* I, iii, 131–132. **12 of all,** in particular: "Last night of all,/ When yond same star that's westward from the pole . . ." *Ham,* I, i, 38–39.

Alla nostra casa ben venuto . . . , [Italian] Welcome to our house [much-honored Signor Petruchio]. *Shrew,* I, ii, 25–26.

Alla stoccata, *n.* [Italian] a thrust in fencing: "O calm, dishonourable, vile submission:/ Alla stoccata carries it away!" *Rom & Jul,* III, i, 72–73.

allay, *v.* **1** to dilute; weaken: "I do not like 'But yet,' it does allay/ The good precedence . . ." *Ant & Cleo,* II, v, 50–51. **2** to moderate: "If with the sap of reason you would quench,/ Or but allay the fire of passion." *Hen 8,* I, i, 148–149.
—*n.* **3** means of lessening; here, ref. to Leontes' grief: ". . . to whose feeling sorrows I/ might be some allay . . ." *W Tale,* IV, ii, 7–8.

allaying, *adj.* that dilutes or weakens; here, with water: ". . . one/ that loves a cup of hot wine, with not a drop of/ allaying Tiber in't . . ." *Cor,* II, i, 46–48.

allayment, *n.* that which lessens or alleviates: "The like allayment could I give my grief." *Tr & Cr,* IV, iv, 8.

allegiant, *adj.* loyal: "For your great graces . . . I/ Can nothing render but allegiant thanks . . ." *Hen 8,* III, ii, 174–176.

All-hallond Eve, *n.* All Hallow Even; Halloween: ". . . was't not at Hallowmas,/ Master Froth?"/ "All-hallond Eve." *Meas,* II, i, 123–125.

All-hallowmas, *n.* All Saints' Day, Nov. 1st: ". . . did you not lend it to Alice/ Shortcake upon All-hallowmas last . . ." *Wives,* I, i, 184–185.

All-hallown summer, *n.* Indian summer; here, in fig. use, the summer of old age: "Farewell, All-hallown summer!" *1 Hen 4,* I, ii, 154–155.

all hid, ref. to the children's game of hide-and-seek: "All hid, all hid; an old infant play." *Love's L,* IV, iii, 75.

allicholy, *n.* Quickly's blunder for "melancholy": ". . . but, indeed, she is given too much to allicholy and/ musing; but for you—well—go to." *Wives,* I, iv, 147–148.

allied, *adj.* **well allied,** of a good family; here, found or known in the best families: "Yes, in good sooth, the vice is of a great kindred;/ it is well allied . . ." *Meas,* III, ii, 97–98.

alligant, *adj.* prob. Quickly's mispron. of "elegant": ". . . in silk and gold, and in such alligant/ terms . . ." *Wives,* II, ii, 64–65.

all is one, no matter; it's of no consequence: "Are you so hasty now? Well, all is one." *M Ado,* V, i, 49.

all-licensed, *adj.* permitted to say or do anything: "Not only, Sir, this your all-licens'd Fool,/ But other of your insolent retinue . . ." *Lear,* I, iv, 209–210.

all-oblivious enmity, *n.* oblivion that is destructive to everything: "'Gainst death and all-oblivious enmity/ Shall you pace forth . . ." *Sonn 55,* 9–10.

all one, [there's] no difference; no matter: "As much as an apple doth an oyster, and/ all one." *Shrew,* IV, ii, 101–102.

Allons! [French] Come on! Let's go!: "*Allons! allons!* Sow'd cockle reap'd no corn . . ." *Love's L,* IV, iii, 379.

allot, *v.* to destine: "Thou art allotted to be ta'en by me." *1 Hen 6,* V, iii, 55.

allottery, *n.* share or portion, as by inheritance: ". . . give me the poor allottery my father left me . . ." *As You,* I, i, 73.

allow, *v.* **1** to accept; acknowledge: "To Bolingbroke are we sworn subjects now,/ Whose state and honour I for aye allow." *Rich 2,* V, ii, 39–40. **2** to approve (of): ". . . if your sweet sway/ Allow obedience . . . Make it your cause . . ." *Lear,* II, iv, 192–193. **3** to invest or endow: ". . . thou shalt be met with thanks,/ Allowed with absolute power . . ." *Timon,* V, i, 160–161. **4** to cause to be acknowledged as; prove: "That will allow me very worth his service." *T Night,* I, ii, 59. **5 allow not,** not to allow: "Allow not nature more than nature needs,/ Man's life is cheap as beast's." *Lear,* II, iv, 268–269.

allowance, *n.* **1** acknowledgment; admission: ". . . the censure of the which one must in your/ allowance o'erweigh a whole theatre of others." *Ham,* III, ii, 27–28. **2** approval or permission: "That you protect this course, and put it on/ By your allowance . . ." *Lear,* I, iv, 216–217. **3 and your allowance,** and [if] it is done with your approval: "If this be known to you, and your allowance,/ We then have done you bold and saucy wrongs." *Oth,* I, i, 127–128. **4 of expert and approved allowance,** of generally acknowledged and proven skill: ". . . his pilot/ Of very expert and approv'd allowance . . ." *Oth,* II, i, 48–49. **5 of no allowance,** that would never be acknowledged [by]: "Of no allowance to your bosom's truth." *Cor,* III, ii, 57.

allowed, *adj.* approved; licensed or given permission: "There is no slander in an allowed fool,/ though he do nothing but rail . . ." *T Night,* I, v, 93–94.

allowed for, *adj.* approved as: "For this damsel, I must keep her at the park; she is/ allowed for the day-woman." *Love's L,* I, ii, 122–123.

all-thing, *adv.* entirely; wholly: "It had been as a gap in our great feast,/ And all-thing unbecoming." *Mac,* III, i, 12–13.

allured, *adj.* tempted: ". . . make desire vomit emptiness,/ Not so allur'd to feed." *Cymb,* I, vii, 45–46.

ally, *n.* relative; kinsman: "This gentleman, the Prince's near ally . . . hath got this mortal hurt . . ." *Rom & Jul,* III, i, 111–112.

allycholy, *adj.* misuse for **melancholy:** ". . . methinks you're allycholy. I/ pray you, why is it?" *Two Gent,* IV, ii, 26–27.

Almain, *n.* German: ". . . he drinks you with facility your Dane dead/ drunk; he sweats not to overthrow your Almain . . ." *Oth,* II, iii, 76–77.

almanac, *n.* book containing a calendar, anniversaries, forecasts, church feasts, etc.: "Here comes the almanac of my true date [record of my exact birthday]." *Errors,* I, ii, 41.

almost, *adv.* **1 almost in,** in most of: "Together with all famous colleges/ Almost in Christendom . . ." *Hen 8,* III, ii, 66–67. **2 cannot . . . almost,** can hardly: "You cannot reason [talk] almost with a man . . ." *Rich 3,* II, iii, 39. **3 not almost,** scarcely; hardly more than: "And yet his trespass . . . is not almost a fault/ To incur a private check [reprimand] . . ." *Oth,* III, iii, 65–68.

alms, *n.* good deed: "And he should, it were an alms to hang him." *M Ado,* II, iii, 155.

alms-basket, *n.* basket of table scraps given to the poor: "O, they have lived long on the alms-basket of words." *Love's L,* V, i, 37.

alms-deed, *n.* charitable act: ". . . murder is thy alms-deed;/ Petitioners for blood thou ne'er put'st back." *3 Hen 6,* V, v, 77–78.

alms-drink, *n.* leavings in a drinking cup, intended for servants or beggars: "They have made him drink alms-drink." *Ant & Cleo,* II, vii, 5.

aloes, *n. pl.* bitter experiences: "The aloes of all forces, shocks, and fears." *Lover's Comp,* 273.

aloft, *adv.* on the upper stage: "Enter the Tribunes and Senators aloft . . ." [SD] *T Andr,* I, i, 1.

alone, *adj.* **1 come alone.** See **come** (def. 20). **2 let me alone,** trust me; leave it to me: "Go thou to Juliet, help to deck up her./ I'll not to bed tonight, let me alone." *Rom & Jul,* IV, ii, 41–42.

along, *adv.* **1** prostrate; stretched out, esp. on the ground: "When he lies along . . . his tale pronounc'd shall bury/ His reasons with his body." *Cor,* V, vi, 57–59. —*v.* **2** to go along: "Regard thy danger, and along with me." *Two Gent,* III, i, 256.

aloof, *adv.* **stand aloof,** to stay at a distance: "Give me thy torch, boy. Hence and stand aloof." *Rom & Jul,* V, iii, 1.

alow, alow, loo, loo, *poss.* refrain of song or nonsense syllables with nursery rhyme: "Pillicock sat on Pillicock hill:/ Alow, alow, loo, loo!" *Lear,* III, iv, 76–77.

alter, *v.* **1** to grow weaker: "Heard he the good news yet?"/ "He alter'd much upon the hearing it." *2 Hen 4,* IV, v, 11–12. **2** to change adversely: "Whose fresh complexion and whose heart together/ Affliction alters." *W Tale,* IV, iv, 575–576. **3 be altered,** change his mind: "Provost, my brother Angelo will not be altered;/ Claudio must die tomorrow." *Meas,* III, ii, 201.

alteration, *n.* changeableness; vacillation: ". . . he's full of alteration/ And self-reproving . . ." *Lear,* V, i, 3–4.

altering rheums, *n.* debilitating diseases: ". . . is he not stupid/ With age and alt'ring rheums?" *W Tale,* IV, iv, 399–400.

Althaea, *n.* (in Greek myth.) mother of Meleager; at his birth the Fates decreed his life would end with a firebrand they had placed in the fire; Althaea snatched it from the fire and quenched it, but years later, in a fit of anger over his killing of her brothers, she hurled the brand back into the fire and caused his death: ". . . the fatal brand Althaea burnt/ Unto the prince's heart of Calydon." *2 Hen 6,* I, 1, 235–236.

Althaea's dream, *n.* confusion with Hecuba, who dreamed that she had given birth to a firebrand: "Away, you rascally Althaea's dream, away!" *2 Hen 4,* II, ii, 83.

altitude, *n.* the same degree [as]: ". . . to be partly proud, which/ he is, even to the altitude of his virtue." *Cor,* I, i, 38–39.

altogether's acquaintance, *n.* See **acquaintance** (def. 2).

Amaimon, *n.* a devil: "Terms! Names! Amaimon/ sounds well . . ." *Wives,* II, ii, 285–286.

amain, *adv.* **1** at full speed: "Two ships from far, making [proceeding] amain to us . . ." *Errors,* I, i, 92. **2** in force; here, in full voice: "'A Talbot! a Talbot!' cried out amain . . ." *1 Hen 6,* I, i, 128. **3 make amain,** to hasten: "Sick-thoughted Venus makes amain unto him . . ." *Ven & Ad,* 5.

Amamon, *n.* evil spirit of Welsh myth.: ". . . he of Wales that gave Amamon the bastinado,/ and made Lucifer cuckold . . ." *1 Hen 4,* II, iv, 332–333.

amaze, *v.* **1** to perplex or confuse: "You amaze me ladies. I would have told you of/ good wrestling . . ." *As You,* I, ii, 101–102. **2** to dismay: "I beseech your Majesty, make up,/ Lest your retirement do amaze your friends." *1 Hen 4,* V, iv, 4–5. —*n.* **3** [pl.] amazement; astonishment: "His face's own margent did quote such amazes . . ." *Love's L,* II, i, 245.

amazed, *adj.* **1** bewildered; confused: "You stand amaz'd,/ But be of comfort." *T Night,* III, iv, 345–346. **2** stupefied or distraught: "Enter Aumerle amazed." [SD] *Rich 2,* V, iii, 23. **3**

amazed with matter, bewildered by so much business: ". . . for the counsel of my son and queen,/ I am amaz'd with matter." *Cymb,* IV, iii, 27–28.

amazedly, *adv.* in a confused or perplexed manner: "My lord, I shall reply amazedly . . ." *M N Dream,* IV, i, 145.

amazement, *n.* **1** bewilderment: "But look, amazement on thy mother sits." *Ham,* III, iv, 112. **2 flame amazement,** to cause terror by appearing as fire; here, Ariel prob. assumes form of St. Elmo's fire: ". . . now on the beak,/ Now in the waist, the deck, in every cabin,/ I flam'd amazement . . ." *Temp,* I, ii, 196–198.

amazing, *adj.* stupefying; rendering one senseless: "And let thy blows . . . Fall like amazing thunder on . . . thy adverse pernicious enemy!" *Rich 2,* I, iii, 80–82.

Amazon, *n.* (in Greek myth.) one of a race of belligerent female warriors who fought the Greeks: ". . . your own ladies and pale-visag'd maids/ Like Amazons come tripping after drums . . ." *K John,* V, ii, 154–155.

Amazonian, *adj.* **1** being or resembling an Amazon: "To triumph like an Amazonian trull/ Upon their woes whom Fortune captivates!" *3 Hen 6,* I, iv, 114–115. **2** beardless: "When with his Amazonian chin he drove/ The bristled lips before him . . ." *Cor,* II, ii, 91–92.

ambassador, *n.* identity assumed by Hamlet on the voyage to England: "There's a letter for/ you, sir. It came from th'ambassador that was bound/ for England—" *Ham,* IV, vi, 8–10.

ambassage, *n.* message: "To thee I send this written ambassage . . ." *Sonn 26,* 3.

ambition's debt, *n.* debt owed to Caesar's ambition: ". . . be not affrighted./ Fly not; stand still; ambition's debt is paid." *J Caes,* III, i, 82–83.

ambitious, *adj.* **this ambitious foul infirmity,** this foul infirmity, ambition: ". . . this ambitious foul infirmity,/ In having much, torments us with defect . . ." *Luc,* 150–151.

amble, *v.* **1** (of a person) to saunter; parade or promenade: "The skipping King, he ambled up and down . . ." *1 Hen 4,* III, ii, 60. **2** to walk with an affected gait: "You jig and amble, and you lisp, you nickname/ God's creatures . . ." *Ham,* III, i, 146–147.

ambling, *n.* affected way of walking or dancing; mincing: "Give me a torch, I am not for this ambling." *Rom & Jul,* I, iv, 11.

ambling gelding, *n.* riding horse: "I will rather/ trust . . . a thief to walk my ambling/ gelding . . ." *Wives,* II, ii, 290–294.

ambuscado, *n.* ambuscade or ambush: ". . . then dreams he of . . . breaches, ambuscados, Spanish blades . . ." *Rom & Jul,* I, iv, 83–84.

ambush, *n.* **1** concealed armed escort: "And see the ambush of our friends be strong . . ." *T Andr,* V, iii, 9. **2 in the ambush,** under cover: "Who may in th'ambush of my name strike home . . ." *Meas,* I, iii, 41.

amend, *v.* to improve or recover, as in health or fortunes: ". . . at his touch,/ Such sanctity hath Heaven given his hand,/ They presently amend." *Mac,* IV, iii, 143–145.

amended, *past part.* prob. wordplay here on "repaired" and "improved": ". . . well you know this is a pitiful case [situation]."/ "Ay, by my troth, the case [situation or his instrument case] may be amended." *Rom & Jul,* IV, v, 98–99.

a-mending, *adj.* out of tune or in the process of being tuned: "'Tis like a chime a-mending . . ." *Tr & Cr,* I, iii, 159.

amendment, *n.* recovery; here, a return to health: "What hope is there of his majesty's amendment?" *All's W,* I, i, 11.

amends, *n. pl.* **1** misuse for *amendment;* recovery: "Now Lord be thanked for my good amends." *Shrew,* Ind., ii, 98. **2 restore amends,** to reciprocate by making amends: "Give me your hands, if we be friends,/ And Robin shall restore amends." *M N Dream,* V, i, 423–424.

amerce, *v.* to punish or penalize: "I'll amerce you with so strong a fine/ That you shall all repent the loss of mine." *Rom & Jul,* III, i, 192–193.

ames-ace, *n.* double aces [the lowest throw at dice]; here, an understatement as intended humor: "I had rather be in this choice than throw ames-ace/ for my life." *All's W,* II, iii, 79.

amiable, *adj.* **1** lovely; pleasing: "Come sit thee down upon this flowery bed,/ While I thy amiable cheeks do coy . . ." *M N Dream,* IV, i, 1–2. **2** desirable; lovable: "'Twould make her amiable, and subdue my father/ Entirely to her love . . ." *Oth,* III, iv, 57–58.

amiss, *n.* **1** wrong; misstep; fault or faults: "Myself corrupting, salving thy amiss . . ." *Sonn 35,* 7. **2** calamity; misfortune: "Each toy seems prologue to some great amiss." *Ham,* IV, v, 18.

amity, *n.* friendship; here, between Bassanio and Antonio: "You have a noble and a true conceit [understanding]/ Of god-like amity . . ." *Merch,* III, iv, 2–3.

amorous, *adj.* devoted; loving: "Lorenzo and his amorous Jessica." *Merch,* II, viii, 9.

amort, *adj.* dejected; heartsick: "How fares my Kate? What, sweeting, all amort?" *Shrew,* IV, iii, 36.

Amphimacus, *n.* iden. only as a Greek duke [or sometimes earl] and a companion of Ajax: "Amphimacus and Thoas deadly hurt;/ Patroclus ta'en or slain . . ." *Tr & Cr,* V, v, 12–13.

ample, *adv.* **1** amply: "You see, my lord, how ample y'are belov'd." *Timon,* I, ii, 126. **2** well; fully: "I know your hostess/ As ample as myself." *All's W,* III, v, 42–43.

amply, *adv.* unconditionally; unequivocally: "And rather choose to hide them in a net/ Than amply to imbar their crooked titles . . ." *Hen 5,* I, ii, 93–94.

Ampthill, *n.* royal residence of Katherine after separation from Henry: "Held a late court at Dunstable, six miles off/ From Ampthill where the princess lay [resided] . . ." *Hen 8,* IV, i, 27–28.

Amurath, *n.* Turkish sultan of the 16th cent. who, upon succeeding his father, had his brothers murdered: "Not Amurath an Amu-rath succeeds,/ But Harry Harry. " *2 Hen 4,* V, ii, 48–49.

an, *prep.* **1** if: ". . . if thou encounter any such, apprehend/ him, an thou dost me love." *Hen 5,* IV, vii, 162–163. **2** on: "And each particular hair to stand an end/ Like quills upon the fretful porpentine." *Ham,* I, v, 19–20.

anatomize, *v.* to analyze in great detail; characterize or dissect: ". . . should I anatomize him to thee as he is, I must blush and weep . . ." *As You,* I, i, 154–155.

anatomy, *n.* skeleton: ". . . one Pinch, a hungry lean-fac'd villain;/ A mere anatomy, a mountebank . . ." *Errors,* V, i, 238–239.

Anchises, *n.* a Trojan and the father of Aeneas; carried by his son from the burning Troy: ". . . as Aeneas, our great ancestor,/ Did from the flames of Troy upon his shoulder/ The old Anchises bear . . ." *J Caes,* I, ii, 111–113.

anchor¹, *n.* anchorite; hermit: "An anchor's cheer in prison be my scope . . ." *Ham,* III, ii, 214.

anchor², *n.* **anchor is deep,** Falstaff's plans are unalterable; or perh. implying that he is already beyond his depth: "The anchor is deep: will that humour pass?" *Wives,* I, iii, 48.

ancient, *n.* **1** [often cap.] corruption of **ensign: a.** title of the standard-bearer in a military company: "Sir, Ancient Pistol's below, and would speak with you." *2 Hen 4,* II, iv, 67–68. **b.** flag or ensign: ". . . ten times more dishonourable-ragged than an old fazed ancient . . ." *1 Hen 4,* IV, ii, 30–31. **2 ancient of war,** experienced generals: "Let's then determine/ With th' ancient of war on our proceeding." *Lear,* V, i, 31–32.

ancient damnation, *n.* cursed (wicked, damned) old woman: "Ancient damnation! O most wicked fiend . . ." *Rom & Jul,* III, v, 235.

ancientest, *adj.* **ancientest order,** recorded time: "Let me pass/ The same I am, ere ancient'st order was . . ." *W Tale,* IV, i, 9–10.

ancientry, *n.* **1** old-fashioned manners, courtliness, etc.: ". . . mannerly-modest as a measure, full of state/ and ancientry . . ." *M Ado,* II, i, 70–71. **2** old people: ". . . nothing in the between but getting/ wenches with child, wronging the ancientry . . ." *W Tale,* III, iii, 61–62.

and or **an,** *conj.* **1** if: "Are you of fourscore pounds a year?/ Yes, and't please you, sir." *Meas,* II, i, 192–193. **2** what with; when there is: "What needs all that, and a pair of stocks in the town?" *Errors,* III, i, 60.

and if, *conj.* if: ". . . a sheep doth very often stray,/ And if the shepherd be awhile away." *Two Gent,* I, i, 74–75.

and it like you, if it please you: "First, and it like you, the house is a respected/ house . . ." *Meas,* II, i, 159–160.

Andren, *n.* **vale of Andren,** valley in N France (Picardy); town of Guynes, controlled by British, was on one side and Arde (now Ardres), belonging to the French, was opposite: ". . . those two lights of men/ Met in the vale of Andren." "'Twixt Guynes and Arde . . ." *Hen 8,* I, i, 6–7.

Andrew, *n.* prob. ref. to a Spanish galleon captured by the English at Cadiz in 1596: "And see my wealthy Andrew dock'd in sand/ Vailing her high top lower than her ribs . . ." *Merch,* I, i, 27–28.

Andronici, *n. pl.* members of the Andronicus family: "The poor remainder of Andronici/ Will hand in hand all headlong hurl ourselves . . ." *T Andr,* V, iii, 131–132.

and 'twere, *conj.* as though he were: ". . . he will weep you and/ 'twere a man born in April." *Tr & Cr,* I, ii, 175–176.

angel, *n.* **1** gold coin stamped with the likeness of the archangel Michael, worth half a pound sterling: "Rich she shall be, that's certain . . . noble, or not I for an angel . . ." *M Ado,* II, iii, 30–33. **2** trusted companion; also, guiding influence: "For Brutus, as you know, was Caesar's angel." *J Caes,* III, ii, 183. **3** evil spirit; demon: "And let the Angel, whom thou still

hast serv'd/ Tell thee . . ." *Mac,* V, viii, 14–15. **4 ancient angel,** fine gentleman of the old mark: ". . . at last I spied/ An ancient angel coming down the hill . . ." *Shrew,* IV, ii, 60–61. **5 imprisoned angels,** gold coins hoarded by the abbots: ". . . see thou shake the bags/ Of hoarding abbots; imprison'd angels/ Set at liberty . . ." *K John,* III, ii, 17–19.

Angelica, *n.* identity not clear; poss. given name of Lady Capulet: "Look to the bak'd meats, good Angelica:/ Spare not for cost." *Rom & Jul,* IV, iv, 5–6.

anger, *n.* **take the chance of anger,** risk fighting while you are angry: "Nay then, come on, and take the chance of anger." *Lear,* III, vii, 78.

angerly, *adv.* angrily: "How angerly I taught my brow to frown . . ." *Two Gent,* I, ii, 62.

angle¹, *n.* **1** baited fishhook: "Thrown out his angle for my proper life/ And with such coz'nage . . ." *Ham,* V, ii, 66–67. **2** fishing tackle; rod and line: "Give me mine angle, we'll to the river there . . ." *Ant & Cleo,* II, v, 10.
—*v.* **3** to bait (fish); here, fig. use: "She knew her distance and did angle for me . . ." *All's W,* V, iii, 211.

angle², *n.* corner or nook: "Whom I left cooling of the air with sighs/ In an odd angle of the isle . . ." *Temp,* I, ii, 222–223.

Anheers, *n.* poss. anglicized form of the Dutch *mynheers,* gentlemen or sirs: ". . . and thy name shall be/ Brook. It is a merry knight. —Will you go,/ Anheers?" *Wives,* II, i, 207–209.

an-hungry, *adj.* var. of A-HUNGRY: "They said they were an-hungry, sigh'd forth proverbs . . ." *Cor,* I, i, 204.

a-night, *adv.* at night: "I broke my sword upon a stone, and bid him take/ that for coming a-night to Jane Smile . . ." *As You,* II, iv, 44–45.

Anjou, *n.* province in the Loire Valley, W France: "France. Plains in Anjou." [SD] *1 Hen 6,* V, ii, 1.

Anna, *n.* [in Vergil's "Aeneid"] sister and confidante of Dido, Queen of Carthage: ". . . to me as secret and as dear/ As Anna to the Queen of Carthage was . . ." *Shrew,* I, i, 153–154.

annexion, *n.* addition: "With the annexions of fair gems enrich'd . . ." *Lover's Comp,* 208.

annexment, *n.* attachment: "Each small annexment . . ./ Attends the boist'rous ruin." *Ham,* III, iii, 21–22.

annothanize, *v.* perh. an old spelling of "anatomize," to explain; perh. a whimsical coinage for "annotate," to gloss: ". . .

and he it was that might rightly say, *veni, vidi, vici;*/ which to annothanize in the vulgar . . . he came, saw, and overcame." *Love's L,* IV, i, 68–70.

annoy, *n.* **1** injury; hurt: "And rape, I fear, was root of thy annoy." *T Andr,* IV, i, 49. **2** ordeal; tribulation: "Farewell, sour annoy!/ For here, I hope, begins our lasting joy." *3 Hen 6,* V, vii, 45–46. **3** something that offends: "Or else receiv'st with pleasure thine annoy?" *Sonn 8,* 4.
—*v.* **4** to harm: ". . . I met a lion,/ Who glaz'd upon me, and went surly by,/ Without annoying me." *J Caes,* I, iii, 20–22.

annoyance, *n.* harm or injury; danger: "Remove from her the means of all annoyance . . ." *Mac,* V, i, 73.

anon, *adv.* **1** soon; presently; shortly: "'You are welcome,' with this shrill addition, 'Anon,/ anon, sir!'" *1 Hen 4,* II, iv, 26–27. **2** later: "[Aside to Men.] Forbear me till anon." *Ant & Cleo,* II, vii, 39. **3** at once; immediately: "One calls within:/ 'Juliet' [SD]"/ "Anon, anon!/ Come let's away, the strangers all are gone. *Exeunt.*" *Rom & Jul,* I, v, 148. **4** every now and then: "This Sir John, cousin, that comes hither anon about/ soldiers?" *2 Hen 4,* III, ii, 26–27.
—*n.* **5 till anon,** for a moment: "Forbear me till anon.—/ This wine for Lepidus!" *Ant & Cleo,* II, vii, 38–39.

another, *pron.* **You are such another,** You are really something! [often used sarcastically or contemptuously] *Tr & Cr,* I, ii, 276.

answer, *v.* **1** to answer for: ". . . it is no more/ Than my poor life must answer." *Rich 2,* V, ii, 82–83. **2** to match; correspond to: ". . . pray God our cheer/ May answer my good will, and your good welcome here." *Errors,* III, i, 19–20. **3** to pay: "Good sir, say whe'er [whether] you'll answer me or no . . ." *Errors,* IV, i, 60. **4** to endure; suffer: "To the conflicting elements expos'd,/ Answer mere [raw] nature . . ." *Timon,* IV, iii, 232–233. **5** to explain: ". . . for the robbery, lad, how is that answered?" *1 Hen 4,* III, iii, 175. **6** to respond to another's challenge to a duel: "Win me and wear me, let him answer me." *M Ado,* V, i, 82. **7 Answer, clerk,** say "amen" [so be it] in the manner of a clerk during church service: "God keep him out of my sight when the/ dance is done! Answer, clerk." *M Ado,* II, i, 100–101.
—*n.* **8** answer of formal charges; trial: "Obey I charge thee,/ And follow to thine answer." *Cor,* III, i, 174–175. **9 put us to our answer,** make us retaliate: "I would revenges . . . would seek us through [out]/ And put us to our answer." *Cymb,* IV, ii, 159–161. **10 quite from the answer of his degree,** unable to answer your challenge because of his high rank: "It may be his enemy is a gentleman of great/ sort, quite from the answer of his degree." *Hen 5,* IV, vii, 139–140. **11 your answer,** what

you may be answerable for: ". . . added to the faults of mine,/ And nothing of your answer." *Meas,* II, iv, 72–73.

answerable, *adj.* **1** commensurate; suitable or equivalent: ". . . all things answerable to this portion." *Shrew,* II, i, 352. **2** consequent; corresponding: ". . . it was a violent commencement, and/ thou shalt see an answerable sequestration [a correspondingly sudden ending] . . ." *Oth,* I, iii, 345–346.

an't, 1 if it: "Me, an't shall please you; I am Anthony Dull." *Love's L,* I, i, 264. **2 an't like,** if it please: ". . . we steal by line and level, an't like your/ grace." *Temp,* IV, i, 239–240.

Anthropophagi, *n.* man-eaters; cannibals: "The Anthropophagi, and men whose heads/ Do grow beneath their shoulders . . ." *Oth,* I, iii, 144–145.

Anthropophaginian, *n.* cannibal: "Go,/ knock and call; he'll speak like an Anthropophaginian/ unto thee; knock, I say." *Wives,* IV, v, 7–9.

Antiates, *n.* citizens [here, soldiers] of Antium: "Their bands i'th'vaward are the Antiates/ Of their best trust . . ." *Cor,* I, vi, 53–54.

antic, *n.* **1** grotesque figure, as a gargoyle: "If black, why, Nature, drawing of an antic,/ Made a foul blot . . ." *M Ado,* III, i, 63–64. **2** [sometimes cap.] jester, clown, or buffoon: ". . . there the antic sits,/ Scoffing his state and grinning at his pomp . . ." *Rich 2,* III, ii, 162–163. **3** pageant of grotesque or fantastic characters: ". . . present the princess . . ./ with some . . . show,/ or pageant, or antic, or firework." *Love's L,* V, i, 102–104.
—*adj.* **4** grotesque or bizarre; quixotic: "As I perchance hereafter shall think meet/ To put an antic disposition on—" *Ham,* I, v, 179–180. **5** quaint; old-fashioned: "Now, good Cesario, but that piece of song,/ That old and antic song we heard last night . . ." *T Night,* II, iv, 2–3. **6** fantastic; capricious: "I'll charm the air to give a sound,/ While you perform your antic round [dance] . . ." *Mac,* IV, i, 129–130.
—*v.* **7** to make a fool of: ". . . the wild disguise hath almost/ Antick'd us all." *Ant & Cleo,* II, vii, 123–124.

antic face, *n.* mask: "What, dares the slave/ Come hither, cover'd with an antic face . . ." *Rom & Jul,* I, v, 54–55.

anticipate, *v.* to frustrate or forestall: "Time, thou anticipat'st my dread exploits . . ." *Mac,* IV, i, 144.

anticly, *adv.* in the grotesque manner of buffoons: "Go anticly, and show outward hideousness . . ." *M Ado,* V, i, 96.

Antiopa, *n.* Amazon, said to be a daughter of Mars; lover of Theseus and later abandoned: ". . . make him with fair Aegles break his faith,/ With Ariadne and Antiopa?" *M N Dream*, II, i, 79–80.

Antipodes, *n. pl.* land or peoples on the opposite side of the earth; here, the Irish: "... Bolingbroke,/ Who all this while hath revell'd in the night,/ Whilst we were wand'ring with the Antipodes ..." *Rich 2*, III, ii, 47–49.

antiquary, *adj.* ancient: "Here's Nestor,/ Instructed by the antiquary times ..." *Tr & Cr*, II, iii, 250–251.

antique, *adj.* **1** ancient; here, also understood as "antic," ridiculous: "I never may believe/ These antique fables, nor these fairy toys." *M N Dream*, V, i, 2–3. **2** poss. wordplay of "antique" [ancient] and "antic" [capricious, quixotic]: "O! carve not with thy hours my love's fair brow,/ Nor draw no lines there with thine antique pen ..." *Sonn 19*, 9–10.

antique hours, *n.* ancient time(s): "In him those holy antique hours are seen ..." *Sonn 68*, 9.

antique Roman, *n.* See **Roman** (def. 2).

antique time, *n.* ancient or old-fashioned customs: "The dust on antique time would lie unswept ..." *Cor*, II, iii, 118.

antiquity, *n.* long standing: "Bawd is he doubtless,/ and of antiquity, too: bawd born." *Meas*, III, ii, 65–66.

Antium, *n.* capital of the Volscians, in Latium: "A goodly city is this Antium. City,/ 'Tis I that made thy widows ..." *Cor*, IV, iv, 1–2.

Antoniad, *n.* flagship of Egyptian fleet: "The Antoniad, the Eqyptian admiral,/ With all their sixty fly ..." *Ant & Cleo*, III, x, 2–3.

antre, *n.* cave; cavern: "Wherein of antres vast, and deserts idle ..." *Oth*, I, iii, 140.

anvil, *n.* **anvil of my sword**, body of Coriolanus, against which the sword of Aufidius has been sharpened: "Here I clip/ The anvil of my sword, and do contest/ As hotly and as nobly with thy love ..." *Cor*, IV, v, 110–112.

any, *pron.* anything: "As any the most vulgar thing to sense [most common of human experiences] ..." *Ham*, I, ii, 99.

anything, *pron.* **It is that anything now,** prob. should be corrected to "Is that anything now? [Does all that mean anything now?]" *Merch*, I, i, 113.

ap, *n.* (as part of a name) son of: "And Rice ap Thomas, with a valiant crew ..." *Rich 3*, IV, v, 15.

apace, *adv.* **1** swiftly; quickly: "Gallop apace, you fiery-footed steeds ..." *R & J*, III, ii, 1. **2** thoughtlessly: "You are pleasant, sir, and speak apace." *Meas*, III, ii, 109.
—*interj.* **3** [used as a command] Hurry! Get a move on!: "Peter!"/ "Anon."/ "Before, and apace." *Rom & Jul*, II, iv, 210–212.

apart, *adv.* in another place: "Resolve yourselves apart;/ I'll come to you anon." *Mac*, III, i, 137–138.

ape, *n.* **1** monkey: "Because that I am little like an ape,/ He thinks that you should bear me on your shoulders!" *Rich 3*, III, i, 130–131. **2** fool or idler: "And to the English court assemble now/ From every region, apes of idleness!" *2 Hen 4*, IV, v, 121–122. **3 lead apes in hell,** believed the ultimate fate of unmarried women [who lacked children to lead them into heaven]: "And for [because of] your love to her lead apes in [to] hell." *Shrew*, II, i, 34.

ape-bearer, *n.* performer who entertained with a monkey: "I know this man well; he hath/ been since an ape-bearer ..." *W Tale*, IV, iii, 91–92.

apish, *adj.* behaving like an ape; loutish: "This apish and unmannerly approach ..." *K John*, V, ii, 131.

Apollo, *n.* (in classic myth.) the sun god; here, as the patron of learning: "A passport too! Apollo, perfect/ me in the characters!" *Per*, III, ii, 68–69.

Apollodorus, *n.* friend of Cleopatra, who smuggled her into Caesar's presence rolled up in a mattress: "And I have heard Apollodorus carried—" *Ant & Cleo*, II, vi, 68.

apoplexed, *adj.* paralyzed: "... sure that sense/ Is apoplex'd, for madness would not err ..." *Ham*, III, iv, 72–73.

apoplexy, *n.* paralysis: "... his Highness is fallen into/ this same whoreson apoplexy." *2 Hen 4*, I, ii, 106–107.

apostrophus, *n.* apostrophe; mark ['] indicating omission of a vowel: "You find not the apostrophus, and so miss the/ accent ..." *Love's L*, IV, ii, 115.

appall, *v.* **1** to disconcert; dismay: "Property was thus appalled,/ That the self was not the same ..." *Phoen*, 37–38. **2** to make pale: "Methinks your looks are sad, your cheer appall'd." *1 Hen 6*, I, ii, 48.

appalled, *adj.* instilled with fear: "... the appalled air/ May pierce the head of the great combatant,/ And hale him hither." *Tr & Cr*, IV, v, 4–6.

apparel, *v.* **1** to dress: "... all shall eat and drink on my score, and I will/ apparel them all in one livery ..." *2 Hen 6*, IV, ii,

70–71. **2** to cover: ". . . remember/ thy courtesy—I beseech thee, apparel thy head . . ." *Love's L,* V, i, 89–90.

apparent, *adj.* **1** obvious; manifest: "Thieves are not judg'd but they are by to hear,/ Although apparent guilt be seen in them . . ." *Rich 2,* IV, i, 123–124. **2** inevitable; imminent: "If death be so apparent, then both fly." *1 Hen 6,* IV, v, 44. **3** now occurring; currently on display: "It may be these apparent prodigies,/ The unaccustom'd terror of this night . . ." *J Caes,* II, i, 198–199.
—*n.* **4** heir apparent: "I'll draw it as apparent to the crown . . ." *3 Hen 6,* II, ii, 64.

apparently, *adv.* openly; also, flagrantly: "I would not spare my brother in this case/ If he should scorn me so apparently." *Errors,* IV, i, 79.

appeach, *v.* **1** to accuse publicly; denounce: "Now by mine honour, by my life, by my troth,/ I will appeach the villain." *Rich 2,* V, ii, 78–79. **2** to inform against or betray one: ". . . disclose/ The state of your affection, for your passions/ Have to the full appeach'd." *All's W,* I, iii, 184–186.

appeal, *n.* **1** formal charge or accusation: ". . . the boist'rous late appeal,/ Which then our leisure would not let us hear . . ." *Rich 2,* I, i, 4–5.
—*v.* **2** to accuse: ". . . hast thou sounded him,/ If he appeal the Duke on ancient malice . . ." *Rich 2,* I, i, 8–9.

appealed, *adj.* charged or accused, as a crime: ". . . as for the rest appeal'd,/ It issues from the rancour of a villain . . ." *Rich 2,* I, i, 142–143.

appearance, *n.* simulation intended to deceive; decoy: "The bloody Douglas . . . Had three times slain th'appearance of the King . . ." *2 Hen 4,* I, i, 127–128.

appeared, *adj.* apparent; discernible: ". . . your favour [identity] is well appeared by your tongue." *Cor,* IV, iii, 9.

appearer, *n.* stranger: "This is your wife."/ "Reverend appearer, no . . ." *Per,* V, iii, 18.

appellant, *n.* **1** the accuser, esp. in a case of treason: ". . . free from other misbegotten hate,/ Come I appellant to this princely presence." *Rich 2,* I, i, 33–34. **2** (in single combat) the challenger: "This is the day appointed for the combat;/ And ready are the appellant and defendant . . ." *2 Hen 6,* II, iii, 48–49.

appendix, *n.* prob. character's misuse for "appendage" [Bianca]: ". . . bid the priest be ready to come against you come/ with your appendix." *Shrew,* IV, iv, 99–100.

apperil, *n.* rare form of *peril:* "Let me stay at thine apperil, Timon . . ." *Timon,* I, ii, 33.

appertaining, *adj.* **1** becoming; appropriate: ". . . the reason that I have to love thee/ Doth much excuse the appertaining rage/ To such a greeting . . ." *Rom & Jul,* III, i, 61–63.
—*n.* **2** [usually pl.] attributes: "His real habitude gave life and grace/ To appertainings and to ornament . . ." *Lover's Comp,* 114–115. **3** [pl.] official duties: ". . . we lay by/ Our appertainings, visiting of him." *Tr & Cr,* II, iii, 81–82.

appertinent, *adj.* **1** pertaining or relating; appropriate (to): ". . . all the/ other gifts appertinent to man . . . are not worth a gooseberry." *2 Hen 4,* I, ii, 170–172.
—*n.* **2** [pl.] rights and privileges of rank: ". . . how apt our love was to accord/ To furnish him with all appertinents . . ." *Hen 5,* II, ii, 86–87.

appetite, *n.* sexual desire: ". . . why, she would hang on him,/ As if increase of appetite had grown/ By what it fed on . . ." *Ham,* I, ii, 143–145.

applauding, *adj.* crowded with cheering citizens: ". . . like great triumphers/ In their applauding gates." *Timon,* V, i, 195–196.

apple, *n.* pupil of the eye: "Do not you . . . laugh upon the apple of her eye [share intimate humor]?" *Love's L,* V, ii, 474–475.

apple-john, *n.* apple that wrinkles when ripe but keeps well: "I am withered like an old apple-john." *1 Hen 4,* III, iii, 4.

appliance, *n.* **1** treatment; medication; cure: "Diseases desperate grown/ By desperate appliance are reliev'd,/ Or not at all." *Ham,* IV, iii, 9–11. **2** [Usually pl.] trappings; appurtenances: ". . . With all appliances and means to boot,/ Deny it to a King?" *2 Hen 4,* III, i, 29–30. **3** compliance: "Thou art too noble to conserve a life/ In base appliances [by unworthy means]." *Meas,* III, i, 87–88.

application, *n.* reference; allusion: "And in this application to the sun,/ Bid her be free and general as the sun . . ." *Edw 3,* II, i, 163–164.

apply, *v.* **1** to study; apply oneself to: ". . . that part of philosophy/ Will I apply that treats of happiness . . ." *Shrew,* I, i, 18–19. **2** to be given: "Let your remembrance apply to Banquo . . ." *Mac,* III, ii, 30.

appoint, *v.* **1** to command or decree: "Goes the King hence to-day?"/ "He does:—he did appoint so." *Mac,* II, iii, 54. **2** to grant; bestow on: ". . . for that/ I do appoint him store of provender." *J Caes,* IV, i, 29–30. **3** to place; position: ". . . so unsettled,/ To appoint myself in this vexation . . ." *W Tale*, I, ii, 325–326.

appointed, *past part.* **nuptial appointed,** the wedding day set: "She should this Angelo have married: was affianced/ to her oath, and the nuptial appointed." *Meas*, III, i, 213–214.

appointment, *n.* **1** outfitting: ". . . a pirate of/ very warlike appointment gave us chase." *Ham*, IV, vi, 14–15. **2** [often pl.] military equipment: "That from this castle's tottered battlements/ Our fair appointments may be well perus'd." *Rich 2*, III, iii, 52–53. **3** weapon; here, sword: "I'll prove it in my shackles, with these hands/ Void of appointment . . ." *Kinsmen*, III, i, 39–40. **4** military readiness; battle order: ". . . we'll set forth/ In best appointment all our regiments." *K John*, II, i, 295–296. **5** [pl.] business affairs; purposes: "And my appointments have in them a need/ Greater than shows itself at the first view . . ." *All's W*, II, v, 67–68. **6** preparation; provision: "Therefore your best appointment make with speed;/ Tomorrow you set on." *Meas*, III, i, 59–60. **7** direction; instructions: "That good fellow . . . follows my appointment . . ." *Hen 8*, II, ii, 132–133.

apprehend, *v.* **1** to lay hold of; seize upon: "He apprehends a world of figures [figures of speech] here . . ." *1 Hen 4*, I, iii, 207. **2** to arrest: "Condemned villain, I do apprehend thee./ Obey, and go with me, for thou must die." *Rom & Jul*, V, iii, 56–57. **3** to perceive; to understand intuitively: "Such shaping fantasies, that apprehend/ More than cool reason ever comprehends." *M N Dream*, V, i, 5–6.

apprehension, *n.* **1** meaning or interpretation: "That's a lascivious apprehension." *Timon*, I, i, 207. **2** ability to understand; perception or, sometimes, quick-wittedness: "God help me, how long have you/ professed apprehension?" *M Ado*, III, iv, 62–63. **3** opinion; notion or idea: "I'll note you in my book of memory,/ To scourge you for this apprehension . . ." *1 Hen 6*, II, iv, 101–102. **4** act of taking into custody; arrest: ". . . go we, brothers, to the man that took him,/ To question of his apprehension." *3 Hen 6*, III, ii, 121–122.

apprehensive, *adj.* **1** (of a person) intelligent; able to reason: "And men are flesh and blood, and apprehensive . . ." *J Caes*, III, i, 67. **2** responsive; perceptive: ". . . apprehensive,/ quick, forgetive, full of nimble, fiery, and delectable/ shapes . . ." *2 Hen 4*, IV, iii, 97–99.

approach, *n.* **1** arrival; appearance: ". . . redoubted Burgundy,/ By whose approach the regions of Artois,/ Walloon, and Picardy, are friends to us." *1 Hen 6*, II, ii, 8–10. **2** attack: "In confutation of which rude approach . . . I crave the benefit of law of arms." *1 Hen 6*, IV, i, 98–100.

approbation, *n.* probationary period of a novitiate: "This day my sister should the cloister enter,/ And there receive her approbation." *Meas*, I, ii, 167–168.

approof, *n.* **1** approval; confirmation: "So in approof lives not his epitaph [nowhere is his epitaph so fully confirmed]/ As in your royal speech." *All's W*, I, ii, 50–51. **2 of valiant approof,** of proved valor: ". . . I hope your lordship thinks not him a soldier."/ "Yes . . . and of very valiant approof." *All's W*, II, v, 1–2.

approve, *v.* **1** to put (a person or thing) to the test or proof: "Nay, task me to my word, approve me, lord." *1 Hen 4*, IV, i, 9. **2** to try or test; here, also, enjoy sexually: ". . . even so doth she abuse me,/ Suffering my friend for my sake to approve her." *Sonn 42*, 7–8. **3** to learn; discover: ". . . and I desperate now approve/ Desire is death . . ." *Sonn 147*, 7–8. **4** to show; demonstrate: "The temple-haunting martlet, does approve,/ By his loved mansionry . . ." *Mac*, I, vi, 4–5. **5** to verify or corroborate: ". . . if again this apparition come,/ He may approve our eyes . . ." *Ham*, I, i, 31–32. **6** to commend: "Yet in faith if you did, it would/ not much approve me." *Ham*, V, ii, 133–134.

approved, *adj.* **1** tried; tested: "My trusty servant well approv'd in all . . ." *Shrew*, I, i, 7. **2** proven; demonstrated: ". . . he is/ of a noble strain, of approved valour, and confirmed/ honesty." *M Ado*, II, i, 355–357. **3 approved in,** found guilty of: ". . . from true evidence, of good esteem,/ He be approv'd in practice culpable." *2 Hen 6*, III, ii, 20–21. **4 still approved,** everlastingly confirmed: "O 'tis the curse in love, and still approv'd,/ When women cannot love where they're belov'd." *Two Gent*, V, iv, 43–44.

approver, *n.* person who tests the courage of another: "Their discipline . . . will make known/ To their approvers . . ." *Cymb*, II, iv, 23–25.

apricock, *n.* **1** apricot tree: "Go, bind thou up young dangling apricocks . . ." *Rich 2*, III, iv, 29. **2** its fruit: "Feed him with apricocks and dewberries . . ." *M N Dream*, III, i, 159.

April, *n.* month of presumed sadness because of its abundant showers, here equated with tears: ". . . he will weep you and/ 'twere a man born in April." *Tr & Cr*, I, ii, 175–176.

apron-men, *n.* tradesmen; menial workers: "You have made good work,/ You, and your apron-men . . ." *Cor*, IV, vi, 93–95.

apt, *adj.* **1** ready; prepared: "Live a thousand years,/ I shall not find myself so apt to die . . ." *J Caes*, III, i, 159–160. **2** comprehending: "I find thee apt./ And duller shouldst thou be than the fat weed . . ." *Ham*, I, v, 31–32. **3** impressionable; susceptible: "She is young and apt . . ." *Timon*, I, i, 135. **4** inclined to be deceived: "Why dost thou show to the apt thoughts of men/ The things that are not?" *J Caes* V, iii, 68–69. **5** fitting; pertinent: ". . . told no more/ Than what he found himself was apt and true." *Oth*, V, ii, 177–178.

aptly, *adv.* properly; suitably: "Leave me, and then the story aptly ends . . ." *Ven & Ad*, 715.

aqua-vitae, *n.* alcoholic spirits: ". . . I have bought/ The oil, the balsamum and aqua-vitae." *Errors*, IV, i, 89–90.

aqua-vitae bottle, *n.* ref. to the Irishman's supposed predilection for strong spirits: "I will rather/ trust a Fleming with my butter . . . an Irishman with my/ aqua-vitae bottle . . ." *Wives*, II, ii, 290–293.

Aquilon, *n.* another name for **Boreas.**

Aquitaine, *n.* large and immensely rich province in SW France: "The French king's daughter with yourself to speak . . . About surrender up of Aquitaine . . ." *Love's L*, I, i, 134–136.

Arabian bird, *n.* phoenix; here, a unique specimen: "O Antony, O thou Arabian bird!" *Ant & Cleo*, III, ii, 12.

Arabian tree, *n.* said to be the throne of the phoenix: "On the sole Arabian tree/ Herald sad and trumpet be . . ." *Phoen*, 2–3.

araise, *v.* to raise from the dead: ". . . whose simple touch/ Is powerful [enough] to araise King Pippen . . ." *All's W*, II, i, 74–75.

arbitrator, *n.* arbiter; one who offers a solution to or resolves an issue: "Out idle words, servants to shallow fools,/ Unprofitable sounds, weak arbitrators!" *Luc*, 1016–1017.

arbitrement, *n.* **1** judgment or adjudication: ". . . we of the off'ring side/ Must keep aloof from strict arbitrement . . ." *1 Hen 4*, IV, i, 69–70. **2** decisive [armed] encounter: "The arbitrement is like to be bloody." *Lear*, IV, vii, 94. **3 mortal arbitrement,** a settlement reached only by combat to the death: "I know the knight is incensed against you, even/ to a mortal arbitrement . . ." *T Night*, III, iv, 264–265.

arch¹, *n.* **1** rainbow: ". . . the queen o' th' sky,/ Whose wat'ry arch and messenger am I . . ." *Temp*, IV, i, 70–71. **2** sky: "Hath nature given them eyes/ To see this vaulted arch . . ." *Cymb*, I, vii, 32–33.

arch², *n.* **arch and patron,** chief patron: "The noble Duke my master,/ My worthy arch and patron, comes to-night . . ." *Lear*, II, i, 58–59.

Ardea, *n.* town S of Rome; here, besieged by Tarquin: "From the besieged Ardea all in post . . ." *Luc*, 1.

are, *v.* often used in place of "have": "You are light [have happened to fall] into my hands, where you are like/ to live." *Per*, IV, ii, 68–69.

argal, *adv.* misuse of Latin *ergo*, therefore: ". . . it is to act,/ to do, to perform; argal, she drowned herself/ wittingly." *Ham*, V, i, 11–13.

argentine, *adj.* silvery; here, shining like silver: "Celestial Dian, goddess argentine,/ I will obey thee." *Per*, V, i, 248–249.

Argier, *n.* old name of *Algiers*: "Where was she born? speak; tell me."/ "Sir, in Argier." *Temp*, I, ii, 260–261.

argo, *adv.* misuse of Latin *ergo*, therefore: "ergo": "Argo, their thread of life is spun." *2 Hen 6*, IV, ii, 29.

argosy, *n.* large merchant vessel: "That she shall have, besides an argosy . . ." *Shrew*, II, i, 367.

argue, *v.* to be a sign or indication of: ". . . argues a great sickness in his judgment that makes it." *Timon*, V, i, 28–29.

argument, *n.* **1** reason; cause: "Grounded upon no other argument/ But that the people praise her for her virtues . . ." *As You*, I, ii, 269–270. **2** theme or subject; also, plot, as that of a play: "I should not seek an absent argument/ Of my revenge . . ." *As You*, III, i, 3–4. **3** topic, as of conversation: ". . . they/ are yet but ear-bussing arguments." *Lear*, II, i, 8–9. **4** subject under discussion: ". . . I was come to the whole depth of my tale and/ meant indeed to occupy the argument no longer." *Rom & Jul*, II, iv, 98–99. **5** proof; evidence: "I shall be forsworn, which is/ a great argument of falsehood, if I love." *Love's L*, I, ii, 159–160. **6** intelligent conversation; also, keenness of reasoning: "Signior Benedick,/ For shape, for bearing, argument, and valour,/ Goes foremost in report through Italy." *M Ado*, III, i, 95–97. **7** challenge; here, opponents: "And sheath'd their swords for lack of argument." *Hen 5*, III, i, 21. **8 arguments of state,** weighty, esp. political, matters: "Let thy tongue tang arguments of state . . ." *T Night*, II, v, 150. **9 thy lovely argument,** the theme of your lovableness: ". . . thy lovely argument/ Deserves the travail of a worthier pen . . ." *Sonn 79*, 5–6.

Argus, *n.* 100-eyed monster, watchman of the Greek gods: ". . . one that will do the deed/ Though Argus were her eunuch and her guard . . ." *Love's L*, III, i, 193–194.

Ariachne, *n.* Arachne, peasant girl who dared to compare her own weaving skills to those of Minerva; in her fury the goddess turned the girl into a spider: "Admits no orifex for a point as subtle/ As Ariachne's broken woof to enter." *Tr & Cr*, V, ii, 150–151.

Ariadne, *n.* daughter of King Minos of Crete; abducted by Theseus and later abandoned: ". . . make him with fair Aegles break his faith,/ With Ariadne and Antiopa?" *M N Dream*, II, i, 79–80.

Aries, *n.* also called **the Ram,** sign of the zodiac: "The Bull . . . gave Aries such a knock/ That down fell both the Ram's horns in the court . . ." *T Andr*, IV, iii, 70–71.

Arion, *n.* (in Greek legend) musician who was saved by a dolphin when pirates threatened to kill him: ". . . like Arion on the dolphin's back/ I saw him hold acquaintance with the waves . . ." *T Night*, I, ii, 15–16.

arithmetic, *n.* **book of arithmetic,** a book of instruction; here, of fencing: "A braggart, a/ rogue, a villain, that fights by the book of arithmetic . . ." *Rom & Jul*, III, i, 102–103.

arithmetician, *n.* one good at figures; here, rather than soldiering: "And what was he?/ Forsooth, a great arithmetician . . ." *Oth*, I, i, 18–19.

arm, *v.* **arm him,** carry him in your arms: "And make him with our pikes and partisans/ A grave: come, arm him." *Cymb*, IV, ii, 399–400.

armado, *n.* var. of *armada*, fleet of warships [galleons]: ". . . Spain, who sent/ whole armadoes of carracks to be ballast at her/ nose." *Errors*, III, ii, 134–136.

Armagnac, *n.* district in Gascony, in SW France: "Have you perus'd the letters from the Pope,/ The Emperor, and the Earl of Armagnac?" *1 Hen 6*, V, i, 1–2.

armed, *adj.* **1** steel-tipped: "Their armed staves in charge, their beavers down . . ." *2 Hen 4*, IV, i, 120. **2** having taken up arms; here, in wordplay with sense of "suffering skin eruptions," the effects of venereal disease (the "French disease"): "Where France?"/ "In her forehead, armed and reverted, making/ war against her heir." *Errors*, III, ii, 120–122. **3** resolved: "If you are arm'd to do, as sworn to do,/ Subscribe to your deep oaths . . ." *Love's L*, I, i, 22–23.

arm-gaunt, *adj.* poss. indicates a horse made lean by bearing soldiers in full armor, though appar. a very spirited horse: "So he nodded/ And soberly did mount an arm-gaunt steed . . ." *Ant & Cleo*, I, v, 47–48.

Armigero, *n.* Latin word for esquire: ". . . a gentleman born,/ Master Parson, who writes himself 'Armigero' in/ any bill . . ." *Wives*, I, i, 8–10.

arming of the verity, confirmation of the truth; verification of the facts: ". . . the particular confirmations, point/ from point, to the full arming of the verity." *All's W*, IV, iii, 59–60.

armipotent, *adj.* powerful in arms: an epithet of Mars: "The armipotent Mars, of lances the almighty,/ Gave Hector a gift,—" *Love's L*, V, ii, 637–638.

armor, *n.* **1** suit of armor: ". . . he would have/ walked ten mile afoot to see a good armour . . ." *M Ado*, II, iii, 15–16. **2 carry armor,** prob. wordplay on "equipped with a penis": "Pray God she prove not masculine ere long,/ If underneath the standard of the French/ She carry armour as she hath begun." *1 Hen 6*, II, i, 22–24.

armorer, *n.* servant who dresses his master in armor: "He chid Andromache and struck his armourer . . ." *Tr & Cr*, I, ii, 6.

armory, *n.* room or place where arms and armor were stored: "Come, go with me into mine armoury:/ Lucius, I'll fit thee . . ." *T Andr*, IV, i, 113–114.

arms, *n. pl.* **1** armor: ". . . clap their female joints/ In stiff unwieldy arms against thy crown . . ." *Rich 2*, III, ii, 114–115. **2** wordplay on coat-of-arms and a man's arm: ". . . I'll cuff you if you strike again."/ "So may you lose your arms." *Shrew*, II, i, 218–219. **3** might or force; here, children regarded as part of a prince's power: ". . . an issue I might propagate,/ Are arms to princes and bring joys to subjects." *Per*, I, ii, 73–74.

arms crossed, *n.* See **folded arms.**

a-row, *adv.* one after the other: "My master and his man are both broke loose,/ Beaten the maids a-row, and bound the doctor . . ." *Errors*, V, i, 169–170.

aroynt or **aroint,** *v.* away! begone!: "'Aroynt thee, witch!' the rump-fed ronyon cries." *Mac*, I, iii, 6.

arraign, *v.* **1** to accuse: "Will nothing stick our person to arraign/ In ear and ear." *Ham*, IV, v, 93–94. **2** to examine: "I'll teach you how you shall arraign your conscience . . ." *Meas*, II, iii, 21.

arrant, *adj.* absolute; out-and-out: ". . . a couple of as arrant/ knaves as any in Messina." *M Ado*, III, v, 30–31.

arras, *n.* heavy curtain or tapestry, used to cover a wall: "Go hide thee behind the arras, the rest walk up/ above." *1 Hen 4*, II, iv, 493–494.

arras counterpoints, *n. pl.* bedcovers (counterpanes) of tapestries woven in Arras, city of N France: "In cypress chests my arras counterpoints . . ." *Shrew*, II, i, 344.

array, *n.* **in fair array,** in full battle dress: ". . . he sent me forth to muster men,/ Which I accordingly have done, and bring them hither/ In fair array . . ." *Edw 3,* II, ii, 4–6.

arrearages, *n.* overdue tribute: "He'll grant the tribute: send th' arrearages,/ Or look upon our Romans . . ." *Cymb,* II, iv, 13–14.

arrest, *v.* **1** to accept as security: "We arrest your word . . ." *Love's L,* II, i, 159. **2 arrest your words,** hold you to your word: "I do arrest your words. Be that you are,/ That is, a woman . . ." *Meas,* II, iv, 133–134.
—*n.* **3** [usually pl.] orders revoking a previous command: ". . . sends out arrests/ On Fortinbras; which he, in brief, obeys . . ." *Ham,* II, ii, 67–68.

arrivance, *n.* **more arrivance,** additional arrivals: "For every minute is expectancy/ Of more arrivance." *Oth,* II, i, 41–42.

arrive, *v.* **am arrived for,** (I) have arrived in: "To see fair Padua, nursery of arts,/ I am arriv'd for fruitful Lombardy . . ." *Shrew,* I, i, 2–3.

arrouse, *v.* to besprinkle: "The blissful dew of heaven does arrouse you." *Kinsmen,* V, iv, 104.

art, *n.* **1** great skill, ability, or dexterity; here, studied charm or behavior: "O, teach me how you look, and with what art/ You sway the motion [inclination] of Demetrius' heart." *M N Dream,* I, i, 192–193. **2** learning; study: ". . . as pregnant in/ As art and practice hath enriched any . . ." *Meas,* I, i, 11–12. **3** way or method: "There's no art/ To find the mind's construction in the face . . ." *Mac,* I, iv, 11–12. **4** artifice or stratagem: "And take thou my oblation . . . Which is not mix'd with seconds, knows no art . . ." *Sonn 125,* 12–13. **5** rhetorical flourishes; here, understood as "artifice": "More matter with less art."/ "Madam, I swear I use no art at all." *Ham,* II, ii, 95–96. **6** reliance on philosophy to bear adversity: "I have as much of this in art as you,/ But yet my nature could not bear it so." *J Caes,* IV, iii, 193–194. **7** experience; also, knowledge gained by such experience: "Who, by the art of known and feeling sorrows,/ Am pregnant to good pity." *Lear,* IV, vi, 223–224. **8** design or plan: "Be it art or hap,/ He hath spoken true." *Ant & Cleo,* II, iii, 31–32. **9** the black arts; magic: "And bring him out that is but woman's son/ Can trace me in the tedious ways of art . . ." *1 Hen 4,* III, i, 44–45. **10 art and nature,** skill [as a prostitute] and natural appeal [as a woman]: "Never could the strumpet/ With all her double vigour, art and nature,/ Once stir my temper . . ." *Meas,* II, ii, 183–185. **11 by art,** deviously; cunningly: "Use power with power, and slay me not by art." *Sonn 139,* 4. **12 choke their art,** hinder their [swimming] skill: "As two spent swimmers, that do cling together/ And choke their art." *Mac,* I, ii, 8–9.

Arthur's bosom, *n.* Hostess's misuse for "Abraham's bosom": "Nay, sure, he's not in hell: he's in Arthur's/ bosom . . ." *Hen 5,* II, iii, 9–10.

Arthur's show, *n.* exhibition of archery skills, in which participants dressed as a character from the Round Table: "I remember at Mile-End Green . . . I was then Sir Dagonet in Arthur's/ show . . ." *2 Hen 4,* III, ii, 274–276.

article, *n.* **1** prominence or worth: "I take him to be a soul of great article . . ." *Ham,* V, ii, 116. **2** [usually pl] detailed list or schedule, as of charges or demands: ". . . the summary of all our griefs to show in articles,/ Which long ere this we offer'd to the King . . ." *2 Hen 4,* IV, i, 74–75. **3** precise terms or conditions: "You have broken/ The article of your oath . . ." *Ant & Cleo,* II, ii, 81–82. **4** stipulation: ". . . his surly nature/ Which easily endures not article . . ." *Cor,* II, iii, 193–194. **5 article of thy gentry,** the matter of your rank: ". . . and so thou shouldst not alter the/ article of thy gentry." *Wives,* II, i, 50–51. **6 articles of the combination,** terms of the treaty: ". . . this cunning cardinal/ The articles o' th' combination drew/ As himself pleas'd . . ." *Hen 8,* I, i, 169–170.

articulate, *adj.* **1** set forth in a list or inventory: "These things indeed you have articulate,/ Proclaim'd at market crosses, read in churches . . ." *1 Hen 4,* V, i, 72–73.
—*v.* **2** to set forth terms for peace: ". . . send us to Rome/ The best, with whom we may articulate/ For their own good and ours." *Cor,* I, ix, 75–76.

artificer, *n.* artisan; workman: "Another lean unwash'd artificer . . ." *K John,* IV, ii, 201.

artificial, *adj.* **1** creative: "We, Hermia, like two artificial gods,/ Have with our needles created both one flower . . ." *M N Dream,* III, ii, 203–204. **2** skillful: "If that thy prosperous and artificial feat/ Can draw him . . ." *Per,* V, i, 72–73. **3** pretended; feigned: "And wet my cheeks with artificial tears . . ." *3 Hen 6,* III, ii, 184.

artificial strife, *n.* contending of art and nature: ". . . artificial strife/ Lives in these touches, livelier than life." *Timon,* I, i, 37–38.

artire, *n.* artery; here, French sense of "sinew," "tendon": "My fate cries out/ And makes each petty artire . . . As hardy as the Nemean lion's nerve." *Ham,* I, iv, 82–83.

artist, *n.* graduate in the arts; scholar; here, one trained in the medical arts: "To be relinquish'd of the artists—" *All's W,* II, iii, 10.

artless jealousy, *n.* uncontrolled suspicion: "So full of artless jealousy is guilt . . ." *Ham,* IV, v, 19.

arts-man, *n.* scholar: "Arts-man, preambulate: we will be singled from the/ barbarous." *Love's L,* V, i, 73–74.

as, *conj.* **1** that: "As very infants prattle of thy pride [arrogance]." *1 Hen 6,* III, i, 16. **2** whenever: "And sister, as the winds give benefit/ And convoy is assistant, do not sleep . . ." *Ham,* I, iii, 2–3. **3** as if; as though: ". . . as the year/ Had found some months asleep and leap'd them over." *2 Hen 4,* IV, iv, 123–124. **4** even (when): "If you'll patch a quarrel,/ As matter whole you have to make it with . . ." *Ant & Cleo,* II, ii, 52–53. **5** to the extent that: "Not so, but as we change [exchange] our courtesies." *All's W,* III, ii, 97. **6 as that,** in that; inasmuch as: ". . . but lest you do repent,/ As that the sin hath brought you to this shame . . ." *Meas,* II, iii, 30–31. **7 as to one,** as you can be to someone: ". . . as welcome as to one/ That would be rid of such an enemy—" *Tr & Cr,* IV, v, 162–163.
—*prep.* **8** like: "When I perceive that men as plants increase . . ." *Sonn 15,* 5. **9** in place of: ". . . must be us'd/ With checks as flatteries, when they are seen abus'd [deluded]." *Lear,* I, iii, 20–21.

Ascanius, *n.* son of Aeneas: "To sit and witch me, as Ascanius did/ When he to madding Dido would unfold/ His father's acts . . ." *2 Hen 6,* III, ii, 115–117.

Ascension Day, *n.* Thursday, 40 days after Easter, when Christ is believed to have ascended into Heaven: "On this Ascension-day, remember well,/ Upon your oath of service to the pope,/ Go I to make the French lay down their arms." *K John,* V, I, 22–24.

ash[1], *n.* lance with a shaft of ash: "My grained ash an hundred times hath broke . . ." *Cor,* IV, v, 109.

ash[2], *n.* city ashes, ashes of their destroyed city: "The pillars of his hearse shall be their bones,/ The mould that covers him, their city ashes . . ." *Edw 3,* V, i, 170–171.

Asher-house, *n.* Esher, residence of the Bishop of Winchester [one of Wolsey's titles]: ". . . confine yourself/ To Asher-house, my Lord of Winchester's,/ Till you hear further from his highness." *Hen 8,* III, ii, 230–232.

Ashford, *n.* town in SE England [reputed birthplace of Jack Cade]: "Where's Dick, the butcher of Ashford?" *2 Hen 6,* IV, iii, 1.

ashy, *adj.* ashen; pale: "And dying eyes gleam'd forth their ashy lights . . ." *Luc,* 1378.

asinico, *n.* small ass [fr. Spanish]: ". . . an asinico may tutor thee." *Tr & Cr,* II, i, 47.

ask, *v.* **1** to require or demand: "That will ask some tears in the true performing of it." *M N Dream,* I, ii, 21. **2 not thy asking,** without your having to ask: "What wouldst thou beg, Laertes,/ That shall not be my offer, not thy asking?" *Ham,* I, ii, 45–46.

askance, *adv.* **1** scornfully: "Thou canst not frown, thou canst not look askance . . ." *Shrew,* II, i, 241.
—*v.* **2** turn aside; avert: ". . . from their own misdeeds askance their eyes!" *Luc,* 637.

askant, *prep.* aslant; slanting over: "There is a willow grows askant the brook . . ." *Ham,* IV, vii, 165.

Asnath, *n.* name of the evil spirit; appar. an anagram of "Sathan" [Satan]: "Asnath!/ By the eternal God, whose name and power/ Thou tremblest at . . ." *2 Hen 6,* I, iv, 23–25.

aspect, *n.* **1** appearance; sometimes applied to the relative positions of the stars and planets and their astrological influence: "Alack, in me, what strange effect/ Would they work in mild aspect [if they regarded me tenderly]?" *As You,* IV, iii, 52–53. **2** one's look or air; mien: "If you will jest with me, know my aspect,/ And fashion your demeanour to my looks . . ." *Errors,* II, ii, 32. **3** [often pl.] glance or look: "With pure aspects did him peculiar duties." *Luc,* 14.

aspersion, *n.* blessing [lit., a sprinkling that promotes fertility]: "No sweet aspersion shall the heavens let fall/ To make this contract grow . . ." *Temp,* IV, i, 18–19.

aspic, *n.* asp; here, its poison: "Have I the aspic in my lips? Dost fall?" *Ant & Cleo,* V, ii, 292.

aspicious, *adj.* misuse for "suspicious": ". . . our watch, sir, have indeed comprehended/ two aspicious persons . . ." *M Ado,* III, v, 43–44.

aspire, *v.* **1** to rise up; rise high: "For who digs hills because they do aspire . . ." *Per,* I, iv, 5. **2** to rise up to or into: "Romeo, brave Mercutio is dead,/ That gallant spirit hath aspir'd the clouds . . ." *Rom & Jul,* III, i, 118–119.

aspiring, *adj.* **1** ambitious: "Mounted upon a hot and fiery steed/ Which his aspiring rider seem'd to know . . ." *Rich 2,* V, ii, 8–9. **2** rising; mounting: "Show boldness and aspiring confidence!" *K John,* V, i, 56.

aspray, *n.* var. of **osprey,** fish hawk; fr. belief that fish, on seeing the osprey's approach, were paralyzed with fear and let themselves be taken: ". . . your actions,/ Soon as they move, as asprays do the fish,/ Subdue before they touch." *Kinsmen,* I, i, 137–139.

a-squint, *adv.* cross-eyed; here, the effect of jealousy: "That eye that told you so look'd but a-squint." *Lear,* V, iii, 73.

ass, *n.* **1 ass and ox,** a fool and a cuckold: "To an ass were nothing: he is both/ ass and ox . . ." *Tr & Cr,* V, i, 58–59. **2 ass in compound,** wordplay on "-as" suffix in compound words and "ass," fool: ". . . I find the ass in/ compound with the major part of your syllables." *Cor,* II, i, 57–58.

assail, *v.* to make amorous siege to: "'Accost' is front her,/ board her, woo her, assail her." *T Night,* I, iii, 55–56.

assault, *n.* **of general assault,** common to all young men: "A savageness in unreclaimed blood,/ Of general assault." *Ham,* II, i, 34–35.

assay, *n.* **1** test or trial; also, challenge: "Makes vow before his uncle never more/ To give th'assay of arms against your Majesty . . ." *Ham,* II, ii, 70–71. **2** maximum or supreme effort: "Help, angels! Make assay./ Bow, stubborn knees; and heart with strings of steel . . ." *Ham,* III, iii, 69–70. **3** assault: "Galling the gleaned land with hot assays . . ." *Hen 5,* I, ii, 151. —*v.* **4** to determine another's interest regarding: "Did you assay him/ To any pastime?" *Ham,* III, i, 14–15. **5** to attempt; try: "The rebels have assay'd to win the Tower." *2 Hen 6,* IV, v, 8. **6** to test or determine; also, try to persuade: "Implore her . . . that she make friends/ To the strict deputy: bid herself assay him." *Meas,* I, ii, 170–171.

assay of reason, test of common sense: "This cannot be/ By no assay of reason . . ." *Oth,* I, iii, 17–18.

assays of bias, *n.* devious attempts to achieve a goal [term in bowls]: ". . . with assays of bias,/ By indirections find directions out." *Ham,* II, i, 65–66.

assemblance, *n.* general appearance of a person; frame: "Care I for the limb, the thews, the stature,/ bulk, and big assemblance of a man?" *2 Hen 4,* III, ii, 253–254.

assembly, *n.* **1** assembled group; company of friends or associates: "Haply in private."/ "And in assemblies too." *Errors,* V, i, 59–60. **2** festivity or revel: ". . . assemblies,/ Where youth, and cost, witless bravery keeps." *Meas,* I, iii, 9–10.

assigns, *n. pl.* accessories; appendages or appurtenances: ". . . six French rapiers and poniards, with their/ assigns . . ." *Ham,* V, ii, 146–147.

assistance, *n.* inspiration: "And found such fair assistance in my verse . . ." *Sonn 78,* 2.

associate, *v.* to accompany: "Going to find a barefoot brother out,/ . . . to associate me,/ Here in this city visiting the sick . . ." *Rom & Jul,* V, ii, 5–7.

assubjugate, *v.* to depreciate or debase: "Shall not so stale his palm . . . Nor, by my will, assubjugate his merit . . ." *Tr & Cr,* II, iii, 192–193.

assurance, *n.* **1** certainty: ". . . rather like a dream than an assurance . . ." *Temp,* I, ii, 45. **2** deed guaranteeing possession: "They are sheep and calves which seek out assurance/ in that." *Ham,* V, i, 114–115. **3** guarantees of money and property that accompanied a betrothal: "Where then do you know best/ We be affied and such assurance ta'en . . ." *Shrew,* IV, iv, 48–49. **4** safety; security: "Look your heart be firm,/ Or else his head's assurance is but frail." *Rich 3,* IV, iv, 495–496.

assure, *v.* **assure her of,** provide for her: "I'll assure her of/ Her widowhood . . ." *Shrew,* II, i, 123–124.

assured, *adj.* **1** promised in marriage; betrothed: ". . . this drudge or diviner laid claim to me, called me/ Dromio, swore I was assured to her . . ." *Errors,* III, ii, 138–140. **2** assured of; here, man's spiritual essence: "Most ignorant of what he's most assur'd—/ His glassy essence . . ." *Meas,* II, ii, 120–121. **3** in truth; actual: "The ills that were not, grew to faults assured . . ." *Sonn 118,* 10.

assured bondage, *n.* [bonds of] matrimony: ". . . will's free hours languish for/ Assured bondage?" *Cymb,* I, vii, 72–73.

Assyrian, *adj.* **Assyrian slings,** ref. to the ancient Assyrians and their reputed skill with slingshots: ". . . as swift as stones/ Enforced from the old Assyrian slings." *Hen 5,* IV, vii, 63–64.

astonish, *v.* **1** to stun or terrify: "When the most mighty gods by tokens send/ Such dreadful heralds to astonish us." *J Caes,* I, iii, 55–56. **2** to strike dumb; silence: "No, neither he, nor his compeers by night/ Giving him aid, my verse astonished." *Sonn 86,* 7–8.

Astraea, *n.* goddess of justice, who eventually forsook the earth because of its corruption and was given a place among the stars: "Divinest creature, Astraea's daughter,/ How shall I honour thee for this success?" *1 Hen 6,* I, vi, 4–5.

astronomer, *n.* astrologer: "O, learn'd indeed were that astronomer/ That knew the stars as I his characters [handwriting] . . ." *Cymb,* III, ii, 27–28.

astronomy, *n.* astrology: ". . . methinks I have astronomy,/ But not to tell of good or evil luck . . ." *Sonn 14,* 1–2.

asunder, *adv.* apart: "Pluck them asunder." *Ham,* V, i, 257.

as who should say, as if to say: As who should say, "I am Sir Oracle,/ And when I ope my lips, let no dog bark." *Merch,* I, i, 93–94.

at', at the: "... it shall be said so again, while Stephano/ breathes at' nostrils." *Temp,* II, ii, 63–64.

Atalanta, *n.* ref. to swift-footed huntress of Greek mythology: "You have a nimble wit; I think 'twas made of/ Atalanta's heels." *As You,* III, ii, 271–272.

Ate, *n.* daughter of Zeus and goddess of vengeance, also strife and discord: "... you shall find her the infernal Ate in good apparel." *M Ado,* II, i, 239.

at first, *adv.* right off; right away: "... in an hour, was't not?/ Or less; at first?" *Cymb,* II, iv, 166–167.

at hand, *adj.* ready (given as a response): "'At hand, quoth pick-purse.'" *1 Hen 4,* II, i, 47.

at high wish, as much or as fully as one could wish: "The one is filling still, never complete,/ The other, at high wish." *Timon,* IV, iii, 246–247.

athversary, *n.* adversary [Shakespeare's rendering of Fluellen's Welsh accent when speaking English]: "... th'/ athversary ... is digt [digged] himself four yard under the countermines." *Hen 5,* III, ii, 64–66.

athwart, *adv.* **1** unexpectedly: "... when all athwart there came/ A post from Wales ..." *1 Hen 4,* I, i, 36–37. **2** awry: "The baby beats the nurse, and quite athwart/ Goes all decorum." *Meas,* I, iii, 30–31.

Atlas, *n.* (in class. myth.) one of the Titans [Elder Gods] and brother of Prometheus; supported the world on his shoulders: "Thou art no Atlas for so great a weight ..." *3 Hen 6,* V, i, 36.

atomi, *n. pl.* tiny creatures: "Drawn with a team of little atomi/ Over men's noses as they lie asleep." *Rom & Jul,* I, iv, 57–58.

atomy, *n.* **1** atom; the minutest particle: "It is as easy to count atomies as to resolve the propositions of a lover." *As You,* III, ii, 228–229. **2** misuse for "anatomy," skeleton: "Goodman death, goodman bones!"/ "Thou atomy, thou!" *2 Hen 4,* V, iv, 28–29.

at once, *adv.* [let us proceed] promptly: "My lords, at once ..." *2 Hen 6,* III, i, 66.

atone, *v.* **1** to reconcile or appease: "... and, to atone your fears/ With my more noble meaning, not a man/ Shall pass his quarter ..." *Timon,* V, iv, 58–60. **2** to become reconciled: "He and Aufidius can no more atone/ Than violent'st contrariety." *Cor,* IV, vi, 73–74.

at one, *adv.* in sympathy: "... thy speaking/ of my tongue, and I thine ... must needs be granted to be much at one." *Hen 5,* V, ii, 198–200.

atonement, *n.* reconciliation: "If we do now make our atonement well,/ Our peace will, like a broken limb united,/ Grow stronger for the breaking." *2 Hen 4,* IV, i, 221–223.

Atropos, *n.* Fate who cut the thread of life: "... Untwind the Sisters Three! Come, Atropos, I say!" *2 Hen 4,* II, iv, 195.

attach, *v.* **1** to arrest; take into custody: "... you, Lord Archbishop, and you, Lord Mowbray,/ Of capital treason I attach you both." *2 Hen 4,* IV, ii, 108–109. **2** take hold of: "Then homeward every man attach the hand/ Of his fair mistress ..." *Love's L,* IV, iii, 371–372. **3** to seize: "I cannot blame thee,/ Who am myself attach'd with weariness ..." *Temp,* III, iii, 4–5. **4 attached with,** affected by: "May worthy Troilus be half attach'd/ with that which here his passion doth express?" *Tr & Cr,* V, ii, 160–161.

attachment, *n.* arrest or imprisonment; here, used fig.: "And give as soft attachment to thy senses/ As infants empty of all thought." *Tr & Cr,* IV, ii, 5–6.

attain, *v.* **hardly attained,** hard to obtain: "... these oracles/ Are hardly attain'd, and hardly understood." *2 Hen 6,* I, iv, 68–69.

attainder, *n.* **1** condemnation; disgrace: "... he that breaks them in the least degree/ Stands in attainder of eternal shame ..." *Love's L,* I, i, 155–156. **2** accusation: "... have mine honour soil'd/ With the attainder of his slanderous lips." *Rich 2,* IV, i, 23–24. **3 attainder of suspects,** taint of suspicion: "He liv'd from all [without any] attainder of suspects." *Rich 3,* III, v, 32.

attaint, *adj.* **1** disgraced: "You are attaint with faults and perjury ..." *Love's L,* V, ii, 811. **2** infected: "My tender youth was never yet attaint/ With any passion of inflaming love ..." *1 Hen 6,* V, v, 81–82.
—*n.* **3** vice; also, disgrace or dishonor: "What simple thief brags of his own attaint?" *Errors,* III, ii, 16. **4** impeachment or indictment: "... and, in thy attaint,/ This gilded serpent. [Pointing to Goneril]" *Lear,* V, iii, 84–85. **5** infection: "The marrow-eating sickness whose attaint/ Disorder breeds ..." *Ven & Ad,* 741–742. **6** blemish: "... nor any man an/ attaint but he carries some stain of it." *Tr & Cr,* I, ii, 25–26. **7 overbears attaint,** resists any sign of fatigue: "But freshly looks and overbears attaint/ With cheerful semblance ..." *Hen 5,* IV, Chor., 39–40.
—*v.* **8** to condemn for treason or a felony: "I must offend before I be attainted ..." *2 Hen 6,* II, iv, 59. **9** to disgrace: "... a

story/ Of faults conceal'd, wherein I am attainted . . ." *Sonn 88*, 6–7.

attainted, *adj.* stained or corrupted; here, with dishonor: "And by his treason stand'st not thou attainted . . ." *1 Hen 6*, II, iv, 92.

attainture, *n.* disgrace; dishonor: "Hume's knavery will be the Duchess' wrack,/ And her attainture will be Humphrey's fall." *2 Hen 6*, I, ii, 105–106.

attaxed, *past part.* blamed: "You are much more attax'd for want of wisdom/ Than prais'd for harmful mildness." *Lear*, I, iv, 353–354.

attempt, *n.* **1** endeavor or activity; exploit: "Such poor, such bare, such lewd, such mean attempts . . ." *1 Hen 4*, III, ii, 13. **2** assault: "The maid will I frame, and make fit for his attempt." *Meas*, III, i, 256–257.
—*v.* **3** to tempt or urge: "Dear sir, of force I must attempt you further . . ." *Merch*, IV, i, 417. **4** to win over: ". . . neither my coat, integrity, nor/ persuasion can with ease attempt you . . ." *Meas*, IV, ii, 188–189. **5** to assail; attack: ". . . got praises of the King/ For him attempting who was self-subdu'd . . ." *Lear*, II, ii, 122–123.

attemptable, *adj.* seducible: ". . . less attemptable than any the rarest of our ladies in/ France." *Cymb*, I, v, 58–59.

attend, *v.* **1** to await: "Attending but the signal to begin." *Rich 2*, I, iii, 116. **2** to wait on; be an attendant to: ". . . twins both alike/ . . . brought up to attend my sons." *Errors*, I, i, 55–57. **3** to pay attention to; heed: "What said my man, when my betossed soul/ Did not attend him, as we rode?" *Rom & Jul*, V, iii, 76–77. **4** to be present: "And we will fear no poison, which attends/ In place of greater state." *Cymb*, III, iii, 77–78. **5 attending for a check,** waiting around [the court] for a rebuke: "O, this life/ Is nobler than attending for a check . . ." *Cymb*, III, iii, 21–22. **6 attend upon,** to wait for: "The solemn feast/ Shall more attend upon the coming space . . ." *All's W*, II, iii, 180–181. **7 neither is attended,** each is alone: "The crow doth sing as sweetly as the lark/ When neither is attended . . ." *Merch*, V, i, 102–103.

attendance, *n.* attention: "For if the touch of sweet concordant strings/ Could force attendance in the ears of hell . . ." *Edw 3*, II, i, 76–77.

attended, *past part.* **1** waited on: ". . . to speak to you like an honest man,/ I am most dreadfully attended." *Ham*, II, ii, 268–269. **2** awaited; expected: "I am attended at the cypress grove." *Cor*, I, x, 30.

attendure, *n.* var. of **attainder;** accusation: "'Tis likely/ By all conjectures: first Kildare's attendure . . ." *Hen 8*, II, i, 40–41.

attent, *adj.* attentive: "Season your admiration for a while/ With an attent ear . . ." *Ham*, I, ii, 192–193.

attest, *n.* **1** testimony: "That doth invert th'attest of eyes and ears . . ." *Tr & Cr*, V, ii, 121.
—*v.* **2** to symbolize; take the place of: ". . . since a crooked figure may/ Attest in little place a million . . ." *Hen 5*, Prol. 15–16.

attorney, *n.* **1** proxy or deputy: "Then in mine own person, I die."/ "No, faith, die by attorney." *As You*, IV, i, 88–89. **2 the heart's attorney,** the tongue; speech: "But when the heart's attorney once is mute,/ The client breaks . . ." *Ven & Ad*, 335–336.

attorneyed, *past part.* **1** acting as an agent: "Not changing heart with habit, I am still/ Attorney'd at your service." *Meas*, V, 382–383. **2** carried on by proxy: ". . . their encounters . . . have been royally attorneyed with interchange/ of gifts . . ." *W Tale*, I, i, 26–28.

attorneyship, *n.* agent or proxy: "Marriage is a matter of more worth/ Than to be dealt in by attorneyship . . ." *1 Hen 6*, V, v, 55–56.

attractive, *adj.* beguiling; here in wordplay with "magnetic": "No, good mother, here's metal more attractive." *Ham*, III, ii, 108.

attribute, *n.* **1** reputation; honor: "And for an honest attribute cry out/ 'she died by foul play.'" *Per*, IV, iii, 18–19. **2 attribute to, a.** symbol of: "His sceptre shows the force of temporal power,/ The attribute to awe and majesty . . ." *Merch*, IV, i, 186–187. **b.** characteristic of: "It is enthroned in the hearts of kings,/ It is an attribute to God himself . . ." *Merch*, IV, i, 190–191.

attribution, *n.* citation or mention of one's merits; credit; praise: "If speaking truth/ . . . were not thought flattery,/ Such attribution should the Douglas have . . ." *1 Hen 4*, IV, i, 1–3.

attributive, *adj.* ascribing qualities: "And the will dotes that is attributive . . ." *Tr & Cr*, II, ii, 59.

audacious, *adj.* confident; animated: ". . . your reasons at dinner/ have been . . . audacious without/ impudency . . ." *Love's L*, V, i, 2–5.

audible, *adj.* keen-eared: ". . . it's sprightly walking, audible,/ and full of vent." *Cor*, IV, v, 229–230.

audience, *n.* **1 have audience,** to be heard: "Shall I have audience?" *Love's L,* V, i, 125. **2 of audience,** neither of hearing: "The queen/ Of audience nor desire shall fail . . ." *Ant & Cleo,* III, xii, 20–21.
—*v.* **3** [used as a command] Listen! Pay attention!: "List to your tribunes. Audience! Peace, I say!" *Cor,* III, iii, 40.

audit, *n.* **1** account: "And how his audit stands who knows save heaven?" *Ham,* III, iii, 82. **2** an accounting: ". . . what is theirs, in compt,/ To make their audit at your Highness' pleasure . . ." *Mac,* I, vi, 26–27. **3** an accounting for one's life: ". . . when Nature calls thee to be gone,/ What acceptable audit canst thou leave?" *Sonn 4,* 11–12. **4** final settlement; here, the one that nature must make with time: "Her audit, though delayed, answered must be . . ." *Sonn 126,* 11.

auditory, *n.* audience; hearers: "Then, gracious auditory, be it known to you,/ That Chiron and the damn'd Demetrius/ Were they that murdered our emperor's brother . . ." *T Andr,* V, iii, 96–98.

auger-hole, *n.* small cranny or nook; here, poss. a dagger hole: ". . . our fate, hid in an auger-hole,/ May rush, and seize us?" *Mac,* II, iii, 123–124.

auger's bore, *n.* hole made by a boring tool; here, a very small space: "Your franchises, whereon you stood, confin'd/ Into an auger's bore." *Cor,* IV, vi, 87–88.

aught, *n.* **1** anything: "This is the man that can, in aught you would [anything you wish],/ Resolve you." *Per,* V, i, 12–13. **2** any such things: "No, not I./ I never gave you aught." *Ham,* III, i, 95–96. **3 in neither aught, or in extremity,** either nothing of either one or too much of both: "For women's fear and love hold quantity,/ In neither aught, or in extremity." *Ham,* III, ii, 162–163.

augur, *n.* **1** prophet; soothsayer: "And the sad [gloomy] augurs mock their own presage . . ." *Sonn 107,* 6.
—*v.* **2** to prophesy: ". . . my auguring hope/ Says it will come to the full." *Ant & Cleo,* II, i, 10–11.

augure, *n.* augury; prediction: "Augures, and understood relations, have . . . brought forth/ The secret'st man of blood." *Mac,* III, iv, 123–125.

augurer, *n.* person who professes to interpret omens and portents: "And the persuasion of his augurers,/ May hold him from the Capitol to-day." *J Caes,* II, i, 200–201.

augury, *n.* ability to predict the future; the act of prophesying: "We defy augury. There is special providence/ in the fall of a sparrow." *Ham,* V, ii, 215–216.

Aulis, *n.* harbor in E Greece: ". . . at the banks of Aulis meet us with/ The forces you can raise . . ." *Kinsmen,* I, i, 212–213.

aunchiant, *adj.* Fluellen's Welsh-accented pron. of "ancient": ". . . of great expedition [erudition] and/ knowledge in th' aunchiant wars . . ." *Hen 5,* III, ii, 81–82.

aunchient lieutenant, *n.* poss. a sub-lieutenant: "There is an/ aunchient lieutenant there at the pridge [bridge] . . ." *Hen 5,* III, vi, 12–13.

aunt, *n.* **1** old woman: "The wisest aunt, telling the saddest tale . . ." *M N Dream,* II, i, 51. **2** doxy; whore: ". . . summer songs for me and my aunts,/ While we lie tumbling in the hay." *W Tale,* IV, iii, 11–12. **3 old aunt,** ref. to Hesione, sister of Priam and mother of Ajax; saved by Hercules from being sacrificed to a sea monster and given as wife to Telamon: "And for an old aunt whom the Greeks held captive,/ He brought a Grecian queen . . ." *Tr & Cr,* II, ii, 78–79.

Aurora, *n.* Roman goddess of the dawn: ". . . the all-cheering sun/ . . . begin to draw/ The shady curtains from Aurora's bed . . ." *Rom & Jul,* I, i, 132–134.

auspicious, *adj.* joyful; cheerful: "With an auspicious and a dropping eye . . ." *Ham,* I, ii, 11.

auspicious mistress, *n.* favorable or favoring goddess: ". . . conjuring the moon/ To stand [his] auspicious mistress." *Lear,* II, i, 39–40.

austere, *adj.* severe: ". . . quenching my/ familiar smile with an austere regard of control—" *T Night,* II, v, 66–67.

authentic, *adj.* recognized and respected: ". . . of great admittance, authentic in your place/ and person . . ." *Wives,* II, ii, 219–220.

author, *n.* **1** creator or originator: "I did but act, he's author of thy slander." *Ven & Ad,* 1006. **2** begetter: ". . . stand/ As if a man were author of himself . . ." *Cor,* V, iii, 35–36.

authority, *n.* **1** dictates; power; influence: ". . . 'gainst th' authority of manners, pray'd you/ To hold your hand more close." *Timon,* II, ii, 142–143. **2** the nobility; ruling class: "What authority surfeits on would relieve us." *Cor,* I, i, 15. **3** justification; precedent: "Thieves for their robbery have authority,/ When judges steal themselves." *Meas,* II, ii, 176–177.

authorize, *v.* to justify or excuse: "Authorising thy trespass with compare . . ." *Sonn 35,* 6.

authorized, *adj.* sanctioned; permitted: "A woman's story at a winter's fire,/ Authoris'd by her grandam." *Mac,* III, iv, 64–65.

Auvergne, *n.* mountainous province in S central France: "The virtuous lady, Countess of Auvergne . . . entreats . . . thou would'st vouchsafe/ To visit her poor castle . . ." *1 Hen 6,* II, ii, 38–41.

avail, *n.* **1** profit; advantage: "I charge thee,/ As heaven shall work in me for thine avail,/ To tell me truly." *All's W,* I, iii, 178–179.
—*v.* **2** to benefit; profit: "But how out of this can/ she avail?" *Meas,* III, i, 233–234.

avaunt, *v.* **1** away! begone!: "Avaunt, perplexity! What shall we do/ If they return in their own shapes to woo?" *Love's L,* V, ii, 298–299.
—*n.* **2 give her the avaunt,** bid her go: "To give her the avaunt, it is a pity/ Would move a monster!" *Hen 8,* II, iii, 10–11.

Ave, *interj.* [Latin] Hail!; used as a salutation: "I do not relish well/ Their loud applause and *Aves* vehement . . ." *Meas,* I, ii, 69–70.

Ave-Maries, *n.* Hail Marys [Latin version of a Roman Catholic prayer]: ". . . all his mind is bent to holiness,/ To number Ave-Maries on his beads . . ." *2 Hen 6,* I, iii, 55–56.

averring, *pres. part.* [or, perh., pres. indic.] affirming; declaring as truthful: ". . . averring notes/ Of chamber-hanging, pictures, this her bracelet . . ." *Cymb,* V, v, 203–204.

avised, *adj.* advised; careful: "Be avised, sir, and pass good humours . . ." *Wives,* I, i, 150.

avoid, *v.* **1** to leave [often used as a command]; away! begone!: "Satan avoid, I charge thee tempt me not." *Errors,* IV, iii, 46. **2** to sidestep; also, nullify [legal term]: ". . . he will avoid your accusation—he/ made trial of you only." *Meas,* III, i, 195–196. **3 avoid hence,** begone [from here]!: "Thou basest thing, avoid hence, from my sight!" *Cymb,* I, ii, 56.

avouch, *v.* **1** to declare; affirm: "Demetrius, I'll avouch it to his head,/ Made love to Nedar's daughter, Helena . . ." *M N Dream,* I, i, l06–l07. **2** to justify: "I could . . . sweep him from my sight,/ And bid my will avouch it . . ." *Mac,* III, i, 117–119. **3** to confirm; verify: ". . . you have made no offence if the/ Duke avouch the justice of your dealing?" *Meas,* IV, ii, 184–185.
—*n.* **4** confirmation; assurance: "I might not this believe/ Without the sensible and true avouch/ Of mine own eyes." *Ham,* I, i, 59–61.

avouchment, *v.* Fluellen seems to mean "testify or witness": ". . . will avouchment/ that this is the glove of Alençon that your/ majesty is give me . . ." *Hen 5,* IV, viii, 37–38.

await, *v.* to expect; be on the lookout [for]: "Posterity, await for wretched years . . ." *1 Hen 6,* I, i, 48.

awake, *v.* **1** to arouse; bestir: "My master is awak'd by great occasion . . ." *Timon,* II, i, 24. **2** to activate or reactivate [for me]: ". . . this new governor/ Awakes me all the enrolled penalties . . ." *Meas,* I, ii, 154–155.

away, *adv.* **1** [to] here; this way: "Come, bring them away." *Meas,* II, i, 41. **2 away about it,** go and do it: "Presently we'll try: come, let's away about it . . ." *1 Hen 6,* I, ii, 149. **3 make thee away,** put an end to you: ". . . thou diest in/ thine unthankfulness, and thine ignorance makes/ thee away." *All's W,* I, i, 206–208.

away with, *v.* to put up with; tolerate: "She never could away with me." *2 Hen 4,* III, ii, 196.

awe, *n.* **1** respect; obedience: "Domestic awe, night-rest and neighbourhood . . ." *Timon,* IV, i, 17. **2** object of respect or obedience: "Now by my sceptre's awe I make a vow . . ." *Rich 2,* I, i, 118. **3** authority: "France being ours, we'll bend it to our awe . . ." *Hen 5,* I, ii, 224. **4 in awe, a.** under authority or subjugation: ". . . debating to and fro/ How France and Frenchmen might be kept in awe." *2 Hen 6,* I, i, 90. **b.** at a respectful distance: "Which to prevent he made a law,/ To keep her still [always], and men in awe . . ." *Per,* I, Chor., 35–36. **5 under one man's awe,** in awe of one man: "Shall Rome stand under one man's awe?" *J Caes,* II, i, 52.
—*v.* **6** to restrain or prevent through fear: "Shall quips and sentences/ . . . awe a man from the career of his humour?" *M Ado,* II, iii, 231–233. **7** to keep in subjection: "Since thou, created to be aw'd by man,/ Wast born to bear?" *Rich 2,* V, v, 91–92.

awed resistance, *n.* fear of resisting: "Pure shame and aw'd resistance made him fret . . ." *Ven & Ad,* 69.

aweful, *adj.* old form of **awful**; commanding fear or respect: "We come within our aweful banks [bounds of obedience] again,/ And knit our powers to the arm of peace." *2 Hen 4,* IV, i, 176–177.

aweless, *adj.* inspiring no awe [because of the king's youth]: "Insulting tyranny begins to jut/ Upon the innocent and aweless throne." *Rich 3,* II, iv, 51–52.

aweless lion, *n.* ref. to legend and origin of nickname "Coeur-de-lion," wherein Richard, unarmed, thrust his hand down a lion's throat and ripped out its heart: "The aweless lion could not wage the fight,/ Nor keep his princely heart from Richard's hand." *K John,* I, i, 266–267.

awful, *adj.* **1** worthy of or compelling respect: "A better prince and benign lord/ That will prove awful both in deed and word." *Per,* II, Chor., 3–4. **2** awe-inspiring: ". . . pluck the diadem from faint Henry's head,/ And wring the awful sceptre from his fist . . ." *3 Hen 6,* II, i, 153–154.

awkward, *adj.* **1** adverse; contrary: ". . . twice by awkward wind from England's bank/ Drove back again unto my native clime?" *2 Hen 6,* III, ii, 82–83. **2** perverse; devious: "'Tis no sinister nor no awkward claim . . ." *Hen 5,* II, iv, 85.

awry, *adv.* obliquely: "Like perspectives . . . ey'd awry,/ Distinguish form." *Rich 2,* II, ii, 18–20.

axletree, *n.* axis: ". . . strong as the axletree/ On which heaven rides . . ." *Tr & Cr,* I, iii, 66–67.

ay[1], *adv.* yes: "Two o'clock is your hour?/ Ay, sweet Rosalind." *As You,* IV, i, 176–177.

ay[2], *interj.* **ay me,** alas!: "Ay me, what act/ That roars so loud and thunders in the index?" *Ham,* III, iv, 51–52.

aye, *adv.* **1** ever; always; forever, esp. in the phrase "for aye": ". . . rich conceit/ Taught thee to make vast Neptune weep for aye." *Timon,* V, iv, 77–78. **2 aye good night,** farewell forever: "I am come/ To bid my King and master aye good night . . ." *Lear,* V, iii, 234–235

B

babbler, See **brabbler** (def. 2).

Baccare! *interj.* [pseudo-Latin] Back! Stand back!: "Baccare! You are marvellous forward." *Shrew,* II, i, 73.

Bacchanals, *n. pl.* **1** female worshipers of Bacchus, who tore the poet Orpheus to pieces during a drunken orgy: "'The riot of the tipsy Bacchanals,/ Tearing the Thracian singer in their rage'?" *M N Dream,* V, i, 48–49. **2** dances in honor of Bacchus, god of wine: "Shall we dance now the Egyptian Bacchanals,/ And celebrate our drink?" *Ant & Cleo,* II, vii, 103–104.

Bacchus, *n.* Greek god of wine [Roman, **Dionysus**]: "Love's tongue proves dainty Bacchus gross in taste." *Love's L,* IV, iii, 335.

back, *v.* **1** to ride (a horse): "Well, I will back him straight." *1 Hen 4,* II, iii, 72. **2** to go back; return: "Thou shalt not back till I have borne this corse/ Into the market-place . . ." *J Caes,* III, i, 291–292. **3** to lend support or backing to: "Thou back'st reproach against long-living laud . . ." *Luc,* 622.
—*n.* **4** backup plan: "Therefore this project/ Should have a back or second . . ." *Ham,* IV, vii, 151–152. **5 a your back,** over your head; that is, I'll accompany you inside: "Nay, faith, I'll see the church a your back, and/ then come back to my master's . . ." *Shrew,* V, i, 4–5. **6 behind the back,** when one's back is turned: "No glory lives behind the back of such [such people have nothing good said about them when their backs are turned]." *M Ado,* III, i, 110.
—*adv.* **7** on his way back: "He is not here."/ "No, my good Lord; I met him back again." *Lear,* IV, ii, 89–90.

backbitten, *adj.* infested with lice: "No worse than they are backbitten, sir, for they/ have marvellous foul linen." *2 Hen 4,* V, i, 31–32.

backed, *adj.* **1** (of a horse) broken in to a rider: "The colt that's back'd and burden'd being young,/ Loseth his pride . . ." *Ven*

& Ad, 419–420. **2** riding on an animal's back: "Great Jupiter, upon his eagle back'd . . ." *Cymb,* V, v, 428.

back-friend, *n.* false friend: "How now? Back-friends! Shepherd, go off a little." *As You,* III, ii, 155.

backside, *n.* **backside the town,** the less familiar parts; here, not the main body: "His steel was in debt, it went o' th' backside the town." *Cymb,* I, iii, 12.

backsword man, *n.* expert at singlestick, fencing done with a stick rather than a sword: "I knew him a good backsword/ man. How doth the good knight?" *2 Hen 4,* III, ii, 62–63.

back-trick, *n.* backward step in the galliard: "I think I have the back-trick simply as/ strong as any man in Illyria." *T Night,* I, iii, 120–121.

backward, *n.* **1** the past: "What seest thou else/ In the dark backward and abysm of time?" *Temp,* I, ii, 49–50.
—*adj.* **2** situated in back: ". . . his backward voice is to utter foul speeches . . ." *Temp,* II, ii, 93. **3** hesitant; unwilling: "Perish the man whose mind is backward now!" *Hen 5,* IV, iii, 72.

backwardly, *adv.* unfavorably: "And does he think so backwardly of me now . . ." *Timon,* III, iii, 20.

back-wounding, *adj.* backbiting or back-stabbing: "Backwounding calumny/ The whitest virtue strikes." *Meas,* III, ii, 180–181.

bacon, *n.* fat pig (term of abuse for a person): "I would your store were here! On, bacons, on!" *1 Hen 4,* II, ii, 85–86.

bacon-fed knave, *n.* clumsy rustic; clodhopper: "Ah, whoreson caterpillars, bacon-fed knaves, they/ hate us youth!" *1 Hen 4,* II, ii, 81–82.

bad, *n.* bad thing or things: "Creating [of] every bad a perfect best . . ." *Sonn 114,* 7.

badest, *n.* old form of **bade:** "For doting, not for loving, pupil mine."/ "And bad'st me bury love." *Rom & Jul,* II, iii, 78–79.

badge, *n.* **1** symbol or emblem [that is, his plain words]: "Honest plain words best pierce the ear of grief;/ And by these badges understand the king." *Love's L,* V, ii, 745–746. **2** emblem specifying one's employment, esp. as a menial: ". . . joy could not show itself modest enough without a/ badge of bitterness." *M Ado,* I, i, 21–22.

badged, *adj.* marked with or as if with a badge: "Their hands and faces were all badg'd with blood . . ." *Mac,* II, iii, 102.

baes, *v.* appar. imitation of a lamb that becomes a bear's growl: "He's a lamb indeed, that baes like a bear." *Cor,* II, i, 10.

baffle, *v.* **1** to hang up (a person) by the heels as a mark of disgrace: ". . . an I do/ not, call me villain and baffle me." *1 Hen 4,* I, ii, 97–98. **2** to treat with contempt; ridicule: "Alas, poor fool, how have they baffled thee!" *T Night,* V, i, 368.

bag, *n.* **1** [usually pl.] moneybags: "And that his bags shall prove." *Shrew,* I, ii, 176. **2 bear bags,** guard their moneybags: "But fathers that bear bags/ Shall see their children kind." *Lear,* II, iv, 50–51.

baggage, *n.* term of contempt for a girl or woman; minx; wanton; good-for-nothing: "Out, you green-sickness carrion! Out, you baggage!" *Rom & Jul,* III, v, 156.

bail, *v.* **1** to furnish or act as bail for: "First, Provost, let me bail these gentle three." *Meas,* V, i, 355. **2** to confine: "But then my friend's heart let my poor heart bail." *Sonn 133,* 10. **3 bail it,** [to] purchase its release: "That blow did bail it from the deep unrest/ Of that polluted prison where it breathed." *Luc,* 1725–1726.

bait[1], *v.* to taunt or torment: "Alas! poor Maccabaeus, how hath he been baited." *Love's L,* V, ii, 625.

bait[2], *v.* to entice; lure: "Do their gay vestments his affections bait?" *Errors,* II, i, 94.

baiting-place, *n.* bear pit, meaning the battlefield; refs. to bear-baiting reflect Warwick's family emblem of bear chained to a staff: "And manacle the bear'ard [bearward] in their chains,/ If thou dar'st bring them to the baiting-place." *2 Hen 6,* V, i, 149–150.

Bajazeth's mule, *n.* poss. mistaken allusion to Balaam's ass of the Old Testament; when Balaam beat the ass, the angel of the Lord reprimanded him through the ass's mouth: "Tongue, I must . . . buy myself another [tongue] of Bajazeth's mule if/ you prattle me into these perils." *All's W,* IV, i, 41–43.

baked, *adj.* hardened; encrusted: "To do me business in the veins o' th' earth/ When it is bak'd with frost." *Temp,* I, ii, 255–256.

balance, *n.* [used as sing. or pl.] scale: ". . . are there balance here to weigh/ The flesh?" *Merch,* IV, i, 251–252.

bald, *adj.* **1** slight; inconsequential: "This bald unjointed chat of his . . ." *1 Hen 4,* I, iii, 64. **2** bareheaded; appar. indication that Elizabethan men wore their hats at dinner: ". . . no question asked him by any of the senators/ but they stand bald before him." *Cor,* IV, v, 198–199.

baldrick, *n.* belt across the chest for carrying the hunter's horn: "I will have a recheat winded in my forehead, or hang my bugle in an invisible baldrick . . ." *M Ado,* I, i, 223–224.

bale, *n.* misfortune; sorrow; disaster: "Rome and her rats are at the point of battle;/ The one side must have bale." *Cor,* I, i, 161–162.

baleful, *adj.* poisonous; pernicious: ". . . boiling choler chokes . . . my poison'd voice/ By sight of these our baleful enemies." *1 Hen 6,* V, iv, 120–122.

balk, *v.* to disregard; ignore: "Balk logic with acquaintance that you have . . ." *Shrew,* I, i, 34.

balked, *adj.* piled or heaped up [lit., lying or piled in ridges]: "Ten thousand bold Scots, two and twenty knights,/ Balk'd in their own blood . . ." *1 Hen 4,* I, i, 68–69.

ball, *n.* **1** [pl.] wordplay on "eyeballs" and "cannon balls": "The fatal balls of murdering basilisks . . ." *Hen 5,* V, ii, 17. **2 these balls bound,** that's the spirit!; here, ref. to leather tennis balls rebounding on a hard court in an energetic game: "Why, these balls bound; there's noise in it." *All's W,* II, iii, 293. **3 two-fold balls and treble sceptres,** prob. ref. to double coronation of James I as King of England and Scotland: ". . . and some I see,/ That two-fold balls [orbs] and treble sceptres carry." *Mac,* IV, i, 120–121.

ballad, *n.* **1** poem: ". . . a woeful ballad/ Made to his mistress' eyebrow." *As You,* II, vii, 148–149. **2** tale or story set to the music of a popular song: "I will get Peter Quince to write a ballad of this dream . . ." *M N Dream,* IV, i, 213–214. **3** ref. to ballad as trivial and inferior rhyming: ". . . a speaker is but a/ prater; a rhyme is but a ballad." *Hen 5,* V, ii, 162–163.

ballad-monger, *n.* contemptuous term for "ballad-maker," a rhymester or maker of street ballads: "I had rather be a kitten and cry 'mew'/ Than one of these same metre ballad-mongers . . ." *1 Hen 4,* III, i, 123–124.

ballow[1], *n.* cudgel: ". . . keep out, che vor' ye [I warrant you], or ise [I'll] try whither your/ costard [head] or my ballow be the harder." *Lear,* IV, vi, 242–243.

ballow[2], *v.* perh. anglicized form of French *bailler,* fetch: "Rugby, ballow me some/ paper. Tarry you a little-a while." *Wives,* I, iv, 82–83.

balm, *v.* to soothe; heal or restore: "This rest might yet have balm'd thy broken sinews . . ." *Lear,* III, vi, 101.

balmy, *adj.* **1** fragrant: "A balmy breath, that doth almost persuade/ Justice herself to break her sword . . ." *Oth,* V, ii, 16–17. **2** peaceful: "Now with the drops of this most balmy time/ My love looks fresh . . ." *Sonn 107,* 9–10.

balsamum, *n.* balsam, an aromatic resin used as a balm: ". . . I have bought/ The oil, the balsamum and aqua-vitae." *Errors,* IV, i, 89–90.

ban, *n.* **1** curse: "Take thou that too, with multiplying bans!" *Timon,* IV, i, 34.
—*v.* **2** to curse: "Adonis sits,/ Banning his boisterous and unruly beast . . ." *Ven & Ad,* 325–326.

Banbury cheese, *n.* notoriously thin cheese: "You Banbury cheese!"/ "Ay, it is no matter." *Wives,* I, i, 118–119.

band, *n.* **1** bond; obligation: ". . . the end of life cancels all bands . . ." *1 Hen 4,* III, ii, 157. **2** [pl.] troops: "Bring him through the bands." *Ant & Cleo,* III, xii, 25. **3** wordplay on "band," a company of soldiers, and "bond": "Ay, sir, the sergeant of the band; he that brings/ any man to answer it that breaks his band . . ." *Errors,* IV, iii, 29–30. **4 infant bands,** swaddling clothes: "Henry the Sixth, in infant bands crown'd King . . ." *Hen 5,* Chor. (Epil.) 9.

banditto, *n.* bandit; outlaw: "A Roman sworder and banditto slave/ Murder'd sweet Tully . . ." *2 Hen 6,* IV, i, 135–136.

ban-dog, *n.* watchdog, esp. a ferocious dog on a chain: "The time when screech-owls cry, and ban-dogs howl . . ." *2 Hen 6,* I, iv, 18.

bandy, *v.* **1** to strive or contend (with): "I will bandy with thee in faction." *As You,* V, i, 54–55. **2** to strike or impel, as a ball: "My words would bandy her to my sweet love,/ And his to me." *Rom & Jul,* II, v, 14–15. **3** to exchange blows or sword thrusts; brawl: "The Prince expressly hath/ Forbid this bandying in Verona streets." *Rom & Jul,* III, i, 87–88. **4 bandy looks,** to return a severe look with one of insolence: "Do you bandy looks with me, you rascal?" *Lear,* I, iv, 89.

bane, *n.* **1** destruction or ruin: ". . . and bane to those/ That for my surety will refuse the boys!" *2 Hen 6,* V, i, 120–121.

2 means of destruction or ruin; also, destroyer: "Lest Rome herself be bane unto herself . . ." *T Andr,* V, iii, 73.
—*v.* **3** to poison: "What if my house be troubled with a rat,/ And I . . . give ten thousand ducats/ To have it ban'd?" *Merch,* IV, i, 44–46.

banes, *n. pl.* See **banns.**

bang, *n.* **bear me a bang,** See **bear** (def. 20).

bank, *n.* **1** [usually pl.] bounds; here, of obedience: "We come within our aweful banks again . . ." *2 Hen 4,* IV, i, 176. **2 o'er the bank,** beyond the bounds or margins: "Whiles they are o'er the bank of their obedience,/ Thus will they bear down all things." *More,* II, iv, 39–40.
—*v.* **3** to sail close to the banks of: "Have I not heard these islanders shout out/ 'Vive le roi!' as I have bank'd their towns?" *K John,* V, ii, 103–104.

banket, *n.* banquet: "Scene ii, a Banket." [SD] *T Andr,* III, ii, 1.

bankrout, *adj.* **1** bankrupt; insolvent: "Be York the next that must be bankrout so!" *Rich 2,* II, i, 151.
—*n.* **2** bankrupt person: "But blessed bankrout, that by love so thriveth!" *Ven & Ad,* 466.

bankrupt, *adj.* lacking; scarcely present: "Big Mars seems bankrupt in their beggar'd host,/ And faintly through a rusty beaver peeps . . ." *Hen 5,* IV, ii, 43–44.

banneret, *n.* small flag; here, worn as a trophy: ". . . the scarfs and the bannerets about/ thee did manifoldly dissuade me from believing thee . . ." *All's W,* II, iii, 202–203.

banning, *adj.* **1** cursing: "Fell banning hag, enchantress, hold thy tongue!" *1 Hen 6,* V, iii, 42. **2** foaming: "For do but stand upon the banning shore . . ." *Oth,* II, i, 11.

banns or **banes,** *n. pl.* announcement in church on three successive Sundays that a couple intends to marry: ". . . I'll crave the day/ When I shall ask the banns, and when be married." *Shrew,* II, i, 179–180.

banquet, *n.* light refreshment, as of sweets, fruit, and wine, following the main feast: ". . . prepare not to be gone,/ We have a trifling foolish banquet towards." *Rom & Jul,* I, v, 120–121.

bar, *v.* **1** to thwart; deny: ". . . pitying/ The pangs of barr'd affections . . ." *Cymb,* I, ii, 12–13. **2** to ignore; fail to consult: "Nor have we herein barr'd/ Your better wisdoms . . ." *Ham,* I, ii, 14–15. **3** to block: "Purpose so barr'd, it follows/ Nothing is done to purpose." *Cor,* III, i, 147–148. **4 be barred of rest,** to be kept from sleeping: "In his bedchamber to be barr'd of rest." *Ven & Ad,* 784.

—*n.* **5** court or other place of judgment: "To bring your most imperial majesties/ Unto this bar and royal interview..." *Hen 5,* V, ii, 26–27. **6 bar in law,** *n.* legal impediment: "... since this bar in law makes us/ friends, it shall be so far forth friendly maintained..." *Shrew,* I, i, 135–136. **7 bring to the bar,** to bring (a matter) before a court: "... at which time we will bring the device to the bar,/ and crown thee for a finder of madmen." *T Night,* III, iv, 141–142. **8 under truest bars,** under most trustworthy lock and key: "Each trifle under truest bars to thrust..." *Sonn 48,* 2.

barbarism, *n.* ignorance; philistinism: "I have for barbarism spoke more/ Than for that angel knowledge..." *Love's L,* I, i, 112–113.

Barbary, *n.* **1** coastal region of western North Africa: "... your white canvas doublet will/ sully. In Barbary, sir, it cannot come to so much." *1 Hen 4,* II, iv, 73–74. **2** breed of Arabian horse prized for its swiftness: "The King, sir, hath wagered with him six Barbary/ horses..." *Ham,* V, ii, 144–145.

Barbary cock-pigeon, male dove of the Barbary coast, generally aggressive and possessive: "I will be/ more jealous of thee than a Barbary cock-pigeon/ over his hen..." *As You,* IV, i, 142–143.

Barbary hen, *n.* guinea hen; also, disparaging term for a woman, esp. a prostitute: "He'll not swagger with a Barbary hen, if her feathers/ turn back in any show of resistance." *2 Hen 4,* II, iv, 97–98.

Barbason, *n.* perh. nickname of the Devil [poss. confused with Beelzebub]: "I am not Barbason; you cannot conjure me." *Hen 5,* II, i, 53.

barbed, *adj.* armored: "His glittering arms he will commend to rust,/ His barbed steeds to stables..." *Rich 2,* III, iii, 116–117.

barber-monger, *n.* constant patron of the barber's shop: "You whoreson cullionly barber-monger, draw." *Lear,* II, ii, 33.

bare¹, *adj.* **1** worthless; wretched: "Such poor, such bare, such lewd, such mean attempts..." *1 Hen 4,* III, ii, 13. **2** threadbare: "... it appears by their bare liveries that they live by/ your bare words." *Two Gent,* II, iv, 41–42. **3 all bare,** in, of, or by itself: "The argument [subject], all bare, is of more worth/ Than when it hath my added praise beside." *Sonn 103,* 3–4.
—*v.* **4** to shave: "Or the baring of my beard, and to say it was in/ stratagem." *All's W,* IV, i, 49–50. **5 bare the raven's eye,** the raven, it was said, slept facing east so as to be awakened by the rising sun; Iachimo, perh., likens himself to the raven, also a predator: "Swift, swift, you dragons of the night, that dawning/ May bare the raven's eye!" *Cymb,* II, ii, 48–49.

—*n.* **6** bareness: "Whose bare out-bragg'd the web it seem'd to wear..." *Lover's Comp,* 95.

bare², *v.* old past tense of **bear;** bore: "Who bare my letter then to Romeo?" *Rom & Jul,* V, ii, 13.

bare-faced, *adj.* undisguised; naked: "... I could/ With bare-fac'd power sweep him from my sight..." *Mac,* III, i, 117–118.

barefoot brother, *n.* fellow Franciscan: "Going to find a barefoot brother out,/ One of our order..." *Rom & Jul,* V, ii, 5–6.

bare-gnawn, *adj.* devoured to the bone: "... my name is lost;/ By treason's tooth bare-gnawn, and canker-bit..." *Lear,* V, iii, 121–122.

bare-ribbed, *adj.* resembling a skeleton: "... and in his forehead sits/ A bare-ribb'd death..." *K John,* V, ii, 176–177.

barful strife, *n.* undertaking full of hindrances: "... yet, a barful strife!/ Whoe'er I woo, myself would be his wife." *T Night,* I, iv, 41–42.

bargain, *n.* **1** business agreement; deal: "... he hath disgrac'd me... thwarted my bargains..." *Merch,* III, i, 48–51. **2 sell (someone) a bargain,** to take advantage of or make a fool of (someone); here, in wordplay with "goose" [prostitute]: "The boy hath sold him a bargain, a goose, that's flat." *Love's L,* III, i, 98.

Bargulus, *n.* pirate slain in battle by Philip of Macedon, mentioned in Cicero's *De Officiis:* "... this villain here... threatens more/ Than Bargulus, the strong Illyrian pirate." *2 Hen 6,* IV, i, 105–107.

bark, *n.* **1** small sailing vessel: "If any bark put forth, come to the mart..." *Errors,* III, ii, 149.
—*v.* **2** to form a bark or heavy crust: "... a most instant tetter bark'd about,/ Most lazar-like, with vile and loathsome crust..." *Ham,* I, v, 71–72. **3** to remove the bark from: "Would bark your honour from that trunk you bear..." *Meas,* III, i, 71. **4** to destroy by stripping the bark from: "... and this pine is bark'd,/ That overtopp'd them all." *Ant & Cleo,* IV, xii, 23–24.

barm, *n.* **bear no barm,** (of a beverage) to fail to ferment; also, to go flat: "And bootless make the breathless housewife churn,/ And sometime make the drink to bear no barm..." *M N Dream,* II, i, 37–38.

barn¹, *n.* wordplay on "barn" and "bairn" [child]: "... if your/ husband have stables enough, you'll see he shall/ lack no barns." *M Ado,* III, iv, 43–45.

barn², *v.* to store in a barn: "And useless barns the harvest of his wits . . ." *Luc,* 859.

barne, *n.* dialect word for "child"; var. of Scottish "bairn": "Mercy on 's, a barne!/ A very pretty barne! A boy or a child, I wonder?" *W Tale,* III, iii, 69–70.

Barnet, *n.* town a few miles N of London: "I will away towards Barnet presently/ And bid thee battle . . ." *3 Hen 6,* V, i, 113–114.

Barrabas, *n.* (in the Bible) robber released instead of Christ when Pilate bowed to the will of the mob; also, scoundrelly protagonist of Marlowe's "Jew of Malta." [Here and in Marlowe the first syllable of the name is stressed.]: "Would any of the stock of Barrabas/ Had been her husband, rather than a Christian." *Merch,* IV, i, 292–293.

barred, *adj.* thwarted; frustrated: ". . . pitying/ The pangs of barr'd affections . . ." *Cymb,* I, ii, 12–13.

barren, *adj.* **1** dull; ignorant: "The shallowest thick-skin of that barren sort . . ." *M N Dream,* III, ii, 13. **2** worthless: "Upon my head they plac'd a fruitless crown,/ And put a barren sceptre in my gripe . . ." *Mac,* III, i, 60–61. **3** empty; here, of jests or wit: ". . . marry, now I let go your hand, I am barren." *T Night,* I, iii, 77–78.

barren-spirited, *adj.* lacking originality: "He must be taught, and train'd, and bid go forth:/ A barren-spirited fellow . . ." *J Caes,* IV, i, 35–36.

barricado, *n.* **1** barricade or fortification; hence, something impenetrable and opaque: "Why, it hath bay-windows transparent as/ barricadoes . . ." *T Night,* IV, ii, 37–38. —*v.* **2** to fortify; erect a barricade around (something): "Man is enemy to virginity; how may/ we barricado it against him?" *All's W,* I, i, 110–111.

Bartholomew, *adj.* of Bartholomew Fair, held on St. Bartholomew's Day, Aug. 24th: "Thou whoreson little tidy Bartholomew boar-pig . . ." *2 Hen 4,* II, iv, 227.

Bartholomew-tide, *n.* around the time of St. Bartholomew's Day, mid- to-late August: ". . . like flies at/ Bartholomewtide . . ." *Hen 5,* V, ii, 326–327.

Basan, *n.* **hill of Basan,** Biblical place of bulls and oxen; Antony regards himself as the greatest of cuckolds: "O that I were/ Upon the hill of Basan, to outroar/ The horned herd . . ." *Ant & Cleo,* III, xiii, 126–128.

base¹, *adj.* **1** cowardly; also, mean or despicable: "I'll ne'er bear a base mind—and't/ be my destiny, so; and't be not, so." *2 Hen 4,* III, ii, 230–231. **2** worthless: "Small have continual

plodders ever won,/ Save base authority from others' books." *Love's L,* I, i, 86–87. **3** vile; Edmund assumes, erroneously, that "bastard" comes from the word "base": "Why bastard? Wherefore base?" *Lear,* I, ii, 6.

base², *n.* **1** one of a pair of skirtlike garments worn by a mounted knight: "Only, my friend, I yet am unprovided of a pair of/ bases." *Per,* II, i, 159–160. **2 bid the base,** to take or sing the bass part; also, to promote the cause of a particular figure in the game of prisoner's base: "Indeed I bid the base for Proteus." *Two Gent,* I, ii, 98.

base³, *n.* **1 bid the wind a base,** challenges the wind to a chase [race]: "To bid the wind a base he now prepares,/ And where he run or fly, they know not whether . . ." *Ven & Ad,* 303–304. **2** See **country base.**

base⁴ *n.* **1 base and pillar,** foundation and chief support; here, ref. to Hector, chief defender of Troy: "I wonder now how yonder city stands/ When we have here her base and pillar by us?" *Tr & Cr,* IV, v, 210–211. **2 on base and ground enough,** with sufficient reason: "Antonio never yet was thief, or pirate,/ Though I confess, on base and ground enough,/ Orsino's enemy." *T Night,* V, i, 72–74.

base court, outer courtyard of a castle: "My lord, in the base court he doth attend/ To speak with you . . ." *Rich 2,* III, iii, 176–177.

basely, *adv.* in a cowardly manner: "They basely fly, and dare not stay the field." *Ven & Ad,* 894.

base matter, *n.* materials needed to kindle a fire: "What trash is Rome,/ What rubbish, and what offal, when it serves/ For the base matter to illuminate/ So vile a thing as Caesar!" *J Caes,* I, iii, 108–111.

baseness, *n.* menial labors: ". . . some kinds of baseness/ Are nobly undergone . . ." *Temp,* III, i, 2–3.

basest, *adj.* darkest: "Anon permit the basest clouds to ride . . ." *Sonn 33,* 5.

bashfulness, *n.* embarrassment; shamefacedness: "Have you no modesty, no maiden shame,/ No touch of bashfulness?" *M N Dream,* III, ii, 285–286.

Basilisco-like, *adj.* ref. to contemporary play, *Soliman and Perseda,* by Thomas Kyd, in which a braggart knight is addressed as "knave" by his servant: "Knight, knight, good mother, Basilisco-like . . ." *K John,* I, i, 244.

basilisk, *n.* **1** (in legend) reptile possessed of a fatal stare: "Here, take this too;/ [Gives the ring.] It is a basilisk unto mine eye,/ Kills me to look on't." *Cymb,* II, iv, 106–107. **2** large cannon: ". . . thou hast talk'd/ . . . Of basilisks, of cannon, culverin . . ." *1 Hen 4,* II, iii, 51–54. **3** wordplay on the two senses, "cannon" and "mythical reptile": "The fatal balls of murdering basilisks . . ." *Hen 5,* V, ii, 17.

Basimecu, *n.* **Mounsier Basimecu,** abusive name for the French Dauphin and his fawning manners, based on the French words *baise mon cul* [kiss my ass]: "What canst thou answer to my Majesty for giving up/ of Normandy unto Mounsieur Basimecu, the Dauphin/ of France?" *2 Hen 6,* IV, vii, 25–27.

Basingstoke, *n.* town SW of London, in Hampshire: "Where lay the King tonight?"/ "At Basingstoke, my lord." *2 Hen 4,* II, i, 165–166.

basis, *n.* **1** base; here, that of Pompey's statue: "How many times shall Caesar bleed in sport,/ That now on Pompey's basis lies along . . ." *J Caes,* III, i, 114–115. **2** bottom or foundation: ". . . th' shore, that o'er his [its] wave-worn basis bowed,/ As stooping to relieve him . . ." *Temp,* II, i, 116–117. **3 mountain's basis,** foothill: "Though we upon this mountain's basis by/ Took stand for idle speculation . . ." *Hen 5,* IV, ii, 30–31.

basket-hilt, *adj.* (of a sword) fitted with basketlike hilt of steel to protect the hand (considered old-fashioned): "Away,/ you bottle-ale rascal, you basket-hilt stale juggler,/ you!" *2 Hen 4,* II, iv, 127–129.

bass, *v.* **1** to proclaim in a deep voice: ". . . the thunder . . . pronounc'd/ The name of Prosper: it did bass my trespass." *Temp,* III, iii, 97–99.
—*n.* **2** wordplay on "bass part" and "base conduct": "The mean is drown'd with your unruly bass." *Two Gent,* I, ii, 97.

Basta, *pron.* [Italian] enough; no more: "Basta, content thee, for I have it full." *Shrew,* I, i, 198.

bastard, *n.* **1** sweetened Spanish wine: "Score a pint of bastard in the Half-moon . . ." *1 Hen 4,* II, iv, 27. **2 bastard to the time,** person who is out of step with the times, hence unfashionable: "For he is but a bastard to the time/ That doth not smack of observation . . ." *K John,* I, i, 207–208. **3 drink brown and white bastard,** wordplay on "drink the Spanish wine" and "beget bastards of all races": ". . . we shall have all the world drink brown and white/ bastard." *Meas,* III, ii, 3–4.
—*adj.* **4** imitation or artificial: "Shame hath a bastard fame, well managed . . ." *Errors,* III, ii, 19. **5 bastard signs of fair,** false appearances of beauty; here, false hair: "Before these bastard signs of fair were born,/ Or durst inhabit on a living brow . . ." *Sonn 68,* 3–4.

bastardizing, *n.* conception out of wedlock: ". . . the maidenliest star in the firmament twinkled/ on my bastardizing." *Lear,* I, ii, 139–140.

bastard of Venus, *n.* Cupid was the offspring of Venus by Mercury [not by Vulcan, her husband]: "That same wicked bastard of Venus, that was/ begot of thought . . ." *As You,* IV, i, 201–202.

bastards and syllables, *n.* illegitimate words: ". . . bastards and syllables/ Of no allowance to your bosom's truth." *Cor,* III, ii, 56–57.

bastards of dung, *n.* artificial garden products: "Nay, it has infected [the city] with the palsy, for these bastards of dung—as you know they grow in dung—have infected us . . ." *More,* II, iv, 12–13.

bastinado, *n.* beating or thrashing, esp. on the soles of the feet: "I will deal in poison with thee, or in bastinado, or in steel." *As You,* V, i, 53–54.

basting, *n.* beating or thrashing; here, wordplay with cooking sense of basting meat: ". . . I think the meat wants that I have."/ ". . . what's that?"/ "Basting." *Errors,* II, ii, 55–57.

bat, *n.* **1** cudgel; club: "Where go you/ With bats and clubs?" *Cor,* I, i, 54–55. **2 grained bat,** staff showing the wood's grain: "So slides he down upon [lets himself down by means of] his grained bat . . ." *Lover's Comp,* 64.

bate[1], *v.* **1** to underrate; put too low a value on: "Who bates mine honour shall not know my coin." *Timon,* III, iii, 28. **2** to abate; hold back: ". . . rather than she will bate one breath of her accustomed crossness." *M Ado,* II, iii, 172. **3** to reduce; decrease: "I cannot be bated one doit of a thousand pieces." *Per,* IV, ii, 48. **4** to remit: ". . . ev'ry dram of it; and I will not bate/ thee a scruple." *All's W,* II, iii, 218–219. **5** to omit or neglect: "Of my instruction hast thou nothing bated/ In what thou hadst to say . . ." *Temp,* III, iii, 85–86. **6** to lose weight; grow thin: ". . . am I not fallen away vilely since this last/ action? Do I not bate?" *1 Hen 4,* III, iii, 1–2. **7** to depress or deject; also, sense of diminish: "These griefs and losses have so bated me/ That I shall hardly spare a pound of flesh . . ." *Merch,* III, iii, 32–33. **8** to except: "Were the world mine, Demetrius being bated,/ The rest I'd give to be to you translated." *M N Dream,* I, i, 190–191. **9** to let off [the hook]; make allowances for: "Bate me some, and/ I will pay you some . . ." *2 Hen 4,* Epil. 14–15. **10** to dull: "That honour which shall bate his scythe's keen edge . . ." *Love's L,* I, i, 6.
—*n.* **11** trouble; strife: ". . . and breeds no bate [causes no trouble] with telling of discreet [polite] stories . . ." *2 Hen 4,* II, iv, 247.

bate², *v.* (in falconry) to flutter or beat the wings: ". . . plum'd like estridges that with the wind/ Bated, like eagles having lately bath'd . . ." *1 Hen 4,* IV, i, 98–99.

bate-breeding, *adj.* causing strife; making mischief: "This sour informer, this bate-breeding spy . . ." *Ven & Ad,* 655.

bated, *adj.* dejected: "Those bated that inherit but the fall/ Of the last monarchy . . ." *All's W,* II, i, 13–14.

bateless, *adj.* refusing to abate: ". . . unhapp'ly set/ This bateless edge on his keen appetite . . ." *Luc,* 8–9.

bat-fowling, *n.* hunting of birds at night with clubs (bats); here, using the moon as a lantern: ". . . you would lift/ the moon out of her sphere . . ."/ "We would so, and then go a bat-fowling." *Temp,* II, i, 177–180.

batler or **batlet,** *n.* wooden board, or bat, used to beat clothes during washing: ". . . I remember the kissing of her batler . . ." *As You,* II, iv, 45–46.

battalia, *n.* fighting forces: "Why, our battalia trebles that account!" *Rich 3,* V, iii, 11.

batten, *v.* **1** to gorge or glut: "Could you on this fair mountain leave to feed/ And batten on this moor?" *Ham,* III, iv, 66–67. **2 batten on cold bits,** gorge yourself on cold scraps: "Follow your function, go, and batten on cold bits." *Cor,* IV, v, 34.

battery, *n.* **1** assault; bombardment: "Where is best place to make our battery next." *1 Hen 6,* I, iv, 64. **2** breaking down of defenses: "Dismiss your vows . . . your flatt'ry,/ For where a heart is hard they make no batt'ry." *Ven & Ad,* 425–426. **3** misuse for "slander": "Prove this . . . or I'll have mine action of battery on thee." *Meas,* II, i, 175–176.

battle, *n.* **1** military force arrayed for battle: "What may the King's whole battle reach unto?" *1 Hen 4,* IV, i, 129. **2 sign of battle,** red flag: "The enemy comes on in gallant show;/ Their bloody sign of battle is hung out . . ." *J Caes,* V, i, 14.

battled, *past part.* (of fighting men) deployed for battle: "Before us in the valley lies the king . . . His party stronger battled than our whole." *Edw 3,* IV, iv, 12–14.

batty, *adj.* batlike: ". . . death-counterfeiting sleep/ With leaden legs and batty wings doth creep." *M N Dream,* III, ii, 364–365.

bauble, *n.* **1** carved stick carried by a court jester; here, also sexual wordplay: ". . . this drivelling love is like a great natural [idiot]/ that runs lolling up and down to hide his bauble in/ a hole." *Rom & Jul,* II, iv, 91–93.
—*adj.* **2** insignificant; toylike: "How many shallow bauble boats dare sail . . ." *Tr & Cr,* I, iii, 35.

baubling, *adj.* miserably small; insignificant: "A baubling vessel was he captain of . . ." *T Night,* V, i, 52.

bavin, *n.* brushwood used for kindling: "With shallow jesters, and rash bavin [flared up like ignited kindling] wits,/ Soon kindled and soon burnt . . ." *1 Hen 4,* III, ii, 61.

bawcock, *n.* fine fellow [from French beau coq]: "Why, how now my bawcock? How dost thou,/ chuck?" *T Night,* III, iv, 114–115.

bawd¹, *n.* **1** pander or procurer: ". . . to be bawd to a bell-wether, and to betray a she-lamb . . ." *As You,* III, ii, 78–79. **2** prostitute or brothel keeper: "It is her habit only that is honest,/ Herself's a bawd." *Timon,* IV, iii, 115–116.

bawd², *n.* dial. word for **hare;** rabbit, with obvious punning on "whore": "She will endite him to some supper./ A bawd! A bawd! A bawd! So ho." *Rom & Jul,* II, iv, 127–128.

bawdry, *n.* unchastity; lasciviousness: "We must be married or we must live in bawdry." *As You,* III, iii, 88.

bawdy-house, *n.* brothel: "Come, I am for no more bawdy-houses." *Per,* IV, v, 6.

bawl out, *v.* to cry or call out; here, allusion to the bastards he begets in his "low" haunts: ". . . those that bawl out the ruins of/ thy linen [your cast-off clothes] . . ." *2 Hen 4,* II, ii, 23–24.

bay¹, *n.* **1** (in hunting) last stand of the quarry: "He should have found his uncle Gaunt a father/ To rouse his wrongs and chase them to the bay." *Rich 2,* II, iii, 126–127. **2** fit of barking and howling: "Uncouple here and let us make a bay . . ." *T Andr,* II, ii, 3. **3 at (a) bay,** (in hunting) brought to bay; cornered: "I would we had a thousand Roman dames/ At such a bay . . ." *T Andr,* IV, ii, 41–42.
—*v.* **4** to chase; pursue: "He leaves his back unarm'd, the French and Welsh/ Baying him at the heels . . ." *2 Hen 4,* I, iii, 79–80. **5** to bring to bay; (in hunting) to corner with hounds: ". . . in a wood of Crete they bay'd the bear/ With hounds of Sparta . . ." *M N Dream,* IV, i, 112–113.

bay², *n.* (in a house) space under a gable or around a bay window: "I'll rent the fairest house in it/ after [for] three pence a bay." *Meas,* II, i, 238–239.

bay³, *n.* **bay of death,** treacherous inlet destructive to ships: "And I in such a desp'rate bay of death,/ Like a poor bark of sails and tackling reft [deprived] . . ." *Rich 3,* IV, iv, 233–234.

bay⁴, *n.* laurel: ". . . wearing on their heads garlands of bays . . ." [SD] *Hen 8,* IV, ii, 82.

bay curtal, *n.* bay horse with a docked tail: "I'd give bay curtal and his furniture . . ." *All's W,* II, iii, 59.

Baynard's Castle, *n.* Thameside residence of Richard in London: "If you thrive well, bring them to Baynard's Castle . . ." *Rich 3,* III, v, 97.

be, *v.* **1 be it so,** if; supposing that: "Be it so she will not here . . . Consent to marry with Demetrius . . ." *M N Dream,* I, i, 39. **2 be to be,** have to be; need to be: "I see no reason why a king of years/ Should be to be protected like a child." *2 Hen 6,* II, iii, 28–29. **3 be with them,** be as conciliatory as possible: "And thus far having stretch'd it—here be with them—/ Thy knee bussing the stones . . ." *Cor,* III, ii, 74–75. **4 for ever being,** ever to be: "Too like the sire for ever being good." *T Andr,* V, i, 50. **5 let that be,** "done" understood here: "The eye wink at the hand; yet let that be,/ Which the eye fears, when it is done, to see." *Mac,* I, iv, 52–53.

beached, *adj.* having or surrounded by a beach: ". . . the beached verge of the salt flood . . ." *Timon,* V, i, 215.

beadle, *n.* minor officer who dealt with petty offenses of the parish, often administering whippings, etc.: "Enter Beadles [dragging in] Hostess Quickly and Doll Tearsheet." [SD] *2 Hen 4,* V, iii.

beadsman, *n.* old man given a pension to pray for his benefactor: "Thy very beadsmen learn to bend their bows . . . against thy state . . ." *Rich 2,* III, ii, 116–117.

beagles, *n.* poss. ref. to Alcibiades' women as hunting dogs: "Get thee away, and take/ Thy beagles with thee." *Timon,* IV, iii, 176–177.

beak, *n.* ship's prow: "I boarded the King's ship; now on the beak,/ Now in the waist, the deck, in every cabin . . ." *Temp,* I, ii, 196–197.

beam, *n.* **1** crossbar on a balance from which the two scales are suspended: "And poise the cause in Justice' equal scales,/ Whose beam stands sure . . ." *2 Hen 6,* II, i, 196–197. **2** lance: ". . . stands colossus-wise, waving his beam,/ Upon the pashed corses of the kings . . ." *Tr & Cr,* V, v, 9–10. **3** [pl.] sight; gaze: "As fast as objects to his beams assemble?" *Sonn 114,* 8. **4** extent; reach: ". . . the precipitation might down stretch/ Below the beam of sight . . ." *Cor,* III, ii, 4–5. **5 turn the beam,** (on a balance) to tilt the crossbar bearing the two scales: ". . . thy madness shall be paid with weight/ Till our scale turn the beam." *Ham,* IV, v, 156–157. **6 weigh thee to the beam,** to outweigh so as to upend the crossbar: "We, poising us in her defective scale,/ Shall weigh thee to the beam . . ." *All's W,* II, iii, 154–155.

bear, *v.* **1** to take or carry away: "Nothing I'll bear from thee/ But nakedness, thou detestable town!" *Timon,* IV, i, 32–33. **2** to be patient (used as a command): "What you want in meat/ we'll have in drink: but you/ must bear; the heart's all." *2 Hen 4,* V, iii, 28–29. **3** to keep in mind: ". . . to bear the inventory/ of thy shirts—" *2 Hen 4,* II, ii, 16–17. **4** to manage; conduct or comport: "'Thus must thou speak, and thus thy body bear' . . ." *Love's L,* V, ii, 100. **5** to conduct or comport oneself: ". . . instruct me/ How I may formally in person bear/ Like a true friar." *Meas,* I, iii, 46–48. **6** to be worth: "His word might bear my wealth at any time." *Errors,* V, i, 8. **7** to escort: "The violets, cowslips, and the primroses/ Bear to my closet." *Cymb,* I, vi, 83–84. **8** to gain possession of: "His honesty rewards him in itself;/ It must not bear my daughter." *Timon,* I, i, 133–134. **9** to stand or put up with something: "We'll bear, with your lordship." *Timon,* I, i, 180. **10** to carry; support or sustain [with sexual innuendo]: ". . . my horse is my mistress."/ "Your mistress bears well." *Hen 5,* III, vii, 45–46. **11 bear all down,** to subdue any opposition: ". . . a woman that/ Bears all down with her brain . . ." *Cymb,* II, i, 52–53. **12 bear away,** (of a ship) to get under way: ". . . there's a bark of Epidamnum/ That stays but till her owner comes aboard,/ And then she bears away." *Errors,* IV, i, 86–88. **13 bear down,** to oppress; crush: "If this will not suffice, it must appear/ That malice bears down truth." *Merch,* IV, i, 209–210. **14 bear him,** [to] carry himself: "Between two horses, which doth bear him best . . ." *1 Hen 6,* II, iv, 14. **15 bear in hand,** to lead (someone) on, esp. with false hopes; delude or deceive: "What, bear her in hand until/ they come to take hands . . ." *M Ado,* IV, i, 302–303. **16 bear it,** to escape with one's life: "But if your father had been victor there,/ He ne'er had borne it out of Coventry . . ." *2 Hen 4,* IV, i, 134–135. **17 bear it out,** [to] make it endurable: ". . . and for turning away, let summer bear it out." *T Night,* I, v, 19–20. **18 bear it that,** conduct yourself in such a way that: ". . . but being in,/ Bear't that th'opposed may beware of thee." *Ham,* I, iii, 66–67. **19 bear me,** ref. to practice of putting a monkey on the back of a bear at fairs; poss. ref. to fools' [jesters'] practice of carrying a monkey on their backs; also, ref. to Richard's hunchback: "Because that I am little like an ape,/ He thinks that you should bear me on your shoulders!" *Rich 3,* III, i, 130–131. **20 bear me a bang,** get a beating from me: "You'll bear me a bang for that, I fear." *J Caes,* III, iii, 18. **21 bear me hard,** has a grudge against me: "Caesar doth bear me hard; but he loves Brutus." *J Caes,* I, ii, 310. **22 bear more toward,** to be nearer: "My father's bears more toward the market-place." *Shrew,* V, i, 8. **23 bear my life off,** get me out of here alive: "I will respect thee as a father if/ Thou bear'st my life off." *W Tale,* I, ii, 461–462. **24 bear off,** to ward off: "Here's neither bush nor shrub, to bear off any/ weather at all . . ." *Temp,* II, ii, 18–19. **25 bear oneself,** to behave (oneself): ". . . you will some good instruction give/ How I may bear me here . . ." *Temp,* I, ii, 427–428. **26 bear out, a.**

to support; stand up for: "... and if/ I cannot once or twice in a quarter bear out a knave/ against an honest man, I have but a very little credit/ with your worship." *2 Hen 4,* V, i, 43–46. **b.** to justify: "I hope your warrant will bear out the deed." *K John,* IV, i, 6. **c.** to endure or survive: "I'll say his greatness may bear out the shame ..." *Edw 3,* II, i, 364. **27 bear the knave,** submit to being called "knave": "... that for th'poorest piece [coin]/ Will bear the knave by th'volume." *Cor,* III, iii, 32–33. **28 bear up, and board 'em,** a nautical command ["Stand firm and attack!"]; here, an exhortation to drinkers: "... bear up, and/ board 'em. Servant-monster, drink to me." *Temp,* III, ii, 2–3. **29 bear with,** wordplay on "put up with" and "carry messages for": "Well, I perceive I must be fain to bear with you." *Two Gent,* I, i, 116.

bear'ard, *n.* bearward: "We'll bait thy bears to death,/ And manacle the bear'ard in their chains ..." *2 Hen 6,* V, i, 153–154.

bear-baiting, *n.* sport of setting dogs on a chained bear: "... would I/ had bestowed that time in the tongues that I have/ in fencing, dancing, and bear-baiting." *T Night,* I, iii, 90–92.

beard, *v.* **1** to challenge or defy, as by plucking by the beard: "No man so potent breathes upon the ground/ But I will beard him." *1 Hen 4,* IV, i, 11–12.
—*n.* **2** symbol of a man's maturity: "But what to me, my love? ... A wife?"/ "A beard, fair health, and honesty ..." *Love's L,* V, ii, 816–817. **3 in his beard,** to his face: "I will/ verify as much in his beard ..." *Hen 5,* III, ii, 74–75.

bearer, *n.* horse: "... excuse the slow offence/ Of my dull bearer ..." *Sonn 51,* 1–2.

bearherd or **bear-herd,** *n.* keeper of a trained bear: "... true valour is turned/ bearherd ..." *2 Hen 4,* I, ii, 168–169.

bearing, *n.* **1** behavior: "With thy brave bearing should I be in love ..." *2 Hen 6,* V, ii, 20. **2** act of sustaining or enduring; endurance: "If there be/ Such valour in the bearing, what make we/ Abroad?" *Timon,* III, v, 46–48. **3** suffering: "... the mind much sufference doth o'erskip,/ When grief hath mates, and bearing fellowship [when misery has companionship]." *Lear,* III, vi, 109–110.

bearing-cloth, *n.* christening robe: "Thy scarlet robes, as a child's bearing-cloth,/ I'll use to carry thee out of this place." *1 Hen 6,* I, iii, 42–43.

bear-like, *adj.* like a bear tied to a stake [in bear-baiting] that must defend itself against attacking dogs: "They have tied me to a stake: I cannot fly,/ But, bear-like, I must fight the course." *Mac,* V, vii, 1–2.

bear the burden, *v.* wordplay on "bear the responsibility" with "bear the weight [of a husband]": "I am the drudge, and toil in your delight,/ But you shall bear the burden soon at night." *Rom & Jul,* II, v, 76–77.

bearward or **bear'ard,** *n.* keeper of bears and, usually, monkeys: "... I will even take sixpence in earnest of the bearward and/ lead his apes into hell." *M Ado,* II, i, 36–37.

beast, *n.* **1 beast with many heads,** the multitude; masses; crowd: "The beast/ With many heads butts me away." *Cor,* IV, i, 1–2. **2 beast with two backs,** sexual intercourse [phrase from Rabelais]: "... your daughter,/ and the Moor, are now making the beast with two/ backs." *Oth,* I, i, 115–117.

beastly, *adj.* **1** vulgar: "... in the beastliest sense, you are Pompey/ the Great." *Meas,* II, i, 215–216. **2** beastlike; brutal; inhuman: "We have seen nothing:/ We are beastly ..." *Cymb,* III, iii, 39–40.
—*adv.* **3** in the manner of a beast: "... what I would have spoke/ Was beastly dumb'd by him." *Ant & Cleo,* I, v, 49–50.

beat, *v.* **1** to drive: "Our enemies have beat us to the pit./ It is more worthy to leap in ourselves ..." *J Caes,* V, v, 23. **2** to strike: "The bell then beating one—" *Ham,* I, i, 42. **3** to soften with padding: "... beat Cut's saddle, put a few/ flocks in the point ..." *1 Hen 4,* II, i, 5–6. **4** (in falconry) to flap the wings: "... as we watch these kites/ That bate and beat and will not be obedient." *Shrew,* IV, i, 182–183. **5** to ponder: "... thine eyes and thoughts/ Beat on a crown, the treasure of thy heart ..." *2 Hen 6,* II, i, 20. **6** wordplay on beating of Lear's painful thoughts and beating of the storm: "... this tempest in my mind/ Doth from my senses take all feeling else/ Save what beats there ..." *Lear,* III, iv, 12–14. **7 beat me out,** defeated me outright: "Thou hast beat me out/ Twelve several times ..." *Cor,* IV, v, 122–123.
—*past part.* **8 beat from his best ward,** forced out of his best defense: "... say this to him,/ He's beat from his best ward." *W Tale,* I, ii, 32–33.

beated, *adj.* beaten; battered: "Beated and chopp'd with tann'd antiquity ..." *Sonn 62,* 10.

beaten way, *n.* well-traveled path: "But in the beaten/ way of friendship, what make you at Elsinore?" *Ham,* II, ii, 269–270.

beauties, *n.* charms; attractions: "And all those beauties whereof now he's king ..." *Sonn 63,* 6.

beautified, *adj.* beautiful; graced with beauty: "To the celestial and my soul's idol, the most/ beautified Ophelia ..." *Ham,* II, ii, 109–110.

beaver, *n.* visor or face guard of a helmet: "I saw young Harry with his beaver on,/ His cushes [hip armor] on his thighs . . ." *1 Hen 4,* IV, i, 104–105.

because, *conj.* so that; in order that: "Because the girl should not survive her shame . . ." *T Andr,* V, iii, 41.

bechance, *v.* to happen; occur: "All happiness bechance to thee in Milan." *Two Gent,* I, i, 61.

beck, *n.* **1** bow or curtsy: "Serving of becks and jutting-out of bums!" *Timon,* I, ii, 233. **2** beckoning; here, a nod or other significant action interpreted as a summons or command: "Thy beck might from the bidding of the gods/ Command me." *Ant & Cleo,* III, xi, 60–61. **3 at one's beck,** waiting to be summoned; here, to be committed: ". . . with more offences at/ my beck than I have thoughts to put them in . . ." *Ham,* III, i, 125–126.
—*v.* **4** to beckon; summon or command: "Whose eye beck'd forth my wars, and call'd them home . . ." *Ant & Cleo,* IV, xii, 26.

become, *v.* **1** to befit: "Vincentio's son . . ./ It shall become to serve all hopes conceiv'd . . ." *Shrew,* I, i, 14–15. **2** to adorn; add splendor to: ". . . glister like the god of war/ When he intendeth to become the field . . ." *K John,* V, i, 54–55. **3** to show deference to; honor: ". . . convey me to the princely Edward/ That . . . I may become him with saluting him." *Edw 3,* IV, vi, 58–60. **4 as it becomes,** as befits it: ". . . set this diamond safe/ In golden palaces, as it becomes." *1 Hen 6,* V, iii, 169–170. **5 become of,** to grace: "Yet so they mourn, becoming of their woe . . ." *Sonn 127,* 13. **6 does become,** is only for [the]: "Patience is sottish, and impatience does/ Become a dog that's mad . . ." *Ant & Cleo,* IV, xv, 79–80. **7 is become,** has gone or got to: "I cannot joy until I be resolv'd/ Where our right valiant father is become [has taken himself]." *3 Hen 6,* II, i, 9–10.

becomed, *adj.* suitable; appropriate or becoming: "I met the youthful lord at Laurence' cell,/ And gave him what becomed love I might . . ." *Rom & Jul,* IV, ii, 25–26.

becomings, *n.* mood changes: ". . . my becomings kill me, when they do not/ Eye [appear] well to you." *Ant & Cleo,* I, iii, 96–97.

bed, *n.* **1 brought to bed,** (in childbirth) delivered: ". . . how a usurer's/ wife was brought to bed of twenty money-bags at a/ burden [birth] . . ." *W Tale,* IV, iv, 263–265. **2 came unto my beds,** poss., grew old: "But when I came unto my beds . . . With toss-pots still 'had drunken heads . . ." *T Night,* V, i, 400–402. **3 go to bed,** bed rest was thought to be the only cure for mental derangement; here, the suggestion is misconstrued: "Wilt thou go to bed, Malvolio?"/ "To bed? Ay, sweetheart . . ." *T Night,* III, iv, 30–31.

bed-blotting, *adj.* defiling the marriage bed: ". . . a most heavy curse/ When thou convert'st from honour's golden name/ To the black faction of bed-blotting shame." *Edw 3,* II, i, 456–458.

bed-chamber, *n.* **of his bed-chamber,** personal attendant: "The king . . . Breeds him, and makes him of his bed-chamber . . ." *Cymb,* I, i, 40–42.

bedded, *adj.* lying flat: "Your bedded hair, like life in excrements,/ Start up and stand an [on] end." *Ham,* III, iv, 121–122.

bedfellow, *n.* constant companion; ref. to Lord Scroop: ". . . his bedfellow,/ Whom he hath dull'd and cloy'd with gracious favours . . ." *Hen 5,* II, ii, 8–9.

bed-hangers, *n.* See **hanger** (def. 1).

bedlam, *adj.* mad; lunatic: "Did instigate the bedlam brain-sick Duchess/ By wicked means to frame our sovereign's fall." *2 Hen 6,* III, i, 51–52.

Bedlam, *n.* **1** London hospital for lunatics, St. Mary of Bethlehem: "To Bedlam with him! Is the man grown mad!" *2 Hen 6,* V, i, 131. **2** lunatic [term of abuse]: "Bedlam, have done." *K John,* II, i, 183.

bedrid, *adj.* bedridden: "Afflict him in his bed with bedrid groans . . ." *Luc,* 975.

bed-right, *n.* conjugal right(s): ". . . no bed-right shall be paid/ Till Hymen's torch be lighted . . ." *Temp,* IV, i, 96–97.

bed-swerver, *n.* person who betrays the marriage bed; adulterer: ". . . one that knows,/ What she should shame to know herself . . . that she's/ A bed-swerver . . ." *W Tale,* II, i, 90–93.

bed-vow, *n.* prob. marriage vow: "In act thy bed-vow broke and new faith torn . . ." *Sonn 152,* 3.

bedward, *adv.* toward bed: "And tapers burn'd to bedward." *Cor,* I, vi, 32.

bed-work, *n.* planning that could be done while resting in bed: "They call this bed-work, mapp'ry, closet-war . . ." *Tr & Cr,* I, iii, 205.

beef, *n.* **1** [usually pl.] cattle, esp. fattened cattle: ". . . and now has he land and beefs." *2 Hen 4,* III, ii, 322. **2** [used as pl.] prostitutes: ". . . she hath eaten [used] up all her beef, and she is/ herself in the tub." *Meas,* III, ii, 54–55.

beef-witted, *adj.* dull-witted; stupid: "The plague of Greece upon thee, thou mongrel/ beef-witted lord!" *Tr & Cr,* II, i, 12–13.

been, *v.* **1** old pl. of **be**; are: "Where when men been, there's seldom ease . . ." *Per,* II, Chor., 28. **2** has been; prob. error for ". . .'s been . . .": "My education been in arts and arms . . ." *Per,* II, iii, 82

beetle, *n.* **1** large hammer used as a pile-driver and requiring three men to operate it: "If I do, fillip me with a three-man beetle." *2 Hen 4,* I, ii, 229.
—*v.* **2** to jut out; overhang: ". . . the dreadful summit of the cliff/ That beetles o'er his base into the sea . . ." *Ham,* I, iv, 70–71.

beetle brows, *n. pl.* thick, overhanging eyebrows; here, a description of Mercutio's mask: "Here are beetle brows shall blush for me." *Rom & Jul,* I, iv, 32.

beetle-headed, *adj.* blockheaded: "A whoreson beetle-headed, flap-ear'd knave!" *Shrew,* IV, i, 144.

befall, *v.* **1** to perish [used in oaths]: ". . . so befall my soul/ As this is false he burdens me withal." *Errors,* V, i, 208–209. **2 befall what will befall,** Let happen what will; come what may: ". . . well, befall what will befall,/ I'll jest a twelvemonth in an hospital." *Love's L,* V, ii, 862–863.

before, *interj.* **1** [used as a command] Proceed! Go ahead!: "Before! And greet his Grace.-My lord, we come." *2 Hen 4,* IV, i, 228.
—*adj.* **2** ahead or in front: "Thou art so far before,/ That swiftest wing of recompense is slow/ To overtake thee . . ." *Mac,* I, iv, 16–17.
—*adv.* **3 before and after,** into the future and back toward the past: "Sure he that made us with such large discourse,/ Looking before and after . . ." *Ham,* IV, iv, 36–37. **4 which shall go before,** who shall precede whom: "Much like a press of people at a door,/ Throng her inventions, which shall go before." *Luc,* 1301–1302.
—*prep.* **5** to a greater extent than: ". . . who this should be,/ Doth miracle itself, lov'd before me." *Cymb,* IV, ii, 28–29. **6 Before me,** Upon my soul: a mild oath: "Before me, she's a good wench." *T Night,* II, iii, 178.

beforehand, *adj.* early in arriving or bringing: ". . . let us pay the time but needful woe,/ Since it hath been beforehand with our griefs." *K John,* V, vii, 110–111.

beforetime, *adv.* previously: "He has the stamp of Martius, and I have/ Beforetime seen him thus." *Cor,* I, vi, 23–24.

befortune, *v.* to befall: "I wish all good befortune you." *Two Gent,* IV, iii, 41.

befriend, *v.* to give comfort or solace to: "That you were once unkind befriends me now . . ." *Sonn 120,* 1.

beg, *v.* **1** to fool; hoodwink: "You cannot beg us, sir, I can assure you, sir; we know/ what we know . . ." *Love's L,* V, ii, 490. **2** to request or demand the full force of: "I beg the law, the law upon his head!" *M N Dream,* IV, i, 154. **3 no less beg,** beg no less: ". . . majesty, to keep decorum, must/ No less beg than a kingdom . . ." *Ant & Cleo,* V, ii, 17–18.

beget, *v.* to procreate; here, in contrast to "give a second life to": "O, come hither,/ Thou that beget'st him that did thee beget . . ." *Per,* V, i, 194–195.

beggar, *v.* **of matter beggar'd,** bereft of facts: "Wherein necessity, of matter beggar'd . . ." *Ham,* IV, v, 92.

beggarly, *adj.* **1** pitifully small: ". . . and about his shelves/ A beggarly account of empty boxes . . ." *Rom & Jul,* V, i, 44–45. **2** reduced to begging; desperately poor: "I have been begging sixteen years in court/ (Am yet a courtier beggarly) . . ." *Hen 8,* II, iii, 82–83.

beggary, *n.* contemptible meanness; degradation: "Not I,/ Inclin'd to this intelligence, pronounce/ The beggary of his change . . ." *Cymb,* I, vii, 113–115.

begin, *v.* **does first begin,** takes the first taste, as a monarch's taster: "If it be poisoned, 'tis the lesser sin/ That mine eye loves it and does first begin." *Sonn 114,* 13–14.

begnaw, *v.* to eat away; also, corrode: "A curse begnaw at very root on's heart,/ That is not glad to see thee!" *Cor,* II, i, 184–185.

begnawn, *past part.* eaten; chewed up: ". . . stark spoiled with the staggers, begnawn with/ the bots . . ." *Shrew,* III, ii, 52–53.

Be God's sonties, By God's saints [a mild oath, here used by an elderly rustic]: "Be God's sonties 'twill be a hard way to hit . . ." *Merch,* II, ii, 42.

beguild, *v.* var. of **beguile**: "To me came Tarquin armed to beguild [posing as a friend]/ With outward honesty . . ." *Luc,* 1544–1545.

beguile, *v.* **1** to capture by the use of guile: "If thou wert the lion, the fox would beguile thee . . ." *Timon,* IV, iii, 329–330. **2** to trick or cheat: "poor ropes, you are beguil'd,/ Both you and I, for Romeo is exil'd." *Rom & Jul,* III, ii, 132–133. **3** to deceive: "His power went out in such distractions as/ Beguil'd all spies." *Ant & Cleo,* III, vii, 76–77. **4** to cause to lose; also, to rob: ". . . a stain/ Upon the beauty of all parts besides,/ Beguiling them of commendation." *1 Hen 4,* III, i, 183. **5** to drive or entice away: ". . . fain I would beguile/ The tedious day with sleep." *Ham,* III, ii, 221–222. **6 beguile the supposition,** See

supposition (def. 2). **7 beguile the time,** to deceive the world (here, the assembled guests): "To beguile the time,/ Look like the time . . ." *Mac,* I, v, 62–63.

behalf, *n.* **in my behalf,** to my advantage: ". . . to intercept the Queen,/ Bearing the King in my behalf along . . ." *3 Hen 6,* II, i, 114–115.

behavior, *n.* **1** [pl.] person's powers of expression: ". . . all his behaviours did make their retire/ To the court [longing looks] of his eye . . ." *Love's L,* II, i, 233–234. **2 in my behavior,** in or through my own person: "Thus, after greeting, speaks the King of France/ In my behaviour to the majesty . . ." *K John,* I, i, 2–3.

beheld, *v.* participated in; more likely a sarcastic ref. to those soldiers who watched the victory from a safe distance: ". . . stand upon my common part with those/ That have beheld the doing." *Cor,* I, ix, 39–40.

behest, *n.* command or urging: ". . . I have learnt me to repent the sin/ Of disobedient opposition/ To you and your behests . . ." *Rom & Jul,* IV, ii, 17–19.

behind, *adv.* **1** afterward: "Before, a joy propos'd; behind, a dream." *Sonn 129,* 12. **2** to follow: "There's more behind that is more gratulate [gratifying]." *Meas,* V, i, 526.

behind-door-work, *n.* tryst achieved by the lover's hiding behind the door in his beloved's bedroom: "This has been some/ stair-work, some trunk-work, some behind-door-work . . ." *W Tale,* III, iii, 73–75.

behind-hand, *adj.* tardy: ". . . interpreters/ Of my behind-hand slackness!" *W Tale,* V, i, 149–150.

beholding, *adj.* **1** beholden; indebted: "Little are we beholding to your love . . ." *Rich 2,* IV, i, 160.
—*n.* **2** look; regard: "Something not worth in me such rich beholding/ As they have often given." *Tr & Cr,* III, iii, 91–92.

behoof, *n.* **1** benefit or advantage: "This tongue hath parley'd unto foreign kings/ For your behoof—" *2 Hen 6,* IV, vii, 74–75. **2 in our behoof,** for our own good: "For fear of harms that preach in our behoof." *Lover's Comp,* 165.

behove or **behoove,** *v.* **1** to manage or control: "He did behove his anger, ere 'twas spent . . ." *Timon,* III, v, 22.
—*n.* **2** advantage: "Methought it was very sweet:/ To contract—O—the time for—a—my behove . . ." *Ham,* V, i, 62–63.

behoveful, *adj.* fitting; appropriate: ". . . we have cull'd such necessaries/ As are behoveful for our state tomorrow." *Rom & Jul,* IV, iii, 7–8.

behowl, *v.* to howl at: "Now the hungry lion roars,/ And the wolf behowls the moon . . ." *M N Dream,* V, i, 357–358.

being, *n.* **1 for ever being,** to ever be: "Too like the sire for ever being good." *T Andr,* V, i, 50. **2 in being,** alive: ". . . the Oracle/ Gave hope thou wast in being . . ." *W Tale,* V, iii, 126–127. **3 not in being,** no longer alive: "If/ The cause were not in being . . ." *W Tale,* II, iii, 2–3.
—*conj.* **4** since; inasmuch as: ". . . you loiter here too long, being you/ are to take soldiers up in counties as you go." *2 Hen 4,* II, i, 181–182.

being that, *conj.* since; inasmuch as: "Being that I flow in grief,/ The smallest twine may lead me." *M Ado,* IV, i, 249–250.

Bel, *n.* (in the Apocrypha) false god [Baal], whose priests were overthrown by Daniel: ". . . sometime like god Bel's priests in/ the old church-window . . ." *M Ado,* III, iii, 131–132.

belching, *adj.* blowing; spouting: ". . . the belching whale/ And humming water must o'erwhelm thy corpse . . ." *Per,* III, i, 62–63.

beldam, *n.* **1** old hag; used as a term of contempt for an older woman: "Beldam, I think we watch'd you at an inch [very closely]." *2 Hen 6,* I, iv, 41.
—*adj.* **2** like a woman of advanced years, esp. a grandmother (used as a title of respect): "Shakes the old beldam earth, and topples down/ Steeples and moss-grown towers." *1 Hen 4,* III, i, 29–30.

Belgia, *n.* Low Countries, Holland and Belgium: "Where stood Belgia, the Netherlands?"/ "O, sir, I did not look so low." *Errors,* III, ii, 137–138.

belie, *v.* **1** to misrepresent with lies; slander: "Thou dost belie him, Percy, thou dost belie him . . ." *1 Hen 4,* I, iii, 112. **2** to prove false: ". . . she concludes the picture was belied." *Luc,* 1533. **3** to penetrate with lies: ". . . whose breath . . . doth belie/ All corners of the world." *Cymb,* III, iv, 36–38.

believed, *past part.* believed to exist: "Let pity not be believ'd!" *Lear,* IV, iii, 30.

belike, *adv.* most likely; in all probability: "Belike, then my appetite was not princely got . . ." *2 Hen 4,* II, ii, 9.

bell, *n.* **1** passing-bell, announcing a death: "This sight of death is as a bell/ That warns my old age to a sepulchre." *Rom & Jul,* V, iii, 205–206. **2** perh. a gossip, with woman's tongue likened to the clapper of a bell: ". . . you are pictures out o' doors;/ Bells in your parlours . . ." *Oth,* II, i, 109–110. **3 bell and burial,** tolling of a church bell as part of a burial ceremony (here in consecrated ground despite Ophelia's "doubt-ful" death): "Yet here she is allow'd her virgin crants . . . and the bringing home/ Of bell and burial." *Ham,* V, i, 225–227. **4 shake his bells,** allusion to the bells fastened to the leg of a falcon: "Neither the King, nor he that loves him best . . . Dares stir a wing if Warwick shake his bells." *3 Hen 6,* I, i, 45–47.

bell, book, and candle, *n.* ritual of excommunication; here, the threat of such: "Bell, book, and candle shall not drive me back/ When gold and silver becks me to come on . . ." *K John,* III, ii, 22–23.

bellman, *n.* watchman who at midnight rang a bell outside the cell of a prisoner condemned to die the next morning; a summons to prayers: "It was the owl that shriek'd, the fa-tal bellman,/ Which gives the stern'st good-night." *Mac,* II, ii, 3–4.

Bellona, *n.* Roman goddess of war; here, fanciful ref. to Mac-beth as her bridegroom: ". . . Bellona's bridegroom, lapp'd in proof,/ Confronted him . . ." *Mac,* I, ii, 55–56.

bell-wether, *n.* **1** sheep that leads the flock and wears a bell around its neck: ". . . to be bawd to a bell-wether, and to betray a she-lamb . . ." *As You,* III, ii, 78–79. **2** Ford, in Falstaff's view, is the [castrated] gang leader: ". . . an intolerable fright, to be detected with a jealous/ rotten [diseased] bell-wether . . ." *Wives,* III, v, 99–101.

belly, *v.* to fill; billow: "Your breath with full consent bellied his sails . . ." *Tr & Cr,* II, ii, 75.

belly-pinched, *adj.* malnourished; gaunt: "The lion and the belly-pinched wolf/ Keep their fur dry . . ." *Lear,* III, i, 13–14.

Belmont, *n.* country residence of Portia, appar. at some dis-tance from Venice and accessible only by sea: ". . . her sunny locks/ Hang on her temples like a golden fleece,/ Which makes her seat of Belmont Colchos' strond . . ." *Merch,* I, i, 169–171.

belong, *v.* **belong to,** [to] be employed in: "'Good master porter, I belong to th'larder [pantry].'" *Hen 8,* V, iii, 4.

belonging, *adj.* **1** appropriate; here, having to do with con-juration: "Here do the ceremonies belonging, and make the circle . . ." [SD] *2 Hen 6,* I, iv, 22. —*n.* **2** [pl.] virtuous qualities: "Thyself and thy belongings/ Are not thine own so proper . . ." *Meas,* I, i, 29–30. **3 trim belonging,** equipment belonging to him: "My noble steed . . . I give him,/ With all his trim belonging . . ." *Cor,* I, ix, 60–61.

beloved, *n.* dearest friend: "This man, Aufidius,/ Was my belov'd in Rome . . ." *Cor,* V, ii, 90–91.

below stairs, *adv.* (in) the servants' quarters: "Why, shall I/ always keep below stairs?" *M Ado,* V, ii, 9–10.

Belzebub, *n.* prince of devils; Satan: "Who's there, i' th' name of Belzebub?" *Mac,* II, iii, 3–4.

bemadding, *adj.* maddening: ". . . how unnatural and be-madding sorrow/ The King hath cause to plain." *Lear,* III, i, 38–39.

be-met, *interj.* **well be-met,** same as "well met," a standard, if perfunctory, greeting: "Our very loving sister, well be-met." *Lear,* V, i, 20.

bemete, *v.* to measure: "I shall so bemete thee with thy yard/ As thou shalt think on prating whilst thou liv'st." *Shrew,* IV, iii, 113–114.

bemock, *v.* to mock: "Bemock the modest moon." *Cor,* I, i, 256.

bemoiled, *adj.* begrimed; covered with dirt and mud: ". . . how she was bemoiled, how he left her/ with the horse upon her . . ." *Shrew,* IV, i, 67–68.

be-monster, *v.* to change into a monster: "Thou changed and self-cover'd thing, for shame,/ Be-monster not thy feature." *Lear,* IV, ii, 62–63.

bench, *n.* **1** seat of judges; here, the senate: ". . . who puts his 'shall' . . . against a graver bench/ Than ever frown'd in Greece." *Cor,* III, i, 104–106. —*v.* **2** to sit on a bench: "And thou, his yoke-fellow of equity,/ Bench by his side." *Lear,* III, vi, 38–39.

bencher, *n.* judge: ". . . a/ perfecter giber for the table than a necessary [indispensable] bencher in/ the Capitol." *Cor,* II, i, 80–82.

bench-hole, *n.* hole on the seat of a privy: "We'll beat 'em into bench-holes. I have yet/ Room for six scotches more." *Ant & Cleo,* IV, vii, 9–10.

bend, *n.* **1** glance or inclination: "And that same eye whose bend doth awe the world/ Did lose his lustre . . ." *J Caes,* I, ii, 122–123. —*v.* **2** to direct; aim: ". . . the revenging Gods/ 'Gainst par-ricides did all the thunder bend . . ." *Lear,* II, i, 45–46. **3** to in-cline: "My thoughts and wishes bend again toward France . . ." *Ham,* I, ii, 55. **4** to bow: ". . . the nobles bended/ As to Jove's statue . . ." *Cor,* II, i, 263–264. **5** to arch; here, like a rainbow: "His crest that prouder than blue Iris bends." *Tr & Cr,* I, iii, 380. **6** to change or alter: "Which alters when it alteration finds,/ Or bends with the remover to remove." *Sonn 116,* 3–4. **7 bend all offices,** devoted my entire duty: ". . . never aim'd so high to love your daughter,/ But bent all offices to honour her." *Per,* II, v, 47–48. **8 bend her humor,** change her attitude: "... which she after,/ Except she bend her humour, shall be assur'd/ To taste of too." *Cymb,* I, vi, 80–82. **9 bend on,** to threaten; menace: "Each one with ireful passion ... Met us again, and madly bent on us,/ Chas'd us away ..." *Errors,* V, i, 151–153. **10 bend one's brows,** to frown or scowl: "See how the ugly witch doth bend her brows ..." *1 Hen 6,* V, iii, 34. **11 bend up,** to stretch: "I am settled, and bend up/ Each corporal agent to this terrible feat." *Mac,* I, vii, 80–81. **12 bend you,** [may you] be inclined: "... we beseech you bend you to remain/ Here in the cheer and comfort of our eye ..." *Ham,* I, ii, 115–116.

bending, *pres. part.* **1** bowing before your judgment: "Our bending author hath pursu'd the story ..." *Hen 5,* Epil. 2. —*adj.* **2** curved: "Love's not Time's fool, though rosy lips and cheeks/ Within his bending sickle's compass [range] come ..." *Sonn 116,* 9–10.

beneath, *adj.* located beneath Heaven: "... this beneath world doth embrace and hug/ With amplest entertainment." *Timon,* I, i, 44–45.

Benedicite, [Latin] Bless you [used in greeting or parting]: "Grace go with you: *Benedicite!*" *Meas,* II, iii, 39.

benedictus, *n.* ref. to *carduus benedictus,* the "blessed thistle": "*Benedictus!* why *benedictus*? you have some moral/ in this *benedictus.*" *M Ado,* III, iv, 72–73.

benefactor, *n.* misuse for "malefactor": "... do bring in here before your good/ honour two notorious benefactors." *Meas,* II, i, 49–50.

benefice, *n.* ecclesiastical appointment providing an income: "Then dreams he of another benefice." *Rom & Jul,* I, iv, 81.

benefit, *n.* **1** profit: "I am invited, sir, to certain merchants,/ Of whom I hope to make much benefit." *Errors,* I, ii, 24–25. **2** kind, loving, or beneficial act: "Turn all her mother's pains and benefits/ To laughter and contempt ..." *Lear,* I, iv, 295–296.

benetted, *past part.* caught in a net; trapped; snared: "Being thus benetted round with villainies—" *Ham,* V, ii, 29.

benevolence, *n.* forced loan made to the monarch by a wealthy subject: "And daily new exactions are devis'd./ As blanks, benevolences, and I wot not what—" *Rich 2,* II, i, 249–250.

benison, *n.* blessing: "The good in conversation,/ To whom I give my benison,/ Is still at Tharsus ..." *Per,* II, Chor., 9–11.

bent, *n.* **1** natural inclination: "Two of them have the very bent of honour ..." *M Ado,* IV, i, 186. **2** intention: "If that thy bent of love be honourable ... send me word tomorrow ..." *Rom & Jul,* II, ii, 143–144. **3** wordplay on "glance" and "line of fire": "Your eyes, which hitherto have borne in them,/ Against the French, that met them in their bent ..." *Hen 5,* V, ii, 15–16. **4** arch: "Eternity was in our lips, and eyes,/ Bliss in our brows' bent ..." *Ant & Cleo,* I, iii, 35–36. **5 full bent with,** intent on: "How Thaliard came full bent with sin/ And hid intent to murder him ..." *Per,* II, Chor., 23–24. **6 high bent,** (of a bow) bent back and ready to shoot: "... my revenges were high bent upon him/ And watch'd the time to shoot." *All's W,* V, iii, 10–11. **7 hold the bent,** to stand the strain: "Then let thy love be younger than thyself,/ Or thy affection cannot hold the bent ..." *T Night,* II, iv, 36–37. **8 in the full bent,** to one's greatest ability: "... here give up ourselves in the full bent/ To lay our service freely at your feet ..." *Ham,* II, ii, 30–31. **9 the true bent,** the desired direction: "For I can give his humour the true bent ..." *J Caes,* II, i, 210. **10 top of my bent,** [to] my utmost limit: "They fool me [force me to play the fool] to the top of my bent." *Ham,* III, ii, 375. —*adj.* **11** inclined: "A sort of naughty persons, lewdly bent ..." *2 Hen 6,* II, i, 159. **12** eager: "... now I am bent to know,/ By the worst means, the worst." *Mac,* III, iv, 133–134. **13 bent my deeds to cross,** determined to thwart my actions: "Now, while the world is bent my deeds to cross ..." *Sonn 90,* 2.

Bentivolii, *n. pl.* powerful medieval family, though actually of Bologna: "A merchant of great traffic through the world,/ Vincentio, come of the Bentivolii." *Shrew,* I, i, 12–13.

benumbed, *adj.* desensitized by lust: "... great minds, of partial indulgence/ To their benumbed wills ..." *Tr & Cr,* II, ii, 179–180.

ben venuto, [Italian] **1** welcome: "I will, on my privilege ... undertake your *ben venuto* ..." *Love's L,* IV, ii, 149–151. **2** welcomer; host: "Petruchio, I shall be your *ben venuto.*" *Shrew,* I, ii, 280.

be one's speed, *v.* to bring one good luck: "Well, I am school'd—good manners be your speed!" *1 Hen 4,* III, i, 184.

bepray, *v.* misuse for "pray," beseech: "I bepray you, let/ me borrow my arms again." *Love's L,* V, ii, 687–688.

berattle, *v.* to mock; disdain or disparage: "These are now the fashion, and/ so berattle the common stages—so they call them—" *Ham,* II, ii, 339–340.

berayed, *adj.* befouled: "Lord Bassianus lies beray'd in blood,/ All on a heap ..." *T Andr,* II, iii, 222–223.

bereave¹, *v.* to deprive: "I'll not bereave you of your servant." *Per,* IV, i, 30.

bereave², *v.* to spoil; take away: "Which the hot tyrant stains and soon bereaves . . ." *Ven & Ad,* 797.

bereft, *v.* **1** to deprive (someone) of something: ". . . all your interest in those territories/ Is utterly bereft you: all is lost." *2 Hen 6,* III, i, 84–85. **2** past part. of BEREAVE¹; deprived: "But if thou live to see like right bereft [see yourself likewise deprived of rights] . . ." *Errors,* II, i, 40.
—*adj.* **3** lost: "Beauty's effect with beauty were bereft . . ." *Sonn 5,* 11. **4** gone; taken away or stolen: "I think his understanding is bereft." *3 Hen 6,* II, vi, 60.

Bergomask, *n.* rustic dance, said to be modeled on those of Bergamo, Italy: "Will it please you to/ see the epilogue, or to hear a Bergomask dance . . . ?" *M N Dream,* 338–340.

berhyme, *v.* to compose verses to or about: ". . . marry, she had a better love/ to berhyme her . . ." *Rom & Jul,* II, iv, 41–42.

Berkeley, *n.* castle W of London, nr. Bristol: "Gentlemen, go muster up your men,/ And meet me presently at Berkeley . . ." *Rich 2,* II, ii, 117–118.

Bermoothes, *n.* the Bermudas [Bermuda]; here, appar. spelled phonetically from Spanish pron.: "Thou call'dst me up at midnight to fetch dew/ From the still-vex'd Bermoothes . . ." *Temp,* I, ii, 228–229.

Berwick, *n.* town and fortress on the Scottish border: "Mount you, my lord; towards Berwick post amain." *3 Hen 6,* II, v, 128.

bescreened, *adj.* hidden; obscured: "What man art thou that thus bescreen'd in night/ So stumblest on my counsel?" *Rom & Jul,* II, ii, 52–53.

beseech, *n.* action of a suppliant: "Achievement is command; ungain'd, beseech." *Tr & Cr,* I, ii, 298.

beseeched, *past part.* misuse for "besieged": "The town is beseeched, and the trumpet call us/ to the breach . . ." *Hen 5,* III, ii, 111–112.

beseecher, *n.* plea or entreaty; also, one who begs: "Let no unkind, no fair beseechers kill . . ." *Sonn 135,* 13.

beseek, *v.* dial. var. of BESEECH: "I beseek you now, aggravate your choler." *2 Hen 4,* II, iv, 159.

beseem, *v.* to be [more] becoming to; befit: "It would beseem the Lord Northumberland/ To say 'King Richard.'" *Rich 2,* III, iii, 7–8.

beseeming, *n.* appearance: "The soldier that did company these three/ In poor beseeming . . ." *Cymb,* V, v, 409–410.

beset, *adj.* **1** surrounded: "The thicket is beset, he cannot 'scape." *Two Gent,* V, iii, 10. **2** assailed; attacked: "They must'ring to the quiet cabinet . . . Do tell her she is dreadfully beset . . ." *Luc,* 442–444. **3 hard beset,** engulfed in serious matters: "Now, daughter Silvia, you are hard beset." *Two Gent,* II, iv, 44.

beshrew, *v.* **1** to curse or berate; also, censure; a plague on: ". . . beshrew my hand/ If it should give your age such cause of fear." *M Ado,* V, i, 55–56. **2 beshrew me,** used as a mild oath with the general sense of "May evil befall me": "Beshrew me, the knight's in admirable fooling." *T Night,* II, iii, 81.

beside, *adv.* **1** besides: "Beside, my lord . . . The Earl of Armagnac . . . Proffers his only daughter to your Grace . . ." *1 Hen 6,* V, i, 15–19. **2** otherwise: ". . . one day in a week to touch no food,/ And but one meal on every day beside . . ." *Love's L,* I, i, 39–40.

beslubber, *v.* to smear: ". . . to beslubber our garments/ with it, and swear it was the blood of true men." *1 Hen 4,* II, iv, 306–307.

besom, *n.* broom of bound twigs: "I am the besom that must sweep the court clean of such/ filth as thou art." *2 Hen 6,* IV, vii, 28–30.

Besonian or **bezonian,** *n.* **1** recruit or rookie; also, by inference, ignoramus: "Under which king, Besonian? Speak, or die." *2 Hen 4,* V, iii, 110. **2** beggar [term of contempt]; here, scoundrel: "Great men oft die by vile bezonians." *2 Hen 6,* IV, i, 134.

besort, *v.* **1** to suit; be becoming to: ". . . such men as may besort your age,/ Which know themselves and you." *Lear,* I, iv, 259–260.
—*n.* **2** suitable companions: ". . . such accommodation and besort/ As levels with her breeding." *Oth,* I, iii, 238–239

bespeak, *v.* **1** to address; speak to: "Whilst he . . . Bespake them thus, 'I thank you, countrymen.'" *Rich 2,* V, ii, 18–20. **2** to order; engage or reserve: "I have bespoke/ supper tomorrow night in East-cheap . . ." *1 Hen 4,* I, ii, 125–126. **3** to request: "Then fairly I bespoke the officer/ To go in person with me to my house." *Errors,* V, i, 233–234.

bespice, *v.* to add spice to; here, to poison: ". . . might'st bespice a cup,/ To give mine enemy a lasting wink . . ." *W Tale,* I, ii, 316–317.

best, *n.* **1 the best,** the best elders [those capable of negotiating terms]: ". . . send us to Rome/ The best, with whom we may articulate/ For their own good and ours." *Cor,* I, ix, 74–75. **2 the Best,** Jesus; ref. here to His betrayal by Judas: ". . . my name/ Be yok'd with his that did betray the Best!" *W Tale,* I, ii, 418–419.

best-conditioned, *adj.* best-natured: "The dearest friend to me, the kindest man,/ The best-condition'd . . ." *Merch,* III, ii, 291–292.

bested or **bestead,** *adj.* placed in such circumstances; situated: "I never a fellow worse bested,/ Or more afraid to fight . . ." *2 Hen 6,* II, iii, 56–57.

best-moving, *adj.* most persuasive: ". . . we single you/ As our best-moving fair solicitor." *Love's L,* II, i, 28–29.

bestow, *v.* **1** to employ; use: "And buy a rope's end; that will I bestow/ Among my wife and her confederates . . ." *Errors,* IV, i, 16–17. **2** to behave; comport: "The boy is fair . . . and bestows himself/ Like a ripe sister." *As You,* IV, iii, 85–87. **3** to pay out; advance (funds): "I would/ have bestowed the thousand pound I borrowed of/ you." *2 Hen 4,* V, v, 11–13. **4** to lodge; quarter or house: "Good my lord, will you see the players well/ bestowed?" *Ham,* II, ii, 518–519. **5** to hide; conceal: "Sir, can you tell/ Where he bestows himself?" *Mac,* III, vi, 23–24. **6** to provide: ". . . you see I have given her physic,/ And you must needs bestow her funeral . . ." *T Andr,* IV, ii, 163–164. **7 bestow of,** to give to: "How shall I feast him? What bestow of him?" *T Night,* III, iv, 2. **8 bestow this place on us,** Leave us alone: "Bestow this place on us a little while. [Exeunt Rosencrantz and Guildenstern.]" *Ham,* IV, i, 4. **9 bestow yourself,** take your position: ". . . bestow yourself with speed:/ The French are bravely in their battles set . . ." *Hen 5,* IV, iii, 68–69.

bestowing, *n.* use or employment: "And all my powers do their bestowing lose . . ." *Tr & Cr,* III, ii, 36.

bestraught, *adj.* var. of **distraught;** mad: "What! I am not/ bestraught. Here's—" *Shrew,* Ind., ii, 25–26.

bestrew, *v.* to cover or spread with rushes, carpets, etc.: "Say thou wilt walk; we will bestrew the ground." *Shrew,* Ind., ii, 41.

bestrid, *v.* old past tense of **bestride;** bestrode. **1** to ride on the back of: "Never bestrid a horse, save one that had/ A rider like myself . . ." *Cymb,* IV, iv, 38–39. **2** (in battle) to stand guard over a wounded comrade: "When I bestrid thee in the wars, and took/ Deep scars to save thy life . . ." *Errors,* V, i, 192–193.

beteem, *v.* **1** to grant; furnish: ". . . which I could well/ Beteem them from the tempest of my eyes." *M N Dream,* I, i, 130–131. **2** to permit; allow: ". . . so loving to my mother/ That he might not beteem the winds of heaven/ Visit her face too roughly." *Ham,* I, ii, 140–142.

bethink, *v.* **1** to devise: ". . . with patience calm the storm,/ While we bethink a means to break it off." *3 Hen 6,* III, iii, 38–39. **2 bethink you,** (to) consider; think about it [used esp. as a warning or admonition] : ". . . what is mine shall never do thee good./ Trust to't, bethink you. I'll not be forsworn." *Rom & Jul,* III, v, 194–195.

bethought, *past part.* of **bethink. 1** considered: ". . . something touching the Lord Hamlet."/ "Marry, well bethought." *Ham,* I, iii, 89–90. **2 am bethought,** intend; mean (to): ". . . and am bethought/ To take the basest and most poorest shape/ That ever penury . . . Brought near to beast . . ." *Lear,* II, iii, 6–9.

betid, *v.* old past tense and past part. of **betide;** happened or befallen: ". . . let them tell thee tales/ Of woeful ages long ago betid . . ." *Rich 2,* V, i, 41–42.

betide, *v.* **1** to occur: ". . . what news else/ Betideth here in absence of thy friend . . ." *Two Gent,* I, i, 58–59. **2** to happen to; befall: "More health and happiness betide my liege . . ." *Rich 2,* III, ii, 91. **3 betide on,** become of: "If he were dead, what would betide on me?" *Rich 3,* I, iii, 6.

betideth, *v.* third pers. sing. of **betide;** happens: ". . . what news else/ Betideth here in absence of thy friend . . ." *Two Gent,* I, i, 58–59.

betime or **betimes,** *adv.* **1** early: "Be with me betimes in the morning;/ and so, good morrow, Peto." *1 Hen 4,* II, iv, 541–542. **2** quickly: "He tires betimes that spurs too fast betimes [early] . . ." *Rich 2,* II, i, 36. **3 betimes before,** early and ahead of us: "Bid him set on his powers betimes before,/ And we will follow." *J Caes,* IV, iii, 304.

betossed, *adj.* agitated; turbulent: "What said my man, when my betossed soul/ Did not attend him, as we rode?" *Rom & Jul,* V, iii, 76–77.

betray, *v.* to ensnare: "And York, and impious Beaufort . . . Have all lim'd bushes to betray thy wings . . ." *2 Hen 6,* II, iv, 53–54.

betrayed, *past part.* caught or trapped; here, ref. to Spenser's *The Faerie Queene,* in which a lion stands before a tree luring a unicorn to charge him; when the lion steps aside at the last moment, the unicorn is impaled on the tree, victim of the lion: ". . . for he loves to hear/ That unicorns may be betray'd with trees . . ." *J Caes*, II, i, 203–204.

better, *adj.* **1 still better, and worse,** even more bitter and worse behaved. *Ham*, III, ii, 245.
—*adv.* **2** at a more suitable time: "He could never come better . . ." *W Tale*, IV, iv, 189.

bettered, *adj.* reputed to be superior: "But since he is better'd, we have therefore odds." *Ham*, V, ii, 260.

bettering, *n.* greater achievement(s): "Compare them with the bettering of the time . . ." *Sonn 32*, 5.

better part of man, *n.* the spirit: "Accursed be that tongue that tells me so,/ For it hath cow'd my better part of man . . ." *Mac*, V, viii, 17–18.

better place, *n.* higher rank: "A many fools that stand in better place,/ Garnish'd like him . . ." *Merch*, III, v, 62–63.

better worth, worth more; more valuable or important: "His health was never better worth than now." *1 Hen 4*, IV, i, 27.

betumbled, *adj.* disorderly: ". . . from her betumbled couch she starteth,/ To find some desp'rate instrument of death . . ." *Luc*, 1037–1038.

betwixt, *prep.* **betwixt us twain,** between the two of us: "The bitter clamour of two eager tongues,/ Can arbitrate this cause betwixt us twain . . ." *Rich 2*, I, i, 49–50.

bevel, *adj.* slanting; deviating from straightness or uprightness: "I may be straight, though they themselves be bevel . . ." *Sonn 121*, 11.

Bevis, *n.* Bevis of Southampton, hero of a medieval romance: ". . . former fabulous story . . . got credit/ That Bevis was believ'd." *Hen 8*, I, i, 36–38.

bevy, *n.* **1** flock: ". . . many more of the same bevy that I/ know the drossy age dotes on . . ." *Ham*, V, ii, 185–186. **2** fair company; here, of beautiful ladies: ". . . none here he hopes,/ In all this noble bevy, has brought with her/ One care abroad . . ." *Hen 8,* I, iv, 3–5.

bewailed, *adj.* lamentable: "Lest my bewailed guilt should do thee shame . . ." *Sonn 36*, 10.

bewailing, *adj.* grieving: "Thy ambition . . . robb'd this bewailing land/ Of noble Buckingham . . ." *Hen 8*, III, ii, 254–256.

beweep, *v.* to weep for: "I all alone beweep my outcast state . . ." *Sonn 29*, 2.

bewet, *adj.* soaked; drenched: "His napkin, with his true tears all bewet . . ." *T Andr*, III, i, 146.

bewhore, *v.* to call (a woman) a whore: "Alas, Iago, my lord hath so bewhor'd her . . ." *Oth*, IV, ii, 117.

bewitch, *v.* to charm by or as if by witchcraft: "Heavens grant that Warwick's words bewitch him not!" *3 Hen 6*, III, iii, 112.

bewitchment, *n.* spellbinding charm: "I will counterfeit the bewitchment/ of some popular man . . ." *Cor*, II, iii, 100–101.

bewray, *v.* **1** to reveal or expose; make known: "Write down thy mind, bewray thy meaning so . . ." *T Andr*, II, iv, 3. **2** var. of **betray:** ". . . the paleness of this flower/ Bewray'd the faintness of my master's heart." *1 Hen 6*, IV, i, 106–107.

bezonian, *n.* See **Besonian.**

bias, *n.* **1** natural inclination; bent: "Study his bias leaves and makes his book thine eyes . . ." *Love's L*, IV, ii, 105. **2** (in the game of bowls) a lead weight on one side of a bowl, giving it a curved trajectory; here, fig. use: "Commodity, the bias of the world . . ." *K John*, II, i, 574. **3 against the bias,** unusually crooked; on an unnatural or destructive course: "'Twill make me think the world is full of rubs/ And that my fortune runs against the bias." *Rich 2*, III, iv, 4–5. **4 falls from bias of nature,** behaves contrary to the natural instincts of a father: ". . . the King falls from bias of nature; there's father/ against child." *Lear*, I, ii, 115–117.
—*adv.* **5 bias and thwart,** off course and awry: ". . . trial did draw/ Bias and thwart, not answering the aim . . ." *Tr & Cr*, I, iii, 14–15.

bias-drawing, *n.* divergence; here, from truth and honesty: ". . . faith and troth,/ Strain'd purely from all hollow bias-drawing,/ Bids thee . . . welcome." *Tr & Cr*, IV, v, 168.

bid, *v.* **1** to invite: ". . . then thou mightst kill 'em—and bid me to 'em." *Timon*, I, ii, 81. **2** to pray [to]: ". . . you shall bid God 'ild us for your pains . . ." *Mac*, I, vi, 13–14. **3 I bid for you as I do buy.** I should bid for your hand in the same way that I would buy anything. *Cymb*, III, vii, 43.
—*past part.* **4** invited: "I am not bid to wait upon this bride." *T Andr*, I, i, 338.

biddy, *n.* chick [term of endearment]; also, a call to summon chickens: "Ay, biddy, come with me." *T Night*, III, iv, 117.

bide, *v.* **1** to remain; endure: ". . . yet the gold bides still/ That others touch . . ." *Errors*, II, i, 110–111. **2** to speak at length: "To bide upon't: thou art not honest . . ." *W Tale*, I, ii, 242.

bide the touch, *v.* to be put to the test: ". . . the fortune of ten thousand men/ Must bide the touch . . ." *1 Hen 4,* IV, iv, 9–10.

biding, *n.* shelter; abode: "Give me your hand,/ I'll lead you to some biding." *Lear,* IV, vi, 224–225.

bier, *n.* cart used in harvesting: ". . . summer's green all girded up in sheaves/ Borne on the bier . . ." *Sonn 12,* 7–8.

big, *adj.* **1** menacing: "Nay, look not big, nor stamp, nor stare, nor fret . . ." *Shrew,* III, ii, 226. **2** loud: "Whilst I was big in clamour came there in a man . . ." *Lear,* V, iii, 208. **3** proud or haughty: ". . . and Buckingham/ Shall lessen this big look." *Hen 8,* I, i, 118–119.

biggen or **biggin,** *n.* nightcap of coarse homespun material: ". . . he whose brow with homely biggen bound/ Snores out the watch of night." *2 Hen 4,* IV, v, 26–27.

bilberry, *n.* large blueberry; whortleberry: "There pinch the maids as blue as bilberry . . ." *Wives,* V, v, 46.

bilbo, *n.* sword of fine steel; Bilboa [from Spanish city Bilbao]: "I combat challenge of this latten bilbo." *Wives,* I, i, 146.

bilboes, *n. pl.* iron shackles for restraining prisoners aboard ship: "Methought I lay/ Worse than the mutines in the bilboes." *Ham,* V, ii, 5–6.

bill¹, *n.* **1** written statement; here, a series of accusations: "Gloucester offers to put up a bill; Winchester snatches it, tears it." [SD] *1 Hen 6,* III, i, 1. **2** handbill or other written or printed advertisement: "He set up his bills here in Messina and challenged/ Cupid at the flight . . ." *M Ado,* I, i, 35–36. **3** list: "I will draw a bill of properties, such as our play wants." *M N Dream,* I, ii, 98–99. **4** written message, esp. orders: ". . . give these bills/ Unto the legions on the other side." *J Caes,* V, ii, 1–2. **5 bills for money by exchange,** bills of exchange; promissory notes: "I have bills for money by exchange/ From Florence, and must here deliver them." *Shrew,* IV, ii, 89–90.

bill², *n.* wooden shaft topped with a curved blade, used both as a pruning implement and as a weapon: ". . . have a care that your bills be not stolen." *M Ado,* III, iii, 41.

bill³, *v.* to kiss: "What, billing again?" *Tr & Cr,* III, ii, 57.

billet¹, *n.* block of wood used as a club: ". . . they shall beat out my brains with billets." *Meas,* IV, iii, 54.

billet², *v.* to enroll (a soldier) in an army: ". . . the centurions and their charges/ distinctly [separately] billeted . . ." *Cor,* IV, iii, 44–45.

bin, *v.* unaccented form of **been:** "We have bin praying for our husbands' welfare . . ." *Merch,* V, i, 114.

bind, *v.* **1** to obligate; make beholden: "Your lordship ever binds him." *Timon,* I, i, 107. **2** to force; compel: "I bind . . . the world to weet [know]/ We stand up peerless." *Ant & Cleo,* I, i, 38–40. **3** to confine: "If there were reason for these miseries,/ Then into limits could I bind my woes . . ." *T Andr,* III, i, 219–220.

bird, *n.* **1** young; offspring: "Nay, if thou be that princely eagle's bird,/ Show thy descent by gazing 'gainst the sun . . ." *3 Hen 6,* II, i, 91–92. **2 well flown bird,** cry when falcon has made a successful kill; here, prob. addressed to the arrow: "O! well flown bird; i' th' clout, i' th' clout . . ." *Lear,* IV, vi, 92–93.

bird-bolt, *n.* blunt-tipped arrow used in hunting birds: "my uncle's fool . . . subscribed for Cupid, and challenged/ him at the bird-bolt." *M Ado,* I, i, 37–38.

bird of dawning, *n.* the cock: "This bird of dawning singeth all night long . . ." *Ham,* I, i, 165.

bird of night, *n.* screech owl: "And yesterday the bird of night did sit,/ Even at noon-day, upon the market-place . . ." *J Caes,* I, iii, 26–27.

Birnam, *n.* forest and high hill near Perth, legendary site of Macbeth's castle: "Macbeth shall never vanquish'd be, until/ Great Birnam wood to high Dunsinane hill/ Shall come against him." *Mac,* IV, i, 92–94.

birth, *n.* **1** rank; station: "What time we will our celebration keep/ According to my birth." *T Night,* IV, iii, 30–31. **2 i' th' rear 'our birth,** below me in birth: "She is as forward of her breeding [above her actual rank] as/ She is i' th' rear 'our [of our] birth." *W Tale,* IV, iv, 581–582.

birthdom, *n.* one's native land: "Hold fast the mortal sword, and like good men/ Bestride our downfall birthdom." *Mac,* IV, iii, 3–4.

birth-hour's blot, *n.* birthmark: "Worse than a slavish wipe or birth-hour's blot . . ." *Luc,* 537.

birthright, *n.* everything one owns: "Bearing their birthrights proudly on their backs [as elegant uniforms] . . ." *K John,* II, i, 70.

bis coctus, *adj.* [Latin] twice-cooked [twice-repeated]: "Twice-sod simplicity, *bis coctus!*" *Love's L,* IV, ii, 21.

bisson, *adj.* **1** partially blind: "What harm can your bisson/ conspectuities glean out of this character . . ." *Cor,* II, i, 63–64. **2 bisson rheum,** *n.* blinding tears: "Run barefoot up and down, threat'ning the flames/ With bisson rheum . . ." *Ham,* II, ii, 501–502.

bite, *v.* **1 bite of** (or **at**) to rail or inveigh against: "No marvel though you bite so sharp of reasons,/ You are empty of them." *Tr & Cr,* II, ii, 33–34. **2 bite the law by th'nose,** show contempt for the law: "That thus can make him bite the law by th'nose . . ." *Meas,* III, i, 108.

biting, *adj.* wounding; painful: "If this sweet lady lie not guiltless here/ Under some biting error." *M Ado,* IV, i, 169–170.

bitter, *adj.* **1** sharp; stinging or biting: "Have at you for a bitter jest or two." *Shrew,* V, ii, 45. **2** painful or disagreeable; also, mortifying: ". . . it cannot be/ But I am pigeon-liver'd and lack gall/ To make oppression bitter . . ." *Ham,* II, ii, 572–574.

bitumed, *adj.* sealed and made watertight with pitch: ". . . we have a chest beneath the hatches, caulked/ and bitumed ready." *Per,* III, i, 70–71.

blab, *v.* **1** to utter; also, chatter: ". . . that delightful engine of her thoughts,/ That blabb'd them with such pleasing eloquence . . ." *T Andr,* III, i, 81–82. **2** to betray: "Beaufort's red sparkling eyes blab his heart's malice . . ." *2 Hen 6,* III, i, 154.

blabbing, *adj.* disclosing secrets: "The gaudy, blabbing, and remorseful day . . ." *2 Hen 6,* IV, i, 1.

black, *adj.* **1** dark-complexioned; swarthy: "If black, why, Nature, drawing of an antic,/ Made a foul blot . . ." *M Ado,* III, i, 63–64. **2** indicating a woman with dark hair and eyes: "In the old age black was not counted fair . . ." *Sonn 127,* 1. **3** homely or ugly: "Though ne'er so black, say they have angels' faces . . ." *Two Gent,* III, i, 103. **4** practicing the black art of witchcraft: "How now, you secret, black, and midnight hags!" *Mac,* IV, i, 48. **5** evil or wicked: "The devil damn thee black, thou cream-fac'd loon!" *Mac,* V, iii, 11. **6 black in my mind,** melancholy, thought to be caused by the presence of black bile: "Not black in my mind, though yellow in my legs." *T Night,* III, iv, 26.
—*adv.* **7** in an evil or sinister manner: "Look'd black upon me; struck me with her tongue . . ." *Lear,* II, iv, 161.
—*n.* **8** [pl.] black clothes: ". . . but were they false/ As o'er-dy'd [dyed with another color] blacks, as wind, as waters . . ." *W Tale,* I, ii, 131–132.

black and blue, *adv.* thoroughly; completely: ". . . we'll have the bear again, and we/ will fool him black and blue . . ." *T Night,* II, v, 9–10.

black brow, *n.* ref. to the threatening blackness of night: "Why, here walk I in the black brow of night,/ To find you out." *K John,* V, vi, 17–18.

Black-Friars, *n.* London monastery of mendicant friars; nickname (because of their black garb) for the Dominican friars: "The most convenient place . . . For such receipt of learning is Black-Friars . . ." *Hen 8,* II, ii, 137–138.

Blackheath, *n.* large, open, uncultivated plot of land near London. [SD] *2 Hen 6,* IV, ii, 1.

Black-Monday, *n.* day after Easter, so-called from the devastatingly cold weather on that day in 1360: ". . . it was not/ for nothing that my nose fell a-bleeding on Black-Monday last . . ." *Merch,* II, v, 23–25.

black mouth, *n.* evil, slanderous mouth: "He [anyone] had a black mouth that said other [otherwise] of him." *Hen 8,* I, iii, 58.

black prince, *n.* the devil; Satan: "The black prince, sir, alias the prince of darkness,/ alias the devil." *All's W,* IV, v, 39–40.

black vesper's pageants, *n.* spectacles brought on by the approach of evening: "Thou hast seen these signs,/ They are black vesper's pageants." *Ant & Cleo,* IV, xiv, 7–8.

blade, *n.* **1** fencer: "By Jesu, a very good/ blade, a very tall man, a very good whore!" *Rom & Jul,* II, iv, 29–30. **2** inexperience; immaturity: ". . . make it/ Natural rebellion done i' th' blade of youth,/ When oil and fire . . . O'erbears it and burns on." *All's W,* V, iii, 5–8.

bladed, *adj.* leafed out; leafy: ". . . Phoebe doth behold/ Her silver visage in the wat'ry glass,/ Decking with liquid pearl the bladed grass . . ." *M N Dream,* I, i, 209–211.

blain, *n.* [usually pl.] blisters or sores: "Itches, blains,/ Sow all th' Athenian bosoms . . ." *Timon,* IV, i, 28–29.

blameful, *adj.* guilty; reprehensible: ". . . with bloody blameful blade,/ He bravely broach'd his boiling bloody breast . . ." *M N Dream,* V, i, 145–146.

blank¹, *n.* **1** blank charter: "And daily new exactions are devis'd./ As blanks, benevolences, and I wot not what—" *Rich 2,* II, i, 249–250. **2** target: "As level as the cannon to his blank . . ." *Ham,* IV, i, 42. **3 blank and level,** bull's-eye of the target and the aim or range needed to hit it: ". . . the harlot king/ Is quite beyond mine arm, out of the blank/ And level of my brain . . ." *W Tale,* II, iii, 4–6. **4 within the blank of,** as the target for: "As I have spoken for you . . . And stood within the blank of his displeasure . . ." *Oth,* III, iv, 124–125.

blank², *v.* to make pale: "Each opposite, that blanks the face of joy,/ Meet what I would have well and it destroy . . ." *Ham,* III, ii, 215–216.

blank charter, *n.* document authorizing the king's agents to collect large sums from wealthy subjects, the amount to be filled in by the agent: "Our substitutes at home shall have blank charters . . . for large sums of gold . . ." *Rich 2,* I, iv, 48–50.

blaspheme, *v.* to slander; disparage; vilify: ". . . the truest issue of thy throne/ By his own interdiction stands accus'd,/ And does blaspheme his breed?" *Mac,* IV, iii, 106–108.

blasphemy, *n.* blasphemous fellow: "Now, blasphemy,/ That swear'st grace o'erboard, not an oath on shore?" *Temp,* V, i, 218–219.

blast, *n.* **1** violent rush of freezing air: "Blasts and fogs upon thee!" *Lear,* I, iv, 308. **2** prob. the uproar expected to follow Duncan's murder: "Pity, like a naked new-born babe,/ Striding the blast . . ." *Mac,* I, vii, 21–22. **3** [pl.] perils; calamities: "They that stand high have many blasts to shake them . . ." *Rich 3,* I, iii, 259.
—*v.* **4** to strike fatally; wither or shrivel up: "I'll cross it though it blast me." *Ham,* I, i, 130. **5** to infect; contaminate: ". . . like a mildew'd ear/ Blasting his wholesome brother." *Ham,* III, iv, 64–65. **6** to wither: ". . . the young and tender wit/ Is turn'd to folly, blasting in the bud . . ." *Two Gent,* I, i, 47–48. **7 blast in proof,** to blow up when being tested, in the manner of a cannon: "Therefore this project/ Should have a back or second that might hold/ If this did blast in proof." *Ham,* IV, vii, 151–153.

blasted, *adj.* **1** withered; blighted: ". . . be men like blasted/ woods . . ." *Timon,* IV, iii, 535. **2** barren: ". . . why/ Upon this blasted heath you stop our way . . ." *Mac,* I, iii, 76–77.

blasting, *adj.* blighting; infecting; corrupting: ". . . in me you behold/ The injury of many a blasting hour . . ." *Lover's Comp,* 71–72.

blastment, *n.* blight: ". . . in the morn and liquid dew of youth/ Contagious blastments are most imminent." *Ham,* I, iii, 41–42.

blaze, *v.* to blazon; proclaim or announce: "Where thou shalt live till we can find a time/ To blaze your marriage . . ." *Rom & Jul,* III, iii, 149–150.

blazon, *n.* **1** detailed description, as that used in heraldry: "I' faith, lady, I think your blazon to be true . . ." *M Ado,* II, i, 278. **2** armorial bearings; coat of arms: "Each fair instalment, coat, and sev'ral crest,/ With loyal blazon, evermore be blest . . ." *Wives,* V, v, 64–65. **3 give five-fold blazon,** (to) verify five times over [that you are a gentleman]: "Thy tongue, thy face, thy limbs, actions, and spirit/ Do give thee five-fold blazon." *T Night,* I, v, 296–297.

—*v.* **4** to proclaim: "Ah, Juliet, if . . . thy skill be more/ To blazon it, then sweeten with thy breath/ This neighbour air . . ." *Rom & Jul,* II, vi, 24–27.

bleak[1], *adj.* chilly; cold: "Yet thou/ liest in the bleak air." *As You,* II, vi, 14–15.

bleak[2], *v.* var. of *bleat:* "Why he hath made the ewe bleak for the lamb . . ." *Merch,* IV, i, 74.

blear, *v.* to blur or cloud; here, to confuse or deceive: "While counterfeit supposes blear'd thine eyne." *Shrew,* V, i, 107.

bleared, *adj.* **1** tear-stained; weeping: "With bleared visages come forth to view/ The issue of th' exploit . . ." *Merch,* III, ii, 59–60. **2 bleared sights,** those with blurred vision: ". . . the bleared sights/ Are spectacled to see him." *Cor,* II, i, 203–204.

bleed, *v.* to let blood as a cure for disease: ". . . Have brought ourselves into a burning fever,/ And we must bleed for it." *2 Hen 4,* IV, i, 56–57.

bleeding, *adj.* **1** unhealed; here, unresolved: ". . . dismiss the controversy/ bleeding, the more entangled by your hearing." *Cor,* II, i, 76–77. **2 the bleeding and the grim alarm,** the bloody and brutal call to battle: ". . . their dear causes [deeply felt wrongs]/ Would, to the bleeding and the grim alarm,/ Excite the mortified man [summon the dead]." *Mac,* V, ii, 3–5.

bleeding and the grim alarm, *n.* bloody death struggles of the battlefield: ". . . their dear causes/ Would, to the bleeding and the grim alarm/ Excite the mortified man." *Mac,* V, ii, 3–5.

bleeding groans, *n.* belief that each lovesick sigh drew a drop of blood from the heart: "Feeling it break, with bleeding groans they pine . . ." *Lover's Comp,* 275.

blemished stock, *n.* ref. to Edward's supposed illegitimacy: "The lineal glory of your royal House,/ To the corruption of a blemish'd stock . . ." *Rich 3,* III, vii, 120–121.

blench, *v.* **1** to start; flinch: "If a [he] do blench,/ I know my course." *Ham,* II, ii, 593–594. **2** to deviate from the course of reason: "Would I do this?/ Could man so blench?" *W Tale,* I, ii, 332–333. **3 lesser blench,** flinch to a lesser degree: "Patience herself, what goddess e'er she be,/ Doth lesser blench at suff'rance than I do." *Tr & Cr,* I, i, 27–28.
—*n.* **4** lapse; aberration: "These blenches gave my heart another youth . . ." *Sonn 110,* 7.

blent, a past part. of **blend;** mixed or mingled: "Where every something being blent together,/ Turns to a wild of nothing . . ." *Merch,* III, ii, 181–182.

bless, *v.* to protect: "Heaven bless thee from/ a tutor . . ." *Tr & Cr,* II, iii, 30–31.

blessed, *adj.* **1** happy; pleased: "Which the rather/ We shall be bless'd to do . . ." *Cor,* II, ii, 57–58. **2 so blessed never,** never so blessed: "What wretched errors hath my heart committed,/ Whilst it hath thought itself so blessed never!" *Sonn 119,* 5–6.

blessed-fair, *adj.* happy as well as beautiful; fortunate: "But what's so blessed-fair that fears no blot?" *Sonn 92,* 13.

blessed part, *n.* the soul: "He gave his honours to the world again,/ His blessed part to heaven . . ." *Hen 8,* IV, ii, 29–30.

blest, *adj.* **1 desirous to be blest,** truly repentant: "And when you are desirous to be blest,/ I'll blessing beg of you." *Ham,* III, iv, 173–174. **2 twice blest,** providing a twofold blessing: ". . . it is twice blest,/ It blesseth him that gives, and him that takes . . ." *Merch,* IV, i, 182–183.

blind, *adj.* **1** heedless; indifferent: "And blind oblivion swallow'd cities up . . ." *Tr & Cr,* III, ii, 185. **2** same sense, but blind with lust: ". . . look to see/ The blind and bloody soldier with foul hand/ Defile the locks of your shrill-shrieking daughters . . ." *Hen 5,* III, iii, 33–35. **3** sluggish; here, because of cool weather: ". . . like flies at/ Bartholomew-tide, blind, though they have their/ eyes . . ." *Hen 5,* V, ii, 326–327.

blind boy, *n.* the love god Cupid: "Her and her blind boy's scandal'd company/ I have forsworn." *Temp,* IV, i, 90–91.

blind Cupid, *n.* traditionally the sign over a brothel: "No, do thy worst, blind Cupid; I'll not love." *Lear,* IV, vi, 139.

blinded god, *n.* Cupid, the blind god of love: "If this fond Love were not a blinded god?" *Two Gent,* IV, iv, 194.

blind fortune, *n.* mere luck: "Will you be put in mind of his blind fortune . . ." *Cor,* V, vi, 117.

blind harper's song, *n.* blind harpers and fiddlers could often be hired to compose a rhymed ballad in honor of a beloved: ". . . never come in visor to my friend,/ Nor woo in rhyme, like a blind harper's song . . ." *Love's L,* V, ii, 404–405.

blind priest, Wolsey likened to Fortune in his indifference to rank and character: "That blind priest, like the eldest son of fortune,/ Turns what he list [deals out what he likes]." *Hen 8,* II, ii, 20–21.

blind-worm, *n.* small snakelike lizard: "Newts and blind-worms, do no wrong . . ." *M N Dream,* II, ii, 11.

blinking, *adj.* blind; an epithet of Cupid: ". . . pretty, fond adoptious christendoms/ That blinking Cupid gossips." *All's W,* I, i, 170–171.

blister, *n.* **1** brand mark of shame on the forehead of a prostitute: ". . . takes off the rose/ From the fair forehead of an innocent love/ And sets a blister there . . ." *Ham,* III, iv, 42–44. —*v.* **2 blistered her report,** branded her reputation: "Who, falling in the flaws of her own youth,/ Hath blister'd her report." *Meas,* II, iii, 11–12.

blistered breeches, *n.* short breeches, puffed out in the manner of a blister: ". . . renouncing clean/ The faith they have in tennis and tall stockings,/ Short blister'd breeches . . ." *Hen 8,* I, iii, 29–31.

blithe, *adj., adv.* cheerful; merry: "And now sweet emperor, be blithe again,/ And bury all thy fear in my devices." *T Andr,* IV, iv, 111–112.

block, *n.* **1** mold for shaping a hat: "he wears his faith but as the/ fashion of his hat, it ever changes with the next block." *M Ado,* I, i, 69–70. **2** blockhead: "For thy conceit is soaking, will draw in/ More than the common blocks . . ." *W Tale,* I, ii, 224–225. **3** poss. ref. to stump serving as a mounting block; perh. ref. to his "hat," the wreath of flowers: "This' a good block!" *Lear,* IV, vi, 185.

blockish, *adj.* dull-witted; stupid: ". . . by device let blockish Ajax draw/ The sort to fight with Hector." *Tr & Cr,* I, iii, 375–376.

blood, *n.* **1** kinsman; here, offspring [sons of Pompey]: "And do you now strew flowers in his way,/ That comes in triumph over Pompey's blood?" *J Caes,* I, i, 50–51. **2** fashionable young man; gallant: ". . . Pompey hath made the challenge."/ "Sweet bloods, I both may and will." *Love's L,* V, ii, 697–699. **3** a blood relationship: "I rather will subject me to the malice/ Of a diverted [unnatural] blood and bloody brother." *As You,* II, iii, 36–37. **4** one's basic nature: "Undone by goodness; strange, unusual blood . . ." *Timon,* IV, ii, 38. **5** vigorous spirit; mettle: "Though sometimes it show greatness, courage, blood . . ." *1 Hen 4,* III, i, 175. **6** desire; passion: ". . . beauty is a witch/ Against whose charms faith melteth into blood." *M Ado,* II, i, 167–168. **7** sensual nature: ". . . though in my nature reigned/ All frailties that besiege all kinds of blood . . ." *Sonn 109,* 9–10. **8** blush or blushes: "Could she here deny/ The story that is printed in her blood?" *M Ado,* IV, i, 121–122. **9** bloodshed: "The King is merciful, if you revolt."/ "But angry . . . and inclin'd to blood,/ If you go forward . . ." *2 Hen 6,* IV, ii, 119–121. **10 be let blood,** assassinated: "I know not, gentlemen, what you intend,/ Who else must be let blood, who else is rank . . ." *J Caes,* III, i, 151–152. **11 blood and life,** great courage and energy: ". . . high in name and power,/ Higher than both in blood and life . . ." *Ant & Cleo,* I, ii, 187–188. **12 Blood, thou art blood,** such passions, however disguised, are shared by all men: "Wrench awe from fools, and tie the wiser souls/ To thy false seeming! Blood, thou art blood." *Meas,* II, iv, 14–15. **13 consume your blood,** waste or fritter away your blood with sighs of woe: "Do not consume your blood with sorrowing:/ Have you a nurse of me!" *Per,* IV, i, 23–24. **14 half made of Hector's blood,** Hector is Priam's son; Ajax is the son of Hesione, Priam's sister: "This Ajax is half made of Hector's blood;/ In love whereof, half Hector stays at home . . ." *Tr & Cr,* IV, v, 83–84. **15 in blood,** in fine physical condition; full of vigor [hunting term]: "The deer was, as you know, *sanguis,* in blood . . ." *Love's L,* IV, ii, 3. **16 lack blood,** turn pale: ". . . the borders maritime/ Lack blood to think on't . . ." *Ant & Cleo,* I, iv, 51–52. **17 worst in blood,** most ferocious; also, most desperate: "Thou rascal, that art worst in blood to run . . ." *Cor,* I, i, 158.

—*v.* **18 let it blood,** bleed it; ref. to blood-letting in treatment of ills: "Sick at the heart."/ "Alack! let it blood." *Love's L,* II, i, 184–185.

blood-boltered, *adj.* having the hair matted with blood: ". . . the blood-bolter'd Banquo smiles upon me . . ." *Mac,* IV, i, 123.

blood-consuming or **blood-drinking** or **blood-sucking,** *adj.* (of sighs) believed to cost the heart one drop of blood each: "Might liquid tears . . . Or blood-consuming sighs recall his life,/ I would be blind with weeping, sick with groans . . ." *2 Hen 6,* III, ii, 59–61.

bloody, *adj.* **1** dangerous; portending bloodshed: ". . . and in such bloody distance,/ That every minute of his being . . ." *Mac,* III, i, 115–116. **2** causing bloodshed: "And do him homage as obedient subjects,/ And I'll withdraw me and my bloody power . . ." *1 Hen 6,* IV, ii, 7–8.

bloody argument, *n.* reason for bloodshed: ". . . the quality of the time and quarrel/ Might well have given us bloody argument." *T Night,* III, iii, 31–32.

bloody fire, *n.* fire in the blood: "Lust is but a bloody fire,/ Kindled with unchaste desire . . ." *Wives,* V, v, 96–97.

bloody flag, *n.* **set up the bloody flag against,** declare war on ["bloody flag" ref. to the red flag of battle]: ". . . make faces like mummers,/ set up the bloody flag against all patience . . ." *Cor,* II, i, 74–75.

bloody-minded, *adj.* bloodthirsty: "Yet let not this make thee be bloody-minded . . ." *2 Hen 6,* IV, i, 36.

bloody succeeding, *n.* aftermath of bloodshed: "A most harsh one, and not to be understood without/ bloody succeeding." *All's W,* II, iii, 190–191.

bloody veins, *n.* bloodthirsty soldiers: ". . . the Trojan horse was stuff'd within/ With bloody veins expecting overthrow . . ." *Per,* I, iv, 94–95.

blossom, *n.* young courtier: "Whose rarest havings [endowments] made the blossoms dote . . ." *Lover's Comp,* 235.

blot, *n.* **1** mishap or disgrace: "But what's so blessed-fair that fears no blot?" *Sonn 92,* 13. **2** blemish; stain: "Full of unpleasing blots and sightless stains . . ." *K John,* II, ii, 45.

—*v.* **3** to mar; blemish: "She passes praise; then praise too short doth blot." *Love's L,* IV, iii, 237. **4** to slander: "There's a good mother, boy, that blots thy father." *K John,* II, 1, 132.

blow¹, *v.* **1** (of winds) to blow adversely to sailing ships: "And the very ports they blow,/ All the quarters that they know . . ." *Mac,* I, iii, 15–16. **2** to puff (a person) up; make conceited: ". . . now he's deeply in: look how imagination/ blows him." *T Night,* II, v, 42–43. **3** to swell to bursting: "This blows my heart:/ If swift thought break it not . . ." *Ant & Cleo,* IV, vi, 34–35. **4** to gasp for breath; pant; puff: "Enter a Messenger, blowing." [SD] *3 Hen 6,* II, i, 43. **5** (of an insect) to deposit eggs on; befoul: ". . . let the water-flies/ Blow me into abhorring [loathsomeness] . . ." *Ant & Cleo,* V, ii, 59–60. **6** same in fig. use: ". . . these summer flies/ Have blown me full of maggot ostentation . . ." *Love's L,* V, ii, 408–409. **7 blow on,** to criticize; censure: "I must have liberty . . . To blow on whom I please . . ." *As You,* II, vii, 47–49. **8 blow our nails,** See **nail** (def. 2).

—*n.* **9** explosive noise; blast: ". . . not half so great a blow to hear/ As will a chestnut in a farmer's fire . . ." *Shrew,* I, ii, 207–208. **10 blow of the law,** legal repercussions: ". . . that keeps you from the blow of/ the law." *T Night,* III, iv, 154–155.

blow², *v.* (of a flower) to bloom; open up: ". . . the most forward bud/ Is eaten by the canker ere it blow . . ." *Two Gent,* I, i, 45–46.

blowing, *n.* the laying of eggs; here, by the blowfly: ". . . as summer's flies, are in the shambles,/ That quicken even with blowing . . ." *Oth,* IV, ii, 67–68.

blown¹, *adj.* **1** filled out by the wind: ". . . toward Ephesus/ Turn our blown sails . . ." *Per,* V, i, 252–253. **2** short-winded: "How now, blown Jack? How now, quilt?" *1 Hen 4,* IV, ii, 49. **3** overblown; puffed-up: "No blown ambition doth our arms incite . . ." *Lear,* IV, iv, 27. **4** swollen; here, with fly bites: ". . . where he is to behold him,/ with flies blown to death." *W Tale,* IV, iv, 792–793.

blown², *adj.* **1** in full bloom: "That unmatch'd form and feature of blown youth/ Blasted with ecstasy." *Ham,* III, i, 161–162. **2 well blown,** beautifully realized; ref. here to night blooming into day: "The morn is fair: good morrow, general."/ "'Tis well blown, lads." *Ant & Cleo,* IV, iv, 24–25.

blown³, *adj., past part.* having left a trail of slime: "Here on her breast,/ There is a vent of blood, and something blown . . ." *Ant & Cleo,* V, ii, 346–347.

blown up, *past part.* prob. ref. to sexual orgasm: "Virginity being blown down man will quicklier be/ blown up . . ." *All's W,* I, i, 121–122.

blowse, *n.* sluttish woman, usually ruddy and fat-faced; here, applied to infant: "Sweet blowse, you are a beauteous blossom, sure." *T Andr,* IV, ii, 72.

blubbered, *adj.* weeping; having a tear-stained face: "O, run Doll, run . . . She comes/ blubbered." *2 Hen 4,* II, iv, 386–387.

blue-bottle, *adj.* dressed in a blue coat, as a beadle: ". . . you blue-bottle/ rogue, you filthy famished correctioner . . ." *2 Hen 4,* V, iv, 20–21.

blue-cap, *n.* Scotchman, typically wearing a blue hat or cap: ". . . well, he is there too,/ and one Mordake, and a thousand blue-caps more." *1 Hen 4,* II, iv, 352–353.

blue eye, *n.* rings or shadows under the eye, due to lack of sleep: ". . . a blue eye and sunken, which you have not . . ." *As You,* III, ii, 363–364.

blue-eyed, *adj.* having the blue eye or, more likely, a blue cast to the eyelids, regarded as a sign of pregnancy: "This blue-ey'd hag was hither brought with child . . ." *Temp,* I, ii, 269.

blunt, *v.* **1** to fail to reciprocate; also, to rebuff: ". . . blunt not his love,/ Nor lose the good advantage of his grace . . ." *2 Hen 4,* IV, iv, 27–28. **2** to stop or attempt to stop: "By blunting us to make our wits more keen." *Lover's Comp,* 161.
—*adj.* **3** rude; coarse: "Hiding his bitter jests in blunt behaviour." *Shrew,* III, ii, 13. **4** dull-witted; stupid; ref. here to the rabble: ". . . the blunt monster with uncounted heads,/ The still-discordant wavering multitude . . ." *2 Hen 4,* Induc., 18–19. **5** wordplay on "lacking a point" and "lacking comprehension": "Base slave, thy words are blunt, and so art thou." *2 Hen 6,* IV, i, 67. **6** Dogberry's mistake for "sharp": ". . . his wits are not so/ blunt as, God help, I would desire they were . . ." *M Ado,* III, v, 10–11.

blunted, *adj.* neglected or abandoned: "This visitation/ Is but to whet thy almost blunted purpose." *Ham,* III, iv, 110–111.

blunt monster, *n.* crowd; rabble: ". . . the blunt monster with uncounted heads,/ The still-discordant wav'ring multitude . . ." *2 Hen 4,* Ind., 18–19.

blur, *v.* **1** to smear or stain; also, disfigure: "Such an act/ That blurs the grace and blush of modesty . . ." *Ham,* III, iv, 40–41.
—*n.* **2** blot or stain: "This blur to youth, this sorrow to the sage . . ." *Luc,* 222.

blurt, *v.* **1** to treat one with contempt: ". . . all the world will blurt and scorn at us." *Edw 3,* IV, vi, 45. **2 blurt at,** to sneer at: ". . . cast their gazes on Marina's face,/ Whilst ours was blurted at and held a malkin . . ." *Per,* IV, iii, 33–34.

blushing, *adj.* glowing: "And bears his blushing honours thick upon him . . ." *Hen 8,* III, ii, 354.

bluster, *n.* storm: ". . . the skies look grimly,/ And threaten present [imminent] blusters." *W Tale,* III, iii, 3–4.

blusterer, *n.* swaggering fellow: "Sometime a blusterer, that the ruffle knew/ Of court . . ." *Lover's Comp,* 58–59.

blustering, *adj.* tempestuous: "And make fair weather in your blust'ring land." *K John,* V, i, 21.

boar, *n.* Richard's heraldic device; here, the symbol stands for Richard himself: "Good angels guard thee from the boar's annoy." *Rich 3,* V, iii, 157.

board, *v.* **1** to address or accost; here, wordplay on boarding a vessel in war and making amorous advances: "I am sure he is in the fleet; I/ would he had boarded me." *M Ado,* II, i, 132–133.
—*n.* **2** table, esp. dining table: "Here's money for my meat,/ I would have left it on the board . . ." *Cymb,* III, vii, 22–23. **3 at board,** at table: "'Tis double wrong to truant with your bed,/ And let her read it in thy looks at board . . ." *Errors,* III, ii, 17–18.

boar of Thessaly, *n.* See **Thessaly** (def. 2).

boar-pig, *n.* young boar for roasting, a delicacy associated with the Bartholomew Fair: "Thou whoreson little tidy Bartholomew boar-pig . . ." *2 Hen 4,* II, iv, 227.

boast, *n.* **1** display: ". . . wherefore look'st thou sad/ When everything doth make a gleeful boast?" *T Andr,* II, iii, 10–11.
—*v.* **2** to praise; boast about: "O Ferdinand,/ Do not smile at me that I boast her off [so highly] . . ." *Temp,* IV, i, 8–9.

bob¹, *n.* **1** malicious jest; gibe: ". . . Not to seem senseless of the bob." *As You,* II, vii, 55.
—*v.* **2** to cheat: "You shall not bob us out of our melody . . ." *Tr & Cr,* III, i, 67. **3 bob from,** to cheat (someone) out of:

"He calls me to a restitution large,/ For gold and jewels, that I bobb'd from him . . ." *Oth,* V, i, 15–16.

bob², *v.* to strike; beat with the fists: "I have bobbed/ his brain more than he has beat my bones." *Tr & Cr,* II, i, 71–72.

bode, *v.* **1** to mean or signify: "My sight is very dull, whate'er it bodes." *T Andr,* II, iii, 195. **2** to prophesy disaster, as a raven is said to do: "Would I could meet that rogue Diomed!—I/ would croak like a raven: I would bode . . ." *Tr & Cr,* V, ii, 188–189.

bodement, *n.* prophecy: "Sweet bodements! good!/ Rebellious dead, rise never, till the wood/ Of Birnam rise . . ." *Mac,* IV, i, 96–98.

boding, *adj.* warning of death or calamity: "And boding screech-owls make the consort full!" *2 Hen 6,* III, ii, 326.

bodkin¹, *n.* long, decorative pin for ladies' hair; also, a short dagger: "When he himself might his quietus make/ With a bare bodkin." *Ham,* III, i, 75–76.

bodkin², *n.* See **God's bodkin.**

body, *n.* **1** vital part; substance: ". . . the very age/ and body of the time his form and pressure." *Ham,* III, ii, 23–24. **2** person: "A deflower'd maid;/ And by an eminent body . . ." *Meas,* IV, iv, 19–20. **3 body a' me,** by my [very] body [lit., body of me]; a mild oath: "Body a' me; where is it?" *Hen 8,* V, ii, 21. **4 the common body,** the populace; common people: ". . . the common body,/ By you reliev'd, would force me to my duty." *Per,* III, iii, 21–22.

body forth, *v.* to embody; give material form to: "And as imagina-tion bodies forth/ The forms of things unknown . . ." *M N Dream,* V, i, 14–15.

bodykins, *n.* [By God's] little body [mild oath]: "Bodykins, Master Page, though I now be old . . ." *Wives,* II, iii, 41.

boggle, *v.* to start or flinch, as a horse does: "You boggle shrewdly [violently]; every feather starts you [makes you jump]." *All's W,* V, iii, 231.

boggler, *n.* person who wavers; also, a shifty person: "You have been a boggler ever . . ." *Ant & Cleo,* III, xiii, 110.

bogs, *n.* ref. to the bogs of Ireland; here, in poss. wordplay with slang sense of "latrine": "Marry, sir, in her buttocks; I found it out by/ the bogs." *Errors,* III, ii, 115–116.

Bohemia, *n.* king of Bohemia: ". . . you shall see . . . great difference/ betwixt our Bohemia and your Sicilia." *W Tale,* I, i, 3–4.

Bohemian-Tartar, *n.* perh. a wild man; appar. a concocted epithet, combining the exotic with the abusive: "Here's a Bohemian-Tartar tarries the coming/ down of thy fat woman." *Wives,* IV, v, 18–19.

boiled, *adj.* seething and therefore useless: "A solemn air . . . cure thy brains,/ Now useless, boil'd within thy skull!" *Temp,* V, i, 58–60.

boiled-brains, *n.* hotheaded youth or youths: "Would any but these/ boiled-brains of nineteen and two-and-twenty hunt/ this weather?" *W Tale,* III, iii, 63–65.

boiled stuff, *n.* prostitutes who have taken the sweating-tub treatment for syphilis: "Such boil'd stuff/ As well might poison poison!" *Cymb,* I, vii, 125–126.

boisterous, *adj.* **1** irritating: "Then, feeling what small things are boisterous there,/ Your vild intent must needs seem horrible." *K John,* IV, i, 94–95. **2** menacing; threatening: ". . . with a base and boist'rous sword enforce/ A thievish living on the common road?" *As You,* II, iii, 32–33. **3** violent: ". . . an honour snatch'd with boist'rous hand . . ." *2 Hen 4,* IV, v, 191. **4** cataclysmic; tumultuous: "Each small annexment . . . Attends the boist'rous ruin." *Ham,* III, iii, 21–22. **5** vicious; savage: "O Clifford, boisterous Clifford! thou hast slain/ The flower of Europe for his chivalry . . ." *3 Hen 6,* II, i, 70–71.

boisterously, *adv.* violently: "A sceptre snatch'd with an unruly hand/ Must be as boisterously maintain'd as gain'd . . ." *K John,* III, iii, 135–136.

boitine, *n.* **une boitine verde,** [French] a small green box: "Pray you go/ and vetch [fetch] me in my closet *une boitine verde*—" *Wives,* I, iv, 40–41.

bold, *adj.* **1** confident; assured: "Bold of your worthiness, we single you/ As our best-moving fair solicitor." *Love's L,* II, i, 28–29. **2** intrusive: "I think we are too bold upon your rest . . ." *J Caes,* II, i, 86. **3** rude; impudent: "Men so disorder'd, so debosh'd, and bold . . ." *Lear,* I, iv, 250. **4 be bold with,** presume to ask: "I will only be bold/ with Benedick for his company . . ." *M Ado,* III, ii, 7–8. **5 make bold a.** to play freely: ". . . one of your nine/ lives. That I mean to make bold withal . . ." *Rom & Jul,* III, i, 76–77. **b.** Bottom's ref. to use of cobwebs to stanch the flow of blood: ". . . if I cut my finger, I shall make bold/ with you." *M N Dream,* III, i, 176–177.
—*v.* **6** to make bold; embolden: "It touches us . . . Not bolds the King, with others, whom I fear . . ." *Lear,* V, i, 25–26.

bold beating, *adj.* poss. brazenly insistent: ". . . your red-lattice/ phrases, and your bold beating oaths . . ." *Wives,* II, ii, 25–26.

bolins, *n. pl.* bowlines [of a ship's rigging]: "Slack the bolins there! Thou wilt not, wilt thou?/ Blow, and split thyself." *Per,* III, i, 43–44.

bollen, *adj.* swollen; here, with rage: "Here one being throng'd bears back, all boll'n and red . . ." *Luc,* 1417.

bolster, *v.* to go to bed together [lit., share a pillow]: "If ever mortal eyes did see them bolster . . ." *Oth,* III, iii, 405.

bolt¹, *n.* **1** arrow, esp. one that is short and blunt: "Yet mark'd I where the bolt of Cupid fell . . ." *M N Dream,* II, i, 165. **2** witty retort of a court fool compared to arrow; ref. here to saying that a fool's bolt (arrow) is soon spent: "According to the fool's bolt sir, and such dulcet/ diseases." **3** [usually pl.] fetters: "Away with/ him to prison! Lay bolts enough upon him . . ." *Meas,* V, i, 343–344. —*v.* **4 bolt up,** to lock up: ". . . that thing that ends all other deeds,/ Which shackles accidents, and bolts up change [misfortune] . . ." *Ant & Cleo,* V, i, 5–6.

bolt², *v.* to sift: ". . . or the fann'd snow that's bolted/ By th' northern blasts twice o'er." *W Tale,* IV, iv, 365–366.

bolted, *adj.* refined [lit., sifted]: ". . . he has been bred i' th' wars . . . and is ill school'd/ In bolted language . . ." *Cor,* III, i, 317–319.

bolter, *n.* sieve for meal, made of coarse cloth: "I have given them away to/ bakers' wives; they have made bolters of them." *1 Hen 4,* III, iii, 67–68.

bolting-hutch, *n.* bin into which flour was sifted: ". . . that bolting-hutch of beastliness, that swollen parcel/ of dropsies . . ." *1 Hen 4,* II, iv, 443–444.

bolts and shackles! call for fetters to bind a prisoner; here, only the audience hears Sir Toby's call. *T Night,* II, v, 56.

bombard, *n.* **1** large leather jug for holding wine: ". . . that huge bombard of sack, that/ stuffed cloak-bag of guts . . ." *1 Hen 4,* II, iv, 445–446. **2** drunkard: "And here ye lie baiting of bombards when/ Ye should do service." *Hen 8,* V, iii, 80–81.

bombast, *n.* cotton batting, used to pad out garments; also, grandiose boasting and bluster: ". . . my sweet creature of bombast, how long is't/ ago, Jack, since thou sawest thine own knee?" *1 Hen 4,* II, iv, 323–324.

bombast circumstance, *n.* blustering circumlocution: "Evades them, with a bombast circumstance,/ Horribly stuff'd with epithets of war . . ." *Oth,* I, i, 13–14.

Bona, *n.* **Lady Bona,** sister (actually, sister-in-law) of Louis XI, king of France: ". . . whence shall Warwick cut the sea to France,/ And ask the Lady Bona for thy queen." *3 Hen 6,* II, vi, 89–90.

bona-robas, *n. pl.* lit., "the good stuff," i.e., the best whores: ". . . we knew where the bona-robas/ were, and had the best of them all at commandment." *2 Hen 4,* III, ii, 22–23.

bona terra, mala gens, [Latin] good country, terrible people: "What say you of Kent?"/ "Nothing but this: 'tis 'bona terra, mala gens.'" *2 Hen 6,* IV, vii, 53–54.

bond, *n.* **1** claim, deed, or fact of ownership; here, Banquo's claim to life: "Cancel, and tear to pieces, that great bond/ Which keeps me pale!" *Mac,* III, ii, 49–50. **2** legal agreement, esp. a promissory note: "Take the bonds along with you,/ And have the dates in." *Timon,* II, i, 34–35. **3** wordplay on sworn statement (replacing a man's promise) and fetters (for the criminal who has broken his promise): ". . . words are very rascals, since bonds disgraced/ them." *T Night,* III, i, 20–21. **4** duty; here, filial obligation: "According to my bond; no more nor less." *Lear,* I, i, 93. **5 bond of air,** eloquence of Nestor, which will link all Greek ears: "Should with a bond of air . . . knit all the Greekish ears/ To his experienc'd tongue . . ." *Tr & Cr,* I, iii, 66–68. **6 cold bonds,** prob. the fetters that bind Posthumus to life: ". . . take this life,/ And cancel these cold bonds." *Cymb,* V, iv, 27–28.

bondage, *n.* **1** binding up into a parcel; here, just as he is bound up as a slave to love: ". . . enthralled as I am, it/ will also be the bondage of certain ribbons and/ gloves." *W Tale,* IV, iv, 234–236. **2 idle and fond bondage,** pointless and foolish servitude: "I begin to/ find an idle and fond bondage in the oppression of aged/ tyranny . . ." *Lear,* I, ii, 49–51.

bondmaid, *n.* young female servant, legally bound to serve without wages; Bianca enters here with her hands bound: "Good sister, wrong me not, nor wrong yourself,/ To make a bondmaid and a slave of me." *Shrew,* II, i, 1–2.

bondman, *n.* servant legally bound to serve without wages; slave: "And is not that your bondman Dromio?" *Errors,* V, i, 288.

bone, *n.* **1** bobbin made of bone, used in lacemaking: "And the free maids that weave their thread with bones . . ." *T Night,* II, iv, 45. **2** frame; build: "So did this horse excel . . . in courage, colour, pace and bone." *Ven & Ad,* 293–294. **3** [pl.] See **tongs and bones. 4 By these ten bones,** oath attested to by raising the two hands, indicating the ten fingers: "By these ten bones, my lords, he did speak them to/ me in the garret one night . . ." *2 Hen 6,* I, iii, 190–191.

boneache, *n.* See **Neapolitan boneache.**

bones, *n.* wordplay with French *bon(s),* good: ". . . who stand so much on the new form that they cannot/ sit at ease on the old bench? O their bones, their/ bones!" *Rom & Jul,* II, iv, 34–36.

Bon, fort bon, [French] Good! Very good. *Love's L,* V, i, 27.

bonjour, *n.* good-day; here, a welcome befitting the emperor's rank: "With horn and hound we'll give your grace bonjour." *T Andr,* I, i, 494.

bonnet, *n.* **1** hat or cap: "And with his bonnet hides his angry brow . . ." *Ven & Ad,* 339.
—*v.* **2** to doff one's cap: ". . . those/ who, having been supple and courteous to the/ people, bonneted . . ." *Cor,* II, ii, 25–27. Cf. **unbonneted.**

bonny, *adj.* fine-looking; here, "strapping" is also implied: ". . . for you are call'd plain Kate,/ And bonny Kate, and sometimes Kate the curst . . ." *Shrew,* II, i, 185–186.

bonos dies, misuse of Latin *bonus dies,* good day: "*Bonos dies,* Sir Toby: for as the old hermit of/ Prague . . . very wittily/ said . . ." *T Night,* IV, ii, 13–15.

book, *n.* **1** the Bible or a prayer book, used in swearing oaths: "I'll be sworn upon all the books in/ England . . ." *1 Hen 4,* II, iv, 49–50. **2** written agreement; compact: "By that time will our book I think be drawn." *1 Hen 4,* III, i, 217. **3** memory or knowledge: "Who has a book of all that monarchs do . . ." *Per,* I, i, 95. **4** learning; education: ". . . my book preferr'd [recommended] me to the King . . ." *2 Hen 6,* IV, vii, 69. **5** [pl] volumes of poetry: "O! let my books be then the eloquence/ And dumb presagers of my speaking breast . . ." *Sonn 23,* 9–10. **6** diary; tables: "Made him my book, wherein my soul recorded/ The history of all her secret thoughts." *Rich 3,* III, v, 27–28. **7 by the book,** according to the rules of etiquette, i.e., politely: "You kiss by th'book." *Rom & Jul,* I, v, 109. **8 in your books,** in your favor: "A herald, Kate? O, put me in thy books." *Shrew,* II, i, 222. **9 ply one's book,** to study: "Keep house and ply his book, welcome his friends . . ." *Shrew,* I, i, 196. **10 without book,** [learned] by heart: "Perhaps you have learned it without book." *Rom & Jul,* I, ii, 59.
—*v.* **11** to record: "That we may wander o'er this bloody field/ To book our dead . . ." *Hen 5,* IV, vii, 74–75. **12 book down,** to mark down in an account book: "Book both my wilfulness and errors down . . ." *Sonn 117,* 9.

bookish, *adj.* **1** scholarly rather than assertive; here, also weak and timid: ". . . I'll make him yield the crown,/ Whose bookish rule hath pull'd fair England down." *2 Hen 6,* I, 1, 259–260. **2 bookish theoric,** theory learned from books rather than from experience: "Nor the devision [deployment] of a battle knows,/ More than a spinster, unless the bookish theoric . . ." *Oth,* I, i, 23–24.

book-man, *n.* scholar: "This civil war of wits were much better us'd/ On Navarre and his book-men . . ." *Love's L,* II, i, 225–226.

book-mate, *n.* a fellow student: ". . . a Monarcho, and one that makes sport/ To the prince and his book-mates." *Love's L,* IV, i, 100–101.

book oath, *n.* oath taken on the Bible: "I put thee now to thy book oath, deny it if thou canst." *2 Hen 4,* II, i, 101.

book of memory, *n.* memorandum book; also, chronicles: "Blotting your names from books of memory . . ." *2 Hen 6,* I, i, 99.

book of praises, *n.* collection of the finest qualities: "Her face the book of praises . . ." *Per,* I, i, 16.

boon, *n.* special favor: "My boon I make it [I beg it as a special favor] that you know me not . . ." *Lear,* IV, vii, 10.

boor, *n.* peasant: "I am a gentleman? Let boors and/ franklins say it, I'll swear it." *W Tale,* V, ii, 159–160.

boot[1], *n.* **1** help [for it]; use: "Norfolk, throw down we bid, there is no boot." *Rich 2,* I, i, 164. **2** profit or advantage: "I'll give you boot, I'll give you three for one." *Tr & Cr,* IV, v, 40. **3** something added to give full value: "Young York, he is but boot, because both they/ Match'd not the high perfection of my loss." *Rich 3,* IV, iv, 65–66. **4** [pl.] booty; spoils: ". . . they ride up and down on her, and make her their boots." *1 Hen 4,* II, i, 81. **5 make boot of,** take advantage of: "Give him no breath, but now/ Make boot of his distraction . . ." *Ant & Cleo,* IV, i, 8–9. **6 make boot upon,** prey upon; take booty or plunder from: "Others, like soldiers, armed in their stings,/ Make boot upon the summer's velvet buds . . ." *Hen 5,* I, ii, 193–194.
—*v.* **7** to be of help to; avail: "It boots thee not to be compassionate [self-pitying] . . ." *Rich 2,* I, iii, 174. **8** to reward: "And I will boot thee with what gift beside/ Thy modesty can beg." *Ant & Cleo,* II, v, 71–72. **9 to boot, and boot,** thank you and reward you: "The bounty and the benison of Heaven/ To boot, and boot!" *Lear,* IV, vi, 226–227.

boot[2], *n.* **1 give (someone) the boots,** make fun of: "Over the boots?/ Nay, give me not the boots . . ." *Two Gent,* I, i, 27. **2 over shoes, over boots,** engaged in reckless pursuit: "For he was more than over shoes in love./ 'Tis true; for you are over boots in love . . ." *Two Gent,* I, i, 24–25.
—*v.* **3** to put on boots: "Boot, boot, Master/ Shallow!" *2 Hen 4,* V, iv, 130–131.

booted, *adj.* wearing riding boots; here indicating a long journey: "Enter Balthasar, Romeo's man, booted." [SD] *Rom & Jul,* V, i, 12.

boot-hose, *n.* [sing. or pl.] coarse stockings for wearing with boots: ". . . with a linen stock on one leg, and a kersey/ boot-hose on the other . . ." *Shrew,* III, ii, 64–65.

booties, *n.* windfalls: "If I had a mind to be honest, I see Fortune would not/ suffer me: she drops booties in my mouth." *W Tale,* IV, iv, 832–833.

bootless, *adj.* **1** pointless; unnecessary: "And bootless 'tis to tell you we will go . . ." *1 Hen 4,* I, i, 29. **2** unsuccessful; unavailing: ". . . I sent him/ Bootless home, and weather-beaten back." *1 Hen 4,* III, i, 62–63. **3 bootless is your sight,** there is no point in your seeing him: "But bootless is your sight; he will not speak/ To any." *Per,* V, i, 33–34.
—*adv.* **4** vainly; unavailingly: ". . . and sometimes labour in the quern,/ And bootless make the breathless housewife churn . . ." *M N Dream,* II, i, 36–37.

bo-peep, *n.* children's game: "That such a king should play bo-peep . . ." *Lear,* I, iv, 184.

bordered, *past part.* kept within bounds: "That nature . . . Cannot be border'd certain [securely] in itself." *Lear,* IV, ii, 32–33.

borderer, *n.* settler in a border region; here, one who makes raids across the border: ". . . to defend/ Our inland from the pilfering borderers." *Hen 5,* I, ii, 141–142.

bore, *n.* **1** width of a cannon's mouth; here likened to a matter of great import, for which words are like inadequate shot: "I have words to speak in thine ear will/ make thee dumb; yet are they much too light for the bore of/ the matter." *Ham,* IV, vi, 22–24. **2 bores of hearing,** the ears: "Love's counsellor should fill the bores of hearing,/ To th' smothering of the sense [of hearing] . . ." *Cymb,* III, ii, 58.
—*v.* **3** to deceive; cheat: ". . . at this instant/ He bores me with some trick . . ." *Hen 8,* I, i, 127–128.

Boreas, *n.* (in Greek myth.) the North Wind: "But let the ruffian Boreas once enrage/ The gentle Thetis . . ." *Tr & Cr,* I, iii, 38–39.

boresprit, *n.* bowsprit, the spar projecting forward of a ship's prow: ". . . on the topmast,/ The yards and boresprit, would I flame distinctly . . ." *Temp,* I, ii, 199–200.

born, *past part.* **1** shaped; made to conform: "And rather make them born to our desire . . ." *Sonn 123,* 7. **2 as she is born,** in accord with her [royal] birth: ". . . give her princely

training, that she may/ Be manner'd as she is born." *Per,* III, iii, 16–17. **3 born in an hour,** born as twins: "He left behind him myself and a sister,/ both born in an hour . . ." *T Night,* II, i, 18–19. **4 not born where't grows,** not natural but assumed: "Put on for villainy; not born where't grows,/ But worn a bait for ladies." *Cymb,* III, iv, 57–58.

borne, *past part.* of **bear. 1** managed; carried out: ". . . only, I say,/ Things have been strangely borne." *Mac,* III, vi, 2–3. **2 borne in hand,** used for another's advantage; here, Fortinbras's: "That so his sickness, age, and impotence/ Was falsely borne in hand . . ." *Ham,* II, ii, 66–67. **3 borne up,** carried out; executed: "'Tis well borne up." *Meas,* IV, i, 48. **4 hence borne out,** carried out abroad: ". . . action hence borne out/ May waste the memory of the former days." *2 Hen 4,* IV, v, 214–215.

borrowed, *adj.* assumed; feigned; spurious: "This borrow'd passion stands for true-ow'd [sincere] woe . . ." *Per,* IV, iv, 24.

borrowing prayers, *n.* requests for aid: "Would in so just a business shut his bosom/ Against our borrowing prayers." *All's W,* III, i, 8–9.

bosky, *adj.* covered with trees and shrubs: "And with each end of thy blue bow dost crown/ My bosky acres and my unshrubb'd down . . ." *Temp,* IV, i, 80–81.

bosom, *n.* **1** the heart: "The broken bosoms that to me belong . . ." *Lover's Comp,* 254. **2** intimate confidence: ". . . you have your father's bosom there/ And speak his very heart." *W Tale,* IV, iv, 564–565. **3 bosom multiplied,** the masses; mob: "How shall this bosom multiplied digest/ The senate's courtesy?" *Cor,* III, i, 130–131. **4 harder bosoms,** coarser persons: ". . . betray its folly . . . and make itself a pastime/ To harder bosoms!" *W Tale,* I, ii, 151–153. **5 have your bosom,** have your desires fulfilled: ". . . you shall have your bosom on this wretch, Grace of the Duke . . ." *Meas,* IV, iii, 134–135. **6 in their bosoms,** aware of their secret thoughts: "Tut, I am in their bosoms, and I know/ Wherefore they do it." *J Caes,* V, i, 7–8. **7 my bosom's lord,** my love: "My bosom's lord sits lightly in his throne . . ." *Rom & Jul,* V, i, 3. **8 of her bosom,** in her confidence: ". . . most speaking looks/ To noble Edmund. I know you are of her bosom." *Lear,* IV, v, 25–26. **9 the common bosom,** affections of the multitude: "To pluck the common bosom on his side . . ." *Lear,* V, iii, 50.
—*v.* **10** to share a physical intimacy; here, engage in coitus: "I am doubtful [suspicious] that you have been conjunct [joined]/ And bosom'd with her . . ." *Lear,* V, i, 12–13. **11 bosom up,** to take to heart; take seriously: "Bosom up my counsel,/ You'll find it wholesome." *Hen 8,* I, i, 112–113.
—*adj.* **12 bosom interest,** deepest concerns: "No more that Thane of Cawdor shall deceive/ Our bosom interest." *Mac,* I,

ii, 65–66. **13 bosom lover,** confidential friend: ". . . this Antonio/ Being the bosom lover of my lord,/ Must needs be like my lord." *Merch,* III, iv, 16–18.

bossed, *adj.* embossed: "Turkey cushions boss'd with pearl . . ." *Shrew,* II, i, 346.

Bosworth, *n.* town near Leicester in central England: "Here pitch our tent, even here in Bosworth field." *Rich 3,* V, iii, 1.

botch, *v.* **1 botch and bungle up,** clumsily attempt to conceal: "Do botch and bungle up damnation/ With patches . . ." *Hen 5,* II, ii, 115–116. **2 botch up, a.** to concoct clumsily: ". . . hear thou there how many fruitless pranks/ This ruffian hath botch'd up . . ." *T Night,* IV, i, 54–55. **b.** to patch together: "They aim at it,/ And botch the words up fit to their own thoughts . . ." *Ham,* IV, v, 9–10.
—*n.* **3** sore or boil: "Thou crusty [scabbed] botch of nature, what's the news?" *Tr & Cr,* V, i, 5.

botcher, *n.* mender of garments, shoes, etc.; patcher: ". . . if he mend, he is no longer dishonest;/ if he cannot, let the botcher mend him." *T Night,* I, v, 43–44.

botchy core, *n.* ulcerous boil; here, poss. wordplay with "bungled heart": ". . . did not the/ general run then? Were not that a botchy core?" *Tr & Cr,* II, i, 5–6.

bots, *n. pl.* **1** worms: ". . . that is the next way to give poor jades the bots . . ." *1 Hen 4,* II, i, 9. **2 bots on't,** a plague on it: ". . . like a poor man's right in the law; 'twill hardly/ come out. Ha, bots on't . . ." *Per,* II, i, 116–117.

bottle, *n.* **1** wicker basket; a twiggen-bottle: ". . . hang me in a bottle like a cat and shoot at me . . ." *M Ado,* I, i, 238. **2** bundle: "Methinks I have a great desire to a/ bottle of hay . . ." *M N Dream,* IV, i, 32–33. **3** vulgar slang for female genitals: "Why should he die, sir?"/ "Why? For filling a bottle with a tun-dish [funnel, i.e. penis]." *Meas,* III, ii, 165–166.

bottle-ale, *adj.* poss. an epithet meaning "cheap" or "drunken": "Away,/ you bottle-ale rascal, you basket-hilt stale juggler, you!" *2 Hen 4,* II, iv, 127–129.

bottle-ale house, *n.* disreputable tavern: ". . . my lady has a white hand,/ and the Myrmidons are no bottle-ale houses." *T Night,* II, iii, 28–29.

bottled spider, *n.* perh. Richard's deformed body was somewhat bottle-shaped; here, a bottle filled with venom: "Why strew'st thou sugar on that bottled spider . . ." *Rich 3,* I, iii, 242.

bottom, *n.* **1** valley: "It shall not wind with such a deep indent,/ To rob me of so rich a bottom here." *1 Hen 4,* III, i,

100–101. **2** clew on which spun thread is wound: ". . . to be great/ Is, when the thread of hazard [life] is once spun,/ A bottom great wound up, greatly undone." *More,* III, ii, 19–21. **3** spool or bobbin: ". . . sew me in/ the skirts of it, and beat me to death with a bottom/ of brown thread." *Shrew,* IV, iii, 133–135. **4** ship's keel; hence, the ship itself: ". . . the most noble bottom of our fleet . . ." *T Night,* V, i, 55. **5** the full scope: "When your/ lordship sees the bottom of his success in't . . ." *All's W,* III, vi, 33–34. **6** core or heart: "But the bottom of the news is, our general/ is cut i'th'middle . . ." *Cor,* IV, v, 202–203. **7 look into the bottom of,** to investigate thoroughly: ". . . it concerns me/ To look into the bottom of my place [situation]." *Meas,* I, i, 77–78. **8 search the bottom,** to penetrate to the depths: "For mirth doth search the bottom of annoy . . ." *Luc,* 1109.
—*adj.* **9** of the valley; also, poss. ref. to pubic hair: "Sweet bottom grass and high delightful plain . . ." *Ven & Ad,* 236.
—*v.* **10** to wind (thread, etc.) onto a core; here, to transfer Silvia's love for Valentine to Sir Thurio: ". . . as you unwind her love from him . . . You must provide to bottom it on me . . ." *Two Gent,* III, ii, 51–53. **11** to probe to the bottom of: ". . . can take no greater wound,/ Nor tent, to bottom that." *Cymb,* III, iv, 116–117.

boudge, *v.* var. of **budge:** "Cousin, I charge you/ Boudge not from Athens." *Kinsmen,* I, i, 223.

bought, *v. past part.* **1 be bought and sold,** to be deceived or betrayed: "It would make a man mad as a buck to be so bought and sold." *Errors,* III, i, 72. **2 be bought up,** to be sold out: "Till honour be bought up, and no sword worn/ But one to dance with." *All's W,* II, i, 32–33.

bounce, imit. of gunshot; bang!: "'Bounce,' would a say; and/ away again would a go . . ." *2 Hen 4,* III, ii, 279–280.

bound¹, *n.* **1** boundary, or an area enclosed by a boundary; limit or limits: "When that this body did contain a spirit,/ A kingdom for it was too small a bound . . ." *1 Hen 4,* V, iv, 88–89. **2** [usually pl.] the boundaries of a country, tract of land, etc.: ". . . his cote, his flocks, and bounds of feed [pastures]/ Are now on sale . . ." *As You,* II, iv, 81–82. **3** one of the banks of a stream: ". . . like the current flies/ Each bound it chases." *Timon,* I, i, 24–25. **4** restrictions of womanly behavior: ". . . thy lord . . . shrunk thee into/ The bound thou wast o'erflowing . . ." *Kinsmen,* I, i, 81–84. **5 bound of land,** private ownership of land: ". . . no kind of traffic/ Would I admit . . . Bourn, bound of land, tilth, vineyard, none . . ." *Temp,* II, i, 144–148.
—*v.* **6** to force; limit: "To whose high will we bound our calm contents [force ourselves to be content]." *Rich 2,* V, ii, 38. **7** to enclose: "Whose veins bound richer blood than Lady Blanche?" *K John,* II, i, 431. **8** to confine: "O God, I could be

bounded in a nutshell and count/ myself a king of infinite space . . ." *Ham,* II, ii, 254–255. **9 bounded in a pale,** fenced in: "How are we park'd and bounded in a pale—" *1 Hen 6,* IV, ii, 45.

bound², *v.* **1** past part. of **bind,** fixed; here, in a painting: "At last she sees a wretched image bound . . ." *Luc,* 1501. **2** committed: ". . . like a man to double business bound,/ I stand in pause . . ." *Ham,* III, iii, 41–42. **3** forced; compelled: "Who have you offended, masters, that you are/ thus bound to your answer?" *M Ado,* V, i, 221–222.

bound³, *v.* **1** to rebound: ". . . grief boundeth where it falls,/ Not with the empty hollowness [of a ball], but weight." *Rich 2,* I, ii, 58–59. **2** to cause to leap: "Or if I might buffet/ for my love, or bound my horse for her favours . . ." *Hen 5,* V, ii, 142–143.
—*n.* **3** leap, as in dancing: ". . . borrow Cupid's wings/ And soar with them above a common [ordinary] bound." *Rom & Jul,* I, iv, 17–18.

bounden, *old past part. of* **bind.** indebted: "I am much bounden to your majesty." *K John,* III, ii, 39.

bound up, *past part.* dressed; costumed: "How would he look, to see his work, so noble,/ Vilely bound up?" *W Tale,* IV, iv, 21–22.

bountiful, *adv.* bountifully: ". . . counterfeit the bewitchment/ of some popular man, and give it bountiful to the/ desirers." *Cor,* II, iii, 100–102.

bounty, *n.* **1** kindness; goodness: ". . . you would be prouder of the work/ Than customary bounty can enforce you." *Merch,* III, iv, 8–9. **2** generosity: ". . . derive a liberty/ From heartiness, from bounty, fertile bosom . . ." *W Tale,* I, ii, 112–113.

Bourbon, *n.* Duke of Bourbon: "And he that will not follow Bourbon now,/ Let him go hence . . ." *Hen 5,* IV, v, 12–13.

bourn¹, *n.* **1** frontier: "Making, to take our imagination,/ From bourn to bourn, region to region." *Per,* IV, iv, 3–4. **2** precincts; confines: "The undiscover'd country, from whose bourn/ No traveller returns . . ." *Ham,* III, i, 79–80. **3** boundary; here, the ownership of private property: "Letters should not be known . . . Bourn, bound of land, tilth, vineyard, none . . ." *Temp,* II, i, 146–148.

bourn², *n.* brook: "Come o'er the bourn, Bessy, to me,—" [lst line is song quote, remainder is Fool's improvisation] *Lear,* III, vi, 26–29.

bout, *n.* **walk a bout,** to dance a turn: ". . . ladies that have their toes/ Unplagu'd with corns will walk a bout with you." *Rom & Jul,* I, v, 16–17.

bow¹, *v.* **1** to bend; curve or shape like a bow: "I did but tell her she mistook her frets,/ And bow'd her hand to teach her fingering . . ." *Shrew,* II, i, 149–150. **2** to willfully misinterpret: "And God forbid . . . That you should fashion, wrest, or bow your reading . . ." *Hen 5,* I, ii, 13–14.
—*n.* **3** yoke for fastening two oxen together at the neck: "As the ox hath his bow sir, the horse his curb, and/ the falcon her bells, so man hath his desires . . ." *As You,* III, iii, 71–72. **4 cut bow strings,** See **hold** (def. 21).

bow², *v.* **1** to yield; here, to flee: "You fled for vantage, every one will swear;/ But if I bow, they'll say it was for fear." *1 Hen 6,* IV, v, 28–29. **2 bows you,** makes you bow: ". . . and bows you/ To a morning's holy office." *Cymb,* III, iii, 3–4.

bow-back, *n.* arched back; here, of the boar: "On his bow-back he hath a battle set . . ." *Ven & Ad,* 619.

bow-boy, *n.* Cupid: ". . . the very pin of his heart cleft with the/ blind bow-boy's butt-shaft." *Rom & Jul,* II, iv, 15–16.

bow-case, *n.* leather case for an unstrung bow: ". . . you sheath, you bow-case, you vile standing/ tuck!" *1 Hen 4,* II, iv, 243–244.

bowed, *adj.* bent; here, worthless: "'Tis strange; a threepence bow'd would hire me/ Old as I am, to queen it . . ." *Hen 8,* II, iii, 36–37.

bowels, *n. pl.* **1** offspring: "For thine own bowels which do call thee sire . . ." *Meas,* III, i, 29. **2** mercy; compassion: ". . . thou thing of no bowels thou!" *Tr & Cr,* II, i, 52. **3 softer bowels,** more gentle or compassionate nature: "There is no lady of more softer bowels,/ More spongy to suck in the sense of fear . . ." *Tr & Cr,* II, ii, 11–12.

bower, *v.* **1** to lodge; also, conceal: "O nature what hadst thou to do in hell/ When thou didst bower the spirit of a fiend . . ." *Rom & Jul,* III, ii, 80–81.
—*n.* **2** arbor; also, poss., a bedchamber: ". . . thou hadst rather/ Follow thine enemy in a fiery gulf/ Than flatter him in a bower." *Cor,* III, ii, 90–92.

bow-hand, *n.* **wide o' the bow-hand,** (in archery) to the left of the target: "Wide o' the bow-hand! i'faith, your hand is out." *Love's L,* IV, i, 134.

bowl, *n.* **1** ball used in the game of bowls [lawn bowling]: "Thus the bowl should run,/ And not unluckily against the bias." *Shrew,* IV, v, 24–25. **2** [pl.] lawn bowling: "What sport

shall we devise here in this garden . . ."/ "Madam, we'll play at bowls." *Rich 2,* III, iv, 1–3.
—*v.* **3** to play at bowls: "She's too hard for you at pricks, sir: challenge her to bowl." *Love's L,* IV, 1, 139. **4 bowled to death with turnips,** be killed by having turnips hurled at one: "I had rather be set quick i' th' earth,/ And bowl'd to death with turnips!" *Wives,* III, iv, 84–85.

bowler, *n.* person who plays bowls: "He is a marvellous good neighbour, faith, and a/ very good bowler . . ." *Love's L,* V, ii, 577–578.

box, *n.* poss. ref. to the female genitals: "He wears his honour in a box unseen/ That hugs his kicky-wicky here at home . . ." *All's W,* II, iii, 275–276.

box-tree, *n.* ornamental evergreen shrub: "Get ye all three into the box-tree. Malvolio's/ coming down this walk . . ." *T Night,* II, v, 15–16.

boy, *n.* **1** male servant: "My boy shall fetch the scrivener presently." *Shrew,* IV, iv, 59. **2** [cap.] Falstaff's page, a gift from Prince Hal: "Enter the Boy." [SD] *Hen 5,* II, i, 80. **3** term of contempt for either sex: "Fare you well, boy . . . I will/ leave you now to your gossip-like humour." *M Ado,* V, i, 182–183. **4 the boy,** Cupid: "The boy for trial needs would touch my breast . . ." *Sonn 153,* 10.
—*v.* **5** to impersonate on the stage as a boy; ref. here to Eliz. practice [in England] of women's parts being played by boys or young men: ". . . and I shall see/ Some squeaking Cleopatra boy my greatness . . ." *Ant & Cleo,* V, ii, 218–219.

boy-queller, *n.* slaughterer of boys [lit., boy-killer]: "Where is Hector?/ Come, come, thou boy-queller, show thy face . . ." *Tr & Cr,* V, v, 44–45.

brabble, *n.* squabble or quarrel; brawl: ". . . by the gods that warlike Goths adore,/ This petty brabble will undo us all." *T Andr,* II, i, 61–62.

brabbler, *n.* **1** quarreler or brawler: "We hold our time too precious to be spent/ With such a brabbler." *K John,* V, ii, 161–162. **2** Also, **babbler,** [usually cap.] hound that yelps as though following a scent but has in fact lost it: "He/ will spend his mouth and promise, like Brabbler/ the hound . . ." *Tr & Cr,* V, i, 90–91.

brace, *n.* **1** armor to cover the arm: "' . . . it hath been a shield/ 'Twixt me and death;'—and pointed to his brace—" *Per,* II, i, 125–126. **2** readiness: "For that it stands not in such warlike brace . . ." *Oth,* I, iii, 24.

braced, *adj.* (of a drum) tightened; ready to be played: ". . . even at hand a drum is ready brac'd/ That shall reverberate all, as loud as thine . . ." *K John,* V, ii, 169–170.

brach, *n.* **1** female hunting dog; bitch: "I had rather hear Lady my brach howl in Irish." *1 Hen 4,* III, i, 230. **2** male sexual companion. Cf. **male varlet:** "I will hold my peace when Achilles' brach bids/ me, shall I?" *Tr & Cr,* II, i, 116–117.

braggardism, *n.* braggadocio; boasting: "Why, Valentine, what braggardism is this?" *Two Gent,* II, iv, 159.

bragged, *adj.* boastful: "That was the whip of your bragg'd progeny [race] . . ." *Cor,* I, viii, 12.

bragging, *adj.* blustering; hence, menacing or threatening: "Threaten the threat'ner, and outface the brow/ Of bragging horror . . ." *K John,* V, i, 49–50.

braid[1], *v.* contracted form of **upbraid;** shame: "Few love to hear the sins they love to act;/ 'Twould braid yourself too near for me to tell it."

braid[2], *adj.* braided; twisted or plaited; here, devious: "Since Frenchmen are so braid,/ Marry that will, I live and die a maid." *All's W,* IV, ii, 73–74.

brain, *n.* **1** [pl.] the work or efforts of one's brains; here, a collective effort: ". . . beside forfeiting/ Our own brains and the opinion that we bring . . ." *Hen 8,* Prol. 19–20.
—*v.* **2** to dash out the brains of; destroy or defeat: "It was the swift celerity of his death . . . That brain'd my purpose." *Meas,* V, i, 392–394. **3** to comprehend; understand: ". . . such stuff as madmen/ Tongue, and brain not . . ." *Cymb,* V, iv, 146–147.

Brainford, *n.* village near Windsor: "Pray you, sir, was 't not the wise woman of Brainford?" *Wives,* IV, v, 24–25.

brainish apprehension, *n.* crazed imagination: "And in this brainish apprehension kills/ The unseen good old man." *Ham,* IV, i, 11–12.

brainsick, *adj.* foolish; mad: "Good Lord, what madness rules in brainsick men . . ." *1 Hen 6,* IV, i, 111.

brake[1], *v.* old past tense of **break:** "But till this afternoon his passion/ Ne'er brake into extremity of rage." *Errors,* V, i, 47–48.

brake[2], *n.* **1** [often pl.] bushes; thicket: "I'll run from thee and hide me in the brakes . . ." *M N Dream,* II, i, 227. **2 brakes of ice,** perh. misuse for "breaks" [some glide over breaks in the ice and are never called to account]; also, may orig. have been "brakes [thickets] of vice": "Some run from brakes of ice and answer none . . ." *Meas,* II, i, 39.

bran, *n.* **1** husks of grain: "Nature hath meal, and bran; contempt, and grace." *Cymb,* IV, ii, 27. **2** coarse bread of bran: "I am fain/ to dine and sup with water and bran . . ." *Meas,* IV, iii, 151–152.

branch, *n.* **1** part; particular: ". . . his own hand may strike his honour down/ That violates the smallest branch herein . . ." *Love's L,* I, i, 20–21.
—*v.* **2** to expand: ". . . an affection/ which cannot choose but branch now." *W Tale,* I, i, 23–24.

branched, *adj.* embroidered with representations of leafy branches: "Calling my officers about me, in my branched/ velvet gown . . ." *T Night,* II, v, 47–48.

branchless, *adj.* shorn of honors: ". . . better I were not yours/ Than yours so branchless." *Ant & Cleo,* III, iv, 23–24.

brand, *n.* **1** burning log: "For why, the senseless brands will sympathize/ . . . And in compassion weep the fire out . . ." *Rich 2,* V, i, 46–48. **2** firebrand; torch: ". . . each on one foot standing, nicely/ Depending on their brands." *Cymb,* II, iv, 90–91. **3** stigma: ". . . to lose it by his country/ Were to us all that do't and suffer it/ A brand to th'end o'th'world." *Cor,* III, i, 299–301.

brandish, *v.* to flourish; flash: "Comets, importing change of times and states,/ Brandish your crystal tresses in the sky . . ." *1 Hen 6,* I, i, 2–3.

brass, *n.* **1** overconfidence; brazen assurance: "Can any face of brass hold longer out?" *Love's L,* V, ii, 395. **2 brass eternal,** brass objects made to last forever: "And brass eternal slave to mortal rage . . ." *Sonn 64,* 4. **3 in brass,** engraved in brass: ". . . such/ As Agamemnon and the hand of Greece/ Should hold up high in brass . . ." *Tr & Cr,* I, iii, 62–64.

brassy, *adj.* insensitive: "And pluck commiseration of his state/ From brassy bosoms . . ." *Merch,* IV, i, 30–31.

brat, *n.* puny or worthless creature: ". . . they follow him/ Against us brats, with no less confidence/ Than boys pursuing summer butterflies . . ." *Cor,* IV, vi, 93–95.

brave, *adj.* **1** noble; lordly or majestic: "And hast thou kill'd him sleeping? O brave touch!" *M N Dream,* III, ii, 70. **2** consisting of or reserved for brave men: ". . . a braver place/ In my heart's love hath no man than yourself . . ." *1 Hen 4,* IV, i, 7–8. **3** beautiful; fine; splendid: "Believe me, sir,/ It carries a brave form. But 'tis a spirit." *Temp,* I, ii, 413–414. **4** gallant: ". . . and his brave fleet/ With silken streamers the young Phoebus fanning . . ." *Hen 5,* III, Chor., 5–6. **5** severe; deservedly harsh: "I'll devise thee brave punishments for him." *M Ado,* V, iv, 126. **6** brazen; insolent; overbearing: "What! Buckingham

and Clifford, are ye so brave?" *2 Hen 6,* IV, viii, 20. **7** elegantly dressed: "Enter Tranio brave, and Biondello." [SD] *Shrew,* I, ii, 216.
—*v.* **8** to defy or dare: "We must be brief when traitors brave the field." *Rich 3,* IV, iii, 57. **9** to insult: "How I am brav'd and must perforce endure it!" *1 Hen 6,* II, iv, 115. **10** to dress splendidly; here in wordplay with "defy": "Thou hast braved many men, brave/ not me: I will neither be faced [bullied] nor braved." *Shrew,* IV, iii, 125–126.
—*n.* **11** [often pl.] **a.** blustering; boastful or defiant threats: ". . . thou dost overween in all,/ And so in this, to bear me down with braves." *T Andr,* II, i, 29–30. **b.** insults: "Sirrah, I will not bear these braves of thine." *Shrew,* III, i, 15.

braved, *past part.* defied; insulted: "Brav'd in mine own house with a skein of thread?" *Shrew,* IV, iii, 111.

bravely, *adv.* **1** adeptly or stylishly: ". . . you must kneel;/ then kiss his foot . . . ; see you do it bravely." *T Andr,* IV, iii, 108–111. **2** splendidly; elegantly: "And revel it as bravely as the best,/ With silken coats and caps, and golden rings . . ." *Shrew,* IV, iii, 54–55. **3** nobly; beautifully: "How bravely thou becom'st thy bed!" *Cymb,* II, ii, 15.

bravely taken, *adj.* well received; highly regarded: "He's bravely taken here. He stole from France . . . for the king had married him/ Against his liking." *All's W,* III, v, 52–54.

brave respect, *n.* gallant consideration [for the best interests of one's country]: "O, what a noble combat hast thou fought/ Between compulsion and a brave respect!" *K John,* V, ii, 43–44.

bravery, *n.* **1** costly and often showy apparel: ". . . he of basest function,/ That says his bravery is not on my cost . . ." *As You,* II, vii, 79–80. **2** display; ostentation: ". . . assemblies,/ Where youth, and cost, witless bravery keeps." *Meas,* I, iii, 9–10. **3** showy excess; bravado: "But sure the bravery of his grief did put me/ Into a tow'ring passion." *Ham,* V, ii, 79–80. **4** splendor: "Hiding thy bravery in their rotten smoke?" *Sonn 33,* 4.

braving, *adj.* defiant: "Have fought with equal fortune, and continue/ A braving war." *All's W,* I, ii, 2–3.

brawl¹, *v.* **1** to flow noisily: ". . . the brook that brawls along this wood . . ." *As You,* II, i, 32. **2 as the times do brawl,** as the turbulent times make necessary: ". . . his divisions, as the times do brawl,/ Are in three heads . . ." *2 Hen 4,* I, iii, 70–71. **3 brawl down,** to batter down: "Till their soul-fearing clamours have brawl'd down/ The flinty ribs of this contemptuous city . . ." *K John,* II, i, 383–384.

brawl², *n.* See **French brawl.**

brawling, *adj.* noisy; clamorous: ". . . whose advice/ Hath often still'd my brawling discontent." *Meas,* IV, i, 9.

brawn, *n.* **1** fat swine: "I'll play Percy, and that damned/ brawn shall play Dame Mortimer his wife." *1 Hen 4,* II, iv, 107–108. **2** [often pl] fleshy or muscular part; here, the arms: "And in my vambrace [armor] put my wither'd brawns . . ." *Tr & Cr,* I, iii, 296.
—*adj.* **3** fleshy; fat [used in combined form]: ". . . the pin-buttock, the quatch-buttock, the brawn-buttock,/ or any buttock." *All's W,* II, ii, 17–18.

braze, *v.* to harden; lit., to cover with brass: "If damned custom have not braz'd it so,/ That it be proof and bulwark against sense." *Ham,* III, iv, 37–38.

brazen, *adj.* **1** made of brass; also, of brassy sound; cacophonous: "I had rather hear a brazen canstick turn'd . . ." *1 Hen 4,* III, i, 125. **2** impregnable, as though encased in brass or bronze: ". . . curs'd the gentle gusts/ And he that loos'd them forth their brazen caves . . ." *2 Hen 6,* III, ii, 87–88. **3** noisy; shameless: ". . . the midnight bell/ Did, with his iron tongue and brazen mouth . . ." *K John,* III, ii, 47–48.

brazier, *n.* person who works in brass: ". . . a fellow/ somewhat near the door, he should be a brazier by/ his face . . ." *Hen 8,* V, iii, 38–40.

breach, *n.* **1** break forced in a defensive line: ". . . then dreams he of . . . breaches, ambuscados, Spanish blades . . ." *Rom & Jul,* I, iv, 83–84. **2** refusal to participate, celebrate, etc.: ". . . a custom/ More honour'd in the breach than the observance." *Ham,* I, iv, 15–16. **3** breaking waves: ". . . some hour before you took me/ from the breach of the sea . . ." *T Night,* II, i, 21–22. **4 make the breach,** to break down the defenses: "To make the breach and enter this sweet city." *Luc,* 469.

bread and cheese, *n.* allusion to Nym's fare as a follower of Falstaff: "Adieu. I love not the humour of bread and/ cheese. Adieu." *Wives,* II, i, 132–133.

break, *v.* **1** to disclose: "What beast was't then,/ That made you break this enterprise to me?" *Mac,* I, vii, 47–48. **2** to break a promise: ". . . if like an ill venture it come unluckily/ home, I break . . ." *2 Hen 4,* Epil., 11–12. **3** to cease; cut short: "Rome's emperor, and nephew, break the parle . . ." *T Andr,* V, iii, 19. **4** to interrupt: ". . . here is good broken music [music played by several varied instruments]."/ "You have broke it, cousin . . ." *Tr & Cr,* III, i, 48–49. **5** to train, as in breaking in a horse: "Why then, thou canst not break her to the lute?" *Shrew,* II, i, 147. **6** to declare bankruptcy: ". . . divers of Antonio's creditors . . . that swear, he cannot choose/ but break." *Merch,* III, i, 103–105. **7** to burst: "From ancient grudge break to new mutiny . . ." *Rom & Jul,* Prol., 3. **8 break a jest,** to crack a joke:

"Patroclus/ Upon a lazy bed the livelong day/ Breaks scurril jests . . ." *Tr & Cr,* I, iii, 146–148. **9 break any breaking,** to attempt to break in: "Break any breaking here and I'll break your knave's pate." *Errors,* III, i, 74. **10 break a word,** to exchange words: "A man may break a word with you, sir, and words are but wind . . ." *Errors,* III, i, 75. **11 break from,** to escape from: ". . . Rainold Lord Cobham . . . That late broke from the Duke of Exeter . . ." *Rich 2,* II, i, 279–281. **12 break his day,** to fail to repay an obligation on time: "If he should break his day what should I gain/ By the exaction of the forfeiture?" *Merch,* I, iii, 159–160. **13 break off,** to adjourn; stop discussions: "And so break off; the day is almost spent." *2 Hen 6,* III, i, 325. **14 break our minds,** disclose our thinking: "But we shall meet and break our minds at large [at length]." *1 Hen 6,* I, iii, 80. **15 break up, a.** to open by force; break open: "Break up the gates, I'll be your warrantize." *1 Hen 6,* I, iii, 13. **b.** to break the seal on (a letter, etc.): "And it shall please you to break up this, it shall/ seem to signify." *Merch,* II, iv, 10–11. **16 break with,** to broach the subject to; inform: "If thou dost love fair Hero, cherish it/ And I will break with her . . ." *M Ado,* I, i, 288–289.

break cross, *v.* to break one's lance across or athwart the shield of an opponent, in the manner of a novice: ". . . give him another staff; this last was/ broke cross." *M Ado,* V, i, 137–138.

breaking, *n.* **1** bankruptcy: ". . . this breaking of his has been but a try for his friends." *Timon,* V, i, 9. **2** discipline; here, the breaking in of a horse: "It seems thou want'st breaking; out upon thee, hind." *Errors,* III, i, 77.
—*adj.* **3 breaking gulf,** swirling whirlpool: ". . . as easy mayst thou fall/ A drop of water in the breaking gulf . . ." *Errors,* II, ii, 125–126.

break-neck, *n.* fatal business: ". . . to do't, or no, is certain/ To me a break-neck." *W Tale,* I, ii, 362–363.

break time, *v.* to fail to perform in the allotted time [two days]: "If I break time, or flinch in property . . . unpitied let me die . . ." *All's W,* II, i, 186–187.

break words, *v.* wordplay on "fail to keep promises" and "use words instead of weapons": ". . . a' breaks words,/ and keeps whole weapons." *Hen 5,* III, ii, 36–37.

breast, *n.* singing voice: "By my troth, the fool has an excellent breast." *T Night,* II, iii, 19.

breath, *n.* **1** sound: "Through brazen trumpet send the breath of parle/ Into his ruin'd ears . . ." *Rich 2,* III, iii, 33–35. **2** spoken words; speech: ". . . sweeten with thy breath/ This neighbour air . . ." *Rom & Jul,* II, vi, 26–27. **3** singing: ". . . such dulcet and harmonious breath/ That the rude sea grew civil at her song . . ." *M N Dream,* II, i, 151–152. **4** the voice: "A love that makes breath poor and speech unable . . ." *Lear*, I, i, 60. **5** spoken approval; here, votes: "Nor showing . . . his wounds/ To th'people, beg their stinking breaths." *Cor*, II, i, 233–234. **6** ability or, perh., right to speak: "What earthy name to interrogatories/ Can taste the free breath of a sacred king?" *K John*, III, i, 73–74. **7** sound of one's voice; presence: "Or know what ground's made happy by his breath." *Per*, II, iv, 28. **8** exercise: ". . . he hopes it is no other/ But for your health and your digestion sake,/ An after-dinner's breath." *Tr & Cr*, II, iii, 112–114. **9** word or report; here, the force of such good report: "So am I driven by breath of her renown/ Either to suffer shipwreck, or arrive . . ." *1 Hen 6*, V, v, 7–8.

breathe, *v.* **1** to say or utter; sometimes, fig., to absorb with the breath: "He's truly valiant that can wisely suffer/ The worst that man can breathe . . ." *Timon*, III, v, 32–33. **2** to pause for breath, esp. while drinking: ". . . and when/ you breathe in your watering they cry 'Hem!' . . ." *1 Hen 4*, II, iv, 15–16. **3** to rest: "We breathe too long: come, cousin Westmoreland,/ Our duty this way lies . . ." *1 Hen 4*, V, iv, 14–15. **4** (esp. of an animal) to let rest; allow to catch its breath: "Breathe Merriman, the poor cur is emboss'd . . ." *Shrew*, Induc., i, 15. **5** (esp. of athletes) to exercise or warm up: "I beseech your Grace, I am not yet well breathed." *As You*, I, ii, 205–206. **6** to speak: "Having ever seen in the prenominate crimes/ The youth you breathe of guilty . . ." *Ham*, II, i, 44–45. **7 breathe oneself,** to get one's exercise: "I think thou wast/ created for men to breathe themselves upon thee [get their exercise by beating you]." *All's W*, II, iii, 251–252.

breathed, *adj.* **1** accustomed: "A most incomparable man, breath'd, as it were,/ To an untirable and continuate goodness." *Timon*, I, i, 10–11. **2** in fine physical condition: "A man so breath'd that certain he would fight . . ." *Love's L*, V, ii, 646.

breather, *n.* **1** a human being: "I will chide no breather in the world but myself . . ." *As You*, III, ii, 275. **2** speaker; here, the one who has spread gossip: ". . . no particular scandal once can touch,/ But it confounds [destroys] the breather." *Meas*, IV, iv, 25–26.

breathing, *n.* **1** interval (of time); period: ". . . you shake your head at so long a breathing . . ." *M Ado*, II, i, 339. **2** exercise; here, dancing: "Come, sir, here's a lady that wants breathing too . . ." *Per*, II, iii, 100. **3** speech; utterance: "I am sorry to give breathing to my purpose . . ." *Ant & Cleo*, I, iii, 14. —*adj.* **4** used or set aside for exercise: "If it please his/ Majesty, it is the breathing time of day with me." *Ham*, V, ii, 170–171. **5 in a breathing while,** in one breath: "Bud, and be blasted, in a breathing while . . ." *Ven & Ad*, 1142.

breathing courtesy, *n.* greeting of mere words: "It must appear in other ways than words,/ Therefore I scant this breathing courtesy." *Merch*, V, i, 141.

Brecknock, *n.* Buckingham's residence in Wales: ". . . let me think on Hastings, and be gone/ To Brecknock while my fearful head is on." *Rich 3*, IV, ii, 121–122.

bred, *adj.* **1** related: ". . . the burnish'd sun,/ To whom I am a neighbour, and near bred." *Merch*, II, i, 2–3. **2 bred of alms,** raised by charity: "The contract you pretend with that base wretch,/ One bred of alms . . ." *Cymb*, II, iii, 112–113.

bred out, *past part.* exhausted through inferior breeding: "Our madams mock at us, and plainly say/ Our mettle is bred out . . ." *Hen 5*, III, v, 28–29.

breech, *n.* **1** [pl.] breeches: ". . . you might still have worn the petticoat/ And ne'er have stol'n the breech from Lancaster." *3 Hen 6*, V, v, 23–24. —*v.* **2** to cover in the manner of breeches: ". . . their daggers/ Unmannerly breech'd with gore." *Mac*, II, iii, 115–116.

breeching scholar, *n.* schoolboy subject to birching [whipping]: "I am no breeching scholar in the schools . . ." *Shrew*, III, i, 18.

breed, *v.* **1** to bring up or, esp., to educate: ". . . charged my brother on his blessing to breed me well . . ." *As You*, I, i, 3–4. **2** to beget or produce; cause: ". . . not an hour! In the day's glorious walk . . . can breed me quiet?" *Per*, I, ii, 4–6. **3** to quicken or stir: "She speaks, and 'tis such sense/ That my sense breeds with it." *Meas*, II, ii, 142–143. **4 bred in broils,** See **broil** (def. 3). **5 breeds no bate,** gives no offense: ". . . breeds no bate with telling of discreet stories . . ." *2 Hen 4*, IV, iv, 247. —*n.* **6** kind; sort: "Nay, good my lord, this courtesy is not of the right/ breed." *Ham*, III, ii, 306–307. **7** interest; profit: ". . . for when did friendship take/ A breed for barren metal of his friend?" *Merch*, I, iii, 128–129. **8** offspring: "And nothing 'gainst Time's scythe can make defence/ Save breed, to brave [defy] him when he takes thee hence." *Sonn 12*, 13–14.

breed-bate, *n.* troublemaker: "I warrant you, no tell-tale/ nor no breed-bate." *Wives*, I, iv, 10–11.

breeder, *n.* female: "You love the breeder better than the male." *3 Hen 6*, II, i, 42.

breeding, *n.* origin: "Honest gentleman, I know not your breeding." *2 Hen 4*, V, iii, 104.

breese, *n.* gadfly: "The herd hath more annoyance by the breese . . ." *Tr & Cr*, I, iii, 48.

Bretagne, *n.* Brittany: "He, mistrusting them,/ Hois'd sail, and made his course again for Bretagne." *Rich 3,* IV, iv, 527.

Breton, *n.* **the Breton Richmond,** Richmond in exile in Brittany; here, a derisive term: ". . . for I know the Breton Richmond aims/ At young Elizabeth, my brother's daughter . . ." *Rich 3,* IV, iii, 40–41.

brewer's horse, *n.* old, decrepit horse: "And I have not forgotten what/ the inside of a church is made of, I am . . . a brewer's horse . . ." *1 Hen 4,* III, iii, 7–9.

Briareus, *n.* (in the Iliad) 100-armed monster that spewed fire from 50 mouths: ". . . everything/ so out of joint that he is a gouty Briareus, many/ hands and no use . . ." *Tr & Cr,* I, ii, 28–30.

bribed buck, *n.* poached deer that had to be divided quickly among the poachers before the theft was discovered: "Divide me like a bribed buck, each a haunch . . ." *Wives,* V, v, 24.

bridal, *n.* honeymoon: "Nor of them look for such observances/ As fits the bridal . . ." *Oth,* III, iv, 147–148.

bride, *n.* **1** here with meaning of bridegroom: "Doth she not count her blest . . . that we have wrought/ So worthy a gentleman to be her bride?" *Rom & Jul,* III, v, 143–145.
—*v.* **2 bride it,** to play the bride: "Shall sweet Bianca practise how to bride it?" *Shrew,* III, ii, 249.

bride-habited, *adj.* dressed as a bride: "I am bride-habited,/ But maiden-hearted." *Kinsmen,* V, i, 150–151.

Bridgnorth or **Bridgenorth,** *n.* town SE of Shrewsbury, on the Severn River: "Our meeting is Bridgnorth, and, Harry, you/ Shall march through Gloucestershire . . ." *1 Hen 4,* III, ii, 175–176.

bridle, *n.* **1** rein or restraint: ". . . know he is the bridle of your will." *Errors,* II, i, 13.
—*v.* **2** to restrain: "This is it that makes me bridle passion [overpowering emotions]/ And bear with mildness my misfortune's cross . . ." *3 Hen 6,* IV, iv, 19–20.

brief, *n.* **1** short list: "There is a brief how many sports are ripe . . ." *M N Dream,* V, i, 42. **2** concise summary: ". . . the hand of time/ Shall draw this brief into as huge a volume." *K John,* II, 1, 102–103.
—*adj.* **3** quick; hasty: "We must be brief, when traitors brave the field." *Rich 3,* IV, iii, 57. **4** terse; curt or brusque: "Go, write it in a martial hand, be curst and/ brief . . ." *T Night,* III, ii, 40–41. **5 a briefer sort,** a faster way: "To teach you gamut in a briefer sort . . ." *Shrew,* III, i, 65. **6 the brief and the tedious of**

it, the long and the short of it: ". . . 'tis very strange; that is the brief/ and the tedious of it . . ." *All's W,* II, iii, 28–29.
—*adv.* **7** briefly; in short: "Brief, he must hence depart to Tyre." *Per,* III, Chor., 39.

briefest, *adj.* swiftest: ". . . we have no friend/ But resolution, and the briefest end." *Ant & Cleo,* IV, xv, 90–91.

brief in hand, *adj.* requiring immediate attention: "A thousand businesses [matters] are brief in hand . . ." *K John,* IV, iii, 158.

briefly, *adv.* **1** quickly: "Let's briefly put on manly readiness,/ And meet i' th' hall together." *Mac,* II, iii, 133–134. **2** shortly; in a moment: "Go, put on thy defences."/ "Briefly, sir." *Ant & Cleo,* IV, iv, 10.

brier, *n.* rosebush: "From off this brier pluck a white rose with me." *1 Hen 6,* II, iv, 30.

bright, *adj.* **1** of great beauty: "For I have sworn thee fair, and thought thee bright . . ." *Sonn 147,* 13. **2** shining with newness and lack of use: "Your sword is bright, sir; put it up again." *K John,* IV, iii, 79. **3 bright in dark directed,** [eyes that see] clearly in darkness: ". . . they look on thee,/ And darkly bright, are bright in dark directed." *Sonn 43,* 3–4.

bright eyes, *n.* beauty: "But thou, contracted to thine own bright eyes . . ." *Sonn 1,* 5.

brinded, *adj.* brindled; streaked: "Thrice the brinded cat hath mew'd." *Mac,* IV, i, 1.

brine-pit, *n.* salt deposit: ". . . show'd thee all the qualities o' th' isle,/ The fresh springs, brine-pits, barren place and fertile . . ." *Temp,* I, ii, 339–340.

bring, *v.* **1** to escort; accompany: "I'll bring you thither, my lord, if you'll vouchsafe me." *M Ado,* III, ii, 3. **2 bring away, a.** to fetch; bring back: "Go, fellow, get thee home, provide some carts/ And bring away the armour that is there." *Rich 2,* II, ii, 106–107. **b.** bring here: ". . . a fellow of the self-same colour/ Our sister speaks of. Come, bring away the stocks." *Lear,* II, ii, 138–139. **3 bring him in,** to restore (a person) to favor: ". . . to have so much to do/ To bring him in?" *Oth,* III, iii, 74–75. **4 bring him off,** to rescue him: "I'll be ta'en too/ Or bring him off." *Tr & Cr,* V, vi, 24–25. **5 bring out,** to lead to; pave the way for: ". . . if I make not this cheat bring/ out another . . . let me/ be unrolled . . ." *W Tale,* IV, iii, 116–118. **6 brings me out,** puts me off; makes me forget my speech: "They do not mark me, and that brings me out." *Love's L,* V, ii, 173. **7 bring you something,** to escort you a short distance: "Yet give leave, my lord,/ That we may bring you something on the way." *Meas,* I, i, 60–61.

bringing home, *n.* burial ceremony: "... she is allow'd her virgin crants [garlands] ... and the bringing home/ Of bell and burial." *Ham,* V, i, 225–227.

bringings-forth, *n.* achievements in public office: "Let him be but testimonied in/ his own bringings-forth ..." *Meas,* III, ii, 140–141.

brisk, *adj., adv.* **shine so brisk,** to stand out by being attired so smartly: "... for he made me mad/ To see him shine so brisk, and smell so sweet ..." *1 Hen 4,* I, iii, 52–53.

brisky, *adj.* lively; energetic: "Most brisky juvenal, and eke most lovely Jew ..." *M N Dream,* III, i, 90.

bristle, *v.* [often with *up*] to pump up; stiffen: "Boy, bristle thy courage up ..." *Hen 5* II, iii, 5.

Bristow, *n.* Bristol, a port city in SW England: "... we must win your grace to go with us/ To Bristow castle ..." *Rich 2,* II, iii, 162–163.

Briton, *n.* [used as adj.] British: "So merry and so gamesome: he is call'd/ The Briton reveller." *Cymb,* I, vii, 60–61.

Brittaine, *n.* Brittany, in France: "I have from le Port Blanc,/ A bay in Brittaine, receiv'd intelligence ..." *Rich 2,* II, i, 277–278.

brittle, *adj.* fragile: "I better brook the loss of brittle life/ Than those proud titles thou hast won of me." *1 Hen 4,* V, iv, 77–78.

broach, *v.* **1** to set flowing: "For what hath broach'd this tumult but thy pride?" *3 Hen 6,* II, ii, 159. **2** to stab: "He bravely broach'd his boiling bloody breast ..." *M N Dream,* V, i, 146. **3** to impale; stick: "I'll broach the tadpole on my rapier's point ..." *T Andr,* IV, ii, 85.

broached, *adj.* **1** tapped in the manner of a keg and, hence, let loose: "... a portent/ Of broached mischief to the unborn times?" *1 Hen 4,* V, i, 20–21. **2** impaled; spitted: "Bringing rebellion broached on his sword ..." *Hen 5,* V, Chor. 32.

broad, *adj.* **1** wide; here, also wordplay with "obvious" and "gross": "O here's a wit of cheveril, that stretches from an/ inch narrow to an ell broad." *Rom & Jul,* II, iv, 83–84. **2** frank; blunt: "... from broad words ... I hear/ Macduff lives in disgrace." *Mac,* III, vi, 21–23. **3** unrestrained; outrageous: "Tell him his pranks have been too broad to bear with ..." *Ham,* III, iv, 2. **4** big; large: "... in full as proud a place/ As broad Achilles ..." *Tr & Cr,* I, iii, 189–190.

broad blown, *adj.* in full bloom: "With all his crimes broad blown, as flush as May ..." *Ham,* III, iii, 81.

broad-fronted, *adj.* having a wide forehead; also, perh. a ref. to his baldness: "Broad-fronted Caesar,/ When thou wast here above the ground ..." *Ant & Cleo,* I, v, 29–30.

brock, *n.* badger, regarded as a smelly animal: "Marry, hang thee, brock!" *T Night,* II, v, 105.

broil, *n.* **1** strife or turmoil; also, battle: "... breathe short-winded accents of new broils/ To be commenc'd in stronds afar remote." *1 Hen 4,* I, i, 3–4. **2** quarrel: "... these domestic and particular [private] broils/ Are not the question here." *Lear,* V, i, 30–31. **3 bred in broils,** grown up on the battlefield: "Thou art their soldier, and being bred in broils,/ Hast not the soft way ..." *Cor,* III, ii, 81–82.
—*v.* **4** to bask; thrive: "... the great Myrmidon,/ Who broils in loud applause ..." *Tr & Cr,* I, iii, 378–379. **5** to sweat with heat: "Where have you been broiling?" *Hen 8,* IV, i, 56.

broke[1], *v.* to deal or trade (in): "He ... brokes with all that can ... Corrupt the tender honour of a maid ..." *All's W,* III, v, 70–72.

broke[2], *v.* past tense of **break**; interrupted: "You have broke it, cousin, and by my life you/ shall make it whole again ..." *Tr & Cr,* III, i, 49–50.

broken, *adj.* **1** insolvent; financially ruined: "The king's grown bankrout [bankrupt] like a broken man." *Rich 2,* II, i, 257. **2** estranged; fallen out: "Shall he marry her?"/ "No, neither."/ "What, are they broken?" *Two Gent,* II, v, 15–17. **3** interrupted: "You have now a broken banquet, but we'll mend it." *Hen 8,* I, iv, 61. **4** bleeding: "... the skin is good/ for your broken coxcomb." *Hen 5,* V, i, 55–56.

broken meats, *n.* leavings; scraps: "A knave, a rascal, an eater of broken meats ..." *Lear,* II, ii, 13.

broken music, *n.* music performed by different types of instruments: "Fair/ prince, here is good broken music." *Tr & Cr,* III, i, 47–48.

broker, *n.* **1** agent or go-between: "Now, by my modesty, a goodly broker!" *Two Gent,* I, ii, 41. **2** bawd or pander: "... they are brokers/ Not of that dye which their investments show ..." *Ham,* I, iii, 127–128.

broker-lackey, *n.* pander; bawd: "Hence, broker-lackey! Ignomy [ignominy] and shame/ Pursue thy life ..." *Tr & Cr,* V, x, 33–34.

broking pawn, *n.* pawnbroker(s) who held the realm in pledge: "Redeem from broking pawn the blemish'd crown ..." *Rich 2,* II, i, 293.

brooch, *n.* **1** decorative emblem; ornament: "... 'tis a sign of love; and love to Richard/ Is a strange brooch in this all-hating world." *Rich 2*, V, v, 65–66.
—*v.* **2** to bedeck; adorn: "... not the imperious show/ Of the full-fortun'd Caesar ever shall/ Be brooch'd with me ..." *Ant & Cleo*, IV, xv, 23–25.

brooch of lead, *n.* badge or medallion showing one's authority: "Ay, and in a brooch of lead."/ "Ay, and worn in the cap of a toothdrawer." *Love's L*, V, ii, 612–613.

brood, *n.* **sit on brood,** to ponder; brood over; here, likened to a hen sitting on hatching eggs: "There's something in his soul/ O'er which his melancholy sits on brood ..." *Ham*, III, i, 166–167.

brooded, *adj.* brooding or, perh., on guard, in the manner of a hen protecting eggs: "Then, in despite of brooded watchful day,/ I would into thy bosom pour my thoughts ..." *K John*, III, ii, 62–63.

brook, *v.* to tolerate or endure: "How brooks your grace the air,/ After your late tossing on the breaking seas?" *Rich 2*, III, ii, 2–3.

broomstaff, close quarters; here, in street fighting: "... at length they came to th' broomstaff to me, I defied 'em still ..." *Hen 8*, V, iii, 53–54.

brother, *n.* **1** associate; colleague: "Provost, my brother Angelo will not be altered ..." *Meas*, III, ii, 201. **2** member of the King's Council [monarch's advisers and the supreme governing body]: "... you, a brother of us!/ It fits we thus proceed ..." *Hen 8*, V, i, 106–107.

brotherhood, *n.* **1** fact of being brothers: "Finds brotherhood in thee no sharper spur?" *Rich 2*, I, ii, 9. **2** guild or society of workers: "Degrees in schools, and brotherhoods in cities ..." *Tr & Cr*, I, iii, 104.

brother-in-law, *n.* husband of Bolingbroke's sister Elizabeth, John Holland, Earl of Huntingdon (formerly Duke of Exeter): "But for our trusty brother-in-law and the abbot,/ With all the rest of that consorted [conniving] crew ..." *Rich 2*, V, iii, 135–136.

brothers' wager, *n.* friendly wager [in the manner of brothers]: "I embrace it freely,/ And will this brothers' wager frankly play." *Ham*, V, ii, 248–249.

brought to bed, *adj.* delivered of a child: "Not far, one Muly lives, my countryman;/ His wife but yesternight was brought to bed." *T Andr*, IV, ii, 153–154.

brow, *n.* **1** aspect or countenance; the area above the eyes, regarded as the seat of facial expressions: "But speak you this with a sad brow ...?" *M Ado*, I, i, 169–170. **2** the head: "You still wrangle with her, Boyet, and she strikes at the/ brow [aims true; hits home]." *Love's L*, IV, i, 118. **3** [pl] ref. to Leontes' fear of growing the cuckold's horns: "O, that is entertainment/ My bosom likes not, nor my brows." *W Tale*, I, ii, 118–119. **4** crest (of a hill); ridge; prominence: "... on the brow o' the sea/ Stand ranks of people, and they cry 'A sail!'" *Oth*, II, i, 53–54. **5 bend one's brow,** to frown; scowl: "And who durst smile when Warwick bent his brow?" *3 Hen 6*, V, ii, 22. **6 break one's brow,** to cut one's forehead: "She could have run and waddled all about;/ For even the day before she broke her brow ..." *Rom & Jul*, I, iii, 37–38. **7 grow out of one's brows,** physical aspect as evidence of the brain's workings; here, the growing evidence of Hamlet's plot against Claudius: "... may not endure/ Hazard so near us as doth hourly grow/ Out of his brows." *Ham*, III, iii, 5–7. **8 underneath the brows,** downhearted; dejected: "The Countess Salisbury and her father ... and all, look underneath the brows." *Edw 3*, II, ii, 18–19.

brow-bound, *past part.* [had] the head adorned: "... and for his meed/ Was brow-bound with the oak." *Cor*, II, ii, 97–98.

brown, *adj.* **1** (of a woman) having dark hair and eyes: "... methinks she's too low [short] for a high/ praise, too brown for a fair praise ..." *M Ado*, I, i, 159–160. **2** ref. prob. to a whore or one unusually ugly: "... when the brown wench/ Lay kissing in your arms, lord cardinal." *Hen 8*, III, ii, 295–296.

brown bill, *n.* **1** bill [pike or halberd] with a varnished shaft to prevent rust: "... but for a sallet [helmet], my brain-pan had/ been cleft with a brown bill ..." *2 Hen 6*, IV, x, 11–12. **2** soldier armed with such a bill: "I'll prove it on a giant. Bring up the brown bills." *Lear*, IV, vi, 91.

Brownist, *n.* follower of Robert Browne, leader of an extremely conservative Puritan sect in early 17th cent.: "I had as lief be a Brownist as a/ politician." *T Night*, III, ii, 30–31.

browse, *v.* to snack; nibble: "There is cold meat i' th' cave, we'll browse on that ..." *Cymb*, III, vii, 11.

bruise, *v.* **1** to crush; destroy: "... the law shall bruise 'em." *Timon*, III, v, 4.
—*n.* **2** hurt(s); distress: "... with grey hairs and bruise of many days ..." *M Ado*, V, i, 65.

bruised, *adj.* dented; battered: "With bruised arms [armor] and wreaths of victory." *Luc*, 110.

bruit, *n.* **1** rumor; report: "One that rejoices in the common wrack,/ As common bruit doth put it." *Timon*, V, i, 191–192.

—*v.* **2** to spread by rumor; report: ". . . his death . . . Being bruited once, took fire and heat away . . ." *2 Hen 4,* I, i, 112–114. **3** to announce noisily; here, by cannon fire: "And the King's rouse the heaven shall bruit again,/ Re-speaking earthly thunder." *Ham,* I, ii, 127–128.

Brundusium, *n.* ancient name of Brindisi, port city in SE Italy: ". . . from Tarentum, and Brundusium/ He could so quickly cut the Ionian sea . . ." *Ant & Cleo,* III, vii, 21–22.

brush, *n.* bruise; here, an attack: "Aged contusions and all brush of time . . ." *2 Hen 6,* V, iii, 3.

brutish sting, *n.* carnal passion; lust: ". . . a libertine,/ As sensual as the brutish sting itself . . ." *As You,* II, vii, 65–66.

Brutus, *n.* **1** Lucius Junius Brutus, father of Lucrece, was the nephew of Tarquin the Proud [fl. 6th cent. B.C.], father of Lucrece's assailant. The elder Tarquin, known as the tyrant of Rome, had murdered Brutus's elder brother: "And from the purple fountain Brutus drew/ The murd'rous knife . . ." *Luc,* 1734–1735. **2 Brutus' bastard hand,** Brutus was thought to be Caesar's bastard son: "Brutus' bastard hand/ Stabb'd Julius Caesar . . ." *2 Hen 6,* IV, i, 136–137. **3 Roman Brutus,** [in early Roman history] nephew of the tyrannical King Tarquin ("the Proud"), who saved his life by pretending to be dull-witted ["brutus" in Latin]: ". . . you shall find his vanities forespent/ Were but the outside of the Roman Brutus . . ." *Hen 5,* II, iv, 36–37.

bubble, *n.* poseur, humbug, or cheat: "On my life, my lord, a bubble." *All's W,* III, vi, 5.

bubukle, *n.* boil; prob. Fluellen's confusion of "bubo" [abscess] and "carbuncle": ". . . his/ face is all bubukles, and whelks, and knobs . . ." *Hen 5,* III, vi, 104–105.

buck[1], *n.* **mad as a buck,** perh. related to "horn-mad": "It would make a man mad as a buck to be so bought and sold." *Errors,* III, i, 72.

buck[2], *n.* quantity of clothes washed with buck [lye]: ". . . not able to travel with her/ furr'd pack, she washes bucks here at home." *2 Hen 6,* IV, ii, 45–46.

buck-basket, *n.* large hamper for dirty clothes: "Quickly, quickly, is the buck-basket—" *Wives,* III, iii, 2.

bucking, *n.* washing: ". . . throw foul/ linen upon him, as if it were going to bucking . . ." *Wives,* III, iii, 120–121.

buckle, *v.* **1** to enclose or encompass: "He cannot buckle his distemper'd cause/ Within the belt of rule." *Mac,* V, iii, 15–16. **2 buckle with, a.** to fight with swords at close quarters: "In single combat thou shalt buckle with me . . ." *1 Hen 6,* I, ii, 95.

b. to attack; here, overcome: ". . . all our general force/ Might with a sally of the very town/ Be buckled with . . ." *1 Hen 6,* IV, iv, 3–5.

buckler, *n.* **1** small, round shield: ". . . my buckler cut through/ and through, my sword hacked like a handsaw . . ." *1 Hen 4,* II, iv, 165–166. **2 give one the bucklers,** to give up one's shield; hence, to surrender: "A most manly wit, Margaret . . . I give/ thee the bucklers." *M Ado,* V, ii, 15–17.
—*v.* **3** to protect; shield: ". . . they shall not touch thee, Kate./ I'll buckler thee against a million." *Shrew,* III, ii, 236–237.

Bucklersbury, *n.* district of London where herbs were sold: ". . . come like women in men's apparel, and smell like Bucklersbury . . ." *Wives,* III, iii, 65–66.

buckram, *n.* **1** coarse fabric, as linen stiffened with glue: "I have cases of buckram for the/ nonce . . ." *1 Hen 4,* I, ii, 174–175.
—*adj.* **2** made of or seeming to be made of buckram: ". . . thou serge, nay, thou buckram lord!" *2 Hen 6,* IV, vii, 23.

buck-washing, *n.* laundry; Ford picks it up in wordplay with "getting rid of my cuckold's horns": "You were best meddle with buck-washing!" *Wives,* III, iii, 144.

bud, *n.* a young, usually immature person: "I have assembled . . . The choicest buds of all our English blood . . ." *Edw 3,* II, ii, 82–83.

budded out, *past part.* come to pass: ". . . aboded/ The sudden breach on't."/ "Which is budded out . . ." *Hen 8,* I, i, 93–94.

budge, *v.* to flinch; yield or give way; also, retreat: "Must I budge?/ Must I observe you? Must I stand and crouch . . ." *J Caes,* IV, iii, 44–45.

budger, *n.* person who flinches or retreats: "Let the first budger die the other's slave . . ." *Cor,* I, viii, 5.

budget, *n.* **1 sow-skin budget,** pigskin bag; here, for carrying the tools of the tinker's trade: "If tinkers may have leave to live,/ And bear the sow-skin budget . . ." *W Tale,* IV, iii, 19–20.
—*interj.* **2** combines with "mum" to form "mumbudget," command to keep silent; from name of children's game and related to "Mum's the word": "I come to her/ in white, and cry 'mum'; she cries 'budget'; and by/ that we know one another." *Wives,* V, ii, 5–7.

buff, *n.* leather, usually ox hide: ". . . is not a buff jerkin a most sweet robe of durance?" *1 Hen 4,* I, ii, 42.

buffet, *v.* **1** to engage in boxing: ". . . if I might buffet/ for my love, or bound my horse for her favours . . ." *Hen 5,* V, ii, 142–143.
—*n.* **2 go to buffets,** come to blows: "O, I could divide myself, and go to buffets . . ." *1 Hen 4,* II, iii, 32. **3 stand the buffet,** to exchange blows: ". . . and stand the buffet/ With knaves that smells of sweat . . ." *Ant & Cleo,* I, iv, 20–21.

buffeting, *n.* fighting: ". . . if there come a hot June, and/ this civil buffeting hold . . ." *1 Hen 4,* II, iv, 357–358.

bug, *n.* **1** bugbear or bogey; source or cause of fear: "With ho! such bugs and goblins in my life . . ." *Ham,* V, ii, 22. **2** fiend; terror: "Those that would die, or ere resist, are grown/ The mortal bugs o' th' field." *Cymb,* V, iii, 50–51.

bugbear, *n.* goblin or gremlin: "Would he not . . . let it sleep? A bugbear take him!" *Tr & Cr,* IV, ii, 32–33.

bugle, *n.* tubelike bead of black glass [here in attrib. use]: "'Tis not . . . Your bugle eyeballs, nor your cheek of cream/ That can entame my spirits . . ." *As You,* III, v, 46–48.

bugle-bracelet, *n.* bracelet of bugle beads: "Bugle-bracelet, necklace amber,/ Perfume for a lady's chamber . . ." *W Tale,* IV, iv, 224–225.

building, *n.* place; location: "This jewel holds his building on my arm." *Per,* II, i, 155.

bulk¹, *n.* **1** the human body: ". . . a sigh so piteous and profound/ As it did seem to shatter all his bulk . . ." *Ham,* II, i, 94–96. **2** great size; in reply, Timon puns on "bulk" [body]: "The monstrous bulk of this ingratitude . . ." *Timon,* V, i, 64.

bulk², *n.* shop stall: ". . . stalls, bulks, windows,/ Are smother'd up, leads fill'd and ridges hors'd . . ." *Cor,* II, i, 208–209.

bulky, *adj.* of great size; tall or massive: "How bloodily the sun begins to peer/ Above yon bulky hill!" *1 Hen 4,* V, I, 1–2.

Bull, *n.* **the Bull,** See **Taurus** (def. 1).

bull-beef, *n., pl.* **bull-beeves,** English beef; here, according to the French, the staple of the English diet: "They want their porridge and their fat bull-beeves . . ." *1 Hen 6,* I, ii, 9.

bullet, *n.* cannonball: ". . . instead of bullets wrapp'd in fire . . . They shoot but calm words folded up in smoke . . ." *K John,* II, i, 227–229.

bully, *n., adj.* **1** friendly term of address meaning "good fellow": "What sayest thou, bully Bottom?" *M N Dream,* III, i, 7. **2** See **rook** (def. 2).

bully stale, *n.* perh. Host's title of mock courtesy [akin to "Master Doctor"] for the physician: "My Galen? My heart of elder? Ha, is/ he dead, bully stale? Is he dead?" *Wives,* II, iii, 27–28.

bulwark, *n.* shelter; refuge: ". . . some, making the wars their bulwark . . ." *Hen 5,* IV, i, 169.

bum, *n.* backside; posterior: "Serving of becks and jutting-out of bums!" *Timon,* I, ii, 233.

bum-baily, *n.* bailiff (arresting officer) who sneaks up behind his prey [slang term]: ". . . scout me for him at the corner/ of the orchard, like a bum-baily." *T Night,* III, iv, 177–178.

bumper, *n.* glass filled with wine: "[To Silence, seeing him take off a bumper] Why, now/ you have done me right." *2 Hen 4,* V, iii, 70–71.

Bunch of Grapes, *n.* name of room in tavern: ". . . 'twas in the/ Bunch of Grapes, where indeed you have a delight/ to sit . . ." *Meas,* II, i, 127–129.

bung, *n.* (in thieves' jargon) purse stealer or pickpocket: "Away, you cutpurse rascal, you filthy bung, away!" *2 Hen 4,* II, iv, 125.

bunting, *n.* bird that resembles the lark but is not a songbird; here, a wry joke: "Then my dial goes not true; I took this lark for a/ bunting." *All's W,* II, v, 5–6.

buoy, *v.* to rise or swell: "The sea . . . would have buoy'd up,/ And quench'd the stelled fires . . ." *Lear,* III, vii, 58–60.

Burdeaux, *n.* Bordeaux, birthplace of Richard II: "The mightiest of thy greatest enemies,/ Richard of Burdeaux, by me hither brought." *Rich 2,* V, vi, 32–33.

burden, *n.* **1** refrain, often of nonsense syllables: "I would sing my song without a burden." *As You,* III, ii, 243. **2** accompaniment to a song, esp. the bass part: "Clap's into 'Light o' Love'; that goes without a/ burden." *M Ado,* III, iv, 42. **3** wordplay on "load, cargo" and "musical bass line": "Heavy? Belike it hath some burden then?" *Two Gent,* I, ii, 85. **4** birth: "Thou hadst a wife . . . That bore thee at a burden two fair sons?" *W Tale,* IV, iv, 342–343.

burgonet, *n.* lightweight steel cap worn by soldiers of Burgundy: "And that I'll write upon thy burgonet . . ." *2 Hen 6,* V, i, 201.

buried, *past part.* ref. to the title of king that will be taken from Edward, appar. by death: "The lustful Edward's title buried—" *3 Hen 6,* III, ii, 129.

burly-boned, *adj.* bulky; husky: ". . . cut not/ out the burly-bon'd clown in chines of beef . . ." *2 Hen 6,* IV, x, 55–56.

burn, *v.* **1** to heat and spice (wine): "Come, come, I'll go burn some sack, 'tis too late/ to go to bed now." *T Night,* II, iii, 190–191. **2** to infect, esp. with venereal disease: ". . . she's in hell already, and burns/ poor souls." *2 Hen 4,* II, iv, 335–336. **3** to inflame: "You see we have burnt our cheeks [with drinking]." *Ant & Cleo,* II, vii, 121. **4 burn daylight,** to waste time: "We burn daylight. Here, read, read . . ." *Wives,* II, i, 52.

burnet, *n.* wild herb having a brown flower: ". . . brought sweetly forth/ The freckled cowslip, burnet, and green clover . . ." *Hen 5,* V, ii, 48–49.

burning, *adj.* eager for amorous play: "My flesh is soft and plump, my marrow burning." *Ven & Ad,* 142.

burning bear, *n.* Little Bear, the constellation of the Little Dipper, with the pole star at the tip of its tail: "Seems to cast water on the burning bear,/ And quench the guards of the ever-fixed pole . . ." *Oth,* II, i, 14–15.

burning devil, *n.* devil from the fires of Hell; also, poss., a ref. to venereal disease: ". . . wars and lechery!/ Nothing else holds fashion. A burning devil take/ them!" *Tr & Cr,* V, ii, 193–195.

burning-glass, *n.* lens used to start a fire by focusing the rays of the sun: ". . . the appetite of her eye did/ seem to scorch me up like a burning-glass!" *Wives,* I, iii, 62–63.

burning lake, *n.* prob. Phlegethon, the fiery river of Hades: "I'll dive into the burning lake below,/ And pull her out of Acheron by the heels." *T Andr,* IV, iii, 43–44.

burning zone, *n.* part of the sky through which the sun moves: ". . . till our ground,/ Singeing his pate against the burning zone,/ Make Ossa like a wart." *Ham,* V, i, 276–278.

burnt in the hand, branded on the hand with a "T" for "thief": ". . . methinks he should stand in fear of fire,/ being burnt i' th' hand for stealing of sheep." *2 Hen 6,* IV, ii, 59–60.

burnt sack, *n.* poss. mulled wine or wine to which burnt sugar has been added: "I'll give you a pottle of burnt/ sack to give me recourse to him . . ." *Wives,* II, i, 203–204.

burst his head, *v.* [very nearly] had his head broken by crowding in among the officials: ". . . and then he burst his head for crowding/ among the marshal's men." *2 Hen 4,* III, ii, 317–318.

burst of speaking, *n.* speaking in spurts: ". . . the snatches in his voice,/ And burst of speaking were as his . . ." *Cymb,* IV, ii, 105–106.

burthen, *n.* **1** var. of **burden;** load or quantity; here, of hair: ". . . thatch/ Your poor thin roofs [heads] with burthens of the dead . . ." *Timon,* IV, iii, 146–147. **2** crop; yield: "Plants with goodly burthen bowing . . ." *Temp,* IV, i, 113. **3** refrain; also, an "undersong" that accompanies the main voices: "And sweet sprites bear/ The burthen. Hark, hark." *Temp,* I, ii, 382–383. **4** cargo; here, understood as intellectual or moral worth: ". . . did manifoldly dissuade me from believing thee/ a vessel of too great a burthen." *All's W,* II, iii, 203–204. **5 burthen dispersedly,** [SD] Refrain sounds from all sides: "Hark, hark./ [Burthen dispersedly. From within] Bow-wow./ The watch dogs bark . . ." *Temp,* I, ii, 384–385.

burthenous, *adj.* burdensome or oppressive: "He hath not money for these Irish wars,/ His burthenous taxations notwithstand-ing . . ." *Rich 2,* II, i, 259–260.

Burton, *n.* Also, **Burton-on-Trent,** town in NW England on Trent river: "Methinks my moiety, north from Burton here,/ In quantity equals not one of yours . . ." *1 Hen 4,* III, i, 92–93.

Burton-heath, *n.* prob. the village of Barton-on-the-Heath, near Stratford: "Am not I/ Christopher Sly, old Sly's son of Burton-heath . . ." *Shrew,* Ind., ii, 17–18.

bury, *v.* to keep hidden or secret: "You shall . . . take the sacrament/ To bury mine intents . . ." *Rich 2,* IV, i, 328–329.

Bury, *n.* Bury St. Edmunds, a town in Suffolk, in SE England: ". . . his Majesty's Parliament,/ Holden at Bury the first of this next month." *2 Hen 6,* II, iv, 70–71.

bush, *n.* ref. to use of branched ivy to designate a wine shop; sense is that good wine does not have to be extolled: "If it be true that good wine needs no/ bush . . ." *As You,* Epil., 200–201.

busilest, *adv.* superl. of "busily"; here, appar. a double superlative: "But these sweet thoughts do even refresh my labours,/ Most busilest [actively] when I do it [work hard]." *Temp,* III, i, 14–15.

business, *n.* **1** worry; preoccupation: "O, full of careful [anxious] business are his looks!" *Rich 2,* II, ii, 75. **2** [pl] business or political matters: "Thou, having/ made me businesses, which none without thee can/ sufficiently manage . . ." *W Tale,* IV, ii, 13–15. **3 business of estate,** See **estate** (def. 5).

buskined, *adj.* dressed in hunting boots: ". . . the bouncing Amazon,/ Your buskin'd mistress and your warrior love . . ." *M N Dream,* II, i, 70–71.

buss, *v.* **1** to touch with or as if with the lips: ". . . here be with them—/ Thy knee bussing the stones . . ." *Cor,* III, ii, 74–75. **2** to kiss lustfully: "Come, grin on me, and I will think thou smil'st,/ And buss thee as thy wife." *K John,* III, iii, 34–35.

bustle, *v.* to be showily busy or active: "God take King Edward to his mercy,/ And leave the world for me to bustle in." *Rich 3,* I, i, 151–152.

bustling rumor, *n.* distant tumult or faint roar: "I heard a bustling rumour, like a fray,/ And the wind brings it from the Capitol." *J Caes,* II, iv, 19–20.

busy, *adj.* meddling, prying, or bothering: "Be it on lion, bear, or wolf, or bull,/ On meddling monkey, or on busy ape . . ." *M N Dream,* II, i, 180–181.

but, *prep.* **1** but or except for; without: ". . . my honour is at pawn,/ And, but my going, nothing can redeem it." *2 Hen 4,* II, iii, 7–8. **2** than: ". . . this weak and idle theme,/ No more yielding but a dream . . ." *M N Dream,* V, i, 413–414. **3 but that,** only that one time: "But that in all my life, when I was a youth." *2 Hen 6,* II, i, 99.
—*adv.* **4** even: "—here,/ But here, upon this bank and shoal of time . . ." *Mac,* I, vii, 5–6. **5** only: ". . . but that piece of song,/ That old and antic song we heard last night . . ." *T Night,* II, iv, 2–3. **6** merely; simply; just: "Well, I will marry one day but to try." *Errors,* II, i, 42. **7** just now: "They are gone but to meet the Duke, villain . . ." *Wives,* IV, v, 66. **8 but so,** worth very little: ". . . if he say it is so, he is, in telling/ true, but so." *Love's L,* I, i, 221–222.
—*conj.* **9** if: "I would be sorry, my lord, but it should be thus." *2 Hen 4,* IV, iii, 30. **10** if only: "Well, I will marry one day but to try." *Errors,* II, i, 42. **11** unless: ". . . for, but I be deceiv'd,/ Our fine musician groweth amorous." *Shrew,* III, i, 60–61. **12** that . . . not: ". . . virtue cannot/ so inoculate our old stock but we shall relish of it." *Ham,* III, i, 118–119. **13 But . . . nor,** Neither . . . nor: "But my five wits, nor my five senses, can/ Dissuade one foolish heart from serving thee . . ." *Sonn 141,* 9–10. **14 but then,** even if it proves distasteful: "Tell me, but truly, but then speak the truth . . ." *Lear,* V, i, 8.

butcherly, *adj.* murderous; savage: "What stratagems, how fell, how butcherly . . ." *3 Hen 6,* II, v, 89.

butcher's cur, *n.* ref. to Wolsey as the son of a butcher: "This butcher's cur is venom-mouth'd, and I/ Have not the power to muzzle him . . ." *Hen 8,* I, i, 120–121.

butchery, *n.* slaughterhouse: "This is no place: this house is but a butchery." *As You,* II, iii, 27.

butt¹, *n.* **1** prob. ref. to horned head, with poss. wordplay on "buttocks": "An hasty-witted body/ Would say your head and butt were head and horn." *Shrew,* V, ii, 40–41. **2** mark aimed at; target or goal: "I am your butt, and I abide your shot." *3 Hen 6,* I, iv, 29.
—*v.* **3 butt together,** to clash, esp. to engage in a combat of wits: "Believe me, sir, they butt together well." *Shrew,* V, ii, 39.

butt², *n.* **1** large cask for wine, ale, etc.: ". . . when the butt is out [empty], we will drink/ water; not a drop before . . ." *Temp,* III, ii, 1–2. **2** tub, derog. term for a boat: ". . . they prepared/ A rotten carcass of a butt, not rigg'd,/ Nor tackle, sail, nor mast . . ." *Temp,* I, ii, 145–147.

butt-end, *n.* conclusion: "That is the butt-end of a mother's blessing . . ." *Rich 3,* II, ii, 110.

butter, *v.* to spread or cook with butter; here, of a particularly smelly sort: "I will henceforth eat/ no fish of Fortune's butt'ring [no fish that Fortune can serve up]." *All's W,* V, ii, 7–8.

butter-woman, *n.* women who sold butter were generally shrill and talkative: "Tongue, I must put you into a butter-woman's/ mouth . . ." *All's W,* IV, i, 41–42.

buttery, *n.* pantry or larder: "Go, sirrah, take them to the buttery,/ And give them friendly welcome every one." *Shrew,* Ind., i, 100–101.

buttery bar, *n.* ledge atop the half door to the pantry or larder, on which drinks were placed for serving; Maria's invitation is flirtatious, though Sir Andrew is oblivious: "I pray you bring/ your hand to th' buttery bar and let it drink." *T Night,* I, iii, 68–69.

buttock, *n.* **buttock of the night,** late night: ". . . one that converses/ more with the buttock of the night . . ." *Cor,* II, i, 50–51.

button, *n.* **1** bud: "The canker galls the infants of the spring/ Too oft before their buttons be disclos'd . . ." *Ham,* I, iii, 39–40. **2 in his buttons,** in his very nature: ". . . 'tis in his buttons he will/ carry 't." *Wives,* III, ii, 63–64. **3 the very button,** the highest point: ". . . on Fortune's/ cap we are not the very button." *Ham,* II, ii, 228–229.

buttoned, *adj.* decorated with metal studs: "Nor from their buttoned tawny leathern belts/ Dismiss their biting whinyards . . ." *Edw 3,* I, ii, 32–33.

button-hole, *n.* **take one a button-hole lower,** to help one undress, with implication of humiliating one: "Master, let me take you a button-hole lower. Do/ you not see Pompey is un-casing [undressing] for the combat?" *Love's L,* V, ii, 692–693.

butt-shaft, *n.* barbless target arrow: "Cupid's butt-shaft/ is too hard for Hercules' club . . ." *Love's L,* I, ii, 165–166.

buxom, *adj.* **1** lively; vivacious: "So buxom, blithe and full of face/ As heaven had lent her all his grace . . ." *Per,* I, Chor., 23–24. **2** sturdy; reliable: ". . . a soldier firm and sound of heart,/ And of buxom valour . . ." *Hen 5,* III, vi, 25–26.

buy, *v.* **1** to be deceived by: "The Lord of Stafford dear [costly] today hath bought/ Thy likeness, for instead of thee, King Harry,/ This sword hath ended him . . ." *1 Hen 4,* V, iii, 7–9. **2 buy out, a.** to redeem or ransom: ". . . not being able to buy out his life . . . Dies ere the weary sun set in the west." *Errors,* I, ii, 5–7. **b.** to compensate for: "An honour in him which buys out his fault . . ." *Timon,* III, v, 17.

buz or **buzz,** *v.* **1** to whisper: "Have hired me to undermine the Duchess,/ And buz these conjurations in her brain." *2 Hen 6,* I, ii, 98–99. **2** to gossip; spread rumors: "Yet look to have them buzz to offend thine ears." *3 Hen 6,* II, vi, 95. —*n.* **3** rumor: ". . . that on every dream,/ Each buzz, each fancy, each complaint . . ." *Lear,* I, iv, 334–335.

buzz, *interj.* exclamation of contempt, annoyance, etc.: ". . . as heavy as my weight should be."/ "Should be? Should—buzz!" *Shrew,* II, i, 205–206.

buzzard, *n.* in fig. sense, a fool: "Well ta'en, and like a buzzard." *Shrew,* II, i, 206.

buzzer, *n.* spreader of rumors; gossip: ". . . keeps himself in clouds,/ And wants not buzzers to infect his ear . . ." *Ham,* IV, v, 89–90.

by, *prep.* **1** about; concerning: "I would not have him know so much by me." *Love's L,* IV, iii, 147. **2** under: ". . . hast not thou full often stroke a doe,/ And borne her cleanly by the keeper's nose?" *T Andr,* II, i, 93–94. **3** by means of; with: "To hear by the nose, it is dulcet in contagion." *T Night,* II, iii, 57. —*adj.* **4** near: "For gazing on your beams, fair sun, being by." *Errors,* III, ii, 56. —*adv.* **5** nearby: ". . . go with me, and with this holy man,/ Into the chantry by . . ." *T Night,* IV, iii, 23–24.

by and by, just a moment; here, in answer to a knocking: "[Knocking.]—By and by.—/ I hope it is some pardon or reprieve/ For the most gentle Claudio." *Meas,* IV, ii, 68–70.

by-dependances, *n.* side issues: ". . . all the other by-dependances,/ From chance to chance [incident to incident]." *Cymb,* V, v, 391–392.

by-drinking, *n.* incidental drinking; drinks between meals: "You owe money here besides, Sir John,/ for your diet, and by-drinkings . . ." *1 Hen 4,* III, iii, 70–71.

by God's mother, a mild oath: "Now, by God's mother, I'll shave/ your crown for this . . ." *2 Hen 6,* II, i, 53–54.

by-peep, *v.* to glance sideways: ". . . then by-peeping in an eye/ Base and illustrous as the smoky light . . ." *Cymb,* I, vii, 108–109.

by'r lady, Also, **by' lady.** contraction of "by Our Lady" [a mild oath]: ". . . nay by'r lady/ I am not such a fool to think what I list . . ." *M Ado,* III, iv, 76–77.

byrlakin or **by'r lakin,** by Our [dear little] Lady (a mild oath): "Byrlakin, a parlous fear." *M N Dream,* III, i, 12.

by-room, *n.* adjoining or nearby room: ". . . do thou stand in some by-room,/ while I question my puny drawer . . ." *1 Hen 4,* II, iv, 29–30.

by the day, in the morning: "An it be not four by the day I'll be/ hanged . . ." *1 Hen 4,* II, i, 1–2.

by (the) mass, mild oath: "Flat burglary as ever was committed./ Yea, by mass, that it is." *M Ado,* IV, ii, 47–48.

by the rood, by Christ's crucifix [mild oath]: ". . . nay, by th'rood,/ She could have run and waddled all about . . ." *Rom & Jul,* I, iii, 36–37.

by the way, *adv.* in a roundabout way; indirectly: "I heard it by the way; but I will send." *Mac,* III, iv, 129.

by-word, *n.* object of scorn or derision: ". . . whose cowardice/ Hath made us by-words to our enemies." *3 Hen 6,* I, i, 41–42.

by your leave, *n.* words preceding a gentleman's kissing a lady's cheek: ". . . we love him highly,/ And shall continue our graces towards him./ By your leave, hostess." *Mac,* I, vi, 29–31.

Byzantium, *n.* ancient name of "Constantinople" [present-day Istanbul]: "His service done/ At Lacedaemon and Byzantium/ Were a sufficient briber for his life." *Timon,* III, v, 60–61.

cabilero, *n.* var. of **cabaliero**; a gallant; fashionable young blade: "I'll drink to Master Bardolph, and to all/ the cabileros about London." *2 Hen 4,* V, iii, 56–57.

cabin, *v.* **1** to lodge: "I'll make you feed on berries and on roots,/ And cabin in a cave . . ." *T Andr,* IV, ii, 178–180.
—*n.* **2** cave or lair: "Oh let him keep his loathsome cabin still!" *Ven & Ad,* 637.

cabinet, *n.* **1** nest: "Lo here the gentle lark . . . From his moist cabinet mounts up on high . . ." *Ven & Ad,* 853–854. **2** the heart: ". . . the quiet cabinet/ Where their dear governess and lady lies . . ." *Luc,* 442–443. **3** refuge or sanctuary: "Then in the summer arbour sit by me,/ Make it our council house or cabinet . . ." *Edw 3,* II, i, 61–62.

cable, *n.* scope; leeway: ". . . put upon you what restraint, and grievance,/ That law . . . Will give him cable." *Oth,* I, ii, 15–17.

Cacaliban, *n.* extra syllable in "Caliban" may be a hiccup indicating that Caliban is drunk: ". . . 'Ban, 'Ban, Cacaliban/ Has a new master . . ." *Temp,* II, ii, 184–185.

cacodemon, *n.* evil spirit; devil: "Hie thee to hell for shame, and leave this world,/ Thou cacodemon . . ." *Rich 3,* I, iii, 143–144.

caddis, *n.* a worsted tape; caddis ribbon or caddis-garter: ". . . inkles, caddisses, cambrics, lawns: why, he/ sings 'em over as [if] they were gods . . ." *W Tale,* IV, iv, 209–210.

caddis-garter, *adj.* wearing garters of caddis ribbon: ". . . not-pated, agate-ring, puke-stocking, caddis-garter . . ." *1 Hen 4,* II, iv, 69.

cade, *n.* barrel of herring: "Or rather, of stealing a cade of her-rings." *2 Hen 6,* IV, ii, 32.

cadent, *adj.* falling: "With cadent tears fret channels in her cheeks . . ." *Lear,* I, iv, 294.

Cadmus, *n.* founder of Thebes: "I was with Hercules and Cad-mus once,/ When in a wood of Crete they bay'd the bear . . ." *M N Dream,* IV, i, 111–112.

caduceus, *n.* staff carried by Mercury as messenger of Jupiter; endowed with magical powers: "Mercury, lose all the serpen-tine craft of/ thy caduceus . . ." *Tr & Cr,* II, iii, 12–13.

Cadwallader, *n.* last Welsh king [fl. 12th cent.]: "Not for Cad-wallader and all his goats." *Hen 5,* V, i, 29.

Caesar, *n.* **1 at the wheels of Caesar,** ref. to Pompey's sons defeated by Caesar and led in triumph behind his chariot: "How now, noble Pompey! What, at the wheels of/ Caesar?" *Meas,* III, ii, 42–43. **2 Caesar and his fortune,** ref. to story [in Plutarch] that Caesar, aboard ship in an approaching storm, quieted an anxious captain with the words "Fear not, thou hast Caesar and his fortune with thee": ". . . that proud insult-ing ship/ Which Caesar and his fortune bare at once [bore together]." *1 Hen 6,* I, ii, 138–139.

Caesarion, *n.* son of Cleopatra, said to have been fathered by Julius Caesar: ". . . at the feet sat/ Caesarion, whom they call my father's son [Octavius was Julius Caesar's adopted son] . . ." *Ant & Cleo,* III, vi, 5–6.

cage, *n.* **1** jail; here, a temporary holding pen for vagabonds, pickpockets, whores, etc.: ". . . his father had/ never a house but the cage." *2 Hen 6,* IV, ii, 49–50. **2 cage of rushes,** jail eas-ily escaped from: ". . . in which/ cage of rushes I am sure you are not prisoner." *As You,* III, ii, 360–361.

Cain, *n.* Adam's firstborn and the first murderer: "But let one spirit of the first-born Cain/ Reign in all bosoms . . ." *2 Hen 4,* I, i, 157–158.

Cain-colored, *adj.* yellow or yellowish-red, traditionally the color of Cain's beard, as in morality plays: ". . . a little wee face, with a/ little yellow beard—a Cain-coloured beard." *Wives,* I, iv, 20–21.

caitiff, *n.* **1** wretched humble person, esp. a slave: "O thou caitiff! O thou varlet! O thou wicked/ Hannibal!" *Meas,* II, i, 171–172.
—*adj.* **2** pitiable; miserable; hapless: "Here lives a caitiff wretch would sell it him." *Rom & Jul,* V, i, 52.

caitive, *adj.* var. of CAITIFF; base; wretched: "A caitive recreant to my cousin Herford!" *Rich 2,* I, ii, 53.

cake, *n.* **Our cake is dough,** Our endeavor is a failure: "Our cake's dough on/ both sides. Farewell." *Shrew,* I, i, 108–109.

cake of roses, *n.* cake of compressed rose petals, used as perfume: "Remnants of packthread, and old cakes of roses/ Were thinly scatter'd to make up a show." *Rom & Jul,* V, i, 47–48.

cakes and ale, *n. pl.* things associated with festivities, which the Puritans railed against: "Dost thou think because thou art virtuous,/ there shall be no more cakes and ale?" *T Night,* II, iii, 114–115.

Calaber, *n.* Calabria, a region in S Italy: "The Dukes of Orleans, Calaber, Bretagne, and Alençon . . ." *2 Hen 6,* I, 1, 7.

calculate, *v.* to prophesy: "Why old men, fools, and children calculate,/ Why all these things change from their ordinance . . ." *J Caes,* I, iii, 65–66.

calendar, *n.* **1** record or register; here, ref. to Dromios as a living record of the brothers Antipholus [since all were born within the same hour]: ". . . my children both,/ And you, the calendars of their nativity,/ Go to a gossips' feast and joy with me . . ." *Errors,* V, i, 403–405. **2** almanac: "Give me a calendar—/ Who saw the sun today?" *Rich 3,* V, iii, 277–278.

calf, *n.* fool; blockhead: "Brutus killed me."/ "It was a brute part of him to kill so capital a calf/ there." *Ham,* III, ii, 103–105.

calf's head, *n.* fool or dolt: "I thank him, he hath bid me to a calf's head and capon . . ." *M Ado,* V, i, 152–153.

Calipolis or **Calypolis,** *n.* muddled quote from contemporary play by Peele: "Then feed and be fat, my fair Calipolis!" *2 Hen 4,* II, iv, 175.

caliver, *n.* light musket used by infantrymen: ". . . such as fear the/ report of a caliver worse than a struck fowl . . ." *1 Hen 4,* IV, ii, 18–19.

calkin, *n.* part of a horseshoe: "Trotting the stones of Athens, which the calkins/ Did rather tell than trample . . ." *Kinsmen,* V, iv, 55–56.

call, *v.* **1 call in question,** to bring to mind: "Examine other beauties."/ "'Tis the way to call hers, exquisite, in question more." *Rom & Jul,* I, i, 226–227. **2 call on him for't,** call him to account for it; demand a reckoning: ". . . the dryness of his bones/ Call on him for't." *Ant & Cleo,* I, iv, 27–28. **3 call to,** call on; pay a visit to: "I weigh my friend's affection with mine own . . . I'll call to you." *Timon,* I, ii, 214–215. **4 call upon,** require action of: ". . . our time does call upon's." *Mac,* III, i, 36. **5 call upon his own,** to call in his obligations: "My master is awak'd by great occasion/ To call upon his own . . ." *Timon,* II, ii, 24–25. **6 call you up,** require of you: ". . . his gracious promise, which you might/ As cause had call'd you up, have held him to . . ." *Cor,* II, iii, 191–192.
—*n.* **7** bait; enticement; decoy: ". . . if but a dozen French/ Were there in arms, they would be as a call/ To train ten thousand English to their side." *K John,* III, iii, 173–175.

callat or **callet,** *n.* strumpet; trull: "Contemptuous base-born callet as she is . . ." *2 Hen 6,* I, iii, 83.

Callice, *n.* old name of **Calais:** "Three parts of that receipt I had for Callice/ Disburs'd I duly . . ." *Rich 2,* I, i, 126–127.

calm, *adj.* **1** pacifying; lulling: "They shoot but calm words folded up in smoke . . ." *K John,* II, i, 229.
—*n.* **2** misuse for "qualm," a sudden attack of faintness, queasiness, etc.: "Sick of a calm, yea, good faith." *2 Hen 4,* II, iv, 36.
—*v.* **3** to becalm: "Like to a ship that, having scap'd a tempest,/ Is straightway calm'd . . ." *2 Hen 6,* IV, ix, 32–33.

calumniating, *adj.* (of Time) misrepresenting the past by erasing evidence: "Love, friendship, charity, are subjects all/ To envious and calumniating Time." *Tr & Cr,* III, iii, 173–174.

calves'-guts, *n.* strings of musical instruments: ". . . horsehairs, and calves'-guts, nor the/ voice of unpaved eunuch to boot . . ." *Cymb,* II, iii, 28–29.

calve's-skin, *n.* ref. to calf as symbol of meekness and cowardice: "And hang a calve's-skin on those recreant limbs." *K John,* III, i, 55.

Calydon, *n.* ancient city-state in central Greece: ". . . the fatal brand Althaea burnt/ Unto the prince's heart of Calydon." *2 Hen 6,* I, 1, 235–236.

Cambio, *n.* name assumed by Lucentio while wooing Bianca: "It shall go hard if Cambio go without her." *Shrew,* IV, iv, 104.

Cambria, *n.* Wales: "Take notice that I am in/ Cambria at Milford-Haven . . ." *Cymb,* III, ii, 43–44.

cambric, *n.* fine white linen used in embroidery: ". . . when she would with sharp neele wound/ The cambric . . ." *Per,* IV, Chor., 23–24.

Cambyses, *n.* ancient king of Persia: ". . . I must speak in passion, and I will do/ it in King Cambyses' vein" [ref. to a bombastic play of the preceding generation]. *1 Hen 4,* II, iv, 381–382.

came, *past tense,* **1** were to come; should come: "Though Paris came, in hope to speed alone." *Shrew,* I, ii, 245. **2** became, with "who" understood: "And sue a friend came debtor for my sake . . ." *Sonn 134,* 11.

camel, *n.* animal used to transport heavy burdens: "Achilles? A drayman, a porter, a very camel." *Tr & Cr,* I, ii, 253.

camp, *v.* to lodge: "Had our great palace the capacity/ To camp this host . . ." *Ant & Cleo,* IV, viii, 32–33.

camping, *adj.* pitching a tent or tents: ". . . with camping foes to live/ Where death and danger dogs the heels of worth." *All's W,* III, iv, 14–15.

can¹, *v.* **1** to be able to do: "Try what repentance can. What can it not?" *Ham,* III, iii, 65. **2** to be skilled in; know: "Let the priest in surplice white,/ That defunctive music can . . ." *Phoen,* 13–14. **3 can well,** See **well** (def. 2).

can², *n.* ale pot; tankard: "A false conclusion: I hate it as an unfilled can." *T Night,* II, iii, 6.

can³, *v.* old form of *'gan;* began to: "And every one with claps can sound . . ." *Per,* III, Chor., 36.

canary, *n.* **1** [often pl.] sweet white wine of the Canary Islands: "But i'faith you have drunk too much canaries . . ." *2 Hen 4,* II, iv, 26. **2** lively jiglike dance: ". . . make you dance canary/ With sprightly fire and motion . . ." *All's W,* II, i, 73–74. **3** [often pl.] poss. a state of confusion: ". . . you have brought her into such a canaries as 'tis wonderful. The best courtier of them all . . . could never have brought her to such a canary." *Wives,* II, ii, 56–60.
—*v.* **4** to dance in a lively manner, esp. to perform the canary: ". . . to jig off a tune at the/ tongue's end, canary to it with your feet . . ." *Love's L,* III, i, 9–10.

cancelled, *adj.* paid in full; here, with tears: "And weep afresh love's long since cancell'd woe . . ." *Sonn 30,* 7.

Cancer, *n.* the Crab, sign and constellation of the zodiac, which the Sun enters at the beginning of summer; symbol of intense heat: ". . . add more coals to Cancer when he burns/ With entertaining great Hyperion [the Sun]." *Tr & Cr,* II, iii, 197–198.

candidatus, *adj.* [Latin] dressed in a white mantle, the garb of those seeking election: "Be *candidatus* then, and put it on,/ And help to set a head on headless Rome." *T Andr,* I, i, 185–186.

candied, *adj.* **1** sugared; sweetened, hence hypocritical: "No, let the candied tongue lick absurd pomp . . ." *Ham,* III, ii, 60. **2** encrusted or coated so as to resemble sugar: ". . . the cold brook,/ Candied with ice . . ." *Timon,* IV, iii, 227–228.

candle, *n.* [usually pl.] stars: ". . . not so bright/ As those gold candles fixed in heaven's air . . ." *Sonn 21,* 11–12.

candle-case, *n.* receptacle for candle ends; here, a pair of old boots: ". . . a pair of old breeches thrice turned; a pair of/ boots that have been candle-cases . . ." *Shrew,* III, ii, 42–43.

candle-mine, *n.* great mass of tallow: "You whoreson candle-mine you, how vilely did/ you speak of me . . ." *2 Hen 4,* II, iv, 297–298.

candle-waster, *n.* bookworm; scholar [contemptuous term]: ". . . make misfortune drunk/ With candle-wasters . . ." *M Ado,* V, i, 18.

candy, *adj.* sugary or sugared-over: ". . . what a candy deal [amount] of courtesy/ This fawning greyhound then did proffer me!" *1 Hen 4,* I, iii, 247–248.

Candy, *n.* Candia, or Crete: ". . . this is that Antonio/ That took the Phoenix and her fraught from Candy . . ." *T Night,* V, i, 58–59.

canker, *n.* **1** wild rose, often contrasted with a garden rose: "I had rather be a canker in a hedge than a rose/ in his grace . . ." *M Ado,* I, iii, 25–26. **2** cankerworm, an insect destructive to plants: "And plant this thorn, this canker Bolingbroke?" *1 Hen 4,* I, iii, 174. **3** sore; here, an evil: "And heal the inveterate [persistent] canker of one wound/ By making many." *K John,* V, ii, 14–15. **4** spreading infection; cancerous growth: "And is't not to be damn'd/ To let this canker of our nature come/ In further evil?" *Ham,* V, ii, 68–70.

canker-bit, *adj.* eaten by worms: ". . . my name is lost;/ By treason's tooth bare-gnawn, and canker-bit . . ." *Lear,* V, iii, 121–122.

canker-blooms, *n.* wild rose, regarded as a weed: "The canker-blooms have full as deep a dye/ As the perfumed tincture of the roses . . ." *Sonn 54,* 5–6.

canker-blossom, *n.* worm in the bud: "You juggler! You canker-blossom!/ You thief of love!" *M N Dream,* III, ii, 282–283.

cankered, *adj.* **1** rusty or rusted: "The canker'd heaps of strange-achievèd gold . . ." *2 Hen 4,* IV, v, 71. **2** corroded with hate; malignant: ". . . in hands as old,/ Canker'd with peace, to part your canker'd hate." *Rom & Jul,* I, i, 92–93. **3** evil; corrupt: ". . . a wicked will;/ A woman's will; a cank'red grandam's will!" *K John,* II, 1, 193–194.

canker-sorrow, *n.* grief that gnaws like a worm: "But now will canker-sorrow eat my bud/ And chase the native beauty from his cheek . . ." *K John,* III, iii, 82–83.

Cannibals, *n.* misuse for "Hannibals": "Shall pack-horses,/ . . . Compare with Caesars and with Cannibals . . . ?" *2 Hen 4,* II, iv, 160–163.

cannikin, *n.* drinking mug [a diminutive]: "And let me the cannikin clink, clink . . ." *Oth,* II, iii, 64.

canon, *n.* **1** custom or law: "At home, upon my brother's guard, even there,/ Against the hospitable canon . . ." *Cor,* I, x, 25–26. **2** Church law, hence God's law: "Or that the Everlasting had not fix'd/ His canon 'gainst self-slaughter." *Ham,* I, ii, 131–132.

canonized, *adj.* buried with sacred rites: ". . . tell/ Why thy canoniz'd bones, hearsèd in death,/ Have burst their cerements . . ." *Ham,* I, iv, 46–47.

canopy, *n.* **1** sky: "Where dwell'st thou?"/ "Under the canopy?" *Cor,* IV, v, 38–39. **2 bear the canopy,** (in a procession) to carry a canopy over one of high rank; here, to honor one publicly: "Were't aught to me I bore the canopy,/ With my extern the outward honouring . . ." *Sonn 125,* 1–2.

canst possible, *v.* inversion of "possibly can": "Ask me what question thou canst possible,/ And I will answer unpremeditated . . ." *1 Hen 6,* I, ii, 87–88.

canstick, *n.* candlestick: "I had rather hear a brazen canstick turn'd . . ." *1 Hen 4,* III, i, 125.

can't, *v.* **can't no other,** can it not be otherwise?: "Can't no other/ But . . . he must be my brother?" *All's W,* I, iii, 160–161.

cantle, *n.* section or segment; slice: ". . . cuts me from the best of all my land/ A huge half-moon, a monstrous cantle out." *1 Hen 4,* III, i, 95–96.

canton, *n.* song, esp. a love song: "Write loyal cantons of contemnèd love,/ And sing them loud even in the dead of night . . ." *T Night,* I, v, 274–275.

canus, *n.* [Latin] misuse for **canis,** dog: "Great Hercules . . ./ Whose club kill'd Cerberus, that three-headed *canus* . . ." *Love's L,* V, ii, 583–584.

canvas or **canvass,** *v.* **1** to toss in a blanket or canvas sheet, esp. as punishment; here, take to task, deal with severely: "I'll canvas thee in thy broad cardinal's hat,/ If thou proceed in this thy insolence." *1 Hen 6,* I, iii, 36–37. **2** preceding in word-play with "solicit between the [canvas] sheets": "And thou dost,/ I'll canvass thee between a pair of sheets." *2 Hen 4,* II, iv, 220–221.

canzonet, *n.* short song or poem: ". . . let me supervise the canzonet. Here are only/ numbers ratified . . ." *Love's L,* IV, ii, 115–116.

cap, *n.* **1** most outstanding of its kind; chief: "Thou art the cap of all the fools alive." *Timon,* IV, iii, 360. **2 caps and legs,** the doffing of caps and the making of legs [bows]: "You are ambitious for poor knaves' caps and legs . . ." *Cor,* II, i, 68. **3 cap of the time,** most fashionable manner: ". . . they wear/ themselves in the cap of the time . . ." *All's W,* II, i, 51–52. **4 gain the cap of,** have the deference of [their tailors]: "Such gain the cap of him that makes him fine . . ." *Cymb,* III, iii, 25. **5 held my cap off to,** been a devoted servant of: "I have ever held my cap off to thy fortunes." *Ant & Cleo,* II, vii, 58. **6 Take my cap, Jupiter,** appar. accompanied by throwing his hat into the air [actors wore Elizabethan, not Roman, costumes]: "Take my cap, Jupiter, and I thank thee. Hoo!/ Martius coming home?" *Cor,* II, i, 104–105. **7 throw their caps at,** have little chance of collecting: "Faith, I perceive our masters may throw their caps/ at their money . . ." *Timon,* III, iv, 99–100. **8 wear his cap with suspicion,** suspect that his cap conceals horns: ". . . hath not the world one/ man but he will wear his cap with suspicion?" *M Ado,* I, i, 183–184. —*v.* **9** to remove one's cap as a sign of respect: ". . . three great ones of the city . . . Oft capp'd to him . . ." *Oth,* I, i, 8–10.

capable, *adj.* **1** able to understand or appreciate: ". . . who for the most part are capable/ of nothing but inexplicable dumb-shows and noise." *Ham,* III, ii, 11–12. **2** able to feel, hence receptive or responsive: "His form and cause conjoin'd,/ preaching to stones,/ Would make them capable." *Ham,* III, iv, 126–127. **3** legitimized; made a legal heir: "Loyal and natural boy, I'll work the means/ To make thee capable." *Lear,* II, i, 84–85. **4** capacious; wide or comprehensive: ". . . my bloody thoughts . . . Shall ne'er look back . . . Till that a capable and wide revenge/ Swallow them up." *Oth,* III, iii, 464–467. **5** visible; apparent: "The cicatrice and capable impressure/ Thy palm some moment keeps . . ." *As You,* III, v, 23–24. **6 capable of, a.** able to be influenced by: ". . . heart too capable/ Of every line and trick of his sweet favour." *All's W,* I, i, 93–94. **b.** vulnerable to: "You were advis'd his flesh was capable/ Of wounds and scars . . ." *2 Hen 4.*

capacity, *n.* **1** ability or sense: ". . . the behaviour of the young gentleman gives him out to/ be of good capacity and breeding . . ." *T Night,* III, iv, 186–187. **2 formal capacity,** normal intelligence: "Why,/ this is evident to any formal capacity . . ." *T Night,* II, v, 117–118. **3 to my capacity,** in my opinion: "Love . . . and tongue-tied simplicity/ In least speak most, to my capacity." *M N Dream,* V, i, 104–105.
—*adj.* **4** parson's misuse for "capable": "I will/ description the matter to you, if you be capacity of/ it." *Wives,* I, i, 195–197.

cap and knee, used esp. in the adverbial phrase, "with cap and knee," with doffing of caps and bending of knees [bowing or kneeling]: "The more and less [rich and poor] came in with cap and knee . . ." *1 Hen 4,* IV, iii, 68.

cap-à-pie or cap-a-pe, *adv.* head to foot: ". . . a figure like your father/ Armed at point exactly, cap-à-pie . . ." *Ham,* I, ii, 199–200.

caparison, *n.* **1** harness, esp. rich ornamental trappings: "What cares he now for . . . rich caparisons or trappings gay?" *Ven & Ad,* 285–286. **2** manner of dress; clothes; here, a suit of rags: "With die and/ drab I purchased this caparison . . ." *W Tale,* IV, iii, 26–27.
—*v.* **3** to fit with trappings: "Come, bustle, bustle! Caparison my horse." *Rich 3,* V, iii, 290.

Capels, *n.* Capulets: "The day is hot, the Capels are abroad . . ." *Rom & Jul,* III, i, 2.

caper, *v.* **1** to dance; here, challenge to a contest of dancing: ". . . he that will/ caper with me for a thousand marks . . ." *2 Hen 4,* I, ii, 191–192. **2 cut a caper,** to execute a leaping step in the galliard; wordplay by Sir Toby on caper (spice), ref. to a caper sauce for mutton: "Faith, I can cut a caper."/ "And I can cut the mutton to't." *T Night,* I, iii, 118–119. **3 fall a-capering,** begin to dance: ". . . if a throstle sing, he/ falls straight a-cap'ring . . ." *Merch,* I, ii, 57–58.

capering, *adj.* merry; playful (here used sarcastically): ". . . but I will catch him./ So tell the cap'ring boy, and get thee gone." *Edw 3,* IV, iv, 99–100.

Capet, *n.* See **Hugh Capet.**

capital, *adj.* **1** highest or most illustrious; supreme: "Holds from all soldiers chief majority/ And military title capital . . ." *1 Hen 4,* III, ii, 109–110. **2** mortal; killing: "I would buy you/

T'instruct me 'gainst a capital grief indeed . . ." *Kinsmen,* I, i, 122–123. **3** punishable by death: ". . . these feats,/ So crimeful and so capital in nature . . ." *Ham,* IV, vii, 6–7.

capite, *n.* See **in capite.**

capitulate, *v.* to make a pact or agreement: "Percy, Northumber-land . . . Capitulate against us and are up." *1 Hen 4,* III, ii, 118–120.

capocchia, *n.* knobbed stick [fr. Ital., "pinhead, simpleton"]; here, used in obscene wordplay: "Ah, poor capocchia! Has't not slept tonight? Would he not . . . let it sleep?" *Tr & Cr,* IV, ii, 31–33.

capon, *n.* **1** term of abuse for a dullard: "I thank him, he hath bid me to a calf's/ head and a capon . . ." *M Ado,* V, i, 152–153. **2** French slang for "love letter" or "message": "Boyet, you can carve;/ Break up [open] this capon." *Love's L,* IV, i, 56–57.

Cappadocia, *n.* country in Asia Minor: "Bocchus, the king of Libya, Archelaus/ Of Cappadocia . . ." *Ant & Cleo,* III, vi, 69–70.

capriccio, *n.* [Ital.] caprice: "Will this capriccio hold in thee, art sure?" *All's W,* II, iii, 289.

captain, *adj.* principal or finest: "Like stones of worth . . . Or captain jewels in the carcanet." *Sonn 52,* 7–8.

captain ill, *n.* the dominance of evil; here, having made good its slave: "And captive good attending captain ill . . ." *Sonn 66,* 12.

captain of compliments, *n.* master of the rules of procedure; here, Tybalt as a master in the art of fencing: ". . . he's the courageous/ captain of compliments: he fights as you sing prick-song . . ." *Rom & Jul,* II, iv, 19–21.

captious, *adj.* receptive; also, capacious: "Yet in this captious and inteemable sieve/ I still pour in the waters of my love . . ." *All's W,* I, iii, 197–198.

captivate, *v.* **1** to take captive; subdue or humble: "To triumph like an Amazonian trull/ Upon their woes whom Fortune captivates!" *3 Hen 6,* I, iv, 114–115.
—*past part.* **2** captured: ". . . slain our citizens,/ And sent our sons and husbands captivate." *1 Hen 6,* II, iii, 40–41.

captive, *adj.* **1** defeated; overcome; also, wretched: "When many times the captive Grecian falls . . ." *Tr & Cr,* V, iii, 40.
—*v.* **2** to capture; take captive: ". . . all our princes captiv'd by the hand/ Of that black name . . ." *Hen 5,* II, iv, 55–56.

captivity, *n.* servitude or slavery: "Given to captivity me and my hopes . . ." *Oth,* IV, ii, 52.

car, *n.* **1** chariot or horse-drawn cart: "Though our silence be drawn from us with cars,/ yet peace!" *T Night,* II, v, 64–65. **2** chariot of Apollo, the sun god: ". . . when the morning sun shall raise his car/ Above the border of this horizon . . ." *3 Hen 6,* IV, vii, 80–81.

caracts, *n. pl.* emblems; insignia: "In all his dressings, caracts, titles, forms . . ." *Meas,* V, i, 59.

carat, *n.* purity; hence, value: "Other, less fine in carat, is more precious . . ." *2 Hen 4,* IV, v, 161.

caraways, *n. pl.* caraway seed; also, cakes containing caraway seeds: ". . . we will eat a last year's pippin of mine own graffing,/ with a dish of caraways . . ." *2 Hen 4,* V, iii, 2–3.

carbonado, *n.* **1** piece of meat, fish, etc., slashed in several places before broiling: ". . . let him make a carbonado of me." *1 Hen 4,* V, iii, 58.
—*v.* **2** to slash as or in the manner of a carbonado: "Draw,/ you rogue, or I'll so carbonado your shanks . . ." *Lear,* II, ii, 37–38.

carbonadoed face, *n.* face on which syphilitic sores have been lanced and covered with patches of velvet: "A scar nobly got, or a noble scar, is a good liv'ry of/ honour . . ."/ "But it is your carbonado'd face." *All's W,* IV, v, 95–97.

carbuncle, *n.* deep-red gemstone, prob. the ruby, believed to shine in the dark; here, in wordplay with sense of "ulcerous sore, boil": ". . . her nose, all o'er-embellished/ with rubies, carbuncles, sapphires . . ." *Errors,* III, ii, 132–133.

carbuncled, *adj.* set with gems: "He has deserv'd it, were it carbuncled/ Like holy Phoebus' car." *Ant & Cleo,* IV, viii, 28–29.

carcanet, *n.* jeweled necklace: "Say that I linger'd with you at your shop/ To see the making of her carcanet . . ." *Errors,* III, i, 3–4.

card¹, *v.* to adulterate: "The skipping King . . . carded his state,/ Mingled his royalty with cap'ring fools . . ." *1 Hen 4,* III, ii, 60–63.

card², *n.* **1 by the card,** as precise as the card of the mariner's compass: "We must speak by the/ card or equivocation will undo us." *Ham,* V, i, 133–134. **2 card of ten,** relatively low card in a high-stakes game: "Yet I have fac'd it with a card of ten." *Shrew,* II, i, 398. **3 card or calendar,** model or essence; here, of gentlemanly behavior: ". . . speak feeling of him, he is the card/ calendar of gentry . . ." *Ham,* V, ii, 109–110.

cardecue, *n.* Anglicized pron. and spelling of French *quart d'écu,* quarter of a crown [silver piece]: "Sir, for a cardecue he will sell the fee-simple of his/ salvation . . ." *All's W,* IV, iii, 269–270.

carder, *n.* weaver's assistant, one who cleans and combs out the wool: "The spinsters, carders, fullers, weavers . . . compell'd by hunger . . ." *Hen 8,* I, ii, 33–34.

cardinally, *adv.* misuse for "carnally": ". . . if she had been a/ woman cardinally given . . ." *Meas,* II, i, 78–79.

Cardinal of York, *n.* Wolsey: "All this was order'd by the good discretion/ Of the right reverend Cardinal of York." *Hen 8,* I, i, 50–51.

cardmaker, *n.* maker of cards [combs] for preparing wool for spinning: ". . . by education a cardmaker, by/ profession a tinker?" *Shrew,* Ind., ii, 19–20.

carduus benedictus, [Latin] holy thistle, a medicinal herb; also, pun on "Benedick": "Get you some of this distilled *carduus benedictus,*/ and lay it to your heart . . ." *M Ado,* III, iv, 68–69.

care¹, *n.* **1** wish; inclination: "I have more care to stay than will to go." *Rom & Jul,* III, v, 23. **2** concern, regard, or consideration; here, one's chief concern: "Day, night . . . still my care hath been/ To have her match'd." *Rom & Jul,* III, v, 176–178. **3** anxiety: ". . . their first conception by mis-dread,/ Have after-nourishment and life by care . . ." *Per,* I, ii, 13–14. **4 make a care of,** be concerned about: ". . . at least if you make a care/ Of happy holding her." *W Tale,* IV, iv, 356–357.
—*v.* **5** to take particular care; make certain: ". . . what was first but fear what might be done,/ Grows elder now and cares it be not done." *Per,* I, ii, 15–16. **6 care for nothing,** to have no worries: "I warrant thou art a merry fellow, and car'st for/ nothing." *T Night,* III, i, 26–27. **7 care to be deceived,** care not whether I am deceived: "I do not greatly care to be deceiv'd/ That have no use for trusting." *Ant & Cleo,* V, ii, 14–15.

care², *n.* prob. misprint for "crare," a trading vessel: ". . . to show what coast thy sluggish care/ Might'st easil'est harbour in?" *Cymb,* IV, ii, 205–206.

career, *n.* **1** course; direction: ". . . these paper bullets of the brain awe a man from/ the career of his humour [inclination]?" *M Ado,* II, iii, 232–233. **2** charge at full speed, in or as if in a tournament: "Sir, I shall meet your wit in the career, and you/ charge it against me." *M Ado,* V, i, 134–135. **3 fierce career,** unchecked gallop: "When down the hill he holds his fierce career?" *Hen 5,* III, iii, 23. **4 humors and careers,** capricious behavior: "The king is a good king: but . . . he passes some humours and careers." *Hen 5,* II, i, 125–126. **5 passed**

the careers, got wildly out of hand: "And being fap, sir, was, as they say, cashiered;/ and so conclusions passed the careers." *Wives,* I, i, 160–161.

careful, *adj.* **1** worried; troubled: "O, full of careful business are his looks!" *Rich 2,* II, ii, 75. **2** full of concern or consideration; solicitous: "Well, well, thou hast a careful father, child . . ." *Rom & Jul,* III, v, 107. **3** prudent: ". . . feed his humour kindly as we may,/ Till time beget some careful remedy." *T Andr,* IV, iii, 29–30. **4** industrious; diligent: ". . . as fairly as to/ say a careful man and a great scholar." *T Night,* IV, ii, 9–10. **5** strict: ". . . that have more time/ For vainer hours, and tutors not so careful." *Temp,* I, ii, 173–174.

careless, *adj.* free from worry or care: "Sleep she as sound as careless infancy . . ." *Wives,* V, v, 53.

carelessly, *adv.* in a carefree manner; casually: ". . . many young gentlemen flock to him every day, and fleet the time carelessly . . ." *As You,* I, i, 117–118.

caret, *v.* **1** [Latin] it is lacking: ". . . but, for the elegancy, facility, and/ golden cadence of poesy, *caret.*" *Love's L,* IV, ii, 117–118. **2** wordplay on preceding and "carrot" [penis]: "Remember, William: focative [vocative] is *caret.*" *Wives,* IV, i, 45.

care-tuned, *adj.* tuned to news of grief and misfortune: "More health and happiness betide my liege/ Than can my care-tun'd tongue deliver him." *Rich 2,* III, ii, 91–92.

carl, *n.* churl; peasant: ". . . the air on't/ Revengingly enfeebles me, or could this carl . . . have subdued me . . ." *Cymb,* V, ii, 3–5.

carlot, *n.* base fellow; churl: ". . . he hath bought the cottage and the bounds/ That old carlot once was master of." *As You,* III, v, 107–108.

carman, *n.* carter: ". . . sung those tunes/ to the overscutched housewives that he heard the/ carmen whistle . . ." *2 Hen 4,* III, ii, 310–312.

Carnarvonshire, *n.* barren county in Wales: "I myself/ Would for Carnarvonshire, although there long'd/ No more to th'crown but that . . ." *Hen 8,* II, iii, 47–49.

carnation, *adj.* flesh-colored; pink: ". . . how much carnation ribbon may a/ man buy for a remuneration?" *Love's L,* III, i, 140–141.

carouse, *n.* **1** toast or health [lit., a filled drinking cup drunk off]: "And quaff carouses to our mistress' health . . ." *Shrew,* I, ii, 275.
—*v.* **2** to drink a toast: "The Queen carouses to thy fortune, Hamlet." *Ham,* V, ii, 292.

carp, *n.* wordplay on "scavenger fish" and "one who complains": "Pray you sir, use the carp as you may . . ." *All's W,* V, ii, 22.

carper, *n.* cynic; fault-finder: "Shame not these woods/ By putting on the cunning of a carper . . ." *Timon,* IV, iii, 210–211.

carpet, *n.* **1** [often pl.] fine carpets, used esp. as table coverings: "Be the . . . carpets laid, and everything in order?" *Shrew,* IV, i, 44–45. **2 on carpet consideration,** (of a knighthood) given at court rather than on the battlefield; here, poss. one that has been bought: "He is knight, dubbed with unhatched rapier,/ and on carpet consideration . . ." *T Night,* III, iv, 237–238.

carpet-monger, *n.* prob. ref. to those knights whose experience was more at home, esp. in the bedroom, than on the battlefield: ". . . a whole bookful of these quondam carpet-mongers . . ." *M Ado,* V, ii, 31.

carrack, *n.* **1** large galleon, built as a merchant ship but convertible to a warship: ". . . Spain, who sent/ whole armadoes of carracks to be ballast at her/ nose." *Errors,* III, ii, 134–136. **2** such a vessel prized as a treasure ship: ". . . he to-night hath boarded a land carrack:/ If it prove lawful prize, he's made for ever." *Oth,* I, ii, 50–51.

carriage, *n.* **1** behavior; conduct: ". . . his right noble mind, illustrious virtue,/ And honourable carriage . . ." *Timon,* III, ii, 83. **2** bearing or demeanor: "Teach sin the carriage of a holy saint . . ." *Errors,* III, ii, 14. **3** wordplay on senses of "good bearing," "accepting a lover's weight," and "bearing a child": "This is the hag . . ./ That presses them and learns them first to bear,/ Making them women of good carriage." *Rom & Jul,* I, iv, 92–94. **4** intent; purport: ". . . by the same cov'nant/ And carriage of the article design'd,/ His fell to Hamlet." *Ham,* I, i, 96–98. **5** affected word for "hanger," a strap for attaching a sword to the girdle: "Three of the/ carriages, in faith, are very dear to fancy . . ." *Ham,* V, ii, 147–148. **6** wagon or cart for transporting army baggage: ". . . many carriages he hath dispatch'd/ To the sea-side . . ." *K John,* V, vii, 90–91. **7** wheeled support for a cannon: "Sometimes her levell'd eyes their carriage ride,/ As they did battery to the spheres intend . . ." *Lover's Comp,* 22–23. **8** removal or disappearance: "Lest being miss'd, I be suspected of/ Your carriage from the court." *Cymb,* III, iv, 188–189.

carried, *v.* carried out; managed or realized: ". . . this well carried shall on her behalf/ Change slander to remorse . . ." *M Ado,* IV, i, 210–211.

carrier, *n.* person who delivers letters and messages; go-between: "Why, villain, art not thou the carrier?"/ "Ay, of my pigeons, sir . . ." *T Andr,* IV, iii, 85–86.

carrion, *n.* **1** person as weak and inactive as a corpse: "Old feeble carrions, and such suffering souls/ That welcome wrongs . . ." *J Caes,* II, i, 130–131. **2** seducer; lecher: "Out upon it old carrion! rebels it at these years?" *Merch,* III, i, 32. **3 carrion Death,** skeleton, esp. a death's head; skull and crossbones: "A carrion Death, within whose empty eye/ There is a written scroll . . ." *Merch,* II, vii, 63–64. **4 island carrions,** English soldiers likened to walking corpses: "Yon island carrions, desperate of their bones . . ." *Hen 5,* IV, ii, 39.

carry, *v.* **1** to convey: "Go carry Sir John Falstaff to the Fleet . . ." *2 Hen 4,* V, v, 91. **2** to put up with; endure: "I will carry no crotchets. I'll re you, I'll/ fa you. Do you note me?" *Rom & Jul,* IV, v, 116–117. **3** to conduct; here, in wordplay with "bear, support": "How does he carry himself?"/ "I have told your lordship already: the stocks/ carry him." *All's W,* IV, iii, 101–103. **4** to continue to wield: ". . . if our father carry authority with such/ disposition as he bears . . ." *Lear,* I, i, 303–304. **5** to manage: "Why, all this business/ Our reverend Cardinal carried." *Hen 8,* I, i, 99–100. **6** to conquer: "Lays down his wanton siege . . . Resolv'd to carry her . . ." *All's W,* III, vii, 18–19. **7 carry her,** convince her of: ". . . if you can carry her your desires towards/ her." *Wives,* I, i, 211–212. **8 carry it,** [to] keep things going; win the day; prevail: ". . . we may carry it thus for our pleasure, and his penance . . ." *T Night,* III, iv, 138–139. **9 carry it away,** to triumph: "Do the boys carry it away?" *Ham,* II, ii, 357.

carry-tale, *n.* tale-bearer; tattletail or gossiper: "Some carry-tale, some please-man, some slight zany . . ." *Love's L,* V, ii, 463.

cart, *n.* **1** vehicle that carried prisoners to their execution: "If I become not a cart as well as/ another man, a plague on my bringing up!" *1 Hen 4,* II, iv, 490–491. **2 to cart,** loading a cart or carts with the harvest, prob. with added sense of def. 3: "They that reap must sheaf and bind,/ Then to cart with Rosalind." *As You,* III, ii, 105–106.
—*v.* **3** to draw (an offender) through the streets in an open cart as punishment; prostitutes were sometimes tied to the back of the cart and beaten along the way: ". . . to court her at your pleasure."/ "To cart her rather. She's too rough for me." *Shrew,* I, i, 54–55.

carter, *n.* driver of a cart: "Let me be no assistant for a state,/ But keep a farm and carters." *Ham,* II, ii, 166–167.

Carthage queen, *n.* Dido, who fell in love with Aeneas and committed suicide by self-immolation when he abandoned

her: ". . . by that fire which burn'd the Carthage queen/ When the false Trojan under sail was seen . . ." *M N Dream,* I, i, 173–174.

carve, *v.* **1** to plan or design: ". . . now will he lie ten nights awake carving the fashion/ of a new doublet." *M Ado,* II, iii, 17–18. **2** to choose: "He may not, as unvalu'd persons do,/ Carve for himself . . ." *Ham,* I, iii, 19–20. **3** to court with the utmost skill and courtesy: "A' can carve too, and lisp: why, this is he/ That kiss'd his hand away in courtesy . . ." *Love's L,* V, ii, 323–324. **4** to display good manners: ". . . she discourses,/ she carves, she gives the leer of invitation . . ." *Wives,* I, iii, 41–42.

case[1], *n.* **1** outer garment: "I have cases of buckram for the/ nonce . . ." *1 Hen 4,* I, ii, 174–175. **2** costume or disguise: "O, they were all in lamentable cases!" *Love's L,* V, ii, 273. **3** mask: "Give me a case to put my visage in:/ A visor for a visor." *Rom & Jul,* I, iv, 29–30. **4** skin; hide of an animal, esp. a fox: "O thou dissembling cub! What wilt thou be/ When time hath sow'd a grizzle on thy case?" *T Night,* V, i, 162–163. **5** body; here, dead body: "This case of that huge spirit now is cold." *Ant & Cleo,* IV, xv, 89. **6** container; here, wordplay with "matter" and contrast between "container" and "contents": "I do not know the matter; he is 'rested [arrested] on the case." *Errors,* IV, ii, 42. **7** external appearance: ". . . eternal love, in love's fresh case,/ Weighs not the dust and injury of age . . ." *Sonn 108,* 9–10. **8** eye socket: "Read."/ "What! with the case of eyes?" *Lear,* IV, vi, 144–145. **9** wordplay on Latin or grammatical case and female pudenda: "Vengeance of Ginny's case; fie on her! Never/ name her, child, if she be a whore." *Wives,* IV, i, 53–54.
—*v.* **10** to conceal; shut up: "If thou wouldst not entomb thyself alive/ And case thy reputation in thy tent . . ." *Tr & Cr,* III, iii, 186–187. **11** to put a mask on: "Case ye, case ye, on with your vizards . . ." *1 Hen 4,* II, ii, 51. **12** to skin (an animal); here, to strip of disguise: "We'll make you some sport with the fox ere/ we case him . . ." *All's W,* III, vi, 98–99.

case[2], *n.* **1** state or condition; here, wordplay with "costume" sense: "O, they were all in lamentable cases!/ The king was weeping-ripe for a good word." *Love's L,* V, ii, 273. **2** set: ". . . for mine own part, I have not a case of lives . . ." *Hen 5,* III, ii, 4. **3** one's rank or circumstances: "Accomplish'd in himself, not in his case . . ." *Lover's Comp,* 116. **4 case of favor,** matter concerning beauty: "For idiots in this case of favour, would/ Be wisely definite . . ." *Cymb,* I, vii, 42–43. **5 if case,** if it should happen that; in case: "If case some one of you would fly from us . . ." *3 Hen 6,* V, iv, 34. **6 in case to,** in condition to: "I am in case to/ justle [wrestle] a constable." *Temp,* III, ii, 24–25. **7 in good case,** in comfortable circumstances; well-off: "She hath been in good case, and the truth is, poverty/ hath distracted her." *2 Hen 4,* II, i, 103–105.

cased, *adj.* prob. "caged": ". . . thou mayst hold a serpent by the tongue,/ A cased lion by the mortal [deadly] paw . . ." *K John,* III, i, 184–185.

cashier, *v.* to dismiss: "Discard, bully Hercules, cashier: let them wag . . ." *Wives,* I, iii, 6.

cashiered, *adj.* dismissed; sacked: "How? What does his cashier'd worship mutter?" *Timon,* III, iv, 60.

casing, *adj.* enclosing; enveloping: "As broad and general as the casing air . . ." *Mac,* III, iv, 22.

cask, *n.* casket for money, jewels, etc.: "A jewel, lock'd into the woefull'st cask/ That ever did contain a thing of worth." *2 Hen 6,* III, ii, 408–409.

casket, *n.* **1** small chest for money, jewels, etc.: "Here catch this casket, it is worth the pains." *Merch,* II, vi, 33. **2** the beautiful daughter of Antiochus: "I lov'd you, and could still,/ Were not this glorious casket stor'd with ill." *Per,* I, i, 77–78.
—*v.* **3** to store in a small chest: "I have writ my letters, casketed my treasure . . ." *All's W,* II, v, 23.

casque, *n.* **1** helmet: "Fall like amazing thunder on the casque/ Of thy adverse pernicious enemy!" *Rich 2,* I, iii, 80–81. **2 from the casque to the cushion,** from the helmet [battlefield] to a seat in the senate: ". . . not moving/ From th'casque to th'cushion, but commanding [ordering] peace . . ." *Cor,* IV, vii, 42–43.

Cassibelan, *n.* Cymbeline's uncle: ". . . did join his honour/ Against the Romans with Cassibelan . . ." *Cymb,* I, i, 29–30.

cassock, *n.* military cloak: ". . . dare not shake the snow from off their/ cassocks lest they shake themselves to pieces." *All's W,* IV, iii, 164–165.

cast, *adj.* **1** cast off; discarded: "He hath bought a pair of cast lips of Diana." *As You,* III, iv, 14. **2 cast in his mood,** dismissed in a moment of [Othello's] anger: ". . . you are/ but now cast in his mood . . ." *Oth,* II, iii, 264–265.
—*n.* **3** throw of the dice: "To set the exact wealth of all our states/ All at one cast?" *1 Hen 4,* IV, i, 46–47.
—*v.* **4** to add up; reckon: "Here is now the smith's note for shoeing/ and plough-irons."/ "Let it be cast and paid." *2 Hen 4,* V, i, 16–18. **5** (in wrestling) to throw one's opponent off or down; here, also wordplay with "to vomit": ". . . though he took up my legs sometime, yet I made a shift to cast him." *Mac,* II, iii, 41–42. **6** to examine or analyze: "If thou couldst, Doctor, cast/ The water [urine] of my land, find her disease . . ." *Mac,* V, iii, 50–51. **7** (of the sea) to cast up on shore: "We all were sea-swallow'd, though some cast again . . ." *Temp,* II, i, 246. **8** to dismiss [lit., discard]: "I do know the state . . . Cannot with

safety cast him . . ." *Oth,* I, i, 147–149. **9 cast accompt,** See **accompt** (def. 6). **10 cast away,** to doom; destroy: ". . . do not cast/ away an honest man for a villain's accusation." *2 Hen 6,* I, iii, 204–205. **11 cast by,** to throw aside: ". . . thrice disturb'd the quiet of our streets/ And made Verona's ancient citizens/ Cast by their grave-beseeming ornaments . . ." *Rom & Jul,* I, i, 89–91. **12 cast th'event,** to calculate the chances for success: "You cast th'event of war, my noble lord,/ And summ'd the account of chance . . ." *2 Hen 4,* I, i, 166–167. **13 cast the gorge,** See **gorge** (def. 2). **14 cast the water,** See **water** (def. 4). **15 cast up,** to vomit: ". . . till he cast bells, steeple, church, and parish up/ again." *Per,* II, i, 42–43.
—*past part.* **16** cast off or lost: "Your colt's tooth is not cast yet?" *Hen 8,* I, iii, 48. **17** dismissed: ". . . he made him/ Brave me upon the watch, whereon it came/ That I was cast . . ." *Oth,* V, ii, 327–328. **18** thrown up on shore: "We all were sea-swallow'd, though some cast again . . ." *Temp,* II, i, 246. **19** vomited; also, dug out: "His filth within being cast, he would appear/ A pond as deep as hell." *Meas,* III, i, 92–93. **20 cast away,** shipwrecked: "Antonio (as I/ heard in Genoa) . . . hath an argosy cast away coming from Tripolis." *Merch,* III, i, 89–92.

Castalian-king-Urinal, *n.* Castalian (prob. misuse for Castilian) is ref. to the hated Spanish king [Philip II of Castile] during the threat of the Spanish Armada; perh. [you are] the Spanish king of chamber pots: "Thou art a Castalian-king-Urinal: Hector of/ Greece, my boy!" *Wives,* II, iii, 31–32.

casted slough, *n.* ref. to the snake's shedding its skin: ". . . and newly move/ With casted slough and fresh legerity." *Hen 5,* IV, i, 22–23.

Castiliano vulgo, *n.* prob. an order to Maria to fetch wine, poss. a common Spanish wine: "What, wench! *Castiliano/ vulgo:* for here comes Sir Andrew Agueface." *T Night,* I, iii, 42–43.

castle, *n.* something providing more than the usual protection for the head: ". . . and Diomed,/ Stand fast, and wear a castle on thy head!" *Tr & Cr,* V, ii, 185–186.

castle-ditch, *n.* poss. the moat surrounding Windsor Castle: "Come, come, we'll couch i' th' castle-ditch till we/ see the light of our fairies." *Wives,* V, ii, 1–2.

casual, *adj.* **1** appar. by chance; unpremeditated: "Of accidental judgments, casual slaughters,/ Of deaths put on by cunning and forc'd cause . . ." *Ham,* V, ii, 387–388. **2** vulnerable to mischance: ". . . so your brace of unprizable/ estimations, the one is but frail and the other casual . . ." *Cymb,* I, v, 87–88.

casualty, *n.* **1** occurrence; happening: "And to the world and awkward casualties/ Bound me in servitude." *Per,* V, i, 93–94.

2 mishap or misfortune: "Even in the force and road of casualty." *Merch,* II, ix, 30. 3 [often pl.] chance; accident: ". . . stripp'd her from his benediction, turn'd her/ To foreign casualties . . ." *Lear,* IV, iii, 44–45.

cat, *n.* 1 wildcat: "Be it ounce, or cat, or bear,/ Pard, or boar with bristled hair . . ." *M N Dream,* II, ii, 29–30. 2 civet cat: "Thou ow'st the worm no silk . . . the cat no perfume." *Lear,* III, iv, 106–107. 3 allusion to the proverb, "Liquor will make a cat speak": "Come on your ways; open your mouth; here is that/ which will give language to you, 'cat . . ." *Temp,* II, ii, 84–85. 4 **cat i' th' adage,** ref. to prov. cat that would eat a fish but wouldn't get her feet wet: "Letting 'I dare not' wait upon 'I would,'/ Like the poor cat i' th' adage?" *Mac,* I, vii, 44–45. 5 **tear a cat,** to rave and rant; engage in bombast: "I could/ play Ercles rarely, or a part to tear a cat in, to make/ all split." *M N Dream,* I, ii, 24–26.

Cataian, *n.* var. of "Cathayan," one from Cathay; that is, a Chinaman; here, appar., a person who cannot be trusted: "My lady's a Cataian, we are politicians . . ." *T Night,* II, iii, 76.

catalog, *n.* general order of things: "Ay, in the catalogue ye go for men . . ." *Mac,* III, i, 91.

cat-a-mountain, *adj.* like a wildcat: ". . . your cat-a-mountain looks, your red-lattice/ phrases . . ." *Wives,* II, ii, 25–26.

cataplasm, *n.* plaster, esp. of medicinal herbs: ". . . no cataplasm so rare,/ Collected from all simples that have virtue . . ." *Ham,* IV, vii, 142–143.

cataract, *n.* [usually pl.] floodgates of heaven: "You cataracts and hurricanoes, spout/ Till you have drench'd our steeples, drown'd the cocks!" *Lear,* III, ii, 2–3.

catastrophe, *n.* 1 slang term for the backside: "Away, you scullion! . . . I'll tickle your catastrophe!" *2 Hen 4,* II, i, 58–59. 2 (in a play) the event that brings on the climax; outcome; conclusion: "The catastrophe is a nuptial: on/ whose side? the king's . . ." *Love's L,* IV, i, 77–78.

catch, *n.* 1 musical round, usually with bawdy words: "Welcome, ass. Now let's have a catch." *T Night,* II, iii, 18. 2 **troll the catch,** to sing a round: "Let us be jocund: will you troll the catch/ You taught me but while-ere?" *Temp,* III, ii, 115–116. —*v.* 3 to catch up to; overtake: "And sail so expeditious, that shall catch/ Your royal fleet far off." *Temp,* V, i, 315–316. 4 to grab: "And have is have, however men do catch." *K John,* I, i, 173. 5 to seize the mind: "Thy wit is as quick as the greyhound's mouth, it catches." *M Ado,* V, ii, 11–12. 6 **catch a clap,** See **clap** (def. 16). 7 **catch the air,** to gasp for breath: ". . . a grievous sickness took him,/ That makes him gasp, and stare, and catch the air . . ." *2 Hen 6,* III, ii, 369–370.

catched, *past part.* 1 stolen; snatched: "And cruel Death hath catch'd it from my sight." *Rom & Jul,* IV, v, 48. 2 caught out: "My fear hath catch'd your fondness . . ." *All's W,* I, iii, 165.

catch the nearest way, See **way** (def. 10).

cate-log, *n.* wordplay on "catalog," list, and poss. "Kate," the name of Launce's lady friend: "Here/ is the cate-log of her conditions." *Two Gent,* III, i, 271–272.

cater-cousin, *n.* close friend: "His master and he . . . are scarce cater-cousins . . ." *Merch,* II, ii, 123–124.

caterpillar, *n.* person who preys upon society; leech; parasite: "All scholars, lawyers, courtiers, gentlemen,/ They call false caterpillars, and intend their death." *2 Hen 6,* IV, iv, 35–36.

cates, *n. pl.* delicacies: "I had rather live/ . . . in a windmill, far,/ Than feed on cates and have him talk to me . . ." *1 Hen 4,* III, i, 155–157.

catling, *n.* name of a lute string; here used whimsically as a person's surname: "Why 'music with her silver sound'?/ What say you, Simon Catling?" *Rom & Jul,* IV, v, 126–127.

Cato, *n.* 1 Marcus ("the Younger"), Roman statesman and Brutus's father-in-law; fought with Pompey and committed suicide when Caesar vanquished them: "I did blame Cato for the death/ Which he did give himself . . ." *J Caes,* V, i, 102–103. 2 his son, Brutus's brother-in-law: "I am the son of Marcus Cato, ho!/ A foe to tyrants, and my country's friend." *J Caes,* V, iv, 4–5.

cat o' mountain, *n.* wildcat or, sometimes, leopard: ". . . and more pinch-spotted make them/ Than pard or cat o' mountain." *Temp,* IV, i, 260–261.

Caucasus, *n.* for stealing the sacred fire from heaven, Zeus ordered Prometheus chained to a peak in the Caucasus Mountains: ". . . faster bound to Aaron's charming eyes/ Than is Prometheus tied to Caucasus." *T Andr,* II, i, 16–17.

caudle, *n.* 1 warm, thin gruel, sometimes mixed with wine, given esp. to invalids or the elderly: ". . . where lies thy pain?/ And where my liege's? all about the breast:/ A caudle, ho!" *Love's L,* IV, iii, 169–171. —*v.* 2 to serve with a caudle: "Will the cold brook/ . . . caudle thy morning taste . . ." *Timon,* IV, iii, 227–228.

cause, *n.* 1 problem; worry: "And 'twere my cause, I should go hang myself." *T Andr,* II, iv, 9. 2 subject matter; business: "But of that to-morrow,/ When, therewithal, we shall have cause of State . . ." *Mac,* III, i, 32–33. 3 obsession or derangement: "He cannot buckle his distemper'd cause/ Within the belt of rule." *Mac,* V, ii, 15–16. 4 offense or charge: "I pardon that

man's life. What was thy cause?" *Lear,* IV, vi, 112. **5** disputed matter; contest; debate: "O madness of discourse,/ That cause sets up with and against itself!" *Tr & Cr,* V, ii, 141–142. **6** occasion: ". . . his gracious promise, which you might/ As cause had call'd you up, have held him to . . ." *Cor,* II, iii, 191–192. **7 all cause unborn,** with no justification: "Th'accusation/ Which they have often made against the senate,/ All cause unborn . . ." *Cor,* III, i, 126–128. **8 as cause will be obeyed,** as necessity may require: ". . . the rest/ Shall bear the business in some other fight,/ As cause will be obey'd." *Cor,* I, vi, 81–82. **9 cause you come,** the cause you come here to defend: "As well appeareth by the cause you come,/ Namely, to appeal each other of high treason . . ." *Rich 2,* I, i, 26–27. **10 give my cause,** (in law) submit my case: "I give my cause, who best can justify." *Per,* I, Chor., 42. **11 have no other cause,** have no reason to be otherwise: "They can be meek that have no other cause." *Errors,* II, i, 33. **12 heavy causes,** serious grievances: ". . . with others, whom, I fear,/ Most just and heavy causes make oppose." *Lear,* V, i, 27.
—*v.* **13** to give cause, as for an action: ". . . the Jew having/ done me wrong, doth cause me as my father . . . shall frutify unto you." *Merch,* II, ii, 125–127.

causeless, *adj.* that cannot be explained; inexplicable: ". . . we have our philosophical/ persons to make modern and familiar, things/ supernatural and causeless." *All's W,* II, iii, 1–3.

cautel, *n.* deceitful action: "And now no soil nor cautel doth besmirch/ The virtue of his will . . ." *Ham,* I, iii, 15–16.

cautelous, *adj.* deceitful: "Swear priests and cowards, and men cautelous,/ Old feeble carrions, and such suffering souls . . ." *J Caes,* II, i, 129–130.

cauterizing, *n.* cauterizing agent: ". . . each false [word]/ Be as a cauterizing to the root o' th' tongue . . ." *Timon,* V, i, 131–132.

Cavalery, *n.* rustic rendering of "cavaliero" [cavalero, a dashing military gentleman]: "Nothing, good mounsieur, but to help Cavalery/ Cobweb to scratch." *M N Dream,* IV, i, 22–23.

cavaliero, *n.* knight on horseback; gallant; here, used humorously [fr. Spanish]: "Thou'rt a gentleman.—/ Cavaliero Justice, I say!" *Wives,* II, i, 185–186.

cavalleria, *n.* body of cavaliers or knights; here, a reference to the clientele: ". . . she'll disfurnish us of/ all our cavalleria, and make our swearers priests." *Per,* IV, vi, 11–12.

cave, *v.* to live in a cave: "It may be heard at court that such as we/ Cave here, hunt here . . ." *Cymb,* IV, ii, 137–138.

cave-keeper, *n.* one who lives in caves: "I thought I was a cave-keeper,/ And cook to honest creatures." *Cymb,* IV, ii, 298–299.

cave-keeping, *adj.* living or hiding in caves: "Cave-keeping evils that obscurely sleep . . ." *Luc,* 1250.

Caveto, *v.* beware: "Therefore, Caveto be thy counsellor." *Hen 5,* II, iii, 54.

cavil, *n.* **1** trivial or superficial objection; quibble: "That's but a cavil. He is old, I young." *Shrew,* II, i, 383.
—*v.* **2** to quarrel or quibble: "In vain I cavil with mine infamy . . ." *Luc,* 1025.

caw, *v.* to call, as a chough [jackdaw]: "Or russet-pated choughs . . . Rising and cawing at the gun's report . . ." *M N Dream,* III, ii, 21–22.

cease, *v.* to stop or silence: "Importune him for my moneys;/ be not ceas'd . . ." *Timon,* II, i, 16.

Cedius, *n.* brother of Epistrophus; both iden. as Greek "kings" and both slain by Hector: ". . . stands colossus-wise . . . Upon the pashed corses of the kings/ Epistrophus and Cedius." *Tr & Cr,* V, v, 9–11.

ceinture, *n.* belt or sash: "Now happy he whose cloak and ceinture can/ Hold out this tempest." *K John,* IV, iii, 155–156.

celestial sign, *n.* sign of the zodiac: "There stay, until the twelve celestial signs/ Have brought about the annual reckoning." *Love's L,* V, ii, 789–790.

cellarage, *n.* underground room; cellar: ". . . you hear this fellow in the cellarage./ Consent to swear." *Ham,* I, v, 159–160.

cement, *n.* **in their cement,** to ashes or cinders: "Your temples burned in their cement . . ." *Cor,* IV, vi, 86.

censer, *n.* covered pan in which incense or perfume was burned: ". . . you thin man in a censer, I will/ have you as soundly swinged for this . . ." *2 Hen 4,* V, iv, 19–20.

censure, *v.* **1** to appraise or judge: "I hear how I am censured: they/ say I will bear myself proudly . . ." *M Ado,* II, iii, 216–217. **2** to pass judgment: ". . . 'tis a passing shame/ That I . . . Should censure thus on lovely gentlemen." *Two Gent,* I, ii, 17–19. **3** to pass sentence on; here, condemn: "Has censur'd him already;/ And, as I hear, the Provost hath a warrant/ For's execution." *Meas,* I, iv, 72–74. **4 censure well,** to approve: "Say you consent and censure well the deed . . ." *2 Hen 6,* III, i, 275.
—*n.* **5** judgment; opinion: ". . . the censure of the which one must in your/ allowance o'erweigh a whole theatre of others."

Ham, III, ii, 27–28. **6** punishment: "... to you, lord governor,/ Remains the censure of this hellish villain ..." *Oth,* V, ii, 369. **7 court'sy at the censure,** bow to the rebuker: "... what's worse,/ Must court'sy at the censure." *Cymb,* III, iii, 54–55. **8 general censure,** popular opinion: "His virtues else ... Shall in the general censure take corruption ..." *Ham,* I, iv, 33–35.

Centaurs, *n. pl.* race of creatures half man and half horse; fierce battle with the Lapithae when the Centaurs, guests at a marriage feast, attempted to abduct the women: "... make this banket ... More stern and bloody than the Centaurs' feast." *T Andr,* V, ii, 202–203.

center, *n.* the very core of the earth: "As iron to adamant, as earth to th'centre ..." *Tr & Cr,* III, ii, 177.

century, *n.* detachment of 100 soldiers [in ancient Rome under the command of a centurion]: "A century send forth;/ Search every acre in the high-grown field ..." *Lear,* IV, iv, 6–7.

Cerberus, *n.* (in Greek myth.) **1** three-headed dog guarding the entrance to Hades: "Nay, rather damn them with/ King Cerberus, and let the welkin roar!" *2 Hen 4,* II, iv, 164–165. **2** same as guardian of Proserpina, queen of Hades; jealous of her beauty, he attacked all her would-be rescuers: "... as full of envy at his greatness/ as Cerberus is at Proserpina/s beauty—" *Tr & Cr,* II, i, 34–36.

cerecloth, *n.* shroud of waxed cloth: "... it were too gross/ To rib her cerecloth in the obscure grave ..." *Merch,* II, vii, 50–51.

cerements, *n. pl.* burial garments; shroud: "Why thy canoniz'd bones, hearsed in death,/ Have burst their cerements ..." *Ham,* I, iv, 47–48.

ceremonious, *adj.* observing formalities precisely: "You are too senseless-obstinate, my lord,/ Too ceremonious and traditional." *Rich 3,* III, i, 44–45.

ceremony, *n.* **1** [usually pl.] decorations; ornaments: "Disrobe the images,/ If you do find them deck'd with ceremonies." *J Caes,* I, i, 64–65. **2** ritual: "Set on, and leave no ceremony out." *J Caes,* I, ii, 11. **3** politeness; civility: "When love begins to sicken and decay/ It useth an enforced ceremony." *J Caes,* IV, i, 20–21. **4** divination; also, an omen or portent thus disclosed: "... the main opinion he held once/ Of fantasy, of dreams, and ceremonies." *J Caes,* II, i, 196–197. **5** sacred token, symbol, or pledge: "... wanted the modesty/ To urge the thing held as a ceremony?" *Merch,* V, i, 205–206.

Ceres, *n.* Roman goddess of agriculture: "Approach, rich Ceres, her to entertain." *Temp,* IV, i, 75.

'cern, *n.* var. of **concern**: "Why,/ sir, what 'cerns it you [what concern is it of yours] if I wear pearl and gold?" *Shrew,* V, i, 66–67.

certain, *adj.* **1** firm or fixed: "... a lodg'd hate, and a certain loathing/ I bear Antonio ..." *Merch,* IV, i, 60–61. **2 certain o'er incertainty,** certain after a period of uncertainty: "When I was certain o'er incertainty,/ Crowning the present, doubting of the rest?" *Sonn 115,* 11–12.
—*adv.* **3** certainly: "This apoplexy will certain be his end." *2 Hen 4,* IV, iv, 130.

certes, *adv.* certainly: "And, certes, the text most infallibly concludes it." *Love's L,* IV, ii, 156.

certificate, *n.* royal document, esp. a license granted by the sovereign: "'... to the son of the King nearest his father,/ Harry Prince of Wales, greeting.'"/ "Why, this is a cer-tificate!" *2 Hen 4,* II, ii, 113–115.

certify, *v.* **1** to inform: "... foreign princes shall be certified ... King Henry's peers and chief nobility/ Destroy'd themselves, and lost the realm of France!" *1 Hen 6,* IV, i, 144–147. **2** to swear to; promise: "... Antonio certified the duke/ They were not with Bassanio in his ship." *Merch,* II, viii, 10–11.

cess[1], *n.* **out of (all) cess,** excessively; beyond reason: "... poor jade is wrung in the withers/ out of all cess." *1 Hen 4,* II, i, 6–7.

cess[2], *n.* cessation; decease: "The cess of majesty [death of a monarch]/ Dies not alone ..." *Ham,* III, iii, 15–16.

cesse, *v.* form of **cease**: "Or, ere they meet, in me, O nature, cesse!" *All's W,* V, iii, 72.

cestron, *n.* See **cistern.**

chafe, *v.* **1** to rage (at): "The troubled Tiber chafing with her shores ..." *J Caes,* I, ii, 100. **2** to make furious; gall or provoke: "I chafe you, if I tarry. Let me go." *Shrew,* II, i, 235.
—*n.* **3** fret; annoyance; fury: "How this Herculean Roman does become/ The carriage of his chafe [how becomingly he conducts himself in his rage]." *Ant & Cleo,* I, iii, 84–85.

chafed, *adj.* **1** irritated: "Rage like an angry boar chafed with sweat?" *Shrew,* I, ii, 201. **2** enraged: "... if you brave the Moor,/ The chafed boar ... The ocean swells not so as Aaron storms ..." *T Andr,* IV, ii, 137–139.

chaff and bran, *n.* worthless things (lit., seed coverings): "Asses, fools, dolts, chaff and bran ..." *Tr & Cr,* I, ii, 245.

chaffless, *adj.* faultless: "... the gods made you/ (Unlike all others) chaffless." *Cymb,* I, vii, 177–178.

chaffy, *adj.* worthless: "A very thief in love, a chaffy lord . . ." *Kinsmen,* III, i, 41.

chafing, *n.* anger; rage: "All swoln with chafing, down Adonis sits . . ." *Ven & Ad,* 325.

chain, *n.* **1** necklace; here, the carcanet mentioned earlier: ". . . get you home/ And fetch the chain, by this [time] I know 'tis made . . ." *Errors,* III, i, 114–115. **2 rub your chain with crumbs,** ref. to Malvolio's chain identifying him as steward of the household (and oblique ref. to his officiousness): "Go sir, rub your chain with/ crumbs [so as to polish it]." *T Night,* II, iii, 118–119. **3 shakes a chain,** behaves like a typical ghost: ". . . and shakes a chain/ In a most hideous and dreadful manner." *Wives,* IV, iv, 33–34.

chair, *n.* **1** throne: "His dukedom and his chair with me is left." *3 Hen 6,* II, i, 90. **2** seat of authority; here, a public official: "And power . . . Hath not a tomb so evident as a chair/ T'extol [justify] what it hath done." *Cor,* IV, vii, 51–53. **3 public chair,** pulpit or rostrum; here, the public platform in the Forum: ". . . let us hear Mark Antony."/ "Let him go up into the public chair." *J Caes,* III, ii, 64–65.

chair-days, *n.* time of retirement and rest: "And, in thy reverence and thy chair-days . . ." *2 Hen 6,* V, ii, 48.

chairs of order, *n.* (in St. George's Chapel, Windsor) stalls assigned to members of the Order of the Garter: "The several chairs of order look you scour/ With juice of balm and every precious flower . . ." *Wives,* V, v, 62–63.

chalice, *n.* drinking cup: "I'll have prepar'd him/ A chalice for the nonce . . ." *Ham,* IV, vii, 158–159.

chaliced, *adj.* cup-shaped: "His steeds to water at those springs/ On chalic'd flowers that lies . . ." *Cymb,* II, iii, 21–22.

chalk, *v.* to mark out: ". . . whose grace/ Chalks successors their way . . ." *Hen 8,* I, i, 59–60.

chalky cliffs, *n. pl.* the teeth: "I looked for the chalky cliffs, but I could find/ no whiteness in them." *Errors,* III, ii, 124–125.

challenge, *v.* **1** to claim; demand: "When she shall challenge this, you will reject her." *Love's L,* V, ii, 438. **2** to contend; also, lay claim: "Where nature doth with merit challenge." *Lear,* I, i, 53. **3** to accuse: ". . . when wert thou wont to walk alone,/ Dishonoured thus, and challenged of wrongs?" *T Andr,* I, i, 339–340. **4 challenge (someone) the field,** to challenge (a person) to a duel: ". . . to challenge him the field, and/ then to break promise with him . . ." *T Night,* II, iii, 126–127. —*n.* **5** claim: "Of benefit proceeding from our king/ And not of any challenge of desert . . ." *1 Hen 6,* V, iv, 152–153. **6** objec-

tion [legal term]: "You are mine enemy, and make my challenge/ You shall not be my judge." *Hen 8,* II, iv, 75–76.

Cham, *n.* title of Mongolian emperors; Khan: ". . . fetch you a hair off the great Cham's beard . . ." *M Ado,* II, i, 252.

chamber, *n.* **1** bedroom: "Cousins, I hope the days are near at hand,/ That chambers will be safe [for sleeping]." *Mac,* V, iv, 1–2. **2** the same in sexual wordplay: "My lord, come you again into my chamber./ You smile and mock me, as if I meant naughtily." *Tr & Cr,* IV, ii, 37. **3** [pl] small cannon; here, a salute: "Drum and trumpet; chambers discharg'd." [SD] *Hen 8,* I, iv, 48. **4 of our chamber,** a trusted servant: "Thaliard,/ You are of our chamber . . ." *Per,* I, ib, 153. —*v.* **5** to lodge: "Even in the best blood chamber'd in his bosom." *Rich 2,* I, i, 149.

chamber-counsels, *n.* personal confidences: "I have trusted thee, Camillo,/ With all the nearest things to my heart, as well/ My chamber-counsels . . ." *W Tale,* I, ii, 235–237.

chamberer, *n.* affected or dissolute courtier: ". . . have not those soft parts of conversation/ That chamberers have . . ." *Oth,* III, iii, 268–269.

chamberlain, *n.* manservant; valet: ". . . think'st/ That the bleak air, thy boisterous chamberlain,/ Will put thy shirt on warm?" *Timon,* IV, iii, 224–225.

chamber-lye, *n.* urine: ". . . your chamber-lye/ breeds fleas like a loach." *1 Hen 4,* II, i, 19–20.

chamblet, *n.* camlet, a fine cloth of silk and angora: "You i'th'chamblet, get up o'th'rail [get off the railing] . . ." *Hen 8,* V, iii, 88.

chameleon, *n.* **of the chameleon's dish,** air, on which the chameleon was believed to subsist: "Excellent, i'faith, of the chameleon's dish. I eat the/ air, promise-crammed." *Ham,* III, ii, 93–94.

champaign or champain, *n.* **1** expanse of the countryside: "Daylight and champaign discovers not more!" *T Night,* II, v, 160. **2** unwooded plain: "With shadowy forests and with champains rich'd . . ." *Lear,* I, i, 64.

Champaigne, *n.* town of Compiègne, in N France, near Rheims: "Guienne, Champaigne, Rheims, Rouen, Orleans,/ Paris, Guysors, Poictiers, are all quite lost." *1 Hen 6,* I, i, 60–61.

champaign plain, *n.* open, level area: "Their smoothness, like a goodly champaign plain,/ Lays open all the little worms that creep . . ." *Luc,* 1247.

champion, *n.* warrior; hero: "A stouter champion never handled sword." *1 Hen 6,* III, iv, 19.

chance, *n.* **1** one's lot or fortune: "Both stood like old acquaintance . . . Met far from home, wond'ring each other's chance." *Luc,* 1595–1596. **2** good fortune or luck: ". . . now it is my chance to find thee out,/ Must I behold thy timeless cruel death?" *1 Hen 6,* V, iv, 4–5. **3** risk: "Think what a chance thou changest on . . ." *Cymb,* I, vi, 68. **4** misfortune: ". . . made a push at chance and sufferance." *M Ado,* V, i, 38. **5** accident: "Not of this country, though my chance is now/ To use it for my time [serve my occasion]." *Meas,* III, ii, 211–212. **6** event; happening: "Ah what an unkind hour/ Is guilty of this lamentable chance?" *Rom & Jul,* V, iii, 145–146. **7 chance of anger,** See **anger. 8 wounded chance,** battered fortunes: "I'll yet follow/ The wounded chance of Antony, though my reason/ Sits in the wind against me." *Ant & Cleo,* III, x, 35–37.
—*v.* **9** to come to pass; succeed or occur: "A more unhappy lady,/ If this division chance, ne'er stood between . . ." *Ant & Cleo,* III, iv, 12–13. **10 how chance,** how does it happen?; how did it come about?: "How chance thou art return'd so soon?" *Errors,* I, ii, 42.

chanced, *past part.* that happened or took place: "Sad stories chanced in the times of old." *T Andr,* III, ii, 83.

chance's mocks, *n.* mockeries of fate: ". . . how chance's mocks/ And changes fill the cup of alteration . . ." *2 Hen 4,* III, i, 51–52.

change, *v.* **1** to exchange or match: ". . . the best part of an hour/ In changing hardiment with great Glendower." *1 Hen 4,* I, iii, 99–100. **2** to interchange: "Will you vouchsafe with me to change a word?" *Love's L,* V, ii, 238. **3** to alter or transform: "Dark-working sorcerers that change the mind . . ." *Errors,* I, ii, 99. **4** to switch affections: "Hortensio will be quit with thee by changing." *Shrew,* III, i, 90. **5** to switch loyalties: "Think what a chance [risk] thou changest on . . ." *Cymb,* I, vi, 68. **6 changed eyes,** exchanged [amorous] looks; fallen in love: "At the first sight/ They have chang'd eyes." *Temp,* I, ii, 443–444. **7 change our courtesies,** exchange my courtesies for yours: "Not so, but as we change our courtesies." *All's W,* III, ii, 97. **8 change the cod's head,** to make a foolish exchange that benefits neither side: "She that in wisdom never was so frail/ To change the cod's head for the salmon's tail . . ." [Partridge suggests that cod's head is penis, salmon's tail is pudenda] *Oth,* II, i, 154–155. **9 change you,** change your mood; be of good cheer: "Change you, madam:/ The worthy Leonatus is in safety . . ." *Cymb,* I, vii, 11–12.
—*n.* **10** change of mind or attitude: "In his own change, or by ill officers,/ Hath given me some worthy cause to wish/ Things done undone . . ." *J Caes,* IV, ii, 7–9. **11** change or reversal of fortune: "It is but change, Titinius; for Octavius/ Is overthrown by noble Brutus' power . . ." *J Caes,* V, iii, 51–52. **12** used in wordplay on changes of the moon and changes [figures] in a dance: "Then, in our measure do but vouchsafe one change." *Love's L,* V, ii, 209.

changeable taffeta, *n.* watered [opalescent] silk: "Now the melancholy god protect thee, and the/ tailor make thy doublet of changeable taffeta . . ." *T Night,* II, iv, 73–74.

changed, *adj.* transformed: "Thou changed and self-cover'd thing . . ." *Lear,* IV, ii, 62.

changeling, *n.* **1** turncoat: ". . . some fine colour that may please the eye/ Of fickle changelings . . ." *1 Hen 4,* V, i, 75–76. **2** child left by fairies, sometimes exchanged for another: "A lovely boy, stol'n from an Indian king—/ She never had so sweet a changeling . . ." *M N Dream,* II, i, 22–23.

change of lust, *n.* quest for sexual variety: ". . . urge his hateful luxury/ And bestial appetite in change of lust . . ." *Rich 3,* III, v, 79–80.

changing piece, *n.* inconstant wench: ". . . go, give that changing piece/ To him that flourish'd for her with his sword." *T Andr,* I, i, 309–310.

channel, *n.* gutter: "Cut me off the villain's/ head! Throw the quean in the channel!" *2 Hen 4,* II, i, 45–46.

chanson, *n.* ballad: "The first row [stanza] of the pious chanson will show you . . ." *Ham,* II, ii, 415.

chanticleer, *n.* cock; rooster: "Hark, hark! I hear/ The strain of strutting chanticleer . . ." *Temp,* I, ii, 387–388.

chantry, *n.* **1** religious house; here, the inhabitants offer up prayers for the dead: "I have built/ Two chantries, where the sad and solemn priests/ Sing still for Richard's soul." *Hen 5,* IV, ii, 306–308. **2** private chapel, usually attached to a great house: "Now go with me, and with this holy man,/ Into the chantry by . . ." *T Night,* IV, iii, 23–24.

chaos, *n.* shapeless mass: "To disproportion me in every part,/ Like to a chaos . . ." *3 Hen 6,* III, ii, 160–161.

chape, *n.* (on a scabbard) metal end to protect the tip of the sword: ". . . the practice [of war] in the chape of his/ dagger." *All's W,* IV, iii, 139–140.

chapel, *v.* to bury or entomb: ". . . give us the bones/ Of our dead kings, that we may chapel them . . ." *Kinsmen,* I, i, 49–50.

chapeless, *adj.* (of a scabbard) lacking a chape: ". . . an old rusty sword ta'en out of the/ town armoury, with a broken hilt, and chapeless . . ." *Shrew,* III, ii, 44–45.

chaplain, *n.* that which beautifies or perfects: "Whether is her beauty by her words divine,/ Or are her words sweet chaplains to her beauty?" *Edw 3,* II, i, 278–279.

chapless, *adj.* lacking a lower jaw: ". . . dead men's rattling bones,/ With reeky shanks and yellow chapless skulls." *Rom & Jul,* IV, i, 82–83.

chapman, *n.* merchant or trader; also, hawker or haggler: "Beauty is bought by judgment of the eye,/ Not utter'd by base sale of chapmen's tongues." *Love's L,* II, i, 15–16.

chaps¹, *n. pl.* cheeks or jaws; "chops" or "choppers": "I'll thrust my knife in your mouldy/ chaps and you play the saucy cuttle with me." *2 Hen 4,* II, iv, 126–127.

chaps², *n. pl.* wrinkles [lit., cracks in the skin]: "But if my frosty signs [white hair] and chaps of age . . . Cannot induce you to attend my words . . ." *T Andr,* V, iii, 77–79.

character, *v.* **1** to describe in writing: "And in their barks my thoughts I'll character . . ." *As You,* III, ii, 6. **2** to engrave or inscribe (here fig.): "And these few precepts in thy memory/ Look thou character." *Ham,* I, iii, 58–59.
—*n.* **3** handwriting: "Madam, this letter . . . Lay with you in your coffer . . . Know you the character?" *Per,* III, iv, 1–3. **4** [usually pl.] signs or characteristics: ". . . written down old with all the characters/ of age?" *2 Hen 4,* I, ii, 178–179. **5** [often pl.] letters or shapes: "But his neat cookery! he cut our roots in characters . . ." *Cymb,* IV, ii, 49. **6** [pl.] written records: "I say, without characters fame lives long." *Rich 3,* III, i, 81. **7** behavior: "There is a kind of character in thy life/ That . . . doth thy history/ Fully unfold." *Meas,* I, i, 27–29. **8 character too gross,** [her] condition too obvious; here, pregnancy: "The stealth of our most mutual entertainment/ With character too gross is writ on Juliet." *Meas,* I, ii, 143–144. **9 in the character,** true-to-life: ". . . if you report him truly."/ "I paint him in the character." *Cor,* V, iv, 26–27.

charactered, *adj.* written; inscribed: ". . . thy tables, are within my brain/ Full character'd with lasting memory . . ." *Sonn 122,* 1–2.

characterless, *adj.* with all written records vanished: "And mighty states characterless are grated/ To dusty nothing . . ." *Tr & Cr,* III, ii, 186–187.

charactery, *n.* **1** meaning: "All my engagements I will construe to thee,/ All the charactery of my sad brows." *J Caes,*

II, i, 307–308. **2** writing; script: "Fairies use flowers for their charactery." *Wives,* V, v, 74.

Charbon, *n.* prob. Anglicization of "chair bonne" [good flesh], a ref. to the Puritans, who ate meat and ignored fast days: ". . . young Charbon the puritan and old Poysam the/ papist . . ." *All's W,* I, iii, 50–51.

chare, *n.* [usually pl.] tasks; chores: ". . . the maid that milks,/ And does the meanest chares." *Ant & Cleo,* IV, xv, 74–75.

charge, *n.* **1** responsibility; duty or employment: "I'm weary of this charge, the gods can witness . . ." *Timon,* III, iv, 26. **2** burden; trouble: "With such a hell of pain and world of charge . . ." *Tr & Cr,* IV, i, 58. **3** instructions: "Well, give them their charge, neighbour Dogberry." *M Ado,* III, iii, 7. **4** command; order: "A good and virtuous nature may recoil,/ In an imperial charge." *Mac,* IV, iii, 19–20. **5** cost or expense: ". . . a little charge will trench him here . . ." *1 Hen 4,* III, i, 108. **6** assessment, as for one's share of an expense: ". . . for the most part such/ To whom as great a charge . . ." *Hen 8,* I, i, 76–77. **7** importance: "The letter was not nice but full of charge . . ." *Rom & Jul,* V, ii, 18. **8** spending money; cash: "For your expenses and sufficient charge,/ Among the people gather up a tenth." *1 Hen 6,* V, v, 92–93. **9 ask charge,** to require an expenditure of money: ". . . these great affairs do ask some charge . . ." *Rich 2,* II, i, 159. **10 be at charges for,** to buy: "I'll be at charges for a looking-glass . . ." *Rich 3,* I, ii, 260. **11 cut off some charge,** to avoid paying a stipulated amount; hence, to divert funds: "Fetch the will hither, and we shall determine/ How to cut off some charge in legacies." *J Caes,* IV, i, 8–9. **12 give the charge,** to be on the attack: ". . . proclaim no shame/ When the compulsive ardour gives the charge . . ." *Ham,* III, iv, 85–86. **13 have in charge,** to be commissioned: "I had in charge at my depart for France,/ As procurator to your Excellence,/ To marry Princess Margaret for your Grace . . ." *2 Hen 6,* I, i, 2–4. **14 in charge,** (esp. of lances) at the ready; fixed for charging: "Their armed staves in charge, their beavers down . . ." *2 Hen 4,* IV, i, 120. **15 on charge,** because I am ordered to: "And know you, lord,/ I'll nothing do on charge . . ." *Tr & Cr,* IV, iv, 130–131. **16 on your charge,** at your expense: "Have by some surgeon Shylock on your charge,/ To stop his wounds, lest he do bleed to death." *Merch,* IV, i, 253–254. **17 parcels of charge,** items of considerable worth: "I hope so, sir; for I have about me many parcels of/ charge." *W Tale,* IV, iv, 258–259. **18 upon this charge,** as you charge [the enemy]: ". . . upon this charge/ Cry, 'God for Harry, England, and Saint George!'" *Hen 5,* III, i, 33–34.
—*v.* **19** to offer a toast to: "Here, Pistol, I charge/ you with a cup of sack . . ." *2 Hen 4,* II, iv, 109–110. **20** to aim or level: "What are they/ That charge their breath [words] against us?" *Love's L,* V, ii, 87–88. **21** to entrust: ". . . I beat him,/ And charg'd him with a thousand marks in gold . . ." *Errors,* III, i, 7–8.

22 to burden: "What a sigh is there! The heart is sorely [heavily] charg'd." *Mac*, V, i, 51. **23** to entreat: ". . . here/ I charge your charity withal; leaving her/ The infant of your care . . ." *Per*, III, iii, 13–15. **24** to bedeck or festoon [his cuckold's horns]; here, in the manner of a sacrificial ox: ". . . this husband, which, you say, must charge his horns/ with garlands!" *Ant & Cleo*, I, ii, 4–5. **25** to attack; assail: "But being [until we are] charg'd, we will be still by land . . ." *Ant & Cleo*, IV, xi, 1. **26** to assault sexually: "Then to you, Mistress Dorothy! I will charge you." *2 Hen 4*, II, iv, 119. **27** to place under oath: "Let us go in,/ And charge us there . . . And we will answer all things faithfully." *Merch*, V, i, 297–299. **28 charge him home,** press home the charge against him: "In this point charge him home, that he affects/ Tyrannical power." *Cor*, III, iii, 1–2. **29 charge home,** attack the heart of the enemy's defenses: "Mend and charge home,/ Or . . . I'll leave the foe/ And make my wars on you." *Cor*, I, iv, 38–40.

chargeful, *adj.* costly; expensive: "The fineness of the gold, and chargeful fashion,/ Which doth amount to three odd ducats more . . ." *Errors*, IV, i, 29–30.

charge-house, *n.* school, perh. one for charges of the parish: "Do you not educate youth at the charge-house/ on the top of the mountain?" *Love's L*, V, i, 74–75.

charge of foot, *n.* commission to command a company of foot soldiers (infantry): "I'll procure this fat rogue a charge of/ foot . . ." *1 Hen 4*, II, iv, 538–539.

chariest, *adj.* superl. Of CHARY; most cautious or vigilant: "The chariest maid is prodigal enough/ If she unmask her beauty to the moon." *Ham*, I, iii, 36–37.

chariness, *n.* careful preservation: ". . . villainy against/ him that may not sully the chariness of our honesty." *Wives*, II, i, 95–96.

charitable, *adj.* **1** affectionate; loving: "Why have you that charitable title from thousands . . ." *Timon*, I, ii, 89. **2** compatible with Christian charity: "Let him be furnished/ with divines, and have all charitable preparation." *Meas*, III, ii, 202–203.

charity, *n.* **1** compassion; humanity; brotherly love: "For charity itself fulfils the [Biblical] law;/ And who can sever love from charity?" *Love's L*, IV, iii, 360–361. **2** action for the public good: "He that knows better how to tame a shrew,/ Now let him speak: 'tis charity to show." *Shrew*, IV, i, 197–198. **3** proper burial ceremony: "The dead with charity enclos'd in clay." *Hen 5*, IV, viii, 126. **4 exchange charity,** forgive each other: "Let's exchange charity./ I am no less in blood than thou art, Edmund . . ." *Lear*, V, iii, 166–167.

Charlemain, *n.* Charlemagne; actually Charles I ("the Bald") [Holinshed's error, copied by Shakespeare]: ". . . heir to th' Lady Lingare,/ Daughter to Charlemain . . ." *Hen 5*, I, ii, 74–75.

Charles the Emperor, *n.* Charles V, King of Spain and Holy Roman Emperor [also Queen Katherine's nephew]; feared an alliance between France and England and bribed Wolsey to aid his cause: "Charles the Emperor,/ Under pretence to see the queen his aunt . . ." *Hen 8*, I, i, 176–177.

Charles the Great, *n.* Charlemagne, king (768–814) of the Franks: "Where Charles the Great having subdu'd the Saxons . . . settled certain French . . ." *Hen 5*, I, ii, 46–47.

Charles' wain, *n.* Great Bear constellation: "Charles' wain is over the new chimney . . ." *1 Hen 4*, II, i, 2.

charm, *v.* **1** to entreat: ". . . upon my knees,/ I charm you . . . That you unfold to me . . . Why you are heavy . . ." *J Caes*, II, i, 270–275. **2** to influence; also, force to obey: "But I will charm him first to keep his tongue." *Shrew*, I, i, 209. **3** to still; silence: "Peace, wilful boy, or I will charm your tongue." *3 Hen 6*, V, v, 31. **4** to save by or as if by a charm: "I, in mine own woe charm'd . . ." *Cymb*, V, iii, 68.
—*n.* **5** charmer; enchantress [Cleopatra]: "For when I am reveng'd upon my charm,/ I have done all." *Ant & Cleo*, IV, xii, 16–17.

charmer, *n.* person who casts a spell: "O you heavenly charmers,/ What things you make of us!" *Kinsmen*, V, iv, 131–132.

charming, *adj.* **1** having the power of a magic charm: "Now help, ye charming spells and periapts . . ." *1 Hen 6*, V, iii, 2. **2** commanding or inspiring: "Accommodated by the place,/ more charming,/ With their own nobleness . . ." *Cymb*, V, iii, 32–33.

charneco, *n.* sweet wine of Portugal: "And here, neighbour, here's a cup of charneco." *2 Hen 6*, II, iii, 62.

charnel-house, *n.* church repository for human bones uncovered when digging new graves: ". . . hide me nightly in a charnel-house/ O'ercover'd quite with dead men's rattling bones . . ." *Rom & Jul*, IV, i, 81–82.

Charon, *n.* (in classical myth.) boatman who ferried dead souls across the river Styx to the Elysian Fields: "O be thou my Charon,/ And give me swift transportance to those fields . . ." *Tr & Cr*, III, ii, 9–10.

charter, *n.* **1** [in law] right or privilege: "The charter of thy worth gives thee releasing . . ." *Sonn 87*, 3. **2** freedom; liberty: ". . . as large a charter as the wind . . ." *As You*, II, vii, 48. **3** permission: "And let me find a charter in your voice . . ." *Oth,* I, iii, 245. **4 bold charter,** audacious claim; here, on the hostess's hospitality: "Lady, of that I have made a bold charter . . ." *All's W,* IV, v, 88.

—*v.* **5** to reserve: ". . . like as if that God/ Owed not nor made not you, nor that the elements/ Were not all appropriate to your comforts,/ But charter'd unto them?" *More,* II, iv, 135–138.

chartered libertine, *n.* licensed freeman: ". . . when he speaks,/ The air, a charter'd libertine, is still . . ." *Hen 5,* I, i, 47–48.

Chartreux, *n.* Carthusian order of France: "A monk o'th'Chartreux." *Hen 8,* I, i, 221.

chary, *adv.* carefully: "Bearing thy heart, which I will keep so chary . . ." *Sonn 22,* 11.

Charybdis, *n.* violent whirlpool opposite the rock of Scylla; sea passage lay between the two perils: ". . . when I shun Scylla (your father),/ I fall into Charybdis (your mother) . . ." *Merch,* III, v, 14–15.

chase, *n.* **1** hunt; also, hunting ground: "I have dogs, my lord,/ Will rouse the proudest panther in the chase . . ." *T Andr,* II, ii, 20–21. **2** prey or quarry: "Nay, Warwick, single out some other chase;/ For I myself will hunt this wolf to death." *3 Hen 6,* II, iv, 12–13. **3** chain of arguments; line of reasoning: "By this kind of chase, I should hate him . . ." *As You,* I, iii, 29. **4** wordplay on "pursuit of missed returns in tennis" and "wrangling over claims to the [French] crown": ". . . all the courts of France will be disturb'd/ With chases." *Hen 5,* I, ii, 265–266. **5 hold in chase,** to pursue: ". . . where is he,/ That holds in chase mine honour up and down?" *K John,* I, i, 222–223. **6 in chase of,** in pursuit of: "I did send . . . A ring in chase of you." *T Night,* III, i, 113–115.

chat, *v.* to chatter about: "Your prattling nurse . . . lets her baby cry/ While she chats him." *Cor,* II, i, 204–206.

chaudron, *n.* animal's entrails: "Add thereto a tiger's chaudron,/ For th' ingredience of our cauldron." *Mac,* IV, i, 33–34.

chawed, *adj.* chewed: "And in their pale dull mouths the gimmal'd bit/ Lies foul with chaw'd grass, still and motionless . . ." *Hen 5,* IV, ii, 49–50.

che, *pron.* **che vor' ye,** I warrant you: ". . . keep out, che vor' ye, or ise [I'll] try whither your/ costard [head] or my ballow [cudgel] be the harder." *Lear,* IV, vi, 242–243.

cheap, *adj.* requiring little effort: "The goodness that is cheap in beauty makes/ beauty brief in goodness . . ." *Meas,* III, i 180–181.

cheapen, *v.* to bargain for; haggle over: "Rich she shall be, that's certain . . . virtuous, or I'll never cheapen her . . ." *M Ado,* II, iii, 30–31.

Cheapside, *n.* chief commercial area of Shakespearean London, near St. Paul's Cathedral: "All the realm shall be in common,/ and in Cheapside shall my palfrey go to grass." *2 Hen 6,* IV, ii, 65–66.

cheat, *n.* **silly cheat,** petty thievery: ". . . my revenue is the silly cheat." *W Tale,* IV, iii, 27–28.

cheater, *n.* **1** sharper; swindler: "Cheater, call you him? I will bar no honest man/ my house, nor no cheater . . ." *2 Hen 4,* II, iv, 100–101. **2** wordplay on "escheater," official who supervised estates [escheats] confiscated by the crown: "I will be/ cheaters to them both, and they shall be exchequers/ to me . . ." *Wives,* I, iii, 65–67. **3 tame cheater,** decoy, who lures victims for a swindler: "He's no swaggerer, hostess, a tame cheater, i'faith . . ." *2 Hen 4,* II, iv, 95.

check, *n.* **1** rebuke; censure: "Nay, you might keep that check for it . . ." *As You,* IV, i, 159. **2** [often pl] restraints or restrictions: ". . . so devote to Aristotle's checks/ As Ovid be an outcast quite abjur'd." *Shrew,* I, i, 32–33.

—*v.* **3** to rebuke or reprimand: "I have/ checked him for it, and the young lion repents . . ." *2 Hen 4,* I, ii, 195–196. **4** to manage or control: ". . . hadst thou never given consent/ That Phaëthon should check thy fiery steeds . . ." *3 Hen 6,* II, vi, 11–12. **5 check at,** (in falconry) **a.** to veer from the pursuit of prey; be diverted: "If he be now return'd,/ As checking at his voyage . . ." *Ham,* IV, vii, 60–61. **b.** here, to attack other prey: "And with what wing the staniel checks at it!" *T Night,* II, v, 115.

cheer, *n.* **1** amusement; entertainment: "I will meet you, so I may have good cheer." *M Ado,* V, i, 150. **2** banquet; feast: "Our wedding cheer to a sad burial feast . . ." *Rom & Jul,* IV, v, 87. **3** dinner fare: ". . . pray God our cheer/ May answer my good will, and your good welcome here." *Errors,* III, i, 19–20. **4** countenance; disposition: "Though chance of war hath wrought this change of cheer,/ Thou com'st not to be made a scorn in Rome . . ." *T Andr,* I, i, 264–265. **5** way or standard of living: "An anchor's cheer in prison be my scope . . ." *Ham,* III, ii, 214. **6 give the cheer,** to be a welcoming host: "My royal Lord,/ You do not give the cheer: the feast is sold . . ." *Mac,* III, iv, 31–32. **7 What cheer?** How is it with you?: "Boatswain!"/ "Here, master: what cheer?" *Temp,* I, i, 1–2. **8 with so dull a**

cheer, in such a dreary fashion: "Or, if they sing, 'tis with so dull a cheer . . ." *Sonn 97,* 13.
—*v.* **9** to encourage; spur on: ". . . a cry more tuneable/ Was never holla'd to, nor cheer'd with horn . . ." *M N Dream,* IV, i, 123–124. **10 how cheerest thou?** Same as **What cheer?** [def. 7]

cheerly *adj.,* **1** cheerful: "Thou lookst cheerly, and I'll be with thee quickly." *As You,* II, vi, 13–14.
—*adv.* **2** cheerfully: ". . . lusty, young, and cheerly drawing breath." *Rich 2,* I, iii, 66. **3** briskly; sharply: "Heigh, my hearts! cheerly, cheerly, my hearts!" *Temp,* I, i, 5.
—*interj.* **4** cry of encouragement: "Cheerly, my lord, how fares your grace?" *1 Hen 4,* V, iv, 43. **5** Onward!: "Cheerly to sea; the signs of war advance . . ." *Hen 5,* II, ii, 192.

cheese, *n.* **1** food thought to aid digestion: "Why, my cheese, my digestion, why hast thou not/ served thyself in to my table . . ." *Tr & Cr,* II, iii, 44–45. **2** thought to be a favorite food of Wales: "'Tis time I were/ choked with a piece of toasted cheese." *Wives,* V, v, 139–140.

cheese and garlic, *n.* diet of the very poor: "I had rather live/ With cheese and garlic in a windmill . . ." *1 Hen 4,* III, i, 155–156.

chequin or **chequeen,** *n.* anglicization of *zecchino,* a gold coin of Italy: "Three or four thousand chequins were as pretty a/ proportion to live quietly . . ." *Per,* IV, ii, 24–25.

cherish, *v.* **1** to foster; encourage: "He has been known to commit outrages/ And cherish factions . . ." *Timon,* III, v, 73–74. **2** to support; believe in: "If you but knew how you the purpose cherish/ Whiles thus you mock it!" *Temp,* II, i, 219–220.

cherry-pit, *n.* child's game in which cherry pits are tossed into a small hole; Sir Toby here treats Malvolio like a child: ". . . 'tis not/ for gravity to play at cherry-pit with Satan." *T Night,* III, iv, 117–118.

Chertsey, *n.* abbey on the Thames, near London: "Come now towards Chertsey with your holy load . . ." *Rich 3,* I, ii, 29.

cherub, *n.,* pl. **cherubim,** one of an order of angels, next below seraphim; Hamlet says Claudius's purposes are known to Heaven: "So is it, if thou knew'st our purposes."/ "I see a cherub that sees them." *Ham,* IV, iii, 50–51.

cherubin, *adj.* angelic: "Hath in her more destruction than thy sword,/ For all her cherubin look." *Timon,* IV, iii, 63–64.

cherubins, *n.* old plural of **cherub:** "But in his motion like an angel sings,/ Still quiring to the young-ey'd cherubins . . ." *Merch,* V, i, 61–62.

Cheshu, *n.* Jesu [Fluellen's Welsh-accented English]: "By Cheshu, I think a' will plow up all/ if there is not better directions." *Hen 5,* III, ii, 67–68.

chest, *n.* treasury: "And so repose, sweet gold, for their unrest/ That have their alms out of the empress' chest." *T Andr,* II, iii, 8–9.

cheval volant, *n.* [French] Pegasus, the flying horse: ". . . le cheval volant, the Pegasus, chez/ les narines de feu [nostrils of fire]!" *Hen 5,* III, vii, 14–15.

cheveril, *n.* **1** kidskin, a fine leather that stretches easily: "O here's a wit of cheveril, that stretches from an/ inch narrow to an ell broad." *Rom & Jul,* II, iv, 83–84.
—*adj.* **2 soft cheveril conscience,** ref. to elasticity of kidskin: ". . . the capacity/ Of your soft cheveril conscience . . . If you might please to stretch it." *Hen 8,* II, iii, 31–33.

chewet, *n.* jackdaw; also, familiar term for a chatterer: "Peace, chewet, peace!" *1 Hen 4,* V, i, 29.

chid, *v.* past part. of CHIDE; scolded; ordered sharply: "For Margaret my queen, and Clifford too,/ Have chid me from the battle . . ." *3 Hen 6,* II, v, 16–17.

chidden, *v.* past part. of **chide;** chided; rebuked: "And yet I was last chidden for being too slow." *Two Gent,* II, i, 13.

chide, *v.* to quarrel: "We shall chide downright if I longer stay." *M N Dream,* II, i, 145.

chiding, *n.* **1** crying of hounds; baying: ". . . never did I hear/ Such gallant chiding . . ." *M N Dream,* IV, i, 113–114.
—*adj.* **2** noisy; tempestuous: "Thou hast as chiding a nativity/ As fire, air, water, earth, and heaven can make . . ." *Per,* III, i, 32–33.

chief, *adj., adv.* here, in disputed passage, prob. functions as adv.; chiefly: "And they in France . . . Are [of a] most select and generous chief in that." *Ham,* I, iii, 73–74.

chiefest, *adj.* highest-ranking: "Bid him . . . bring with him/ Some of the chiefest princes of the Goths . . ." *T Andr,* V, ii, 124–125.

chien, *n.* [French] dog: "Le chien est retourné . . ." appar. from the Bible [2 Peter 2:22], "The dog is turned to his own vomit again; and the sow that was washed to [her wallowing in] the mire." *Hen 5,* III, vii, 65–66.

child, *n.* **1** title given a man-at-arms who has not yet been granted knighthood: "Child Rowland to the dark tower came . . ." *Lear,* III, iv, 186. **2 with child,** rounded or humped:

"Stoop, I say;/ Her shoulder is with child." *Love's L,* IV, iii, 86–87.
—*v.* **3** to have a child or children; here, cruel children [Goneril and Regan]: ". . . that which makes me bend makes the king bow;/ He childed as I father'd!" *Lear,* III, vi, 112–113.

child-bed privilege, *n.* privilege of resting in seclusion after childbirth: "The child-bed privilege denied, which 'longs/ To women of all fashion . . ." *W Tale,* III, ii, 103–104.

child-changed, *adj.* changed into a child: "Th' untuned and jarring senses, O! wind up/ Of this child-changed father." *Lear,* IV, vii, 16–17.

Childeric, *n.* Merovingian king, deposed c.751 by Pepin: "King Pepin, which deposed Childeric,/ Did, as heir general . . ." *Hen 5,* I, ii, 65–66.

childhood, *n.* **bond of childhood,** duty of a child to its parents: "The offices of nature, bond of childhood,/ Effects of courtesy . . ." *Lear,* II, iv, 180–181.

childing, *adj.* fertile; fruitful; teeming: "The childing autumn, angry winter, change/ Their wonted liveries . . ." *M N Dream,* II, i, 112–113.

child-like, *adj.* filial: "Edmund, I hear that you have shown your father/ A child-like office [service]." *Lear,* II, i, 105–106.

chill, *v.* I'll [Edgar speaks in stage dialect used for rustics]: "Chill not let go, zir, without vurther 'casion." *Lear,* IV, vi, 236.

chill and tender, *adj.* used to comfort and ease: ". . . the many/ will be too chill and tender, and they'll be for the/ flow'ry way . . ." *All's W,* IV, v, 49–51.

chimes at midnight, *n.* prob. no precise meaning, only the sense of shared memories: "We have heard the chimes at midnight, Master/ Shallow." *2 Hen 4,* III, ii, 209–210.

chimney, *n.* fireplace: ". . . we leak in your chimney, and your chamber-lye/ breeds fleas like a loach." *1 Hen 4,* II, i, 19–20.

chine, *n.* **1** saddle or roast: ". . . cut not/ out the burly-bon'd clown in chines of beef . . ." *2 Hen 6,* IV, x, 55–56. **2** perh. ref. to backs and shoulders cudgeled: "Let me ne'er hope to see a chine again . . ." *Hen 8,* V, iii, 25.

chink, *n.* **have the chinks,** have plenty of cash or ready money: ". . . he that can lay hold of her/ Shall have the chinks." *Rom & Jul,* I, v, 115–116.

Chi non ti vede, non ti pretia, [Venice, Old Ital.] who sees thee not, praises thee not. *Love's L,* IV, ii, 94.

chip[1]**,** *n.* moving keys of a virginal or spinet: "To be so tickl'd they would change their state/ And situation with those dancing chips . . ." *Sonn 128,* 9–10.

chip[2]**,** *v.* to remove the crust from (stale bread), the duty of a pantler: ". . . a would ha' made a/ good pantler, a would ha' chipped bread well." *2 Hen 4,* II, iv, 234–235.

chirrah, *n.* prob. dial. rendering of "sirrah": "Chirrah!"/ *Quare* chirrah, not sirrah? *Love's L,* V, i, 31–32.

chirurgeonly, *adv.* like a good surgeon: ". . . you rub the sore,/ When you should bring the plaster . . . And most chirurgeonly." *Temp,* II, i, 135–136.

chivalry, *n.* valor, esp. in battle: "The flower of Europe for his chivalry . . ." *3 Hen 6,* II, i, 71.

choice, *n.* **1** regard; estimation: "This ring he holds/ In most rich choice . . ." *All's W,* III, vii, 25–26. **2 some quantity of choice,** minimal ability to make a choice: ". . . it reserv'd some quantity of choice/ To serve in such a difference [so obvious a difference]." *Ham,* III, iv, 75–76.
—*adj.* **3** fine; excellent: ". . . ye choice spirits that admonish me . . ." *1 Hen 6,* V, iii, 3.

choice hour, *n.* suitable time: ". . . a choice hour/ To hear from him a matter of some moment . . ." *Hen 8,* I, ii, 162–163.

choir, *n.* **1 bare ruined choirs,** standing ruins of churches: "Bare ruin'd choirs, where late the sweet birds sang." *Sonn 73,* 4. **2** See **quire** (def. 2).
—*v.* **3 choir with,** to be in harmony with: "My throat of war be turn'd,/ Which choired with my drum . . ." *Cor,* III, ii, 112–113.

choke, *v.* **1** to hinder; obstruct: "As two spent swimmers, that do cling together/ And choke their art [skill in swimming]." *Mac,* I, ii, 8–9. **2** to quell; put down: "I stood i'th'level/ Of a full-charg'd confederacy, and give thanks/ To you that chok'd it." *Hen 8,* I, ii, 2–4.

choler, *n.* anger: ". . . boiling choler chokes/ The hollow passage of my poison'd voice . . ." *1 Hen 6,* V, iv, 120–121.

choleric, *adj.* **1** hot-tempered; irascible [thought to be caused by improper diet, including overdone meat]: "I pray you eat none of it . . . Lest it make you choleric, and purchase me another dry basting." *Errors,* II, ii, 59–62. **2** (of food) causing bile and, hence, bad temper: "I fear it is too choleric a meat." *Shrew,* IV, iii, 19.

chollors, *n.* parson appar. means "choler," but is melancholy rather than angry: "Pless my soul, how full of chollors I am, and/ trempling of mind . . ." *Wives,* III, i, 11–12.

choose, *v.* **choose me for them,** deputize me to serve for them: "As they are chosen, they are glad to choose me for them . . ." *Meas,* II, i, 265–266.

chop, *v.* **chop on,** interrupt with: "That I, poor man, might eftsoons come between/ And chop on some cold [chaste] thought!" *Kinsmen,* III, i, 12–13.

chop-fallen, *adj.* dejected; also, lit., chopless [without a lower jaw]: "Not one now to mock/ your own grinning? Quite chop-fallen?" *Ham,* V, i, 185–186.

chopine, *n.* shoe with a thick sole, worn to give added height; here, merely a pleasantry about the boy actor's having grown: ". . . your ladyship/ is nearer to heaven than when I saw you last by/ the altitude of a chopine." *Ham,* II, ii, 421–423.

chopless, *adj.* missing the jaw: ". . . my Lady Worm's, chopless,/ and knocked about the mazard wih a sexton's spade." *Ham,* V, i, 87–88.

chopped, *adj.* chapped: "Beated and chopp'd with tann'd antiquity . . ." *Sonn 62,* 10.

chopped logic, *n.* choplogic; plausible but deceptive reasoning: "How, how, how, how? Chopp'd logic? What is this?" *Rom & Jul,* III, v, 149.

chopping, *adj.* changing the meanings [of words]: "Speak 'pardon' as 'tis current in our land,/ The chopping French we do not understand." *Rich 2,* V, iii, 121–122.

choppy, *adj.* chapped; scaly: "By each at once her choppy finger laying/ Upon her skinny lips . . ." *Mac,* I, iii, 44–45.

chops¹, *n.* fat cheeks, esp. a fat-cheeked face or person: "Come on, you whoreson chops! Ah, rogue, i'faith, I/ love thee." *2 Hen 4,* II, iv, 215–216.

chops², *n.* cracks in the skin, esp. the face: "Her cheeks with chops and wrinkles were disguis'd . . ." *Luc,* 1452.

chopt or **chopped,** *adj.* **1** chapped: ". . . the cow's dugs that her pretty chopt hands had milked . . ." *As You,* II, iv, 46–47. **2** dried-up; shriveled: "O, give me always/ a little, lean, old, chopt, bald shot [marksman]." *2 Hen 4,* III, ii, 269–270.

chorus, *n.* character in some plays who explains the action, background, etc., of a play: "You are as good as a chorus, my lord." *Ham,* III, ii, 240.

chose, *v.* old past part. of **choose. chose out,** selected: "O what a time have you chose out, brave Caius,/ To wear a kerchief [appear to be ill]!" *J Caes,* II, i, 314–315.

chosen, *adj.* choice: ". . . her sweet harmony/ And other chosen attractions . . ." *Per,* V, i, 44–45.

chough, *n.* **1** starling or grackle: "As wild geese that the creeping fowler eye,/ Or russet-pated choughs . . ." *M N Dream,* III, ii, 20–21. **2** jackdaw, a small crow: "By magot-pies, and choughs, and rooks, brought forth/ The secret'st man of blood." *Mac,* III, iv, 124–125. **3** same, with sense of fool or simpleton: ". . . a whoo-bub against his/ daughter and the king's son, and scared my choughs/ from the chaff . . ." *W Tale,* IV, iv, 617–619. **4 make a chough of as deep chat,** teach a jackdaw to speak just as well: ". . . lords that can prate/ As amply . . . As this Gonzalo; I myself could make/ A chough of as deep chat." *Temp,* II, i, 258–261.

Chrish, *n.* mispron. of "Christ": "By Chrish, la! tish ['tis] ill done: the work ish [is] give/ over . . ." *Hen 5,* III, ii, 91–92.

christen, *adj.* Christian: ". . . there is ne'er a king/ christen could be better bit . . ." *1 Hen 4,* II, i, 15–16.

christendom, *n.* [sometimes cap.] **1** Christian name; here, nickname or pet name: ". . . with a world/ Of pretty, fond, adoptious christendoms . . ." *All's W,* I, i, 169–170. **2 By my christendom,** As I am a Christian [a mild oath]: "By my christendom,/ So I were out of prison and kept sheep . . ." *K John,* IV, i, 16–17. **3 worn out Christendom,** exhausted all the fashions in the Christian world: "Their clothes are after such a pagan cut to't/ That sure th'have [they have] worn out Christendom . . ." *Hen 8,* I, iii, 14–15.

Christian, *n.* ordinary human being: ". . . neither having th'accent of Christians,/ nor the gait of Christian, pagan, nor man . . ." *Ham,* III, ii, 31–32.

christom child, *n.* newly baptized child dressed in white robe [chrism-cloth or chrisom-cloth]; Hostess's confusion with "Christian": "'A/ made a finer end, and went away an it had been/ any christom child . . ." *Hen 5,* II, iii, 10–12.

chronicle, *n.* **1** record, esp. historical record of brave deeds; one's place in history: "I, and my sword, will earn our chronicle . . ." *Ant & Cleo,* III, xiii, 175. **2** person regarded as such a repository: "Let me embrace thee, good old chronicle . . ." *Tr & Cr,* IV, v, 201.
—*v.* **3** to record in history books: "This sport, well carried, shall be chronicled." *M N Dream,* III, ii, 240. **4** to keep track of, esp. in household accounts: "To suckle fools, and chronicle small beer." *Oth,* II, i, 160.

chrysolite, *n.* topaz: ". . . make me such another world,/ Of one entire and perfect chrysolite . . ." *Oth,* V, ii, 145–146.

chuck, *n.* chick [term of endearment]: ". . . the king would have me present the princess, sweet/ chuck, with some . . . show . . ." *Love's L,* V, i, 102–103.

'chud, *v.* **and 'chud,** if I could: "And 'chud ha' bin zwagger'd [swaggered] out of/ my life . . ." *Lear,* IV, vi, 239–240.

chuff, *n.* var. of **chough;** coarse, boorish fellow; also, a wealthy miser: "No, ye/ fat chuffs, I would your store were here!" *1 Hen 4,* II, ii, 84–85.

churchlike humor, *n.* pious disposition: "Nor wear the diadem upon his head,/ Whose church-like humour fits not for a crown." *2 Hen 6,* I, 1, 247–248.

churl, *n.* **1** miser: "O churl. Drunk all, and left no friendly drop/ To help me after?" *Rom & Jul,* V, iii, 163–164. **2** disagreeable fellow; boor: "Churl, upon thy eyes I throw/ All the power this charm doth owe . . ." *M N Dream,* II, ii, 77–78. **3** (used affectionately) rascal; scoundrel: "Within thine own bud buriest thy content,/ And, tender churl, mak'st waste in niggarding." *Sonn 1,* 11–12. **4 like a churl,** so rudely: "Lavinia, though you left me like a churl,/ I found a friend . . ." *T Andr,* I, i, 486–487.

churlish, *adj.* **1** rough or rude; also, inferior: "The interruption of their churlish drums/ Cuts off more circumstance [discussion]: they are at hand . . ." *K John,* II, i, 76–77. **2** niggardly or grudging: "Though churlish thoughts themselves should be your judge . . ." *K John,* II, i, 519.

cicatrice, *n.* **1** ref., appar., to past devastation wrought by Denmark on England: "Since yet thy cicatrice looks raw and red/ After the Danish sword . . ." *Ham,* IV, iii, 63–64. **2** imprint or impression resembling a scar: ". . . lean upon a rush,/ The cicatrice and capable impressure/ Thy palm some moment keeps . . ." *As You,* III, v, 22–24.

Ciceter, *n.* Cirencester: ". . . the rebels have consum'd with fire/ Our town of Ciceter in Gloucestershire . . ." *Rich 2,* V, vi, 2–3.

Cilicia, *n.* country in Asia Minor: ". . . to Ptolemy he assign'd/ Syria, Cilicia, and Phoenicia . . ." *Ant & Cleo,* III, vi, 15–16.

Cimmerian, *n.* [according to Homer] any of the "black" people from the dark, remote, and gloomy North: "Believe me, queen, your swart Cimmerian/ Doth make your honour of his body's hue . . ." *T Andr,* II, iii, 72–73.

cinders, *n. pl.* **1** stars; celestial objects seen in the sky: "I in the clear sky of fame o'ershine/ you as much as the full moon doth the cinders/ of the element . . ." *2 Hen 4,* IV, iii, 50–52. **2** hot coals; fire hidden in the ashes: "Prithee go hence,/ Or I shall show the cinders of my spirits . . ." *Ant & Cleo,* V, ii, 171–172.

cinque-pace, *n.* lively dance of five steps followed by a leap or jump: ". . . repenting is as a Scotch jig, a measure,/ and a cinque-pace . . ." *M Ado,* II, i, 67–68.

Cinque-ports, *n.* association, dating from the 13th cent., of British seaport towns (Dover, Sandwich, Romney, Hastings, and Hythe) that received special privileges in return for their efforts to strengthen coastal defenses: "A canopy, born by four of the Cinque-ports, under it the Queen . . ." [SD] *Hen 8,* IV, i, 37.

cinque-spotted, *adj.* consisting of five dots: "On her left breast/ A mole cinque-spotted . . ." *Cymb,* II, ii, 37–38.

cipher, *n.* **1** person or thing of little or no worth: "A most fine figure!"/ "To prove you a cipher." *Love's L,* I, ii, 51–52. **2** simile of the cipher, which has no intrinsic value, but when added to other numbers can multiply the value endlessly: ". . . like a cipher/ (Yet standing in rich place) I multiply/ With one 'We thank you' many thousands moe . . ." *W Tale,* I, ii, 6–8. **3 cipher of a function,** worthless duty or charge: "Mine were the very cipher of a function/ To fine the faults whose fine stands in record . . ." *Meas,* II, ii, 39–40.
—*v.* **4** to read; make out: ". . . the illiterate that know not how/ To cipher what is writ in learned books . . ." *Luc,* 810–811. **5** to register; express: "The face of either cipher'd either's heart . . ." *Luc,* 1396. **6 cipher me,** describe [to] me: "To cipher me how fondly I did dote . . ." *Luc,* 207.

Circe's cup, *n.* (in the *Odyssey*) cup given Ulysses' men by the sorceress Circe, which transformed them into swine: "I think you all have drunk of Circe's cup . . ." *Errors,* V, i, 271.

circle, *n.* **1** wordplay on "magic circle" of the conjurer and "vagina": "To raise a spirit in his mistress' circle/ Of some strange nature . . ." *Rom & Jul,* II, i, 24–25. **2** crown: "Cleopatra . . . of thee craves/ The circle of the Ptolemies for her heirs . . ." *Ant & Cleo,* III, xii, 17–18. **3** perimeter; boundary: "To whip this dwarfish war, this pigmy arms,/ From out the circle of his territories." *K John,* V, ii, 135–136.

circuit, *n.* **golden circuit,** monarch's crown: ". . . the golden circuit on my head,/ Like to the glorious sun's transparent beams . . ." *2 Hen 6,* III, i, 352–353.

circumference, *n.* periphery: "He is no crescent, and his horns are invisible within/ the circumference." *M N Dream,* V, i, 233–234.

circummured, *adj.* surrounded [by a wall]; enclosed: "He hath a garden circummur'd with brick . . ." *Meas,* IV, i, 28.

circumscribe, *v.* to restrain or subdue: "From where he circumscribed with his sword,/ And brought to yoke, the enemies of Rome." *T Andr,* I, i, 68–69.

circumscription, *n.* restraint or confinement: ". . . my unhoused free condition/ Put into circumscription . . ." *Oth,* I, ii, 26–27.

circumstance, *n.* **1** [often pl.] facts; details or particulars: "With circumstance and oaths so to deny/ This chain . . ." *Errors,* V, i, 16–17. **2** discussion: "The interruption of their churlish drums/ Cuts off more circumstance . . ." *K John,* II, i, 76–77. **3** fancy phrases; here, flattery: "You know me well, and herein spend but time/ To wind about my love with circumstance . . ." *Merch,* I, i, 153–154. **4** roundabout logic: "So, by your circumstance, you call me fool." *Two Gent,* I, i, 36. **5** devious argument: "You know me well, and herein spend but time/ To wind about my love with circumstance . . ." *Merch,* I, i, 153–154. **6** something that may happen; a contingency or accident: "Or breed [renew] itself so out of circumstance [on the slightest provocation] . . ." *Oth,* III, iii, 16. **7** ceremony; pageantry: "Pride, pomp, and circumstance of glorious war!" *Oth,* III, iii, 360. **8 in our circumstance,** to our mortal senses: ". . . in our circumstance and course of thought/ 'Tis heavy with him." *Ham,* III, iii, 83–84. **9 out of circumstance,** unceremonious: ". . . his approach/ (So out of circumstance, and sudden) . . ." *W Tale,* V, i, 89–90. **10 stay the circumstance,** to await the details: "Is thy news good or bad? Answer to that,/ Say either, and I'll stay the circumstance." *Rom & Jul,* II, v, 35–36.

circumstanc'd, *past part.* forced to yield to circumstances [and accept your terms]: "'Tis very good, I must be circumstanc'd." *Oth,* III, iv, 199.

circumvent God, *v.* ref. to Cain's action in the Bible: "This might be the pate of a politician which this ass now/ o'er-offices, one that would circumvent God . . ." *Ham,* V, i, 76–78.

circumvention, *n.* powers or opportunity to circumvent: "What ever have been thought on in this state/ That could be brought to bodily act, ere Rome/ Had circumvention?" *Cor,* I, ii, 4–6.

cistern or **cestron,** *n.* reservoir; hence, a store: "Your matrons, and your maids, could not fill up/ The cistern of my lust . . ." *Mac,* IV, iii, 62–63.

citadel, *n.* fortress near a city: ". . . meet me by and by at the citadel . . ." *Oth,* II, i, 278.

cital, *n.* recital; (legal) summons or citation; also, impeachment: "And, which became him like a prince indeed,/ He made a blushing cital of himself . . ." *1 Hen 4,* V, ii, 60–61.

cite, *v.* **1** to incite or urge: "And had I not been cited so by them,/ Yet did I purpose as they do entreat . . ." *2 Hen 6,* III, ii, 280–281. **2** to summon for a court appearance: "She was often cited by them, but appear'd not . . ." *Hen 8,* IV, i, 29. **3 cite up,** to recall: ". . . we look'd toward England,/ And cited up a thousand heavy times . . ." *Rich 3,* I, iv, 13–14.

citizen, *adj.* city-bred; effete or effeminate: "But not so citizen a wanton [spoiled child] as/ To seem to die ere sick . . ." *Cymb,* IV, ii, 8–9.

cittern-head, *n.* (on a cittern, stringed musical instrument resem-bling the lute or guitar) carved head, usually grotesque, at the end of the fingerboard: ". . . thou hast no face."/ "What is this?"/ "A cittern-head." *Love's L,* V, ii, 603–605.

city, *n.* chastity: "'And long upon these terms I held my city . . .'" *Lover's Comp,* 176.

City feast, *n.* formal banquet, appar. in the manner of the City of London [an obvious anachronism]: "Make not a City feast of it, to let the meat cool . . ." *Timon,* III, vi, 66–67.

civet, *n.* strong, musky perfume, made from a glandular secretion of the civet cat: ". . . a rubs himself with civet; can you smell/ him out by that?" *M Ado,* III, ii, 46–47.

civil, *adj.* **1** well-behaved: "He is sad and civil,/ And suits well for a servant with my fortunes . . ." *T Night,* III, iv, 5–6. **2** sober; serious-minded: "Where's Malvolio? He is sad and civil . . ." *T Night,* III, iv, 5. **3** same in wordplay with "Seville" [orange]: ". . . civil as an orange, and something/ of that jealous complexion." *M Ado,* II, i, 276–277. **4** solemn; also, respectable: "Come, civil night,/ Thou sober-suited matron, all in black . . ." *Rom & Jul,* III, ii, 10–11. **5** resulting from civil war: ". . . who hath brought the fatal engine in/ That gives our Troy, our Rome, the civil wound." *T Andr,* V, iii, 86–87. **6** of the citizens: "There's many a beast then in a populous city,/ And many a civil monster." *Oth,* IV, i, 63–64. **7 civil blood,** bloodshed of civil upheaval: "Where civil blood makes civil hands unclean." *Rom & Jul,* Prol., 4. **8 civil bounds,** limits of courtesy or polite behavior: ". . . leap all civil bounds,/ Rather than make unprofited return." *T Night,* I, iv, 21–22. **9 civil doctor,** doctor of civil law: "No woman had it, but a civil doctor,/ Which did refuse three thousand ducats of me . . ." *Merch,* V, i, 210–211. **10 civil fears,** decorous or seemly concerns: "Shook off my sober guards and civil fears." *Lover's Comp,* 298. **11 civil swords,** swords raised in civil unrest: "Our Italy/ Shines o'er with civil swords . . ." *Ant & Cleo,* I, iii, 44–45.

civility, *n.* **observance of civility,** attention to good manners: "Use all the observance of civility/ Like one well studied in a sad ostent . . ." *Merch,* II, ii, 186–187.

clack-dish, *n.* beggar's bowl having a cover that could be clacked to attract attention: ". . . his use was to put a ducat in her clack-dish . . ." *Meas,* III, ii, 123–124.

claim, *v.* to assert or press a claim: "God forbid your Grace should be forsworn."/ "I shall be, if I claim by open war." *3 Hen 6,* I, ii, 18–19.

clamber, *v.* to climb or crawl up: "Clamb'ring the walls to eye him." *Cor,* II, i, 208.

clamor, *n.* **1** noisy grief: ". . . an hour in clamour and a quarter/ in rheum." *M Ado,* V, ii, 76–77. **2** outcry: "The venom [venomous] clamours of a jealous woman . . ." *Errors,* V, i, 69. **3 clamor moistened,** outcries moistened with tears: ". . . she shook/ The holy water from her heavenly eyes,/ And clamour moisten'd, then away she started . . ." *Lear,* IV, iii, 30–32. —*v.* **4** to silence; shut up: ". . . clamor your tongues,/ and not a word more." *W Tale,* IV, iv, 249–250.

clamorous, *adj.* loud and insistent: "Be clamorous, and leap all civil bounds . . ." *T Night,* I, iv, 21.

clap, *v.* **1** to begin: "Shall we clap into't roundly, without hawking or spitting . . . ?" *As You,* V, iii, 9–10. **2** to thrust: ". . . boys, with women's voices,/ . . . clap their female joints/ In stiff unwieldy arms . . ." *Rich 2,* III, ii, 113–115. **3** to pat: "This hand hath made him proud with clapping him" *Rich 2,* V, v, 86. **4** to applaud: ". . . little eyases, that/ cry out on the top of question, and are most tyrannically/ clapped for't." *Ham,* II, ii, 337–339. **5** to pledge [by means of a handclasp]: "Ere I could make thee open thy white hand,/ And clap thyself my love . . ." *W Tale,* I, ii, 103–104. **6 clap hands and a bargain,** join hands and the bargain is sealed: "Give me your answer . . . and so clap hands and a bargain. How say/ you, lady?" *Hen 5,* V, ii, 130–132. **7 clap into,** to get on with: "I would desire you to clap into/ your prayers; for look you, the warrant's come." *Meas,* IV, iii, 40–41. **8 clap me,** to slam down: ". . . when he/ enters the confines of a tavern, claps me his sword/ upon the table . . ." *Rom & Jul,* III, i, 5–7. **9 clap on,** to present to [lit., attach to]: ". . . this all-changing word,/ Clapp'd on the outward eye of fickle France . . ." *K John,* II, i, 582–583. **10 clapped him o' th' shoulder,** given him an encouraging pat: ". . . it may be said of him that Cupid/ hath clapped him o' th' shoulder . . ." *As You,* IV, i, 45–46. **11 clap thyself my love,** pledge yourself [by means of a handclasp] to love me: "Ere I could make thee open thy white hand,/ And clap thyself my love . . ." *W Tale,* I, ii, 103–104. **12 clap to,** to slam shut: "Hostess, clap to the doors!" *1 Hen 4,* II, iv, 272–273. **13 clap up,** to settle; agree on [lit., slap together]: "Was ever match clapp'd up so suddenly?" *Shrew,* II, i, 318. **14 clap up close,** to confine under close guard: "Away with them! let them be clapp'd up close,/ And kept asunder [apart]." *2 Hen 6,* I, iv, 49–50. **15 clap up**

together, to combine: ". . . all of you clapp'd up together in/ An Antony . . ." *Ant & Cleo,* IV, ii, 17–18. —*n.* **16 catch a clap,** prob. wordplay on "slap" and slang word for gonorrhea: "Fight closer or, good faith, you'll catch a clap." *3 Hen 6,* III, ii, 23.

clap i'th'clout, *v.* to hit the bull's-eye: "A [he] would/ have clapped i'th'clout at twelve score [yards] . . ." *2 Hen 4,* III, ii, 45–46.

clapper-claw, *v.* to thrash or maul: "Now they are clapper-clawing one another, I'll/ go look on." *Tr & Cr,* V, iv, 1–2.

Claribel, *n.* daughter of Alonso: ". . . in one voyage/ Did Claribel her husband find at Tunis . . ." *Temp,* V, i, 208–209.

clasp, *v.* to cling: "And, clasping to the mast, endur'd a sea/ That almost burst the deck." *Per,* IV, i, 55–56.

clasping, *n.* [often pl.] embrace; here, incestuous sexual alliance: ". . . now you're both a father and a son,/ By your uncomely claspings with your child . . ." *Per,* I, i, 128–129.

clause, *n.* conclusion; also, premise or proposition: "Do not extort thy reasons from this clause . . ." *T Night,* III, i, 155.

claw, *v.* to stroke or flatter: ". . . laugh when I am merry, and claw no man in his humour." *M Ado,* I, iii, 17.

clay, *n.* **1** the earth; here, the grave: "Then kings' misdeeds cannot be hid in clay." *Luc,* 609. **2 clay and clay,** human beings; man and his fellow man: "But clay and clay differs in dignity [rank],/ Whose dust is both alike [both alike in death]." *Cymb,* IV, ii, 4–5.

clean, *adv.* **1** completely or entirely; quite: "A happy gentleman . . . By you unhappied and disfigured clean . . ." *Rich 2,* III, i, 9–10. —*adj.* **2** polished: "I will never trust a man again for keeping his/ sword clean . . ." *All's W,* IV, iii, 141–142. **3** quite apart; entirely different: ". . . men may construe things, after their fashion,/ Clean from the purpose of the things themselves." *J Caes,* I, iii, 34–35.

cleanly, *adj.* adroit; dexterous: ". . . wherein neat and cleanly, but to carve a/ capon and eat it?" *1 Hen 4,* II, iv, 450–451.

clean-timbered, *adj.* well-built: "I think Hector was not so clean-timbered." *Love's L,* V, ii, 631.

clear, *adj.* **1** innocent; pure and unsullied: "You cannot make gross sins look clear . . ." *Timon,* III, v, 39. **2** blameless: ". . . whose wraths to guard you from . . . is nothing but heart-sorrow/ And a clear life ensuing." *Temp,* III, iii, 79–82. **3** bright; full: "Come away; it is almost clear dawn." *Meas,* IV, ii, 209.

4 calm or serene; unruffled: "Say that she frown, I'll say she looks as clear/ As morning roses newly wash'd with dew." *Shrew,* II, i, 172–173.

—*adv.* **5** with an innocent look: "Only look up clear;/ To alter favour ever is to fear." *Mac,* I, v, 71–72.

clearest, *adj.* purest; finest: "Think that the clearest Gods . . . have preserved thee." *Lear,* IV, vi, 73–74.

clearly, *adv.* without interference, here from the enemy: "After such bloody toil, we bid good-night,/ And wound our tott'ring colours clearly up . . ." *K John,* V, v, 6–7.

clearness, *n.* blamelessness: ". . . always thought/ That I require a clearness . . ." *Mac,* III, i, 131–132.

cleave to my consent, *v.* swear allegiance to my cause; also, be advised by me: "If you shall cleave to my consent, when 'tis [when it may be required]/ It shall make honour for you." *Mac,* II, i, 25–26.

clef, *n.* wordplay on "musical clef" and slang term "cleft," pudenda: "And any man may sing her, if he can take her/ clef: she's noted." *Tr & Cr,* V, ii, 10–11.

cleft, *adj.* double; twofold: "O cleft effect! cold modesty, hot wrath . . ." *Lover's Comp,* 293.

Clement's Inn, *n.* law college, similar to but less select than the Inns of Court: "I was once/ of Clement's Inn, where I think they will talk of mad/ Shallow yet." *2 Hen 4,* III, ii, 13–14.

clepe, *v.* to call or name: "They clepe us drunkards, and with swinish phrase/ Soil our addition . . ." *Ham,* I, iv, 19–20.

clepeth, *v.* calleth: ". . . he/ clepeth a calf, cauf; half, hauf . . ." *Love's L,* V, i, 21–22.

clept, past tense and past part. of **clepe;** called; named: "Shoughs, water-rugs, and demi-wolves, are clept/ All by the name of dogs . . ." *Mac,* III, i, 93–94.

clerestory, *n.* high interior wall with windows near the ceiling for admitting light: ". . . the clerestories toward the/ south-north are as lustrous as ebony . . ." *T Night,* IV, ii, 38–39.

clerk, *n.* **1** scholar; man of learning: ". . . great clerks have purposed/ To greet me with premeditated welcomes . . ." *M N Dream,* V, i, 93–94. **2** cleric: "All the clerks/ (I mean the learned ones in Christian kingdoms) . . ." *Hen 8,* II, ii, 91–92.

clerk-like experienced, *adj.* having the experience of an educated man: "As you are certainly a gentleman, thereto/ Clerk-like experienc'd . . ." *W Tale,* I, ii, 391–392.

clerkly, *adj.* **1** scholarly; intelligent or learned: "Thou art clerkly, thou art clerkly, Sir John." *Wives,* IV, v, 54.

—*adv.* **2** in a scholarly manner: "I thank you, gentle servant. 'Tis very clerkly done." *Two Gent,* II, i, 101. **3 clerkly couched,** cleverly phrased: "Hath he not twit our sovereign lady here/ With ignominious words, though clerkly couch'd . . ." *2 Hen 6,* III, i, 178–179.

clew, *n.* ball of thread, wound as it is spun; here, used ironically: "Speak, is't so?/ If it be so, you have wound a goodly clew [you've created a fine situation] . . ." *All's W,* I, iii, 176–177.

client, *n.* person who enlists the help of a lawyer or advocate in obtaining justice under the law: "To trembling clients be you mediators . . ." *Luc,* 1020.

climate, *n.* **1** region; immediate area: ". . . they are portentous things/ Unto the Climate that they point upon." *J Caes,* I, iii, 31–32. **2** sky overhead: "And by this hand I swear,/ That sways the earth this climate overlooks . . ." *K John,* II, i, 343–344.

—*v.* **3** to live or visit in a particular region: "The blessed gods/ Purge all infection from our air whilst you/ Do climate here!" *W Tale,* V, i, 167–169.

climature, *n.* region; clime: ". . . heaven and earth together demonstrated/ Unto our climatures and countrymen." *Ham,* I, i, 126–127.

clime, *n.* land; region: "Where shivering cold and sickness pines the clime . . ." *Rich 2,* V, i, 77.

cling, *v.* to wither; shrivel: "Upon the next tree shalt thou hang alive,/ Till famine cling thee . . ." *Mac,* V, v, 39–40.

clinquant, *adj.* aglitter: "To-day the French,/ All clinquant all in gold, like heathen gods . . ." *Hen 8,* I, i, 18–19.

clip, *v.* **1** to brush with the wings; hence, to embrace: "Who with their drowsy, slow, and flagging [drooping] wings/ Clip dead men's graves . . ." *2 Hen 6,* IV, i, 5–6. **2** to clasp or enclose; embrace: "No grave upon the earth shall clip in it/ A pair so famous . . ." *Ant & Cleo,* V, ii, 357–358.

clipped[1], *adj.* abridged; curtailed: "Nor more nor clipp'd, but so [precise]." *Lear,* IV, vii, 6.

clipped[2], *adj.* embraced; hugged about: "Unknown to you, unsought, were clipp'd about/ With this most tender air." *Cymb,* V, v, 452–453.

clipped in, *adj.* encircled: ". . . clipp'd in with the sea/ That chides the banks of England . . ." *1 Hen 4,* III, i, 41–42.

clipper, *n.* wordplay on "one who clips gold coins" and "one who kills French soldiers": ". . . and to-morrow the/ king himself will be a clipper." *Hen 5,* IV, i, 234–235.

cloak, *v.* **cloak itself on,** to use as an excuse (for): ". . . and basest theft is that/ Which cannot cloak itself on poverty." *Edw 3,* II, ii, 79–80.

cloak-bag, *n.* bag or valise for carrying cloaks or other clothes: ". . . that huge bombard of sack, that/ stuffed cloak-bag of guts . . ." *1 Hen 4,* II, iv, 445–446.

clock, *n.* **tell the clock,** See **tell** (def. 10).

clodpole, *n.* dunce; blockhead: "Therefore this letter . . . will breed no terror in the youth: he/ will find it comes from a clodpole." *T Night,* III, iv, 189–191.

clog, *n.* **1** block of wood attached to the leg of an animal to prevent escape: "I am trusted with a/ muzzle and enfranchised with a clog . . ." *M Ado,* I, iii, 30–31. **2** ref. to his new wife; the "ball and chain": "Here comes my clog." *All's W,* II, v, 53. **3** mental weight or burden: "With clog of conscience and sour melancholy/ Hath yielded up his body to the grave." *Rich 2,* V, vi, 20–21.
—*v.* **4** to burden or encumber: "'You'll rue the time/ That clogs me with this answer.'" *Mac,* III, vi, 42–43.

clogging, *adj.* oppressive; vexatious: "The clogging burthen of a guilty soul." *Rich 2,* I, iii, 200.

cloistress, *n.* inhabitant of a cloister; nun: "But like a cloistress she will veiled walk . . ." *T Night,* I, i, 28.

close¹, *adj.* **1** private; secluded: ". . . give me leave,/ In this close walk, to satisfy myself,/ In craving your opinion . . ." *2 Hen 6,* II, ii, 2–4. **2** sly; underhanded: "And my consent ne'er ask'd herein before!/ This is close dealing." *2 Hen 6,* II, iv, 72–73. **3** shut fast: ". . . to close prison he commanded her . . ." *Two Gent,* III, i, 235. **4** secret: ". . . close pent-up guilts,/ Rive your concealing continents . . ." *Lear,* III, ii, 57–58. **5 close as oak,** tight as the grain of oak: "To seal her father's eyes up, close as oak . . ." *Oth,* III, iii, 213. **6 keep close, a.** let it remain secret: "What there is else/ keep close, we'll read it at more advantage." *1 Hen 4,* II, iv, 534–535. **b.** don't go out; stay close to home: "Let housewifery appear; keep close, I thee command." *Hen 5,* II, iii, 62. **7 stand close,** remain concealed: "Stand close awhile, for here comes one in haste." *J Caes,* I, iii, 131.
—*adv.* **8** surreptitiously; secretly: "An onion will do well for such a shift,/ Which in a napkin being close convey'd . . ." *Shrew,* Ind., i, 124–125. **9** close together; also, quietly and inconspicuously: "My masters, let's stand close: my Lord Protector/ will come this way by and by . . ." *2 Hen 6,* I, iii, 1–2.

—*n.* **10** yard or garden: "I have a tree which grows here in my close . . ." *Timon,* V, i, 204. **11** hand-to-hand combat: ". . . the intestine shock/ And furious close of civil butchery . . ." *1 Hen 4,* I, i, 12–13.
—*v.* **12** to conceal oneself; lie or remain hidden: "Close, in the name of jesting! [As the men/ hide, she drops a letter.]" *T Night,* II, v, 20–21. **13** to embrace: "Marry, after they closed in earnest, they parted very/ fairly in jest." *Two Gent,* II, v, 12. **14** to bury; entomb: "My father and Lavinia shall forthwith/ Be closed in our household's monument." *T Andr,* V, iii, 193–194. **15** to heal: "We have scorch'd the snake, not kill'd it;/ She'll close, and be herself . . ." *Mac,* III, ii, 13–14. **16 close with, a.** to engage in hand-to-hand combat: "If I can close with him, I care not for his thrust." *2 Hen 4,* II, i, 18. **b.** to come to terms or an agreement with: "See now whether pure fear . . . doth not make thee wrong this virtuous gentlewoman/ to close with us." *2 Hen 4,* II, iv, 322–324.

close², *n.* musical cadence: "Congreeing in a full and natural close,/ Like music." *Hen 5,* I, ii, 182–183.

close aspect, *n.* suspicious look: ". . . that close aspect of his/ Do show the mood of a much troubled breast . . ." *K John,* IV, ii, 72–73.

closed, *past part.* enclosed: ". . . the gift which bounteous Nature/ Hath in him clos'd . . ." *Mac,* III, i, 97–98.

close dealing, *n.* conniving; underhand plotting: "And my consent ne'er ask'd herein before!/ This is close dealing." *2 Hen 6,* II, iv, 72–73.

close enacts, *n. pl.* secret workings: ". . . treacherous hue, that will betray with blushing/ The close enacts and counsels of thy heart!" *T Andr,* IV, ii, 117–118.

close fire, *n.* prob. ref. to her undisclosed venereal disease: "Let your close fire predominate his smoke . . ." *Timon,* IV, iii, 144.

closely, *adv.* **1** secretly: "Meaning to keep her closely at my cell/ Till I conveniently could send to Romeo." *Rom & Jul,* V, iii, 254–255. **2** privately: ". . . we have closely sent for Hamlet hither/ That he . . . may here/ Affront Ophelia." *Ham,* III, i, 29–31. **3** unseen; hidden: "I'll closely step aside,/ And list their babble, blunt and full of pride." *Edw 3,* I, ii, 16–17.

closeness, *n.* solitude; seclusion: ". . . all dedicated/ To closeness and the bettering of my mind . . ." *Temp,* I, ii, 89–90.

close patience, *n.* tight-lipped resignation: "Show your wisdom, daughter,/ In your close patience." *Meas,* IV, iii, 117–118.

close-stool, *n.* stool with a chamber pot underneath; also, a privy: ". . . your lion, that holds his poll-axe sitting on a close-stool, will be given to Ajax . . ." *Love's L,* V, ii, 571–572.

closet, *n.* **1** private bedroom or chamber; also, study: "Nurse, will you go with me into my closet,/ To help me sort such needful ornaments/ As you think fit . . ." *Rom & Jul,* IV, ii, 33–35. **2** locked box for valuables: "I have seen/ her rise from her bed . . . unlock her closet, take forth paper . . ." *Mac,* V, i, 3–5.

Clotharius, *n.* Clothair or Clotaire, Frankish [French] king of the 6th cent.: ". . . you would swear directly/ Their very noses had been counsellors/ To Pepin or Clotharius . . ." *Hen 8,* I, iii, 8–10.

clothier's yard, *n.* arrow, whose standard length was 37 inches, that of the cloth yard: "That fellow handles his bow/ like a crow-keeper: draw me a clothier's yard." *Lear,* IV, vi, 87–88.

cloth of honor, *n.* canopy, or cloth of state: "They that bear/ The cloth of honour over her, are four barons . . ." *Hen 8,* IV, i, 47–48.

cloth of state, *n.* canopy symbolizing great rank: "The King takes place/ under the cloth of state." [SD] *Hen 8,* II, iv, 1.

clotpoll, *n.* var. of **clodpole. 1** blockhead: "What says the fellow there? Call the clotpoll back." *Lear,* I, iv, 50. **2** wooden head; here, ref. to Cloten's stupidity: "I have sent Cloten's clotpoll down the stream . . ." *Cymb,* IV, ii, 184.

cloud, *n.* **1** blemish: "Blushing to be encount'red with a cloud." *T Andr,* II, iv, 32. **2 cloud in autumn,** cloud that may betoken bad weather: "O, he smiles valiantly . . . and 'twere a cloud in autumn." *Tr & Cr,* I, ii, 127–129. **3 in clouds,** surrounded by suspicion and uncertainty: "Feeds on this wonder, keeps himself in clouds,/ And wants not buzzers to infect his ear . . ." *Ham,* IV, v, 89–90.
—*v.* **4** to slander: "I would not be a stander-by, to hear/ My sovereign mistress clouded so . . ." *W Tale,* I, ii, 279–280.

clouded, *adj.* covered with a veil: "My face is but a moon, and clouded too." *Love's L,* V, ii, 203.

cloudy, *adj.* **1** sullen or resentful: ". . . render'd such aspect/ As cloudy men use to their adversaries . . ." *1 Hen 4,* III, ii, 82–83. **2** gloomy or sorrowful: "You cloudy princes and heart-sorrowing peers . . ." *Rich 3,* II, ii, 112.

clout, *n.* **1** piece of [white] cloth: ". . . she looks as pale/ as any clout in the versal [entire] world." *Rom & Jul,* II, iv, 201–202. **2** bandage: ". . . we had droven them home/ With clouts about their heads." *Ant & Cleo,* IV, vi, 5–6. **3** white-headed pin in the

center of the bull's-eye, by which the target was affixed: "Indeed, a' must shoot nearer, or he'll ne'er hit the clout." *Love's L,* IV, i, 135. **4** target aimed at: "O! well flown bird; i' th' clout, i' th' clout . . ." *Lear,* IV, vi, 92–93. **5** [pl.] clothes: "That great baby you see there is not yet out/ of his swaddling-clouts." *Ham,* II, ii, 378–379. **6 babe of clouts,** rag doll: "If I were mad, I should forget my son,/ Or madly think a babe of clouts were he." *K John,* III, iii, 57–58. **7 clap i'th'clout,** (in archery) hit the bull's-eye: "A would/ have clapped i'th'clout at twelve score . . ." *2 Hen 4,* III, ii, 45–46.

clouted shoon, *n. pl.* hobnailed shoes; also, a rustic: "Spare none but such as go in clouted shoon,/ For they are thrifty honest men . . ." *2 Hen 6,* IV, ii, 178–179.

cloven, *adj.* split up; cut in two: "List what work he makes/ Amongst your cloven army." *Cor,* I, iv, 20–21.

clown, *n.* rustic fellow: "Enter the Clown, with a basket, and two pigeons in it." [SD] *T Andr,* IV, iii, 76.

cloy, *v.* **1** to surfeit; glut: ". . . thy uncle is removing hence,/ As princes do their courts when they are cloy'd/ With long continuance in a settled place." *1 Hen 6,* II, v, 104–106. **2** (of a bird) to scratch with the claws: ". . . his royal bird . . . cloys his beak,/ As when his god is pleased." *Cymb,* V, iv, 117–119.
—*past part.* **3 so cloyed importantly,** so urgently occupied: ". . . have both their eyes/ And ears so cloy'd importantly as now . . ." *Cymb,* IV, iv, 18–19.

cloyed, *adj.* **the cloyed will,** lust; also, lustful man: "The cloyed will—/ That satiate yet unsatisfied desire . . ." *Cymb,* I, vii, 47–48.

cloyless, *adj.* impossible to tire of: "Epicurean cooks/ Sharpen with cloyless sauce his appetite . . ." *Ant & Cleo,* II, i, 24–25.

cloyment, *n.* distaste or revulsion: ". . . the palate,/ That suffers surfeit, cloyment, and revolt . . ." *T Night,* II, iv, 99–100.

Clubs! *interj.* **1** (in London) cry for the watch to bring clubs to break up a street fight: "Clubs, clubs! these lovers will not keep the peace." *T Andr,* II, i, 37. **2** call for apprentices to come to someone's aid: "I miss'd the/ meteor once, and hit that woman, who cried out/ 'Clubs' . . ." *Hen 8,* V, iii, 48–50.

cluster, *n.* crowd; mob: ". . . like beasts/ and cowardly nobles, gave way unto your clusters . . ." *Cor,* IV, vi, 122–123.

clutch, *v.* to close; here, refuse: "Not that I have the power to clutch my hand,/ When his fair angels would salute my palm . . ." *K John,* II, i, 589–590.

clutched, *adj.* clutching money; also, with obvious sexual innuendo: ". . . newly made woman to/ be had now, for putting the hand in the pocket and/ extracting [it] clutched?" *Meas,* III, ii, 44–46.

clyster-pipe, *n.* tube or syringe for administering an enema: ". . . yet again, your fingers/ at your lips? would they were clyster pipes for/ your sake . . ." *Oth,* II, i, 175–177.

coach, *n.* carriage; here, Ophelia's delusion that her coach awaits: "Come,/ my coach. Good night, ladies, good night." *Ham,* IV, v, 71–72.

coacher, *n.* Apollo, the sun god, who daily drove the chariot of the sun across the sky: "Ere twice the horses of the sun shall bring/ Their fiery coacher his diurnal ring . . ." *All's W,* II, i, 160–161.

coach-fellow, *n.* one of a pair of horses yoked together to draw a coach; hence, companion: "I have grated upon/ my good friends for three reprieves for you and your/ coach-fellow Nym . . ." *Wives,* II, ii, 5–7.

co-act, *v.* to act together; interact: "But if I tell how these two did co-act,/ Shall I not lie, in publishing a truth?" *Tr & Cr,* V, ii, 117–118.

coactive, *adj.* acting in concurrence; here, engaging in lust: "With what's unreal thou coactive art,/ And fellow'st nothing . . ." *W Tale,* I, ii, 141–142.

coagulate, *adj.* congealed: "And thus o'ersized with coagulate gore . . ." *Ham,* II, ii, 458.

coal, *n.* **1** charcoal; also, cinders: ". . . that have wrack'd for Rome/ To make coals cheap . . ." *Cor,* V, i, 16–17. **2 carry coals,** do menial work; also, show cowardice: "I knew by that piece of/ service the men would carry coals." *Hen 5,* III, ii, 48–49.

coast, *v.* **1** to glide: "And all in haste she coasteth to the cry." *Ven & Ad,* 870.
—*n.* **2** quarter; sector: "Yet have I gold flies from another coast . . ." *2 Hen 6,* I, ii, 93. **3** shore; also, port or harbor: ". . . show what coast thy sluggish care [crare]/ Might'st easi'est harbour in?" *Cymb,* IV, ii, 205–206.

coat, *n.* **1** coat of arms: "The King hath many marching in his coats." *1 Hen 4,* V, iii, 25. **2** confusion with "cod"; prob. a mispron.: "The luce is the fresh [freshwater] fish; the salt [saltwater] fish is an old coat [cod]." *Wives,* I, i, 21.

cobbled, *adj.* shoddily patched: ". . . such as stand not in their liking/ Below their cobbled shoes." *Cor,* I, i, 194–195.

cobloaf, *n.* small loaf of bread with a round head: "Cobloaf!"/ "He would pun thee into shivers with his fist . . ." *Tr & Cr,* II, i, 39–40.

cobweb, *n.* applied to a cut to stanch the flow of blood: ". . . good Master/ Cobweb: if I cut my finger, I shall make bold / with you." *M N Dream,* III, i, 175–177.

cock[1], *n.* **1** woodcock, proverbially a foolish bird; here, the shepherd is assumed to be a simpleton: "[Aside] If the springe hold, the cock's mine." *W Tale,* IV, iii, 35. **2 drowned the cocks,** inundated the weathercocks atop the church steeples: ". . . spout [rain]/ Till you have drench'd our steeples, drown'd the cocks!" *Lear,* III, ii, 2–3. **3 old cock,** Gonzalo, the "honest old Councellor": "Which, of he or Adrian, for a good wager, first/ begins to crow?"/ "The old cock." *Temp,* II, i, 27–29.

cock[2], *n.* **cock is up,** [his] pistol is in the cocked position; here, in obviously bawdy wordplay: "Pistol's cock is up,/ And flashing fire will follow." *Hen 5,* II, i, 51–52.

cock[3], *n.* spigot or tap on a wine cask: "I have retir'd me to a wasteful cock/ And set mine eyes at flow." *Timon,* II, ii, 166–167.

cock[4], *n.* cockboat, a ship's boat: "Diminish'd to her cock, her cock a buoy . . ." *Lear,* IV, vi, 19.

Cock, *n.* corruption of "God"; prob. also vulgar wordplay on sense of "penis": "Young men will do't if they come to't—/ By Cock, they are to blame." *Ham,* IV, v, 58–59.

cock a diddle dow, imit. of rooster crowing: "The strain of strutting chanticleer/ Cry—[burthen dispersedly.] Cock a diddle dow." *Temp,* I, ii, 388–389.

cock-a-hoop, *n.* **set cock-a-hoop,** to throw off all restraint: "You'll make a mutiny among my guests,/ You will set cock-a-hoop, you'll be the man!" *Rom & Jul,* I, v, 79–80.

cock and pie, *interj.* mild oath of the approx. meaning "[By] God and the holy book of services"; used esp. by rustics: "By cock and pie, sir, you shall not away to-night." *2 Hen 4,* V, i, 1.

cockatrice, *n.* basilisk, a fabled serpent whose stare was fatal: ". . . that bare vowel 'I' shall poison more/ Than the death-darting eye of cockatrice." *Rom & Jul,* III, ii, 46–47.

cockered, *adj.* pampered: ". . . shall a beardless boy,/ A cock'red silken wanton, brave our fields . . ." *K John,* V, i, 69–70.

cockerel, *n.* young lord Adrian: "Which, of he or Adrian . . . first/ begins to crow?"/ "The old cock."/ "The cockerel." *Temp,* II, i, 27–30.

cockle¹, *n.* type of weed: "Sow'd cockle reap'd no corn . . ." *Love's L,* IV, iii, 379.

cockle², *n.* cockleshell: "Sail seas in cockles, have and wish but for't . . ." *Per,* IV, iv, 2.

cockled, *adj.* encased in shell: "Love's feeling is more soft and sensible/ Than are the tender horns of cockled snails . . ." *Love's L,* IV, iii, 333–334.

cockle hat, *n.* hat decorated with a cockleshell, symbol of the shrine of St. James of Compostella, as evidence of the pilgrim's having visited the shrine: "By his cockle hat and staff/ And his sandal shoon." *Ham,* IV, v, 25–26.

cockney, *n.* **1** mollycoddle; also, a fop: "I am afraid this great lubber, the world,/ will prove a cockney." *T Night,* IV, i, 14–15. **2** city-dweller, esp. a Londoner; here, appar. a squeamish woman: "Cry to it, Nuncle, as the cockney did to the eels . . ." *Lear,* II, iv, 122.

cockscomb, *n.* fool's cap: "Shall I/ have a cockscomb of frieze?" *Wives,* V, v, 138–139.

cockshut time, *n.* time when poultry were put away for the night; dusk: "Much about cockshut time . . . Went through the army cheering up the soldiers." *Rich 3,* V, iii, 71–72.

Cock's passion, *interj.* God's passion [an oath]: "Cock's passion, silence! I hear my master." *Shrew,* IV, i, 106.

Cocytus, *n.* river in Hades; here, Hades itself: "Out of this fell devouring receptacle,/ As hateful as Cocytus' misty mouth." *T Andr,* II, iii, 235–236.

cod, *n.* pod or husk, esp. the peapod, often used as a love token: ". . . I remember the wooing of a peascod instead of her, from whom I took two cods . . ." *As You,* II, iv, 48–49.

codding, *adj.* lustful; also, deceitful: "That codding spirit had they from their mother . . ." *T Andr,* V, i, 99.

codling, *n.* unripe apple: ". . . as a squash is before 'tis a peascod, or a/ codling when 'tis almost an apple." *T Night,* I, v, 159–160.

codpiece or **cod-piece,** *n.* **1** decorative flap covering the crotch of a man's breeches: ". . . like the/ shaven Hercules . . . where his codpiece seems as massy as his club?" *M Ado,* III, iii, 132–134. **2** ref. to customary prominence of such covering on a fool's costume: "Marry, here's grace and a cod-piece; that's/ a wise man and a Fool." *Lear,* III, ii, 40–41. **3** the penis: "Why, what a ruthless thing is this . . . for the/ rebellion of a codpiece to take away the life of a/ man!" *Meas,* III, ii, 110–112.

coelo, *n.* [Latin] sky; heaven: ". . . now hangeth like a jewel in/ the ear of *coelo,* the sky, the welkin, the heaven . . ." *Love's L,* IV, ii, 4–5.

Coeur-de-lion, *n.* See **aweless lion.**

coffer, *n.* **1** coffin: ". . . this letter and some certain jewels/ Lay with you in your coffer . . ." *Per,* III, iv, 1–2. **2** chest for money or other valuables: "If there be anypody in the house, and in the/ chambers, and in the coffers . . ." *Wives,* III, iii, 194–195. **3** [pl] luggage; baggage: "I prithee, good Iago,/ Go to the bay, and disembark my coffers . . ." *Oth,* II, i, 207–208. **4 general coffers,** public treasury [lit., the "treasure chests"]: "He hath brought many captives home to Rome,/ Whose ransoms did the general coffers fill . . ." *J Caes,* III, ii, 90–91.

coffin, *n.* pie crust, perh. in ref. to its domed top: "And of the paste a coffin I will rear . . ." *T Andr,* V, ii, 188.

coffined, *adj.* placed or carried in a coffin: "Wouldst thou have laugh'd had I come coffin'd home . . ." *Cor,* II, i, 175.

cog, *v.* to deceive, as by tricks or flattery; cheat: "Since you can cog, I'll play no more with you." *Love's L,* V, ii, 235.

cogging, *adj.* deceitful; cheating: ". . . to be revenge on this same/ scall, scurvy, cogging companion . . ." *Wives,* III, i, 110–111.

cognizance, *n.* identifying emblem worn by servants, esp. of a great house: ". . . great men shall press/ For tinctures, stains, relics, and cognizance." *J Caes,* II, ii, 88–89.

cohere, *v.* to agree; tally or coincide: ". . . till each circumstance/ Of place, time, fortune, do cohere and jump/ That I am Viola . . ." *T Night,* V, i, 249–251.

coherent, *adj.* in accord; suitable: "That time and place with this deceit so lawful/ May prove coherent." *All's W,* III, vii, 38–39.

coif, *n.* nightcap: ". . . hence, thou sickly coif!/ Thou art a guard too wanton for the head . . ." *2 Hen 4,* I, i, 147–148.

coign, *n.* **1** corner: "By the four opposing coigns/ Which the world together joins . . ." *Per,* III, Chor., 17–18. **2** cornerstone: "See you yond coign o'th'Capitol, yond cornerstone?" *Cor,* V, iv, 1–2. **3 coign of vantage,** *n.* well-situated or convenient corner: ". . . no jutty, frieze,/ Buttress, nor coign of vantage, but this bird/ Hath made his pendent bed . . ." *Mac,* I, vi, 6–8.

coil, *n.* **1** confusion; turmoil; fuss or hubbub: "What a coil's here,/ Serving of becks and jutting-out of bums!" *Timon,* I, ii, 232–233. **2 keep a coil, a.** to make a fuss: "What need we fight and sweat and keep a coil,/ When railing crows outscold our adversaries?" *Edw 3,* IV, vi, 11–12. **b.** to be fussed over: "I am commanded here, and kept a coil with/ 'Too young'. . ." *All's W,* II, i, 27–28. **3 old coil,** great to-do or rumpus: ". . . yonder's/ old coil at home." *M Ado,* V, ii, 88–89. **4 this mortal coil,** the turbulence of human existence: "When we have shuffled off this mortal coil . . ." *Ham,* III, i, 67.

coin, *v.* **coin heaven's image,** beget children; here, illegitimately: "Their saucy sweetness that do coin heaven's image/ In stamps that are forbid." *Meas,* II, iv, 45–46.

coining, *n.* minting of coins; also, poss. wordplay on slang sense, "begetting children": "No, they cannot touch me for coining; I am/ the king himself." *Lear,* IV, vi, 83–84.

coistrel, *n.* knave; scoundrel: ". . . the damned door-keeper to every/ Coistrel that comes inquiring for his Tib . . ." *Per,* IV, vi, 164–165.

Colbrand, *n.* giant overcome by Guy of Warwick in old romances: ". . . old Sir Robert's son?/ Colbrand the giant, that same mighty man?" *K John,* I, i, 224–225.

Colchos, *n.* Colchis, land where Jason captured the golden fleece: "Which makes her seat of Belmont Colchos' strond,/ And many Jasons come in quest of her." *Merch,* I, i, 171–172.

cold, *adj.* **1** unwilling; also, cowardly: "He's like/ to be a cold soldier." *2 Hen 4,* III, ii, 122–123. **2** impartial: "After this cold considerance sentence me . . ." *2 Hen 4,* V, ii, 98. **3** indifferent; apathetic: "The nobles they are fled, the commons cold . . ." *Rich 2,* II, ii, 88. **4** collected; tranquil: "Who, moving others, are themselves as stone,/ Unmoved, cold, and to temptation slow . . ." *Sonn 94,* 3–4. **5** filled with cold fear: ". . . Norweyan banners flout the sky,/ And fan our people cold." *Mac,* I, ii, 50–51. **6** bleak; gloomy; hopeless: "A cold premeditation for my purpose!" *3 Hen 6,* III, ii, 133. **7** chaste; modest: "But our cold maids do dead men's fingers call them." *Ham,* IV, vii, 170. **8** cancelled; voided or nullified: "Fare you well, your suit is cold." *Merch,* II, vii, 73. **9** naked: "Cold wisdom waiting on superfluous [overdressed] folly." *All's W,* I, i, 103. **10 cold bonds,** See **bond** (def. 6). **11 cold for action,** cooled off for lack of action: ". . . another half stand laughing by,/ All out of work, and cold for action!" *Hen 5,* I, ii, 113–114.

cold demeanor, *n.* lack of enthusiasm in battle: ". . . I perceive/ But cold demeanour in Octavius' wing . . ." *J Caes,* V, ii, 3–4.

cold dishes, *n.* leftovers: "One bred of alms, and foster'd with [fed on] cold dishes . . ." *Cymb,* II, iii, 112–113.

coldest, *adj.* least favorable: "Though no man be assur'd what grace to find,/ You stand in coldest expectation." *2 Hen 4,* V, ii, 30–31.

coldly, *adv.* **1** patiently: "Bear it coldly but till midnight, and let/ the issue show itself." *M Ado,* III, ii, 118–119. **2** rationally: "If he were mad, he would not plead so coldly." *Errors,* V, i, 273.

Colebrook, *n.* village near Windsor: ". . . has cozened all the hosts of/ Readins, of Maidenhead, of Colebrook . . ." *Wives,* IV, v, 72–73.

colic, *n.* trapped or pent-up wind: "Out-swell the colic of puff'd Aquilon [the North wind]." *Tr & Cr,* IV, v, 9.

collateral, *adj.* **1** acting as an accessory: "If by direct or by collateral hand/ They find us touch'd . . ." *Ham,* IV, v, 203–204. **2** indirect; here, emanating from a higher sphere: "In his bright radiance and collateral light/ Must I be comforted . . ." *All's W,* I, i, 86–87.

Collatinus, *n.* Roman name of Collatine: "But now he throws that shallow habit by . . . To check the tears in Collatinus' eyes." *Luc,* 1814–1817.

Collatium, *n.* home of Collatine and his wife, Lucrece: ". . . leaves the Roman host/ And to Collatium bears the lightless fire . . ." *Luc,* 3–4.

colleagued, *adj.* joined: "Colleagued with this dream of his advantage . . ." *Ham,* I, ii, 21.

collected, *adj.* **be collected,** calm down: "Be collected:/ No more amazement: tell your piteous heart/ There's no harm done." *Temp,* I, ii, 13–15.

collection, *n.* **1** a gathering or putting together; here, of conversational fragments: "Yet the unshaped use of it doth move/ The hearers to collection." *Ham,* IV, v, 8–9. **2** sense or understanding; deduction: ". . . so from sense in hardness, that I can/ Make no collection of it." *Cymb,* V, v, 432–433.

college, *n.* learned society or chapter: ". . . a college of witcrackers/ cannot flout me out of my humour." *M Ado,* V, iv, 99–100.

collied, *adj.* **1** blackened [lit. "coal-blackened"]: "Brief as the lightning in the collied night . . ." *M N Dream,* I, i, 145. **2** clouded or beclouded: ". . . passion having my best judgement collied/ Assays to lead the way." *Oth,* II, iii, 197–198.

collier, *n.* **1** person who mines or sells coal; also, one who makes and sells charcoal: "And since her time are colliers counted bright." *Love's L,* IV, iii, 263. **2** such a person, usually blackened and dirty, compared to the devil, who was represented as hell-blackened: ". . . 'tis not/ for gravity to play at cherry-pit with Satan. Hang/ him, foul collier!" *T Night,* III, iv, 117–119.

collop, *n.* **1** piece; part: "God knows thou art a collop of my flesh . . ." *1 Hen 6,* V, iv, 18. **2** part of myself: "Look on me with your welkin eye: sweet villain!/ Most dear'st, my collop!" *W Tale,* I, ii, 136–137.

collusion, *n.* misuse for "allusion": "'Tis true indeed: the collusion holds in the exchange." *Love's L,* IV, ii, 41.

Colme-kill, *n.* isle in the Hebrides; burial ground of ancient Scottish kings: "Where is Duncan's body?"/ "Carried to Colme-kill . . ." *Mac,* II, iv, 32–33.

coloquintida, *n.* colocynth, or "bitter apple," used to make a purgative: "The food that to him now is as luscious as locusts,/ shall be to him shortly as acerb as the coloquintida." *Oth,* I, iii, 349–350.

color, *n.* **1** kind, sort, or nature: ". . . you have lost much good sport."/ "Sport? Of what colour?" *As You,* I, ii, 92–93. **2** pretext; alibi: "'Tis no/ matter if I do halt; I have the wars for my colour . . ." *2 Hen 4,* I, ii, 246–247. **3** pretense; also, wordplay on "collar" [noose]: "This that you heard/ was but a colour." *2 Hen 4,* V, v, 85–86. **4** paint; veneer; artificial coloring: "'Truth needs no colour . . . Beauty no pencil . .'" *Sonn 101,* 6–7. **5** [pl.] banners, ensigns, etc., esp. of an army or cause: ". . . those that weep this/ lamentable divorce under her colours . . ." *Cymb,* I, v, 17–18. **6 advance the colors,** take the initiative [for my cause]: "I must advance the colours of my love . . ." *Wives,* III, iv, 79. **7 against all color,** without any pretense of fairness: "Caesar's ambition . . . against all colour here/ Did put the yoke upon's . . ." *Cymb,* III, i, 49–52. **8 bear no color for,** be substantiated by: "And since the quarrel/ Will bear no colour for the thing he is . . ." *J Caes,* II, i, 28–29. **9 fear no colors,** to fear nothing or no one [proverbial expression]; also, wordplay on "collar" [noose]: ". . . he that is well hanged in this/ world needs to fear no colours." *T Night,* I, v, 5–6. **10 hold not color with,** to be inappropriate for: "You must not marvel, Helen, at my course,/ Which holds not colour with the time . . ." *All's W,* II, v, 58–59. **11 show no color,** to offer no excuse: "If I find not/ what I seek, show no colour for my extremity . . ." *Wives,* IV, ii, 147–148. **12 want true color,** to lack the proper aspect: "Then what I have to do/ Will want true colour—tears perchance for blood." *Ham,* III, iv, 129–130. —*v.* **13** to make believable: "That show of such an exercise may colour/ Your loneliness." *Ham,* III, i, 45–46. **14** to disguise: ". . . you are partly a bawd, Pompey,/ howsoever you colour it in being a tapster . . ." *Meas,* II, i, 216–217.

colorable colors, *n.* plausible excuses: "Sir, tell not me of the father; I do fear colourable/ colours." *Love's L,* IV, ii, 143–144.

colored, *adj.* **colored ill,** dark-complexioned: "My worser spirit a woman, colour'd ill." *Pass Pil,* II, 4.

coloring, *n.* **passes coloring,** goes beyond any justification [lit., surpasses any skill of dyeing]: "Here's such ado to make no stain a stain/ As passes colouring." *W Tale,* II, ii, 19–20.

colt, *n.* **1** young and inexperienced fellow: "Ay that's a colt indeed, for he doth nothing but talk/ of his horse . . ." *Merch,* I, ii, 39–40. —*v.* **2** to trick; deceive: "What a/ plague mean ye to colt me thus?" *1 Hen 4,* II, ii, 36–37. **3** to mount sexually; cover: "She hath been colted by him." *Cymb,* II, iv, 133.

colt's tooth, *n.* youthful indiscretions; here, sexual desire, esp. in older men: "Your colt's tooth is not cast [discarded] yet?" *Hen 8,* I, iii, 48.

Comagene, *n.* kingdom in Syria: "Mithridates, king/ Of Comagene, Polemon and Amyntas . . ." *Ant & Cleo,* III, vi, 73–74.

co-mate, *n.* companion: "Now my co-mates and brothers in exile . . ." *As You,* II, i, 1.

combinate, *adj.* bound by oath: ". . . with both, [she lost] her/ combinate husband, this well-seeming Angelo." *Meas,* III, i, 222–223.

combine, *v.* to bind; unite: "And friendship shall combine, and brotherhood . . ." *Hen 5,* II, i, 109.

combined, *past part.* bound: "For my poor self,/ I am combined by a sacred vow . . ." *Meas,* IV, iii, 143–144.

combless cock, *n.* humbled and spiritless cock: "A combless cock, so Kate will be my hen." *Shrew,* II, i, 224.

combustion, *n.* turmoil; tumult: ". . . prophesying with accents terrible/ Of dire combustion, and confus'd events . . ." *Mac,* II, iii, 58–59.

come, *v.* **1** to yield; come around: "He will relent;/ He's coming: I perceive't." *Meas,* II, ii, 125–126. **2 come again,** come at me again; here, with a stinging reply: "Nay, come again,/ Good Kate. I am a gentleman—" *Shrew,* II, i, 216–217. **3 come away, a.** come here; come along (used as a command): "What, ostler! Come away, and be hanged . . ." *1 Hen 4,* II, i, 21. **b.** Hurry up!: "Look how thou stirr'st now! come away, or I'll/ fetch'th with a wanion." *Per,* II, i, 16–17. **4 come better,** to arrive at a more opportune moment: "He could never come

better: he shall come in." *W Tale,* IV, iv, 189. **5 come current,** See **current**[2] (def. 3). **6 come me, a.** get or move along: "Come me to what was done to her." *Meas,* II, i, 117. **b.** infringe on my rights: "See how this river comes me cranking in,/ And cuts me from the best of all my land . . ." *1 Hen 4,* III, I, 94–95. **7 come near,** begin to understand: "O ho, do you come near me now?" *T Night,* III, iv, 64. **8 come o'er us,** tax us: ". . . we understand him well,/ How he comes o'er us with our wilder days . . ." *Hen 5,* I, ii, 266–267. **9 come off, a.** escape: "No, he's settled/ (Not to come off) in his displeasure." *Hen 8,* III, ii, 22–23. **b.** leave the field of battle [at the end of a day's fighting]; disengage: "O, bravely came we off,/ When with a volley of our needless shot . . . we bid good-night . . ." *K John,* V, v, 5. **c.** pay up: "I have turned away my other guests./ They must come off . . ." *Wives,* IV, iii, 10–11. **10 come on,** (of a military force) to advance: ". . . marry, in coming on he has/ the cramp [muscular spasm]." *All's W,* IV, iii, 281–282. **11 come over it,** to outdo or excel; here, in wordplay with "top sexually": "In so high a style, Margaret, that no man living/ shall come over it . . ." *M Ado,* V, ii, 7–8. **12 come roundly,** to speak plainly: ". . . shall I then come roundly to thee . . ." *Shrew,* I, ii, 58. **13 come sooner by,** to acquire earlier: ". . . superfluity comes sooner by white hairs, but/ competency lives longer." *Merch,* I, ii, 8–9. **14 come to,** end up in the same condition as: "His neck will come to your waist—a cord, sir." *Meas,* III, ii, 39. **15 come to it,** reach maturity: "Th'other's not come to't, you shall tell me . . ." *Tr & Cr,* I, ii, 84. **16 come unto it,** sense of preceding, with wordplay on calf becoming bull and able to provide "service": ". . . for your part,/ Bullcalf, grow till you come unto it." *2 Hen 4,* III, ii, 246–247. **17 come up, a.** become fashionable: ". . . it was/ never merry world in England since gentlemen came up." *2 Hen 6,* IV, ii, 7–9. **b.** term of sharp rebuke: "Are you so hot? Marry, come up, I trow." *Rom & Jul,* II, v, 63. **18 come (on) your ways, a.** come along now: "Look to't, I charge you. Come your ways." *Ham,* I, iv, 135. **b.** come here (used as an imperative): "Come on your ways; open your mouth; here is that which will give language to you, cat . . ." *Temp,* II, ii, 84–85. **19 let it come,** let (the drinking cup, etc.) be passed around: "Let it come, i'faith, and I'll pledge you all . . ." *2 Hen 6,* II, iii, 65. **20 to come alone,** that he would come alone: "yet is't not probable/ To come alone . . ."*Cymb,* IV, ii, 141–142.
—*past part.* **21** conferred: "New honours come upon him . . . cleave not to their mould . . ." *Mac,* I, iii, 145–146.

come, bird, come, *interj.* falconer's cry to recall his bird; here, an answering call: "Hillo, ho, ho, boy. Come, bird, come." *Ham,* I, v, 118.

comedian, *n.* actor: "Are you a comedian?"/ "No, my profound heart . . ." *T Night,* I, v, 183–184.

comely, *adj.* certain; here, with compliment to Margaret's beauty: ". . . in most comely truth thou/ deservest it." *M Ado,* V, ii, 7–8.

comely-distant, *adv.* at a discreet distance: "And comely-distant sits he by her side . . ." *Lover's Comp,* 65.

comer, *n.* one newly arrived; newcomer: ". . . with his arms out-stretch'd, as he would fly,/ Grasps in the comer." *Tr & Cr,* III, iii, 167–168.

comet, *n.* celestial phenomenon regarded as signaling disaster: "As if they saw some wondrous monument,/ Some comet, or unusual prodigy?" *Shrew,* III, ii, 93–94.

comfect, *n.* var. of *confect;* sweetmeat or comfit: ". . . Count Comfect, a sweet gallant/ surely!" *M Ado,* IV, i, 315.

comfit-maker, *n.* candy-maker; confectioner: "Heart, you swear like a/ comfit-maker's wife . . ." *1 Hen 4,* III, i, 241–242.

comfort, *v.* to minister to; encourage: ". . . that dares/ Less appear so, in comforting your evils . . ." *W Tale,* II, iii, 55–56.

comfortable, *adj.* **1** easy in one's mind; agreeable; cheerful: "For my sake be comfortable; hold death awhile at the arm's end." *As You,* II, vi, 8–10. **2** comforting; consoling: "I have another daughter/ Who, I am sure, is kind and comfortable." *Lear,* I, iv, 314–315.

comfort of retirement, *n.* protected position of retreat: "A comfort of retirement lives in this." *1 Hen 4,* IV, i, 56.

coming-in, *n.* income; profits or benefits: ". . . aleven widows and nine maids is a/ simple [modest] coming-in for one man . . ." *Merch,* II, ii, 154–155.

coming on, *n.* military action of advancing: ". . . marry, in coming on he has/ the cramp." *All's W,* IV, iii, 281–282.

coming-on, *adj.* encouraging: ". . . I will be your Rosalind in a more coming-on disposition . . ." *As You,* IV, i, 107.

command, *n.* **1** authority; right to exercise power: "Go, fool, and whom thou keep'st command [your servants]." *Shrew,* II, i, 251. **2** military use: ". . . a soldier-like/ word, and a word of exceeding good command, by/ heaven." *2 Hen 4,* III, ii, 74–75. **3** dictatorial rule; oppression: "'Achievement is command; ungain'd, beseech.'" **4 better thee in their command,** have authority over you [who are a slave]: "Neither of these are so bad as thou art,/ Since they do better thee in their command." *Per,* IV, vi, 160–161. **5 deal in her command,** exercise her [the moon's] authority: ". . . one so strong/ That could control the moon . . . And deal in her command, without her power." *Temp,* V, i, 269–271. **6 in command,** when or as commanded: "Those he commands move only in command . . ." *Mac,* V, ii, 19.

—*v.* **7 command at,** receive cooperation from: ". . . at every house I'll call,/ I may command at most . . ." *Oth,* I, i, 181–182. **8 commanded here,** ordered to remain here: "I am commanded here, and kept a coil with/ 'Too young'. . ." *All's W,* II, i, 27–28.

commandement, *n.* old form (and pron.) of **commandment:** "Let his deservings and my love withal/ Be valued 'gainst your wife's commandement." *Merch,* IV, i, 446–447.

commandment, *n.* **at commandment,** at one's will; whenever one wants: ". . . we knew where the bona-robas/ were, and had the best of them all at commandment." *2 Hen 4,* III, ii, 22–23.

commeddled, *adj.* commingled: ". . . blest are those/ Whose blood and judgment are so well commeddled . . ." *Ham,* III, ii, 69.

commence, *v.* to put into use; activate: ". . . and learning [is] a mere/ hoard of gold . . . till sack commences it/ and sets it in act and use." *2 Hen 4,* IV, iii, 113–115.

commencement, *n.* enterprise or undertaking: ". . . as if/ The passage and whole stream of this commencement/ Rode on his tide." *Tr & Cr,* II, iii, 132–134.

commend, *v.* **1** to send the regards of: "'I commend me to thee . . .'" *2 Hen 4,* II, ii, 119. **2** to think well of: "'I commend thee . . .'" *2 Hen 4,* II, ii, 119. **3** to commit; consign or entrust: "His glittering arms he will commend to rust,/ His barbed steeds to stables . . ." *Rich 2,* III, iii, 116–117. **4** to entrust: "Sir, I do know you;/ And dare . . . Commend a dear [important] thing to you." *Lear,* III, i, 17–19. **5** to offer; present: ". . . this even-handed Justice/ Commends th' ingredience of our poison'd chalice/ To our own lips." *Mac,* I, vii, 10–12. **6** to introduce: "Let me commend thee first to those that shall/ Say yea to thy desires." *Cor,* IV, v, 145–146. **7** wordplay on Osric's "commend" [offer] and Hamlet's reply of "commend" [praise], appar. ref. to Osric's bow: "I commend my duty to your lordship."/ "A does well to commend it himself . . ." *Ham,* V, ii, 179–181. **8** to be equal to: "Farewell, and let your haste commend your duty." *Ham,* I, ii, 39. **9 commend them and condemn them,** "Commend them and condemn them to her service,/ Or to their own perdition [I would commend such qualities to her service or condemn them to their own perdition]." *W Tale,* IV, iv, 378–379.

—*n.* **10** [pl.] regards or greetings; also, compliments: "With all the gracious utterance that thou hast/ Speak to his gentle hearing kind commends." *Rich 2,* III, iii, 125–126.

commendable, *adj.* praiseworthy; here, stressed on first syllable: "And commendable prov'd, let's die in pride." *1 Hen 6,* IV, vi, 57.

commendation, *n.* **1** introduction: "I have your commendation for my more/ free entertainment." *Cymb,* I, v, 151–152. **2** [pl] greetings: ". . . 'tis a word or two/ Of commendations sent from Valentine . . ." *Two Gent,* I, iii, 52–53.

comment, *v.* **1** to expand; elaborate: "Say that thou didst forsake me for some fault,/ And I will comment upon that offence . . ." *Sonn* 89, 1–2.

—*n.* **2 the very comment of thy soul,** your keenest powers of observation: "Even with the very comment of thy soul/ Observe my uncle." *Ham,* III, ii, 79–80.

commenting, *n.* discussion: "I have learn'd that fearful commenting/ Is leaden servitor to dull delay . . ." *Rich 3,* IV, iii, 51–52.

commerce, *n.* business sense implied, but Hamlet picks up on the word's sexual connotation: "Could beauty, my lord, have better commerce than/ with honesty [chastity]?" *Ham,* III, i, 109–110.

commission, *n.* **1** a usually royal warrant permitting an official to exercise authority: "There is our commission,/ From which we would not have you warp [deviate]." *Meas,* I, i, 13–14. **2** warrant permitting the collecting of taxes: ". . . there have been commissions/ Sent down among 'em . . ." *Hen 8,* I, ii, 20–21. **3** warrant; also, status: "You are more saucy with lords/ and honourable personages than the commission of/ your birth and virtue gives you heraldry." *All's W,* II, iii, 256–258. **4** soldiers under one's command: ". . . take/ Th'one half of my commission, and set down/ As best thou art experienc'd . . ." *Cor,* IV, v, 138–140. **5 from my commission,** beyond the scope of my instructions: ". . . what is yours to bestow is not yours to/ reserve. But this is from my commission." *T Night,* I, v, 189–190. **6 in commission,** charged with a particular duty: "Or not/ Those in commission yet return'd?" *Mac,* I, iv, 1–2. **7 in commission with,** of the same profession as: ". . . it is my cousin Silence, in commission/ with me." *2 Hen 4,* III, ii, 87–88. **8 of the commission,** commissioned as a judge: "You are o' th' commission,/ Sit you too." *Lear,* III, vi, 39–40. **9 seal a commission,** to grant legal authority or permission: "Omission to do what is necessary/ Seals a commission to a blank of danger . . ." *Tr & Cr,* III, iii, 229–230.

commit, *v.* **1** to send to jail or prison: ". . . the nobleman that committed the/ Prince for striking him about Bardolph." *2 Hen 4,* I, ii, 55–56. **2 commit not,** "adultery" understood here: ". . . commit not/ with man's sworn spouse . . ." *Lear,* III, iv, 81–82. **3 commit to doubt,** to distrust: "I committed/

The daring'st counsel which I had to doubt . . ." *Hen 8*, II, iv, 212–213.

commix, *v.* to mingle: ". . . to commix/ With winds that sailors rail at." *Cymb,* IV, ii, 55–56.

commixtion, *n.* mixture or blending of elements: "Were thy commixtion Greek and Trojan so . . ." *Tr & Cr,* IV, v, 123.

commixture, *n.* **1** blend or blending: "Dismask'd, their damask sweet commixture shown,/ Are angels vailing clouds, or roses blown." *Love's L,* V, ii, 296–297. **2** compound: "And, now I fall, thy tough commixture melts . . ." *3 Hen 6,* II, vi, 6.

commodious, *adj.* accommodating: ". . . the parrot will not do/ more for an almond than he for a commodious/ drab." *Tr & Cr,* V, ii, 191–193.

commodity, *n.* **1** supply or consignment; quantity: "I would to God thou and I knew where a/ commodity of good names were to be bought . . ." *1 Hen 4,* I, ii, 80–81. **2** [often pl] merchandise: "Neither have I money, nor commodity/ To raise a present sum . . ." *Merch,* I, i, 178–179. **3** [pl] loan in which the borrower had to accept often worthless "commodities" [products] along with the actual money, then was forced to pay interest on the entire value of the loan (as set by the lender): ". . . he's in/ for a commodity of brown paper and old ginger,/ nine score and seventeen pounds . . ." *Meas,* IV, iii, 4–6. **4** profit or gain; advantage: ". . . the commodity wages not with the danger . . ." *Per,* IV, ii, 29. **5** personal advantage; benefit: "I will turn/ diseases to commodity." *2 Hen 4,* I, ii, 249–250. **6** self-interest; expedience: "That smooth-fac'd gentleman, tickling commodity,/ Commodity, the bias of the world . . ." *K John,* II, i, 573–574.

common, *n.* **1** park or meadow shared by all citizens: "My lips are no common, though several they be." *Love's L,* II, i, 222. **2** [pl.] commoners; the common people, as disting. from the nobility: "The nobles they are fled, the commons cold . . ." *Rich 2,* II, ii, 88. **3** [pl.] public pasturelands: "Like to the empty ass, to shake his ears,/ And graze in commons." *J Caes,* IV, i, 26–27.
—*adj.* **4** usual; universal; here, doubtless with wordplay on "vulgar": "Ay, madam, it is common." *Ham,* I, ii, 74. **5** low; base; dejected: ". . . he would unto the stews,/ And from the common'st creature pluck a glove . . ." *Rich 2,* V, iii, 16–17. **6** ordinary; of no particular distinction: ". . . if they should grow themselves to common/ players—as it is most like . . ." *Ham,* II, ii, 346–347. **7** public: ". . . the common ferry/ Which trades to Venice . . ." *Merch,* III, iv, 53–54. **8 in common,** shared by all: "All the realm shall be in common . . ." *2 Hen 6,* IV, ii, 65. **9 the common,** ordinary expectations: ". . . your son/ Will or exceed the common, or be caught . . ." *Cor,* IV, i, 31–32.

commonalty, *n.* common people: "He's a very dog to the commonalty." *Cor,* I, i, 27–28.

common body, *n.* common people: "This common body,/ Like to a vagabond flag upon the stream . . ." *Ant & Cleo,* I, iv, 44–45.

commoner, *n.* **1** prostitute: "Committed! O thou public commoner!" *Oth,* IV, ii, 75. **2 vital commoners,** vital fluids of the body: ". . . and then the vital commoners, and/ inland petty spirits, muster me all to their captain, the heart . . ." *2 Hen 4,* IV, iii, 108–110.

common-hackney'd, *adj.* commonplace; overfamiliar: "So common-hackney'd in the eyes of men,/ So stale and cheap to vulgar company . . ." *1 Hen 4,* III, ii, 40–41.

common house, *n.* brothel: ". . . good people . . . that do nothing but use their/ abuses in common houses . . ." *Measures,* II, i, 41–43.

common-kissing, *adj.* kissing [affecting] all alike: ". . . the greedy touch/ Of Common-kissing Titan [the sun] . . ." *Cymb,* III, iv, 164–165.

commonplace, *n.* a book of thoughts, impressions, etc., to be readily referred to: "Then render back this commonplace of prayer/ To do himself good in adversity." *Edw 3,* IV, iv, 116–117.

common proof, *n.* matter of universal experience: "But 'tis a common proof,/ That lowliness is young ambition's ladder . . ." *J Caes,* II, i, 21–22.

common pulpits, *n.* the public platforms, esp. those in the Forum: "Some to the common pulpits, and cry out,/ 'Liberty, freedom, and enfranchisement!'" *J Caes,* III, i, 80–81.

common sense, *n.* **1** ordinary intelligence: "Things hid and barr'd, you mean, from common sense?" *Love's L,* I, i, 57. **2 in common sense,** as all must be aware of: "The time misorder'd doth, in common sense,/ Crowd us and crush us to this monstrous form . . ." *2 Hen 4,* IV, ii, 33–34.

common shores, *n. pl.* lawful dumping areas along the river: "Empty/ Old receptacles, or common shores, of filth . . ." *Per,* IV, vi, 173–174.

common sort, *n.* ordinary soldiers: "Now march we hence: discharge the common sort/ With pay and thanks . . ." *3 Hen 6,* V, v, 85–86.

commons' suit, *n.* petition by Commons [historically, following Bolingbroke's coronation] for formal arraignment of

Richard II and a specification of charges: "May it please you, lords to grant the commons' suit?" *Rich 2*, IV, i, 154.

common talk, *n.* ordinary conversation: "And practise rhetoric in your common talk . . ." *Shrew*, I, i, 35.

commonweal, *n.* old form of **commonwealth**: "Swear like a ruffian, and demean himself/ Unlike the ruler of a commonweal." *2 Hen 6*, I, i, 187–188.

commonwealth, *n.* lower class, comprising the common people: "Here comes a member of the commonwealth." *Love's L*, IV, i, 41.

commotion, *n.* riot; insurrection: ". . . if damn'd commotion so appear'd/ In his true, native, and most proper shape . . ." *2 Hen 4*, IV, i, 36–37.

commune, *v.* **1** to confer: "I would commune with you of such things/ That want no ear but yours." *Meas*, IV, iii, 103–104. **2 commune with,** to share in: "Laertes, I must commune with your grief,/ Or you deny me right." *Ham*, IV, v, 199–200.

communicate, *v.* to associate; share a nature: "Thou dost make possible things not so held,/ Communicat'st with dreams . . ." *W Tale*, I, ii, 139–140.

community, *n.* commonness; overfamiliarity: ". . . sick and blunted with community,/ Afford no extraordinary gaze . . ." *1 Hen 4*, III, ii, 77–78.

commutual, *adv.* as one; mutually: ". . . Hymen did our hands/ Unite commutual in most sacred bands." *Ham*, III, ii, 154–155.

comonty, *n.* Sly's misuse for "comedy" [or perh. his drunken pron.]: "Is not a comonty/ A Christmas gambol or a tumbling-trick?" *Shrew*, Ind., ii, 137–138.

compact[1], *adj.* **1** made up; composed: "If he, compact of jars, grow musical,/ We shall have shortly discord in the spheres." *As You*, II, vii, 5–6. **2** well arranged: "Conceit deceitful, so compact, so kind . . ." *Luc*, 1423.
—*v.* **3** to compound; mix: "The poisonous simple sometime is compacted/ In a pure compound . . ." *Luc*, 530–531. **4** to consolidate; buttress or strengthen: "And thereto add such reasons of your own/ As may compact it more." *Lear*, I, iv, 348–349.

compact[2], *n.* **1** plot; conspiracy: "What is the course and drift [the gist] of your compact?" *Errors*, II, ii, 161.
—*adj.* **2** in league; here, with the king: "When he, compact, and flattering his displeasure,/ Tripp'd me behind . . ." *Lear*, II, ii, 119–120.

companion, *n.* **1** fellow; rascal; knave: "What an equivocal companion is this!" *All's W*, V, iii, 246–247. **2** [often pl.] cohort; fellow ruffian (contemp. use): "'. . . receive,' says he, 'no swaggering/ companions'; there comes none here." *2 Hen 4*, II, iv, 91–92.

company, *n.* **1** companion: "I would gladly have him see his company anatomiz'd [dissected] . . ." *All's W*, IV, iii, 30–31. **2 from company,** in solitude; alone: "And so conduct me where from company/ I may revolve and ruminate my grief." *1 Hen 6*, V, v, 100–101. **3 more company,** a call for assistance: "More company; the fiend is strong within him." *Errors*, IV, iv, 105.

comparative, *adj.* **1** abounding in comparisons; also, quick at making comparisons: "Thou . . . art indeed the most comparative rascalliest sweet young prince." *1 Hen 4*, I, ii, 78.
—*n.* **2** person who makes insulting comparisons: ". . . stand the push/ Of every beardless vain comparative . . ." *1 Hen 4*, III, ii, 66–67.

compare, *n.* **1** comparison: ". . . a princess/ To equal any single crown o'th'earth/ I'th'justice of compare [in any just comparison]!" *Per*, IV, iii, 7–9. **2 big compare,** comparison(s) with monumental subjects: ". . . their rhymes,/ Full of protest, of oath, and big compare . . ." *Tr & Cr*, III, ii, 172–173.

comparison, *n.* **1** taunting simile: ". . . a man replete with mocks;/ Full of comparisons and wounding flouts . . ." *Love's L*, V, ii, 835–836. **2** quibbling about terms; here, concerning settlement of hostilities: "Stand'st thou aloof upon comparison?" *1 Hen 6*, V, iv, 150. **3 break a comparison,** make an unflattering joke: ". . . he'll but break a comparison or two on/ me . . ." *M Ado*, II, i, 136–137.

compartner, *n.* partner and companion: "Enter Dogberry and his compartner [Verges], with the Watch" [SD] *M Ado*, III, iii, 1.

compass, *n.* **1** circle or circumference: "A thousand flatterers sit within thy crown,/ Whose compass is no bigger than thy head . . ." *Rich 2*, II, i, 100–101. **2** limits; confines: "Why should we, in the compass of a pale,/ Keep law and form . . ." *Rich 2*, III, iv, 40–41. **3** range or extent: "Though Fortune's malice overthrow my state,/ My mind exceeds the compass of her wheel." *3 Hen 6*, IV, iii, 47. **4** full extent: ". . . where I did begin, there shall I end./ My life is run his compass." *J Caes*, V, iii, 24–25. **5** reach; capability: "To do this is within the compass of a man . . ." *Oth*, III, iv, 17. **6 in good compass,** within limits: ". . . lived well, and/ in good compass . . ." *1 Hen 4*, III, iii, 17–18. **7 out of (all) compass, a.** in disorder: ". . . and now I live out of all order, out/ of all compass." *1 Hen 4*, III, iii, 18–19. **b.** obese: ". . . you are so fat, Sir John, that you must needs/ be out of all compass . . ." *1 Hen 4*, III, iii,

20–21. 8 two hundred compasses, annual circling of the sun; evidence that the sibyl was 200 years old: "... had number'd in the world/ The sun to make two hundred compasses..." *Oth,* III, iv, 68–69.
—*v.* **9** to encompass; here, wordplay on "encircle with the arms" and "conquer": "... Dowsabel did claim me for her husband;/ She is too big I hope for me to compass." *Errors,* IV, i, 111–112. **10** to carry out; achieve: "That were hard to compass,/ Because she will admit no kind of suit..." *T Night,* I, ii, 44–45. **11** to win; win over: "If I can check my erring love, I will;/ If not, to compass her I'll use my skill." *Two Gent,* II, iv, 209–210. **12** to obtain: "... the fault/ My father made in compassing the crown!" *Hen 5,* IV, i, 299–300. **13** to go about with: "... then he compassed a motion [puppet show] of the Prodigal/ Son, and married a tinker's wife..." *W Tale,* IV, iii, 93–94. **14** to bend; here, into a circle: "... to be compassed like a/ good bilbo in the circumference of a peck, hilt to/ point..." *Wives,* III, v, 101–103.

compassed, *adj.* **1** circular or semicircular: "I said a gown... 'With a small compassed cape." *Shrew,* IV, iii, 135–137. **2** arched: "... his braided hanging mane/ Upon his compass'd crest now stand on end..." *Ven & Ad,* 271–272.

compassed window, *n.* a semicircular bay window: "... she came to him/ th'other day into the compassed window..." *Tr & Cr,* I, ii, 111–112.

compassion, *v.* to show pity for: "... can you hear a good man groan/ And... not compassion him?" *T Andr,* IV, i, 123–124.

compassionate, *adj.* self-pitying: "It boots thee not to be compassionate..." *Rich 2,* I, iii, 174.

compeer, *n.* **1** friend or associate: "No, neither he, nor his compeers by night,/ Giving him aid, my verse astonished." *Sonn 86,* 7–8.
—*v.* **2** to equal: "In my rights,/ By me invested, he compeers the best." *Lear,* V, iii, 69–70.

compel, *v.* **1** to demand or exact: "... in our marches/ through the country there be nothing compelled/ from the villages..." *Hen 5,* III, vi, 112–113. **2** to force acceptance of (an offer, terms, etc.): "Say you not then, our offer is compell'd." *2 Hen 4,* IV, i, 158.

compelled fortune, *n.* fate that one is forced to bear: "... (fie, fie, fie upon/ This compell'd fortune)..." *Hen 8,* II, iii, 86–87.

compelled restraint, *n.* unavoidable necessity: "... puts it off to [because of] a compell'd restraint..." *All's W,* II, iv, 41.

compelled sins, *n.* ref. to old Christian saying that a compelled sin is not a sin: "... our compell'd sins/ Stand more for number than for accompt [final accounting]." *Meas,* II, iv, 57–58.

competence of life, *n.* means of livelihood; here, an allowance: "For competence of life I will allow you,/ That lack of means enforce you not to evils..." *2 Hen 4,* V, v, 66–67.

competency, *n.* **1** modest means: "... superfluity comes sooner by white hairs, but/ competency lives longer." *Merch,* I, ii, 8–9. **2** sufficient supply; here, of life-giving properties: "... small inferior veins/ From me receive that natural competency..." *Cor* I, i, 137–138.

competent, *adj.* **1** adequate; here, equivalent: "Against the which a moiety competent/ Was gaged by our King..." *Ham,* I, i, 93–94. **2** providing sufficient justification (for an action): "... his indignation derives itself out of a/ very competent injury..." *T Night,* III, iv, 249–250.

competitor, *n.* **1** associate; fellow; also, confederate: "... he and his competitors in oath/ Were all address'd to meet you..." *Love's L,* II, i, 82–83. **2** friendly rival: "That thou my brother, my competitor... my mate in empire..." *Ant & Cleo,* V, i, 42–43.

compile, *v.* to compose: "Yet be most proud of that which I compile..." *Sonn 78,* 9.

complement, *n.* **1** appearance: "Garnish'd and deck'd in modest complement,/ Not working with the eye without the ear [not relying on either the eye or ear alone]..." *Hen 5,* II, ii, 134. **2** [often pl.] refined behavior; also, accomplishments: "A man of complements, whom right and wrong/ Have chose as umpire of their mutiny..." *Love's L,* I, i, 167–168.

complement extern, *n.* external manifestation of innate feelings: "For when my outward action does demonstrate/ The native act, and figure of my heart,/ In complement extern..." *Oth,* I, i, 61–63.

complete, *adj.* **1** perfect; perfected: "He is complete in feature and in mind..." *Two Gent,* II, iv, 68. **2** fully defended with or as if with a suit of armor; here, invincible: "Believe not that the dribbling dart of love/ Can pierce a complete bosom." *Meas,* I, iii, 2–3.

complete steel, *n.* See **steel** (def. 4).

complexion, *n.* **1** general appearance; physique: "Thou art no man, though of a man's complexion..." *Ven & Ad,* 215. **2** skin color; here, race or nationality: "You shall fare well;/ you shall have the/ difference [variety] of all complexions."

Per, IV, i, 75–76. **3** wordplay on "appearance" and "behavior": "O omnipotent love, how near the god drew/ to the complexion of a goose!" *Wives,* V, v, 7–8. **4** physical makeup; constitution: "But yet methinks it is very sultry and hot for my/ complexion." *Ham,* V, ii, 97–98. **5** person's disposition or temperament: "Good my complexion! Dost thou think . . . I have a doublet and hose in my disposition?" *As You,* III, ii, 191–193. **6** one of the humors, which governed the disposition: "By their o'ergrowth [dominance] of some complexion,/ Oft breaking down the pales and forts of reason . . ." *Ham,* I, iv, 27–28. **7** mood or whim: "For thy complexion shifts to strange effects/ After the moon." *Meas,* III, i, 24–25. **8** radiance; splendor; magnificence: ". . . it discolours the complexion/ of my greatness to acknowledge it." *2 Hen 4,* II, ii, 4–5.

complice, *n.* accomplice: ". . . Bristow castle, which they say is held/ By Bushy, Bagot, and their complices . . ." *Rich 2,* II, iii, 163–164.

compliment, *n.* **1** polite leave-taking: "Stay not thy compliment; I forgive/ thy duty: adieu." *Love's L,* IV, ii, 137–138. **2** conventional, modest behavior: "But farewell, compliment./ Dost thou love me? I know thou wilt say 'Ay' . . ." *Rom & Jul,* II, ii, 89–90. **3** courtesy; civility: "The time will not allow the compliment/ Which very manners urges." *Lear,* V, iii, 233–234.

complimental assault, *n.* series of courtly and ceremonial speeches: "I will make a complimental/ assault upon him, for my business seethes." *Tr & Cr,* III, i, 38–39.

complot, *n.* **1** conspiracy: "Then all too late I bring this fatal writ,/ The complot of this timeless tragedy . . ." *T Andr,* II, iii, 264–265.
—*v.* **2** to plot or conspire: ". . . all the treasons for these eighteen years/ Complotted and contrived in this land . . ." *Rich 2,* I, i, 95–96.

comply, *v.* **comply with,** to pay elaborate compliments to; bow to: "A did comply with his [i.e., his nurse's] dug before a sucked it." *Ham,* V, ii, 184.

compose, *v.* to reach an agreement: "If we compose well here, to Parthia . . ." *Ant & Cleo,* II, ii, 15.

composition, *n.* **1** body; constitution; also, condition: ". . . how is't with aged Gaunt?"/ "O, how that name befits my composition!" *Rich 2,* II, i, 72–73. **2** truce; terms of peace: "Sweno, the Norways' King, craves composition . . ." *Mac,* I, ii, 61. **3** bargain or agreement: ". . . thinks himself made in the unchaste composition." *All's W,* IV, iii, 16–17. **4** makeup of one's character; poss. wordplay on "truce": ". . . the composition that your valour and fear makes/ in you is a virtue of a good wing . . ." *All's W,* I, i, 199–200. **5** consistency: "There is

no composition in these news,/ That gives them credit." *Oth,* I, iii, 1–2. **6 our swifter composition,** our coming to terms quicker than anticipated: ". . . and that it was which caus'd/ Our swifter composition." *Cor,* III, i, 2–3.

composture, *n.* var. of **compost:** ". . . the earth's a thief,/ That feeds and breeds by a composture stol'n . . ." *Timon,* IV, iii, 443–444.

composure, *n.* unity or alliance: ". . . it was a strong composure a/ fool could disunite." *Tr & Cr,* II, iii, 102–103.

compound, *n.* **1** lump or mass: "Thou whoreson mad compound of majesty . . ." *2 Hen 4,* II, iv, 291.
—*v.* **2** to mix: "Only compound me with forgotten dust." *2 Hen 4,* IV, v, 115. **3** to settle: "Rise, Grumio, rise. We will compound this quarrel." *Shrew,* I, ii, 27. **4** to decide or determine: "As manhood shall compound: push home. [They draw.]" *Hen 5,* II, i, 98. **5** to reach an agreement; settle terms: "If you think it meet, compound with/ him by the year, and let him abide here with you . . ." *Meas,* IV, ii, 21–22. **6** to engage in sexual intercourse: "My father compounded with my mother under/ the dragon's tail . . ." *Lear,* I, ii, 135–136.
—*adj.* **7** compounded of the four elements: "Heaven's face does glow/ O'er this solidity and compound mass [the earth]/ With tristful visage . . ." *Ham,* III, iv, 48–50. **8** mixed; combined: ". . . paying too much rent,/ For compound sweet forgoing simple savour . . ." *Sonn 125,* 6–7.

compounds strange, *n.* outlandishly concocted words: ". . . glance aside/ To new-found methods and to compounds strange?" *Sonn 76,* 3–4.

comprehend, *v.* misuse for "apprehend": "This is your charge:/ you shall comprehend all vagrom men . . ." *M Ado,* III, iii, 24–25.

comprimise, *n.* var. of **compromise:** "Shall we, upon the footing of our land,/ Send fair-play orders and make comprimise . . ." *K John,* V, i, 66–67.

comprised, *past part.* included; here, listed: "She is our capital demand, compris'd/ Within the fore-rank of our articles." *Hen 5,* V, ii, 96–97.

compromise, *n.* **grow to compromise,** to be on the verge of settlement: ". . . now the matter grows to compromise,/ Stand'st thou aloof upon comparison?" *1 Hen 6,* V, iv, 149–150.

compt, *n.* **1** account; accounting; here, poss. a heavenly reckoning: "That thou didst love her, strikes some scores away/ From the great compt . . ." *All's W,* V, iii, 56–57. **2** See **count**[1]. **3 in compt,** subject to a reckoning: ". . . what is theirs, in

compt,/ To make their audit at your Highness' pleasure..."
Mac, I, vi, 26–27.

comptible, *adj.* sensitive; vulnerable to criticism: "I am very/ comptible, even to the least sinister usage." *T Night*, I, v, 176–177.

comptless, *adj.* incalculable: "And one sweet kiss shall pay this comptless debt." *Ven & Ad*, 84.

comptroller, *n.* steward in the royal household: "For I was spoke to, with Sir Henry Guilford,/ This night to be comptrollers." *Hen 8*, I, iii, 66–67.

compulsive ardor, *n.* unrestrained lust: "... proclaim no shame/ When the compulsive ardour gives the charge..." *Ham*, III, iv, 85–86.

computation, *n.* reckoning or guesswork: "... the heedful slave/ Is wander'd forth in care to seek me out/ By computation [as I assume] and mine host's report." *Errors*, II, ii, 2–4.

con, *v.* **1** to learn by heart; memorize: "You are full of pretty answers. Have you... conned them out of rings?" *As You*, III, ii, 266–268. **2** to offer, express, or acknowledge: "Yet thanks I must you con/ That you are thieves profess'd..." *Timon*, IV, iii, 428–429. **3 cons state without book**, memorizes the fine expressions of persons in high positions: "... an affectioned/ ass, that cons state without book..." *T Night*, II, iii, 147–148.

concealed, *adj.* secret: "And what says/ My conceal'd lady [wife] to our cancell'd love?" *Rom & Jul*, III, iii, 96–97.

concealment, *n.* **1** suppression of one's true feelings: "... let concealment like a worm i' th' bud/ Feed on her damask cheek..." *T Night*, II, iv, 112–113. **2** [pl.] secret or occult arts: "Exceedingly well read, and profited/ In strange concealments..." *1 Hen 4*, III, i, 160–161. **3 in ignorant concealment**, concealment that keeps me ignorant; also, concealment while [you are] pretending ignorance: "If you know aught... imprison 't not!/ In ignorant concealment." *W Tale*, I, ii, 395–397. **4 name concealments**, to tell matters that should not be revealed: "... him I do not love that... names concealments in/ The boldest language." *Kinsmen*, V, i, 122–124.

conceit, *n.* **1** intelligence or wit: "... I know you are a gentleman of good conceit." *As You*, V, ii, 53–54. **2** understanding; thought: "Conceit more rich in matter than in words/ Brags of his substance..." *Rom & Jul*, II, vi, 30–31. **3** idea; also, imagination or illusion: "Conceit in weakest bodies strongest works." *Ham*, III, iv, 114. **4** morbid thoughts; brooding: "Conceit upon her father." *Ham*, IV, v, 45. **5** meaning: "Why sir, what's your conceit in that?" *Shrew*, IV, iii, 157. **6** fears; dire thoughts or imaginings: "Come, sister, I am press'd down

with conceit..." *Errors*, IV, ii, 65. **7** [usually pl.] elaborate trifles, as jewelry: "... stol'n the impression of her fantasy,/ With bracelets of thy hair, rings, gauds, conceits..." *M N Dream*, I, i, 32–33. **8 approve the fair conceit**, confirm the good opinion; judgment: "Lady,/ I shall not fail t'approve the fair conceit/ The king hath of you." *Hen 8*, II, iii, 73–75. **9 first conceit**, original impulse or concept: "Finding the first conceit of love there bred." *Sonn 108*, 13. **10 gross conceit**, limited understanding of mortals when compared to that of the gods: "Lay open to my earthy gross conceit... The folded meaning of your words' deceit." *Errors*, III, ii, 34–36. **11 of liberal conceit**, of lavish design: "... most delicate carriages, and of/ very liberal conceit." *Ham*, V, ii, 149–150. **12 quaint conceit**, ingenious use of [his] imagination: "... though he seem with forged quaint conceit/ To set a gloss upon his bold intent..." *1 Hen 6*, IV, i, 102–103.
—*v.* **13** to understand; conceive: "... our great need of him/ You have right well conceited." *J Caes*, I, iii, 161–162. **14** to think of; judge: "... one of two bad ways you must conceit me,/ Either a coward, or a flatterer." *J Caes*, III, i, 192–193.

conceit and fear, *n.* fearful thoughts: "The prince your son, with mere conceit and fear/ Of the queen's speed [fate], is gone." *W Tale*, III, ii, 144–145.

conceited, *adj.* **1** witty: "Well [very] conceited, Davy—about thy business, Davy." *2 Hen 4*, V, i, 33. **2** ingenious: "He was gotten [begotten] in drink: is not the humour/ conceited?" *Wives*, I, iii, 21–22. **3 be horribly conceited**, to be horrified or terrified: "He is as horribly conceited of him, and pants/ and looks pale..." *T Night*, III, iv, 299–300.

conceited characters, *n.* extravagant designs: "Oft did she heave her napkin to her eyne,/ Which on it had conceited characters..." *Lover's Comp*, 15–16.

conceitless, *adj.* witless: "Think'st thou I am so shallow, so conceitless,/ To be seduced by thy flattery..." *Two Gent*, IV, ii, 93–94.

conceive, *v.* **1** to imagine; guess: "... what he is indeed/ More suits you to conceive than I to speak of." *As You*, I, ii, 256–257. **2** to understand: "'How/ comes that?' says he that takes upon him [pretends] not to/ conceive." *2 Hen 4*, II, ii, 107–109. **3** same sense in wordplay with "become pregnant": "Thus I conceive by him [that is what I take him to be]." *Shrew*, V, ii, 22. **4** to experience; feel: "... such a pleasure as incaged birds/ Conceive when... They quite forget their loss of liberty." *3 Hen 6*, IV, vi, 12–15. **5** think about what I have said: "Conceive, and fare thee well." *Lear*, IV, ii, 24. **6 conceive the fairest**, to have the highest opinion: "I hope his/ honour will conceive the fairest of me..." *Timon*, III, ii, 52–53.

conception, *n.* [often pl] thought or idea: "Conceptions only proper to myself,/ Which give some soil, perhaps, to my behaviours . . ." *J Caes,* I, ii, 40–41.

conceptious, *adj.* likely to conceive; prolific: "Ensear thy fertile and conceptious womb." *Timon,* IV, iii, 189.

concernancy, *n.* importance; relevance: "The concernancy, sir? Why do we wrap the gentleman/ in our more rawer breath?" *Ham,* V, ii, 122–123.

concerning, *n.* **1** [usually pl.] considerations: "We shall write to you,/ As time and our concernings shall importune [dictate] . . ." *Meas,* I, i, 55–56. **2 dear concernings,** vital matters: "For who . . . Would from a paddock, from a bat, a gib,/ Such dear concernings hide?" *Ham,* III, iv, 191–193.

conclude, *v.* **1** to prove the truth of something: "This argues what her kind of life hath been,/ Wicked and vile; and so her death concludes." *1 Hen 6,* V, iv, 15–16. **2** to reach a decision: "Cannot conclude but by the yea and no/ Of general ignorance . . ." *Cor,* III, i, 144–145.

conclusion, *n.* **1** consummated act: "Nay, this was but his dream."/ "But this denoted a foregone conclusion." *Oth,* III, iii, 433–434. **2** experiment: "That mother tries a merciless conclusion . . ." *Luc,* 1160. **3** end or termination; here, the riddle with the wordplay on "resolution" [death]: "Scorning advice, read the conclusion then . . ." *Per,* I, i, 57. **4 conclusions infinite,** numerous experiments: "She hath pursued conclusions infinite/ Of easy ways to die." *Ant & Cleo,* V, ii, 353–354. **5 conclusions to be as kisses,** poss. offered by Clown as an example of paradox, with kisses regarded as a consummation, or conclusion rather than a beginning: ". . . conclusions to be as kisses, if your four negatives/ make your two affirmatives . . ." *T Night,* V, i, 20–21. **6 try conclusions,** to attempt to repeat an experiment: ". . . and like the famous ape,/ To try conclusions, in the basket creep . . ." *Ham,* III, iv, 196–197.

Concolinel, *n.* prob. a song title: "Warble, child: make passionate my sense of hearing."/ "[sings]. Concolinel." *Love's L,* III, i, 1–2.

concord, *n.* **1** harmony: "But for the concord of my state and time,/ Had not an ear to hear my true time broke . . ." *Rich 2,* V, v, 47–48. **2** a simultaneous sounding, as of musical notes: "The man that hath no music in himself,/ Nor is not moved with concord of sweet sounds . . ." *Merch,* V, i, 83–84.

concupiscible, *adj.* lustful; lecherous: ". . . by gift of my chaste body/ To his concupiscible intemperate lust . . ." *Meas,* V, i, 100–101.

concupy, *n.* prob. a var. of (a) **concuby** (concubine) or (b) **concupiscence** (lust): "He'll tickle it for his concupy." *Tr & Cr,* V, ii, 176.

condemned, *adj.* useless or inept; here, more likely, damned: "Officious, and not valiant, you have sham'd me/ In your condemned seconds." *Cor,* I, viii, 14–15.

condescend, *v.* to agree; consent: "In earnest of a further benefit,/ So you do condescend to help me now." *1 Hen 6,* V, iii, 16–17.

condign, *adj.* well-deserved: "Speak you this in my praise, master?"/ "In thy condign praise." *Love's L,* I, ii, 24–25.

condition, *n.* **1** status, rank or, sometimes, profession: "This throne, this Fortune, and this hill . . . would be well express'd/ In our condition." *Timon,* I, i, 75–79. **2** [often pl.] circumstances; here, way of life: "Quiet and gentle thy conditions! for/ Thou art the rudeliest welcome to this world . . ." *Per,* III, i, 29–30. **3** temperament; disposition: ". . . not alone the imperfections of long-engraffed condition . . ." *Lear,* I, i, 297. **4** [usually pl.] one's true nature or quality; character: "Spare your oaths:/ I'll trust to your conditions." *Timon,* IV, iii, 140–141. **5** contract or compact: "Mark his condition, and th' event; then tell me/ If this might be a brother." *Temp,* I, ii, 117–118. **6 make conditions,** to determine strategy: "I am a soldier, I,/ Older in practice, abler than yourself/ To make conditions." *J Caes,* IV, iii, 30–32. **7 on such slight conditions,** so easily; here, rather than fight for her: "To make such means for her . . . And leave her on such slight conditions." *Two Gent,* V, iv, 135–136.
—*conj.* **8** even if; here, in order to prove it: "—Condition I had gone barefoot to India." *Tr & Cr,* I, ii, 74.

conditionally, *adv.* on or with condition [that]: "Conditionally that here thou take thine oath/ To cease this civil war . . ." *3 Hen 6,* I, i, 202–203.

conditioned, *adj.* limited or restricted: "But thus condition'd: thou shalt build from men . . ." *Timon,* IV, iii, 530.

condole, *v.* **1** to grieve; sorrow: "They seem to condole with her." *Ham,* III, ii, 133 [dumb-show]. **2** same, but "with" understood: "Let us condole the knight; for, lambkins, we will live." *Hen 5,* II, i, 127. **3** appar. misuse of word to mean "arouse pity": "I will/ move storms, I will condole in some measure." *M N Dream,* I, ii, 22–23.

condolement, *n.* **1** grief or grieving: ". . . to persever/ In obstinate condolement is a course/ Of impious stubbornness . . ." *Ham,* I, ii, 92–94. **2** perh. a quasi-elegant misuse for "dole" [one's share or portion], as well as a request for a tip: ". . .

there are certain condolements, certain/ vails. I hope, sir, if you thrive, you'll remember . . ." *Per,* II, i, 149–150.

condoling, *adj.* appar. misuse for "mournful; lamenting; pathetic": "This is Ercles' vein, a tyrant's vein: a lover is more/ condoling." *M N Dream,* I, ii, 36–37.

conduce, *v.* to carry on; continue: "Within my soul there doth conduce a fight/ Of this strange nature . . ." *Tr & Cr,* V, ii, 146–147.

conduct, *n.* **1** command; leadership: "Address'd a mighty power, which were on foot/ In his own conduct . . ." *As You,* V, iv, 155–156. **2** escort; also, protection: ". . . she and my aunt Percy/ Shall follow in your conduct speedily." *1 Hen 4,* III, i, 190–191. **3** guide or counselor; also, example: "Away to heaven respective lenity,/ And fire-ey'd fury be my conduct now!" *Rom & Jul,* III, i, 125–126. **4** guidance: "Thy wit, that ornament to shape and love,/ Misshapen in the conduct of them both . . ." *Rom & Jul,* III, iii, 129–130. **5** permission; allowance: ". . . and under your fair conduct . . . entreat/ An hour of revels with 'em." *Hen 8,* I, iv, 70–72.
—*v.* **6** to lead; command: "Back, Edmund, to my brother;/ Hasten his musters and conduct his powers . . ." *Lear,* IV, ii, 15–16.

conductor, *n.* leader; commander: "Who is conductor of his people?" *Lear,* IV, vii, 88.

conduit, *n.* fountain; here, a shower of tears: "How now, a conduit, girl? What, still in tears?" *Rom & Jul,* III, v, 129.

confection, *n.* compounded drug: ". . . our great king himself doth woo me oft/ For my confections . . ." *Cymb,* I, vi, 14–15.

confederacy, *n.* conspiracy: "I stood i'th'level/ Of a full-charg'd confederacy . . ." *Hen 8,* I, ii, 2–3.

confederate, *v.* to join in a confederation: ". . . confederates,/ So dry he was for sway, wi' th' King of Naples." *Temp,* I, ii, 111–112.

confederate season, *n.* opportune time [acting] as one's ally: ". . . and time agreeing,/ Confederate season, else no creature seeing . . ." *Ham,* III, ii, 249–250.

conference, *n.* **1** conversation; talk: "I cannot speak to her, yet she urg'd conference." *As You,* I, ii, 248. **2** debate or discussion: ". . . we have seen him in the Capitol,/ Being cross'd in conference by some senators." *J Caes,* I, ii, 185–186.

confession, *n.* admission; avowal: "That loves his mistress more than in confession/ With truant vows . . ." *Tr & Cr,* I, iii, 268–269.

confidence, *n.* **have confidence,** talk together; exchange confidences; or perh. she means "conference": "I will tell your worship more of the wart the next time we have/ confidence . . ." *Wives,* I, iv, 153–154.

confident, *adj.* **1** trusting: "Rome, be as just and gracious unto me/ As I am confident and kind to thee." *T Andr,* I, i, 60–61. **2** boldly assured: "It is not a confident brow [aspect], nor the throng of/ words that come . . ." *2 Hen 4,* II, i, 109–110.

confine, *v.* **1** to regulate or control (oneself); here, appar. "to dress up": ". . . you must confine yourself within the/ modest limits of order."/ "Confine? I'll confine myself no finer than I am." *T Night,* I, iii, 8–10. **2** to restrict: "Confin'd to exhibition! All this done/ Upon the gad!" *Lear,* I, ii, 25–26. **3** to bind: "A god in love, to whom I am confined." *Sonn 110,* 12.
—*n.* **4** limit of life or boundary of the flesh: "Nature in you stands on the very verge/ Of her confine . . ." *Lear,* II, iv, 148–149. **5** [pl.] places of confinement: "A goodly one, in which there are many confines . . ." *Ham,* II, ii, 245.

confined doom, *n.* limitations of mortality: "Supposed as forfeit to a confined doom." *Sonn 107,* 4.

confineless, *adj.* boundless; measureless: "Esteem him as a lamb, being compar'd/ With my confineless harms." *Mac,* IV, iii, 54–55.

confiners, *n.* inhabitants: "The senate hath stirr'd up the confiners/ And gentlemen of Italy . . ." *Cymb,* IV, ii, 337–338.

confines, *n. pl.* **1** territories; domain or realm: ". . . they have let the dangerous enemy/ Measure our confines with such peaceful steps?" *Rich 2,* III, ii, 124–125. **2** countries; nations: "Now, neighbour confines, purge you of your scum!" *2 Hen 4,* IV, v, 123.

confirm, *v.* to strengthen: "As his alliance will confirm our peace . . ." *1 Hen 6,* V, v, 42.

confirmed, *adj.* determined; confident: "You must . . . give her to young Claudio./ Which I will do with confirm'd countenance [manner]." *M Ado,* V, iv, 15–17.

confirmity, *n.* [often pl.] misuse for "infirmity": ". . . you cannot/ one bear with another's confirmities." *2 Hen 4,* II, iv, 56–57.

confiscate, *past part.* confiscated: "His goods confiscate to the Duke's dispose . . ." *Errors,* I, i, 20.

confixed, *adj.* firmly fixed: ". . . for ever be confixed here,/ A marble monument." *Meas,* V, i, 231–232.

conflicting, *pres. part.* contending; battling: ". . . whose bare unhoused trunks,/ To the conflicting elements expos'd . . ." *Timon*, IV, iii, 231–232.

conformable, *adj.* compliant or obedient; also, submissive: "And bring you from a wild Kate to a Kate/ Conformable as other household Kates." *Shrew*, II, i, 270–271.

confound, *v.* **1** to overcome or subdue; here, with delight: "The wiry concord that mine ear confounds . . ." *Sonn 128*, 4. **2** to ruin or destroy; damn [used as a curse]: "The gods confound—hear me, you good gods all—/ Th' Athenians both within and out that wall . . ." *Timon*, IV, i, 37–38. **3** to consume or exhaust; use up: "He did confound the best part of an hour/ In changing hardiment with great Glendower." *1 Hen 4*, I, iii, 99–100. **4** to dismiss from one's mind: ". . . whereto being bound,/ The interim, pray you, all confound." *Per*, V, ii, 13–14. **5** to be thrown into confusion: "Appals her senses and her spirit confounds." *Ven & Ad*, 882. **6** to waste; fritter away: "Let's not confound the time with conference harsh . . ." *Ant & Cleo*, I, i, 45. **7 confound oneself**, to lose one's identity: "Who, falling there to find his fellow forth,/ (Unseen, inquisitive) confounds himself." *Errors*, I, ii, 37–38.

confounded, *adj.* collapsed; ruined; destroyed: "Their form confounded makes most form in mirth,/ When great things labouring perish in their birth." *Love's L*, V, ii, 515–516.

confounding, *adj.* **1** calamitous; ruinous: ". . . customs and laws,/ Decline to your confounding contraries . . ." *Timon*, IV, i, 19–20. **2** destructive; deadly: ". . . by thy virtue/ Set them into confounding odds [rivalry] . . ." *Timon*, IV, iii, 393–394.

confused, *past part.* mixed together indistinguishably: ". . . the mad mothers with their howls confus'd/ Do break the clouds . . ." *Hen 5*, III, iii, 39–40.

confusion, *n.* **1** calamity; ruin; devastation: ". . . thou wilt use the wars as thy redress/ And not as our confusion . . ." *Timon*, V, iv, 51–52. **2** [often pl.] outburst of grief: "Confusion's cure lives not/ In these confusions." *Rom & Jul*, IV, v, 65–66. **3** chaos: ". . . how soon confusion/ May enter 'twixt the gap of both . . ." *Cor*, III, i, 109–110.

confutation, *n.* act of refuting; a refutation: "In confutation of which rude approach . . . I crave the benefit of law of arms." *1 Hen 6*, IV, i, 98–100.

confute, *v.* to get the better of; silence: "My sisterly remorse confutes mine honour . . ." *Meas*, V, i, 103.

congee or **congy**, *v.* to bow or curtsy: "They first/ congee unto her, then dance . . ." [SD] *Hen 8*, IV, ii, 82.

conger, *n.* large eel; also, abusive term for a man: "Hang yourself, you muddy conger, hang yourself!" *2 Hen 4*, II, iv, 53.

congest, *v.* to gather together: "Must for your victory us all congest . . ." *Lover's Comp*, 258.

congied, *v.* past part. of **congee**; taken leave (of): "I have congied with the duke, done my adieu with his/ nearest . . ." *All's W*, IV, iii, 84–85.

congratulate, *v.* to greet; visit or pay respects to: ". . . it is the king's most sweet pleasure and affection/ to congratulate the princess at her pavilion . . ." *Love's L*, V, i, 79–80.

congree, *v.* to agree: "Congreeing in a full and natural close,/ Like music." *Hen 5*, I, ii, 182–183.

congreet, *v.* to greet each other: ". . . face to face, and royal eye to eye,/ You have congreeted . . ." *Hen 5*, V, ii, 30–31.

congregated college, *n.* assembly of the leading physicians: "The congregated college have concluded/ That labouring art can never ransom nature . . ." *All's W*, II, i, 116–117.

congregated sands, *n.* sandbars: "The gutter'd rocks, and congregated sands,/ Traitors ensteep'd, to clog the guiltless keel . . ." *Oth*, II, i, 69–70.

congregation, *n.* **1** mass: ". . . it appeareth nothing to me but a foul and pestilent/ congregation of vapours." *Ham*, II, ii, 302–303. **2** [pl.] public assemblies: "To buy and sell with groats, to show bare heads/ In congregations . . ." *Cor*, III, ii, 10–11.

congrue, *v.* to agree or accord (with): ". . . imports at full,/ By letters congruing to that effect,/ The present death of Hamlet." *Ham*, IV, iii, 66–68.

congruent, *adj.* congruous; suitable or appropriate: "I spoke it . . . as a congruent epitheton/ appertaining to thy young days . . ." *Love's L*, I, ii, 13–14.

conject, *v.* to imagine: "I entreat you then,/ From one that so imperfectly conjects,/ You'd take no notice . . ." *Oth*, III, iii, 152–154.

conjecture, *n.* suspicion or doubt: ". . . I'll lock up all the gates of love,/ And on my eyelids shall conjecture hang . . ." *M Ado*, IV, i, 105–106.

conjoin, *v.* to unite; here, conspire together: "Now I perceive they have conjoin'd all three/ To fashion this false sport in spite of me." *M N Dream*, III, ii, 193–194.

conjointly, *adv.* together; at the same time: "When these prodigies/ Do so conjointly meet . . ." *J Caes*, I, iii, 28–29.

conjunct, *adj.* joined together; here, in a sexual liaison: "I am doubtful that you have been conjunct/ And bosom'd with her . . ." *Lear,* V, i, 12–13.

conjunction, *n.* **1** assembled forces: "Yet doth he give us bold advertisement/ That with our small conjunction we should on . . ." *1 Hen 4,* IV, i, 36–37. **2** union; alliance: "Their spirits/ are so married in conjunction . . ." *2 Hen 4,* V, i, 65–66. **3** marriage: "Now all my joy/ Trace [follow] the conjunction." *Hen 8,* III, ii, 44–45.

conjunctive, *adj.* inseparably joined: "She is so conjunctive to my life and soul . . ." *Ham,* IV, vii, 14.

conjuration, *n.* **1** solemn appeal or entreaty: "I do defy thy conjuration/ And apprehend thee for a felon here." *Rom & Jul,* V, iii, 68–69. **2** spell or charm: ". . . to undermine the Duchess,/ And buz these conjurations in her brain." *2 Hen 6,* I, ii, 98–99.

conjure, *v.* **1** to summon (up) by or as if by magic: "See . . . all these spirits thy power/ Hath conjur'd to attend!" *Timon,* I, i, 5–7. **2** to summon up the spirits in: "Stiffen the sinews, conjure up the blood . . ." *Hen 5,* III, i, 7. **3** to cast a spell upon: ". . . whose phrase of sorrow/ Conjures the wand'ring stars and makes them stand . . ." *Ham,* V, i, 248–249. **4** to beg divine assistance or intervention: "She conjures: away with her! Would she had/ never come within my doors!" *Per,* IV, vi, 147–148. **5** to urge; beg or implore: ". . . but he hath conjur'd me beyond them, and I must needs appear." *Timon,* III, vi, 11–12. **6** to call upon or order solemnly: "I conjure thee to leave me and be gone." *Errors,* IV, iii, 65. **7** to control; check: "Devil or devil's dam, I'll conjure thee . . ." *1 Hen 6,* I, v, 5.

conjurer, *n.* learned man who could cast out evil spirits; exorcist: "Good Doctor Pinch, you are a conjurer;/ Establish him in his true sense again . . ." *Errors,* IV, iv, 45–46.

conjuro te, *v.* [Latin] I conjure you: "Bolingbroke or/ Southwell reads, *Conjuro te,* etc." [SD] *2 Hen 6,* I, iv, 22.

connive, *v.* **connive at,** to indulge: "Sure the gods do this year connive/ at us . . ." *W Tale,* IV, iv, 676–677.

conquering part, *n.* victorious side; also, perh., share of victory: "What heart receives from hence a conquering part/ To steel a strong opinion to themselves?—" *Tr & Cr,* I, iii, 352–353.

conscience, *n.* **1** moral awareness; here, in wordplay with "carnal knowledge": "Love is too young to know what conscience is,/ Yet who knows not conscience is born of love?" *Sonn 151,* 1–2. **2 a' conscience,** on my conscience: ". . . there's two unwholesome, a'/ conscience." *Per,* IV, ii, 19–20.

consecrate, *adj.* dedicated: ". . . suffer not dishonour to approach/ The imperial seat, to virtue consecrate . . ." *T Andr,* I, i, 13–14.

consent¹, *v.* **1** to agree: "Consent upon a sure foundation,/ Question surveyors, know our own estate . . ." *2 Hen 4,* I, iii, 52–53. **2 consent unto,** to conspire together so as to cause: "You all consented unto Salisbury's death . . ." *1 Hen 6,* I, v, 34.
—*n.* **3** understanding; also, conspiracy: "I see the trick on 't: here was a consent . . . to dash it like a Christmas comedy." *Love's L,* V, ii, 460–462. **4** consenting person: "Consents bewitch'd, ere he desire, have granted . . ." *Lover's Comp,* 131.

consent², *n.* **1** agreement; unity: "For government . . . Put into parts, doth keep in one consent [remain in harmony] . . ." *Hen 5,* I, ii, 180–181. **2** goal: ". . . many things, having full reference/ To one consent [sharing a common goal] may work contrariously . . ." *Hen 5,* I, ii, 205–206.

consequence, *n.* **1** consequences; aftermath: ". . . if th'assassination/ Could trammel up the consequence, and catch/ With his surcease success . . ." *Mac,* I, vii, 2–4. **2** that which attends; attachment or connection: "Each small annexment, petty consequence,/ Attends the boist'rous ruin." *Ham,* III, iii, 21–22. **3 consequence of dread,** frightening consequences: "Bearing a state of mighty moment in't/ And consequence of dread . . ." *Hen 8,* II, iv, 211–212. **4 deepest consequence,** most serious matters: "The instruments of Darkness . . ./ Win us with honest trifles, to betray's/ In deepest consequence." *Mac,* I, iii, 124–126. **5 in this consequence,** in the following manner; to this effect: ". . . be assur'd/ He closes with you in this consequence: . . ." *Ham,* II, i, 45–46.

consequently, *adv.* subsequently: ". . . consequently, like a traitor coward,/ Sluic'd out his innocent soul through streams of blood . . ." *Rich 2,* I, i, 102–103.

conserve, *n.* **1** sweetmeat, usually of candied fruit: "Will't please your honour taste of these conserves?" *Shrew,* Ind., ii, 3. **2 conserves of beef,** beef preserved by salting and hanging: "And if you give me any conserves, give me conserves of beef." *Shrew,* Ind., ii, 6–7.

consider, *v.* **1** to reward: ". . . if I have not enough/ considered . . . to be more thankful/ to thee shall be my study [endeavor] . . ." *W Tale,* IV, ii, 17–19. **2 something gently considered,** for a generous consideration [bribe]: ". . . being something gently considered, I'll bring/ you where he is aboard . . ." *W Tale,* IV, iv, 797–798.

considerance, *n.* consideration: "After this cold considerance sentence me . . ." *2 Hen 4,* V, ii, 98.

considerate, *adj.* **1** reflecting in silence: ". . . therefore speak no more."/ "Go to, then: your considerate stone [I'll keep quiet, but I'll be thinking a lot]." *Ant & Cleo,* II, ii, 109–110. **2** thoughtful; prudent: ". . . none are for me/ That look into me with considerate eyes." *Rich 3,* IV, ii, 30.

consideration, *n.* **1** thought or the ability to think: ". . . greases his pure mind,/ That from it all consideration slips—" *Timon,* IV, iii, 198. **2** morbid thoughts: "Let's to supper, come,/ And drown consideration." *Ant & Cleo,* IV, ii, 44–45.

considered, *adj.* permitting consideration: ". . . at our more consider'd time we'll read . . ." *Ham,* II, ii, 81.

consign, *v.* **1** to agree (with); endorse: "And, God consigning to my good intents . . ." *2 Hen 4,* V, ii, 143. **2** to yield or submit: ". . . all lovers must/ Consign to thee and come to dust." *Cymb,* IV, ii, 274–275.

consist, *v.* **1** to insist on; be adamant concerning: ". . . such large terms, and so absolute,/ As our conditions shall consist upon . . ." *2 Hen 4,* IV, i, 186–187. **2** to be disposed: "Welcome is peace, if he on [toward] peace consist . . ." *Per,* I, iv, 83. **3** to reside: "Fair one, all goodness that consists in beauty,/ Expect even here . . ." *Per,* V, i, 70–71. **4** to be expected or anticipated: "Though in and of him there be much consisting . . ." *Tr & Cr,* III, iii, 116.

consistory, *n.* council chamber; here, fund of wisdom: "My other self, my counsel's consistory . . ." *Rich 3,* II, ii, 151.

consonancy, *n.* **1** similarity; correspondence: "But let me conjure you,/ by the rights of our fellowship, by the consonancy of/ our youth . . ." *Ham,* II, ii, 283–285. **2** consistency: ". . . there is no consonancy in the/ sequel; that suffers under probation . . ." *T Night,* II, v, 130–131.

consonant, *n.* nonentity, since a consonant cannot be sounded without an accompanying vowel: "*Quis, quis,* thou consonant?" *Love's L,* V, i, 49.

consort, *n.* **1** band or company: "Wilt thou be of our consort?/ Say 'ay', and be the captain of us all . . ." *Two Gent,* IV, i, 64–65. **2** band of musicians: "And boding screech-owls make the consort full!" *2 Hen 6,* III, ii, 326.
—*v.* **3** to accompany: "Sweet health and fair desires consort your grace!" *Love's L,* II, i, 177. **4** to keep (someone) company: ". . . I'll meet with you upon the mart,/ And afterward consort you till bed-time . . ." *Errors,* I, ii, 27–28. **5** wordplay on "keep company" and "group of hired musicians": "Consort? What, dost thou make us minstrels?" *Rom & Jul,* III, i, 45.

consorted, *adj.* associated as conspirators; conniving: ". . . our trusty brother-in-law and the abbot,/ With all the rest of that consorted crew . . ." *Rich 2,* V, iii, 135–136.

conspectuity, *n.* sightedness; perception [evidently a coinage by Menenius]: "What harm can your bisson/ conspectuities glean out of this character . . ." *Cor,* II, i, 63–64.

conspirant, *adj.* conspiring; plotting: "Conspirant 'gainst this high illustrious prince . . ." *Lear,* V, iii, 135.

conspire, *v.* misuse for "consult" or "conclude": "And they have conspired together,—I will not say/ you shall see a masque . . ." *Merch,* II, v, 22–23.

conspirer, *n.* conspirator: ". . . take no care/ Who chafes, who frets, or where conspirers are . . ." *Mac,* IV, i, 90–91.

constancy, *n.* firmness of mind; certainty; self-control: "O constancy, be strong upon my side . . ." *J Caes,* II, iv, 6.

constant, *adj.* **1** loyal: ". . . who resists/ Are mock'd for valiant ignorance,/ And perish constant fools." *Cor,* IV, vi, 104–106. **2** steady; level-headed: ". . . nothing in the world/ Could turn so much the constitution/ Of any constant man . . ." *Merch,* III, ii, 244–246. **3** reliable; here, ready to serve: "It is your former promise."/ "Sir, it is,/ And I am constant." *Cor,* I, i, 237–238. **4 be constant,** get hold of yourself: "Cassius or Caesar never shall turn back,/ For I will slay myself."/ "Cassius, be constant . . ." *J Caes,* III, i, 21–22. **5 constant pleasure,** firm decision: ". . . he's full of alteration/ And self-reproving; bring his constant pleasure." *Lear,* V, i, 3–4. **6 constant question,** logical or coherent questioning: ". . . make the trial of it in any constant/ question." *T Night,* IV, ii, 49–50. **7 constant temper,** resolute mind: "You keep a constant temper." *Cor,* V, ii, 92.

Constantine, *n.* 4th cent. Roman emperor, who adopted Christianity: "Helen, the mother of great Constantine . . ." *1 Hen 6,* I, ii, 142.

constantly, *adv.* **1** firmly; with resolution: ". . . I am fresh of spirit, and resolv'd/ To meet all perils very constantly." *J Caes,* V, i, 91–92. **2** consistently: "The devil a Puritan that he is, or anything/ constantly . . ." *T Night,* II, iii, 146–147. **3** assuredly: "I do constantly believe you . . ." *Meas,* IV, i, 21.

constant will, *n.* firm intention: "We have this hour a constant will to publish [announce]/ Our daughters' several dowers . . ." *Lear,* I, i, 43–44.

constellation, *n.* (in astrology) the celestial influences in one's horoscope: "I know thy constellation is right apt/ For this affair." *T Night,* I, iv, 35–36.

conster, *v.* **1** var. of **construe**; explain: "I will conster to them whence you/ come . . ." *T Night*, III, i, 57–58. **2** to interpret; translate: "He in the worst sense consters their denial." *Luc*, 324. **3 conster to,** to inform: "I will conster to them whence you/ come . . ." *T Night*, III, i, 57–58.

constrain, *v.* **1** Sir Andrew prob. means "cause" rather than "force": "'Tis not the first time I have constrained one to/ call me knave." *T Night*, II, iii, 68–69. **2 constrain the garb,** See **garb.**

constraint, *n.* military force; war: "Or else what follows?"/ "Bloody constraint . . ." *Hen 5*, II, iv, 96–97.

constringed, *adj.* compressed; drawn together: "Constring'd in mass by the almighty sun . . ." *Tr & Cr*, V, ii, 172.

construction, *n.* **1** disposition; character: "There's no art/ To find the mind's construction in the face . . ." *Mac*, I, iv, 11–12. **2** interpretation; manner of construing something: "I will plant you two . . . where he shall find the/ letter: observe his construction of it." *T Night*, II, iii, 173–175. **3 good construction,** justification: "And my pretext to strike at him admits/ A good construction." *Cor*, V, vi, 20–21. **4 hard construction,** severe judgment: "Under your hard construction must I sit . . ." *T Night*, III, i, 117.

construe, *v.* to interpret or explain; also, understand; comprehend: "Construe my speeches better, if you may." *Love's L*, V, ii, 341.

consult, *v.* **1** to conspire together: "Like many clouds consulting for foul weather." *Ven & Ad*, 972. **2 not consulting,** independently: "Every man . . . not consulting, broke/ Into a general prophecy . . ." *Hen 8*, I, i, 89–92.

consume, *v.* **1** to overindulge; here with sexual innuendo: "O, he hath kept an evil diet long,/ And over-much consum'd his royal person . . ." *Rich 3*, I, ii, 139–140. **2 consume your blood,** See **blood** (def. 13).

consummate, *past part.* consummated: "I do but stay till your marriage be consummate . . ." *M Ado*, III, ii, 1.

consummation, *n.* conclusion or termination: ". . . 'tis a consummation/ Devoutly to be wish'd." *Ham*, III, i, 63–64.

consumption, *n.* **1** lovesickness: "I yield . . . partly to save your life, for I was told you were in a consumption." *M Ado*, V, iv, 94–96. **2** any wasting disease; often applied to venereal disease: "Consumptions sow/ In hollow bones of man . . ." *Timon*, IV, iii, 153–154.

contagion, *n.* **1** infection or pestilence; also, poison: "I'll touch my point/ With this contagion, that if I gall him slightly,/ It may be death." *Ham*, IV, vii, 145–147. **2 dulcet in conta gion,** sweetly stinking: "To hear by [with] the nose, it is dulcet in contagion." *T Night*, II, iii, 57.

contagious, *adj.* **1** filthy; disease-spreading: "Thy Doll/ . . . Is in base durance and contagious prison . . ." *2 Hen 4*, V, v, 33–34. **2** noxious; poisonous: ". . . the winds . . ./ As in revenge have suck'd up from the sea/ Contagious fogs . . ." *M N Dream*, II, i, 88–90. **3** catching or infectious; here, foul or stinking: "A contagious breath."/ "Very sweet and contagious, i' faith." *T Night*, II, iii, 55–56.

contain, *v.* to keep; retain: "If you had known the virtue of the ring . . . Or your own honour to contain the ring . . ." *Merch*, V, i, 199–201.

containing, *adj.* **as much containing as,** of equal importance with: "Last, and as much containing as all these . . ." *Ham*, IV, v, 87.

contemn, *v.* **1** to scorn or despise: "Yet better thus, and known to be contemn'd,/ Than, still contemn'd and flatter'd, to be worst." *Lear*, IV, i, 1–2. **2** to despise the fact that: "As if he did contemn what he requested/ Should be in them [within their power] to give." *Cor*, II, ii, 157–158.

contemned, *adj.* scornfully rejected; despised: "Write cantons of contemned love,/ And sing them loud even in the dead of night . . ." *T Night*, I, v, 274–275.

contemnedest, *adj.* superl. of **contemned**: ". . . such as basest and contemn'st wretches . . . Are punish'd with . . ." *Lear*, II, ii, 143–145.

contemplative, *adj.* devoted to pondering: "Still and contemplative in living art." *Love's L*, I, i, 14.

contemplative idiot, *n.* empty-headed fool: "I know this letter will make a contemplative/ idiot of him." *T Night*, II, v, 19–20.

contempt, *n.* object of contempt: ". . . it cannot but turn him/ into a notable contempt." *T Night*, II, v, 203–204.

contemptible, *adj.* **1** contemptuous; given to scorn: ". . . for the man,/ as you know all, hath a contemptible spirit." *M Ado*, II, iii, 175–176. **2** humble; lowly: ". . . our Lady gracious hath it pleas'd/ To shine on my contemptible estate." *1 Hen 6*, I, ii, 74–75.

contempt of empire, *n.* scorn of an emperor: ". . . a maid too virtuous/ For the contempt of empire [even an emperor to scorn]." *All's W*, III, ii, 30–31.

contempt of question, *n.* See **question** (def. 6).

contempts, *n. pl.* misuse for "contents": "Sir, the contempts thereof are as touching me." *Love's L,* I, i, 188.

contemptuous, *adj.* contemptible; deserving of contempt: "Contemptuous base-born callet as she is . . ." *2 Hen 6,* I, iii, 83.

contend, *v.* **1** to fight: "Now kiss, embrace, contend, do what you will." *Two Gent,* I, ii, 130. **2** to strive determinedly: "One that, above all other strifes, contended especially/ to know himself." *Meas,* III, ii, 226–227.

contending, *adj.* warring or warlike: "What is she but a foul contending rebel,/ And graceless traitor to her loving lord?" *Shrew,* V, ii, 160–161.

content, *v.* **1** to satisfy: "Fear not, Baptista, we will content you, go to." *Shrew,* V, i, 124. **2** to be gratifying or satisfying: "Gramercies, lad. Go forward, this contents." *Shrew,* I, i, 163. **3** to remunerate: "Come the next sabbath and I will content you." *Rich 3,* III, ii, 109. **4 make content with his fortunes fit,** be just as happy as his fortunes allow: "He that has and a little tiny wit . . . Must make content with his fortunes fit . . ." *Lear,* III, ii, 74–76.
—*adj.* **5 could be content,** would really prefer: "They could be content/ To visit other places . . ." *J Caes,* V, i, 8–9.
—*n.* **6** pleasure: "The unborn event/ I do commend to your content . . ." *Per,* IV, Chor., 45–46. **7 true contents,** contentment; here, upon learning the truth: "To join in Hymen's bands,/ If truth holds true contents." *As You,* V, iv, 128–129.
–*interj.* **8** agreed!: "Shall I? Content! This chair shall be my state [throne], this/ dagger my sceptre . . ." *1 Hen 4,* II, iv, 373–374.

contention, *n.* **when contention and occasion meet,** when an opportunity arises for us to meet in combat: "But when contention and occasion meet,/ By Jove, I'll play the hunter for thy life . . ." *Tr & Cr,* IV, i, 17–18.

contestation, *n.* contention or controversy; here, armed insurrection: ". . . their contestation/ Was theme for you, you were the word of war." *Ant & Cleo,* II, ii, 43–44.

continence, *n.* restrained use of power: ". . . suffer not dishonour to approach/ The imperial seat . . . To justice, continence, and nobility . . ." *T Andr,* I, i, 13–15.

continent, *n.* **1** the shore or bank of a stream: "Gelding the opposed continent as much/ As on the other side it takes from you." *1 Hen 4,* III, i, 106–107. **2** dry land; terra firma: "Make mountains level, and the continent,/ Weary of solid firmness, melt itself . . ." *2 Hen 4,* III, i, 47–48. **3** container or vessel; here, also sum or quintessence: "Ay, my continent of beauty." *Love's L,* IV, i, 110. **4 concealing continents,** enclo-

sure that hides one: ". . . close pent-up guilts,/ Rive your concealing continents . . ." *Lear,* III, ii, 57–58.
—*adj.* **5** that restrain; also, chaste: "All continent impediments would o'erbear . . ." *Mac,* IV, iii, 64.

continent canon, *n.* canon decreeing continence: ". . . sorted and consorted, contrary to thy established/ proclaimed edict and continent canon . . ." *Love's L,* I, i, 252–253.

continent forbearance, *n.* restrained attitude and a withdrawn presence: "I pray you have a continent/ forbearance till the speed of his rage goes slower . . ." *Lear,* I, ii, 172–173.

continuance, *n.* duration: "Continuance tames the one; the other wild . . ." *Luc,* 1097.

continuantly, *adv.* prob. misuse for "continually": "A comes continuantly to Pie Corner . . . to buy a saddle . . ." *2 Hen 4,* II, i, 25–26.

continuate, *adj.* continued at length; continuous: ". . . an untirable and continuate goodness." *Timon,* I, i, 11.

continue, *v.* to keep or retain: ". . . how shall we continue Claudio,/ To save me from the danger that might come . . ." *Meas,* IV, iii, 83–84.

continuer, *n.* person who has persistence and endurance: "I would my horse had the speed of your tongue/ and so good a continuer." *M Ado,* I, i, 130–131.

contract, *v.* to shorten, hence to pass agreeably: "Methought it was very sweet:/ To contract—O—the time for—a—my behove . . ." *Ham,* V, i, 62–63.

contracted, *adj.* **1** betrothed: ". . . where two contracted new/ Come daily to the banks . . ." *Sonn 56,* 10–11. **2** the same in fig. sense: "But thou, contracted to thine own bright eyes . . ." *Sonn 1,* 5.

contracting, *n.* betrothal: "Pay with falsehood [deception] false exacting,/ And perform an old contracting." *Meas,* III, ii, 274–275.

contraction, *n.* signing of a contract, esp. a marriage contract: "O, such a deed/ As from the body of contraction plucks/ The very soul . . ." *Ham,* III, iv, 45–47.

contradiction, *n.* objection: ". . . may (without contradiction) suffer the report." *Cymb,* I, v, 52.

contrariety, *n.* **1** opposition; here, ref. to two people who are extreme opposites: "He and Aufidius can no more atone/ Than violent'st contrariety." *Cor,* IV, vi, 73–74. **2** [pl.] contrary statements; contradictions: "He will be here, and yet he is not here:/ How can these contrarieties agree?" *1 Hen 6,* II, iii, 57–58.

contrarious, *adj., adv.* adverse[ly]; also, inconsistent or contradictory: ". . . and most contrarious [spitefully] quest/ Upon [report on] thy doings . . ." *Meas,* IV, i, 62–63.

contrariously, *adv.* in opposite directions; discordantly: ". . . many things, having full reference/ To one consent, may work contrariously . . ." *Hen 5,* I, ii, 205–206.

contrary, *n.* **1** opposite condition: "Decline to your confounding contraries . . ." *Timon,* IV, i, 20. **2** [often pl] contrary or perverse behavior: "Is't good to soothe him in these contraries?" *Errors,* IV, iv, 77. **3** person or thing of opposite qualities; here, like a bad child begotten of a good parent: "Like a good parent, did beget of him/ A falsehood in its contrary, as great/ As my trust was . . ." *Temp,* I, ii, 94–96. **4** opposite or contrary procedure: "I' th' commonwealth I would by contraries/ Execute all things . . ." *Temp,* II, i, 143–144.
—*adj.* **5** different: "My/ merry host hath had the measuring of their/ weapons, and . . . appointed them/ contrary places . . ." *Wives,* II, i, 195–197. **6 contrary parts,** opposing sides: ". . . banding themselves in contrary parts,/ Do pelt so fast at one another's pate . . ." *1 Hen 6,* III, i, 81–82.
—*v.* **7** to defy or disobey: "You must contrary me. Marry, 'tis time—" *Rom & Jul,* I, v, 84–85.
—*adv.* **8** in a contradictory way: "And wouldst thou turn our offers contary?" *1 Hen 4,* V, v, 4.

contrive¹, *v.* **1** to conspire: "If thou read this, O Caesar, thou may'st live;/ If not, the Fates with traitors do contrive." *J Caes,* II, iii, 13–14. **2** to arrange: ". . . as a branch and member of this royalty,/ By whom this great assembly is contriv'd . . ." *Hen 5,* V, ii, 5–6.

contrive², *v.* to pass the time: "Please ye we may contrive this afternoon . . ." *Shrew,* I, ii, 274.

contriving, *adj.* working on one's behalf: ". . . the letters too/ Of many our contriving friends in Rome . . ." *Ant & Cleo,* I, ii, 179–180.

control, *n.* **1** check or constraint; force: "The proud control of fierce and bloody war . . ." *K John,* I, i, 17. **2** authority: ". . . quenching my/ familiar smile with an austere regard of control . . ." *T Night,* II, v, 66–67.

controlled, *past part.* **1** checked; stopped: "I made unto the noise, when soon I heard/ The crying babe controll'd with this discourse . . ." *T Andr,* V, i, 25–26. **2** overpowered: ". . . peeping forth this tumult to behold,/ Are by his flaming torch dimm'd and controll'd." *Luc,* 447–448.

controller, *n.* critic or detractor; censor: "Saucy controller of my private steps!" *T Andr,* II, iii, 60.

controlment, *n.* restraint or check: ". . . you must not make the full show of this/ till you may do it without controlment." *M Ado,* I, iii, 18–19.

controversy, *n.* rivalry: "The torrent roar'd, and we did buffet it/ With lusty sinews, throwing it aside,/ And stemming it with hearts of controversy." *J Caes,* I, ii, 106–108.

contumelious, *adj.* **1** haughty: "He dares not calm his contumelious spirit . . ." *2 Hen 6,* III, ii, 203. **2** insulting; slanderous: "With scoffs and scorns and contumelious taunts." *1 Hen 6,* I, iv, 38.

contumeliously, *adv.* insolently; contemptuously: ". . . that you . . ./ Thus contumeliously should break the peace!" *1 Hen 6,* I, iii, 57–58.

contumely, *n.* haughtiness or disdain: "Th'oppressor's wrong, the proud man's contumely . . ." *Ham,* III, i, 71.

contusions, *n. pl.* hurts: "That winter lion, who in rage forgets/ Aged contusions and all brush of time . . ." *2 Hen 6,* V, iii, 2–3.

Con tutto il cuore ben trovato, [Italian] With all my heart, well met. *Shrew,* I, ii, 24.

convenience, *n.* **1** that which is fit and proper; here, because of Bertram's age and status: "The duke will lay upon him all the honour/ That good convenience claims." *All's W,* III, ii, 71–72. **2** [pl.] advantages; suitabilities: ". . . now, for/ want of these requir'd conveniences . . ." *Oth,* II, i, 229–230.

conveniency, *n.* var. of **convenience:** ". . . thou keepest from me/ all conveniency than suppliest me with the least advantage/ of hope . . ." *Oth,* IV, ii, 178–180.

convenient, *adj.* **1** suitable; fitting: ". . . here's a marvellous convenient place/ for our rehearsal." *M N Dream,* III, i, 2–3. **2** becoming or proper: ". . . it shall be convenient, Master/ Hume, that you be by her aloft . . ." *2 Hen 6,* I, iv, 7–8. **3** fit; capable: "Dispatch the most convenient messenger." *All's W,* III, iv, 34. **4** adequate: ". . . take/ Convenient numbers to make good the city . . ." *Cor,* I, v, 11–12.

convent, *v.* **1** to be suitable or fitting: "When . . . golden time convents,/ A solemn combination shall be made/ Of our dear souls." *T Night,* V, i, 381–383. **2** to summon or order to appear, as for trial: ". . . 'hath commanded/ To-morrow morning to the council board/ He be convented." *Hen 8,* V, i, 50–52. **3** to convene: "We are convented/ Upon a pleasing treaty . . ." *Cor,* II, ii, 54–55.

conventicle, *n.* **1** a meeting place: "Since green our thoughts, green be the conventicle/ Where we will ease us by disburd'ning them." *Edw 3,* II, i, 63–64. **2** clandestine meeting: ". . . all of you have laid your heads together—/ Myself had notice of your conventicles . . ." *2 Hen 6,* III, i, 166.

conversant, *adj.* **alike conversant,** equally versed [in]: ". . . above him in birth, alike conversant in general services . . ." *Cymb,* IV, i, 12.

conversation, *n.* **1** conduct; behavior: "The good in conversation . . . Is still at Tharsus . . ." *Per,* II, Chor., 9–11. **2** [pl] manners: ". . . all are banish'd till their conversations/ Appear more wise . . ." *2 Hen 4,* V, v, 100–101. **3** interplay or interchange: ". . . the king/ Had from the conversation of my thoughts/ Haply been absent then." *All's W,* I, iii, 228–229. **4** sexual relations: "I mean his conversation with Shore's wife . . ." *Rich 3,* III, v, 31.

converse, *n.* **1** conversation: "Your party in converse, him you would sound . . ." *Ham,* II, i, 44. **2 converse of breath,** social intercourse: "If over-boldly we have borne ourselves/ In the converse of breath . . ." *Love's L,* V, ii, 726–727.

—*v.* **3** to be acquainted: ". . . one that converses/ more with the buttock of the night . . ." *Cor,* II, i, 50–51.

conversion, *n.* elevated status or, perh., conversation [with inferiors]: "'Tis too respective and too sociable/ For your conversion." *K John,* I, i, 188–189.

convert, *v.* **1** to change; alter: "Thy overflow of good converts to bad . . ." *Rich 2,* V, iii, 62. **2** to transform: "May I be so converted and see with these eyes?" *M Ado,* II, iii, 22. **3** to reform: "The devil fiddle 'em . . . For sure there's no converting of 'em . . ." *Hen 8,* I, iii, 42–43. **4** to turn away: "The eyes, 'fore duteous, now converted are . . ." *Sonn 7,* 11.

convertite, *n.* **1** convert: ". . . since you are a gentle convertite/ My tongue shall hush again this storm of war . . ." *K John,* V, i, 19–20. **2** person converted to the religious life: "Out of these convertites,/ There is much matter to be heard and learn'd." *As You,* V, iv, 183–184. **3 heavy convertite,** sorrowful penitent: "He thence departs a heavy convertite . . ." *Luc,* 743.

convey, *v.* **1** to arrange or indulge in secret: ". . . you may/ Convey your pleasures in a spacious plenty . . ." *Mac,* IV, iii, 70–71. **2** to steal [euphem.]: "O, good! Convey! Conveyers are you all,/ That rise thus nimbly by a true king's fall." *Rich 2,* IV, i, 317–318. **3** to hide; conceal: "Behind the arras I'll convey myself/ To hear the process." *Ham,* III, iii, 28–29. **4** to escort away from here: "For God's sake, lords, convey my tristful Queen,/ For tears do stop the floodgates of her eyes." *1 Hen 4,* II, iv, 388–389.

conveyance, *n.* **1** nimbleness or dexterity, as in jugglery: ". . . huddling jest upon jest with such impossible conveyance upon me . . ." *M Ado,* II, i, 228–229. **2** deceit or trickery; fraud: "I am come to survey the Tower this day;/ Since Henry's death, I fear, there is conveyance." *1 Hen 6,* I, iii, 1–2. **3** escort: "Fortinbras/ Craves the conveyance of [for] a promis'd march/ Over his kingdom." *Ham,* IV, iv, 2–4. **4** removal by force; disposal [of]: ". . . and for her sake/ Mad'st quick conveyance with her good aunt Anne." *Rich 3,* IV, iv, 282–283.

conveyer, *n.* thief [euphem.]: "Conveyers are you all,/ That rise thus nimbly by a true king's fall." *Rich 2,* IV, i, 317–318.

conveying gusts, *n.* [sounds] carried by the wind: "By interims and conveying gusts we have heard/ The charges of our friends." *Cor,* I, vi, 5–6.

convict, *adj.* convicted: "Before I be convict by course of law . . ." *Rich 3,* I, iv, 176.

convicted, *adj.* overwhelmed; doomed: "A whole armado of convicted sail/ Is scatter'd and disjoin'd . . ." *K John,* III, iii, 2–3.

convince, *v.* **1** to prove: "The holy suit which fain it would convince . . ." *Love's L,* V, ii, 738. **2** to defeat: ". . . their malady convinces/ The great assay of art [test of medical skills] . . ." *Mac,* IV, iii, 142–143. **3** to overcome: ". . . his two chamberlains/ Will I with wine and wassail so convince . . ." *Mac,* I, vii, 64–65. **4** to refute; prove false: ". . . time of both this truth shall ne'er convince,/ Thou show'dst a subject's shine, I a true prince' [prince's]." *Per,* I, ii, 124. **5** to convict: "Else might the world convince of levity/ As well my undertakings as your counsels." *Tr & Cr,* II, ii, 131–132.

convive, *v.* to feast: ". . . go to my tent;/ There in the full convive we . . ." *Tr & Cr,* IV, v, 270–271.

convoy, *n.* **1 convoy is assistant,** [a] means of conveyance is available: ". . . as the winds give benefit/ And convoy is assistant, do not sleep . . ." *Ham,* I, iii, 2–3. **2 entertain one's convoy,** to hire one's means of conveyance: ". . . writ to my/ lady mother I am returning, entertain'd my convoy . . ." *All's W,* IV, iii, 85–86.

cony, *n.* wild rabbit, esp. a young one: "As the cony that you see dwell where she is kindled." *As You,* III, ii, 332.

cony-catch, *v.* to trick or deceive; dupe; gull: "Take heed, Signor Baptista, lest you be cony-catched/ in this business." *Shrew,* V, i, 90–91.

cony-catching, *n.* **1** [lit., rabbit-stealing] trickery; knavery; also, wordplay on "catch" of preceding line: "Come, you are so full of cony-catching." *Shrew,* IV, i, 38.
—*adj.* **2** cheating: "... your cony-catching rascals, Bardolph,/ Nym, and Pistol." *Wives,* I, i, 116–117.

cook, *n.* **let thine eye be thy cook,** let me seem more attractive to you than I really am: "If thou canst love a fellow of this/ temper, Kate . . . let thine eye be thy cook." *Hen 5,* V, ii, 149–152.

cooled, *past part.* quailed; recoiled: "The time has been, my senses would have cool'd/ To hear a night-shriek . . ." *Mac,* V, v, 10–11.

cooling card, *n.* card played by one's opponent that ruins one's chances of winning: "There all is marr'd; there lies a cooling card." *1 Hen 6,* V, iii, 84.

coop, *v.* to confine or enclose; here, as a means of defense: "Alas, I am not coop'd here for defence!" *3 Hen 6,* V, i, 112.

copatain hat, *n.* high-crowned hat, somewhat resembling a sugar loaf: "A silken doublet, a velvet/ hose, a scarlet cloak, and a copatain hat!" *Shrew,* V, i, 58–59.

cope¹, *v.* **1** to encounter; deal with: "I love to cope him in these sullen fits . . ." *As You,* II, i, 67. **2** to fight (with): ". . . he yesterday coped Hector in the battle/ and struck him down . . ." *Tr & Cr,* I, ii, 34–35. **3** to be an equal match for: "And here's a lord . . . Ajax shall cope the best." *Tr & Cr,* II, iii, 263–264. **4** to recompense; requite: "Three thousand ducats due unto the Jew/ We freely cope your courteous pains withal." *Merch,* IV, i, 407–408. **5 cope with,** to meet with; deal with: "He is a man, and, Clifford, cope with him." *3 Hen 6,* I, iii, 24.

cope², *n.* vault of heaven; sky: ". . . not worth a breakfast in the cheapest country under the cope . . ." *Per,* IV, vi, 122–123.

copesmate, *n.* companion: "Mis-shapen time, copesmate of ugly night . . ." *Luc,* 925.

Cophetua, *n.* **1** legendary African ruler of immense wealth: "O base Assyrian knight, what is thy news?/ Let King Cophetua know the truth thereof." *2 Hen 4,* V, iii, 98–99. **2** popular ballad concerning Cophetua's love for Zenelophon, a beggar maid: "The magnanimous/ and most illustrate king Cophetua set eye upon/ the . . . beggar Zenelophon . . ." *Love's L,* IV, i, 65–67.

copped, *adj.* peaked: "The blind mole casts/ Copp'd hills towards heaven . . ." *Per,* I, i, 101–102.

copper, *n.* copper coin, usually a penny or halfpenny: ". . . our copper buys no better treasure." *Love's L,* IV, iii, 382.

copulative, *n.* [usually pl.] persons about to be married: humorous use: "I press in here sir, amongst the rest of the country copulatives . . ." *As You,* V, iv, 54–55.

copy, *n.* **1** topic or theme: "It was the copy of our conference . . ." *Errors,* V, i, 62. **2** child; heir: "If you will lead these graces to the grave/ And leave the world no copy." *T Night,* I, v, 245–256. **3** example: "Such a man/ Might be a copy to these younger times . . ." *All's W,* I, ii, 45–46.

coragio, *n.* courage [from Italian *coraggio*]: "Coragio,/ bully-monster, coragio!" *Temp,* V, i, 257–258.

Coram, *n.* quorum; ref. to required minimum of two justices necessary to try felony cases: "In the county of Gloucester, Justice of Peace and/ Coram." *Wives,* I, i, 5–6.

coranto, *n.* quick dance with a running step: "Why dost thou not go to church in a galliard, and/ come home in a coranto?" *T Night,* I, iii, 125–126.

cordial, *n.* **1** restorative, as a medicine or drink that revives the spirits: "Come, cordial, and not poison, go with me/ To Juliet's grave, for there must I use thee." *Rom & Jul,* V, i, 85–86. **2** something that comforts: "Kind Rome, that hast thus lovingly reserv'd/ The cordial of mine age to glad my heart." *T Andr,* I, i, 165–166.
—*adj.* **3** able to revive the spirits; restorative: "I do not know/ What is more cordial." *Cymb,* I, vi, 63–64.

co-responsive, *adj.* corresponding; dovetailing: ". . . with massy staples/ And co-responsive and fulfilling bolts . . ." *Tr & Cr,* Prol., 17–18.

Corin, *n.* traditional shepherd's name in pastoral poetry: "And in the shape of Corin, sat all day/ Playing on pipes of corn, and versing love . . ." *M N Dream,* II, i, 66–67.

Corinth, *n.* city of ancient Greece noted for its licentiousness; here, slang term for "brothel" or district of brothels: "Would we could see you at Corinth!" *Timon,* II, i, 73.

Corinthian, *n.* merry and usually debauched companion: "I am no proud Jack like Falstaff,/ but a Corinthian, a lad of mettle . . ." *1 Hen 4,* II, iv, 11–12.

Coriolanus, *n.* Roman general who, after being banished, gathered an army of Volscians and attacked Rome: "Who threats, in course of his revenge, to do/ As much as ever Coriolanus did." *T Andr,* IV, iv, 67–68.

Corioles, *n.* seat of Volscian government: "[Enter Tullus Aufidius with Senators of Corioles.]" [SD] *Cor,* I, ii, 1.

co-rival, *v.* to vie or compete with: ". . . the saucy boat/ Whose weak untimber'd sides but even now/ Co-rivall'd greatness?" *Tr & Cr,* I, iii, 42–44.

corky, *adj.* withered with age: "Bind fast his corky arms." *Lear,* III, vii, 29.

cormorant, *n.* **1** seabird; here, regarded as a symbol of gluttony: "Light vanity, insatiate cormorant,/ Consuming means, soon preys upon itself." *Rich 2,* II, i, 38–39. —*adj.* **2** rapacious; ravenous: "When, spite of cormorant devouring Time,/ Th'endeavour of this present breath may buy/ That honour . . ." *Love's L,* I, i, 4–5.

corn, *n.* **1** generalized word for "grain": "Sow'd cockle reap'd no corn . . ." *Love's L,* IV, iii, 379. **2 pipes of corn,** music pipes made from oat straws: "And in the shape of Corin, sat all day/ Playing on pipes of corn, and versing love . . ." *M N Dream,* II, i, 66–67.

Cornelia, *n.* Roman mother, revered for her careful education of her two sons, the Gracchi: "Ah, boy, Cornelia never with more care/ Read to her sons . . ." *T Andr,* IV, i, 12–13.

corner, *n.* **of all the corners,** the four corners of the earth: "And winds of all the corners kiss'd your sails . . ." *Cymb,* II, iv, 28

corner-cap, *n.* cap with square corners, as that worn by graduates, magistrates, etc.: "Thou mak'st the triumviry, the corner-cap of society . . ." *Love's L,* IV, iii, 50.

cornet, *n.* troop of horse soldiers: ". . . that Somerset, who in proud heart/ Doth stop my cornets, were in Talbot's place!" *1 Hen 6,* IV, iii, 24–25.

cornuto, *n.* horned beast; hence, cuckold: ". . . the peaking cornuto her/ husband . . . dwelling in a continual/ larum of jealousy . . ." *Wives,* III, v, 64–66.

corollary, *n.* excess; surfeit: "Now come, my Ariel! bring a corollary,/ Rather than want a spirit . . ." *Temp,* IV, i, 57–58.

coronal, *n.* coronet, usually indicating the wearer's rank: "The old Duchess of Norfolk, in a coronal of gold . . ." [SD] *Hen 8,* IV, i, 36.

coronation day, *n.* anniversary of the monarch's coronation, an annual holiday: ". . . ringing in the King's affairs upon his coronation/ day, sir." *2 Hen 4,* III, ii, 178–179.

coronet, *n.* crown indicating rank below that of king: "Adorn his temples with a coronet,/ And yet . . . Retain but privilege of a private man?" *1 Hen 6,* V, iv, 134–136.

corporal, *n.* officer in Cupid's army [whimsical use]: ". . . the wonder in a mortal eye!"/ "By earth, she is not, corporal; there you lie." *Love's L,* IV, iii, 82–83.

corporate, *adj.* as though [uttered by] one person: "They answer in a joint and corporate voice . . ." *Timon,* II, ii, 218.

Corporate, *n.* misuse for "Corporal": "Good Master Corporate Bardolph, stand my/ friend . . ." *2 Hen 4,* III, ii, 215–216.

corpse, *n.* [used as sing. or pl.] bodies as distinct from souls: "My lord your son had only but the corpse,/ But shadows and the shows of men, to fight . . ." *2 Hen 4,* I, i, 192–193.

corpulent, *adj.* having a large, though not necessarily obese, body: "A goodly portly man, i'faith, and a corpulent . . ." *1 Hen 4,* II, iv, 416.

correct, *v.* **1** to deal out justice: "Where some, like magistrates, correct at home . . ." *Hen 5,* I, ii, 191. **2** to chastise: "Where's Troilus? . . . I would correct him." *Tr & Cr,* V, vi, 2–3. **3** to punish: "To show his sorrow he'd correct himself . . ." *Per,* I, iii, 22.

corrected, *adj.* rebuked; chastised: "Your knees to me? to your corrected son?" *Cor,* V, iii, 57.

correction, *n.* **1** punishment: "As it shall follow in my correction; and God defend/ the right!" *Love's L,* I, i, 210–211. **2** privilege of punishing [Troilus]: "Were I the general, thou shouldst have my office [rank]/ Ere [before you took from me] that correction." *Tr & Cr,* V, vi, 4–5. **3 correct correction,** correct what must be corrected; also, punish what is punishable: "No bitterness that I will bitter think,/ Nor double penance to correct correction." *Sonn 111,* 11–12. **4 under correction,** prob. rustic oath, with general meaning of "may I be punished": "Under correction, sir, we know whereuntil it doth/ amount." *Love's L,* V, ii, 493.

correctioner, *n.* coinage for "correction officer": ". . . you filthy famished correctioner, if you/ be not swinged I'll forswear half-kirtles." *2 Hen 4,* V, iv, 21–22.

correspondent, *adj.* agreeable or compliant; obedient: "I will be correspondent to command,/ And do my spriting gently." *Temp,* I, ii, 297–298.

corrigible, *adj.* **1** submissive; obedient: "His corrigible neck, his face subdued . . ." *Ant & Cleo,* IV, xiv, 74. **2** corrective; correcting: ". . . the power, and/ corrigible authority [control] of this, lies in our wills." *Oth,* I, iii, 325–326.

corrival, *n.* partner: "So he that doth redeem her thence might wear/ Without corrival all her dignities . . ." *1 Hen 4,* I, iii, 204–205.

corroborate, *adj.* See **fracted** (def. 2).

corrosive, *adj.* acting like a bitter medicine: "Care is no cure,/ but rather corrosive,/ For things that are not to be remedied." *1 Hen 6,* III, iii, 3–4.

corruption, *n.* misrepresentation: "His virtues else . . . Shall in the general censure take corruption . . ." *Ham,* I, iv, 33–35.

corse, *n.* corpse: "Here lies a wretched corse, of wretched soul bereft . . ." *Timon,* V, iv, 70.

corslet, *n.* armor covering body between neck and waist; cuirass: "He is able to pierce a corslet with his/ eye . . ." *Cor,* V, iv, 20–21.

cost, *n.* **1** costly undertaking: "Gives o'er, and leaves his part-created cost . . ." *2 Hen 4,* I, iii, 60. **2** lavish display or expenditure: "Where youth, and cost, witless bravery keeps." *Meas,* I, iii, 10. **3** trouble; bother: "The fashion of the world is to avoid/ cost, and you encounter it." *M Ado,* I, I, 89–90. **4 my proper cost,** my own expense: "One day shall crown th' alliance on't . . . Here at my house, and at my proper cost." *T Night,* V, i, 317–318. **5 upon my cost,** at my expense: "Nor care I who doth feed upon my cost . . ." *Hen 5,* IV, iii, 25.
—*v.* **6** to be worth: "Did these bones cost [Are these bones worth] no more the breeding but to play/ at loggets with 'em?" *Ham,* V, i, 90–91.

costard, *n.* large, ribbed apple; also, slang term for the head: "A wonder, master! here's a costard broken [cut] in a shin." *Love's L,* III, i, 67.

costermonger, *n.* fruit peddler, often a term of abuse: ". . . virtue is of so little regard in these/ costermongers' times . . ." *2 Hen 4,* I, ii, 167–168.

costly, *adj.* richly adorned; lavish: "To show how costly summer was at hand . . ." *Merch,* II, ix, 94.

co-supreme, *n.* person who shares power; joint ruler: ". . . the Phoenix and the Dove,/ Co-supremes and stars of love . . ." *Phoen,* 50–51.

cote¹, *n.* cot or cottage: ". . . his cote, his flocks, and bounds of feed/ Are now on sale . . ." *As You,* II, iv, 81–82.

cote², *v.* to overtake or pass: "We coted them on the way,/ and hither are they/ coming to offer you service." *Ham,* II, ii, 316–317.

cote³, *v.* to cover with or as if with paint: "Coting the other hill in such array/ That all his gilded upright pikes do seem/ Straight trees of gold . . ." *Edw 3,* IV, iv, 24–26.

cot-quean, *n.* man who meddles in women's business [speech may belong to Lady Capulet rather than Nurse]: "Go, you cot-quean, go,/ Get you to bed." *Rom & Jul,* IV, iv, 6–7.

Cotshall or **Cotsall,** *n.* var. of **Cotswold,** hilly region of Gloucestershire; here, prob. indicates Elizabethan pronunciation: ". . . what a weary way/ From Ravenspurgh to Cotshall will be found/ In Ross and Willoughby . . ." *Rich 2,* II, iii, 8–10.

Cotsole, *adj.* from the Cotswold, a hilly region of central England: ". . . black George Barnes, and Francis Pickbone,/ and Will Squele, a Cotsole man . . ." *2 Hen 4,* III, ii, 19–20.

couch, *v.* **1** to fix a (lance) in the attack position: "A braver soldier never couched lance . . ." *1 Hen 6,* III, ii, 134. **2** (of an animal) to hide in its lair: "This night, wherein the cub-drawn bear would couch . . ." *Lear,* III, i, 12. **3** to crouch; lie hidden: "Come, come, we'll couch i' th' castle-ditch till we/ see the light of our fairies." *Wives,* V, ii, 1–2. **4** to cause to crouch or cower: ". . . like a falcon tow'ring in the skies,/ Coucheth the fowl below . . ." *Luc,* 506–507. **5** to lie in bed (with): "If I court moe women, you'll couch with moe men." *Oth,* IV, iii, 56.

couched, *adj.* expressed: ". . . securely I espy/ Virtue with valour couched in thine eye." *Rich 2,* I, iii, 97–98.

couching, *n.* **1** low bow: "These couchings and these lowly courtesies/ Might fire the blood of ordinary men . . ." *J Caes,* III, i, 36–37.
—*adj.* **2** humorous use for "couchant," heraldic term for "lying down": "A couching lion and a ramping cat . . ." *1 Hen 4,* III, i, 147.

coulter, *n.* blade at the head of a plow: ". . . the coulter rusts/ That should deracinate such savagery . . ." *Hen 5,* V, ii, 46–47.

council, *n.* **in council,** engaged in debate; here, a moral dilemma: "The genius and the mortal instruments/ Are then in council . . ." *J Caes,* II, i, 66–67.

Council, *n.* confusion between ecclesiastical and government Council: "It is not meet the Council hear a riot; there is no/ fear of Got [God] in a riot." *Wives,* I, i, 33–34.

counsel, *n.* **1** deliberation or reflection: ". . . let her wear it out with/ good counsel." *M Ado,* II, iii, 194–195. **2** advice: "I'll show thee some attires, and have thy counsel/ Which is the best to furnish me tomorrow." *M Ado,* III, i, 102–103. **3** confidential note or letter: "And to her white hand see thou do commend/ This seal'd-up counsel." *Love's L,* III, i, 162–163. **4** [often pl.] a confidence; private thoughts: "Their several counsels they unbosom shall/ To loves mistook, and so be mock'd withal . . ." *Love's L,* V, ii, 141–142. **5 in counsel,** sharing a secret: "To climb celestial Silvia's chamber-window,/ Myself in counsel, his competitor." *Two Gent,* II, vi, 34–35. **6 keep counsel,** to keep a secret: "The players cannot/ keep counsel: they'll tell all." *Ham,* III, ii, 137–138. **7 never admitting counsel o'th'war,** not seeking the counsel of other officers regarding the war: "Breaking his oath and resolution . . . never admitting/ Counsel o'th'war . . ." *Cor,* V, vi, 96–97. **8 soul of counsel,** one's most secret feelings: ". . . your silence . . . from my weakness draws/ My very soul of counsel." *Tr & Cr,* III, ii, 130–132.

counsellor, *n.* **1** councillor; Gonzalo was a member of the King's council: "You are a/ counsellor; if you can command these elements to/ silence . . ." *Temp,* I, i, 21–22. **2 counsellors to fear,** the means of instilling fear in others: ". . . those linen cheeks of thine/ Are counsellors to fear." *Mac,* V, iii, 16–17.

count[1], *n.* **1** var. of **compt;** accounting; reckoning: "The other motive/ Why to a public count I might not go . . ." *Ham,* IV, vii, 16–17. **2 at count,** on the Day of Reckoning: ". . . when we shall meet at count,/ This look of thine will hurl my soul from heaven . . ." *Oth,* V, ii, 274–275. **3 out of all count,** incalculable: ". . . the one is painted, and the other out/ of all count." *Two Gent,* II, i, 54–55. —*v.* **4** to judge [as]: "Which in their wills count bad what I think good?" *Sonn 121,* 8. **5 count of,** to appreciate; esteem: ". . . so painted to make her fair that no man/ counts of her beauty." *Two Gent,* II, i, 57–58.

count[2], *n.* gown; Katharine appar. mistakes the English word for French "conne" [cunt]: "Le foot, et le count? O Seigneur Dieu!" *Hen 5,* III, iv, 52.

counted, *adj.* accounted; esteemed: "Nor mother, wife, nor England's counted Queen." *Rich 3,* IV, i, 46.

countenance, *n.* **1** behavior or manner: ". . . the something that nature gave me his countenance seems to take from me." *As You,* I, i, 17–18. **2** person's face or, sometimes, one's general aspect or appearance: ". . . and almost chide God for making you that countenance you are . . ." *As You,* IV, i, 34–35. **3** reputation; standing: "I have been content, sir, you should/ lay my countenance to pawn . . ." *Wives,* II, ii, 4–5. **4** support or encouragement: ". . . the poor abuses of the time want/ countenance." *1 Hen 4,* I, ii, 151–152. **5** favor; rewards or benefits: "Ay, sir, that soaks up the King's countenance, his/ rewards, his authorities." *Ham,* IV, ii, 14–15. **6** privilege; right: "And the more pity that/ great folk should have countenance in this world to/ drown or hang themselves . . ." *Ham,* V, i, 26–28. **7** authority: "Now then, we'll use/ His countenance for the battle . . ." *Lear,* V, i, 62–63. **8 hold one's countenance,** to maintain a straight face: "O the Father, how he holds his countenance!" *1 Hen 4,* II, iv, 387. **9 out of countenance,**

disconcerted; rattled: "This pert Berowne was out of countenance quite." *Love's L,* V, ii, 272. **10 sleep day out of countenance,** insult the day by sleeping through it: ". . . we did sleep day out of countenance; and/ made the night light with drinking." *Ant & Cleo,* II, ii, 177–178. —*v.* **11** to support; lend encouragement to: "Led on by bloody youth . . . And countenanc'd by boys and beggary . . ." *2 Hen 4,* IV, i, 33–35. **12** to accept responsibility for: ". . . this vile deed/ We must with all our majesty and skill/ Both countenance and excuse." *Ham,* IV, i, 30–32. **13** to favor: "I beseech you, sir, to countenance William Visor of/ Woncot against Clement Perkes a'th'Hill." *2 Hen 4,* V, i, 34–35. **14** to be suitable for; here also, to behold or view: "As from your graves rise up, and walk like sprites,/ To countenance this horror!" *Mac,* II, iii, 80–81. **15** to greet; pay one's respects to: "You must meet my master to/ countenance my mistress." *Shrew,* IV, i, 88–89.

counter[1], *n.* **1** coinlike piece of metal used for reckoning: "What, for a counter, would I do but good? *As You,* II, vii, 63. **2** contemp. term for a coin: "When Marcus Brutus grows so covetous,/ To lock such rascal counters from his friends . . ." *J Caes,* IV, iii, 79–80.

counter[2], *adj.* following a scent in the wrong direction: "O, this is counter, you false Danish dogs." *Ham,* IV, v, 110.

counter-caster, *n.* person who requires counters to reckon sums: ". . . must be lee'd, and calm'd,/ By . . . this counter-caster . . ." *Oth,* I, i, 29–31.

counterchange, *n.* mutual exchange: ". . . hitting/ Each object with a joy: the counterchange/ Is severally in all." *Cymb,* V, v, 396–398.

counterfeit, *v.* **1** to pretend; feign: ". . . as if the tragedy/ Were play'd in jest by counterfeiting actors?" *3 Hen 6,* II, iii, 27–28. **2** to reflect: "Why did he then thus counterfeit her looks?" *Edw 3,* II, i, 13. —*n.* **3** picture or portrait, regarded as a counterfeit likeness: "Thou draw'st a counterfeit/ Best in all Athens . . ." *Timon,* V, i, 79–80. **4** reflected image; here, Lucrece's weeping maid: ". . . mild patience bid fair Lucrece speak/ To the poor counterfeit of her complaining." *Luc,* 1268–1269. **5** counterfeit coin; here, bearing the king's image: ". . . a counterfeit/ Resembling majesty, which, being touch'd and tried,/ Proves valueless . . ." *K John,* III, i, 25–27. **6** imitation: "I fear thou art another counterfeit,/ And yet, in faith, thou bearest thee like a king . . ." *1 Hen 4,* V, iv, 34–35. **7** false representation of the truth: "Thou draw'st a counterfeit/ Best in all Athens . . ." *Timon,* V, i, 79–80. —*adj.* **8** false; deceitful: "While counterfeit supposes blear'd thine eyne [eyes]." *Shrew,* V, i, 107.

counterfeit presentment, *n.* painted likeness; here, prob. a miniature worn on a chain: "The counterfeit presentment of two brothers." *Ham,* III, iv, 54.

Counter-gate, *n.* gate of debtor's prison [the Counter], notorious for its stench: ". . . walk by the/ Counter-gate, which is as hateful to me as the reek/ of a lime-kill [kiln]." *Wives,* III, iii, 72–73.

countermand, *v.* to prevent or prohibit: ". . . one that countermands/ The passages of alleys, creeks and narrow lands . . ." *Errors,* IV, ii, 37–38.

counterpoise or counter-poise, *n.* **1** opposing force of equal strength: ". . . your/ whole plot too light, for the counterpoise of so great/ an opposition." *1 Hen 4,* II, iii, 12–14.
—*v.* **2** to match with an equal amount or sum; balance: "What you bestow, in him I'll counterpoise . . ." *Timon,* I, i, 148. **3 be singly counter-poised,** be matched by any one person: "The man I speak of cannot in the world/ Be singly counter-pois'd." *Cor,* II, ii, 86–87.

counter-reflect, *n.* that which reflects back; here, that changes the direction of heat: "Your sorrow beats so ardently upon me/ That it shall make a counter-reflect 'gainst/ My brother's heart . . ." *Kinsmen,* I, i, 126–128.

counterseal, *v.* to affix one's seal to a document already sealed by another: "A better witness . . . which we,/ On like conditions, will have counterseal'd." *Cor,* V, iii, 204–205.

countervail, *v.* to counterbalance; equal or match: ". . . come what sorrow can,/ It cannot countervail the exchange of joy . . ." *Rom & Jul,* II, vi, 3–4.

countless glory, *n.* her lovely qualities, as numerous as stars: "Her face, like heaven, enticeth thee to view/ Her countless glory, which desert must gain . . ." *Per,* I, i, 31–32.

country, *adj.* **1** simple; of no particular importance: "Sure he's a gallant gentleman."/ "He's but a country gentleman . . ." *Per,* II, iii, 32–33. **2** country's: "If in your country wars you chance to die . . ." *Cymb,* IV, iv, 51.

country base, *n.* prisoner's base, a children's game: ". . . lads more like to run/ The country base than to commit such slaughter . . ." *Cymb,* V, iii, 19–20.

country forms, *n.* types of countrymen [she has been used to]: "May fall to match you with her country forms,/ And happily repent." *Oth,* III, iii, 241–242.

countryman, *n.* **What countryman?** Where do you come from?: "No, say'st me so, friend? What countryman?" *Shrew,* I, ii, 188.

country matters, *n.* something indecent; that is, sexual relations: "Do you think I meant country matters?" *Ham,* III, ii, 115.

Count's master, *n.* ref. to the king: "Count's master is of/ another style." *All's W,* II, iii, 194–195.

County, *n.* var. of **count:** "County Claudio, when mean you to go to/ church?" *M Ado,* II, i, 332–333.

couple, *v.* **1** to embrace; here, sexually: ". . . a lady wiser, fairer, truer,/ Than ever Greek did couple in his arms . . ." *Tr & Cr,* I, iii, 274–275.
—*n.* **2 in couples,** leashed together like a pair of hounds: "I'll go in couples with her;/ Than when I feel and see her no farther trust her . . ." *W Tale,* II, i, 135–136.

Couple a gorge! Pistol's pseudo-French, appar. a rendering of "Cut my throat?": "'Couple a gorge!'/ That is the word. I thee defy again." *Hen 5,* II, i, 71–72.

couplement, *n.* **1** couple: "I wish you the peace/ of mind, most royal couplement!" *Love's L,* V, ii, 526–527. **2** coupling; linkage: "Making a couplement of proud compare . . ." *Sonn 21,* 5.

couplet, *n.* See **golden couplets.**

courage, *n.* **1** determination or inclination: "I'd such a courage to do him good." *Timon,* III, iii, 26. **2** young blade; gallant: ". . . do not dull thy palm with entertainment/ Of each new-hatch'd, unfledg'd courage." *Ham,* I, iii, 64–65. **3 hot courage,** sexual energy; lust: "His eye . . . Shows his hot courage and his high desire." *Ven & Ad,* 275–276.

course, *v.* **1** to chase or pursue: ". . . big round tears/ Cours'd one another down his innocent nose . . ." *As You,* II, i, 38–39. **2** to go hunting: "Say thou wilt course, thy greyhounds are as swift/ As breathed stags . . ." *Shrew,* Ind., ii, 48–49.
—*n.* **3** event or proceeding: "Here at more leisure may your Highness read,/ With every course in his particular." *2 Hen 4,* IV, iv, 89–90. **4** procedure; custom: ". . . you know the course is common." *Meas,* IV, ii, 177. **5** footrace: "Stand you directly in Antonius' way/ When he doth run his course." *J Caes,* I, ii, 3–4. **6** (in horsemanship) ability to run or race: "What rounds, what bounds, what course, what stop he makes!" *Lover's Comp,* 109. **7** serving of food; here likened to sleep: ". . . great Nature's second [main] course,/ Chief nourisher in life's feast . . ." *Mac,* II, ii, 38–39. **8** ship's sail: "Lay her a-hold, a-hold! set her two courses; off to/ sea again; lay her off." *Temp,* I, i, 49–50. **9** (in bear-baiting) a round or period of fighting: "They have tied me to a stake: I cannot fly,/ But, bear-like, I must fight the course." *Mac,* V, vii, 1–2. **10 course of direct session,** normal legal process: "To prison, till fit time/

Of law, and course of direct session,/ Call thee to answer." *Oth*, I, ii, 85–87. **11 Nature's second course,** sleep likened to the main part of a meal: "Balm of hurt minds, great Nature's second course,/ Chief nourisher in life's feast . . ." *Mac*, II, ii, 38–39. **12 run a certain course,** to adopt a safe plan of action: ". . . [to] derive from him better/ testimony of his intent, you should run a certain/ course . . ." *Lear*, I, ii, 82–84.

courser, *n.* riding-horse, esp. a charger: ". . . you gave good words the other day of a bay courser I rode on." *Timon*, I, ii, 208–209.

courser's hair, *n.* fr. the belief that horsehairs placed on a body of water would turn into eels or even poisonous snakes: ". . . like the courser's hair, hath yet but life,/ And not a serpent's poison." *Ant & Cleo*, I, ii, 191–192.

coursing snatchers, *n.* raiders on horseback; marauders: "We do not mean the coursing snatchers only . . ." *Hen 5*, I, ii, 143.

court, *n.* **1** amorous attentions, esp. longing looks: ". . . all his behaviours did make their retire/ To the court of his eye . . ." *Love's L*, II, i, 233–234. **2** heart regarded as the seat of the brain's reason: "I send it through the rivers of your blood/ Even to the court, the heart, to th'seat of th'brain . . ." *Cor*, I, i, 134–135.
—*v.* **3** to take advantage of: "If now I court not, but omit, my fortunes/ Will ever after droop." *Temp*, I, ii, 183–184. **4 court it,** to play the suitor; engage in courtship: "Then why should he despair that knows to court it/ With words, fair looks, and liberality?" *T Andr*, II, i, 91–92.

court and guard of safety, *n.* the very guardhouse that should provide [general] protection: "To manage private and domestic quarrels,/ In night, and on the court and guard of safety?" *Oth*, II, iii, 206–207.

court-contempt, *n.* courtier's disdain: ". . . reflect I not on thy/ baseness, court-contempt?" *W Tale*, IV, iv, 733–734.

court-cupboard, *n.* sideboard: "Away with the joint-stools, remove the court-cupboard,/ look to the plate." *Rom & Jul*, I, v, 6–7.

courtesy, *n.* **1** manners; politeness: "O, that's as much as you would be denied/ Of your fair courtesy." *Per*, II, iii, 105–106. **2** elaborate politeness, esp. as a salutation or introduction: "Sure you have some hideous matter to deliver,/ when the courtesy of it is so fearful." *T Night*, I, v, 208–209. **3** a bow or curtsy: "I would . . . ransom him to any French courtier for a new-devised/ courtesy." *Love's L*, I, ii, 57–59. **4** cultivated life: ". . . hopeless/ To have the courtesy your cradle promis'd . . ." *Cymb*, IV, iv, 27–28. **5** conventions; traditions: "The/ cour-

tesy of nations allows you my better . . ." *As You*, I, i, 45–46. **6 leave your courtesy,** put on your hat [no need to remain bareheaded out of courtesy]: "Pray/ you, leave your courtesy, good mounsieur." *M N Dream*, IV, i, 19–20.
—*v.* **7 court'sy at the censure,** bow to the rebuker: "Doth ill deserve by doing well: what's worse,/ Must court'sy at the censure." *Cymb*, III, iii, 54–55.

courthand, *n.* style of handwriting used in legal documents: "Nay, he can make obligations, and write courthand." *2 Hen 6*, IV, ii, 88.

court holy-water, *n.* flattery: ". . . court holy-water in a dry house is/ better than this rain-water out o' door." *Lear*, III, ii, 10–11.

courtier, *n.* man who courts or woos; here, used ironically: ". . . courtiers of beauteous freedom . . ." *Ant & Cleo*, II, vi, 17.

courtly, *adj.* flattering and insincere in the manner of a courtier: "So tell the courtly wanton [rascal], and be gone." *Edw 3*, IV, iv, 122.

court of guard, *n.* guardhouse or guardroom: ". . . by some apparent sign/ Let us have knowledge at the court of guard." *1 Hen 6*, II, i, 3–4.

courtship, *n.* **1** courtly, or elegant, manners: ". . . one that knew courtship too well, for there he fell in love." *As You*, III, ii, 337–338. **2** state or condition or a courtier: "More honourable state, more courtship lives/ In carrion flies than Romeo." *Rom & Jul*, III, iii, 34–35.

cousin, *n.* term of endearment for any near relative: "How now, brother, where is my cousin, your son?" *M Ado*, I, ii, 1.

cousin-german, *n.* a first cousin: "Thou art, great lord, my father's sister's son,/ A cousin-german to great Priam's seed . . ." *Tr & Cr*, IV, v, 119–120.

cout, *v.* prob. misprint for "scout"; poss. var. of "colt": "Flout 'em and cout 'em,/ And scout 'em and flout 'em . . ." *Temp*, III, ii, 119–120.

covenant, *n.* bargain; compact: ". . . as, by the same cov'nant . . . His fell to Hamlet." *Ham*, I, i, 96–98.

covent, *n.* old form of CONVENT; body of religious associates, esp. a monastery: "One of our covent, and his confessor/ Gives me this instance." *Meas*, IV, iii, 128–129.

Coventry, *n.* town NW of London: site of lists and trials by combat: ". . . your lives shall answer it,/ At Coventry upon Saint Lambert's day." *Rich 2*, I, i, 198–199.

cover, *v.* **1** to set or lay the table: "Sirs, cover the while: the/ Duke will drink under this tree." *As You,* II, v, 28–29. **2** to put on one's cap or hat, customarily removed in the presence of a superior: "How many then should cover that stand bare!" *Merch,* II, ix, 44. **3** wordplay with both of the preceding, prob. with the bawdy implication of sexual service: "Will you cover then sir?"/ "Not so sir neither, I know my duty." *Merch,* III, v, 48–49. **4 cover one's head,** to cease showing respect, as by replacing one's cap or hat: "Cover your heads, and mock not flesh and blood/ With solemn reverence . . ." *Rich 2,* III, ii, 171–172.

cover'd fire, *n.* fire that is kept burning slowly with a protective covering: ". . . let Benedick, like cover'd fire,/ Consume away in sighs, waste inwardly." *M Ado,* III, i, 77–78.

covert, *n.* **1** thicket: ". . . you must retire yourself/ Into some covert . . ." *W Tale,* IV, iv, 649–650.
—*adj.* **2 covert bosom,** my secret heart: "I should wrong it/ To lock it in the wards of covert bosom . . ." *Meas,* V, i, 11. **3 covert matters,** secret threats; hidden dangers: ". . . let us presently go sit in council,/ How covert matters may be best disclos'd [uncovered] . . ." *J Caes,* IV, i, 45–46.

coverture, *n.* **1** shade; shadow; cover: "And now what rests but, in night's coverture . . ." *3 Hen 6,* IV, ii, 13. **2** See **ovator.**

covet, *v.* to desire: ". . . rather hide me from my greatness . . . Than in my greatness covet to be hid [protected by my greatness] . . ." *Rich 3,* III, vii, 160–162.

coward, *n.* **1 great-siz'd coward,** ref. to Achilles: ". . . and thou great-siz'd coward,/ No space of earth shall sunder our two hates . . ." *Tr & Cr,* V, x, 26–27.
—*adv.* **2** cowardly: "My tongue is made of steel, and it shall beg/ My mercy on his coward burgonet." *Edw 3,* IV, iv, 82–83.
—*v.* **3** to make cowardly: "That have so cowarded and chas'd your blood/ Out of appearance?" *Hen 5,* II, ii, 75–76.

Coward of France, *n.* the Dauphin: "Coward of France, how much he wrongs his fame . . ." *1 Hen 6,* II, i, 16.

cowardship, *n.* cowardice; cowardliness: ". . . and for/ his cowardship, ask Fabian." *T Night,* III, iv, 397–398.

cower i' the hams, *v.* to bend in the knees; squat: ". . . do you know/ the French knight that cowers i' the hams?" *Per,* IV, ii, 102–103.

cowish, *adj.* cowardly: "It is the cowish terror of his spirit . . ." *Lear,* IV, ii, 12.

cowl-staff, *n.* pole put through handles of tub, basket, etc., and carried by two persons: "Go take up these clothes here quickly. Where's the/ cowl-staff?" *Wives,* III, iii, 135–136.

coxcomb, *n.* **1** crested cap of a professional fool: "What is your crest, a coxcomb?" *Shrew,* II, i, 223. **2** fool: "Come, let them be opinioned./ . . . Off, coxcomb!" *M Ado,* IV, ii, 64–66. **3** the head; crown: "'Has broke my head across, and has given Sir/ Toby a bloody coxcomb too." *T Night,* V, i, 173–174.

Cox my passion! God's my passion! [a mild oath]: "Cox my passion!/ Give me your hand. How does your drum?" *All's W,* V, ii, 39–40.

coy, *adj.* **1** fiercely independent; also, disdainful: "I know her spirits are as coy and wild/ As haggards of the rock." *M Ado,* III, i, 35–36. **2** cool; reserved: "Yet was he servile to my coy disdain." *Ven & Ad,* 112.
—*v.* **3** to caress [a term in falconry]: "Come sit thee down upon this flowery bed,/ While I thy amiable cheeks do coy . . ." *M N Dream,* IV, i, 1–2. **4** to disdain; refuse: "Nay, if he coy'd/ To hear Cominius speak, I'll keep at home." *Cor,* V, i, 6–7.

coz, *n.* abbr. of "cousin," though often used as a term of endearment for friends as well as relatives: "I pray thee, Rosalind, sweet my coz, be merry." *As You,* I, ii, 1.

cozen, *v.* to cheat or deceive: ". . . who is thus like to be/ cozened with the semblance of a maid . . ." *M Ado,* II, ii, 38–39.

cozenage, *n.* **1** deception; treachery: "Thrown out his angle [fishhook] for my proper life/ And with such coz'nage . . ." *Ham,* V, ii, 66–67. **2** cheating; double-dealing: "They say this town is full of cozenage . . ." *Errors,* I, ii, 97.

cozened thoughts, *n.* delusions; here, prompted by lust: "When saucy trusting of the cozen'd thoughts/ Defiles the pitchy night . . ." *All's W,* IV, iv, 23–24.

cozener, *n.* deceiver; cheat: "O, the devil take such cozeners!" *1 Hen 4,* I, iii, 251.

cozen-Germans, *n.* wordplay on "cousins-german" [blood relatives] and "cozening [cheating] Germans": ". . . there is three/ cozen-Germans that has cozened all the hosts of/ Readins . . ." *Wives,* IV, v, 71–73.

cozening, *adj.* deceitful; cheating: "I will despair, and be at enmity/ With cozening Hope . . ." *Rich 2,* II, ii, 68–69.

cozier, *n.* mender, as of old clothes, shoes, or utensils: ". . . ye squeak out your coziers' catches without any/ mitigation or remorse of voice?" *T Night,* II, iii, 91–92.

crab, *n.* **1** crab apple: ". . . let me bring thee where crabs grow . . ." *Temp,* II, ii, 167. **2** sour person: ". . . and anon falleth like a crab on the face of *terra,* the soil . . ." *Love's L,* IV, ii, 6.

crabbed, *adj.* **1** petulant; peevish; sullen: "O, she is/ Ten times more gentle than her father's crabbed,/ And he's compos'd of harshness." *Temp,* III, i, 7–9. **2** harsh: "Something too crabbed that way, friar." *Meas,* III, ii, 95.

crab-tree or crabtree, *n.* **1** [lit.] crab-apple tree; here, persons of a crabbed or sour disposition: "We have some old crabtrees here at home that will not/ Be grafted to your relish." *Cor,* II, i, 187–188.
—*adj.* **2** made of wood from the crabapple tree: "Fetch me a dozen crab-tree/ staves, and strong ones . . ." *Hen 8,* V, iii, 6–7.

crack, *n.* **1** lively boy; also, a young rascal: "I see him break/ Scoggin's head . . . when a was a/ crack, not thus high . . ." *2 Hen 4,* III, ii, 29–30. **2** charge of powder, shot, cannon-ball, etc.: "As cannons overcharg'd with double cracks . . ." *Mac,* I, ii, 37. **3** flaw: ". . . I cannot/ Believe this crack to be in my dread mistress . . ." *W Tale,* I, ii, 321–322. **4 crack of doom,** very moment of eternal damnation: ". . . will the line stretch out to th' crack of doom?" *Mac,* IV, i, 117.
—*v.* **5** Also, **crake,** to boast: "And Ethiops of their sweet complexion crack." *Love's L,* IV, iii, 264. **6** to break; also, to betray: ". . . one heinous article . . . cracking the strong warrant of an oath . . ." *Rich 2,* IV, i, 233–235. **7** to weaken or collapse: "My charms crack not; my spirits obey . . ." *Temp,* V, i, 2. **8** to burst: ". . . he cracks his gorge, his sides,/ With violent hefts." *W Tale,* II, i, 44–45. **9 crack the wind of (a horse),** to break the wind of: ". . . not to crack the wind of the poor phrase,/ Running it thus—you'll tender me [make me look like] a fool." *Ham,* I, iii, 108–109.

cracked within the ring, *adj.* See **ring** (def. 7).

cracker, *n.* braggart; blusterer: "What cracker is this same that deafs our ears . . ." *K John,* II, i, 147.

crack-hemp, *n.* gallows bird [a term of abuse]: "[*To Biondello.*] Come hither, crack-hemp." *Shrew,* V, i, 40.

cradle, *n.* **in their dumb cradles,** before such thoughts can be expressed: "Keeps place with thought and almost, like the gods,/ Do thoughts unveil in their dumb cradles." *Tr & Cr,* III, iii, 198–199.

craft, *n.* **1** plot or scheme: "O, 'tis most sweet/ When in one line two crafts directly meet." *Ham,* III, iv, 211–212. **2** cunning or deceitfulness: "Or will not else thy craft so quickly grow." *T Night,* V, i, 164.

—*v.* **3 crafted fair,** done a fine job [used ironically]: "You and your crafts! You have crafted fair!" *Cor,* IV, vi, 119.

craft of will, *n.* skill of persuasion: "He had the dialect and different skill,/ Catching all passions in his craft of will . . ." *Lover's Comp,* 125–126.

crafty, *adj.* **1** sly or cunning; also, shrewd: "But with a crafty madness keeps aloof . . ." *Ham,* III, i, 8.
—*adv.* **2** craftily; deceptively: ". . . either you are ignorant,/ Or seem so, crafty . . ." *Meas,* II, iv, 74–75.

crafty-sick, *adj.* feigning illness: "Where Hotspur's father, old Northumberland,/ Lies crafty-sick." *2 Hen 4,* Induc., 36–37.

crake or crack, *v.* to speak boastfully: ". . . our brags/ Were crak'd of kitchen-trulls . . ." *Cymb,* V, v, 176–177.

crammed, *adj.* stuffed or force-fed; here, with reservations: ". . . would they but fat their thoughts/ With this cramm'd reason . . ." *Tr & Cr,* II, ii, 48–49.

cramp, *n.* **not Stephano, but a cramp,** poss. wordplay on "stefano," an Italian slang word for "stomach": "O, touch me not;—I am not Stephano, but a cramp." *Temp,* V, i, 286.

cramps, *n. pl.* **old cramps,** continuous cramps, as those experienced by old people: "I'll rack thee with old cramps,/ Fill all thy bones with aches . . ." *Temp,* I, ii, 371–372.

crank, *v.* **1** to wind; twist and turn; zigzag: ". . . this river comes me cranking in [comes winding into my part]/ And cuts me from the best of all my land . . ." *1 Hen 4,* III, i, 94–95.
—*n.* **2 cranks and offices,** twisting passages and compartments: "And through the cranks and offices of man,/ The strongest nerves and small inferior veins . . ." *Cor,* I, i, 136.

crannied, *adj.* cracked: ". . . a wall as I would have you think/ That had in it a crannied hole, or chink . . ." *M N Dream,* V, i, 156–157.

crants, *n.* wreath or garland, symbol of maidenhood: "Yet here she is allow'd her virgin crants,/ Her maiden strewments . . ." *Ham,* V, i, 225–226.

crase, *v.* to graze: "That being dead, like to the bullet's crasing,/ Break out into a second course of mischief . . ." *Hen 5,* IV, iii, 105–106.

crave, *v.* **1** to demand; require: "It is the bright day that brings forth the adder,/ And that craves wary walking." *J Caes,* II, i, 14–15. **2** to demand to know: "If she deny to wed, I'll crave the day . . ." *Shrew,* II, i, 179. **3** to ask; request: ". . . you said you could not beg."/ "I did but crave." *Per,* II, i, 85–86.

craven, *n.* **1** cock with no fighting spirit: "No cock of mine, you crow too like a craven." *Shrew,* II, i, 225.
—*v.* **2** to make cowardly: "There is a prohibition so divine/ That cravens my weak hand." *Cymb,* III, iv, 78–79.

craver, *n.* beggar: ". . . then I'll turn craver too, and so I shall/ 'scape whipping." *Per,* II, i, 87–88.

crazed, *adj.* flawed; invalid: ". . . Lysander, yield/ Thy crazed title [claim] to my certain right." *M N Dream,* I, i, 91–92.

crazy, *adj.* infirm; feeble: ". . . some better place,/ Fitter for sickness and for crazy age." *1 Hen 6,* III, ii, 88–89.

cream and mantle, *v.* to develop a scumlike covering on the surface: "There are a sort of men whose visages/ Do cream and mantle like a standing pond . . ." *Merch,* I, i, 88–89.

create, *past part.* **1** created: "O anything of nothing first create!" *Rom & Jul,* I, i, 175. **2** made up [of]; composed [of]: ". . . do serve you/ With hearts create of duty and of zeal." *Hen 5,* II, ii, 30–31.

creature, *n.* **1** unfortunate fellow: "And the creature run from the cur?" *Lear,* IV, vi, 158. **2** servant or dependent; also, puppet or instrument: "A creature of the queen's, Lady Anne Bullen." *Hen 8,* III, ii, 36.

creature of sale, *n.* prostitute: "Why, the house you dwell in proclaims you to be a/ creature of sale." *Per,* IV, vi, 76–77.

creature of thy place, *n.* Leontes' euphem. for "whore": "O thou thing—/ Which I'll not call a creature of thy place . . ." *W Tale,* II, i, 82–83.

creatures of note, *n.* notorious objects: "That mercy which fierce fire and iron extends—/ Creatures of note for mercy lacking uses [objects notorious for lacking any employment of mercy]!" *K John,* IV, i, 119–120.

credence, *n.* trust; faith: ". . . we . . . lay our best love and credence/ Upon thy promising fortune." *All's W,* III, iii, 1–3.

credent, *adj.* **1** willing to believe; credulous: ". . . weigh what loss your honour may sustain/ If with too credent ear you list his songs . . ." *Ham,* I, iii, 29–30. **2** believable; credible: ". . . then 'tis very credent/ Thou may'st co-join with something . . ." *W Tale,* I, ii, 142–143. **3 so credent bulk,** such an overwhelming amount of trust or credibility: "For my authority bears so credent bulk/ That no particular scandal once can touch . . ." *Meas,* IV, iv, 24–25.

credit, *n.* **1** reputation or repute: "Tomorrow, sir, I wrestle for my credit . . ." *As You,* I, i, 125. **2** information or report: ". . . there I found this credit,/ That he did range the town to seek me out." *T Night,* IV, iii, 6–7. **3** believability; credibility: "And what does else want credit, come to me,/ And I'll be sworn 'tis true . . ." *Temp,* III, iii, 25–26. **4** good opinion held by others: "I was in that/ credit with them at that time . . ." *All's W,* V, iii, 256–257. **5** trust: "The credit that thy lady hath of thee/ Deserves thy trust . . ." *Cymb,* I, vii, 157–158. **6 compact of credit,** full of trust: "Alas, poor women, make us but believe/ (Being compact of credit) that you love us . . ." *Errors,* III, ii, 21–22. **7 grown to credit,** risen to high esteem: "Such as were grown to credit by the wars . . ." *1 Hen 6,* IV, i, 36. **8 hold the credit,** to maintain the high reputation: ". . . you must hold the credit of/ your father." *All's W,* I, i, 75–76.
—*v.* **9** to honor: "I call them forth to credit her." *Shrew,* IV, i, 94.

credulous, *adj.* impressionable; also, deceived by: ". . . we are soft as our complexions are,/ And credulous to false prints." *Meas,* II, iv, 128–129.

creek, *n.* narrow, winding passage: ". . . one that countermands/ The passages of alleys, creeks and narrow lands . . ." *Errors,* IV, ii, 37–38.

creep, *v.* **1** wordplay on "move stealthily" and "move haltingly": ". . . are you crept before us?"/ "Ay . . . for you know that love/ Will creep in service where it cannot go [move easily]." *Two Gent,* IV, ii, 18–20. **2 how creeps acquaintance?** how did he creep into your acquaintance [or you into his]?: ". . . how comes/ it he is to sojourn with you? how creeps acquaintance?" *Cymb,* I, v, 21–23.

crescent, *adj.* growing or increasing: ". . . nature crescent does not grow alone . . ." *Ham,* I, iii, 11.

crescent note, *n.* growing reputation: "I have seen him in Britain; he was then/ of a crescent note . . ." *Cymb,* I, v, 1–2.

crescive, *adj.* growing: "Unseen, yet crescive in his faculty." *Hen 5,* I, i, 66.

cresset, *n.* iron basket holding flammable material, used as a torch, beacon, etc.: "The front of heaven was full of fiery shapes,/ Of burning cressets [stars or meteors] . . ." *1 Hen 4,* III, i, 12–13.

Cressid or **Cressida,** *n.* (in medieval legend) young Trojan woman betrothed to Troilus, son of King Priam, but who deserts him for the Greek warrior Diomedes: "And sigh'd his soul toward the Grecian tents/ Where Cressid lay that night." *Merch,* V, i, 5–6.

Cressid's uncle, *n.* See **Pandarus.**

Cressy, *n.* Crécy, a region in N France; defeat here in 1346 by English forces under Edward III: "Witness our too much memorable shame/ When Cressy battle fatally was struck [fought] . . ." *Hen 5,* II, iv, 53–54.

crest, *n.* **1** crowning achievement or highest point of perfection: "And beauty's crest becomes the heavens well." *Love's L,* IV, iii, 252. **2** the head: "Let fall thy blade on vulnerable crests . . ." *Mac,* V, viii, 11. **3** horse's raised head and neck: "They fall their crests, and like deceitful jades/ Sink in the trial." *J Caes,* IV, ii, 26–27. **4** helmet: ". . . the burning crest/ Of the old, feeble and day-wearied sun . . ." *K John,* V, iv, 34–35. **5** heraldic device, the distinguishing emblem of a coat of arms, worn esp. on a knight's helmet or shield: "And all the budding honours on thy crest/ I'll crop to make a garland for my head." *1 Hen 4,* V, iv, 71–72. **6** pride; self-esteem: "But when they shall see, sir, his crest up/ again, and the man in blood . . ." *Cor,* IV, v, 216–217. **7 fall one's crest,** to lower one's head in defeat; here, an insincere man is compared to a worthless horse: "They fall their crests, and like deceitful jades/ Sink in the trial." *J Caes,* IV, ii, 26–27. **8 strike upon someone's crest,** to treat someone dishonorably: "Marcus, even thou hast stroke upon my crest . . ." *T Andr,* I, i, 364. —*v.* **9** to serve as a crest for: ". . . his rear'd arm/ Crested the world . . ." *Ant & Cleo,* V, ii, 82–83.

crest-fallen, *adj.* humbled or humiliated: "Shall I seem crest-fallen in my father's sight?" *Rich 2,* I, i, 188.

crestless, *adj.* having no heraldic crest; here, deprived of lands and titles: "Spring crestless yeomen from so deep a root?" *1 Hen 6,* II, iv, 85.

crest-wounding, *adj.* insulting to a family's honor: "O unfelt sore, crest-wounding private scar!" *Luc,* 828.

Crete, *n.* **1 hound of Crete,** perh. ref. to earlier line "cur of Iceland": "O hound of Crete, think'st thou my spouse to get?" *Hen 5,* II, i, 73. **2 sire of Crete,** Talbot likens himself to Daedalus and his son to Icarus and the ancient pair's escape from the Cretan labyrinth: "Then follow thou thy desperate sire of Crete,/ Thou Icarus . . ." *1 Hen 6,* IV, vi, 54–55.

crew, *n.* **1** band or party: "Come, go with us, we'll bring thee to our crews . . ." *Two Gent,* IV, i, 74. **2** company; outfit: ". . . a Cornish name: art thou of Cornish crew?" *Hen 5,* IV, i, 50.

crib, *n.* **1** hut or hovel: "Why rather, sleep, liest thou in smoky cribs . . ." *2 Hen 4,* III, i, 9. **2** manger; food box for livestock: "Let a/ beast be lord of beasts and his crib shall stand at the/ king's mess." *Ham,* V, ii, 86–87.

cribbed, *adj.* caged: "But now, I am cabin'd, cribb'd, confin'd,/ bound in/ To saucy doubts and fears." *Mac,* III, iv, 23–24.

crickets, *n.* ref. to ladies of the court and their chattering: "I will tell it softly,/ Yond crickets shall not hear it." *W Tale,* II, i, 30–31.

cried game, *interj.* said to be a term in bear-baiting, or perh. a hunting cry equiv. to "the hunt is on!": "Mistress/ Anne Page is . . . a-feasting; and thou/ shalt woo her. Cried game; said I well?" *Wives,* II, iii, 81–83.

crier, *n.* **Hear the crier!** ref. to the crier's call in a court of justice: "Peace!"/ "Hear the crier!"/ "What the devil art thou?" *K John,* II, i, 134.

crime, *n.* **1** sin or offense: "My blood is mingled with the crime of lust . . ." *Errors,* II, ii, 141. **2** harm or ill: ". . . to you it doth belong/ Yourself to pardon of self-doing crime." *Sonn 58,* 11–12. **3 each several crime,** every separate sin: "I have no relish of them; but abound/ In the division of each several crime . . ." *Mac,* IV, iii, 95–96.

crimeful, *adj.* like a criminal: ". . . these feats,/ So crimeful and so capital in nature . . ." *Ham,* IV, vii, 6–7.

cripple, *v.* to disable; here, by removing all the inhabitants: ". . . bear thee from the knowledge of thyself—/ And cripple thee—unto a pagan [heathen] shore . . ." *K John,* V, ii, 35–36.

crisp, *adj.* **1** covered with swirling clouds: "With all th' abhorred births below crisp heaven." *Timon,* IV, iii, 185. **2** (of the hair) tightly curled: "And hid his crisp head in the hollow bank,/ Bloodstained with these valiant combatants." *1 Hen 4,* I, iii, 105–106. **3** covered with tiny waves; rippling: "Leave your crisp channels, and on this green land/ Answer your summons . . ." *Temp,* IV, i, 130–131.

crisped, *adj.* curled or curly: ". . . those crisped snaky golden locks/ Which make such wanton gambols with the wind . . ." *Merch,* III, ii, 92–93.

Crispian, *n.* **feast of Crispian,** Oct. 25th, feast day in honor of the Roman martyrs, the brothers Crispin and Crispian, patron saints of shoemakers: "This day is call'd the feast of Crispian . . ." *Hen 5,* IV, iii, 40.

critic, *n.* **1** cynic or misanthrope: "And critic Timon laugh at idle toys!" *Love's L,* IV, iii, 167. **2** one prone to pass judgment; a fault-finder: ". . . stubborn critics, apt, without a theme/ For depravation . . ." *Tr & Cr,* V, iii, 130–131.

critical, *adj.* censorious: "That is some satire, keen and critical,/ Not sorting with a nuptial ceremony." *M N Dream,* V, i, 54–55.

crocodile, *n.* the crocodile was thought to snare its victims by shedding tears: ". . . Gloucester's show/ Beguiles him as the mournful crocodile/ With sorrow snares relenting passengers . . ." *2 Hen 6,* III, i, 225–227.

crone, *n.* withered old woman: "Take up the bastard,/ Take 't up, I say; give 't to thy crone." *W Tale,* II, iii, 75–76.

crook-back, *adj.* hunchbacked: "And where's that valiant crook-back prodigy [freak] . . ." *3 Hen 6,* I, iv, 75.

crooked, *adj.* **1** curved; bent: "Coucheth the fowl below with his wings' shade,/ Whose crooked beak threats . . ." *Luc,* 507–508. **2** hostile; fiendish: "Crooked eclipses 'gainst his glory fight . . ." *Sonn 60,* 7. **3** false; fraudulent: ". . . amply to imbar their crooked titles/ Usurp'd from you and your progenitors." *Hen 5,* II, ii, 94–95.

crooked figure, *n.* cipher; zero (here, as in mathmatics, a few ciphers may stand for a large number): "O, pardon! since a crooked figure may/ Attest in little place a million . . ." *Hen 5,* Prol. 15–16.

crooked knife, *n.* scythe: "So thou prevent'st his scythe and crooked knife." *Sonn 100,* 14.

crop, *n.* **1** harvest: ". . . the rich crop/ Of sea and land . . ." *Cymb,* I, vii, 33–34.
—*v.* **2** to bear fruit; here, a child [ref. to Cleopatra's child Caesarion by Caesar]: "He plough'd her, and she cropp'd." *Ant & Cleo,* II, ii, 228. **3 crop the ears,** wordplay here on sense of "curtail" [crop, i.e., cut], appar. implying the ears of an ass: ". . . not for/ any standers-by to curtail his oaths. Ha?"/ "No, my lord; [Aside] nor crop the ears of them." *Cymb,* II, i, 11–13.

crop-ear, *n.* short-eared horse: "What horse? A roan, a crop-ear is it not?" *1 Hen 4,* II, iii, 70.

Crosby Place, *n.* Richard's London residence: "And presently repair to Crosby Place . . ." *Rich 3,* I, ii, 216.

cross¹, *v.* **1** to contradict; here, in wordplay with "crossed off a list of debtors": "There is no crossing him in's humour . . ." *Timon,* I, ii, 156. **2** to cross the path of; confront; accost: "I'll cross it though it blast me." *Ham,* I, i, 130. **3** to interrupt: "What cursed foot wanders this way tonight,/ To cross my obsequies and true love's rite?" *Rom & Jul,* V, iii, 19–20. **4** to frustrate or thwart: "A man I am, cross'd with adversity . . ." *Two Gent,* IV, i, 12. **5 cross one's arms,** to fold one's arms as an indication of melancholy: "To cross their arms and hang their hands with mine . . ." *Luc,* 793.
—*n.* **6** instance of thwarting or foiling: "Any bar, any cross, any impediment will be medicinable to me." *M Ado,* II, ii, 4–5. **7** trial or hardship; vexation; annoyance: "The happiest youth, viewing his progress through,/ What perils past, what crosses to ensue . . ." *2 Hen 4,* III, i, 54–55. **8 bear crosses,**

favorite pun, combining "to suffer hardships" with "to carry money": "Not a penny, not a penny; you are too impatient/ to bear crosses." *2 Hen 4,* I, ii, 226–227.
—*adj.* **9** contrary; perverse; willful: ". . . move the heavens to smile upon my state,/ Which . . . is cross and full of sin." *Rom & Jul,* IV, iii, 4–5. **10** forked or jagged: "And when the cross blue lightning seem'd to open/ The breast of heaven, I did present myself . . ." *J Caes,* I, iii, 50–51.
—*adv.* **11** See **break cross.**
—*interj.* **12** vexation! [exclam. of annoyance, frustration, etc.]: "O cross! too high to be enthrall'd to low." *M N Dream,* I, i, 136.

cross², *n.* silver coin, from the cross stamped on each; [pl.] money: "He speaks the mere contrary: crosses love not him." *Love's L,* I, ii, 33.

cross-gartered, *adj.* wearing cross-garters, criss-crossed tapes that held the stockings in place between the knee and ankle: "Remember who commended thy/ yellow stockings, and wished to see thee ever cross-gartered . . ." *T Night,* II, v, 152–154.

crossing, *n.* opposition; contradiction: "Cousin, of many men/ I do not bear these crossings . . ." *1 Hen 4,* III, i, 32–33.

crossly, *adv.* adversely: "Thy friends are fled to wait upon thy foes,/ And crossly to thy good all fortune goes." *Rich 2,* II, iv, 23–24.

cross-row, *n.* alphabet [fr. cross prefixed to it in primers]: "He hearkens after prophecies and dreams,/ And from the cross-row plucks the letter G . . ." *Rich 3,* I, i, 54–55.

cross-ways, *n. pl.* crossroads: "Damned spirits all,/ That in cross-ways and floods have burial . . ." *M N Dream,* III, ii, 382–383.

crost, *past part.* var. of **crossed** (see **cross**); thwarted: ". . . and if my fortune be not crost,/ I have a father, you a daughter, lost." *Merch,* II, v, 55–56.

crotchet, *n.* **1** whimsy or caprice; here, in wordplay with "notes" [musical quarter notes]: "Why, these are very crotchets that he speaks!" *M Ado,* II, iii, 56. **2** wordplay on "whim" and the musical term for "quarter note": "I will carry [put up with] no crotchets. I'll re you, I'll fa you. Do you note me?" *Rom & Jul,* IV, v, 116–117. **3** [often pl.] eccentric ideas or ways: ". . . the Duke had crotchets in him." *Meas,* III, ii, 124.

crow¹, *v.* **1** to laugh uproariously; guffaw: "My lungs began to crow like chanticleer . . ." *As You,* II, vii, 30.
—*n.* **2** the French cock [term of contempt]; also, poss. wordplay on the crow or raven as ill omens: ". . . to thrill [tremble]

and shake/ Even at the crying of your nation's crow . . ." *K John*, V, ii, 143–144.

crow², *n.* crowbar: "Well, I'll break in; go, borrow me a crow." *Errors*, III, i, 80.

crow-flower, *n.* prob. the buttercup: "Therewith fantastic garlands did she make/ Of crow-flowers, nettles, daisies, and long purples . . ." *Ham*, IV, vii, 167–168.

crowkeeper, *n.* scarecrow: "Bearing a Tartar's painted bow of lath,/ Scaring the ladies like a crowkeeper . . ." *Rom & Jul*, I, iv, 5–6.

crown, *n.* **1** formerly, a silver coin of England, worth five shillings: ". . . mine's three thousand crowns;/ What's yours?" *Timon*, III, iv, 29–30. **2** the head: "Ten thousand bloody crowns of mothers' sons/ Shall ill become the flower of England's face . . ." *Rich 2*, III, iii, 96–97. **3 crowns and crownets,** kings and lesser royalty: ". . . in his livery/ Walk'd crowns and crownets . . ." *Ant & Cleo*, V, ii, 90–91. **4 crowns in the sun,** prob. ref. to "crowns of the sun," gold coins of France used in England: "I know he will/ come in our shadow, to scatter his crowns in the/ sun." *Per*, IV, ii, 109–111. **5 cut French crowns,** wordplay on "behead" and "trim gold from coins": ". . . it is no English/ treason to cut French crowns . . ." *Hen 5*, IV, i, 233–234.
—*v.* **6** to glorify; praise: ". . . and crown thee for a finder of madmen." *T Night*, III, iv, 142. **7 crown up,** to complete or perfect: "As true as Troilus' shall crown up the verse/ And sanctify the numbers." *Tr & Cr*, III, ii, 180–181.

crowned, *adj.* having achieved the peak of perfection: "Or any of these all, or all, or more,/ Entitled in thy parts do crowned sit . . ." *Sonn 37*, 6–7.

crowner, *n.* var. of **coroner:** "The crowner hath sat on her and finds it Christian/ burial." *Ham*, V, i, 4–5.

crownet, *n.* **1** a coronet; wreath: "There on the pendent boughs her crownet weeds/ Clamb'ring to hang . . ." *Ham*, IV, vii, 171–172. **2** [fig. use] reward for one's labors: "Whose bosom was my crownet, my chief end . . ." *Ant & Cleo*, IV, xii, 27.

crown imperial, *n.* fritillaria, a type of lily: ". . . bold oxlips and/ The crown imperial; lilies of all kinds . . ." *W Tale*, IV, iv, 125–126.

crudy, *adj.* old form of **curdy;** curdlike; thick: ". . . all the foolish and dull and crudy/ vapours which environ it . . ." *2 Hen 4*, IV, iii, 96–97.

cruel, *adj.* **1** extremely difficult; painful: ". . . their intents,/ Extremely stretch'd and conn'd with cruel pain [effort] . . ." *M N Dream*, V, i, 79–80.
—*n.* **2** [pl.] cruel people collectively: "All cruels else subscribe: but I shall see/ The winged vengeance overtake such children." *Lear*, III, vii, 64–65.

crupper, *n.* leather strap, looped under the horse's tail, for holding the saddle in place: "To pay the saddler for my mistress' crupper . . ." *Errors*, I, ii, 56.

crusado, *n.* Portuguese gold coin stamped with a cross: "I had rather lose my purse/ Full of crusadoes . . ." *Oth*, III, iv, 21–22.

crush, *v.* **1** to drink; quaff: ". . . if you be not of the house of/ Montagues I pray come and crush a cup of wine." *Rom & Jul*, I, ii, 81–82. **2** to force: ". . . to crush this a little, it would bow to/ me . . ." *T Night*, II, v, 140–141.

crushed necessity, *n.* need that has been eradicated: "Yet that is but a crush'd necessity,/ Since we have locks to safeguard necessaries . . ." *Hen 5*, I, ii, 175–176.

crusty, *adj.* scabbed: "Thou crusty botch [sore] of nature, what's the news?" *Tr & Cr*, V, i, 5.

crutch, *n.* wordplay on "old age" and "crotch"; also, poss. ref. to slang "clap": ". . . you will have leave/ Till youth take leave and leave you to the crutch." *3 Hen 6*, III, ii, 34–35.

cry, *n.* **1** a pack (of hounds): ". . . a cry more tuneable/ Was never holla'd to, nor cheer'd with horn . . ." *M N Dream*, IV, i, 123–124. **2** a company: "Would not this, sir . . . get me a fellowship in a cry/ of players?" *Ham*, III, ii, 269–271. **3** subject of conversation: "The cry went once on thee,/ And still it might . . ." *Tr & Cr*, III, iii, 184–185.
—*v.* **4** to beg for: "Cry the man mercy, love him, take his offer . . ." *As You*, III, v, 61. **5** to cry out in pain; here, in childbirth: "Divinest patroness, and midwife gentle/ To those that cry by night . . ." *Per*, III, i, 11–12. **6** to howl like dogs following a scent: "How cheerfully on the false trail they cry." *Ham*, IV, v, 109. **7** to proclaim: "Now this masque/ Was cried incomparable . . ." *Hen 8*, I, i, 26–27. **8 cry away,** ref. to the plover's shrill cry, enticing trespassers away from its nest: "Far from her nest the lapwing [plover] cries away . . ." *Errors*, IV, ii, 27. **9 cry in the top of,** to carry more authority than; surpass: ". . . others, whose judgments in such matters cried in/ the top of mine . . ." *Ham*, II, ii, 434–435. **10 cry on, a.** to cry out or proclaim, as in shock or outrage: "This quarry cries on havoc." *Ham*, V, ii, 369. **b.** to howl against: ". . . his mangled Myrmidons/ That noseless, handless, hack'd and chipp'd, come to him,/ Crying on Hector." *Tr & Cr*, V, v, 33–35. **c.** to encourage by yelps or shouts: ". . . their souls whose bodies

Richard murder'd/ Came to my tent and cried on victory." *Rich 3,* V, iii, 231–232. **11 cry out of,** to rail against: "They say he cried out of sack." *Hen 5,* II, iii, 28. **12 cry up,** to praise: ". . . what worst, as oft/ Hitting a grosser quality, is cried up/ For [as] our best act." *Hen 8,* I, ii, 83–85.

cry aim, *v.* to give encouragement [from archery, to shout encouragement to the contestants]: "It ill beseems this presence to cry aim/ To these ill-tuned repetitions." *K John,* II, i, 196–197.

cry havoc, *v.* See **havoc** (def. 2).

crystal, *n.* **1** [pl.] the eyes: "Go, clear [wipe] thy crystals." *Hen 5,* II, iii, 55.
—*adj.* **2 crystal beads,** tears; also, perh., prayers with rosary beads: "Ay, with these crystal beads heaven shall be brib'd/ To do him justice and revenge on you." *K John,* II, 1, 171–172. **3 crystal eyes,** a penetrating glance: "A closet never pierc'd with crystal eyes . . ." *Sonn 46,* 6. **4 crystal tresses,** comet tail likened to bright, flowing hair: "Comets . . . Brandish your crystal tresses in the sky . . ." *1 Hen 6,* I, i, 2–3.

cry you mercy, Also, **cry mercy:(I)** beg your pardon: "Cry mercy, lords and watchful gentlemen,/ That you have ta'en a tardy sluggard here." *Rich 3,* V, iii, 225–226.

cry your worship mercy, I beg your honor's pardon: "I cry your worships mercy, heartily. I beseech your/ worship's name?" *M N Dream,* III, i, 172–173.

cub, *n.* a cunning or conniving young man (from the fox's supposed cunning): "O thou dissembling cub! What wilt thou be/ When time hath sow'd a grizzle on thy case?" *T Night,* V, i, 162–163.

cub-drawn, *adj.* (of a female mammal) sucked by its young and therefore hungry: "This night, wherein the cub-drawn bear would couch . . ." *Lear,* III, i, 12.

cubiculo, *n.* bedroom; here, prob. "cubicle" [whimsical borrowing from Latin/Italian]: "We'll call thee at thy cubiculo. Go!" *T Night,* III, ii, 50.

cubit, *n.* unit of length, based on length of forearm from elbow to fingertips, about 18 inches: "A space whose ev'ry cubit/ Seems to cry out . . ." *Temp,* II, i, 252–253.

cuckoo or cuckoo-bird, *n.* superstition that the cuckoo's song brought bad luck [cuckoldry] when heard by a married man: "Cuckoo, cuckoo: O word of fear,/ Unpleasing to a married ear!" *Love's L,* V, ii, 893–894.

cuckoo-flower, *n.* poss. the cowslip: "Crown'd with rank fumiter . . . With hardocks, hemlock, nettles, cuckoo-flowers . . ." *Lear,* IV, iv, 3–4.

cucullus non facit monachum, [Latin] the cowl does not make the monk: "Lady, *cucullus/ non facit monachum:* that's as much to say, as I wear/ not motley in my brain." *T Night,* I, v, 53–54.

cuff, *n.* **go to cuffs,** to attack each other: ". . . the poet and the player went to cuffs in the/ question." *Ham,* II, ii, 353–354.

cull, *v.* **1** to collect; pick or gather: "In tatter'd weeds, with overwhelming brows,/ Culling of simples." *Rom & Jul,* V, i, 39–40. **2** to pick out; choose; select: ". . . in this covert will we make our stand,/ Culling the principal of all the deer." *3 Hen 6,* III, i, 3–4.

culled, *adj.* selected; choice: "Of all complexions the cull'd sovereignty/ Do meet, as at a fair, in her fair cheek . . ." *Love's L,* IV, iii, 230–231.

cullion, *n.* a rogue; rascal [vulgar term of abuse]: ". . . such a one as leaves a gentleman/ and makes a god of such a cullion." *Shrew,* IV, ii, 19–20.

cullionly, *adv.* in a base or vile manner; rascally: "You whoreson cullionly barber-monger, draw." *Lear,* II, ii, 33.

culverin, *n.* a long cannon of relatively small bore: ". . . thou hast talk'd . . . Of basilisks, of cannon, culverin . . ." *1 Hen 4,* II, iii, 51–54.

cumber, *v.* to encumber; burden: ". . . fierce civil strife/ Shall cumber all the parts of Italy . . ." *J Caes,* III, i, 263–264.

cum privilegio, [Latin] with immunity: "They may *cum privilegio* 'oui' away/ The lag end of their lewdness . . ." *Hen 8,* I, iii, 34–35.

cum privilegio ad imprimendum solum, [Latin] with the sole right to print [denoted a printer's rights to a particular book]: "Take you assurance of her,/ *cum privilegio ad imprimendum solum.* To th' church!" *Shrew,* IV, iv, 88–89.

cunning, *n.* **1** knowledge; skill or inventiveness: "Shame not these woods/ By putting on the cunning of a carper." *Timon,* IV, iii, 210–211. **2 cunning in dumbness,** the silence [of Troilus] elicits Cressida's most secret thoughts: "See, see, your silence,/ Cunning in dumbness, from my weakness draws/ My very soul of counsel." *Tr & Cr,* III, ii, 130–132. **3 in cunning,** to give the appearance of antagonism: "In cunning I must draw my sword upon you . . ." *Lear,* II, i, 30.
—*adj.* **4** ingenious; clever: "The learned constable/ is too cunning to be understood." *M Ado,* V, i, 222–223. **5** knowledge-

able; skilled: "Sirrah, go hire me twenty cunning cooks." *Rom & Jul*, IV, ii, 2. **6** skillfully made: ". . . like a cunning instrument cas'd up—" *Rich 2*, I, iii, 163–165. **7** skilled at deception: "The seeming truth which cunning times [occasions] put on/ To entrap the wisest." *Merch*, III, ii, 100–101.

cupbearer, *n.* a lackey who serves wine: ". . . and thou/ His cupbearer . . . might'st bespice a cup,/ To give mine enemy a lasting wink . . ." *W Tale*, I, ii, 312–317.

cupboard, *v.* to store away: ". . . idle and unactive,/ Still cupboarding the viand . . ." *Cor*, I, i, 98–99.

Cupid, *n.* Roman god of love, son of Venus: "Tell me, heavenly bow,/ If Venus or her son . . . Do now attend the queen?" *Temp*, IV, i, 86–88.

Cupid's tables, *n.* love letters: "Though forfeiters you cast in prison, yet/ You clasp young Cupid's tables." *Cymb*, III, ii, 38–39.

curb¹, *v.* to bow: "Yea, curb and woo for leave to do him good." *Ham*, III, iv, 157.

curb², *n.* check or restraint [fr. strap or chain fastened to bit in horse's mouth]: ". . . cracking ten thousand curbs/ Of more strong link asunder . . ." *Cor*, I, i, 69–70.

curbed time, *n.* period of abstinence: "Which they distil now in the curbed time,/ To make the coming hour o'erflow with joy . . ." *All's W*, II, iv, 43–44.

curd, *v.* to curdle: ". . . it doth posset/ And curd, like eager droppings into milk . . ." *Ham*, I, v, 68–69.

curds, *n. pl.* simple food of milk curds: ". . . the shepherd's homely curds,/ His cold thin drink out of his leather bottle . . ." *3 Hen 6*, II, v, 47–48.

curdy, *v.* to congeal: ". . . chaste as the icicle/ That's curdied by the frost from purest snow . . ." *Cor*, V, iii, 65–66.

cure, *n.* **1** duty; also, spiritual care [used humorously]: "For my little cure/ Let me alone [I'm perfectly capable of attending to it]." *Hen 8*, I, iv, 33–34. **2 stand in bold cure,** remain healthily optimistic: "Therefore my hopes, not surfeited to death,/ Stand in bold cure." *Oth*, II, i, 50–51. **3 stand in hard cure,** will hardly ever be cured: ". . . thy broken sinews/ Which, if convenience will not allow,/ Stand in hard cure." *Lear*, III, vi, 101–103.

cureless, *adj.* **1** incurable: "Repair thy wit good youth, or it will fall/ To cureless ruin." *Merch*, IV, i, 141–142. **2** fatal: "Bootless are plaints, and cureless are my wounds . . ." *3 Hen 6*, II, vi, 23.

curfew, *n.* usually sounded at 9 p.m.: "This is the foul Flibbertigibbet: he begins at/ curfew, and walks till the first cock [midnight] . . ." *Lear*, III, iv, 118–119.

curfew bell, *n.* bell that announces curfew also rings shortly before daybreak: "The curfew bell hath rung, 'tis three o'clock." *Rom & Jul*, IV, iv, 4.

curiosity, *n.* **1** fastidiousness, as in food or dress: ". . . they mock'd thee for too much curiosity . . ." *Timon*, IV, iii, 303–304. **2 jealous curiosity,** overscrupulous attention to one's dignity: ". . . I have rather blamed as mine own/ jealous curiosity than as a very pretence and/ purpose of unkindness . . ." *Lear*, I, iv, 72–73.

curious, *adj.* **1** severely critical: "If my slight Muse do please these curious days . . ." *Sonn 38*, 13. **2** picayune; niggling: ". . . curious I cannot be with you,/ Signor Baptista, of whom I hear so well." *Shrew*, IV, iv, 36–37. **3** exquisite: "Her face the book of praises, where is read/ Nothing but curious pleasures . . ." *Per*, I, i, 16–17. **4** beautifully embroidered: "Your younger princely son . . . was lapp'd/ In a most curious mantle . . ." *Cymb*, V, v, 361–362. **5** careful; meticulous: "Frank nature, rather curious than in haste,/ Hath well compos'd thee." *All's W*, I, ii, 20–21. **6** choice; fancy: "Those mothers who . . . Thought nought too curious . . ." *Per*, I, iv, 42–43. **7** distressing: "I am so fraught with curious business . . ." *W Tale*, IV, iv, 515. **8 curious, being strange,** anxious, since I am a stranger: "And I am something curious, being strange,/ To have them in safe stowage . . ." *Cymb*, I, vii, 191–192.

curious-good, *adj.* elaborately expressed; overrefined: "This is curious-good, this blunt and ill." *Lucrece*, 1300.

curious-knotted, *adj.* intricately laid out; labyrinthine: ". . . by east from the/ west corner of thy curious-knotted garden . . ." *Love's L*, I, i, 241–242.

curiously, *adv.* **1** artfully; skillfully: ". . . the which if I do not carve most/ curiously, say my knife's naught." *M Ado*, V, i, 153–154. **2** literally or precisely: "'Twere to consider too curiously to consider so." *Ham*, V, i, 199. **3** elaborately: "'The sleeves curiously cut.'" *Shrew*, IV, iii, 141.

curled, *adj.* ref. to Antony's curled hair: "If she first meet the curled Antony,/ He'll make demand of her . . ." *Ant & Cleo*, V, ii, 300–301.

curled hair, *n.* regarded as typical of the luxury-loving nobility: "Let him have time to tear his curled hair . . ." *Luc*, 981.

currance, *n.* strong current; torrent: "Never came reformation in a flood,/ With such a heady [headlong] currance . . ." *Hen 5*, I, i, 33–34.

current¹, *n.* **1** [usually pl.] course or direction; trend: "And all the currents of a heady fight." *1 Hen 4*, II, iii, 56. **2** [pl] courses of human events: "In the corrupted currents of this world . . ." *Ham*, III, iii, 57. **3 turn your current in a ditch**, take advantage of you at every opportunity [irrigation metaphor]: "To say he'll turn your current in a ditch/ And make your channel his?" *Cor*, III, i, 95–96.

current², *adj.* **1** genuine; negotiable: ". . . unpay the villainy you have done with her . . . with current repentance." *2 Hen 4*, II, i, 118–120. **2** decisive: "Thy word is current with him [i.e., time] for my death . . ." *Rich 2*, I, iii, 321. **3 come (or go) current**, be accepted as genuine: ". . . let not his report/ Come current for an accusation/ Betwixt my love and your high Majesty." *1 Hen 4*, I, iii, 66–68. **4 pass them current**, make them acceptable as legal tender [pun here on crown meaning "head, coin"]: "We must have bloody noses, and crack'd crowns,/ And pass them current too." *1 Hen 4*, II, iii, 94–95.

currish, *adj.* resembling or typical of a dog; here, also sense of "vicious; malicious": "A good swift simile, but something currish." *Shrew*, V, ii, 54.

curry, *v.* to flatter; curry favor (with): "I would curry with/ Master Shallow that no man could better command/ his servants." *2 Hen 4*, V, i, 70–72.

cursitory, *adj.* cursory: "I have but with a cursitory eye/ O'erglanc'd the articles . . ." *Hen 5*, V, ii, 77–78.

curst, *adj.* **1** cross, disagreeable, or shrewish; also, cantankerous: "In faith, she's too curst." *M Ado*, II, i, 18. **2** ferocious: "Go, write it in a martial hand, be curst and/ brief . . ." *T Night*, III, ii, 40–41. **3** mean; vicious: ". . . they are never curst but when/ they are hungry . . ." *W Tale*, III, iii, 128–129. **4** evil or injurious; malignant: "I would invent as bitter searching terms,/ As curst, as harsh, and horrible to hear . . ." *2 Hen 6*, III, ii, 310–311.

curster, *adj.* compar. of **curst**: "Curster than she? Why, 'tis impossible." *Shrew*, III, ii, 152.

curstness, *n.* bitterness; ill humor: "Touch you the sourest points with sweetest terms,/ Nor curstness grow to the matter [let not bitterness be added to a discussion of our differences]." *Ant & Cleo*, II, ii, 24–25.

cur'sy, *v.* **1** "curtsy" here spelled as pronounced: "And she [Rome] whom mighty kingdoms cur'sy to . . . Do shameful execution on herself." *T Andr*, V, iii, 74–76.
—*n.* **2 Christian cur'sy**, act of Christian charity [benevolence or generosity]: ". . . he was wont to lend/ money for [as] a Christian cur'sy, let him look to his bond!" *Merch*, III, i, 43–44.

curtain, *n.* **1** banner; pennant: "Their ragged curtains poorly are let loose . . ." *Hen V*, IV, ii, 41. **2** ref. to placing a curtain over pictures to prevent fading or protect from dust: "Wherefore/ have these gifts a curtain before 'em?" *T Night*, I, iii, 122–123. **3 draw this curtain**, lift your veil: "Come,/ draw this curtain, and let's see your picture—" *Tr & Cr*, III, ii, 45–46.

curtained, *adj.* enclosed with curtains; here, a reference to the bed: "Nature seems dead, and wicked dreams abuse/ The curtain'd sleep . . ." *Mac*, II, i, 50–51.

curtal dog, *n.* dock-tailed dog: "She had transform'd me to a curtal dog, and made me/ turn i'th'wheel." *Errors*, III, ii, 145.

curtle-axe, *n.* cutlass: "A gallant curtle-axe upon my thigh . . ." *As You*, I, iii, 113.

curtsies, *n. pl.* overrefined manners, esp. in an obsequious effort to obtain favors: ". . . manner is melted into curtsies, valour into compliment . . ." *M Ado*, IV, i, 318.

curtsy, *n.* **1** bow or a salute with the hand: "Marry, hang you!"/ "And your curtsy, for a ring-carrier!" *All's W*, III, v, 90–91.
—*v.* **2** (of a man) to bow, esp. servilely: "To fight against me under Percy's pay,/ To dog his heels, and curtsy at his frowns . . ." *1 Hen 4*, III, ii, 126–127.

curvet, *n.* **1** high prance of a horse, in which all four legs are off the ground at one time: "Which should sustain the bound and high curvet/ Of Mars's fiery steed." *All's W*, II, iii, 278–279.
—*v.* **2** (of a horse) to prance: "Cry holla to the tongue . . . it curvets unseasonably." *As You*, III, ii, 240–241.

cush, *n.* cuisse (phonetic spelling); piece of armor covering the thigh: "I saw young Harry with his beaver on,/ His cushes on his thighs . . ." *1 Hen 4*, IV, i, 104–105.

cushion, *n.* **lay cushions**, to spread cushions used for seating of high-ranking officials: "Enter two Officers, to lay cushions, as it were in the Capitol." [SD] *Cor*, II, ii, 1.

Custalorum, *n.* abridg. of *custos rotulorum*, keeper of the rolls: "Ay, cousin Slender, and Custalorum." *Wives*, I, i, 7.

custard, *n.* **leaped into the custard**, ref. to highlight of [London] city entertainments when a jester jumped into a huge custard: ". . . run into't, boots and spurs/ and all, like him that leap'd into the custard . . ." *All's W*, II, v, 36–37.

custard-coffin, *n.* piecrust: "It is a paltry cap,/ A custard-coffin, a bauble, a silken pie." *Shrew*, IV, iii, 81–82.

custom, *n.* **1** customers; clientele: ". . . report what a/ sojourner we have; you'll lose nothing by custom." *Per*, IV, ii, 135–136.

2 habit; here, habitual wrongdoing: "If damned custom have not braz'd it so,/ That it be proof and bulwark against sense." *Ham*, III, iv, 37–38. **3** regular practice; duty or responsibility: "... had/ he himself eternity ... would beguile Nature of her custom ..." *W Tale*, V, ii, 96–98.

customed, *adj.* customary; usual: "No common wind, no customed event,/ But they will pluck away his [its] natural cause ..." *K John*, III, iii, 154–155.

customer, *n.* prostitute: "I think thee now some common customer." *All's W*, V, iii, 280.

custom of fell deeds, being accustomed to [experiencing] cruel deeds: "All pity chok'd with custom of fell deeds ..." *J Caes*, III, i, 269.

custom-shrunk, *adj.* short of customers; losing business; going broke: "... what with the gallows, and what with poverty, I am/ custom-shrunk." *Meas*, I, ii, 76–77.

cut, *adj.* **1** carved or sculptured: "Why should a man whose blood is warm within,/ Sit like his grandsire, cut in alablaster?" *Merch*, I, i, 83–84. **2 come cut and long-tail,** no matter what happens; fr. usual practice of docking the tails of dogs and horses: "Ay, that I will, come cut and long-tail, under the/ degree of a squire." *Wives*, III, iv, 46–47.
—*n.* **3** horse with a docked tail; also, perh., gelding: "... if thou hast her not i' th' end, call me cut." *T Night*, II, iii, 186–187. **4** emotional blow, prob. with bawdy wordplay on "cut" and "case": "If there were/ no more women but Fulvia, then had you indeed a/ cut ..." *Ant & Cleo*, I, ii, 163–165.
—*v.* **5** (of a ship) to cut through or across: "He could so quickly cut the Ionian sea,/ And take in Toryne?" *Ant & Cleo*, III, vii, 22–23. **6** trim; pare; shave: "... but it is no English/ treason to cut French crowns ..." *Hen 5*, IV, i, 233–234. **7 cut i'th'middle,** divided in half like a joint of meat: "... our general/ is cut i'th'middle, and but one half of what he was/ yesterday ..." *Cor*, IV, v, 202–204. **8 cuts him off,** kills him: "Preferment falls on him that cuts him off." *Lear*, IV, v, 38. **9 cut out,** because of her feelings for him, Perdita deduces that Florizel feels the same toward her [metaphor from tailoring]: "By th' pattern of mine own thoughts I cut out/ The purity of his." *W Tale*, IV, iv, 383–384. **10 cut the sea,** See **sea.**

Cut, *n.* nickname for a curtal horse, one with a docked tail: "... beat Cut's saddle, put a few/ flocks in the point ..." *1 Hen 4*, II, i, 5–6.

C.U.T., appar. an unconscious indecency on Malvolio's part, "cut" being vulgar slang for the female genitals: "... these be her very C's, her U's, and her T's,/ and thus makes she her great P's." *T Night*, II, v, 88–89.

cutler, *n.* person who makes cutlery: "... whose posy was/ For all the world like cutler's poetry/ Upon a knife ..." *Merch*, V, i, 148–150.

cutpurse or **cut-purse,** *n.* thief who steals purses by cutting the cords that attach them to a person's belt: "Away, you cut-purse rascal, you filthy bung, away!" *2 Hen 4*, II, iv, 125.

cuts, *n. pl.* slits, as in a sleeve, to expose the lining, often of silver or gold cloth: "... cloth o' gold, and cuts, and laced with/ silver ..." *M Ado*, III, iv, 18–19.

cutter, *n.* sculptor: "... the cutter/ Was as another Nature, dumb ..." *Cymb*, II, iv, 83–84.

cuttle, *n.* cutpurse; also, bully or cutthroat [lit., the knife used by a cutpurse]: "I'll thrust my knife in your mouldy/ chaps and you play the saucy cuttle with me." *2 Hen 4*, II, iv, 126–127.

Cyclops, *n. pl.* race of one-eyed giants in Homer's "Odyssey": "... no cedars we;/ No big-bon'd men fram'd of the Cyclops' size ..." *T Andr*, IV, iii, 45–46.

Cydnus, *n.* river in S Asia Minor, on which the city of Tarsus was located: "When she first met Mark Antony, she purs'd up/ his heart upon the river of Cydnus." *Ant & Cleo*, II, ii, 186–187.

cyme, *n.* prob. the tops of colewort, used as a purgative; poss., too, the herb senna: "What rhubarb, cyme or what purgative drug,/ Would scour these English hence?" *Mac*, V, iii, 55–56.

Cynthia, *n.* moon goddess; here, the moon itself: "... yon grey is not the morning's eye,/ 'Tis but the pale reflex of Cynthia's brow." *Rom & Jul*, III, v, 19–20.

cypress[1], *n.* **1** tree associated with death and thought suitable only for graveyards: "Their sweetest shade a grove of cypress trees!" *2 Hen 6*, III, ii, 322. **2** coffin of cypress wood: "Come away, come away death,/ And in sad cypress let me be laid." *T Night*, II, iv, 51–52.

cypress[2], *n.* black, transparent fabric; crepe: "... a cypress, not a bosom,/ Hides my heart ..." *T Night*, III, i, 123–124.

Cytherea, *n.* Venus: "And Cytherea all in sedges hid ..." *Shrew*, Ind., ii, 52.

~ D ~

'd, *v.* would; prob. pron. as separate syllable: "... as you 'd thrust a cork into a/ hogs-head." *W Tale,* III, iii, 92–94.

dace, *n.* small freshwater fish used esp. for bait: "If the young dace be a bait for the old pike, I see no/ reason ... but I may snap at him ..." *2 Hen 4,* III, ii, 325–326.

Dachet Mead, *n.* meadow near the Thames in Windsor: "... carry it among the whitsters in Datchet Mead, and/ there empty it..." *Wives,* III, iii, 12–13.

dad, *n.* Vice, in the old morality plays, was often the Devil's son: "Like a mad lad, 'Pare thy nails, dad./ Adieu, goodman devil!'" *T Night,* IV, ii, 131–132.

Daedalus, *n.* father of Icarus and architect of the Cretan labyrinth: "I, Daedalus; my poor boy, Icarus ... The sun that sear'd the wings of my sweet boy,/ Thy brother Edward ..." *3 Hen 6,* V, vi, 21–24.

daff, *v.* [past & past part.: **daft** or **daffed**] **1** to toss aside: "I would have daffed all other respects and made her/ half myself." *M Ado,* II, iii, 165–166. **2** doff; take off; put off: "... till we do please/ To daff 't for our repose ..." *Ant & Cleo,* IV, iv, 12–13.

dagger, *n.* **dagger of lath,** the wooden dagger brandished by Vice in the old morality plays and often used to pare the Devil's nails: "Who, with dagger of lath, in his rage ... Cries, 'Ah, ha!' to the devil ..." *T Night,* IV, ii, 128–130.

Daintry, *n.* town, now called Daventry, N of London: "By this at Daintry, with a puissant troop." *3 Hen 6,* V, i, 6.

dainty, *adj.* **1** petty; trivial: "... the King is weary/ Of dainty and such picking grievances..." *2 Hen 4,* IV, i, 197–198. **2** refined; elegant: "Armado to th'one side, O! a most dainty man ..." *Love's L,* IV, i, 145. **3** unduly concerned [about]: "Having his ear full of his airy fame,/ Grows dainty of his

worth ..." *Tr & Cr,* I, iii, 144–145. **4 make dainty,** to act shy or coy: "She that makes dainty,/ She I'll swear hath corns." *Rom & Jul,* I, v, 19–20.
—*n.* **5** delicacy; sweetmeat: "... my super-dainty Kate,/ For dainties are all Kates ..." *Shrew,* II, i, 188–189.

dalliance, *n.* **1** delaying tactic used to gain time: "You use this dalliance to excuse/ Your breach of promise to the Porpentine ..." *Errors,* IV, i, 48–49. **2** instance of idling away time; trifling: "And keep not back your powers in dalliance." *1 Hen 6,* V, ii, 5.

dally, *v.* **1** to engage in amorous play: "I could interpret between you and your love if I/ could see the puppets dallying." *Ham,* III, ii, 241–242. **2** to speak agreeably with no intention of complying; trifle: "Take heed you dally not before your King ..." *Rich 3,* II, i, 12. **3 dally nicely with words,** to engage in subtle wordplay: "... they that dally nicely with/ words may quickly make them wanton." *T Night,* III, i, 14–15. **4 dally with,** to trifle with: "Grief dallied with, nor law nor limit knows." *Luc,* 1120.

Dalmatians, *n.* inhabitants of Dalmatia, a province on the E coast of the Adriatic Sea: "... the common men are now in action/ 'Gainst the Pannonians and Dalmatians ..." *Cymb,* III, viii, 2–3.

dam, *n.* **1** female parent; mother: "Nay, she is worse, she is the devil's dam ..." *Errors,* IV, iii, 49. **2** female dog; bitch: "... a kind of puppy/ To th' old dam treason ..." *Hen 8,* I, i, 175–176. **3 Can thy dam?** Is it possible your mother has been unfaithful?: "... sweet villain!/ Most dear'st, my collop! Can thy dam?—may't be?—" *W Tale,* I, ii, 136–137.

Damascus, *n.* ancient city, said to have been founded on the place where Cain slew his brother Abel: "This be Damascus, be thou cursed Cain,/ To slay thy brother Abel, if thou wilt." *1 Hen 6,* I, iii, 39–40.

damask cheek, *n.* pinkish white skin of a woman's cheek: ". . . let concealment like a worm i' th' bud/ Feed on her damask cheek . . ." *T Night,* II, iv, 112–113.

damasked, *adj.* variegated red or pink with white: "I have seen roses damask'd, red and white . . ." *Sonn 130,* 5.

dame, *n.* **1** noblewoman; lady: ". . . the fairest dame/ That liv'd, that lov'd, that lik'd, that look'd with cheer." *M N Dream,* V, i, 282–283. **2** woman; wife [affectionate term of address]: "Fare thee well, dame, whate'er becomes of me:/ This is a soldier's kiss . . ." *Ant & Cleo,* IV, iv, 29–30. **3** mistress; madam [used as a scolding term of address]: "Why, how now, dame, whence grows this insolence?" *Shrew,* II, i, 23. **4 old dame,** "old woman"; wife: "My old dame will be undone/ now for one to do her husbandry and her drudgery." *2 Hen 4,* III, ii, 112–113.

damn, *v.* **1** to condemn: ". . . damns himself to do, and dares better be/ damn'd than to do't." *All's W,* III, vi, 84–85. **2 damn'd in a fair wife,** perh. obsessively in love, though Cassio appears not to be married: "One Michael Cassio . . . A fellow almost damn'd in a fair wife . . ." *Oth,* I, i, 20–21.

damnable, *adj.* **1** serving wicked purposes: ". . . a magician, most profound in his art and yet not damnable." *As You,* V, ii, 61–62. **2** regarded as a mortal sin: "Is it not meant damnable in us to be trumpeters/ of our unlawful intents?" *All's W,* IV, iii, 25–26.
—*adv.* **3** damnably: "That did but show thee, of [for] a fool, inconstant/ And damnable ingrateful . . ." *W Tale,* III, ii, 186–187.

Damon, *n.* legendary companion of Pythias: "For thou dost know, O Damon dear,/ This realm dismantled was . . ." *Ham,* III, ii, 275–276.

damosella, *n.* old form of **damsel:** "But, damosella virgin, was this directed to you?" *Love's L,* IV, ii, 123.

damp, *n.* mist or fog: "With rotten damps ravish the morning air . . ." *Luc,* 778.

dan, *n.* var. of **don:** master or sir (used as a respectful form of address): "This signor junior, giant-dwarf, dan Cupid . . ." *Love's L,* III, i, 175.

dance, *v.* **1 dance attendance,** am kept waiting: "Welcome, my lord: I dance attendance here." *Rich 3,* III, vii, 55. **2 dance barefoot,** custom that an older unmarried sister danced barefoot on the day of her younger sister's wedding: ". . . she must have a husband,/ I must dance barefoot on her wedding-day . . ." *Shrew,* II, i, 32–33. **3 dance the hay,** See **hay**[1].

dancing, *adj.* bouncing; here, storm-tossed: ". . . convey thy deity/ Aboard our dancing boat . . ." *Per,* III, i, 12–13.

dancing horse, *n.* prob. ref. to Morocco, a famous performing horse of the day: ". . . how easy it is/ to . . . study three years/ in two words, the dancing horse will tell you." *Love's L,* I, ii, 48–50.

dancing-rapier, *n.* sword worn only as part of one's costume, esp. for dancing: ". . . our mother, unadvis'd,/ Gave you a dancing-rapier by your side . . ." *T Andr,* II, i, 38–39.

Dane, *n.* king of Denmark; here, the newly crowned Claudius: "you cannot speak of reason to the Dane/ And lose your voice." *Ham,* I, ii, 44–45.

danger, *n.* **1** harm; here, repercussions: "If you deny it, let the danger light/ Upon your charter and your city's freedom!" *Merch,* IV, i, 38–39. **2** risk; hazard: "To eject him hence/ Were but our danger . . ." *Cor,* III, i, 284–285. **3 within his danger,** in his power: "You stand within his danger, do you not?" *Merch,* IV, i, 176.
—*v.* **4** to endanger: ". . . whose quality, going on,/ The sides o' the world may danger." *Ant & Cleo,* I, ii, 189–190.

dangerous, *adj.* **1** threatening; menacing: "By unkind usage, dangerous countenance [looks] . . ." *1 Hen 4,* V, i, 69. **2** inviolable; rigorous: "For that's an article within our law/ As dangerous as the rest." *Per,* I, i, 89–90. **3 dangerous year,** year of the plague [prob. 1593, the year this poem was composed]: "To drive infection from the dangerous year . . ." *Ven & Ad,* 508.
—*adv.* **4** seriously; gravely: "Duke of Buckingham,/ Is either slain or wounded dangerous . . ." *3 Hen 6,* I, i, 10–11.

Daniel, *n.* (in the Apocrypha) the young defender of Susannah against the elders who falsely accused her of adultery: "A Daniel come to judgment . . . O wise young judge how I do honour thee!" *Merch,* IV, i, 219–220.

Dansker, *n.* Dane: "Inquire me first what Danskers are in Paris . . ." *Ham,* II, i, 7.

Daphne, *n.* nymph, daughter of the river-god Peneus, who fled Apollo's advances and was transformed by her father into a laurel tree: ". . . the story shall be chang'd:/ Apollo flies, and Daphne holds the chase . . ." *M N Dream,* II, i, 230–231.

Dardan, *n.* **1** another name for Dardania, the country where Troy was located: ". . . from the strond of Dardan where they fought . . ." *Luc,* 1436.
—*adj.* **2** Trojan: "Now on Dardan plains/ The . . . Greeks do pitch/ Their brave pavilions . . ." *Tr & Cr,* Prol., 13–15.

Dardanian, *adj.* Trojan: "I stand for sacrifice,/ The rest aloof are the Dardanian wives . . ." *Merch,* III, ii, 57–58.

dare¹, *v.* **1** to defy: "Conscience and grace, to the profoundest pit!/ I dare damnation." *Ham,* IV, v, 132–133. **2** to frighten; terrify: "For our approach shall so much dare the field/ That England shall couch down in fear . . ." *Hen 5,* IV, ii, 36–37. **3 dare better,** would rather: ". . . damns himself to do, and dares better be/ damn'd than to do't." *All's W,* III, vi, 84–85.

dare², *v.* **dare us with his cap,** to dazzle us with his red hat; ref. to method of snaring larks by holding their attention with a red cloth while they are netted from behind: ". . . let his grace go forward,/ And dare us with his cap, like larks." *Hen 8,* III, ii, 281–282.

dareful, *adj., adv.* full of daring; boldly: "We might have met them dareful, beard to beard . . ." *Mac,* V, v, 6.

daring of, *adj.* eager for: "Their neighing coursers daring of the spur . . ." *2 Hen 4,* IV, i, 119.

Darius, *n.* king of Persia, defeated by Alexander the Great, who used a jeweled coffer of Darius' to carry the poems of Homer with him: ". . . an urn more precious/ Than the rich jewel-coffer of Darius . . ." *1 Hen 6,* I, vi, 24–25.

dark, *adj.* **dark and vicious place,** scene of Gloucester's adultery: "The dark and vicious place where thee he got/ Cost him his eyes." *Lear,* V, iii, 172–173.

dark corners, *n.* **duke of dark corners,** *n.* ref. to Duke's absence, which Lucio assumes is for an assignation: "Isabel, I loved thy brother;/ if the old fantastical duke of dark corners had been/ at home, he had lived." *Meas,* IV, iii, 155–157.

darken, *v.* **1** to debase: "Darkening thy power to lend base subjects light?" *Sonn 100,* 4. **2** to sully: ". . . careless heirs/ May the two latter darken and expend . . ." *Per,* III, ii, 28–29. **3** to dim; becloud; obscure: ". . . their blaze/ Shall darken him for ever." *Cor,* II, i, 256–257.

darker, *adj.* secret; undisclosed: "Meantime, we shall express our darker purpose." *Lear,* I, i, 36.

dark house, *n.* gloomy abode: "Wars is no strife/ To the dark house and the detested wife." *All's W,* II, iii, 287–288.

darkling, *adv.* in the dark: "O wilt thou darkling leave me? Do not so." *M N Dream,* II, ii, 85.

darkly, *adv.* **1** secretly: "I will tell you a/ thing, but you shall let it dwell darkly with you." *All's W,* IV, iii, 9–10. **2** subtly; slyly: "I will go darkly to work with her." *Meas,* V, i, 277.

darkness, *n.* **1** spiritual ignorance and, hence, damnation: ". . . if they speak more or less than truth, they/ are villains, and the sons of darkness." *1 Hen 4,* II, iv, 169–170. **2** death: "Clarence, whom I, indeed, have cast in darkness . . ." *Rich 3,* I, iii, 327. **3 act (or deed) of darkness,** fornication: ". . . serv'd/ the lust of my mistress' heart, and did the act of/ darkness with her . . ." *Lear,* III, iv, 86–88.

dark night, *n.* sound sleep: "And make a dark night too of half the day . . ." *Love's L,* I, i, 45.

dark room and bound, conventional treatment for those regarded as insane: "Come, we'll have him [confine him] in a dark room and/ bound." *T Night,* III, iv, 136–137.

darling, *n.* favorite thing, person, etc.: ". . . as the dearest issue [result] of his practice,/ And of his old experience th' only darling . . ." *All's W,* II, i, 105–106.

darnel, *n.* weedy grass; tares: "Good morrow, gallants! Want ye corn for bread? . . . 'Twas full of darnel . . ." *1 Hen 6,* III, ii, 41–44.

darraign, *v.* to set in order: "Darraign your battle [army], for they are at hand." *3 Hen 6,* II, ii, 72.

dart, *n.* [pl.] arrows: "Filling the air with swords advanc'd [raised] and darts . . ." *Cor,* I, vi, 61.

Dartford, *n.* town in Kent, in SE England: "Fields between Dartford and Blackheath." [SD] *2 Hen 6,* V, i, 1.

dash, *n.* **1** mark or stain; here, indicative of disgrace: "Some loathsome dash the herald will contrive . . ." *Luc,* 206. **2 at first dash,** from the very beginning: "She takes upon her bravely at first dash." *1 Hen 6,* I, ii, 71.
—*v.* **3** to jeer at; frustrate or ruin: "To dash it like a Christmas comedy." *Love's L,* V, ii, 462.

dashed, *adj.* discouraged; dejected: ". . . a foolish mild/ man; an honest man, look you, and soon dashed!" *Love's L,* V, ii, 575–576.

Datchet Mead, *n.* mead [meadow] along the Thames near Windsor Park: ". . . carry it among the whitsters in Datchet Mead, and/ there empty it in the muddy ditch . . ." *Wives,* III, iii, 12–13.

date¹, *n.* **1** duration; term or extent: "To my determin'd time thou gav'st new date." *1 Hen 6,* IV, vi, 9. **2** [often pl.] one's term of life: "Diana's temple is not distant far,/ Where you may abide till your date expire." *Per,* III, iv, 12–13. **3** date on a promissory note: "Take the bonds along with you,/ And have the dates in [make certain each agreement is dated]." *Timon,* II, i, 34–35. **4 date is out,** past one's best: ". . . then to be baked with/ No date in the pie, for then the man's date is out." *Tr & Cr*, I, ii, 261–262. **5 doom and date,** doomsday; calamitous end: "Thy end is truth's and beauty's doom and date." *Sonn 14*, 14. **6 of one date,** the same age; here, young: "So long as youth and thou are of one date . . ." *Sonn 22*, 2. **7 the date is out,** the time has expired: "The date is out of [for] such prolixity [long-windedness]." *Rom & Jul*, I, iv, 3.

date², *n.* the fruit, often used as a sweetener; here, in wordplay with "apparent age": "Your date is better/ in your pie and your porridge than in your cheek . . ." *All's W*, I, i, 154–155.

dateless, *adj.* everlasting; eternal: ". . . seal with a righteous kiss/ A dateless bargain to engrossing Death." *Rom & Jul*, V, iii, 114–115.

daub, *n.* **daub it,** to dissemble; here, to impersonate Poor Tom: "Poor Tom's a-cold. [Aside.] I cannot daub it further." *Lear*, IV, i, 51.

daubery, *n.* false pretenses: "She works by charms, by spells, by/ th' figure, and such daubery as this is . . ." *Wives*, IV, ii, 162–163.

daughter-beamed, *adj.* wordplay on "sun-beamed" [sun, i.e. son]: "You were best call it 'daughter-beamed eyes.'" *Love's L*, V, ii, 172.

Dauphin, *n.* **1** eldest son and principal heir of a French king: "Myself . . . Am sure I scar'd the Dauphin and his trull . . ." *1 Hen 6*, II, ii, 26–28. **2 the Dauphin's Grace,** His Grace the Dauphin: "I muse we met not with the Dauphin's Grace . . ." *1 Hen 6*, II, ii, 19.

Daventry, *n.* town NW of London: ". . . the shirt to say the truth/ stolen from my host at Saint Albans, or the red-nose/ innkeeper of Daventry." *1 Hen 4*, IV, ii, 45–47.

daw, *n.* **1** jackdaw, regarded as a lazy, stupid bird: ". . . so much as you may take upon a knife's/ point and choke a daw withal." *M Ado*, II, iii, 245–246. **2** [pl.] See **doves.**

day, *n.* **1** the sun: ". . . not an hour/ In the day's glorious walk or peaceful night . . ." *Per*, I, i, 4–5. **2** [pl.] time: "This done, see that you take no longer days,/ But send the midwife presently to me." *T Andr*, IV, ii, 166–167. **3** [pl.] age; here, youth: "Painting my age with beauty of thy days." *Sonn 62*, 14. **4 by day and night,** mild oath: "By day and night,/ He's traitor to th'height [to the greatest degree]!" *Hen 8*, I, ii, 213–214. **5 days outworn,** times past; bygone days: "Thus is his cheek the map of days outworn . . ." *Sonn 68*, 1. **6 keep one's day,** to meet one's obligation at the appointed time: "Let good Antonio look he keep his day/ Or he shall pay for this." *Merch*, II, viii, 25–26. **7 of all the day,** during the day: "And not be seen to wink [nap] of all the day . . ." *Love's L*, I, i, 43. **8 of so young days,** from the earliest years: "That, being of so young days brought up with him . . ." *Ham*, II, ii, 11. **9 the day,** victory: "Come on, brave soldiers: doubt not of the day . . ." *3 Hen 6*, IV, vii, 87. **10 this many a day,** these past several days, weeks, etc.: "Good my lord,/ How does your honour for this many a day?" *Ham*, III, i, 90–91.

day-bed, *n.* couch or sofa: ". . . having come from a day-bed, where/ I have left Olivia sleeping—" *T Night*, II, v, 48–49.

day of season, *n.* one particular mood or attitude: "I am not a day of season,/ For thou may'st see a sunshine and a hail/ In me at once." *All's W*, V, iii, 32–34.

day o' the world, *n.* brightest creature in the world; Cleopatra: "O thou day o' the world,/ Chain mine arm'd neck . . ." *Ant & Cleo*, IV, viii, 13–14.

day-star, *n.* (often pl.) the eyes likened to two bright stars: "For here two day-stars that mine eyes would see/ More than the sun steals mine own light from me." *Edw 3*, I, ii, 133–134.

day-woman, *n.* dairy woman; milkmaid: "For this damsel, I must keep her at the park; she is/ allowed for the day-woman." *Love's L*, I, ii, 123–124.

dazzle, *v.* **1** to blur; glaze over: ". . . thy sight is young,/ And thou shalt read when mine [eyes] begin to dazzle." *T Andr*, III, ii, 84–85. **2 dazzle mine eyes,** Do my eyes blur?: "Dazzle mine eyes, or do I see three suns?" *3 Hen 6*, II, i, 25.

dead, *adj.* **1** deathly; deathlike: ". . . till so much blood thither come again,/ Have I not reason to look pale and dead?" *Rich 2*, III, ii, 78–79. **2** deadly; lethal: "So should a murderer look, so dead, so grim." *M N Dream*, III, ii, 57. **3** dark; ominous: "In that dead time when Gloucester's death was plotted . . ." *Rich 2*, IV, i, 10. **4** of the quietest time of night: "Thus twice before, and jump at this dead hour . . ." *Ham*, I, i, 68. **5** (of sleep) abnormally heavy; deep: ". . . and strike more dead/ Than common sleep, of all these five the sense." *M N Dream*, IV, i, 80–81. **6 strike one dead,** to stun into silence: "Was it his spirit, by spirits taught to write/ Above a mortal pitch, that struck me dead?" *Sonn 86*, 5–6.

deadly, *adj.* **1** dying or, as here, suffering intensely: "If I did love you in my master's flame,/ With such a suff'ring, such a deadly life . . ." *T Night*, I, v, 268–269. **2** resembling death: ". . . both man and master is possess'd,/ I know it by their pale and deadly looks . . ." *Errors*, IV, iv, 91. **3 come to deadly use,** result in burning, the only use for a dead branch: "She that herself will sliver . . . perforce must wither/ And come to deadly use." *Lear*, IV, ii, 34–36.

deadly-standing, *adj.* fixed in a murderous stare: "What signifies my deadly-standing eye,/ My silence and my cloudy melancholy . . ." *T Andr,* II, iii, 32–33.

deadly theme, *n.* subject for mortal combat: "Name her not now, sir; she's a deadly theme." *Tr & Cr,* IV, v, 180.

dead march, *n.* **1** funeral procession; cortege: "Dead March. Enter the Funeral of King Henry the Fifth, attended/ on by the Duke of Bedford . . ." [SD] *l Hen 6,* I, i, l. **2** slow and solemn music to accompany a funeral procession: "Exeunt, bearing the body of Martius. A dead march sounded." [SD] *Cor,* V, vi, 154.

deaf, *v.* to make deaf; deafen: "What cracker is this same that deafs our ears?" *K John,* II, i, 147.

deafing, *adj.* deafening: "With deafing clamour in the slippery clouds . . ." *2 Hen 4,* III, i, 24.

deal¹, *n.* **1** amount or quantity: ". . . what a candy deal of courtesy/ This fawning greyhound then did proffer me!" *1 Hen 4,* I, iii, 247–248. **2 such a deal of man,** such a fine example of a man: "And put upon him [made himself out to be] such a deal of man . . ." *Lear,* II, ii, 121.

deal², *v.* **1** to take action: "God above/ Deal between thee and me!" *Mac,* IV, iii, 120–121. **2 deal in her command,** See **command** (def. 5). **3 deal upon,** to proceed against: ". . . my sweet sleep's disturbers,/ Are they that I would have thee deal upon." *Rich 3,* IV, ii, 72–73. **4 deal withal,** to copulate with: ". . . have you that a man may deal withal, and/ defy the surgeon?" *Per,* IV, vi, 24–25.

dealing, *n.* treatment: "But were my worth, as is my conscience, firm,/ You should find better dealing." *T Night,* III, iii, 17–18.

dear¹, *adj.* **1** extremely important; cherished: "What yesternight our Council did decree/ In forwarding this dear expedience." *1 Hen 4,* I, i, 32–33. **2** highly regarded; noble or honorable: "And many mo [more] corrivals and dear men/ Of estimation and command in arms." *1 Hen 4,* IV, iv, 31–32. **3** loving: "A solemn combination shall be made/ Of our dear souls." *T Night,* V, i, 382–383. **4** wordplay on "beloved" and "costly": "Is she a Capulet?/ O dear account. My life is my foe's debt." *Rom & Jul,* I, v, 116–117. **5** rare; scarce: "Be now as prodigal of all dear [best] grace/ As Nature was in making graces dear . . ." *Love's L,* II, i, 9–10. **6** deeply sincere; heartfelt: "I should not make so dear a show of zeal . . ." *1 Hen 4,* V, iv, 93–94. **7** fervent; ardent: "Consort with me in loud and dear petition . . ." *Tr & Cr,* V, iii, 9. **8** confidential; secret: "I do know you;/ And dare . . . Commend a dear thing to you." *Lear,* III, i, 17–19. **9** extremely personal: "A precious ring, a ring that I

must use/ In dear employment." *Rom & Jul,* V, iii, 31–32. **10 dear to fancy,** pleasing to the taste: "Three of the/ carriages, in faith, are very dear to fancy . . ." *Ham,* V, ii, 147–148. —*adv.* **11** deeply; sincerely or devotedly; here, wordplay with "lavishly": "Youngling, thou canst not love so dear as I." *Shrew,* II, i, 330. **12** at great cost: "The Lord of Stafford dear today hath bought/ Thy likeness, for instead of thee, King Harry,/ This sword hath ended him . . ." *1 Hen 4,* V, iii, 7–9.

dear², *adj.* extreme; grievous; dire: ". . . what other means is left unto us/ In our dear peril." *Timon,* V, i, 226–227.

dear account, *n.* heavy obligation: ". . . my sovereign liege was in my debt/ Upon remainder of a dear account . . ." *Rich 2,* I, i, 129–130.

dear cause, *n.* urgent matter: "Some dear cause/ Will in concealment wrap me up awhile . . ." *Lear,* IV, iii, 52–53.

dear discretion, *n.* worthy discrimination: "O dear discretion, how his words are suited!" *Merch,* III, v, 59.

deared, *adj.* beloved: ". . . the ebb'd man . . . Comes dear'd by being lack'd." *Ant & Cleo,* I, iv, 43–44.

dearest¹, *adj.* **1** most valuable or precious; noblest: "And that's the dearest grace it renders you . . ." *1 Hen 4,* III, i, 176. **2** best; most; greatest: "You, son John . . . Towards York shall bend you with your dearest speed . . ." *1 Hen 4,* V, v, 35–36.

dearest² *adj.* **1** worst; vilest: "Would I had met my dearest foe in heaven/ Or ever I had seen that day, Horatio." *Ham,* I, ii, 182–183. **2** most painful or grievous: ". . . cost me the dearest groans of a mother . . ." *All's W,* IV, v, 11.

dear expense, *n.* costly gain: ". . . and for this intelligence/ If I have thanks, it is a dear expense." *M N Dream,* I, i, 248–249.

dearly, *adv.* deeply; grievously: "How dearly would it touch thee to the quick,/ Shouldst thou but hear I were licentious?" *Errors,* II, ii, 130–131.

dearn, *adj.* dire or dread: "If wolves had at thy gate howl'd that dearn time . . ." *Lear,* III, vii, 62.

dearth, *n.* **1** scarcity: ". . . his infusion of such dearth and rareness as, to/ make true diction of him . . ." *Ham,* V, ii, 117–118. **2** famine: "For the dearth,/ The gods, not the patricians, make it . . ." *Cor,* I, i, 71–72.

dear times', *n.* person's most productive years: "And with old woes new wail my dear times' waste . . ." *Sonn 30,* 4.

death, *n.* **1** consummation of love [poetic overstatement]: "He gains by death that hath such means to die . . ." *Errors,* III, ii,

51. **2 take my death,** swear upon my life: "I will take my death I never meant him any ill . . ." *2 Hen 6*, II, iii, 85–86.
—*interj.* **3** [usually cap.] var. of **'Sdeath** [by God's death], a mild oath: "Death my lord,/ Their clothes are after such a pagan cut to't . . ." *Hen 8*, I, iii, 13–14.

deathful, *adj.* fatal; deadly: "Though parting be a fretful corrosive,/ It is applied to a deathful wound." *2 Hen 6*, III, ii, 402–403.

death-practiced, *adj.* whose death has been plotted: "With this ungracious paper strike the sight/ Of the death-practis'd Duke." *Lear*, IV, vi, 278–279.

death's face, *n.* death's-head; a human skull: "The head of a bodkin."/ "A death's face in a ring." *Love's L*, V, ii, 606–607.

death's-head, *n.* skull and crossbones, often carved on old tombstones: "I had rather be married/ to a death's-head with a bone in his mouth . . ." *Merch*, I, ii, 49–50.

deathsman, *n.* executioner: ". . . have him so cut off/ As, deathsmen, you have rid this sweet young prince!" *3 Hen 6*, V, v, 64–65.

death's second self, *n.* sleep: "Death's second self that seals up all in rest . . ." *Sonn 73*, 8.

death-token, *n.* [often pl.] visible evidence of a fatal malady, usually the plague; here, a fatal pride: ". . . the death-tokens of it/ Cry 'No recovery.'" *Tr & Cr*, II, iii, 178–179.

death to nature, *n.* mortal wound: ". . . twenty trenched gashes on his head;/ The least a death to nature." *Mac*, III, iv, 26–27.

debar, *v.* to deprive: "That am debarr'd the benefit of rest?" *Sonn 28*, 2.

debate, *n.* **1** dispute or quarrel; here, armed conflict: ". . . this debate that bleedeth at our doors . . ." *2 Hen 4*, IV, iv, 2.
—*v.* **2** to settle: "Two thousand souls and twenty thousand ducats/ Will not debate the question of this straw!" *Ham*, IV, iv, 25–26.

debatement, *n.* **1** argument or discussion: "Without debatement further more or less,/ He should those bearers put to sudden death . . ." *Ham*, V, ii, 45–46. **2** consideration; here, soul-searching: ". . . after much debatement,/ My sisterly remorse confutes mine honour . . ." *Meas*, V, i, 102–103.

debating, *n.* discussion: "Then childish fear avaunt, debating die!" *Luc*, 274.

debile, *adj.* very weak; feeble: "In a most weak—"/ "And debile minister . . ." *All's W*, II, iii, 33–34.

debitor and creditor, *n.* account book; also, accountant: "O, the charity/ of a penny cord [hangman's noose]! . . . you/ have no true debitor and creditor but it . . ." *Cymb*, V, iv, 167–169.

debonair, *adj.* gentle; gracious: "Courtiers as free, as debonair, unarm'd/ As bending angels . . ." *Tr & Cr*, I, iii, 234–235.

Deborah, *n.* (in the Bible) Hebrew prophetess who led her people in the defeat of their Canaanite oppressors: ". . . thou art an Amazon,/ And fightest with the sword of Deborah." *1 Hen 6*, I, ii, 104–105.

deboshed, *adj.* debauched; debased; corrupt(ed); here, prob. with a "French" pronunciation: "Why, thou debosh'd fish, thou,/ was there ever man a coward that hath drunk so/ much sack . . ." *Temp*, III, ii, 25–27.

debt, *n.* **1** payment; recompense: ". . . you did exceed/ The barren tender of a poet's debt . . ." *Sonn 83*, 3–4. **2 in debt,** ref. to debtor who keeps to the back streets; Cloten's sword avoided the main thoroughfare, i.e., the body of Posthumus: "His steel was in debt, it went o' th' backside the town." *Cymb*, I, iii, 12.

debuty, *n.* misuse of "deputy"; the chief officer of a ward and responsible for maintaining order: "I was before/ Master Tisick the debuty t'other day . . ." *2 Hen 4*, II, iv, 82–83.

decay, *n.* **1** ruin; downfall: ". . . with what wings shall his affections fly/ Towards fronting peril and oppos'd decay!" *2 Hen 4*, IV, iv, 65–66. **2 great decay,** final image of Lear: "What comfort to this great decay may come/ Shall be appli'd . . ." *Lear*, V, iii, 297–298.
—*v.* **3** to weaken; falter: "And in mine own love's strength seem to decay . . ." *Sonn 23*, 7. **4** to destroy: "And every day that comes comes to decay/ A day's work in him." *Cymb*, I, vi, 56–57.

decayed, *adj.* perished; vanished: ". . . my decayed fair [beauty]/ A sunny look of his would soon repair . . ." *Errors*, II, i, 98–99.

deceit, *n.* confusing, hence misleading, meaning: "The folded meaning of your words' deceit." *Errors*, III, ii, 36.

deceitful, *adj.* tending to deceive or mislead; here, by artistry: "Conceit deceitful, so compact, so kind [natural] . . ." *Luc*, 1423.

deceivable, *adj.* deceitful; deceptive: "Show me thy humble heart, and not thy knee,/ Whose duty is deceivable and false." *Rich 2*, II, iii, 83–84.

deceive, *v.* **1** to cheat: "Thou of thyself thy sweet self dost deceive." *Sonn 4,* 10. **2** to while away; beguile: ". . . thoughts of love,/ Which time and thoughts so sweetly doth deceive . . ." *Sonn 39,* 11–12.

deceived, *past part.* **1** mistaken: "Thou art deceiv'd: 'tis not thy southern power . . ." *3 Hen 6,* I, i, 159. **2** disappointed: "Only they/ That come to hear a merry bawdy play . . . Will be deceiv'd . . ." *Hen 8,* Prol. 13–17. **3 be not deceived,** do not misjudge me: "Cassius,/ Be not deceiv'd: if I have veil'd my look . . ." *J Caes,* I, ii, 35–36. **4 care to be deceived,** care whether or not I am deceived: "I do not greatly care to be deceiv'd/ That have no use for trusting." *Ant & Cleo,* V, ii, 14–15.

deceptious, *adj.* deceiving or deluding: "As if those organs had deceptious functions,/ Created only to calumniate." *Tr & Cr,* V, ii, 122–123.

decern, *v.* misuse for "concern": ". . . I would have some confidence with/ you, that decerns you nearly." *M Ado,* III, v, 2–3.

decimation, *n.* the slaughter of one soldier, civilian, etc., out of every ten: "By decimation and a tithed death . . . take thou the destin'd tenth . . ." *Timon,* V, iv, 31–33.

decipher, *v.* to identify: "The white will decipher her well/ enough." *Wives,* V, ii, 9–10.

deciphered, *adj.* detected; found out: ". . . Lucius: what's the news?"/ "That you are both decipher'd, that's the news . . ." *T Andr,* IV, ii, 7–8.

deck[1], *v.* **1** to strew; adorn: "Thou didst smile . . . When I have deck'd the sea with drops full salt . . ." *Temp,* I, ii, 153–155. **2 deck up,** to adorn; bedeck: "Go thou to Juliet, help to deck up her." *Rom & Jul,* IV, ii, 41.

deck[2], *n.* prob. the ship's after deck or poop: "Now in the waist, the deck, in every cabin . . ." *Temp,* I, ii, 197.

declension, *n.* decline from a high standard: "Seduc'd the pitch and height of his degree/ To base declension . . ." *Rich 3,* III, vii, 187–188.

decline, *v.* **1** to incline; feel drawn: "Far more, far more to you do I decline . . ." *Errors,* III, ii, 44. **2** to bend: ". . . rubies, carbuncles, sapphires, declining their/ rich aspect to the hot breath of Spain . . ." *Errors,* III, ii, 133–134. **3** to sink morally: ". . . and to decline/ Upon a wretch whose natural gifts were poor/ To those of mine." *Ham,* I, v, 50–52. **4** to rest: "He takes her up,/ and declines his head upon her neck." *Ham,* III, ii, 133 [dumb-show]. **5** to recite or set forth in prescribed order: "I'll decline the whole question. Agamemnon/ commands

Achilles, Achilles is my lord . . ." *Tr & Cr,* II, iii, 55–56. **6** to descend; fall: "When thou hast hung thy advanced sword i'th'air,/ Not letting it decline on the declin'd [wounded enemy] . . ." *Tr & Cr,* IV, v, 187–188.

declined, *adj.* **1** fallen in fortunes: "To lay his gay comparisons apart/ And answer me declin'd, sword against sword . . ." *Ant & Cleo,* III, xiii, 26–27.
—*n.* **2** [used as pl.] warriors wounded in combat; here, enemy wounded: "When thou hast hung thy advanced sword i'th'air,/ Not letting it decline on the declin'd . . ." *Tr & Cr,* IV, v, 187–188.

decoct, *v.* to heat up: "Can sodden [boiled] water . . . Decoct their cold blood to such valiant heat?" *Hen 5,* III, v, 18–20.

decrease, *v.* Slender's misuse for "increase": ". . . yet heaven may/ decrease it upon better acquaintance . . ." *Wives,* I, i, 226–227.

decreasing, *adj.* shrinking: "Have you not . . . a decreasing leg, an/ increasing belly?" *2 Hen 4,* I, ii, 179–181.

decree, *v.* **1** to decide or determine: ". . . therefore I have decreed not to sing in my cage." *M Ado,* I, iii, 31–32.
—*n.* **2** decision or resolution: "Is it your trick to make me ope the door,/ That so my sad decrees may fly away . . ." *T Andr,* V, ii, 10–11.

dedicate, *past part.* dedicated: "He that is truly dedicate to war/ Hath no self-love . . ." *2 Hen 6,* V, ii, 37–38.

deed, *n.* **1** action; performance: "As he in his particular act and place/ May give his saying deed . . ." *Ham,* I, iii, 26–27. **2** [pl.] same in wordplay with "property titles" and other evidence of wealth: "'Tis deeds must win the prize . . ." *Shrew,* II, i, 335. **3** [often pl.] sexual relations; fornication: ". . . give her deeds; but she'll/ bereave [deprive] you o'th'deeds too . . ." *Tr & Cr,* III, ii, 55–56. **4** [pl.] wordplay bet. "brave actions" and "property titles": "'Tis deeds must win the prize . . ." *Shrew,* II, i, 335. **5 as good deed as drink,** "And/ 'twere not as good deed as drink to break the pate on/ thee, I am a very villain [if it didn't make as much sense to hit you over the head as to take a drink, I'm a real rascal]." *1 Hen 4,* II, i, 27–29. **6 became his deed,** performed to the most exacting standards: "Whether the horse by him became his deed . . ." *Lover's Comp,* 111. **7 deed of kind,** copulation: "And in the doing of the deed of kind/ He stuck them up before the fulsome ewes . . ." *Merch,* I, iii, 80–81. **8 deeds of darkness,** copulation: "If she'd do the deeds of darkness, thou wouldst say." *Per,* IV, vi, 29. **9 make no deed,** to do nothing; take no part (in): ". . . do you think he will make no deed at all of this/ that so seriously he does address himself unto?" *All's W,* III, vi, 91–92. **10 My deeds upon my head!** I ask no mercy: "My deeds upon my head! I crave the law,/ The penalty and forfeit of my bond." *Merch,* IV, i, 203–204.

deedless, *adj.* **deedless in his tongue,** not talking about his deeds: ". . . firm of word,/ Speaking in deeds, and deedless in his tongue . . ." *Tr & Cr,* IV, v, 97–98.

deem, *v.* **1** to regard as appropriate or effective: ". . . to esteem/ A senseless help, when help past sense we deem [we judge any help to be beyond reason]." *All's W,* II, i, 122–123.
—*n.* **2** idea; thought: "I, true! How now, what wicked deem is this?" *Tr & Cr,* IV, iv, 58.

deep, *adj.* **1** (of music or sounds) loud or sonorous: ". . . the tongues of dying men/ Inforce attention like deep harmony." *Rich 2,* II, i, 5–6. **2** learned; serious or profound: "Deep clerks she dumbs . . ." *Per,* V, Chor., 5. **3** darkest: "Deep night, dark night, the silent of the night . . ." *2 Hen 6,* I, iv, 15. **4** secret; occult: "And bring him out that is but woman's son/ Can . . . hold me pace in deep experiments." *1 Hen 4,* III, i, 44–46.
—*adv.* **5** deeply; extremely: "That trick of state/ Was a deep envious [vicious] one." *Hen 8,* II, i, 44–45.
—*n.* **6** deepest part, esp. of a body of water: "Make tigers tame, and huge leviathans/ Forsake unsounded deeps, to dance on sands." *Two Gent,* III, ii, 79–80.

deep-brained, *adj.* ingenious: ". . . deep-brain'd sonnets,/ that did amplify/ Each stone's dear nature . . ." *Lover's Comp,* 209–210.

deep designs, *n.* See **design**[1] (def. 5).

deep-fet, *adj.* deep-fetched: ". . . a rabble that rejoice/ To see my tears and hear my deep-fet groans." *2 Hen 6,* II, iv, 33.

deep-mouthed, *adj.* (esp. of dogs) having a loud, deep bark: "And couple Clowder with the deep-mouth'd brach [bitch]." *Shrew,* Ind., i, 16.

deep-revolving, *adj.* deep-pondering; profound: "The deep-revolving, witty Buckingham/ No more shall be the neighbour to my counsels." *Rich 3,* IV, ii, 42–43.

deer, *n.* **1** [sing. or pl.] used in wordplay with "dear(s)": "'Tis well, sir, that you hunted for yourself./ 'Tis thought your deer does hold you at a bay." *Shrew,* V, ii, 55–56. **2** any animals; game: "But mice and rats and such small deer . . ." *Lear,* III, iv, 142.

deface, *v.* to destroy: "Pay him six thousand, and deface the bond . . ." *Merch,* III, ii, 298.

defame, *n.* infamy: "Blind muffled bawd, dark harbour for defame . . ." *Luc,* 768.

default, *n.* **1** sin; offense: ". . . we that know what 'tis to fast and pray,/ Are penitent for your default to-day." *Errors,* I, ii, 51–52. **2 in the default,** when the need arises: ". . . that I may/ say, in the default, 'He is a man I know.'" *All's W,* II, iii, 225–226.

defeat, *v.* **1** to defraud [a legal term]; cheat: "They would have stol'n away . . . Thereby to have defeated you and me . . ." *M N Dream,* IV, i, 155–156. **2** to deprive: "Till Nature . . . by addition me of thee defeated . . ." *Sonn 20,* 10–11. **3** to frustrate: "Thou strik'st not me, 'tis Caesar thou defeat'st." *Ant & Cleo,* IV, xiv, 68. **4 defeat thy favor,** disguise your appearance [face]: ". . . follow/ these wars, defeat thy favour with an usurp'd/ beard . . ." *Oth,* I, iii, 340–342.
—*n.* **5** ruin; destruction or annihilation: "Upon whose property and most dear life/ A damn'd defeat was made." *Ham,* II, ii, 565–566.

defeature, *n.* **1** disfigurement: ". . . careful hours with time's deformed hand/ Have written strange defeatures in my face . . ." *Errors,* V, i, 299–300. **2** [pl] ruins; disrepair: "Then is he the ground/ Of my defeatures . . ." *Errors,* II, i, 97–98.

defect, *n.* **1** insufficiency or inadequacy: "Being unprepar'd,/ Our will became the servant to defect . . ." *Mac,* II, i, 17–18. **2** misuse for "effect": ". . . he himself/ must speak through, saying thus, or to the same/ defect . . ." *M N Dream,* III, i, 36–38. **3** same as preceding, though "gist" or "crux" is the sense intended: "That is the very defect of the matter sir." *Merch,* II, ii, 136.

defence, *n.* See **defense.**

defend, *v.* **1** to forbid: ". . . ingaged by my oath/ (Which God defend a knight should violate!) . . ." *Rich 2,* I, iii, 17–18. **2 defend the interim,** to deal with the present situation: "What shall defend the interim, and at length/ How goes our reck'ning?" *Timon,* II, ii, 153–154.

defendant, *adj.* capable of offering a defense: "To line and new repair our towns of war/ With men of courage and with means defendant . . ." *Hen 5,* II, iv, 7–8.

defender, *n.* **great defender,** the god Jupiter: "Thou great defender of this Capitol,/ Stand gracious to the rites that we intend." *T Andr,* I, i, 77–78.

defense or defence, *n.* **purpose of defense,** intention of defending oneself or one's cause: ". . . let it at least be said/ They saw we had a purpose of defence." *K John,* V, i, 75–76.

defensible, *adj.* able to offer a defense: "Enter our gates; dispose of us and ours;/ For we no longer are defensible." *Hen 5,* III, iii, 49–50.

deficient, *adj.* **1** defective: "(Being not deficient, blind, or lame of sense,)" *Oth,* I, iii, 63. **2 deficient sight,** failing eye-sight: "I'll look no more,/ Lest my brain turn, and the deficient sight/ Topple down headlong." *Lear,* IV, vi, 22–24.

defiled, *adj.* slandered; defamed: "One Hero died defil'd, but I do live . . ." *M Ado,* V, iv, 63.

definite, *adj.* **be wisely definite,** make a wise decision: "For idiots in this case of favour, would/ Be wisely definite . . ." *Cymb,* I, vii, 42–43.

definitive, *adj.* **we are definitive,** my decision is final: "I crave no other, nor no better man."/ "Never crave him; we are de-finitive." *Meas,* V, i, 424–425.

deflower, *v.* prob. misuse for "devour": "O wherefore, Nature, didst thou lions frame,/ Since lion vile hath here deflower'd my dear?" *M N Dream,* V, i, 280–281.

deform, *v.* to change or alter: "Your beauty, ladies,/ Hath much deform'd us . . ." *Love's L,* V, ii, 748–749.

deformed, *adj.* **1** causing deformity: ". . . careful hours with time's deformed hand/ Have written strange defeatures in my face . . ." *Errors,* V, i, 299–300. **2** (of a beloved) transformed in the eyes of a lover: "You never saw her since she was de-formed." *Two Gent,* II, i, 60.

defunct, *adj.* modern sense of "dead" seems unreasonable; perh. here given meaning of "calmed," "cooled," etc.: "Nor to comply with heat, the young affects [youthful passions]/ In my [me?] defunct, and proper satisfaction . . ." *Oth,* I, iii, 263–264.

defunction, *n.* death; decease: "Until four hundred one and twenty years/ After defunction of King Pharamond . . ." *Hen 5,* I, ii, 57–58.

defunctive, *adj.* funereal: "Let the priest in surplice white,/ That defunctive music can . . ." *Phoen,* 13–14.

defuse, *v.* to disguise: "If but as well I other accents borrow,/ That can my speech defuse . . ." *Lear,* I, iv, 1–2.

defy, *v.* **1** to distrust: "I do defy/ The tongues of soothers . . ." *1 Hen 4,* IV, i, 6–7. **2** to reject: "I had myself twenty angels given me/ this morning; but I defy all angels . . ." *Wives,* II, ii, 68–69. **3** to object to: ". . . beards that pleased me, complexions that liked me, and breaths that I defied not." *As You,* Epil. 216–217. **4 defy the matter,** ignore the sense [when it interferes with the wit]: "Garnish'd like him, that for a tricksy word/ Defy the matter . . ." *Merch,* III, v, 63–64. **5 defy the surgeon,** to avoid disease: ". . . have you [something] that a man may deal withal, and/ defy the surgeon?" *Per,* IV, vi, 24–25.

degenerate, *adj.* **1** corrupt; base: "Oft have I heard that grief softens the mind,/ And makes it fearful and degenerate . . ." *2 Hen 6,* IV, iv, 1–2. **2** betraying one's class or rank: "A recreant and most degenerate traitor . . ." *Rich 2,* I, i, 144.

degree, *n.* **1** rank; standing: ". . . I know not the degree of/ the Worthy, but I am to stand for him." *Love's L,* V, ii, 503–504. **2** place in a hierarchy; precedence: "The heavens themselves, the planets, and this centre/ Observe degree, priority, and place . . ." *Tr & Cr,* I, iii, 85–86. **3** a step (up): "I pity you."/ "That's a degree to love." *T Night,* III, i, 124–125. **4 degrees in schools,** academic rank: "Degrees in schools, and broth-erhoods in cities . . ." *Tr & Cr,* I, iii, 104. **5 in the degree of this fortune,** in line for this blessing: ". . . who stands so emi-nently in/ the degree of this fortune as Cassio does?" *Oth,* II, i, 235–236.

degrees in schools, *n.* academic ranking: "Degrees in schools, and brotherhoods in cities . . ." *Tr & Cr,* I, iii, 104.

deign, *v.* **1** to condescend to accept: "I fear my Julia would not deign my lines . . ." *Two Gent,* I, i, 146. **2** to accept without disdain: ". . . thy palate then did deign/ The roughest berry, on the rudest hedge . . ." *Ant & Cleo,* I, iv, 63–64.

deity, *n.* divine powers: "Divinest patroness . . . convey thy deity/ Aboard our dancing boat . . ." *Per,* III, i, 11–13.

deject, *adj.* **1** dejected: ". . . reason and respect/ Make livers pale, and lustihood deject." *Tr & Cr,* II, ii, 49–50. —*v.* **2** to decrease or lessen: ". . . nor once deject the courage of our minds/ Because Cassandra's mad . . ." *Tr & Cr,* II, ii, 122–123.

delay, *n.* [often pl.] postponement; here, of what seemed to be an imminent death warrant: ". . . piteous plainings of the pretty babes . . . Forc'd me to seek delays for them and me . . ." *Errors,* I, i, 72–74.

deliberate, *adj.* guided by logic, not by love: "O these deliber-ate fools! when they do choose,/ They have the wisdom by their wit to lose." *Merch,* II, ix, 80–81.

delicate, *adj.* **1** refined; noble: "Witness this army of such mass and charge,/ Led by a delicate and tender prince . . ." *Ham,* IV, iv, 47–48. **2** elegantly crafted: ". . . very responsive to the hilts, most delicate carriages, and of/ very liberal conceit." *Ham,* V, ii, 149–150. **3** sensitive to pain; vulnerable: "When the mind's free/ The body's delicate . . ." *Lear,* III, iv, 11–12. —*n.* **4** [usually pl.] luxuries; also, delicacies: "All which secure and sweetly he enjoys,/ Is far beyond a prince's delicates—" *3 Hen 6,* II, v, 50–51.

delighted, *adj.* **1** experiencing (or used to experiencing) delight: ". . . and the delighted spirit/ To bath in fiery floods . . ." *Meas*, III, i, 120–121. **2** delightful: "If virtue no delighted beauty lack,/ Your son-in-law is far more fair than black." *Oth*, I, iii, 289–290.

delineate, *past part.* pictured or imagined: "Still do I see in him delineate/ His mother's visage: those his eyes are hers . . ." *Edw 3*, II, ii, 86–87.

deliver, *v.* **1** to report or communicate [to]: "More health and happiness betide my liege/ Than can my care-tun'd tongue deliver him." *Rich 2*, III, ii, 91–92. **2** to reveal: "O that I serv'd that lady,/ And might not be deliver'd to the world . . ." *T Night*, I, ii, 41–42. **3** to set free: "If he may be conveniently delivered,/ I would he were . . ." *T Night*, IV, ii, 70–71. **4** to state; declare: "Ay, and a subtle; as he most learnedly deliver'd." *Temp*, II, i, 44. **5** to send away; Bertram will be assuming adult responsibilities: "In delivering my son from me, I bury a second/ husband." *All's W*, I, i, 1–2. **6 deliver up,** to release; turn over: "My uncle is return'd;/ Deliver up my Lord of Westmoreland." *1 Hen 4*, V, ii, 27–28.

Delphos, *n.* Delphi and the Delphic oracle: "To sacred Delphos, to Apollo's temple . . ." *W Tale*, II, i, 183.

delve, *v.* **1** to dig: "And delves the parallels [furrows] in beauty's brow . . ." *Sonn 60*, 10. **2 delve him to the root,** give a precise account of his lineage: "What's his name and birth?"/ "I cannot delve him to the root . . ." *Cymb*, I, i, 27–28.

delver, *n.* digger; here, a grave-digger: "Nay, but hear you, Goodman Delver—" *Ham*, V, i, 14.

demand, *v.* **1** to ask; question: "Where/ when? what visor? why demand you this?" *Love's L*, V, ii, 386. **2** to learn; ascertain: "Methinks our pleasure might have been demanded,/ Ere you had spoke so far." *Lear*, V, iii, 63. **3 demanding after,** asking about: ". . . even but now, demanding after you,/ Denied me to come in . . ." *Lear*, III, ii, 65–66.
—*n.* **4** question; query: ". . . any/ thing you know than comes from her demand/ out of the letter." *Lear*, I, v, 3–4. **5 not your demand,** not worth your question: "My good lord,/ Not your demand . . ." *Hen 8*, II, iii, 51–52.

demanded of, *past part.* questioned by: "Besides, to be demanded of a sponge—what replication/ should be made by the son of a king?" *Ham*, IV, ii, 11–12.

demean, *v.* **demean oneself,** to behave: "Now out of doubt Antipholus is mad,/ Else would he never so demean himself . . ." *Errors*, IV, iii, 78–79.

demeanor, *n.* **cold demeanor,** lack of fighting spirit: ". . . I perceive/ But cold demeanour in Octavius' wing . . ." *J Caes*, V, ii, 3–4.

demerits, *n.* merits; just deserts: "Opinion, that so sticks on Martius, shall/ Of his demerits rob Cominius." *Cor*, I, i, 270–271.

demesnes, *n. pl.* domains; estates: ". . . her fine foot, straight leg, and quivering thigh,/ And the demesnes that there adjacent lie . . ." *Rom & Jul*, II, i, 19–20.

demi-cannon, *n.* large cannon: "What's this? A sleeve? 'Tis like a demi-cannon." *Shrew*, IV, iii, 88.

demi-coronal, *n.* small coronet: "Marquess Dorset . . . on his head a/ demi-coronal of gold." [SD] *Hen 8*, IV, i, 36.

demi-natured, *adj.* possessed of half the nature of another: "As had he been incorps'd and demi-natur'd/ With the brave beast." *Ham*, IV, vii, 86–87.

demi-puppets, *n.* seeming puppets; that is, the tiny elves: ". . . you demi-puppets that/ By moonshine do the green sour ringlets make . . ." *Temp*, V, i, 36–37.

demise, *v.* to convey; transmit: ". . . what honour,/ Canst thou demise to any child of mine?" *Rich 3*, IV, iv, 247–248.

demonstrative, *adj.* proving clearly: "In every branch truly demonstrative . . ." *Hen 5*, II, iv, 89.

demsel, *n.* misuse for "damsel," young woman: "I was taken with none, sir: I was taken with a/ demsel." *Love's L*, I, i, 282–283.

demure, *adj.* **1** solemn; grave: ". . . to no creature living but/ To me should utter, with demure confidence . . ." *Hen 8*, I, ii, 166–167.
—*v.* **2** to look demurely: "Your wife Octavia . . . shall acquire no honour/ Demuring upon me . . ." *Ant & Cleo*, IV, xv, 27–29.

demurely, *adv.* solemnly; gravely: "Hark the drums/ Demurely wake the sleepers." *Ant & Cleo*, IV, ix, 29–30.

denay, *n.* denial: "My love can give no place, bide [endure] no denay." *T Night*, II, iv, 125.

denayed, *v.* old past part. of DENY; refused: "Then let him be denay'd the regentship." *2 Hen 6*, I, iii, 104.

denier, *n.* copper coin, the tenth part of a penny; hence, the smallest possible amount: "Let them coin his nose, let them coin his cheeks,/ I'll not pay a denier." *1 Hen 4*, III, iii, 76–77.

Denmark, *n.* king of Denmark; Claudius here refers to himself: "No jocund health that Denmark drinks today/ But the great cannon to the clouds shall tell . . ." *Ham,* I, ii, 125–126.

denote, *v.* to mark or indicate; single out: "The better to denote her to the Doctor . . ." *Wives,* IV, vi, 38.

denotement, *n.* **1** noting; observation: ". . . given up himself to the/ contemplation, mark and denotement of her parts/ and graces." *Oth,* II, iii, 307–309. **2 close denotements,** [in some editions "dilations"] manifestations of secret thoughts or concerns: ". . . but in a man that's just,/ They are close denotements, working from the heart . . ." *Oth,* III, iii, 126–127.

denounce, *v.* **1** to call down: "I will denounce a curse upon his head." *K John,* III, i, 245. **2** to declare; proclaim: "If [the war were] not denounc'd against us, why should not we/ Be there in person?" *Ant & Cleo,* III, vii, 5–6.

denunciation, *n.* formal declaration; here, either the banns or the wedding ceremony: ". . . we do the denunciation lack/ Of outward order." *Meas,* I, ii, 137–138.

deny, *v.* **1** to refuse: "If you deny to dance, let's hold more chat." *Love's L,* V, ii, 228. **2** to disavow; cancel: "My acts, decrees, and statutes I deny." *Rich 2,* IV, i, 213. **3 For shame! deny,** How can you insist: "For shame! deny that thou bear'st love to any . . ." *Sonn* 10, 1.

depart, *v.* **1** to give up; surrender: "To have his title live in Aquitaine;/ Which we much rather had depart withal . . ." *Love's L,* II, i, 145–146. —*n.* **2** departure: "I had in charge at my depart for France . . ." *2 Hen 6,* I, i, 2.

departure, *n.* death: ". . . the Dauphin's drum . . . Sings heavy music to thy timorous soul,/ And mine shall ring thy dire departure out." *1 Hen 6,* IV, ii, 39–41.

depend, *v.* **1** to impend; be a threat: "In me moe [more] woes than words are now depending . . ." *Luc,* 1615. **2** to accompany a person as a dependent: ". . . the remainders, that shall still depend,/ To be such men as may besort your age . . ." *Lear,* I, iv, 258–259. **3** to lean: ". . . Cupids/ Of silver, each on one foot standing, nicely/ Depending on their brands [torches]." *Cymb,* II, iv, 89–91.

dependency, *n.* sequence; succession: "Such a dependency of thing on thing,/ As e'er I heard in madness." *Meas,* V, i, 65–66.

dependent or dependant, *n.* **1** [often pl.] household servants: ". . . a great abatement of kindness/ appears as in the general dependants . . ." *Lear,* I, iv, 63–64. **2 free dependant,** guiltless or blameless follower: "I am your free dependant." *Meas,* IV, iii, 90.

depender, *n.* person who depends on another; dependent: "What shalt thou expect,/ To be depender on a thing that leans?" *Cymb,* I, vi, 57–58.

deplore, *v.* to bemoan; lament: ". . . never more/ Will I my master's tears to you deplore." *T Night,* III, i, 163–164.

depose, *v.* **1** to take a deposition from: ". . . formally, according to our law,/ Depose him in the justice of his cause." *Rich 2,* I, iii, 29–30. **2** to give a deposition; swear: "I'll depose I had him in mine arms/ With all th'effect of love." *Meas,* V, i, 197–198.

depositary, *n.* trustee: "Made you my guardians, my depositaries . . ." *Lear,* II, iv, 253.

depravation, *n.* disparagement or scorn; also, defamation or slander: ". . . stubborn critics, apt, without a theme/ For depravation . . ." *Tr & Cr,* V, ii, 130–131.

deprave, *v.* to belittle or slander: "Who lives that's not depraved or depraves?" *Timon,* I, ii, 136.

depressed, *adj.* humbled: "Depress'd he is already, and depos'd/ 'Tis doubt he will be." *Rich 2,* III, iv, 68–69.

deputation, *n.* **1** appointment of another to act in one's place: ". . . his friends by deputation could not/ So soon be drawn . . ." *1 Hen 4,* IV, i, 32–33. **2** exalted position; eminence: "Sometime, great Agamemnon,/ Thy topless deputation he puts on . . ." *Tr & Cr,* I, iii, 151–152.

deputed, *adj.* **deputed sword,** sword of office, symbolizing a deputy's power: "Not the king's crown, nor the deputed sword . . ." *Meas,* II, ii, 60.

deputy's wife of the ward, *n.* wife of the deputy of the ward, usually a model of respectability: ". . . for womanhood, Maid Marian may be/ the deputy's wife of the ward to thee." *1 Hen 4,* III, iii, 112–113.

derision, *n.* mockery: "When they next wake, all this derision/ Shall seem a dream . . ." *M N Dream,* III, ii, 370–371.

derivative, *n.* something to be passed on to succeeding generations: ". . . for honour,/ 'Tis a derivative from me to mine . . ." *W Tale,* III, ii, 43–44.

derive, *v.* to explain or describe [how a conclusion was reached]: ". . . and, as aforesaid, Patroclus is a fool."/ "Derive this: come." *Tr & Cr,* II, iii, 62–63.

dern, *adj.* (of land) wild and uninhabited; also, dark and dreary: "By many a dern and painful perch/ Of Pericles the careful search . . ." *Per,* III, Chor., 15–16.

derogate, *v.* **1** to lose face or dignity: "You cannot derogate, my lord." *Cymb,* II, i, 44.
—*adj.* **2** debased: "And from her derogate body never spring/ A babe to honour her!" *Lear,* I, iv, 288–289.

derogately, *adv.* disparagingly: ". . . more laugh'd at, that I should/ Once name you derogately . . ." *Ant & Cleo,* II, ii, 33–34.

derogation, *n.* loss of face or dignity: "Is it fit I went to look upon him? Is there no derogation in't?" *Cymb,* II, i, 42–43.

desartless, *adj.* misuse of "deserving": ". . . who think you the most desartless man to be/ constable?" *M Ado,* III, iii, 9–10.

descant, *n.* **1** (in music) the treble part, esp. variations on a melody: ". . . you are too flat;/ And mar the concord with too harsh a descant . . ." *Two Gent,* I, ii, 94–95. **2** improvization; here, argument or variation: "For on that ground I'll build a holy descant." *Rich 3,* III, vii, 48.
—*v.* **3** to improvize harmoniously over a theme; extemporize: "While thou on Tereus descants better skill." *Luc,* 1134.

descension, *n.* descent, esp. on the social scale: "From a god to a bull? A heavy descension!" *2 Hen 4,* II, ii, 166.

descent, *v.* **1** old past part. of *descend;* descended: "Are we not both Plantagenets by birth,/ And from two brothers lineally descent?" *3 Hen 6,* I, i, 125–126.
—*n.* **2** lineage; heritage: ". . . slander Valentine,/ With falsehood, cowardice, and poor descent . . ." *Two Gent,* III, ii, 31–32. **3** lowest part; here, the sole of the foot: "To the descent and dust below thy foot,/ A most toad-spotted traitor." *Lear,* V, iii, 137–138.

description, *v.* parson's misuse for "describe": "Master Slender, I will/ description the matter to you . . ." *Wives,* I, i, 195–196.

descry, *v.* **1** to reveal; make known: "What's past and what's to come she can descry." *1 Hen 6,* I, ii, 57. **2** to espy; behold: "We have descried, upon our neighbouring shore,/ A portly sail of ships . . ." *Per,* I, iv, 60–61. **3** to discover: "We were descried: they'll mock us now downright." *Love's L,* V, ii, 389.
—*n.* **4** view or discovery; here, of enemy troops: ". . . the main descry/ Stands on the hourly thought [any hour now]." *Lear,* IV, vi, 214–215.

desert, *n.* **1** persons of merit or great worth: "As, to behold desert a beggar born . . ." *Sonn 66,* 2. **2** [usually pl.] persons of varying worth or capacity: "The base o' th' mount/ Is rank'd with all deserts . . ." *Timon,* I, i, 66–67. **3 without desert,** without my, your, etc., deserving it: "My wife (but I protest, without desert)/ Hath oftentimes upbraided me withal . . ." *Errors,* III, i, 112–113.
—*adj.* **4** uninhabited: "To trust the opportunity of night/ And the ill counsel of a desert place . . ." *M N Dream,* II, i, 217–218.

deserve, *v.* **1** to earn: "Is't not enough . . . That I did never . . . Deserve a sweet look from Demetrius' eye . . ." *M N Dream,* II, ii, 124–126. **2** to requite; reward: "On, good Roderigo, I'll deserve your pains." *Oth,* I, i, 183–184. **3 study deserving,** strive to be worthy: "I . . . sue [seek] to know you better."/ "Sir, I shall study deserving." *Lear,* I, i, 30–31.

deserved, *adj.* deserving: ". . . our renowned Rome, whose gratitude/ Towards her deserved children is enroll'd/ In Jove's own book . . ." *Cor,* III, i, 288–290.

deserving, *n.* action deserving of a reward: "This seems a fair deserving, and must draw me/ That which my father loses . . ." *Lear,* III, iii, 25–26.

design[1], *n.* **1** goal or destination; here, an intended victim: "With Tarquin's ravishing strides, towards his design/ Moves like a ghost." *Mac,* II, i, 55, 56. **2** enterprise: "Gonzalo . . . who being then appointed/ Master of this design . . ." *Temp,* I, ii, 161–163. **3** [pl.] proceedings: ". . . the marshal and such officers/ Appointed to direct these fair designs." *Rich 2,* I, iii, 44–45. **4** intention: "His giving out [declarations] were of an infinite distance/ From his true-meant design." *Meas,* I, iv, 54–55. **5 deep designs,** enterprises of great importance: ". . . the Mayor and aldermen,/ In deep designs . . . Are come to have some conference . . ." *Rich 3,* III, vii, 65–68.

design[2], *v.* to designate; specify: ". . . as, by the same cov'nant/ And carriage of the article design'd . . ." *Ham,* I, i, 96–97.

designments, *n.* purposes; designs: ". . . serv'd his designments/ In mine own person . . ." *Cor,* V, vi, 35–36.

desire, *n.* **1** [often pl.] objective or purpose: "Most fair return of greetings and desires." *Ham,* II, ii, 60. **2** an unfulfilled or frustrated longing: ". . . but most miserable/ Is the desire that's glorious." *Cymb,* I, vii, 6–7
—*v.* **3** to ask; request: ". . . desire Gratiano to come anon to my lodging." *Merch,* II, ii, 112.

desirous to be blest, *adj.* truly repentant: "And when you are desirous to be blest,/ I'll blessing beg of you." *Ham,* III, iv, 173–174.

desolation, *n.* destitution: "O, there were desolation of gaolers/ and gallowses!" *Cymb,* V, iv, 206–207.

despatch, *v.* See **dispatch** (def. 1).

desperate, *adj.* **1** involving risk or danger: "... tutored in the rudiments/ Of many desperate studies ..." *As You,* V, iv, 31–32. **2** (of debts) uncollectible: "... these debts may well be call'd desperate ones, for a madman owes 'em." *Timon,* III, iv, 100–101. **3** reckless: "As dissolute as desperate! But yet/ Through both I see some sparks of better hope ..." *Rich 2,* V, iii, 20–21. **4** bold: "Sir Paris, I will make a desperate tender/ Of my child's love." *Rom & Jul,* III, iv, 12–13. **5 desperate of shame and state,** recklessly indifferent to reputation or to civil behavior: "Here in the streets, desperate of shame and state,/ In private brabble did we apprehend him." *T Night,* V, i, 62–63. **6 desperate of their bones,** despairing of saving themselves: "Yon island carrions, desperate of their bones ..." *Hen 5,* IV, ii, 39. **7 desperate train,** retinue of irresponsible men: "Shut up your doors;/ He is attended with a desperate train ..." *Lear,* II, iv, 306–307.

desperate assurance, *n.* certainty without hope: "... you should put your lord/ into a desperate assurance she will none of him." *T Night,* II, i, 6–7.

desperately, *adv.* out of desperation or despair: "Your eldest daughters have fordone themselves,/ And desperately are dead." *Lear,* V, iii, 291–292.

despised, *adj.* **my despised time,** the rest of my wretched life: "And what's to come, of my despised time,/ Is nought but bitterness." *Oth,* I, i, 161–162.

despite, *v.* **1** to spite: "Only to despite them I will endeavour anything." *M Ado,* II, ii, 31.
—*n.* **2** scorn or contempt: "Thou wast ever an obstinate heretic in the/ despite of beauty." *M Ado,* I, i, 217–218. **3** shame: "In vain I spurn at my confirm'd despite ..." *Luc,* 1026. **4** abuse: "... my lord hath so bewhor'd her,/ Thrown such despite, and heavy terms upon her ..." *Oth,* IV, ii, 117–118. **5 in despite, a.** in spite of everything; here, despite a reluctance to cry: "An onion ... in a napkin being close convey'd,/ Shall in despite enforce a watery eye." *Shrew,* Ind., i, 124–126. **b.** out of spite: "And in despite I'll cram thee with more food." *Rom & Jul,* V, iii, 48. **6 in despite of,** contrary to; in defiance of: "... I will depart in quiet,/ And in despite of mirth mean to be merry." *Errors,* III, i, 107–108. **7 in high despite,** with excessive malice: "... the Queen,/ Who crown'd the gracious Duke in high despite,/ Laugh'd in his face ..." *3 Hen 6,* II, i, 58–60. **8 in my despite,** despite my wishes: "What, would you bury him in my despite?" *T Andr,* I, i, 361. **9 of all despite,**

full of malice: "Foul fiend of France and hag of all despite ..." *1 Hen 6,* III, ii, 52.

despiteful, *adj.* hateful; cruel or malicious: "O despiteful love, unconstant womankind!" *Shrew,* IV, ii, 14.

Destinies, *n. pl.* the three Fates, who spun the thread of life, determined its length, then cut it off at the appointed time: "Or till the Destinies do cut his thread of life." *Per,* I, ii, 108.

detain, *v.* **1** to keep back; withhold: "Would that alone [only] a toy he would detain,/ So he would keep fair quarter with his bed ..." *Errors,* II, i, 107–108. **2** to confiscate: "... he frets/ That Lepidus ... Should be depos'd, and, being [so], that we detain/ All his revenue." *Ant & Cleo,* III, vi, 27–30.

detect, *v.* **1** to expose; reveal: "Sham'st thou not, knowing whence thou art extraught,/ To let thy tongue detect thy base-born heart?" *3 Hen 6,* II, ii, 142–143. **2** to suspect or accuse: "I have never heard the absent Duke much detected/ for women ..." *Meas,* III, ii, 118–119.

detention, *n.* withholding of payment or a failure to pay: "... clamorous demands of debt ... And the detention of long since due debts ..." *Timon,* II, i, 44.

determinate, *v.* **1** put an end to; terminate: "The sly slow hours shall not determinate/ The dateless limit of thy dear exile ..." *Rich 2,* I, iii, 150–151.
—*adj.* **2** expired; at an end: "My bonds in [claims on] thee are all determinate." *Sonn 87,* 4. **3** intended; planned: "... my determinate voyage is mere/ extravagancy." *T Night,* II, i, 10–11. **4** decisive: "... some accident, wherein none can be so determinate/ as the removing of Cassio. *Oth,* IV, ii, 226–227. **5 determinate resolution,** final decision or settlement: "Ere a determinate resolution, he ... did require a respite ..." *Hen 8,* II, iv, 174–175.

determination, *n.* **1** mind; intention: "... would to God/ You were of our determination!" *1 Hen 4,* IV, iii, 32–33. **2** termination; end [legal term]: "So should that beauty which you hold in lease/ Find no determination ..." *Sonn 13,* 5–6.

determine, *v.* **1** to conclude; put an end to: "Till his friend sickness have determin'd me?" *2 Hen 4,* IV, v, 81. **2** to settle on; decide: "But what we do determine, oft we break." *Ham,* III, ii, 182. **3** to come to an end; dissolve or melt: "... the first stone/ Drop in my neck: as it determines, so/ Dissolve my life ..." *Ant & Cleo,* III, xiii, 160–162. **4** to be determined or concluded: "Must all determine here?" *Cor,* III, iii, 43. **5 determine of,** to decide on: "... the cause why we are met/ Is to determine of the coronation." *Rich 3,* III, iv, 1–2.

determined, *adj.* **1** planned; agreed-on: "... tell my lord the emperor/ How I have govern'd our determin'd jest?" *T Andr,* V, ii, 138–139. **2 determined respite,** predetermined time to which Buckingham's punishment has been postponed: "This, this All-Souls' day to my fearful soul/ Is the determin'd respite of my wrongs ..." *Rich 3,* V, i, 18–19.

detest, *v.* misuse for "protest" [swear]: "My wife, sir, whom I detest before heaven ..." *Meas,* II, i, 68.

detested, *adj.* detestable: "Glory grows guilty of detested crimes ..." *Love's L,* IV, i, 31.

detraction, *n.* **1** adverse criticism: "... happy are they that/ hear their detractions and can put them to mending." *M Ado,* II, iii, 220–221. **2** slander; calumny: "Detraction will not suf-fer/ it. Therefore I'll none of it." *1 Hen 4,* V, i, 139–140. **3** trou-ble; misfortune: "... you/ might see more detraction at your heels than/ fortunes before you." *T Night,* II, v, 136–138.

Deucalion, *n.* Noah of the classical world, survivor of the Great Flood: "Not hold thee of our blood, no, not our kin,/ Farre than Deucalion off ..." *W Tale,* IV, iv, 431–432.

deuce-ace, *n.* throw of the dice producing two and one: "I am sure you know how much the gross sum/ of deuce-ace amounts to." *Love's L,* I, ii, 42–43.

devest, *v.* to undress: "... like bride and groom,/ Devesting them to bed ..." *Oth,* II, iii, 171–172.

device, *n.* **1** plan or scheme: "... if we meet in the city, we shall be dogged with/ company, and our devices known." *M N Dream,* I, ii, 96–97. **2** story or plot: "That is an old device, and it was play'd/ When I from Thebes came last a conquer-or." *M N Dream,* V, i, 50–51. **3** any scheming or any fanciful contrivance: "But I will forward with/ my device." *Love's L,* V, ii, 655–656. **4** distinctive emblem, usually with a motto, dis-played on a knight's shield: "'Tis now your honour, daughter, to entertain/ The labour of each knight in his device." *Per,* II, ii, 14–15. **5** manner, disposition, or intent: "Yet he's gentle ... full of noble device ..." *As You,* I, i, 164–165. **6** stage mecha-nism: "Enter Ariel, like a Harpy; claps his wings/ upon the table; and, with a quaint device, the banquet vanishes." [SD] *Temp,* III, iii, 52. **7 device and practice,** plots and intrigues: "I shall perish/ Under device and practice." *Hen 8,* I, i, 203–204. **8 habit and device,** dress and heraldic insignia; here, evidence of his new knighthood: "And not alone in habit and device,/ Exterior form, outward accoutrement ..." *K John,* I, i, 210–211.

devil, *n.* **1 devil in the old play,** stock character of the Devil in the old morality plays; he was subdued by Vice, wielding a wooden dagger, and humiliated by having his nails clipped:

"... this roaring devil i' th' old play, that every one/ may pare his nails, with a wooden dagger ..." *Hen 5,* IV, iv, 73–74. **2 the devil,** exclam. of disgust or impatience; here Dromio cannot resist a pun on their supposed demonic possession: "Be mad, good master; cry 'the devil.'" *Errors,* IV, iv, 125. **3 the devil's grace,** His Grace the Devil: "A goodly prize, fit for the devil's grace!" *1 Hen 6,* V, iii, 33. **4 what a devil's name,** what in the devil's name: "Why, what a devil's name, tailor, call'st thou this?" *Shrew,* IV, iii, 92. **5 with the devil's name,** with the devil's help: "What an unweighed/ behaviour hath this Flemish drunkard picked—/with the devil's name—out of my conversation ..." *Wives,* II, i, 22–24.

devilish-holy, *adj.* wicked, because of your cunning; sacred, because of your vow: "When truth kills truth, O devilish-holy fray!" *M N Dream,* III, ii, 129.

devise, *v.* **1** to imagine or conceive; understand: "... I never injuried thee,/ But love thee better than thou canst de vise ..." *Rom & Jul,* III, i, 67–68. **2** to plan: "Through Athens' gates have we devis'd to steal." *M N Dream,* I, i, 213. **3** to offer; bestow on: "He cannot but with measure fit the honours/ Which we devise him." *Cor,* II, ii, 123–124. **4 devise me,** explain [it] to me: "And in a postscript here he says 'Alone.'/ Can you devise me?" *Ham,* IV, vii, 51–52. **5 devised well for her,** invented a flattering description of her: "There she appear'd indeed; or my reporter/ devis'd well for her." *Ant & Cleo,* II, ii, 188–189. **6 What devise you on?** What have you decided to do?: "My lord, where are you? What devise you on?/ Shall we give over Orleans, or no?" *1 Hen 6,* I, ii, 124–125.

devision, *n.* deployment of troops [in a battle]: "That nev-er set a squadron in the field,/ Nor the devision of a battle knows ..." *Oth,* I, i, 22–23.

devote, *adj.* devoted: "... so devote to Aristotle's checks/ As Ovid be an outcast quite abjur'd." *Shrew,* I, i, 32–33.

devotion, *n.* devoutness or piety: "... with devotion's visage/ And pious action we do sugar o'er/ The devil himself." *Ham,* III, i, 47–49.

devour, *v.* **devour their reason,** appar. ref. to the open-mouthed astonishment of the lords: "I perceive, these lords ... do so much admire/ That they devour their reason ..." *Temp,* V, i, 153–155.

devouring, *adj.* ravishing; captivating or entralling: "Bravely the figure of this Harpy hast thou/ Perform'd, my Ariel; a grace it had devouring ..." *Temp,* III, iii, 83–84.

dew, *n.* **1** tears: "The night of dew that on my cheeks down flows ..." *Love's L,* IV, iii, 27. **2** [pl.] blessings; also, perh.

wordplay on "dues": "A hand as fruitful as the land that feeds us;/ His dews fall everywhere." *Hen 8*, I, iii, 56–57.

dewberry, *n.* blackberry: "Feed him with apricocks and dewberries . . ." *M N Dream*, III, i, 159.

dew-drop, *n.* common term for a pearl; also, ref. to wearing of ear ornaments by men: "I must go seek some dew-drops here,/ And hang a pearl in every cowslip's ear." *M N Dream*, II, i, 14–15.

dewlap, *n.* loose skin at the throat: "And when she drinks, against her lips I bob,/ And on her wither'd dewlap pour the ale." *M N Dream*, II, i, 49–50.

dexter, *adj., adv.* **1** right; on or to the right side (an implied ref. to a coat of arms): ". . . my mother's blood/ Runs on the dexter cheek . . ." *Tr & Cr*, IV, v, 126–127. Cf. **sinister**. **2** proper; appropriate: "To give the smooth and dexter way to me/ That owe it him by nature." *More*, III, ii, 11–12.

dexteriously, *adv.* dexterously: ". . . give me/ leave to prove you a fool."/ "Can you do it?"/ "Dexteriously, good madonna." *T Night*, I, v, 55–58.

diable, *n.* [French] devil: "*O diable, diable!* Vat [what] is in my closet?" *Wives*, I, iv, 62.

Diablo, *n.* [Spanish] devil: "Who's that that rings the bell?—Diablo . . . ho,/ The town will rise . . ." *Oth*, II, iii, 152–153.

diadem, *n.* royal crown: ". . . a worthless king,/ Having neither subject, wealth, nor diadem." *2 Hen 6*, IV, i, 80–81.

dial, *n.* clock or watch; also, a sundial: "And then he drew a dial from his poke [pocket] . . ." *As You*, II, vii, 20.

dialect, *n.* manner of expression: "There is a prone and speechless dialect/ Such as move men . . ." *Meas*, I, ii, 173–174.

dialogue, *v.* **1** to converse; here, carry on an imaginary conversation: "How dost, fool?/ Dost dialogue with thy shadow?" *Timon*, II, i, 55–56. **2** to write in the form of a dialogue: "And dialogued for him what he would say . . ." *Lover's Comp*, 132.

diameter, *n.* extent; length and breadth: "Whose whisper o'er the world's diameter . . . may miss our name . . ." *Ham*, IV, i, 41–43.

Dian, *n.* var. of **Diana**: ". . . the consecrated snow/ That lies on Dian's lap!" *Timon*, IV, iii, 388–389.

Diana, *n.* **1** goddess of chastity and the moon: "I will die as chaste as/ Diana, unless I be obtained by the manner of my/ father's will." *Merch*, I, ii, 102–104. **2 Diana's waiting-women**, the stars, attending on Diana the moon: "By all Diana's waiting-women yond,/ And by herself, I will not tell you whose." *Tr & Cr*, V, ii, 91–92. **3 wear Diana's livery**, to vow chastity: "One twelve moons more she'll wear Diana's livery . . ." *Per*, II, v, 10.

diapason, *n.* bass accompaniment coupled with melody: "So I at each sad strain will strain a tear/ And with deep groans the diapason bear . . ." *Luc*, 1132.

diaper, *n.* towel: "Another bear the ewer, the third a diaper . . ." *Shrew*, Ind., i, 55.

dicer, *n.* person who gambles with dice: ". . . makes marriage vows/ As false as dicers' oaths—" *Ham*, III, iv, 44–45.

Dick, *n.* fool; blockhead: ". . . some Dick,/ That smiles his cheek in years, and knows the trick/ To make my lady laugh . . ." *Love's L*, V, ii, 464–466.

dickens, *n.* **what the dickens**, 16th-cent. expression of uncertain meaning, prob. the equiv. of "what the heck": "I cannot tell what the dickens his name is/ my husband had him of." *Wives*, III, ii, 16–17.

Dickon, *n.* contemptuous nickname for "Richard": "For Dickon thy master is bought and sold." *Rich 3*, V, iii, 306.

diction, *n.* **make true diction of**, [to] speak truly of: ". . . to make true diction of him, his semblable is his mirror . . ." *Ham*, V, ii, 117–118.

Dictynna, *n.* ancient Roman name of **DIANA**: "Dictynna, goodman Dull; Dictynna, goodman Dull." *Love's L*, IV, ii, 35.

Dido, *n.* (in Vergil's "Aeneid") a queen of Carthage who immolated herself after being abandoned by Aeneas: ". . . he [Aeneas] did discourse/ To love-sick Dido's sad-attending ear/ The story of that baleful burning night . . ." *T Andr*, V, iii, 81–83.

die[1], *v.* **1** common sexual innuendo, wherein death is compared to experiencing an orgasm: "I will live in thy heart, die in thy lap, and be buried/ in thy eyes . . ." *M Ado*, V, ii, 94–95. **2** to prepare constantly for death: ". . . the Queen . . . Died every day she liv'd." *Mac*, IV, iii, 109–111. **3 die on**, to fight to the death with: "I'll die on him that says so but yourself." *Two Gent*, II, iv, 109. **4 die the death**, to be put to death: "She hath betray'd me, and shall die the death." *Ant & Cleo*, IV, xiv, 26. **5 only dying**, dying alone: ". . . whom to leave/ Is only bitter to him, only dying . . ." *Hen 8*, II, i, 73–74.

die[2], *n.* **1** one of a pair of dice: "With die and/ drab [whores] I purchased this caparison [rags] . . ." *W Tale*, IV, iii, 26–27.

2 wordplay on this sense and "expire": "No die, but an ace [throw of one with a die] for him; for he is but one." *M N Dream*, V, i, 296.

die, v. Also, **d' ye.** do ye; do you: "Why, die take it; and the gods give thee good/ on't!" *Per*, II, i, 145–146.

diet, n. 1 food, esp. that provided at a meal: "Your diet shall be in all places alike." *Timon*, III, vi, 65. **2 for diet,** with regard to what he eats: "Your worm is your only emperor for diet . . ." *Ham*, IV, iii, 21. **3 kept an evil diet,** engaged in sexual excesses: "O, he hath kept an evil diet long,/ And over-much consum'd his royal person . . ." *Rich 3*, I, i, 139–140. **4 nice and wat'rish diet,** [require] meager nourishment: "The policy may either last so long,/ Or feed upon such nice and wat'rish diet . . ." *Oth*, III, iii, 14–15.
—*v.* **5** to feed; nourish: "I will attend my husband, be his nurse,/ Diet his sickness . . ." *Errors*, V, i, 98–99. **6** to restrict; limit or keep: "Not till after midnight, for he is dieted to his/ hour [appointed time]." *All's W*, IV, iii, 28–29. **7** to deprive: "You that have turn'd off a first so noble wife/ May justly diet me." *All's W*, V, iii, 219–220. **8 dieted in,** fed on: "As if I lov'd my little should be dieted/ in praises sauc'd with lies." *Cor*, I, ix, 51–52. **9 dieted to my request,** dined so as to be receptive to my request: "Therefore I'll watch him/ Till he be dieted to my request . . ." *Cor*, V, i, 56–57. **10 diet me with,** permit me to have: "Thou art all the comfort/ The gods will diet me with." *Cymb*, III, iv, 181–182.

dieter, n. person who prepares food according to the rules of medicine: ". . . sauced our broths, as Juno had been sick,/ And he her dieter." *Cymb*, IV, ii, 50–51.

Dieu de batailles! [French] God of battles! [a mild oath]: "Dieu de batailles! where [from where] have they this mettle?" *Hen 5*, III, v, 15.

Dieu vivant! [French] the living God [a mild oath]: "O Dieu vivant! shall a few sprays of us,/ The emptying of our fathers' luxury . . ." *Hen 5*, III, v, 5–6.

Di faciant laudis summa sit ista tuae! [Latin] The gods grant that this may be your greatest deed [the murder of an innocent]. *3 Hen 6*, I, iii, 47.

difference, n. 1 conflict: "Vexed I am/ Of late with passions of some difference . . ." *J Caes*, I, ii, 38–39. **2** quarrel; argument: "What is your difference? speak." *Lear*, II, ii, 51. **3** personal characteristic: ". . . an absolute gentleman, full of most excellent/ differences . . ." *Ham*, V, ii, 107–108. **4** mark or degree of distinction [a term in heraldry for distinguishing different members or branches of a family]: "You must wear your rue/ with a difference." *Ham*, IV, v, 180–181. **5** difference in rank or station; here, between prince and peasant girl: "To me

the difference forges dread . . ." *W Tale*, IV, iv, 17. **6** variety: ". . . you shall have the difference/ of all complexions [races]." *Per*, IV, ii, 75–76. **7** variation: ". . . my verse to constancy confined,/ One thing expressing, leaves out difference." *Sonn 105*, 7–8. **8 difference and decay,** change and decline [of fortune]: "That from your first of difference and decay,/ Have follow'd your sad steps,—" *Lear*, V, iii, 288. **9 make difference,** to tell the difference; discriminate [among]: ". . . as long as I have an eye to make difference of/ men's liking . . ." *Wives*, II, i, 54–55. **10 teach you differences,** teach you your place: "Come, sir, arise, away! I'll teach you differences:/ away, away!" *Lear*, I, iv, 94–95.

differency, n. var. of **difference:** "There is differency between a grub and a butterfly . . ." *Cor*, V, iv, 11.

differing multitudes, n. the common people of lower rank; here, flattery by the mob: "That nothing-gift of differing multitudes . . ." *Cymb*, III, viii, 57–58.

diffidence, n. 1 distrust; suspicion: "We have been guided by thee hitherto,/ And of thy cunning had no diffidence . . ." *1 Hen 6*, III, iii, 9–10. **2 needless diffidences,** groundless suspicions: ". . . needless/ diffidences, banishment of friends, dissipation/ of cohorts . . ." *Lear*, I, ii, 154–156.

diffused, adj. 1 wild; disordered: ". . . swearing and stern looks, diffus'd attire,/ And every thing that seems unnatural." *Hen 5*, V, ii, 61–62. **2** spread about, in the manner of a contagion: "Vouchsafe, diffus'd infection of a man . . ." *Rich 3*, I, ii, 78. **3** (of a song) with the parts divided equally among participants: "Let them from forth a sawpit rush at once/ With some diffused song . . ." *Wives*, IV, iv, 53–54.

dig, v. to dig up: "For who digs hills because they do aspire . . ." *Per*, I, iv, 5.

digest, v. 1 to incorporate; assimilate: "Come on, my son, in whom my house's name/ Must be digested . . ." *All's W*, V, iii, 73–74. **2** to accept or endure: ". . . our feasts/ In every mess have folly, and the feeders/ Digest it with a custom . . ." *W Tale*, IV, iv, 10–12. **3** to "stomach"; condone or overlook: "But will the king/ Digest this letter of the cardinal's?" *Hen 8*, III, ii, 52–53. **4** to analyze: ". . . digest things rightly/ Touching the weal o'th'common . . ." *Cor*, I, i, 149–150. **5** to arrange: "We may digest our complots in some form [proper order]." *Rich 3*, III, i, 200. **6** to dissipate; get rid of: "Go cheerfully together and digest/ Your angry choler on your enemies." *1 Hen 6*, IV, i, 167–168.

digested, adj. shaped; arranged: ". . . an excellent play, well digested in/ the scenes . . ." *Ham*, II, ii, 435–436.

digged, *v.* past part. of **dig;** dug: "Thy grave is digg'd already in the earth." *2 Hen 6,* IV, x, 51.

dignity, *n.* **1** value; estimation or worth: "I would not have such a heart in my bosom, for/ the dignity of the whole body." *Mac,* V, i, 52–53. **2** state of highest worth or excellence: ". . . her fair cheek;/ Where several worthies make one dignity . . ." *Love's L,* IV, iii, 231–232. **3** elevated rank: "To furnish Rome and to prepare the ways/ You have for dignities . . ." *Hen 8,* III, ii, 328–329. **4** dignitary: "In spite of Pope or dignities of church,/ Here by the cheeks I'll drag thee up and down." *1 Hen 6,* I, iii, 50–51.

digress, *v.* to deviate; differ: "Thy noble shape is but a form of wax/ Digressing from the valour of a man . . ." *Rom & Jul,* III, iii, 125–126.

digressing, *adj.* wayward; transgressing: ". . . thy abundant goodness shall excuse/ This deadly blot in thy digressing son." *Rich 2,* V, iii, 63–64.

digt, *v.* past part. of **dig;** dug: ". . . th'/ athversary [adversary] . . . is digt himself four yard under the countermines." *Hen 5,* III, ii, 64–66.

dig-you-den, give you good even: "God dig-you-den all! Pray you, which is the head/ lady?" *Love's L,* IV, i, 42.

dilate, *v.* to explain or relate in length; amplify: "Do me the favour to dilate at full/ What have befall'n of them . . ." *Errors,* I, i, 122–123.

dilated, *adj.* **1** detailed: ". . . no further personal power . . . than the scope/ Of these dilated articles allow." *Ham,* I, ii, 36–38. **2** copious; extensive: ". . . like a bourn, a pale, a shore,/ confines/ Thy spacious and dilated parts." *Tr & Cr,* II, iii, 249–250.

dilation, *n.* See **denotement** (def. 2).

dildoes and fadings, *n.* appar. words used in the refrains of the song and misunderstood by the servant; "dildo" [penis] and "fading" [orgasm], in direct contradiction to the "delicate" refrain: ". . . with such delicate burdens/ of dildoes and fadings, jump her and thump her . . ." *W Tale,* IV, iv, 196–197.

dilemma, *n.* argument for or against a particular course of action: "I will presently pen/ down my dilemmas, encourage myself in my certainty . . ." *All's W,* III, vi, 70–71.

diligence, *n.* alertness; attention: "I will receive it, sir, with all diligence of spirit." *Ham,* V, ii, 92.

diluculo surgere, [Latin] maxim from schoolboy's grammar, *Diluculo surgere saluberrimum est,* Rising early is very healthy: ". . . not to be abed after/ midnight, is to be up betimes; and *diluculo surgere,*/ thou know'st—" *T Night,* II, iii, 1–3.

dimension, *n.* **1** physical form; appearance: "And in dimension, and the shape of nature,/ A gracious person." *T Night,* I, v, 265–266. **2** [pl.] proportions: ". . . hath not a Jew hands, organs, dimensions,/ senses, affections, passions?" *Merch,* III, i, 53–54.

diminitive, *adj.* var. of **diminutive:** "The most diminitive of birds, will fight,/ Her young ones in her nest, against the owl." *Mac,* IV, ii, 10–11.

diminutive, *n.* insignificant or worthless thing or person: "Most monster-like [as a curiosity] be shown/ For poor'st diminutives, for dolts . . ." *Ant & Cleo,* IV, xii, 36–37.

dine, *v.* Valentine here means that he has feasted on Silvia's beauty: "'Tis dinner time."/ "I have dined." *Two Gent,* II, i, 160–161.

dinner, *n.* **something at the latter end of a dinner,** provider of amusement with his [the traveler's] tall tales: "A good traveller is something at the latter/ end of a dinner, but one that lies three thirds . . ." *All's W,* II, v, 27–28.

dinner time, *n.* usually noon; dinner was the principal meal of the day: "Within this hour it will be dinner time;/ Till that I'll view the manners of the town . . ." *Errors,* I, ii, 11–12.

dint, *n.* stroke; impression: "O, now you weep, and I perceive you feel/ The dint of pity." *J Caes,* III, ii, 195–196.

Diomede, *n.* Also, **Diomed, Diomedes.** Greek warrior of the Trojan War; with Ulysses he killed King Rhesus and captured his horses before the Thracian king could come to the aid of the Trojans: ". . . as Ulysses and stout Diomede . . . stole to Rhesus' tents,/ And brought from thence the Thracian fatal steeds . . ." *3 Hen 6,* IV, ii, 19–21.

Dionysus, *n.* See **Bacchus.**

dire, *adj.* dreadful; horrible: "Thy natural magic and dire property [nature]/ On wholesome life usurps immediately." *Ham,* III, ii, 253–254.

direct, *v.* to hand over; entrust or assign: "Your rule direct to any; if to me,/ Day serves not light more faithful than I'll be." *Per,* I, ii, 109–110.

direction, *n.* **1** [usually pl.] truth; here, the desired information: "And thus do we of wisdom and of reach . . . By indirections find directions out." *Ham,* II, i, 64–66. **2** guidance or instruction: "I am not solely led/ By nice [precise] direction of a maiden's eyes . . ." *Merch,* II, i, 13–14. **3 giving direction,** overseeing a group of laborers; here, in wordplay with "planning a robbery": ". . . thou variest no more from picking of/ purses than giving direction doth from labouring . . ." *1 Hen 4,* II, i, 49–50. **4 to the direction just,** exactly according to instructions: ". . . he delivers/ Our offices [duties], and what we have to do,/ To the direction just." *Mac,* III, iii, 2–4.

directitude, *n.* evidently a blunder; the servant tries for an impressive word, poss. "disrepute": ". . . which friends . . . durst not . . . show themselves,/ as we term it, his friends, whilst he's in directitude." *Cor,* IV, v, 212–214.

directive, *adj.* able to be directed: ". . . swords and bows/ Directive by the limbs." *Tr & Cr,* I, iii, 355–356.

direness, *n.* horror: "Direness, familiar to my slaughterous thoughts,/ Cannot once start me." *Mac,* V, v, 14–15.

dirt-rotten, *adj.* putrefied; prob. indicative of hepatitis or cirrhosis: ". . . lethargies, cold/ palsies, raw eyes, dirt-rotten livers, whissing lungs . . ." *Tr & Cr,* V, i, 18–19.

dirty gods, *n.* the gods of gold and silver [money]: ". . . 'tis no better reckon'd, but of those/ Who worship dirty gods." *Cymb,* III, vii, 27–28.

Dis, *n.* **1** Pluto, ruler of the underworld, who had abducted Ceres' daughter Persephone to be his queen: ". . . they did plot/ The means that dusky [gloomy] Dis my daughter got . . ." *Temp,* IV, i, 88–89. **2 Dis's waggon,** Pluto's chariot: "For the flowers now that, frighted, thou let'st fall/ From Dis's waggon!" *W Tale,* IV, iv, 117–118.

disability, *n.* unworthiness; here, mock modesty: "Leave off discourse of disability." *Two Gent,* II, iv, 104.

disable, *v.* **1** to disparage; slight: "Fie, de la Pole! disable not thyself;/ Hast not a tongue?" *1 Hen 6,* V, iii, 67–68. **2** to ridicule; make fun of: ". . . disable all the benefits of your own country . . ." *As You,* IV, i, 32–33. **3** to deplete: "'Tis not unknown to you Antonio/ How much I have disabled mine estate . . ." *Merch,* I, i, 122–123.

disanimate, *v.* to discourage; intimidate: "The presence of a king engenders love/ Amongst his subjects . . . As it disanimates his enemies." *1 Hen 6,* III, i, 181–183.

disannul, *v.* to abolish; cancel: "Against my crown, my oath, my dignity,/ Which princes, would they, may not disannul . . ." *Errors,* I, i, 143–144.

disappointed, *adj.* having made no spiritual preparation for death: "Cut off even in the blossoms of my sin,/ Unhousel'd, disappointed, unanel'd . . ." *Ham,* I, v, 76–77.

disaster, *n.* **1** (often pl.) misfortunes; also, unfavorable circum stances: ". . . checks and disasters/ Grow in the veins of actions highest rear'd . . ." *Tr & Cr,* I, iii, 5–6.
—*v.* **2** to injure or disfigure: ". . . the holes where eyes/ should be, which pitifully disaster the cheeks." *Ant & Cleo,* II, vii, 15–16.

disbench, *v.* to drive (a person) from his seat; unseat: "Sir, I hope/ My words disbench'd you not?" *Cor,* II, ii, 70–71.

discandy, *v.* to melt: "By the discandying of this pelleted storm,/ Lie graveless . . ." *Ant & Cleo,* III, xiii, 165–166.

discase, *v.* to undress; here, to change out of his [Prospero's] magician's robes: "I will discase me, and myself present/ As I was sometime [duke of] Milan . . ." *Temp,* V, i, 85–86.

discharge, *v.* **1** to pay off an obligation to (another): "Would we were all discharg'd!" *Timon,* II, i, 14. **2** to perform: "I will discharge it [the role] in either your straw-colour beard . . . or your French-crown-colour beard . . ." *M N Dream,* I, ii, 86–88.
—*n.* **3** payment; fulfillment of an obligation: "My Lord of Somerset will keep me here,/ Without discharge, money, or furniture . . ." *2 Hen 6,* I, iii, 168–169. **4** sigh likened to the discharge of a weapon: "We two, that with so many thousand sighs/ Did buy each other, must poorly sell ourselves/ With the rude brevity and discharge of one." *Tr & Cr,* IV, iv, 38–40. **5** act of dismissing: "Then let those foot trudge hence upon those horse,/ According to our discharge . . ." *Edw 3,* II, ii, 32–33.

discipled, *past part.* **be discipled of,** to have as pupils: "He did look far/ Into the service of the time, and was/ Discipled of the bravest." *All's W,* I, ii, 26–28.

discipline, *n.* **1** instruction; learning: "This discipline shows thou hast been in love." *Two Gent,* III, ii, 87. **2** training or experience in military matters: "Call for our chiefest men of discipline,/ To cull the plots of best advantages . . ." *K John,* II, i, 39–40. **3** [pl.] rules or protocol: ". . . the mines is/ not according to the disciplines of the war . . ." *Hen 5,* III, ii, 62–63.

disclaim, *v.* **1** Faulconbridge's misuse for "renounce": "I have disclaim'd Sir Robert and my land;/ Legitimation, name and all is gone." *K John,* I, i, 247–248. **2 disclaim in,** to disown; disavow [lit., disclaims any part in you]: ". . . nature disclaims in thee:/ a tailor made thee." *Lear,* II, ii, 54–55.

disclosed, *past part.* hatched: "... as patient as the female dove/ When that her golden couplets are disclos'd ..." *Ham,* V, i, 281–282.

discomfited, *adj.* discouraged: "Well, go with me, and be not so discomfited." *Shrew,* II, i, 163.

discomfort, *v.* to discourage: "My lord, you do discomfort all the host." *Tr & Cr,* V, x, 10.

discomfortable, *adj.* causing discomfort; discouraging: "Discomfortable cousin! know'st thou not/ That when the searching eye of heaven is hid ..." *Rich 2,* III, ii, 36–37.

discommend, *v.* to disapprove: "... go out of my dialect, which you discommend/ so much." *Lear,* II, ii, 110–111.

discontent, *n.* discontented person; malcontent: "... to the ports/ The discontents repair ..." *Ant & Cleo,* I, iv, 38–39.

discontented, *adj.* still craving battle: "... let us know/ If 'twill tie up [hold back] thy discontented sword ..." *Ant & Cleo,* II, vi, 5–6.

discontenting, *adj.* angry: "And with my best endeavours ... Your discontenting father strive to qualify [appease] ..." *W Tale,* IV, iv, 532–533.

discontinue, *v.* to leave; finish with: "... men shall swear I have discontinued school/ Above a twelvemonth ..." *Merch,* III, iv, 75–76.

discourse, *v.* **1** to relate or recount: "The manner of their taking may appear/ At large discoursed in this paper here." *Rich 2,* V, vi, 9–10.
—*n.* **2** familiar behavior: "... your honesty should/ admit no discourse to your beauty." *Ham,* III, i, 107–108. **3** reasoning; comprehension or understanding: "Sure he that made us with such large discourse ... gave us not/ That capability ... To fust in us unus'd." *Ham,* IV, iv, 36–39. **4 discourse of reason,** ability to reason: "... a beast that wants discourse of reason/ Would have mourn'd longer ..." *Ham,* I, ii, 150–151. **5 discourse of thought,** thought processes: "If e'er my will did trespass 'gainst his love/ Either in discourse of thought or actual deed ..." *Oth,* IV, ii, 154–155.

discover, *v.* **1** to reveal; show or disclose: "... the Prince discovered to Claudio that he/ loved my niece your daughter ..." *M Ado,* I, ii, 10–11. **2** to identify or recognize: "... by no means I may discover them/ By any mark of favour." *J Caes,* II, i, 75–76.

discoverer, *n.* scout: "... send discoverers forth/ To know the numbers of our enemies." *2 Hen 4,* IV, i, 3–4.

discovery, *n.* **1** disclosure; act of revealing or exposing: "... a discovery of/ the infinite flatteries that follow youth and opulency." *Timon,* V, i, 34–35. **2** reconnaissance reports: "... make discovery/ Err in report of us." *Mac,* V, iv, 6–7.

discreet, *adj.* **1** discerning; circumspect; wise or prudent: "Love is a ... madness most discreet,/ A choking gall, and a preserving sweet." *Rom & Jul,* I, i, 188–192. **2** polite; here, prob. used sarcastically, since all of Poins's stories are indiscreet: "... breeds no bate with telling of discreet stories ..." *2 Hen 4,* II, iv, 247.

discretion, *n.* **1** reason or common sense: "Yet so far hath discretion fought with nature ..." *Ham,* I, ii, 5. **2** opinion or judgment of others: "I have/ seen the day of wrong through the little hole of discretion ..." *Love's L,* V, ii, 715–716. **3** regard or consideration: "... they would have no more discretion/ but to hang us." *M N Dream,* I, ii, 75–76. **4** person of reason or common sense: "... some discretion that discerns your state/ Better than you yourself." *Lear,* II, iv, 150–151. **5 adventure one's discretion,** to risk one's reputation [here, for good sense] by becoming angry at such foolishness: "Nay, good my lord, be not angry."/ "No, I warrant you; I will not adventure my discretion/ so weakly." *Temp,* II, i, 181–183. **6 best discretions of a woman,** parson's grammatical jumble for "most discreet women": "'Tis one of the best discretions of a 'oman as ever/ I did look upon." *Wives,* IV, iv, 1–2. **7 O dear discretion!** How rare [is] true discrimination!: "O dear discretion, how his words are suited!" *Merch,* III, v, 59.
—*adj.* **8** parson's misuse for "sensible": "It is a fery [very] discretion answer ..." *Wives,* I, i, 232.

discuss, *v.* **1** to disclose; declare or inform: "... you may discuss unto the duke, look/ you ..." *Hen 5,* III, ii, 65–66. **2** [as a command] speak up: "Speak, breathe, discuss; brief, short ..." *Wives,* IV, v, 2.

disdain, *n.* disgrace; humiliation: "... the disdain and shame/ whereof hath ever since kept Hector fasting and/ waking." *Tr & Cr,* I, ii, 35–37.

disdained, *adj.* **1** disdainful: "... the jeering and disdain'd contempt/ Of this proud King ..." *1 Hen 4,* I, iii, 181–182. **2** scorned: "Like lies, disdain'd in the reporting." *Per,* V, i, 119.

disease, *v.* to make uneasy: "... as she is now, she will but/ disease our better mirth." *Cor,* I, iii, 103–104.

diseased, *adj.* unsettled realm likened to diseased body: "... we are all diseas'd,/ And with our surfeiting ... Have brought ourselves into a burning fever ..." *2 Hen 4,* IV, i, 54–56.

disedge, *v.* **be disedged by,** to have the edge of the appetite taken off by; be surfeited by: ". . . when thou shalt be disedg'd by her/ That now thou tirest on . . ." *Cymb,* III, iv, 95–96.

disfigure, *v.* **1** to mar the dignity or majesty of: "A happy gentleman in blood and lineaments,/ By you unhappied and disfigured clean . . ." *Rich 2,* III, i, 9–10. **2** appar. misuse for "figure" [portray] or "prefigure" [picture]: ". . . say he comes to disfigure or to/ present the person of Moonshine." *M N Dream,* III, i, 56–57.

disfurnish, *v.* to deprive; here, to rob: ". . . if you should here disfurnish me,/ You take the sum and substance that I have." *Two Gent,* IV, i, 14–15.

disgest, *v.* var. of **digest:** "This rudeness is a sauce to his good wit,/ Which gives men stomach to disgest his words . . ." *J Caes,* I, ii, 297–298.

disgrace, *n.* **1** degradation or humiliation; also, desperation: ". . . yet you must not think/ to fob off our disgrace with a tale . . ." *Cor,* I, i, 92–93. **2** degeneration; decay: "And then grace us in the disgrace of death . . ." *Love's L,* I, i, 3. **3 take this disgrace off me,** [on whom] I can retaliate: ". . . thou hast a son shall take this disgrace off me . . ." *All's W,* II, iii, 231.

disgracious, *adj.* displeasing; offensive: "I do suspect I have done some offence/ That seems disgracious in the City's eye." *Rich 3,* III, vii, 110–111.

disguise, *n.* **1** state of intoxication; also, drunken revelry: ". . . the wild disguise hath almost/ Antick'd us all." *Ant & Cleo,* II, vii, 123–124.
—*v.* **2** to conceal: "Disguise fair nature with hard-favour'd rage . . ." *Hen 5,* III, i, 8.

disguising, *n.* act or instance of concealing: "I'll give her father notice/ Of their disguising and pretended flight . . ." *Two Gent,* II, vi, 36–37.

dish, *n.* **1 the dish pays the shot,** the meal is well worth the cost: "So if I prove a good repast to the spectators, the/ dish pays the shot [reckoning]." *Cymb,* V, iv, 156–157.
—*v.* **2** to serve up, as or as if at table: "I know not how it tastes, though it be dish'd/ For me to try how . . ." *W Tale,* III, ii, 72–73.

dishabited, *adj.* dislodged: "By this time from their fixed beds of lime/ Had been dishabited, and wide havoc made . . ." *K John,* II, i, 219–220.

dishclout, *n.* dishcloth: ". . . a dishclout of Jaquenetta's, and that a' wears next/ his heart for a favour." *Love's L,* V, ii, 705–706.

dishonest, *adj.* **1** unreliable; badly behaved: "I'll no more of you./ Besides, you grow dishonest." *T Night,* I, v, 38–39. **2** dishonorable: "A very dishonest paltry boy, and more a coward/ than a hare . . ." *T Night,* III, iv, 395–396. **3** telling a lie or lies: "Fie, thou dishonest Satan!" *T Night,* IV, ii, 32. **4 dishonest manners,** loose behavior: ". . . holding in disdain the German women/ For some dishonest manners of their life . . ." *Hen 5,* I, ii, 48–49.

dishonor, *n.* **1** insult: "Do what you will, dishonour shall be humour [regarded as only a burst of temper]." *J Caes,* IV, iii, 108. **2** dishonorable state of affairs [yielding to the demands of the masses]: "Your dishonour/ Mangles true judgement, and bereaves the state . . ." *Cor,* III, i, 156–157.

dishonored rub, *n.* shameful obstacle: ". . . nor has Coriolanus/ Deserv'd this so dishonour'd rub . . ." *Cor,* III, i, 58–59.

dis-horn, *v.* to disarm; here, to expose Falstaff's true character: "We'll all present ourselves, dis-horn the spirit . . ." *Wives,* IV, iv, 63.

disjoin, *v.* to separate; divorce: "Th'abuse of greatness is when it disjoins/ Remorse from power . . ." *J Caes,* II, i, 18–19.

disjoint, *adj.* **1** in disarray; disorganized: ". . . thinking by our late dear brother's death/ Our state to be disjoint and out of frame . . ." *Ham,* I, ii, 19–20.
—*v.* **2** to fall or come apart: "But let the frame of things disjoint, both the worlds suffer . . ." *Mac,* III, ii, 16.

disjunction, *n.* separation: "There's no disjunction to be made, but by . . . your ruin." *W Tale,* IV, iv, 530–531.

disliken, *v.* to disguise: ". . . and (as you can) disliken/ The truth of your own seeming . . ." *W Tale,* IV, iv, 652–653.

dislimn, *v.* to distort or efface; blot out: "The rack dislimns, and makes it indistinct/ As water is in water." *Ant & Cleo,* IV, xiv, 10–11.

dislodge, *v.* to withdraw; take leave: "Dislodge, dislodge: it is the King of England." *Edw 3,* I, ii, 56.

disloyal, *adj.* unfaithful: "I came hither to tell you . . . the lady is disloyal." *M Ado,* III, ii, 91–93.

disloyalty, *n.* **become disloyalty,** carry your unfaithfulness with grace: "Look sweet, speak fair, become disloyalty . . ." *Errors,* III, ii, 11.

dismal, *adj.* **1** vicious; savage: "Norway himself . . . Assisted by that most disloyal traitor,/ The Thane of Cawdor, began a dismal conflict . . ." *Mac,* I, ii, 51–54. **2** disastrous: ". . . this night I'll spend/ Unto a dismal and a fatal end . . ." *Mac,* III, v, 20–21. **3** sorrowful: ". . . my fell of hair/ Would at a dismal treatise rouse, and stir . . ." *Mac*, V, v, 11–12. **4** fateful; sinister or ill-boding: "My dismal scene I needs must act alone." *Rom & Jul*, IV, iii, 19.

dismantle, *v.* to undress: "Dismantle you, and (as you can) disliken/ The truth of your own seeming . . ." *W Tale*, IV, iv, 652–653.

dismantled, *past part.* stripped; deprived: "This realm dismantled was/ Of Jove himself . . ." *Ham*, III, ii, 276–277.

disme, *n.* (pron. "dime") a tenth part: "Every tithe soul 'mongst many thousand dismes/ Hath been as dear as Helen . . ." *Tr & Cr*, II, ii, 19–20.

dismiss, *v.* to free: "But life, being weary of these worldly bars,/ Never lacks power to dismiss itself." *J Caes*, I, iii, 96–97.

dismission, *n.* **1** dismissal; here, orders to return to Rome: "You must not stay here longer, your dismission/ Is come from Caesar . . ." *Ant & Cleo*, I, i, 26–27. **2** rejection: "Save when command to your dismission tends . . ." *Cymb*, II, iii, 51.

dismount, *v.* **1** to lower [fig. use]: "This said, his watery eyes he did dismount . . ." *Lover's Comp*, 281. **2 dismount thy tuck,** [to] unsheathe your sword: "Dismount thy tuck, be yare in thy preparation, for thy assailant is quick . . ." *T Night*, III, iv, 226–227.

disnatured, *adj.* unnatural; lacking any natural affection: "And be a thwart disnatur'd torment to her!" *Lear*, I, iv, 292.

disorbed, *adj.* removed from its sphere: "And fly like chidden Mercury from Jove,/ Or like a star disorb'd?" *Tr & Cr*, II, ii, 45–46.

disorder, *n.* loss of self-control: "You have displac'd the mirth, broke the good meeting/ With most admir'd disorder." *Mac*, III, iv, 108–109.

disordered, *adj.* **1** disorderly: "Men so disorder'd, so debosh'd, and bold . . ." *Lear*, I, iv, 250. **2** irregular; also, out-of-tune: "And here have I the daintiness of ear/ To check time broke in a disordered string . . ." *Rich 2*, V, v, 45–46.

disparagement, *n.* dishonor; disgrace: ". . . passed sentence may not be recall'd/ But to our honour's great disparagement . . ." *Errors*, I, i, 147–148.

dispark, *v.* to remove the enclosures from (private grounds); throw open: ". . . you have fed upon my signories,/ Dispark'd my parks and fell'd my forest woods . . ." *Rich 2*, III, i, 22–23.

dispatch, *v.* **1** also, **despatch,** to hurry (usually used as a command): "'Twill be two o'clock ere they come from/ the coronation. Dispatch, dispatch." *2 Hen 4*, V, v, 3–4. **2** to deprive: "Thus was I, sleeping, by a brother's hand/ Of life, of crown, of queen at once dispatch'd . . ." *Ham*, I, v, 74–75. **3** to answer decisively: "Dispatch us with all speed, lest that our king/ Come here himself . . ." *Hen 5*, II, iv, 141–142. **4** to deal with quickly: "I your commission will forthwith dispatch . . ." *Ham*, III, iii, 3. **5** to prepare; make ready: "And whilst a field should be dispatch'd and fought,/ You are disputing of [about] your generals . . ." *1 Hen 6*, I, i, 72–73. **6** to put to death; kill: "Not in this land shall he remain uncaught;/ And found—dispatch." *Lear*, II, i, 57–58. **7** to settle matters promptly: ". . . at that place call/ upon me; and dispatch with Angelo, that it may be/ quickly." *Meas*, III, i, 266–268. —*n.* **8** care; management; here also, prob. wordplay on "kill; get rid of": ". . . you shall put/ This night's great business into my dispatch . . ." *Mac*, I, v, 66–67. **9** prompt settlement: ". . . to have a dispatch of/ complaints, and to deliver us from devices hereafter . . ." *Meas*, IV, iv, 10–11. **10** leave to go; dismissal: "Yet give us our dispatch:/ I am husht until our city be afire . . ." *Cor*, V, iii, 180–181. **11 attend dispatch,** (to) await orders where to be sent: ". . . the several messengers/ From hence attend dispatch." *Lear*, II, i, 124–125. **12 terrible dispatch,** unseemly haste: "What needed then that terrible dispatch of/ it into your pocket?" *Lear*, I, ii, 32–33.

dispensation, *n.* plausible excuse for an action: ". . . with good thoughts makes dispensation,/ Urging the worser sense for vantage still . . ." *Luc*, 248–249.

dispense, *v.* **dispense with, a.** to forgive or excuse: "Mark how with my neglect [disregard] I do dispense . . ." *Sonn 112*, 12. **b.** to forgo: "Might you dispense with your leisure, I would . . . have some speech with you . . ." *Meas*, III, i, 153–154.

disperse, *v.* to circulate: "And under thee their poesy disperse." *Sonn 78*, 4.

dispersedly, *adv.* See **burthen** (def. 5).

dispiteous, *adj.* pitiless; merciless: "How now, foolish rheum!/ Turning dispiteous torture out of door!" *K John*, IV, i, 33–34.

displant, *v.* to transplant; relocate: "Unless philosophy can make a Juliet,/ Displant a town, reverse a Prince's doom . . ." *Rom & Jul*, III, iii, 58–59.

display, *v.* **1** to spread (out): "Upon the world dim darkness doth display . . ." *Luc*, 118. **2** to bloom; come into full bloom: "For women are as roses whose fair flower/ Being once display'd, doth fall [perish] that very hour." *T Night*, II, iv, 38–39.

displeasure, *n.* **1** harm or injury: "Hast thou delight to see a wretched man/ Do outrage and displeasure to himself?" *Errors,* IV, iv, 113–114. **2** loss of favor: "I am sorry/ For your displeasure, but all will soon be well . . ." *Oth,* III, i, 42–43.

disponge, *v.* to drop as though squeezed from a sponge: "The poisonous damp of night disponge upon me . . ." *Ant & Cleo,* IV, ix, 13.

disport, *n.* pastime; diversion: "That my disports corrupt and taint my business . . ." *Oth,* I, iii, 271.

dispose, *v.* **1** to seat (oneself): ". . . an idle banquet attends you;/ Please you to dispose yourselves." *Timon,* I, ii, 151–152. **2** to deposit: ". . . tell me how thou hast dispos'd thy charge." *Errors,* I, ii, 73. **3** to make terms [with]: ". . . you did suspect/ She had dispos'd with Caesar . . ." *Ant & Cleo,* IV, xiv, 122–123. **4** to regulate; settle or arrange: "To the disposing of it nought rebell'd . . ." *Hen 8,* I, i, 43. **5 dispose of,** to take care of; make arrangements for: "Come, cousin,/ I'll dispose of you." *Rich 2,* II, ii, 116–117. **6 dispose oneself,** to behave accordingly: ". . . I'll hear from thee,/ And by whose letters I'll dispose myself." *Per,* I, ii, 116–117.
—*n.* **7** disposal: "His goods confiscate to the Duke's dispose . . ." *Errors,* I, i, 20. **8** inclination: ". . . carries on the stream of his dispose/ Without observance or respect . . ." *Tr & Cr,* II, iii, 165–166. **9** manner: "He has a person and a smooth dispose,/ To be suspected . . ." *Oth,* I, iii, 395–396. **10 at thy dispose,** in your care; at your disposal: "All that is mine I leave at thy dispose . . ." *Two Gent,* II, vii, 86.

disposed, *adj.* **1** inclined to be merry: "Come to our pavilion: Boyet is dispos'd." *Love's L,* II, i, 249. **2** made [good] use of: "So hot a speed with such advice dispos'd . . ." *K John,* III, iii, 11. **3** placed: "His blows are well dispos'd. There, Ajax!" *Tr & Cr,* IV, v, 115.

disposer, *n.* **1** one whose heart is at the disposal of another: "I'll lay my life, with my disposer Cressida." *Tr & Cr,* III, i, 84. **2** person who owes allegiance to another; here, in wordplay with preceding: "No, no, no such matter, you are wide: come,/ your disposer is sick." *Tr & Cr,* III, i, 85–86.

disposition, *n.* **1** one's nature; here, esp., mental stability: "So horridly to shake our disposition/ With thoughts beyond the reaches of our souls?" *Ham,* I, iv, 55–56. **2** [often pl] inclination: "How stands your dispositions to be married?" *Rom & Jul,* I, iii, 65. **3** general quality; way of thinking and behaving: ". . . to practise his judgement [experiment] with the disposition/ of natures." *Meas,* III, i, 162–163.

disprized, *adj.* despised; rejected: "The pangs of dispriz'd love, the law's delay . . ." *Ham,* III, i, 72.

disproperty, *v.* to deprive of; take away: ". . . silenc'd their pleaders, and/ Dispropertied their freedoms . . ." *Cor,* II, i, 245–246.

disproportion, *n.* **1** unfitness; irregularity or abnormality: "Fie, we may smell in such a will most rank,/ Foul disproportion . . ." *Oth,* III, iii, 236–237.
—*v.* **2** to deprive of symmetry: "To disproportion me in every part . . ." *3 Hen 6,* III, ii, 160.

dispursed, *past part.* disbursed: ". . . many a pound of mine own proper store . . . Have I dispursed to the garrisons . . ." *2 Hen 6,* III, i, 115–117.

disputable, *adj.* disposed to argue; disputatious: "He is too disputable for my company." *As You,* II, v, 31–32.

dispute, *v.* **1** to discuss: "Let me dispute with thee of thy estate." *Rom & Jul,* III, iii, 63. **2** to bear or strive against (grief, etc.): "Dispute it like a man."/ "I shall do so;/ But I must also feel it as a man . . ." *Mac,* IV, iii, 220–221. **3 disputed on,** argued in a court of law: "I'll have 't disputed on;/ 'Tis probable, and palpable to thinking." *Oth,* I, ii, 75–76.

disquantity, *v.* to reduce the number of: ". . . be then desir'd . . . A little to disquantity your train . . ." *Lear,* I, iv, 255–257.

disquiet, *adj.* impatient; upset or angry: "I pray you, husband, be not so disquiet." *Shrew,* IV, i, 155.

disquietly, *adv.* disquietingly; disturbingly: ". . . and all ruinous disorders follow us disquietly to our/ graves." *Lear,* I, ii, 119–120.

disrobe, *v.* to undeck; remove the decorations from: "Disrobe the images [statues]/ If you do find them deck'd with ceremonies." *J Caes,* I, i, 64–65.

disseat, *v.* to unseat; here, dethrone: "This push/ Will cheer me ever, or disseat me now." *Mac,* V, iii, 20–21.

dissemble, *v.* **1** to disguise; hide: "Dissemble not your hatred: swear your love." *Rich 3,* II, i, 8. **2** to disguise oneself; also, to play the hypocrite: "I will dissemble myself/ in't, and I would I were the first that ever dissembled/ in such a gown." *T Night,* IV, ii, 4–6.

dissembly, *n.* misuse for "assembly": "Is our whole dissembly appeared?" *M Ado,* IV, ii, 1.

dissentious, *adj.* causing discord; discordant: "This carrytale, dissentious jealousy . . ." *Ven & Ad,* 657.

dissever, *v.* **1** to separate: ". . . to dissever so/ Our great self and our credit . . ." *All's W,* II, i, 121–122. **2** to part, as from a body: "At Crécy field our clouds of warlike smoke/ Choked up those French mouths, and dissevered them . . ." *Edw 3*, IV, iv, 4–5.

dissipation, *n.* **dissipation of cohorts,** desertion of troops: ". . . banishment of friends, dissipation/ of cohorts, nuptial breaches, and I know not what." *Lear*, I, ii, 155–156.

dissolutely, *adv.* Slender's misuse for "resolutely": ". . . that I am freely dissolved [resolved], and dissolutely." *Wives*, I, i, 231.

dissolution, *n.* **1** destruction; death: ". . . so great a fever on goodness/ that the dissolution of it must cure it." *Meas*, III, ii, 216–217. **2** action of dissolving: ". . . a man of continual dissolution and/ thaw . . ." *Wives*, III, v, 107–108. **3 hath dissolution,** dissolves: "Against love's fire fear's frost hath dissolution . . ." *Luc*, 355.

dissolved, *past part.* **1** Slender's blunder for "resolved": "I will marry/ her; that I am freely dissolved . . ." *Wives*, I, i, 230–231. **2** See **resolved** (def. 2).

distaff, *n.* **1** the staff from which the flax or wool is drawn in spinning: ". . . it hangs like flax on a distaff . . ." *T Night*, I, iii, 99. **2** same, regarded as the symbol for a woman: ". . . nobleness, which could have turn'd/ A distaff to a lance [man] . . ." *Cymb*, V, iii, 33–34.

distaff-women, *n.* women who spin: ". . . distaff-women manage rusty bills/ Against thy seat . . ." *Rich 2*, III, ii, 118–119.

distain, *v.* **1** to stain or blemish; here, by comparison with her beauty: "She did distain my child, and stood between/ Her and her fortunes." *Per*, IV, iii, 31–32. **2** to defile; dishonor: "The silver-shining queen he would distain . . ." *Luc*, 786.

distance, *n.* **1** relative closeness; hence, enmity [a term in fencing]: ". . . in such bloody distance,/ That every minute of his being thrusts/ Against my near'st of life . . ." *Mac*, III, i, 115–117. **2** difference in rank; here, a becoming sense of inferiority: "She knew her distance and did angle for me . . ." *All's W*, V, iii, 211. **3 in a wary distance,** ready to take offense: ". . . noble swelling spirits,/ That hold their honour in a wary distance . . ." *Oth*, II, iii, 51–52.

distaste, *v.* **1** to find distasteful: "If he distaste it, let him to my sister . . ." *Lear*, I, iii, 15. **2** to make distasteful: ". . . her brain-sick raptures/ Cannot distaste the goodness of a quarrel . . ." *Tr & Cr*, II, ii, 123–124.

distasted, *adj.* distasteful; bitter: "Distasted with the salt of broken tears." *Tr & Cr*, IV, iv, 47.

distemper, *n.* **1** mental or emotional disturbance: "Upon the heat and flame of thy distemper/ Sprinkle cool patience." *Ham*, III, iv, 123–124. **2 proceeding on distemper,** resulting from drunkenness: "If little faults, proceeding on distemper,/ Shall not be wink'd at . . ." *Hen 5*, II, ii, 54–55. —*v.* **3** to disorder; derange or infect: ". . . the malignancy of my fate might perhaps/ distemper yours . . ." *T Night*, II, i, 4–5.

distemperature, *n.* **1** disorder, either in worldly affairs or in the universe: "At your birth/ Our grandam earth, having this distemp'rature,/ In passion shook." *1 Hen 4*, III, i, 30–32. **2** ailment: "And at her heels a huge infectious troop/ Of pale distemperatures and foes to life?" *Errors*, V, i, 81–82. **3** unnatural weather; here also, an upset in the natural order [def. 1]: "And thorough this distemperature we see/ The seasons alter . . ." *M N Dream*, II, i, 106–107. **4** mental disorder or disturbance: "Upon what ground is his distemperature?" *Per*, V, i, 27.

distempered, *adj.* **1** unquestionably, though not mortally, ill: "It is but as a body yet distemper'd . . ." *2 Hen 4*, III, i, 41. **2** upset; disturbed: ". . . it argues a distemper'd head/ So soon to bid good morrow to thy bed." *Rom & Jul*, II, iii, 29–30. **3** angry; here in wordplay with "drunk": "The King, sir . . . Is in his retirement marvellous distempered." *Ham*, III, ii, 291–293. **4** diseased: "He cannot buckle his distemper'd cause/ Within the belt of rule." *Mac*, V, iii, 15–16. **5** (of weather) stormy; turbulent: "No scope of nature, no distemper'd day,/ No common wind, no customed event . . ." *K John*, III, iii, 154–155. **6** double meaning of emotional upset and disagreeable weather: ". . . this distempered messenger of wet,/ The many-colour'd Iris, rounds thine eye?" *All's W*, I, iii, 146–147.

distempering, *adj.* intoxicating: "Being full of supper, and distempering draughts . . ." *Oth*, I, i, 99.

distilled, *adj.* **1** finest or purest; here, prob. rose water: "Balm his foul head in warm distilled waters . . ." *Shrew*, Ind., i, 46. **2** melted: ". . . whilst they, distill'd/ Almost to jelly with the act of fear,/ Stand dumb . . ." *Ham*, I, ii, 204–206. **3** ref. to rose preserved in perfume rather than withering on the vine: "But earthlier happy is the rose distill'd/ Than that which . . . Grows, lives, and dies, in single blessedness." *M N Dream*, I, i, 76–78.

distilling, *adj.* able to permeate the body: "Take thou this vial, being then in bed,/ And this distilling liquor drink thou off . . ." *Rom & Jul*, IV, i, 93–94.

distinct, *n.* person or thing that is separate and distinct: "Two distincts, division none;/ Number there in love was slain." *Phoen*, 27–28.

distinctly, *adv.* **1** at different times: "The yards and boresprit,/ would I flame distinctly,/ Then meet and join." *Temp,* I, ii, 200–201. **2** separately; individually: ". . . the centurions and their charges/ distinctly billeted . . ." *Cor,* IV, iii, 44–45.

distinguish, *v.* to be discriminating in: "And could of men distinguish her election . . ." *Ham,* III, ii, 64.

distinguishment, *n.* **mannerly distinguishment,** a polite or proper distinction: "And mannerly distinguishment leave out/ Betwixt the prince and beggar." *W Tale,* II, i, 86–87.

distract, *adj.* **1** distracted; mad; insane: "The fellow is distract, and so am I . . ." *Errors,* IV, iii, 40. **2** distraught: "With this she fell distract,/ And . . . swallow'd fire." *J Caes,* IV, iii, 154–155. **3** different; separate: ". . . and to your audit comes/ Their distract parcels [items] in combined sums." *Lover's Comp,* 230–231.
—*v.* **4** to divide: "Distract your army, which doth most consist/ Of war-mark'd footmen . . ." *Ant & Cleo,* III, vii, 43–44.

distracted, *adj.* **1** maddened; put beside oneself: "Ay, thou poor ghost, whiles memory holds a seat/ In this distracted globe." *Ham,* I, v, 96–97. **2** unstable; illogical: "He's lov'd of the distracted multitude,/ Who like not in their judgment but their eyes . . ." *Ham,* IV, iii, 4–5. **3** broken; broken up: "But to the brightest beams/ Distracted clouds give way . . ." *All's W,* V, iii, 34–35.

distraction, *n.* **1** madness; insanity: ". . . in conclusion put strange speech upon me,/ I know not what 'twas, but distraction." *T Night,* V, i, 65–66. **2** emotional upset; frenzy: "Madam, this is a mere [sheer] distraction . . ." *Hen 8,* III, i, 112. **3** small detachment, as of soldiers or ships: "His power went out in such distractions as/ Beguil'd all spies." *Ant & Cleo,* III, vii, 76–77.

distrain, *v.* to seize; confiscate [legal term]: "My father's goods are all distrain'd and sold . . ." *Rich 2,* II, iii, 130.

distressful, *adj.* earned by hard work: "Gets him to rest, cramm'd with distressful bread . . ." *Hen 5,* IV, i, 276.

distrust, *v.* to fear for; be anxious about: "So far from cheer and from your former state,/ That I distrust you." *Ham,* III, ii, 159–160.

disvouch, *v.* to disavow; contradict: "Every letter he hath writ hath disvouched [the] other." *Meas,* IV, iv, 1.

ditch-dog, *n.* dead dog found in a ditch: ". . . eats cow-dung for sallets; swallows the/ old rat and the ditch-dog . . ." *Lear,* III, iv, 135–136.

ditched, *adj.* closed in by a ditch: "Where was this lane?"/ "Close by the battle, ditch'd, and wall'd with turf . . ." *Cymb,* V, iii, 13–14.

ditcher, *n.* digger: "There is no ancient/ gentlemen but gardeners, ditchers, and grave-makers . . ." *Ham,* V, i, 29–30.

ditty, *n.* words of a song: "The ditty does remember my drown'd father." *Temp,* I, ii, 408.

diurnal ring, *n.* daily circuit; here, that of the sun: "Ere twice the horses of the sun shall bring/ Their fiery coacher his diurnal ring . . ." *All's W,* II, i, 160–161.

dive-dapper, *n.* small grebe: "Like a dive-dapper peering through a wave . . ." *Ven & Ad,* 86.

divel, *n.* var. of **devil**: ". . . that same purpose-changer, that sly divel,/ That broker . . ." *K John,* II, i, 567–568.

divers, *adj.* various: ". . . changes fill the cup of alteration/ With divers liquors!" *2 Hen 4,* III, i, 52–53.

Dives, *n.* rich man in the Gospel of Luke: ". . . I think upon hell-fire and/ Dives that lived in purple . . ." *1 Hen 4,* III, iii, 30–31.

dividable, *adj.* dividing; separating; or, perh., separated, i.e., distant: "Peaceful commerce from dividable shores . . ." *Tr & Cr,* I, iii, 105.

dividant, *adj.* divisible; separable: "Whose procreation, residence and birth/ Scarce is dividant . . ." *Timon,* IV, iii, 4–5.

divide, *v.* **1** to share: "Her grievance with his hearing to divide . . ." *Lover's Comp,* 67. **2 divide in all,** share in all the honors: "Make good this ostentation, and you shall/ Divide in all with us." *Cor,* I, vi, 86–87. **3 divide our equalness,** split our partnership: ". . . that our stars,/ Unreconciliable, should divide/ Our equalness to this." *Ant & Cleo,* V, i, 46–48. **4 divides him,** his conversation is divided between the two subjects: ". . . o'er and o'er divides him/ 'Twixt his unkindness and his kindness . . ." *W Tale,* IV, iv, 552–553.

divided, *adj.* **1** shared: ". . . pledges the breath of him in a divided draught [shared drink]" *Timon,* I, ii, 47–48. **2** separate; here, opposing purposes: "For we tomorrow hold divided Councils . . ." *Rich 3,* III, i, 179. **3** incomplete: "And she a fair divided excellence . . ." *K John,* II, i, 439. **4** half-uttered: "Yet sometime a/ divided sigh, martyr'd as 'twere i' th' deliverance . . ." *Kinsmen,* II, i, 40–41.

dividual, *adj.* **in sex dividual,** between persons of the opposite sex: ". . . the true love 'tween maid and maid may be/ More than in sex dividual." *Kinsmen,* I, iii, 81–82.

divination, *n.* intuition of disaster; prophecy: "Tell thou an earl his divination lies . . ." *2 Hen 4,* I, i, 88.

divine, *adj.* **1** immortal: "Or my divine soul answer it in heaven." *Rich 2,* I, i, 38. **2** of unparalleled excellence: ". . . an operation more divine/ Than breath or pen can give expressure to." *Tr & Cr,* III, iii, 202–203.
—*n.* **3** clergyman: ". . . it is a good divine that follows his/ own instructions . . ." *Merch,* I, ii, 14–15. **4 great divine,** high priest: "Thus by Apollo's great divine seal'd up . . ." *W Tale,* III, i, 19.

diviner, *n.* witch: ". . . this drudge or diviner laid claim to me . . ." *Errors,* III, ii, 139.

divinity, *n.* **1** theology: "But to have divinity preach'd there!" *Per,* IV, v, 4. **2 no good divinity,** bad theology, Lear says, because it contradicts the Bible: " 'Ay' and 'no' too was no/ good divinity." *Lear,* IV, vi, 101–102.

division, *n.* **1** category or categories: "Rightly reasoned, and in his own division . . ." *M Ado,* V, i, 219. **2** subdividing; various aspects: ". . . abound/ In the division of each several crime . . ." *Mac,* IV, iii, 95–96. **3** (in music) florid embellishment, as a run: "Sung by a fair queen in a summer's bow'r/ With ravishing division to her lute." *1 Hen 4,* III, i, 203–204. **4** wordplay on musical sense with "action of dividing": "Some say the lark makes sweet division./ This doth not so, for she divideth us." *Rom & Jul,* III, v, 29–30. **5** discord or difference; disunity: "O! these eclipses/ do portend these divisions." *Lear,* I, ii, 143–144. **6 divisions in state,** factions in government: ". . . divisions in state; menaces and/ maledictions against King and nobles . . ." *Lear,* I, ii, 153–154.

divorce, *n.* act of disowning: "Mark your divorce, young sir,/ Whom son I dare not call . . ." *W Tale,* IV, iv, 418–419.

divulge, *v.* **1** to reveal itself: ". . . like the owner of a foul disease,/ To keep it from divulging . . ." *Ham,* IV, i, 21–22. **2 well divulged,** well spoken of: ". . . of fresh and stainless youth;/ In voices well divulg'd, free . . ." *T Night,* I, v, 263, 264.

dizzy, *v.* to stun: "Shall dizzy with more clamour Neptune's ear . . ." *Tr & Cr,* V, ii, 173.

do, *v.* **1** to have sexual relations with [Pompey deliberately misconstrues the intended meaning]: "What has he done?"/ "A woman." *Meas,* I, ii, 80–81. **2 do it, a.** kiss each other [ref. to Imogen's lips]: "Rubies unparagon'd,/ How dearly they do't . . ." *Cymb,* II, ii, 17–18. **b.** put it into words: ". . . which lames report to follow it,/ and undoes description to do it." *W Tale,* V, ii, 58–59. **3 do withal,** help it: "Which I denying, they fell sick and died:/ I could not do withal . . ." *Merch,* III, iv, 71–72. **4 fain be doing,** rather get on with it: "O pardon me, Signor Gremio, I would fain be doing." *Shrew,* II, i, 74. **5 I not doing this,** had I not done this: "Yet I not doing this, the fool had borne/ My head, as I do his." *Cymb,* IV, ii, 116–117. **6 not doing it, and being done,** death (for not doing it) and reward (when it was done): "I with death, and with/ Reward, did threaten and encourage him,/ Not doing it, and being done." *W Tale,* III, ii, 163–165. **7 what had he to do,** what business was it of his: "For what had he to do to chide at me?" *As You,* III, v, 129.

docks, *n. pl.* weedy plants; here, a wry joke is intended: "Had I plantation of this isle, my lord,—"/ "He'd sow 't with nettle-seed."/ "Or docks, or mallows." *Temp,* II, i, 139–140.

doctor, *n.* learned man: used as a model of intelligence: "He is then a giant to an ape; but then is an ape a/ doctor to such a man." *M Ado,* V, i, 198–199.

doctor-like, *adj.* having the ability and authority to teach a skill: "And folly, doctor-like, controlling skill . . ." *Sonn 66,* 10.

Doctor Shaa, *n.* var. of **Shaw;** brother of Mayor: "Go, Lovell, with all speed, to Doctor Shaa . . ." *Rich 3,* III, v, 102.

doctrine, *n.* **pay a doctrine,** to teach a lesson: "I'll pay that doctrine or else die in debt." *Rom & Jul,* I, i, 236.

document, *n.* lesson; instruction: "A document in madness: thoughts and/ remembrance fitted." *Ham,* IV, v, 176–177.

do de, *interj.* simulation of shivering, chattering of teeth, etc.: "Tom's a-cold. O! do de,/ do de, do de." *Lear,* III, iv, 58–59.

doer, *n.* brothel customer: ". . . I think forty more, all/ great doers in our trade . . ." *Meas,* IV, iii, 18–19.

doff, *v.* **1** to take off; remove: "You have deceiv'd our trust,/ And made us doff our easy robes of peace . . ." *1 Hen 4,* V, i, 11–12. **2** put one off: "Every day thou doffest me with some device, Iago . . ." *Oth,* IV, ii, 177. **3** See **daff** (def. 2).

dog, *n.* **1 dog and the bush,** man in the moon and his dog were banished there for gathering firewood on Sunday; he is seen as perpetually bearing a bundle of thornbush: "My mistress show'd me thee, and thy dog, and thy bush." *Temp,* II, ii, 141. **2 dog will have his day,** ref. to the proverb that everyone will have his share of good fortune eventually; Hamlet is saying that his turn to be believed will come: "The cat will mew, and dog will have his day." *Ham,* V, i, 287. **3 give a dog,** ref. to story that Queen Elizabeth, granting a favor to one whose dog she had requested and received, was asked for the return of the dog: "This is to give a dog, and in recompense desire/ my dog again." *T Night,* V, i, 5–6.

—*adj.* **4 dog at,** good or adept at: "And you love me, let's do't: I am dog at a/ catch." *T Night*, II, iii, 62–63.

dog-ape, *n.* baboon: ". . . that they call compliment is like the encounter of two dog-apes." *As You*, II, v, 23–24.

dog-days, *n.* hot days of early August, likened to the red glow of the man's nose: ". . . he should be a brazier by/ his face, for . . . twenty of the dog-days/ now reign in's nose . . ." *Hen 8*, V, iii, 39–41.

dog-fox, *n.* male fox; allusion to the cunning of Ulysses: ". . . that stale old mouse-eaten dry/ cheese Nestor, and that same dog-fox Ulysses—" *Tr & Cr*, V, v, 10–11.

dog-hole, *n.* small, wretched place fit only for a dog: "France is a dog-hole and it no more merits/ The tread of a man's foot . . ." *All's W*, II, iii, 270–271.

dog's-leather, *n.* leather used for making gloves: "He shall have the skins of our enemies to make/ dog's-leather of." *2 Hen 6*, IV, ii, 23–24.

dogs of war, *n. pl.* destructive forces of war: "Cry havoc and let slip the dogs of war . . ." *J Caes*, III, i, 273.

dog-weary, *adj.* dog-tired: "I have watch'd so long/ That I am dog-weary . . ." *Shrew*, IV, ii, 59–60.

doing, *pres. part.* engaging in sexual intercourse: ". . . for doing I am past, as I will [pass] by thee . . ." *All's W*, II, iii, 229–230.

doit, *n.* **1** tiny amount [formerly a small Dutch coin worth a fraction of a penny]: "Not so well as plain-dealing, which will not cast a man a doit." *Timon*, I, i, 210. **2 dissension of a doit,** disagreement over nothing at all: ". . . shall within this hour,/ On a dissension of a doit, break out/ To bitterest enmity . . ." *Cor*, IV, iv, 16–18. **3 irons of a doit,** swords worth no more than a doit: "Cushions, leaden spoons,/ Irons of a doit . . ." *Cor*, I, v, 5–6.

dole¹, *n.* **1** one's fortune or lot; destiny: "Now, my masters, happy man be his dole, say I . . ." *1 Hen 4*, II, ii, 73. **2** action of distributing or dealing out: "It was your presurmise/ That in the dole of blows your son might drop." *2 Hen 4*, I, i, 168–169. **3 dole of honor,** dealing out of honors, titles, etc.: "What great creation and what dole of honour/ Flies where you bid it . . ." *All's W*, II, iii, 169–170. **4 happy man be's dole,** good luck to the one who is successful: "No, my lord, I'll fight."/ "You will? Why, happy man be's dole!" *W Tale*, I, ii, 162–163.

dole², *n.* **1** grief; lamentation: "Omit we all their dole and woe." *Per*, III, Chor., 42. **2** grievous occasion or spectacle: "But mark, poor knight,/ What dreadful dole is here?" *M N Dream*, V, i, 266–267.

dollar, *n.* **1** English word for "thaler," a European coin; here, in wordplay with "dolor": "Comes to th' entertainer—"/ "A dollar."/ "Dolour comes to him, indeed . . ." *Temp*, II, i, 17–19. **2** word first used in the 16th century; here, an anachronism: "Nor would we deign him burial of his men/ Till he disbursed . . . Ten thousand dollars to our general use." *Mac*, I, ii, 62–64.

dolor, *n.* **1** grief; here, wordplay with "dollar": ". . . thou shalt have as many dolours/ for thy daughters as thou canst tell [count] in a year." *Lear*, II, iv, 54–55. **2 syllable of dolor,** cry of grief: "As if it felt with Scotland, and yell'd out/ Like syllable of dolour." *Mac*, IV, iii, 7–8.

Dolphin, *n.* **1** old var. of **Dauphin:** heir to the French throne: ". . . look upon the years/ Of Lewis [Louis] the Dolphin and that lovely maid . . ." *K John*, II, i, 424–425. **2** poss. song refrain and ref. to "Dauphin," regarded as the earthly incarnation of the Devil: "Dolphin my/ boy, boy; sessa! let him trot by." *Lear*, III, iv, 101–102.

dolphin-like, *adj.* being part of the element, but able to rise above it when necessary: ". . . his delights/ Were dolphin-like, they show'd his back above/ The element they lived in . . ." *Ant & Cleo*, V, ii, 88–90.

dolt, *n.* fool: "Most monster-like be shown/ For poor'st diminutives, for dolts . . ." *Ant & Cleo*, IV, xii, 36–37.

domestic, *n.* menial; lackey: ". . . and your words/ (Domestics to you) serve your will as't please/ Yourself pronounce their office [your words are no sooner pronounced than they are acted upon]." *Hen 8*, II, iv, 111–113.

domestic awe, *n.* reverence and respect due parents: "Domestic awe, night-rest and neighbourhood . . ." *Timon*, IV, i, 17.

dominations, *n.* dominions: "The dominations, royalties and rights/ Of this oppressed boy . . ." *K John*, II, i, 176–177.

dominator, *n.* **1** ruler; monarch: "Great deputy, the welkin's vice-gerent,/ and sole dominator of Navarre . . ." *Love's L*, I, i, 216–217. **2** (in astrology) one's ruling sign or "planet": ". . . though Venus govern your desires,/ Saturn is dominator over mine . . ." *T Andr*, II, iii, 30–31.

domineer, *v.* to enjoy or indulge oneself; here, "yourselves": "Go to the feast, revel and domineer . . ." *Shrew*, III, ii, 222.

dominical, *n.* large red "S" marking Sundays in the old almanacs: "My red dominical, my golden letter:/ O! that your face were not so full of O's." *Love's L*, V, ii, 44–45.

Doncaster, *n.* town N of London, near Manchester: "Forgot your oath to us at Doncaster,/ And being fed by us, you us'd us so . . ." *1 Hen 4,* V, I, 58–59.

done, *past part.* had sexual relations with: "Thou hast undone our mother."/ "Villain, I have done thy mother." *T Andr,* IV, ii, 75–76.

doom, *n.* **1** judgment or decree; sentence: "I bring thee tidings of the Prince's doom." *Rom & Jul,* III, iii, 8. **2** doomsday; Judgment Day: ". . . look on death itself!—up, up, and see/ The great doom's image!" *Mac,* II, iii, 78–79. **3 as against the doom,** as if anticipating eternal judgment: "Heaven's face does glow . . . With tristful visage, as against the doom,/ Is thought-sick at the act." *Ham,* III, iv, 48–51.

doomsday, *n.* extinction; here, of the moon: ". . . and the moist star . . . Was sick almost to doomsday with eclipse." *Ham,* I, i, 121–123.

door, *n.* **1** locality or quarter (used fig.): "Is the wind in that door, i'faith, must/ we all march?" *1 Hen 4,* III, iii, 86–87. **2 forth of doors,** out of doors: "I have no will to wander forth of doors,/ Yet something leads me forth." *J Caes,* III, iii, 3–4. **3 without doors,** outside [the bedroom]: ". . . sits at dinner, and will make/ No wars without doors." *Ant & Cleo,* II, i, 12–13.

doo's, *v.* Fluellen's pron. of "does": "Your grace doo's me as great honours as can be/ desired in the hearts of his subjects . . ." *Hen 5,* IV, vii, 164–165.

Doreus, *n.* earl attending Ajax: ". . . bastard Margarelon/ Hath Doreus prisoner . . ." *Tr & Cr,* V, v, 7–8.

Doricles, *n.* Florizel's bucolic pseudonym: "O Doricles,/ Your praises are too large . . ." *W Tale,* IV, iv, 146–147.

dormouse, *adj.* as a modifier, prob. of negligible size; hence, extremely weak: ". . . only to exasperate you, to awake your dormouse/ valour . . ." *T Night,* III, ii, 17–18.

dost, *v.* 2nd pers. sing. of **do:** "Thou dost lie in't, to be in't and say 'tis thine." *Ham,* V, i, 122.

do't, *v.* See **do** (def. 2a).

dotage, *n.* excessive or, sometimes, foolish affection: "I would she had bestowed this dotage on me . . ." *M Ado,* II, iii, 164.

dotant, *n.* old person; dotard: ". . . such a decayed dotant as you/ seem to be?" *Cor,* V, ii, 43–44.

dotard, *n.* old fool: "Thou dotard! thou art woman-tir'd, unroosted . . ." *W Tale,* II, iii, 74.

dote, *v.* to act or speak irrationally: "Good uncle, can you dote,/ To hide such malice with such holiness?" *2 Hen 6,* II, i, 25–26.

doth, *v.* 3rd pers. sing. of **do;** does: "For here he doth demand to have repaid/ A hundred thousand crowns . . ." *Love's L,* II, i, 142–143.

doting, *pres. part., adj.* **1** acting or speaking foolishly: "Peace, doting wizard, peace; I am not mad." *Errors,* IV, iv, 56. **2** overfond; loving excessively: "Such hazard now must doting Tarquin make . . ." *Luc,* 155.

double, *v.* **1** to thicken; here, indistinct speech caused by drinking: ". . . this knave's tongue begins to double." *2 Hen 6,* II, iii, 89.
—*adj.* **2** twofold; also, perh. "confusing" or "ambiguous": "I understand you not: my griefs are double." *Love's L,* V, ii, 744. **3** doubly powerful: "A lady/ So fair . . . Would make the great'st king double . . ." *Cymb,* I, vii, 119–121. **4** deliberately misleading; ambiguous: "He would say untruths, and be ever double/ Both in his words and meaning." *Hen 8,* IV, ii, 38–39. **5 double as the duke's,** assumption here that the Duke of Venice held the deciding vote [in effect, a double vote] and that Brabantio would have the benefit of this: "And hath in his effect a voice potential/ As double as the duke's . . ." *Oth,* I, ii, 13–14.

double beer, *n.* beer of extra strength: "And here's a pot of good double beer, neighbour:/ drink . . ." *2 Hen 6,* II, iii, 63–64.

double business, *n.* pursuit of two objectives; here, following two courses of action: ". . . like a man to double business bound,/ I stand in pause . . ." *Ham,* III, iii, 41–42.

doubled, *adj.* redoubled: ". . . his doubled spirit/ Requicken'd what in flesh was fatigate [fatigued] . . ." *Cor,* II, ii, 116–117.

double-dealer, *n.* unfaithful spouse: "I might have cudgelled thee out of/ thy single life, to make thee a double-dealer . . ." *M Ado,* V, iv, 112–113.

double-dealing, *n.* wordplay on "tipping twice" and "duplicity": "But that it would be double-dealing, sir, I/ would you could make it another." *T Night,* V, i, 27–28.

double ducat, *n.* ducat having twice the value of an ordinary ducat: ". . . two sealed bags of ducats,/ Of double ducats, stol'n from me by my daughter!" *Merch,* II, viii, 18–19.

double-fatal yew, *n.* ref. to the poisonous leaves and use of the wood in making death-dealing weapons: "Thy very beadsmen learn to bend their bows/ Of double-fatal yew against thy state . . ." *Rich 2*, III, ii, 116–117.

double gilt, *n.* richness; magnificence [from the practice of double-dipping gold plate]: ". . . the double gilt of this opportunity you let/ time wash off . . ." *T Night*, III, ii, 23–24.

double set, *adv.* twice around: "He'll watch the horologe [clock] a double set,/ If drink rock not his cradle." *Oth*, II, iii, 123–124.

double surety, *n.* the pledge of both religious and patriotic devotion: "He is a man/ Who with a double surety binds his followers." *2 Hen 4*, I, i, 190–191.

doublet, *n.* short, tight-fitting jacket, often elaborately cut and decorated: ". . . now will he lie ten nights awake carving the fashion/ of a new doublet." *M Ado*, II, iii, 17–18.

double tongue, *n.* the forked tongue of deceit: a pun on the tongue of a mask and the "false face," or visor: "You have a double tongue within your mask . . ." *Love's L*, V, ii, 245.

double-vantage, *v.* to doubly profit: "Doing thee vantage, double-vantage me." *Sonn 88*, 12.

double voucher, *n.* certificate of title to property guaranteed by two persons: ". . . a great buyer of land . . . with his double vouchers, his/ recoveries." *Ham*, V, i, 102–104.

doubling of files, *n.* simple military drill: ". . . he had/ the honour to be the officer . . . to instruct for the doubling of files." *All's W*, IV, iii, 260–261.

doubt, *v.* **1** to suspect: "Had we fought, I doubt we should have been too/ young for them." *M Ado*, V, i, 118–119. **2** to fear: "Yea, but I doubt they will be too hard for us." *1 Hen 4*, I, ii, 176.
—*n.* **3** suspicion; guess or conjecture: "'Tis a shrewd doubt, though it be but a dream . . ." *Oth*, III, iii, 435. **4 in doubt,** confusingly: ". . . speaks things in doubt/ That carry but half sense." *Ham*, IV, v, 6–7. **5 out of doubt,** beyond doubt: "Now out of doubt Antipholus is mad . . ." *Errors*, IV, iii, 78. **6 'tis doubt,** no doubt: "Depress'd he is already, and depos'd/ 'Tis doubt he will be." *Rich 2*, III, iv, 68–69.

doubtful, *adj.* **1** causing fear; dreadful: "A doubtful warrant of immediate death . . ." *Errors*, I, i, 68. **2** suspicious: "Her obsequies have been as far enlarg'd/ As we have warranty. Her death was doubtful . . ." *Ham*, V, i, 219–220. **3** of dubious outcome: "Let me be umpire in this doubtful strife." *1 Hen 6*, IV, i, 151. **4** anxious; apprehensive: "For till I see them here, by doubtful fear/ My joy of liberty is half eclips'd." *3 Hen 6*, IV, vi, 62–63.

doubtfully, *adv.* **1** ambiguously: "Spake he so doubtfully, thou couldst not feel his meaning?" *Errors*, II, i, 50. **2** frighteningly [in wordplay with previous sense]: ". . . he struck so plainly . . . and withal so doubtfully, that I could/ scarce understand them." *Errors*, II, i, 52–53. **3** uncertainly; anxiously: "For being ignorant to whom it goes,/ I writ at random, very doubtfully." *Two Gent*, II, I, 103–104.

doubtless, *adj.* free from fear: "And, pretty child, sleep doubtless and secure . . ." *K John*, IV, i, 129.

doughty-handed, *adj.* stalwart; valiant: "I thank you all,/ For doughty-handed are you . . . you have shown all Hectors." *Ant & Cleo*, IV, viii, 4–7.

dout, *v.* to blot out; extinguish: "Doth all the noble substance often dout/ To his own scandal." *Ham*, I, iv, 37–38.

dove-drawn, *adj.* ref. to the chariot of Venus, which was drawn by doves: "I met her deity/ Cutting the clouds towards Paphos, and her son/ Dove-drawn with her." *Temp*, IV, i, 92–94.

doves, *n.* in most editions "daws": ". . . I will wear my heart upon my sleeve,/ For doves to peck at . . ." *Oth*, I, i, 64–65.

dowager, *n.* widow living on an income from her husband's estate: "Like to a step-dame or a dowager/ Long withering out a young man's revenue." *M N Dream*, I, i, 5–6.

dowlas, *n.* coarse linen: "I bought you/ a dozen of shirts to your back./ Dowlas, filthy dowlas." *1 Hen 4*, III, iii, 65–67.

dowle, *n.* small feather: ". . . may as well/ Wound the loud winds . . . as diminish/ One dowle that's in my plume . . ." *Temp*, III, iii, 62–65.

down¹, *adv.* **1** downright; outright; with no hesitation: "There did this perjur'd goldsmith swear me down/ That I this day of him receiv'd the chain . . ." *Errors*, V, i, 227–228. **2** as the result of a fall: ". . . in the basket creep,/ And break your own neck down." *Ham*, III, iv, 197–198. **3** to [be brought to] a reduced status; also, to [suffer] defeat: "Nay, then I see that Edward needs must down." *3 Hen 6*, IV, iii, 42. **4** out of the way; gone: "She being down,/ I have the placing of the British crown." *Cymb*, III, v, 65–66. **5 be down together,** to fight on the ground: "We have been down together in my sleep . . ." *Cor*, IV, v, 125.
—*adj.* **6** lying down: "What, dress'd, and in your clothes, and down again?" *Rom & Jul*, IV, v, 12.
—*v.* **7** to fail; suffer defeat: "'Tis like that Richmond with the rest shall down." *3 Hen 6*, IV, vi, 100.

down², *interj.* meaningless syllable used to fill out song refrains: "[Singing] And down, down, adown-a, etc." *Wives,* I, iv, 39.

downfall, *adj.* downfallen: ". . . and like good men/ Bestride our downfall birthdom [native land]." *Mac,* IV, iii, 3–4.

down-gyved, *adj.* fallen; collapsed: ". . . his stockings foul'd,/ Ungarter'd and down-gyved to his ankle . . ." *Ham,* II, i, 79–80.

down-razed, *adj.* torn down: "When sometime lofty towers I see down-raz'd . . ." *Sonn 64,* 3.

downright, *adv.* **1** clearly or openly; also, without letup or without mercy: "We were descried: they'll mock us now downright." *Love's L,* V, ii, 389.
—*adj.* **2** straight on, with a slightly downward tilt: ". . . therefore, Peter, have at/ thee with a downright blow." *2 Hen 6,* II, iii, 87–88. **3** straight down; vertical: "I cleft his beaver with a downright blow . . ." *3 Hen 6,* I, i, 12. **4** plain; ordinary: ". . . this Angelo was not made by man and woman,/ after this downright way of creation . . ." *Meas,* III, ii, 100–101. **5 downright violence,** flagrant disregard of convention: "My downright violence, and scorn of fortunes . . ." *Oth,* I, iii, 249.

down-roping, *pres. part.* dribbling down: "The gum downroping from their pale-dead eyes . . ." *Hen 5,* IV, ii, 48.

Downs, *n. pl.* roadstead along the E coast of Kent: ". . . whilst our pinnace anchors in the Downs . . ." *2 Hen 6,* IV, i, 9.

down sleeve, *n.* sleeve extending to the wrist: ". . . down sleeves, side sleeves,/ and skirts, round underborne . . ." *M Ado,* III, iv, 19–20.

downtrodden equity, *n.* trampled right: "For this downtrodden equity we tread/ In warlike march these greens before your town . . ." *K John,* II, i, 241–242.

downward hath succeeded, has been handed or passed down: ". . . a ring the county wears/ That downward hath succeeded in his house/ From son to son . . ." *All's W,* III, vii, 22–23.

downy, *adj.* soft; peaceful: "Shake off this downy sleep, death's counterfeit . . ." *Mac,* II, iii, 77.

dowry, *n.* gift; endowment: ". . . often known/ To be the dowry of a second head,/ The skull that bred them in the sepulchre." *Merch,* III, ii, 94–96.

doxy, *n.* beggar's woman; also, a female beggar: "When daffodils begin to peer,/ With heigh! the doxy over the dale . . ." *W Tale,* IV, iii, 1–2.

dozy, *v.* to dizzy; make giddy: ". . . to divide him inventorially would/ dozy th'arithmetic of memory . . ." *Ham,* V, ii, 113–114.

drab, *n.* slut; prostitute: "Finger of birth-strangled babe,/ Ditch-deliver'd by a drab . . ." *Mac,* IV, i, 30–31.

drabbing, *n.* consorting with prostitutes; whoring: "Ay, or drinking, fencing, swearing,/ Quarrelling, drabbing—you may go so far." *Ham,* II, i, 25–26.

drachma, *n.* Greek coin; here, a worthless coin: "See here these movers, that do prize their hours/ At a crack'd drachma!" *Cor,* I, v, 4–5.

draff, *n.* food for swine; swill: ". . . lately/ come from swine-keeping, from eating draff and/ husks." *1 Hen 4,* IV, ii, 34–36.

dragons, *n.* drawers of Night's chariot: ". . . night's swift dragons cut the clouds full fast . . ." *M N Dream,* III, ii, 379.

dragon's tail, *n.* constellation Draco, in the northern sky: "My father compounded with my mother under/ the dragon's tail . . ." *Lear,* I, ii, 135–136.

dram, *n.* **1** poison: "Those that with cords, knives, drams, precipitance,/ Weary of this world's light . . ." *Kinsmen,* I, i, 142–143. **2 dram of a scruple,** smallest amount; tiniest particle: ". . . no dram of a scruple, no scruple of a/ scruple, no obstacle, no incredulous or unsafe circumstance . . ." *T Night,* III, iv, 79–81. **3 make a dram of a scruple,** to experience a particle of doubt: ". . . the/ wise may make some dram of a scruple, or indeed a/ scruple itself." *2 Hen 4,* I, ii, 128–130.

draught, *n.* **1** amount drunk at one gulp: ". . . one draught above heat makes him a fool . . ." *T Night,* I, v, 133. **2** sewer, cesspool, or, often, a privy: "Hang them or stab them, drown them in a draught . . ." *Timon,* V, i, 101.

drave, *v.* old past tense of **drive:** "I drave my suitor from his mad humour of love to a living humour of madness [from being obsessed with love to being certifiably mad]." *As You,* III, ii, 406–407.

draw, *v.* **1** to draw up; compose: ". . . resolv'd/ To draw conditions of a friendly peace . . ." *1 Hen 6,* V, i, 37–38. **2** to disembowel (a person) after hanging; here, in wordplay with drawing [pulling (a tooth)]: "You must hang it first, and draw it afterwards." *M Ado,* III, ii, 23. **3** to assemble or levy (an army): "That such an army could be drawn in France . . ." *K John,* IV, ii, 118. **4** to take or collect: "If every ducat . . . Were in six parts, and every part a ducat,/ I would not draw them . . ." *Merch,* IV, i, 85–87. **5** to follow, as an inclination; be attracted: "But nature to her bias drew in that." *T Night,* V, i, 258. **6** (of musicians) to begin playing, as by drawing a bow across the strings of an instrument: "I will bid thee draw, as we do the minstrels—draw to pleasure us." *M Ado,* V, i, 128–129. **7** to pull back: "This absence of your father's draws a curtain/ That shows the ignorant a kind of fear . . ." *1 Hen 4,* IV, i, 73–74. **8** to withdraw; rescind or cancel: "Go, wash thy face, and/ draw the action." *2 Hen 4,* II, i, 147–148. **9** to drag: "Hooking both right and wrong to th'appetite,/ To follow as it draws!" *Meas,* II, iv, 175–176. **10** to draw liquor from a barrel or cask: "I will entertain [hire] Bardolph; he shall draw, he shall/ tap." *Wives,* I, iii, 10–11. **11 draw me much about,** take me in a roundabout way: "My purposes do draw me much about,/ You'll win two days upon me." *Ant & Cleo,* II, iv, 8–9. **12 drawn your number,** assembled your supporters: ". . . when you have drawn your number,/ Repair to th'Capitol." *Cor,* II, iii, 251–252. **13 draw on,** to threaten (a person) by drawing one's sword: "My Lord your son drew on my master." *Cymb,* I, ii, 91. **14 draw (someone) on,** to attract or entice (someone): ". . . so by your companies/ To draw him on to pleasures and to gather,/ So much as from occasion you may glean . . ." *Ham,* II, ii, 14–16. **15 draw out,** to choose; select: "Artesius, that best knowest/ How to draw out, fit to this enterprise . . ." *Kinsmen,* I, i, 159–160. **16 draw something near,** to fit with; be very similar to: ". . . it draws something near to the/ speech we had to such a purpose." *Meas,* I, ii, 71–72. **17 draw to that point,** See **point** (def. 12). **18 draw toward an end,** finish one's dealings [with]: "Come, sir, to draw toward an end with you." *Ham,* III, iv, 218.

draw cuts, *v.* to draw lots or straws: "We'll draw cuts for the senior; till then, lead thou first." *Errors,* V, i, 422.

draw dry-foot, *v.* to track game entirely by the scent: "A hound that runs counter, and yet draws dry-foot well . . ." *Errors,* IV, ii, 39.

drawer, *n.* tapster; also, waiter or server: "Put on two leathern jerkins and aprons, and wait/ upon him at his table as drawers." *2 Hen 4,* II, ii, 164–165.

drawing days out, *v.* attempting to prolong life: "That we shall die, we know; 'tis but the time/ And drawing days out, that men stand upon." *J Caes,* III, i, 99–100.

drawling, *adj.* drawing out one's words, esp. in an affected manner: "I never heard such a drawling, affecting rogue." *Wives,* II, i, 137.

drawn, *past part.* **1** drawn together: ". . . his friends by deputation could not/ So soon be drawn . . ." *1 Hen 4,* IV, i, 32–33. **2** etched; here, fig. use: "And you must live, drawn by your own sweet skill." *Sonn 16,* 14. **3** won: ". . . a fool,/ That seest a game play'd home, the rich stake drawn . . ." *W Tale,* I, ii,

247–248. **4** emptied: ". . . the/ purse too light, being drawn of heaviness." *Cymb,* V, iv, 165–166.
—*adj.* **5** having the sword drawn: "Here, villain, drawn and ready. Where art thou?" *M N Dream,* III, ii, 402. **6** (of a dead fox) disemboweled and used to mark a false trail: ". . . no more truth in thee than in a drawn/ fox . . ." *1 Hen 4,* III, iii, 111–112. **7 right drawn,** (of a sword) drawn in a righteous cause: "What my tongue speaks my right drawn sword may prove." *Rich 2,* I, i, 46.

drawn in little, *adj.* reduced to the smallest size or compacted into the smallest space: "If all the devils of hell be drawn in little . . ." *T Night,* III, iv, 85–86.

drawn to head, assembled: "The powers that he already hath in Gallia/ Will soon be drawn to head . . ." *Cymb,* III, v, 24–25.

draw short breath, *v.* to fight; engage in a duel: "O, would . . . that no man might draw short breath today/ But I and Harry Monmouth!" *1 Hen 4,* V, ii, 47–49.

drayman, *n.* driver of a dray, a brewer's cart: "Achilles? A drayman, a porter, a very camel." *Tr & Cr,* I, ii, 253.

dread, *adj.* deeply revered: "Welcome, my lord; welcome, dread queen . . ." *T Andr,* V, iii, 26.

dread-bolted, *adj.* accompanied by the dread thunderbolt: "To stand against the deep dread-bolted thunder?" *Lear,* IV, vii, 33.

dreadful, *adj.* **1** inspiring fear or dread; dreaded: "Hear your own dignity so much profan'd,/ See your most dreadful laws so loosely slighted . . ." *2 Hen 4,* V, ii, 93–94. **2** filled with dread; fearful: "This to me/ In dreadful secrecy impart they did . . ." *Ham,* I, ii, 206–207.

dream, *n.* **1 as offended in a dream,** offended without conscious intent: "He hath but as offended in a dream;/ All sects, all ages smack of this vice . . ." *Meas,* II, ii, 4–5.
—*v.* **2 dream on,** to think about: "Then never dream on infamy, but go." *Two Gent,* II, vii, 64.

dreg, *n.* **1** [pl.] last bit: "I will here shroud till the/ dregs of the storm be past." *Temp,* II, ii, 41–42. **2 too curious dreg,** tiny blemish or obstacle; here, imagined by Cressida: "What too curious dreg espies my/ sweet lady in the fountain of our love?" *Tr & Cr,* III, ii, 64–65.

dregg'd, *past part.* checked; hindered: "When that his action's dregg'd with mind assur'd/ 'Tis bad he goes about." *Kinsmen,* I, ii, 97–98.

drench, *n.* **1** drink; also, a purge or other dose of medicine: " 'Give my roan/ horse a drench,' says he . . ." *1 Hen 4,* II, iv, 104–105.
—*v.* **2** to cover with blood: "Made the all-honour'd . . . Brutus,/ With the arm'd rest . . . To drench the Capitol . . ." *Ant & Cleo,* II, vi, 16–18.

drenched, *adj.* immersed: "O where am I? . . . in the ocean drench'd, or in the fire?" *Ven & Ad,* 493–494.

dress, *v.* **1** to cultivate; maintain: "O, what pity is it/ That he had not so trimm'd and dress'd his land/ As we this garden!" *Rich 2,* III, iv, 55–57. **2** (in cookery) to make ready; prepare: ". . . a woman is a dish for the gods, if the devil/ dress her not." *Ant & Cleo,* V, ii, 273–274. **3 dressed to,** prepared for: ". . . hem and stroke thy beard,/ As he being dress'd to some oration." *Tr & Cr,* I, iii, 165–166. **4 dress us fairly,** prepare ourselves adequately: ". . . admonishing/ That we should dress us fairly for our end." *Hen 5,* IV, i, 9, 10.

dresser, *n.* sideboard, table, etc., on which food is set for serving: "How durst you, villains, bring it from the dresser/ And serve it thus . . ." *Shrew,* IV, i, 150–151.

dressings, *n. pl.* **1** vestments: ". . . even so may Angelo,/ In all his dressings . . . Be an arch-villain." *Meas,* V, i, 58–60. **2** elaborations: "They are but dressings of a former sight." *Sonn 123,* 4.

dribbling dart, *n.* arrow shot with insufficient force to reach its target: "Believe not that the dribbling dart of love/ Can pierce a complete bosom." *Meas,* I, iii, 2–3.

drift, *n.* **1** intent or intentions: "In the meantime, against thou shalt awake,/ Shall Romeo by my letters know our drift . . ." *Rom & Jul,* IV, i, 113–114. **2** scheme or plot: "If this should fail,/ And that our drift look through our bad performance . . ." *Ham,* IV, vii, 149–150. **3** aim; meaning: "My free drift/ Halts not particularly . . ." *Timon,* I, i, 45–46. **4** shower: "Our thunder [cannon] from the south/ Shall rain their drift of bullets on this town." *K John,* II, i, 411–412.

drink, *n.* **1** prob. posset, a bedtime drink, usually of hot spiced wine and milk: "Go, bid thy mistress, when my drink is ready,/ She strike upon the bell." *Mac,* II, i, 31–32.
—*v.* **2** to inhale: "In their thick breaths . . . shall we be enclouded,/ And forc'd to drink their vapour." *Ant & Cleo,* V, ii, 210–212. **3 drink after (someone),** fr. belief that one could catch the pox [venereal disease] by drinking from the same cup as another: "I will . . . learn to begin thy health; but . . . forget to drink after thee." *Meas,* I, ii, 35–37. **4 drink in,** to imbibe; quaff: "I think I shall drink in pipe-wine first . . ." *Wives,* III, ii, 82. **5 drink to (another),** to drink the health of (another); here, to poison one's own drink as well: "If thou

hadst drunk to him, 't had been a kindness/ Becoming well thy fact [deed]." *Per,* IV, iii, 11–12.

drive, *v.* **1** to rush: ". . . the hounds/ Should drive upon thy new-transformed limbs,/ Unmannerly intruder as thou art." *T Andr,* II, iii, 66–67. **2** old past tense of **drive** [pron. "driv"]: "A troubled mind drive me to walk abroad . . ." *Rom & Jul,* I, i, 118. **3 drive unto,** to reduce to: "Which humbleness may drive unto a fine." *Merch,* IV, i, 368.

driving, *adj.* driven by the wind: "When you and those poor number sav'd with you/ Hung on our driving boat . . ." *T Night,* I, ii, 10–11.

drollery, *n.* **1** comic painting: ". . . and for thy walls, a pretty slight drollery . . ." *2 Hen 4,* II, i, 141–142. **2** puppet show; here, one with living puppets: "What were these?"/ "A living drollery." *Temp,* III, iii, 20–21.

drone, *n.* beetle: "Drones suck not eagles' blood but rob beehives." *2 Hen 6,* IV, i, 108.

droop, *v.* **1** to suffer a decline, esp. of health: "Sick now? Droop now? This sickness doth infect/ The very life-blood of our enterprise . . ." *1 Hen 4,* IV, i, 28–29. **2** to be depressed; languish: "Anon, as patient as the female dove . . . His silence will sit drooping." *Ham,* V, i, 281–283.

drooping, *adj.* ref. to sun sinking in the west: "I, from the Orient to the drooping West . . ." *2 Hen 4,* Induc., 3.

drop, *n.* **1** [pl.] dewdrops: "Now with the drops of this most balmy time . . ." *Sonn 107,* 9. **2 drops of salt,** tears [those shed by Volumnia and Virgilia]: ". . . given up,/ For certain drops of salt, your city Rome . . ." *Cor,* V, vi, 92–93.

droplet, *n.* [often pl.] tear: ". . . those our droplets which/ From niggard nature fall . . ." *Timon,* V, iv, 76–77.

dropping, *adj.* **1** dripping; drenched: "And with a dropping industry they skip/ From stem to stern . . ." *Per,* IV, i, 62–63. **2** tearful; weeping: ". . . as 'twere with a defeated joy,/ With an auspicious and a dropping eye . . ." *Ham,* I, ii, 10–11.

dropsied, *adj.* swollen; inflated: "Where great additions swell's and virtue none,/ It is a dropsied honour." *All's W,* II, iii, 127–128.

drossy, *adj.* frivolous; empty-headed or worthless: ". . . many more of the same bevy that I/ know the drossy age dotes on . . ." *Ham,* V, ii, 185–186.

drouth, *n.* dryness; here, thirst: ". . . crickets at the oven's mouth/ Sing the blither for their drouth." *Per,* III, Chor., 7–8.

droven, *v.* old past part. of **drive; driven:** "Had we done so at first, we had droven them home/ With clouts about their heads." *Ant & Cleo,* IV, vi, 5–6.

drover, *n.* cattle-dealer or cattle-driver: "Why, that's spoken like an honest drover . . ." *M Ado,* II, i, 181.

drown, *v.* **drowned the cocks,** See **cock**[1] (def. 2).

drowned, *adj.* **1** (esp. of the eyes) inundated with tears: "And these who, often drown'd, could never die,/ Transparent heretics, be burnt for liars." *Rom & Jul,* I, ii, 92–93. **2 drowned in the last rain,** gone out of fashion; poss. ref. to enthusiasm having been dampened: "Is't not/ drowned i'th'last rain? Ha? What say'st thou, trot?" *Meas,* III, ii, 47–48.

drowning mark, *n.* ref. to the proverb, "He that is born to be hanged will never drown": ". . . methinks he/ hath no drowning mark upon him; his complexion/ is perfect gallows." *Temp,* I, i, 28–30.

drowsy, *adj.* sleep-inducing: "Nor all the drowsy syrups of the world . . ." *Oth,* III, iii, 337.

drudge, *n.* menial [term of abuse]: ". . . these paltry, servile, abject drudges." *2 Hen 6,* IV, i, 104.

drug, *n.* **1** menial; drudge: ". . . such as may the passive drugs of it/ Freely command . . ." *Timon,* IV, iii, 256–257. **2** poison-yielding plant: "Here grow no damned drugs, here are no storms,/ No noise, but silence and eternal sleep." *T Andr,* I, i, 154–155.

drug-damned, *adj.* damned because of its many poisonings: "That drug-damn'd Italy hath out-craftied him . . ." *Cymb,* III, iv, 15.

drum, *n.* **1** a place of assembly for troops, after being summoned by a drum: "O, I could wish this tavern were my drum." *1 Hen 4,* III, iii, 205. **2** drummer: "He's a good drum, my lord, but a naughty [dreadful] orator." *All's W,* V, iii, 249. **3** sound of the drum as a sign of military preparedness: "Where's thy drum?" *Lear,* IV, ii, 55.
—*v.* **4** to summon: ". . . to confound such time,/ That drums him from his sport . . ." *Ant & Cleo,* I, iv, 28–29.

drumble, *v.* to dawdle; dillydally: "Look, how you drumble! Carry them to/ the laundress in Datchet Mead; quickly, come." *Wives,* III, iii, 136–137.

dry, *adj.* **1** dull; boring: "This jest is dry to me. My gentle sweet,/ Your wit makes wise things foolish . . ." *Love's L,* V, ii, 373–374. **2** lacking wit: "Go to, y'are a dry fool: I'll no more of you." *T Night,* I, v, 38. **3** vacuous or obtuse: ". . . were his brain as barren/ As banks of Libya . . . 'Tis dry enough . . ." *Tr & Cr,*

I, iii, 327–329. **4** thirsty; here, eager or greedy: "So dry he was for sway, wi' th' King of Naples/ To give him annual tribute, do him homage . . ." *Temp,* I, ii, 112–113.

dry basting, *n.* beating in which the skin is not broken: "Lest it make you choleric, and purchase me/ another dry basting." *Errors,* II, ii, 61–62.

dry-beat, *v.* to thrash or cudgel; bruise without drawing blood: ". . . one of your nine/ lives. That I mean to make bold withal, and . . . dry-beat the rest of the eight." *Rom & Jul,* III, i, 76–78.

dry-beaten, *adj.* bruised but not bloody: "By heaven, all dry-beaten with pure scoff!" *Love's L,* V, ii, 263.

dry hand, *n.* regarded as a sign of aging: "Here's his dry hand up and down:/ you are he, you are he." *M Ado,* II, i, 108–109.

ducat, *n.* **1** gold or, sometimes, silver coin used in various European countries; worth perh. one-third of a pound sterling: "Be cunning in the working this,/ and thy fee is a thousand ducats." *M Ado,* II, ii, 52–53. **2 dead for a ducat,** the fee [here claimed by Hamlet] for killing a rat: "How now? A rat! Dead for a ducat, dead." *Ham,* III, iv, 23.

duck, *v.* to bow; make obeisance: ". . . the learned pate/ Ducks to the golden fool . . ." *Timon,* IV, iii, 18.

dudgeon, *n.* handle, as of a dagger: "And on thy blade, and dudgeon, gouts of blood . . ." *Mac,* II, i, 46.

due[1], *adj.* **1 due to,** possessed by: ". . . is it a fee-grief,/ Due to some single breast?" *Mac,* IV, iii, 196–197. **2 due unto,** which should have been delivered by means of: "So that my errand due unto my tongue . . . I bare home upon my shoulders . . ." *Errors,* II, i, 72–73.
—*n.* **3** [usually pl.] debts or other obligations: ". . . what remains will hardly stop the mouth/ Of present dues." *Timon,* II, ii, 151–152. **4** [pl.] rightful claims: "The offices of nature, bond of childhood,/ Effects of courtesy, dues of gratitude . . ." *Lear,* II, iv, 180–181. **5** justice: ". . . not ever/ The justice and the truth of th'question carries/ The due o'th'verdict [a just verdict] with it . . ." *Hen 8,* V, i, 129–131.

due[2], *v.* endue; honor or glorify: "This is the latest [last] glory of thy praise,/ That I, thy enemy, due thee withal . . ." *1 Hen 6,* IV, ii, 33–34.

duello, *n.* rules governing dueling: ". . . the passado he/ respects not, the duello he regards not . . ." *Love's L,* I, ii, 168–169.

duer paid, *adj.* more promptly paid [when due]: ". . . duer paid to the hearer than/ the Turk's tribute." *2 Hen 4,* III, ii, 301–302.

dug, *n.* teat: "Shall thy old dugs once more a traitor rear?" *Rich 2,* V, iii, 88.

duke, *v.* **duke it,** to assume the role of a duke: "Lord Angelo dukes it well in his absence . . ." *Meas,* III, ii, 91.

dulcet diseases, *n.* ref. to the fool's arrow (bolt) that may cause anger or pain: "According to the fool's bolt sir, and such dulcet/ diseases." *As You,* IV, iv, 63–64.

dulcet in contagion, *adj.* sweetly stinking: "To hear by the nose, it is dulcet in contagion." *T Night,* II, iii, 57.

dull, *adj.* **1** insensitive; indifferent: "O thou dull god, why li'st thou with the vile/ In loathsome beds . . ." *2 Hen 4,* III, i, 15–16. **2** without feeling: "The woods are ruthless, dreadful, deaf, and dull . . ." *T Andr,* II, i, 128. **3** drowsy or, often, producing drowsiness: "Let there be no noise made . . . Unless some dull and favourable hand/ Will whisper music to my weary spirit." *2 Hen 4,* IV, v, 1–2. **4** dim; obscured: "My sight is very dull, whate'er it bodes." *T Andr,* II, iii, 195. **5** slow-witted; obtuse or stupid: "You are dull, Casca, and those sparks of life/ That should be in a Roman you do want . . ." *J Caes,* I, iii, 57–58. **6** untrained; inexperienced: "Like a dull actor now/ I have forgot my part . . ." *Cor,* V, iii, 40–41. **7** quiet; stilled: "Now our sands are almost run;/ More a little, and then dumb." *Per,* V, ii, 1–2. **8** heavy: "If the dull substance of my flesh were thought . . ." *Sonn 44,* 1. **9** sullen; surly: ". . . where the dull tribunes,/ That with the fusty plebeians hate thine honours . . ." *Cor,* I, ix, 6–7.
—*v.* **10** to tire: ". . . his bedfellow,/ Whom he hath dull'd and cloy'd with gracious favours . . ." *Hen 5,* II, ii, 9.

dullard, *n.* **make a dullard of the world,** assume that everyone else is stupid: "And thou must make a dullard of the world,/ If they not thought [wouldn't think] the profits of my death . . ." *Lear,* II, i, 74–75.

dulled, *adj.* lifeless; inert: ". . . the rarest dream that e'er dull'd sleep/ Did mock sad fools withal . . ." *Per,* V, i, 161–162.

duller Britain, *n.* perh. fr. belief that brains operated more sluggishly in northern climates: ". . . mine Italian brain/ Gan in your duller Britain operate/ Most vilely . . ." *Cymb,* V, v, 196–197.

dull sight, *n.* dreary spectacle; or perh. a ref. to Lear's failing eyesight: "This is a dull sight. Are you not Kent?" *Lear,* V, iii, 282.

dulness, *n.* drowsiness: "Thou art inclin'd to sleep; 'tis a good dulness,/ And give it way . . ." *Temp,* I, ii, 185–186.

dumb, *adj.* **1** silent: "Dumb jewels often in their silent kind . . . do move a woman's mind." *Two Gent,* III, i, 90–91. **2** (of a poet) lacking a theme or subject: "For who's so dumb that cannot write to thee . . ." *Sonn 38,* 7. **3** [but] without the power of speech: ". . . the cutter/ Was as another Nature, dumb . . ." *Cymb,* II, iv, 83–84.
—*v.* **4** to silence: "Deep clerks she dumbs . . ." *Per,* V, Chor., 5.
—*adv.* **5** into silence: ". . . presuming them to have some force,/ Or sentencing for aye their vigor dumb . . ." *Kinsmen,* I, i, 194–195.

dumb-discoursive, *adj.* communicating without speech: "There lurks a still and dumb-discoursive devil/ That tempts most cunningly." *Tr & Cr,* IV, iv, 89–90.

dumbness, *n.* silence; muteness: "To th' dumbness of the gesture/ One might interpret." *Timon,* I, i, 33–34.

dumb-show, *n.* **1** story enacted in pantomime: ". . . that's the scene that I would see, which will be/ merely a dumb-show." *M Ado,* II, iii, 209–210. **2** short pantomime that is a synopsis of the play that follows: ". . . capable/ of nothing but inexplicable dumb-shows and noise." *Ham,* III, ii, 11–12.

dump, *n.* **1** sad tune or song; here, a contradiction in terms: "O play me some merry dump to comfort me." *Rom & Jul,* IV, v, 105. **2** [pl] sadness or melancholy: "Sing no more ditties, sing no moe,/ Of dumps so dull and heavy . . ." *M Ado,* II, iii, 70–71. **3 in one's dumps,** in a glum or depressed mood: "Why, how now, daughter Katherine? In your dumps?" *Shrew,* II, i, 277.

dun, *adj.* **1** brown [used here of mice]; here also, wordplay with Romeo's "done": "Tut, dun's the mouse, the constable's own word [mice, like constables, are silent and inconspicuous]." *Rom & Jul,* I, iv, 40. **2** dark; swarthy: "If snow be white, why then her breasts are dun . . ." *Sonn 130,* 3.
—*n.* **3** perh. wordplay on "Dun," common name for a horse (regardless of color) and "done," ref. to common problem of being stuck in mud: "If thou art dun, we'll draw thee from the mire/ Of . . . love, wherein thou stickest . . ." *Rom & Jul,* I, iv, 41–42.

dung, *n.* food grown in manure: ". . . never palates more the dung,/ The beggar's nurse, and Caesar's." *Ant & Cleo,* V, ii, 7–8.

dunghill, *adj.* **1** term of abuse: "Shall I be flouted thus by dunghill grooms?" *1 Hen 6,* I, iii, 14.
—*n.* **2** abusive term of address: "Out, dunghill!" *Lear,* IV, vi, 245.

dungy, *adj.* covered with or made of dung: "... our dungy earth alike/ Feeds beast as man ..." *Ant & Cleo,* I, i, 35–36.

dunnest, *adj.* darkest: "... pall thee in the dunnest smoke of Hell ..." *Mac,* I, v, 51.

Dunsmore, *n.* town NW of London: "By this at Dunsmore, marching hitherward." *3 Hen 6,* V, i, 3.

Dunstable, *n.* town N of London: "The Archbishop/ Of Canterbury ... Held a late court at Dunstable ..." *Hen 8,* IV, i, 24–27.

dup, *v.* to open: "Then up he rose, and donn'd his clo'es,/ And dupp'd the chamber door ..." *Ham,* IV, v, 52–53.

durance, *n.* **1** confinement; imprisonment: "... he upon some action/ Is now in durance, at Malvolio's suit ..." *T Night,* V, i, 273–274. **2** wordplay on leather coat of arresting sergeant and imprisonment: "... is not a buff jerkin a most sweet robe of durance?" *1 Hen 4,* I, ii, 42.

durst, *v.* past tense of **dare:** "So, I am free; yet would not so have been,/ Durst I have done my will." *J Caes,* V, iii, 47–48.

dusky, *adj.* **1** extinguished: "Here dies the dusky torch of Mortimer ..." *1 Hen 6,* II, v, 122. **2** dim or obscure; also, gloomy: "... they did plot/ The means that dusky Dis [Pluto] my daughter got ..." *Temp,* IV, i, 88–89.

dust, *n.* particle of dust: "Why have those banish'd and forbidden legs/ Dar'd once to touch a dust of England's ground?" *Rich 2,* II, iii, 89–90.

Dutch dish, *n.* Dutch cooking was thought to contain much oil and grease: "... I was more than/ half stewed in grease, like a Dutch dish ..." *Wives,* III, v, 109–110.

duteous, *adj.* dutiful: "The eyes, 'fore duteous, now converted are ..." *Sonn 7,* 11.

duty, *n.* **1** curtsy: "Stay not thy compliment; I forgive/ thy duty: adieu." *Love's L,* IV, ii, 137–138. **2** obeisance, as the act of kneeling or bowing: "Show me thy humble heart, and not thy knee,/ Whose duty is deceivable and false." *Rich 2,* II, iii, 83–84. **3** wordplay on "obedience" and "bowing": "I commend my duty to your lordship."/ "Yours./ A does well to commend it himself, there are no/ tongues else for's turn." *Ham,* V, ii, 179–182. **4** compensation due one: "Do thy duty, and have thy duty ..." *Shrew,* IV, i, 32. **5** [pl.] honor and respect due: "He gave you all the duties of a man ..." *1 Hen 4,* V, ii, 55. **6 express our duty,** (to) pay our respects: "If that his Majesty would aught with us,/ We shall express our duty in his eye ..." *Ham,* IV, iv, 5–6. **7 in personal duty,** like servants in attendance: "In personal duty, following where he haunted ..." *Lover's Comp,* 120.

dwell, *v.* **1** to remain: "I'll rather dwell in my necessity ..." *Merch,* I, iii, 151. **2** to rely: "... she dwells so securely on/ the excellency of her honour ..." *Wives,* II, ii, 233–234.

dweller, *n.* person who seeks favors from the rich and powerful: "Have I not seen dwellers on form and favour/ Lose all, and more ..." *Sonn 125,* 5–6.

dyeing scarlet, *v.* prob. to become red-faced as a result of heavy drinking: "They call drinking deep 'dyeing scarlet,' and when/ you breathe in your watering they cry 'Hem!' ..." *1 Hen 4,* II, iv, 15–16.

dying fall, *n.* final, or concluding, musical pattern; poss. also a descending melody with diminuendo: "That strain again, it had a dying fall ..." *T Night,* I, i, 4.

— E —

each, *pron.* **1 at each,** one atop the other: "Ten masts at each make not the altitude/ Which thou hast perpendicularly fell . . ." *Lear,* IV, vi, 53–54. **2 each at other,** at each other: "Make mouths upon me when I turn my back,/ Wink each at other . . ." *M N Dream,* III, ii, 238–239.

each under each, each one harmoniously linked with every other for a melodious effect: ". . . match'd in mouth like bells,/ Each under each: a cry more tuneable/ Was never holla'd to . . ." *M N Dream,* IV, i, 122–124.

eager, *adj.* **1** vehement; impetuous: "What shrill-voic'd suppliant makes this eager cry?" *Rich 2,* V, iii, 73. **2** sharp; biting: "It is a nipping and an eager air." *Ham,* I, iv, 2. **3** harsh; bitter: "If so thou think'st, vex him with eager words." *3 Hen 6,* II, vi, 68. **4** of vinegar or other acid: ". . . with a sudden vigour it doth posset/ And curd, like eager droppings into milk . . ." *Ham,* I, v, 68–69.

eagle-sighted, *adj.* having the power of an eagle, unique among birds, to gaze at the sun: "What peremptory eagle-sighted eye/ Dares look upon the heaven of her brow . . ." *Love's L,* IV, iii, 222–223.

ean, *v.* to yean; bring forth young: "So many weeks ere the poor fools will ean . . ." *3 Hen 6,* II, v, 36.

eaning time, *n.* time of childbirth: "I well remember, even on my eaning time . . ." *Per,* III, iv, 5.

eanling, *n.* newborn lamb: ". . . all the eanlings which were streak'd and pied/ Should fall as Jacob's hire . . ." *Merch,* I, iii, 74–75.

ear¹, *n.* **1** ear of corn or other grain: ". . . like a mildew'd ear/ Blasting his wholesome brother." *Ham,* III, iv, 64–65. **2 by the ears,** quarreling: "The Florentines and Senoys are by th' ears . . ." *All's W,* I, ii, 1. **3 ears more deaf than adders,** See **adder. 4 hears with ears,** poss. Biblical ref. to 44th Psalm ["We

have heard with our ears, O God . . ."]: "Pistol!"/ "He hears with ears." *Wives,* I, i, 133–134. **5 his proper ear,** his own hearing: "To accuse this worthy man . . . And in the witness of his proper ear . . ." *Meas,* V, I, 305–306. **6 in ear and ear,** in one ear after the other: "Will nothing stick our person to arraign/ In ear and ear." *Ham,* IV, v, 93–94. **7 in the ear,** within hearing or earshot: "And I'll be plac'd, so please you, in the ear/ Of all their conference." *Ham,* III, i, 186–187. **8 light of ear,** listening to gossip and scandal: ". . . false of heart, light of ear, bloody of/ hand . . ." *Lear,* III, iv, 93–94. **9 o'er ears,** up to or over my ears [in water]: "I will fetch off my bottle, though I be o'er ears for/ my labour." *Temp,* IV, i, 213–214.

ear², *v.* to plow: ". . . let them go/ To ear the land that hath some hope to grow . . ." *Rich 2,* III, ii, 211–212.

ear-bussing, *adj.* whispered [lit., ear-kissing]: ". . . they are yet but ear-bussing arguments [topics]." *Lear,* II, i, 8–9.

earing, *n.* plowing: "When our quick minds lie still, and our ills told us/ Is as our earing." *Ant & Cleo,* I, ii, 107–108.

earliest, *adj.* **with your earliest,** at your earliest convenience: ". . . to-morrow with your earliest,/ Let me have speech with you . . ." *Oth,* II, iii, 7–8.

early days, *n.* early in the morning: "No trumpet answers."/ "'Tis but [still] early days." *Tr & Cr,* IV, v, 12.

earn, *v.* to grieve; mourn: "That every like is not the same, O Caesar!/ The heart of Brutus earns to think upon." *J Caes,* II, ii, 128–129.

earnest, *n.* **1** sincerity; seriousness: ". . . there is too great testimony in your complexion that it was a passion of earnest." *As You,* IV, iii, 169–171. **2** pledge or promise: "This supernatural soliciting/ Cannot be ill . . . If ill, why hath it given me earnest of success . . ." *Mac,* I, iii, 130–132. **3** money given as part payment; deposit: ". . . and from his coffers/ Receiv'd the golden earnest of our death . . ." *Hen 5*, II, ii, 168–169. **4** wordplay on preceding senses: "But did you perceive/ her earnest?"/ "She gave me none, except an angry word." *Two Gent*, II, i, 147–149. **5 in earnest,** as payment in advance: ". . . I will even take sixpence in earnest of the bearward . . ." *M Ado*, II, i, 35–36.

—*adj.* **6** sincere; here, wordplay on "serious" and "earnest money," down payment on a bargain: ". . . now your jest is earnest,/ Upon what bargain do you give it me?" *Errors*, II, ii, 24–25.

earth, *n.* **1** human body: "My will that marks thee for my earth's delight . . ." *Luc*, 487. **2 of earth and water wrought,** [the body] made of the slow and heavy elements rather than the nimble elements of air and fire: ". . . so much of earth and water wrought,/ I must attend time's leisure with my moan . . ." *Sonn 44*, 11–12.

—*v.* **3** to bury in the earth: "Who shall be of as little memory/ When he is earth'd . . ." *Temp*, II, i, 228–229.

earth-delving conies, *n.* burrowing rabbits: ". . . sometime where earth-delving conies keep,/ To stop the loud pursuers in their yell . . ." *Ven & Ad*, 687–688.

earthlier happy, *adj.* happier on earth: "But earthlier happy is the rose distill'd . . ." *M N Dream*, I, i, 76.

earthquake, *n.* riot; tumult: "And great affections wrastling in thy bosom/ Doth make an earthquake of nobility." *K John*, V, ii, 41–42.

earthy, *adj.* earthly: "What earthy name to interrogatories/ Can taste the free breath of a sacred king?" *K John*, III, i, 73–74.

ease, *v.* **1** to free from anxiety: "Nor I, nor any man . . . With nothing shall be pleas'd, till he be eas'd/ With being nothing." *Rich 2*, V, v, 39–41.

—*n.* **2** something to relieve the pain and discomfort of venereal disease: "Till then I'll sweat and seek about for eases . . ." *Tr & Cr*, V, x, 56. **3 at what ease,** how easily: ". . . at what ease/ Might corrupt minds procure knaves as corrupt/ To swear against you?" *Hen 8*, V, i, 131–133.

easeful, *adj.* providing comfort: "That will encounter with our glorious sun/ Ere he attain his easeful western bed . . ." *3 Hen 6*, V, iii, 5–6.

easier, *adj.* **1** easier-working or, perh., better-fitting: "What, is my beaver easier than it was . . ." *Rich 3*, V, iii, 51. **2 easier for,** more open to: "I would your spirit were easier for advice . . ." *W Tale*, IV, iv, 506.

easiness, *n.* **1** indifference: "If we suffer/ Out of our easiness and childish pity . . ." *Hen 8*, V, ii, 58–59. **2 property of easiness,** ability to do something without being distracted by the [grim] nature of the activity: "Custom hath made it in him a property of easiness." *Ham*, V, i, 67.

Eastcheap, *n.* street on London's South Bank, site of the Boar's Head Tavern: "I am a poor widow of Eastcheap, and he is/ arrested at my suit." *2 Hen 4*, II, i, 68–69.

easy, *adj.* **1** minor; insignificant: "My lord, these faults are easy, quickly answer'd . . ." *2 Hen 6*, III, i, 133. **2** readily persuaded or managed; tractable: "And when he thinks, good easy man, full surely/ His greatness is a-ripening . . ." *Hen 8*, III, ii, 356–357. **3** requiring little exertion: ". . . her judgement,/ which else an easy battery might lay flat . . ." *Cymb*, I, v, 19–20.

—*adv.* **4** easily: "To show an unfelt sorrow is an office/ Which the false man does easy." *Mac*, II, iii, 136–137.

easy-borrowed, *adj.* done in imitation of his betters: "This is a slave, whose easy-borrowed pride/ Dwells in the fickle grace of her he follows." *Lear*, II, iv, 187–188.

easy fines, *n.* light penalties: "What faults he made before the last . . . Might have found easy fines . . ." *Cor*, V, vi, 64–65.

eat, *v.* **1** to devour: "The weeds . . . / That seem'd in eating him to hold him up . . ." *Rich 2*, III, iv, 50–51. **2** old past tense of **eat;** ate; also, was eating: "A vengeful canker eat him up to death." *Sonn 99*, 13. **3** old past part. of **eat** [pron. "et"]: "That jade hath eat bread from my royal hand . . ." *Rich 2*, V, v, 85. **4 swear and eat it,** be forced to eat the words one has sworn to: "By my sword, Beatrice, thou lovest me."/ "Do not swear and eat it." *M Ado*, IV, i, 273–274.

eaux, *n.* **les eaux et la terre!** [French] over water and earth! *Hen 5*, IV, ii, 4.

ebb, *v.* to retreat or fall back; here, decline or decay: ". . . to ebb/ Hereditary sloth instructs me." *Temp*, II, i, 217–218.

ebbed, *adj.* removed from power: ". . . the ebb'd man, ne'er lov'd till ne'er worth love [having lost his power],/ Comes dear'd [becomes beloved], by being lack'd [out of the public consciousness]." *Ant & Cleo*, I, iv, 43–44.

ebbing, *adj.* lazy; unambitious: "Ebbing men . . . do so near the bottom run/ By their own fear or sloth." *Temp*, II, i, 221–223.

ebon, *adj.* black; ebony-colored: "Rouse up Revenge from ebon den . . ." *2 Hen 4*, V, v, 37.

Ebrew, *n.* misuse of "Hebrew": ". . . they were bound, every man of them,/ or I am a Jew else: an Ebrew Jew." *1 Hen 4*, II, iv, 176–177.

ecce signum, a Latin motto, "Behold the sign": ". . . my sword hacked like a handsaw—/ *ecce signum! 1 Hen 4,* II, iv, 166–167.

eche, *v.* old form of EKE; extend or piece out: "And time that is so briefly spent/ With your fine fancies quaintly eche . . ." *Per,* III, Chor., 12–13.

echo, *n.* gossip; rumor: ". . . whilst the babbling echo mocks the hounds,/ Replying shrilly to the well-tun'd horns . . ." *T Andr,* II, iii, 17–18.

Echo, *n.* (in Greek legend) a nymph so in love with Narcissus that she pined away till nothing was left but her voice: "Bondage is hoarse and may not speak aloud,/ Else would I tear the cave where Echo lies . . ." *Rom & Jul,* II, ii, 160–161.

ecstasy, *n.* **1** excess of emotion; agitation: ". . . the ecstasy hath so much overborne her that my/ daughter is sometime afeard . . ." *M Ado,* II, iii, 148–149. **2** delusion or hallucination: ". . . madness would not err/ Nor sense to ecstasy was ne'er so thrall'd . . ." *Ham,* III, iv, 73–74. **3** fit of madness; frenzy: ". . . how fiery, and how sharp he looks."/ "Mark now he trembles in his ecstasy." *Errors,* IV, iv, 48–49.

edge, *n.* **1** sword: "And consecrate commotion's bitter edge?" *2 Hen 4,* IV, i, 93. **2** sharpness, as of a cutting edge; here, keenness of perception: "Chiron, thy years wants wit, thy wits wants edge . . ." *T Andr,* II, i, 26. **3** keenness of desire: ". . . blunt his natural edge/ With profits of the mind, study and fast." *Meas,* I, iv, 60–61. **4** sense of "cutting edge" in wordplay with "strong sexual desire": ". . . my lord, you are keen."/ "It would cost you a groaning to take off my edge." *Ham,* III, ii, 243–244. **5** encouragement; spur: ". . . give him a further edge,/ And drive his purpose into these delights." *Ham,* III, i, 26–27. **6 edge of traitors,** the edge [sharpness] of traitors' swords: "Abate [blunt] the edge of traitors, gracious Lord . . ." *Rich 3,* V, v, 35.

edgeless, *adj.* blunted; useless: "Tomorrow in the battle think on me,/ And fall thy edgeless sword: despair and die." *Rich 3,* V, iii, 163–164.

edict, *n.* decree; here, a reward: "Make thine own edict for thy pains, which we/ Will answer as a law." *Ant & Cleo,* III, xii, 32–33.

edify, *v.* to gratify; please: "My love with words and errors still she feeds,/ But edifies another with her deeds." *Tr & Cr,* V, iii, 111–112.

eel-skin, *n.* tall, thin person: "'Sblood, you starveling, you eel-skin, you dried/ neat's-tongue . . ." *1 Hen 4,* II, iv, 240–241.

e'en, *adv.* **1** var. of **even:** ". . . we were Christians/ enow before, e'en as many as could well live one by/ another . . ." *Merch,* III, v, 19–21. **2** even now: "A certain convocation of politic worms are e'en at him." *Ham,* IV, iii, 19–20.

e'en to't, *v.* to go at something with full intensity: "We'll e'en to't/ like French falconers, fly at anything we see." *Ham,* II, ii, 425–246.

e'er, *adv.* var. of **ever:** "If e'er the Jew her father come to heaven,/ It will be for his gentle daughter's sake . . ." *Merch,* II, iv, 33–34.

e'er-remaining, *adj.* perpetually lighted: "Where, for a monument upon thy bones,/ And e'er-remaining lamps . . ." *Per,* III, i, 61–62.

effect, *n.* **1** intent; purpose: ". . . blacker in their effect/ Than in their countenance." *As You,* IV, iii, 35–36. **2** creation; here, offspring: "Beauty's effect with beauty were bereft . . ." *Sonn 5,* 11. **3** [often pl.] an action or deed: "Lest with this piteous action you convert/ My stern effects." *Ham,* III, iv, 128–129. **4** [pl.] trappings; outward show: ". . . my power,/ Pre-eminence, and all the large [impressive] effects/ That troop with majesty." *Lear,* I, i, 130–132. **5** [usually pl.] **a.** manifestations: "For thy complexion shifts to strange effects/ After the moon." *Meas,* III, i, 24–25. **b.** misuse for "affects"; desires: "Which in a moment doth confound and kill/ All pure effects . . ." *Luc,* 250–251. **6 between the effect and it,** between the achievement of my purpose and the purpose itself: "That no compunctious visitings of Nature/ Shake my fell purpose, nor keep peace between/ Th'effect and it!" *Mac,* I, v, 45–47. **7 effects of courtesy,** courteous actions: "The offices of nature, bond of childhood,/ Effects of courtesy . . ." *Lear,* II, iv, 180–181. **8 in effect,** in fact or in truth: "Me for my dumb thoughts, speaking in effect." *Sonn 85,* 14. **9 in the effect (of),** as befits one: ". . . answer in th'effect of your reputation . . ." *2 Hen 4,* II, i, 129. **10 prove effects,** (to) be realized or fulfilled: "Our wishes on the way/ May prove effects." *Lear,* IV, ii, 14–15. **11 to effect, a.** to the purpose: "I have written to effect;/ There's not a god left unsolicited." *T Andr,* IV, iii, 59–60. **b.** in importance: "Few words, but, to effect, more than all yet . . ." *Lear,* III, i, 52–53. **12 touch their effects,** are realized: "Caesar, thy thoughts/ Touch their effects in this . . ." *Ant & Cleo,* V, ii, 328–329.

effected, *adj.* realized: "The ancient proverb will be well effected:/ A staff is quickly found to beat a dog!" *2 Hen 6,* III, i, 170–171.

effectless, *adj.* vain or ineffectual; unavailing: "In bootless prayer have they been held up,/ And they have serv'd me to effectless use." *T Andr,* III, i, 75–76.

effectual, *adj.* decisive; to the point: "Reprove my allegation . . . / Or else conclude my words effectual." *2 Hen 6,* III, i, 40–41.

effectually, *adv.* precisely; decisively: "Your bidding shall I do effectually." *T Andr,* IV, iv, 107.

effeminate, *adj.* **1** weak; cowardly: "None do you like but an effeminate prince,/ Whom like a school-boy you may over-awe." *1 Hen 6,* I, i, 35–36. **2** self-indulgent; also, capricious: "While he, young wanton, and effeminate boy,/ Takes on the point of honour to support/ So dissolute a crew." *Rich 2,* V, iii, 10–12. **3** tender or tender-hearted; soft: ". . . your tenderness of heart,/ And gentle, kind, effeminate remorse . . ." *Rich 3,* III, vii, 209–210.

effuse, *n.* loss; outflow or outpouring: ". . . much effuse of blood doth make me faint." *3 Hen 6,* II, vi, 28.

eftest, *adj.* appar. coinage for "fittest" or "aptest": ". . . you must call forth the watch that are their accusers."/ "Yea, marry, that's the eftest way." *M Ado,* IV, ii, 32–33.

eftsoons, *adv.* by and by; presently: ". . . toward Ephesus/ Turn our blown sails: eftsoons I'll tell thee why." *Per,* V, i, 252–253.

egal or **egall,** *adj.* vars. of **equal:** ". . . and, for the extent/ Of egal justice, us'd in such contempt?" *T Andr,* IV, iv, 3–4.

egg, *n.* **1** unhatched traitor: "What, you egg!/ Young fry of treachery!" *Mac,* IV, ii, 82–83. **2 take eggs for money,** to accept something of less value: "Mine honest friend,/ Will you take eggs for money?" *W Tale,* I, ii, 160–161.

eglantine, *n.* woodbrier, a white or pink rose: "With sweet musk-roses, and with eglantine . . ." *M N Dream,* II, i, 252.

egma, *n.* misuse for "enigma": "No egma, no riddle, no l'envoy; no salve in the mail,/ sir." *Love's L,* III, i, 69–70.

Ego et Rex meus, [Latin] my king and I; it was inferred that Wolsey had placed himself on a level with, or even above, the king: ". . . that in all you writ to Rome, or else/ To foreign princes, *Ego et Rex meus*/ Was still inscrib'd . . ." *Hen 8,* III, ii, 313–315.

egregious, *adj.* enormous: ". . . thou diest on point of fox,/ Except, O signieur, thou do give to me/ Egregious ransom." *Hen 5,* IV, iv, 9–11.

egress and regress, *n.* freedom to come and go [legal term]: "My hand, bully; thou shalt have egress and/ regress—said I well?" *Wives,* II, i, 206–207.

Egypt, *n.* Cleopatra: ". . . thou shouldst know/ There were a heart in Egypt." *Ant & Cleo,* I, iii, 40–41.

Egyptians in their fog, (in the Bible) the plague of darkness that Moses caused to descend upon the Egyptians: ". . . thou art more puzzled than/ the Egyptians in their fog." *T Night,* IV, ii, 44–45.

Egyptian thief, *n.* (in fiction) the robber chieftain Thyamis, in love with his captive Chariclea, attempts to kill her first when he is about to be captured, but in the dark kills someone else: "Like to th' Egyptian thief at point of death,/ Kill I love?" *T Night,* V, i, 116–117.

Eie, *n.* town SW of London, near Winchester: "Hast thou as yet conferr'd/ With Margery Jourdain, the witch of Eie . . ." *2 Hen 6,* I, ii, 74–75.

eight and six, *n.* standard meter for ballads, a line of eight syllables followed by one of six, etc.: "Well, we will have such a prologue; and it shall be/ written in eight and six." *M N Dream,* III, i, 22–23.

eisel, *n.* **1** vinegar: "Woo't drink up eisel, eat a crocodile?" *Ham,* V, i, 271. **2 potions of eisel,** vinegar drunk in the belief that it would ward off the plague: ". . . like a willing patient, I will drink/ Potions of eisel 'gainst my strong infection . . ." *Sonn 111,* 9–10.

either's, *poss. adj.* each other's: "They are both in either's pow'rs . . ." *Temp,* I, ii, 453.

eke[1], *adv.* also: "Most brisky juvenal, and eke most lovely Jew . . ." *M N Dream,* III, i, 90.

eke[2], *v.* **eke out,** to piece out: ". . . to eke out that/ Wherein toward me my homely stars have fail'd . . ." *All's W,* II, v, 74–75.

elbow, *v.* **1** to haunt; harass: "A sovereign shame so elbows him . . ." *Lear,* IV, iii, 43.
—*n.* **2 out at elbow,** threadbare; also, lacking wits: "Why dost thou not speak, Elbow?"/ "He cannot, sir: he's out at elbow." *Meas,* II, i, 59–60.

eld, *n.* **1** old age: ". . . thy blessed youth/ Becomes as aged, and doth beg the alms/ Of palsied eld . . ." *Meas,* III, i, 34–36. **2** those of earlier generations: "The superstitious idle-headed eld . . ." *Wives,* IV, iv, 36.

elder[1], *n.* ref. to senators and patricians of Rome: "Most reverend and grave elders . . ." *Cor,* II, ii, 42.

elder[2], *n.* succeeding one: "To second ills with ills, each elder worse . . ." *Cymb,* V, i, 14.

elder[3], *n.* **heart of elder,** humorous var. on "heart of oak" (with opp. meaning): "What says my/ Aesculapius? My Galen? My heart of elder?" *Wives,* II, iii, 26–27.

elder-gun, *n.* a popgun, usually made of elder wood: "That's a perilous shot out/ of an elder-gun . . ." *Hen 5,* IV, i, 203–204.

eld'st, *adj.* eldest; oldest or longest: "Your eld'st acquaintance cannot be three hours . . ." *Temp,* V, i, 186.

elect, *v.* to accept or acknowledge: "That you elect no other king but him . . ." *1 Hen 6,* IV, i, 4.

election, *n.* **1** choice: "And could of men distinguish her election . . ." *Ham,* III, ii, 64. **2** basis for choosing: "And choice . . . Makes merit her election . . ." *Tr & Cr,* I, iii, 348–349. **3** word-play on "free choice" and theological sense of predestination: "[Aside] If it be a sin to make a true election, she/ is damn'd." *Cymb,* I, iii, 25–26. **4 in election,** as a candidate: ". . . the people of Rome . . . Send thee . . . This palliament . . . And name thee in election for the empire . . ." *T Andr,* I, i, 179–183.

element, *n.* **1** the sky and stars; also, air or atmosphere: ". . . the element shows [appears] to him as it doth/ to me . . ." *Hen 5,* IV, i, 103–104. **2** base human nature; Malvolio here considers himself a higher form of creation: ". . . you are idle, shallow/ things, I am not of your element . . ." *T Night,* III, iv, 124–125. **3** natural or proper place: ". . . down, thou climbing sorrow!/ Thy element's below." *Lear,* II, iv, 57–58. **4** part or share; perh. proper sphere: "One certes, that promises no element [unlikely to be concerned]/ In such a business." *Hen 8,* I, i, 48–49. **5** [pl.] wind and waves of the storm at sea: ". . . let the heavens/ Give him defence against their elements . . ." *Oth,* II, i, 44–45. **6** [pl.] life: "It lives by that which/ nourisheth it, and the elements once out of it, it/ transmigrates." *Ant & Cleo,* II, vii, 43–45. **7 beyond our element,** beyond our understanding: ". . . such daubery as this is, beyond our/ element; we know nothing." *Wives,* IV, ii, 163–164. **8 four elements,** earth, air, fire, and water: regarded as the constituents of all matter: "Does not our life consist of/ the four elements?" *T Night,* II, iii, 9–10.

eleven and twenty long, *adj.* precisely right: ". . . and Petruchio is the master,/ That teacheth tricks eleven and twenty long . . ." *Shrew,* IV, ii, 56–57.

elf, *v.* to tangle or mat into elf-locks: "Blanket my loins, elf all my hairs in knots,/ And with presented nakedness outface/ The winds . . ." *Lear,* II, iii, 10–12.

elf-locks, *n. pl.* matted hair of slovenly people, thought to be the work of elves and which brought misfortune to those who untangled it: "This is that very Mab/ That . . . bakes the elf-locks in foul sluttish hairs . . ." *Rom & Jul,* I, iv, 88–90.

Elizium, *n.* See **Elysium.**

ell, *n.* **1** (in measure) yard and a quarter (45 inches): "Now as I am a true woman, holland of eight shillings/ an ell!" *1 Hen 4,* III, iii, 69–70. **2** letter "L"; also, the Latin symbol for "50": "The dogs did yell; put 'ell to sore, then sorel jumps/ from thicket . . ." *Love's L,* IV, ii, 57.

else, *adv.* **1** besides: "What's his will else?" *All's W,* II, iv, 45. **2** otherwise; on the other hand: "Your betters sir."/ "Else are they very wretched." *As You,* II, iv, 65–66. **3** merely; simply: ". . . we fat all/ creatures else to fat us . . ." *Ham,* IV, iii, 21–22. **4** in any case: "A witty mother, witless else her son." *Shrew,* II, i, 258. **5 All leave us else,** Everyone else leave us: "All leave us else; but let your cares o'erlook . . ." *Per,* I, ii, 49. **6 else so,** or else; even worse: ". . . else so thy cheek pays shame/ When shrill-tongued Fulvia scolds." *Ant & Cleo,* I, i, 31–32.

Eltham, *n.* royal residence SE of London: "To Eltham will I, where the young King is,/ Being ordain'd his special governor . . ." *1 Hen 6,* I, i, 170–171.

elvish-marked, *adj.* marked by elves at birth; deformed: "Thou elvish-mark'd, abortive, rooting hog . . ." *Rich 3,* I, iii, 228.

Ely House, *n.* palace of the Bishop of Ely in London. [SD] *Rich 2,* II, i, 1.

Elysium or **Elizium,** *n.* (in classical myth.) abode of the blessed after death; heaven or a state of bliss; here, poetic contrast to "Illyria": "And what should I do in Illyria?/ My brother he is in Elysium." *T Night,* I, ii, 3–4.

emballing, *n.* royal investiture with the golden orb [ball]; sexual innuendo [intercourse] evidently intended: ". . . for little England/ You'd venture an emballing: I myself/ Would for Carnarvonshire . . ." *Hen 8,* II, iii, 46–48.

embarked, *adj.* put aboard ship: "My necessaries are embark'd. Farewell." *Ham,* I, iii, 1.

embarquement, *n.* hindrance or restraint: "The prayers of priests, nor times of sacrifice—/ Embarquements all of fury . . ." *Cor,* I, x, 21–22.

embassade, *n.* embassage; mission: "When you disgrac'd me in my embassade,/ Then I degraded you from being King . . ." *3 Hen 6,* IV, iii, 32–33.

embassage, *n.* **1** mission; commission: "I have almost matter enough in me for such an embassage . . ." *M Ado,* I, i, 259. **2** message: ". . . a pretty knavish page,/ That well by heart hath conn'd his embassage . . ." *Love's L,* V, ii, 97–98.

embassy, *n.* **1** message; communication: "Silence, good mother; hear the embassy." *K John,* I, i, 6. **2 in embassy, a.** in the role or function of ambassador: ". . . here comes in embassy/ The French king's daughter . . ." *Love's L,* I, i, 133–134. **b.** as messenger: "In tender embassy of love to thee . . ." *Sonn 45,* 6. **c.** as a message: "In embassy to his mother; his body's hostage/ For his return." *Cymb,* IV, ii, 185–186.

embattailed, *past part.* placed in readiness for battle: ". . . many thousand warlike French/ That were embattailed and rank'd in Kent . . ." *K John,* IV, ii, 199–200.

embattle, *v.* to be arrayed [readied] for battle: ". . . they say we shall embattle/ By the second hour i' the morn." *Ant & Cleo,* IV, ix, 3–4.

embayed, *adj.* (of a ship) anchored in a bay: "If that the Turkish fleet/ Be not enshelter'd, and embay'd, they are drown'd . . ." *Oth,* II, i, 17–18.

ember-eve, *n.* evening preceding ember day (quarterly period of prayer and fasting): "It hath been sung at festivals,/ On ember-eves and holy-ales . . ." *Per,* I, Chor., 5–6.

embodied, *past part.* incorporated into one body; here, by marriage vows: "For I by vow am so embodied yours . . ." *All's W,* V, iii, 172.

emboss, *v.* to corner (prey): ". . . we have almost emboss'd him; you shall see his/ fall tonight . . ." *All's W,* III, vi, 95–96.

embossed¹, *adj.* swollen: ". . . thou art a boil,/ A plague-sore, or embossed carbuncle . . ." *Lear,* II, iv, 225–226.

embossed², *adj., past part.* foaming at the mouth from over-exertion: "Breathe Merriman, the poor cur is emboss'd . . ." *Shrew,* Ind., i, 15.

embounded, *past part.* enclosed: ". . . that sweet breath/ Which was embounded in this beauteous clay . . ." *K John,* IV, iii, 136–137.

embowelled, *adj.* **1** disemboweled, as preparation for burial: "Embowell'd will I see thee by and by,/ Till then in blood by noble Percy lie." *1 Hen 4,* V, iv, 108–109. **2** emptied, drained, or exhausted: ". . . the schools,/ Embowel'd of their doctrine, have left off/ The danger to itself?" *All's W,* I, iii, 235–237.

embraced, *adj.* accepted or clung to: ". . . let us go and find him out/ And quicken his embraced heaviness . . ." *Merch,* II, viii, 51–52.

embracement, *n.* embrace: "Beating his kind embracements with her heels." *Ven & Ad,* 312.

embrasure, *n.* embrace: ". . . forcibly prevents/ Our lock'd embrasures, strangles our dear vows . . ." *Tr & Cr,* IV, iv, 35–36.

eminence, *n.* **1** special consideration or favor: "Present him eminence, both with eye and tongue . . ." *Mac,* III, ii, 31. **2** feeling of superiority: "Whether the tyranny be in his place [office],/ Or in his eminence that fills it up,/ I stagger in . . ." *Meas,* I, ii, 152–154. **3 have the eminence of,** be regarded as superior to: "You should not have the eminence of him,/ But be as Ajax." *Tr & Cr,* II, iii, 255–256.

Emmanuel, *n.* God [be] with us; a salutation on letters and documents: "Emmanuel."/ "They use to write it on the top of letters." *2 Hen 6,* IV, ii, 93–94.

empatron, *v.* to become the patron of; patronize: "Since I their altar, you empatron me." *Lover's Comp,* 224.

emperal, *n.* misuse for "emperor": ". . . a matter of brawl betwixt/ my uncle and one of the emperal's men." *T Andr,* IV, iii, 91–92.

emperious, *adj.* imperious; lordly: "Th' emperious seas breed monsters; for the dish/ Poor tributary rivers as sweet fish . . ." *Cymb,* IV, ii, 35.

empery, *n.* **1** empire: "A lady/ So fair, and fasten'd to an empery . . ." *Cymb,* I, vii, 119–120. **2** sovereignty: "Princes, that strive by factions and by friends/ Ambitiously for rule and empery . . ." *T Andr,* I, i, 18–19.

empire, *n.* **1** kingdom: "Is the King dead? The empire unpossess'd?" *Rich 3,* IV, iv, 470. **2** dominance: "Thy blood and virtue/ Contend for empire in thee . . ." *All's W,* I, i, 58–59.

empiric, *n.* charlatan; "quack": "To prostitute our past-cure malady/ To empirics . . ." *All's W,* II, i, 120–121.

empiricutic, *adj.* fraudulent: "The most sovereign prescription in/ Galen is but empiricutic . . ." *Cor,* II, i, 115–116.

empleached, *adj.* intertwined: ". . . their hair,/ With twisted metal amorously empleached . . ." *Lover's Comp,* 204–205.

employ, *v.* to set to work: "Employ thee, then, sweet virgin, for our good." *1 Hen 6,* III, iii, 16.

employment or **imployment,** *n.* **1** business; matter: "[Seeing the letter] What employment have we/ here?" *T Night,* II, v, 82–83. **2** use: ". . . your Highness' soldiers,/ The which he hath detain'd for lewd imployments . . ." *Rich 2,* I, i, 89–90.

empress, *n.* ref. here to Cleopatra as Antony's widow: "Most noble empress, you have heard of me?" *Ant & Cleo,* V, ii, 71.

empty, *adj.* hungry; famished: "Were 't not all one an empty eagle were set/ To guard the chicken from a hungry kite . . ." *2 Hen 6,* III, i, 248–249.

emptying, *n.* outpouring: "The emptying of our fathers' luxury [lust],/ Our scions, put in wild and savage stock . . ." *Hen 5,* III, v, 6–7.

emulate, *adj.* determined to excel; jealous: "Fortinbras of Norway,/ Thereto prick'd on by a most emulate pride . . ." *Ham,* I, i, 85–86.

emulation, *n.* **1** professional rivalry or jealousy: ". . . neither the scholar's melancholy, which is emulation; nor the musician's, which is fantastical." *As You,* IV, i, 10–11. **2** resentment of authority: ". . . grows to an envious fever/ Of pale and bloodless emulation." *Tr & Cr,* I, iii, 133–134. **3** contention; struggle, esp. for power: "The obligation of our blood forbids/ A gory emulation 'twixt us twain." *Tr & Cr,* IV, v, 121–122. **4** attempt to outdo one another in shouting: ". . . they threw their caps . . . Shouting their emulation." *Cor,* I, i, 211–213.

emulous, *adj.* **1** envious or competitive: ". . . a good quarrel to draw emulous factions,/ and bleed to death upon." *Tr & Cr,* II, iii, 75–76. **2** greedy for praise: "He is not emulous, as Achilles is." *Tr & Cr,* II, iii, 231. **3** ambitious: "But in mine emulous honour let him die/ With every joint a wound . . ." *Tr & Cr,* IV, i, 29–30.

enacture, *n.* putting into action; performance: "The violence of either grief or joy/ Their own enactures with themselves destroy." *Ham,* III, ii, 191–192.

encave, *v.* to conceal: ". . . encave yourself,/ And mark the jeers . . . That dwell in every region of his face . . ." *Oth,* IV, i, 81–83.

Enceladus, *n.* (in early Greek legend) a Titan and son of Typhon; waged war against the Olympian gods: ". . . not Enceladus,/ Nor great Alcides . . . Shall seize this prey out of his father's hands." *T Andr,* IV, ii, 93–96.

enchafed, *adj.* **1** stirred to anger; riled: ". . . and yet, as rough,/ (Their royal blood enchaf'd) as the rud'st wind . . ." *Cymb,* IV, ii, 173–174. **2** (of waters) stirred up; roiled: "I never did like molestation view/ On the enchafed flood." *Oth,* II, i, 16–17.

enchantingly, *adv.* in a manner that charms or enchants: "Yet he's gentle, . . . of all sorts enchantingly beloved . . ." *As You,* I, i, 164–166.

enchantment, *n.* **1** charm or spell: "I did send,/ After the last enchantment you did [cast] here . . ." *T Night,* III, i, 113–114. **2** ref. to Perdita's bewitching beauty and her sorcerer's power over Florizel: "And you, enchantment,—/ Worthy enough a herdsman . . ." *W Tale,* IV, iv, 435–436.

enchantress, *n.* witch; sorceress: "Fell banning hag, enchantress, hold thy tongue!" *1 Hen 6,* V, iii, 42.

enchased, *adj.* embellished; enriched: "King Henry's diadem,/ Enchas'd with all the honours of the world?" *2 Hen 6,* I, ii, 7–8.

encieled, *adj.* shielded: "Proclaim an enciel'd beauty ten times louder/ Than beauty could, display'd." *Meas,* II, iv, 80–81.

encloud, *v.* to enclose or entrap: "In their thick breaths . . . shall we be enclouded,/ And forc'd to drink their vapour." *Ant & Cleo,* V, ii, 210–212.

encompass, *v.* to take advantage of; "get round": "Ah, ha,/ Mistress Ford and Mistress Page, have I encompassed/ you?" *Wives,* II, ii, 146–148.

encompassment, *n.* roundabout method: ". . . and finding/ By this encompassment and drift of question/ That they do know my son . . ." *Ham,* II, i, 9–11.

encouch, *v.* to embellish: "And when thou writest of tears, encouch the word/ Before and after with such sweet laments,/ That it may raise drops in a Tartar's eye . . ." *Edw 3,* II, i, 69–71.

encounter, *v.* **1** to assail; attack: "He shall be encount'red with a man as good as himself." *2 Hen 6,* IV, ii, 109–110. **2** to be in conflict; fight or do battle: "Let not your hate encounter with my love . . ." *All's W,* I, iii, 203. **3** to approach; go towards: "Will you encounter the house?" *T Night,* III, i, 75. **4** to relate or respond to: "See, they encounter thee with their hearts' thanks." *Mac,* III, iv, 9. **5 encounter me,** join with me [in]: "At the sixth hour of morn, at noon, at midnight,/ T' encounter me with orisons [prayers] . . ." *Cymb,* I, iv, 31–32.
—*n.* **6** manner of accosting; address: "The loose encounters of lascivious men . . ." *Two Gent,* II, vii, 41. **7** lovers' tryst: ". . . in the instant of our/ encounter, after we had embraced . . ." *Wives,* III, v, 66–67.

encumbered, *adj.* (of the arms) crossed or folded: "With arms encumber'd thus, or this head-shake,/ Or by pronouncing of some doubtful phrase . . ." *Ham,* I, v, 182–183.

end[1], *n.* **1** the person responsible [for]: "Certainly/ The cardinal is the end of this." *Hen 8,* II, i, 39–40. **2 an end, a.** [let's] make an end of it: "Down! an end:/ This is the last." *Cor,* V, iii, 171–172. **b.** on end: "Your bedded hair . . . Start up and stand an end." *Ham,* III, iv, 121–122.
—*v.* **3** to finish what one has started: "Son, let your mother end." *Cymb,* III, i, 40. **4 end it,** be an end in itself: ". . . and is content/ To spend the time to end it." *Cor,* II, ii, 128–129.

end², *v.* to gather in; harvest: "... holp to reap the fame/ Which he did end [as] all his ..." *Cor,* V, vi, 36–37.

endamage, *v.* to injure; do mischief to: "And lay new platforms to endamage them." *1 Hen 6,* II, i, 77.

endamagement, *n.* detriment; harm or injury: "These flags of France ... Have hither march'd to your endamagement." *K John,* II, i, 207–209.

endart, *v.* to send or unleash like a dart: "... no more deep will I endart mine eye/ Than your consent gives strength to make it fly." *Rom & Jul,* I, iii, 98–99.

endeared, *adj.* **1** enriched: "Thy bosom is endeared with all hearts ..." *Sonn 31,* 1. **2** indebted or beholden: "We are so virtuously bound,/ So infinitely endear'd—" *Timon,* I, ii, 226–228.

ended, *adj.* **ended action,** recently completed [military] campaign: "When you went onward on this ended action ..." *M Ado,* I, i, 277.

ender, *n.* conclusion: "That is, to you, my origin and ender ..." *Lover's Comp,* 222.

ending, *adj.* dying: "This bitter taste/ Yields his engrossments to the ending father." *2 Hen 4,* IV, v, 78–79.

ending anthem, *n.* funeral hymn: "... breathe it in mine ear,/ As ending anthem of my endless dolour." *Two Gent,* III, i, 239–240.

ending doom, *n.* doomsday and the end of the world: "Even in the eyes of all posterity/ That wear this world out to the ending doom." *Sonn 55,* 11–12.

endite, *v.* humorous misuse for "invite": "She will endite him to some supper." *Rom & Jul,* II, iv, 127.

endowments, *n. pl.* property wrongfully seized: "Base men by his endowments are made great." *Rich 2,* II, iii, 138.

endue, *v.* to endow: "These banish'd men, that I have kept withal,/ Are men endu'd with worthy qualities ..." *Two Gent,* V, iv, 150–151.

endure, *v.* to allow; here, because of overconfidence: "... the confident tyrant/ Keeps still in Dunsinane, and will endure/ Our setting down before 't." *Mac,* V, iv, 8–10.

Endymion, *n.* (in Greek myth.) beautiful youth with whom the moon goddess [Selene/Artemis] fell in love and caused to sleep perpetually on Mount Latmos: "Peace!—how the moon sleeps with Endymion,/ And would not be awak'd!" *Merch,* V, i, 109–110.

enemy, *n.* [usually cap.] Satan: "... and mine eternal jewel/ Given to the common Enemy of man ..." *Mac,* III, i, 67–68.

enew, *v.* to drive into water: "Nips youth i'th'head and follies doth enew/ As falcon doth the fowl ..." *Meas,* III, i, 90–91.

enfeoff, *v.* (in law) to surrender possession of: "Grew a companion to the common streets,/ Enfeoff'd himself to popularity ..." *1 Hen 4,* III, ii, 68–69.

enfoldings, *n.pl.* garments: "Seest thou/ not the air of the court in these enfoldings?" *W Tale,* IV, iv, 730–731.

enforce, *v.* **1** to urge; also, oblige: "To enforce the pained impotent to smile." *Love's L,* V, ii, 846. **2** to urge on: "... you would be prouder of the work/ Than customary bounty can enforce you." *Merch,* III, iv, 8–9. **3** to take by force; here, to ravish or rape: "To slay his daughter with his own right hand,/ Because she was enforc'd, stain'd, and deflow'r'd?" *T Andr,* V, iii, 37–38. **4** to stress; emphasize: "... nor his offences/ enforc'd, for which he suffered death." *J Caes,* III, ii, 40–41. **5** to state as evidence; swear: "We shall entreat you to abide here till he come, and/ enforce them against him." *Meas,* V, i, 264–265. **6 enforce him with,** accuse him of: "Enforce him with his envy to [ill will toward] the people ..." *Cor,* III, iii, 3.

enforced, *adj.* **1** forced; strained: "When love begins to sicken and decay/ It useth an enforced ceremony." *J Caes,* IV, ii, 20–21. **2** ravished; raped: "Yield to my love; if not, enforced hated,/ Instead of love's coy touch, shall rudely tear thee ..." *Luc,* 668–669.
—*past part.* **3** released; discharged: "... as swift as stones/ Enforced from the old Assyrian slings." *Hen 5,* IV, vii, 63–64.

enforcement, *n.* **1** action of being forced into motion: "And as the thing that's heavy in itself/ Upon enforcement flies with greatest speed ..." *2 Hen 4,* I, i, 119–120. **2** sexual abuse; rape: "Th'unsatiate greediness of his desire,/ And his enforcement of the city wives ..." *Rich 3,* III, vii, 7–8.

enfranched, *adj.* enfranchised; freed: "... tell him he has/ Hipparchus, my enfranched bondman ..." *Ant & Cleo,* III, xiii, 148–149.

enfranchise, *v.* to set free; release; here, restore to one's rights: "... being enfranchis'd, bid him come to me." *Timon,* I, i, 109.

enfranchisement, *n.* **1** setting free: "Then I ... heartily request/ Th' enfranchisement of Arthur ..." *K John,* IV, ii, 47–52. **2** freedom; liberty: "... ere they will have me go to ward,/

They'll pawn their swords for my enfranchisement." *2 Hen 6,* V, i, 112–113.

enfreed, *adj.* set free: ". . . there to render him,/ For the enfreed Antenor, the fair Cressid." *Tr & Cr,* IV, i, 38–39.

enfreedom, *v.* to release; set free: "I mean setting thee at liberty,/ enfreedoming thy person . . ." *Love's L,* III, i, 120–121.

engage, *v.* to pledge; vow or promise: "This to be true,/ I do engage my life." *As You,* V, iv, 163–164.

engaged, *adj.* **1** pledged as security; mortgaged: "Let all my land be sold./ 'Tis all engag'd . . ." *Timon,* II, ii, 149–150. **2** held as hostage: ". . . suffer'd his kinsman March/ . . . to be engag'd in Wales . . ." *1 Hen 4,* IV, iii, 93–95. **3** caught; trapped or entangled: "O limed soul, that struggling to be free/ Art more engag'd!" *Ham,* III, iii, 68–69.

engendered, *adj.* conceived: "I ha't [have it], it is engender'd; Hell and night/ Must bring this monstrous birth to the world's light." *Oth,* I, iii, 401–402.

engendering, *n.* act of begetting; copulation: "I do hate a proud man as I do hate the engendering/ of toads." *Tr & Cr,* II, iii, 160–161.

engild, *v.* to make resplendent: "Fair Helena, who more engilds the night/ Than all yon fiery oes and eyes of light." *M N Dream,* III, ii, 187–188.

engine, *n.* **1** construction; mechanism; here, the Wooden Horse: ". . . who hath brought the fatal engine in/ That gives our Troy, our Rome, the civil wound." *T Andr,* V, iii, 86–87. **2** machine of war: ". . . treason, felony,/ Sword, pike, knife, gun, or need of any engine,/ Would I not have . . ." *Temp,* II, i, 156–159. **3** cannon: "O ye mortal engines, whose wide throats/ The immortal Jove's great clamour counterfeit . . ." *Oth,* III, iii, 361–362. **4** device; any devising: ". . . their promises, enticements,/ oaths, tokens, and all these engines of lust . . ." *All's W,* III, v, 18–19. **5** instrument of torture: ". . . take me from this world with treachery,/ and devise engines for [against] my life." *Oth,* IV, ii, 217–218. **6 engine of her thoughts,** tongue; power of speech: "Once more the engine of her thoughts began . . ." *Ven & Ad,* 367. **7 file our engines,** See **file**[3] (def. 2).

enginer, *n.* **1** one who contrives the machines of war: ". . . 'tis the sport to have the enginer/ Hoist with his own petard . . ." *Ham,* III, iv, 208–209. **2** strategist or plotter: "Then there's Achilles:/ a rare enginer." *Tr & Cr,* II, iii, 7–8.

engirt, *v.* **1** to encompass or enclose: "So white a friend engirts so white a foe." *Ven & Ad,* 364.

—*past part.* **2** encompassed; engulfed: "This siege that hath engirt his marriage . . ." *Luc,* 221.

England, *n.* King of England: ". . . from gracious England, have I offer/ Of goodly thousands . . ." *Mac,* IV, iii, 43–44.

English, *n. pl.* Englishmen: "When English measure backward their own ground/ In faint retire." *K John,* V, v, 3–4.

Englished, *past part.* put into English: ". . . her behaviour, to be Englished/ rightly, is, 'I am Sir John Falstaff's.'" *Wives,* I, iii, 44–45.

englut, *v.* to gulp down: "How many prodigal bits have slaves and peasants/ This night englutted!" *Timon,* II, ii, 169–170.

englutted, *past part.* swallowed [up]: "For certainly thou art so near the gulf/ Thou needs must be englutted." *Hen V,* IV, iii, 82–83.

engraff, *v.* var. of **engraft**; attach: ". . . you have been so lewd, and so much/ engraffed to Falstaff." *2 Hen 4,* II, ii, 58–59.

engraft, *v.* **engraft you new,** inject new life into you by grafting; here, give you immortality through my verse: ". . . all in war with Time for love of you,/ As he takes from you, I engraft you new." *Sonn 15,* 14.

engross, *v.* **1** to monopolize: "If thou engrossest all the griefs are thine/ Thou robb'st me of a moiety [fair share]." *All's W,* III, ii, 65–66. **2** to make the most of; seize or grab: ". . . followed her with a doting/ observance; engrossed opportunities to meet her . . ." *Wives,* II, ii, 189–190.

engrossed, *adj.* written out in full: ". . . the indictment of the good Lord Hastings,/ Which in a set hand fairly is engross'd . . ." *Rich 3,* III, vi, 1–2.

engrossing, *adj.* commandeering or monopolizing all: ". . . seal with a righteous kiss/ A dateless bargain to engrossing Death." *Rom & Jul,* V, iii, 114–115.

engross up, *v.* to buy up or collect; amass: "Percy is but my factor . . . To engross up glorious deeds on my behalf . . ." *1 Hen 4,* III, ii, 147–148.

enguard, *v.* to protect: "He may enguard his dotage with their powers . . ." *Lear,* I, iv, 336.

enjoined penitent, *n.* sinner bound by oath to undertake a pilgrimage: ". . . of enjoin'd penitents/ There's four or five, to Great Saint Jaques bound . . ." *All's W,* III, v, 93–94.

enjoy, *v.* to seek enjoyment: "The one in fear to lose what they enjoy,/ The other to enjoy by [after resorting to] rage and war." *Rich 2,* II, iv, 13–14.

enkindle, *v.* to arouse hope in: "That, trusted home,/ Might yet enkindle you unto the crown . . ." *Mac,* I, iii, 120–121.

enlarge, *v.* **1** to set free: "Discomfited great Douglas, ta'en him once,/ Enlarged him, and made a friend of him . . ." *1 Hen 4,* III, ii, 114–115. **2** to enhance; strengthen or magnify: "And doth enlarge his rising with the blood/ Of fair King Richard . . ." *2 Hen 4,* I, i, 204–205.

enlarged, *adj.* **evermore enlarged,** always at large: "To tie up envy evermore enlarg'd . . ." *Sonn 70,* 12.

enlargement, *n.* **1** freedom; release or liberation: "Go, tenderness of years; take this key,/ give enlargement to the swain . . ." *Love's L,* III, i, 3–4. **2** freedom of choice or action: ". . . curb'd from that enlargement, by/ The consequence o' th' crown . . ." *Cymb,* II, iii, 119–120.

enlighten, *v.* to give added luster to: "And, to enlighten thee, gave eyes to blindness . . ." *Sonn 152,* 11.

enlinked, *past part.* connected: ". . . all fell feats/ Enlink'd to waste and desolation?" *Hen 5,* III, iii, 17–18.

enormous, *adj.* disordered; abnormal; also, wicked: "From this enormous state [of affairs], seeking to give/ Losses their remedies." *Lear,* II, ii, 169–170.

enow, *adv.* var. of **enough:** ". . . we were Christians/ enow before, e'en as many as could well live one by/ another . . ." *Merch,* III, v, 19–21.

enpatron, *v.* **you enpatron me,** you are the patron saint of me: "Since I their altar, you enpatron me." *Lover's Comp,* 224.

enquire, *v.* **enquire you forth,** [to] seek you out; find out where you live: "Go on before; I shall enquire you forth." *Two Gent,* II, iv, 182.

enrank, *v.* (of soldiers) to draw up in ranks; make ready for fighting: "No leisure had he to enrank his men . . ." *1 Hen 6,* I, i, 115.

enrich, *v.* to give value to; make precious: "But herein mean I to enrich my pain,/ To have his sight thither and back again." *M N Dream,* I, i, 250–251.

enridged, *adj.* furrowed: "Horns whelk'd and wav'd like the enridged sea . . ." *Lear,* IV, vi, 71.

enring, *v.* to twist around; entwine: ". . . the female ivy so/ Enrings the barky fingers of the elm." *M N Dream,* IV, i, 42–43.

enroll, *v.* **1** to list as part of a formal agreement: "As not to see a woman in that term,/ Which I hope well is not enrolled there . . ." *Love's L,* I, i, 37–38. **2** to enter into the official records: "The question of/ his death is enroll'd in the Capitol . . ." *J Caes,* III, ii, 38–39.

enrolled, *adj.* (of laws, regulations, etc.) official; enacted into law: ". . . this new governor/ Awakes me all the enrolled penalties . . ." *Meas,* I, ii, 154–155.

enround, *v.* to surround: "How dread an army hath enrounded him . . ." *Hen 5,* IV, Chor., 36.

enscheduled, *adj.* written out: "Whose tenours and particular effects/ You have, enschedul'd briefly, in your hands." *Hen 5,* V, ii, 72–73.

ensconce, *v.* to conceal; hide: "She shall not see me: I will ensconce me behind the/ arras." *Wives,* III, iii, 82–83.

enseamed, *adj.* grease-stained: "Nay, but to live/ In the rank sweat of an enseamed bed . . ." *Ham,* III, iv, 91–92.

ensear, *v.* to wither or dry up: "Ensear thy fertile and conceptious womb . . ." *Timon,* IV, iii, 189.

ensinewed or **insinewed,** *adj.* to lend one's strength or force to: "All members of our cause . . . That are ensinew'd to this action . . ." *2 Hen 4,* IV, i, 171–172.

enskied, *adj.* living in heaven: "I hold you as a thing enskied and sainted . . ." *Meas,* I, iv, 34.

ensteeped, *adj.* submerged: "Traitors ensteep'd, to clog the guiltless keel . . ." *Oth,* II, i, 70.

ensue, *v.* to follow: "Let not to-morrow then ensue to-day . . ." *Rich 2,* II, i, 197.

entail, *n.* right of inheritance by future heirs: ". . . cut th' entail/ from all remainders, and a perpetual succession for it/ perpetually." *All's W,* IV, iii, 270–272.

enter, *v.* **1** to file a legal action against; charge: "Yea, good Master Snare, I have entered him and/ all." *2 Hen 4,* II, i, 9–10. —*n.* **2** entrance: ". . . his enter and exit shall be strangling a/ snake . . ." *Love's L,* V, i, 126–127.

entertain, *v.* **1** to receive or admit, as a guest or gift: "Let the presents/ Be worthily entertain'd." *Timon,* I, ii, 182–183. **2** to engage or hire; employ: "Being entertained for [as] a perfumer, As I was/ smoking a musty room . . ." *M Ado,* I, iii, 54–55. **3**

to think about; mull over: "But entertain it . . . I am the man/ Will give thee all the world." *Ant & Cleo,* II, vii, 63–65. **4** to accept; believe: "Until I know this sure uncertainty,/ I'll entertain the offer'd fallacy." *Errors,* II, ii, 185–186. **5** to maintain: "And do a wilful stillness entertain . . ." *Merch,* I, i, 90. **6** to take into or keep in service; Pistol advises Falstaff to counter Ford's angels with his own devils: "As many devils entertain; and to her, boy, say I." *Wives,* I, iii, 51. **7** to deal with; treat: "Yet tell'st thou not how thou wert entertain'd." *1 Hen 6,* I, iv, 37. **8** (of time) to spend; while away: "The weary time she cannot entertain . . ." *Luc,* 1361. **9** to cherish: "Lest thou a feverous life shouldst entertain . . ." *Meas,* III, i, 74.
—*n.* **10** entertainment: ". . . until then your entertain shall be/ As doth befit our honour and your worth." *Per,* I, i, 120–121.

entertainment, *n.* **1** hospitality: ". . . the gentle Duke,/ Who gave me fresh array and entertainment . . ." *As You,* IV, iii, 142–143. **2** courteous greeting; here, an attempt at reconciliation: "The Queen desires you to use some gentle entertainment/ to Laertes before you fall to play." *Ham,* V, ii, 202–203. **3** reception: "The rudeness that hath appeared in me have I/ learned from my entertainment." *T Night,* I, v, 217–218. **4** service or employment; pay: "He must think us some band of strangers i' th'/ adversary's entertainment." *All's W,* IV, i, 14–15. **5** acceptance: ". . . advised him for th'entertainment of death." *Meas,* III, ii, 207. **6 strain her entertainment,** press for his reinstatement: "Note if your lady strain her [his?] entertainment/ With any strong or vehement importunity . . ." *Oth,* III, iii, 254–255. **7 in th'entertainment,** (of soldiers) mobilized: ". . . the centurions and their charges/ distinctly billeted, already in th'entertainment . . ." *Cor,* IV, iii, 44–45.

enthralled, *adj.* **1** made a captive: "What though I be enthrall'd?" *1 Hen 6,* V, iii, 101. **2** made a servant (to): "O cross! too high to be enthrall'd to low." *M N Dream,* I, i, 136.

enticing bird, *n.* decoy: ". . . a quire of such enticing birds/ That she will light to listen to their lays . . ." *2 Hen 6,* I, iii, 89–90.

entire, *adj.* **1** sincere; pure: "I have often heard/ Of your entire affection to Bianca . . ." *Shrew,* IV, ii, 22–23. **2** without defect; flawless: "A carbuncle [gem] entire, as big as thou art . . ." *Cor,* I, iv, 55.

entirely, *adj.* sincerely; heartily: "They are entirely welcome." *Merch,* III, ii, 224.

entitled, *adj.* justly claiming the highest rank: "Entitled in thy parts do crowned sit . . ." *Sonn 37,* 7.

entituled, *adj.* having a claim [derived from]: "But beauty in that white entituled/ From Venus' doves . . ." *Luc,* 57–58.

entrails, *n. pl.* inside or interior: ". . . like a taper in some monument . . . shows the ragged entrails of this pit . . ." *T Andr,* II, iii, 228–230.

entrance, *n.* entrance fee: "And for an entrance to my entertainment/ I do present you with a man of mine . . ." *Shrew,* II, i, 54–55.

entranced, *adj.* in a faint or swoon; unconscious: "She hath not been entranc'd above five hours . . ." *Per,* III, ii, 96.

entreat, *n.* **1** entreaty: "Yield at [to] entreats, and then let me alone . . ." *T Andr,* I, i, 449.
—*v.* **2** to treat; use: "Entreat her fair, and by my soul, fair Greek,/ If e'er thou stand at mercy of my sword . . ." *Tr & Cr,* IV, iv, 111–112. **3 be entreated to,** to regard as a plea: "Which do not be entreated to, but weigh/ What it is worth embrac'd [in your own interests]." *Ant & Cleo,* II, vi, 32–33.

entwist, *v.* to entwine; twist around: "So doth the woodbine the sweet honeysuckle/ Gently entwist . . ." *M N Dream,* IV, i, 41–42.

envenom, *v.* to cover with venom; here, react hatefully toward: ". . . this report of his/ Did Hamlet so envenom with his envy . . ." *Ham,* IV, vii, 101–102.

envious, *adj.* **1** hateful; spiteful; malicious: "As is the bud bit with an envious worm . . ." *Rom & Jul,* I, i, 149. **2** treacherous: ". . . often did I strive/ To yield the ghost, but still the envious flood/ Stopp'd in my soul . . ." *Rich 3,* I, iv, 36–38.

envire, *v.* var. of **environ:** "To have escaped the danger of my foes/ And to be ten times worse envired by friends!" *Edw 3,* II, I, 414–415.

environ, *v.* to surround; envelop or engulf: ". . . darkness and the gloomy shade of death/ Environ you . . ." *1 Hen 6,* V, iv, 89–90.

envy, *v.* **1** to begrudge; resent: ". . . and even those some/ Envy your great deservings and good name . . ." *1 Hen 4,* IV, iii, 34–35. **2** to hate; despise: "Is it for him you do envy me so?" *Shrew,* II, i, 18. **3** to show or be indicative of malice toward: ". . . such as become a soldier,/ Rather than envy you." *Cor,* III, iii, 56–57.
—*n.* **4** malice; ill will: "If he outlive the envy of this day . . ." *1 Hen 4,* V, ii, 66. **5** [cap.] the deadly sin personified as one consumed with hate: "With full as many signs of deadly hate,/ As lean-fac'd Envy in her loathsome cave." *2 Hen 6,* III, ii, 313–314. **6** the envy it [your fame] creates: "Not Afric [Africa] owns a serpent I abhor/ More than thy fame and envy." *Cor,* I, viii, 3–4.

enwheel, *v.* to encircle: ". . . and on every hand,/ Enwheel thee round!" *Oth,* II, i, 86–87.

enwombed, *adj.* conceived in the womb and born of the womb: ". . . put you in the catalogue of those/ That were enwombed mine." *All's W,* I, iii, 138–139.

Ephesian, *n.* **1** boon companion: "Art thou there? It is thine host,/ thine Ephesian, calls." *Wives,* IV, v, 15–16. **2** drinking companion: "What company?"/ "Ephesians, my lord, of the old church." *2 Hen 4,* II, ii, 141–142.

Ephesus, *n.* ancient city in W Asia Minor. [SD] *Per,* III, ii, 1.

epicure, *n.* person given to overeating and soft living; here, one who is therefore useless as a soldier: "Then fly, false Thanes,/ And mingle with the English epicures . . ." *Mac,* V, iii, 7–8.

Epicurean, *adj.* lustful; sensual: "What a damned Epicurean rascal is this?" *Wives,* II, ii, 276.

epicurism, *n.* [often cap.] self-indulgence; gluttony; riotous living: ". . . epicurism and lust/ Makes it more like a tavern or a brothel/ Than a grac'd palace." *Lear,* I, iv, 252–254.

Epicurus, *n.* Greek philosopher who held that the gods had no interest in human affairs and that omens should be disregarded: ". . . I held Epicurus strong,/ And his opinion; now I change my mind . . ." *J Caes,* V, i, 77–78.

epileptic, *adj.* pale and nervous; appar. Oswald's face twitches with nervousness: "A plague upon your epileptic visage!" *Lear,* II, ii, 82.

Epistrophus, *n.* brother of Cedius; both iden. as Greek "kings" and both slain by Hector: ". . . stands colossus-wise . . . Upon the pashed corses of the kings/ Epistrophus and Cedius." *Tr & Cr,* V, v, 9–11.

epitaph, *n.* short poem or other memorial affixed to the monument of a deceased: "Hang mournful epitaphs, and do all rites/ That appertain unto a burial." *M Ado,* IV, i, 207–208.

epitheton, *n.* old form of EPITHET: "I spoke it . . . as a congruent epitheton/ appertaining to thy young days . . ." *Love's L,* I, ii, 13–14.

epithets, *n.* fine phrases; here, perh., terminology: ". . . bombast circumstance,/ Horribly stuff'd with epithets of war . . ." *Oth,* I, i, 13–14.

epitome, *n.* ref. to Coriolanus' son as a reduced version of himself: "This is a poor epitome of yours,/ Which . . . May show like all yourself." *Cor,* V, iii, 68–70.

equal, *adj.* **1** exact; precise: ". . . let the forfeit/ Be nominated for an equal pound/ Of your fair flesh . . ." *Merch,* I, iii, 144–146. —*adv.* **2** equally: ". . . for he is equal rav'nous/ As he is subtle . . ." *Hen 8,* I, i, 159–160.

equinox, *n.* **just equinox,** an exact counterpart [good and bad are also in equal proportion]: "'Tis to his virtue a just equinox . . ." *Oth,* II, iii, 117.

equipage, *n.* equipment or accoutrements; here, literary production: "To march in ranks of better equipage . . ." *Sonn 32,* 12.

equity, *n.* **1** sound judgment: ". . . and the Prince and Poins be not two/ arrant cowards there's no equity stirring . . ." *1 Hen 4,* II, ii, 94–95. **2** justice: "And thou, his yoke-fellow of equity,/ Bench by his side." *Lear,* III, vi, 38–39.

equivocation, *n.* ambiguity; quibbling: "To doubt th' equivocation of the fiend,/ That lies like truth . . ." *Mac,* V, v, 43–44.

equivocator, *n.* allusion to the Jesuits, in particular a Father Garnet, hanged for conspiracy in the Gunpowder Plot of 1605: "Faith, here's an equivocator, that could swear in/ both the scales against either scale . . ." *Mac,* II, iii, 9–10.

Ercles, *n.* Hercules: "I could/ play Ercles rarely, or a part to tear a cat in . . ." *M N Dream,* I, ii, 24–25.

ere, *conj.* **1** Also, **or ere;** before: "I would/ Have sunk the sea within the earth, or ere/ It should the good ship so have swallow'd . . ." *Temp,* I, ii, 10–12. —*prep.* **2** before; here, before seeing: "And saw the lion's shadow ere himself,/ And ran dismayed away." *Merch,* V, i, 8–9.

Erebus, *n.* (in Greek myth.) place of eternal darkness through which the dead first pass on their way to Hades: ". . . to th'infernal deep, with Erebus and/ tortures vile also!" *2 Hen 4,* II, iv, 154–155.

erection, *n.* Quickly's blunder for "direction" [instructions]; Falstaff promptly quibbles on the word: "She does so take on with her men; they mistook their/ erection."/ "So did I mine . . ." *Wives,* III, v, 35–37.

erewhile, *adv.* short while ago; earlier on: "That young swain that you saw here but erewhile . . ." *As You,* II, iv, 87.

ergo, *conj.* therefore; a word in logic much favored among clowns: "But I pray you ergo old man, ergo I beseech you . . ." *Merch,* II, ii, 54.

eringo, *n.* candied root of the sea holly, regarded as an aphrodisiac: ". . . let it thunder to the tune of 'Greensleeves,'/ hail kissing-comfits, and snow eringoes . . ." *Wives,* V, v, 19–20.

ermite, *n.* See **hermit.**

ern, *v.* to grieve: "O, how it ern'd my heart . . . When Boling-broke rode on roan Barbary—" *Rich 2,* V, v, 76–78.

errand, *n.* **were as good go a mile on his errand,** things will go badly with him: "If he be a whoremonger and comes before him, he/ were as good go a mile on his errand." *Meas,* III, ii, 35–36.

erring, *adj.* wandering: ". . . how brief the life of man/ Runs his erring pilgrimage . . ." *As You,* III, ii, 126–127.

erroneous, *adj.* lacking virtue; here, criminal: "What stratagems, how fell, how butcherly,/ Erroneous, mutinous, and unnatural . . ." *3 Hen 6,* II, v, 89–90.

error, *n.* **1** delusion: ". . . death remember'd should be like a mirror,/ Who tells us life's but breath, to trust it [to be in] error." *Per,* I, i, 46–47. **2** deception; lie: "They shoot but calm words . . . To make a faithless error in your ears . . ." *K John,* II, i, 229–230. **3** [usually pl] lapses in judgment: ". . . my earthy gross conceit,/ Smother'd in errors, feeble, shallow, weak . . ." *Errors,* III, ii, 34–35. **4** transgression; sin: "What damned error but some sober brow/ Will bless it . . ." *Merch,* III, ii, 78–79. **5 error of the moon,** straying of the moon from its normal course: "It is the very error of the moon,/ She comes more near the earth than she was wont . . ." *Oth,* V, ii, 110–111. **6 in error,** mistakenly: "We are again forsworn, in will [deliberately] and error." *Love's L,* V, ii, 471.

erst, *adv.* **1** erstwhile; formerly: "Thy company, which erst was irksome to me,/ I will endure . . ." *As You,* III, v, 95–96. **2** once; one time: "Or slunk not Saturnine, as Tarquin erst,/ That left the camp to sin in Lucrece' bed?" *T Andr,* IV, i, 63–64.

eruption, *n.* violent commotion: ". . . the curate and your sweet self are good at/ such eruptions and sudden breaking out of mirth . . ." *Love's L,* V, i, 105–106.

escape, *n.* **1** sin or transgression: "Rome will despise her for this foul escape." *T Andr,* IV, ii, 113. **2** sally; thrust or burst: ". . . thousand escapes of wit/ Make thee the father of their idle dream . . ." *Meas,* IV, i, 63–64.

escapend, *pres. part.* escaping [old form]: "All perishen of men, of pelf,/ Ne aught escapend but himself . . ." *Per,* II, Chor., 35–36.

escot, *v.* to support or maintain; provide for: "What, are they children? Who maintains 'em?/ How are they escotted?" *Ham,* II, ii, 343–344.

esperance, *n.* **1** hope: "The lowest and most dejected thing of Fortune,/ Stands still [always] in esperance . . ." *Lear,* IV, i,

3–4. **2** [cap.] used as a motto, here of the Percys: "Now, Esperance! Percy! And set on,/ Sound all the lofty instruments of war . . ." *1 Hen 4,* V, ii, 95–96.

espial, *n.* spy: "Her father and myself, lawful espials . . ." *Ham,* III, i, 32.

espouse, *v.* to marry: "Doll Tearsheet she by name, and her espouse . . ." *Hen 5,* II, i, 77.

esquire, *n.* [usually pron. as one syllable] **1** gentleman, ranking just below a knight: "I am Robert Shallow, sir, a poor esquire of this/ county . . ." *2 Hen 4,* III, ii, 56–57. **2** [usually cap.] title of dignity applied here to a justice of the peace: ". . . he shall not abuse Robert Shallow,/ Esquire." *Wives,* I, i, 3–4.

essay, *n.* trial or test: ". . . he wrote/ this but as an essay or taste of my virtue." *Lear,* I, ii, 45–46.

estate, *n.* **1** situation or condition; rank; status: "Let me dispute with thee of thy estate." *Rom & Jul,* III, iii, 63. **2** one's fortunes; possessions or property: "Then do we sin against our own estate . . ." *Timon,* V, i, 40. **3** [often pl] class of persons: ". . . wounding flouts,/ Which you on all estates will execute . . ." *Love's L,* V, ii, 836–837. **4** state of one's soul; spiritual state: ". . . have made suit/ That their good souls may be appeas'd with slaughter/ Of you their captives . . . So think of your estate." *Cymb,* V, v, 71–74. **5 business of estate,** affairs of state: ". . . business of estate, in which we come/ To know your royal pleasure." *Hen 8,* II, ii, 69–70. **6 establish our estate,** settle the succession: "We will establish our estate upon/ Our eldest, Malcolm . . ." *Mac,* I, iv, 37–38. **7 gives me an estate of,** endows me with: "It gives me an estate of seven/ years' health . . ." *Cor,* II, i, 113–114.
—*v.* **8** to bestow; settle: "And some donation freely to estate/ On the blest lovers." *Temp,* IV, i, 85–86.

estate of the world, *n.* universal order: "I 'gin to be aweary of the sun,/ And wish th' estate o' th' world were now undone." *Mac,* V, v, 49–50.

esteem, *v.* **1** to consider: "Who for this seven years hath esteemed him/ No better than a poor and loathsome beggar." *Shrew,* Ind., i, 120–121. **2** to trust or put faith in: ". . . to esteem/ A senseless help, when help past sense we deem." *All's W,* II, i, 122–123.
—*n.* **3** total value: "We lost a jewel of [in] her, and our esteem/ Was made much poorer by it . . ." *All's W,* V, iii, 1–2. **4** judgment; also, worth: ". . . not born fair, no beauty lack,/ Sland'ring creation with a false esteem . . ." *Sonn 127,* 11–12.

estimable, *adj.* full of esteem and admiration: ". . . I could not with such estimable wonder/ overfar believe that . . ." *T Night,* II, i, 26–27.

estimate, *n.* **1** rank; class, position, or standing: ". . . in it are the Lords of York, Berkeley, and Seymour—/ None else of name and noble estimate." *Rich 2*, II, iii, 55–56. **2** worth; value: ". . . for all that life can rate/ Worth name of life in thee hath estimate [must be brought into account] . . ." *All's W*, II, i, 178–179. **3** honor; reputation: "More holy and profound, than mine own life,/ My dear wife's estimate . . ." *Cor*, III, iii, 113–114.

estimation, *n.* **1** guess; conjecture: "I speak not this in estimation . . ." *1 Hen 4*, I, iii, 266. **2** esteem; reputation: ". . . a man of good repute, carriage, bearing, and estimation." *Love's L*, I, i, 262–263. **3** object of great value: "Beggar the estimation which you priz'd/ Richer than sea and land?" *Tr & Cr*, II, ii, 92–93. **4** good graces: ". . . without any further deed to have/ them at all into their estimation . . ." *Cor*, II, ii, 27–28.

estridge, *n.* **1** ostrich: "All furnish'd, all in arms;/ All plum'd like estridges . . ." *1 Hen 4*, IV, i, 97–98. **2** goshawk: ". . . and in that mood/ The dove will peck the estridge . . ." *Ant & Cleo*, III, xiii, 196–197.

Et bonum quo antiquius eo melius, [Latin] And the older a good thing is, the better. *Per*, I, Chor., 10.

eternal, *adj.* **1** relating to eternal matters: "But this eternal blazon must not be/ To ears of flesh and blood." *Ham*, I, v, 21–22. **2** everlasting; endless: "I would it were hell-pains for thy sake, and my poor/ doing eternal . . ." *All's W*, II, iii, 228–229. **3** forever memorable: "For her life [being alive] in Rome/ Would be eternal in our triumph . . ." *Ant & Cleo*, V, i, 65–66.

eternal jewel, *n.* immortal soul: ". . . and mine eternal jewel/ Given to the common Enemy of man . . ." *Mac*, III, i, 67–68.

eterne, *adj.* able to last forever; eternal; everlasting: "But in them Nature's copy's not eterne." *Mac*, III, ii, 38.

eternize, *v.* to immortalize: "Saint Albans battle, won by famous York,/ Shall be eterniz'd in all age to come." *2 Hen 6*, V, iii, 30–31.

Ethiop or **Ethiope,** *n.* **1** Ethiopian or any black person: ". . . she hangs upon the cheek of night/ As a rich jewel in an Ethiop's ear—" *Rom & Jul*, I, v, 44–45. **2** blackamoor; here, ref. to Hermia's dark hair and eyes: "Lysander, whereto tends all this?"/ "Away, you Ethiope!" *M N Dream*, III, ii, 257–258. **3** in attrib. use, darkly sinister: "Such Ethiop words, blacker in their effect/ Than in their countenance." *As You*, IV, iii, 35–36. **4** example of ugliness: "Thou for whom Jove would swear/ Juno but an Ethiop were . . ." *Love's L*, IV, iii, 114–115.

Ethiopian, *n.* fanciful term for the Frenchman, whose coloring appar. is swarthy: "Is he dead, my Ethiopian?/ Is he dead, my Francisco?" *Wives*, II, iii, 25–26.

Europa, *n.* **1** Europe: "And all Europa shall rejoice at thee . . ." *M Ado*, V, iv, 45. **2** beautiful princess abducted by Zeus (Jupiter), who had assumed the form of a white bull: ". . . rejoice at thee,/ As once Europa did at lusty Jove . . ." *M Ado*, V, iv, 45–46.

evasion, *n.* [usually pl.] arguments, often evasive, in defense of oneself: ". . . what modicums of wit he utters—/ his evasions have ears thus long [like those of an ass]." *Tr & Cr*, II, i, 70–71.

even, *adj.* **1** direct; straightforward: "Is there any way to show such friendship?"/ "A very even way, but no such friend." *M Ado*, IV, i, 262–263. **2** equal: "All must be even in our government." *Rich 2*, III, iv, 36. **3** even-handed; impartial: ". . . pause there Morocco,/ And weigh thy value with an even hand . . ." *Merch*, II, vii, 24–25. **4** steadfast: ". . . do not stain/ The even virtue of our enterprise . . ." *J Caes*, II, i, 132–133. **5** level: ". . . lead your battle softly on/ Upon the left hand of the even field." *J Caes*, V, i, 16–17. **6** plain; exact: "Let us from point to point this story know/ To make the even truth in pleasure flow." *All's W*, V, iii, 319–320. **7** calm; unruffled: "How smooth and even they do bear themselves!" *Hen 5*, II, ii, 3. **8 even with the earth,** level with the ground: "Who in a moment even with the earth/ Shall lay your stately . . . towers . . ." *1 Hen 6*, IV, ii, 12–13. **9 go even,** to match; correspond: "Were you a woman, as the rest goes even . . ." *T Night*, V, i, 237. **10 make it even,** to fulfill a request or keep a bargain: "But will you make it even?"/ "Ay, by my sceptre and my hopes of heaven." *All's W*, II, i, 100–101. **11 make us even with you,** reward you amply [for your various services]: "We shall not spend a large expense of time,/ Before we reckon with your several loves,/ And make us even with you." *Mac*, V, ix, 26–28.

—*adv.* **12** carefully; discreetly or circumspectly: "For, bear ourselves as even as we can,/ The King will always think him in our debt . . ." *1 Hen 4*, I, iii, 279–280. **13** simply; just: "By my consent, we'll even let them alone." *1 Hen 6*, I, ii, 44. **14** in accord (with): ". . . there nought hath pass'd/ But even with law against the wilful sons/ Of old Andronicus." *T Andr*, IV, iv, 7–9. **15** steadily; equably: ". . . he could not/ Carry his honours even." *Cor*, IV, vii, 36–37. **16** quite: "My affairs/ Do even drag me homeward . . ." *W Tale*, I, ii, 23–24. **17** equally; likewise: ". . . where I,/ Even in theirs and in the commons' ears,/ Will vouch the truth of it." *Cor*, V, vi, 3–5. **18** at the same time or moment: "But let your love even with my life decay . . ." *Sonn 71*, 12. **19** at this very moment: "She's e'en setting on water to scald such chickens/ as you are." *Timon*, II, ii, 72–73. **20** where else but: "Ev'n to the hall, to hear what shall become/ Of the great Duke of Buckingham." *Hen 8*, II, i, 2–3. **21 even since then,** at that very time: "And even since then hath Richard been obscur'd . . ." *1 Hen 6*, II, v, 26. **22 even with,** equal to: "From me, whose love was of that dignity/ That it went hand in hand even with the vow/ I made to her in marriage . . ." *Ham,* I, v, 48–50.

—*v.* **23** to take advantage of; profit by: ". . . we'll even/ All that good time will give us." *Cymb,* III, iv, 183–184. **24 even o'er,** to fill in; account for: ". . . yet it is danger/ To make him even o'er the time he has lost." *Lear,* IV, vii, 79–80. **25 even your content,** to serve you satisfactorily; also, live up to your expectations of me: ". . . the care I have had to even your content/ I wish might be found in the calendar of my past/ endeavours . . ." *All's W,* I, iii, 2–4.

—*n.* **26** evening: ". . . she did intend confession/ At Patrick's cell this even . . ." *Two Gent,* V, ii, 40–41. **27 the even of it,** the truth of the matter: "The king hath run bad humours on the knight;/ that's the even of it." *Hen 5,* II, i, 121–122.

even-Christen, *n.* fellow Christian: ". . . have countenance in this world to/ drown or hang themselves more than their even-Christen." *Ham,* V, i, 27–29.

evenly, *adv.* directly: ". . . evenly deriv'd/ From his most fam'd of famous ancestors . . ." *Hen 5,* II, iv, 91–92.

even-pleached, *adj.* intertwined: ". . . her hedges even-pleach'd,/ Like prisoners wildly overgrown with hair . . ." *Hen 5,* V, ii, 42–43.

event, *n.* **1** outcome; result: "Against ill chances men are ever merry,/ But heaviness foreruns the good event." *2 Hen 4,* IV, ii, 81–82. **2** consequence; penalty: "expose/ Those tender limbs of thine to the event/ Of the none-sparing war?" *All's W,* III, ii, 103–105. **3** result of one's business endeavors: ". . . leave we him to/ his events, with a prayer they may prove prosperous . . ." *Meas,* III, ii, 231–232. **4 th' event,** we'll see what happens: "Well, well; th' event. [Exeunt.]" *Lear,* I, iv, 358. **5 the true event,** the final outcome; here, of the battle: "Let our just censures/ Attend the true event . . ." *Mac,* V, iv, 14–15.

ever, *adv.* **1** at all times; always: "What is the reason that you use me thus?/ I lov'd you ever." *Ham,* V, i, 284–285. **2** always the same: "Menenius, ever, ever." *Cor,* II, i, 191.

ever among, *adv.* all the while: "And lusty lads roam here and there,/ So merrily,/ And ever among so merrily." *2 Hen 4,* V, iii, 20–22.

everlasting garment, *n.* ref. to the catchpole's leather coat: "A devil in an everlasting garment hath him,/ One whose hard heart is button'd up with steel . . ." *Errors,* IV, ii, 33–34.

evermore, *adj.* **1** continual; everlasting: "And frantic-mad with evermore unrest . . ." *Sonn 147,* 10.
—*adv.* **2** at any future time: "I may not evermore acknowledge thee,/ Lest my bewailed guilt should do thee shame . . ." *Sonn 36,* 9–10.

ever when, at any moment that: "Expecting ever when some envious surge/ Will in his [its] brinish bowels swallow him." *T Andr,* III, i, 96–97.

every, *pron.* **1** everyone: ". . . every of this happy number/ That have endur'd shrewd days and nights with us . . ." *As You,* V, iv, 171–172. **2** every one of: "I'll resolve you . . . of every/ These happen'd accidents . . ." *Temp,* V, i, 248–250.

Eve's apple, *n.* Biblical allusion illustrating the deceptiveness of appearances: "How like Eve's apple doth thy beauty grow,/ If thy sweet virtue answer [match] not thy show [appearance]!" *Sonn 93,* 13–14.

evident, *adj.* certain; inevitable: "We must find/ An evident calamity, though we had/ Our wish . . ." *Cor,* V, iii, 111–113.

evil[1], *n.* **1** harm: "Let my disclaiming from a purpos'd evil/ Free me so far in your most generous thoughts . . ." *Ham,* V, ii, 237–238. **2** disease: ". . . who desires most that/ Which would increase his evil." *Cor,* I, i, 177–178.
—*adj.* **3** unwholesome or harmful: "O, he hath kept an evil diet long . . ." *Rich 3,* I, i, 139.
—*adv.* **4** wrongfully: ". . . were he evil us'd, he would outgo/ His father . . ." *Hen 8,* I, ii, 207–208.

evil[2], *n.* privy or perh. brothel: "Shall we desire to raze the sanctuary/ And pitch our evils there?" *Meas,* II, ii, 171–172.

evilly, *adv.* badly; ill: "This act so evilly borne shall cool the hearts/ Of all his people . . ." *K John,* III, iii, 149–150.

evitate, *v.* to avoid: ". . . she doth evitate and shun/ A thousand irreligious cursed hours . . ." *Wives,* V, v, 225–226.

exact, *adj.* entire; total: "To set the exact wealth of all our states/ All at one cast?" *1 Hen 4,* IV, i, 46–47.

exaction, *n.* demand; here, a compulsory tax: ". . . they vent reproaches/ Most bitterly on you, as putter on/ Of these exactions . . ." *Hen 8,* I, ii, 23–25.

exactly, *adv.* expressly; specifically: "I did confess it, and exactly begg'd/ Your grace's pardon . . ." *Rich 2,* I, i, 140–141.

exalted, *past part.* **1** lifted high: "Th'ambitious ocean swell and rage and foam,/ To be exalted with [as high as] the threat'ning clouds . . ." *J Caes,* I, iii, 7–8.
—*adj.* **2 most exalted,** highest: ". . . weep your tears/ Into the channel, till the lowest stream/ Do kiss the most exalted shores of all." *J Caes,* I, i, 58–60.

examination, *v.* **1** written deposition: "The Duke of Buckingham's surveyor, ha?/ Where's his examination?" *Hen 8,* I, i, 115–116. —*v.* **2** misuse for "examine": ". . . we are now to examination these men." *M Ado,* III, v, 55.

examine, *v.* to question; express doubt about: ". . . a reserved honesty, and that/ I have not heard examin'd." *All's W,* III, v, 62–63.

example, *v.* **1** to give an example of; show a precedent for: "I'll example you with thievery . . ." *Timon,* IV, iii, 438. —*n.* **2** precedent: "There is example for't. The Lady of the Strachy/ married the yeoman of the wardrobe." *T Night,* II, v, 39–40.

exampled, *adj.* furnished with a precedent: ". . . so every step,/ Exampled by the first pace that is sick/ Of his superior . . ." *Tr & Cr,* I, iii, 131–133.

exasperate, *past part.* exasperated; angered: "And this report/ Hath so exasperate the King, that he/ Prepares for some attempt of war." *Mac,* III, vi, 37–39.

exceed, *v.* to excel; be superior: ". . . the Duchess of Milan's/ gown that they praise so./ O, that exceeds, they say." *M Ado,* III, iv, 14–16.

excellent, *adj.* **1** splendid [often used ironically]: "Excellent falsehood!" *Ant & Cleo,* I, i, 40. **2** unequaled or unexcelled: "That excellent grand tyrant of the earth . . ." *Rich 3,* IV, iv, 51.

excelling, *adj.* excellent: "Thou cunning pattern of excelling nature . . ." *Oth,* V, ii, 11.

except, *v.* **1** to give as an excuse: ". . . my high blood's royalty,/ Which fear, not reverence, makes thee to except." *Rich 2,* I, i, 71–72. **2** to raise objections or impediments to: ". . . with the vantage of mine own excuse/ Hath he excepted most against my love." *Two Gent,* I, iii, 82–83. **3 except against,** to take exception to: "Sweet, except not any,/ Except thou wilt except against my love." *Two Gent,* II, iv, 149–150. **4 except, before excepted,** paraphrase of legal term, "excepting the [before-mentioned] exceptions": ". . . my lady takes great exceptions/ to your ill hours."/ "Why, let her except, before excepted." *T Night,* I, iii, 5–7. —*conj.* **5** unless: "I cannot tell, except they are busied about a/ counterfeit assurance." *Shrew,* IV, iv, 87–88. —*past part.* **6** made an exception of; excepted: "Richard except, those whom we fight against/ Had rather have us win than him they follow." *Rich 3,* V, iii, 244–245.

exception, *n.* **1** disapproval or outrage: "What I have done/ That might your nature, honour, and exception/ Roughly awake . . ." *Ham,* V, ii, 226–228. **2** disagreement: "How modest in exception, and withal/ How terrible in constant resolu-

tion . . ." *Hen 5,* II, iv, 34–35. **3** [pl.] objections: "'Tis positive 'gainst all exceptions, lords . . ." *Hen 5,* IV, ii, 25.

exceptless, *adj.* making no exceptions: "Forgive my general and exceptless rashness . . ." *Timon,* IV, iii, 499.

excess, *n.* interest; profit: "I neither lend nor borrow/ By taking nor by giving of excess . . ." *Merch,* I, iii, 56–57.

exchange, *n.* **1** something given [or here, sacrificed] in return for another: "A plot upon her virtuous husband's life,/ And the exchange my brother!" *Lear,* IV, vi, 274–275. **2** disguise: "I am glad 'tis night . . . For I am much asham'd of my exchange . . ." *Merch,* II, vi, 34–35. **3 hold in the exchange,** still prove true when "Adam" is substituted for "Cain": "I say the allusion holds/ in the exchange." *Love's L,* IV, ii, 42–43. **4 right great exchange,** [in] exchange for a captive [Trojan] of note: "Oft have you . . . Desir'd my Cressid in right great exchange . . ." *Tr & Cr,* III, iii, 20–21. —*v.* **5** to change; alter: "Just to the time, not with the time exchanged . . ." *Sonn 109,* 7.

exchequer, *n.* treasury; here, resources: "For she hath no exchequer now but his . . ." *Sonn 67,* 11.

excitement, *n.* exhortation: "Excitements to the field, or speech for truce . . ." *Tr & Cr,* I, iii, 182.

exclaim, *n.* **1** [usually pl.] pleas or urgings: ". . . the part [share] I had in Woodstock's blood/ Doth more solicit me than your exclaims . . ." *Rich 2,* I, ii, 1–2. **2** outcry or protest: "There is enough written upon this earth/ To stir a mutiny . . . / And arm the minds of infants to exclaims." *T Andr,* IV, i, 84–86. —*v.* **3 exclaim on,** to reproach: "Let it presage the ruin of your love,/ And be my vantage to exclaim on you." *Merch,* III, ii, 173–174.

exclamation, *n.* **1** angry complaint: ". . . satisfy her so/ That we shall stop her exclamation." *K John,* II, i, 557–558. **2** reproach or rebuke: ". . . or else you suffer/ Too hard an exclamation." *Hen 8,* I, ii, 51–52. **3** prob. misuse for "acclamation": ". . . I hear as good exclamation on your worship as of/ any man in the city." *M Ado,* III, v, 24–25.

excommunicate, *past part.* excommunicated; excluded from a religion and from the community: "That he hath broke his faith with God and man,/ And from them both stands excommunicate." *Edw 3,* II, i, 333–334.

excommunication, *n.* misuse for "examination": "Only get/ the learned writer to set down our excommunication . . ." *M Ado,* III, v, 58–59.

excrement, *n.* something growing out of the body, as hair or nails: ". . . and with his royal finger, thus, dally with my/ excrement, with my mustachio . . ." *Love's L,* V, i, 95–96.

excursion, *n.* crossing of the stage by attacking troops: "An Alarum. [Enter] Talbot in an excursion." [SD] *1 Hen 6,* III, ii, 35.

excuse, *v.* **1** to explain: ". . . she will well excuse/ Why . . . the doors are made against you." *Errors,* III, i, 92–93. **2** to clear (oneself) of guilt: "Pray God the Duke of York excuse himself!" *2 Hen 6,* I, iii, 178. **3 excuse me,** I beg to disagree: "No, Hector is not a better/ man than Troilus."/ "Excuse me." *Tr & Cr,* I, ii, 79–80.
—*n.* **4 make my old excuse,** justify my old age: "'This fair child of mine/ Shall sum my count and make my old excuse' . . ." *Sonn 2,* 10–11.

executed, *past part.* slit; done prior to hanging: ". . . his nose is executed, and his fire's/ out." *Hen 5,* III, vi, 108–109.

execution, *n.* **1** putting into action; here, the passions of his heart: ". . . scarce I can refrain/ The execution of my big-swoln heart . . ." *3 Hen 6,* II, ii, 110–111. **2** function; operation: "Or those that with the fineness of their souls/ By reason guide his [its] execution." *Tr & Cr,* I, iii, 209–210.

executioner, *n.* person who executes [dispenses] justice: "The gods my justice/ Take from my hand, and they themselves become/ The executioners." *Kinsmen,* V, iv, 120–122.

executor, *n.* **1** survivor; here, one's offspring: "Thy unused beauty . . . Which, used, lives the executor to be." *Sonn 4,* 13–14. **2** executioner: "Delivering o'er to executors pale/ The lazy yawning drone." *Hen 5,* I, ii, 203–204. **3** person who disposes of anything left behind by the dead; here, fig. sense: ". . . their executors, the knavish crows,/ Fly o'er them all . . ." *Hen 5,* IV, ii, 51–52.

exempt, *adj.* **1** estranged; alienated: "Be it my wrong, you are from me exempt,/ But wrong not that wrong with a more [worse] contempt." *Errors,* II, ii, 171–172. **2** excluded; barred: ". . . stand'st not thou attainted,/ Corrupted, and exempt from ancient gentry?" *1 Hen 6,* II, iv, 92–93.

exequies, *n. pl.* funeral ceremonies: ". . . let's not forget/ The noble Duke of Bedford, late deceas'd,/ But see his exequies fulfill'd in Rouen . . ." *1 Hen 6,* III, ii, 131–133.

exercise, *n.* **1** practice and refinement of gentlemanly skills: ". . . to choke his days/ With barbarous ignorance, and deny his youth/ The rich advantage of good exercise?" *K John,* IV, ii, 58–60. **2** usual activity: "He's all my exercise, my mirth, my matter . . ." *W Tale,* I, ii, 166. **3** sermon: "I am in your debt for

your last exercise . . ." *Rich 3,* III, ii, 108. **4** religious devotion: "That show of such an exercise may colour/ Your loneliness." *Ham,* III, i, 45–46.
—*v.* **5** to work mischief: ". . . urchins/ Shall, for that vast of night that they may work,/ All exercise on thee . . ." *Temp,* I, ii, 328–330. **6** to perform sports and public entertainments: "I' the common show-place, where they exercise." *Ant & Cleo,* III, vi, 12.

Exeter, *n.* town SW of London, in Devon: "When last I was at Exeter,/ The Mayor in courtesy show'd me the castle . . ." *Rich 3,* IV, ii, 101–102.

Exeunt, [from Latin for "they exit"] stage direction, indicating that two or more characters leave the stage or, at the end of a scene, that all characters exit: "[Exeunt all but Queen and Suffolk.]" *2 Hen 6,* III, ii, 298.

Exeunt omnes, [from Latin for "all exit"] stage direction, indicating that all characters leave the stage. *All's W,* III, iii, 11.

exhalation, *n.* meteor: "The exhalations whizzing in the air/ Give so much light that I may read by them." *J Caes,* II, i, 44–45.

exhale[1], *v.* to draw forth one's sword [Pistol's misuse]: "The grave doth gape, and doting death is near;/ Therefore exhale." *Hen 5,* II, i, 61–62.

exhale[2], *v.* to draw out; cause to flow: "For 'tis thy presence that exhales this blood . . ." *Rich 3,* I, ii, 58.

exhaled, *adj.* expelled, as by the sun, and sent off course: "And be no more an exhal'd meteor,/ A prodigy of fear . . ." *1 Hen 4,* V, i, 19–20.

exhaust, *v.* to draw forth: "Spare not the babe/ Whose dimpled smiles from fools exhaust their mercy . . ." *Timon,* IV, iii, 120–121.

exhibit, *v.* **1** to present, as for consideration: "Accept this scroll, most gracious sovereign,/ Which . . . We do exhibit to your Majesty." *1 Hen 6,* III, i, 149–151. **2** misuse for "inhibit": "Adieu! tears exhibit my tongue, most beautiful/ pagan, most sweet Jew!" *Merch,* II, iii, 10–11.

exhibiters, *n.* sponsors or promoters: ". . . swaying more upon our part/ Than cherishing th' exhibiters against us . . ." *Hen 5,* I, i, 73–74.

exhibition, *n.* **1** an allowance: "And the King gone to-night!/ prescrib'd his power!/ Confin'd to exhibition!" *Lear,* I, ii, 24–25. **2** misuse for "instruction" or "authority": ". . . we have the exhibition to/ examine." *M Ado,* IV, ii, 5–6. **3** maintenance: "Due reference of place, and exhibition . . ." *Oth,* I, iii, 237.

exigent, *n.* **1** critical moment; emergency: "Why do you cross me in this exigent?" *J Caes,* V, i, 19. **2** end; termination: "These eyes . . . Wax dim, as drawing to their exigent . . ." *1 Hen 6,* II, v, 8–9.

exiled, *adj.* exiled from: "And Equity exil'd your Highness' land." *2 Hen 6,* III, i, 146.

exion, *n.* action [prob. indication of her pron.]: ". . . since my/ exion is entered . . . let him be brought in to his answer." *2 Hen 4,* II, i, 28–30.

exorciser, *n.* See **exorcist.**

exorcism, *n.* summoning of spirits; conjuration: ". . . will/ her ladyship behold and hear our exorcisms?" *2 Hen 6,* I, iv, 3–4.

exorcist or **exorciser,** *n.* one empowered to summon spirits: "Thou, like an exorcist, hast conjur'd up/ My mortified spirit." *J Caes,* II, i, 323–324.

expect, *v.* **1** to await: "Sweet soul let's in, and there expect their coming." *Merch,* V, i, 49. **2** to anticipate: ". . . bloody veins [soldiers] expecting overthrow . . ." *Per,* I, iv, 94. —*n.* **3** expectation: ". . . be't of less expect/ That matter needless, of importless burden,/ Divide thy lips . . ." *Tr & Cr,* I, iii, 70–72.

expectance, *n.* anticipation; here, wondering: "There is expectance here from both the sides/ What further you will do." *Tr & Cr,* IV, v, 145–146.

expectancy, *n.* Hamlet as heir to the Danish throne: "Th'expectancy and rose of the fair state . . ." *Ham,* III, i, 154.

expectation, *n.* fears: "Thou hast seal'd up [confirmed] my expectation." *2 Hen 4,* IV, v, 103.

expected good, *n.* anticipated praise: ". . . that I fear/ All the expected good w'are like to hear/ For this play at this time . . ." *Hen 8,* Epil.7–9.

expecter, *n.* person who is waiting to hear: ". . . signify this loving interview/ To the expecters of our Trojan part . . ." *Tr & Cr,* IV, v, 155.

expedience, *n.* **1** expedition; haste or urgency: "I shall break/ The cause of our expedience to the queen . . ." *Ant & Cleo,* I, ii, 175–176. **2** urgent enterprise: "What yesternight our Council did decree/ In forwarding this dear expedience." *1 Hen 4,* I, i, 32–33.

expedient, *adj.* **1** expeditious; speedy: "Expedient manage must be made, my liege . . ." *Rich 2,* I, iv, 39. **2 expedient head,** swift headway: "This sudden, mighty, and expedient head/ That they have made . . . is wonderful." *Edw 3,* IV, iv, 10–11.

expediently, *adv.* expeditiously; with haste: "Make an extent upon his house and lands./ Do this expediently . . ." *As You,* III, i, 17–18.

expedition, *n.* **1** the march of an army: ". . . a mighty power,/ Bending their expedition toward Philippi." *J Caes,* IV, iii, 168–169. **2** venture; endeavor: ". . . you shall be employ'd/ To hasten on his expedition." *Two Gent,* I, iii, 76–77. **3** speed or haste: ". . . his expedition promises/ Present approach. *Timon,* V, ii, 3–4. **4** progress; setting forth: "Who intercepts me in my expedition?" *Rich 3,* IV, iv, 136. **5** blind fury: "Th' expedition of my violent love/ Outrun the pauser, reason." *Mac,* II, iii, 110–111. **6** motion; action: ". . . deliver/ Our puissance into the hand of God,/ Putting it straight in expedition." *Hen 5,* II, ii, 189–191. **7** poss. Fluellen means "expertise" or "erudition": ". . . of great expedition and/ knowledge in th' aunchiant [ancient] wars . . ." *Hen 5,* III, ii, 81–82.

expeditious, *adj.* speedy; hasty: "Our abbeys and our priories shall pay/ This expeditious charge." *K John,* I, i, 48–49.

expense, *n.* **1** loss: "And moan the expense of many a vanish'd sight . . ." *Sonn 30,* 8. **2** dissipation: "And husband nature's riches from expense . . ." *Sonn 94,* 6. **3 expense and waste,** wasteful spending; squandering: "'Tis they have put him on the old man's death,/ To have th' expense and waste of his revenues." *Lear,* II, i, 99–100.

experimental, *adj.* based on experience: ". . . my observations,/ Which with experimental seal doth warrant/ The tenor of my book . . ." *M Ado,* IV, i, 165–167.

expiate, *v.* **1** to end: "Then look [expect] I death my days should expiate." *Sonn 22,* 4. —*adj.* **2** fully come: "Make haste: the hour of death is expiate." *Rich 3,* III, iii, 24.

exploit, *n.* deed or action; here, sport: "A trim exploit, a manly enterprise,/ To conjure tears up in a poor maid's eyes . . ." *M N Dream,* III, ii, 157–158.

exposition, *n.* **1** interpretation: "Thou hast most kindly hit it."/ "A most courteous exposition." *Rom & Jul,* II, iv, 58–59. **2** misuse for **disposition;** inclination or desire: "I have an exposition of [for] sleep come upon me." *M N Dream,* IV, i, 38.

expositor, *n.* commentator; voice: ". . . his fair tongue (conceit's expositor)/ Delivers in such apt and gracious words . . ." *Love's L,* II, i, 72–73.

expostulate, *v.* to discuss or examine; here, to engage in a philosophical inquiry: ". . . to expostulate/ What majesty should be, what duty is . . ." *Ham,* II, ii, 86–87.

exposture, *n.* exposure: "More than a wild exposture to each chance/ That starts i'th'way before thee." *Cor,* IV, i, 36–37.

exposure, *n.* exposed, hazardous, or dangerous position [of an army]: "To match us in comparisons with dirt/ To weaken and discredit our exposure . . ." *Tr & Cr,* I, iii, 194–195.

expound, *v.* to explain: "Which read and not expounded, 'tis decreed,/ As these before thee thou thyself shalt bleed." *Per,* I, i, 58–59.

express[1], *adj.* exact; precise: ". . . in form/ and moving how express and admirable . . ." *Ham,* II, ii, 304–305.

express[2], *v.* to declare: "Scorn'd a fair colour or express'd it stol'n . . ." *All's W,* V, iii, 50.

expressed, *past part.* shown; revealed: "If you be one [a woman]—as you are well express'd/ By all external warrants—show it now . . ." *Meas,* II, iv, 135–136.

expressure, *n.* **1** expression: ". . . the manner of his gait, the/ expressure of his eye, forehead, and complexion . . ." *T Night,* II, iii, 157–158. **2** impression or imprint: "Th' expressure that it bears, green let it be . . ." *Wives,* V, v, 68.

exsufflicate, *adj.* windy or overblown; empty; unsubstantiated: "When I shall turn the business of my soul/ To such exsufflicate and blown surmises . . ." *Oth,* III, iii, 185–186.

extant, *adj.* **1** alive; living: "That you yourself, being extant, well might show . . ." *Sonn 83,* 6. **2** present: "But in this extant moment, faith and troth . . . Bids thee . . . welcome." *Tr & Cr,* IV, v, 167–170. **3** wordplay on "still existing" and "stand out": ". . . I am made an ass."/ "Ay, and an ox too: both the proofs are extant." *Wives,* V, v, 120–121.

extasy, *n.* var. of ecstasy: "O love be moderate, allay thy extasy,/ In measure rain thy joy . . ." *Merch,* III, ii, 111–112.

extemporal, *adj.* extempore; able to speak extemporaneously: "Assist me, some/ extemporal god of rhyme . . ." *Love's L,* I, ii, 172–173.

extemporally, *adv.* in an improvised manner; extemporaneously: "And sings extemporally a woeful ditty . . ." *Ven & Ad,* 836.

extempore, *adj.* **1** extemporaneous: "It is extempore, from my mother-wit . . ." *Shrew,* II, i, 257.

—*adv.* **2** in an extemporaneous manner: "You may do it extempore, for it is nothing but/ roaring." *M N Dream,* I, ii, 64–65.

extend, *v.* **1** to attack or invade: "Labienus . . . hath with his Parthian force/ Extended Asia . . ." *Ant & Cleo,* I, ii, 96–98. **2** to spread: ". . . the report of her is extended/ more than can be thought to begin from such/ a cottage [it must concern a person of some importance]." *W Tale,* IV, ii, 43–45. **3 extend my manners,** stretch my show of courtesy [by kissing Emilia]: "let it not gall your patience, good Iago,/ That I extend my manners . . ." *Oth,* II, i, 97–98. **4 wonderfully to extend him,** greatly increase his reputation: ". . . the approbation of those that weep this/ lamentable divorce . . . are wonderfully/ to extend him . . ." *Cymb,* I, v, 17–19.

extent, *n.* **1** exercise: ". . . and, for the extent/ Of egal [equal] justice, us'd in such contempt?" *T Andr,* IV, iv, 3–4. **2** act of violence; attack: "Let thy fair wisdom . . . sway/ In this uncivil and unjust extent . . ." *T Night,* IV, i, 51–52. **3** behavior; here, toward the players: ". . . lest my extent to the players . . . should more appear/ like entertainment than yours." *Ham,* II, ii, 369–371. **4 make an extent upon,** [to] seize by means of a legal writ: "And let my officers . . . Make an extent upon his house and lands." *As You,* III, i, 16–17.

extenuate, *v.* **1** to lessen or excuse: ". . . she did embrace me as a husband,/ And so extenuate the 'forehand sin." *M Ado,* IV, i, 49–50. **2** to disparage; depreciate: ". . . his glory not/ extenuated, wherein he was worthy . . ." *J Caes,* III, ii, 39–40.

extermine, *v.* exterminate: ". . . your sorrow and my grief/ Were both extermined." *As You,* III, v, 88–89.

extern, *n.* exterior: "With my extern the outward honouring . . ." *Sonn 125,* 2.

extincture, *n.* extinction; quenching: "Both fire from hence and chill extincture hath." *Lover's Comp,* 294.

extinguish, *v.* to eclipse; obscure or obliterate: ". . . her virtues that surmount,/ And natural graces that extinguish art . . ." *1 Hen 6,* V, iii, 192.

extirp, *v.* to extirpate; rip out; eradicate: ". . . but it is impossible to extirp it quite,/ friar, till eating and drinking be put down." *Meas,* III, ii, 98–99.

extirped, *past part.* extirpated; eradicated; ripped out: "Nor should that nation boast it so with us,/ But be extirped from our provinces." *1 Hen 6,* III, iii, 23–24.

extol, *v.* to explain or justify: "And power . . . Hath not a tomb so evident as a chair/ T'extol what it hath done." *Cor,* IV, vii, 51–53.

extort, *v.* **1** to seize by force: ". . . if thou hast uphoarded in thy life/ Extorted treasure in the womb of earth . . ." *Ham,* I, i, 139–140. **2** to wring or wrest: "None of noble sort/ Would so offend a virgin, and extort/ A poor soul's patience . . ." *M N Dream,* III, ii, 159–160.

extracting, *adj.* tending to distract: "A most extracting frenzy of mine own/ From my remembrance clearly banish'd his." *T Night,* V, i, 279–280.

extraught, *past part.* derived; here, descended: "Sham'st thou not, knowing whence thou art extraught,/ To let thy tongue detect thy base-born heart?" *3 Hen 6,* II, ii, 142–143.

extravagancy, *n.* vagrancy; wandering; here, a voyage with no predetermined destination: ". . . my determinate voyage is mere extravagancy." *T Night,* II, i, 10–11.

extravagant, *adj.* **1** wandering outside its proper confines: "Th'extravagant and erring spirit hies/ To his confine . . ." *Ham,* I, i, 159–160. **2** ref. to Othello as an alien and a roamer or vagabond: "Tying her duty . . . In an extravagant and wheeling stranger . . ." *Oth,* I, i, 135–136.

extremes, *n. pl.* **1** extremities, esp. the body's limbs: ". . . makes its course from the inwards to the parts' extremes . . ." *2 Hen 4,* IV, iii, 105. **2** exaggerations: "To chide at your extremes, it not becomes me—" *W Tale,* IV, iv, 6. **3 extremes beyond extremity,** calamities or suffering in the greatest degree: "With some mischance cross Tarquin in his flight;/ Devise extremes beyond extremity . . ." *Luc,* 968–969.

extremest, *adj.* last or entire; utmost: "My purse, my person,/ My extremest means/ Lie all unlock'd to your occasions." *Merch,* I, i, 138–139.

extremity, *n.* **1** utter calamity: "Like Patience gazing on kings' graves, and smiling/ Extremity out of act." *Per,* V, i, 138–139. **2 in extremity,** to the greatest degree: "Then, what it was that next came in her eye,/ Which she must dote on in extremity." *M N Dream,* III, ii, 2–3. **3 take off some extremity,** lessen the shock: "Speak, man, thy tongue/ May take off some extremity . . ." *Cymb,* III, iv, 16–17.

eyas, *n.* an unfledged hawk: ". . . an eyrie of children, little eyases, that/ cry out on the top of question . . ." *Ham,* II, ii, 337–338.

eyas-musket, *n.* young sparrow hawk: "How now, my eyas-musket, what news with/ you?" *Wives,* III, iii, 19–20.

eye, *n.* **1** a patch or spot: "The ground, indeed, is tawny."/ "With an eye of green in 't." *Temp,* II, i, 52–53. **2** [pl.] spectators; here, appar. the devils of Tom [Edgar]: "Look where he stands and glares! Want'st/ thou eyes at trial, madam?" *Lear,* III, vi, 24–25. **3** spy: "I have eyes under my service which/ look upon his removedness [absence from court] . . ." *W Tale,* IV, ii, 36–37. **4 change eyes,** to exchange loving glances: "At the first sight/ They have chang'd eyes." *Temp,* I, ii, 443–444. **5 eye of heaven,** the sun: "Sometime too hot the eye of heaven shines . . ." *Sonn 18,* 5. **6 eye of Helen's needle,** bawdy ref. to sexually servicing Helen: "As will stop [fill] the eye of Helen's needle, for whom/ he comes to fight." *Tr & Cr,* II, i, 82–83. **7 eyes half out,** eyes half-blind from venereal disease: "Your eyes, half out, weep out at Pandar's fall . . ." *Tr & Cr,* V, x, 49. **8 eyes over,** overseeing eyes; hence, spies: "For I do fear eyes over . . ." *W Tale,* IV, iv, 654. **9 eye without the ear,** neither eye nor ear alone: "Not working with the eye without the ear . . ." *Hen 5,* II, ii, 135. **10 have an eye of (someone),** to keep an eye on; watch carefully: "Nay, then I have an eye of you." *Ham,* II, ii, 290. **11 in eye of,** be witness to: ". . . converse with noblemen,/ And be in eye of every exercise . . ." *Two Gent,* I, iii, 31–32. **12 in his eye,** in his presence; in person: "If that his Majesty would aught with us,/ We shall express our duty in his eye . . ." *Ham,* IV, iv, 5–6. **13 in the eyes,** within [her] sight: "Her gentlewomen, like . . . So many mermaids, tended her i' the eyes . . ." *Ant & Cleo,* Ii, ii, 206–207. **14 worn your eyes out in the service,** sly ref. to Mistress Overdone's service on behalf of Blind Cupid: ". . . there will be pity taken on you; you that/ have worn your eyes almost out in the service . . ." *Meas,* I, ii, 101–102.
—*v.* **15** to appear: ". . . my becomings kill me, when they do not/ Eye well to you." *Ant & Cleo,* I, iii, 96–97. **16 eye thee,** take you as their guide: "Like a great sea-mark standing every flaw/ And saving those that eye thee!" *Cor,* V, iii, 74–75.

eyeless, *adj.* blind: ". . . the impetuous blasts, with eyeless rage,/ Catch in their fury . . ." *Lear,* III, i, 8–9.

eyewink, *n.* glance; notice: ". . . they could never get an eyewink/ of her . . ." *Wives,* II, ii, 67–68.

eyne, *n.* **1** old pl. of **eye:** "If the scorn of your bright eyne/ Have power to raise such love in mine . . ." *As You,* IV, iii, 50–51. **2 pink eyne,** small or half-shut eyes: "Come, thou monarch of the vine,/ Plumpy Bacchus with pink eyne!" *Ant & Cleo,* II, vii, 112–113.

eyrie, *n.* var of **aerie;** nest, esp. that of a predator, in a high, inaccessible place: ". . . there is, sir, an eyrie of children, little eyases, that/ cry out on the top of question . . ." *Ham,* II, ii, 337–338.

F

fa, *n.* fourth tone in the musical scale, here used whimsically as a verb: "I'll re you, I'll/ fa you. Do you note me?" *Rom & Jul,* IV, v, 116–117.

fable, *n.* **1** lie, esp. in the phrase *sans fable* [truly]: "... did she not herself revile me there?"/ "Sans fable, she herself revil'd you there." *Errors,* IV, iv, 70–71. **2 that's a fable,** ref. to belief that the devil had cloven hooves; if Iago is truly the devil Othello's sword cannot kill him: "I look down towards his feet, but that's a fable,/ If that thou be'st a devil, I cannot kill thee." *Oth,* V, ii, 287–288.
—*v.* **3** to lie; tell falsehoods: "He fables not; I hear the enemy." *1 Hen 6,* IV, ii, 42. **4** to tell fictitious tales: "Let Aesop fable in a winter's night..." *3 Hen 6,* V, v, 25.

fabric, *n.* **1** composition; here, prob., the human body: "With other muniments and petty helps/ In this our fabric..." *Cor,* I, i, 117–118. **2 falling fabric,** collapsing building: "And manhood is call'd foolery when it stands/ Against a falling fabric." *Cor,* III, i, 244–245.

fabulous, *adj.* like a fable, esp. in being absurd: "I see report is fabulous and false..." *1 Hen 6,* II, iii, 17.

face, *n.* **1** appearance; show: "... thinking by this face/ To fasten in our thoughts that they have courage..." *J Caes,* V, i, 10–11. **2 faces fit for masks,** faces as fair as any hidden behind masks for protection: "With faces fit for masks, or rather fairer/ Than those for preservation cas'd, or shame..." *Cymb,* V, iii, 21–22. **3 full of face,** beautiful: "So buxom, blithe and full of face/ As heaven had lent her all his grace..." *Per,* I, Chor., 23–24. **4 put a strange face on,** to lend an assumed appearance to [not to admit]: "To put a strange face on his own perfection." *M Ado,* II, iii, 47. **5 with his face backward,** retreating while looking back over his shoulder; ref. to lion (passant regardant) in heraldry: "And thou shalt hunt a lion that will fly/ With his face backward." *Tr & Cr,* IV, i, 20–21.
—*v.* **6** to trim; decorate or adorn: "To face the garment of rebellion/ With some fine colour..." *1 Hen 4,* V, i, 74–75. **7**

to bully; here, in wordplay with preceding: "Thou hast faced many things... Face not me." *Shrew,* IV, iii, 123–125. **8** to profess one thing and do another; deceive: "Fair Margaret knows/ That Suffolk doth not flatter, face, or feign." *1 Hen 6,* V, iii, 141–142. **9 face it,** to bluff; brazen it out: "Yet I have fac'd it with a card of ten." *Shrew,* II, i, 398. **10 face it out,** put on a brave front: "... a' faces it out, but fights not." *Hen 5,* III, ii, 34. **11 face (someone) down,** to insist boldly or brazenly to (another): "But here's a villain that would face me down/ He met me on the mart..." *Errors,* III, i, 6–7. **12 face (someone) out of,** to deny brazenly any knowledge of: "... his false cunning... Taught him to face me out of his acquaintance..." *T Night,* V, i, 84–86. **13 face the matter out,** [to] bully or bluff one's way through: "... a swearing Jack,/ That thinks with oaths to face the matter out." *Shrew,* II, i, 281–282.

faced, *past part.* **faced out of my way,** put to shame: "I will not say so for fear I should be faced out/ of my way." *Hen 5,* III, vii, 85–86.

facere, *v.* [Latin] to make; offer or provide: "*facere,*/ as it were replication [explanation]..." *Love's L,* IV, ii, 14–15.

face-royal, *n.* ten-shilling coin, called a "royal," stamped with the king's head: "He/ may keep it still at a face-royal, for a barber shall/ never earn sixpence out of it." *2 Hen 4,* I, ii, 23–25.

facile question, *n.* less effort: "So may he with more facile question bear it [carry it off]..." *Oth,* I, iii, 23.

Facile, misuse for "Fauste," Faustus; the poet Mantuanus is misquoted here, prob. Shakespeare's jibe at the character's schoolboy Latin: [in translation] "... while all your flock lies chewing their cud in the cool shade..." *Love's L,* IV, ii, 90.

facility, *n.* fluency: "... but, for the elegancy, facility, and/ golden cadence of poesy, *caret.*" *Love's L,* IV, ii, 117–118.

facinerious, *adj.* var. of facinorous; very wicked: ". . . he's of a most facinerious/ spirit that will not acknowledge it to be the—" *All's W,* II, iii, 29–30.

facing, *n.* **stands for the facing,** the trimming [fox = craftiness] is just as acceptable as the garment [lambskin = innocency]: ". . . to signify that craft,/ being richer than innocency,/ stands for the facing." *Meas,* III, ii, 9–10.

fact, *n.* **1** deed; action: "If thou hadst drunk to him, 't had been a kindness/ Becoming well thy fact." *Per,* IV, iii, 11–12. **2** crime; sin: ". . . indeed, his fact till now . . . came not to an undoubtful proof." *Meas,* IV, ii, 134–135. **3 in the fact,** in the act (of committing a crime): "Dealing with witches and with conjurers:/ Whom we have apprehended in the fact . . ." *2 Hen 6,* II, i, 164–165.

faction, *n.* **1** band or party; alliance; here, members of the conspiracy: "Let 'em enter./ They are the faction." *J Caes,* II, i, 76–77. **2** company; fellowship: "I will keep where there is/ wit stirring, and leave the faction of fools." *Tr & Cr,* II, i, 120–121. **3** favoritism; instance of taking sides: "Made emulous missions 'mongst the gods themselves,/ And drave great Mars to faction." *Tr & Cr,* III, iii, 189–190. **4** [often pl.] intrigues or conspiracies; dissension or, sometimes, rebellion: "I will bandy with thee in faction." *As You,* V, i, 54–55.

factionary, *adj.* loyally partisan: ". . . always factionary on the party of your general." *Cor,* V, ii, 29.

factious, *adj.* **1** rebellious: ". . . let him to the Tower,/ And chop away that factious pate of his." *2 Hen 6,* V, i, 134–135. **2** being part of a faction; here, the conspiracy to murder Caesar: "Be factious [form a faction] for redress of all these griefs . . ." *J Caes,* I, iii, 118.

factious numbers, *n.* supporters of a cause; a rebellious army or faction: "Make up no factious numbers for the matter . . ." *2 Hen 6,* II, i, 43.

factor, *n.* agent; a buyer or go-between: "Percy is but my factor . . . To engross up glorious deeds on my behalf . . ." *1 Hen 4,* III, ii, 147–148.

faculty, *n.* **1** [often pl.] inborn quality or characteristic: "Why all these things change from their ordinance,/ Their natures, and pre-formed faculties . . ." *J Caes,* I, iii, 66–67. **2** [pl.] royal powers: ". . . this Duncan/ Hath borne his faculties so meek . . ." *Mac,* I, vii, 16–17. **3 faculties inclusive,** properties considered as a whole: ". . . notes whose faculties inclusive were/ More than they were in note [greater than the sum of their ingredients]." *All's W,* I, iii, 221–222.

fadge, *v.* to work out; turn out: "How will this fadge? My master loves her dearly,/ And I, poor monster, fond as much on him . . ." *T Night* II, ii, 32–33.

fadom or **faddom,** *n.* var. of **fathom:** "Full fadom five thy father lies;/ Of his bones are coral made . . ." *Temp,* I, ii, 399–400.

faggot, *n.* bundle of sticks or twigs: "What fool hath added water to the sea,/ Or brought a faggot to bright-burning Troy?" *T Andr,* III, i, 68–69.

fail, *n.* failure; here, to produce an heir: "How grounded he his title to the crown/ Upon our fail?" *Hen 8,* I, ii, 144–145.

failing, *n.* failing stength; weakness: "Is yond despis'd and ruinous man my lord?/ Full of decay and failing?" *Timon,* IV, iii, 462–463.

fain, *adv.* **1** gladly; willingly: "I would fain dissuade him, but he/ will not be entreated." *As You,* I, ii, 149–150. —*adj.* **2** obliged; content: "I must be fain/ to pawn both my plate and the tapestry of my/ dining-chambers." *2 Hen 4,* II, i, 138–140. **3** fond; keen (on): "Yea, man and birds are fain of climbing high." *2 Hen 6,* II, i, 8.

faining, *adj.* (of a voice) soft; mezza voce: "With faining voice verses of feigning [pretended] love . . ." *M N Dream,* I, i, 31.

faint, *adj.* **1** weak or exhausted; fainthearted: ". . . this strong right hand of mine/ Can pluck the diadem from faint Henry's head . . ." *3 Hen 6,* II, ii, 152–153. **2** pale: ". . . where often you and I/ Upon faint primrose beds were wont to lie . . ." *M N Dream,* I, i, 214–215. **3** causing faintness: "I have a faint cold fear thrills through my veins . . ." *Rom & Jul,* IV, iii, 15. **4** (of sleep) light; easily awakened: "In thy faint slumbers I by thee have watch'd . . ." *1 Hen 4,* II, iii, 48. **5** trivial: ". . . ceremony was but devis'd at first/ To set a gloss on faint deeds . . ." *Timon,* I, ii, 15–16. —*v.* **6** to lose courage; show fear: "Why faint you, lords?/ My title's good, and better far than his." *3 Hen 6,* I, i, 133–134. **7** to become discouraged or disheartened: "O! how I faint when I of you do write . . ." *Sonn 80,* 1. **8 it faints me,** it causes me to feel faint: ". . . it faints me/ To think what follows." *Hen 8,* II, iii, 103–104.

faintly, *adv.* **1** faintheartedly: "Woe doth the heavier sit/ Where it perceives it is but faintly borne." *Rich 2,* I, iii, 280–281. **2** slightly; to a small extent: "I have told you what I have seen and heard;/ but faintly, nothing like the image and horror of it . . ." *Lear,* I, ii, 181–182. **3** hintingly: "I faintly broke with thee of Arthur's death . . ." *K John,* IV, ii, 227.

fair¹, *adj.* **1** beautiful; handsome: ". . . those that she makes fair, she scarce makes honest . . ." *As You,* I, ii, 36–37. **2** blond; pale: "What says she to my face?"/ "She says it is a fair one." *Two Gent,* V, ii, 8–9. **3** appropriate and usually generous: ". . . let them be receiv'd,/ Not without fair reward." *Timon,* I, ii, 188–189. **4** reasonable: ". . . why do you start, and seem to fear/ Things that do sound so fair?" *Mac,* I, iii, 51–52. **5** harmless; friendly: "I have fair meanings, sir."/ "And fair words to them." *Ant & Cleo,* II, vi, 66. **6** evenly matched: "To try the fair adventure of tomorrow." *K John,* V, v, 22. **7** just; even-handed: ". . . we single you/ As our best-moving fair solicitor." *Love's L,* II, i, 28–29. **8 fair befall,** good luck to: "And so farewell; and fair befall thy hopes . . ." *1 Hen 6,* II, v, 112–113. **9 fair o' Friday,** as beautiful on a fast day as Helen is in her Sunday best: "And she were not kin to me,/ she would be as fair o' Friday as Helen is o'/ Sunday." *Tr & Cr,* I, i, 75–77. **10 in fair (or good) terms,** in speech rather than in fact: "I will scour you/ with my rapier, as I may, in fair terms . . ." *Hen 5,* II, i, 55–56. **11 keep you fair,** keep you in fine clothes: "You will have Gremio to keep you fair." *Shrew,* II, i, 17. **12 take thy fair hour,** enjoy your youth while you may: "Take thy fair hour, Laertes, time be thine . . ." *Ham,* I, ii, 62. —*adv.* **13** kindly; courteously: "First he did praise my beauty, then my speech."/ "Did'st speak him fair?" *Errors,* IV, ii, 15–16. **14** in an elegant hand: "I sat me down,/ Devis'd a new commission, wrote it fair—" *Ham,* V, ii, 31–32. **15** justly; reasonably: "We will not now be troubled with reply:/ We offer fair, take it advisedly." *1 Hen 4,* V, I, 113–114. **16 stand fair,** stand still: "Stand fair, I pray thee; let me look on thee." *Tr & Cr,* IV, v, 234. —*n.* **17** beauty: "Let no face be kept in mind/ But the fair of Rosalind." *As You,* III, ii, 92–93. **18** beautiful woman: "I am compar'd to twenty thousand fairs." *Love's L,* V, ii, 37. **19** favor; fortune: "Now fair befall your mask!" *Love's L,* II, i, 123. **20 fair fall (or befall),** good luck to: "Fair fall the face it covers!" *Love's L,* II, i, 124. —*v.* **21** to make beautiful; here, by artificial means: "Fairing the foul with art's false borrowed face . . ." *Sonn 127,* 6.

fair², *n.* **buy in a fair,** to buy secondhand, or often stolen, goods at a fair is here considered preferable: "I will buy me a son-in-law in a fair, and toll [pay a tax] for this." *All's W,* V, iii, 147.

fair according, *adj.* readily agreeing: ". . . within her scope of choice/ Lies my consent and fair according voice." *Rom & Jul,* I, ii, 18–19.

fairer, *adj.* **1** more desirable; even better: "And she is fair, and (fairer than that word),/ Of wondrous virtues . . ." *Merch,* I, i, 162–163. **2 fairer than honest,** more amusing than decent: "Sir, your company is fairer than honest; rest you well." *Meas,* IV, iii, 174.

fairest, *adj.* most favorable or effective: "A stand where you may make the fairest shoot." *Love's L,* IV, i, 10.

fair-faced league, *n.* kindly agreement: ". . . I shall show you peace and fair-fac'd league . . ." *K John,* II, i, 417.

fairing, *n.* a present: ". . . we shall be rich ere we depart,/ If fairings come thus plentifully in . . ." *Love's L,* V, ii, 1–2.

fairly, *adv.* **1** warmly; kindly; gladly: "My lord, there are certain nobles . . . come to visit you./ They are fairly welcome." *Timon,* I, ii, 170–172. **2** skillfully; effectively; appealingly: "How fairly this lord strives to appear foul!" *Timon,* III, iii, 33. **3** finely; elegantly or handsomely: "I have perus'd the note . . . I'll have them very fairly bound—" *Shrew,* I, ii, 143–145. **4** properly; here, honorably: ". . . my chief care/ Is to come fairly off from the great debts/ Wherein my time . . . Hath left me gag'd . . ." *Merch,* I, i, 127–130. **5** kindly; gently: ". . . they parted very/ fairly in jest." *Two Gent,* II, v, 11–12. **6** completely; quite: "Would I were fairly out on't." *Hen 8,* V, ii, 143. **7 stand full fairly,** to stand a fair chance of victory: "Up and away! Our soldiers stand full fairly for the day." *1 Hen 4,* V, iii, 28–29.

fair nature, *n.* agreeable disposition or personality: "Disguise fair nature with hard-favour'd rage . . ." *Hen 5,* III, i, 8.

fair-play, *n.* code of chivalry: "According to the fair-play of the world,/ Let me have audience . . ." *K John,* V, ii, 118–119.

fair show, *n.* impressive appearance: "And your fair show shall suck away their souls . . ." *Hen 5,* IV, ii, 17.

fairy, *n.* **1** enchantress; captivating woman; also, bringer of good fortune: "To this great fairy I'll commend thy acts . . ." *Ant & Cleo,* IV, viii, 12. **2** [pl.] evil spirits: "To your protection I commend me, gods,/ From fairies and the tempters of the night . . ." *Cymb,* II, ii, 8–9. **3** poss. an illusion: "But that it eats our victuals, I should think/ Here were a fairy." *Cymb,* III, vii, 13–14.

faith, *n.* **1** pledge, as of intent to marry: ". . . being else by faith enforc'd/ To call young Claudio to a reckoning for it." *M Ado,* V, iv, 8–9. **2** trust: "In act thy bed-vow broke and new faith torn . . ." *Sonn 152,* 3. **3 in (good) faith,** in truth: "Sir, in good faith, in sincere verity . . ." *Lear,* II, ii, 106. —*interj.* **4** by my faith (a mild oath): "You are/ grandjurors, are ye? We'll jure ye, faith." *1 Hen 4,* II, ii, 86–87.

'faith, *interj.* in faith; by my faith: ". . . 'faith/ I shall unfold equal discourtesy/ To your best kindness . . ." *Cymb,* II, iii, 94–96.

faith-breach, *n.* act(s) of treason: "Now minutely revolts upbraid his faith-breach . . ." *Mac,* V, ii, 18.

faithed, *adj.* believed or believable; creditable: ". . . would the reposal/ Of any trust, virtue, or worth in thee/ Make thy words faith'd?" *Lear,* II, i, 68–70.

faithfully, *adv.* honestly; sincerely: "If that you were the good Sir Rowland's son,/ As you have whisper'd faithfully you were . . ." *As You,* II, vii, 194–195.

faithless, *adj.* **1** not of the Christian faith; unbelieving: "Unless she do it under this excuse,/ That she is issue to a faithless Jew . . ." *Merch,* II, iv, 36–37. **2 faithless error,** treacherous lie: "They shoot but calm words . . . To make a faithless error in your ears . . ." *K John,* II, i, 229–230.

faitor, *n.* rogue; impostor or cheat: "Down,/ down, dogs! Down, faitors!" *2 Hen 4,* II, iv, 155–156.

falchion, *n.* sword; here, one with a curved blade: "The face of an old Roman coin, scarce seen."/ "The pommel of Caesar's falchion." *Love's L,* V, ii, 608–609.

fall, *v.* **1** to let fall; drop: "Here did she fall a tear; here in this place/ I'll set a bank of rue . . ." *Rich 2,* III, iv, 104–105. **2** to alight: "Coming from Sardis, on our former ensign/ Two mighty eagles fell . . ." *J Caes,* V, i, 80–81. **3** to give birth to: "Who then conceiving, did in eaning time/ Fall parti-colour'd lambs . . ." *Merch,* I, iii, 82–83. **4** to befall: "Fair [good luck] fall the bones that took the pains for me!" *K John,* I, i, 78. **5** to occur: ". . . had your watch been good/ This sudden mischief never could have fallen." *1 Hen 6,* II, i, 58–59. **6** to fall vacant: "When better fall, for your avails they fell [will have fallen vacant]." *All's W,* III, i, 22. **7** to let or cause to fall: ". . . rather cut a little,/ Than fall, and bruise to death." *Meas,* II, i, 5–6. **8** to decay or perish: ". . . roses, whose fair flower/ Being once display'd, doth fall that very hour." *T Night,* II, iv, 38–39. **9** to go astray; lapse: ". . . almost spent with hunger,/ I am fall'n in [into] this offence." *Cymb,* III, vii, 335–36. **10 fall among,** to come by chance among: "Be sprightly, for you fall 'mongst friends." *Cymb,* III, vii, 47. **11 fall besides,** to lose [lit., fall out of]: "Alas, sir, how fell you besides your five wits?" *T Night,* IV, ii, 89. **12 fall for,** to perish because of: "Two such young handsome men/ Shall never fall for me . . ." *Kinsmen,* IV, ii, 3–4. **13 fall from,** to desert: ". . . as for Clarence . . . He's very likely now to fall from him . . ." *3 Hen 6,* III, iii, 208–209. **14 fall in,** to become friendly; here, with bawdy wordplay: "Falling in after falling out may make them three." *Tr & Cr,* III, i, 99. **15 fall off, a.** to tire or weary: "Inconstancy falls off, ere it begins." *Two Gent,* V, iv, 112. **b.** (of a soldier) to desert; rebel: "He never did fall off, my sovereign liege,/ But by the chance of war . . ." *1 Hen 4,* I, iii, 93–94. **16 fall out, a.** to happen;

come to pass: ". . . for it so falls out/ That what we have we prize not to the worth . . ." *M Ado,* IV, i, 217–218. **b.** to turn out: ". . . by bad courses may be understood/ That their events can never fall out good." *Rich 2,* II, i, 213–214. **c.** to quarrel: "'There falling out at tennis', or perchance/ 'I saw him enter such a house of sale'—" *Ham,* II, i, 59–60. **17 fall over,** to desert; bolt: "And dost thou now fall over to my foes?" *K John,* III, i, 53. **18 fall to,** to begin: "Play music, and you brides and bridegrooms all . . . to th' measures fall [begin the dancing]." *As You,* V, iv, 177–178. **19 fall upon,** to rush at violently; set upon; assail: "He fell upon me, ere admitted, then . . ." *Ant & Cleo,* II, ii, 75.
—*n.* **20 at fall,** in a time of financial troubles [actually a period of devalued currency]: "They answer in a joint and corporate voice/ That now they are at fall . . ." *Timon,* II, ii, 208–209.

fallacy, *n.* delusion: "Until I know this sure uncertainty,/ I'll entertain the offer'd fallacy." *Errors,* II, ii, 185–186.

fall and cease, *n.* Doomsday and the end of earthly existence: "Is this the promis'd end?"/ "Or image of that horror?"/ "Fall and cease." *Lear,* V, iii, 263–264.

fallen-off, *adj.* rebellious: ". . . to undertake our wars against/ The fall'n-off Britons . . ." *Cymb,* III, viii, 5–6.

fall foul, *v.* to have a falling out; quarrel: "Shall we fall foul for toys?" *2 Hen 4,* II, iv, 166.

falliable, *adj.* misuse for "fallible," though intended meaning is doubtless "infallible": ". . . but this is/ most falliable, the worm's an odd worm." *Ant & Cleo,* V, ii, 256–257.

falling-from, *n.* act of forsaking or falling away: "The mere want of gold, and the falling-from of his friends . . ." *Timon,* IV, iii, 403.

falling-sickness, *n.* epilepsy: "He fell down in the marketplace, and foam'd at/ mouth, and was speechless."/ "'Tis very like; he hath the falling-sickness." *J Caes,* I, ii, 249–251.

fallow¹, *n.* arable land uncultivated: ". . . our vineyards, fallows, meads, and hedges . . . grow to wildness . . ." *Hen 5,* V, ii, 54–55.

fallow², *adj.* pale brown: "How does your fallow greyhound, sir?" *Wives,* I, i, 81.

falorous, *adj.* Fluellen's pron. of "valorous": "Captain Jamy is a marvellous falorous gentleman . . ." *Hen 5,* III, ii, 80.

false, *adj.* **1** ill-tuned; out of tune: "The strings, my lord, are false."/ "He thinks he still is at his instrument." *J Caes,* IV, iii, 290–291. **2** untrustworthy; treacherous: "Descend to darkness and the burning lake:/ False fiend, avoid!" *2 Hen 6,* I, iv, 38–39.

—*n.* **3** eyes that misinterpret or misrepresent: "... volumes of report/ Run with these false ..." *Meas,* IV, i, 61–62.

—*v.* **4** to betray: "... and makes/ Diana's rangers false themselves ..." *Cymb,* II, iii, 67–68.

—*adv.* **5** falsely: "I should be false/ persuaded I had daughters." *Lear,* I, iv, 241–242. **6 play false,** to engage in adultery: "I am much afeard my lady his mother played false/ with a smith." *Merch,* I, ii, 41–43.

false fire, *n.* firing of blank cartridges, hence make-believe: "What, frighted with false fire?" *Ham,* III, ii, 260.

false gallop, canter or trot: "This is the very false gallop of verses ..." *As You,* III, ii, 111.

false gaze, *n.* looking in the wrong direction: "... 'tis a pageant,/ To keep us in false gaze ..." *Oth,* I, iii, 18–19.

falsehood, *n.* **1** deception; treachery: "So disguise shall by th'disguised/ Pay with falsehood false exacting ..." *Meas,* III, ii, 273–274. **2 hands of falsehood,** thievish hands: "That to my use it might unused stay/ From hands of falsehood ..." *Sonn 48,* 3–4.

falsely, *adv.* treacherously: "... truth the while/ Doth falsely blind the eyesight of his look ..." *Love's L,* I, i, 75–76.

false transgression, *n.* unfaithfulness to the beloved: "Her true perfection, or my false transgression,/ That makes me reasonless, to reason thus?" *Two Gent,* II, iv, 193–194.

falsing, *adj.* deceptive: "Sure ones, then."/ "Nay, not sure in a thing falsing." *Errors,* II, ii, 92–93.

fame, *n.* **1** reputation: "I am in good name and fame with the/ very best." *2 Hen 4,* II, iv, 73–74. **2** mere rumor or gossip; hearsay: "Too much to know is to know nought but fame ..." *Love's L,* I, i, 92. **3** high praise: "That very envy and the tongue of loss/ Cried fame and honour on him." *T Night,* V, i, 56–57. **4 house of Fame,** place where everything is known and spread by rumor: "The emperor's court is like the house of Fame,/ The palace full of tongues ..." *T Andr,* II, i, 126–127.

—*v.* **5** to make famous: "And such a counterpart shall fame his wit ..." *Sonn 84,* 11.

famed, *adj.* **1** rumored: "They are fam'd to be a pair of absolute men." *Kinsmen,* II, i, 26. **2 famed for,** deemed; reputed [as]: "Your Grace hath still been fam'd for virtuous ..." *3 Hen 6,* IV, vi, 26. **3 famed with,** celebrated for: "When went there by an age, since the great flood,/ But it was fam'd with more than with one man?" *J Caes,* I, ii, 150–151.

fame's eternal date, *n.* everlasting fame or renown: "... outlive thy father's days,/ And fame's eternal date, for virtue's praise." *T Andr,* I, i, 167–168.

familiar, *n.* **1** attendant spirit, usually the devil: "Love is a familiar; Love is a devil ..." *Love's L,* I, ii, 162. **2** close friend: "Sir, the king is a noble gentleman, and my familiar ..." *Love's L,* V, i, 87.

—*adj.* **3** kindly or friendly: "I extend my hand to him thus,/ quenching my/ familiar smile ..." *T Night,* II, v, 66–67. **4** customary; habitual: "... 'tis my familiar sin,/ With maids to seem the lapwing ..." *Meas,* I, iv, 31–32. **5 familiar at first,** on friendly terms immediately: "... I thank/ him, makes no stranger of me; we are familiar at/ first." *Cymb,* I, v, 97–99. **6 familiar instances,** signs or tokens of friendship: "With courtesy and with respect enough,/ But not with such familiar instances ..." *J Caes,* IV, ii, 15–16.

famine, sword, and fire, *n.* the three hounds [attendants] of war: "Leash'd in like hounds, should famine, sword, and fire/ Crouch for employment." *Hen 5,* Prol., 7–8.

famoused, *adj.* made famous: "The painful warrior famoused for fight ..." *Sonn 25,* 9.

famously, *adv.* so as to become famous: "... what he hath done famously,/ he did it to that end ..." *Cor,* I, i, 35–36.

fan, *v.* **1** to winnow; test: "The love I bear him/ Made me to fan you thus ..." *Cymb,* I, vii, 176–177.

—*n.* **2 bear another's fan,** to accompany a lady, carrying her fan, in the manner of a true gallant: "To see him walk before a lady, and to bear her fan!" *Love's L,* IV, i, 146.

fan and wind, *n.* whirling air: "Even in the fan and wind of your fair sword ..." *Tr & Cr,* V, iii, 41.

fanatical, *adj.* extravagant; also, frantic: "I abhor such fanatical/ phantasimes, such insociable and point-devise/ companions ..." *Love's L,* V, i, 17–19.

fancy, *v.* **1** to love; fall or be in love (with): "... should she fancy, it should/ be one of my complexion." *T Night,* II, v, 25–26.

—*n.* **2** personal liking or inclination: "Speaking my fancy: Signior Benedick,/ For shape, for bearing ... Goes foremost in report through Italy." *M Ado,* III, i, 95–97. **3** love or, often, thoughts of love: "Chewing the food of sweet and bitter fancy ..." *As You,* IV, iii, 101. **4** the heart as the seat of love: "... when in other habits you are seen,/ Orsino's mistress, and my fancy's queen." *T Night,* V, i, 386–387. **5** one's own true love: "Be advis'd."/ "I am: and by my fancy." *W Tale,* IV, iv, 482–483. **6** affectation; here, in wordplay with "affection": "... a fancy that he hath to strange disguises ..." *M Ado,* III, ii, 30. **7** eccentricity or ornateness: "Costly thy habit as thy purse can buy,/ But not express'd in fancy . . ." *Ham*, I, iii, 70–71. **8** (in music) a fantasia, esp. an impromptu love song: ". . . tunes . . . he heard the/ carmen whistle, and sware they were his fancies or/ his good-nights." *2 Hen 4*, III, ii, 310–313. **9** mind; concentration: "Nor shall not when my fancy's on my play." *Hen 8*, V, i, 60. **10 afflicted fancy,** girl suffering the afflictions of love: "Towards this afflicted fancy fastly drew . . ." *Lover's Comp*, 61. **11 the humour of forty fancies,** poss. a wildly whimsical ornament used to decorate Petruchio's hat: ". . . an old hat, and the humour of forty fancies/ pricked [pinned] in't for a feather . . ." *Shrew*, III, ii, 66–67.

fancy-free, *adj.* immune to thoughts of love: "And the imperial votress passed on,/ In maiden meditation, fancy-free . . ." *M N Dream*, II, i, 163–164.

fancy-monger, *n.* peddler of love, esp. a lovesick swain: "If I could meet that fancy-monger,/ I would give him some good counsel . . ." *As You*, III, ii, 354–355.

fancy-sick, *adj.* lovesick: "All fancy-sick she is, and pale of cheer . . ." *M N Dream*, III, ii, 96.

fane, *n.* temple; here, the temple oracle: "For notes of sorrow out of tune are worse/ Than priests and fanes that lie." *Cymb*, IV, ii, 241–242.

fang, *v.* to seize or attack with the fangs, as a dog does: "Destruction fang mankind! Earth, yield me roots." *Timon*, IV, iii, 23.

fangled, *adj.* given to finery; also, foppish: "Be not, as is our fangled world, a garment/ Nobler than that it covers." *Cymb*, V, iv, 134–135.

fanned and winnowed, *adj.* tried and carefully selected: ". . . carries them through and through the most fanned and winnowed opinions . . ." *Ham*, V, ii, 188–189.

fantasied, *adj.* **strangely fantasied,** full of curious notions: "I find the people strangely fantasied;/ Possess'd with rumours, full of idle dreams . . ." *K John*, IV, ii, 144–145.

fantastic, *adj.* imagined: "Or wallow naked in December snow/ By thinking on fantastic summer's heat?" *Rich 2*, I, iii, 298–299.

fantastical, *adj.* **1** imaginary: "Are ye fantastical, or that indeed/ Which outwardly ye show?" *Mac*, I, iii, 53–54. **2** full of fanciful notions or ideas; capricious and, sometimes, irrational: "At which time would I, being but a moonish youth, grieve, be . . . proud, fantastical, apish, shallow . . ." *As You*, III, ii, 397–400. **3 high fantastical,** highly imaginative; that is, love is the most imaginative of all the passions: "So full of shapes is fancy,/ That it alone is high fantastical." *T Night*, I, i, 14–15.

fantastically, *adv.* capriciously: ". . . she is so idly king'd/ Her sceptre so fantastically borne [power exercised so capriciously] . . ." *Hen 5*, II, iv, 26–27.

fantasy, *n.* **1** illusion: "That, for a fantasy and trick of fame,/ Go to their graves like beds . . ." *Ham*, IV, iv, 61–62. **2** [often pl] imagination or fancy; also, day dreams: "With faining voice verses of feigning love,/ And stol'n the impression of her fantasy . . ." *M N Dream*, I, i, 31–32. **3** [pl.] whims: ". . . the which he pricks and wounds/ With many legions of strange fantasies . . ." *K John*, V, vii, 17–18. **4** erotic desire: "How many actions most ridiculous/ Hast thou been drawn to by thy fantasy?" *As You*, II, iv, 28–29.

fap, *adj.* drunk: "And being fap, sir, was, as they say, cashiered . . ." *Wives*, I, i, 160.

far, *adv.* **1** exceedingly: ". . . by His Majesty I swear,/ Whose far unworthy deputy I am . . ." *2 Hen 6*, III, ii, 284–285. **2** far away: "I had rather live . . . in a windmill, far,/ Than feed on cates and have him talk to me . . ." *1 Hen 4*, III, i, 155–157. **3** farther: "To mingle friendship far, is mingling bloods." *W Tale*, I, ii, 109–110. **4 as far as we call hers,** in the most obvious sense of that expression: ". . . you have been conjunct/ And bosom'd with her, as far as we call hers." *Lear*, V, i, 12–13. **5 speak him far,** praise him exceedingly: "You speak him far."/ "I do extend him, sir, within himself . . ." *Cymb*, I, i, 24–25. —*adj.* **6** harsh; severe: ". . . your late censure/ Both of his truth and him (which was too far) . . ." *Hen 8*, III, i, 64–65.

farborough or **tharborough,** *n.* misuse for "thirdborough," a low-ranking constable: "I myself reprehend his own person, for I am his/ grace's farborough . . ." *Love's L*, I, i, 182–183.

farced, *adj.* stuffed; extended or inflated: "The farced title running 'fore the king . . ." *Hen 5*, IV, i, 269.

fardel, *n.* [often pl.] burden [lit., bundle], as a heavy pack carried on the back: "Who would fardels bear,/ To grunt and sweat under a weary life . . ." *Ham*, III, i, 76–77.

fare, *v.* **1** to get on; thrive; here, understood as meaning "eat": "How fares our cousin Hamlet?"/ "Excellent, i'faith, of the chameleon's dish." *Ham*, III, ii, 92–93. **2** to become; here, to fall: "As tender nurse her babe from faring ill." *Sonn 22*, 12. —*n.* **3 ill fare,** bitter pun on "bad luck" and "bad [poisoned] food": "How fares your majesty?"/ "Poison'd, ill fare; dead, forsook, cast off . . ." *K John*, V, vii, 34–35. **4 What fare?** How are things going?: "How now, fair lords! What fare? What news abroad?" *3 Hen 6*, II, i, 95.

far-fet, *adj.* far-fetched; elaborate: "If York, with all his far-fet policy,/ Had been the Regent there instead of me . . ." *2 Hen 6*, III, i, 293–294.

farm, *n.* **1 in farm,** leased out: "The Earl of Wiltshire hath the realm in farm." *Rich 2*, II, i, 256.
—*v.* **2** to lease out; here, to guarantee loans with tax revenues: "We are inforc'd to farm our royal realm . . ." *Rich 2*, I, iv, 45. **3** to lease; here, at an annual rent: "To pay five ducats—five—I would not farm it . . ." *Ham*, IV, iv, 20.

farre, *adv.* old form of **farther;** more removed: "Not hold thee of our blood, no, not our kin,/ Farre than Deucalion off . . ." *W Tale*, IV, iv, 431–432.

farrow, *n.* animal's litter: "Pour in sow's blood, that hath eaten/ Her nine farrow . . ." *Mac*, IV, i, 64–65.

farther, *adj.* additional: "Make no moe offers, use no farther means . . ." *Merch*, IV, i, 81.

farthest, *adj.* **at the farthest, a.** at the end of one's journey: "Travel you far on, or are you at the farthest?" *Shrew*, IV, ii, 73. **b.** at the latest: ". . . let it be so hasted that supper be/ ready at the farthest by five of the clock . . ." *Merch*, II, ii, 109–110.

farthingale, *n.* dress extended by hoops at the hipline; worn by fine ladies of the Elizabethan era: "When didst thou see me heave up my leg, and/ make water against a gentlewoman's farthingale?" *Two Gent*, IV, iv, 37–39.

fartuous, *adj.* Quickly's blunder for "virtuous": ". . . let me tell you in/ your ear, she's as fartuous a civil modest wife . . ." *Wives*, II, ii, 91–92.

fashion[1], *n.* **1** appearance; aspect: "You have . . . Set a fair fashion on our entertainment . . ." *Timon*, I, ii, 142–143. **2** workmanship; design: "The . . . chargeful fashion,/ Which doth amount to three odd ducats more . . ." *Errors*, IV, i, 29–30. **3** semblance or pretence: ". . . thou but leadest this fashion of thy malice/ To the last hour of act . . ." *Merch*, IV, i, 18–19. **4** customary or expected way of behaving: "For Hamlet, and the trifling of his favour,/ Hold it a fashion and a toy in blood . . ." *Ham*, I, iii, 5–6. **5** wordplay on "manner, way" and "expected behavior": ". . . he hath importun'd me with love/ In honourable fashion."/ "Ay, fashion you may call it." *Ham*, I, iii, 110–112. **6** nature or characteristics: "By heaven I will,/ Or let me lose the fashion of a man." *Hen 8*, IV, ii, 158–159. **7** kind or sort: "I scorn thee and thy fashion, peevish boy." *1 Hen 6*, II, iv 76. **8 fashion of himself,** his usual behavior: "Whereon his brains still beating puts him thus/ From fashion of himself." *Ham*, III, i, 176–177. **9 for fashion,** in imitation of another or others: ". . . the pretty babes,/ That mourn'd for fashion, ignorant what to fear . . ." *Errors*, I, i, 72–73. **10 our fashion**

calls, [the times] require us to become familiar with ["smiling pomp" and "thralled discontent"]: "Whereto the inviting time our fashion calls . . ." *Sonn 124*, 8.
—*v.* **11** to contrive: "Where you, and Douglas, and our powers at once,/ As I will fashion it, shall happily meet . . ." *1 Hen 4*, I, iii, 290–291. **12** to mold the opinions of: "Send him but hither, and I'll fashion him." *J Caes*, II, i, 220. **13 fashion fit,** to make serve one's own ends: "All with me's meet that I can fashion fit." *Lear*, I, ii, 191. **14 fashion in,** to inject or introduce: "But 'Be thou true' say I to fashion in/ My sequent protestation . . ." *Tr & Cr*, IV, iv, 64–65. **15 fashion it thus,** phrase it this way: "Fashion it thus: that what he is, augmented,/ Would run to these and these extremities . . ." *J Caes*, II, i, 30–31.

fashion[2], *n.* **the fashions,** small swellings or tumors on a horse's body: ". . . infected/ with the fashions, full of wind-galls . . ." *Shrew*, III, ii, 49–50.

fashion-mongers, *n.* fellows who affect the latest fashion in manners or dress: ". . . these strange flies,/ these fashion-mongers, these 'pardon-me's . . ." *Rom & Jul*, II, iv, 32–33.

fashion-monging, *adj.* overconcerned with the latest fashions; dandified: "Scambling, outfacing, fashion-monging boys . . ." *M Ado*, V, i, 94.

Fa, sol, la, mi, [Italian] notes of the musical scale; Edmund here appar. sings to himself: "Oh! these eclipses/ do portend these divisions. *Fa, sol, la, mi*." *Lear*, I, ii, 143–144.

fast, *adv.* **1** firmly; unalterably: ". . . thou art so fast mine enemy." *2 Hen 6*, V, ii, 21. **2** by reason of vows exchanged; here, not solemnized: "You know the lady; she is fast my wife . . ." *Meas*, I, ii, 136. **3** fast asleep: "Mistress! What, mistress! Juliet! Fast, I warrant her, she." *Rom & Jul*, IV, v, 1.
—*adj.* **4** true: "Wilt thou be fast to my hopes?" *Oth*, I, iii, 363. **5** firm; unalterable: ". . . 'tis our fast intent/ To shake all cares and business from our age . . ." *Lear*, I, i, 38–39. **6** shut tight: "All fast? What means this? Ho!/ Who waits there?" *Hen 8*, V, ii, 3–4. **7 make fast,** to confine: ". . . whom we raise/ We will make fast within a hallow'd verge." *2 Hen 6*, I, iv, 22.

fast and loose, *n.* cheating game: "I will fast, being loose."/ "No, sir, that were fast and loose: thou shalt to/ prison." *Love's L*, I, ii, 146–148.

fast bind, fast find, proverb with appar. meaning of [that which is] bound securely [will be] found quickly: "Fast bind, fast find,—/ A proverb never stale in thrifty mind." *Merch*, II, v, 53–54.

fastened, *adj.* confirmed; hardened: "O strange and fast'ned villain!" *Lear*, II, i, 78.

faster, *adv.* more swiftly and decisively: "Give my love fame faster than Time wastes life . . ." *Sonn 100,* 13.

fast-growing, *adj.* rapidly moving: ". . . to Marina bend your mind,/ Whom our fast-growing scene [play] must find/ At Tharsus [Tarsus] . . ." *Per,* IV, Chor., 5–6.

fasting, *adj.* starved; here, for love: "This will I send . . . That shall express my true love's fasting pain." *Love's L,* IV, iii, 118–119.

fat[1] **,** *adj.* **1** stale; stuffy; close or muggy: ". . . come out of that fat room, and lend/ me thy hand to laugh a little." *1 Hen 4,* II, iv, 1–2. **2** sweaty; also, out of condition: "Our son shall win."/ "He's fat and scant of breath." *Ham,* V, ii, 290. **3** fertile: "Most subject is the fattest soil to weeds . . ." *2 Hen 4,* IV, iv, 54. **4 fat and fulsome,** vulgar and disgusting: "It is as fat and fulsome to mine ear/ As howling after music." *T Night,* V, i, 107–108. **5 feed fat,** to nourish well: "If I can catch him once upon the hip,/ I will feed fat the ancient grudge I bear him." *Merch,* I, iii, 41–42.
—*v.* **6** to nourish: "O, how this villainy/ Doth fat me with the very thoughts of it!" *T Andr* III, i, 202–203.
—*n.* **7** wealth; abundance or surplus: "Your country's fat shall pay your pains the hire . . ." *Rich 3,* V, iii, 259.

fat[2] **,** *n.* dial. var. of **vat:** "In thy fats our cares be drown'd . . ." *Ant & Cleo,* II, vii, 114.

fatal, *adj.* **1** menacing; ominous: "Here never shines the sun: here nothing breeds,/ Unless the nightly owl or fatal raven . . ." *T Andr,* II, iii, 96–97. **2** bringing death; ref. here to the evil omen of predatory birds: ". . . their shadows seem/ A canopy most fatal . . ." *J Caes,* V, i, 87–88. **3** being an instrument of destiny: "And brought from thence the Thracian fatal steeds . . ." *3 Hen 6,* IV, ii, 21. **4 fatal and neglected,** ignored to our detriment: ". . . late examples/ Left by the fatal and neglected English/ Upon our fields." *Hen 5,* II, iv, 12–14.

fated, *adj.* fateful; controlling man's fate: ". . . the fated sky/ Gives us free scope . . ." *All's W,* I, i, 213–214.

Fates, *n.* (in Greek myth.) minor goddesses, Clotho, who spun the thread of life; Lachesis, who determined its length; and Atropos, who cut it: "O Fates, come, come!/ Cut thread and thrum . . ." *M N Dream,* V, i, 274–275.

father, *n.* **1** term of respect for an older man: "Let not my worser spirit tempt me again/ To die before you please./ Well pray you, father." *Lear* IV, vi, 214–215. **2** father-in-law; here, intended father-in-law: "My father Capulet will have it so,/ And I am nothing slow to slack his haste." *Rom & Jul,* IV, i, 2–3. **3** source; object: ". . . thousand escapes of wit/ Make thee the father of their idle dream . . ." *Meas,* IV, i, 63–64. **4 my**

father's, my father-in-law's house: "My father's bears more toward the market-place." *Shrew,* V, i, 8.
—*v.* **5** to have a father; here, a cruel father [Gloucester]: ". . . that which makes me bend makes the king bow;/ He childed as I father'd!" *Lear,* III, vi, 111–112.

father's badge, *n.* See **housed badge.**

fathom, *n.* **1** depth; caliber: "Another of his fathom they have not/ To lead their business . . ." *Oth,* I, i, 152–153. **2 fathom and half,** sailor's cry when ship is taking on water; here, the hovel is being flooded: "Fathom and half, fathom and half!/ Poor Tom!" *Lear,* III, iv, 37–38.

fathom-line, *n.* sounding line; lead line: "Where fathom-line could never touch the ground . . ." *1 Hen 4,* I, iii, 202.

fatigate, *adj.* fatigued: ". . . straight his doubled spirit [redoubled energy]/ Requicken'd what in flesh was fatigate . . ." *Cor,* II, ii, 116–117.

fatness, *n.* grossness; sensuality: "For in the fatness of these pursy times/ Virtue itself of vice must pardon beg . . ." *Ham,* III, iv, 155–156.

faucet-seller, *n.* vendor of taps for wine barrels: ". . . hearing/ a cause between an orange-wife and a faucet-seller . . ." *Cor,* II, i, 69–70.

fault, *n.* **1** error: "O monstrous fault to harbour such a thought!" *3 Hen 6,* III, ii, 164. **2** offense: ". . . and for that vild [vile] fault/ Two of her brothers were condemn'd to death . . ." *T Andr,* V, ii, 172–173. **3 a fault alone,** a single misstep: "Some run from brakes of ice [vice?] and answer none,/ And some condemned for a fault alone." *Meas,* II, i, 39–40. **4 coldest fault,** the faintest scent [that a hunting dog can follow]: "Silver made it good/ At the hedge corner, in the coldest fault?" *Shrew,* Ind., i, 17–18. **5 for fault of a worse,** alt. of phrase "for want of a better": "I am the youngest of that name, for/ fault of a worse." *Rom & Jul,* II, iv, 121–122. **6 let it be his fault,** let it be his offense [rather than himself] that is condemned: "I do beseech you, let it be his fault,/ And not my brother." *Meas,* II, ii, 35–36. **7 make faults,** to commit offenses: ". . . the king have mercies/ More than I dare make faults." *Hen 8,* II, i, 70–71. **8 take a fault upon me,** to assume blame for an offense: ". . . to take a fault upon me that he did . . ." *Two Gent,* IV, iv, 14.

fault and glimpse, *n.* imperfect idea [of how to proceed with his new responsibilities]: "Whether it be the fault and glimpse of newness,/ Of whether that the body public be/ A horse . . ." *Meas,* I, ii, 147–149.

faultful, *adj.* having sinned: "So fares it with this faultful lord of Rome . . ." *Luc,* 715.

favor, *n.* **1** face; countenance; here, in wordplay with "benefits": "Yet I well remember/ The favours of these men." *Rich 2,* IV, i, 167–168. **2** appearance; aspect: "An if my face were but as fair as yours,/ My favour were as great . . ." *Love's L,* V, ii, 32–33. **3** identity: ". . . your favour is well appeared by your tongue." *Cor,* IV, iii, 9. **4** charm; graciousness: "Thought and affliction, passion, hell itself/ She turns to favour and to prettiness." *Ham,* IV, v, 185–186. **5** [pl.] **a.** features: "And stain my favours in a bloody mask,/ Which, wash'd away, shall scour my shame with it . . ." *1 Hen 4,* III, ii, 136–137. **b.** the same in wordplay with "sexual favors": "Then you live about her waist, or in the middle of/ her favours?"/ "Faith, her privates we." *Ham,* II, ii, 232–234. **c.** scarf or handkerchief, usually a token of a lady's favor: "But let my favours hide thy mangled face . . ." *1 Hen 4,* V, iv, 95. **6** gift; love token: "But, Rosaline, you have a favour too:/ Who sent it? and what is it?" *Love's L,* V, ii, 30–31. **7** token of royal favor: "In their gold coats spots you see;/ Those be rubies, fairy favours . . ." *M N Dream,* II, i, 11–12. **8** pardon: "Give me your favour: my dull brain was wrought/ With things forgotten." *Mac,* I, iii, 150–151. **9** goodwill: "The Spaniard tied by blood and favour to her . . ." *Hen 8,* II, ii, 89. **10 by your favor,** by your leave: "But, by your favour,/ How near's the other army?" *Lear,* IV, vi, 212–213. **11 give me favor,** give me your attention: "Pray give me favour sir . . ." *Hen 8,* I, i, 168. **12 in favor,** favoring us: "Fortune in favour makes him lag behind." *1 Hen 6,* III, iii, 34. **13 under favor,** by your leave: "My lords, then, under favour, pardon me . . ." *Timon,* III, v, 41.

favorable, *adj.* kindly; gentle: ". . . some dull and favourable hand/ Will whisper music to my weary spirit." *2 Hen 4,* IV, v, 2–3.

favorer, *n.* friend: ". . . they bring us peace,/ And come to us as favourers, not as foes." *Per,* I, iv, 72–73.

favorite, *n.* one granted special favors: ". . . you both have vow'd revenge/ On him, his sons, his favourites, and his friends." *3 Hen 6,* I, i, 55–56.

fawn, *n.* **1** flattering action: ". . . spend a fawn upon 'em/ For the inheritance of their loves . . ." *Cor,* III, ii, 67–68.
—*v.* **2** (of an animal) to wag the tail: ". . . take heed of yonder dog!/ Look when he fawns, he bites . . ." *Rich 3,* I, iii, 289–290.

fay, *n.* faith: "Ah sirrah, by my fay, it waxes late,/ I'll to my rest." *Rom & Jul,* I, v, 125–126.

fazed, *adj.* frayed: ". . . ten times more dishonourable-ragged than an old fazed ancient . . ." *1 Hen 4,* IV, ii, 30–31.

fear, *v.* **1** to be afraid for; be anxious or apprehensive about: "Let him go, Gertrude. Do not fear our person." *Ham,* IV, v, 122. **2** to instill fear in; frighten; terrify: "I tell thee lady this aspect of mine/ Hath fear'd the valiant . . ." *Merch,* II, i, 8–9. **3** previous sense confused with (or in wordplay with) "to be afraid of": "Hortensio fears his widow."/ "Then never trust me if I be afeard." *Shrew,* V, ii, 16–17. **4** to imagine: "The thief doth fear each bush an officer." *3 Hen 6,* V, vi, 12. **5 fear boys with bugs!** [as soon] frighten children with hobgoblins!: ". . . not half so great a blow to hear/ As will a chestnut in a farmer's fire?/ Tush, tush, fear boys with bugs!" *Shrew,* I, ii, 207–209. **6 fear not,** do not be afraid for: "Fear not thy sons, they shall do well enough." *T Andr,* II, iii, 305. **7 fear you,** [I'm] afraid for you: ". . . therefore (I promise you),/ I fear you . . ." *Merch,* III, v, 2–3.
—*n.* **8** concern; anxiety: "Most holy and religious fear it is/ To keep those many many bodies safe . . ." *Ham,* III, iii, 8–9. **9** cause for fear: "There is no fear in him; let him not die . . ." *J Caes,* II, i, 190. **10** object of one's fear: "For we will fetters put about this fear/ Which now goes too free-footed." *Ham,* III, iii, 25–26. **11 fear of trust,** afraid to trust myself: "So I, for fear of trust, forget to say/ The perfect ceremony of love's rite . . ." *Sonn 23,* 5–6.

feared, *past part.* **1** feared for: "He was much fear'd by his physicians." *1 Hen 4,* IV, i, 24. **2** it is feared that: "They say in great extremity, and fear'd/ She'll with the labour end." *Hen 8,* V, i, 19–20.

feared hopes, *n.* hopes stifled by fear: ". . . in these fear'd hopes,/ I barely gratify your love . . ." *Cymb,* II, iv, 6–7.

fearful, *adj.* **1** timid; also, cowardly: "And think how such an apprehension/ May turn the tide of fearful faction . . ." *1 Hen 4,* IV, i, 66–67. **2** frightened or apprehensive: "Did but convey unto our fearful minds/ A doubtful warrant of immediate death . . ." *Errors,* I, i, 67–68. **3** frightening or alarming; fearsome: "A man no mightier than thyself, or me . . . yet prodigious grown,/ And fearful, as these strange eruptions are." *J Caes,* I, iii, 76–78. **4 fearful commenting,** *n.* nervous talk: "I have learn'd that fearful commenting/ Is leaden servitor to dull delay . . ." *Rich 3,* IV, iii, 51–52.

fearfully, *adv.* so as to instill fear: "My master . . . fearfully did menace me with death/ If I did stay . . ." *Rom & Jul,* V, iii, 132–133.

feast-finding, *adj.* ref. to minstrels who sought out feasts where they would be paid to entertain: "Feast-finding minstrels tuning my defame . . ." *Luc,* 817.

feasting, *adj.* festive: ". . . her beauty makes/ This vault a feasting presence, full of light." *Rom & Jul,* V, iii, 85–86.

feat, *n.* **1** deed or exploit; here, a vile deed: "But tell me/ Why you proceeded not against these feats . . ." *Ham,* IV, vii, 5–6. **2 high feats,** noble exploits: ". . . nor call'd upon/ For high feats done to th'crown . . ." *Hen 8,* I, i, 60–61.
—*v.* **3** to reflect shortcomings and serve as model; also, poss. wordplay on "defeat": ". . . to th' more mature/ A glass that feated them . . ." *Cymb,* I, i, 48–49.
—*adj.* **4** deft; dexterous: "So tender over his occasions, true,/ So feat, so nurse-like . . ." *Cymb,* V, v, 87–88.

feater, *adv.* more trimly or handsomely: "And look how well my garments sit upon me;/ Much feater than before . . ." *Temp,* II, i, 267–268.

feather, *n.* **1** kind or sort; also, disposition or turn of mind: "I am not of that feather to shake off/ My friend when he must need me." *Timon,* I, i, 103–104. **2 forest of feathers,** ref. to the multitudinous feathers used by players to enhance their hats and costumes: ". . . a forest of feathers . . . with Provincial/ roses on my razed shoes . . ." *Ham,* III, ii, 269–271. **3 molt no feather,** run no risk of disclosure: ". . . your secrecy to the King and/ Queen moult no feather." *Ham,* II, ii, 294–295.

feathered, *adj.* **in feather'd briefness,** in the briefest time: "In feather'd briefness sails are fill'd . . ." *Per,* V, ii, 15.

featly, *adv.* nimbly; gracefully: "She dances featly."/ "So she does any thing . . ." *W Tale,* IV, iv, 178–179.

feature, *n.* **1** form or appearance: ". . . to show virtue/ her feature, scorn her own image . . ." *Ham,* III, ii, 22–23. **2** physical beauty: ". . . for feature, laming/ The shrine of Venus . . ." *Cymb,* V, v, 163–164. **3 good feature,** pleasing appearance; handsomeness; here, the belief that fine features indicated a noble spirit: "Thou hast, Sebastian, done good feature shame." *T Night,* III, iv, 375. **4 how features are abroad,** what people look like in the outside world: ". . . how features are abroad,/ I am skilless of . . ." *Temp,* III, i, 52–53.

featureless, *adj.* (of a person) homely or ugly: ". . . those whom nature hath not made for store,/ Harsh, featureless and rude . . ." *Sonn 11,* 9–10.

fecks, *n.* **i' fecks,** in faith: "Art thou my boy?"/ "Ay, my good lord."/ "I' fecks . . ." *W Tale,* I, ii, 120.

federary, *n.* confederate; accomplice: ". . . she's a traitor, and Camillo is/ A federary with her . . ." *W Tale,* II, i, 89–90.

fee, *n.* **1** payment for services; recompense: "Here is thy fee, arrest him officer." *Errors,* IV, i, 77. **2** privilege; rights: ". . . the youth, mistook by me,/ Pleading for a lover's fee." *M N Dream,* III, ii, 112–113. **3** repayment; requital or recompense: "But that your trespass now becomes a fee . . ." *Sonn 120,* 13.

4 in fee, outright: "Nor will it yield to Norway or the Pole/ A ranker [richer] rate should it be sold in fee." *Ham,* IV, iv, 21–22. **5 pay your fees,** pay the fees exacted from a prisoner before his release: ". . . so you shall pay your fees/ When you depart, and save your thanks?" *W Tale,* I, ii, 53–54.
—*v.* **6** to pay for; hire: ". . . go Tubal, fee me/ an officer, bespeak him a fortnight before . . ." *Merch,* III, i, 115–116. **7** to pay; reward: "Thou would'st be fee'd, I see, to make me sport . . ." *3 Hen 6,* I, iv, 92. **8** to pay off; bribe: "For mine own ends (indeed to gain the popedom/ And fee my friends in Rome)." *Hen 8,* III, ii, 212–213.

feeble, *v.* to weaken; make feeble: "And feebling such as stand not in their liking . . ." *Cor,* I, i, 194.

feed, *v.* to merely eat: ". . . to feed were best at home . . ." *Mac,* III, iv, 34.

fee'd, *adj.* paid a fee or given a tip; here, for spying: "There's not a one of them, but in his house/ I keep a servant fee'd." *Mac,* III, iv, 130–131.

feeder, *n.* **1** shepherd: "I will your very faithful feeder be . . ." *As You,* II, iv, 97. **2** servant [contemptuous term]: ". . . to be abus'd/ By one that looks on feeders?" *Ant & Cleo,* III, xiii, 108–109.

feed fat, *v.* See **fat**[1] (def. 5).

feeding, *n.* **1** pasturelands: "They call him Doricles; and boasts himself/ To have a worthy feeding . . ." *W Tale,* IV, iv, 170–171. **2 frame my feeding,** adjust my diet: "To bitter sauces did I frame my feeding . . ." *Sonn 118,* 6.

fee-farm, *n.* **in fee-farm,** owned in perpetuity; here, of extended duration: "How now, a kiss in fee-farm!" *Tr & Cr,* III, ii, 49.

fee-grief, *n.* private grief: "The general cause? or is it a fee-grief,/ Due to some single breast?" *Mac,* IV, iii, 196–197.

feel, *v.* to realize the results of one's [unwise] actions: "He will not hear [heed], till feel." *Timon,* II, ii, 7.

feeling[1] *adj.* **1** heartfelt: "Yet let me weep for such a feeling loss." *Rom & Jul,* III, v, 74. **2 feeling disputation,** exchange of feelings rather than words: "I understand thy kisses, and thou mine,/ And that's a feeling disputation . . ." *1 Hen 4,* III, i, 198–199.

feeling[2] *n.* knowledge or experience: "Thou hast no feeling of it, Moth: I will speak that/ l'envoy." *Love's L,* III, i, 111–112.

feelingly, *adv.* **1** so as to do justice: "Indeed, to speak feelingly of him, he is the card or/ calendar of gentry . . ." *Ham,* V, ii,

109–111. **2** by means of one's own feelings: "These are counsellors/ That feelingly persuade me what I am." *As You,* II, i, 10–11. **3** wordplay on "gropingly" and "emotionally": "...yet you see how this world goes."/ "I see it feelingly." *Lear,* IV, vi, 149–150. **4** to the point: "Do I speak feelingly now?" *Meas,* I, ii, 33.

fee simple or **fee-simple,** *n.* **1** absolute ownership [legal term]: "...any man/ should buy the fee simple of my life for an hour and/ a quarter." *Rom & Jul,* III, i, 31–33. **2** one's property; domain: "Here's the lord of the soil come to seize me...for entering his fee-simple without leave." *2 Hen 6,* IV, x, 24–25.

feet, *n.* **1 going shall be us'd with feet,** walking will be done with the feet: "Then comes the time, who lives to see't,/ That going shall be us'd with feet." *Lear,* III, ii, 93–94. **2** See **secret feet.**

feeze or **pheeze** or **pheese,** *v.* to get even with; "fix": "I'll feeze you, in faith." *Shrew,* Ind., i, 1.

feign, *v.* **1** to invent: "...Elysium/ And all that poets feign of bliss and joy." *3 Hen 6,* I, ii, 30–31. **2** to allege; also, misrepresent: "Look in thy last work, where thou hast feign'd him a worthy fellow." *Timon,* I, i, 221–222. **3** to make oneself appear: "But old folks, many feign as they were dead—" *Rom & Jul,* II, v, 16.

feigned, *adj.* fictitious: "It is the more like to be feigned; I pray you/ keep it in [refrain from saying it]." *T Night,* I, v, 197–198.

feigning, *adj.* **1** See **faining.**
—*n.* **2 lowly feigning,** pretended humility: "'Twas never merry world/ Since lowly feigning was call'd [was first taken for a] compliment..." *T Night,* III, i, 100–101.

felicitate, *adj.* made happy: "I am alone felicitate/ In your dear highness' love." *Lear,* I, i, 75–76.

felicity, *n.* eternal bliss: "If thou didst ever hold me in thy heart,/ Absent thee from felicity awhile..." *Ham,* V, ii, 351–352.

fell¹, *n.* **1** fleece: "...their fells you know are greasy." *As You,* III, ii, 51–52. **2 fell of hair,** hair on the scalp: "...my fell of hair/ Would at a dismal treatise rouse, and stir..." *Mac,* V, v, 11–12.

fell², *adj.* **1** fierce; also, cruel or ruthless: "By whose fell working I was first advanc'd..." *2 Hen 4,* IV, v, 206. **2** deadly; destructive or lethal: "This fell whore of thine/ Hath in her more destruction than thy sword..." *Timon,* IV, iii, 62–63.

fell³, *v.* **1** past part. of FALL: "Ten masts at each make not the altitude/ Which thou hast perpendicularly fell..." *Lear,* IV, vi, 53–54. **2** future perfect of FALL; will have fallen: "When better fall, for your avails they fell [you will get them]." *All's W,* III, i, 22–23. **3 fell thee down,** cut thee down [with my sword]: "Stand, villain, stand, or I'll fell thee down." *2 Hen 6,* IV, ii, 109.

fell anatomy, *n.* savage skeleton [Death's representation]: "And rouse from sleep that fell anatomy..." *K John,* III, iii, 40.

fell-lurking, *adj.* waiting to do harm; skulking; treacherous: "...with the very shaking of their chains/ They may astonish these fell-lurking curs..." *2 Hen 6,* V, i, 145–146.

fellow, *n.* **1** companion; here, wife: "...to be your fellow/ You may deny me; but I'll be your servant,/ Whether you will or no." *Temp,* III, i, 84–86. **2** equal: "It is impossible that ever Rome/ Should breed thy fellow." *J Caes,* V, iii, 100–101. **3** male person [often used contemptuously]: "The fellow loaden with irons wiser than the judge..." *Timon,* III, v, 51. **4** servant: "I am more bound to you than your fellows, for they/ are but lightly rewarded." *Love's L,* I, ii, 142–143. **5** fellow servingman: "What service is here! I/ think our fellows are asleep." *Cor,* IV, v, 1–2.
—*v.* **6** to pair with: "With what's unreal thou coactive art,/ And fellow'st nothing..." *W Tale,* I, ii, 141–142.

fellowly, *adj.* brotherly or commiserating: "Mine eyes, ev'n sociable to the show of thine,/ Fall fellowly drops." *Temp,* V, i, 63–64.

fellowship, *n.* **1** partnership or alliance: "...letters of entreaty, which imported/ His fellowship i' th' cause against your city..." *Timon,* V, ii, 11–12. **2 fears his fellowship,** will not risk his companionship: "We would not die in that man's company/ That fears his fellowship to die with us." *Hen 5,* IV, iii, 38–39.

felly, *n.* rim of a wheel: "Break all the spokes and fellies from her wheel..." *Ham,* II, ii, 491.

fen, *n.* swamp or bog: "As wicked dew as e'er my mother brush'd/ With raven's feather from unwholesome fen/ Drop on you both!" *Temp,* I, ii, 323–325.

fence, *n.* **1** act of fencing; also, swordplay or swordsmanship: "I'll prove it on his body if he dare,/ Despite his nice fence [skill at fencing]..." *M Ado,* V, i, 74–75. **2** defense: "Let us be back'd with God and with the seas/ Which he hath given for fence impregnable..." *3 Hen 6,* IV, i, 42–43.
—*v.* **3** to protect or defend; shield: "Where's Captain Margaret, to fence you now?" *3 Hen 6,* II, vi, 75.

fenny, *adj.* of the swamps: "Fillet of a fenny snake,/ In the cauldron boil and bake . . ." *Mac,* IV, i, 12–13.

fen-sucked fogs, *n.* noisome fogs sucked up from fens by the sun: "You fen-suck'd fogs, drawn by the pow'rful sun,/ To fall and blister her!" *Lear,* II, iv, 168–169.

feodary, *n.* Also, **fedary, federary.** confederate or associate; accomplice: "If not a feodary but only he/ Owe and succeed thy weakness [if no one but he has this weakness you speak of]." *Meas,* II, iv, 122–123.

fere, *n.* spouse or mate: ". . . swear with me, as with the woeful fere/ And father of that chaste dishonoured dame . . ." *T Andr,* IV, i, 89–90.

fern-seed, *n.* said to be visible only on Midsummer Eve (June 23rd); if gathered then, it conferred invisibility on the finder: ". . . we have the receipt of/ fern-seed, we walk invisible." *1 Hen 4,* II, i, 85–86.

Ferrara, *n.* principality in N Italy: ". . . to conclude . . . A league between his highness and Ferrara." *Hen 8,* III, ii, 321–323.

ferret, *v.* to worry or harass in the manner of a ferret: "I'll fer him, and firk him, and/ ferret him." *Hen 5,* IV, iv, 28–29.

ferryman, *n.* (in classical myth.) Charon, the aged boatman who ferried dead souls across the river of the underworld: "With that sour ferryman which poets write of . . ." *Rich 3,* I, iv, 46.

fertile, *adj.* profuse; abundant: "How does he love me?"/ "With adorations, fertile tears . . ." *T Night,* I, v, 258–259.

fertile bosom, *n.* warmheartedness: ". . . derive a liberty/ From heartiness, from bounty, fertile bosom . . ." *W Tale,* I, ii, 112–113.

festinate, *adj.* hasty; speedy: "Advise the Duke . . . to a most festinate preparation . . ." *Lear,* III, vii, 9–11.

festinately, *adv.* quickly; right away: ". . . take this key,/ give enlargement to the swain, bring him festinately/ hither . . ." *Love's L,* III, i, 3–5.

festival, *adj.* **1** joyous; carefree: "I cannot woo in festival terms." *M Ado,* V, ii, 40. **2** used or intended for celebration; festive: "All things that we ordained festival/ Turn from their office to black funeral . . ." *Rom & Jul,* IV, v, 84–85.

fet, *v.* old past part. of **fetch;** fetched; derived or inherited: ". . . you noblest English!/ Whose blood is fet from fathers of war-proof . . ." *Hen 5,* III, i, 17–18.

fetch, *v.* **1** to derive: ". . . all the treasons . . . Fetch from false Mowbray their first head and spring . . ." *Rich 2,* I, i, 95–97. **2** to seize; lay hold of: ". . . come away, or I'll/ fetch'th [thee] with a wanion [vengeance]." *Per,* II, i, 16–17. **3** to execute; perform: ". . . race of youthful and unhandled colts/ Fetching mad bounds [wild leaps] . . ." *Merch,* V, i, 72–73. **4** to make or take: "I'll fetch a turn about the garden . . ." *Cymb,* I, ii, 12. **5** to draw [in]: ". . . she fetches her breath as short as a/ new-ta'en sparrow." *Tr & Cr,* III, ii, 32–33. **6 fetch about,** (in sailing) to change direction: ". . . like a shifted wind unto a sail,/ It makes the course of thoughts to fetch about . . ." *K John,* IV, ii, 23–24. **7 fetch in, a.** to cajole into disclosing the truth: "You speak this to fetch me in, my lord." *M Ado,* I, i, 206. **b.** to capture: ". . . there are,/ Of those that serv'd Mark Antony but late,/ Enough to fetch him in." *Ant & Cleo,* IV, i, 13–14. **8 fetch off, a.** to take advantage of; here, fleece: "As I return, I will fetch off these justices." *2 Hen 4,* III, ii, 295. **b.** to rescue; retrieve: ". . . let him fetch off his/ drum, which you hear him so confidently undertake/ to do." *All's W,* III, vi, 17–19. **c.** to get out of the way; here, appar. to kill: "I do; and will fetch off Bohemia for't . . ." *W Tale,* I, ii, 334.

fetch of warrant, *n.* a justified trick or stratagem: "Marry, sir, here's my drift,/ And I believe it is a fetch of warrant." *Ham,* II, i, 38–39. Also, **fetch of wit.**

fetter, *v.* to bind together: "But rather reason thus with reason fetter . . ." *T Night,* III, i, 157.

fettle, *v.* to prepare: ". . . fettle your fine joints 'gainst Thursday next/ To go with Paris to Saint Peter's Church . . ." *Rom & Jul,* III, v, 153–154.

fever, *n.* **so great a fever on goodness,** fr. the old belief that death was the only cure for fever; here, the death of goodness: ". . . there is so great a fever on goodness/ that the dissolution of it must cure it." *Meas,* III, ii, 216–217.

feverous, *adj.* **1** feverish: "Lest thou a feverous life shouldst entertain . . ." *Meas,* III, i, 74. **2** prob. ref. to the fevers and shakes of ague; here, implying earthquake: ". . . some say,/ the earth/ Was feverous, and did shake." *Mac,* II, iii, 61–62.

few, *pron.* **in few,** in a few words; briefly: "In few, his death . . . Being bruited once, took fire and heat away . . ." *2 Hen 4,* I, i, 112–114.

fewer, *adv.* softer; lower: ". . . in the name of Jesu Christ, speak fewer." *Hen 5,* IV, i, 65.

fewness and truth, *n.* truth in few words; here, briefly and truly: "Fewness and truth, 'tis thus:/ Your brother and his lover have embrac'd . . ." *Meas,* I, iv, 39–40.

fia, *v.* get along! [exhortation from the Ital. *via*]: "'Fia!' says the fiend, 'away!' says/ the fiend . . ." *Merch,* II, ii, 10–11.

fickle, *adj.* excited or agitated: "Ere long espied a fickle maid full pale . . ." *Lover's Comp,* 5.

fico, *n.* fig; usually accomp. by an obscene gesture: "'Steal'! Foh, a fico for the/ phrase!" *Wives,* I, iii, 27–28.

fiction, *n.* imaginative invention: "And, for thy fiction,/ Why, thy verse swells with stuff so fine and smooth . . ." *Timon,* V, i, 82–83.

fiddle, *n.* lit., a violin; here, in sexual context, prob. meaning is further wordplay on "act of intercourse" and "penis": "A French song and a fiddle has no fellow [equal]." *Hen 8,* I, iii, 41.

fiddler, *n.* **the fiddler Apollo,** derog. ref. to Apollo the musician, though usually identified with the lute: ". . . unless the fiddler/ Apollo get his sinews to make catlings on." *Tr & Cr,* III, iii, 301–302.

fiddle-stick or **fiddlestick,** *n.* **1** bow with which a stringed instrument is played: "Heigh, heigh, the devil rides upon a fiddle-stick [a great to-do about nothing] . . ." *1 Hen 4,* II, iv, 481. **2** same used in wordplay with "rapier": "Here's my fiddlestick, here's that shall make you dance. Zounds, consort!" *Rom & Jul,* III, i, 47–48.

fidelicet, *adv.* the parson's misuse for "videlicet," namely: ". . . three umpires in this matter . . . that is, Master Page (fidelicet Master Page); and/ there is myself (fidelicet myself) . . ." *Wives,* I, i, 125–127.

fidelity, *n.* **By my fidelity,** by or upon my faith [a mild oath]: "By my fidelity, this is not well, Master Ford; this/ wrongs you." *Wives,* IV, ii, 141–142.

'fidiussed, *v.* past part. of made-up verb on name of Aufidius, with sense of "beaten, thrashed": "I would not have been so/ 'fidiussed for all the chests in Corioles . . ." *Cor,* II, i, 129–130.

fie, *interj.* **1** expression of disgust: "Fie, fie upon her! she's able to freeze the god/ Priapus . . ." *Per,* IV, vi, 3–4. **2 fie away,** get thee gone: "Fie away, fie away breath [life] . . ." *T Night,* II, iv, 53.

field, *n.* **1** battle: ". . . a Persian prince/ That won three fields of Sultan Solyman . . ." *Merch,* II, i, 25–26. **2** wordplay on "background of coat of arms" and "meadow": ". . . the field is honourable, and/ there was he born, under a hedge . . ." *2 Hen 6,* IV, ii, 48–49. **3 get the field,** to win the battle: "Help me this once, that France may get the field." *1 Hen 6,* V, iii, 12.

4 high-grown field, crop grown to maturity [the time here is appar. late summer]: "Search every acre in the high-grown field,/ And bring him to our eye." *Lear,* IV, iv, 7–8.

field-bed, *n.* prob. ref. to sleeping on the ground: "I'll to my truckle-bed./ This field-bed is too cold for me to sleep." *Rom & Jul,* II, i, 39–40.

fielded, *adj.* (of a soldier) on the field of battle: "That we with smoking swords may march from hence/ To help our fielded friends." *Cor,* I, iv, 11–12.

field of feasts, *n.* Pompey wants Cleopatra to tether Antony near her, where he will not be tempted to stray: "Tie up the libertine in a field of feasts . . ." *Ant & Cleo,* II, i, 23.

fiend, *n.* **1** demon or devil: ". . . bowl the round nave down the hill of heaven/ As low as to the fiends." *Ham,* II, ii, 492–493. **2** the evil spirit supposedly inhabiting Malvolio and causing his insanity: "Out, hyperbolical fiend! how vexest thou this/ man!" *T Night,* IV, ii, 26–27. **3 the fiend,** Satan, the Devil: "But to the girdle do the Gods inherit,/ Beneath is all the fiend's . . ." *Lear,* IV, vi, 128–129.

fierce, *adj.* **1** vigorous: ". . . in the lusty stealth of nature take/ More composition and fierce quality . . ." *Lear,* I, ii, 11–12. **2** keenly or sorely felt: "O the fierce wretchedness that glory brings us!" *Timon,* IV, ii, 30. **3** extreme or excessive: ". . . think no more of this night's accidents/ But as the fierce vexation of a dream." *M N Dream,* IV, i, 67–68.

fiery, *adj.* ardent; spirited: ". . . full of nimble, fiery, and delectable/ shapes . . ." *2 Hen 4,* IV, iii, 98–99.

fiery numbers, *n.* ref. to the lovers' sonnets, verses, etc.: "Such fiery numbers as the prompting eyes/ Of beauty's tutors have enriched you with?" *Love's L,* IV, iii, 318–319.

Fife, *n.* county in E Scotland: "Will you to Scone?"/ "No cousin; I'll to Fife." *Mac,* II, iv, 34–35.

fift, *pron.* var. of FIFTH: "Four fixed, and the fift did whirl about . . ." *K John,* IV, ii, 183.

fifteenth, *n.* tax of 15% on income and property [Suffolk was granted 10%]: "That Suffolk should demand a whole fifteenth/ For costs and charges in transporting her!" *2 Hen 6,* I, 1, 132–133.

fifth, *adj.* **fifth hour of the sun,** 11 a.m.: "Hector, by the fifth hour of the sun,/ Will . . . call some knights to arms . . ." *Tr & Cr,* II, i, 124–126.

fig or **figo,** *n.* **1** word of contempt: "Die and be damn'd; and figo for thy friendship!" *Hen V,* III, vi, 58. **2 a fig for,** to hell

with: ". . . I'll pledge you all; and a fig/ for Peter!" *2 Hen 6*, II, iii, 65–66. **3 The fig of Spain!** emphatic form of preceding: "Die and be damn'd; and figo for thy friendship! . . ./ The fig of Spain!" *Hen 5*, III, vi, 58–60.
—*v.* **4** to insult (another) by thrusting the thumb between the first two fingers: "When Pistol lies, do this, and fig me, like/ The bragging Spaniard." *2 Hen 4*, V, iii, 115–116.

fight, *n.* **1** [usually pl.] canvas screens hoisted to shield sailors in combat: "Clap on more sails, pursue; up with your fights . . ." *Wives*, II, ii, 131. **2 fights and fireworks,** dueling and whoring: "With all their honourable points of ignorance/ Pertaining thereunto, as fights and fireworks . . ." *Hen 8*, I, iii, 26–27.

fig's-end, *n.* **Blest fig's end!** expression of contempt or annoyance; rubbish!: "Blest fig's-end! the wine she drinks is made of/ grapes . . ." *Oth*, II, i, 249–250.

figure, *n.* **1** [usually pl.] amount or value: "And write in thee the figures of their love . . ." *Timon*, V, i, 153. **2** letter of an alphabet or a system of lettering: "Our captain hath in every figure skill . . ." *Timon*, V, iii, 7. **3** shape, figure, or fantasy: "He apprehends a world of figures here . . ." *1 Hen 4*, I, iii, 207. **4** symbol: "They were but sweet, but figures of delight . . ." *Sonn 98*, 11. **5** a dream image; nightmare: "Thou hast no figures nor no fantasies/ Which busy care draws in the brains of men . . ." *J Caes*, II, i, 231–232. **6** drawing or design: ". . . when we see the figure of the house,/ Then must we rate the cost of the erection . . ." *2 Hen 4*, I, iii, 43–44. **7** [often pl.] carvings on the chimneypiece: "Th' adornment of her bed; the arras, figures,/ Why, such, and such . . ." *Cymb*, II, ii, 26–27. **8** figure of speech; simile or metaphor: "What is the figure? what is the figure?"/ "Horns." *Love's L*, V, i, 58–59. **9** wordplay on "rhetorical device" and "number": "Why, she woos you by a figure."/ "What figure?"/ "By a letter, I should say." *Two Gent*, II, i, 140–142. **10** impression or image; here, as a deputy: "What figure of us, think you, he will bear?" *Meas*, I, i, 16. **11** image molded in wax: "The native act, and figure of my heart,/ In complement extern . . ." *Oth*, I, i, 62–63. **12** [often pl.] similarity; parallel: "Harry of Monmouth's/ life is come after it indifferent well; for/ there is figures in all things." *Hen 5*, IV, vii, 33–35. **13 by the figure,** using charts and diagrams; also, perh., using wax figures for casting spells: "She works by charms, by spells, by/ th' figure, and such daubery . . ." *Wives*, IV, ii, 162–163. **14 for the figure's sake,** because of the [sovereign's] figure stamped thereon: "Thought light [lacking the proper weight in gold or silver], take [accept] pieces for the figure's sake . . ." *Cymb*, V, iv, 25. **15 throw a figure,** to fling a figure of speech: ". . . and she stand/ him but a little, he will throw a figure in her face . . ." *Shrew*, I, ii, 111–112.
—*v.* **16** to represent; portray: "There is a history in all men's lives/ Figuring the nature of the times deceas'd . . ." *2 Hen 4*,

III, i, 80–81. **17** to symbolize: "Wings, and no eyes, figure unheedy haste." *M N Dream*, I, i, 237. **18** to disclose; foreshadow: "In this the heaven figures some event." *3 Hen 6*, II, i, 32. **19** to imagine: "Thou art always figuring diseases in me . . ." *Meas*, I, ii, 49.

figured, *adj.* ornamented: "My figur'd goblets for a dish of wood . . ." *Rich 2*, III, iii, 150.

filching age, *n.* ref. to the keen competition among writers for a wealthy patron: ". . . and anon/ Doubting [suspecting] the filching age will steal his treasure . . ." *Sonn 75*, 5–6.

file¹, *n.* **1** register or list: ". . . the valu'd file/ Distinguishes the swift, the slow, the subtle . . ." *Mac*, III, i, 94–95. **2** line or wire, as in a military officer's tent, to which messages were attached: ". . . either it is there or it/ is upon a file . . . in my tent." *All's W*, IV, iii, 196–198. **3** line of assembled troops: "For three performers are the file when all/ The rest do nothing . . ." *Cymb*, V, iii, 30–31. **4** [usually pl.] list or roster of troops: ". . . are his files/ As full as thy report?" *Timon*, V, ii, 1–2. **5 file and quality,** rank and condition: ". . . grant/ The file and quality I hold I may/ Continue in thy band." *Kinsmen*, V, i, 160–162. **6 files and musters,** troop formations: "That o'er the files and musters of the war . . ." *Ant & Cleo*, I, i, 3. **7 greater file of the subject,** majority of his subjects: ". . . the greater file of the subject held the Duke/ to be wise." *Meas*, III, ii, 133–134.
—*v.* **8** to keep pace: "My endeavours/ Have ever come too short of my desires,/ Yet fil'd with my abilities . . ." *Hen 8*, III, ii, 169–171.

file², *v.* to defile: "If't be so,/ For Banquo's issue have I fil'd my mind . . ." *Mac*, III, i, 63–64.

file³, *v.* **1** to smooth with or as if with a file; polish or refine: ". . . his humour is lofty,/ his tongue filed . . ." *Love's L*, V, i, 9–10. **2 file our engines,** [to] sharpen our wits: "And she shall file our engines with advice . . ." *T Andr*, II, i, 123.

fill, *n.* [usually pl.] the shafts for drawing a wagon or cart: ". . . and you draw backward we'll put you/ i'th'fills." *Tr & Cr*, III, ii, 44–45.

fillet, *n.* slice: "Fillet of a fenny snake,/ In the cauldron boil and bake . . ." *Mac*, IV, i, 12–13.

fill-horse, *n.* cart horse: ". . . thou hast got more hair on thy chin, than Dobbin/ my fill-horse has on his tail." *Merch*, II, ii, 90–91.

fillip, *v.* **1** to flip or flick; strike: "If I do, fillip me with a three-man beetle." *2 Hen 4*, I, ii, 229. **2** to strike against: "Then let the pebbles on the hungry beach/ Fillip the stars." *Cor*, V, iii, 58–

59. **3** to touch on a sensitive subject: "You fillip me o'th'head." *Tr & Cr,* IV, v, 45.

film, *n.* spider's thread; gossamer: "Her whip of cricket's bone, the lash of film . . ." *Rom & Jul,* I, iv, 66.

filthy, *adj.* revolting; trashy: "A velvet dish! Fie, fie! 'Tis lewd and filthy." *Shrew,* IV, iii, 65.

filthy-mantled, *adj.* covered with dirty scum: ". . . at last I left them/ I' th'filthy-mantled pool beyond your cell . . ." *Temp,* IV, i, 181–182.

filz, *n.* misuse for French "fils," son: "Notre très cher/ filz Henry, Roy [Roi] d'Angleterre, Héritier de France . . ." *Hen 5,* V, ii, 357–358.

finch egg, *n.* a small egg of little use; here, term of abuse: "Out, gall!"/ "Finch egg!" *Tr & Cr,* V, i, 34–35.

find, *v.* **1** to discover the truth about; find (someone) out: "If she find him not,/ To England send him . . ." *Ham,* III, i, 187–188. **2** to furnish: "To find his title with some shows of truth . . ." *Hen 5,* I, ii, 72. **3** suffer; experience: "In corporal sufferance finds a pang as great/ As when a giant dies." *Meas,* III, i, 79–80. **4 find easy fines,** to suffer minor penalties: "What faults he made before the last, I think/ Might have found easy fines . . ." *Cor,* V, vi, 64–65. **5 find forth,** to seek out: "Who, falling there to find his fellow forth,/ (Unseen, inquisitive) confounds himself." *Errors,* I, ii, 37–38. **6 find me,** find in my hand [in palm-reading]: "Find me to/ marry with Octavius Caesar . . ." *Ant & Cleo,* I, ii, 28–29. **7 find thee out,** to locate you: ". . . now it is my chance to find thee out,/ Must I behold thy timeless cruel death?" *1 Hen 6,* V, iv, 4–5. **8 found 'em,** found them out: ". . . there I found 'em, there I smelt 'em out." *Lear,* IV, vi, 105. **9 found them in mine honesty,** regarded my honesty as the best system of bookkeeping: ". . . you would throw them off,/ And say you found them in mine honesty." *Timon,* II, ii, 138–139.

finder of madmen, one empowered to pass judgment on a person's sanity: ". . . we will bring the device to the bar,/ and crown thee for a finder of madmen." *T Night,* III, iv, 141–142.

find-fault, *n.* overcritical person: ". . . and the liberty that/ follows our places stops the mouth of all find-faults,/ as I will do yours . . ." *Hen 5,* V, ii, 287–289.

fine¹, *n.* **1** conclusion: ". . . and the fine is . . . I will live a bachelor." *M Ado,* I, i, 227–228. **2** fee; sum of money: ". . . to pay a fine for a periwig, and recover the lost hair of another man." *Errors,* II, ii, 74–75. **3 in fine,** in the end; in short: ". . . in fine,/ Makes vow before his uncle never more/ To give th'assay of

arms . . ." *Ham,* II, ii, 69–71. **4 the fine's the crown,** the end [of life] crowns all: "All's well that ends well; still the fine's the crown." *All's W,* IV, iv, 35.
—*adj.* **5** elegantly dressed: "I will be sure my Katherine shall be fine." *Shrew,* II, i, 310. **6** of elegant or subtle craftsmanship: ". . . and by very much more handsome than fine." *Ham,* II, ii, 441. **7** extremely sensitive: "Nature [human nature] is fine in love, and where 'tis fine/ It sends some precious instance of itself . . ." *Ham,* IV, v, 161–162. **8** sly, cunning, or deceptive: ". . . thou art too fine in thy evidence;/ therefore, stand aside." *All's W,* V, iii, 262–263. **9** pure; purged of impurities: "The grief is fine, full, perfect, that I taste . . ." *Tr & Cr,* IV, iv, 3. **10** clear; free of sediment: "A cup of wine that's brisk and fine . . ." *2 Hen 4,* V, iii, 44.
—*v.* **11** to conclude; bring to an end: "Time's office is to fine the hate of foes . . ." *Luc,* 936.
—*adv.* **12** mincingly; preciously: ". . . to speak/ dout, fine, when he should say doubt . . ." *Love's L,* V, i, 19–20.

fine², *v.* to wager; stake: "Know'st thou not/ That I have fin'd these bones of mine for ransom?" *Hen 5,* IV, vii, 70–71.

fine³, *adv.* subtly: "How fine this tyrant/ Can tickle where she wounds!" *Cymb,* I, ii, 15–16.

fine and recovery, *n.* [in law] processes for transferring the ownership of property: "There's no time for a man to recover his hair/ that grows bald by nature."/ "May he not do it by fine and recovery?" *Errors,* II, ii, 71–73.

fine-baited, *adj.* irresistibly tempting: ". . . lead him on with a fine-baited delay/ till he hath pawned his horses to mine host . . ." *Wives,* II, i, 92–93.

fine hand, *n.* fine mess: "Y'have made a fine hand, fellows!" *Hen 8,* V, iii, 69.

fineless, *adj.* boundless; endless: "But riches, fineless, is as poor as winter/ To him that ever fears he shall be poor . . ." *Oth,* III, iii, 177.

finely, *adv.* **1** cleverly; skillfully: "We will turn it finely off, sir; we will take some care." *Love's L,* V, ii, 506. **2** excellently: "Spirits are not finely touch'd/ But to fine issues . . ." *Meas,* I, i, 35–36.

fineness, *n.* full capacity: ". . . those that with the fineness of their souls/ By reason guide his execution." *Tr & Cr,* I, iii, 209–210.

finger, *n.* **1** width of a finger used as a unit of measure: "No, I'll be sworn, unless you call three fingers in/ the ribs bare." *1 Hen 4,* IV, ii, 73–74. **2 at my fingers' ends,** at the ready: "Ay, sir, I have them at my fingers' ends . . ." *T Night,* I, iii, 77. **3 lay**

thy finger thus, put your finger to your lips: "Lay thy finger thus, and let thy soul be instructed . . ." *Oth,* II, i, 220. **4 put finger in the eye,** childhood expression meaning "cry-baby!": "A pretty peat! it is best put finger in the eye, and she knew why [if she could only find an excuse]." *Shrew,* I, i, 78–79. **5 put my finger in the fire,** [there's no need to] put one's finger in the fire [if one doesn't need to]: "This is all, indeed, la, but I'll ne'er put my finger/ in the fire, and need not." *Wives,* I, iv, 80–81. **6 with finger and thumb,** to snap the fingers: "Another, with his finger and his thumb,/ Cry'd 'Via! we will do't, come what will come'. . ." *Love's L,* V, ii, 111–112.
—*v.* **7** to steal; filch: "Grop'd I to find out them, had my desire,/ Finger'd their packet, and in fine withdrew . . ." *Ham,* V, ii, 14–15.

finical, *adj.* overfastidious; foppish: ". . . glass-gazing, superserviceable, finical rogue . . ." *Lear,* II, ii, 17.

finny, *adj.* having fins: "How from the finny subject [inhabitants] of the sea . . ." *Per,* II, i, 48.

Finsbury, *n.* Finsbury Fields, a favorite walking place for Londoners: "As if thou never walk'st further than Finsbury." *1 Hen 4,* III, i, 246.

firago, *n.* misuse for "virago," a sharp-tongued, aggressive woman: "Why, man, he's a very devil, I have not seen/ such a firago." *T Night,* III, iv, 278–279.

fire, *n.* **1** ruddy complexion: "Thou hadst/ fire and sword on thy side, and yet thou ran'st away . . ." *1 Hen 4,* II, iv, 312–313. **2** prob. will-o'-the-wisp: "Sometime a horse I'll be, sometime a hound,/ A hog, a headless bear, sometime a fire . . ." *M N Dream,* III, i, 103–104. **3 give fire,** to shoot: "Fear we broadsides? No, let the fiend give fire!" *2 Hen 4,* II, iv, 178. **4 Muse of fire.** See **Muse** (def. 3).
—*v.* **5** to kindle: "Takes prisoner the wild motion of mine eye,/ Firing it only here . . ." *Cymb,* I, vii, 103–104. **6** to catch foxes by inserting firebrands into their burrows: "He that parts us shall bring a brand from heaven,/ And fire us hence like foxes." *Lear,* V, iii, 22–23. **7 fire out,** to drive out with or as if with fire; also, to exhaust sexually; also, poss., to infect with venereal disease: "I shall not know . . . Till my bad angel fire my good one out." *Pass Pil,* II, 13–14; repeated in *Sonn 144,* 13–14.

fired, *adj.* lighted; ignited: ". . . like a beacon fir'd t'amaze your eyes." *Per,* I, iv, 87.

fire-drake, *n.* fiery dragon; also, a meteor or, sometimes, a firework: ". . . that fire-drake/ did I hit three times on the head, and three/ times was his nose discharg'd against me . . ." *Hen 8,* V, iii, 42–44.

fire-eyed maid, *n.* Bellona, goddess of war: "They come like sacrifices in their trim,/ And to the fire-ey'd maid of smoky war/ . . . will we offer them." *1 Hen 4,* IV, i, 113–115.

fire-new, *adj.* brand-new; bright in the manner of a freshly minted coin: "A man of fire-new words, fashion's own knight." *Love's L,* I, i, 177.

firing, *n.* firewood; fuel: "No more dams I'll make for fish;/ Nor fetch in firing . . ." *Temp,* II, ii, 180–181.

firk, *v.* to whip; beat: "I'll fer him, and firk him, and/ ferret him." *Hen 5,* IV, iv, 28–29.

firm, *adj.* **1** steady; unshaken: "But were my worth, as is my conscience, firm,/ You should find better dealing." *T Night,* III, iii, 17–18. **2** constant; faithful: "Say the firm Roman to great Egypt sends/ This treasure of an oyster . . ." *Ant & Cleo* I, v, 43–44.

first, *adv.* **1** before (me): "Pisa . . . Gave me my being and my father first . . ." *Shrew,* I, i, 10–11. **2** already: "To fetch his daughter home, who first is gone." *Per,* IV, iv, 20. **3 at first and last,** from start to finish; here, to one and all: ". . . at first/ And last, the hearty welcome." *Mac,* III, iv, 1–2.
—*n.* **4** beginning: "And many unrough youths . . . Protest their first of manhood." *Mac,* V, ii, 10–11. **5** first hearing, presentation, introduction of a subject, etc.: "Upon our first, he sent out to suppress/ His nephew's levies . . ." *Ham,* II, ii, 61–62.

first cause, second cause, etc. technical reasons for a duel: "The first and second cause will not serve my turn . . ." *Love's L,* I, ii, 167–168.

first cock, *n.* first cockcrow; midnight: ". . . ne'er a king/ christen could be better bit than I have been since/ the first cock." *1 Hen 4,* II, i, 15–17.

first decree, *n.* fundamental law: "And turn pre-ordinance and first decree/ Into the law of children." *J Caes,* III, i, 38–39.

first house, *n.* first rank; also, the best fencing school: ". . . a duellist, a duellist, a gentleman of the very first house . . ." *Rom & Jul,* II, iv, 24.

first head, *n.* **buck of the first head,** mature buck with fully developed antlers: ". . . varied, like a scholar at the least: but sir, I assure/ ye, it was a buck of the first head." *Love's L,* IV, ii, 9–10.

firstling, *n.* **1** [often pl.] first fruits, offspring, or the like: ". . . our play/ Leaps o'er the vaunt and firstlings of those broils . . ." *Tr & Cr,* Prol., 26–27. **2** [pl.] one's first impulses; also, one's first actions [which result]: "The very firstlings of my heart shall be/ The firstlings of my hand." *Mac*, IV, i, 147–148.

First Nature, *n.* nature at the beginning of the world: "Born to uphold creation in that honor/ First Nature styl'd it in . . ." *Kinsmen*, I, i, 82–83.

first proportion, *n.* greatest proportion; first magnitude: ". . . Northumberland,/ Whose power was in the first proportion . . ." *1 Hen 4*, IV, iv, 14–15.

fisher, *n.* fisherman: "These fishers tell the infirmities of men . . ." *Per*, II, i, 49.

fishmonger, *n.* person who sells fish: "Yet he knew me not at first; a said I was a/ fishmonger." *Ham*, II, ii, 188–189.

fisnomy, *n.* Clown's mistake for "physiognomy": ". . . 'a has an English name; but his fisnomy is/ more hotter in France than there." *All's W*, IV, v, 36–37.

fist, *v.* to grasp: "Unbuckling helms, fisting each other's throat . . ." *Cor*, IV, v, 126.

fisting, *n.* beating; cuffing: "To the choleric fisting of every rogue/ Thy ear is liable . . ." *Per*, IV, vi, 166–167.

fit¹, *v.* **1** to outfit; equip: "Come, go with me into mine armoury:/ Lucius, I'll fit thee . . ." *T Andr*, IV, i, 113–114. **2** to suit; accord with; here, used ironically: "If it be a day/ fits you, search out of the calendar . . ." *Per*, II, i, 53–54. **3** to make suitable or appropriate: "I had a thing to say,/ But I will fit it with some better tune." *K John*, III, ii, 35–36. **4** fitted; here, with sexual wordplay: "Why should his mistress who was made by/ him that made the tailor, not be fit too?" *Cymb*, IV, i, 3–4. **5 I'll fit you,** I'll satisfy you fully: "Nay, I'll fit you,/ And not be all day neither." *All's W*, II, i, 89–90.
—*n.* **6** triple wordplay on "tailor's fitting," "fits and starts," and "act of intercourse": ". . . 'tis said a woman's/ fitness comes by fits." *Cymb*, IV, i, 5–6.
—*adj.* **7** ready; prepared: "Tell Valeria/ We are fit to bid her welcome." *Cor*, I, iii, 43–44.

fit², *n.* grimace; an affected way of twisting the features to show disdain: ". . . all the good our English/ Have got by the late voyage is but merely/ A fit or two o'th'face . . ." *Hen 8*, I, iii, 5–7.

fit³, *n.* spell [lit., attack of disease or lunacy]: ". . . (for I feel/ The last fit of my greatness) . . ." *Hen 8*, III, i, 77–78.

fit⁴, *n.* short strain of music: "Well said, my lord; well, you say so in fits." *Tr & Cr*, III, i, 56.

fitchew, *n.* polecat; also, slang term for prostitute: "[nor] The fitchew nor the soiled horse goes to't/ With a more riotous appetite." *Lear*, IV, vi, 124–125.

fitchook, *n.* fitchew: "To be a dog, a mule, a cat, a fitchook, a/ toad, a lizard . . ." *Tr & Cr*, V, i, 60–61.

fitful, *adj.* subject to fits or seizures; here, intermittent: "After life's fitful fever he sleeps well . . ." *Mac*, III, ii, 23.

fitly, *adv.* **1** conveniently: "My steward?"/ "Here, my lord."/ "So fitly?" *Timon*, III, iv, 104–106. **2 fitly like,** seem suitable to: "If aught within that little-seeming substance . . . may fitly like your Grace . . ." *Lear*, I, i, 198–200.

fitment, *n.* **1** that which is proper and fitting; one's duty: "When she/ should do for clients her fitment and do me the kindness/ of our profession . . ." *Per*, IV, vi, 5–7. **2** makeshift; disguise: ". . . 'twas a fitment for/ The purpose I then follow'd." *Cymb*, V, v, 410–411.

fitness, *n.* **1** readiness; convenience: "If his fitness speaks, mine is ready [I await his pleasure]." *Ham*, V, ii, 198. **2** sexual inclination: ". . . 'tis said a woman's/ fitness comes by fits." *Cymb*, IV, i, 5–6.

fits o' th' season, *n. pl.* turbulence of the times: "He is noble, wise, judicious, and best knows/ The fits o' th' season." *Mac*, IV, ii, 16–17.

fitted, *adj.* **1** equipped or supplied: "Well fitted in arts, glorious in arms . . .": *Love's L*, II, i, 45. **2** (of a play) cast; having an actor assigned to each role: "And I hope here/ is a play fitted." *M N Dream*, I, ii, 60–61. **3** suitable; here, well cast: "There is not one word apt, one player fitted." *M N Dream*, V, i, 65. **4** placed or situated appropriately: "A document in madness: thoughts and/ remembrance fitted." *Ham*, IV, v, 176–177.

fittest, *adj.* most suitable: "This course I fittest choose,/ For forty ducats is too much to lose." *Errors*, IV, iii, 92–93.

five-finger-tied, *adj.* done by human hands or poss. those of the devil; here, in contrast to the heavenly bond Troilus thought he and Cressida shared: "And with another knot, five-finger-tied,/ The fractions of her faith . . ." *Tr & Cr*, V, ii, 156–157.

five-fold blazon, *n.* See **blazon** (def. 3).

fives, *n. pl.* disease among horses, characterized by swellings behind the ears: ". . . past cure of the fives, stark spoiled with the staggers . . ." *Shrew*, III, ii, 51–52.

five wits, *n.* differentiated from the five senses and usually enumerated as common wit, imagination, fantasy, estimation, and memory: "Bless thy five wits! Tom's a-cold. O! do de,/ do de, do de." *Lear*, III, iv, 58–59.

fixed, *adj.* **1** certain: "O, 'tis a worthy lord."/ "Nay, that's most fix'd." *Timon*, I, i, 8–9. **2** constant: "Hector, whose patience/ Is as a virtue fix'd . . ." *Tr & Cr*, I, ii, 4–5.

fixed figure, *n.* Othello likens his public humiliation to a numeral on a clock, to which the hands point: ". . . to make me/ A fixed figure, for the time of scorn/ To point his slow unmoving fingers at . . ." *Oth*, IV, ii, 54–56.

fixure, *n.* **1** fixed position; also, stability: ". . . deracinate/ The unity and married calm of states/ Quite from their fixure!" *Tr & Cr*, I, iii, 99–101. **2** same, with addit. sense of set or focus, which add lifelikeness and make the eye seem to move: "The fixure of her eye has motion in 't . . ." *W Tale*, V, iii, 67.

flag, *n.* kind of iris, perh. the water iris: "Like to a vagabond flag upon the stream . . ." *Ant & Cleo*, I, iv, 45.

flagging, *adj.* drooping: "Who with their drowsy, slow, and flagging wings . . ." *2 Hen 6*, IV, i, 5.

flame, *n.* **1** passion; intensity: "If I did love you in my master's flame . . ." *T Night*, I, v, 268.
—*v.* **2 flamed amazement,** See **amazement** (def. 2).

flamen, *n.* priest, esp. one of ancient Rome: "Hoar the flamen,/ That scolds against the quality of flesh . . ." *Timon*, IV, iii, 157–158.

flaming, *adj.* lusty; hot-blooded: "To flaming youth let virtue be as wax/ And melt in her own fire . . ." *Ham*, III, iv, 84–85.

flanker, *n.* (often pl.) one or more soldiers stationed on either side of a column of soldiers to guard the line of march: "These wings, these flankers, and these squadrons/ Argue in thee defective discipline . . ." *Edw 3*, II, i, 187–188.

flap-dragon, *n.* **1** drinking game in which a lighted candle end was floated in a drink, the object being to down the drink without burning oneself or extinguishing the candle: ". . . drinks off candles' ends for flap-dragons, and rides the wild mare with the boys . . ." *2 Hen 4*, II, iv, 243–244.
—*v.* to swallow: "But to make an end of the ship, to see how/ the sea flap-dragoned it . . ." *W Tale*, III, iii, 97–98.

flap-jack, *n.* a pancake; griddle cake: ". . . we'll have flesh for holidays, fish for/ fasting-days, and moreo'er puddings and flap-jacks . . ." *Per*, II, i, 81–82.

flaring, *pres. part.* fluttering: "With ribands pendant flaring 'bout her head . . ." *Wives*, IV, vi, 41.

flash, *n.* **1** burst of high spirits: "The flash and outbreak of a fiery mind,/ A savageness in unreclaimed blood . . ." *Ham*, II, i, 33–34.
—*v.* **2** to break out: ". . . every hour/ He flashes into one gross crime or other . . ." *Lear*, I, iii, 4–5. **3** to shine; dazzle the eye [as]: ". . . a naked gull,/ Which flashes now a phoenix." *Timon*, II, i, 31–32.

flat, *adj.* **1** absolute; outright; plain: "The flat transgression of a schoolboy . . ." *M Ado*, II, i, 207. **2** dull; obtuse: "The flat unraised spirits that hath dar'd/ On this unworthy scaffold to bring forth/ So great an object . . ." *Hen 5*, Prol., 9–11. **3** blunt; curt: "You, minion, are too saucy./ Nay, now you are too flat . . ." *Two Gent*, I, ii, 93–94. **4** certain; indisputable: "I'll not/ march through Coventry with them, that's flat . . ." *1 Hen 4*, IV, ii, 38–39.
—*n.* **5** flat piece of land: "Now pile your dust upon the quick and dead,/ Till of this flat a mountain you have made . . ." *Ham*, V, i, 244–245. **6** [pl.] lowlands: "The ocean, overpeering of his list,/ Eats not the flats with more impetuous haste . . ." *Ham*, IV, v, 99–100. **7** [pl.] swampland: "All the infections . . . From bogs, fens, flats, on Prosper fall . . ." *Temp*, II, ii, 1–2.

flat-long, *adv.* so as to strike with the flat side, rather than the edge: "What a blow was there given!"/ "An it had not fallen flat-long." *Temp*, II, i, 175–176.

flatness, *n.* completeness; hopelessness: ". . . that he did but see/ The flatness of my misery . . ." *W Tale*, III, ii, 121–122.

flatter, *v.* **1** to cover or gloss over: "So should I give consent to flatter sin." *1 Hen 6*, V, v, 25. **2 flatter up,** to indulge (in): "To flatter up these powers of mine with rest . . ." *Love's L*, V, ii, 806. **3 flatter with, a.** to engage in flattery: "Should dying men flatter with those that live?" *Rich 2*, II, i, 88. **b.** to encourage: "Desire him not to flatter with his lord,/ Nor hold him up with hopes . . ." *T Night*, I, v, 307–308.

flatterer, *n.* deceiver; here, the eye may have deceived the mind: ". . . fear to find/ Mine eye too great a flatterer for my mind." *T Night*, I, v, 312–313.

flattering, *adj.* gratifying; encouraging: "If I may trust the flattering truth of sleep/ My dreams presage some joyful news at hand." *Rom & Jul*, V, i, 1–2.

flaunts, *n.,pl.* fine clothes: ". . . how/ Should I, in these my borrowed flaunts, behold/ The sternness of his presence?" *W Tale*, IV, iv, 22–24.

flaw[1], *n.* **1** sudden gust of wind; squall: "I do not fear the flaw;/ It hath done to me the worst." *Per*, III, i, 39–40. **2** burst of passion [fig. use of preceding def.]: "O! these flaws and starts ... would well become/ A woman's story at a winter's fire ..." *Mac*, III, iv, 62–64.

flaw², *n.* **1** [pl.] fragments: "... this heart/ Shall break into a hundred thousand flaws/ Or ere I'll weep." *Lear*, II, iv, 286–288. **2 becomes his flaw**, bears up under his disgrace: "Observe how Antony becomes his flaw,/ And what thou think'st his very action speaks ..." *Ant & Cleo*, III, xii, 34–35. —*v.* **3** to break [with]; violate (a treaty, etc.): "For France hath flaw'd the league [peace] ..." *Hen 8*, I, i, 95.

flawed, *adj.* cracked; here, with grief [Gloucester has died offstage; Edgar is now Earl of Gloucester]: "... but his flaw'd heart,/ Alack, too weak the conflict to support!" *Lear*, V, iii, 196–197.

flaxen, *adj.* pale yellow, as the color of flax: "His beard was as white as snow,/ All flaxen was his poll [head]." *Ham*, IV, v, 192–193.

flax-wench, *n.* girl hired to dress flax: "As rank as any flax-wench that puts to ..." *W Tale*, I, ii, 277.

flayed, *adj.* undressed: "Nay, prithee, dispatch: the gentleman is half/ flayed already." *W Tale*, IV, iv, 641–642.

fleckled, *adj.* dappled; spotted: "... darkness fleckled like a drunkard reels/ From forth day's pathway ..." *Rom & Jul*, II, ii, 190–191.

fled, *v.* past tense of FLY; flew: "... arrows fled not swifter toward their aim ..." *2 Hen 4*, I, i, 123.

fledge, *adj.* covered with down, as a young bird: "... the Prince your master, whose chin is not yet fledge." *2 Hen 4*, I, ii, 19.

fleer, *v.* **1** to sneer or mock: "Tush, tush, man, never fleer and jest at me!" *M Ado*, V, i, 58. **2** to grin: "One rubb'd his elbow thus, and fleer'd, and swore/ A better speech was never spoke before ..." *Love's L*, V, ii, 109–110.

fleet, *v.* **1** to pass or spend (time): "... many young gentlemen flock to him every day, and fleet the time carelessly ..." *As You*, I, i, 117–118. **2** to depart rapidly; fly: "Even from the gallows did his fell soul fleet ..." *Merch*, IV, i, 135. **3** to float: "... our sever'd navy too/ Have knit again, and fleet, threatening most sea-like." *Ant & Cleo*, III, xiii, 170–171. —*n.* **4** band of soldiers, returned from combat: "I am sure he is in the fleet; I/ would he had boarded me." *M Ado*, II, i, 132–133.

Fleet, *n.* **the Fleet**, London prison: "Go carry Sir John Falstaff to the Fleet ..." *2 Hen 4*, V, v, 91.

fleeting, *adj.* inconstant; changeable: "... now the fleeting moon/ No planet is of mine." *Ant & Cleo*, V, ii, 239–240.

Fleming, *n.* inhabitant of the Low Countries, who supposedly subsisted on butter: "I will rather/ trust a Fleming with my butter ..." *Wives*, II, ii, 290–291.

Flemish, *adj.* alluding to the supposedly heavy drinking in the Low Countries: "What an unweighed/ behaviour hath this Flemish drunkard picked—" *Wives*, II, i, 22–23.

flesh, *v.* **1** to initiate (a youth, novice, etc.) into the use of a sword [from the practice of giving a hound a taste of the kill to make him eager for the hunt]: "... come,/ I'll flesh ye; come on, young master." *Lear*, II, ii, 45–46. **2** (of a weapon) to use in battle for the first time: "... full bravely hast thou flesh'd/ Thy maiden sword." *1 Hen 4*, V, iv, 129–130. **3 fleshed upon us**, emboldened in war by feeding upon our flesh: "The kindred of him hath been flesh'd upon us ..." *Hen 5*, II, iv, 50. **4 flesh his will**, reward or feed his lust: "... this/ night he fleshes his will in the spoil of her honour ..." *All's W*, IV, iii, 14–15. —*n.* **5** meat: "And praise God for the merry year,/ When flesh is cheap and females dear ..." *2 Hen 4*, V, iii, 18–19. **6** human nature: "I shall follow it as the flesh and fortune/ shall better determine." *Meas*, II, i, 250–251. **7 get thyself in flesh**, grow fat: "Fare-well, buy food, and get thyself in flesh." *Rom & Jul*, V, i, 84.

flesh and blood, *n.* offspring: "Our flesh and blood, my lord, is grown so vile,/ That it doth hate what gets it." *Lear*, III, iv, 149–150.

flesh and fell, *adv.* flesh and skin; hence, entirely; altogether: "The good [triumphant] years shall devour them, flesh and fell,/ Ere they shall make us weep ..." *Lear*, V, iii, 24–25.

fleshed, *adj.* **1** hardened to slaughter: "Albeit they were flesh'd villains, bloody dogs ..." *Rich 3*, IV, iii, 6. **2** made eager; emboldened: "... the head/ Which princes, flesh'd with conquest, aim to hit." *2 Hen 4*, I, i, 148–149.

flesh-fly, *n.* insect that feeds on flesh and deposits eggs in it: "... would no more endure/ This wooden slavery than to suffer/ The flesh-fly blow my mouth." *Temp*, III, i, 61–63.

fleshly land, *n.* the body: "Nay, in the body of this fleshly land ... this confine of blood and breath ..." *K John*, IV, ii, 245–246.

fleshment, *n.* act of fleshing; here, reacting to the excitement of being fleshed: "And, in the fleshment of this dread exploit,/ Drew on me here again." *Lear*, II, ii, 124–125.

fleshmonger, *n.* fornicator: "And was the Duke a fleshmonger . . . as you then reported him to be?" *Meas,* V, i, 331–333.

fleur-de-luce, *n.* fleur-de-lys [iris], symbol of the French crown: ". . . have I a sword,/ On which I'll toss the fleur-de-luce of France." *2 Hen 6,* V, i, 10–11.

flewed, *adj.* having large, drooping chaps: "My hounds are bred out of the Spartan kind,/ So flew'd, so sanded . . ." *M N Dream,* IV, i, 118–119.

flexure, *n.* **1** bowing: "Will it give place to flexure and low-bending?" *Hen 5,* IV, i, 261. **2 not for flexure,** fr. the old belief that the elephant, like the proud man, could not bend his knee: "His legs are legs for necessity, not for flexure." *Tr & Cr,* II, iii, 108.

Flibbertigibbet, *n.* one of the demons or devils that haunt Tom [Edgar]: "This is the foul Flibbertigibbet: he begins at/ curfew, and walks till the first cock . . ." *Lear,* III, iv, 118–119.

flidge, *adj.* var. of **fledged;** (of a bird) ready to leave the nest: "And Shylock (for his own part) knew the bird was/ flidge . . ." *Merch,* III, i, 26–27.

flier, *n.* soldier who retreats: "Though you it seems come from the fliers." *Cymb,* V, iii, 2.

flight, *n.* contest between archers shooting for distance; flight shooting: "He set up his bills here in Messina and challenged/ Cupid at the flight . . ." *M Ado,* I, i, 35–36.

flighty, *adj.* swift; instantaneous: "The flighty purpose never is o'ertook,/ Unless the deed go with it." *Mac,* IV, i, 145–146.

flinch in property, *v.* to fall short in fulfilling a bargain: "If I break time, or flinch in property . . . unpitied let me die . . ." *All's W,* II, i, 186–187.

flint, *n.* **1** hard stone; here, appar., of the ground: ". . . with no softer cushion than the flint,/ I kneel before thee . . ." *Cor,* V, iii, 53–54. **2 snore upon the flint,** sleep comfortably on a bed of stones: ". . . weariness/ Can snore upon the flint, when resty sloth/ Finds the down-pillow hard." *Cymb,* III, vii, 6–8. —*adj.* **3** var. of **flinty:** "To whose flint bosom my condemned lord/ Is doom'd a prisoner . . ." *Rich 2,* V, i, 3–4.

Flint Castle, *n.* fortress in NW England, near Chester: "Go to Flint Castle, there I'll pine away—" *Rich 2,* III, ii, 209.

flinty, *adj.* **1** of hard, flintlike stone: "Let us resolve to scale their flinty bulwarks." *1 Hen 6,* II, i, 27. **2** mean-spirited or hard-hearted: "Yet notwithstanding, being incens'd, he's flint,/ As humorous as winter . . ." *2 Hen 4,* IV, iv, 33–34.

flirt-gill, *n.* loose woman: "Scurvy knave! I am none of his flirt-gills, I am none/ of his skains-mates." *Rom & Jul,* II, iv, 150–151.

flock[1], *n.* tuft of wool: ". . . beat Cut's saddle, put a few/ flocks in the point . . ." *1 Hen 4,* II, i, 5–6.

flock[2], *n.* company; here, fellow revelers: ". . . they could do no less . . . But leave their flocks . . ." *Hen 8,* I, iv, 68–70.

flood, *n.* **1** the sea: "What if it tempt you toward the flood, my lord . . ." *Ham,* I, iv, 69. **2** any body of water: "Damned spirits all,/ That in crossways and floods have burial . . ." *M N Dream,* III, ii, 382–383. **3** person's prime: "His youth in flood,/ I'll prove this troth with my three drops of blood." *Tr & Cr,* I, iii, 298–299. **4 great flood,** deluge sent by Zeus to annihilate the wicked world: "When went there by an age, since the great flood,/ But it was fam'd with more than with one man?" *J Caes,* I, ii, 150–151.

Flora, *n.* goddess of flowers: ". . . no shepherdess, but Flora/ Peering in April's front." *W Tale,* IV, iv, 2–3.

Florentine, *n.* **the Florentine,** Duke of Florence: ". . . the Florentine will move us/ For speedy aid . . ." *All's W,* I, ii, 6–7.

Florentius, *n.* knight who dutifully marries an ugly old woman; on their wedding night she turns into a beautiful maiden: "Be she as foul as was Florentius' love,/ As old as Sibyl . . ." *Shrew,* I, ii, 68–69.

flote, *n.* flood; sea: ". . . they all have met again,/ And are upon the Mediterranean flote . . ." *Temp,* I, ii, 233–234.

flourish, *n.* **1** [usually cap.] stage direction, indicating a fanfare of trumpets to announce an entrance: "Flourish. Enter Duke Frederick, lords . . ." *As You,* I, ii, 138. **2** elaboration: "To this effect, sir, after what flourish your nature/ will." *Ham,* V, ii, 177–178. **3** glow; bloom: "Time doth transfix the flourish set on youth . . ." *Sonn 60,* 9. **4** embellishment; decoration: "Poor painted queen, vain flourish of my fortune . . ." *Rich 3,* I, iii, 241. —*v.* **5** to engage in combat: ". . . go, give that changing piece/ To him that flourish'd for her with his sword." *T Andr,* I, i, 309–310. **6** to remove the guilt of; absolve: ". . . the justice of your title to him/ Doth flourish the deceit." *Meas,* IV, i, 74–75. **7** to bloom or blossom: ". . . this pale and angry rose . . . Will I forever wear,/ Until it wither with me to my grave,/ Or flourish to the height of my degree." *1 Hen 6,* II, iv, 107–111.

flout, *v.* **1** to mock; jest: ". . . Nature hath given us wit to flout at Fortune . . ." *As You,* I, ii, 43–44. **2** to be an affront to; insult: "Her silence flouts me, and I'll be reveng'd." *Shrew,* II, i, 29.

—*n.* **3** mocking speech; a jest or verbal thrust: "Bruise me with scorn, confound me with a flout . . ." *Love's L,* V, ii, 397.

flouting Jack, *n.* person who mocks or scoffs (term of contempt): ". . . or do you play the flouting Jack/ to tell us Cupid is a good hare-finder . . . ?" *M Ado,* I, i, 170–171.

flow, *v.* **1** to advance, as an incoming tide; here, to increase one's fortunes: "I am standing water."/ "I'll teach you how to flow." *Temp,* II, i, 216–217. **2** to overflow; here, be carried away by emotions: "You flow to great distraction: come, my lord." *Tr & Cr,* V, ii, 41.
—*n.* **3 take the flow,** to measure the volume: ". . . they take the flow o' the Nile/ By certain scales . . ." *Ant & Cleo,* II, vii, 17–18.

flower-de-luces, *n. pl.* fleurs-de-lis; the fleur-de-lis or fleur-de-lys [iris] was the emblem of France, which had been incorporated on Henry V's coat of arms: "Cropp'd are the flower-de-luces in your arms . . ." *1 Hen 6,* I, i, 80.

flowering, *adj.* youthful: "O serpent heart, hid with a flowering face." *Rom & Jul,* III, ii, 73.

flowery way, *n.* attractive way [through the broad gate] leading to damnation; poss. ref. to the "primrose path": ". . . they'll be for the/ flow'ry way that leads to the broad gate and the/ great fire." *All's W,* IV, v, 50–51.

flowing, *adj.* generous; magnificent: "Does purpose honour to you no less flowing/ Than Marchioness of Pembroke . . ." *Hen 8,* II, iii, 62–63.

flurted, *past. part.* cast aside; rejected: ". . . and now flurted/ By peace, for whom he fought . . ." *Kinsmen,* I, ii, 18–19.

flush, *adj.* **1** in full vigor; also, lusty: "With all his crimes broad blown, as flush as May . . ." *Ham,* III, iii, 81. **2** ripe; auspicious: "Now the time is flush . . ." *Timon,* V, iv, 8.

flushing, *n.* redness; here, inflammation: "Ere yet the salt of most unrighteous tears/ Had left the flushing in her galled eyes . . ." *Ham,* I, ii, 154–155.

flutter, *v.* to put to flight: ". . . like an eagle in a dove-cote, I/ Flutter'd your Volscians in Corioles." *Cor,* V, vi, 114–115.

flux, *n.* **1** flow (of people); crowd: ". . . misery doth part/ The flux of company." *As You,* II, i, 51–52. **2** discharge, as from the body: "Civet is of a baser birth than tar, the very uncleanly flux of a cat." *As You,* III, ii, 65–66.

fluxive, *adj.* flowing: "These often bath'd she in her fluxive eyes . . ." *Lover's Comp,* 50.

fly, *v.* **1** to flee [from]: "The great man down, you mark his favourite flies . . ." *Ham,* III, ii, 199. **2** to escape or avoid: "O Jove! I think/ Foundations fly the wretched . . ." *Cymb,* III, vi, 6–7. **3 fly off,** to become estranged: "To join our kingdoms, and our hearts, and never/ Fly off our loves again!" *Ant & Cleo,* II, ii, 152–153. **4 fly out of itself,** deviate from its normal course: "My valour's poison'd . . . for him [it]/ Shall fly out of itself." *Cor,* I, x, 17–19.

fly-blowing, *n.* **not fear fly-blowing,** Trinculo, being drunk, can expect no harm from flies, which could infest unpickled meat: "I have been in such a pickle . . . I shall not fear fly-blowing." *Temp,* V, i, 282–284.

flying, *n.* **flying at the brook,** hawking at a river or brook [where water fowl gathered]: "Believe me, lords, for flying at the brook,/ I saw not better sport . . ." *2 Hen 6,* II, i, 1–2.

fo, *interj.* See **foh.**

fob, *v.* **fob off,** to put off by deceit: ". . . you must not think/ to fob off our disgrace with a tale . . ." *Cor,* I, i, 92–93.

focative, *adj.* parson's mispron. of "vocative" [indicating one addressed]; combined with "case" makes bawdy pun: "What is the/ focative case, William?" *Wives,* IV, i, 42–43.

foeman, *n.* enemy soldier: ". . . the foeman may with as/ great aim [may just as well] level at the edge of a penknife." *2 Hen 4,* III, ii, 261–262.

foh or **fo,** *interj.* exclam. of disgust: "And fall a-cursing like a very drab,/ A scullion! Fie upon't! Foh!" *Ham,* II, ii, 582–583.

foil[1], *n.* rapier used in fencing: ". . . blunt as the fencer's foils, which hit,/ but hurt not." *M Ado,* V, ii, 13–14.

foil[2], *n.* **1** defeat; setback: "One sudden foil shall never breed distrust." *1 Hen 6,* III, iii, 11. **2** stain or disgrace: ". . . yet must Antony/ No way excuse his foils, when we do bear/ So great weight in his lightness." *Ant & Cleo,* I, iv, 23–25. **3 give the foil [to],** to conquer: "Then take my soul; my body, soul, and all,/ Before that England give the French the foil." *1 Hen 6,* V, iii, 22–23. **4 put it to the foil,** to challenge it [the virtue] and threaten to defeat it: ". . . some defect in her/ Did quarrel with the noblest grace she ow'd,/ And put it to the foil . . ." *Temp,* III, i, 44–46.
—*v.* **5** to overthrow; defeat: "For that I have not wash'd my nose that bled,/ Or foil'd some debile wretch . . ." *Cor,* I, ix, 47–48. **6** to thwart; frustrate: ". . . when light-wing'd toys,/ And feather'd Cupid, foils with wanton dullness/ My speculative and active instruments . . ." *Oth,* I, iii, 268–270. **7** to foul; stain: ". . . and must not foil/ The precious note [eminence] of it . . ." *Cymb,* II, iii, 120–121.

foil³, *n.* thin sheet of metal set behind a jewel for added luster: "The sullen passage of thy weary steps/ Esteem as foil . . . to set/ The precious jewel of thy home return." *Rich 2*, I, iii, 265–267.

foin, *v.* **1** to thrust, esp. in swordplay: ". . . he will foin like any devil, he will spare neither man, woman, nor child." *2 Hen 4*, II, i, 16–17. **2** the same, used frequently in sexual innuendo: ". . . when wilt thou leave fighting a-days, and foining/ a-nights . . ." *2 Hen 4*, II, iv, 228–229.
—*n.* **3** (in fencing) a thrust: "Come; no matter vor [for]/ your foins." *Lear*, IV, vi, 246–247.

foining, *adj.* defensive, rather than attacking; timid or cowardly: "Sir boy, I'll whip you from your foining fence . . ." *M Ado*, V, i, 84.

foison, *n.* rich harvest; hence, esp. in pl., abundance: "Scotland hath foisons to fill up your will . . ." *Mac*, IV, iii, 88.

fold, *v.* **1** to hide; conceal: "I will not . . . fold my fault in cleanly-coin'd excuses . . ." *Luc*, 1072–1073. **2 folds in this orb**, encompasses this globe: ". . . and his fame folds in/ This orb o'th'earth." *Cor*, V, vi, 124–125.
—*n.* **3** embrace: ". . . wanton Cupid/ Shall from your neck unloose his amorous fold . . ." *Tr & Cr*, III, iii, 221–222.

folded, *adj.* hidden; obscure: "The folded meaning of your words' deceit." *Errors*, III, ii, 36.

folded arms, *n.* arms crossed over the breast, betokening the melancholy lover: "Regent of love rhymes, lord of folded arms,/ The anointed sovereign of sighs and groans . . ." *Love's L*, III, i, 176–177.

folio, *n.* **in folio,** in one book; a folio was a book of the largest size: "Devise, wit; write, pen; for I am for whole/ volumes in folio." *Love's L*, I, ii, 174–175.

follow, *v.* **1** to be a follower: "To follow in a house where twice so many/ Have a command to tend you?" *Lear*, II, iv, 264–265. **2** to concern: "Now, fair one, does your business follow us?" *All's W*, II, i, 98. **3** to copy: ". . . she, with pretty and with swimming gait/ Following . . . Would imitate . . ." *M N Dream*, II, i, 130–132. **4 follow our places,** is the privilege of royalty: ". . . and the liberty that/ follows our places stops the mouth of all find-faults . . ." *Hen 5*, V, ii, 287–288. **5 follow your function,** go about your business: "Follow your function, go, and batten on cold bits." *Cor*, IV, v, 34.

followed, *adj.* (of a goal) pursued to its successful conclusion: "O, such a day,/ So fought, so follow'd, and so fairly won . . ." *2 Hen 4*, I, i, 20–21.

follower, *n.* **1** attendant spirit; familiar: "Beware my follower. Peace, Smulkin! peace,/ thou fiend!" *Lear*, III, iv, 144–145. **2** result: ". . . our shame in this/ Are dogg'd with two strange followers." *Tr & Cr*, I, iii, 364–365.

folly, *n.* **1** foolishness: "To Athens will I bear my folly back,/ And follow you no further." *M N Dream*, III, ii, 314–315. **2** stupidity: "And folly—doctor-like [pontificating]—controlling skill . . ." *Sonn 66*, 10. **3** wantonness: ". . . he gives/ her folly motion and advantage . . ." *Wives*, III, ii, 30–31. **4** lust or depravity: "Her sad behaviour feeds his vulture folly . . ." *Luc*, 556. **5** ref. by Laertes to his tears: "I have a speech o' fire that fain would blaze/ But that this folly douts [extinguishes] it." *Ham*, IV, vii, 189–190. **6 his folly's show,** Brutus's appearance of simplemindedness [he had feigned idiocy to escape the fate of his elder brother]: "Brutus . . . Began to clothe his wit in state and pride,/ Burying in Lucrece' wound his folly's show." *Luc*, 1807–1810.

folly-fallen, *adj.* fallen or lapsed into folly: "But wise men, folly-fall'n, quite taint their wit." *T Night*, III, i, 69.

fond, *adj.* **1** doting; infatuated: "How many fond fools serve mad jealousy?" *Errors*, II, i, 116. **2** foolish: "Grant I may never prove so fond,/ To trust man on his oath or bond . . ." *Timon*, I, ii, 64–65. **3** foolishly prized: "Not with fond sickles of the tested gold,/ Or stones . . ." *Meas*, II, ii, 150–151. **4 fond of,** desiring: ". . . she, poor hen, fond of no second brood . . ." *Cor*, V, iii, 162. **5 fond of issue,** prob. despairing of further issue: "Then old, and fond of issue, took such sorrow/ That he quit being [died] . . ." *Cymb*, I, i, 37–38.
—*adv.* **6** foolishly: "Was this fair face the cause, quoth she,/ Why the Grecians sacked Troy?/ Fond done, done fond . . ." *All's W*, I, iii, 67–69.

fondling, *n.* foolish one [a term of endearment]: "'Fondling,' she saith, 'since I have hemm'd thee here/ Within the circuit of this ivory pale . . .'" *Ven & Ad*, 229–230.

fondly, *adv.* foolishly, wildly, or distractedly: "Sorrow and grief of heart/ Makes him speak fondly like a frantic man . . ." *Rich 2*, III, iii, 184–185.

fondness, *n.* **obsequious fondness,** foolish (or mindless) loyalty: ". . . and in obsequious fondness/ Crowd to his presence . . ." *Meas*, II, iv, 28–29.

food and diet, *n.* feed or fodder for the military expedition: ". . . lawless resolutes/ For food and diet to some enterprise . . ." *Ham*, I, i, 101–102.

fool¹, *n.* **1** sweet, unsuspecting innocent: "Tut! She's a lamb, a dove, a fool [compared] to him." *Shrew*, III, ii, 155. **2** toy or plaything; also, a dupe: ". . . we fools of nature/ So horridly to shake our disposition . . ." *Ham,* I, iv, 54–55. **3** term of endearment; here, for Cordelia: "And my poor fool is hang'd! No, no, no life!" *Lear,* V, iii, 305. **4 a fool go with thy soul,** may you be remembered as a fool: "A fool go with thy soul, whither it goes!/ A borrow'd title hast thou bought too dear." *1 Hen 4,* V, iii, 22–23.

—*v.* **5** to mock; play the fool with: ". . . and we/ will fool him black and blue—" *T Night,* II, v, 9–10. **6** to obtain by foolery: "You can fool no more money out of me . . ." *T Night,* V, i, 39. **7 fool me,** force me to play the fool: "[Aside] They fool me to the top of my bent." *Ham,* III, ii, 375. **8 fool me not so much,** make me not such a fool as (to): "If it be you that stirs these daughters' hearts . . . fool me not so much/ To bear it tamely . . ." *Lear,* II, iv, 276–278.

fool², *n.* sweetened custard; here, with obvious pun: "Why, thou full dish of fool, from Troy." *Tr & Cr,* V, i, 9.

fool and feather, *n.* foolishness and fashion; poss. ref. to men's fashion of plumed hats: ". . . leave those remnants/ Of fool and feather that they got in France . . ." *Hen 8,* I, iii, 24–25.

fool-begged, *adj.* labeled a fool; foolish: "This fool-begg'd patience in thee will be left." *Errors,* II, i, 41.

foolery, *n.* folly; foolishness: "And manhood is call'd foolery when it stands/ Against a falling fabric." *Cor,* III, i, 244–245.

foolish, *adj.* modest or humble: "We have a trifling foolish banquet towards." *Rom & Jul,* I, v, 121.

foolish-compounded, *adj.* foolishly made; here, of clay: "The brain/ of this foolish-compounded clay, man, is not able to/ invent anything that intends to laughter more than I/ invent . . ." *2 Hen 4,* I, ii, 5–7.

foolish thing, *n.* mischievous child: "A foolish thing was but a toy . . ." *T Night,* V, i, 390.

foot, *n.* **1** ability to move or, sometimes, to dance: ". . . a good leg and a good foot, uncle, and money/ enough in his purse . . ." *M Ado,* II, i, 13–14. **2** foot soldiers; infantrymen: ". . . our foot/ Upon the hills adjoining to the city/ Shall stay with us . . ." *Ant & Cleo,* IV, x, 4–6. **3** footing; here, status: "A foot of honour better than I was,/ But many a many foot of land the worse." *K John,* I, i, 182–183. **4 at foot,** close behind: "Follow him at foot. Tempt him with speed aboard . . ." *Ham,* IV, iii, 57. **5 attend the foot,** to follow or serve: "The king hath dispossess'd himself of us:/ We will not line his thin bestained cloak/ With our pure honours, nor attend the foot/ That leaves the print of blood where'er it walks." *K John,* IV, iii, 23–27. **6 le foot,** Katharine appar. mistakes the English word "foot" for French "foutre" [fuck]: "Le foot, et le count? O Seigneur Dieu!" *Hen 5,* III, iv, 52. **7 My foot my tutor?**

Am I to be instructed by my inferior? [Prospero's reaction to his daughter's pleas on behalf of Ferdinand]: "What! I say,/ My foot my tutor? Put thy sword up, traitor . . ." *Temp,* I, ii, 472–473. **8 on foot, a.** in motion; begun: "Methinks I see this hurly all on foot . . ." *K John,* III, iii, 169. **b.** standing; here, undefeated: "And 'tis this fever that keeps Troy on foot . . ." *Tr & Cr,* I, iii, 135. **9 set foot under thy table,** See **table** (def. 6). **10 the better foot before,** as fast as possible: "Nay, but make haste: the better foot before!" *K John,* IV, ii, 170.

—*v.* **11** (on a stocking) to add a foot to: "I'll sew nether-stocks, and mend/ them and foot them too." *1 Hen 4,* II, iv, 113–114. **12** to kick: "You that did void your rheum upon my beard,/ And foot me as you spurn a stranger cur . . ." *Merch,* I, iii, 112–113. **13** (of an eagle) to grab with the talons: ". . . the holy eagle/ Stoop'd, as to foot us . . ." *Cymb,* V, iv, 115–116. **14** to walk about: "Take heed; have open eye; for thieves do foot by night . . ." *Wives,* II, i, 120. **15 foot it,** to dance: "Foot it featly here and there . . ." *Temp,* I, ii, 381.

football, *n.* round, inflated, leather-covered bladder, propelled with the feet in competitive games: "Am I so round with you . . . That like a football you do spurn me thus?" *Errors,* II, i, 82–83.

foot-ball player, *n.* any of a group of young ruffians who played soccerlike games in the streets of London and were regarded as nuisances: "I'll not be strucken, my Lord."/ "Nor tripp'd neither, you base foot-ball player." *Lear,* I, iv, 90–91.

foot-boy or **footboy,** *n.* servant who followed on foot his master riding on horseback; lackey: "Like peasant foot-boys do they keep the walls . . ." *1 Hen 6,* III, ii, 69.

foot-cloth, *n.* **1** ornamental cloth covering the back of a horse and extending to the ground on both sides: "Thou dost ride in a/ foot-cloth, dost thou not?" *2 Hen 6,* IV, vii, 44–45.
—*adj.* **2** decorated with such trappings: "And bare-head plodded by my foot-cloth mule . . ." *2 Hen 6,* IV, i, 54.

footed, *adj.* landed; here, ref. to French army on English soil: ". . . there is part/ of a power already footed . . ." *Lear,* III, iii, 13–14.

footing, *n.* **1** footsteps or footfall: "But hark, I hear the footing of a man." *Merch,* V, i, 24. **2** dancing: ". . . these fresh nymphs encounter every one/ In country footing." *Temp,* IV, i, 137–138. **3** foothold; also, wordplay on "charity without funding": ". . . there your charity would have lacked/ footing." *W Tale,* III, iii, 109–110.

foot-landraker, *n.* another name for *footpad,* a highwayman who works on foot: "I am joined with no foot-landrakers,/ no long-staff sixpenny strikers . . ." *1 Hen 4,* II, i, 72–73.

footman, *n.* foot soldier: "Distract your army, which doth most consist/ Of war-mark'd footmen . . ." *Ant & Cleo,* III, vii, 43–44.

foot of fear, *n.* panic-stricken flight: ". . . all his men/ Upon the foot of fear, fled with the rest . . ." *1 Hen 4,* V, v, 19–20.

foot of motion, *n.* beginning of an action: "Nor our strong sorrow/ Upon the foot of motion." *Mac,* II, iii, 124–125.

fop, *n.* **1** fool: ". . . a whole tribe of fops,/ Got 'tween asleep and wake?" *Lear,* I, ii, 14–15.
—*v.* **2** var. of **fob;** to dupe; swindle: "I say 'tis very scurvy, and begin/ to find myself fopp'd in it." *Oth,* IV, ii, 195–196.

foppery, *n.* **1** foolishness: "I had as lief have the foppery of freedom/ as the morality of imprisonment." *Meas,* I, ii, 125–126. **2** folly; stupidity: "This is the excellent foppery of the world . . ." *Lear,* I, ii, 124. **3** deceit: ". . . drove the grossness of the foppery into a/ received belief . . ." *Wives,* V, v, 125–126.

foppish, *adj.* foolish: "For wise men are grown foppish,/ And know not how their wits to wear . . ." *Lear,* I, iv, 174–175.

for, *conj.* **1** because: "And for I know your reverend ages love/ Security . . ." *Timon,* III, v, 81–82. **2** so that: "And, for I should not deal in her soft laws,/ She did corrupt frail Nature . . ." *3 Hen 6,* III, ii, 154–155. **3 for and,** perh. sense of "and what's more": "A pickaxe and a spade, a spade,/ For and a shrouding-sheet . . ." *Ham,* V, i, 92–93. **4 for because,** because: "And for because the world is populous,/ And here is not a creature but myself . . ." *Rich II,* V, v, 3–4. **5 for that, a.** because: "The other part reserv'd I by consent,/ For that my sovereign liege was in my debt . . ." *Rich 2,* I, i, 128–129. **b.** in order that: "For that our kingdom's earth should not be soil'd/ With that dear blood which it hath fostered . . ." *Rich 2,* I, iii, 125–126. **6 for the,** for the lack of the: ". . . for the counsel of my son and queen,/ I am amaz'd with matter." *Cymb,* IV, iii, 27–28. **7 for to,** to: ". . . though bride and bridegroom wants [are lacking]/ For to supply the places at the table . . ." *Shrew,* III, ii, 244–245. **8 for why,** because: "For why, the fools are mad, if left alone." *Two Gent,* III, i, 99.
—*prep.* **9** because of; due to: "In bed he slept not for my urging it,/ At board he fed not for my urging it . . ." *Errors,* V, i, 63–64. **10** by: "Master, for my hand,/ Both our inventions meet and jump in one." *Shrew,* I, i, 189–190. **11** with respect to: "Your worm is your only emperor for diet . . ." *Ham,* IV, iii, 21. **12** from: ". . . advise thee to desist/ For going on death's net . . ." *Per,* I, i, 40–41. **13** during; throughout: ". . . urchins/ Shall, for that vast of night that they may work,/ All exercise on thee . . ." *Temp,* I, ii, 328–330. **14** [so as] to summon: "Come, stretch thy chest, and let thy eyes spout blood:/ Thou blowest for Hector." *Tr & Cr,* IV, v, 10–11. **15** as being: ". . . here abjure/

The taints and blames I laid upon myself,/ For strangers to my nature." *Mac,* IV, iii, 123–125. **16** in the same way as; in the character of: "For canker vice the sweetest buds doth love . . ." *Sonn 70,* 7. **17** as for: ". . . for our hearts/ He knows no more of mine than I of yours . . ." *Rich 3,* III, iv, 10–11. **18** rather than; in place of: "In duty lower than the ground I kneel,/ And for my dull knees bow my feeling heart . . ." *Edw 3,* I, ii, 107–108. **19** the reason for; purpose of: "Now for ourself, and for this time of meeting . . ." *Ham,* I, ii, 26. **20** because of the lack of: ". . . we shall/ not shortly have a rasher on the coals for money." *Merch,* III, v, 22–23. **21** that which precedes: ". . . so bad a prayer as his/ Was never yet for sleep." *Ant & Cleo,* IV, ix, 26–27. **22 for me,** on my part: ". . . what store of parting tears were shed?"/ "Faith, none for me . . ." *Rich 2,* I, iv, 5–6. **23 I am for thee,** I am ready for you: "I am for thee straight. Take thou the bill, give me/ thy mete-yard . . ." *Shrew,* IV, iii, 149–150.
—*interj.* **24 for O,** alas!: ". . . 'For O, for O, the hobby-horse is forgot." *Ham,* III, ii, 133.

forage, *v.* **1** to prey on: "Stood smiling to behold his lion's whelp/ Forage in blood of French nobility." *Hen 5,* I, ii, 109–110. **2** to seek [prey] beyond the local confines: ". . . forage, and run/ To meet displeasure farther from the doors . . ." *K John,* V, i, 59–60.

foragement, *n.* prey or quarry: "The lion doth become his bloody jaws,/ And grace his foragement by being mild . . ." *Edw 3,* II, i, 396–397.

forager, *n.* (usually pl.) members of an army assigned to search for provisions: ". . . not like the hive/ To whom the foragers shall all repair . . ." *Tr & Cr,* I, iii, 81–82.

forbear, *v.* **1** to suffer; put up with: ". . . let me entreat you/ To forbear the absence of your king . . ." *Per,* II, iv, 45–46. **2** to cease or abstain from: "My lords, forbear this talk; here comes the King." *3 Hen 6,* IV, i, 6. **3** to avoid; stay away from: "[Aside to Men.] Forbear me till anon." *Ant & Cleo,* II, vii, 39. **4** to withdraw; here, an order: "Forbear, Seleucus. [Exit Seleucus.]" *Ant & Cleo,* V, ii, 174. **5 forbear him,** [to] get away from him; leave him alone: "O, he is mad, Laertes."/ "For love of God forbear him." *Ham,* V, i, 267–268.

forbid, *adj.* **1** under a spell or curse; cursed: "He shall live a man forbid." *Mac,* I, iii, 21.
—*v.* **2** forbidden: "This courtesy, forbid thee, shall the Duke/ Instantly know . . ." *Lear,* III, iii, 23–24.

forbod, *v.* old past tense of **forbid;** forbade: "My bloody judge forbod my tongue to speak . . ." *Luc,* 1648.

forbode, *v.* old past part. of **forbid;** forbidden: "To be forebode the sweets that seems so good . . ." *Lover's Comp,* 164.

force[1], *n.* **1 of force,** of necessity; perforce: "Good reasons must of force give place to better." *J Caes,* IV, iii, 202.
—*v.* **2** to value: "For me, I force not argument a straw [care nothing for argument] . . ." *Luc,* 1021. **3** to enforce: ". . . thus can make him bite the law by th'nose/ When he would force it?" *Meas,* III, i, 108–109. **4 force not,** to find it easy (to do something): "Your oath once broke, you force not to forswear." *Love's L,* V, ii, 440.

force[2], *v.* **1** to stuff: "Force him/ with praises—pour in, pour in, his ambition is dry." *Tr & Cr,* II, iii, 223–224. **2** to compel; perh. also an element of preceding "stuff": "Linger your patience on; and we'll digest/ Th' abuse of distance; force a play." *Hen 5,* II, Chor., 31–32.

forced, *adj.* **1** reinforced: "Were they not forc'd with those that should be ours . . ." *Mac,* V, v, 5. **2** stuffed: ". . . should wit/ larded with malice and malice forced with wit/ turn him to?" *Tr & Cr,* V, i, 56–58. **3** contrived: "Of deaths put on by cunning and forc'd cause . . ." *Ham,* V, ii, 388. **4** wrongfully imposed: ". . . that forced baseness/ Which he has put upon 't!" *W Tale,* II, iii, 78–79. **5** farfetched: "With these forc'd thoughts, I prithee, darken not/ The mirth o' th' feast." *W Tale,* IV, iv, 41–42.

forceless, *adj.* **1** lacking strength or force; weak: "These forceless flowers like sturdy trees support me." *Ven & Ad,* 152. **2** done with reckless ease; effortless: ". . . redeeming of himself/ With such a careless [easygoing] force and forceless care . . ." *Tr & Cr,* V, vi, 39–40.

force perforce, *adv.* **1** by force of circumstances; inevitably or unavoidably: "The King that lov'd him . . . Was force perforce compell'd to banish him . . ." *2 Hen 4,* IV, i, 115–116. **2** by force or violence: ". . . and force perforce/ Keep Stephen Langton, chosen archbishop/ Of Canterbury, from that holy see . . ." *K John,* III, i, 68–70.

fordid, *v.* past tense of **fordo;** destroyed; killed: "To lay the blame upon her own despair,/ That she fordid herself." *Lear,* V, iii, 254–255.

fordo, *v.* to undo; destroy: ". . . the very ecstasy of love,/ Whose violent property fordoes itself . . ." *Ham,* II, i, 102–103.

fordone, past part. of **fordo. 1** exhausted: "Whilst the heavy ploughman snores,/ All with weary task fordone." *M N Dream,* V, i, 359–360. **2** destroyed; killed: "Your eldest daughters have fordone themselves . . ." *Lear,* V, iii, 291.

fore-bemoaned, *adj.* previously lamented: "The sad account of fore-bemoaned moan . . ." *Sonn 30,* ll.

forecast, *n.* foresight: "Alas, that Warwick had no more forecast . . ." *3 Hen 6,* V, i, 42.

fore-end, *n.* earlier part or period: ". . . paid/ More pious debts to heaven than in all/ The fore-end of my time." *Cymb,* III, iii, 71–73.

foregone, *adj.* past; bygone; also, vanished: "Then can I grieve at grievances foregone . . ." *Sonn 30,* 9.

foregone conclusion, *n.* earlier consummation; here, an act that has already been committed: "Nay, this was but his dream."/ "But this denoted a foregone conclusion." *Oth,* III, iii, 433–434.

forehand or **fore-hand,** *n.* **1** more favorable circumstances: "Had the fore-hand and vantage of a king." *Hen 5,* IV, i, 286. **2** main source of strength; "right hand": "The great Achilles, whom opinion crowns/ The sinew and the forehand of our host . . ." *Tr & Cr,* I, iii, 142–143.

forehand shaft, *n.* arrow aimed directly at the target: ". . . and carried/ you a forehand shaft a fourteen and fourteen and a/ half [score yards] . . ." *2 Hen 4,* III, ii, 46–48.

forehead, *n.* **forehead of the morning,** early hours of the day: ". . . converses/ more with the buttock of the night than with the/ forehead of the morning." *Cor,* II, i, 51–52.

forehorse, *n.* leader of a group of horses, often brightly decorated: "I shall stay here the forehorse to a smock . . ." *All's W,* II, i, 30.

foreign, *adj.* **1** unrelated by blood: "I love the king your father and yourself/ With more than foreign heart." *Per,* IV, i, 32–33. **2** one employed abroad: "And fearing he would rise . . . Kept him a foreign man still [regularly employed abroad] . . ." *Hen 8,* II, ii, 127–128.

fore-past, *adj.* previous; former: "My fore-past proofs . . . Shall tax my fears of little vanity . . ." *All's W,* V, iii, 121–122.

fore-rank, *n.* that or those foremost: "She is our capital demand, compris'd/ Within the fore-rank of our articles." *Hen 5,* V, ii, 96–97.

forerun, *v.* to serve as a forerunner to; precede or herald: "For revels, dances, masks, and merry hours,/ Forerun fair Love . . ." *Love's L,* IV, iii, 375–376.

forerunner, *n.* messenger: ". . . there is a forerunner come from a fifth,/ the Prince of Morocco . . ." *Merch,* I, ii, 118–119.

foresaid, *adj.* aforesaid; mentioned before: ". . . to recover of us by strong hand/ And terms compulsatory those foresaid lands . . ." *Ham,* I, i, 105–106.

foresay, *v.* to will; order: "Let ordinance/ Come as the gods foresay it . . ." *Cymb,* IV, ii, 145–146.

foreshow, *v.* to divulge; indicate: ". . . your looks foreshow/ You have a gentle heart." *Per,* IV, i, 85–86.

foreskirt, *n.* front bottom part of a coat, esp. a man's doublet: ". . . honour's train/ Is longer than his foreskirt [blessings to come will be even greater than these] . . ." *Hen 8,* II, iii, 97–98.

forespent, *past part.* **1** previously bestowed: "And towards himself, his goodness forespent on us,/ We must extend our notice." *Cymb,* II, iii, 58–59. **2** See **forspent** (def. 1). **3 vanities forespent,** early or former follies: ". . . you shall find his vanities forespent/ Were but the outside of the Roman Brutus . . ." *Hen 5,* II, iv, 36–37.

fore-spurrer, *n.* forerunner; harbinger: "A day in April never came so sweet . . . As this fore-spurrer comes before his lord." *Merch,* II, ix, 93–95.

forest, *adj.* living in the forest; untamed: "Whose hand is that the forest bear doth lick?" *3 Hen 6,* II, ii, 13.

forestall, *v.* to deprive; here, prove fatal to: ". . . may/ This night forestall him of [before] the coming day!" *Cymb,* III, v, 69–70.

Forest of Arden, *n.* fanciful place, perh. hinting at the area in Warwickshire known as Arden, near Shakespeare's birthplace: "Why, whither shall we go?"/ "To seek my uncle in the Forest of Arden." *As You,* I, iii, 102–103.

forestalled remission, *n.* beggarly pardon asked before an offense has been committed: "And never shall you see that I will beg/ A ragged and forestall'd remission." *2 Hen 4,* V, ii, 37–38.

forethink, *v.* to anticipate; count on: ". . . the soul of every man/ Prophetically do forethink thy fall." *1 Hen 4,* III, ii, 37–38.

fore-vouched, *adj.* previously affirmed: ". . . your fore-vouch'd affection/ Fall into taint . . ." *Lear,* I, i, 220–221.

foreward, *n.* forefront; vanguard: "My foreward shall be drawn out all in length . . ." *Rich 3,* V, iii, 294.

forewarning, *adj.* **well forewarning,** accurately predicting: "What boded this, but well forewarning wind . . ." *2 Hen 6,* III, ii, 84.

forfeit, *adj.* **1** subject [to]: "Supposed as forfeit to a confined doom." *Sonn 107,* 4. **2** in a state of forfeiture: "Why this bond is forfeit,/ And lawfully by this the Jew may claim/ A pound of flesh . . ." *Merch,* IV, i, 226–228. **3** guilty of a transgression: "Why, all the souls that were, were forfeit once . . ." *Meas,* II, ii, 73.
—*n.* **4** person condemned to death: "Your brother is a forfeit of the law . . ." *Meas,* II, ii, 71. **5** remission of the forfeit: ". . . what is it thou demand'st."/ "The forfeit, Sovereign, of my servant's life . . ." *Rich 3,* II, i, 99–100. **6** man mortally wounded in combat: ". . . I have seen thee . . . spur thy Phrygian steed,/ Despising many forfeits and subduements . . ." *Tr & Cr,* IV, v, 184–186. **7** penalty; here, ref. to humorous lists of fines or punishments posted by barbers for rowdy behavior in their shops: ". . . the strong statutes/ Stand like the forfeits in a barber's shop,/ As much in mock as mark." *Meas,* V, i, 318–320.

forfeited, *adj.* having one's property, estates, etc., confiscated: ". . . suffer'd his kinsman March . . . to be engag'd in Wales,/ There without ransom to lie forfeited . . ." *1 Hen 4,* IV, iii, 93–96.

forfend, *v.* to forbid: "O forfend it, God,/ That in a Christian climate souls refin'd/ Should show so heinous . . . a deed!" *Rich 2,* IV, i, 129–131.

forfended, *adj.* forbidden; ref. here to Goneril's bed: "But have you never found my brother's way/ To the forfended place?" *Lear,* V, i, 10–11.

forge, *v.* **1** to counterfeit: "Till forging nature be condemn'd of treason . . ." *Ven & Ad,* 729. **2** to invent; concoct: "Whate'er I forge to feed his brain-sick humours,/ Do you uphold . . ." *T Andr,* V, ii, 71–72.

forged process, *n.* false, esp. fabricated, account: ". . . the whole ear of Denmark/ Is by a forged process of my death/ Rankly abus'd . . ." *Ham,* I, v, 36–38.

forgery, *n.* **1** invention; concoction; fabrication: "These are the forgeries of jealousy . . ." *M N Dream,* II, i, 81. **2** deception or lie: ". . . untutor'd youth,/ Unskilful in the world's false forgeries." *Pass Pil,* I, 3–4. **3** act of imagining: "That I in forgery of shapes and tricks/ Come short of what he did." *Ham,* IV, vii, 88–89.

forget, *v.* to lose sight of: "The latter end of his commonwealth forgets the/ beginning." *Temp,* II, i, 153–154.

forgetive, *adj.* inventive; creative or imaginative: ". . . quick, forgetive, full of nimble, fiery, and delectable/ shapes . . ." *2 Hen 4,* IV, iii, 98–99.

fork, *n.* **1** forked tongue: "Adder's fork, and blind-worm's sting,/ Lizard's leg, and howlet's wing . . ." *Mac,* IV, i, 16–17. **2** pointed head of an arrow: "Let it fall rather, though the fork invade/ The region of my heart . . ." *Lear,* I, i, 144–145. **3** [pl.] the legs: ". . . yond simp'ring dame,/ Whose face between her forks presages snow [appears as chaste as ice] . . ." *Lear,* IV, vi, 120–121.

forked, *adj.* **1** two-legged: ". . . a poor, bare, forked animal/ as thou art." *Lear,* III, iv, 110–111. **2** preceding in wordplay with "horned" [cuckolded]: ". . . 'which of these hairs is Paris/ my husband?' 'The forked one,' quoth he . . ." *Tr & Cr,* I, ii, 165–166. **3** double-dealing: ". . . o'er head and ears a fork'd one." *W Tale,* I, ii, 186. **4 forked plague,** cuckold's disease: "Even then this forked plague is fated to us,/ When we do quicken . . ." *Oth,* III, iii, 280–281.

forlorn, *adj.* **1** thin; meager: "A was so forlorn, that his/ dimensions to any thick sight [dimmed vision] were invisible . . ." *2 Hen 4,* III, ii, 306–307. **2** outcast: "To hovel thee with swine and rogues forlorn . . ." *Lear,* IV, vii, 39. **3** wretched; vile: "Speak, Captain, shall I stab the forlorn swain?" *2 Hen 6,* IV, i, 65. **4 in thine own law forlorn,** unhappy in love, where she [Venus] makes the rules: "Poor queen of love, in thine own law forlorn . . ." *Ven & Ad,* 251.

—*n.* **5** one forsaken or abandoned; an outcast: ". . . a banish'd man,/ And forc'd to live in Scotland a forlorn . . ." *3 Hen 6,* III, iii, 25–26.

form, *n.* **1** law and order: "For now a time is come to mock at form . . ." *2 Hen 4,* IV, v, 118. **2** formal manners; strict etiquette: "This is the ape of form, monsieur the nice . . ." *Love's L,* V, ii, 325. **3** dignity: "O place, O form,/ How often dost thou with thy case, thy habit,/ Wrench awe from fools . . ." *Meas,* II, iv, 12–14. **4** behavior; demeanor: "Brutus, this sober form of yours hides wrongs . . ." *J Caes,* IV, ii, 40. **5** ideal manly behavior: "The glass of fashion and the mould of form . . ." *Ham,* III, i, 155. **6** external appearance: "Nothing of that wonderful promise, to read/ him by his form . . ." *T Night,* III, iv, 268–269. **7** semblance or likeness: "Thou canst not, love, disgrace me half so ill,/ To set a form upon desired change . . ." *Sonn 89,* 5–6. **8** image or reflection: ". . . the glasses where they view themselves,/ Which are as easy broke as they make forms." *Meas,* II, iv, 124–125. **9** [often pl.] an image carried in the mind; memory: "All saws of books, all forms, all pressures past/ That youth and observation copied there . . ." *Ham,* I, v, 100–101. **10** painting, drawing, or other likeness: "There take it prince, and if my form lie there/ Then I am yours!"

Merch, II, vii, 61–62. **11** ritual or ceremony in wordplay with "method or result": "Their form confounded makes most form in mirth . . ." *Love's L,* V, ii, 513–514. **12** [usually pl.] ceremonies: "In all his dressings, caracts, titles, forms . . ." *Meas,* V, i, 59. **13** proper manner, shape, or pattern: ". . . this ornament/ [which] Makes me look dismal will I clip to form . . ." *Per,* V, iii, 73–74. **14** order; here, arrangement of her hair: "I will not keep this form upon my head,/ When there is such disorder in my wit." *K John,* III, iii, 101–102. **15** bench: "I was seen with her in the manor-house, sitting with/ her upon the form . . ." *Love's L,* I, i, 203–204. **16** formality; here, according to law: ". . . we may not pass upon his life/ Without the form of justice . . ." *Lear,* III, vii, 24–25. **17** mere show: "That sir which serves and seeks for gain,/ And follows but for form . . ." *Lear,* II, iv, 78–79. **18** social position; rank; station: ". . . whom I from meaner form/ Have bench'd and rear'd to worship . . ." *W Tale,* I, ii, 313–314. **19 bring into form,** to make acceptable or even admirable: ". . . as if they labour'd/ To bring manslaughter into form . . ." *Timon,* III, v, 26–27. **20 form and favor,** prescribed behavior and status: "Have I not seen dwellers on form and favour/ Lose all . . ." *Sonn 125,* 5–6. **21 his form and pressure,** its exact representation; lit., an impression stamped in wax: ". . . the very age/ and body of the time his [its] form and pressure." *Ham,* III, ii, 23–24. **22 set one's form,** to impress or imprint oneself: "How easy is it for the proper false/ In women's waxen hearts to set their forms!" *T Night,* II, i, 28–29. **23 take form,** take a stamped impression, as hot metal does: "Now 'twill take form, the heats are gone to-morrow." *Kinsmen,* I, i, 152. **24 well-balanced form,** observance of formalities: "By cold gradation and well-balanc'd form,/ We shall proceed with Angelo." *Meas,* IV, iii, 99–100. **25 with each other's form,** from each other's point of view: ". . . but eye to eye oppos'd/ Salutes each other with each other's form . . ." *Tr & Cr,* III, iii, 107–108.

formal, *adj.* **1** normal or sane: ". . . I will not let him stir/ Till I have us'd the approved means I have . . . To make of him a formal man again." *Errors,* V, i, 102–105. **2** meticulous; precise: "Are you so formal, sir? Well, I must wait—" *Shrew,* III, i, 59.

formal capacity, *n.* See **capacity** (def. 2).

formal constancy, *n.* dignified bearing: ". . . bear it as our Roman actors do,/ With untir'd spirits and formal constancy . . ." *J Caes,* II, i, 226–227.

former, *adj.* foremost: ". . . on our former ensign/ Two mighty eagles fell . . ." *J Caes,* V, i, 80–81.

Forres, *n.* Scottish town, northeast of Inverness: "How far is't call'd to Forres?" *Mac,* I, iii, 39.

forsake, *v.* **1** to deny: "Thou hast power to choose, and they none to forsake." *All's W,* II, iii, 56. **2** to refuse: "Shall lay your stately and air-braving towers,/ If you forsake the offer of their love." *1 Hen 6,* IV, ii, 13–14. **3** to leave [the body]: ". . . till my soul forsake/ Shall cry for blessings on him." *Hen 8,* II, i, 89–90.

forslow, *v.* to delay: "Forslow no longer; make we hence amain." *3 Hen 6,* II, iii, 56.

forsooth, *adv.* truly: "He will forsooth have all my prisoners . . ." *I Hen 4,* I, iii, 138.

forspeak, *v.* to speak [out] against: "Thou hast forspoke my being in these wars . . ." *Ant & Cleo,* III, vii, 3.

forspent, *adj.* **1** exhausted: "After him came spurring hard/ A gentleman almost forspent with speed . . ." *2 Hen 4,* I, i, 36–37. **2** See **forespent** (def. 1).

forswear, *v.* **1** to renounce; swear off: "I have forsworn his company/ hourly . . ." *1 Hen 4,* II, ii, 15–16. **2** to deny, esp. under oath: ". . . he mended thus,/ By now forswearing that he is forsworn." *1 Hen 4,* V, ii, 37–38. **3 forswear't,** swear not to do it: ". . . since/ Nor brass, nor stone, nor parchment bears not one,/ Let villainy itself forswear't." *W Tale,* I, ii, 359–361. **4 forswore myself,** cheated: "I never/ prospered since I forswore myself at primero." *Wives,* IV, v, 95–96.

forsworn, *adj.* **1** guilty of breaking one's vow; perjured: "In loving thee thou knowst I am forsworn." *Sonn 152,* 1. **2** falsely sworn: "Of his oath-breaking; which he mended thus,/ By now forswearing that he is forsworn . . ." *1 Hen 4,* V, ii, 37–38. **3** denied; refused: "Trust to't, bethink you. I'll not be forsworn." *Rom & Jul,* III, v, 195.

forted, *adj.* fortified: "A forted residence 'gainst the tooth of time . . ." *Meas,* V, i, 13.

forth, *v.* **1** to go forth; depart: "So soon as dinner's done, we'll forth again . . ." *Timon,* II, i, 17.
—*adv.* **2** out; away [from home, etc.]: "Say he dines forth, and let no creature enter." *Errors,* II, ii, 210. **3** from this place; here, from the cave: ". . . the boy Fidele's sickness/ Did make my way long forth." *Cymb,* IV, ii, 148–149. **4** put or set forth: ". . . his best force/ Is forth to man his galleys." *Ant & Cleo,* IV, xi, 2–3. **5 forth of,** out of; away from: "To breakfast once, forth of my company." *Rich 3,* IV, iv, 177. **6 go forth of,** precede: ". . . if our virtues/ Did not go forth of us, 'twere all alike . . ." *Meas,* I, i, 33–34. **7 lock (someone) forth,** to lock (someone) out: "Say, wherefore didst thou lock me forth to-day . . ." *Errors,* IV, iv, 93. **8 make forth,** to go forward: "Make forth; the generals would have some words." *J Caes,* V, i, 25.

—*prep.* **9** beyond; out of: ". . . raise this tedious siege/ And drive the English forth the bounds of France." *1 Hen 6,* I, ii, 53–54.

forthcoming, *adj.* **1** used in court as evidence: "We'll see your trinkets here all forthcoming." *2 Hen 6,* I, iv, 52. **2** arrested and soon to be tried: "Your lady is forthcoming yet at London." *2 Hen 6,* II, i, 171.

forth-right or forthright, *n.* straight path, in contrast to a "meander" [winding path]: ". . . here's a maze trod, indeed,/ Through forth-rights and meanders!" *Temp,* III, iii, 2–3.

forthwith, *adv.* at once; without delay: "Take leave and part, for you must part forthwith." *Rich 2,* V, i, 70.

fortify, *v.* **1** to make plans; build expectations: ". . . or else/ We fortify in paper and in figures . . ." *2 Hen 4,* I, iii, 55–56. **2** to shield; protect: ". . . a platted hive of straw,/ Which fortified her visage from the sun . . ." *Lover's Comp,* 8–9.

fortitude, *n.* **1** strength; here, prob., fortifications: "Othello, the fortitude of the place is/ best known to you . . ." *Oth,* I, iii, 222–223. **2 arm's fortitude,** armed might: "Despairing of his own arm's fortitude,/ To join with witches and the help of hell!" *1 Hen 6,* II, i, 17–18.

fortuna de la guerra, [Italian] the fortune(s) of war: ". . . we will put it, as/ they say, to *fortuna de la guerra.*" *Love's L,* V, ii, 525–526.

fortunate, *adj.* blessed by fortune; here, victorious: "Then on, my lords; and France be fortunate." *1 Hen 6,* V, ii, 21.

fortune, *n.* **1** story of one's life; one's past: "The residue of your fortune,/ Go to my cave and tell me." *As You,* II, vii, 199–200. **2** chance or accident: "Petruchio means but well,/ Whatever fortune stays him from his word." *Shrew,* III, ii, 22–23. **3** good luck: ". . . fortune now/ To my heart's hope!" *Merch,* II, ix, 19–20. **4** [pl.] triumphs: "O, such a day . . . Came not till now to dignify the times/ Since Caesar's fortunes!" *2 Hen 4,* I, i, 20–23. **5** [cap.] fate, whose spinning wheel randomly determines earthly events; here, likened to a housewife: "Let us sit and mock the good hussif Fortune from/ her wheel . . ." *As You,* I, ii, 30–31. **6 at Fortune's alms,** as a small act of Fortune's charity: ". . . content your lord, who hath receiv'd you/ At Fortune's alms . . ." *Lear,* I, i, 277–278. **7 eldest son of fortune,** ref. to Wolsey's behavior like Fortune's eldest son, dictating others' fates: ". . . like the eldest son of fortune,/ Turns what he list." *Hen 8,* II, ii, 20–21. **8 fortune on,** advantage or victory over: "But what art thou/ That hast this fortune on me?" *Lear,* V, iii, 164–165. **9 hold (someone) under fortune,** to prevent (a person) from achieving his just deserts: ". . . it was he, in the times past, which held you/ So under fortune, which you thought had been/ Our innocent self?" *Mac*, III, i, 76–78. **10 in fortune's tender,** when good fortune is offered: "A whining mammet, in her fortune's tender,/ To answer 'I'll not wed . . . '" *Rom & Jul*, III, v, 183–185. **11 put to one's fortune,** force one to take his chances: ". . . would put you to your fortune and/ The hazard of much blood." *Cor*, III, ii, 60–61. **12 take thy fortunes up,** happily receive your fortunes: "Cesario, take thy fortunes up,/ Be that thou know'st thou art . . ." *T Night*, V, i, 146–147. **13 work myself a former fortune,** restore my fortunes to their former height: "[Aside] I am glad thou hast set thy mercy and thy honour/ At difference in thee. Out of that I'll work/ Myself a former fortune." *Cor*, V, iii, 200–202. —*v.* **14** to occur: "That you will wonder what hath fortuned." *Two Gent*, V, iv, 167. **15** to award the proper fortune to: ". . . therefore, dear/ Isis, keep decorum, and fortune him accordingly!" *Ant & Cleo*, I, ii, 70–71.

fortune's dearest spite, *n.* fate's most malicious blow: "So I, made lame by fortune's dearest spite . . ." *Sonn 37*, 3.

forty pence, *n.* usual amount of small bet or fee: "How tastes it/ Is it bitter? Forty pence, no [I'll wager 40 pence it's not] . . ." *Hen 8*, II, iii, 89.

forward, *adj.* **1** blooming early; hence, premature: "A violet in the youth of primy nature,/ Forward, not permanent . . ." *Ham*, I, iii, 7–8. **2** promising or precocious; also, bold and impudent: "A very forward March-chick!" *M Ado*, I, iii, 52. **3** aggressive; fearless: ". . . his forward spirit/ Would lift him where most trade of danger rang'd." *2 Hen 4*, I, i, 173–174. **4** willing; inclined or eager: "Nor do we find him forward to be sounded . . ." *Ham*, III, i, 7. **5** prepared for future contingencies: "Our expectation that it would be thus/ Hath made us forward." *Cymb*, III, v, 28–29. **6** situated in front: "His forward voice, now, is to speak well of his/ friend . . ." *Temp*, II, ii, 92–93. **7** facing or exposed to the enemy: "Whoever charges on his forward breast . . ." *All's W*, III, ii, 113. **8** preparing: "A kind and voluntary gift thou proferest,/ That I was forward to have begged of thee." *Edw 3*, II, i, 300–301. **9 forward of,** intent on: "I have not been . . . forward of revenge, though they much err'd." *3 Hen 6*, IV, viii, 44–46. **10 forward upon his party,** enthusiastically supporting his cause: "Ay . . . and hopes to find you forward/ Upon his party for the gain thereof . . ." *Rich 3*, III, ii, 45–46.

forwardness, *n.* **1** eagerness; zeal: "Gloucester, why doubt'st thou of my forwardness?" *1 Hen 6*, I, i, 100. **2** readiness: "This forwardness/ Makes our hopes fair." *Cymb*, IV, ii, 342–343.

forward top, *n.* lock of hair at the front of the head; forelock: "Let's take the instant by the forward top . . ." *All's W*, V, iii, 39.

forwearied, *adj.* **forwearied in,** worn out by: ". . . whose labour'd spirits/ Forwearied in this action of swift speed . . ." *K John*, II, i, 232–233.

foster, *v.* to nurse; rear; nourish: ". . . like a lion foster'd up at hand,/ It may lie gently at the foot of peace . . ." *K John*, V, ii, 75–76.

fostering, *adj.* sustaining: ". . . my soul's earth's/ God, and body's fostering patron." *Love's L*, I, i, 217–218.

foster-nurse, *n.* support or sustenance; here, pension: "I have five hundred crowns . . . Which I did store to be my foster-nurse . . ." *As You*, II, iii, 38–40.

foul, *adj.* **1** plain-looking; homely; ugly: "I am not a slut, though I thank the gods I am foul." *As You*, III, iii, 33. **2** same in wordplay with "unclean, odious": ". . . this black-fac'd night, desire's foul nurse . . ." *Ven & Ad*, 773. **3** muddy; mired: "Will she/ hold out water in foul way?" *1 Hen 4*, II, i, 82–83. **4** evil: "Those articles, my lord, are in the king's hand [possession]:/ But thus much, they are foul ones." *Hen 8*, III, ii, 299–300. —*adv.* **5** foully; wrongfully: "To plague thee for thy foul misleading me." *3 Hen 6*, V, i, 100. **6 fall foul,** fall out; disagree or argue: "Shall we fall foul for toys [trifles]?" *2 Hen 4*, II, iv, 166. **7 grow foul with,** to discharge a pistol at: "If you grow foul with me, Pistol, I will scour you/ with my rapier . . ." *Hen 5*, II, i, 55–56.

fouled, *adj.* dirty; befouled: "No hat upon his head, his stockings foul'd . . ." *Ham*, II, i, 79.

foul fiend, *n.* fiendishly clever Devil: "Who gives any thing to poor Tom? whom the/ foul fiend hath led through fire . . ." *Lear*, III, iv, 50–51.

foulness, *n.* **1** wickedness; also, feelings of guilt: ". . . the honour of it/ Does pay the act of it, as i'th'contrary/ The foulness is the punishment." *Hen 8*, III, ii, 181–183. **2** ugliness: "Well, praised be the gods for thy foulness . . ." *As You*, III, iii, 34.

foul show, *n.* hypocrisy: "See how belief may suffer by foul show!" *Per*, IV, iv, 23.

foul way, *n.* muddy road(s): "Will she/ hold out water in foul way?" *1 Hen 4*, II, i, 82–83.

foul way out, *adj.* in financial straits: "If I cannot recover your niece, I am a foul way/ out." *T Night*, II, iii, 184–185.

foundation, *n.* **1** family, house, or household: "God save the foundation!" *M Ado*, V, i, 312. **2** religious house dispensing care or aid: "I think/ Foundations fly [escape] the wretched . . ." *Cymb*, III, vi, 6–7.

founded, *adj.* established; immovable: "Whole as marble, founded as the rock . . ." *Mac,* III, iv, 21.

founder, *v.* to make lame: "I have foundered/ nine score and odd posts [horses]; and here, travel-tainted as/ I am . . ." *2 Hen 4,* IV, iii, 35–37.

four, *pron.* **the other four,** remaining senses: ". . . what banquet wert thou to the taste,/ Being nurse and feeder of the other four!" *Ven & Ad,* 445–446.

four elements, *n.* See **element** (def. 8).

fourscore, *n.* eightieth; perh. an example of Autolycus' humor: ". . . a fish that appeared upon/ the coast on Wednesday the fourscore of April . . ." *W Tale,* IV, iv, 276–277.

four terms, *n.* See **term** (def. 4).

foutre, *n.* vulgar version of "A fig for . . .": "A foutre for the world and worldlings base!" *2 Hen 4,* V, iii, 96.

fowl, *n.* **1 fowl of tyrant wing,** bird of prey: "From this session interdict/ Every fowl of tyrant wing . . ." *Phoen,* 9–10. **2 put up fowl,** to raise game, as in hunting: "Had not your man put up the fowl so suddenly,/ We had had more sport." *2 Hen 6,* II, i, 48–49.

fowler, *n.* person who hunts birds: "As wild geese that the creeping fowler eye . . ." *M N Dream,* III, ii, 20.

fox, *n.* **1** sword [fr. maker's mark stamped on some fine swords]: "O Signieur Dew, thou diest on point of fox . . ." *Hen 5,* IV, iv, 9. **2 my royal fox,** ref. to the fable of the fox and the grapes; the fox, unable to reach the grapes, said they were sour: "O, will you eat/ No grapes, my royal fox?" *All's W,* II, i, 68–69.

foxship, *n.* despicable cunning, typical of the fox; here, in sharp retort to Sicinius's "mankind": "Hadst thou foxship/ To banish him that struck more blows for Rome . . ." *Cor,* IV, ii, 18–19.

fracted, *adj.* **1** (esp. of a promise or agreement) broken; unkept: ". . . my reliances on his fracted dates [broken promises]/ Have smit my credit." *Timon,* II, i, 22–23. **2 fracted and corrobo rate,** may ref. to Falstaff's broken and now contrite heart; perh. his heart is crushed and now "corrupted" [full of ill humors]: ". . . thou hast spoke the right;/ His heart is fracted and corroborate." *Hen 5,* II, i, 123–124.

fraction, *n.* **1** fragment: "After distasteful looks, and these hard fractions . . ." *Timon,* II, ii, 215. **2** division; splitting up: ". . . their fraction is more our wish/ than their faction . . ." *Tr & Cr,* II, iii, 101–102.

fragment, *n.* **1** scrap [term of contempt]: ". . . here's a letter for thee."/ "From whence, fragment?" *Tr & Cr,* V, i, 7–8. **2** [often pl.] scraps of food that prevent starvation: "Like fragments in hard voyages became/ The life o' th' need . . ." *Cymb,* V, iii, 44–45.

frame, *v.* **1** to arrange: "It is needful that/ you frame the season [contrive the occasion] for your own harvest." *M Ado,* I, iii, 23–24. **2** to create; originate: "Nature never fram'd a woman's heart/ Of prouder stuff than that of Beatrice." *M Ado,* III, i, 49–50. **3** to devise; imagine or conjecture: ". . . the great figure of a council frames/ By self-unable motion . . ." *All's W,* III, i, 12–13. **4** to accustom or conform: ". . . they thought it good you hear a play/ And frame your mind to mirth . . ." *Shrew,* Ind., ii, 134–135. **5** to direct one's course: "The beauty of this sinful dame/ Made many princes thither frame . . ." *Per,* I, Chor., 31–32. **6** to prepare; ready: "The maid will I frame, and make fit for his attempt." *Meas,* III, i, 256–257. **7** to perform; execute: ". . . those flower-soft hands,/ That yarely frame the office." *Ant & Cleo,* II, ii, 210–211. **8** to shape; form; fashion: ". . . thou wilt frame/ Thyself, forsooth, hereafter theirs, so far/ As thou hast power and person." *Cor,* III, ii, 84–86. **9 frame to,** to arrange for; adapt to: "I framed to the harp/ Many an English ditty lovely well . . ." *1 Hen 4,* III, i, 118–119. **10 frame to oneself,** to form in one's mind: "Yet had he framed/ to himself . . . many/ deceiving promises of life . . ." *Meas,* III, ii, 238–240. —*n.* **11** structure; framework: ". . . were the whole frame here,/ It is of such a spacious lofty pitch . . ." *1 Hen 6,* II, iii, 53–54. **12** plan or design: "Chid I for that at frugal Nature's frame?" *M Ado,* IV, i, 128. **13** sensible or logical form: "Good my lord, put your discourse into some frame . . ." *Ham,* III, ii, 300. **14 frame my feeding.** See **feeding** (def. 2). **15 frame of sense,** structure of reasoning: "Her madness hath the oddest frame of sense . . ." *Meas,* V, i, 64. **16 frame of things,** universe, comprising both earth and heaven: "But let the frame of things disjoint, both the worlds suffer . . ." *Mac,* III, ii, 16. **17 out of frame,** out of order: "A woman that is like a German clock,/ Still a-repairing, ever out of frame . . ." *Love's L,* III, i, 185–186.

frampold, *adj.* disagreeable: ". . . she leads a very frampold life with him, good heart." *Wives,* II, ii, 86.

franchise, *n.* **1** free exercise: ". . . whose repair, and franchise,/ Shall (by the power we hold) be our good deed . . ." *Cymb,* III, i, 57–58. **2** [pl.] citizen's rights: "Your franchises, whereon you stood, confin'd/ Into an auger's bore." *Cor,* IV, vi, 86–87.

franchised, *adj.* blameless or uncorrupted; unblemished: ". . . still keep/ My bosom franchis'd, and allegiance clear . . ." *Mac,* II, i, 27–28.

Francisco, *n.* prob. a fanciful rendering of "Frenchman": "Is he dead, my Ethiopian?/ Is he dead, my Francisco?" *Wives,* II, iii, 25–26.

frank, *n.* **1** pen for hogs; pigsty: "Doth the old boar feed in the old/ frank?" *2 Hen 4,* II, ii, 138–139.
—*adj.* **2** generous: "For what purpose, love?"/ "But to be frank and give it thee again . . ." *Rom & Jul,* II, ii, 130–131.
—*v.* **3** (of a pig) to pen up for fattening: "Marry, as for Clarence . . . He is frank'd up to fatting for his pains." *Rich 3,* I, iii, 313–314.

frank donation, *n.* freely-offered gift: ". . . the native/ Of our so frank donation." *Cor,* III, i, 128–129.

franklin, *n.* freeholder, ranking below the gentry; here, a rich landowner: ". . . there's a franklin in the/ Wild of Kent hath brought three hundred marks . . ." *1 Hen 4,* II, i, 53–54.

frankly, *adv.* **1** with an open or untroubled mind: "I embrace it freely,/ And will this brothers' wager frankly play." *Ham,* V, ii, 248–249. **2** freely; without restraint: "Speak frankly as the wind." *Tr & Cr,* I, iii, 252.

frantic, *adj.* mad; lunatic; crazy: "If that I do not dream, or be not frantic . . ." *As You,* I, iii, 45.

Frateretto, *n.* one of Tom's [Edgar's] demons or devils: "Frateretto calls me, and tells me Nero is an/ angler in the Lake of Darkness." *Lear,* III, vi, 6–7.

fraud, *n.* **1** falseness or faithlessness: "The fraud of England, not the force of France,/ Hath now entrapp'd the noble-minded Talbot . . ." *1 Hen 6,* IV, iv, 36–37. **2** deception: ". . . at once dispatch/ This little business of a silly [ridiculous] fraud." *Edw 3,* IV, v, 54–55.

fraudful, *adj.* deceitful or treacherous: ". . . the welfare of us all/ Hangs on the cutting short that fraudful man." *2 Hen 6,* III, i, 80–81.

fraught, *n.* **1** freight; cargo: ". . . the bark that hath discharg'd his fraught/ Returns with precious lading to the bay . . ." *T Andr,* I, i, 71–72.
—*v.* **2** to burden: "If after this command thou fraught the court . . . thou diest." *Cymb,* I, ii, 57–58.
—*adj.* **3** fully provided: ". . . your good wisdom,/ Whereof I know you are fraught . . ." *Lear,* I, iv, 228–229. **4** loaded: ". . . sent their ships/ Fraught with the ministers and instruments/ Of cruel war . . ." *Tr & Cr,* Prol., 3–5.

fraughtage, *n.* baggage; also, cargo: "Our fraughtage, sir,/ I have convey'd aboard . . ." *Errors,* IV, i, 88–89.

fraughting, *adj.* constituting the freight: ". . . ere/ It should the good ship so have swallow'd, and/ The fraughting souls within her." *Temp,* I, ii, 11–13.

fray, *n.* **1 part the fray,** to break up the fight: "Signor Hortensio, come you to part the fray?" *Shrew,* I, ii, 23.
—*v.* **2** to frighten: ". . . fetches her wind so short, as if she were frayed/ with a spirit!" *Tr & Cr,* III, ii, 30–31.

freckles, *n.* spots on the "freckled cowslip": "Those be rubies, fairy favours,/ In those freckles live their savours." *M N Dream,* II, i, 12–13.

free, *adj.* **1** of noble character; generous; magnanimous: ". . . in grateful virtue I am bound/ To your free heart . . ." *Timon,* I, ii, 5–6. **2** untouched by the plague or by love: "These lords are visited; you are not free . . ." *Love's L,* V, ii, 422–423. **3** guiltless; innocent: "Make mad the guilty and appal the free . . ." *Ham,* II, ii, 558. **4** relieved from painful thoughts; at ease: "When the mind's free/ The body's delicate [vulnerable] . . ." *Lear,* III, iv, 11–12. **5** unrestrained: ". . . whiles the jolly Briton . . . laughs from's free lungs . . ." *Cymb,* I, vii, 67–68. **6** carefree; happy: ". . . suffers most i' th' mind,/ Leaving free things and happy shows behind . . ." *Lear,* III, vi, 107–108. **7** free-spoken; frank; open: ". . . give me leave/ To have free speech with you . . ." *Meas,* I, i, 76–77.
—*adv.* **8** freely; unstintingly: "Our will became the servant to defect,/ Which else should free have wrought." *Mac,* II, i, 18–19.
—*v.* **9** to clear of blame; absolve: "As he hath spices of them all, not all,/ For I dare so far free him . . ." *Cor,* IV, vii, 46–47.

free awe, *n.* voluntary submission: ". . . thy free awe/ Pays homage to us . . ." *Ham,* IV, iii, 64–65.

free duty, *n.* unqualified loyalty: "Your trusty and most valiant servitor,/ With his free duty recommends you thus . . ." *Oth,* I, iii, 40–41.

free entertainment, *n.* generous hospitality: ". . . provided I have your commendation for my more/ free entertainment." *Cymb,* I, v, 151–152.

free-footed, *adj.* unrestrained: "For we will fetters put about this fear/ Which now goes too free-footed." *Ham,* III, iii, 25–26.

free hearts, *n.* [speak our] thoughts freely: ". . . let us speak/ Our free hearts each to other." *Mac,* I, iii, 155–156.

freelier, *adv.* more freely: "I should freelier rejoice in that absence . . ." *Cor,* I, iii, 3.

free march, *n.* a quick march, poss. not in step: "Strike [sound] a free march to Troy!" *Tr & Cr,* V, x, 30.

freeness, *n.* generosity: "We'll learn our freeness of a son-in-law . . ." *Cymb,* V, v, 422.

freestone, *n.* yellowish sandstone; here, used adjectivally: "She has a leathern hand,/ A freestone-colour'd hand." *As You,* IV, iii, 24–25.

Freetown, *n.* castle of the Capulets in the old story adapted by Shakespeare [trans. of *Villa Franca*]: ". . . come you this afternoon . . . To old Freetown, our common judgement-place." *Rom & Jul,* I, i, 98–100.

French brawl, *n.* popular dance imported from France: "Master, will you win your love with a French/ brawl?" *Love's L,* III, i, 7.

French crown, *n.* **1** coin worth four shillings, or one-fifth of a pound, in Shakespeare's England: ". . . here's four Harry ten shillings in French/ crowns for you." *2 Hen 4,* III, ii, 216–217. **2** used in puns, referring to a bald pate, thought to be the result of syphilis, the so-called "French disease": "Re-muneration! why/ it is a fairer name than French crown." *Love's L,* III, i, 136–137. **3 cut French crowns,** wordplay on "trim gold coins" and "kill French soldiers": ". . . it is no English/ treason to cut French crowns . . ." *Hen 5,* IV, i, 233–234.

French-crown-color, *adj.* golden, from the color of the French goldpiece écu [crown]: ". . . your French-crown-co-lour beard, your/ perfect yellow." *M N Dream,* I, ii, 88–89.

French hose, *n. pl.* short full breeches covering the hips; tailors were often accused of stealing material in the making of these: ". . . here's an English tailor/ come hither for stealing out of a French hose . . ." *Mac,* II, iii, 14–15.

Frenchman, *n.* ref. to the alliance between Scotland and France in late 16th cent.: "I think the Frenchman became his surety, and seal'd/ under for another." *Merch,* I, ii, 78–79.

French nod, *n.* an affected bow: "Smile in men's faces, smooth, deceive and cog,/ Duck with French nods and apish courtesy . . ." *Rich 3,* I, iii, 48–49.

French slop, *n.* baggy breeches: "Signor/ Romeo, bonjour. There's a French salutation to/ your French slop." *Rom & Jul,* II, iv, 44–46.

French thrift, *n.* perh. the employment of one page rather than a retinue is thought by Falstaff to be the French manner: "French thrift, you rogues—myself and skirted page." *Wives,* I, iii, 80.

frenzy, *n.* **1** violent agitation of the mind; here, a trancelike distraction: "And his untimely frenzy thus awaketh . . ." *Luc,* 1675. **2** lunacy; madness: "And melancholy is the nurse of frenzy." *Shrew,* Ind., ii, 133.

frequent, *v.* to hang about; consort: ". . . he daily doth frequent/ With unrestrained loose companions . . ." *Rich 2,* V, iii, 6–7.

fresh, *adj.* **1** keen; eager: "O spirit of love, how quick [lively] and fresh art thou . . ." *T Night,* I, i, 9. **2** young and lovely: ". . . kisses the hands/ Of your fresh princess . . ." *W Tale,* IV, iv, 551–552.
—*n.* **3 quick freshes,** rapidly flowing springs: "I'll not show him/ Where the quick freshes are." *Temp,* III, ii, 65–66.

fresh cups, *n.* refreshing wine cups: ". . . he hides him in fresh cups, soft beds . . ." *Cymb,* V, iii, 71.

freshly, *adj.* fresh; vigorous: "Looks he as freshly as he did the/ day he wrestled?" *As You,* III, ii, 225–226.

fret[1], *n.* **1** any of several ridges on a lute's fingerboard to indicate placement of the fingers: "I did but tell her she mistook her frets . . ." *Shrew,* II, i, 149. See also **fret**[2] (def. 3).
—*v.* **2** to furnish with frets: ". . . though you fret me, you cannot/ play upon me." *Ham,* III, ii, 362–363.

fret[2], *v.* **1** to disturb, agitate, or vex: "Do not fret yourself/ too much in the action, mounsieur . . ." *M N Dream,* IV, i, 13–14. **2** to become angry; rage: "His eyes like glow-worms shine when he doth fret . . ." *Ven & Ad,,* 621.
—*n.* **3** annoyance or irritation; here, the musical sense willfully misconstrued: "'Frets, call you these?' quoth she, 'I'll fume with them.'" *Shrew,* II, i, 152.

fret[3], *v.* **1** to wear away; erode: ". . . to drop them still upon one place,/ Till they have fretted us a pair of graves . . ." *Rich 2,* III, iii, 166–167. **2** to go to waste; also, wordplay on "be peevish": "'Twas a commodity lay fretting by you . . ." *Shrew,* II, i, 321. **3** to ferment; also, corrode: ". . . a strong distillation with stinking clothes that/ fretted in their own grease . . ." *Wives,* III, v, 104–105.

fret[4], *v.* to adorn or ornament: ". . . yon grey lines/ That fret the clouds are messengers of day." *J Caes,* II, i, 103–104.

fretted, *adj.* full of problems; checkered: "His fretted fortunes give him hope and fear/ Of what he has, and has not." *Ant & Cleo,* IV, xii, 8–9.

fretten, *past part.* of **fret**[2], var. of **fretted:** ". . . to make no noise/ When they are fretten with the gusts of heaven . . ." *Merch,* IV, i, 76–77.

fretting, *adj.* eroding; eating away: "Command these fretting waters from your eyes/ With a light heart . . ." *Meas,* IV, iii, 146–147.

fretting gust, *n.* violent gust of wind: "As doth a sail, fill'd with a fretting gust,/ Command an argosy to stem the waves." *3 Hen 6,* II, vi, 35–36.

friend, *n.* **1** sweetheart or lover: "Nor never come in visor to my friend,/ Nor woo in rhyme . . ." *Love's L,* V, ii, 404–405. **2** cousin or other relative; kinsman: "So shall you feel the loss but not the friend/ Which you weep for." *Rom & Jul,* III, v, 75–76. **3** [pl.] family; kinfolk: "A good-limbed fellow,/ young, strong, and of good friends." *2 Hen 4,* III, ii, 102–103. **4 have to friend,** have as a friend; have on one's side: ". . . had I admittance, and opportunity/ to friend." *Cymb,* I, v, 102–103 —*v.* **5** to be friendly; make friends: ". . . and what I can redress,/ As I shall find the time to friend, I will." *Mac,* IV, iii, 9–10. **6** to help; aid: "Not friended by his wish to your high person [that the king die without issue] . . ." *Hen 8,* I, ii, 140. **7 be friended with,** take advantage of: ". . . be friended/ With aptness of the season [when opportunities present themselves] . . ." *Cymb,* II, iii, 46–47. **8 friend or end,** bring favorable circumstances or terminate one's life: "Well, the gods are above, time must/ friend or end." *Tr & Cr,* I, ii, 77–78.

friending, *n.* friendship: ". . . what so poor a man as Hamlet is/ May do t'express his love and friending to you . . ." *Ham,* I, v, 192–193.

frieze, *n.* coarse woollen material, thought to be widely used in Wales and Ireland: "Shall I have a cockscomb of frieze?" *Wives,* V, v, 139.

frighted, *adj.* frightened or feeling the effects of fear: "Find we a time for frighted peace to pant . . ." *1 Hen 4,* I, i, 2.

frippery, *n.* shop where old clothes are sold: ". . . we know what belongs to a frippery." *Temp,* IV, i, 225.

Frogmore, *n.* village on outskirts of Windsor: "Cavaliero Slender, go you through the town to/ Frogmore." *Wives,* II, iii, 70–71.

frolic, *adj.* merry: "And we fairies . . . Following darkness like a dream,/ Now are frolic . . ." *M N Dream,* V, i, 369–373.

from, *prep.* **1** out of: ". . . how dar'st thou trust/ So great a charge from thine own custody?" *Errors,* I, ii, 60–61. **2** away, esp. far away, from: ". . . 'tis ever common/ That men are merriest when they are from home." *Hen 5,* I, ii, 271–272. **3** aside from; other than: "If aught possess thee from me, it is dross . . ." *Errors,* II, ii, 177. **4** against: "And yet thou wilt/ tutor me from quarrelling!" *Rom & Jul,* III, i, 29–30. **5** contrary

to: ". . . not to be so odd and from all fashions/ As Beatrice is . . ." *M Ado,* III, i, 72–73. **6 from it,** budge or swerve from it: "Signior Iachimo will not from it." *Cymb,* I, v, 169.

from forth, away from: "As when brave Gaunt, thy father, and myself,/ Rescued the Black Prince . . . From forth the ranks of many thousand French . . ." *Rich 2,* II, iii, 99–101.

front, *n.* **1** the face or forehead: ". . . at my nativity/ The front of heaven was full of fiery shapes . . ." *1 Hen 4,* III, i, 11–12. **2** the early part: "As Philomel in summer's front doth sing . . ." *Sonn 102,* 7. **3 front to front,** face to face: ". . . front to front,/ Bring thou this fiend of Scotland, and myself . . ." *Mac,* IV, iii, 232–233. —*v.* **4** to confront: "Sirs, you four shall front them in the narrow lane . . ." *1 Hen 4,* II, ii, 57. **5** to oppose: "Could not with graceful [approving] eyes attend those wars/ Which fronted mine own peace." *Ant & Cleo,* II, ii, 60–61. **6** to appear in front; Wolsey is saying he appears to have more authority than he actually has: ". . . and front but in that file/ Where others tell steps with me." *Hen 8,* I, ii, 42–43.

frontier, *n.* **1** brow or forehead; here, a contradictory or disagreeable expression: ". . . majesty might never yet endure/ The moody frontier of a servant brow." *1 Hen 4,* I, iii, 17–18. **2** fortress or fortification; also, a barricade: "And thou hast talk'd . . . Of palisadoes, frontiers, parapets . . ." *1 Hen 4,* II, iii, 51–53.

frontlet, *n.* band worn around the head; here, appar. a deep frown: "How now, daughter! what makes that frontlet/ on?" *Lear,* I, iv, 197–198.

frost, *n.* older persons; here, their sexual passions: "Since frost itself as actively doth burn/ And reason panders will." *Ham,* III, iv, 87–88.

frosty signs, *n. pl.* aged appearance; here, white hair: "But if my frosty signs and chaps of age . . . Cannot induce you to attend my words . . ." *T Andr,* V, iii, 77–79.

froth, *n.* **1** something trifling and self-indulgent: "A dream, a breath, a froth of fleeting joy." *Luc,* 212. —*v.* **2** to foam beer [so that the customer got more foam than beer]: "Let me see/ thee froth and lime." *Wives,* I, iii, 13–14.

froward, *adj.* **1** fretful; peevish: "Or like the froward infant still'd with dandling . . ." *Ven & Ad,* 562. **2** obstinate; stubborn: "Affection . . . woos best when most his choice is froward." *Ven & Ad,* 569–570.

frozen, *adj.* cold or cowardly: "Throw in the frozen bosoms of our part/ Hot coals of vengeance!" *2 Hen 6,* V, ii, 35–36.

fruit, *n.* dessert course: "My news shall be the fruit to that great feast." *Ham,* II, ii, 52.

fruitful, *adj.* **1** fertile: "To see fair Padua . . . I am arriv'd for fruitful Lombardy . . ." *Shrew,* I, i, 2–3. **2** plenteous; copious: ". . . one fruitful meal would set/ me to't [lust]." *Meas,* IV, iii, 153–154. **3** generous; bountiful: ". . . she's fram'd as fruitful/ As the free elements . . ." *Oth,* II, iii, 332–333.

fruitless, *adj.* **1** empty; idle: "Bray forth their conquest and our overthrow,/ Even in the barren, bleak, and fruitless air." *Edw 3,* I, ii, 13–14. **2** barren; lacking offspring: "Therefore despite of fruitless chastity . . ." *Ven & Ad,* 751.

frush, *v.* to beat or pound; batter: "I like thy armour well:/ I'll frush it and unlock the rivets all . . ." *Tr & Cr,* V, vi, 28–29.

frustrate, *adj.* **1** baffled: "Being so frustrate, tell him, he mocks/ The pauses that he makes [makes his delays seem ridiculous]." *Ant & Cleo,* V, i, 2–3. **2** futile; vain: ". . . and the sea mocks/ Our frustrate search on land." *Temp,* III, iii, 9–10. —*v.* **3** to cancel; annul: "To frustrate both his oath and what beside/ May make against the house of Lancaster." *3 Hen 6,* II, i, 175–176.

frutify, *v.* misuse for "testify" or "certify": ". . . the Jew having/ done me wrong, doth cause me as my father . . . shall frutify unto you." *Merch,* II, ii, 125–127.

fry, *n.* **1** spawn, esp. a swarm of tiny fish: "Young fry of treachery!" *Mac,* IV, ii, 83. **2 fry of fornication,** swarm of bastards: "Bless me, what a fry/ of fornication is at door!" *Hen 8,* V, iii, 34–35.

fub, *v.* var of **fob;** to cheat: ". . . and resolution thus fubbed as it/ is with the rusty curb of old father Antic the law?" *1 Hen 4,* I, ii, 58–59.

fubbed off, *past part.* var. of **fobbed off;** put off: ". . . fubbed off/ from this day to that day, that it is a shame to be/ thought on." *2 Hen 4,* II, i, 33–35.

fugitive, *n.* deserter: "But let the world rank me in register [on record]/ A master-leaver, and a fugitive . . ." *Ant & Cleo,* IV, ix, 21–22.

fulfilled, *adj.* filled full; filled up: "Poor women's faults, that they are so fulfill'd/ With men's abuses!" *Luc,* 1258–1259.

full, *adv.* **1** completely; fully: ". . . she is not so divine,/ So full replete with choice of all delights . . ." *1 Hen 6,* V, v, 16–17. **2** very; exceedingly or excessively: "I am more better/ Than Prospero, master of a full poor cell . . ." *Temp,* I, ii, 19–20. **3 full oft,** very often; frequently: ". . . I have heard my grandsire say full oft,/ Extremity of griefs would make

men mad." *T Andr,* IV, i, 18–19. **4 full so,** equally or every bit as: "No face is fair that is not full so black." *Love's L,* IV, iii, 249. **5 have it full,** to have something fully planned or clearly thought out: "*Basta,* content thee, for I have it full." *Shrew,* I, i, 198. —*adj.* **6 at full,** fully; completely: "But what at full I know, thou know'st no part . . ." *All's W,* II, i, 131. —*n.* **7 full of view,** complete satisfaction of my eyes: ". . . to behold his visage/ Even to my full of view." *Tr & Cr,* III, iii, 239–240. **8 in the full,** to the utmost; in the highest degree: ". . . all you peers of Greece, go to my tent;/ There in the full convive we . . ." *Tr & Cr,* IV, v, 270–271.

full-acorned, *adj.* well-fed; stuffed; wordplay on "boar" and "boor": "Like a full-acorn'd boar, a German one,/ Cried 'O!' and mounted . . ." *Cymb,* II, iv, 168–169.

fullam, *n.* false dice, perh. loaded: "Let vultures gripe thy guts, for gourd and fullam holds . . ." *Wives,* I, iii, 81.

fuller, *n.* weaver's assistant, one who cleans and thickens the finished cloth: "The spinsters, carders, fullers, weavers . . . compell'd by hunger . . ." *Hen 8,* I, ii, 33–34.

fullest, *adj.* most blest by Fortune: "One that performs/ The bidding of the fullest man . . ." *Ant & Cleo,* III, xiii, 86–87.

full-fraught, *adj.* **1** entirely filled: ". . . wailful sonnets . . . full-fraught with serviceable vows." *Two Gent,* III, ii, 69–70. **2** endowed with the finest qualities: "To mark the full-fraught man and best indued/ With some suspicion." *Hen V,* II, ii, 139–140.

full oft, *adv.* constantly; continually: ". . . I have heard my grandsire say full oft,/ Extremity of griefs would make men mad." *T Andr,* IV, i, 18–19.

full stop, *n.* (in punctuation) period; here, the point of the story: "Come, the full stop [get to the point]." *Merch,* III, i, 15.

full time, *n.* natural course of time: "Which by th'interpretation of full time/ May show like all yourself." *Cor,* V, iii, 69–70.

fulsome, *adj.* **1** lustful; wanton: "He stuck them up before the fulsome ewes . . ." *Merch,* I, iii, 81. **2** disgusting: "I, that was wash'd to death with fulsome wine . . ." *Rich 3,* V, iii, 133.

fumble, *v.* **fumble up,** to utter awkwardly: "With distinct breath and consign'd kisses to them,/ He fumbles up into a loose adieu . . ." *Tr & Cr,* IV, iv, 44–45.

fume, *n.* **1** passionate outburst; rage: "He stamps, and bites the poor flies in his fume." *Ven & Ad,* 316. **2** vapor; here, a cloud impeding reason: ". . . their rising senses/ Begin to chase the ignorant fumes that mantle/ Their clearer reason." *Temp,* V, i, 66–68. **3** ref. to the belief that intoxication resulted when the fumes of alcohol rose from the stomach to the brain: "... memory, the warder of the brain,/ Shall be a fume, and the receipt of reason/ A limbeck [still] only ..." *Mac,* I, vii, 66–68.

—*v.* **4** to rage: "'Frets, call you these?' quoth she, 'I'll fume with them.'" *Shrew,* II, i, 152. **5** (of wine fumes) to mount to the brain and cause drunkenness: "Tie up the libertine in a field of feasts,/ Keep his brain fuming ..." *Ant & Cleo,* II, i, 23–24.

fumiter, *n.* common herb, the fumitory: "Crown'd with rank fumiter and furrow-weeds,/ With hardocks, hemlock, nettles, cuckoo-flowers ..." *Lear,* IV, iv, 3–4.

fumitory, *n.* wild grass: "... her fallow leas/ The darnel, hemlock and rank fumitory/ Doth root upon ..." *Hen 5,* V, ii, 44–46.

function, *n.* **1** employment; duties: "Or what is he of basest function ..." *As You,* II, vii, 79. **2** action; mental or physical activity: "Shakes so my single state of man,/ That function is smother'd in surmise ..." *Mac,* I, iii, 140–141. **3 a.** occupation; here, the duties of a priest: "I am not tall enough to/ become the function well ..." *T Night,* IV, ii, 6–7. **b.** trade: "Our tradesmen singing in their shops and going/ About their functions friendly." *Cor,* IV, vi, 8–9. **4** instincts: "Even as her appetite shall play the god/ With his weak function." *Oth,* II, iii, 338–339.

furbish, *v.* to add luster to; make bright: "And furbish new the name of John a Gaunt ..." *Rich 2,* I, iii, 76.

furies, *n. pl.* (in Greek myth.) grotesque superhuman creatures [usually three] who pursued and punished sinners: "... he was mad for her and talk'd of Satan and of Limbo/ and of furies and I know not what ..." *All's W,* V, iii, 255–256.

furious, *adj.* cruel: "And giddy Fortune's furious fickle wheel ..." *Hen 5,* III, vi, 27.

furlong, *n.* unit of distance equal to 220 yards or one-fifth kilometer: "Now would I give a thousand furlongs of sea for an/ acre of barren ground ..." *Temp,* I, i, 64–65.

furnace, *v.* to exhale or roar like a furnace: "He furnaces/ The thick [numerous] sighs from him ..." *Cymb,* I, vii, 66–67.

furnish, *v.* **1** to dress; put on: "I'll show thee some attires, and have thy counsel/ Which is the best to furnish me tomorrow." *M Ado,* III, i, 102–103. **2** to supply; equip: "'Tis now but four of clock, we have two hours/ To furnish us ..." *Merch,* II, iv, 8–9. **3 furnish forth,** to replenish; provision: "Thrift, thrift, Horatio. The funeral bak'd meats/ Did coldly furnish forth the marriage tables." *Ham,* I, ii, 180–181.

furnished, *adj.* wearing full armor: "All furnish'd, all in arms;/ All plum'd like estridges [ostriches] ..." *1 Hen 4,* IV, i, 97–98.

furnishings, *n. pl.* pretexts: "... something deeper,/ Whereof perchance these are but furnishings—" *Lear,* III, i, 28–29.

furniture, *n.* **1** equipment: "... and there receive/ Money and order for their furniture." *1 Hen 4,* III, iii, 200–201. **2** furnishings; a costume or outfit: "... neither art thou the worse/ For this poor furniture and mean array." *Shrew,* IV, iii, 176–177. **3** trappings; adornments: "I'd give bay curtal and his furniture ..." *All's W,* II, iii, 59.

furred pack, *n.* knapsack of skin, with the hair or fur on the outside: "... not able to travel with her/ furr'd pack, she washes bucks here at home." *2 Hen 6,* IV, ii, 45–46.

furrow-weed, *n.* weed growing in furrows after plowing: "Crown'd with rank fumiter and furrow-weeds,/ With hardocks, hemlock ..." *Lear,* IV, iv, 3–4.

further, *n.* **1** additional business: "... now you have left your voices,/ I have no further with you." *Cor,* II, iii, 170–171.
—*adv.* **2** more; to a greater degree: "I muse [wonder] my mother/ Does not approve me further ..." *Cor,* III, ii, 7–8.

further aid, *n.* additional help; others to help you: "Friends both, go join you with some further aid." *Ham,* IV, i, 33.

furtherance, *n.* assistance: "Cannot my body nor blood-sacrifice/ Entreat you to your wonted furtherance?" *1 Hen 6,* V, iii, 20–21.

fury, *n.* **1** madness: "I know my noble aunt ... would not, but in fury, fright my youth ..." *T Andr,* IV, i, 22–24. **2** artistic, esp. poetic, inspiration: "Spend'st thou thy fury on some worthless song ..." *Sonn 100,* 3.

Fury, *n.* [in Roman myth.] one of three lesser gods of the underworld, who relentlessly pursued evildoers in Hades: "Thou shouldst come like a Fury crown'd with snakes ..." *Ant & Cleo,* II, v, 40.

furze, *n.* gorse, a shrub that thrives on barren ground: "... an acre of barren ground, long heath, broom, furze,/ anything." *Temp,* I, i, 65–66.

fust, *v.* to become musty or moldy: "... gave us not/ That capability and godlike reason/ To fust in us unus'd." *Ham,* IV, iv, 37–39.

fustian, *adj.* **1** ranting; raving: ". . . thrust him downstairs, I cannot/ endure such a fustian rascal." *2 Hen 4,* II, iv, 184–185. **2** high-flown; also, nonsensical: "A fustian riddle!" *T Night,* II, v, 110.
—*n.* **3** coarse material of cotton and flax; here, servants' uniforms of this material: "Is supper ready, the house/ trimmed . . . the/ servingmen in their new fustian, their white/ stockings . . ." *Shrew,* IV, i, 40–43. **4 discourse fustian,** talk nonsense: ". . . discourse fustian/ with one's own shadow?" *Oth,* II, iii, 272–273.

fustilarian, *n.* misuse of "fustilugs," a fat, frowsy woman: "Away, you scullion! you rampallian! you fustilarian!" *2 Hen 4,* II, i, 58–59.

fusty, *adj.* **1** stale; trite or hackneyed: "At this fusty stuff/ The large Achilles . . . laughs out a loud applause . . ." *Tr & Cr,* I, iii, 161–163. **2** moldy; rotten: ". . . a were as good [he might as well] crack a fusty nut with no/ kernel." *Tr & Cr,* II, i, 103–104.

fut, *interj.* exclam. of impatience or disgust: "Fut! I should have been that I am/ had the maidenliest star in the firmament twinkled/ on my bastardizing." *Lear,* I, ii, 138–140.

futurely, *adv.* in the future: ". . . all the actions that I have foregone,/ Or futurely can cope." *Kinsmen,* I, i, 173–174.

G

gabble, *n.* **gabble enough and good enough,** just keep babbling, and it will serve well enough. *All's W,* IV, i, 19–20.

gaberdine, *n.* long, loose outer garment worn by Jewish men in some countries: "You call me misbeliever, cut-throat dog,/ And spet upon my Jewish gaberdine . . ." *Merch,* I, iii, 106–107.

gad, *n.* **1** spike used as a stylus: "And with a gad of steel will write these words,/ And lay it by . . ." *T Andr,* IV, i, 103–104. **2 upon the gad,** all at once; suddenly: "All this done/ Upon the gad!" *Lear,* I, ii, 25–26.

gage, *v.* **1** to pledge or engage: "That men of your nobility and power/ Did gage them both in an unjust behalf . . ." *1 Hen 4,* I, iii, 170–171. **2** to wager; risk: ". . . such thwarting strife/ That one for all or all for one we gage . . ." *Luc,* 143–144. **3** to bind: "Both taxing me, and gaging me to keep/ An oath that I have sworn." *Tr & Cr,* V, i, 40–41.
—*n.* **4** glove or a gauntlet: "Pale trembling coward, there I throw my gage . . ." *Rich 2,* I, i, 69. **5 under gage,** in a state of challenge to combat: "Your differences shall all rest under gage/ Till we assign you to your days of trial." *Rich 2,* IV, i, 105–106.

gaged, *adj.* pledged; indebted: ". . . the great debts/ Wherein my time . . . Hath left me gag'd . . ." *Merch,* I, i, 128–130.

gain, *v.* **gain the cap of,** See **cap** (def. 4).

gaingiving, *n.* misgiving: ". . . it is such a kind of gaingiving/ as would perhaps trouble a woman." *Ham,* V, ii, 212.

gainsay, *v.* **1** to contradict; dispute or deny: "You are too great to be by me gainsaid . . ." *2 Hen 4,* I, i, 91. **2** to forbid: ". . . but the just gods gainsay/ That any drop thou borrow'dst from thy mother . . ." *Tr & Cr,* IV, v, 131–132. **3 I'll no gainsaying,** I'll accept no denial: "We'll part the time between 's then: and in that/ I'll no gainsaying." *W Tale,* I, ii, 18–19.

'gainst, *prep.* short form of **against;** in preparation for: "I will unto Venice,/ To buy apparel 'gainst the wedding-day." *Shrew,* II, i, 307–308.

gait, *n.* **1** advance or proceeding: ". . . we have here writ/ To Norway, uncle of young Fortinbras . . . to suppress/ His further gait herein . . ." *Ham,* I, ii, 27–31. **2** manner of walking; here, regal manner: "Highest queen of state,/ Great Juno comes; I know her by her gait." *Temp,* IV, i, 101–102. **3 address thy gait,** direct your footsteps: ". . . address thy gait unto her,/ Be not denied access . . ." *T Night,* I, iv, 15–16. **4 go (or take) your gait,** go your way: "Good gentleman, go your gait, and let poor/ volk [folk] pass." *Lear,* IV, vi, 238–239.

gale and vary, *n.* changing wind: ". . . turn their halcyon beaks/ With every gale and vary of their masters . . ." *Lear,* II, ii, 79–80.

Galen, *n.* Greek physician and writer of the 2d cent. A.D.: "I have read the cause of/ his effects in Galen . . ." *2 Hen 4,* I, ii, 115–116.

gall, *n.* **1** sore or sore spot: "Thou griev'st my gall." *Love's L,* V, ii, 237. **2** bile; also, bitterness of mind [used in puns with "sore"]: "Gall! bitter."/ "Therefore meet." *Love's L,* V, ii, 237. **3** bitterness; rancor; ill will: ". . . it cannot be/ But I am pigeon-liver'd and lack gall/ To make oppression bitter . . ." *Ham,* II, ii, 573–574. **4** bitter or tragic experience: "You have the honey still, but these the gall . . ." *Tr & Cr,* II, ii, 145. **5** bitter, vituperative person: "Out, gall!" *Tr & Cr,* V, i, 34. **6** spirit; temper: "Why, we have galls: and though we have some grace,/ Yet have we some revenge." *Oth,* IV, iii, 92–93. **7 tie the gall up,** to restrain the venom: "What king so strong/ Can tie the gall up in the slanderous tongue?" *Meas,* III, ii, 181–182.
—*v.* **8** to make sore by rubbing; chafe: ". . . the gout galls the/ one, and the pox pinches the other . . ." *2 Hen 4,* I, ii, 231–232. **9** to harass; annoy: "Galling the gleaned land with hot assays . . ." *Hen 5,* I, ii, 151. **10** to harm or injure: "The canker galls the infants of the spring . . ." *Ham,* I, iii, 39. **11** to deplete:

"... my state [estate] being gall'd with my expense ..." *Wives*, III, iv, 5. **12 to graze:** "The Bull, being gall'd, gave Aries such a knock/ That down fell both the Ram's horns in the court ..." *T Andr*, IV, iii, 70–71. **13 to scoff:** "I have seen you gleeking and galling at/ this gentleman twice or thrice." *Hen 5*, V, i, 77–78.

gallant, *adj.* **1** splendid; beautiful: "... never did I hear/ Such gallant chiding ..." *M N Dream*, IV, i, 113–114. **2** fine; noble: "... you must needs bestow her funeral;/ The fields are near, and you are gallant grooms." *T Andr*, IV, ii, 164–165. —*n.* **3** gentleman, esp. a young man of fashion: "Come, where be these gallants? Who's at home?" *Shrew*, III, ii, 84.

gallantry, *n.* gallants; nobility: "Hector, Deiphobus, Helenus, Antenor, and all/ the gallantry of Troy." *Tr & Cr*, III, i, 131–132.

gallant-springing, *adj.* showing a life of great promise: "When gallant-springing, brave Plantagenet ... was struck dead by thee?" *Rich 3*, I, iv, 210–211.

galled, *adj.* **1** irritated; made sore by or as if by chafing: "... they that are most galled with my folly,/ They most must laugh." *As You*, II, vii, 50–51. **2** worn away: "... their ranks began/ To break upon the galled shore ..." *Luc*, 1440. **3** infected; here, with venereal disease: "Some galled goose of Winchester would hiss." *Tr & Cr*, V, x, 55.

gallery, *n.* walkway, corridor, or the like; here, in the royal palace: "Scene 1—[A gallery in the court.]" [SD] *Hen 8*, V, i, 1.

Gallia, *n.* **1** Latin name of Gaul [France]: "Whose life was England's glory, Gallia's wonder." *1 Hen 6*, IV, vii, 48. **2 Gallia and Gaul,** Wales [fr. French *Galles*] and France: "Peace, I say, Gallia and Gaul, French and Welsh,/ soul-curer and body-curer." *Wives*, III, i, 89–90. —*adj.* **3** of Gaul; French: "... patches will I get unto these cudgell'd scars,/ And swear I got them in the Gallia wars." *Hen 5*, V, i, 92–93.

Gallian, *adj.* belonging to Gaul [France]; French: "I am possess'd/ With more than half the Gallian territories ..." *1 Hen 6*, V, iv, 138–139.

galliard, *n.* lively dance, featuring a "caper," or leaping step: "What is thy excellence in a galliard, knight?" *T Night*, I, iii, 117.

galliass, *n.* large, swift galley: "... my father hath no less/ Than three great argosies, besides two galliasses ..." *Shrew*, II, i, 370–371.

gallimaufry, *n.* medley or hodgepodge: "... a dance which the/ wenches say is a gallimaufry of gambols ..." *W Tale*, IV, iv, 328–329.

galling, *pres. part.* blistering: "... galling/ His kingly hands, haling ropes ..." *Per*, IV, i, 53–54.

gallow, *v.* to terrify: "... the wrathful skies/ Gallow the very wanderers of the dark ..." *Lear*, III, ii, 43–44.

Galloway nags, *n.* Irish [perh. Galway] horses of little use for riding; in fig. use, "nag" means "prostitute": "Know we not Galloway/ nags?" *2 Hen 4*, II, iv, 186–187.

gallowglass, *n.* Irish horse-soldier, armed with an ax: "The merciless Macdonwald ... from the western isles/ Of Kernes and Gallowglasses is supplied ..." *Mac*, I, ii, 9–13.

gallows, *n.* **1** gallows bird; rogue: "Ay, and a shrewd unhappy gallows too." *Love's L*, V, ii, 12. —*adj.* **2** having the look of a gallows bird: "... he hath no drowning mark upon him; his complexion/ is perfect gallows." *Temp*, I, i, 28–30.

gambol, *n.* **1** skipping or frisking about; caper: "Where be your gibes now, your gambols,/ your songs, your flashes of merriment ..." *Ham*, V, i, 183–184. **2** frolic: "Is not a comonty [comedy]/ A Christmas gambol or a tumbling-trick?" *Shrew*, Ind., ii, 137–138. **3 gambol faculties,** playful inclinations: "... breeds no bate with telling of discreet stories, and/ such other gambol faculties ..." *2 Hen 4*, II, iv, 247–248. —*v.* **4** to start; shy: "And I the matter will re-word, which madness/ Would gambol from." *Ham*, III, iv, 145–146.

game, *n.* **1** sport: "As waggish boys, in game, themselves forswear ..." *M N Dream*, I, i, 240. **2** hunting of wild game: "... if about this hour he make this way,/ Under the colour of his usual game ..." *3 Hen 6*, 10–11. **3** sexual playfulness: "And I'll warrant her full of game." *Oth*, II, iii, 19. **4 know the game,** wordplay on "game of love" and tracking wild game: "He knows the game: how true he keeps the wind!" *3 Hen 6*, III, ii, 14. **5 the game,** the game of love; here, prostitution: "... set them down/ For sluttish spoils of opportunity/ And daughters of the game." *Tr & Cr*, IV, v, 61–63.

gamesome, *adj.* **1** sportive; frolicsome: "I am not gamesome: I do lack some part/ Of that quick spirit that is in Antony." *J Caes*, I, ii, 27–28. **2** same in wordplay with "sexually loose": "So merry and so gamesome: he is call'd/ The Briton [British] reveller." *Cymb*, I, vii, 60–61.

gamester, *n.* **1** sportsman or, often, a gambler: "Now will I stir this gamester. I hope I shall see an end of him ..." *As You*,

I, i, 161–162. **2** prostitute: "Were you a gamester at/ five or at seven?" *Per,* IV, vi, 73–74.

gaming, *n.* gambling: "'There was a gaming', 'there o'ertook in's rouse' . . ." *Ham,* II, i, 58–59.

gammon, *n.* bottom, or leg, half of cured pork: "I have a gammon of bacon, and two razes of/ ginger . . ." *1 Hen 4,* II, i, 23–24.

gamut, *n.* the musical scale: "I must begin with rudiments of art,/ To teach you gamut . . ." *Shrew,* III, i, 64–65.

gan or **'gan,** elided form of **began [to]:** "The bloody Douglas . . . Gan vail his stomach [lose his courage] . . ." *2 Hen 4,* I, i, 127–129.

Ganymede, *n.* (in Greek myth.) handsome youth abducted by Zeus to be his cupbearer on Mount Olympus: "Just such another wanton Ganymede/ Set Jove afire with, and enforc'd the god/ Snatch up the goodly boy and set him by him . . ." *Kinsmen,* IV, ii, 15–17.

gaol, *n.* var. of **jail:** ". . . break open the/ gaols and let out the prisoners." *2 Hen 6,* IV, iii, 14–15.

gaoler, *n.* var. of **jailer:** ". . . seldom when/ The steeled gaoler is the friend of men." *Meas,* IV, ii, 84–85.

gap, *n.* **1** [often pl.] a leap or jump in time; here, a telescoping of several years: ". . . learn of me, who stand i' th' gaps to teach you/ The stages of our story." *Per,* IV, iv, 8–9. **2** interpolation of a bawdy remark into a ballad, esp. a duet between man and maid: ". . . where some stretch-mouthed rascal would . . . mean mischief and break a foul gap into/ the matter . . ." *W Tale,* IV, iv, 198–200. **3 gap and trade,** an open way: "Stands in the gap and trade of moe [more] preferments . . ." *Hen 8,* V, i, 36.

gape, *v.* to wait expectantly with open-mouthed eagerness: "Now old desire doth in his deathbed lie/ And young affection gapes to be his heir . . ." *Rom & Jul,* II, Prol., 2.

gar, *n.* Frenchman's pron. of "God": ". . . by/ gar, it is a shallenge [challenge]." *Wives,* I, iv, 102–103.

garb, *n.* **constrain the garb,** to distort the style (of plain speech): ". . . doth affect/ A saucy roughness, and contrains the garb/ Quite from his [its] nature . . ." *Lear,* II, ii, 97–99.

garboil, *n.* [often pl] tumult or disturbance: ". . . at thy sovereign leisure read/ The garboils she awak'd . . ." *Ant & Cleo,* I, iii, 60–61.

garden, *n.* **1 maiden gardens,** virginal gardens; here, marriageable virgins: "And many maiden gardens, yet unset [unplanted] . . ." *Sonn 16,* 6. **2 world's best garden,** France: "By which the world's best garden he achieved . . ." *Hen 5,* Epil. 7.

Gargantua, *n.* ref. to Rabelais' giant hero: "You must borrow me Gargantua's mouth first. 'Tis a word too great for any mouth . . ." *As You,* III, ii, 221–222.

garland, *n.* **1** king's crown: "So thou the garland wear'st successively." *2 Hen 4,* IV, v, 201. **2** crowning achievement or glory: "O, wither'd is the garland of the war . . ." *Ant & Cleo,* IV, xv, 64. **3** hero or idol: "And call him noble that was now your hate,/ Him vile that was your garland." *Cor,* I, i, 182–183.

garner, *n.* granary: "Earth's increase, foison plenty,/ Barns and garners never empty . . ." *Temp,* IV, i, 110–111.

garnish, *n.* clothing: "So are you (sweet)/ Even in the lovely garnish of a boy." *Merch,* II, vi, 44–45.

garnished, *adj.* clothed or furnished: "Garnish'd like him, that for a tricksy word/ Defy the matter . . ." *Merch,* III, v, 63–64.

Garter, *n.* appar. ref. to an inn of that name in Windsor: ". . . and the three/ party is (lastly and finally) mine host of the Garter." *Wives,* I, i, 127–128.

Gascony, *n.* province in SW France: "Plains in Gascony." [SD] *1 Hen 6,* IV, iii, 1.

gaskins, *n. pl.* breeches: "That if one break, the other will hold: or if both/ break, your gaskins fall." *T Night,* I, v, 23–24.

gasp, *n.* **at last gasp,** all but dead: "His fortunes all lie speechless, and his name/ Is at last gasp." *Cymb,* I, vi, 52–53.

gasted, *adj.* startled; frightened: "Or whether gasted by the noise I made,/ Full suddenly he fled." *Lear,* II, i, 55–56.

gat, *v.* short form of **begat;** old form of **begot:** ". . . and our daughter . . . Sits here like Beauty's child, whom Nature gat . . ." *Per,* II, ii, 4–6.

gate, *n.* **1** barrier: "Who [which] glaz'd with crystal gate the glowing roses . . ." *Lover's Comp,* 286. **2 out at gates,** through the [city's] gates: "Come, come, let's see him out at gates!" *Cor,* III, iii, 142.

gather, *v.* to learn or infer: "Thou art my heir; the rest I wish thee gather . . ." *1 Hen 6,* II, v, 96.

gathered, *adj.* (of a flower) picked; plucked: ". . . as doth the honey-dew/ Upon a gath'red lily almost withered." *T Andr,* III, i, 112–113.

gaud, *n.* [often pl.] gaudy trinket; trifle: ". . . stol'n the impression of her fantasy,/ With bracelets of thy hair, rings, gauds, conceits . . ." *M N Dream,* I, i, 32–33.

gauded, *adj.* Also, **gawded.** made-up; painted: "Commit the war of white and damask in/ Their nicely gauded cheeks . . ." *Cor,* II, i, 214–215.

gaudy, *adj.* **1** bright; brilliant: "Under whose brim the gaudy sun would peep . . ." *Ven & Ad,* 1088. **2** festive; joyous; also, sportive or rowdy: "Come,/ Let's have one other gaudy night . . ." *Ant & Cleo,* III, xiii, 182–183.

Gaul, *n.* ancient country of W Europe; coextensive with modern-day France and Belgium. "Peace, I say, Gallia and Gaul, French and Welsh,/ soul-curer and body-curer." *Wives,* III, i, 89–90.

Gaultree Forest, *n.* royal forest NW of York: "What is this forest call'd?"/ "'Tis Gaultree Forest, and't shall please your Grace." *2 Hen 4,* IV, i, 1–2.

Gaunt, *n.* Duke of Lancaster also called "John of Gaunt" because of his birthplace: Ghent, in Flanders: "Old John of Gaunt, time-honoured Lancaster . . ." *Rich 2,* I, i, 1.

gauntlet, *n.* man's glove; here, thrown down as a challenge to combat: "There's my gauntlet;/ I'll prove it on a giant." *Lear,* IV, vi, 90–91.

gawded, *adj.* See **gauded.**

gawds, *n. pl.* baubles; ornaments or trifles: "But for these other gawds,/ Unbind my hands, I'll pull them off myself . . ." *Shrew,* II, i, 3–4.

gay, *adj.* ornately dressed: "Never lack'd gold, and yet went never gay . . ." *Oth,* II, i, 150.

gay comparisons, *n.* showy trappings: "I dare him therefore/ To lay his gay comparisons apart . . ." *Ant & Cleo,* III, xiii, 25–26.

gayness, *n.* elegant attire; here, ref. to the uniforms of the French soldiers: "Our gayness and our gilt are all besmirch'd/ With rainy marching . . ." *Hen 5,* IV, iii, 110–111.

gay skins, *n.* pleasing appearances: "The more do thou in serpents' natures think them,/ Fear their gay skins with thought of their sharp state . . ." *More,* III, ii, 17–18.

gaze, *v.* **1** to stare, esp. in astonishment: "You look pale, and gaze,/ And put on fear . . ." *J Caes,* I, iii, 59–60. **2** to imitate one's superiors; here, in a vain effort to be accepted by them: "Pitiful thrivers in their gazing spent?" *Sonn 125,* 8.
—*n.* **3** object of one's gaze: "The lovely gaze where every eye doth dwell . . ." *Sonn 5,* 2. **4 in false gaze,** looking in the wrong

direction: ". . . 'tis a pageant,/ To keep us in false gaze . . ." *Oth,* I, iii, 18–19. **5 stand at gaze,** (of a deer) to stand still with a bewildered look: "As the poor frighted deer that stands at gaze . . ." *Luc,* 1149.

gear, *n.* **1** clothing; costume: ". . . what fools were here,/ Disguis'd like Muscovites, in shapeless gear . . ." *Love's L,* V, ii, 302–303. **2** equipment: "And Cupid grant all tongue-tied maidens here/ Bed, chamber, pander to provide this gear!" *Tr & Cr,* III, ii, 209–210. **3** matter; purpose or business; also, stuff: "Here's goodly gear."/ "A sail! a sail!" *Rom & Jul,* II, iv, 100–101. **4** chatter; blather: "Fare you well, I'll grow a talker for this [because of all this] gear." *Merch,* I, i, 110. **5** nonsense; silliness; foolishness: "Will this gear ne'er be mended?" *Tr & Cr,* I, i, 6. **6 to this gear,** on with the business: "To this/ gear, the sooner the better." *2 Hen 6,* I, iv, 13–14.

geck, *n.* fool; gull or dupe: ". . . made the most notorious geck and gull/ That e'er invention play'd on?" *T Night,* V, i, 342–343.

geld, *v.* to rob; take a vital part of: "Gelding the opposed continent as much/ As on the other side it takes from you." *1 Hen 4,* III, i, 106–107.

gelded, *adj.* blighted; despoiled; impaired: ". . . we much rather . . . have the money by our father lent,/ Than Aquitaine, so gelded as it is." *Love's L,* II, i, 146–148.

gelt, *past part.* var. of GELDED: "Would he were gelt that had it for my part . . ." *Merch,* V, i, 144.

geminy, *n.* twin pair: ". . . like a geminy of baboons . . ." *Wives,* II, ii, 8.

gender, *n.* **1 thy sable gender mak'st,** crows were said to procreate by contact between their bills: ". . . thy sable gender mak'st/ With the breath thou giv'st and tak'st . . ." *Phoen,* 18–19.
—*v.* **2** to procreate: "Or keep it as a cistern for foul toads/ To knot and gender in!" *Oth,* IV, ii, 62–63.

general, *adj.* **1** usual or customary: ". . . I knew it the most general way,/ To them to use your signet and your name . . ." *Timon,* II, ii, 204–205. **2** common; public; here, referring to the audience: "He would drown the stage with tears,/ And cleave the general ear with horrid speech . . ." *Ham,* II, ii, 556–557. **3** universal: "Who redeems nature from the general curse . . ." *Lear,* IV, vi, 207. **4** unanimous: "Every man . . . not consulting, broke/ Into a general prophecy . . ." *Hen 8,* I, i, 89–92. **5** open; friendly: "Bid her be free and general as the sun,/ Who smiles upon the basest weed that grows . . ." *Edw 3,* II, i, 164–165.

—*adv.* **6** widely; universally: ". . . not a soldier . . . Should go so general current through the world." *1 Hen 4,* IV, i, 4–5.
—*n.* **7 be general** take command: "And then will I be general of your woes . . ." *Rom & Jul,* V, iii, 218.

general assault, *n.* a common fault: "A savageness in unreclaimed blood,/ Of general assault." *Ham,* II, i, 34–35.

general censure, *n.* public or popular opinion: "Shall in the general censure take corruption [misrepresentation] . . ." *Ham,* I, iv, 35.

general dependants, *n.pl.* common retainers [lowest-ranking servants]: ". . . there's a great abatement of kindness . . . in the general dependants . . ." *Lear,* I, iv, 63–64.

general gender, *n.* common people: ". . . the great love the general gender bear him . . ." *Ham,* IV, vii, 18.

general honest thought, *n.* honorable respect for the community: "He only, in a general honest thought . . . made one of them." *J Caes,* V, v, 71–72.

generally, *adv.* **1** prob. misuse for "severally," though "separately" or "individually" seems to be intended: "You were best to call them generally, man by man,/ according to the scrip." *M N Dream,* I, ii, 2–3. **2** universally: ". . . as to be—"/ "Generally thankful." *All's W,* II, iii, 36–38.

general offense, *n.* public nuisance: "Methink'st thou art a general offence and/ every man should beat thee." *All's W,* II, iii, 250–251.

general services, *n.* military service: ". . . alike conversant in general services,/ and more remarkable in single oppositions . . ." *Cymb,* IV, i, 12–13.

general state, *n.* See **state** (def. 22).

general subject, *n.* common people; crowd: "The general subject to a well-wish'd king/ Quit their own part . . ." *Meas,* II, iv, 27–28.

generation, *n.* **1** offspring; successive generations: "And heir from heir shall hold this quarrel up/ Whiles England shall have generation." *2 Hen 4,* IV, ii, 48–49. **2 yonder generation,** distant peoples: "Ere twice the sun hath made his journal greeting [daily round]/ To yonder generation . . ." *Meas,* IV, iii, 88–89.

generosity, *n.* the nobles: ". . . a petition granted them, a strange one,/ To break the heart of generosity . . ." *Cor,* I, i, 209–210.

generous, *adj.* **1** noble: "This is not generous, not gentle, not humble." *Love's L,* V, ii, 623. **2** of the nobility; here, recognizably so: "And they in France . . . Are [of a] most select and generous chief in that." *Ham,* I, iii, 73–74. **3 generous and gravest,** the most noble and highest ranking: "The generous and gravest citizens/ Have hent the gates . . ." *Meas,* IV, vi, 13–14.

genius, *n.* **1** [sometimes cap.] guardian spirit: "One of these men is *genius* to the other . . ." *Errors,* V, i, 332. **2** embodiment; soul: ". . . a was the/ very genius of famine . . ." *2 Hen 4,* III, ii, 307–308.

gennet, *n.* small Spanish horse; jennet: ". . . you'll have/ coursers for cousins, and gennets for germans." *Oth,* I, i, 112–113.

gentility, *n.* good manners: "A dangerous law against gentility!" *Love's L,* I, i, 127.

gentle, *adj.* **1** of noble birth; well-born: "The gentle Archbishop of York is up . . ." *2 Hen 4,* I, i, 189. **2** courteous; polite: "This is not generous, not gentle, not humble." *Love's L,* V, ii, 623. **3** tender; also, refined or elegant: "Return, forgetful Muse, and straight redeem/ In gentle numbers [verses] time so idly spent . . ." *Sonn 100,* 5–6. **4** peaceful; occurring in a time of peace: "Health to you, valiant sir,/ During all question of the gentle truce . . ." *Tr & Cr,* IV, i, 11–12. **5 as gentle,** as a courtesy: "As gentle tell me, of what honour [repute] was/ This Cressida in Troy?" *Tr & Cr,* IV, v, 286–287. **6 being gentle wounded,** to remain noble when struck down by fortune: ". . . being gentle wounded, craves/ A noble cunning." *Cor,* IV, i, 8–9.
—*n.* **7** one of gentle birth; gentleman; noble: "Now (by my hood) a gentle, and no Jew." *Merch,* II, vi, 51. **8** [pl.] gentlefolk: "Away! the gentles are at their/ game, and we will to our recreation." *Love's L,* IV, ii, 158–159.
—*v.* **9** to raise to the rank of gentleman: "This day shall gentle his condition . . ." *Hen 5,* IV, iii, 63.

gentlemen of companies, *n.* soldiers ranking above sergeants and below officers: ". . . my whole charge consists of ancients, corporals, lieutenants, gentlemen of companies—" *1 Hen 4,* IV, ii, 23–24.

gentleness, *n.* **1** noble conduct or action: "I give thee thanks in part of thy deserts,/ And will with deeds requite thy gentleness . . ." *T Andr,* I, i, 236–237. **2** blessing; favor: "The gentleness of all the gods go with thee!" *T Night,* II, i, 43.

gentler, *adj.* nobler; of better birth: "Whilst by a slave, no gentler than my dog . . ." *Hen 5,* IV, v, 15.

gentlewoman, *n.* woman, usually of noble birth, who attends a woman of high rank: "Sirrah, tell my gentlewoman I would speak with/ her—Helen I mean." *All's W,* I, iii, 65–66.

gently, *adv.* willingly: "I will be correspondent to command,/ And do my spriting gently." *Temp,* I, ii, 297–298.

gentry, *n.* **1** courtesy; gentlemanliness: "To show us so much gentry and good will/ As to expend your time with us awhile . . ." *Ham,* Ii, ii, 22–23. **2** rank; social standing: ". . . and so thou shouldst not alter the/ article [matter] of thy gentry." *Wives,* II, i, 50–51. **3** members of the nobility: "I have a file [list]/ Of all the gentry . . ." *Mac,* V, ii, 8–9.

George, *n.* insignia of the Order of the Garter, showing St. George and the dragon: "Look on my George; I am a gentleman." *2 Hen 6,* IV, i, 29.

german, *adj.* **1** pertinent; Hamlet indicates that "carriage" is a more suitable word when discussing cannon: "The phrase would be more german to the matter/ if we could carry a cannon by our sides . . ." *Ham,* V, ii, 155, 156.
—*n.* **2** german cousin; a blood relative: ". . . you'll have/ coursers for cousins, and gennets for germans." *Oth,* I, i, 112–113.

German devil, *n.* ref. to Marlowe's play "Doctor Faustus" and its German characters: ". . . set spurs and away,/ like three German devils, three Doctor Faustuses." *Wives,* IV, v, 64–65.

germane, *adj.* closely related; akin: ". . . wert thou a leopard, thou wert germane to the lion . . ." *Timon,* IV, iii, 341–342.

Germany, *n.* **upper Germany,** prob. ref. to peasant revolts in Saxony, esp. in 1520s at beginning of Reformation: "Commotions, uproars . . . as of late days our neighbours,/ The upper Germany, can dearly witness . . ." *Hen 8,* V, ii, 62–64.

germens, *n. pl.* the seed that produces all of nature, including man: ". . . though the treasure/ Of Nature's germens tumble all together . . ." *Mac,* IV, i, 58–59.

gest¹, *n.* [often pl.] deed; exploit: ". . . run one before,/ And let the queen know of our gests . . ." *Ant & Cleo,* IV, viii, 1–2.

gest², *n.* period of stay; appointed day [for departure]: "To let him there a month behind the gest/ Prefix'd for's parting . . ." *W Tale,* I, ii, 41–42.

get, *v.* **1** to beget: "I would rather have one of your father's getting." *M Ado,* II, i, 303. **2** to beget offspring: "Thou wast begot, to get it is thy duty." *Ven & Ad,* 168. **3** to be begotten: "Now . . . were I to get again,/ Madam, I would not wish a better father." *K John,* I, i, 259–260. **4** to obtain or make money: ". . . is it a shame to get/ when we are old?" *Per,* IV, ii, 26–27. **5 got off,** fled; escaped: "Titus Lartius writes, they fought together, but/

Aufidius got off." *Cor,* II, i, 126–127. **6 got upon me,** gained over me: "Have by their brave instruction got upon me/ A nobleness in record." *Ant & Cleo,* IV, xiv, 98–99.

getting, *n.* wordplay here on "securing" and "begetting": "I would rather have one of your father's getting." *M Ado,* II, i, 303.

ghastly, *adj.* **1** white-faced: ". . . a hundred ghastly women,/ Transformed with their fear . . ." *J Caes,* I, iii, 23–24. **2** terrifying: ". . . like a jewel hung in ghastly night . . ." *Sonn 27,* 11.

ghost, *n.* **1** spirit of a dead person: "Henry the Fifth, thy ghost I invoke . . ." *1 Hen 6,* I, i, 52. **2** dead body: "Oft have I seen a timely-parted ghost,/ Of ashy semblance . . ." *2 Hen 6,* III, ii, 160–161. **3 yield the ghost,** to "give up the ghost"; die: "These news would cause him once more yield the ghost." *1 Hen 6,* I, i, 67.
—*v.* **4** to haunt: ". . . since Julius Caesar,/ Who at Philippi the good Brutus ghosted . . ." *Ant & Cleo,* II, vi, 12–13.

ghostly, *adj.* serving as a spiritual guide: "Hence will I to my ghostly Sire's close cell,/ His help to crave and my dear hap to tell." *Rom & Jul,* II, ii, 192–193.

gi', *v.* contraction of "give ye": "God gi' good e'en [good evening]; I pray, sir, can you read?": *Rom & Jul,* I, ii, 57.

giant, *n.* **1** protector; bodyguard; perh. a humorous allusion to Maria's small size: "Some mollification for your giant, sweet/ lady!" *T Night,* I, v, 206–207. **2 a giant's strength,** ref. to the giants' rebellion against Jove in Greek myth.; despite their superhuman strength, the giants lacked wisdom and compassion: "O, it is excellent/ To have a giant's strength, but it is tyrannous/ To use it like a giant." *Meas,* II, ii, 108–110.

gib, *n.* **1** tomcat: "For who . . . Would from a paddock, from a bat, a gib,/ Such dear concernings hide?" *Ham,* III, iv, 191–193. **2** Also, **gib cat,** castrated male cat: "'Sblood, I am as melancholy/ as a gib cat . . ." *1 Hen 4,* I, ii, 71–72.

gibbet, *n.* **1** gallows: ". . . grease, that's sweaten/ From the murderer's gibbet . . ." *Mac,* IV, i, 65–66.
—*v.* **2** to hang: ". . . come off and on swifter than he that gibbets/ on the brewer's bucket." *2 Hen 4,* III, ii, 258–259.

gibbet-maker, *n.* builder of scaffolds for public hangings; the Clown appar. hears "gibbet-er" in place of "Jupiter": "Ho, the gibbet-maker? He says that he hath taken/ them down again . . ." *T Andr,* IV, iii, 79–80.

gibe, *v.* **1** to sneer or scoff: "Why, that's the way to choke a gibing spirit . . ." *Love's L,* V, ii, 850.

—*n.* **2** sneer or scoff: ". . . you/ are wise, and full of gibes and vlouting-stocks . . ." *Wives,* IV, v, 74–75.

giber, *n.* **perfecter giber for the table,** much wittier table companion: ". . . you are well understood to be a/ perfecter giber for the table than a necessary bencher in/ the Capitol." *Cor,* II, i, 80–82.

giddily, *adv.* lightly; inconsequentially: "The parts that fortune hath bestow'd upon her,/ Tell her I hold as giddily as fortune . . ." *T Night,* II, iv, 84–85.

giddiness, *n.* impulsiveness; rashness: "Neither call the giddiness of it in question . . . nor her sudden consenting." *As You,* V, ii, 5–7.

giddy, *adj.* **1** unstable or untrustworthy; precarious: "An habitation giddy and unsure/ Hath he that buildeth on the vulgar heart." *2 Hen 4,* I, iii, 89–90. **2** mad; insane: "I fear, I fear, 'twill prove a giddy world." *Rich 3,* II, iii, 5. **3** fickle, esp. in one's loyalties: "He can at pleasure stint their melody;/ Even so mayest thou the giddy men of Rome." *T Andr,* IV, iv, 86–87. **4** capricious: "And giddy Fortune's furious fickle wheel . . ." *Hen 5,* III, vi, 27. **5** acting with uncontrolled fury: "Do pelt so fast at one another's pate/ That many have their giddy brains knock'd out . . ." *1 Hen 6,* III, i, 82–83. **6** foolish: ". . . arm thy constant and thy nobler parts/ Against these giddy loose suggestions . . ." *K John,* III, i, 217–218. **7 giddy censure,** unstable popular opinion: ". . . and giddy censure/ Will then cry out of Martius . . ." *Cor,* I, i, 267–268.

gift, *n.* act of giving: "Who dies that bears not one spurn to their graves/ Of their friends' gift?" *Timon,* I, ii, 137–138.

gig, *n.* toy top, often spun by striking [whipping]: "To see a great Hercules whipping a gig . . ." *Love's L,* IV, iii, 164.

giglot or **giglet,** *adj.* **1** wanton: "'Young Talbot was not born/ To be the pillage of a giglot wench.'" *1 Hen 6,* IV, vii, 40–41. **2 O giglot fortune!** Oh fortune thou strumpet!: "The fam'd Cassibelan, who was once at point/ (O giglot fortune!) to master Caesar's sword . . ." *Cymb,* III, i, 31–32.
—*n.* **3** loose woman; a wanton: "Away with those giglets too,/ and/ with the other confederate companion!" *Meas,* V, i, 345–346.

gild, *v.* **1** to supply with gold; enrich: "I will make fast the doors and gild myself/ With some moe ducats . . ." *Merch,* II, vi, 49–50. **2** to paint; here, to smear with blood [the colors "red" and "gold" often being used interchangeably]: "If he do bleed,/ I'll gild the faces of the grooms withal . . ." *Mac,* II, ii, 54–55. **3** to redden; here, to become flushed: ". . . where should they/ Find this grand liquor that hath gilded 'em?—" *Temp,* V, i, 279–280. **4** to shine on like rays of the sun: ". . .

sometimes the beam of her view gilded my foot,/ sometimes my portly belly." *Wives,* I, iii, 57–58. **5** to restore color to: ". . . their own nobleness, which could have turn'd/ A distaff to a lance, gilded pale looks . . ." *Cymb,* V, iii, 33–34.

gilded, *adj.* **1** bright or embellished; also, noble or worthy: "And gilded honour shamefully misplac'd . . ." *Sonn 66,* 5. **2** covered with bright scum: ". . . the gilded puddle/ Which beasts would cough at . . ." *Ant & Cleo,* I, iv, 62–63. **3** superficially attractive: ". . . and, in thy attaint,/ This gilded serpent." *Lear,* V, iii, 84–85.

gilded hand, *n.* hand full of or representing wealth; also, a hand ready to dispense gold for services: "Offence's gilded hand may shove by justice . . ." *Ham,* III, iii, 58.

gillyvor, *n.* the pink, a clove-scented flower: ". . . the fairest flowers o' th' season/ Are our carnations and streak'd gillyvors . . ." *W Tale,* IV, iv, 81–82.

gilt[1], *n.* **1** gold, in wordplay with "guilt": "Have, for the gilt of France,—O guilt indeed!—/ Confirm'd conspiracy with fearful France . . ." *Hen 5,* II, Chor., 26–27. **2 gilt o'er-dusted,** gold covered up with dust: "And give to dust that is a little gilt/ More laud than gilt o'er-dusted." *Tr & Cr,* III, iii, 178–179.

gilt[2], *adj.* made golden; here, spread with egg yolk: "The armipotent Mars . . . Gave Hector a gift,—"/ "A gilt nutmeg." *Love's L,* V, ii, 637–638.

gilt counterfeit, *n.* counterfeit coin, usually called a "slip": "If I could a' remembered a gilt counterfeit, thou/ couldst not have slipped out of my contemplation . . ." *Tr & Cr,* II, iii, 26–27.

gilt twopence, *n.* twopenny bit gilded to counterfeit a gold half crown: ". . . if you do not all show like gilt/ twopences to me [compared to me] . . ." *2 Hen 4,* IV, iii, 49–50.

gimmaled, *adj.* **1** consisting of two jointed pieces; twinned: "And in their pale dull mouths the gimmal'd bit . . ." *Hen 5,* IV, ii, 49. **2** made of chain mail: ". . . their nimble spurs . . . their jacks [jackets] of gimmaled mail . . ." *Edw 3,* I, ii, 28–29.

gimmers, *n.* prob. gimmals, part of a clock's mechanism: "I think by some odd gimmers or device/ Their arms are set, like clocks, still to strike on . . ." *1 Hen 6,* I, ii, 41–42.

gin, *n.* snare or trap: "Poor bird! thou'dst never fear the net, nor line,/ The pit-fall, nor the gin." *Mac,* IV, ii, 35.

ging, *n.* gang: ". . . there's a knot, a/ ging, a pack, a conspiracy against me." *Wives,* IV, ii, 108–109.

ginger, *n.* **1** spice used to flavor ale: "Yes, by Saint Anne, and ginger shall be hot i' th'/ mouth too." *T Night,* II, iii, 116–117. **2** munching of ginger was appar. associated with old house-wives, or "gossips": "I would she were as lying a gossip in that, as ever/ knapp'd ginger . . ." *Merch,* III, i, 8–9.

gins, *v.* begins: "The glow-worm shows the matin to be near/ And gins to pale his uneffectual fire." *Ham,* I, v, 89–90.

gipes, *n.* gibes [a mispron.]: ". . . he was full of jests, and gipes, and knaveries, and/ mocks . . ." *Hen 5,* IV, vii, 52–53.

gipsy, *n.* var. of **gypsy;** Gypsies were incorrectly believed to have originated in Egypt: "And is become the bellows and the fan/ To cool a gipsy's lust." *Ant & Cleo,* I, i, 9–10.

gird[1], *v.* **1** to gibe [at]; make fun of: "Men of all sorts take a pride to gird at me." *2 Hen 4,* I, ii, 5. —*n.* **2** jibe or taunt: "I thank thee for that gird, good Tranio." *Shrew,* V, ii, 58. **3** reproof or rebuke: "Sweet King! The Bishop hath a kindly gird." *1 Hen 6,* III, i, 131.

gird[2], *v.* to encircle; surround: "Girding with grievous siege castles and towns . . ." *Hen 5,* I, ii, 152.

girded, *adj.* encircled; besieged: "With fatal mouths gaping on girded Harfleur." *Hen 5,* III, Chor., 27.

girdle, *n.* **1** belt worn around the waist, often having a pouch, keys, sword, etc., attached to it: "The whoreson/ smooth-pates do now wear nothing but high shoes/ and bunches of keys at their girdles . . ." *2 Hen 4,* I, ii, 37–39. **2** waist or waistline [wordplay on "bill" as "weapon"]: "Knock me down with 'em: cleave me to the girdle." *Timon,* III, iv, 89. **3** circumference; enclosed space: "Suppose within the girdle of these walls/ Are now confin'd two mighty monarchies . . ." *Hen 5,* Prol. 19–20. **4 turn his girdle,** poss. suggestion that Claudio can simply swallow his anger: "If he be, he knows how to turn his girdle." *M Ado,* V, i, 141. —*v.* **5** to enclose: "O thou wall/ That girdles in those wolves . . ." *Timon,* IV, i, 1–2.

girlond, *n.* var. of **garland:** "Wear the girlond/ With joy that you have won." *Kinsmen,* V, iii, 130–131.

girt, *v.* **1** var. of GIRD: "I girt thee with the valiant sword of York . . ." *1 Hen 6,* III, i, 171. **2 girt in,** surrounded by: "Like to his island girt in with the ocean . . ." *3 Hen 6,* IV, viii, 20.

girth, *n.* harness strap around the horse's midsection: ". . . one girth/ six times pieced, and a woman's crupper of velure . . ." *Shrew,* III, ii, 57–58.

Gis, *n.* corruption of "Jesus": "By Gis and by Saint Charity,/ Alack and fie for shame . . ." *Ham,* IV, v, 58–59.

Gisors, *n.* See **Guysors.**

give, *v.* **1** to display: "Renounce your style, give sheep in lions' stead . . ." *1 Hen 6,* I, v, 29. **2** to represent as: ". . . men's reports/ Give him much wrong'd." *Ant & Cleo,* I, iv, 39–40. **3** to share; here, pass on to offspring: ". . . why dost thou abuse/ The bounteous largess given thee to give?" *Sonn 4,* 5–6. **4** to tell or warn; reveal to: "My mind gave me,/ In seeking tales and informations . . ." *Hen 8,* V, ii, 143–144. **5** to ascribe: "To give full growth to that which still doth grow." *Sonn 115,* 14. **6 give away,** to abandon: "For thy solicitor shall rather die/ Than give thy cause away." *Oth,* III, iii, 27–28. **7 give back,** to stand back; here, an order: "Thurio, give back; or else embrace thy death . . ." *Two Gent,* V, iv, 124. **8 give in,** to depose; swear to (as): ". . . compell'd/ Even to the teeth and forehead of our faults/ To give in evidence." *Ham,* III, iii, 62–64. **9 give it way,** give in to it: ". . . 'tis a good dulness,/ And give it way . . ." *Temp,* I, ii, 185–186. **10 give off,** to give over; end or cease: "Follow the noise so far as we have quarter./ Let's see how it will give off." *Ant & Cleo,* IV, iii, 20–21. **11 give out, a.** to disclose information (about): "it is the . . . disposition/ of Beatrice that puts the world into her person, and/ so gives me out." *M Ado,* II, i, 193–195. **b.** (to) let it be known that: "Therefore give out you are of Epidamnum,/ Lest that your goods too soon be confiscate . . ." *Errors,* I, ii, 1–2. **12 give over** or **give o'er, a.** to cease; give up (on) or abandon: "We pray you for your own sake to . . . give over this attempt." *As You,* I, ii, 167–168. **b.** to renounce: "I had no judgement when to her I swore."/ "Nor none . . . now you give her o'er." *M N Dream,* III, ii, 134–135. **c.** to take leave of; quit: "To give you over at this first encounter,/ Unless you will accompany me thither." *Shrew,* I, ii, 104–105. **d.** to retire: "Three or four thousand chequins were as pretty a/ proportion to live quietly, and so give over." *Per,* IV, ii, 24–25. **e.** to divulge: ". . . talk not to me, my mind is heavy./ I will give over all." *Wives,* IV, vi, 1–2. **13 give way,** to give scope or opportunity: ". . . (though now the time/ Gives way to us) . . ." *Hen 8,* III, ii, 15–16.

given, *adj.* **1** disposed: "He is a noble Roman, and well given." *J Caes,* I, ii, 194. **2** inclined: ". . . if she had been a/ woman cardinally [carnally] given . . ." *Meas,* II, i, 78–79. —*past part.* **3 would have given,** would like to be given: ". . . have given largely [generously] to many to know/ what she would have given . . ." *Wives,* II, ii, 193–194.

give the cheer, *n.* See **cheer** (def. 6).

Give you good morrow! May God grant you a good tomorrow, equiv. to "good-night" [conventional words of parting]. *Lear,* II, ii, 158.

giving out, *n.* declared intention[s]: "His giving out were of an infinite distance/ From his true-meant design [actual intention]." *Meas,* I, iv, 54–55.

glad, *v.* **1** to gladden: ". . . ancient Gower is come . . . To glad your ear, and please your eyes." *Per,* I, Chor., 2–4. **2** to brighten or cheer: ". . . to glad her presence,/ The senate-house of planets all did sit . . ." *Per,* I, i, 10–11.
—*n.* **3** gladness: "Till fortune, tir'd with doing bad,/ Threw him ashore, to give him glad . . ." *Per,* II, Chor., 37–38.

gladding, *n.* act or instance of gladdening: ". . . to the gladding of/ Your highness with an heir." *Hen 8,* V, i, 71–72.

glance, *n.* **1** jest or innuendo: ". . . the squand'ring glances of the fool." *As You,* II, vii, 57.
—*v.* **2** to hint (at): "In company I often glanc'd at it . . ." *Errors,* V, i, 66. **3** to cast doubt or discredit (on): "How canst thou thus, for shame, Titania,/ Glance at my credit with Hippolyta . . ." *M N Dream,* II, i, 74–75.

glanders, *n. pl.* disease among horses, char. by swellings of the upper neck: ". . . possessed with the glanders and like to mose/ in the chine . . ." *Shrew,* III, ii, 48–49.

glass, *n.* **1** model, paragon, or ideal: "He was indeed the glass/ Wherein the noble youth did dress themselves." *2 Hen 4,* II, iii, 21–22. **2** mirror; looking glass: ". . . then thou will keep/ My tears for glasses, and still make me weep." *Love's L,* IV, iii, 36–37. **3** magic mirror for viewing the future: "A show of eight Kings, the last with a glass in his hand; Banquo following." [SD] *Mac,* IV, i, 111. **4** same, but perh. a crystal ball: ". . . like a prophet/ Looks in a glass that shows what future evils . . ." *Meas,* II, ii, 95–96. **5** "perspective" glass that distorts an image; here, the twins, who seem like a distortion of nature: "If this be so, as yet the glass seems true . . ." *T Night,* V, i, 263. **6** hourglass: "What is the time o' th' day?" "Past the mid season./ At least two glasses [two o'clock]." *Temp,* I, ii, 239–240. **7** [pl.] tears likened to mirrors that reflect the soul: "Uncle, even in the glasses of thine eyes/ I see thy grieved heart." *Rich 2,* I, iii, 208–209. **8** [pl.] eyeballs: ". . . and schoolboys' tears take up/ The glasses of my sight!" *Cor,* III, ii, 116–117. **9** pattern: "My poor chin too, for 'tis not scissor'd just/ To such a favor ite's glass?" *Kinsmen,* I, ii, 54–55. **10 living in my glass,** alive every time I gaze into my mirror: "I my brother know/ Yet living in my glass . . ." *T Night,* III, iv, 389–390. **11 running of one glass,** time elapsed while sand runs from top to bottom in an hourglass: ". . . she would not live/ The running of one glass." *W Tale,* I, ii, 305–306.
—*v.* **12** to encase or enclose in glass: "As jewels in crystal . . . tend'ring their own worth from where they were glass'd." *Love's L,* II, i, 242–243.

glass-fac'd, *adj.* reflecting like a looking-glass the opinions of another: ". . . from the glass-fac'd flatterer/ To Apemantus, that few things loves better/ Than to abhor himself . . ." *Timon,* I, i, 59–61.

glass-gazing, *adj.* self-admiring; vain: ". . . glass-gazing,/ super-serviceable, finical rogue . . ." *Lear,* II, ii, 16–17.

glassy, *adj.* mirrorlike; here, man's soul, reflecting his godlike essence: "Most ignorant of what he's most assur'd—/ His glassy essence . . ." *Meas,* II, ii, 120–121.

glaze, *v.* **1** to stare or glare: "Against the Capitol I met a lion,/ Who glaz'd upon me, and went surly by . . ." *J Caes,* I, iii, 20–21. **2** to cover or furnish with glass: "That hath his [its] windows glazed with thine eyes." *Sonn 24,* 8.

gleam, *v.* to dart, as rays of light: "And dying eyes gleam'd forth their ashy lights . . ." *Luc,* 1378.

glean, *v.* to gather; here, to acquire: ". . . that goodness/ Of gleaning all the land's wealth into one . . ." *Hen 8,* III, ii, 283–284.

gleaned, *adj.* emptied of its defenders: "Galling the gleaned land with hot assays . . ." *Hen 5,* I, ii, 151.

gleeful, *adj.* merry; happy: ". . . wherefore look'st thou sad/ When everything doth make a gleeful boast?" *T Andr,* II, iii, 10–11.

gleek, *n.* **1** gibe or scoff; gesture of contempt: "What will you give us?"/ "No money, on my faith, but the gleek!" *Rom & Jul,* IV, v, 111–112.
—*v.* **2** to jest or jeer; make gibes: "Nay, I can gleek upon occasion." *M N Dream,* III, i, 141.

Glendor, *n.* Owen Glendower [See *l Hen 4.*]: "Come, lords, away,/ To fight with Glendor and his complices . . ." *Rich 2,* III, i, 42–43.

glib, *v.* to geld; castrate: "I had rather glib myself, than they/ Should not produce fair issue." *W Tale,* II, i, 149–150.

glimpses of the moon, See **moon** (def. 2).

glister, *v.* **1** to shine: ". . . how he glisters/ Thorough [through] my rust!" *W Tale,* III, ii, 170–171. **2** to glitter or glint: "His eye, which scornfully glisters like fire,/ Shows his hot courage . . ." *Ven & Ad,* 275–276.

glistering, *adj.* **1** appar. coinage by Shakespeare, combining elements of "bright" [glitter] and "hot" [blistering]: "Down, down I come, like glist'ring Phaeton,/ Wanting the manage of unruly jades." *Rich 2,* III, iii, 178–179. **2** showy and false: ". . .

go 235

forms, being fetch'd/ From glist'ring semblances of piety . . ." *Hen 5*, II, ii, 116–117.

—*n.* **3** sparkle or glitter: ". . . make stale/ The glistering of this present . . ." *W Tale*, IV, i, 13–14.

globe, *n.* **1** the head: ". . . whiles memory holds a seat/ In this distracted globe." *Ham*, I, v, 96–97. **2 the globe,** earth: ". . . when the searching eye of heaven is hid/ Behind the globe and lights the lower world . . ." *Rich 2*, III, ii, 37–38.

glooming, *adj.* gloomy; dismal: "A glooming peace this morning with it brings . . ." *Rom & Jul*, V, iii, 304.

glorious, *adj.* ref. to high aspirations, or perh. ref. to those of exalted rank: ". . . most miserable/ Is the desire that's glorious." *Cymb*, I, vii, 6–7.

glory, *n.* **1** splendor or fame; also, perh. [if Arthur's hand is meant], a halo: "Never to be infected with delight . . . Till I have set a glory to this hand . . ." *K John*, IV, iii, 69–71. **2** vainglory; vanity: "Glory grows guilty of detested crimes . . ." *Love's L*, IV, i, 31. **3** credit; honor; good repute: "Which shall be most my glory, being dumb . . ." *Sonn 83*, 10.

glose, *v.* See **gloze.**

gloss, *n.* **1** fine appearance: "To set a gloss upon his bold intent . . ." *1 Hen 6*, IV, i, 103. **2** look of newness: "'Tis a commodity will lose the gloss with lying . . ." *All's W*, I, i, 149. **3** smooth, plausible manner: "I fear me, lords, for all this flattering gloss,/ He will be found a dangerous Protector." *2 Hen 6*, I, 1, 162–163.

Gloucestershire, *n.* county W of London: "Our meeting is Bridgnorth, and, Harry, you/ Shall march through Gloucestershire . . ." *1 Hen 4*, III, ii, 175–176.

gloves in my cap, *n.* favors given by his mistress: ". . . curl'd my hair, wore gloves in my cap . . ." *Lear*, III, iv, 86.

glowing, *pres. part.* smoldering; ready to burst into flame: "This lies glowing . . . and is almost mature for the violent breaking out." *Cor*, IV, iii, 25–27.

gloze or **glose,** *v.* **1** to comment: "And on the cause and question now in hand/ Have gloz'd, but superficially . . ." *Tr & Cr*, II, ii, 165–166. **2** to flatter: ". . . they whom youth and ease have taught to glose . . ." *Rich 2*, II, i, 10. **3** to fence verbally; hedge: "Heaven, that I had thy head! he has found the meaning;/ But I will gloze with him." *Per*, I, i, 110–111. **4** to gloss; interpret: "Which Salic land the French unjustly gloze/ To be the realm of France . . ." *Hen 5*, I, ii, 40–41.

—*n.* **5** [pl.] verbal sparring; wordplay; also, bawdy puns: "Now to plain-dealing; lay these glozes by . . ." *Love's L*, IV, iii, 366.

glut, *v.* to swallow: "He'll be hang'd yet,/ Though every drop of water swear against it,/ And gape at wid'st to glut him." *Temp*, I, i, 57–59.

glutton, *v.* to eat greedily: "Thus do I pine and surfeit day by day,/ Or gluttoning on all, or all away." *Sonn 75*, 13–14.

gnarl, *v.* to snarl: ". . . wolves are gnarling who shall gnaw thee first." *2 Hen 6*, III, i, 192.

gnarling, *adj.* snarling; growling: "For gnarling sorrow hath less power to bite . . ." *Rich 2*, I, iii, 292.

gnat, *n.* example of an insignificant creature: ". . . with what strict patience have I sat,/ To see a king transformed to a gnat . . ." *Love's L*, IV, iii, 162–163.

go, *v.* **1** to walk: "We'll not run, Monsieur Monster."/ "Nor go neither . . ." *Temp*, III, ii, 17–18. **2** to carry oneself: ". . . and how he looks, and how he goes! O/ admirable youth . . ." *Tr & Cr*, I, ii, 237–238. **3** to accord; agree or coincide: "All my reports go with the modest truth . . ." *Lear*, IV, vii, 5. **4** going: "Returning were as tedious as go o'er." *Mac*, III, iv, 137. **5** poss. to become pregnant, or to make a satisfactory sexual partner: "O, let him marry a/ woman that cannot go, sweet Isis, I beseech thee . . ." *Ant & Cleo*, I, ii, 60–61. **6 go about, a.** to attempt; set about: "I wonder that thou . . . goest about to aply a moral medicine to a mortifying mischief." *M Ado*, I, iii, 10–12. **b.** to move hither and thither: "His horses go about."/ "Almost a mile . . ." *Mac*, III, iii, 11–12. **7 go about her,** [to] set about marrying her: "Hap what hap may, I'll roundly go about her . . ." *Shrew*, IV, iv, 103. **8 go about to,** to intend: "Ay, good brother, or go about to think." *W Tale*, IV, iv, 219. **9 go about with,** to deal with; get around: "A marvellous witty fellow . . . but I will/ go about with him." *M Ado*, IV, ii, 24–25. **10 go alone,** to walk without assistance, esp. without a cane or crutches: "If ever he go alone again, I'll never wrestle for prize more." *As You*, I, i, 158–159. **11 go before,** to surpass: "If that thy gentry, Britain, go before/ This lout, as he exceeds our lords . . ." *Cymb*, V, ii, 8–9. **12 go beyond,** to get the better of; overreach: "Cromwell,/ The king has gone beyond me . . ." *Hen 8*, III, ii, 407–408. **13 go by,** dismissive phrase with approx. meaning of "let it go" or "let it pass": "Go by, Saint Jeronimy, go to thy/ cold bed and warm thee." *Shrew*, Ind., i, 7–8. **14 go down,** go downstairs: "Pray thee go down, good ancient." *2 Hen 4*, II, iv, 148. **15 go down upon,** to capture; bring down: "Go down upon him, you have power enough,/ And in a captive chariot into Rouen/ Bring him our prisoner." *Hen V*, III, v, 53–54. **16 go great,** to become pregnant: "Go great with tigers, dragons, wolves and bears . . ." *Timon*, IV, iii, 191. **17 go in the song,** to understand or be in harmony with another: "Come, in what key shall a man/ take you to go in the song?" *M Ado*, I, i, 172–173. **18 go off,** [in the theatre] to exit; here, to die [exit from life's stage]: "I would the friends we miss were safe arriv'd."/ "Some must go off . . ." *Mac,* V, viii, 1–2. **19 go out,** (of a hawk) to attack game: ". . . the wind was very high,/ And, ten to one, old Joan had not gone out." *2 Hen 6,* II, i, 3–4. **20 go through,** to make an offer; strike a bargain: "Master, I have gone through for this piece you see." *Per,* IV, ii, 41. **21 go thy ways,** Be off with you; off you go: "Go thy/ ways, wench, serve God." *Rom & Jul,* II, v, 44–45. **22 go to, a.** come now (exclam. of impatience or exasperation): "Ay, fashion you may call it. Go to, go to." *Ham,* I, iii, 112. **b.** you needn't worry: "Fear not, Baptista, we will content you, go to." *Shrew,* V, i, 124. **c.** to go along with; follow: "I would/ have sworn his disposition would have gone to the/ truth of his words . . ." *Wives,* II, i, 57–59. **d.** get on with it: "Mistress Ford and Mistress Page, have I encompassed/ you? Go to; via!" *Wives,* II, ii, 147–148. **23 go to't,** to engage in sexual relations: "Did you go to't so young?" *Per,* IV, vi, 73. **24 go under,** to continue; go along with: ". . . if he fail,/ Yet go we under our opinion still . . ." *Tr & Cr,* I, iii, 382–383. **25 go up,** to return to its sheath: "When think you that the sword goes up again?" *J Caes,* V, i, 52. **26 go with me,** go along with my plan: "Things bad begun make strong themselves by ill [wickedness]./ So, pr'ythee, go with me." *Mac,* III, ii, 55–56. **27 go your gait,** See **gait** (def. 4). **28 how go,** what's the going rate for: "How now, how now, how go maidenheads?" *Tr & Cr,* IV, ii, 23.

goad, *n.* pointed instrument; prod: ". . . sully/ The purity and whiteness of my sheets . . . which being spotted/ Is goads, thorns, nettles . . ." *W Tale,* I, ii, 326–329.

goat, *n.* **1** fr. belief that the Devil often assumed the form of a goat: "Am I ridden with a Welsh goat too?" *Wives,* V, v, 138. **2** [often pl.] derisive term for the Welsh subjects of Cadwallader: "Not for Cadwallader and all his goats." *Hen 5,* V, i, 29.

goatish, *adj.* lustful: ". . . to lay/ his goatish disposition to the charge of a star!" *Lear,* I, ii, 133–134.

gobbet, *n.* piece of raw flesh: ". . . overgorg'd/ With gobbets of thy mother's [England's] bleeding heart." *2 Hen 6,* IV, i, 83–84.

goblin, *n.* demon or devil: "Be thou a spirit of health or goblin damn'd [evil spirit] . . ." *Ham,* I, iv, 40.

god, *n.* **1 give like gods,** to show godlike qualities; here, by sparing another's life: ". . . let him learn to know, when maidens sue,/ Men give like gods . . ." *Meas,* I, iv, 80–81.
—*v.* **2 godded me,** made a god of me: "Lov'd me above the measure of a father,/ Nay, godded me indeed." *Cor,* V, iii, 10–11.

God-a-mercy, God have mercy [used in polite responses]: "How does my good Lord Hamlet?"/ "Well, God-a-mercy." *Ham,* II, ii, 171–172.

God and our right, English fighting motto; here, spoken by Philip appar. to emphasize his alignment with England: ". . . at the other hill/ Command the rest to stand. God and our right!" *K John,* II, i, 298–299.

God before, God leading us: ". . . for, God before,/ We'll chide this Dauphin at his father's door." *Hen 5,* I, ii, 307–308.

God bless the mark, *interj.* expression of frustration, roughly the equiv. of "Heaven help me!": "And I, God bless the mark, his worship's ancient." *Oth,* I, i, 33.

God buy you or God bye you or God buy ye or God buy to you, God be with you; good-bye: "God buy you: let's meet as little as we can." *As You,* III, ii, 253.

God defend, God forbid: ". . . God defend the lute/ should be like the case!" *M Ado,* II, i, 86–87.

God defend the right!, Prayer offered before trial by combat: "As it shall follow in my correction; and God defend/ the right!" *Love's L,* I, i, 210–211.

godden, *n.* good evening: "God and Saint Stephen give you godden." *T Andr,* IV, iv, 42.

goddess, *n.* **That goddess blind,** Fortune: "That goddess blind,/ That stands upon the rolling restless stone,—" *Hen 5,* III, vi, 28–29.

godhead, *n.* divinity: "'Why, thy godhead laid apart,/ Warr'st thou with a woman's heart?'" *As You,* IV, iii, 44–45.

God 'i' good e'en, var. of "God [give] ye good e'en"; here, exclam. of impatience and reproach, prob. equiv. to "Go! Goodnight!": "I speak no treason."/ "O God 'i' good e'en!" *Rom & Jul,* III, v, 172.

God 'ild you, God yield [reward] you: "You are very well met. God 'ild you for/ your last company." *As You,* III, iii, 67–68.

God mend me, may God improve my condition: ". . . and so God mend/ me, and by all pretty oaths that are not dangerous . . ." *As You,* IV, i, 178–179.

God morrow, contraction of "God give ye good morrow": "God morrow, lords./ O, tell me, did you see Aaron the Moor?" *T Andr,* IV, ii, 51–52.

god of soldiers, *n.* Mars: "The god of soldiers . . . inform/ Thy thoughts with nobleness . . ." *Cor,* V, iii, 70–72.

God's bodkin, *n.* [by] God's little body [mild oath]: "My lord, I will use them according to their desert."/ "God's bodkin, man, much better." *Ham,* II, ii, 523–524.

God's bread, *n.* consecrated bread of Communion; here, a mild oath: "God's bread, it makes me mad! Day, night . . . still my care hath been/ To have her match'd." *Rom & Jul,* III, v, 176–178.

God send (you) good shipping! Have a good voyage [or trip]; also, a wish for success in any venture: "I have seen them in the church together. God send/ 'em good shipping!" *Shrew,* V, i, 36–37.

Godsforbot, *interj.* old form of "God forbid!": "Marry, Godsforbot! for he'll take vantages." *3 Hen 6,* III, ii, 25.

God's lid, By God's eyelid [mild oath]: "God's lid, his richness/ And costliness of spirit look'd through him . . ." *Kinsmen,* V, iii, 96–97.

God's light, By God's light; by the light of the sun [mild oath]: "God's light, I was never/ called so in mine own house before." *1 Hen 4,* III, iii, 60–61.

God's me, God save me [mild oath]: "God's me! my horse!/ What say'st thou, Kate?" *1 Hen 4,* II, iii, 95–96.

God's my life, God save my life! [mild oath]: "God's my life, where's the sexton?" *M Ado,* IV, ii, 67.

God wot, God knows: "Stood the state so? No, no, good friends, God wot." *Rich 3,* II, iii, 18.

God ye good morrow [good e'en], God give you good morning [good evening]: "God ye good morrow, gentlemen."/ "God ye good e'en, fair gentlewoman." *Rom & Jul,* II, iv, 108–109.

goer-back, *n.* person who retreats: "Myself by with a needle, that I might prick/ The goer-back." *Cymb,* I, ii, 99–100.

goers backward, *n.* inferior beings: "Which, followed well, would demonstrate them now/ But [merely] goers backward." *All's W,* I, ii, 47–48.

gogs-wouns, *n.* [By] God's wounds [an oath]: "'Ay, by gogs-wouns,' quoth he, and swore so loud/ That all amaz'd the priest let fall the book . . ." *Shrew,* III, ii, 158–159.

going, *n.* **going shall be used with feet,** walking will be done with the feet: "Then comes the time . . . That going shall be us'd with feet." *Lear,* III, ii, 93–94.

going-out, *n.* excursion or expedition: "Upon this French going-out, took he upon him . . ." *Hen 8,* I, i, 73.

gold, *n.* **sit in gold,** to sit on a throne; perh. here in fig. sense, suggesting his disdain: ". . . he does sit in gold, his eye/ Red as 'twould burn Rome . . ." *Cor,* V, i, 63–64.

golden, *adj.* **1** resplendent; also, auspicious: ". . . follow'd him/ Even at the heels in golden multitudes." *1 Hen 4,* IV, iii, 72–73. **2** royal; here also, precious: "Here lay Duncan,/ His silver skin lac'd with his golden blood . . ." *Mac,* II, iii, 111–112.

golden age, *n.* age of innocence: "Which virtue gave the golden age to gild/ Their silver cheeks . . ." *Luc,* 60–61.

golden couplets, *n.* pairs of eggs laid by the dove; here, ref. to the golden down of the hatchlings: ". . . as patient as the female dove/ When that her golden couplets are disclos'd . . ." *Ham,* V, i, 281–282.

golden head, *n.* golden tip of Cupid's arrow, reserved for true love: "I swear to thee by Cupid's strongest bow,/ By his best arrow with the golden head . . ." *M N Dream,* I, i, 169–170.

golden letter, *n.* letter marking each Sunday on the old calendars [and a reference to Katharine's fair complexion or light-colored hair]: ". . . let me not die your debtor,/ My red dominical, my golden letter . . ." *Love's L,* V, ii, 43–44.

goldenly, *adv.* glowingly: ". . . report speaks goldenly of his profit . . ." *As You,* I, i, 5–6.

golden round, *n.* royal crown: ". . . chastise with the valour of my tongue/ All that impedes thee from the golden round . . ." *Mac,* I, v, 27–28.

golden shaft, *n.* Cupid's gold-tipped arrow, which caused love: "How will she love, when the rich golden shaft/ Hath kill'd the flock of all affections . . ." *T Night,* I, i, 35–36.

golden time, *n.* time when Richard will have the crown: ". . . no hopeful branch may spring,/ To cross me from the golden time I look for!" *3 Hen 6,* III, ii, 126–127.

golden world, *n.* days gone by; the good old days: "They . . . fleet the time carelessly as they did in the golden world." *As You,* I, i, 118–119.

Golgotha, *n.* place of execution in Palestine; scene of the Crucifixion: ". . . this land be call'd/ The field of Golgotha and dead men's skulls—" *Rich 2,* IV, i, 143–144.

Goliases, *n. pl.* of Goliath: "For none but Samsons and Goliases/ It sendeth forth to skirmish." *1 Hen 6,* I, ii, 33–34.

gone, *adj.* **1** ruined; done for [wordplay on previous "gone" (departed)]: "Fellow Hector, she is gone; she is two months on/ her way [pregnant]." *Love's L,* V, ii, 664–665.

—*past part.* **2** gained: "For where there is advantage to be gone,/ Both more and less have given him the revolt . . ." *Mac,* V, iv, 11–12.

good, *adj.* **1** substantial; well-to-do: "I press [conscript] me none but/ good householders . . ." *1 Hen 4,* IV, ii, 14–15. **2** sound; considered or thoughtful: "Our reasons are so full of good regard [deliberation] . . ." *J Caes,* III, i, 224. **3** justifiable; acceptable: "Was this inserted to make interest good?" *Merch,* I, iii, 89. **4** high in rank: "Thou art a traitor and a miscreant,/ Too good to be so, and too bad to live . . ." *Rich 2,* I, i, 39–40. **5 do good,** to succeed: "If we mean to thrive and do good, break open the/ gaols and let out the prisoners." *2 Hen 6,* IV, iii, 14–15. **6 in good time,** expression of indignation: ". . . marry, garlic to/ mend her kissing with [garlic would make her mouth sweeter than it is]!"/ "Now, in good time!" *W Tale,* IV, iv, 163–165. **7 make that good,** explain that; also, prove that: ". . . he that is well hanged in this/ world needs to fear no colours."/ "Make that good." *T Night,* I, v, 5–7. **8 our goods,** our own good: "Which for our goods we do no further ask . . ." *K John,* IV, ii, 64. **9 you were as good to,** you might as well: "To Saturn, Caius, not to Saturnine;/ You were as good to shoot against the wind." *T Andr,* IV, iii, 56–57.
—*n.* **10** good fellow; (my) good man: "Nay, good, be patient." *Temp,* I, i, 15. **11 do good on,** to benefit; help or aid: "Who can do good on him?/ Well, go; prepare yourself." *Meas,* IV, ii, 66–67. **12 our goods,** our personal benefits: "Which for our goods we do no further ask . . ." *K John,* IV, ii, 64.
—*interj.* **13 good now,** exclam. of dismay; oh please! not again!: "Ay, good now, love, love, nothing but love." *Tr & Cr,* III, i, 108.

good and good store, good ones and many of them: "Of all the horses—/ Whereof we have ta'en good, and good store . . ." *Cor,* I, ix, 31–32.

good cheap, *adv.* cheaply: ". . . bought me lights as good/ cheap at the dearest chandler's in Europe." *1 Hen 4,* III, iii, 44–45.

good-conceited, *adj.* (of music) full of elaborate invention: "First, a/ very excellent good-conceited thing . . ." *Cymb,* II, iii, 15–16.

Good dawning, God give you a good day [salutation spoken shortly before dawn]: "Good dawning to thee, friend: art of this house?" *Lear,* II, ii, 1.

good deed, *adv.* indeed; truly: ". . . yet, good deed, Leontes/ I love thee not a jar o' th' clock behind/ What lady she her lord." *W Tale,* I, ii, 43–44.

Good den, [God give you] good evening: "God save you!"/ "Good den, brother." *M Ado,* III, ii, 71–72.

good dild you, God reward you [corruption of "God yield you"]: "How do you, pretty lady?"/ "Well, good dild you." *Ham,* IV, v, 41–42.

good even, good evening: a greeting used anytime after midday: "Good even, Varro; what, you come for money?" *Timon,* II, i, 10.

goodlier, *adj.* finer; more worthy or upright: ". . . if he were honester/ He were much goodlier." *All's W,* III, v, 79–80.

goodliest, *adv.* in the finest or fairest manner: ". . . patience and sorrow strove/ Who should express her goodliest." *Lear,* IV, iii, 17–18.

goodly, *adj.* fair or handsome; fine: ". . . those his goodly eyes,/ That o'er the files and musters of the war . . ." *Ant & Cleo,* I, i, 2–3.

goodman, *n.* **1** husband [term used by the lower classes]: "My men should call me 'lord,' I am your goodman." *Shrew,* Ind., ii, 106. **2** title of respect given to those below the rank of gentleman, esp. yeomen and farmers: "By'r lady, I think a be, but goodman Puff of Barson." *2 Hen 4,* V, iii, 87. **3** term of chastisement, as for ill-bred conduct: "He shall be endur'd./ What, goodman boy! I say he shall! Go to . . ." *Rom & Jul,* I, v, 75–76.

good morrow, *n.* greeting; salutation: "Till I be gentle, stay thou for thy good morrow . . ." *Timon,* I, i, 181.

goodness, *n.* **1** success: ". . . the chance of goodness/ Be like our warranted quarrel." *Mac,* IV, iii, 136–137. **2 die for goodness,** go to their deaths as martyrs: "Which die for goodness who have liv'd for crime." *Sonn 124,* 14.

good-night, *n.* musical composition, as a lullaby, used to serenade a beloved at night: ". . . tunes . . . he heard the/ carmen whistle, and sware they were his fancies or/ his good-nights . . ." *2 Hen 4,* III, ii, 310–313.

good night our part, say farewell to our part of the bargain: "Is this your speeding? Nay then, good night our part." *Shrew,* II, i, 294.

good now, *interj.* exclam. of entreaty, similar to "good sirs" or "please you": "Good now, sit down, and tell me . . . Why this same strict and most observant watch . . ." *Ham,* I, i, 73–74.

good sooth or **good troth,** in truth; truly: "Good troth, you do me wrong, good sooth, you do . . ." *M N Dream,* II, ii, 128.

Goodwins, the, *n.* See **Goodwin Sands.**

Goodwin Sands, *n.* treacherous area of the Channel, off the coast of SE England: ". . . the great supply/ That was expected by the Dolphin here,/ Are wrack'd three nights ago on Goodwin Sands." *K John,* V, iii, 9–11.

good-year, *n.* **what the good-year,** meaningless expression, roughly equivalent to "What the heck, deuce, dickens, etc.": "What the good-year, my lord, why are you thus/ out of measure sad?" *M Ado,* I, iii, 1–2.

goose, *n.* **1** prostitute: "The boy hath sold him a bargain, a goose, that's flat." *Love's L,* III, i, 98. **2** fool; blockhead; here, also poss. wordplay with "prostitute": "Thou wast never with me for anything, when/ thou wast not there for the goose." *Rom & Jul,* II, iv, 76–77. **3** tailor's pressing iron; also, poss. wordplay with "venereal swelling": ". . . here you may roast [heat] your goose." *Mac,* II, iii, 16.

goose-quills, *n. pl.* writers' pens, hence the quips or barbs of writers: ". . . many wearing rapiers are afraid of goose-quills/ and dare scarce come thither." *Ham,* II, ii, 341–342.

gorbellied, *adj.* big-bellied: "Hang ye, gorbellied knaves, are ye undone?" *1 Hen 4,* II, ii, 84.

Gorboduc, *n.* legendary British king, protagonist of a 1562 play; Clown here improvises a quasi-authority: ". . . for as the old hermit of/ Prague . . . very wittily/ said to a niece of King Gorboduc . . ." *T Night,* IV, ii, 13–15.

Gordian knot, *n.* intricate knot tied by Gordius, king of the Phrygians; ancients believed whoever could untie it would rule Asia; Alexander the Great cut the knot and declared himself ruler of Asia: "Turn him to any cause of policy,/ The Gordian knot of it he will unloose . . ." *Hen 5,* I, i, 45–46.

gore, *v.* to defile; befoul: "Gored mine own thoughts, sold cheap what is most dear . . ." *Sonn 110,* 3.

gore-blood, *n.* clotted blood: "Pale, pale as ashes, all bedaub'd in blood,/ All in gore-blood." *Rom & Jul,* III, ii, 55–56.

gorge, *n.* **1** throat: ". . . how/ abhorred in my imagination it is. My gorge rises [feels constricted] at it." *Ham,* V, i, 180–182. **2 cast or heave the gorge,** to vomit; retch: "She whom the spital-house and ulcerous sores/ Would cast the gorge at . . ." *Timon,* IV, iii, 40–41.

gorget, *n.* protective armor for the throat: "And with a palsy fumbling on his gorget/ Shake in and out the rivet . . ." *Tr & Cr,* I, iii, 174–175.

Gorgon, *n.* **1** (in Greek myth.) winged, dragonlike creature whose gaze turned people to stone: "Approach the chamber, and destroy your sight/ With a new Gorgon." *Mac,* II,

iii, 72–73. **2** prob. Medusa, whose gaze turned men to stone: "Though he be painted one way like a Gorgon,/ The other way's a Mars." *Ant & Cleo,* II, v, 116–117.

gosling, *n.* foolish, inexperienced person [lit., a young goose]; here, a girl: "Marry, whip thee, gosling; I think I shall have/ something to do with you." *Per,* IV, ii, 82–83.

gospelled, *adj.* devoutly religious: "Are you so gospell'd,/ To pray for this good man, and for his issue . . ." *Mac,* III, i, 87–88.

goss, *n.* gorse, a spiny shrub: ". . . through/ Tooth'd briers, sharp furzes, pricking goss, and thorns . . ." *Temp,* IV, i, 180–181.

gossamers, *n.* webs or threads spun by spiders: "A lover may bestride the gossamers/ That idles in the wanton summer air . . ." *Rom & Jul,* II, vi, 18–19.

gossip, *n.* **1** familiar term of address used among women; "neighbor": "Did not goodwife Keech the butcher's/ wife come in then and call me gossip Quickly?" *2 Hen 4,* II, i, 91–92. **2** [pl.] godparents; here, for one or more illegitimate children: ". . . yet 'tis not/ a maid, for she hath had gossips . . ." *Two Gent,* III, i, 267–268. **3 babbling gossip of the air,** Echo, a chattering nymph condemned by Hera to repeat only the words of others: "And make the babbling gossip of the air/ Cry out 'Olivia!' . . ." *T Night,* I, v, 277–278. —*v.* **4** to christen; here, sponsor in the manner of a godparent: ". . . pretty, fond, adoptious christendoms/ That blinking Cupid gossips." *All's W,* I, i, 170–171. **5** to take part in merrymaking: "With all my heart, I'll gossip at this feast." *Errors,* V, i, 407.

gossip Report, *n.* another name for "Dame Rumor": ". . . where the carcases of many a/ tall ship lie buried . . . if my gossip Report/ be an honest woman of her word." *Merch,* III, i, 5–7.

gossip's bowl, *n.* gathering of gossips: "Peace, you mumbling fool!/ Utter your gravity o'er a gossip's bowl . . ." *Rom & Jul,* III, v, 173–174.

gossips' feast, *n.* baptismal feast: "Go to a gossips' feast, and joy with me,/ After so long grief, such felicity." *Errors,* V, i, 405–406.

got, *v.* **1** begot: "Would he deny his letter, said he? I never got him." *Lear,* II, i, 78. **2** won; conquered: "The army of the Queen hath got the field . . ." *3 Hen 6,* I, iv, 1.

gots, *v.* var. of **gottest:** ". . . by what means gots thou to be releas'd?" *1 Hen 6,* I, iv, 24.

gourd, *n.* false dice, perh. hollow: "Let vultures gripe thy guts, for gourd and fullam holds . . ." *Wives,* I, iii, 81.

gout, *n.* drop: "And on thy blade, and dudgeon, gouts of blood . . ." *Mac,* II, i, 46.

gouty, *adj.* infirm; decrepit: ". . . the true gouty landlord which doth owe them." *Lover's Comp,* 140.

govern, *v.* **1** to arrange; manage: ". . . tell my lord the emperor/ How I have govern'd our determin'd jest?" *T Andr,* V, ii, 138–139. **2** to control; restrain: "Go after her: she's desperate; govern her." *Lear,* V, iii, 161. **3** to enable: "And that which governs me to go about . . ." *Sonn 113,* 2.

governess, *n.* female ruler: ". . . the quiet cabinet/ Where their dear governess and lady lies . . ." *Luc,* 442–443.

government, *n.* **1** command; authority: "Who leads his power?/ Under whose government come they along?" *1 Hen 4,* IV, i, 18–19. **2** control; management: "Each part depriv'd of supple government/ Shall stiff and stark and cold appear, like death . . ." *Rom & Jul,* IV, i, 102–103. **3** self-control; good conduct: "'Tis government that makes them seem divine . . ." *3 Hen 6,* I, iv, 132. **4** act of governing: "Of government the properties to unfold/ Would seem in me t'affect speech and discourse . . ." *Meas,* I, i, 3–4. **5** period of rule: ". . . his fact [crime] till now in the government of Lord/ Angelo came not to an undoubtful proof." *Meas,* IV, ii, 134–135. **6** wordplay on "bad conduct" and "poor governing": "I will open my lips in vain, or discover [reveal]/ his government." *Meas,* III, i, 192–193. **7 in government,** under control: ". . . like a child/ on a recorder; a sound, but not in government." *M N Dream,* V, i, 122–123.

Gower, John, 14th cent. English poet: "To sing a song that old was sung,/ From ashes ancient Gower is come . . ." *Per,* I, Chor., 1–2.

gown, *n.* dressing gown: "Enter old Capulet in his gown . . ." [SD] *Rom & Jul,* I, i, 72.

grace, *n.* **1** [pl.] a person's pleasing qualities or attractive features: ". . . to some kind of men,/ Their graces serve them but as enemies . . ." *As You,* II, iii, 10–11. **2** honor; homage: "I will/ make the King do you grace." *2 Hen 4,* V, v, 5–6. **3** distinction: ". . . that loose grace/ Which shallow laughing hearers give to fools." *Love's L,* V, ii, 851–852. **4** favor; kindly regard: "Thy grace being gain'd cures all disgrace in me." *Love's L,* IV, iii, 64. **5** act of kindness or a favor: And not a man of them shall have the grace,/ Despite of suit, to see a lady's face." *Love's L,* V, ii, 128–129. **6** [often cap.] divine grace: "And sundry blessings hang about his throne;/ That speak him full of grace." *Mac,* IV, iii, 158–159. **7** virtue: "I think the boy hath

grace in him, he blushes." *Two Gent,* V, iv, 161. **8** honorific title; here, in a comic form: "Think what thou wilt, I am thy lover's grace . . ." *M N Dream,* V, i, 193. **9** [cap.] God; heavenly Goodness: ". . . what needful else/ That calls upon us, by the grace of Grace . . ." *Mac,* V, viii, 37–38. **10** generosity; humanity: "Your grace, that fed my country with your corn . . ." *Per,* III, iii, 18. **11** [often pl.] any of the three goddesses, daughters of Zeus, who represented beauty, elegance, and charm: "Had I a sister/ were a grace, or a daughter a goddess, he should/ take his choice." *Tr & Cr,* I, ii, 239–240. **12 best grace,** chief excellence: "I think the/ best grace of wit will shortly turn into silence . . ." *Merch,* III, v, 40–41. **13 grace grow,** ref. to rue, the herb of grace: "Grace grow where those drops fall, my hearty friends . . ." *Ant & Cleo,* IV, ii, 38. **14 grace of kings** honor to sovereignty [ref. to Henry]: "And by their hands this grace of kings must die . . ." *Hen 5,* II, Chor., 28. **15 Grace to boot!** Heaven help me!: "Your precious self had then not cross'd the eyes/ Of my young play-fellow."/ "Grace to boot!" *W Tale,* I, ii, 79–80. **16 grace to stand,** [to have the] grace to stand [remain] upright: "Grace to stand, and virtue, go . . ." *Meas,* III, ii, 257. **17 herb of grace,** the bitter herb rue: "Here did she fall a tear; here in this place/ I'll set a bank of rue, sour herb of grace." *Rich 2,* III, iv, 104–105. **18 in grace,** in favor: "What though I be not so in grace as you,/ So hung upon with love, so fortunate . . ." *M N Dream,* III, ii, 232–233. **19 in grace of,** to grace or honor: ". . . they rose up early . . . and hearing our intent,/ Came here in grace of our solemnity." *M N Dream,* IV, i, 131–133. **20 in the state of grace,** wordplay between "sins forgiven" and "addressed as 'Your Grace'": "You are in the state of grace?"/ "Not so, friend: honour and lordship are/ my titles." *Tr & Cr,* III, i, 14–16. **21 of grace exact,** of a most graceful precision: "All our abilities, gifts, natures, shapes,/ Severals and generals of grace exact . . ." *Tr & Cr,* I, iii, 179–180. **22 put your grace in your pocket,** set aside your rank and [here] succumb to human impulses: "Put your grace in your pocket, sir, for this once,/ and let your flesh and blood obey it [my counsel]." *T Night,* V, i, 30–31. **23 state of grace,** free of sin: "You are in the state of grace?"/ "Grace? Not so, friend: honour and lordship are/ my titles." *Tr & Cr,* III, i, 14–16. **24 thou outrun'st grace,** grace will never catch up with you: "Answer not; I am gone."/ "E'en so thou outrun'st grace." *Timon,* II, ii, 90–91. **25 with a grace,** with a show of respect, as in kneeling: "Sirrah, can you with a grace deliver up a supplication?" *T Andr,* IV, iii, 105. **26 with present grace,** by one's present title: "My noble partner/ You greet with present grace . . ." *Mac,* I, iii, 54–55.

—*v.* **27** to favor; show favoritism toward: ". . . all their prayers and love/ Were set on Hereford, whom they . . . bless'd and grac'd . . ." *2 Hen 4,* IV, i, 137–139. **28** to beautify: "Yet eyes this cunning want to grace their art . . ." *Sonn 24,* 13. **29** to pay respect to: ". . . stay here with Antony./ Do grace to Caesar's corpse, and grace his speech/ Tending to Caesar's glories . . ."

J Caes, III, ii, 58–60. **30** to distinguish; do honor to: "... if he do not mightily grace himself on thee, he/ will practise against thee by poison ..." *As You,* I, i, 147–148. **31** to show mercy toward: "The lion doth become his bloody jaws,/ And grace his foragement [prey] by being mild ..." *Edw 3,* II, i, 396–397. **32 grace occasions,** to justify [their] actions: "That the time's enemies may not have this/ To grace occasions, let it be our suit ..." *K John,* IV, ii, 61–62.

graced, *adj.* **1** gracious; also, honored or honoring: "Here had we now our country's honour roof'd,/ Were the grac'd person of our Banquo present ..." *Mac,* III, iv, 39–40. **2** dignified; honorable: "... more like a tavern or a brothel/ Than a grac'd palace." *Lear,* I, iv, 253–254.

graceful, *adj.* sympathetic; approving: "Could not with graceful eyes attend those wars/ Which fronted mine own peace." *Ant & Cleo,* II, ii, 60–61.

graceless, *adj.* disrespectful or irreverent; here, wicked, an epithet addressed to Joan: "Graceless, wilt thou deny thy parentage?" *1 Hen 6,* V, iv, 14.

gracious, *adj.* **1** graceful: "And in dimension, and the shape of nature,/ A gracious person." *T Night,* I, v, 265–266. **2** attractive or appealing: "Peradventure, to make it/ the more gracious, I shall sing it at her [Thisbe's] death." *M N Dream,* IV, i, 216–217. **3** full of or showing grace: "... if his rule were true, he should be gracious." *Rich 3,* II, iv, 20. **4** acceptable: "If ever Bassianus ... Were gracious in the eyes of royal Rome ..." *T Andr,* I, i, 10–11. **5** amusing; delightful: "... thou wast in very gracious fooling last/ night, when thou spok'st of Pigrogromitus ..." *T Night,* II, iii, 22–23. **6** fortunate; blessed: "Thy state is the more gracious, for 'tis a vice to/ know him." *Ham,* V, ii, 85–86. **7** doing honor: "O, now you weep, and I perceive you feel/ The dint of pity. These are but gracious drops." *J Caes,* III, ii, 195–196. **8** holy or pious; virtuous: "... if his rule were true, he should be gracious." *Rich 3,* II, iv, 20.
—*n.* **9** short form of "your gracious majesty": "Gracious, so please you,/ We will bestow ourselves." *Ham,* III, i, 43–44.

graciously, *adv.* by heavenly grace: "... in nothing good,/ But graciously to know I am no better." *Meas,* II, iv, 76–77.

gradation, *n.* **1** seniority; here, promotion based on this: "Preferment goes by letter and affection,/ Not by the old gradation ..." *Oth,* I, i, 36–37. **2 by cold gradation,** with solemn procedure: "... and from thence,/ By cold gradation and well-balanc'd form,/ We shall proceed with Angelo." *Meas,* IV, iii, 98–100.

graff, *v.* **1** var. of **graft:** "I'll graff it with you, and then I shall graff it with a medlar." *As You,* III, ii, 115–116.

—*n.* **2** grafted plant: "... the most just God/ For every graff would send a caterpillar ..." *Per,* V, i, 58–59.

graft, *v.* to implant; here, fig. use as "adopted" or "taken into": "A servant grafted in my serious trust ..." *W Tale,* I, ii, 246.

grafter, *n.* tree from which the scion has been taken: "Spirt up so suddenly into the clouds,/ And overlook their grafters?" *Hen 5,* III, v, 8–9.

grain, *n.* **in grain,** fast-dyed; ingrained or indelible: "That's a fault that water will mend."/ "No sir, 'tis in grain; Noah's flood could not do it." *Errors,* III, ii, 104–105.

grained[1], *adj.* ingrained; indelible: "I see such black and grained spots/ As will not leave their tinct." *Ham,* III, iv, 90–91.

grained[2], *adj.* **1** (of wood) having or showing a grain: "... that body, where against/ My grained ash an hundred times hath broke ..." *Cor,* IV, v, 108–109. **2** furrowed; deeply wrinkled: "Though now this grained face of mine be hid ..." *Errors,* V, i, 311.

gramercy, *n.* [often pl.] thank-you: "Gramercies, good fool. How does your mistress?" *Timon,* II, i, 71.

grandam, *n.* grandmother: "She might ha' been a grandam ere she died ..." *Love's L,* V, ii, 17.

grandfather, *n.* Edward III, actually Henry's great-grandfather: "Your grandfather of famous memory ... and your great-uncle Edward the/ Plack [Black] Prince of Wales ..." *Hen 5,* IV, vii, 94–96.

grandjuror, *n.* man of wealth and high standing: "You are/ grandjurors, are ye? We'll jure ye, faith." *1 Hen 4,* II, ii, 86–87.

grandsire, *n.* grandfather; here, Mercutio pretends he and Benvolio are old men complaining about the young: "Why, is/ not this a lamentable thing, grandsire, that we/ should be thus afflicted ..." *Rom & Jul,* II, iv, 30–32.

grandsire phrase, *n.* proverb or old saying: "... I am proverb'd with a grandsire phrase—/ I'll be a candle-holder and look on." *Rom & Jul,* I, iv, 37–38.

grange, *n.* country house; here, one occupied by a religious order: "... there at the moated grange/ resides this dejected Mariana ..." *Meas,* III, i, 265–266.

grant, *v.* **1 grant scarce,** scarcely admit of any: "Without the which a soldier and his sword/ Grants scarce distinction." *Ant & Cleo,* III, i, 28–29. **2 grant to,** to consent or accede to: "The soldiers should have toss'd me on their pikes/ Before I would have granted to that act . . ." *3 Hen 6*, I, i, 251–252.

grapple, *n.* close-in fighting between ships, esp. hand-to-hand combat: ". . . we put on a compelled valour, and in the/ grapple I boarded them." *Ham*, IV, vi, 16–17.

grasp, *v.* **grasp in,** to embrace: "And with his arms out-stretch'd, as he would fly,/ Grasps in the comer." *Tr & Cr*, III, iii, 167–168.

grass, *n.* ref. to proverb, "While the grass is growing, the horse starves": "Ay, sir, but while the grass grows—the proverb is/ something musty [somewhat stale]." *Ham*, III, ii, 334–335.

grate¹, *v.* **1** to disturb; upset: ". . . this confusion,/ Grating so harshly all his days of quiet . . ." *Ham*, III, i, 2–3. **2** to vex or bore: "Grates me, the sum [gist]." *Ant & Cleo*, I, i, 18. **3 grate upon,** be a nuisance to: "I have grated upon/ my good friends for three reprieves for you . . ." *Wives*, II, ii, 5–6.

grate², *n.* bars of a prison: ". . . else you had looked through/ the grate, like a geminy of baboons . . ." *Wives*, II, ii, 7–8.

grateful, *adj.* agreeable or gratifying; acceptable: "Neighbour, this is a gift very grateful, I am sure of it." *Shrew*, II, i, 76.

gratify, *v.* **1** to reward: "You must, as we do, gratify this gentleman . . ." *Shrew*, I, ii, 271. **2** to express gratitude [for]: ". . . when any shall not gratify,/ Or pay you with unthankfulness in thought . . ." *Per*, I, iv, 101–102. **3** to requite: ". . . in these fear'd hopes,/ I barely gratify your love . . ." *Cymb*, II, iv, 6–7.

gratillity, *n.* Clown's whimsical variant of *gratuity*: "I did impeticos thy gratillity: for Malvolio's/ nose is no whipstock . . ." *T Night*, II, iii, 27–28.

gratulate, *v.* **1** to greet or welcome: "Dear aunt, descend and gratulate his highness." *Edw 3*, I, ii, 87. **2** to honor: ". . . come freely to gratulate thy plenteous bosom." *Timon*, I, ii, 120–121. **3** to be thankful for: "To gratify the good Andronicus,/ And gratulate his safe return to Rome . . ." *T Andr*, I, i, 220–221. —*adj.* **4** gratifying: "There's more behind that is more gratulate." *Meas*, V, i, 526.

grave, *v.* **1** to serve as a grave for: ". . . let this damn you,/ And ditches grave you all!" *Timon*, IV, iii, 167–168. **2** to place in a grave: ". . . lie full low, grav'd in the hollow ground." *Rich 2*, III, ii, 140. **3** var. of **engrave:** "Let's see once more this saying grav'd in gold . . ." *Merch*, II, vii, 36. —*adj.* **4** worthy; respected or venerable: "Pisa renowned for grave citizens/ Gave me my being . . ." *Shrew*, I, i, 10–11. **5** thoughtful; discerning: ". . . your good advice/ (Which still hath been both grave and prosperous) . . ." *Mac*, III, i, 20–21.

6 deadly; lethal: "O this false soul of Egypt! this grave charm [witch] . . ." *Ant & Cleo*, IV, xii, 25. **7** wordplay on Mercutio's "deadly serious" condition: "Ask for/ me tomorrow and you shall find me a grave man." *Rom & Jul*, III, i, 98–99. —*n.* **8 by the grave and thee,** if you die childless, your beauty will be consumed by you, then by the grave: ". . . or else this glutton be:/ To eat the world's due, by the grave and thee." *Sonn 1*, 13–14. **9 grave of your deserving,** the final resting place of your merits: "You shall not be/ The grave of your deserving [you must not keep these great deeds to yourself]; Rome must know . . ." *Cor*, I, ix, 19–20.

grave-beseeming ornaments, *adj.* suitably serious appurtenances [for peace-loving old people], such as walking staffs: ". . . made Verona's ancient citizens/ Cast by their grave-beseeming ornaments/ To wield old partisans . . ." *Rom & Jul*, I, i, 90–92.

gravel, *adj.* **1** hard as stone: "Unfit to live or die! O gravel heart." *Meas*, IV, iii, 63. —*n.* **2 loads o' gravel i'th'back,** kidney stones:. ". . . loads o' gravel i'th'back, lethargies, cold/ palsies, raw eyes, dirt-rotten livers . . ." *Tr & Cr*, V, i, 18–19.

gravel-blind, *adj.* appar. Launcelot's coinage for his father's condition, more than sand-blind [partially blind] but not stone-blind [fully blind]: ". . . my true-begotten father,/ who being more than sand-blind, high gravel-blind,/ knows me not . . ." *Merch*, II, ii, 33–35.

gravelled, *adj.* stuck or run aground; figuratively, at a loss for words: ". . . when you were gravelled for lack of matter, you might take occasion to kiss." *As You*, IV, i, 70–72.

graveness, *n.* seriousness or reserve; also, deference or venerableness: ". . . settled age his sables and his weeds/ Importing health and graveness." *Ham*, IV, vii, 79–80.

grave ornaments, *n. pl.* robes of high office; here, those of cardinal: "The sum of money which I promised . . . his Holiness/ For clothing me in these grave ornaments." *1 Hen 6*, V, i, 52–54.

graver, *adj.* worthier; more venerable: ". . . we two will walk, my lord,/ And leave you to your graver steps." *W Tale*, I, ii, 172–173.

gravity, *n.* **1** wisdom; sage advice; here, used ironically: "Peace, you mumbling fool!/ Utter your gravity o'er a gossip's bowl . . ." *Rom & Jul*, III, v, 173–174. **2** dignity; self-respect: ". . . having received wrong by some person, is at most/ odds with his own gravity . . ." *Wives*, III, i, 50–51. **3** dignified or serious person: ". . . 'tis not/ for gravity to play at cherry-pit with Satan." *T Night*, III, iv, 117–118.

gravy, *n.* melted fat of hot meat; ref. to Falstaff's girth; also, in wordplay with "gravity," both pron. with a long *a*: "There is not a white hair in your face but/ should have his effect of gravity."/ "His effect of gravy, gravy, gravy." *2 Hen 4,* I, ii, 159–161.

Graymalkin, *n.* common name for a gray cat; here, the witch's familiar: "I come, Graymalkin!" *Mac,* I, i, 8.

greasily, *adv.* obscenely; indecently: "Come, come, you talk greasily; your lips grow foul." *Love's L,* IV, i, 138.

greasy, *adj.* fat; slovenly: "Let's consult together against this greasy/ knight." *Wives,* II, i, 104–105.

great, *adj.* **1** filled with sorrow; heavy; oppressed: "My heart is great, but it must break with silence,/ Ere't be disburdened with a liberal tongue." *Rich 2,* II, i, 228–229. **2** pregnant, esp. about to give birth: "Sir, she came in great with child . . ." *Meas,* II, i, 88. **3** strict or harsh: ". . . his life is parallel'd/ Even with the stroke and line of his great justice." *Meas,* IV, ii, 77–78. **4 great of heart,** overflowing with emotion: "This did I fear . . . For he was great of heart." *Oth,* V, ii, 362.
—*adv.* **5** in high or exalted position: ". . . think you see them great,/ And follow'd with the general throng . . ." *Hen 8,* Prol. 27–28.

great-belly doublet, *n.* doublet fashionably padded in the lower part with several pounds of bombast [cotton wadding]: ". . . turned/ away the fat knight with the great-belly doublet . . ." *Hen 5,* IV, vii, 49–50.

great chamber, *n.* prob. main hall or living room: "I would I might/ never come in mine own great chamber again else . . ." *Wives,* I, i, 138–139.

great deal, *n.* party or accessory (to): "So should I be a great/ deal of his act [present deed]." *All's W,* IV, iii, 43–44.

great defender, *n.* ref. to god Jupiter [called "Jupiter Capitolinus"]: "Thou great defender of this Capitol,/ Stand gracious to the rites that we intend." *T Andr,* I, i, 77–78.

greater time, *n.* See **time** (def. 19).

great like, *adv.* very likely: "Say that he thrive, as 'tis great like he will . . ." *2 Hen 6,* III, i, 379.

greatly, *adv.* nobly or magnificently: "Rightly to be great/ Is not to stir without great argument,/ But greatly to find quarrel in a straw/ When honour's at the stake." *Ham,* IV, iv, 53–56.

great men, *n.* the nobility: ". . . build their evils on the graves of great men." *Hen 8,* II, i, 67.

great morning, *n.* broad daylight: "It is great morning; and the hour prefix'd/ For her delivery to this valiant Greek . . ." *Tr & Cr,* IV, iii, 1–2.

greatness, *n.* **1** power or force: "And in the greatness of my word, you die." *As You,* I, iii, 85. **2 I send him the greatness he has got,** I bow to him in submission: "Pray you, tell him/ I am his fortune's vassal, and I send him/ The greatness he has got." *Ant & Cleo,* V, ii, 28–30.

great way, *adj.* for the most part: "Think him a great way fool, solely a coward . . ." *All's W,* I, i, 99.

Grecian, *n.* a Greek: "The Grecians keep our aunt." *Tr & Cr,* II, ii, 81.

gree, *v.* agree: "I cannot hope Caesar and Antony shall well gree together . . ." *Ant & Cleo,* II, i, 38–39.

greeing, *adj.* agreeable; satisfying: "Mine eye well knows what with his gust [taste] is greeing . . ." *Sonn 114,* 11.

Greek, *n.* clown or merrymaker: "I prithee, foolish Greek, depart from me." *T Night,* IV, i, 18.

Greekish, *adj.* old adjectival form of **Greek**: ". . . knit all the Greekish ears/ To his experienc'd tongue . . ." *Tr & Cr,* I, iii, 67–68.

green, *adj.* **1** raw; unhealed: ". . . I told thee they were ill/ for a green wound?" *2 Hen 4,* II, i, 95–96. **2** fresh or new; vivid; intense: "Though yet of Hamlet our dear brother's death/ The memory be green . . ." *Ham,* I, ii, 1–2. **3** inexperienced: "He surely affected her for her wit."/ "It was so, sir, for she had a green wit." *Love's L,* I, ii, 83–84. **4** young; youthful: ". . . everything I look on seemeth green." *Shrew,* IV, v, 46. **5** (of eyes) indicative of youthful vigor: "An eagle, madam,/ Hath not so green, so quick, so fair an eye/ As Paris hath." *Rom & Jul,* III, v, 219–221.
—*n.* **6** new plot of grass marking a grave: "I will rob Tellus of her weed,/ To strew thy green with flowers . . ." *Per,* IV, i, 13–14.

green and pale, *adj.* appearing hung over: "And wakes it now, to look so green and pale/ At what it did so freely?" *Mac,* I, vii, 37–38.

green goose, *n.* young goose; gosling; also, a naive, inexperienced person: "The spring is near, when green geese are a-breeding." *Love's L,* I, i, 97.

greenly, *adv.* **1** sheepishly: "I cannot look greenly nor gasp out my eloquence . . ." *Hen 5,* V, ii, 146. **2** foolishly: ". . . we have done but greenly/ In hugger-mugger to inter him . . ." *Ham,* IV, v, 83–84.

green mantle, *n.* scum: "... drinks the green/ mantle of the standing pool ..." *Lear,* III, iv, 136–137.

green-sickness, *n.* **1** kind of anemia thought to afflict unmarried girls: "... thin drink doth so over-cool their/ blood ... that they fall/ into a kind of male green-sickness ..." *2 Hen 4,* IV, iii, 89–91. **2** excessive modesty resulting from sexual inexperience: "Now, the pox upon her green-sickness for me!" *Per,* IV, vi, 13.
—*adj.* **3** immature and, hence, foolish: "Out, you green-sickness carrion! Out, you baggage!" *Rom & Jul,* III, v, 156.

green sour ringlets, *n.* See **ringlets** (def. 2).

greet, *v.* **1** to look at: "... when we greet, with eyes best seeing, heaven's fiery eye ..." *Love's L,* V, ii, 374–375. **2** to satisfy: "It greets me as an enterprise of kindness/ Perform'd to your sole daughter." *Per,* IV, iii, 38–39. **3 greets me well,** sends me greetings by a worthy representative: "... Pindarus is come/ To do you salutation from his master."/ "He greets me well." *J Caes,* IV, ii, 4–6. **4 greet the time,** be ready for the emergency: "... your haste/ Is now urged on you."/ "We will greet the time." *Lear,* V, i, 53–54.

greeting, *n.* precise words; here, accusation: "Now Thomas Mowbray do I turn to thee,/ And mark my greeting well ..." *Rich 2,* I, i, 35–36.

grey, *adj.* indicating early morning, just before sunrise: "The hunt is up, the morn is bright and grey ..." *T Andr,* II, ii, 1.

grey eye, *n.* blue eyes; regarded as a compliment: "Thisbe, a grey eye or so, but not to the purpose." *Rom & Jul,* II, iv, 43–44.

greyhound, *n.* ref. to Hector's swiftness as a runner: "... it runs against Hector."/ "Ay, and Hector's a greyhound." *Love's L,* V, ii, 650–652.

grief, *n.* **1** pain; smarting, as of wounds: "I then ... Out of my grief and my impatience/ Answer'd neglectingly ..." *1 Hen 4,* I, iii, 48–51. **2** grievance; complaint: "Thy grief is but thy absence for a time." *Rich 2,* I, iii, 258. **3** [pl.] grievances: "When we are wrong'd and would unfold our griefs ..." *2 Hen 4,* IV, i, 77. **4** instance of suffering: "... let us pay the time but needful woe,/ Since it hath been beforehand with our griefs." *K John,* V, vii, 110–111.

grief-shot, *adj.* grief-stricken: "... as a discontented friend, grief-shot/ With his unkindness?" *Cor,* V, i, 44–45.

grievance, *n.* **1** source of sorrow: "I'll know his grievance or be much denied." *Rom & Jul,* I, i, 155. **2** lamentation; suffering: "... the night's dead silence/ Will well become such sweet complaining grievance." *Two Gent,* III, ii, 84–85.

grieve, *v.* **1** to grieve for: "I thought it princely charity to grieve them." *Per,* I, ii, 100. **2** to chafe; cause pain to by rubbing: "Thou griev'st my gall." *Love's L,* V, ii, 237. **3** to annoy or afflict: "It shall no longer grieve without reproof." *Per,* II, iv, 19.

griffin, *n.* fabled beast, having the lion's body and the eagle's head and wings: "A clip-wing'd griffin and a moulten raven ..." *1 Hen 4,* III, i, 146.

grin, *v.* to bare the teeth: "Small curs are not regarded when they grin ..." *2 Hen 6,* III, i, 18.

grind, *v.* to sharpen: "Mine appetite I never more will grind/ On newer proof [new experiences] ..." *Sonn 110,* 10–11.

gripe[1]**,** *v.* **1** to grip; also, to grab or seize: "You took occasion to be quickly woo'd/ To gripe the general sway into your hand ..." *1 Hen 4,* V, i, 56–57. **2** to take or lead by the hand: "We live not to be grip'd by meaner persons." *Hen 8,* II, ii, 135.
—*n.* **3** grasp or grip: "Upon my head they plac'd a fruitless crown,/ And put a barren sceptre in my gripe ..." *Mac,* III, i, 60–61. **4** [usually pl.] clutches: "I take my cause/ Out of the gripes of cruel men ..." *Hen 8,* V, ii, 133–134. **5 join gripes,** to clasp hands: "... join gripes, with hands/ Made hard with hourly falsehood ..." *Cymb,* I, vii, 106–107.

gripe[2]**,** *n.* griffin of fable or poss. the eagle: "Like a white hind under the gripe's sharp claws ..." *Luc,* 543.

grise or **grize,** *n.* step; level or degree: "... for every grise of fortune/ Is smooth'd by that below." *Timon,* IV, iii, 16–17.

grisled, *adj.* grisly; dreary; grim: "... the grisled north/ Disgorges such a tempest forth ..." *Per,* III, Chor., 47–48.

Grissel, *n.* [in the "Decameron" of Boccaccio] Griselda, a woman of extraordinary patience, meekness, and humility: "For patience she will prove a second Grissel ..." *Shrew,* II, i, 288.

grize, *n.* See **grise.**

grizzle, *n.* gray hair: "O thou dissembling cub! What wilt thou be/ When time hath sow'd a grizzle on thy case [hide]?" *T Night,* V, i, 162–163.

grizzled, *adj.* streaked with grey: "His beard was grizzled, no?" *Ham,* I, ii, 240.

groaning, *n.* pain of losing one's maidenhead: "It would cost you a groaning to take off my edge." *Ham,* III, ii, 244.

groat, *n.* **1** coin worth four pence: "What money is in my purse?/ Seven groats and two pence." *2 Hen 4,* I, ii, 235–236. **2 ten groats too dear,** wordplay on "royal" and "noble," also units of money, the latter worth 10 groats less than the former: "Hail, royal prince!"/ "Thanks, noble peer;/ The cheapest of us is ten groats too dear." *Rich 2,* V, v, 67–68.

groom, *n.* **1** fellow or chap: "... you must needs bestow her funeral;/ The fields are near, and you are gallant grooms." *T Andr,* IV, ii, 164–165. **2** bridegroom: "I should woo hard, but be your groom in honesty..." *Cymb,* III, vii, 42. **3 vulgar groom,** base fellow [term of contempt]: "And sooner dance upon a bloody pole/ Than stand uncover'd to the vulgar groom." *2 Hen 6,* IV, i, 127–128.

gross, *adj.* **1** large; here, obvious: "Examples gross as earth exhort me..." *Ham,* IV, iv, 46. **2** monstrous: "O villain!"/ "Most heathenish, and most gross!" *Oth,* V, ii, 314.
—*n.* **3** full amount: "... by the near guess of my memory/ I cannot instantly raise up the gross..." *Merch,* I, ii, 49–50. **4 by gross,** wholesale: "And we that sell by gross.../ Have not the grace to grace it with such show." *Love's L,* V, ii, 319–320. **5 gross and scope,** general conclusion or theory: "... in the gross and scope of my opinion,/ This bodes some strange eruption to our state." *Ham,* I, i, 71–72. **6 gross in sense,** obvious: "... if 'tis not gross in sense,/ That thou has practis'd on her with foul charms..." *Oth,* I, ii, 72–73. **7 in gross,** See **term** (def. 6).

grossly, *adv.* **1** obviously: "How ill agrees it with your gravity/ To counterfeit thus grossly with your slave..." *Errors,* II, ii, 168–169. **2** having no spiritual preparation for death: "A took my father grossly, full of bread,/ With all his crimes broad blown..." *Ham,* III, iii, 80–81. **3** indelicately: "Speak not so grossly, you are all amaz'd..." *Merch,* V, i, 266. **4** wordplay on "badly" and "obesely": "Let them say 'tis grossly done; so it be/ fairly done, no matter." *Wives,* II, ii, 137–138. **5** ineptly: "Though you and all the kings of Christendom/ Are led so grossly by this meddling priest..." *K John,* III, i, 88–89.

grossness, *n.* **1** corporeality: "... I will purge thy mortal grossness so,/ That thou shalt like an airy spirit go." *M N Dream,* III, i, 153–154. **2** mass; bulk; extent: "... perspicuous as substance [wealth]/ Whose grossness little characters sum up..." *Tr & Cr,* I, iii, 324–325.

ground, *n.* **1** background: "... like bright metal on a sullen ground..." *1 Hen 4,* I, ii, 207. **2** foundation or basis: "For when would you, my lord, or you, or you,/ Have found the ground of study's excellence..." *Love's L,* IV, iii, 295–296. **3**

the first, or basic, tone of a musical scale: "*Gamut* I am, the ground of all accord—" *Shrew,* III, i, 71. **4** reason or cause: "... the true ground of all these piteous woes/ We cannot without circumstance descry." *Rom & Jul,* V, iii, 179–180. **5** country; land: "Or know what ground's made happy by his breath." *Per,* II, iv, 28. **6** grave; here, a common grave: "... let them throw/ Millions of acres on us, till our ground ... Make Ossa like a wart." *Ham,* V, i, 275–279. **7** (in music) a bass passage over which variations in melody and harmony are constantly wrought: "Ah, what a world of descant makes my soul/ Upon this voluntary ground of love!" *Edw 3,* II, i, 123–124. **8 get ground of,** to gain an advantage over: "With five times so much conversation, I should get/ ground of your fair mistress..." *Cymb,* I, v, 100–101. **9 lose the grounds,** to reveal oneself unintentionally: "I know not how I shall assure you further/ But I shall lose the grounds I work upon." *All's W,* III, vii, 2–3. **10 on the ground,** on earth; in the world: "... the wicked'st caitiff on the ground..." *Meas,* V, i, 56.
—*v.* **11** to base: "How grounded he his title to the crown..." *Hen 8,* I, ii, 144.

grounded, *adj.* firmly rooted or established: "From wayward sickness, and no grounded malice." *Rich 3,* I, iii, 29.

groundlings, *n. pl.* members of the audience who stood in the yard surrounding the stage: "... tear a passion to tatters, to very rags, to split the ears/ of the groundlings..." *Ham,* III, ii, 10–11.

ground-piece, *n.* sketch or drawing: "If that you were/ The ground-piece of some painter, I would buy you/ T'instruct me..." *Kinsmen,* I, i, 121–123.

grove, *n.* wood: "Make thy sad grove in my dishevel'd hair..." *Luc,* 1129.

grovel, *v.* to lie prone; here, in death: "Many a widow's husband grovelling lies..." *K John,* II, i, 305.

grow, *v.* **1** to become: "And grew a seething bath, which yet men prove/ Against strange maladies a sovereign cure." *Sonn* 153, 7–8. **2** to become due: "... the sum that I do owe to you/ Is growing to me by Antipholus..." *Errors,* IV, i, 7–8. **3** to become pregnant: "No less, nay bigger. Women grow by men." *Rom & Jul,* I, iii, 95. **4** to encroach: "Here, as I point my sword, the sun arises,/ Which is a great way growing on the south..." *J Caes,* II, i, 106–107. **5** to grow [become] older: "... how goes the world?"/ "It wears [wears out], sir, as it grows." *Timon,* I, i, 2–3. **6 grow to, a.** to be part of: "I lay aside that which/ grows to me?" *2 Hen 4,* I, ii, 86–87. **b.** [have] become attached to: "I grow to you, and our parting is a tortur'd body." *All's W,* II, i, 36. **c.** of an unpleasant taste; said of milk burned in the pan: "... my father did something smack, something/ grow to; he had a kind of taste . . ." *Merch,* II, ii, 16–17. **7 grow to a point,** See **point** (def. 14). **8 grow upon,** to annoy; become troublesome to: "Begin you to grow upon me?" *As You,* I, i, 5.

growth, *n.* **1** events and developments: ". . . I slide/ O'er sixteen years, and leave the growth untried/ Of that wide gap . . ." *W Tale,* IV, i, 5–7. **2** size or stature: ". . . my little son/ And three or four more of their growth . . ." *Wives,* IV, iv, 47–48. **3 in growth of,** in the course of development (of): "And stops her pipe in growth of riper days." *Sonn 102, 8.*

grub, *n.* **1** boring insect that here acts as "joiner" [carpenter]: "Made by the joiner squirrel or old grub . . . the fairies' coach-makers . . ." *Rom & Jul,* I, iv, 60–61.
—*v.* **2 grub up,** to dig up by the roots: ". . . but for the stock, Sir Thomas,/ I wish it grubb'd up now." *Hen 8,* V, i, 22–23.

grudge, *v.* to begrudge; give reluctantly: "For they have grudg'd us contribution." *J Caes,* IV, iii, 205.

grudging stomachs, *n.* resentful pride: "How will their grudging stomachs be provok'd/ To wilful disobedience . . ." *1 Hen 6,* IV, i, 141–142.

Gualtier, *n.* French form of *Walter:* "Thy name is Gualtier, being rightly sounded." *2 Hen 6,* IV, i, 37.

guard, *v.* **1** to protect; keep safe: "Draw not thy sword to guard iniquity . . ." *Luc,* 626. **2** to embellish; decorate: "To guard a title that was rich before . . ." *K John,* IV, ii, 10–11. **3** to bear witness to: "To guard the lawful reasons on thy part . . ." *Sonn 49,* 12.
—*n.* **4** standard-bearer [in some editions "guidon," pennant]: "I stay but for my guard. On to the field!" *Hen 5,* IV, ii, 60. **5** guardhouse: "Whoe'er keeps me, let my heart be his guard . . ." *Sonn 133,* 11. **6** protection: "Where I find him, were it/ At home, upon [under] my brother's guard . . ." *Cor,* I, x, 24–25. **7** [usually pl.] decoration or embroidery on a garment, esp. gold braid: "O! rhymes are guards on wanton Cupid's hose:/ Disfigure not his shop [codpiece]." *Love's L,* IV, iii, 55–56. **8** fig. use of preceding for seemingly virtuous appearance: "The damnedst body to invest and cover/ In precise guards!" *Meas,* III, i, 95–96. **9 at a guard,** alert and ready to defend oneself: "Lord Angelo is precise;/ Stands at a guard with Envy . . ." *Meas,* I, iii, 50–51. **10 out of one's guard,** at a loss for words; here, witty repartee: "Look you now, he's out of his guard already:/ unless you laugh . . . he is gagged." *T Night,* I, v, 84–86.

guardage, *n.* guardianship [by her father]: "Run from her guardage to the sooty bosom/ Of such a thing as thou?" *Oth,* I, ii, 70–71.

guardant, *n.* guard; protector: ". . . my angry guardant stood alone,/ Tendering my ruin . . ." *1 Hen 6,* IV, vii, 9–10.

guarded, *adj.* decorated or embellished: ". . . the body of your discourse/ is sometime guarded with fragments . . ." *M Ado,* I, i, 265–266.

gudgeon, *n.* small fish that is easily caught; hence, a person who is easily duped: "But fish not with this melancholy bait/ For this fool gudgeon, this opinion . . ." *Merch,* I, i, 101–102.

guerdon, *n.* **1** reward or recompense: "Death, in guerdon of her wrongs,/ Gives her fame which never dies . . ." *M Ado,* V, iii, 5–6. **2** gratuity; tip: "And to her white hand see thou do commend/ This seal'd-up counsel. There's thy guerdon: go." *Love's L,* III, i, 162–163.
—*v.* **3** to reward: "My Lord Protector will . . . See you well guerdon'd for these good deserts." *2 Hen 6,* I, iv, 44–45.

guess, *n.* **1** conjecture; hypothesis: "It is not so with Him that all things knows/ As 'tis with us that square our guess by shows [shape our conjectures by outward appearances]." *All's W,* II, i, 148–149.
—*v.* **2** to hazard a guess: ". . . I have found/ Myself in my incertain grounds to fail/ As often as I guess'd." *All's W,* III, i, 14–16.

guessingly, *adv.* done without knowledge of the facts: "I have a letter guessingly set down . . ." *Lear,* III, vii, 47.

guests, *n.* tears: ". . . seem'd not to know/ What guests were in her eyes . . ." *Lear,* IV, iii, 21–22.

guest-wise sojourned, like a guest that has stayed for a time: "My heart to her but as guest-wise sojourn'd,/ And now to Helen is it home return'd . . ." *M N Dream,* III, ii, 171–172.

guide, *n.* here, the vial of poison that will lead Romeo to death: "Come, bitter conduct, come unsavoury guide,/ Thou desperate pilot . . ." *Rom & Jul,* V, iii, 116–117.

guider, *n.* guide: "Our guider, come; to the Roman camp conduct us." *Cor,* I, vii, 7.

Guienne, *n.* former prov. in SW France: "Guienne, Champaigne, Rheims, Rouen, Orleans,/ Paris, Guysors, Poictiers, are all quite lost." *1 Hen 6,* I, i, 60–61.

guilder, *n.* gold coin of the Netherlands; here, a generic term for "money": ". . . our well-dealing countrymen,/ Who, wanting guilders to redeem their lives/ Have seal'd his rigorous statutes with their bloods . . ." *Errors,* I, i, 7–9.

Guildhall, *n.* town hall of London: "Look for the news that the Guildhall affords." *Rich 3,* III, v, 101.

guiled, *adj.* treacherously alluring: "Thus ornament is but the guiled shore/ To a most dangerous sea . . ." *Merch,* III, ii, 97–98.

guileful, *adj.* **1** deceitful; treacherous: "A third thinks . . . By guileful fair words peace may be obtain'd." *1 Hen 6,* I, i, 76–77. **2** deceptive: "I train'd thy brethren to that guileful hole . . ." *T Andr,* V, i, 104.

guinea-hen, *n.* mildly contemptuous term for a girl or woman; "skirt": ". . . ere I would/ say I would drown myself, for the love of a guinea-hen,/ I would change my humanity with a baboon." *Oth,* I, iii, 314–316.

Guinever, *n.* queen to King Arthur; also, symbol of an unfaithful woman: ". . . one as old, that was a/ woman when Queen Guinever of Britain was a little/ wench . . ." *Love's L,* IV, i, 123–125.

guise, *n.* custom; customary behavior: "This is her very guise; and,/ upon my life, fast asleep." *Mac,* V, i, 18–19.

gules, *n.* (in heraldry) the color red: "With man's blood paint the ground, gules, gules." *Timon,* IV, iii, 60.

gulf, *n.* **1** gullet; also, a ravenous appetite: "Witches' mummy; maw, and gulf,/ Of the ravin'd salt-sea shark . . ." *Mac,* IV, i, 22–23. **2** vortex; whirlpool: ". . . but like a gulf doth draw/ What's near it with it." *Ham,* III, iii, 16–17.

gull, *n.* **1** one easily deceived; dupe or fool: "An ass-head, and a coxcomb,/ and a knave, a thin-faced knave, a gull?" *T Night,* V, i, 204–205. **2** trick or hoax: "I should think this a gull, but that the/ white-bearded fellow speaks it." *M Ado,* II, iii, 118–119.

—*v.* **3** to fool or dupe; cheat: "Which nightly gulls him with intelligence . . ." *Sonn 86,* 10.

gull-catcher, *n.* trapper of gullible fools; here, ref. to Maria: "Here comes my noble gull-catcher." *T Night,* II, v, 187.

gummed velvet, *n.* cheap velvet painted with gum to give it a gloss, causing it to fray [fret] more quickly: "I have removed Falstaff's/ horse, and he frets like a gummed velvet." *1 Hen 4,* II, ii, 1–2.

gun-stones, *n.* stones used as cannon balls: ". . . tell the pleasant prince this mock of his/ Hath turn'd his balls to gun-stones . . ." *Hen 5,* I, ii, 281–282.

gurnet, *n.* small fish pickled (soused) and prized as a delicacy: "If I be not ashamed of my soldiers, I am a soused/ gurnet . . ." *1 Hen 4,* IV, ii, 11–12.

gust, *n.* **1** taste: "Mine eye well knows what with his [its] gust is 'greeing . . ." *Sonn 114,* 11. **2** gusto; relish: ". . . he hath the gift of a coward to allay the gust he/ hath in quarrelling . . ." *T Night,* I, iii, 31–32. **3** attribute: "To kill, I grant, is sin's extremest gust . . ." *Timon,* III, v, 55.
—*v.* **4** to perceive; become aware of: ". . . 'tis far gone,/ When I shall gust it last." *W Tale,* I, ii, 218–219.

guts-griping, *n.* prob. colic or colitis: "Now the rotten diseases/ of the south, the guts-griping, ruptures . . ." *Tr & Cr,* V, i, 16–17.

guttered, *adj.* jagged: "The gutter'd rocks, and congregated sands,/ Traitors ensteep'd, to clog the guiltless keel . . ." *Oth,* II, i, 69–70.

Guysors or **Gisors,** *n.* a city and stronghold in N central France: "Guienne, Champaigne, Rheims, Rouen, Orleans,/ Paris, Guysors, Poictiers, are all quite lost." *1 Hen 6,* I, i, 60–61.

gypsy or **gipsy,** *n.* gypsies were thought to be Egyptian [a term of contempt]; here, wordplay on additional sense of "slut": ". . . Cleopatra a/ gypsy, Helen and Hero hildings and harlots . . ." *Rom & Jul,* II, iv, 42–43.

gyve, *n.* **1** [often pl.] fetter; shackle; here, a leg fetter: ". . . the villains march wide betwixt the legs as if they/ had gyves on . . ." *1 Hen 4,* IV, ii, 40–41. **2** the same, understood as imprisonment: ". . . if you/ will take it on you to assist him, it shall redeem you/ from your gyves . . ." *Meas,* IV, ii, 8–10. **3** fault or weakness: ". . . the great love the general gender bear him,/ Who . . . Convert his gyves to graces . . ." *Ham,* IV, vii, 18–21.

H

H, *n.* wordplay on shape of letter and shared pron. of "H" and "ache" [aitch]: "I had a wound here that was [shaped] like a T,/ But now 'tis made an H [hurt]." *Ant & Cleo,* IV, vi, 7–8.

ha, *interj.* exclam. of contempt or annoyance: "Ha, ha! keep time—how sour sweet music is/ When time is broke and no proportion kept!" *Rich 2,* V, v, 42–43.

ha', *v.* contraction of "have": "Ha' with you [let's go]" *Oth,* I, ii, 53.

habiliment, *n.* **1** disguise: ". . . in this strange and sad habiliment,/ I will encounter with Andronicus . . ." *T Andr,* V, ii, 1–2. **2** [pl.] dress; vestments: ". . . why he cometh hither/ Thus plated in habiliments of war . . ." *Rich 2,* I, iii, 27–28.

habit, *n.* **1** clothing or manner of dressing: "My father, in his habit as he liv'd!" *Ham,* III, iv, 137. **2** here, a herald's coat, or tabard, decorated with his coat of arms: "You know me by my habit." *Hen 5,* III, vi, 118. **3** manner; behavior: "If thou didst put this sour cold habit on/ To castigate thy pride . . ." *Timon,* IV, iii, 241–242.
—*v.* **4** to dress: "She shall be habited as it becomes/ The partner of your bed." *W Tale,* IV, iv, 547–548.

habitation, *n.* dwelling: ". . . to eat of the habitation which your/ prophet the Nazarite conjured the devil into . . ." *Merch,* I, iii, 29–30.

habited, *adj.* dressed: "Enter King and others as masquers, habited like shepherds . . ." [SD] *Hen 8,* I, iv, 63.

habit of doctors, *n.* long furred gown and black cap of a doctor of laws: ". . . next them two scribes in the/ habit of doctors . . ." [SD] *Hen 8,* II, iv, 1.

habit of encounter, *n.* stylishly superficial social intercourse: ". . . the tune of/ the time and, out of an habit of encounter, a kind of/ yeasty collection . . ." *Ham,* V, ii, 186–188.

habitude, *n.* **real habitude,** true nature: "His real habitude gave life and grace/ To appertainings . . ." *Lover's Comp,* 114–115.

hack, *n.* **1** gash or dent: "Look you/ what hacks are on his helmet . . ." *Tr & Cr,* I, ii, 206–207.
—*v.* **2** perh. to be promiscuous [fig. sense of attack with one's sword plus sexual innuendo]: "These knights will hack; and so thou shouldst not alter the/ article of thy gentry." *Wives,* II, i, 49–51. **3** to mangle: ". . . let them keep/ their limbs whole, and hack our English." *Wives,* III, i, 71–72. **4 hack and hew,** to engage in war against: "The sin is more to hack and hew poor men,/ Than to embrace in an unlawful bed . . ." *Edw 3,* II, ii, 112–113.

hackney, *n.* riding horse; also, a prostitute: ". . . the hobby-horse is but a colt,—and/ your love perhaps a hackney [*aside*]." *Love's L,* III, i, 29–30.

h'ad, *v.* contraction of "he had": "I'd rather than the worth of thrice the sum,/ H'ad sent to me first . . ." *Timon,* III, iii, 24–25.

hade land, *n.* headland: ". . . and again, sir—shall we sow the hade land with/ wheat?" *2 Hen 4,* V, i, 12–13.

hag, *n.* **1** ugly, evil woman; here, ref. to the witch Sycorax: "This blue-ey'd hag was hither brought with child . . ." *Temp,* I, ii, 269. **2 hags of hell,** the Furies: "And wedded be thou to the hags of hell . . ." *2 Hen 6,* IV, i, 78.

Hagar's offspring, *n.* Ishmael, son of Hagar, a gentile servant, and Abraham; outcast or vagabond: "What says that fool of Hagar's offspring? ha?" *Merch,* II, v, 43.

hag-born, *adj.* born of a hag; here, of the witch Sycorax: "A freckled whelp hag-born—not honour'd with/ A human shape." *Temp,* I, ii, 283–284.

haggard, *n.* **1** young female hawk: ". . . her spirits are as coy and wild/ As haggards of the rock." *M Ado,* III, i, 35–36. **2** untrained hawk; also, one poorly trained: "And like the haggard, check at [be diverted by] every feather/ That comes before his eye." *T Night,* III, i, 65–66. **3 man my haggard,** to tame my wild hawk: "Another way I have to man my haggard,/ To make her come and know her keeper's call . . ." *Shrew,* IV, i, 180–181.

—*adj.* **4** wild; unruly [term in falconry]: ". . . if I do prove her haggard . . . I'ld whistle her off . . ." *Oth,* III, iii, 264–266.

haggish, *adj.* like a hag in being ugly or repulsive: "But on us both did haggish age steal on . . ." *All's W,* I, ii, 29.

haggled, *past part.* mangled; maimed: ". . . and York, all haggled over,/ Comes to him, where in gore he lay insteep'd . . ." *Hen 5,* IV, vi, 11–12.

hag-seed, *n.* child of a hag; here, the witch Sycorax: "Hagseed, hence!/ Fetch us in fuel . . ." *Temp,* I, ii, 367.

hair, *n.* **1** nature; kind or sort: "The quality and hair of our attempt/ Brooks no division . . ." *1 Hen 4,* IV, i, 61–62. **2** very small amount; bit, whit, or jot: "God may/ finish it when He will, 'tis not a hair amiss yet." *2 Hen 4,* I, ii, 22–23. **3** wordplay on "hair" and "hare," following Launce's hunting call: "There's not a hair on 's head but/ 'tis a Valentine." *Two Gent,* III, i, 191–192. **4 against the hair, a.** against one's wishes; here, in obscene wordplay with "pubic hair": "Thou desirest me to stop in my tale against the hair." *Rom & Jul,* II, iv, 95. **b.** contrary to his nature: "He is melancholy/ without cause and merry against the hair . . ." *Tr & Cr,* I, ii, 26–27. **5 men of hair,** prob. guests dressed in skins to resemble satyrs: ". . . that have/ made themselves all men of hair, they call themselves/ Saltiers . . ." *W Tale,* IV, iv, 326–328. **6 to a hair,** to the last detail: "You'll remember your brother's/ excuse?"/ "To a hair." *Tr & Cr,* III, i, 138–140.

halberd, *n.* **1** battle-ax mounted on a long spear or pole: "Come, stand by me, fear nothing; guard with halberds." *Errors,* V, i, 185. **2** soldier armed with a halberd; halberdier: "Enter the corse of Henry the Sixth with Halberds to guard it . . ." *Rich 3,* I, ii, [SD].

halberdier, *n.* See **halberd** (def. 2).

halcyon beaks, *n.* the kingfisher, it was thought, could be hung up and its bill would point in the direction of the wind; here, readily adjusting to every mood: ". . . turn their halcyon beaks/ With every gale and vary of their masters . . ." *Lear,* II, ii, 79–80.

halcyon's days, *n. pl.* period of fine weather, fine enough [it was said] for the halcyon [kingfisher] to nest on the sea: "Ex-pect Saint Martin's summer, halcyon's days,/ Since I have entered into these wars." *1 Hen 6,* I, ii, 131–132.

hale, *v.* **1** to haul or drag; carry off: ". . . Hal'd thither/ By most mechanical and dirty hand." *2 Hen 4,* V, v, 35–36. **2** to draw or pull: "Is it not strange that sheep's guts should hale souls/ out of men's bodies?" *M Ado,* II, iii, 59–60. **3** to maul; manhandle or abuse: "Thus strangers may be haled and abused. O/ monstrous villain!" *Shrew,* V, i, 98–99.

half, *n.* **1 be your half, a.** be your wife ["better half"]: "Let's part the word."/ "No, I'll not be your half . . ." *Love's L,* V, ii, 249. **b.** share your bet that: "Son, I'll be your half Bianca comes." *Shrew,* V, ii, 79.

—*adj.* **2 half to half the world,** half the world [at war] with the other half: "Were half to half the world by th'ears . . ." *Cor,* I, i, 232.

half-cap, *n.* salutation given in part: "With certain half-caps, and cold-moving nods . . ." *Timon,* II, ii, 216.

half-cheek or half-face, profile; side face: "Saint George's half-cheek in a brooch." *Love's L,* V, ii, 611.

half-cheeked bit, *n.* horse's bit, either unattached on one side or improperly attached: ". . . a half-cheeked bit/ and a headstall of sheep's leather . . ." *Shrew,* III, ii, 54–55.

half-fac'd, *adj.* insufficient; inadequate: "But out upon this half-fac'd fellowship [sharing of honors]!" *1 Hen 4,* I, iii, 206.

half-fac'd sun, *n.* sun emerging from a cloud, the emblem of Edward III: ". . . whose hopeful colours/ Advance our half-fac'd sun, striving to shine . . ." *2 Hen 6,* IV, i, 96–97.

half-face, *n.* profile: "Because he hath a half-face, like my father!" *K John,* I, i, 92.

half-kirtle, *n.* skirt (bottom half of a kirtle): ". . . if you/ be not swinged I'll forswear half-kirtles." *2 Hen 4,* V, iv, 21–22.

half-part, *interj.* [we'll go] equal shares: "Half-part, mates, half-part! Come, let's have her/ aboard suddenly." *Per,* IV, i, 94–95.

halfpenny, *n.* **too dear a halfpenny,** too costly at a halfpenny; worth very little: "And sure, dear friends, my thanks are too/ dear a halfpenny." *Ham,* II, ii, 273–274.

halfpenny purse, *n.* small purse for holding the tiny halfpenny coins: ". . . thou halfpenny/ purse of wit, thou pigeon-egg of discretion." *Love's L,* V, i, 66–67.

half-sight, *n.* glance: "Half-sights saw/ That Arcite was no babe." *Kinsmen,* V, iii, 95–96.

half-sword, *n.* length of half a sword: "I am a rogue if I were not at half-sword [very close quarters] with a/ dozen of them . . ." *1 Hen 4,* II, iv, 162–163.

half-worker, *n.* collaborator; partner: "Is there no way for men to be [come into being], but women/ Must be half-workers?" *Cymb,* II, iv, 153–154.

half-world, *n.* hemisphere enclosed in night: "Now o'er the one half-world/ Nature seems dead . . ." *Mac,* II, i, 49–50.

halidom, *n.* See **holidame.**

haling, *pres. part.* hauling; pulling: ". . . galling/ His kingly hands, haling ropes . . ." *Per,* IV, i, 53–54.

hall, *n.* **1** guild of craftsmen; here, of panders: "As many as be here of Pandar's hall . . ." *Tr & Cr, V, x, 48.* **2** Westminster Hall, where Buckingham's trial was held: "Ev'n to the hall, to hear what shall become/ Of the great Duke of Buckingham." *Hen 8,* II, i, 2–3. **3 A hall!** Clear the floor!: "A hall, a hall, give room! And foot it girls!" *Rom & Jul,* I, v, 26.

halloo, *v.* to cry or call out; here, in exultation: "Halloo your name to the reverberate hills . . ." *T Night,* I, v, 276

hallow, *v.* to revere; sanctify: "Even as when first I hallowed thy fair name . . ." *Sonn 108,* 8.

hallowed verge, *n.* magic circle: "We will make fast within a hallow'd verge." *2 Hen 6,* I, iv, 22.

hallowing, *n.* shouting: "Noise and hallowing, as people a-Maying." [SD] shout: *Kinsmen,* III, i, 1.

Hallowmas, *n.* All Saints' Day (Nov. 1); in some areas, the custom of begging alms by promising to pray for the giver: ". . . to speak puling,/ like a beggar at Hallowmas." *Two Gent,* II, i, 24–25.

halt, *v.* to limp: "Cripple our senators, that their limbs may halt/ As lamely as their manners!" *Timon,* IV, i, 24–25.

halter, *n.* hangman's rope: "A halter, soldiers, hang him on this tree . . ." *T Andr,* V, i, 47.

halting, *adj.* lame or limp; hence, clumsy and inexpert: ". . . A halting sonnet of his own pure brain,/ Fashion'd to Beatrice." *M Ado,* V, iv, 87–88.

ham, *n.* **1** [pl.] the knee joints: ". . . they have a plentiful lack of wit,/ together with most weak hams . . ." *Ham,* II, ii, 199–200. **2 bow in the hams,** to bend the thighs in curtsying; here, Mercutio implies that Romeo's sexual exertions have made bowing difficult: ". . . such a case as yours/ constrains a man to bow in the hams." *Rom & Jul,* II, iv, 54–55.

Hames Castle, *n.* stronghold on the French coast, opp. Dover: "Away with Oxford to Hames Castle straight . . ." *3 Hen 6,* V, v, 2.

hammer, *v.* **1** to devise; contrive: "And wilt thou still be hammering treachery . . ." *2 Hen 6,* I, ii, 47. **2** to deliberate: "Nor need'st thou much importune me to that/ Whereon this month I have been hammering." *Two Gent,* I, iii, 17–18.

Hampton, *n.* Southampton: ". . . sworn unto the practices of France,/ To kill us here in Hampton . . ." *Hen 5,* II, ii, 90–91.

hamstring, *n.* the legs [lit., knees], prob. because of the posing and strutting: "And like a strutting player, whose conceit [wit]/ Lies in his hamstring . . ." *Tr & Cr,* I, iii, 153–154.

hand, *n.* **1** handwriting: "I will this night,/ In several hands, in at his windows throw,/ Writings . . ." *J Caes,* I, ii, 312–315. **2** part; participation: "Else shall you not have any hand at all/ About [in] his funeral." *J Caes,* III, i, 248–249. **3** physical action: ". . . esteem no act/ But that of hand." *Tr & Cr,* I, iii, 199–200. **4 at any hand,** in any case: "All books of love, see that at any hand—" *Shrew,* I, ii, 145. **5 at hand,** at the start (of a contest, etc.): ". . . like horses hot at hand,/ Make gallant show and promise of their mettle . . ." *J Caes,* IV, ii, 23–24. **6 at two hands,** fighting with the fists: "Nay, he's at two hands with me, and that my/ two ears can witness." *Errors,* II, i, 45–46. **7 by the hand,** in or at hand: ". . . we should not step too far/ Till we had his assistance by the hand . . ." *2 Hen 4,* I, iii, 20–21. **8 careless hand of pride,** indifferent to personal appearance: "Her hair, nor loose nor tied in formal plat,/ Proclaim'd in her a careless hand of pride . . ." *Lover's Comp,* 29–30. **9 for thy hand,** ellip. for "for stealing the whiteness of thy hand": "The lily I condemned for thy hand . . ." *Sonn 99,* 6. **10 give us your hands,** give us your applause: "Give me your hands, if we be friends . . ." *M N Dream,* V, i, 423. **11 hands at it,** signatures to it: "Five justices' hands at it, and witnesses more than/ my pack will hold." *W Tale,* IV, iv, 284–285. **12 hands, not hearts,** ref. to the new manners, when hands are joined, but hearts remain free: "But our new heraldry is hands, not hearts." *Oth,* III, iv, 43. **13 here's my hand,** offering the hand as bond; here, as sign of betrothal: ". . . with a heart as willing/ As bondage e'er [ever was] of freedom: here's my hand." *Temp,* III, i, 88–89. **14 holds hand with,** is the equal of: "As she in beauty, education, blood,/ Holds hand with any princess of the world." *K John,* II, i, 493–494. **15 in any hand,** in any case; whatever happens: ". . . let him fetch off his drum in/ any hand." *All's W,* III, vi, 40–41. **16 in hand,** to deal with: "Fair lady, do you think/ you have fools in hand?" *T Night,* I, iii, 63–64. **17 in thy hand,** with yourself as escort: "Go, fetch the countess hither

in thy hand . . ." *Edw 3, II, ii, 109.* **18 made fair hands,** made a fine mess of things: "You have made fair hands,/ You and your crafts!" *Cor,* IV, vi, 118–119. **19 man or fellow of his hands,** a good fighter: ". . . I am a second brother, and . . . a proper/ fellow of my hands . . ." *2 Hen 4,* II, ii, 63–64. **20 my hand,** here is my hand on it [as an expression of agreement]: ". . . to such a man/ That is no fleering tell-tale. Hold, my hand . . ." *J Caes,* I, iii, 116–117. **21 of all hands,** by all means: "Therefore, of all hands must we be forsworn." *Love's L,* IV, iii, 215. **22 of his hands,** for fighting: ". . . he is as tall [valiant] a man of his hands/ as any is between this and his head . . ." *Wives,* I, iv, 23–24. **23 open hand,** generous nature; here, prob. in word-play with sense of threatening gesture, as Sebastian threatens to strike him: ". . . if you tarry longer,/ I shall give worse pay-ment."/ "By my troth, thou hast an open hand." *T Night,* IV, i, 19–21. **24 out of hand, a.** at once; without delay: ". . . gather we our forces out of hand,/ And set upon our boasting en-emy." *1 Hen 6,* III, ii, 102–103. **b.** on the spur of the moment: "I'll find some cunning practice out of hand/ To scatter and disperse the giddy Goths . . ." *T Andr,* V, ii, 77–78. **25 shake hands,** to take leave: "Which ne'er shook hands, nor bade farewell to him . . ." *Mac,* I, ii, 21. **26 your hand,** invitation to go arm in arm (to avoid any question of precedence): "Your hand, Leonato, we will go together." *M Ado,* I, i, 147.
—*v.* **27** to conduct the business of (love); woo: "Sooth, when I was young/ And handed love . . ." *W Tale,* IV, iv, 348–349.

hand-fast, *n.* **1** marriage contract: ". . . the remembrancer of her to hold/ The hand-fast to her lord." *Cymb,* I, vi, 77–78. **2 in hand-fast,** under arrest: "If that shepherd be not in hand-fast, let him fly . . ." *W Tale,* IV, iv, 769.

handicraft man, *n.* artisan: ". . . he hath simply the best wit of any handicraft/ man in Athens." *M N Dream,* IV, ii, 9–10.

hand-in-hand, *adj.* of equality rather than superiority: "As fair, and as good—a kind of hand-in-hand/ comparison—had been something too fair . . ." *Cymb,* I, v, 67–68.

handkercher, *n.* handkerchief: "When your head did but ache,/ I knit my handkercher about your brows . . ." *K John,* IV, i, 41–42.

handsaw, *n.* See **hawk** (def. 1).

handsome, *adj.* suitable; apt or proper: ". . . and by very much more handsome than fine." *Ham,* II, ii, 441.

handsomely, *adv.* conveniently: "And if we miss to meet him handsomely,/ Sweet huntsman, Bassianus 'tis we mean . . ." *T Andr,* II, iii, 268–269.

handy-dandy, *interj.* take your choice [words from a chil-dren's game]: ". . . change places, and,/ handy-dandy, which is the justice, which is the/ thief?" *Lear,* IV, vi, 154–156.

hang, *v.* **1 hang by the walls,** See **wall** (def. 1). **2 hang off,** [Usually a command] Let go!: "Hang off, thou cat, thou burr! Vile thing, let loose . . ." *M N Dream,* III, ii, 260. **3 hang to-gether,** somehow survive: ". . . and as idle as she may hang together, for want/ of company." *Wives,* III, ii, 11–12.

hanger, *n.* **1** hanging, esp. a piece of tapestry: ". . . the German hunting, in waterwork, is/ worth a thousand of these bed-hangers . . ." *2 Hen 4* II, i, 143–144. **2** strap by which a sword or dagger was attached to the girdle: ". . . six French rapiers and poniards, with their/ assigns, as girdle, hanger, and so." *Ham,* V, ii, 146–147.

hangman, *n.* **1** generalized term for "executioner"; part of the hangman's bloody job was to eviscerate and quarter his victims: "One cried, 'God bless us!' and, 'Amen,' the other,/ As they had seen me with these hangman's hands." *Mac,* II, ii, 26–27. **2** [pl.] ref. to hangmen's being entitled to clothing of those they executed: ". . . doublets that hangmen would/ Bury with those that wore them . . ." *Cor,* I, v, 6–7. **3 little hangman,** term of affection for Cupid, usually referred to as a rogue or rascal: "He hath twice or thrice cut Cupid's bow-string, and the/ little hangman dare not shoot at him." *M Ado,* III, ii, 10–11.

hangman boys, *n.* fellows deserving of the hangman: ". . . the other squirrel was stolen from me by the/ hangman boys in the market-place . . ." *Two Gent,* IV, iv, 54–55.

Hannibal, *n.* misuse for "cannibal": "O thou caitiff! O thou varlet! O thou wicked/ Hannibal!" *Meas,* II, i, 171–172.

hap, *n.* **1** happenstance: "Be it art [scheme] or hap,/ He hath spoken true." *Ant & Cleo,* II, iii, 31–32. **2** luck; fortune; chance: "See, by good hap, yonder's my lord . . ." *Timon,* III, ii, 24. **3 by haps,** by chance: "If it prove so, then loving goes by haps . . ." *M Ado,* III, i, 105.
—*v.* **4** to happen: "Make them . . . ready for this hint/ When we shall hap to give't them." *Cor,* III, iii, 23–24. **5 haps it,** does it happen: ". . . how haps it I seek not to advance . . ." *1 Hen 6,* III, i, 31. **6 hap what hap may,** let happen what will; whatever happens: "Hap what hap may, I'll roundly go about her . . ." *Shrew,* IV, iv, 103.

haply, *adv.* perhaps; perchance: "I will kiss thy lips./ Haply some poison yet doth hang on them . . ." *Rom & Jul,* V, iii, 164–165.

happier, *adj.* more talented: "Exceeded by the height of hap-pier men." *Sonn 32, 8.*

happiest, *adj.* most sophisticated or discriminating: ". . . you are known/ The first and happiest hearers [audience] of the town . . ." *Hen 8,* Prol. 23–24.

happily, *adv.* haply; by chance: ". . . old Gremio is hearkening still,/ And happily we might be interrupted." *Shrew,* IV, iv, 53–54.

happiness, *n.* **1** ease and luxury as a way of life: "To diet rank minds sick of happiness . . ." *2 Hen 4,* IV, i, 64. **2** appropriateness: ". . . a happiness that often/ madness hits on . . ." *Ham,* II, ii, 209–210.

happy, *adj.* **1** opportune; fortunate: "You wish me health in very happy season,/ For I am on the sudden something ill." *2 Hen 4,* IV, ii, 79–80. **2** accomplished: ". . . desire his service: tell him/ Wherein you're happy . . ." *Cymb,* III, iv, 175–176. **3 in happy time,** good! indeed! how fortunate! [vague term of assent or approval]: "Madam, in happy time. What day is that?" *Rom & Jul,* III, v, 111.
—*v.* **4** to make happy: ". . . happies those that pay the willing [willingly repay the] loan . . ." *Sonn 6,* 6.

happy hour, *n.* opportune moment: ". . . omit [lose] no happy hour/ That may give furth'rance to our expedition . . ." *Hen 5,* I, ii, 300–301.

happy title, *n.* right to be called happy: "O! what a happy title do I find . . ." *Sonn 92,* 11.

haps, *v.* **haps it,** does it happen that: ". . . how haps it I seek not to advance/ Or raise myself . . ." *1 Hen 6,* III, i, 31–32.

harbinger, *n.* **1** Venus, the morning star, arising in the eastern sky: "And yonder shines Aurora's harbinger . . ." *M N Dream,* III, ii, 380. **2** household officer sent ahead to secure lodgings for the monarch and his/her retinue: "I'll be myself the harbinger, and make joyful/ The hearing of my wife . . ." *Mac,* I, iv, 45–46.

harbor, *v.* **1** to remain; lodge: ". . . if the wind blow any way from shore/ I will not harbour in this town to-night." *Errors,* III, ii, 147–148.
—*n.* **2** shelter: "Why I desire thee/ To give me secret harbour hath a purpose . . ." *Meas,* I, iii, 3–4.

hard, *adj.* **1** reluctant: ". . . at last/ Upon his will I seal'd my hard consent." *Ham,* I, ii, 59–60. **2** calloused: ". . . there's no better sign of a brave/ mind than a hard hand." *2 Hen 6,* IV, ii, 19–20. **3** harsh; cruel: "Repose you there while I to this hard house . . . return and force/ Their scanted courtesy." *Lear,* III, ii, 63–67. **4 too hard,** too much; too difficult: "You are too hard for me [too much for me to handle]." *Love's L,* II, i, 258.

—*adv.* **5 bear (someone) hard,** to bear ill will toward: "Caius Ligarius doth bear Caesar hard,/ Who rated him for speaking well of Pompey . . ." *J Caes,* II, i, 215–216. **6 hard upon,** very soon; quickly; immediately: "Indeed, my lord, it follow'd hard upon." *Ham,* I, ii, 179. **7 that goes hard,** that is very serious business: "My life, sir? How, I pray? For that goes hard." *Shrew,* IV, ii, 80.

hard-believing, *adj.* doubting or skeptical: "O hard-believing love, how strange it seems/ Not to believe . . ." *Ven & Ad,* 985–986.

hard beset, *adj.* ardently pursued [by young men]: "Now, daughter Silvia, you are hard beset." *Two Gent,* II, iv, 44.

hardening *n.* **hardening of my brows,** growing of cuckold's horns on my forehead: "And that to the infection of my brains/ And hard'ning of my brows." *W Tale,* I, ii, 145–146.

harder bosoms, *n.* persons of less tender [or scrupulous] natures: ". . . make itself a pastime/ To harder bosoms!" *W Tale,* I, ii, 152–153.

hard-favored, *adj.* **1** plain, homely, or ugly: "Would you not have me honest?/ No truly, unless thou wert hard-favoured . . ." *As You,* III, iii, 24–25. **2** grimly determined: "Disguise fair nature with hard-favour'd rage . . ." *Hen 5,* III, i, 8.

hard fractions, *n.* harsh words or phrases: "After distasteful looks, and these hard fractions . . ." *Timon,* II, ii, 215.

hard-handed, *adj.* working as a manual laborer: "Hard-handed men that work in Athens here,/ Which never labour'd in their minds till now . . ." *M N Dream,* V, i, 72–73.

hardiment, *n.* **1** bravery, boldness, or hardihood: ". . . the best part of an hour/ In changing [matching] hardiment with great Glendower." *1 Hen 4,* I, iii, 99–100. **2** prob. wordplay with preceding and "erection": "For thus popp'd Paris in his hardiment,/ And parted thus you and your argument." *Tr & Cr,* IV, v, 27–28.

hardly, *adv.* **1** with difficulty: ". . . I could be sad, and sad indeed too."/ "Very hardly [not very easily], upon such a subject." *2 Hen 4,* II, ii, 41–42. **2** hesitantly or unwillingly: "Go with me to my tent, where you shall see/ How hardly I was drawn into this war . . ." *Ant & Cleo,* V, i, 73–74. **3** barely: "So it far'd . . . between these kinsmen; till heavens did/ Make hardly one the winner." *Kinsmen,* V, iii, 128–129. **4** badly: "We house i' th' rock, yet use thee not so hardly/ As prouder livers do." *Cymb, III, iii, 8–9.* **5 come hardly off,** be done with great difficulty: "Now trust me, madam, it came hardly off." *Two Gent,* II, i, 102. **6 hardly conceive,** think harshly: "The grieved commons/ Hardly conceive of me . . ." *Hen 8*, I, ii, 104–105.

hardness, *n.* **1** want; deprivation; hardship: ". . . hardness ever/ Of hardiness is mother." *Cymb*, III, vi, 21–22. **2** difficulty; complexity or abstruseness: ". . . so from sense in hardness, that I can/ Make no collection of it." *Cymb*, V, v, 432–433.

hardock, *n.* Also, **hardoke.** coarse weedy plant, prob. the burdock: "Crown'd with rank fumiter and furrow-weeds,/ With hardocks, hemlock . . ." *Lear*, IV, iv, 3–4.

hard point, *n.* **at some hard point,** in extreme difficulty: "That drug-damn'd Italy hath out-craftied him,/ And he's at some hard point." *Cymb*, III, iv, 15–16.

hard rein, *n.* lack of cooperation; resistance; opposition: ". . . the hard rein which both of them have borne/ Against the old kind King . . ." *Lear*, III, i, 27–28.

hard-ruled, *adj.* managed with difficulty: ". . . not wholesome to/ Our cause, that she should lie i'th'bosom of/ Our hard-rul'd king." *Hen 8*, III, ii, 99–101.

hardy, *adj.* bold; forward: ". . . that you be never so hardy to/ come again in his affairs . . ." *T Night*, II, i, 8–9.

hare, *n.* another word for **prostitute;** here, wordplay on "whore" and "hoar": "No hare, sir, unless a hare, sir, in a lenten pie, that/ is something stale and hoar . . ." *Rom & Jul*, II, iv, 130–131.

hare-brained, *adj.* reckless and dangerous: ". . . they are hare-brain'd slaves,/ And hunger will enforce them be more eager . . ." *1 Hen 6*, II, ii, 37–38.

hare-finder, *n.* keen-eyed spotter: ". . . do you play the flouting Jack,/ to tell us Cupid is a good hare-finder . . ." *M Ado*, I, i, 170–171.

Harfleur, *n.* port at mouth of the Seine, in NW France: "With fatal mouths gaping on girded Harfleur." *Hen 5*, III, Chor., 27.

Ha'rfordwest, *n.* Haverfordwest, town in Wales: "At Pembroke, or at Ha'rfordwest in Wales." *Rich 3*, IV, v, 10.

hark, *v.* [to] listen: "Why, hark ye, hark ye, and are you such fools/ To square [quarrel] for this?" *T Andr*, II, i, 99–100.

harlot, *n.* **1** lewd fellow; low companion: ". . . she shut the doors upon me/ While she with harlots feasted in my house." *Errors*, V, i, 204–205.
—*adj.* **2** lewd; lecherous: ". . . for the harlot king/ Is quite beyond mine arm . . ." *W Tale*, II, iii, 4–5

harlotry, *adj.* **1** knavish; scurvy; trashy; here, with some element of admiration: ". . . as like one of these harlotry/ players as ever I see!" *1 Hen 4*, II, iv, 390–391.
—*n.* **2** foolish girl; silly thing (term of impatience or frustration but not abuse): ". . . a peevish, self-willed/ harlotry, one that no persuasion can do good upon." *1 Hen 4*, III, i, 192–193.

harm, *n.* **1** evil; wickedness: "Esteem him as a lamb, being compar'd/ With my confineless harms." *Mac*, IV, iii, 54–55. **2** [often pl.] injury: "My spirit can no longer bear these harms." *1 Hen 6*, IV, vii, 30. **3 object of all harm,** the sight of any kind of danger: "And reason flies the object of all harm." *Tr & Cr*, II, ii, 41. **4 think no harm,** sleep peacefully: "When I was wont to think no harm all night . . ." *Love's L*, I, i, 44.

harmless, *adj.* meaning no harm; innocent: "A napkin steeped in the harmless blood/ Of sweet young Rutland . . ." *3 Hen 6*, II, i, 62–63.

harmony, *n.* **1** music: ". . . the tongues of dying men/ Inforce attention like deep harmony." *Rich 2*, II, i, 4–5. **2** ability to appreciate the music of the spheres: "Such harmony is in immortal souls . . ." *Merch*, V, i, 63.

harness, *n.* armor: "Great men should drink with harness on their throats." *Timon*, I, ii, 52.

harnessed, *adj.* dressed up in armor: "This harness'd masque and unadvised revel . . ." *K John*, V, ii, 132.

harp, *v.* to guess; discover: "Thou hast harp'd my fear aright." *Mac*, IV, i, 74.

harper, *n.* person who plays the harp: "Nor woo in rhyme, like a blind harper's song . . ." *Love's L*, V, ii, 405.

Harpier, *n.* third witch's familiar: "Harpier cries:—'Tis time, 'tis time." *Mac*, IV, i, 3.

harpy, *n.* (in Greek myth.) malevolent creature, part woman and part predatory bird: "Enter Ariel like a Harpy; claps his wings/ upon the table; and, with a quaint device, the banquet vanishes." [SD] *Temp*, III, iii, 52.

harrow, *v.* to distress; torment: "It harrows me with fear and wonder." *Ham*, I, i, 47.

Harry groat, *n.* a four-penny coin: ". . . he that will not see a red herring at a Harry groat . . . list to me" *More*, II, iv, 1–3.

Harry ten shilling, *n.* coin worth about five shillings by the 1590s: ". . . here's four Harry ten shillings in French/ crowns for you [the sum of one pound] . . ." *2 Hen 4*, III, ii, 216–217.

harsh, *adj.* of unpleasing appearance: ". . . those whom nature hath not made for store [procreation],/ Harsh, featureless and rude . . ." *Sonn 11,* 9–10.

harshness, *n.* discord; disobedience: "With cunning hast thou filch'd my daughter's heart,/ Turn'd her obedience . . . To stubborn harshness." *M N Dream,* I, i, 36–38.

hart, *n.* **1** male deer; stag: "To-morrow, and it please your majesty/ To hunt the panther and the hart with me . . ." *T Andr,* I, i, 492–493. **2** same in wordplay with "heart": "O world, thou wast the forest to this hart;/ And this indeed, O world, the heart of thee." *J Caes,* III, i, 207–208.

harvest-home, *n.* **1** end of the harvesting season; celebrates the bringing in of the corn: ". . . like a stubble-land at harvest-home." *1 Hen 4,* I, iii, 34. **2** chance to turn a profit; here, a sexual conquest: "I will use/ her as the key of the cuckoldly rogue's coffer, and/ there's my harvest-home." *Wives,* II, ii, 262–264.

'has, *v.* contraction of "he has": ". . . 'has wherewithal: in him/ Sparing would show a worse sin . . ." *Hen 8,* I, iii, 59–60.

hast, *v.* 2nd pers. sing. of *have*: "Try all the friends thou hast in Ephesus . . ." *Errors,* I, i, 152.

haste, *n.* **1 in haste whereof,** so as to settle [the matter] as quickly as possible: "In haste whereof most heartily I pray/ Your Highness to assign our trial day." *Rich 2,* I, i, 150–151. **2 put it to the haste,** make haste: ". . . it is provided,/ Go put it to the haste." *Ant & Cleo,* V, ii, 194–195.
—*v.* **3** to hasten; hurry up: ". . . but let it be so hasted that supper be/ ready at the farthest by five of the clock . . ." *Merch,* II, ii, 109–110. **4 Haste you again,** Hurry back. *All's W,* II, ii, 65.

hasty, *adj.* rash; reckless: "With hasty Germans and blunt Hollanders . . ." *3 Hen 6,* IV, viii, 2.

hat, *n.* **1** ref. to custom of wearing one's hat at meals but taking it off while grace was said: ". . . while grace is saying hood mine eyes/ Thus with my hat . . ." *Merch,* II, ii, 184–185. **2 my hat to a halfpenny,** popular wager: "My hat to a halfpenny, Pompey proves the best/ Worthy." *Love's L,* V, ii, 556–557.

ha't, *v.* contraction of "have it": "Whate'er the ocean pales, or sky inclips,/ Is thine, if thou wilt ha't." *Ant & Cleo,* II, vii, 68–69.

hatch, *n.* **1** bottom half of a divided door: "Either get thee from the door or sit down at the hatch . . ." *Errors,* III, i, 33. **2** opening in the deck of a ship covered by planks: ". . . my brother Gloucester,/ Who from my cabin tempted me to walk/ Upon the hatches . . ." *Rich 3,* I, iv, 11–13. **3 o'er the**

hatch, conceived illegitimately [from an old proverb]: "In at the window, or else o'er the hatch . . ." *K John,* I, i, 171. **4 take the hatch,** to retreat quickly, as if by leaping over the hatch of a door: "To cudgel you and make you take the hatch . . ." *K John,* V, ii, 138. **5 the hatch and the disclose,** identity of the hatchlings emerging from the eggs; here, discovery of the truth: "And I do doubt [suspect] the hatch and the disclose/ Will be some danger . . ." *Ham,* III, i, 168–169.
—*v.* **6** to close the hatch (of a door): ". . . 'twere not amiss to keep our door hatch'd." *Per,* IV, ii, 31.

hatched, *adj.* etched or engraved: "As Agamemnon . . . Should hold up high in brass; and such again/ As venerable Nestor, hatch'd in silver . . ." *Tr & Cr,* I, iii, 63–65.

hatchment, *n.* tablet or device showing a person's coat of arms, carried in the funeral procession and placed permanently over the tomb: "No trophy, sword, nor hatchment o'er his bones . . ." *Ham,* IV, v, 211.

hate, *n.* offense or displeasure given: "More grief to hide than hate to utter love." *Ham,* II, i, 119.

hateful, *adj.* feeling or expressing hatred: ". . . little office/ The hateful commons will perform for us,/ Except like curs to tear us all to pieces." *Rich 2,* II, ii 136–138.

hath, *v.* **1** 3rd pers. sing. of *have*; has: "He hath bore/ me on his back a thousand times . . ." *Ham,* V, i, 179–180. **2** gets; acquires: ". . . he shall pay for him that/ hath him and that soundly." *Temp,* II, ii, 79–80.

haud credo, [Latin] I do not believe it: "Sir Nathaniel, *haud credo.*" *Love's L,* IV, ii, 11.

haught, *adj.* haughty: "No lord of thine, thou haught insulting man . . ." *Rich 2,* IV, i, 254.

haughty, *adj.* **1** high-spirited; adventurous: ". . . as in this haughty great attempt/ They laboured to plant the rightful heir . . ." *1 Hen 6,* II, v, 79–80. **2** noble; lofty: "Valiant and virtuous, full of haughty courage . . ." *1 Hen 6,* IV, i, 35.

haunch, *n.* **1** hip: "Divide me like a bribed [stolen] buck, each a haunch . . ." *Wives,* V, v, 24. **2** [fig. use] end; latter part: ". . . a summer bird,/ Which ever in the haunch of winter sings/ The lifting up of day." *2 Hen 4,* IV, iv, 91–93.

haunt, *v.* **1** to frequent: "Our court, you know, is haunted/ With a refined traveller of Spain . . ." *Love's L,* I, i, 161–162. **2** to follow; pursue: ". . . that bloody strain/ That haunted us in our familiar paths . . ." *Hen 5,* II, iv, 51–52.
—*n.* **3** See **public haunt. 4 all the haunt be ours,** we shall be the center of attention: "Dido, and her Aeneas, shall want

troops,/ And all the haunt be ours." *Ant & Cleo*, IV, xiv, 53–54.
5 open haunts, gathering places for the common people: ". . .
never noted in him . . . Any retirement, any sequestration/
From open haunts . . ." *Hen 5*, I, i, 57–59. **6 out of haunt,**
away from others [so as not to harm them]: "It will be laid
to us, whose providence/ Should have kept . . . out of haunt/
This mad young man." *Ham*, IV, i, 17–19.

haunted, *adj.* much frequented: "What night-rule now about
this haunted grove?" *M N Dream*, III, ii, 5.

hautboy, *n.* woodwind instrument, forerunner of the modern oboe; also, player of such an instrument: "Hautboys playing loud music." [SD] *Timon*, I, ii, 1.

have, *v.* **1** to understand: "You have me, have you not?" *Ham*,
II, i, 68. **2 have after,** to follow (someone): "Let's follow. 'Tis
not fit thus to obey him."/ "Have after." *Ham*, I, iv, 88–89. **3
have at you,** I'll answer you: "Have at you with a proverb—
shall I set in my staff?" *Errors*, III, i, 51. **4 have away,** to get
rid of: ". . . thou shalt go to the wars in a gown; we will/ have
away thy cold . . ." *2 Hen 4*, III, ii, 180–181. **5 have old,** hear
a lot of: ". . . we shall have old swearing/ That they did give
the rings away to men . . ." *Merch*, IV, ii, 15–16. **6 have them,**
get themselves; here, ingratiate themselves: ". . . without any
further deed to have/ them at all into their estimation . . ."
Cor, II, ii, 27–28. **7 have to,** here's to: "Have to my widow!
And if she be froward,/ Then hast thou taught Hortensio to
be untoward." *Shrew*, IV, v, 77–78. **8 have to bed,** to escort to
bed: ". . . light them at the fiery glow-worms' eyes,/ To have
my love to bed, and to arise . . ." *M N Dream*, III, i, 163–164.
9 have to do with, to be concerned about: "Nor need you . . .
have to do/ With any scruple." *Meas*, I, i, 63–64. **10 have with
thee,** I'm coming [I'll go with thee]: "Good Costard, go with
me."/ "Have with thee, my girl." *Love's L*, IV, ii, 139–140. **11 I
have it,** facetious ref. to receiving a mortal wound, here from
being dubbed a knight: "What! I am dubb'd! I have it on my
shoulder." *K John*, I, i, 245. **12 you have of these,** there are
some: "You have of these pedlars that have more in them/
than you'd think, sister." *W Tale*, IV, iv, 217–218.

having, *n.* [often pl.] possessions; substance or property; also,
endowment(s): ". . . if it be a just and true report that goes of
his having." *Timon*, V, i, 16.

havior, *n.* var. of **behavior;** conduct; demeanor: ". . . furbish
new the name of John a Gaunt,/ Even in the lusty haviour of
his son." *Rich 2*, I, iii, 76–77.

havoc, *n.* **1** slaughter; massacre: "This quarry cries on havoc."
Ham, V, ii, 369. **2 cry havoc,** war cry: orig. the monarch's signal for wholesale slaughter and plunder, its being understood
that an invading monarch showed no mercy to an enemy:

"Cry havoc and let slip the dogs of war . . ." *J Caes*, III, i, 273.
3 wide havoc, gaping hole: ". . . wide havoc made/ For bloody
power to rush upon your peace." *K John*, II, i, 220–221.
—*v.* **4** to ravage; destroy: "To tame and havoc more than she
can eat." *Hen 5*, I, ii, 173.

hawk, *n.* **1 know a hawk from a handsaw,** to be lucid and
perceptive; here, to recognize deceit ["hawk" may also be No.
country dial. for "pickax"; "handsaw" often interp. as "hern-
shaw," heron]: "I am but mad north-north-west. When the
wind is/ southerly, I know a hawk from a handsaw." *Ham*, II,
ii, 374–375.
—*v.* **2 hawk at,** to attack (prey) as or as if a hawk: "A falcon . . .
Was by a mousing owl hawk'd at, and kill'd." *Mac*, II, iv, 12–
13.

hawking, *adj.* sharp or keen as a hawk's: ". . . to sit and draw/
His arched brows, his hawking eye . . ." *All's W*, I, i, 91–92.

hawthorn-bud, *n.* Falstaff's term of contempt for young, inexperienced swains: ". . . these lisping hawthorn-buds that
come like/ women in men's apparel . . ." *Wives*, III, iii, 65–66.

hay[1], *n.* winding country dance; also, **dance the hay,** to twist
and turn without making any progress: ". . . I will play on the
tabor to the Worthies, and let them dance the/ hay." *Love's L*,
V, i, 143–145.

hay[2], *n.* sword thrust that strikes the opponent: "Ah, the im-
mortal/ passado, the punto reverso, the hay!" *Rom & Jul*, II,
iv, 25–26.

hazard, *n.* **1** chance or risk; wager; gamble: "to set so rich a
main/ On the nice hazard of one doubtful hour?" *1 Hen 4*, IV,
i, 47–48. **2 edge of hazard,** limit of personal danger: "We'll
strive to bear it for your worthy sake/ To th'extreme edge of
hazard." *All's W*, III, iii, 5–6. **3 go to hazard,** to make a bet:
"Who will go to hazard with me for twenty/ prisoners?" *Hen
5*, III, vii, 88–89. **4 on the hazard,** at stake: "The storm is up,
and all is on the hazard." *J Caes*, V, i, 68. **5 put in hazard,** to
risk: "This mutiny were better put in hazard . . ." *Cor*, II, iii,
254. **6 sets all on hazard,** puts everything at risk: "Now expectation, tickling skittish spirits/ On one and other side . . .
Sets all on hazard." *Tr & Cr*, Prol. 20–22. **7 thread of hazard,**
the thread of life: ". . . to be great/ Is, when the thread of hazard is once spun,/ A bottom great wound up, greatly undone."
More, III, ii, 19–21.
—*v.* **8 hazarded to thy grace,** dependent upon your favor:
". . . craves/ The circle [crown] of the Ptolemies for her heirs,/
Now hazarded to thy grace." *Ant & Cleo*, III, xii, 17–19.

he, *n.* man; person: ". . . but Mantua's law/ Is death to any he
that utters them." *Rom & Jul*, V, i, 66–67.

head, *n.* **1** chief; commander: "Thy husband is thy lord, thy life, thy keeper,/ Thy head, thy sovereign . . ." *Shrew,* V, ii, 147–148. **2** organizer: "The ringleader and head of all this rout . . ." *2 Hen 6,* II, i, 162. **3** army or armed force; here, in wordplay with "human head": "To save our heads by raising of a head . . ." *1 Hen 4,* I, iii, 278. **4** advance by rebellious forces: ". . . young Laertes, in a riotous head,/ O'erbears your officers." *Ham,* IV, v, 101–102. **5** (in horsemanship) unchecked freedom: "And given unto the house of York such head/ As thou shalt reign but by their sufferance." *3 Hen 6,* I, i, 240–241. **6** one's title: ". . . he would/ Have been so brief with you to shorten you,/ For taking so the head [title of "king"], your whole head's length." *Rich 2,* III, iii, 12–14. **7** source; origin: ". . . all the treasons . . . Fetch from false Mowbray their first head and spring . . ." *Rich 2,* I, i, 95–97. **8** surface of a body of water: "And hid his crisp head in the hollow bank . . ." *1 Hen 4,* I, iii, 105. **9** headland; promontory: ". . . from the head of Actium/ Beat the approaching Caesar." *Ant & Cleo,* III, vii, 51–52. **10 at head,** head-on [a term in bear-baiting]: "As true a dog as ever fought at head." *T Andr,* V, i, 102. **11 for my head,** for fear of losing my head; fr. belief that a full belly incited lust: "I dare not for/ my head fill my belly . . ." *Meas,* IV, iii, 152–153. **12 gather head,** to collect an army: ". . . get you to Smithfield and gather head . . ." *2 Hen 6,* IV, v, 9. **13 heads of steel,** staglike soldiers fighting with steel lances in place of "horns": ". . . moody-mad and desperate stags,/ Turn on the bloody hounds with heads of steel . . ." *1 Hen 6,* IV, ii, 50–51. **14 hold up head,** to maintain a military force: "Whether our present five and twenty thousand/ May hold up head without Northumberland." *2 Hen 4,* I, iii, 16–17. **15 in head,** as a military force: ". . . the act/ For which we have in head assembled them?" *Hen 5,* II, ii, 17–18. **16 make (a) head,** to raise an army: "If we without his help can make a head . . ." *1 Hen 4,* IV, i, 80. **17 of the first head,** referring to a five-year-old buck, with its first full head of antlers: ". . . sir, I assure/ ye, it was a buck of the first head." *Love's L,* IV, ii, 9–10. **18 set upon the head of,** to make part of: ". . . and set quarrelling/ Upon the head of valour . . ." *Timon,* III, v, 27–28 **19 take head,** to rush away; flee: "Makes it take head from all indifference [impartiality] . . ." *K John,* II, i, 579. **20 to one's head,** to one's face: "Demetrius, I'll avouch it to his head,/ Made love to Nedar's daughter, Helena . . ." *M N Dream,* I, i, 106–107. **21 turn head,** [to] stand at bay [command in hunting]: "Turn head, and stop pursuit . . ." *Hen 5,* II, iv, 69.

—*v.* **22** to behead: "If you head and hang all that offend that way . . ." *Meas,* II, i, 235.

headed, *past part.* beheaded: "Was not thy father . . . For treason headed in our late king's days?" *1 Hen 6,* II, iv, 90–91.

heading, *n.* beheading: "There is pretty orders beginning, I can tell you. It is/ but heading and hanging." *Meas,* II, i, 233–234.

headless, *adj.* lacking a leader: "And help to set a head on headless Rome." *T Andr,* I, i, 186.

headlong, *adv.* at length with the head dragging: "Hence will I drag thee headlong by the heels/ Unto a dunghill . . ." *2 Hen 6,* IV, x, 79–80.

head-lugged bear, *n.* bear pulled by a rope around its neck: ". . . a gracious aged man,/ Whose reverence even the head-lugg'd bear would lick . . ." *Lear,* IV, ii, 41–42.

head of safety, *n.* protective army: "And in conclusion drove us to seek out/ This head of safety . . ." *1 Hen 4,* IV, iii, 102–103.

head of theft, *n.* ears of a thief: "When the suspicious [apprehensive] head of theft is stopp'd . . ." *Love's L,* IV, iii, 332.

head-piece, *n.* brain [lit., helmet]: "He that has a house to put's head in has a good/ head-piece." *Lear,* III, ii, 25–26.

headsman, *n.* executioner: "Enter the Duke of Ephesus, and the Merchant/ of Syracuse barehead, with the Headsman and other Officers." [SD] *Errors,* V, i, 130.

headstall, *n.* (on a harness) the bridle strap around the horse's head: ". . . a headstall of sheep's leather, which, being/ restrained to keep him from stumbling, hath been/ often burst . . ." *Shrew,* III, ii, 55–57.

heady, *adj.* **1** fierce; relentless: "And all the currents of a heady fight." *1 Hen 4,* II, iii, 56. **2** heedless; reckless or unruly: ". . . the filthy and contagious clouds/ Of heady murder, spoil, and villainy." *Hen 5,* III, iii, 31–32.

heady-rash, *adj.* overhasty: "Neither disturb'd with the effect of wine,/ Nor heady-rash, provok'd with raging ire . . ." *Errors,* V, i, 215–216.

health, *n.* **1** toast to someone's health; also, a cup of wine drunk at such a toast: "My lord, in heart; and let the health go round." *Timon,* I, ii, 53. **2** prosperity; stability: ". . . his sables and his weeds/ Importing health and graveness." *Ham,* IV, vii, 79–80. **3 begin thy health,** to begin drinking healths to you: "I will, out of thine own confession,/ learn to begin thy health . . ." *Meas,* I, ii, 35–36.

healthful, *adj.* health-giving; salutary: "At length another ship . . . Gave healthful welcome to their ship-wrack'd guests . . ." *Errors,* I, i, 112–114.

heap, *n.* **1** group or gathering: ". . . Among this princely heap—if any here . . . Hold me a foe—" *Rich 3,* II, i, 54–56. **2 all the whole heap,** entire body; you yourself: ". . . because thine eye/ Presumes to reach, all the whole heap must die." *Per,* I, i, 33–34. **3 drawn upon a heap,** huddled together; collected into a mass: "And there were drawn/ Upon a heap a hundred ghastly women . . ." *J Caes,* I, iii, 22–23. **4 on heaps,** all together: "Let us on heaps go offer up our lives." *Hen 5,* IV, v, 18.

hear, *v.* **1 do you hear,** Listen; pay attention: "Do you hear, my mad wenches?" *Love's L,* II, i, 256. **2 hear by the nose.** See **nose** (def. 1). **3 hear ourselves,** to confer: "Get thee gone; tomorrow/ We'll hear ourselves again." *Mac,* III, iv, 30–31.

heard, *past part.* **1 have him heard,** to make certain he is heard [as a warning]: "The threshold grates the door to have him heard . . ." *Luc,* 306. **2 heard of,** perh. equiv. to "more or less"; poss. "made famous": ". . . battles thrice six/ I have seen and heard of . . ." *Cor,* II, iii, 127–128.

hearing, *n.* something heard: "'Tis a good hearing [It's always nice to hear] when children are toward [obedient]." *Shrew,* V, ii, 183.

hearken, *v.* **1** to wait (for); pay attention (to): "Prove that ever I dress myself handsome/ till thy return,—Well, hearken a' th'end [i.e., before judging me]." *2 Hen 4,* II, iv, 276–277. **2 hearken after,** to inquire about: "He hearkens after prophecies and dreams,/ And from the cross-row plucks the letter G . . ." *Rich 3,* I, i, 54–55. **3 hearken for,** to await; also, to desire: ". . . they did me too much injury/ That ever said I hearken'd for your death." *1 Hen 4,* V, iv, 50–51.

hearse, *n.* coffin together with platform or mountings; bier: "Stand from the hearse! stand from the body!" *J Caes,* III, ii, 167.

hearsed, *adj.* entombed; buried: "Why thy canoniz'd bones, hearsed in death,/ Have burst their cerements . . ." *Ham,* I, iv, 47–48.

heart, *n.* **1** good intentions: ". . . you/ must bear; the heart's all." *2 Hen 4,* V, iii, 28–29. **2** person, esp. a good-hearted fellow: "Where are these lads? Where are these hearts?" *M N Dream,* IV, ii, 25. **3** the heart as the organ of wisdom as well as courage: "Why, had your bodies/ No heart among you?" *Cor,* II, iii, 201–202. **4 for his heart,** to save his life: ". . . and this her son/ Cannot take two from twenty, for his heart,/ And leave eighteen." *Cymb,* II, i, 53–55. **5 heart of elder,** appar. misfire as fanciful variation on "heart of oak"; gives opp. sense: "What says my/ Aesculapius? My Galen? My heart of elder?" *Wives,* II, iii, 26–27. **6 heart of loss,** complete or utter loss: "Like a right gipsy, hath at fast and loose/ Beguil'd me, to the very heart of loss." *Ant & Cleo,* IV, xii, 28–29. **7 men of heart,** courageous men [soldiers]:

". . . men of heart/ Look'd wond'ring each at others." *Cor,* V, vi, 99–100. **8 my profound heart,** mild oath or protestation that one is telling the truth: "Are you a comedian?"/ "No, my profound heart . . ." *T Night,* I, v, 183–184. **9 not half way to her heart,** of no interest to her: ". . . you shall never need to fear./ Iwis [indeed] it is not half way to her heart." *Shrew,* I, i, 61–62. **10 out of heart,** in poor physical condition: "I shall be out of heart shortly, and then I shall have/ no strength to repent." *1 Hen 4,* III, iii, 6–7. **11 put (someone) in heart,** to give someone courage: "Petruchio, this has put me in heart./ Have to my widow!" *Shrew,* IV, v, 76–77. **12 to your heart,** to your heart's content [complete satisfaction]: "And you shall have . . . revenges to your heart,/ And general honour." *Meas,* IV, iii, 134–136.

heart and place, *n.* very center: ". . . all the grace,/ Which makes her both the heart and place/ Of general wonder [widespread admiration]." *Per,* IV, Chor., 9–11.

heart-breaking, *n.* heart-breaking matter: ". . . it is a heart-breaking to see a handsome/ man loose-wiv'd . . ." *Ant & Cleo,* I, ii, 68–69.

heart-burned or **heartburnt,** *adj.* suffering from indigestion: "I never can see/ him but I am heart-burned an hour after." *M Ado,* II, i, 3–4.

hearted, *adj.* deeply rooted; heartfelt: ". . . my cause is hearted, thine has no/ less reason . . ." *Oth,* I, iii, 366–367.

hearted throne, *n.* love's throne deep in the heart: "Yield up, O love, thy crown, and hearted throne . . ." *Oth,* III, iii, 455.

heartiness, *n.* sincerity: "This entertainment [hospitality]/ May a free [innocent] face put on, derive a liberty/ From heartiness . . ." *W Tale,* I, ii, 111–113.

heartless hinds, *n.* wordplay on "cowardly underlings" and "female deer unprotected by stag [hartless]": "What, art thou drawn among these heartless hinds?" *Rom & Jul,* I, i, 63.

heartly, *adv.* heartily; earnestly: "I pray you pardon me;/ pray heartly pardon me." *Wives,* III, iii, 210–211.

heart-sorrow, *n.* remorse; repentance: ". . . whose wraths to guard you from . . . is nothing but heart-sorrow/ And a clear life ensuing." *Temp,* III, iii, 79–82.

hearts' proceeding, *n.* blood feud between Capulets and Montagues: "I have an interest in your hearts' proceeding;/ My blood for your rude brawls doth lie a-bleeding." *Rom & Jul,* III, i, 190–191.

heart's table, *n.* notebook or sketchbook of the heart: "... to sit and draw/ His arched brows, his hawking eye, his curls,/ In our heart's table ..." *All's W,* I, i, 91–93.

heart-strook, *adj.* striking the heart: "... labours to out-jest/ His heart-strook injuries." *Lear,* III, i, 16–17.

heat, *n.* **1** anger, esp. outraged or excited words: "... your Grace hath screen'd and stood between/ Much heat and him." *Ham,* III, iv, 3–4. **2** importance or urgency: "It is a business of some heat ..." *Oth,* I, ii, 40. **3** lust: "Nor to comply with heat the young affects ..." *Oth,* I, iii, 263. **4 above heat,** beyond the point at which the body feels a cozy warmth: "... one draught above heat makes him a fool ..." *T Night,* I, v, 133. **5 i' th' heat,** quickly: "We must do something, and i' th' heat [strike while the iron is hot]." *Lear,* I, i, 308. **6 seven years' heat,** seven summers [have passed]: "The element itself, till seven years' heat,/ Shall not behold her face ..." *T Night,* I, i, 26–27. **7 take the heat,** to strike while the iron is hot: "My lord, he will ... turn all to a merriment, if you take not the heat." *2 Hen 4,* II, iv, 295–296.
—*v.* **8** to race across: "You may ride 's/ With one soft kiss a thousand furlongs ere/ With spur we heat an acre." *W Tale,* I, ii, 94–96. **9** to cause to sweat: "Nay, we shall heat you thoroughly anon." *2 Hen 6,* V, i, 159.

heathenish, *adj.* savage; barbarous: "O villain!"/ "Most heathenish, and most gross!" *Oth,* V, ii, 314.

heat-oppressed, *adj.* fevered: "... a false creation,/ Proceeding from the heat-oppressed brain?" *Mac,* II, i, 38–39.

heave, *v.* **1** to raise or lift: "This shoulder was ordain'd so thick to heave ..." *3 Hen 6,* V, vii, 23. **2** to throw out: "My sighs like whirlwinds labour hence to heave thee ..." *Luc,* 586. **3** to speak with difficulty: "... once or twice she heav'd the name of 'father' ..." *Lear,* IV, iii, 26. **4 heaved to head,** raised to [my] mouth: "O, would/ Our viands had been poison'd (or at least/ Those which I heaved to head) ..." *Cymb,* V, v, 155–157.

heaved-up, *adj.* raised: "Her joy with heav'd-up hand she doth express ..." *Luc,* 111.

heaven, *n.* **1** [often cap. and pl.] "But, gentle Heavens,/ Cut short all intermission [delay] ..." *Mac,* IV, iii, 231–232. **2 affairs to heaven,** business with heaven: "Lord Angelo, having affairs to heaven,/ Intends you for his swift ambassador ..." *Meas,* III, i, 56–57. **3 eye of heaven,** the sun: "Sometime too hot the eye of heaven shines ..." *Sonn 18,* 5. **4 for the heavens,** for heaven's sake: "... 'for the heavens rouse up a brave mind'/ says the fiend, 'and run.'" *Merch,* II, ii, 11–12. **5 Heaven in my mouth,** giving only lip service to religion: "Heaven in my mouth,/ As if I did but only chew his name ..." *Meas,* II, iv, 3–4. **6 shape of heaven,** angelic form; here, intended to deceive: "But virtue, as it never will be mov'd,/ Though lewdness court it in a shape of heaven ..." *Ham,* I, v, 53–54.

heavenly bow, *n.* Iris, goddess of the rainbow: "Tell me, heavenly bow,/ If Venus or her son ... Do now attend the queen" *Temp,* IV, i, 86–88.

heavenly business, *n.* religious duties or worship: "... nothing but heavenly business/ Should rob my bed-mate of my company." *Tr & Cr,* IV, i, 5–6.

heavenly-harness'd team, *n.* horses of the sun-god Apollo: "The hour before the heavenly-harness'd team/ Begins his golden progress in the east." *1 Hen 4,* III, i, 214–215.

heaven's fiery eye, *n.* the sun: "... when we greet,/ With eyes best seeing, heaven's fiery eye ..." *Love's L,* V, ii, 374–375.

heaven to earth, *n.* wager of heaven against earth: "For, heaven to earth, some of us never shall/ A second time do such a courtesy." *1 Hen 4,* V, ii, 99–100.

heavily, *adv.* reluctantly; also, sorrowfully: "... to a strange, hollow, and/ confused noise, they heavily vanish." [SD] *Temp,* IV, i, 138.

heaviness, *n.* sadness; melancholy: "You promis'd, when you parted with the king,/ To lay aside life-harming heaviness ..." *Rich 2,* II, ii, 2–3.

heavy, *adj.* **1** unfortunate; unhappy: "Why, this [is] a heavy chance [situation] 'twixt him and you ..." *Shrew,* I, ii, 45. **2** dejected; depressed: "... you unfold to me, your self, your half,/ Why you are heavy ..." *J Caes,* II, i, 274–275. **3** sorrowful; grieving: "Here come the heavy issue [sons] of dead Harry." *2 Hen 4,* V, ii, 14. **4** hard or severe; grievous: "But in our circumstance and course of thought/ 'Tis heavy with him." *Ham,* III, iii, 83–84. **5** tedious; tiresome: "Is love so light ... That thou should think it heavy unto thee?" *Ven & Ad,* 155–156. **6** drowsy; sleepy: "Intending weariness with heavy sprite ..." *Luc,* 121.

heavy-gaited, *adj.* slow; sluggish: "... let thy spiders that suck up thy venom/ And heavy-gaited toads lie in their way ..." *Rich 2,* III, ii, 14–15.

heavy-headed, *adj.* dull-witted because of drunkenness: "This heavy-headed revel east and west/ Makes us traduc'd and tax'd of other nations ..." *Ham,* I, iv, 17–18.

heavy satisfaction, *n.* condition in which one is convinced but saddened: "... she ceas'd/ In heavy satisfaction, and would never/ Receive the ring again." *All's W,* V, iii, 99–101.

hebenon, *n.* prob. henbane, a poisonous plant of the nightshade family: "Upon my secure hour thy uncle stole/ With juice of cursed hebenon in a vial . . ." *Ham,* I, v, 61–62.

Hecate, *n.* goddess in three forms: Diana on earth; Hecate when presiding in Hades over night and the arts of witchcraft; and, in heaven, Luna [Moon] or Selene [or sometimes Phoebe or Cynthia]: "And we fairies, that do run/ By the triple Hecate's team . . ." *M N Dream,* V, i, 369–370.

hectic, *n.* chronic fever: "For like the hectic in my blood he rages . . ." *Ham,* IV, iii, 69.

Hector, *n.* Trojan warrior, son of Priam and the chief defender of Troy: "Thou art as valorous as Hector of Troy,/ worth five of Agamemnon . . ." *2 Hen 4,* II, iv, 216–217.

Hecuba, *n.* (in the Iliad) wife of Priam and mother of Hector, slain in battle by Achilles: "And I have read that Hecuba of Troy/ Ran mad for sorrow . . ." *T Andr,* IV, i, 20–21.

hedge, *v.* **1** to turn or veer: ". . . if you give way,/ Or hedge aside from the direct forthright . . ." *Tr & Cr,* III, iii, 157–158. **2** to deviate from an honest course [thieves' jargon]: ". . . hiding mine/ honour in my necessity, am fain to shuffle, to hedge,/ and to lurch . . ." *Wives,* II, ii, 22–24. **3 hedge out,** to deprive: "Nay, this shall not hedge us out: we'll hear you/ sing, certainly." *Tr & Cr,* III, i, 59–60.
—*n.* **4 look upon the hedge,** step behind the hedge to urinate: "I will but look upon the hedge/ and follow you." *W Tale,* IV, iv, 827–828.

hedge-born, *adj.* born under a hedge; of very low birth: ". . . quite degraded, like a hedge-born swain . . ." *1 Hen 6,* IV, i, 43.

hedgehog, *n.* sneering ref. to Richard's crest, a wild boar: "Dost grant me, hedgehog! Then God grant me too . . ." *Rich 3,* I, ii, 104.

hedge-pig, *n.* hedgehog: "Thrice, and once the hedge-pig whin'd." *Mac,* IV, i, 2.

hedge-priest, *n.* contemptuous term for an illiterate country priest: "The pedant, the braggart, the hedge-priest, the/ fool, and the boy . . ." *Love's L,* V, ii, 536–537.

heed, *n.* **1** guide or guardian: ". . . that eye shall be his heed,/ And give him light that it was blinded by." *Love's L,* I, i, 82–83. **2** attention or care: "I am sorry that with better heed and judgment/ I had not quoted him." *Ham,* II, i, 111–112. **3** concern: ". . . a heed/ Was in his countenance." *Hen 8,* III, ii, 80–81.

—*v.* **4 if heed me,** if you pay attention to what I'm saying: "I am more serious than my custom: you/ Must be so too, if heed me . . ." *Temp,* II, i, 214–215.

heedfullest reservation, *n.* utmost care: ". . . he will'd me/ In [with] heedfull'st reservation to bestow them . . ." *All's W,* I, iii, 219–220.

heedfully, *adv.* **1** watchfully; attentively: ". . . here sit I in the sky,/ And wretched fools' secrets heedfully o'er-eye." *Love's L,* IV, iii, 76–77. **2** cautiously; warily: ". . . heedfully doth view/ The sight which makes supposed terror true." *Luc,* 454–455.

heel, *n.* **1 at heel of,** immediately following: "At heel of that, defy him." *Ant & Cleo,* II, ii, 158. **2 by my heel,** oath by which one vows not to retreat: "By my head, here comes the Capulets."/ "By my heel, I care not." *Rom & Jul,* III, i, 35–36. **3 by the heels,** [put] in prison; also, in stocks: "To punish you by the heels would amend the/ attention of your ears . . ." *2 Hen 4,* I, ii, 122–123. **4 out at heels, a.** penniless [lit., with soles worn through]: "Well, sirs, I am almost out at heels."/ "Why, then, let kibes [blisters] ensue." *Wives,* I, iii, 29–30. **b.** into a wretched condition: "A good man's fortune may grow out at heels . . ." *Lear,* II, ii, 157. **5 trust their heels,** to retreat hurriedly: ". . . justice had, with valour arm'd,/ Compell'd these skipping Kernes to trust their heels . . ." *Mac,* I, ii, 29–30.
—*v.* **6** to foot; dance: "I cannot sing,/ Nor heel the high lavolt . . ." *Tr & Cr,* IV, iv, 84–85.

heft, *n.* heaving; retching: ". . . he cracks his gorge, his sides,/ With violent hefts." *W Tale,* II, i, 44–45.

heigh, *interj.* cry of encouragement or exhortation: "Heigh, heigh, the devil rides upon a fiddle-stick,/ what's the matter?" *1 Hen 4,* II, iv, 481–482.

heigh-ho, *interj.* sighlike expression of weariness, resignation, etc.: "I may sit in a/ corner and cry 'Heigh-ho for a husband!'" *M Ado,* II, i, 300–301.

height, *n.* **1** attainments: "Exceeded by the height of happier men." *Sonn 32,* 8. **2 at height,** in the best way possible: ". . . it takes/ From our achievements, though perform'd at height . . ." *Ham,* I, iv, 20–21. **3 his height be taken,** its [the ship's] height can be ascertained by navigational instruments: "It is the star to every wandering bark,/ Whose worth's unknown, although his height be taken." *Sonn 116,* 7–8. **4 in (or to) the height,** to the highest degree: "Is a not approved in the height a villain, that hath/ slandered . . . my kinswoman?" *M Ado,* IV, i, 300–301.

heighth, *n.* var. of **height;** highest or greatest degree: "This is the very top,/ The heighth, the crest, or crest unto the crest . . ." *K John,* IV, iii, 45–46.

heinous, *adj.* **heinous respect of grief,** wicked fondness for grief: "You hold too heinous a respect of grief." *K John*, III, iii, 90.

heinously, *adv.* atrociously; outrageously: "O for a fine thief of the age of/ two and twenty or thereabouts: I am heinously unprovided." *1 Hen 4*, III, iii, 187–188.

heir, *n.* **1** here, in wordplay with "hair" and allusion to hair loss in venereal disease: "Where France?"/ "In her forehead, armed and reverted, making/ war against her heir." *Errors*, III, ii, 120–122. **2 beauty's successive heir,** [black has] succeeded to the term "beautiful": "But now is black beauty's successive heir,/ And beauty slandered with a bastard shame . . ." *Sonn 127*, 3–4.

held, *past part.* **1** to be held; scheduled or planned: ". . . I saw the prince,/ And told him of those triumphs held at Oxford." *Rich 2*, V, iii, 13–14. **2** thought; assumed: "Thou dost make possible things not so held . . ." *W Tale*, I, ii, 139. **3 held out,** See **hold** (def. 22).

Helen, *n.* **1** daughter of Zeus and Leda and the ancient world's greatest beauty; her abduction by Paris triggered the Trojan War: "Helen of Greece was fairer far than thou,/ Although thy husband may be Menelaus . . ." *3 Hen 6*, II, ii, 146–147. **2** Saint Helena, mother of the emperor Constantine; said to have discovered the True Cross and the sepulchre of Christ: "Helen, the mother of great Constantine,/ Nor yet [nor even] Saint Philip's daughters, were like thee." *1 Hen 6*, I, ii, 142–143. **3** Flute's blunder for "Hero": "And I like Helen, till the Fates me kill." *M N Dream*, V, i, 195.

Helicons, *n. pl.* Greek mountains sacred to the Muses: often confused with Muses themselves: "Shall dunghill curs confront the Helicons?" *2 Hen 4*, V, iii, 101.

hell, *n.* **in another's hell,** engaged in sexual relations: "I guess one angel in another's hell . . ." *Pass Pil*, II, 12.

hell-hated, *adj.* hated as much as a good Christian hates Hell: "With the hell-hated lie o'erwhelm thy heart . . ." *Lear*, V, iii, 147.

hell-hound, *n.* fiend; devil: "Turn, Hell-hound, turn!" *Mac*, V, viii, 3.

hell-kite, *n.* prob. a vulture; here, a ref. to Macbeth: "O Hell-kite!—All?/ What, all my pretty chickens, and their dam,/ At one fell swoop?" *Mac*, IV, iii, 217–219.

hell-pains, *n.* the torments of hell: "I would it were hell-pains for thy sake . . ." *All's W*, II, iii, 228.

helm¹, *n.* helmet: "For every honour sitting on his helm . . . and on my head/ My shames redoubled!" *1 Hen 4*, III, ii, 142–144.

helm², *v.* to guide or steer; here, manage: ". . . the business he hath/ helmed must . . . give him a/ better proclamation." *Meas*, III, ii, 138–140.

help, *n.* **1** aid or remedy: ". . . such as was never/ S'incapable [so incapable] of help." *Cor*, IV, vi, 120–121. **2 at help,** in the most helpful quarter: "The bark is ready, and the wind at help . . ." *Ham*, IV, iii, 44. **3 so never-needed help,** help [that was] never needed so much: "If you refuse your aid/ In this so never-needed help . . ." *Cor*, V, i, 33–34.
—*v.* **4** to cure: "Love doth to her eyes repair,/ To help him of his blindness . . ." *Two Gent*, IV, ii, 45–46.

helpless, *adj.* useless: "As those poor birds that helpless berries saw." *Ven & Ad*, 603.

hem¹, *interj.* **1** the sound of clearing one's throat (used to encourage one's drinking companions): ". . . and when/ you breathe in your watering they cry 'Hem!' . . ." *1 Hen 4*, II, iv, 15–16.
—*v.* **2** to mutter, stammer, or cry incoherently: "She speaks much of her father . . . and hems, and beats her heart . . ." *Ham*, IV, v, 4–5. **3** to clear [out] or disperse, as by clearing the throat: ". . . these burs are in/ my heart."/ "Hem them away." *As You*, I, iii, 17–18.

hem², *v.* to enclose; shut in or up: ". . . 'since I have hemm'd thee here/ Within the circuit of this ivory pale . . .'" *Ven & Ad*, 229–230.

hempen caudle, *n.* a noose; Say is to be hanged and beheaded: "Ye shall have a hempen caudle then, and pap with/ a hatchet." *2 Hen 6*, IV, vii, 85–86.

hempen homespun, *n.* homespun cloth of hemp; here, the uncouth rustics attired thus: "What hempen homespuns have we swaggering here . . ." *M N Dream*, III, i, 73.

hempseed, *n.* person who deserves to be hanged: a gallows-bird: "Do, do, thou rogue! Do,/ thou hempseed!" *2 Hen 4*, II, i, 56–57.

hence, *v.* away! begone!: "Hence! home, you idle creatures, get you home . . ." *J Caes*, I, i, 1.

henchman, *n.* chief page: "I do but beg a little changeling boy/ To be my henchman." *M N Dream*, II, i, 120–121.

Henry Monmouth, *n.* Henry V: "Since Henry Monmouth first began to reign . . . This loathsome sequestration have I had . . ." *1 Hen 6*, II, v, 23–25.

Henry III, *n.* son of John, who succeeded his father in 1216 at the age of nine: ". . . the lords are all come back,/ And brought Prince Henry in their company . . ." *K John,* V, vi, 33–34.

hent, *n.* **1** opportunity; poss. var. of HINT: "Up, sword, and know thou a more horrid hent . . ." *Ham,* III, iii, 88.
—*v.* **2** to take up positions at: "The generous and gravest citizens/ Have hent the gates . . ." *Meas,* IV, vi, 13–14. **3** to grasp; hence, leap over: "Jog on, jog on, the foot-path way,/ And merrily hent the stile-a . . ." *W Tale,* IV, iii, 119–120.

her, *pron.* **to her,** compared to her: "Thy mind to her is now as low as were/ Thy fortunes." *Cymb,* III, ii, 10–11.

herald, *n.* **1** ref. to herald's place in Eliz. funeral processions, proclaiming titles, honors, etc., of the deceased: "Let him be regarded/ As the most noble corse that ever herald/ Did follow to his urn [tomb]." *Cor,* V, vi, 142–144. **2 in the herald's book,** registered with the College of Heralds as a gentleman: "A herald, Kate? O, put me in thy books." *Shrew,* II, i, 222.
—*adj.* **3** flying ahead: "My herald thoughts in thy pure bosom rest them . . ." *Two Gent,* III, i, 144.

heraldry, *n.* authority; entitlement: "You are more saucy with lords/ and honourable personages than the commission of/ your birth and virtue gives you heraldry." *All's W,* II, iii, 256–258.

herb, *n.* **herb of grace,** rue, a bitter herb used in medicine: ". . . she was the sweet-marjoram of the sallet,/ or, rather, the herb of grace." *All's W,* IV, v, 15–16.

Herculean, *adj.* descended from Hercules: "How this Herculean Roman does become/ The carriage of his chafe [how becomingly he conducts himself in his rage]." *Ant & Cleo,* I, iii, 84–85.

Hercules and his load, Hercules depicted as carrying the world on his back: "Ay, that they do, my lord, Hercules and his load too." *Ham,* II, ii, 358.

here, *n.* **1** the present (material) world: "—here,/ But here, upon this bank and shoal of time . . ." *Mac,* I, vii, 5–6.
—*adv.* **2** appar. at the bottom, as Edmund was before his fortunes appeared to rise: "The wheel is come full circle; I am here." *Lear,* V, iii, 174.

hereafter time, *n., adv.* (in) future time: "I myself have many tears to wash/ Hereafter time, for time past wrong'd by thee." *Rich 3,* IV, iv, 389–390.

here and everywhere, ref. to the ubiquity of divine beings: "Nor can there be that deity in my nature/ Of here and everywhere." *T Night,* V, i, 225–226.

here-approach, *n.* arrival: "Whither, indeed, before thy here-approach,/ Old Siward . . . was setting forth." *Mac,* IV, iii, 133–135.

hereby, *adv.* nearby: "I will visit thee at the lodge."/ "That's hereby." *Love's L,* I, ii, 126–127.

hereditary, *adj.* being part of one's (low) birthright: ". . . put stuff/ To some she-beggar and compounded thee/ Poor rogue hereditary." *Timon,* IV, iii, 274–276.

hereditary sloth, *n.* natural or inherent laziness: "I'll teach you how to flow."/ "Do so: to ebb/ Hereditary sloth instructs me." *Temp,* II, i, 217–218.

herein, *adv.* in this [matter]: "And yet would herein others' eyes were worse . . ." *Errors,* IV, ii, 26.

here-remain, *n.* stay; visit or residence: "A most miraculous work . . . Which often, since my here-remain in England,/ I have seen him do." *Mac,* IV, iii, 147–149.

heresy in fair, *n.* heresy against beauty: ". . . my beauty will be saved by merit./ O heresy in fair, fit for these days!" *Love's L,* IV, i, 21–22.

Hermes, *n.* Zeus's son and messenger; invented lyre from a tortoise's shell: ". . . the basest horn of his hoof is more/ musical than the pipe of Hermes." *Hen 5,* III, vii, 17–18.

hermit or **ermite,** *n.* beadsman: ". . . for those of old,/ And the late dignities heap'd up to them,/ We rest your hermits." *Mac,* I, vi, 19–20.

Hero, *n.* **1** (in Greek myth.) priestess of Aphrodite at Sestus; Leander, in love with her, nightly swam the Hellespont to be with her: ". . . a ladder quaintly made of cords . . . Would serve to scale another Hero's tower . . ." *Two Gent,* III, i, 117–119. **2 Hero itself,** the very name, "Hero," from preceding, the personification of faithful love: "Hero itself can blot out Hero's virtue." *M Ado,* IV, i, 82.

Herod, *n.* Biblical ruler, traditionally represented in mystery plays as a ranting tyrant: "It out-Herods Herod. Pray you avoid it." *Ham,* III, ii, 14.

Herod of Jewry, *n.* typical example of the raging tyrant [See **Herod**]: ". . . let me have a child at fifty, to whom/ Herod of Jewry may do homage." *Ant & Cleo,* I, ii, 27–28.

Hesperides, *n. pl.* (in Greek myth.) daughters of Hesperus, who guarded the orchard of golden apples [not, as here, the orchard itself]; Hercules' final labor was to steal the apples: "For valour, is not Love a Hercules,/ Still climbing trees in the Hesperides?" *Love's L,* IV, iii, 336–337.

Hesperus, *n.* evening star Venus: "Moist Hesperus hath quench'd her sleepy lamp . . ." *All's W,* II, i, 163.

hest, *n.* behest; order or command: ". . . when men restrain their breath/ On some great sudden hest." *1 Hen 4,* II, iii, 62–63.

heyday, *n.* **heyday in the blood,** the highest pitch of sexual energy: ". . . at your age/ The heyday in the blood is tame . . ." *Ham,* III, iv, 68–69.

hey nonny, nonny, *interj.* meaningless exclam. usually indicative of cheerful indifference: "Converting all your sounds of woe/ Into Hey nonny, nonny." *M Ado,* II, iii, 68–69.

Hibocrates, *n.* parson's blunder for "Hippocrates," renowned physician of ancient Greece: "He has no more knowledge in Hibocrates and/ Galen . . ." *Wives,* III, i, 62–63.

Hic et ubique?, [Latin] Here and everywhere?: "*Hic et ubique?* Then we'll shift our ground." *Ham,* I, v, 164.

Hic ibat Simois, [Latin] Here ran the river Simois; [fol. by, trans.] here is the Sigeian country; here stood the lofty palace of old Priam. [from Ovid's "Heroides"] *Shrew,* III, i, 28–29.

Hic jacet, [Latin] Here lies . . . [opening words of an epitaph]: "I would have that drum or another, or *hic jacet.*" *All's W,* III, vi, 59.

hide, *v.* **1** to overlook: ". . . to excuse or hide/ The liberal opposition of our spirits . . ." *Love's L,* V, ii, 724–725. **2** to withhold: "If thou dost seek to have what thou dost hide . . ." *Sonn 142,* 13. to cover: "And, by the ground they hide, I judge their number/ Upon or near the rate of thirty thousand." *2 Hen 4,* IV, i, 21–22.

hideous, *adj.* frightful; horrifying: "Revisits thus the glimpses of the moon,/ making night hideous . . ." *Ham,* I, iv, 53–54.

hie, *v.* [usually in commands] hasten; hurry: ". . . yield possession to my holy prayers,/ And to thy state of darkness hie thee straight." *Errors,* IV, iv, 53–54.

Hiems, *n.* personification of winter: "This side is *Hiems,* Winter, this *Ver,* the Spring . . ." *Love's L,* V, ii, 883.

high, *adj.* **1** true; precise: ". . . the high east/ Stands, as the Capitol, directly here." *J Caes,* II, i, 110–111. **2** important: ". . . Her ashes, in an urn . . . Transported shall be at high festivals . . ." *1 Hen 6,* I, vi, 25–26. **3** lofty; elevated: "Sad, high, and working, full of state and woe . . ." *Hen 8,* Prol. 3. **4** high-flown or pretentious: ". . . her without-door form/ (Which on my faith deserves high speech) . . ." *W Tale,* II, i, 69–70. **5** greatest; exceeding: "My high charms work,/ And these mine en-

emies are all knit up . . ." *Temp,* III, iii, 88–89. **6** extreme; here, grievous: "Though with their high wrongs I am struck to th'/ quick . . ." *Temp,* V, i, 24–25.
—*adv.* **7** highly: "So full of shapes is fancy,/ That it alone is high fantastical." *T Night,* I, i, 14–15. **8** deeply: "My high-repented blames . . . pardon to me." *All's W,* V, iii, 36–37.
—*n.* **9 on high,** aloud: "Thine eyes, that taught the dumb on high to sing . . ." *Sonn 78,* 5.

high and low, *n.* false dice, capable of throwing either high or low numbers: "And high and low beguiles the rich and poor . . ." *Wives,* I, iii, 82.

high-battled, *adj.* commanding magnificent armies: "High-battled Caesar will/ Unstate his happiness . . ." *Ant & Cleo,* III, xiii, 29–30.

high bent, *adj.* (in the manner of a bow) bent to the maximum: ". . . my revenges were high bent upon him/ And watch'd the time to shoot." *All's W,* V, iii, 10–11.

high cross, *n.* cross usually erected in the center of a town's marketplace: "But I had as lief . . . be whipped at the high cross every morning." *Shrew,* I, i, 131–133.

high-day, *n.* **1** holiday: "Freedom, high-day! high-day, freedom! freedom,/ high-day, freedom!" *Temp,* II, ii, 186–187.
—*adj.* **2** suitable for festive occasions: "Thou spend'st such high-day wit in praising him . . ." *Merch,* II, ix, 98.

high-engendered battles, *n.* armies begotten on high: ". . . join/ Your high-engender'd battles 'gainst a head/ So old and white as this." *Lear,* III, ii, 22–24.

higher, *adv.* poss. (a) into a higher rank in the military, or (b) north, into the more mountainous regions of Italy: "Will he/ travel higher, or return again into France?" *All's W,* IV, iii, 39–40.

highest degree, *n.* strongest language or terms: ". . . tell the traitor in the highest degree [as forcefully as possible]/ He hath abus'd your powers." *Cor,* V, vi, 85–86.

high feeding, *n.* rich food: ". . . like a horse/ Full of high feeding, madly hath broke loose . . ." *2 Hen 4,* I, i, 9–10.

high hearts, *n.* lofty expressions of love: ". . . this kingly seal,/ And plighter of high hearts!" *Ant & Cleo,* III, xiii, 125–126.

high-lone, *adv.* completely alone; without aid or support: "For then she could stand high-lone, nay, by th'rood . . ." *Rom & Jul,* I, iii, 36.

highly, *adv.* **1** elegantly: ". . . thy tongue/ Makes Welsh as sweet as ditties highly penn'd . . ." *1 Hen 4,* III, i, 201–202. **2**

ambitiously: ". . . what thou wouldst highly,/ That wouldst thou holily . . ." *Mac*, I, v, 20–21. **3** to a great degree: ". . . wondrous things/ That highly may advantage thee to hear . . ." *T Andr*, V, i, 55–56.

high-minded, *adj.* arrogant: "But I will chastise this high-minded strumpet." *1 Hen 6*, I, v, 12.

high noises, *n.* impending conflict between Cornwall and Albany; also, invasion by France: "Mark the high noises, and thyself bewray . . ." *Lear*, III, vi, 114.

high note, *n.* notice of those in high places: ". . . and high note's/ Ta'en of your many virtues . . ." *Hen 8*, II, iii, 59–60.

high order, *n.* dignified ceremony: "Come, Dolabella, see/ High order, in this great solemnity." *Ant & Cleo*, V, ii, 363–364.

high-proof, *adj.* of the highest degree: ". . . we are high-proof melancholy, and would fain have it/ beaten away." *M Ado*, V, i, 123–124.

high-sighted, *adj.* able to see from a great height, as a predatory bird: "So let high-sighted tyranny range on,/ Till each man drop by lottery." *J Caes*, II, i, 118–119.

high-stomached, *adj.* haughty; also, hot-tempered: "High-stomach'd are they both and full of ire,/ In rage, deaf as the sea, hasty as fire." *Rich 2*, I, i, 18–19.

hight, *v.* is named or called: "This child of fancy, that Armado hight . . ." *Love's L*, I, i, 169.

high terms, *n.* lofty expressions; here, extravagant claims: "Thou hast astonish'd me with thy high terms." *1 Hen 6*, I, ii, 93.

high tides, *n.* chief festivals: "That it in golden letters should be set/ Among the high tides in the calendar?" *K John*, III, i, 11–12.

high-vaunting, *adj.* boastful; conceited: "And you, high-vaunting Charles of Normandy,/ That once today sent me a horse to fly . . ." *Edw 3*, IV, vii, 3–4.

high-witted, *adj.* clever; cunning: "Why, thus it shall become/ High-witted Tamora to gloze with all . . ." *T Andr*, IV, iv, 34–35.

hild, *v.* old past tense of **hold;** held: "O let it not be hild/ Poor women's faults . . ." *Luc*, 1257–1258.

hilding, *adj.* **1** worthless: "He was some hilding fellow that had stol'n/ The horse he rode on . . ." *2 Hen 4*, I, i, 57–58.

—n. **2** good-for-nothing; here, a coward: "If your lordship find him not a hilding, hold/ me no more in your respect." *All's W*, III, vi, 3–4. **3** slut: ". . . Cleopatra a/ gypsy, Helen and Hero hildings and harlots . . ." *Rom & Jul*, II, iv, 42–43. **4 hilding for a livery,** a fellow fit only for the livery of a servant: ". . . a base slave,/ A hilding for a livery, a squire's cloth,/ A pantler . . ." *Cymb*, II, iii, 121–123.

hillo, *interj.* hunting call in falconry: "Hillo, ho, ho, my lord." *Ham*, I, v, 117.

hilts, *n. pl.* the hilt of one's sword (used in oath-taking because of its resemblance to a cross): "Seven, by these hilts, or I am a villain else." *1 Hen 4*, II, iv, 202.

him, *pron.* himself: ". . . after this, let Caesar seat him sure,/ For we will shake him, or worse days endure." *J Caes*, I, ii, 318–319.

himself, *pron.* **1** oneself: ". . . to know a man well were to/ know himself." *Ham*, V, ii, 137–138. **2 like himself,** presented in a manner worthy of his greatness: "Then should the war-like Harry, like himself,/ Assume the port of Mars . . ." *Hen 5*, Prol., 5–6. **3 out of himself,** outside his own mind: "And never seek for aid out of himself . . ." *Hen 8*, I, ii, 114.

himself to mar, *n.* man himself mars [God's handiwork]: "What a man are you?"/ "One, gentlewoman, that God hath made,/ himself to mar." *Rom & Jul*, II, iv, 113–115.

hind[1], *n.* **1** peasant: "Rebellious hinds, the filth and scum of Kent . . ." *2 Hen 6*, IV, ii, 116. **2** servant, esp. a farm laborer: "He lets me feed with his hinds . . ." *As You*, I, i, 18–19.

hind[2], *n.* female red deer, regarded as the essence of timidity: ". . . you are a shallow cowardly hind, and you/ lie . . ." *1 Hen 4*, II, iii, 15.

hinder, *v.* **1** to prevent from making or obtaining: ". . . he hath disgrac'd me, and/ hind'red me half a million, laugh'd at my losses,/ mock'd my gains . . ." *Merch*, III, i, 48–50. **2** to neglect; ignore or slight: ". . . which to hinder/ Were (in your love) a whip to me . . ." *W Tale*, I, ii, 24–25.

hindering, *adj.* believed to stunt the growth of children and animals: "You minimus, of hindering knot-grass made . . ." *M N Dream*, III, ii, 329.

hindmost, *adj.* **1** last; here, the last to arrive: "'Tis not his wont to be the hindmost man . . ." *2 Hen 6*, III, i, 2.
–adv. **2** at the end: ". . . whose love to you/ (Though words come hindmost) holds his rank before . . ." *Sonn 85*, 11–12.

hinge, *n.* **1** pivot: "That the probation bear no hinge, nor loop,/ To hang a doubt on . . ." *Oth*, III, iii, 371–372.

—*v.* **2** to bend: "Hinge thy knee,/ And let his very breath . . . Blow off thy cap . . ." *Timon,* IV, iii, 213–215.

hint, *n.* **1** occasion or opportunity: "When the best hint was given him, he not took't,/ Or did it from his teeth." *Ant & Cleo,* III, iv, 9–10. **2** cue; turn: "It was my hint to speak, such was the process . . ." *Oth,* I, iii, 142.

hip¹, *n.* fruit of the wild rose: "The oaks bear mast, the briers scarlet hips . . ." *Timon,* IV, iii, 422.

hip², *n.* **on or upon the hip,** at a disadvantage [wrestling term]: "If I can catch him once upon the hip,/ I will feed fat the ancient grudge I bear him." *Merch,* I, iii, 41–42.

hipped, *adj.* (of a horse) lame in the hip: ". . . his horse hipped—with an/ old mothy saddle and stirrups of no kindred—" *Shrew,* III, ii, 46–47.

hire, *n.* wages; "thrifty hire" was the amount saved from wages: "I have five hundred crowns,/ The thrifty hire I sav'd under your father . . ." *As You,* II, iii, 38–39.

Hiren, *n.* dial. pron. of "iron"; also, fig. term for "whore": "Down, faitors! Have we not Hiren/ here? [Draws his sword.]" *2 Hen 4,* II, iv, 156–157.

his, *adj.* **1** its: "So high above his limits swells the rage/ Of Bolingbroke . . ." *Rich 2,* III, ii, 109–110. **2** this [or that] person's: "Desire his jewels, and this other's house . . ." *Mac,* IV, iii, 80. **3** its own: "A lady to the worthiest sir that ever/ Country call'd his . . ." *Cymb,* I, vii, 160–161.

hiss, *v.* to cause (a person) to be hissed; here, because of stale news: "What's the newest grief?/ That of an hour's age doth hiss the speaker . . ." *Mac,* IV, iii, 174–175.

history, *n.* **1** story; account: "It is a kind of history." *Shrew,* Ind., ii, 140. **2** communication: ". . . a tardiness in nature/ Which often leaves the history unspoke/ That it intends to do?" *Lear,* I, i, 235–237.
—*v.* **3** to record: ". . . keep no tell-tale to his memory/ That may repeat and history his loss . . ." *2 Hen 4,* IV, i, 202–203.

hit, *v.* **1** to hit on; guess: ". . . what your name is else I know not,/ Nor by what wonder you do hit of mine . . ." *Errors,* III, ii, 29–30. **2** to agree: "Pray you, let us hit together . . ." *Lear,* I, i, 303. **3** (of a glance) to strike: ". . . her master hitting/ Each object with a joy . . ." *Cymb,* V, v, 396–397. **4** to fit; here, with sexual innuendo: "She'll find a white, that shall her blackness hit." *Oth,* II, i, 133. **5** [past part.] succeeded: "Hath all his ventures fail'd? What not one hit?" *Merch,* III, ii, 266. **6 hit or miss,** succeed or fail: "But, hit or miss,/ Our project's life this shape of sense assumes . . ." *Tr & Cr,* I, iii, 384–385. **7 hitting**

a grosser quality, appealing to grosser natures: ". . . as oft/ Hitting a grosser quality, is cried up [praised]/ For our best act." *Hen 8,* I, ii, 83–85. **8 'tis hit,** that hit [struck] home: "He blushes and 'tis hit." *All's W,* V, iii, 194.

hitherward or **hitherwards,** *adv.* toward this place: "The Earl of Westmoreland seven thousand strong/ Is marching hitherwards . . ." *1 Hen 4,* IV, i, 88–89.

hit it, *v.* end of a popular round, with bawdy innuendo: "Shall I come upon thee with an old saying . . . as touching the hit it?" *Love's L,* IV, i, 121–122.

hive, *v.* to reside; lodge: ". . . drones hive not with me . . ." *Merch,* II, v, 47.

hizzing, *pres. part.* hissing: "To have a thousand with red burning spits/ Come hizzing in upon 'em—" *Lear,* III, vi, 15–16.

ho, *interj.* exclam. of mild surprise, similar to "oh": "Ho, the gibbet-maker? He says that he hath taken/ them down again . . ." *T Andr,* IV, iii, 79–80.

hoa, *interj.* old form of **ho:** "What hoa! Peace here; grace and good/ company!" *Meas,* III, i, 43–44.

hoar, *adj.* **1** gray with age; moldy; here, pun on "whore": ". . . something stale and hoar ere it be spent." *Rom & Jul,* II, iv, 131.
—*v.* **2** to make moldy; also, strike down with leprosy: "Hoar the flamen,/ That scolds against the quality of flesh . . ." *Timon,* IV, iii, 157–158.

hoarded, *adj.* stored; saved, esp. for just such an occasion: ". . . the hoarded plague o'th'gods/ Requite your love!" *Cor,* IV, ii, 11–12.

Hob and Dick, *n.* every Tom, Dick, and Harry: "To beg of Hob and Dick that does appear/ Their needless vouches?" *Cor,* II, iii, 115–116.

hobby-horse, *n.* **1** buffoon: "I have . . . wise words to speak to you, which these hobby-horses/ must not hear." *M Ado,* III, ii, 64–66. **2** participant in the morris-dance, whose costume imitated a horse: "But O, but O,—"/ "The hobby-horse is forgot." *Love's L,* III, i, 26–27. **3** prostitute: "Call'st thou my love hobby-horse?" *Love's L,* III, i, 28. **4** example of something quickly forgotten; perh. linked with preceding: ". . . or else shall/ a suffer not thinking on, with the hobby-horse . . ." *Ham,* III, ii, 131–132.

Hoberdidance, *n.* another of Tom's demons: "Five fiends have been in poor Tom at once;/ as Obidicut, of lust; Hoberdidance, prince of/ dumbness . . ." *Lear,* IV, i, 58–60.

Hob, nob, [a motto] Have [or] have not: "Hob, nob, is his/ word: give't [death] or take't." *T Night,* III, iv, 242–243.

hodge-pudding, *n.* large pork sausage [hodge was pig's entrails]: "What, a hodge-pudding? A bag of flax?" *Wives,* V, v, 152.

hogshead, *n.* **1** dim-witted person: "Marry, master schoolmaster, he that is likest to a/ hogshead." *Love's L,* IV, ii, 82–83. **2 pierce a hogshead,** to get drunk: "Of piercing a hogshead! a good lustre of conceit in/ a turf of earth . . ." *Love's L,* IV, ii, 84–85.

hoise, *v.* to hoist; eject: "We'll quickly hoise Duke Humphrey from his seat." *2 Hen 6,* I, 1, 168.

hoist with his own petard, blown up with a device of his own making: ". . . 'tis the sport to have the enginer/ Hoist with his own petard . . ." *Ham,* III, iv, 208–209.

Holborn, *n.* district of London where Bishop of Ely's residence was located: ". . . when I was last in Holborn/ I saw good strawberries in your garden there . . ." *Rich 3,* III, iv, 31–32.

hold, *v.* **1** to continue; last: "Still in motion/ Of raging waste? It cannot hold . . ." *Timon,* II, i, 3–4. **2** to remain; stay: "I will hold friends with you, lady." *M Ado,* I, i, 83. **3** to prove true; prevail: "Let vultures gripe thy guts, for gourd and fullam holds . . ." *Wives,* I, iii, 81. **4** [used imperatively in offering something] Here! Take it!: "Hold, take these keys and fetch more spices, Nurse." *Rom & Jul,* IV, iv, 1. **5** to maintain: "He that . . . is at all times good/ must of necessity hold his virtue to you . . ." *All's W,* I, i, 7–8. **6** to bear; withstand: ". . . the ripest mulberry/ That will not hold the handling . . ." *Cor,* III, ii, 79–80. **7** to remain intact; keep from breaking: "Iron may hold with her, but never lutes." *Shrew,* II, i, 146. **8** to wager; bet: "I hold you a penny,/ A horse and a man/ Is more than one . . ." *Shrew,* III, ii, 80–82. **9** to regard: "He loves you well that holds his life of [as dependent on] you." *Per,* II, ii, 22. **10** to have or share: "We should hold day with the Antipodes,/ If you would walk in absence of the sun." *Merch,* V, i, 127–128. **11** to withhold: "Till you compound whose right is worthiest,/ We for the worthiest hold the right from both." *K John,* II, i, 281–282. **12** to hold back; refrain: ". . . 'tis ill hap/ If they hold, when their ladies bid 'em clap." *Hen 8,* Epil., 13–14. **13** to keep; look after: ". . . at least if you make a care/ Of happy holding her." *W Tale,* IV, iv, 356–357. **14** to go through with a commitment: "Prithee no more prattling; go. I'll hold." *Wives,* V, i, 1. **15** to survive; outlast: ". . . many pocky corses nowadays that will scarce hold/ the laying in . . ." *Ham,* V, i, 160–161. **16 hold in,** to keep silent; also, to keep at a thing until completed: ". . . such as can hold in, such as will strike sooner than/ speak . . ."

1 Hen 4, II, i, 76–77. **17 hold it ever,** [I] have always agreed with that: "I hold it ever,/ Virtue and cunning were endowments greater/ Than nobleness and riches . . ." *Per,* III, ii, 26–28. **18 hold it up,** keep going; keep it up: "[Aside.] He hath ta'en th'infection; hold it up." *M Ado,* II, iii, 121. **19 hold not off,** [to] hold nothing back: "If you love me,/ hold not off." *Ham,* II, ii, 290–291. **20 hold on,** to proceed with: "And bid the lords hold on their play at chess . . ." *Edw 3,* II, i, 50. **21 hold or cut bow-strings,** poss. stick to the agreement or pay the penalty: "At the Duke's oak we meet."/ "Enough: hold, or cut bow-strings." *M N Dream,* I, ii, 102–103. **22 hold out, a.** to last; endure: "Hold out my horse, and I will first be there." *Rich 2,* II, i, 300. **b.** to continue or persist (as): "She would not hold out enemy for ever . . ." *Merch,* IV, i, 443. **23 holds him much to have,** proves most advantageous to him: "The fellow has a deal of that too much,/ Which holds him much to have." *All's W,* III, ii, 90–91. **24 hold (someone) up, a.** to support; endorse: "The proudest he that holds up Lancaster,/ Dares stir a wing if Warwick shake his bells." *3 Hen 6,* I, i, 46–47. **b.** to encourage with flattering words: "Desire him not to flatter with his lord,/ Nor hold him up with hopes . . ." *T Night,* I, v, 307–308. **25 holds you well,** thinks highly of you: "For my brother, I think he holds you well . . ." *M Ado,* III, ii, 86. **26 hold thee that,** take this as a tip: "Th'art a tall fellow. Hold thee that to [for a] drink." *Shrew,* IV, iv, 17. **27 hold ye play,** See **play** (def. 8).
—*n.* **28** stronghold, as a fortress or castle; also, a walled city: "Between that royal field of Shrewsbury/ And this worm-eaten hold of ragged stone . . ." *2 Hen 4,* Induc. 34–35. **29** prison cell: ". . . put them in secret holds,/ Both Barnardine and Claudio." *Meas,* IV, iii, 86–87. **30** lair; den: "Here is a path to 't: 'tis some savage hold . . ." *Cymb,* III, vi, 18. **31** safekeeping; custody: "King Richard he is in the mighty hold/ Of Bolingbroke." *Rich 2,* III, iv, 83–84. **32 that last hold,** the mind viewed as the last stronghold against death: ". . . many legions of strange fantasies,/ Which, in their throng and press to that last hold,/ Confound themselves." *K John,* V, vii, 18–20.

hold-door trade, *n.* trade of a bawd or pimp: "Brethren and sisters of the hold-door trade . . ." *Tr & Cr,* V, x, 52.

holden, *v.* old past part. of **hold;** here, to be held: ". . . his Majesty's Parliament,/ Holden at Bury the first of this next month." *2 Hen 6,* II, iv, 70–71.

hold-fast, *n.* allusion to saying, "Brag is a good dog, but Hold-fast is a better": "And hold-fast is the only dog, my duck . . ." *Hen 5,* II, iii, 53.

holding, *n.* **1** meaning or consistency: "This has no holding,/ To swear by Him whom I protest to love . . ." *All's W,* IV, ii, 27–28. **2** refrain of a song: "The holding every man shall bear as loud/ As his strong sides can volley." *Ant & Cleo*, II, vii, 110–111.

—*pres part.* **3 as holding of the pope,** as coming from the hand of the pope: "Take again/ From this my hand, as holding of the pope,/ Your sovereign greatness and authority." *K John*, V, i, 2–3.

hold one's countenance, *v.* to maintain a straight (serious) face: "O the Father, how he holds his countenance!" *1 Hen 4*, II, iv, 387.

hold or cut bow-strings, poss. current saying, with the approx. meaning of "hold to the agreement or suffer the penalty": "At the Duke's oak we meet."/ "Enough: hold, or cut bow-strings." *M N Dream*, I, ii, 103–104.

hole, *n.* **1 hole in his coat,** opportunity to expose him: ". . . if I find a hole in his coat I/ will tell him my mind." *Hen 5*, III, vi, 85–86. **2 hole in one's best coat,** var. of preceding; blemish on one's hitherto unblemished character: ". . . awake, Master Ford:/ there's a hole made in your best coat, Master Ford." *Wives*, III, v, 130–131. **3 hole of discretion,** See **discretion** (def. 2).

holidame or **halidom,** *n.* orig. an oath [by Our Lady] sworn on a holy relic; here, with sense of "salvation": "And by my holidame,/ The pretty wretch left crying and said 'Ay.'" *Rom & Jul*, I, iii, 43–44.

holiday, *adj.* **1** fancy or affected, not everyday: "With many holiday and lady terms/ He question'd me . . ." *1 Hen 4*, I, iii, 45–46. **2 speaks holiday,** converses merrily: ". . . he writes verses, he/ speaks holiday, he smells April and May." *Wives*, III, ii, 61–62.

holiday-time, *n.* high point; heyday: "What, have I scaped love-letters in the/ holiday-time of my beauty . . ." *Wives*, II, i, 1–2.

holily, *adv.* in a most righteous manner: ". . . what thou wouldst highly,/ That wouldst thou holily . . ." *Mac*, I, v, 20–21.

holla or **holloa,** *interj.* **1** cry used to halt a horse: "Cry holla to the tongue, I prithee." *As You*, III, ii, 240. **2** exclam. of surprise: "Holla, holla!/ That eye that told you so look'd but a-squint." *Lear*, V, iii, 72–73.

—*v.* **3** to pursue in the manner of a hunt: "If I fly [flee], Martius,/ Holloa me like a hare." *Cor*, I, viii, 6–7.

holland, *n.* fine linen, made chiefly in Holland: "Now as I am a true woman, holland of eight shillings/ an ell!" *1 Hen 4*, III, iii, 69–70.

hollow, *adj.* **1** shallow or insincere; empty or superficial: ". . . hollow men, like horses hot at hand,/ Make gallant show and promise of their mettle . . ." *J Caes*, IV, ii, 23–24. **2** sunken; here, also emptied of feeling: "To view with hollow eye and wrinkled brow/ An age of poverty . . ." *Merch*, IV, i, 266–267. **3** misuse for "holla," a shout to attract someone's attention: "Shall pack-horses,/ And hollow pamper'd jades of Asia . . . Compare with Caesars . . . ?" *2 Hen 4*, II, iv, 160–163. **4** ref. to hollow bones, a supposed symptom of venereal disease: ". . . thy bones are hollow;/ impiety has made a feast of thee." *Meas*, I, ii, 52–53. **5** wordplay on "empty" and "unproductive": "And look how [however] many Grecian tents do stand/ Hollow upon this plain, so many hollow factions." *Tr & Cr*, I, iii, 79–80.

—*v.* **6** to halloo; Launcelot here is imitating a post horn and uttering hunting cries: "Master Lorenzo,/ sola, sola!"/ "Leave hollowing man,—here!" *Merch*, V, i, 41–44.

Hollowmas, *n.* Hallowmas, or All Saints' Day, Nov. 1; here, the unadorned season of late fall: "She came adorned hither like sweet May,/ Sent back like Hollowmas or short'st of day." *Rich 2*, V, i, 79–80.

hollow mine, *n.* great cavern within the earth, home of the winds: "The bawdy wind, that kisses all it meets,/ Is hush'd within the hollow mine of earth . . ." *Oth*, IV, ii, 80–81.

hollowness, *n.* wordplay on "hollow sound" and "insincerity": "Nor are those empty-hearted whose low sounds/ Reverb no hollowness." *Lear*, I, i, 153–154.

Holmedon, also Humbleton, *n.* a town in Northumberland, near the Scottish border; English defeated Scots here 1402: "Young Harry Percy and brave Archibald . . . At Holmedon met, where they did spend/ A sad and bloody hour . . ." *1 Hen 4*, I, i, 53–56.

holp, *v.* **1** old past tense of **help:** "Sly frantic wretch, that holp'st to make me great,/ In hope thyself should govern Rome and me." *T Andr*, IV, iv, 59–60. **2** short form of **holpen,** old past part. of **help:** "You had musty victual, and he hath holp to eat it . . ." *M Ado*, I, i, 45. **3** aided; cured: "Turn giddy, and be holp by backward turning." *Rom & Jul*, I, ii, 47.

holy, *adj.* **1** devoted; poss. error for "wholly": "As I was then,/ Advertising and holy to your business . . ." *Meas*, V, i, 380–381. **2** in wordplay with "holey" [full of holes]: "And he will bless that cross with other beating;/ Between you I shall have a holy head." *Errors*, II, i, 79–80.

holy-ale, *n.* rural festival at which ale was sold to raise money for the church or charities: "It hath been sung at festivals,/ On ember-eves and holy-ales . . ." *Per*, I, Chor., 5–6.

holy cords, *n. pl.* holy bonds of matrimony: "Like rats, oft bite the holy cords a-twain . . ." *Lear,* II, ii, 75.

holy-cruel, *adj.* cruel because of her holy chastity: "Be not so holy-cruel; love is holy . . ." *All's W,* IV, ii, 32.

holy office, *n.* prayers: ". . . bows you/ To a morning's holy office." *Cymb,* III, iii, 3–4.

Holy-rood day, *n.* September 14th, the Exaltation of the Cross: "On Holy-rood day, the gallant Hotspur there,/ Young Harry Percy, and brave Archibald . . . At Holmedon met . . ." *1 Hen 4,* I, i, 52–55.

homage, *n.* act of homage required when a monarch had granted one's rightful inheritance: "Call in the letters patents that he hath . . . and deny his off'red homage . . ." *Rich 2,* II, i, 202–204.

homager, *n.* vassal: ". . . that blood of thine/ Is Caesar's homager . . ." *Ant & Cleo,* I, i, 30–31.

home, *n.* **1 from home,** away from home: ". . . 'tis ever common/ That men are merriest when they are from home." *Hen 5,* I, ii, 271–272. **2 latest home,** final resting place; the grave: "These that I bring unto their latest home . . ." *T Andr,* I, i, 83.
—*adj.* **3** domestic; internal: "Marshal, command our officers-at-arms/ Be ready to direct these home alarms." *Rich 2,* I, i, 204–205.
—*adv.* **4** fully; completely: "That, trusted home,/ Might yet enkindle you unto the crown . . ." *Mac,* I, iii, 120–121. **5** directly; to the point: "Speak to me home, mince not the general tongue . . ." *Ant & Cleo,* I, ii, 102. **6** in all seriousness: ". . . or else a fool,/ That seest a game play'd home . . ." *W Tale,* I, ii, 247–248. **7 come home,** (of an anchor) to fail to hold: "You had much ado to make his anchor hold:/ When you cast out, it still came home." *W Tale,* I, ii, 213–214. **8 come home by me,** come back to taunt me: "Though my mocks come home by me, I will now/ be merry." *Love's L,* V, ii, 627–628. **9 Desire them home,** Ask them to go home: ". . . signify this loving interview/ To the expecters of our Trojan part:/ Desire them home." *Tr & Cr,* IV, v, 154–156. **10 home and home,** thoroughly; without letup [intensive expression]: ". . . and to the head of Angelo/ Accuse him home and home." *Meas,* IV, iii, 42–43. **11 lay home to,** to criticize sharply: "Look you lay home to him,/ Tell him his pranks have been too broad to bear with . . ." *Ham,* III, iv, 1–2.

homely, *adj.* **1** simple; straightforward: "Be plain, good son, and homely in thy drift . . ." *Rom & Jul,* II, iii, 51. **2** modest; humble: "And like rich hangings in a homely house,/ So was his will in his old feeble body . . ." *2 Hen 6,* V, iii, 12–13.

homely meat, *n.* simple food: "I think, sir, you can eat none of this homely meat." *All's W,* II, ii, 44.

homely stars, *n.* humble birth or parentage: ". . . to eke out that/ Wherein toward me my homely stars have fail'd/ To equal my great fortune." *All's W,* II, v, 74–76.

homicide, *n.* slayer; assassin: "Salisbury is a desperate homicide;/ He fighteth as one weary of his life . . ." *1 Hen 6,* I, ii, 25–26.

honest, *adj.* **1** chaste; virtuous: ". . . those that she makes fair, she scarce makes honest . . ." *As You,* I, ii, 36–37. **2** honorable; worthy or decent: "I thank you honest gentlemen, good night." *Rom & Jul,* I, v, 123. **3** harmless; blameless: "I'll devise some honest slanders/ To stain my cousin with . . ." *M Ado,* III, i, 84–85. **4 as honest as I am,** for all my presumed honesty: ". . . I'll set down the pegs that make this music,/ As honest as I am." *Oth,* II, i, 200–201.

honester, *adj.* more decent or honorable: ". . . if he were honester/ He were much goodlier." *All's W,* III, v, 79–80.

honestest defense, *n.* utmost defense of chastity: ". . . she is arm'd for him and keeps her guard/ In honestest defence." *All's W,* III, v, 73–74.

honest gentleman, *n.* term of address, equiv. to "good sir": "Your name, honest gentleman?" *M N Dream,* III, i, 177.

honestly, *adv.* **show honestly,** appear honorable: ". . . 'tis/ not amiss we tender our loves to him . . . it will show honestly in us . . ." *Timon,* V, i, 12–14.

honesty, *n.* **1** openhandedness; also, profligacy: "Every man has his fault, and honesty is his." *Timon,* III, i, 27–28. **2** integrity; uprightness or decency: ". . . he is/ of a noble strain,/ of approved valour, and confirmed/ honesty." *M Ado,* II, i, 355–357. **3 in honesty,** in truth; indeed; also, in any case: "I should woo hard, but be your groom in honesty . . ." *Cymb,* III, vii, 42.

honey, *v.* to exchange endearments: "Stew'd in corruption, honeying and making love/ Over the nasty sty!" *Ham,* III, iv, 93–94.

honey-heavy dew, *n.* sleep that is sweet, deep, and refreshing: "Enjoy the honey-heavy dew of slumber . . ." *J Caes,* II, i, 230.

honeyseed, *n., adj.* prob. misuse for "homicide" or "homicidal": "Ah, thou/ honeyseed rogue! thou art a honeyseed . . ." *2 Hen 4,* II, i, 50–51.

honey-stalks, *n.* stalks of clover: "... yet more dangerous,/ Than baits to fish, or honey-stalks to sheep..." *T Andr,* IV, iv, 90–91.

honeysuckle, *adj.* prob. misuse for "homicidal": "Ah, thou honeysuckle villain,/ wilt thou kill God's officers and the King's?" *2 Hen 4,* II, i, 49–50.

Honi soit qui mal y pense, Shamed be he who thinks ill of it; French motto of the Order of the Garter: "And *Honi soit qui mal y pense* write/ In em'rald tufts, flowers purple..." *Wives,* V, v, 70–71.

honor, *n.* **1** honored duty: "'Tis now your honour, daughter, to entertain/ The labour of each knight..." *Per,* II, ii, 14–15. **2** reputation; good name: "Which, to preserve mine honour, I'll perform." *Per,* II, ii, 16. **3** [pl.] titles: "He gave his honours to the world again,/ His blessed part to heaven..." *Hen 8,* IV, ii, 29–30. **4 bring one's honor off,** to acquit oneself with honor: "... who may you else oppose/ That can from Hector bring his honour off/ If not Achilles?" *Tr & Cr,* I, iii, 333–334. **5 free honors,** rewards given and received honorably, not as payment for crimes: "Do faithful homage, and receive free honours,/ All which we pine for now." *Mac,* III, vi, 36–37. **6 in honor he required,** because of his position he was entitled to: "I lov'd him as in honour he requir'd..." *W Tale,* III, ii, 63. **7 make them honors,** do themselves honors: "... the clearest Gods, who make them honours/ Of men's impossibilities [accomplishing things that men cannot]..." *Lear,* IV, vi, 73–74. **8 stand within the eye of honor,** (to) be honorable: "And if it stand as you yourself still do,/ Within the eye of honour, be assur'd..." *Merch,* I, i, 136–137. **9 this is her honor!** [don't forget that] this is her honor we're talking about: "This is her honour!/ Let it be granted you have seen all this..." *Cymb,* II, iv, 91–92. **10 use honor,** to plead in opposition: "We here below/ Recall not what we give, and therein may/ Use honour with you." *Per,* III, i, 24–26.

honorable, *adv.* honorably: "I would have the soil of her fair rape/ Wip'd off in honourable keeping her." *Tr & Cr,* II, ii, 149–150.

honorably, *adv.* **ordered honorably,** accorded every honor: "Within my tent his bones to-night shall lie,/ Most like a soldier, order'd honourably." *J Caes,* V, v, 78–79.

honored, *adj.* honorable: "Do you not love my sister?"/ "In honour'd love." *Lear,* V, i, 9.

honorificabilitudinitatibus, [Latin] in the condition of being loaded with honors [longest Latin word and a favorite joke among scholars]: "I marvel thy master hath not eaten thee for a word;/ for thou art not so long by the head as *honorificabilitudinitatibus*..." *Love's L,* V, i, 39–40.

honor-owing, *adj.* honor-owning; honorable: "Yoke-fellow to his honour-owing wounds..." *Hen 5,* IV, vi, 9.

hoo, *interj.* exultant cry: "Hoo! says 'a. There's my cap."/ "Hoo! Noble captain, come." *Ant & Cleo,* II, vii, 133–134.

hood, *v.* **1** to cover; hide [term in falconry]: "Hood my unmann'd blood, bating in my cheeks,/ With thy black mantle..." *Rom & Jul,* III, ii, 14–15. —*n.* **2 by my hood,** an affirmation of no precise meaning: "Now (by my hood) a gentle, and no Jew." *Merch,* II, vi, 51. **3 hoods make not monks,** from prov., it takes more than a hood to make a monk: "They should be good men... But all hoods make not monks." *Hen 8,* III, i, 22–23.

hooded, *adj.* concealed [term in falconry]: "... never any body saw it/ but his lackey: 'tis a hooded valour..." *Hen 5,* III, vii, 111–112.

hoodman-blind, *n.* game of blindman's buff: "What devil was't/ That thus hath cozen'd you at hoodman-blind?" *Ham,* III, iv, 76–77.

hoodwink, *v.* **1** to blindfold: "We'll have no Cupid hoodwink'd with a scarf..." *Rom & Jul,* I, iv, 4. **2** to render harmless or ineffectual: "... the prize I'll bring thee to/ Shall hoodwink this mischance..." *Temp,* IV, i, 205–206.

hook-nosed fellow of Rome, *n.* ref. to Julius Caesar: "... that I may justly say, with the hook-nosed/ fellow of Rome, three words, 'I came, saw,/ and overcame'." *2 King Henry IV,* IV, iii, 41–42.

hook of wiving, *n.* bait for marriage: "... besides that hook of wiving,/ Fairness, which strikes the eye." *Cymb,* V, v, 167–168.

hook on, *v.* to attach oneself to another: "Go, with her, with her!/ Hook on, hook on [Don't let her change her mind]!" *2 Hen 4,* II, i, 159–160.

hoop[1], *n.* **1** measuring band on ale pot: "... the three-hoop'd pot/ shall have ten hoops [contain more than three times as much]..." *2 Hen 6,* IV, ii, 63–64. **2 grown into a hoop,** bent double: "The foul witch Sycorax, who with age and envy/ Was grown into a hoop?" *Temp,* I, ii, 258–259. —*v.* **3** to encircle: "Or hoop his body more with thy embraces..." *W Tale,* IV, iv, 440.

hoop[2], *v.* **1** to cry out in astonishment: "That admiration did not hoop at them..." *Hen 5,* II, ii, 108. **2** See **whoop.**

hop, *v.* to skip about: "Hop in [during] his walks, and gambol in his eyes..." *M N Dream,* III, i, 158.

hope, *n.* **1** [pl.] expectations; here, Hamlet's expectations of succeeding his father as the new king: "He that hath kill'd my king and whor'd my mother,/ Popp'd in between th'election and my hopes..." *Ham,* V, ii, 64–65. **2** likelihood or possibility: "Let her go;/ There's no hope she'll return." *Per,* IV, i, 97–98. **3 hope of action,** See **action** (def. 6). **4 out of hope of all but,** with no expectation of anything except: "Out of hope of all, but my share of the feast." *Shrew,* V, i, 129.

hopeful, *adj.* [what I hope will be a] successful: "To th'hopeful execution do I leave you/ Of your commissions." *Meas,* I, i, 59–60.

hopeless, *adj.* lacking hope; despairing: "Hopeless to find, yet loth to leave unsought..." *Errors,* I, i, 135.

Hoppedance, *n.* one of Tom's [Edgar's] demons or devils: "Hoppedance cries in Tom's/ belly for two white herring." *Lear,* III, vi, 31–32.

horn, *n.* **1** poss. ref. to horn of plenty: "... by how much defence is/ better than no skill, by so much is a horn more/ precious than to want." *As You,* III, iii, 55–57. **2** horn(s) of cuckoldry; here, in wordplay with sense of "erect penis," as Grumio implies he has cuckolded Curtis: "Am I but three inches? Why, thy horn is a foot, and/ so long am I at the least." *Shrew,* IV, i, 24–25. **3** horn, usually of an ox, carried by beggars to hold drink given them as alms: "Poor Tom, thy horn is dry." *Lear,* III, vi, 75–76. **4** hunting horn; prob. wordplay also on cuckold's horn(s): "Well, a horn for my money,/ when all's done." *M Ado,* II, iii, 60–61. **5 give horns,** to butt with the horns; also, to cuckold: "Will you give horns, chaste lady? do not so." *Love's L,* V, ii, 252. **6 horn and noise,** noisy horn; ref. to earlier mention of Triton: "... being but/ The horn and noise o'th'monster's..." *Cor,* III, i, 93–94.

horn-beast, *n.* cuckold: "... we have no temple/ but the wood, no assembly but horn-beasts." *As You,* III, iii, 43–44.

horned, *adj.* referring to the points of the crescent moon: "This lantern doth the horned moon present—" *M N Dream,* V, i, 231.

horning, *pres. part.* cuckolding; making your husband a cuckold: "Under your patience, gentle empress,/ 'Tis thought you have a goodly gift in horning..." *T Andr,* II, iii, 66–67.

horn-mad, *adj.* enraged in the manner of a charging bull; also, raving mad at being made a cuckold: "If this should ever happen, thou wouldst be horn-mad." *M Ado,* I, i, 249.

horn of abundance, *n.* horn of plenty, or cornucopia; also, in punning, the horn(s) of the cuckold: "... he hath the horn of abundance, and the lightness/ of his wife shines through it..." *2 Hen 4,* I, ii, 46–47.

horn-ring, *n.* ring made of horn, thought to have magic properties: "... shoe-tie, bracelet, horn-ring/, to keep my pack from fasting..." *W Tale,* IV, iv, 600–601.

horologe, *n.* clock: "He'll watch the horologe a double set [twice round]..." *Oth,* II, iii, 123.

horrid, *adj.* horrified; terrified: "... pursy insolence shall break his wind/ With fear and horrid flight." *Timon,* V, iv, 12–13.

horse, *n.* **1** understood as "horses": "Charles' wain is over the new chimney, and/ yet our horse not packed." *1 Hen 4,* II, i, 2–3. **2** troops on horseback; cavalry: "Your uncle Worcester's horse came but today..." *1 Hen 4,* IV, iii, 21. **3** stupid person; blockhead: "... Hal, if I tell thee a/ lie, spit in my face, call me horse." *1 Hen 4,* II, iv, 189–190. **4 come from horse,** to dismount: "Thou told'st me when we came from horse, the place/ Was near at hand..." *Cymb,* III, iv, 1–2. **5 horses of the sun,** horses drawing the chariot of the sun god [Apollo]: "Ere twice the horses of the sun shall bring/ Their fiery coacher his diurnal ring..." *All's W,* II, i, 160–161. **6 take horse with,** to join (another person) on horseback: "... he sends to know... If you will presently take horse with him/ And with all speed post with him toward the north..." *Rich 3,* III, ii, 14–16. **7 the ominous horse,** wooden horse in which the Greek army entered Troy: "Black as his purpose... When he lay couched in the ominous horse..." *Ham,* II, ii, 449–450.
—*v.* **8** to mount a horse; here, to set or place: "... horsing foot on foot?" *W Tale,* I, ii, 288.

horsed, *adj.* seated or transported on a horse: "... hors'd/ Upon the sightless couriers of the air [winds]..." *Mac,* I, vii, 22–23.

horse-drench, *n.* dose of horse medicine: "... to this preservative,/ of no better report than a horse-drench." *Cor,* II, i, 116–117.

horse-hairs, *n.* bows for stringed musical instruments: "... horse-hairs, and calves'-guts, nor the/ voice of unpaved eunuch to boot..." *Cymb,* II, iii, 28–29.

horse-leech, *n.* large leech used in medicine: "... like horse-leeches, my boys,/ To suck, to suck, the very blood to suck!" *Hen 5,* II, iii, 56–57.

horse-way, *n.* bridle path: "Both stile and gate, horse-way and foot-path." *Lear,* IV, i, 55.

hose and doublet, *n.* basic male clothing of breeches and jacket; here, lacking the cloak of more elegant gentlemen: ". . . thou ought'st not to let thy horse wear a/ cloak, when honester men than thou go in their hose/ and doublets." *2 Hen 6,* IV, vii, 47–49.

host¹, *v.* **1** to lodge: "Go, bear it to the Centaur, where we host . . ." *Errors,* I, ii, 9.
—*n.* **2** person or thing providing shelter: ". . . take the shadow of this tree/ For your good host . . ." *Lear,* V, ii, 1–2. **3 at host,** at one's lodgings: "Your goods that lay at host, sir, in the Centaur." *Errors,* V, i, 410.

host², *n.* an army; here, enemy lines: ". . . best you saf'd the bringer/ Out of the host . . ." *Ant & Cleo,* IV, vi, 26–27.

hostess, *n.* woman who operates an inn: ". . . ruminates like an hostess that/ hath no arithmetic but her brain . . ." *Tr & Cr,* III, iii, 251–252.

hostler, *n.* servant, as at an inn, who looks after horses: ". . . as an hostler, that for th'poorest piece/ Will bear the knave by th'volume." *Cor,* III, iii, 32–33.

hot, *adj.* **1** eager; anxious: "O God's lady dear,/ Are you so hot?" *Rom & Jul,* II, v, 62–63. **2** angry; insulting: ". . . to you that were so hot at sea,/ Disgracing of these colours that I wear . . ." *1 Hen 6,* III, iv, 28–29. **3** ardent; fiery: "I tell thee, my master is become a hot lover." *Two Gent,* II, v, 43. **4** furious; also, violent: "Galling the gleaned land with hot assays . . ." *Hen 5,* I, ii, 151. **5** lecherous: ". . . that of coward hares, hot goats, and venison!" *Cymb,* IV, iv, 37. **6 hot at hand,** lively at the beginning; eager to start: ". . . hollow men, like horses hot at hand,/ Make gallant show and promise of their mettle . . ." *J Caes,* IV, ii, 23–24.

hot-house, *n.* bathhouse; often, a euphem. for brothel: ". . . she professes/ a hot-house; which I think is a very ill house/ too." *Meas,* II, i, 64–66.

hotly, *adv.* urgently: ". . . you have been hotly call'd for . . ." *Oth,* I, ii, 44.

hour, *n.* **1** appointment: "'Tis like, my lord, you will not keep your hour." *2 Hen 6,* ii, i, 173. **2** time of suffering before death: ". . . let not that part of nature . . . be of any power/To expel sickness, but prolong his hour!" *Timon,* III, i, 63. **3** [pl.] the passage of time: "When hours have drain'd his blood and fill'd his brow . . ." *Sonn 63,* 3. **4 break hours,** to fail to keep appointments: ". . . lovers break not hours,/ Unless it be to come before their time . . ." *Two Gent,* V, i, 4–5. **5 fair hour,** the best time of life: "Take thy fair hour, Laertes, time be thine . . ." *Ham,* I, ii, 62. **6 my hour,** dawn; daybreak: "My hour is almost come/ When I . . . Must render up myself." *Ham,* I, v, 2–4.

7 the hourly thought, any hour now: ". . . the main descry/ Stands on the hourly thought." *Lear,* IV, vi, 214–215. **8 upon your hour,** at the appointed time: "You come most carefully upon your hour." *Ham,* I, i, 6.

house, *n.* **1** wordplay on "domicile" and astrological sense for area of the zodiac: "For Venus smiles not in a house of tears." *Rom & Jul,* IV, i, 8. **2** inn or alehouse: "And rail upon the hostess of the house,/ And say you would present her at the leet . . ." *Shrew,* Ind., ii, 87–88. **3** house of prostitution: "All houses in the suburbs of Vienna must be plucked down." *Meas,* I, ii, 88. **4** scabbard: "This dagger hath mista'en, for lo, his house/ Is empty on the back of Montague . . ." *Rom & Jul,* V, iii, 202–203. **5** a room: "Say'st thou that house is dark?" *T Night,* IV, ii, 35. **6** household; family or family relations: "Do you but mark how this becomes the house . . ." *Lear,* II, iv, 154. **7** title or responsibility: "To be a king is of a younger [more recent] house/ Than to be married . . ." *Edw 3,* II, i, 263–264. **8 keep the house,** wordplay on "stay home" and "stay in prison": ". . . you will turn good husband now, Pompey; you will/ keep the house." *Meas,* III, ii, 68–69.
—*v.* **9** to find a home: "The cod-piece that will house/ Before the head has any . . ." *Lear,* III, ii, 27–28.

house-clogs, *n.* fetters: "Had I a sword,/ And these house-clogs away—" *Kinsmen,* III, i, 42–43.

housed badge or **household badge,** *n.* family emblem: "Might I but know thee by thy housed badge." *2 Hen 6,* V, i, 202. Sometimes, **father's badge.**

household harmony, *n.* melodious music throughout the house: "At last by notes of household harmony/ They quite forget their loss of liberty." *3 Hen 6,* IV, vi, 14–15.

household's grave, *n.* family tomb, hung with their coats of arms: "O foul dishonour to my household's grave!" *Luc,* 198.

household stuff, *n.* furnishings; also, domestic matters: ". . . my good lord, it is more pleasing stuff."/ "What, household stuff?" *Shrew,* Ind., ii, 140.

housekeeper, *n.* **1** one offering hospitality; a host: ". . . to be said an honest/ man and a good housekeeper goes as fairly as to/ say a careful man . . ." *T Night,* IV, ii, 8–10. **2** watchdog: "Distinguishes the swift, the slow, the subtle,/ The housekeeper, the hunter . . ." *Mac,* III, i, 95–96. **3** person who remains indoors or at home: "How do you both? You are manifest housekeepers." *Cor,* I, iii, 51.

house-keeping, *n.* hospitality: "I hear your grace hath sworn out [forsworn] house-keeping . . ." *Love's L,* II, i, 103.

house of resort, brothel; in London, located beyond the city limits and not subject to city laws: "But shall all our houses of resort in the suburbs be/ pulled down?" *Meas,* I, ii, 93–94.

housewife, *n.* slang term for "hussy" or, often, a prostitute: ". . . sung those tunes/ to the overscutched housewives that he heard the/ carmen whistle . . ." *2 Hen 4,* III, ii, 310–312.

housewifery, *n.* duties as well as the virtues of a housewife: "Let housewifery appear; keep close, I thee command." *Hen 5,* II, iii, 62.

hovel, *v.* to house in a hovel or shed: "To hovel thee with swine and rogues forlorn . . ." *Lear,* IV, vii, 39.

hovel-post, *n.* post supporting a shed: "Do I look like a cudgel or a hovel-post, a/ staff, or a prop?" *Merch,* II, ii, 65–66.

hovering temporizer, *n.* a wavering compromiser: "Or else a hovering temporizer that/ Canst with thine eyes at once see good and evil . . ." *W Tale,* I, ii, 302–303.

how, *adv.* **1** however: "I never yet saw man,/ How wise, how noble, young, how rarely featur'd . . ." *M Ado,* III, i, 59–60. **2** how much? what is the cost of?: "How/ a good yoke of bullocks at Stamford fair?" *2 Hen 4,* III, ii, 37–38.

howbeit, *adv.* nevertheless: ". . . you shall perceive/ Whether I blush or no: howbeit, I thank you." *Cor,* I, ix, 67–68.

how ever, *conj.* in any case; either way: "How ever, but a folly bought with wit,/ Or else a wit by folly vanquished." *Two Gent,* I, i, 34–35.

how go? *v.* See **go** (def. 28).

howl, *v.* to suffer the torments of hell: ". . . contrary to the law, for the which I think thou wilt/ howl." *2 Hen 4,* II, iv, 342–343.

howlet, *n.* owlet: "Lizard's leg, and howlet's wing . . ." *Mac,* IV, i, 17.

howling, *pres. part.* **1** keening; lamenting: ". . . he did redeem/ The virgin tribute, paid by howling Troy/ To the sea-monster . . ." *Merch,* III, ii, 55–57. **2** screaming with torment in hell: "A minist'ring angel shall my sister be/ When thou liest howling." *Ham,* V, i, 234–235. **3 howling after music,** appar. ref. to the response of some dogs to loud or high-pitched music: "It is as fat and fulsome to mine ear/ As howling after [at] music." *T Night,* V, i, 107–108.

how much, *adv.* **1** how little; so little: "By how much of me their reproach contains . . ." *Lover's Comp,* 189. **2** as much as:

"You are the better at proverbs, by how much/ 'A fool's bolt is soon shot.'" *Hen 5,* III, vii, 122–123.

howsoever or **howsoe'er,** *adv.* in any case; in whatever way: "And gold confound [damn] you howsoe'er!" *Timon,* IV, iii, 452.

howsomever or **howsome'er,** *adv.* var. of HOWSOEVER; in whatever way: "But howsomever thou pursuest this act,/ Taint not thy mind . . ." *Ham,* I, v, 84–85.

hox, *v.* to hamstring; cripple: ". . . thou art a coward,/ Which hoxes honesty behind . . ." *W Tale,* I, ii, 243–244.

hoy, *n.* small coastal vessel: ". . . then were you hindered by the sergeant to tarry for the/ hoy *Delay.*" *Errors,* IV, iii, 37–38.

hoyday, *interj.* exclam. of surprise or, as here, impatience: "Hoyday, a riddle! Neither good nor bad—" *Rich 3,* IV, iv, 459.

huddle, *v.* to heap or pile in a jumble: ". . . huddling jest upon/ jest with such impossible conveyance . . ." *M Ado,* II, i, 228–229.

hue, *n.* appearance or complexion; looks: "A man in hue, all hues in his controlling . . ." *Sonn 20,* 7.

hue and cry, *n.* pursuit of a suspect or fugitive, often with cries for help: "A hue and cry/ Hath follow'd certain men unto this house." *1 Hen 4,* II, iv, 500–501.

huge, *adj.* important; eminent: "If I were a huge man, I should fear to drink at meals . . ." *Timon,* I, ii, 49–50.

hugger-mugger, *n.* secrecy: ". . . we have done but greenly/ In hugger-mugger to inter him . . ." *Ham,* IV, v, 83–84.

Hugh Capet, *n.* king of France [987–996]: "Hugh Capet also, who usurp'd the crown/ Of Charles the Duke of Lorraine . . ." *Hen 5,* I, ii, 69–70.

hugy, *adj.,* var. of **huge:** ". . . the sea,/ Whose hugy vastures can digest the ill . . ." *Edw 3,* II, i, 402–403.

hulk, *n.* large merchant ship; also, a large, clumsy man: "And Harry Monmouth's brawn, the hulk Sir John,/ Is prisoner to your son." *2 Hen 4,* I, i, 19–20.

hull, *v.* **1** (of a ship) to remain stationary with sails furled: "No, good swabber, I am to hull here a little/ longer." *T Night,* I, v, 205–206. **2** to drift with the wind: ". . . thus hulling in/ The wild sea of my conscience . . ." *Hen 8,* II, iv, 197–198.

hum, *interj.* **1** exclam. indicating deliberation: "Hum—I have heard/ That guilty creatures sitting at a play . . ." *Ham,* II, ii, 584–585.
—*v.* **2** to make such a sound, expressive of impatience and often contempt: ". . . to bite his lip/ And hum at good Cominius, much unhearts me." *Cor,* V, i, 48–49.
—*n.* **3 his hum is a battery,** his hum sounds like a barrage of gunfire: ". . . talks like a knell, and his hum is a battery." *Cor,* V, iv, 21.

humane, *adj.* human; civilized or sensible: "It is the humane way. The other course/ Will prove too bloody . . ." *Cor,* III, i, 324–325.

humanity, *n.* **1** any human being: "A rarer spirit never/ Did steer humanity . . ." *Ant & Cleo,* V, i, 31–32. **2** human nature: "What nearer debt in all humanity/ Than wife is to the husband?" *Tr & Cr,* II, ii, 176–177.

humble, *adj.* **1** kind: "This is not generous, not gentle, not humble." *Love's L,* V, ii, 623. **2** courteous; complimentary: "A heavy heart bears not a humble tongue." *Love's L,* V, ii, 729.

humble-bee, *n.* bumblebee: "The honey-bags steal from the humble-bees . . ." *M N Dream,* III, i, 161.

humbleness, *n.* repentance: "The other half comes to the general state,/ Which humbleness may drive unto [reduce to] a fine." *Merch,* IV, i, 367–368.

Humbleton, *n.* See **Holmedon.**

Humh! *interj.* prob. an imitation of the howling wind: "Through/ the sharp hawthorn blow the winds. Humh!" *Lear,* III, iv, 45–46.

humidity, *n.* ref. to Falstaff, prob. describing him as a foul sack of fluid matter: ". . . we'll use this unwholesome/ humidity, this gross watery pumpion . . ." *Wives,* III, iii, 35–36.

humility, *n.* patient suffering; forbearance [here used sarcastically]: "If a Jew wrong a Christian, what is his [the Christian's] humility?/ revenge!" *Merch,* III, i, 62–63.

humor, *n.* **1** quirk of temperament; whim or mood: ". . . y'have got a humour there/ Does not become a man . . ." *Timon,* I, ii, 26–27. **2** disposition; nature: "I thank God/ . . . I am of your humour for that . . ." *M Ado,* I, i, 119–120. **3** inclination; intention: ". . . these paper bullets of the brain awe a man from/ the career of his humour?" *M Ado,* II, iii, 232–233. **4** fluid; liquid; moisture: ". . . presently through all thy veins shall run/ A cold and drowsy humour . . ." *Rom & Jul,* IV, i, 95–96. **5** [usually pl.] damp weather; dampness: ". . . is it physical/ To walk unbraced and suck up the humours/ Of the dank morning?"

J Caes, II, i, 261–263. **6 bend her humor.** See **bend** (def. 8). **7 good humors indeed!** fine carryings-on: "These be good humours indeed!" *2 Hen 4,* II, iv, 160. **8 have an humor,** am in the mood: "I have an humour to knock you indifferently [moderately] well." *Hen 5,* II, i, 54. **9 humors and conceits,** moods and opinions: ". . . for your coming in to dinner/ sir, why let it be as humours and conceits shall/ govern." *Merch,* III, v, 56–58. **10 pass good humors,** be careful what you say: "Be advised, sir, and pass good humours . . ." *Wives,* I, i, 150. **11 run bad humors on,** shown his ill will toward: "The king hath run bad humours on the knight . . ." *Hen 5,* II, i, 121. **12 the humor of it,** just how things are: ". . . if you/ would walk off, I would prick your guts a little . . . and that's the humour/ of it." *Hen 5,* II, i, 56–59. **13 unsettled humors,** discontented men: "With them a bastard of the king's deceas'd,/ And all th'unsettled humours of the land . . ." *K John,* II, i, 65–66.

humored, *adj.* dealing with Falstaff's intentions: "I/ should have borne the humoured letter to her . . ." *Wives,* II, i, 126–127.

humor of forty fancies, *n.* appar. an ornament, poss. a bouquet of ribbons: ". . . an old hat, and the humour of forty fancies/ pricked [pinned] in't for a feather . . ." *Shrew,* III, ii, 66–67.

humor of state, *n.* See **state** (def. 19).

humorous, *adj.* **1** moody or melancholy; also, temperamental: ". . . he misconsters all that you have done./ The Duke is humorous . . ." *As You,* I, ii, 255–256. **2** full of whims; capricious: ". . . 'tis no marvel he is so humorous,/ By'r lady, he is a good musician." *1 Hen 4,* III, i, 225–226. **3** full of humors (damp): ". . . he hath hid himself among these trees/ To be consorted with the humorous night." *Rom & Jul,* II, i, 31. **4** given to temper tantrums: ". . . the humorous man shall end his part in peace . . ." *Ham,* II, ii, 321.

Humphrey Hower or **Humphrey Hour,** *n.* unexplained sarcasm, perh. ref. to "dining with Duke Humphrey," which was to go hungry: ". . . none but Humphrey Hower, that call'd your Grace/ To breakfast once . . ." *Rich 3,* IV, iv, 176–177.

hundred, *n.* **a hundred lacking one,** 99 years, the customary length of a lease: ". . . thou shalt have/ licence to kill for a hundred lacking one." *2 Hen 6,* IV, iii, 6–7.

Hundred Merry Tales, 16th-cent. collection of humorous tales: "I had my good wit/ out of the 'Hundred Merry Tales'—" *M Ado,* II, i, 119–120.

hundred-pound, *adj.* poss. ref. to minimum estate of one who aspired to the status of gentleman: ". . . a base, proud . . .

hundred-pound, filthy worsted-stocking knave . . ." *Lear,* II, ii, 13–15.

hundreth, *n.* var. of **hundred**: "This monument five hundreth years hath stood . . ." *T Andr,* I, i, 350.

Hungarian, *adj.* common term of abuse, perh. from associations with "hungry" and "beggar": "O base Hungarian wight, wilt thou the spigot/ wield?" *Wives,* I, iii, 19–20.

Hungary, *n.* **King of Hungary's,** wordplay on "hungry," a topical ref. to Hungary's devastating war with Turkey: "Heaven grant us its peace, but not the King of/ Hungary's!" *Meas,* I, ii, 4–5.

hungerly, *adv.* sparsely: "Having no other reason/ But that his beard grew thin and hungerly . . ." *Shrew,* III, ii, 172–173.

hungry, *adj.* barren; sterile: ". . . let the pebbles on the hungry beach/ Fillip the stars." *Cor,* V, iii, 58–59.

hunt, *n.* game killed by hunter: "Boys, we'll go dress our hunt." *Cymb,* III, vii, 62.

hunt counter, *v.* to follow the scent in reverse; be off the scent: "If thou tak'st leave, thou wert better be hanged. You/ hunt counter." *2 Hen 4,* I, ii, 88–89.

hunter's peal, *n.* blowing of horns and, usually, barking of dogs to summon hunters for the hunt: ". . . rouse the prince, and ring a hunter's peal,/ That all the court may echo with the noise." *T Andr,* II, ii, 5–6.

hunting, *n.* (in painting) a hunting scene: ". . . the German [German-style] hunting, in waterwork, is/ worth a thousand of these bed-hangers . . ." *2 Hen 4,* II, i, 143–144.

hunt's-up, *n.* early morning song to arouse hunters; also, song to serenade a new bride on her first morning as a wife: ". . . arm from arm that voice doth us affray,/ Hunting thee hence with hunt's-up to the day." *Rom & Jul,* III, v, 33–34.

hurdle, *n.* wooden frame on which criminals were dragged to execution: ". . . fettle your fine joints 'gainst Thursday next/ To go with Paris to Saint Peter's Church,/ Or I will drag thee on a hurdle thither." *Rom & Jul,* III, v, 153–155.

hurly, *n.* tumult; turbulence: ". . . That with the hurly death itself awakes?" *2 Hen 4,* III, i, 25.

hurlyburly, *n.* **1** noise, uproar, etc.; here, of battle: "When the hurlyburly's done,/ When the battle's lost and won." *Mac* I, i, 3–4.

—*adj.* **2** promoting confusion and turmoil: ". . . rub the elbow at the news/ Of hurlyburly innovation . . ." *1 Hen 4,* V, i, 77–78.

hurricano, *n.* waterspout: "You cataracts and hurricanoes, spout/ Till you have drench'd our steeples . . ." *Lear,* III, ii, 2–3.

hurry, *n.* disorder; commotion: ". . . quietness of the people, which before/ Were in wild hurry." *Cor,* IV, vi, 3–4.

hurt behind, *adj.* wounded while in retreat: ". . . the strait [narrow] pass was damm'd/ With dead men, hurt behind . . ." *Cymb,* V, iii, 11–12.

hurtle, *v.* to clash noisily: "The noise of battle hurtled in the air . . ." *J Caes,* II, ii, 22.

hurtling, *n.* noisy conflict; clashing: ". . . in which hurtling/ From miserable slumber I awak'd." *As You,* IV, iii, 131–132.

husband, *v.* **1** to cultivate (land): ". . . he hath like lean, sterile, and/ bare land manured, husbanded, and tilled, with/ excellent endeavour . . ." *2 Hen 4,* IV, iii, 117–119. **2** put into effect; carry out precisely: "Well, husband your device; I'll to the vicar." *Wives,* IV, vi, 51.
—*n.* **3** husbandman; farm steward or manager: "This Davy . . . is your serving-man and your husband." *2 Hen 4,* V, iii, 10–11.

husbandry, *n.* **1** careful or, esp., thrifty management; economy: "If you suspect my husbandry or falsehood . . ." *Timon,* II, ii, 159. **2** same in wordplay with "state of being a husband": "Which husbandry in honour [honorable] might uphold/ Against the stormy gusts of winter's day . . ." *Sonn 13,* 10–11. **3** eagerness to work, esp. to be up early and doing: "That is the cause we trouble you so early;/ 'Tis not our husbandry." *Per,* III, ii, 19–20. **4** farm work or management: "My old dame will be undone/ now for one to do her husbandry . . ." *2 Hen 4,* III, ii, 112–113.

hush, *adj.* hushed; quiet or silent: ". . . and the orb below/ As hush as death . . ." *Ham,* II, ii, 481–482.

hussif, *n.* colloquial form of **housewife**: "Let us sit and mock the good hussif Fortune from her wheel . . ." *As You,* I, ii, 30–31.

huswife, *n.* var. of **housewife**; hussy: ". . . let me rail so high,/ That the false huswife Fortune break her wheel . . ." *Ant & Cleo,* IV, xv, 43–44.

Hybla, *n.* town in Sicily, famous for its honey: "But for your words, they rob the Hybla bees,/ And leave them honeyless." *J Caes,* V, i, 34–35.

Hydra, *n.* **1** [Greek myth.] the multiheaded beast slain by Hercules; when one head was severed, two others grew in its place: "Another king! They grow like Hydra's heads." *1 Hen 4,* V, iv, 24. **2** the mob, likened here to a many-headed monster: ". . . why . . . have you thus/ Given Hydra here to choose an officer . . ." *Cor,* III, i, 90–92.

hyen, *n.* hyena: "I will laugh like a/ hyen, and that when thou art inclined to sleep." *As You,* IV, i, 147–148.

Hymen, *n.* Greek god of marriage: ". . . thou bright defiler/ Of Hymen's purest bed . . ." *Timon,* IV, iii, 385–386.

Hymenaeus, *n.* Roman god of marriage: ". . . tapers burn so bright, and everything/ In readiness for Hymenaeus stand . . ." *T Andr,* I, i, 324–325.

hyperbolical, *adj.* greatly exaggerated; here, used by Clown simply as a quasi-learned word: "Out, hyperbolical fiend! how vexest thou this!/ man!" *T Night,* IV, ii, 26–27.

Hyperion, *n.* (in classical myth.) a Titan, father of the sun and moon; occasionally personified as the sun itself: ". . . crisp heaven/ Whereon Hyperion's quick'ning fire doth shine . . ." *Timon,* IV, iii, 185–186.

hypocrite, *n.* prob. misuse for "imposter": "Nay, and / you be a cursing [lying] hypocrite once, you must be looked to." *M Ado,* V, i, 204–205.

Hyrcan, *adj.* of Hyrcania: "Approach thou like the rugged Russian bear,/ The arm'd rhinoceros, or th' Hyrcan tiger . . ." *Mac,* III, iv, 99–100.

Hyrcania, *n.* land south of the Caspian Sea, said to be inhabited by tigers: "But you are more inhuman . . . than tigers of Hyrcania." *3 Hen 6,* I, iv, 154–155.

Hyrcanian, *adj.* Hyrcan: "The rugged Pyrrhus, like th' Hyrcanian beast—" *Ham,* II, ii, 446.

Hysterica passio, *n.* [Latin] Also called **mother,** lit., "passionate hysteria," a feeling of suffocation brought on by constrictions in the throat: "O! how this mother swells up toward my heart;/ *Hysterica passio!* down, thou climbing sorrow!" *Lear,* II, iv, 56–57.

~ I ~

Icarus, *n.* (in Greek myth.) escaped with his father, Daedalus, from the Cretan labyrinth by fashioning wings; Icarus ignored his father's advice and flew upward toward the sun, melting the wings' glue and casting him into the sea: "Then follow thou thy desperate sire of Crete,/ Thou Icarus . . ." *1 Hen 6,* IV, vi, 54–55.

ice, *n.* **brakes of ice,** poss. a misprint for "brakes [thickets] of vice": "Some run from brakes of ice [vice?] and answer none [are never held accountable] . . ." *Meas,* II, i, 39.

ice-brook's temper, *n.* ref. to Spanish method of tempering steel in ice-cold water: "It is a sword of Spain, the ice-brook's temper . . ." *Oth,* V, ii, 254.

Iceland dog, *n.* See **prick-eared.**

idea, *n.* **the right idea,** the very image: "Being the right idea of your father . . ." *Rich 3,* III, vii, 13.

ides of March, *n. pl.* March 15th on the Roman calendar: "The ides of March are come."/ "Ay, Caesar, but not gone." *J Caes,* III, i, 1–2.

idiot, *n.* **play the idiots,** make no effort to ingratiate themselves with Fortune: "While others play the idiots in her eyes!" *Tr & Cr,* III, iii, 135.

idle, *adj.* **1** unused; empty: "And every man hence to his idle bed." *J Caes,* II, i, 117. **2** useless; worthless: "Usurping ivy, briar, or idle moss . . ." *Errors,* II, ii, 178. **3** barren; lifeless: "Wherein of antres vast, and deserts idle . . ." *Oth,* I, iii, 140. **4** frivolous; shallow; irresponsible: ". . . one Count Rossillion,/ a foolish idle boy, but for all that very ruttish." *All's W,* IV, iii, 206–207. **5** foolish; silly: "Come, come, you answer with an idle tongue." *Ham,* III, iv, 10. **6** uncomprehending: "If I had . . . look'd upon this love with idle sight—" *Ham,* II, ii, 136–138. **7** playing the madman: "They are coming to the play. I must be idle./ Get you a place." *Ham,* III, ii, 90–91. **8**

modest or, often, trifling: "Ladies, there is an idle banquet attends you . . ." *Timon,* I, ii, 151.

idle dream, *n.* fantasy: ". . . thousand escapes of wit/ Make thee the father of their idle dream . . ." *Meas,* IV, i, 63–64.

idle fire, *n.* senseless lust: ". . . yet, in his idle fire,/ To buy his will it would not seem too dear . . ." *All's W,* III, vii, 26–27.

idle markets, *n. pl.* trifling or casual purchases: ". . . your store,/ I think, is not for idle markets, sir." *T Night,* III, iii, 45–46.

idleness, *n.* **1** use of leisure time; pastime: "Well sir, for want of other idleness, I'll bide/ your proof." *T Night,* I, v, 62–63. **2** frivolousness or foolishness; vanity: "But that your royalty/ Holds idleness your subject, I should take you/ For idleness itself." *Ant & Cleo,* I, iii, 91–93.

idle rank, *n.* mere jottings; here, contrasted with memory: "Which shall above that idle rank remain . . ." *Sonn 122,* 3.

idly, *adv.* **1** indifferently: ". . . the eyes of men,/ After a well-grac'd actor leaves the stage,/ Are idly bent on him that enters next . . ." *Rich 2,* V, ii, 23–25. **2** foolishly: "King Pharamond,/ Idly suppos'd the founder of this law . . ." *Hen 5,* I, ii, 58–59. **3** frivolously: ". . . she is so idly king'd,/ Her sceptre so fantastically borne . . ." *Hen 5,* II, iv, 26–27. **4** without paying sufficient attention: ". . . but this from rumour's tongue/ I idly heard . . ." *K John,* IV, ii, 123–124.

if, *conj.* ellip. of "to see if": "If Time have any wrinkle graven there . . ." *Sonn 100,* 10.

i'fecks, *interj.* in faith: "I'fecks:/ Why that's my bawcock." *W Tale,* I, ii, 120–121.

ignis fatuus, [Latin] will-o'-the-wisp: ". . . if I did not think thou hadst been an *ignis fatuus,* or a/ ball of wildfire . . ." *1 Hen 4,* III, iii, 38–39.

275

ignomy, *n.* var. of **ignominy;** disgrace: "I blush to think upon this ignomy." *T Andr,* IV, ii, 115.

ignorance, *n.* **1** a fool: "I had rather/ be a tick in a sheep than such a valiant [brazen] ignorance." *Tr & Cr,* III, iii, 309–310. **2 honorable points of ignorance,** ignorant [idea] of honorable conduct: ". . . they got in France,/ With all their honourable points of ignorance . . ." *Hen 8,* I, iii, 25–26.

ignorant, *adj.* unknowing; unsuspecting: "Alas, what ignorant sin have I committed?" *Oth,* IV, ii, 72.

Ilion, *n.* Greek name of Troy; also, used poetically for the city of Troy: "The armipotent Mars . . . Gave Hector a gift, the heir of Ilion . . ." *Love's L,* V, ii, 644–645.

Ilium, *n.* English form of **Ilion;** here, the palace of Priam and the citadel of Troy: "Between our Ilium and where she resides,/ Let it be call'd the wild and wand'ring flood . . ." *Tr & Cr,* I, i, 101–102.

ill, *n.* **1** evil; wickedness: "What folly 'tis to hazard life for ill!" *Timon,* III, v, 38.
—*adj.* **2** ill-meaning or ill-trained: "In his own change, or by ill officers,/ Hath given me some worthy cause to wish/ Things done undone . . ." *J Caes,* IV, ii, 7–8. **3** evil or wicked (used in puns with "infirm" sense): "Now He that made me knows I see thee ill,/ Ill in myself to see, and in thee, seeing ill." *Rich 2,* II, i, 93–94. **4** inept: "I am ill at these numbers [verses]." *Ham,* II, ii, 119. **5** ref. to house of ill fame [brothel]: ". . . she professes a hot-house; which I think is a very ill house too." *Meas,* II, i, 65–66. **6 all ill,** altogether inadequate: "I cannot mend it . . . Because my power is weak and all ill left." *Rich 2,* II, iii, 152–153.
—*adv.* **7** badly: ". . . would you believe my oaths/ When I did love you ill?" *All's W,* IV, ii, 26–27.

ill-breeding, *adj.* ready to believe or spread evil: ". . . she may strew/ Dangerous conjectures in ill-breeding minds." *Ham,* IV, v, 14–15.

ill conditions, *n. pl.* unpleasant qualities: "I warrant, one that knows him not."/ "Yes, and his ill conditions . . ." *M Ado,* III, ii, 59–60.

ill-erected, *adj.* built for or serving evil purposes [believed to have been built by Caesar, but actually constructed some 1,000 years later]: ". . . this is the way/ To Julius Caesar's ill-erected tower . . ." *Rich 2,* V, i, 1–2.

ill-favored, *adj.* **1** ugly; homely: "Pardon me, sir; it was a black ill-favour'd fly/ Like to the empress' Moor . . ." *T Andr,* III, ii, 66–67. **2** unbecoming: "Out, out, Lucetta, that will be ill-favour'd." *Two Gent,* II, vii, 54.

ill-favoredly, *adv.* **1** in an ugly manner: ". . . those that she makes honest, she makes very ill-favouredly." *As You,* I, ii, 37–38. **2** unfortunately; disagreeably: "And sped you, sir?"/ "Very ill-favouredly, Master Brook." *Wives,* III, v, 61–62.

ill-inhabited, *adj.* meagerly or insufficiently lodged: "O knowledge ill-inhabited, worse than/ Jove in a thatched house!" *As You,* III, iii, 7–8.

illness, *n.* wickedness; evil: "Art not without ambition, but without/ The illness should attend it . . ." *Mac,* I, v, 19–20.

ill-nurtured, *adj.* ill-bred; badly behaved or wicked: "Presumptuous dame! ill-nurtur'd Eleanor!" *2 Hen 6,* I, ii, 42.

ill-seeming, *adj.* of unpleasing or disagreeable appearance: ". . . like a fountain troubled,/ Muddy, ill-seeming, thick, bereft of beauty . . ." *Shrew,* V, ii, 143–144.

ill sorted, *adj.* defamed; corrupted: ". . . the word 'occupy', which was an/ excellent good word before it was ill sorted . . ." *2 Hen 4,* II, iv, 145–146.

ill to friend, not in any way your friends: "Sir, for my thoughts, you have them ill to friend . . ." *All's W,* V, iii, 181.

illume, *v.* to illuminate: ". . . t'illume that part of heaven/ Where now it burns . . ." *Ham,* I, i, 40–41.

illustrate, *adj.* illustrious: ". . . illustrate king Cophetua set eye upon/ the . . . beggar Zenelophon . . ." *Love's L,* IV, i, 66–67.

illustrous, *adj.* not lustrous; dull; lackluster: "Base and illustrous as the smoky light/ That's fed with stinking tallow . . ." *Cymb,* I, vii, 109–110.

ill-wresting, *adj.* putting the worst possible face on everything: ". . . this ill-wresting world is grown so bad,/ Mad slanderers by mad ears believed be." *Sonn 140,* 11–12.

Illyria, *n.* poss. the E coast of the Adriatic Sea; in any case, an imaginary kingdom: "What country, friends, is this?"/ "This is Illyria, lady." *T Night,* I, ii, 1–2.

image, *n.* **1** gilded statue: "Glittering in golden coats like images . . ." *1 Hen 4,* IV, i, 100. **2** reflection; here Hamlet sees his own cause reflected in Laertes' outrage: "For by the image of my cause I see/ The portraiture of his." *Ham,* V, ii, 77–78. **3** the exact likeness of something: "Is this the promis'd end?"/ "Or image of that horror?" *Lear,* V, iii, 263–264. **4** an appearance; evidence: "Without some image of th'affected merit [excellence in the object of affection]." *Tr & Cr,* II, ii, 61. **5** a person's appearance; here, equated with moral beauty: "And to his image, which methought did promise/ Most venerable worth, did I devotion." *T Night,* III, iv, 371–372. **6** concept;

idea: "The image of it gives me content already . . ." *Meas,* III, i, 260. **7** personification; quintessence: "Image of Pride, why should I hold my peace?" *2 Hen 6,* I, iii, 176.

image and horror, *n.* horrible truth: "I have told you what I have seen and heard;/ but faintly, nothing like the image and horror of it . . ." *Lear,* I, ii, 181–182.

imaginary, *adj.* affected by imagination: ". . . my rage was blind,/ And foul imaginary eyes of blood/ Presented thee more hideous than thou art." *K John,* IV, ii, 264–266.

imagination, *n.* **1** impulsiveness that lacks a sense of reality: ". . . with great imagination/ Proper to madmen . . . leap'd into destruction." *2 Hen 4,* I, iii, 31–33. **2 wrong imaginations,** illusions: ". . . woes by wrong imaginations lose/ The knowledge of themselves." *Lear,* IV, vi, 285–286. **3** See **study of imagination.**

imagined, *adj.* **1** all possible [lit., as fast as one can imagine]: "Bring them (I pray thee) with imagin'd speed . . ." *Merch,* III, iv, 52. **2 imagined wing.** See **wing** (def. 3).

imbar, *v.* to exclude or rule out: "And rather choose to hide them in a net/ Than amply [unconditionally] to imbar their crooked titles . . ." *Hen 5,* I, ii, 93–94.

imbrue, *v.* **1** to stain one's sword with blood: "What! shall we have incision? shall we imbrue? [Snatches up his sword.]" *2 Hen 4,* II, iv, 192. **2** to shed the blood of: "Come, blade, my breast imbrue!" *M N Dream,* V, i, 331.

imitari, *v.* [Latin] to imitate: "*Imitari* is nothing; so doth the hound his/ master, the ape his keeper . . ." *Love's L,* IV, ii, 121–122.

immanity, *n.* inhumanity; cruelty; savagery: "That such immanity and bloody strife/ Should reign among professors of one faith." *1 Hen 6,* V, i, 13–14.

immask, *v.* to disguise; hide: "I have cases of buckram . . . to immask our noted outward garments." *1 Hen 4,* I, ii, 174–175.

immaterial, *adj.* worthless: "Why art thou then exasperate, thou idle/ immaterial skein of sleave silk . . ." *Tr & Cr,* V, i, 29–30.

immediacy, *n.* fact that Edmund is acting as Regan's deputy: "The which immediacy may well stand up,/ And call itself your brother." *Lear,* V, iii, 66–67.

imminence, *n.* impending doom: "But dare all imminence that gods and men/ Address their dangers in." *Tr & Cr,* V, x, 13–14.

immodest, *adj.* immoderate; excess: "Proclaim'd a strumpet, with immodest hatred . . ." *W Tale,* III, ii, 102.

immoment, *adj.* inconsequential: "Immoment toys, things of such dignity/ As we greet modern friends withal . . ." *Ant & Cleo,* V, ii, 165–166.

immortal, *adj.* lethal; deadly: ". . . I would not be the party/ that should desire you to touch him, for his biting is/ immortal . . ." *Ant & Cleo,* V, ii, 244–246.

immortal longings, *n.* longings for immortality: "Give me my robe, put on my crown, I have/ Immortal longings in me." *Ant & Cleo,* V, ii, 279–280.

immortal title, *n.* title of immortality: ". . . the heavens, envying earth's good hap,/ Add an immortal title to your crown!" *Rich 2,* I, i, 23–24.

immure, *n.* wall or walled enclosure: ". . . within whose strong immures/ The ravish'd Helen . . . With wanton Paris sleeps . . ." *Tr & Cr,* Prol., 8–10.

immured, *adj.* enclosed in or as if in a wall: "Or shall I think in silver she's immur'd . . ." *Merch,* II, vii, 52.

imp[1], *n.* **1** child; youngster; also, upstart: "Why! sadness is one and the self-same thing, dear imp." *Love's L,* I, ii, 5. **2** royal descendant: "The heavens thee guard and keep, most royal imp of fame!" *2 Hen 4,* V, v, 42.

imp[2], *v.* imp out, [falconry] to engraft feathers in (a wing) so as to improve a bird's flight: "Imp out our drooping country's broken wing . . ." *Rich 2,* II, i, 292.

impaint, *v.* to cover with or as if with paint: "And never yet did insurrection want/ Such water-colours to impaint his cause . . ." *1 Hen 4,* V, I, 79–80.

impaled, *adj.* crown likened to a fence surrounding the head: ". . . my misshap'd trunk that bears this head/ Be round impaled with a glorious crown." *3 Hen 6,* III, ii, 170–171.

impare, *adj.* immature or ill-considered; also, unjust: "Yet gives he not till judgement guide his bounty,/ Nor dignifies an impare thought with breath . . ." *Tr & Cr,* IV, v, 102–103.

impart, *v.* to provide: "But this no slaughterhouse no tool imparteth . . ." *Luc,* 1039.

impartial, *adj.* uninvolved; indifferent: "Whereat th'impartial gazer late did wonder . . ." *Ven & Ad,* 748.

impartment, *n.* communication: "It beckons you to go away with it,/ As if it some impartment did desire . . ." *Ham*, I, iv, 58–59.

impatient, *adj.* hotly angry: ". . . know ye not in Rome/ How furious and impatient they be . . ." *T Andr*, II, i, 75–76.

impawn, *v.* to pledge; stake: ". . . let there be impawn'd/ Some surety for a safe return again . . ." *1 Hen 4*, IV, iii, 108–109.

impawned, *adj.* given as a pledge: ". . . this trunk; which you/ Shall bear along impawn'd, away to-night!" *W Tale*, I, ii, 435–436.

impeach, *v.* **1** to accuse or charge: "I am disgrac'd, impeach'd, and baffl'd here . . ." *Rich 2*, I, i, 170. **2** to malign; slander: ". . . a true soul/ When most impeach'd stands least in thy control." *Sonn 125*, 13–14. **3** to challenge; also, imperil: ". . . if it be denied,/ Will much impeach the justice of the state . . ." *Merch*, III, iii, 28–29. **4 impeach one's height,** to prove traitor to one's high birth: "Shall I . . . with pale beggar-fear impeach my height/ Before this out-dar'd dastard?" *Rich 2*, I, i, 188–190.
—*n.* **5** charge or accusation: "Why, what an intricate impeach is this?" *Errors*, V, i, 270. **6** reproach: "And ten to one is no impeach of valour." *3 Hen 6*, I, iv, 60.

impeachment, *n.* hindrance or impediment; detriment: ". . . let him spend his time no more at home;/ Which would be great impeachment to his age . . ." *Two Gent*, I, iii, 14–15.

impediment, *n.* obstruction or, as here, opposition: ". . . cracking ten thousand curbs/ Of more strong link asunder than can ever/ Appear in your impediment." *Cor*, I, i, 69–71.

imperator, *n.* Latin word for **emperor:** "She is as imperator over me, and I to her . . ." *Edw 3*, II, ii, 40.

imperfect, *adj.* incomplete: "Stay, you imperfect speakers, tell me more." *Mac*, I, iii, 70.

imperial, *adj.* royal: "A good and virtuous nature may recoil,/ In an imperial charge [command]." *Mac*, IV, iii, 19–20.

Imperial's, *adj.* misuse for "Emperor's": ". . . am going with Sir Proteus to the Imperial's court." *Two Gent*, II, iii, 4.

imperious, *adj.* imperial: "My sword, my chariot, and my prisoners;/ Presents well worthy Rome's imperious lord . . ." *T Andr*, I, i, 249–250.

imperseverant, *adj.* lacking perception or discrimination; imperceptive: ". . . yet this imperseverant thing loves him in my despite." *Cymb*, IV, i, 14.

impertinency, *n.* foolishness; nonsense: "O! matter and impertinency [sense and nonsense] mix'd;/ Reason in madness." *Lear*, IV, vi, 176–177.

impertinent, *adj.* **1** irrelevant; inappropriate: "I'll bring thee to the present business . . . without the which, this story/ Were most impertinent." *Temp*, I, ii, 136–138. **2** misuse for "pertinent": "In very brief, the suit is impertinent to myself . . ." *Merch*, II, ii, 130.

impeticos, *v.* to pocket: "I did impeticos thy gratillity . . ." *T Night*, II, iii, 27.

impetuous, *adj.* violent; ferocious: "The ocean, overpeering of his list,/ Eats not the flats with more impetuous haste . . ." *Ham*, IV, v, 99–100.

impiety, *n.* **impiety hath wrought,** iniquity has brought [him]: "So from [out of] himself impiety hath wrought . . ." *Luc*, 341.

impious war, *n.* rebellion; civil war: "What is it then to me,/ if impious war . . . Do, with his smirch'd complexion, all fell feats/ Enlink'd to waste and desolation?" *Hen 5*, III, iii, 15–18.

impleach, *v.* to entwine: "With twisted metal amorously impleach'd . . ." *Lover's Comp*, 205.

implorator, *n.* pleader; importuner: ". . . mere implorators of unholy suits . . ." *Ham*, I, iii, 129.

imployment, *n.* See **employment.**

import, *v.* **1** to be of importance; signify: "If you knew/ How much they do import you would make haste." *1 Hen 4*, IV, iv, 4–5. **2** to concern: "This letter is mistook; it importeth none here . . ." *Love's L*, IV, i, 58. **3** to express; indicate: "Belike this show imports the argument of the play." *Ham*, III, ii, 136. **4** to suggest; imply: "To keep an adjunct to remember thee/ Were to import forgetfulness in me." *Sonn 122*, 13–14. **5 import offending,** imply that I had offended you: "To be your prisoner should import offending . . ." *W Tale*, I, ii, 57.
—*n.* **6** importance; consequence: "The letter was not nice but full of charge,/ Of dear import . . ." *Rom & Jul*, V, ii, 18–19.

importance, *n.* **1** act of importuning; insistence: "Maria writ/ The letter, at Sir Toby's great importance . . ." *T Night*, V, i, 361–362. **2** matter or subject: ". . . upon importance of so/ slight and trivial a nature." *Cymb*, I, v, 39–40. **3** significance; import: ". . . but the wisest/ beholder . . . could not say/ if th' importance were joy or sorrow . . ." *W Tale*, V, ii, 16–18.

important, *adj.* **1** urgent: ". . . lets go by/ Th'important acting of your dread command?" *Ham*, III, iv, 108–109. **2** importunate; insistent: "If the Prince be too important/ tell him there is measure in everything . . ." *M Ado,* II, i, 64–65.

important blood, *n.* urgent passion: "Now his important blood will naught deny/ That she'll demand . . ." *All's W,* III, vii, 21–22.

importing, *adj.* earnest; urgent: ". . . her business looks in her/ With an importing visage . . ." *All's W,* V, iii, 135–136.

importless, *adj.* trivial: "That matter needless, of importless burden . . ." *Tr & Cr,* I, iii, 71.

importment, *n.* import; meaning; also, consequence: "(Which . . . comes in/ Like old importment's bastard)" *Kinsmen,* I, iii, 79–80.

importunacy, *n.* act of urging persistently; importunity: ". . . and art thou not asham'd/ To wrong him with thy importunacy?" *Two Gent,* IV, ii, 107–108.

importune, *v.* **1** to request urgently: "Tell him the daughter of the King of France . . . Importunes personal conference with his grace." *Love's L,* II, i, 30–32. **2** to urge on; hurl or impel: "My herald thoughts in thy pure bosom rest them,/ While I, their king, that thither them importune . . ." *Two Gent,* III, i, 144–145. **3** to beg to delay: "I am dying, Egypt, dying; only/ I here importune death awhile . . ." *Ant & Cleo,* IV, xv, 18–19. **4** to dictate or demand: "We shall write to you,/ As time and our concernings shall importune . . ." *Meas,* I, i, 55–56.

importuned, *adj.* importunate; urgent or persistent: "Therefore great France/ My mourning and importun'd tears hath pitied." *Lear,* IV, iv, 25–26.

importunity, *n.* urgent request: ". . . he is furnished/ with my opinion, which . . . comes with/ him at my importunity . . ." *Merch,* IV, i, 155–158.

impose, *v.* **1** to subject: "Impose me to what penance your invention/ Can lay upon my sin." *M Ado,* V, i, 267–268. —*n.* **2** command: "According to your ladyship's impose,/ I am thus early come . . ." *Two Gent,* IV, iii, 8–9.

imposition, *n.* **1** order; command: "I do desire you/ Not to deny this imposition . . ." *Merch,* III, iv, 32–33. **2** accusation: ". . . which else would stand under grievous/ imposition, as for the enjoying of thy life . . ." *Meas,* I, ii, 178–179. **3** original sin imposed on mankind: ". . . we should have answer'd heaven/ Boldly 'not guilty,' the imposition clear'd/ Hereditary ours [removing our taint of hereditary sin]." *W Tale,* I, ii, 73–75.

impossibility, *n.* **1** task impossible to achieve: ". . . the clearest Gods, who make them honours/ Of men's impossibilities . . ." *Lear,* IV, vi, 73–74. **2** something unsuitable or incongruous:

"Thou visible god,/ That sold'rest [unites] close impossibilities." *Timon,* IV, iii, 389–390.

impostume or **imposthume,** *n.* abscess: "This is th'impostume of much wealth and peace . . ." *Ham,* IV, iv, 27.

impotent, *adj.* disabled; helpless: "Who, impotent and bedrid, scarcely hears/ Of this . . ." *Ham,* I, ii, 29–30.

imprese, *n.* heraldic device: "Rac'd out my imprese, leaving me no sign . . . To show the world I am a gentleman." *Rich 2,* III, i, 25–27.

impress¹, *v.* **1** to force into [military] service; conscript: "Who can impress the forest; bid the tree/ Unfix his earth-bound root?" *Mac,* IV, i, 95–96. —*n.* **2** impressment; conscription: "Why such impress of shipwrights . . ." *Ham,* I, i, 78.

impress², *v.* **1** to imprint: "As easy may'st thou the intrenchant air/ With thy keen sword impress . . ." *Mac,* V, viii, 9–10. —*n.* **2** impression: "This weak impress of love is as a figure/ Trenched in ice . . ." *Two Gent,* III, ii, 6–7.

impressed, *adj.* enlisted; conscripted: ". . . under whose blessed cross/ We are impressed and engag'd to fight—" *1 Hen 4,* I, i, 20–21.

impression, *n.* **1** figure or embodiment: "With faining voice verses of feigning love,/ And stol'n the impression of her fantasy . . ." *M N Dream,* I, i, 31–32. **2** dent or scar, as if from beating or branding: "Your love and pity doth th'impression fill/ Which vulgar scandal stamped upon my brow . . ." *Sonn 112,* 1–2.

impressure, *n.* imprint or impression, as one made by a seal in soft wax: ". . . the impressure her Lucrece, with which she uses/ to seal . . ." *T Night,* II, v, 95–96.

imprimis, *adv.* [Latin] in the first place; firstly: "Now I begin. *Imprimis,* we came down a/ foul hill, my master riding behind my mistress—" *Shrew,* IV, i, 59–60.

improve, *v.* to turn to one's advantage: ". . . his means,/ If he improve them, may well stretch so far . . ." *J Caes,* II, i, 158–159.

improvident, *adj.* lacking foresight; rash, heedless, or careless: "Improvident soldiers! had your watch been good/ This sudden mischief never could have fallen." *1 Hen 6,* II, i, 58–59.

impugn, *v.* to oppose; fault: ". . . the Venetian law/ Cannot impugn you as you do proceed." *Merch,* IV, i, 174–175.

imputation, *n.* reputation; repute; here, either good or bad: "Our imputation shall be oddly pois'd/ In this vile action . . ." *Tr & Cr,* I, iii, 339–340.

in, *adv.* **1** in the same predicament [in love]: "By the world, I would not care a pin if the other three/ were in." *Love's L,* IV, iii, 17–18. **2** in prison: ". . . Doll is in." *2 Hen 4,* V, v, 38. **3 in that,** (used as conj.) inasmuch as; because: ". . . but in that thou art like to be my kinsman, live unbruised/ and love my cousin." *M Ado,* V, iv, 109–110.
—*prep.* **4** in regard to; also, against: "O heresy in fair [beauty], fit for these days!" *Love's L,* IV, i, 22. **5** on: "Or in the beached margent of the sea . . ." *M N Dream,* II, i, 85. **6** under: ". . . like a child/ on a recorder; a sound, but not in government." *M N Dream,* V, i, 122–123. **7** for: "Observe his inclination in yourself." *Ham,* II, i, 71. **8** in view of; considering: "I con him no thanks for't, in the nature he/ delivers it." *All's W,* IV, iii, 148–149. **9** during: "Nay, we will slink away in sup-per-time . . ." *Merch,* II, iii, 1. **10** into: ". . . almost spent with hunger,/ I am fall'n in this offence." *Cymb,* III, vii, 35–36. **11** owing to: "Troy in our weakness stands, not in her strength." *Tr & Cr,* I, iii, 137. **12** with; in the appearance of: ". . . the cun-ning of her passion/ Invites me in this churlish messenger." *T Night,* II, ii, 21–22.
—*v.* **13** [with "go" understood] to go inside: "But I/ will in, to be revenged for this villainy." *Shrew,* V, i, 124–125. **14** to bring in; harvest: "He that ears [plows] my land spares my team, and gives me/ leave to in the crop . . ." *All's W,* I, iii, 42–43.

in-a-door, *adv.* indoors: "Leave thy drink and thy whore,/ And keep in-a-door . . ." *Lear,* I, iv, 130–131.

inaidible estate, *n.* incurable condition: ". . . labouring art can never ransom nature/ From her inaidible estate." *All's W,* II, i, 117–118.

incapable, *adj.* incapable of feeling or understanding; insen-sible; uncomprehending: "As one incapable of her own dis-tress . . ." *Ham,* IV, vii, 177.

in capite, [Latin] in chief; by direct grant from the Crown [legal term]: "Men shall hold of me/ in capite . . ." *2 Hen 6,* IV, vii, 117–118.

incardinate, *adj.* misuse for "incarnate": "We took/ him for a coward, but he's the very devil incardinate." *T Night,* V, i, 178–180.

incarnadine, *v.* to turn red; here, with blood: ". . . this my hand will rather/ The multitudinous seas incarnadine . . ." *Mac,* II, ii, 60–61.

incarnation, *n.* misuse for adj. "incarnate": ". . . certainly/ the Jew is the very devil incarnation . . ." *Merch,* II, ii, 25–26.

incense, *n.* **1** power to ascend to heaven in the manner of incense: "And breathing to his breathless excellence/ The in-cense of a vow, a holy vow . . ." *K John,* IV, iii, 66–67.
—*v.* **2** to incite or instigate; also, hire: ". . . how Don John your brother incensed/ me to slander the Lady Hero . . ." *M Ado,* V, i, 230–231.

incensed, *adj.* **1** fiery; flaming: "Between the pass and fell incensed points/ Of mighty opposites." *Ham,* V, ii, 61–62. **2** provoked: "Part them; they are incensed." *Ham,* V, ii, 307.

incensement, *n.* anger; rage: ". . . his incensement at this mo-ment is so/ implacable that satisfaction can be none . . ." *T Night,* III, iv, 240–241.

incertain, *adj.* **1** var. of **uncertain:** ". . . the affairs of men rests still [always] incertain . . ." *J Caes,* V, i, 96. **2** doubtful; dubi-ous: "Of those that lawless and incertain thought/ Imagine howling . . ." *Meas,* III, i, 126–127.

incertainties, *n.* uncertainties: "Incertainties now crown themselves assured [doubtful outcomes have now been hap-pily resolved] . . ." *Sonn 107,* 7.

incessantly, *adv.* Also [in some texts], **successantly,** quickly; at once: "Then go incessantly, and plead to him." *T Andr,* IV, iv, 113.

incest, *n.* ref. to religious prohibition against sexual relations between in-laws: "Let not the royal bed of Denmark be/ A couch for luxury and damned incest." *Ham,* I, v, 82–83.

inch¹, *n.* **1** [pl.] size: "I would I had thy inches, thou shouldst know/ There were a heart in Egypt." *Ant & Cleo,* I, iii, 40–41. **2 at an inch,** very closely; without letup: "Beldam, I think we watch'd you at an inch." *2 Hen 6,* I, iv, 41. **3 even to his inches,** thoroughly; intimately; here, his exact height: "Thus says Ae-neas, one that knows the youth/ Even to his inches . . ." *Tr & Cr,* IV, v, 110–111.

inch², *n.* See **Saint Colme's Inch.**

inch-meal, *n.* **by inch-meal,** by inches; inch by inch: "All the infections . . . on Prosper fall, and make him/ By inch-meal a disease!" *Temp,* II, ii, 1–3.

inch-thick, *adv.* assuredly; beyond doubt: "Inch-thick, knee-deep; o'er head and ears a fork'd one." *W Tale,* I, ii, 186.

incidency, *n.* harmful incident likely to occur: "What inci-dency thou dost guess of harm/ Is creeping toward me . . ." *W Tale,* I, ii, 403–404.

incident, *adj.* **1** preying (upon): "Plagues incident to men,/ Your potent and infectious fevers heap . . ." *Timon,* IV, i,

21–22. **2** likely to occur: ". . . other incident throes/ That nature's fragile vessel doth sustain . . ." *Timon,* V, i, 199–200.

incision, *n.* **1** blood-letting: "What! shall we have incision? shall we imbrue? [Snatches up his sword.]" *2 Hen 4,* II, iv, 192. **2 make incision,** *a.* to spur on [the horses]: "Mount them, and make incision in their hides . . ." *Hen 5,* IV, ii, 9. **b.** poss. to season, as to add knowledge or experience: "God make incision in thee, thou art raw [inexperienced]!" *As You,* III, ii, 70.

incite, *v.* to impel; also, to serve or enforce: "No blown ambition doth our arms incite . . ." *Lear,* IV, iv, 27.

inclination, *n.* **1** nature or quality; tendency: "Men judge by the complexion of the sky/ The state and inclination of the day . . ." *Rich 2,* III, ii, 194–195. **2** temperament; disposition: "Report the feature of Octavia; her years,/ Her inclination . . ." *Ant & Cleo,* II, v, 112–113.

incline, *v.* **incline to,** to take the part or side of: ". . . we must incline to/ the King." *Lear,* III, iii, 14–15.

inclining, *n.* liking; partiality: ". . . if you give him not John Drum's entertainment,/ your inclining cannot be removed." *All's W,* III, vi, 36–37.

inclip, *v.* to embrace: "Whate'er the ocean pales, or sky inclips,/ Is thine . . ." *Ant & Cleo,* II, vii, 68–69.

include, *v.* **1** to conclude: ". . . we will include all jars,/ With triumphs, mirth, and rare solemnity." *Two Gent,* V, iv, 158–159. **2** to subsume: "Then everything includes itself in [becomes part of] power,/ power into will . . ." *Tr & Cr,* I, iii, 119–120.

inclusive verge, *n.* See **verge** (def. 3).

income, *n.* **pay the income,** to be the price of accomplishing: "Pain pays the income of each precious thing . . ." *Luc,* 334.

inconsiderate, *adj.* **1** reckless: "Rash, inconsiderate, fiery voluntaries . . ." *K John,* II, i, 67.
—*n.* **2** thoughtless, dull-witted person: "Doth the inconsiderate take salve for l'envoy, and the word / l'envoy for a salve?" *Love's L,* III, i, 74–76.

inconstant, *adj.* **1** fickle; capricious: "O swear not by the moon, th'inconstant moon . . ." *Rom & Jul,* II, ii, 109–110. **2** unstable; unreliable: "That did but show thee, of [for] a fool, inconstant/ And damnable ingrateful . . ." *W Tale,* III, ii, 186–187.

inconstant toy, *n.* whimsical change of mind: ". . . this shall free thee from this present shame,/ If no inconstant toy . . . Abate thy valour in the acting it." *Rom & Jul,* IV, i, 118–119.

incontinency, *n.* **1** habitual lewdness; licentiousness: "You must not put another scandal on him,/ That he is open to incontinency—" *Ham,* II, i, 29–30. **2** unchastity; infidelity: "Iachimo,/ Thou didst accuse him of incontinency . . ." *Cymb,* III, iv, 47–48.

incontinent, *adv.* **1** at once; immediately; here, prob. with sexual innuendo: ". . . they made a pair of stairs to marriage, which they will climb incontinent . . ." *As You,* V, ii, 36–37.

—*adj.* **2** lacking restraint, esp. in sexual appetite: "Matrons, turn incontinent!/ Obedience fail in children!" *Timon,* IV, i, 3–4.

incontinently, *adv.* at once; immediately: "I will incontinently drown myself." *Oth,* I, iii, 305.

inconvenience, *n.* harm; trouble; also, evil: "To intercept this inconvenience,/ A piece of ordnance 'gainst it I have plac'd . . ." *1 Hen 6,* I, iv, 14–15.

incony, *adj.* (in terms of address): fine; rare; lovely: "My sweet ounce of man's flesh! my incony Jew!" *Love's L,* III, i, 131.

incorporal, *adj.* incorporeal; bodiless: ". . . you do bend your eye on vacancy,/ And with th'incorporal air do hold discourse?" *Ham,* III, iv, 117–118.

incorporate, *adj.* **1** being of the same body [with another]: "That undividable, incorporate,/ Am better than thy dear self's better part." *Errors,* II, ii, 122–123. **2** in league: ". . . it is Casca, one incorporate/ To [with] our attempts." *J Caes,* I, iii, 134–135. **3** naturalized; made a citizen: "Titus, I am incorporate in Rome,/ A Roman now adopted happily . . ." *T Andr,* I, i, 462–463.

incorpsed, *adj.* made one or united [with]: "As had he been incorps'd and demi-natur'd/ With the brave beast." *Ham,* IV, vii, 86–87.

incorrect, *adj.* undisciplined; hence, lacking reverence or humility: "It shows a will most incorrect to heaven . . ." *Ham,* I, ii, 95.

increase, *n.* **1** crop(s); produce: "And that thy summer bred us no increase,/ We set the axe to thy usurping root . . ." *3 Hen 6,* II, ii, 164–165. **2** interest; profit; dividend; here, fig. use: ". . . if thou dost plead for him/ Thou wilt but add increase unto my wrath." *2 Hen 6,* III, ii, 291–292. **3** progeny; offspring: "You do it for increase: O strange excuse . . ." *Ven & Ad,* 791. **4 increase and die,** to rise and fall: ". . . like inconstant clouds/

That rack upon the carriage of the winds,/ Increase and die in his disturbed cheeks." *Edw 3,* II, i, 3–5. **5 quicken your increase,** give life to your descendants: "To quicken your increase, I will beget/ Mine issue of your blood upon your daughter." *Rich 3,* IV, iv, 297–298.

increaseful, *adj.* ever-increasing; fertile or fruitful: "To cheer the ploughman with increaseful crops . . ." *Luc,* 958.

incursion, *n.* military skirmish: "When thou art/ forth in the incursions thou strikest as slow as/ another." *Tr & Cr,* II, i, 29–31.

Inde or **Ind,** *n.* India, regarded as an exotic and near-mythical country: ". . . like a rude and savage man of Inde . . . Bows not his vassal head . . ." *Love's L,* IV, iii, 218–220.

indent, *v.* **1** to run a zigzag course: "Turn, and return, indenting with the way." *Ven & Ad,* 704. **2** to make an agreement, as by indenture: "Shall we buy treason, and indent with fears . . ." *1 Hen 4,* I, iii, 86.

indenture, *n.* **1** legal agreement, esp. one between apprentice and master stipulating a period of service, usually seven years: ". . . darest thou be so valiant as to/ play the coward with thy indenture . . ." *1 Hen 4,* II, iv, 46–47. **2** something having the legal or binding force of a contract: ". . . if a king bid a man be a villain,/ he's bound by the indenture of his oath to be one." *Per,* I, iii, 7–8. **3 by indenture,** as an indentured apprentice: "Serve by indenture to the common hangman . . ." *Per,* IV, vi, 175. **4 pair of indentures,** a deed cut in half with a jagged edge so that fitting it together would prove its authenticity: "Will his vouchers vouch him no more of/ his purchases . . . than the length/ and breadth of a pair of indentures?" *Ham,* V, i, 106–108.

index, *n.* **1** beginning, hence preface or introduction: "Ay me, what act/ That roars so loud and thunders in the index?" *Ham,* III, iv, 51–52. **2** that which points the way: "As index to the story we late talk'd of . . ." *Rich 3,* II, ii, 149.

India, *n.* **1** symbol of a fabulously wealthy place: ". . . and tomorrow they/ Made Britain India . . ." *Hen 8,* I, i, 20–21. **2** here, used as an example of a romantic, far-off place: "Her bed is India; there she lies, a pearl." *Tr & Cr,* I, i, 100.

Indian, *n.* **1** American Indian, many of whom were exhibited as curiosities in London in the early 1600's: ". . . have we/ some strange Indian with the great tool come to/ court . . ." *Hen 8,* V, iii, 32–34. **2 base Indian,** poss. ref. to folk tale: "Like the base Indian, threw a pearl away,/ Richer than all his tribe . . ." *Oth,* V, ii, 348–349.

Indian-like, *adj.* prob. ref. to American Indians, assumed to be sun worshipers: "Thus, Indian-like . . . I adore/ The sun that looks upon his worshipper/ But knows of him no more." *All's W,* I, iii, 199–202.

Indies, *n.* prob. India, regarded as a place of incredible wealth: "Our king has all the Indies in his arms . . ." *Hen 8,* IV, i, 45.

indifferency, *n.* **1** average or ordinary kind, size, etc.: "And I had but a belly of any indifferency,/ I were simply the most active fellow in/ Europe . . ." *2 Hen 4,* IV, iii, 20–22. **2** impartiality: "Makes it take head from all indifferency . . ." *K John,* II, i, 579.

indifferent, *adj.* **1** impartial; unbiased: "Look on my wrongs with an indifferent eye." *Rich 2,* II, iii, 115. **2** not different; matching or identical: ". . . their blue coats brushed, and their/ garters of an indifferent knit." *Shrew,* IV, i, 81–82. **3** neither good nor bad: "Therefore the office is indifferent,/ Being entreated to it by your friend." *Two Gent,* III, ii, 44–45. **4** neither the best nor the worst; average: "Good lads, how do you both?"/ "As the indifferent children of the earth." *Ham,* II, ii, 225–227.
—*adv.* **5** moderately; reasonably: "Helenus? No—yes, he'll fight indifferent well—" *Tr & Cr,* I, ii, 226.

indifferently, *adv.* **1** impartially: "Set honour in one eye, and death i' th'other,/ And I will look on both indifferently . . ." *J Caes,* I, ii, 85–86. **2** reasonably well: "I hope we have reformed that indifferently with/ us." *Ham,* III, ii, 36–37.

indigest, *n.* **1** chaos; confusion: ". . . you are born/ To set a form upon that indigest . . ." *K John,* V, vii, 25–26.
—*adj.* **2** formless; chaotic: "To make of monsters and things indigest/ Such cherubins as your sweet self resemble . . ." *Sonn 114,* 5–6.

indigested, *adj.* lacking form or shape: "Hence, heap of wrath, foul indigested lump . . ." *2 Hen 6,* V, i, 157.

indign, *adj.* shameful; unworthy: "And all indign and base adversities/ Make head against my reputation!" *Oth,* I, iii, 273–274.

indirect, *adj.* **1** (of a title) not acquired by direct descent: ". . . to pry/ Into his title, the which we find/ Too indirect for long continuance." *1 Hen 4,* IV, iii, 103–105. **2** devious; deceitful or treacherous: "God knows, my son,/ By what by-paths and indirect crook'd ways/ I met this crown . . ." *2 Hen 4,* IV, v, 183–185.

indirection, *n.* deceit; deviousness: ". . . to wring/ From the hard hands of peasants their vile trash/ By any indirection." *J Caes,* IV, iii, 73–75.

indirectly, *adv.* **1** evasively or inattentively: "I answer'd indirectly, as I said . . ." *1 Hen 4,* I, iii, 65. **2** wrongfully; unjustly: ". . . repent each drop of blood/ That hot rash haste so indirectly shed." *K John,* II, i, 48–49.

indistinct regard, *n.* appearance of two things merging as one: "Even till we make the main and the aerial blue/ An indistinct regard." *Oth,* II, i, 39–40.

indistinguishable, *adj.* of no value or use; worthless: "Why, no, you ruinous butt, you whoreson/ indistinguishable cur, no." *Tr & Cr,* V, i, 27–28.

indistinguished, *adj.* **indistinguished space,** limitless range; that which ranges beyond the powers of sight: "O indistinguish'd space of woman's will [lust]!/ A plot upon her virtuous husband's life . . ." *Lear,* IV, vi, 272–273.

indite, *v.* to write; compose: "What plume of feathers is he that indited this letter?" *Love's L,* IV, i, 95.

indited, *past part.* prob. misuse for "invited": ". . . and he is indited/ to dinner to the Lubber's Head in Lumbert Street . . ." *2 Hen 4,* II, i, 26–27.

indrenched, *adj.* engulfed; swamped or drowned: "Reply not in how many fathoms deep/ They lie indrench'd." *Tr & Cr,* I, i, 50–51.

indubitate, *adj.* true; authentic; unquestioned: ". . . king Cophetua set eye upon/ the pernicious and indubitate beggar Zenelophon . . ." *Love's L,* IV, i, 66–67.

inducement, *n.* **1** enticements; allurements or seductions: "My son corrupts a well-derived nature/ With his inducement." *All's W,* III, ii, 88–89. **2** that which persuades or impels one to act: "Then mark th'inducement: thus it came; give heed to't . . ." *Hen 8,* II, iv, 167.

induction, *n.* **1** beginning; opening: "And our induction full of prosperous hope." *1 Hen 4,* III, i, 2. **2** [pl] preparations: "Plots have I laid, inductions dangerous . . ." *Rich 3,* I, i, 32. **3** prologue: "A dire induction am I witness to . . ." *Rich 3,* IV, iv, 5.

indue, *v.* **1** to furnish; supply: "And more, more strong than lesser is my fear,/ I shall indue you with . . ." *K John,* IV, ii, 42–43. **2** to imbue [with]: "And it indues our other healthful members/ Even to that sense of pain . . ." *Oth,* III, iv, 144–145.

indued, *adj.* **1** endowed: ". . . he is best indued in the small [of the leg]." *Love's L,* V, ii, 634. **2** accustomed; habituated: ". . . like a creature native and indued/ Unto that element." *Ham,* IV, vii, 178–179.

indurance, *n.* imprisonment: ". . . bring together/ Yourself and your accusers, and to have heard you/ Without indurance further." *Hen 8,* V, i, 119–121.

indurate, *adj.* callous; unfeeling: "Thou stern, indurate, flinty, rough, remorseless." *3 Hen 6,* I, iv, 142.

industrious, *adj.* **1** painstaking; thorough: "Here is a dear, a true industrious friend . . ." *1 Hen 4,* I, i, 62. **2 industrious scenes,** ingenious preparations: "As in a theatre, whence they gape and point/ At your industrious scenes and acts of death." *K John,* II, i, 375–376.

industriously, *adv.* deliberately: ". . . if industriously/ I play'd the fool, it was my negligence . . ." *W Tale,* I, ii, 256–257.

industry, *n.* devoted gallantry: "Thine in the dearest design of industry . . ." *Love's L,* IV, i, 87.

inequality, *n.* the fact of our unequal ranks: ". . . do not banish reason [do not assume I am unreasonable]/ For inequality . . ." *Meas,* V, i, 67–68.

inevitable, *adj.* unavoidable; inescapable: ". . . he gives me the stuck in/ with such a mortal motion that it is inevitable . . ." *T Night,* III, iv, 280–281.

inexecrable, *adj.* prob. a coinage with sense of "utterly detestable" [that cannot be execrated enough]; may also be misprint for "inexorable," immovable or inflexible: "O be thou damn'd, inexecrable dog!" *Merch,* IV, i, 128.

inexplicable, *adj.* unintelligible: ". . . capable/ of nothing but inexplicable dumb-shows and noise." *Ham,* III, ii, 11–12.

infallible, *adj.* certain; undoubted: ". . . to accuse/ your mothers, which is most infallible disobedience." *All's W,* I, i, 134–135.

infamonize, *v.* misuse for "infamize," to slander: "Dost thou infamonize me among potentates?/ Thou shalt die." *Love's L,* V, ii, 670–671.

infant, *n.* young plant; also, bud: ". . . an envious sneaping frost/ That bites the first-born infants of the spring." *Love's L,* I, i, 100–101.

infant bands, *n.* See **band** (def. 4).

infant play, *n.* child's game: "All hid, all hid; an old infant play." *Love's L,* IV, iii, 75.

infect, *v.* **1** to poison; contaminate: ". . . one may drink, depart,/ And yet partake no venom (for his knowledge/ Is not infected) . . ." *W Tale,* II, i, 40–42.

—*past part.* **2** infected: "And in the imitation of these twain . . . many are infect." *Tr & Cr,* I, iii, 185–187.

infected, *past part.* **1** affected; also, contaminated: "No more infected with my country's love/ Than when I parted hence [departed from Antium] . . ." *Cor,* V, vi, 72–73.
—*adj.* **2** sham: "This is in thee a nature but infected . . ." *Timon,* IV, iii, 204. **3** infectious: "'O, that infected moisture of his eye!'" *Lover's Comp,* 323.

infection, *n.* **1** plague; also, moral corruption: "This fortress built by Nature for herself/ Against infection and the hand of war . . ." *Rich 2,* II, i, 43–44. **2** misuse for "affection," keen desire: "He hath a great infection sir, (as one would say) to/ serve." *Merch,* II, ii, 119–120. **3** moral corruption: "Ah! wherefore with infection should he live . . ." *Sonn 67,* 1.

infectiously, *adv.* as if by infection; here, by ascribing fine qualities to the object of desire: ". . . the will dotes that is attributive/ To what infectiously itself affects . . ." *Tr & Cr,* II, ii, 59–60.

infer, *v.* **1** to report: ". . . known to commit outrages/ And cherish factions; 'tis inferr'd to us . . ." *Timon,* III, v, 73–74. **2** to bring together and put forward: "Full well hath Clifford play'd the orator,/ Inferring arguments of mighty force." *3 Hen 6,* II, ii, 44–45. **3** to allege or assert: "Infer the bastardy of Edward's children . . ." *Rich 3,* III, v, 74.

infest, *v.* to harass; annoy: "Do not infest your mind with beating on/ The strangeness of this business . . ." *Temp,* V, i, 246–247.

infinite, *adj.* **1** the worst possible: "Of man and beast the infinite malady/ Crust you quite o'er!" *Timon,* III, vi, 94–95.
—*n.* **2** greatest or furthest extent: ". . . it is past the infinite of thought." *M Ado,* II, iii, 102. **3** infinity: "Will you with counters sum/ The past-proportion of his infinite . . ." *Tr & Cr,* II, ii, 28–29.

infinitive, *adj.* prob. misuse for "infinite": "I warrant you, he's an/ infinitive thing upon my score." *2 Hen 4,* II, i, 22–23.

infirmities, *n.* **assuming man's infirmities,** taking on human form [once more]: "From ashes ancient Gower is come,/ Assuming man's infirmities . . ." *Per,* I, Chor., 2–3.

infix, *v.* to imprint: ". . . the impression of [in] mine eye infixing,/ Contempt his scornful perspective did lend me . . ." *All's W,* V, iii, 47–48.

inflamed, *adj.* engulfed in the flames of war and rebellion: ". . . use all your power/ To stop their marches 'fore we are inflam'd." *K John,* V, i, 6–7.

inflammation, *n.* the warming effects of liquor; excitation: "They are generally/ fools and cowards . . . but for inflammation." *2 Hen 4,* IV, iii, 92–94.

inflict, *v.* afflict: "For every graff would send a caterpillar,/ And so inflict our province." *Per,* V, i, 59–60.

influence, *n.* poss. inspiration: ". . . a gibing spirit,/ Whose influence is begot of that loose grace . . ." *Love's L,* V, ii, 850–851.

inform, *v.* **1** to assume a shape: "It is the bloody business which informs/ Thus to mine eyes." *Mac,* II, i, 48–49. **2** to report; divulge or confess: "Haply thou may'st inform/ Something to save thy life." *All's W,* IV, i, 82–83. **3** to grant or imbue: ". . . with what patience/ Your wisdom may inform you." *Cymb,* I, ii, 9–10. **4 inform against,** to accuse: "How all occasions do inform against me . . ." *Ham,* IV, iv, 32.

informal, *adj.* mentally disturbed: "These poor informal women are no more/ But instruments . . ." *Meas,* V, i, 235–236.

infortunate, *adj.* unfortunate: ". . . this is thy eldest son's son,/ Infortunate in nothing but in thee . . ." *K John,* II, i, 177–178.

infringe, *v.* to violate: "Nor wittingly have I infring'd my vow." *3 Hen 6,* II, ii, 8.

infuse, *v.* to pour or shed: "With those clear rays which she infus'd on me . . ." *1 Hen 6,* I, ii, 85.

infusion, *n.* essence: "I take him to be a soul of great article/ and his infusion of such dearth and rareness . . ." *Ham,* V, ii, 116–117.

ingage, *v.* to accept as a challenge; here, to combat: ". . . there is my honour's pawn;/ Ingage it to the trial if thou darest." *Rich 2,* IV, i, 70–71.

ingaged, *adj.* not engaged; unattached: "Noble she was, and thought/ I stood ingag'd . . ." *All's W,* V, iii, 95–96.

ingenious, *adj.* **1** intellectual; liberal: "A course of learning and ingenious studies." *Shrew,* I, i, 9. **2** conscious: ". . . I stand up, and have ingenious feeling/ Of my huge sorrows!" *Lear,* IV, vi, 282–283. **3 ingenious sense,** keen intelligence: ". . . that cursed head/ Whose wicked deed thy most ingenious sense/ Depriv'd thee of." *Ham,* V, i, 240–242.

ingeniously, *adv.* frankly; sincerely: ". . . ingeniously I speak,/ No blame belongs to thee." *Timon,* II, ii, 225–226.

ingraft, *adj.* var. of **ingrafted;** innate; ingrained: ". . . one of an ingraft infirmity . . ." *Oth,* II, iii, 133.

ingrafted, *adj.* deeply felt; ingrained: "Yet I fear him;/ For in the ingrafted love he bears to Caesar—" *J Caes,* II, i, 183–184.

ingrate or **ingrateful,** *adj.* ungrateful: "Will not so graceless be to be ingrate." *Shrew,* I, ii, 268.

ingredience, *n.* old pl. of **ingredient**: ". . . th' ingredience of our poison'd chalice . . ." *Mac,* I, vii, 11.

ingross, *v.* to amass; here, to grab or gather up: "Your mariners are muleters, reapers, people/ Ingross'd by swift impress." *Ant & Cleo,* IIi, vii, 35–36.

inhabit, *v.* **1** to be filled with: "If trembling I inhabit then, protest me/ The baby of a girl." *Mac,* III, iv, 104–105. **2** to dwell: ". . . so eating Love/ Inhabits in the finest wits of all." *Two Gent,* I, i, 44.

inhabitable, *adj.* uninhabitable: "Even to the frozen ridges of the Alps,/ Or any other ground inhabitable . . ." *Rich 2,* I, i, 64–65.

In hac spe vivo, [Latin] In this hope I live. *Per,* II, ii, 43.

inhearse, *v.* to bury; here, remain unexpressed: "Was it the proud full sail of his great verse . . . That did my ripe thoughts in my brain inhearse . . ." *Sonn 86,* 1–3.

inhearsed, *adj.* enclosed in or [here] as if in a coffin: "See where he lies inhearsed in the arms/ Of the most bloody nurser of his harms." *1 Hen 6,* IV, vii, 45–46.

in heart, used as a toast, meaning "with all my heart": "My lord, in heart; and let the health go round." *Timon,* I, ii, 53.

inherent, *adj.* ingrained; inborn or inbred: ". . . by my body's action teach my mind/ A most inherent baseness." *Cor,* III, ii, 122–123.

inherit, *v.* **1** to possess; have or enjoy the possession of: "Gaunt am I for the grave . . . Whose hollow womb inherits nought but bones." *Rich 2,* II, i, 82–83. **2** to receive or experience: "Among fresh female buds shall you this night/ Inherit at my house." *Rom & Jul,* I, ii, 29–30. **3** to cause (one) to be the inheritor of; arouse in (one): "It must be great that can inherit us/ So much as of a thought of ill in him." *Rich 2,* I, i, 85–86. **4** to occupy: ". . . the great globe itself,/ Yea, all which it inherit [everything that occupies the earth], shall dissolve . . ." *Temp,* IV, i, 153–154. **5** to win or win over: "This, or else nothing, will inherit her." *Two Gent,* III, ii, 86. **6** wordplay on twins [letters] inheriting the knighthood; Page says that Ford's is doubtless older [received first]: ". . . but let thine inherit first, for I protest mine/ never shall." *Wives,* II, i, 70–71.

inheritance, *n.* act of acquiring or obtaining: ". . . the inheritance of their loves and safeguard/ Of what that want might ruin." *Cor,* III, ii, 68–69.

inheritor, *n.* **1** owner: ". . . the sole inheritor/ Of all perfections that a man may owe,/ Matchless Navarre . . ." *Love's L,* II, i, 5–7. **2** heir: "You . . . out of whorish loins/ Are pleas'd to breed out your inheritors." *Tr & Cr,* IV, i, 64–65.

inhibited, *adj.* prohibited: ". . . self-love which is the most/ inhibited sin in the canon." *All's W,* I, i, 142–143.

inhibition, *n.* legal restriction on the number of performances a city company could give: "I think their inhibition comes by the means of the/ late innovation." *Ham,* II, ii, 330–331.

inhooped, *adj.* confined within a hoop; here, forced to fight: ". . . and his quails ever/ Beat mine, inhoop'd, at odds." *Ant & Cleo,* II, iii, 36–37.

iniquity, *n.* (often cap.) figure in the old morality plays: ". . . that reverend vice, that grey iniquity, that father ruffian, that vanity in/ years . . ." *1 Hen 4,* II, iv, 457–459.

initiate, *adj.* characteristic of a novice: "My strange and self-abuse/ Is the initiate fear, that wants hard use . . ." *Mac,* III, iv, 141–142.

injoint, *v.* to join; unite: "The Ottomites . . . Steering with due course, toward the isle of Rhodes,/ Have there injointed with an after [reserve] fleet—" *Oth,* I, iii, 33–35.

injunction, *n.* **1 by great injunctions,** for urgent reasons: ". . . by great injunctions I am bound/ To enter publicly." *Meas,* IV, iii, 95–96. **2 upon a sore injunction,** with the warning that failure to do so will bring grievous consequences: "I must remove/ Some thousands of these logs, and pile them up,/ Upon a sore injunction . . ." *Temp,* III, i, 9–11.

injurious, *adj.* **1** malicious; slanderous; insulting: "Like a false traitor, and injurious villain . . ." *Rich 2,* I, i, 91. **2** awkward; burdensome: "Injurious distance should not stop my way . . ." *Sonn 44,* 2.

injury, *n.* **1** any wrong, insult, loss, etc.: ". . . if thy/ pocket were enriched with any other injuries but/ these . . ." *1 Hen 4,* III, iii, 159–161. **2** slander; vilification: "In some . . . religious life,/ Out of all eyes, tongues, minds, and injuries." *M Ado,* IV, i, 242–243. **3** [pl] reference to Theseus' war against the Amazons, resulting in his capture of their queen: "Hippolyta, I woo'd thee with my sword,/ And won thy love doing thee injuries . . ." *M N Dream,* I, i, 16–17. **4 buy my injuries,** interpret my wrongs as favors: "I never do him wrong/ But he does buy my injuries, to be friends . . ." *Cymb,* I, ii, 35–36.

—v. 5 to injure: "I do protest I never injuried thee . . ." *Rom & Jul*, III, i, 67.

ink-horn, *n.* portable container for ink, often a section of horn: ". . . hang him with his pen and/ ink-horn about his neck." *2 Hen 6*, IV, ii, 103–104.

inkhorn mate, *n.* scholarly drudge: "So kind a father of the commonweal,/ To be disgraced by an inkhorn mate . . ." *1 Hen 6*, III, i, 98–99.

inkle, *n.* linen tape: "'What's the price of/ this inkle?' 'One penny': 'No, I'll give you a/ remuneration' . . ." *Love's L*, III, i, 134–136.

inland, *adj.* **inland bred**, of gentle birth; raised in refined circumstances [i.e., in or near cities, the centers of civilization]: "Yet am I inland bred,/ And know some nurture." *As You*, II, vii, 97–98.

in lieu of, despite; in return for: "That cannot so much as a blossom yield,/ In lieu of all thy pains . . ." *As You*, II, iii, 64–65.

inly, *adv.* **1** inwardly: "I have inly wept,/ Or should have spoke ere this." *Temp*, V, i, 200–201.
—*adj.* **2** inward: "To see how inly sorrow gripes his soul." *3 Hen 6*, I, iv, 171.

innocent, *n.* **1** idiot; simpleton: ". . . a dumb innocent that could not say/ him nay." *All's W*, IV, iii, 182–183. **2** same used as term of address to Fool: "Pray, innocent,/ and beware the foul fiend." *Lear*, III, vi, 7–8.

innovation, *n.* **1** uprising; insurrection; poss. an allusion to the Essex rebellion of 1601: "I think their inhibition comes by the means of the/ late innovation." *Ham*, II, ii, 330–331. **2** commotion: "I ha' drunk but one cup to-night . . . and behold what innovation it/ makes here [in my head] . . ." *Oth*, II, iii, 35–37.

innovator, *n.* revolutionary; rebel: "Go call the people; in whose name myself/ Attach thee as a traitorous innovator . . ." *Cor*, III, i, 172–173.

Inns of Court, *n. pl.* London law colleges, where select students finished their legal studies: "A must then to the Inns o'Court shortly . . ." *2 Hen 4*, III, ii, 12.

inoculate, *v.* to graft onto; engraft: ". . . for virtue cannot/ so inoculate our old stock [basically sinful nature] but we shall relish of it." *Ham*, III, i, 117–118.

in one's books, in the favor or good graces of another: "I see, lady, the gentleman is not in your books." *M Ado*, I, i, 71.

inordinate, *adj.* intemperate or excessive: ". . . such inordinate and low desires . . ." *1 Hen 4*, III, ii, 12.

inquire out, *v.* to seek out: "I press me none but/ good householders . . . inquire me out/ contracted bachelors . . ." *1 Hen 4*, IV, ii, 14–16.

inquisitive, *adj.* eager for information: "Who, falling there . . . (Unseen, inquisitive) confounds himself." *Errors*, I, ii, 37–38.

insane root, hallucinogenic or toxic substance, poss. henbane, hemlock, or belladonna (deadly nightshade): "Were such things here . . . Or have we eaten on the insane root,/ That takes the reason prisoner?" *Mac*, I, iii, 83–85.

insanie, *n.* insanity: "This is abhominable,/ which he would call abominable, it insinuateth me of/ insanie . . ." *Love's L*, V, i, 24–25.

insatiate, *adj.* insatiable, esp. greedy: "Light vanity, insatiate cormorant,/ Consuming means, soon preys upon itself." *Rich 2*, II, i, 38–39.

inscrolled, *adj.* written down here: "Had you been as wise as bold . . . Your answer had not been inscroll'd [you would have received a different answer]." *Merch*, II, vii, 71–72.

insculped, *past part.* engraved: ". . . the figure of an angel/ Stamp'd in gold, but that's insculp'd upon . . ." *Merch*, II, vii, 56–57.

insculpture, *n.* inscription: "And on his grave-stone this insculpture which/ With wax I brought away . . ." *Timon*, V, iv, 67.

insensible, *adj.* **1** not perceived by the senses: "'Tis insensible,/ then? Yea, to the dead." *1 Hen 4*, V, i, 137–138. **2** indifferent; here, understood as "stupid": "Save when command to your dismission tends,/ And therein you are senseless."/ "Senseless? Not so." *Cymb*, II, iii, 51–52.

inseparate, *adj.* that cannot be divided; inseparable: ". . . that a thing inseparate/ Divides more wider than the sky and earth . . ." *Tr & Cr*, V, ii, 147–148.

insert, *v.* to inject or introduce; here, into the conversation: "Was this inserted to make interest good?" *Merch*, I, iii, 89.

inset, *v.* to set into, as a jewel set into gold or silver: "I will inset you, neither in gold/ nor silver, but in vile apparel . . ." *2 Hen 4*, I, ii, 16–17.

inshell, *v.* to tuck inside a shell: "Thrusts forth his horns again into the world,/ Which were inshell'd when Martius stood for Rome . . ." *Cor*, IV, vi, 44–45.

inshipped, *adj.* embarked: "... see them guarded/ And safely brought to Dover; where, inshipp'd,/ Commit them to the fortune of the sea." *1 Hen 6,* V, i, 48–50.

insinewed, *adj.* See **ensinewed.**

insinuate, *v.* **1** to ingratiate (oneself): "What a case am I in then, that ... cannot insinuate with you in the behalf of a good play?" *As You,* V, iv, 204–206. **2** to flatter or toady: "... to see so great a lord/ Basely insinuate and send us gifts." *T Andr,* IV, ii, 37–38. **3** to suggest; make or cause: "This is abhominable,/ which he would call abominable, it insinuateth me of/ insanie ..." [either "suggests insanity to me" or "makes me frantic"] *Love's L,* V, i, 24–25. **4** to coax; wheedle: "Think'st thou, for that/ I insinuate, or toaze from thee thy business ..." *W Tale,* IV, iv, 734–735.

insisture, *n.* persistence on its (or their) course: "The heavens themselves, the planets, and this centre/ Observe degree, priority, and place,/ Insisture, course ..." *Tr & Cr,* I, iii, 85–87.

insociable, *adj.* not companionable; unfriendly; also, intolerable: "I abhor such fanatical/ phantasimes, such insociable and point-devise/ companions ..." *Love's L,* V, i, 17–19.

insolence, *n.* overbearing pride: "Why, Suffolk, England knows thine insolence." *2 Hen 6,* II, i, 31.

insomuch, *conj.* **insomuch it shall be known,** so that it may be made known: "Yet, insomuch it shall be known that we/ As well can master our affections [passions]/ As conquer other[s] by the dint of sword ..." *Edw 3,* V, i, 50–52.

inspiration, *n.* intuition or supernatural means: "How can she thus then call us by our names?—/ Unless it be by inspiration." *Errors,* II, ii, 166–167.

instalment, *n.* individual stall: "Each fair instalment, coat, and sev'ral crest,/ With loyal blazon, evermore be blest ..." *Wives,* V, v, 64–65.

instance, *n.* **1** illustration or example: "Full of wise saws, and modern [commonplace] instances ..." *As You,* II, vii, 156. **2** prior instance; precedent: "Yet doth this accident ... So far exceed all instance, all discourse ..." *T Night,* IV, iii, 12–13. **3** proof; piece of evidence: "I have receiv'd/ A certain instance that Glendower is dead." *2 Hen 4,* III, i, 102–103. **4** sign or indication: "Before the always-wind-obeying deep/ Gave any tragic instance of our harm ..." *Errors,* I, i, 63–64. **5** urging; insistence: "... the examples/ Of every minute's instance ... Hath put us in these ill-beseeming arms ..." *2 Hen 4,* IV, i, 82–84. **6** reason or motive: "The instances that second mar-

riage move ..." *Ham,* III, ii, 177. **7** token: "It sends some precious instance of itself/ After the thing it loves." *Ham,* IV, v, 162–163.

instant, *adv.* **1** instantly; immediately: "... give 't these fellows/ To whom 'tis instant due." *Timon,* II, ii, 233–234. —*n.* **2 at an instant,** at once; simultaneously: "And did he send you both these letters at an/ instant?" *Wives,* IV, iv, 3–4. **3 in the instant,** at this very moment: "... I feel now/ The future in the instant." *Mac,* I, v, 57–58. —*adj.* **4** assembled quickly: "... your good tongue/ More than the instant army we can make ..." *Cor,* V, i, 36–37. **5 craves the instant use,** must be taken care of at once: "Your needful counsel to our businesses,/ Which craves the instant use." *Lear,* II, i, 127–128.

instantly, *adv.* simultaneously: "As if he master'd there a double spirit/ Of teaching and of learning instantly." *1 Hen 4,* V, ii, 63–64.

instate, *v.* **instate and widow,** to endow [you] as Claudio's widow with his estate: "We do instate and widow you withal ..." *Meas,* V, i, 422.

insteeped, *past part.* soaked or drenched: "... and York, all haggled over,/ Comes to him, where in gore he lay insteep'd ..." *Hen 5,* IV, vi, 11–12.

instigation, *n.* urge or motive to act: "... what need we/ Commune with you of this, but rather follow/ Our forceful instigation?" *W Tale,* II, i, 161–163.

institutions, *n.pl.* social and political customs, usages, and practices: "The nature of our people,/ Our city's institutions, and the terms/ For common justice ..." *Meas,* I, i, 9–11.

instruction, *n.* **1** [often pl.] sound advice: "... let instructions enter/ Where folly now possesses?" *Cymb,* I, vi, 47–48. **2** [usually pl] precepts or principles: "I cannot say 'tis pity/ She lacks instructions ..." *W Tale,* IV, iv, 582–583. **3** reason; cause: "Nature would/ not invest herself in such shadowing passion without/ some instruction." *Oth,* IV, i, 39–41. **4 brave instruction,** noble example: "Have by their brave instruction got upon me/ A nobleness in record." *Ant & Cleo,* IV, xiv, 98–99. **5 instruction of his frailty,** [the] prompting[s] of human weakness: "Yet had he framed/ to himself, by the instruction of his frailty ..." *Meas,* III, ii, 238–239.

instrument, *n.* **1** musical instrument; here, prob. a lute or harp: "Canst thou hold up thy heavy eyes awhile,/ And touch thy instrument a strain or two?" *J Caes,* IV, iii, 255–256. **2** [pl] prob. ref. to the fingers: "... and see withal/ The instruments that feel." *W Tale,* II, i, 153–154. **3 put on their instruments,**

to take up arms: "Macbeth/ Is ripe for shaking, and the Powers above/ Put on their instruments." *Mac,* IV, iii, 237–239.

instrumental, *adj.* serviceable: "The hand more instrumental to the mouth . . ." *Ham,* I, ii, 48.

insubstantial, *adj.* having no body or substance: "And, like this insubstantial pageant faded,/ Leave not a rack behind." *Temp,* IV, i, 155–156.

insufficiency, *n.* defects; imperfections: "O, from what power hast thou this powerful might/ With insufficiency my heart to sway?" *Sonn* 150, 1–2.

insult, *v.* to triumph [over]: ". . . I will insult on him;/ Flattering myself as if it were the Moor . . ." *T Andr,* III, ii, 71–72.

insulting, *adj.* **1** triumphant, esp. in a gloating or boastful manner: ". . . I might have let alone/ The insulting hand of Douglas over you . . ." *1 Hen 4,* V, iv, 52–53. **2** indifferent to danger: "Now am I like that proud insulting ship/ Which Caesar and his fortune bare at once." *1 Hen 6,* I, ii, 138–139. —*pres. part.* **3** exulting; gloating: "And so he walks, insulting o'er his prey . . ." *3 Hen 6,* I, iii, 14.

insultment, *n.* scornful triumph: ". . . my speech of insultment ended on his dead body . . ." *Cymb,* III, v, 142.

insuppressive, *adj.* insuppressible; unquenchable: ". . . do not stain/ The even virtue of our enterprise,/ Nor th'insuppressive mettle of our spirits . . ." *J Caes,* II, i, 132–134.

inteemable, *adj.* unretentive; also, irretrievable: "Yet in this captious and inteemable sieve/ I still pour in the waters of my love . . ." *All's W,* I, iii, 197–198.

Integer vitae, sclerisque . . . , [Latin] He who is virtuous in life has no need of the Moor's javelins or bows [from an Ode of Horace]. *T Andr,* IV, ii, 20–21.

intellect, *n.* contents or meaning; also, level of intelligence: "I will look again on the intellect of the letter, for the/ nomination of the party . . ." *Love's L,* IV, ii, 128–129.

intelligence, *n.* **1** talk; communication: "If with myself I hold intelligence . . ." *As You,* I, iii, 43. **2** news; information: "I can give you intelligence of an intended marriage." *M Ado,* I, iii, 42. **3** spies or informers; also, secret information: "Disgrac'd me in my happy victories,/ Sought to entrap me by intelligence . . ." *1 Hen 4,* IV, iii, 97–98.

intelligencer, *n.* **1** agent or messenger: "The very opener and intelligencer/ Between the grace . . . of heaven,/ And our dull workings?" *2 Hen 4,* IV, ii, 20–22. **2** spy; subversive agent:

"Richard yet lives, hell's black intelligencer . . ." *Rich 3,* IV, iv, 71.

intelligencing, *adj.* acting as a go-between; here, for Hermione and Polixenes: "A most intelligencing bawd!" *W Tale,* II, iii, 67–68.

intelligent, *adj.* **1** informative: "Our posts shall/ be swift and intelligent betwixt us." *Lear,* III, vii, 11–12. **2** intelligible: "Do you know, and dare not?/ Be intelligent to me . . ." *W Tale,* I, ii, 377–378. **3 intelligent of,** furnishing information (about): ". . . Which are to France the spies and speculations/ Intelligent of our state." *Lear,* III, i, 24–25.

intelligent party, *n.* willing conspirator: ". . . approves him an intelligent party to the advantages/ of France." *Lear,* III, v, 11–12.

intemperance, *n.* unrestrained or dissolute behavior: "I do beseech your Majesty may salve/ The long-grown wounds of my intemperance . . ." *1 Hen 4,* III, ii, 155–156.

intemperate, *adj.* uncontrollable; raging: ". . . by gift of my chaste body/ To his concupiscible intemperate lust . . ." *Meas,* V, i, 100–101.

intend, *v.* **1** to pretend: ". . . intending other serious matters . . . They froze me into silence." *Timon,* II, ii, 214–217. **2** to tend or lead: ". . . man is not able to/ invent anything that intends to laughter more than I/ invent . . ." *2 Hen 4,* I, ii, 6–8. **3** to direct: ". . . to Tharsus/ Intend my travel, where I'll hear from thee . . ." *Per,* I, ii, 115–116. **4** to try to restore: "And happy newness, that intends old right!" *K John,* V, iv, 61. **5** appar. misuse for "attend": "Do intend vat [what] I speak? A green-a box." *Wives,* I, iv, 42.

intendment, *n.* **1** intent or intention: ". . . you must stay him from his intendment . . ." *As You,* I, i, 132. **2** [pl.] words intended to be spoken: "And now her sobs do her intendments break." *Ven & Ad,* 222.

intent, *n.* **1** cause; reason: ". . . the arms are fair/ When the intent of bearing them is just." *1 Hen 4,* V, ii, 87–88. **2 made intent,** plan or procedure: "Yet to be known shortens my made intent . . ." *Lear,* IV, vii, 9. **3 of our intent,** for matters to go according to our wishes: "Which, since you come too late of our intent . . ." *Rich 3,* III, v, 68.

intention, *n.* bent or aim; also, intensity: "Affection! thy intention stabs the centre . . ." *W Tale,* I, ii, 138.

intentively, *adv.* attentively; also, consecutively or continuously: "Whereof by parcel she had something heard,/ But not intentively . . ." *Oth,* I, iii, 154–155.

intercept, *v.* to interrupt: "And, being intercepted in your sport,/ Great reason that my noble lord be rated . . ." *T Andr,* II, iii, 80–81.

intercepter, *n.* person who intercepts or ambushes another: ". . . but thy intercepter . . . attends thee at the orchard-end." *T Night,* III, iv, 224–226.

intercession, *n.* a halt; here, to making war: "Here, English lords, we do proclaim a rest,/ An intercession of our painful arms . . ." *Edw 3,* V, i, 236–237.

interchangeably, *adv.* **1** first by one, then by the other(s): ". . . our indentures tripartite . . . being sealed interchangeably . . ." *1 Hen 4,* III, i, 76–77. **2** in turn; in response: ". . . in myself I boldly will defend,/ And interchangeably hurl down my gage . . ." *Rich 2,* I, i, 145–146. **3** mutually or reciprocally; ref. here to indentures, an agreement binding two persons; here, sealed with a kiss: "What, billing again? Here's/ 'In witness whereof the parties interchangeably—'" *Tr & Cr,* III, ii, 57–58.

interchangement, *n.* mutual exchange: "Attested by the holy close of lips,/ Strengthen'd by interchangement of your rings . . ." *T Night,* V, i, 156–157.

interchange of state, *n.* susceptibility to change in condition: "When I have seen such interchange of state,/ Or state itself confounded, to decay . . ." *Sonn 64,* 9–10.

interdiction, *n.* action of restraining or prohibiting: ". . . the truest issue of thy throne/ By his own interdiction stands accus'd,/ And does blaspheme his breed?" *Mac,* IV, iii, 106–108.

interessed, *adj.* concerned; having a share or part: ". . . to whose young love/ The vines of France and milk of Burgundy/ Strive to be interess'd . . ." *Lear,* I, i, 83–85.

interest, *n.* **1** right or claim: "Replies her husband, 'do not take away/ My sorrow's interest . . .'" *Luc,* 1796–1797. **2** possession: ". . . we will divest us both of rule,/ Interest of territory, cares of state . . ." *Lear,* I, i, 49–50.

inter'gatory, *n.* [spelled as pron.] **1** (in a court of law) a question put to a witness under oath: "Let us go in,/ And charge us there upon inter'gatories,/ And we will answer all things faithfully." *Merch,* V, i, 297–299. **2** See **interrogatory.**

interim, *n.* **1** pause or interlude: "For interim to our studies shall relate/ . . . the worth of many a knight . . ." *Love's L,* I, i, 170–171. **2 by interims,** at intervals: "By interims and conveying gusts we have heard/ The charges of our friends." *Cor,* I, vi, 5–6.

interjoin, *v.* **interjoin their issues,** allow their children to intermarry: ". . . shall grow dear friends/ And interjoin their issues." *Cor,* IV, iv, 21–22.

interlude, *n.* brief play, usually one performed during an interval between festivities: "Here is the scroll of every man's name which is/ thought fit . . . to play in our interlude . . ." *M N Dream,* I, ii, 4–5.

intermission, *n.* **1** delay or postponement: "Cut short all intermission; front to front,/ Bring thou this fiend of Scotland, and myself . . ." *Mac,* IV, iii, 232–233. **2** act of putting aside or ignoring something; here, Kent's business is shoved aside: "Deliver'd letters, spite of intermission,/ Which presently [at once] they read . . ." *Lear,* II, iv, 33–34.

intermissive, *adj.* occurring at intervals; here, given a respite by the death of Henry V: "Wounds will I lend the French . . . To weep their intermissive miseries." *1 Hen 6,* I, i, 87–88.

intermit, *v.* to delay or postpone: "Pray to the gods to intermit the plague . . ." *J Caes,* I, i, 54.

intermixed, *past part.* adulterated: "But best is best [each is best alone], if never intermixed . . ." *Sonn 101,* 8.

interpret, *v.* (in a puppet show) to speak dialogue from behind the scene; narrate: "I could interpret between you and your love if I/ could see the puppets dallying." *Ham,* III, ii, 241–242.

interpretation, *n.* **1** action of revealing and fulfilling: "Which by th'interpretation of full time/ May show like all yourself." *Cor,* V, iii, 69–70. **2 abuse interpretation,** misinterpret; get the wrong idea: "If your lass/ Interpretation should abuse, and call this/ Your lack of love . . ." *W Tale,* IV, iv, 353–355.

interpreter, *n.* commentator: ". . . these thy offices . . . are as interpreters/ Of my behind-hand slackness!" *W Tale,* V, i, 148–150.

interrogatory, *n.* **name to interrogatories,** the right to demand answers [to questions put to an accused]: "What earthy [earthly] name to interrogatories/ Can taste the free breath of a sacred king?" *K John,* III, i, 73–74.

interrupted waters, *n.* floodwaters overflowing their banks: "Whose rage doth rend/ Like interrupted waters . . ." *Cor,* III, i, 246–247.

interruption, *n.* attempt to stop an action: "And bloody England into England gone,/ O'erbearing interruption, spite of France?" *K John,* III, iii, 8–9.

intertissued, *adj.* interwoven: "The intertissued robe of gold and pearl . . ." *Hen 5,* IV, i, 268.

intervallum, *n.* intermission or interval between any two law terms during the year: ". . . four terms, or two/ actions, and a shall laugh without intervallums." *2 Hen 4,* V, i, 77–78.

interview, *n.* meeting of the French and English kings mentioned previously: ". . . th'interview/ That swallowed so much treasure . . ." *Hen 8,* I, i, 165–166.

intestate, *adj.* (fig. use) dead and not passed on to others: "Airy succeeders of intestate joys . . ." *Rich 3,* IV, iv, 128.

intestine, *adj.* (esp. of a country) internal; domestic: ". . . the intestine shock/ And furious close of civil butchery . . ." *1 Hen 4,* I, i, 12–13.

in that, *conj.* because; inasmuch as: ". . . but in that thou art like to be my kinsman, live unbruised/, and love my cousin." *M Ado,* V, iv, 109–110.

intil, *prep.* into: "But age with his stealing steps/ Hath claw'd me in his clutch,/ And hath shipp'd me intil the land [ground]." *Ham,* V, i, 70–72.

intimate, *v.* 1 to make mention of: ". . . your father here doth intimate/ The payment of a hundred thousand crowns . . ." *Love's L,* II, i, 128–129. 2 to suggest; cause to think of: ". . . and the spirit of humours intimate/ reading aloud to him!" *T Night,* II, v, 85–86.

intitled, *adj.* having a legal claim (on): ". . . let our hands part;/ Neither intitled in the other's heart." *Love's L,* V, ii, 803–804.

intituled, *adj.* old spelling of **entitled:** ". . . a companion of the king's, who is intituled,/ nominated, or called, Don Adriano de Armado." *Love's L,* V, i, 7–8.

into, *prep.* unto: ". . . like one/ Who having into truth, by telling of it [often incorrectly],/ Made such a sinner of his memory . . ." *Temp,* I, ii, 100–101.

intolerable, *adj.* excessive; immense: "Old, cold, withered, and of intolerable entrails [enormous belly]?" *Wives,* V, v, 154.

intoxicates, *adj.* Fluellen's confusion with "intoxicated': ". . . being a little intoxicates in his prains [brains] . . ." *Hen 5,* IV, vii, 39.

intreasured, *adj.* gathered and stored, as in a treasury: ". . . in their seeds/ And weak beginnings lie intreasured." *2 Hen 4,* III, i, 84–85.

intreat, *v.* to treat: ". . . you say the queen is at your house;/ For God's sake fairly let her be intreated . . ." *Rich 2,* III, i, 36–37.

intrenchant, *adj.* that cannot be cut: "As easy may'st thou the intrenchant air/ With thy keen sword impress . . ." *Mac,* V, viii, 9–10.

intrince, *adj.* intricately knotted; bound together: "Like rats, oft bite the holy cords a-twain/ Which are too intrince t' unloose . . ." *Lear,* II, ii, 75–76.

intrinsicate, *adj.* appar. an elaboration of "intricate" or "intrince"; perh. also, "intrinsical": "With thy sharp teeth this knot intrinsicate/ Of life at once untie . . ." *Ant & Cleo,* V, ii, 303–304.

inurned, *adj.* buried; entombed: ". . . why the sepulchre/ Wherein we saw thee quietly inurn'd/ Hath op'd his ponderous and marble jaws . . ." *Ham,* I, iv, 48–50.

invectively, *adv.* with verbal abuse, often for mock serious effect: "Thus most invectively he pierceth through/ The body of country, city, court . . ." *As You,* II, i, 58–59.

invention, *n.* 1 ability to plan; inventiveness: "Time hath not yet so dried this blood of mine/ Nor age so eat up my invention . . ." *M Ado,* IV, i, 193–194. 2 ability to fabricate excuses or plausible answers: "You love my son. Invention is asham'd/ Against the proclamation of thy passion/ To say thou dost not." *All's W,* I, iii, 168–170. 3 scheme or plan: "Both our inventions meet and jump in one." *Shrew,* I, i, 190. 4 novelty: "Those palates who . . . Must have inventions to delight the taste . . ." *Per,* I, iv, 39–40. 5 elaborate preparation: "If thou canst accuse/ Or aught intend'st to lay unto my charge,/ Do it without invention, suddenly [extemporaneously] . . ." *1 Hen 6,* III, i, 3–5. 6 fancy; imagination: "Whilst my invention, hearing not my tongue,/ Anchors on Isabel . . ." *Meas,* II, iv, 3–4. 7 creative imagination; also, a work of the imagination: "O, for a Muse of fire, that would ascend/ The brightest heaven of invention . . ." *Hen 5,* Prol., 1–2. **8 accuse me by invention,** invent accusations against me: "Let them accuse me by invention: I/ Will answer in mine honour." *Cor,* III, ii, 143–144.

inventorially, *adv.* item by item in the manner of a catalog: ". . . to divide him inventorially would/ dozy [dizzy] th'arithmetic of memory . . ." *Ham,* V, ii, 113–114.

inventory, *n.* catalog: ". . . an inventory to particularise [itemize] their abundance . . ." *Cor,* I, i, 20.

invert, *v.* to turn or change: ". . . invert/ What best is boded me to mischief!" *Temp,* III, i, 70–71.

invest, *v.* **1** to equip: "... to invest/ Their sons with arts and martial exercises..." *2 Hen 4,* IV, v, 72–73. **2** to urge on; press: "The time invests you; go, your servants tend." *Ham,* I, iii, 83. **3** to dress (something) up; make to seem more attractive: "... how, in stripping it,/ You more invest it!" *Temp,* II, i, 220–221.

invested, *adj.* empowered: "Our substitutes in absence well invested..." *2 Hen 4,* IV, iv, 6.

investments, *n. pl.* vestments; robes or garments: "Whose white investments figure innocence..." *2 Hen 4,* IV, i, 45.

inveterate, *adj.* of long standing: "On some apparent danger seen in him ... no inveterate malice." *Rich 2,* I, i, 13–14.

invised, *adj.* poss. invisible or unseen: "Whereto his invis'd properties did tend..." *Lover's Comp,* 212.

invisible, *adj.* unseen; hence, unknowable: "Makes mouths at the invisible event [outcome]..." *Ham,* IV, iv, 50.

invite, *v.* to lure or entice: "... the cunning of her passion/ Invites me in this churlish messenger." *T Night,* II, ii, 21–22.

inviting, *n.* invitation: "He hath sent me an earnest/ inviting..." *Timon,* III, vi, 9–10.

Invitis nubibus, [Latin] in spite of clouds: "... our half-fac'd sun, striving to shine,/ Under the which is writ 'Invitis nubibus." *2 Hen 6,* IV, i, 97–98.

invocate, *v.* var. of invoke: "Henry the Fifth, thy ghost I invocate..." *l Hen 6,* I, i, 52.

invocation, *n.* supplication: "... that fell anatomy ... Which scorns a modern [commonplace] invocation." *K John,* III, iii, 40–42.

inward, *adj.* **1** internal; home: "And were these inward wars once out of hand,/ We would, dear lords, unto the Holy Land." *2 Hen 4,* III, i, 107–108. **2** private; confidential: "For what is inward/ between us, let it pass..." *Love's L,* V, i, 88–89. **3** intimate: "Who is most inward with the noble Duke?" *Rich 3,* III, iv, 8.

—*n.* **4** intimate companion: "Sir, I was an inward of his." *Meas,* III, ii, 127. **5** the inside: "To kiss the tender inward of thy hand..." *Sonn 128,* 6.

inwardness, *n.* innermost feelings, loyalties, etc.: "... you know my inwardness and love/ Is very much unto the Prince and Claudio..." *M Ado,* IV, i, 245–246.

Io, *n.* Greek maiden beloved of Jupiter, who changed her into a cow in an attempt to shield her from Juno's jealous wrath: "We'll show thee Io as she was a maid..." *Shrew,* Ind., ii, 55.

Ionia, *n.* country in Greek Asia Minor: "His conquering banner shook, from Syria/ To Lydia, and to Ionia..." *Ant & Cleo,* I, ii, 99–100.

Ipswich, *n.* **1** seaport in SE England; ref. here to Wolsey's birthplace: "And from a mouth of honour quite cry down/ This Ipswich fellow's insolence..." *Hen 8,* I, i, 137–138. **2** college founded here by Wolsey; closed down after his fall from power: "Those twins of learning that he rais'd in you,/ Ipswich and Oxford..." *Hen 8,* IV, ii, 58–59.

Ira furor brevis est, [Latin] Anger is a brief madness [quote from Horace]. *Timon,* I, ii, 28.

ireful, *adj.* enraged: "With fiery eyes sparkling for very wrath,/ And bloody steel grasp'd in their ireful hands..." *3 Hen 6,* II, v, 131–132.

Iris, *n.* Roman goddess of the rainbow and messenger to Juno: "Enter Iris." [SD] *Temp,* IV, i, 59.

Irish rat, *n.* ref. to old belief that an Irish magician could kill rats with a rhymed spell: "I was never so berhymed since Pythagoras'/ time that I was an Irish rat..." *As You,* III, ii, 173–174.

iron, *n.* **1** sword: "... for meddle you must, that's certain, or forswear/ to wear iron about you." *T Night,* III, iv, 255–256. —*adj.* **2** harsh; cruel: "And heard thee murmur tales of iron wars..." *1 Hen 4,* II, iii, 49.

iron age, *n.* unfeeling or hardhearted times; also, cruel world: "Ah, none but in this iron age would do it!" *K John,* IV, i, 60.

iron man, *n.* man in armor; also, a man of inflexible will: "... to see you here an iron man,/ Cheering a rout of rebels..." *2 Hen 4,* IV, ii, 8–9.

iron-witted, *adj.* unfeeling; here, dull-witted: "I will converse with iron-witted fools/ And unrespective boys..." *Rich 3,* IV, ii, 28–29.

irreconciled, *adj.* unforgiven; unabsolved: "... die in many irreconciled iniquities..." *Hen 5,* IV, i, 156.

irregular, *adj.* unruly or, sometimes, lawless: "... to fight/ Against the irregular and wild Glendower..." *1 Hen 4,* I, i, 39–40.

irregulous, *adj.* indifferent to rules; lawless: "Thou,/ Conspir'd with that irregulous devil, Cloten..." *Cymb,* IV, ii, 314–315.

irremoveable, *adj.* inflexible: "He's irremoveable,/ Resolv'd for flight." *W Tale,* IV, iv, 508–509.

is, *v.* occas. used in place of **has:** ". . . he is retir'd to Antium." *Cor,* III, i, 11.

Isbel, *n.* generic name for a waiting woman: "Our old/ lings and our Isbels a' th' country are nothing like/ your old ling and your Isbels a' th' court." *All's W,* III, ii, 12–14.

ise, *v.* I shall: ". . . keep out . . . or ise try whither your/ costard or my ballow be the harder." *Lear,* IV, vi, 242–243.

Isis, *n.* Egyptian goddess of the earth and moon: "O, let him marry a/ woman that cannot go, sweet Isis . . ." *Ant & Cleo,* I, ii, 60–61.

island kings, *n.* Greek leaders in the Trojan War: ". . . you shall do more/ Than all the island kings—disarm great Hector." *Tr & Cr,* III, i, 149–150.

issue, *n.* **1** result; outcome; consequences: "For he that brought them . . . did take horse,/ Uncertain of the issue any way." *1 Hen 4,* I, i, 59–61. **2** [often pl.] purpose; end: "Spirits are not finely touch'd/ But to fine issues . . ." *Meas,* I, i, 35–36. **3** disclosure; revelation: ". . . a part, whose issue/ Will hiss me to my grave . . ." *W Tale,* I, ii, 188–189. **4** point of an argument, action, etc.: ". . . what/ cunning match have you made with this jest of the/ drawer: come, what's the issue?" *1 Hen 4,* II, iv, 87–89. **5** action; deed: ". . . there shall I try . . . how the people take/ The cruel issue of these bloody men . . ." *J Caes,* III, i, 292–294. **6** [usually pl.] offspring; children: "Else one self mate and make could not beget/ Such different is-sues." *Lear,* IV, iii, 35–36. **7** sons: ". . . our issues/ (Who if he live, will scarce be gentlemen) . . ." *Hen 8,* III, ii, 291–292. **8** rich vegetation: "Delve there and find this issue and their pride/ To spring from ordure and corruption's side." *Edw 3,* I, ii, 154–155. **9 dearest issue,** most precious product: ". . . the dearest issue of his practice . . ." *All's W,* II, i, 105.
—*v.* **10 issue out,** to stream or sally forth: ". . . we are well fortified,/ And strong enough to issue out and fight." *1 Hen 6,* IV, ii, 19–20.

it, *adj.* **1** its: ". . . fed the cuckoo so long,/ That it's had it head bit off by it young." *Lear,* I, iv, 224–225. **2** same used as baby talk; here, indirectly (and contemptuously) to Eleanor: ". . . go to it grandam, child;/ Give grandam kingdom, and it grandam will/ Give it a plum . . ." *K John,* II, 1, 160–162.

iteration, *n.* habit of quoting or repeating another's words: "O, thou hast damnable iteration, and art indeed able/ to corrupt a saint . . ." *1 Hen 4,* I, ii, 88–89.

its, *adj.* its own: ". . . till the last/ Made former wonders, its." *Hen 8,* I, i, 17–18.

itself, *n.* its own child: "Love loving not itself none other can." *Rich 2,* V, iii, 86.

ivy-tods, *n.* ivy bushes: "Hard-hair'd, and curl'd, thick twin'd like ivy-tods,/ Not to undo with thunder." *Kinsmen,* IV, ii, 104–105.

iwis or **Iwis,** *adv.* assuredly; indeed: ". . . you shall never need to fear./ Iwis it is not half way to her heart [of no interest to her]." *Shrew,* I, i, 61–62.

J

jack¹, *n.* **1** soldier's quilted jacket; here, wordplay on Falstaff's nickname "Jack": "How now, blown [swollen] Jack? How now, quilt?" *1 Hen 4, IV, ii, 49.* **2** similar garment of linked [gimmaled] mail: ". . . their nimble spurs . . . their jacks of gimmaled mail . . ." *Edw 3, I, ii, 28–29.*

jack², *n.* **1** (in the game of bowls) the target ball [bowl], often struck and jostled by the other balls: "Since every Jack became a gentleman/ There's many a gentle person made a jack." *Rich 3, I, iii, 72–73.* **2 kiss the jack**, to bring one's ball [bowl] alongside the jack: "When I kissed/ the jack upon an upcast, to be hit away!" *Cymb, II, i, 1–2.*

jack³, *n.* [pl.] misuse here as spinet keys: "Do I envy those jacks that nimble leap/ To kiss the tender inward of thy hand . . ." *Sonn 128, 5–6.*

Jack, *n.* **1** servingman; here, also wordplay on leather tankard: "Be the Jacks fair within, the Jills fair without . . ." *Shrew, IV, i, 44.* **2** knave; rascal; fellow (term of contempt): "Boys, apes, braggarts, Jacks, milksops!" *M Ado, V, i, 91.* **3** term of contempt for lower classes, esp. noisy, ill-mannered persons: ". . . his simple truth must be abus'd/ With silken, sly, insinuating Jacks?" *Rich 3, I, iii, 52–53.* **4 Jack guardant**, knave of a sentry: ". . . you/ shall perceive that a Jack guardant cannot office me . . ." *Cor, V, ii, 60–61.*

Jack-a-Lent, *n.* gaily dressed straw puppet at which children throw stones during Lent: "You little Jack-a-Lent, have you been true/ to us?" *Wives, III, iii, 23–24.*

jackanapes or **jack-an-apes**, *n.* **1** monkey; hence, fool or idiot: "I could lay on like a butcher and sit like a jack-an-apes,/ never off [like a monkey, securely on my horse, and never be thrown]." *Hen 5, V, ii, 144–145.* **2** prob. some representation of an evil sprite: ". . . and I/ will be like a jack-an-apes also, to burn the knight/ with my taber." *Wives, IV, iv, 66–68.*

Jack, boy, ho, boy! First line of a popular catch: "Why, 'Jack, boy, ho, boy!' and as much news as/ wilt thou." *Shrew, IV, i, 36–37.*

Jack-dog, *n.* mongrel: "Scurvy Jack-dog priest! By gar, me/ vill cut his ears." *Wives, II, iii, 59–60.*

jack'nape, *n.* jackanapes; monkey; fool: "You jack'nape, give-a this letter to Sir Hugh . . ." *Wives, I, iv, 102.*

Jack of the clock, *n.* dwarf figure that struck the bell in some old clocks: ". . . my time/ Runs posting on in Bolingbroke's proud joy,/ While I stand fooling here, his Jack of the clock." *Rich 2, V, v, 58–60.*

Jack out of office, *n.* one ousted from his office: "I am left out; for me nothing remains;/ But long I will not be Jack out of office." *1 Hen 6, 174–175.*

Jack-sauce, *n.* impudent fellow; rascal: ". . . as arrant a villain and a Jack-sauce as/ ever his black shoe trod upon God's ground . . ." *Hen 5, IV, vii, 145–146.*

Jack-slave, *n.* lackey; flunky: ". . . every Jack-slave hath his bellyful of fighting . . ." *Cymb, II, i, 20.*

Jacob, *n.* **1** Old Testament patriarch: "When Jacob graz'd his uncle Laban's sheep . . ." *Merch, I, iii, 66.* **2 by Jacob's staff**, mild oath: "By Jacob's staff I swear/ I have no mind of feasting forth to-night . . ." *Merch, II, v, 36–37.*

jade, *n.* **1** term of contempt for a worthless or an unruly horse: "That jade hath eat bread from my royal hand . . ." *Rich 2, V, v, 85.* **2** same applied to the dragons that draw night's chariot across the sky: ". . . loud-howling wolves arouse the jades/ That drag the tragic melancholy night . . ." *2 Hen 6, IV, i, 3–4.* **3** term of abuse or contempt for either a man or a woman: "Women are made to bear . . ."/ "No such jade as you, if me you mean." *Shrew, II, i, 200–201.*

—*v.* **4** to deceive or trick: "I do not now fool myself, to let imagination/ jade me . . ." *T Night,* II, v, 164–165. **5** to drive out like a worthless horse: "The ne'er-yet-beaten horse [cavalry] of Parthia/ We have jaded out o' the field." *Ant & Cleo,* III, i, 33–34. **6** to treat contemptuously: "To be thus jaded by a piece of scarlet . . ." *Hen 8,* III, ii, 280.

jaded, *adj.* lowborn (term of contempt): "The honourable blood of Lancaster,/ Must not be shed by such a jaded groom." *2 Hen 6,* IV, i, 51–52.

jade's trick, *n.* **1** mischievous habit of a jade, such as slipping out of its collar: "You always end with a jade's trick, I know you of old." *M Ado,* I, i, 134. **2** [pl.] wordplay on tricks by an "unruly horse" or a "knave": "If I put any tricks upon 'em, sir, they shall be jades'/ tricks, which are their own right by the law of/ nature." *All's W,* IV, v, 57–59.

jakes, *n. pl.* privy; outhouse: "I will tread/ this unbolted villain into mortar, and daub the/ wall of a jakes with him." *Lear,* II, ii, 65–67.

Jamanie, *n.* prob. the doctor's pron. of "Germany": ". . . you/ make grand preparation for a Duke de Jamanie . . ." *Wives,* IV, v, 81–82.

jangle, *v.* to speak harshly or angrily; dispute; clash: "Good wits will be jangling . . . / This civil war of wits were much better us'd/ on Navarre . . ." *Love's L,* II, i, 224–226.

jangling, *n.* wrangling; dispute or discord: ". . . so far am I glad it so did sort,/ As this their jangling I esteem a sport." *M N Dream,* III, ii, 352–353.

Janus, *n.* Roman god having two faces, one young and the other old: "Now by two-headed Janus,/ Nature hath fram'd strange fellows in her time . . ." *Merch,* I, i, 50–51.

Japhet, *n.* son of Noah and father of the Europeans: "Nay, they will be kin to us, or they will fetch it/ from Japhet." *2 Hen 4,* II, ii, 111–112.

jar, *n.* **1** [often pl.] discord; disagreement or quarreling: "If he, compact [composed] of jars, grow musical,/ We shall have shortly discord in the spheres." *As You,* II, vii, 5–6. **2 at jars,** at odds; into disagreement: "And Humphrey with the peers be fall'n at jars . . ." *2 Hen 6,* I, i, 254. **3 jar o' th' clock,** tick of the clock: "I love thee not a jar o' th' clock behind [less than]/ What lady she her lord [any lady, whoever she is, loves her husband]." *W Tale,* I, ii, 43–44. **4 live at jar,** to quarrel among yourselves: ". . . whilst you live at jar,/ The fearful [cowardly] French . . . Should make a start o'er seas . . ." *2 Hen 6,* IV, viii, 41–43.

—*v.* **5** to tick off or away (the minutes or seconds): ". . . with sighs they jar/ Their watches on unto mine eyes, the outward watch . . ." *Rich 2,* V, v, 51–52. **6** to clash; quarrel: "For shame, be friends, and join for that you jar . . ." *T Andr,* II, i, 103.

Jarteer, *n.* Frenchman's pron. of "Garter": "I have appointed mine host/ of de Jarteer to measure our weapon." *Wives,* I, iv, 112–113.

Jason, *n.* hero of Greek myth who, with his band of Argonauts, led an expedition to Colchis and retrieved the golden fleece: ". . . her sunny locks/ Hang on her temples like a golden fleece . . . And many Jasons come in quest of her." *Merch,* I, i, 170–172.

jaunce, *n.* **1** a prancing about; exhausting journey: "Fie, how my bones ache. What a jaunce have I!" *Rom & Jul,* II, v, 26.
—*v.* **2** to work or be worked hard; trudge: "Beshrew your heart for sending me about/ To catch my death with jauncing up and down." *Rom & Jul,* II, v, 52–53.

jauncing, *adj.* moving or bouncing up and down, as in riding a horse: "And yet I bear a burthen like an ass,/ Spurr'd, gall'd, and tir'd by jauncing Bolingbroke." *Rich 2,* V, v, 93–94.

jaundies, *n.* [used as pl.] perh. symptoms of jaundice; more likely paleness and fatigue: "Princes:/ What grief hath set these jaundies on your cheeks?" *Tr & Cr,* I, iii, 1–2.

jay, *n.* whore, esp. one who is treacherous: "Some jay of Italy . . . hath betray'd him." *Cymb,* III, iv, 50–51.

jealous, *adj.* **1** watchful; vigilant: "O night . . . Let not the jealous day behold that face . . ." *Luc,* 799–800. **2** curious: "But if thou jealous dost return to pry/ In what I farther shall intend to do . . ." *Rom & Jul,* V, iii, 33–34. **3** suspicious: "And be not jealous on [of] me, gentle Brutus . . ." *J Caes,* I, ii, 70. **4** doubtful: "That you do love me, I am nothing jealous . . ." *J Caes,* I, ii, 160. **5** concerned; anxious: ". . . your nobles, jealous of your absence . . ." *Hen 5,* IV, i, 291. **6 not jealous,** implying she has every reason to be: ". . . his noble Queen/ Well struck in years, fair, and not jealous." *Rich 3,* I, i, 91–92.

jealous-hood, *n.* personification of jealousy; Lady Jealousy: "A jealous-hood, a jealous-hood!" *Rom & Jul,* IV, iv, 13.

jealous of catching, *adj.* frightened of being caught: ". . . lo the unback'd breeder . . . Jealous of catching, swiftly doth forsake him . . ." *Ven & Ad,* 320–321.

jealousy, *n.* **1** [often pl.] suspicion; mistrust: "Let not my jealousies be your dishonours,/ But mine own safeties . . ." *Mac,* IV, iii, 29–30. **2** concern; anxiety: "And not all love to see you . . . But jealousy what might befall your travel . . ." *T*

Night, III, iii, 6–8. **3** critical judgment: "... oft my jealousy/ Shapes faults that are not ..." *Oth,* III, iii, 151–152. **4** Quickly's mistake for "jealous": "... the sweet woman/ leads an ill life with him: he's a very jealousy man ..." *Wives,* II, ii, 84–85. **5 jealousy does yet depend,** [my] suspicion still hangs over you: "We'll slip [release] you for a season, but our jealousy/ Does yet depend." *Cymb,* IV, iii, 22–23.

jennet, *n.* Spanish mare: "A breeding jennet, lusty, young and proud ..." *Ven & Ad,* 260.

Jephthah, *n.* leader of Israel's forces against the Ammonites; promised God that if successful he would sacrifice the first creature he met upon his return home, which proved to be his daughter and only child: "O Jephthah, judge of Israel, what a treasure hadst/ thou!" *Ham,* II, ii, 399–400.

jerkin, *n.* man's jacket: "... is not a buff jerkin a most sweet robe of durance?" *1 Hen 4,* I, ii, 42.

jerks of invention, *n.* thrusts or sallies of wit: "*Naso* ... for smelling/ out the odoriferous flowers of fancy, the jerks of/ invention?" *Love's L,* IV, ii, 119–121.

Jerusalem, *n.* New Jerusalem, final abode of the blessed; heaven: "So part we sadly in this troublous world,/ To meet with joy in sweet Jerusalem." *3 Hen 6,* V, v, 7–8.

jesses, *n.* (usually pl.) leg straps securing the falcon to a leash: "Though that her jesses were my dear heart-strings ..." *Oth,* III, iii, 265.

jest, *n.* **1** make-believe; pretending: "No, no, they do but jest—poison in jest. No offence/ i'th' world." *Ham,* III, ii, 229–230. **2 break a jest upon,** to play a joke on: "Like pleasant travellers, to break a jest/ Upon the company you overtake?" *Shrew,* IV, v, 71–72.

Jesu, *n.* Jesus [used as a mild oath]: "By Jesu, a very good/ blade, a very tall man, a very good whore!" *Rom & Jul,* II, iv, 29–30.

jet¹, *v.* to encroach: "... think you not now dangerous/ It is to jet upon a prince's right?" *T Andr,* II, i, 63–64.

jet², *v.* to strut: "Whose men and dames so jetted and adorn'd ..." *Per,* I, iv, 26.

Jew, *n.* **1** impersonal term of abuse, roughly equiv. to rascal, scoundrel, or unbeliever: "... if I do not love her, I am a Jew." *M Ado,* II, iii, 253–254. **2** prob. a repetition of first syllable of "juvenal" [juvenile] to force rhyme with "hue" : "Most brisky juvenal, and eke [also] most lovely Jew ..." *M N Dream,* III, i, 90.

jewel, *n.* ornament set with one or more gemstones; also, a beloved person (a source of punning): "... send you back/ again to your master for a jewel,—the juvenal the/ Prince your master ..." *2 Hen 4,* I, ii, 17–19.

Jewes, *n.* prob. same as "Jewess'": "There will come a Christian by/ Will be worth a Jewes eye." *Merch,* II, v, 41–42.

Jewry, *n.* land of the Jews; Judaea or Jerusalem: "... as far from home ... As is the sepulchre in stubborn Jewry ..." *Rich 2,* II, i, 53–55.

Jezebel, *n.* (in the Bible) widow of King Ahab; she tried to impose the cult of Baal on the Israelites and was killed; here, Malvolio's insufferable pride is likened to hers: "Fie on him, Jezebel!" *T Night,* II, v, 41.

jig, *n.* **1** entertainment of dancing and singing, performed after a play: "He's for a jig or a tale of bawdry, or he sleeps." *Ham,* II, ii, 496. **2 skipping jigs,** wild, unruly dances to bawdy songs or ballads: "How much they will deride us in the North,/ And, in their vile uncivil skipping jigs,/ Bray forth their conquest and our overthrow ..." *Edw 3,* I, ii, 11–13. —*adj.* **3** comporting oneself [here, to rhyme] in the manner of one doing a jig: "What should the wars do with these jigging fools?" *J Caes,* IV, iii, 136. —*v.* **4** to move in a jerky manner, as one doing a jig: "You jig and amble, and you lisp ..." *Ham,* III, i, 146. **5 jig off,** to play or sing (a tune) in the manner of a jig: "... to jig off a tune at the/ tongue's end, canary to it with your feet ..." *Love's L,* III, i, 9–10.

jig-maker, *n.* person who composes jigs, that is musical entertainments to follow play performances: "O God, your only [best] jig-maker." *Ham,* III, ii, 123.

Jill, *n.* maidservant; also, wordplay on small metal drinking vessel: "Be the Jacks fair within, the Jills fair without ..." *Shrew,* IV, i, 44.

Joan, *n.* **1** typical name of a country girl: "Some men must love my lady, and some Joan." *Love's L,* III, i, 200. **2** name of an older hawk: "... ten to one, old Joan had not gone out [flown at the game]." *2 Hen 6,* II, i, 4.

jocund, *adj.* **1** merry; joyful: "No jocund health that Denmark drinks today/ But the great cannon to the clouds shall tell ..." *Ham,* I, ii, 125–126. **2** lively; energetic: "Night's candles are burnt out, and jocund day/ Stands tiptoe on the misty mountain tops." *Rom & Jul,* III, v, 9–10.

jog, *v.* to be on one's way: "You may be jogging whiles your boots are green [without wasting more time]." *Shrew,* III, ii, 209.

John-a-dreams, *n.* nickname for a woolgatherer or day-dreamer: ". . . peak/ Like John-a-dreams, unpregnant of my cause . . ." *Ham,* II, ii, 562–563.

John Drum's entertainment, *n.* dismissal from the corps: ". . . if you give him not John Drum's entertainment/ your inclining cannot be removed." *All's W,* III, vi, 36–38.

join, *v.* **1** to join forces; unite, esp. to gain a common objective: "For shame, be friends, and join for that you jar . . ." *T Andr,* II, i, 103. **2 join in souls,** to join together; unite: "Can you not hate me . . . But you must join in souls to mock me too?" *M N Dream,* III, ii, 149–150.

joinder, *n.* act of joining: ". . . eternal bond of love,/ Confirm'd by mutual joinder of your hands . . ." *T Night,* V, i, 154–155.

joiner, *n.* worker who fits pieces of wood together for doors, windows, chairs, etc.: "Snug the joiner, you the lion's part." *M N Dream,* I, ii, 60.

joiner squirrel, *n.* the fairy-tale carpentry team of the gnawing squirrel and the boring grub: "Her chariot is an empty hazelnut/ Made by the joiner squirrel or old grub . . ." *Rom & Jul,* I, iv, 59–60.

joint, *n.* **1** limb of the body: ". . . he hath the joints of everything, but everything/ so out of joint . . ." *Tr & Cr,* I, ii, 28–29. **2 out of joint,** in disarray; chaotic: "The time is out of joint. O cursed spite,/ That ever I was born to set it right." *Ham,* I, v, 196–197. —*v.* **3** to join; unite: ". . . the time's state/ Made friends of them, jointing their force 'gainst Caesar . . ." *Ant & Cleo,* I, ii, 88–89.

jointress, *n.* a woman regarded as a joint sovereign: ". . . our sometime sister, now our queen,/ Th'imperial jointress to this warlike state . . ." *Ham,* I, ii, 8–9.

joint-ring, *n.* ring made in interlocking halves: "I would not do such a thing for/ a joint-ring . . ." *Oth,* IV, iii, 71–72.

joint-servant, *n.* fellow servant; here, partner: "I took him,/ Made him joint-servant with me . . ." *Cor,* V, vi, 31–32.

joint-stool, *n.* three- or four-legged stool made by a joiner, the parts cut to measure and fitted together: "Thy state is taken for a joint-stool . . ." *1 Hen 4,* II, iv, 375.

jointure, *n.* marriage portion set aside by husband for wife's maintenance after his death; protected by law from seizure: ". . . a better jointure I think than you make a woman." *As You,* IV, i, 53–54.

jollity, *n.* **1** debauchery; sexual pleasure: here, linked with venereal disease and the loss of a man's hair: "The plainer dealer [dealings with prostitutes], the sooner lost; yet he/ loseth it in a kind of jollity." *Errors,* II, ii, 87–88. **2** finery; frippery: "And needy nothing trimm'd in jollity . . ." *Sonn 66,* 3.

jolly, *adj.* **1** lustful; lecherous: ". . . whiles the jolly Briton/ (Your lord, I mean) laughs from's free lungs . . ." *Cymb,* I, vii, 67–68. —*adv.* **2** very; exceedingly: "'Tis like you'll prove a jolly surly groom . . ." *Shrew,* III, ii, 211.

jolthead or **jolt-head,** *n.* blockhead: "You heedless joltheads and unmanner'd slaves!" *Shrew,* IV, i, 153.

jordan, *n.* chamber pot: ". . . they will allow us ne'er a jordan, and then/ we leak in your chimney . . ." *1 Hen 4,* II, i, 18–19.

jot, *n.* **no jot,** not in the least: "You do mistake me, sir."/ "No, sir, no jot: I know your favour well . . ." *T Night,* III, iv, 336–337.

journal, *adj.* **1** daily or morning: "Ere the sun hath made his journal greeting . . ." *Meas,* IV, iii, 88. **2 journal course,** daily routine: ". . . so please you, leave me,/ Stick to your journal course . . ." *Cymb,* IV, ii, 9–10.

journey, *n.* death: "I have a journey, sir, shortly to go . . ." *Lear,* V, iii, 321.

journey-bated, *adj.* exhausted from traveling: "So are the horses of the enemy/ In general journey-bated and brought low." *1 Hen 4,* IV, iii, 25–26.

journeyman, *n.* common laborer: ". . . I have thought some of/ Nature's journeymen had made men, and not made/ them well . . ." *Ham,* III, ii, 33–35.

Jove in a thatched house, ref. to Jove and Mercury disguising themselves on earthly visit and being repeatedly turned away until taken in by poor couple and shown great courtesy: "O knowledge ill-inhabited, worse than/ Jove in a thatched house!" *As You,* III, iii, 7–8.

Jove's spreading tree, *n.* oak tree: "Whose top branch over-peer'd Jove's spreading tree . . ." *3 Hen 6,* V, ii, 14.

jowl, *v.* **1** to throw with force; dash: "How the knave jowls it to th' ground, as if 'twere/ Cain's jawbone . . ." *Ham,* V, i, 75–76. **2** to knock or dash together; clash: ". . . they may jowl horns/ together like any deer i' th' herd." *All's W,* I, iii, 52–53.

joy, *v.* **1** to experience joy: "Poor fellow never joyed since the price of oats/ rose . . ." *1 Hen 4,* II, i, 11–12. **2** to bring joy to: "Yet neither pleasure's art can joy my spirits . . ." *Per,* I, ii, 10.

3 to have the enjoyment of: ". . . let us hence,/ And let her joy her raven-coloured love . . ." *T Andr*, II, iii, 82–83.
—*n.* **4** (as an endearment) dear; pet: "Yea, joy, our chains and our jewels." *2 Hen 4*, II, iv, 47.

Judas Maccabaeus, *n.* 2d cent. B.C. Jewish patriot: "He presents Hector of Troy; the swain, Pompey . . . the pedant, Judas Maccabaeus." *Love's L*, V, ii, 529–531.

judge, *v.* to guess: "To what, I pray?"/ "Judge."/ "To three thousand dolours a year." *Meas*, I, ii, 44–46.

judgment, *n.* **1** good sense; understanding: "Take our good meaning, for our judgement sits/ Five times in that ere once in our five wits [there's five times as much sense in what I mean as in what I say]." *Rom & Jul*, I, iv, 46–47. **2** ruling or opinion: "Judgment."/ "A hit, a very palpable hit." *Ham*, V, ii, 281–282. **3** dispensing of justice; here, by divine authority: "Of carnal, bloody, and unnatural acts,/ Of accidental judgments, casual slaughters . . ." *Ham*, V, ii, 386–387. **4** Judgment Day: "So, till the judgment that yourself [when you yourself] arise . . ." *Sonn 55*, 13. **5 have judgment,** to have sentence passed or be punished: "But in these cases,/ We still have judgment here . . ." *Mac*, I, vii, 7–8. **6 on better judgment making,** on better consideration [being made by you]: "So thy great gift, upon misprision growing,/ Comes home again, on better judgment making." *Sonn 87*, 11–12. **7 practice his judgment,** to experiment: ". . . he hath made an assay of her/ virtue, to practise his judgement with the disposition/ of natures." *Meas*, III, i, 161–163. **8 rebel to judgment,** rebel against their better judgment: "Pawn their experience to their present pleasure,/ And so rebel to judgment." *Ant & Cleo*, I, iv, 32–33.

judicious, *adj.* judicial; here, showing sound judgment: "His last offences to us/ Shall have judicious hearing." *Cor*, V, vi, 125–126.

juggle, *v.* **1** to copulate: "She and the Dauphin have been juggling . . ." *1 Hen 6*, V, iv, 68. **2 juggle with,** to play tricks or practice deception on: "How came he dead? I'll not be juggled with." *Ham*, IV, v, 130.

juggler, *n.* **1** deceiver or trickster: "Away,/ you bottle-ale rascal, you basket-hilt stale juggler,/ you!" *2 Hen 4*, II, iv, 127–129. **2** sorcerer: ". . . a mountebank,/ A thread-bare juggler and a fortune-teller . . ." *Errors*, V, i, 239–240.

juggling, *adj.* playing tricks; practicing deception: "And be these juggling fiends no more believ'd . . ." *Mac*, V, viii, 19.

jump, *v.* **1** to agree; coincide: ". . . in some sort it jumps with my humour . . ." *1 Hen 4*, I, ii, 66. **2** to risk; take one's chances with: "We'd jump the life to come . . ." *Mac*, I, vii, 7. **3 jump**

the after-inquiry, to risk the Final Judgment: ". . . jump the after-inquiry on your own/ peril . . ." *Cymb*, V, iv, 184–185.
—*adv.* **4** precisely; exactly: "Thus twice before, and jump at this dead hour . . ." *Ham*, I, i, 68.
—*n.* **5** stake or hazard: ". . . our fortune lies/ Upon this jump." *Ant & Cleo*, III, viii, 5–6.

junket, *n.* [often pl.] dainties; sweetmeats: "You know there wants no junkets at the feast." *Shrew*, III, ii, 246.

jure, *v.* to give the oath to (a juror): "You are/ grandjurors, are ye? We'll jure ye, faith." *1 Hen 4*, II, ii, 86–87.

just¹, *adv.* **1** just so; exactly; precisely: "Rosalind is your love's name?/ Yes, just." *As You*, III, ii, 259–260.
—*adj.* **2** precise; exact: "Monday, my dear son, which is hence a/ just seven-night . . ." *M Ado*, II, i, 336–337. **3** morally right; righteous: "How malicious is my fortune, that I must repent/ to be just!" *Lear*, III, v, 9–10. **4 'Tis just,** It is true: "'Tis just;/ And it is very much lamented, Brutus . . ." *J Caes*, I, ii, 53–54.

just², *n.* joust; tournament: "What news from Oxford? Do these justs and triumphs hold?" *Rich 2*, V, ii, 52.

just distance, *n.* halfway between two points or objects: "Pleaseth your lordship/ To meet his Grace just distance 'tween our armies." *2 Hen 4*, IV, i, 225–226.

justice, *n.* **1 indeed Justice,** justice personified or, more likely, justice without mercy: ". . . he hath forced me to tell him he/ is indeed Justice." *Meas*, III, ii, 247–248. **2 justice of compare,** See **compare** (def. 1).

justicer, *n.* judge; justice: "Come, sit thou here, most learned justicer . . ." *Lear*, III, vi, 21.

justify, **1** to prove or establish: "I could pluck his highness' frown upon you,/ And justify you traitors . . ." *Temp*, V, i, 127–128. **2** to verify: ". . . and now she sings in heaven."/ "How is this justified?" *All's W*, IV, iii, 51–52. **3** to judge; poss. to acquit: "I give my cause, who best can justify." *Per*, I, Chor., 42. **4** to vindicate; atone for: ". . . we will be justified in our loves . . ." *W Tale*, I, ii, 8–9.

justle, *v.* **1** var. of **jostle:** "Let not the cloud of sorrow justle it . . ." *Love's L*, V, ii, 740. **2** to wrestle; fight: "I am in case to/ justle a constable." *Temp*, III, ii, 24–25. **3** to force; wrench: ". . . howsoe'er you have/ Been justled from your senses . . ." *Temp*, V, i, 157–158.

justling, *adj.* var. of **jostling;** clashing or struggling; also, disturbed: ". . . how has he the leisure to be sick/ In such a justling time?" *1 Hen 4*, IV, i, 18.

justly, *adv.* exactly; precisely: "I have in equal balance justly weigh'd/ What wrongs our arms may do . . ." *2 Hen 4,* IV, i, 67–68.

just proof, *n.* proof of innocence: "When false opinion . . . In thy just proof repeals and reconciles thee." *Lear,* III, vi, 115–116.

jut, *v.* to encroach; menace: "Insulting tyranny begins to jut/ Upon the innocent and aweless throne." *Rich 3,* II, iv, 51–52.

jutty, *n.* 1 projection, as of a building or roof support: ". . . no jutty, frieze,/ Buttress, nor coign of vantage . . ." *Mac,* I, vi, 6–7.
—*v.* 2 to jut out; project out over: ". . . as doth a galled rock/ O'erhang and jutty his confounded base . . ." *Hen 5,* III, i, 13.

juvenal, *n.* juvenile; a young man: ". . . send you back/ again to your master for a jewel,—the juvenal the/ Prince your master . . ." *2 Hen 4,* I, ii, 17–19.

K

kam, *adj.* twisted; awry: "This is clean [completely] kam." *Cor,* III, i, 301.

Kated, *adj.* either "provided with a Kate" or "afflicted with a Kate": "I warrant him, Petruchio is Kated." *Shrew,* III, ii, 243.

Kate Hall, *n.* poss. a suggestion by Petruchio that the house is known by this name, an allusion to Kate's notoriety: "Kate of Kate Hall, my super-dainty Kate . . ." *Shrew,* II, i, 188.

Kates, *n.* wordplay with "cates," delicacies or sweetmeats: ". . . my super-dainty Kate,/ For dainties are all Kates . . ." *Shrew,* II, i, 188–189.

kecksies, *n.* dried stems of hemlock: ". . . nothing teems/ But hateful docks, rough thistles, kecksies, burrs . . ." *Hen 5,* V, ii, 51–52.

keech, *n.* large ball of animal fat: "That such a keech can with his very bulk/ Take up the rays o'th'beneficial sun . . ." *Hen 8,* I, i, 55–56.

keel, *v.* to stir or otherwise cool (cooking food) to prevent boiling over: "Tu-who, a merry note,/ While greasy Joan doth keel the pot." *Love's L,* V, ii, 911–912.

keen, *adj.* **1** bitter; rancorous: "O, when she is angry, she is keen and shrewd . . ." *M N Dream,* III, ii, 323. **2** same in wordplay with "lecherous": ". . . my lord, you are keen."/ "It would cost you a groaning to take off my edge." *Ham,* III, ii, 243–244. **3** cruel; savage: "A creature that did bear the shape of man/ So keen and greedy to confound a man." *Merch,* III, ii, 274–275. **4** sharp: "Let us be keen, and rather cut a little,/ Than fall, and bruise to death." *Measure,* II, i, 5–6.

keep, *v.* **1** to guard: "Who cannot keep [hang on to] his wealth must keep [watch over] his house." *Timon,* III, iii, 43. **2** to hoard: "Keep it not; you cannot/ choose but lose by't." *All's W,* I, i, 143–144. **3** to remain or stay (in): "Many do keep their chambers are not sick . . ." *Timon,* III, iv, 71. **4** to stay close to: "Base muleteers of France!/ Like peasant foot-boys do they keep the walls . . ." *1 Hen 6,* III, ii, 68–69. **5** to live; reside: "This Armado is a Spaniard, that keeps here in court . . ." *Love's L,* IV, i, 99. **6** to make; here, "keeps making": "Who is that at the door that keeps all this noise?" *Errors,* III, i, 61. **7** to restrain oneself [or itself]; behave: ". . . 'tis a foul thing, when a cur cannot keep himself in/ all companies . . ." *Two Gent,* IV, iv, 10–11. **8 keep close,** to remain in confinement: "She pray'd me to excuse her keeping close . . ." *Cymb,* III, v, 46. **9 keep it in,** refrain from uttering it: "It is the more like to be feigned; I pray you/ keep it in." *T Night,* I, v, 197–198. **10 keep itself,** to be unoccupied: "But at this hour the house doth keep itself,/ There's none within." *As You,* IV, iii, 81–82. **11 keep off,** to detain; restrain: ". . . tell me true I charge you,/ Not fearing the displeasure of your master,/ Which on your just proceeding I'll keep off—" *All's W,* V, iii, 233–235. **12 keep on,** to go on ahead [without me]: "I do beseech you, good my lords, keep on . . ." *Timon,* II, ii, 39. **13 keep one's day,** See **day** (def. 6). **14 keep with, a.** to keep company with: ". . . keep with Bohemia,/ And with your queen." *W Tale,* I, ii, 344–345. **b.** Also, **keep withal,** live with or among: "It [he] is the most impenetrable cur/ That ever kept with men" *Merch,* III, iii, 18–19. **15 keep your way** See **way** (def. 21).
—*n.* **16** custody; safekeeping: "For in Baptista's keep my treasure is." *Shrew,* I, ii, 117.

keeper, *n.* **1** jailer or guard: "So I leave you/ To the protection of the prosperous gods,/ As thieves to keepers." *Timon,* V, i, 181–183. **2** nurse: ". . . breaks like a fire/ Out of his keeper's arms . . ." *2 Hen 4,* I, i, 142–143. **3** gamekeeper: "Enter two Keepers, with cross-bows in their hands." [SD] *3 Hen 6,* III, i, 1.

keep house, *v.* to remain indoors: "A goodly day not to keep house with such/ Whose roof's as low as ours!" *Cymb,* III, iii, 1–2.

keeping, *adj.* that one must abide by: "... having sworn too hard a keeping oath,/ Study to break it and not break my troth." *Love's L,* I, i, 65–66.

Keiser, *n.* form of German "Kaiser" appar. to rhyme with "Caesar": "Thou'rt an emperor, Caesar, Keiser, and Pheazar." *Wives,* I, iii, 9.

ken, *n.* **1** sight, esp. the limit of one's vision [c.20 miles]: "For lo, within a ken our army lies ..." *2 Hen 4,* IV, i, 151. —*v.* **2** to discern; make out: "As far as I could ken thy chalky cliffs ..." *2 Hen 6,* III, ii, 100. **3** to know; be acquainted with: "I ken the wight: he is of substance good." *Wives,* I, iii, 35.

Kendal green, *n.* coarse wool cloth: "... three misbegotten/ knaves in Kendal green came at my back ..." *1 Hen 4,* II, iv, 216–217.

Kenilworth, *n.* See **Killingworth.**

kennel, *n.* gutter: "Go, hop me over every kennel home ..." *Shrew,* IV, iii, 98.

kept, *adj.* guarded: "Had all your quarters been as safely kept ..." *1 Hen 6,* II, ii, 75.

kerchief, *n.* scarf or muffler tied around the head of a sick person: "O what a time have you chose out, brave Caius,/ To wear a kerchief!" *J Caes,* II, i, 314–315.

kern or **Kerne,** *n.* light-armed Irish foot soldier, usually a mercenary [a term of humor and sometimes contempt]: "We must supplant those rough rug-headed kerns ..." *Rich 2,* II, i, 156.

kernel, *n.* seed; here, ref. to young son: "How like, methought, I then was to this kernel ..." *W Tale,* I, ii, 159.

kersey, *n.* coarse homespun; here, simple and down-to-earth: "Henceforth my wooing mind shall be express'd/ In russet yeas and honest kersey noes ..." *Love's L,* V, ii, 412–413.

kettle, *n.* kettledrum(s): "And let the kettle to the trumpet speak,/ The trumpet to the cannoneer without ..." *Ham,* V, ii, 272–273.

key, *n.* **1** tone (of voice): "Shall I bend low, and in a bondman's key/ With bated breath, and whisp'ring humbleness ..." *Merch,* I, iii, 118–119. **2** key of office; also, tuning to a musical key: "... having both the key/ Of officer and office, set all hearts i' th' state/ To what tune pleas'd his ear ..." *Temp,* I, ii, 83–85. **3 turn the key,** open the door (to): "Fortune, that arrant whore,/ Ne'er turns the key to th' poor." *Lear,* II, iv, 52–53.

key-cold, *adj.* cold as metal; used esp. of death: "And then in key-cold Lucrece' bleeding stream/ He falls ..." *Luc,* 1774–1775.

kibe, *n.* sore on the heel: "... the toe of the peasant/ comes so near the heel of the courtier he galls his/ kibe." *Ham,* V, i, 136–138.

kick, *v.* **kick at,** to spurn: "Our spoils he kick'd at ..." *Cor,* II, ii, 124.

kickshaw, *n.* **1** sidedish; dainty or trifle: "... a couple of/ short-legged hens, a joint of mutton, and any pretty/ little tiny kickshaws ..." *2 Hen 4,* V, i, 24–26. **2** [pl.] trivial pastimes: "Art thou good at these kickshawses, knight?" *T Night,* I, iii, 113.

kicky-wicky, *n.* appar. coined endearment for one's wife; poss. based on *quelque chose* [Fr., "something"], as is "kick-shaw": "He wears his honour in a box unseen/ That hugs his kicky-wicky here at home ..." *All's W,* II, iii, 275–276.

kid-fox, *n.* cub, hence a novice; one easily outwitted: "We'll fit the kid-fox with a pennyworth." *M Ado,* II, iii, 42.

kidney, *n.* type; sort: "... a man/ of my kidney—think of that—that am as subject to/ heat as butter ..." *Wives,* III, v, 105–107.

kill, *v.* to overcome; here, with sleep: "To bed, to bed! Sleep kill those pretty eyes ..." *Tr & Cr,* IV, ii, 4.

kill-courtesy, *n.* rude person: "Pretty soul, she durst not lie/ Near this lack-love, this kill-courtesy." *M N Dream,* II, ii, 75–76.

killen, *v.* old form of **kill:** "... he strives/ To killen bad, keep good alive ..." *Per,* II, Chor., 19–20.

kill-hole, *n.* See **kiln-hole.**

Killingworth, *n.* Kenilworth, town in central England: "My gracious lord, retire to Killingworth,/ Until a power be rais'd to put them down." *2 Hen 6,* IV, iv, 38–39.

kiln-hole, *n.* firehole of a kiln; also, opening of an oven: "... when you are/ going to bed, or kiln-hole, to whistle of these secrets ..." *W Tale,* IV, iv, 246–247.

Kimmalton, *n.* Kimbalton [prob. spelled as pronounced], castle in E central England: "Since which she was remov'd to Kimmalton,/ Where she remains now sick." *Hen 8,* IV, i, 34–35.

kind, *n.* **1** one's nature: "Whether that thy youth and kind/ Will the faithful offer take . . ." *As You*, IV, iii, 59–60. **2** role or task, esp. one dictated by a person's nature: ". . . my meaner ministers/ Their several kinds have done." *Temp*, III, iii, 87–88. **3** manner or type: "But in this kind to come, in braving arms . . . it may not be." *Rich 2*, II, iii, 142–144. **4** family or relations: "A little more than kin, and less than kind." *Ham*, I, ii, 65. **5** breed or strain: "My hounds are bred out of the Spartan kind . . ." *M N Dream*, IV, i, 118. **6 after kind,** to behave according to one's nature: "If the cat will after kind,/ So be sure will Rosalind." *As You*, III, ii, 101–102. **7 by kind,** naturally: "Your cuckoo sings by kind." *All's W*, I, iii, 61. **8 do his kind,** behave according to its nature: "You must think this . . . that the worm/ will do his kind." *Ant & Cleo*, V, ii, 261–262. **9 in their kind,** in actuality: "She shall see deeds of honor in their kind . . ." *Kinsmen*, V, iii, 12. **10 in this kind, a** in such a matter: "But in this kind, wanting your father's voice . . ." *M N Dream*, I, i, 54. **b** of this sort: "He says they can do nothing in this kind." *M N Dream*, V, i, 88. **11 strange kinds,** dissimilar natures: "The weak oppress'd, th'impression of strange kinds/ Is form'd in them by force . . ." *Luc*, 1242–1243.
—*adj.* **12** true to one's nature; instinctive: "A kind overflow of kindness . . ." *M Ado*, I, i, 25. **13** generous; open-handed: "Never mind/ Was to be so unwise, to be so kind." *Timon*, II, i, 5–6. **14** loving; affectionate: "Drew me from kind embracements of my spouse . . ." *Errors*, I, i, 43. **15** natural; lifelike: "Conceit deceitful, so compact, so kind . . ." *Luc*, 1423. **16** proper; fitting: "I have a kind soul that would give thanks/ And knows not how to do it but with tears." *K John*, V, vii, 108–109. **17 kind and natural,** affectionate and loyal [according to the law of nature]: "Were all thy children kind and natural!" *Hen 5*, II, Chor., 19. **18 kind event,** favorable outcome: ". . . bear witness to this sound,/ And crown what I profess with kind event . . ." *Temp*, III, i, 68–69.

kindle[1], *v.* **1** to lure; entice: "Nothing remains but that I kindle/ the boy thither . . ." *As You*, I, i, 170–171. **2** to incite: ". . . How that ambitious Constance would not cease/ Till she had kindled France . . ." *K John*, I, i, 32–33.

kindle[2], *v.* to bring forth, as young; be born: "As the cony that you see dwell where she is kindled." *As You*, III, ii, 332.

kindless, *adj.* unnatural; here, bereft of familial loyalty or affection: "Remorseless, treacherous, lecherous, kindless villain!" *Ham*, II, ii, 577.

kindly, *adj.* **1** natural: "'Tis lack of kindly warmth they are not kind . . ." *Timon*, II, ii, 221.
—*adv.* **2** willingly; properly: ". . . spends what he borrows kindly in your company." *Two Gent*, II, iv, 36. **3** wordplay on "graciously" and "truly": "Meaning to curtsy."/ "Thou hast most kindly hit it." *Rom & Jul*, II, iv, 56–57. **4** welcome; by

all means: "Let him come, and kindly." *Shrew*, Ind., i, 12. **5** convincingly: "This do, and do it kindly, gentle sirs." *Shrew*, Ind., i, 64.

kindness, *n.* tenderness: "Fare ye well at once; my bosom is full of kindness . . ." *T Night*, II, i, 38.

kindred, *n.* **1** kinship: "Disclaiming here the kindred of the king,/ And lay aside my high blood's royalty . . ." *Rich 2*, I, i, 70–71. **2 of a great kindred,** of a large family: "Yes, in good sooth, the vice is of a great kindred . . ." *Meas*, III, ii, 97. **3 of no kindred,** that do not match: ". . . his horse hipped—with an/ old mothy saddle and stirrups of no kindred—" *Shrew*, III, ii, 46–47.

kine, *n. pl.* old plural of **cow:** ". . . if to be fat/ be to be hated, then Pharaoh's lean kine are to be/ loved." *1 Hen 4*, II, iv, 466–468.

kingdomed, *adj.* like a kingdom in which civil war rages: ". . . 'twixt his mental and his active parts/ Kingdom'd Achilles in commotion rages . . ." *Tr & Cr*, II, iii, 175–176.

King of kings, *n.* God: "He was a king bless'd of the King of kings." *1 Hen 6*, I, i, 28.

King of Scots, *n.* David II, captured in 1346 while Edward III was in France; imprisoned in London but never taken to France: ". . . not only well defended,/ But taken and impounded as a stray/ The King of Scots . . ." *Hen 5*, I, ii, 159–161.

kinsman, *n.* any [male] relative; here, a first cousin: "Let's after him . . . It is a peerless kinsman." *Mac*, I, iv, 56–58.

kirtle, *n.* gown with a very full skirt: "What stuff wilt have a kirtle of?" *2 Hen 4*, II, iv, 271.

kiss, *v.* **1 kiss one's hand,** gesture of courtesy or respect, as by a French gallant to his lady: "To see him kiss his hand! and how most sweetly a' will swear!" *Love's L*, IV, i, 147. **2 kiss the earth,** prostrate themselves: "Never saw I/ Wretches so quake: they kneel, they kiss the earth . . ." *W Tale*, V, i, 197–198. **3 kiss the fingers, a.** to kiss one's fingers as a peaceful overture: "I kiss these fingers for eternal peace." *1 Hen 6*, V, iii, 49. **b.** same as a courtly gesture: ". . . it had been better you had not kiss'd/ your three fingers so oft . . ." *Oth*, II, i, 172–173.

kissing carrion, *n.* rotted flesh kissed by the sun and breeding maggots; also, human flesh available for carnal pleasure: "For if the sun breed maggots in a dead dog, being a/ good kissing carrion . . ." *Ham*, II, ii, 181–182.

kissing-comfits, *n.* sweetmeats perfumed to sweeten the breath: ". . . hail kissing-comfits, and snow eringoes . . ." *Wives*, V, v, 20.

kiss the book, *v.* to take a drink from a bottle: "I can swim like a/ duck, I'll be sworn."/ "Here, kiss the book." *Temp,* II, ii, 129–131.

kiss the mistress, *n.* (in lawn bowling) to touch lightly the jack [target ball]: "So, so; rub/ on and kiss the mistress." *Tr & Cr,* III, ii, 48–49.

kitchen, *v.* to entertain (a person) in the kitchen: "There is a fat friend at your master's house,/ That kitchen'd me for you to-day at dinner . . ." *Errors,* V, i, 415.

kitchen-trull, *n.* kitchen-maid available for sexual use: ". . . our brags/ Were crak'd [boastful] of kitchen-trulls . . ." *Cymb,* V, v, 176–177.

kitchen-vestal, *n.* kitchen-maid humorously compared to a vestal virgin [charged in antiquity with keeping the temple fires burning]: "Certes she did, the kitchen-vestal scorn'd you." *Errors,* IV, iv, 73.

kite, *n.* **1** hawk; here, any bird of prey: ". . . our monuments/ Shall be the maws of kites." *Mac,* III, iv, 71–72. **2** bird of prey regarded contemptuously as a scavenger and the embodiment of evil: "[To Goneril.] Detested kite! thou liest." *Lear,* I, iv, 271. **3** whore: "Approach there! Ah, you kite! Now, gods and devils . . ." *Ant & Cleo,* III, xiii, 89.

knack, *n.* **1** [usually pl.] knickknacks: "Knacks, trifles, nosegays, sweetmeats (messengers/ Of strong prevailment in unharden'd youth) . . ." *M N Dream,* I, i, 34–35. **2** worthless thing; ref. here to Perdita: ". . . thou dost but sigh/ That thou no more shalt see this knack . . ." *W Tale,* IV, iv, 428–429. **3** [pl.] flowers [lit., ornaments]: "Th' enamell'd knacks o' th' mead or garden!" *Kinsmen,* III, i, 7.

knap, *v.* **1** to nibble; munch: ". . . as lying a gossip in that, as ever/ knapp'd ginger . . ." *Merch,* III, i, 8–9. **2** to strike or rap: ". . . she knapp'd/ 'em o' th' coxcombs with a stick . . ." *Lear,* II, iv, 123–124.

knave, *n.* **1** rogue; villain: ". . . if a Christian do not play/ the knave and get thee, I am much deceived . . ." *Merch,* II, iii, 11–12. **2** young male servant; boy; here, used affectionately: "What, thou speak'st drowsily?/ Poor knave, I blame thee not . . ." *J Caes,* IV, iii, 239–240. **3** male servant or other menial of any age: ". . . all I kept were knaves, to serve in meat to villains." *Timon,* IV, iii, 482. **4 bear the knave,** put up with being called "knave": ". . . for th'poorest piece/ Will bear the knave by th'volume [repeatedly]." *Cor,* III, iii, 32–33. **5 call (someone) knave,** to challenge (a person) to a duel: "'Tis not the first time I have constrained one to/ call me knave." *T Night,* II, iii, 68–69.

knavery, *n.* **1** mischief or mischance; here, at the hands of Hamlet's escorts: "They bear the mandate, they must sweep my way/ And marshal me to knavery." *Ham,* III, iv, 206–207. **2** michievous trick: "This is a knavery of them/ to make me afeard." *M N Dream,* III, i, 107–108. **3** [often pl.] tricks of dress; stylish adornments: "With amber bracelets, beads, and all this knavery." *Shrew,* IV, iii, 58.

knavish, *adj.* roguish; mischievous: "A knavish speech sleeps in a foolish ear." *Ham,* IV, ii, 22.

knead, *v.* **knead up,** to gather up; also, form or mold: "The civil citizens kneading up the honey . . ." *Hen 5,* I, ii, 199.

kneaded, *adj.* **kneaded clod,** lump of clay; clump of dirt: "This sensible warm motion to become/ A kneaded clod . . ." *Meas,* III, i, 119–120.

knee, *v.* **1** to kneel before: "I could as well be brought/ To knee his throne . . ." *Lear,* II, iv, 215–216. **2** to crawl on one's knees: "A mile before his tent fall down, and knee/ The way into his mercy." *Cor,* V, 5–6.
—*n.* **3** courtesy of kneeling: "And give them title, knee and approbation . . ." *Timon,* IV, iii, 37. **4** (often pl.) knee-timber; oak beams used in ship-building: ". . . the splitting wind/ Makes flexible the knees of knotted oaks . . ." *Tr & Cr,* I, iii, 49–50.

knell, *n.* tolling of a funeral bell: ". . . talks like a knell, and his hum is a battery." *Cor,* V, iv, 21.

knife, *n.* **lay knife aboard,** to establish or press one's claim: "O, there is a nobleman in town, one Paris, that would fain/ lay knife aboard . . ." *Rom & Jul,* II, iv, 196–198.

knight, *n.* follower; also, votary: "Pardon, goddess of the night,/ Those that slew thy virgin knight . . ." *M Ado,* V, iii, 13–14.

knight-errant, *n.* (applied to a woman) a streetwalker by night: "Come, come, you she knight-errant, come!" *2 Hen 4,* V, iv, 23.

knit, *v.* **1** to tie or knot: "If thou hadst hands to help thee knit the cord." *T Andr,* II, iv, 10. **2** to join; combine: "By that which knitteth souls and prospers loves . . ." *M N Dream,* I, i, 172. **3 knit a knot,** to mend; salvage: "No, he shall not knit a knot in his/ fortunes with the finger of my substance . . ." *Wives,* III, ii, 68–69. **4 knit up, a.** to tie together; fasten: "Sleep, that knits up the ravell'd sleave of care . . ." *Mac,* II, ii, 36. **b.** bound up; engrossed: "And these mine enemies are all knit up/ In their distractions . . ." *Temp,* III, iii, 89–90.
—*n.* **5** style; design: ". . . their blue coats brushed, and their/ garters of an indifferent [matching] knit." *Shrew,* IV, i, 81–82.

knock, *v.* **1** to strike: "As rushing out of doors, to be resolv'd/ If Brutus so unkindly knock'd or no . . ." *J Caes,* III, ii, 181–182. **2 knock it,** to strike up [music]: ". . . let's dream/ Who's best in favour. Let the music knock it." *Hen 8,* I, iv, 107–108.
—*n.* **3** blow, esp. with the fist; cuff: "A thing/ More slavish did I ne'er than answering/ A slave without a knock." *Cymb,* IV, ii, 72–74. **4** beating: "Gallows and knock are too powerful/ on the highway . . ." *W Tale,* IV, iii, 28–29.

knog, *v.* Parson's pron. of "knock": "I will knog his/ urinals [testicles] about his knave's costard . . ." *Wives,* III, i, 13–14.

knoll, *v.* var. of **knell;** to summon by a bell or bells; toll: "If ever been where bells have knoll'd to church . . ." *As You,* II, vii, 114.

knot, *n.* **1** small group: "His ancient knot of dangerous adversaries/ Tomorrow are let blood at Pomfret castle . . ." *Rich 3,* III, i, 182–183. **2** bunch or gang: "You knot of mouth-friends!" *Timon,* III, vi, 84. **3** intricate pattern of flowerbeds: "Her knots disordered, and her wholesome herbs/ Swarming with caterpillars?" *Rich 2,* III, iv, 46–47. **4** marriage: ". . . Richmond aims/ At young Elizabeth, my brother's daughter,/ And by that knot looks proudly on the crown . . ." *Rich 3,* IV, iii, 40–42.
—*v.* **5** to cluster: "Or keep it as a cistern, for foul toads/ To knot and gender [procreate] in!" *Oth,* IV, ii, 62–63.

knot-grass, *n.* clinging weed, thought to stunt the growth of animals and children: "You minimus, of hindering knot-grass made . . ." *M N Dream,* III, ii, 329.

knotty-pated, *adj.* blockheaded: "Why, thou/ clay-brained guts, thou knotty-pated fool . . ." *1 Hen 4,* II, iv, 221–222.

know, *v.* **1** to learn; bother to find out: ". . . he will neither know how to maintain it,/ Nor cease his flow of riot." *Timon,* II, i, 2–3. **2** know how: "Then why should he despair that knows to court it/ With words, fair looks, and liberality?" *T Andr,* II, i, 91–92. **3** to indulge; bear with: "I'll know his humour, when he knows his time [the appropriate time]." *J Caes,* IV, iii, 135. **4** to await: "Up, sword, and know thou a more horrid hent [opportunity] . . ." *Ham,* III, iii, 87. **5** wordplay on "learn" and "have carnal knowledge of": "I am come to

know your pleasure."/ "[aside] That you might know it, would much better please me . . ." *Meas,* II, iv, 31–33. **6 I know what,** I mean what I say: "This trick may chance to scathe you. I know what." *Rom & Jul,* I, v, 83. **7 know for,** be aware of: ". . . he might have/ moe diseases than he knew for." *2 Hen 4,* I, ii, 3–4. **8 knowing all measures,** See **measure** (def. 11). **9 know more hereafter,** (to) hear about this later: "I am not of your element: you shall/ know more hereafter." *T Night,* III, iv, 125–126. **10 know of,** take into consideration: "Therefore, fair Hermia, question your desires,/ Know of your youth, examine well your blood . . ." *M N Dream,* I, i, 67–68. **11 let us know,** to pay attention to: ". . . let us know/ Our indiscretion sometime serves us well . . ." *Ham,* V, ii, 7–8. **12 yet to know,** not generally known: ". . . 'tis yet to know—/ Which, when I know that boasting is an honour,/ I shall provulgate—" *Oth,* I, ii, 19–21.

knowing, *adj.* **1** knowledgeable; discerning: "Sith you have heard, and with a knowing ear . . ." *Ham,* IV, vii, 3.
—*n.* **2** knowledge, experience or refinement: ". . . as suits, with gentlemen of your knowing,/ to a stranger of his quality." *Cymb,* I, v, 27–28.

knowingly, *adv.* confidently; assuredly: "Dost thou believe't?"/ "Ay, madam, knowingly." *All's W,* I, iii, 244–245.

knowledge, *n.* source of knowledge [about]: "Gower is a good captain, and is good knowledge,/ and literatured in the wars." *Hen 5,* IV, vii, 153–154.

known, *adj.* **1** undisguised; deliberate: "To bear love's wrong than hate's known injury." *Sonn 40,* 12. **2** declared; proclaimed: "Or do you purpose/ A victor shall be known—" *Tr & Cr,* IV, v, 66–67. **3 known and feeling sorrows,** deep sorrows I have experienced: ". . . by the art of [instructed by] known and feeling sorrows,/ Am pregnant to good pity." *Lear,* IV, vi, 223–224.

known aright, *adj.* known by my right name: "When I am known aright, you shall not grieve/ Lending me this acquaintance." *Lear,* IV, iii, 54–55.

known together, *v.* been acquainted: "Sir, we have known together in Orleans." *Cymb,* I, v, 33.

— L —

la, *interj.* **1** meaningless word used to emphasize what follows or has preceded it: "... your colour ... is as red as any rose, in good/ truth, la!" *2 Hen 4,* II, iv, 25–26. **2 la you,** *exclam.* to gain another's attention; look you; look here: "La you, and you speak ill of the devil, how he/ takes it at heart!" *T Night,* III, iv, 101–102.

label, *n.* **1** strip of parchment attached to a document for affixing the seal; here, a deed that cancels the first [marriage] contract: "And ere this hand, by thee to Romeo's seal'd,/ Shall be the label to another deed ..." *Rom & Jul,* IV, i, 56–57. —*v.* **2** to attach; esp. to stick or paste: "It shall be/ inventoried, and every particle and utensil/ labelled to my will." *T Night,* I, v, 248–250.

labor, *v.* **1** to be anxious; agonize: "Whom whilst I labour'd of a [out of] love to see ..." *Errors,* I, i, 130. **2** to make mischief; here, to grind things not meant to be ground and to keep milk from being churned into butter: "Skim milk, and sometimes labour in the quern,/ And bootless make the breathless housewife churn ..." *M N Dream,* II, i, 36–37. **3** to work for: "... swore with sobs/ That he would labour my delivery." *Rich 3,* I, iv, 235–236. —*n.* **4** intense effort or painful exertion; here, in pursuing sports for pleasure: "There be some sports are painful, and their labour/ Delight in them sets off [effort is compensated for by the pleasure they give] ..." *Temp,* III, i, 1–2. **5** [pl] service: "... thy master, whom thou lov'st,/ Shall find thee full of labours." *Lear,* I, iv, 6–7. **6** diligence: "Have you observ'd him/ Since our great lord departed?"/ "With much labor ..." *Kinsmen,* I, iii, 33–34.

labored, *adj.* accomplished; complete: "And you are her labour'd scholar." *Per,* II, iii, 17.

laboring, *adj.* struggling to give birth: "Even in the birth of our own labouring breath." *Tr & Cr,* IV, iv, 37.

laborsome, *adj.* requiring great pains; elaborate: "... forget/ Your laboursome and dainty trims ..." *Cymb,* III, iv, 165–166.

labras, *n.* Pistol's pseudo-Latin for "lips": "Word of denial in thy labras here!" *Wives,* I, i, 147.

lace, *v.* **1** to adorn: "That sin by him advantage should achieve/ And lace itself with his society?" *Sonn 67,* 3–4. —*n.* **2 cut my lace,** to cut the laces of one's bodice as an indication of one's vexation or, here, grief: "Cut my lace, Charmian, come,/ But let it be ..." *Ant & Cleo,* I, iii, 71–72.

Lacedaemon, *n.* ancient name of Sparta: "To Lacedaemon did my land extend." *Timon,* II, ii, 155.

laced mutton, *n.* woman in a tightly laced bodice; often a term for "loose woman," but prob. understood here as "attractive young woman": "I (a lost mutton) gave your letter to her (a/ laced mutton) ..." *Two Gent,* I, i, 95–96.

lack, *v.* **1** to regret the absence of; here, do without: "Alas, dear love, I cannot lack thee two hours." *As You,* IV, i, 169. —*n.* **2 our lack,** all that remains for us to do: "... our power is ready;/ Our lack is nothing but our leave." *Mac,* IV, iii, 236–237.

'lack, *interj.* alack: "'Lack, to what end?" *Cymb,* V, iii, 59.

lacked, *adj.* missed: "I shall be lov'd when I am lack'd." *Cor,* IV, i, 15.

lackey, *n.* **1** servant who ran errands and often ran ahead of his master's horse or other conveyance; running footman: "In a retreat/ he outruns any lackey ..." *All's W,* IV, iii, 280–281. —*v.* **2** to follow subserviently in the manner of a lackey: "Goes to, and back, lackeying the varying tide ..." *Ant & Cleo,* I, iv, 46.

lack-linen, *adj.* having no shirt: ". . . you poor, base, rascally, cheating, lack-linen/mate!" *2 Hen 4,* II, iv, 121–122.

lack-love, *n.* one unable to love: "Pretty soul, she durst not lie/ Near this lack-love . . ." *M N Dream,* II, ii, 75–76.

lack-lustre, *adj.* solemn; mirthless: ". . . he drew a dial from his poke,/ And looking on it, with lack-lustre eye,/ Says very wisely, 'It is ten o'clock . . .'" *As You,* II, vii, 20–22.

lad, *n.* fellow [term of address, not necessarily to one younger]: "Thy counsel, lad, smells of no cowardice." *T Andr,* II, i, 132.

ladder-tackle, *n.* rope ladder: "And from the ladder-tackle washes off/ A canvas-climber." *Per,* IV, i, 60–61.

lade, *v.* to ladle (out); empty: "Saying he'll lade it dry to have his way . . ." *3 Hen 6,* III, ii, 139.

lading, *n.* cargo: ". . . o'erlook/ What shipping and what lading's in our haven . . ." *Per,* I, ii, 49–50.

lady, *n.* **1** any woman: ". . . swear before you choose, if you choose wrong/ Never to speak to lady afterward . . ." *Merch,* II, i, 40–41. **2 lady, ladies, woman,** any lady, all ladies, all womankind: "And that she hath all courtly parts more exquisite/ Than lady, ladies, woman . . ." *Cymb,* III, v, 72–73.

Lady Fame, *n.* personification of gossip: "Troth, my lord, I have played the part of Lady Fame." *M Ado,* II, i, 198.

Lady Lucy, *n.* charge that Edward had been betrothed to Elizabeth Lucy and was arranging a dynastic marriage in France, both of which invalidated his marriage to Elizabeth Grey; here, an attempt to bastardize Edward's heirs: ". . . with his contract with Lady Lucy,/ And his contract by deputy in France . . ." *Rich 3,* III, vii, 5–6.

Lady Margery, *n.* hen; synon. with "Dame Partlet": "You that have been so tenderly officious/ With Lady Margery . . ." *W Tale,* II, iii, 158–159.

Lady of the Strachy, *n.* not identified; prob. Shakespeare's coinage: "The Lady of the Strachy/ married the yeoman of the wardrobe." *T Night,* II, v, 39–40.

La fin couronne les oeuvres, [French] The end crowns [all] one's deeds. *2 Hen 6,* V, ii, 28.

lag, *adv.* **1** tardily: ". . . the countermand,/ That came too lag to see him buried." *Rich 3,* II, i, 90–91.
—*adj.* **2** late; final: ". . . gout and rheum, that in lag hours attend/ For grey approachers . . ." *Kinsmen,* V, iv, 8–9. **3 lag of**

a, younger than [lit., behind]: "I am some twelve or fourteen moonshines/ Lag of a brother?" *Lear,* I, ii, 5–6.

lag end, *n.* tail end: "They may . . . 'oui' away/ The lag end of their lewdness [lechery] . . ." *Hen 8,* I, iii, 34–35.

laid[1], *past part.* set with traps or snares: "I hid me in these woods and durst not peep out, for all/ the country is laid for me . . ." *2 Hen 6,* IV, x, 3–4.

laid[2], *past part.* **1 and your head were laid,** if you were dead: "[Aside] I'll blast his harvest, and your head were laid . . ." *3 Hen 6,* V, vii, 21. **2 laid up,** See **lay[1]** (def. 17).

Lake of Darkness, *n.* (in Greek myth.) the stygian lake of Hades: "Fraterretto calls me, and tells me Nero is an/ angler in the Lake of Darkness." *Lear,* III, vi, 6–7.

lakin, *n.* Ladykin, dim. of "Lady," esp. in the phrase "By 'r lakin" [by Our Lady, a mild oath]: "By 'r lakin, I can go no further, sir . . ." *Temp,* III, iii, 1.

lame, *v.* **1** to cause to seem crippled or deformed [by comparison]: ". . . for feature [beautiful form], laming/ The shrine of Venus . . ." *Cymb,* V, v, 163–164. **2 lame the foot of,** to hobble or cripple [fig. use]: "Unless, by using means, I lame the foot/ Of our design." *Cor,* IV, vii, 7–8.
—*adj.* **3 lame of sense,** impaired in strength: "(Being not deficient, blind, or lame of sense,)" *Oth,* I, iii, 63.

lamenting doings, *n. pl.* lamentable affairs; lamentations: "How would he hang his slender gilded wings,/ And buzz lamenting doings in the air!" *T Andr,* III, ii, 61–62.

Lammas-tide, *n.* August 1, a church festival of early harvest: "She's not fourteen. How long is it now/ To Lammas-tide?" *Rom & Jul,* I, iii, 14–15.

lamp, *n.* [usually pl.] the eyes: "My wasting lamps some fading glimmer left . . ." *Errors,* V, i, 315.

lampass, *n.* swellings in a horse's gums and in the roof of its mouth: ". . . troubled with the lampass, infected/ with the fashions, full of windgalls . . ." *Shrew,* III, ii, 49–50.

Lancaster, *n.* Bolingbroke insists on being addressed as the Duke of Lancaster, his rightful title following the death of his father: "My lord, my answer is—to Lancaster . . . And I must find that title in your tongue . . ." *Rich 2,* II, iii, 70–72.

lance, *n.* spear; here, armed soldier: "And turn our impress'd lances in our eyes/ Which do command them." *Lear,* V, iii, 51–52.

lanched, *adj.* old form of **lanced;** pierced: ". . . he charges home/ My unprovided body, lanch'd mine arm . . ." *Lear,* II, i, 51–52.

land, *n.* **1 a several land,** a different route: "The Duke has lost Hippolyta; each took/ A several land." *Kinsmen,* III, i, 1–2. **2 lands,** poss. mistake for **launds,** clearings in wooded areas: "The passages of alleys, creeks and narrow lands . . ." *Errors,* IV, ii, 38.

land-damn, *v.* perh. to thrash soundly: ". . . would I knew the villain,/ I would land-damn him." *W Tale,* II, i, 142–143.

landed, *adj.* possessed of lands: "That Slender, though well landed, is an idiot . . ." *Wives,* IV, iv, 85.

land-fish, *n.* something removed from its element, hence un-natural: "He's grown a very land-fish/, languageless, a mon-ster." *Tr & Cr,* III, iii, 262–263.

landmen, *n.* soldiers: "I have an absolute hope/ Our landmen will stand up." *Ant & Cleo,* IV, iii, 9–10.

land-service, *n.* **1** military service: ". . . my learned counsel in the/ laws of this land-service . . ." *2 Hen 4,* I, ii, 133–134. **2** events on land; here, as disting. from the storm and ship-wreck at sea: "And then for the land-service, to see how/ the bear tore out his shoulder-bone . . ." *W Tale,* III, iii, 94–95.

lane, *n.* **1** path; here, of slaughtered bodies: "Three times did Richard make a lane to me . . ." *3 Hen 6,* I, iv, 9. **2** pass; here, escape route: "We have th'advantage of the ground;/ The lane is guarded . . ." *Cymb,* V, ii, 11–12.

language, *n.* **1** expressiveness; here, expressive of wanton-ness: "Fie, fie upon her!/ There's language in her eye, her cheek, her lip—" *Tr & Cr,* IV, v, 55. **2 with lustful language broken,** words that interrupt the kisses: "And kissing speaks, with lustful language broken . . ." *Ven & Ad,* 47.

languish, *v.* **1** to pine; here, also in wordplay with "become sexually frustrated": ". . . will's free hours languish for/ As-sured bondage [bonds of matrimony]?" *Cymb,* I, vii, 72–73. —*n.* **2** wasting-away; lingering disease: "What, of death, too,/ That rids our dogs of languish?" *Ant & Cleo,* V, ii, 41–42.

languishing, *n.* **1** lingering illness: "To cure the desperate languishings whereof/ The king is render'd lost [thought to be dying]." *All's W,* I, iii, 224–225. —*adj.* **2** lingering; torturous: ". . . these most poisonous com-pounds,/ Which are the movers of a languishing death . . ." *Cymb,* I, vi, 8–9.

languor, *n.* grief: ". . . in the dust I write/ My heart's deep lan-guor and my soul's sad tears." *T Andr,* III, i, 12–13.

lank, *v.* to grow thin: ". . . borne so like a soldier, that thy cheek/ So much as lank'd not." *Ant & Cleo,* I, iv, 70–71.

lanthorn, *n.* lantern: ". . . yet cannot he/ see, though he have his own lanthorn to light him." *2 Hen 4,* I, ii, 47–48.

lap, *v.* **1** to wrap: "Your younger princely son . . . was lapp'd/ In a most curious mantle . . ." *Cymb,* V, v, 361–362. **2 lapped in proof,** clad in battle-tested armor: ". . . that Bellona's bridegroom, lapp'd in proof,/ Confronted him . . ." *Mac,* I, ii, 55–56. —*n.* **3 proud lap,** bosom of the earth: "Or from their proud lap pluck them where they grew . . ." *Sonn 98,* 8.

Lapland, *n.* northern land believed to be inhabited by witch-es and sorcerers: "Sure these are but imaginary wiles,/ And Lapland sorcerers inhabit here." *Errors,* IV, iii, 10–11.

lapse, *n.* **1** moral collapse: ". . . the staggers and the careless lapse/ Of youth and ignorance . . ." *All's W,* II, iii, 163–164. —*v.* **2** to slip into falsehood: ". . . with all the size that verity [truthfulness]/ Would without lapsing suffer [allow]." *Cor,* V, ii, 18–19. **3** to apprehend; take prisoner: ". . . if I be lapsed in this place,/ I shall pay dear." *T Night,* III, iii, 36–37. **4 lapse in fulness,** to lie when prosperous: "To lapse in fulness/ Is sorer than to lie for need . . ." *Cymb,* III, vi, 12–13.

lapsed, *adj.* **lapsed in time and passion,** negligent in both prompt ness and resolve: ". . . laps'd in time and passion, lets go by/ Th'important acting of your dread command?" *Ham,* III, iv, 108–109.

lapwing, *n.* **1** large bird of the plover family, noted for its swift running close to the ground: ". . . look where Beatrice like a lapwing runs/ Close by the ground, to hear our conference." *M Ado,* III, i, 24–25. **2** ref. to the hatchling, which runs about as soon as it emerges from the egg, proverbially with part of the shell still on its head; here, Osric has at last donned his hat: "This lapwing runs away with the shell on his head." *Ham,* V, ii, 183. **3** ref. to the lapwing's straying far from its nest: ". . . 'tis my familiar sin,/ With maids to seem the lapwing, and to jest/ Tongue far from heart . . ." *Meas,* I, iv, 31–32.

lard, *v.* to enrich or fatten; here, with blood: "In which array, brave soldier, doth he lie,/ Larding the plain . . ." *Hen 5,* IV, vi, 7–8.

larded, *adj.* **1** strewn; adorned: "Larded with sweet flowers/ Which bewept to the grave did not go . . ." *Ham,* IV, v, 38–39. **2** garnished: ". . . an exact command,/ Larded with many sev-eral sorts of reasons . . ." *Ham,* V, ii, 19–20. **3** mixed together: "The mirth whereof so larded with my matter . . ." *Wives,* IV, vi, 14.

large, *adj.* **1** broad; improper or coarse: ". . . it seems not in him by some large jests he/ will make." *M Ado,* II, iii, 191–192. **2** wordplay on "lengthy" and "indecent" or "erect": "Thou wouldst else have made thy tale large." *Rom & Jul,* II, iv, 96. **3** impressive; fine-sounding: "And your large speeches may your deeds approve." *Lear,* I, i, 184. **4** unrestrained; free or licentious: "Only the adulterous Antony, most large/ In his abominations . . ." *Ant & Cleo,* III, vi, 93–94. **5** complete: "This little abstract doth contain that large/ Which died in Geoffrey . . ." *K John,* II, 1, 101–102.
—*adv.* **6 at large, a.** in their full size: "The baby figure of the giant mass/ Of things to come at large." *Tr & Cr,* I, iii, 345–346. **b.** at length; in full: "A gentleman of mine I have dispatch'd/ With letters of your love to her at large." *Rich 2,* III, i, 40–41.

largely, *adv.* **1** fully; in detail: "I'll tell you largely of fair Hero's death." *M Ado,* V, iv, 69. **2** generously: ". . . have given largely to many to know/ what she would have given . . ." *Wives,* II, ii, 193–194.

largess, *n.* gift; offering: "Over and beside/ Signor Baptista's liberality./ I'll mend it with a largess." *Shrew,* I, ii, 147–149.

larron, *n.* [French] thief: "Villainy,/ larron! [Pulling Simple out] Rugby, my rapier!" *Wives,* I, iv, 62–63.

'larum or **larum,** *n.* [often pl] alarums; call to arms: "Remaineth nought but to inter our brethren,/ And with loud 'larums welcome them to Rome." *T Andr,* I, i, 146–147.

lash, *v.* **1** to punish; scourge: ". . . headstrong liberty is lash'd with woe." *Errors,* II, i, 15.
—*n.* **2** cord of a whip: "Her whip of cricket's bone, the lash of film [gossamer] . . ." *Rom & Jul,* I, iv, 66.

lass-lorn, *adj.* forsaken by his lady: "Whose shadow the dismissed bachelor loves,/ Being lass-lorn . . ." *Temp,* IV, i, 67–68.

last, *v.* **1 last love,** to continue or survive as love: "But that it bear this trial and last love . . ." *Love's L,* V, ii, 795.
—*adv.* **2** at the end; finally: "If thou wilt leave me, do not leave me last . . ." *Sonn 90,* 9.

last day, *n.* Judgment Day: "O! let the vile world end,/ And the premised flames of the last day . . ." *2 Hen 6,* V, ii, 40–41.

latch, *v.* **1** to anoint; dab; smear: ". . . hast thou yet latch'd the Athenian's eyes/ With the love-juice, as I did bid thee do?" *M N Dream,* III, ii, 36–37. **2** to catch: ". . . words,/ That would be howl'd out in the desert air,/ Where hearing should not latch them." *Mac,* IV, iii, 192–194. **3** to catch sight of: "For it no form delivers to the heart/ Of bird, of flower, or shape which it doth latch . . ." *Sonn 113,* 5–6.

late, *adv.* **1** lately; recently: "And late, five thousand; to Varro and to Isidore/ He owes nine thousand . . ." *Timon,* II, i, 1–2. **2 late ago,** recently; short time ago: ". . . the vows/ We made each other but so late ago." *T Night,* V, i, 212–213. **3 too late,** most recently: ". . . but now grow fearful,/ By what yourself too late have spoke and done . . ." *Lear,* I, iv, 214–215.
—*adj.* **4** recent: ". . . the boist'rous late appeal,/ Which then our leisure would not let us hear . . ." *Rich 2,* I, i, 4–5. **5** lately or recently appointed: "And now to our French causes:/ Who are the late commissioners?" *Hen 5,* II, ii, 60–61.

late-betrayed, *adj.* which has just now been betrayed: "As sure as in this late-betrayed town/ Great Coeur-de-lion's heart was buried . . ." *1 Hen 6,* III, ii, 82–83.

lated, *adj.* belated, as a traveler overtaken by darkness; delayed or tardy: "Now spurs the lated traveller apace,/ To gain the timely inn . . ." *Mac,* III, iii, 6–7.

late footed, *adj.* lately landed: ". . . the traitors/ Late footed in the kingdom?" *Lear,* III, vii, 44–45.

lately, *adv.* recently; not long ago: "I saw you lately,/ When you caught hurt in parting two that fought." *Per,* IV, i, 86–87.

latest, *pron.* **1** last part: "The latest of my wealth I'll share amongst you." *Timon,* IV, ii, 23.
—*adj.* **2** last; final: ". . . the very latest counsel/ That ever I shall breathe." *2 Hen 4,* IV, v, 182–183.

lath, *n.* **1** wood: "If I do not beat thee out of thy kingdom/ with a dagger of lath . . ." *1 Hen 4,* II, iv, 133–134. **2** wooden sword, as that used by actors or as a child's toy: ". . . have your lath glued within your sheath/ Till you know better how to handle it." *T Andr,* II, i, 41–42.

latten bilbo, *n.* one with an inferior sword made of a base alloy [latten] resembling brass: "I combat challenge of this latten bilbo." *Wives,* I, i, 146.

latter, *adj.* **1** very last: "And in his bosom spend my latter gasp." *1 Hen 6,* II, v, 38. **2** later; more recent: "These well express in thee thy latter spirits." *Timon,* V, iv, 74.

latter-born, *adj.* (of twins) being the second born: "My wife, more careful for the latter-born,/ Had fasten'd him unto a small spare mast . . ." *Errors,* I, i, 78–79.

latter end, *n.* Bottom's redundancy for "end" or "finale": "I will sing it in the latter end/ of a play, before the Duke." *M N Dream,* IV, i, 215–216.

latter spring, *n.* late spring; here, in fig. use, spry old age: "Farewell, the latter spring!" *1 Hen 4,* I, ii, 154.

laud, *n.* **1** praise: "Thou back'st reproach against long-living laud . . ." *Luc,* 622. **2** hymn of praise: ". . . mermaid-like awhile they bore her up,/ Which time she chanted snatches of old lauds . . ." *Ham,* IV, vii, 175–176.

laugh, *v.* **1** to happily look forward to: "For what we lack/ We laugh, for what we have are sorry . . ." *Kinsmen,* V, iv, 132–133. **2 laugh mortal,** [the gods would] laugh themselves into being mortal; also, perh., laugh at men as men do at apes: ". . . who, with our spleens [emotions],/ Would all themselves laugh mortal." *Meas,* II, ii, 123–124.

laughter, *n.* **1** source or object of laughter; one not to be taken seriously: "Were I a common laughter . . . then hold me danger ous." *J Caes,* I, ii, 71–77. **2** first to laugh wins; from old proverb, "He laughs that wins": "The wager?"/ "A laughter."/ "A match!" *Temp,* II, i, 31–33. **3 return to laughter,** to change for the better: "The lamentable change is from the best;/ The worst returns to laughter." *Lear,* IV, i, 5–6.

launch, *v.* to lance: "O Antony,/ I have follow'd thee to this, but we do launch/ Diseases in our bodies." *Ant & Cleo,* V, i, 35–37.

laund, *n.* open, grassy area surrounded by woods; glade: "For through this laund anon the deer will come . . ." *3 Hen 6,* III, i, 2.

laundry, *n.* parson's blunder for "laundress": ". . . which is in the manner of his nurse . . . or his cook; or his laundry . . ." *Wives,* I, ii, 3–4.

Laus Deo, bone intelligo, [Latin] Praise God, I understand well. *Love's L,* V, i, 26.

Lavatch, *n.* appar. the Clown's surname, poss. La Vache given an Anglicized pronunciation: "Good Master Lavatch, give my Lord Lafew this/ letter . . ." *All's W,* V, ii, 1–2.

lave, *v.* to wash: "Basins and ewers to lave her dainty hands . . ." *Shrew,* II, i, 341.

lavish, *adj.* **1** unrestrained; also, profligate or licentious: ". . . rage and hot blood are his counsellors,/ When means and lavish manners meet together . . ." *2 Hen 4,* IV, iv, 63–64. **2** insolent; rebellious: "Confronted him . . . rebellious arm 'gainst arm,/ Curbing his lavish spirit . . ." *Mac,* I, ii, 56–58. **3** overready or overgenerous: "And choke the lavish tongue when it doth utter/ The breath of falsehood not charactered there!" *Edw 3,* II, i, 307–308.

lavolt, *n.* **the high lavolt,** the lavolta, a dance for two persons, char. by high leaps: "I cannot sing,/ Nor heel the high lavolt . . ." *Tr & Cr,* IV, iv, 84–85.

law, *n.* **1 answer of the law,** answer in a court of law to the charges brought against them: "Their faults are open:/ Arrest them to the answer of the law . . ." *Hen 5,* II, ii, 142–143. **2 blow of the law,** punishment for breaking a law: "A good note; that keeps you from the blow of/ the law." *T Night,* III, iv, 154–155. **3 form of law,** established order of legal procedure: "Did he not, contrary to form of law,/ Devise strange deaths for small offences done?" *2 Hen 6,* III, i, 58–59. **4 let the law go whistle,** we will be beyond the reach of the law: ". . . this being/ done, let the law go whistle . . ." *W Tale,* IV, iv, 697–698. **5 pull the law upon you,** to feel the full force of the law: "Whether you had not sometime in your life/ Err'd in this point . . . And pull'd the law upon you." *Meas,* II, i, 14–16. —*interj.* **6** prob. a corrupt form of "la": "And to begin: Wench,/ —so God help me, law!—"*Love's L,* V, ii, 414.

lawless, *adj.* **1** unrestrained; unruly: ". . . to be worse than worst/ Of those that lawless and incertain thought/ Imagine howling . . ." *Meas,* III, i, 125–127. **2** mad; crazy: "In his lawless fit,/ Behind the arras hearing something stir,/ Whips out his rapier . . ." *Ham,* IV, i, 8–9. **3** not conforming to Christian doctrine: ". . . to be worse than worst/ Of those that lawless and incertain thought/ Imagine howling . . ." *Meas,* III, i, 125–126.

lawn, *n.* fine linen fabric: "Like lawn being spread upon the blushing rose . . ." *Ven & Ad,* 590.

law of arms, *n.* law whereby fighting within the monarch's residence was punishable by death: ". . . the law of arms is such/ That whoso draws a sword, 'tis present [immediate] death . . ." *1 Hen 6,* III, iv, 38–39.

law of nature, *n.* survival of the fittest: "I see no/ reason in the law of nature but I may snap at him . . ." *2 Hen 4,* III, ii, 325–326.

law of writ, *n.* prob. ref. to those plays adhering to classic rules of composition: "For the law of writ, and the liberty, these are/ the only men." *Ham,* II, ii, 397–398.

lawyer, *n.* here, a person hired to petition on behalf of another: "I will make/ One of her women lawyer to me . . ." *Cymb,* II, iii, 72–73.

lay¹, *v.* **1** past tense of **lie,** to lodge; live: "I remember at Mile-End Green, when I lay at/ Clement's Inn . . ." *2 Hen 4,* III, ii, 274–275. **2** to bet; wager: "I'll lay my head to any good man's hat . . ." *Love's L,* I, i, 299. **3** to apply: "Lay not that flattering unction to your soul . . ." *Ham,* III, iv, 147. **4** to allay; keep down: "To use his eyes for garden water-pots,/ Ay, and lay-ing autumn's dust." *Lear,* IV, vi, 198–199. **5** to knock down: "Who in a moment even with the earth/ Shall lay your stately and air-braving towers . . ." *1 Hen 6,* IV, ii, 12–13. **6 lay about him,** to strike out in all directions: ". . . he'll lay/ about him today, I can tell them that . . ." *Tr & Cr,* I, ii, 56–57. **7 lay by a.** Put down (your weapons); the command of a robber to his victim: ". . . got with swearing/ 'Lay by!', and spent with cry-ing 'Bring in!'" *1 Hen 4,* I, ii, 35–36. **b.** to put aside; renounce: ". . . laying by/ That nothing-gift of differing multitudes . . ." *Cymb,* III, vii, 57–58. **8 lay by the heels,** to put in the stocks: "If the king blame me for't, I'll lay ye all/ By th' heels . . ." *Hen 8,* V, iii, 77–78. **9 lay (someone) down, a.** to convince by the use of: "I will lay him down such reasons for this adventure/ that he shall go." *1 Hen 4,* I, ii, 145–146. **b.** to seduce: ". . . the sly whoresons/ Have got a speeding trick to lay down la-dies." *Hen 8,* I, iii, 39–40. **10 lay fair,** to smooth; put in order: "Have you laid fair the bed?" *2 Hen 6,* III, ii, 11. **11 lay for,** to ambush: "I'll cheer up/ My discontented troops, and lay for hearts" [attempt to win sympathizers]. *Timon,* III, v, 115–116. **12 lay home to,** See **home** (def. 11). **13 lay her off,** steer the ship away from shore: "Lay her a-hold, a-hold! set her two courses; off to/ sea again; lay her off." *Temp,* I, i, 49–50. **14 lay it on,** do it well: "I would I could see/ this taborer; he lays it on." *Temp,* III, ii, 148–149. **15 lay on,** to strike; attack; exchange blows: ". . . lay on, Macduff,/ And damn'd be him that first cries, 'Hold, enough!'" *Mac,* V, viii, 33–34. **16 lay out, a.** to advance money for expenses out of one's pocket: "Will you give me money, captain?/ Lay out, lay out." *1 Hen 4,* IV, ii, 5. **b.** to wager: "And laid mine honour too unchary out . . ." *T Night,* III, iv, 204. **17 lay up,** to pack or store away: ". . . you shall see him laugh till/ his face be like a wet cloak ill laid up." *2 Hen 4,* V, i, 81–82.

—*n.* **18** wager; bet: "My soul and body on the action both!"/ "A dreadful lay!" *2 Hen 6,* V, ii, 26–27.

lay², *n.* song: "She sings like one immortal, and she dances/ As goddess-like to her admired lays." *Per,* V, Chor., 4.

lay³, *n.* layman: ". . . had he been lay, my lord . . . I had swing'd him soundly." *Meas,* V, i, 131–133.

layer-up, *n.* preserver: ". . . old age, that ill layer-up of beau-ty . . ." *Hen 5,* V, ii, 242.

laying on, *n.* mighty exchange of blows: ". . . there's no jest-ing,/ there's laying on, take't off who will . . ." *Tr & Cr,* I, ii, 208–209.

lay-to, *v.* to busy; set to work: "Monster, lay-to your fingers: help to bear this away . . ." *Temp,* IV, i, 250.

lazar, *n.* leper; in general use, a beggar [fr. Lazarus, name of Biblical leper]: "I'll/ be sworn and sworn upon't, she never shrouded/ any but lazars." *Tr & Cr,* II, iii, 33–35.

lazar kite, *n.* leprous whore: "Fetch forth the lazar kite of Cressid's kind . . ." *Hen 5,* II, i, 76.

lazar-like, *adj.* resembling a leper [fr. Lazarus, Biblical lep-er]: "Most lazar-like, with vile and loathsome crust/ All my smooth body." *Ham,* I, v, 72–73.

lazy, *adj.* (of time) sluggish; slow to pass: "How shall we be-guile/ The lazy time, if not with some delight?" *M N Dream,* V, i, 40–41.

lea, *n.* pasture; grassland: ". . . thy rich leas/ Of wheat, rye, barley, vetches, oats, and pease . . ." *Temp,* IV, i, 60–61.

lead¹, *n.* **1** inner coffin of lead: ". . . the loss of those great towns/ Will make him burst his lead and rise from death." *1 Hen 6,* I, i, 63–64. **2** [pl.] roofs covered with lead sheeting: "You have help to . . . melt the city leads upon your pates . . ." *Cor,* IV, vi, 82–83.

lead², *v.* **1** to keep up; maintain: ". . . thou but leadest this fashion of thy malice/ To the last hour of act . . ." *Merch,* IV, i, 18–19. **2** to lead to: "Delay leads impotent and snail-pac'd beggary . . ." *Rich 3,* IV, iii, 53. **3 lead away,** to lead astray; beguile or seduce: "How many gazers mightst thou lead away . . ." *Sonn 96,* 11.

leaden, *adj.* **1** blunt; blunted: "To you our swords have leaden points, Mark Antony . . ." *J Caes,* III, i, 173. **2** heavy, as with sleep: "O murd'rous slumber!/ Layest thou thy leaden mace upon my boy . . ." *J Caes,* IV, iii, 266–267. **3** lacking spirit or enthusiasm: "If he be leaden, icy, cold, unwilling,/ Be thou so too . . ." *Rich 3,* III, i, 176–177.

leaden sword, *n.* mock weapon, as a stage prop: "You leer upon me, do you? there's an eye/ Wounds like a leaden sword." *Love's L,* V, ii, 480–481.

leaders, *n.* those leading the dance: "We must follow the/ leaders." *M Ado,* II, i, 140–141.

leading, *n.* command of troops; generalship: "Being men of such great leading as you are . . ." *1 Hen 4,* IV, iii, 17.

leaf, *n.* sheet, as of metal: "I will go get a leaf of brass,/ And with a gad of steel will write these words . . ." *T Andr,* IV, i, 102–103.

leaf of pity, *n.* list of things exciting pity: ". . . those milk-paps . . . Are not within the leaf of pity writ . . ." *Timon,* IV, iii, 117–119.

league¹, *n.* **1** friendship; alliance; mutual love: "I am sworn brother, sweet/ To grim Necessity, and he and I/ Will keep a league till death." *Rich 2,* V, i, 20–22. **2** agreement, esp. a treaty concluding hostilities: "We come to be informed . . . What the conditions of that league must be." *1 Hen 6,* V, iv, 118–119.

league², *n.* **1** unit of measuring distance, roughly 3 to 4 miles: "A league from Epidamnum had we sail'd . . ." *Errors,* I, i, 62. **2 ten leagues beyond man's life,** considerably farther than a man may live to travel; used here as hyperbole: ". . . she that dwells/ Ten leagues beyond man's life . . ." *Temp,* II, i, 241–242.

leagued, *adj.* crossed; folded: "His arms thus leagu'd, I thought he slept . . ." *Cymb,* IV, ii, 213.

leaguer, *n.* camp [military jargon]: ". . . he shall suppose . . . he is carried into the leaguer of the adversaries . . ." *All's W,* III, vi, 23–24.

leak, *v.* to urinate: ". . . we leak in your chimney, and your chamber-lye/ breeds fleas like a loach." *1 Hen 4,* II, i, 19–20.

lean¹, *v.* **1** to be on the verge of falling: "To be depender on a thing that leans?" *Cymb,* I, vi, 58. **2 lean on,** (to) pertain to: ". . . for everything is seal'd and done/ That else leans on th'affair." *Ham,* IV, iii, 59–60. **3 lean to,** to incline to the profession of: ". . . bawd I'll turn,/ And something lean to cutpurse of quick hand." *Hen 5,* V, i, 89–90. **4 lean unto,** to obey: ". . . 'twere good/ You lean'd unto his sentence . . ." *Cymb,* I, ii, 8–9. **5 lean upon,** prob. character's misuse for "support" or "uphold": "I do lean upon/ justice, sir . . ." *Measure,* II, i, 48–49.

lean², *adj.* **1** meager; scanty: "Out of my lean and low ability/ I'll lend you something." *T Night,* III, iv, 352–353. **2** barren: ". . . he hath like lean, sterile, and/ bare land manured . . ." *2 Hen 4,* IV, iii, 117–118.

Leander, *n.* (in Greek legend) a youth who nightly swam the Hellespont to visit his lover Hero: ". . . in loving, Leander the good/ swimmer, Troilus the first employer of pandars . . ." *M Ado,* V, ii, 29–30.

lean-looked, *adj.* of a lean and, often, menacing appearance: ". . . lean-look'd prophets whisper fearful change . . ." *Rich 2,* II, iv, 11.

leap, *v.* **1** to be delighted: "What, doth his highness leap to hear these news?" *Edw 3,* II, ii, 13. **2** to skip or dance about: "How will he scorn! how will he spend his wit!/ How will he triumph, leap, and laugh at it!" *Love's L,* IV, iii, 144–145. **3** to copulate with: "And some such strange bull leap'd your

father's cow . . ." *M Ado,* V, iv, 49. **4 leap into,** to win; achieve: ". . . I should/ quickly leap into a wife." *Hen 5,* V, ii, 141–142.

leaped into my seat, had intercourse with my wife: "For that I do suspect the lustful Moor/ Hath leap'd into my seat . . ." *Oth,* II, i, 290–291.

leaping-house, *n.* brothel: "Unless hours were cups of sack . . . and dials/ the signs of leaping-houses . . ." *1 Hen 4,* I, ii, 7–9.

leaping time, *n.* time of [active] youth: "To have turn'd my leaping time into a crutch,/ Than have seen this." *Cymb,* IV, ii, 200–201.

learn, *v.* **1** to teach: "Sweet Prince, you learn me noble thankfulness." *M Ado,* IV, i, 29. **2** to tell; inform (someone) of: "Toadstool! Learn me the proclamation." *Tr & Cr,* II, i, 21.

learned, *adj.* educated; here, in the skills of governing: "If you are learn'd/ Be not as common fools . . ." *Cor,* III, i, 98–99.

lease, *n.* **1** term or span; lifetime: "And summer's lease hath all too short a date . . ." *Sonn 18,* 4. **2 hold in lease,** to have possession of temporarily: "So should that beauty which you hold in lease/ Find no determination . . ." *Sonn 13,* 5–6. **3 out by lease,** let or rented out: "Considers she my possessions?"/ "O, ay; and pities them . . . That they are out by lease." *Two Gent,* V, ii, 25–29.

lease of Nature, *n.* one's normal span of life: ". . . our highplac'd Macbeth/ Shall live the lease of Nature . . ." *Mac,* IV, i, 98–99.

leash, *n.* a trio; set of three: "I am sworn brother to a/ leash of drawers . . ." *1 Hen 4,* II, iv, 6–7.

leasing, *n.* lying [necessary when speaking well of fools; Mercury was the god of cheats]: "Now Mercury endue thee with leasing, for thou/ speak'st well of fools!" *T Night,* I, v, 97–98.

least, *adv.* **at least,** as a last resort: "What do we then but draw anew the model/ In fewer offices, or at least desist/ To build at all?" *2 Hen 4,* I, iii, 46–48.

leather-coat, *n.* russet apple: "There's a dish of leather-coats for/ you." *2 Hen 4,* V, iii, 39–40.

leave¹, *v.* **1** to leave off; stop: ". . . weeping made you break the story off,/ Of our two cousins' coming into London."/ "Where did I leave?" *Rich 2,* V, ii, 2–4. **2** to abandon: "This fool-begg'd patience in thee will be left." *Errors,* II, i, 41. **3 leaves and takes,** spares some and kills others: "Here, there, and everywhere, he leaves and takes . . ." *Tr & Cr,* V, v, 26. **4 leave to do,** (to) cease to function: "My operant powers their functions leave to do . . ." *Ham,* III, ii, 169. **5 leave unexecuted,** make no use of: "... leave unexecuted/ Your own renowned knowledge ..." *Ant & Cleo*, III, vii, 44–45.

leave², *n.* **1** leave-taking: "... our power is ready;/ Our lack is nothing but our leave." *Mac*, IV, iii, 236–237. **2 by your leave:** "Leave, gentle wax; and, manners, blame us not ..." *Lear*, IV, vi, 261. **3 give me leave a while,** polite dismissal: "You may go walk, and give me leave a while." *Shrew*, III, i, 57. **4 good leave have you,** we will leave you alone: "Ay, good leave have you; for you will have leave/ Till youth take leave and leave you to the crutch." *3 Hen 6*, III, ii, 34–35. **5 leave exceeds commission,** desire [usually] exceeds fulfillment: "Things out of hope are compass'd oft with vent'ring,/ Chiefly in love, whose leave exceeds commission ..." *Ven & Ad*, 567–568. **6 you will have leave,** you will take liberties: "... you will have leave/ Till youth take leave and leave you to the crutch." *3 Hen 6*, III, ii, 34–35.

leaven, *n.* **lay the leaven,** to bring disgrace (in the manner of soured dough that spoils other dough): "... so thou, Posthumus/ Wilt lay the leaven on all proper [honorable] men ..." *Cymb*, III, iv, 62–63.

leavened, *adj.* considered: "We have with a leaven'd and prepared choice ..." *Meas*, I, i, 51.

leavy, *adj.* leafy: "The fraud of men was ever so,/ Since summer first was leavy." *M Ado*, II, iii, 72–73.

lechery, *n.* **1** misuse for "treachery": "... the most dangerous piece of/ lechery that ever was known ..." *M Ado*, III, iii, 161–162. **2 lechery eats itself,** fr. belief that sexual indulgence shortened one's life: "... yet in a sort lechery eats itself." *Tr & Cr*, V, iv, 35.

lecture, *n.* **1** lesson; instruction: "So by my former lecture and advice/ Shall you my son." *Ham*, II, i, 67–68. **2 read a lecture,** give a public reading: "Would it not shame thee ... To read a lecture of them?" *Rich 2*, IV, i, 231–232.

Leda, *n.* wife of the King of Sparta and mother [by Zeus, disguised as a swan] of Helen of Troy: "Fair Leda's daughter had a thousand wooers ..." *Shrew*, I, ii, 242.

leech, *n.* physician: "... make each/ Prescribe to other, as each other's leech." *Timon*, V, iv, 83–84.

lee'd and calm'd, *adj.* (of a sailing ship) robbed of the wind in her sails and becalmed: "And I, of whom his eyes had seen the proof ... must be lee'd, and calm'd,/ By debitor and creditor ..." *Oth*, I, i, 28–30.

leer, *n.* **1** look; appearance: "... he hath a Rosalind of a better leer than you." *As You*, IV, i, 63–64. **2** complexion: "Here's a young lad fram'd of another leer ..." *T Andr*, IV, ii, 119.
—*v.* **3** to look affectionately or longingly: "I will leer upon him as/ a comes by ..." *2 Hen 4*, V, v, 5–6.

leese, *v.* old form of **lose:** "But flowers distill'd, though they with winter meet,/ Leese but their show ..." *Sonn 5*, 13–14.

leet, *n.* **1** manorial court presided over by the lord of the estate: "And rail upon the hostess of the house,/ And say you would present her at the leet ..." *Shrew*, Ind., ii, 87–88. **2 keep leets,** hold court: "... who has a breast so pure,/ But some uncleanly apprehensions/ Keep leets and law-days ..." *Oth*, III, iii, 142–144.

left, *past. part.* **1** passed: "The rank of osiers ... Left on your right hand, brings you to the place." *As You*, IV, iii, 79–80. **2** given up; dispensed with: "Will not this malice, Somerset, be left?" *1 Hen 6*, IV, i, 108. **3** regarded as: "The ostentation of our love; which, left unshown,/ Is often left unlov'd ..." *Ant & Cleo*, III, vi, 52–53. **4 left off,** abandoned; given up: "... the schools,/ Embowel'd of their doctrine, have left off/ The danger to itself?" *All's W*, I, iii, 235–237. **5 left out,** excepted: "... outwent her,/ Motion and breath left out." *Cymb*, II, iv, 84–85.

leg¹, *n.* **1** bow: "I will do/ it in King Cambyses' vein."/ "Well, here is my leg." *1 Hen 4*, II, iv, 382–383. **2** graceful leg, either for dancing or for making courtesies: "I had rather than forty shillings I had such a leg ..." *T Night*, II, iii, 19–20. **3** manner of walking: "They have all new legs, and lame ones ..." *Hen 8*, I, iii, 11. **4 make a leg,** to bow, usually with the right leg drawn back; make an obeisance: "You make a leg, and Bolingbroke says 'ay'." *Rich 2*, III, iii, 175. **5 sign of the Leg,** sign over a bootmaker's shop, displaying a booted leg: "... wears his/ boots very smooth like unto the sign of the Leg ..." *2 Hen 4*, II, iv, 245–246. **6 take up another's legs,** to secure a hold in wrestling; here, describing the effects of alcohol: "... though he took up my legs sometime, yet I made a shift to cast him." *Mac*, II, iii, 41–42.

leg², *n.* pack; crowd: "... the Senators of Athens, together with the common leg of people ..." *Timon*, III, vi, 77–78.

legate, *n.* the Pope's deputy: "... without the king's assent or knowledge/ You wrought to be a legate ..." *Hen 8*, III, ii, 310–311.

legative, *adj.* **power legative,** powers pertaining to a papal legate: "... all those things you have done of late/ By your power legative ..." *Hen 8*, III, ii, 338–339.

lege, domine, [Latin] read, master: "Let me hear a staff, a stanze, a verse: *lege, domine*." *Love's L,* IV, ii, 100.

legerity, *n.* quickness; nimbleness: ". . . and newly move/ With casted slough and fresh legerity." *Hen 5,* IV, i, 22–23.

legion, *n.* great number: ". . . he hath a legion of angels [gold coins]." *Wives,* I, iii, 50.

Legion, *n.* (in the Bible) the unclean spirit cast out of a man by Jesus, recounted in Mark: "If . . . Legion/ himself possessed him, yet I'll speak to him." *T Night,* III, iv, 85–87.

legitimation, *n.* legitimacy: "I have disclaim'd Sir Robert and my land;/ Legitimation, name and all is gone." *K John,* I, i, 252–253.

Leicester, *n.* city NW of London: ". . . this foul swine/ Is now . . . Near to the town of Leicester . . ." *Rich 3,* V, ii, 10–12.

leiger, *n.* resident ambassador: "Intends you for his swift ambassador,/ Where you shall be an everlasting leiger." *Meas,* III, i, 57–58.

leisure, *n.* **1** unoccupied time; convenience: ". . . the boist'rous late appeal,/ Which then our leisure would not let us hear . . ." *Rich 2,* I, i, 4–5. **2 at leisure,** inclined or disposed: "Hear ye, captain, are you not at leisure?" *1 Hen 6,* V, iii, 97. **3 by leisure,** hardly at all; barely: "I'll trust by leisure him that mocks me once;/ Thee never, nor thy traitorous haughty sons . . ." *T Andr,* I, i, 301–302. **4 by my good leisure,** as time permitted me: ". . . many deceiving promises of life, which I, by my good/ leisure, have discredited to him . . ." *Meas,* III, ii, 239–241. **5 no leisure bated,** without wasting any time: "That on the supervise, no leisure bated . . . My head should be struck off." *Ham,* V, ii, 23–25.

leman, *n.* sweetheart; also, illicit lover: "And drink unto thee, leman mine . . ." *2 Hen 4,* V, iii, 45.

lendings, *n. pl.* **1** money advanced to soldiers in lieu of pay: "That Mowbray hath receiv'd eight thousand nobles/ In name of lendings for your Highness' soldiers . . ." *Rich 2,* I, i, 88–89. **2** borrowed articles; here, animal skins: "Off, off, you lendings! Come;/ unbutton here. [Tearing off his clothes.]" *Lear,* III, iv, 111–112.

length, *n.* **1** range: ". . . if I can get him within my pistol's/ length, I'll make him sure enough . . ." *Per,* I, i, 167. **2** duration of life: ". . . for now/ All length is torture: since the torch is out . . ." *Ant & Cleo,* IV, xiv, 45–46. **3** pace: ". . . for the horse/ Would make his length a mile, if't pleas'd his rider . . ." *Kinsmen,* V, iv, 56–57. **4 have all a length,** all have the same length: "These foils have all a length?" *Ham,* V, ii, 262. **5 such another length,** the same or similar length: "I'll get me one of such another length." *Two Gent,* III, i, 133.

lenity, *n.* mildness; also, meekness; acquiescence: ". . . King Henry gives consent,/ Of mere compassion and of lenity . . ." *1 Hen 6,* V, iv, 124–125.

Lent, *n.* no butchering was allowed during Lent except by special permission: ". . . the Lent shall be as long again as it is; thou shalt have/ licence to kill for a hundred lacking one." *2 Hen 6,* IV, iii, 6–7.

lenten, *adj.* lean, spare, or meager; hence, inadequate: "A good lenten answer. I can tell thee where that/ saying was born . . ." *T Night,* I, v, 9–10.

Lenten entertainment, *n.* frugal or ungenerous reception: ". . . what/ Lenten entertainment the players shall receive from you." *Ham,* II, ii, 314–316.

l'envoy, *n.* explanation or commentary: "Some enigma, some riddle: come, thy l'envoy; begin." *Love's L,* III, i, 68.

Leonati, *n. pl.* those bearing the name "Leonatus," esp. the father and brothers of Leonatus Posthumus: "Gods, put the strength o' th' Leonati in me!" *Cymb,* V, i, 31.

leperous, *adj.* causing symptoms like those of leprosy: "And in the porches of my ears did pour/ The leperous distilment . . ." *Ham,* I, v, 63–64.

lessen, *v.* **lessens and sets off,** dimishes but at the same time enhances: "When you above perceive me like a crow,/ That it is place [position] which lessens and sets off . . ." *Cymb,* III, iii, 12–13.

lesser, *adv.* to a less degree: "Patience herself . . . Doth lesser blench at suff'rance than I do." *Tr & Cr,* I, i, 27–28.

lesson, *v.* to instruct; teach: "Well hast thou lesson'd us; this shall we do." *T Andr,* V, ii, 110.

lest, *conj.* for fear that: "Well, may you see things well done there:—adieu!—/ Lest our old robes sit easier than our new!" *Mac,* II, iv, 37–38.

let[1], *v.* **1** to hinder or prevent: "Or else what lets it but he would be here [prevents him from being here]?" *Errors,* II, i, 105.
—*n.* **2** obstacle; hindrance: ". . . these lets attend the time,/ Like little frosts that sometime threat the spring . . ." *Luc,* 330–331.

let², *v.* **1** to allow to remain: ". . . I'll give him my commission/ To let him there a month . . ." *W Tale,* I, ii, 40–41. **2 let me alone,** See **alone.**

let-alone, *n.* power to forbid: "The let-alone lies not in your good will." *Lear,* V, iii, 80.

let go, *v.* Enough of that! No more!: "I would have had you put your power well on/ Before you had worn it out."/ "Let go." *Cor,* III, ii, 17–18.

lethargied, *past part.* dulled; made numb; paralyzed: "Either his notion weakens, his discernings/ Are lethargied . . ." *Lear,* I, iv, 236–237.

lethargy, *n.* **1** drunken stupor: "Cousin, cousin, how have you come so early by/ this lethargy?" *T Night,* I, v, 124–125. **2** apoplexy or epilepsy: ". . . loads o' gravel i'th'back, lethargies, cold/ palsies, raw eyes . . ." *Tr & Cr,* V, i, 18–19.

Lethe, *n.* **1** river of forgetfulness in Hades: "Was this easy?/ May this be wash'd in Lethe and forgotten?" *2 Hen 4,* V, ii, 71–72. **2** [l.c.] flow of blood likened to the river of Hell, a stream of death: ". . . here thy hunters stand,/ Sign'd in thy spoil, and crimson'd in thy lethe." *J Caes,* III, i, 205–206. **3** forgetfulness; oblivion: "Till that the conquering wine hath steep'd our sense/ In soft and delicate Lethe." *Ant & Cleo,* II, vii, 106–107.

let it (or that) pass, Forget about it: ". . . among other importunate and most serious designs,/ and of great import indeed, too, but let that/ pass . . ." *Love's L,* V, i, 91–93.

letter, *n.* **1** [pl.] **a.** handwriting; penmanship: "Any thing like?"/ "Much in the letters, nothing in the praise." *Love's L,* V, ii, 39–40. **b.** learning; literacy: ". . . no kind of traffic/ Would I admit . . . Letters should not be known . . ." *Temp,* II, i, 144–146. **c.** written communication; a letter: "There's letters from my mother; what th' import is/ I know not yet." *All's W,* II, iii, 272–273. **2** summons: ". . . and his own letter . . . Must fetch him in he papers [makes a note of]." *Hen 8,* I, i, 78–80. **3 affect the letter,** to use alliteration: "I will something affect the letter; for it argues/ facility." *Love's L,* IV, ii, 53. **4 by letter and affection,** on the basis of recommendations and personal inclinations: "Preferment goes by letter and affection,/ Not by the old gradation . . ." *Oth,* I, i, 36–37.

letters patents, *n. pl.* document or documents granting a particular right or power; here, permission to sue to obtain a rightful inheritance: "If you do wrongfully seize Herford's rights/ Call in the letters patents that he hath . . ." *Rich 2,* II, i, 201–202.

level, *v.* **1** to aim; take aim [at]: "And that's the mark I know you level at." *Per,* II, iii, 113. **2** to guess: ". . . according to my/ description level at my affection." *Merch,* I, ii, 36–37.
—*adj.* **3** fair; unbiased: "It is not a confident brow, nor the throng of/ words . . . can thrust me from a level consideration." *2 Hen 4,* II, i, 109–112. **4** conforming to that which is normal or expected: "There's nothing level in our cursed natures/ But direct villainy." *Timon,* IV, iii, 19–20. **5** direct or straight: "It shall as level to your judgment 'pear/ As day does to your eye." *Ham,* IV, v, 151–152. **6 level to,** in accord with: "And every thing lies level to our wish . . ." *2 Hen 4,* IV, iv, 7.
—*adv.* **7** clearly: "It shall as level to your judgment 'pear/ As day does to your eye." *Ham,* IV, v, 151–152.
—*n.* **8** act of aiming or pointing a weapon: "As if that name,/ Shot from the deadly level of a gun . . ." *Rom & Jul,* III, iii, 101–102. **9** line of fire; target: "I stood i'th'level/ Of a full-charg'd confederacy . . ." *Hen 8,* I, ii, 2–3. **10 hold one's level,** put oneself on the same level as: ". . . rude society, As thou art match'd withal, and grafted to,/ hold their level with thy princely heart?" *1 Hen 4,* III, ii, 14–17. **11 level of your frown,** the compass of your displeasure: "Bring me within the level of your frown,/ But shoot not at me in your wakened hate . . ." *Sonn 117,* 11–12.

leveled, *adj.* aimed at a specific target: ". . . no level'd malice/ Infects one comma in the course I hold . . ." *Timon,* i, i, 47–48.

leviathan, *n.* Biblical name for the whale: "Fetch me this herb . . . Ere the leviathan can swim a league." *M N Dream,* II, i, 173–174.

levied succors, *n. pl.* recruited soldiers: "Let not your private discord keep away/ The levied succors that should lend him aid . . ." *1 Hen 6,* IV, iv, 22–23.

levity, *n.* frivolousness; wanton or irresponsible conduct: "For that her reputation was disvalu'd/ In levity . . ." *Meas,* V, i, 220–221.

levy, *n.* **1** raising of an army: "Malice domestic, foreign levy, nothing/ Can touch him further!" *Mac,* III, ii, 24–26. **2** army that has been raised: "With those legions . . . whereunto your levy/ Must be supplyant [suppliant] . . ." *Cymb,* III, viii, 12–14. **3 benefit of our levies,** advantage that our armies give us: ". . . but there to end/ Where he was to begin, and give away/ The benefit of our levies . . ." *Cor,* V, vi, 65–67.
—*v.* **4** to demand and obtain payment of: "If they do this,/ As, if God please, they shall, my ransom then/ Will soon be levied." *Hen 5,* IV, iii, 119–121. **5** to enlist the aid of (heads of state together with their armies): ". . . who now are levying/ The kings o' the earth for war." *Ant & Cleo,* III, vi, 67–68.

lewd, *adj.* **1** addicted to low companions and loose living: "... because you have been so lewd, and so much/ engraffed to Falstaff." *2 Hen 4,* II, ii, 58–59. **2** wicked; corrupt; evil: "We'll talk with Margaret,/ How her acquaintance grew with this lewd fellow." *M Ado,* V, i, 325–326. **3** base; improper: "The which he hath detain'd for lewd imployments..." *Rich 2,* I, i, 90. **4** cheap-looking; tacky: "A velvet dish! Fie, fie! 'Tis lewd and filthy." *Shrew,* IV, iii, 65. **5** stupid; unfounded: "But you must trouble him with lewd complaints." *Rich 3,* I, iii, 61.

lewdly, *adv.* in a vile or monstrous manner: "A sort of naughty persons, lewdly bent..." *2 Hen 6,* II, i, 159.

lewdster, *n.* lecher [prob. Mistress Page's coinage]: "Against such lewdsters and their lechery/ Those that betray them do no treachery." *Wives,* V, iii, 21–22.

lewd-tongued, *adj.* sharp-tongued; foul-mouthed: "... 't shall not only be/ Death to thyself, but to thy lewd-tongu'd wife..." *W Tale,* II, iii, 170–171.

Lewis the Tenth, *n.* actually Louis IX, king (1226–70) of France: "Also King Lewis the Tenth,/ Who was sole heir to the usurper Capet..." *Hen 5,* I, ii, 77–78.

liable, *adj.* **1** suitable: "The posterior of the day... is liable,/ congruent, and measurable for the afternoon..." *Love's L,* V, i, 83–84. **2** subordinate or subservient: "And reason to my love is liable." *J Caes,* II, ii, 104. **3 liable to,** belonging to; owned by: "Those are her own, still liable to her,/ And who inherits her hath those with all." *Edw 3,* I, ii, 46–47.

libbard, *n.* head of a leopard or lion on a coat of arms [sometimes worn on the elbow or knee]: "I Pompey am,—"/ "With libbard's head on knee." *Love's L,* V, ii, 542.

liberal, *adj.* **1** unchecked; unrestrained: "My heart is great, but it must break with silence,/ Ere't be disburdened with a liberal tongue." *Rich 2,* II, i, 228–229. **2** outspoken; here, foul-mouthed: "... long purples,/ That liberal shepherds give a grosser name..." *Ham,* IV, vii, 168–169. **3** wanton; licentious: "Who hath indeed, most like a liberal villain,/ Confess'd the vile encounters they have had..." *M Ado,* IV, i, 92–93. **4** lavish: "... most delicate carriages, and of/ very liberal conceit." *Ham,* V, ii, 149–150. **5** generous; here, in wordplay with "sexually promiscuous": "I will become as liberal as you,/ I'll not deny him any thing I have..." *Merch,* V, i, 226–227.

liberal Arts, *n. pl.* academic studies: "... so reputed/ In dignity, and for the liberal Arts/ Without a parallel..." *Temp,* I, ii, 72–74.

liberality, *n.* generosity; munificence: "... knows to court it/ With words, fair looks, and liberality?" *T Andr,* II, i, 91–92.

liberal opposition, *n.* unrestrained contrariness: "... to excuse or hide/ The liberal opposition of our spirits..." *Love's L,* V, ii, 724–725.

liberties, *n. pl.* royal rights; prerogatives: "But should he wrong my liberties in my absence?" *Per,* I, ii, 112.

liberty, *n.* **1** lack of restraint; licentiousness: "Those pretty wrongs that liberty commits..." *Sonn 41,* 1. **2 the liberty,** prob. ref. to plays that ignored the classic unities, etc.: "For the law of writ, and the liberty, these are/ the only men." *Ham,* II, ii, 397–398.

Libya, *n.* **banks of Libya,** "Libya" was vaguely synon. with N Africa, all of which was assumed to be barren desert: "Achilles, were his brain as barren/ As banks of Libya..." *Tr & Cr,* I, iii, 327–328.

license or **licence,** *n.* **1** vice; licentiousness: "For the fifth Harry from curb'd licence plucks/ The muzzle of restraint..." *2 Hen 4,* IV, v, 130–131. **2** permissive freedom; liberty: "I know your virtue hath a licence in't..." *Meas,* II, iv, 144. **3 license of free foot,** liberty to roam anywhere: "... headed evils/ That thou with licence of free foot hast caught..." *As You,* II, vii, 67–68.

Lichas, *n.* **1** servant to Hercules: "If Hercules and Lichas play at dice/ Which is the better man..." *Merch,* II, i, 32–33. **2** same, who innocently delivered the poisoned shirt of Nessus to Hercules and was flung by his master into the sea: "Let me lodge Lichas on the horns o' the moon..." *Ant & Cleo,* IV, xii, 45.

lictor, *n.* minor public official in ancient Rome: "... saucy lictors/ Will catch at us like strumpets, and scald rhymers/ Ballad us out o' tune." *Ant & Cleo,* V, ii, 213–215.

lid, *n.* **By God's lid,** By God's eyelid [a mild oath]: "By God's lid it does one's/ heart good." *Tr & Cr,* I, ii, 213–214.

lie¹, *v.* **1** to stay; remain: "She must lie here on mere necessity." *Love's L,* I, i, 147. **2** to lodge; reside: "There doth my father lie; and there this night/ We'll pass the business privately and well." *Shrew,* IV, iv, 56–57. **3** to recline; here, in wordplay with "prevaricate": "... you'll lie, like dogs, and yet/ say nothing neither." *Temp,* III, ii, 18–19. **4 lie along,** to lie prostrate [dead]: "When he lies along,/ After your way his tale pronounc'd..." *Cor,* V, vi, 57–58. **5 lie by,** to sleep next to; also, in wordplay, understood as "to lie with" [sleep with]: "So thou may'st say the king lies by a beggar, if a/ beggar dwell near him..." *T Night,* III, i, 8–9. **6 lie for you,** ambig. reply, meaning "take your place" or "tell lies about you": "I will deliver you, or else lie for you." *Rich 3,* I, i, 115. **7 lie in,** to be in confinement, awaiting the birth of a child: "... you must go visit the good lady that lies in." *Cor*, I, iii, 77. **8 lies you on,** is your duty: "... now it lies you on to speak/ To th'people ..." *Cor*, III, ii, 52–53. **9 lie under,** to suffer the consequences of: "... let him, like an engine/ Not portable, lie under this report ..." *Tr & Cr*, II, iii, 136–137.

lie², *v.* **1** wordplay on "falsehood" and "lying with a man": "... a very/ honest woman, but something given to lie, as a/ woman should not do, but in the way of honesty ..." *Ant & Cleo*, V, ii, 250–252. **2 lie in the throat,** to lie flagrantly: "Well, I do nothing in the/ world but lie, and lie in my throat." *Love's L*, IV, iii, 10–11.
—*n.* **3 give (someone) the lie,** to call (a person) a liar; also, to knock someone flat; here, also wordplay with "lye" (urine): "... in conclusion, equivocates him in a sleep, and, giving him the lie,/ leaves him." *Mac*, II, iii, 35–37. **4 give the lie to,** cause to deny or disbelieve: "... my heart to sway,/ To make me give the lie to my true sight ..." *Sonn 150*, 2–3.

lief, *adv.* **had as lief,** would be just as happy if; would just as soon: "... but if you mouth it as many of your players do, I had as lief the town-crier spoke my lines." *Ham*, III, ii, 2–4.

liefest, *adj.* dearest: "... with your best endeavour have stirr'd up/ My liefest liege to be mine enemy." *2 Hen 6*, III, i, 163–164.

liege, *n.* sovereign: "Remember, sir, my liege [your majesty],/ The kings your ancestors ..." *Cymb*, III, i, 17–18.

liegeman, *n.* loyal subject; sworn follower: "... swore the/ devil his true liegeman upon the cross of a Welsh/ hook ..." *1 Hen 4*, II, iv, 333–334.

lieger, *n.,* resident ambassador; also, supporter or defender: "I have given him that ... shall quite unpeople her/ Of liegers for her sweet [husband] ..." *Cymb*, I, vi, 78–80.

lien, *past part.* var. of **lain:** "I heard of an Egyptian/ That had nine hours lien dead ..." *Per*, III, ii, 86–87.

lieu, *n.* **in lieu of,** in return for: "For that same scrubbed boy ... In lieu of this, last night did lie with me." *Merch*, V, i, 261–262.

lieutenantry, *n.* **dealt on lieutenantry,** fought by proxy: "... 'twas I/ That the mad Brutus ended: he alone/ Dealt on lieutenantry ..." *Ant & Cleo*, III, xi, 37–39.

life, *n.* **1** essence: "Let their exhal'd unwholesome breaths make sick/ The life of purity ..." *Luc*, 779–780. **2** fact of being alive: "For her life in Rome/ Would be eternal in our triumph ..." *Ant & Cleo*, V, i, 65–66. **3** success; triumph: "Our project's life this shape of sense assumes ..." *Tr & Cr*, I, iii,

385. **4 a life,** on my life: "I love a ballad in print, a/ life, for then we are sure they are true." *W Tale*, IV, iv, 261–262. **5 beyond man's life,** farther than a man may live to travel: "... she that dwells/ Ten leagues beyond man's life ..." *Temp*, II, i, 241–242. **6 in my life,** while I remained alive: "With ho! such bugs and goblins in my life ..." *Ham*, V, ii, 22. **7 there's life in't,** perh. akin to "While there's life, there's hope": "I have heard her swear't. Tut, there's life in't,/ man." *T Night*, I, iii, 108–109. **8 to the life,** convincingly; realistically: "... put me now to such a part which never/ I shall discharge to th'life." *Cor*, III, ii, 105–106.

lift, *v.* used as past tense; lifted: "He ne'er lift up his hand but conquered." *1 Hen 6*, I, i, 16.

lifter, *n.* wordplay on "one who lifts weights" and "thief": "Is he so young [inexperienced] a man, and so old [accomplished] a lifter?" *Tr & Cr*, I, ii, 119.

lig, *v.* Fluellen's Welsh pron. of "lie": "... ay'll de gud service, or I'll lig/ i' th' grund for it ..." *Hen 5*, III, ii, 118–119.

liggens, *n.* poss. an incoherent pron. of "legs" (used as part of an oath): "By God's liggens, I thank thee; the knave will stick/ by thee ..." *2 Hen 4*, V, iii, 63–64.

light¹, *adj.* **1** wanton: "And that's great marvel, loving a light wench." *Love's L*, I, ii, 116. **2** foolish; giddy; frivolous: "Light wenches may prove plagues to men forsworn ..." *Love's L*, IV, iii, 381. **3** same in wordplay with "candlelight": "What, must I hold a candle to my shames?—/ They in themselves (goodsooth) are too too light." *Merch*, II, vi, 41–42. **4** trivial; here, in wordplay with "lightweight": "O, then I see you will part but with light gifts ..." *Rich 3*, III, i, 118. **5** careless; indifferent: "Light vanity, insatiate cormorant,/ Consuming means, soon preys upon itself." *Rich 2*, II, i, 38–39. **6** cheerful: "And so may you, for a light heart lives long." *Love's L*, V, ii, 18. **7 set me light,** to regard me lightly: "When thou shalt be dispos'd to set me light ..." *Sonn 88*, 1.
—*n.* **8** (used as pl.) light-headed, frivolous persons: "Distinction, with a broad and powerful fan/ Puffing at all, winnows the light away ..." *Tr & Cr*, I, iii, 27–28.

light², *v.* **1** to alight; dismount: "Now, Titinius! Now some light. O, he lights too!/ He's ta'en!" *J Caes*, V, iii, 31–32. **2** to land or fall: "You are [have] light into my hands, where you are like/ to live." *Per*, IV, ii, 68–69.

light³, *n.* **1** [pl.] sight: "O that ... your own eyes had the lights they were wont to have ..." *Two Gent*, II, i, 67–68. **2** illumination; enlightenment: "And that hath dazzled my reason's light ..." *Two Gent*, II, iv, 206. **3** inspiration; here, for the poet: "For who's so dumb, that cannot write to thee,/ When thou thyself dost give invention light?" *Sonn 38*, 7–8. **4 clear**

lights, unmistakable signs or indications: "Why you have given me such clear lights of favour . . ." *T Night,* V, i, 335. **5 lights of men,** glorious or luminous beings: ". . . those two lights of men/ Met in the vale of Andren." *Hen 8,* I, i, 6–7.
—*v.* **6** to dawn: "And that shall be the day, whene'er it lights . . ." *1 Hen 4,* III, ii, 138.
—*adv.* **7** quickly; also, poss., in lightweight armor: "Before the sun rose he was harness'd light . . ." *Tr & Cr,* I, ii, 8.

lighten, *v.* **1** to flash like lightning: ". . . behold, his eye,/ As bright as is the eagle's, lightens forth . . ." *Rich II,* III, iii, 68–69. **2** to enlighten: "Now the Lord lighten thee, thou art a great/ fool." *2 Hen 4,* II, i, 189–190.

lighter, *adj.* lesser: "To put on yellow stockings, and to frown/ Upon Sir Toby, and the lighter people . . ." *T Night,* V, i, 337–338.

lightest, *adj.* wordplay on "lightest in appearance" and "lightest in morals": ". . . a miracle in nature,/ Making them lightest that wear most of it . . ." *Merch,* III, ii, 90–91.

lightless, *adj.* showing no light; smoldering: ". . . bears the lightless fire,/ Which in pale embers hid . . ." *Luc,* 4–5.

light lights by day, *v.* to waste time as well as light: "I mean sir, in delay/ We waste our lights in vain, light lights by day." *Rom & Jul,* I, iv, 44–45.

lightly, *adv.* generally; usually: "Short summers lightly have a forward spring." *Rich 3,* III, i, 94.

lightness, *n.* **1** wantonness; infidelity: ". . . he hath the horn of abundance, and the lightness/ of his wife shines through it . . ." *2 Hen 4,* I, ii, 46–47. **2** light-headedness; also, delirium: "Thence to a watch, thence into a weakness,/ Thence to a lightness . . ." *Ham,* II, ii, 148–149.

lightning, *n.* animation, proverbially occurring shortly before death: "How oft when men are at the point of death/ Have they been merry! Which their keepers call/ A lightning . . ." *Rom & Jul,* V, iii, 88–90.

light of ear, *adj.* See **ear**[1] (def. 8).

light-wing'd, *adj.* volatile; capricious: ". . . when light-wing'd toys,/ And feather'd Cupid, foils with wanton dullness . . ." *Oth,* I, iii, 268–269.

ligned, *adj.* aligned; connected: "A gentleman of noble parentage,/ Of fair demesnes, youthful and nobly lign'd . . ." *Rom & Jul,* III, v, 179–180.

like[1], *v.* **1** to look or seem: "By/ my troth, you like well, and bear your years very/ well." *2 Hen 4,* III, ii, 83. **2** to please: "His countenance likes me not." *Lear,* II, ii, 91. **3 and it like you,** if it please you: "Then at my lodging, and it like you." *Shrew,* IV, iv, 55. **4 like it your grace,** I beg pardon, your grace [apology prefacing a warning]: "Like it your grace,/ The state takes notice of the private difference/ Betwixt you and the Cardinal." *Hen 8,* I, i, 100–102. **5 like of,** be fond of; heartily approve of: "But like of each thing that in season grows." *Love's L,* I, i, 107. **6 like to me,** as much as [you love] me: "Thou never should'st love woman like to me." *T Night,* V, i, 266. **7 so like you,** if it please you: "So like you, sir, ambassadors from Rome . . ." *Cymb,* II, iii, 53.

like[2], *adv.* **1** similarly: "Whilst I had been like heedful of the other." *Errors,* I, i, 82. **2** equally: ". . . the enterprise whereof/ Shall be to you, as us, like glorious." *Hen 5,* II, ii, 182–183. **3** likely: ". . . tell what hath happened . . . And how she's like to be Lucentio's wife." *Shrew,* IV, iv, 64–66.
—*adj.* **4** likely [on the verge of passing]: ". . . that self bill is urg'd,/ Which in the eleventh year of the last king's reign/ Was like . . ." *Hen 5,* I, 1–3. **5** same: ". . . to visit Bohemia, on/ the like occasion whereon my services are now on/ foot . . ." *W Tale,* I, i, 1–3.
—*prep.* **6** so much as: "And yet no man like he doth grieve my heart." *Rom & Jul,* III, v, 83. **7** disguised as: "I . . . have oft made sport;/ And like a forester the groves may tread . . ." *M N Dream,* III, ii, 389–390. **8 like to,** in the manner of: ". . . convers'd with such/ As, like to pitch, defile nobility . . ." *2 Hen 6,* II, i, 187–188.
—*v.* **9** to liken; compare: "And like me to the peasant boys of France . . ." *1 Hen 6,* IV, vi, 48.

liker, *adj.* more so: ". . . but the time is long."/ "The liker you; few taller are so young." *Love's L,* V, ii, 827–828.

likest, *adj.* most like; most resembling: "And earthly power doth then show [appear] likest God's/ When mercy seasons justice . . ." *Merch,* IV, i, 192–193.

liking, *n.* **1** desire: ". . . these round enchanting pits,/ Open'd their mouths to swallow Venus' liking . . ." *Ven & Ad,* 247–248. **2** physical condition; physique: ". . . as long as I have an eye to make difference of/ men's liking . . ." *Wives,* II, i, 54–55. **3 in some liking,** in good physical condition: ". . . I'll repent,/ and that suddenly, while I am in some liking . . ." *1 Hen 4,* III, iii, 4–5.

lily-livered, *adj.* white-livered (the liver being the seat of courage); hence, cowardly: "Go, prick thy face, and over-red thy fear,/ Thou lily-liver'd boy." *Mac,* V, iii, 14–15.

Limander, *n.* Bottom's blunder for "Leander": ". . . I am thy lover's grace;/ And like Limander am I trusty still." *M N Dream,* V, i, 193–194.

limb, *n.* **1** person regarded as a "member" of the body politic: ". . . let us choose such limbs of noble counsel . . ." *2 Hen 4,* V, ii, 135. **2** frame of the body: ". . . neither heat, affection, limb, nor beauty/ To make thy riches pleasant." *Meas,* III, i, 37–38. **3 limbs of Limehouse,** rogues of the dockyards: ". . . no audience but the . . . limbs of Limehouse . . . are able to endure." *Hen 8,* V, iii, 60–62.

limbeck, *n.* alembic; (formerly) the top part of a still, which condensed the vapors of alcohol: ". . . memory, the warder of the brain,/ Shall be a fume, and the receipt of reason/ A limbeck only . . ." *Mac,* I, vii, 66–68.

limber, *adj.* limp; flabby: "You put me off with limber vows . . ." *W Tale,* I, ii, 47.

limb-meal, *adv.* limb from limb: "O, that I had her here, to tear her limb-meal!" *Cymb,* II, iv, 147.

limbo, *n.* **1** wordplay on religious sense of "abode of unbaptized souls" and slang term for "prison": ". . . He's in Tartar limbo, worse than hell." *Errors,* IV, ii, 32. **2** Parolles appar. means hell: ". . . he was mad for her and talk'd of Satan and of Limbo/ and of furies and I know not what . . ." *All's W,* V, iii, 255–256.

Limbo Patrum, *n.* [Latin] prison; lit., abode on the fringes of hell for those who died before the coming of Christ: "I have some/ of 'em in *Limbo Patrum,* and there they are like to/ dance these three days . . ." *Hen 8,* V, iii, 62–64.

lime, *n.* **1** additive to wine to lighten the color and make it sparkling: "You rogue, here's lime in this sack . . ." *1 Hen 4,* II, iv, 121. **2** birdlime, a sticky substance used to catch birds; because of their "sticky" fingers, thieves were said to have lime on their fingers: ". . . come, put some lime upon your fingers,/ and away with the rest." *Temp,* IV, i, 245–246. **3 lay lime,** to spread birdlime on tree branches to trap songbirds; here, fig. use: "You must lay lime, to tangle her desires . . ." *Two Gent,* III, ii, 68.
—*v.* **4** to catch (a bird) with birdlime: "I have limed her,/ but it is Jove's doing, and Jove make me thankful!" *T Night,* III, iv, 74–75. **5** to add lime juice to cheap wine to disguise the sour taste: "Let me see/ thee froth and lime." *Wives,* I, iii, 13–14.

limed, *adj.* caught with lime, as one traps a bird: "She's lim'd, I warrant you! We have caught her,/ madam." *M Ado,* III, i, 104.

lime-kill, *n.* var. of **Lime-kiln:** ". . . which is as hateful to me as the reek/ of a lime-kill." *Wives,* III, iii, 72–73.

lime-kiln, *n.* **lime-kilns i'th'palm,** arthritis: ". . . bladders full of impostume, sciaticas, lime-kilns/ i'th'palm . . ." *Tr & Cr,* V, i, 20–21.

lime-twigs, *n.* branches or twigs smeared with birdlime to trap small birds: "Like lime-twigs set to catch my winged soul." *2 Hen 6,* III, iii, 16.

limit, *n.* **1** tract or other area of bounded land: "The Archdeacon hath divided it/ Into three limits very equally . . ." *1 Hen 4,* III, i, 68–69. **2** extended area; also, value: "Finding thy worth a limit past [beyond] my praise . . ." *Sonn 82,* 6. **3** specified date or time: "Between which time of the contract and limit of the/ solemnity . . ." *Meas,* III, i, 215–216. **4 out of limit,** beyond the bounds of allegiance: "So long as out of limit and true rule/ You stand against anointed majesty." *1 Hen 4,* IV, iii, 39–40.
—*v.* **5** to allow as a limit: ". . . I'll limit thee this day/ To seek thy health by beneficial help . . ." *Errors,* I, i, 150–151. **6** to specify; appoint or stipulate: "Having the hour limited,/ and an express command under penalty . . ." *Meas,* IV, ii, 164–165.

limitation, *n.* required time: "You have stood your limitation, and the tribunes/ Endue you with the people's voice . . ." *Cor,* II, iii, 137–138.

limited, *adj.* **1** appointed: "I'll make so bold to call,/ For 'tis my limited service." *Mac,* II, iii, 52–53. **2** specified: "Having the hour limited,/ and an express command under penalty . . ." *Meas,* IV, ii, 164–165. **3** restricted or exclusive: ". . . there is boundless theft/ In limited professions." *Timon,* IV, iii, 430–431.

limn, *v.* to etch, also to sketch or paint: ". . . his effigies/ Most truly limn'd and living in your face . . ." *As You,* II, vii, 196–197.

limping sway, *n.* halting or stumbling authority: "And strength by limping sway disabled . . ." *Sonn 66,* 5.

Lincoln Washes, *n.* flooded marshlands near the sea in Lincolnshire: ". . . half my power this night . . . are taken by the tide;/ These Lincoln Washes have devoured them . . ." *K John,* V, vi, 39–41.

line¹, *n.* **1** degree or station: "To show the line and the predicament/ Wherein you range under this subtle King!" *1 Hen 4,* I, iii, 166–167. **2** [often pl] fits of jealousy: ". . . woman, your husband is in his old lines/ again . . ." *Wives,* IV, ii, 17–18. **3** [pl.] pathways: "Nor shall death brag thou wander'st in his shade,/ When in eternal lines to time thou grow'st . . ." *Sonn 18,* 11–12. **4** range; scope: "And with full line of his authority,/ Governs Lord Angelo . . ." *Meas,* I, iv, 56–57. **5** line of descent; pedigree: "He sends you this most memorable line,/ In every branch truly demonstrative . . ." *Hen 5,* II, iv, 88–89. **6** descendants: "Such hap have all the line of John of Gaunt!" *3 Hen 6,* I, i, 19. **7 by line and level,** by the rules; orderly or precisely: ". . . we steal by line and level, and't like your grace." *Temp,* IV, i, 239–240. **8 deep-premeditated lines,** prepared written statement: "Com'st thou with deep-premeditated lines,/ With written pamphlets studiously devis'd . . ." *1 Hen 6,* III, i, 1–2. **9 give line,** to pay out line, as in fishing: "[Aside] I am angling now,/ Though you perceive me not how I give line." *W Tale,* I, ii, 180–181. **10 line of order,** rule or principle governing function: "Office, and custom, in all line of order." *Tr & Cr,* I, iii, 88. **11 lines of life,** living lines; here, offspring: "So should the lines of life that life repair [renew] . . ." *Sonn 16,* 9. **12 meet in one line,** unite as one force: "Now powers from home and discontents at home/ Meet in one line . . ." *K John,* IV, iii, 151–152. **13 under the line, a.** [living] on the equator: ". . . all that stand about him are/ under the line, they need no other penance . . ." *Hen 8,* V, iii, 41–42. **b.** poss. ref. to belief that those crossing the equator often developed fevers and lost their hair: "Now is the jerkin under the line: now,/ jerkin, you are like to lose your hair . . ." *Temp,* IV, i, 236–237. —*v.* **14** to draw; sketch: "All the pictures fairest lin'd/ Are but black to Rosalind." *As You,* III, ii, 90–91.

line², *n.* prob. a lime tree: "Come, hang them on this line." *Temp,* IV, i, 193.

line³, *v.* **1** to support or strengthen; reinforce: ". . . my brother Mortimer . . . hath sent for you/ To line his enterprise." *1 Hen 4,* II, iii, 82–84. **2** to fill or supply: "And then, the justice,/ In fair round belly, with good capon lin'd . . ." *As You,* II, vii, 153–154. **3 line someone's hand,** to bribe (a person): ". . . what/ If I do line one of their hands?" *Cymb,* II, iii, 65–66.

line⁴, *v.* to provide with a lining; here, in wordplay with "cover" [to copulate with]: "Winter'd garments must be lin'd,/ So must slender Rosalind." *As You,* III, ii, 103–104.

lineal, *adj.* **1** done by right of inheritance: ". . . if France in peace permit/ Our just and lineal entrance to our own . . ." *K John,* II, i, 84–85. **2 lineal of,** descended from: "Queen Isabel, his grandmother,/ Was lineal of the Lady Ermengare . . ." *Hen 5,* I, ii, 81–82.

lineament, *n.* feature, esp. of the face: ". . . such a grief for such,/ In every lineament, branch, shape, and form." *M Ado,* V, i, 13–14.

lined, *adj.* **1** padded: "Pluck the lin'd crutch from thy old limping sire . . ." *Timon,* IV, i, 14. **2 better lined,** more wealthy: "I am given out to be better lin'd than it/ can appear . . ." *Kinsmen,* II, i, 5–6.

line-grove, *n.* prob. a grove of lime trees: ". . . all prisoners, sir,/ In the line-grove which weather-fends your cell . . ." *Temp,* V, i, 9–10.

linen, *adj.* pale or white: ". . . those linen cheeks of thine/ Are counsellors to fear." *Mac,* V, iii, 16–17.

ling, *n.* salted cod; here, prob. with vulgar slang sense of "penis" and general sense of "lecherous old men": "Our old/ lings and our Isbels a' th' country are nothing like/ your old ling and your Isbels a' th' court." *All's W,* III, ii, 12–14.

linger, *v.* **1** to postpone the realization of: ". . . how slow/ This old moon wanes! She lingers my desires . . ." *M N Dream,* I, i, 3–4. **2 linger out,** to draw out; protract: "To linger out a purpos'd [intended] overthrow." *Sonn 90,* 8.

lingering, *adj.* protracted; drawn out: "One would have lingering wars, with little cost . . ." *1 Hen 6,* I, i, 74.

lining, *n.* contents: "The lining of his coffers shall make coats/ To deck our soldiers for these Irish wars." *Rich 2,* I, iv, 61–62.

link, *n.* **1** flare for lighting one's way: "Thou hast saved me a thousand marks in/ links and torches . . ." *1 Hen 4,* III, iii, 41–42. **2** smoke from such a flare used to touch up the faded spots on a black hat: "There was no link to colour Peter's hat . . ." *Shrew,* IV, i, 121.

linsey-woolsey, *n.* cloth of blended linen and wool; hence, a hodgepodge of words, languages, etc.: "But what linsey-woolsey hast thou to speak to/ us again?" *All's W,* IV, i, 11–12.

linstock, *n.* forked staff for holding the gunner's match: "Enter the Boy [seen only by the audience] with a linstock, and exit." [SD] *1 Hen 6,* I, iv, 55.

lion, *n.* **1** (in heraldry) the symbol of English kings: "Give me his gage; lions make leopards tame." *Rich 2,* I, i, 174. **2** the lion regarded as a merciful beast, perh. because of its reputed nobility: ". . . you have a vice of mercy in you,/ Which better fits a lion than a man." *Tr & Cr,* V, iii, 37–38.

lion-mettled, *adj.* having the courage of a lion: "Be lion-mettled, proud, and take no care/ Who chafes, who frets . . ." *Mac,* IV, i, 90–91.

lion-sick, *adj.* ref. to mythical pride of the lion: "He is not sick."/ "Yes, lion-sick—sick of proud heart." *Tr & Cr,* II, iii, 88–89.

lip, *n.* **1 hang the lip,** to sulk: "He hangs the lip at something: you know all,/ Lord Pandarus." *Tr & Cr,* III, i, 135–136. **2 make a lip,** to sneer: ". . . in which time I will make a lip at/ the physician." *Cor,* II, i, 114–115.

—*v.* **3** to kiss: "... a hand that kings/ Have lipp'd, and trembled kissing." *Ant & Cleo,* II, v, 29–30.

Lipsbury pinfold, *n.* poss. ref. to holding Oswald between his teeth [and perh. shaking him like a dog], since Lipsbury appears to mean "mouth," and a pinfold was a holding pen for stray livestock; Kent may mean a pen to hold such impudent knaves as Oswald: "If I had thee in Lipsbury pinfold, I would/ make thee care for me." *Lear,* II, ii, 8–9.

liquor, *n.* **1** (esp. in cooking) any liquid: "The fire that mounts the liquor till't run [boil] o'er ..." *Hen 8,* I, i, 144.
—*v.* **2** to bribe; also, to ply with alcoholic liquor: "... justice hath liquored her: we/ steal as in a castle, cock-sure ..." *1 Hen 4,* II, i, 84–85. **3** to grease; oil: "... they would melt me ... and liquor fishermen's boots with me ..." *Wives,* IV, v, 92–93.

lisp, *v.* **1** to speak in an affected manner: "You jig and amble, and you lisp, you nickname/ God's creatures ..." *Ham,* III, i, 146–147. **2** to affect a foreign accent: "Farewell Monsieur Traveller. Look you lisp, and wear strange suits ..." *As You,* IV, i, 31–32. **3** to whisper intimately; coo: "... look whether the fiery Trigon his man be not lisping to his master's old tables ..." *2 Hen 4,* II, iv, 253–264.

list¹, *v.* **1** to listen (to): "I will debate this matter at more leisure,/ And teach your ears to list me with more heed." *Errors,* IV, i, 101–102. **2** [used as a command] listen; pay attention: "List, list, O list!/ If thou didst ever thy dear father love—" *Ham,* I, v, 22–23.

list², *n.* **1** [often pl.] edge or outer limit; boundary: "The very list, the very utmost bound/ Of all our fortunes." *1 Hen 4,* IV, i, 51–52. **2** destination; objective: "I mean, she is the/ list of my voyage." *T Night,* III, i, 77–78. **3** barriers: "Dear Kate, you and I cannot be confined within/ the weak list of a country's fashion ..." *Hen 5,* V, ii, 285–286. **4** edge or selvage on a piece of cloth: "... as there may between the lists and the/ velvet. Thou art the list." *Meas,* I, ii, 28–29. **5** strip of cloth: "... a kersey/ boot-hose on the other [leg], gartered with a red and blue list ..." *Shrew,* III, ii, 64–66. **6** [pl.] the enclosed grounds on which combats were fought: "The lists at Coventry" [SD] *Rich 2,* I, iii, 1.

list³, *n.* register containing soldiers' names: "... here and there/ Shark'd up a list of lawless resolutes ..." *Ham,* I, i, 100–101.

list⁴, *v.* **1** to like; please; want, choose, or care to: "I will frown as I pass by, and let them take it as/ they list." *Rom & Jul,* I, i 38–39. **2 if you list,** if you please; poss. wordplay on nautical "list," to lean from the vertical: "Your lieutenant, if you list; he's no standard." *Temp,* III, ii, 16. **3 turns what he list,** has

from Fortune what he wants: "That blind priest, like the eldest son of fortune,/ Turns what he list." *Hen 8,* II, ii, 20–21.
—*n.* **4** wish; desire: "... for when I ha' list to sleep—" *Oth,* II, i, 104.

list'ning, *pres. part.* listening to: "List'ning their fear, I could not say, 'Amen.'" *Mac,* II, ii, 28.

literatured, *adj.* informed [about]: "Gower is a good captain, and is good knowledge,/ and literatured in the wars." *Hen 5,* IV, vii, 153–154.

lither, *adj.* supple; yielding: "Coupled in bonds of perpetuity,/ Two Talbots winged through the lither sky ..." *1 Hen 6,* IV, vii, 20–21.

litigious, *adj.* interrupted by frequent bickering: "... and Tyrus stands/ In a litigious peace." *Per,* III, iii, 3.

Litio, *n.* Hortensio's assumed name: "But let it rest. Now, Litio, to you." *Shrew,* III, i, 54.

litter, *n.* **1** bedding of straw, etc., for animals: "To crouch in litter of your stable planks ..." *K John,* V, ii, 140. **2** portable curtained bed, carried usually by two servants: "Set on toward Swinstead; to my litter straight:/ Weakness possesseth me, and I am faint." *K John,* V, iii, 16–17.
—*v.* **3** to give birth to; here, in sense of an animal: "... the son that she did litter here,/ A freckled whelp hag-born ..." *Temp,* I, ii, 282–283. **4 littered under Mercury,** born when the planet Mercury was in the ascendant: "My father named me Autolycus; who,/ being as I am, littered under Mercury ..." *W Tale,* IV, iii, 24–25.

little, *adj.* **1** some; of a proper amount: "... may be restor'd/ With good advice and little medicine." *2 Hen 4,* III, i, 42–43. **2** thin: "... my leg is too long?"/ "No, that it is too little." *Two Gent,* V, ii, 4–5. **3 as little by,** reply to "set" of previous line [set music to the words], understood by Julia as "set store by": "As little by such toys [set as little store by such trifles] as may be possible ..." *Two Gent,* I, ii, 82. **4 little good,** [worth] little good: "So fare you well, my little good lord cardinal." *Hen 8,* III, ii, 349.
—*n.* **5** small worth; scant merit: "As if I lov'd my little should be dieted/ In praises sauc'd with lies." *Cor,* I, ix, 51–52. **6 in little, a.** in miniature: "... give twenty, forty, fifty, a/ hundred ducats apiece for his picture in little." *Ham,* II, ii, 361–362. **b.** in one woman: "The quintessence of every sprite/ Heaven would in little show." *As You,* III, ii, 136–137.

live, *v.* **1** to float: "... a strong mast that liv'd upon the sea ..." *T Night,* I, ii, 14. **2** to survive; here, through offspring: "... what could death do, if thou shouldst depart,/ Leaving thee living in posterity?" *Sonn 6,* 11–12. **3 here live,** [to] remain

alive: ". . . but, love, you are/ No longer yours than you your-self here live . . ." *Sonn 13*, 1–2. **4 live by,** to gain a livelihood by (doing or performing something); also, to live next to: "Dost thou/ live by thy tabor?"/ "No, sir, I live by the church." *T Night*, III, i, 1–3. **5 lives not,** is not present; hence, the re-ports are lies: "Sir, the Duke is marvellous little beholding to/ your reports; but the best is, he lives not in them." *Meas*, IV, iii, 158–159. **6 Will I live?** Of course! You bet!: "But will you woo this wildcat?"/ "Will I live?" *Shrew*, I, ii, 195.
—*n.* **7** var. of **life:** ". . . and will weep/ My date of life out for his sweet live's loss." *K John*, IV, iii, 105–106.

livelihood, *n.* liveliness; animation: "What of his heart per-ceive you in his face/ By any livelihood he show'd today?" *Rich 3*, III, iv, 54–55.

lively, *adj.* **1** living: ". . . what shall I do/ Now I behold thy lively body so?" *T Andr*, III, i, 104–105. **2** striking; vivid: "A pattern, president [precedent], and lively warrant/ For me . . . to perform the like." *T Andr*, V, iii, 44–45.
—*adv.* **3** in a lifelike [truthful] manner: ". . . th' art indeed the best;/ Thou counterfeit'st most lively." *Timon*, V, i, 80–81.

liver[1], *n.* **1** body organ regarded as seat of the passions, esp. love or anger: ". . . this way will I take upon me to wash your liver as clean as a sound sheep's heart . . ." *As You*, III, ii, 410–411. **2 liver white as milk,** proof of cowardice: "How many cowards . . . Who inward search'd, have livers white as milk?" *Merch*, III, ii, 83–86.

liver[2], *n.* **1** ordinary person: ". . . 'tis better to be lowly born,/ And range with humble livers [be ranked among the com-mon people] in content . . ." *Hen 8*, II, iii, 19–20. **2** living person; human being: ". . . prithee think/ There's livers out of Britain." *Cymb*, III, iv, 141–142.

liver vein, *n.* manner of love [because the liver is the seat of passionate love]: "This is the liver vein, which makes flesh a deity . . ." *Love's L*, IV, iii, 71.

livery, *n.* **1** inherited property: "He came but to be Duke of Lancaster,/ To sue his livery [claim his inheritance], and beg his peace . . ." *1 Hen 4*, IV, iii, 61–62. **2** [often pl.] apparel: "The childing autumn, angry winter, change/ Their wonted liver-ies . . ." *M N Dream*, II, i, 112–113. **3** outward appearance; semblance: "Did livery falseness in a pride of truth." *Lover's Comp*, 105. **4** badge: "A scar nobly got . . . is a good liv'ry of/ honour." *All's W*, IV, v, 95–96. **5 destined livery,** natural role of women: "If you be one [a woman] . . . show it now,/ By putting on the destin'd livery." *Meas*, II, iv, 135–137. **6 in liv-eries,** as servants: "Kept hearts in liveries, but mine own was free . . ." *Lover's Comp*, 195.

Livia, *n.* Octavius Caesar's wife: "Some nobler token I have kept apart/ For Livia and Octavia . . ." *Ant & Cleo*, V, ii, 167–168.

living, *n.* **1** property; estates: "I will die,/ And leave him all: life, living, all is Death's." *Rom & Jul*, IV, v, 39–40.
—*adj.* **2** everlasting: "This grave shall have a living monu-ment." *Ham*, V, i, 292.

living art, *n.* prob. ref. to the ancients' "art of living": "Still and contemplative in living art." *Love's L*, I, i, 14.

living drollery, *n.* See **drollery** (def. 2).

living flowers, *n.* offspring; progeny: "With virtuous wish would bear you living flowers . . ." *Sonn 16*, 7.

lo or **loe,** *interj.* look! behold!: "Lo you! here she comes. This is her very guise; and,/ upon my life, fast asleep." *Mac*, V, i, 18–19.

loach, *n.* small foodfish, sometimes used as bait: ". . . your chamber-lye/ breeds fleas like a loach." *1 Hen 4*, II, i, 19–20.

load, *n.* **1** burden of woes: "I had my load before, now press'd with bearing . . ." *Ven & Ad*, 430.
—*v.* **2** to reward: ". . . it will show honestly in us, and . . . load our purposes . . ." *Timon*, V, i, 14–15. **3** to burden: ". . . 'tis a cruelty/ To load a falling man." *Hen 8*, V, ii, 110–111.
—*past part.* **4 loaden me,** loaded myself: "For I have loaden me with many spoils . . ." *1 Hen 6*, II, i, 80.

loaden, *adj.* loaded; laden: "A post from Wales, loaden with heavy news . . ." *1 Hen 4*, I, i, 37.

loam, *n.* mixture of wet clay, etc., used to plaster walls: ". . . let him/ have some plaster, or some loam, or some roughcast/ about him, to signify wall . . ." *M N Dream*, III, i, 63–65.

loathly, *adj.* **1** loathsome (often applied to malformed off-spring): ". . . they do observe/ Unfather'd heirs and loathly births of nature." *2 Hen 4*, IV, iv, 121–122.
—*adv.* **2** aversely; strongly: "Seeing how loathly opposite I stood/ To his unnatural purpose . . ." *Lear*, II, i, 49–50. **3** dis-gustingly: ". . . bestrew/ The union of your bed with weeds so loathly/ That you shall hate it both . . ." *Temp*, IV, i, 20–22. **4** with abhorrence: ". . . my father's eye/ Should hold her loath-ly . . ." *Oth*, III, iv, 59–60.

loathness, *n.* reluctance or hesitation: "Pray you, look not sad,/ Nor make replies of loathness . . ." *Ant & Cleo*, III, xi, 17–18.

lob, *n.* **1** bumpkin: "Farewell, thou lob of [among] spirits; I'll be gone . . ." *M N Dream*, II, i, 16.

—*v.* **2** to droop: "... and their poor jades/ Lob down their heads, dropping the hides and hips ..." *Hen 5,* IV, ii, 46–47.

lock *v.* **1** to lock up; lock away: "When Marcus Brutus grows so covetous,/ To lock such rascal counters from his friends ..." *J Caes,* IV, iii, 79–80. **2 lock away from,** be locked away from [by]: "Sport and repose lock from me day and night ..." *Ham,* III, ii, 212.
—*n.* **3 locks of counsel,** seals on private or secret documents: "... blest be/ You bees that make these locks of counsel!" *Cymb,* III, ii, 35–36.

lockram, *n.* collar of cheap linen: "The kitchen malkin pins/ Her richest lockram 'bout her reechy neck ..." *Cor,* II, i, 206–207.

locust, *n.* appar. a sweet fruit of Eastern countries: "The food that to him now is as luscious as locusts,/ shall be to him shortly as acerb as the coloquintida." *Oth,* I, iii, 349–350.

lodestar or **lode-star,** *n.* guiding star: "Your eyes are lode-stars, and your tongue's sweet air/ More tuneable than lark to shepherd's ear ..." *M N Dream,* I, i, 183–184.

lodge, *n.* **1** hut or cottage, esp. of a gamekeeper: "I found him here as melancholy as a lodge/ in a warren." *M Ado,* II, i, 199–200.
—*v.* **2** to harbor; entertain: "... by whose power I well might lodge a fear/ To be again displac'd ..." *2 Hen 4,* IV, v, 207–208. **3** to beat down; flatten: "Our sighs and they shall lodge the summer corn,/ And make a dearth in this revolting land." *Rich 2,* III, iii, 162–163. **4** to remain; stay the night: "And, soldiers, stay and lodge by me this night." *3 Hen 6,* I, i, 32.

lodged, *adj.* deep-seated: "So I can give no reason ... More than a lodg'd hate ..." *Merch,* IV, I, 59–60.

lodging, *n.* **1** stocks, which hold Kent prisoner: "Take vantage, heavy eyes, not to behold/ This shameful lodging." *Lear,* II, ii, 171–172. **2** destruction, as of crops by a storm: "Look on the tragic lodging of this bed ..." *Oth,* V, ii, 364.

loe, *interj.* See **lo.**

loffe, *v.* old form of **laugh:** "And then the whole quire hold their hips and loffe ..." *M N Dream,* II, i, 55.

lofty, *adj.* **1** proud; haughty: "... his humour is lofty, his discourse/ peremptory ..." *Love's L,* V, i, 9–10. **2** elegant; stylish: "Saying our grace is only in our heels,/ And that we are most lofty runaways [cowards]." *Hen V,* III, vi, 34–35.

loggerhead, *n.* dolt; blockhead: "With three or four loggerheads, amongst three or/ fourscore hogsheads." *1 Hen 4,* II, iv, 4–5.

logger-headed, *adj.* blockheaded; stupid: "You logger-headed and unpolish'd grooms!" *Shrew,* IV, i, 112.

loggets or **loggats,** *n.* game in which shaped pieces of wood (loggets) were tossed at a stake in the ground: "Did these bones cost no more the breeding but to play/ at loggets with 'em?" *Ham,* V, i, 90–91.

loiterer, *n.* idler: "O illiterate loiterer! It was the son of thy grandmother." *Two Gent,* III, i, 290–291.

loll, *v.* (of the tongue) to thrust out: "... the enemy full-hearted,/ Lolling the tongue with slaught'ring ..." *Cymb,* V, iii, 7–8.

lolling, *adj.* with the tongue hanging out: "... like a great natural/ that runs lolling up and down ..." *Rom & Jul,* II, iv, 91–92.

London Stone, *n.* large rounded stone in Cannon Street; landmark from ancient times: "And here, sitting/ upon London Stone, I charge and command ..." *2 Hen 6,* IV, vi, 1–2.

loneliness, *n.* **1** act of hiding away; seclusion: "... now I see/ The myst'ry of your loneliness ..." *All's W,* I, iii, 165–166. **2** fact of being by oneself: "That show of such an exercise may colour/ Your loneliness." *Ham,* III, i, 45–46.

lonely, *adj.* secluded; hidden: "So her dead likeness ... Excels whatever ... hand of man hath done; therefore I keep it/ Lonely, apart." *W Tale,* V, iii, 15–18.

long¹, *adj.* **1** trying; wearisome: "... the boy Fidele's sickness/ Did make my way long forth [from the cave]." *Cymb,* IV, ii, 148–149.
—*v.* **2 long till,** to await eagerly: "I long till Edward fall by war's mischance ..." *3 Hen 6,* III, iii, 254.
—*adv.* **3** after a long time: "At last, though long, our jarring notes agree ..." *Shrew,* V, ii, 1.
—*n.* **4 long life:** "... [you] that prefer/ A noble life before [to] a long ..." *Cor,* III, i, 151–152.

long², *prep.* **1 long all of,** all because of: "Maine, Blois, Poictiers, and Tours, are won away,/ Long all of Somerset and his delay." *1 Hen 6,* IV, iii, 45–46. **2 long of,** because of: "'Tis long of you that spur me with [your fault for asking me] such questions." *Love's L,* II, i, 118. Also, **'long of.**

long³, *v.* Also, **'long.** var. of **belong:** "By law of nature and of nations, longs/ To him and to his heirs ..." *Hen 5,* II, iv, 80–81.

long-engraffed, *adj.* long-ingrained; deep-seated: "... not alone the imperfections of long-engraffed condition [disposition] ..." *Lear,* I, i, 297.

long heath, *n.* prob. heather, a shrub that thrives on barren ground: "I would give a thousand furlongs of sea for an/ acre of barren ground, long heath, broom, furze,/ anything." *Temp,* I, i, 64–66.

longing, *adj.* motivated by longing: ". . . what I stand in need of,/ To furnish me upon my longing journey." *Two Gent,* II, vii, 84–85.

longly, *adv.* at great length; also, attentively or unrelentingly: "Master, you look'd so longly on the maid . . ." *Shrew,* I, i, 165.

long purple, *n.* prob. the wild orchid, a tall spike of purple flowers: ". . . long purples,/ That liberal shepherds give a grosser name,/ But our cold maids do dead men's fingers call them." *Ham,* IV, vii, 168–170.

long since, *adv.* long past; long ago: "In days long since, before these last so bad." *Sonn 67,* 14.

long-staff sixpenny strikers, *n.* highwaymen who used a long pole tipped with a hook to pull victims from their horses: "I am joined with no foot-landrakers,/ no long-staff sixpenny strikers . . ." *1 Hen 4,* II, i, 72–73.

long sword, *n.* long and heavy English sword; here, an old-fashioned weapon that Capulet can no longer manage: "Give me my long sword, ho!"/ "A crutch, a crutch! Why call you for a sword?" *Rom & Jul,* I, i, 73–74.

long-tongued, *adj.* bragging or chattering: "Why, how now, long-tongu'd Warwick! dare you speak?" *3 Hen 6,* II, ii, 102.

'loo, *interj.* cry of encouragement, esp. to hounds: "Now, bull! Now, dog! 'Loo, Paris, 'loo!" *Tr & Cr,* V, vii, 10.

loofed, *adj.* disengaged; here, from the battle: "She once being loof'd . . . Antony/ Claps on his sea-wing . . ." *Ant & Cleo,* III, x, 18–20.

look, *v.* **1** to expect: "I'll look to like, if looking liking move . . ." *Rom & Jul,* I, iii, 97. **2** to be seen or detected: "If this should fail,/ And that our drift [scheme] look through our bad performance . . ." *Ham,* IV, vii, 149–150. **3** to be certain or careful; take care: "Let good Antonio look he keep his day/ Or he shall pay for this." *Merch,* II, viii, 25–26. **4** to search for; find: "I must go look my twigs. He shall be caught." *All's W,* III, vi, 103. **5** to appear likely; promise: ". . . that is there which looks/ With us [with our help] to break his neck." *Cor,* III, iii, 29–30. **6** introductory word to emphasize what follows: "Look, whom she best endow'd she gave the more . . ." *Sonn 11,* 11. **7 look about,** (to) get moving; get busy (usually given as an order): "Go to; I say he shall have no wrong. Look

about,/ Davy." *2 Hen 4,* V, i, 49–50. **8 look against,** to gaze at directly: ". . . the folly of my/ soul dares not present itself; she is too bright to be/ looked against." *Wives,* II, ii, 234–236. **9 look beyond,** to mistake or misjudge (a person): "My gracious lord, you look beyond him quite." *2 Hen 4,* IV, iv, 67. **10 look big,** (to) appear to threaten: "A rendezvous, a home to fly unto,/ If that the devil and mischance look big . . ." *1 Hen 4,* IV, i, 57–58. **11 look far,** to have great understanding or insight: "He did look far/ Into the service of the time . . ." *All's W,* I, ii, 26–27. **12 look for,** to await: "I know they are in Rome together/ Looking for Antony . . ." *Ant & Cleo,* II, i, 19–20. **13 look I,** I will expect or anticipate: "But when in thee time's furrows I behold,/ Then look I death my days should expiate . . ." *Sonn 22,* 3–4. **14 look into,** to consider: ". . . look into Master Froth/ here, sir; a man of fourscore pound a year . . ." *Meas,* II, i, 121–122. **15 look like the time,** show a countenance appropriate to the occasion: "To beguile the time,/ Look like the time; bear welcome in your eye . . ." *Mac,* I, v, 63–64. **16 look on,** to be a witness to: "I am sorry/ To see you ta'en from liberty, to look on/ The business present." *Hen 8,* I, i, 204–206. **17 look one out,** to repay or reciprocate with: "I'll look you out a good turn, Servilius." *Timon,* III, ii, 60. **18 look out,** to blush: "He tells her something/ That makes her blood look out . . ." *W Tale,* IV, iv, 159–160. **19 looks us,** appears to us: "She looks us like/ A thing more made of malice than of duty . . ." *Cymb,* III, v, 32–33. **20 look through, a.** to perceive the motive behind (an action): "He is a great observer, and he looks/ Quite through the deeds of men." *J Caes,* I, ii, 199–200. **b.** be apparent in: ". . . his richness/ And costliness of spirit look'd through him." *Kinsmen,* V, iii, 96–97. **21 look to,** take care of: "Away with the joint-stools, remove the court-cupboard,/ look to the plate." *Rom & Jul,* I, v, 6–7. **22 look to know,** expect to hear: ". . . and do look to know/ What doth befall you here." *Meas,* I, i, 57–58. **23 look up,** to take heart, courage, etc.: "Only look up clear;/ To alter favour ever is to fear." *Mac,* I, v, 71–72. **24 look you (or thou),** be sure to; don't fail to: ". . . and look you eat no more/ Than will preserve just so much strength in us . . ." *T Andr,* III, ii, 1–2. **25 look you out,** to search out for you: "I'll look you out a good turn,/ Servilius." *Timon,* III, ii, 60–61.

—*n.* **26** [pl.] glances: "Her pretty looks have been mine enemies . . ." *Sonn 139,* 10. **27 make their looks by his,** adopt a superior's attitudes as their own: ". . . for he would shine on those/ That make their looks by his . . ." *Ant & Cleo,* I, v, 55–56.

looked after, *adj.* kept watch upon: "Is lechery so look'd after?" *Meas,* I, ii, 133.

looked on, *adj.* respected; regarded: "For yet I am not look'd on in the world." *3 Hen 6,* V, vii, 22.

look how, *conj.* just as; in the same way that: "Look how a bird lies tangled in a net,/ So fasten'd in her arms Adonis lies . . ." *Ven & Ad,* 67–68.

look what, *pron.* whatever; that which: "Look what will serve is fit . . ." *M Ado,* I, i, 298.

look when, *pron.* whenever: "Look when his infant fortune came to age . . ." *1 Hen 4,* I, iii, 249.

loon, *n.* rascal; knave: "The devil damn thee black, thou cream-fac'd loon!" *Mac,* V, iii, 11.

loop[1], *n.* loop-hole; hole, esp. in a wall, for peering through: "And stop all sight-holes;, every loop from whence/ The eye of reason may pry in upon us . . ." *1 Hen 4,* IV, i, 71–72.

loop[2], *n.* doubled piece of wire, rope, etc., forming a loop; here, fig. use: "That the probation bear no hinge, nor loop,/ To hang a doubt on . . ." *Oth,* III, iii, 371–372.

looped and windowed, *adj.* full of holes, rents, etc.: "How shall your houseless heads and unfed sides,/ Your loop'd and window'd raggedness, defend you . . ." *Lear,* III, iv, 30–32.

loop-hole, *n.* one of a series of small peepholes in a fortification: "The very eyes of men through loop-holes thrust . . ." *Luc,* 1383.

loose, *n.* **1** release of an arrow: ". . . often, at his very loose, de-cides/ That which long process could not arbitrate . . ." *Love's L,* V, ii, 734–735.
—*adj.* **2** lacking in restraint: "Where you are liberal of your loves and counsels,/ Be sure you be not loose . . ." *Hen 8,* II, i, 126–127. **3** wanton; dissolute: ". . . that loose grace/ Which shallow laughing hearers give to fools." *Love's L,* V, ii, 851–852. **4** negligent; indifferent: "With distinct breath and consign'd kisses to them,/ He fumbles up into a loose adieu . . ." *Tr & Cr,* IV, iv, 44–45.
—*v.* **5** to release ["lose" meaning "forget" may have been intended, with sense of "to forgive or forgo"]: "Thou wilt not only loose the forfeiture [forfeit],/ But . . . Forgive a moiety [part] of the principal . . ." *Merch,* IV, i, 24–26. **6** to release an arrow: "To it, boy! Marcus, loose when I bid." *T Andr,* IV, iii, 58. **7 loose forth,** to release from: "What did I then, but curs'd the gentle gusts/ And he that loos'd them forth their brazen caves . . ." *2 Hen 6,* III, ii, 87–88.

loosely, *adv.* carelessly; indifferently: ". . . a prince should not be so loosely studied as to/ remember so weak a composition." *2 Hen 4,* II, ii, 7–8.

loose regard indifferent looks: ". . . and, princes all,/ Lay negligent and loose regard upon him." *Tr & Cr,* III, iii, 40–41.

loose shot, *n.* throwers not attached to a company: ". . . a file of boys behind 'em, loose shot, deliver'd such a/ shower of pebbles . . ." *Hen 8,* V, iii, 55–56.

loose-wived, *adj.* having a wanton wife: ". . . it is a heart-breaking to see a handsome/ man loose-wiv'd . . ." *Ant & Cleo,* I, ii, 68–69.

lord, *v.* **1** to make (a person) a lord: "He being thus lorded,/ Not only with what my revenue yielded,/ But what my power might else exact . . ." *Temp,* I, ii, 97–99. **2 lord it,** to play the master; give oneself airs: "I see them lording it in London streets . . ." *2 Hen 6,* IV, viii, 45.

Lord have mercy on us, words placed over the door of a house infected with the plague: "Write 'Lord have mercy on us' on those three;/ They are infected, in their hearts it lies . . ." *Love's L,* V, ii, 419–420.

lording, *n.* **1** very young lord: ". . . my lord's tricks, and yours, when you were boys./ You were pretty lordings then?" *W Tale,* I, ii, 61–62. **2** [pl] old form of address, equiv. to "gentlemen" or "my lords": "Lordings, farewell; and say, when I am gone,/ I prophesied France will be lost ere long." *2 Hen 6,* I, 1, 144–145.

Lord of Hosts, *n.* God: "The battles of the Lord of Hosts he fought;/ The Church's prayers made him so prosperous." *1 Hen 6,* I, i, 31–32.

Lord's sake, *n.* **for the Lord's sake,** prisoners' cry to passersby for food: ". . . all great doers in our trade, and are now 'for the Lord's/ sake.'" *Meas,* IV, iii, 19–20.

Lord's tokens, *n.* plague spots; death-tokens: ". . . you are not free,/ For the Lord's tokens on you do I see." *Love's L,* V, ii, 422–423.

lose, *v.* **1** to forget: "Hear what I say, and then go home and lose me." *Hen 8,* II, i, 57. **2** to forgo; give up: ". . . she will not lose her wonted greatness/ To use so rude behaviour." *Hen 8,* IV, ii, 102–103. **3** to waste: "You cannot speak of reason to the Dane/ And lose your voice." *Ham,* I, ii, 44–45. **4 lose by 'em,** urge on them to no avail: ". . . like the virtues/ Which our divines lose by 'em." *Cor,* II, iii, 59–60. **5 lose oneself,** to roam; stroll aimlessly: ". . . I will go lose myself,/ And wander up and down to view the city." *Errors,* I, ii, 30–31.

losing suit, *n.* Shylock's ref. to the three thousand ducats he has lost: "I follow thus/ A losing suit against him!" *Merch,* IV, i, 61–62.

loss, *n.* **1** death; destruction: "Poor thing, condemn'd to loss!" *W Tale,* II, iii, 191. **2 in the loss of question,** See **question** (def. 8).

lost, *adj.* useless; idle: "Do you go back dismay'd? 'tis a lost fear . . ." *Oth,* V, ii, 270.

lot, *n.* **lots to blanks,** more than likely: ". . . it is lots to blanks/ My name hath touch'd your ears . . ." *Cor,* V, ii, 10–11.

lottery, *n.* **1** chance: "So let high-sighted tyranny range on,/ Till each man drop by lottery." *J Caes,* II, i, 118–119. **2** marriage regarded as a lottery or a game of chance: ". . . we might have a good woman born but or [either] every/ blazing star or at an earthquake, 'twould mend the/ lottery well . . ." *All's W,* I, iii, 83–85. **3** gift or allotment; prize: "Octavia is/ A blessed lottery to him." *Ant & Cleo,* II, ii, 242–243.

loud, *adj.* **1 so loud a wind,** the strong wind of public sentiment: ". . . my arrows,/ Too slightly timber'd for so loud a wind . . ." *Ham,* IV, vii, 21–22.
—*n.* **2** loudness: ". . . there's no answer/ That will be given to th' loud of noise we make." *Cymb,* III, v, 43–44.

lour, *v.* to lower; look sullen; menace or threaten: "This louring tempest of your home-bred hate . . ." *Rich 2,* I, iii, 187.

louse, *n.* **1** confusion with "luce" [pike] and with coat = coat of arms: "The dozen white louses do become an old coat/ well . . ." *Wives,* I, i, 18–19.
—*v.* **2** to have lice: "The head and he shall louse;/ So beggars marry many." *Lear,* III, ii, 29–30.

lousy, *adj.* low; contemptible [lit., infested with lice]; here, understood as "a contemptible person": ". . . is this captain in the Duke of Florence's/ camp?"/ "Upon my knowledge he is, and lousy." *All's W,* IV, iii, 186–188.

lout, *n.* **1 general louts,** fools of the community: "And you will rather show our general louts/ How you can frown . . ." *Cor,* III, ii, 66–67.
—*v.* **2** to make a fool of: "And I am louted by a traitor villain/ And cannot help the noble chevalier." *1 Hen 6,* IV, iii, 13–14.

love, *n.* **1** act of love or devotion: "But if I cannot win you to this love,/ Go search like nobles . . ." *Per,* II, iv, 49–50. **2** one beloved; lover: ". . . this is pity now . . . there should be/ In such a love so vile a lout as he!" *K John,* II, i, 507–509. **3** feelings of love: "If my dear love were but the child of state [accidental] . . ." *Sonn 124,* 1. **4 for your love,** as a token of friendship: "And (for your love) I'll take this ring from you . . ." *Merch,* IV, i, 423. **5 in love,** in the name of friendship: "I'll take no more,/ And you in love shall not deny me this!" *Merch,* IV, i, 424–425. **6 in your love,** despite your love: ". . . which to hin-

der/ Were (in your love) a whip to me . . ." *W Tale,* I, ii, 24–25. **7 make love,** to woo; here, solicit help: ". . . thence it is/ That I to your assistance do make love . . ." *Mac,* III, i, 122–123. **8 my love and fear,** love and fear of me: "My love and fear glu'd many friends to thee . . ." *3 Hen 6,* II, vi, 5. **9 of all loves,** for heaven's sake: "Speak, of all loves! I swoon almost with fear." *M N Dream,* II, ii, 153. **10 out of love,** from the knowledge of love: "Therefore this maxim out of love I teach . . ." *Tr & Cr,* I, ii, 297. **11 why to love,** why you should love me: "Since why to love I can allege no cause." *Sonn 49,* 14.
—*v.* **12** to desire that; want: "As if I lov'd my little [merit] should be dieted/ In praises sauc'd with lies." *Cor,* I, ix, 51–52.

Love, *n.* Venus, goddess of love: "Therefore do nimblepinion'd doves draw Love . . ." *Rom & Jul,* II, v, 7.

love-book, *n.* manual of love: "And on a love-book pray for my success?" *Two Gent,* I, i, 19.

loved, *adj.* preferred; favorite: "The temple-haunting martlet, does approve,/ By his loved mansionry . . ." *Mac,* I, vi, 4–5.

love-day, *n.* day of forgiveness and peacemaking: "You are my guest, Lavinia, and your friends./ This day shall be a love-day, Tamora." *T Andr,* I, i, 490–491.

love-feat, *n.* lover's suit; courtship: "And every one his love-feat will advance/ Unto his several mistress . . ." *Love's L,* V, ii, 123–124.

love in idleness, belief that love is generated by idleness: ". . . while idly I stood looking on,/ I found the effect of love in idleness . . ." *Shrew,* I, i, 150–151.

love-in-idleness, *n.* another name for the pansy: ". . . now purple with love's wound:/ And maidens call it 'love-in-idleness.'" *M N Dream,* II, i, 167–168.

love-lay, *n.* love song: ". . . who but women do our love-lays greet?" *Edw 3,* II, i, 97.

lovely, *adj.* **1** loving: ". . . bid good morrow to my bride,/ And seal the title with a lovely kiss." *Shrew,* III, ii, 120–121. **2** handsome: "In praise of ladies dead and lovely knights . . ." *Sonn 106,* 4.

lovely well, *adv.* quite capably: ". . . being but young I framed to the harp/ Many an English ditty lovely well . . ." *1 Hen 4,* III, i, 118–119.

love-monger, *n.* dealer in or purveyor of love: "Thou art an old love-monger, and speak'st skilfully." *Love's L,* II, i, 253.

love of soul, *n.* true loyalty or allegiance: "Swearing allegiance and the love of soul/ To stranger blood, to foreign royalty." *K John*, V, i, 10–11.

lover, *n.* **1** devoted friend; comrade: "'The mighty gods defend thee! Thy lover, Artemidorus.'" *J Caes*, II, iii, 7. **2** person who is in love; here, those with loved ones back in Greece: "This shall be told our lovers, Lord Aeneas." *Tr & Cr*, I, iii, 283.

lovered, *adj.* provided with a lover: "Who, young and simple, would not be so lover'd?" *Lover's Comp*, 320.

lovers' food, *n.* each other's company: ". . . we must starve our sight/ From lovers' food, till morrow deep midnight." *M N Dream*, I, i, 222–223.

love-springs, *n. pl.* tender shoots and buds of love: "Even in the spring of love, thy love-springs rot?" *Errors*, III, ii, 3.

love's use, *n.* lovemaking; also, poss. wordplay with "interest [offspring] on expenditure": "Mine be thy love, and thy love's use their treasure." *Sonn 20*, 14.

loving, *adj.* loyal; faithful: ". . . three or four loving lords have put themselves into voluntary exile with him . . ." *As You*, I, i, 100–101.

loving likelihood, *n.* warmly anticipated possibility: "As, by a lower but by loving likelihood . . ." *Hen 5*, V, Chor. 29.

loving motion, *n.* favorable urging: "Your loving motion toward the common body . . ." *Cor*, II, ii, 53.

low¹, *adj.* **1** not tall; short or comparatively so: "The woman low,/ And browner than her brother." *As You*, IV, iii, 87–88. **2** lowly; humble: ". . . in low simplicity/ He lends out money gratis . . ." *Merch*, I, iii, 38–39. **3** degrading; humiliating: ". . . your purpos'd low correction/ Is such as basest and contemned'st wretches . . . Are punish'd with . . ." *Lear*, II, ii, 142–145. **4** impoverished: "I hope it is not so low with him as he/ made it seem . . ." *Timon*, III, vi, 5–6. **5 low name,** status of a commoner: ". . . between their titles, and low name,/ There's nothing differs but the outward fame." *Rich 3*, I, iv, 82–83.
—*adv.* **6** in a humble manner: ". . . living low where Fortune cannot hurt me . . ." *3 Hen 6*, IV, vi, 20.
—*n.* **7** person or persons of low rank: "Then happy low, lie down!" *2 Hen 4*, III, i, 30.

low², *v.* to moo: ". . . the dam runs lowing up and down,/ Looking the way her harmless young one went . . ." *2 Hen 6*, III, i, 214–215.

low countries, *n.* pun on Low Countries and the lower (or "nether") regions of the body: ". . . the rest of thy low coun-

tries/ have made a shift to eat up thy holland." *2 Hen 4*, II, ii, 21–22.

low-crooked, *adj.* low-bowing: "I mean sweet words,/ Low-crooked curtsies, and base spaniel fawning." *J Caes*, III, i, 43–44.

lower¹, *v.* to frown or look sullen; here, a sign of jealousy: "What low'ring star now envies thy estate . . ." *2 Hen 6*, III, i, 206.

lower², *adj.* **1** humbler: "As, by a lower but by loving likelihood . . ." *Hen 5*, V, Chor. 29. **2** shorter: "Arcite is the/ lower of the twain . . ." *Kinsmen*, II, i, 49–50.

lowest, *adj.* faintest; softest: "A lover's ear will hear the lowest sound . . ." *Love's L*, IV, iii, 331.

lowliness, *n.* pretended humility: ". . . 'tis a common proof,/ That lowliness is young ambition's ladder . . ." *J Caes*, II, i, 21–22.

lowly, *adj.* **1** humble: "And lowly words were ransom for their fault." *2 Hen 6*, III, i, 127.
—*adv.* **2** in a position of humility: "And, lowly at his stirrup,/ comes afoot/ King John of France together with his son/ In captive bonds . . ." *Edw 3*, V, I, 181–183.

lown, *n.* base fellow; lout: "We should have both lord and lown, if the peevish/ baggage would but give way to customers." *Per*, IV, vi, 17–18.

low sounds, *n.* murmurings or softly spoken words: "Nor are those empty-hearted whose low sounds/ Reverb no hollowness." *Lear*, I, i, 153–154.

low steps, *n.* humble [or humbler] positions: "You have by fortune . . . Gone slightly o'er low steps [have been promoted quickly], and now are mounted/ Where powers are your retainers . . ." *Hen 8*, II, iv, 109–111.

loyal, *adj.* showing the devotion of a lover: "Write loyal cantons of contemned love . . ." *T Night*, I, v, 274.

loyalty, *n.* affection for parent [nature] here contrasted with [and subordinated to] loyalty to sovereign [Duke of Cornwall]: "How, my lord, I may be censured, that nature/ thus gives way to loyalty . . ." *Lear*, III, v, 2–3.

lozel, *n.* scoundrel: ". . . lozel, thou art worthy to be hang'd,/ That wilt not stay her tongue." *W Tale*, II, iii, 108–109.

lubber, *n.* **1** clumsy fool; oaf or lout: "I am afraid this great lubber, the world,/ will prove a cockney." *T Night*, IV, i, 14–15. **2 measure your lubber's length,** sprawl your oafish carcass [on the floor]: "If you will measure your/ lubber's length again, tarry; but away!" *Lear*, I, iv, 95–96.

lubberly, *adj.* churlish; loutish: "I came yonder at Eton to marry Mistress Anne/ Page, and she's a great lubberly boy." *Wives*, V, v, 183–184.

luce, *n.* pike [fish]; here, misunderstood as "louse": ". . . they/ may give the dozen white luces in their coat [coat of arms]." *Wives*, I, i, 15–16.

Lucifer, *n.* Satan; here, ref. to his being cast out of Heaven for demanding equality with God: "And when he falls, he falls like Lucifer,/ Never to hope again." *Hen 8*, III, ii, 371–372.

Lucina, *n.* Roman goddess of childbirth: "At whose conception, till Lucina reign'd,/ Nature this dowry gave . . ." *Per*, I, i, 9–10.

lucre, *n.* **for lucre of,** out of greed for: "Shall I, for lucre of the rest unvanquish'd,/ Detract so much from that prerogative . . ." *1 Hen 6*, V, iv, 141–142.

Lucrece, *n.* **1** [Latin, *Lucretia*] virtuous Roman matron who committed suicide after being raped by Sextus Tarquinius, son of Tarquinius Superbus, Rome's last king: "Take this of me: Lucrece was not more chaste/ Than this Lavinia, Bassianus' love." *T Andr*, II, i, 108–109. **2** signet ring whose seal bears the image of Lucrece, used in sealing letters: "By your leave, wax. Soft! and/ the impressure her Lucrece, with which she uses/ to seal . . ." *T Night*, II, v, 94–96.

Lucretius, *n.* another name for Lucius Junius Brutus, father of Lucrece: "'Daughter, dear daughter,' old Lucretius cries . . ." *Luc*, 1751.

Ludlow, *n.* castle in Shropshire, on the Welsh border: "Forthwith from Ludlow the young Prince be fet [fetched]/ Hither to London . . ." *Rich 3*, II, ii, 121–122.

Lud's town, *n.* London; from King Lud, Cymbeline's grandfather: "Made Lud's town with rejoicing-fires bright,/ And Britons strut with courage." *Cymb*, III, i, 33–34.

lug, *v.* to tug or pull; yank: "Why, this/ Will lug your priests and servants from your sides . . ." *Timon*, IV, iii, 31–32.

luggage, *n.* encumbering baggage; impedimenta: ". . . what do you mean/ To dote thus on such luggage?" *Temp*, IV, i, 230–231.

lugged, *adj.* (esp. of a bear) baited; torn or attacked by dogs: "I am as melancholy/ as a gib cat, or a lugged bear." *1 Hen 4*, I, ii, 71–72.

lullaby, *n.* sweet repose; may it rest easily: "Marry, sir, lullaby to your bounty till I come/ again." *T Night*, V, i, 43–44.

lumpish, *adj.* dejected; depressed: ". . . she is lumpish, heavy, melancholy . . ." *Two Gent*, III, ii, 62.

Luna, *n.* Roman goddess of the moon; also, the moon itself: "A title to Phoebe, to Luna, to the moon." *Love's L*, IV, ii, 37.

lunes, *n.* fits of lunacy: "These dangerous, unsafe lunes i' th' king, beshrew them!" *W Tale*, II, ii, 30.

lungs, *n.* seat [organ] of laughter: "With a kind of smile,/ Which ne'er came from the lungs . . ." *Cor*, I, i, 106–107.

Lupercal, *n.* Lupercalia, Roman festival held on Feb. 15th: "May we do so?/ You know it is the feast of Lupercal." *J Caes*, I, i, 66–67.

lurch, *v.* **1** to pilfer [thieves' jargon]: ". . . hiding mine/ honour in my necessity, am fain to shuffle, to hedge,/ and to lurch . . ." *Wives*, II, ii, 22–24. **2** to steal or rob: ". . . in the brunt of seventeen battles since/ He lurch'd all swords of the garland." *Cor*, II, ii, 100–101.

lure, *n.* device or bait used by the falconer to entice the hawk to return to him: "And till she stoop she must not be fullgorg'd,/ For then she never looks upon her lure." *Shrew*, IV, i, 178–179.

lurk, *v.* to conceal oneself: "What [whatever] will hap more to-night, safe 'scape the King!/ Lurk, lurk." *Lear*, III, vi, 117–118.

lust, *n.* **1** enjoyment; pleasure; delight: "Gazing upon the Greeks with little lust . . ." *Luc*, 1384. **2 change of lust,** quest for sexual variety: ". . . his hateful luxury/ And bestial appetite in change of lust . . ." *Rich 3*, III, v, 79–80.

lust-dieted, *adj.* sated with pleasure: ". . . the superfluous and lust-dieted man,/ That slaves your ordinance . . ." *Lear*, IV, i, 67–68.

luster of conceit, *n.* spark of wit: ". . . a good lustre of conceit in/ a turf of earth . . ." *Love's L*, IV, ii, 84–85.

lustihood, *n.* courage; valor: ". . . reason and respect/ Make livers pale, and lustihood deject." *Tr & Cr*, II, ii, 49–50.

lustique, *adj., adv.* lusty; lustily: "Here comes the king."/ "Lustique, as the Dutchman [German] says." *All's W*, II, iii, 39–41.

lusty, *adj.* **1** (of a man) strong; able-bodied; vigorous: "Where's your yeoman? Is't a lusty yeoman? Will a/ stand to't?" *2 Hen 4,* II, i, 3–4. **2** (of a girl or woman) lively, energetic, and forceful: "Now, by the world, it is a lusty wench." *Shrew,* II, i, 160.

Lux tua vita mihi, [Latin] Your light is life to me. *Per,* II, ii, 21.

luxurious, *adj.* lustful; lecherous; debauched: "She knows the heat of a luxurious bed . . ." *M Ado,* IV, i, 40.

luxuriously, *adv.* lustfully: ". . . what hotter hours . . . you have/ Luxuriously pick'd out." *Ant & Cleo,* III, xiii, 118–120.

luxury, *n.* **1** lust; debauchery: "Let not the royal bed of Denmark be/ A couch for luxury and damned incest." *Ham,* I, v, 82–83. **2** [cap.] personification of the deadly sin of lust: "How the devil Luxury, with his fat rump and/ potato finger, tickles these together!" *Tr & Cr,* V, ii, 55–56.

lyam, *n.* **in lyam,** on a leash: "Kill them, cut their throats, possess their houses,/ And lead the majesty of law in lyam . . ." *More,* II, iv, 120–121.

Lycaonia, *n.* kingdom in Asia Minor: "The kings of Mede and Lycaonia . . ." *Ant & Cleo,* III, vi, 75.

Lycurguses, *n.* pl. of "Lycurgus," famous lawgiver of ancient Greece: "Meeting two such/ wealsmen as you are—I cannot call you Lycurguses . . ." *Cor,* II, i, 53–54.

Lydia, *n.* country in Asia Minor: "His conquering banner shook, from Syria/ To Lydia, and to Ionia . . ." *Ant & Cleo,* I, ii, 99–100.

lym, *n.* bloodhound: "Hound or spaniel, brach or lym . . ." *Lear,* III, vi, 69.

Lynn, *n.* seaport NE of London: "To Lynn, my lord?/ And ship from thence to Flanders?" *3 Hen 6,* IV, v, 20–21.

— M —

mace, *n.* clublike staff of office carried by an arresting officer: ". . . he that sets up his rest to do/ more exploits with his mace than a morris-pike." *Errors,* IV, iii, 26–27.

Machiavel, *n.* **1** Niccolò Machiavelli, 16th cent. Italian political philosopher, who wrote that desirable ends justified any means: "And set the murderous Machiavel to school." *3 Hen 6,* III, ii, 193. **2** person without moral or religious principles; anachronistic ref. [some 85 years prior] to the writings of N. Machiavelli: "Alençon, that notorious Machiavel!" *1 Hen 6,* V, iv, 74.

machination, *n.* intrigue; conspiracy: "Your business of the world hath so an end,/ And machination ceases." *Lear,* V, i, 45–46.

machine, *n.* human body: "Thine evermore, most dear lady, whilst this/ machine is [belongs] to him . . ." *Ham,* II, ii, 122–123.

maculate, *adj.* spotted; hence, tainted or impure: "Most maculate thoughts, master, are masked/ under such colours." *Love's L,* I, ii, 86–87.

maculation, *n.* stain; here, the result of infidelity: ". . . I will throw my glove to Death himself/ That there's no maculation in thy heart . . ." *Tr & Cr,* IV, iv, 62–63.

mad, *v.* **1** to madden: "This music mads me. Let it sound no more . . ." *Rich 2,* V, v, 61. **2** to excite; inflame: "Madding my eagerness with her restraint . . ." *All's W,* V, iii, 212.
—*adj.* **3** driven by passion; here, lust: "As they were mad unto the wood they hie them . . ." *Ven & Ad,* 323. **4** wild; excited: "Fetching [performing] mad bounds, bellowing and neighing loud . . ." *Merch,* V, i, 73. **5 mad north-north-west,** mad only when it suits his [Hamlet's] purpose: "I am but mad north-north-west. When the wind is/ southerly, I know a hawk from a handsaw." *Ham,* II, ii, 374–375. **6 of the mad,** experienced by madmen: "Not a soul/ But felt a fever of the mad . . ." *Temp,* I, ii, 208–209.

Madam Mitigation, *n.* nickname for the bawd Mistress Overdone, who quells sexual desire: "Behold, behold, where Madam Mitigation comes!" *Meas,* I, ii, 41.

mad-bred, *adj.* brought about by insane mismanagement [by Henry]: ". . . the glorious sun's transparent beams,/ Do calm the fury of this mad-bred flaw." *2 Hen 6,* III, i, 353–354.

madcap, *n.* wild, eccentric fellow: "Why, what a madcap hath heaven lent us here!" *K John,* I, i, 84.

madded, *past part.* driven mad: "a father, and a gracious aged man . . . have you madded." *Lear,* IV, ii, 41–43.

madding, *adj.* **1** going or becoming mad: ". . . as Ascanius did/ When he to madding Dido would unfold/ His father's acts . . ." *2 Hen 6,* III, ii, 115–117. **2** causing madness; maddening: ". . . the distraction of this madding fever!" *Sonn 119,* 8.

made, *past part.* **1** closed; shut: ". . . she will well excuse/ Why at this time the doors are made against you." *Errors,* III, i, 92–93. **2 made away,** done away (with); killed: "Ne'er let my heart know merry cheer indeed/ Till all the Andronici be made away." *T Andr,* II, iii, 188–189. **3 made for,** made to resemble: "He/ sits in his state as a thing made for Alexander." *Cor,* V, iv, 21–22. **4 so made on,** made so much of: "Why, he is so made on here within as if he/ were son and heir to Mars . . ." *Cor,* IV, v, 196–197.
—*adj.* **5** successful; having one's fortune made: "If our sport had gone forward, we had all been/ made men." *M N Dream,* IV, ii, 17–18.

made-up, *adj.* thoroughgoing; complete: ". . . remain assur'd/ That he's a made-up villain." *Timon,* V, i, 96–97.

mad fellow, *n.* a wit; wag: "A mad fellow . . . told me/ I had unloaded all the gibbets and pressed the dead/ bodies." *1 Hen 4,* IV, ii, 36–38.

madman, *n.* **1** droll fellow; jester: "Behaviour, what wert thou/ Till this madman show'd thee?" *Love's L,* V, ii, 337–338. **2** mad talk; craziness: "Fetch him off, I pray you: he speaks nothing/ but madman. Fie on him!" *T Night,* I, v, 106–107.

madonna, *n.* my lady: a term of address: "Two faults, ma-donna, that drink and good/ counsel will amend . . ." *T Night,* I, v, 40–41.

ma foi, il fait fort chaud . . . , [French] my word, it's very hot. I'm going to the court to see the big doings. *Wives,* I, iv, 46–47.

magic of bounty, *n.* magic power of generosity: "See,/ Magic of bounty, all these spirits thy power/ Hath conjur'd to at-tend!" *Timon,* I, i, 6–7.

magnanimious, *adj.* var. of **magnanimous:** ". . . be magnani-mious in the enterprise and go on . . ." *All's W,* III, vi, 63.

magnanimity, *n.* heroic bravery: "Should, if a coward heard her speak these words,/ Infuse his breast with magnanim-ity . . ." *3 Hen 6,* V, iv, 40–41.

magnanimous, *adj.* **1** courageous; brave: "Thou wilt be as valiant as the wrathful/ dove, or most magnanimous mouse." *2 Hen 4,* III, ii, 157–158. **2** glorious; noble: "A spur to valiant and magnanimous deeds . . ." *Tr & Cr,* II, ii, 201.

Magni dominator poli . . . , [Latin] God of the great heavens, Art thou so slow to see crimes, so slow to hear them? [from Seneca's *Phaedra*] *T Andr,* IV, i, 81–82.

magnificent, *adj.* proud; haughty: "Than whom no mortal so magnificent!" *Love's L,* III, i, 173.

magnifico, *n.* community leader; city father: "Twenty mer-chants,/ The duke himself, and the magnificoes/ Of greatest port have all persuaded with him . . ." *Merch,* III, ii, 278–280.

magot-pie, *n.* magpie: "By magot-pies, and choughs, and rooks, brought forth/ The secret'st man of blood." *Mac,* III, iv, 124–125.

Mahu, *n.* one of Tom's [Edgar's] demons or devils: "The Prince of Darkness is a gentleman; Modo/ he's called, and Mahu." *Lear,* III, iv, 147–148.

maid, *n.* young of some fish; here, sexual wordplay: "Is there a maid with child by him?"/ "No: but there's a woman with maid by him." *Meas,* I, ii, 84–85.

maid and man, *n.* male virgin: "You are betroth'd both to a maid and man." *T Night,* V, i, 261.

maiden, *adj.* **1** "virginal" or "chaste," depending on context: "Her breasts . . . A pair of maiden worlds unconquered;/ Save of their lord . . ." *Luc,* 407–409. **2** free of bloodshed: "A maid-en battle, then? O, I perceive you." *Tr & Cr,* IV, v, 87. **3 her maiden loss,** the loss of her virginity: ". . . her tender shame/ Will not proclaim against her maiden loss . . ." *Meas,* IV, iv, 21–22.

Maidenhead, *n.* village near Windsor: ". . . three/ cozen-Ger-mans that has cozened all the hosts of/ Readins, Maidenhead, of Colbrook . . ." *Wives,* IV, v, 71–73.

maidenhood, *n.* maidenhead; virginity: "The ireful Bastard Orleans, that drew blood/ From thee, my boy, and had the maidenhood/ Of thy first fight . . ." *1 Hen 6,* IV, vi, 16–17.

maidenliest, *adj.* most chaste or virginal: "I should have been that I am/ had the maidenliest star in the firmament twin-kled/ on my bastardizing." *Lear,* I, ii, 138–140.

maiden-tongued, *adj.* soft-spoken: "For maiden-tongu'd he was, and thereof free . . ." *Love's Comp,* 100.

Maid Marian, character of morris dances, often played with rowdy humor by a man in woman's clothes: ". . . and for wom-anhood, Maid Marian may be/ the deputy's wife of the ward to thee." *1 Hen 4,* III, iii, 112–113.

maid-pale, *adj.* white as a maiden's complexion: "Change the complexion of her maid-pale peace/ To scarlet indigna-tion . . ." *Rich 2,* III, iii, 98–99.

maid's part, *n.* (in a descant) the soprano part, usually that of a maiden resisting the persistent suit of the tenor: "Play the maid's part: still answer nay, and take it." *Rich 3,* III, vii, 50.

mail[1], *n.* **a rusty mail,** suit of rusty armor: "Quite out of fash-ion, like a rusty mail/ In monumental mockery." *Tr & Cr,* III, iii, 152–153.

mail[2], *n.* **1** pouch or bag: "No egma [enigma], no riddle, no l'envoy; no salve in the mail,/ sir." *Love's L,* III, i, 69–70. —*v.* **2** to wrap; envelop: "Mail'd up in shame, with papers on my back . . ." *2 Hen 6,* II, iv, 31.

mailed, *adj.* dressed in armor: "The mailed Mars shall on his altar sit/ Up to the ears in blood." *1 Hen 4,* IV, i, 116–117.

maim, *n.* **1** injury; hurt: "A dearer merit [reward], not so deep a maim . . ." *Rich 2,* I, iii, 156. **2** mutilation: ". . . Duke of Gloucester scarce himself,/ That bears so shrewd a maim . . ." *2 Hen 6,* II, iii, 40–41. **3 maims of shame,** shameful desecrations: ". . . stop those maims/ Of shame seen through thy country . . ." *Cor,* IV, v, 87–88.

maimed rites, *n. pl.* curtailed or abbreviated ceremony: "Who is this they follow?/ And with such maimed rites?" *Ham,* V, i, 211–212.

main[1], *n.* **1** chief reason; principal cause: ". . . no other but the main,/ His father's death and our o'er-hasty marriage." *Ham,* II, ii, 56–57. **2** land; mainland: "Or swell the curled waters 'bove the main . . ." *Lear,* III, i, 6. **3** ocean: "I cannot 'twixt the heaven and the main/ Descry a sail." *Oth,* II, i, 3–4. **4** force; strength: "We must with all our main of power stand fast . . ." *Tr & Cr.* II, iii, 262. **5** center; here, the full force: "Nativity, one in the main of light . . ." *Sonn 60,* 5.
—*adj.* **6** strong; unequivocal: "Quite from [contrary to] the main opinion he held once . . ." *J Caes,* II, i, 196–197. **7** general: ". . . no further/ Than the main voice of Denmark goes withal." *Ham,* I, iii, 27–28.
—*v.* **8** wordplay on "Maine" [French province] and "maimed": ". . . thereby is England main'd/ and fain to go with a staff . . ." *2 Hen 6,* IV, ii, 155–156.

main[2], *n.* gambling stake: "to set so rich a main/ On the nice hazard of one doubtful hour?" *1 Hen 4,* IV, i, 47–48.

main chance, *n.* **1** likely outcome of events: ". . . a man may prophesy,/ With a near aim, of the main chance of things/ As yet not come to life . . ." *2 Hen 4,* III, i, 82–84. **2** (in the dice game of hazard) the stake being gambled for: "Main chance, father, you meant; but I meant Maine,/ Which I will win from France, or else be slain." *2 Hen 6,* I, i, 213–214.

main-course, *n.* mainsail (of a ship): "Bring her to try with main-course." *Temp,* I, i, 35.

Maine, *n.* province in NW France: ". . . though her father be the King of Naples,/ Duke of Anjou and Maine, yet is he poor . . ." *1 Hen 6,* V, iii, 94–95.

mainly, *adv.* **1** to a powerful extent; strongly: ". . . by your safety, wisdom, all things else/ You mainly were stirr'd up." *Ham,* IV, vii, 8–9. **2** with great force or vigor; violently: "These four came all afront, and mainly thrust at/ me . . ." *1 Hen 4,* II, iv, 196–197. **3** fully; completely: ". . . I am mainly ignorant/ What place this is . . ." *Lear,* IV, vii, 65–66.

mainport, *n.* small offering; tribute: "If of my freedom 'tis the mainport, take/ No stricter render of me than my all." *Cymb,* V, iv, 16–17.

main soldier, *n.* chief military leader: "Higher than both in blood and life, stands up/ For main soldier . . ." *Ant & Cleo,* I, ii, 188–189.

maintain, *v.* to represent: ". . . the one maintained by the owl, the other by the cuckoo." *Love's L,* V, ii, 884.

maintenance, *n.* **lustier maintenance,** unrelenting attack: "I saw him hold Lord Percy at the point/ With lustier maintenance than I did look for/ Of such an ungrown warrior." *1 Hen 4,* V, iv, 20–22.

main-top, *n.* top of the mainmast; here, ref. to the head of Posthumus: "From this most bravest vessel of the world/ Struck the main-top!" *Cymb,* IV, ii, 319–320.

majestical, *adj.* **1** princely; noble: "Presence majestical would put him out . . ." *Love's L,* V, ii, 102. **2** stately or pompous: ". . . his humour is lofty, his/ gait majestical . . ." *Love's L,* V, i, 9–11. **3** **being majestical,** because of its majesty: "We do it wrong,/ being so majestical,/ To offer it the show of violence . . ." *Ham,* I, i, 148–149.

majesty, *n.* **1** one's royal person: ". . . the king's majesty/ Commends his good opinion of you . . ." *Hen 8,* II, iii, 60–61. **2** **double majesty,** an even greater force: "And given grace a double majesty." *Sonn 78,* 8.

major, *n.* major premise: "And thou a natural coward without instinct./ I deny your major." *1 Hen 4,* II, iv, 488–489.

majority, *n.* supremacy; preeminence: "Whose hot incursions and great name in arms,/ Holds from all soldiers chief majority . . ." *1 Hen 4,* III, ii, 108–109.

make[1], *v.* **1** to do: "Now sir, what make you here?" *As You,* I, i, 29. **2** to fasten or lock; make fast: "Make the doors upon a woman's wit, and it will out at the casement . . ." *As You,* IV, i, 153–154. **3** to express; voice: "And ever and anon they made a doubt [fear] . . ." *Love's L,* V, ii, 101. **4** to induce: "What wicked and dissembling glass of mine/ Made me compare with Hermia's sphery eyne?" *M N Dream,* II, ii, 97–98. **5** to consider; think: "Make it no wonder. If you knew my business,/ You would entreat me rather go than stay." *Shrew,* III, ii, 189–190. **6** to count; be important: "I think the policy [political ends] of that purpose made more in/ the marriage than the love of the parties." *Ant & Cleo,* II, vi, 115–116. **7** to cause: "If thinking on me then should make you woe." *Sonn 71,* 8. **8** to give; host: "This night he makes a supper, and a great one . . ." *Hen 8,* I, iii, 52. **9** to interfere: "I will teach a scurvy jack-a-nape priest to/ meddle or make." *Wives,* I, iv, 104–105. **10** to give to; bestow on: "He will make you a hundred and fifty pounds/ jointure." *Wives,* III, iv, 48–49. **11** **is make,** will or is to provide: "Ay, and her father is make her a petter [better] penny." *Wives,* I, i, 55. **12** **made them for us,** made them sympathetic to our plight: ". . . we thought it meet to hide our love/ Till time had made them for us . . ." *Meas,* I, ii, 141–142. **13** **make after,** to pursue; go after: "Rouse him, make after him, poison his delight . . ." *Oth,* I, i, 68. **14 make away, a.** to do away with; end: "And all to make away my guiltless life." *2 Hen 6,* III, i, 167. **b.** to kill: "How these were they that made away his brother." *T Andr,* II, iii, 208. **15 make from,** watch out for; be careful of: "The bow is bent and drawn; make from the shaft." *Lear,* I, i, 143. **16 make no farther,** to attempt nothing else: ". . . for my part/ I'll not meddle nor make no farther." Also, **make no more.** *Tr & Cr,* I, i, 13–14. **17 make of,** to offer in place of: "What proof shall I make of that?" *M Ado,* II, ii, 27. **18 make one,** to participate: ". . . 'tis not that time of/ moon with me to make one in so skipping a/ dialogue." *T Night,* I, v, 201–203. **19 make that good,** See **good** (def. 7). **20 make thee away,** to destroy you: ". . . thine ignorance makes/ thee away." *All's W,* I, i, 207–208. **21 make to,** to go toward; advance on: "Look how he makes to Caesar: mark him." *J Caes,* III, i, 18. **22 make up, a.** (in warfare) to go to the front lines: "I beseech your Majesty, make up,/ Lest your retirement do amaze your friends." *1 Hen 4,* V, iv, 4–5. **b.** to proceed; go directly: "Make up to Clifton, I'll to Sir Nicholas Gawsey." *1 Hen 4,* V, iv, 57. **c.** to hasten; hurry: "Hubert, keep this boy. Philip, make up . . ." *K John,* III, ii, 5. **d.** to conclude: "But, to make up my all too long compare . . ." *Edw 3,* I, ii, 156. **23 make with,** to contend or grapple with: ". . . the less you meddle or make with them, why, the more is for your honesty." *M Ado,* III, iii, 51–52. **24 what make you,** what are you doing?: "And what make you from [away from] Wittenberg, Horatio?" *Ham,* I, ii, 164.

make², *n.* spouse: "Else one self mate and make could not beget/ Such different issues." *Lear,* IV, iii, 35–36.

makeless, *adj.* mateless; here, lacking a mate of equal quality: "The world will wail thee like a makeless wife . . ." *Sonn 9,* 4.

make-peace, *n.* peacemaker: "To be a make-peace shall become my age." *Rich 2,* I, i, 160.

making, *n.* form or build; physical aspect or appearance: "Either I mistake your shape and making quite,/ Or else you are . . . Call'd Robin Goodfellow." *M N Dream,* II, i, 32–34.

malady, *n.* love generally viewed as an illness: ". . . not an eye that sees you but is a physician to/ comment on your malady." *Two Gent,* II, i, 39–40.

malady of France, *n.* venereal disease: "News have I that my Doll is dead i' th' spital/ Of malady of France . . ." *Hen 5,* V, i, 85–86.

malapert, *adj.* rude; impudent: "Peace, Master Marquess: you are malapert . . ." *Rich 3,* I, iii, 255.

male varlet, *n.* male concubine or prostitute: ". . . thou art said to be Achilles' male varlet." *Tr & Cr,* V, i, 14.

malice, *n.* power to inflict injury: "Our cannons' malice vainly shall be spent . . ." *K John,* II, i, 251.

maliciously, *adv.* **1** savagely: "I will be treble-sinew'd, hearted, breath'd,/ And fight maliciously . . ." *Ant & Cleo,* III, xiii, 178–179. **2** violently: ". . . a ling'ring dram, that should not work/ Maliciously . . ." *W Tale,* I, ii, 320–321.

malign, *v.* to affect adversely: "Though wayward fortune did malign my state . . ." *Per,* V, i, 89.

malignancy, *n.* [in astrology] a sinister influence: ". . . the malignancy of my fate might perhaps/ distemper yours . . ." *T Night,* II, i, 4–5.

malignant, *adj.* bringing evil; causing harm: "O malignant and ill-boding stars!" *1 Hen 6,* IV, v, 6.

malkin, *n.* **1** slut; slattern: "Whilst ours was blurted at and held a malkin/ Not worth the time of day." *Per,* IV, iii, 34–35. **2** wench; here, scullery maid: "The kitchen malkin pins/ Her richest lockram 'bout her reechy neck . . ." *Cor,* II, i, 206–207.

mallows, *n. pl.* weedy plants: "He'd sow 't with nettle-seed."/ "Or docks, or mallows." *Temp,* II, i, 140.

malmsey, *n.* strong, sweet wine of southern Europe: ". . . an if you grow so nice,/ Metheglin, wort, and malmsey . . ." *Love's L,* V, ii, 232–233.

malthorse or **malt-horse,** *n.* workhorse, hence a big, stupid creature: "Mome, malthorse, capon, coxcomb,/ idiot, patch . . ." *Errors,* III, i, 32.

maltworm or **malt-worm,** *n.* heavy drinker; tippler: ". . . none of these mad/ mustachio purple-hued maltworms . . ." *1 Hen 4,* II, i, 73–74.

mammering, *pres. part.* hesitating: "What you could ask me, that I should deny?/ Or stand so mammering on?" *Oth,* III, iii, 70–71.

mammet, *n.* doll or puppet [perh. likening Kate to one]; some editors: female breast: ". . . this is no world/ To play with mammets . . ." *1 Hen 4,* II, iii, 92–93.

mammock, *v.* to tear to pieces: "Oh, I warrant how he mammocked it!" *Cor,* I, iii, 65.

man, *n.* **1** manhood: "Being scarce made up,/ I mean, to man . . ." *Cymb,* IV, ii, 109–110. **2** courage; daring: ". . . Having more man than wit about me, [I] drew." *Lear,* II, ii, 232. **3** wordplay on "mankind" [perh. "manly"] and "servant": "To any Count; to all Counts; to what is man."/ "To what is Count's man . . ." *All's W,* II, iii, 193–194. **4 be the man,** [to]

play at being a man; give orders without authority: "You'll make a mutiny among my guests,/ You will set cock-a-hoop, you'll be the man!" *Rom & Jul*, I, v, 79–80. **5 man of blood,** murderer: "By magot-pies, and choughs, and rooks, brought forth/ The secret'st man of blood." *Mac*, III, iv, 124–125. **6 man of occupation,** laborer or tradesman, hence one possessed of the proper tools: "And I had been a man of any occupation,/ if I would not have taken him at a word . . ." *J Caes*, I, ii, 263–264. **7 man of salt** See **salt** (def. 5). **8 my man,** the man I was looking for; understood here as meaning "man-servant": ". . . here comes my man."/ "But I'll be hang'd, sir, if he wear your livery." *Rom & Jul*, III, i, 55–56. **9 since I was man,** ever since I was born: "Since I was man/ Such sheets of fire such bursts of horrid thunder . . ." *All's W*, III, ii, 45–46. **10 stolen a man already made,** committed a murder: "To pardon him that hath from nature stolen/ A man already made . . ." *Meas*, II, iv, 43–44. **11 such a deal of man,** such a big hero of a man: ". . . put upon him [made himself out] such a deal of man,/ That worthied him . . ." *Lear*, II, ii, 121–122. **12 write man,** declare myself to be a man: "I must tell thee, sirrah, I write man; to which title/ age cannot bring thee." *All's W*, II, iii, 197–198.
—*v.* **13 man my haggard,** See **haggard** (def. 3).

manacle, *n.* shackle; here, a bracelet: "For my sake wear this,/ It is a manacle of love . . ." *Cymb*, I, ii, 52–53.

manage, *n.* **1** arrangements; handling: "Expedient manage must be made, my liege . . ." *Rich 2*, I, iv, 39. **2** training and discipline of a horse: ". . . they are taught their manage, and to that end riders dearly hired . . ." *As You*, I, i, 12–13. **3** exhibition of horsemanship, esp. on the tilting ground: "Full merrily/ Hath this brave manage, this career, been run." *Love's L*, V, ii, 481–482. **4** leaders or rulers: ". . . now the manage of two kingdoms must/ With fearful-bloody issue arbitrate." *K John*, I, i, 37–38. **5 taught their manage,** (of horses) trained for riding: ". . . they are taught their manage, and to that end/ riders dearly hired . . ." *As You*, I, i, 12–13.
—*v.* **6** to wield; brandish: ". . . distaff-women manage rusty bills/ Against thy seat . . ." *Rich 2*, III, ii, 118–119. **7** to put (a horse) through its paces: "He will not manage her, although he mount her . . ." *Ven & Ad*, 598.

manager, *n.* skilled handler of arms, esp. the rapier: "Adieu, valour! rust, rapier! . . . for your/ manager is in love . . ." *Love's L*, I, ii, 171–172.

man-at-arms, *n.* soldier: "What a maidenly man-at-arms are you/ become!" *2 Hen 4*, II, ii, 73–74.

mandragora, *n.* juice of the mandrake plant, used to induce sleep: "Give me to drink mandragora . . . That I might sleep out this great gap of time/ My Antony is away." *Ant & Cleo*, I, v, 4–6.

mandrake, *n.* **1** medicinal plant with forked root said to resemble the human form; associated with sexual prowess and when pulled from the earth it was believed to emit a shriek that caused madness or death: "And shrieks like mandrakes torn out of the earth,/ That living mortals, hearing them, run mad—" *Rom & Jul*, IV, iii, 47–48. **2** term of abuse: "Thou whoreson/ mandrake, thou art fitter to be worn in my cap than/ to wait at my heels." *2 Hen 4*, I, ii, 13–15.

Manent, *pl. v.,* **manet,** *sing. v.,* [SD] Remain(s) [on stage]: "Sennet. Exeunt. Manent Brutus and Cassius." *J Caes*, I, ii, 24.

manhood, *n.* **1** bravery; daring: "Ulysses and stout Diomede/ With sleight and manhood stole to Rhesus' tents . . ." *3 Hen 6*, IV, ii, 19–20. **2 saving your manhoods,** appar. Hostess's attempt to find a masculine equiv. for the apologetic "saving your ladyship": "A comes continuantly to Pie Corner—saving/ your manhoods—to buy a saddle . . ." *2 Hen 4*, II, i, 25–26.

manifest, *adj.* obviously just: "The Duke's unjust/ Thus to retort your manifest appeal . . ." *Meas*, V, i, 298–299.

manifoldly, *adv.* in many ways: ". . . the bannerets about/ thee did manifoldly dissuade me from believing thee . . ." *All's W*, II, iii, 202–203.

manifold record, *n.* full and varied record(s): ". . . what particular rarity, what strange,/ Which manifold record not matches [lacks any precedent]?" *Timon*, I, i, 4–5.

manikin, *n.* puppet: "This is a dear manikin to you, Sir Toby." *T Night*, III, ii, 51.

mankind, *adj.* male; also, ferocious: "Out!/ A mankind witch! Hence with her, out o' door . . ." *W Tale*, II, iii, 66–67.

manned, *adj.* served; waited on: "I was never manned with an/ agate till now . . ." *2 Hen 4*, I, ii, 15–16.

manner[1], *n.* **1** fashion or style: "My lady, to the manner of the days,/ In courtesy gives undeserving praise." *Love's L*, V, ii, 365–366. **2** [pl.] **a.** way of living: ". . . rage and hot blood are his counsellors,/ When means and lavish manners meet together . . ." *2 Hen 4*, IV, iv, 63–64. **b.** usual characteristics: "The seasons change their manners, as the year/ Had found some months asleep and leap'd them over." *2 Hen 4*, IV, iv, 123–124. **c.** behavior: "He is as disproportion'd in his manners/ As in his shape." *Temp*, V, i, 290–291. **d.** morals: ". . . if thou never saw'st good/ manners, then thy manners must be wicked . . ." *As You*, III, ii, 40–41. **e.** becoming modesty: "O!

how thy worth with manners may I sing . . ." *Sonn 39,* 1. **3 a million of manners,** beautiful manners; elegant behavior: "[Aside] O, 'give-ye-good-ev'n! Here's a million of/ manners." *Two Gent,* II, i, 92–93. **4 in manner,** in a manner of speaking; as it were: "You have in manner . . . / Made a divorce betwixt his queen and him . . ." *Rich 2,* III, i, 11–12. **5 manners of my mother,** manners more childlike than manly: ". . . so near the manners of my mother,/ . . . mine eyes will tell/ tales of me." *T Night,* II, i, 38–40. **6 no manner person,** no person whatever: ". . . no manner person/ Have, any time, recourse unto the Princes." *Rich 3,* III, v, 107–108. **7 to the manner born,** accustomed from birth to such ways: ". . . though I am native here/ And to the manner born, it is a custom/ More honour'd in the breach than the observance." *Ham,* I, iv, 14–16.
—*v.* **8** to rear; train or bring up: "To give her princely training, that she may/ Be manner'd as she is born." *Per,* III, iii, 16–17.

manner², *n.* something stolen; esp. in the phrase "taken [arrested] with the manner": ". . . thou stolest a cup of sack eighteen years/ ago, and wert taken with the manner . . ." *1 Hen 4,* II, iv, 310–311.

mannerly, *adj.* modest; respectful: "Good pilgrim, you do wrong your hand too much,/ Which mannerly devotion shows in this . . ." *Rom & Jul,* I, v, 96–97.

Manningtree, *n.* town in Essex [England], famous for its cattle market and its fairs: ". . . that roasted Manningtree/ ox with the pudding in his belly . . ." *1 Hen 4,* II, iv, 446–447.

man-of-war, *n.* warship: "And leave you not a man-of-war unsearch'd . . ." *T Andr,* IV, iii, 22.

manor, *n.* **laying manors,** putting the wealth of their estates [on their backs in the form of rich clothing]: "O many/ Have broke their backs with laying manors on 'em/ For this great journey." *Hen 8,* I, i, 83–85.

mansionry, *n.* building; here, nest-construction: ". . . does approve [show],/ By his loved mansionry, that the heaven's breath/ Smells wooingly here . . ." *Mac,* I, vi, 4–6.

mantle, *v.* to cover; here, to obscure: ". . . their rising senses/ Begin to chase the ignorant fumes that mantle/ Their clearer reason." *Temp,* V, i, 66–68.

Mantuan, *n.* ref. to Mantuanus [d. 1516], Italian poet: "Ah! good old Mantuan. I may speak of/ thee as the traveller doth of Venice . . ." *Love's L,* IV, ii, 91–92.

manual seal, *n.* seal affixed by hand; also, something having such authority: "There is my gage, the manual seal of death,/ That marks thee out for hell." *Rich 2,* IV, i, 25–26.

manu cita, [Latin] with ready hand: "Lend me your horn to make one, and I will whip/ about your infamy *manu cita.*" *Love's L,* V, i, 61–62.

manus, *n.* [Latin] hand: ". . . when he was a babe . . . Thus did he strangle serpents in his *manus.*" *Love's L,* V, ii, 585–586.

many, *adj.* **a many,** a great many: "A many fools that stand in better place . . ." *Merch,* III, v, 62.

map, *n.* **1** picture or embodiment: "Thou map of woe, that thus dost talk in signs,/ When thy poor heart beats with outrageous beating . . ." *T Andr,* III, ii, 12–13. **2 map of death,** sleep as the picture of death: "Showing life's triumph in the map of death . . ." *Luc,* 402. **3 map of my microcosm,** my face as a picture of the little universe [fr. philosophical view of man as a miniature universe]: "If you see this in/ the map of my microcosm, follows it that I am/ known well enough too?" *Cor,* II, i, 61–63.

mar, *v.* to spoil or ruin; Evans may misunderstand "marrying" as "marring" or may ref. to proverb "Marrying is marring": "I may quarter, coz."/ "You may, by marrying."/ "It is marring indeed, if he quarter it." *Wives,* I, i, 22–24.

marble, *adj.* **1** perh. hard and unrelenting; poss. ref. to mottled cloud covering: "Now by yond marble heaven . . . I here engage my words." *Oth,* III, iii, 467–469.
–*n.* **2** person who is unmoved or unfeeling: ". . . and he, a marble to her tears,/ is washed with them, but relents not." *Meas,* III, i, 229–230.

marble-breasted, *adj.* stonelike; unyielding and unrelenting: "Live you the marble-breasted tyrant still." *T Night,* V, i, 122.

marble-constant, *adj.* firm [resolved] as marble: "I have nothing/ Of woman in me: now from head to foot/ I am marble-constant . . ." *Ant & Cleo,* V, ii, 237–239.

marbled mansion, *n.* the sky mottled with clouds; also, Heaven: ". . . the marbled mansion all above . . ." *Timon,* IV, iii, 193.

marble heaven, *n.* perh. Othello's view of heaven as unyielding and unrelenting: "Now by yond marble heaven . . . I here engage [pledge] my words." *Oth,* III, iii, 467–468.

Marcellus, *n.* Latinate form of *Marseilles:* "His grace is at Marcellus, to which place/ We have convenient convoy." *All's W,* IV, iv, 9–10.

march, *n.* sound of marching from offstage, usually the sound of drumbeats: "A march afar." [SD] *All's W,* III, v, 37.

March-chick, *n.* young man or woman; youngster: "A very forward March-chick!" *M Ado,* I, iii, 52.

Marches, *n. pl.* [sometimes l.c.] border country; here between Wales and England, W of Shrewsbury: "For in the Marches here we heard you were,/ Making another head to fight again." *3 Hen 6,* II, i, 140–141.

marchpane, *n.* marzipan: "Good thou, save me a/ piece of marchpane . . ." *Rom & Jul,* I, v, 7–8.

Marcus Crassus, *n.* member (with Pompey and Caesar) of first Roman triumvirate; defeated and treacherously killed by forces of Orodes, 53 B.C.: "Thy Pacorus, Orodes,/ Pays this for Marcus Crassus." *Ant & Cleo,* III, i, 4–5.

mare¹, *n.* nightmare: a spirit that bestrode one during sleep: "I will ride thee/ a-nights like the mare." *2 Hen 4,* II, i, 74–75.

mare², *n.* **tired mare,** ref. to the proverbial tiredness of horses; here, appar. confused with proverb that patience is a mare ready to bolt: ". . . though/ patience be a tired mare, yet she will plod." *Hen 5,* II, i, 24–25.

margent, *n.* **1** margin; perimeter: "His face's own margent did quote [register] such amazes . . ." *Love's L,* II, i, 245. **2** edge: "Or in the beached margent of the sea . . ." *M N Dream,* II, i, 85. **3** bank; shore: "Upon whose weeping margent she was set . . ." *Lover's Comp,* 39.

margin, *n.* ref. to explanatory notes often printed in the margin of books: "I knew you must be edified by the margin ere you/ had done." *Ham,* V, ii, 152–153.

mark¹, *n.* **1** target or goal: "Before proud Athens he's set down by this,/ Whose fall the mark of his ambition is." *Timon,* V, iii, 9–10. **2** reach or capacity: "You are abus'd/ Beyond the mark of thought . . ." *Ant & Cleo,* III, vi, 86–87. **3** guide or beacon: "He was the mark and glass, copy and book,/ That fashion'd others." *2 Hen 4,* II, iii, 31–32. **4** [usually pl.] **a.** outward signs or manifestations: ". . . by the marks of sovereignty,/ knowledge, and reason, I should be false/ persuaded I had daughters." *Lear,* I, iv, 240–242. **b.** outstanding characteristics: ". . . take you the marks of her, the colour of her/ hair, complexion . . ." *Per,* IV, ii, 53–54. **5** observance, as of a law or rule: ". . . the strong statutes/ Stand like the forfeits in a barber's shop,/ As much in mock as mark." *Meas,* V, i, 318–320. **6 a mark so bloody,** ref. to marking with the blood of a deer those in on the kill; regarded as a mark of bravery: ". . . they durst not . . . nor set/ A mark so bloody on the business . . ." *Temp,* I, ii, 140–142. **7 a mark to thyself,** mark used in place of a signature: "Dost thou use to write thy name? Or/ has thou a mark to thyself, like an honest/ plain-dealing man?" *2 Hen 6,* IV, ii, 96–98. **8 bless the mark,** an apologetic aside; here,

for an indelicate remark: ". . . he had not been there/ (bless the mark) a pissing while . . ." *Two Gent,* IV, iv, 18–19. **9 hit the mark,** achieve its goal; here, sense of "target" in wordplay with "pudenda": "If love be blind, love cannot hit the mark." *Rom & Jul,* II, i, 33. **10 mark of favor,** identifying feature: ". . . by no means I may discover them/ By any mark of favour." *J Caes,* II, i, 75–76.

—*v.* **11** to remark; observe: ". . . had they mark'd him/In parcels as I did, would have gone near/ To fall in love with him . . ." *As You,* III, v, 124–126. **12** to listen or pay attention to; heed: "Signior Benedick: nobody marks you." *M Ado,* I, i, 108. **13** to designate; elect: "Peace, I have done. God mark thee to his grace . . ." *Rom & Jul,* I, iii, 59.

–*past part.* **14** stamped; branded: "But like a foul misshapen stigmatic,/ Mark'd by the Destinies to be avoided . . ." *3 Hen 6,* II, ii, 136–137.

mark², *n.* amount (not a coin) equal to two-thirds of a pound sterling: ". . . a franklin in the/ Wild of Kent hath brought three hundred marks/ with him in gold . . ." *1 Hen 4,* II, i, 53–55.

marked for the gallows, fr. belief that the position of a mole on the face or body foretold the manner of a person's death: "Rebellious hinds, the filth and scum of Kent,/ Mark'd for the gallows . . ." *2 Hen 6,* IV, ii, 116–117.

market, *n.* marketability; also, purchase or profit: "What is a man/ If his chief good and market of his time/ Be but to sleep and feed?" *Ham,* IV, iv, 33–35.

market-day, *n.* a day, usually once a week, when products, wares, etc., were brought to the central market place of a town and sold or bartered: ". . . I have seen him/ whipp'd three market-days together [for being a vagabond]." *2 Hen 6,* IV, ii, 54–55.

market-maid, *n.* female servant sent to market: ". . . you are come/ A market-maid to Rome . . ." *Ant & Cleo,* III, vi, 50–51.

marl, *n.* clay or earth: ". . . make an/ account of her life to a clod of wayward marl?" *M Ado,* II, i, 57–58.

marmoset, *n.* small monkey, said to be prized for its flesh: "Show thee a jay's nest, and instruct thee how/ To snare the nimble marmoset . . ." *Temp,* II, ii, 169–170.

marred, *adj.* from old proverb [referring to a maiden], "Soon married is soon marred"; spoiled; ruined: "A young man married is a man that's marr'd." *All's W,* II, iii, 294.

married, *adj.* harmoniously linked or proportioned: "Examine every married lineament [feature]/ And see how one another lends content . . ." *Rom & Jul,* I, iii, 83–84.

marrow, *n.* **1** vigor; virility: ". . . hugs his kicky-wicky here at home,/ Spending his manly marrow in her arms . . ." *All's W,* II, iii, 276–277. **2** strength, vitality, or courage: ". . . crouching marrow, in the bearer strong,/ Cries, of itself, 'No more.'" *Timon,* V, iv, 9–10.

marrow-eating sickness, *n.* progressive disease, poss. cancer or syphilis: "The marrow-eating sickness whose attaint/ Disorder breeds . . ." *Ven & Ad,* 741–742.

marry, *interj.* **1** Mary; by the Virgin (mild oath, used esp. to emphasize an assertion): "Marry I prithee do, to make sport withal." *As You,* I, ii, 25. **2 Marry, and did,** I certainly did: "Marry, and did. But if you be remember'd,/ I did not bid you mar it . . ." *Shrew,* IV, iii, 96–97.

marry trap, *interj.* exclam. of triumph when a wrong is avenged: "I will say/ 'marry trap with you', if you run the nuthook's/ humour on me . . ." *Wives,* I, i, 150–152.

Mars, *n.* **1** Roman god of war: "This earth of majesty, this seat of Mars . . ." *Rich 2,* II, i, 41. **2** person who is most warlike: "Thou art the Mars of Malcontents." *Wives,* I, iii, 99. **3 Big Mars,** warlike spirit: "Big Mars seems bankrupt in their beggar'd host . . ." *Hen 5,* IV, ii, 43. **4 Mars his idiot,** a fool good only for making war: "Mars his idiot! do, rudeness: do, camel: do, do!" *Tr & Cr,* II, i, 56.

marshal, *n.* **1** Lord Marshal, the king's officer presiding at a trial by combat: "Marshal, command our officers-at-arms/ Be ready to direct these home alarms." *Rich 2,* I, i, 204–205. **2** controlling or governing force [lit. the commanding officer]: "Reason becomes the marshal to my will . . ." *M N Dream,* II, ii, 119.
—*v.* **3** to lead; conduct: "Thou marshall'st me the way that I was going . . ." *Mac,* II, i, 42.

Marshalsea, *n.* prison on London's South Bank: "I'll find/ A Marshalsea shall hold ye play these two months." *Hen 8,* V, iii, 84–85.

mart, *v.* **1** to market; trade or traffic in: "To sell and mart your offices for gold/ To undeservers." *J Caes,* IV, iii, 11–12. **2** to do business: ". . . you have let him go,/ And nothing marted with him." *W Tale,* IV, iv, 352–353. **3** to bargain; haggle: "A saucy stranger in his court to mart/ As in a Romish stew . . ." *Cymb,* I, vii, 151–152.
—*n.* **4** pact or agreement; bargain: ". . . now I play a merchant's part,/ And venture madly on a desperate mart." *Shrew,* II, i, 319–320. **5** period of selling; chance to make money: "We lost too much money this mart by being/ too wenchless." *Per,* IV, ii, 4–5.

martial man, *n.* soldier: "A martial man to be soft fancy's slave!" *Luc,* 200.

martlemas, *n.* Martinmas, ref. to St. Martin's Summer, a brief period of warm weather in late fall: "And how doth the/ martlemas your master?" *2 Hen 4,* II, ii, 96–97.

martlet, *n.* martin, regarded as a foolish bird that built its nest in unprotected places: ". . . like the martlet/ Builds in the weather on the outward wall . . ." *Merch,* II, ix, 28–29.

martyr, *v.* to mutilate; disfigure: "Speak, gentle sister, who hath mart'red thee?" *T Andr,* III, i, 81.

marvel, *n.* **1 kill the marvel,** to put an end to the [your] astonishment: ". . . a tribute . . . Is left untender'd."/ "And, to kill the marvel,/ Shall be so ever." *Cymb,* III, i, 8–11. **2 'tis marvel,** it is remarkable or astonishing: "'Tis marvel . . . You might have heard it else proclaim'd about [you didn't hear it proclaimed publicly]." *Shrew,* IV, ii, 86–87.

marvell's, *adj.* prob. old form (and perh. pron.) of MARVELOUS: ". . . indeed she has a marvell's white/ hand . . ." *Tr & Cr,* I, ii, 138–139.

marvelous, *adv.* incredibly; exceedingly: "No worse than they are backbitten, sir, for they/ have marvellous foul linen." *2 Hen 4,* V, i, 31–32.

Mary-bud, *n.* marigold: "And winking Mary-buds begin to ope their golden eyes . . ." *Cymb,* II, iii, 23.

mask, *n.* **1** silk covering to protect a woman's face from sunburn: ". . . my mask to defend my/ beauty . . ." *Tr & Cr,* I, ii, 267–268.
—*v.* **2 mask one's brows,** to pull one's hat down over one's eyes as an indication of grief: "To mask their brows and hide their infamy . . ." *Luc,* 794.

masked, *adj.* of a deceptively calm appearance: ". . . give you up to the mask'd Neptune and/ The gentlest winds of heaven . . ." *Per,* III, iii, 36–37.

masker, *n.* person who participates in a revelry; here, the meaning is armed soldiers: ". . . tell false Edward . . . That Lewis of France is sending over maskers/ To revel it with him . . ." *3 Hen 6,* III, iii, 223–225.

masque, *n.* elaborate entertainment, often allegorical, performed by masked actors; here, used ironically: "This harness'd masque and unadvised revel . . ." *K John,* V, ii, 132.

masquing stuff, *n.* costume(s) fit for a masque: "O mercy, God! What masquing stuff is here?" *Shrew,* IV, iii, 87.

mass, *n.* size: "Witness this army of such mass and charge [cost] . . ." *Ham,* IV, iv, 47.

Mass or **'Mass,** by the Mass (a mild oath): "Mass, and my elbow itched . . ." *M Ado,* III, iii, 97.

massy, *adj.* of great size and/or weight; massive: ". . . his codpiece seems as massy as his club?" *M Ado,* III, iii, 134.

mast, *n.* acorns, beechnuts, etc., of the forest, serving as animal food: "The oaks bear mast, the briers scarlet hips . . ." *Timon,* IV, iii, 422.

master, *n.* **1** teacher: "Each following day/ Became the next day's master . . ." *Hen 8,* I, i, 16–17.
—*v.* **2** to possess: ". . . he would not leave it,/ Nor pluck it from his finger, for the wealth/ That the world masters." *Merch,* V, i, 172–174.

master-leaver, *n.* servant who runs away from his master: ". . . let the world rank me in register/ A master-leaver, and a fugitive . . ." *Ant & Cleo,* IV, ix, 21–22.

master-reason, *n.* chief or principal reason: ". . . she has me her quirks, her/ reasons, her master-reasons, her prayers . . ." *Per,* IV, vi, 7–8.

mastic, *adj.* abusive; railing or reviling: "When rank Thersites opes his mastic jaws . . ." *Tr & Cr,* I, iii, 73.

match, *n.* **1** game or contest: ". . . what cunning match have you made with this jest of the/ drawer . . ." *1 Hen 4,* II, iv, 88–89. **2** agreement: "Cadwal and I/ Will play the cook and servant, 'tis our match . . ." *Cymb,* III, vii, 2–3. **3** marriage or betrothal: "The gain I seek is quiet in the match." *Shrew,* II, i, 323. **4** assignation: ". . . this is the body/ That took away the match from Isabel . . ." *Meas,* V, i, 210. **5 a match!,** [in striking a bargain] done!: "A match, sir. There's in all two worthy voices/ begged." *Cor,* II, iii, 80–81. **6 cry a match,** to claim a victory: "Switch and spurs, switch and spurs, or I'll cry a/ match!" *Rom & Jul,* II, iv, 70–71. **7 set a match,** to plan a robbery [thieves' jargon]: "Now shall we know if Gadshill have set a/ match." *1 Hen 4,* I, ii, 103–104.
—*v.* **8** to marry; make a match: ". . . truly I hold it a sin to match in my kindred." *M Ado,* II, i, 60. **9** to be or furnish a precedent: "Which manifold record not matches [lack precedent]?" *Timon,* I, i, 5. **10** to compare: "May fall to match you with her country forms . . ." *Oth,* III, iii, 241.

match and weight, *n.* equal amount: ". . . the match and weight/ Of such a winnow'd purity in love . . ." *Tr & Cr,* III, ii, 164–165.

matched, *adj.* married or betrothed: "I am content, in a good father's care,/ To have him match'd . . ." *Shrew,* IV, iv, 31–32.

matched in mouth, *adj.* referring to the harmonious braying of the hounds, likened to music: "Slow in pursuit, but match'd in mouth like bells,/ Each under each . . ." *M N Dream,* IV, i, 122–123.

mate¹, *n.* **1** fellow; chap (used contemptuously): ". . . you poor, base, rascally, cheating, lack-linen/ mate!" *2 Hen 4,* II, iv, 121–122. **2** [often pl.] boisterous companion(s); here, wordplay with sense of "husband": "No mates for you/ Unless you were of gentler, milder mould." *Shrew,* I, i, 59–60. **3 mate and make,** husband and wife: "Else one self mate and make could not beget/ Such different issues." *Lear,* IV, iii, 35–36.

mate², *v.* **1** to astonish; bewilder: "My mind she has mated, and amaz'd my sight." *Mac,* V, i, 75. **2** to checkmate; defeat or disable: ". . . for that is good deceit/ Which mates him first that first intends deceit." *2 Hen 6,* III, i, 265.

mated, *adj.* overcome; amazed or bewildered; here, in wordplay with "married" sense: ". . . are you mad that you do reason so?"/ "Not mad, but mated, how I do not know." *Errors,* III, ii, 53–54.

material, *adj.* **1** full of sense or cleverness: "A material fool!" *As You,* III, iii, 28. **2** important; pressing: "He would not stay at your petitions; made/ His business more material." *W Tale,* I, ii, 215–216. **3** essential: "I have outstood my time, which is material/ To th' tender of our present." *Cymb,* I, vii, 207–208.

matin, *n.* morning; here, dawn: "The glow-worm shows the matin to be near . . ." *Ham,* I, v, 89.

matron, *n.* respectable elderly woman: ". . . your wives, your daughters,/ Your matrons, and your maids . . ." *Mac,* IV, iii, 61–62.

matter, *n.* **1** good sense; ideas: "I love to cope him in these sullen fits,/ For then he's full of matter." *As You,* II, i, 67–68. **2** substance; contents or meaning: "I was born/ to speak all mirth and no matter." *M Ado,* II, i, 310–311. **3** interest: "He's all my exercise, my mirth, my matter . . ." *W Tale,* I, ii, 166. **4** poetic inspiration: "Then lack'd I matter; that enfeebled mine." *Sonn 86,* 14. **5** something of great concern; problem: "The setting of thine eye and cheek proclaim/ A matter from thee . . ." *Temp,* II, i, 224–225. **6** amount: "The matter, I hope, is not great, sir, begging but/ a beggar . . ." *T Night,* III, i, 55–

56. **7** business affairs; pressing mattters: "Now for the [lack of] counsel of my son and queen,/ I am amaz'd with matter." *Cymb*, IV, iii, 27–28. **8** something of consequence; here, a possible reward: "To him will I present/ them: there may be matter in it." *W Tale*, IV, iv, 842–843. **9** grounds for complaint; here, in wordplay with "gray matter": "Slender, I broke your/ head: what matter have you against me?" *Wives*, I, i, 113–114. **10 defy the matter,** to scorn sense: "A many fools . . . that for a tricksy word/ Defy the matter . . ." *Merch*, III, v, 62–64. **11 from the matter,** more than deserved: ". . . words him (I doubt not) a great deal from the/ matter." *Cymb*, I, v, 14–15. **12 matter and impertinency,** sense and nonsense: "O! matter and impertinency mix'd;/ Reason in madness." *Lear*, IV, vi, 176–177. **13 of matter beggared,** lacking facts: "Wherein necessity, of matter beggar'd,/ Will nothing stick our person to arraign . . ." *Ham*, IV, v, 92–93. **14 pick strong matter of,** find good reason for: ". . . kiss the lips of unacquainted change,/ And pick strong matter of revolt and wrath." *K John*, III, iii, 166–167. **15 to the matter,** to the point: "The phrase is to the matter." *Meas*, V, i, 93.

mattock, *n.* pickax: "Enter Romeo and Balthasar with a torch, a mattock and a crow of iron." [SD] *Rom & Jul*, V, iii, 22.

mature in knowledge, *adj.* old enough to know better: "As we rate [scold] boys, who being mature in knowledge,/ Pawn their experience . . ." *Ant & Cleo*, I, iv, 31–32.

maturity, *n.* ripeness: ". . . the seeded pride/ That hath to this maturity blown up/ In rank Achilles . . ." *Tr & Cr*, I, iii, 315–317.

Maudlin, *n.* Magdalene [appar. spelled as pronounced]: "Send forth your amorous token for fair Maudlin." *All's W*, V, iii, 68.

maugre, *prep.* in spite of: "This maugre all the world will I keep safe . . ." *T Andr*, IV, ii, 110.

maund, *n.* basket: "A thousand favours from a maund she drew . . ." *Lover's Comp*, 36.

ma vie! by my very life! [mild oath, from French]: ". . . ma vie! if they march along/ Unfought withal, but I will sell my dukedom . . ." *Hen 5*, III, v, 11–12.

maw, *n.* **1** stomach; belly: "Methinks your maw, like mine, should be your clock . . ." *Errors*, I, ii, 66. **2** gullet or craw; here, likened to that of a voracious beast: "Thou detestable maw, thou womb of death/ Gorg'd with the dearest morsel of the earth . . ." *Rom & Jul*, V, iii, 45–46.

may, *v.* **1** can; are you able?: "May you stead me? Will you pleasure me?" *Merch*, I, iii, 6. **2 as you may,** in whatever way you can: "For your desire to know what is between us,/ O'ermaster't as you may." *Ham*, I, v, 145–146. **3 may see,** you may see what: "May see the sea hath cast upon your coast—" *Per*, II, i, 56. **4 you may, you may,** *a.* get along with you; you're pulling my leg: "By my troth, sweet lord,/ thou hast a fine forehead."/ "Ay, you may, you may." *Tr & Cr*, III, i, 102–103. **b.** go on, have your little joke: "You are never without your tricks; you may,/ you may." *Cor*, II, iii, 35–36.

May, *n.* **morn of May,** May Day and its annual observances: "Where I did meet thee once with Helena/ To do observance to a morn of May . . ." *M N Dream*, I, i, 166–167.

may-day morning, *n.* morning of May 1, an important spring festival: ". . . to make 'em sleep/ On may-day morning, which will never be . . ." *Hen 8*, V, iii, 13–14.

May-morn, *n.* youthful prime: ". . . in the very May-morn of his youth . . ." *Hen 5*, I, ii, 120.

May morning, *n.* **More matter for a May morning!** material fit for a holiday entertainment in May. *T Night*, III, iv, 144.

mazard or **mazzard,** *n.* drinking bowl; here, slang term for "head": ". . . my Lady Worm's, chopless, and knocked about the mazard with a sexton's spade." *Ham*, V, i, 87–88.

maze, *v.* to trap in or as if in a maze; here, to bewilder or confuse: "A little herd of England's timorous deer,/ Maz'd with a yelping kennel of French curs!" *1 Hen 6*, IV, ii, 46–47.

mazed, *adj.* bewildered: ". . . the mazed world,/ By their increase, now knows not which is which." *M N Dream*, II, i, 113–114.

me, *pron.* **me rather had,** I had rather: "Me rather had my heart might feel your love . . ." *Rich 2*, III, iii, 192.

meacock, *adj.* timid; apathetic: "How tame . . . A meacock wretch can make the curstest shrew." *Shrew*, II, i, 305–306.

mead, *n.* flat, grassy land; meadow: "One hour's storm will drown the fragrant meads . . ." *T Andr*, II, iv, 54.

meal, *n.* flour: "Nature hath meal, and bran [husks]; contempt, and grace." *Cymb*, IV, ii, 27.

mealed, *past part.* mixed; compounded; some editors: stained or tainted: ". . . were he meal'd with that/ Which he corrects, then were he tyrannous . . ." *Meas*, IV, ii, 81–82.

mealy, *adj.* powdery: ". . . for men, like butterflies,/ Show not their mealy wings but to the summer . . ." *Tr & Cr*, III, iii, 78–79.

mean¹, *adj.* **1** lowly; humble: ". . . show Lord Timon that mean eyes have seen/ The foot above the head." *Timon,* I, i, 95–96. **2** ordinary; common (as disting. from noble or royal): "That which in mean men we intitle patience/ Is pale cold cowardice in noble breasts." *Rich 2,* I, ii, 33–34. **3** contemptible: "A very mean meaning . . . / And I am mean, indeed, respecting you." *Shrew,* V, ii, 31–32. **4 mean and gentle all,** those of humble as well as gentle birth: "His liberal eye doth give to every one . . . that mean and gentle all . . ." *Hen 5,* IV, Chor., 44–45.

mean², *n.* **1** means: ". . . make the Douglas' son your only mean/ For powers in Scotland . . ." *1 Hen 4,* I, iii, 257–258. **2** limit; moderation: "Shall we disturb him, since he keeps no mean?" *1 Hen 6,* I, ii, 121. **3** opportunity: ". . . there's some of ye, I see . . . Would try him to the utmost, had ye mean . . ." *Hen 8,* V, ii, 178–180. **4** [pl.] authority: "Our brother is imprison'd by your means . . ." *Rich 3,* I, iii, 78. **5** (in music) the middle, or tenor, part: ". . . nay, he can sing/ A mean most meanly . . ." *Love's L,* V, ii, 327–328. **6** male who sings the tenor part: ". . . they are most of them means and basses but one/ puritan amongst them . . ." *W Tale,* IV, iii, 43–44. **7 make such means,** to take such pains: "To make such means for her . . . And leave her on such slight conditions." *Two Gent,* V, iv, 135–136.

mean³, *v.* to lament: "And thus she means, videlicet—" *M N Dream,* V, i, 310.

mean affairs, *n.* humble or routine business: "If one of mean affairs/ May plod it in a week . . ." *Cymb,* III, ii, 51–52.

meander, *n.* winding path; Gonzalo here likens the course taken to that of a maze: ". . . here's a maze trod, indeed,/ Through forth-rights and meanders!" *Temp,* III, iii, 2–3.

meaner, *adj.* (of a person) belonging to a lower rank or class; poorer; humbler: "Youngling, learn thou to make some meaner choice . . ." *T Andr,* II, i, 73.

meanest, *adj.* most humble: "So honour peereth in the meanest habit [outfit]." *Shrew,* IV, iii, 171.

meaning, *n.* intention: "I am no honest/ man if there be any good meaning toward you . . ." *Lear,* I, ii, 179–180.

meanly¹, *adv.* poorly; badly: ". . . nay, he can sing/ A mean [middle voice] most meanly . . ." *Love's L,* V, ii, 327–328.

meanly², *adv.* **not meanly,** in no small degree; considerably: "My wife, not meanly proudly of two such boys . . ." *Errors,* I, i, 58.

means, *n.* **1** profitable employment: ". . . he that wants money, means, and content is without three good friends . . ." *As You,*

III, ii, 24–25. **2** that which is necessary to sustain life: "Light vanity, insatiate cormorant,/ Consuming means, soon preys upon itself." *Rich 2,* II, i, 38–39. **3** access: ". . . when thou shalt have overlooked/ this, give these fellows some means to the King." *Ham,* IV, vi, 13–14. **4** go-between or pimp: "Ay, sir, by Mistress Overdone's means; but as she/ spit in his face, so she defied him." *Meas,* II, i, 82–83. **5** attempts to placate or reconcile; mediation: "What means do you make to him?" *Cymb,* II, iv, 3. **6 for means,** how something is to be carried out: "Well, Juliet, I will lie with thee tonight. Let's see for means." *Rom & Jul,* V, i, 34–35. **7 make such means,** go to so much trouble: ". . . base art thou/ To make such means for her, as thou hast done . . ." *Two Gent,* V, iv, 134–135. **8 means secure us,** See **secure** (def. 4). **9 means will make us means,** [how our] financial means can provide means of transportation: "I will come after you with what good speed/ Our means will make us means." *All's W,* V, i, 33–34.

measles, *n.* plague spots: "Coin words till their decay, against those measles/ Which we disdain should tetter us . . ." *Cor,* III, i, 77–78.

measurable, *adj.* meet or appropriate: "The posterior of the day . . . is liable,/ congruent, and measurable for the afternoon . . ." *Love's L,* V, i, 83–84.

measure, *n.* **1** dance or period of dancing: "Play music, and you brides and bridegrooms all,/ to th' measures fall." *As You,* V, iv, 177–178. **2** slow, stately formal dance: ". . . repenting is as a Scotch jig, a measure,/ and a cinque-pace . . ." *M Ado,* II, i, 67–68. **3** [pl.] musical accompaniment; here, for a wedding feast: "Shall braying trumpets and loud churlish drums . . . be measures to our pomp?" *K John,* III, i, 229–230. **4** limit or moderation: ". . . my poor heart no measure keeps in grief . . ." *Rich 2,* III, iv, 8. **5** activity; conduct: ". . . you have gone on, and fill'd the time/ With all licentious measure . . ." *Timon,* V, iv, 3–4. **6** treatment; handling: "He professes to have received no sinister measure/ from his judge . . ." *Meas,* III, ii, 236–237. **7** portion; here, of recompense: "My life will be too short,/ And every measure fail me." *Lear,* IV, vii, 2–3. **8** eminent suitability: "He cannot but with measure fit the honours/ Which we devise him." *Cor,* II, ii, 123–124. **9 after the measure as,** to the extent that; insofar [as]: "Must have that thanks from Rome after the measure/ As you intended well." *Cor,* V, i, 46–47. **10 in measure,** with all due ceremony: "We will perform in measure, time, and place." *Mac,* V, viii, 39. **11 knowing all measures,** acquainted with all kinds of fortune: "Knowing all measures, the full Caesar will/ Answer his emptiness . . ." *Ant & Cleo,* III, xiii, 35–36. **12 measure of my wrath,** distance my sword can reach: "Come not within the measure of my wrath . . ." *Two Gent,* V, iv, 125.

—*v.* **13** to travel through; traverse: ". . . they have let the dangerous enemy/ Measure our confines with such peaceful steps?" *Rich 2,* III, ii, 124–125. **14** to appraise; estimate: "But let them measure us by what they will . . ." *Rom & Jul,* I, iv, 9. **15** to allot; deal out: "We'll measure them a measure [dance] and be gone." *Rom & Jul,* I, iv, 10. **16 measure our weapon,** to act as second in a duel [and measure the opponent's rapier to guard against any unfair advantage]: "I have appointed mine host/ of de Jarteer to measure our weapon." *Wives,* I, iv, 112–113.

meat, *n.* food: "All viands that I eat do seem unsavoury,/ Wishing him my meat." *Per,* II, iii, 31–32.

mechanic, *adj.* **1** formal or elaborate; also, conventional: ". . . worthy shameful check it were, to stand/ On more mechanic compliment . . ." *Ant & Cleo,* IV, iv, 31–32. **2** laboring; forced to do manual labor: ". . . mechanic slaves/ With greasy aprons, rules, and hammers shall/ Uplift us to the view." *Ant & Cleo,* V, ii, 208–210.
–*n.* **3** workingman; mechanical: "Dismiss my soldiers, or capitulate/ Again with Rome's mechanics." *Cor,* V, iii, 82–83.

mechanical, *adj.* **1** of a laborer or workingman: "Hal'd thither/ By most mechanical and dirty hand." *2 Hen 4,* V, v, 35–36. **2** belonging to the laboring class: "Being mechanical, you ought not walk/ Upon a labouring day . . ." *J Caes,* I, i, 3–4. **3** common; vulgar: "Hang him, mechanical salt-butter rogue!" *Wives,* II, ii, 267.
—*n.* **4** workingman: "A crew of patches, rude mechanicals . . . Were met together to rehearse a play . . ." *M N Dream,* III, ii, 9–11.

meddle, *v.* **1** to get oneself involved: ". . . for meddle you must, that's certain, or forswear/ to wear iron about you." *T Night,* III, iv, 255–256. **2** to concern yourself; here, wordplay on "have sexual intercourse": "Do you meddle with my master?"/ "Ay; 'tis an honester service than to meddle with thy/ mistress." *Cor,* IV, v, 47–49.

meddler, *n.* go-between in commercial transactions: "Money's a meddler,/ That doth utter all men's ware-a." *W Tale,* IV, iv, 323–324.

meddling, *adj.* intruding; bothering or pestering: ". . . the busy meddling fiend/ That lays strong siege unto this wretch's soul . . ." *2 Hen 6,* III iii, 21–22.

Mede, *n.* Media: "The kings of Mede and Lycaonia . . ." *Ant & Cleo,* III, vi, 75.

Media, *n.* Asian country, appar. near or adjoining Mesopotamia: "Spur through Media,/ Mesopotamia, and the shelters whither/ The routed fly." *Ant & Cleo,* III, i, 7–9.

Medice, teipsum, [Latin] incomplete quote from the Vulgate: Physician [heal] thyself: "*Medice, teipsum*—/ Protector, see to't well, protect yourself." *2 Hen 6,* II, i, 54–55.

medicinable, *adj.* **1** medicinal or salutary: "Any bar, any cross, any impediment will be/ medicinable to me." *M Ado,* II, ii, 4–5. **2** having healing properties: ". . . whose med'cinable eye/ Corrects the influence of evil planets . . ." *Tr & Cr,* I, iii, 91–92.

medicine¹, *n.* **1** [often pl.] potion, esp. a love potion: "If the rascal have not given me medicines to make me love/ him, I'll be hanged." *1 Hen 4,* II, ii, 17–19. **2** poison: "Sick!/ O, sick!"/ "[Aside.] If not, I'll ne'er trust medicine." *Lear,* V, iii, 96–97.
—*v.* **3** to act as medicine upon: "Nor all the drowsy syrups of the world,/ Shall ever medicine thee to that sweet sleep . . ." *Oth,* III, iii, 336–337.

medicine², *n.* physician: "Yet coming from him, that great med'cine hath/ With his tinct gilded thee." *Ant & Cleo,* I, v, 36–37.

meditance, *n.* meditation: ". . . your first thought is more/ Than others' labored meditance . . ." *Kinsmen,* I, i, 135–136.

meditation, *n.* prayer: "Close up his eyes . . . And let us all to meditation." *2 Hen 6,* III, iii, 31–33.

medlar, *n.* **1** small brown fruit, similar to the apple but soft when ripe: ". . . you'll be rotten ere you be half ripe, and that's the right virtue of the medlar." *As You,* III, ii, 117–118. **2** wordplay with "prostitute," slang sense of the word: "And wish his mistress were that kind of fruit/ As maids call medlars when they laugh alone." *Rom & Jul,* II, i, 35–36.

meed, *n.* **1** merit: ". . . we, the sons of brave Plantagenet,/ Each one already blazing by our meeds . . ." *3 Hen 6,* II, i, 35–36. **2** reward or recompense: "No meed but he repays/ Seven-fold above itself . . ." *Timon,* I, i, 276–277. **3** service: ". . . in the imputation/ laid on him, by them in his meed, he's unfellowed." *Ham,* V, ii, 139–140. **4 meed for meed,** just deserts; here, "measure for measure": "There's meed for meed, death for a deadly deed." *T Andr,* V, iii, 66.

meet, *adj.* **1** even; equal: ". . . he'll be meet with you, I doubt it not." *M Ado,* I, i, 43. **2** right and proper: "Is it possible disdain should die, while she hath/ such meet food . . . ?" *M Ado,* I, i, 110–111. **3** wise; prudent: ". . . her friends [family],/ From whom we thought it meet to hide our love . . ." *Meas,* I, ii, 140–141.
—*adv.* **4** properly; fittingly: "All yet seems well, and if it end so meet . . ." *All's Well,* V, iii, 327.

meeter, *adj.* compar. of **meet;** fitter; more suitable: "He therefore sends you, meeter for your spirit,/ This tun of treasure . . ." *Hen 5*, I, ii, 254–255.

meetly, *adj.* pretty good; not bad: "You can do better yet; but this is meetly." *Ant & Cleo,* I, iii, 81.

meetness, *n.* appropriateness: "And sick of welfare found a kind of meetness/ To be diseased . . ." *Sonn 118,* 7–8.

Mehercle! [Latin] By Hercules! [mild oath]: "*Mehercle!* if their sons be ingenious, they shall want/ no instruction . . ." *Love's L,* IV, ii, 75–76.

meiny or **meinie,** *n.* **1** attendants; retinue: ". . . on whose contents/ They summon'd up their meiny, straight took horse . . ." *Lear,* II, iv, 34–35. **2** multitude; here, mob, crew or herd: "For the mutable, rank-scented meinie, let them/ Regard me as I do not flatter . . ." *Cor,* III, i, 65–66.

melancholy, *n.* **1** gloominess; depression; sullenness: "Or if that surly spirit, melancholy,/ Had bak'd thy blood and made it heavy, thick . . ." *K John,* III, ii, 52–53. **2** pleasantry, since melancholy was regarded as a cold humor: ". . . if I lose a scruple of this sport,/ let me be boiled to death with melancholy." *T Night,* II, v, 2–3.

melancholy god, *n.* Saturn, Roman god of agriculture; perh. reference is to the "changeableness" of the harvest: "Now the melancholy god protect thee, and the/ tailor make thy doublet of changeable taffeta . . ." *T Night,* II, iv, 73–74.

mell, *v.* to mix or mingle (with); here, to engage in sexual relations: "Men are to mell with, boys are not to kiss . . ." *All's W,* IV, iii, 220.

mellow, *adj.* ripe; suitable: ". . . night not be deliver'd to the world,/ Till I had made mine own occasion mellow . . ." *T Night,* I, ii, 42–43.

melt in showers, dissolve in tears: ". . . come and learn of us/ To melt in showers . . ." *T Andr,* V, iii, 160–161.

member, *n.* **1** person who shares; sharer: "The slave, a member of the country's peace . . ." *Hen 5,* IV, i, 287. **2** person who is part of a conspiracy: ". . . no more/ But instruments of some more mightier member/ That sets them on." *Meas,* V, i, 235–237. **3** limb or part, poss. in bawdy wordplay: ". . . when old robes are worn/ out, there are members to make new." *Ant & Cleo,* I, ii, 162–163.

memento mori, [Latin] reminder of [one's] mortality: "I make as good use of it as many a/ man doth of a death's-head, or a *memento mori.*" *1 Hen 4,* III, iii, 28–29.

memorial, *adj.* **1** full of memories: ". . . takes my glove,/ And gives memorial dainty kisses to it,/ As I kiss thee . . ." *Tr & Cr,* V, ii, 79–81.
—*n.* **2** [pl.] ancient monuments; antiquities: ". . . let us satisfy our eyes/ With the memorials and the things of fame/ That do renown this city." *T Night,* III, iii, 22–24.

memorize, *v.* to make memorable; memorialize: ". . . they meant to bathe in reeking wounds,/ Or memorize another Golgotha . . ." *Mac,* I, ii, 40–41.

memory, *n.* **1** [pl.] tokens or souvenirs; reminders: "These weeds are memories of those worser hours . . ." *Lear,* IV, vii, 7. **2 a noble memory!** a fine memorial!: ". . . have wrack'd for Rome/ To make coals cheap: a noble memory!" *Cor,* V, i, 16–17. **3 of memory,** not forgotten: "I have some rights of memory in this kingdom . . ." *Ham,* V, ii, 394. **4 out of memory,** until vanished from the memory: "And wear their brave state out of memory . . ." *Sonn 15,* 8.

mend, *v.* **1** to augment or improve: "And we will mend thy wages." *As You,* II, iv, 92. **2** to improve on; surpass: ". . . and, in ushering,/ Mend him who can . . ." *Love's L,* V, ii, 328–329. **3** [as a command] strengthen your defenses: "Mend and charge home,/ Or . . . I'll leave the foe/ And make my wars on you." *Cor,* I, iv, 38–40. **4 mend upon the world,** to improve in the eyes of the world: ". . . they are people such/ That mend upon the world." *Cymb,* II, iv, 25–26.
—*n.* **5** [pl.] prob. ref. to cosmetics: ". . . and she be not,/ she has the mends in her own hands." *Tr & Cr,* I, i, 67–68.

Menelaus, *n.* husband of Helen and brother of Agamemnon: "Helen of Greece was fairer far than thou,/ Although thy husband may be Menelaus . . ." *3 Hen 6,* II, ii, 146–147.

Menon, *n.* Achilles' cousin: "The fierce Polydamas/ Hath beat down Menon . . ." *Tr & Cr,* V, v, 6–7.

Mephostophilus, *n.* Mephistophilis [Mephistopheles], the Devil in Marlowe's *Tragical History of Dr. Faustus:* "How now, Mephostophilus?"/ "Ay, it is no matter." *Wives,* I, i, 120–121.

Me pompae provexit apex, [Latin] The crown of victory has carried me forward. *Per,* II, ii, 30.

mercatante, *n.* [Italian] merchant: "Master, a mercatante, or a pedant,/ I know not what . . ." *Shrew,* IV, ii, 63–64.

mercenary, *n.* common soldier who served for pay: ". . . in these ten thousand they have lost,/ There are but sixteen hundred mercenaries . . ." *Hen 5,* IV, viii, 89–90.

mercer, *n.* dealer in fabrics: ". . . at the/ suit of Master Three-pile the mercer, for some four/ suits of peach-coloured satin . . ." *Meas,* IV, iii, 9–11.

merchandise, *n.* **make merchandise,** to conduct business, esp. to drive a bargain: ". . . were he out of/ Venice I can make what merchandise I will . . ." *Merch,* III, i, 117–118.

merchandised, *adj.* offered, or as though offered, for sale: "That love is merchandised, whose rich esteeming/ The owner's tongue doth publish everywhere." *Sonn 102,* 3–4.

merchant, *n.* [when distinguished from "gentleman"] fellow [often a term of contempt]: "I pray you, sir, what saucy merchant was this,/ that was so full of his ropery?" *Rom & Jul,* II, iv, 142–143.

merchant-marring, *adj.* destructive to merchant vessels: "And not one vessel scape the dreadful touch/ Of merchant-marring rocks?" *Merch,* III, ii, 269–270.

Mercury, *n.* **1** son of Jupiter and messenger of the gods, who wore winged sandals: "I saw young Harry . . . Rise from the ground like feather'd Mercury . . ." *1 Hen 4,* IV, i, 104–106. **2** same, revered for his cunning and regarded as the god of thieves, cheats, and liars: "Now Mercury endue thee with leasing, for thou/ speak'st well of fools!" *T Night,* I, v, 97–98.

mercy, *n.* **1** ability to act at pleasure; discretion: ". . . all estates . . . That lie within the mercy of your wit . . ." *Love's L,* V, ii, 837–838. **2** forgiveness: "Let all my sins lack mercy!" *M Ado,* IV, i, 180. **3 by mercy,** using a merciful interpretation: "But in defence, by mercy, 'tis most just." *Timon,* III, v, 56. **4 I cry you mercy,** I beg your pardon [lit., beg mercy of you]: "I cry you mercy, sir, and well could wish/ You had not found me here so musical." *Meas,* IV, i, 10–11. **5 in mercy,** at another's discretion: "He may enguard his dotage with their powers,/ And hold our lives in mercy [at his mercy]." *Lear,* I, iv, 336–337.

mere, *adj.* **1** absolute; complete; utter: "Last scene of all . . . Is second childishness and mere oblivion . . ." *As You,* II, vii, 163–165. **2** most essential; bare: "I . . . will love nought/ But even the mere necessities upon 't." *Timon,* IV, iii, 378–379. **3** substantial; considerable: ". . . that pity begets you/ a good opinion, and that opinion a mere profit." *Per,* IV, ii, 119–120. **4 at the merest loss,** when the scent was completely lost: "Belman is as good as he, my lord./ He cried upon it at the merest loss . . ." *Shrew,* Ind., i, 20–21. **5 upon his mere request,** entirely at his request: "Upon his mere reqest . . . came I hither . . ." *Meas,* V, i, 154–156. —*adv.* **6** absolutely: "Ay, surely, mere the truth; I know his lady." *All's W,* III, v, 55.

mered, *adj.* [lit., fenced or marked off from the others] **the mered question,** cause of the dispute and the only issue to be settled: "When half to half the world oppos'd, he being/ The mered question." *Ant & Cleo,* III, xiii, 9–10.

merely, *adv.* **1** fully or entirely; utterly: ". . . things rank and gross in nature/ Possess it merely." *Ham,* I, ii, 136–137. **2 merely awry,** absolutely wrong: "Merely awry. When he did love his country,/ It honour'd him." *Cor,* III, i, 302–303.

mere the truth, absolutely true: "Ay, surely, mere the truth; I know his lady." *All's W,* III, v, 55.

merit, *n.* **1** proven worth; past services: "[Aside to Pompey] If for the sake of merit thou wilt hear me." *Ant & Cleo,* II, vii, 55. **2** reward: "A dearer merit, not so deep a maim [injury] . . ." *Rich 2,* I, iii, 156. **3** worthy people: ". . . the spurns/ That patient merit of the unworthy takes . . ." *Ham,* III, i, 73–74. **4** demonstrated affection: "Where nature doth with merit challenge." *Lear,* I, i, 53.

Merlin, *n.* (in legend) magician at the court of King Arthur [after the time of Lear]: "This prophecy Merlin shall make; for I live before his time." *Lear,* III, ii, 95.

Mermaid, *n.* Siren of ancient literature, whose singing lured mariner's ships onto the rocks: "I'll drown more sailors than the Mermaid shall . . ." *3 Hen 6,* III, ii, 186.

mermaid's song, *n.* comparison to the sirens' song in Homer's *Odyssey,* thought to lure men to destruction: ". . . lest myself be guilty to self-wrong,/ I'll stop mine ears against the mermaid's song." *Errors,* III, ii, 162–163.

Merops, *n.* husband of Clymene, who was the mother, by Apollo, of Phaëton: "Why, Phaëton, for thou art Merops' son/ Wilt thou aspire to guide the heavenly car?" *Two Gent,* III, i, 153–154.

merry, *adj.* **1** in good spirits: ". . . commend me to my lord;/ Say I am merry . . ." *J Caes,* II, iv, 44–45. **2** done as a lark: "Then meet me forthwith at the notary's,/ Give him direction for this merry bond—" *Merch,* I, iii, 168–169. **3 merry Greek,** wanton: "I think Helen loves him better/ than Paris."/ "Then she's a merry Greek indeed." *Tr & Cr,* I, ii, 108–110.

mervailous, *adj.* marvelous [perh. Shakespeare's spelling]: "The 'solus' in thy most mervailous face . . ." *Hen 5,* II, i, 46.

me seemeth or meseemeth, it seems to me: "Me seemeth then it is no policy,/ Respecting what a rancorous mind he bears . . ." *2 Hen 6,* III, i, 23–24.

mesh, *n.* [often pl.] net for trapping animals: ". . . such a hare is madness the youth, to skip/ o'er the meshes of good counsel the cripple . . ." *Merch,* I, ii, 19–20.

meshed, *adj.* mashed [term in brewing]: ". . . she drinks no other drink but tears,/ Brew'd with her sorrow, mesh'd upon her cheeks." *T Andr,* III, ii, 37–38.

mess, *n.* **1** dish or serving of food: "The bounteous housewife nature on each bush/ Lays her full mess before you." *Timon,* IV, iii, 423–424. **2** small amount, esp. enough to prepare a dish or one serving: ". . . goodwife Keech the butcher's/ wife . . . coming in to borrow a mess of vinegar . . ." *2 Hen 4,* II, i, 91–93. **3** group or party of four, esp. at table: ". . . you three fools lack'd me, fool, to make/ up the mess . . ." *Love's L,* IV, iii, 203. **4** [pl.] bits; tiny pieces: "I will chop her into messes . . . Cuckold me!" *Oth,* IV, i, 196. **5** mispron. of "Mass": "By the mess, ere theise eyes of mine take themselves/ to slomber ay'll de gud service . . ." *Hen 5,* III, ii, 117–118. **6 lower messes,** persons of lower rank: ". . . lower messes/ Perchance are to this business purblind?" *W Tale,* I, ii, 227–228.

message, *n.* **of message,** with a message; as a messenger: "I go of message from the Queen to France." *2 Hen 6,* IV, i, 113.

Messaline, *n.* poss. Messina, in Sicily, but more likely Shakespeare's invention: ". . . my father was/ that Sebastian of Messaline whom I know you have heard of." *T Night,* II, i, 16–17.

messenger, *n.* Quickly's error for "message": ". . . you say well. But I have another messenger/ to your worship . . ." *Wives,* II, ii, 89–90.

messenger of wet, *n.* telltale signs of tears: ". . . what's the matter,/ That this distempered messenger of wet . . . rounds thine eye?" *All's W,* I, iii, 145–147.

met, *past part.* are met with: "Martius Caius Coriolanus, whom/ We met here . . ." *Cor,* II, ii, 46–47.

metal, *n.* material: "Not till God make men of some other metal than earth." *M Ado,* II, i, 55.

metal of India, *n.* gold: "Here comes the little villain. How now, my/ metal of India?" *T Night,* II, v, 13–14.

metamorphose, *v.* to cause a change in: "Thou, Julia, thou hast metamorphos'd me . . ." *Two Gent,* I, i, 66.

metamorphosed, *past part.* petrified: "In brief, our soldiers . . . stand like metamorphosed images,/ Bloodless and pale . . ." *Edw 3,* IV, v, 36–38.

metaphysical, *adj.* supernatural: "Which fate and metaphysical aid doth seem/ To have thee crown'd withal." *Mac,* I, v, 29–30.

mete, *v.* **1** to appraise or judge: ". . . his Grace must mete the lives of other,/ Turning past evils to advantages." *2 Hen 4,* IV, iv, 77–78. **2** to measure (by) or take aim (at): "Let the mark have a prick in't, to mete at, if it may be." *Love's L,* IV, i, 133.

meteor, *n.* **1** [often pl.] an emotion: "What observation mad'st thou in this case,/ Of his heart's meteors tilting in his face?" *Errors,* IV, ii, 5–6. **2** prob. a meteor shower or a comet, both of which were regarded as evil omens: ". . . like the meteors of a troubled heaven . . ." *1 Hen 4,* I, i, 10.

meter, *n.* **1** trivial rhyming verse; doggerel; here, in attrib. use with pejor. sense of "versifying": "I had rather be a kitten and cry 'mew'/ Than one of these same metre ballad-mongers . . ." *1 Hen 4,* III, i, 123–124. **2** [pl.] verses in such doggerel: "Lascivious metres, to whose venom [venomous] sound/ The open ear of youth doth always listen . . ." *Rich 2,* II, i, 19–20. **3** melody; passage or strain: ". . . a poet's rage/ And stretched [exaggerated] metre of an antique song . . ." *Sonn 17,* 11–12. **4 in meter,** in verse; also, implies "in a song" or "in a play": ". . . I think thou never wast where/ grace was said."/ "No? A dozen times at least."/ "What, in metre?" *Meas,* I, ii, 18–21.

mete-yard, *n.* yardstick: "Take thou the bill, give me/ thy mete-yard, and spare not me." *Shrew,* IV, iii, 149–150.

metheglin, *n.* Welsh drink of fermented honey, water, and herbs: ". . . an if you grow so nice,/ Metheglin, wort, and malmsey . . ." *Love's L,* V, ii, 232–233.

methinks, *v.* it seems to me: "Methinks your looks are sad, your cheer appall'd." *1 Hen 6,* I, ii, 48.

method, *n.* **1** logic; sense: "Though this be madness, yet there is method/ in't." *Ham,* II, ii, 205–206. **2** summary; here, of charges: "Think not . . . I have forg'd, or am not able/ Verbatim to rehearse my method penn'd." *1 Hen 6,* III, i, 10–13. **3** manner of behaving: "To leave this keen encounter of our wits,/ And fall something into a slower method . . ." *Rich 3,* I, ii, 119–120. **4 by the method,** in the same style or metaphor: "To answer by the method, in the first of his/ heart." *T Night,* I, v, 229–230. **5 hold the method,** to employ the [proper] technique: "You do not hold the method, to enforce/ The like from him." *Ant & Cleo,* I, iii, 7–8.

methought, also, **methoughts** or **me thoughts,** *v.* I thought: "I pass'd, methought, the melancholy flood,/ With that sour ferryman which poets write of . . ." *Rich 3,* I, iv, 45–46.

mettle, *n.* **1** matter or substance; gist: ". . . therein suits/ His folly to the mettle of my speech." *As You,* II, vii, 82. **2** courage: "O, this boy/ Lends mettle to us all!" *1 Hen 4,* V, iv, 23. **3** wordplay on "courage" and "metal" [prison chains]: "I will pray, Pompey, to increase your bondage; if you/ take it not patiently, why, your mettle is the more!" *Meas,* III, ii, 72–73. **4** essence: ". . . his blood was thine! that bed, that womb,/ That mettle, that self mould . . ." *Rich 2,* I, ii, 22–23. **5** temperament; disposition: "He was quick [lively] mettle when he went to school" *J Caes,* I, ii, 293.

mew, *v.* **1** appar. Goneril imitates a cat's mewing, as an insult to Albany's faintheartedness: "Marry, your manhood—mew!" *Lear,* IV, ii, 68. **2 mew up,** [in falconry] to shut or coop up; confine: "Tonight she's mew'd up to her heaviness." *Rom & Jul,* III, iv, 11.

mewl, *v.* to cry faintly; whimper: "At first the infant,/ Mewling and puking in the nurse's arms." *As You,* II, vii, 143–144.

Michaelmas, *n.* Feast of St. Michael, Sept. 29: ". . . upon Allhallowmas last, a fortnight/ afore Michaelmas?" *Wives,* I, i, 185–186.

micher, *n.* [rhymes with *pitcher*] truant, esp. one who leaves duties to gather blackberries: "Shall the/ blessed sun of heaven prove a micher, and eat/ blackberries?" *1 Hen 4,* II, iv, 403–404.

miching malicho, *n.* sly but insidious mischief: "Marry, this is miching malicho. It means mischief." *Ham,* III, ii, 135.

mickle, *adj.* **1** much; great: "The one ne'er got me credit, the other mickle blame . . ." *Errors,* III, i, 45. **2 more mickle,** greater: ". . . more mickle was the pain,/ That nothing could be used to turn them both to gain . . ." *Pass Pil,* XV, 9–10.

Midas, *n.* myth. king of Phrygia whose wish was granted causing everything he touched to turn into gold, including his food: "Therefore thou gaudy gold,/ Hard food for Midas, I will none of thee . . ." *Merch,* III, ii, 101–102.

midnight, *n.* middle of the night [it was 1 A.M. at beginning of scene]: "'Tis midnight Charles;/ Prithee to bed . . ." *Hen 8,* V, i, 72–73.

midnight mushrooms, *n.* believed to be created at midnight by elves: ". . . you whose pastime/ Is to make midnight mushrooms . . ." *Temp,* V, i, 38–39.

mid season, *n.* noon: "What is the time o' th' day?"/ "Past the mid season." *Temp,* I, ii, 239.

midsummer madness, *n.* regarded as a common malady, brought on by the summer moon: "Why, this is very midsummer madness." *T Night,* III, iv, 55.

midway, *adv.* in mid-course; before [messages] reach their destination: "And make a batt'ry through his deafen'd ports,/ Which now are midway stopp'd." *Per,* V, i, 46–47.

midwife, *n.* **1** Queen Mab, the fairy charged with delivering men's dreams: "O then I see Queen Mab hath been with you./ She is the fairies' midwife . . ." *Rom & Jul,* I, iv, 53–54. **2** old woman [term of contempt]: "With Lady Margery, your midwife there,/ To save this bastard's life . . ." *W Tale,* II, iii, 159–160.

might, *n.* **1** will or intention: ". . . noble respect/ Takes it in might, not merit." *M N Dream,* V, i, 91–92. —*v.* **2 if might,** if [it were] possible: "Where what is done in action, more, if might,/ Shall be discover'd . . ." *Per,* V, Chor., 23–24.

mightful, *adj.* mighty; powerful: "My lords, you know, as know the mightful gods . . ." *T Andr,* IV, iv, 5.

mighty suit, *n.* urgent petition: "Be not you spoke with but by mighty suit." *Rich 3,* III, vii, 45.

Milan, *n.* **1** title of Duke of Milan: ". . . confer fair Milan,/ With all the honours, on my brother . . ." *Temp,* I, ii, 126–127. **2 Absolute Milan,** actual title of Duke of Milan, as disting. from merely usurping the prerogatives: "To have no screen between this part he play'd/ And him he play'd it for, he needs will be/ Absolute Milan." *Temp,* I, ii, 107–109.

milch, *n.* **made milch,** [to] moisten; lit., turn to milk: "The instant burst of clamour that she made . . . Would have made milch the burning eyes of heaven . . ." *Ham,* II, ii, 511–513.

milch-kine, *n. pl.* **1** milk cows [dairy cattle]: ". . . and takes [bewitches] the cattle,/ And makes milch-kine yield blood . . ." *Wives,* IV, iv, 32–33. **2 milch-kine to the pail,** dairy cattle, producing milk to be sold: "Then at my farm/ I have a hundred milch-kine to the pail . . ." *Shrew,* II, i, 349–350.

mild, *adj.* tender; gentle: "But be thou mild, and blush not at my shame . . ." *2 Hen 6,* II, iv, 48.

mild companion, *n.* companion of [or associated with] such a gentle nature: ". . . and testy wrath/ Could never be her mild companion." *Per,* I, i, 18–19.

milder, *adj.* compar. of **mild**; better disposed [toward something or someone]: "I find her milder than she was,/ And yet she takes exceptions at your person." *Two Gent,* V, ii, 2–3.

mildewed, *adj.* blighted; contaminated: ". . . like a mildew'd ear/ Blasting his wholesome brother." *Ham,* III, iv, 64–65.

mildly, *adv.* done as mildly: ". . . what we did was mildly as we might . . ." *T Andr,* I, i, 475.

Mile-End Green, *n.* military training ground, also fairgrounds, in E London: "I remember at Mile-End Green, when I lay at/ Clement's Inn . . ." *2 Hen 4,* III, ii, 274–275.

Milford-Haven, *n.* port in SW Wales: "Take notice that I am in/ Cambria at Milford-Haven . . ." *Cymb,* III, ii, 43–44.

milk, *n.* submission or conciliation; also, lack of resolve: "I should/ Pour the sweet milk of concord into Hell . . ." *Mac,* IV, iii, 97–98.

milk-livered, *adj.* cowardly; fainthearted: "Milk-liver'd man!/ That bear'st a cheek for blows, a head for wrongs . . ." *Lear,* IV, ii, 50–51.

milk of human kindness, *n.* lack of resolve in human nature: ". . . I fear thy nature:/ It is too full o' th' milk of human kindness . . ." *Mac,* I, v, 16–17.

milk-pap, *n.* female breast: ". . . those milk-paps,/ That through the window-bars bore at men's eyes . . ." *Timon,* IV, iii, 117–118.

millioned, *adj.* innumerable: "But reckoning Time, whose million'd accidents/ Creep in 'twixt vows . . ." *Sonn 115,* 5–6.

million of manners, *n.* See **manner**[1] (def. 3).

mill-sixpence, *n.* stamped coin having a corrugated edge: ". . . seven groats in mill-sixpences, and two Edward/ shovel-boards . . ." *Wives,* I, i, 140–141.

millstone, *n.* fr. the saying that hard-hearted people could not shed real tears: "Queen Hecuba/ laughed that her eyes ran o'er—"/ "With millstones." *Tr & Cr,* I, ii, 144–146.

Milo, *n.* legendary Greek athlete who reputedly slew a young bull with a blow of his fist and ate him: ". . . for thy vigour,/ Bull-bearing Milo his addition yield/ To sinewy Ajax." *Tr & Cr,* II, iii, 246–248.

mimic, *n.* mime or actor: "Anon, his Thisbe must be answered,/ And forth my mimic comes." *M N Dream,* III, ii, 18–19.

mince, *v.* **1** to walk with small, affected steps; here, to go quickly: "Away, I say, time wears; hold up your head, and/ mince." *Wives,* V, i, 7–8. **2** to lessen the seriousness of; extenuate; mitigate: "I know, Iago,/ Thy honesty and love doth mince this matter . . ." *Oth,* II, iii, 237–238. **3 minces virtue,**

coyly affects the appearance of virtue: "Behold yond simp'ring dame . . . That minces virtue . . ." *Lear,* IV, vi, 120–122.

minced, *adj.* separated into so many parts, as Pandarus has just done: ". . . the spice and salt that season/ a man?"/ "Ay, a minced man . . ." *Tr & Cr,* I, ii, 259–261.

mincing, *n.* **1** affectation: ". . . which gifts/ (Saving your mincing) [your affectation notwithstanding] the capacity/ Of your soft cheveril conscience would receive . . ." *Hen 8,* II, iii, 30–31. —*adj.* **2** affected: "And that would set my teeth nothing on edge,/ Nothing so much as mincing poetry . . ." *1 Hen 4,* III, i, 127–128.

mind, *v.* **1** to notice: "I'll fall flat;/ Perchance he will not mind me." *Temp,* II, ii, 16–17. **2** to heed; pay attention: "Never mind/ Was to be so unwise, to be so kind." *Timon,* II, i, 5–6. **3** to brood upon: ". . . her tears/ Which, too much minded by herself alone,/ May be put from her by society." *Rom & Jul,* IV, i, 13–14. **4** to intend: "We do not come, as minding to content you . . ." *M N Dream,* V, i, 113. **5** to imagine; bring to mind: "Minding true things by what their mock'ries be." *Hen 5,* IV, Chor., 53. **6** to remind: "Fight valiantly to-day:/ And yet I do thee wrong to mind thee of it . . ." *Hen 5,* IV, iii, 12–13. —*n.* **7** memory; here, recorded history: "O! that record could with a backward look . . . Show me your image in some antique book,/ Since mind at first in character was done!" *Sonn 59,* 5–8. **8** intent; intentions: ". . . his mind and place [high office]/ Infecting one another, yea reciprocally . . ." *Hen 8,* I, i, 161–162. **9 for his mind,** because of his generous inclinations: "That man might ne'er be wretched for his mind." *Timon,* I, ii, 160. **10 have mind upon,** to have regard for; remember: "Have mind upon your health; tempt me no farther." *J Caes,* IV, iii, 36. **11 not in the mind,** to be of the opinion (that): "I am not in the mind but I were better to be married of him than of another . . ." *As You,* III, iii, 81–82.

minded, *adj.* **minded so,** of such a mind; here, determined not to marry and have offspring: "If all were minded so the times should cease . . ." *Sonn 11,* 7.

mine[1], *adj.* **1** my: "Mine eyes are full of tears, I cannot see." *Rich 2,* IV, i, 244. —*pron.* **2** my eyes: ". . . thy sight is young,/ And thou shalt read when mine begin to dazzle." *T Andr,* III, ii, 84–85. **3** for me; that is, as an answer to my question: "I have nothing with this answer, Hamlet. These/ words are not mine." *Ham,* III, ii, 95–96. **4** my vision: "My most true mind thus maketh mine untrue." *Sonn 113,* 14. **5** my business: "Go to; let that be mine . . ." *Meas,* II, ii, 12. **6 mine being yours,** my life being of your making: "You rather [you should be happy to take my lightweight life], mine being yours . . ." *Cymb,* V, iv, 26. —*n.* **7** I or self: "Either was the other's mine." *Phoen,* 36.

mine², *n.* **1** [often pl.] excavation, as under the wall of a besieged fortress: "Captain Fluellen, you must come presently to/ the mines . . ." *Hen 5,* III, ii, 58–59. **2** wealth of gold, jewels, etc., produced by a mine: ". . . every man that stood/ Show'd like a mine." *Hen 8,* I, i, 21–22.
—*v.* **3** to undermine: "He . . . mines my gentility with my education." *As You,* I, i, 18–20.

mine own man, my own master: ". . . I did but seal once to/ a thing, and I was never mine own man since." *2 Hen 6,* IV, ii, 78–79.

mineral, *n.* mine: ". . . his very madness, like some ore/ Among a mineral of metals base . . ." *Ham,* IV, i, 25–26.

Minerva, *n.* Greek goddess of wisdom: "Hark, Tranio, thou may'st hear Minerva speak." *Shrew,* I, i, 84.

minikin, *adj.* dainty: "And for one blast of thy minikin mouth [on your shepherd's pipe],/ Thy sheep shall take no harm." *Lear,* III, vi, 44–45.

minim rest, *n.* shortest rest in Tudor music: "He rests/ his minim rests, one, two, and the third in your/ bosom . . ." *Rom & Jul,* II, iv, 21–23.

Minime, [Latin] by no means; not in the least: "Is not lead a metal heavy, dull, and slow?"/ "*Minime,* honest master . . ." *Love's L,* III, i, 56–57.

minimus, *n.* tiny, inconsequential thing: "Get you gone, you dwarf;/ You minimus, of hindering knot-grass made . . ." *M N Dream,* III, ii, 328–329.

minion, *n.* **1** a darling or favorite [often used contemptuously]: "Is this th' Athenian minion whom the world/ Voic'd so regardfully?" *Timon,* IV, iii, 82–83. **2** hussy; minx: "Do you hear, you minion, you'll let us in I trow?": *Errors,* III, i, 54. **3 hot minion,** ref. to Venus as the lustful mistress of Mars, Roman god of war: "Mars's hot minion is return'd again . . ." *Temp,* IV, i, 98.

minister, *v.* **1** to rule or govern: "Pluck the grave wrinkled senate from the bench,/ And minister in their steads!" *Timon,* IV, i, 5–6. **2** to provide: "I do well believe your highness; and did it to minister/ occasion [opportunity] to these gentlemen . . ." *Temp,* II, i, 167–168. **3** to prescribe or order: "That ministers thine own death if I die." *All's W,* II, i, 185. **4** to serve or wait on (another): "To him the other two shall minister . . ." *Cymb,* III, iii, 76. **5 minister communication,** to furnish the occasion for a conference: "What did this vanity/ But minister communication of/ A most poor issue?" *Hen 8,* I, i, 85–87.
—*n.* **6** agent, deputy, or servant; here, enemy agent: ". . . ministers for th' purpose hurried thence/ Me and thy crying self."

Temp, I, ii, 131–132. **7** monarch regarded as God's earthly deputy: "Let heaven revenge, for I may never lift/ An angry arm against His minister." *Rich 2,* I, ii, 40–41. **8 murthering ministers,** evil spirits: "And take my milk for gall, you murth'ring ministers . . ." *Mac,* I, v, 48. **9 servile ministers,** cringing servants: ". . . yet I call you servile ministers,/ That will with two pernicious daughters join . . ." *Lear,* III, ii, 21–22.

minnow, *n.* small or insignificant person or thing (used as a term of contempt): ". . . there/ did I see that low-spirited swain, that base minnow/ of thy mirth.—" *Love's L,* I, i, 242–244.

minority, *n.* **1** childhood; here, ref. to previously mentioned "golden age" [of innocence]: "Proving from world's minority their right." *Luc,* 67. **2 in minority,** as a child: ". . . he shall present Hercules/ in minority . . ." *Love's L,* V, i, 125–126.

minstrel, *n.* **1** musician; ref. to drawing bows across instruments: "I will bid thee draw, as we do the/ minstrels—draw to pleasure us." *M Ado,* V, i, 128–129. **2** term of contempt, since minstrels were often regarded as rogues and vagabonds: "What will you give us?"/ ". . . I will give you the minstrel." *Rom & Jul,* IV, v, 111–113.

minstrelsy, *n.* playing and singing of minstrels: ". . . every room/ Hath blaz'd with lights and bray'd with minstrelsy . . ." *Timon,* II, ii, 165.

minute, *n.* **at a minute's rest,** as quickly as possible: "The good humour is to steal at a minute's rest." *Wives,* I, iii, 26.

minute-jack, *n.* figure on a clock that strikes the hour: term of contempt, esp. for a faithless friend: ". . . Cap-and-knee slaves, vapours, and minute-jacks!" *Timon,* III, vi, 93.

minutely, *adj.* frequent or constant [lit., occurring every minute]: "Now minutely revolts upbraid his faith-breach." *Mac,* V, ii, 18.

minute-while, *n.* **every minute-while,** every moment; continuously: ". . . a guard of chosen shot I had,/ That walk'd about me every minute-while . . ." *1 Hen 6,* I, iv, 52–53.

minx, *n.* saucy wench; hussy: ". . . good Sir Toby, get/ him to pray."/ "My prayers, minx!" *T Night,* III, iv, 120–122.

Mi perdonato, [Italian] pardon me; forgive me: "*Mi perdonato,* gentle master mine." *Shrew,* I, i, 25.

mirable, *adj.* admirable; marvelous: "Not Neoptolemus so mirable . . ." *Tr & Cr,* IV, v, 141.

miracle, *v.* to reveal as a miracle: "I'm not their father, yet who this should be,/ Doth miracle itself . . ." *Cymb,* IV, ii, 28–29.

mire, *v.* to sink in mire: "Paint till a horse may mire upon your face . . ." *Timon,* IV, iii, 150.

mirror, *n.* model; paragon: "Following the mirror of all Christian kings . . ." *Hen 5,* II, Chor. 6.

Misanthropos, *n.* hater of mankind: "I am *Misanthropos,* and hate mankind." *Timon,* IV, iii, 54.

misbecome, *v.* to act in a way unworthy of; violate: ". . . speak in your state/ What I have done that misbecame my place . . ." *2 Hen 4,* V, ii, 99–100.

misbeliever, *n.* infidel; heathen or nonbeliever [non-Christian]: "You call me misbeliever, cut-throat dog,/ And spet upon my Jewish gaberdine . . ." *Merch,* I, iii, 106–107.

misbelieving, *adj.* infidel: "Go, go into old Titus' sorrowful house,/ And hither hale that misbelieving Moor . . ." *T Andr,* V, iii, 142–143.

miscarry, *v.* **1** to fail; be in short supply: "Hang me by the neck if horns that year miscarry." *Love's L,* IV, i, 113. **2** to come to harm: "I would not have him miscarry for the half/ of my dowry." *T Night,* III, iv, 62–63. **3** to die; here, in infancy: "Better ten thousand base-born Cades miscarry/ Than you should stoop unto a Frenchman's mercy." *2 Hen 6,* IV, viii, 47–48.

mischance, *n.* misfortune: "And never come mischance between us twain." *Ham,* III, ii, 223.

mischief, *v.* **1** to cause mischief to; harm: ". . . and rather woo/ Those that would mischief me than those that do!" *Timon,* IV, iii, 470–471.
—*n.* **2** harm; injury: ". . . do not believe/ But [anything except that] I shall do thee mischief in the wood." *M N Dream,* II, i, 236–237. **3** calamity; misfortune: ". . . they are but felt, and seen with mischief's eyes . . ." *Per,* I, iv, 8. **4** ill; disease: ". . . to apply a/ moral medicine [bromides] to a mortifying mischief [deadly disease]. *M Ado,* I, iii, 11–12.

misconceived, *adj.* misunderstood; here, perh. also ref. to her illegitimacy: "No, misconceived Joan of Aire hath been/ A virgin from her tender infancy . . ." *1 Hen 6,* V, iv, 49–50.

misconster, *v.* var. of **misconstrue.** ". . . such is now the Duke's condition/ That he misconsters all that you have done." *As You,* I, ii, 254–255.

misconstruction, *n.* misunderstanding; misapprehension: "It pleas'd the King his master very late/ To strike at me, upon his misconstruction . . ." *Lear,* II, ii, 117–118.

misconstrued *adj.* misunderstood or misrepresented: "So much misconstru'd in his wantonness." *1 Hen 4,* V, ii, 68.

miscreant, *n.* **1** one who is misbegotten: "Curse, miscreant, when thou comest to the stake." *1 Hen 6,* V, iii, 44. **2** malefactor; villain: "Thou art a traitor and a miscreant . . ." *Rich 2,* I, i, 39.

miscreate, *adj.* illegitimate; spurious: ". . . charge your understanding soul/ With opening titles miscreate [urging spurious claims] . . ." *Hen 5,* I, ii, 15–16.

misdoubt *n.* **1** [usually pl.] fears: "He cannot so precisely weed this land/ As his misdoubts present occasion." *2 Hen 4,* IV, i, 205–206.
—*v.* Also, **misdoubteth. 2** to mistrust or suspect: "Our Person misdoubts it; 'twas treason, he said." *Love's L,* IV, iii, 191.

mis-dread, *n.* a fear of evil: ". . . the passions of the mind,/ That have their first conception by mis-dread . . ." *Per,* I, ii, 12–13.

misgive, *v.* **1** to make fearful: "So doth my heart misgive me, in these conflicts . . ." *3 Hen 6,* IV, vi, 94. **2** to have a premonition of [evil]: ". . . my mind misgives/ Some consequence yet hanging in the stars/ Shall bitterly begin his fearful date/ With this night's revels . . ." *Rom & Jul,* I, iv, 106–109.

misgovernment, *n.* immoral conduct: "Thus, pretty lady,/ I am sorry for thy much [great] misgovernment." *M Ado,* IV, i, 98–99.

misgraffed, *adj.* badly matched or paired: "Or else misgraffed in respect of years—" *M N Dream,* I, i, 137.

mishap, *n.* **1** [often pl.] misfortune: "Even so she languisheth in her mishaps . . ." *Ven & Ad,* 603. **2 planets of mishap,** planets that bring misfortune: "What! shall we curse the planets of mishap/ That plotted thus our glory's overthrow?" *1 Hen 6,* I, i, 23–24.

mishaved, *adj.* misbehaved: ". . . like a mishav'd and a sullen wench/ Thou pouts upon thy fortune and thy love." *Rom & Jul,* III, iii, 142–143.

misleader, *n.* person who leads another or others astray; bad influence: "I banish thee, on pain of death,/ As I have done the rest of my misleaders . . ." *2 Hen 4,* V, v, 63–64.

mislike, *v.* **1** to dislike; disapprove of: "'Tis not my speeches that you do mislike,/ But 'tis my presence . . ." *2 Hen 6,* I, 1, 139–140.
—*n.* **2** dislike; disapproval: "Setting your scorns and your mislike aside . . ." *3 Hen 6,* IV, i, 23.

misorder, *v.* to disturb; cause disorder in: "The time misorder'd doth, in common sense,/ Crowd us and crush us to this monstrous form . . ." *2 Hen 4,* IV, ii, 33–34.

misplace, *v.* to misuse words, esp. to twist their meaning and (as here) invert their order: "Do you hear how he misplaces?" *Meas,* II, i, 87.

misprision¹, *n.* **1** misunderstanding; misconception: "There is some strange misprision in the princes." *M Ado,* IV, i, 185. **2** mistake: ". . . why, then incision/ Would let her out in saucers: sweet misprision!" *Love's L,* IV, iii, 94–95. **3 upon misprision growing,** arising from a misunderstanding: "So thy great gift, upon misprision growing . . ." *Sonn 87,* 11.

misprision², *n.* disdain; contempt: "That dost in vile misprision shackle up/ My love and her desert . . ." *All's Well,* II, iii, 152–153.

misprize, *v.* to show contempt for: "Disdain and scorn ride sparkling in her eyes,/ Misprising what they look on . . ." *M Ado,* III, i, 51–52.

misprized, *adj.* **1** rejected as worthless: ". . . in the heart of the world . . . I am altogether misprised." *As You,* I, i, 166–169. **2** mistaken: "You spend your passion on a mispris'd mood . . ." *M N Dream,* III, ii, 74.

misproud, *adj.* haughty: "Impairing Henry, strengthening misproud York." *3 Hen 6,* II, vi, 7.

miss, *v.* **1** to lose: ". . . thy record never can be miss'd." *Sonn 122,* 8. **2** to fail to win: "Who ever strove/ To show her merit that did miss her love?" *All's W,* I, i, 222–223. **3** to get along or do without: "We cannot miss him: he does make our fire,/ Fetch in our wood . . ." *Temp,* I, ii, 313–314.
—*n.* **4** misbehavior: "He saith she is immodest, blames her miss . . ." *Ven & Ad,* 53.

missed, *adj.* lost: "Of thee, thy record never can be missed." *Sonn 122,* 8.

missingly, *adv.* regretfully (from not seeing him): ". . . but I/ have (missingly) noted, he is of late much retired/ from court . . ." *W Tale,* IV, ii, 31–33.

missive, *n.* messenger: "Whiles I stood rapt in the wonder of it, came/ missives from the King . . ." *Mac,* I, v, 6–7.

mistake, *v.* to misunderstand; misjudge: "Why, thou whoreson ass, thou mistak'st me." *Two Gent,* II, v, 41.

mistaking, *n.* mistake; blunder: "I have done thee worthy service;/ Told thee no lies, made no mistakings . . ." *Temp,* I, ii, 247–248.

mistempered, *adj.* **1** disordered; agitated: "This inundation of mistemp'red humour/ Rests by you only to be qualified . . ." *K John,* V, i, 12–13. **2** angry; here, wordplay on "well-tempered weapons" used for "ill-tempered ends": "On pain of torture from those bloody hands/ Throw your mistemper'd weapons to the ground . . ." *Rom & Jul,* I, i, 84–85.

misthink, *v.* to misjudge; think ill of: "How will the country . . . Misthink the King and not be satisfied!" *3 Hen 6,* II, v, 107–108.

mistook, *v.* mistaken; here, wrongly delivered: "This letter is mistook; it importeth none here . . ." *Love's L,* IV, i, 58.

mistreading, *n.* misstep; mistake: ". . . the rod of heaven,/ To punish my mistreadings." *1 Hen 4,* III, ii, 10–11.

mistress, *n.* **1** authoress; creator; teacher: ". . . the art and practic part of life/ Must be the mistress to this theoric . . ." *Hen 5,* I, i, 51–52.
—*adj.* **2** chief; principal; poss. also, wordplay on "mistress" and "lover" (approx. pron. of "Louvre"): "He'll make your Paris Louvre shake for it,/ Were it the mistress-court of mighty Europe . . ." *Hen 5,* II, iv, 132–133.

Mistress Mall, *n.* Mall means "little Mary"; prob. ref. to any picture covered by a curtain to protect it from dust: "Are they/ like to take dust, like Mistress Mall's picture?" *T Night,* I, iii, 123–124.

mistress minion, *n.* spoiled child; minx or hussy: "Mistress minion you,/ Thank me no thankings nor proud me no prouds . . ." *Rom & Jul,* III, v, 151–152.

mistress's command, *n.* prob. Goneril's hint that she will soon give Edmund an order to kill her husband: ". . . ere long you are like to hear,/ If you dare venture in your own behalf,/ A mistress's command." *Lear,* IV, ii, 19–21.

Mistress Shore, *n.* [not a character in the play] appar. the King's mistress; after the King's death said to be kept by Hastings: ". . . night-walking heralds/ That trudge betwixt the King and Mistress Shore." *Rich 3,* I, i, 72–73.

mistrust, *v.* **1** to suspect: "This is an accident of hourly proof/ Which I mistrusted not." *M Ado,* II, i, 169–170. **2** to perceive: ". . . many a thousand/ Which now mistrust no parcel of my fear . . ." *3 Hen 6,* V, vi, 37–38.
—*n.* **3** doubt or fear: "Mistrust of my success hath done this deed." *J Caes,* V, iii, 65.

mistrustful, *adj.* causing fear; frightening: "Their light blown out in some mistrustful wood . . ." *Ven & Ad,* 826.

misuse, *v.* **1** to deceive or delude: "Proof enough to misuse the Prince, to vex Claudio,/ to undo Hero, and kill Leonato." *M Ado*, II, ii, 28–29. **2** to misrepresent; speak falsely of: "For all my vows are oaths but to misuse thee . . ." *Sonn 152*, 7. —*n.* **3** violation; abuse; desecration: "Upon whose dead corpse there was such misuse . . ." *1 Hen 4*, I, i, 43.

mitigation, *n.* act of moderating: ". . . my good lord,/ How now for mitigation of this bill . . ." *Hen 5*, I, ii, 69–70.

mixed, *adj.* balanced: ". . . the elements [humors]/ So mix'd in him, that Nature might . . . say to all the world, 'This was a man!'" *J Caes*, V, v, 73–75.

mo, *adj.* old form of **more,** usually used with numbers: "What, hath the firmament mo suns than one?" *T Andr*, V, iii, 17.

moan, *n.* **1** complaint or grief: "You cloudy princes . . . That bear this heavy mutual load of moan . . ." *Rich 3*, II, ii, 112–113. **2** make moan, to complain: "I oft deliver'd from his forfeitures/ Many that have at times made moan to me . . ." *Merch*, III, iii, 22–23. **3** record with moan, to sing mournfully: "She sung, and made the night-bird mute/ That still records with moan . . ." *Per*, IV, Chor., 26–27.

mobbled, *adj.* having the head or face covered by a muffler: "But who—ah, woe!—had seen the mobbled queen—" *Ham*, II, ii, 498.

mock, *n.* **1** sneering remark; jibe: ". . . it were a mock/ Apt to be render'd, for some one to say,/ 'Break up the Senate till another time . . .'" *J Caes*, II, ii, 96–98. **2** [often pl.] sneers; derision or mockery: ". . . the world's large tongue/ Proclaims you for a man replete with mocks . . ." *Love's L*, V, ii, 834–835. —*v.* **3** to imitate: ". . . prepare/ To see the life as lively mock'd/ as ever/ Still sleep mock'd death . . ." *W Tale*, V, iii, 18–20. **4 mocks the pauses,** [his] delays are pointless: "Being so frustrate, tell him, he mocks/ The pauses that he makes." *Ant & Cleo*, V, i, 2–3. **5 mock the time,** deceive all observers: "Away, and mock the time with fairest show . . ." *Mac*, I, vii, 82.

mocking, *n.* imitation; simulation or representation: "It is a pretty mocking of the life." *Timon*, I, i, 35.

Mock-water, *n.* Host's fanciful nickname for Caius, prob. with wordplay on "make-water": "A word, Mounseur Mock-Water . . . Mock-water, in our English tongue, is valour,/ bully." *Wives*, II, iii, 53–57.

model, *n.* **1** mold or shape, as the mound of earth covering a grave: ". . . that small model of the barren earth/ Which serves as paste and cover to our bones." *Rich 2*, III, ii, 153–154. **2** here, Richard regarded as an example of ruined majesty: "Ah, thou, the model where old Troy did stand!" *Rich 2*, V, i, 11.

modern, *adj.* ordinary; common or commonplace: "Thy father or thy mother, nay or both,/ Which modern lamentation might have mov'd?" *Rom & Jul*, III, ii, 119–120.

modern grace, *n.* rather commonplace attractiveness [prettiness]: "Her inf'nite cunning with her modern grace/ Subdu'd me to her rate [terms] . . ." *All's W*, V, iii, 215–216.

modest, *adj.* **1** moderate; reasonable: ". . . you must confine yourself within the/ modest limits of order." *T Night*, I, iii, 8–9. **2** mild; temperate: "I call thee by the/ most modest terms, for I am one of those gentle/ ones . . ." *T Night*, IV, ii, 32–34.

modest eyes, *n.* humble or unassuming looks: "Your wife Octavia, with her modest eyes . . ." *Ant & Cleo*, IV, xv, 27.

modestly, *adv.* without exaggeration: ". . . and modestly I think/ The fall of every Phrygian stone will cost/ A drop of Grecian blood." *Tr & Cr*, IV, v, 221–223.

modest warrant, *n.* restricted authority: "Do not cry havoc where you should but hunt/ With modest warrant." *Cor*, III, i, 272–273.

modesty, *n.* **1** chastity: "Think true love acted [consummated] simple modesty." *Rom & Jul*, III, ii, 16. **2** moderation: "The enemies of Caesar shall say this;/ Then, in a friend, it is cold modesty." *J Caes*, III, i, 212–213. **3** mildness: "Deliver this with modesty to th' queen." *Hen 8*, II, ii, 136. **4** [pl.] powers of self-control or self-restraint: "But I am doubtful of your modesties . . ." *Shrew*, Ind., i, 92. **5** propriety; appropriateness: ". . . and the sobriety of it, and/ the modesty of it, to be otherwise." *Hen 5*, IV, i, 74–75.

Modo, *n.* one of Tom's [Edgar's] demons or devils: "The Prince of Darkness is a gentleman; Modo/ he's called, and Mahu." *Lear*, III, iv, 147–148.

module, *n.* **1** model; here, of a proper soldier: ". . . this counterfeit module has deceiv'd me like a/ double-meaning prophesier." *All's W*, IV, iii, 96–97. **2** a counterfeit: ". . . all this thou seest is but a clod/ And module of confounded royalty." *K John*, V, vii, 57–58.

moe, *pron.* **1** old form of **more:** "Look, moe!/ You see this confluence, this great flood of visitors." *Timon*, I, i, 41–42. **2** more persons; others: "Charges she moe than me?" *Meas*, V, i, 199.

moiety, *n.* **1** share or part, often more or less than a half: "Methinks my moiety . . . In quantity equals not one of yours . . ." *1 Hen 4*, III, i, 92–93. **2 make choice of either's moiety,** cause either to prefer his share to the other's: ". . . equalities are so/ weigh'd [balanced] that curiosity in neither [scrutiny on the part of either one] can make choice/ of either's moiety." *Lear,* I, i, 5–7.

moist star, *n.* moon: ". . . the moist star,/ Upon whose influence Neptune's empire stands . . ." *Ham,* I, i, 121–122.

mold¹, *n.* **1** soft earth; soil: "The pillars of his hearse shall be their bones,/ The mould that covers him, their city ashes . . ." *Edw 3,* V, i, 170–171. **2 men of mold,** earthly men; mere mortals: "Be merciful, great duke, to men of mould!" *Hen 5,* III, ii, 22.

mold², *n.* **1** form or pattern: "The glass of fashion and the mould of form . . ." *Ham,* III, i, 155.
—*v.* **2 mold up,** go into the making of: "All princely graces/ That mould up such a mighty piece as this is . . ." *Hen 8,* V, iv, 25–26.

moldwarp, *n.* mole: ". . . sometimes he angers me/ With telling me of the moldwarp and the ant . . ." *1 Hen 4,* III, i, 142–143.

mole of nature, *n.* natural defect or blemish: ". . . for some vicious [vile] mole of nature in them . . ." *Ham,* I, iv, 24.

molestation, *n.* disturbance: "I never did like molestation view . . ." *Oth,* II, i, 16.

molt no feather, *v.* See **feather** (def. 3).

mome, *n.* blockhead: "Mome, malthorse, capon, coxcomb,/ idiot patch . . ." *Errors,* III, i, 32.

moment, *adj.* **1 moment leisure,** a leisure moment: ". . . so slander any moment leisure/ As to give words or talk with the Lord Hamlet." *Ham,* I, iii, 133–134.
—*n.* **2** importance: "To hear from him a matter of some moment . . ." *Hen 8,* I, ii, 163. **3 mighty moment,** extreme importance: "Bearing [concerning] a state of mighty moment in't . . ." *Hen 8,* II, iv, 211. **4 poorer moment,** lesser cause: "I have seen her/ die twenty times upon far poorer moment . . ." *Ant & Cleo,* I, ii, 138–139.

momentany, *adj.* momentary: ". . . momentany as a sound,/ Swift as a shadow, short as any dream . . ." *M N Dream,* I, i, 143–144.

monarch, *n.* **monarch of the north,** the Devil, along with his evil spirits, thought to inhabit the far northern regions: "Under the lordly monarch of the north,/ Appear and aid me in this enterprise!" *1 Hen 6,* V, iii, 6–7.

monarchize, *v.* to play at being a monarch: "Allowing him a breath, a little scene,/ To monarchize, be fear'd, and kill with looks . . ." *Rich 2,* III, ii, 164–165.

Monarcho, *n.* famed Italian eccentric, a hanger-on at the court of Queen Elizabeth: "A phantasime, a Monarcho, and one that makes sport/ To the prince and his book-mates." *Love's L,* IV, i, 100–101.

money, *n.* **1 for money,** for ready money; for any amount of money: ". . . we shall/ not shortly have a rasher on the coals for money." *Merch,* III, v, 22–23. **2 some piece of money,** small amount of money; here, a few coins: "I do it for some piece of money, and go through with/ all." *Meas,* II, i, 267–268.

Monmouth, *n.* Also, **Monmouthshire,** county in SE Wales, often considered part of England; birthplace of Henry V: "Ay, he was porn [born] at Monmouth, Captain Gower." *Hen 5,* IV, vii, 12.

monster, *n.* **1** horned cuckold: ". . . for wise men know well enough what monsters/ you make of them." *Ham,* III, i, 140–141. **2** freak exhibited to crowds: ". . . besides your cheer, you shall have/ sport: I will show you a monster." *Wives,* III, ii, 73–74.
—*v.* **3** to inflate beyond reason: ". . . idly sit/ To hear my nothings [small deeds] monster'd." *Cor,* II, ii, 76–77.

monstrous, *adj.* **1** that only seems large: "The smallest monstrous mouse that creeps on floor . . ." *M N Dream,* V, i, 215. **2** unnatural; abnormal: ". . . heaven hath infus'd them with these spirits/ To make them instruments of fear and warning/ Unto some monstrous state." *J Caes,* I, iii, 69–71.
—*adv.* **3** horribly; shockingly: "Thou this to hazard needs must intimate/ Skill infinite, or monstrous desperate [reckless]." *All's W,* II, i, 182–183.

monstrous state, *n.* unnatural state of affairs: ". . . fear and warning/ Unto some monstrous state." *J Caes,* I, iii, 70–71.

monstruosity, *n.* old form of **monstrosity;** most shocking paradox: "This is the monstruosity in/ love, lady . . ." *Tr & Cr,* III, ii, 79–80.

montant, *n.* (in fencing) upward thrust: ". . . to see/ thee pass thy punto, thy stock . . . thy montant." *Wives,* II, iii, 23–25.

month's mind, *n.* longing; strong inclination: "I see you have a month's mind to them." *Two Gent,* I, ii, 137.

monument, *n.* **1** any type of memorial for the dead: ". . . he shall live no/ longer in monument than the bell rings, and the/ widow weeps." *M Ado,* V, ii, 72–74. **2** grave or tomb: ". . . our monuments/ Shall be the maws of kites." *Mac,* III, iv, 71–72. **3** statue decorating a tomb: "And be her sense but as a monument,/ Thus in a chapel lying." *Cymb,* II, ii, 32–33. **4** any strange sight regarded as a portent: ". . . wherefore gaze this goodly company,/ As if they saw some wondrous monument . . ." *Shrew,* III, ii, 92–93. **5 woeful monuments,** *n. pl.* signs of grief; here, the Queen's tears: "Nor let the rain of heaven wet this place,/ To wash away my woeful monuments." *2 Hen 6,* III, ii, 340–341.

monumental, *adj.* serving to remind him of his heritage: ". . . he/ hath given her his monumental ring . . ." *All's W,* IV, iii, 15–16.

mood¹, *n.* **1** anger; fury: ". . . a gentleman,/ Who, in my mood,/ I stabb'd unto the heart." *Two Gent,* IV, i, 50–51. **2** outward expression, as of a state of mind: "Together with all forms,/ moods, shapes of grief . . ." *Ham,* I, ii, 82.

mood², *n.* musical mode: "And now my death/ Changes the mood . . ." *2 Hen 4,* IV, v, 198–199.

moody, *adj.* **1** sullen or ill-natured; surly: ". . . moody beggars/ starving for a time/ Of pellmell havoc and confusion." *1 Hen 4,* V, i, 81–82. **2** choleric; raging; furious: ". . . as soon moved/ to be moody,/ and as soon moody to be moved." *Rom & Jul,* III, i, 12–13. **3** melancholy: ". . . music, moody food/ Of us/ that trade in love." *Ant & Cleo,* II, v, 1–2.

moody-mad, *adj.* wildly angered: ". . . moody-mad and/ desperate stags,/ Turn on the bloody hounds with heads of/ steel . . ." *1 Hen 6,* IV, ii, 50–51.

moon, *n.* **1** virgin goddess Diana: ". . . I might see young/ Cupid's fiery shaft/ Quench'd in the chaste beams of the watery moon . . ." *M N Dream,* II, i, 161–162. **2 glimpses of the moon,** sporadic moonlight: "That thou, dead corse, again in/ complete steel/ Revisits thus the glimpses of the moon . . ." *Ham,* I, iv, 52–53. **3 time of moon,** time of the month when odd behavior (lunacy) could be expected: ". . . 'tis not that/ time of/ moon with me to make one in so skipping a/ dialogue." *T Night,* I, v, 201–203.

moon-calf, *n.* freak or monstrosity, resulting from the influence of the moon: "How can'st/ thou to be the siege of this/ moon-calf? can he vent/ Trinculos?" *Temp,* II, ii, 106–108.

moonish, *adj.* changeable, moody, or fickle: "At which time/ would I, being a moonish youth, grieve . . ." *As You,* III, ii, 397–398.

moonshine, *n.* **1** period of one month: "For that I am some/ twelve or fourteen moonshines/ Lag of a brother?" *Lear,* I, ii, 5–6. **2 moonshine in the water,** foolishness; nothing of consequence: "O vain petitioner! beg a greater matter;/ Thou now/ requests but moonshine in the water." *Love's L,* V, ii, 207–208. **3 sop o' th' moonshine,** ref. to ground drenched in moonlight; perh. Kent means that he will kill Oswald and let him/ steep in moonlight in the manner of sops. "I'll make a sop o'/ the moonshine of you." *Lear* II, ii, 30. Cf. **sop.**

Moor, *n.* **1** native of NW Africa, usually assumed to be a/ black man (or woman): "Enter Tamora alone to the Moor."/ [SD] *T Andr,* II, iii, 10. **2** [l.c.] perh. Claudius is compared to/ a barren plain; or may be an indication that he was of swarthy/ complexion: "Could you on this fair mountain leave to feed/ And batten on this moor?" *Ham,* III, iv, 66–67.

Moor-ditch, *n.* large open sewer in London, and an area associated with melancholy: "What sayest thou to a hare, or the/ melancholy of/ Moor-ditch?" *1 Hen 4,* I, ii, 75–76.

Moorfields, *n.* resort area on the outskirts of London; also/ said to be exercise ground for citizen militia: "Is this Moorfields to muster in?" *Hen 8,* V, iii, 32.

mop, *n.* grimace: "Each one, tripping on his toe,/ Will be here/ with mop and mow." *Temp,* IV, i, 46–47.

mope, *v.* to be in a daze or stupor; act without mental direction: "Or but a sickly part of one true sense/ Could not so/ mope." *Ham,* III, iv, 80–81.

mopping and mowing, *v.* making faces: ". . . Flibbertigibbet,/ of mopping and mowing; who/ since possesses chambermaids and waiting-women." *Lear,* IV, i, 61–62.

moral, *n.* **1** hidden meaning: "Why *benedictus?* You have/ some moral/ in this *benedictus.*" *M Ado,* III, iv, 72–73.
—*adj.* **2** somber; grave: "When I did hear/ The motley fool/ thus moral on the time,/ My lungs began to crow like chanticleer . . ." *As You,* II, vii, 28–30.

moraler, *n.* moralizer: "Come, you are too severe a moraler . . ." *Oth,* II, iii, 290.

morality, *n.* correction; moral instruction: "I had as lief have/ the foppery of freedom/ as the morality of imprisonment." *Meas,* I, ii, 125–126.

moralize, *v.* to interpret, esp. so as to expound a moral: "Did/ he not moralize this spectacle?" *As You,* II, i, 44.

Mor du vinager! By the crucifixion! [mild oath, lit., in anglicized French, "Death of vinegar!"] *All's W,* II, iii, 44.

more, *adj.* **1** greater; worse: ". . . wrong not that wrong with a/ more contempt." *Errors,* II, ii, 171–172.
—*pron.* **2 more and less,** the nobles as well as the commoners: "Both more and less have given him the revolt . . ." *Mac,* V, iv, 12. **3 more hath more expressed,** more eloquently has/ expressed deeper feelings: ". . . look for recompense/ More/ than that tongue that more hath more expressed." *Sonn 23,* 11–12. **4 more nor less,** neither more nor less: "More nor less/ to others paying/ Than by self-offences weighing." *Meas,* III,

ii, 258–259. **5 more or less,** more or less important: "Made more or less by thy continual haste . . ." *Sonn 123,* 12.

more-having, *n.* increase in wealth: "And my more-having would be as a sauce/ To make me hunger more . . ." *Mac,* IV, iii, 81–82.

moreover or **moreo'er,** *adv.* besides: "Moreover that we much did long to see you,/ The need we have to use you did provoke/ Our hasty sending." *Ham,* II, ii, 2–4.

Morisco, *n.* morris dancer: ". . . I have seen/ Him caper upright like a wild Morisco . . ." *2 Hen 6,* III, i, 364–365.

morning, *n.* **1** rosy freshness of a new day: ". . . whose youth and freshness/ Wrinkles Apollo's, and makes stale the morning." *Tr & Cr,* II, ii, 79–80. **2** [cap.] the goddess Aurora: "I with the Morning's love have oft made sport . . ." *M N Dream,* III, ii, 389.

morning's dream, *n.* morning dreams were believed to come true: ". . . I'll requite it/ With sweet rehearsal of my morning's dream." *2 Hen 6,* I, ii, 23–24.

morris, *n.* spirited dance, traditionally performed on May Day: "As fit . . . as a pancake for Shrove/ Tuesday, a morris for May-day . . ." *All's W,* II, ii, 20–23.

morris-pike, *n.* kind of pike thought to be of Moorish origin: ". . . he that sets up his rest to do/ more exploits with his mace than a morris-pike." *Errors,* IV, iii, 26–27.

mort, *n.* (in hunting) death of the deer, as announced on the hunting horn: ". . . and then to sigh, as 'twere/ The mort o' th' deer . . ." *W Tale,* I, ii, 117–118.

mortal, *adj.* **1** deadly; lethal; murderous: "Come, you Spirits/ That tend on mortal thoughts, unsex me here . . ." *Mac,* I, v, 40–41. **2 is mortal,** would be fatal: ". . . now this matter must be look'd to,/ For her relapse is mortal." *Per,* III, ii, 112–113. **3 mortal in folly,** foolish in a human way: ". . . as all is mortal [subject to death] in nature, so is all nature/ in love mortal in folly." *As You,* II, iv, 52–53.
—*adv.* **4** mortally; fatally: "Most dangerously you have with him prevail'd,/ If not most mortal to him." *Cor,* V, iii, 188–189.

mortal act, *n.* earthly life: "He finished indeed his mortal act/ That day that made my sister thirteen years." *T Night,* V, i, 245–246.

mortal coil, *n.* turmoil and confusion of mortal life: ". . . what dreams may come,/ When we have shuffled off this mortal coil . . ." *Ham,* III, i, 66–67.

mortal custom, *n.* natural time and circumstances of death: ". . . pay his breath/ To time, and mortal custom." *Mac,* IV, i, 99–100.

mortal fault, *n.* deadly sin: "And by their mortal fault brought in subjection/ Her immortality . . ." *Luc,* 724–725.

mortal instruments, *n. pl.* agents of the body that carry out the dictates of the will: "The genius and the mortal instruments/ Are then in council . . ." *J Caes,* II, i, 66–67.

mortality, *n.* **1** mortal beings; humankind: "No might nor greatness in mortality/ Can censure 'scape." *Meas,* III, ii, 179–180. **2** human experience: ". . . from this instant,/ There's nothing serious in mortality . . ." *Mac,* II, iii, 92–93. **3** death; also, sentence of death: "Here, on my knee, I beg mortality,/ Rather than life preserv'd with infamy." *1 Hen 6,* IV, v, 32–33.

mortal moon, *n.* Queen Elizabeth; here, ref. to threat to her life by the alleged conspiracy [1593–94] of her physician, Dr. Lopez: "The mortal moon hath her eclipse endured . . ." *Sonn 107,* 5.

mortal murthers, *n. pl.* wounds, any one of which would be called deadly: ". . . now they rise again,/ With twenty mortal murthers on their crowns . . ." *Mac,* III, iv, 79–80.

mortal preparation, *n.* ref. either to the readying of his death-dealing arms or receiving the last sacrament in preparation for death: "I will presently pen/ down my dilemmas . . . put myself into my mortal preparation . . ." *All's W,* III, vi, 70–72.

mortal rage, *n.* ravages of time: "And brass eternal slave to mortal rage . . ." *Sonn 64,* 4.

mortal-staring, *adj.* of a deadly glare: "Of bloody strokes and mortal-staring war." *Rich 3,* V, iii, 91.

mortal stars, *n.* eyes; here, those of Lucrece: "Where mortal stars as bright as heaven's beauties . . ." *Luc,* 13.

mortal times, *n.* human lives: "The purest treasure mortal times afford/ Is spotless reputation . . ." *Rich 2,* I, i, 177–178.

mortal vigor, *n.* deadly force or power: "Now nature cares not for thy mortal vigour . . ." *Ven & Ad,* 953.

mortal wretch, *n.* deadly creature: "Come, thou mortal wretch,/ With thy sharp teeth . . ." *Ant & Cleo,* V, ii, 302–303.

Mort Dieu!, *interj.* [French] By God's death! [an oath]: ". . . are the cities, that I got with wounds,/ Deliver'd up again with peaceful words?/ *Mort Dieu!*" *2 Hen 6,* I, 1, 120–122.

mortgaged, *adj.* bound; here, perh. legally: "And I myself am mortgaged to thy will . . ." *Sonn 134,* 2.

mortified, *adj.* **1** dead or insensible: "Thou, like an exorcist, hast conjur'd up/ My mortified spirit." *J Caes,* II, i, 323–324. **2** indifferent to desires and temptations: "Dumain is mortified:/ The grosser manner of these world's delights/ He throws upon the gross world's baser slaves . . ." *Love's L,* I, i, 28–30.

mortifying, *adj.* mortal; deadly: ". . . to apply a/ moral medicine to a mortifying mischief [deadly disease]." *M Ado,* I, iii, 11–12.

mortifying groans, *n.* groans (also sighs) were thought to deplete the heart of blood: ". . . let my liver rather heat with wine/ Than my heart cool with mortifying groans." *Merch,* I, i, 81–82.

mose in the chine, poss. ref. to *mort d'eschine,* French name for glanders (or a similar disease); in any case, the horse's symptoms are near fatal: ". . . possessed with the glanders and like to mose/ in the chine . . ." *Shrew,* III, ii, 48–49.

most, *adj.* **1** longest possible: "I have possess'd him my most stay/ Can be but brief . . ." *Meas,* IV, i, 44–45.
–*n.* **2** greatest extent; utmost: "And to the most of praise add something more . . ." *Sonn 85,* 10.

most in sight, See **sight** (def. 4).

most master, *n.* person having the most authority; here, the queen: "Though in this place most master wear no breeches . . ." *2 Hen 6,* I, iii, 146.

mot, *n.* motto, as on a coat of arms: "And Tarquin's eye may read the mot afar . . ." *Luc,* 830.

mote, *n.* tiny particle, as a speck of dust: "You found his mote; the king your mote did see . . ." *Love's L,* IV, iii, 158.

mother, *n.* **1** See **Hysterica passio. 2 thy mother's,** England's: ". . . overgorg'd/ With gobbets of thy mother's bleeding heart." *2 Hen 6,* IV, i, 83–84.

motion, *n.* **1** direction or inclination: "O, teach me . . . with what art/ You sway the motion of Demetrius' heart." *M N Dream,* I, i, 192–193. **2** practice continuing without letup: "Still in motion/ Of raging waste?" *Timon,* II, i, 3–4. **3** resolution or volition; will: "Abus'd her delicate youth, with drugs or minerals,/ That weakens motion . . ." *Oth,* I, ii, 74–75. **4** [often pl.] impulse: ". . . a foolish/ extravagant spirit, full of forms, figures . . . motions, revolutions . . ." *Love's L,* IV, ii, 64–66. **5** emotion: "For such as I am, all true lovers are,/ Unstaid and skittish in all motions else . . ." *T Night,* II, iv, 17–18. **6** proposal: "Tell me, Andronicus, doth this motion please thee?"

T Andr, I, i, 243. **7** request or urging: "My wife . . . Made daily motions for our home return . . ." *Errors,* I, i, 58–59. **8** [in astronomy] orbit or sphere: "We in your motion turn, and you may move us." *Errors,* III, ii, 24. **9** [fencing] thrust: ". . . in fell motion,/ With his prepared sword he charges home/ My unprovided body . . ." *Lear,* II, i, 50–52. **10** puppet show: ". . . then he compassed a motion of the Prodigal/ Son, and married a tinker's wife . . ." *W Tale,* IV, iii, 93–94. **11** wordplay on "graceful movement" and "puppet show": "[Aside] O excellent motion! O exceeding puppet!" *Two Gent,* II, i, 89. **12** provocation or urging: ". . . he gives her folly motion and advantage . . ." *Wives,* III, ii, 30–31. **13** [pl.] bowel movements: "Shall/ I lose my doctor? No, he gives me the potions and/ the motions." *Wives,* III, i, 93–95. **14 in my motion,** in my involuntary thoughts: "I see it in/ My motion, have it not in my tongue . . ." *Ant & Cleo,* II, iii, 12–13. **15 inward motion,** strong inclination or leaning: "But from the inward motion to deliver/ Sweet, sweet, sweet poison . . ." *K John,* I, i, 212–213. **16 in what motion,** with whatever speed: ". . . in what motion age will give me leave [my old age permits]." *All's W,* II, iii, 230. **17 motions of the sense,** sexual urges: ". . . one who never feels/ The wanton stings and motions of the sense . . ." *Meas,* I, iv, 58–59. **18 motion ungenerative,** puppet (either sexless or impotent male): "And he is a/ motion ungenerative; that's infallible." *Meas,* III, ii, 107–108. **19 too trivial motion,** slightest provocation: ". . . favouring the first complaint, hasty and tinder-like/ upon too trivial motion . . ." *Cor,* II, i, 49–50. **20 upon the foot of motion,** ready to act: "Nor our strong sorrow/ Upon the foot of motion." *Mac,* II, iii, 124–125.
—*v.* **21** to propose: "One that still [always] motions war, and never peace . . ." *1 Hen 6,* I, iii, 63.

motive, *n.* **1** cause or reason; also, an instigator: "Nor are they living/ Who were the motives that you first went out . . ." *Timon,* V, iv, 26–27. **2** instrument: ". . . my teeth shall tear/ The slavish motive [i.e., the tongue] of recanting fear . . ." *Rich 2,* I, i, 192–193. **3 your three motives,** the motives of you three: "These,/ And your three motives to the battle . . ." *Cymb,* V, v, 388–389.

motley, *adj.* dressed in motley, garb of the professional fool: "I met a fool i' th'forest,/ A motley fool . . ." *As You,* II, vii, 12–13.

mought, *v.* old form of **might;** here, means "could": ". . . and more he spoke;/ Which sounded like a cannon in a vault/ That mought not be distinguish'd . . ." *3 Hen 6,* V, ii, 43–45.

mounch, *v.* old var. of **munch:** "A sailor's wife had chestnuts in her lap,/ And mounch'd, and mounch'd . . ." *Mac,* I, iii, 4–5.

mount, *v.* **1** to cause to rise: "The fire that mounts the liquor [liquid] till't run o'er . . ." *Hen 8,* I, i, 144. **2** to be advanced or promoted: "Therefore let me/ have right, and let desert mount." *2 Hen 4,* IV, iii, 54–55. **3 mount her pitch,** to mount to the highest point of her flight [term in falconry]: ". . . mount her pitch whom thou in triumph long/ Hast prisoner held . . ." *T Andr,* II, i, 14–15.

—*n.* **4 mount of all the age,** absolute pinnacle: "Whose worth . . . Stood challenger on mount of all the age/ For her perfections." *Ham,* IV, vii, 27–29.

Mount, *n.* **the Mount,** See **Mount Misena.**

mountain, *adj.* perh. ref. to Edward III's imposing size; perh. ref. to his birth in mountainous region of Wales: "Whiles that his mountain sire, on mountain standing . . ." *Hen 5,* II, iv, 57.

mountaineer, *n.* derog., since mountain dwellers were often outlaws: "Soft, what are you/ That fly me thus? Some villain mountaineers?" *Cymb,* IV, ii, 70–71.

mountain foreigner, *n.* Welshman [stranger from the Welsh mountains]: "Ha, thou mountain foreigner!" *Wives,* I, i, 144.

mountain's basis, *n.* foothill: "Though we upon this mountain's basis by/ Took stand for idle speculation . . ." *Hen 5,* IV, ii, 30–31.

mountain-squire, *n.* squire of barren land; here, poor Welshman: "You called me yesterday mountain-squire,/ but I will make you to-day a squire/ of low degree." *Hen 5,* V, i, 36–38.

mountant, *adj.* held or lifted up: "Hold up, you sluts,/ Your aprons mountant." *Timon,* IV, iii, 136–137.

Mountanto, *n.* humorous name for a fencer, from "montanto" = thrust: "I pray you, is Signior Mountanto returned from the wars or no?" *M Ado,* I, i, 28–29.

mountebank, *v.* to gain by cheap tricks: "I'll mountebank their loves,/ Cog their hearts from them . . ." *Cor,* III, ii, 132–133.

mounted, *adj.* **higher mounted,** soar higher [term in falconry]: ". . . though his affections/ are higher mounted than ours . . ." *Hen 5,* IV, i, 106–107.

mounting mind, *n.* lofty spirit; also, occupied thought: "Whoe'er a' was, a' show'd a mounting mind." *Love's L,* IV, i, 4.

Mount Misena, *n.* promontory in SW Italy: "Where lies he?"/ "About the Mount Misena." *Ant & Cleo,* II, ii, 160–161.

Mount Pelion, *n.* **1 lie under Mount Pelion,** ref. to Greek myth. and collapse of two mountains, Pelion and Ossa, bury-ing the giants who had tried to attack Mount Olympus: "I had rather be a giantess, and lie under Mount/ Pelion." *Wives,* II, i, 76–77. **2 See Pelion.**

mournful crocodile, *n.* ref. to myth that the crocodile lures its victims by tears and a mournful aspect: ". . . Gloucester's show/ Beguiles him as the mournful crocodile . . ." *2 Hen 6,* III, i, 225–226.

mourning house, *n.* appar. the residence of the Princess will be dedicated to mourning for the next year: ". . . till that instant [one year], shut/ My woeful self up in a mourning house . . ." *Love's L,* V, ii, 799–800.

mouse, *n.* **1** term of endearment: "What's your dark meaning, mouse, of this light word?" *Love's L,* V, ii, 19.

—*v.* **2** to tear in the manner of a cat tearing a mouse: "And now he feasts, mousing the flesh of men . . ." *K John,* II, i, 354.

moused, *adj.* mauled in the manner of a cat worrying a mouse: "Well moused, Lion!" *M N Dream,* V, i, 258.

mouse-hunt, *n.* chaser of pretty women [mice]: "Ay, you have been a mouse-hunt in your time . . ." *Rom & Jul,* IV, iv, 11.

mouth, *n.* **1** dog's bark: "Between two dogs, which hath the deeper mouth . . ." *1 Hen 6,* II, iv, 12. **2 make mouths,** to prac-tice smiling, frowning, etc., in front of a mirror: ". . . there was never yet fair woman but she/ made mouths in a glass." *Lear,* III, ii, 35–36. **3 make mouths at,** to mock or ridicule, esp. by making faces behind another's back: ". . . those that would make mouths at him/ while my father lived . . ." *Ham,* II, ii, 360–361. **4 my mouth no more were broken,** perh. means he still has most of his teeth: "My mouth no more were broken than these boys' . . ." *All's W,* II, iii, 60. **5 spend their mouths,** See **spend.**

—*v.* **6** to boast; talk big: "Nay, and thou'lt mouth,/ I'll rant as well as thou." *Ham,* V, i, 278–279. **7 mouth with,** to kiss: ". . . he would mouth with a beggar though she smelt [of] brown/ bread and garlic . . ." *Meas,* III, ii, 177–178.

mouthed, *adj.* yawning; gaping: "Of mouthed graves will give thee memory . . ." *Sonn 77,* 6.

mouth-friend, *n.* person who merely professes friendship: "You knot of mouth-friends!" *Timon,* III, vi, 85.

mouth-honor, *n.* insincere agreement, flattery, etc.; lip ser-vice: ". . . but in their stead,/ Curses, not loud, but deep, mouth-honour . . ." *Mac,* V, iii, 26–27.

mouth of outrage, *n.* anguished outcries: "Seal up the mouth of outrage for a while/ Till we can clear these ambiguities . . ." *Rom & Jul,* V, iii, 215–216.

movable or **moveable,** *n.* piece of furniture; also, other personal property: "The plate, coin, revenues, and moveables,/ Whereof our uncle Gaunt did stand possess'd." *Rich 2,* II, i, 161–162.

move, *v.* **1** to call upon; appeal to: "To me she speaks, she moves me for her/ theme . . ." *Errors,* II, ii, 181–182. **2** to petition; entreat: ". . . the Florentine will move us/ For speedy aid . . ." *All's W,* I, ii, 6–7. **3** to arouse or awaken; also, excite: "Thy father or thy mother, nay or both,/ Which modern lamentation might have mov'd?" *Rom & Jul,* III, ii, 119–120. **4** to persuade; convince: "Things have fallen out, sir, so unluckily/ That we have had no time to move our daughter." *Rom & Jul,* III, iv, 1–2. **5** to change another's mind: "If I could pray to move, prayers would move me . . ." *J Caes,* III, i, 59. **6** to bother or disturb: "Be she as foul as was Florentius' love,/ As old as Sibyl . . . She moves me not . . ." *Shrew,* I, ii, 68–71. **7** to prevail on: ". . . yet I'll move him/ To walk this way . . ." *Cymb,* I, ii, 34–35. **8** to incite or provoke: "His brother warr'd upon him, although I think/ Not mov'd by Antony." *Ant & Cleo,* II, i, 41–42. **9** to propose; offer for consideration: "The instances that second marriage move/ Are base respects of thrift . . ." *Ham,* III, ii, 177–178. **10 heaven still move about her,** may God always be near her: "This royal infant (heaven still move about her) . . ." *Hen 8,* V, iv, 17.

moved, *past part.* **1** provoked: ". . . as soon moved to be moody,/ and as soon moody to be moved." *Rom & Jul,* III, i, 12–13. **2** angry; emotionally distraught: "You look/ As if you held a brow of much distraction:/ Are you mov'd, my lord?" *W Tale,* I, ii, 148–150.

mover, *n.* **1** active person; here, used ironically of soldiers who grab at plunder instead of fighting: "See here these movers, that do prize their hours/ At a crack'd drachma!" *Cor,* I, v, 4–5. **2** activator; instrument: ". . . compounds,/ Which are the movers of a languishing death . . ." *Cymb,* I, vi, 8–9.

moving, *n.* ability to move: "For so much moving hath a poet's pen./ Then, if thou be a poet, move thou so . . ." *Edw 3,* II, i, 73–74.

mow, *v.* **1** to make faces; grimace: ". . . like apes, that mow and chatter at me,/ And after bite me . . ." *Temp,* II, ii, 9–10. —*n.* **2** wry or mocking face; grimace: ". . . enter the Shapes again,/ and dance, with mocks and mows . . ." [SD] *Temp,* III, iii, 82.

moy, *n.* bushel; wordplay on French *moi,* "me," and English measure: "Moy shall not serve; I will have forty moys . . ." *Hen 5,* IV, iv, 13.

much, *n.* **1** without much, hence little: "Thy mother's son! . . . and thy father's/ shadow . . . but much of the father's/ substance!" *2 Hen 4,* III, ii, 128–131. **2 it is much,** it's a sorry business: "'Tis much when sceptres are in children's hands . . ." *1 Hen 6,* IV, i, 192. **3 much he should,** probably more than he would do: ". . . take thought, and die for Caesar./ And that were much he should . . ." *J Caes,* II, i, 187–188. —*adj.* **4** used ironically to mean nothing at all: "How say you now, is it not past two o'clock? And/ here much Orlando!" *As You,* IV, iii, 1–2. —*interj.* **5** Incredible! I don't believe it!: "God's light, with/ two points on your shoulder? Much!" *2 Hen 4,* II, iv, 129–130.

much unlike, [it is] very unlikely: "Though much unlike/ You should be so transported . . ." *Kinsmen,* I, i, 186–187.

much upon, 1 very nearly: "Much upon this [this way]/ 'tis . . ." *Love's L,* V, ii, 472. **2** at approximately: "By my count/ I was your mother much upon these years . . ." *Rom & Jul,* I, iii, 71–72.

mudded, *adj.* embedded in mud: "And with him there lie mudded." *Temp,* III, iii, 102.

muddied, *adj.* bewildered; confused: ". . . the people muddied,/ Thick and unwholesome in their thoughts . . ." *Ham,* IV, v, 81–82.

muddy, *adj.* **1** muddleheaded; dim-witted: "Farewell,/ you muddy knave." *1 Hen 4,* II, i, 94–95. **2** mentally disturbed: "Dost think I am so muddy, so unsettled . . ." *W Tale,* I, ii, 325. **3** dirty; dirty-minded: "A pox damn you, you muddy rascal, is that all the/ comfort you give me?" *2 Hen 4,* II, iv, 39–40.

muddy-mettled, dull-spirited; irresolute: "Yet I,/ A dull and muddy-mettled rascal . . ." *Ham,* II, ii, 561–562.

muddy vesture, *n.* clay enclosure [human body] of the soul: "But whilst this muddy vesture of decay/ Doth grossly close it in, we cannot hear it . . ." *Merch,* V, i, 64–65.

muffle, *v.* **1** to wrap or cover: "And in his mantle muffling up his face . . . great Caesar fell." *J Caes,* III, ii, 189–191. **2** to conceal: "Muffle me, night, awhile. [Paris retires.]" *Rom & Jul,* V, iii, 21.

muffled, *adj.* **1** with the head covered: "Enter Steward in a cloak, muffled." [SD] *Timon,* III, iv, 40. **2** blindfolded [allusion to Cupid's blindness]: "Alas that love whose view is muffled still/ Should without eyes see pathways to his will." *Rom & Jul*, I, i, 169–170.

muleteer or **muleter,** *n.* mule-driver: "Base muleteers of France!/ Like peasant foot-boys do they keep the walls . . ." *1 Hen 6*, III, ii, 68–69.

mulier, *n.* [Latin] woman; wife: "We term it *mulier*: which *mulier* I divine/ Is this most constant wife . . ." *Cymb*, V, v, 449–450.

mulled, *adj.* dulled or stupefied: "Peace is a very apoplexy, lethargy;/ mulled, deaf, sleepy, insensible . . ." *Cor,* IV, v, 230–231.

Mulmutius, *n.* first King of Britain: "Our ancestor was that Mulmutius which/ Ordain'd our laws . . ." *Cymb*, III, i, 55–56.

multiplying medicine, *n.* magic elixir for multiplying gold endlessly: "Plutus himself,/ That knows the tinct and multiplying med'cine . . ." *All's W*, V, iii, 101–102.

multiplying spawn, *n.* burgeoning offspring; here, breeders of children: "Your multiplying spawn how can he flatter—" *Cor,* II, ii, 78.

multipotent, *adj.* omnipotent; all-powerful: ". . . and this sinister/ Bounds in my father's—by Jove multipotent . . ." *Tr & Cr*, V, v, 127–128.

multitudinous tongue, *n.* voice of the tribunes in government affairs, regarded as representing the common people: ". . . at once pluck out/ The multitudinous tongue . . ." *Cor,* III, i, 154–155.

mum, *n.* silence: "Go to,/ mum, you are he . . ." *M Ado*, II, i, 112–113.

mumble-news, *n.* prattler or chatterbox: "Some mumble-news, some trencher-knight, some Dick . . ." *Love's L,* V, ii, 464.

mummer, *n.* performer in a dumb-show: ". . . pinched with the colic, you make faces like mummers . . ." *Cor,* II, i, 74.

mummy, *n.* magic drug made from embalmed bodies: "And it was dyed in mummy, which the skilful/ Conserve of maidens' hearts." *Oth*, III, iv, 72–73.

muniments, *n.* defenses; fortifications: "Our steed the leg, the tongue our trumpeter,/ With other muniments and petty [minor] helps . . ." *Cor,* I, i, 116–117.

munition, *n.* materials to make war: "I'll to the Tower with all the haste I can/ To view th' artillery and munition . . ." *1 Hen 6*, I, i, 167–168.

murder, *v.* **1** to rip off: "God let me not live, but I will murder your ruff for/ this." *2 Hen 4*, II, iv, 131–132. **2 murder me for my love,** [to] cause my death over grieving for you: "If you will not murder me for my love, let me be/ your servant." *T Night*, II, i, 34–35.

murdering-piece, *n.* cannon that fired a barrage of metal fragments: ". . . this,/ Like to a murd'ring-piece, in many places/ Gives me superfluous death." *Ham*, IV, v, 94–96.

mure, *n.* wall: ". . . wrought the mure that should confine it in/ So thin that life looks through and will break out." *2 Hen 4*, IV, iv, 119–120.

murmur, *n.* rumor; gossip: ". . . then 'twas fresh in murmur . . . That he did seek the love of fair Olivia." *T Night*, I, ii, 32–34.

murrain, *n.* infectious disease of cattle; the cattle plague: "A murrain on your monster, and the/ devil take your fingers!" *Temp*, III, ii, 78–79.

murrion, *adj.* killed by murrain: "The fold [pen] stands empty in the drowned field,/ And crows are fatted with the murrion flock . . ." *M N Dream*, II, i, 96–97.

murther, *n.* **1** old spelling of **murder**: "Then thieves and robbers range abroad unseen/ In murthers and in outrage boldly here . . ." *Rich 2*, III, ii, 39–40. **2 commit murther in healing wounds,** [to] kill the patient when treating wounds that would heal by themselves: "When we debate/ Our trivial difference loud, we do commit/ Murther in healing wounds." *Ant & Cleo*, II, ii, 20–22.

murtherer, *n.* old spelling of **murderer**: "Some bring the murthered body, some the murtherers . . ." *T Andr*, II, iii, 300.

muscadel, *n.* muscatel, a sweet wine made from the muscat grape; drunk with sops as a toast after the wedding ceremony: ". . . quaff'd off the muscadel,/ And threw the sops all in the sexton's face . . ." *Shrew*, III, ii, 170–171.

muse, *v.* **1** to marvel; be amazed: "I muse you make so slight a question." *2 Hen 4*, IV, i, 167. **2** to wonder (at): "I cannot too much muse/ Such shapes, such gesture, and such sound . . ." *Temp*, III, iii, 36–37.

Muse, *n.* **1** any of the nine Greek goddesses presiding over the arts: "Be thou the tenth Muse, ten times more in worth/ Than those old nine which rimers invoke . . ." *Sonn 38*, 9–10. **2** poet's ability to summon inspiration from his Muse: "If my slight Muse do please these curious days . . ." *Sonn 38*, 13. **3 Muse of fire,** a Muse capable of bringing inspiration from the heavens, fire being the lightest, purest, brightest, and most sublime (creative) of the earthly elements: "O, for a Muse of fire, that would ascend/ The brightest heaven of invention . . ." *Hen 5*, Prol. 1–2.

mushroom, *n.* **midnight mushrooms,** because they sprang up overnight, mushrooms were believed to be the work of elves: ". . . you whose pastime/ Is to make midnight mushrooms . . ." *Temp*, V, i, 38–39.

music, *n.* **1** band of musicians: "The County will be here with music straight . . ." *Rom & Jul*, IV, iv, 21. **2 music from the spheres,** See **sphere** (def. 5). **3 music to hear,** you whose voice is like music: "Music to hear, why hear'st thou music sadly?" *Sonn 8*, 1.

musit, *n.* hole or gap in a fence, hedge, etc.: "The many musits through the which he goes/ Are like a labyrinth . . ." *Ven & Ad*, 683–684.

Musko, *n.* prob. Muscovite: "I know you are the Muskos' regiment,/ And I shall lose my life for want of language." *All's W*, IV, i, 69–70.

musk-rose, *n.* large white rose with a musklike fragrance: "With sweet musk-roses, and with eglantine . . ." *M N Dream*, II, i, 252.

muss, *n.* scramble, as small boys after coins: "Like boys unto a muss, kings would start forth/ And cry 'Your will?'" *Ant & Cleo*, III, xiii, 91–92.

mussel-shell, *n.* prob. ref. to Simple's open-mouthed dimness: "Ay, marry, was it, mussel-shell: what would you/ with her?" *Wives*, IV, v, 26–27.

must, *v.* **1** be obligated to go, travel, etc.: "I must a dozen mile tonight." **2 you must not,** you dare not: "Pray you, peruse that letter./ You must not now deny it is your hand . . ." *T Night*, V, i, 329–330.

mustardseed, *n.* celebrated for its ability to endure adversity: "Good Master Mustardseed, I know your patience/ well." *M N Dream*, III, i, 184–185.

muster, *v.* **1** to assemble; gather; rally: "They must'ring to the quiet cabinet/ Where their dear governess and lady lies . . ." *Luc*, 442–443.
—*n.* **2** [usually pl.] troops: ". . . those his goodly eyes,/ That o'er the files and musters of the war . . ." *Ant & Cleo*, I, i, 2–3.

muster-book, *n.* roll containing the names of men conscripted for military service: ". . . we have a number of shadows fill up the muster-book." *2 Hen 4*, III, ii, 134.

muster-file, *n.* total number of men in a military unit: ". . . the muster-file, rotten and sound . . . amounts not to fifteen thousand poll . . ." *All's W*, IV, iii, 162–163.

musty, *adj.* **1** stale; moldy: ". . . let thy musty vapours march so thick . . . his smother'd light/ May set at noon . . ." *Luc*, 782–784. **2** trite; hackneyed; here, not worth finishing: ". . . but while the grass grows—the proverb is/ something musty." *Ham*, III, ii, 334–335.

mutability, *n.* inconstancy: ". . . change of prides, disdain,/ Nice longings, slanders, mutability . . ." *Cymb*, II, iv, 177–178.

mutable, *adj.* changeable; unstable or unreliable: "For the mutable, rank-scented meinie [multitude] . . ." *Cor*, III, i, 65.

mutation, *n.* changeableness; also, instability: ". . . his honour/ Was nothing but mutation, ay, and that/ From one bad thing to worse . . ." *Cymb*, IV, ii, 132–134.

mutine, *v.* **1** to mutiny; rebel: "Rebellious hell,/ If thou canst mutine in a matron's bones . . ." *Ham*, III, iv, 82–83.
—*n.* **2** rebel or mutineer: "Do like the mutines of Jerusalem,/ Be friends awhile . . ." *K John*, II, i, 378–379.

mutiner, *n.* var. of *mutineer;* here, to fit meter: "Worshipful mutiners,/ Your valour puts well forth . . ." *Cor*, I, i, 249–250.

mutiny, *n.* **1** insurrection or rebellion: "Myself have calm'd their spleenful mutiny . . ." *2 Hen 6*, III, ii, 127. **2** uproar; commotion: "Where's Publius?"/ "Here, quite confounded with this mutiny." *J Caes*, III, i, 85–86. **3** discord: ". . . disturbing jealousy . . . Gives false alarms, suggesteth mutiny . . ." *Ven & Ad*, 649–651.

mutton, *n.* **1** wordplay on "meat" and slang word for "prostitute": "The/ Duke, I say to thee again, would eat mutton on Fridays." *Meas*, III, ii, 174–175. **2** See **laced mutton.**

mutual, *adj.* **1** common; done together: "The skies, the fountains, every region near/ Seem'd all one mutual cry . . ." *M N Dream*, IV, i, 115–116. **2** united: "O, let me teach you how to knit again/ This scattered corn into one mutual sheaf . . ." *T Andr*, V, iii, 70–71.

mutual closure, *n.* common end: "And on the ragged stones beat forth our souls,/ And make a mutual closure of our house." *T Andr*, V, iii, 133–134.

mutual conference, *n.* intimate conversation: "The mutual conference that my mind hath had/ By day, by night, waking, and in my dreams . . ." *2 Hen 6,* I, 1, 25–26.

mutually, *adv.* at the same time; all together: "Pinch him fairies, mutually;/ Pinch him for his villainy . . ." *Wives,* V, v, 100–101.

mutual pair, two people equally in love: ". . . when such a mutual pair,/ And such a twain can do't . . ." *Ant & Cleo,* I, i, 37–38.

Myrmidon, *n.* **1** [pl.] a people of Thessaly, in E Greece; Myrmidon soldiers were led by their king Achilles in the Trojan War; here, poss. a reference to a London tavern: ". . . my lady has a white hand,/ and the Myrmidons are no bottle-ale houses." *T Night,* II, iii, 28–29. **2 the great Myrmidon,** Achilles: "For that will physic the great Myrmidon,/ Who broils in loud applause . . ." *Tr & Cr,* I, iii, 378–379.

myself, *pron.* wordplay on "[you] my other self" and "my own self": "'Tis thee, myself,—that for [in] myself I praise . . ." *Sonn 62,* 13.

mystery, *n.* **1** profession or skilled trade; calling: "Instruction, manners, mysteries and trades . . ." *Timon,* IV, i, 18. **2** skill or craft: "If you/ think your mystery in stratagem can bring this/ instrument of honour again . . ." *All's W,* III, vi, 60–62. **3 mysteries,** secret rituals: ". . . by the sacred radiance of the sun,/ The mysteries of Hecate and the night . . ." *Lear,* I, i, 109–110.

Mytilene, *n.* town on the island of Lesbos: "Mytilene. In front of a Brothel." [SD] *Per,* IV, ii, 1.

N

Nabuchadnezzar, *n.* Nebuchadnezzar; (in the Bible) Babylonian king who, in his madness, ate grass; prob. wordplay based on similarity of pron. of "grace" and "grass": "I am no great Nabuchadnezzar, sir; I have not much/ skill in grass." *All's W,* IV, v, 18–19.

nail, *n.* **1** measurement for cloth; 2 1/4 inches (1/16 yard): "Thou yard, three-quarters, half-yard, quarter, nail . . ." *Shrew,* IV, iii, 109. **2 blow one's nail(s), a.** to blow one's breath on nails and hands to warm them: "When icicles hang by the wall,/ And Dick the shepherd blows his nail . . ." *Love's L,* V, ii, 904–905. **b.** to wait patiently in the cold; hence, twiddle our thumbs: ". . . we may blow our nails together,/ and fast it fairly out [starve]." *Shrew,* I, i, 107–108.

naked, *adj.* **1** simple, bare, or unfurnished; also, austere: ". . . but go with speed/ To some forlorn and naked hermitage . . ." *Love's L,* V, ii, 786–787. **2** merely mentioned: ". . . dine, sup, and sleep/ Upon the very naked name of Love." *Two Gent,* II, iv, 136–137. **3** unarmed; here, not wearing a sword: "Or, naked as I am, I will assault thee." *Oth,* V, ii, 259. **4** with no personal belongings: ". . . you shall know I am set naked on/ your kingdom." *Ham,* IV, vii, 42–43. **5** defenseless: ". . . he would not in mine age [last years]/ Have left me naked to mine enemies." *Hen 8,* III, ii, 456–457. **6 stand naked,** to wear only the outer garment (toga) when addressing the people: ". . . for I cannot/ Put on the gown, stand naked, and entreat them . . ." *Cor,* II, ii, 136–137.

name, *n.* **1** reputation: ". . . and for a name/ Now puts the drowsy and neglected act/ Freshly on me . . ." *Meas,* I, ii, 159–160. **2** honor or glory: ". . . he gives my son the/ whole name of the war . . ." *Cor,* II, i, 133–134. **3** term of address: "Sir, my good friend, I'll change that name with you." *Ham,* I, ii, 163. **4** identity; family or stock: ". . . right and wrong,/ Between whose endless jar [collision] justice resides,/ Should lose their names . . ." *Tr & Cr,* I, iii, 116–118. **5 against his name,** causing loss to his (royal) authority: "Had his great name profaned with their scorns,/ And gave his countenance against his name . . ." *1 Hen 4,* III, ii, 64–65. **6 only in my name,** at the mere mention of my name: "Wretched shall France be only in my name." *1 Hen 6,* I, iv, 96.

—*v.* **7** to have a name; can be named: "All faults that name, nay, that hell knows . . ." *Cymb,* II, iv, 179. **8** to choose; elect: "He is already nam'd, and gone to Scone/ To be invested." *Mac,* II, iv, 31–32. **9** to announce; proclaim: "The country cocks do crow, the clocks do toll,/ And the third hour of drowsy morning name." *Hen 5,* IV, Chor., 15–16.

nameless, *adj.* **1** more than can be named: "Item, she hath many nameless virtues." *Two Gent,* III, i, 311. **2** (of a child) not entitled to the family name: "Thy issue blurr'd with nameless bastardy." *Luc,* 522.

Nan, *n.* **such another Nan,** imprecise expression, roughly equiv. to "such a girl!": "Good faith, it [she] is such/ another Nan . . ." *Wives,* I, iv, 143–144.

nap, *n.* fuzzy or nubby surface on cloth: ". . . to dress/ the commonwealth, and turn it, and set a new nap/ upon it." *2 Hen 6,* IV, ii, 4–6.

napkin, *n.* handkerchief: ". . . to that youth he calls his Rosalind/ He sends this bloody napkin." *As You,* IV, iii, 92–93.

Naples, *n.* king of Naples: "A single thing . . . that wonders/ To hear thee speak of Naples." *Temp,* I, ii, 435–436.

napless vesture, *n.* threadbare toga traditionally worn by one humbly seeking public office: ". . . never would he/ Appear i'th'market-place, nor on him put/ The napless vesture of humility . . ." *Cor,* II, i, 230–232.

Narcissus, *n.* (in Greek myth.) youth of surpassing beauty who fell in love with his own reflection: "Narcissus so himself himself forsook,/ And died to kiss his shadow in the brook." *Ven & Ad,* 161–162.

narines, *n.* **chez les narines de feu,** [French] with the fiery nostrils: ". . . le cheval volant, the Pegasus, chez/ les narines de feu!" *Hen 5,* III, vii, 14–15.

narrow gate, *n.* ref. to Jesus' illustration of the narrow gate to salvation and the broad gate to destruction: "I am for the house with the narrow/ gate, which I take to be too little for pomp to enter . . ." *All's W,* IV, v, 47–48.

narrowly, *adv.* attentively; closely or sharply: ". . . thou wilt be, if my cousin do not/ look exceeding narrowly to thee." *M Ado,* V, iv, 114–115.

Naso, *adj.* "Nosed"; ref. to the Latin poet Ovid's name, Publius Ovidius Naso: "Ovidius Naso was/ the man . . . *Naso,* but for smelling/ out the odoriferous flowers of fancy . . ." *Love's L,* IV, ii, 118–120.

nation, *n.* race or people; here, Jewish race: ". . . he hath disgrac'd me, and/ hind'red me half a million, laugh'd at my losses,/ mock'd at my gains, scorned my nation . . ." *Merch,* III, i, 48–50.

native, *adj.* **1** rightful; legitimate: ". . . ere her native king/ Shall falter under foul rebellion's arms." *Rich 2,* III, ii, 25–26. **2** (of rank and privilege) entitled to by reason of one's (high) birth: "The senators shall bear contempt hereditary,/ The beggar native honour." *Timon,* IV, iii, 10–11. **3** natural: ". . . no pulse/ Shall keep his native progress, but surcease . . ." *Rom & Jul,* IV, i, 97–98. **4** innate: "For when my outward action does demonstrate/ The native act . . ." *Oth,* I, i, 61–62. **5** closely related: "The head is not more native to the heart . . ." *Ham,* I, ii, 47. **6 in native colors,** naturally: "Suits not in native colours with the truth . . ." *Hen 5,* I, ii, 17. **7 native of,** reason for: ". . . could never be the native/ Of our so frank donation." *Cor,* III, i, 128–129.

native blood, *n.* natural coloring: "For native blood is counted painting now . . ." *Love's L,* IV, iii, 259.

native hue, *n.* natural, hence ruddy, complexion or coloring: "And thus the native hue of resolution/ Is sicklied o'er with the pale cast of thought . . ." *Ham,* III, i, 84–85.

native lords, *n.* noblemen; masters: "Poor [poor-spirited] we may call them in their native lords." *Hen 5,* III, v, 26.

native things, *n.* beings of the same rank or status: "To join like likes, and kiss like native things." *All's W,* I, i, 219.

nativity, *n.* **1** birth; also, time, place, or circumstances of birth: ". . . at my nativity/ The front of heaven was full of fiery shapes . . ." *1 Hen 4,* III, i, 11–12. **2** newborn child: "Nativity,

once in the main of light,/ Crawls to maturity . . ." *Sonn 60,* 5–6.

natural, *adj.* **1** related by blood: ". . . a secret and villainous contriver against me his natural brother." *As You,* I, i, 143. —*n.* **2** idiot: ". . . Fortune makes Nature's natural the cutter-off of Nature's wit." *As You,* I, ii, 47–48.

natural breath, *n.* human speech: ". . . scarce think/ Their eyes do offices of truth, their words/ Are natural breath . . ." *Temp,* V, i, 155–157.

natural cause, *n.* cause natural to them both: ". . . two yoke-devils [devils coupled together] sworn to either's purpose,/ Working so grossly [obviously] in a natural cause . . ." *Hen 5,* II, ii, 106–107.

natural fool of Fortune, born to be the plaything of Fortune: "What! a prisoner? I am even/ The natural fool of Fortune." *Lear,* IV, vi, 192–193.

naturalize, *v.* to familiarize: ". . . my instruction shall serve to naturalize thee . . ." *All's W,* I, i, 204.

natural touch, *n.* natural affection(s): "He loves us not:/ He wants [lacks] the natural touch . . ." *Mac,* IV, ii, 8–9.

nature, *n.* **1** natural affection; here, fatherly affection: ". . . my end/ Was wrought by nature, not by vile offence . . ." *Errors,* I, i, 33–34. **2** entitlement by birth: "Where nature doth with merit challenge." *Lear,* I, i, 53. **3** controlling force of the universe: ". . . gentle people, give me aim awhile,/ For nature puts me to a heavy task." *T Andr,* V, iii, 149–150. **4** individual constitution; also, personal character: "A great perturbation in nature, to receive at once/ the benefit of sleep, and do the effects of watching!" *Mac,* V, i, 9–10. **5** way; manner: "I con him no thanks for't, in the nature he/ delivers it." *All's W,* IV, iii, 148–149. **6** one's natural powers: ". . . nothing could have subdu'd nature/ To such a lowness but his unkind daughters." *Lear,* III, iv, 70–71. **7** one's self or person: "And yet my nature never in the fight/ To do in slander." *Meas,* I, iii, 42–43. **8** natural feelings or inclinations; here, those of a son: "How, my lord, I may be censured, that nature/ thus gives way to loyalty . . ." *Lear,* III, v, 2–3. **9 a death to nature,** sufficient to cause death: ". . . twenty trenched gashes on his head;/ The least a death to nature." *Mac,* III, iv, 26–27. **10 days of nature,** time of human existence: "Till the foul crimes done in my days of nature/ Are burnt and purg'd away." *Ham,* I, v, 12–13. **11 in nature,** with regard to my personal feelings: "I am satisfied in nature . . ." *Ham,* V, ii, 240. **12 nature's above art,** poss. Lear's belief that a natural-born king is above any kind of counterfeiting: "Nature's above art in that respect." *Lear,* IV, vi, 86. **13 touch of nature,** natural trait: "One touch of nature makes the whole world kin—" *Tr & Cr,* III, iii, 175.

Nature, *n.* **1** law of survival, or every man for himself: "Thou, Nature, art my goddess; to thy law/ My services are bound." *Lear,* I, ii, 1–2. **2 Nature seems dead,** ref. to the stillness of night: "Now o'er the one half-world/ Nature seems dead, and wicked dreams abuse/The curtain'd sleep . . ." *Mac,* II, i, 49–51.

Nature's copy, *n.* man as reproduced by Nature; also, poss. wordplay with legal sense of "land tenure": "But in them Nature's copy's not eterne." *Mac,* III, ii, 38.

Nature's mischief, *n.* calamities in nature caused by evil spirits: "Wherever in your sightless substances/ You wait on Nature's mischief!" *Mac,* I, v, 49–50.

Nature's molds, *n.* molds in which Nature shapes men: "Crack Nature's moulds, all germens spill at once/ That makes ingrateful man!" *Lear,* III, ii, 8–9.

nature's outward, *n.* appearance bestowed by nature: "Of one by nature's outwards so commended . . ." *Lover's Comp,* 80.

naught or **nought,** *adj.* **1** nothing; used often as a term of abuse: "Marry sir, be better employed, and be naught awhile [the devil take you]." *As You,* I, i, 35–36. **2** of no consequence; worthless: ". . . in respect that it is a shepherd's life, it is naught." *As You,* III, ii, 14–15. **3** wicked; disgusting: "No faith, no honesty in men. All perjur'd,/ All forsworn, all naught, all dissemblers." *Rom & Jul,* III, ii, 86–87. **4 all to naught, a.** thoroughly vile: "It was not she that call'd him all to naught . . ." *Ven & Ad,* 993. **b.** with the odds overwhelmingly in my favor: "His cocks do win the battle still [always] of mine/ When it is all to nought . . ." *Ant & Cleo,* II, iii, 35–36.
—*pron.* **5** nothing: "Jack shall have Jill,/ Nought shall go ill . . ." *M N Dream,* III, ii, 461–462. **6** wordplay on "nought" [nothing] and "naught" [wickedness]: "He that doth naught with her . . . Were best to do it secretly, alone." *Rich 3,* I, i, 98–99.
—*n.* **7** shame; wickedness; (jokingly) naughtiness: "You must say paragon. A paramour is, God bless/ us, a thing of naught." *M N Dream,* IV, ii, 13–14. **8** inconsequential matter: "My lord desires you presently . . ."/ "'Twill be naught . . ." *Ant & Cleo,* III, v, 21–22. **9 Naught, naught, all naught,** Everything has come to nothing: "Naught, naught, all naught! I can behold no longer." *Ant & Cleo,* III, x, 1–2.

naughty, *adj.* **1** worthless; good-for-nothing: "What trade, thou knave? thou naughty knave, what trade?" *J Caes,* I, i, 15. **2** evil; vile; wicked: "O these naughty times/ Put bars between the owners and their rights!" *Merch,* III, ii, 18–19. **3** dreadful; wretched: "He's a good drum, my lord, but a naughty orator." *All's W,* V, iii, 249.

Navarre, *n.* kingdom bet. France and Spain in W Pyrenees: "Navarre shall be the wonder of the world . . ." *Love's L,* I, i, 12.

nave, *n.* **1** navel: ". . . he unseam'd him from the nave to th' chops . . ." *Mac,* I, ii, 22. **2** hub, with wordplay on "knave" as well as Falstaff's girth: "Would not this nave of a wheel have his ears cut/ off?" *2 Hen 4,* II, iv, 253–254.

navel, *n.* very existence: "Even when the navel of the state was touch'd [threatened] . . ." *Cor,* III, i, 122.

nay-ward, *n.* contrary: ". . . you would believe my saying,/ How e'er you lean to th' nay-ward." *W Tale,* II, i, 63–64.

nayword or **nay-word,** *n.* **1** password: ". . . have a nay-word, that you may know one another's/ mind . . ." *Wives,* II, ii, 121–122. **2 gull him into a nayword,** make him look so foolish he will be a laughingstock [become a byword]: If I do not gull him into/ a nayword, and make him a common recreation . . ." *T Night,* II, iii, 135–136.

Nazarite, *n.* var. of **Nazarene;** here, ref. to Biblical story of Jesus' casting devils into swine: ". . . the habitation which your/ prophet the Nazarite conjured the devil into . . ." *Merch,* I, iii, 29–30.

ne, *conj.* **1** nor: ". . . ne worse of worst, extended/ With vildest torture, let my life be ended." *All's W,* II, i, 172–173. **2** See **ne aught.**

neaf, *n.* dial. word for *fist:* "Sweet knight, I kiss thy neaf." *2 Hen 4,* II, iv, 182.

Neapolitan boneache, *n.* syphilis, popularly supposed to have originated in Naples: ". . . the vengeance on/ the whole camp—or rather, the Neapolitan boneache . . ." *Tr & Cr,* II, iii, 18–19.

near, *adv.* **1** closely or intimately: "I beseech your honour . . . it does concern you near." *Timon,* I, ii, 173–174. **2 look too near unto,** inquire too closely into: "Lest rest and lying still might make them look/ Too near unto my state." *2 Hen 4,* IV, v, 211–212. **3 very near upon,** any minute now; at any moment: ". . . very near upon/ The Duke is ent'ring . . ." *Meas,* IV, vi, 14–15.
—*adj.* **4** important or urgent: ". . . an earnest/ inviting, which many my near occasions did urge/ me to put off . . ." *Timon,* III, vi, 9–11. **5 the near in blood,** the nearer the kinship: "There's daggers in men's smiles: the near in blood,/ The nearer bloody [the greater the chance of being murdered]." *Mac,* II, iii, 138–139.

near bred, *adj.* closely allied: ". . . the burnish'd sun,/ To whom I am a neighbour, and near bred." *Merch,* II, i, 2–3.

nearest, *adj.* shortest; most direct: "What need'st thou run so many miles about/ When thou mayst tell thy tale the nearest way?" *Rich 3,* IV, iv, 460–461.

nearest of life, *n.* one's most vital parts, esp. the heart: ". . . every minute of his being thrusts/ Against my near'st of life . . ." *Mac,* III, i, 116–117.

near-legged, *adj.* (of a horse) knock-kneed: ". . . near-legged before [in front], and with a half-cheeked bit . . ." *Shrew,* III, ii, 54.

nearly, *adv.* **1** closely; intimately: ". . . I would have some confidence with/ you, that decerns you nearly." *M Ado,* III, v, 2–3. **2** close at hand or very soon: "I doubt, some danger does approach you nearly . . ." *Mac,* IV, ii, 66. **3 nearly that,** that closely: "Of something nearly that concerns yourselves." *M N Dream,* I, i, 126.

neat¹, *n.* (sing. or pl.) **1** ox: "What say you to a neat's foot?" *Shrew,* IV, iii, 17. **2** oxen: ". . . he bore him in the thickest troop/ As doth a lion in a herd of neat . . ." *3 Hen 6,* II, i, 13–14. **3 not neat but cleanly,** wordplay on meanings of "oxen" and "clean"; Leontes rejects the word because of its association with horns: "We must be neat; not neat, but cleanly, captain . . ." *W Tale,* I, ii, 123.

neat², *adj.* **1** foppish; also, absolute; pure: ". . . stand, rogue, stand; you/ neat slave, strike." *Lear,* II, ii, 41–42. **2** delicate; also, incomparable: "Sluttery, to such neat excellence oppos'd,/ Should make desire vomit emptiness . . ." *Cymb,* I, vii, 44–45.

neat-herd, *n.* person who tends cows; cowherd: "Would I were/ A neat-herd's daughter . . ." *Cymb,* I, ii, 79–80.

neat's leather, *n.* cowhide; oxhide: "As proper men as ever trod upon neat's leather have/ gone upon my handiwork." *J Caes,* I, i, 25–26.

neat's tongue, *n.* ox tongue, often dried and spiced for eating: ". . . silence is only commendable/ In a neat's tongue dried, and a maid not vendible." *Merch,* I, i, 111–112.

ne aught, *pron.* nothing; no one [old form]: "All perishen of men, of pelf,/ Ne aught escapend [escaping] but himself . . ." *Per,* II, Chor., 35–36.

neb, *n.* woman's face: "How she holds up the neb, the bill to him!" *W Tale,* I, ii, 183.

Nebuchadnezzar, *n.* See **Nabuchadnezzar.**

necessaries, *n. pl.* luggage; baggage: "My necessaries are embark'd. Farewell." *Ham,* I, iii, 1.

necessary, *adj.* inevitable: ". . . death, a necessary end,/ Will come when it will come." *J Caes,* II, ii, 36–37.

necessitied, *adj.* in need (of): "I bade her, if her fortunes ever stood/ Necessitied to help, that by this token/ I would relieve her." *All's W,* V, iii, 84–86.

necessity, *n.* **1** need; great hardship: "Be quiet then, as men should be/ Till he hath pass'd necessity." *Per,* II, Chor., 5–6. **2 art of our necessities,** necessity has power to change things for us: "The art of our necessities is strange,/ And can make vile things precious." *Lear,* III, ii, 70–71. **3 upon my necessity,** when (and as) I need it: "I have a sword, and it shall bite upon my necessity." *Wives,* II, i, 128.

neck, *n.* **in the neck of,** on top of; immediately after: "And in the neck of that task'd the whole state . . ." *1 Hen 4,* IV, iii, 92.

need, *n.* **1 at your most need,** in your direst extremity: "So grace and mercy at your most need help you." *Ham,* I, v, 188. **2 for a need,** if necessary: "You could for a need/ study a speech of some dozen or sixteen lines . . ." *Ham,* II, ii, 534–535. —*v.* **3 A must needs,** He must [has to] be: "Valiant I am."/ "A must needs, for beggary is valiant." *2 Hen 6,* IV, ii, 51–52. **4 what needs?** what's the use or point of?: ". . . but what needs either your 'mum'/ or her 'budget'?" *Wives,* V, ii, 8–9.

needful, *adj.* **1** lacking necessary elements: "And for your brother, he was lately sent . . . With aid of soldiers to this needful war." *3 Hen 6,* II, i, 145–147. **2** exactly what is needed: "They shall be no more than needful there if/ they were more than they can commend [even if they recommended him in the strongest terms]." *All's W,* IV, iii, 77–78.

needl or **neeld,** *n.* needle [pron. as one syllable]: "Their thimbles into armed gauntlets change,/ Their needl's to lances . . ." *K John,* V, ii, 156–157.

needless, *adj.* not needed; superfluous: "When with a volley of our needless shot . . . we bid good-night . . ." *K John,* V, v, 5–6.

needly, *adv.* necessarily: ". . . sour woe delights in fellowship/ And needly will be rank'd with other griefs . . ." *Rom & Jul,* III, ii, 116–117.

needy, *adj., n.* much-needed; also, those in need: "And these our ships . . . Are stor'd with corn to make your needy bread . . ." *Per,* I, iv, 92–95.

needy nothing, *n.* naked unworthiness: "And needy nothing trimm'd in jollity . . ." *Sonn 66,* 3.

neele, *n.* needle: ". . . when she would with sharp neele wound/ The cambric . . ." *Per,* IV, Chor., 23–24.

ne'er the near, *adj.* never the nearer: "Better far off than near,/ be ne'er the near." *Rich 2,* V, i, 88.

neeze, *v.* old form of **sneeze:** ". . . waxen in their mirth, and neeze, and swear/ A merrier hour was never wasted there." *M N Dream,* II, i, 56–57.

negative, *n.* **four negatives make two affirmatives,** appar. the Clown uses this as an example of paradox, implying that four hesitant lips combine to make two positive kisses: ". . . if your four negatives/ make your two affirmatives, why then the worse for/ my friends . . ." *T Night,* V, i, 20–21.

neglect, *v.* **1** to disregard; ignore: "Which of the peers/ Have uncontemn'd gone by him, or at least/ Strangely neglected?" *Hen 8,* III, ii, 9–11. **2** to cause (something) to be neglected: ". . . I trust/ My absence doth neglect no great design . . ." *Rich 3,* III, iv, 23–24.

neglected, *adj.* **1** unrequited: "The origin and commencement of his grief/ Sprung from neglected love." *Ham,* III, i, 179–180. **2** ignored: "Have uncontemn'd gone by him, or at least/ Strangely neglected?" *Hen 8,* III, ii, 10–11.

neglectingly, *adv.* slightingly; indifferently: "Out of my grief and my impatience/ Answer'd neglectingly, I know not what . . ." *1 Hen 4,* I, iii, 50–51.

neglection, *n.* **1** neglect: "If neglection/ Should therein make me vile, the common body . . . would force me to my duty." *Per,* III, iii, 20–22. **2** disregard: "And this neglection of degree it is . . ." *Tr & Cr,* I, iii, 127.

negligence, *n.* contempt or indifference: ". . . both the worlds I give to negligence,/ Let come what comes . . ." *Ham,* IV, v, 134–135.

negligent danger, *n.* danger incurred through negligence: "Till we perceiv'd both how you were wrong led,/ And we in negligent danger." *Ant & Cleo,* III, vi, 80–81.

neighbored, *adj.* **1** familiar [with]: ". . . being of so young days brought up with him,/ And sith so neighbour'd to his youth and haviour . . ." *Ham,* II, ii, 11–12. **2** helped in time of need: "Be as well neighbour'd, pitied, and reliev'd,/ As thou my sometime daughter." *Lear,* I, i, 119–120.

neighborhood, *n.* neighborliness: "Domestic awe, night-rest and neighbourhood . . ." *Timon,* IV, i, 17.

ne intelligis domine? [Latin] Do you understand, Master? *Love's L,* V, i, 25.

neither, *adv.* **1** word added to emphasize the negative meaning that precedes it: ". . . one hope in it that can do you any good, and/ that is but a kind of bastard hope neither." *Merch,* III, v, 6–7.
—*pron.* **2 neither loves,** loves neither Mark Antony nor Caesar: ". . . but he neither loves,/ Nor either cares for him." *Ant & Cleo,* II, i, 15–16.

Nemean lion, *n.* (in Greek myth.) savage beast slain by Hercules as the first of his labors: "Thus dost thou hear the Nemean lion roar/ 'Gainst thee, thou lamb . . ." *Love's L,* IV, i, 89–90.

Nemesis, *n.* (in Greek myth.) goddess of avenging justice: ". . . the Frenchmen's only Scourge,/ Your kingdom's Terror and black Nemesis?" *1 Hen 6,* IV, vii, 77–78.

Neoptolemus, *n.* **1** See **Pyrrhus. 2** (in some editions) another name for **Achilles:** "Not Neoptolemus so mirable,/ On whose bright crest Fame with her loud'st Oyes/ Cries 'This is he' . . ." *Tr & Cr,* IV, v, 141–143.

nephews, *n.* grandsons: ". . . you'll/ have your nephews neigh to you . . ." *Oth,* I, i, 111–112.

Neptune, *n.* **1** Roman sea god: ". . . the moist star,/ Upon whose influence Neptune's empire stands . . ." *Ham,* I, i, 121–122. **2** the sea itself: ". . . rich conceit/ Taught thee to make vast Neptune weep for aye." *Timon,* V, iv, 77–78. **3 ebbing Neptune,** outgoing tide: ". . . ye that on the sands with printless foot/ Do chase the ebbing Neptune . . ." *Temp,* V, i, 34–35.

Nereides, *n.* sea nymphs, the 50 daughters of the sea-god Nereus [all of whom had human form, not the body of mermaids]: "Her gentlewomen, like the Nereides,/ So many mermaids, tended her i' the eyes . . ." *Ant & Cleo,* II, ii, 206–207.

Nero, *n.* Roman emperor, lst cent. A.D., who had his mother put to death; regarded as the personification of cruelty: "Let not ever/ The soul of Nero enter this firm bosom . . ." *Ham,* III, ii, 384–385.

Nero-like, *adj.* Nero is said to have ordered the burning of Rome and played the lute [in some accounts, the harp] while the city burned: ". . . and, Nero-like,/ Play on the lute, beholding the towns burn." *1 Hen 6,* I, iv, 94–95.

nerve, *n.* **1** seat of the body's strength: ". . . makes each petty artire [artery] in this body/ As hardy as the Nemean lion's nerve." *Ham,* I, iv, 82–83. **2** [usually pl.] sinews; tendons: "Thy nerves are in their infancy again,/ And have no vigour in them." *Temp,* I, ii, 487–488.

Nervii, *n. pl.* Belgian tribe of ancient Gaul, subdued by Caesar in 57 B.C.: "'Twas on a summer's evening in his tent,/ That day he overcame the Nervii." *J Caes,* III, ii, 174–175.

nervy, *adj.* sinewy; strong or muscular: "Death, that dark spirit, in's nervy arm doth lie . . ." *Cor,* II, i, 159.

Nessus, *n.* **1** (in Greek myth.) a centaur who attempted to rape Deianira, wife of Hercules, and was slain by Hercules: ". . . for rapes and ravishments he parallels Nessus." *All's W,* IV, iii, 241–242. **2 shirt of Nessus,** bloodstained shirt of Nessus, which he sent to Deianira, assuring her it could be used as a love charm; when she later gave it to Hercules, it caused his agonized death: "The shirt of Nessus is upon me, teach me,/ Alcides, thou mine ancestor, thy rage." *Ant & Cleo,* IV, xii, 43–44.

nest of spicery, *n.* womb likened to nest of spices where the phoenix was believed to be periodically consumed and reborn: "Where, in that nest of spicery, they will breed/ Selves of themselves . . ." *Rich 3,* IV, iv, 424–425.

Nestor, *n.* most venerable of Greek generals in the Trojan War and the essence of gravity; also, renowned as an orator: "And Nestor play at push-pin with the boys . . ." *Love's L,* IV, iii, 166.

net, *n.* **hide them in a net,** take refuge in a mass of obvious contradictions: "And rather choose to hide them in a net/ Than amply to imbar their crooked titles . . ." *Hen 5,* I, ii, 93–94.

nether, *adj.* earthly; here, committed here on earth: "You justicers, that these our nether crimes/ So speedily can venge!" *Lear,* IV, ii, 79–80.

nether-stocks, *n. pl.* **1** stockings, cut from material and sewed: "I'll sew nether-stocks, and mend/ them and foot them too." *1 Hen 4,* II, iv, 113–114. **2** wordplay on nether-stocks and wooden stocks: ". . . when a man's over-lusty at legs, then he wears/ wooden nether-stocks." *Lear,* II, iv, 10–11.

nettled, *adj.* beaten with or as if with nettles: "I am whipp'd and scourg'd with rods,/ Nettled, and stung with pismires . . ." *1 Hen 4,* I, iii, 236–237.

nettle-seed, *n.* wry joke about planting nettles, a weed covered with stinging hairs: "Had I plantation of this isle, my lord . . ."/ "He'd sow 't with nettle-seed." *Temp,* II, i, 139–140.

neuter, *adj.* neutral: "I would attach you all . . . But since I cannot . . . I do remain as neuter." *Rich 2,* II, iii, 155–158.

neutral, *n.* inaction; passiveness: "And like a neutral to his will and matter . . ." *Ham,* II, ii, 477.

never so, *adv.* ever so much; more than ever: "Who would give a bird the lie, though he cry/ 'cuckoo' never so?" *M N Dream,* III, i, 130–131.

Nevil, *n.* **1** Neville, the family name of Salisbury and Warwick: "The reverence of mine age, and Nevil's name,/ Is of no little force, if I command." *2 Hen 6,* I, 1, 198–199. **2 Nevils' parts,** York is Salisbury's brother-in-law and allies himself with the Neville faction: ". . . therefore I will take the Nevils' parts/ And make a show of love to proud Duke Humphrey . . ." *2 Hen 6,* I, 1, 241–242.

new, *adv.* **1** newly: "Came there a certain lord, neat and trimly dress'd,/ Fresh as a bridegroom, and his chin new reap'd . . ." *1 Hen 4,* I, iii, 32–33. **2** again: "And new pervert a reconciled maid." *Lover's Comp,* 329.

new-devised courtesy, *n.* latest compliment, bow, curtsy, or the like, esp. from the French court: "I would take Desire prisoner, and ransom/ him to any French courtier for a new-devised courtesy." *Love's L,* I, ii, 57–59.

new-fangled, *adj.* **1** new or novel (used contemptuously): "At Christmas I no more desire a rose/ Than wish a snow in May's new-fangled shows . . ." *Love's L,* I, i, 105–106. **2** eager for novelty: ". . . more new-fangled than an ape, more giddy in my desires than a monkey." *As You,* IV, i, 144–145. **3 new-fangled ill,** ugly though considered fashionable: "Some in their garments, though new-fangled ill . . ." *Sonn 91,* 3.

new form, *n.* latest fashion: ". . . who stand so much on the new form that they cannot/ sit at ease on the old bench . . ." *Rom & Jul,* II, iv, 34–35.

Newgate, *n.* London prison for felons: ". . . must we all march?/ Yea, two and two, Newgate fashion [chained together]." *1 Hen 4,* III, iii, 87–88.

Newhaven, *n.* port in S England, on the English Channel: "Scour to Newhaven: some there stay [wait] for me." *Edw 3,* II, ii, 203.

newly, *adv.* **newly with the time,** at the beginning [of our new regime]: "What's more to do,/ Which would be planted newly with the time . . ." *Mac,* V, ix, 30–31.

new pride, *n.* novelty; invention: "Why is my verse so barren of new pride . . ." *Sonn 76,* 1.

news, *n.* See **what news?**

newsmonger, *n.* bearer of tales; tattler; informer: "Which oft the ear of greatness needs must hear,/ By smiling pick-thanks, and base newsmongers . . ." *1 Hen 4,* III, ii, 24–25.

new-store, *v.* to restore; reinvigorate: "To new-store France with bastard warriors." *Hen 5,* III, v, 31.

newt, *n.* small, lizardlike animal: "Newts and blind-worms, do no wrong . . ." *M N Dream,* II, ii, 11.

new-ta'en, *adj.* newly caught: ". . . she fetches her breath as short as a new-ta'en/ sparrow." *Tr & Cr,* III, ii, 32–33.

new-tuned, *adj.* newly invented: ". . . the phrase of war, which they trick up with/ new-tuned oaths . . ." *Hen V,* III, vi, 76–77.

new-varnished, *adj.* freshly painted; here, so as to superficially resemble nobility: ". . . honour/ Pick'd from the chaff and ruin of the times,/ To be new-varnish'd!" *Merch,* II, ix, 48–49.

next, *adj.* **1** quickest; easiest: ". . . that is the next way to give poor jades the bots . . ." *1 Hen 4,* II, i, 9. **2** nearest; shortest: "Let my sheep go: come, good/ boy, the next way home." *W Tale,* III, iii, 124–125. **3** other: "And my next self thou harder hast engrossed . . ." *Sonn 133,* 6.

nibbling, *adj.* enjoyed in small bits: ". . . and as pigeons bill, so wedlock would be nibbling." *As You,* III, iii, 72–73.

nice, *adj.* **1** affected; overrefined: ". . . neither the scholar's melancholy, which is emulation . . . nor the lady's, which is nice . . ." *As You,* IV, i, 10–14. **2** delicate; also, risky: "to set so rich a main/ On the nice hazard of one doubtful hour?" *1 Hen 4,* IV, i, 47–48. **3** unmanly; effeminate: "Hence, therefore, thou nice crutch!" *2 Hen 4,* I, i, 145. **4** precise; exact: "O relation,/ Too nice, and yet too true!" *Mac,* IV, iii, 173–174. **5** skillful: "I'll prove it on his body if he dare,/ Despite his nice fence . . ." *M Ado,* V, i, 74–75. **6** untroubled; carefree: ". . . when mine hours/ Were nice and lucky . . ." *Ant & Cleo,* III, xiii, 179–180. **7** particular; unique: "Never, O never, do his ghost the wrong/ To hold your honour more precise and nice . . ." *2 Hen 4,* II, iii, 39–40. **8** trivial; insignificant: "Romeo, that spoke him fair,/ bid him bethink/ How nice the quarrel was . . ." *Rom & Jul,* III, i, 155–156. **9** flighty; capricious: "I am not so nice/ To change true rules for odd inventions." *Shrew,* III, i, 78–79. **10 make nice of,** to be fussy about: "And he that stands upon a slipp'ry place/ Makes nice of no vild hold to stay him up [is not particular what means he employs to support himself] . . ." *K John,* III, iii, 137–138. **11 nice and coy,** shy: ". . . but she is nice, and coy,/ And nought esteems my aged eloquence." *Two Gent,* III, i, 82–83.

nice longing, *n.* lustful appetites: "Ambitions, covetings . . . Nice longing, slanders, mutability . . ." *Cymb,* II, iv, 177–178.

nicely, *adv.* **1** subtly or, perh., extravagantly: "Can sick men play so nicely with their names?" *Rich 2,* II, i, 84. **2** scrupulously: "Let not conscience . . . thy bosom/ Enslave too nicely . . ." *Per,* IV, i, 4–6. **3** daintily: ". . . two winking Cupids/ Of silver, each on one foot standing, nicely/ Depending on their brands." *Cymb,* II, iv, 89–91. **4 too nicely urg'd,** overscrupulous or overprecise: "Haply a woman's voice may do some good/ When articles too nicely urg'd be stood [insisted] on." *Hen 5,* V, ii, 93–94.

niceness, *n.* fastidiousness; also, daintiness: ". . . change/ Command into obedience: fear, and niceness . . . into a waggish courage . . ." *Cymb,* III, iv, 156–159.

nicety, *n.* affectation of shyness or reserve; coyness: "Lay by all nicety and prolixious blushes . . ." *Meas,* II, iv, 161.

nick, *v.* **1** to cut the hair of: "My master preaches patience to him, and the while/ His man with scissors nicks him like a fool [so as to look like a jester] . . ." *Errors,* V, i, 174–175. **2** to get the better of: "The itch of his affection should not then/ Have nick'd his captainship . . ." *Ant & Cleo,* III, xiii, 7–8.
—*n.* **3 out of all nick,** beyond all reckoning: "Launce his man told me, he loved/ her out of all nick." *Two Gent,* IV, ii, 72–73.

nickname, *v.* **1 nickname God's creatures,** perh. ref. to fashion of calling courtiers by pet names; pos. ref. to affectations that turn human beings into caricatures: ". . . you nickname/ God's creatures, and make your wantonness/ your ignorance." *Ham,* III, i, 146–148. **2** to misname; miscall: "You nickname virtue; vice you should have spoke . . ." *Love's L,* V, ii, 349.

niesse, *n.* See **nyas.**

niggard, *v.* **1** to oblige or supply sparingly or grudgingly: "And nature must obey necessity,/ Which we will niggard with a little rest." *J Caes,* IV, iii, 226–227. **2** to begrudge; be stinting with: "Then, dear my liege, now niggard not thy state . . ." *Edw 3,* I, ii, 123.
—*n.* **3** stingy person; miser: "Then, beauteous niggard, why dost thou abuse/ The bounteous largess given thee to give?" *Sonn 4,* 6–7.
—*adj.* **4** niggardly; miserly: "Niggard of question [regarding conversation], but of our demands/ Most free in his reply." *Ham,* III, i, 13–14.

night, *n.* **1 soon at night,** towards evening: "I shall be sent for/ soon at night." *2 Hen 4,* V, v, 89–90. **2 this night,** last night: "My troublous dreams this night doth make me sad." *2 Hen 6,* I, ii, 22.

night-bird, *n.* nightingale: "She sung, and made the night-bird mute/ That still records with moan . . ." *Per,* IV, Chor., 26–27.

nighted, *adj.* **1** resembling night; dark or gloomy: "Good Hamlet, cast thy nighted colour off . . ." *Ham,* I, ii, 68. **2** being in darkness; here, because of his blindness: "Edmund, I think, is gone,/ In pity of his misery, to dispatch/ His nighted life . . ." *Lear,* IV, v, 11–13.

night-gown, *n.* dressing gown: "By my troth 's but a night-gown in respect of/ yours . . ." *M Ado,* III, iv, 17–18.

nightingale, *n.* **nightingales answer daws,** as instructed, Malvolio is being "surly with servants": "How do you, Malvolio?"/ "At your request? Yes, nightingales answer daws!" *T Night,* III, iv, 34–35.

nightly, *adv.* at night: "I will corrupt the Grecian sentinels/ To give thee nightly visitation." *Tr & Cr,* IV, iv, 70–72.

night-mare, *n.* demon that terrorizes people in their sleep: "He met the night-mare, and her nine-fold . . ." *Lear,* III, iv, 124.

night-raven, *n.* bird whose night-cry portended ill: "I had as/ lief have heard the night-raven, come what plague/ could have come after it." *M Ado,* II, iii, 82–83.

night-rule, *n.* nighttime sport or mischief: "How now, mad spirit?/ What night-rule now about this haunted grove?" *M N Dream,* III, ii, 4–5.

night-tripping, *adj.* tripping about in the night: ". . . some night-tripping fairy had exchang'd/ In cradle-clothes our children where they lay . . ." *1 Hen 4,* I, i, 86–87.

night-walking heralds, *n.* secret emissaries; here, appar., discreet go-betweens: ". . . there is no man secure,/ But the Queen's kindred, and night-walking heralds . . ." *Rich 3,* I, i, 71–72.

nill, *v.* will not: "I nill relate, action may/ Conveniently the rest convey . . ." *Per,* III, Chor., 55–56.

Nilus, *n.* river Nile: "My grief was at the height before thou cam'st,/ And now like Nilus it disdaineth bounds." *T Andr,* III, i, 70–71.

nimble, *adj.* moving quickly: "And winds of all the corners kiss'd your sails,/ To make your vessel nimble." *Cymb,* II, iv, 28–29.

nimble-pinion'd, *adj.* swiftly flying: "Therefore do nimble-pinion'd doves draw Love . . ." *Rom & Jul,* II, v, 7.

nimbly, *adv.* briskly: ". . . the air/ Nimbly and sweetly recommends itself/ Unto our gentle senses." *Mac,* I, vi, 2–3.

nine-fold, *n.* poss. a ref. to offspring: "He met the night-mare, and her nine-fold . . ." *Lear,* III, iv, 124.

nine-men's morris, *n.* outdoor game played on concentric squares; here, the outlines of the marked-off area for the game: "The nine-men's-morris is fill'd up with mud . . ." *M N Dream,* II, i, 98.

Nine Worthies, *n. pl.* most illustrious figures of history: "Thou art . . . ten times better/ than the Nine Worthies." *2 Hen 4,* II, iv, 216–218.

Ninny, *n.* misuse for "Ninus": "Wilt thou at Ninny's tomb meet me straightway?" *M N Dream,* V, i, 200.

Ninus, *n.* king of Assyria: ". . . these lovers think no scorn/ To meet at Ninus' tomb, there, there to woo." *M N Dream,* V, i, 136–137.

Niobe, *n.* [in classical myth.] arrogant daughter of Tantalus; avenging her insults, Apollo and Artemis slew her sons; grief turned her to stone, but she continued to weep inconsolably: ". . . she follow'd my poor father's body,/ Like Niobe, all tears . . ." *Ham,* I, ii, 148–149.

nit, *n.* speck; louse or louse's egg [contemptuous term for a person]: "Ah! heavens, it is a most pathetical nit." *Love's L,* IV, i, 149.

noble, *n.* **1** English gold coin, worth about one-third of a pound sterling: "Rich she shall be, that's certain . . . noble, or not I for an angel." *M Ado,* II, iii, 30–33. **2** wordplay on "royal" and "noble"; as coins, the noble was worth 10 groats less than the royal: "Hail, royal prince!"/ "Thanks, noble peer;/ The cheapest of us is ten groats too dear." *Rich 2,* V, v, 67–68. —*adj.* **3** of a noble family: "The last true duties of thy noble son." *T Andr,* V, iii, 155.

noble carelessness, *n.* indifference of the nobility: ". . . out of his noble carelessness/ lets them plainly see't." *Cor,* II, ii, 14–15.

noble knot, *n.* bond by which Coriolanus was bound to Rome: ". . . and not unknit himself/ The noble knot he made." *Cor,* IV, ii, 31–32.

nobleness, *n.* nobility; status of a noble birth: "Virtue and cunning were endowments greater/ Than nobleness and riches . . ." *Per,* III, ii, 27–28.

noblesse, *n.* nobility: "... then true noblesse would/ Learn him forbearance from so foul a wrong." *Rich 2,* IV, i, 119–120.

noble touch, *n.* proven nobility: "Come, my sweet wife, my dearest mother, and/ My friends of noble touch ..." *Cor,* IV, i, 48–49.

nod, *n.* **give you the nod,** call you a fool: "... you shall/ see him nod at me."/ "Will he give you the nod?" *Tr & Cr,* I, ii, 196–198.

noddle, *n.* slang term for "head": "To comb your noddle with a three-legg'd stool ..." *Shrew,* I, i, 64.

noddy, *adj.* blockhead; simpleton: "Nod—ay: why, that's 'noddy." *Two Gent,* I, i, 109.

noise, *n.* **1** rumor; gossip or hearsay: "Cleopatra catching but the/ least noise of this, dies instantly." *Ant & Cleo,* I, ii, 137–138. **2** abusive term for a band of musicians: "... see if/ thou canst find out Sneak's noise. Mistress Tearsheet/ would fain hear some music." *2 Hen 4,* II, iv, 10–12.
—*v.* **3 noise it,** to make a great noise; be clamorous: "And gives his potent regiment to a trull,/ That noises it against us." *Ant & Cleo,* III, vi, 95–96.

noiseless, *adj.* **our noiseless land,** our country that has made no preparations for war: "Where's thy drum;/ France spreads his banners in our noiseless land ..." *Lear,* IV, ii, 55–56.

noisome, *adj.* offensive; disgusting: "He could not stay to pick them in a pile/ Of noisome musty chaff." *Cor,* V, i, 25–26.

nole, *n.* head: "An ass's nole I fixed on his head." *M N Dream,* III, ii, 17.

nominate, to name or call; enumerate: "To nominate them all, it is impossible." *2 Hen 6,* II, i, 129.

nominated, *past part.* stipulated [as]: "... let the forfeit/ Be nominated for an equal pound/ Of your fair flesh ..." *Merch,* I, iii, 144–146.

nomination, *n.* **1** naming or disclosure: "I will look again ... for the/ nomination of the party writing to the person written/ unto ..." *Love's L,* IV, ii, 128–130. **2** mention: "What imports the nomination of this gentleman?" *Ham,* V, ii, 127.

no more, 1 nothing more: "To die—to sleep,/ No more ..." *Ham,* III, i, 60–61. **2** absolutely not: "Before the time be out? No more!" *Temp,* I, ii, 246.

nonage, *n.* minority: "In him there is a hope of government,/ Which, in his nonage, council under him ..." *Rich 3,* II, iii, 12–13.

nonce, *n.* **1** occasion: "I have cases of buckram for the/ nonce ..." *1 Hen 4,* I, ii, 174–175. **2 for the nonce,** as the situation demands: "This is a riddling merchant for the nonce;/ He will be here, and yet he is not here ..." *1 Hen 6,* II, iii, 56–57.

non-come, *n.* prob. misuse of "non compos" [not of sound mind] for "nonplus" [perplexed state]: "... here's that/ shall drive some of them to a non-come." *M Ado,* III, v, 57–58.

none, *pron.* **1** not a man, but either more or less than one: "I dare do all that may become a man;/ Who dares do more, is none." *Mac,* I, vii, 46–47. **2** let no one: "None wed the second but [those] who kill'd the first." *Ham,* III, ii, 175.

Non nobis, [Latin] Psalm 115:1, "Not unto us, O Lord, not unto us ...": "Do we all holy rites:/ Let there be sung *Non nobis* and *Te Deum* ..." *Hen 5,* IV, viii, 124–125.

nonpareil, *n.* person or thing without equal; paragon: "Yet he's good that did the like for Fleance:/ If thou didst it, thou art the nonpareil." *Mac,* III, iv, 17–18.

nonsuit, *v.* to refuse or rebuff: "And in conclusion,/ Nonsuits my mediators ..." *Oth,* I, i, 15–16.

nook-shotten, *adj.* full of nooks and corners: "... that nook-shotten isle of Albion." *Hen 5,* III, v, 14.

noon, *n.* prime of life: "So thou, thyself outgoing in thy noon ..." *Sonn 7,* 13.

noontide prick, *n.* point on a sundial indicating noon: "... tumbled from his car,/ And made an evening at the noontide prick." *3 Hen 6,* I, iv, 33–34.

nor, *conj.* **1 nor ... nor, a.** neither ... nor: "But now nor Lucius nor Lavinia lives/ But in oblivion and hateful griefs." *T Andr,* III, i, 294–295. **b.** neither (as) ... nor (as): "Nor friends, nor foes, to me welcome you are." *Rich 2,* II, iii, 169. **2 nor yet,** nor even: "Helen, the mother of great Constantine,/ Nor yet Saint Philip's daughters, were like thee." *1 Hen 6,* I, ii, 142–143.

north, *n.* **1** colder regions; here, less receptive areas: "... you are now sailed into the north/ of my lady's opinion ..." *T Night,* III, ii, 24–25. **2** north wind: "... entreat the north/ To make his bleak winds kiss my parched lips ..." *K John,* V, vii, 39–40. **3 breathing of the north,** the tumultuous wind from the north: "... like the tyrannous breathing of the north,/ Shakes all our buds from growing." *Cymb,* I, iv, 36–37.

Northampton, *n.* town N of London in Northamptonshire: "And at Northampton they do rest tonight . . ." *Rich 3,* II, iv, 2.

northen, *adj.* old var. of **northern:** ". . . the angry northen wind/ Will blow these sands like Sibyl's leaves abroad . . ." *T Andr,* IV, i, 104–105.

northern man, *n.* ref. to the long staves carried by northern highwaymen: "I will not fight with a pole, like a northern man . . ." *Love's L,* V, ii, 686.

Norway, *n.* king of Norway; here, Fortinbras's father: ". . . the very armour he had on/ When he th'ambitious Norway combated." *Ham,* I, i, 63–64.

Norweyan, *adj.* of Norway; Norwegian: ". . . the Norweyan Lord, surveying vantage . . . Began a fresh assault." *Mac,* I, ii, 31–33.

nose, *n.* **1 hear by the nose,** [if we could] hear with our noses: "To hear by the nose, it is dulcet in contagion." *T Night,* II, iii, 57. **2 speak i' the nose,** perh. ref. to the nasal twang of Neapolitan speech: ". . . ha' your instruments been at Naples,/ that they speak i' the nose thus?" *Oth,* III, i, 3–4. **3 wear our own noses,** disparaging ref. to the Roman nose: ". . . we will nothing pay/ for wearing our own noses." *Cymb,* III, i, 13–14. —*v.* **4** to smell; detect the odor of: ". . . you shall nose him as you go up the stairs into/ the lobby." *Ham,* IV, iii, 36–37.

nose-herb, *n.* herb prized for its scent rather than its flavor: "They are not herbs, you knave; they are nose-herbs." *All's W,* IV, v, 17.

nose-painting, *n.* reddening of the nose, presumably as a result of heavy drinking: "What three things does drink especially provoke?"/ "Marry, Sir, nose-painting, sleep, and urine." *Mac,* II, iii, 27–28.

not, *adv.* **1** not even: ". . . she will admit no kind of suit,/ No, not the Duke's." *T Night,* I, ii, 45–46. **2** not only: "Given hostile strokes, and that not in the presence/ Of dreaded justice . . ." *Cor,* III, iii, 97–98.

notable, *adj.* **1** notorious: "Notable pirate, thou salt-water thief,/ What foolish boldness brought thee to their mercies . . ." *T Night,* V, i, 67. **2** observable: "And mark the . . . notable scorns,/ That dwell in every region of his face . . ." *Oth,* IV, i, 82–83.

not-appearance, *n.* failure to appear in court: ". . . for not-appearance, and/ The king's late scruple . . . she was divorc'd . . ." *Hen 8,* IV, i, 30–32.

notary, *n.* clerk or secretary; here, recorder: "Dim register and notary of shame . . ." *Luc,* 765.

note, *v.* **1** to look at with particular interest: "I noted her not, but I looked on her." *M Ado,* I, i, 152. **2** to dishonor; stigmatize: "You have condemn'd and noted Lucius Pella/ For taking bribes here of the Sardians . . ." *J Caes,* IV, iii, 2–3. **3** to take note of; here, stare at: "If much you note him,/ You shall offend him, and extend his passion . . ." *Mac,* III, iv, 55–56. **4 fairly note,** to regard with favor: ". . . and heavens so shine,/ That they may fairly note this act of mine!" *T Night,* IV, iii, 34–35. **5 worthily note,** to show respect for: "I desire to find him so, that I may worthily note/ him." *Per,* IV, vi, 49–50. —*n.* **6** sign or indication: ". . . the sweet youth's in love."/ "The greatest [most obvious] note of it is his melancholy." *Much Ado,* III, ii, 48–49. **7** eminence; mark of distinction: "No note upon my parents, his all noble." *All's W,* I, iii, 152. **8** repute; reputation: "He is one of the noblest note, to whose/ kindnesses I am infinitely tied." *Cymb,* I, vii, 22–23. **9** stigma; brand or accusation: ". . . the more to aggravate the note,/ With a foul traitor's name stuff I thy throat . . ." *Rich 2,* I, i, 43–44. **10** song; melody: "Mine ear is much enamour'd of thy note . . ." *M N Dream,* III, i, 133. **11** list; here, a reading list: "I have perus'd the note . . . I'll have them very fairly bound—" *Shrew,* I, ii, 143–144. **12** act of remarking; notice: ". . . shall find I love my country,/ Even to the note o' th' king . . ." *Cymb,* IV, iii, 43–44. **13** observation: "Nine changes of the watery star hath been/ The shepherd's note . . ." *W Tale,* I, ii, 1–2. **14** information or knowledge; communication: ". . . she that from Naples/ Can have no note, unless the sun were post . . ." *Temp,* II, i, 242–243. **15** bill: "Here is now the smith's note for shoeing/ and plough-irons." *2 Hen 4,* V, i, 16–17. **16** mark or notation; here, of censure: ". . . my posterity sham'd with the note,/ Shall curse my bones . . ." *Luc,* 208–209. **17** birthmark: ". . . some natural notes about her body . . ." *Cymb,* II, ii, 28. **18** any distinctive feature: ". . . many will not buy/ His goodness with this note . . ." *Kinsmen,* V, iv, 52–53. **19 by note,** [authorized] in writing; here, the scroll: ". . . fair lady, by your leave,/ I come by note to give, and to receive . . ." *Merch,* III, ii, 139–140. **20 come to note,** become generally known: "Whiles you are willing it shall come to note . . ." *T Night,* IV, iii, 29. **21 note of expectation,** guest list: ". . . the rest/ That are within the note of expectation,/ Already are i' th' court." *Mac,* III, iii, 9–11. **22 out of a note,** from a memorandum: ". . . answer to what I shall ask you out of a note." *All's W,* IV, iii, 124. **23 out of my note,** not on my list: ". . . dates, none—that's out of my note . . ." *W Tale,* IV, iii, 46. **24 warrant of my note,** the justification of my knowing you: "Sir, I do know you;/ And dare, upon the warrant of my note,/ Commend a dear thing to you." *Lear,* III, i, 17–19.

noted, *adj.* **1** familiar; easily identifiable: "I have cases of buckram . . . to immask our noted outward garments." *1 Hen 4,* I, ii, 174–175. **2** notorious: "The king my brother shall have note of this."/ "Ay, for these slips have made him noted long . . ." *T Andr,* II, iii, 85–86. **3** wordplay on "musical notes" and "notorious": "Any man may sing her, if he can take her/ clef: she's noted." *Tr & Cr,* V, ii, 10–11.

noted weed, *n.* See **weed** (def. 4).

nothing, *adj.* **1** dead: "Nor I, nor any man . . . With nothing shall be pleas'd, till he be eas'd/ With being nothing." *Rich 2,* V, v, 39–41. **2** of no value: "By adding one thing to my purpose nothing . . ." *Sonn 20,* 12.
—*adv.* **3** not at all; in no way: ". . . nothing impaired,/ but all disordered." *M N Dream,* V, i, 124–125.
—*pron.* **4** no one: ". . . nothing,/ But [him] who knows nothing, is once [ever] seen to smile . . ." *Mac,* IV, iii, 166–167. **5 be nothing of,** have nothing to do with; be no part of: "Let this fellow/ Be nothing of our strife . . ." *Ant & Cleo,* II, ii, 79–80. **6 have nothing with,** do not understand: "I have nothing with this answer, Hamlet." *Ham,* III, ii, 95. **7 make nothing of,** to treat with no respect; here, do violence to; maul: ". . . the impetuous blasts, with eyeless rage,/ Catch in their fury, and make nothing of . . ." *Lear,* III, i, 8–9.
—*n.* **8** nonsense: "Her speech is nothing,/ Yet the unshaped use of it doth move/ The hearers to collection." *Ham,* IV, v, 7–9. **9** slightest or most trivial thing: ". . . of such/ sensible and nimble lungs that they always use to/ laugh at nothing." *Temp,* II, i, 168–170. **10 a.** wordplay with "noting" [spying] of similar pron.: "There's not a note of mine that's worth the noting . . . Note notes, forsooth, and nothing!" *M Ado,* II, iii, 55–57. **b.** triviality; also, wordplay on "noting" [tune] of similar pron.: ". . . no hearing,/ no feeling, but my sir's song, and admiring the nothing/ of it." *W Tale,* IV, iv, 613–615. **11 nothing but,** no other way except: ". . . whose wraths to guard you from . . . is nothing but heart-sorrow/ And a clear life ensuing." *Temp,* III, iii, 79–82. **12 nothing of your answer,** no part of what you must answer for: "To have it added to the faults of mine,/ And nothing of your answer." *Meas,* II, iv, 72–73. **13 nothing to a man,** does not reveal the true man: "Thou knowest/ that the fashion of a doublet . . . is/ nothing to a man." *M Ado,* III, iii, 114–116.

nothing-gift, *n.* worthless gift; here, flattery or adulation: ". . . laying by/ That nothing-gift of differing multitudes . . ." *Cymb,* III, vii, 57–58.

notice, *n.* **1** care; attention: ". . . bring but five-and-twenty; to no more/ Will I give place or notice." *Lear,* II, iv, 250–251. **2** information: "Belike they had some notice of the people [about the people's response] . . ." *J Caes,* III, ii, 272.

notify, *v.* **gives you to notify,** poss. "wants you to know" or Quickly's confusion with "gives you notice that": ". . . and she/ gives you to notify that her husband will be absence/ from his house between ten and eleven." *Wives,* II, ii, 78–80.

notion, *n.* mind; intellect or intelligence: ". . . that might,/ To half a soul, and [even] to a notion craz'd,/ Say, 'Thus did Banquo.'" *Mac,* III, i, 81–83.

not-pated, *adj.* having the hair closely cropped: "Wilt thou rob this leathern-jerkin, crystal-button,/ not-pated, agate-ring . . ." *1 Hen 4,* II, iv, 68–69.

not with oneself, *adj.* beside oneself; emotionally overwrought: "He is not with himself; let us withdraw." *T Andr,* I, i, 368.

notwithstanding, *adv.* nevertheless: "Antony, that revels long a-nights,/ Is notwithstanding up." *J Caes,* II, ii, 116–117.

nought, *pron.* See **naught.**

nourish, *n.* act of nursing; a feeding; also, nurse: "When at their mothers' moist eyes babes shall suck,/ Our isle be made a nourish of salt tears . . ." *1 Hen 6,* I, i, 49–50.

novelty, *n.* **novelty is only in request,** only the most up-to-date things are wanted these days: "Novelty is/ only in request, and it is as dangerous . . ." *Meas,* III, ii, 217–218.

no-verb, *n.* word instructing a person what not to do: ". . . he gives me the proverbs and/ the no-verbs." *Wives,* III, i, 96–97.

Novi hominem tanquam te, [Latin] I know the man as well as I know you. *Love's L,* V, i, 9.

novum, *n.* dice game, also called *novum quinque,* whose principal throws were nine [novum] and five [quinque]: "Abate [except for a] throw at novum, and the whole world again/ Cannot pick out five such . . ." *Love's L,* V, ii, 538–539.

now, *adv.* **1** at once; immediately: "Get linen: now this matter must be look'd to . . ." *Per,* III, ii, 112. **2** just now; a short while ago: "She will sit you [sit about]—you heard my daughter tell you now." *M Ado,* II, iii, 110–111. **3 but now,** a moment ago: "But now the blood of twenty thousand men/ Did triumph in my face . . ." *Rich 2,* III, ii, 76–77. **4 right now,** just now: "Came he right now to sing a raven's note . . ." *2 Hen 6,* III, ii, 39.

now-born brief, *n.* newly completed agreement or contract: ". . . whose ceremony/ Shall seem expedient [expeditious] on the now-born brief,/ And be perform'd tonight." *All's W,* II, iii, 178–180.

noyance, *n.* harm or injury: "With all the strength and armour of the mind/ To keep itself from noyance . . ." *Ham,* III, iii, 12–13.

number, *n.* **1** large number [of persons]; here, used ironically: ". . . it gives a good report to a number to be [for being] chaste." *Per,* IV, vi, 38. **2** [often pl.] verses; poetry; also, stanzas or measures: ". . . let him bring forth/ Eternal numbers to outlive long date." *Sonn 38,* 11–12.
—*v.* **3** to versify: "Think, speak, cast, write, sing, number, hoo,/ His love to Antony." *Ant & Cleo,* III, ii, 17–18.

numbered, *adj.* providing in great numbers: ". . . the twinn'd stones/ Upon the number'd beach . . ." *Cymb,* I, vii, 35–36.

numbering, *n.* estimate; appraisal: "The numbers true; and,/ were the numbering too,/ I were the fairest goddess on the ground . . ." *Love's L,* V, ii, 35–36.

numbering clock, *n.* imagined clock by which time itself displays the hours: "For now hath time made me his numb'ring clock . . ." *Rich 2,* V, v, 50.

numberless, *adj.* of great number; innumerable: ". . . numberless upon me stuck, as leaves . . ." *Timon,* IV, iii, 265.

numbers, *n. pl.* **1** verses: "These numbers will I tear, and write in prose." *Love's L,* IV, iii, 54. **2** poetic meter: "The numbers true; and, were the numbering too,/ I were the fairest goddess on the ground . . ." *Love's L,* V, ii, 35.

nuncio, *n.* messenger: "She will attend it better in thy youth,/ Than in a nuncio's of more grave aspect." *T Night,* I, iv, 27–28.

nuncle, *n.* var. of **uncle**; fool's address to his master: "How now, Nuncle! Would/ I had two coxcombs and two daughters!" *Lear,* I, iv, 110–111.

nunnery, *n.* word has slang sense of "brothel," but context suggests Hamlet means lit. sense: "Get thee to a nunnery. Why, wouldst thou be a/ breeder of sinners?" *Ham,* III, i, 121–122.

nurse, *n.* **1** source of nourishment: ". . . never palates more the dung,/ The beggar's nurse, and Caesar's." *Ant & Cleo,* V, ii, 7–8.
—*v.* **2** to sustain or prolong: ". . . longing still/ For that which longer nurseth the disease . . ." *Sonn 147,* 1–2.

nursery, *n.* tender care: ". . . thought to set my rest/ On her kind nursery." *Lear,* I, i, 123–124.

nursh-a, *n.* nurse, though Caius prob. means "housekeeper": ". . . my nursh-a/ Quickly tell me so mush." *Wives,* III, ii, 58–59.

nursing, *n.* rearing: ". . . he would have paid for the/ nursing a thousand." *Meas,* III, ii, 114–115.

nurture, *n.* good breeding: "Yet am I inland bred,/ And know some nurture." *As You,* II, vii, 97–98.

nut-hook or **nuthook,** *n.* sheriff's deputy, who arrests people for debt, etc.; catchpole or beadle [lit., a hooked stick for pulling nuts off trees]: "Nut-hook, nut-hook, you lie!" *2 Hen 4,* V, iv, 8.

nuzzle up, *v.* to nurture; bring up: "Those mothers who, to nuzzle up their babes/ Thought nought too curious . . ." *Per,* I, iv, 42.

nyas or **niesse,** *n.* young hawk that has not left the nest: "Romeo."/ "My nyas."/ "What o'clock tomorrow . . . ?" *Rom & Jul,* II, ii, 167.

O

O¹, *n.*, pl. **O's** or **oes. 1** cipher; nothing: ". . . now thou art an O/ without a figure." *Lear,* I, iv, 200–201. **2** something having a round shape: "A sun and moon, which kept their course, and lighted/ The little O, the earth." *Ant & Cleo,* V, ii, 80–81. **3** [pl.] circles or orbs; here, stars: "Fair Helena, who more engilds the night/ Than all yon fiery oes and eyes of light." *M N Dream,* III, ii, 187–188. **4** spot, blemish, pimple, or, often, a pockmark: "O! that your face were not so full of O's." *Love's L,* V, ii, 45. **5** prob. ref. to hangman's noose: "And 'O' shall end, I hope." *T Night,* II, v, 133.

6 See **wooden O.**

O², *n.* moan or groan; also, fit of moaning or groaning: "For Juliet's sake . . . rise and stand./ Why should you fall into so deep an O?" *Rom & Jul,* III, iii, 89–90.

o', *prep.* **1** of: "What is the time o' th' day?" *Temp,* I, ii, 239. **2** on: "If he took you a box o' th' ear, you/ might have your action of slander too." *Meas,* II, i, 194–195. **3** in: "Then come, o' God's name; I fear no woman." *1 Hen 6,* I, ii, 102.

oak, *n.* **bound with oak,** decorated with a garland of oak leaves for bravery: "To a cruel war I sent him, from whence he/ returned, his brows bound with oak." *Cor,* I, iii, 14–15.

oars, *n.* rowboat; partitive construction, in which the part stands for the whole: ". . . thy master is/ shipped, and thou art to post after with oars." *Two Gent,* II, iii, 33–34.

oathable, *adj.* not worthy of being put under oath: "You are not oathable,/ Although I know you'll swear . . ." *Timon,* IV, iii, 137–138.

oath of credit, *n.* oath that must be believed: ". . . swear by your double self,/ And there's an oath of credit." *Merch,* V, i, 245–246.

oats, *n.* **oats have eaten the horses,** the horses have had all the oats they can eat: "Ay, sir, they be ready; the oats have eaten the/ horses." *Shrew,* III, ii, 203–204.

ob., abbrev. for "obolus," a halfpenny: "Item bread . . . ob." *1 Hen 4,* II, iv, 532.

obduracy, *n.* lack of remorse for immoral conduct: ". . . thou thinkest me as far in the devil's/ book as thou and Falstaff, for obduracy and persistency." *2 Hen 4,* II, ii, 43–44.

obedience, *n.* act of obedience, as kneeling or bowing: "If I affect it more/ Than as your honour and as your renown,/ Let me no more from this obedience rise . . ." *2 Hen 4,* IV, v, 144–146.

obedient orb, *n.* celestial body moving in a predetermined sphere (fig. use): "Will you again unknit/ This churlish knot of all-abhorred war,/ And move in that obedient orb again . . ." *1 Hen 4,* V, i, 15–17.

obey, *v.* to be cured by: ". . . his dissolute disease/ will scarce obey this medicine." *Wives,* III, iii, 177–178.

Obidicut, *n.* one of the demons haunting Poor Tom: "Five fiends have been in poor Tom at once;/ as Obidicut, of lust . . ." *Lear,* IV, i, 58–59.

object, *n.* **1** objection; protest: "Swear against objects. Put armour on thine ears and on thine eyes . . ." *Timon,* IV, iii, 124–125. **2** sight; view: "Doth not the object cheer your heart, my lord?" *3 Hen 6,* II, ii, 4. **3** object of pity; sight; spectacle: "And with this horrible object, from low farms,/ Poor pelting villages . . ." *Lear,* II, iii, 17–18. **4 make us their object,** look at us: "They would not/ make us their object." *Kinsmen,* II, i, 51–52. **5 variable objects,** new sights; here, to a traveler: "With variable objects, shall expel/ This something settled matter in his heart . . ." *Ham,* III, i, 174–175.

—*v.* **6** to bring a specific charge: "Cousin of Herford, what dost thou object/ Against the Duke of Norfolk, Thomas Mowbray?" *Rich 2*, I, i, 28–29. **7** to reproach someone with: "Perhaps thou wilt object my holy oath . . ." *3 Hen 6*, V, i, 92.

oblation, *n.* offering: "For these, of force, must your oblations [offerings to you] be . . ." *Lover's Comp*, 223.

obligation, *n.* contract or bond: "Nay, he can make obligations, and write courthand." *2 Hen 6*, IV, ii, 88.

obliged faith, *n.* vow bound by contract: "O ten times faster Venus' pigeons fly/ To seal love's bonds new-made, than they are wont/ To keep obliged faith unforfeited!" *Merch*, II, vi, 5–7.

oblique, *adj.* more symbolic than actual: ". . . the primitive/ statue and oblique memorial of cuckolds . . ." *Tr & Cr*, V, i, 53–54.

obliquy, *n.* prob. var. of "obliquity," deviation from the normal or expected: ". . . the learned pate/ Ducks to the golden fool; all's obliquy . . ." *Timon*, IV, iii, 17–18.

oblivion, *n.* **1** forgetfulness: "Now whether it be/ Bestial oblivion, or some craven scruple . . ." *Ham*, IV, iv, 39–40. **2** indifference to other considerations: "Planting oblivion, beating reason back . . ." *Ven & Ad*, 557. **3 razed oblivion,** oblivion that erases thoughts and images: "Till each to razed oblivion yield his part . . ." *Sonn 122*, 7.

oblivious, *adj.* causing one to forget: "And with some sweet oblivious antidote/ Cleanse the stuff'd bosom of that perilous stuff . . ." *Mac*, V, iii, 43–44.

obloquy, *n.* **1** verbal abuse: ". . . did upbraid me with my father's death;/ Which obloquy set bars before my tongue . . ." *1 Hen 6*, II, v, 48–49. **2** disgrace: "It is an honour 'longing to our house . . . Which were the greatest obloquy i' th' world/ In me to lose." *All's W*, IV, ii, 42–45.

obscenely, *adv.* **1** poss. misuse for "seemly" [though "obscenely" better fits the context]: "When it comes so smoothly off, so obscenely as it were,/ so fit." *Love's L*, IV, i, 144. **2** prob. misuse for "unobtrusively" or "obscurely"; in any case, Bottom's meaning appears to be "privately": "We will meet, and there we may rehearse most obscenely/ and courageously." *M N Dream*, I, ii, 100–101.

obscure, *adj.* **1** dark; deprived of light: ". . . it were too gross/ To rib her cerecloth in the obscure grave . . ." *Merch*, II, vii, 50–51. **2** the bird of darkness; here, the screech owl: "New hatch'd to th'woeful time, the obscure bird/ Clamour'd the livelong night . . ." *Mac*, II, iii, 60–61.

—*v.* **3** to debase; degrade: "And even since then [at that very time] hath Richard been obscur'd . . ." *1 Hen 6*, II, v, 26.

obscured, *adj.* disguised: "Who hath most fortunately been inform'd/ Of my obscured course . . ." *Lear*, II, ii, 167–168.

obscurely, *adv.* in the dark: "Cave-keeping evils that obscurely sleep . . ." *Luc*, 1250.

obsequious, *adj.* **1** devoted; loyal: ". . . let me be obsequious in thy heart . . ." *Sonn 125*, 9. **2** befitting an obsequy [funeral]; dutiful: ". . . uncle, draw you near/ To shed obsequious tears upon this trunk." *T Andr*, V, iii, 151–152.

obsequiously, *adv.* in the manner appropriate to a funeral [obsequies]: "Whilst I awhile obsequiously lament . . ." *Rich 3*, I, ii, 3.

obsequy, *n.* funeral: "Keep the obsequy so strict." *Phoenix*, 12.

observance, *n.* **1** respect: ". . . all made of wishes,/ All adoration, duty and observance . . ." *As You*, V, ii, 94–95. **2** dutiful attention: ". . . ever shall/ With true observance seek to eke out that/ Wherein . . . my homely stars have fail'd . . ." *All's W*, II, v, 73–75. **3** instructions or the like that must be observed: "Are there no other tokens/ Between you 'greed, concerning her observance?" *Meas*, IV, i, 41–42. **4** exactitude; precision; here, lifelikeness: "Such sweet observance in this work was had . . ." *Luc*, 1385.

observant, *n.* obsequious attendant; toady: ". . . twenty silly-ducking observants,/ That stretch their duties nicely." *Lear*, II, ii, 104–105.

observation, *n.* **1** act of observing; observance: "For now our observation is perform'd . . ." *M N Dream*, IV, i, 103. **2** word-play on preceding sense and "obsequiousness": ". . . he is but a bastard to the time/ That doth not smack of observation . . ." *K John*, I, i, 207–208. **3 observation strange,** particular care or attention: ". . . so, with good life/ And observation strange, my meaner ministers/ Their several kinds have done." *Temp*, III, iii, 86–88.

observed, *adj.* **1** treated with respect; also, humored: ". . . he is gracious, if he be observ'd . . ." *2 Hen 4*, IV, iv, 30. **2** honored; revered or respected: "Th'observ'd of all observers, quite, quite down!" *Ham*, III, i, 156.

observing, *adj.* respectful; here, indulgent: "And underwrite in an observing kind/ His humorous predominance . . ." *Tr & Cr*, II, iii, 130–131.

obsque hoc nihil est, misuse for *absque . . .*; Latin motto meaning "Apart from this there is nothing.": "'Tis *semper* *idem*, for *obsque hoc nihil est;* 'tis all in every/ part." *2 Hen 4,* V, v, 28–29.

obstacle, *adj.* prob. misuse for "obstinate": "Fie, Joan, that thou wilt be so obstacle!" *1 Hen 6,* V, iv, 17.

obstruct, *n.* See **abstract** (def. 3).

obstruction, *n.* **1** hindrance or obstacle: "Why, she may/ command me ... There/ is no obstruction in this." *T Night,* II, v, 116–119. **2** lack of light; shutting out of light: "... the clerestories ... are as lustrous as ebony: and yet/ complainest thou of obstruction?" *T Night,* IV, ii, 38–40. **3 cold obstruction,** cessation of body's vital functions; death: "To lie in cold obstruction, and to rot ..." *Meas,* III, i, 118.

obtain and ask, *v.* to have for the asking: "Titus, thou shalt obtain and ask the empery." *T Andr,* I, i, 201.

occasion, *n.* **1** opportunity; circumstance: "... nature, stronger than his just occasion,/ Made him give battle ..." *As You,* IV, iii, 129–130. **2** political expedience; what is immediately necessary to achieve a desired end: "Antony will use his/ affection where it is. He married but his occasion/ here." *Ant & Cleo,* II, vi, 127–129. **3** responsibility; cause: "O that woman that cannot make her fault her husband's occasion ..." *As You,* IV, i, 164–165. **4** need or requirement: "My master is awak'd by great occasion ..." *Timon,* II, i, 24. **5** reason or justification: "I well allow the occasion of our arms ..." *2 Hen 4,* I, iii, 5. **6** [often pl.] **a.** matters: "Occasions, noble Gloucester, of some prize [importance] ..." *Lear,* II, i, 120. **b.** events; circumstances: "... enforc'd from our most quiet there/ By the rough torrent of occasion ..." *2 Hen 4,* IV, i, 71–72. **c.** duties: "... so duteous, diligent,/ So tender over his occasions ..." *Cymb,* V, v, 86–87. **7** emergency: "We must awake endeavour for defence,/ For courage mounteth with occasion ..." *K John,* II, i, 81–82. **8 many my near occasions,** my many urgent commitments: "... an earnest/ inviting, which many my near occasions did urge/ me to put off ..." *Timon,* III, vi, 9–11. **9 on great occasion,** on a matter of some urgency: "I would on great occasion speak with you." *Oth,* IV, i, 58. **10 quarrel with occasion,** to quibble [pun] at every opportunity: "Yet more quarrelling with occasion! wilt thou show/ the whole wealth of thy wit in an instant?" *Merch,* III, v, 50–51. **11 sharp occasions,** urgent needs: "... goaded with most sharp occasions ..." *All's W,* V, i, 14. **12 sort occasion,** to find an opportunity: "I'll sort occasion ... To part the Queen's proud kindred from the Prince." *Rich 3,* II, ii, 148–150. **13 very little thief of occasion,** the most trivial circumstance: "... a very little thief of/ occasion will rob you of a great deal of patience." *Cor,* II, i, 27–28.

occulted, *adj.* hidden or concealed: "If his occulted guilt/ Do not itself unkennel in one speech ..." *Ham,* III, ii, 80–81.

occupation, *n.* **1** [often pl.] any of the trades or handicrafts: "Now the red pestilence strike all trades in Rome,/ And occupations perish!" *Cor,* IV, i, 13–14. **2 man of any occupation,** [any] workingman: "And I had been a man of any occupation,/ if I would not have taken him at a word ..." *J Caes,* I, ii, 263–264.

occupy, *v.* to penetrate sexually: "... I was come to the whole depth of my tale and/ meant indeed to occupy the argument no longer." *Rom & Jul,* II, iv, 98–99.

occurrence, *n.* events of one's life: "All the occurrence of my fortune since/ Hath been between this lady and this lord." *T Night,* V, i, 255–256.

occurrent, *n.* occurrence; event: "So tell him, with th'occurrents more and less/ Which have solicited—" *Ham,* V, ii, 362–363.

Octavius Caesar, grand-nephew and heir of Julius Caesar; became emperor Augustus: "You serve Octavius Caesar, do you not?/ Caesar did write for him to come to Rome." *J Caes,* III, i, 276–278.

odd, *adj.* **1** not accounted for: "There are yet missing of your company/ Some few odd lads ..." *Temp,* V, i, 254–255. **2** fanciful: "I am not so nice/ To change true rules for odd inventions [new schemes]." *Shrew,* III, i, 78–79. **3 be odd,** to engage in combat; fight: "The general state, I fear,/ Can scarce entreat you to be odd with him." *Tr & Cr,* IV, v, 263–264.

odd-even, *adj.* ref. to the time around midnight, when it's a tossup whether it's still the present day or the next: "At this odd-even and dull watch o' the night ..." *Oth,* I, i, 123.

odds, *n. pl.* **1** amount of difference between two quantities: "This and my food are equals, there's no odds ..." *Timon,* I, ii, 60. **2** confrontation, esp. rivalry: "Set them into confounding odds, that beasts/ May have the world in empire!" *Timon,* IV, iii, 394–395. **3** most likely; almost a certainty: "'Twas odds, belike, when valiant Warwick fled ..." *3 Hen 6,* II, i, 148. **4** distinction; here, between great and common men: "... young boys and girls/ Are level now with men: the odds is gone ..." *Ant & Cleo,* IV, xv, 65–66. **5** hostility: "... for I desire/ Nothing but odds with England ..." *Hen 5,* II, iv, 128–129. **6 at odds,** with the odds in my favor: "... his quails ever/ Beat mine, inhoop'd, at odds." *Ant & Cleo,* II, iii, 36–37. **7 at odds with,** contending or disputing with: "What is the night?/ Almost at odds with morning, which is which." *Mac,* III, iv, 126. **8 at the odds,** on the odd hits; here, nine out of twelve: "Since he went into France, I have/ been in continual practice. I shall win at the odds." *Ham*, V, ii, 206–207. **9 have the odds of,** to have the advantage over: "Thou hast the odds of me; therefore no more." *T Andr*, V, ii, 19. **10 put odds among,** to set to fighting or squabbling: "Thou common whore of mankind, that puts odds/ Among the rout of nations . . ." *Timon*, IV, iii, 43–44. **11 stay the odds,** to put an end to quarreling; also, in gambling, to change the odds: ". . . the goose came out of door,/ Staying the odds by adding four [a fourth]." *Love's L*, III, i, 94–95. **12 take the odds,** to have the advantage: "I am content that he shall take the odds/ Of his great name and estimation . . ." *1 Hen 4*, V, i, 97–98.

—*adj.* **13** single; lacking a wife: ". . . for you know 'tis true/ That you are odd, and he [Paris] is even with you." *Tr & Cr*, IV, v, 43–44.

odorous, *adj.* misuse for "odious": "Comparisons are odorous . . ." *M Ado*, III, v, 15.

Od's heartlings, *interj.* by God's little heart [a mild oath]: "Od's heartlings, that's a pretty jest/ indeed!" *Wives*, III, iv, 56–57.

'Od's lifelings, *interj.* by God's little life [a mild oath]: "'Od's lifelings, here he is! You broke my head/ for nothing . . ." *T Night*, V, i, 182–183.

Od's me, *interj.* prob. an ellipsis of "God save me" [a mild oath]: "Od's me, *que ai je/ oublié?* [what have I forgotten?]" *Wives*, I, iv, 57–58.

'Od's my will, as God is my will [mild oath]: "'Od's my will,/ Her love is not the hare that I do hunt . . ." *As You*, IV, iii, 17–18.

Od's nouns, *interj.* [pron. "noonz"] Quickly's blunder for "Od's wounds" [by God's wounds], a mild oath: "Truly I thought there had been one number more,/ because they say 'Od's nouns." *Wives*, IV, i, 19–20.

'Ods pittikins, *interj.* God's pity [a diminutive form]: "'Ods pittikins: can it be six mile yet?" *Cymb*, IV, ii, 293.

Od's plessed will, *interj.* God's blessed will [a mild oath]: "Od's plessed will, I will not be absence at the/ grace." *Wives*, I, i, 242–243.

oeilliads or **oeilliades** *n.* loving or provocative glances: "She gave strange oeilliads and most speaking looks/ To noble Edmund." *Lear*, IV, v, 25–26.

o'erbear, *v.* **1** to beat down; turn back: "O'erbearing interruption [any attempt to stop him], spite of France?" . . . *K John*, III, iii, 9. **2** to overpower; subdue: ". . . young Laertes, in a riotous head,/ O'erbears your officers." *Ham*, IV, v, 101–102.

3 to overrun; invade: ". . . pouring war/ Into the bowels of ungrateful Rome,/ Like a bold flood o'erbear't." *Cor*, IV, v, 131–132.

o'erborne, *past part.* of **overbear**; overwhelmed; defeated: ". . . some their friends/ O'erborne i' th' former wave . . ." *Cymb*, V, iii, 47–48.

o'er-change, *v.* to transform: ". . . my steeled sense o'er-changes right or wrong." *Sonn 112*, 8.

o'er-charged, *adj.* overburdened: "I love not to see wretchedness o'er-charg'd,/ And duty in his service perishing." *M N Dream*, V, i, 85–86.

o'er-cloyed, *adj.* overrun; filled to overflowing: ". . . base lackey peasants,/ Whom their o'er-cloyed country vomits forth . . ." *Rich 3*, V, iii, 318–319.

o'er-count, *v.* to outnumber; here, in wordplay with "to cheat": "At land thou know'st/ How much we do o'er-count thee."/ "At land, indeed,/ Thou dost o'er-count me of my father's house . . ." *Ant & Cleo*, II, vi, 25–27.

o'ercrow, *v.* to overpower; lit., like a victorious fighting cock: "The potent poison quite o'ercrows my spirit." *Ham*, V, ii, 358.

o'er-dyed, *adj.* dyed with another color; ref. to black clothes re-dyed with another color; the black eventually shows through and "betrays" the lighter color: ". . . but were they false/ As o'er-dy'd blacks, as wind, as waters . . ." *W Tale*, I, ii, 131–132.

o'er ears, *adj.* submerged: "I will fetch off my bottle, though I be o'er ears for/ my labour." *Temp*, IV, i, 213–214.

o'er-eaten faith, *n.* begnawed vows; perh. an excess (in her vows of love) has caused them to dwindle: ". . . the bits, and greasy relics/ Of her o'er-eaten faith are given to Diomed." *Tr & Cr*, V, ii, 158–159.

o'er-eye, *v.* to spy on: ". . . here sit I in the sky,/ And wretched fools' secrets heedfully o'er-eye." *Love's L*, IV, iii, 77.

o'er-flourish, *v.* to embellish or decorate excessively: ". . . the beauteous evil/ Are empty trunks, o'er-flourish'd by the devil." *T Night*, III, iv, 378–379.

o'er-fraught, *adj.* overburdened: "Whispers the o'er-fraught heart, and bids it break." *Mac*, IV, iii, 210.

o'er-galled, *adj.* made sore: "Their eyes o'er-galled with recourse of tears . . ." *Tr & Cr*, V, iii, 55.

o'er-green, *v.* to cover up or over with, or as if with, new grass; gloss over: "So you o'er-green my bad, my good allow?" *Sonn 112,* 4.

o'ergrown, *adj.* grown out of memory: ". . . yourself/ So out of thought, and thereto so o'ergrown . . ." *Cymb,* IV, iv, 32–33.

o'ergrowth, *n.* overdevelopment; dominance: "By their o'ergrowth of some complexion,/ Oft breaking down the pales and forts of reason . . ." *Ham,* I, iv, 27–28.

o'erleaven, *v.* to corrupt: ". . . some habit, that too much o'erleavens/ The form of plausive manners . . ." *Ham,* I, iv, 29–30.

o'erlook, *v.* **1** to regard, peruse, or read: "Reason . . . leads me to your eyes, where I o'erlook/ Love's stories . . ." *M N Dream,* II, ii, 119–121. **2** to determine or find out; survey: ". . . but let your cares o'erlook/ What shipping and what lading's in our haven . . ." *Per,* I, ii, 49–50.

o'ermaster, *v.* **1** to gain an understanding of: "For your desire to know what is between us,/ O'ermaster't as you may." *Ham,* I, v, 145–146. **2** to usurp: ". . . living blood doth in these temples beat,/ Which owe the crown that thou o'ermasterest?" *K John,* II, i, 108–109.

o'er-night's, *adj.* last night's: ". . . caudle thy morning taste/ To cure thy o'er-night's surfeit?" *Timon,* IV, iii, 228–229.

o'er-office, *v.* to lord it over (another) by virtue of one's office: "This/ might be the pate of a politician which this ass now/ o'er-offices . . ." *Ham,* V, i, 76–78.

o'erparted, *adj.* given a too difficult part: ". . . but for Alisander,—alas! you/ see how 'tis,—a little o'erparted." *Love's L,* V, ii, 578–579.

o'erpeer, *v.* to look over; be seen over [it]: "And mountainous error be too highly heap'd/ For truth to o'erpeer." *Cor,* II, iii, 119–120.

o'erperch, *v.* to fly over: "With love's light wings did I o'erperch these walls . . ." *Rom & Jul,* II, ii, 66.

o'er-picture, *v.* to outdo; surpass: "O'er-picturing that Venus where we see/ The fancy outwork nature." *Ant & Cleo,* II, ii, 200–201.

o'er-posting, *v.* var. of "over-post(ing)," to get away with or escape from (something): "You may/ thank th'unquiet time for your quiet o'er-posting/ that action." *2 Hen 4,* I, ii, 148–150.

o'erpressed, *adj.* **1** overwhelmed; overcome: "And yet the fire of life kindle again/ The o'erpress'd spirits." *Per,* III, ii, 85–86.

2 exhausted or depleted: ". . . thy might/ Is more than my o'erpressed defence can bide?" *Sonn 139,* 7–8.

o'erprize, *v.* to exceed in worth: "With that which, but by being so retir'd,/ O'er-priz'd all popular rate . . ." *Temp,* I, ii, 91–92.

o'er-rank, *adj.* excessively populated: "O great corrector of enormous times,/ Shaker of o'er-rank states . . ." *Kinsmen,* V, i, 62–63.

o'er-raught or **o'erraught,** *adj.* **1** overreached; swindled or fleeced: ". . . by some device or other/ The villain is o'er-raught of all my money." *Errors,* I, ii, 95–96. **2** caught up to; overtook: ". . . certain players/ We o'erraught on the way." *Ham,* III, i, 16–17.

o'er-read, *v.* to read over: ". . . bid them o'er-read these letters/ And well consider of them." *2 Hen 4,* III, i, 2–3.

o'erset, *adj.* overturned; vanquished: "And since we are o'erset, venture again." *2 Hen 4,* I, i, 185.

o'ershade, *v.* to cover with darkness or gloom: "Fear o'ershades me . . ." *W Tale,* I, ii, 457.

o'ershot, *adj.* **1** astray; in error: "But are you not asham'd? nay, are you not,/ All three of you, to be thus much o'ershot?" *Love's L,* IV, iii, 156–157.
—*past part.* **2** overreached; gone too far: "Will you stay awhile?/ I have o'ershot myself to tell you of it." *J Caes,* III, ii, 151–152.

o'ersized, *adj.* covered or smeared as if with sizing; here, with congealed blood: "Roasted in wrath and fire,/ And thus o'ersized with coagulate gore . . ." *Ham,* II, ii, 457–458.

o'erslip, *v.* to slip by: "And when that hour o'erslips me in the day . . ." *Two Gent,* II, ii, 9.

o'erspend, *v.* to exhaust: "We would, till gloomy winter were o'erspent,/ Dispose our men in garrison a while . . ." *Edw 3,* V, i, 61–62.

o'erstare, *v.* to outstare; look fiercer than: "I would o'erstare the sternest eyes that look . . ." *Merch,* II, i, 27.

o'erstrawed, *adj.* strewn (over): ". . . the top o'erstraw'd/ With sweets that shall the truest sight beguile . . ." *Ven & Ad,* 1143–1144.

o'erstunk, *v.* appar. past tense of **o'erstink;** smelled worse than: "There dancing up to th' chins, that the foul lake/ O'erstunk their feet." *Temp,* IV, i, 183–184.

o'ersway, *v.* to overrule: "But sad mortality o'ersways their power . . ." *Sonn 65,* 2.

o'erswell, *v.* to overflow: "Shall leave his native channel and o'erswell . . . even thy confining shores . . ." *K John,* II, i, 337–338.

o'erteemed, *adj.* worn out with childbearing: ". . . and, for a robe,/ About her lank and all o'erteemed loins/ A blanket . . ." *Ham,* II, ii, 503–505.

o'ertook, *past part.* **1** overtaken; hence, captured: "The flighty purpose never is o'ertook,/ Unless the deed go with it." *Mac,* IV, i, 145–146. **2** become drunk: ". . . There was a gaming, there o'ertook in's rouse . . ." *Ham,* II, i, 58.

o'erwatched, *adj.* worn out from lack of sleep: "All weary and o'erwatch'd,/ Take vantage heavy eyes, not to behold/ This shameful lodging." *Lear,* II, ii, 170–172.

o'erween, *v.* to be arrogant; presume: "My eye's too quick, my heart o'erweens too much . . ." *3 Hen 6,* III, ii, 144.

o'erweening, *adj.* hard to control; here, arrogant and foolhardy: "Oft have I seen a hot o'erweening cur/ Run back and bite, because he was withheld . . ." *2 Hen 6,* V, i, 151–152.

o'erwhelm, *v.* **1** to overhang: ". . . let the brow o'erwhelm it/ As fearfully as doth a galled rock . . ." *Hen 5,* III, i, 11–12. **2** to cover or enclose; engulf: ". . . the belching whale/ And humming water must o'erwhelm thy corpse . . ." *Per,* III, i, 62–63.

o'erworn or **o'er-worn,** *adj.* worn out; worn down; spent: "O'erworn, despised, rheumatic and cold . . ." *Ven & Ad,* 135.

o'er-wrested, *adj.* strained: "Such to-be-pitied and o'er-wrested seeming/ He acts thy greatness in . . ." *Tr & Cr,* I, iii, 157–158.

oes, *n.* See **O**[1] (def. 3).

of, *prep.* **1** on: "A vulgar comment will be made of it . . ." *Errors,* III, i, 100. **2** redundant use after "like": "I no more desire a rose/ . . . But like of each thing that in season grows." *Love's L,* I, i, 105–107. **3** by: "O that a lady, of one man refus'd,/ Should of another therefore be abus'd!" *M N Dream,* II, ii, 132–133. **4** at: ". . . of the city's cost, the pissing-conduit run nothing but/ claret wine . . ." *2 Hen 6,* IV, vi, 2–4. **5** by means of: "And thus do we of wisdom and of reach,/ With windlasses and with assays of bias . . ." *Ham,* II, i, 64–65. **6** from: "Secure of thunder's crack or lightning flash . . ." *T Andr,* II, i, 3. **7** for: "Well aim'd of such a young one." *Shrew,* II, i, 231. **8** as being dependent on: "He loves you well that holds his life of you." *Per,* II, ii, 22. **9** in: "I charge your charity withal; leaving her/ The infant of your care . . ." *Per,* III, iii, 14–15. **10** in the person of: "You shall find of the king a husband, madam . . ." *All's W,* I, i, 6. **11** concerning or regarding; in response to: "Niggard of question, but of our demands/ Most free in his reply." *Ham,* III, i, 13–14. **12** because of; as a result of: ". . . and of that natural luck,/ He beats thee 'gainst the odds." *Ant & Cleo,* II, iii, 25–26. **13** therein: "If not complete of, say he is not she [he lacks only her] . . ." *K John,* II, i, 434. **14** with: "The merciless Macdonwald . . . from the western isles/ Of Kernes and Gallowglasses is supplied . . ." *Mac,* I, ii, 9–13.

off, *adv.* **1** so much; so highly; here, used as an intensive: "O Ferdinand,/ Do not smile at me that I boast her off . . ." *Temp,* IV, i, 8–9.
—*adj.* **2** irrelevant; beside the point: "That's off, that's off!/ I would you rather had been silent." *Cor,* II, ii, 60–61. **3 be off,** take off my hat: "I will practise the/ insinuating nod, and be off to them most counterfeitly . . ." *Cor,* II, iii, 98–100. **4 I'll off,** [here with "be" understood] to leave; go away: ". . . on mine own accord I'll off;/ But first, I'll do my errand." *W Tale,* II, iii, 63–64.

offal, *n.* **1** guts; entrails: ". . . ere this!/ I should ha' fatted all the region kites/ With this slave's offal." *Ham,* II, ii, 574–576. **2** wood chips, splinters, etc., used to start a fire: "What trash is Rome,/ What rubbish, and what offal, when it serves . . . to illuminate/ So vile a thing as Caesar!" *J Caes,* I, iii, 108–111.

offence, *n.* See **offense.**

offend, *v.* to injure: "Thou but offend'st thy lungs to speak so loud . . ." *Merch,* IV, i, 140.

offendress, *n.* fem. form of **offender;** poss. whimsical coinage by Parolles: ". . . buried in highways out of all/ sanctified limit, as a desperate offendress against/ nature." *All's W,* I, i, 137–139.

offense *n.* **1** harm; damage or detriment: "So shall he waste his means, weary his soldiers,/ Doing himself offence . . ." *J Caes,* IV, iii, 199–200. **2** offensiveness; here in wordplay with sense of "crime": "Is there no offence in't?"/ "No, no, they do but jest—poison in jest. No offence/ i'th' world." *Ham,* III, ii, 227–230. **3** offensive matter: "For one poor grain or two, to leave unburnt/ And still to nose th'offence." *Cor,* V, i, 27–28. **4** grievance; wrong or injustice: "Now that their souls are topful of offence." *K John,* III, iii, 180.

offer, *v.* **1** to menace or threaten: ". . . his power, like to a fangless lion,/ May offer, but not hold." *2 Hen 4,* IV, i, 218–219. **2** to attempt: "Gloucester offers to put up a bill; Winchester snatches it, tears it." [SD] *1 Hen 6,* III, i, 1. **3** to venture; presume: "I offer'd to awaken his regard/ For's private friends." *Cor,* V, i, 23–24. **4 offer fairly,** bring a fine present: "Thou offer'st fairly to thy brothers' wedding . . ." *As You,* V, iv, 166.

5 offer nothing, don't start anything [don't fight]: "Good lieutenant! good corporal! offer nothing/ here." *Hen 5*, II, i, 38–39.

offered mercy, *n.* Heaven's mercy extended to sinners: ". . . 'twere a paper lost/ As offer'd mercy is." *Cymb*, I, iv, 3–4.

offering, *adj.* **1** (in warfare) taking the offensive; challenging: ". . . well you know we of the off'ring side/ Must keep aloof from strict arbitrement . . ." *1 Hen 4*, IV, i, 69–70.
—*n.* **2** [pl.] rituals: "Witchcraft celebrates/ Pale Hecate's off'rings . . ." *Mac*, II, i, 51–52.

office, *n.* **1** service, favor, or accommodation: "I will do any modest office, my lord, to help my/ cousin to a good husband." *M Ado*, II, i, 352–353. **2** duty; task; business or assignment: "This is thy office;/ Bear thee well in it . . ." *M Ado*, III, i, 13–14. **3** function or purpose: "This precious stone set in the silver sea,/ Which serves it in the office of a wall . . ." *Rich 2*, II, i, 46–47. **4** officeholders; functionaries or bureaucrats: "The insolence of office, and the spurns/ That patient merit of th'unworthy takes . . ." *Ham*, III, i, 73–74. **5** [usually pl.] the rooms of a house set aside for service, as the kitchen, scullery, and wine cellar: "When all our offices have been oppress'd [overrun]/ With riotous feeders . . ." *Timon*, II, ii, 162–163. **6** [pl.] friendly greetings: ". . . these thy offices . . . are as interpreters/ Of my behind-hand slackness!" *W Tale*, V, i, 148–150. **7 bend all offices.** See **bend** (def. 7). **8 close offices,** secret matters: "Yea, him I do not love that tells close offices/ The foulest way . . ." *Kinsmen*, V, i, 122–123. **9 do offices of truth,** to perform their true function: ". . . they devour their reason, and scarce think/ Their eyes do offices of truth . . ." *Temp*, V, i, 155–156. **10 ill office,** unfriendly dealings: ". . . never may ill office, or fell jealousy . . . Thrust in between the paction [compact] of these kingdoms . . ." *Hen 5*, V, ii, 381–383. **11 the office,** each official: ". . . the office did/ Distinctly his full function." *Hen 8*, I, i, 44–45.
—*v.* **12** to perform household chores: "The air of paradise did fan the house/ And angels offic'd all." *All's W*, III, ii, 125–126. **13** to officiously keep [from]: ". . . a Jack guardant cannot office me/ from my son Coriolanus." *Cor*, V, ii, 61–62.

office-badge, *n.* symbol of authority as Protector: "Methought this staff, mine office-badge in court,/ Was broke in twain . . ." *2 Hen 6*, I, ii, 25–26.

officed, *adj.* holding a position: "So stands this squire/ Offic'd with me . . ." *W Tale*, I, ii, 171–172.

officer, *n.* **1** subordinate: "Your master . . . by ill officers,/ Hath given me some worthy cause to wish/ Things done undone . . ." *J Caes*, IV, i, 7–9. **2** household servant: ". . . the servingmen in their new fustian, their white/ stockings, and every

officer his wedding-garment/ on?" *Shrew*, IV, i, 41–44. **3** officer of the court, esp. a sheriff's assistant, empowered to make arrests for debt: ". . . go Tubal, fee me/ an officer, bespeak him a fortnight before . . ." *Merch*, III, i, 115–116.

official marks, *n.* insignia of office: ". . . remains/ That, in th'official marks invested, you/ Anon do meet the senate." *Cor*, II, iii, 138–140.

officious, *adj.* **1** busy; intent: "Come, come, be every one officious/ To make this banket . . ." *T Andr*, V, ii, 201–202. **2** meddling; interfering: "Officious, and not valiant, you have sham'd me . . ." *Cor*, I, viii, 14.

of force, *adv.* by necessity; perforce: "Will this content you, Kate?/ It must, of force." *1 Hen 4*, II, iii, 118.

offspring, *n.* rightful heirs; here, not direct descendants: "God shall forgive you Coeur-de-lion's death/ The rather that you give his offspring life . . ." *K John*, II, i, 12–13.

oft, *adv.* **1** often; frequently: "Oft have you . . . Desir'd my Cressid in right great exchange . . ." *Tr & Cr*, III, iii, 20–21.
—*adj.* **2** frequent: "By oft predict [portents] that I in heaven find." *Sonn 14*, 8.

often, *adj.* frequent: ". . . my often rumination wraps/ me in a most humorous sadness." *As You*, IV, i, 18–19.

of the, in: ". . . and of the season too, it shall appear." *Wives*, III, iii, 147.

oft-subdued, *adj.* usually defeated: "Sheep run not half so treacherous from the wolf . . . As you fly from your oft-subdued slaves." *1 Hen 6*, I, v, 30–32.

oil and flax, *n.* materials for starting a fire: "And beauty, that the tyrant oft reclaims,/ Shall to my flaming wrath be oil and flax." *2 Hen 6*, V, ii, 54–55.

oil and root, *n.* the bare essentials to sustain life: "Like madness is the glory of this life,/ As this pomp shows to a little oil and root." *Timon*, I, ii, 130–131.

old, *adj.* **1** experienced; also, hardened: "Doth not she think me an old murderer/ Now I have stain'd the childhood of our joy . . ." *Rom & Jul*, III, iii, 93–94. **2** copious; plentiful: "Master, master, news! And such old news as you/ never heard of." *Shrew*, III, ii, 30–31. **3** occurring in old age: "'This fair child of mine/ Shall sum my count, and make my old excuse' . . ." *Sonn 2*, 10,11. **4 have old,** to get a lot of [practice or experience]: "If a man were/ Porter of Hell Gate, he should have old turning the/ key." *Mac*, II, iii, 1–2. **5 old and antic,** here "antic" means "antique"; hence, quaint and old-fashioned: "That old and antic song we heard last night . . ." *T Night*, II, iv, 3.

—*adv.* **6** of old: "To sing a song that old was sung . . ." *Per,* I, Chor., 1.

old or **'old,** *n.* wold; an open upland area: "Swithold footed thrice the old;/ He met the night-mare, and her nine-fold . . ." *Lear,* III, iv, 123–124.

old age, *n.* former times; the good old days: ". . . it is silly sooth,/ And dallies with the innocence of love,/ Like the old age." *T Night,* II, iv, 46–48.

old Brutus, *n.* Lucius Junius Brutus, who had expelled Tarquin from Rome; Brutus claimed descent from him: ". . . set this up with wax/ Upon old Brutus' statue . . ." *J Caes,* I, iii, 145–146.

old coil, *n.* great to-do; big rumpus: ". . . you must come to your uncle—yonder's/ old coil at home." *M Ado,* V, ii, 88–89.

old ends, *n.* conventional amenities; also, old scraps of wit: "Ere you flout old ends any further, examine your conscience . . ." *M Ado,* I, i, 267–268.

old-faced walls, *n.* old-style walls were considered more solidly built; also, venerable: "'Tis not the roundure of your old-fac'd walls/ Can hide you . . ." *K John,* II, i, 259–260.

old utis, *n.* great time; rare fun: "By the mass, here will be old utis . . ." *2 Hen 4,* II, iv, 19.

olive, *n.* **1** olive branch of peace, often implying compassionate mercy: ". . . And I will use the olive with my sword . . ." *Timon,* V, iv, 82. **2 olives of endless age,** permanent peace: "And peace proclaims olives of endless age." *Sonn 107,* 8.

Oliver, *n.* **all Olivers and Rolands,** ref. to Charlemagne's most legendary knights: "Foissart . . . records/ England all Olivers and Rolands bred . . ." *1 Hen 6,* I, ii, 29–30.

Olympus, *n.* **1** mountain in NE Greece, home of the Greek gods: "Now climbeth Tamora Olympus' top,/ Safe out of fortune's shot . . ." *T Andr,* II, i, 1–2. **2 lift up Olympus,** to attempt the impossible; here, to try to change Caesar's mind, which is unshakable: "O Caesar—"/ "Hence! Wilt thou lift up Olympus?" *J Caes,* III, i, 74.

ominous, *adj.* **1** cursed with bad luck: "Let me be Duke of Clarence . . . For Gloucester's dukedom is too ominous." *3 Hen 6,* II, vi, 106–107. **2** fateful; deadly: "The rugged Pyrrhus . . . did the night resemble/ When he lay couched in the ominous horse . . ." *Ham,* II, ii, 450.

omit, *v.* **1** to fail to take advantage of: "There is a tide in the affairs of men . . . Omitted, all the voyage of their life/ Is bound in shallows and in miseries." *J Caes,* IV, iii, 217–220. **2** to ne-

glect; ignore or disregard: ". . . omit him not, blunt not his love . . ." *2 Hen 4,* IV, iv, 27.

omittance, *n.* **omittance is no quittance,** ref. to legal term, failure to respond to a claim does not indicate one's acceptance of it: "I marvel why I answer'd not again./ But that's all one. Omittance is no quittance." *As You,* III, v, 132–133.

omne bene, [Latin] all's well: "But, *omne bene,* say I . . . Many can brook the weather that love not the wind." *Love's L,* IV, ii, 31–32.

on, *v.* **1** to proceed; advance; march on: "That with our small conjunction we should on . . ." *1 Hen 4,* IV, i, 37.
—*prep.* **2** at: "Ne'er may I . . . sleep on night,/ But she tells to your highness simple truth." *Errors,* V, i, 210–211. **3** of: "Such whales have I heard on a'th' [of on the]/ land . . ." *Per,* II, i, 32–33. **4** from: ". . . his Majesty/ shall have tribute on me . . ." *Ham,* II, ii, 318–319. **5** for: ". . . nor no matter in/ the phrase that might indict the author of affection . . ." *Ham,* II, ii, 438–439. **6** by; by reason of: ". . . as if we were/ villains on necessity . . ." *Lear,* I, ii, 127–128. **7** to: "My Lord, you have one eye left/ To see some mischief [injury] on him." *Lear,* III, vii, 80–81. **8** according to: "He bears him on the place's privilege . . ." *1 Hen 6,* II, iv, 86.
—*interj.* **9** [as a command] go ahead: "On, speak to him." *Cymb,* V, v, 134.

once, *adv.* **1** actually; for a fact: used as an intensive: "Have I once liv'd to see two honest men?" *Timon,* V, i, 55. **2** ever; at all; in any way: "Direness, familiar to my slaughterous thoughts,/ Cannot once start me." *Mac,* V, v, 14–15. **3** once and for all: ". . . 'tis once, thou lovest/ And I will fit thee with the remedy." *M Ado,* I, i, 298–299. **4** once or one time when: ". . . for once we stood up about the/ corn, he himself stuck not to call us the many-headed/ multitude." *Cor,* II, iii, 15–17. **5 once this,** in summation: "Once this,—your long experience of her wisdom . . . Plead on her part some cause . . ." *Errors,* III, i, 89–91.

one, *pron.* **1** someone; one of you: "Go one and call the Jew into the court." *Merch,* IV, i, 14. **2** the other [fourth] one: "Help, three o'th'chiefest soldiers. I'll be one." *Cor,* V, vi, 148. **3 all one,** no matter; [it's] all the same: "I have a beard/ coming."/ "That's all one: you shall play it in a mask . . ." *M N Dream,* I, ii, 43–45. **4 all's one for that,** in any case; be that as it may: "Here will I lie tonight—/ But where tomorrow? Well, all's one for that." *Rich 3,* V, iii, 7–8. **5 one at other's,** at one another's: "Swords out, and tilting one at other's breast . . ." *Oth,* II, iii, 174. **6 one of thine,** a child of yours: "In one of thine, from that which thou departest [that prime which you are leaving] . . ." *Sonn 11,* 2. **7 one on another,** one after another: "One on another's neck do witness bear . . ." *Sonn 131,*

11. **8 say 'one',** perh. to begin to count; poss. ref. to a single sword thrust: "And a man's life's no more than to say 'one'." *Ham,* V, ii, 74.

one self, *adj.* same or identical: "Else one self mate and make [partner] could not beget/ Such different issues." *Lear,* IV, iii, 35–36.

one-trunk-inheriting, *adj.* owning only one trunk of possessions: ". . . super-serviceable, finical rogue; one-trunk-inheriting slave . . ." *Lear,* II, ii, 17–18.

oneyer, *n.* See **onyer.**

onion, *n.* **tears live in an onion,** enough tears [for this occasion] can be found in an onion: ". . . the tears live in/ an onion, that should water this sorrow." *Ant & Cleo,* I, ii, 167–168.

onion-eyed, *adj.* tending to weep: "Look, they weep,/ And I, an ass, am onion-ey'd . . ." *Ant & Cleo,* IV, ii, 34–35.

only, *adj.* **1** sole: ". . . only his gift [his sole gift] is in devising impossible slanders." *M Ado,* II, i, 128. **2** very best: "For the law of writ, and the liberty, these are/ the only men." *Ham,* II, ii, 397–398.
—*adv.* **3** merely; barely: "I must thank him only,/ Lest my remembrance suffer ill report . . ." *Ant & Cleo,* II, ii, 156–157.

on's, contraction of "of his": "Banquo's buried: he cannot come out on's grave." *Mac,* V, i, 60–61.

onset, *n.* beginning: "And for an onset . . . Lavinia will I make my empress . . ." *T Andr,* I, i, 238–240.

on't, contraction of "of it": ". . . if I had a monopoly out, they would have part/ on't . . ." *Lear,* I, iv, 159–160.

onyer or **oneyer,** *n.* poss. a dial. variant of "one"; perh. anglicized form of Dutch *oneer groot,* infinitely great [ones], or *mynheer,* gentleman or sir: ". . . with nobility, and tranquillity, burgomasters and great onyers,/ such as can hold in . . ." *1 Hen 4,* II, i, 75–76.

ooze and bottom, *n.* oozy bottom: ". . . as rich with praise/ As is the ooze and bottom of the sea . . ." *Hen 5,* I, ii, 163–164.

ope, *v., adj., adv.* open: "Who drown'd their enmity in my true tears,/ And op'd their arms to embrace me as a friend . . ." *T Andr,* V, iii, 108–109.

open, *adj.* **1** generous; unstinting: "Having often of your open bounty tasted . . ." *Timon,* V, i, 57. **2** apparent; obvious: "How covert matters may be best disclos'd,/ And open perils surest answered." *J Caes,* IV, i, 46–47. **3** public: ". . . it is an open

room, and good for/ winter." *Meas,* II, i, 130–131. **4 open haunts,** See **haunt** (def. 5).
—*v.* **5** to reveal; disclose: "The petty wrens of Tharsus will fly hence,/ And open this to Pericles." *Per,* IV, iii, 22–23. **6** to urge; put forward: ". . . charge your understanding soul/ With opening titles miscreate [spurious claims] . . ." *Hen 5,* I, ii, 15–16. **7** (of hounds) to cry when following a scent: ". . . never trust me when I open/ again." *Wives,* IV, ii, 184–185.

open air, *n.* ref. to proverbially harmful effects of fresh air on invalids: ". . . hurried/ Here, to this place, i' th' open air . . ." *W Tale,* III, ii, 104–105.

open-arse, *n.* vulgar name of the medlar fruit, because of its supposed resemblance to the female genitalia: "O that she were/ An open-arse and thou a poperin pear!" *Rom & Jul,* II, i, 37–38.

opener, *n.* person who reveals or interprets: "The very opener and intelligencer/ Between the grace . . . of heaven,/ And our dull workings?" *2 Hen 4,* IV, ii, 20–22.

open night, *n.* night in the open: "The tyranny of the open night's too rough/ For nature to endure." *Lear,* III, iv, 2–3.

operance, *n.* act of operating; operation: "That know not what nor why, yet do effect/ Rare issues by their operance . . ." *Kinsmen,* I, iii, 62–63.

operant, *adj.* potent; effective: ". . . sauce his palate/ With thy most operant poison." *Timon,* IV, iii, 24–25.

operant powers, *n. pl.* one's faculties; vital functions: "My operant powers their functions leave to do . . ." *Ham,* III, ii, 169.

operate, *v.* **operate another way,** [Her actions] give the lie to her words: ". . . mere words, no matter from the heart;/ Th'effect doth operate another way." *Tr & Cr,* V, iii, 108–109.

operation, *n.* **1** intoxicating effect of alcohol: ". . . by the operation of the second cup draws/ him on the drawer . . ." *Rom & Jul,* III, i, 8–9. **2** influence or effect: "By all the operation of the orbs/ From whom we do exist and cease to be . . ." *Lear,* I, i, 111–112. **3** [often pl.] feelings or perh. schemes: "I have operations which be humours of revenge." *Wives,* I, iii, 85.

operative, *adj.* useful or effective: ". . . many simples [herbs] operative, whose power/ Will close the eye of anguish." *Lear,* IV, iv, 13–14.

opinion, *n.* **1** conceit and, often, self-assertiveness: "Pride, haughtiness, opinion, and disdain . . ." *1 Hen 4,* III, i, 179. **2** public opinion; reputation: "Opinion, that did help me to the crown,/ Had still kept loyal to possession . . ." *1 Hen 4,* III, ii, 42–43. **3** adverse opinion: "How have I been behav'd, that he might stick/ The smallest opinion, on my greatest abuse?" *Oth,* IV, ii, 110–111. **4** consequence; prestige: "It lends a lustre and more great opinion,/ A larger dare to our great enterprise . . ." *1 Hen 4,* IV, i, 77–78. **5** intention: "Our own brains and the opinion that we bring . . ." *Hen 8,* Prol. 20. **6 main opinion,** entire reputation: ". . . we did our main opinion crush/ In taint of our best man." *Tr & Cr,* I, iii, 373–374. **7 our opinion,** our self-regard: ". . . but let us rear/ The higher our opinion . . ." *Ant & Cleo,* II, i, 35–36. **8 rich opinion,** enviable reputation: ". . . spend your rich opinion, for the name/ Of a night-brawler?" *Oth,* II, iii, 186–187.

opinioned, *adj.* misuse for "pinioned": ". . . let these men be bound/ and brought to Leonato's . . . Come, let them be opinioned." *M Ado,* IV, ii, 61–64.

opportunity, *n.* favorable circumstances: "To trust the opportunity of night . . ." *M N Dream,* II, i, 217.

oppose, *v.* **1** to offer as an opponent: ". . . who may you else oppose/ That can from Hector bring his honour off/ If not Achilles?" *Tr & Cr,* I, iii, 333–334. **2 oppose the bolt,** lock the door: "And, in conclusion to oppose the bolt/ Against my coming in . . ." *Lear,* II, iv, 178–179.

opposed, *adj.* **1** opposite: "Gelding the opposed continent as much/ As on the other side it takes from you." *1 Hen 4,* III, i, 106–107. **2** confronting like an enemy: ". . . with what wings shall his affections fly/ Towards fronting peril and oppos'd decay!" *2 Hen 4,* IV, iv, 65–66. **3** contrasted: "Sluttery, to such neat excellence oppos'd . . ." *Cymb,* I, vii, 44. **4 eye to eye opposed,** staring into each other's eyes: ". . . but eye to eye oppos'd/ Salutes each other with each other's form . . ." *Tr & Cr,* III, iii, 107–108.

opposed winds, *n.* opposite sides of the earth: ". . . embraced, as it were, from/ the ends of opposed winds." *W Tale,* I, i, 30–31.

opposeless, *adj.* all-powerful; invincible: "To quarrel with your great opposeless wills . . ." *Lear,* IV, vi, 38.

opposite, *n.* **1** adverse elements or factors, esp. the overall cost: "How able such a work to undergo,/ To weigh against his opposite . . ." *2 Hen 4,* I, iii, 54–55. **2** opponent or enemy; adversary: ". . . your attempts may overlive the hazard/ And fearful meeting of their opposite." *2 Hen 4,* IV, i, 15–16. —*adj.* **3** contrary; overbearing or quarrelsome: "Be opposite with a kinsman, surly with/ servants." *T Night,* II, v, 149–150. **4** opposed: "Seeing how loathly opposite I stood/ To his unnatural purpose . . ." *Lear,* II, i, 49–50.

opposite intent, *n.* antagonism or opposition; here, rebellion: ". . . mere instinct of love and loyalty,/ Free from a stubborn opposite intent . . ." *2 Hen 6,* III, ii, 249–250.

oppress, *v.* to defeat; crush: ". . . by oppressing and betraying me,/ Thou mightst have sooner got another service . . ." *Timon,* IV, iii, 507–508.

oppressed, *adj.* **1** overrun; packed: "When all our offices have been oppress'd/ With riotous feeders . . ." *Timon,* II, ii, 162–163. **2** stunned; overwhelmed: ". . . thrice he walk'd/ By their oppress'd and fear-surprised eyes . . ." *Ham,* I, ii, 202–203.

oppression, *n.* **1** opposition: ". . . our oppression/ Exceeds what we expected." *Ant & Cleo,* IV, vi, 2–3. **2** tyranny: ". . . lack gall/ To make oppression bitter . . ." *Ham,* II, ii, 573–574.

oppugnancy, *n.* **mere oppugnancy,** absolute conflict; utter chaos: "Each thing melts/ In mere oppugnancy . . ." *Tr & Cr,* I, iii, 110–111.

or[1], *conj.* var. of ERE; before: "Or I could make a prologue to my brains,/ They had begun the play . . ." *Ham,* V, ii, 30–31.

or[2], *conj.* **1 or ere,** before: ". . . and return/ Or ere your pulse twice beat." *Temp,* V, i, 102–103. **2 or for,** either for: "I must be laugh'd at,/ If or for nothing, or a little . . ." *Ant & Cleo,* II, ii, 30–31. **3 or . . . or,** either . . . or: "Or Charles, or something weaker masters thee." *As You,* I, ii, 250.

oracle, *n.* truth; wisdom: "We shall hear music, wit, and oracle." *Tr & Cr,* I, iii, 74.

orange-tawny, *adj.* of a tan color: ". . . your orange-tawny beard, your purple-in-grain/ beard, or your French-crown-colour beard . . ." *M N Dream,* I, ii, 87–88.

orator, *n.* speaker, esp. one who pleads on behalf of another: "He's a good drum, my lord, but a naughty orator." *All's W,* V, iii, 249.

oratory, *n.* act of pleading: "Her modest eloquence with sighs is mixed,/ Which to her oratory adds more grace." *Luc,* 563–564.

orb, *n.* **1** moon or its sphere; ref. to Diana, goddess of the moon and of chastity: "You seem to me as Dian in her orb . . ." *M Ado,* IV, i, 57. **2** [often pl.] ring or circle; here, fairy rings: "And I serve the Fairy Queen,/ To dew her orbs upon the green." *M N Dream,* II, i, 8–9. **3** sphere of activity: "But in our orbs we'll live so round and safe . . ." *Per,* I, ii, 122. **4** the earth: "The bold winds speechless, and the orb below/ As hush as death . . ." *Ham,* II, ii, 481–482.

orbed, *adj.* **orbed continent,** spherical container; here, the celestial sphere that contains the fiery sun: "And all those swearings keep as true in soul/ As doth that orbed continent the fire/ That severs day from night." *T Night,* V, i, 268–270.

orchard, *n.* garden: "Enter Brutus in his Orchard." [SD] *J Caes,* II, i, 1.

order, *n.* **1** manner; way in which something takes place: "Until they hear the order of his death." *2 Hen 6,* III, ii, 128. **2** finish or outcome; results: "Will you go see the order of the course?" *J Caes,* I, ii, 25. **3** prescribed ritual: "And but that great command o'ersways the order,/ She should in ground unsanctified been lodg'd . . ." *Ham,* V, i, 221–222. **4** measures; steps; methods or procedures: "I'll order take my mother shall not hear." *All's W,* IV, ii, 55. **5** proposal: ". . . having our fair order written down . . ." *K John,* V, ii, 4. **6 by order of law,** legitimately: "I have a son, Sir, by order of law, some/ year elder . . ." *Lear,* I, i, 19–20. **7 in order,** respectful; diplomatic: ". . . reproof, obedient and in order,/ Fits kings, as they are men . . ." *Per,* I, ii, 43–44. **8 take order for, a.** to make a settlement or reparation for: "Whilst to take order for the wrongs I went . . ." *Errors,* V, i, 146. **b.** to put in order; arrange: ". . . provide me soldiers, lords,/ Whiles I take order for mine own affairs." *2 Hen 6,* III, i, 319–320. **c.** to attend to: "If your worship will take order for the drabs and the/ knaves, you need not to fear the bawds." *Meas,* II, i, 231–232.
—*v.* **9** to manage; arrange: "'Tis vile unless it may be quaintly ordered . . ." *Merch,* II, iv, 6.

ordering, *n.* responsibility of making arrangements: "Have thou the ordering of this present time." *K John,* V, i, 77.

orderly, *adv.* **1** according to the rules [of procedure]: "Ask him his name, and orderly proceed/ To swear him in the justice of his cause." *Rich 2,* I, iii, 9–10. **2** in a proper manner; here, more ceremoniously or diplomatically: "You are too blunt, go to it orderly." *Shrew,* II, i, 45.

ordinance, *n.* **1** natural and established order: "Why all these things change from their ordinance,/ Their natures, and preformed faculties . . ." *J Caes,* I, iii, 66–67. **2** ordnance; cannon: ". . . return your mock/ In second accent of his ordinance." *Hen 5,* II, iv, 125–126. **3** rank; order of precedence: "When one but [merely] of my ordinance stood up/ To speak of peace or war." *Cor,* III, ii, 12–13. **4** future as ordained by Fate: "Let ordinance/ Come as the gods foresay it . . ." *Cymb,* IV, ii, 145–146. **5 ordinance of times,** established custom: ". . . honours that pertain/ By custom and the ordinance of times . . ." *Hen 5,* II, iv, 82–83.

ordinant, *adj.* directing or guiding: "Why, even in that was heaven ordinant." *Ham,* V, ii, 48.

ordinary, *adj.* **1** commonplace; routine: "To stale with ordinary oaths my love/ To every new protester . . ." *J Caes,* I, ii, 72–73.
—*n.* **2** meal, usually one taken in a tavern; also, mealtime: "I did think thee for two ordinaries to be a pretty wise/ fellow . . ." *All's W,* II, iii, 200–201.

ordure, *n.* manure: "As gardeners do with ordure hide those roots . . ." *Hen 5,* II, iv, 39.

ore, *n.* precious metal, esp. gold: ". . . his very madness, like some ore/ Among a mineral of metals base . . ." *Ham,* IV, i, 25–26.

organ, *n.* **1** human faculty; personal aspect: "And every lovely organ of her life/ Shall come apparell'd in more precious habit . . ." *M Ado,* IV, i, 226–227. **2** means of communication: "For murder, though it have no tongue, will speak/ With most miraculous organ." *Ham,* II, ii, 589–590. **3** agent or instrument, esp. of a plot: ". . . if you could devise it so/ That I might be the organ." *Ham,* IV, vii, 68–69. **4** [pl.] instruments: "And given his deputation all the organs/ Of our own power." *Meas,* I, i, 20–21. **5 organs of her fantasy,** dreams; here, give her sweet dreams: "Raise up the organs of her fantasy,/ Sleep she as sound as careless infancy . . ." *Wives,* V, v, 52–53.

orgulous, *adj.* proud; haughty: "The princes orgulous, their high blood chaf'd . . ." *Tr & Cr,* Prol., 2.

orient, *adj.* **1** lustrous: "Last thing he did . . . He kiss'd . . . This orient pearl." *Ant & Cleo,* I, v, 39–41.
—*n.* **2** the east: "Lo! in the orient when the gracious light/ Lifts up his burning head . . ." *Sonn 7,* 1–2.

oriental, *adj.* resembling the dawn in its radiance: "His cheeks put on their scarlet ornaments,/ But no more like her oriental red/ Than brick to coral . . ." *Edw 3,* II, i, 10–12.

orient drop, *n.* pearl; here, a tear: "Yet sometimes falls an orient drop beside . . ." *Ven & Ad,* 981.

orifex, *n.* orifice: "Admits no orifex for a point as subtle/ As Ariachne's broken woof to enter." *Tr & Cr,* V, ii, 150–151.

orison, *n.* [usually pl.] prayers: ". . . I have need of many orisons/ To move the heavens to smile upon my state . . ." *Rom & Jul,* IV, iii, 3–4.

ornament, *n.* **1** musical accompaniment: "And gave the tongue a helpful ornament . . ." *1 Hen 4,* III, i, 120. **2** decoration or embellishment; here, extenuating or exonerating words: "Will bless it, and approve it with a text,/ Hiding the grossness with fair ornament?" *Merch,* III, ii, 79–80. **3** beard; here, Pericles' overgrown hair and beard: ". . . this ornament/

[which] Makes me look dismal will I clip to form . . ." *Per,* V, iii, 73–74.

ornament of life, *n.* king's crown: "Would'st thou have that/ Which thou esteem'st the ornament of life,/ And live a coward . . ." *Mac,* I, vii, 41–42.

Orodes, *n.* King of Parthia: "Thy Pacorus, Orodes,/ Pays this for Marcus Crassus." *Ant & Cleo,* III, i, 4–5.

Orpheus, *n.* (in Greek myth.) Thracian musician whose playing (of the lute) and singing charmed even the rocks and trees and could change the course of a river: ". . . the poet/ Did feign that Orpheus drew trees, stones, and floods . . ." *Merch,* V, i, 79–80.

ort, *n.* **1** scrap or remnant: ". . . some poor fragment, some slender ort of his remainder." *Timon,* IV, iii, 402. **2** [pl.] refuse; leavings: "The fractions of her faith, orts of her love . . ." *Tr & Cr,* V, ii, 157.

orthography, *n.* coinage and/or use of overelaborate words and phrases: "He was wont to speak plain and to/ the purpose . . . and now is he turned orthography . . ." *M Ado,* II, iii, 18–20.

osier, *n.* willow tree: "The rank of osiers by the murmuring stream . . ." *As You,* IV, iii, 79.

osier cage, *n.* wicker basket: "I must upfill this osier cage of ours/ With baleful weeds . . ." *Rom & Jul,* II, iii, 3.

Ossa, *n.* mountain near Mount Olympus; in Greek myth., Mount Pelion was piled on top of it by giants seeking to overthrow the Olympian gods: ". . . till our ground,/ Singeing his pate against the burning zone,/ Make Ossa like a wart." *Ham,* V, i, 276–278.

ostent, *n.* **1** abridged form of **ostentation;** display: ". . . he'll o'erspread the land,/ And with th'ostent of war will look so huge . . ." *Per,* I, ii, 25–26. **2** appearance: "Like one well studied in a sad [sober] ostent/ To please his grandam . . ." *Merch,* II, ii, 187–188. **3** outward expression: ". . . employ your chiefest thoughts/ To courtship, and such fair ostents of love . . ." *Merch,* II, viii, 43–44.

ostentation, *n.* **1** traditional ceremony: "No noble rite, nor formal ostentation—" *Ham,* IV, v, 212. **2** outward manifestation: ". . . keeping such vile company as thou art hath in reason/ taken from me all ostentation of sorrow." *2 Hen 4,* II, ii, 47–48. **3** threatening action: "Frighting her pale-fac'd villages with war/ And ostentation of despised arms?" *Rich 2,* II, iii, 93–94. **4** vain show or display: ". . . these summer flies/ Have blown me full of maggot ostentation . . ." *Love's L,*

V, ii, 408–409. **5** spectacular entertainment, as a pageant or masque: ". . . present the princess . . . with some delightful ostentation, or show . . ." *Love's L,* V, i, 102–103.

ostler, *n.* var. of **hostler:** ". . . four by the day . . . yet our horse not packed. What, ostler!" *1 Hen 4,* II, i, 1–3.

other, *n.* **1** opposite side: "Vaulting ambition, which o'er-leaps itself/ And falls on th' other—" *Mac,* I, vii, 27–28. —*pron.* **2** another; here, the rival poet: "I think good thoughts, while others write good words . . ." *Sonn 85,* 5. **3** others: "And her withholds from me and other more . . ." *Shrew,* I, ii, 120. **4 each at others,** at one another: ". . . men of heart [valiant men]/ Look'd wond'ring each at others." *Cor,* V, vi, 99–100. —*adv.* **5** otherwise: "Who dares receive it other,/ As we shall make our griefs and clamour roar . . ." *Mac,* I, vii, 78–79. **6 can't no other,** can it not be otherwise?: "So I were not his sister. Can't no other/ But, I your daughter, he must be my brother?" *All's W,* I, iii, 160–161.

othergates, *adv.* in another way: ". . . if he had not been in drink, he would/ have tickled you othergates than he did." *T Night,* V, i, 191–192.

other some, *pron.* **1** some or certain others: "Some say he is with the Emperor of Russia; other/ some, he is in Rome . . ." *Meas,* III, ii, 85–86. **2** others [of my own]: ". . . thou hast some children . . . I, being but a bachelor,/ Have other some." *3 Hen 6,* III, ii, 102–104.

otherwhere, *adv.* elsewhere: "I know his eye doth homage otherwhere . . ." *Errors,* II, i, 104.

o'th's, contraction of "of these": ". . . and what one thing, what another, that I shall/ leave you one o'th's days . . ." *Tr & Cr,* V, iii, 103–104.

Ottomite, *n.* Turk: "The Ottomites . . . Steering with due course, toward the isle of Rhodes . . ." *Oth,* I, iii, 33–34.

ouch, *n.* jewel or brooch; also, a carbuncle or skin sore (a favorite pun): ". . . our chains and our jewels."/ "'Your brooches, pearls, and ouches'. . ." *2 Hen 4,* II, iv, 47–48.

ought, *v.* old form of **owed:** ". . . said this other day/ you ought him a thousand pound." *1 Hen 4,* III, iii, 132–133.

oui, *v.* [French] yes; here, the English courtiers may ape the French and indulge their lechery to the limit: "They may . . . 'oui' away/ The lag end of their lewdness, and be laugh'd at." *Hen 8,* I, iii, 34–35.

Oui, mette le au mon pocket: dépeche, [French & English] Yes, put it in my pocket: hurry up. *Wives,* I, iv, 49.

ounce, *n.* lynx: "Be it ounce, or cat, or bear,/ Pard, or boar with bristled hair . . ." *M N Dream,* II, ii, 29–30.

ouph, *n.* elf or elfin child: ". . . three or four more of their growth we'll dress/ Like urchins, ouphs, and fairies . . ." *Wives,* IV, iv, 48–49.

our, *adj.* of our country; Roman: "Our Tarquin thus/ Did softly press the rushes . . ." *Cymb,* II, ii, 12–13.

'our, contraction of "of our" [of my]: "She is as forward of her breeding as/ She is i' th' rear 'our birth." *W Tale,* IV, iv, 581–582.

ours, *pron.* **1** our minds [are in accord]: "And ours with thine, befall what fortune will." *T Andr,* V, iii, 3. **2 ours as yours,** as familiar to us as it is to you: "All the commerce that you have had with Troy/ As perfectly is ours as yours . . ." *Tr & Cr,* III, iii, 204–205.

ourselves, *n.* **of ourselves,** by nature: "Since, of ourselves, ourselves are choleric . . ." *Shrew,* IV, i, 161.

ousel cock, *n.* blackbird: "The ousel cock, so black of hue,/ With orange-tawny bill . . ." *M N Dream,* III, i, 120–121.

out, *prep.* **1** from out; out of: ". . . those that bawl out the ru-ins of/ thy linen shall inherit his kingdom . . ." *2 Hen 4,* II, ii, 23–24.

—*adv.* **2** out of memory: ". . . I make no doubt/ The rest will ne'er come in, if he be out." *Love's L,* V, ii, 151–152. **3** fully; quite: ". . . for then thou wast not/ Out three years old." *Temp,* I, ii, 40–41. **4** in foreign lands: "He hath been out nine years, and away he shall/ again." *Lear,* I, i, 32–33. **5** in my possession; granted to me: ". . . if I had a monopoly out, they would have part/ on't . . ." *Lear,* I, iv, 158–159. **6** over; at an end: ". . . our hour/ Is fully out." *Ant & Cleo,* IV, ix, 31–32. **7** [step] out of ranks: "Stand fast, Titinius; we must out and talk." *J Caes,* V, i, 22. **8** in disagreement: "Nay, you need not fear us Loren-zo, Launcelot and I/ are out . . ." *Merch,* III, v, 28–29. **9 beat (someone) out,** to overpower (someone) in battle: "Thou hast beat me out/ Twelve several times . . ." *Cor,* IV, v, 122–123. **10 I'll ne'er out,** I'll never refuse a drink: "I am not so well as I should be: but I'll ne'er out." *Ant & Cleo,* II, vii, 30. **11 out of, a.** except with; without using: "I will never/ buy and sell out of this word." *Love's L,* III, i, 137–138. **b.** beyond; free from: "I am out of fear/ Of death or death's hand for this one half year." *1 Hen 4,* IV, i, 135–136. **c.** lost; strayed from: ". . . you must inquire your way,/ Which you are out of . . ." *Cor,* III, i, 53–54. **12 out on, a.** exclam. of indignation or condemnation: "Out on thee villain, wherefore dost thou mad me?" *Errors,* IV, iv, 124. **b.** away from: "Would I were fairly [honorably] out on't." *Hen 8,* V, ii, 143.

—*adj.* **13** angry; here, wordplay with "worn-out": "Nay, I be-seech you, sir, be not out with me; yet, if/ you be out, sir, I can mend you." *J Caes,* I, i, 16–17. **14** bearing arms; engaged in rebellion: ". . . there ran a rumour/ Of many worthy fellows that were out . . ." *Mac,* IV, iii, 182–183. **15** empty; depleted: ". . . when the butt is out, we will drink/ water; not a drop before . . ." *Temp,* III, ii, 1–2. **16** finished; done: ". . . our hour/ Is fully out." *Ant & Cleo,* IV, ix, 331–32. **17** wrong; in error: "O, I am out,/ That mercy does . . ." *W Tale,* II, i, 72–73. **18** not functioning; extinguished: "Seems seeing, but effectually is out . . ." *Sonn 113,* 4.

—*interj.* **19** uttered as a rebuke: "Out, you green-sickness car-rion! Out, you baggage!" *Rom & Jul,* III, v, 156. **20 out alas!** intensive combining two exclamations: "But, out alas! here have we found him dead." *T Andr,* II, iii, 258. **21 out, out!** cry of indignation: "Out, out! My lords . . . 'tis not so;/ I did beget her, all the parish knows . . ." *1 Hen 6,* V, iv, 10–11. **22 Out upon't,** exclamation of impatient dismissal: "I know Anne's mind as well as another does.—Out/ upon't . . ." *Wives,* I, iv, 158–159. **23 Out with't!** Lend it out at interest: "Out with't! Within the year it/ will make itself two . . ." *All's W,* I, i, 144–145.

—*v.* **24** come out; emerge: ". . . your wit will not so soon out as another/ man's will . . ." *Cor,* II, iii, 27–28.

out alack, *interj.* expression of dejection; alas!: "But out alack, he was but one hour mine . . ." *Sonn 33,* 11.

out-brag, *v.* to surpass: "Whose bare out-bragg'd the web it seem'd to wear . . ." *Lover's Comp,* 95.

outbrave, *v.* **outbraves his dignity,** surpasses him in worth: "The basest weed outbraves his dignity . . ." *Sonn 94,* 12.

outbreathed, *adj.* caused to be out of breath: "Rend'ring faint quittance, wearied, and outbreath'd,/ To Harry Mon-mouth . . ." *2 Hen 4,* I, i, 108–109.

out-crafty, *v.* to overcome with cunning: "That drug-damn'd Italy hath out-craftied him . . ." *Cymb,* III, iv, 15.

out-dared, *adj.* cowed; daunted: "Shall I . . . with pale beggar-fear impeach my height/ Before this out-dar'd dastard?" *Rich 2,* I, i, 188–190.

out-dwell, *v.* to stay beyond; stay away longer than: "And it is marvel he out-dwells his hour . . ." *Merch,* II, vi, 3.

outface, *v.* **1** to brave: ". . . outface/ The winds and persecu-tions of the sky." *Lear,* II, iii, 11–12. **2** to mock and, hence, to put one out of countenance: ". . . we have given thee faces."/ "But you have outfaced them all." *Love's L,* V, ii, 616–617. **3 outfaced infant state,** defied the young king's majesty: "Outfaced infant state, and done a rape/ Upon the maiden virtue of the crown." *K John,* II, i, 97–98.

outfacing, *adj.* impudent and defiant: "Scambling, outfacing, fashion-monging boys . . ." *M Ado,* V, i, 94.

out-go or **outgo,** *v.* **1** to exceed: "He out-goes/ The very heart of kindness." *Timon,* I, i, 273. **2** to leave behind; out-distance: ". . . the time shall not/ Out-go my thinking on you." *Ant & Cleo,* III, ii, 60–61. **3** to decline: "So thou, thyself outgoing in thy noon . . ." *Sonn 7,* 13.

outlive, *v.* to remain alive; survive: "Let not this wasp outlive, us both to sting." *T Andr,* II, iii, 132.

outlook, *v.* to outface; stare down: "To outlook conquest and to win renown/ Even in the jaws of danger and of death." *K John,* V, ii, 115–116.

out of (all) cess, See **cess**[1].

out of door or **out o'door,** *adv.* **1** away from home: ". . . their business still lies out o'door." *Errors,* II, i, 11.
—*adj.* **2** visible; perh. exposed: "All of her that is out of door most rich!" *Cymb,* I, vii, 15.

out of measure, *adv.* unusually; unnecessarily: ". . . why are you thus/ out of measure sad?" *M Ado,* I, iii, 1–2.

out of suits with, out of favor with: ". . . one out of suits with fortune,/ That could give more but that her hand lacks means." *As You,* I, ii, 236–237.

out o' question, beyond question; undoubtedly: ". . . out o' question, you were/ born in a merry hour." *M Ado,* II, i, 313–314.

out o' th' way, See **way** (def. 24).

out-paramour, *v.* **out-paramour the Turk,** to outdo the Turkish Sultan in number of mistresses: "Wine lov'd I deeply,/ dice dearly, and in woman out-paramour'd the/ Turk . . ." *Lear,* III, iv, 91–92.

out-peer, *v.* to surpass: "That nothing-gift of differing multitudes,/ Could not out-peer these twain." *Cymb,* III, vii, 58–59.

outrage, *n.* act or acts of violence: ". . . the rancorous outrage of your Duke/ To merchants, our well-dealing countrymen . . ." *Errors,* I, i, 6–7.

outrageous, *adj.* **1** cruel and erratic; wanton: ". . . to suffer/ The slings and arrows of outrageous fortune . . ." *Ham,* III, i, 57–58. **2** violent or excessive; abandoned: "I never heard

a passion so confus'd,/ So strange, outrageous, and so variable . . ." *Merch,* II, viii, 12–13.

outsell, *v.* to exceed in value: "Her pretty action did outsell her gift . . ." *Cymb,* II, iv, 102.

outsides, *n.* [usually pl.] external appearances: ". . . make his wrongs his outsides,/ To wear them like his raiment, carelessly . . ." *Timon,* III, v, 33–34.

out-speak, *v.* to exceed; be excessive for: ". . . it out-speaks/ Possession of a subject." *Hen 8,* III, ii, 127–128.

out-stare, *v.* to face down: ". . . he's gone to th' king:/ I'll follow and out-stare him." *Hen 8,* I, i, 128–129.

outstood, *past part.* of **outstand;** outstayed: "I have outstood my time . . ." *Cymb,* I, vii, 207.

outstretched, *adj.* elongated; appearing larger than life: ". . . our monarchs/ and outstretched heroes the beggars' shadows." *Ham,* II, ii, 263–264.

outswear, *v.* to overcome with swearing; also, to forswear: "I think scorn to sigh: methinks I should/ outswear Cupid." *Love's L,* I, ii, 59–60.

out-tongue, *v.* to have greater regard than: "My services . . . Shall out-tongue his complaints . . ." *Oth,* I, ii, 18–19.

outvied, *adj.* outbid; outdone: ". . . the maid is mine from all the world/ By your firm promise. Gremio is outvied." *Shrew,* II, i, 377–378.

out-wall, *n.* exterior appearance: "For confirmation that I am much more/ Than my out-wall, open this purse . . ." *Lear,* III, i, 44–45.

outward, *n.* **1** external appearance: "Outliving beauty's outward, with a mind . . ." *Tr & Cr,* III, ii, 160.
—*adj.* **2** outside; external: "Where time and outward form [appearance] would show it dead." *Sonn 108,* 14.

outward happiness, *n.* handsome appearance: "He hath indeed a good outward happiness." *M Ado,* II, iii, 178.

outward man, *n.* outsider: ". . . like a common and an outward man . . ." *All's W,* III, i, 11.

outward worth, *n.* property or possessions: "He that helps him take all my outward worth." *Lear,* IV, iv, 10.

outwear, *v.* **1** to outlast: "Her song was tedious, and outwore the night . . ." *Ven & Ad,* 841. **2** to waste: "The sun is high, and we outwear the day." *Hen 5,* IV, ii, 63.

outwent, *v.* past tense of **outgo;** outdid; surpassed: ". . . outwent her,/ Motion and breath left out [excepted]." *Cymb,* II, iv, 84–85.

outwork, *v.* to surpass; outdo: ". . . that Venus where we see/ The fancy outwork nature." *Ant & Cleo,* II, ii, 200–201.

outworn buried age, *n.* buried ages of the past: "The rich, proud cost of outworn buried age . . ." *Sonn 64,* 2.

outworth, *v.* to exceed in value: "A beggar's book [learning]/ Outworths a noble's blood." *Hen 8,* I, i, 122–123.

ovator, *n.* one given an ovation [in some editions "overture" or "coverture"]: "When steel [men of steel] grows/ Soft as the parasite's silk [courtiers], let him be made/ An ovator for th'wars!" *Cor,* I, ix, 44–46.

over and over, *adv.* head over heels: ". . . they were never so truly turned/ over and over as my poor self in love." *M Ado,* V, ii, 33–34.

overawe, *v.* to keep in complete subjection: "None do you like but an effeminate prince,/ Whom like a school-boy you may overawe." *1 Hen 6,* I, i, 35–36.

overbear, *v.* **1** to ignore: "We breath'd our counsel: but it pleas'd your highness/ To overbear it . . ." *K John,* IV, ii, 36–37. **2** to overrule: "Egeus, I will overbear your will;/ For in the temple . . . These couples shall eternally be knit." *M N Dream,* IV, i, 178–180.

overblown, *adj.* blown over; evaporated: "To smile at scapes and perils overblown." *Shrew,* V, ii, 3.

overboard, *v.* to go overboard; be jettisoned: "Sir, your queen must overboard; the sea works/ high, the wind is loud . . ." *Per,* III, i, 47–48.

overborne, *past part.* of **overbear. 1** overruled: "Ay, so the bishop be not overborne." *1 Hen 6,* III, i, 53. **2** overwhelmed; overcome: ". . . the ecstasy hath so much overborne her that my/ daughter is sometime afeard . . ." *M Ado,* II, iii, 148–149. **3** overflowed: "Hath every pelting river made so proud/ That they have overborne their continents." *M N Dream,* II, i, 91–92.

overbulk, *v.* to overwhelm: "Or, shedding, breed a nursery of like evil/ To overbulk us all." *Tr & Cr,* I, iii, 318–319.

over-charged, *adj.* overcrowded; overloaded: "If the ground be over-charged, you were best stick/ her." *Two Gent,* I, i, 99–100.

overcome, *v.* **1** to pass overhead of: "Can such things be,/ And overcome us like a summer's cloud . . ." *Mac,* III, iv, 109–110. **2** to conquer: ". . . make a conquest of unhappy men,/ Whereas no glory's got to overcome." *Per,* I, iv, 69–70.

overfar, *adv.* to any great extent: "I could not with such estimable wonder/ overfar believe that . . ." *T Night,* II, i, 26–27.

overfly, *v.* to fly farther or faster [than]: "Outstripping crows that strive to overfly them." *Ven & Ad,* 324.

overglance, *v.* to read or look over: "I will overglance the superscript." *Love's L,* IV, ii, 126.

over-go or **overgo,** *v.* to go beyond; exceed or surpass: ". . . there appears a face/ That over-goes my blunt invention quite . . ." *Sonn 103,* 6–7.

overgone, *adj.* overcome or overpowered (by): "Sad-hearted men, much overgone with care,/ Here sits a king more woeful than you are." *3 Hen 6,* II, v, 123.

over-handled, *adj.* overused; overfamiliar: ". . . you will fall again/ Into your idle over-handled theme." *Ven & Ad,* 769–770.

overhold, *v.* to overestimate: ". . . add/ That if he overhold his price so much/ We'll none of him . . ." *Tr & Cr,* II, iii, 134–136.

overlive, *v.* to survive: ". . . concludes in hearty prayers/ That your attempts may overlive the hazard . . ." *2 Hen 4,* IV, i, 14–15.

overlook, *v.* **1** to overtop; look down upon: "Gallops the zodiac in his glistering coach,/ And overlooks the highest-peering hills . . ." *T Andr,* II, i, 7–8. **2** to read; peruse: ". . . when thou shalt have overlooked/ this, give these fellows some means to the King." *Ham,* IV, vi, 12–13.

over-lusty, *adj.* **1** too full of high spirits; over-joyful: "The confident and over-lusty French/ Do the low-rated English play at dice . . ." *Hen 5,* IV, Chorus, 18–19. **2 over-lusty at legs,** given to wandering; also, poss. ref. to one who has run away from service: ". . . when a man's over-lusty at legs, then he wears/ wooden nether-stocks." *Lear,* II, iv, 10–11.

over-matching, *adj.* overpowering: ". . . swim against the tide/ And spend her strength with over-matching waves." *3 Hen 6,* I, iv, 20–21.

over-name, *v.* to read off a list of: "I pray thee over-name them, and as thou namest/ them, I will describe them . . ." *Merch,* I, ii, 35–36.

overnight, *n.* **at overnight,** last evening; last night: "If I had given you this at overnight/ She might have been o'erta'en . . ." *All's W,* III, iv, 23–24.

overpass, *v.* to spend; pass: "In prison hast thou spent a pilgrimage,/ And like a hermit overpass'd thy days." *1 Hen 6,* II, v, 116–117.

overpeer or **over-peer,** *v.* **1** to look down on; tower over: ". . . the pageants of the sea,/ Do overpeer the petty traffickers/ That cur'sy to them . . ." *Merch,* I, i, 11–13. **2** to overflow [with redundant "of"]: "The ocean, overpeering of his list [boundary],/ Eats not the flats with more impetuous haste . . ." *Ham,* IV, v, 99–100.

overplus, *n.* surplus: ". . . sent all thy treasure, with/ His bounty overplus." *Ant & Cleo,* IV, vi, 21–22.

over-red, *v.* to cover with red; here, with blood: "Go, prick thy face, and over-red thy fear,/ Thou lily-liver'd boy." *Mac,* V, iii, 14–15.

over-ride, *v.* to overtake; catch up to on horseback: "My lord, I over-rode him on the way,/ And he is furnish'd with no certainties . . ." *2 Hen 4,* I, i, 30–31.

overscutched, *adj.* exhausted by use; worn-out: ". . . sung those tunes/ to the overscutched housewives that he heard the/ carmen whistle . . ." *2 Hen 4,* III, ii, 310–312.

oversee, *v.* to be the executor of: "Thou Collatine, shalt oversee this will . . ." *Luc,* 1205.

overseen, *adj.* deceived; betrayed: "How was I overseen that thou shalt see it!" *Luc,* 1206.

overset, *v.* to upset or overturn: ". . . the winds thy sighs . . . Without a sudden calm will overset/ Thy tempest-tossed body." *Rom & Jul,* III, v, 134–137.

overshade, *v.* to cover with shade: ". . . the elder-tree/ Which overshades the mouth of that same pit . . ." *T Andr,* II, iii, 272–273.

overshine or **over-shine,** *v.* **1** to outshine: ". . . like the stately Phoebe 'mongst her nymphs/ Dost overshine the gallan'st dames of Rome . . ." *T Andr,* I, i, 316–317. **2** to illumine; shine upon: ". . . join our lights together,/ And over-shine the earth . . ." *3 Hen 6,* II, i, 37–38.

over-shoes, *adv.* over the tops of one's shoes: ". . . she sweats, a man may/ go over-shoes in the grime of it." *Errors,* III, ii, 101–102.

overshot, *adj.* **1** wide of the mark; off target: "So study evermore is overshot . . ." *Love's L,* I, i, 141. **2** bested in shoot-

ing: "'Tis not the first time you were overshot." *Hen 5,* III, vii, 125.

overslip, *v.* to pass unheeded; escape or evade: "Which all this time hath overslipp'd her thought . . ." *Luc,* 1576.

over-swear, *v.* to swear again; reaffirm: "And all those sayings will I over-swear/ And all those swearings keep as true . . ." *T Night,* V, i, 267–268.

overtake, *v.* to catch up with: "Hear me one word."/ "I'll overtake you." *Lear,* V, i, 39.

overthrow, *n.* annihilation: "Whose misadventur'd piteous overthrows/ Doth with their death bury their parents' strife." *Rom & Jul,* Prol., 7–8.

over-top, *v.* (of a plant) to grow too tall; here, to exceed one's authority: ". . . who t' advance, and who/ To trash for overtopping . . ." *Temp,* I, ii, 80–81.

overture, *n.* **1** discovery; disclosure: ". . . it was he/ That made the overture of thy treasons to us . . ." *Lear,* III, vii, 87–88. **2** fanfare; ado: "And I wish, my liege,/ You had . . . tried it,/ Without more overture." *W Tale,* II, i, 170–172. **3** See **ovator.**

overwatch, *v.* to stay awake later than is customary: "I fear we shall outsleep the coming morn,/ As much as we this night have overwatch'd." *M N Dream,* V, i, 351–352.

over-weathered, *adj.* weatherbeaten: "With over-weather'd ribs and ragged sails—" *Merch,* II, vi, 18.

overween, *v.* to be presumptuous or conceited: "Mowbray, you overween to take it so." *2 Hen 4,* IV, i, 149.

overweening, *adj.* haughty; presumptuous: ". . . hurl down my gage/ Upon this overweening traitor's foot . . ." *Rich 2,* I, i, 146–147.

overwhelm, *v.* **1** to roll over on and crush: "I do here walk before thee like a sow that hath/ overwhelmed all her litter but one." *2 Hen 4,* I, ii, 10–11. **2** See **o'erwhelm.**

overwhelming, *adj.* overhanging: "In tatter'd weeds, with overwhelming brows . . ." *Rom & Jul,* V, i, 39.

Ovid, *n.* ref. here to the Roman poet's banishment: "As Ovid be an outcast quite abjur'd." *Shrew,* I, i, 33.

owd, *adj.* prob. var. of auld, old: "Then take thine owd cloak about thee." *Oth,* II, iii, 90.

owe, *v.* **1** to have; own or possess: "Churl, upon thy eyes I throw/ All the power this charm doth owe . . ." *M N Dream,*

II, ii, 77–78. **2** to mean or signify (to): "I care not for their names, they owe me/ nothing." *As You,* II, v, 19–20. **3** to own: ". . . ourselves we do not owe./ What is decreed, must be: and be this so." *T Night,* I, v, 314–315. **4 one time will owe another,** a more auspicious time will present itself: "Put not your worthy rage into your tongue./ One time will owe another." *Cor,* III, i, 239–240.

owed, *adj.* owned; sincere or genuine: "O! all that borrow'd motion seeming ow'd . . ." *Lover's Comp,* 327.

owedst, *v.* [you] enjoyed: ". . . that sweet sleep/ Which thou owedst yesterday." *Oth,* III, iii, 337–338.

owest, *v.* [you] own: "Lend less than thou owest . . ." *Lear,* I, iv, 126.

owl, screech owl, regarded as a portent of death: "It was the owl that shriek'd, the fatal bellman,/ Which gives the stern'st good-night." *Mac,* II, ii, 3–4.

ox, *n.* fool: "I am made an ass."/ "Ay, and an ox too . . ." *Wives,* V, v, 120–121.

Oxford, *n.* ref. to Cardinal College, founded by Wolsey as part of the University; name later changed to Christ Church: "Those twins of learning that he rais'd in you,/ Ipswich and Oxford . . ." *Hen 8,* IV, ii, 58–59.

ox-head, *n.* symbol of cuckoldry: "I would set an ox-head to your lion's hide,/ And make a monster of you." *K John,* II, i, 292–293.

oxlip, *n.* small white flower, resembling both the cowslip and the primrose: "Where oxlips and the nodding violet grows . . ." *M N Dream,* II, i, 250.

oyes, *n.* [often cap.] the cry of "Hear ye!": "On whose bright crest Fame with her loud'st Oyes/ Cries 'This is he' . . ." *Tr & Cr,* IV, v, 142–143.

P

pace, *n.* **1** manner of walking; carriage: ". . . her eyes as jewel-like/ And cas'd as richly; in pace another Juno . . ." *Per,* V, i, 110–111. **2** (in the training of a horse) discipline, esp. holding to a desirable gait; here, applied to the Clown: ". . . indeed he has no pace, but runs where he will." *All's W,* IV, v, 63–64. **3** movement: ". . . like a dial-hand/ Steal from his figure, and no pace perceived . . ." *Sonn 104,* 9–10. **4 hold pace in,** to keep pace with: ". . . hold me pace in deep experiments." *1 Hen 4,* III, i, 46.
—*v.* **5** to manage or direct [term in horsemanship]: "If you can pace your wisdom/ In that good path that I would wish it go . . ." *Meas,* IV, iii, 132–133. **6** to walk: ". . . one would take it,/ That never see [saw] 'em pace before . . ." *Hen 8,* I, iii, 11–12.

paced, *past part.* schooled; trained [as in the training of horses]: "My lord, she's not pac'd yet; you must take some/ pains to work her to your manage." *Per,* IV, vi, 62–63.

pack[1] *v.* **1** to gather one's belongings and depart: often used as a command: "Hence, pack! There's gold; you came for gold, ye slaves." *Timon,* V, i, 111. **2 be packing,** begone!: "Be packing, therefore, thou that wast a knight . . ." *1 Hen 6,* IV, i, 46. **3 set one packing,** cause one to depart in haste: "This man shall set me packing." *Ham,* III, iv, 213.

pack[2] *v.* **1** to scheme or conspire: "What are you packing, sirrah?/ Come hither: ah, you precious pandar!" *Cymb,* III, v, 81–82. **2** to make a deal; reach an accommodation: "Go pack with him, and give the mother gold,/ And tell them both the circumstance of all . . ." *T Andr,* IV, ii, 156–157. **3 pack cards with,** to stack the cards against someone in league with [another]: ". . . she, Eros, has/ Pack'd cards with Caesar, and false-play'd my glory . . ." *Ant & Cleo,* IV, xiv, 18–19.
—*n.* **4 packs and sects,** cliques and factions: ". . . packs and sects of great ones/ That ebb and flow by th' moon." *Lear,* V, iii, 18–19.

packed, *past part.* **1** involved, esp. as an accomplice: ". . . Margaret,/ Who I believe was pack'd in all this wrong . . ." *M Ado,* V, i, 292–293. **2 packed with,** in league with: "That goldsmith there, were he not pack'd with her,/ Could witness it . . ." *Errors,* V, i, 219–220.

packing, *n.* **1** plotting: "Here's packing, with a witness, to deceive us all." *Shrew,* V, i, 108. **2** plot or intrigue: "What hath been seen,/ Either in snuffs and packings of the Dukes . . ." *Lear,* III, i, 25–26.
—*adj.* **3** furtive; underhand: "This packing evil, we both shall tremble for it." *Edw 3,* II, ii, 165.

pack of matter, *n.* messenger's news likened to items in a peddler's pack: "Pour out the pack of matter to mine ear . . ." *Ant & Cleo,* II, v, 53.

packthread, *n.* twine or cord used to tie up packages: "Remnants of packthread and old cakes of roses/ Were thinly scatter'd to make up a show." *Rom & Jul,* V, i, 47–48.

Pacorus, *n.* son of Orodes, King of Parthia: "Thy Pacorus, Orodes,/ Pays this for Marcus Crassus." *Ant & Cleo,* III, i, 4–5.

paction, *n.* compact: ". . . never may ill office . . . Thrust in between the paction of these kingdoms . . ." *Hen 5,* V, ii, 381–383.

paddle, *v.* **1** to finger or handle amorously; fondle: ". . . paddling in your neck with his damn'd fingers . . ." *Ham,* III, iv, 187. **2 paddling palms,** amorous clasping of hands: "But to be paddling palms . . . As now they are . . ." *W Tale,* I, ii, 115–116.

Paddock, *n.* dialect word for "toad"; here, the witch's familiar: "I come, Graymalkin!"/ "Paddock calls." *Mac,* I, i, 8–9.

pagan, *adj.* **1** unenlightened; unbelieving: "What a pagan rascal is this, an infidel!" *1 Hen 4,* II, iii, 29.

—*n.* **2** strumpet; courtesan: "... Mistress Doll Tearsheet."/ "What pagan may that be?" *2 Hen 4*, II, ii, 145–146.

page, *n.* **1** young male servant: "He whin'd and roar'd away your victory,/ That pages blush'd at him ..." *Cor*, V, vi, 98–99.
—*v.* **2** to follow, as a page: "... page thy heels/ And skip when thou point'st out?" *Timon*, IV, iii, 226–227.

pageant, *n.* **1** ships compared to elaborate floats in street parades of London: "Like signiors and rich burghers on the flood,/ Or as it were the pageants of the sea ..." *Merch*, I, i, 10–11. **2** mere show: "... 'tis a pageant,/ To keep us in false gaze ..." *Oth*, I, iii, 18–19.
—*v.* **3** to mimic: "And with ridiculous and awkward action ... He pageants us." *Tr & Cr*, I, iii, 149–151.

pageants of delight, *n.* staged entertainments popular around Pentecost: "... for at Pentecost,/ When all our pageants of delight were play'd ..." *Two Gent*, IV, iv, 156–157.

paid home, *v.* repaid in full: "All my services/ You have paid home ..." *W Tale*, V, iii, 3–4.

pain, *n.* **1** hard labor; intense effort: "Which with pain purchas'd doth inherit pain [discomfort] ..." *Love's L*, I, i, 73. **2** suffering; torment: "Unless the Lady Bona quite [relieve] his pain." *3 Hen 6*, III, iii, 128. **3** [pl.] **a.** efforts; trouble: "Kind gentlemen, your pains/ Are register'd where every day I turn ..." *Mac*, I, iii, 151–152. **b.** chores; tasks: "Since thou dost give me pains,/ Let me remember thee what thou hast promis'd ..." *Temp*, I, ii, 242–243. **c.** menstrual cramps: "... may your pains, six months [of the year],/ Be quite contrary [abnormally painful]." *Timon*, IV, iii, 145–146. **4** punishment: "... she that makes me sin awards me pain." *Sonn 141*, 14. **5** penalty; here, the death penalty: "And his offence is ... Accountant to the law upon that pain." *Meas*, II, iv, 85–86. **6 in which your pain,** in which endeavor your efforts will be: "... when we have found the King, in which your pain/ That way [direction], I'll this ..." *Lear*, III, i, 53–54. **7 usual pain,** daily toil: "Was it not to refresh the mind of man/ After his studies or his usual pain?" *Shrew*, III, i, 11–12.

pained impotent, *n.* [construed as pl.] those made helpless by pain: "With all the fierce endeavour of your wit/ To enforce the pained impotent to smile." *Love's L*, V, ii, 845–846.

painful, *adj.* **1** hardworking; also, experiencing pain: "The painful warrior famoused [renowned] for fight ..." *Sonn 25*, 9. **2** laborious; difficult: "Till painful study shall outwear three years,/ No woman may approach his silent court ..." *Love's L*, II, i, 23–24.

paint, *v.* **1** to use cosmetics, esp. excessively: "Does Bridget paint still, Pompey? Ha?" *Meas*, III, ii, 76. **2** to apply cosmetics (to): "... when was he wont to wash his face?/ Yea, or to paint himself?" *M Ado*, III, ii, 50–51. **3** to disguise: "Painting my age with beauty of thy days [youth]." *Sonn 62*, 14. **4** to flatter: "Nay, never paint me now:/ Where fair is not, praise cannot mend the brow." *Love's L*, IV, i, 16–17. **5 paint out,** to detail; enumerate: "The word is too good to paint out her wickedness." *M Ado*, III, ii, 98. **6 paint your face,** to besmear your face with blood from my scratches: "To comb your noddle with a three-legg'd stool,/ And paint your face ..." *Shrew*, I, i, 64–65.

painted, *adj.* **1** false; insincere: "... my beauty, though but mean,/ Needs not the painted flourish of your praise ..." *Love's L*, II, i, 13–14. **2** artificial; unreal or make-believe: "Poor painted queen, vain flourish of my fortune ..." *Rich 3*, I, iii, 241. **3** painted on a board as a lure to sightseers: "Were I in England now ... and/ had but this fish painted ..." *Temp*, II, ii, 28–29.

painted cloth, *n.* cloth painted to resemble a tapestry, often embellished with proverbs, moral precepts, etc., and used as wall decoration: "... slaves/ as ragged as Lazarus in the painted cloth ..." *1 Hen 4*, IV, ii, 24–25.

painted counterfeit, *n.* portrait: "Much liker [a closer resemblance] than your painted counterfeit ..." *Sonn 16*, 9.

painted imagery, *n.* effect resembling a painted cloth: "You would have thought ... that all the walls/ With painted imagery had said at once/ '... Welcome, Bolingbroke!'" *Rich 2*, V, ii, 12–17.

painting, *n.* **1** use of cosmetics: "For native blood is counted painting now ..." *Love's L*, IV, iii, 259. **2** representation; hence, manifestation: "This is the very painting of your fear ..." *Mac*, III, iv, 60. **3** exact likeness: "Some jay of Italy/ (Whose mother was her painting) hath betray'd him ..." *Cymb*, III, iv, 50–51.

pair of shears, *n.* from the proverb. "we two are cut from the same cloth": "Well, there went but a pair of shears between us." *Meas*, I, ii, 27.

pair of spectacles, *n.* doubly sad sight; that is, two tragic lovers: "What a pair of spectacles is here! Let me embrace, too." *Tr & Cr*, IV, iv, 13.

Pair-Taunt, *n.* winning hand in the obsolete card game of Post and Pair: "So Pair-Taunt like would I o'ersway his state/ That he should be my fool, and I his fate." *Love's L*, V, ii, 67–68.

pajock, *n.* prob. the peacock, regarded as a pompous and lecherous bird: "This realm dismantled was/ Of Jove himself, and now reigns here/ A very, very—pajock." [The expected end rhyme, apparently, was "ass"] *Ham*, III, ii, 276–278.

palabras, *n. pl.* [Spanish] short form of *pocas palabras,* few words: "Comparisons are odorous: *palabras,* neighbour/ Verges." *M Ado,* III, v, 15–16.

Palamedes, *n.* leader of Greek forces; succeeded Agamemnon as commander: "Patroclus ta'en or slain; and Palamedes/ Sore hurt and bruis'd . . ." *Tr & Cr,* V, v, 13–14.

palate, *v.* to taste or savor: ". . . never palates more the dung,/ The beggar's nurse, and Caesar's. *Ant & Cleo,* V, ii, 7–8.

pale¹, *n.* **1** fence; here, the encompassing arms of Venus: "'I have hemm'd thee here/ Within the circuit of this ivory pale . . .'" *Ven & Ad,* 229–230. **2** enclosure; here, England, whose white cliffs turn back the sea: ". . . that pale, that white-fac'd shore,/ Whose foot spurns back the ocean's roaring tides . . ." *K John,* II, 1, 23–24. **3** paling; also, enclosed grounds or a walled garden: "Why should we, in the compass of a pale,/ Keep law and form . . ." *Rich 2,* III, iv, 40–41. **4 pales and forts,** defenses; here, those that protect reason: "Oft breaking down the pales and forts of reason . . ." *Ham,* I, iv, 28.
—*v.* **5** to enclose with or as if with a fence: "And will you pale your head in Henry's glory . . ." *3 Hen 6,* I, iv, 103. **6 pale in,** to encircle or surround; here, in the manner of fence stakes: "Behold, the English beach/ Pales in the flood with men, with wives, and boys . . ." *Hen 5,* V, Chor. 9–10.

pale², *adj.* **1** humbled; here, the constant reminder that Macbeth is a mere human: "Cancel, and tear to pieces, that great bond/ Which keeps me pale!" *Mac,* III, ii, 49–50. **2** unmoved; unimpressed: "Then, if you can/ Be pale, I beg but leave to air this jewel: see!" *Cymb,* II, iv, 95–96.
—*n.* **3** pallor; perh. also wordplay on "confinement": "For the red blood reigns in the winter's pale." *W Tale,* IV, iii, 4.

paled, *adj.* pale; pallid: "Of paled pearls and rubies red as blood . . ." *Lover's Comp,* 198.

pale policy, *n.* intrigue born of fear; desperation: ". . . and. with pale policy/ Seek to divert the English purposes." *Hen 5,* II, Chor., 14–15.

palfrey, *n.* saddle horse, esp. one considered gentle enough for a woman to ride: "Provide two proper palfreys, black as jet,/ To hale thy vengeful waggon swift away . . ." *T Andr,* V, ii, 50–51.

palisadoes, *n. pl.* defense of iron-pointed stakes driven into the ground: "And thou hast talk'd/ . . . Of palisadoes, frontiers, parapets . . ." *1 Hen 4,* II, iii, 51–53.

pall¹, *v.* to wrap; enshroud: ". . . pall thee in the dunnest smoke of Hell . . ." *Mac,* I, v, 51.

pall², *v.* to falter: "Our indiscretion sometime serves us well/ When our deep plots do pall . . ." *Ham,* V, ii, 8–9.

Pallas, *n.* Athena, Greek goddess of wisdom [Roman: Minerva]: "Apollo, Pallas, Jove, or Mercury,/ Inspire me, that I may this treason find!" *T Andr,* IV, i, 66–67.

palled, *adj.* dwindled or faded: "[Aside] For this,/ I'll never follow thy pall'd fortunes more." *Ant & Cleo,* II, vii, 81–82.

pallet, *n.* rough or makeshift bed: ". . . liest thou in smoky cribs,/ Upon uneasy pallets stretching thee . . ." *2 Hen 4,* III, i, 9–10.

palliament, *n.* ceremonial mantle; cloak: ". . . the people of Rome . . . Send thee by me . . . This palliament of white and spotless hue . . ." *T Andr,* I, i, 179–182.

palm¹, *n.* **1** palm tree, Biblical symbol of flourishing righteousness: "You shall see him a palm in Athens again . . ." *Timon,* V, i, 11. **2** reward: ". . . what he shall receive of us in duty/ Gives us more palm in beauty than we have . . ." *Tr & Cr,* III, i, 152–153. **3 bear the palm,** to be victorious [lit., to carry off the palm of victory]: ". . . it doth amaze me/ A man of such a feeble temper should/ So get the start of the majestic world,/ And bear the palm alone." *J Caes,* I, ii, 127–130. **4 stale one's palm,** to degrade one's reputation; here, laurels: ". . . this thrice worthy and right valiant lord/ Shall not so stale his palm, nobly acquir'd . . ." *Tr & Cr,* II, iii, 191–192.

palm², *n.* **1** [usually pl.] upraised supplicating hands: ". . . the virginal palms of your daughters . . ." *Cor,* V, ii, 42. **2 dull thy palm,** to wear out one's hand; here, in indiscriminate welcoming: ". . . do not dull thy palm with entertainment/ Of each new-hatch'd, unfledg'd courage." *Ham,* I, iii, 64–65.

palmer, *n.* pilgrim: "My sceptre for a palmer's walking staff . . ." *Rich 2,* III, iii, 150.

palmy, *adj.* flourishing; exalted: "In the most high and palmy state of Rome . . ." *Ham,* I, i, 116.

palpable, *adj.* obvious; clear: "I see thee yet, in form as palpable/ As this which now I draw." *Mac,* II, i, 40–41.

palpable-gross, *adj.* obviously crude: "This palpable-gross play hath well beguil'd/ The heavy gait [slow pace] of night." *M N Dream,* V, i, 353–354.

palsy, *n.* **cold palsies,** paralysis: ". . . lethargies, cold/ palsies, raw eyes, dirt-rotten livers, whissing lungs . . ." *Tr & Cr,* V, i, 18–19.

palter, *v.* to deceive; evade a truthful answer: ". . . what other bond/ Than secret Romans, that have spoke the word,/ And will not palter?" *J Caes,* II, i, 124–126.

paltry, *adj.* vile; contemptible: "A very dishonest paltry boy, and more a coward/ than a hare . . ." *T Night,* III, iv, 395–396.

paly, *adj.* pale: "Fain would I go to chafe his paly lips/ With twenty thousand kisses . . ." *2 Hen 6,* III, ii, 140–141.

pampered, *adj.* overindulged, esp. in sensual delights: ". . . those pamper'd animals/ That rage in savage sensuality." *M Ado,* IV, i, 60–61.

pamphlet, *n.* written statement; here, a list of accusations: "Com'st thou with deep-premeditated lines,/ With written pamphlets studiously devis'd . . ." *1 Hen 6,* III, i, 1–2.

pandar, *n.* var. of **pander;** procurer or go-between in amorous affairs: "Troilus the first employer of pandars . . ." *M Ado,* V, ii, 30.

Pandar, *n.* wordplay on name of Pandarus and "pander": "Ourself the merchant, and this sailing Pandar/ Our doubtful hope . . ." *Tr & Cr,* I, i, 103–104.

Pandarus, *n.* uncle of Cressida; acted as go-between in Troilus' courtship of her; here, the Clown is courting another tip: "I would play Lord Pandarus of Phrygia, sir, to/ bring a Cressida to this Troilus." *T Night,* III, i, 52–53.

pander, *v.* to procure for; here, indulge; cater to the whim of: "Since frost itself as actively doth burn/ And reason panders will." *Ham,* III, iv, 87–88.

pang, *v.* to torture: ". . . how thy memory/ Will then be pang'd by me." *Cymb,* III, iv, 96–97.

panging, *adj.* painful: ". . . 'tis a sufferance [suffering] panging/ As soul and body's severing." *Hen 8,* II, iii, 15–16.

pannier, *n.* large basket, usually carried on a horse or mule: "The turkeys in my pannier are/ quite starved." *1 Hen 4,* II, i, 25–26.

Pannonians, *n.* inhabitants of Roman province of Pannonia, in SE Europe, more or less coextensive with present-day Hungary: ". . . the common men are now in action/ 'Gainst the Pannonians and Dalmatians . . ." *Cymb,* III, viii, 2–3.

pant, *n.* [usually pl.] heartbeats; palpitations: ". . . leap thou . . . Through proof of harness to my heart, and there/ Ride on the pants triumphing!" *Ant & Cleo,* IV, viii, 14–16.

pantaloon, *n.* foolish old man, a stock character from medieval Italian comedy: "The sixth age shifts/ Into the lean and slipper'd pantaloon . . ." *As You,* II, vii, 157–158.

pantler, *n.* pantry servant: ". . . a would have made a/ good pantler, a would ha' chipped bread well." *2 Hen 4,* II, iv, 234–235.

pap[1], *n.* nipple or teat: ". . . sweet Cupid: thou hast/ thumped him with thy bird-bolt under the left pap [in the heart]." *Love's L,* IV, iii, 21–22.

pap[2], *n.* **pap with a hatchet,** extension of pap meaning "baby food"; alluding to saying that pap with a spoon is often fol. by pap with a hatchet [beheading]: "Ye shall have a hempen caudle then, and pap with/ a hatchet." *2 Hen 6,* IV, vii, 85–86.

paper, *n.* **1** piece of writing: "For every vulgar paper to rehearse?" *Sonn 38,* 4. **2** wrapping: "Look'd he/ O' th' inside of the paper?" *Hen 8,* III, ii, 77–78. **3 in paper,** as promissory notes: "I fear me thou wilt give away thyself in paper shortly." *Timon,* I, ii, 243. **4 wear papers,** (of a prisoner in the pillory) to wear a placard, usually on the back, proclaiming one's offense: "Why, he comes in like a perjure, wearing papers." *Love's L,* IV, iii, 45.
—*v.* **5** to enter on a list: "Must fetch him in he papers [can call in anyone whose name he puts on the list] . . ." *Hen 8,* I, i, 80.

Paphlagonia, *n.* country in Asia Minor: "Philadelphos, king/ Of Paphlagonia: the Thracian king Adallas . . ." *Ant & Cleo,* III, vi, 70–71.

Paphos, *n.* town on the island of Cyprus, reputed birthplace of Venus, to whom the dove was sacred: ". . . so/ With dove of Paphos might the crow/ Vie feathers white." *Per,* IV, Chor., 31–33.

Paracelsus, *n.* Swiss physician of the 16th cent.: "So I say—both of Galen and Paracelsus." *All's W,* II, iii, 11.

paradox, *n.* object of ridicule; mockery; travesty: ". . . what is or is not, serves/ As stuff for these two to make paradoxes." *Tr & Cr,* I, iii, 183–184.

paragon, *n.* **1** example of perfection; here, incomparable beauty: ". . . when he shall come and find/ Our paragon to all reports thus blasted . . ." *Per,* IV, i, 34–35.
—*v.* **2** to surpass: ". . . a maid/ That paragons description . . ." *Oth,* II, i, 61–62. **3** to compare with: "If thou with Caesar paragon again/ My man of men." *Ant & Cleo,* I, v, 71–72. **4** to hold up as unrivaled: ". . . the primest [finest] creature/ That's paragon'd o'th'world." *Hen 8,* II, iv, 227–228.

parallel, *n.* **1** deep wrinkle; furrow: "And delves the parallels in beauty's brow . . ." *Sonn 60,* 10.
—*v.* **2** to liken; compare: "My young remembrance cannot parallel/ A fellow to it." *Mac,* II, iii, 63–64.

paraquito, *n.* small parrot, esp. a parakeet (term of endearment): "Come, come, you paraquito, answer me . . ." *1 Hen 4,* II, iii, 86.

Parca, *n.* (in Roman myth.) any of the Parcae, the three Fates, who spun the thread of life, determined its length, then cut it when one's destiny was fulfilled: ". . . dost thou thirst, base Trojan/ To have me fold up Parca's fatal web [kill you]?" *Hen 5,* V, i, 19–21.

parcel *n.* **1** item on a bill: ". . . his eloquence the/ parcel of a reckoning." *1 Hen 4,* II, iv, 98–99. **2** [pl.] **a.** details: "I sent your Grace/ The parcels and particulars of our grief . . ." *2 Hen 4,* IV, ii, 35–36. **b.** separate items or features: ". . . had they mark'd him/ In parcels as I did, would have gone near/ To fall in love with him . . ." *As You,* III, v, 124–126. **3** essential element: "It is a branch and parcel of mine oath . . ." *Errors,* V, i, 106. **4** group or party: "I am glad this parcel of wooers are so/ reasonable . . ." *Merch,* I, ii, 104–105. **5** part; also, bit or fraction: ". . . many a thousand/ Which now mistrust no parcel of my fear . . ." *3 Hen 6,* V, vi, 37–38.
—*adj.* **6** partly or part-time: "A tapster, sir; parcel bawd; one that/ serves a bad woman . . ." *Meas,* II, i, 62–63.
—*v.* **7** to divide and give out in small portions: "Their woes are parcell'd, mine is general." *Rich 3,* II, ii, 81.

parcel-gilt, *adj.* partly gilded: "Thou didst swear to me upon a parcel-gilt/ goblet . . ." *2 Hen 4,* II, i, 84–85.

pard, *n.* leopard: "Full of strange oaths, and bearded like the pard . . ." *As You,* II, vii, 150.

pardon, *n.* **1** permission; here, to withdraw: ". . . your pardon and my return shall be the end of my business." *Ham,* III, ii, 309–310. **2 under your pardon,** if you'll allow me to finish: "Under your pardon. You must note beside/ That we have tried the utmost of our friends . . ." *J Caes,* IV, iii, 212–213.
—*v.* **3** to excuse: "Even now about it. I will pardon you." *Two Gent,* III, ii, 97. **4 pardon me,** I beg to disagree: "He is elder."/ "Pardon me, pardon me." *Tr & Cr,* I, ii, 82–83.

pardon-me's, *n.* fellows who affect foreign manners: ". . . these strange flies,/ these fashion-mongers, these 'pardon-me's' . . ." *Rom & Jul,* II, iv, 32–33.

parfect, *v.* dial. pron. of "perfect"; misuse for "perform" or "present": ". . . for mine own/ part, I am, as they say, but to parfect one man in/ one poor man . . ." *Love's L,* V, ii, 499–500.

Paris, *n.* (in Greek legend) son of Priam, the king of Troy; he abducted Helen, wife of Menelaus, the king of Sparta, precipitating the Trojan War: ". . . thus he goes,/ As did the youthful Paris once to Greece;/ With hope to find the like event in love . . ." *1 Hen 6,* V, v, 103–105.

Paris-balls, *n.* tennis balls: "As matching to his youth and vanity,/ I did present him with the Paris-balls." *Hen 5,* II, iv, 130–131.

Parish-garden, *n.* site of bull-baiting in London and notorious for noisy crowds: "You'll leave your noise anon ye rascals: do you take/ the court for Parish-garden?" *Hen 8,* V, iii, 1–2.

parish top, *n.* large top kept spinning with a whip; used as means of recreation when parishoners were prevented by weather from working outside: ". . . will not drink to my niece till his brains turn o'/ th' toe, like a parish top." *T Night,* I, iii, 41–42.

Paris Louvre, *n.* seat of the French royal court: "He'll make your Paris Louvre shake for it . . ." *Hen 5,* II, iv, 132.

paritor, *n.* apparitor, minor official of an ecclesiastical court, who issued summonses for moral offenses: "Sole imperator and great general/ Of trotting paritors . . ." *Love's L,* III, i, 180–181.

park, *n.* **1** enclosed tract of land adjoining a castle or country mansion: "That roan shall be my throne . . . Bid Butler lead him forth into the park." *1 Hen 4,* II, iii, 71–73. **2** tract of land enclosed by royal decree to protect game: "Over park, over pale,/ Thorough flood, thorough fire,/ I do wander everywhere . . ." *M N Dream,* II, i, 2–4.
—*v.* **3** to enclose; encircle: "How are we park'd and bounded in a pale—" *1 Hen 6,* IV, ii, 45.

parle, short form of **parley,** pron. as one syllable. *v.* **1** to talk; hold a discussion: "Their purpose is to parle, to court and dance . . ." *Love's L,* V, ii, 122.
—*n.* **2** talk or chat: ". . . the fair resort of gentlemen/ That every day with parle encounter me . . ." *Two Gent,* I, ii, 3–4. **3** parley; summons to a truce conference: ". . . sound so base a parle, my teeth shall tear/ The slavish motive of recanting fear . . ." *Rich 2,* I, i, 192–193. **4** discussion or other encounter between contending forces; also, negotiations: ". . . the nature of our quarrel yet never brooked/ parle . . ." *Shrew,* I, i, 114–115. **5** argument; dispute; here, verbal abuse: "Rome's emperor, and nephew, break the parle . . ." *T Andr,* V, iii, 19.

parley, *n.* **1** conference, under truce, between warring parties, often announced by trumpets: used as a stage direction. **2** manner of speaking: ". . . but for shame/ In such a parley should I answer thee." *1 Hen 4,* III, i, 196–197.
—*v.* **3 parley to,** to confer with; try to reach an understanding with: ". . . because you are a banish'd man . . . we parley to you . . ." *Two Gent,* IV, i, 59–60.

parling, *adj.* speaking: ". . . she that never cop'd with stranger eyes,/ Could pick no meaning from their parling looks . . ." *Luc,* 99–100.

parlous, *adj.* **1** alarming: "By'r lakin, a parlous fear." *M N Dream,* III, i, 12. **2** clever or cunning; here, precocious: "A parlous boy: go to, you are too shrewd." *Rich 3,* II, iv, 35. **3** same in wordplay with "perilous": "O, 'tis a parlous boy,/ Bold, quick, ingenious, forward, capable . . ." *Rich 3,* III, i, 154–155.

parmacity, *n.* spermaceti, a fatty substance from whales used to make a healing ointment: ". . . the sovereignest thing on earth/ Was parmacity for an inward bruise . . ." *1 Hen 4,* I, iii, 56–57.

parrot, *n.* **speak parrot,** to talk gibberish: "Drunk? and speak parrot? and/ squabble? swagger? swear?" *Oth,* II, iii, 271–272.

parrot-teacher, *n.* person who repeats trite phrases: "Well, you are a rare parrot-teacher." *M Ado,* I, i, 128.

part, *v.* **1** depart [from]: ". . . 'thus misery doth part/ The flux of company.'" *As You,* II, i, 51–52. **2** to halve; divide: ". . . a fair lord calf."/ "Let's part the word." *Love's L,* V, ii, 248–249. **3** to separate: "Let this sad interim like the ocean be/ Which parts the shore . . ." *Sonn 56,* 9–10. **4** to share: ". . . let's away,/ To part the glories of this happy day." *J Caes,* V, v, 80–81. **5 part away,** to go away; depart: ". . . if the trial of the law o'ertake ye,/ You'll part away disgrac'd." *Hen 8,* III, i, 96–97. **6 part bread,** to break bread; share a meal: ". . . the fellow that sits next/ him, now parts bread with him . . ." *Timon,* I, ii, 46–47. **7 part the time,** to split in half the difference in time: "We'll part the time between 's then . . ." *W Tale,* I, ii, 18. **8 part with,** to depart from: ". . . he was with me then,/ Who parted with me to go fetch a chain . . ." *Errors,* V, i, 220–221.
—*n.* **9** role; function; charge: "It is our part and promise to th' Athenians/ To speak with Timon." *Timon,* V, i, 119–120. **10** [often pl.] action or instance of conduct: ". . . some stubborn and uncourteous parts/ We had conceiv'd against him." *T Night,* V, i, 360–361. **11** [pl.] person's good qualities; also, good looks, appearance, etc.: "A man of sovereign [superlative] parts he is esteem'd,/ Well fitted in arts, glorious in arms . . ." *Love's L,* II, i, 44–45. **12** natural trait: "It is the part of men to fear and tremble/ When the most mighty gods . . . send/ Such dreadful heralds to astonish us." *J Caes,* I, iii, 54–56. **13** share, as in a business: "Is this your speeding? Nay then, good night our part." *Shrew,* II, i, 294. **14** [often pl.] voices or instruments required to render a musical composition: "My lessons make no music in three parts." *Shrew,* III, i, 58. **15** [often pl.] tasks; duties: "You have among you many a purchas'd slave,/ Which . . . You use in abject and in slavish parts . . ." *Merch,* IV, i, 90–92. **16** side or faction; here,

forces: "Throw in the frozen bosoms of our part/ Hot coals of vengeance!" *2 Hen 6,* V, ii, 35–36. **17** behalf: "Upon thy part I can set down a story/ Of faults concealed . . ." *Sonn 88,* 6–7. **18** [pl.] endowments; here, wealth and rank: "The parts that fortune hath bestow'd upon her . . ." *T Night,* II, iv, 84. **19 a conquering part,** share in victory: "What heart receives from hence a conquering part . . ." *Tr & Cr,* I, iii, 352. **20 contrary parts,** opposing sides: "And, banding themselves in contrary parts,/ Do pelt . . . at one another's pate . . ." *1 Hen 6,* III, i, 81–82. **21 in good part,** with kindness: "But though my cates be mean, take them in good part . . ." *Errors,* III, i, 28. **22 not in part,** not partially [but completely]: "And was my own fee-simple, not in part . . ." *Lover's Comp,* 144. **23 on part and part,** on one side or the other: "While we were interchanging thrusts and blows/ Came more and more, and fought on part and part . . ." *Rom & Jul,* I, i, 111–112. **24 out of my part,** not part of my speech: "I can say little more than I have studied, and/ that question's out of my part." *T Night,* I, v, 179–180. **25 part of men,** natural reaction: "It is the part of men to fear and tremble . . ." *J Caes,* I, iii, 54. **26 quit their own part,** abandon their [proper] function [as spectators]: "Quit their own part, and in obsequious fondness/ Crowd to his presence . . ." *Meas,* II, iv, 28–29. **27 take my part,** say the words I should say: "You take my part from me, sir . . ." *Cor,* IV, iii, 51. **28 to have part in someone's blood,** to have a blood relationship to another: ". . . the part I had in Woodstock's blood [the relationship of brother]/ Doth more solicit me than your exclaims . . ." *Rich 2,* I, ii, 1–2.

partake, *v.* **1** to communicate; impart: ". . . our mind partakes/ Her private actions to your secrecy . . ." *Per,* I, i, 153–154. **2** to take sides: "When I against myself with thee partake?" *Sonn 149,* 2. **3** to share: ". . . his false cunning/ (Not meaning to partake with me in danger) . . ." *T Night,* V, i, 84–85.

partaker, *n.* supporter or sympathizer: "For your partaker Pole, and you yourself,/ I'll note you in my book of memory . . ." *1 Hen 6,* II, iv, 100–101.

part-created, *adj.* half-finished; partly done: ". . . half-through,/ Gives o'er, and leaves his part-created cost . . ." *2 Hen 4,* I, iii, 59–60.

parted, *adj.* **1** unfocused; out of focus: "Methinks I see these things with parted eye . . ." *M N Dream,* IV, i, 188. **2** divided; shared: "The old proverb is very well parted between my/ master Shylock and you sir . . ." *Merch,* II, ii, 142–143.

Parthia, *n.* **1** country in NE Persia: "In Parthia did I take thee prisoner . . ." *J Caes,* V, iii, 37. **2 darting Parthia,** allusion to Parthian soldiers, who attacked swiftly on horseback, shooting arrows from close range and as they retreated: "Now, darting Parthia, art thou struck . . ." *Ant & Cleo,* III, i, 1.

Parthian, *n.* famed Parthian soldier, loosing arrows while retreating: "Or like the Parthian I shall flying fight . . ." *Cymb,* I, vii, 20.

partial, *adj.* **1** showing partiality: "Canst thou, O partial sleep,/ give thy repose/ To the wet sea-boy . . ." *2 Hen 4,* III, i, 26–27. **2 come in partial,** to be introduced, esp. in a court of law, in favor of the accused: "Let mine own judgement pattern out my death,/ And nothing come in partial." *Meas,* II, i, 30–31.

partialize, *v.* to cause to become partial; compromise: "Such neighbor nearness . . . Should nothing privilege him nor partialize/ The unstooping firmness of my upright soul." *Rich 2,* I, i, 119–121.

partially, *adv.* through partiality: "Their own transgressions partially they smother." *Luc,* 634.

partial slander, *n.* charge of partiality: "A partial slander sought I to avoid,/ And in the sentence my own life destroy'd." *Rich 2,* I, iii, 241–242.

participate, *v.* to share or have in common with others: "I . . . am in that dimension grossly clad/ Which from the womb I did participate." *T Night,* V, i, 235–236.

participation, *n.* association; fellowship: ". . . thou hast lost thy princely privilege/ With vile participation." *1 Hen 4,* III, ii, 86–87.

particle, *n.* **every particle and utensil,** each particular item: "It shall be/ inventoried, and every particle and utensil/ labelled to my will." *T Night,* I, v, 248–250.

parti-colored, *adj.* variegated; multi-colored: ". . . the upper turf of earth doth boast/ His pride, perfumes, and parti-colored cost [splendor] . . ." *Edw 3,* I, ii, 152–153.

particular, *n.* **1** private gain or advantage: ". . . him that, his particular to foresee,/ Smells from the general weal." *Timon,* IV, iii, 161–162. **2** private or special duty: ". . . nor does/ The ministration and required office/ On my particular [my particular duties as a new husband]." *All's W,* II, v, 59–61. **3 by particulars,** to each person individually: "He's to make his requests by particulars . . ." *Cor,* II, iii, 44–45. **4 for his particular,** insofar as he personally is concerned: "For his particular, I'll receive him gladly . . ." *Lear,* II, iv, 294. **5 for your particular,** with respect to your own interest: "Yet I wish, sir,/ I mean for your particular, you had not/ Join'd in commission with him . . ." *Cor,* IV, vii, 12–14. **6 in love's particular,** especially in regard to a personal relationship: ". . . your bond of duty,/ As 'twere in love's particular, be more/ To me your friend, than any." *Hen 8,* III, ii, 188–190. **7 in most dear particular,** in a close personal relationship: ". . . was sometime

his general, who lov'd him/ In a most dear particular." *Cor,* V, i, 2–3. **8 in thine own particular,** insofar as you yourself are concerned: "O Antony . . . Forgive me in thine own particular . . ." *Ant & Cleo,* IV, ix, 18–20. **9 my more particular,** my personal concern: "My more particular . . . Is Fulvia's death." *Ant & Cleo,* I, iii, 54–56.
—*adj.* **10** personal or private: "I will have it in a/ particular ballad else [one about me personally], with mine own picture on the/ top on't." *2 Hen 4,* IV, iii, 46–48. **11** same in wordplay with "general": "Where's our general?"/ "Here I am, thou particular fellow." *2 Hen 6,* IV, ii, 105–106. **12** limited; specific or individual: ". . . the success,/ Although particular, shall give a scantling/ Of good or bad . . ." *Tr & Cr,* I, iii, 340–342. **13** separate; single: ". . . what a hell of witchcraft lies/ In the small orb of one particular tear . . ." *Lover's Comp,* 288–289.

particularities, *n. pl.* inconsequential details; trifles: "Particularities and petty sounds/ To cease . . ." *2 Hen 6,* V, ii, 44–45.

particularize, *v.* to itemize: ". . . the leanness that afflicts us . . . is as an inventory to particularise their abundance . . ." *Cor,* I, i, 18–20.

partisan, *n.* lance topped with a wide, swordlike blade: "Shall I strike at it with my partisan?" *Ham,* I, i, 143.

partition, *n.* act of discriminating; distinction: ". . . can we not/ Partition make with spectacles so precious . . ." *Cymb,* I, vii, 36–37.

Partlet, *n.* Chanticleer's wife in the fable of Reynard the Fox, used as a familiar name for any hen or a fussy woman: "How now, dame Partlet the hen, have you enquired/ yet who picked my pocket?" *1 Hen 4,* III, iii, 50–51.

party, *n.* **1** troops or followers: "For from his metal was his party steel'd . . ." *2 Hen 4,* I, i, 116. **2** political cause, side of an issue, or the like: ". . . she had kindled France, and all the world,/ Upon the right and party of her son?" *K John,* I, i, 33–34. **3** [pl.] factions: "Lest parties . . . break out/ And sack great Rome with Romans." *Cor,* III, i, 312–313. **4 party and party,** one litigant and the other: "When you are hearing a/ matter between party and party . . ." *Cor,* II, i, 72–73. **5 upon his party, a.** on his side: ". . . all your northern castles yielded up,/ And all your southern gentlemen in arms/ Upon his party." *Rich 2,* III, ii, 201–203. **b.** concerning his cause: ". . . have you nothing said/ Upon his party 'gainst the Duke of Albany?" *Lear,* II, i, 26–27.

party-coated, *adj.* dressed in motley: "Which party-coated presence of loose love/ Put on by us . . ." *Love's L,* V, ii, 758–759.

party-verdict, *n.* verdict arrived at by voting; also, one person's share of such a verdict: "Thy son is banish'd upon good advice,/ Whereto thy tongue a party-verdict gave . . ." *Rich 2*, I, iii, 233–234.

pash[1], *v.* to strike or smash: "If I go to him, with my armed fist/ I'll pash him o'er the face." *Tr & Cr*, II, iii, 203–204.

pash[2], *n.* the head: "Thou want'st a rough [shaggy] pash and the shoots [horns] that I have/ To be full like me . . ." *W Tale*, I, ii, 128–129.

pashed, *adj.* battered: ". . . stands colossus-wise, waving his beam,/ Upon the pashed corses of the kings . . ." *Tr & Cr*, V, v, 9–10.

pass, *v.* **1** to grant; settle on: ". . . like a father you will deal with him,/ And pass my daughter a sufficient dower . . ." *Shrew*, IV, iv, 44–45. **2** to give in pledge: "Your oaths are pass'd; and now subscribe your names . . ." *Love's L*, I, i, 19. **3** to experience; endure or suffer: "She lov'd me for the dangers I had pass'd . . ." *Oth*, I, iii, 167. **4** to indulge in: "The king is a good king: but . . . he passes some humours and careers [eccentric behavior]." *Hen 5*, II, i, 125–126. **5** to portray or impersonate: ". . . this swain, because of his/ great limb or joint, shall pass Pompey the Great . . ." *Love's L*, V, i, 119–120. **6** to surpass; excell: "A most incomparable man . . . He passes." *Timon*, I, i, 10–12. **7** to be [amusing] beyond description: ". . . and Helen so blushed, and Paris so chafed, and/ all the rest so laughed that it passed." *Tr & Cr*, I, ii, 168–169. **8** to utter: ". . . and that not pass'd [uttered by] me but/ By learned approbation of the judges . . ." *Hen 8*, I, ii, 70–71. **9** to die: "Thus might he pass indeed; yet he revives." *Lear*, IV, vi, 47. **10** to be accepted: "Let me pass! The same I am, ere ancient'st order was . . ." *W Tale*, IV, i, 9–10. **11** to surpass understanding; be intolerable: "Why, this passes, Master Ford; you are not to go/ loose any longer, you must be pinioned." *Wives*, IV, ii, 113–114. **12** to pass up; omit: "Please you/ That I may pass this doing." *Cor*, II, ii, 138–139. **13** to pass over; overlook: ". . . some strange indignity,/ Which patience could not pass." *Oth*, II, iii, 236–237. **14 I pass not**, I care not: "As for these silken-coated slaves, I pass not . . ." *2 Hen 6*, IV, ii, 122. **15 pass on**, to pass judgment on: "What knows the laws/ That thieves do pass on thieves?" *Meas*, II, i, 22–23. **16 pass upon, a.** [in fencing] to thrust at; here, fig. use, to attack with words; attempt to make a fool of: "Nay, and thou pass upon me, I'll no more with/ thee." *T Night*, III, i, 43–44. **b.** to be played or imposed upon: "This practice hath most shrewdly pass'd upon thee." *T Night*, V, i, 351. —*n.* **17** sword thrust: "'Tis dangerous when the baser nature comes/ Between the pass and fell incensed points . . ." *Ham*, V, ii, 60–61. **18** [often pl.] actions; here, trespasses: ". . . your Grace, like power divine,/ Hath looked upon my passes." *Meas*, V, i, 367–368. **19** end; objective: "For to no other pass my verses tend/ Than of your graces and your gifts to tell." *Sonn 103*, 11–12. **20 at that pass**, in that situation: "I should

kick, being kick'd, and being at that pass,/ You would keep from my heels, and beware of an ass." *Errors*, III, i, 17–18. **21 a worthy pass**, good reputation: ". . . I do know him well; and common speech/ Gives him a worthy pass." *All's W*, II, v, 52–53. **22 pass of pate**, witty thrust [a fencing term]: "'Steal by line and level' is an excellent/ pass of pate . . ." *Temp*, IV, i, 243–244.

passado, *n.* sword thrust: ". . . the passado he/ respects not, the duello he regards not . . ." *Love's L*, I, ii, 168–169.

passage, *n.* **1** traffic: "Now in the stirring [busy] passage of the day,/ A vulgar comment will be made . . ." *Errors*, III, i, 99–100. **2** passerby: "What ho, no watch, no passage? murder, murder!" *Oth*, V, i, 37. **3** act, occurrence, or expression: ". . . no Christian that means to be saved . . . can ever believe such impossible passages of/ grossness." *T Night*, III, ii, 68–70. **4 passages, a.** proceedings: ". . . but oft have hinder'd, oft/ The passages made toward it . . ." *Hen 8*, II, iv, 162–163. **b.** experiences: "But thou dost in thy passages of life/ Make me believe that thou art only mark'd/ For the hot vengeance and the rod of heaven . . ." *1 Hen 4*, III, ii, 8–10. **5 act of common passage**, common occurrence: "It is no act of common passage, but/ A strain of rareness . . ." *Cymb*, III, iv, 93–94. **6 passage and whole stream**, outcome and complete success: ". . . as if/ The passage and whole stream of this commencement/ Rode on his tide." *Tr & Cr*, II, iii, 132–134.

passages of proof, *n.* experience over the years: ". . . I see, in passages of proof,/ Time qualifies the spark and fire of it." *Ham*, IV, vii, 111–112.

passant, *adj.* [in heraldry] looking to the [its] right; also, poss., adverbial use as "exceedingly": ". . . it agrees well, passant; it is a familiar beast to/ man . . ." *Wives*, I, i, 19–20.

passed, *adj.* just now uttered: "I would . . . on thy knee/ Make thee beg pardon for thy passed speech . . ." *2 Hen 6*, III, ii, 219–220.

passed on, passed by; missed: ". . . the imperial votress passed on,/ In maiden meditation, fancy-free." *M N Dream*, II, i, 163–164.

passenger, *n.* **1** passerby: "Even such, they say, as stand in narrow lanes . . . and rob our passengers . . ." *Rich 2*, V, iii, 8–9. **2** traveler: "Fellows, stand fast: I see a passenger." *Two Gent*, IV, i, 1.

passing, *adv.* **1** surpassingly; exceedingly: "Cousin, you apprehend passing shrewdly." *M Ado*, II, i, 74. —*adj.* **2** surpassing: "O passing traitor, perjur'd and unjust!" *3 Hen 6*, V, i, 109. **3** extreme or excessive: "Your own present folly, and her passing deformity . . ." *Two Gent*, II, i, 71.

passing bell, *n.* bell tolling after a person has died: ". . . his grief may be compared well/ To one sore sick, that hears the passing bell." *Ven & Ad,* 701–702.

passion, *n.* **1** emotion: "And strain their cheeks to idle merriment,/ A passion hateful to my purposes . . ." *K John,* III, ii, 56–57. **2** outburst of violent emotion: "I never heard a passion so confus'd/ So strange, outrageous, and so variable . . ." *Merch,* II, viii, 12–13. **3** great suffering or agitation: ". . . grandam earth, having this distemp'rature,/ In passion shook." *1 Hen 4,* III, i, 31–32. **4** sorrow: "This music crept by me upon the waters,/ Allaying both their fury and my passion . . ." *Temp,* I, ii, 394–395. **5** mood: ". . . how every passion fully strives/ To make itself, in thee, fair and admired!" *Ant & Cleo,* I, i, 50–51.
—*v.* **6** to grieve; sorrow: ". . . but with this I passion to say wherewith,—" *Love's L,* I, i, 254–255.

passionate, *adj.* **1** compassionate: "I hope this passionate/ humour of mine will change." *Rich 3,* I, iv, 113–114.
—*v.* **2** to express with great emotion: "Thy niece and I . . . cannot passionate our ten-fold grief . . ." *T Andr,* III, ii, 5–7.

pass of practice, *n.* (in fencing) a sly, treacherous thrust: ". . . and in a pass of practice/ Requite him for your father." *Ham,* IV, vii, 137–138.

passport, *n.* **1** a permit; permission: "Why then, give sin a passport to offend/ And youth the dangerous rein of liberty . . ." *Edw 3,* II, i, 423–424. **2** license to travel; here, permission to wander from home: "Look on his letter, madam; here's my passport . . ." *All's W,* III, ii, 55.

passy measures pavin, *n.* brisker Italian version of the pavane; appar. ironic ref. to lack of help to be expected from Dick Surgeon: "Then he's a rogue, and a passy measures pavin:/ I hate a drunken rogue." *T Night,* V, i, 198–199.

past, *prep.* more than: ". . . he has not past three or four hairs on/ his chin—" *Tr & Cr,* I, ii, 113–114.

past-cure, *adj.* incurable: "To prostitute our past-cure malady/ To empirics . . ." *All's W,* II, i, 120–121.

paste, *n.* pastry covering of a pie; piecrust: ". . . that small model of the barren earth/ Which serves as paste and cover to our bones." *Rich 2,* III, ii, 153–154.

pastern, *n.* hoof: "I will not change my/ horse with any that treads but on four pasterns." *Hen 5,* III, vii, 11–12.

pastime, *n.* amusement: "You must not think . . . That we can let our beard be shook with danger/ And think it pastime." *Ham,* IV, vii, 30–33.

past-proportion, *n.* immeasurable amount: "Will you with counters sum/ The past-proportion of his infinite . . ." *Tr & Cr,* II, ii, 28–29.

pastry, *n.* pastry kitchen; bakehouse: "They call for dates and quinces in the pastry." *Rom & Jul,* IV, iv, 2.

pasture, *n.* rearing; upbringing: ". . . show us here/ The mettle [quality] of your pasture . . ." *Hen 5,* III, i, 26–27.

pasty, *n.* [pron. as past-e] meat pie: ". . . of the paste a coffin I will rear,/ And make two pasties of your shameful heads . . ." *T Andr,* V, ii, 188–189.

pat, *adv.* (as a reply) right; exactly or precisely: "Are we all met?"/ "Pat, pat . . ." *M N Dream,* III, i, 1–2.

Patay, *n.* town in S Orléans, N central France: "This dastard, at the battle of Patay . . . did run away . . ." *1 Hen 6,* IV, i, 19–23.

patch, *v.* **1** to cover (over): "Patch grief with proverbs, make misfortune drunk . . ." *M Ado,* V, i, 17. **2** to patch together; make up of patches: "If you'll patch a quarrel . . . It must not be with this [such weak matter as this]." *Ant & Cleo,* II, ii, 52–54.
—*n.* **3** jester; ref. to Trinculo's motley attire as well as the following sense: "What a pied ninny's this! Thou scurvy patch!" *Temp,* III, ii, 62. **4** fool; buffoon: "So were there a patch set on learning, to see him in a/ school . . ." *Love's L,* IV, ii, 30. **5 patches, colors, and with forms,** shabby ornaments, false pretexts, and showy outward forms: ". . . bungle up damnation/ With patches, colours, and with forms . . ." *Hen 5,* II, ii, 115–116.

patch-breech, *n.* patched breeches; here, a nickname: "What, Patch-breech, I say!" *Per,* II, i, 14.

patched fool, *n.* professional fool dressed in motley: ". . . man is but a patched fool if he/ will offer to say what methought I had." *M N Dream,* IV, i, 208–209.

patchery, *n.* **1** knavery: "Know his gross patchery, love him, feed him . . ." *Timon,* V, i, 95. **2** trickery; cheating: "Here is such patchery, such juggling, and such/ knavery!" *Tr & Cr,* II, iii, 73–74.

pate, *n.* crown of the head regarded as the seat of intellect: "Fat paunches have lean pates . . ." *Love's L,* I, i, 26.

paten, *n.* shallow dish; plate: ". . . look how the floor of heaven/ Is thick inlaid with patens of bright gold . . ." *Merch,* V, i, 58–59.

patent, *n.* **1** privilege or entitlement: "So will I grow, so live, so die, my lord,/ Ere I will yield my virgin patent up . . ." *M*

N Dream, I, i, 79–80. **2** liberty; license: ". . . by his authority he remains here,/ which he thinks is a patent for his sauciness . . ." *All's W,* IV, v, 62–63. **3** right or grant of ownership: "The cause of this fair gift in me is wanting,/ And so my patent back again is swerving." *Sonn 87,* 7–8.

path, *v.* to pursue an intended course: ". . . if thou path, thy native semblance on,/ Not Erebus itself were dim enough/ To hide thee from prevention." *J Caes,* II, i, 83–85.

pathetical, *adj.* **1** moving; touching: "Sweet invocation of a child; most pretty and pathetical!" *Love's L,* I, ii, 90. **2** [used as an intensive] disgusting; revolting: "I will think you the most/ pathetical break-promise . . ." *As You,* IV, i, 181–182.

patience, *n.* **1** indulgence, hence permission: "Be the players ready?"/ "Ay, my lord, they stay upon your patience." *Ham,* III, ii, 105–106. **2** calmness or composure; self-control: "Upon the heat and flame of thy distemper/ Sprinkle cool patience." *Ham,* III, iv, 123–124. **3 under your patience,** with your indulgence; if I may say so: "Under your patience, gentle empress,/ 'Tis thought you have a goodly gift in horning . . ." *T Andr,* II, iii, 66–67. **4 wake your patience,** disturb your calm: "Gentlemen both, we will not wake your patience." *M Ado,* V, i, 102.

Patience, *n.* statue personifying grief, often affixed to a tomb: "And with a green and yellow melancholy/ She sat like Patience on a monument,/ Smiling at grief." *T Night,* II, iv, 114–116.

patient, *v.* **1** to calm: "Patient yourself, madam, and pardon me." *T Andr,* I, i, 121.
—*adj.* **2** composed; here, restrained and impassive: "Why art thou patient, man? thou should'st be mad . . ." *3 Hen 6,* I, iv, 89.

patron, *n.* **1** benefactor; protector: "Confess who set thee up and pluck'd thee down,/ Call Warwick patron, and be penitent . . ." *3 Hen 6,* V, i, 26–27. **2** supporter; follower: "Noble patricians, patrons of my right [to succeed] . . ." *T Andr,* I, i, 1.

patronage, *v.* to protect or defend; cover up: ". . . as an outlaw in a castle keeps,/ And useth it—to patronage his theft." *1 Hen 6,* III, i, 47–48.

pattern, *n.* **1** example or model: ". . . their memory/ Shall as a pattern or a measure live . . ." *2 Hen 4,* IV, iv, 75–76. **2** product: "Thou cunning pattern of excelling nature . . ." *Oth,* V, ii, 11. **3** precedent; here, for his own behavior: "Pattern in himself to know . . ." *Meas,* III, ii, 256.
—*v.* **4** to match; serve as a precedent (for): ". . . which is more/ Than history can pattern . . ." *W Tale,* III, ii, 35–36. **5 patterned by,** in the same way: "Pattern'd by that the poet here

describes,/ By nature made for murthers and for rapes." *T Andr,* IV, i, 57–58. **6 pattern out,** to serve as a precedent for: "Let mine own judgement pattern out my death . . ." *Meas,* II, i, 30.

pauca, *adj.* few; here, in few words: ". . . the quondam Quickly/ For the only she; and—pauca, there's enough." *Hen 5,* II, i, 78–79.

paucas pallabris, *n. pl.* Latinate corruption of the Spanish *pocas palabras,* few words: "Therefore *paucas pallabris,* let the world slide [go by]. Sessa!" *Shrew,* Ind., i, 5.

pauca verba, *n. pl.* [Latin] few words: "Sir, I do invite you too: you shall not say/ me nay: *pauca verba." Love's L,* IV, ii, 157–158.

Paul's, *n.* St. Paul's Cathedral in London: "This oily rascal is known as well as Paul's . . ." *1 Hen 4,* II, iv, 519.

paunch, *n.* **1** belly; guts: "'Zounds! ye fat paunch, an ye call/ me coward, I'll stab thee." *1 Hen 4,* II, iv, 141–142.
—*v.* **2** to stab the belly of: "Batter his skull, or paunch him with a stake . . ." *Temp,* III, ii, 88.

pause, *v.* **1** to delay an action; here, take time to consider before getting married: "Patience unmov'd! no marvel though she pause . . ." *Errors,* II, i, 32. **2 pause upon,** to take time to consider; reflect upon: "Other offenders we will pause upon." *1 Hen 4,* V, v, 15.
—*n.* **3 deliberate pause,** carefully considered change; here, removal: "To bear all smooth and even,/ This sudden sending him away must seem/ Deliberate pause." *Ham,* IV, iii, 7–9.

pauser, *n.* something that causes a delay: "Th' expedition [unthinking haste] of my violent love/ Outrun the pauser, reason." *Mac,* II, iii, 110–111.

pausingly, *adv.* with pauses or interruptions: ". . . with demure confidence/ This pausingly ensued . . ." *Hen 8,* I, ii, 167–168.

paved, *adj.* **paved bed,** sealed tomb: "Her brother's ghost his paved bed would break . . ." *Meas,* V, i, 433.

pavement, *n.* ground, pathway, or street: "Lie there for pavement for the abject rear . . ." *Tr & Cr,* III, iii, 162.

pavilion, *n.* **1** tent, used for temporary quarters: ". . . it is the king's most sweet pleasure and affection/ to congratulate the princess at her pavilion . . ." *Love's L,* V, i, 79–80. **2** [on shipboard] an area curtained off for privacy: "A Pavilion on/ deck, with a curtain before it; Pericles within it, reclined on a couch . . ." [SD] *Per,* V, i, 1.

pavilioned, *adj.* housed in tents: "Whose hearts have left their bodies here in England/ And lie pavilion'd in the fields of France." *Hen 5*, I, ii, 128–129.

pawn, *v.* **1** to pledge or promise; also, stake: "Will you thus break your faith?"/ "I pawn'd thee none." *2 Hen 4*, IV, ii, 112. **2 pawn down,** to lay down as a pledge: "I dare pawn down my/ life for him . . ." *Lear*, I, ii, 87–88.
—*n.* **3** pledge, as a gage thrown down: "If guilty dread have left thee so much strength/ As to take up mine honour's pawn, then stoop." *Rich 2*, I, i, 73–74. **4** stake or pledge that can be sacrificed: "My life I never held but as a pawn/ To wage against thine enemies . . ." *Lear*, I, i, 155–156. **5** [usually pl.] objects taken as security for a loan; also, poss. wordplay on the chess piece: "To lie like pawns lock'd up in chests and trunks . . ." *K John*, V, ii, 141. **6 at pawn,** in a condition of being pledged: "Alas, sweet wife, my honour is at pawn . . ." *2 Hen 4*, II, iii, 7. **7 lay to pawn,** to borrow [money] on the strength of; trade on: "I have been content, sir, you should/ lay my countenance [reputation] to pawn . . ." *Wives*, II, ii, 4–5.

pax, *n.* metal plate, stamped with a representation of the Crucifixion, that is kissed first by the celebrant [the kiss of peace], then by the congregation: ". . . he hath stol'n a pax, and hanged must a' be." *Hen 5*, III, vi, 40–41.

pay, *v.* **1** to settle with; also, to kill: "Two I am sure I have paid, two rogues in/ buckram suits." *1 Hen 4*, II, iv, 188–189. **2 pay down by weight,** to pay exactly what is owed; here, pay heavily: "Thus can the demi-god, Authority,/ Make us pay down for our offence by weight." *Meas*, I, ii, 112–113. **3 pay us home,** to repay us fully; here, give us our deserts: "And think we think ourselves unsatisfy'd,/ Till he hath found a time to pay us home . . ." *1 Hen 4*, I, iii, 281–282. **4 pay your fees,** [to] pay fees to jailers upon release from prison [fig. use]: "Force me to keep you as a prisoner,/ Not like a guest: so you shall pay your fees/ When you depart . . ." *W Tale*, I, ii, 52–54.

paysan, *n.* [French] peasant: "I/ ha' married *un garçon*, a boy;/ *un paysan*, by gar . . ." *Wives*, V, v, 203–204.

peace, *n.* **1 for the peace of you,** for your sake: "And for the peace of you I hold such strife . . ." *Sonn 75*, 3. **2 keep peace,** to act as peacemaker: "That no compunctious visitings of Nature/ Shake my fell purpose, nor keep peace between/ Th'effect and it!" *Mac*, I, v, 45–47. **3 peace of the presence,** serenity appropriate to the king's presence: ". . . if you can command these elements to/ silence, and work the peace of the presence, we will/ not hand a rope more . . ." *Temp*, I, i, 21–23.
—*v.* **4** to quiet down: ". . . when/ the thunder would not peace at my bidding . . ." *Lear*, IV, vi, 104. **5** to cease: "Peace your tattlings!" *Wives*, IV, i, 21.

peach, *v.* **1** to turn informer; give incriminating evidence: "If I be ta'en, I'll peach for this . . ." *1 Hen 4*, II, ii, 43. **2** to accuse of being: ". . . at the suit of Master Three-pile the mercer . . . which now peaches/ him a beggar." *Meas*, IV, iii, 9–12.

peak, *v.* to grow thin and emaciated: "Weary sev'n-nights nine times nine,/ Shall he dwindle, peak, and pine . . ." *Mac*, I, iii, 22–23.

peaking, *adj.* sneaking: ". . . the peaking cornuto her/ husband . . . in a continual/ larum of jealousy . . ." *Wives*, III, v, 64–66.

peal, *n.* torrent of words: "Peace! the peal begins." *Love's L*, V, i, 42.

pear, *v.* **is pear,** Fluellen appar. means "will bear": "I hope your majesty is pear/ me testimony and witness . . ." *Hen 5*, IV, viii, 36–37.

'pear, *v.* appear: "It shall as level to your judgment 'pear/ As day does to your eye." *Ham*, IV, v, 151–152.

pearl, *n.* **1** jeweled earring, often an adornment of fashionable men; here, adornment of the cowslip-bodyguards: "I must go seek some dew-drops here,/ And hang a pearl in every cowslip's ear." *M N Dream*, II, i, 14–15. **2** highest-ranking members (used as a collective): "I see thee compass'd with thy kingdom's pearl . . ." *Mac*, V, viii, 22. **3** person or thing of great worth: "Black men are pearls, in beauteous ladies' eyes." *Two Gent*, V, ii, 12. **4** [pl.] tears; also, cataracts: "[Aside] 'Tis true, such pearls as put out ladies' eyes . . ." *Two Gent*, V, ii, 13.

peasant, *n.* servant: "I did obey, and sent my peasant home/ For certain ducats . . ." *Errors*, V, i, 231–232.

peascod, *n.* **1** pea pod; here, the pea plant: "I remember the wooing of a peascod instead of her . . ." *As You*, II, iv, 48. **2 peascod-time,** early summer, when peas are podding: "I have known thee these/ twenty-nine years, come peascod-time . . ." *2 Hen 4*, II, iv, 379–380.

pease, *n.* pl. of **pea**: ". . . thy rich leas/ Of wheat, rye, barley, vetches, oats, and pease . . ." *Temp*, IV, i, 60–61.

peat[1], *n.* pet; spoiled favorite: "A pretty peat! it is best put finger in the eye, and/ she knew why." *Shrew*, I, i, 78–79.

peat[2], *v.* Fluellen's pron. of "beat": ". . . I will make him eat some part of my leek,/ or I will peat his pate four days." *Hen 5*, V, i, 41–42.

pebble, *n.* [used as pl.] pebbled beach: "The murmuring surge,/ That on th' unnumber'd idle pebble chafes . . ." *Lear*, IV, vi, 20–21.

peck¹, *v.* to pitch: ". . . get up o'th'rail,/ I'll peck you o'er the pales else." *Hen 8,* V, iii, 88–89.

peck², *n.* container holding a peck [8 quarts]: ". . . to be compassed like a/ good bilbo in the circumference of a peck, hilt to/ point . . ." *Wives,* III, v, 101–103.

peck up, *v.* to gather in the manner of a bird: "This fellow pecks up wit, as pigeons pease . . ." *Love's L,* V, ii, 315.

peculiar, *adj.* **1** individual: "The single and peculiar life is bound/ With all the strength and armour of the mind . . ." *Ham,* III, iii, 11–12. **2** exclusive: "With pure aspects did him peculiar duties." *Luc,* 14. **3** private: "Groping for trouts, in a peculiar river." *Meas,* I, ii, 83.

peculiar care, *n.* personal cares or troubles: "Augustus lives to think on't: and so much/ For my peculiar care." *Cymb,* V, v, 82–83.

pedant, *n.* schoolmaster: "A domineering pedant o'er the boy . . ." *Love's L,* III, i, 172.

pedascule, *n.* appar. coinage, with the approx. meaning of "[miserable] little pedant": "Pedascule, I'll watch you better yet." *Shrew,* III, i, 48.

peeled, *adj.* having the head shaved; tonsured: "Peel'd priest, dost thou command me be shut out?" *1 Hen 6,* I, iii, 30.

peep, *v.* **peep to,** to glimpse at: ". . . treason can but peep to what it would . . ." *Ham,* IV, v, 124.

peer¹, *n.* **1** nobleman: "The mighty and redoubted Prince of Wales . . . Triumphant rideth like a Roman peer . . ." *Edw 3,* V, i, 177–180. **2** mate or companion; here, a wife of equal status: "This king unto him took a peer,/ Who died and left a female heir . . ." *Per,* I, Chor., 21–22.

peer², *v.* to appear; come into view: "For yet a many of your horsemen peer/ And gallop o'er the field." *Hen 5,* IV, vii, 87–88.

peer³, *v.* to rise over or above: "Like a proud river peering o'er his bounds . . ." *K John,* II, ii, 23.

peereth, *v.* appeareth; appears: ". . . as the sun breaks through the darkest clouds,/ So honour peereth in the meanest habit." *Shrew,* IV, iii, 170–171.

peerless, *adj.* having no rival: "I bind . . . the world to weet [witness]/ We stand up peerless [our love is without rival]." *Ant & Cleo,* I, i, 38–40.

Peesel, *n.* prob. deliberate mispron. of "Pistol" to allow pun on "pizzle" [penis]: "Good Captain Peesel, be quiet, 'tis very late i'faith . . ." *2 Hen 4,* II, iv, 158–159.

peevish, *adj.* **1** foolish or senseless; silly: "'Tis but a peevish boy—yet he talks well . . ." *As You,* III, v, 110. **2** impulsive or headstrong; hotheaded: "The gods are deaf to hot and peevish vows . . ." *Tr & Cr,* V, iii, 16. **3** contrary; wayward: "And be not peevish found in great designs." [in some editions, "peevish-fond," obstinately foolish] *Rich 3,* IV, iv, 417.

peg, *n.* **set down the pegs,** (on a stringed musical instrument) to loosen the pegs, thereby slackening tension on the strings and lowering the pitch; here, create discord: "I'll set down the pegs that make this music,/ As honest as I am." *Oth,* II, i, 200–201.

Peg-a-Ramsey, *n.* poss. ref. to a bawdy ballad and the implication that Malvolio is like a meddlesome old woman: "My lady's a Cataian, we are politicians, Malvolio's a Peg-a-Ramsey . . ." *T Night,* II, iii, 76–77.

Pegasus, *n.* **1** winged horse of Perseus: "As if an angel dropp'd down from the clouds/ To turn and wind a fiery Pegasus . . ." *1 Hen 4,* IV, i, 108–109. **2** inn, prob. identified by a sign showing the winged horse: ". . . in Genoa,/ Where we were lodgers at the Pegasus." *Shrew,* IV, iv, 4–5.

peise, *v.* **1** poss. to weigh down (time) so as to keep it from passing too quickly or to extend (time): "I speak too long, but 'tis to peise the time,/ To eche [eke] it . . ." *Merch,* III, ii, 22–23. **2** to balance: "The world, who of itself is peised well . . ." *K John,* II, i, 575. **3** **peise down,** to burden: ". . . take a nap/ Lest leaden slumber peise me down tomorrow . . ." *Rich 3,* V, iii, 105–106.

pelf, *n.* **1** possessions: "All perishen of men, of pelf,/ Ne aught escapend but himself . . ." *Per,* II, Chor., 35–36. **2** booty; spoils; sometimes, money or cash: "Immortal gods, I crave no pelf . . ." *Timon,* I, ii, 62.

pelican, *n.* **1** bird believed to nourish its young on its own blood and the young to be ungrateful: a traditional story of sacrifice and ingratitude: "That blood already, like the pelican,/ Hast thou tapp'd out and drunkenly carous'd . . ." *Rich 2,* II, i, 126–127.
—*adj.* **2** ungrateful; here, Lear compares himself to the pelican in his sacrifice for his young: ". . . 'twas this flesh begot/ Those pelican daughters." *Lear,* III, iv, 74–75.

Pelion, *n.* (in Greek myth.) mountain which the giants, in their war against the gods, piled on top of Mount Ossa in a vain effort to reach the top of Mount Olympus: "Till of this flat a mountain you have made/ T'o'ertop old Pelion or the skyish head/ Of blue Olympus." *Ham,* V, i, 245–247.

pellet, *v.* to fall in pellets: ". . . the brine/ That seasoned woe had pelleted in tears . . ." *Lover's Comp,* 17–18.

pelleted, *adj.* sending down pellets, i.e., of hail: "By the discandying of this pelleted storm,/ Lie graveless . . ." *Ant & Cleo,* III, xiii, 165–166.

pell-mell, *adv.* **1** at close quarters, esp. in hand-to-hand combat: "March on! Join bravely. Let us to it pell-mell—" *Rich 3,* V, iii, 313. **2** in confused disorder; here, suggesting a free-for-all fight: "Why then defy each other, and pell-mell/ Make work upon ourselves . . ." *K John,* II, i, 406–407.

Peloponnesus, *n.* S mainland of Greece: "Toward Peloponnesus are they fled." *Ant & Cleo,* III, x, 31.

Pelops, *n.* son of Tantalus, revived by the gods and given a new shoulder of ivory: "What a brow . . . Arch'd like the greatey'd Juno's, but far sweeter,/ Smoother than Pelops' shoulder!" *Kinsmen,* IV, ii, 18–21.

pelt, *v.* to curse: "Another smother'd seems to pelt and swear . . ." *Luc,* 1418.

pelting, *adj.* paltry; insignificant: ". . . this dear dear land . . . Is now leas'd out . . . Like to a tenement or pelting farm." *Rich 2,* II, i, 57–60.

pen, *n.* **1** wordplay on "pen" and "penis": ". . . let not me take him then,/ For if I do, I'll mar the young clerk's pen." *Merch,* V, i, 236–237. **2 sharp as a pen,** Falstaff's nose likened to the sharpness of a quill [regarded as a sign of approaching death]: ". . . for his nose was/ as sharp as a pen, and a' babbled of green fields." *Hen 5,* II, iii, 16–17.
—*v.* **3** to write down: ". . . I will presently pen/ down my dilemmas . . ." *All's W,* III, vi, 70–71.

pence, *n.* pl. of **penny:** "Bardolph stole a lute-case . . . and sold it for three half-pence." *Hen 5,* III, ii, 45–46.

pencil, *n.* artist's paintbrush, esp. one having a fine point: "Truth needs no colour, with his colour fix'd:/ Beauty no pencil, beauty's truth to lay . . ." *Sonn 101,* 6–7.

pencilled, *adj.* merely sketched: "She shall see deeds of honor in their kind/ Which sometime show well, pencill'd." *Kinsmen,* V, iii, 12–13.

pendent or **pendant,** *adj.* **1** suspended in space: ". . . blown with restless violence round about/ The pendent world . . ." *Meas,* III, i, 124–125. **2** hanging down: "With ribands pendant flaring 'bout her head . . ." *Wives,* IV, vi, 41.

pendent bed, *n.* the hanging nest of the martin or swift: ". . . this bird/ Hath made his pendent bed, and procreant cradle . . ." *Mac,* I, vi, 7–8.

Pendragon, *n.* (in British legend) Uther Pendragon, father of King Arthur: ". . . stout Pendragon in his litter sick/ Came to the field and vanquished his foes." *1 Hen 6,* III, ii, 95–96.

Pene gelidus timor occupat artus, [Latin] Cold fear seizes my limbs. *2 Hen 6,* IV, i, 116.

penetrate, *v.* touch her heart: "I am advised to give/ her music a mornings, they say it will penetrate." *Cymb,* II, iii, 11–12.

penetrative, *adj.* penetrating; piercing: "His corrigible neck, his face subdued/ To penetrative shame . . ." *Ant & Cleo,* IV, xiv, 74–75.

penitent, *adj.* doing penance, esp. in being punished: "But we that know what 'tis to fast and pray,/ Are penitent for your default to-day." *Errors,* I, ii, 51–52.

penned, *adj.* written or composed for a special occasion: ". . . to the death we will not move a foot:/ Nor to their penn'd speech render we no grace . . ." *Love's L,* V, ii, 146–147.

penning, *n.* style of writing: "Read thou this challenge; mark but the penning of it." *Lear,* IV, vi, 140.

pennon, *n.* small flag; pennant: ". . . sweeps through our land/ With pennons painted in the blood of Harfleur . . ." *Hen V,* III, v, 48–49.

penny, *n.* **1** pennyworth; amount a penny can buy: "How has thou purchased this experience?"/ "By my penny of observation." *Love's L,* III, i, 24–25. **2** money; wealth; inheritance: "Ay, and her father is make her a petter [better] penny." *Wives,* I, i, 55.

penny cord, *n.* pennyworth of rope [for hanging]: "O, the charity/ of a penny cord!" *Cymb,* V, iv, 167–168.

pennyworth, *n.* **1** small amount, allowance, etc.: "What, not a word? You take your pennyworths now." *Rom & Jul,* IV, v, 4. **2** bargain or money's worth, often more than was bargained for: "We'll fit the kid-fox with a pennyworth." *M Ado,* II, iii, 42. **3 make cheap pennyworths,** to sell for next to nothing: "Pirates may make cheap pennyworths of their pillage . . ." *2 Hen 6,* I, 1, 223.

pensioner, *n.* royal bodyguard, likened to those of Queen Elizabeth, who were tall and handsome; as here, they wore coats richly decorated with gold and jewels: "The cowslips tall her pensioners be,/ In their gold coats spots you see . . ." *M N Dream,* II, i, 10–11.

pensived, *adj.* saddened; melancholy: "Of pensiv'd and subdu'd desires the tender . . ." *Lover's Comp,* 219.

pent, *v.* past part. of PEN **1** shut away [from]: "Being pent from liberty as I am now—" *Rich 3,* I, iv, 250. **2** imprisoned: "Vagabond exile, flaying, pent to linger/ But with a grain a day . . ." *Cor,* III, iii, 89–90.

Pentapolis, *n.* ancient city on the coast of Asia Minor: "The Sea-side, Pentapolis." [SD] *Per,* II, i, 1.

Pentecost, *n.* Whitsunday, the 7th Sunday following Easter, a time [Whitsuntide] of plays and outdoor entertainments: "'Tis since the nuptial of Lucentio,/ Come Pentecost as quickly as it will . . ." *Rom & Jul,* I, v, 35–36.

Penthesilea, *n.* Queen of the Amazons; prob. a tribute to her daring as well as a good-humored jibe at her small size: "Good night, Penthesilea." *T Night,* II, iii, 177.

penthouse, *n.* **1** [on street side of house] portion of upper floor that jutted out over ground floor; also, overhanging roof, as of a porch or shed: "Stand thee close then under this penthouse, for it/ drizzles rain . . ." *M Ado,* III, iii, 101–102. **2** eyelid likened to the preceding: "Sleep shall neither night nor day/ Hang upon his penthouse lid . . ." *Mac,* I, iii, 19–20.

penthouse-like, *adj.* resembling a penthouse; (esp. of a hat) low or pulled down over the eyes, in the manner of a lover: ". . . your hat penthouse-like o'er the shop of your eyes . . ." *Love's L,* III, i, 15.

pent-up, *adj.* confined; also, frustrated: "So looks the pent-up lion o'er the wretch/ That trembles under his devouring paws . . ." *3 Hen 6,* I, iii, 12–13.

people, *n. pl.* common people; commoners: ". . . the people of Rome . . . have by common voice,/ Chosen Andronicus . . ." *T Andr,* I, i, 20–23.

Pepin, *n.* 8th cent. king of France and father of Charlemagne: ". . . an old saying, that was/ a man when King Pepin of France was a little boy . . ." *Love's L,* IV, i, 120–121.

peppered, *past part.* finished off: "I am peppered, I warrant, for this world." *Rom & Jul,* III, i, 100.

pepper-gingerbread, *n.* something having only a mildly tangy flavor and therefore weak and indecisive: ". . . leave 'In sooth'/ And such protest of pepper-gingerbread, to velvet-guards [those in holiday finery], and Sunday citizens." *1 Hen 4,* III, i, 248–249.

peradventure, *adv.* **1** perhaps; perchance: "Peradventure, to make it/ the more gracious, I shall sing it at her [Thisbe's]

death." *M N Dream,* IV, i, 216–217. **2** by chance or accident; as it happened: ". . . the lion would suspect thee, when peradventure thou wert accus'd by the ass . . ." *Timon,* IV, iii, 331–332. **3** probably; most likely: "Peradventure I will with ye to the court." *2 Hen 4,* III, ii, 290.

perch, *n.* stretch of land: "By many a dern and painful perch/ Of Pericles the careful search . . ." *Per,* III, Chor., 15–16.

perchance, *adv.* **1** possibly; perhaps: "Perchance some single vantages you took,/ When my indisposition put you back . . ." *Timon,* II, ii, 133–134. **2** wordplay on preceding and "by mere chance": "Perchance he is not drown'd: what think you, sailors?"/ "It is perchance that you yourself were sav'd." *T Night,* I, ii, 5–6.

perdie, *interj.* var. of **Perdy**; certainly [a mild oath]: "My lady is unkind, perdie." *T Night,* IV, ii, 78.

perdition, *n.* **1** loss: "Sir, his definement suffers no perdition in you . . ." *Ham,* V, ii, 112. **2** ruin or destruction: ". . . where reason can revolt/ Without perdition . . ." *Tr & Cr,* V, ii, 143–144.

perdu, *n.* sentry assigned to a dangerous post; hence, "lost one": ". . . to watch—poor *perdu!*—/ With this thin helm?" *Lear,* IV, vii, 35–36.

perdurable, *adj.* everlasting; durable: "I confess me knit to thy deserving, with cables/ of perdurable toughness . . ." *Oth,* I, iii, 338–339.

perdurably, *adv.* everlastingly: "Why would he for the momentary trick/ Be perdurably fin'd [punished]?" *Meas,* III, i, 113–114.

perdy, *adv.* assuredly [from French *pardieu,* by God]: "Were not my doors lock'd up, and I shut out?"/ "Perdy, your doors were lock'd, and you shut out." *Errors,* IV, iv, 68–69.

peregrinate, *adj.* strange or foreign: "He is too picked, too spruce . . . too peregrinate,/ as I may call it." *Love's L,* V, i, 12–14.

peremptorily, *adv.* positively; decisively: ". . . then peremptorily I speak it,/ there is virtue in that Falstaff . . ." *1 Hen 4,* II, iv, 423–424.

peremptory, *adj.* **1** determined; resolute: "What peremptory eagle-sighted eye/ Dares look upon the heaven of her brow . . ." *Love's L,* IV, iii, 222–223. **2** imperious or overbearing: ". . . his humour is lofty, his discourse/ peremptory . . ." *Love's L,* V, i, 9–10. **3** final; decisive: ". . . we will suddenly/ Pass our accept and peremptory answer." *Hen 5,* V, ii, 81–82.

perfect, *adj.* **1** word perfect: "... I hope I was perfect./ I made a little fault in 'Great.'" *Love's L,* V, ii, 554–555. **2** thoroughly acquainted or knowledgeable: "I am not to you known,/ Though in your state of honour I am perfect." *Mac,* IV, ii, 64–65. **3** expert; skilled: "In thy dumb action will I be as perfect/ As begging hermits in their holy prayers ..." *T Andr,* III, ii, 40–41. **4** certain: "Thou art perfect, then, our ship hath touch'd upon/ The deserts of Bohemia?" *W Tale,* III, iii, 1–2. **5 I am perfect what,** I'll tell you precisely what [I've done]: "What hast thou done?"/ "I am perfect what: cut off one Cloten's head ..." *Cymb,* IV, ii, 117–118. **6 perfect age,** legal age; maturity: "... sons at perfect age, and/ fathers declin'd, the father should be as ward/ to the son ..." *Lear,* I, ii, 72–74. —*v.* **7** to instruct; enlighten: "A passport too! Apollo, perfect/ me in the characters!" *Per,* III, ii, 68–69.

perfected, *adj.* experienced: "Being once perfected how to grant suits,/ How to deny them ..." *Temp,* I, ii, 79–80.

perfecter giber, *n.* See **giber.**

perfectest, *adj.* best; most reliable: "... I have learn'd by the perfect'st report, they have/ more in them than mortal knowledge." *Mac,* I, v, 2–3.

perfectness, *n.* ripeness: "The Prince will, in the perfectness of time [at the proper time],/ Cast off his followers ..." *2 Hen 4,* IV, iv, 74–75.

perfect soul, *n.* clear conscience: "... my perfect soul,/ Shall manifest me rightly ..." *Oth,* I, ii, 31–32.

perforce, *adv.* by the use of force; forcibly: "... for what he hath taken away from thy father perforce ..." *As You,* I, ii, 18–19.

perform, *v.* to execute; here, to sculpt: "... a piece ... newly performed by/ that rare Italian master, Julio Romano ..." *W Tale,* V, ii, 94–96.

perfume, *n.* **1** fragrance; sweetness; here, fig. use: "The perfume and suppliance of a minute,/ No more." *Ham,* I, iii, 9–10. **2** perfumed woman, esp. a mistress or prostitute: "Thy flatterers yet wear silk, drink wine ... Hug their diseas'd perfumes ..." *Timon,* IV, iii, 208–209. **3 died in perfume,** fr. belief that phoenix was consumed in fire of aromatic wood, then rose from the ashes: "... commit it/ To the like innocent cradle, where phoenix-like/ They died in perfume." *Kinsmen,* I, iii, 69–71.

perfumer, *n.* fumigator: "Being entertained for a perfumer, as I was/ smoking a musty room ..." *M Ado,* I, iii, 54–55.

Perge, *v.* [Latin] proceed: "*Perge,* good Master Holofernes, *Perge* ..." *Love's L,* IV, ii, 51.

periapt, *n.* amulet, usually worn around the neck to ward off evil or danger: "Now help, ye charming spells and periapts ..." *1 Hen 6,* V, iii, 2.

Perigouna, *n.* Also called **Perigenia,** daughter of the outlaw Sinnis, slain by the young Theseus; an early mistress of Theseus: "Didst not thou lead him through the glimmering night/ From Perigouna, whom he ravished ..." *M N Dream,* II, i, 77–78.

peril, *n.* **to his utmost peril,** at the risk of his life: "... he shall answer by a lawful form—/ In peace—to his utmost peril." *Cor,* III, i, 322–323.

perilous, *adj.* deadly; lethal: "That's a perilous shot out/ of an elder-gun [popgun] ..." *Hen 5,* IV, i, 203–204.

period, *v.* **1** put an end to: "Your honourable letter he desires ... which failing/ Periods his comfort." *Timon,* I, i, 100–102. —*n.* **2** stop or halt; end; conclusion: "Upon thy sight/ My worldly business makes a period." *2 Hen 4,* IV, v, 229–230. **3** goal or purpose: "There's his period,/ To sheath his knife in us ..." *Hen 8,* I, ii, 209–210.

perish, *v.* to destroy; kill: "Because thy flinty heart ... Might in thy palace perish Margaret." *2 Hen 6,* III, ii, 98–99.

perishen, *v.* old pl. of **perish:** "All perishen of men, of pelf,/ Ne aught escapend but himself ..." *Per,* II, Chor., 35–36.

periwig-pated, *adj.* bewigged; here, used as an instance of artificiality: "... to hear a robustious periwig-pated fellow/ tear a passion to tatters ..." *Ham,* III, ii, 9–10.

perjure, *n.* **1** perjurer: "Why, he comes in like a perjure, wearing papers." *Love's L,* IV, iii, 45. —*v.* **2** to seduce or undermine: "... want will perjure/ The ne'er-touch'd vestal ..." *Ant & Cleo,* III, xii, 30–31.

perjured, *adj.* forsworn; having broken his oath: "Now, perjur'd Henry, wilt thou kneel for grace,/ And set thy diadem upon my head ..." *3 Hen 6,* II, ii, 81–82.

perjured note, *n.* paper or placard proclaiming the perjurer's offense: "Ill, to example ill,/ Would from my forehead wipe a perjur'd note ..." *Love's L,* IV, iii, 121–122.

perk up, *v.* to deck out: "... 'tis better to be lowly born ... Than to be perk'd up in a glist'ring grief/ And wear a golden sorrow." *Hen 8,* II, iii, 19–22.

per-lady, *n.* by Our Lady: "Yes, per-lady: if he has a quarter of your coat,/ there is but three skirts for yourself ..." *Wives,* I, i, 26–27.

permissive pass, *n.* permission to continue: "... for we bid this be done,/ When evil deeds have their permissive pass..." *Meas,* I, iii, 37–38.

pernicious, *adj.* treacherous: "Pernicious Protector... That smooth'st it so with king and commonweal!" *2 Hen 6,* II, i, 21–22.

perpend, *v.* to consider; ponder or reflect: "Learn of the wise and perpend." *As You,* III, ii, 64–65.

perpetual doom, *n.* Last Judgment: "Strew good luck, ouphs, on every sacred room/ That it may stand till the perpetual doom..." *Wives,* V, v, 58–59.

perplexed, *adj.* distressed: "One but painted thus/ Would be interpreted a thing perplex'd..." *Cymb,* III, iv, 6–7.

per se, *adv.* [Latin] to the fullest extent; absolutely: "They say he is a very man *per se*/ And stands alone." *Tr & Cr,* I, ii, 15–16.

persecute, *v.* to endure; suffer: "... he hath persecuted time with hope..." *All's W,* I, i, 13.

Perseus, *n.* son of Danaë by Zeus and slayer of Medusa; ref. here is to his winged horse Pegasus: "Bounding between the two moist elements/ Like Perseus' horse." *Tr & Cr,* I, iii, 40–41.

persever, *v.* **1** earlier form of persevere: "But to persever/ In obstinate condolement is a course/ Of impious stubbornness." *Ham,* I, ii, 92–94. **2** go ahead; keep it up: "Ay, do! Persever: counterfeit sad looks,/ Make mouths upon me when I turn my back..." *M N Dream,* III, ii, 237–238.

persisted, *adj.* worked for persistently: "And strange it is,/ That nature must compel us to lament/ Our most persisted deeds." *Ant & Cleo,* V, i, 28–30.

person, *n.* **1** external appearance: "He has a person and a smooth dispose,/ To be suspected..." *Oth,* I, iii, 395–396. **2** one of handsome appearance: "... honour would become such a person... no better than picture-like to hang/ by th'wall..." *Cor,* I, iii, 10–12. **3** prob. misuse for "parson": "Good master Person, be so good as read me this/ letter: it was given me by Costard..." *Love's L,* IV, iii, 87–88. **4 make my person yours,** put yourself in my place: "Good reverend father, make my person yours,/ And tell me how you would bestow yourself." *K John,* III, i, 150–151.

personage, *n.* one's appearance or, sometimes, figure: "And with her personage, her tall personage,/ Her height, forsooth, she hath prevail'd with him." *M N Dream,* III, ii, 292–293.

personal, *adj.* personally involved: "... the absent King... left behind him here,/ When he was personal in the Irish war." *1 Hen 4,* IV, iii, 86–88.

personate, *v.* to describe or represent, as in writing: "... by the colour of his beard, the/ shape of his leg... he shall find himself most feelingly [minutely] personated." *T Night,* II, iii, 156–159.

personating, *n.* representation: "... a personating of himself;/ a satire/ against the softness of prosperity..." *Timon,* V, i, 33–34.

perspective, *n.* prism or other glass that distorts or shows multiple images of an object; here, such an optical illusion in nature: "One face, one voice, one habit, and two persons!/ A natural perspective, that is, and is not!" *T Night,* V, i, 214–215.

perspectively, *adv.* in a distorted view: "Yes, my lord, you see them perspectively,/ the cities turned into a maid..." *Hen 5,* V, ii, 337–338.

perspicuous, *adj.* apparent or obvious: "... perspicuous as substance/ Whose grossness little characters sum up..." *Tr & Cr,* I, iii, 324–325.

Per Stygia, per manes vehor, [Latin] I am in Hell; lit., Across the Styx I am borne and among the shades of the dead [line from Seneca]: "... till I find the stream/ To cool this heat, a charm to calm these fits,/ *Per Stygia, per manes vehor.*" *T Andr,* II, i, 133–135.

persuade, *v.* **1** to argue persuasively for: "Hadst thou thy wits and didst persuade revenge..." *Ham,* IV, v, 167. **2** to plead (with): "... the magnificoes/ Of greatest port have all persuaded with him..." *Merch,* III, ii, 279–280. **3 best persuaded of himself,** highly conceited: "... the best persuaded of himself,/ so crammed (as he thinks) with excellencies..." *T Night,* II, iii, 149–150.

persuasion, *n.* **1** thought, idea, or way of thinking: "A good persuasion; therefore hear me, Hermia." *M N Dream,* I, i, 156. **2** belief or understanding: "I have a servant comes with me along... whose persuasion is/ I come about my brother." *Meas,* IV, i, 46–48. **3 by the persuasion,** on the evidence: "It should not be, by the persuasion of his new/ feasting." *Timon,* III, vi, 7–8.

pert, *adj.* hearty or vigorous; also, fervent or ardent: "This pert Berowne was out of countenance quite." *Love's L,* V, ii, 272.

pertly, *adv.* **1** quickly; smartly: "... appear, and pertly!/ No tongue! all eyes! be silent." *Temp,* IV, i, 58–59. **2** boldly; also, perh., overconfidently: "For yonder walls that pertly front your town ..." *Tr & Cr,* IV, v, 218.

perturbation, *n.* disturbance; disorder: "A great perturbation in nature [the constitution], to receive at once/ the benefit of sleep ..." *Mac,* V, i, 9–10.

peruse, *v.* to inspect; survey: "... I'll view the manners of the town,/ Peruse the traders, gaze upon the buildings ..." *Errors,* I, ii, 12–13.

pervert, *v.* **1** to seduce: "He hath perverted a young gentlewoman/ here in Florence ..." *All's W,* IV, iii, 13–14. **2** to misdirect: "... trust not my holy order,/ If I pervert your course." *Meas,* IV, iii, 147–148. **3** to divert: "Let's follow him, and pervert the present wrath/ He hath against himself." *Cymb,* II, iv, 151–152.

pester, *v.* to crowd or obstruct: "... behold/ Dissentious numbers pest'ring streets ..." *Cor,* IV, vi, 6–7.

pestered, *adj.* plagued; tormented: "Who then shall blame/ His pester'd senses to recoil and start ..." *Mac,* V, ii, 22–23.

pestiferous, *adj.* noxious; deadly: "Thy lewd, pestiferous, and dissentious pranks ..." *1 Hen 6,* III, i, 15.

pestilence, *n.* plague or other contagious disease: "... to walk alone, like one that had the pestilence ..." *Two Gent,* II, i, 20.

pestilent, *adj.* **1** extremely disagreeable: "What a pestilent knave is this same." *Rom & Jul,* IV, v, 139. **2** distressing: "... wants not buzzers to infect his ear/ With pestilent speeches of his father's death ..." *Ham,* IV, v, 90–91.

pestilent scythe, *n.* scythe wielded by Death during the plague; Antony promises to kill a comparable number in battle: "I'll make death love me; for I will contend/ Even with his pestilent scythe." *Ant & Cleo,* III, xiii, 193–194.

petard, *n.* explosive device: "... 'tis the sport to have the enginer/ Hoist [blown up] with his own petard ..." *Ham,* III, iv, 208–209.

petitionary, *adj.* pleading; urging: "... with most petitionary vehemence, tell me who it is." *As You,* III, ii, 186–187.

Petrarch, *n.* 14th cent. Italian poet: "Now is he for the/ numbers that Petrarch flowed in." *Rom & Jul,* II, iv, 39–40.

petter, *adj.* Evans's misuse for "better"; expression "better penny" evidently means "an additional sum": "Ay, and her father is make her a petter penny." *Wives,* I, i, 55.

pettiness, *n.* inadequate means: "... which in weight to re-answer, his pettiness would/ bow under." *Hen 5,* III, vi, 133–134.

pettitoes, *n.* pig's trotters; here, human feet: "... he would not stir his pettitoes till he had both/ tune and words ..." *W Tale,* IV, iv, 608–609.

petty, *adj.* **1** small or tiny; here, the superstition that concealed murders were revealed by little birds: "Be one of those that thinks/ The petty wrens of Tharsus will ... open this to Pericles." *Per,* IV, iii, 21–23. **2** inconsequential: "I was of late as petty to his ends,/ As is the morn-dew ... To his grand sea." *Ant & Cleo,* III, xii, 8–10. **3** lesser; minor: "... a meeting of the petty gods,/ And you the queen on 't." *W Tale,* IV, iv, 4–5.

petty consequence, *n.* smallest connection: "Each small annexment, petty consequence,/ Attends the boist'rous ruin." *Ham,* III, iii, 21–22.

petty officer, *n.* insignificant official: "For every pelting petty officer/ Would use his heaven for thunder ..." *Meas,* II, ii, 113–114.

petty spirits, *n.* vital fluids of the body: "... and then the vital commoners, and/ inland petty spirits, muster me all to their captain,/ the heart ..." *2 Hen 4,* IV, iii, 108–110.

pew, *n.* seat, usually in church; here, a series of temptations to suicide, leading to the Devil's claiming of a damned soul: "... hath laid knives under his/ pillow, and halters in his pew ..." *Lear,* III, iv, 53–54.

pew-fellow, *n.* one who shares a pew; here, a fellow mourner: "Preys on the issue of his mother's body,/ And makes her pew-fellow with others' moan." *Rich 3,* IV, iv, 57–58.

Phaeton or **Phaëton** or **Phaëthon** *n.* **1** son of Apollo, the sun god: he stole his father's chariot, which ran out of control, and was struck down by Zeus: "Down, down I come, like glist'ring Phaeton,/ Wanting the manage of unruly jades." *Rich 2,* III, iii, 178–179. **2** epithet used for York, whose emblem was the sun: "Now Phaëthon hath tumbled from his car ..." *3 Hen 6,* I, iv, 33.

phantasime, *n.* person full of fanciful, hence foolish, notions; coxcomb: "A phantasime, a Monarcho, and one that makes sport/ To the prince and his book-mates." *Love's L,* IV, i, 100–101.

phantasma, *n.* nightmare; hallucination: "... all the interim is/ Like a phantasma, or a hideous dream ..." *J Caes,* II, i, 64–65.

Pharamond, *n.* legendary Salic [Frankish] king: "There is no bar . . . But this, which they produce from Pharamond . . ." *Hen 5,* I, ii, 35–37.

Pharsalia, *n.* ancient city and district in NE Greece: ". . . to wage this battle at Pharsalia,/ Where Caesar fought with Pompey." *Ant & Cleo,* III, vii, 31–32.

Pheazar, *n.* perh. misuse of "vizier" ["viceroy" in Turkish]; poss. nonsense word to rhyme with "Caesar" and "Keiser": "Thou'rt an emperor, Caesar, Keiser, and Pheazar." *Wives,* I, iii, 9.

Phebe, *v.* to treat badly; abuse: "She Phebes me. Mark how the tyrant writes." *As You,* IV, iii, 39.

pheeze or **pheese,** *v.* See **feeze.**

Phibbus, *n.* appar. Bottom's pron. of "Phoebus": ". . . break the locks/ Of prison-gates;/ And Phibbus' car/ Shall shine from far . . ." *M N Dream,* I, ii, 29–32.

Philemon, old man of Greek legend who gave shelter to Zeus (Jove): "My visor is Philemon's roof;/ Within the house is Jove." *M Ado,* II, i, 88–89.

Philip and Jacob, *n.* May lst, the feast day of St. Philip and St. James: "His child is a year and a quarter old come Philip/ and Jacob." *Meas,* III, ii, 195–196.

Philippan, *n.* appar. name of Antony's sword, used to defeat Brutus at Philippi: "Then put my tires and mantles on him,/ whilst/ I wore his sword Philippan." *Ant & Cleo,* II, v, 22–23.

Philippi, *n.* town in northeastern Greece (Macedonia): ". . . Octavius and Mark Antony/ Come down upon us with a mighty power,/ Bending their expedition toward Philippi." *J Caes,* IV, iii, 167–169.

Phillida, *n.* tradit. name of shepherdess in pastoral poetry: "Play on pipes of corn, and versing love/ To amorous Phillida." *M N Dream,* II, i, 67–68.

Philomel, *n.* **1** daughter of King Pandion of Athens, who was raped by Tereus, king of Thrace; he then cut out her tongue to prevent her exposing him: "This is the day of doom for Bassianus;/ His Philomel must lose her tongue to-day . . ." *T Andr,* II, iii, 42–43. **2** nightingale [fr. Roman belief that gods had turned her into a songbird]: "Philomel, with melody,/ Sing in our sweet lullaby . . ." *M N Dream,* II, ii, 13–14.

philosopher's stone, *n.* either of the legendary secrets (a) for transmuting base metals into gold, or (b) for attaining perpetual youth: ". . . and't shall go hard/ but I'll make him a philosopher's two stones to me." *2 Hen 4,* III, ii, 323–324.

philosophy, *n.* here, ref. to the Stoic philosophy, which denied the influence of chance evils: "Of your philosophy you make no use,/ If you give place to accidental evils." *J Caes,* IV, iii, 144–145.

phlegmatic, *adj.* Quickly appar. means just the opposite, prob. "choleric": "I beseech you, be not so phlegmatic. Hear the/ truth of it . . ." *Wives,* I, iv, 69–70.

Phoebe, *n.* moon goddess or the moon itself: "A title to Phoebe, to Luna, to the moon." *Love's L,* IV, ii, 37.

Phoebus, *n.* **1** another name for the sun-god Apollo or, often, the sun itself: ". . . we that/ take purses go by the moon and the seven stars, and/ not by Phoebus." *1 Hen 4,* I, ii, 13–15. **2 wheels of Phoebus,** the sun god's chariot: ". . . look, the gentle day,/ Before the wheels of Phoebus . . . Dapples the drowsy east with spots of grey." *M Ado,* V, iii, 25–27. **3 young Phoebus,** the rising sun: "With silken streamers the young Phoebus fanning . . ." *Hen 5,* III, Chor. 6.

Phoebus' cart or **wheel,** *n.* the sun god's chariot: "Full thirty times hath Phoebus' cart gone round . . ." *Ham,* III, ii, 150.

phoenix, *n.* **1** person or thing that is rare or unique; here, likened to the legendary bird: "There shall your master have a thousand loves,/ A mother, and a mistress, and a friend,/ A phoenix . . ." *All's W,* I, i, 162–164.
—*adj.* **2** beginning to form; also, matchless: "His phoenix down [beard] began but to appear/ Like unshorn velvet . . ." *Lover's Comp,* 93.

phoenix' throne, *n.* perh. ref. to nest of spices on which the unique bird was said to immolate itself every 500 years: ". . . in Arabia/ There is one tree, the phoenix' throne . . ." *Temp,* III, iii, 22–23.

phrase, *v.* **1** to describe: "When these suns/ (For so they phrase 'em) by their heralds challeng'd/ The noble spirits to arms . . ." *Hen 8,* I, i, 33–35.
—*n.* **2** words, terms or statements: "They clepe us drunkards, and with swinish phrase/ Soil our addition . . ." *Ham,* I, iv, 19–20. **3 phrase of sorrow,** pompous words of grief: ". . . whose phrase of sorrow/ Conjures the wand'ring stars . . ." *Ham,* V, i, 248–249.

phraseless, *adj.* beyond words; indescribable: "'O! then, advance of yours that phraseless hand . . ." *Lover's Comp,* 225.

Phrygia, *n.* ancient country in NW Asia Minor: ". . . from th'Athenian bay/ Put forth toward Phrygia and their vow is made/ To ransack Troy . . ." *Tr & Cr,* Prol., 6–7.

Phrygian, *adj.* of Phrygia: ". . . piteous looks to Phrygian shepherds lent . . ." *Luc,* 1502.

Phrygian Turk, *n.* term of abuse: "Tester I'll have in pouch when thou shalt lack,/ Base Phrygian Turk!" *Wives,* I, iii, 83–84.

physic, *v.* **1** to cure or punish: "I will physic your rankness . . ." *As You,* I, i, 86. **2** to act as a remedy for: "For that will physic the great Myrmidon,/ Who broils in loud applause . . ." *Tr & Cr,* I, iii, 378–379. **3** to preserve the health of; strengthen: "Some griefs are med'cinable, that is one of them,/ For it doth physic love . . ." *Cymb,* III, ii, 33–34. **4 physics the subject,** energizes the entire country: ". . . a gallant child; one that, indeed physics the subject,/ makes old hearts fresh . . ." *W Tale,* I, i, 38–39. —*n.* **5** medicine; medications: "I will not cast away my physic but on those that are sick." *As You,* III, ii, 349–350. **6** remedy: "And I will see what physic the tavern affords." *1 Hen 6,* III, i, 148. **7** medical opinion: "Desire is death, which physic did except." *Sonn 147,* 8. **8** healing power; here, the sacrament of marriage: "Both our remedies/ Within thy help and holy physic lies." *Rom & Jul,* II, iii, 47–48. **9** instance of purging; here, prayer as catharsis: "This physic but prolongs thy sickly days." *Ham,* III, iii, 96. **10** science of medicine: "The sceptre, learning, physic, must/ All follow this and come to dust." *Cymb,* IV, ii, 268–269.

physical, *adj.* conducive to health; healthful: ". . . is it physical/ To walk unbraced and suck up the humours/ Of the dank morning?" *J Caes,* II, i, 261–263.

pia mater, *n.* **1** membrane enclosing the brain: ". . . nourished in the/ womb of *pia mater,* and delivered upon the mellowing/ of occasion." *Love's L,* IV, ii, 67–69. **2** loosely, the brain: ". . . for here he comes, one of thy kin has a/ most weak *pia mater.*" *T Night,* I, v, 115–116.

pick, *v.* **1** to pitch; hurl: ". . . as high/ As I could pick my lance." *Cor,* I, i, 198–199. **2** to look for; search out: "He could not stay to pick them in a pile/ Of noisome musty chaff." *Cor,* V, i, 24–25. **3 pick bad from bad,** [not to be] corrupted by bad examples: "Not to pick bad from bad, but by bad mend [use them to improve]!" *Oth,* IV, iii, 105. —*n.* **4** See **pike** (def. 1).

picked, *adj.* **1** fastidious or overrefined: "He is too picked,/ too spruce, too affected . . ." *Love's L,* V, i, 12–13. **2** convenient: ". . . at pick'd leisure . . . I'll resolve you . . . of every/ These happen'd accidents . . ." *Temp,* V, i, 247–250. **3 picked man of countries,** poss. well picked (with his toothpick) or selected among his well-traveled companions: "Why then I suck my teeth and catechize/ My picked man of countries . . ." *K John,* I, i, 192–193.

pickers and stealers, *n. pl.* the hands: "My lord, you once did love me."/ "And do still, by these pickers and stealers." *Ham,* III, ii, 326–327.

picking, *adj.* **1** given to nit-picking; finicky: ". . . the King is weary/ Of dainty and such picking grievances . . ." *2 Hen 4,* IV, i, 197–198.
—*pres. part.* **2 picking on's teeth,** picking of his teeth; affectation prob. not experienced before by the rustics: ". . . a great man, I'll warrant; I know by the picking/ on's teeth." *W Tale,* IV, iv, 753–754.

pick-lock, *n.* skeleton key or a device for picking locks; perh. an oblique ref. to a chastity belt, since Pompey has been identified as a procurer: ". . . we have found upon/ him, sir, a strange pick-lock . . ." *Meas,* III, ii, 15–16.

pick-purse, *n.* pickpocket or purse snatcher; fig., a cheater: ". . . you, my liege, and I,/ Are pick-purses in love, and we deserve to die." *Love's L,* IV, iii, 204–205.

pickthank, *n.* person who curries favor by informing on others: ". . . the ear of greatness needs must hear,/ By smiling pickthanks, and base newsmongers . . ." *1 Hen 4,* III, ii, 24–25.

Pickt-hatch, *n.* crime-ridden section of London: ". . . to your manor of Pickt-hatch, go!" *Wives,* II, ii, 17.

picture, *n.* **1** outward form; appearance: "'Tis but her picture I have yet beheld . . ." *Two Gent,* II, iv, 205. **2** lifeless or soulless form: "Without the which we are pictures, or mere beasts . . ." *Ham,* IV, v, 86. **3** painted face [heavily made-up]: "Come on, come on, you are pictures out o' doors . . ." *Oth,* II, i, 109. **4** painted statue: ". . . the kings/ and princes, our kindred, are going to see the/ queen's picture." *W Tale,* V, ii, 172–175. **5 best in picture,** best-looking; here, most suitable for stealing: ". . . by which means I saw whose purse was best in picture . . ." *W Tale,* IV, iv, 604–605.

picture of Nobody, *n.* well-known drawing of a man with arms, legs, and head, but no body: "This is the tune of our catch, played by the picture/ of Nobody. *Temp,* III, ii, 125.

pie[1], *n.* magpie [regarded as a bird of ill omen]: "And chattering pies in dismal discords sung . . ." *3 Hen 6,* V, vi, 48.

pie[2], *n.* See **cock and pie.**

piece, *n.* **1** firearm: ". . . and a [he] would/ manage you his piece thus, and a would about . . ." *2 Hen 4,* III, ii, 276–277. **2** ideal specimen; masterpiece: "Thy mother was a piece of virtue, and/ She said thou wast my daughter . . ." *Temp,* I, ii, 56–57. **3** piece of flesh; here, with obvious ref. to Marina as a sexual object: "Master, I have gone through for this piece you

see." *Per,* IV, ii, 41. **4** coin: ". . . an hostler, that for th'poorest piece/ Will bear the knave by th'volume." *Cor,* III, iii, 32–33. **5 flat tamed piece,** cask of spoiled wine; here, in wordplay with preceding sense: "He, like a puling cuckold, would drink up/ The lees and dregs of a flat tamed piece . . ." *Tr & Cr,* IV, i, 62–63. **6 piece of beauty rarer,** woman of greater beauty: "Their transformations/ Were never for a piece of beauty rarer [than you] . . ." *W Tale,* IV, iv, 31–32.
—*v.* **7** to enhance; augment: ". . . yet their purpos'd trim/ Piec'd not his grace . . ." *Lover's Comp,* 118–119. **8 piece it out,** to mend it; make amends: ". . . you shall piece it out/ with a piece of your performance." *Tr & Cr,* III, i, 50–51. **9 piece out,** to strengthen; intensify: "He pieces out his wife's inclination; he gives/ her folly motion and advantage . . ." *Wives,* III, ii, 30–31. **10 piece up,** to parcel up; here, make part [of]: "To take off so much grief from you as he/ Will piece up in himself." *W Tale,* V, iii, 55–56.

Pie Corner, *n.* street corner in London, surrounded by many foul-smelling food shops: "A comes continually to Pie Corner—saving/ your manhoods . . ." *2 Hen 4,* II, i, 25–26.

pied, *adj.* **1** variegated; parti-colored: "When daisies pied and violets blue . . ." *Love's L,* V, ii, 886. **2** dressed in motley: "What a pied ninny's [fool's] this! Thou scurvy patch!" *Temp,* III, ii, 62.

piedness, *n.* variegated color: "There is an art which, in their piedness, shares/ With great creating nature." *W Tale,* IV, iv, 87–88.

pierce, *v.* to move by emotion: "Did your letters pierce the queen to any demonstration/ of grief?" *Lear,* IV, iii, 10–11.

piercing, *n.* **1** severe; stringent: ". . . more/ piercing statutes daily, to chain up and restrain the/ poor." *Cor,* I, i, 82–83. **2** touching; moving: ". . . I'll commend her volubility,/ And say she uttereth piercing eloquence." *Shrew,* II, i, 175–176.

piety, *n.* misuse for "impiety": "No, thou villain, thou art full of/ piety . . ." *M Ado,* IV, ii, 75–76.

pig, *n.* **a gaping pig,** roasted pig, which seems to stare when it is served: "As there is no firm reason to be rend'red/ Why he cannot abide a gaping pig . . ." *Merch,* IV, i, 53–54.

pigeon-egg, *n.* used as an example of smallness: ". . . thou half-penny/ purse of wit, thou pigeon-egg of discretion." *Love's L,* V, i, 66–67.

pigeon-livered, *adj.* lacking courage or resolution: ". . . it cannot be/ But I am pigeon-liver'd and lack gall . . ." *Ham,* II, ii, 573.

pight, *adj.* **1** old past part. of **pitch:** ". . . you vile abominable tents,/ Thus proudly pight upon our Phrygian plains . . ." *Tr*

& Cr, V, x, 23–24. **2** resolved; determined: "When I dissuaded him from his intent,/ And found him pight to do it . . ." *Lear,* II, i, 64–65.

pig-nut, *n.* peanut or earthnut: "And I with my long nails will dig thee pig-nuts . . ." *Temp,* II, ii, 168.

Pigrogromitus, *n.* name appar. coined by the Clown: ". . . thou was in very gracious fooling last/ night, when thou spok'st of Pigrogromitus . . ." *T Night,* II, iii, 22–23.

pike, *n.* **1** long lance tipped with a spear; here, obvious sexual innuendo: ". . . to serve/ bravely is to come halting off, you know; to come/ off the breach, with his pike bent bravely . . ." *2 Hen 4,* II, iv, 48–50. **2** spike, esp. one in the center of a round shield: ". . . you must put in the/ pikes with a vice . . ." *M Ado,* V, ii, 19–20. **3** pitchfork: "Let us revenge/ this with our pikes, ere we become rakes." *Cor,* I, i, 21–22.

pilch, *n.* leather jacket; here, a nickname: "What, ho, Pilch!"/ "Ha, come and bring away the nets!" *Per,* II, i, 12–13.

pilchard, *n.* small fish resembling a herring: ". . . fools/ are as like husbands as pilchards are to herrings . . ." *T Night,* III, i, 34–35.

pilcher, *n.* leather scabbard: "Will you pluck your sword out of his pilcher by the/ ears?" *Rom & Jul,* III, i, 79–80.

pile, *n.* **two pile and a half,** joke by the Clown, who invents a pile between two and three for the thickness of velvet: "His left cheek is a cheek of two pile and a half,/ but his right cheek is worn bare." *All's W,* IV, v, 93–94.

pilgrimage, *n.* any long, tiring journey: "Most miserable hour that e'er time saw/ In lasting labour [ceaseless toil] of his pilgrimage." *Rom & Jul,* IV, v, 44–45.

pill, *v.* **1** to strip bare: "The commons hath he pill'd with grievous taxes . . ." *Rich 2,* II, i, 246. **2** to pillage; plunder: "Large-handed robbers your grave masters are,/ And pill by law." *Timon,* IV, i, 11–12.

pilled, *adj.* bald, often the result of mercury treatment for venereal disease [so-called "French disease"]: ". . . be piled as thou art/ pilled, for a French velvet." *Meas,* I, ii, 32–33.

Pillicock, *n.* poss. a nursery rhyme, with second line a refrain; brought to Tom's [Edgar's] mind by "pelican"; also, used as an endearment and as a slang term for "penis": "Pillicock sat on Pillicock hill [pudenda?]:/ Alow, alow, loo, loo!" *Lear,* III, iv, 76–77.

pillory, *n.* form of punishment, consisting of a large board with holes that shackled the prisoner's head and hands as he stood on a platform in public view: "And there I stood amazed for a while,/ As on a pillory, looking through the lute . . ." *Shrew,* II, i, 155–156.

pilot, *n.* captain of a merchant vessel: "I am no pilot, yet wert thou as far/ As that vast shore wash'd with the farthest sea,/ I should adventure for such merchandise." *Rom & Jul,* II, ii, 82–84.

pin, *n.* **1** most worthless trifle: "If you should need a pin,/ You could not with more tame a tongue desire it." *Meas,* II, ii, 45–46. **2** exact center, as on a target: ". . . the very pin of his heart cleft with the/ blind bow-boy's butt-shaft." *Rom & Jul,* II, iv, 15–16. **3 a codpiece to stick pins on,** codpieces were sometimes ornamented with jeweled pins: "A round hose . . . now 's not worth a pin/ Unless you have a cod-piece to stick pins on." *Two Gent,* II, vii, 55–56. **4 a pin,** something quite irrelevant: "But not kissed your keeper's daughter?"/ "Tut, a pin . . ." *Wives,* I, i, 105–106. **5 tell a pin,** don't tease; also, prob. wordplay on pin [penis]: "Fo, fo, come, tell a pin; you are forsworn." *Tr & Cr,* V, ii, 22.

pin and web, *n.* disease of cataracts: ". . . and all eyes/ Blind with the pin and web . . ." *W Tale,* I, ii, 290–291.

pin-buttock, *n.* buttocks that are pointed in the manner of a pin: ". . . the pin-buttock, the quatch-buttock, the brawn-buttock,/ or any buttock." *All's W,* II, ii, 17–18.

pinch, *n.* **1** nip, as by pursuing hounds: "Not rascal-like to fall down with a pinch . . ." *1 Hen 6,* IV, ii, 49. **2 necessity's sharp pinch,** the pain of poverty: "To be a comrade with the wolf and owl,/ Necessity's sharp pinch!" *Lear,* II, iv, 212–213.
—*v.* **3** to pain or torment: ". . . gout galls the one, and the pox pinches the other . . ." *2 Hen 4,* I, ii, 231–232. **4 pinch one another,** to risk offending one another: "As they pinch one another by the disposition [because of their differing temperaments],/ he cries out 'No more' . . ." *Ant & Cleo,* II, vii, 6–7. **5 pinch wanton on your cheek,** (to) leave pinch marks on your cheek that betray you as a wanton: "Let the bloat King tempt you to bed,/ Pinch wanton on your cheek . . ." *Ham,* III, iv, 184–185.

pinched, *adj.* tormented; anguished: "He has discover'd my design, and I/ Remain a pinch'd thing . . ." *W Tale,* II, i, 50–51.

pinching, *adj.* cramped or confining; here also, uncomfortably cold: "How/ In this our pinching cave shall we discourse/ The freezing hours away?" *Cymb,* III, iii, 37–39.

pinch-spotted, *adj.* covered with spots caused by pinching: ". . . and more pinch-spotted make them/ Than pard [leopard] or cat o' mountain." *Temp,* IV, i, 260–261.

pine, *v.* **1** to afflict: "I towards the north,/ Where shivering cold and sickness pines the clime . . ." *Rich 2,* V, i, 76–77. **2** to dwindle; fade: "And let that pine to aggravate thy store . . ." *Sonn 146,* 10. **3 pine the maw,** to starve the stomach: ". . . poor birds deceiv'd with painted grapes/ Do surfeit by the eye and pine the maw . . ." *Ven & Ad,* 601–602.
—*n.* **4** Antony refers to himself: ". . . and this pine is bark'd,/ That overtopp'd them all." *Ant & Cleo,* IV, xii, 23–24.

pinfold, *n.* town enclosure for stray cattle: "You mistake; I mean the pound, a pinfold." *Two Gent,* I, i, 104.

pinion, *v.* to incapacitate by binding the elbows: "Go seek the traitor Gloucester,/ Pinion him like a thief . . ." *Lear,* III, vii, 22–23.

pinioned, *adj.* like a bird whose wings have been clipped: "Know, sir, that I/ Will not wait pinion'd at your master's court . . ." *Ant & Cleo,* V, ii, 52–53.

pink, *n.* **1** essence or paragon: "Nay, I am the very pink of courtesy." *Rom & Jul,* II, iv, 59. **2** the flower dianthus: "Pink for flower."/ . . . "Why, then is my pump well flowered." *Rom & Jul,* II, iv, 60–62.

pinked porringer, *n.* woman's cap likened to an overturned porringer: ". . . rail'd/ upon me till her pink'd porringer fell off her head . . ." *Hen 8,* V, iii, 46–48.

pink eyne, *n.* See **eyne** (def. 2).

pinnace, *n.* small, light sailing vessel: ". . . whilst our pinnace anchors in the Downs . . ." *2 Hen 6,* IV, i, 9.

pinse, *v.* to torment or torture: ". . . serve Got [God], and leave your/ desires, and fairies will not pinse you." *Wives,* V, v, 130–131.

pint-pot, *n.* pot for serving a pint of ale (used as a nickname for the Hostess): "Peace, good pint-pot, peace, good ticklebrain." *1 Hen 4,* II, iv, 392.

pioned and twilled, *adj.* prob. eroded by action of the water and strengthened along the top with interwoven branches: "Thy banks with pioned and twilled brims,/ Which spongy April at thy hest betrims . . ." *Temp,* IV, i, 64–65.

pioner, *n.* laborer who digs; here, a miner [military term]: "Well said, old mole. Canst work i'th' earth so fast?/ A worthy pioner!" *Ham,* I, v, 170–171.

pious, *adj.* sacred or holy: "The first row [stanza] of the pious chanson will show you more . . ." *Ham,* II, ii, 415–416.

pip, *n.* **a pip out,** (in the card game of Thirty-one) one over the winning count; here, poss. a loss of reason as well: ". . . being perhaps, for aught I see, two and/ thirty, a pip out?" *Shrew,* I, ii, 32–33.

pipe, *n.* **1** musical instrument resembling a flute or recorder: "Rumour is a pipe/ Blown by surmises . . ." *2 Hen 4,* Induc., 15–16. **2** immature voice; here, a "boyish" treble: ". . . thy small pipe/ Is as the maiden's organ, shrill and sound . . ." *T Night,* I, iv, 32–33. **3** vein of the body: ". . . when we have stuff'd/ These pipes and these conveyances of our blood . . ." *Cor,* V, i, 53–54.
—*v.* **4** to seek in vain: "This wicked emperor may have shipp'd her hence;/ And kinsmen, then we may go pipe for justice." *T Andr,* IV, iii, 23–24.

pipe-wine, *n.* wine from a cask; also, wordplay on musical pipe that was played for dancing: "I think I shall drink in pipe-wine first with/ him; I'll make him dance." *Wives,* III, ii, 82–83.

piping time, *n.* a time when the weak music of pipes was heard, not the drums and trumpets of war: ". . . this weak piping time of peace . . ." *Rich 3,* I, i, 24.

Pippen, *n.* Pepin, King of the Franks [France] 751–768; father of Charlemagne: ". . . powerful to araise King Pippen, nay,/ To give great Charlemain a pen in's hand . . ." *All's W,* II, i, 75–76.

pippin, *n.* type of apple; here, eaten as dessert: "I will make an end of my/ dinner; there's pippins and cheese to come." *Wives,* I, ii, 11–12.

pirate, *n.* pirate ship: ". . . a pirate of/ very warlike appointment gave us chase." *Ham,* IV, vi, 14–15.

piring, *pres. part.* of pire; peering; "poking around": "Piring in maps for ports, and piers and roads . . ." *Merch,* I, i, 19.

pismire, *n.* ant: "I am . . . stung with pismires, when I hear/ Of this vile politician Bolingbroke." *1 Hen 4,* I, iii, 236–238.

pissing-conduit, *n.* small stream near the Royal Exchange: "I charge and command that . . . the pissing-conduit run nothing but/ claret wine this first year of our reign." *2 Hen 6,* IV, vi, 2–4.

pissing while, *n.* time required to urinate; a short while: ". . . he had not been there . . . a pissing while, but all the chamber/ smelt him." *Two Gent,* IV, iv, 18–20.

pistol, *n.* obvious anachronism, but not uncommon: ". . . if I can get him within my pistol's length [range], I'll make him sure enough." *Per,* I, i, 167.

pit, *n.* pit into which a wild animal was driven and captured; here, also the connotation of a grave: "Our enemies have beat us to the pit." *J Caes,* V, v, 23.

pitch[1], *n.* the pitch-black eyes of Rosaline: "I am toiling in a pitch,/ —pitch that defiles . . ." *Love's L,* IV, iii, 2–3.

pitch[2], *n.* **1** highest point in a falcon's flight before swooping to attack prey: "How high a pitch his resolution soars!" *Rich 2,* I, i, 109. **2** rank or status [exten. of falconry sense]: ". . . all men's honours/ Lie like one lump before him, to be fashion'd/ Into what pitch he please." *Hen 8,* II, ii, 47–49. **3** high worth; value: ". . . nought enters there,/ Of what validity and pitch soe'er . . ." *T Night,* I, i, 11–12.

pitch[3], *v.* **1** **pitch a field,** to arm a field with sharp stakes to impede the advance of enemy horse soldiers: ". . . the very parings of our nails/ Shall pitch a field when we are dead." *1 Hen 6,* III, ii, 102–103. **2** **pitch a toil,** to set a snare; spread a net to trap game: ". . . they have pitched a toil; I am toiling in a pitch . . ." *Love's L,* IV, iii, 2.

pitch and pay, *v.* cash down, no credit: "Let senses rule, the word is 'Pitch and pay' . . ." *Hen 5,* II, iii, 50.

pitchy, *adj.* black as pitch: "I will sort [select] a pitchy day for thee . . ." *3 Hen 6,* V, vi, 85.

piteously, *adv.* so as to arouse pity: "Ruthful to hear, yet piteously perform'd . . ." *T Andr,* V, i, 66.

pit-fall, *n.* pit dug to trap animals: ". . . thou'dst never fear the net, nor lime,/ The pit-fall, nor the gin." *Mac,* IV, ii, 34–35.

pith, *n.* **1** essence: "Perhaps you mark'd not what's the pith of all [the most vital part]." *Shrew,* I, i, 166. **2** strength: "Either past or not arriv'd to pith and puissance . . ." *Hen 5,* III, Chor., 21. **3** **pith and marrow,** most important elements: ". . . it takes/ From our achievements . . . The pith and marrow of our attribute." *Ham,* I, iv, 20–22.

pithless, *adj.* weakened; emaciated: ". . . pithless arms, like to a wither'd vine . . ." *1 Hen 6,* II, v, 11.

pitiful, *adj.* **1** full of pity; feeling pity: "Our hearts you see not; they are pitiful . . ." *J Caes,* III, i, 169. **2** showing pity; pitying: "O, be to me, though thy hard heart say no,/ Nothing so kind, but something pitiful." *T Andr,* II, iii, 155–156.

pitiful-hearted, *adj.* soft-hearted: "Didst thou never see Titan kiss a dish of butter/ (pitiful-hearted Titan!) . . ." *1 Hen 4,* II, iv, 117–118.

pitifully, *adv.* showing pity; mercifully: "As you are great, be pitifully good." *Timon,* III, v, 53.

Pitty-ward, *adv.* toward the Petty [or Little] Park: "Marry, sir, the Pitty-ward, the Park-ward, every/ way..." *Wives,* III, i, 5–6.

Piùe per dolcezza che per forza, [Italian] Rather by gentleness than by force. *Per,* II, ii, 27.

place, *v.* **1** to elevate to a position of dignity: "...place thieves,/ And give them title, knee and approbation..." *Timon,* IV, iii, 36–37.
—*n.* **2** office or rank; official position: "First, what is your place?" *Per,* V, i, 20. **3** high standing; here, among friends: "I'm angry at him/ That might have known my place." *Timon,* III, iii, 15–16. **4 follow our places.** See **follow** (def. 4). **5 give no place,** to refuse to yield; not restrain itself: "My love can give no place, bide no denay." *T Night,* II, iv, 125. **6 give place, a.** make way; get out of the way: "What, is the fellow mad?"/ "Sirrah, give place." *J Caes,* III, i, 10. **b.** to yield to: "Nor gives to necessary wrinkles place..." *Sonn 108,* 11. **7 in place,** nearby; at hand: "And yet here's one in place I cannot pardon." *Meas,* V, i, 497. **8 in place where,** in a suitable place; here, for armed combat: "This is true that I say; and I had thee in place/ where, thou shouldst know it." *Shrew,* IV, iii, 147–148. **9 keep place,** to keep pace; agree: "Keeps place with thought, and... Do thoughts unveil in their dumb cradles." *Tr & Cr,* III, iii, 198–199. **10 of another place,** of a different [or equal] rank: "Who [those who] were below him/ He us'd as creatures of another place..." *All's W,* I, ii, 41–42. **11 take place,** to gain acceptance: "...these fix'd evils so fit in him/ That they take place when virtue's steely bones/ Looks bleak i' th' cold wind..." *All's W,* I, i, 100–102.

placket, *n.* opening in a petticoat, giving access to a pocket; also, in bawdy sense, a woman: "Dread prince of plackets, king of codpieces..." *Love's L,* III, i, 179.

plague, *n.* **1** curse: "If thou dost marry, I'll give thee this plague for thy/ dowry..." *Ham,* III, i, 136–137. **2** vexation; torment: "Wherefore should I/ Stand in the plague of custom..." *Lear,* I, ii, 2–3. **3** physical or mental distress: "Only my plague thus far I count my gain,/ That she that makes me sin, awards me pain." *Sonn 141,* 13–14. **4 monarch's plague,** flattery: "Drink up the monarch's plague, this flattery?" *Sonn 114,* 2. **5 plague of,** a plague on: "Plague of your policy..." *Hen 8,* III, ii, 259.
—*v.* **6** to vex or annoy; also, tease: "Ay, come: O Jove, do come: I shall be plagu'd." *Tr & Cr,* V, ii, 104. **7** to punish: "By heaven, brat, I'll plague ye for that word." *3 Hen 6,* V, v, 27.

plaguy proud, *adj.* infected with the plague of pride: "He is so plaguy proud that the death-tokens of it/ Cry 'No recovery.'" *Tr & Cr,* II, iii, 178–179.

plain¹, *adj.* **1** plainspoken: "...'tis our will/ That some plain man recount their purposes..." *Love's L,* V, ii, 176–177. **2** level: "Follow me then/ To plainer ground." *M N Dream,* III, ii, 403–404. **3** clear; easily understood: "...the song we had last night./ Mark it, Cesario, it is old and plain..." *T Night,* II, iv, 42–43. **4 plain and free,** frank and unreserved: "And that my love may appear plain and free..." *Two Gent,* V, iv, 82.
—*adv.* **5** clearly; so as to leave no doubt: "...to confirm it plain,/ You gave me this..." *Love's L,* V, ii, 452–453.

plain², *v.* to complain: "After our sentence plaining comes too late." *Rich 2,* I, iii, 175.

plain³, *v.* to explain: "What's dumb in show I'll plain with speech." *Per,* III, Chor., 14.

plain dealer, *n.* one free of deceit, esp. an honest merchant: "Why, thou didst conclude hairy men plain/ dealers without wit." *Errors,* II, ii, 85–86.

plaining, *n.* [often pl.] wailing: "Weeping before for what she saw must come,/ And piteous plainings of the pretty babes..." *Errors,* I, i, 71–72.

plainly, *adv.* honestly; straightforwardly: "You must report to th'Volscian lords how plainly/ I have borne this business." *Cor,* V, iii, 3–4.

plainness, *n.* **1** honest dealing: "Thy deeds, thy plainness, and thy house-keeping,/ Hath won the greatest favour of the commons..." *2 Hen 6,* I, 1, 190–191. **2** sincerity; openness; frankness: "Let pride, which she calls plainness, marry her." *Lear,* I, i, 129. **3 in plainness,** frankly; openly: "And now in plainness do confess to thee..." *Shrew,* I, i, 152.

plain-song, *n.* **1** simple tune or melody: "An honest country lord as I am... may bring his plain-song,/ And have an hour of hearing..." *Hen 8,* I, iii, 44–46. **2** plain truth: "...the humour of it is too hot, that is the very plain-song of it." *Hen 5,* III, ii, 5–6.
—*adj.* **3** singing a simple or unvaried song: "The plain-song cuckoo gray,/ Whose note full many a man doth mark..." *M N Dream,* III, i, 126–127.

plaint, *n.* complaint: "Bootless are plaints, and cureless are my wounds..." *3 Hen 6,* II, vi, 23.

plaintful, *adj.* mournful: "A plaintful story from a sist'ring vale..." *Lover's Comp,* 2.

plaintiff, *n.* misuse for "defendant": "Come, bring away the plaintiffs." *M Ado,* V, i, 247.

plait, *v.* to braid; here, thought to be the work of elves: "This is that very Mab/ That plaits the manes of horses in the night . . ." *Rom & Jul,* I, iv, 83–84.

plaited, *adj.* See **plighted.**

planched, *adj.* made of planks: "And to that vineyard is a planched gate . . ." *Meas,* IV, i, 30.

planet, *n.* **1** ref. to astrological belief in the harmful influence of certain planets: "As if some planet had unwitted men . . ." *Oth,* II, iii, 173. **2 strike like a planet,** to affect like a planet in sinister aspect: ". . . with a sudden reinforcement struck/ Corioles like a planet." *Cor,* II, ii, 113–114.

planetary, *adj.* caused by the influence of the planets: "Be as a planetary plague . . ." *Timon,* IV, iii, 110.

plant, *v.* **1** to establish: "Planting oblivion, beating reason back . . ." *Ven & Ad,* 557.
—*n.* **2** [pl.] soles of the feet; here, in wordplay with growing plants: "Some o' their plants/ are ill-rooted already, the least wind i' the world/ will blow them down." *Ant & Cleo,* II, vii, 1–3.

plantage, *n.* **as plantage to the moon,** as cultivated plants are influenced by the phases of the moon: "As true as steel, as plantage to the moon . . ." *Tr & Cr,* III, ii, 175.

plantain, *n.* plantain leaf, thought to heal cuts and bruises: "O, sir, plantain, a plain plantain! no l'envoy . . ." *Love's L,* III, i, 70.

plantation, *n.* intended meaning is "colonization," but misunderstood, perh. intentionally, as "planting": "Had I plantation of this isle, my lord,—"/ "He'd sow 't with nettle-seed." *Temp,* II, i, 139–140.

plantin, *n.* See **plantain.**

plash, *n.* shallow pool: ". . . he that leaves/ A shallow plash to plunge him in the deep . . ." *Shrew,* I, i, 22–23.

Plashy, *n.* country residence of Gloucester in Essex, SE England: "With all good speed at Plashy visit me." *Rich 2,* I, ii, 66.

plat, *n.* knot [of hair]: "Her hair, nor loose nor tied in formal plat . . ." *Lover's Comp,* 29.

plate, *n.* **1** dishes, utensils, etc., plated with silver or gold: "The plate, coin, revenues, and moveables,/ Whereof our uncle Gaunt did stand possess'd." *Rich 2,* II, i, 161–162. **2** silver coin: ". . . realms and islands were/ As plates dropp'd from his pocket." *Ant & Cleo,* V, ii, 91–92. **3** armor: ". . . the braving Duke of Normandy,/ Hath trimmed the mountain on our right hand up/ In shining plate . . ." *Edw 3,* IV, iv, 15–17.

plated, *adj.* dressed in armor: ". . . why he cometh hither/ Thus plated in habiliments of war . . ." *Rich 2,* I, iii, 27–28.

platform, *n.* plan; strategy or plot: "And lay new platforms to endamage them." *1 Hen 6,* II, i, 77.

platted hive, *n.* woven hat: "Upon her head a platted hive of straw . . ." *Lover's Comp,* 8.

plausibly, *adv.* with applause; here, willingly or unanimously: "The Romans plausibly did give consent . . ." *Luc,* 1854.

plausive, *adj.* **1** pleasing; acceptable: ". . . some habit, that too much o'er leavens/ The form of plausive manners . . ." *Ham,* I, iv, 29–30. **2** commendable; praiseworthy: ". . . his plausive words/ He scatter'd not in ears, but grafted them/ To grow there and to bear . . ." *All's W,* I, ii, 53–55. **3** plausible; also, specious: "It/ must be a very plausive invention that carries it." *All's W,* IV, i, 25–26.

Plautus, *n.* Roman writer of comedies, d. 2nd cent. B.C.: "Seneca cannot be too heavy, nor Plautus too/ light." *Ham,* II, ii, 396–397.

play, *v.* **1** to wager: "We'll play with them the first boy for a thousand/ ducats." *Merch,* III, ii, 213–214. **2** to gamble for: "The confident and over-lusty French/ Do the low-rated English play at dice . . ." *Hen 5,* IV, Chor., 18–19. **3** to deploy; perh. "ply," with sense of "urge on" is meant: "Good boatswain have care. Where's the master?/ Play the men." *Temp,* I, i, 9–10. **4 play false,** to engage in adultery: "I am much afeard my lady his mother played false/ with a smith." *Merch,* I, ii, 42–43. **5 play it off,** *v.* drink it down; get on with it: ". . . when you breathe in your watering . . . they bid you 'Play it off!' . . ." *1 Hen 4,* II, iv, 15–17. **6 play upon,** train the guns upon [artillery term]: "I'd play incessantly upon these jades . . ." *K John,* II, i, 385.
—*n.* **7** entertainment; spectacle: "Shall's have a play of this?" *Cymb,* V, v, 228. **8 hold ye play,** keep you busy: "I'll find/ A Marshalsea shall hold ye play these two months." *Hen 8,* V, iii, 84–85. **9 make one's play,** [in cards] to win a trick; here, used with sexual innuendo: "You are a merry gamester/ My Lord Sands."/ "Yes, if I make my play . . ." *Hen 8,* I, iv, 45–46. **10 out of play,** sexually inactive: "An honest country lord as I am, beaten/ A long time out of play . . ." *Hen 8,* I, iii, 44–45.

player, *n.* actor; here, perh., one who only pretends: "Players in your housewifery; and housewives in your beds." *Oth,* II, i, 112.

playing-day, *n.* school holiday: "Look, where his master/ comes; 'tis a playing-day, I see." *Wives,* IV, i, 6–7.

play one's prize, *v.* to win one's match [a term in fencing]: "So, Bassianus, you have play'd your prize . . ." *T Andr,* I, i, 399.

play the desk or table-book, *v.* to share another's secrets: "If I had play'd the desk or table-book,/ Or given my heart a winking mute and dumb . . ." *Ham,* II, ii, 136–137.

plea, *n.* **1** object of pleading: ". . . the plea of no less weight/ Than Aquitaine, a dowry for a queen." *Love's L,* II, i, 7–8. **2 hold a plea,** to try an action in a court of law; here, to sustain a cause: "How with this rage shall beauty hold a plea . . ." *Sonn 65,* 3.

pleached, *adj.* **1** (esp. of branches) interlaced; intertwined: "walking in a thick-pleached alley in mine orchard . . ." *M Ado,* I, ii, 8–9. **2** folded; here, prob. bound together: "Thy master thus with pleach'd arms, bending down/ His corrigible neck . . ." *Ant & Cleo,* IV, xiv, 73–74.

plead, *v.* **1** to argue; attest to: "Know then, I here . . . Plead a new state [condition] in thy unrivall'd merit . . ." *Two Gent,* V, iv, 140–142. **2** to deliver an oration: "There pleading might you see grave Nestor stand . . ." *Luc,* 1401.

pleasance, *n.* merriment: "Crabbed age and youth cannot live together:/ Youth is full of pleasance, age is full of care . . ." *Pass Pil,* XII, 1–2.

pleasant, *adj.* **1** merry; prankish: "Like pleasant travellers, to break a jest/ Upon the company you overtake?" *Shrew,* IV, v, 71–72. **2** in a joking mood; facetious: "You are pleasant, sir, and speak apace." *Meas,* III, ii, 109. **3** given to pleasantries, esp. at another's expense: "And tell the pleasant prince this mock of his/ Hath turn'd his balls to gun-stones . . ." *Hen 5,* I, ii, 281–282.

pleasantly, *adv.* easily; simply: "Think'st thou to catch my life so pleasantly . . ." *Tr & Cr,* IV, v, 248.

please, *v.* **1** to recompense; satisfy: "Establish him in his true sense again,/ And I will please you what you will demand." *Errors,* IV, iv, 46–47. **2 please you,** if you agree: "Please you to do't,/ I'll take it as a peril to my soul . . ." *Meas,* II, iv, 64–65.

please-man, *n.* toady; sycophant: "Some carry-tale, some please-man, some slight zany . . ." *Love's L,* V, ii, 463.

pleasing, *adj.* convincing: ". . . the devil hath power/ T'assume a pleasing shape . . ." *Ham,* II, ii, 595–596.

pleasing punishment, *n.* pregnancy: ". . . almost at fainting under/ The pleasing punishment that women bear . . ." *Errors,* I, i, 45–46.

pleasure, *n.* **1** desire or intention; will: "His Highness' pleasure is to talk with him." *2 Hen 6,* II, i, 73. **2 common plea-**sures, public parks: ". . . common pleasures,/ To walk abroad and recreate yourselves." *J Caes,* III, ii, 252–253. **3 their greater pleasures,** decision of those in higher authority: ". . . good guard [guard them closely],/ Until their greater pleasures first be known/ That are to censure them." *Lear,* V, iii, 2–3. **4 use your pleasure,** behave according to your own inclination: ". . . if I might but see you at my death: notwithstanding, use/ your pleasure . . ." *Merch,* III, ii, 318–319.

plebeii, *n. pl.* plebeians; common people: "If he should still malignantly remain/ Fast foe to th'plebeii . . ." *Cor,* II, iii, 181–182.

plebs, *n.* See **tribunal plebs.**

pledge, *n.* surety or bail: "Petruchio, patience, I am Grumio's pledge." *Shrew,* I, ii, 44.

plenteous, *adv.* plenteously: ". . . she breeds sweets as plenteous as the sun . . ." *Edw 3,* II, i, 159.

plenty, *n.* [often pl.] abundance; here, of the necessaries and comforts of life: ". . . the naked, poor, and mangled Peace,/ Dear nurse of arts, plenties, and joyful births . . ." *Hen 5,* V, ii, 34–35.

pleurisy or **plurisy,** *n.* plethora or superabundance: "For goodness, growing to a pleurisy,/ Dies in his own too-much." *Ham,* IV, vii, 116–117.

plight, *n.* **1** wedding vow or pledge: "The lord whose hand must take my plight shall carry/ Half my love . . ." *Lear,* I, i, 101–102. **2** state or condition: "How can I then return in happy plight . . ." *Sonn 28,* 1. **3** healthy condition: "To keep her constancy in plight and youth . . ." *Tr & Cr,* III, ii, 159. **4 plight troth,** to give one's promise; here, not to do harm: "Bid her alight,/ And her troth plight . . ." *Lear,* III, iv, 125–126.

plighted, *adj.* cleverly concealed [in some editions **plaited,** pleated, enfolded]: "Time shall unfold what plighted cunning hides . . ." *Lear,* I, i, 280.

plighter, *n.* pledger: ". . . this kingly seal,/ And plighter of high hearts!" *Ant & Cleo,* III, xiii, 125–126.

plot, *n.* small, esp. secluded, area; spot: "And many unfrequented plots there are!/ Fitted by kind for rape and villainy . . ." *T Andr,* II, i, 116–117.

plot-proof, *adj.* impervious to conspiracies: ". . . out of the blank/ And level of my brain: plot-proof . . ." *W Tale,* II, iii, 5–6.

plough, *n.* **1 hold the plough,** to engage in farming: "I have vowed to Jaquenetta to hold the/ plough for her sweet love three year." *Love's L,* V, ii, 875–876.
—*v.* **2** wordplay on "to work (the earth)" and "to have sexual relations with": "She made great Caesar lay his sword to bed;/ He plough'd her, and she cropp'd." *Ant & Cleo,* II, ii, 227–228.

plow, *v.* Fluellen's pron. of "blow": "By Cheshu [Jesu], I think a' will plow up all/ if there is not better directions." *Hen 5,* III, ii, 67–68.

pluck, *v.* **1** to pull down so as to cover: "... their hats are pluck'd about their ears,/ And half their faces buried in their cloaks ..." *J Caes,* II, i, 73–74. **2** to pull down or cause to crash in ruins: "May all the building in my fancy pluck/ Upon my hateful life ..." *Lear,* IV, ii, 85–86. **3 plucked him after,** caused him to follow shortly [in death]: "But not without that harmful stroke, which since/ Hath pluck'd him after." *Lear,* IV, ii, 77–78. **4 pluck off a little,** come down a notch [in rank]: "... pluck off a little,/ I would not be a young count in your way/ For more than blushing comes to [blushing will be as far as you get with him] ..." *Hen 8,* II, iii, 40–42. **5 pluck on,** to encourage; induce or excite: "How ... it was follow'd/ May rather pluck on laughter than revenge ..." *T Night,* V, i, 364–365. **6 pluck one,** (in a lottery) to draw (a winning number); here, to draw a winner as a marriage partner: "... a man may draw his heart out ere 'a [he]/ pluck one." *All's W,* I, iii, 85–86.

pluck another's beard, gross insult: "[Regan plucks his beard.]/ By the kind Gods, 'tis most ignobly done/ To pluck me by the beard." *Lear,* III, vii, 34–36.

plummet, *n.* nautical sounding device; Falstaff may mean his ignorance is now being sounded by others more ignorant; poss. pun on "plumbet," a type of flannel, and further ref. to "Welshman": "I am not able to answer the Welsh/ flannel; ignorance itself is a plummet o'er me; use/ me as you will." *Wives,* V, v, 163–165.

plurisy, *n.* See **pleurisy.**

Pluto, *n.* Greek god of the underworld: "To Pluto's damned lake,/ by this hand, to th'infernal deep ..." *2 Hen 4,* II, iv, 153–154.

Pluto's mine, *n.* [traditional] confusion of Pluto with Plutus, the god of wealth: "... within, a heart/ Dearer than Pluto's mine, richer than gold ..." *J Caes,* IV, iii, 100–101.

Plutus, *n.* Roman god of wealth: "Plutus himself,/ That knows the tinct and multiplying med'cine ..." *All's W,* V, iii, 101–102.

ply one's book, See **book (def. 9).**

pocket, *v.* **1 pocket up,** to conceal: "Ay, or very falsely pocket up his report." *Temp,* II, i, 65. **2 pocketing up of wrongs,** putting up with insults; also, receiving stolen goods: "... take from/ another's pocket to put into mine; for it is plain/ pocketing up of wrongs." *Hen 5,* III, ii, 52–54.

pocky, *adj.* afflicted with venereal disease: "... we have/ many pocky corses nowadays that will scarce hold/ the laying in ..." *Ham,* V, i, 159–161.

poem unlimited, *n. poss.* a play that does not observe the classic unities of time, place, etc.; *perh.* a work that touches all the preceding categories: "... tragical-comical-historical-pastoral, scene individable, or poem unlimited." *Ham,* II, ii, 394–396.

poet, *n. prob.* ref. to Ovid, who wrote of Orpheus in his *Metamorphoses:* "... therefore the poet/ Did feign that Orpheus drew trees, stones, and floods ..." *Merch,* V, i, 79–80.

Poictiers, *n.* town of Poitiers, in W central France: "Guienne, Champaigne, Rheims, Rouen, Orleans,/ Paris, Guysors, Poictiers, are all quite lost." *l Hen 6,* I, i, 60–61.

point, *n.* **1** cord or lace, esp. for securing hose to the doublet: "... for a silken point/ I'll give my barony, never talk of it." *2 Hen 4,* I, i, 53–54. **2** same, with wordplay on point = argument: "... I am resolved on two points."/ "That if one break, the other will hold: or if both/ break, your gaskins fall." *T Night,* I, v, 22–24; also, *W Tale,* IV, iv, 207–208. **3** thong sewn on clothing for attaching armor to the body: "God's light, with/ two points on your shoulder?" *2 Hen 4,* II, iv, 129–130. **4** apex; summit: "And, touching now the point of human skill ..." *M N Dream,* II, ii, 118. **5** position attained by the falcon in relation to the prey just before attacking: "But what a point, my lord, your falcon made ..." *2 Hen 6,* II, i, 5. **6** [pl.] punctuation marks; also, small matters [niceties]: "This fellow doth not stand upon [concern himself with] points." *M N Dream,* V, i, 118. **7** tip of a sword: "'Tis dangerous when the baser nature comes/ Between the pass and fell incensed points/ Of might opposites." *Ham,* V, ii, 60–62. **8** [pl.] orders; instructions: "Tullus Aufidius ... obeys his points/ As if he were his officer." *Cor,* IV, vi, 125–127. **9 at a point,** in readiness: "Old Siward, with ten thousand warlike men,/ Already at a point, was setting forth." *Mac,* 134–135. **10 at point, a.** precisely; in every detail: "... a figure like your father/ Armed at point exactly, cap-à-pie ..." *Ham,* I, ii, 199–200. **b.** armed: "... to let him keep/ At point a hundred knights ..." *Lear,* I, iv, 333–334. **c.** ready: "... have secret feet/ In some of our best ports, and are at point/ To show their open banner." *Lear,* III, i, 32–34. **d.** on the point or verge [of]: "... was once at point ... to master Caesar's sword ..." *Cymb,* III, i, 31–32. **11 at the point,** at swordpoint: "I saw him hold Lord Percy at

the point . . ." *1 Hen 4,* V, iv, 20. **12 draw to that point,** [to] be bestowed on that person [me]: "Let your best love draw to that point which seeks/ Best to preserve it . . ." *Ant & Cleo,* III, iv, 21–22. **13 full point,** (in punctuation) period; full stop: "Come we to full points here? And are etceteras nothings?" *2 Hen 4,* II, iv, 180. **14 grow to a point,** to reach a conclusion: ". . . read the names of the actors; and so grow/ to a point." *M N Dream,* I, ii, 9–10. **15 no point,** by no means; not at all: "Dumain was at my service, and his sword:/ No point, quoth I: my servant straight was mute." *Love's L,* V, ii, 276–277. **16 point and period,** end and purpose: "My point and period will be throughly wrought,/ Or well or ill, as this day's battle's fought." *Lear,* IV, vii, 95–96. **17 point of war,** signal to attack, usually sounded on the trumpet: ". . . your tongue divine/ To a loud trumpet and a point of war?" *2 Hen 4,* IV, i, 51–52. **18 point of wisdom,** action showing wisdom: "You may, sir; 'tis a point of wisdom. Fare you well." *Rich 3,* I, iv, 98. **19 ties his points,** ref. to a menial who helps his master dress by lacing his hose to his doublet; here, ref. to Caesar's servant: "To flatter Caesar, would you mingle eyes/ With one that ties his [Caesar's] points?" *Ant & Cleo,* III, xiii, 156–157. **20 to full points,** to a complete stop: "Come we to full points here?" *2 Hen 4,* II, iv, 180. **21 to point,** at point; in every detail: "Hast thou, spirit,/ Perform'd to point the tempest that I bade thee?" *Temp,* I, ii, 193–194.
—*v.* **22** to prompt or impel: ". . . tend'ring their own worth from where they were glass'd,/ Did point you to buy them . . ." *Love's L,* II, i, 243–244. **23** to lead: ". . . most poor matters/ Point to rich ends." *Temp,* III, i, 3–4. **24** to appoint: "Whoever plots the sin, thou poinst ['point'st] the season." *Luc,* 879.

point-blank, *n.* range or reach of a gun: ". . . now art/ thou within point-blank of our jurisdiction regal." *2 Hen 6,* IV, vii, 23–24.

point-device or **point-devise,** *adj.* **1** meticulous or overprecise: ". . . you are point-device in your accoutrements . . ." *As You,* III, ii, 372–373.
—*adv.* **2** precisely; absolutely: "I will wash off/ gross acquaintance, I will be point-device the very/ man." *T Night,* II, v, 162–164.

pointing-stock, *n.* butt of ridicule; laughingstock: ". . . I, his forlorn duchess,/ Was made a wonder and a pointing-stock/ To every idle rascal follower." *2 Hen 6,* II, iv, 45–46.

poise, *v.* **1** to weigh: ". . . call these foul offenders to their answers,/ And poise the cause in Justice' equal scales . . ." *2 Hen 6,* II, i, 195–196.
—*n.* **2** weight: "Pleas'd you to do't . . . Were equal poise of sin and charity." *Meas,* II, iv, 67–68. **3** blow; impact: "For the great swinge and rudeness of his poise . . ." *Tr & Cr,* I, iii, 207.

poised, *adj.* balanced: ". . . you saw her fair, none else being by:/ Herself pois'd with herself in either eye." *Rom & Jul,* I, ii, 96–97.

poison, *n.* **sweet poison,** flattery: "Sweet, sweet, sweet poison for the age's tooth [appetite] . . ." *K John,* I, i, 213.

poke, *n.* large bag or pocket: "And then he drew a dial from his poke . . ." *As You,* II, vii, 20.

poking-stick, *n.* metal rod heated and used to iron and stiffen the neck ruff: "Pins, and poking-sticks of steel,/ What maids lack from head to heel . . ." *W Tale,* IV, iv, 228–229.

Polack, *n.* **1** king of Poland, hence the Polish people: ". . . to Him appear'd/ To be a preparation 'gainst the Polack . . ." *Ham,* II, ii, 62–63. **2** [pl.] Poles; here, Polish soldiers: ". . . in an angry parle/ He smote the sledded Polacks on the ice." *Ham,* I, i, 65–66.

pole, *n.* **1** polestar; North Star: "When yond same star that's westward from the pole,/ Had made his course . . ." *Ham,* I, i, 39–40. **2** Antony regarded as either the soldier's standard-bearer or his polestar: "O, wither'd is the garland of the war,/ The soldier's pole is fall'n . . ." *Ant & Cleo,* IV, xv, 64–65.

Pole, *n.* **de la Pole,** family name of the Duke of Suffolk: "Fie, de la Pole! disable not thyself . . ." *1 Hen 6,* V, iii, 67.

polecats, *n.* slang for "prostitutes"; Quickly's misunderstanding of *pulcher,* Latin word for "beautiful": "Polecats? There are fairer things than polecats,/ sure." *Wives,* IV, i, 23–24.

pole-clipped, *adj.* See **poll-clipt.**

policy, *n.* **1** clever schemes; craftiness, cunning, or intrigue: "I will o'er-run thee with policy." *As You,* V, i, 55. **2** strategy; wise procedure [often in wordplay with the preceding]: ". . . and 'tis some policy/ To have one show worse than the king's and his company." *Love's L,* V, ii, 508–509. **3** statecraft: ". . . this brain of mine/ Hunts not the trail [follows the scent] of policy so sure/ As it hath us'd to do . . ." *Ham,* II, ii, 46–48. **4** immediate ends, often to be served ruthlessly: "Men must learn now with pity to dispense,/ For policy sits above conscience." *Timon,* III, ii, 88–89. **5** prudence; here, adopted on a short-term basis: "It fears not policy . . . Which works on leases of short-numbered hours . . ." *Sonn 124,* 9–10. **6 policy and reverence of age,** idea (or foolish practice) of revering old people: "This policy and reverence of age makes the/ world bitter to the best of our times . . ." *Lear,* I, ii, 47–48. **7 the policy,** prob. ref. to the principles of statecraft laid down by Machiavelli, characterized by low cunning: "Smacks it not something of the policy?" *K John,* II, i, 396.

politic, *adj.* **1** prudent or wise; also, clever or cunning: "... all alone stands hugely politic,/ That it nor grows with heat nor drowns with showers [not affected by changes in fortune]." *Sonn 124,* 10–11. **2** crafty or scheming: "... neither the scholar's melancholy, which is emulation ... nor the lawyer's, which is politic ..." *As You,* IV, i, 10–14. **3** carefully or meticulously contrived: "... maintained so politic/ a state of evil that they will not admit any good part ..." *M Ado,* V, ii, 58–59. **4** dealing with the art of politics: "I will be proud, I will read politic/ authors, I will baffle Sir Toby ..." *T Night,* II, v, 161–162. **5** necessary for the sake of appearance: "He shall in strangest stand no farther off/ Than in a politic distance." *Oth,* III, iii, 12–13.

politician, *n.* schemer, trickster, or intriguer: "This might be the pate of a politician which this ass now/ o'er-offices ..." *Ham,* V, i, 76–78.

politicly, *adv.* cleverly; shrewdly: "Thus have I politicly begun my reign ..." *Shrew,* IV, i, 175.

politic regard, *n.* look of wise understanding or concern; here, assumed: "... bites his lip with a politic regard, as/ who should say 'There were wit in this head, and/ 'twould out'—" *Tr & Cr,* III, iii, 253–255.

Polixenes, *n.* iden. only as a Greek "duke," slain in battle by Hector: "Polixenes is slain;/ Amphimacus and Thoas deadly hurt ..." *Tr & Cr,* V, v, 11–12.

poll, *n.* [sing. or pl.] **1** person's head, esp. the hair: "... the withered elder hath not his poll/ clawed like a parrot." *2 Hen 4,* II, iv, 256–257. **2** person: "... the muster-file, rotten and sound ... amounts not to fifteen thousand poll ..." *All's W,* IV, iii, 162–163. **3 by the poll,** individually [lit., by the head]: "... a catalogue/ Of all the voices that we have procur'd,/ Set down by th'poll?" *Cor,* III, iii, 8–9. **4 the greater poll,** the greater majority [number of heads]: "We are the greater poll, and in true fear/ They gave us our demands." *Cor,* III, i, 132–133.

poll-axe, *n.* poleax or battle-ax: "... your lion, that holds his poll-axe/ sitting on a close-stool, will be given to Ajax ..." *Love's L,* V, ii, 571–572.

poll-clipt, *adj.* with the top growth pruned [some editions: "pole-clipped," vines caressing the poles]: "... thy poll-clipt vineyard;/ And thy sea-marge, sterile and rocky-hard ..." *Temp,* IV, i, 68–69.

polled, *adj.* **1** cleared: "He will mow all down before him, and leave his/ passage polled." *Cor,* IV, v, 207–208. **2** bald: "... the poll'd bachelor,/ Whose youth, like wanton boys through bonfires,/ Have skipp'd thy flame ..." *Kinsmen,* V, i, 85–87.

pollution, *n.* misuse for "allusion": "And I say the pollution holds in the exchange ..." *Love's L,* IV, ii, 44.

poltroon, *n.* abject coward: "Patience is for poltroons, such as he ..." *3 Hen 6,* I, i, 62.

Polydamas, *n.* bastard son of Priam: "The fierce Polydamas/ Hath beat down Menon ..." *Tr & Cr,* V, v, 6–7.

pomewater, *n.* type of white, juicy apple: "... ripe/ as the pomewater, who now hangeth like a jewel in/ the ear of *coelo* ..." *Love's L,* IV, ii, 3–5.

Pomfret, *n.* castle [actually Pontefract castle] in Yorkshire where Richard II was murdered: "... the blood/ Of fair King Richard, scrap'd from Pomfret stones ..." *2 Hen 4,* I, i, 204–205.

pomp, *n.* **1** ceremonial splendor, esp. a grand procession: "Turn melancholy forth to funerals;/ The pale companion [bloodless fellow] is not for our pomp." *M N Dream,* I, i, 14–15. **2** ceremonial feast; here, wedding feast: "Shall braying trumpets and loud churlish drums ... be measures to our pomp?" *K John,* III, i, 229–230. **3** those who live in splendor: "Take physic [cure yourself], Pomp;/ Expose thyself to feel what wretches feel ..." *Lear,* III, iv, 33–34.

Pompey, *n.* **1** poss. wordplay on "puppy": "Go to kennel, Pompey, go." *Meas,* III, ii, 82. **2 great Pompey,** actually Cneius [Gnaeus], oldest son of Pompey the Great: "... and great Pompey/ Would stand and make his eyes grow in my brow ..." *Ant & Cleo,* I, v, 31–32.

Pompey's porch, *n.* portico of the theater built by Pompey in 55 B.C.: "And I do know, by this they stay for me/ In Pompey's porch ..." *J Caes,* I, iii, 125–126.

Pompion, *n.* dial. word for *pumpkin;* misuse for Pompey: "I am, as they say, but to parfect one man in/ one poor man, Pompion the Great, sir." *Love's L,* V, ii, 499–500.

pompous, *adj.* splendid; magnificent; showy: "The Duke hath put on a religious life,/ And thrown into neglect the pompous court?" *As You,* V, iv, 180–181.

ponderous, *adj.* weighty; heavy: "I am sure my love's/ More ponderous than my tongue." *Lear,* I, i, 77–78.

poniard, *n.* dagger: "She speaks poniards, and every/ word stabs ..." *M Ado,* II, i, 231–232.

Pont, *n.* Pontus, a country in Asia Minor: "King Manchus of Arabia, King of Pont ..." *Ant & Cleo,* III, vi, 72.

Pontic sea, *n.* Black Sea: "Like to the Pontic sea,/ Whose icy current . . . Ne'er feels retiring ebb . . ." *Oth,* III, iii, 460–462.

poop, *v.* to infect; here, with venereal disease: "Ay, she quickly poop'd him; she made him roast-meat/ for worms." *Per,* IV, ii, 22–23.

poor, *adj.* **1** pitiable: "As rich shall Romeo's by his lady's lie,/ Poor sacrifices of our enmity." *Rom & Jul,* V, iii, 302–303. **2** insignificant; worthless: "It is my birth-day,/ I had thought t' have held it poor." *Ant & Cleo,* III, xiii, 185–186. **3 poor a,** a mere: ". . . bequeathed me by will but poor a thousand crowns . . ." *As You,* I, i, 2.

poor I, *n.* I, poor woman: "Poor I was slain when Bassianus died." *T Andr,* II, iii, 171.

poor itch, *n.* superficiality; here, ignorance or empty-headedness: "That, rubbing the poor itch of your opinion,/ Make yourselves scabs?" *Cor,* I, i, 164–165.

Poor John, *n.* dried and salted hake, a cheap fish eaten esp. during Lent: "'Tis well thou art not fish; if thou hadst, thou/ hadst been Poor John." *Rom & Jul,* I, i, 29–30.

poor likelihoods, *n.* dubious grounds for a conclusion: "These are thin habits, and poor likelihoods/ Of modern [ordinary] seemings . . ." *Oth,* I, iii, 108–109.

poorly, *adv.* meanly; inadequately, considering his status: "[Enter Gloucester, led by an old Man.] My father, poorly led?" *Lear,* IV, i, 10.

poor matters, *n.* menial tasks: ". . . most poor matters/ Point to rich ends." *Temp,* III, i, 3–4.

poor Tom, *n.* name by which Bedlam beggars were known: "Poor Turlygod! poor Tom!/ That's something yet: Edgar I nothing am." *Lear,* II, iii, 21.

pop, *v.* to thrust (in) or enter; here, prob. with sexual ref.: "For thus popp'd Paris in his hardiment . . ." *Tr & Cr,* IV, v, 28.

poperin pear, *n.* Flemish pear thought to resemble the male genitalia: "O that she were/ An open-arse and thou a poperin pear!" *Rom & Jul,* II, i, 37–38.

popinjay *n.* parrot, hence a prattling, affected person: ". . . all smarting with my wounds being cold,/ To be so pester'd with a popinjay . . ." *1 Hen 4,* I, iii, 48–49.

popular, *adj.* representing the people: ". . . who puts his 'shall',/ His popular 'shall', against a graver bench . . ." *Cor,* III, i, 104–105.

popularity, *n.* mingling with common people; also, with low company: "Grew a companion to the common streets,/ Enfeoff'd himself to popularity . . ." *1 Hen 4,* III, ii, 68–69.

popular man, *n.* man of the people; demagogue: "I will counterfeit the bewitchment/ of some popular man . . ." *Cor,* II, iii, 100–101.

porch, *n.* entryway; opening: "And in the porches of my ears did pour/ The leperous distilment . . ." *Ham,* I, v, 63–64.

poring, *adj.* making one strain to see: "When creeping murmur and the poring dark/ Fills the wide vessel of the universe." *Hen 5,* IV, Chor., 2–3.

porpentine, *n.* porcupine: "And each particular hair to stand an [on] end/ Like quills upon the fretful porpentine." *Ham,* I, v, 19–20.

porridge, *n.* thin soup; broth: ". . . the other, that at dinner they should not drop/ in his porridge." *Errors,* II, ii, 97–98.

porringer, *n.* small metal dish for serving soft or liquid food: "Why, this was moulded on a porringer!" *Shrew,* IV, iii, 64.

port[1], *n.* **1** one's style or manner of living: "Keep house, and port, and servants, as I should . . ." *Shrew,* I, i, 203. **2** deportment; appearance, esp. as an indication of social class: "*Priami,* is my man/ Tranio—*regia,* bearing my port—" *Shrew,* III, i, 34–35. **3** dignity; esteem: ". . . the magnificoes/ Of greatest port have all persuaded with him . . ." *Merch,* III, ii, 279–280.

port[2], *n.* portal; city gate: "At the Saint Francis here beside the port." *All's W,* III, v, 36.

portable, *adj.* bearable: "How light and portable my pain seems now . . ." *Lear,* III, vi, 111.

portage[1], *n.* freight; a crew member's or passenger's baggage: "Even at the first thy loss is more than can/ Thy portage quit . . ." *Per,* III, i, 35–36.

portage[2], *n.* portholes: ". . . lend the eye a terrible aspect;/ Let it pry through the portage of the head . . ." *Hen 5,* III, i, 9–10.

portance, *n.* attitude; bearing or demeanor: ". . . your loves . . . took from you/ Th'apprehension of his present portance . . ." *Cor,* II, iii, 220–222.

portentous, *adj.* of bad omen; ominous: ". . . they are portentous things/ Unto the climate that they point upon." *J Caes,* I, iii, 31–32.

porter, *n.* doorkeeper; also, bearer of heavy burdens: "Achilles? A drayman, a porter, a very camel." *Tr & Cr,* I, ii, 253.

portion, *n.* **1** legal settlement, esp. as part of a marriage agreement: "... all things answerable to this portion." *Shrew,* II, i, 352. **2** the totality of one's possessions; estate: "What piles of wealth hath he accumulated/ To his own portion!" *Hen 8,* III, ii, 107–108.

portly, *adj.* **1** imposing or magnificent: "... that same greatness too which our own hands/ Have holp to make so portly." *1 Hen 4,* I, iii, 12–13. **2** well-behaved; of good deportment: "... let him alone,/ A [he] bears him like a portly gentleman..." *Rom & Jul,* I, v, 64–65.

pose *v.* to put a difficult question to: "Then I shall pose you quickly./ Which had you rather..." *Meas,* II, iv, 51–52.

position, *n.* assertion; also, hypothesis: "... as it is a most pregnant [obvious]/ and unforc'd position..." *Oth,* II, i, 234–235.

positive, *adj.* absolute; complete: "... and this Patroclus is a fool positive." *Tr & Cr,* II, iii, 67.

possess, *v.* **1** to inform: "Possess us, possess us, tell us something of him." *T Night,* II, iii, 139. **2** to instill [in]; endow or imbue: "... have, out of malice/ To the good queen, possess'd him with a scruple [doubt]..." *Hen 8,* II, i, 157–158. **3 possess it,** go ahead [and offer your toast]: "Possess it, I'll make answer..." *Ant & Cleo,* II, vii, 100.

possessed, *adj.* punning on "possessed of the monarchy" and "possessed by evil": "From forth thy reach he would have laid thy shame,/ Deposing thee before thou wert possess'd..." *Rich 2,* II, i, 106–107.

possession, *n.* **1** fact of possession; also, the person having possession: "Opinion, that did help me to the crown,/ Had still kept loyal to possession..." *1 Hen 4,* III, ii, 42–43. **2 in possession,** [given] when married: "... one half of my lands,/ And in possession twenty thousand crowns." *Shrew,* II, i, 121–122.

posset, *n.* **1** hot drink of milk curdled with ale or wine and often spiced: "Go; and we'll have a posset for 't soon at night..." *Wives,* I, iv, 7.
—*v.* **2** to thicken or curdle like a posset: "And with a sudden vigour it doth posset/ And curd, like eager droppings into milk..." *Ham,* I, v, 68–69.

possibility, *n.* limit; capacity: "... to the possibility of thy/ soldiership [I] will subscribe for thee." *All's W,* III, vi, 78–79.

possible, *adj.* latent or potential: "I would revenges,/ That possible strength might meet, would seek us through [out]..." *Cymb,* IV, ii, 159–160.

possitable, *adv.* parson's misuse for "positively": "You must speak/ possitable, if you can carry her..." *Wives,* I, i, 216–217.

post[1], *n.* **1** messenger; courier; here, wordplay on "doorpost": "'Twas the/ boy that stole your meat, and you'll beat the post." *M Ado,* II, i, 185–186. **2** post horse: "I have foundered/ nine score and odd posts..." *2 Hen 4,* IV, iii, 35–36. **3** haste: "The Mayor towards Guildhall hies him in all post." *Rich 3,* III, v, 72. **4 in post,** hastily: "Away with me in post to Ravenspurgh..." *Rich 2,* II, i, 296. **5 post with post,** one messenger immediately after the other: "As thick as hail,/ Came post with post..." *Mac,* I, iii, 97–98. **6 take post,** to travel as fast as possible by hiring post horses: "I saw her laid low in her kindred's vault/ And presently took post to tell it you." *Rom & Jul,* V, i, 20–21.
—*v.* **7** to travel with great haste; gallop: "... and posted day and night/ To meet you on the way..." *1 Hen 4,* V, i, 35–36. **8** to send in haste: "Is posted as the agent of our cardinal,/ To second all his plot." *Hen 8,* III, ii, 59–60. **9 post off,** to postpone: "I have not stopp'd mine ears to their demands,/ Nor posted off their suits with slow delays..." *3 Hen 6,* IV, viii, 39–40.
—*adv.* **10** posthaste: "... if I be not sent away post,/ I will see you again ere I go." *2 Hen 4,* II, iv, 374–375.

post[2], *n.* **1** doorpost where tavern reckonings were chalked up: "If I return I shall be post indeed,/ For she will scour your fault upon my pate." *Errors,* I, ii, 64–65. **2** See **sheriff's post.**

posted over, *past part.* hurried through; gotten out of the way: "His guilt should be but idly posted over/ Because his purpose is not executed." *2 Hen 6,* III, i, 255–256.

poster, *n.* person who travels at great speed: "The Weïrd Sisters, hand in hand,/ Posters of the sea and land..." *Mac,* I, iii, 32–33.

posterior, *n.* [often pl.] whimsical or affected use for "the latter part": "... to congratulate the princess at her pavilion in the/ posteriors of this day..." *Love's L,* V, i, 80–81.

postern, *n.* **1** small opening: "... as hard to come as for a camel/ To thread the postern of a small needle's eye." *Rich 2,* V, v, 16–17. **2** small gate or door, usually at the back or side: "... go on, good Eglamour,/ Out at the postern by the abbey wall..." *Two Gent,* V, i, 8–9. **3** secondary, or rear, gate in or out of a city: "... will by twos and threes, at several posterns,/ Clear them o' th' city." *W Tale,* I, ii, 438–439.

post-haste, *n.* widespread activity [lit., great speed]: "... the chief head/ Of this post-haste and rummage in the land." *Ham,* I, i, 109–110.

post-horse or **posthorse,** *n.* fast horse, used esp. by messengers: "Making the wind my post-horse..." *2 Hen 4,* Induc., 4.

posting, *adj.* **1** passing quickly: "But this exceeding posting day and night/ Must wear your spirits low." *All's W,* V, i, 1–2.

2 traveling quickly: ". . . whose breath/ Rides on the posting winds . . ." *Cymb,* III, iv, 36–37.

postmaster, *n.* man in charge of post-horses or messengers: ". . . would I might never stir—and/ 'tis a postmaster's boy!" *Wives,* V, v, 187–188.

post post-haste, *n.* greatest possible speed: "Write from us, wish him post post-haste, dispatch." *Oth,* I, iii, 46.

posture, *n.* form; kind: "Antony,/ The posture of your blows are yet unknown . . ." *J Caes,* V, i, 32–33.

posy *n.* **posy of a ring,** short motto engraved inside a ring: "Is this a prologue, or the posy of a ring?" *Ham,* III, ii, 147.

pot *n.* **to the pot,** to the cooking pot [to his death]: "See, they have shut him in."/ "To th'pot, I warrant him." *Cor,* I, iv, 47.

potato, *n.* the sweet (or Spanish) potato was thought to be an aphrodisiac: "Let the sky rain/ potatoes . . ." *Wives,* V, v, 18–19.

potato finger, *n.* prob. whimsical term for "penis" [See **potato**]; "little finger" was a Biblical euphem. for "penis": ". . . Luxury, with his fat rump and/ potato finger . . ." *Tr & Cr,* V, ii, 56.

potch, *v.* to thrust; jab or poke: "True sword to sword, I'll potch at him some way . . ." *Cor,* I, x, 15.

potency, *n.* power of office: "I would to heaven I had your potency,/ And you were Isabel!" *Meas,* II, ii, 67–68.

potent, *n.* **equal potents,** potentates of equal rank: ". . . back to the stained field,/ You equal potents, fiery kindled spirits!" *K John,* II, i, 357–358.

potential, *adj.* potent; powerful: ". . . the profits of my death/ Were very pregnant and potential spirits . . ." *Lear,* II, i, 75–76.

pother, *n.* confusion; uproar: "Such a pother,/ As if that whatsoever god who leads him/ Were slily crept into his human powers . . ." *Cor,* II, i, 216–218.

potting, *n.* drinking; tippling: "I learn'd it in England, where indeed they are most/ potent in potting . . ." *Oth,* II, iii, 71–72.

pottle, *n.* measure of two quarts; also, a pottle-pot: "I'll give you a pottle of burnt/ sack to give me recourse to him . . ." *Wives,* II, i, 203–204.

pottle-deep, *adv.* to the very bottom [of the pottle]: "Potations pottle-deep, and he's to watch . . ." *Oth,* II, iii, 50.

pottle-pot, *n.* tankard of two-quart capacity: "Is't such a matter to get a pottle-pot's maidenhead?" *2 Hen 4,* II, ii, 74–75.

poulter, *n.* poulterer: ". . . hang me up by the/ heels for a rabbit-sucker, or a poulter's hare." *1 Hen 4,* II, iv, 430–431.

pouncet-box, *n.* small box for aromatic powders, inhaled to counteract foul odors: "A pouncet-box, which ever and anon/ He gave his nose . . ." *1 Hen 4,* I, iii, 37–38.

pound[1], *n.* **1** perh. ref. to the "thousand marks" of *Errors,* I, ii; also, poss. wordplay of "pound" and "beating," which Dromio may well expect after tying up his mistress: "I buy a thousand pound a year, I buy a rope!" *Errors,* IV, i, 21. **2 three thousand pounds,** according to weight, three thousand pounds of gold or silver: ". . . granted Rome a tribute,/ Yearly three thousand pounds . . ." *Cymb,* III, i, 8–9.

pound[2], *n.* **1** a public enclosure, esp. for stray animals: "You mistake; I mean the pound, a pinfold." *Two Gent,* I, i, 104. —*v.* **2** to enclose in a pound; pen up; also, wordplay on "beat": "Nay, in that you are astray; 'twere best pound you." *Two Gent,* I, i, 101.

pour, *v.* **pour it out,** [to] outdo oneself; here, be exceedingly generous: "He out-goes/ The very heart of kindness."/ "He pours it out." *Timon,* I, i, 273–275.

pow, waw! *interj.* exclam. of impatience or derision; poof!: "The gods grant them true."/ "True? pow, waw!" *Cor,* II, i, 139–140.

powder, *v.* **1** to sprinkle with salt as part of the pickling process: "I'll give/ you leave to powder me and eat me too tomorrow." *1 Hen 4,* V, iv, 110–111. —*n.* **2** gunpowder: "These violent delights have violent ends/ And in their triumph die, like fire and powder . . ." *Rom & Jul,* II, vi, 9–10.

powdered bawd, *n.* ref. to use of the pickling tub as a sweating tub: "Ever your fresh whore, and your powdered bawd;/ an/ unshunned consequence . . ." *Meas,* III, ii, 57–58.

powdering-tub, *n.* sweating tub for treating venereal disease: "And from the powdering-tub of infamy/ Fetch forth the lazar kite . . ." *Hen 5,* II, i, 75–76.

power, *n.* **1** [often pl.] army; military force: "My father hath a power; inquire of him . . ." *Rich 2,* III, ii, 186. **2** capability: "Be able for thine enemy/ Rather in power than use . . ." *All's W,* I, i, 61–62. **3** charm: ". . . she did make defect perfection,/ And, breathless, power breathe forth." *Ant & Cleo,* II, ii, 231–232. **4 every power that moves,** every movement he makes: ". . . what thou think'st his very action speaks/ In every power that moves." *Ant & Cleo,* III, xii, 35–36. **5 have power of,** to exert control over: ". . . my mother, having/ power of his testiness, shall turn all into my commendations." *Cymb,* IV, i, 20–22. **6**

in his power, at his command: ". . . deliver all the intelligence/ in his power against you . . ." *All's W,* III, vi, 28–29. **7 past power,** without power; powerless: "My art is not past power, nor you past cure [incurable]." *All's W,* II, i, 157. **8 press a power,** to raise an army: "They have press'd a power, but it is not known/ Whether for east or west." *Cor,* I, ii, 9–10. **9 to my power,** to the best of my ability: "I will prove so, sir, to my power." *W Tale,* V, ii, 169. **10 with power,** directly; openly: "Use power with power, and slay me not by art." *Sonn 139,* 4.

power and person, *n.* authority and innate ability: ". . . so far/ As thou hast [to the full extent of your] power and person." *Cor,* III, ii, 85–86.

powers from home, *n.* foreign powers [powers away from home]: "Now powers from home and discontents at home/ Meet in one line . . ." *K John,* IV, iii, 151–152.

pox, *n.* **1** syphilis; also, smallpox or plague: ". . . gout galls the/ one, and the pox pinches the other . . ." *2 Hen 4,* I, ii, 231–232. **2** curse: "The pox of [on] such antic lisping affecting phantasimes . . ." *Rom & Jul,* II, iv, 28.

Poysam, *n.* prob. an anglicization of the French "poisson" [fish]; here, a contrast between meat-eating Puritans and fish-eating Catholics: ". . . young Charbon the puritan and old Poysam the/ papist, howsome'er their hearts are sever'd in religion,/ their heads are both one . . ." *All's W,* I, iii, 50–52.

prabble, *n.* Fluellen's pron. of "brabble," squabble: ". . . keep/ you out of prawls, and prabbles, and quarrels . . ." *Hen 5,* IV, viii, 66–67.

practic, *adj.* learned; acquired by experience: ". . . the art and practic part of life . . ." *Hen 5,* I, i, 51.

practice, *n.* **1** [often pl.] a plot or conspiracy; scheme; connivance: "I overheard him, and his practices . . . this house is but a butchery." *As You,* II, iii, 26–27. **2** performing of a treacherous deed: "Yea, and paid me richly for the practice of it." *M Ado,* V, i, 242. **3** trickery; deception: "How may likeness made in crimes,/ Making practice on the times . . ." *Meas,* III, ii, 266–267. **4** profession: "This is a practice/ As full of labour as a wise man's art . . ." *T Night,* III, i, 66–67. **5** ability, skill, or art: "This disease is beyond my practice . . ." *Mac,* V, i, 55. **6 proceed in practice,** to go ahead with instruction: "Proceed in practice with my younger daughter . . ." *Shrew,* II, i, 164. —*v.* **7** to conspire or plot: ". . . he will practise against thee by poison . . ." *As You,* I, i, 148. **8** to train; allow to get used to: "Practice your eyes with tears!" *Tr & Cr,* II, ii, 109. **9 practice on, a.** to play a trick on: "Sirs, I will practise on this drunken man." *Shrew,* Ind., i, 34. **b.** to plot against: ". . . under covert and convenient seeming/ Has practis'd on man's life . . ." *Lear,* III, ii, 56–57. **10 practice upon,** to seduce: "I never practiced/ Upon man's wife . . ." *Kinsmen,* V, i, 100–101.

practiced, *adj.* deliberate; calculated: ". . . and making practis'd smiles/ As in a looking-glass . . ." *W Tale,* I, ii, 116–117.

practicer, *n.* practitioner of the arts; here, the healing arts; a physician: "Sweet practiser, thy physic I will try . . ." *All's W,* II, i, 184.

practisant, *n.* co-conspirator: "Here enter'd Pucelle and her practisants . . ." *1 Hen 6,* III, ii, 20.

Praeclarissimus, *adj.* [Latin] most illustrious: "Praeclarissimus filius noster/ Henricus, Rex Angliae, et Haeres Franciae [Our most illustrious son, Henry, King of England, and heir of France]." *Hen 5,* V, ii, 359–360.

praemunire, *n.* [Latin] to forewarn; law forbidding an appeal to Rome over the jurisdiction of an English court: ". . . all those things you have done of late . . . Fall into the th'compass of a praemunire . . ." *Hen 8,* III, ii, 338–340.

praetor, *n.* chief judge in Rome; here, ref. to Brutus: ". . . take this paper,/ And look you lay it in the praetor's chair,/ Where Brutus may but find it . . ." *J Caes,* I, iii, 142–144.

praise, *n.* **1** content of a letter or document: "Much in the letters, nothing in the praise." *Love's L,* V, ii, 40. **2 book of praises,** standard phrase for a woman's beautiful face: "Her face the book of praises, where is read/ Nothing but curious pleasures . . ." *Per,* I, i, 16–17. —*v.* **3** to appraise: "Were you/ sent hither to praise me?" *T Night,* I, v, 252–253. **4** same, with additional sense of to sip or taste: "Item, she will often praise her liquor." *Two Gent,* III, i, 336.

prank *v.* **1** to adorn: "But 'tis that miracle and queen of gems/ That nature pranks her in, attracts my soul." *T Night,* II, iv, 86–87. **2 prank them,** [to] dress themselves up: "I do despise them:/ For they do prank them in authority . . ." *Cor,* III, i, 22–23. —*n.* **3** mischievous trick: "This admiration, Sir, is much o' th' savour/ Of other your new pranks." *Lear,* I, iv, 245–246.

pranked up, *adj.* dressed up: ". . . and me, poor lowly maid,/ Most goddess-like prank'd up . . ." *W Tale,* IV, iv, 9–10.

prat, *v.* perh. to kick in the buttocks; poss. to practice trickery on: "I'll prat her. [Beating him] Out of my door, you/ witch, you rag . . ." *Wives,* IV, ii, 170–171.

prate, *v.* **1** to hawk; extol extravagantly or deceptively: "Disguised cheaters, prating mountebanks [quacks hawking remedies] . . ." *Errors,* I, ii, 101. **2** to babble; talk idly: "Marry, sir, because silver hath a sweet sound."/ "[He] Prates. What say you, Hugh Rebeck?" *Rom & Jul,* IV, v, 128–129.

prave, *n.* brave; Fluellen's Welsh-accented English, confusing p's and b's: ". . . 'a uttered as prave words at the/ pridge as you shall see in a summer's day." *Hen 5*, III, vi, 64–65.

pray, *v.* **1** to petition or beg favors [of others]: "If I could pray to move, prayers would move me . . ." *J Caes*, III, i, 59. **2 pray to a fault,** to cajole into committing a fault: "It were a shame to call her back again,/ And pray her to a fault for which I chid her." *Two Gent*, I, ii, 51–52.

prayer, *n.* entreaty or supplication; petition: "I will . . . never rise until my tears and prayers/ Have won his grace . . ." *Errors*, V, i, 114–116.

preambulate, *v.* to walk on ahead [with another]: "Arts-man, preambulate: we will be singled from the/ barbarous." *Love's L*, V, i, 73–74.

precedence, *n.* **1** something stated or written previously: "Some obscure precedence that hath tofore been sain." *Love's L*, III, i, 80. **2 good precedence,** good news you have just uttered: "I do not like 'But yet,' it does allay/ The good precedence . . ." *Ant & Cleo*, II, v, 50–51.

precedent, *n.* **1** example or sample; also, specimen or proof: "Step aside, and I'll show thee a precedent." *1 Hen 4*, II, iv, 33. **2** original document; appar. a draft of the Magna Carta, though the oath of the lords preceded it by a year [1214] and the French invasion followed it by a year [1216], here compressed for dramatic effect: "Return the precedent to these lords again . . ." *K John*, V, ii, 3.

—*adj.* **3** occurring in the past, esp. one's youth: "Our own precedent passions do instruct us . . ." *Timon*, I, i, 136. **4** previous: ". . . not twentieth part the tithe/ Of your precedent lord . . ." *Ham*, III, iv, 97–98.

precept, *n.* **1** [often pl.] order; writ: "Marry, sir, thus: those precepts cannot be served . . ." *2 Hen 4*, V, i, 11. **2** [usually pl.] sound advice: "I will bestow some precepts of [on] this virgin,/ Worthy the note." *All's W*, III, v, 99–100. **3 all of precept,** by detailed directions: "In action all of precept, he did show me/ The way twice o'er." *Meas*, IV, i, 40–41.

preceptial, *adj.* consisting of precepts: "Their counsel turns to passion, which before/ Would give preceptial medicine to rage . . ." *M Ado*, V, i, 23–24.

precinct, *n.* area under personal control: "Within her quarter and mine own precinct/ I was employ'd . . ." *1 Hen 6*, II, i, 68–69.

precious, *adj.* **1** acutely sensitive: ". . . can we not/ Partition make with spectacles [eyes] so precious/ 'Twixt fair, and foul?" *Cymb*, I, vii, 36–38. **2** used ironically; dirty or scurvy:

". . . ah, you precious pandar! Villain,/ Where is thy lady?" *Cymb*, III, v, 82–83.

preciously, *adv.* carefully or wisely: "The time 'twixt six and now/ Must by us both be spent most preciously." *Temp*, I, ii, 240–241.

precipitance, *n.* leaping from heights: "Those that with cords, knives, drams, precipitance,/ Weary of this world's light . . ." *Kinsmen*, I, i, 142–143.

precipitation, *n.* **1** steepness: ". . . the precipitation might down stretch/ Below the beam of sight . . ." *Cor*, III, ii, 4–5. **2** execution by throwing a person off the Tarpeian rock: ". . . banish him our city,/ In peril of precipitation/ From off the rock Tarpeian . . ." *Cor*, III, iii, 101–103.

precise, *adj.* morally strict; puritanical: "Lord Angelo is precise;/ Stands at a guard with Envy . . ." *Meas*, I, iii, 50–51.

precisian, *n.* puritanical guide in spiritual matters: ". . . though Love/ use Reason for his precisian . . ." *Wives*, II, i, 4–5.

precurrer, *n.* precursor; forerunner: "But thou shrieking harbinger,/ Foul precurrer of the fiend . . ." *Phoen*, 5–6.

precurse, *n.* a foreshadowing or forewarning: ". . . the like precurse of fear'd events,/ As harbingers preceding still the fates . . ." *Ham*, I, i, 124–125.

predeceased valor, *n.* valor of fallen warriors: ". . . worn as a/ memorable trophy of predeceased valour . . ." *Hen 5*, V, i, 74–75.

predestinate, *adj.* predestined; unavoidable or inescapable: "some gentleman or other shall scape a predestinate/ scratched face." *M Ado*, I, i, 124–125.

predict, *n.* prediction or prophecy; here, signs or portents: "By oft [frequent] predict that I in heaven find." *Sonn 14*, 8.

predominance, *n.* superiority; here, haughtiness: "And underwrite in an observing kind/ His humorous predominance . . ." *Tr & Cr*, II, iii, 130–131.

predominate, *v.* [fr. astrology] to be in the ascendancy, as a ruling planet: ". . . thou shalt know I will predominate/ over the peasant . . ." *Wives*, II, ii, 270–271.

preeches, *past part.* parson's blunder for "breeched," whipped: ". . . if you forget your *quies* . . . and your *quods*, you must be preeches." *Wives*, IV, i, 68–69.

prefer, *v.* **1** to proffer; present: "Why then preferr'd you not your sums and bills/ When your false masters eat of my lord's meat?" *Timon*, III, iv, 49–50. **2** to recommend: "Fellow, wilt thou bestow thy time with me?"/ "Ay, if Messala will prefer me to you." *J Caes*, V, v, 61–62. **3** to advance; further: "Under the colour of commending him,/ I have access my own love to prefer." *Two Gent,* IV, ii, 3–4. **4** to reward: ". . . say it is done,/ And I will love thee, and prefer thee for it." *Rich 3,* IV, ii, 79–80. **5** to set down in detail; specify [legal term]: ". . . in writing I preferr'd/ The manner of thy vile outrageous crimes . . ." *1 Hen 6,* III, i, 10–11. **6 prefers itself,** takes precedence over anything else: "Our haste from hence is of so quick condition/ That it prefers itself . . ." *Meas,* I, i, 53–54.

preferment, *n.* promotion: "I speak against my present profit,/ but my wish hath a preferment in't." *Cymb,* V, iv, 207–208.

preferred, *adj.* recommended; put forward for acceptance or advancement: ". . . the short and the long is, our play is/ preferred." *M N Dream,* IV, ii, 36–37.

prefixed, *adj.* prearranged: "At the prefixed hour of her waking/ Came I to take her from her kindred's vault . . ." *Rom & Jul,* V, iii, 252–253.

pre-formed, *adj.* inherent; original: "Why all these things change from their ordinance,/ Their natures, and pre-formed faculties . . ." *J Caes,* I, iii, 66–67.

pregnancy, *n.* quick-wittedness; sharpness of intellect: ". . . pregnancy is made a tapster, and his/ quick wit wasted in giving reckonings [making out bills]." *2 Hen 4,* I, ii, 169–170.

pregnant¹, *adj.* **1** clever, resourceful, and, often, devious: ". . . a wickedness,/ Wherein the pregnant enemy [the Devil] does much." *T Night,* II, ii, 26–27. **2** apt; quick-witted: "How pregnant/sometimes his replies are . . ." *Ham,* II, ii, 208–209. **3** willing; obliging: ". . . the pregnant hinges of the knee . . ." *Ham,* III, ii, 61. **4** receptive; disposed: ". . . but to your own/ most pregnant and vouchsafed ear." *T Night,* III, i, 90–91. **5** suggestible; easily influenced: "And cursed Dionyza hath/ The pregnant instrument of wrath/ Prest for this blow." *Per,* IV, Chor., 43–45. **6** well-versed; experienced: ". . . the terms/ For common justice, y'are as pregnant in/ As art [theory] and practice hath enriched any . . ." *Meas,* I, i, 10–12.

pregnant², *adj.* **1** very probable: "'Twere pregnant they should square between themselves . . ." *Ant & Cleo,* II, i, 45. **2** evident or obvious: "'Tis very pregnant,/ The jewel that we find, we stoop and take't . . ." *Meas,* II, i, 23. **3 pregnant by circumstance,** made convincing by facts or evidence: "Most true, if ever truth were pregnant by/ circumstance . . ." *W Tale,* V, ii, 31–32.

pregnantly, *adv.* aptly; clearly: "That shall demonstrate . . . More pregnantly than words." *Timon,* I, i, 93–94.

prejudicate, *v.* to prejudge: ". . . our dearest friend/ Prejudicates the business, and would seem/ To have us make denial." *All's W,* I, ii, 7–9.

prejudice, *v.* to harm; injure: "Now let us on, my lords . . . And seek how we may prejudice the foe." *1 Hen 6,* III, iii, 90–91.

premised, *adj.* predestined: "O! let the vile world end,/ And the premised flames of the last day/ Knit earth and heaven together . . ." *2 Hen 6,* V, ii, 40–42.

premises *n. pl.* **1 in lieu o' th' premises,** in return for the [specified] conditions: ". . . he, in lieu o' th' premises/ Of homage and I know not how much tribute,/ Should presently extirpate me and mine . . ." *Temp,* I, ii, 123–125. **2 premises observed,** conditions satisfied: "Here is my hand; the premises observ'd,/ Thy will by my performance shall be serv'd . . ." *All's W,* II, i, 200–201. **3 upon the premises,** considering the evidence: "'T has done upon the premises but justice . . ." *Hen 8,* II, i, 63.

prenominate, *adj.* **1** aforementioned: "Having ever seen in the prenominate crimes/ The youth you breathe of guilty . . ." *Ham,* II, i, 44–45.

—*v.* **2** to name or detail ahead of time: ". . . to prenominate in nice [precise] conjecture/ Where thou wilt hit me dead?" *Tr & Cr,* IV, v, 248–249.

prentice, *n.* apprentice: ". . . at the other door, his man with/ a drum and sand-bag, and prentices drinking to him." [SD] *2 Hen 6,* II, iii, 58.

pre-ordinance, *n.* established rule or law: "And turn pre-ordinance and first decree/ Into the law of children." *J Caes,* III, i, 38–39.

preparation, *n.* **1** armed readiness: ". . . our preparation stands/ In expectation of them." *Lear,* IV, iv, 22–23. **2** [pl.] endowments or accomplishments: ". . . your many war-like,/ court-like, and learned preparations." *Wives,* II, ii, 220–221.

prepare, *v.* **1** to move or advance: "The Dolphin is preparing hitherward . . ." *K John,* V, vii, 59.

—*n.* **2** preparation: "Go levy men and make prepare for war . . ." *3 Hen 6,* IV, i, 129.

prepared, *adj.* prob. sharpened for the occasion: ". . . and let/ Patient Octavia plough thy visage up/ With her prepared nails." *Ant & Cleo,* IV, xii, 37–39.

preposterous, *adj.* **1** contrary to nature and good sense: "O preposterous/ And frantic outrage, end thy damned spleen . . ." *Rich 3,* II, iv, 63–64. **2** unseemly; unsuitable: ". . . where, I mean, I did encounter that obscene and most preposterous event . . ." *Love's L,* I, i, 236–238.

preposterous discoveries, *n.* evidence of depraved acts: ". . . take and take again such/ preposterous discoveries!" *Tr & Cr,* V, i, 22–23.

preposterously, *adv.* unnaturally or unreasonably: ". . . whatsoever cunning fiend it was/ That wrought upon thee so preposterously . . ." *Hen 5,* II, ii, 111–112.

prerogative, *n.* **1** precedence: "Then give me leave to have prerogative . . ." *Shrew,* III, i, 6. **2 old prerogative,** tradition giving sovereign right to the commons: "Insisting on the old prerogative/ And power i' th' truth o' th' cause." *Cor,* III, iii, 17–18.

prerogatived, *adj.* privileged: ". . . 'tis the plague of great ones,/ Prerogativ'd are they less than the base . . ." *Oth,* III, iii, 277–278.

presage, *n.* **1** omen, herald, or portent: "Be thou the trumpet of our wrath/ And sullen [grim] presage of your own decay." *K John,* I, i, 27–28. **2** prediction; forecast: "And the sad augurs mock their own presage . . ." *Sonn 107,* 6.

prescience, *n.* foresight; here, any attempts to exercise foresight: "Forestall [obstruct] prescience, and esteem no act/ But that of hand." *Tr & Cr,* I, iii, 199–200.

prescribe, *v.* to limit: "And the King gone to-night! prescrib'd his power!" *Lear,* I, ii, 24.

prescript, *adj.* **1** prescribed; requisite: ". . . which is the prescript praise and/ perfection of a good and particular [monogamous] mistress." *Hen 5,* III, vii, 47–48. —*n.* **2** written orders or instructions: "Do not exceed/ The prescript of this scroll . . ." *Ant & Cleo,* III, viii, 4–5.

presence, *n.* **1** air or appearance: "Which party-coated presence of loose love/ Put on by us . . ." *Love's L,* V, ii, 758–759. **2** noble bearing; dignity: "Now he goes/ With no less presence, but with much more love . . ." *Merch,* III, ii, 53–54. **3** personal appearance: "The two kings . . . were now best, now worst,/ As presence did present them . . ." *Hen 8,* I, i, 28–30. **4** presence chamber: ". . . her beauty makes/ This vault a feasting presence, full of light." *Rom & Jul,* V, iii, 85–86. **5** the [august] people assembled: "This presence knows . . . How I am punish'd with a sore distraction." *Ham,* V, ii, 224–225. **6 in presence,** [to be] present: ". . . you were in presence then,/ And you can witness with me this is true." *Rich 2,* IV, i, 62–63. **7 keep in presence of,** remain in attendance on: ". . . keep in presence of his majesty,/ And do your best to make his highness merry." *Edw 3,* II, i, 372–373.

presence chamber, *n.* reception room where a monarch receives state visitors: "Scene II. The Same. The Presence Chamber." [SD]. *Hen 5,* II, ii, 1.

present, *adj.* **1** immediate: "And if a man did need a poison now,/ Whose sale is present death in Mantua . . ." *Rom & Jul,* V, i, 50–51. **2** impulsive; spur-of-the-moment: "Pardon what I have spoke,/ For 'tis a studied, not a present thought . . ." *Ant & Cleo,* II, ii, 137–138. —*v.* **3** to represent: "The majesty and power of law and justice,/ The image of the King whom I presented . . ." *2 Hen 4,* V, ii, 78–79. **4** prob. misuse for "impersonate": ". . . say he comes to disfigure or to/ present the person of Moonshine." *M N Dream,* III, i, 56–57. **5** bring charges against in a manorial court: ". . . say you would present her at the leet,/ Because she brought stone jugs and no seal'd quarts." *Shrew,* Ind., ii, 88–89. —*n.* **6** document or presentment: "God bless the king!"/ "What present hast thou there?" *Love's L,* IV, iii, 186. **7 my present,** my present wealth: "My having is not much;/ I'll make division of my present with you." *T Night,* III, iv, 353–354. **8 this present,** on this present occasion: "Shall I be charg'd no further than this present?" *Cor,* III, iii, 42.

presentation, *n.* semblance or representation: ". . . under the presentation of that he shoots his wit." *As You,* V, iv, 106.

present death, *n.* immediate execution: ". . . a poison now,/ Whose sale is present death in Mantua . . ." *Rom & Jul,* V, i, 50–51.

presented, *adj.* exposed; bold: "And with presented nakedness outface/ The winds . . ." *Lear,* II, iii, 11–12.

presenter, *n.* person who introduces a play, speaks the prologue, etc.; here, those who have provided the entertainment for Sly: "The Presenters above speak." [SD] *Shrew,* I, i, 247.

presently, *adv.* at once; immediately: "Go presently, and take this ring with thee . . ." *Two Gent,* IV, iv, 70.

presentment, *n.* act of presenting; presentation: "When comes your book forth?/ Upon the heels of my presentment, sir." *Timon,* I, i, 26–27.

present moan, *n.* immediate outburst of grief: ". . . do I not spend/ Revenge upon myself with present moan?" *Sonn 149,* 7–8.

present parts, *n.* remaining troops: ". . . uncurable discomfit/ Reigns in the hearts of all our present parts." *2 Hen 6,* V, ii, 86–87.

present push, *n.* See **push** (def. 4).

present sum, *n.* ready money; cash: "Neither have I money, nor commodity/ To raise a present sum . . ." *Merch,* I, i, 178–179.

preservation, *n.* divine protection: ". . . by great preservation,/ We live to tell it . . ." *Rich 3,* III, v, 35–36.

preserve, *v.* to protect another's life: "Nurses are not the fates,/ To foster it [is?], not ever to preserve." *Per,* IV, iii, 14–15.

preserved, *adj.* protected from the world; that is, nun's prayers: ". . . prayers from preserved souls,/ From fasting maids, whose minds are dedicate/ to nothing temporal." *Meas,* II, ii, 154–156.

president, *n.* var. spelling of **precedent:** "My brother Gloucester . . . May be a president . . . That thou respect'st not spilling Edward's blood." *Rich 2,* II, i, 128–131.

press[1]**,** *n.* **1** crowd; throng: "Who is it in the press that calls on me?" *J Caes,* I, ii, 15. **2** cupboard for clothing; wardrobe: "If there be anypody in the house, and in the/ chambers, and in the coffers, and in the presses . . ." *Wives,* III, iii, 194–195. —*v.* **3** to weight down (a branch of a shrub) and force propagation: "Griefs . . . lie heavy in my breast,/ Which thou wilt propagate to have it press'd/ With more of thine." *Rom & Jul,* I, i, 185–186. **4** to hurry; rush: "What manners is in this,/ To press before thy father to a grave?" *Rom & Jul,* V, iii, 213–214. **5** to beg for something; trouble or bother: "God forbid I should be so bold to press to heaven in my/ young days." *T Andr,* IV, iii, 89–90.

press[2]**,** *n.* **1** impressment; right to conscript soldiers, granted by royal commission: "I have misused the King's press damnably." *1 Hen 4,* IV, ii, 12. —*v.* **2** to conscript: ". . . every man that Bolingbroke hath press'd/ To lift shrewd steel against our golden crown . . ." *Rich 2,* III, ii, 58–59.

pressed, *adj.* weighed down; here with woes: "I had my load before, now press'd with bearing . . ." *Ven & Ad,* 430.

pressing, *n.* pressure: ". . . under her breast/ (Worthy her pressing) [worthy of the pressure of her breast] lies a mole . . ." *Cymb,* II, iv, 134–135.

press-money, *n.* bonus money paid to a new recruit: "Nature's above art in that respect. There's/ your press-money." *Lear,* IV, vi, 86–87.

press to death, *v.* to execute by pressing with weights, the penalty in England for remaining silent and refusing to plead either guilty or not guilty to a charge: "O, I am press'd to death through want of speaking!" *Rich 2,* III, iv, 72.

pressure, *n.* **1** [often pl.] mental impression: "All saws of books, all forms, all pressures past/ That youth and observation copied there . . ." *Ham,* I, v, 100–101. **2 his form**

and pressure, its precise image, as in a wax impression: "to show . . . the very age and body of the time his form and pressure." *Ham,* III, ii, 22–24.

prest, *adj.* **1** prepared: "The pregnant instrument of wrath/ Prest for this blow." *Per,* IV, Chor., 44–45. **2** ready or willing: "Then do but say to me what I should do . . . And I am prest unto it . . ." *Merch,* I, i, 158–160.

Prester John, *n.* legendary king of eastern Africa: ". . . bring you the length of Prester John's foot . . ." *M Ado,* II, i, 251.

presupposed, *past part.* suggested or intimated earlier: ". . . then cam'st in smiling,/ And in such forms which here were presuppos'd/ Upon thee in the letter." *T Night,* V, i, 348–350.

presurmise, *n.* apprehension; suspicion: "It was your presurmise/ That in the dole of blows your son might drop." *2 Hen 4,* I, i, 168–169.

pretence, *n.* See **pretense.**

pretend, *v.* **1** to claim; maintain: ". . . in the Capitol and senate's right,/ Whom you pretend to honour and adore . . ." *T Andr,* I, i, 41–42. **2** to intend; plan: "And none your foes but such as shall pretend/ Malicious practices against his state . . ." *1 Hen 6,* IV, i, 6–7.

pretended, *adj.* intended; planned: "I'll give her father notice/ Of their disguising and pretended flight . . ." *Two Gent,* II, vi, 36–37.

pretense or **pretence,** *n.* **1** a design; plan: "Against the undivulg'd pretence I fight/ Of treasonous malice." *Mac,* II, iii, 131–132. **2** intention; purpose: "Her pretence is a pilgrimage to Saint/ Jaques le Grand . . ." *All's W,* IV, iii, 46–47. **3 a very pretence,** a true intent [to be rude]: ". . . a very pretence and/ purpose of unkindness . . ." *Lear,* I, iv, 73–74.

prettily, *adv.* cleverly; skillfully: "Lysander riddles very prettily." *M N Dream,* II, ii, 52.

pretty, *adj.* **1** clever; ingenious: "And pretty traps to catch the petty thieves." *Hen 5,* I, ii, 177. **2** admirable; fine; excellent: "I am . . . as pretty a piece of flesh as any is in Messina . . ." *M Ado,* IV, ii, 77–79. **3** advantageous: ". . . you should tread a course/ Pretty, and full of view . . ." *Cymb,* III, iv, 148–149. **4** petty; trivial: "Those pretty wrongs that liberty commits/ When I am sometime absent from thy heart . . ." *Sonn 41,* 1–2.

prevailment, *n.* influence: "Knacks, trifles, nosegays, sweetmeats (messengers/ Of strong prevailment in unharden'd youth) . . ." *M N Dream,* I, i, 34–35.

prevent, *v.* **1** to evade or escape: "She hath prevented me . . . This bird you aim'd at, though you hit her not . . ." *Shrew,* V, ii, 49–50. **2** to anticipate: "I will answer you with gait and entrance; but we/ are prevented." *T Night,* III, i, 84–85. **3** to frustrate; thwart: "So thou prevent'st his scythe and crooked knife." *Sonn 100,* 14.

prevention, *n.* **1** intervention or interference: "My resolution is more nimbler far/ Than thy prevention can be in my rescue . . ." *Edw 3,* II, ii, 178–179. **2** discovery and defeat: ". . . if thou path, thy native semblance on,/ Not Erebus itself were dim enough/ To hide thee from prevention." *J Caes,* II, i, 83–85. **3** anticipation of an enemy's plans: ". . . fear not thou, until thy foot be snar'd,/ Nor never seek prevention of thy foes." *2 Hen 6,* II, iv, 56–57. **4** [usually pl.] defensive strategies: "Achievements, plots, orders, preventions,/ Excitements to the field, or speech for truce . . ." *Tr & Cr,* I, iii, 181–182.

prey, *n.* **1** spoils; booty: ". . . the French might have a good prey of us/ if he knew of it . . ." *Hen 5,* IV, iv, 78–79.
—*v.* **2** to prey upon: ". . . throw her forth to beasts and birds to prey." *T Andr,* V, iii, 180. **3 prey at fortune,** get along as best she could: "I'ld whistle her off, and let her down the wind,/ To prey at fortune." *Oth,* III, iii, 266–267.

preyful, *adj.* intent on killing game: "The preyful princess pierc'd and prick'd a pretty/ pleasing pricket . . ." *Love's L,* IV, ii, 54–55.

Priam, *n.* king of Troy, killed in the Trojan War: ". . . 'twas Aeneas' tale'/ to Dido—and thereabout of it especially when he/ speaks of Priam's slaughter." *Ham,* II, ii, 442–444.

Priapus, *n.* Roman god of fertility and male potency: ". . . she's able to freeze the god/ Priapus, and undo a whole generation." *Per,* IV, vi, 3–4.

pribbles and prabbles, *n.* perh. fanciful var. on "brabbles" [quarrels]: "It were a goot [good] motion if we leave our pribbles/ and prabbles . . ." *Wives,* I, i, 51–52.

price, *n.* **held in idle price,** regarded as useless or worthless: "I have ever lov'd the life remov'd,/ And held in idle price to haunt assemblies . . ." *Meas,* I, iii, 8–9.

prick, *v.* **1** to mark or check (off), as on a list: "'Tis the more time thou wert used . . . Prick him." *2 Hen 4,* III, ii, 106–110. **2** to stab; here, with obvious sexual wordplay: "Prick love for pricking and you beat love down [conquer desire by satisfying it]." *Rom & Jul,* I, iv, 28. **3** to sting or itch: "By the pricking of my thumbs,/ Something wicked this way comes." *Mac,* IV, i, 44–45. **4** to pin: ". . . and the humour of forty fancies/ pricked in't for a feather . . ." *Shrew,* III, ii, 66–67. **5** to force or goad: "'Tis some odd humour pricks him to this fashion."

Shrew, III, ii, 70. **6** to ride fast: ". . . as we were pricking on the hills . . . marching hitherward,/ We might descry a mighty host of men." *Edw 3,* I, ii, 48–50. **7 prick down,** *v.* to mark or check off (an item on a list, etc.): "The fiend hath pricked down Bardolph irrecoverable . . ." *2 Hen 4,* II, iv, 329. **8 prick thee out,** wordplay on "marked you out as special" and "equipped you with a penis": "But since she [Nature] pricked thee out for women's pleasure . . ." *Sonn 20,* 13.
—*n.* **9** center, or bull's-eye, of a target; also, a pun on prick [penis]: "Let the mark have a prick in't, to mete at . . ." *Love's L,* IV, i, 133. **10** any target marked with a bull's-eye: "She's too hard for you at pricks, sir: challenge her to/ bowl." *Love's L,* IV, i, 139. **11** point or mark on a clock or dial indicating the hour; here, also with sexual innuendo: ". . . the bawdy hand of the/ dial is now upon the prick of noon." *Rom & Jul,* II, iv, 111–112. **12** mark or tick; also, a small amount: "And in such indexes, although small pricks/ To their subsequent volumes . . ." *Tr & Cr,* I, iii, 343–344. **13** a skewer: "Strike in their numb'd and mortified bare arms/ Pins, wooden pricks, nails . . ." *Lear,* II, iii, 15–16.

prick-eared, *adj.* having pointed ears; also, Icelandic dogs were believed to have disagreeable dispositions: "Pish for thee, Iceland dog! thou prick-eared cur of/ Iceland!" *Hen 5,* II, i, 40–41.

pricket, *n.* two-year-old deer: "'Twas not a *haud credo,* 'twas a pricket." *Love's L,* IV, ii, 12.

pricksong, *n.* music sung from a printed score and therefore assumed to be precise; here, wordplay with prick [stab]: ". . . he fights as you sing pricksong,/ keeps time, distance and proportion." *Rom & Jul,* II, iv, 20–21.

pride, *n.* **1** full military force: "Beat down Alençon, Orleans, Burgundy,/ And from the pride of Gallia rescu'd thee." *1 Hen 6,* IV, vi, 14–15. **2** height; climax: ". . . in the very heat/ And pride of their contention . . ." *1 Hen 4,* I, i, 59–60. **3** prime [of one's life]: "And for they cannot, die in their own pride." *Rich 2,* V, v, 22. **4** splendor; beauty: "By new unfolding his imprison'd pride." *Sonn 52,* 11–12. **5** sumptuous clothing and ornaments: ". . . the madams too . . . did almost sweat to bear/ The pride upon them . . ." *Hen 8,* I, i, 23–25. **6** source of pride: "And, having thee, of all men's pride I boast [my boast is the equal of anyone's] . . ." *Sonn 91,* 12. **7** arrogance: "This priest has no pride in him?" *Hen 8,* II, ii, 81. **8** eager sexual desire; lust: "Wooing his purity with her fair pride." *Pass Pil,* II, 8. **9** erection: "Proud of this pride,/ He is contented thy poor drudge to be . . ." *Sonn 151,* 10–11. **10 change of prides,** succession of extravagances: "Ambitions, covetings, change of prides, disdain . . ." *Cymb,* II, iv, 177. **11 wither in their pride,** decline in beauty: "Let two more summers wither in their pride . . ." *Rom & Jul,* I, ii, 10.

priest, *n.* **be his priest,** give the victim the last rites [in the manner of a priest]; here, to murder him: "... to preserve my sovereign from his foe,/ Say but the word and I will be his priest." *2 Hen 6,* III, i, 271–272.

priest and clerk, *n.* (in a religious service) prayers said by the priest, followed by responses led by the clerk: "God save the king! Will no man say amen?/ Am I both priest and clerk?" *Rich 2,* IV, i, 172–173.

prig, *n.* thief: "Out upon him! prig, for my life, prig..." *W Tale,* IV, iii, 98.

primal eldest curse, *n.* God's curse on Cain for slaying his brother Abel: "It hath the primal eldest curse upon't—/ A brother's murder." *Ham,* III, iii, 37.

primal state, *n.* beginnings of organized society: "It hath been taught us from the primal state..." *Ant & Cleo,* I, iv, 41.

prime, *adj.* **1** being first in rank: "And Prospero the prime duke, being so reputed/ In dignity..." *Temp,* I, ii, 72–73. **2** lustful: "Were they as prime as goats, as hot as monkeys..." *Oth,* III, iii, 409.
—*n.* **3** height of perfection; here, youth: "... all/ That happiness and prime can happy call." *All's W,* II, i, 180–181. **4** springtime: "To add a more rejoicing to the prime..." *Luc,* 332.

primer, *adj.* more urgent: "There is no primer baseness [wickedness that needs more urgent attention]." *Hen 8,* I, ii, 67.

primero, *n.* [sometimes cap.] card game with some similarities to poker: "Came you from the king, my lord?"/ "I did Sir Thomas, and left him at Primero..." *Hen 8,* V, i, 6–7.

primest, *adj.* finest; most excellent: "(Katherine our Queen) before the primest creature/ That's paragon'd o'th'world." *Hen 8,* II, iv, 227–228.

primogenity, *n.* primogeniture; inheritance rights of the firstborn: "The primogenity and due of birth..." *Tr & Cr,* I, iii, 106.

Primo, secundo, tertio, *adv.* [Latin] firstly, secondly, thirdly; perh. ref. to a children's game, or to the "old saying" that follows: "*Primo, secundo, tertio,* is a good play, and the/ old saying is 'The third pays for all'..." *T Night,* V, i, 34–35.

primy, *adj.* springlike; youthful: "A violet in the youth of primy nature..." *Ham,* I, iii, 7.

prince, *v.* **prince it,** to act the prince: "Nature prompts them/ In simple and low things to prince it..." *Cymb,* III, iii, 84–85.

prince', *adj.* prince's: "Thou show'dst a subject's shine, I a true prince'." *Per,* I, ii, 124.

Prince of Cats, *n.* in the fable of "Reynard the Fox," the Prince of Cat's name is Tybert, sometimes anglicized as "Tibault" or "Tibalt": "Why, what is Tybalt?"/ "More than Prince of Cats." *Rom & Jul,* II, iv, 18–19.

prince of darkness, *n.* the devil; Satan: "The black prince, sir, alias the prince of darkness,/ alias the devil." *All's W,* IV, v, 39–40.

prince of fiends, *n.* the devil; Satan: "... impious war,/ Array'd in flames like to the prince of fiends..." *Hen 5,* III, iii, 15–16.

prince of the world, *n.* the devil; Satan: "... sure he is the prince of the world; let his nobility/ remain in's court..." *All's W,* IV, v, 46–47.

principal, *n.* **1** employer; boss: "Why, hath your principal made known unto you/ who I am?" *Per,* IV, vi, 81–82. **2** partner; here, sexual partner: "What she should shame to know herself/ But with her most vile principal..." *W Tale,* II, i, 91–92. **3** [pl.] the framework of a structure: "The very principals/ Did seem to rend and all to topple." *Per,* III, ii, 16–17.
—*adj.* **4** best; choicest: "... in this covert will we make our stand,/ Culling the principal of all the deer." *3 Hen 6,* III, i, 3–4.

principality, *n.* one of the nine orders of angels: "... if not divine,/ Yet let her be a principality,/ Sovereign to all the creatures on the earth." *Two Gent,* II, iv, 146–148.

princox, *n.* insolent boy: "You are a princox, go/ Be quiet, or... I'll make you quiet." *Rom & Jul,* I, v, 85–87.

print, *n.* **1** imprint: "... thou wilt needs thrust thy neck into a/ yoke, wear the print of it..." *M Ado,* I, i, 186–187. **2** impression [printing term]: "Abhorred slave,/ Which any print of goodness wilt not take..." *Temp,* I, ii, 353–354. **3 in print,** precisely; very carefully: "Most sweet/ gardon [guerdon]! I will do it, sir, in print." *Love's L,* III, i, 165–166.
—*v.* **4 print off,** to conceive an exact likeness of: "For she did print your royal father off,/ Conceiving you." *W Tale,* V, i, 124–125.

Priscian, *n.* Latin grammarian of the 6th century: "Priscian a little scratched; 'twill/ serve." *Love's L,* V, i, 27.

prisoner's base, *n.* See **country base.**

prisonment, *n.* imprisonment: "I'll well requite thy kindness,/ For that it made my prisonment a pleasure..." *3 Hen 6,* IV, vi, 10–11.

pristine, *adj.* perfect, as before: "... find her disease,/ And purge it to a sound and pristine health..." *Mac,* V, iii, 51–52.

prithee, *interj.* shortened form of "(I) pray thee": "Prithee, no more: thou dost talk nothing to me." *Temp,* II, i, 166.

private, *adj.* **1** solitary; secluded: ". . . in respect that it is private, it is a very vile life." *As You,* III, ii, 16–17. **2** individual: "When every private widow well may keep/ By children's eyes her husband's shape in mind." *Sonn 9,* 7–8.
—*n.* **3** private conversation or communication: "The Count Melun . . . Whose private with me of the Dolphin's love . . ." *K John,* IV, iii, 15–16. **4** [pl.] bawdy wordplay on "commoners" and "genitals": "Then you live about her waist, or in the middle of/ her favours?"/ "Faith, her privates we." *Ham,* II, ii, 232–234. **5** privacy: "Let me enjoy my private./ Go off." *T Night,* III, iv, 90–91.

privately, *adv.* wordplay on "in private" and "genitally": "Marry, sir, I think if you handled her privately/ she would sooner confess . . ." *Meas,* V, i, 274.

private plot, *n.* secluded area: ". . . in this private plot be we the first/ That shall salute our rightful sovereign . . ." *2 Hen 6,* II, ii, 59–60.

private stomaching, *n.* See **stomach** (def. 13).

prived, *adj.* deprived; bereft: ". . . the prived maidens' groans,/ For husbands, fathers, and betrothed lovers . . ." *Hen 5,* II, iv, 107–108.

privilege, *v.* **1** to protect; exempt: "He took this place for sanctuary,/ And it shall privilege him from your hands . . ." *Errors,* V, i, 94–95. **2** to allow; authorize: ". . . you yourself may privilege your time/ To what you will . . ." *Sonn 58,* 10–11.
—*n.* **3** immunity from arrest, prosecution, etc.; asylum: "He bears him [behaves himself] on the place's privilege . . ." *1 Hen 6,* II, iv, 86. **4** guarantee; assurance: "Your virtue is my privilege . . ." *M N Dream,* II, i, 220. **5** here, stay of execution if Joan confesses she is pregnant: "Then, Joan, discover thine infirmity/ That warranteth by law to be thy privilege . . ." *1 Hen 6,* V, iv, 60–61. **6 large privilege,** extensive or far-reaching advantage, immunity, etc.: "Take heed, dear heart, of this large privilege . . ." *Sonn 95,* 13. **7 shape privilege,** to provide immunity: "Nor [neither] age nor honour shall shape privilege." *T Andr,* IV, iv, 57.

privileged, *adj.* **1** sanctified or set apart for private or royal use: "Draw, men, for all this privileged place—" *1 Hen 6,* I, iii, 46. **2** recognized as a fool and therefore immune from punishment: "Peace, fool, I have not done."/ "He is a privileged man: proceed, Thersites." *Tr & Cr,* II, iii, 59–60.

privily, *adv.* privately; secretly: "Thou, Richard, shalt to the Duke of Norfolk straight/ And tell him privily of our intent." *3 Hen 6,* I, ii, 38–39.

privity, *n.* act of informing or being informed: "Why the devil . . . took he upon him/ (Without the privity o'th'king) . . ." *Hen 8,* I, i, 72–74.

privy, *adj.* **1** private: ". . . his face is Lucifer's privy-kitchen . . ." *2 Hen 4,* II, iv, 330. **2** secret: ". . . this drudge or diviner . . . told me what/ privy marks I had about me . . ." *Errors,* III, ii, 139–141.

privy-kitchen, *n.* private kitchen; appar. meant as the hottest part of hell: ". . . his face is Lucifer's privy-kitchen . . ." *2 Hen 4,* II, iv, 330.

privy order, *n.* **take some privy order,** issue some private instructions: "Now will I go to take some privy order/ To draw the brats of Clarence out of sight . . ." *Rich 3,* III, v, 105–106.

prize, *n.* **1** match; contest: "Like one of two contending in a prize/ That thinks he hath done well in people's eyes . . ." *Merch,* III, ii, 141–142. **2** gain or advantage; privilege: "It is war's prize to take all vantages . . ." *3 Hen 6,* I, iv, 59. **3** worth; importance: "Occasions, noble Gloucester, of some prize . . ." *Lear,* II, i, 120. **4 make prize,** to vie in a contest: "Caesar's no merchant, to make prize with you/ Of things that merchants sold." *Ant & Cleo,* V, ii, 182–183.
—*v.* **5** to appraise; size up: "And any thing that may not misbecome/ The mighty sender, doth he prize you at." *Hen 5,* II, iv, 118–119. **6** to regard; pay attention to: "Not prizing her poor infant's discontent . . ." *Sonn 143,* 8.

prized, *adj.* reputed; esteemed: "Having so swift and excellent a wit/ As she is priz'd to have . . ." *M Ado,* III, i, 89–90.

prizer, *n.* prize-winner, esp. a prizefighter: "Why would you be so fond to overcome/ The bonny prizer of the humorous Duke?" *As You,* II, iii, 7–8.

probable need, *n.* plausible excuse: "Strength'ned with what apology you think/ May make it probable need." *All's W,* II, iv, 48–49.

probal, *adj.* in agreement or harmony [with]: "When this advice is free I give, and honest,/ Probal to thinking . . ." *Oth,* II, iii, 328–329.

probation, *n.* **1** testing or examination: ". . . there is no consonancy in the/ sequel; that suffers under probation . . ." *T Night,* II, v, 130–131. **2** proof: ". . . of the truth herein/ This present object made probation." *Ham,* I, i, 160–161. **3** noviatiate: "I—in probation of a sisterhood—/ Was sent to by my brother . . ." *Meas,* V, i, 75–76. **4 pass in probation,** to review the proof: ". . . pass'd in probation with you,/ How you were borne in hand . . ." *Mac,* III, i, 79–80.

proceeded, *adj.* advanced in a course of study; also, graduated with a degree and, hence, to have proved oneself a scholar: "Proceeded well, to stop all good proceeding!" *Love's L,* I, i, 95.

proceeder, *n.* scholar who advances to a higher academic degree: "Quick proceeders, marry! . . . your mistress Bianca/ Lov'd none in the world so well as Lucentio." *Shrew,* IV, ii, 11–13.

proceeding, *n.* **1** advancement: ". . . my dear dear love/ To [my deepest concern for] your proceeding bids me tell you this . . ." *J Caes,* II, ii, 102–104. **2** [pl.] progress of events; here, the succession: "What plain proceedings is more plain than this?" *2 Hen 6,* II, ii, 52. **3** [pl.] actions; movements: "Follow me, sirs, and my proceedings eye . . ." *Tr & Cr,* V, vii, 7.

process, *n.* **1** course, as of a journey; also, flight of an arrow: ". . . your company . . . hath very much beguil'd/ The tediousness and process of my travel." *Rich 2* II, iii, 10–12. **2** proceedings; here, a conversation: "Behind the arras I'll convey myself/ To hear the process." *Ham,* III, iii, 28–29. **3** legal proceedings: "Proceed by process,/ Lest parties . . . break out/ And sack great Rome . . ." *Cor,* III, i, 311–313. **4** summons in a legal proceeding: "Where's Fulvia's process? Caesar's I would say. Both?" *Ant & Cleo,* I, i, 28. **5** story; tale: "Tell her the process of Antonio's end . . ." *Merch,* IV, i, 270. **6** gist; essence: "Witness the process of your speech . . ." *Tr & Cr,* IV, i, 9. **7** progression: "In process of the seasons have I seen . . ." *Sonn 104,* 6.

proclaim, *v.* to denounce; expose: "I will proclaim thee, Angelo, look for't." *Meas,* II, iv, 150.

proclaimed prize, *n.* outlaw with a price on his head: "A proclaim'd prize! Most happy!" *Lear,* IV, vi, 227.

proclamation, *n.* **1** reputation: ". . . must upon a warranted need give him a/ better proclamation." *Meas,* III, ii, 139–140. **2** announcement by crier: "The dearest ring in Venice will I give you,/ And find it out by proclamation . . ." *Merch,* IV, i, 431–432.

proconsul, *n.* governor of an ancient Roman province, often a high-ranking military commander: "He creates/ Lucius proconsul; and to you the tribunes . . ." *Cymb,* III, viii, 7–8.

procrastinate, *v.* to postpone: "Hopeless and helpless doth Egeon wend,/ But to procrastinate his lifeless end." *Errors,* I, i, 147–148.

procreant cradle, *n.* the nest of the martin or swift: ". . . this bird/ Hath made his pendent bed, and procreant cradle . . ." *Mac,* I, vi, 7–8.

procreants, *n.* persons engaged in copulation: "Leave procreants alone, and shut the door . . ." *Oth,* IV, ii, 28.

procurator, *n.* proxy or agent: ". . . in charge at my depart for France,/ As procurator to your Excellence . . ." *2 Hen 6,* I, i, 2–3.

procure, *v.* **1** to make certain; contrive: ". . . procure/ That Lady Margaret do vouchsafe to come . . . to England and be crown'd/ King Henry's faithful and anointed queen." *1 Hen 6,* V, v, 88–91. **2** to cause; bring about: "I am sorry that such sorrow I procure . . ." *Meas,* V, i, 472.

prodigious, *adj.* **1** ominous; portentous; also, gigantic and unnatural: "Prodigious birth of love it is to me/ That I must love a loathed enemy." *Rom & Jul,* I, v, 139–140. **2** misuse for "prodigal": "I have/ received my proportion, like the prodigious son . . ." *Two Gent,* II, iii, 2–3. **3** monstrous; deformed; hence, portending evil: "Lame, foolish, crooked, swart, prodigious,/ Patch'd with foul moles and eye-offending marks . . ." *K John,* II, ii, 46–47.

prodigiously, *adv.* in an ugly or vicious manner: "Pray that their burthens may not fall this day,/ Lest that their hopes prodigiously be cross'd." *K John,* III, i, 16–17.

prodigy, *n.* **1** event portending evil: "That so the shadows be not unappeas'd,/ Nor we disturb'd with prodigies on earth." *T Andr,* I, i, 100–101. **2** monster or freak; here, newly born: "Now hath my soul brought forth her prodigy . . ." *Rich 2,* II, ii, 64.

proditor, *n.* traitor: ". . . thou most usurping proditor,/ And not Protector, of the King or realm." *1 Hen 6,* I, iii, 31–32.

produce, *v.* **1** to bring forth; offer to view: ". . . I may/ Produce his body to the market-place,/ And . . . Speak in the order [course] of his funeral." *J Caes,* III, i, 227–230. **2** to be required to appear in court and give evidence: "It seems not meet . . . To be produc'd . . . Against the Moor . . ." *Oth,* I, i, 145–147. **3 produce forth,** to bring to justice: "Producing forth the cruel ministers/ Of this dead butcher, and his fiend-like Queen . . ." *Mac,* V, ix, 34–35.

Proface! *v.* Begin! Set to! (said by a host to guests at the beginning of a meal) [fr. Old French "bon prou vous fasse" May it do you good!]: "Proface!/ What you want in meat, we'll have in drink . . ." *2 Hen 4,* V, iii, 27–28.

profanation, *n.* prob. misuse for "profession": ". . . void of all profanation in the world, that good/ Christians ought to have." *Meas,* II, i, 55–56.

profane, *v.* **1** to waste: "O, let no noble eye profane a tear/ For me, if I be gor'd with Mowbray's spear!" *Rich 2,* I, iii, 59–60. **2** to desecrate; defile: "If I profane with my unworthiest hand/ This holy shrine, the gentle sin is this . . ." *Rom & Jul,* I, v, 92–93.

—*adj.* **3** worldly: "Our holy lives must win a new world's crown/ Which our profane hours here have thrown down." *Rich 2,* V, i, 24–25.

profess, *v.* **1** to have as one's skill or profession: "I thank him that he cuts me from my tale,/ For I profess not talking . . ." *1 Hen 4,* V, ii, 90–91. **2** to operate; here, sense of "falsely profess," inasmuch as most "hot-houses" [bathhouses] were actually brothels: ". . . now she professes/ a hot-house; which I think is a very ill house/ too." *Meas,* II, i, 64–66. **3** to profess affection: "He is dishonour'd by a man which ever/ Profess'd to him . . ." *W Tale,* I, ii, 455–456. **4 profess oneself,** make professions of friendship, esp. indiscriminately: ". . . if you know/ That I profess myself in banqueting/ To all the rout, then hold me dangerous." *J Caes,* I, ii, 75–77.

professor, *n.* person who professes Christianity: "Woe upon ye,/ And all such false professors." *Hen 8,* III, i, 114–115.

profit, *n.* success; also, progress or improvement: ". . . report speaks goldenly of his profit . . ." *As You,* I, i, 5–6.

profited, *adj.* experienced; proficient; skilled: "Exceedingly well read, and profited/ In strange concealments . . ." *1 Hen 4,* III, i, 160–161.

profitless, *adj.* (of a person) unable or unwilling to derive a profit; here, to sire offspring: "Profitless usurer, why dost thou use/ So great a sum of sums yet canst not live?" *Sonn 4,* 7–8.

profound, *adj.* **1** of great significance; also, full of hidden meanings: "Upon the corner of the moon/ There hangs a vap'rous drop profound . . ." *Mac,* III, v, 23–24. **2** of great depth; deep: "In so profound abysm I throw all care/ Of others' voices . . ." *Sonn 112,* 9–10.

profoundest pit, *n.* the "bottomless pit" of the Bible (Revelation): "Conscience and grace, to the profoundest pit!" *Ham,* IV, v, 132.

progeny, *n.* **1** issue; race: "And this same progeny of evils comes/ From our debate . . ." *M N Dream,* II, i, 115–116. **2** ancestry: "That was the whip of your bragg'd [boastful] progeny . . ." *Cor,* I, viii, 12.

Progne, *n.* (in Greek myth.) wife of Tereus, who raped her sister Philomel; in revenge she slew her son by Tereus and served him a dish made of his son's flesh: "For worse than Philomel you us'd my daughter,/ And worse than Progne I will be reveng'd." *T Andr,* V, ii, 194–195.

progression, *n.* **by way of progression,** proceeding from one person to another, hand to hand, etc.: ". . . a letter to a sequent of the stranger queen's,/ which, accidentally, or by the way of progression,/ hath miscarried." *Love's L,* IV, ii, 133–135.

prohibit, *v.* misuse for "grant": ". . . if a merry/ meeting may be wished, God prohibit it! *M Ado,* V, i, 319–320.

project, *n.* **1** idea or concept: "She cannot love,/Nor take no shape nor project of affection . . ." *M Ado,* III, i, 54–55. **2** expectation or anticipation: "Flatt'ring himself in project of a power . . ." *2 Hen 4,* I, iii, 29.
—*v.* **3** to set forth: "I cannot project mine own cause so well/ To make it clear . . ." *Ant & Cleo,* V, ii, 120–121.

projection, *n.* design; plan; scale: "Which of a weak and niggardly projection/ Doth, like a miser, spoil his coat with scanting/ A little cloth." *Hen V,* II, iv, 46–48.

prolixious, *adj.* tiresome; time-wasting: "Lay by all nicety and prolixious blushes . . ." *Meas,* II, iv, 161.

prolixity, *n.* **slip of prolixity,** lapse into long-windedness: ". . . it is true,/ without any slips of prolixity, or crossing the plain/ highway of talk . . ." *Merch,* III, i, 10–12.

prolonged, *past part.* put off; postponed: "I myself am not so well provided/ As else I would be, were the day prolong'd." *Rich 3,* III, iv, 44–45.

Promethean, *adj.* pertaining to Prometheus; here, divine: "I know not where is that Promethean heat/ That can thy light relume . . ." *Oth,* V, ii, 12–13.

Promethean fire, *n.* ref. to the Greek legend of Prometheus, who stole the sacred fire from heaven and gave it to man: ". . . the ground, the books, the academes,/ From whence doth spring the true Promethean fire." *Love's L,* IV, iii, 299–300.

Prometheus, *n.* Titan who stole the sacred fire from heaven and was punished by Zeus by being chained to a mountain top in the Caucasus: "And faster bound to Aaron's charming eyes/ Than is Prometheus tied to Caucasus." *T Andr,* II, i, 16–17.

promise-crammed, *adj.* referring to the promises with which Claudius has filled the air: "I eat the/ air, promise-crammed. You cannot feed capons so." *Ham,* III, ii, 93–94.

promised end, *n.* end of the world, according to Biblical prophecy: "Is this the promis'd end?"/ "Or image of that horror?" *Lear,* V, iii, 263–264.

promontory, *n.* the earth here likened to a land mass jutting into a void: ". . . this goodly frame the earth seems to/ me a sterile promontory . . ." *Ham,* II, ii, 298–299.

prompt, *v.* **1** to remind; here, in the manner of a theater prompter: "I have/ Prompted you in the ebb of your estate . . ." *Timon,* II, ii, 144–145. **2** to incite or restore to: "Hence, bash-

ful cunning!/ And prompt me plain and holy innocence!" *Temp,* III, i, 81–82.
—*adj.* **3** willing; well-disposed: "I have observed thee always for a towardly prompt spirit . . ." *Timon,* III, i, 34–35.

prompted, *adj.* ready; here, eager: ". . . my prompted sword/ Falling on Diomed." *Tr & Cr,* V, ii, 174–175.

prompture, *n.* act of inciting or urging: "Though he hath fall'n by prompture of the blood . . ." *Meas,* II, iv, 177.

prone, *adj.* **1** eagerly prepared: "O that prone lust should stain so pure a bed!" *Luc,* 684. **2** submissive and, hence, effective: ". . . in her youth/ There is a prone and speechless dialect/ Such as move men . . ." *Meas,* I, ii, 172–174. **3** receptive; responsive: "Nor tender feeling to base touches prone . . ." *Sonn 141,* 6.

pronounced, *adj.* spoken: "Good sentences, and well pronounc'd." *Merch,* I, ii, 10.

proof, *n.* **1** impenetrability or invulnerability: "Whose proof nor yells of mothers, maids, nor babes . . . Shall pierce a jot." *Timon,* IV, iii, 126–128. **2** action of doing or performing: "A bliss in proof, and proved, a very woe . . ." *Sonn 129,* 11. **3** experience; test: "Now what my love is, proof hath made you know . . ." *Ham,* III, ii, 164. **4** example: "The country gives me proof and precedent/ Of Bedlam beggars . . ." *Lear,* II, iii, 13–14. **5** argument in defense [of]: "Nay, if the devil have given thee proofs for sin,/ Thou wilt prove his." *Meas,* III, ii, 29–30. **6 be of proof,** "impenetrable, like tested armor" in wordplay with "threadbare," probably due to frequent whipping: "He need not fear the sword, for his coat/ is of proof." *2 Hen 6,* IV, ii, 57–58. **7 come to proof,** turn out well; stand the test: "There's never none of these demure boys come/ to any proof . . ." *2 Hen 4,* IV, iii, 88–89. **8 in proof,** when actually experienced: "Alas that love so gentle in his view/ Should be so tyrannous and rough in proof." *Rom & Jul,* I, i, 167–168. **9 lapped in proof.** See **lap** (def. 2). **10 proof and bulwark,** impenetrable defense: "If damned custom have not braz'd it so,/ That it be proof and bulwark against sense." *Ham,* III, iv, 37–38. **11 proof eterne,** eternal invulnerability: ". . . Mars's armour, forg'd for proof eterne . . ." *Ham,* II, ii, 486. **12 proof of harness,** tested [impenetrable] armor: ". . . leap thou, attire and all,/ Through proof of harness to my heart . . ." *Ant & Cleo,* IV, viii, 14–15. **13 proofs new-bleeding,** examples of those recently betrayed or injured: "Experience for me many bulwarks builded/ Of proofs new-bleeding . . ." *Lover's Comp,* 152–153. **14 put in proof,** to put to the test: "It were a delicate stratagem to shoe/ A troop of horse with felt; I'll put 't in proof . . ." *Lear,* IV, vi, 186–187.
—*adj.* **15** impenetrable: "With hearts more proof than shields." *Cor,* I, iv, 25.

prop, *n.* support; here, tradition and custom, which must be the supports of such "words": "And, as the world were now but to begin,/ Antiquity forgot, custom not known—/ The ratifiers and props of every word—" *Ham,* IV, v, 103–105.

propagate, *v.* to increase or expand [image from gardening]: "Which thou wilt propagate to have it press'd/ With more of thine." *Rom & Jul,* I, i, 185–186.

propagation, *n.* breeding; period of gestation [fig. use]: "Only for propagation of a dower/ Remaining in the coffer of her friends . . ." *Meas,* I, ii, 139–140.

propend, *v.* to incline; tend to agree [with]: "I propend to you/ In resolution to keep Helen still . . ." *Tr & Cr,* II, ii, 191–192.

propension, *n.* inclination: ". . . your full consent/ Gave wings to my propension . . ." *Tr & Cr,* II, ii, 133–134.

proper, *adj.* **1** own; very own: ". . . a man so bold/ That dares do justice on my proper son . . ." *2 Hen 4,* V, ii, 108–109. **2** used with "own" as an intensifier: "Thy spirit walks abroad, and turns our swords/ In our own proper entrails." *J Caes,* V, iii, 95–96. **3** fine; splendid; admirable: ". . . she concluded with a sigh, thou was the properest/ man in Italy." *M Ado,* V, i, 169–170. **4** handsome; sturdy and well-proportioned: "Three proper young men, of excellent growth/ and presence—" *As You,* I, ii, 111–112. **5** true; virtuous or respectable: ". . . an advertisement/ to a proper maid in Florence, one Diana . . ." *All's W,* IV, iii, 204–205. **6** belonging; pertaining: ". . . with such vehemency he should pursue/ Faults proper to himself." *Meas,* V, i, 112–113. **7** personal; private: "In my defunct, and proper satisfaction . . ." *Oth,* I, iii, 264. **8 my proper cost,** my own expense: ". . . crown th' alliance on't . . . Here at my house, and at my proper cost." *T Night,* V, i, 317–318. **9 O proper stuff!** [used ironically] A fine situation indeed!: "O proper stuff!/ This is the very painting of your fear . . ." *Mac,* III, iv, 59–60.
—*adv.* **10** exclusively: "Thyself and thy belongings/ Are not thine own so proper as to waste . . ." *Meas,* I, i, 29–30.

proper false, *n. pl.* men who are handsome but deceitful: "How easy is it for the proper false/ In women's waxen hearts to set their forms! [impress themselves on women's receptive hearts]" *T Night,* II, i, 28–29.

properly, *adv.* precisely; accurately: "Or if you will, to speak more properly,/ I will enforce it eas'ly to my love." *K John,* II, i, 514–515.

proper stream, *n.* the predetermined course of his life: ". . . in his proper stream o'erflows himself." *All's W,* IV, iii, 24.

property, *n.* **1** quality; nature: "Sweet love, I see, changing his property,/ Turns to the sourest and most deadly hate." *Rich 2,* III, ii, 135–136. **2** a useful object; tool: "Do not talk of him/ But as a property." *J Caes,* IV, i, 39–40. **3** exclusive

ownership: "Property was thus appalled/ That the self was not the same . . ." *Phoen,* 37–38. **4** [pl.] necessary qualities; qualifications: "Of government the properties to unfold/ Would seem in me t'affect speech and discourse . . ." *Meas,* I, i, 3–4. **5 property of blood,** mutuality of blood; close kinship: "Here I disclaim all my paternal care,/ Propinquity and property of blood . . ." *Lear,* I, i, 113–114.
—*v.* **6** to take possession of; appropriate: ". . . his large fortune . . . Subdues and properties to his love and tendance." *Timon,* I, i, 56–58. **7** to use as property: "I am too high-born to be propertied . . ." *K John,* V, ii, 79. **8** to store away, as a piece of furniture: "They have here propertied me: keep me in darkness . . ." *T Night,* IV, ii, 94. **9** to have the qualities [of]: ". . . his voice was propertied/ As all the tuned spheres . . ." *Ant & Cleo,* V, ii, 83–84.

prophesy, *v.* to suggest or indicate: "Methought thy very gait did prophesy/ A royal nobleness." *Lear,* V, iii, 173–174.

prophet, *n.* omen: "Now shine it like a comet of revenge,/ A prophet to the fall of all our foes!" *1 Hen 6* III, ii, 31–32.

prophetic, *adj.* prob. indicating Hamlet's previous guess at his uncle's true character (not his suspicion that his father's death was murder): "O my prophetic soul! My uncle!" *Ham,* I, v, 41.

propinquity, *n.* closeness; here, of relationship: "Here I disclaim all my paternal care,/ Propinquity and property of blood . . ." *Lear,* I, i, 113–114.

Propontic, *n.* Sea of Marmora: "Ne'er feels retiring ebb, but keeps due on/ To the Propontic, and the Hellespont . . ." *Oth,* III, iii, 462–463.

proportion, *n.* **1** amount or estimate: "Upon or near the rate of thirty thousand."/ "The just proportion [exact number] that we gave them out." *2 Hen 4,* IV, i, 22–23. **2** share; portion; allotment: "Three or four thousand chequins were as pretty a/ proportion to live quietly . . ." *Per,* IV, ii, 24–25. **3** [pl.] required forces, here military forces: ". . . 'tis best to weigh [judge]/ The enemy more mighty than he seems:/ So the proportions of defence are fill'd . . ." *Hen 5,* II, iv, 43–45. **4** bride's portion; dowry: ". . . her promised proportions/ Came short of composition . . ." *Meas,* V, i, 218–219. **5** relation: ". . . the realms of England, France, and Ireland/ Bear that proportion to my flesh and blood . . ." *2 Hen 6,* I, i, 233–234. **6** (in music) rhythm; meter: ". . . how sour sweet music is/ When time is broke and no proportion kept!" *Rich 2,* V, v, 42–43. **7** natural order: "But thou, 'gainst all proportion, didst bring in/ Wonder to wait on treason . . ." *Hen 5,* II, ii, 109–110. **8** shape; physical form or appearance: "Well shalt thou know her by thine own proportion,/ For up and down she doth resemble

thee . . ." *T Andr,* V, ii, 106–107. **9 lay down our proportions,** estimate the military resources needed: "We must not only arm t' invade the French,/ But lay down our proportions to defend/ Against the Scot . . ." *Hen 5,* I, ii, 136–138. **10 proportion of subjection,** proper duties of a subject: ". . . the king that led them to it, who to disobey/ were against all proportion of subjection." *Hen 5,* IV, i, 148–149.
—*v.* **11** to be in proportion to: ". . . his ransom, which/ must proportion the losses we have borne . . ." *Hen 5,* III, vi, 130–131.

proportionable, *adj.* proportional: "For us to levy power/ Proportionable to the enemy/ Is all unpossible." *Rich 2,* II, ii, 123–125.

proportioned, *adj.* **1** (of time) regularly divided between night and day: "Make war against proportion'd course of time . . ." *Luc,* 774. **2** adjusted; measured: ". . . our size of sorrow,/ Proportion'd to our cause, must be as great/ As that which makes it." *Ant & Cleo,* IV, xv, 4–6. **3** made; fashioned: "Proportion'd as one's thought would wish a man . . ." *Rom & Jul,* III, v, 182.

propose, *v.* **1** to talk; converse: "There shalt thou find my cousin Beatrice/ Proposing with the Prince and Claudio." *M Ado,* III, i, 2–3. **2** to imagine: "Be now the father, and propose a son . . ." *2 Hen 4,* V, ii, 92.
—*n.* **3** subject for discussion; also, proposal or proposition: "There will she hide her/ To listen our propose." *M Ado,* III, i, 11–12.

propound, *v.* to ask; inquire of: "A spirit . . . shall make answer to such questions/ As by your Grace shall be propounded him." *2 Hen 6,* I, ii, 79–81.

propriety, *n.* one's identity or true self: ". . . it is the baseness of thy fear/ That makes thee strangle thy propriety." *T Night,* V, i, 144–145.

propugnation, *n.* defense: "What propugnation is in one man's valour . . ." *Tr & Cr,* II, ii, 137.

prorogue, *v.* **1** to postpone or suspend: "I hear thou must—and nothing may prorogue it—/ On Thursday next be married to this County." *Rom & Jul,* IV, i, 47–48. **2** to prolong: ". . . nor taken sustenance/ But to prorogue his grief." *Per,* V, i, 25–26.

proscription, *n.* action of condemning to death without legal trial and sentence: ". . . who should be prick'd to die/ In our black sentence and proscription." *J Caes,* IV, i, 16–17.

prosecution, *n.* **inevitable prosecution,** inescapable pursuit: ". . . see behind me/ The inevitable prosecution of/ Disgrace and horror . . ." *Ant & Cleo,* IV, xiv, 64–66.

Proserpina, *n.* goddess of the underworld, wife of Pluto: ". . . as full of envy at his greatness/ as Cerberus is at Proserpina's beauty—" *Tr & Cr,* II, i, 34–35.

prospect, *n.* aspect; scene; view: "It were a tedious difficulty, I think,/ To bring 'em to that prospect . . ." *Oth,* III, iii, 403–404.

prosperity, *n.* success: "A jest's prosperity lies in the ear/ Of him that hears it . . ." *Love's L,* V, ii, 853–854.

prosperous, *adj.* **1** bringing prosperity; propitious: "So I leave you/ To the protection of the prosperous gods . . ." *Timon,* V, i, 181–182. **2** successful; fortunate: "Get you gone. Be strong and prosperous/ In this resolve." *Rom & Jul,* IV, i, 122–123. **3** valuable; rewarding: ". . . your good advice/ (Which still hath been both grave and prosperous) . . ." *Mac,* III, i, 20–21. **4** effective: ". . . she hath prosperous art/ When she will play with reason and discourse . . ." *Meas,* I, ii, 174–175.

prosperously, *adv.* successfully: ". . . which reason and sanity could not/ so prosperously be delivered of." *Ham,* II, ii, 210–211.

prostitute, *v.,* to expose to unskilled opinion: "To prostitute our past-cure malady/ To empirics . . ." *All's W,* II, i, 120–121.

Protector, *n.* regent of England during the minority of the heir to the throne [Henry VI was 9 months old at the time of his father's death]: "Gloucester, whate'er we like, thou art Protector,/ And lookest to command the Prince and realm." *1 Hen 6,* I, i, 37–38.

protest, *v.* **1** to give a solemn promise; vow: ". . . he protests/ he will not hurt you." *T Night,* III, iv, 305–306. **2** to declare or proclaim; also, denounce: "Do me right, or I will protest/ your cowardice." *M Ado,* V, i, 146–147. **3** to admit; profess: "You have stayed me in a happy hour, I was about/ to protest I loved you." *M Ado,* IV, i, 282–283. **4** to declare one's love: "I will tell her, sir, that you do protest—which, as/ I take it, is a gentleman-like offer." *Rom & Jul,* II, iv, 174–175.

protestation, *n.* oath or vow: "And to his protestation urg'd the rest . . ." *Luc,* 1844.

protester, *n.* person who professes love or friendship: "To stale with ordinary oaths my love/ To every new protester . . ." *J Caes,* I, ii, 72–73.

Proteus, *n.* the Old Man of the Sea, who eluded capture by constantly changing his shape: "I can add colours to the chameleon,/ Change shapes with Proteus for advantages . . ." *3 Hen 6,* III, ii, 191–192.

protractive, *adj.* extended; drawn out: ". . . the protractive trials of great Jove/ To find persistive constancy in men . . ." *Tr & Cr,* I, iii, 20–21.

proud, *adj.* **1** devoted to luxury: "Report of fashions in proud Italy . . ." *Rich 2,* II, i, 21. **2** wanton; poss., also, lascivious: "Item, she is proud."/ ". . . it was Eve's legacy, and cannot/ be ta'en from her." *Two Gent,* III, i, 329–331. **3** boasting proudly: "And, proud of many, lives upon his gains." *Sonn 67,* 12. **4** (of a stream) swollen beyond its bounds: "Like a proud river peering o'er his bounds . . ." *K John,* II, ii, 23. **5** arrogant; rebellious: "The one affrights you,/ The other makes you proud." *Cor,* I, i, 168–169. **6 proud control,** overpowering force: "The proud control of fierce and bloody war . . ." *K John,* I, i, 17. **7 proud of this pride,** swollen with sexual ardor: "Proud of this pride,/ He is contented thy poor drudge to be . . ." *Sonn 151,* 10–11.

prouder, *adj.* stronger; fiercer: "Our party may well meet [could well handle] a prouder foe." *K John,* V, i, 79.

proud livery, *n.* elegant clothes; gorgeous attire: "Thy youth's proud livery, so gazed on now . . ." *Sonn 2,* 3.

proudly, *adv.* with authority; forcefully: "Question her proudly; let thy looks be stern . . ." *1 Hen 6,* I, ii, 62.

proud-pied, *adj.* magnificently colored or variegated: "When proud-pied April, dress'd in all his trim . . ." *Sonn 98,* 2.

provand, *n.* feed; provender: ". . . camels in their war, who have their provand . . ." *Cor,* II, i, 249.

prove, *v.* **1** to try; put to the test: ". . . even now/ To tie the rider she begins to prove . . ." *Ven & Ad,* 39–40. **2** to ascertain; see for oneself: "Shall we go prove what's to be done?" *M Ado,* I, iii, 69. **3** to experience: "You have seen and prov'd a fairer former fortune/ Than that which is to approach." *Ant & Cleo,* I, ii, 33–34. **4** to attempt to prove; argue: "Indeed it does stink in some sort, sir. But yet, sir, I/ would prove—" *Meas,* III, ii, 27–28. **5** to turn out to be: "Nay, if the devil have given thee proofs for sin,/ Thou wilt prove his." *Meas,* III, ii, 29–30. **6 prove it on,** to fight in armed combat [against]: "There's my gauntlet;/ I'll prove it on a giant." *Lear,* IV, vi, 90–91. **7 prove upon thee,** to settle [with thee] in combat: ". . . that I'll prove upon thee, though thy little/ finger be armed in a thimble." *Shrew,* IV, iii, 145–146.

provide, *v.* to make ready: "We will ourselves provide./ Most holy and religious fear it is . . ." *Ham,* III, iii, 7–8.

provided, *adj.* prepared; supplied: ". . . it will seek me in another place,/ And find me worse provided." *2 Hen 4,* II, iii, 48–49.

providence, *n.* foresight: "It will be laid to us, whose providence/ Should have kept short . . . This mad young man." *Ham,* IV, i, 17–19.

provident, *adj.* prudent; foresighted: "I saw your brother,/ Most provident in peril, bind himself . . . To a strong mast . . ." *T Night,* I, ii, 11–14.

provincial, *adj.* under the ecclesiastical authority of the local province: "His subject am I not,/ Nor here provincial." *Meas,* V, i, 313–314.

Provincial rose, *n.* elaborate roselike decoration, often used on shoes: ". . . with Provincial/ roses on my razed shoes . . ." *Ham,* III, ii, 270–271.

provision, *n.* supply of ready money: "I am sorry, when he sent to borrow of me, that my/ provision was out." *Timon,* III, vi, 15–16.

provocation, *n.* carnal temptation: ". . . let there/ come a tempest of provocation, I will shelter me/ here." *Wives,* V, v, 20–22.

provoke, *v.* **1** to push or hurl; force forward: ". . . as rigour of tempestuous gusts/ Provokes the mightiest hulk against the tide . . ." *1 Hen 6,* V, v, 5–6. **2** to arouse to action; incite: "No had, my lord! why, did you not provoke me?" *K John,* IV, ii, 207.

provoking merit, *n.* personality trait that provokes others to violence; here, a quality in Gloucester that made Edgar want to kill him: ". . . a provoking merit, set a-work by/ a reprovable badness in himself [Edgar]." *Lear,* III, v, 7–8.

provost, *n.* warden or jailer: ". . . the Provost hath a warrant/ For's execution." *Meas,* I, iv, 73–74.

provulgate, *v.* prob. typog. error for promulgate; make known: "Which, when I know that boasting is an honour,/ I shall provulgate—" *Oth,* I, ii, 20–21.

prudence, *n.* **Good Prudence,** Madam Wisdom [an ironic or contemptuous manner of address]: "Hold your tongue,/ Good Prudence! Smatter with your gossips, go." *Rom & Jul,* III, v, 170–171.

prune[1], *n.* **stewed prunes,** favorite refreshment in brothels; also, a slang term for "prostitutes": ". . . longing,/ saving your honours' reverence, for stewed prunes . . ." *Meas,* II, i, 88–89.

prune[2], *v.* (of a bird) to preen (the feathers); similarly, of people, to exhibit pride: ". . . makes him prune himself, and bristle up/ The crest of youth against your dignity." *1 Hen 4,* I, i, 97–98.

pry, *v.* to look carefully: "Speak, and look back, and pry on every side . . ." *Rich 3,* III, v, 6.

psaltery, *n.* stringed instrument, played by plucking; forerunner of the dulcimer: "The trumpets, sackbuts, psalteries and fifes . . ." *Cor,* V, iv, 50.

Ptolemy, *n.* name of 15 Egyptian kings prior to 30 B.C.; here, younger [deceased] brother of Cleopatra, to whom she had been nominally married as a child: ". . . nor the queen of Ptolemy/ More womanly than he . . ." *Ant & Cleo,* I, iv, 6–7.

publican, *n.* (in ancient Rome) tax collector; traditionally overbearing but, as here, ingratiating when requesting a favor: "How like a fawning publican he looks!" *Merch,* I, iii, 36.

publication, *n.* announcement or proclamation: "And in the publication make no strain . . ." *Tr & Cr,* I, iii, 326.

public haunt, *n.* clamor of crowds or, esp., unwelcome strangers: "And this our life, exempt from public haunt . . ." *As You,* II, i, 15.

Publicola, *n.* Roman hero, dead some years prior to action of the play: "The noble sister of Publicola,/ The moon of Rome [ref. to chasteness of Valeria] . . ." *Cor,* V, iii, 64–65.

public weal, *n.* commonwealth; state or nation: "The King from Eltham I intend to steal,/ And sit at chiefest stern of public weal." *1 Hen 6,* I, i, 176–177.

publish, *v.* to proclaim; make known: "Let us on,/ And publish the occasion of our arms." *2 Hen 4,* I, iii, 85–86.

publisher, *n.* person who reveals or makes known: "For love of you . . . Hath made me publisher of this pretence." *Two Gent,* III, i, 46–47.

pucelle, *n.* virgin; here, an epithet: "Joan la Pucelle, commonly called Joan of Aire" [SD] *1 Hen 6,* I, i, 1.

pudder, *n.* din; turmoil; hubbub: ". . . the great Gods,/ That keep this dreadful pudder o'er our heads . . ." *Lear,* III, ii, 49–50.

pudding, *n.* **1** stuffing: ". . . that Manningtree/ ox with the pudding in his belly . . ." *1 Hen 4,* II, iv, 446–447. **2** a sausage, prob. made like the preceding: ". . . we'll have flesh for holidays, fish for/ fasting-days, and moreo'er puddings and flapjacks . . ." *Per,* II, i, 81–83.

puddle, *v.* to muddle; muddy: ". . . something sure of state . . . Hath puddled his clear spirit . . ." *Oth,* III, iv, 137–140.

puddled, *adj.* stirred up; also, befouled: ". . . they threw on him/ Great pails of puddled mire to quench the hair . . ." *Errors,* V, i, 172–173.

pudency, *n.* modesty: ". . . did it with/ A pudency so rosy . . ." *Cymb,* II, iv, 162–163.

pueritia, *n.* [Latin] little child; also, childishness: "Ba, *pueritia,* with a horn added." *Love's L,* V, i, 46.

puff, *v.* **1** to strain: ". . . press among the popular throngs, and puff/ To win a vulgar station." *Cor,* II, i, 212–213. **2** to blast away in the manner of a cannon: "And . . . from his very arm/ Puff'd his own brother . . ." *Oth,* III, iv, 133–134.

puffed, *adj.* swollen; bloated: ". . . like a puff'd and reckless libertine/ Himself the primrose path of dalliance treads . . ." *Ham,* I, iii, 49–50.

pugging, *adj.* prob. thieving [stealing the sheets to pay for a quart of ale]: "Doth set my pugging tooth an edge . . ." *W Tale,* IV, iii, 7.

puisny, *adj.* inexperienced, hence inferior: ". . . as a puisny tilter that spurs his horse but on one side breaks his staff like a noble goose." *As You,* III, iv, 39–40.

puissance, *n.* (usu. pron. as three syll.) military power; army: "Cousin, go draw our puissance together." *K John,* III, i, 265.

puissant, *adj.* powerful; overwhelming: ". . . which in recounting/ His grief grew puissant . . ." *Lear,* V, iii, 215–216.

puke-stocking, *adj.* wearing stockings of puke, a dark grey wool: ". . . not-pated, agate-ring, puke-stocking, caddis-garter . . ." *1 Hen 4,* II, iv, 69.

pulcher, *adj.* [Latin] beautiful: "What is 'fair', William?"/ "*Pulcher.*" *Wives,* IV, i, 21–22.

puling, *adj.* whining; whimpering: ". . . a wretched puling fool,/ A whining mammet . . . To answer 'I'll not wed . . .'" *Rom & Jul,* III, v, 183–185.

pull, *v.* **1 pull in,** to rein in: "I pull in resolution; and begin/ To doubt th' equivocation of the fiend . . ." *Mac,* V, v, 42–43. —*n.* **2** a plucking or pruning: ". . . two pulls at once;/ His lady banish'd, and a limb lopp'd off . . ." *2 Hen 6,* II, iii, 41–42.

pulpit, *n.* See **common pulpits.**

pulsidge, *n.* misuse for "pulse": "Your pulsidge beats as/ extraordinarily as heart would desire . . ." *2 Hen 4,* II, iv, 23–24.

pump, *n.* man's shoe, often decorated with flowerlike perforations: "Pink for flower."/ ". . . Why, then is my pump well flowered." *Rom & Jul,* II, iv, 60–62.

pumpion or **pompion,** *n.* pumpkin or, sometimes, a squash: ". . . we'll use this unwholesome humidity, this gross watery pumpion . . ." *Wives,* III, iii, 35–36.

punk, *n.* prostitute: "As fit as ten groats is for the hand of an attorney, as/ your French crown for your taffety punk . . ." *All's W,* II, ii, 20–21.

punto, *n.* (in fencing) direct thrust with the point of the sword: ". . . to see thee there, to see/ thee pass thy punto, thy stock, thy reverse . . ." *Wives,* II, iii, 23–24.

punto reverso, *n.* back-handed sword thrust: "Ah, the immortal/ passado, the punto reverso, the hay!" *Rom & Jul,* II, iv, 25–26.

puny, *adj.* petty; piddling: "Lest that thy wives with spits, and boys with stones,/ In puny battle slay me." *Cor,* IV, iv, 5–6.

pupil, *adj.* immature: "Time's pencil, or my pupil pen . . ." *Sonn 16,* 10.

pupil age, *n.* **1** one's school years; childhood: ". . . since the old days of goodman Adam/ to the pupil age of this present twelve o'clock at midnight." *1 Hen 4,* II, iv, 91–93. **2** apprenticeship: "His pupil age/ Man-enter'd thus, he waxed like a sea . . ." *Cor,* II, ii, 98–99.

puppet, *n.* **1** doll-like woman with no mind of her own: "Fie, fie, you counterfeit! You puppet you!" *M N Dream,* III, ii, 288. **2** ref. to the popularity of Eliz. puppet shows: "Thou, an Egyptian puppet shall be shown/ In Rome as well as I . . ." *Ant & Cleo,* V, ii, 207–208.

pur, *n.* jack [knave] in the card game of *post and pair;* also, wordplay on the purr of a cat and a piece of animal excrement: "Here is a pur of Fortune's, sir, or of Fortune's cat, but/ not a musk-cat, that has fall'n into the unclean fishpond . . ." *All's W,* V, ii, 19–20.

purblind, *adj.* **1** totally blind: "This wimpled, whining, purblind, wayward boy . . ." *Love's L,* III, i, 174. **2** partially blind; dim-sighted: "Speak to my gossip Venus one fair word,/ One nickname for her purblind son and heir . . ." *Rom & Jul,* II, i, 11–12.

purchase, *n.* **1** (in thieves' jargon) plunder: ". . . thou shalt have a share in our/ purchase, as I am a true man." *1 Hen 4,* II, i, 90–91. **2** gain or profit: "The purchase is to make men glorious . . ." *Per,* I, Chor., 9. **3 fourteen years' purchase,** ref. to value of land equal to 12 years' rent; here, a high price: ". . . get themselves a/ good report—after [based on] fourteen years' purchase." *T Night,* IV, i, 22–23. —*v.* **4** to acquire: "Go, say I sent thee forth to purchase honour . . ." *Rich 2,* I, iii, 282. **5** to earn: "Ay . . . and not without/ his true purchasing." *Cor,* II, i, 137–138. **6** to win or win over: "Do this, and purchase us thy lasting friends." *T Andr,* II, iii, 275. **7 purchase out,** to buy off; redeem: "Nor tears nor prayers shall purchase out abuses." *Rom & Jul,* III, i, 195.

pure, *adj.* **1** clear; lucid: ". . . his pure brain . . . Doth by the idle comments that it makes/ Foretell the ending of mortality." *K John,* V, vii, 2–5.

—*adv.* **2** purely; solely: "For his sake/ Did I expose myself (pure for his love)/ Into the danger of this adverse town . . ." *T Night,* V, i, 80–82.

purgation, *n.* **1** proof of one's innocence; exoneration: "If their purgation did consist in words,/ They are as innocent as grace itself." *As You,* I, iii, 49–50. **2** acquittal: "Proceed in justice, which shall have due course,/ Even to the guilt or the purgation." *W Tale,* III, ii, 6–7. **3** means of liberation; here in wordplay with bound [constipated], etc.: ". . . thou wert immured, restrained,/ captivated, bound."/ "True, true, and now you will be my purgation and/ let me loose." *Love's L,* III, i, 121–124. **4** proof of a claim or an assertion: "If any man doubt that, let him put me to my purgation." *As You,* V, iv, 43. **5 put someone to his purgation,** to eliminate excess humor [bile] from the body: ". . . for for me to put him to/ his purgation would perhaps plunge him into more/ choler." *Ham,* III, ii, 297–299.

purge, *v.* **1** to repent; reform: "If I do grow great, I'll grow/ less, for I'll purge . . ." *1 Hen 4,* V, iv, 162–163. **2** to disperse; clear: "Love is a smoke made with the fume of sighs;/ Being purg'd, a fire sparkling in lovers' eyes . . ." *Rom & Jul,* I, i, 188–189. **3** to cleanse or purify, esp. of guilt: "You cannot with such freedom purge yourself . . ." *Hen 8,* V, i, 102. **4** to take a seasonal purgative to ward off illness: "We sicken to shun sickness when we purge . . ." *Sonn 118,* 4. **5** to civilize: ". . . i' th' olden time,/ Ere humane statute purg'd the gentle weal . . ." *Mac,* III, iv, 74–75. **6** to discharge; exude: ". . . their faces are/ wrinkled, their eyes purging thick amber and plum-tree gum . . ." *Ham,* II, ii, 197–199.

—*n.* **7** blood shed by Malcolm and his followers to cleanse the land: "And with him pour we, in our country's purge,/ Each drop of us." *Mac,* V, iii, 28–29.

purged, *adj.* refined; here, impartial: "Not working with the eye without the ear,/ And but in purged judgment trusting neither?" *Hen 5,* II, ii, 135–136.

purger, *n.* healer: "We shall be call'd purgers, not murderers." *J Caes,* II, i, 180.

puritan, *n.* male singer with a high voice: ". . . they are most of them means and bases but one/ puritan amongst them . . ." *W Tale,* IV, iii, 43–44.

purl, *v.* to swirl upward: "Thin winding breath which purl'd up to the sky." *Luc,* 1407.

purlieu, *n.* [usually pl.] cleared land bordering, or sometimes within a forest: "Where in the purlieus of this forest stands/ A sheep-cote fenc'd about with olive-trees?" *As You,* IV, iii, 76–77.

purple, *adj.* blood-red: "With purple falchion, painted to the hilt/ In blood of those that had encounter'd him . . ." *3 Hen 6,* I, iv, 12–13.

purpled, *adj.* drenched in blood: "Now, whilst your purpled hands do reek and smoke . . ." *J Caes,* III, i, 158.

purple-hued, *adj.* (of the face) dark red or purple due to heavy drinking: ". . . none of these mad/ mustachio purple-hued malt-worms . . ." *1 Hen 4,* II, i, 73–74.

purple-in-grain, *adj.* of a reddish color: ". . . your purple-in-grain/ beard, or your French-crown-colour beard . . ." *M N Dream,* I, ii, 87–88.

purpose, *v.* **1** to intend; expect: ". . . since I do/ purpose to marry, I will think nothing to any purpose/ that the world can say against it . . ." *M Ado,* V, iv, 103–105. **2** to design or create: "What can be avoided/ Whose end is purpos'd by the mighty gods?" *J Caes,* II, ii, 26–27. **3** to promise; here, had the intention of giving in marriage: "His daughter . . . (whom/ He purpos'd to his wife's sole son . . .)" *Cymb,* I, i, 4–5. **4 purpose not,** have no intention: "I will not praise that purpose not to sell." *Sonn 21,* 14.

—*n.* **5** the truth: ". . . or any such proverb so little kin to the purpose." *Hen 5,* III, vii, 69. **6** impulse or intention: "The flighty purpose never is o'ertook,/ Unless the deed go with it." *Mac,* IV, i, 145–146. **7 in my purpose bred,** a part of all my plans: "You are so strongly in my purpose bred . . ." *Sonn 112,* 13. **8 make your own purpose,** carry out your own plan: ". . . make your own purpose,/ How in my strength you please." *Lear,* II, i, 111–112. **9 nothing of my purpose,** nothing I did intentionally: ". . . it is something of my/ negligence, nothing of my purpose." *T Night,* III, iv, 259–260. **10 of purpose to,** with the intention of: ". . . come again/ to supper to him of purpose of have him spend less . . ." *Timon,* III, i, 24–25. **11 to the purpose, a.** worth mentioning: "Thisbe/ a grey eye or so, but not to the purpose." *Rom & Jul,* II, iv, 43–44. **b.** close to the truth: ". . . my misgiving still/ Falls shrewdly to the purpose." *J Caes,* III, i, 145–146.

purposed, *adj.* **1** destined; directed: "How purpos'd, sir, I pray you?"/ "Against some part of Poland." *Ham,* IV, iv, 10–11. **2** intentional: "Let my disclaiming from a purpos'd evil [harm]/ Free me so far in your most generous thoughts . . ." *Ham,* V, ii, 237–238. **3** proposed: ". . . your purpos'd low correction/

Is such as basest and contemnèd'st wretches . . . Are punish'd with . . ." *Lear* II, ii, 142–145. **4 a purposed thing,** a contrived situation; conspiracy: "It is a purpos'd thing, and grows by plot . . ." *Cor,* III, i, 37–38.

Purr, *n.* demon or devil seen by Tom [Edgar]; perh. a familiar: "Purr, the cat is grey." *Lear,* III, vi, 46.

purse, *n.* **1** the great seal in its carrying case; here, symbol of Wolsey's office as Lord Chancellor: "Enter Cardinal Wolsey, the purse borne before him . . ." [SD] *Hen 8,* I, i, 114. **2 upon your purse,** using your money: "Whiles he is vaulting variable ramps,/ In your despite, upon your purse . . ." *Cymb,* I, vii, 134–135. —*v.* **3** to make up a purse of: "And I will go and purse the ducats straight . . ." *Merch,* I, iii, 170. **4 purse up,** to put into her purse; pocket: "When she first met Mark Antony, she purs'd up/ his heart upon the river of Cydnus." *Ant & Cleo,* II, ii, 186–187.

pursent, *v.* dial. pron. of **present**; here, "represents": "No, sir; but it is vara fine,/ For every one pursents three." *Love's L,* V, ii, 487–488.

pursue, *v.* to persecute: "That with such vehemency he should pursue/ Faults proper to himself." *Meas,* V, i, 112–113.

pursuivant, *n.* **1** herald; here, a harbinger or forerunner: "And these grey locks, the pursuivants of Death . . ." *1 Hen 6,* II, v, 5. **2** junior officer: ". . . send for his master with a/ pursuivant presently." *2 Hen 6,* i, iii, 34–35.

pursy, *adj.* fat, esp. overfat; paunchy, flabby, or bloated: "And pursy insolence shall break his wind/ With fear and horrid flight." *Timon,* V, iv, 12–13.

purveyor, *n.* court official who travels ahead of the monarch to secure provisions [Cf. **harbinger**]: "We cours'd him at the heels, and had a purpose/ To be his purveyor . . ." *Mac,* I, vi, 21–22.

push, *n.* **1** military thrust; attack: "This push/ Will cheer me ever, or disseat me now." *Mac,* V, iii, 20. **2** critical stage or time: "Lest they desire (upon this push) to trouble/ Your joys with like relation." *W Tale,* V, iii, 129–130. **3 make a push at,** to defy or scorn: "However they have writ the style of gods,/ And made a push at chance and sufferance [suffering]." *M Ado,* V, i, 37–38. **4 present push,** prompt action; lit., immediate test: "We'll put the matter to the present push." *Ham,* V, i, 290. **5 stand the push of,** be able to stand up to: "Go to, I stand the push of your one thing that you/ will tell." *2 Hen 4,* II, ii, 36–37. —*interj.* **6** exclam. of impatience: "Push, did you see my cap?" *Timon,* III, vi, 104.

push-pin, *n.* child's game in which a pin is pushed in an effort to cross the pin of an opponent: "And Nestor play at push-pin with the boys . . ." *Love's L,* IV, iii, 166.

put, *v.* **1** to separate: "Whereon his brains still beating puts him thus/ From fashion of himself." *Ham,* III, i, 176–177. **2 put apart,** to remove; oust: "For Humphrey being dead . . . And Henry put apart, the next for me." *2 Hen 6,* III, i, 382–383. **3 put back,** to turn back or away: "Coming from thee I could not put him back . . ." *Luc,* 843. **4 put beside,** to suffer a memory lapse in: "As an unperfect actor on the stage . . . is put beside his part . . ." *Sonn 23,* 1–2. **5 put down,** to repress or suppress; abolish: "'Twas never merry world since, of two usuries, the/ merriest was put down . . ." *Meas,* III, ii, 6–7. **6 put (someone) down, a.** to get the better of; best; here, in wordplay with "to bed": "A hundred marks, my Kate does put her down."/ "That's my office." *Shrew,* V, ii, 35–36. **b.** wordplay on "to squelch" and "to render unconscious with drink": ". . . when/ did I see thee so put down?"/ "Never . . . unless you see canary/ put me down." *T Night,* I, iii, 80–82. **7 put forth, a.** to sail; depart by ship: "Come, we will all put forth, body and goods." *2 Hen 4,* I, i, 186. **b.** to leave; sail or depart from: ". . . order for sea is given,/ They have put forth the haven . . ." *Ant & Cleo,* IV, x, 6–7. **c.** to come to the fore, esp. to occupy one: ". . . that may blow/ No sneaping winds at home, to make us say/ 'This is put forth too truly [with good reason].'" *W Tale,* I, ii, 12–14. **d.** to show itself; appear: ". . . his folly, fear,/ Among the infinite doings of the world,/ Sometime puts forth." *W Tale,* I, ii, 252–254. **8 put in,** to make a bid: ". . . they had gone down too,/ but that a burgher put in for them." *Meas,* I, ii, 91–92. **9 put it off,** make a go of it; pull it off; here, in wordplay with "put off": ". . . if God have lent a man any manners/ he may easily put it off at court . . ." *All's W,* II, ii, 8–9. **10 put it on,** to encourage or instigate it: "That you protect this course, and put it on/ By your allowance . . ." *Lear,* I, iv, 216–217. **11 put it up,** to submit [lit., to sheathe one's sword]: "What, madam, be dishonoured openly,/ And basely put it up without revenge?" *T Andr,* I, i, 432–433. **12 put off, a.** to shrug off; dismiss: "Why, what place make you special,/ when you put off that with such contempt?" *All's W,* II, ii, 5–6. **b.** poss. a term in fencing, meaning to parry; fend off or evade: "Why, she that bears the bow./ Finely put off!" *Love's L,* IV, i, 110–111. **13 put (someone) off,** to get rid of or discard (someone): "Hath my behaviour given to your displeasure,/ That thus you should proceed to put me off . . ." *Hen 8,* II, iv, 18–19. **14 put on, a.** to betray; give away: "Let not our looks put on our purposes . . ." *J Caes,* II, i, 225. **b.** to press or force on (someone): "If it be so—as so 'tis put on me,/ And that in way of caution . . ." *Ham,* I, iii, 94–95. **c.** to assume: ". . . each hand hath put on nature's power . . ." *Sonn 127,* 5. **d.** to bring about; instigate: "Of deaths put on by cunning and forc'd cause . . ." *Ham,* V, ii, 388. **e.** to put to the

test: "For he was likely, had he been put on,/ To have prov'd most royal . . ." *Ham,* V, ii, 402–403. **f.** poss. a term in fencing, meaning to thrust or strike: "Hang me by the neck if horns that year miscarry./ Finely put on!" *Love's L,* IV, i, 113–114. **15 put out,** to show; display: "Pray you put up your dagger and put out your wit." *Rom & Jul,* IV, v, 119. **16 put (someone) out, a.** to interrupt (someone): "I have put you out:/ But to your protestation: let me hear/ What you profess." *W Tale,* IV, iv, 368–370. **b.** to cause (a person) to forget lines, a speech, etc.; confuse or embarrass: "And ever and anon they made a doubt/ Presence majestical would put him out . . ." *Love's L,* V, ii, 101–102. **17 puts me,** puts; use of [ethical] dative in informal speech, poss. with sense of "just imagine" or "for my benefit": "But to prove to you that Helen loves him, she/ came and puts me her white hand to his cloven/ chin—" *Tr & Cr,* I, ii, 120–122. **18 put to,** to engage in coitus: "As rank as any flax-wench that puts to/ Before her troth-plight . . ." *W Tale,* I, ii, 277–278. **19 put (someone) to, a.** to enlist (a conscript) as: "I cannot put him/ to a private soldier, that is the leader of so many/ thousands." *2 Hen 4,* III, ii, 163–164. **b.** to incite someone to: "There's in him stuff that puts him to these ends . . ." *Hen 8,* I, i, 58. **c.** to assign: "You have put me now to such a part [role] . . ." *Cor,* III, ii, 105. **d.** to impose on: "For nature puts me to a heavy task." *T Andr,* V, iii, 150. **20 put together,** set opposite each other [in a duel]: ". . . it had been pity/ you should have been put together, with so mortal a/ purpose . . ." *Cymb,* I, v, 37–39. **21 put to it, a.** to put (someone) to the test: "Nay, good my lord, put him to't;/ let him have/ his way." *All's W,* III, vi, 1. **b.** to be inflexible or unrelenting about: "Lord Angelo dukes it well in his absence: he puts/ transgression to't." *Meas,* III, ii, 91–92. **22 put up,** sheathe your sword: "Nor would your noble mother . . . Be so dishonoured . . . For shame, put up." *T Andr,* II, i, 51–53. **23 put us to our answer,** force us to respond [retaliate]: ". . . would seek us through/ And put us to our answer." *Cymb,* IV, ii, 160–161. **24 put well forth,** to make a good show: "Worshipful mutiners,/ Your valour puts well forth . . ." *Cor,* I, i, 249–250. **25 put you o'er,** to refer or commend: "But for the certain knowledge of that truth/ I put you o'er to heaven and to my mother . . ." *K John,* I, 1, 61–62. **26 put you upon it,** to burden you with it: ". . . they do you/ wrong to put you so oft upon't." *Meas,* II, i, 262–263.
—*past part.* **27 put to know,** forced to admit: "Since I am put to know that your own science [knowledge]/ Exceeds . . ." *Meas,* I, i, 5–6.

putrefied core, *n.* corrupt or defiled body; ref. to Greek that Hector has pursued and slain for his fine armor: "Most putrefied core, so fair without . . ." *Tr & Cr,* V, viii, 1.

putter-out, *n.* merchant, etc., with whom a traveler deposited money before a voyage; if he returned safely, he received five times the amount, otherwise the sum was forfeited: "Each putter-out of five for one will bring us/ Good warrant . . ." *Temp,* III, iii, 48–49.

putting-on, *n.* an urging; here, a command and threat: ". . . thinking me remiss/ in mine office, awakens me with this unwonted/ putting-on . . ." *Meas,* IV, ii, 113–115.

puttock, *n.* kite, a lesser hawk; term sometimes applied to the common buzzard: "I chose an eagle,/ And did avoid a puttock." *Cymb,* I, ii, 70–71.

puzzel, *n.* drab; slut [pun on Fr. *pucelle,* maid]: "Puzzel or Pucelle, dolphin or dogfish,/ Your hearts I'll stamp out with my horse's heels . . ." *1 Hen 6,* I, iv, 106–107.

Pygmalion, *n.* sculptor of Greek mythology whose statue of a young woman comes to life: "What, is there/ none of Pygmalion's images newly made woman to/ be had now . . ." *Meas,* III, ii, 43–45.

pyramid, *n.* [pl.] large buildings: "Thy pyramids built up with newer might . . ." *Sonn 123,* 2.

pyramis, *n.* pyramid [fr. Latin]: "A statelier pyramis to her I'll rear/ Than Rhodope's of Memphis ever was . . ." *1 Hen 6,* I, vi, 21–22.

pyramises, *n.* prob. a drunken mistake for "pyramides," Latin pl. of "pyramis": "I have heard the Ptolemies'/ pyramises are very goodly things . . ." *Ant & Cleo,* II, vii, 33–34.

Pyramus and Thisbe, *n.* legendary young Babylonian couple whose love ended tragically: "'The most lamentable comedy,/ and most cruel death of Pyramus and Thisbe." *M N Dream,* I, ii, 11–12.

Pyrenean, *n.* the Pyrenees: "And talking of the Alps and Apennines./ The Pyrenean and the river Po. . . ." *K John,* I, i, 202–203.

Pyrrhus, *n.* Also called **Neoptolemus,** son of Achilles; slayer of Priam in the Trojan War: "The rugged Pyrrhus, like th'Hyrcanian beast—" *Ham,* II, ii, 446.

Pythagoras, *n.* philosopher of ancient Greece, who taught that the souls of the dead inhabited other beings: "To hold opinion with Pythagoras,/ That souls of animals infuse themselves/ Into the trunks of men. . . ." *Merch,* IV, i, 131–133.

— Q —

quadrant, *n.* **in quadrant wise,** arranged in a quadrant, a quarter of a circle: "Here stood a battle of ten thousand horse,/ There twice as many pikes in quadrant wise . . ." *Edw 3,* V, i, 136–137.

quail¹, *v.* **1** to slacken; weaken or relent: "And let not search and inquisition quail/ To bring again these foolish runaways." *As You,* II, ii, 20–21. **2** to discourage: "The twentieth part/ Of those that live are men enow to quail/ The feeble handful on the adverse part." *Edw 3,* IV, vi, 48–50. **3** to overpower: "Quail, crush, conclude, and quell." *M N Dream,* V, i, 276.

quail², *n.* [slang] prostitute: "Here's Agamemnon: an honest fellow enough,/ and one that loves quails . . ." *Tr & Cr,* V, i, 50–51.

quaint, *adj.* **1** intricate; elaborate or complicated: ". . . the quaint mazes in the wanton green/ For lack of tread are undistinguishable." *M N Dream,* II, i, 99–100. **2** dainty; pretty: "The clamorous owl, that nightly hoots and wonders/ At our quaint spirits." *M N Dream,* II, ii, 6–7. **3** elegant; stylish: "I never saw a better-fashion'd gown,/ More quaint, more pleasing . . ." *Shrew,* IV, iii, 101–102. **4** clever; artful or quick-witted: "The quaint musician, amorous Litio . . ." *Shrew,* III, ii, 145. **5** ingenious: "Enter Ariel like a Harpy; claps his wings/ upon the table; and, with a quaint device [mechanism], the banquet vanishes." [SD] *Temp,* III, iii, 52.
—*adv.* **6** prettily: "That quaint in green she shall be loose enrob'd . . ." *Wives,* IV, vi, 40.

quaintly, *adv.* skillfully; ingeniously: "And time that is so briefly spent/ With your fine fancies quaintly eche . . ." *Per,* III, Chor., 12–13.

quaked, *adj.* terrified: ". . . where ladies shall be frighted,/ And, gladly quak'd, hear more . . ." *Cor,* I, ix, 5–6.

qualification, *n.* pacification; appeasement: ". . . whose qualification shall come/ into no true trust again, but by the displanting of/ Cassio." *Oth,* II, i, 270–272.

qualified, *adj.* **1** endowed with many fine qualities: ". . . so qualified as may beseem/ The spouse of any noble gentleman." *Shrew,* IV, v, 65–66. **2** diluted: "I ha' drunk but one cup to-night, and that was/ craftily qualified too . . ." *Oth,* II, iii, 35–36.

qualify, *v.* **1** to moderate or lessen; here, make less severe or disagreeable: "All this amazement can I qualify . . ." *M Ado,* V, iv, 67. **2** to calm or appease: "And with my best endeavours . . . Your discontenting father strive to qualify . . ." *W Tale,* IV, iv, 532–533.

quality, *n.* **1** nature; character: "The quality of mercy is not strain'd . . ." *Merch,* IV, i, 180. **2** circumstances: ". . . the quality of the time and quarrel/ Might well have given us bloody argument." *T Night,* III, iii, 31–32. **3** company or fellowship; also, profession: ". . . you are not of our quality,/ But stand against us like an enemy." *1 Hen 4,* IV, iii, 36–37. **4** one's profession: "Will they pursue the quality/ no longer than they can sing?" *Ham,* II, ii, 344–345. **5** way; manner: ". . . you know yourself,/ Hate counsels not in such a quality . . ." *Merch,* III, ii, 5–6. **6** skill; also, powers or gifts: ". . . to thy strong bidding task/ Ariel and all his quality." *Temp,* I, ii, 192–193. **7** [pl.] accomplishments: "She hath more qualities than a water-spaniel . . ." *Two Gent,* III, i, 270. **8** virtues; also, good and bad characteristics: ". . . and then I lov'd thee,/ And show'd thee all the qualities o' th' isle . . ." *Temp,* I, ii, 338–339. **9** rank: "Your name? your quality? and why you answer/ This present summons?" *Lear,* V, iii, 120–121. **10 quality wherefore,** state of affairs relating to it: "Rouse him, and give him note of our approach,/ With the whole quality wherefore . . ." *Tr & Cr,* IV, i, 44–45. **11 without less quality,** of no apparent quality: "to fortify her judgement . . . for/ taking a beggar without less quality." *Cymb,* I, v, 19–21.

qualm, *n.* **1** sick feeling; nausea: "Get you some of this distilled *carduus benedictus* . . . it is the only thing for a/ qualm." *M Ado,* III, iv, 68–70. **2** in puns with "come"; perhaps both pronounced more like "calm": "And trow you what he call'd me?"/ "Qualm, perhaps."/ ". . . Go, sickness as thou art!" *Love's L,* V, ii, 279–280.

Qualtitie calmie custure me! *appar.* Pistol's nonsensical pseudo-French: "Qualtitie calmie custure me! Art thou a gentleman? What is thy name?" *Hen 5,* IV, iv, 4–5.

quantity, *n.* **1** trifling amount [used contemptuously]: "Forty thousand brothers/ Could not with all their quantity of love/ Make up my sum." *Ham,* V, i, 264–266. **2** sufficient size: ". . . he is not quantity enough for/ that Worthy's thumb . . ." *Love's L,* V, i, 122–123. **3 hold quantity,** [to] be of like proportion: "For women's fear and love hold quantity . . ." *Ham,* III, ii, 162.

quare, *adv.* [Latin] why?: "*Quare* chirrah, not sirrah?" *Love's L,* V, i, 32.

quarrel, *n.* **1** cause for complaint; grievance: ". . . since the quarrel/ Will bear no colour for the thing he is,/ Fashion it thus . . ." *J Caes,* II, i, 28–30. **2** cause tried by warfare: ". . . the chance of goodness/ Be like our warranted quarrel." *Mac,* IV, iii, 136–137. **3** quarreler: "Yet if that quarrel, fortune, do divorce/ It from the bearer . . ." *Hen 8,* II, iii, 14–15. **4 quarrelling with occasion,** quibbling at every opportunity: "Yet more quarrelling with occasion! wilt thou show/ the whole wealth of thy wit . . ." *Merch,* III, v, 50–51.

quarrelous, *adj.* quarrelsome; quick-tempered: ". . . saucy, and/ As quarrelous as the weasel . . ." *Cymb,* III, iv, 160–161.

quarry, *n.* **1** animals killed in a hunt: ". . . on the quarry of these murther'd deer . . ." *Mac,* IV, iii, 206. **2** heap of slaughtered: "This quarry cries on havoc. O proud Death . . ." *Ham,* V, ii, 369.

quarter, *n.* **1** part of an army: "These quarters, squadrons, and these regiments,/ Before, behind us, and on either hand,/ Are but a power." *Edw 3,* IV, iv, 50–52. **2** area of military duty, assignment, authority, etc.: ". . . not a man/ Shall pass his quarter . . ." *Timon,* V, iv, 59–60. **3 in quarter, and in terms,** amiably carrying out their guard duty: ". . . friends all but now, even now,/ In quarter, and in terms, like bride and groom . . ." *Oth,* II, iii, 170–171. **4 keep fair quarter,** to have the proper regard for: "Would that alone a toy he would detain,/ So he would keep fair quarter with his bed . . ." *Errors,* II, i, 107–108. **5 keep good quarter,** to keep a close watch: "Well; keep good quarter and good care to-night . . ." *K John,* V, v, 20. —*v.* **6** to cut a human body in four parts, esp. after hanging: "Lean Famine, quartering Steel, and climbing Fire . . ." *1 Hen 6,* IV, ii, 11. **7** to add another's coat of arms to one's own by

marrying; placed in one quarter of the escutcheon: "I may quarter, coz."/ "You may, by marrying." *Wives,* I, i, 22–23.

quartered fires, *n.* campfires in their quarters: ". . . when they hear their Roman horses neigh,/ Behold their quarter'd fires . . ." *Cymb,* IV, iv, 17–18.

quart-pot, *n.* drinking vessel holding a quart: ". . . it hath serv'd/ me instead of a quart-pot to drink in . . ." *2 Hen 6,* IV, x, 13–14.

quat, *n.* fool [lit., pimple or boil]: "I have rubb'd this young quat almost to the sense . . ." *Oth,* V, i, 11.

quatch-buttock, *n.* appar. a coinage; perh. wide and flat, squashed or squat buttock: ". . . the pin-buttock, the quatch-buttock, the brawn-buttock,/ or any buttock." *All's W,* II, ii, 17–18.

que ai je oublié, [French] what did I forget?: "Od's me, *que ai je/ oublié*?" *Wives,* I, iv, 57–58.

quean, *n.* slut; strumpet: "Cut me off the villain's/ head! Throw the quean in the channel!" *2 Hen 4,* II, i, 45–46.

queasiness, *n.* feeling of uneasiness, reluctance or revulsion; a heavy heart: "And they did fight with queasiness, constrain'd,/ As men drink potions . . ." *2 Hen 4,* I, i, 196–197.

queasy, *adj.* **1** in fig. use, difficult to please; overcritical: ". . . in despite of his/ quick wit and his queasy stomach, he shall fall in/ love with Beatrice." *M Ado,* II, i, 360–362. **2** requiring delicate handling or treatment: ". . . I have one thing, of a queasy question,/ Which I must act." *Lear,* II, i, 18–19.

queen, *v.* **queen it,** to be a queen; here, in wordplay with "quean," strumpet: ". . . a threepence bow'd would hire me/ Old as I am, to queen it . . ." *Hen 8,* II, iii, 36–37.

Queen Mab, *n.* prob. original coinage by Shakespeare, with wordplay on both queen/quean and slang meaning of mab [slut]: "O then I see Queen Mab hath been with you." *Rom & Jul,* I, iv, 53.

queen of heaven, *n.* the goddess Juno, protector of marriages: "Now by the jealous queen of heaven, that kiss/ I carried from thee . . ." *Cor,* V, iii, 46–47.

queen of shades, *n.* the goddess Diana, who ruled over the moon and chastity: "'More fair and chaste than is the queen of shades.'" *Edw 3,* II, i, 142.

Queen of Troy, *n.* Hecuba, who killed the sons of Polymnestor, king of Thrace, in revenge for the slaying of her son Polydorus: "The self-same gods that arm'd the Queen of Troy/

With opportunity of sharp revenge/ Upon the Thracian tyrant . . ." *T Andr*, I, i, 136–137.

quell, *v.* **1** to defeat; overcome: ". . . your oaths to Henry sworn,/ Either to quell the Dauphin utterly,/ Or bring him in obedience to your yoke." *1 Hen 6*, I, i, 162–164. **2** to slay: "Quail, crush, conclude, and quell." *M N Dream*, V, i, 276. —*n.* **3** murder; assassination: ". . . who shall bear the guilt/ Of our great quell?" *Mac*, I, vii, 72–73.

queller, *n.* misuse for "killer": ". . . thou art a honeyseed, a man/ queller, and a woman queller." *2 Hen 4*, II, i, 51–52.

quench, *v.* to cool down: "Dost thou think in time/ She will not quench . . ." *Cymb*, I, vi, 46–47.

quern, *n.* hand-grinder for grain, seeds, etc.; also, var. of "churn": "Are not you he/ That frights the maidens . . . and sometimes labour in the quern . . ." *M N Dream*, II, i, 34–36.

quest¹, *n.* **1** var. of **inquest:** "Ay, marry is't, crowner's quest law." *Ham*, V, i, 22. **2** jury: "To 'cide this title is impannelled/ A quest of thoughts, all tenants to the heart . . ." *Sonn 46*, 9–10. **3** judicial inquiry: "What lawful quest have giv'n their verdict up . . ." *Rich 3*, I, iv, 173.

quest², *v.* (of hounds) to seek game; also, to bark upon sighting it; here, false rumors likened to hounds on the wrong scent: ". . . volumes of report/ Run with these false [hostile eyes], and most contrarious quest/ Upon [give tongue to] thy doings . . ." *Meas*, IV, i, 61–63.

questant, *n.* seeker; here, wooer: "Not to woo honour, but to wed it, when/ The bravest questant shrinks . . ." *All's W*, II, i, 15–16.

question, *n.* **1** cause; subject: ". . . so like the King/ That was and is the question of these wars." *Ham*, I, i, 113–114. **2** examination or investigation: ". . . against her will, as it appears/ In the true course of all the question." *M Ado*, V, iv, 5–6. **3** questioning; interrogation: "I pray you, speak not . . . Question enrages him." *Mac*, III, iv, 116–117. **4** talk(s) or discussion; also, negotiations: "Health to you, valiant sir,/ During all question of the gentle truce . . ." *Tr & Cr*, IV, i, 11–12. **5 first in question,** first in seniority: "Old Escalus,/ Though first in question, is thy secondary." *Meas*, I, i, 45–46. **6 in contempt of question,** beyond any doubt; unquestionably: "It is in contempt/ of question her hand." *T Night*, II, v, 89–90. **7 in question,** being investigated: "Falstaff, and't please your lordship./ He that was in question for the robbery?" *2 Hen 4*, I, ii, 59–60. **8 in the loss of question,** for the sake of argument: "As I subscribe not that, nor any other,/ But in the loss of question—" *Meas*, II, iv, 89–90. **9 in the question,** concerning the issue: ". . . the poet and the player went to cuffs in the/ ques-

tion." *Ham*, II, ii, 353–354. **10 make I as little question,** have I as little doubt: ". . . make I as little question/ As [that] he is proud to do't." *Cor*, II, i, 228–229. **11 move the question,** to assert the authority: ". . . lest perchance he think/ We dare not move the question of our place [rank] . . ." *Tr & Cr*, II, iii, 83–84. **12 niggard of question,** lacking or without much inquisitiveness: "Niggard of question, but of our demands/ Most free in his reply." *Ham*, III, i, 13–14. **13 no question make,** doubt not: ". . . and I no question make/ To have it of my trust, or for my sake." *Merch*, I, i, 184–185. **14 on the top of question,** in shrill contention: ". . . little eyases, that/ cry out on the top of question . . ." *Ham*, II, ii, 337–338. **15 out of question,** unquestionably; undeniably: "And out of question . . . Glory grows guilty of detested crimes . . ." *Love's L*, IV, i, 30–31. —*v.* **16** to reason: "I pray you think you question with the Jew . . ." *Merch*, IV, i, 70. **17** to debate; argue: "And let your reason with your choler question . . ." *Hen 8*, I, i, 130. **18** to suspect: ". . . yourself/ So out of thought . . . Cannot be question'd." *Cymb*, IV, iv, 32–34.

questionable, *adj.* appearing to invite questions: "Thou com'st in such a questionable shape/ That I will speak to thee." *Ham*, I, iv, 43–44.

questionless, *adv.* doubtless: "She, questionless, with her sweet harmony . . . would allure,/ And make a batt'ry through his deafen'd ports . . ." *Per*, V, i, 44–46.

questrist, *n.* seeker: "Some five or six and thirty of his knights,/ Hot questrists after him, met him at gate . . ." *Lear*, III, vii, 16–17.

Queubus, *n.* mock geographical name, appar. coined by the Clown: ". . . the Vapians passing the equinoctial of Queubus . . ." *T Night*, II, iii, 24.

quick, *adj.* **1** lively: "But is there no quick recreation granted?" *Love's L*, I, i, 160. **2** alive: "Be buried quick with her, and so will I." *Ham*, V, i, 274. **3** sharp; tart or stinging: "You must not be so quick." *Love's L*, II, i, 117. **4** pregnant: ". . . the poor/ wench is cast away: she's quick; the child brags in/ her belly already . . ." *Love's L*, V, ii, 667–669. **5** fresh; invigorating: "On the sea-margent/ Walk with Leonine; the air is quick there . . ." *Per*, IV, i, 26–27. **6** sensitive; perceptive: "You have a quick ear." *Two Gent*, IV, ii, 61. **7** quick-witted: "The quick comedians/ Extemporally will stage us . . ." *Ant & Cleo*, V, ii, 215–216. **8** forceful; emphatic: ". . . give way, dull clouds, to my quick curses . . ." *Rich 3*, I, iii, 196. —*n.* **9 the quick,** the living: "'Tis/ for the dead, not for the quick: therefore thou liest." *Ham*, V, i, 122–123.

quicken, *v.* **1** to enliven: "Music and poesy use to quicken you . . ." *Shrew,* I, i, 36. **2** to come to life: "These hairs, which thou dost ravish from my chin,/ Will quicken, and accuse thee . . ." *Lear,* III, vii, 38–39. **3** to enter life; be born: "Even then this forked plague is fated to us,/ When we do quicken . . ." *Oth,* III, iii, 280–281. **4** to fertilize: "By the fire [sun]/ That quickens Nilus' slime . . ." *Ant & Cleo,* I, iii, 68–69.

quick freshes, *n.* quick-flowing streams: ". . . for I'll not show him/ Where the quick freshes are." *Temp,* III, ii, 65–66.

quick object, *n.* brief glance: "Of his [the eye's] quick objects hath the mind no part . . ." *Sonn 113,* 7.

quick-shifting, *adj.* rapidly changing: ". . . there appears/ Quick-shifting antics, ugly in her eyes." *Luc,* 458–459.

quiddity, *n.* quibble; pun: ". . . how now, mad wag? What, in thy quips/ and thy quiddities?" *1 Hen 4,* I, ii, 43–44.

quid for quo, tit for tat [quid pro quo]: "I cry you mercy, 'tis but *quid* for *quo.*" *1 Hen 6,* V, iii, 109.

quietus, *n.* settlement or discharge, as of a debt: "Her audit . . . answer'd must be,/ And her quietus is to render thee." *Sonn 126,* 11–12.

quill, *n.* **1** piping note or voice [lit., a small reed for a musical pipe]: "The throstle, with his note so true,/ The wren with little quill—" *M N Dream,* III, i, 122–123. **2 in the quill,** all together: ". . . my Lord Protector/ will come this way by and by, and then we may/ deliver our supplications in the quill." *2 Hen 6,* I, iii, 1–3.

quillet, *n.* **1** quibbling distinction: ". . . he may never more false title plead,/ Nor sound his quillets shrilly." *Timon,* IV, iii, 156–157. **2** [pl.] fine points; subtleties or technicalities: "And do not stand on quillets how to slay him . . ." *2 Hen 6,* III, i, 261.

quillity, *n.* quibbling argument or subtle distinction [interchangeable with "quillet"]: "Where be his quiddities now, his quillities . . ." *Ham,* V, i, 97.

quilt, *n.* thick protective covering for the body, worn in place of armor; also, humorous term for a fat person: "How now, blown Jack? How now, quilt?" *1 Hen 4,* IV, ii, 49.

Qui me alit, me extinguit, [quasi-Latin] Who [what?] feeds me extinguishes me. *Per,* II, ii, 33.

Quinapalus, *n.* name coined by the clown: "For what says Quinapalus?/ 'Better a witty fool than a foolish wit.'" *T Night,* I, v, 33–34.

quintain, *n.* post, representing a man, used in tilting practice: ". . . that which here stands up/ Is but a quintain . . ." *As You,* I, ii, 240–241.

quintessence, *n.* **1** most refined essence: "Will I Rosalinda write,/ Teaching all that read to know/ The quintessence of every sprite . . ." *As You,* III, ii, 134–136. **2 quintessence of dust,** man here regarded as the perfection of elements: ". . . and yet, to me, what is this quintessence of dust?" *Ham,* II, ii, 308.

quip, *n.* retort or sarcasm; also, taunt: ". . . notwithstanding all her sudden quips . . ." *Two Gent,* IV, ii, 12.

quire, *n.* **1** company; gathering: "And then the whole quire hold their hips and loffe . . ." *M N Dream,* II, i, 55. **2** var. of **choir;** place where singers are gathered: ". . . our cage/ We make a quire, as doth the prison'd bird . . ." *Cymb,* III, iii, 42–43.
—*v.* **3** to sing in concert and in tune: ". . . like an angel sings,/ Still quiring to the young-ey'd cherubins . . ." *Merch,* V, i, 61–62.

quirk, *n.* **1** whim or caprice: ". . . belike this is a man of that quirk." *T Night,* III, iv, 247–248. **2** witty remark; quip: "I may chance have some odd quirks and remnants/ of wit broken on me . . ." *M Ado,* II, iii, 227–228. **3** quibble: ". . . she has me her quirks, her/ reasons, her master-reasons . . ." *Per,* IV, vi, 7–8. **4** sudden turn; switch: "I have felt so many quirks of joy and grief . . ." *All's W,* III, ii, 48.

quis, *pron.* [Latin] who?: "*Quis, quis,* thou consonant?" *Love's L,* V, i, 49.

quit, *v.* **1** to acquit or absolve: "Till thou canst quit thee . . . Of what we think against thee." *As You,* III, i, 11–12. **2** to settle; pay: "To quit the penalty and to ransom him." *Errors,* I, i, 22. **3** to remit; cancel: ". . . a thousand marks be levied/ To quit the penalty . . ." *Errors,* I, i, 21–22. **4** to requite; reward or repay: "Farewell, be trusty, and I'll quit thy pains . . ." *Rom & Jul,* II, iv, 188. **5** to release from an obligation; set free: "Your master quits you; and for your service done him . . . Here is my hand . . ." *T Night,* V, i, 320–324. **6** to avenge; pay back: "Ability in means and choice of friends,/ To quit me of them throughly." *M Ado,* IV, i, 199–200. **7** to leave; depart from: "How many would the peaceful city quit/ To welcome him!" *Hen 5,* V, Chor., 33–34. **8 God quit you!,** God reward you; a beggar's response to giver: "To let a fellow that will take rewards,/ And say, 'God quit you!'" *Ant & Cleo,* III, xiii, 123–124. **9 quit being,** died: "Then old, and fond of issue, took such sorrow/ That he quit being . . ." *Cymb,* I, i, 37–38. **10 quit me,** [to] get even with me: "He may at pleasure whip, or hang, or torture,/ As he shall like to quit me." *Ant & Cleo,* III, xiii,

150–151. 11 quit you of, avenge yourselves for [such]: "For your great seats [for the sake of your great positions] now quit you of great shames . . ." *Hen 5,* III, v, 47.
—*adj.* **12** rid or free of a person or thing: "Long live so, and so die! I am quit." *Timon,* IV, iii, 399. **13** forgiven: "No, I think thou art not [damned], I think thou art quit for/ that." *2 Hen 4,* II, iv, 339. **14** exempt (from): ". . . he that dies this year is quit for the next." *2 Hen 4,* III, ii, 233. **15** paid; repaid; compensated for: "Even at the first thy loss is more than can/ Thy portage quit . . ." *Per,* III, i, 35–36.

quite, *v.* to requite; relieve or recompense; also, to outdo: ". . . to quite their griefs/ Tell thou the lamentable tale of me . . ." *Rich 2,* V, i, 43–44.

quittance, *n.* **1** repayment: ". . . no gift to him/ But breeds the giver a return exceeding/ All use of quittance." *Timon,* I, i, 278–279. **2** release from debt or other obligation: ". . . writes himself 'Armigero' in/ any bill, warrant, quittance, or obligation—" *Wives,* I, i, 9–10. **3** return or exchange of blows: "Rend'ring faint quittance, wearied, and out-breath'd . . ." *2 Hen 4,* I, i, 108.
—*v.* **4** to repay; here, to retaliate for: "Embrace we then this opportunity,/ As fitting best to quittance their deceit . . ." *1 Hen 6,* II, i, 13–14.

quiver, *adj.* nimble: ". . . there was a little quiver fellow, and a would/ manage you his piece thus . . ." *2 Hen 4,* III, ii, 276–277.

quoif, *n.* coif; woman's close-fitting cap: "Golden quoifs and stomachers/ For my lads to give their dears . . ." *W Tale,* IV, iv, 226–227.

quoit, *v.* **1** to pitch or toss; also, hurl: "Quoit him down, Bardolph, like a shove-groat shilling." *2 Hen 4,* II, iv, 188.
—*n.* **2** [pl.] game in which rings of steel or rope are tossed at a stake or upright pin: "Because their legs are both of a bigness, and a plays/ at quoits well . . ." *2 Hen 4,* II, iv, 241–242.

quondam, *adj.* **1** former; sometime: ". . . a whole bookful of these quondam carpet-mongers . . ." *M Ado,* V, ii, 31. **2 this quondam day,** the other day: "I did converse this quondam day/ with a companion of the king's . . ." *Love's L,* V, i, 6–7.

quoniam, *conj.* [Latin] since: "*Quoniam* he seemeth in minority,/ *Ergo* I come with this apology." *Love's L,* V, ii, 587–588.

quote, *v.* **1** to note; make note of: "His face's own margent did quote such amazes . . ." *Love's L,* II, i, 245. **2** to observe; also, scrutinize: "What curious eye doth quote deformities?" *Rom & Jul,* I, iv, 31. **3** wordplay on "quote" and "coat" [pron. alike]: "And how quote you my folly?"/ "I quote it in your jerkin." *Two Gent,* II, iv, 18–19. **4** be compared to; liken: "Her amber hairs for foul have amber quoted [made amber drab or ugly by comparison]." *Love's L,* IV, iii, 84. **5** to interpret or construe: "Our letters, madam, show'd much more than jest."/ . . . "We did not quote them so." *Love's L,* V, ii, 777–778. **6** to regard; set down (as): "He's quoted for a most perfidious slave . . ." *All's W,* V, iii, 204.

quoted and signed, *adj.* noted and singled out; designated: "Quoted and sign'd to do a deed of shame . . ." *K John,* IV, ii, 222.

quoth, *v.* say; says [used as both present and past tenses]: "What! did these rent lines show some love of thine?"/ "Did they? quoth you." *Love's L,* IV, iii, 216–217.

quoth-a or **quoth'a,** *v.* quoth he; says he: "Die, quoth-a? Now gods forbid't . . ." *Per,* II, i, 78.

quotidian, *n.* recurring fever ["daily fever"] or shivering associated with malaria or an ague, here applied to love: ". . . he seems to have the quotidian of love upon him." *As You,* III, ii, 356.

quotidian tertian, *n.* See **tertian**

~ R ~

rabbit-sucker, *n.* baby rabbit: ". . . hang me up by the/ heels for a rabbit-sucker, or a poulter's hare." *1 Hen 4,* II, iv, 430–431.

rabble, *n.* lesser spirits; here, prob. Caliban and his fellows: "Go bring the rabble,/ O'er whom I give thee power, here to this place . . ." *Temp,* IV, i, 37–38.

rabblement, *n.* rabble; crowd or mob of commoners: ". . . the rabblement/ hooted, and clapp'd their chopt hands, and threw/ up their sweaty night-caps . . ." *J Caes,* I, ii, 240–242.

race¹, *n.* **1** root: ". . . a race or two of ginger . . ." *W Tale,* IV, iii, 47.
—*v.* **2** to erase [lit., to root out]: ". . . 'tis not my meaning/ To race one title of your honour out." *Rich 2,* II, iii, 74–75. **3** Also, **race out,** to raze; destroy: "Rac'd out my imprese, leaving me no sign . . . To show the world I am a gentleman." *Rich 2,* III, i, 25–27.

race², *n.* taste or flavor: ". . . none our parts so poor,/ But was a race of heaven." *Ant & Cleo,* I, iii, 36–37.

race³, *n.* **1** course: ". . . if the midnight bell . . . Sound on into the drowsy race of night . . ." *K John,* III, ii, 47–49. **2** strain; natural disposition: "And now I give my sensual race the rein . . ." *Meas,* II, iv, 159.

race⁴, *n.* **1** See **raze** (def. 1). **2** breed; also, drove or pack: ". . . a wild and wanton herd/ Or race of youthful and unhandled colts . . ." *Merch,* V, i, 71–72.

rack¹, *v.* **1** to torment or torture, esp. by stretching on the rack: "You must be purged to [till] your sins are rack'd . . ." *Love's L,* V, ii, 810. **2** to stretch; strain: "Try what my credit can in Venice do,—/ That shall be rack'd even to the uttermost . . ." *Merch,* I, i, 180–181. **3** to be driven: ". . . inconstant clouds/ That rack upon the carriage of the winds . . ." *Edw 3,* II, i, 3–4. **4** to stretch out; inflate or overestimate: ". . . being lack'd and

lost,/ Why then we rack the value . . ." *M Ado,* IV, i, 219–220. **5** to distort: "Make thee the father of their idle dream/ And rack thee in their fancies." *Meas,* IV, i, 64–65. **6** to ruin; impoverish: "The commons has thou rack'd; the clergy's bags/ Are lank and lean with thy extortions." *2 Hen 6,* I, iii, 128–129.

rack², *n.* **1** clouds of the upper air: "A silence in the heavens, the rack stand still . . ." *Ham,* II, ii, 480. **2** something, as a cloud, that obscures; obstruction: "Anon permit the basest clouds to ride/ With ugly rack on his celestial face . . ." *Sonn 33,* 5–6. **3** remnant or trace: "And, like this insubstantial pageant faded,/ Leave not a rack behind." *Temp,* IV, i, 155–156.

racker, *n.* tormentor or torturer: ". . . such insociable and point-devise/ companions; such rackers of orthography . . ." *Love's L,* V, i, 18–19.

racking, *adj.* (of clouds) driven forward; swirling: ". . . each one a perfect sun;/ Not separated with the racking clouds . . ." *3 Hen 6,* II, i, 26–27.

rag, *n.* **1** rogue or baggage (contemptuous term): ". . . thy father (that poor rag)/ Must be thy subject . . ." *Timon,* IV, iii, 273–274. **2** scrap or remnant: ". . . But surely, master, not a rag of money." *Errors,* IV, iv, 84.

rage, *n.* **1** fever or infection; also, poetic fury: "Yet I have a trick/ Of the old rage . . ." *Love's L,* V, ii, 416–417. **2** madness; insanity: "Besides this present instance of his rage,/ Is a mad tale he told to-day at dinner . . ." *Errors,* IV, iii, 84–85. **3** emotional frenzy: "Lest his ungovern'd rage dissolve the life/ That wants the means to lead it." *Lear,* IV, iv, 19–20. **4** wild, reckless jest: "So is Alcides beaten by his rage . . ." *Merch,* II, i, 35. **5** exaggeration or fantasizing: "And your true rights be termed a poet's rage . . ." *Sonn 17,* 11. **6** destructive force: "How with this rage shall beauty hold a plea . . ." *Sonn 65,* 3.

ragged, *adj.* **1** rugged; rough: ". . . the flinty ribs/ Of this hard world, my ragged prison walls . . ." *Rich 2,* V, v, 20–21. **2** shaggy or jagged; also, pronged: "Walk round about an oak, with great ragg'd horns . . ." *Wives,* IV, iv, 31.

raggedest, *adj.* roughest; most dangerous or devastating: "The ragged'st hour that time and spite dare bring . . ." *2 Hen 4,* I, i, 151.

raging-wood, *adj.* in a mad rage: "How the young whelp of Talbot's, raging-wood,/ Did flesh his puny sword in Frenchmen's blood!" *1 Hen 6,* IV, vii, 35–36.

Rah, tah, tah, imit. of drumbeats, used to give commands to infantrymen: "'Rah,/ tah, tah,' would a say . . ." *2 Hen 4,* III, ii, 278–279.

rail, *v.* **rail upon,** to scold; abuse: ". . . rail'd/ upon me till her pink'd porringer fell off her head . . ." *Hen 8,* V, iii, 46–47.

railer, *n.* scold or shrew; ref. to Prince as the image of his mother: "Take that, the likeness of this railer here." *3 Hen 6,* V, v, 38.

rain, *n.* **rain, to lay this wind,** fr. belief that wind subsided when rain began to fall: "Rain, to lay [allay] this wind, or/ my heart will be blown up by th'root." *Tr & Cr,* IV, iv, 52–53.

raise, *v.* **1** to build; cause to be built: "Those twins of learning that he rais'd in you,/ Ipswich and Oxford . . ." *Hen 8,* IV, ii, 58–59. **2** to rouse; stir up: "We are to speak in public; for this business/ Will raise us all." *W Tale,* II, i, 197–198. **3** to arouse: "If thy unworthiness raised love in me,/ More worthy I to be beloved of thee." *Sonn 150,* 13–14. **4 raise up,** wordplay on "cause to materialize" and "cause to have an erection": ". . . in his mistress' name/ I conjure only but to raise up him." *Rom & Jul,* II, i, 28–29.

raise a siege, *v.* to relieve a besieged town or place: "Let's raise the siege: why live we idly here?" *1 Hen 6,* I, ii, 13.

raised, *adj.* elevated; prestigious: ". . . my estate deserves an heir more rais'd . . ." *Timon,* I, i, 122.

raisin, *n.* **raisins o' th' sun,** sun-dried raisins; here, as disting. from currants: ". . . four pound of prunes, and as many of raisins o' th'/ sun." *W Tale,* IV, iii, 48–49.

raising, *n.* spreading of rumors: "'Tis this slave . . . his raising,/ Nothing but his report." *Cor,* IV, vi, 60–62.

rake, *n.* **1** very thin person likened to a rake: "Let us revenge/ this with our pikes [pitchforks], ere we become rakes." *Cor,* I, i, 21–22.
—*v.* **2** to search, as if with a rake: ". . . if you hide the crown/ Even in your hearts, there will he rake for it . . ." *Hen 5,* II,

iv, 97–98. **3 rake up,** to cover; cover up: "Here in the sands,/ Thee I'll rake up . . ." *Lear,* IV, vi, 275–276.

ram, *n.* **1** battering-ram: "Great-bellied women,/ That had not half a week to go, like rams/ In the old time of war . . ." *Hen 8,* IV, i, 76–78.
—*v.* **2 ram up,** to bar or block: ". . . till that time/ Have we ramm'd up our gates against the world." *K John,* II, i, 271–272.

Ram, *n.* **the Ram,** See **Aries.**

ramp, *n.* whore: "Live . . . betwixt cold sheets,/ Whiles he is vaulting variable ramps . . ." *Cymb,* I, vii, 133–134.

rampallian, *n.* ruffian or rascal (sometimes used of women): "Away, you scullion! you rampallian!": *2 Hen 4,* II, i, 58.

ramping, *adj.* **1** (in heraldry) rampant; upreared; rearing: "A couching lion and a ramping cat . . ." *1 Hen 4,* III, i, 147. **2** rampaging; ref. to the lion's skin which Austria [Limoges] wears: "What a fool art thou,/ A ramping fool, to brag, and stamp, and swear/ Upon my party [in support of my cause]!" *K John,* III, i, 47–49.

rampired, *adj.* (of fortifications) protected with ramparts: "Set but thy foot/ Against our rampir'd gates . . ." *Timon,* V, iv, 46–47.

random, *adv.* **at random, a.** untended; unsupervised or unprotected: ". . . my factor's death,/ And the great care of goods at random left . . ." *Errors,* I, i, 41–42. **b.** foolishly; recklessly: "He talks at random; sure, the man is mad." *1 Hen 6,* V, iii, 85.

range, *v.* **1** to wander or rove, esp. in search of something: "And Caesar's spirit, ranging for revenge . . ." *J Caes,* III, i, 270. **2** to stray: "If once I find thee ranging,/ Hortensio will be quit with thee . . ." *Shrew,* III, i, 89–90. **3** to roam about or through: ". . . there I found this credit,/ That he did range the town to seek me out." *T Night,* IV, iii, 6–7. **4** to rank: ". . . the line and the predicament/ Wherein you range under this subtle King!" *1 Hen 4,* I, iii, 166–167.
—*n.* **5** [pl.] ranks of fighting ships in battle position: ". . . that great face of war, whose several ranges/ Frighted each other?" *Ant & Cleo,* III, xiii, 5–6.

ranged, *adj.* ordered; also, far-ranging: "Let Rome in Tiber melt, and the wide arch/ Of the rang'd empire fall!" *Ant & Cleo,* I, i, 33–34.

ranger, *n.* gamekeeper or forester, one of Diana's chaste followers: ". . . and makes/ Diana's rangers false themselves . . ." *Cymb,* II, iii, 67–68.

rank¹, *n.* **1** row or line, as of people, one behind the other: ". . . the right butter-women's rank to market." *As You,* III, ii, 96. **2**

degree, as of dignity: ". . . not being the worst/ Stands in some rank of praise." *Lear*, II, iv, 259–260. **3 hold on one's rank,** to maintain one's position: "I do know but one/ That unassailable holds on his rank,/ Unshak'd of motion . . ." *J Caes*, III, i, 68–70.

—*v.* **4** to form a line (at or around): "The base o' th' mount/ Is rank'd with all deserts . . ." *Timon*, I, i, 66–67. **5** to include, as in a series: ". . . sour woe delights in fellowship/ And needly will be rank'd with other griefs . . ." *Rom & Jul*, III, ii, 116–117.

rank[2], *adj.* **1** foul; offensive: ". . . things rank and gross in nature/ Possess it merely." *Ham*, I, ii, 136–137. **2** filled with disease and ready for bloodletting [a periodic remedy]: "Who else must be let blood, who else is rank:/ If I myself, there is no hour so fit . . ." *J Caes*, III, i, 152–153. **3** puffed up; swollen: ". . . the seeded pride/ That hath to this maturity blown up/ In rank Achilles . . ." *Tr & Cr*, I, iii, 315–317. **4** in heat: ". . . the ewes being rank/ In end of autumn turned to the rams . . ." *Merch*, I, iii, 75–76. **5** (of a stream) filled to overflowing: "Rain added to a river that is rank/ Perforce will force it overflow the bank." *Ven & Ad*, 71–72. **6 ranker than,** superior to; greater than: "I should think my honesty ranker than my wit." *As You*, IV, i, 81. **7 rank garb,** grossest manner: "Abuse him to the Moor, in the rank garb . . ." *Oth*, II, i, 301. **8 rank of goodness,** excess of goodness; cloying goodness: ". . . brought to medicine a healthful state/ Which, rank of goodness, would by ill be cured." *Sonn 118*, 11–12.

—*adv.* **9** thickly; heavily: "How rank soever [however thickly] rounded in with danger." *Tr & Cr*, I, iii, 196. **10** in great number; overabundantly: "While other jests are something rank on foot . . ." *Wives*, IV, vi, 22.

ranked, *past part.* (of soldiers) set forth in lines for battle: ". . . many thousand warlike French/ That were embattailed and rank'd in Kent . . ." *K John*, IV, ii, 199–200.

ranker rate, *n.* richer price: "Nor will it yield to Norway or the Pole/ A ranker ráte . . ." *Ham*, IV, iv, 21–22.

rankle, *v.* to cause to fester: "His venom tooth will rankle to the death." *Rich 3*, I, iii, 291.

rankness, *n.* offensiveness, as haughtiness or rebelliousness: "I will physic your rankness . . ." *As You*, I, i, 86.

ransacked, *adj.* **1** carried off as plunder: "What treason were it to the ransack'd queen . . ." *Tr & Cr*, II, ii, 151. **2 ransacked treasury,** violated chastity: ". . . her, whose ransacked treasury hath tasked/ The vain endeavour of so many pens." *Edw 3*, II, ii,

ransom, *n.* **1** atonement; redemption: ". . . the ransom of my bold attempt/ Shall be this cold corpse on the earth's cold face . . ." *Rich 3*, V, iii, 266–267.

—*v.* **2** to deliver: ". . . labouring art can never ransom nature/ From her inaidible estate." *All's W*, II, i, 116–117. **3** to atone for; redeem: "But that your trespass now becomes a fee;/ Mine ransoms yours, and yours must ransom me." *Sonn 120*, 13–14.

rap, *v.* to transport; possess: "What, dear sir,/ Thus raps you? Are you well?" *Cymb*, I, vii, 50–51.

rape, *n.* abduction: "I would have the soil of her fair rape/ Wip'd off in honourable keeping her." *Tr & Cr*, II, ii, 149–150.

rapier, *n.* sword with long, narrow blade, a weapon considered part of the fashionable man's costume: "O well-knit Samson! . . . I do/ excell thee in my rapier as much as thou didst me in/ carrying gates." *Love's L*, I, ii, 69–70.

rapine, *n.* rape: "I'll do this heavy task,/ So thou destroy Rapine and Murder there." *T Andr*, V, ii, 58–59.

rapt, *adj.* **1** absorbed; intent: "You are rapt, sir, in some work, some dedication/ To the great lord." *Timon*, I, i, 19. **2** moved by poetic rapture: "I am rapt, and cannot cover/ The monstrous bulk of this ingratitude . . ." *Timon*, V, i, 63–64.

rapture, *n.* tumult; fury: "And spite of all the rapture of the sea/ This jewel holds his building on my arm." *Per*, II, i, 154–155.

rare, *adj.* **1** fine; splendid: ". . . to tell us Cupid is a good hare-finder, and Vulcan/ a rare carpenter?" *M Ado*, I, i, 171–172. **2 none rare,** nothing unusual; not much of note: "What is the news i' th' court?"/ "None rare, my lord." *W Tale*, I, ii, 367.

rarely, *adv.* **1** excellently; splendidly: "I'd wish no better choice, and think me rarely wed." *Per*, V, i, 69. **2** extremely; extraordinarily: ". . . and these thy offices,/ So rarely kind . . ." *W Tale*, V, i, 148–149.

rareness, *n.* **strain of rareness,** result of rare qualities: "It is no act of common passage, but/ A strain of rareness . . ." *Cymb*, III, iv, 93–94.

rariety, *n.* var. of **rarity;** rare or exceptional trait or character: "The register of all rarieties/ Since leathern Adam till this youngest hour." *Edw 3*, II, ii, 114–115.

rarity, *n.* rare excellence: "Beauty, truth and rarity,/ Grace in all simplicity . . ." *Phoen*, 53–54.

rascal, *n.* **1** young deer, esp. one badly nourished: "The noblest deer hath them as huge as the rascal." *As You*, III, iii, 50–51. **2** member of a pack, here appar. of hounds: "Thou rascal, that art worst in blood [of the lowest breed] to run . . ." *Cor*, I, i, 158.

—*adj.* **3** worthless; good-for-nothing: ". . . Was made a wonder and a pointing-stock/ To every idle rascal follower." *2 Hen 6,* II, iv, 46–47. **4** wretched; miserable: "When Marcus Brutus grows so covetous,/ To lock such rascal counters [coins] from his friends . . ." *J Caes,* IV, iii, 79–80.

rased, *past part.* razed; torn down: "Now is the mure [wall] rased between the two neighbours." *M N Dream,* V, i, 204.

rash[1], *adj.* **1** easily ignited: "With shallow jesters, and rash bavin [like kindling] wits . . ." *1 Hen 4,* III, ii, 61. **2** violent; destructive: ". . . it do work as strong/ As aconitum or rash gunpowder." *2 Hen 4,* IV, iv, 47–48.

rash[2], *v.* to sink; bury: "In his anointed flesh rash boarish fangs." *Lear,* III, vii, 57.

rasher, *n.* slice of bacon, usually cooked at the fireplace; considered a beggarly meal: ". . . we shall not shortly have a rasher on the coals for money." *Merch,* III, v, 22–23.

rat-catcher, *n.* allusion to "Good King of Cats," Mercutio's nickname for Tybalt: "Tybalt, you rat-catcher, will you walk?" *Rom & Jul,* III, i, 74.

rate[1], *v.* **1** to berate; curse or revile: ". . . an old/ lord of the Council rated me the other day in the/ street about you, sir . . ." *1 Hen 4,* I, ii, 81–83. **2** to drive away by rebuking or denouncing: "Rated mine uncle from the Council-board . . ." *1 Hen 4,* IV, iii, 99.

rate[2], *v.* **1** to set a value on: "Rate me at what thou wilt, thou shalt be paid." *2 Hen 6,* IV, i, 30. **2** to apportion; allot [a share of expense, etc.]: ". . . we had not rated him/ His part o' the isle." *Ant & Cleo,* III, vi, 25–26. —*n.* **3** value and esteem: "There shall no figure at such rate be set/ As that of true and faithful Juliet." *Rom & Jul,* V, iii, 300–301. **4** style of living: "Nor do I now make moan to be abridg'd/ From such a noble rate . . ." *Merch,* I, i, 126–127. **5** sum charged or asked; terms; price: "Three months from twelve, then let me see the rate." *Merch,* I, iii, 99. **6** estimation; belief or opinion: "My son is lost, and, in my rate, she too . . ." *Temp,* II, i, 105. **7 at the rate,** for such an amount: "I'll serve you, sir, five hundred at the rate." *Errors,* IV, iv, 14. **8 popular rate,** vulgar opinion: "With that which, but by being so retir'd,/ O'er-priz'd all popular rate . . ." *Temp,* I, ii, 91–92.

rated, *adj.* **1** important; valued: ". . . Glendower's absence thence,/ Who with them was a rated sinew too . . ." *1 Hen 4,* IV, iv, 16–17. **2** assessed at its full or proper value: "Paying the fine of rated treachery . . ." *K John,* V, iv, 37.

rather, *adv.* **1 the rather, a.** the more: "God shall forgive you Coeur-de-lion's death/ The rather that you give his offspring life . . ." *K John,* II, i, 12–13. **b.** the sooner; faster: ". . . and I return'd the rather,/ For that I heard the clink and fall of swords . . ." *Oth,* II, iii, 224–225. **2 you rather,** you should do this even more readily: "You rather, mine being yours [the stamp on my life is your doing] . . ." *Cymb,* V, iv, 26.

ratherest, *adv.* most of all [appar. Holofernes' quasi-learned coinage]: ". . . or/ rather unlettered, or ratherest, unconfirmed fashion . . ." *Love's L,* IV, ii, 17–18.

ratified, *n.* (of verses) correctly proportioned [set in meter]: ". . . let me supervise the canzonet. Here are only/ numbers [verses] ratified . . ." *Love's L,* IV, ii, 116–117.

ratifiers and props, *n.* tradition and custom, the links of past and present: "Antiquity forgot, custom not known—/ The ratifiers and props of every word [slogan]—" *Ham,* IV, v, 104–105.

rational hind, *n.* intelligent rustic: "Boy, I do love that country girl that I took in the/ park with the rational hind Costard . . ." *Love's L,* I, ii, 110–111.

Ratolorum, *n.* Slender fails to understand that "Custalorum" is condensed form of Latin *custor rotulorum* [keeper of the rolls]: "Ay, cousin Slender, and Custalorum."/ "Ay, and Ratolorum too; and a gentleman born . . ." *Wives,* I, i, 7–8.

ratsbane, *n.* rat poison: "I had as lief they would/ put ratsbane in my mouth as offer to stop it with/ security." *2 Hen 4,* I, ii, 41–43.

raught, *v.* **1** old past tense of **reach**; reached; attained: ". . . a month old when Adam was no more;/ And raught not to five weeks when he came to five-score." *Love's L,* IV, ii, 38–39. **2** to seize; steal away: "The hand of death hath raught him." *Ant & Cleo,* IV, ix, 29.

rave, *v.* to rage or explode: ". . . not frenzy, not/ Absolute madness could so far have rav'd,/ To bring him here alone . . ." *Cymb,* IV, ii, 134–136.

ravel, *v.* **ravel out,** to unravel; here, reveal: "Make you to ravel all this matter out . . ." *Ham,* III, iv, 188.

raven, *n.* **1** ominous bird, whose presence and/or croaking portended evil, death, etc.: "The raven himself is hoarse,/ That croaks the fatal entrance of Duncan . . ." *Mac,* I, v, 38–39. **2** use of bird for wordplay on "fowl" and "foul": "An amber-coloured raven was well noted." *Love's L,* IV, iii, 85. **3 ancient ravens' wings,** ravens were thought to be very long-lived, perh. three times the life of man: "To pluck the quills from ancient ravens' wings . . ." *Luc,* 949. —*v.* **4** See **ravin.**

raven's note, *n.* raven's croaking, said to portend death or disaster: "Came he right now to sing a raven's note,/ Whose dismal tune bereft my vital powers . . ." *2 Hen 6,* III, ii, 39–40.

Ravenspurgh or **Ravenspur,** *n.* (formerly) North Sea port in N England, E of York: ". . . we being thus arriv'd/ From Ravenspurgh haven before the gates of York . . ." *3 Hen 6,* IV, vii, 7–8.

ravin, *adj.* **1** ravening or ravenous: "Better 'twere/ I met the ravin lion when he roar'd/ With sharp constraint of hunger . . ." *All's W,* III, ii, 116–117.
—*v.* **2 ravin down,** to eat greedily: "Like rats that ravin down their proper bane . . ." *Meas,* I, ii, 119–120. **3 ravin up,** to gobble; devour: "Thriftless Ambition, that will ravin up/ Thine own life's means!" *Mac,* II, iv, 28–29.

ravined, *adj.* ravening or ravenous; also, glutted: "Witches' mummy; maw, and gulf,/ Of the ravin'd salt-sea shark . . ." *Mac,* IV, i, 23–24.

ravish, *v.* to pull out; uproot: "These hairs, which thou dost ravish from my chin . . ." *Lear,* III, vii, 38.

raw, *adj.* **1** green; inexperienced: ". . . instruct her what/ she has to do, that she may not be raw in her entertainment." *Per,* IV, ii, 50–52. **2** adolescent; sophomoric: "I have within my mind/ A thousand raw tricks of these bragging Jacks . . ." *Merch,* III, iv, 76–77. **3 more rawer breath,** [our] cruder or more untutored descriptions: "Why do we wrap the gentleman/ in our more rawer breath?" *Ham,* V, ii, 122–123.

rawly, *adv.* without provision: ". . . some crying for a surgeon . . . some upon their/ children rawly left." *Hen 5,* IV, i, 142–143.

rawness, *n.* undefended or unprotected state: "Why in that rawness left you wife and child . . ." *Mac,* IV, iii, 26.

rayed, *adj.* **1** afflicted; blighted or defiled: ". . . rayed with the yellows, past cure of the/ fives . . ." *Shrew,* III, ii, 51–52. **2** dirtied; muddied: "Was ever man so beaten? Was ever man/ so rayed?" *Shrew,* IV, i, 2–3.

raze, *n.* **1** old form of **race;** root: "I have a gammon of bacon, and two razes of/ ginger . . ." *1 Hen 4,* II, i, 23–24.
—*v.* **2** to erase; obliterate: ". . . as from thence/ Sorrow were ever raz'd, and testy wrath/ Could never be her mild companion." *Per,* I, i, 17–18. **3 raze off,** to pull off: "He dreamt the boar had razed off his helm . . ." *Rich 3,* III, ii, 10. **4 raze out,** to cut out; erase: "To frustrate prophecies, and to raze out/ Rotten opinion . . ." *2 Hen 4,* V, ii, 127–128.

razed, *adj.* razored; here, decorated with slashes or slits: ". . . with Provincial/ roses on my razed shoes . . ." *Ham,* III, ii, 270–271.

razure, *n.* obliteration: ". . . the tooth of time/ And razure of oblivion." *Meas,* V, i, 13–14.

re, *n.* second tone of the musical scale, here used whimsically as a verb: "I'll re you, I'll/ fa you. Do you note me?" *Rom & Jul,* IV, v, 116–117.

reach, *n.* **1** extent: ". . . the moral of my wit/ Is 'Plain and true';/ there's all the reach of it." *Tr & Cr,* IV, iv, 105–106. **2** comprehension or understanding; also, mental capacity: "And thus do we of wisdom and of reach . . . By indirections find directions out." *Ham,* II, i, 64–66.
—*v.* **3 reach at the moon,** ref. to dog baying at the moon: "And dogged York, that reaches at the moon . . ." *2 Hen 6,* III, i, 158. **4 reach unto,** to attain: "By marrying her which I must reach unto." *Rich 3,* I, i, 159.

reaching hands, *n.* long reach; here, meant figuratively, as an indication of power and influence: "Great men have reaching hands: oft have I struck/ Those that I never saw, and struck them dead." *2 Hen 6,* IV, vii, 77–78.

read, *v.* **1** to understand; regard: ". . . that you read/ The Cardinal's malice and his potency/ Together . . ." *Hen 8,* I, i, 104–106. **2** to learn: ". . . those about her/ From her shall read the perfect ways of honour . . ." *Hen 8,* V, iv, 36–37. **3** to perceive or acknowledge the meaning of: ". . . a precedent/ Which not to read would show the Britons cold [indifferent] . . ." *Cymb,* III, i, 76. **4 read to,** to tutor; instruct: "Where is he living . . . Which calls me pupil or hath read to me?" *1 Hen 4,* III, i, 41–43.

read a lecture, *v.* to give a public reading (of); read out publicly: "Would it not shame thee, in so fair a troop,/ To read a lecture of them?" *Rich 2,* IV, i, 231–232.

readiness, *n.* ease or facility: "I thought, by the readiness in the office, you had/ continued in it some time." *Meas,* II, i, 258–259.

Readins, *n.* Reading, a village near Windsor: ". . . there is three/ cozen-Germans that has cozened all the hosts of/ Readins . . ." *Wives,* IV, v, 71–73.

re-answer, *v.* to make restitution for: ". . . which in weight to re-answer, his pettiness [slender means] would/ bow under." *Hen 5,* III, vi, 133–134.

reaped, *adj.* closely cropped or trimmed: "Fresh as a bridegroom, and his chin new reap'd . . ." *1 Hen 4,* I, iii, 33.

rear, *v.* **1** to erect; build up: "And with your blood and it I'll make a paste,/ And of the paste a coffin I will rear . . ." *T Andr,* V, ii, 187–188. **2** to raise; increase: ". . . but let us rear/ The higher our opinion [self-regard] . . ." *Ant & Cleo,* II, i, 35–36. **3 rear up,** to lift up: "Rear up his body; wring him by the nose." *2 Hen 6,* III, ii, 33.
—*n.* **4 abject rear,** inferior troops following behind: "Lie there for pavement for the abject rear . . ." *Tr & Cr,* III, iii, 162.

rearward, *n.* aftermath [lit., rearguard]: "Myself would on the rearward of reproaches/ Strike at thy life." *M Ado,* IV, i, 126–127.

reason, *v.* **1** to talk; converse: ". . . who perceiveth our natural wits too dull to reason of such goddesses . . ." *As You,* I, ii, 50–51. **2** to discuss: "Why is this reason'd [why do we waste time discussing this]?" *Lear,* V, i, 28. **3** wordplay on "talk" versus "debate": "What are you reasoning with yourself?"/ "Nay, I was rhyming; 'tis you that have the reason [faculty of mind]." *Two Gent,* II, i, 134–136. **4** to argue on behalf of; plead: "Does reason our petition with more strength/ Than thou hast to deny't." *Cor,* V, iii, 176–177. **5 reason coldly,** to discuss calmly: "Either withdraw unto some private place,/ Or reason coldly of your grievances . . ." *Rom & Jul,* III, i, 50–51. **6 reason with,** to consider; take into account: "Let's reason with the worst that may befall." *J Caes,* V, i, 97.
—*n.* **7** good sense; here, your wits: "If you be mad, be gone:/ if you have reason, be brief . . ." *T Night,* I, v, 200–201. **8** discourse; conversation: ". . . your reasons at dinner/ have been sharp and sententious . . ." *Love's L,* V, i, 2–3. **9 in (or in all) reason,** by all that's reasonable: ". . . but yet in courtesy, in all reason, we/ must stay the time." *M N Dream,* V, i, 244–245. **10 more than reason,** beyond measure; here, unreasonably large, hence, pregnant: "It is much [a sorry business] that the Moor should be more than/ reason . . ." *Merch,* III, v, 37–38. **11 speak of reason,** make a reasonable request: "You cannot speak of reason to the Dane/ And lose your voice." *Ham,* I, ii, 44–45. **12 with such loud reason,** with general endorsement: ". . . for he's embark'd/ With such loud reason, to the Cyprus wars . . ." *Oth,* I, i, 149–150.

reasonable, *adj.* consisting of or displaying reason: ". . . the approaching tide/ Will shortly fill the reasonable shore . . ." *Temp,* V, i, 80–81.

reason panders will, *n.* reason corrupts [panders to] desire instead of controlling it: "Since frost itself as actively doth burn/ And reason panders will." *Ham,* III, iv, 87–88.

reave, *v.* to deprive; rob: "To reave the orphan of his patrimony . . ." *2 Hen 6,* V, i, 187.

rebate, *v.* to make dull; curb: "But doth rebate and blunt his natural edge/ With profits of the mind . . ." *Meas,* I, iv, 60–61.

rebato, *n.* woman's high collar or ruff, supported in back by a wire frame: "Troth, I think your other rebato were better." *M Ado,* III, iv, 6.

rebeck, *n.* three-stringed fiddle; here used whimsically as a person's surname: "What say you, Hugh Rebeck?"/ "I say 'silver sound' because musicians sound for silver." *Rom & Jul,* IV, v, 129–131.

rebel, *v.* to experience lust: "Out upon it old carrion! rebels it [the flesh] at these years?" *Merch,* III, i, 32.

rebel blood, *n.* rebellious, hence unstable, disposition: "Be not fond [foolish],/ To think that Caesar bears such rebel blood . . ." *J Caes,* III, i, 39–40.

rebellious hell, *n.* uncontrollable sexual passion: "Rebellious hell,/ If thou canst mutine in a matron's bones . . ." *Ham,* III, iv, 82–83.

rebel powers, *n.* rebellious flesh [also faculties]: ". . . these rebel powers that thee array . . ." *Sonn 146,* 2.

rebel to judgment, *v.* to act despite one's better judgment: "Pawn their experience to their present pleasure,/ And so rebel to judgment." *Ant & Cleo,* I, iv, 32–33.

rebukable, *adj.* deserving of rebuke; disgraceful: "This is a soldier's kiss: rebukeable . . ." *Ant & Cleo,* IV, iv, 30.

rebuke, *v.* to hold in check; restrain or intimidate: ". . . under him/ My Genius is rebuk'd . . ." *Mac,* III, i, 54–55.

rebused, *past part.,* misuse for "abused": "Is there any/ man has rebused your worship?" *Shrew,* I, ii, 6–7.

recall, *v.* to revoke; cancel: ". . . passed sentence may not be recall'd . . ." *Errors,* I, i, 147.

recanter, *n.* person who recants; a penitent: ". . . the public body, which doth seldom/ Play the recanter . . ." *Timon,* V, i, 144–145.

receipt, *n.* **1** recipe; directions for using: ". . . we have the receipt of/ fern-seed; we walk invisible." *1 Hen 4,* II, i, 85–86. **2** sum of money received: "Three parts of that receipt . . . Disburs'd I duly to his Highness' soldiers . . ." *Rich 2,* I, i, 126–127. **3** receptacle: ". . . memory, the warder of the brain,/ Shall be a fume, and the receipt of reason/ A limbeck only . . ." *Mac,* I, vii, 66–68. **4** capacity: "In things of great receipt with ease we prove/ Among a number one is reckoned none." *Sonn 136,* 7–8. **5** that which is received; here, the variety of food taken in: "... the mutinous parts/ That envied his receipt ..." *Cor,* I, i, 110–111. **6 such receipt of learning,** reception [accommodation] of such learned men: "The most convenient place ... For such receipt of learning is Black-Friars ..." *Hen 8,* II, ii, 137–138.

receive, *v.* **1** to learn; be informed about: "Young prince of Tyre, you have at large receiv'd [been fully informed about]/ The danger of the task you undertake." *Per,* I, i, 1–2. **2** to believe or accept [as]: "And once again I do receive thee [as] honest." *Two Gent,* V, iv, 78.

received, *past part.* **1** understood: "To be received plain, I'll speak more gross." *Meas,* II, iv, 82. **2** fashionable: "... eat, speak, and move, under the influence/ of the most receiv'd star ..." *All's W,* II, i, 53–54. **3 what is now received,** the present time: "The same I am, ere ancient'st order was,/ Or what is now receiv'd." *W Tale,* IV, i, 10–11.

receiving, *n.* intelligence; perception: "To one of your receiving/ Enough is shown ..." *T Night,* III, i, 122–123.

receptacle, *n.* prob. a latrine or cesspit: "Empty/ Old receptacles, or common shores [sewers], of filth ..." *Per,* IV, vi, 173–174.

recheat, *n.* horn call to assemble hounds before a hunt: "... I will have a recheat winded in my/ forehead ..." *M Ado,* I, i, 223–224.

reck, *v.* **1** to be concerned; care or bother: "And little recks to find the way to heaven ..." *As You,* II, iv, 79. **2** to heed; pay attention to: "Himself the primrose path of dalliance treads,/ And recks not his own rede [advice]." *Ham,* I, iii, 50–51.

reckon, *v.* **1** to add up or keep track of sums of money: "I have no more to reckon, he to spend." *Timon,* III, iv, 56. **2** double sense of "add up" and "express in verse": "I have not art to/ reckon my groans." *Ham,* II, ii, 119–120. **3 reckon up, a.** to list or enumerate: "... you know no house, nor no such maid,/ Nor no such men as you have reckon'd up ..." *Shrew,* Ind., ii, 92–93. **b.** to expose; reveal: "... they that level/ At my abuses reckon up their own ..." *Sonn 121,* 9–10.

reckoning, *n.* **1** amount due; bill: "... it strikes a man more dead than a great reckoning in a little room [than a large bill for a small entertainment]." *As You,* III, iii, 11–12. **2** matter to be settled: "For this I owe you: here comes other reck'nings." *M Ado,* V, iv, 52. **3** repute; reputation: "Of honourable reckoning are you both,/ And pity 'tis you lived at odds so long." *Rom & Jul,* I, ii, 4–5. **4 sense of reckoning,** ability to count; here, to reckon the odds: "... take from them now/ The sense of reck'ning, if th' opposed numbers/ Pluck their hearts from them." *Hen 5,* IV, i, 296–298.

reclaim, *v.* to subdue: "... beauty, that the tyrant oft reclaims ..." *2 Hen 6,* V, ii, 54.

reclusive, *adj.* secluded; cloistered or sequestered: "In some reclusive and religious life,/ Out of all eyes ..." *M Ado,* IV, i, 242–243.

recognizance, *n.* **1** bond of obligation: "... this fellow might be in's/ time a great buyer of land, with his statutes, his/ recognizances ..." *Ham,* V, i, 101–103. **2** token: "... the recognizance and pledge of love,/ Which I first gave her ..." *Oth,* V, ii, 215–216.

recoil, *v.* **1** to weaken or give way: "A good and virtuous nature may recoil,/ In an imperial charge." *Mac,* IV, iii, 19–20. **2** to degenerate: "... and you/ Recoil from your great stock [prove a disgrace to your great family]." *Cymb,* I, vii, 127–128. **3** to go back in time: "Of my boy's face, methoughts I did recoil/ Twenty-three years ..." *W Tale,* I, ii, 154–155.

recollect, *v.* to gather: "... from their wat'ry empire recollect/ All that may men approve or men detect!" *Per,* II, i, 50–51.

recollected terms, *n. pl.* memorized phrases: "Methought it did relieve my passion much,/ More than light airs and recollected terms ..." *T Night,* II, iv, 4–5.

recomforted, *adj.* **the recomforted,** reassured citizens: "Ne'er through an arch so hurried the blown tide/ As the recomforted through th'gates." *Cor,* V, iv, 48–49.

recomforture, *n.* consolation: "... they will breed/ Selves of themselves, to your recomforture." *Rich 3,* IV, iv, 424–425.

recommend, *v.* to entrust: "... denied me mine own purse,/ Which I had recommended to his use ..." *T Night,* V, i, 88–89.

recompense, *v.* to requite; pay back equally: "... such love/ Could be but [no more than] recompens'd, though you were crown'd/ The nonpareil of beauty!" *T Night,* I, v, 256–258.

reconciled, *adj.* repentant: "Would yet again betray the forebetray'd,/ And new pervert a reconciled maid." *Lover's Comp,* 328–329.

record, *v.* **1** to sing: "... made the night-bird mute/ That still records with moan [mournfully] ..." *Per,* IV, Chor., 26–27. **2 be recorded,** speak for the [heavenly] record: "Let me be recorded by the righteous gods,/ I am as poor as you." *Timon,* IV, ii, 4–5.
—*n.* **3** (often with second syllable stressed) memory or recollection: "O, that record is lively in my soul!" *T Night,* V, i, 244. **4** historical record: "Have by their brave instruction got upon

me/ A nobleness in record." *Ant & Cleo,* IV, xiv, 98–99. **5** recorder: "Still music of records." [SD] *Kinsmen,* V, i, 136.

recordation, *n.* **1** tribute or memorial: "That it may grow and sprout as high as heaven/ For recordation to my noble husband." *2 Hen 4,* II, iii, 60–61. **2** a reminder; here, a record that serves as a reminder: "To make a recordation to my soul/ Of every syllable that here was spoke." *Tr & Cr,* V, ii, 115–116.

recorder¹, *n.* [sometimes cap.] city magistrate: ". . . the people were not us'd/ To be spoke to but by the Recorder." *Rich 3,* III, vii, 29–30.

recorder², *n.* wooden wind instrument resembling the flute or oboe: "Come, some music; come, the recorders." *Ham,* III, ii, 285.

recountment, *n.* account or recital, esp. of adventures: "betwixt us two/ Tears our recountments had most kindly bath'd." *As You,* IV, iii, 139–140.

recourse, *n.* **1** access: ". . . no manner person/ Have, any time, recourse unto the Princes." *Rich 3,* III, v, 107–108. **2** steady flow: "Their eyes o'er-galled with recourse of tears . . ." *Tr & Cr,* V, iii, 55.

recover, *v.* **1** to revive or restore: ". . . I recover'd him, bound up his wound . . ." *As You,* IV, iii, 150. **2** wordplay on "patch" and "cause to get well": ". . . I am, indeed, sir, a surgeon to old shoes:/ when they are in great danger I recover them." *J Caes,* I, i, 23–24. **3** to reach or regain; arrive at; get back to: "I swam, ere/ I could recover the shore, five-and-thirty leagues off and on." *Temp,* III, ii, 12–14. **4** to win over; here, in matrimony: "If I cannot recover your niece, I am a foul way/ out." *T Night,* II, iii, 184–185. **5 recover the wind,** to get downwind of, esp. so as to drive game in the opposite direction: ". . . why do you go about to recover the wind/ of me . . ." *Ham,* III, ii, 337–338.

recovered, *v.* misuse for "uncovered" or "discovered": ". . . we have here recovered the most dangerous piece of/ lechery . . ." *M Ado,* III, iii, 161–162.

recovery, *n.* **1** process for gaining possession of property: ". . . with his statutes, his/ recognizances, his fines, his double vouchers, his/ recoveries." *Ham,* V, i, 102–104. **2** entire gain; here, in wordplay with preceding: "Is this the fine of his fines and the/ recovery of his recoveries . . ." *Ham,* V, i, 104–105.

recreant, *adj.* **1** betraying one's religious principles; faithless: "A recreant and most degenerate traitor . . ." *Rich 2,* I, i, 144. **2** cowardly; false: "Feeble desire, all recreant, poor and meek . . ." *Luc,* 710.
—*n.* **3** coward or unfaithful scoundrel: "Come, recreant, come thou child!/ I'll whip thee with a rod; he is defil'd/ That draws

a sword on thee." *M N Dream,* III, ii, 409–411. **4** a traitor; one who betrays his allegiance: "Hear me, recreant!/ On thine allegiance, hear me!" *Lear,* I, i, 166–167. **5** person who has betrayed his religious principles; apostate: "A caitive recreant to my cousin Herford!" *Rich 2,* I, ii, 53.

recreation, *n.* **1** restoration of spirits: "Once a day I'll visit/ The chapel . . . and tears shed there/ Shall be my recreation." *W Tale,* III, ii, 238–240. **2** laughingstock: "If I do not gull him into/ a nayword, and make him a common [general] recreation . . ." *T Night,* II, iii, 135–136.

rectify, *v.* to set straight; also, to verify: ". . . some oracle/ Must rectify our knowledge." *Temp,* V, i, 244–245.

rectorship of judgment, *n.* dictates of reason: "Or had you tongues to cry/ Against the rectorship of judgement [contrary to common sense]?" *Cor,* II, iii, 202–203.

recure, *v.* to heal or cure: "A smile recures the wounding of a frown." *Ven & Ad,* 465.

red, *n.* **1** color of shame; here, virtue [white] borrows beauty's red in its defense: "When shame assail'd, the red should fence the white." *Luc,* 63.
—*adj.* **2** used as an intensive: "A red murrain [plague] o' thy/ jade's tricks." *Tr & Cr,* II, i, 19–20.

red and white, *n.* colors of beauty and chastity: ". . . unwisely did not let/ To praise the clear unmatched red and white . . ." *Luc,* 10–11.

redbreast, *n.* robin: "'Tis the next way to turn tailor, or be redbreast/ teacher [teach caged birds to sing]." *1 Hen 4,* III, i, 253–254.

reddest, *adj.* bravest: ". . . let us make incision for your love,/ To prove whose blood is reddest, his or mine." *Merch,* II, i, 6–7.

rede, *n.* advice; counsel: "Himself the primrose path of dalliance treads,/ And recks not his own rede." *Ham,* I, iii, 50–51.

redeem, *v.* to free or pardon: ". . . if you/ will take it on you to assist him, it shall redeem you/ from your gyves [shackles] . . ." *Meas,* IV, ii, 8–10.

redeliver, *v.* to give back; return: ". . . I have remembrances of yours/ That I have longed long to redeliver." *Ham,* III, i, 93–94.

redemption, *n.* misuse for "damnation" or "perdition": "Thou wilt be condemned into everlasting/ redemption for this." *M Ado,* IV, ii, 53–54.

Redime te captum quam queas minimo, [Latin] Buy your way out of captivity as cheaply as you can [quote from Terence]. *Shrew,* I, i, 162.

red-lattice, *adj.* more appropriate to the alehouse or tavern: ". . . your red-lattice/ phrases, and your bold beating oaths . . ." *Wives,* II, ii, 25–26.

red-looked, *adj.* flushed: "And never to my red-look'd anger be/ The trumpet any more." *W Tale,* II, ii, 34–35.

redoubted, *adj.* **1** redoubtable; formidable: "And these assume but valour's excrement [outcroppings]/ To render them redoubted." *Merch,* III, ii, 87–88. **2** dreaded; feared: "So far be mine, my most redoubted lord,/ As my true service shall deserve your love." *Rich 2,* III, iii, 198–199. **3** respected or revered: "My most redoubted father,/ It is most meet we arm us 'gainst the foe . . ." *Hen 5,* II, iv, 14–15.

red pestilence, *n.* perh. typhus, because of its red rash; poss. same as "red plague": "Now the red pestilence strike all trades in Rome,/ And occupations perish!" *Cor,* IV, i, 12–13.

red plague, *n.* type of plague producing red sores: "The red plague rid you/ For learning me your language!" *Temp,* I, ii, 366–367.

red-tailed humble-bee, *n.* large, noisy bee; here, ref. to Parolles' gaudy apparel and effusive manner: ". . . more/ advanc'd by the king than by that red-tail'd humble-bee/ I speak of." *All's W,* IV, v, 5–7.

reduce, *v.* to bring back; return: "Which to reduce into our former favour [appearance]/ You are assembled . . ." *Hen 5,* V, ii, 63–64.

reechy, *adj.* **1** grimy; begrimed with smoke: ". . . like Pharaoh's soldiers in the/ reechy painting . . ." *M Ado,* III, iii, 130–131. **2** greasy: "The kitchen malkin pins/ Her richest lockram 'bout her reechy neck . . ." *Cor,* II, i, 206–207. **3** foul; filthy: ". . . for a pair of reechy kisses,/ Or paddling in your neck with his damn'd fingers . . ." *Ham,* III, iv, 186–187.

reed, *n.* **1** something not intended as a weapon: "I had as lief have a reed that will do/ me no service, as a partisan I could not heave." *Ant & Cleo,* II, vii, 12–13. **2 reed is as the oak,** in life the reed survives by being flexible, the oak by its strength; in death both are alike: "To thee the reed is as the oak . . ." *Cymb,* IV, ii, 267.

re-edify, *v.* to rebuild or renovate: "This monument five hundreth years hath stood,/ Which I have sumptuously re-edified . . ." *T Andr,* I, i, 350–351.

reek, *v.* **1** to be exhaled: "And in some perfumes is there more delight/ Than in the breath that from my mistress reeks." *Sonn 130,* 7–8. **2** to steam or smoke: "And draw their honours reeking up to heaven . . ." *Hen 5,* IV, iii, 101. **3** to pour forth, as steam or smoke: "I heard your guilty rhymes, observed your fashion,/ Saw sighs reek from you, noted well your passion . . ." *Love's L,* IV, iii, 136–137. **4** to sweat; here, from acute distress: ". . . you remember/ How under my oppression I did reek . . ." *Hen 8,* II, iv, 205–207.
—*n.* **5** toxic vapor; stench: "You common cry of curs! Whose breath I hate/ As reek o'th'rotten fens . . ." *Cor,* III, iii, 120–121.

reeking, *adj.* [of blood] steaming: "Except they meant to bathe in reeking wounds . . ." *Mac,* I, ii, 40.

reeky, *adj.* that reeks; malodorous: ". . . dead men's rattling bones,/ With reeky shanks and yellow chapless skulls." *Rom & Jul,* IV, i, 82–83.

reel, *v.* **1** to stagger drunkenly (in); here, to perform in staggers: "Keeps wassail, and the swagg'ring upspring reels . . ." *Ham,* I, iv, 9.
—*n.* **2** [pl.] revelry: "Drink thou; increase the reels." *Ant & Cleo,* II, vii, 93.

reeling ripe, *adj.* so drunk as to reel: "And Trinculo is reeling ripe: where should they/ Find this grand liquor that hath gilded 'em?—" *Temp,* V, i, 279–280.

refel, *v.* to refuse; also, to refute: "How he refell'd me, and how I replied . . ." *Meas,* V, i, 97.

refer, *v.* **1** to entrust or commit: "Only refer/ yourself to this advantage . . ." *Meas,* III, i, 245–246. **2** to bestow; give in marriage: "His daughter . . . hath referr'd herself/ Unto a poor but worthy gentleman." *Cymb,* I, i, 4–7. **3 refer me,** submit my complaint: "For I'll refer me to all things of sense . . ." *Oth,* I, ii, 64.

reference, *n.* **1** agreement; unanimity: ". . . many things, having full reference/ To one consent [common goal] . . ." *Hen 5,* I, ii, 205–206. **2** assignment: "Due reference of place, and exhibition . . ." *Oth,* I, iii, 237. **3 hath reference to,** depends on; is at the mercy of: "All that he is hath reference to your highness." *All's W,* V, iii, 29.

refigure, *v.* to copy; reproduce: "Ten times thyself were happier than thou art/ If ten of thine ten times refigured thee . . ." *Sonn 6,* 9–10.

reflect, *v.* to shine: ". . . whose virtues will, I hope,/ Reflect on Rome as Titan's rays on earth . . ." *T Andr,* I, i, 225–226.

reflection, *n.* ref. to the vernal equinox, when the sun appears to turn northward: "As whence the sun 'gins his reflection,/ Shipwracking storms and direful thunders break . . ." *Mac,* I, ii, 25–26.

reflex, *n.* **1** reflection: "I'll say yon grey is not the morning's eye,/ 'Tis but the pale reflex of Cynthia's brow." *Rom & Jul,* III, v, 19–20.
—*v.* **2** to reflect; cast or shine: "May never glorious sun reflex his beams/ Upon the country where you make abode . . ." *1 Hen 6,* V, iv, 87–88.

reform, *v.* misuse for "inform": ". . . our sexton hath reformed Signior Leonato of the/ matter . . ." *M Ado,* V, i, 248–249.

refrain, *v.* to hold back; restrain: ". . . scarce I can refrain/ The execution of my big-swoln heart/ Upon that Clifford . . ." *3 Hen 6,* II, ii, 110–112.

reft, *v.* **1** past part. of **reave;** robbed (of): "Nor my bad life reft me so much of friends . . ." *M Ado,* IV, I, 196. **2** past tense of **reave;** to deprive; take away by force: "Thinking to bar thee of succession as/ Thou refts [reft'st] me of my lands." *Cymb,* III, iii, 102–103.
—*adj.* **3** bereft; deprived: "Like a poor bark of sails and tackling reft . . ." *Rich 3,* IV, iv, 234.

refuge, *v.* to seek [or find] refuge for; excuse: ". . . sitting in the stocks, refuge their shame,/ That many have and others must sit there . . ." *Rich 2,* V, v, 26–27.

refuse, *v.* **1** to renounce or disown: "Hero was in this manner accused, in this very/ manner refused . . ." *M Ado,* IV, ii, 59–60.
—*n.* **2** worst or most worthless part: ". . . in the very refuse of thy deeds/ There is such strength . . ." *Sonn 150,* 6–7.

regard, *n.* **1** respect: ". . . my noble master will appear/ Such as he is, full of regard and honour." *J Caes,* IV, ii, 11–12. **2** thought or deliberation: ". . . the mild glance that sly Ulysses lent/ Show'd deep regard . . ." *Luc,* 1399–1400. **3** consideration: "Where will doth mutiny with wit's [wisdom's] regard." *Rich 2,* II, i, 28. **4** look: ". . . quenching my/ familiar smile with an austere regard of control [severe look of authority]—" *T Night,* II, v, 66–67. **5 demure travel of regard,** gravely looking from one to another: ". . . and after a/ demure travel of regard, telling them I know my/ place . . ." *T Night,* II, v, 52–54. **6 in regard,** since; considering that: ". . . in regard King Henry gives consent,/ Of mere compassion and of lenity . . ." *1 Hen 6,* V, iv, 124–125.
—*v.* **7** to watch; observe: "Regard Titinius,/ And tell me what thou not'st about the field." *J Caes,* V, iii, 21–22. **8** to remember or consider: "Regard thy danger, and along with me." *Two Gent,* III, i, 256.

regardfully, *adv.* with great praise; respectfully: ". . . th' Athenian minion whom the world/ Voic'd so regardfully?" *Timon,* IV, iii, 82–83.

regent, *n.* **1** ruler; monarch: "Why, cousin, wert thou regent of the world,/ It were a shame to let this land by lease . . ." *Rich 2,* II, i, 109–110. **2** [cap.] ref. to Duke of York, the king's regent in the French areas claimed by England: "The Regent hath with Talbot broke his word . . ." *1 Hen 6,* IV, vi, 2.

region, *n.* **1** social class: "He is of too high a region; he/ knows too much." *Wives,* III, ii, 67–68.
—*adj.* **2** of the vicinity; here, of the surrounding air: ". . . ere this/ I should ha' fatted all the region kites/ With this slave's offal." *Ham,* II, ii, 574–576.

regions under earth, *n. pl.* abode of evil spirits, esp. Erebus: ". . . ye familiar spirits that are cull'd/ Out of the powerful regions under earth . . ." *1 Hen 6,* V, iii, 10–11.

register[1], *v.* **1** to record; here, in the memory: ". . . your pains/ Are register'd where every day I turn/ The leaf to read them." *Mac,* I, iii, 151–153.
—*n.* **2 in register,** on permanent record: ". . . let the world rank me in register/ A master-leaver, and a fugitive . . ." *Ant & Cleo,* IV, ix, 21–22.

register[2], *n.* person who maintains a register: "O comfort-killing night . . . Dim register and notary of shame . . ." *Luc,* 764–765.

registered, *adj.* **1** written down: "But say . . . it were not register'd,/ Methinks the truth should live from age to age . . ." *Rich 3,* III, i, 75–76. **2** engraved: "Let fame . . . Live register'd upon our brazen tombs . . ." *Love's L,* I, i, 1–2.

regreet, *v.* **1** to welcome; also, salute: ". . . as at English feasts, so I regreet/ The daintiest last . . ." *Rich 2,* I, iii, 67–68.
—*n.* **2** [usually pl.] greeting: "To signify th'approaching of his lord,/ From whom he bringeth sensible regreets . . ." *Merch,* II, ix, 88–89.

reguerdon, *n.* **1** recognition; reward: ". . . in reguerdon of that duty done/ I gird thee with the valiant sword of York . . ." *1 Hen 6,* III, i, 170–171.
—*v.* **2** to reward: "Yet never have you . . . been reguerdon'd with so much as thanks . . ." *1 Hen 6,* III, iv, 22–23.

rehearsal, *n.* recital or narration: ". . . I'll requite it/ With sweet rehearsal of my morning's dream." *2 Hen 6,* I, ii, 23–24.

rehearse, *v.* **1** to repeat; speak or recite: ". . . hearing how our plaints and prayers do pierce,/ Pity may move thee 'pardon' to rehearse." *Rich 2,* V, iii, 125–126. **2** to describe; report: "Thine own sweet argument, too excellent/ For every vulgar paper to rehearse?" *Sonn 38,* 3–4.

reign, *v.* to triumph; also, persist or exult in: "All men are bad, and in their badness reign." *Sonn 121,* 14.

rein, *v.* **1** (of a horse) to be managed; behave; ref. is to Sir Andrew's horse, Capilet, of which Viola knows nothing: ". . . I'll be as good as my word. He will bear you/ easily, and reins well." *T Night,* III, iv, 332–333.
—*n.* **2 in such a rein,** so haughtily: "Ajax is grown self-will'd, and bears his head/ In such a rein . . ." *Tr & Cr,* I, iii, 188–189. **3 the rein,** free rein: "And now I give my sensual race the rein . . ." *Meas,* II, iv, 159.

reins, *n.* kidneys: ". . . my belly's as cold as if I had swallowed/ snowballs for pills to cool the reins." *Wives,* III, v, 20–21.

rejoicing, *n.* **dues of rejoicing,** joy; elation: "This have/ I thought good to deliver thee . . . that thou might'st not lose the dues/ of rejoicing . . ." *Mac,* I, v, 10–13.

rejoindure, *n.* reunion: ". . . rudely beguiles our lips/ Of all rejoindure . . ." *Tr & Cr,* IV, iv, 34–35.

rejourn, *v.* to adjourn or postpone: ". . . then rejourn the controversy of [amounting to] threepence to a/ second day of audience." *Cor,* II, i, 71–72.

relapse, *n.* **relapse of mortality,** succumbing to death; that is, the soldiers spread death by dying: "Break out into a second course of mischief,/ Killing in relapse of mortality." *Hen 5,* IV, iii, 106–107.

relation, *n.* account; report: "O relation,/ Too nice, and yet too true!" *Mac,* IV, iii, 173–174.

relative, *adj.* convincing or conclusive: "I'll have grounds/ More relative than this. The play's the thing . . ." *Ham,* II, ii, 599–600.

relics, *n. pl.* **1** antiquities; ancient monuments, etc.: "Shall we go see the relics of this town?" *T Night,* III, iii, 19. **2** remnants: "The fragments, scraps, the bits, and greasy relics/ Of her o'er-eaten faith are given to Diomed." *Tr & Cr,* V, ii, 158–159. **3 incensing relics,** disturbing memories; upsetting reminders: "And deeper than oblivion we do bury/ Th' incensing relics of it." *All's W,* V, iii, 24–25.

relier, *n.* that which is or can be relied on: "Not to seducing lust, thy rash relier [which you rashly rely on]." *Luc,* 639.

relieve, *v.* **1** to experience relief: "He cheers the morn, and all the earth relieveth . . ." *Ven & Ad,* 484. **2** to aid; help in distress: ". . . shall to my bosom/ Be as well neighbour'd, pit-

ied, and reliev'd,/ As thou my sometime daughter." *Lear,* I, i, 118–120. **3** to rescue: "Do not yourself such wrong, who are in this/ Reliev'd, but not betray'd." *Ant & Cleo,* V, ii, 40–41

religion, *n.* superstition: ". . . but I see you have some religion in/ you, that you fear." *Cymb,* I, v, 133–134.

religious, *adj.* **1** conscientious; properly directed: "As thou lov'st her/ Thy love's to me religious . . ." *All's W,* II, iii, 182–183. **2** fervent; impassioned: "Religious love put out Religion's eye . . ." *Lover's Comp,* 250.

relinquish, *v.* **relinquished of the artists,** abandoned by the scholars: ". . . 'tis the rarest argument of wonder that hath/ shot out in our latter times."/ "To be relinquish'd of the artists—" *All's W,* II, iii, 7–10.

relish¹, *v.* **1** to retain a taste of or liking for (something): ". . . for virtue cannot/ so inoculate our old stock but we shall relish [still retain a taste] of it." *Ham,* III, i, 117–118. **2** to be pleasing: ". . . it would not have/ relished among my other discredits." *W Tale,* V, ii, 122–123.
—*n.* **3** taste or trace: ". . . about some act/ That has no relish of salvation in't . . ." *Ham,* III, iii, 91–92. **4** kind or sort: ". . . his fears,/ out of doubt, be of the same relish as ours are . . ." *Hen 5,* IV, i, 109–110. **5 What relish is in this?** What does this mean?: "What relish is in this? How runs the stream?" *T Night,* IV, i, 59.

relish², *v.* to sing or warble; render or interpret: ". . . to relish a love-song, like a robin-redbreast . . ." *Two Gent,* II, i, 19.

relume, *v.* to relight; rekindle: ". . . where is that Promethean heat/ That can thy light relume . . ." *Oth,* V, ii, 12–13.

remain¹, *v.* **1** to live (on); inhabit: "Vouchsafe my prayer/ May know if you remain upon this island . . ." *Temp,* I, ii, 425–426.
—*n.* **2 make remain alike,** share the same fate: "Let's fetch him off, or make remain alike." *Cor,* I, iv, 62.

remain², *n.* **all the remain,** all that remains: "All the remain is 'Welcome.'" *Cymb,* III, i, 86.

remediate, *adj.* healing; remedial: ". . . be aidant and remediate/ In the good man's distress!" *Lear,* IV, iv, 17–18.

remedy, *v.* **1** to render; hand over, esp. for punishment: ". . . shall be remedied to your public laws/ At heaviest answer." *Timon,* V, iv, 62–63.
—*n.* **2 no remedy,** there is no help for it: "You must send her/ your page, no remedy." *Wives,* II, ii, 116–117.

remember, *v.* **1** to remind: "For if of joy . . . It doth remember me the more of sorrow . . ." *Rich 2,* III, iv, 13–14. **2** to mention previously: ". . . we will accite,/ As I before remember'd, all our state . . ." *2 Hen 4,* V, ii, 141–142. **3** to acknowledge; reward: "Much deserved on his part, and equally remembered/ by Don Pedro." *M Ado,* I, i, 11–12. **4** to commemorate: ". . . to remember what he does,/ Build his statue to make him glorious." *Per,* II, Chor., 11–12. **5 be remembered, a.** [to] remember; recollect: "But if you be remember'd,/ I did not bid you mar it to the time." *Shrew,* IV, iii, 96–97. **b.** do remember: "O be remember'd, no outrageous thing/ From vassal actors can be wip'd away . . ." *Luc,* 607–608.

remembrance, *n.* **1** memory of someone deceased: "For your father's remembrance, be at accord." *As You,* I, i, 63–64. **2** memory of the past: ". . . rather like a dream than an assurance/ That my remembrance warrants." *Temp,* I, ii, 45–46. **3** attention or consideration: "Let your remembrance apply to Banquo:/ Present him eminence . . ." *Mac,* III, ii, 30. **4** reputation for showing gratitude: "I must thank him only,/ Lest my remembrance suffer ill report . . ." *Ant & Cleo,* II, ii, 156–157.

remembrancer, *n.* person or thing that serves to remind: "Sweet remembrancer!—/ Now, good digestion wait on appetite . . ." *Mac,* III, iv, 36–37.

remission, *n.* forgiveness: ". . . when that decays,/ The guilty rebel for remission prays." *Luc,* 714.

remit, *v.* **1** to give up; surrender: "What, will you have me, or your pearl again?"/ "Neither of either; I remit both twain." *Love's L,* V, ii, 458–459. **2** to forgive; pardon: ". . . to remit/ Their saucy sweetness that do coin heaven's image . . ." *Meas,* II, iv, 44–45.

remorse, *n.* **1** pity; mercy or compassion: "Th'abuse of greatness is when it disjoins/ Remorse from power . . ." *J Caes,* II, i, 18–19. **2** hope or expectation of pity: "Never pray more, abandon all remorse." *Oth,* III, iii, 375–376. **3 remorse of voice,** lowering of [your] voice: ". . . ye squeak out your coziers' catches without any/ mitigation or remorse of voice?" *T Night,* II, iii, 90–92.

remorseful, *adj.* showing pity; compassionate: "The gaudy, blabbing, and remorseful day . . ." *2 Hen 6,* IV, i, 1.

remotion, *n.* **1** act of departing or moving away: "All thy safety were remotion, and/ thy defence absence." *Timon,* IV, iii, 343–344. **2** act of staying away or remaining aloof: ". . . this remotion of the Duke and her/ Is practice [deception] only." *Lear,* II, iv, 114–115.

remove, *n.* **1** exchange; trade: ". . . so shall your loves/ Woo contrary, deceiv'd by these removes." *Love's L,* V, ii, 134–135. **2** change by the royal court from one location to another: ". . . hath for four or five removes come short [late]/ To tender it

herself." *All's W,* V, iii, 131–132. **3** absence: "In our remove, be thou at full ourself." *Meas,* I, i, 43.

—*v.* **4** to go away from a place: ". . . in a night the best part of my power,/ As I upon advantage did remove,/ Were in the Washes all unwarily/ Devoured . . ." *K John,* V, vii, 61–64. **5** to depart in death: "But now thy uncle is removing hence . . ." *1 Hen 6,* II, v, 104.

removed, *adj.* **1** less directly concerned (than): "To lay so dangerous and dear a trust/ On any soul remov'd but on his own." *1 Hen 4,* IV, i, 34–35. **2** private; secluded: "I have ever lov'd the life remov'd . . ." *Meas,* I, iii, 8. **3 removed issue,** Eleanor's grandson, descended indirectly from her, but still harmed by her: "But God hath made her sin and her the plague/ On this removed issue . . ." *K John,* II, i, 185–186. **4 removed thing,** something distant or remote; here, a stranger: "And grew a twenty years' removed thing/ While one would wink . . ." *T Night,* V, i, 87–88. **5 time removed,** period of absence: "And yet this time remov'd was summer's time . . ." *Sonn 97,* 5.

removedness, *n.* absence: "I have eyes under my service which/ look upon his removedness . . ." *W Tale,* IV, ii, 36–37.

remover, *n.* inconstant lover: "Or bends with the remover to remove." *Sonn 116,* 4.

render, *n.* **1** act of divulging; confession: ". . . may drive us to a render/ Where we have liv'd . . ." *Cymb,* IV, iv, 11. **2** exchange: ". . . knows no art/ But mutual render, only me for thee." *Sonn 125,* 11–12. **3** recompense or repayment; also, restitution: ". . . send forth us, to make their sorrowed render . . ." *Timon,* V, i, 148. **4** act of giving up; surrender: "No stricter render of me than my all." *Cymb,* V, iv, 17.

—*v.* **5** to return; give back: "And what have I to give you back . . . ?/ Nothing, unless you render her again." *M Ado,* IV, i, 26–28. **6** to pay back [in kind]; give in return: "And that same prayer, doth teach us all to render/ The deeds of mercy." *Merch,* IV, i, 197–198. **7** to give up; surrender: ". . . she render'd life/ Thy name so buried in her." *Ant & Cleo,* IV, xiv, 33–34. **8 render back,** to repay one's debts: "Bankrupts, hold fast;/ Rather than render back, out with your knives . . ." *Timon,* IV, i, 8–9.

rendered lost, *adj.* assumed to be dying: ". . . the desperate languishings whereof/ The king is render'd lost." *All's W,* I, iii, 224–225.

rendezvous, *n.* **1** poss. misuse for "last resort" or "last word on the subject": ". . . that is my rest, that is the/ rendezvous of it." *Hen 5,* II, i, 16–17. **2** refuge: "And there my rendezvous is quite cut off." *Hen 5,* V, i, 87.

renegado, *n.* person who has forsaken his religion: "Yond gull Malvolio/ is turned heathen, a very renegado . . ." *T Night,* III, ii, 66–67.

renege, *v.* **1** to deny: "Renege, affirm, and turn their halcyon beaks . . ." *Lear,* II, ii, 79. **2 reneges all temper,** refuses or renounces all self-restraint: ". . . his captain's heart . . . reneges all temper . . ." *Ant & Cleo,* I, i, 6–8.

renouncement, *n.* renunciation of the world: "I hold you as a thing enskied and sainted/ By your renouncement . . ." *Meas,* I, iv, 34–35.

renowmed, *adj.* var. of renowned: "Renowmed Titus, more than half my soul,—" *T Andr,* I, i, 373.

renown, *n.* **1** reputation; good name: "To make the noble Leonatus mad,/ By wounding his belief in her renown . . ." *Cymb,* V, v, 201–202. **2 the end is the renown,** the last part [of life] determines the praise: ". . . the fine's the crown./ Whate'er the course, the end is the renown." *All's W,* IV, iv, 35–36.
—*v.* **3** to bring renown to: ". . . the things of fame/ That do renown this city." *T Night,* III, iii, 23–24.

rent¹, *v.* var. of **rend;** tear: "Rent off thy silver hair, thy other hand/ Gnawing with thy teeth . . ." *T Andr,* III, i, 260–261.

rent², *n.* **1** price, as for favors: "Lose all and more by paying too much rent . . ." *Sonn 125,* 6. **2** [usually pl.] revenues: "What are thy rents? what are thy comings-in [income]?" *Hen 5,* IV, i, 249.

repair¹, *v.* **1** to return; come back: "I prithee but repair to me next morning." *Timon,* II, i, 28.
—*n.* **2** coming or arrival: "I will forestall/ their repair hither and say you are not fit." *Ham,* V, ii, 213–214.

repair², *v.* **1** to renew or restore: ". . . he brought his disease/ hither: here he does but repair it." *Per,* IV, ii, 108–109. **2 repairs him with occasion,** is revived with opportunity: ". . . like a gallant in the brow of youth,/ Repairs him with occasion?" *2 Hen 6,* V, iii, 4–5.
—*n.* **3** renewal or perpetuation: "Whose fresh repair if now thou not renewest/ Thou dost beguile the world . . ." *Sonn 3,* 3–4.

repairing nature, *n.* ability to recuperate: ". . . our foes are this time fled,/ Being opposites of such repairing nature." *2 Hen 6,* V, iii, 21–22.

repast, *v.* to feed: "And, like the kind life-rend'ring pelican,/ Repast them with my blood." *Ham,* IV, v, 146–147.

repasture, *n.* meal: "Food for his rage, repasture for his den." *Love's L,* IV, i, 94.

repeal, *v.* **1** to recall [from exile]; return: "The banish'd Bolingbroke repeals himself . . ." *Rich 2,* II, ii, 49. **2** to restore to honor or trust: "When false opinion . . . In thy just proof repeals and reconciles thee." *Lear,* III, vi, 115–116.
—*n.* **3** act of recalling: "I sue for exil'd majesty's repeal . . ." *Luc,* 640.

repeat, *v.* **1** to mention: "The name of help grew odious to repeat." *Per,* I, iv, 31. **2 repeat your will,** state your wish: "Repeat your will and take it." *Hen 8,* I, ii, 13.

repeated, *adj.* often mentioned or recited; reiterated; enumerated: ". . . and those repeated/ Vexations of it!" *Cymb,* I, vi, 4–5.

repetition, *n.* review or recital of past wrongs or grievances: "We are reconcil'd, and the first view shall kill/ All repetition." *All's W,* V, iii, 21–22.

repine, *v.* **1** to feel dejected: "Let Henry fret and all the world repine." *1 Hen 6,* V, iii, 20. **2** to be reluctant or unwilling to grant; begrudge: "But what the repining enemy commends,/ That breath fame blows . . ." *Tr & Cr,* I, iii, 242–243.
—*n.* **3** vexation; discomfort: "Had not his clouded with his brow's repine . . ." *Ven & Ad,* 490.

replenished, *adj.* complete or perfect: "The most replenish'd villain in the world . . ." *W Tale,* II, i, 79.

replication, *n.* **1** reply; response: ". . . what replication/ should be made by the son of a king?" *Ham,* IV, ii, 11–12. **2** echo; reverberation: "That Tiber trembled underneath her banks/ To hear the replication of your sounds . . ." *J Caes,* I, i, 45–46.

report, *n.* **1** repute; reputation: "These wise men that give fools money get themselves a/ good report . . ." *T Night,* IV, i, 21–23. **2** praise: "And therefore have I slept in your report . . ." *Sonn 83,* 5. **3** reporter; here, a participant: "And have my learning from some true reports/ That drew their swords with you." *Ant & Cleo,* II, ii, 47–48. **4** accusation(s): "If he know/ That I am free [guiltless] of your report . . ." *Hen 8,* II, iv, 96–97.
—*v.* **5 likely to report themselves,** [so] lifelike they could almost talk: ". . . never saw I figures/ So likely to report themselves . . ." *Cymb,* II, iv, 82–83.

reportingly, *adv.* from the reports of others: "For others say thou dost deserve, and I/ Believe it better than reportingly." *M Ado,* III, i, 115–116.

reposal, *n.* act of placing or putting: ". . . would the reposal/ Of any trust . . . in thee/ Make thy words faith'd [creditable]?" *Lear,* II, i, 68–70.

repose, *v.* to confide; also, to trust: ". . . lest, reposing too/ far in his virtue . . . he might . . . in a main danger fail you." *All's W,* III, vi, 13–15.

reprehend, *v.* **1** to rebuke; censure: "You should for that have reprehended him." *Errors,* V, i, 57. **2** misuse for "represent": "I myself reprehend his own person, for I am his/ grace's farborough . . ." *Love's L,* I, i, 182–183.

reprisal, *n.* prize; booty: "I am on fire/ To hear this rich reprisal is so nigh . . ." *1 Hen 4,* IV, i, 117–118.

reproach, *n.* misuse for "approach" [presence]: ". . . my young master doth expect/ your reproach." *Merch,* II, v, 19–20.

reprobation or **reprobance,** *n.* **to reprobation,** into eternal damnation: ". . . curse his better angel from his side,/ And fall to reprobation." *Oth,* V, ii, 209–210.

reproof, *n.* **1** punishment, often death: "Those enemies of Timon's and mine own/ Whom you yourselves shall set out for reproof/ Fall, and no more . . ." *Timon,* V, iv, 56–58. **2** rebuttal or disproof: ". . . in the reproof of this/ lives the jest." *1 Hen 4,* I, ii, 184–185.

reprovable, *adj.* blamable; reprehensible: ". . . a provoking merit, set a-work by/ a reproveable badness in himself." *Lear,* III, v, 7–8.

reprove, *v.* to disprove; refute: "Reprove my allegation if you can . . ." *2 Hen 6,* III, i, 40.

repugn, *v.* to reject: ". . . stubbornly he did repugn the truth/ About a certain question in the law . . ." *1 Hen 6,* IV, i, 94–95.

repugnancy, *n.* resistance or retaliation: ". . . let the foes quietly cut their throats/ Without repugnancy?" *Timon,* III, v, 45–46.

repugnant, *adj.* resistant; hostile: "His antique sword,/ Rebellious to his arm, lies where it falls,/ Repugnant to command." *Ham,* II, ii, 465–467.

repured, *adj.* purified; refined: ". . . the wat'ry palate tastes indeed/ Love's thrice-repured nectar?" *Tr & Cr,* III, ii, 19–20.

repute, *v.* **1** to regard; consider: "Sweet smoke of rhetoric!/ He reputes me a cannon . . ." *Love's L,* III, i, 60–61. **2 repute of,** to be proud of; boast of: "Yet, by reputing of his high descent . . . And such high vaunts of his nobility . . ." *2 Hen 6,* III, i, 48–50.

request, *v.* **1 request you off,** ask you to come away [ashore]: "Good brother,/ Let me request you off: our graver business/ Frowns at this levity." *Ant & Cleo,* II, vii, 118–120.

—*n.* **2 for request's sake only,** simply because they had been requested: "Things small as nothing, for request's sake only,/ He makes important . . ." *Tr & Cr,* II, iii, 170–171. **3 in request,** in demand: "I'll try whether my old wit be in request/ With those that have but little . . ." *Cor,* III, i, 249–250. **4 in no request of,** not wanted or required by: ". . . his/ great opposer, Coriolanus, being now in no request/ of his country." *Cor,* IV, iii, 34–36. **5 only in request,** the only thing people want: "Novelty is/ only in request . . ." *Meas,* III, ii, 217–218.

require, *v.* **1** to request: ". . . in best time,/ We will require her welcome." *Mac,* III, iv, 5–6. **2** to beg: "In humblest manner I require your highness,/ That it shall please you . . ." *Hen 8,* II, iv, 142–143.

requit, *past part.* repaid (the deed): ". . . you three/ From Milan did supplant good Prospero:/ Expos'd unto the sea, which hath requit it . . ." *Temp,* III, iii, 69–71.

requite, *v.* **1** to repay: ". . . I requited him for his lie . . ." *Mac,* II, iii, 40. **2** to offset or counteract: ". . . I'll requite it/ With sweet rehearsal of my morning's dream." *2 Hen 6,* I, ii, 23–24.

reremouse, *n.* bat: "Some war with reremice for their leathern wings . . ." *M N Dream,* II, ii, 4.

rescue, *n.* **1 A rescue!** call for help, either from an arresting officer or one trying to avoid arrest: "A rescue! A rescue!"/ "Good people, bring a rescue or two." *2 Hen 4,* II, v, 54–55. **2 honorable rescue and defense,** [those] honorably defending and delivering their country: "Where honourable rescue and defence/ Cries out upon [against] the name of Salisbury!" *K John,* V, ii, 18–19.

reservation, *n.* **1** right or privilege reserved for oneself: "Ourself, by monthly course,/ With reservation of an hundred knights . . ." *Lear,* I, i, 132–133. **2** exception: "Making but reservation of yourselves,/ Still your own foes . . ." *Cor,* III, iii, 130–131. **3 keep a reservation,** to retain a right or privilege: "But kept a reservation to be follow'd/ With such a number." *Lear,* II, iv, 254–255. **4 make some reservation of your wrongs,** (to) leave some of your insults unsaid: "I most unfeignedly beseech your lordship to make/ some reservation of your wrongs." *All's W,* II, iii, 240–241.

reserve, *v.* **1** to preserve; guard or treasure: ". . . reserve/ That excellent complexion, which did steal/ The eyes of young and old." *Per,* IV, i, 39–41. **2** to withhold: ". . . what is yours to bestow is not yours to/ reserve." *T Night,* I, v, 189–190. **3** to except, as part of an agreement: ". . . only reserv'd you claim no interest/ In any of our towns of garrison." *1 Hen 6,* V, iv, 166–167. **4 reserve their character,** preserve their characteristics: "While comments of your praise . . . Reserve their character with golden quill . . ." *Sonn 85,* 2–3. **5 reserved their factor,**

hired as their [hell's] agent: "Only reserv'd their factor to buy souls/ And send them thither." *Rich 3*, IV, iv, 72–73.

reserved honesty, *n.* carefully guarded chastity: ". . . all her deserving/ Is a reserved honesty . . ." *All's W*, III, v, 61–62.

residence, *n.* **1** fact of residing in the city: "Their residence, both/ in reputation and profit, was better both ways." *Ham*, II, ii, 328–329. **2 suffer question for your residence,** [to] be queried as to why you are there: ". . . and out/ of it you'll run again rather than suffer question for/ your residence." *All's W*, II, v, 37–39.

residue, *n.* remainder; rest: "The residue of your fortune,/ Go to my cave and tell me." *As You*, II, vii, 199–200.

resist, *v.* to have no appeal [to]: "These cates resist me, he not thought upon." *Per*, II, iii, 29.

resolute, *n.* **lawless resolute,** cutthroat; assassin: "Shark'd up a list of lawless resolutes/ For food and diet . . ." *Ham*, I, i, 101–102.

resolution, *n.* **1** resolve; courage: ". . . and resolution thus fubbed as it/ is with the rusty curb of old father Antic the law?" *1 Hen 4*, I, ii, 58–59. **2 be in a due resolution,** have [my] uncertainty resolved fully: "I would/ unstate myself to be in a due resolution." *Lear*, I, ii, 102–103.

resolve, *v.* **1** to reach a decision; decide: "How yet resolves the governor of the town?" *Hen 5*, III, iii, 1. **2** to answer; reply to: "Vouchsafe to read the purpose of my coming,/ And suddenly resolve me in my suit." *Love's L*, II, i, 108–109. **3** to free from doubt; reassure: "My lord the emperor, resolve me this:/ Was it well done of rash Virginius/ To slay his daughter . . ." *T Andr*, V, iii, 35–37. **4** to dissolve; melt: "The sea's a thief, whose liquid surge resolves/ The moon into salt tears . . ." *Timon*, IV, iii, 442–443. **5 be resolved,** to know for certain; have it explained to one: ". . . Antony/ May safely come to him, and be resolv'd/ How Caesar hath deserv'd to lie in death . . ." *J Caes*, III, i, 130–132. **6 resolve for,** determine to go to: "I will resolve for Scotland." *2 Hen 4*, II, iii, 67. **7 resolve itself,** to melt away; deliquesce: "O that this too too sullied flesh would melt,/ Thaw and resolve itself into a dew . . ." *Ham*, I, ii, 129–130. **8 resolve yourselves apart,** Go off by yourselves and make up your minds: "Resolve yourselves apart;/ I'll come to you anon." *Mac*, III, i, 137–138.

resolved, *adj.* **1** determined: "And he wants wit that wants resolved will . . ." *Two Gent*, II, vi, 12. **2 resolved to be dissolved,** resigned to being destroyed: "What says my fair love? Is she resolved?/ Resolved to be dissolved, and therefore this:/ Keep but thy word, great king, and I am thine." *Edw 3*, II, ii, 166–168.

resolvedly, *adv.* in a manner to resolve all questions: "Of that and all the progress more and less/ Resolvedly more leisure shall express." *All's W*, V, iii, 325–326.

resort, *n.* **1** access to another's person or presence: "Join with me to forbid him her resort . . ." *Timon*, I, i, 130. **2** company or group: ". . . the fair resort of gentlemen/ That every day with parle encounter me . . ." *Two Gent*, I, ii, 4–5.
—*v.* **3** to gather; repair; betake oneself: ". . . where, as they say,/ At some hours in the night spirits resort—" *Rom & Jul*, IV, iii, 43–44.

resorter, *n.* frequenter; here, a regular customer: ". . . 'tis the better for you that your resorters/ stand upon sound legs." *Per*, IV, vi, 22–23.

re-speak, *v.* to echo: ". . . the King's rouse the heaven shall bruit again,/ Re-speaking earthly thunder." *Ham*, I, ii, 127–128.

respect, *n.* **1** repute; reputation: ". . . many of the best respect in Rome/ (Except immortal Caesar), speaking of Brutus . . . Have wish'd that noble Brutus had his eyes." *J Caes*, I, ii, 58–61. **2** [often pl.] consideration; reluctance to act considering the consequences: ". . . reason and respect/ Make livers pale, and lustihood deject." *Tr & Cr*, II, ii, 49–50. **3** central issue; focal point: "In our two loves there is but one respect . . ." *Sonn 36*, 5. **4** opinion: "I am almost asham'd/ To say what good respect I have of thee." *K John*, III, ii, 37–38. **5** the proper circumstances in which a thing can be judged: "Nothing is good (I see) without respect . . ." *Merch*, V, i, 99. **6** care or attention: "Such harmless creatures have a true respect/ To talk in deeds . . ." *Luc*, 1347–1348. **7** self-respect: ". . . such offers of our peace/ As we with honour and respect may take . . ." *K John*, V, vii, 84–85. **8** basis or consideration: ". . . an ancient tradition, begun/ upon an honourable respect . . ." *Hen 5*, V, i, 73–74. **9** [pl.] reasons: "For my respects are better than they seem . . ." *All's W*, II, v, 66. **10 have respect to,** to bear in mind: "Believe me/ for mine honour, and have respect to mine honour . . ." *J Caes*, III, ii, 14–15. **11 have respect upon,** to pay attention to: "You have too much respect upon the world [business matters] . . ." *Merch*, I, i, 74. **12 in my respect,** in my regard: "His mean'st garment . . . is dearer/ In my respect, than all the hairs above thee . . ." *Cymb*, II, iii, 132–134. **13 in respect,** by comparison: "He was a man; this, in respect, a child . . ." *3 Hen 6*, V, v, 54. **14 in respect of, a.** in comparison to: "Truly, sir, in respect of a fine workman, I am but,/ as you would say, a cobbler." *J Caes*, I, i, 10–11. **b.** because of: "Item, she is not to be kissed [when she is] fasting in respect of her/ breath." *Two Gent*, III, i, 317–318. **15 there's no respect,** it matters not: "So it be new, there's no respect how vile . . ." *Rich 2*, II, i, 25. **16 to my respect,** in my regard: "I have one myself,/ Who shall not be more dear to my respect . . ." *Per*, III, iii, 32–33.

—*v.* **17** to regard: "I have a widow aunt, a dowager/ Of great revenue . . . And she respects me as her only son." *M N Dream,* I, i, 157–160. **18** to value; prize: "That more than all the world I did respect her." *Love's L,* V, ii, 437. **19** to show respect for; here, in wordplay with "to take notice of" or "pay any attention to": "And I am mean [contemptible], indeed, respecting you." *Shrew,* V, ii, 32.

respected, *adj.* misuse for **suspected** (def. 3): ". . . the house is a respected/ house; next, this is a respected fellow; and his mistress/ is a respected woman." *Meas,* II, i, 159–161.

respecting, *prep.* considering; in view of: "Respecting what a rancorous mind he bears . . ." *2 Hen 6,* III, i, 24.

respective, *adj.* **1** careful: ". . . yet for your vehement oaths,/ You should have been respective and have kept it." *Merch,* V, i, 155–156. **2** arousing esteem; also, worth caring about: "What should it be that he respects in her,/ But I can make respective in myself . . ." *Two Gent,* IV, iv, 192–193. **3** respectful: "'Tis too respective and too sociable/ For your conversion." *K John,* I, i, 188–189.

respective lenity, *n.* considerations of leniency or mercy: "Away to heaven respective lenity,/ And fire-ey'd fury be my conduct now!" *Rom & Jul,* III, i, 125–126.

respectively, *adv.* respectfully; with all due respect: ". . . you are very respectively welcome, sir." *Timon,* III, i, 7.

respice finem, [Latin] wordplay on "respect your end [Judgment Day]" and "respect the rope's end," the penalty of crime: "Mistress, *respice finem,* respect your end, or/ rather, to prophesy like the parrot, beware the rope's/ end." *Errors,* IV, iv, 39–41.

respite, *n.* **1** delay: "This respite shook/ The bosom of my conscience . . ." *Hen 8,* II, iv, 179–180.
—*v.* **2** to grant a delay to: "Forty days longer we do respite you . . ." *Per,* I, i, 117.

responsive, *adj.* of matching design: "Three of the/ carriages, in faith, are very dear to fancy, very/ responsive to the hilts . . ." *Ham,* V, ii, 147–149.

rest[1], *n.* **1** peace of mind; also, mental stability: "'Tis his own blame; [he] hath put himself from rest,/ And must needs taste his folly." *Lear,* II, iv, 292–293. **2** renewed vigor: ". . . we, lying still,/ Are full of rest, defence, and nimbleness." *J Caes,* IV, iii, 200–201. **3 do you rest,** to give you peace of mind: "And I most . . . willingly,/ To do you rest, a thousand deaths would die." *T Night,* V, i, 130–131. **4 set up my rest,** made up my mind: ". . . but for mine own part, as I have set up/ my rest to run away . . ." *Merch,* II, ii, 98–99.

—*v.* **5** wordplay on "breathing spell" and "arrest": ". . . the man, sir, that when/ gentlemen are tired gives them a sob, and rests them . . ." *Errors,* IV, iii, 23–24. **6 rest you fair,** conventional greeting: "Rest you fair, good signior . . ." *Merch,* I, iii, 54. **7 rest you merry,** conventional words of leave-taking: "Ye say honestly; rest you merry." *Rom & Jul,* I, ii, 62. **8 there rest,** Hold on to that opinion: "There rest./ Your partner, as I hear, must die tomorrow." *Meas,* II, iii, 36–37.

rest[2], *n.* **1** (in gambling) a last stake or throw: ". . . when I cannot live any longer,/ I will do as I may: that is my rest . . ." *Hen 5,* II, i, 15–16. **2 set up one's rest,** to be fully determined; venture or stake all; here, with more wordplay on "arrest": ". . . he that sets up his rest to do/ more exploits with his mace than a morris-pike." *Errors,* IV, iii, 26–27.

rest[3], *v.* **1** to remain: "What then? What rests?/ Try what repentance can." *Ham,* III, iii, 64–65.
—*n.* **2 armed rest,** remainder of the armed faction: ". . . the all-honour'd, honest Roman, Brutus,/ With the arm'd rest . . ." *Ant & Cleo,* II, vi, 16–17.

re-stem, *v.* to retrace; steer again: ". . . and now they do restem/ Their backward course . . . towards Cyprus . . ." *Oth,* I, iii, 37–39.

restful, *adj.* peaceful; undisturbed: "'Is not my arm of length,/ That reacheth from the restful English court/ As far as Callice, to mine uncle's head?" *Rich 2,* IV, i, 11–13.

resting, *adj.* changeless; stable: ". . . the northern star,/ Of whose true-fix'd and resting quality/ There is no fellow . . ." *J Caes,* III, i, 60–62.

restitution, *n.* Cupid grants the pleasure he previously denied Falstaff: "Why, now is Cupid a child of/ conscience: he makes restitution." *Wives,* V, v, 28–29.

restless, *adj.* ceaseless: ". . . blown with restless violence round about/ The pendent world . . ." *Meas,* III, i, 124–125.

restrain, *v.* to withhold: ". . . the gods will plague thee/ That thou restrain'st from me the duty . . ." *Cor,* V, iii, 166–167.

restrained, *adj.* forbidden; here, illegitimate child compared with counterfeit coin: ". . . to put mettle [metal?] in restrained means/ To make a false one." *Meas,* II, iv, 48–49.

restraint, *n.* prison: "Your gaoler shall deliver you the keys/ That lock up your restraint." *Cymb,* I, ii, 4–5.

resty, *adj.* inactive; also, lazy or sluggish: "A prince call'd Hector . . . Who in this dull and long-continu'd truce/ Is resty grown." *Tr & Cr,* I, iii, 260–262.

resume, *v.* **1** to assume; take: "... resumes no care/ Of what is to continue." *Timon,* II, i, 4–5. **2** to take back: "That opportunity ... to resume/ We have again." *Cymb,* III, i, 15–17.

retail, *v.* **1** to hand down; here, to succeeding generations: "Methinks the truth should live from age to age,/ As 'twere retail'd to all posterity ..." *Rich 3,* III, i, 76–77. **2** tell; relate: "... he is furnish'd with no certainties/ More than he haply may retail from me." *2 Hen 4,* I, i, 31–32.

retention, *n.* **1** ability to retain [or contain] such strong emotion: "... no woman's heart/ So big, to hold so much: they lack retention." *T Night,* II, iv, 96–97. **2** reserve; reservation: "His life I gave him, and did thereto add/ My love, without retention or restraint ..." *T Night,* V, i, 78–79. **3** confinement: "To send the old and miserable King/ To some retention ..." *Lear,* V, iii, 47–48. **4** container or retainer; here, ref. to the tables: "That poor retention could not so much hold ..." *Sonn 122,* 9.

retentive, *adj.* restraining; confining: "... must my house/ Be my retentive enemy, my gaol?" *Timon,* III, iv, 79–80.

retire, *n.* **1** withdrawal: "... all his behaviours did make their retire/ To the court of his eye ..." *Love's L,* II, i, 233–234. **2** retreat: "Oft have I heard his praises in pursuit,/ But ne'er till now his scandal of retire." *3 Hen 6,* II, i, 149–150.
—*v.* **3** to retreat: "Ne'er may he live to see a sunshine day,/ That cries 'Retire,' if Warwick bid him stay." *3 Hen 6,* II, i, 187–188. **4** to draw back: "Each one by him enforc'd, retires his [its] ward ..." *Luc,* 303. **5** to go back (to): "And, with an accent tun'd in self-same key,/ Retires to chiding fortune." *Tr & Cr,* I, iii, 53–54.

retired, *adj.* withdrawn from society: "Hearing you were retir'd, your friends fall'n off ..." *Timon,* V, i, 58.

retirement, *n.* withdrawal from company; act of seeking privacy: "And never noted in him any study,/ Any retirement, any sequestration ..." *Hen 5,* I, i, 57–58.

retort, *v.* **1** to reject; refuse: "The Duke's unjust/ Thus to retort your manifest appeal ..." *Meas,* V, i, 298–299. **2** to give or send back; reflect: "... and they retort that heat again/ To the first giver." *Tr & Cr,* III, iii, 101–102.

retrograde, *adj.* contrary: "For your intent/ In going back to school in Wittenberg,/ It is most retrograde to our desire ..." *Ham,* I, ii, 112–114.

return, *n.* **1** [often pl.] the result of efforts, as on another's behalf: "... I'll pawn my victories, all/ My honour to you, upon his good returns [in the belief that he will make good return]." *Timon,* III, v, 82–83.

—*v.* **2** to inform: "... let the trumpets sound,/ While we return these dukes what we decree." *Rich 2,* I, iii, 121–122.

revel, *v.* **1** to pass, spend, waste, etc., in reveling: "... drink, dance,/ Revel the night, rob, murder, and commit/ The oldest sins the newest kind of ways?" *2 Hen 4,* IV, v, 124–126. **2 revel it,** to feast; participate in revelry: "And revel it as bravely as the best ..." *Shrew,* IV, iii, 54.

revengement, *n.* divine punishment: "... in his secret doom out of my blood/ He'll breed revengement and a scourge for me." *1 Hen 4,* III, ii, 6–7.

Revenge the heavens! Let Heaven take revenge!: "Revenge the heavens for old Andronicus!" *T Andr,* IV, i, 129.

revenue, *n.* **1** source of income: "... your having in beard is a younger brother's revenue." *As You,* III, ii, 367–368. **2** inheritance: "Like to a step-dame or a dowager/ Long withering out a young man's revenue." *M N Dream,* I, i, 5–6. **3** profit or reward; also, advantage or benefit: "... a promis'd glory/ As smiles upon the forehead of this action/ For the wide world's revenue." *Tr & Cr,* II, ii, 205–207.

reverb, *v.* appar. coined var. of **reverberate:** "Nor are those empty-hearted whose low sounds/ Reverb no hollowness." *Lear,* I, i, 153–154.

reverberate, *adj.* reverberating; resounding: "Halloo your name to the reverberate hills ..." *T Night,* I, v, 276.

reverence, *n.* **1** veneration due age: "Repair those violent harms that my two sisters/ Have in thy reverence made!" *Lear,* IV, vii, 28–29. **2** period when one is venerated: "And, in thy reverence and thy chair-days ..." *2 Hen 6,* V, ii, 48. **3 saving your reverence,** apologetic phrase uttered before making a rude or irreverent remark: "I should be ruled by the fiend, who/ (saving your reverence) is the devil himself ..." *Merch,* II, ii, 24–25.

reverend, *adj.* **1** deserving respect: "Very reverend sport, truly: and done in the/ testimony of a good conscience." *Love's L,* IV, ii, 1–2. **2** dignified: "... consequently/ sets down the manner how: as, a sad face, a/ reverend carriage ..." *T Night,* III, iv, 72–73. **3** aged: "You stubborn ancient knave, you reverend braggart,/ We'll teach you." *Lear,* II, ii, 127–128.

reverent, *adj.* **1** var. of **reverend;** revered: "... by my fathers' reverent tomb I vow/ They shall be ready at your highness' will ..." *T Andr,* II, iii, 296–297.
—*adv.* **2** reverently: "How may I reverent worship thee enough?" *1 Hen 6,* I, ii, 145.

reverse, *n.* See **punto reverso.**

reversion, *n.* **1** portion or inheritance to come: "A sweet reversion—we may boldly spend/ Upon the hope of what is to come in." *1 Hen 4,* IV, i, 54–55. **2 in reversion, a.** (of property) in the act of reverting to its original owner: "As were our England in reversion his . . ." *Rich 2,* I, iv, 35. **b.** with the hope of future possession or enjoyment: ". . . no perfection in reversion/ shall have a praise in present." *Tr & Cr,* III, ii, 91–92.

reverted, *adj.* being in revolt; here, in wordplay suggesting a receding hairline, the result of venereal disease (the "French disease"): "Where France?"/ "In her forehead, armed and reverted, making/ war against her heir." *Errors,* III, ii, 120–122.

re-view, *v.* to see again: "I shall re-view Sicilia, for whose sight/ I have a woman's longing." *W Tale,* IV, iv, 666–667.

revokement, *n.* act of revoking; revocation: ". . . let it be nois'd/ That through our intercession this revokement/ And pardon comes . . ." *Hen 8,* I, ii, 105–107.

revolt[1]**,** *n.* **1** revulsion: ". . . the palate,/ That suffers surfeit, cloyment, and revolt . . ." *T Night,* II, iv, 99–100. **2** inconstancy; faithlessness: "Since that my life on thy revolt doth lie . . ." *Sonn 92,* 10.

revolt[2]**,** *n.* **1** rebel: "And you degenerate, you ingrate revolts . . ." *K John,* V, ii, 151.
—*v.* **2** to return to one's previous allegiance: "The King is merciful, if you revolt." *2 Hen 6,* IV, ii, 119.

revolted, *adj.* **1** being a deserter or rebel; rebellious: "To ransom home revolted Mortimer." *1 Hen 4,* I, iii, 91. **2** false-hearted; faithless: "Farewell, revolted fair!" *Tr & Cr,* V, ii, 185.

revolution, *n.* **1** [often pl.] turning over of thoughts or ideas: ". . . a foolish/ extravagant spirit, full of forms, figures, shapes, objects . . . motions, revolutions . . ." *Love's L,* IV, ii, 64–66. **2** turning of the wheel of Fortune; hence, change: "Here's fine revolution and [if] we had the trick to see't." *Ham,* V, i, 89. **3 by revolution lowering,** lessened in intensity by the turn of events [as on Fortune's wheel]: "The present pleasure,/ By revolution lowering, does become/ The opposite of itself . . ." *Ant & Cleo,* I, ii, 121–123.

revolve, *v.* **1** to reflect; consider: "If this fall into thy hand, revolve." *T Night,* II, v, 143. **2** to think over; ponder: "Revolving this will teach thee how to curse." *Rich 3,* IV, iv, 123. **3 revolve and ruminate himself,** [that which] concerns itself or is preoccupied with him: ". . . never suffers matter of the world/ Enter his thoughts, save such as do revolve/ And ruminate himself . . ." *Tr & Cr,* II, iii, 187–189.

re-word, *v.* to echo: ". . . whose concave womb re-worded/ A plaintful story from a sistering vale . . ." *Lover's Comp,* 1–2.

rhapsody, *n.* jumble: ". . . and sweet religion makes/ A rhapsody of words." *Ham,* III, iv, 47–48.

Rhenish, *n.* Rhine wine: "And as he drains his draughts of Rhenish down,/ The kettle-drum and trumpet thus bray out . . ." *Ham,* I, iv, 10–11.

Rhesus, *n.* Thracian prince and Priam's ally in the Trojan war: "With sleight and manhood stole to Rhesus' tents . . ." *3 Hen 6,* IV, ii, 20.

rhetoric, *n.* **1** skill in speaking: "And practise rhetoric in your common talk . . ." *Shrew,* I, i, 35. **2 still rhetoric,** silent eloquence: ". . . the heart's still rhetoric disclosed with eyes . . ." *Love's L,* II, i, 228.

rheum, *n.* **1** tears; crying: ". . . an hour in clamour and a quarter/ in rheum." *M Ado,* V, ii, 76–77. **2** watery discharge from eyes or nose: ". . . I guess it stood in her/ chin, by the salt rheum that ran between France/ and it." *Errors,* III, ii, 125–127. **3** catarrh, a respiratory inflamation: "Do curse the gout, serpigo, and the rheum . . ." *Meas,* III, i, 31. **4** saliva; spittle: ". . . whose low vassal seat/ The Alps doth spit and void his rheum upon . . ." *Hen 5,* III, v, 51–52. **5 salt and sullen rheum,** dismal running cold: "I have a salt and sullen rheum offends me . . ." *Oth,* III, iv, 47.

rheumatic, *adj.* poss. misuse for "choleric": "You are both i'/ good truth as rheumatic as two dry toasts . . ." *2 Hen 4,* II, iv, 55–56.

Rhodope, *n.* Greek courtesan, who married an Egyptian king; some accounts say she used her own wealth to build the great pyramid of Memphis: "A statelier pyramis to her I'll rear/ Than Rhodope's of Memphis ever was . . ." *1 Hen 6,* I, vi, 21–22.

rhubarb, *n.* plant, esp. the root, used as a purgative: "What rhubarb, cyme or what purgative drug,/ Would scour these English hence?" *Mac,* V, iii, 55–56.

rhyme, *n.* [often pl.] poem(s); poetry; verses: "Thou, thou, Lysander, thou hast given her rhymes,/ And interchang'd love-tokens with my child . . ." *M N Dream,* I, i, 28–29.

rhymer, *n.* poet [term of contempt]: ". . . and scald rhymers/ Ballad us out o' tune." *Ant & Cleo,* V, ii, 214–215.

Rialto, *n.* commercial heart of Venice: "What news on the/ Rialto?" *Merch,* I, iii, 33–34.

rib, *v.* to enclose: ". . . it were too gross/ To rib her cerecloth in the obscure grave . . ." *Merch,* II, vii, 50–51.

ribald, *adj.* raucous or rude; here, prob. the omens of calamity: "Wak'd by the lark, hath rous'd the ribald crows . . ." *Tr & Cr,* IV, ii, 9.

ribaudred, *adj.* lewd; lascivious [lit., "easily mounted"]: "Yon ribaudred nag of Egypt,—/ Whom leprosy o'ertake! . . ." *Ant & Cleo,* III, x, 10–11.

rich, *adj.* **1** precious; dear: "This ring he holds/ In most rich choice . . ." *All's W,* III, vii, 25–26. **2 no richer than his honor,** having no wealth except his honor: ". . . to the certain hazard/ Of all incertainties, himself commended,/ No richer than his honour . . ." *W Tale,* III, ii, 168–170.
—*n.* **3** [pl.] rich persons: "If he do, the rich shall have more [rich in foolishness, you will be made even richer]." *Tr & Cr,* I, ii, 200.

richest, *adj.* most experienced: "Whose beauty did astonish the survey/ Of richest eyes . . ." *All's W,* V, iii, 16–17.

Richmond, *n.* here introduced as "young Henry, Earl of Richmond"; later defeats Richard III and ascends throne as Henry VII. *3 Hen 6,* IV, vi, 67.

rid¹, *v.* to destroy: "The red plague rid you/ For learning me your language!" *Temp,* I, ii, 366–367.

rid², *v.* past part. of **ride. 1** ridden: "Brutus and Cassius/ Are [have] rid like madmen through the gates of Rome." *J Caes,* III, ii, 270–271. **2** [in many editions, **ride**] to cover by riding: "How many score of miles may we well rid/ 'Twixt hour, and hour?" *Cymb,* III, ii, 68–69.

riddle, *v.* to speak confusingly; talk in riddles: "This i s a riddling merchant for the nonce . . ." *1 Hen 6,* II, iii, 56.

ride, *v.* **bay where all men ride,** place where any ship can anchor [nautical term]; also, euphem. for "loose woman": "If eyes . . . Be anchored in the bay where all men ride . . ." *Sonn 137,* 5–6.

rider, *n.* trainer: ". . . they are taught their manage, and to that end/ riders dearly hired . . ." *As You,* I, i, 12–13.

ridge, *n.* **1** top or crest; here, of waves: "Whose ridges with the meeting clouds contend . . ." *Ven & Ad,* 820. **2** ridge or apex of a roof: ". . . leads fill'd and ridges hors'd [straddled]/ With variable complexions, all agreeing . . ." *Cor,* II, i, 209–210.

riding-rod, *n.* switch used by a rider: "And if my legs were two such riding-rods . . ." *K John,* I, i, 140.

rid the world, gone from the world; here, executed or murdered: "This Gloucester should be quickly rid the world,/ To rid us from the fear we have of him." *2 Hen 6,* III, i, 233–234.

Rien puis? [French] nothing more?; here, used ironically: "Rien puis? l'air et le feu [why not air and fire, too?]!" *Hen 5,* IV, ii, 5.

rifle, *v.* to rob; strip of valuables: "If not, we'll make you sit, and rifle you." *Two Gent,* IV, i, 4.

rift, *n.* **1** fissure or crevice: ". . . within which rift/ Imprison'd thou didst painfully remain . . ." *Temp,* I, ii, 277–278.
—*v.* **2** to split: ". . . to the dread rattling thunder/ Have I given fire, and rifted Jove's stout oak/ With his own bolt . . ." *Temp,* V, i, 44–46.

riggish, *adj.* wanton; lewd: ". . . the holy priests/ Bless her, when she is riggish." *Ant & Cleo,* II, ii, 239–240.

right, *adj.* **1** true; proper: "I am a right maid for my cowardice . . ." *M N Dream,* III, ii, 302. **2** direct or straight, and often typical: "It is the right butter-women's rank to market." *As You,* III, ii, 95–96. **3** typical: "Like a right gipsy, hath at fast and loose/ Beguil'd me . . ." *Ant & Cleo,* IV, xii, 28–29. **4 right form,** regular or proper order: "Fierce fiery warriors fight upon the clouds/ In ranks and squadrons and right form of war . . ." *J Caes,* II, ii, 19–20.
—*adv.* **5** unmistakably: ". . . I do see the cruel pangs of death/ Right in thine eye." *K John,* V, iv, 59–60. **6** very: "You are right courteous knights." *Per,* II, iii, 27. **7 right on, a.** directly; straight: "I only speak right on." *J Caes,* III, ii, 225. **b.** straight ahead: ". . . sometimes they do extend/ Their view right on . . ." *Lover's Comp,* 25–26. **8 stand too right,** be situated too far to the right [Alexander's neck was said to be twisted somewhat to the left]: "Your nose says, no, you are not; for it stands too right." *Love's L,* V, ii, 561.
—*n.* **9** justice; fairness: "No humble suitors press to speak for right . . ." *3 Hen 6,* III, i, 19. **10** something rightfully belonging to one; due: "Be the death-divining swan,/ Lest the requiem lack his right." *Phoen,* 15–16. **11 in right of,** in support of the rightful claims of: "Knighted in field, slain manfully in arms,/ In right and service of their noble country." *T Andr,* I, i, 196–197. **12 right for right,** just reward of just claims: ". . . say that right for right/ Hath dimm'd your infant morn to aged night." *Rich 3,* IV, iv, 15–16. **13 rights by rights falter,** individual rights must sometimes be sacrificed for the common good: "Rights by rights falter, strengths by strengths do fail." *Cor,* IV, vii, 55.
—*v.* **14** to vindicate: "You scarce can right me throughly, then, to say/ You did mistake." *W Tale,* II, i, 99–100.

right-hand file, *n.* position of the best soldiers in a formation, parade, etc.: "Do you two know how you are/ censured here in the city . . . of us o'th'right-hand file?" *Cor,* II, i, 20–22.

rightly, *adv.* directly: "Like perspectives, which, rightly gaz'd upon,/ Show nothing but confusion . . ." *Rich 2,* II, ii, 18–19.

rigol, *n.* ring or circle; here, the crown: ". . . this is a sleep/ That from this golden rigol hath divorc'd/ So many English kings." *2 Hen 4,* IV, v, 34–36.

rigor, *n.* **1** relentless force or severity: ". . . like as rigour of tempestuous gusts/ Provokes the mightiest hulk against the tide . . ." *1 Hen 6,* V, v, 5–6. **2** cruelty; viciousness: "Or more than common fear of Clifford's rigour . . ." *3 Hen 6,* II, i, 126.

rigorous, *adj.* relentless; merciless: "He shall be thrown down the Tarpeian rock/ With rigorous hands . . ." *Cor,* III, i, 264–265.

rim, *n.* diaphragm: ". . . I will fetch thy rim out at thy throat/ In drops of crimson blood." *Hen 5,* IV, iv, 14–15.

rime, *n.* var. of **rhyme:** "Only I carried winged time/ Post on the lame feet of my rime . . ." *Per,* IV, Chor., 47–48.

rimer, *n.* var. of **rhymer:** "Than those old nine which rimers invocate . . ." *Sonn 38,* 10.

rind, *n.* covering; here, of a budding flower: "Within the infant rind of this weak flower/ Poison hath residence . . ." *Rom & Jul,* II, iii, 19–20.

ring, *v.* **1** to blow: ". . . rouse the prince, and ring a hunter's peal,/ That all the court may echo with the noise." *T Andr,* II, ii, 5–6. **2** to announce: "No funeral rite, nor man in mourning weed,/ No mournful bell shall ring her burial . . ." *T Andr,* V, iii, 196–197. **3 ring in,** to celebrate with the ringing of bells: ". . . a cough, sir, which I caught/ with ringing in the King's affairs . . ." *2 Hen 4,* III, ii, 177–178.
—*n.* **4** [in jousting] the sport of riding at a metal ring and spearing it with a lance: "He that runs fastest gets the ring." *Shrew,* I, i, 140. **5** wordplay on "finger ring" and "female pudenda": ". . . while I live, I'll fear no other thing/ So sore, as keeping safe Nerissa's ring." *Merch,* V, i, 306–307. **6** [pl.] the eye sockets: ". . . and in this habit/ Met I my father with his bleeding rings . . ." *Lear,* V, iii, 187–188. **7 cracked within the ring,** (of a coin) clipped or shaved within the stamped circle (to obtain the precious metal) and not accepted as legal tender; wordplay on loss of female virginity: ". . . like a/ piece of uncurrent gold, be not cracked within the/ ring." *Ham,* II, ii, 423–424.

ring-carrier, *n.* go-between; pimp: "Marry, hang you!"/ "And your curtsy, for a ring-carrier!" *All's W,* III, v, 90–91.

ringlets, *n. pl.* **1** circular dances; fairy dances: "To dance our ringlets in the whistling wind . . ." *M N Dream,* II, i, 86. **2**

green sour ringlets, rings in the grass surrounding mushrooms, supposedly left by the dancing elves, actually caused by the mushroom's roots: ". . . you demi-puppets that/ By moonshine do the green sour ringlets make . . ." *Temp,* V, i, 36–37.

ring-time, *n.* time when wedding rings are exchanged: "In spring-time, the only pretty ring-time . . ." *As You,* V, iii, 17.

Ringwood, *n.* typical name for a hound: "Or go thou, like Sir Actaeon he,/ With Ringwood at thy heels." *Wives,* II, i, 115–116.

riot, *n.* **1** revelry; extravagant entertainment: ". . . he will neither know how to maintain it,/ Nor cease his flow of riot." *Timon,* II, i, 2–3. **2** riotous living; debauchery: ". . . 'gainst the stream of virtue they may strive,/ And drown themselves in riot!" *Timon,* IV, i, 27–28. **3** internal strife; political upheaval: "What wilt thou do when riot is thy care?" *2 Hen 4,* IV, v, 135.

rioter, *n.* person given to riotous living: "He's a sworn rioter;/ he has a sin/ That often drowns him . . ." *Timon,* III, v, 68–69.

riotous, *adj.* **1** unrestrained; here, also seditious: "And therefore shall it charm thy riotous tongue." *2 Hen 6,* IV, i, 64. **2** noisy; tumultuous: ". . . young Laertes, in a riotous head,/ O'erbears your officers." *Ham,* IV, v, 101–102.

ripe, *v.* **1** to grow or become ripe; ripen: "And so from hour to hour, we ripe, and ripe . . ." *As You,* II, vii, 26. **2** to build, increase, or replenish: "He is retir'd to ripe his growing fortunes/ To Scotland . . ." *2 Hen 4,* IV, i, 13–14.
—*adj.* **3** prepared; ready: "There is a brief how many sports are ripe . . ." *M N Dream,* V, i, 42. **4** needing satisfaction at once: "Yet to supply the ripe wants of my friend,/ I'll break a custom . . ." *Merch,* I, iii, 58–59. **5** showing good reason [for]: "Give scandal to the blood o' th' prince, my son . . . Without ripe moving to 't?" *W Tale,* I, ii, 330–332. **6** (of the lips) resembling ripe fruit in being red and full: "O how ripe in show/ Thy lips, those kissing cherries, tempting grow!" *M N Dream,* III, ii, 139–140.

ripely, *adv.* urgently: "It fits us therefore ripely/ Our chariots and our horsemen be in readiness . . ." *Cymb,* III, v, 22–23.

ripeness, *n.* readiness; here, for death: "Men must endure/ Their going hence, even as their coming hither:/ Ripeness is all." *Lear,* V, ii, 9–11.

riper, *adj.* later: "And stops her pipe in growth of riper days . . ." *Sonn 102,* 8.

riping, *n.* fullness; completion: "Slubber not business for my sake, Bassanio,/ But stay the very riping of the time [until your business is properly conducted] . . ." *Merch,* II, viii, 39–40.

ripped, *past part.* discarded or destroyed: "And, for I am richer than to hang by th' walls,/ I must be ripp'd . . ." *Cymb,* III, iv, 53–54.

rise, *v.* to become erect: ". . . flesh stays no farther reason,/ But rising at thy name doth point out thee/ As his triumphant prize." *Sonn 151,* 8–10.

rising, *adj.* thriving; becoming famous, prosperous, great, etc.: "The other . . . yet so famous,/ So excellent in art, and still so rising . . ." *Hen 8,* IV, ii, 61–62.

rivage, *n.* shore; bank: "O, do but think/ You stand upon the rivage and behold/ A city . . ." *Hen 5,* III, Chor., 13–15.

rival, *n.* **1** partner: "Horatio and Marcellus,/ The rivals of my watch . . ." *Ham,* I, i, 13–14. —*v.* **2** to compete: "We first address toward you, who with this king/ Hath rivall'd for our daughter." *Lear,* I, i, 190–191.

rivality, *n.* equality; partnership: "Caesar, having made use of him in the wars 'gainst/ Pompey, presently denied him rivality . . ." *Ant & Cleo,* III, v, 6–7.

rive, *v.* **1** to split: "I have seen tempests, when the scolding winds/ Have riv'd the knotty oaks . . ." *J Caes,* I, iii, 5–6. **2** to fire; discharge: "To rive their dangerous artillery/ Upon no Christian soul but English Talbot." *1 Hen 6,* IV, ii, 29–30. **3 rive not more,** create no greater split: "The soul and body rive not more in parting/ Than greatness going off." *Ant & Cleo,* IV, xiii, 5–6.

rivelled, *adj.* wrinkled or shriveled: ". . . the rivelled/ fee-simple [complete ownership] of the tetter, take and take again . . ." *Tr & Cr,* V, i, 21–22.

Rivo!, *interj.* exhortation to drinkers, poss. of Spanish origin: "Rivo!/ says the drunkard . . ." *1 Hen 4,* II, iv, 108–109.

road, *n.* **1** roadstead or anchorage; harbor: "Go, hie thee presently, post to the road . . ." *Errors,* III, ii, 146. **2** period of riding; stage: "At last, with easy roads, he came to Leicester . . ." *Hen 8,* IV, ii, 17. **3** whore: "This Doll Tearsheet should be some road." *2 Hen 4,* II, ii, 159. **4** inroads; incursion: ". . . the Volsces stand but as at first,/ Ready . . . to make road/ Upon's again." *Cor,* III, i, 4–6. **5 out of the road,** giving up the usual practice: "I'll do anything now that is virtuous; but I am/ out of the road of rutting for ever." *Per,* IV, v, 8–9.

roam, *v.* to surge or sweep: "Say, shall the current of our right roam on?" *K John,* II, i, 335.

roan, *n.* horse, usually having a reddish coat mixed with grey or white: "What horse? A roan, a crop-ear is it not?" *1 Hen 4,* II, iii, 70.

roast, *n.* **rules the roast,** domineers or takes precedence at the feast: ". . . the new-made duke that rules the roast . . ." *2 Hen 6,* I, 1, 108.

robe, *n.* symbol of high office: "O, this life/ Is . . . Richer than doing nothing for a robe . . ." *Cymb,* III, iii, 21–23.

robed, *adj.* Lear mistakes Tom's blanket for a justice's robe: "Thou robed man of justice, take thy place . . ." *Lear,* III, vi, 37.

robustious, *adj.* loud and coarse; here, ranting: ". . . to hear a robustious, periwig-pated fellow/ tear a passion to tatters . . ." *Ham,* III, ii, 9–10.

rock, *v.* to tremble; shake: "Which strook her sad, and then it [her hand] faster rock'd . . ." *Luc,* 262.

rod, *n.* incursion or inroad: ". . . burn their neighbour towns, and so persist/ With eager rods beyond their city, York . . ." *Edw 3,* I, ii, 24–25.

roe, *n.* small, nimble-footed deer: ". . . thy greyhounds are as swift/ As breathed stags, ay, fleeter than the roe." *Shrew,* Ind., ii, 48–49.

rogue, *n.* **1** rascal: "Come hither, you rogue. What, have you forgot/ me?" *Shrew,* V, i, 42–43. **2 settled in rogue,** settled down to being a rogue: ". . . and, having flown over/ many knavish professions, he settled only in rogue." *W Tale,* IV, iii, 95–96.

roguing, *adj.* prob. sense of "roaming" or "roving": "These roguing thieves serve the great pirate Valdes . . ." *Per,* IV, i, 96.

roguish madness, *n.* [being] both a vagabond and madman: ". . . his roguish madness/ Allows itself to any thing [lets him do anything]." *Lear,* III, vii, 103–104.

roisting, *adj.* boisterous: "I have a roisting challenge sent amongst/ The dull and factious nobles of the Greeks . . ." *Tr & Cr,* II, ii, 209–210.

rolling, *pres. part.* (of eyes) roving; wandering: "An eye more bright than theirs, less false in rolling . . ." *Sonn 20,* 5.

rolls, *n.* **Master of the Rolls,** member of the Judicial Committee, the keeper of the rolls, patents, and grants that pass the great seal: ". . . Cromwell,/ Beside that of the jewel-house, is made master/ O'th'rolls, and the king's secretary . . ." *Hen 8,* V, i, 33–35.

Roman, *n.* **1** perh. by association with "triumph" Cassio is hailed as a conquering Roman: "Do you triumph, Roman, do you triumph?" *Oth,* IV, i, 118. **2 antique Roman,** one who would commit suicide at such a moment: "I am more an antique Roman than a Dane./ Here's yet some liquor left." *Ham,* V, ii, 346–347.

Roman Brutus, *n.* See **Brutus** (def. 3).

Roman disciplines, *n.* Roman military tactics; here, conventional warfare: ". . . the true disciplines of the wars, look/ you, of the Roman disciplines . . ." *Hen 5,* III, ii, 76–77.

Roman fool, *n.* ref. to Antony, Brutus, and other noble suicides: "Why should I play the Roman fool, and die/ On mine own sword?" *Mac,* V, viii, 1–2.

Romano, *n.* Julio Romano, painter and sculptor of the early 16th cent.; an anachronism here: ". . . newly performed by/ that rare Italian master, Julio Romano . . ." *W Tale,* V, ii, 95–96.

Romish, *adj.* Roman [used contemptuously]: ". . . to mart/ As in a Romish stew [brothel] . . ." *Cymb,* I, vii, 151–152.

rondure, *n.* earthly sphere: ". . . all things rare/ That heaven's air in this huge rondure hems." *Sonn 21,* 7–8.

ronyon, *n.* [as term of abuse] scabby creature: "'Aroynt thee, witch!' the rump-fed ronyon cries." *Mac,* I, iii, 6.

rood, *n.* cross; crucifix: "an early stirrer, by the/ rood!" *2 Hen 4,* III, ii, 2–3.

roof, *n.* **1** roof of the mouth: "And swearing till my very roof was dry/ With oaths of love . . ." *Merch,* III, ii, 204–205. **2** family fortunes: "Seeking that beauteous roof to ruinate . . ." *Sonn 10,* 7.

roofed, *past part.* housed under one roof: "Here had we now our country's honour roof'd,/ Were the grac'd person of our Banquo present . . ." *Mac,* III, iv, 39–40.

rook, *v.* **1** to crouch; here, perch: "The raven rook'd her on the chimney's top . . ." *3 Hen 6,* V, vi, 47.
—*n.* **2 bully rook,** fine fellow: "What says my bully rook? Speak scholarly and/ wisely." *Wives,* I, iii, 2–3.

rooky, *adj.* inhabited by rooks; here also, dark and ominous: "Light thickens; and the crow/ Makes wing to th' rooky wood . . ." *Mac,* III, ii, 50–51.

room, *n.* **1** place; here, at the table: "And let Bianca take her sister's room." *Shrew,* III, ii, 248.
—*interj.* **2** make room! stand aside!: "But room, fairy! Here comes Oberon." *M N Dream,* II, i, 58.

root, *n.* **cleft the root,** split the very foundation; here, of her heart: "How oft hast thou with perjury cleft the root!" *Two Gent,* V, iv, 102.

rooted, *adj.* sincere; deeply felt: "I could/ not have owed her a more rooted love." *All's W,* IV, v, 11–12.

rootedly, *adv.* wholeheartedly: ". . . they all do hate him/ As rootedly as I." *Temp,* III, ii, 92–93.

rope, *n.* **rope of destiny,** hangman's rope: ". . . make the rope of his destiny our cable, for/ our own doth little advantage." *Temp,* I, i, 31–32.

ropery, *n.* knavery or roguery; lewd jesting: ". . . what saucy merchant was this,/ that was so full of his ropery?" *Rom & Jul,* II, iv, 142–143.

rope's end, *n.* length of rope, esp. one used for whippings, hangings, etc.: "You sent me for a rope's end, sir, as soon . . ." *Errors,* IV, i, 99.

rope tricks, poss. misuse for "rhetoric(s)": ". . . and he begin once, he'll rail in/ his rope-tricks." *Shrew,* I, ii, 110–111.

roping, *adj.* hanging or drooping like rope; also, perh., congealing: "Let us not hang like roping icicles . . ." *Hen 5,* III, v, 23.

Roscius, *n.* Roman actor of the lst cent. B.C.; called the greatest actor of the ancient world: "My lord, I have news to tell you. When Roscius was/ an actor in Rome—" *Ham,* II, ii, 386–387.

rose, *n.* **1** symbol of beauty and perfection, here represented by Hamlet: "Th'expectancy and rose of the fair state . . ." *Ham,* III, i, 154. **2** rosette: ". . . with Provincial/ roses on my razed shoes . . ." *Ham,* III, ii, 270–271. **3 the Rose,** manor house belonging to Buckingham: "The duke being at the Rose, within the parish/ Saint Lawrence Poultney [London] . . ." *Hen 8,* I, ii, 152–153.

rosemary, *n.* herb symbolizing remembrance: "Dry up your tears, and stick your rosemary/ On this fair corse . . ." *Rom & Jul,* IV, v, 79–80.

Rossillion, *n.* French province bordering Spain: "Rossillion. The Count's palace." [SD] *All's W,* I, i, 1.

roted, *adj.* learned by rote; memorized: "But with such words that are but roted in/ Your tongue . . ." *Cor,* III, ii, 55–56.

rotten, *adj.* **1** rusted: "Enter Richard and Buckingham in rotten armour, marvellous ill-favoured." [SD] *Rich 3,* III, v, 1. **2** causing rot: "To lose itself in a fog, where, being three parts/ melted away with rotten dews . . ." *Cor,* II, iii, 31–32. **3** rotting, esp. with disease: ". . . to be detected with a jealous/ rotten bell-wether . . ." *Wives,* III, v, 100–101.

rotten and sound, diseased and healthy: ". . . the muster-file, rotten and sound . . . amounts not to fifteen thousand poll . . ." *All's W,* IV, iii, 162–163.

rotten smoke, *n.* foul odors: "Hiding thy bravery in their rotten smoke?" *Sonn 34,* 4.

rough, *adj.* **1** difficult: "Give even way unto my rough affairs . . ." *2 Hen 4,* II, iii, 2. **2** (of a horse) unbroken: "He hath rid his prologue like a rough colt . . ." *M N Dream,* V, i, 119. **3** harsh; menacing: ". . . be not too rough in terms,/ For he is fierce and cannot brook hard language." *2 Hen 6,* IV, ix, 43–44. **4** violent; uncontrollable: ". . . the fiend/ is rough, and will not be roughly used." *T Night,* III, iv, 112–113. **5** cruel; sadistic: "Thou stern, indurate, flinty, rough, remorseless." *3 Hen 6,* I, iv, 142. **6** dull and unresponsive: ". . . beauty's princely majesty is such/ Confounds the tongue and makes the senses rough." *1 Hen 6,* V, iii, 70–71. **7** shaggy: "Thou want'st a rough pash [head] and the shoots that I have/ To be full like me . . ." *W Tale,* I, ii, 128–129.

rough-cast, *n.* plaster mixed with gravel for coating exterior walls: ". . . let him/ have some plaster, or some loam, or some rough-cast/ about him, to signify wall . . ." *M N Dream,* III, i, 63–65.

rough magic, *n.* command of physical forces, appar. considered rudimentary sorcery: "But this rough magic/ I here abjure . . ." *Temp,* V, i, 50–51.

roughness, *n.* rudeness: ". . . having been prais'd for bluntness, doth affect/ A saucy roughness . . ." *Lear,* II, ii, 97–98.

round¹, *adj.* **1** outspoken; frank or blunt: "He will not hear, till feel./ I must be round with him . . ." *Timon,* II, i, 7–8. **2** harsh; here, in wordplay with "spherical": "Am I so round with you, as you with me,/ That like a football you do spurn me thus?" *Errors,* II, i, 82–83. **3** severe; heavy: ". . . and on your heads/ Clap round fines for neglect . . ." *Hen 8,* V, iii, 78–79. —*v.* **4** to encircle: ". . . within the hollow crown/ That rounds the mortal temples of a king . . ." *Rich 2,* III, ii, 160–161. **5** to surround; hem [in]: "How rank soever rounded in with danger." *Tr & Cr,* I, iii, 196. **6** to grow round in pregnancy:

"The queen your mother rounds apace: we shall/ Present our services to a fine new prince . . ." *W Tale,* II, i, 16–17. —*n.* **7** round dance: "If you will patiently dance in our round,/ And see our moonlight revels, go with us . . ." *M N Dream,* II, i, 140–141. **8** same, but with added meaning of leading the players in a circular [roundabout] way: "I'll lead you about a round!/ Through bog, through bush, through brake, through briar . . ." *M N Dream,* III, i, 101–102. **9** (in horsemanship) circular movement: "What rounds, what bounds, what course, what stop he makes!" *Lover's Comp,* 109. **10 round and top,** crown: "And wears upon his baby brow the round/ And top of sovereignty?" *Mac,* IV, i, 88–89. —*adv.* **11** uprightly; honestly: "But in our orbs we'll live so round and safe . . ." *Per,* I, ii, 122. **12** without hesitation; straight; direct: "No, I went round to work,/ And my young mistress thus I did bespeak . . ." *Ham,* II, ii, 139–140. **13 Does the world go round?** Cymbeline appar. experiences dizziness. *Cymb,* V, v, 232.

round², *v.* to whisper: "And France . . . rounded in the ear/ With that same purpose-changer, that sly divel . . ." *K John,* II, i, 564–567.

roundel, *n.* round dance: "Come, now a roundel and a fairy song . . ." *M N Dream,* II, ii, 1.

roundest, *adj.* bluntest; rudest: "Sir, he answered me in the roundest manner, he would not." *Lear,* I, iv, 56.

round hose, *n.* men's short ballooned trousers covering only the hips: "A round hose, madam, now 's not worth a pin/ Unless you have a cod-piece to stick pins on." *Two Gent,* II, vii, 55–56.

roundly, *adv.* **1** at once; promptly: "Shall we clap into't roundly, without hawking or spitting . . . ?" *As You,* V, iii, 9–10. **2** to the point or subject: "Well, how then? Come, roundly, roundly." *1 Hen 4,* I, ii, 22. **3** plainly or frankly; bluntly: "He that is giddy thinks the world turns round."/ "Roundly replied." *Shrew,* V, ii, 20–21. **4** freely; brazenly: "This tongue that runs so roundly in thy head/ Should run thy head from thy unreverent shoulders." *Rich 2,* II, i, 122–123. **5** outrageously: "That take it on you at the first so roundly." *Shrew,* III, ii, 212. **6 come roundly,** speak plainly: "Petruchio, shall I then come roundly to thee." *Shrew,* I, ii, 58.

round underborne, having the under edge of the skirt lined: ". . . skirts, round underborne with a bluish tinsel . . ." *M Ado,* III, iv, 20.

roundure, *n.* roundness [fr. belief that circular walls were easier to defend]: "'Tis not the roundure of your old-fac'd walls/ Can hide you . . ." *K John,* II, i, 259–260.

rouse[1], *v.* **1** (in hunting) to chase (game) from the lair: "He should have found his uncle Gaunt a father/ To rouse his wrongs and chase them to the bay." *Rich 2*, II, iii, 126–127. **2 rouse me,** to raise (oneself) up: "When I do rouse me in my throne of France . . ." *Hen 5*, I, ii, 275.

rouse[2], *n.* **1** large cup of wine, drunk as a toast; bumper: ". . . the King's rouse the heaven shall bruit again,/ Re-speaking earthly thunder." *Ham*, I, ii, 127–128. **2** bout of drinking: "'. . . There was a gaming,' 'there o'ertook in's rouse' . . ." *Ham*, II, i, 58. **3 take one's rouse,** to carouse: "The King doth wake tonight and takes his rouse . . ." *Ham*, I, iv, 8.

rout, *n.* **1** crowd; here, the invited guests: "And after me, I know, the rout is coming." *Shrew*, III, ii, 179. **2** rabble; common herd: "Thou common whore of mankind, that puts odds/ Among the rout of nations . . ." *Timon*, IV, iii, 43–44. **3** a wicked band or company: ". . . Lady Eleanor, the Protector's wife,/ The ringleader and head of all this rout . . ." *2 Hen 6*, II, i, 161–162.

rover, *n.* rascal; here, used playfully: "Next to thyself, and my young rover, he's/ Apparent to my heart." *W Tale*, I, ii, 176–177.

row, *n.* stanza; here, of a ballad: "The first row of the pious chanson will show you/ more . . ." *Ham*, II, ii, 415–416.

rowel, *n.* wheellike spur: "A rider like myself, who ne'er wore rowel . . ." *Cymb*, IV, iv, 39.

rowel-head, *n.* spiked wheel of a spur: ". . . struck his armed heels/ Against the panting sides of his poor jade/ Up to the rowel-head . . ." *2 Hen 4*, I, i, 44–46.

Rowland, *n.* Roland, nephew of Charlemagne and hero of *The Song of Roland* and other medieval ballads: "Child Rowland to the dark tower came . . ." *Lear*, III, iv, 186.

royal, *n.* **1** gold coin, worth 10 shillings (used often in puns with "noble," a coin of less value): "Give him as much as will make him a royal man . . ." *1 Hen 4*, II, iv, 286.
—*adj.* **2** magnificent: "All was royal;/ To the disposing of it nought rebell'd . . ." *Hen 8*, I, i, 42–43.

royally, *adv.* decisively: ". . . it us concerns/ To answer royally in our defences." *Hen 5*, II, iv, 2–3.

royal mind, *n.* devotion to the king: ". . . the citizens/ I am sure have shown at full their royal minds . . ." *Hen 8*, IV, i, 7–8.

royal occupation, *n.* war, regarded as the work of kings: "That thou couldst see my wars to-day, and knew'st/ The royal occupation . . ." *Ant & Cleo*, IV, iv, 16–17.

royalty, *n.* **1** one's royal person: ". . . to his highness,/ Whose health and royalty I pray for." *Hen 8*, II, iii, 72–73. **2** [pl.] royal prerogatives: "The dominations, royalties and rights/ Of this oppressed boy . . ." *K John*, II, i, 176–177. **3** [pl.] privileges granted to a subject by the monarch: "Seek you to seize . . . The royalties and rights of banish'd Herford?" *Rich 2*, II, i, 189–190.

royalty of nature, *n.* royal blood: ". . . and in his royalty of nature/ Reigns that which would be fear'd . . ." *Mac*, III, i, 48–49.

roynish, *adj.* scurvy; disgusting or contemptible: ". . . the roynish clown, at whom so oft/ Your Grace was wont to laugh . . ." *As You*, II, ii, 8–9.

rub, *n.* **1** [often pl.] (in bowling) bump or other obstacle; in fig. use, difficulty: "'Twill make me think the world is full of rubs . . ." *Rich 2*, III, iv, 4.
—*v.* **2** (in bowling) to move gently or, perh., stealthily: "So, so; rub/ on and kiss the mistress [lightly touch the target ball]." *Tr & Cr*, III, ii, 48–49. **3** to hinder; impede: "Whose disposition . . . Will not be rubb'd nor stopp'd . . ." *Lear*, II, ii, 153–155.

rubbing, *n.* (in the game of bowls) the action of touching another bowl [ball] while in passage: ". . . challenge her to bowl."/ "I fear too much rubbing." *Love's L*, IV, i, 139–140.

rubbish, *n.* refuse or litter used to start a fire: "What trash is Rome,/ What rubbish, and what offal, when it serves . . . to illuminate/ So vile a thing as Caesar!" *J Caes*, I, iii, 108–111.

rubies, *n.* the lips; here, Imogen's: "But kiss, one kiss! Rubies unparagon'd . . ." *Cymb*, II, ii, 17.

rubious, *adj.* of a ruby color; ruby-red: "Diana's lip/ Is not more smooth and rubious . . ." *T Night*, I, iv, 31–32.

rub one's elbow, *v.* to express great satisfaction (presumably caused by an itching elbow): "One rubb'd his elbow thus, and fleer'd, and swore/ A better speech was never spoke before . . ." *Love's L*, V, ii, 109–110.

ruddiness, *n.* redness: "The ruddiness upon her lip is wet;/ You'll mar it if you kiss it . . ." *W Tale*, V, iii, 81–82.

ruddock, *n.* robin redbreast: ". . . the ruddock would/ With charitable bill . . . bring thee all this . . ." *Cymb*, IV, ii, 224–227.

ruddy drops, *n. pl.* blood: "You are . . . As dear to me as are the ruddy drops/ That visit my sad heart." *J Caes*, II, i, 288–290.

rude, *adj.* **1** harsh or brutal: "Thy tooth is not so keen . . . Although thy breath be rude . . ." *As You,* II, vii, 178–179. **2** rough: "And touching hers, make blessed my rude hand." *Rom & Jul,* I, v, 50. **3** ignorant; uncouth: "A crew of patches, rude mechanicals . . . Were met together to rehearse a play . . ." *M N Dream,* III, ii, 9–11. **4** ill-formed: ". . . those whom nature hath not made for store,/ Harsh, featureless and rude . . ." *Sonn 11,* 9–10.

rudeliest, *adj.* harshest; roughest: "Thou art the rudeliest welcome to this world/ That e'er was prince's child." *Per,* III, i, 30–31.

rudeness, *n.* **1** rough behavior: "His rudeness so with his authoriz'd youth . . ." *Love's Comp,* 104. **2** violence: "For the great swinge and rudeness of his poise . . ." *Tr & Cr,* I, iii, 207.

ruder, *adj.* more ungraceful or unpolished: ". . . salute my king/ With ruder terms, such as my wit [mind] affords . . ." *2 Hen 6,* I, i, 30.

rudesby, *n.* rude fellow; ruffian: "To give my hand . . . Unto a mad-brain rudesby, full of spleen . . ." *Shrew,* III, ii, 9–10.

rude will, *n.* sexual desire: "Two such opposed kings encamp them still/ In man as well as herbs: grace and rude will . . ." *Rom & Jul,* II, iii, 23–24.

rue, *n.* **1** bitter herb associated with repentance and divine grace: ". . . here in this place/ I'll set a bank of rue, sour herb of grace." *Rich 2,* III, iv, 104–105.
—*v.* **2** to grieve for; lament: "Was ever son so rued a father's death?" *3 Hen 6,* II, v, 109.

ruff, *n.* **1** elaborate ruffled collar: "God let me not live, but I will murder your ruff for/ this." *2 Hen 4,* II, iv, 131–132. **2** such collar as a symbol of stiff, unyielding attitudes: "Authority quite silenc'd by your brawl,/ And you in ruff of your opinions cloth'd . . ." *More,* II, iv, 78–79.

ruffian, *n.* **1** person of low character; one given to vices: "Did see her . . . Talk with a ruffian at her chamber-window . . ." *M Ado,* IV, i, 90–91.
—*v.* **2** to rage; bluster: "If it ha' ruffian'd so upon the sea . . ." *Oth,* II, i, 7.

ruffle¹, *v.* **1** to swagger, esp. in a rowdy or disorderly manner: "One fit to bandy with thy lawless sons,/ To ruffle in the commonwealth of Rome." *T Andr,* I, i, 312–313. **2** to be turbulent; bluster: ". . . the night comes on, and the bleak winds/ Do sorely ruffle . . ." *Lear,* II, iv, 302–303. **3** to treat roughly or violently: ". . . my hospitable favours/ You should not ruffle thus." *Lear,* III, vii, 40–41.

—*n.* **4** stir; bustle: ". . . the ruffle knew/ Of court, of city . . ." *Lover's Comp,* 58–59.

ruffle², *v.* **ruffle up,** to rouse to anger: ". . . there were an Antony/ Would ruffle up your spirits . . ." *J Caes,* III, ii, 229–230.

rugged, *adj.* wild or unruly; also, scowling: "Gentle my Lord, sleek o'er your rugged looks . . ." *Mac,* III, ii, 27.

rug-headed, *adj.* shaggy-haired: "We must supplant those rough rug-headed kerns . . ." *Rich 2,* II, i, 156.

ruin, *n.* **1** rubbish; refuse: ". . . how much honour/ Pick'd from the chaff and ruin of the times . . ." *Merch,* II, ix, 47–48. **2** downfall; here, collapse with wounds: ". . . my angry guardant stood alone,/ Tendering my ruin . . ." *1 Hen 6,* IV, vii, 9–10. **3 come all to ruin,** if worst comes to worst: "Come all to ruin; let/ Thy mother rather feel thy pride . . ." *Cor,* III, ii, 125–126.

ruinate, *v.* to ruin; destroy: "I will not ruinate my father's house,/ Who gave his blood to lime the stones together . . ." *3 Hen 6,* V, i, 86–87.

ruinous, *adj.* **1** ruined; wasted or destroyed: "Is yond despis'd and ruinous man my lord?" *Timon,* IV, iii, 462. **2** (of a wine cask) leaky or broken: ". . . you ruinous butt, you whoreson/ indistinguishable cur . . ." *Tr & Cr,* V, i, 27–28.

rule, *n.* **1** control of one's behavior: "He cannot buckle his distemper'd cause/ Within the belt of rule." *Mac,* V, ii, 15–16. **2** royal power: "A cutpurse of the empire and the rule . . ." *Ham,* III, iv, 99. **3** proper order or form: ". . . in such rule, that the Venetian law/ Cannot impugn you as you do proceed." *Merch,* IV, i, 174–175. **4** ruler or measure: ". . . slaves/ With greasy aprons, rules, and hammers shall/ Uplift us to the view." *Ant & Cleo,* V, ii, 208–210. **5 by the rule,** wordplay on "according to the law" and "as if made with a carpenter's ruler": "I have not kept my square, but that to come/ Shall all be done by the rule." *Ant & Cleo,* II, iii, 6–7.

ruminate, *v.* to think over carefully; consider: ". . . what I know/ Is ruminated, plotted, and set down . . ." *1 Hen 4,* I, iii, 267–268.

rummage, *n.* bustle; turmoil: ". . . the chief head/ Of this post-haste and rummage in the land." *Ham,* I, i, 109–110.

rumor, *n.* **1** noisy confusion; din: ". . . I pray you, bear me hence/ From forth the noise and rumour of the field . . ." *K John,* V, iv, 44–45. **2** repute or reputation: "Great is the rumour of this dreadful knight . . ." *1 Hen 6,* II, iii, 7.

rumorer, *n.* person who spreads rumors; here, a bringer of bad news: "Go see this rumourer whipp'd." *Cor,* IV, VI, 47.

rump-fed, *adj.* prob. big-bottomed; also, var. explained as "nut-fed" and "offal-fed": "'Aroynt thee, witch!' the rump-fed ronyon cries." *Mac,* I, iii, 6.

run, *v.* **1** to run away; retreat; also, poss. wordplay on "urinate": "We'll not run, Monsieur Monster."/ "Nor go neither . . ." *Temp,* III, ii, 17–18. **2** to function or operate; here, poss. in wordplay with "retreat": "What can go well, when we have run so ill?" *K John,* III, iii, 5. **3** to take or pursue: "And did entreat your highness to this course/ Which you are running here." *Hen 8,* II, iv, 214–215. **4 run by,** to dodge or ignore: "Which have for long run by the hideous law/ As mice by lions . . ." *Meas,* I, iv, 63–64. **5 run counter,** to follow the scent of game in the opposite direction; here, wordplay with "Counter," debtors prison: "A hound that runs counter, and yet draws dry-foot well . . ." *Errors,* IV, ii, 39. **6 runs me,** to extend on my side: "But mark how he bears his course, and runs me up/With like advantage on the other side . . ." *1 Hen 4,* III, i, 104–105.

runagate, *n.* **1** runaway; fugitive: "I cannot find those runagates, that villain/ Hath mock'd me." *Cymb,* IV, ii, 62–63. **2** renegade or outcast: "I'll send to one in Mantua,/ Where that same banish'd runagate doth live . . ." *Rom & Jul,* III, v, 88–89. **3** unfaithful husband: "More noble than that runagate to your bed . . ." *Cymb,* I, vii, 137.

runaway, *n.* **1** coward: ". . . our grace is only in our heels,/ And that we are most lofty [graceful] runaways." *Hen 5,* III, v, 34–35. **2** perh. referring to Phaeton and the sun god's runaway chariot: "Spread thy close curtain, love-performing night,/ That runaway's eyes may wink . . ." *Rom & Jul,* III, ii, 5–6.

running, *pres. part.* running out; emptying: "That satiate yet unsatisfied desire, that tub/ Both fill'd and running . . ." *Cymb,* I, vii, 48–49.

running banquet, *n.* **1** hasty meal; here, in wordplay with "sexual indulgence": "But half my lay-thoughts in him, some of these/ Should find a running banquet ere they rested . . ." *Hen 8,* I, iv, 11–12. **2** wordplay on extended feasting and the entertainment of two prisoners being whipped through the streets: ". . . like to/ dance these three days; besides the running banquet/ of two beadles that is to come." *Hen 8,* V, iii, 64–65.

runnion, *n.* ronyon; a scabby, mangy creature: ". . . you baggage, you polecat, you/ runnion, out, out!" *Wives,* IV, ii, 171–172.

rupture, *n.* breach of an agreement: "It is a rupture that you may easily heal . . ." *Meas,* III, i, 235.

rush, *n.* **1** long-stemmed marsh grass: "He's walking in the garden—thus, and spurns/ The rush that lies before him . . ." *Ant & Cleo,* III, v, 16–17. **2** [usually pl.] this grass used as a floor covering: "Is supper ready, the house/ trimmed, rushes strewed . . ." *Shrew,* IV, i, 40–41.

rush-candle, *n.* makeshift candle of a rush dipped in tallow or grease: ". . . if you please to call it a rush-candle,/ Henceforth I vow it shall be so for me." *Shrew,* IV, v, 14–15.

rush'd, *past part.* pushed or thrust; poss. misreading of "brush'd": ". . . the kind Prince,/ Taking thy part, hath rush'd aside the law . . ." *Rom & Jul,* III, iii, 25–26.

rushling, *adj.* Quickly's blunder for "rustling": ". . . and so rushling, I/ warrant you, in silk and gold . . ." *Wives,* II, ii, 63–64.

rushy, *adj.* full of or edged with rushes: ". . . by rushy brook,/ Or in the beached margent of the sea . . ." *M N Dream,* II, i, 84–85.

russet, *n.* **1** reddish-brown homespun: "Henceforth my wooing mind shall be express'd/ In russet yeas and honest kersey noes . . ." *Love's L,* V, ii, 412–413.
—*adj.* **2** of a generally reddish-brown color: ". . . the morn in russet mantle clad . . ." *Ham,* I, i, 171.

russet-pated, *adj.* ref. to jackdaw, whose head varies in color from dull brown to gray: "As wild geese that the creeping fowler eye,/ Or russet-pated choughs . . ." *M N Dream,* III, ii, 20–21.

rustically, *adv.* like a peasant: ". . . he keeps/ me rustically at home . . ." *As You,* I, i, 6–7.

ruth, *n.* **1** pity; compassion: "Looking with pretty ruth upon my pain." *Sonn 132,* 4. **2** another name for **rue;** here associated with pity: "Rue, even for ruth . . . In the remembrance of a weeping queen." *Rich 2,* III, iv, 106–107.

ruthful, *adj.* pitiful; woeful: "Ruthful to hear, yet piteously perform'd . . ." *T Andr,* V, i, 66.

Rutland, *n.* Earl of Rutland, Aumerle's title after being deprived of his dukedom: "Aumerle that was,/ But that is lost for being Richard's friend . . . you must call him Rutland now." *Rich 2,* V, ii, 41–43.

rutting, *n.* copulation: ". . . I am/ out of the road of rutting for ever." *Per,* IV, v, 9.

ruttish, *adj.* lustful: ". . . one Count Rossillion,/ a foolish idle boy, but for all that very ruttish." *All's W,* IV, iii, 206–207.

S

s', contraction of **so:** "... such as was never/ S'incapable of help." *Cor,* IV, vi, 120–121.

's, contraction of **us:** "Let's [go] to the Capitol." *Cor,* IV, vi, 160.

sa, *interj.* (in hunting) a call, esp. to urge hounds forward in the chase: "Come and you get it,/ you shall get it by running. Sa, sa, sa, sa." *Lear,* IV, vi, 203–204.

Saba, *n.* Queen of Sheba, who journeyed far to share King Solomon's wisdom: "Saba was never/ More covetous of wisdom and fair virtue ..." *Hen 8,* V, iv, 23–24.

sable, *n.* **1** black color: "His beard was grizzled, no?"/ "It was ... A sable silver'd." *Ham,* I, ii, 240–242. **2** [pl.] usually black or dark-colored garments; sometimes, sable-trimmed garments: "... youth no less becomes/ The light and careless livery that it wears/ Than settled age his sables and his weeds ..." *Ham,* IV, vii, 77–79. **3 suit of sables,** sable-trimmed gown worn esp. by wealthy older men: "... let the devil wear black, for I'll/ have a suit of sables." *Ham,* III, ii, 127–128.

sable ground, *n.* black background, as on a coat of arms: "My sable ground of sin I will not paint ..." *Luc,* 1074.

sack¹, *n.* white wine of Spain: "... not in ashes and sackcloth, but in/ new silk and old sack." *2 Hen 4,* I, ii, 197–198.

sack², *v.* to loot, plunder, and destroy: "Was this fair face the cause, quoth she,/ Why the Grecians sacked Troy?" *All's W,* I, iii, 67–68.

sack³, *n.* **more sacks to the mill,** more work yet to do; more trouble to come [proverb]: "More sacks to the mill! O heavens! I have my wish ..." *Love's L,* IV, iii, 78.

sackbut, *n.* bass wind instrument, forerunner of the trombone: "The trumpets, sackbuts, psalteries and fifes ..." *Cor,* V, iv, 50.

Sackerson, *n.* famous bear of the day: "I have seen/ Sackerson loose twenty times ..." *Wives,* I, i, 270–271.

sacrament, *n.* **take the sacrament,** swear an oath; take a solemn vow: "A dozen of them here have ta'en the sacrament ... To kill the king at Oxford." *Rich 2,* V, ii, 97.

sacred, *adj.* dedicated: "... her sacred wit/ To villainy and vengeance consecrate ..." *T Andr,* II, i, 120–121.

sacrificing, *adj.* epithet of Abel, who made sacrifices to God and was in turn slaughtered by his brother Cain: "Which blood, like sacrificing Abel's, cries/ Even from the tongueless caverns of the earth ..." *Rich 2,* I, i, 104–105.

sacring bell, *n.* bell used in the Mass; here, prob. post-Reformation sense of bell announcing morning prayers: "I'll startle you/ Worse than the sacring bell, when the brown wench/ Lay kissing in your arms, lord cardinal." *Hen 8,* III, ii, 294–296.

sad, *adj.* **1** serious; sober; grave: "But speak you this with a sad brow ...?" *M Ado,* I, i, 169–170. **2** dreary; dismal: "Thus, in this strange and sad habiliment,/ I will encounter with Andronicus ..." *T Andr,* V, ii, 1–2. **3** melancholy: "Which is the way [fashion]? Is it/ sad, and few words?" *Meas,* III, ii, 49–50.

sad decrees, *n.* serious decisions: "... to make me ope the door,/ That so my sad decrees may fly away ..." *T Andr,* V, ii, 10–11.

saddle-bow, *n.* fore part of a saddle: "And rein his proud head to the saddle-bow ..." *Ven & Ad,* 14.

sadly, *adv.* soberly, seriously, or gravely: "This can be no trick: the conference/ was sadly borne ..." *M Ado,* II, iii, 212–213.

sadness, *n.* **in (good) sadness,** seriously; in all seriousness: "Now, in good sadness, son Petruchio,/ I think thou hast the veriest shrew of all." *Shrew,* V, ii, 63–64.

safe, *adj.* **1** certain; sure: "I had thought, by making this well known unto you,/ To have found a safe redress . . ." *Lear,* I, iv, 213–214.
—*adv.* **2 safe and nicely,** cautiously and legally correct: "What safe and nicely I might well delay/ By rule of knighthood . . ." *Lear,* V, iii, 144–145. **3 safe toward,** so as to protect and insure: ". . . do but what they should, by doing everything/ Safe toward your love and honour." *Mac,* I, iv, 26–27.
—*v.* **4** to cause to feel safe concerning: ". . . that which most with you should safe my going,/ Is Fulvia's death." *Ant & Cleo,* I, iii, 55–56. **5** to conduct to safety: ". . . best you saf'd the bringer/ Out of the host . . ." *Ant & Cleo,* IV, vi, 26–27.

safe discretion, *n.* sound judgment: "Nor do I think the man of safe discretion/ That does affect it." *Meas,* I, i, 71–72.

safeguard, *n.* **on safeguard,** under safe-conduct: "On safeguard he came to me . . ." *Cor,* III, i, 9.

safer, *adj.* sounder; saner: "The safer sense will ne'er accommodate/ His master thus." *Lear,* IV, vi, 81–82.

safety, *n.* **1** safekeeping; detention: "Deliver him to safety, and return . . ." *K John,* IV, ii, 158. **2 in safety,** securely; under restraint: "Hold him in safety till the Prince come hither." *Rom & Jul,* V, iii, 182.

saffron, *n.* yellowish brown spice, used to color as well as lend flavor; ref. here to Parolles's cowardly color as well as his unwholesome influence on inexperienced youths: ". . . whose villainous saffron would have/ made all the unbak'd and doughy youth of a nation/ in his colour." *All's W,* IV, v, 2–4.

sage, *adj.* **1** solemn; somber: "We should profane the service of the dead/ To sing sage requiem and such rest to her . . ." *Ham,* V, i, 230. **2** prob. the sense of "be frank but be prudent": "How's this? how's this? Some more; be sage." *Per,* IV, vi, 94.
—*n.* **3 the sage,** those who are wise and serious: "This blur to youth, this sorrow to the sage . . ." *Luc,* 222.

Sagittar or **Sagittary,** *n.* inn whose sign showed Sagittary shooting an arrow [astrological sign of Sagittarius]: "Lead to the Sagittar the raised search,/ And there will I be with him." *Oth,* I, i, 158–159.

Sagittary, *n.* centaur that fought on the side of the Trojans: ". . . the dreadful Sagittary/ Appals our numbers." *Tr & Cr,* V, v, 14–15.

said, *past. part.* **1** had my say: "When I have said, make answer to us both." *K John,* II, i, 235. **2 well said,** well done: "So, so; come, give me that: this way; well said." *Ant & Cleo,* IV, iv, 28. **3 you have said now,** you've got the right idea; now

you're talking!: ". . . if not, assure yourself I'll seek satisfaction of you."/ "You have said now[!]" *Oth,* IV, ii, 201–202.

sail, *n.* **1** ship: "I have sixty sails, Caesar none better." *Ant & Cleo,* III, vii, 49. **2** fleet: "We have descried . . . A portly sail of ships make hitherward." *Per,* I, iv, 60–61. **3** prob. ref. to the Nurse's costume, poss. a black dress and white headdress: "Here's goodly gear . . . A sail! a sail!" *Rom & Jul,* II, iv, 100–101. **4** sailing; voyage: ". . . auspicious gales,/ And sail so expeditious, that shall catch/ Your royal fleet far off." *Temp,* V, i, 314–316. **5 my sail of greatness,** my powers under full sail: "I will keep my state,/ Be like a king and show my sail of greatness . . ." *Hen 5,* I, ii, 273–274. **6 strike sail,** to lower sails as the signal of a ship's surrender; here, humble oneself: "How many nobles then should hold their places/ That must strike sail to spirits of vile sort!" *2 Hen 4,* V, ii, 17–18.

sain, *v.* past part. of say; said: "Some obscure precedence that hath tofore been sain." *Love's L,* III, i, 80.

saint, *n.* **1** stone statue of a saint: "For saints have hands that pilgrims' hands do touch . . ." *Rom & Jul,* I, v, 98. **2** sanctimonious person: "Saints in your injuries [when you say spiteful things] . . ." *Oth,* II, i, 111.

Saint Albans, *n.* town NW of London: ". . . 'tis his Highness' pleasure/ You do prepare to ride unto Saint Albans . . ." *2 Hen 6,* I, ii, 56–57.

Saint Anne, *n.* mother of the Virgin Mary; a favorite oath: "Yes, by Saint Anne, do I. A good matter, surely." *Shrew,* I, i, 249.

Saint Bennet, *n.* Saint Benedict; perh. refers to church across the Thames from the Globe Theatre: ". . . or the bells of/ Saint Bennet, sir, may put you in mind—one, two,/ three." *T Night,* V, i, 36–38.

Saint Clare, *n.* founder of a 13th-century order of nuns at Assisi, noted for its strictness: ". . . wishing a more strict restraint/ Upon the sisters stood, the votarists of Saint Clare." *Meas,* I, iv, 4–5.

Saint Colme's Inch, *n.* Inchcomb, a small island near Edinburgh, in the Firth of Forth: ". . . he disbursed at Saint Colme's Inch/ Ten thousand dollars to our general use." *Mac,* I, ii, 63–64.

Saint Davy's day, *n.* March 1st, St. David's day, commemorating Welsh victory over the Saxons, when Welshmen wore leeks on their caps, as ordered by their patron saint, David: "Tell him, I'll knock his leek about his pate/ Upon Saint Davy's day." *Hen 5,* IV, i, 54–55.

Saint Denis, *n.* **1** patron saint of France: "Saint Denis to Saint Cupid! What are they/ That charge their breath against us?" *Love's L,* V, ii, 87–88. **2** the feast of Saint Denis, October 9th: "No longer on Saint Denis will we cry . . ." *1 Hen 6,* I, vi, 28.

Saint Edmundsbury, *n.* Bury St. Edmunds, ancient town in SE England: "Lords, I will meet him at Saint Edmundsbury . . ." *K John,* IV, iii, 11.

Saint Francis, *n.* inn with a figure of the saint painted on its sign: "At the Saint Francis here beside the port." *All's W,* III, v, 36.

Saint George, *n.* patron saint of England: "Mine innocence and Saint George to thrive!" *Rich 2,* I, iii, 84.

Saint George's Feast, *n.* April 23rd: "Bonfires in France forthwith I am to make/ To keep our great Saint George's feast withal." *1 Hen 6,* I, i, 153–154.

Saint George's Field, *n.* large open space on London's South Bank: "Soldiers, I thank you all; disperse yourselves:/ Meet me to-morrow in Saint George's Field . . ." *2 Hen 6,* V, i, 45–46.

Saint Jamy, *n.* prob. ref. to the apostle James in a ballad of the day: "Nay, by Saint Jamy,/ I hold you a penny . . ." *Shrew,* III, ii, 79–80.

Saint Jaques', *n.* prob. the shrine at Santiago de Compostela in NW Spain; "I am Saint Jaques' pilgrim, thither gone." *All's W,* III, iv, 4.

Saint Jeronimy, *n.* prob. confusion with "Saint Jerome": "Go by, Saint Jeronimy, go to thy/ cold bed and warm thee." *Shrew,* Ind. i, 7–8.

Saint Lambert's day, *n.* September 17th: ". . . your lives shall answer it,/ At Coventry upon Saint Lambert's day." *Rich 2,* I, i, 198–199.

Saint Martin's summer, *n.* Nov. 11, a feast marking Indian summer: "Expect Saint Martin's summer, halcyon's days,/ Since I have entered into these wars." *1 Hen 6,* I, ii, 131–132.

Saint Nicholas, *n.* patron saint of scholars: "[Giving him the paper] There; and Saint Nicholas be/ thy speed." *Two Gent,* III, i, 293–294.

Saint Nicholas' clerk or clergyman, *n.* highwayman: "Sirrah, if they meet not with Saint Nicholas' clerks,/ I'll give thee this neck." *1 Hen 4,* II, i, 60–61.

Saint Philip's daughters, *n.* four daughters of Philip, the evangelist, who were gifted with prophecy: "Nor yet Saint Philip's daughters, were like thee." *1 Hen 6,* I, ii, 143.

sake, *n.* **1 for my sake,** for the sake of friendship; here, a friendly loan: ". . . and I no question make/ To have it of my trust, or for my sake." *Merch,* I, i, 184–185. **2 for such a sake,** in a similar situation: "What I should do again for such a sake." *Lover's Comp,* 322.

Sala, *n.* river in E Germany; present-day, Saale: ". . . the land Salic is in Germany,/ Between the floods of Sala and of Elbe . . ." *Hen 5,* I, ii, 44–45.

salad days, *n.* period of youthful immaturity: "My salad days,/ When I was green in judgment, cold in blood . . ." *Ant & Cleo,* I, v, 73–74.

salamander, *n.* type of lizard believed to be able to live in fire: "I have maintained that salamander [nose] of yours with fire any/ time this two and thirty years . . ." *1 Hen 4,* III, iii, 46–47.

sale-work, *n.* something made, grown, etc., to be sold: "I see no more in you than in the ordinary/ Of Nature's sale-work." *As You,* III, v, 42–43.

Salic or **Salique,** *adj.* ref. to an early Frankish [French] law barring women from succeeding to the crown: "Why the law Salic that they have in France/ Or [either] should, or should not, bar us in our claim." *Hen 5,* I, ii, 11–12.

Salisbury, *n.* town SW of London, in Wiltshire: "And meet me suddenly at Salisbury." *Rich 3,* IV, iv, 451.

sallet¹, *n.* **1** salad, with wordplay on additional sense [fr. French] of "helmet": "Wherefore . . . have I climb'd into this garden, to see if I can/ eat grass, or pick a sallet . . . for many a time, but for a sallet, my brain-pan had/ been cleft with a brown bill . . ." *2 Hen 6,* IV, x, 6–12. **2** [pl.] salad greens: "We may pick/ a thousand sallets ere we light on such another herb." *All's W,* IV, v, 13–14. **3** witty, esp. bawdy, remark: ". . . there were no sallets in the/ lines to make the matter savoury . . ." *Ham,* II, ii, 437–438.

sallet², *n.* helmet; here, in wordplay with "salad": ". . . but for a sallet, my brain-pan had/ been cleft with a brown bill . . ." *2 Hen 6,* IV, x, 11–12.

sallied, *adj.* See **sullied** (def. 2).

sally, *n.* bursting forth of attacking troops from a besieged place: "No notes of sally, for the heavens, sweet brother." *Tr & Cr,* V, iii, 14.

salt, *adj.* **1** lustful; also, lecherous or lascivious: "Make use of thy salt hours . . ." *Timon,* IV, iii, 86. **2** bitter: ". . . the pride and salt scorn of his eyes . . ." *Tr & Cr,* I, iii, 371.

—*n.* **3** youthful exuberance: "We have some salt of our youth in us." *Wives,* II, iii, 50. **4 drops of salt,** tears; here, those of his mother and wife: ". . . given up,/ For certain drops of salt, your city Rome . . ." *Cor,* V, vi, 92–93. **5 man of salt,** man of tears: "Why this would make a man a man of salt . . ." *Lear,* IV, vi, 197.

salt-butter, *adj.* having inferior tastes: "Hang him, mechanical salt-butter rogue!" *Wives,* II, ii, 267.

Saltiers, *n.* poss. coinage combining "satyrs" and "sault" [jump]: ". . . have made themselves all men of hair, they call themselves/ Saltiers . . ." *W Tale,* IV, iv, 327–328.

saltness, *n.* zest, esp. as the result of experience: ". . . some smack of age in you,/ some relish of the saltness of time . . ." *2 Hen 4,* I, ii, 96–97.

salt wash, *n.* ocean's tides: "Neptune's salt wash and Tellus' orbed ground . . ." *Ham,* III, ii, 151.

salt-water girdle, *n.* seas surrounding Britain: ". . . if you seek us afterwards . . . you shall find us in our salt-water/ girdle . . ." *Cymb,* III, i, 79–81.

salute, *v.* **1** to greet; hail: "But if the prince do live, let us salute him . . ." *Per,* II, iv, 27. **2 salute my blood,** pleasure me: "Would I had no being/ If this salute my blood a jot . . ." *Hen 8,* II, iii, 102–103.

salvage, *n.* misuse for "savage": "Do you/ put tricks upon 's with salvages and men of Ind, ha?" *Temp,* II, ii, 58–59.

salve, *n.* **1** remedy; here, prob. an apology or repentance: "For no man well of such a salve can speak . . ." *Sonn 34,* 7. —*v.* **2** to smooth or soften; make less harsh or abrupt: "But lest my liking might too sudden seem/ I would have salv'd it with a longer treatise." *M Ado,* I, i, 294–295.

same, *pron.* she; the one: ". . . tell me now what lady is the same/ To whom you swore a secret pilgrimage . . ." *Merch,* I, i, 119–120.

Samingo, *n.* tag line from a popular drinking song; perh. a slurring of "San Domingo"; also, poss. ref. to Latin "mingo," I urinate: "Do me right [match me drink for drink],/ And dub me knight:/ Samingo." *2 Hen 4,* V, iii, 72–74.

sampire, *n.* samphire, an aromatic herb that was sometimes pickled: ". . . half way down/ Hangs one that gathers sampire, dreadful trade!" *Lear,* IV, vi, 14–15.

sample, *n.* example: ". . . most prais'd, most lov'd;/ A sample to the youngest . . ." *Cymb,* I, i, 47–48.

sampler, *n.* a piece of embroidery containing a quotation, maxim, etc.: "We, Hermia . . . Have with our needles created both one flower,/ Both on one sampler . . ." *M N Dream,* III, ii, 203–205.

Samsons and Goliases, *n.* ref. to the Biblical strongmen, Samson and Goliath: "For none but Samsons and Goliases/ It sendeth forth to skirmish." *1 Hen 6,* I, ii, 33–34.

sancta majestas, [Latin] sacred majesty: "Ah! sancta majestas, who'd not buy thee dear?" *2 Hen 6,* V, i, 5.

sanctify, *v.* **sanctifies himself,** blesses himself [as though he has touched something holy]: "Our general himself/ makes a mistress of him, sanctifies himself with's/ hand . . ." *Cor,* IV, v, 199–201.

sanctimony, *n.* **1** [usually pl.] sacred things: "If souls guide vows, if vows be sanctimonies . . ." *Tr & Cr,* V, ii, 138. **2** quality of being sacred or holy: "If sanctimony be the gods' delight . . ." *Tr & Cr,* V, ii, 139. **3** solemn rite; here, wedding: "If/ sanctimony, and a frail vow, betwixt an erring barbarian,/ and a super-subtle Venetian . . ." *Oth,* I, iii, 355–357.

sanctuarize, *v.* to protect from punishment: "No place indeed should murder sanctuarize . . ." *Ham,* IV, vii, 126.

sand, *n.* [pl.] sand in an hourglass: ". . . nimbler than the sands/ That run i' th' clock's behalf." *Cymb,* III, ii, 73–74.

Sandal Castle, *n.* located in Yorkshire, near Wakefield. *3 Hen 6,* [SD] I, ii, 1.

sand-bag, *n.* sand-filled bag used as a weapon: ". . . he enters bearing his staff with a sand-bag/ fastened to it . . ." *2 Hen 6,* II, iii, 58.

sand-blind, *adj.* partially blind: ". . . this is my true-begotten father,/ who being more than sand-blind . . . knows me not . . ." *Merch,* II, ii, 33–35.

sanded, *adj.* of a sandy color: "My hounds are bred out of the Spartan kind,/ So flew'd, so sanded . . ." *M N Dream,* IV, i, 118–119.

sanguine, *adj.* **1** giving the appearance of courage, valor, and the like: "This sanguine/ coward, this bed-presser, this horse-back-breaker . . ." *1 Hen 4,* II, iv, 237–238. **2** ruddy-faced (in contrast to black): ". . . ye sanguine, shallow-hearted boys!/ Ye white-lim'd walls!" *T Andr,* IV, ii, 97–98. **3** blood-red: "Guiderius had/ Upon his neck a mole, a sanguine star . . ." *Cymb,* V, v, 364–365.

sans, *prep.* without: ". . . the throat shall cut,/ And mince it sans remorse." *Timon,* IV, iii, 123–124.

sap, *n.* life or vitality; here, assurance of success: "I am bound to you:/ There is some sap in this." *W Tale,* IV, iv, 565–566.

sappy, *adj.* full of sap: "Torches are made to light . . . and sappy plants to bear . . ." *Ven & Ad,* 165.

sarcenet or **sarsenet,** *n.* silk cloth of the finest and most delicate texture: "And givest such sarcenet [lightweight] surety for thy oaths . . ." *1 Hen 4,* III, i, 245.

Sardis, *n.* ancient city in western Asia Minor: "Coming from Sardis, on our former ensign/ Two mighty eagles fell . . ." *J Caes,* V, i, 80–81.

sarsenet, *n.* See **sarcenet.**

Sarum, *n.* Salisbury; the site of Camelot was thought to be in nearby Winchester and inhabited by flocks of geese: "Goose, if I had you upon Sarum plain,/ I'd drive ye cackling home to Camelot." *Lear,* II, ii, 84–85.

sate, *v.* old past tense of **set;** ignored; other editors give as "shent," rebuked or reviled: "He sate our messengers, and we lay by/ Our appertainings, visiting of him." *Tr & Cr,* II, iii, 81–82.

satire, *n.* **be a satire to decay,** inspire me with a satire on the ruins of time: "If Time have any wrinkle graven there;/ If any, be a satire to decay . . ." *Sonn 100,* 10–11.

satirical, *adj.* ironic; sardonic: "The nightingale sings of adulterate wrong,/ And that, compared, is too satirical . . ." *Edw 3,* II, I, 111–112.

satisfaction, *n.* **1** recompense; amends: "Edward, what satisfaction canst thou make/ For bearing arms, for stirring up my subjects . . ." *3 Hen 6,* V, v, 14–15. **2 heavy satisfaction,** sad realization; here, of the hopelessness of the situation: ". . . she ceas'd/ In heavy satisfaction, and would never/ Receive the ring again." *All's W,* V, iii, 99–101.

satisfice, *v.* old var. of **satisfy:** "So should I rob my sweet sons of their fee:/ No, let them satisfice their lust on thee." *T Andr,* II, iii, 179–180.

satisfy, *v.* **1** to confirm; verify or corroborate: "I will set down what comes/ from her, to satisfy my remembrance . . ." *Mac,* V, i, 31–32. **2** to comfort; mollify: "How will my mother . . . Take on with me and ne'er be satisfied!" *3 Hen 6,* II, v, 103–104. **3** to recompense or repay: "There must I be unloos'd, although not there/ At once and fully satisfied . . ." *Hen 8,* II, iv, 145–146.

Satis quid sufficit, [Latin] Whatever satisfies suffices. *Love's L,* V, i, 1.

Saturn, *n.* **1** [in Roman myth.] father of the god Jupiter: "To Saturn, Caius, not to Saturnine;/ You were as good to shoot against the wind." *T Andr,* IV, iii, 55–56. **2** [in astrology] the sign and planet governing gloomy, cold, and unfeeling people: ". . . though Venus govern your desires,/ Saturn is dominator over mine . . ." *T Andr,* II, iii, 30–31.

satyr, *n.* (in Greek mythology) a lecherous creature, usually represented as half man and half goat: "So excellent a king, that was to this/ Hyperion to a satyr . . ." *Ham,* I, ii, 139–140.

sauce, *v.* to charge (someone) exorbitantly: "They shall have my horses, but I'll make them pay;/ I'll sauce them." *Wives,* IV, iii, 8–9.

saucy, *adj.* **1** insolent; badly behaved: "Go to, go to./ You are a saucy boy. Is't so indeed?" *Rom & Jul,* I, v, 81–82. **2** annoying or tormenting: ". . . I am cabin'd, cribb'd, confin'd, bound in/ To saucy doubts and fears." *Mac,* III, iv, 23–24. **3** wanton; lascivious: "When saucy trusting of the cozen'd thoughts/ Defiles the pitchy night . . ." *All's W,* IV, iv, 23–24. **4 saucy roughness,** impudent rudeness: ". . . doth affect/ A saucy roughness, and constrains the garb . . ." *Lear,* II, ii, 97–98. **5 saucy sweetness,** illicit sexual pleasure: ". . . to remit/ Their saucy sweetness that do coin heaven's image . . ." *Meas,* II, iv, 44–45.

save, *conj.* **1** except for the fact: ". . . save/ that he comes not along with her." *All's W,* III, ii, 1–2.
—*prep.* **2** except: ". . . never none/ Shall mistress be of it, save I alone." *T Night,* III, i, 161–162.

save thee, May God save thee [used as a salutation]: "Save thee, Curan."/ "And you, sir." *Lear,* II, i, 1–2.

saving, *prep.* with no disrespect to: "Saving your tale, Petruchio, I pray/ Let us that are poor petitioners speak too." *Shrew,* II, i, 71–72.

saving your reverence, respectful apology: "I think you would/ have me say, saving your reverence, 'a husband.'" *M Ado,* III, iv, 29–30.

savor, *n.* **1** fragrance or perfume: "In those freckles live their savours." *M N Dream,* II, i, 13. **2 simple savor,** simple tastes, as plain food: "For compound sweet forgoing simple savour . . ." *Sonn 125,* 7.
—*v.* **3 savor nobly,** to have a certain nobility: ". . . a savage jealousy/ That sometime savours nobly." *T Night,* V, i, 117–118.

savory, *adj.* pungent; zestful: ". . . there were no sallets in the/ lines to make the matter savoury . . ." *Ham,* II, ii, 436–437.

Savoy, *n.* palace in London, near the Inns of Court [actually destroyed 1381 in the Peasants' Revolt and not rebuilt till the early 1500's]: "Now go some and pull down the Savoy;/ others to the Inns of Court . . ." *2 Hen 6,* IV, vii, 1–2.

saw¹, *n.* platitude pointing up a moral; wise saying: "When all aloud the wind doth blow,/ And coughing drowns the parson's saw . . ." *Love's L,* V, ii, 913–914.

saw², *n.* sighs likened to a carpenter's saw that pushes grief away yet promptly draws it back again: "Even so his sighs,/ his sorrows make a saw,/ To push grief on and back the same/ grief draw." *Luc,* 1672–1673.

saw³, past tense of **see;** saw each other: "How have ye done/ Since last we saw in France?" *Hen 8,* I, i, 1–2.

sawn, *past part.* of **see;** seen; in some editions, "sown," spread, as seed: "For on his visage was in little drawn/ What largeness thinks in Paradise was sawn." *Lover's Comp,* 90–91.

sawpit, *n.* open pit over which wood was sawed: "Let them from forth a sawpit rush at once . . ." *Wives,* IV, iv, 53.

sawyer, *n.* worker who saws lumber: "Enter Cade, Dick Butcher, Smith the Weaver, and a/ Sawyer, with infinite numbers." [SD] *2 Hen 6,* IV, ii, 30.

say¹, *v.* **1** to speak; talk: "Young lad, come forth; I have to say with you." *K John,* IV, i, 8. **2 as who should say,** as though to say: "As who should say, 'I am Sir Oracle,/ And when I ope my lips, let no dog bark.'" *Merch,* I, i, 93–94. **3 How sayest thou?** What do you make of this?: "How say'st thou, that Macduff denies his person,/ At our great bidding?" *Mac,* III, iv, 127–128. **4 say'st me so?** Do you really mean that?: "No, say'st me so, friend? What countryman?" *Shrew,* I, ii, 188. **5 what 'tis to say,** what I'm trying to say; what I mean: "Your honour knows what 'tis to say well enough." *Per,* IV, vi, 30. —*n.* **6** taste or trace: ". . . thy tongue some say of breeding breathes . . ." *Lear,* V, iii, 143.

say², *n.* heavy silk fabric, similar to serge; here, wordplay with name of Lord Say: "Ah, thou/ say, thou serge, nay, thou buckram lord!" *2 Hen 6,* IV, vii, 22–23.

'say'd, *past part.* shortened form of **assayed;** attempted: "Of all, 'say'd yet, may'st thou prove prosperous!/ Of all, 'say'd yet, I wish thee happiness." *Per,* I, i, 60–61.

saying, *n.* way of talking: "Talk with a man out at a window!/ A proper/ saying!" *M Ado,* IV, i, 308–309.

'Sblood, *interj.* (by God)'s blood (a mild oath): "'Sblood, I am as melancholy/ as a gib cat, or a lugged bear." *1 Hen 4,* I, ii, 71–72.

scab, *n.* rascal; scoundrel; also, wordplay on Wart's name: "Well said, i'faith,/ Wart, th'art a good scab." *2 Hen 4,* III, ii, 270–271.

scaffold, *n.* wooden stage: ". . . hath dar'd/ On this unworthy scaffold to bring forth/ So great an object . . ." *Hen 5,* Prol. 9–11.

scaffoldage, *n.* wooden framework of the stage: ". . . the wooden dialogue and sound/ 'Twixt his stretch'd footing and the scaffoldage . . ." *Tr & Cr,* I, iii, 156.

scald, *adj.* scurvy or scabby; contemptible: ". . . and scald rhymers [poets]/ Ballad us out o' tune." *Ant & Cleo,* V, ii, 214–215.

scale¹, *n.* **1 equal scale,** equal measure: "In equal scale weighing delight and dole . . ." *Ham,* I, ii, 13. —*v.* **2** to weigh [and discover lacking moral character]: ". . . the poor Mariana advantaged, and the corrupt deputy/ scaled." *Meas,* III, i, 255–256.

scale², *n.* **1** graduated amount: ". . . they take the flow of the Nile/ By certain scales i' the pyramid . . ." —*v.* **2** to move upward: "Whose ranks of blue veins, as his hand did scale . . ." *Luc,* 440.

scaled sculls, *n.* schools of fish: ". . . like scaled sculls/ Before the belching whale . . ." *Tr & Cr,* V, v, 22–23.

scall, *adj.* var. of **scald;** contemptible: ". . . to be revenge on this same/ scall, scurvy, cogging companion . . ." *Wives,* III, i, 110–111.

scalp, *n.* head or skull: "And gentle Puck, take this transformed scalp/ From off the head of this Athenian swain . . ." *M N Dream,* IV, i, 63–64.

scaly, *adj.* (of armor) made of overlapping pieces of metal: "A scaly gauntlet now with joints of steel/ Must glove this hand . . ." *2 Hen 4,* I, i, 146–147.

scamble, *v.* to scramble: ". . . and England now is left/ To tug and scamble . . ." *K John,* IV, iii, 145–146.

scambling, *adj.* **1** disorderly; contentious: ". . . the scambling and unquiet time/ Did push it out of farther question." *Hen 5,* I, i, 4–5. —*n.* **2** struggling; scuffling: "I get thee with scambling, and/ thou must therefore needs prove a good/ soldier-breeder." *Hen 5,* V, ii, 213–215.

scamel, *n.* poss. type of shellfish [sea-mel] or a young seabird [sea-mell]: ". . . sometimes I'll get thee/ Young scamels from the rock." *Temp,* II, ii, 171–172.

scan, *v.* to weigh or consider; study; examine: "Strange things I have in head . . . Which must be acted, ere they may be scann'd." *Mac,* III, iv, 138–139.

scandal, *n.* **1** disrepute or disgrace: "The dram of evil/ Doth all the noble substance often dout/ To his own scandal." *Ham,* I, iv, 38.
—*v.* **2** to slander: "Scandal'd the suppliants for the people, call'd them/ Time-pleasers, flatterers . . ." *Cor,* III, i, 43–44.

scandaled, *adj.* scandalous; here, because of Cupid's mischievous capers: "Her and her blind boy's scandal'd company/ I have forsworn." *Temp,* IV, i, 90–91.

scandalized, *adj.* being the cause of scandal; disgraced: "I fear me it will make me scandalis'd." *Two Gent,* II, vii, 61.

scant, *adj.* **1** sparing; withholding: "From this time/ Be something scanter of your maiden presence . . ." *Ham,* I, iii, 120–121.
—*v.* **2** to restrict: "But if my father had not scanted me . . ." *Merch,* II, i, 17. **3** to make brief: "Therefore I scant this breathing courtesy." *Merch,* V, i, 141. **4** to reduce or cut: ". . . to cut off my train,/ To bandy hasty words, to scant my sizes . . ." *Lear,* II, iv, 176–177. **5** to stint on: "Doth, like a miser, spoil his coat with scanting/ A little cloth." *Hen 5,* II, iv, 47–48.

scanted, *adj.* offering little with reluctance; grudging: ". . . return and force/ Their scanted courtesy." *Lear,* III, ii, 66–67.

scantling, *n.* degree; sample: ". . . for the success . . . shall give a scantling/ Of good or bad unto the general . . ." *Tr & Cr,* I, iii, 340–342.

scape or **'scape,** *v.* **1** to escape: ". . . but if we haply scape . . . We shall to London get, where you are lov'd . . ." *2 Hen 6,* V, ii, 79–81.
—*n.* **2** [pl.] [narrow] escapes: "To smile at scapes and perils overblown." *Shrew,* V, ii, 3. **3** sexual transgression or escapade: "'For day,' quoth she, 'night's 'scapes doth open lay . . .'" *Luc,* 747.

scaped, *past part.* escaped: "Most royal Sir . . . Fleance is scap'd." *Mac,* III, iv, 19.

scar, *n.* **1** wound: "When I bestrid thee in the wars, and took/ Deep scars to save thy life . . ." *Errors,* V, I, 191–192. **2 have scar for,** to deserve because of battle wounds: ". . . hath/ More of thee merited than a band of Clotens/ Had ever scar for." *Cymb,* V, v, 303–305. **3 scar to scorn,** a wound resulting from an insult: "Let Paris bleed, 'tis but a scar to scorn . . ." *Tr & Cr,* I, i, 111.

scarce, *adv.* seldom; rarely: ". . . those that she makes fair, she scarce makes honest . . ." *As You,* I, ii, 36–37.

scarce-bearded, *adj.* slighting ref. to Octavius's youth [he was actually 23]: ". . . who knows/ If the scarce-bearded Caesar have not sent/ His powerful mandate to you . . ." *Ant & Cleo,* I, i, 21–22.

scarf, *v.* **1** to wrap around: "Up from my cabin,/ My sea-gown scarf'd about me . . ." *Ham,* V, ii, 12–13. **2 scarf up,** to blindfold: "Come, seeling Night,/ Scarf up the tender eye of pitiful Day . . ." *Mac,* III, ii, 46–47.

scarfed, *adj.* decorated or adorned, here with flags: "How like a younger or a prodigal/ The scarfed bark puts from her native bay—" *Merch,* II, vi, 14–15.

scarre, *n.* var. of scare; fright; panic: "I see that men make rope's [?] in such a scarre,/ That we'll forsake ourselves." *All's W,* IV, ii, 38–39.

scathe, *v.* **1** to harm or injure: "You are a saucy boy . . . This trick may chance to scathe you." *Rom & Jul,* I, v, 82–83.
—*n.* **2** Also, **scath,** harm or injury: ". . . wherein Rome hath done you any scath,/ Let him make treble satisfaction." *T Andr,* V, i, 7–8.

scathful grapple, *n.* destructive attack: "A baubling vessel was he captain of . . . With which such scathful grapple did he make . . ." *T Night,* V, i, 52–54.

scattering, *adj.* haphazard: "Out of my scattering and unsure observance . . ." *Oth,* III, iii, 155.

scauld, *adj.* rotten; scurvy: "The rascally, scauld, beggarly,/ lousy, pragging [bragging] knave, Pistol . . ." *Hen 5,* V, i, 5–6.

scene, *n.* **1** play or spectacle: "Have, by the very cunning of the scene,/ Been struck so to the soul . . ." *Ham,* II, ii, 586–587. **2 fill the scene,** play the part: "A queen in jest, only to fill the scene." *Rich 3,* IV, iv, 91.

scene individable, *n.* poss. a play that observes the classic unities of time, place, etc.; perh. a play outside the preceding categories: ". . . tragical-comical-historical-pastoral, scene individable, or poem unlimited." *Ham,* II, ii, 394–396.

scepter, *n.* **1** the scepter as a symbol of a monarch's power: "Her sceptre so fantastically [erratically] borne/ By a vain, giddy, shallow, humorous youth . . ." *Hen 5,* II, iv, 27–28. **2** the monarch wielding a scepter: "The kings of Mede and Lycaonia,/ With a more larger list of sceptres." *Ant & Cleo,* III, vi, 75–76.

scepter's awe, *n.* reverence due a monarch, symbolized by his scepter: "Now by my sceptre's awe I make a vow . . ." *Rich 2,* I, i, 118.

schedule, *n.* **1** letter, petition, or other document; paper: "Hail, Caesar! Read this schedule." *J Caes,* III, i, 3. **2** list or inventory: "I will give/ out divers schedules of my beauty." *T Night,* I, v, 247–248. **3** summary or summarizing statement: "By this short schedule Collatine may know/ Her grief . . ." *Luc,* 1312–1313.

scholar, *n.* person who knew Latin and was presumably capable of addressing the devil and performing exorcisms: "I would to God some scholar would conjure her . . ." *M Ado,* II, i, 240–241.

school, *n.* **1** public building: ". . . great tow'rs, trophies, and schools should fall/ For private faults in them." *Timon,* V, iv, 25–26. **2 keep school i' th' church,** to teach school in the church building, for want of a schoolhouse; appar. an illustration of rusticity: "Most villainously; like a pedant that keeps a/ school i' th' church." *T Night,* III, ii, 72–73. **3 set to school,** to teach: "And set the murderous Machiavel to school." *3 Hen 6,* III, ii, 193.
—*v.* **4** to teach; also, to chasten: "Well, I am school'd—good manners be your speed!" *1 Hen 4,* III, i, 184. **5** to control; discipline: "My dearest coz,/ I pray you, school yourself . . ." *Mac,* IV, ii, 14–15.

schooling, *n.* advice or admonition: ". . . you shall go with me:/ I have some private schooling for you both." *M N Dream,* I, i, 115–116.

school of night, *n.* prob. allusion to a group of writers known as the "School of Atheism": "Black is the badge of hell,/ The hue of dungeons and the school of night . . ." *Love's L,* IV, iii, 250–251.

sciatica, *n.* thought to be a symptom of venereal disease and an affliction among bawds: "How now, which of your hips has the most profound/ sciatica?" *Meas,* I, ii, 54–55.

science, *n.* **1** expert knowledge: "Since I am put to know [forced to admit] that your own science/ Exceeds . . ." *Meas,* I, i, 5–6. **2** skill or craft: ". . . do not learn for want of time,/ The sciences that should become our country . . ." *Hen 5,* V, ii, 57–58. **3 the sciences,** the various branches of knowledge: ". . . a man of mine . . . To instruct her fully in those sciences,/ Whereof I know she is not ignorant." *Shrew,* II, i, 55–57.

scimitar, *n.* sword having a curved blade, used esp. in the Middle East: "He dies upon my scimitar's sharp point/ That touches this my first-born son and heir." *T Andr,* IV, ii, 91–92.

scion, *n.* offshoot [lit., shoot for grafting]: ". . . I take this, that you call love, to be a/ sect, or scion." *Oth,* I, iii, 332–333.

scoff, *v.* **scoffing his state,** jeering at his regality: ". . . there the antic sits,/ Scoffing his [the king's] state and grinning at his pomp . . ." *Rich 2,* III, ii, 162–163.

scoffer, *n.* an ill-natured person: "Foul is most foul, being foul to be a scoffer [It's bad enough that you're ill-favored, why compound the problem by being ill-natured too?]" *As You,* III, v, 62.

sconce[1], *n.* the head [slang]: ". . . answer me . . . Or I shall break that merry sconce of yours . . ." *Errors,* I, ii, 77–79.

sconce[2], *n.* **1** fortification or earthwork: ". . . at such and such a sconce, at/ such a breach, at such a convoy . . ." *Hen 5,* III, vi, 72–73. **2** defensive screen or barrier; here, wordplay with "sconce," head: ". . . and you use these/ blows long, I must get a sconce for my head . . ." *Errors,* II, ii, 36–37.

Scone, *n.* ancient capital of the old Scottish kingdom, near Perth: "He is already nam'd [elected], and gone to Scone/ To be invested." *Mac,* II, iv, 31–32.

scope, *n.* **1** aim or purpose: "His coming hither hath no further scope/ Than for his lineal royalties . . ." *Rich 2,* III, iii, 112–113. **2** extent or force of action or, often, revenge: ". . . curbs himself even of his natural scope/ When you come 'cross his humour . . ." *1 Hen 4,* III, i, 165–166. **3** full force or authority: "Now, good my lord, give me the scope of justice." *Meas,* V, i, 233. **4** intellect; here, intellectual attainments: "Desiring this man's art, and that man's scope . . ." *Sonn 29,* 7. **5** liberty; unrestrained action: "So every scope by the immoderate use/ Turns to restraint." *Meas,* I, ii, 119–120. **6** power: "Blessed are you, whose worthiness gives scope . . ." *Sonn 52,* 13. **7 scope of nature,** freakish occurrence in nature: "No natural exhalation in the sky,/ No scope of nature, no distemper'd day . . ." *K John,* III, iii, 153–154.

scorch, *v.* to slash; here, to wound and not kill: "We have scorch'd the snake, not kill'd it:/ She'll close, and be herself . . ." *Mac,* III, ii, 13–14.

score, *v.* **1** to mark down or chalk up (a charge); also, to cut notches in a post: "Score a pint of bastard in the Half-moon . . ." *1 Hen 4,* II, iv, 27. **2** to get the better of; wound: "Ha' you scor'd me? Well." *Oth,* IV, i, 126. **3 score me up,** (to) mark me down: ". . . score me up for the lying'st knave in Christendom." *Shrew,* Ind., ii, 24.
—*n.* **4** bill or tab in a tavern: "I am undone by his going, I warrant you, he's an/ infinitive thing upon my score." *2 Hen 4,* II, i, 22–23. **5 on my score,** at my expense: ". . . there shall be no/ money; all shall eat and drink on my score . . ." *2 Hen*

6, IV, ii, 69–70. **6 on the score,** in debt (for): "If she say I/ am not fourteen pence on the score for sheer ale . . ." *Shrew*, Ind., ii, 22–23. **7 too much for a score,** too moldy to buy: "But a hare that is hoar/ Is too much for a score . . ." *Rom & Jul*, II, iv, 135–136. **8 two tens to a score,** appar. the precept that virtuous conduct reaps monetary rewards: "And thou shalt have more/ Than two tens to a score [twenty shillings to the pound?]." *Lear*, I, iv, 132–133.

score and tally, stick scored as a record of moneys loaned or repaid; split lengthwise, with borrower and lender each retaining an identical half: ". . . our forefathers had/ no other books but the score and the tally . . ." *2 Hen 6*, IV, vii, 32–33.

scorn, *n.* **1** object of scorn: ". . . to show virtue/ her feature, scorn her own image . . ." *Ham*, III, ii, 22–23. **2** insult: ". . . if sickly ears . . . Will hear your idle scorns, continue then . . ." *Love's L*, V, ii, 855–857. **3 take foul scorn,** regard it as a disgrace; "I owe him little duty . . . And take foul scorn to fawn on him by sending." *1 Hen 6*, IV, iv, 34–35. **4 think scorn,** to regard as detestable: "The nobility think scorn to go in leather aprons." *2 Hen 6*, IV, ii, 12.

scot and lot, *adv.* **pay scot and lot,** to pay in full: ". . . that hot/ termagant Scot had paid me, scot and lot too." *1 Hen 4*, V, iv, 112–113.

scotch, *n.* **1** slight cut; nick: "I have yet/ Room for six scotches more." *Ant & Cleo*, IV, vii, 9–10.
—*v.* **2** to slash: ". . . he scotched him and/ notched him like a carbonado." *Cor*, IV, v, 191–192.

scour¹, *v.* **1** to beat or cudgel; here, wordplay with "score": ". . . I shall be post indeed,/ For she will scour your fault upon my pate." *Errors*, I, ii, 64–65. **2** to cleanse: "Never came reformation in a flood,/ With such a heady currance, scouring faults . . ." *Hen 5*, I, i, 33–34.

scour², *v.* to scurry: ". . . never/ Saw I men scour so on their way . . ." *W Tale*, II, i, 34–35.

scourge, *n.* punishment: ". . . th'offender's scourge is weigh'd,/ But never the offence." *Ham*, IV, iii, 6–7.

scourge and minister, *n.* agent of heavenly justice: ". . . but heaven hath pleas'd it so,/ To punish me with this . . . That I must be their scourge and minister." *Ham*, III, iv, 175–177.

scouring, *n.* scurrying about; anxious haste: "The enemy's drum is heard, and fearful scouring/ Doth choke the air with dust." *Timon*, V, ii, 15–16.

scout¹, *v.* to deride; jeer at: "Flout 'em and cout [scout?] 'em,/ And scout 'em and flout 'em . . ." *Temp*, III, ii, 119–120.

scout², *v.* **scout me,** to keep watch: ". . . scout me for him at the corner/ of the orchard, like a bum-baily." *T Night*, III, iv, 177–178.

scrambling, *adj.* rowdy; quarrelsome: "Scrambling, outfacing, fashion-monging boys . . ." *M Ado*, V, i, 94.

screech-owl, *n.* bird's nighttime call was thought to warn of death or calamity: "And boding screech-owls make the consort full!" *2 Hen 6*, III, ii, 326.

screen, *v.* **1** to act as protection: ". . . your Grace hath screen'd and stood between/ Much heat and him." *Ham*, III, iv, 3–4. —*n.* **2** barrier; impediment: "To have no screen between this part he play'd/ And him he play'd it for, he needs will be/ Absolute Milan." *Temp* I, ii, 107–109.

screw, *v.* **1** to tighten; also, force: "But screw your courage to the sticking-place,/ And we'll not fail." *Mac*, I, vii, 61–62. **2** to tear; wrench: "I partly know the instrument/ That screws me from my true place in your favour . . ." *T Night*, V, i, 120–121.

scrimer, *n.* fencer: "The scrimers of their nation/ He swore had neither motion, guard, nor eye . . ." *Ham*, IV, vii, 99–100.

scrip¹, *n.* shepherd's bag or pouch: ". . . an honourable retreat, though not with bag and baggage, yet with scrip and scrippage." *As You*, III, ii, 157–159.

scrip², *n.* misuse for "script": ". . . call them generally, man by man, according to the scrip." *M N Dream*, I, ii, 2–3.

scrivener, *n.* professional scribe skilled in drawing up legal documents: "My boy shall fetch the scrivener presently." *Shrew*, IV, iv, 59.

scrowl, *v.* old form of scrawl; here, to gesticulate: "See how with signs and tokens she can scrowl." *T Andr*, II, iv, 5.

scroyle, *n.* scabby rascal; scoundrel: "By heaven, these scroyles of Angiers flout you, kings . . ." *K John*, II, i, 373.

scrubbed, *adj.* scrubby; small and insignificant: "I gave it to a youth,/ A kind of boy, a little scrubbed boy,/ No higher than thyself . . ." *Merch*, V, i, 161–163.

scruple, *n.* **1** very small unit of weight or measurement; fraction of an ounce: "I know them, yea,/ And what they weigh, even to the utmost scruple . . ." *M Ado*, V, i, 92–93. **2** tiniest bit: ". . . if I lose a scruple of this sport,/ let me be boiled to death with melancholy." *T Night*, II, v, 2–3. **3** doubt or hesitancy (frequent use in puns with sense of definition 1): ". . . the wise may make some dram of a scruple, or indeed a/ scruple itself." *2 Hen 4*, I, ii, 129–130. **4 make scruple,** to express doubt: ". . . whereat I, wretch,/ Made scruple of his praise . . ." *Cymb*, V, v, 181–182.

scrupulous faction, *n.* divided political parties, unwilling to declare their allegiance: "Equality of two domestic powers/ Breed scrupulous faction . . ." *Ant & Cleo,* I, iii, 47–48.

scrupulous wit, *n.* cautious or prudent wisdom: "Away with scrupulous wit! Now arms must rule." *3 Hen 6,* IV, vii, 62.

scud, *v.* to run swiftly: "Sometime he scuds far off, and there he stares . . ." *Ven & Ad*, 301.

scullion, *n.* scullery maid; dishwasher [a term of contempt]: "Away, you scullion! you rampallian!" *2 Hen 4,* II, i, 58.

scurril, *adj.* scurrilous; gross; coarse: ". . . Patroclus/ Upon a lazy bed the livelong day/ Breaks scurril jests . . ." *Tr & Cr,* I, iii, 146–148.

scurvy, *adj.* disgusting; repellent: ". . . a saucy friar,/ A very scurvy fellow." *Meas,* V, i, 138–139.

scuse, *n.* var. of **excuse:** "That scuse serves many men to save their gifts . . ." *Merch,* IV, i, 440.

scut, *n.* tail of a rabbit or deer; here, also slang term for "pudenda": "My doe with the black scut?" *Wives,* V, v, 18.

scutcheon, *n.* display of heraldic devices, arms, etc., esp. at a funeral: "Honour is a mere/ scutcheon—and so ends my catechism." *1 Hen 4,* V, i, 140–141.

Scylla, *n.* rock mass on one side of a narrow passage, opposite the whirlpool Charybdis: ". . . when I shun Scylla (your father),/ I fall into Charybdis (your mother) . . ." *Merch,* III, v, 14–15.

scythe, *n.* Time seen as the Grim Reaper [Death] harvesting souls: "I will be true despite thy scythe and thee." *Sonn 123,* 14.

Scythian, *n.* inhabitant of European Russia, regarded as the abode of barbarians: "The barbarous Scythian,/ Or he that makes his generation messes/ To gorge his appetite . . ." *Lear,* I, i, 116–117.

'Sdeath, *interj.* God's death [a mild oath]: "'Sdeath,/ The rabble should have first unroof'd the city . . ." *Cor,* I, i, 216–217.

sea, *n.* **cut the sea,** to plow through the sea: "From whence shall Warwick cut the sea to France . . ." *3 Hen 6,* II, vi, 89.

sea-coal, *adj.* made with coal brought in by ship, usually from N England: ". . . at the latter end of a sea-coal fire." *Wives,* I, iv, 8.

sea-gown, *n.* outer garment worn by seamen: "Up from my cabin,/ My sea-gown scarf'd about me . . ." *Ham,* V, ii, 12–13.

seal, *v.* **1** to satisfy; fulfill: ". . . till we/ Have seal'd thy full desire." *Timon,* V, iv, 53–54. **2** to affix one's seal to an agreement: ". . . we'll but seal,/ And then to horse immediately." *1 Hen 4,* III, i, 258–259. **3 sealed in my function,** sanctified in the performance of my [priestly] duties: "And all the ceremony of this compact/ Seal'd in my function, by my testimony . . ." *T Night,* V, i, 158–159. **4 seal on,** to attach to a letter or other document: "Writ o' both sides the leaf, margent and all,/ That he was fain to seal on Cupid's name." *Love's L,* V, ii, 8–9. **5 seal under,** to guarantee the obligation of another: "I think the Frenchman became his surety, and seal'd/ under for another." *Merch,* I, ii, 78–79. **6 seal up,** to confirm; justify: ". . . and at my death/ Thou hast seal'd up my expectation." *2 Hen 4,* IV, v, 102–103. —*n.* **7** pledge; troth: "O let me kiss/ This princess of pure white, this seal of bliss!" *M N Dream,* III, ii, 143–144. **8** that which ratifies by putting into action: "To give them seals never my soul consent." *Ham,* III, ii, 390. **9** imprint or impression; here, of the Queen's lips: "O! could this kiss be printed in thy hand,/ That thou might'st think upon these by the seal . . ." *2 Hen 6,* III, ii, 342–343.

sealed, *adj.* **1** (of an agreement) impressed with the signer's seal in softened wax: ". . . our indentures tripartite . . . being sealed interchangeably . . ." *1 Hen 4,* III, i, 76–77. **2 sealed up,** completed; here, a certainty: "Here had the conquest fully been seal'd up/ If Sir John Falstaff had not play'd the coward." *1 Hen 6,* I, i, 130–131.

sealed quarts, *n. pl.* quarts of ale or beer bearing an official seal testifying to their full measure: "And say you would present her at the leet,/ Because she brought stone jugs and no seal'd quarts." *Shrew,* Ind., ii, 88–89.

sealing-day, *n.* marriage day: "The sealing-day betwixt my love and me/ For everlasting bond of fellowship . . ." *M N Dream,* I, i, 84–85.

seal-ring, *n.* a ring whose face is an incised seal: ". . . three or four bonds of/ forty pound apiece, and a seal-ring of my grandfather's." *1 Hen 4,* III, iii, 99–100.

seam, *n.* fat; grease: ". . . the proud lord/ That bastes his arrogance with his own seam . . ." *Tr & Cr,* II, iii, 185–186.

sea-maid, *n.* mermaid: "Some report, a sea-maid spawned him." *Meas,* III, ii, 104.

sea-marge, *n.* ocean's shore: "... thy sea-marge, sterile and rocky-hard,/ Where thou thyself dost air ..." *Temp,* IV, i, 69–70.

sea-margent, *n.* beach bordering the ocean: "On the sea-margent/ Walk with Leonine ..." *Per,* IV, i, 26–27.

sea-mark, *n.* object on shore used as guide by mariners: "Like a great sea-mark standing every flaw [withstanding every squall] ..." *Cor,* V, iii, 74.

sear¹, *v.* **sear up,** to seal as if with sealing wax: "And sear up my embracements from a next [wife]/ With bonds of death!" *Cymb,* I, ii, 47–48.

sear², *n.* See **tickle a th' sear.**

search, *v.* **search out,** poss. to tear out [of the calendar]: "If it be a day/ fits you, search out of the calendar, and nobody look/ after it [will miss it]. *Per,* II, i, 53–55.

searcher, *n.* health inspector; esp., during the plague, one who located dead bodies and reported them: "... the searchers of the town ... Seal'd up the doors and would not let us forth ..." *Rom & Jul,* V, ii, 8–11.

searching, *adj.* (of a wine) quickly intoxicating: "... you have drunk too much/ canaries, and that' a marvellous searching wine ..." *2 Hen 4,* II, iv, 26–27.

sea-room, *n.* open sea: "But sea-room, and the brine and cloudy billow/ kiss the moon, I care not." *Per,* III, i, 45–46.

season, *v.* **1** to prepare; make ready: "... season the slaves/ For tubs and baths ..." *Timon,* IV, iii, 86–87. **2** to lessen; temper: "Season your admiration for a while/ With an attent ear ..." *Ham,* I, ii, 192–193. **3** to mature or ripen: "Farewell, my blessing season this in thee." *Ham,* I, iii, 81. **4** to please or gratify; also, to pamper: "... let their beds/ Be made as soft as yours, and let their palates/ Be season'd with such viands?" *Merch,* IV, i, 95–97. **5** to add relish to: "... that have their honest wills,/ Which seasons comfort." *Cymb,* I, vii, 8–9.
—*n.* **6** that which preserves or sustains; a preservative: "You lack the season of all natures, sleep." *Mac,* III, iv, 140. **7** time; hour: "It then draws near the season/ Wherein the spirit held his wont to walk." *Ham,* I, iv, 5–6. **8** appropriate or proper time: "How many things by season, season'd are/ To their right praise, and true perfection!" *Merch,* V, i, 107–108. **9** a usually short period of time; while: "We'll slip you for a season, but our jealousy/ Does yet depend." *Cymb,* IV, iii, 22–23. **10 day of season,** person with a single mood or characteristic: "I am not a day of season,/ For thou may'st see a sunshine and a hail/ In me at once." *All's W,* V, iii, 32–34. **11 of the season,** in season; here, both the mating season and the rutting

season are implied: "Ay, buck; I warrant you, buck;/ and of the season too, it shall appear." *Wives,* III, iii, 146–147. **12 out of season,** ill-timed; inappropriate: "Come, Dromio, come, these jests are out of season ..." *Errors,* I, ii, 68. **13 season of all natures, to season,** at any particular moment: "Time is a very bankrupt, and owes more than he's worth to season." *Errors,* IV, ii, 58.

seasoned, *adj.* **1** wordplay on "matured" and "salted": "That season'd woe had pelleted in tears ..." *Lover's Comp,* 18. **2** firmly established: "... you have contriv'd to take/ From Rome all season'd office ..." *Cor,* III, iii, 63–64.

sea-sorrow, *n.* sad sea journey: "Sit still, and hear the last of our sea-sorrow." *Temp,* I, ii, 170.

sea's worth, *n.* treasures (as pearls) of the sea: "I would not my unhoused free condition ... confine/ For the sea's worth." *Oth,* I, ii, 26–28.

seat, *n.* **1** place; situation; environment: "He's flung in rage from this ingrateful seat/ Of monstrous friends ..." *Timon,* IV, ii, 45–46. **2** place of habitation; residence: "This earth of majesty, this seat of Mars ..." *Rich 2,* II, i, 41. **3** throne; royal power: "... distaff-women manage rusty bills/ Against thy seat ..." *Rich 2,* III, ii, 118–119. **4** central or governing place; here, the heart, seat of the emotions of love: "It gives a very echo to the seat/ Where love is thron'd." *T Night,* II, iv, 21–22. **5** seat of office; here, the office itself: "Thus we debase/ The nature of our seats ..." *Cor,* III, i, 134–135. **6** person's right; here, sexual rights to another: "Ay me! but yet thou mightst my seat forbear ..." *Sonn 41,* 9. **7 chiefest seat,** center of government: "This Antioch, then, Antiochus the Great/ Built up, this city, for this chiefest seat ..." *Per,* I, Chor., 17–18. **8 For your great seats,** for the sake of your lofty positions: "For your great seats now quit you of great shames ..." *Hen 5,* III, v, 47. **9 kept seat,** took up residence: "Which three [qualities] till now never kept seat in one [person]." *Sonn 105,* 14.
—*v.* **10** to settle: "Subdu'd the Saxons, and did seat the French/ Beyond the river Sala ..." *Hen 5,* I, ii, 62–63.

seated, *adj.* **1** firmly fixed; embedded: "... doth unfix my hair,/ And make my seated heart knock at my ribs ..." *Mac,* I, iii, 135–136. **2** situated; placed: "Some dark deep desert seated from the way ..." *Luc,* 1144.

sea-water green, *adj.* suffering from green-sickness: "Tell me precisely of what complexion."/ "Of the sea-water green, sir." *Love's L,* I, ii, 77–78.

second, *v.* **1** to reinforce; increase or augment: "... 'tis not wisdom thus to second grief/ Against yourself." *M Ado,* V, i, 2–3.

—*n.* **2** assistant or helper; also, supporter: "No seconds [no one to help me]? all myself?" *Lear,* IV, vi, 196. **3** [pl.] chaff or other adulterants: "And take thou my oblation . . . Which is not mixed with seconds . . ." *Sonn 125,* 10–11. **4 be second to me,** support me; back me up: "Nay rather, good my lords, be second to me . . ." *W Tale,* II, iii, 28.

second accent, *n.* echo: ". . . return your mock/ In second accent of his ordinance [ordnance]." *Hen 5,* II, iv, 125–126.

secondary, *n.* associate or assistant: "Old Escalus,/ Though first in question, is thy secondary." *Meas,* I, i, 45–46.

second body, *n.* deputy or representative: ". . . to spurn at your most royal image,/ And mock your workings in a second body?" *2 Hen 4,* V, ii, 89–90.

second brother, *n.* younger son, who receives no inheritance: "The worst that they can say of me is/ that I am a second brother . . ." *2 Hen 4,* II, ii, 62–63.

second cock, *n.* three A.M.: "Come, stir, stir, stir, the second cock hath crow'd!" *Rom & Jul,* IV, iv, 3.

second course, *n.* the main, or meat, course of a feast: "Balm of hurt minds, great Nature's second course . . ." *Mac,* II, ii, 38.

second name of men, *n.* second only to Coriolanus in importance: "Tullus Aufidius,/ The second name of men . . ." *Cor,* IV, vi, 125–126.

second voice, *n.* messenger or go-between: "In second voice we'll not be satisfied . . ." *Tr & Cr,* II, iii, 142.

secret, *adj.* discreet or trustworthy; able to keep a secret: "Is your man secret?" *Rom & Jul,* II, iv, 192.

secretest, *adj.* best concealed: "Augures . . . have . . . brought forth/ The secret'st man of blood [murderer]." *Mac,* III, iv, 123–125.

secret feet, *n.* secret foothold: ". . . have secret feet/ In some of our best ports . . ." *Lear,* III, i, 32–33.

secret policies, *n.* tricks to deceive the enemy: "Search out thy wit for secret policies . . ." *1 Hen 6,* III, iii, 12.

sect, *n.* **1** wordplay on "sex" and "profession or calling": "So is all her sect; and they be once in a calm they are/ sick." *2 Hen 4,* II, iv, 37–38. **2** class or rank: "All sects, all ages smack of this vice . . ." *Meas,* II, ii, 5. **3** branch or offshoot; also, a cutting: ". . . whereof I take this, that you call love, to be a/ sect, or scion." *Oth,* I, iii, 332–333.

sectary, *n.* disciple; also, a follower: "How long have you been a sectary astronomical [of astronomy]?" *Lear,* I, ii, 157.

secure, *adj.* **1** overconfident; unsuspecting: "Open the door,/ Secure, foolhardy king." *Rich 2,* V, iii, 41–42. **2** devoted to rest or relaxation: "Upon my secure hour thy uncle stole/ With juice of cursed hebenon in a vial . . ." *Ham,* I, v, 61–62.
—*v.* **3** to protect: "Heavens secure him." *Ham,* I, v, 115. **4 means secure us,** our prosperity makes us careless or overconfident: "Our means secure us, and our mere defects/ Prove our commodities [advantages]." *Lear,* IV, i, 20–21. **5 secure me to,** rely upon: "I do not so secure me to the error [inconsistency] . . ." *Oth,* I, iii, 10.

securely, *adv.* **1** confidently: ". . . securely I espy/ Virtue with valour couched [expressed] in thine eye." *Rich 2,* I, iii, 97–98. **2** unsuspectingly; overconfidently: "We see the wind sit sore upon our sails,/ And yet we strike not, but securely perish." *Rich 2,* II, i, 265–266.

security, *n.* **1** one legally responsible for another's debt; surety: ". . . procure him better assurance than Bardolph: he would not take his bond and/ yours, he liked not the security." *2 Hen 4,* I, ii, 31–33. **2** indifference or overconfidence; also, irresponsibility: "Well, he may sleep in security,/ for he hath the horn of abundance . . ." *2 Hen 4,* I, ii, 45–46.

sedge, *n.* [usually pl.] reeds or rushlike grasses: "Alas, poor hurt fowl, now will he creep into/ sedges." *M Ado,* II, i, 188–189.

sedged, *adj.* covered or bedecked with sedge: ". . . Naiads, of the windring brooks,/ With your sedg'd crowns and ever-harmless looks . . ." *Temp,* IV, i, 128–129.

sedgy, *adj.* covered with reeds: ". . . on the gentle Severn's sedgy bank,/ In single opposition hand to hand . . ." *1 Hen 4,* I, iii, 97–98.

seduce, *v.* to lead astray; here, win over: "The doubt [suspicion] is that he will seduce the rest." *3 Hen 6,* IV, viii, 37.

see, *v.* **1** to see to; supervise: "Bid him repair to us to Ely House/ To see this business." *Rich 2,* II, i, 216–217. **2** to do: "My Lord, you have one eye left/ To see some mischief on [to] him." *Lear,* III, vii, 80–81. **3** to see each other; meet: "How have ye done/ Since last we saw in France?" *Hen 8,* I, i, 1–2. **4 see away,** to spend in seeing: ". . . may see away their shilling/ Richly in two short hours." *Hen 8,* Prol. 12–13. **5 see that straight,** see to that shortly: "I am the very man,—"/ "I'll see that straight." *Lear,* V, iii, 287. **6 see thou,** be certain to: "Thou shalt not bail them; see thou follow me." *T Andr,* II, iii, 298.

See, *n.* **the See,** Rome, seat of the Roman Catholic Church: ". . . late come from the See/ In special business from his Holiness [the Pope]." *Meas,* III, ii, 213–214.

seed, *n.* **1** offspring; here, noble progeny: "How much low peasantry would then be gleaned/ From the true seed of honour!" *Merch,* II, ix, 46–47. **2** son; ref. to Edward the Black Prince, son of Edward III: "Saw his heroical seed, and smil'd to see him,/ Mangle the work of nature . . ." *Hen 5,* II, iv, 59–60. **3 stand for seed,** like grain left standing to provide seed for another season, these houses will seed other houses [brothels]: "They shall stand for seed: they had gone down too,/ but that a wise burgher put in for them." *Meas,* I, ii, 91–92.
—*v.* **4** to mature; yield fruit: "How will thy shame be seeded in thine age . . ." *Luc,* 603.

seeded, *adj.* gone to seed: ". . . the seeded pride/ That hath to this maturity blown up/ In rank Achilles . . ." *Tr & Cr,* I, iii, 315–317.

seedness, *n.* sowing time: ". . . from the seedness the bare fallow brings/ To teeming foison . . ." *Meas,* I, iv, 42–43.

seedsman, *n.* sower of seed: ". . . the seedsman/ Upon the slime and ooze scatters his grain . . ." *Ant & Cleo,* II, vii, 21–22.

seeds of time, *n.* future events: "If you can look into the seeds of time,/ And say which grain will grow . . ." *Mac,* I, iii, 58–59.

seeing, *n.* **1** appearance: "And steal dead [lifeless] seeing of his living hue?" *Sonn 67,* 6.
—*adj.* **2** perceptive; observant: "Blind fear, that seeing reason leads . . ." *Tr & Cr,* III, ii, 69.

seel, *v.* (in falconry) to sew up (the eyes) of a hawk in early training: ". . . the wise gods seel our eyes,/ In our own filth drop our clear judgements . . ." *Ant & Cleo,* III, xiii, 112–113.

seeling, *adj.* (in falconry) sewing up the bird's eyelids: "Come, seeling Night,/ Scarf up the tender eye of pitiful Day . . ." *Mac,* III, ii, 46–47.

seem, *v.* **1** to pretend or affect: ". . . the sinful father/ Seem'd not to strike, but smooth . . ." *Per,* I, ii, 77–78. **2 would not seem to,** pretended not to: "He would not seem to know me." *Cor,* V, i, 8.

seemer, *n.* person who projects a certain image; here, of selfless morality: "Hence shall we see!/ If power change purpose, what our seemers be." *Meas,* I, iii, 53–54.

seeming, *adj.* **1** apparent: "There is no seeming mercy in the King." *1 Hen 4,* V, ii, 34.

—*n.* **2** appearance; manner or comportment: "And after we will both our judgments join/ In censure of his seeming." *Ham,* III, ii, 86–87. **3** pretense; hypocrisy: ". . . under covert and convenient seeming/ Has practis'd on man's life . . ." *Lear,* III, ii, 56–57.
—*adv.* **4** seemingly; apparently: "O, all that borrowed motion, seeming owed . . ." *Lover's Comp,* 327.

seen, *past part., adj.* **well seen,** thoroughly instructed; expert: ". . . a schoolmaster/ Well seen in music, to instruct Bianca . . ." *Shrew,* I, ii, 132–133.

seethe, *v.* to be urgent [lit., to boil]: "I will make a complimental/ assault upon him, for my business seethes." *Tr & Cr,* III, i, 38–39.

seething, *adj.* boiling: "And grew a seething bath, which yet men prove/ Against strange maladies a sovereign cure." *Sonn 153,* 7–8.

segregation, *n.* dispersal: "A segregation of the Turkish fleet . . ." *Oth,* II, i, 10.

seigniory, *n.* sovereignty; here also, seniority: "If ancient sorrow be most reverend/ Give mine the benefit of seigniory . . ." *Rich 3,* IV, iv, 35–36.

seized, *adj.* possessed: "Did forfeit, with his life, all those his lands/ Which he stood seiz'd of to the conqueror . . ." *Ham,* I, i, 91–92.

Seize thee that list, Let him who wants have you: "Yet if thy thoughts, Bianca, be so humble/ To cast thy wandering eyes on every stale,/ Seize thee that list." *Shrew,* III, i, 87–89.

seizure, *n.* clasp; here, handclasp of friendship: "Unyoke this seizure and this kind regreet?" *K John,* III, i, 167.

seld, *adv.* seldom: "If I might in entreaties find success—/ As seld I have the chance . . ." *Tr & Cr,* IV, v, 148–149.

seld-shown, *adj.* seldom-seen; seldom-appearing: "Seld-shown flamens [priests]/ Do press among the popular throngs . . ." *Cor,* II, i, 211–212.

select, *adj.* particular; hence, distinguished or superior: "And they in France . . . Are [of a] most select and generous chief in that." *Ham,* I, iii, 73–74.

self, *adj.* **1** self-same; identical: "That mettle, that self mould, that fashioned thee . . ." *Rich 2,* I, ii, 23. **2** of one's own: ". . . his fiend-like Queen,/ Who, as 'tis thought, by self and violent hands/ Took off her life . . ." *Mac,* V, viii, 35–37. **3 self instant,** self-sufficient or self-contained: "When we name a man,/ His hand, his foot, his head, hath several strengths,/ And, being all but one self instant strength . . ." *Edw 3,* IV, iv, 52–54.

—*n.* **4 their proper selves,** themselves: ". . . even with such-like valour men hang and drown/ Their proper selves." *Temp,* III, iii, 59–60.

self-abuse, *n.* self-deception: "My strange and self-abuse [strange self-deception]/ Is the initiate fear, that wants hard use . . ." *Mac,* III, iv, 141–142.

self-admission, *n.* self-approbation; here, stubbornly relying on his own judgment: "[Achilles] carries on the stream of his dispose . . . In will peculiar and in self-admission." *Tr & Cr,* II, iii, 165–167.

self-affairs, *n. pl.* my own affairs [concerns]: ". . . being over-full of self-affairs,/ My mind did lose it." *M N Dream,* I, i, 113–114.

self-affected, *adj.* enamored of himself: "If he were proud—"/ "Or strange [distant], or self-affected." *Tr & Cr,* II, iii, 236–239.

self-borne, *adj.* (of arms) taken up for personal goals, not on behalf of one's monarch: ". . . what pricks you on/ To . . . fright our native peace with self-borne arms." *Rich 2,* II, iii, 78–80.

self-bounty, *n.* innate goodness; also, generosity: "I would not have your free and noble nature/ Out of self-bounty be abused . . ." *Oth,* III, iii, 203–204.

self-breath, *n.* one's own words: ". . . speaks not to himself but with a pride/ That quarrels at self-breath [even his own words are inadequate to stroke his pride]." *Tr & Cr,* II, iii, 172–173.

self-comparisons, *n. pl.* equal skills and valor: "Till that Bellona's bridegroom, lapp'd in proof,/ Confronted him with self-comparisons . . ." *Mac,* I, ii, 55–56.

self-covered, *adj.* having the true self obscured by shameless greed; also, poss. that Goneril is a devil with a woman's appearance: "Thou changed and self-cover'd thing, for shame,/ Be-monster not thy feature." *Lear,* IV, ii, 62–63.

self-drawing, *adj.* like the web of a spider, which he himself has spun: ". . . spider-like,/ Out of his self-drawing web . . ." *Hen 8,* I, i, 62–63.

self-exhibition, *n.* very same money: ". . . with that self exhibition/ Which your own coffers yield!" *Cymb,* I, vii, 122–123.

self-figured, *adj.* arranged by themselves: ". . . to knit their souls . . . in self-figur'd knot . . ." *Cymb,* II, iii, 116–118.

self-gracious remembrance, *n.* [act of] kindly remembering without being reminded: ". . . which . . . his/ majesty out of a self-gracious remembrance did first/ propose." *All's W,* IV, v, 70–71.

self-mettle, *n.* [the horse's own] spirit or vigor: "A full hot horse, who being allow'd his way,/ Self-mettle tires him . . ." *Hen 8,* I, i, 133–134.

self-offense, *n.* offense committed by oneself: "More nor less to others paying/ Than by self-offences weighing." *Meas,* III, ii, 258–259.

self-reproving, *n.* self-reproach: ". . . he's full of alteration/ And self-reproving; bring his constant pleasure." *Lear,* V, i, 3–4.

self-subdued, *adj.* (of a person) offering no resistance when attacked: ". . . got praises of the King/ For him attempting who was self-subdu'd . . ." *Lear,* II, ii, 122–123.

self-substantial, *adj.* that consumes its own substance: "Feed'st thy light's flame with self-substantial fuel . . ." *Sonn 1,* 6.

self-unable motion, *n.* one's own inadequate thoughts or imaginings: ". . . the great figure of a council frames/ By self-unable motion . . ." *All's W,* III, i, 12–13.

sell, *v.* to let out of one's sight at any price: ". . . when for a day of kings' entreaties, a mother/ should not sell him an hour from her beholding . . ." *Cor,* I, iii, 8–9.

semblable, *adj.* **1** similar; like: "That were excusable, that and thousands more/ Of semblable import . . ." *Ant & Cleo,* III, iv, 2–3.

—*n.* **2** counterpart; equal: ". . . to make true diction of him, his semblable is his mirror . . ." *Ham,* V, ii, 117–118. **3** likeness or mirrored image: "His semblable, yea himself, Timon disdains." *Timon,* IV, iii, 22.

semblable coherence, *n.* close likeness: "It is a wonderful thing to/ see the semblable coherence of his men's spirits and/ his." *2 Hen 4,* V, i, 61–63.

semblably, *adv.* similarly; in like manner: "Semblably furnish'd like the King himself." *1 Hen 4,* V, iii, 21.

semblance, *n.* **1** face; visage: "Yon sometimes famous princes . . . Tell thee, with speechless tongues and semblance pale . . ." *Per,* I, i, 35–37. **2** appearance; image or likeness: ". . . who is thus like to be/ cozened with the semblance of a maid . . ." *M Ado,* II, ii, 38–39. **3 simple semblance,** innocent appearance: "Under whose simple semblance he hath fed/ Upon fresh beauty . . ." *Ven & Ad,* 795–796. **4 thy native sem-**

blance on, showing your true nature: "For if thou path, thy native semblance on . . ." *J Caes,* II, i, 83.

semblative, *adj.* like or resembling: "And all is semblative a woman's part." *T Night,* I, iv, 34.

semicircled farthingale, *n.* farthingale expanded only at the back: ". . . give an excellent motion to thy gait in a semicircled/ farthingale." *Wives,* III, iii, 57–58.

Semiramis, *n.* beautiful, lustful Assyrian queen, the wife of Ninus: "This goddess, this Semiramis, this nymph,/ This siren that will charm Rome's Saturnine . . ." *T Andr,* II, i, 22–23.

semper idem, Latin motto meaning "ever the same": "'Tis *semper idem, for obsque hoc nihil est;* 'tis all in every part." *2 Hen 4,* V, v, 28–29.

send, *v.* to dispatch a messenger: "Did you send to him, Sir?/ I heard it by the way; but I will send." *Mac,* III, iv, 128–129.

Seneca, *n.* Roman writer of tragedies, lst cent. A.D.: "Seneca cannot be too heavy, nor Plautus too/ light." *Ham,* II, ii, 396–397.

sennet, *n.* trumpet call accompanying an entrance, or sometimes an exit, of a group of characters [disting. from *flourish,* which announced an entrance]: "Sennet. Exeunt. Manent Brutus and Cassius." *J Caes,* [SD] I, ii, 24.

se'nnight's, *adj.* seven night's; week's: "Whose footing here anticipates our thoughts/ A se'nnight's speed . . ." *Oth,* II, i, 76–77.

Senoy, *n.* native of Siena; Sienese: "The Florentines and Senoys are by th' ears . . ." *All's W,* I, ii, 1.

sense, *n.* **1** reason or logic: "For to thy sensual fault I bring in sense . . ." *Sonn 35,* 9. **2** understanding or comprehension; reasoning: ". . . and is as common/ As any the most vulgar thing to sense . . ." *Ham,* I, ii, 98–99. **3** feeling; sensitivity or perception: "A woman of quick [lively] sense." *Tr & Cr,* IV, v, 54. **4** discomfort; trouble: "Impossible be strange attempts to those/ That weigh their pains in sense . . ." *All's W,* I, i, 220–221. **5** sensual appetites: ". . . modesty may more betray our sense/ Than woman's lightness?" *Meas,* II, ii, 169–170. **6 all things of sense,** anyone capable of normal judgment: "For I'll refer me to all things of sense . . ." *Oth,* I, ii, 64. **7 bereaved sense,** ref. to Lear's "stolen" senses: "What can man's wisdom/ In the restoring his bereaved sense? *Lear,* IV, iv, 8–9. **8 heavy sense,** strict interpretation: "Under whose heavy sense your brother's life/ Falls into forfeit . . ." *Meas,* I, iv, 65–66. **9 in sense,** wordplay on "comprehension" and "physical sensation": ". . . take it in what sense thou wilt."/ "They must take it

in sense that feel it." *Rom & Jul,* I, i, 25–26. **10 take the sense,** to understand the true meaning: "O take the sense, sweet, of my innocence!" *M N Dream,* II, ii, 44. **11 to the sense,** to the quick: "I have rubb'd this young quat almost to the sense . . ." *Oth,* V, i, 11.

senseless, *adj.* **1** lacking feeling; insensible: "Then senseless Ilium,/ Seeming to feel this blow . . . Stoops to his base . . ." *Ham,* II, ii, 470–472. **2** incapable of feeling [another's pain]: "I am senseless of your wrath . . ." *Cymb,* I, ii, 66. **3** unaware or indifferent: "Doth very foolishly . . . not to seem senseless of the bob." *As You,* II, vii, 54–55. **4** confusion between preceding [Queen's meaning] and "stupid" [Cloten's misunderstanding]: "Save when command to your dismission tends,/ And therein you are senseless."/ "Senseless? not so." *Cymb,* II, iii, 51–52. **5** misuse for "sensible": "You are thought here to be the most senseless/ and fit man for the constable of the watch . . ." *M Ado,* III, iii, 22–23. **6** not based on reason; unreasonable; foolish: ". . . to esteem/ A senseless help, when help past sense we deem [we judge any help to be beyond reason]." *All's W,* II, i, 122–123.

senseless-obstinate, *adj.* unyielding; inflexible: "You are too senseless-obstinate, my lord,/ Too ceremonious and traditional." *Rich 3,* III, i, 44–45.

sensible, *adj.* **1** able to feel: "If thou wert sensible of courtesy/ I should not make so dear a show of zeal . . ." *1 Hen 4,* V, iv, 93–94. **2** able to be felt; perceptible: "Art thou not, fatal vision, sensible/ To feeling, as to sight?" *Mac,* II, i, 36–37. **3** sensitive; also, intense: "And with affection wondrous sensible/ He wrung Bassanio's hand . . ." *Merch,* II, viii, 48–49. **4** down-to-earth; realistic or hardheaded: ". . . if ever the sensible/ Benedick bear it, pluck off the bull's horns . . ." *M Ado,* I, i, 243–244. **5** evident or obvious; considerable: "To signify th'approaching of his lord,/ From whom he bringeth sensible regreets . . ." *Merch,* II, ix, 88–89.

sensibly, *adv.* **1** as one alive and having feeling: "Who sensibly outdares his senseless sword . . ." *Cor,* I, iv, 53. **2** with great feeling: ". . . how was there a costard broken in a/ shin?"/ "I will tell you sensibly." *Love's L,* III, i, 108–110.

sentence, *n.* **1** pithy saying; saw or maxim: "Shall quips and sentences . . . awe a man from the career of his humour?" *M Ado,* II, iii, 231–233. **2** [pl.] misuse for "senses": "I say the gentleman had/ drunk himself out of his five sentences." *Wives,* I, i, 157–158.

sententious, *adj.* **1** given to clever talk or witty sayings: "By my faith, he is very swift and sententious." *As You,* V, iv, 62. **2** pithy: ". . . your reasons at dinner/ have been sharp and sententious . . ." *Love's L,* V, i, 2–3.

—*n.* **3** prob. misuse for "sentence," a witty saying or proverb: "... she hath the prettiest sententious of it, of you and/ rosemary ..." *Rom & Jul,* II, iv, 207–208.

sentinel, *v.* to stand watch during: "To wake the morn and sentinel the night ..." *Luc,* 942.

se offendendo, mistake for Latin *se defendendo,* in self-defense: "It must be *se offendendo,* it cannot be else." *Ham,* V, i, 9.

separable spite, *n.* frustrating [or mortifying] separation: "Though in our lives a separable spite ..." *Sonn* 36, 6.

Septentrion, *n.* north; precisely, the seven stars of the constellation Great Bear: "Thou art as opposite to every good ... as the south to the Septentrion." *3 Hen 6,* I, iv, 134–136.

sepulchre, *v.* to bury in a sepulchre: "I would divorce me from thy mother's tomb,/ Sepulchring an adult'ress." *Lear,* II, iv, 132–133.

sequel, *n.* **1** what follows [the pause by Valentine]: "A pretty period. Well, I guess the sequel ..." *Two Gent,* II, i, 109. **2** continuation or conclusion: "But/ is there no sequel at the heels of this mother's admiration?" *Ham,* III, ii, 319–320.

sequence of degree, (in) order of rank: "... tell my friends,/ Tell Athens, in the sequence of degree ..." *Timon,* V, i, 206–207.

sequent, *n.* **1** follower: "... here he hath/ framed a letter to a sequent of the stranger queen's ..." *Love's L,* IV, ii, 132–133. —*adj.* **2** following; subsequent: "... and what to this was sequent/ Thou knowest already." *Ham,* V, ii, 54–55. **3** successive: "... the galleys/ Have sent a dozen sequent messengers/ This very night ..." *Oth,* I, ii, 40–42. **4 sequent issue,** the newest heir: "Of six preceding ancestors, that gem/ Conferr'd by testament to th' sequent issue ..." *All's W,* V, iii, 195–196.

sequester, *v.* **1** to separate: "... sequest'ring from me all/ That time, acquaintance, custom, and condition/ Made tame and most familiar to my nature ..." *Tr & Cr,* III, iii, 8–10. —*n.* **2** separation: "... this hand of yours requires/ A sequester from liberty ..." *Oth,* III, iv, 35–36.

sequestered, *adj.* separated; here, cut off from his fellows: "... a poor sequester'd stag,/ That from the hunter's aim had ta'en a hurt ..." *As You,* II, i, 33–34.

sequestration, *n.* **1** imprisonment; here, also loss of lands and titles: "Since Henry Monmouth first began to reign ... This loathsome sequestration have I had ..." *1 Hen 6,* II, v, 23–25. **2** seclusion: "And never noted in him ... any sequestration/ From open haunts and popularity." *Hen 5,* I, i, 57–59. **3** abrupt

ending: "... it was a violent commencement, and/ thou shalt see an answerable sequestration ..." *Oth,* I, iii, 345–346.

sere, *adj.* **1** withered; dried up: "He is deformed, crooked, old and sere ..." *Errors,* IV, ii, 19. —*n.* **2** wilted and faded state: "... my way of life/ Is fall'n into the sere, the yellow leaf ..." *Mac,* V, iii, 22–23.

sergeant, *n.* sheriff's assistant charged with making arrests: "... this fell sergeant, Death,/ Is strict in his arrest ..." *Ham,* V, ii, 341–342.

serious, *adj.* weighty; solemn or momentous: "O heavy lightness, serious vanity ..." *Rom & Jul,* I, i, 176.

sermon, *v.* to lecture or chastise: "Come, sermon me no further." *Timon,* II, ii, 176.

serpent's curse, *n.* (in the Bible) curse laid on serpent by God for tempting Eve to taste the forbidden fruit: "Let heaven requite it with the serpent's curse ..." *Oth,* IV, ii, 16.

serpent's tongue, *n.* hiss; the sound of hissing: "Now to 'scape the serpent's tongue,/ We will make amends ere long ..." *M N Dream,* V, i, 419–420.

serpigo, *n.* creeping skin disease, erroneously thought to be venereal: "Do curse the gout, serpigo, and the rheum/ For ending thee no sooner." *Meas,* III, i, 31–32.

servant, *n.* **1** lover or suitor: "Let me thy servant and not sovereign be ..." *1 Hen 6,* I, ii, 111. **2** slave; here, love-slave: "... the bitterness of absence sour/ When you have bid your servant once adieu." *Sonn* 57, 7–8. **3 your servant,** my master, who is your humble servant: "Cesario is your servant's name, fair princess." *T Night,* III, i, 99. —*v.* **4 are servanted,** have been made servants: "My affairs/ Are servanted to others." *Cor,* V, ii, 80–81.

serve, *v.* **1** to realize; fulfill: "Vincentio's son ... It shall become to serve all hopes conceiv'd ..." *Shrew,* I, i, 14–15. **2** to be suitable or acceptable (with regard to): "... now 'tis not to be/ found; or, if it were, it would neither serve for the/ writing nor the tune." *Love's L,* I, ii, 105–107. **3** to treat: "... when I serve him so, he takes it ill." *Errors,* II, i, 12. **4** to work as a servant: "This was a venture sir that Jacob serv'd for ..." *Merch,* I, iii, 86. **5** to permit; allow: "Certainly, my conscience will serve me to run from/ this Jew my master ..." *Merch,* II, ii, 1–2. **6** wordplay on "give service" and "perform sexual service for": "Ay, so you serve us/ Till we serve you ..." *All's W,* IV, ii, 17–18. **7** to worship: "Serving with looks his sacred majesty ..." *Sonn* 7, 4. **8 serve in,** to perform; serve up: "And while I pause serve in your harmony." *Shrew,* III, i, 14. **9 serve one's turn, a.** to meet one's obligations: "My uses cry to me; I must serve my turn . . ." *Timon,* II, i, 20. **b.** to be of help; Costard replies in bawdy sense: "This maid will not serve your turn, sir." *Love's L,* I, i, 289.

service, *n.* **1** military service vs. sexual service (a frequent pun): ". . . for you, Mouldy, stay at/ home till you are past service . . ." *2 Hen 4,* III, ii, 245–246. **2** worship of the intellect and spirit; here, on (quasi-religious) theme of body as a "temple": ". . . as this temple waxes,/ The inward service of the mind and soul/ Grows wide withal." *Ham,* I, iii, 12–14. **3** food served at a meal: "Your fat king and your lean beggar is but/ variable service—two dishes, but to one table." *Ham,* IV, iii, 23–24. **4** favor, with implication of sexual favors: "What service wilt thou do me if I give them?" *3 Hen 6,* III, ii, 44. **5** employment as a servant; here, in wordplay with "sexual service": "I would cozen the man of his wife and do his service." *All's W,* IV, v, 25. **6** act of obedience: "This service is not service, so being done,/ But being so allow'd [accepted as a token of submission]." *Cymb,* III, iii, 16–17. **7** [pl.] duty: "My services to your Lordship." *Lear,* I, i, 29. **8** military deed or exploit: "I assure you there is very excellent services/ committed at the bridge." *Hen 5,* III, vi, 3–4. **9** profession of prostitution: ". . . he knew the service; and that instructed him/ to mercy." *Meas,* III, ii, 116–117. **10 turn out of service,** dismiss from employment; here, from the French army: ". . . they will pluck/ The gay new coats o'er the French soldiers' heads,/ And turn them out of service." *Hen 5,* IV, iii, 117–119. **11 use of service,** employment of servants: "Letters [learning] should not be known; riches, poverty,/ And use of service, none . . ." *Temp,* II, i, 146–147.

serviceable, *adj.* **1** responsive or obliging: "What would my lord . . . Wherein Olivia may seem serviceable?" *T Night,* V, i, 99–100. **2** diligent or persistent; here, officious: ". . . a serviceable villain;/ As duteous to the vices of thy mistress/ As badness would desire." *Lear,* IV, vi, 253–255. **3** promising devotion: ". . . whose composed rhymes/ Should be full-fraught with serviceable vows." *Two Gent,* III, ii, 69–70.

servile, *adj.* **1** like a slave; slavelike: "Yet, if this servile usage [treatment] once offend,/ Go and be free again . . ." *1 Hen 6,* V, iii, 58–59. **2** subject; under the control [of]: "Servile to all the skyey influences . . ." *Meas,* III, i, 9.

servile ministers, *n.* See **minister** (def. 9).

servitor, *n.* **1** servant: ". . . as servitors to the unjust . . ." *Luc,* 285. **2** common soldier; serviceman: "Thus are poor servitors,/ Constrain'd to watch in darkness, rain, and cold." *1 Hen 6,* II, i, 5–7. **3** soldier in the service of the god of war: "The mighty and redoubted Prince of Wales,/ Great servitor to bloody Mars in arms . . ." *Edw 3,* V, i, 177–178.

Sessa! prob. a dismissive term with the approx. meaning of "no matter" or "get on with it"; poss. corruption of French *c'est ça!,* that's that: "Therefore *paucas pallabris,* let the world slide. Sessa!" *Shrew,* Ind., i, 5.

session, *n.* sitting of a court of justice: ". . . every shop, church, session, hanging,/ yields a careful man work." *W Tale,* IV, iv, 685–686.

Sestos, *n.* Also, **Sestus.** ancient city on the Hellespont, in Turkey; site of the myth of Hero and Leander: "I will through a Hellespont of blood/ To arrive at Sestos, where my Hero lies." *Edw 3,* II, ii, 154–155.

set, *adj.* **1** accurate; technically correct: ". . . rail'd on Lady Fortune in good terms,/ In good set terms . . ." *As You,* II, vii, 16–17. **2** fixed; resolute: ". . . he is set so only to himself/ That nothing but himself . . . Is friendly with him." *Timon,* V, i, 116–118. **3** lacking spontaneity; memorized: "I take these wise men, that crow/ so at these set kind of fools, no better than the/ fools' zanies." *T Night,* I, v, 86–88. **4** closed; also, sunk, in the manner of the setting sun: ". . . thy eyes/ are almost set in thy head." *Temp,* III, ii, 7–8.
—*v.* **5** to value: ". . . gnarling sorrow hath less power to bite/ The man that mocks at it and sets it light." *Rich 2,* I, iii, 292–293. **6** to hazard; gamble: "To set the exact wealth of all our states/ All at one cast?" *1 Hen 4,* IV, i, 46–47. **7** to challenge: "Who sets me else? By heaven, I'll throw at all!" *Rich 2,* IV, i, 57. **8** to close (down): "O, he's drunk, Sir Toby, an hour a-gone; his/ eyes were set at eight i' th' morning." *T Night,* V, i, 196–197. **9** to put music to words: "Give me a note; your ladyship can set." *Two Gent,* I, ii, 81. **10** old past part. of **sit;** seated; Speed's rejoinder to Valentine's "stand": "I would you were set, so your affection would cease." *Two Gent,* II, i, 81. **11** to apply: "And therefore to your fair [beauty] no painting set . . ." *Sonn 83,* 2. **12 coldly set,** [to] undervalue; disregard: ". . . thou mayst not coldly set/ Our sovereign process . . ." *Ham,* IV, iii, 65–66. **13 set abroad,** to unleash; let loose: "To-morrow yield up rule, resign my life,/ And set abroad new business for you all?" *T Andr,* I, i, 191–192. **14 set against,** to set upon; attack: "I see you all are bent/ To set against me for your merriment." *M N Dream,* III, ii, 145–146. **15 set a match,** See **match** (def. 7). **16 set [it] down,** to resolve or determine: "I have in quick determination/ Thus set it down: he shall with speed to England . . ." *Ham,* III, i, 170–171. **17 set down before,** to lay siege to: ". . . the confident tyrant/ Keeps still in Dunsinane, and will endure/ Our setting down before 't." *Mac,* V, iv, 8–10. **18 set him clear,** make him [Devil] look blameless: ". . . but in the end the villainies of man will set him clear." *Timon,* III, iii, 32. **19 set off,** to cancel; nullify: ". . . your demands are just,/ You shall enjoy them, everything set off/ That might so much as think you enemies." *2 Hen 4,* IV, i, 144–146. **20 set on, a.** [usually a command] go ahead; begin or proceed: "Set

on, and leave no ceremony out." *J Caes,* I, ii, 11. **b.** to incite or urge; put up to: "Come, come,/ I know thou wast set on to this." *2 Hen 4,* II, i, 149–150. **c.** attack!: ". . . set on,/ Sound all the lofty instruments of war . . ." *1 Hen 4,* V, ii, 96–97. **d.** to put on the fire: "She's e'en setting on water to scald such chickens/ as you are." *Timon,* II, ii, 72–73. **21 set to,** to reset; mend: "Can honour set to a leg?" *1 Hen 4,* V, i, 131. **22 set up, a.** to cause to spin: "He turned me about . . . as one would set up/ a top." *Cor,* IV, v, 154–156. **b.** firmly resolve to maintain: "O here/ Will I set up my everlasting rest . . ." *Rom & Jul,* V, iii, 109–110. **23 set you forth,** praise you extravagantly: "I shall digest it."/ "Well, I'll set you forth." *Merch,* III, v, 84. —*n.* **24** game of cards: "As sure a card as ever won the set . . ." *T Andr,* V, i, 100.

Setebos, *n.* said to be a devil-god of the Patagonians: "It would control my dam's god, Setebos,/ And make a vassal of him." *Temp,* I, ii, 375–376.

set hand, *n.* formal or legal handwriting: "Here is the indictment . . . Which in a set hand fairly is engross'd . . ." *Rich 3,* III, vi, 1–2.

set my rest, *n.* stake my all; here, a passing (and ironic) ref. to a play in the card game of primero: "I lov'd her most, and thought to set my rest/ On her kind nursery." *Lear,* I, i, 123–124.

set off one's head, *adj.* not counted against one; excepted: "This present enterprise set off his head,/ I do not think a braver gentleman . . . is now alive . . ." *1 Hen 4,* V, i, 88–91.

sets up his rest, *v.* is determined: ". . . he that sets up his rest to do/ more exploits with his mace . . ." *Errors,* IV, iii, 26–27.

setter, *n.* (in thieves' jargon) one paid to point out likely victims: "O, 'tis our setter, I know his voice." *1 Hen 4,* II, ii, 49.

setting, *n.* fixed look: "The setting of thine eye and cheek proclaim/ A matter from thee . . ." *Temp,* II, i, 224–225.

setting of boys' copies, teaching boys to write: "We took him setting of boys' copies." *2 Hen 6,* IV, ii, 84.

settle, *v.* to instill: "'Tis thou that . . . Settlest admired reverence in a slave . . ." *Timon,* V, i, 49–50.

settled, *adj.* composed; also, inscrutable: "Whose settl'd visage and deliberate word/ Nips youth i'th'head . . ." *Meas,* III, i, 89–90.

settled gravity, *n.* necessary seriousness; here, to justify an action: "When love, converted from the thing it was,/ Shall reasons find of settled gravity . . ." *Sonn 49,* 7–8.

settling, *n.* calming down: "Desire him to go in; trouble him no more/ Till further settling." *Lear,* IV, vii, 81–82.

seven-fold shield, *n.* shield of Ajax, made of brass backed by seven layers of hide: "The seven-fold shield of Ajax cannot keep/ The battery from my heart." *Ant & Cleo,* IV, xiv, 38–39.

seven stars, *n.* prob. the stars of Ursa Major [Big Dipper]; in fig. use, "see the seven stars" means to have made quite a night of it: "Sweet knight, I kiss thy neaf. What! we have seen/ the seven stars." *2 Hen 4,* II, iv, 182–183.

seven years' day, *n.* [in] seven years: "I saw not better sport these seven years' day . . ." *2 Hen 6,* II, i, 2.

sever, *v.* to separate; disperse or scatter: "By uproars sever'd, as a flight of fowl/ Scatter'd by winds and high tempestuous gusts . . ." *T Andr,* V, iii, 68–69.

several, *adj.* **1** different; various: ". . . touch them with several fortunes,/ The greater scorns the lesser." *Timon,* IV, iii, 5–6. **2** particular or individual; respective: "And every one his love-feat will advance/ Unto his several mistress . . ." *Love's L,* V, ii, 123–124. **3** separate or separated; hence, private: "My lips are no common, though several they be." *Love's L,* II, i, 222. **4 twelve several times,** on twelve separate occasions: "Thou hast beat me out/ Twelve several times . . ." *Cor,* IV, v, 122–123. —*n.* **5** [pl.] details or particulars: "The severals and unhidden passages/ Of his true titles . . ." *Hen 5,* I, i, 86–87. **6** [usually pl.] individuals: ". . . by some severals/ Of head-piece extraordinary?" *W Tale,* I, ii, 226–227. **7 severals and generals,** individual and collective qualities [of excellence]: "All our abilities, gifts, natures, shapes,/ Severals and generals of grace exact . . ." *Tr & Cr,* I, iii, 179–180.

severally, *adv.* **1** separately; in or from different directions, at different times, etc.: "I will dispatch you severally . . ." *Timon,* II, ii, 191. **2** to or for each person: ". . . the counterchange/ Is severally in all." *Cymb,* V, v, 397–398.

several plot, *n.* an enclosed garden or pasture: "Why should my heart think that a several plot/ Which my heart knows the wide world's common place?" *Sonn 137,* 9–10.

Severn, *n.* river separating England and Wales: "Leave not the worthy Lucius . . . Till he have cross'd the Severn." *Cymb,* III, v, 16–17.

sewer, *n.* servant charged with tasting dishes (to detect poison) before serving to guests: "Enter . . . a Sewer,/ and divers Servants with dishes and service." [SD] *Mac,* I, vii, 1.

sexton, *n.* ref. to sexton's responsibility of a church's clock: "Old time the clock-setter, that bald sexton time . . ." *K John,* III, i, 250.

Sextus Pompeius, *n.* ruler of Sicily and the son of Pompey the Great: "Sextus Pompeius/ Hath given the dare to Caesar, and commands/ The empire of the sea." *Ant & Cleo,* I, ii, 181–182.

'Sfoot, *interj.* By God's foot [a mild oath]: "'Sfoot, I'll learn/ to conjure and raise devils . . ." *Tr & Cr,* II, iii, 5–6.

shade, *n.* **1** darkness: "Nor shall death brag thou wander'st in his shade . . ." *Sonn 18,* 11. **2** image of the memory: "When in dead night thy fair imperfect [hazy] shade/ Through heavy sleep on sightless eyes doth stay!" *Sonn 43,* 11–12. **3** shadow: "Since every one hath, every one, one shade . . ." *Sonn 53,* 3.

shadow, *n.* **1** shady spot: "I'll go find a shadow and sigh till he come." *As You,* IV, i, 206–207. **2** darkness cast by grief: "The shadow of your sorrow hath destroy'd/ The shadow [reflection] of your face." *Rich 2,* IV, i, 292–293. **3** reflected image: "The shadow [darkness] of your sorrow hath destroy'd/ The shadow of your face." *Rich 2,* IV, i, 292–293. **4** picture or portrait: "Long time thy shadow hath been thrall to me,/ For in my gallery thy picture hangs . . ." *1 Hen 6,* II, iii, 35–36. **5** image in one's memory: "As with your shadow I with these did play." *Sonn 98,* 14. **6** [often pl.] products of the imagination, as dreams: ". . . how sweet is love itself possess'd/ When but love's shadows are so rich in joy." *Rom & Jul,* V, i, 10–11. **7** spirit or ghost of the dead; shade: "That so the shadows be not unappeas'd,/ Nor we disturb'd with prodigies on earth." *T Andr,* I, i, 100–101. **8** fictitious name on military roll, allowing captain to keep the pay: "Prick him, for we/ have a number of shadows fill up the muster-book." *2 Hen 4,* III, ii, 133–134. **9 in our shadow,** under our roof: "I know he will/ come in our shadow, to scatter his crowns in the/ sun." *Per,* IV, ii, 109–111. **10 roses of shadow,** imitation [painted] roses: "Why should poor beauty indirectly seek/ Roses of shadow, since his rose is true?" *Sonn 67,* 7–8. **11 thy shadow's form,** your actual presence: "How would thy shadow's form form happy show . . ." *Sonn 43,* 6.
—*v.* **12** to disguise or conceal: ". . . thereby shall we shadow/ The numbers of our host . . ." *Mac,* V, iv, 5–6. **13** to shelter; protect: "The rather that you give his offspring life,/ Shadowing their right under your wings of war . . ." *K John,* II, i, 13–14.

shadowed livery, *adj.* dark distinguishing mark: "The shadowed livery of the burnish'd sun . . ." *Merch,* II, i, 2.

shadowing, *adj.* engulfing; overwhelming: "Nature would/ not invest herself in such shadowing passion without/ some instruction." *Oth,* IV, i, 39–41.

shady stealth, *n.* stealthy shadow: "Thou by thy dial's shady stealth mayst know . . ." *Sonn 77,* 7.

Shafalus to Procrus, blunder by Bottom and Flute for "Cephalus to Procris"; in legend, Cephalus, though abducted by Aurora, remained faithful to his wife Procris: "Not Shafalus to Procrus was so true."/ "As Shafalus to Procrus, I to you." *M N Dream,* V, i, 196–197.

shaft, *n.* **shaft or a bolt,** one way or the other; ref. to shooting with the slim arrow used with a bow or the thicker, shorter arrow used with a crossbow: "I'll make a shaft or a bolt on 't. 'Slid, 'tis but/ venturing." *Wives,* III, iv, 24–25.

shag, *adj.* shaggy: "Round-hoof'd, short-jointed, fetlocks shag and long . . ." *Ven & Ad,* 295.

shake, *v.* **1** to steal or empty: ". . . see thou shake the bags/ Of hoarding abbots . . ." *K John,* III, ii, 17–18. **2 shake out,** to be the cause of; here, the result of a servant's blabbing: ". . . for many a man's/ tongue shakes out his master's undoing." *All's W,* II, iv, 22–23. **3 shake up,** to berate; scold or abuse: ". . . thou shalt hear how he will/ shake me up." *As You,* I, i, 27–28.

shaked, *past part.;* shaken. **1** here, disturbed or upset: "O, when degree [order of precedence] is shak'd . . . The enterprise is sick." *Tr & Cr,* I, iii, 101–103. **2** made to waver or weaken: "A sly and constant knave./ Not to be shak'd . . ." *Cymb,* I, vi, 75–76.

shake hands, *v.* to take leave; bid farewell: ". . . the slave;/ Which ne'er shook hands, nor bade farewell to him . . ." *Mac,* I, ii, 20–21.

shake his bells, *v.* ref. to the bells attached to falcons' legs and the fear that such sound instilled in prey: "Neither the King, nor he that loves him best . . . Dares stir a wing if Warwick shake his bells." *3 Hen 6,* I, i, 45–47.

shale, *n.* shell: "Leaving them but the shales and husks of men." *Hen 5,* IV, ii, 18.

shall, *v.* **1** am to: "Sweet father, if I shall be thought thy son,/ Let me redeem my brothers . . ." *T Andr,* III, i, 179–180. **2** must; have to: ". . . you/ shall seek all day ere you find them . . ." *Merch,* I, i, 116–117. **3 that shall,** who tries to; who thinks he can: "A whoreson dog, that shall palter with us thus." *Tr & Cr,* II, iii, 233.

shallow, *adj.* **1** slight or negligible; also, unworthy: "I'll show my mind,/ According to my shallow simple skill." *Two Gent,* I, ii, 7–8. **2** inexperienced: "Armed in proof, and led by shallow Richmond." *Rich 3,* V, iii, 220. **3** stupid: "The shallowest thick-skin of that barren sort . . . Forsook his scene, and enter'd in a brake . . ." *M N Dream,* III, ii, 13–15. **4** (of a boat) flat-bottomed: "How many shallow bauble boats dare sail . . ." *Tr & Cr,* I, iii, 35. **5 be shallow in great friends,** to be a superficial judge of deep friendships: "Y'are shallow, madam, in great friends . . ." *All's W,* I, iii, 40.

shallowest, *adj.* slightest: "Your shallowest help will hold me up afloat . . ." *Sonn 80,* 9.

shall's, *v.* shall us [we]: "Shall's go hear the vestals sing?" *Per,* IV, v, 7.

shalt, *v.* old 2d pers. sing. of **shall:** "Ah, if thou issueless shalt hap to die . . ." *Sonn 9,* 3.

shambles, *n.* slaughterhouse: "O, ay, as summer's flies, are in the shambles . . ." *Oth,* IV, ii, 67.

shame, *n.* **1** attempt to inflict shame: "Why, what a shame was this?" *Hen 8,* V, ii, 175.
—*v.* **2** to feel ashamed: "I do shame/ To think of what a noble strain you are . . ." *Per,* IV, iii, 23–24. **3** to cause embarrassment to: "Wherein our entertainment shall shame us [because of its inadequacy] . . ." *W Tale,* I, i, 8.

shape, *n.* **1** human form, esp. the body of a man: "Fie, fie, thou sham'st thy shape, thy love, thy wit . . ." *Rom & Jul,* III, iii, 121. **2** appearance; semblance: "It is the lesser blot modesty finds,/ Women to change their shapes, than men their minds." *Two Gent,* V, iv, 107–108. **3** role we have assumed: "Weigh what convenience both of time and means/ May fit us to our shape." *Ham,* IV, vii, 148–149. **4** [often pl.] an imaginary form: "So full of shapes is fancy,/ That it alone is high fantastical." *T Night,* I, i, 14–15. **5 in one's own shape,** undisguised: "Immediately they will again be here/ In their own shapes . . ." *Love's L,* V, ii, 287–288.
—*v.* **6** to form into: "Shape every bush a hideous shapeless devil." *Luc,* 973.

shapeless, *adj.* **1** unshapely or misshapen; also, ugly or uncouth: "Ill-fac'd, worse bodied, shapeless everywhere . . ." *Errors,* IV, ii, 20. **2** aimless; purposeless: "Wear out thy youth with shapeless idleness." *Two Gent* I, I, 8.

shape of heaven, *n.* power of Satan to assume angelic shape: "Though lewdness court it in a shape of heaven . . ." *Ham,* I, v, 54.

shape of likelihood, what was likely to happen: "As by discharge of their artillery,/ And shape of likelihood, the news was told . . ." *1 Hen 4,* I, i, 57–58.

shapes and tricks, *n.* amazing feats of skill: "That I in forgery of shapes and tricks/ Come short of what he did." *Ham,* IV, vii, 88–89.

shaping, *adj.* fertile; prolific: "Such shaping fantasies [imaginations], that apprehend/ More than cool reason ever comprehends." *M N Dream,* V, i, 5–6.

shard, *n.* wing case of an insect: "They are his shards, and he their beetle, so . . ." *Ant & Cleo,* III, ii, 20.

shard-born, *adj.* prob. ref. to the beetle's hatching in dung; also, poss. wordplay with "borne [carried along] on scaly wings": "The shard-born beetle, with his drowsy hums,/ Hath rung Night's yawning peal . . ." *Mac,* III, ii, 42–43.

sharded, *adj.* having the wings encased: ". . . shall we find/ The sharded beetle in a safer hold . . ." *Cymb,* III, iii, 19–20.

shark, *v.* **1** to prey [on]: "For other ruffians/ Would shark on you, and men like ravenous fishes/ Would feed on one another." *More,* II, iv, 84–87. **2 shark up,** to snap up, as a shark gathers food: "Shark'd up a list of lawless resolutes/ For food and diet to some enterprise . . ." *Ham,* I, i, 101–102.

sharp, *adj.* **1** witty; incisive: "If voluble and sharp discourse be marr'd,/ Unkindness blunts it more than marble hard." *Errors,* II, i, 92–93. **2** keen; eager: "But you, Sir Thurio, are not sharp enough/ You must lay lime, to tangle her desires . . ." *Two Gent,* III, ii, 67. **3** subtle; precise or discriminating: ". . . these nice sharp quillets of the law . . ." *1 Hen 6,* II, iv, 17. **4** harsh; disagreeable: "Haply this life is best . . . sweeter to you/ That have a sharper known . . ." *Cymb,* III, iii, 29–31. **5** fierce; angry: "Alas, how fiery, and how sharp he looks." *Errors,* IV, iv, 48. **6** bitter; strong and distasteful: "Sharp physic is the last: but, O you powers/ That gives heaven countless eyes . . ." *Per,* I, i, 73–74. **7** cold: ". . . sun and sharp air/ Lurk'd like two thieves to rob him of his fair." *Ven & Ad,* 1085–1086. **8** hungry or famished: "My falcon now is sharp and passing empty . . ." *Shrew,* IV, i, 177.
—*n.* **9** [usually pl.] high musical notes: "It is the lark that sings so out of tune,/ Straining harsh discords and unpleasing sharps." *Rom & Jul,* III, v, 27–28.

sharp by fast, *adj.* ravenous from fasting: "Even as an empty eagle, sharp by fast,/ Tires with her beak on feathers . . ." *Ven & Ad,* 55–56.

sharpness, *n.* harshness or roughness; also, biting sarcasm: "So like a courtier, contempt nor bitterness/ Were in his pride or sharpness . . ." *All's W,* I, ii, 36–37.

sharp occasions, *n.* urgent necessities: ". . . goaded with most sharp occasions/ Which lay nice manners by . . ." *All's W,* V, i, 14–15.

sharp-provided, *adj.* keenly furnished: "With what a sharp-provided wit he reasons . . ." *Rich 3,* III, i, 132.

sharp state, *n.* deadly nature: "The more do thou in serpents' natures think them,/ Fear their gay skins with thought of their sharp state . . ." *More,* III, ii, 17–18.

shaved, *adj.* given a venereal infection: "Bardolph was shaved and lost many/ a hair . . ." *1 Hen 4,* III, iii, 57–58.

she, *n.* **1** woman: "That she belov'd knows naught that knows not this . . ." *Tr & Cr,* I, ii, 293. **2 she herself,** virtue itself: "The temple/ Of Virtue was she; yea, and she herself." *Cymb,* V, v, 220–221. **3 two such shes,** two women, one fair [Imogen], the other plain: ". . . for apes and monkeys,/ 'Twixt two such shes, would chatter this way . . ." *Cymb,* I, vii, 39–40.

shealed, *adj.* shelled: "That's a sheal'd peascod. [Pointing to Lear]" *Lear,* I, iv, 208.

shearman, *n.* worker who shears the nap from newly woven cloth: "And thou thyself a shearman, art thou not?" *2 Hen 6,* IV, ii, 127.

shears of destiny, *n.* ref. to the Fates of Greek mythology who spun the thread of life, determined its length, then cut it at the appointed time [See **Atropos**]: "Think you I bear the shears of destiny?" *K John,* IV, ii, 91.

sheath, *n.* long case, usually of leather, for a rapier: ". . . you tailor's yard,/ you sheath, you bow-case, you vile standing tuck!" *1 Hen 4,* II, iv, 242–244.

sheaved, *adj.* made of straw: "For some, untuck'd, descended her sheav'd hat . . ." *Lover's Comp,* 31.

shed, *v.* to spill: ". . . he weeps like a wench that had shed her milk . . ." *All's W,* IV, iii, 104.

sheen, *n.* **1** brightness: "And thirty dozen moons with borrow'd sheen . . ." *Ham,* III, ii, 152. **2** splendor: ". . . they never meet in grove or green,/ By fountain clear, or spangled starlight sheen . . ." *M N Dream,* II, i, 28–29.

sheep, *n.* **1** ref. to the schoolchild's memory device for recalling the English vowels: "oueia" was the Spanish word for "sheep": "I will repeat them; a, e, i,—"/ "The sheep: the other

two concludes it; o, u." *Love's L,* V, i, 52–53. **2 play the sheep,** behave like a fool; also, wordplay on similar pron. of "ship" and "sheep": ". . . he is shipp'd already,/ And I have play'd the sheep in losing him." *Two Gent,* I, i, 72–73.

sheep-biter, *n.* sneaking, malicious fellow: ". . . to have the niggardly/ rascally sheep-biter come by some notable shame?" *T Night,* II, v, 4–5.

sheep-biting, *adj.* ref. to the punishment of hanging for killing or stealing a sheep: "Show your sheep-biting face, and be/ hanged an hour!" *Meas,* V, i, 352–353.

sheep-hook, *n.* shepherd's crook: ". . . thou a sceptre's heir,/ That thus affects a sheep-hook!" *W Tale,* IV, iv, 420–421.

sheep's guts, *n.* strings of a musical instrument: "Is it not strange that sheep's guts should hale souls/ out of men's bodies?" *M Ado,* II, iii, 59–61.

sheep-whistling, *adj.* sheep-tending: "An old sheep-whistling rogue, a/ ram-tender . . ." *W Tale,* IV, iv, 777–778.

sheer, *adj.* **1** pure: "Thou sheer, immaculate and silver fountain . . ." *Rich 2,* V, iii, 59. **2** only; nothing but; may also have "undiluted" sense of 1: ". . . fourteen pence on the score for sheer ale . . ." *Shrew,* Ind., ii, 23.

sheet, *v.* to cover [over]: ". . . like the stag, when snow the pasture sheets . . ." *Ant & Cleo,* I, iv, 65.

shelter, *n.* excuse or alibi (for): ". . . his feigned ecstasies/ Shall be no shelter to these outrages . . ." *T Andr,* IV, iv, 21–22.

shelves, *n.* pl. of *shelf;* sandbanks: "Huge rocks, high winds, strong pirates, shelves and sands/ The merchant fears . . ." *Luc,* 335–336.

shelving, *adj.* projecting: "Her chamber is aloft . . . And built so shelving that one cannot climb it . . ." *Two Gent,* III, i, 114–115.

shent, *v.* **1** past part. of archaic **shend,** to rebuke or revile: "How in my words somever [howsoever] she be shent,/ To give them seals never my soul consent." *Ham,* III, ii, 389–390. **2** See **sate.**

sheriff's post, *n.* elaborate post placed outside a sheriff's office as a symbol of authority: ". . . he says he'll stand at/ your door like a sheriff's post . . ." *T Night,* I, v, 149–150.

sherris-sack, *n.* white wine of Spain; sherry: "A good sherris-sack hath a/ twofold operation in it." *2 Hen 4,* IV, iii, 94–95.

shew or **'schew,** *v.* poss. abbrev. form of "eschew"; sense here is "shun or avoid": ". . . those men . . . Will shew no course to keep them from the light." *Per,* I, i, 135–137.

shield, *v.* to forbid; prevent: "God shield I should disturb devotion." *Rom & Jul,* IV, i, 41.

shift, *n.* **1** makeshift arrangement, method, or device; contrivance: ". . . for lovers lacking . . . matter, the cleanliest shift is to kiss." *As You,* IV, i, 73–74. **2** scheme or trick: "I see a man here needs not live by shifts . . ." *Errors,* III, ii, 181. **3** preceding sense in wordplay with "shirt": ". . . the rest of thy low countries/ have made a shift to eat up thy holland." *2 Hen 4,* II, ii, 21–22. **4** deceit; trickery: "Guilty of treason, forgery and shift . . ." *Luc,* 920. **5** wordplay on "trickery" and "chemise": "When he was made a shriver, 'twas for shift." *3 Hen 6,* III, ii, 108. **6 for a shift,** to make do: ". . . thou sing'st well enough for/ a shift." *M Ado,* II, iii, 77–78. **7 make (a) shift,** to manage: ". . . though he took up my legs sometime,/ yet I made a shift to cast him." *Mac,* II, iii, 41–42. **8 puts us to our shifts,** causes us to resort to such trickery: "For it is you that puts us to our shifts . . ." *T Andr,* IV, ii, 177.
—*v.* **9** to change: "Sir, I would advise you to shift a shirt . . ." *Cymb,* I, iii, 1. **10** wordplay on "change one's clothes" and "change one's fate": "My shame will not be shifted with my sheet . . ." *2 Hen 6,* II, iv, 107. **11** to exchange; here, condition or status: "And should we shift estates, yours would be mine." *Ant & Cleo,* V, ii, 151. **12** to depart quickly: "O mistress, mistress, shift and save yourself . . ." *Errors,* V, i, 168. **13** to think of something; find a way out of a predicament: "There is no remedy: I must cony-catch; I must/ shift." *Wives,* I, iii, 31–32. **14 every man shift,** Stephano, in his drunkenness, confuses the saying, "Every man for himself": "Every man shift for all the rest, and let no man take/ care for himself . . ." *Temp,* V, i, 256–257. **15 shift away,** to leave surreptitiously; slip away: "And let us not be dainty of leave-taking,/ But shift away." *Mac,* II, iii, 144–145. **16 shift for one,** shift for myself: "For me, I will make/ shift for one, and so God's curse light upon you all!" *2 Hen 6,* IV, viii, 31–32. **17 shift his being,** change his place of abode: ". . . to shift his being/ Is to exchange one misery with another . . ." *Cymb,* I, vi, 54–55. **18 shift me,** change my clothes: ". . . to ride day and night, and not to . . . have patience to shift me—" *2 Hen 4,* V, v, 20–22.

shifting, *adj.* given to fickleness: "A woman's gentle heart, but not acquainted/ With shifting change, as is false women's fashion . . ." *Sonn 20,* 3–4.

shifts of lowness, *n.* tricks to which one without power is reduced: ". . . send humble treaties, dodge/ And palter in the shifts of lowness . . ." *Ant & Cleo,* III, xi, 62–63.

shilling, *n.* ref. to those in the expensive seats of the Globe Theatre: "I'll undertake may see away their shilling/ Richly in two short hours." *Hen 8,* Prol. 12–13.

shine, *v.* **1 shine down,** to outshine: ". . . like heathen gods/ Shone down the English . . ." *Hen 8,* I, i, 19–20.
—*n.* **2** shining example: "Thou show'dst a subject's shine, I a true prince." *Per,* I, ii, 124.

ship, *v.* to send or dispatch; here, to shove: "But age with his stealing steps/ Hath claw'd me in his clutch,/ And hath shipp'd me intil the land [into the ground] . . ." *Ham,* V, i, 70–72.

shipman, *n.* mariner: "So puts himself unto the shipman's toil [entrusts himself to the perils of a sea voyage] . . ." *Per,* I, iii, 23.

shipman's card, *n.* prob. a compass card: "All the quarters that they know/ I' th' shipman's card." *Mac,* I, iii, 16–17.

shipped, *adj.* aboard ship or embarked: "Launce, away, away; aboard; thy master is/ shipped . . ." *Two Gent,* II, iii, 33–34.

ship-tire, *n.* headdress in the form of a sailing ship: ". . . thou/ hast the right arched beauty of the brow that becomes/ the ship-tire . . ." *Wives,* III, iii, 49–51.

shipwrack, *n.* destruction and ruin, as if by shipwreck: "This siren that will charm Rome's Saturnine,/ And see his shipwrack and his commonweal's." *T Andr,* II, i, 23–24.

shirt and smock, *n.* man and woman, as indicated by their costume: "Here's goodly gear . . . A sail! a sail!"/ "Two. Two. A shirt and a smock." *Rom & Jul,* II, iv, 100–102.

shive, *n.* slice: ". . . and easy it is/ Of a cut loaf to steal a shive . . ." *T Andr,* II, i, 86–87.

shiver, *n.* **1** [often pl] splinter: ". . . there it is, crack'd in an hundred shivers." *Rich 2,* IV, i, 289.
—*v.* **2** to shatter: "So many fathom down precipitating,/ Thou'dst [you would have] shiver'd like an egg . . ." *Lear,* IV, vi, 50–51.

shock, *n.* **1** [pl.] mental or emotional wounds: "The heartache and the thousand natural shocks/ That flesh is heir to . . ." *Ham,* III, i, 62–63.
—*v.* **2** to meet the force of (an enemy) with superior force: "Come the three corners of the world in arms/ And we shall shock them!" *K John,* V, vii, 116–117.

shoe, *n.* **1** See **show** (def. 14). **2 over shoes or boots,** recklessly; head over heels: "For he was more than over shoes in love."/ "'Tis true; for you are over boots in love . . ." *Two Gent,* I, i, 24–25.

shoeing-horn, *n.* shoehorn: ". . . a thrifty shoeing-horn in a chain at his brother's/ leg . . ." *Tr & Cr,* V, i, 55–56.

shog, *v.* **1** to get going; move along: "Shall we shog? the king will be gone from/ Southampton." *Hen 5,* II, iii, 46–47. **2 shog off,** [to] come along: "Will you shog off? I would have you solus [alone]." *Hen 5,* II, i, 44.

shoon, *n.* old pl. of **shoe:** "By his cockle hat and staff/ And his sandal shoon." *Ham,* IV, v, 25–26.

shoot, *n.* **1** act of shooting: "End thy ill aim before thy shoot be ended . . ." *Luc,* 579. **2** offshoot; here, the cuckold's horns: "Thou want'st a rough pash and the shoots that I have/ To be full like me . . ." *W Tale,* I, ii, 128–129.
—*v.* **3 shoot over,** to overshoot the mark: "You have shot over."/ "'Tis not the first time you were overshot [outshot]." *Hen 5,* III, vii, 124–125.

shop, *n.* **1** seat of an organ, as the heart: ". . . your hat penthouse-like o'er the shop of your eyes . . ." *Love's L,* III, i, 15. **2** [slang] codpiece: "O! rhymes are guards on wanton Cupid's hose:/ Disfigure not his shop." *Love's L,* IV, iii, 55–56. **3** store; storehouse: "A shop of all the qualities that man/ Loves woman for . . ." *Cymb,* V, v, 166–167.

shore[1]**,** *n.* **1** boundary or limit: ". . . to the extremest/ shore of my modesty . . ." *Meas,* III, ii, 245–246.
—*v.* **2** to put ashore: ". . . if he think it fit to shore them again . . ." *W Tale,* IV, iv, 838.

shore[2]**,** *n.* sewer: "Empty/ Old receptacles, or common shores, of filth . . ." *Per,* IV, vi, 173–174.

shore[3]**,** *past part.* old form of shorn: "Lay them in gore,/ Since you have shore/ With shears his thread of silk [i.e., life]." *M N Dream,* V, i, 326–328.

short, *adj.* **1** restrained or confined: "It will be laid to us, whose providence/ Should have kept short . . . This mad young man." *Ham,* IV, i, 17–19. **2** lacking or inadequate; here, failing to comply: "And to be short, for not-appearance . . ." *Hen 8,* IV, i, 30. **3** brief; fleeting: ". . . great bases for eternity,/ Which prove more short than waste or ruining?" *Sonn 125,* 3–4. **4** hasty: "Well, madam, we must take a short farewell . . ." *Cymb,* III, iv, 187.
—*adv.* **5 come short,** to arrive too late: ". . . hath for four or five removes come short/ To tender it herself." *All's W,* V, iii, 131–132. **6 take up short,** to dispose of quickly: "Take up the English short, and let them know/ Of what a monarchy you are the head . . ." *Hen 5,* II, iv, 72–73.
—*v.* **7 short my word,** fail to keep my promise: "I shall short my word/ By length'ning my return." *Cymb,* I, vii, 200–201.

short-armed ignorance, *n.* ignorance so pervasive that almost everything is beyond its grasp: ". . . short-armed ignorance itself knows is so abundant/ scarce . . ." *Tr & Cr,* II, iii, 15–16.

shorten, *v.* to interfere with or harm: "Yet to be known shortens my made intent [plan] . . ." *Lear,* IV, vii, 9.

short knife and a throng, cutpurse's requirements: "Go—a short knife/ and a throng [crowd]!—to your manor of Pickt-hatch, go!" *Wives,* II, ii, 16–17.

shortness, *n.* candidness; straightforwardness: "Your plainness and your shortness please me well." *Shrew,* IV, iv, 39.

short'st of day, *n.* shortest day of the year, on or about Dec. 21st: "Sent back like Hollowmas or short'st of day." *Rich 2,* V, i, 80.

short straw, *n.* straw reduced to rubble through heavy use: "To hovel thee with swine and rogues forlorn,/ In short and musty straw?" *Lear,* IV, vii, 39–40.

shot[1]**,** *n.* **1** marksman; perh. also wordplay on remnant of flock after best animals have been selected: "O, give me always/ a little, lean, old, chopt, bald shot." *2 Hen 4,* III, ii, 269–270. **2** act of shooting; discharge: ". . . the hourly shot/ Of angry eyes . . ." *Cymb,* I, ii, 20–21.
—*past part.* **3 well shot,** having hit the target implies good aim (with sexual innuendo): "Near or far off, well won is still well shot . . ." *Hen 5,* I, i, 174.

shot[2]**,** *n.* alehouse reckoning; bill or tab: ". . . never welcome to a/ place till some certain shot be paid . . ." *Two Gent,* II, v, 4–5.

shot-free, *adv.* without paying the bill, esp. at a tavern or inn: "Though I could scape shot-free at London, I fear/ the shot here . . ." *1 Hen 4,* V, iii, 30–31.

shot over, *v.* See **shoot** (def. 3).

shotten, *adj.* (of a fish) having just spawned: ". . . if manhood . . . be/ not forgot upon the face of the earth, then am I a/ shotten herring . . ." *1 Hen 4,* II, iv, 125–127.

shough, *n.* small, long-haired dog: "Shoughs, water-rugs, and demi-wolves, are clept/ All by the name of dogs . . ." *Mac,* III, i, 93–94.

should, *v.* **1** was supposed to: ". . . if you can find the huntsman out/ That should have murthered Bassianus here." *T Andr,* II, iii, 278–279. **2** would undoubtedly: "She should have died hereafter [if not now] . . ." *Mac,* V, v, 17. **3 should he,**

could he have: "Where the devil/ should he learn our language?" *Temp,* II, ii, 67–68.

shoulder, *v.* **1** to attempt to supplant another: "This shouldering of each other in the Court . . ." *1 Hen 6,* IV, i, 189. —*n.* **2** the shoulder as a symbol of strength and support: "Even as thou wilt, sweet Warwick, let it be;/ For in thy shoulder do I build my seat . . ." *3 Hen 6,* II, vi, 99–100.

shoulder-clapper, *n.* bailiff or catchpole: "A back-friend, a shoulder-clapper, one that countermands/ The passages of alleys . . ." *Errors,* IV, ii, 37–38.

shoulder-shotten, *adj.* (of a horse) having a dislocated shoulder: ". . . swayed in the back and shoulder-shotten . . ." *Shrew,* III, ii, 53.

should sure, *v.* certainly ought to be sent: "And such a daughter,/ Should sure to the slaughter . . ." *Lear,* I, iv, 328–329.

shout, *v.* **shout me forth,** praise me; acclaim me: ". . . you shout me forth/ In acclamations hyperbolical . . ." *Cor,* I, ix, 49–50.

shove, *v.* **shove by,** to push aside: "Offence's gilded hand may shove by justice . . ." *Ham,* III, iii, 58.

shove-groat, *n.* ref. to a smooth coin used in the game of shove-groat, played esp. in pubs, in which a coin is slid along a board or table toward a numbered square: "Quoit him down [pitch him down the stairs], Bardolph, like a shove-groat shilling." *2 Hen 4,* II, iv, 188.

shovel-board, *n.* **Edward shovel-board,** shilling from time of Edward VI [some 50 years earlier], worn smooth and favored for use in game of shovel-board [shove-groat]: ". . . two Edward/ shovel-boards that cost me two shilling and two-pence/ apiece . . ." *Wives,* I, i, 140–142.

show, *v.* **1** to appear; come into sight: "And Fortune/ Show'd like a rebel's whore . . ." *Mac,* I, ii, 14–15. **2** to look; seem: ". . . it will show honestly in us, and is very likely to load our purposes . . ." *Timon,* V, i, 14–15. **3** to reveal: "Let his queen-mother all alone entreat him/ To show his grief . . ." *Ham,* III, i, 184–185. **4** to disclose what one knows; here, a method for taming a shrew: "He that knows better . . . Now let him speak: 'tis charity to show." *Shrew,* IV, i, 197–198. **5 better show,** appear to better advantage: ". . . it better show'd with you/ When that your flock, assembled by the bell . . ." *2 Hen 4,* IV, ii, 4–5. **6 show scarce so gross,** appear hardly as big; seem no larger (than): "The crows . . . Show scarce so gross as beetles . . ." *Lear,* IV, vi, 13–14. **7 show you far off,** indicate to you generally or vaguely: "Or shall we sparingly show you far off/ The Dauphin's meaning . . ." *Hen 5,* I, ii, 239–240.

—*n.* **8** act of appearing; here, the mere sight: "Mine eyes, ev'n sociable to the show of thine . . ." *Temp,* V, i, 63. **9** one's aspect or appearance: ". . . alack, alack for woe/ That any harm should stain so fair a show!" *Rich 2,* III, iii, 70–71. **10** false appearance; hypocrisy: "See how belief may suffer by foul show!" *Per,* IV, iv, 23. **11** [often pl.] protestations: "Our shows are more than will [we profess much more than we actually feel] . . ." *T Night,* II, iv, 118. **12** [usually pl.] sights; scenes: "Leaving free things and happy shows behind . . ." *Lear,* III, vi, 108. **13** dumb-show: "Belike this show imports the argument of the play." *Ham,* III, ii, 136. **14** same in wordplay, poss. with the vulgarism "shoe" [vulva], since Ophelia accepts Hamlet's reply as indecent: "Will a tell us what this show meant?"/ "Ay, or any show [shoe?] that you will show him." *Ham,* III, ii, 139–140. **15 in show,** in appearance: "If you were men, as men you are in show . . ." *M N Dream,* III, ii, 151. **16 the show and gaze o'th'time,** the freak show of the day: "Then yield thee, coward,/ And live to be the show and gaze o'th'time . . ." *Mac,* V, vii, 23–24. **17 the show appear,** appearances would make it seem so: "I love not less, though less the show appear . . ." *Sonn 102,* 2.

shower, *n.* **shower sing in the wind,** signs of trouble may sometimes be seen in advance: "A man/ may hear this shower sing in the wind." *Wives,* III, ii, 32–33.

showing, *n.* **1** person's appearance: ". . . an absolute gentleman, full of most excellent/ differences . . . and great showing." *Ham,* V, ii, 107–108. **2 in showing,** in writing; in print: ". . . if you will have it in showing, you shall/ read it in what-do-ye-call there." *All's W,* II, iii, 21–22.

shown, *past part.* judged; interpreted: "By their rank thoughts my deeds must not be shown . . ." *Sonn 121,* 12.

shrape, *v.* to hem, restrict, or confine: "When that a ring of Greeks have shrap'd thee in . . ." *Tr & Cr,* IV, v, 192.

shred, *n.* **1** [pl.] fragments; odds and ends: "With these shreds/ They vented their complainings . . ." *Cor,* I, i, 207–208. **2 shreds and patches,** (something) patched together, hence makeshift or spurious: "A king of shreds and patches—" *Ham,* III, iv, 103.

shreiff, *n.* See **shrieve.**

shrew, *n.* **1** peevish person of either sex: "But like a shrew you first begin to brawl." *Errors,* IV, i, 51. **2** shrewmouse; here, obviously meant as a compliment: "Bless you, fair shrew." *T Night,* I, iii, 46.

shrewd, *adj.* **1** harsh; bitter: ". . . every of this happy number/ That have endur'd shrewd days and nights with us . . ." *As You,* V, iv, 171–172. **2** shrewish; spiteful or malicious: ". . . thou wilt never get thee a/ husband, if thou be so shrewd of thy tongue." *M Ado,* II, i, 16–17. **3** sly; cunning; also, cursed: ". . . you are that shrewd and knavish sprite/ Call'd Robin Good-fellow." *M N Dream,* II, i, 33–34. **4** evil; accursed; harmful or injurious: ". . . every man that Bolingbroke hath press'd/ To lift shrewd steel against our golden crown . . ." *Rich 2,* III, ii, 58–59. **5** severe: "I shall beat you to your tent, and prove a/ shrewd Caesar to you . . ." *Meas,* II, i, 245–246. **6** penetrating; telling: "'Tis a shrewd doubt [suspicion], though it be but a dream . . ." *Oth,* III, iii, 435. **7 shrewd turn,** ill service; act of malice [used ironically]: "Do my lord of Canterbury/ A shrewd turn, and he's your friend for ever [he'll never forget you]." *Hen 8,* V, ii, 210–211.

shrewdly, *adv.* **1** piercingly; spitefully: "The air bites shrewd-ly, it is very cold." *Ham,* I, iv, 1. **2** amazingly or uncomfortably close: ". . . my misgiving still/ Falls shrewdly to the purpose." *J Caes,* III, i, 145–146. **3** mischievously: "This practice hath most shrewdly pass'd upon thee." *T Night,* V, i, 351. **4** sorely; grievously: "He's shrewdly vex'd at something." *All's W,* III, v, 88. **5** violently; sharply: "You boggle shrewdly; every feather starts you." *All's W,* V, iii, 231.

shrewishly, *adv.* shrilly; sharply: "He is/ very well-favoured, and he speaks very shrewishly . . ." *T Night,* I, v, 161–162.

'Shrew me, See **beshrew** (def. 2).

Shrewsbury, *n.* town NW of London, near Wales: ". . . we rose both at an instant, and/ fought a long hour by Shrews-bury clock." *1 Hen 4,* V, iv, 146–147.

shrievaltry, *n.* hospitality of a sheriff: "A [he] keeps a plenti-ful shrievaltry, and 'a made my brother Arthur Watchins Ser-geant Safe's yeoman." *More,* II, iv, 42–43.

shrieve or **shreiff,** *n.* old form of sheriff: "The Earl Northum-berland, and the Lord Bardolph . . . Are by the shrieve of Yorkshire overthrown." *2 Hen 4,* IV, iv, 97–99.

shrieve's fool, *n.* idiot of little means, officially in the care of the sheriff: ". . . whence he was shipp'd for getting the shrieve's fool with child . . ." *All's W,* IV, iii, 181–182.

shrift, *n.* **1** confession: "I would thou wert so happy by thy stay/ To hear true shrift." *Rom & Jul,* I, i, 156–157. **2** confes-sional: "His bed shall seem a school, his board a shrift . . ." *Oth,* III, iii, 24. **3** absolution: "Riddling confession finds but riddling shrift." *Rom & Jul,* II, iii, 52.

shrill-gorged, *adj.* shrill-voiced: ". . . the shrill-gorg'd lark so far/ Cannot be seen or heard . . ." *Lear,* IV, vi, 58–59.

shrimp, *n.* term of contempt for a short person, esp. a man: "It cannot be this weak and writhled shrimp/ Should strike such terror to his enemies." *1 Hen 6,* II, iii, 22–23.

shrink, *v.* **1** to evaporate; slip away: ". . . that this sight should make so deep a wound,/ And yet detested life not shrink thereat . . ." *T Andr,* III, i, 246–247. **2** to collapse; give way: "When he perceiv'd me shrink and on my knee . . ." *1 Hen 6,* IV, vii, 5.

shrive, *v.* to hear the confession of (a person) and grant for-giveness: ". . . I'll dine above with you to-day,/ And shrive you of a thousand idle pranks." *Errors,* II, ii, 207–208.

shriver, *n.* priest who shrives; father confessor: "When he was made a shriver, 'twas for shift." *3 Hen 6,* III, ii, 108.

shriving-time, *n.* time allowed for confession of sins: "He should those bearers put to sudden death,/ Not shriving-time allow'd." *Ham,* V, ii, 46–47.

shroud[1], *v.* **1 a.** to hide; conceal: "Nor how to shroud yourself from enemies?" *3 Hen 6,* IV, iii, 40. **b.** to conceal oneself: "I will here shroud till the/ dregs of the storm be past." *Temp,* II, ii, 41–42.
—*n.* **2** shelter; protection: ". . . put yourself under his shroud,/ The universal landlord." *Ant & Cleo,* III, xiii, 71–72.

shroud[2], *n.* [usually pl.] lines supporting a ship's masts: "The friends of France our shrouds and tacklings?" *3 Hen 6,* V, iv, 18.

shrouding-sheet, *n.* winding-sheet; shroud: "A pickaxe and a spade, a spade,/ For and a shrouding-sheet . . ." *Ham,* V, i, 92–93.

Shrove-tide, *n.* three days preceding Ash Wednesday, the beginning of Lent: "And welcome merry Shrove-tide! Be merry,/ be merry." *2 Hen 4,* V, iii, 34–35.

Shrove Tuesday, *n.* day preceding the start of Lent, when pancakes are traditionally eaten: "As fit as ten groats is for the hand of an attorney . . . as a pancake for Shrove/ Tuesday . . ." *All's W,* II, ii, 20–23.

shrow, *n.* old form of shrew: "A pox of that jest! and I beshrew all shrows!" *Love's L,* V, ii, 46.

shrug, *v.* to show astonishment or disbelief: "Where great pa-tricians shall attend, and shrug . . ." *Cor,* I, ix, 4.

shuffle, *v.* **1** to assume responsibility; shift: ". . . your life, good master,/ Must shuffle for itself." *Cymb,* V, v, 104–105. **2** to prac-tice trickery; cheat [thieves' jargon]: ". . . hiding mine/ honour in my necessity, am fain to shuffle, to hedge . . ." *Wives,* II, ii,

22–23. 3 shuffle off, a. to slough off; cast off: "When we have shuffled off this mortal coil . . ." *Ham*, III, i, 67. **b.** to shrug off: ". . . and oft good turns/ Are shuffled off with such uncurrent pay . . ." *T Night*, III, iii, 15–16.

shuffling, *n.* evasion; deception or trickery: "But 'tis not so above:/ There is no shuffling . . ." *Ham*, III, iii, 60–61.

shun, *v.* **shunn'd to go even,** refused to agree: ". . . rather shunn'd to go even with what I heard than in/ my every action to be guided by others' experiences . . ." *Cymb*, I, v, 42–43.

shunless destiny, *n.* bloody doom impossible to escape: ". . . alone he enter'd/ The mortal gate of th'city, which he painted/ With shunless destiny . . ." *Cor*, II, ii, 110–112.

shut up, *v.* **1** to block; bar: "Unless our halberds did shut up his passage." *3 Hen 6*, IV, iii, 20. **2** to end or conclude: ". . . greets your wife withal, By the name of most kind hostess, and shut up/ In measureless content." *Mac*, II, i, 16–17.
—*past part.* **3** embodied; incorporated: "In whom the tempers and the minds of all/ Should be shut up . . ." *Tr & Cr*, I, iii, 57–58.

shy, *adj.* reserved; also, cautious, circumspect, or suspicious: "A shy fellow was the/ Duke . . ." *Meas*, III, ii, 127–128.

sib, *adj.* related; akin: "Let/ The blood of mine that's sib to him be suck'd/ From me with leeches!" *Kinsmen*, I, ii, 71–73.

Sibyl, *n.* **1** Also **Sibylla,** the Cumaean Sibyl, to whom Apollo granted as many years of life as the number of grains of sand she could hold in her hand: "Be she as foul as was Florentius' love,/ As old as Sibyl . . ." *Shrew*, I, ii, 68–69. **2** Roman prophetess who wrote her prophecies on leaves, which she laid on the ground and were often blown away before they could be read: ". . . the angry northen wind/ Will blow these sands like Sibyl's leaves abroad . . ." *T Andr*, IV, i, 104–105.

Sicil, *n.* Sicily; Margaret's father was king of Sicily: "In presence of the Kings of France and Sicil . . ." *2 Hen 6*, I, 1, 6.

Sicilia, *n.* king of Sicily: ". . . you shall see . . . great difference/ betwixt our Bohemia and your Sicilia." *W Tale*, I, i, 3–4.

Sicils, *n.* Kingdom of the Two Sicilies, Naples and Sicily: "Reignier, her father, to the King of France/ Hath pawn'd the Sicils and Jerusalem . . ." *3 Hen 6*, V, vii, 38–39.

sick, *adj.* **1** afflicted; here, with the sin of pride: "I would not be so sick though for his 'place [I would not have his exalted position at such cost] . . ." *Hen 8*, II, ii, 83. **2 in the sick tune,** like a sick person: "Why, how now? Do you speak in the sick tune?" *M Ado*, III, iv, 39. **3 make sick,** euphem. for "to kill": "But are not some whole that we must make sick?" *J Caes*, II,

i, 328. **4 sick for,** to pine for: ". . . our gentry, who are sick/ For breathing and exploit." *All's W*, I, ii, 16–17. **5 sick of,** sick because of: "I was not sick of any fear from thence." *Sonn 86*, 12.
—*v.* **6** to become sick; sicken: "Say it did so a little time before/ That our great-grandsire Edward sick'd and died." *2 Hen 4*, IV, iv, 127–128.

sicken, *v.* **1** to become surfeited or sated: ". . . tumble all together,/ Even till destruction sicken . . ." *Mac*, IV, i, 59–60. **2** to impair; deplete or disable: ". . . Kinsmen of mine . . . have/ By this so sicken'd their estates . . ." *Hen 8*, I, i, 81–82.

sick interpreters, *n.* envious persons of corrupt judgment: "By sick interpreters . . . is/ Not ours or not allow'd [attributed to others or else condemned] . . ." *Hen 8*, I, ii, 82–83.

sickle, *n.* shekel, a Hebrew coin: "Not with fond sickles of the tested gold,/ Or stones . . ." *Meas*, II, ii, 150–151.

sickle hour, *n.* the hour in which Death (Time) terminates mortal life: "O thou my lovely Boy, who in thy power/ Dost hold time's fickle glass, his sickle hour . . ." *Sonn 126*, 1–2.

sicklemen, *n.* reapers: "You sunburn'd sicklemen, of August weary . . ." *Temp*, IV, i, 134.

sick offense, *n.* worrisome or dangerous illness: "You have some sick offence within your mind . . . I ought to know of . . ." *J Caes*, II, i, 268–270.

sick-service, *n.* **at your sick-service,** attending you when you were sick: "But you at your sick-service had a prince." *K John*, IV, i, 52.

sick-thoughted, *adj.* lovesick: "Sick-thoughted Venus makes amain unto him . . ." *Ven & Ad*, 5.

Sic spectanda fides, [Latin] So must faith be tested. *Per*, II, ii, 38.

Sicyon, *n.* town in Greece, where Antony had taken leave of Fulvia: "From Sicyon how the news? Speak there!" *Ant & Cleo*, I, ii, 110.

side, *n.* **1** faction; segment of the population: "These are a side that would be glad to have/ This true . . ." *Cor*, IV, vi, 151–152. **2** [pl.] trunk of the human body: "How shall your houseless heads and unfed sides . . . defend you/ From seasons such as these?" *Lear*, III, iv, 30–32. **3 sides of nature,** human body or frame: "It cannot be thus long, the sides of nature/ Will not sustain it." *Ant & Cleo*, I, iii, 16–17. **4 wrong side out,** wrong interpretation; misunderstanding: ". . . he call'd me sot,/ And told me I had turn'd the wrong side out . . ." *Lear*, IV, ii, 8–9.

—*v.* **5** to take the side of: ". . . side factions, and give out/ Conjectural marriages . . ." *Cor,* I, i, 192–193.

side-piercing, *adj.* heart-rending: "O thou side-piercing sight!" *Lear,* IV, vi, 85.

side sleeve, *n.* open sleeve, hanging from the shoulder: ". . . down sleeves, side sleeves,/ and skirts, round underborne . . ." *M Ado,* III, iv, 19–20.

siege, *n.* **1** rank or place: ". . . and that, in my regard,/ Of the unworthiest siege." *Ham,* IV, vii, 74–75. **2** seat: ". . . upon the very siege of justice/ Lord Angelo hath . . . Profess'd the contrary." *Meas,* IV, ii, 96–98. **3** excrement: "How cam'st/ thou to be the siege of this moon-calf? can he vent/ Trinculos?" *Temp,* II, ii, 106–108.

Siena, *n.* Duke of Siena: ". . . they come/ Under the conduct of bold Iachimo,/ Siena's brother." *Cymb,* IV, ii, 339–341.

Si fortune me tormente sperato me contento, Pistol's garbled version of Latin/Italian/Spanish motto, meaning "If fortune torments me, hope contents me." *2 Hen 4,* II, iv, 177.

sift, *v.* to question or examine; also, to understand or comprehend: "As near as I could sift him on that argument,/ On some apparent danger seen in him . . ." *Rich 2,* I, i, 12–13.

sight, *n.* **1** image; here, poss. a portrait: ". . . a mortal war,/ How to divide the conquest of thy sight . . ." *Sonn 46,* 1–2. **2** wonder or spectacle: "They are but dressings of a former sight." *Sonn 123,* 4. **3 his sight,** the appearance or presence of him [King Henry V]: "So dreadful will not be as was [nothing will ever be more awesome than] his sight." *1 Hen 6,* I, i, 30. **4 most in sight,** conspicuously: "Come on, then; wear the favours most in sight." *Love's L,* V, ii, 136. **5 not in sight,** invisible or unobserved: "Be bold to play, our sport is not in sight." *Ven & Ad,* 124.

sight-hole, *n.* hole to peer through, as in spying: "And stop all sight-holes, every loop from whence/ The eye of reason may pry in upon us . . ." *1 Hen 4,* IV, i, 71–72.

sightless, *adj.* **1** invisible: "Poor grooms are sightless night, kings glorious day . . ." *Luc.* 1013. **2** ugly; unsightly: "Full of unpleasing blots and sightless stains . . ." *K John,* II, ii, 45. **3 sightless couriers,** invisible messengers; that is, the winds: ". . . heaven's Cherubins, hors'd/ Upon the sightless couriers of the air . . ." *Mac,* I, vii, 22–23.

sight-outrunning, *adj.* swifter than sight: "Jove's lightnings, the precursors/ O' th' dreadful thunder-claps, more momentary/ And sight-outrunning . . ." *Temp,* I, ii, 201–203.

sign, *n.* **1** outward appearance: ". . . then we,/ Following the signs, woo'd but the sign of she." *Love's L,* V, ii, 468–469. **2** evidence; proof: "Give thee her hand for sign of plighted faith." *1 Hen 6,* V, iii, 162. **3** any indication, as a nod or gesture: "But thou didst understand me by my signs/ And didst in signs again parley with sin . . ." *K John,* IV, ii, 237–238. **4** symbol; here, the illusion: "A sign of dignity; a breath, a bubble . . ." *Rich 3,* IV, iv, 90. **5** ensign or banner: "Cheerly to sea; the signs of war advance . . ." *Hen 5* II, ii, 192.

—*v.* **6** to signify; give evidence of: "You sign your place and calling, in full seeming,/ With meekness and humility . . ." *Hen 8,* II, iv, 106–107. **7** to portend: "It signs well, does it not?" *Ant & Cleo,* IV, iii, 13.

signal, *n.* sign or token: ". . . in signal of my love to thee . . . Will I upon thy party wear this rose." *1 Hen 6,* II, iv, 121–123.

signed, *adj.* stained or marked: ". . . here thy hunters stand,/ Sign'd in thy spoil, and crimson'd in thy lethe." *J Caes,* III, i, 205–206.

significant, *n.* **1** token or sign, esp. in the form of a message: ". . . bear this significant to the country maid Jaquenetta." *Love's L,* III, i, 127. **2 dumb significants,** dumb show; gestures without words: "Since you are . . . so loath to speak,/ In dumb significants proclaim your thoughts . . ." *1 Hen 6,* II, iv, 25–26.

signify, *v.* **1** to announce; make known: "We attend his lordship; pray signify so much." *Timon,* III, iv, 38. **2** to have meaning; be self-explanatory: "And it shall please you to break up this, it shall/ seem to signify." *Merch,* II, iv, 10–11.

signior, *n.* term of address from Italian "signore," equiv. to "Mr" or "sir": "I would/ be loath to have you overflowen with a honey-bag,/ signior." *M N Dream,* IV, i, 15–17.

Signior Sooth, *n.* Sir Smoothtalker; Sir Appeasement: "When Signior Sooth here does proclaim a peace,/ He flatters you . . ." *Per,* I, ii, 45–46.

signiory, *n.* governing elders of the city: "My services, which I have done the signiory,/ Shall out-tongue his complaints . . ." *Oth,* I, ii, 18–19.

sign of battle, *n.* See **battle** (def. 2).

sign of blind Cupid, *n.* ref. to painted sign depicting blind Cupid hung over the door of a brothel: ". . . hang me up at the door of a brothel-house for the/ sign of blind Cupid." *M Ado,* I, i, 234–235.

sign of the Leg, *n.* sign over a bootmaker's shop: ". . . wears his/ boots very smooth [close-fitting] like unto the sign of the Leg . . ." *2 Hen 4,* II, iv, 245–246.

signories, *n. pl.* **1** state or "domain" governed by a lord [signior]: ". . . at that time/ Through all the signories it was the first . . ." *Temp,* I, ii, 70–71. **2** estates, together with all rights and privileges: ". . . were you not restor'd/ To all the Duke of Norfolk's signories . . .?" *2 Hen 4,* IV, i, 110–111.

silence, *n.* **put to silence,** executed; put to death: "Marullus and Flavius, for pulling scarfs/ off Caesar's images, are put to silence." *J Caes,* I, ii, 282–283.

silken-coated slaves, *n.* allusion to the fine clothes of Sir Humphrey Stafford and his brother: "As for these silken-coated slaves, I pass [care] not:/ It is to you, good people, that I speak . . ." *2 Hen 6,* IV, ii, 122–123.

silken dalliance, *n.* carnal pleasures, as well as fine clothes: "And silken dalliance in the wardrobe lies . . ." *Hen 5,* II, Chor., 2.

silling, *n.* Fluellen's pron. of "shilling": ". . . 'tis a good silling, I warrant you, or I will change it." *Hen 5,* IV, viii, 74.

silly, *adj.* **1** poor; wretched: "While as the silly owner of the goods/ Weeps over them . . ." *2 Hen 6,* I, 1, 226–227. **2** innocent; helpless or defenseless: "To shepherds looking on their silly sheep . . ." *3 Hen 6,* II, v, 43. **3** simple: "The silly boy,/ believing she is dead,/ Claps her pale cheek . . ." *Ven & Ad,* 467–468. **4** slight; trifling: ". . . a pedigree/ Of threescore and two years—a silly time . . ." *3 Hen 6,* III, iii, 92–93. **5 silly habit,** rustic garb: "There was a fourth man, in a silly habit . . ." *Cymb,* V, iii, 86.

silly-ducking, *adj.* obsequiously bowing: ". . . twenty silly-ducking observants,/ That stretch their duties nicely." *Lear,* II, ii, 104–105.

silly sooth, *n.* plain, simple truth: ". . . it is silly sooth,/ And dallies with the innocence of love,/ Like the old age." *T Night,* II, iv, 46–48.

silly-stately, *adj.* foolishly pretentious or ostentatious: "Here is a silly-stately style indeed!" *1 Hen 6,* IV, vii, 72.

silver, *n.* **hatched in silver,** engraved in silver [prob. ref. to Nestor's white hair]: ". . . and such again/ As venerable Nestor, hatch'd in silver . . ." *Tr & Cr,* I, iii, 64–65.

silver bow, *n.* moon: ". . . perform my bidding, or thou liv'st in woe;/ Do't, and happy; by my silver bow!" *Per,* V, i, 245–246.

silver livery, *n.* **1** grey or white hair: ". . . to achieve/ The silver livery of advised age . . ." *2 Hen 6,* V, ii, 46–47. **2** white virgin robes of Diana, goddess of the moon: "A maid-child call'd Marina; who, O goddess,/ Wears yet thy silver livery." *Per,* V, iii, 6–7.

silverly, *adv.* as bright as silver: ". . . this honourable dew,/ That silverly doth progress on thy cheeks . . ." *K John,* V, ii, 46.

silver water, *n.* column of soldiers in full armor likened to a river: "Unless thou let his silver water keep/ A peaceful progress to the ocean." *K John,* II, i, 339–340.

simile, *n.* **1** symbol or emblem; love-token; here, ref. to the jewels: "Take all these similes to your own command . . ." *Lover's Comp,* 227. **2 want similes,** to lack [further] comparisons: ". . . when their rhymes,/ Full of protest, of oath, and big compare,/ Wants similes . . ." *Tr & Cr,* III, ii, 172–174.

Simois, *n.* river on the Trojan plain: "To Simois' reedy banks the red blood ran . . ." *Luc,* 1437.

simony, *n.* buying or selling of religious offices: ". . . one that by suggestion/ Tied all the kingdom; simony was fair play . . ." *Hen 8,* IV, ii, 35–36.

simple, *n.* **1** basic ingredient or, sometimes, a drug or medicine made of only one ingredient: ". . . a melancholy of mine own, compounded of many simples . . ." *As You,* IV, i, 15–16. **2** medicinal herb: "In tatter'd weeds, with overwhelming brows,/ Culling of simples." *Rom & Jul,* V, i, 39–40. **3** [pl.] medicine made from a single herb or plant; here, addit. comic element with Simple's hiding in the closet: "Dere is some simples in my closet dat I vill not/ for the varld I shall leave behind." *Wives,* I, iv, 58–59. **4 simples operative,** (in medicine) efficacious herbs: ". . . many simples operative, whose power/ Will close the eye of anguish." *Lear,* IV, iv, 14–15.
—*adj.* **5** plain; ordinary or undistinguished: ". . . here's a simple line/ of life, here's a small trifle of wives . . ." *Merch,* II, ii, 152–153. **6** straight; with no additions: "With eggs, sir?"/ "Simple of itself . . ." *Wives,* III, v, 27–28. **7** foolish; silly; unintelligent: "Well, you have made a simple choice. You know/ not how to choose a man." *Rom & Jul,* II, v, 38–39. **8** empty-headed; witless: "Let me go:/ You see how simple and how fond [foolish] I am." *M N Dream,* III, ii, 316–317. **9** humble, with implied meaning of "foolish": ". . . there is but three skirts for yourself, in my simple/ conjectures . . ." *Wives,* I, i, 27–28. **10 simple though I stand here,** equiv. to "as sure as I'm standing here": ". . . he's a Justice of Peace in his/ country, simple though I stand here." *Wives,* I, i, 199–200.

simpleness, *n.* **1** unaffected honesty; simplicity: "And never gives to truth and virtue that/ Which simpleness and merit purchaseth." *M Ado,* III, i, 69–70. **2** foolishness: "What simpleness is this?—I come, I come. [Knock] / Who knocks so hard?" *Rom & Jul,* III, iii, 77–78.

simple savor, *n.* simple tastes; also, simple goodness: "For compound sweet forgoing simple savour . . ." *Sonn 125,* 7.

simple show, *n.* appearance of simplicity or innocence: "And in his simple show he harbours treason." *2 Hen 6,* III, i, 54.

simple time, *n.* summertime, when herbs were gathered and sold: ". . . and smell like Bucklersbury in simple time . . ." *Wives,* III, iii, 66–67.

simplicity, *n.* **1** folly; foolishness: "Thou mak'st the triumviry . . . The shape of love's Tyburn, that hangs up simplicity." *Love's L,* IV, iii, 50–51. **2** innocence: "By the simplicity of Venus' doves . . ." *M N Dream,* I, i, 171. **3** confused by parson with "simple"; fool of a; stupid: "You are a very simplicity 'oman: I pray you,/ peace." *Wives,* IV, i, 25–26. **4 in low simplicity,** because of simple foolishness: ". . . in low simplicity/ He lends out money gratis . . ." *Merch,* I, iii, 38–39.

simply, *adv.* as she is [without any dowry]: ". . . if he take/ her, let him take her simply . . ." *Wives,* III, ii, 69–70.

simular, *adj.* **1** feigned; specious: ". . . I return'd with simular proof enough/ To make the noble Leonatus mad . . ." *Cymb,* V, v, 200–201.
—*n.* **2** person who feigns or counterfeits; simulator: "Thou perjur'd, and thou simular of virtue/ That art incestuous . . ." *Lear,* III, ii, 54–55.

simulation, *n.* disguised meaning; hence, a puzzle: "'M. O.A.I.' This simulation is not as the former . . ." *T Night,* II, v, 139.

since, *conj.* **1** when: "Thou rememb'rest/ Since once I sat upon a promontory . . ." *M N Dream,* II, i, 148–149. **2 since for,** because of: ". . . since for the great desire I had/ To see fair Padua . . ." *Shrew,* I, i, 1–2.
—*adv.* **3** lately: "I did not see him since." *Ant & Cleo,* I, iii, 1.

Sinel, *n.* Macbeth's father: "By Sinel's death I know I am Thane of Glamis . . ." *Mac,* I, iii, 71.

sinew, *n.* **1** source of power or strength: ". . . Glendower's absence thence,/ Who with them was a rated sinew too . . ." *1 Hen 4,* IV, iv, 16–17. **2** [pl.] muscles: "He tumbled down upon his Nemean hide,/ And swore his sinews thaw'd." *Kinsmen,* I, i, 68–69.
—*v.* **3** to join with or as if with sinews: "So shalt thou sinew both these lands together . . ." *3 Hen 6,* II, vi, 91.

sing, *v.* **1** to praise: "They had not skill enough your worth to sing . . ." *Sonn 106,* 12. **2 sing . . . at first sight,** Cressida is as familiar with men as an experienced singer who can sight-read a piece of music: "Yea, so familiar?"/ "She will sing any man at first sight." *Tr & Cr,* V, ii, 8–9.

singing-man, *n.* chorister: ". . . the Prince broke thy head for/ liking his father to a singing-man of Windsor . . ." *2 Hen 4,* II, i, 87–88.

single, *adj.* **1** weak or feeble: ". . . your chin double, your wit single . . ." *2 Hen 4,* I, ii, 182. **2** simple: "All our service/ Were poor and single business . . ." *Mac,* I, vi, 14–16. **3** of one person: "For what, alas, can these my single arms?" *Tr & Cr,* II, ii, 136. **4** continuous; uninterrupted: ". . . at pick'd leisure/ Which shall be shortly single, I'll resolve you . . ." *Temp,* V, i, 247–248. **5 single wilt prove none,** the unmarried state amounts to nothing in the end: "Whose speechless song . . . Sings this to thee: 'Thou single wilt prove none.'" *Sonn 8,* 13–14.
—*v.* **6** to separate or distinguish: "Arts-man, preambulate: we will be singled from the/ barbarous." *Love's L,* V, i, 73–74. **7** to single out and isolate, as a hunter targets one animal in a pack: "Single you thither then this dainty doe,/ And strike her home by force . . ." *T Andr,* II, i, 117–118.

single blessedness, *n.* unwedded bliss: ". . . earthlier happy is the rose distill'd/ Than that which, withering on the virgin thorn,/ Grows, lives, and dies in single blessedness." *M N Dream,* I, i, 76–78.

single fight, *n.* single combat; here, the suggestion of Antony vs. Caesar: "So hath my lord dar'd him to single fight." *Ant & Cleo,* III, vii, 30.

singleness, *n.* **1** silliness; ridiculousness: "O single-soled jest, solely singular for the/ singleness." *Rom & Jul,* II, iv, 67–68. **2** role of a solo performer; also, the unmarried state: ". . . who confounds/ In singleness the parts that thou shouldst bear." *Sonn 8,* 7–8.

single oppositions, *n.* duels; single combats: ". . . alike conversant in general services, and more remarkable in single oppositions . . ." *Cymb,* IV, i, 12–13.

single plot, *n.* piece of earth [i.e., myself]: "Yet were there but this single plot to lose,/ This mould [form] of Martius . . ." *Cor,* III, ii, 102–103.

single-soled, *adj.* thin; feeble: "O single-soled jest, solely singular for the/ singleness." *Rom & Jul,* II, iv, 67–68.

single state of man, *n.* man conceived of as a microcosm, a tiny kingdom, albeit one subject to human frailties: "Shakes so my single state of man,/ That function is smother'd in surmise . . ." *Mac,* I, iii, 140–141.

single ten, *n.* (in playing cards) the ten; the nearest in value to the "royal" cards: ". . . whiles he thought to steal the single ten,/ The king was slily finger'd from the deck! *3 Hen 6,* V, i, 43–44.

single virtue, *n.* unsupported valor: "Trust to thy single virtue; for thy soldiers,/ All levied in my name . . ." *Lear,* V, iii, 103–104.

single voice, *n.* unanimous vote; Wolsey says he merely concurred in the unanimous approval of the judges [the king's council]: "I have no further gone in this than by/ A single voice, and that not pass'd [uttered by] me but/ By learned approbation of the judges . . ." *Hen 8,* I, ii, 69–71.

singly, *adv.* truly; also, solely or uniquely: "Thou singly honest man . . ." *Timon,* IV, iii, 527.

singularity, *n.* **1** uniqueness; here, eccentricity in dress and behavior: ". . . put/ thyself into the trick [trait] of singularity." *T Night,* II, v, 150–151. **2** [often pl.] rarities: ". . . not without much content/ In many singularities . . ." *W Tale,* V, iii, 11–12.

sinister, *adj., adv.* **1** left; on or to the left side: "And this the cranny is, right and sinister . . ." *M N Dream,* V, i, 162. **2** irregular: "'Tis no sinister nor no awkward claim . . ." *Hen 5,* II, iv, 85.

sinister measure, *n.* unjust treatment: "He professes to have received no sinister measure/ from his judge . . ." *Meas,* III, ii, 236–237.

sinister usage, *n.* rudeness; incivility: "I am very/ comptible, even to the least sinister usage." *T Night,* I, v, 176–177.

sink, *n.* **1** drain or cesspool; sewer; pit: "Ay, kennel, puddle, sink, whose filth/ Troubles the silver spring where England drinks . . ." *2 Hen 6,* IV, i, 70–71.
—*v.* **2** to fall; perish: "For every false drop in her bawdy veins/ A Grecian's life hath sunk . . ." *Tr & Cr,* IV, i, 70–71.

sink-a-pace, *n.* cinque-pace [from French *cinque pas*], a dance made up of five steps; also, poss. ribald wordplay on "sink" [sewer]: "I would not so much as make water but in/ a sink-a-pace." *T Night,* I, iii, 127–128.

Sinon, *n.* Greek who persuaded the Trojans to admit the Wooden Horse: "Tell us what Sinon hath bewitch'd our ears . . ." *T Andr,* V, iii, 85.

sir, *n.* **1** title of respect, often used with professions and occupations: "I am one/ that had rather go with sir priest than sir knight . . ." *T Night,* III, iv, 275–276. **2** [often cap.] used ironically: ". . . and at this sport/ Sir Valour [Achilles] dies, cries 'O, enough, Patroclus . . . '" *Tr & Cr,* I, iii, 175–176. **3** man of high social rank: ". . . a slow tongue, in the habit of/ some sir of note . . ." *T Night,* III, iv, 73–74. **4** a gallant: ". . . which now again you are/ most apt to play the sir in . . ." *Oth,* II, i, 173–174. **5** my sir, title of mock respect: ". . . no hearing,/ no feeling, but my sir's song . . ." *W Tale,* IV, iv, 613–614.

Sir boy, *n.* term of address to a younger person or an inferior; here, to a grandson: "Sir boy, let me see your archery . . ." *T Andr,* IV, iii, 2.

Sir Dagonet, *n.* King Arthur's fool: "I was then Sir Dagonet in Arthur's/ show . . ." *2 Hen 4,* III, ii, 275–276.

siren, *n.* [often cap.] any of the mythical maidens whose seductive singing lured mariners to a rocky destruction while traversing the Strait of Messina: "This siren that will charm Rome's Saturnine,/ And see his shipwrack and his commonweal's." *T Andr,* II, i, 23–24.

Sir Guy, *n.* Guy of Warwick, legendary hero, who slew the giant Colbrand: "I am not Samson, nor Sir Guy, nor Colbrand . . ." *Hen 8,* V, iii, 21.

Sir John, *n.* name commonly applied to a priest: "Where are you there, Sir John? nay, fear not, man,/ We are alone . . ." *2 Hen 6,* I, ii, 68–69.

Sir Knob, *n.* nickname for Robert, with wordplay on "Bob" and "knob" [head]: "It would not be Sir Knob in any case." *K John,* I, i, 147.

Sir Prudence, *n.* Antonio's contemptuous nickname for the "honest councellor" Gonzalo: ". . . whiles you . . . To the perpetual wink for aye might put/ This ancient morsel, this Sir Prudence . . ." *Temp,* II, i, 280–281.

sirrah, *n.* term used in addressing inferiors: "Ah, sirrah, a body would think this was well counterfeited." *As You,* IV, iii, 166–167.

sir-reverence, *n.* elided form of "save your reverence," exclam. of apology used to introduce an unpleasant statement: ". . . such a one as a man/ may not speak of, without he say 'sir-reverence' . . ." *Errors,* III, ii, 88–89.

Sir Smile, *n.* smiling villain of fiction: "And his pond fish'd by his next neighbour, by/ Sir Smile, his neighbour . . ." *W Tale,* I, ii, 195–196.

Sir Valor, *n.* slighting ref. to Achilles: ". . . and at this sport/ Sir Valour dies, cries 'O, enough, Patroclus . . .'" *Tr & Cr,* I, iii, 175–176.

sister, *v.* to match or resemble: ". . . even her art sisters the natural roses . . ." *Per,* V, Chor., 7.

sistering, *adj.* neighboring; nearby: "A plaintful story from a sist'ring vale . . ." *Lover's Comp,* 2.

Sisters Three, *n.* the Fates: ". . . Untwind the Sisters Three! Come, Atropos, I say!" *2 Hen 4,* II, iv, 195.

sit, *v.* **1 sit about,** to sit in conference concerning; discuss: ". . . summon him tomorrow to the Tower/ To sit about the coronation." *Rich 3,* III, i, 172–173. **2 sit at,** spend; pay out: "I sit at ten pounds a week." *Wives,* I, iii, 8. **3 sit fast,** be prepared or on guard: "Now, Montague, sit fast; I seek for thee,/ That Warwick's bones may keep thine company." *3 Hen 6,* V, ii, 3–4. **4 sit in gold,** See **gold. 5 sit you out,** [you may] withdraw: "Well, sit you out: go home, Berowne: adieu!" *Love's L,* I, i, 110.

Sit fas aut nefas, [Latin] Be it right or wrong: "*Sit fas aut nefas,* till I find the stream/ To cool this heat . . ." *T Andr,* II, i, 133–134.

sith, *conj.* since; inasmuch as: "Not I, my lord, sith true nobility/ Warrants these words in princely courtesy." *T Andr,* I, i, 271–272.

sithence, *conj.* since: ". . . to acquaint you withal, sithence . . . it concerns you something to know it." *All's W,* I, iii, 114–116.

situate, *adj.* situated; located: "I know where it is situate."/ "Lord, how wise you are!" *Love's L,* I, ii, 128–129.

sixpence a day, *n.* royal pension, granted for the remainder of one's life; considered by an artisan quite generous: "O sweet bully Bottom! Thus hath he lost sixpence a/ day during his life . . ." *M N Dream,* IV, ii, 19–20.

sixpenny, *adj.* worth no more than sixpence; paltry: "I am joined with no foot-landrakers,/ no long-staff sixpenny strikers . . ." *1 Hen 4,* II, i, 72–73.

size, *n.* **1 past the size of,** beyond the capacity of: "But if there be, or ever were one such,/ It's past the size of dreaming . . ." *Ant & Cleo,* V, ii, 96–97. **2 with all the size,** to the fullest extent: ". . . with all the size that verity/ Would without lapsing suffer." *Cor,* V, ii, 18–19.

sized, *past part.* grown to a certain magnitude: "And as my love is siz'd, my fear is so." *Ham,* III, ii, 165.

sizes, *n.* allowances: ". . . to cut off my train,/ To bandy hasty words, to scant my sizes . . ." *Lear,* II, iv, 176–177.

skains-mate, *n.* cutthroat companion; criminal or assassin: "Scurvy knave! I am none of his flirt-gills, I am none/ of his skains-mates." *Rom & Jul,* II, iv, 150–151.

skiff, *v.* to sail over; row across: ". . . they have skiff'd/ Torrents whose roaring tyranny and power . . . was dreadful . . ." *Kinsmen,* I, iii, 37–39.

skill, *n.* **1** judgment: ". . . touching now the point of human skill,/ Reason becomes the marshal to my will." *M N Dream,* II, ii, 118–119. **2** discernment; shrewdness: ". . . yet 'tis greater skill/ In a true hate, to pray they have their will . . ." *Cymb,* II, iv, 184–185. **3** cause; need or reason: ". . . you have/ As little skill to fear as I have purpose/ To put you to 't." *W Tale,* IV, iv, 151–153.
—*v.* **4** to matter; be of concern: ". . . whate'er he be/ It skills not much, we'll fit him to our turn—" *Shrew,* III, ii, 129–130.

skill-contending school, *n.* school in which students are expected to compete in displaying argumentation skills: "Busy yourselves in skill-contending schools,/ Debate where leisure serves with dull debaters . . ." *Luc,* 1018–1019.

skilless, *adj.* **1** inexperienced: "And not all love to see you . . . But jealousy what might befall your travel,/ Being skilless in these parts." *T Night,* III, iii, 6–9. **2** ignorant; uninformed: ". . . how features are abroad,/ I am skilless of . . ." *Temp,* III, i, 52–53.

skillfully, *adv.* from experience; knowledgeably: "Thou art an old love-monger, and speak'st skilfully." *Love's L,* II, i, 253.

skimble-skamble, *adj.* nonsensical: ". . . such a deal of skimble-skamble stuff/ As puts me from my faith." *1 Hen 4,* III, i, 148–149.

skin, *v.* to cover over with new skin: "It will but skin and film the ulcerous place . . ." *Ham,* III, iv, 149.

skin-coat, *n.* the skin, which he threatens to thrash; also, ref. to lion's skin that Austria wears: "I'll smoke your skin-coat, and I catch you right . . ." *K John,* II, i, 139.

skip, *v.* to move quickly, esp. in answer to a command: ". . . page thy heels/ And skip when thou point'st out?" *Timon,* IV, iii, 226–227.

skipper, *n.* heedless, flighty fellow: "Skipper, stand back, 'tis age that nourisheth." *Shrew,* II, i, 332.

skipping, *adj.* **1** frivolous; also, vain or flighty: "The skipping King [Richard II], he ambled up and down . . ." *1 Hen 4,* III, ii, 60. **2** mobile, esp. because of light armaments; here, also inclined to retreat: ". . . justice had . . . Compell'd these skipping Kernes to trust their heels . . ." *Mac*, I, ii, 29–30. **3 skipping jigs.** See **jig** (def. 2).

skirmish, *v.* to do battle: "For none but Samsons and Goliases [Goliaths]/ It sendeth forth to skirmish." *1 Hen 6*, I, ii, 33–34.

skirr, *v.* **1** to scurry: ". . . we will come to them,/ And make them skirr away . . ." *Hen 5*, IV, vii, 62–63. **2** to search carefully; scour: "Send out moe horses, skirr the country round;/ Hang those that talk of fear." *Mac*, V, iii, 35–36.

skirt, *n.* **1** tail of man's coat, divided at back and sides into four tails, or "skirts": ". . . if he has a quarter of your coat,/ there is but three skirts for yourself . . ." *Wives*, I, i, 26–27. **2** [pl.] outlying areas: "Hath in the skirts of Norway here and there/ Shark'd up a list of lawless resolutes . . ." *Ham*, I, i, 100–101.

skirted, *adj.* wearing a skirted doublet: "French thrift, you rogues—myself and skirted page." *Wives*, I, iii, 80.

skittish, *adj.* **1** capricious; fickle: "For such as I am, all true lovers are,/ Unstaid and skittish in all motions else . . ." *T Night*, II, iv, 17–18. **2** animated; vigorous: "Now expectation, tickling skittish spirits . . ." *Tr & Cr*, Prol., 20.

skyey, *adj.* of the stars, planets, etc.: "Servile to all the skyey influences . . ." *Meas*, III, i, 9.

skyish, *adj.* reaching to the sky: "T'o'ertop old Pelion or the skyish head/ Of blue Olympus." *Ham*, V, i, 246–247.

slab, *adj.* glutinous; sticky: "Make the gruel thick and slab . . ." *Mac*, IV, i, 32.

slack, *adj.* **1 come slack,** to provide less (of): "If you come slack of former services,/ You shall do well; the fault of it I'll answer." *Lear*, I, iii, 10–11.
—*v.* **2** to neglect: "If then they chanc'd to slack ye/ We could control them." *Lear*, II, iv, 247–248.

slackness, *n.* neglectfulness; remissness: ". . . these thy offices . . . are as interpreters/ Of my behind-hand slackness!" *W Tale*, V, i, 148–150.

slander, *n.* **1** disgrace or insult: ". . . bid his ears a little while be deaf,/ Till I have told this slander of [to] his blood . . ." *Rich 2*, I, i, 112–113. **2 do in slander,** to slander my name: "And yet my nature never in the fight/ To do in slander." *Meas*, I, iii, 42–43. **3 slanders of the age,** those who prove a disgrace to their own times: ". . . you must learn/ to know such slanders

of the age, or else you may/ be marvellously mistook." *Hen 5*, III, vi, 80–82.
—*v.* **4** to abuse; misuse: ". . . so slander any moment leisure/ As to give words or talk with the Lord Hamlet." *Ham*, I, iii, 133–134.

slanderous, *adj.* disgusting; loathsome: "As sland'rous deaths-man to so base a slave?" *Luc*, 1001.

slaughterman or **slaughter-man,** *n.* **1** murderer: ". . . thou fight'st against thy countrymen,/ And join'st with them will be thy slaughter-men." *1 Hen 6*, III, iii, 74–75. **2** executioner: "For this proud mock I'll be thy slaughterman . . ." *T Andr*, IV, iv, 58. **3** heroic slayer in battle: ". . . ten chas'd by one,/ Are now each one the slaughter-man of twenty . . ." *Cymb*, V, iii, 48–49.

slave, *n.* **1** victim: ". . . flatter themselves/ That they are not the first of fortune's slaves . . ." *Rich 2*, V, v, 23–24. **2** term of contempt or abuse: ". . . they are hare-brain'd slaves,/ And hunger will enforce them be more eager . . ." *1 Hen 6*, I, ii, 37–38.
—*v.* **3 slaves your ordinance,** treats the laws of heaven with no more respect that he would a slave: ". . . the superfluous and lust-dieted man,/ That slaves your ordinance . . ." *Lear*, IV, i, 67–68.

slave of Nature, *n.* person condemned by original sin: "Thou that wast seal'd in thy nativity/ The slave of Nature, and the son of hell . . ." *Rich 3*, I, iii, 229–230.

slaver, *v.* to exchange slobbering kisses with prostitutes: "Slaver with lips as common as the stairs/ That mount the Capitol . . ." *Cymb*, I, vii, 105–106.

sleave, *n.* thread of fine silk: "Sleep, that knits up the ravell'd sleave of care . . ." *Mac*, II, ii, 36.

sleave silk, *n.* raw silk, separated into strands for embroidery: "Why art thou then exasperate, thou idle/ immaterial skein of sleave silk . . ." *Tr & Cr*, V, i, 29–30.

sledded, *adj.* equipped with or traveling on sleds or sledges: ". . . in an angry parle/ He smote the sledded Pollacks on the ice." *Ham*, I, i, 65–66.

sleek, *v.* to smooth: "Gentle my Lord, sleek o'er your rugged looks . . ." *Mac*, III, ii, 27.

sleep, *n.* **1 break one's sleeps,** to lose sleep: "But my revenge will come."/ "Break not your sleeps for that [worrying that you won't have your revenge]." *Ham*, IV, vii, 29–30. **2 dead of sleep,** soundly sleeping: "We were dead of sleep,/ And . . . all clapp'd under hatches . . ." *Temp*, V, i, 230–231. **3 equivocate in a sleep,** to trick (someone) into sleep, then bring nightmares [said of liquor]: ". . . in conclusion, equivocates him in a sleep, and, giving him the lie,/ leaves him." *Mac,* II, iii, 35–37.

—*v.* **4** to miss the point; become meaningless: "A knavish speech sleeps in a foolish ear." *Ham,* IV, ii, 22. **5** to be lax, remiss, or neglectful: "And therefore have I slept in your report . . ." *Sonn 83,* 5. **6** to be at rest [silenced]: ". . . truth can never be confirm'd enough,/ Though doubts did ever sleep." *Per,* V, i, 201–202. **7 sleep out,** to ignore; not be concerned with: ". . . for the life to come, I sleep out the thought of it." *W Tale,* IV, iii, 30. **8 sleep upon,** to be blind to: "The king's eyes, that so long have slept upon/ This bold bad man." *Hen 8,* II, ii, 42–43.

sleepy, *adj.* **1** lazy; careless: "'Tis not sleepy business,/ But must be look'd to speedily, and strongly." *Cymb,* III, v, 26–27. **2** sleep-inducing: "We will give you sleepy/ drinks . . ." *W Tale,* I, i, 13–14. **3** occupied with meditation: "Whiles in the mildness of your sleepy thoughts . . ." *Rich 3,* III, vii, 122.

sleeve-hand, *n.* sleeve cuff: ". . . he so chants/ to the sleeve-hand and the work about the square/ on 't." *W Tale,* IV, iv, 211–213.

sleeveless, *adj.* futile; pointless: ". . . send that/ Greekish whoremasterly villain with the sleeve/ back to the dissembling luxurious drab of [on] a sleeveless/ errand." *Tr & Cr,* V, iv, 6–9.

sleided silk, *n.* silk that has been separated into threads, as by fraying: "Be't when she weav'd the sleided silk/ With fingers long . . ." *Per,* IV, Chor., 21–22.

sleight, *n.* **1** artifice or trickery; cunning: "Ulysses and stout Diomede/ With sleight and manhood stole to Rhesus' tents . . ." *3 Hen 6,* IV, ii, 19–20. **2** [pl.] devices; manipulations: "And that, distill'd by magic sleights,/ Shall raise such artificial sprites . . ." *Mac,* III, v, 26–27.

slenderly, *adv.* insufficiently: ". . . yet he hath ever but/ slenderly known himself." *Lear,* I, i, 293–294.

'Slid, *interj.* by God's eyelid [mild oath]: "'Slid, I'll after him again, and beat him." *T Night,* III, iv, 400.

sliding, *n.* lapse of morals: ". . . rather prov'd the sliding of your brother/ A merriment than a vice." *Meas,* II, iv, 115–116.

'Slight, *interj.* by God's light; a mild oath: "'Slight, I could so beat the rogue!" *T Night,* II, v, 33.

slighted, *v.* perh. "slided"; tossed or dumped unceremoniously: "The rogues/ slighted me into the river with as little remorse [pity] . . ." *Wives,* III, v, 8–9.

slight in sufferance, See **sufferance** (def. 6).

slightly, *adv.* easily or lightly; here, willingly: "You were to blame . . . To part so slightly with your wife's first gift . . ." *Merch,* V, i, 166–167.

slightly handled, *adj.* passed over lightly: ". . . left nothing . . . Untouch'd, or slightly handled in discourse." *Rich 3,* III, vii, 18–19.

slightness, *n.* **unstable slightness,** indecisive trifling: ". . . omit/ Real necessities, and give way the while/ To unstable slight ness." *Cor,* III, i, 145–147.

sling, *n.* leather device for hurling small stones: ". . . to suffer/ The slings and arrows of outrageous fortune . . ." *Ham,* III, i, 57–58.

slip, *n.* **1** error: ". . . for fear of slips,/ Set thy seal manual on my wax-red lips." *Ven & Ad,* 515–516. **2** counterfeit coin: "What counterfeit did/ I give you?"/ "The slip sir, the slip. Can you not conceive?" *Rom & Jul,* II, iv, 48–50. **3** (in botany) a cutting; here, scion or son: ". . . thy sons, fair slips of such a stock." *2 Hen 6,* II, ii, 57. **4** leash: "I see you stand like greyhounds in the slips . . ." *Hen 5,* III, i, 31.

—*v.* **5** to allow to go by unnoticed: "I have almost slipp'd the hour." *Mac,* II, iii, 48. **6** to release; let go: "We'll slip you for a *season* [time] . . ." *Cymb,* IV, iii, 22. **7** to shake loose [from the yoke]: "From which even here I slip my weary head . . ." *Rich 3,* IV, iv, 112. **8 let slip,** to unleash: "Cry havoc and let slip the dogs of war . . ." *J Caes,* III, i, 273.

slippery, *adj.* **1** changing shape or location quickly: ". . . hanging them/ With deafing clamour in the slippery clouds . . ." *2 Hen 4,* III, i, 23–24. **2** fickle; inconstant: "Our slippery people . . . begin to throw/ Pompey the Great, and all his dignities/ Upon his son . . ." *Ant & Cleo,* I, ii, 183–186. **3** wanton; unchaste: "Ha' not you seen, Camillo . . . or heard? . . . or thought? . . . My wife is slippery?" *W Tale,* I, ii, 267–273. **4 slippery standers,** those of uncertain footing [transient fame]: ". . . when they fall, as being slippery standers,/ The love that lean'd on them . . . Doth one pluck down another . . ." *Tr & Cr,* III, iii, 84–86. **5 slippery turns,** treacherous shifts of fortune: "O world, thy slippery turns!" *Cor,* IV, iv, 12.

slip-shod, *adj.* wearing slippers: ". . . I prithee, be merry; thy wit shall not/ go slip-shod [no brains in your heels to undertake such a journey]." *Lear,* I, v, 11–12.

sliver, *v.* **sliver and disbranch,** to slice and cut off; here, Goneril's wish to dissociate herself from her family tree: "She that herself will sliver and disbranch/ From her material sap . . ." *Lear,* IV, ii, 34–35.

slobbery, *adj.* sloppy; slovenly: ". . . a slobb'ry and a dirty farm/ In that nook-shotten isle of Albion." *Hen 5,* III, v, 13–14.

slope, *v.* to bend: ". . . palaces, and pyramids, do slope/ Their heads to their foundations . . ." *Mac,* IV, i, 57–58.

slops, *n. pl.* baggy, knee-length breeches: ". . . a German/ from the waist downward, all slops . . ." *M Ado,* III, ii, 32–33.

slough[1], (pron. sluff), *n.* **1** skin: ". . . as the snake . . . With shining checker'd slough, doth sting a child . . ." *2 Hen 6,* III, i, 228–229. **2 humble slough,** outward humility: ". . . to inure thyself/ to what thou art like to be, cast thy humble slough,/ and/ appear fresh." *T Night,* II, v, 147–149.

slough[2], (pron. slew), *n.* bog: ". . . they threw me off . . . in a slew of mire . . ." *Wives,* IV, v, 63–64.

slovenry, *n.* slovenliness: "And time hath worn us into slovenry . . ." *Hen 5,* IV, iii, 114.

slow, *adj.* **1 nothing slow,** reluctant; not of a mind: "My father Capulet will have it so,/ And I am nothing slow to slack his haste." *Rom & Jul,* IV, i, 2–3. **2 slow in speech,** soft-spoken: "But slow in speech, yet sweet as spring-time flowers." *Shrew,* II, i, 240.

slow offense, *n.* offense of slowness: "Thus can my love excuse the slow offence/ Of my dull bearer . . ." *Sonn 51,* 1–2.

slubber, *v.* **1** to do hastily and carelessly: "Slubber not business for my sake Bassanio,/ But stay the very riping of the time . . ." *Merch,* II, viii, 39–40. **2** to sully; besmear: ". . . be content to/ slubber the gloss of your new fortunes . . ." *Oth,* I, iii, 226–227.

slug-abed, *n.* sleepyhead: "Why, lamb, why, lady, fie! You slug-abed!" *Rom & Jul,* IV, v, 2.

sluggardized, *adj.* made lazy and sluglike: ". . . living dully sluggardis'd at home . . ." *Two Gent,* I, i, 7.

sluice, *v.* to flood; here, to bed: ". . . little thinks she has been sluic'd in 's absence/ And his pond fish'd by his next neighbour . . ." *W Tale,* I, ii, 194–195.

sluttery, *n.* sluttishness: "Sluttery . . . Should make desire vomit emptiness,/ Not so allur'd to feed." *Cymb,* I, vii, 44–46.

sly, *adj.* imperceptible: "The sly slow hours shall not determinate/ The dateless limit of thy dear exile . . ." *Rich 2,* I, iii, 150–151.

smack, *n.* **1** taste; also, trace or suggestion: ". . . your lordship, though not clean/ past your youth, have yet some smack of age in you . . ." *2 Hen 4,* I, ii, 95–96. **2** same in wordplay with "to see through" and "to smoke": ". . . he is but a bastard to the time/ That doth not smack of observation;/ And so am I [unfashionable], whether I smoke or no." *K John,* I, i, 207–209. **3 pull at a smack a' th' contrary,** to swallow a fair taste of the opposite [your own foolishness]: "Well, I shall be wiser."/ "Ev'n as soon as thou canst; for thou hast to pull at a/ smack a' th' contrary." *All's W,* II, iii, 220–222.
—*v.* **4** to have a taste; here, a taste for lechery: ". . . my father did something smack, something/ grow to; he had a kind of taste . . ." *Merch,* II, ii, 16–17. **5 smack of,** to taste of; hence, engage in: "All sects, all ages smack of this vice . . ." *Meas,* II, ii, 5.

small, *adj.* **1** slender: "With fingers long, small, white as milk . . ." *Per,* IV, Chor., 22. **2** weak: "Doth it/ not show vilely in me to desire small beer?" *2 Hen 4,* II, ii, 5–6. **3** shrill; high-pitched: "My throat of war be turn'd . . . into a pipe/ Small as an eunuch . . ." *Cor,* III, ii, 113–114.
—*adv.* **4** high; shrilly: ". . . you shall play it in a mask; and you/ may speak as small as you will." *M N Dream,* I, ii, 45–46. **5 by small and small,** little by little: "I play the torturer by small and small/ To lengthen out the worst that must be spoken . . ." *Rich 2,* III, ii, 198–199.
—*pron.* **6** very little: "Small have continual plodders ever won . . ." *Love's L,* I, i, 86.

small ale, *n.* weak beer of the cheapest quality: "For God's sake, a pot of small ale." *Shrew,* Ind., ii, 1.

small beer, *n.* **1** weak beer: ". . . and I will make it [a] felony to/ drink small beer." *2 Hen 6,* IV, ii, 64–65. **2** trivialities: "To suckle fools, and chronicle small beer." *Oth,* II, i, 160.

smallest, *adj.* **1** thinnest; most delicate: "Being that I flow in grief,/ The smallest twine may lead me." *M Ado,* IV, i, 249–250. **2 in the smallest,** in the least possible way: "I may make my/ case as Claudio's to cross this in the smallest." *Meas,* IV, ii, 166–167.

small time, *n.* a short period of time: "Small time, but in that small most greatly lived/ This star of England . . ." *Hen 5,* V, ii, Chorus 5–6.

Smalus, *n.* poss. "Synalus," Carthaginian captain mentioned in Plutarch: "Where the warlike Smalus,/ That noble honour'd lord, is fear'd and lov'd?" *W Tale,* V, i, 156–157.

smart, *adj.* burning, biting, pricking, or the like: "Their softest touch as smart as lizards' stings!" *2 Hen 6*, III, ii, 324.

smatch, *n.* taste or smack: "Thy life hath had some smatch of honour in it." *J Caes*, V, v, 46.

smatter, *v.* to chatter; prattle: "Hold your tongue,/ Good Prudence! Smatter with your gossips, go." *Rom & Jul*, III, v, 170–171.

smell, *v.* **1** to reek or stink of: ". . . he would mouth with a beggar though she smelt brown/ bread and garlic . . ." *Meas*, III, ii, 177–178. **2 smell out a suit,** (of a courtier) to discover a wealthy client eager to win royal favor: "Sometimes she gallops o'er a courtier's nose/ And then dreams he of smelling out a suit . . ." *Rom & Jul*, I, iv, 77–78. **3 smells April and May,** [he] is as fresh as spring flowers: ". . . he writes verses, he/ speaks holiday, he smells April and May." *Wives*, III, ii, 61–62. **4 smelt like a fool,** wordplay on "smell" and "rank": "Would he/ had been one of my rank!"/ "[Aside] To have smelt like a fool." *Cymb*, II, i, 14–16.

smile, *v.* **1** to influence favorably: ". . . Venus smiles not in a house of tears." *Rom & Jul*, IV, i, 8. **2 smile one's cheek in years,** to smile or laugh one's face into wrinkles: ". . . some Dick,/ That smiles his cheek in years, and knows the trick/ To make my lady laugh . . ." *Love's L*, V, ii, 464–466. —*n.* **3 there shall be smiles,** I will be friendly enough: ". . . when/ time shall serve there shall be smiles . . ." *Hen 5*, II, i, 4–5.

smilet, *n.* little smile: ". . . those happy smilets/ That play'd on her ripe lip . . ." *Lear*, IV, iii, 20–21.

smilingly, *adv.* willingly; gladly: "All the regions/ Do smilingly revolt, and who resists/ Are mock'd . . ." *Cor*, IV, vi, 103–105.

smirched, *adj.* soiled or stained: ". . . like the shaven/ Hercules in the smirched worm-eaten tapestry . . ." *M Ado*, III, iii, 132–133.

smit, *v.* var. of **smitten;** harmed or injured: ". . . my reliances on his fracted dates/ Have smit my credit." *Timon*, II, i, 22–23.

Smithfield, *n.* **1** open-air market for animals in London: "He's gone into Smithfield to buy your worship a/ horse." *2 Hen 4*, I, ii, 50–51. **2** (in the same general area) site used from the Middle Ages for fairs, jousts, executions, etc.: "The witch in Smithfield shall be burn'd to ashes . . ." *2 Hen 6*, II, iii, 7.

smock, *n.* **1** lady's nightdress or undergarment: ". . . there will she sit in her smock till she have writ a/ sheet of paper . . ." *M Ado*, II, iii, 130–131. **2** women in general: "I shall stay here the forehorse to a smock . . ." *All's W*, II, i, 30.

smoile, *v.* to smile at; spelling seems to indicate that a dialect is part of Kent's disguise: "Smoile you my speeches, as I were a Fool?" *Lear*, II, ii, 83.

smoke, *v.* **1** to curry or, perh., to disinfect; also, to beat or thrash: "I'll smoke your skin-coat, and I catch you right . . ." *K John*, II, i, 139. **2** to mist: "But even this night . . . Already smokes about the burning crest . . ." *K John*, V, iv, 33–34. **3** to fumigate, as with incense or perfume: "Being entertained for a perfumer, as I was/ smoking a musty room . . ." *M Ado*, I, iii, 54–55. **4** to suffer: ". . . some of you shall smoke for it in Rome." *T Andr*, IV, ii, 111. **5** to steam: "What means this bloody knife?"/ "'Tis hot, it smokes . . ." *Lear*, V, iii, 223. **6** to thrash, or perh. here, to brand: "I'll smoke your skin-coat, and I catch you right;/ Sirrah, look to't . . ." *K John*, II, 1, 139–140. **7 smoke me,** find me out: "They begin to smoke me, and disgraces have of late/ knock'd too often at my door." *All's W*, IV, i, 27–28. —*n.* **8** illusion or artifice; camouflage: "They shoot but calm words folded up in smoke . . ." *K John*, II, i, 229. **9** poss. ref. to pious breath or foul breath: "Let your close fire predominate his smoke . . ." *Timon*, IV, iii, 144.

smooth, *adj.* **1** pleasant; agreeable: ". . . he hath brought us smooth and welcome news." *1 Hen 4*, I, i, 66. **2** amiable on the surface: "I have been politic with my friend, smooth with mine enemy . . ." *As You*, V, iv, 45–46. —*adv.* **3** smoothly; agreeably: "His Grace looks cheerfully and smooth today . . ." *Rich 3*, III, iv, 48. —*v.* **4** to speak well of: ". . . what tongue shall smooth thy name/ When I thy three-hours wife have mangled it?" *Rom & Jul*, III, ii, 98–99. **5** to flatter: "I can smooth and fill his aged ears/ With golden promises . . ." *T Andr*, IV, iv, 96–97. **6** to gloss over or ignore something: ". . . the sinful father/ Seem'd not to strike, but smooth . . ." *Per*, I, ii, 77–78. **7 smooth it,** to play the flatterer: ". . . dangerous peer,/ That smooth'st it so with king and commonweal!" *2 Hen 6*, II, i, 21–22.

smooth-faced, *adj.* **1** young and immature: "I'll mark no words that smooth-faced wooers say . . ." *Love's L*, V, ii, 820. **2** deceptively pleasing or attractive: "That smooth-fac'd gentleman, tickling commodity . . ." *K John*, II, i, 573.

smoothing, *adj.* full of blandishments; flattering: ". . . let not his smoothing words/ Bewitch your hearts . . ." *2 Hen 6*, I, 1, 155–156.

smooth-pate, *n.* term of abuse for the Roundheads (Puritans) and their closely cropped heads: "The whoreson/ smooth-pates do now wear nothing but high shoes/ and bunches of keys . . ." *2 Hen 4*, I, ii, 37–39.

smother, *n.* **1** dense, choking smoke: "from the smoke into the smother [out of the frying pan into the fire]." *As You,* I, ii, 277.

—*v.* **2** to almost suffocate: "Another smother'd seems to pelt and swear . . ." *Luc,* 1418. **3 smother up,** to stifle or suppress: "These things, come thus to light,/ Smother her spirits up." *M Ado,* IV, i, 111–112.

smug, *adj.* **1** smooth; tranquil or serene: ". . . here the smug and silver Trent shall run/ In a new channel fair and evenly." *1 Hen 4,* III, i, 98–99. **2** finely dressed; spruce; trim: "I will die bravely,/ Like a smug bridegroom." *Lear,* IV, vi, 199–200.

Smulkin, *n.* name given by Poor Tom [Edgar] to his attendant devil: "Beware my follower. Peace, Smulkin! Peace,/ thou fiend!" *Lear,* III, iv, 144–145.

smutch, *v.* to smudge: "Why that's my bawcock. What! hast smutch'd thy nose?" *W Tale,* I, ii, 121.

snaffle, *n.* (in horsemanship) a bit having no curb, used only with gentle horses: "The third o' the world is yours, which with a snaffle/ You may pace easy . . ." *Ant & Cleo,* II, ii, 63–64.

snap, *adv.* at once: "Speak, breathe, discuss; brief, short, quick, snap." *Wives,* IV, v, 2.

snatch, *n.* **1** catch in the voice: ". . . the snatches in his voice,/ And burst of speaking were as his . . ." *Cymb,* IV, ii, 105–106. **2** quick catch or seizure; here, wordplay on added meaning of "snack," understood as sexual innuendo: ". . . it seems some certain snatch or so/ Would serve your·turns."/ "Ay, so the turn were served." *T Andr,* II, i, 95–96. **3** quibble; pun: ". . . leave me your snatches, and yield me a/ direct answer." *Meas,* IV, ii, 5–6.

—*v.* **4** to rob: "I am afear'd the life of Helen, lady,/ Was foully snatch'd." *All's W,* V, iii, 152–153.

sneak-up, *n.* creeping, cowardly thief: "How? the Prince is a Jack, a sneak-up." *1 Hen 4,* III, iii, 83.

sneap, *n.* rebuke or affront: "My lord, I will not undergo this sneap without/ reply." *2 Hen 4,* II, i, 121–122.

sneaped, *adj.* nipped with cold: "And give the sneaped birds more cause to sing." *Luc,* 333.

sneaping, *adj.* (of weather) nipping; biting: "Berowne is like an envious sneaping frost . . ." *Love's L,* I, i, 100.

sneck up! *interj.* Be hanged!: "We did keep time, sir, in our catches. Sneck up!" *T Night,* II, iii, 94.

snip, *n.* snippet; snatch or fragment: ". . . and keep not too long in/ one tune, but a snip and away." *Love's L,* III, i, 18–19.

snipe, *n.* fool; blockhead [term of utter contempt]: "I mine own gain'd knowledge should profane,/ If I would time expend with such a snipe . . ." *Oth,* I, iii, 382–383.

snipped-taffeta, *adj.* wearing material slashed [esp. the upper sleeves] to allow a more colorful lining to show through; ref. to Parolles's vivid attire: ". . . your son was misled with a snipp'd-taffeta/ fellow there . . ." *All's W,* IV, v, 1–2.

snorting, *adj.* snoring: "Awake the snorting citizens with the bell . . ." *Oth,* I, i, 90.

snow-broth, *n.* melted snow: ". . . a man whose blood/ Is very snow-broth . . ." *Meas,* I, iv, 57–58.

snuff, *n.* **1** burning wick of a candle; here, life as a candle that has nearly burned out: "My snuff and loathed part of nature should/ Burn itself out." *Lear,* IV, vi, 39–40. **2** exhausted man likened to a burned-out candle end: "To hide me from the radiant sun, and solace/ I' th' dungeon by a snuff?" *Cymb,* I, vii, 86–87. **3** odor of a smoking candle; also, disgust at such an odor: "There lives within the very flame of love/ A kind of wick or snuff that will abate it . . ." *Ham,* IV, vii, 113–114. **4** quarrel: "What hath been seen,/ Either in snuffs and packings of the Dukes . . ." *Lear,* III, i, 25–26. **5 in snuff,** in need of snuffing [trimming the burned-down wick]: "He dares not come there for the candle; for you see/ it is already in snuff." *M N Dream,* V, i, 240–241. **6 take (something) in snuff,** to take offense at something: "You'll mar the light by taking it in snuff . . ." *Love's L,* V, ii, 22.

so, *conj.* **1** provided that: "So thou wilt send thy gentle heart before,/ To say thou'lt enter friendly." *Timon,* V, iv, 48–49. **2** so long as: "I'll do this heavy task,/ So thou destroy Rapine and Murder there." *T Andr,* V, ii, 58–59. **3** doing so: "These deeds must not be thought/ After these ways: so, it will make us mad." *Mac,* II, ii, 32–33. **4 or so,** or something like that; or some such: "Is she wedded or no?"/ "To her will sir, or so." *Love's L,* II, i, 210–211.

—*interj.* **5** good! excellent!: "Why, so! then am I sure of victory." *3 Hen 6,* IV, i, 145.

—*pron.* **6** as much; the same thing: "You had a father: let your son say so." *Sonn 13,* 14.

—*adv.* **7** similarly: "The words of heaven; on whom it will, it will;/ On whom it will not, so . . ." *Meas,* I, ii, 114–115. **8** sufficiently: "Yet this thy praise cannot be so thy praise . . ." *Sonn 70,* 11. **9** in this way; in such a manner: "Press me not, beseech you, so." *W Tale,* I, ii, 19. **10 I ought so,** I should do so: "Say then: 'tis true, I ought so." *Cor,* III, iii, 62.

soaking, *adj.* able to absorb: "For thy conceit is soaking, will draw in/ More than the common blocks..." *W Tale,* I, ii, 224–225.

sob, *n.* wordplay on usual sense with "sob," a rest given a horse to recover its wind: "... the man, sir, that when/ gentlemen are tired gives them a sob, and rests [arrests] them..." *Errors,* IV, iii, 23–24.

sober, *adj.* **1** truthful; sincere: "Speak'st thou in sober meanings?" *As You,* V, ii, 69. **2 sober guards,** clothes, as proper guardians of virtue: "Shook off my sober guards and civil fears..." *Lover's Comp,* 298.

sobriety, *n.* orderliness; decency: "... and the sobriety of it, and/ the modesty of it, to be otherwise." *Hen 5,* IV, i, 74–75.

sociable, *adj.* sympathetic: "Mine eyes, ev'n sociable to the show of thine..." *Temp,* V, i, 63.

society, *n.* **1** friendship or companionship: "To stop the inundation of her tears/ Which... May be put from her by society." *Rom & Jul,* IV, i, 12–14. **2** company; here, guests: "Ourself will mingle with society,/ And play the humble host." *Mac,* III, iv, 3–4. **3 soft society,** refined manners: "... an absolute gentleman, full of most excellent/ differences, of very soft society..." *Ham,* V, ii, 107–108.

sod, *adj.* **1** sodden; boiled or steeped: "Her eyes though sod in tears, look'd red and raw..." *Luc,* 1592.
—*v.* **2** past part. of **seethe;** boiled: "... or women/ That have sod their infants in... The brine they wept at killing 'em." *Kinsmen,* I, iii, 20–22.

sodden, *adj.* or past part. of **seethe;** boiled or stewed; ref. to stews [brothels], also subjected to the hot-tub treatment for venereal disease: "The stuff we have, a strong wind/ will blow it to pieces, they are so pitifully sodden." *Per,* IV, ii, 17–18.

soever, *adv.* **how...soever,** however; howsoever: "How rank soever [however thickly] rounded in with danger." *Tr & Cr,* I, iii, 196.

so far as to, to the extent that [I may address]: "Norfolk, so far as to mine enemy..." *Rich 2,* I, iii, 193.

so-forth, *n.* so-and-so; prob. euphem. for "cuckold": "... whisp'ring, rounding/ 'Sicilia is a so-forth'..." *W Tale,* I, ii, 217–218.

soft, *adj.* **1** weak: "Alack, alack, that heaven should practise stratagems/ Upon so soft a subject as myself." *Rom & Jul,* III, v, 209–210.
—*adv.* **2** gently: "And in your power soft silencing your son." *2 Hen 4,* V, ii, 97. **3 soft and fair,** here used as a polite request

to stop a moment: "Soft and fair, friar. Which is Beatrice?" *M Ado,* V, iv, 72.
—*v.* **4** [as an imperative] be quiet! stop!: "Soft you now,/ The fair Ophelia!" *Ham,* III, i, 88–89.

soft-conscienced, *adj.* of little or no conscience: "... though soft-conscienced men... say it was for his country, he did it/ to please his mother..." *Cor,* I, i, 36–38.

soft courage, *n.* weak resolve; faintheartedness: "... this soft courage makes your followers faint." *3 Hen 6,* II, ii, 57.

soft laws, *n.* gentle rules of love: "And, for I should not deal in her soft laws,/ She did corrupt frail Nature..." *3 Hen 6,* III, ii, 154–155.

softly, *adv.* slowly: "... though he go as softly as foot can fall, he thinks himself too soon there." *As You,* III, ii, 321–323.

softly-sprighted, *adj.* mild or meek of spirit: "A softly-sprighted man, is he not?" *Wives,* I, iv, 22.

softness, *n.* effeteness; decadence: "... a satire against the softness of prosperity..." *Timon,* V, i, 34.

soft parts of conversation, *n.* social graces: "... have not those soft parts of conversation/ That chamberers have..." *Oth,* III, iii, 268–269.

So ho, *interj.* hunter's cry upon spotting the quarry, esp. a hare: "A bawd! A bawd! A Bawd! So ho." *Rom & Jul,* II, iv, 128.

soil, *n.* basis; also, perh., solution: "The soil is this, that thou dost common grow." *Sonn 69,* 14.

soiled, *adj.* (of a horse) high-spirited or wanton with feeding on rich pasturage: "... nor the soiled horse goes to't/ With a more riotous appetite." *Lear,* IV, vi, 124–125.

soilure, *n.* taint; dishonor: "Not making any scruple of her soilure..." *Tr & Cr,* IV, i, 57.

sojourn, *v.* to reside temporarily as a guest: "... in the mean time sojourn'd at my father's,/ Where how he did prevail I shame to speak..." *K John,* I, i, 103–104.

sojourner, *n.* guest; temporary resident: "... report what a/ sojourner we have; you'll lose nothing by custom." *Per,* IV, ii, 135–136.

Sol, *n.* the Sun: "And therefore is the glorious planet Sol/ In noble eminence enthron'd..." *Tr & Cr,* I, iii, 89–90.

sola, *interj.* hunting cry, similar to "halloo": "[Shout within.] Sola, sola! [Exit Costard.]" *Love's L,* IV, i, 150.

solace, *v.* to find pleasure: "To hide me from the radiant sun, and solace/ I' th' dungeon by a snuff?" *Cymb,* I, vii, 86–87.

sold, *adj.* (of a meal) purchased, not given, because the host does not make the guests feel welcome: "You do not give the cheer: the feast is sold . . ." *Mac,* III, iv, 32.

solder, *v.* to unite and solidify: "As if the world should cleave, and that slain men/ Should solder up the rift." *Ant & Cleo,* III, iv, 31–32.

soldier, *n.* **be soldier to,** to be prepared for: "This attempt/ I am soldier to, and will abide it with/ A prince's courage." *Cymb,* III, iv, 184–186.

sole, *adj.* **1** very; mere: "This tyrant, whose sole name blisters our tongues . . ." *Mac,* IV, iii, 12. **2** unique; also, unifying: "Which, though it alter not love's sole effect . . ." *Sonn 36,* 7. —*adv.* **3** utterly; completely: ". . . that praise, sole pure, transcends." *Tr & Cr,* I, iii, 243.

solely, *adv.* **1** alone: "Leave me solely: go,/ See how he fares." *W Tale,* II, iii, 17–18. **2** (for us) absolutely: ". . . to all our nights and days to come/ Give solely sovereign sway and masterdom." *Mac,* I, v, 69–70.

solely singular, *adj.* unique: ". . . the jest may remain after the wearing solely/ singular." *Rom & Jul,* II, iv, 65–66.

solemn, *adj.* **1** melancholy: ". . . in this spleen ridiculous appears/ To check their folly, passion's solemn tears." *Love's L,* V, ii, 117–118. **2** ceremonial; formal: "Our solemn hymns to sullen dirges change . . ." *Rom & Jul,* IV, v, 88.

solemnity, *n.* [often pl] celebration; festivities: "Come hither, cover'd with an antic face,/ To fleer and scorn at our solemnity?" *Rom & Jul,* I, v, 55–56.

solfa, *v.* to sing, using do, re, mi, etc., for the tones of the scale: "I'll try how you can solfa and sing it." *Shrew,* I, ii, 17.

solicit, *v.* **1** to urge; move or impel: ". . . tell him, with th'occurrents more and less/ Which have solicited [prompted me to give him my vote]—" *Ham,* V, ii, 362–363. **2** to annoy; importune: "Therefore be gone, solicit me no more." *Two Gent,* V, iv, 40.

solid, See **sullied** (def 2).

solidare, *n.* coin of small denomination; perhaps "solidus," a term for shilling: "Here's three solidares for thee; . . . wink at me, and say thou saw'st me not." *Timon,* III, i, 43–44.

solidity, *n.* **this solidity and compound mass,** earth: "Heaven's face does glow/ O'er this solidity and compound mass/ With tristful visage . . ." *Ham,* III, iv, 49–50.

so like you, if it please you: "So like you, sir, ambassadors from Rome . . ." *Cymb,* II, iii, 53.

Solon, *n.* lawgiver of ancient Athens: "But safer triumph is this funeral pomp/ That hath aspir'd to Solon's happiness . . ." *T Andr,* I, i, 176–177.

solus, *adj.* [Latin] alone: "Enter Hotspur solus, reading a letter" [SD] *1 Hen 4,* II, iii, 1.

some, *adv.* about; nearly: "I think 'tis now some seven o'clock . . ." *Shrew,* IV, iii, 184.

some'er, *adv.* use of "howsome'er" with intervening words: "How strange or odd some'er [howsoever] I bear myself—" *Ham,* I, v, 178.

some o'er other some, some [people] as compared with others: "How happy some o'er other some can be!" *M N Dream,* I, i, 226.

something, *adv.* **1** somewhat; rather; more or less: ". . . with a white head, and something a/ round belly." *2 Hen 4,* I, ii, 187–188. **2** at some distance: ". . . for't must be done to-night,/ And something from the palace . . ." *Mac,* III, i, 130–131. **3** in some ways; to some extent: ". . . I have disabled mine estate,/ By something showing a more swelling port . . ." *Merch,* I, i, 123–124. —*adj.* **4** real; substantial: "For nothing hath begot my something grief . . ." *Rich 2,* II, ii, 36.

something about, *adv.* somewhat indirectly: "Something about, a little from the right,/ In at the window, or else o'er the hatch . . ." *K John,* I, i, 170–171.

something into, *adv.* into a somewhat: ". . . leave this keen encounter of our wits,/ And fall something into a slower method [procedure] . . ." *Rich 3,* I, ii, 119–120.

something settled, *adj.* firmly lodged but unidentifiable: "This something settled matter in his heart,/ Whereon his brains still beating puts him thus . . ." *Ham,* III, i, 175–176.

sometime, *adv.* **1** at one time; formerly; once: ". . . you hear what he hath said/ Which was sometime his general . . ." *Cor,* V, i, 1–2. **2** occasionally; from time to time: ". . . a savage jealousy/ That sometime savours nobly." *T Night,* V, i, 117–118. **3** at some future time: "And every fair from fair sometime declines . . ." *Sonn 18,* 7. **4 sometime of,** at sometime during: "There sleeps Titania sometime of the night . . ." *M N Dream,* II, i, 253.

—*adj.* **5** former: "Therefore our sometime sister, now our queen ..." *Ham,* I, ii, 8.

sometimes, *adv.* once; formerly: "... sometimes from her eyes/ I did receive fair speechless messages ..." *Merch,* I, i, 163–164.

somever, *adv.* use of "howsomever" with intervening words: "How in my words somever [howsoever] she be shent,/ To give them seals never my soul consent." *Ham,* III, ii, 389–390.

somewhat, *pron.* something: "Well, somewhat we must do." *Rich 2,* II, ii, 116.

somewhither, *adv.* to some place or other: "Somewhither would she have thee go with her." *T Andr,* IV, i, 11.

Somme, *n.* river in NW France, flowing into the English Channel: "'Tis certain he hath pass'd the river Somme." *Hen 5,* III, v, 1.

son, *n.* **1** tender term of address by older man to younger: "... a Jack guardant cannot office me/ from my son Coriolanus." *Cor,* V, ii, 61–62. **2** son-in-law; here, intended son-in-law: "Wife, go you to her ere you go to bed,/ Acquaint her here of my son Paris' love ..." *Rom & Jul,* III, iv, 15–16. **3** wordplay on "sun" (emblem of Edward IV) and "heir": "Now is the winter of our discontent/ Made glorious summer by this son of York ..." *Rich 3,* I, i, 1–2.

song, *n.* poem; poetic composition: "If with too credent ear you list his songs,/ Or lose your heart ..." *Ham,* I, iii, 30–31.

sonties, *n. pl.* dial. pron. of "saints": "Be [by] God's sonties "twill be a hard way to hit ..." *Merch,* II, ii, 42.

soon at night, *adv.* towards evening: "I shall be sent for/ soon at night." *2 Hen 4,* V, v, 89–90.

soon-believing, *adj.* easily convinced; overcredulous: "... he did plot the Duke of Gloucester's death,/ Suggest his soon-believing adversaries ..." *Rich 2,* I, i, 100–101.

soonest, *adj.* **1** quickest; fastest: "... make your soonest haste;/ So your desires are yours." *Ant & Cleo,* III, iv, 27–28.
—*adv.* **2** most easily or readily: "Your Grace, we think, should soonest know his mind." *Rich 3,* III, iv, 9.

soon-speeding, *adj.* quick-acting: "A dram of poison, such soon-speeding gear/ As will disperse itself through all the veins ..." *Rom & Jul,* V, i, 60–61.

sooth, *n.* **1** truth: "... in good sooth, are you he that hangs the verses on the trees ...?" *As You,* III, ii, 381–382. **2** ap-

peasement; blandishment: "... that e'er this tongue of mine,/ That laid the sentence of dread banishment/ On yon proud man, should take it off again/ With words of sooth!" *Rich 2,* III, iii, 133–136. **3 good sooth,** in truth: "Hell only danceth at so harsh a chime./ Good sooth, I care not for you." *Per,* I, i, 86–87. **4 looks like sooth,** looks like an honest man: "... I have it/ Upon his own report and I believe it;/ He looks like sooth." *W Tale,* IV, iv, 171–173. **5 say (the) sooth,** (to) tell the truth: "... for, to say the sooth ... My people are with sickness much enfeebled ..." *Hen 5,* III, vi, 147–150. **6 sooth to say,** truth to tell: "Sir, sooth so say, you did not dine at home." *Errors,* IV, iv, 67. **7 very sooth,** truly; indeed: "One seve'night longer."/ "Very sooth, to-morrow." *W Tale,* I, ii, 17.
—*adv.* **8** short for "in sooth"; truly: "No, sooth, sir: my determinate voyage is mere/ extravagancy." *T Night,* II, i, 10–11.

soothe, *v.* **1** to humor: "Is't good to soothe him in these contraries?" *Errors,* IV, iv, 77. **2 soothe up,** to flatter: "... thou art perjur'd too,/ And sooth'st up greatness." *K John,* III, i, 46–47.

soother, *n.* flatterer: "I do defy/ The tongues of soothers ..." *1 Hen 4,* IV, i, 6–7.

soothing, *n.* flattery: "... let courts and cities be/ Made all of false-fac'd soothing!" *Cor,* I, ix, 43–44.

soothsayer, *n.* person who foretells the future: "... most absolute Alexas, where's the soothsayer/ that you prais'd so to the queen?" *Ant & Cleo,* I, ii, 2–3.

sop, *n.* **1** small piece of food, as toast or a wafer, dipped in wine, liquor, etc., before eating: "... the bounded waters/ Should lift their bosoms higher than the shores,/ And make a sop of all this solid globe ..." *Tr & Cr,* I, iii, 111–113. **2** [pl.] pieces of cake soaked in a glass of wine; drunk by a wedding party after the service: "... quaff'd off the muscadel,/ And threw the sops all in the sexton's face ..." *Shrew,* III, ii, 170–171.

sophister, *n.* arguer skilled in sophistry; one who reasons deviously: "A subtle traitor needs no sophister." *2 Hen 6,* V, i, 191.

sophisticated, *adj.* adulterated; (of man) wearing clothes not his own: "... here's three on 's are sophisticated;/ thou art the thing itself ..." *Lear,* III, iv, 108–109.

Sophy, *n.* Shah [King] of Persia: "... by this scimitar/ That slew the Sophy, and a Persian prince ..." *Merch,* II, i, 24–25.

sops, *n.* See **sop** (def. 2).

sorceries terrible, *n. pl.* with "too" understood: "For mischiefs manifold, and sorceries terrible/ To enter human hearing [for humans to hear] . . ." *Temp,* I, ii, 264–265.

sore[1], *n.* four-year-old buck deer: "Some say a sore; but not a sore, till now made sore/ with shooting." *Love's L,* IV, ii, 56.

sore[2], *adj.* **1** deplorable: ". . . the sore terms we stand upon with the gods/ will be strong . . ." *Per,* IV, ii, 32–33. **2** grievous: "To lapse in fulness/ Is sorer than to lie for need . . ." *Cymb,* III, vi, 12–13. **3** harsh; severe: "I must remove . . . these logs, and pile them up,/ Upon a sore injunction . . ." *Temp,* III, i, 9–11. **4** causing pain: ". . . out, sword, and/ to a sore purpose!" *Cymb,* IV, i, 22–23. **5 go sore,** suffer punishment; here, a beating: "If you went in pain, master, this knave would go sore." *Errors,* III, i, 65.
—*adv.* **6** sorely; grievously: ". . . while I live, I'll fear no other thing/ So sore, as keeping safe Nerissa's ring." *Merch,* V, i, 306–307.

sorel, *n.* three-year-old buck deer: "The dogs did yell; put 'ell to sore, then sorel jumps/ from thicket . . ." *Love's L,* IV, ii, 57.

sorely, *adv.* heavily; severely: "What a sigh is there! The heart is sorely charg'd." *Mac,* V, i, 51.

sorrow, *n.* ref. to sorrowing Gloucester: "Bad is the trade that must play the fool to sorrow . . ." *Lear,* IV, i, 38.

sorrowed, *adj.* full of or expressing sorrow; sorrowful: ". . . send forth us, to make their sorrowed render . . ." *Timon,* V, i, 148.

sorrow-wreathen knot, *n.* folded arms, regarded as a sign of grief or melancholy: "Marcus, unknit that sorrow-wreathen knot:/ Thy niece and I . . . cannot passionate our ten-fold grief/ With folded arms." *T Andr,* III, ii, 4–7.

sorry, *adj.* sad; causing sadness: ". . . the melancholy vale,/ The place of death and sorry execution . . ." *Errors,* V, i, 120–121.

sort[1], *v.* **1** to turn out; work out: "And if it sort not well, you may conceal her,/ As best befits her wounded reputation." *M Ado,* IV, i, 240–241. **2** to use: ". . . an/ excellent good word before it was ill sorted . . ." *2 Hen 4,* II, iv, 146. **3** to choose; select: ". . . help me sort such needful ornaments/ As you think fit to furnish me tomorrow?" *Rom & Jul,* IV, ii, 34–35. **4** to arrange: "I'll sort some other time to visit you." *1 Hen 6,* II, iii, 26. **5** to order; decree: ". . . if God sort it so/ 'Tis more than we deserve . . ." *Rich 3,* II, iii, 36–37. **6** to class; classify: "I will not sort you with the rest of/ my servants . . ." *Ham,* II, ii, 267–268. **7** to dispose or take care of: "But God sort all: you are welcome home my lord." *Merch,* V, i, 132. **8** to adapt: "I pray thee, sort thy heart to patience . . ." *2 Hen 6,* II, iv, 68.

9 to be fitting: "Why then it sorts; brave warriors, let's away." *3 Hen 6,* II, i, 209. **10** to suit; fit; agree: "His currish riddles sorts not with this place." *3 Hen 6,* V, v, 26. **11** to consort; run (with): "And sometime sorteth with a herd of deer . . ." *Ven & Ad,* 689. **12 sort how it will,** let things turn out how they will: "Sort how it will, I shall have gold for all." *2 Hen 6,* I, ii, 107. **13 sort out,** to choose; select: "One who to put thee from thy heaviness/ Hath sorted out a sudden day of joy . . ." *Rom & Jul,* III, v, 108–109. **14 sort with,** to be suitable for: "That is some satire, keen and critical,/ Not sorting with a nuptial ceremony." *M N Dream,* V, i, 54–55.
—*n.* **15** gang or pack: ". . . salt water blinds them not so much/ But they can see a sort of traitors here." *Rich 2,* IV, i, 245–246. **16** [usually pl.] classes of people; types of workers: "Come, other sorts offend as well as we." *Per,* IV, ii, 34. **17** manner or way: ". . . let's on our way in silent sort . . ." *3 Hen 6,* IV, ii, 28. **18** apparel: "The mayor and all his brethren in best sort . . ." *Hen 5,* V, Chor. 25. **19 a sort of,** a good many: "There are a sort of men whose visages/ Do cream and mantle like a standing pond . . ." *Merch,* I, i, 88–89. **20 in a sort,** in a way: ". . . yet in a sort lechery eats itself." *Tr & Cr,* V, iv, 35. **21 in sort or limitation,** in a limited way or for a specified period [legal term]: "Am I your self/ But, as it were, in sort or limitation . . . ?" *J Caes,* II, i, 282–283. **22 many in sort,** in a large flock: ". . . russet-pated choughs, many in sort . . ." *M N Dream,* III, ii, 21. **23 men of sort and suit,** nobles and their followers: "Give notice to such men of sort and suit/ As are to meet him." *Meas,* IV, iv, 15–16. **24 of great sort,** of noble rank: "It may be his enemy is a gentleman of great/ sort . . ." *Hen 5,* IV, vii, 139–140.

sort[2], *n.* (in gambling) a lot: ". . . let blockish Ajax draw/ The sort to fight with Hector." *Tr & Cr,* I, iii, 375–376.

sortance, *n.* **hold sortance,** to be suitable; accord: ". . . with such powers/ As might hold sortance with his quality . . ." *2 Hen 4,* IV, i, 10–11.

sorted, *adj.* **1** associated: ". . . sorted and consorted, contrary to thy established/ proclaimed edict . . ." *Love's L,* I, i, 252–253. **2** being in agreement: "My will is something sorted with his wish." *Two Gent,* I, iii, 63. **3 sorted to no proof,** come to naught: "Nay then, thou lov'st it not,/ And all my pains is sorted to no proof." *Shrew,* IV, iii, 42–43.

sot, *n.* **1** fool; idiot: "Remember/ First to possess his books; for without them/ He's but a sot, as I am . . ." *Temp,* III, ii, 89–91.
— *v.* **2** to make foolish: "To one that shames the fair and sots the wise . . ." *Edw 3,* II, i, 81.

sotted, *adj.* **I am sotted,** I have become an utter fool: "I am sotted,/ Utterly lost. My virgin's faith has fled me . . ." *Kinsmen,* IV, ii, 45–46.

sottish, *adj.* foolish; stupid: "Patience is sottish, and impatience does/ Become a dog that's mad . . ." *Ant & Cleo,* IV, xv, 79–80.

sought, *v.* past part. of **seek;** searched: "Have I sought every country far and near . . ." *1 Hen 6,* V, iv, 3.

soul, *n.* **1** intellect; intellectual capabilities: ". . . those that with the fineness of their souls/ By reason guide his execution." *Tr & Cr,* I, iii, 209–210. **2** conscience: "If thy soul check thee that I come so near . . ." *Sonn 136,* 1. **3** examination of one's conscience; also, conviction: ". . . we have with special soul/ Elected him our absence to supply . . ." *Meas,* I, i, 17–18. **4** emotions; feelings: "If none of them have soul in such a kind . . ." *Tr & Cr,* I, iii, 284. **5 divine forfeit of his soul upon oath,** swearing by his eternal soul that he was telling the truth: ". . . deliver all the intelligence/ in his power against you, and that with the/ divine forfeit of his soul upon oath . . ." *All's W,* III, vi, 28–30. **6 draw three souls out of one weaver,** music, it was believed, could draw the soul from the body; here is a three-part catch forceful enough to draw three souls out of a weaver (type of worker given to piety and singing psalms while at work): "Shall we rouse the night-owl in a catch that will/ draw three souls out of one weaver?" *T Night,* II, iii, 59–60. **7 love of soul,** true loyalty or allegiance: "Swearing allegiance and the love of soul/ To stranger blood, to foreign royalty." *K John,* V, i, 10–11. **8 no soul,** no lost soul; that is, no loss of life: "I have with such provision in mine Art/ So safely ordered, that there is no soul—" *Temp,* I, ii, 28–29.

soul-fearing, *adj.* soul-terrifying: "Till their soul-fearing clamours have brawl'd down/ The flinty ribs of this contemptuous city . . ." *K John,* II, i, 383–384.

sound¹, *v.* **1** to test the depth, degree, soundness, etc., of: ". . . no reason/ Can sound his state in safety." *Timon,* II, i, 12–13. **2** to question or examine: "Tell me, moreover, hast thou sounded him,/ If he appeal the Duke on ancient malice . . ." *Rich 2,* I, i, 8–9. **3** to ascertain: "By this means shall we sound what skill she hath." *1 Hen 6,* I, ii, 63. **4** to signal: "Death, I fear me,/ Sounding destruction, or some joy too fine . . ." *Tr & Cr,* III, ii, 20–21. **5 sound thy bottom,** discover your true depth: "O melancholy,/ Who ever yet could sound thy bottom . . ." *Cymb,* IV, ii, 203–204.

sound², *adj.* **1** healthy or strong; also, valuable: "The cambric, which she made more sound/ By hurting it . . ." *Per,* IV, Chor., 24–25. **2** previous sense in wordplay with "resound": "Nay, not, as one would say, healthy: but so sound/ as things

that are hollow . . ." *Meas,* I, ii, 51–52. **3** complete; thorough: "Thou odoriferous stench! sound rottenness!" *K John,* III, iii, 26. **4** loyal; here, to traditional or orthodox values: "Do not I know you for a favourer/ Of this new sect? ye are not sound." *Hen 8,* V, ii, 114–115.
—*adv.* **5** soundly: "Let the supposed fairies pinch him sound . . ." *Wives,* IV, iv, 61.

sound³, *v.* **1** to play or sing: "I say 'silver sound' because musicians sound for/ silver." *Rom & Jul,* IV, v, 130–131. **2** previous sense in wordplay with "jingle," the sound of coins in a purse: "It is 'music with her silver sound' because/ musicians have no gold for sounding." *Rom & Jul,* IV, v, 135–136. **3** to proclaim; tout: "Hearing thy mildness prais'd in every town,/ Thy virtues spoke of, and thy beauty sounded . . ." *Shrew,* II, i, 191–192. **4** to call or cry out: ". . . and break my heart/ With sounding 'Troilus.'" *Tr & Cr,* IV, ii, 111–112.

sound⁴, *v.* to swoon: "She sounded almost at my pleasing tale . . ." *T Andr,* V, i, 119.

soundpost, *n.* wooden peg serving as an inner support for the violin; here used whimsically as a person's surname: "Prates too. What say you, James Soundpost?" *Rom & Jul,* IV, v, 132.

sour, *adj.* **1** bitter; harsh: ". . . yet you Pilates/ Have here deliver'd me to my sour cross . . ." *Rich 2,* IV, i, 240–241. **2** distasteful; also, gloomy: ". . . thy sour leisure gave sweet leave/ To entertain the time with thoughts of love . . ." *Sonn 39,* 10–11.

sourly, *adv.* **1** in a humiliating way: "To that sweet thief which sourly robs from me." *Sonn 35,* 14. **2** sullenly; also, morosely: ". . . what woman's son/ Will sourly leave her till she have prevail'd?" *Sonn 41,* 7–8.

sour one's cheeks, *v.* to give evidence of distaste: "His louring brows o'erwhelming his fair sight . . . Souring his cheeks, cries, 'Fie, no more of love! . . .'" *Ven & Ad,* 183–185.

souse, *v.* to pounce or swoop down on: "And like an eagle . . . To souse annoyance that comes near his nest." *K John,* V, ii, 149–150.

south, *n.* **1** (often cap.) the south wind, thought to bring foul weather, esp. fog, and often illness: ". . . wherefore do you follow her/ Like foggy South puffing with wind and rain?" *As You,* III, v, 49–50. **2** southern Europe, esp. Italy, thought to be the source of the pox [syphilis]: "Now the rotten diseases/ of the south, the guts-griping, ruptures . . ." *Tr & Cr,* V, i, 16–17.
—*adv.* **3** south of: "'Tis south the city mills—" *Cor,* I, x, 31.

Southam, *n.* village in SW central England: "At Southam I did leave him with his forces . . ." *3 Hen 6,* V, i, 9.

southern clouds, *n. pl.* foul weather and misfortune were thought to come from the south: "And with the southern clouds contend in tears . . ." *2 Hen 6,* III, ii, 383.

south-fog, *n.* another ref. to foul pestilence from southern climates: "The south-fog rot him!" *Cymb,* II, iii, 130.

South Sea, *n.* endless tedium, as a voyage to the South Seas: "One inch of delay more is/ a South Sea of discovery." *As You,* III, ii, 193–194.

Southwark, *n.* section of London, on the south bank of the Thames: "The rebels are in Southwark; fly, my lord!" *2 Hen 6,* IV, iv, 26.

south-west, *n.* the southwest wind was thought to bring pestilence: ". . . a south-west blow on ye/ And blister you all o'er!" *Temp,* I, ii, 325–326.

sovereign, *n.* **1** prince; lord: "Whilst I, my sovereign, watch the clock for you . . ." *Sonn 57,* 6.
—*adj.* **2** excellent; fine; efficacious: ". . . telling me the sovereignest thing on earth/ Was parmacity for an inward bruise . . ." *1 Hen 4,* I, iii, 56–57. **3** overpowering; overwhelming: "A sovereign shame so elbows him . . ." *Lear,* IV, iii, 43. **4** healing; soothing: "And thus I search it with a sovereign kiss." *Two Gent,* I, ii, 117.

sovereign flower, *n.* rightful monarch; here, restoration of the true heir: ". . . so much as it needs/ To dew the sovereign flower, and drown the weeds." *Mac,* V, ii, 29–30.

sovereign thrones, *n. pl.* liver (which governed passions), the brain (thought), and the heart (emotion): ". . . when liver, brain, and heart,/ These sovereign thrones, are all supplied, and fill'd . . ." *T Night,* I, i, 37–38.

sovereignty, *n.* **general sovereignty,** cure for any disease; panacea: ". . . rare and prov'd effects . . . For general sovereignty . . ." *All's W,* I, iii, 217–219.

sow, *n.* mass: "So charm'd me that methought Alcides was/ To him a sow of lead." *Kinsmen,* V, iii, 119–120.

sowl, *v.* to grab hold of; also, drag: "He'll go, he says,/ and sowl the porter of Rome gates by th'ears." *Cor,* IV, v, 205–206.

sowter, *n.* cobbler; here, a dog's name: "Sowter will cry upon't for all this, though it be/ as rank as a fox." *T Night,* II, v, 124–125.

space, *n.* **1** difference or disparity in rank or status: "The mightiest space in fortune nature brings/ To join like likes . . ." *All's W,* I, i, 218. **2** any restriction of space: "O most potential love! vow, bond, nor space . . ." *Lover's Comp,* 264. **3** reprieve: "Come on; thou art granted space." *All's W,* IV, i, 88. **4** sufficient period of time: ". . . since he went from Egypt, 'tis/ A space for farther travel." *Ant & Cleo,* II, i, 30–31. **5 at further space,** at a later time: ". . . they are ready/ To-morrow, or at further space, t'appear . . ." *Lear,* V, iii, 53–54. **6 good space,** for some time: "So it far'd/ Good space between these kinsmen . . ." *Kinsmen,* V, iii, 128–129. **7 mighty space,** great power: "And sell the mighty space of our large honours [reputation]/ For so much trash . . ." *J Caes,* IV, iii, 25–26.

spacious, *adj.* extensive; far-reaching: ". . . vows revenge as spacious as between [as to include]/ The young'st and oldest thing." *Cor,* IV, vi, 68–69.

spake, *v.* old past tense of **speak:** ". . . renowned Warwick,/ Who spake aloud, 'What scourge for perjury . . . ?'" *Rich 3,* I, iv, 49–50.

span, *n.* **1** measurement of about 9 inches, generally the space between the outstretched thumb and forefinger, often used metaphorically as a short space of time: ". . . the stretching of a span/ Buckles in his sum of age." *As You,* III, ii, 128–129.
—*v.* **2** to measure out: ". . . my life is spann'd already . . ." *Hen 8,* I, i, 223.

span-counter, *n.* game in which players toss coins, attempting to place them within a span of each other: "Henry the Fifth, in whose time boys/ went to span-counter for French crowns . . ." *2 Hen 6,* IV, ii, 150–151.

Spaniard, *n.* Emperor Carlos [Charles]: "The Spaniard tied by blood and favour to her . . ." *Hen 8,* II, ii, 89.

spaniel, *v.* to follow devotedly: "The hearts/ That spaniel'd me at heels, to whom I gave/ Their wishes . . ." *Ant & Cleo,* IV, xii, 20–22.

Spanish blade, *n.* Toledo steel was highly prized for swords, rapiers, etc.: ". . . then dreams he of . . . breaches, ambuscados, Spanish blades . . ." *Rom & Jul,* I, iv, 83–84.

spare, *adj.* **1** frugal; parsimonious: "As it is a spare life . . . it fits my humour well . . ." *As You,* III, ii, 19–20.
—*v.* **2** to avoid: ". . . go with us;/ If not, shun me, and I will spare your haunts." *M N Dream,* II, i, 141–142. **3** refrain from causing sorrow to: ". . . we would not spare heaven as we love it . . ." *Meas,* II, iii, 33. **4 spare for no,** do not spare (the): "Spare for no faggots, let there be enow . . ." *1 Hen 6,* V, iv, 56.

sparing, *adj.* **1** frugal; parsimonious: "It shall be sparing, and too full of riot . . ." *Ven & Ad,* 1147.
—*n.* **2** frugality; niggardliness: "Sparing would show [appear] a worse sin than ill doctrine . . ." *Hen 8,* I, iii, 60.

sparingly, *adv.* hesitantly; discreetly or circumspectly: "Or shall we sparingly show you far off/ The Dauphin's meaning . . ." *Hen 5,* I, ii, 239–240.

spark, *n.* bright, energetic young man: "'Tis not his fault, the spark." *All's W,* II, i, 25.

sparkle, *v.* to emit sparks: "Nay, it perchance will sparkle in your eyes . . ." *K John,* IV, i, 114.

sparrow, *n.* ref. to "Philip" as pet name for sparrow: "Philip?—sparrow!—James,/ There's toys abroad . . ." *K John,* I, i, 231–232.

Spartan, *adj.* **1** referring to hunting hounds of Sparta, appar. those most prized: "My hounds are bred out of the Spartan kind,/ So flew'd, so sanded . . ." *M N Dream,* IV, i, 118–119. **2 Spartan dog,** poss. ref. to Iago's tenacity as well as his meanness: "O Spartan dog,/ More fell than anguish, hunger, or the sea . . ." *Oth,* V, ii, 362–363.

spavins, *n. pl.* horse's disease of the rear leg joint: ". . . sped with spavins, rayed with the yellows . . ." *Shrew,* III, ii, 50–51.

speak, *v.* **1** to tell or report: ". . . and 'tis spoken [rumored],/ To the succeeding royalty he leaves/ The healing benediction." *Mac,* IV, iii, 154–156. **2** to declare or affirm: "And sundry blessings hang about his throne,/ That speak him full of grace." *Mac,* IV, iii, 158–159. **3** to signify; mean: ". . . what thou think'st his very action speaks/ In every power that moves." *Ant & Cleo,* III, xii, 35–36. **4** to describe: ". . . give me leave to speak him,/ And yet with charity." *Hen 8,* IV, ii, 32–33. **5** subjunctive use; here, "let them speak": ". . . and for his passage,/ The soldier's music and the rite of war/ Speak loudly for him." *Ham,* V, ii, 403–405. **6 speak him fair,** humor him: "Yield to his humour, smooth and speak him fair . . ." *T Andr,* V, ii 140. **7 speak him home,** speak of him adequately: "For this last . . . let me say/ I cannot speak him home." *Cor,* II, ii, 101–103. **8 speak sad brow and true maid,** truthfully; in all honesty: "Nay, but the devil take mocking. Speak sad brow/ and true maid." *As You,* III, ii, 210–211. **9 speaks his own standing,** expresses his status [i.e., that of the subject]: "How this grace/ Speaks his own standing!" *Timon,* I, i, 30–31. **10 speak thee out,** adequately describe you: "(If thy rare qualities, sweet gentleness,/ They meekness saintlike . . . could speak thee out)" *Hen 8,* II, iv, 135–138.

specially, *adv.* especially; above all: ". . . that treats of happiness/ By virtue specially to be achiev'd." *Shrew,* I, i, 19–20.

specialty, *n.* **1** legal document, esp. a contract: ". . . the packet is not come/ Where that and other specialties are bound . . ." *Love's L,* II, i, 163–164. **2** distinction: "The specialty of rule hath been neglected . . ." *Tr & Cr,* I, iii, 78.

speciously, *adv.* Quickly's blunder for "specially": "I'll/ be as good as my word, but speciously for Master/ Fenton." *Wives,* III, iv, 104–106.

spectacled, *adj.* equipped with eyeglasses [anachronism of many centuries]: ". . . the bleared sights/ Are spectacled to see him." *Cor,* II, i, 203–204.

spectacles, *n. pl.* the eyes: ". . . bid mine eyes be packing with my heart,/ And call'd them blind and dusky spectacles/ For losing ken of Albion's wished coast." *2 Hen 6,* III, ii, 110–112.

speculation, *n.* **1** power of sight; here, esp. the look of intelligence: "Thou hast no speculation in those eyes,/ Which thou dost glare with." *Mac,* III, iv, 94–95. **2** observer or watcher; here, a spy: "Which are to France the spies and speculations/ Intelligent of our state." *Lear,* III, i, 24–25.

sped, *v.* **1** past part. of **speed;** done for; dispatched: "I am hurt./ A plague o' both your houses. I am sped." *Rom & Jul,* III, i, 91–92. **2** succeeded; here, in sexual conquest: "I was at her/ house the hour she appointed me."/ "And sped you, sir?" *Wives,* III, v, 59–61.

speech, *n.* **1** here, a speech by the leader of a group of masquers when entering a festivity uninvited, usually one with an apology to the host and compliments to the ladies: "What, shall this speech be spoke for our excuse?/ Or shall we on without apology?" *Rom & Jul,* I, iv, 1–2. **2** report; general feeling: "What was the speech among the Londoners . . ." *Hen 8,* I, ii, 154.

speechless, *adj.* silent; here, exhausted or spent: "His fortunes all lie speechless, and his name/ Is at last gasp." *Cymb,* I, vi, 52–53.

speed, *v.* **1** to give good fortune to; cause to succeed: "For let the gods so speed me as I love/ The name of honour more than I fear death." *J Caes,* I, ii, 88–89. **2** to succeed; thrive or prosper: ". . . he that's once denied will hardly speed." *Timon,* III, ii, 62. **3** to accomplish: "It shall be speeded well." *Meas,* IV, v, 10. **4 speed well,** best of luck: "Once more adieu: be valiant, and speed well." *Rich 3,* V, iii, 103.
—*n.* **5** haste; urgency: "How now, good Blunt? Thy looks are full of speed." *1 Hen 4,* III, ii, 162. **6** aid or protection; also, wordplay on Speed's name: "[Giving him the paper] There;/ and Saint Nicholas be/ thy speed." *Two Gent,* III, i, 293–294. **7** fate; fortune or welfare: "The prince your son, with mere conceit and fear/ Of the queen's speed, is gone." *W Tale,* III, ii, 144–145. **8 be your speed,** give you good fortune: "Well, I am school'd—good manners be your speed!" *1 Hen 4,* III, i, 184. **9 have the speed of,** to outrace or outdistance: ". . . our Thane is coming;/ One of my fellows had the speed of him . . ." *Mac,* I, v, 34–35.

speeding, *adj.* **1** effective; sure-fire: ". . . the sly whoresons/ Have got a speeding trick to lay down ladies." *Hen 8,* I, iii, 39–40.
—n. **2** success; here, in wooing: "To-morrow all for speeding do their best." *Per,* II, iii, 115.

spell (someone) backward, to misrepresent and, hence, to disparage: "I never yet saw man . . . But she would spell him backward . . ." *M Ado,* III, i, 59–61.

spelling, *adj.* working spells: "Unchain your spirits now with spelling charms . . ." *1 Hen 6,* V, iii, 31.

spell-stopped, *adj.* inanimate, due to Prospero's magic spell: "There stand/ For you are spell-stopp'd." *Temp,* V, i, 60–61.

spend, *v.* **spend their mouths,** to cry; yelp: "Then they do spend their mouths: echo replies . . ." *Ven & Ad,* 695.

spendthrift sigh, *n.* the sigh, which gave ease, was also thought to drain blood from the heart: "And then this 'should' is like a spendthrift sigh/ That hurts by easing." *Ham,* IV, vii, 121–122.

spent, *adj.* **1** made use of; used up: ". . . you shall go, Mouldy; it is/ time you were spent." *2 Hen 4,* III, ii, 116–117. **2** passed or wasted away: "When tyrants' crests and tombs of brass are spent." *Sonn 107,* 14. **3 The day is spent,** Daylight is well advanced: "What, shall we toward the Tower? The day is spent." *Rich 3,* III, ii, 87.

spet, *v.* pres. and past tense of **spit:** "You call me misbeliever, cut-throat dog,/ And spet upon my Jewish gaberdine . . ." *Merch,* I, iii, 106–107.

sphere, *n.* **1** earth: ". . . all kind of natures/ That labour on the bosom of this sphere . . ." *Timon,* I, i, 67–68. **2** (in Ptolemaic astronomy) the invisible sphere that carried the moon and other celestial objects around the stationary earth: "I do wander everywhere,/ Swifter than the moon's sphere . . ." *M N Dream,* II, i, 6–7. **3** eye socket; here, likened to the preceding: "Make thy two eyes like stars start from their spheres . . ." *Ham,* I, v, 17. **4 called into a huge sphere,** oblique ref. to astronomy; here, Lepidus associates with the great "planets" Caesar and Antony, yet has no comparable authority, a situation likened to eyeless sockets: "To be called into a huge sphere, and not to/ be seen to move in't, are the holes where eyes/ should be . . ." *Ant & Cleo,* II, vii, 14–16. **5 music from the spheres,** music produced by the movement of celestial bodies within their spheres and inaudible to humans: "I had rather hear you to solicit that,/ Than music from the spheres." *T Night,* III, i, 111–112.

sphered, *adj.* set in its own sphere; here, the Sun: ". . . the glorious planet Sol/ In noble eminence enthron'd and spher'd . . ." *Tr & Cr,* I, iii, 89–90.

sphered bias cheek, *n.* trumpeter's cheek puffed out and resembling a sphere as well as a weighted [biased] ball in the game of bowls: "Blow, villain, till thy sphered bias cheek/ Out-swell the colic of puff'd Aquilon." *Tr & Cr,* IV, v, 8–9.

spherical predominance, *n.* strong influence of one particular celestial body: ". . . knaves, thieves, and treachers by spherical predominance . . ." *Lear,* I, ii, 128.

sphery, *adj.* resembling the stars in their spheres; starry: "What wicked and dissembling glass of mine/ Made me compare with Hermia's sphery eyne [eyes]?" *M N Dream,* II, ii, 97–98.

Sphinx, *n.* (in Greek legend) creature, half woman and half lion, that terrorized the people of Thebes; vanquished by Oedipus: "Subtle as Sphinx; as sweet and musical/ As bright Apollo's lute, strung with his hair . . ." *Love's L,* IV, iii, 338–339.

spice, *n.* sample or trace; taste: ". . . for all/ Thy by-gone fooleries were but spices of it." *W Tale,* III, ii, 183–184.

spicery, *n.* See **nest of spicery.**

spies, *n.* pl. of **spy. 1** soldiers sent ahead of an advancing army as reconnaissance; scouts: "When sorrows come, they come not single spies . . ." *Ham,* IV, v, 78. **2** people; here, esp. those with suspicious eyes: "Or on my frailties why are frailer spies,/ Which in their wills count bad what I think good?" *Sonn 121,* 7–8. **3 true spies,** reliable witnesses; that is, the eyes: "If these be true spies which I wear in my head,/ here's a goodly sight." *Temp,* V, i, 259–260.

spilth, *n.* spillage: ". . . our vaults have wept/ With drunken spilth of wine . . ." *Timon,* II, ii, 164.

spin, *v.* **1** to spray: "That their hot blood may spin in English eyes . . ." *Hen 5,* IV, ii, 10. **2 spin off,** to cause (something) to fall off; here, the loss of hair as a result of venereal disease: "I hope to see a housewife take thee between her legs,/ and spin it off." *T Night,* I, iii, 100–101.

spinners' legs, *n.* prob. the daddy longlegs, or crane fly: "Her waggon-spokes made of long spinners' legs,/ The cover of the wings of grasshoppers . . ." *Rom & Jul,* I, iv, 62–63.

spinster, *n.* spinner; person who spins: "The spinsters and the knitters in the sun . . ." *T Night,* II, iv, 44.

spirit, *n.* **1** seat of anger within the human body: "And, not to swell our spirit,/ He shall be executed presently." *Timon,* III, v, 103–104. **2** intuition or divination: "Your spirit is too true, your fears too certain." *2 Hen 4,* I, i, 92. **3** temperament; disposition; personality: "Why, that's the way to choke a gibing spirit . . ." *Love's L,* V, ii, 850. **4** person; here, a courtier: "For she was sought by spirits of richest coat . . ." *Lover's Comp,* 236. **5** mythical or supernatural being, who is the source of continuing trouble: ". . . three such enemies/ again, as that fiend Douglas, that spirit Percy, and/ that devil Glendower?" *1 Hen 4,* II, iv, 363–365. **6** previous sense of "demon" in wordplay with bawdy sense of "penis" or, sometimes, "semen": "'Twould anger him/ To raise a spirit in his mistress' circle . . ." *Rom & Jul,* II, i, 23–24. **7 spirits, a.** feelings or sentiments: "And with his spirits sadly I survive/ To mock the expectation of the world . . ." *2 Hen 4,* V, ii, 125–126. **b.** wits; intellectual resources; ingenuity: "Now, madam, summon up your dearest [best] spirits . . ." *Love's L,* II, i, 1. **c.** inducements; motives; also, temptations: ". . . the profits of my death/ Were very pregnant and potential spirits [spurs?]/ To make thee seek it." *Lear,* II, i, 75–77. **d.** persons; here, the members of an acting company: "The flat unraised spirits that hath dar'd/ On this unworthy scaffold to bring forth/ So great an object . . ." *Hen 5,* Prol., 9–11. **8 spirit of health,** good spirit; angel: "Be thou a spirit of health or goblin damn'd . . ." *Ham,* I, iv, 40. **9 spirit of sense,** any of the bodily emanations that linked body and soul: ". . . and spirit of sense/ Hard as the palm of ploughman." *Tr & Cr,* I, i, 58–59. **10 swell our spirit,** give further vent to our anger: "And, not to swell our spirit,/ He shall be executed presently [at once]." *Timon,* III, v, 103–104.

spiritless, *adj.* downcast; depressed or dejected: ". . . such a man, so faint, so spiritless,/ So dull, so dead in look, so woebegone . . ." *2 Hen 4,* I, i, 70–71.

spiritual convocation, *n.* assembly of the clergy: "I have made an offer to his majesty,/ Upon our spiritual convocation . . ." *Hen 5,* I, i, 75–76.

spiritualty, *n.* clergy: ". . . we of the spiritualty/ Will raise your highness such a mighty sum . . ." *Hen 5,* I, ii, 132–133.

spirt, *v.* to shoot: "Spirt up so suddenly into the clouds . . ." *Hen 5,* III, v, 8.

spit¹, *n.* **1** iron rod on which meat was roasted: "Lest that thy wives with spits, and boys with stones,/ In puny battle slay me." *Cor,* IV, iv, 5–6.
—*v.* **2** to impale: "Seeking out Romeo that did spit his body/ Upon a rapier's point!" *Rom & Jul,* IV, iii, 56–57.

spit², *v.* **1 spit in the hole,** perh. to moisten the peg and keep it from slipping: "Spit in the hole, man, and tune again."

Shrew, III, i, 39. **2 spit white,** prob. to give an indication of good health: "If . . . I brandish anything but a bottle, I would I might/ never spit white again." *2 Hen 4,* I, ii, 210–212.

spital or **spital-house,** *n.* hospital, esp. one for venereal diseases, leprosy, etc.: "She whom the spital-house and ulcerous sores/ Would cast the gorge at . . ." *Timon,* IV, iii, 40–41.

spite, *n.* **1** vexation or grief: "First he denied you had in him no right."/ "He meant he did me none; the more my spite." *Errors,* IV, ii, 7–8. **2** outrage: ". . . letting it there stand/ Till she had laid it and conjur'd it down:/ That were some spite." *Rom & Jul,* II, i, 25–27. **3** malicious act of fate: "But stay! O spite! . . . What dreadful dole is here?" *M N Dream,* V, i, 265–267. **4** malice resulting in mortification: "Hark, what fine change is in the music!"/ "Ay; that change is the spite." *Two Gent,* IV, ii, 66–67. **5 in another's spite,** to the great vexation of; in defiance of: "Him will I tear out of that cruel eye/ Where he sits crowned in his master's spite." *T Night,* V, i, 125–126. **6 in spite of,** just to spite: "Now I perceive they have conjoin'd all three/ To fashion this false sport in spite of me." *M N Dream,* III, ii, 193–194. **7 spite of,** in spite of; despite: "And spite of all the rapture of the sea . . ." *Per,* II, i, 154. **8 spite of spite,** regardless of what happens: "And spite of spite needs must I rest awhile." *3 Hen 6,* II, iii, 5.

splay, *v.* misuse for "spay": "Does your worship mean to geld and splay all the/ youth of the city?" *Meas,* II, i, 227–228.

spleen, *n.* **1** seat of human emotions, esp. anger and passion; synon. with anger, rage, fury, etc.: "It is a cause worthy my spleen and fury,/ That I may strike at Athens." *Timon,* III, v, 114–115. **2** urgency: "With swifter spleen than powder can enforce,/ The mouth of passage shall we fling wide ope . . ." *K John,* II, i, 448–449. **3** hatred or spite; malice: "O preposterous/ And frantic outrage, end thy damned spleen . . ." *Rich 3,* II, iv, 63–64. **4** the spleen regarded as exercising control over excessive mirth or anger: "By virtue, thou enforcest laughter; thy silly thought/ my spleen . . ." *Love's L,* III, i, 72–73. **5** fit of laughing: "If you desire the spleen, and will laugh yourselves/ into stitches, follow me." *T Night,* III, ii, 65–66. **6** outburst of anger or passion: "Thou that art like enough, through vassal fear,/ Base inclination, and the start of spleen,/ To fight against me . . ." *1 Hen 4,* III, ii, 124–126. **7** erratic behavior; caprice: "To give my hand . . . / Unto a mad-brain rudesby, full of spleen . . ." *Shrew,* III, ii, 9–10. **8 spleen of speed,** furious haste: "O, I am scalded with my violent motion,/ And spleen of speed to see your majesty!" *K John,* V, vii, 49–50.

spleenful, *adj.* **1** angry; rebellious: "Myself have calm'd their spleenful mutiny . . ." *2 Hen 6,* III, ii, 127. **2** lustful: "Now will I hence to seek my lovely Moor,/ And let my spleenful sons this trull deflower." *T Andr,* II, iii, 190–191.

spleen ridiculous, *n.* fit of laughter: "... in this spleen ridiculous appears,/ To check their folly, passion's solemn tears." *Love's L,* V, ii, 117–118.

spleeny, *adj.* passionate or hot-headed: "... yet I know her for/ A spleeny Lutheran ..." *Hen 8,* III, ii, 98–99.

splenative, *adj.* full of rage; from the spleen, which caused outbursts of temper: "... though I am not splenative and rash,/ Yet have I in me something dangerous ..." *Ham,* V, i, 254–255.

splinter, *n.* **1** act of breaking: "The Grecian dames are sunburnt and not worth/ The splinter of a lance [engaging in combat]." *Tr & Cr,* I, iii, 281–282.
—*v.* **2** to heal with splints: "This brawl between you and her/ husband, entreat her to splinter ..." *Oth,* II, iii, 313–314.

split, *v.* **make all split,** to cause a great commotion; tear the place apart: "I could/ play Ercles rarely, or a part to tear a cat in, to make/ all split." *M N Dream,* I, ii, 24–26.

spoil, *n.* **1** acts of looting: "... his soldiers fell to spoil,/ Whilst we by Antony are all enclos'd." *J Caes,* V, iii, 7–8. **2** [usually pl.] ravages: "And make Time's spoils despised everywhere." *Sonn 100,* 12. **3 apparent spoil,** imminent destruction: "And no way canst thou turn thee for redress/ But Death doth front thee with apparent spoil ..." *1 Hen 6,* IV, ii, 25–26.
—*v.* **4** to steal; carry off: "Whose hand is that the forest bear doth lick?/ Not his that spoils her young before her face." *3 Hen 6,* II, ii, 13–14.

spoiled, *adj.* doomed; done for: "Run master, run, for God's sake take a house ... in, or we are spoil'd." *Errors,* V, i, 36–37.

spoken, *v.* **he spoken can,** [that] he is able to speak; here, in imitation of the 14th cent. Gower: "... each man/ Thinks all is writ he spoken can ..." *Per,* II, Chor., 11–12.

sponge, *n.* a drunken fellow: "I will do anything, Nerissa,/ ere I will be married to a sponge." *Merch,* I, ii, 94–95.

spongy, *adj.* **1** soaked with alcohol; drunken: "... what not put upon/ His spongy officers, who shall bear the guilt ..." *Mac,* I, vii, 71–73. **2** damp; rainy: "From the spongy south to this part of the west ..." *Cymb,* IV, ii, 349.

spoon, *n.* **1 have a long spoon,** from the proverb, "He that would sup with the Devil must have a long spoon": "This is a devil, and no monster: I will leave him; I/ have no long spoon." *Temp,* II, ii, 99–100. **2 spare your spoons,** ref. to custom of giving a set of "apostle" spoons (with figure of apostle on handle) as a christening gift; king suggests that Cranmer

may prefer to save his money: "Come, come my lord, you'ld spare your spoons ..." *Hen 8,* V, ii, 200.

spoon-meat, *n.* soft food to be eaten with a spoon: "Master, if you do, expect spoon-meat, or bespeak a long spoon." *Errors,* IV, iii, 58–59.

sport, *n.* **1** the hunt; hunting [here in ref. to war]: "Hark what good sport is out of town today?" *Tr & Cr,* I, ii, 113. **2** diversion; pleasure; entertainment: "There is a brief how many sports are ripe ..." *M N Dream,* V, i, 42. **3** amorous dalliance: "... there was good sport at his/ making, and the whoreson must be acknowledged." *Lear,* I, i, 23–24. **4 act of sport,** sexual intercourse: "When the blood/ is made dull with the act of sport, there should be/ again to inflame it ..." *Oth,* II, i, 225–227. **5 book of sport,** handbook for sportsmen: "O, like a book of sport thou'lt read me o'er ..." *Tr & Cr,* IV, v, 238. **6 gentle sport,** sportiveness or playfulness; coltishness: "Some say thy grace is youth and gentle sport ..." *Sonn 96,* 2. **7 make sport with, a.** to engage in amorous dalliance: "I with the Morning's love have oft made sport ..." *M N Dream,* III, ii, 389. **b.** to entertain; enjoy the company of: "Wait on me home, I'll make sport/ with thee." *All's W,* V, iii, 316.
—*v.* **8** to amuse or divert (oneself): "So many hours must I sport myself ..." *3 Hen 6,* II, v, 34. **9** to engage in amorous play: "And for my sake hath learn'd to sport and dance ..." *Ven & Ad,* 105.

sportful, *adj.* **1** amorous; here, wanton: "... then let Kate be chaste and Dian sportful." *Shrew,* II, i, 255. **2** lascivious: "O unbid spite! Is sportful Edward come?" *3 Hen 6,* V, i, 18.

sportive, *adj.* **1** pleasure-loving: "And is it I/ That drive thee from the sportive court ..." *All's W,* III, ii, 105–106. **2 sportive blood,** wanton or licentious habits: "For why should others' false adulterate eyes/ Give salutation to [greet familiarly] my sportive blood?" *Sonn 121,* 5–6. **3 sportive tricks,** sexual capers: "But I, that am not shap'd for sportive tricks ..." *Rich 3,* I, i, 14.

spot, *n.* **1** blemish; disgrace: "Follow his chariot, like the greatest spot/ Of all thy sex." *Ant & Cleo,* IV, xii, 35–36. **2** stain on one's character; vice: "... the spots of thy kindred were/ jurors on thy life." *Timon,* IV, iii, 342–343. **3** wordplay on "stain" [disgrace] and "place": "I must withdraw and weep/ Upon the spot of this enforced cause—" *K John,* V, ii, 29–30. **4** checkmark: "He shall not live. Look, with a spot I damn him." *J Caes,* IV, i, 6. **5** piece of work: "A fine spot, in good/ faith." *Cor,* I, iii, 52–53.
—*v.* **6** to stain or blemish: "Which, like a canker in the fragrant rose,/ Doth spot the beauty of thy budding name!" *Sonn 95,* 2–3.

spots of heaven, *n.* stars: "His faults, in him seem as the spots of heaven,/ More fiery by night's blackness . . ." *Ant & Cleo,* I, iv, 12–13.

spotted, *adj.* **1** guilty; stained or morally blighted: "Terrible hell,/ Make war upon their spotted souls for this!" *Rich 2,* III, ii, 133–134. **2** tainted or infected: ". . . your swart Cimmerian/ Doth make your honour of his body's hue,/ Spotted, detested, and abominable." *T Andr,* II, iii, 72–74.

spousal, *n.* **1** marriage: "So be there 'twixt your kingdoms such a spousal . . ." *Hen 5,* V, ii, 380.
—*adj.* **2** of marriage: "There shall we consummate our spousal rites." *T Andr,* I, i, 337.

spout, *n.* waterspout: "Not the dreadful spout/ Which shipmen do the hurricano call . . ." *Tr & Cr,* V, ii, 170–171.

sprag, *adj.* lively; keen; alert: "He is a good sprag memory." *Wives,* IV, i, 72.

sprat, *n.* small herring; here, an insignificant person: ". . . when his disguise and he is parted tell me/ what a sprat you shall find him . . ." *All's W,* III, vi, 100–101.

sprawl, *v.* to undergo convulsions and strangulation in death by hanging: "First hang the child, that he may see it sprawl . . ." *T Andr,* V, i, 51.

spray, *n.* offshoot; here, bastard: ". . . a few sprays of us,/ The emptying of our fathers' luxury [lust] . . ." *Hen 5,* III, v, 5–6.

spread, *v.* **1** to spread a tablecloth on a table: "Spread, Davy, spread,/ Davy, well said, Davy." *2 Hen 4,* V, iii, 8–9. **2 spread yourselves,** line up in a row: " . . . good Peter Quince, call forth your/ actors by the scroll. Masters, spread yourselves." *M N Dream,* I, ii, 14–15.

sprightful, *adj.* spirited: "Spoke like a sprightful noble gentleman." *K John,* IV, ii, 177.

sprightfully, *adv.* vigorously; full of spirit: "The Duke of Norfolk, sprightfully and bold,/ Stays [awaits] but the summons of the appellant's trumpet." *Rich 2,* I, iii, 3–4.

sprightly, *adj.* **1** displaying great energy or vitality: ". . . we'll hand in hand,/ And with our sprightly port make the ghosts gaze . . ." *Ant & Cleo,* IV, xiv, 51–52. **2** of good cheer: "Most welcome!/ Be sprightly, for you fall 'mongst friends." *Cymb,* III, vii, 46–47.

spring, *n.* **1** source; origin: ". . . clear these ambiguities/ And know their spring, their head, their true descent . . ." *Rom & Jul,* V, iii, 216–217. **2** down: "The tender [soft] spring upon thy tempting lip . . ." *Ven & Ad,* 127. **3** shoot or sprig; also, a

sapling: "To dry the old oak's sap and cherish springs . . ." *Luc,* 950. **4 middle summer's spring,** beginning of midsummer: "And never, since the middle summer's spring,/ Met we on hill, in dale . . ." *M N Dream,* II, i, 82–83.

springe, *n.* snare, esp. for trapping birds: "Ay, springes to catch woodcocks." *Ham,* I, iii, 115.

springhalt, *n.* var. of **stringhalt,** a disease, esp. among horses, causing lameness: ". . . one would take it . . . the spavin,/ A springhalt reign'd among 'em." *Hen 8,* I, iii, 11–13.

springing, *adj.* growing; maturing: "If springing things be any jot diminish'd . . ." *Ven & Ad,* 417.

sprite, *n.* **1** ghost: ". . . the graves, all gaping wide,/ Every one lets forth his [its] sprite . . ." *M N Dream,* V, I, 366–367. **2** spirit [appar. spelled as pronounced]: "Heart of our numbers, soul and only sprite . . ." *Tr & Cr,* I, iii, 56. **3** [often pl.] spirits; morale: "Come, sisters, cheer we up his sprites,/ And show the best of our delights." *Mac,* IV, i, 127–128. **4** mood; humor: "Adonis with a lazy sprite,/ And with a heavy, dark, disliking eye . . ." *Ven & Ad,* 181–182.
—*v.* **5 be sprited with,** to be haunted by: "I am sprited with a fool,/ Frighted, and anger'd worse." *Cymb,* II, iii, 138–139.

spritely, *adj.* sprightly; cheerful; in high spirits: "I will reward thee/ Once for thy spritely comfort, and ten-fold/ For thy good valour." *Ant & Cleo,* IV, ii, 14–16.

spritely shows, *n.* ghostly apparitions: "Appear'd to me, with other spritely shows/ Of mine own kindred." *Cymb,* V, v, 429–430.

spriting, *n.* Ariel's duties as a sprite or spirit: "I will be correspondent to command,/ And do my spriting gently [willingly]." *Temp,* I, ii, 297–298.

spruce, *adj.* **1** overrefined: "He is too picked,/ too spruce, too affected . . ." *Love's L,* V, i, 12–13. **2** smartly turned out; dashing: "Now, my spruce/ companions, is all ready, and all things neat?" *Shrew,* IV, i, 102–103.

spur, *n.* **1** speed: ". . . with that spur as he would to/ the lip of his mistress." *Timon,* III, vi, 64–65. **2** [pl.] roots: ". . . the strong-bas'd promontory/ Have I made shake, and by the spurs pluck'd up/ The pine and cedar . . ." *Temp,* V, i, 46–48. **3 on the spur,** with all possible haste: "Titinius is enclosed round about/ With horsemen, that make to him on the spur . . ." *J Caes,* V, iii, 28–29. **4 set spurs,** applied spurs to their horses; sped away: "they threw me off . . . in a slough of mire; and set spurs and away . . ." *Wives,* IV, v, 63–64.
—*v.* **5** to hasten: "So much they spur their expedition." *Two Gent,* V, i, 6. **6** to goad: "But love will not be spurr'd to what it

loathes." *Two Gent,* V, ii, 7. **7** to incite; here used in wordplay with "speer," north-country word for "address a question to": "'Tis long of you that spur me with such questions." *Love's L,* II, i, 118. **8 spur and stop,** impels you to speak and keeps you from it: ". . . discover to me/ What both you spur and stop." *Cymb,* I, vii, 98–99. **9 spur on,** to urge forward; impel: "That in himself which he spurs on his power/ To qualify in others . . ." *Meas,* IV, ii, 80–81. **10 spur post,** go as fast as possible: "Spur post, and get before him to the king . . ." *Rich 2,* V, ii, 112.

Spurio, *n.* coined name from the Italian word for "spurious": "You shall/ find in the regiment of the Spinii one Captain Spurio . . ." *All's W,* II, i, 40–41.

spurn, *n.* **1** a slight or insult: "Who dies that bears not one spurn to their graves . . ." *Timon,* I, ii, 137.
—*v.* **2** to kick: ". . . I could rend bars of steel/ And spurn in pieces posts of adamant." *1 Hen 6,* I, iv, 50–51. **3 spurn at,** to oppose or defy: "I know no personal cause to spurn at him . . ." *J Caes,* II, i, 11. **4 spurn enviously at straws,** to become angry at trifles [lit., to kick spitefully]: "Spurns enviously at straws, speaks things in doubt/ That carry but half sense." *Ham,* IV, v, 6–7. **5 spurn upon,** to trample underfoot: "I'll strike thee to my foot,/ And spurn upon thee, beggar, for thy boldness." *Rich 3,* I, ii, 41–42.

spy, *n.* **1** indication or, perh., information; here, a cue for the murderers to act: "I will advise you where to plant yourselves,/ Acquaint you with the perfect [precise] spy o' th' time . . ." *Mac,* III, i, 128–129. **2** See **spies** (def. 1).
—*v.* **3** to perceive; see: "By spying and avoiding Fortune's malice . . ." *3 Hen 6,* IV, vi, 28. **4** allusion to children's game of "I spy": "I spy."/ "You spy? What do you spy?" *Tr & Cr,* III, i, 90–91.

squadron, *n.* body of troops: "Set we our squadrons on yond side o' the hill . . ." *Ant & Cleo,* III, ix, 1.

squander, *v.* to scatter about: ". . . other/ ventures he hath squand'red abroad . . ." *Merch,* I, iii, 18–19.

squandering, *adj.* scattered; random: "The wiseman's folly is anatomiz'd/ Even by the squand'ring glances of the fool." *As You,* II, vii, 56–57.

square, *adj.* **1** fair; just: ". . . it is not square to take/ On those that are . . ." *Timon,* V, iv, 36–37.
—*n.* **2** squadron: ". . . and no practice had/ In the brave squares of war . . ." *Ant & Cleo,* III, xi, 39–40. **3** carpenter's square [ruler]; hence, measurement: ". . . the most precious square of sense possesses . . ." *Lear,* I, i, 74. **4** embroidered yoke of a dress: ". . . he so chants/ to the sleeve-hand and the work about the square/ on 't." *W Tale,* IV, iv, 211–213. **5 by**

the square, precisely: ". . . jumps twelve foot and a half by th'/ square." *W Tale,* IV, iv, 339–340. **6 keep one's square,** to keep [one's life] on a straight course: "I have not kept my square,/ but that to come/ Shall all be done by the rule." *Ant & Cleo,* II, iii, 6–7. **7 know by the square,** to know exactly (how to): "Do not you know my lady's foot [how to please my lady] by the square . . ." *Love's L,* V, ii, 474.
—*v.* **8** to quarrel; also, to adopt a hostile stance or attitude; square off: ". . . they never meet in grove or green . . . But they do square . . ." *M N Dream,* II, i, 28–30. **9** to adjust or regulate: "Fie, fie, how franticly I square my talk,/ As if we should forget we had no hands . . ." *T Andr,* III, ii, 31–32. **10** to shape or form: "It is not so with Him that all things knows/ As 'tis with us that square our guess by shows [outward appearances] . . ." *All's W,* II, i, 148–149. **11 square me to,** to be influenced by; follow: "O, that ever I/ Had squar'd me to thy counsel!" *W Tale,* V, i, 51–52. **12 square yourselves,** to fight with each other or among yourselves: ". . . she shall file our engines with advice,/ That will not suffer you to square yourselves . . ." *T Andr,* II, i, 123–124.

square foot round, [had made his] straight foot crooked: ". . . the aged cramp/ Had screw'd his square foot round . . ." *Kinsmen,* V, i, 110–111.

squarer, *n.* quarreling, contentious person; brawler: "Is there no young/ squarer now that will make a voyage with him to the devil?" *M Ado,* I, i, 73–75.

squash, *n.* unripe peapod; here, ref. to his young son: "How like, methought, I then was to this kernel,/ This squash . . ." *W Tale,* I, ii, 159–160.

squeak, *v.* to speak in the shrill, shrieking voice attrib. to ghosts: ". . . the sheeted dead/ Did squeak and gibber in the Roman streets . . ." *Ham,* I, i, 118–119.

squier, *n.* old form of **square** (measuring instrument): "If I travel but four foot by the squier further/ afoot, I shall break my wind." *1 Hen 4,* II, ii, 12–13.

squiny, *v.* **1** to squint; also, to look sideways in the manner of a prostitute: "Dost thou squiny at me?" *Lear,* IV, vi, 138. **2** to cause to squint: ". . . he gives/ the web and the pin, squinies the eye . . ." *Lear,* III, iv, 119–120.

squire, *n.* esquire, a knight's attendant; one ranking by birth just below a knight: "And now is this Vice's dagger/ become a squire . . ." *2 Hen 4,* III, ii, 313–314.

squirrel, *n.* prob. a contemptuous term for a very small dog: ". . . the other squirrel was stolen from me by the/ hangman boys in the market-place . . ." *Two Gent,* IV, iv, 54–55.

stab, *v.* **1** wordplay on "fencing thrust" and "sexual attack": "... take heed of him—he stabbed me in/ mine own house, most beastly in good faith." *2 Hen 4,* II, i, 13–14. **2 stab pots,** poss. ref. to tapster who "nicked" ale pots, indicating a lesser capacity than was required: "... and wild Half-can/ that stabbed pots ..." *Meas,* IV, iii, 17–18.

stable, *adj.* trustworthy; dependable: "... rather let me leave to be a prince/ Than break the stable verdict of a prince ..." *Edw 3,* IV, v, 77–78.

staff, *n.* **1** lance used in tilting: "... give him another staff; this last was/ broke cross." *M Ado,* V, i, 137–138. **2** walking stick: "There is no staff more reverend than one tipped with horn." *M Ado,* V, iv, 122. **3** staff or badge of office: "... the Earl of Worcester/ Hath broken his staff, resign'd his stewardship,/ And all the household servants fled ..." *Rich 2,* II, ii, 58–60. **4** same as "stanza": "Let me hear a staff, a stanze, a verse: *lege, domine.*" *Love's L,* IV, ii, 100. **5 set in one's staff,** to take up residence; make one's self at home; here, with bawdy overtones: "Have at you with a proverb—shall I set in my staff?" *Errors,* III, i, 52.

stage, *n.* **1** platform: "... give order that these bodies/ High on a stage be placed to the view ..." *Ham,* V, ii, 382–383.
—*v.* **2 stage me,** [to] exhibit myself publicly: "I love the people,/ But do not like to stage me to their eyes ..." *Meas,* I, i, 67–68.

staged to the show, *adj.* made a public exhibition of: "Unstate his happiness, and be stag'd to the show/ Against a sworder!" *Ant & Cleo,* III, xiii, 30–31.

stagger, *v.* **stagger in,** to be uncertain; hesitate to say: "Whether the tyranny be in his place,/ Or in his eminence that fills it up,/ I stagger in ..." *Meas,* I, ii, 152–154.

staggering, *n.* hesitation: "... without/ any pause or staggering, take this basket on your/ shoulders." *Wives,* III, iii, 9–11.

staggers, *n. pl.* **1** disease of horses, causing dizziness and a staggering gait: "... stark spoiled with the staggers, begnawn with the bots ..." *Shrew,* III, ii, 52–53. **2** state of giddiness or confusion: "... I will throw thee from my care for ever/ Into the staggers and the careless lapse/ Of youth and ignorance ..." *All's W,* II, iii, 162–164.

stain, *n.* **1** color used in depicting a coat of arms; here, the additional meaning of a handkerchief stained with a martyr's blood: "... great men shall press/ For tinctures, stains, relics, and cognizance." *J Caes,* II, ii, 88–89. **2** trace; remnant: "You have some stain of soldier in you ..." *All's W,* I, i, 109. **3** blot or shadow cast by superior beauty: "Stain to all nymphs, more lovely than a man ..." *Ven & Ad,* 9. **4** loss of dignity or

eminence: "My valour's poison'd/ With only suff'ring stain by him ..." *Cor,* I, x, 17–18. **5** offense; fault or misdeed: "So that myself bring water for my stain ..." *Sonn 109,* 8.
—*v.* **6** to diminish or weaken; discredit: "I'll raise the preparation of a war/ Shall stain your brother ..." *Ant & Cleo,* III, iv, 26–27.

stained, *adj.* corrupted or polluted: "... all kinds of blood,/ That it could so preposterously be stained ..." *Sonn 109,* 10–11.

Staines, *n.* town on the river Thames, on the road to Southampton: "Prithee, honey-sweet husband, let me bring thee/ To Staines." *Hen 5,* II, iii, 1–2.

staining, *adj.* causing disgrace: "... would not put my reputation now/ In any staining act." *All's W,* III, vii, 6–7.

stair-work, *n.* lovers' tryst via the back stairs: "This has been some/ stair-work, some trunk-work, some behind-door-work ..." *W Tale,* III, iii, 73–75.

stake, *n.* **1 at the stake,** like a bear, in the sport of bear-baiting, tied to a stake and surrounded by vicious dogs: "... we are at the stake,/ And bay'd about with many enemies ..." *J Caes,* IV, i, 48–49. **2 to the stake,** to the place of execution: "Bringing the murderous coward to the stake ..." *Lear,* II, i, 62.
—*v.* **3 stake down,** to put down money as a wager; also, bawdy pun by Gratiano on impotence: "What! and stake down?"/ "No, we shall ne'er win at that sport and stake down." *Merch,* III, ii, 215–216.

St. Albans, *n.* **1** See **Saint Albans. 2 St. Albans field,** site of battles between York and Lancastrian forces in the War of the Roses: "... at St. Albans field/ This lady's husband, Sir John Grey, was slain ..." *3 Hen 6,* III, ii, 1–2.

stale[1], *n.* **1** loose woman; wanton; also, a discarded lover: "... he hath wronged his honour in marrying the/ renowned Claudio ... to a contaminated stale ..." *M Ado,* II, ii, 23–25. **2** laughingstock: "Was none in Rome to make a stale/ But Saturnine?" *T Andr,* I, i, 304–305. **3** (in falconry) a decoy bird; bait or lure: "To cast thy wandering eyes on every stale ..." *Shrew,* III, i, 88.

stale[2], *adj.* **1** tasteless; also, useless or pointless: "For now 'tis stale to sigh, to weep and groan ..." *Luc,* 1362. **2** no longer new or fresh: "Poor I am stale, a garment out of fashion ..." *Cymb,* III, iv, 52.
—*v.* **3** to make stale; cheapen: "To stale with ordinary oaths my love/ To every new protester ..." *J Caes,* I, ii, 72–73. **4** to make uninteresting: "I will venture/ To stale't a little more." *Cor,* I, i, 90–91.

stale³, *n.* **1** urine: "Thou didst drink/ The stale of horses . . ." *Ant & Cleo,* I, iv, 61–62. **2** slang term for "doctor" [fr. physician's practice of analyzing urine to diagnose illness]: "Ha, is/ he dead, bully stale? Is he dead?" *Wives,* II, iii, 27–28.

stalk¹, *v.* **1** to pace; walk up and down: "I stalk about her door/ Like a strange soul upon the Stygian banks . . ." *Tr & Cr,* III, i, 7–8.
—*n.* **2** stately manner of walking: "With martial stalk hath he gone by our watch." *Ham,* I, i, 69.

stalk², *n.* **grows to the stalk,** like a rose inseparable from the stem: "Here comes that which grows to the stalk; never/ pluck'd yet . . ." *Per,* IV, vi, 39–40.

stalking-horse, *n.* real or imitation horse, used as cover by a sportsman approaching game: "He uses his folly like a stalking-horse." *As You,* V, iv, 105.

stall, *n.* **1** booth, esp. in a marketplace, where wares were sold: "A crew of patches, rude mechanicals,/ That work for bread upon Athenian stalls . . ." *M N Dream,* III, ii, 9–10.
—*v.* **2** to enclose or confine in or as if in a stall: ". . . stall this in your bosom; and I thank you for your/ honest care." *All's W,* I, iii, 121–122. **3** to live or dwell [lit., to share a stall]: ". . . we could not stall together,/ In the whole world." *Ant & Cleo,* V, i, 39–40. **4** install; here, enthrone: "Deck'd in thy rights, as thou art stall'd in mine . . ." *Rich 3,* I, iii, 206. **5 stalled up,** tied up, as in a stall: "The steed is stalled up, and even now/ To tie the rider she begins to prove . . ." *Ven & Ad,* 39–40.

Stamford, *n.* market town in N central England: site of livestock fair: "How/ a good yoke of bullocks at Stamford fair?" *2 Hen 4,* III, ii, 37–38.

stammer, *v.* to give a deficient report on: "I think fame but stammers/ 'em, they stand a grise above the reach of report." *Kinsmen,* II, i, 27–28.

stamp, *n.* **1** minting, as of a coin: ". . . not a soldier of this season's stamp . . ." *1 Hen 4,* IV, i, 4. **2** stamped gold coin or medallion; here, prob. the "angel" coin: "Hanging a golden stamp about their necks,/ Put on with holy prayers . . ." *Mac,* IV, iii, 153–154. **3** Also, **stump,** perh. refers to stamp of the foot by which Puck effects his magic; or stage stump over which players trip in their haste to escape: "And at our stamp, here o'er and o'er one falls . . ." *M N Dream,* III, ii, 25. **4 stamps that are forbid,** illegitimate children: ". . . that do coin heaven's image/ In stamps that are forbid." *Meas,* II, iv, 45–46. **5 weigh not every stamp,** accept the coin because of the monarch's likeness stamped on it: "'Tween man and man they weigh not every stamp . . ." *Cymb,* V, iv, 24.

stamp the leasing, *n.* set the seal on a lie: ". . . in his praise/ Have almost stamp'd the leasing." *Cor,* V, ii, 21–22.

stand, *v.* **1** to be consistent [with]: ". . . if it stand with honesty,/ Buy thou the cottage . . ." *As You,* II, iv, 89–90. **2** to act the part of; be: "Good Master Corporate Bardolph, stand my/ friend . . ." *2 Hen 4,* III, ii, 215–216. **3** to hold one's ground, as in defending a position: "Thou runn'st before me, shifting every place,/ And dar'st not stand, nor look me in the face." *M N Dream,* III, ii, 423–424. **4** (as an order) **a.** stop; halt: "Stand, sir, and throw us that you have about ye." *Two Gent,* IV, i, 3. **b.** hold off; desist: "Stand, Aufidius,/ And trouble not the peace." *Cor,* V, vi, 126–127. **5** to fight; here, with swords: "I'll prove mine honour . . . Against thee presently, if thou dar'st stand." *Errors,* V, i, 30–31. **6** to be in a specified state or condition: "Say their great enemy is gone and they/ Stand in their ancient strength." *Cor,* IV, ii, 6–7. **7** to stand up to; resist or oppose: ". . . and she stand/ him but a little, he will throw a figure in her face . . ." *Shrew,* I, ii, 111–112. **8** to waste time on: ". . . never stand 'you had rather'/ and 'you had rather' . . ." *Wives,* III, iii, 115–116. **9** to stand still; stop: ". . . makes them stand/ Like wonder-wounded hearers?" *Ham,* V, i, 249–250. **10** to have or maintain an erection: "Me they shall feel while I am able to stand . . ." *Rom & Jul,* I, i, 27. **11** to depend: ". . . the moist star,/ Upon whose influence Neptune's empire stands . . ." *Ham,* I, i, 121–122. **12 stand against,** to withstand: "O! give thyself the thanks, if aught in me/ Worthy perusal stand against thy sight . . ." *Sonn 38,* 5–6. **13 stand by,** to be located next to; also, in wordplay, to be maintained or supported by: ". . . the church stands by thy/ tabor, if thy tabor stand by the church." *T Night,* III, i, 9–10. **14 stand close,** See **close¹** (def. 7). **15 stand close up,** stand up straight: "You great fellow,/ Stand close up, or I'll make your head ache." *Hen 8,* V, iii, 86–87. **16 stand for, a.** to stand up for; support or defend: "Pisanio, thou that stand'st so for Posthumus . . ." *Cymb,* III, v, 57. **b.** to be acceptable as: "I hope this reason stands for my excuse." *Shrew,* Ind., ii, 125. **c.** to take the place of; represent or impersonate: "Must thou needs stand for a villain in thine own work?" *Timon,* V, i, 36–37. **17 stand for his place,** offer himself as a candidate [for consul]: ". . . large cicatrices to show the people when he shall/ stand for his place." *Cor,* II, i, 147–148. **18 stand forth,** come forward; come out of your shelter or retreat: ". . . stand thou forth;/ The time is fair again." *All's W,* V, iii, 35–36. **19 stand in,** to continue [with]; be passed along to: ". . . yet it was said,/ It should not stand in thy posterity . . ." *Mac,* III, i, 3–4. **20 standing by,** yet to come: ". . . poor trespasses,/ More monstrous standing by . . ." *W Tale,* III, ii, 189–190. **21 standing every flaw,** withstanding every gust of wind: "Like a great sea-mark standing every flaw . . ." *Cor,* V, iii, 74. **22 standing water,** moving in no direction: "Well, I am standing water."/ "I'll teach you how to flow." *Temp,* II, i, 216–217. **23 stand in like request,**

are equally necessary: ". . . since that to both/ It stands in like request?" *Cor,* III, ii, 50–51. **24 stand off,** to stand out: ". . . the truth of it stands off as gross/ As black and white . . ." *Hen 5,* II, ii, 103–104. **25 stand on, a.** to demand; insist on: "And if he stand on hostage for his safety . . ." *T Andr,* IV, iv, 105. **b.** to depend on: ". . . my state/ Stands on me to defend, not to debate." *Lear,* V, i, 68–69. **26 stand out, a.** to rebel: "Now for the rebels which stand out in Ireland . . ." *Rich 2,* I, iv, 38. **b.** (of a soldier) to stay out of action: "What, art thou stiff? Standst out?" *Cor,* I, i, 240. **27 stands in act,** is underway: ". . . the Cyprus wars,/ Which even now stands in act . . ." *Oth,* I, i, 150–151. **28 stands me much upon,** is imperative to me: ". . . it stands me much upon/ To stop all hopes whose growth may damage me." *Rich 3,* IV, ii, 58–59. **29 stands our lives upon,** is a matter of life and death: "It only stands/ Our lives upon to use our strongest hands." *Ant & Cleo,* II, i, 50–51. **30 stands so firmly on his wife's frailty,** is firmly convinced his wife could not succumb to frailty: "Though Page be a secure fool, and stands so firmly/ on his wife's frailty . . ." *Wives,* II, i, 222–223. **31 stand the push of,** See **push** (def. 5). **32 stand to, a.** to stand by; stand up for; support: "Good my lord, be good to me, I beseech you stand/ to me." *2 Hen 4,* II, i, 61–62. **b.** to put up with; abide: "A gentleman, Nurse, that . . . will speak more in a minute than he will/ stand to in a month." *Rom & Jul,* II, iv, 144–146. **c.** to fall to; to begin working or, often, eating; also, sexual innuendo is obvious: ". . . much drink . . . makes him/ stand to, and not stand to . . ." *Mac,* II, iii, 31–35. **33 stand to it, a.** to be resolved on a course of action: "And thy mind stand to't, boy, steal away bravely." *All's W,* II, i, 29. **b.** to put up a good fight: "Where's your yeoman? Is't a lusty yeoman? Will a/ stand to't?" *2 Hen 4,* II, i, 3–4. **c.** same in wordplay with "have an erection": ". . . the danger is in standing to't; that's the loss of men,/ though it be the getting of children." *All's W,* III, ii, 40–41. **34 stand up,** to stand up to; defy: "A peasant stand up thus!" *Lear,* III, vii, 79. **35 stand up for,** to make a claim as: "Higher than both in blood and life, stands up/ For the main [chief] soldier . . ." *Ant & Cleo,* I, ii, 188–189. **36 stand upon, a.** to insist on: ". . . to bear a gentleman in/ hand, and then stand upon security!" *2 Hen 4,* I, ii, 36–37. **b.** to concern; be of importance to: "Consider how it stands upon my credit [reputation]." *Errors,* IV, i, 68. **c.** to be dependent upon: "Or else it stood upon the choice of friends—" *M N Dream,* I, i, 139. **d.** to pride oneself on: "This minion stood upon her chastity . . ." *T Andr,* II, iii, 124. **e.** to be incumbent upon (a person): "It stands your grace upon to do him right." *Rich 2,* II, iii, 137. **37 stand with, a.** to accord with: ". . . if it may stand with the tune of your/ voices that I may be consul . . ." *Cor,* II, iii, 84–85. **b.** to accompany: ". . . the drum that stroke the lusty march/ Stands with Prince Edward, your thrice valiant son." *Edw 3,* II, ii, 73–74. **38 whereon you stood,** which you asserted: "Your franchises, whereon you stood, confin'd/ Into an auger's bore." *Cor,* IV, vi, 87–88.

—*n.* **39** position; location: "A stand where you may make the fairest shoot." *Love's L,* IV, i, 10. **40** place to stand: "I have found you out a stand most fit,/ Where you may have such vantage on the Duke/ He shall not pass you." *Meas,* IV, vi, 10–12. **41** hiding place, as in a thicket, where hunters await game: "And in this covert will we make our stand . . ." *3 Hen 6,* III, i, 3. **42 make a stand at,** go no further than: "Since all and every part of what we would/ Doth make a stand at what your highness will [wishes]." *K John,* IV, ii, 38–39. **43 make stand,** to wait: "This is the penthouse under which Lorenzo/ Desired us to make stand." *Merch,* II, vi, 1–2.

stand a comma, *v.* to remain a connecting link; also, wordplay on "as" and "ass": "And stand a comma 'tween their amities [friendship],/ And many such-like 'as'es of great charge . . ." *Ham,* V, ii, 42–43.

standard, *n.* **1** standard-bearer: "By this light, thou shalt be my lieutenant,/ monster, or my standard." *Temp,* III, ii, 14–15. **2** same, with wordplay on "stander" or perh. vertical characteristic of a standard, since Caliban is too drunk to stand: "your lieutenant, if you list; he's no standard." *Temp,* III, ii, 16.

stander-by, *n.* [often pl] an associate or follower: ". . . I have said to some [of] my standers-by/ 'Lo, Jupiter is yonder, dealing life' . . ." *Tr & Cr,* IV, v, 189–190.

standing, *adj.* **1** upright; erect; also, with the tip stuck into the ground: ". . . you sheath, you bow-case, you vile standing/ tuck!" *1 Hen 4,* II, iv, 243–244. **2** stagnant: ". . . men whose visages/ Do cream and mantle like a standing pond . . ." *Merch,* I, i, 88–89. **3 standing water,** neither advancing nor retreating: "Well, I am standing water." *Temp,* II, i, 216.

—*n.* **4 continue the standing of,** [will] last as long as: ". . . whose foundation/ Is pil'd upon his faith, and will continue/ The standing of his body." *W Tale,* I, ii, 429–431.

standing-bed, *n.* bed that rests on legs [as disting. from a truckle-bed]: "There's his chamber, his house, his castle, his/ standing-bed, and truckle-bed . . ." *Wives,* IV, v, 5–6.

standing-bowl, *n.* goblet with feet or one mounted on a pedestal: "Here say we drink this standing-bowl of wine to him." *Per,* II, iii, 65.

stand in hard cure, *v.* may be impossible to cure: "Which, if convenience will not allow,/ Stand in hard cure." *Lear,* III, vi, 102–103.

stand my good lord, act as my patron: "Stand my good lord, pray, in your good report." *2 Hen 4,* IV, iii, 81.

stand the buffet, *n.* to exchange blows: ". . . and stand the buffet/ With knaves that smell of sweat . . ." *Ant & Cleo,* I, iv, 20–21.

staniel, *n.* kestrel, a small falcon: "And with what wing the staniel checks at it!" *T Night,* II, v, 115.

stanzo, *n.* var. of **stanza:** "I do desire you/ to sing. Come, more, another stanzo." *As You,* II, v, 15–16.

staple, *n.* **1** fiber; also, texture: "He draweth out the thread of his verbosity finer than/ the staple of his argument." *Love's L,* V, i, 16–17. **2** iron socket: ". . . with massy staples/ And co-responsive and fulfilling bolts . . ." *Tr & Cr,* Prol., 17–18.

star, *n.* **1** mark or blemish: ". . . the stamp of one defect,/ Being Nature's livery or Fortune's star . . ." *Ham,* I, iv, 31–32. **2 the star,** the North Star or Pole Star: ". . . and you be not turned Turk, there's no/ more sailing by the star." *M Ado,* III, iv, 52–53. **3** [pl.] birth; class or rank: "Shall I so much dishonour my fair stars [high birth]/ On equal terms to give him chastisement?" *Rich 2,* IV, i, 21–22. **4** [pl.] fate; fortune: ". . . that our stars,/ Unreconciliable, should divide/ Our equalness to this." *Ant & Cleo,* V, i, 46–48. **5 out of thy star,** above your social station: "'Lord Hamlet is a prince out of thy star./ This must not be.'" *Ham,* II, ii, 141–142. **6 received star,** (in astrology) the most acknowledged or accepted planet: ". . . there do muster/ true gait, eat, speak, and move, under the influence/ of the most receiv'd star . . ." *All's W,* II, i, 52–54. **7 under the star of,** designed by destiny for: ". . . the excellent/ constitution of thy leg, it was formed under the/ star of a galliard." *T Night,* I, iii, 129–131.

star-blasting, *n.* evil influence of a celestial body: "Bless thee from whirlwinds, star-blasting,/ and taking!" *Lear,* III, iv, 59–60.

Star Chamber, *n.* **1** court of the Privy Council, England's highest judicial body: "I will make a Star/ Chamber matter of it." *Wives,* I, i, 1–2. **2** metaphor for the court of heavenly justice: "When to the great Star-chamber o'er our heads/ The universal sessions calls to 'count/ This packing evil, we both shall tremble for it." *Edw 3,* II, ii, 163–165.

star-crossed, *adj.* doomed by the influence of the stars: "A pair of star-cross'd lovers take their life . . ." *Rom & Jul,* Prol., 6.

staring, *n.* drink-induced rowdiness: "And given to fornications, and to taverns . . . and swearings, and starings . . ." *Wives,* V, v, 158–160.

stark, *adv.* quite; absolutely: ". . . stark spoiled with the staggers, begnawn with/ the bots . . ." *Shrew,* III, ii, 52–53.

starkly, *adv.* stiffly: ". . . guiltless labour/ When it lies starkly in the traveller's bones." *Meas,* IV, ii, 64–65.

start, *v.* **1** to bolt; fly off: "How if your husband start some other where?" *Errors,* II, i, 30. **2** to raise or arouse: ". . . conjure with 'em,/ 'Brutus' will start a spirit as soon as 'Caesar.'" *J Caes,* I, ii, 144–145. **3** to flinch; blench: "Who then shall blame/ His pester'd senses to recoil and start . . ." *Mac,* V, ii, 22–23. **4** to startle; here, because Cesario has her heart, Olivia says her heart was startled too: "He started one poor heart of mine, in thee." *T Night,* IV, i, 58. **5** to disturb: "Upon malicious bravery, dost thou come/ To start my quiet?" *Oth,* I, i, 100–101. **6** to provoke to sudden action: ". . . one cannot speak a word/ But it straight starts you." *Tr & Cr,* V, ii, 100–101. —*n.* **7** outburst or flare-up: "The fearful [cowardly] French . . . Should make a start o'er seas and vanquish you?" *2 Hen 6,* IV, viii, 42–43. **8** impulse; whim: "Such unconstant starts are we like to have from/ him as this of Kent's banishment." *Lear,* I, i, 300–301. **9 by starts,** by choosing or omitting certain events: "Mangling by starts the full course of their glory." *Hen 5,* Epil. 4. **10 get the start of,** to outdo; outstrip: ". . . it doth amaze me/ A man of such a feeble temper should/ So get the start of the majestic world . . ." *J Caes,* I, ii, 128–129. **11 have the start of me,** have the advantage over me: "Well, I am your theme: you have the start of me." *Wives,* V, v, 162.

starting, *n.* startled reactions: "No more o' that, my Lord . . . you/ mar all with this starting." *Mac,* V, i, 43–44.

starting courage, *n.* eagerness to begin: ". . . in appointment fresh and fair/ Anticipating time with starting courage." *Tr & Cr,* IV, v, 1–2.

starting-hole, *n.* hole or burrow in which a hunted animal takes cover: ". . . what starting-hole/ canst thou now find out, to hide thee from this open/ and apparent shame?" *1 Hen 4,* II, iv, 259–261.

startle, *v.* to sound alarmingly: "What fear is this which startles in our ears?" *Rom & Jul,* V, iii, 193.

start-up, *n.* upstart: ". . . that young start-up hath/ all the glory of my overthrow." *M Ado,* I, iii, 62–63.

starve, *v.* **1** to die, as from exhaustion: "I'll starve ere I'll rob a foot/ further . . ." *1 Hen 4,* II, ii, 21–22. **2** to kill; here, with the cold: "The air hath starv'd the roses in her cheeks . . ." *Two Gent,* IV, iv, 152. **3 starve out,** to suffer through; here, in bitter cold: "Never go home: here starve we out the night." *Tr & Cr,* V, x, 2.

starved, *adj.* **1** prob. perishing with cold: "God's body! The turkeys in my pannier are/ quite starved." *1 Hen 4,* II, i, 25–26. **2** inconsequential; trivial: "I cannot fight upon this argument;/ It is too starv'd a subject for my sword." *Tr & Cr*, I, i, 92–93.

starveling, *n.* thin, emaciated and undernourished person: "'Sblood, you starveling, you eel-skin . . ." *1 Hen 4*, II, iv, 240.

state, *n.* **1** condition; means; rank or status: "His promises fly so beyond his state . . ." *Timon*, I, ii, 195. **2** position; duty or responsibility: "And to my state grew stranger, being transported/ And rapt in secret studies." *Temp*, I, ii, 76–77. **3** wealth and possessions along with elevated social position: "To have his pomp and all what [that which] state compounds . . ." *Timon*, IV, ii, 35. **4** dignity; majesty: "Question . . . the late ambassadors,/ With what great state he heard their embassy . . ." *Hen 5*, II, iv, 31–32. **5** power of a monarch: "Death on my state! wherefore/ Should he sit here?" *Lear*, II, iv, 112–113. **6** presence of a monarch: "Then, dear my liege, now niggard not [don't be stinting with] thy state . . ." *Edw 3*, I, ii, 123. **7** state of affairs: ". . . heaven hath infus'd them with these spirits/ To make them instruments of fear and warning/ Unto some monstrous state." *J Caes*, I, iii, 69–71. **8** politics: "My wretchedness unto a row of pins,/ They'll talk of state . . ." *Rich 2*, III, iv, 26–27. **9** [often pl.] estates; here, also, ourselves: "Our states are forfeit: seek not to undo us." *Love's L*, V, ii, 425. **10** formal ceremony: ". . . such necessaries/ As are behoveful for our state tomorrow." *Rom & Jul*, IV, iii, 7–8. **11** pomp; ceremony: "And with the same full state pac'd back again/ To York-place . . ." *Hen 8*, IV, i, 93–94. **12** courtly behavior, esp. elegant phrases: ". . . an affectioned/ ass, that cons state without book, and utters it/ by great swarths . . ." *T Night*, II, iii, 147–149. **13** persons of rank, as those making up Parliament; statesmen: ". . . we will accite,/ As I before remember'd, all our state . . ." *2 Hen 4*, V, ii, 141–142. **14** chair of state; throne: "Having been three months married to her, sitting/ in my state—" *T Night*, II, v, 44–45. **15** canopy over a chair of state: "Hautboys. A small table under a state for the Cardinal . . ." [SD] *Hen 8*, I, iv, 1. **16** frail condition of body and mind; also, status as a dependent: ". . . some discretion that discerns your state/ Better than you yourself." *Lear*, II, iv, 150–151. **17** wordplay on "condition" and "greatness": "When I have seen such interchange of state,/ Or state itself confounded to decay . . ." *Sonn 64*, 9–10. **18** way of standing or posing: "Will praise a hand, a foot, a face, an eye,/ A gait, a state, a brow, a breast, a waist,/ A leg, a limb—?" *Love's L*, IV, iii, 181–183. **19 have the humor of state,** to adopt the manner of a statesman: "And then to have the humour of state;/ and after a/ demure travel of regard . . ." *T Night*, II, v, 52–53. **20 holds his state,** maintains his dignity: ". . . his grace of Canterbury,/ Who holds his state at door 'mongst pursuivants . . ." *Hen 8*, V, ii, 22–23. **21 keep one's state,** to stay apart; here, to remain seated on her throne: "Our hostess keeps her state; but, in best time,/ We will require her welcome." *Mac*,

III, iv, 5–6. **22 the general state,** the military leaders; here, Agamemnon's staff: "The general state, I fear,/ Can scarce entreat you to be odd with him." *Tr & Cr*, IV, v, 263–264.

state of floods, *n.* majesty of the sea: ". . . ebb back to the sea,/ Where it shall mingle with the state of floods . . ." *2 Hen 4*, V, ii, 131–132.

state-statue, *n.* [merely] image of a statesman: "We should take root here, where we sit;/ Or sit state-statues only." *Hen 8*, I, ii, 87–88.

station, *n.* **1** bearing; stance: "A station like the herald Mercury . . ." *Ham*, III, iv, 58. **2** place to stand, as in a crowd: ". . . press among the popular throngs, and puff/ To win a vulgar station." *Cor*, II, i, 212–213.

statist, *n.* **1** public official: "I once did hold it, as our statists do,/ A baseness to write fair . . ." *Ham*, V, ii, 33–34. **2** statesman; diplomat: "Statist though I am none, nor like to be . . ." *Cymb*, II, iv, 16.

statuë or **statua,** var. of statue when pron. as three syllables: "Erect his statuë and worship it . . ." *2 Hen 6*, III, ii, 79.

statute, *n.* **1** obligation secured by property, esp. land: ". . . this fellow might be in's/ time a great buyer of land, with his statutes, his/ recognizances . . ." *Ham*, V, i, 101–103. **2** full value of bonded property: "The statute of thy beauty thou wilt take . . ." *Sonn 134*, 9.

statute-cap, *n.* prob. the plain woolen cap that London apprentices were required to wear: "Well, better wits have worn plain statute-caps." *Love's L*, V, ii, 281.

staunchless, *adj.* insatiable: ". . . there grows/ In my most ill-compos'd affection such/ A staunchless avarice . . ." *Mac*, IV, iii, 76–78.

stave, *n.* var. of **staff;** here, in an old proverb about keeping the Devil at bay: "Truly, Madam, he holds Belzebub at the stave's/ end . . ." *T Night*, V, i, 282–283.

staves, *n.* pl. of **staff;** lance [actually, wooden shaft of lance]: "Their armed staves in charge, their beavers down . . ." *2 Hen 4*, IV, i, 120.

stay¹, *v.* **1** to wait (for); await: "Let me stay the growth of his beard, if/ thou delay me not the knowledge of his chin." *As You*, III, ii, 206–207. **2** to stay for: "I shall return before your lordship thence."/ "Nay, like enough, for I stay dinner there." *Rich 3*, III, ii, 118–119. **3** to give allegiance to: "What will ye do?"/ "Stay the king." *All's W*, II, i, 48–49. **4** to delay: ". . . to stay him not too long,/ I am content, in a good father's care . . ." *Shrew*, IV, iv, 30–31. **5** to restrain; hold in custody:

"A great suspicion. Stay the friar too." *Rom & Jul*, V, iii, 186. **6** to prevent or stop: "I'll be reveng'd/ Most throughly for my father."/ "Who shall stay you?" *Ham*, IV, v, 136. **7** to be fixed indelibly: ". . . thy fair imperfect shade/ Through heavy sleep on sightless eyes doth stay!" *Sonn 43*, 11–12. **8 stay by,** to oppose: ". . . and he had stayed by him, I would not have been so/ 'fidiussed for all the chests in Corioles . . ." *Cor*, II, i, 129–130. **9 stay for,** to await: "The day, my friends, and all things stay for me." *Hen 5*, IV, i, 315. **10 Stay his time,** wait for him to come to his senses: ". . . it portends alone/ The fall of Antony!"/ "I must stay his time." *Ant & Cleo*, III, xiii, 154–155. **11 stay on,** be delayed because of: ". . . my honest friend,/ Who, but for staying on our controversy . . ." *Errors*, V, i, 19–20. **12 stay (the) question,** to await the outcome, judgment, etc.: "He seem'd in running to devour the way,/ Staying no longer question." *2 Hen 4*, I, i, 47–48. **13 stay the odds,** wordplay on "stopped the quarrelling" and "put an end to uneven numbers": ". . . the goose came out of coor,/ And stay'd the odds by adding four [a fourth]." *Love's L*, III, i, 88–89. —*n.* **14** period of waiting: ". . . our dinner/ will not recompense this long stay." *Timon*, III, vi, 31–32. **15** interruption; also, check or hindrance: "Here's a stay/ That shakes the rotten carcass of old death . . ." *K John*, II, i, 455–456. **16 inconstant stay,** ever-changing state: ". . . the conceit [idea] of this inconstant stay/ Sets you most rich in youth before my sight . . ." *Sonn 15*, 9–10.

stay², *n.* **1** prop or support: "Yet are these feet, whose strengthless stay is numb,/ Unable to support this lump of clay . . ." *1 Hen 6*, II, v, 13–14. —*v.* **2** to prop; support: "And he that stands upon a slipp'ry place/ Makes nice of no vild hold to stay him up . . ." *K John*, III, iii, 137–138.

stay awhile, *v.* [to] wait a moment: "Romeo, arise,/ Thou wilt be taken.—Stay awhile.—Stand up." *Rom & Jul*, III, iii, 74–75.

stayed for, *adj.* awaited: "Am I not stay'd for? Tell me."/ "Yes, you are." *J Caes*, I, iii, 139.

stay not, *v.* Don't take time for, stay for, etc.: "Stay not thy compliment; I forgive/ thy duty: adieu." *Love's L*, IV, ii, 137–138.

stead, *v.* **1** to aid or benefit: "My intercession likewise steads my foe." *Rom & Jul*, II, iii, 50. **2** to serve; avail: ". . . it nothing steads us/ To chide him from our eaves . . ." *All's W*, III, vii, 41–42. **3 May you stead me?** Can you help me?: "May you stead me? Will you pleasure me? Shall I/ know your answer?" *Merch*, I, iii, 6–7. **4 stead up,** to keep in your place: "We shall advise this wronged maid/ to stead up your appointment, go in your place." *Meas*, III, i, 250–251.

—*n.* **5** use; benefit; service: "The help of one stands me in little stead." *1 Hen 6*, IV, vi, 31.

steal, *v.* **stolen a man already made,** committed murder: "To pardon him that hath from nature stolen/ A man already made . . ." *Meas*, II, iv, 43–44.

stealth, *n.* **1** act of stealing; thievery: ". . . ingratitude makes it worse than stealth." *Timon*, III, iv, 28. **2 stealth of nature,** illicit sexual relations: "Who in the lusty stealth of nature take/ More composition and fierce quality . . ." *Lear*, I, ii, 11–12.

steel, *n.* **1** sword; here, Cade addresses his own sword: "Steel, if thou turn the edge, or cut not/ out the burly-bon'd clown in chines . . ." *2 Hen 6*, IV, x, 55–56. **2** armor; here, to observe mourning by arming for battle: "The hope thereof makes Clifford mourn in steel." *3 Hen 6*, I, i, 58. **3** man of steel; soldier; warrior: "When steel grows/ Soft as the parasite's silk . . ." *Cor*, I, ix, 44–45. **4 complete steel,** full armor: ". . . thou, dead corse, again in complete steel/ Revisits thus the glimpses of the moon . . ." *Ham*, I, iv, 52–53. **5 wear steel,** [I who] am a soldier; here, should not therefore be regarded as a mere pander: "Shall I Sir Pandarus of Troy become,/ And by my side wear steel?" *Wives*, I, iii, 71–72. —*v.* **6** to brace with steel; here, make determined: "For from his metal was his party steel'd . . ." *2 Hen 4*, I, i, 116. **7** to take confidently: "To steel a strong opinion to themselves?" *Tr & Cr*, I, iii, 353.

steeled, *adj.* hardened: ". . . seldom when/ The steeled gaoler is the friend of men." *Meas*, IV, ii, 84–85.

steeled coat, *n.* body armor of steel: "Give me my steeled coat: I'll fight for France." *1 Hen 6*, I, i, 85.

steeled sense, *n.* firm determination: "That my steeled sense or changes right or wrong [that changes my firm determination, whether right or wrong]." *Sonn 112*, 8.

steep-down, *adj.* precipitous: "Wash me in steep-down gulfs of liquid fire!" *Oth*, V, ii, 281.

steepy, *adj.* precipitous; here, hovering on the edge of a precipice: ". . . when his youthful morn/ Hath travelled on to age's steepy night . . ." *Sonn 63*, 4–5.

steer, *v.* to direct; command: "A rarer spirit never/ Did steer humanity . . ." *Ant & Cleo*, V, i, 31–32.

steerage, *n.* act of piloting: ". . . think his pilot thought;/ So with his steerage shall your thoughts grow on . . ." *Per*, IV, iv, 18–19.

stell, *v.* to paint, etch, or engrave; here, prob. to portray or reveal: "To this well-painted piece is Lucrece come,/ To find a face where all distress is stell'd." *Luc,* 1443–1444.

stelled, *adj.* starry: "The sea . . . would have buoy'd up,/ And quench'd the stelled fires . . ." *Lear,* III, vii, 58–60.

stem, *n.* foremost part of a ship; bow: ". . . bid them blow towards England's blessed shore,/ Or turn our stem upon a dreadful rock." *2 Hen 6,* III, ii, 89–90.

step or **steppe,** *n.* limit of travel; poss. misuse for "steep," indicating a mountain range: "Why art thou here,/ Come from the farthest step of India . . ." *M N Dream,* II, i, 68–69.

step-dame, *n.* stepmother: "Like to a step-dame or a dowager/ Long withering out a young man's revenue." *M N Dream,* I, i, 5–6.

sterling, *adj.* (of money) silver; also, sound or valid: "Pay her the debt you owe her . . . with sterling money . . ." *2 Hen 4,* II, i, 117–119.

stern[1], *adj.* **1** fierce; also, cruel and pitiless: ". . . make this banket, which I wish may prove/ More stern and bloody than the centaurs' feast." *T Andr,* V, ii, 202–203. **2** rough; crude or uncouth: "Thy mother took into her blameful bed/ Some stern untutor'd churl . . ." *2 Hen 6,* III, ii, 211–212. **3 stern'st good-night,** ref. to bell that was rung the night before a prisoner was executed: "It was the owl that shriek'd, the fatal bellman,/ Which gives the stern'st good-night." *Mac,* II, ii, 3–4.

stern[2], *n.* **at chiefest stern,** in the position of greatest power: "The King from Eltham I intend to steal,/ And sit at chiefest stern of public weal." *1 Hen 6,* I, i, 176–177.

sternage, *n.* rear: "Grapple your minds to sternage of [pretend that you follow] this navy . . ." *Hen 5,* III, Chor., 18.

stew, *n.* [usually pl.] brothels; red-light district: "And I could get me but a wife in the/ stews, I were manned, horsed, and wived." *2 Hen 4,* I, ii, 53–54.

steward, *n.* caretaker: "They are the lords and owners of their faces,/ Others but stewards of their excellence." *Sonn 94,* 8.

stewed, *adj.* **1** steeped or drenched: "Stew'd in corruption, honeying and making love/ Over the nasty sty!" *Ham,* III, iv, 93–94. **2** same in wordplay with "stews" [brothels]: "Sodden business: there's a stewed phrase/ indeed!" *Tr & Cr,* III, i, 40–41.

stick, *v.* **1** to hesitate: "She will not stick to round me on th'ear . . ." *P Pil,* XVIII, 51. **2** to stab or slaughter; also, with sexual innuendo: "If the ground be overcharged, you were best stick/ her." *Two Gent,* I, i, 99–100. **3** to stand out; excel: ". . . stick i'th' wars/ Like a great sea-mark . . ." *Cor,* V, iii, 73–74. **4 stick deep,** to be of profound concern; here, in the manner of a thorn: "Our fears in Banquo/ Stick deep . . ." *Mac,* III, i, 48–49. **5 stick fiery off,** to stand out in sharp contrast: "Your skill shall like a star i'th' darkest night/ Stick fiery off indeed." *Ham,* V, ii, 253–254. **6 stick in,** to stand firm in; also, stand out in: ". . . stick i'th'wars/ Like a great sea-mark standing every flaw . . ." *Cor,* V, iii, 73–74. **7 stuck not,** didn't hesitate: ". . . he himself stuck not to call us the many-headed/ multitude." *Cor,* II, iii, 16–17.

sticking-place, *n.* (a) the point to which a peg on a stringed musical instrument had to be tightened to provide the proper pitch, or (b) the point to which the string on a crossbow had to be drawn (or wound) back to provide the proper thrust: "But screw your courage to the sticking-place,/ And we'll not fail." *Mac,* I, vii, 61–62.

stickler-like, *adj.* resembling a stickler, the umpire who parted opponents in friendly combat: "The dragon wing of night o'er-spreads the earth/ And, stickler-like, the armies separates." *Tr & Cr,* V, viii, 17–18.

stiff, *adj.* **1** unbending; unyielding: ". . . how stiff is my vile sense/ That I stand up, and have ingenious feeling . . ." *Lear,* IV, vi, 281–282. **2** stout; sturdy: ". . . make you ready your stiff bats and clubs . . ." *Cor,* I, i, 160. **3** grave: "This is stiff news . . ." *Ant & Cleo,* I, ii, 97.

stiff-borne, *adj.* hard or bravely fought: ". . . none of this . . . could restrain/ The stiff-borne action." *2 Hen 4,* I, i, 175–177.

stifle, *v.* **stifle up,** to suffocate [with *up* as an intensive]: ". . . it shall be as all the ocean,/ Enough to stifle such a villain up." *K John,* IV, iii, 132–133.

stigmatic, *n.* deformity; here, a deformed person: "Foul stigmatic, that's more than thou canst tell." *2 Hen 6,* V, i, 216.

stigmatical, *adj.* deformed: "Stigmatical in making [by nature], worse in mind." *Errors,* IV, ii, 22.

stile, *n.* set of steps for crossing over a fence or wall: "Both stile and gate, horse-way and foot-path." *Lear,* IV, i, 55.

still, *adv.* **1** always; ever; continually; constantly: "We still have slept together,/ Rose at an instant, learn'd, play'd, eat together . . ." *As You,* I, iii, 69–70. **2** yet: "I shall forget, to have thee still stand there . . ." *Rom & Jul,* II, ii, 172. **3** at rest: ". . . stout-hearted, still,/ But when he stirs, a tiger." *Kinsmen,* IV, ii, 130–131.

—*adj.* **4** constant; steady: "I of [from] these will wrest an al-phabet,/ And by still practice learn to know thy meaning." *T Andr,* III, ii, 44–45.

still and anon, *adv.* repeatedly; continually: ". . . like the watchful minutes to the hour,/ Still and anon cheer'd up the heavy time . . ." *K John,* IV, i, 46–47.

still an end, *adv.* forever; everlastingly: "A slave, that still an end turns me to shame!" *Two Gent,* IV, iv, 61.

still-breeding, *adj.* ever or continually breeding: ". . . and these two beget/ A generation of still-breeding thoughts . . ." *Rich 2,* V, v, 7–8.

still-closing, *adj.* (of waters) quickly closing over any opening: ". . . may as well/ Wound the loud winds, or with bemock'd-at stabs/ Kill the still-closing waters . . ." *Temp,* III, iii, 62–64.

still conclusion, *n.* silent judgment: "Your wife Octavia, with her modest eyes,/ And still conclusion . . ." *Ant & Cleo,* IV, xv, 27–28.

stillitory, *n.* still, used esp. in making perfume: ". . . from the stillitory of thy face excelling/ Comes breath perfum'd . . ." *Ven & Ad,* 443.

still-piecing, *adj.* (of the air) closing together unharmed after piercing by every bullet: "Fly with false aim; move the still-piecing air/ That sings with piercing; do not touch my lord." *All's W,* III, ii, 110–111.

still rhetoric, *n.* See **rhetoric** (def. 2).

still-soliciting, *adj.* always begging favors: "A still-soliciting eye, and such a tongue/ That I am glad I have not . . ." *Lear,* I, i, 231–232.

still-stand, *n.* standstill: ". . . the tide swell'd up unto his height,/ That makes a still-stand, running neither way." *2 Hen 4,* II, iii, 63–64.

still-vexed, *adj.* forever stormy: "Thou call'dst me up at mid-night to fetch dew/ From the still-vex'd Bermoothes [Bermu-das] . . ." *Temp,* I, ii, 228–229.

sting, *n.* sexual desire; here, additional implication of "male sexual organ": "But she, sound sleeping . . . Lies at the mercy of his mortal sting." *Luc,* 363–364.

stinking-elder, *n.* perh. ref. to belief that Judas had hanged himself on an elder tree: "And let the stinking-elder, grief, un-twine/ His perishing root . . ." *Cymb,* IV, ii, 59–60.

stint, *v.* to stop or cease; check: "Make war breed peace, make peace stint war . . ." *Timon,* V, iv, 83.

stir, *n.* **1** action, esp. military action: ". . . what stir/ Keeps good old York there with his men of war?" *Rich 2,* II, iii, 51–52. **2** effort or exertion: "If Chance will have me King, why, Chance may crown me,/ Without my stir." *Mac,* I, iii, 144–145.
—*v.* **3** to encourage (another) to be forthcoming: "I could not stir him:/ He said he was gentle [a gentleman], but unfortu-nate . . ." *Cymb,* IV, ii, 38–39. **4** to be aroused; be restless or angry: "You show too much of that/ For which the people stir." *Cor,* III, i, 51–52. **5 Look how thou stirr'st now!** Don't hurry! [used ironically]: "Look how thou stirr'st now! come away [get moving], or I'll/ fetch'th with a wanion." *Per,* II, i, 16–17.

stirring, *adj.* active or energetic: "A stirring dwarf we do al-lowance give/ Before a sleeping giant." *Tr & Cr,* II, iii, 139–140.

stithy, *n.* **1** smithy; blacksmith's shop: "And my imaginations are as foul/ As Vulcan's stithy." *Ham,* III, ii, 83–84.
—*v.* **2** to forge: ". . . by the forge that stithied Mars his helm,/ I'll kill thee everywhere . . ." *Tr & Cr,* IV, v, 254–255.

stoccado, *n.* (in fencing) thrust: ". . . you stand on distance, your passes, stoccadoes,/ and I know not what." *Wives,* II, i, 214–215.

stock¹, *n.* **1** blockhead; dunce; here, wordplay with "stoic": "Let's be no stoics nor no stocks, I pray . . ." *Shrew,* I, i, 31. **2** stocking: ". . . with a linen stock on one leg, and a kersey/ boot-hose on the other . . ." *Shrew,* III, ii, 64–65. **3** dowry; also, wordplay on "stocking" sense: "What need a man care for a stock with a wench . . ." *Two Gent,* III, i, 303. **4** main stem of a plant, in wordplay with branch of a family tree: ". . . but for the stock, Sir Thomas,/ I wish it grubb'd up [uprooted] now." *Hen 8,* V, i, 22–23.
—*v.* **5** to place in stocks as punishment: "Who stock'd my ser-vant? Regan, I have good hope/ Thou didst not know on't." *Lear,* II, iv, 190–191.

stock², *n.* short [informal] form of "stoccado": ". . . to see thee/ traverse . . . to see/ thy punto, thy stock, thy reverse . . ." *Wives,* II, iii, 22–24.

stock-fish or **stockfish,** *n.* dried codfish, so hard that it had to be beaten before it could be boiled: ". . . by this hand, I'll/ turn my mercy out o' doors, and make a stock-fish/ of thee." *Temp,* III, ii, 68–70.

stocking, *n.* **tall stockings,** long stockings: ". . . renouncing clean/ The faith they have in tennis and tall stockings . . ." *Hen 8,* I, iii, 29–30.

stockish, *adj.* showing no feeling, like a block of wood: "Since naught so stockish, hard, and full of rage,/ But music for the time doth change his nature . . ." *Merch,* V, i, 81–82.

stock-punish, *v.* to place in stocks as punishment: ". . . whipp'd/ from tithing to tithing, and stock-punish'd . . ." *Lear,* III, iv, 137–138.

stoic, *n.* follower of stoicism, considered cold and impassive; here, wordplay with "stock," blockhead: "Let's be no stoics nor no stocks, I pray . . ." *Shrew,* I, i, 31.

stole all courtesy, adopted a courteous manner [as though sent by heaven]: "And then I stole all courtesy from heaven . . ." *1 Hen 4,* III, ii, 50.

stolen, *adj.* borrowed, copied, or plagiarized: ". . . warp'd the line of every other favour,/ Scorn'd a fair colour or express'd it stol'n . . ." *All's W,* V, iii, 49–50.

stomach, *n.* **1** appetite: ". . . what is't that takes from thee/ Thy stomach, pleasure, and thy golden sleep?" *1 Hen 4,* II, iii, 41–42. **2** inclination: "Nay, let me praise you while I have a stomach." *Merch,* III, v, 81. **3** boldness or daring: ". . . some enterprise/ That hath a stomach in't . . ." *Ham,* I, i, 102–103. **4** ambition: "He was a man/ Of an unbounded stomach . . ." *Hen 8,* IV, ii, 33–34. **5** in fig. use, one's disposition: ". . . in despite of his/ quick wit and his queasy stomach, he shall fall in/ love with Beatrice." *M Ado,* II, i, 360–362. **6** stomach regarded as the seat of anger: "Lady, I am not well; else I should answer/ From a full-flowing stomach." *Lear,* V, iii, 74–75. **7** [often pl.] resentments: ". . . losers will have leave/ To ease their stomachs with their bitter tongues." *T Andr,* III, i, 232–233. **8 an undergoing stomach,** the courage to endure; the stomach was regarded as the seat of valor: "Thou didst smile . . . which rais'd in me/ An undergoing stomach, to bear up/ Against what should ensue." *Temp,* I, ii, 153–158. **9 close our stomachs up,** to put the final touches to our feast: "My banquet is to close our stomachs up/ After our great good cheer." *Shrew,* V, ii, 10. **10 kill your stomach,** satisfy your appetite; also, quench your anger: "That you might kill your stomach on your meat,/ And not upon your maid." *Two Gent,* I, ii, 68–69. **11 vail your stomachs,** swallow your pride: "Then vail your stomachs, for it is no boot . . ." *Shrew,* V, ii, 177.
—*v.* **12** to resent: "Believe not all, or if you must believe,/ Stomach not all." *Ant & Cleo,* III, iv, 11–12. **13 private stomaching,** indulging personal grievances: "'Tis not a time/ For private stomaching." *Ant & Cleo,* II, ii, 8–9.

stomacher, *n.* ornamented chest covering: "Golden quoifs and stomachers/ For my lads to give their dears . . ." *W Tale,* IV, iv, 226–227.

stone, *n.* **1** testicle: ". . . I warrant it had upon it [her] brow/ A bump as big as a young cockerel's stone . . ." *Rom & Jul,* I, iii, 52–53. **2** [pl.] jewels, prob. with wordplay on preceding: "Give her no token but stones, for she's as hard as/ steel." *Two Gent,* I, i, 134–135.
—*v.* **3** to turn to stone: "O perjur'd woman, thou dost stone thy heart . . ." *Oth,* V, ii, 64.

stone-bow, *n.* crossbow that shoots small stones instead of arrows: "O for a stone-bow to hit him in the eye!" *T Night,* II, v, 46.

stones of sulphur, *n.* thunderbolts: "The gods throw stones of sulphur on me . . ." *Cymb,* V, v, 240.

stonish, *v.* astonish; amaze or bewilder: "O wonderful son, that can so stonish a mother!" *Ham,* III, ii, 319.

Stony Stratford, *n.* market-town NW of London in Buckinghamshire: "Last night, I hear, they lay at Stony Stratford . . ." *Rich 3,* II, iv, 1.

stool, *n.* privy; commode; poss. ref. to Thersites' small misshapen body: "Thou stool for a witch!" *Tr & Cr,* II, i, 44.

stoop, *v.* **1** (in falconry) to swoop down onto the prey; also, to return to the falconer's lure: "And till she stoop she must not be full-gorg'd . . ." *Shrew,* IV, i, 178. **2** to bow: ". . . the king before the Douglas' rage/ Stoop'd his anointed head as low as death." *2 Hen 4,* Induc., 31–32.

stooping, *n.* submissive attitude; yielding: ". . . his stoutness/ When he did stand for consul, which he lost/ By lack of stooping—" *Cor,* V, vi, 27–29.

stop, *n.* **1** obstacle; obstruction: "These be the stops that hinder study quite . . ." *Love's L,* I, i, 70. **2** power of prevention: "I have made my way through more impediments/ Than twenty times your stop . . ." *Oth,* V, ii, 264–265. **3** (in manège) the halting of a horse in full gallop; here, in wordplay with "stop" [period]: "He hath rid his prologue like a rough colt; he knows/ not the stop." *M N Dream,* V, i, 119–120. **4** one of a series of holes on a pipe: the instrument is played by blowing air through the mouthpiece and covering and uncovering the stops with the fingers: "Rumour is a pipe . . . And of so easy and so plain a stop . . ." *2 Hen 4,* Induc. 15–17.
—*v.* **5** to fill: "Has not so much wit . . . As will stop the eye of Helen's needle . . ." *Tr & Cr,* II, i, 80–82. **6** to thwart or block: "John, to stop Arthur's title in the whole,/ Hath willingly departed with a part . . ." *K John,* II, i, 562–563.

stople, *v.* var. of stopple; to stopper: "Shut your mouth, dame,/ Or with this paper shall I stople it." *Lear,* V, iii, 154–155.

store, *n.* **1** person's goods or money: "No, ye/ fat chuffs, I would your store were here!" *1 Hen 4,* II, ii, 84–85. **2** supply of something; here, of money: "I am debating of my present store . . ." *Merch,* I, iii, 48. **3** abundance: "Increasing store with loss and loss with store . . ." *Sonn 64,* 8. **4** material: ". . . whose warp'd looks proclaim/ What store her heart is made on." *Lear,* III, vi, 53–54. **5** procreation: "Let those whom Nature hath not made for store . . . barrenly perish." *Sonn 11,* 9–10 —*v.* **6** to fill; cram or pack: "Here, with a cup that's stor'd unto the brim . . ." *Per,* II, iii, 50. **7** to populate: ". . . as many to the vantage, as would/ store the world they played for." *Oth,* IV, iii, 84–85. **8** to preserve: "O! him she stores, to show what wealth she had . . ." *Sonn 67,* 13.

stored, *adj.* **1** provided; supplied: "I did not think the king so stor'd with friends." *K John,* V, iv, 1. **2** stocked: "Their tables were stor'd full to glad the sight . . ." *Per,* I, iv, 28.

store's account, *n.* [long] list of lovers: "Though in thy store's account I one must be . . ." *Sonn 136,* 10.

story[1], *n.* **1** object of [your] humor: "Sir, make me not your story." *Meas,* I, iv, 30. —*v.* **2** to relate; tell (of): ". . . and stories/ His victories, his triumphs and his glories." *Ven & Ad,* 1013–1014. **3** to give an account of: ". . . rather than story him in his own hearing." *Cymb,* I, v, 32.

story[2], *n.* prob. the bedchamber: ". . . such/ Th' adornment of her bed; the arras, figures . . . and the contents o' th' story." *Cymb,* II, ii, 25–27.

stoup, *n.* large pot: "Go, get thee to Yaughan; fetch me a stoup of liquor." *Ham,* V, i, 60.

stout, *adj.* **1** haughty; disdainful: "Oft have I seen the haughty Cardinal . . . As stout and proud as he were lord of all . . ." *2 Hen 6,* I, I, 184–186. **2** valiant; brave and fearless: "This earth that bears thee dead/ Bears not alive so stout a gentleman." *1 Hen 4,* V, iv, 91–92. **3** firm; resolved; that is, in his new mode of behavior: "I will be strange, stout, in/ yellow stockings, and cross-gartered . . ." *T Night,* II, v, 171–172. **4** bold; daring: "With dreadful pomp of stout invasion!" *K John,* IV, ii, 173.

stoutness, *n.* obstinacy; stubbornness: ". . . let/ Thy mother rather feel thy pride than fear/ Thy dangerous stoutness . . ." *Cor,* III, ii, 125–127.

stover, *n.* winter hay: ". . . where live nibbling sheep,/ And flat meads thatch'd with stover . . ." *Temp,* IV, i, 62–63.

straggling, *adj.* wandering away from assigned duty, esp. to steal or pillage: "He likewise enrich'd poor/ straggling soldiers with great quantity." *Timon,* V, i, 6–7.

straight, *adj.* **1** strong: ". . . other of them may/ have crook'd noses, but to owe [own] such straight arms,/ none." *Cymb,* III, i, 37–39. —*adv.* **2** straightaway; at once; promptly: "No point, quoth I: my servant straight was mute." *Love's L,* V, ii, 277.

straight-pight, *n.* tall and erect: ". . . for feature, laming/ The shrine of Venus, or straight-pight Minerva . . ." *Cymb,* V, v, 163–164.

strain[1], *n.* **1** one's lineage; pedigree: ". . . praise his most vicious strain,/ And call it excellent." *Timon,* IV, iii, 215–216. **2** kind or type: "And other strains of woe, which now seem woe . . ." *Sonn 90,* 13.

strain[2], *n.* **1** impulse or tendency: "As love is full of unbefitting strains . . ." *Love's L,* V, ii, 752. **2** (in music) melody, passage, or tune: "That strain again! it had a dying fall . . ." *T Night,* I, i, 4. **3** utterance or pronouncement: ". . . do not these high strains/ Of divination in our sister work/ Some touches of remorse?" *Tr & Cr,* II, ii, 114–116. **4 make no strain,** do not doubt: "And in the publication make no strain . . ." *Tr & Cr,* I, iii, 326. **5 strain for strain,** emotion for emotion; here, a musical image: "Measure his woe the length and breadth of mine,/ And let it answer every strain for strain . . ." *M Ado,* V, i, 11–12. —*v.* **6** to exceed the normal limits of; exhaust: "Let us return,/ And strain what other means is left unto us . . ." *Timon,* V, i, 225–226. **7** to degrade, warp, or pervert: "Nor aught so good but, strain'd from that fair use,/ Revolts from true birth . . ." *Rom & Jul,* II, iii, 15–16. **8** to embrace: "Our king has all the Indies in his arms . . . when he strains that lady . . ." *Hen 8,* IV, i, 45–46. **9** to transgress: "With what encounter so uncurrent I/ Have strain'd t'appear thus . . ." *W Tale,* III, ii, 49–50.

strained, *adj.* **1** constrained; forced: "The quality [nature] of mercy is not strain'd . . ." *Merch,* IV, i, 180. **2** exaggerated or excessive: ". . . with strain'd pride/ To come betwixt our sentence and our power . . ." *Lear,* I, i, 169–170. **3** refined: "Cressid, I love thee in so strain'd a purity . . ." *Tr & Cr,* IV, iv, 23.

strait, *adj.* **1** niggardly [lit., narrow]: "I beg cold comfort; and you are so strait . . . you deny me that." *K John,* V, vii, 42–43. **2** strict; demanding: "His means most short, his creditors most strait." *Timon,* I, i, 99. —*adv.* **3** strictly; rigorously: "Proceed no straiter 'gainst our uncle Gloucester . . ." *2 Hen 6,* III, ii, 19. —*v.* **4 be straited for,** find it difficult to make: "If your lass . . . call this/ Your lack of love or bounty, you were straited/ For a reply . . ." *W Tale,* IV, iv, 353–356.

straitly, *adv.* strictly: "His Majesty hath straitly given in charge . . ." *Rich 3,* I, i, 85.

straitness, *n.* **straitness of his proceeding,** strictness of his judicial procedures: "If his own life answer the straitness of his proceeding,/ it shall become him well . . ." *Meas*, III, ii, 249–250.

strait strossers, *n.* tight trousers; here, underpants [continuing the sexual innuendo]: ". . . like a kern of Ireland, your French hose/ off, and in your strait strossers." *Hen 5*, III, vii, 54–55.

Strand, *n.* area of fashionable shops and fine residences in London, along the City [north] bank of the Thames: ". . . some forty truncheoners . . . which were the hope o'th'Strand where she was quarter'd . . ." *Hen 8*, V, iii, 50–52.

strange, *adj.* **1** unfamiliar or unacquainted; ignorant: "I know thee well;/ But in thy fortunes am unlearn'd and strange." *Timon*, IV, iii, 56–57. **2** foreign: ". . . from one Monsieur Berowne, one of the/ strange queen's lords." *Love's L*, IV, ii, 124–125. **3** unusual; also, remarkable or extraordinary: "We will with some strange pastime solace them,/ Such as the shortness of the time can shape . . ." *Love's L*, IV, iii, 373–374. **4** uneasy or hesitant; reluctant: "I see a strange confession in thine eye." *2 Hen 4*, I, i, 94. **5** aloof; distant: "Ay, ay, Antipholus, look strange and frown . . ." *Errors*, II, ii, 110. **6** reserved; shy: ". . . till strange love grow bold,/ Think true love acted simple modesty." *Rom & Jul*, III, ii, 15–16. **7** new or fresh: ". . . your reasons at dinner/ have been . . . strange without heresy." *Love's L*, V, i, 2–6. **8** foolish: "Strong reasons make strange actions." *K John*, III, iii, 182. **9 strange and strange,** most strange [an intensive]: "That Angelo is an adulterous thief . . . Is it not strange, and strange?" *Meas*, V, i, 42–44.

strange flies, *n.* parasites; fellows who affect fashionable manners and dress: "Why, is/ not this a lamentable thing, grandsire, that we/ should be thus afflicted with these strange flies . . ." *Rom & Jul*, II, iv, 30–32.

strangely, *adv.* **1** in the manner of a stranger: "Against that time when thou shalt strangely pass . . ." *Sonn 49*, 5. **2** wonderfully; remarkably: ". . . thy vexations/ Were but my trials of thy love, and thou/ Hast strangely stood the test . . ." *Temp*, IV, i, 5–7.

strangeness, *n.* aloofness or pretense: ". . . ungird thy/ strangeness, and tell me what I shall vent to my/ lady." *T Night*, IV, i, 15–17.

stranger, *n.* **1** foreigner: "But, gentle sir, methinks/ you walk like a stranger." *Shrew*, II, i, 85–86. **2** person whose past mistakes have been stricken from the record: "Let him approach/ A stranger, no offender . . ." *All's W*, V, iii, 25–26.
—*adj.* **3** foreign; strange: ". . . he hath/ framed a letter to a sequent of the stranger queen's . . ." *Love's L*, IV, ii, 132–133.

stranger companies, *n.* the company [companionship] of strangers: ". . . thence from Athens turn away our eyes,/ To seek new friends, and stranger companies." *M N Dream*, I, i, 218–219.

stranger sense, *n.* stranger's ear: ". . . she/ thought . . . they touch'd not any/ stranger sense." *All's W*, I, iii, 104–106.

strangest, *n.* most editions have "strangeness" [estrangement]: "He shall in strangest stand no farther off/ Than in a politic distance." *Oth*, III, iii, 12–13.

strangle, *v.* to conceal or suppress: "Alas, it is the baseness of thy fear/ That makes thee strangle thy propriety [true self]." *T Night*, V, i, 144–145.

strangled, *past part.* hanged: "And you three shall be strangled on the gallows." *2 Hen 6*, II, iii, 8.

strappado, *n.* cruel form of torture: ". . . and I were at/ the strappado, or all the racks in the world, I would/ not tell you . . ." *1 Hen 4*, II, iv, 231–233.

stratagem, *n.* **1** deed of violence or bloodshed: "Every minute now/ Should be the father of some stratagem." *2 Hen 4*, I, i, 7–8. **2** [usually pl.] **a.** the art of planning military campaigns: ". . . stratagems forepast with iron pens/ Are texted in thine honourable face." *Edw 3*, IV, iv, 129–130. **b.** tricks, plots, or conspiracies: "Alack, alack, that heaven should practise stratagems/ Upon so soft a subject as myself." *Rom & Jul*, III, v, 209–210.

straw, *n.* trifle: ". . . twenty thousand ducats/ Will not debate the question of this straw!" *Ham*, IV, iv, 25–26.

strawy, *adj.* weak as straw: ". . . the strawy Greeks . . . Fall down before him like a mower's swath." *Tr & Cr*, V, v, 24–25.

stray, *n.* **1** stragglers (used collectively): "Strike up our drums, pursue the scatter'd stray . . ." *2 Hen 4*, IV, ii, 120.
—*v.* **2** to wander; roam: ". . . he hath lost his fellows,/ And strays about to find 'em." *Temp*, I, ii, 419–420.

streak, *v.* to paint or daub; smear: "And with the juice of this I'll streak her eyes . . ." *M N Dream*, II, i, 257.

strength, *n.* **1** power or influence: ". . . make your own purpose,/ How in my strength you please [using my authority in any way you like]." *Lear*, II, i, 111–112. **2 strength of all thy state,** all your strength, as well as the power of your position: "How many gazers mightst thou lead away [astray],/ If thou wouldst use the strength of all thy state!" *Sonn 96*, 11–12. **3 strength of limit,** strength that a woman recovers in a prescribed period after childbirth: ". . . hurried/ Here . . . before/ I have got strength of limit." *W Tale*, III, ii, 104–106.

4 strengths by strengths do fail, power must always give way to greater power: "Rights by rights falter, strengths by strengths do fail." *Cor,* IV, vii, 55.

stretch, *v.* **1** to carry out (an assignment) to the best of one's ability: ". . . twenty silly-ducking observants,/ That stretch their duties nicely." *Lear,* II, ii, 104–105. **2** to extend forward; stretch out; here, ref. to the hand and an act of conciliation: "Go to them, with this bonnet in thy hand,/ And thus far having stretch'd it . . ." *Cor,* III, ii, 73–74. **3** to be extended or drawn out: "There's not a minute of our lives should stretch/ Without some pleasure now." *Ant & Cleo,* I, i, 46–47. **4 stretch it out,** extend [to him] the means that we do have: "Rather our state's defective for requital [lacks means to requite adequately]/ Than we to stretch it out." *Cor,* II, ii, 50–51.

stretched, *adj.* **1** strained: ". . . find sport in their intents,/ Extremely stretch'd and conn'd with cruel pain . . ." *M N Dream,* V, i, 79–80. **2** exaggerated: ". . . a poet's rage/ And stretched metre [strains] of an antique song . . ." *Sonn 17,* 12.

stretch-mouthed, *adj.* foul-mouthed: ". . . where some stretch-mouthed rascal would . . . mean mischief and break a foul gap into/ the matter . . ." *W Tale,* IV, iv, 198–200.

strew, *v.* **1** to give out; plant [in fig. sense]: "And he supposes me travell'd to Poland;/ For so I have strew'd it in the common ear . . ." *Meas,* I, iii, 14–15. **2** to strew flowers on: "I thought thy bride-bed to have deck'd . . . And not have strew'd thy grave." *Ham,* V, i, 238–239.

strewings, *n.* rushes used as a floor covering: "Enter Daughter [with strewings]." *Kinsmen,* [SD] II, i, 14.

strewments, *n. pl.* flowers strewn on the corpse of a maiden: "Yet here she is allow'd her virgin crants,/ Her maiden strewments . . ." *Ham,* V, i, 225–226.

stricken, *past part.,* old usage for **struck;** here, of course, an anachronism: "Peace! count the clock."/ "The clock hath stricken three." *J Caes,* II, i, 192.

strict, *adj.* **1** exact or precise; also, impartial: ". . . we of the off'ring side/ Must keep aloof from strict arbitrement . . ." *1 Hen 4,* IV, i, 69–70. **2** severe; harsh or cruel: "That the strict fates had pleas'd you had brought her hither . . ." *Per,* III, iii, 8. **3** tight; close: "She wildly breaketh from their strict embrace . . ." *Ven & Ad,* 874.

stricture, *n.* strict living: "A man of stricture and firm abstinence—" *Meas,* I, iii, 12.

stride a limit, *v.* to cross a boundary; overstep prescribed limits: "A prison, or a debtor that not dares/ To stride a limit." *Cymb,* III, iii, 34–35.

strife, *n.* **1** intense effort: "But if thou meanest not well/ I do beseech thee . . . To cease thy strife and leave me to my grief." *Rom & Jul,* II, ii, 150–152. **2** dispute or quarrel: "I pray, my lords, let me compound [settle] this strife." *2 Hen 6,* II, i, 59. **3** contention; rivalry: "Now stay your strife; what shall be is dispatch'd." *T Andr,* III, i, 192. **4 at strife,** striving to outdo herself: "Nature that made thee with herself at strife . . ." *Ven & Ad,* 11. **5 the painter's strife,** great effort by the painter to duplicate nature: "The red blood reek'd to show the painter's strife . . ." *Luc,* 1377.

strike, *v.* **1** to commit a robbery: ". . . such as will strike sooner than/ speak, and speak sooner than drink . . ." *1 Hen 4,* II, i, 76–77. **2** to exert evil or fatal influences: "The nights are wholesome, then no planets strike . . ." *Ham,* I, i, 167. **3** to punish: "Prince, pardon me, or strike me, if you please . . ." *Per,* I, ii, 47. **4** to warn or alert: ". . . your maw . . . should be your clock,/ And strike you home [remind you with rumblings] without a messenger." *Errors,* I, ii, 66–67. **5** to fight [either fight with us or avoid hitting us]: "We have met with foes/ That strike beside us." *Mac,* V, vii, 28–29. **6** to lower sails (in double sense with "to strike a blow"): "We see the wind sit sore upon our sails,/ And yet we strike not . . ." *Rich 2,* II, i, 265–266. **7** to complete a stroke; also, perh. ref. to the incessant grinding noise made by the rotating wheel: ". . . thou didst vent thy groans/ As fast as mill-wheels strike." *Temp,* I, ii, 280–281. **8** to impress: ". . . and in the mature time/ With this ungracious paper strike the sight/ Of the death-practis'd Duke." *Lear,* IV, vi, 277–279. **9** to affect or afflict: ". . . high events as these/ Strike those that make them . . ." *Ant & Cleo,* V, ii, 358–359. **10 strike into the hazard,** to capture in the bargain: "We will in France . . . play a set/ Shall strike his father's crown into the hazard." *Hen 5,* I, ii, 262–263. **11 strike sail,** See **sail** (def. 6). **12 strikes more,** causes more damage: ". . . for Pompey's name strikes more/ Than could his war resisted [forces met by our opposition]." *Ant & Cleo,* I, iv, 54–55.

striker, *n.* (in thieves' jargon) a pickpocket or purse-cutter: "I am joined with no foot-landrakers,/ no long-staff sixpenny strikers . . ." *1 Hen 4,* II, i, 72–73.

string, *n.* **1** [pl.] cords for attaching actor's false beards: "Get your apparel together, good/ strings to your beards, new ribbons to your pumps . . ." *M N Dream,* IV, ii, 33–34. **2** stringed musical instrument; also, the music produced by such an instrument: "And here have I the daintiness of ear/ To check time broke in a disordered string . . ." *Rich 2,* V, v, 45–46.

strip, *v.* **1** to downplay or downgrade (something); belittle: ". . . you the purpose cherish/ Whiles thus you mock it! how, in stripping it,/ You more invest it!" *Temp,* II, i, 219–221. **2** to uncover; pull back: "Then will he strip his sleeve and show his scars . . ." *Hen 5,* IV, iii, 47. **3 strip your sword,** unsheathe your sword: ". . . therefore on, or strip your sword stark naked:/ for meddle you must . . ." *T Night,* III, iv, 254–255.

stripes, *n. pl.* lash marks; here, a beating: "Thou most lying slave,/ Whom stripes may move, not kindness!" *Temp,* I, ii, 346–347.

strive, *v.* **1** to put up a fight; struggle or resist: "But if thou strive, poor soul, what art thou then?" *Love's L,* IV, i, 93–94. **2 strive in,** to excel in both: ". . . so rich, that it did strive/ In workmanship and value . . ." *Cymb,* II, iv, 73–74. **3 strive to,** to contend with; struggle against: "Where zeal strives to content, and the contents/ Dies in the zeal of that which it presents . . ." *Love's L,* V, ii, 513–514. **4 strive upon,** to agitate: ". . . daughter and mother/ So strive upon your pulse." *All's W,* I, iii, 163–164.

stroke, *v.,* old past and past part. of **strike. 1** to show disrespect for: "Marcus, even thou hast stroke upon my crest . . ." *T Andr,* I, i, 364. **2** to hit, prob. with bow and arrow: ". . . hast not thou full often stroke a doe,/ And borne her cleanly by the keeper's nose?" *T Andr,* II, i, 93–94. **3** (in music) to play or perform: ". . . the drum that stroke the lusty march/ Stands with Prince Edward, your thrice valiant son." *Edw 3,* II, ii, 73–74.
—*n.* **4** [sometimes pl.] cut, slash, or thrust with a sword, dagger, spear, etc.: "Good words are better than bad strokes, Octavius." *J Caes,* V, i, 29. **5** blow of the fist: "Beating your officers, cursing yourselves,/ Opposing laws with strokes . . ." *Cor,* III, iii, 79–80. **6** [pl.] the action of war: "But certain issue strokes must arbitrate . . ." *Mac,* V, iv, 20. **7 humbled to all strokes,** forced to accept the dealings of Fortune: ". . . thou whom the heav'ns' plagues/ Have humbled to all strokes . . ." *Lear,* IV, i, 64–65.

stroke and line, *n.* strokes of Angelo's pen, which create severe acts of justice: ". . . his life is parallel'd/ Even with the stroke and line of his great justice." *Meas,* IV, ii, 77–78.

strond, *n.* var. of **strand**; shore: ". . . new broils/ To be commenc'd in stronds afar remote." *1 Hen 4,* I, i, 3–4.

strong, *adj.* **1** forcible: ". . . I wot not by what strong escape,/ He broke from those that had the guard of him . . ." *Errors,* V, i, 148–149. **2** victorious: "I strong o'er them, and you o'er me being strong . . ." *Lover's Comp,* 257.

strook, *v.* old past tense of **strike;** struck: "This said, he strook his hand upon his breast . . ." *Luc,* 1842.

strooken, *v.* old past part. of **strike;** struck: "Bows not his vassal head, and strooken blind,/ Kisses the base ground with obedient breast?" *Love's L,* IV, iii, 220–221.

stroy'd, *past part.* destroyed: ". . . what I have left behind/ Stroy'd in dishonour." *Ant & Cleo,* III, xi, 53–54.

struck, *v.* past part. of **strike. 1** advanced: "Myself am struck in years, I must confess . . ." *Shrew,* II, i, 353. **2** fought: "When Cressy battle fatally was struck . . ." *Hen 5,* II, iv, 54. **3 well struck in years,** wisely mature, yet not old: ". . . we say the King/ Is wise and virtuous, and his noble Queen/ Well struck in years . . ." *Rich 3,* I, i, 90–92.

strucken, *v.* **1** old and rare form of **struck:** "The clock hath strucken twelve upon the bell . . ." *Errors,* I, ii, 45.
—*adj.* **2** stricken; wounded: "Why, let the strucken deer go weep . . ." *Ham,* III, ii, 265.

strumpet, *n.* **1** likened to a strumpet because of its [her] changeableness: "Out, out, thou strumpet Fortune!" *Ham,* II, ii, 489.
—*adj.* **2** fickle; untrustworthy: "Hugg'd and embraced by the strumpet wind!" *Merch,* II, vi, 16.

strumpeted, *past. part.* **1** turned into a strumpet; defiled or debauched: "I do digest the poison of thy flesh,/ Being strumpeted by thy contagion." *Errors,* II, ii, 143–144. **2** dishonored; also, defamed or slandered: "And maiden virtue rudely strumpeted . . ." *Sonn 66,* 6.

stubborn, *adj.* **1** haughty; arrogant: ". . . some stubborn and uncourteous parts/ We had conceiv'd against him." *T Night,* V, i, 360–361. **2** rough; rude; harsh: "You stubborn ancient knave, you reverend braggart . . ." *Lear,* II, ii, 127. **3** prob. ref. to the Jews' continued rejection of Christianity: "Renowned for their deeds as far from home . . . As is the sepulchre in stubborn Jewry . . ." *Rich 2,* II, i, 53–55.

stuck, *n.* **1** thrust; here, of a poisoned rapier: "If he by chance escape your venom'd stuck . . ." *Ham,* IV, vii, 160. **2 stuck in,** sword thrust to the body; a thrust home: ". . . he gives me the stuck in/ with such a mortal motion that it is inevitable [inescapable] . . ." *T Night,* III, iv, 280–281.

studied, *adj.* rehearsed; carefully prepared: "As one that had been studied in his death . . ." *Mac,* I, iv, 9.

study, *n.* **1** intention; purpose: "I care not if I have. It is my study." *As You,* V, ii, 78. **2** [often pl.] an endeavor or effort: "All studies here I solemnly defy . . ." *1 Hen 4,* I, iii, 225. **3** field of specialized study: "I'll talk a word with this same learned Theban./ What is your study?" *Lear,* III, iv, 161–162. **4 be slow of study,** (of an actor) to have difficulty learning lines:

"Have you the lion's part written? . . . give it me; for I am slow of study." *M N Dream,* I, ii, 62–63.
—*v.* **5** to be intent on: "Sir, I shall study deserving." *Lear,* I, i, 31.

study of imagination, *n.* contemplation or reflection: "Th'idea of her life shall sweetly creep/ Into his study of imagination . . ." *M Ado,* IV, i, 224–225.

stuff, *n.* **1** baggage; effects: "Therefore away, to get our stuff aboard." *Errors,* IV, iv, 156. **2** raw material: ". . . nature wants [lacks] stuff/ To vie strange forms with fancy . . ." *Ant & Cleo,* V, ii, 97–98. **3** merchandise; here, prostitutes for hire: "The stuff we have, a strong wind/ will blow it to pieces . . ." *Per,* IV, ii, 17–18.

stuffed, *adj.* suffering with a headcold; stuffed up; Margaret answers with sense of "sexually penetrated": "I am stuffed, cousin, I cannot smell."/ "A maid, and stuffed!" *M Ado,* III, iv, 59.

stuffed sufficiency, *n.* unquestioned ability: "Cleomenes and Dion, whom you know/ Of stuff'd sufficiency . . ." *W Tale,* II, i, 184–185.

stumbling, *adj.* causing stumbling [due to darkness]: ". . . an hour or two before/ The stumbling night did part our weary powers?" *K John,* V, v, 17–18.

stump, *n.* wordplay on "stump of a tooth" and "penis": "Your colt's tooth is not cast yet?"/ "No my lord,/ Nor shall not while I have a stump." *Hen 8,* I, iii, 48–49.

stuprum, *n.* [Latin] rape: "*Stuprum. Chiron, Demetrius.*"/ "What, what! the lustful sons of Tamora/ Performers of this heinous, bloody deed?" *T Andr,* IV, i, 78–80.

sturdy, *adj.* brutish and rebellious: "My lords, look where the sturdy rebel sits . . ." *3 Hen 6,* I, i, 50.

sty, *n.* **1** royal bed of Denmark likened to a pigsty because of its licentiousness: "Stew'd in corruption, honeying and making love/ Over the nasty sty!" *Ham,* III, iv, 93–94.
—*v.* **2** to keep in or confine to a sty: ". . . here you sty me/ In this hard rock, whiles you do keep from me/ The rest o' th' island." *Temp,* I, ii, 344–346.

Stygian, *adj.* of the river Styx: "Like a strange soul upon the Stygian banks/ Staying for waftage [waiting for passage]." *Tr & Cr,* III, ii, 8–9.

style, *n.* **1** title or designation: "Am I a queen in title and in style,/ And must be made a subject to a duke?" *2 Hen 6,* I, iii, 48–49. **2** poss. "title" or "reputation"; most editors read this as *soyle,* "soil," native land: "Renounce your style, give sheep

in lions' stead . . ." *1 Hen 6,* I, v, 29. **3** wordplay with "stile" [steps]: ". . . be it as the style shall give us cause to/ climb in the merriness." *Love's L,* I, i, 197–198.

Styx, *n.* (in classical myth.) river of Hades, which the dead could not cross without a suitable burial: "Why suffer'st thou thy sons, unburied yet,/ To hover on the dreadful shore of Styx?" *T Andr,* I, i, 87–88.

sub-contracted, *adj.* betrothed: "'Tis she is sub-contracted to this lord,/ And I, her husband, contradict your banes [banns]." *Lear,* V, iii, 87–88.

subdue, *v.* **1** to reduce: "And almost thence my nature is subdued/ To what it works in . . ." *Sonn 111,* 6–7. **2** to cause to suffer punishment: "To make him worthy whose offence subdues him . . ." *Cor,* I, i, 174.

subduement, *n.* man taken prisoner in combat: ". . . I have seen thee,/ spur thy Phrygian steed,/ Despising many forfeits and subduements . . ." *Tr & Cr,* IV, v, 184–186.

subject, *n.* **1** subjects collectively: "So nightly toils the subject of the land . . ." *Ham,* I, i, 75. **2** inhabitants: "How from the finny subject of the sea . . ." *Per,* II, i, 48. **3 the subject,** my subjects: "Give we our hand,/ And let the subject see . . ." *Meas,* V, i, 14–15.

subjected, *adj.* plays on the meanings (1) vulnerable or liable to (such human needs) and (2) made a subject (in this way): "I live with bread . . . need friends—subjected thus,/ How can you say to me, I am a king?" *Rich 2,* III, ii, 175–177.

submission, *n.* admission of fault: "Find pardon on my true submission." *1 Hen 4,* III, ii, 28.

suborn, *v.* **1** to induce; compel; instigate: "What peer hath been suborn'd to grate on you . . ." *2 Hen 4,* IV, i, 90. **2** to hire to commit a treacherous deed: "What good could they pretend?"/ "They were suborn'd." *Mac,* II, iv, 24. **3 suborn'd the witness,** misunderstood Othello's behavior: "But now I find I had suborn'd the witness,/ And he's indicted falsely." *Oth,* III, iv, 151–152.

subornation, *n.* instigation to treason or other wrongdoing: "The Duchess by his subornation . . . began her devilish practices . . ." *2 Hen 6,* III, i, 45–46.

suborned informer, *n.* paid spy; here, the constant threat of jealousy: "Hence, thou suborn'd informer! a true soul/ When most impeach'd stands least in thy control." *Sonn 125,* 13–14.

subscribe, *v.* **1** to agree; here, to submit or acquiesce [lit., to sign one's name to an agreement]: "If I have fewest, I subscribe in silence." *1 Hen 6,* II, iv, 44. **2** to vouch (for): ". . . my uncle's fool, reading the/ challenge, subscribed for Cupid . . ." *M Ado*, I, i, 36–37. **3** to proclaim or denounce in writing: ". . . I must /shortly hear from him, or I will subscribe him a coward." *M Ado*, V, ii, 54–55. **4** to enter the amount on (a document): ". . . when they shall know what men are rich,/ They shall sub- scribe them [i.e., the charters] for large sums of gold . . ." *Rich 2*, I, iv, 49–50. **5** to acknowledge; admit or confess: ". . . but when I had subscrib'd/ to mine own fortune [married status], and inform'd her fully . . ." *All's W*, V, iii, 96–97. **6** to second; endorse: "Will you subscribe his thought, and say he is?" *Tr & Cr*, II, iii, 149. **7** to submit or yield to: "My love looks fresh, and death to me subscribes . . ." *Sonn 107*, 10. **8** to yield to pity or compassion: "All cruels else subscribe: but I shall see/ The winged vengeance overtake such children." *Lear*, III, vii, 64–65.

subscription, *n.* loyalty; allegiance: "I never gave you king- dom, call'd you children,/ You owe me no subscription . . ." *Lear*, III, ii, 17–18.

subsidy, *n.* tax on property, levied for a special purpose: ". . . he that made us pay . . . one shilling to the pound, the last subsidy." *2 Hen 6*, IV, vii, 19–21.

substance, *n.* wealth; property: "Thy substance, valued at the highest rate,/ Cannot amount unto a hundred marks . . ." *Er- rors*, I, i, 23–24.

substitute, *v.* **1** to delegate; send as deputy: "But who is sub- stituted 'gainst the French/ I have no certain notice." *2 Hen 4*, I, iii, 84–85.
—*n.* **2** the deputy Angelo: "How will you do to content/ this substitute, and to save your brother?" *Meas*, III, i, 186–187. **3** God's deputy, the king: "You have ta'en up,/ Under the coun- terfeited zeal of God,/ The subjects of his substitute, my fa- ther . . ." *2 Hen 4*, IV, ii, 26–28.

substractor, *n.* prob. misuse for "detractor": ". . . they are scoundrels and substractors/ that say so of him." *T Night*, I, iii, 34–35.

subtle, *adj.* **1** sly; clever or cunning: "A subtle knave! But yet it shall not serve." *2 Hen 6*, II, i, 104. **2** crafty or decep- tive; treacherous: "Go, suck the subtle blood o' th' grape . . ." *Timon*, IV, iii, 432. **3** fine; delicate: "Admits no orifex for a point as subtle/ As Ariachne's broken woof to enter." *Tr & Cr*, V, ii, 150–151. **4** (of ground) not as level as it would appear: "Like to a bowl upon a subtle ground . . ." *Cor*, V, ii, 20.

suburbs, *n. pl.* ref. to the outskirts of London, where brothels flourished: "Dwell I but in the suburbs/ of your good plea- sure?" *J Caes*, II, i, 285–286.

subversion, *n.* overthrow; here, destruction: ". . . these great lords . . . Do seek subversion of thy harmless life?" *2 Hen 6*, III, i, 207–208.

succeed, *v.* **1** to inherit; also, pass on to succeeding genera- tions: "If not a feodary but only he/ Owe and succeed thy weakness." *Meas*, II, iv, 122–123. **2** follow; occur subsequent- ly: "Bethought me what was past, what might succeed." *Per*, I, ii, 83.
—*past part.* **3** prob. abridgment of "succeeded": "Let us en- treat, by honour of his name/ Whom worthily you would have now succeed . . ." *T Andr*, I, i, 39–40.

succeeding, *adj.* coming after; later: "To the succeeding royal- ty he leaves/ The healing benediction." *Mac*, IV, iii, 155–156.

success, *n.* **1** succession: "And so success of mischief shall be born . . ." *2 Hen 4*, IV, ii, 47. **2** result or outcome: "Caesar and Lepidus have made wars upon Pompey."/ "This is old, what is the success?" *Ant & Cleo*, III, v, 4–5.

successantly, *adv.* See **incessantly**.

successfully, *adv.* in a way that suggests success: "Alas, he is too young. Yet he looks successfully." *As You*, I, ii, 143.

succession, *n.* **1** rights of inheritance: ". . . no kind of traffic [business]/ Would I admit . . . contract, succession,/ Bourn, bound of land, tilth, vineyard, none . . ." *Temp*, II, i, 144–148. **2** action of generating heirs; here, one slander begetting oth- ers in an unbroken line: "For slander lives upon succession,/ For e'er hous'd where it gets possession [a foothold]." *Errors*, III, i, 105–106. **3** future to which one is most likely to suc- ceed: ". . . their writers do them wrong to make them/ exclaim against their own succession?" *Ham*, II, ii, 348–349. **4 dis- suade succession,** to prevent others [girls] from following the same course: ". . . cannot/ for all that dissuade succession, but that they are/ limed with the twigs that threatens them." *All's W*, III, v, 22–24. **5 to the succession of new days,** from one day to the next: ". . . he hath put me off/ To the succession of new days this month." *Timon*, II, ii, 22–23.

successive, *adj.* having the right to succeed: "Plead my suc- cessive title with your swords . . ." *T Andr*, I, i, 4.

succor, *n.* [usually pl.] additional troops; reinforcements: "Send succours, lords, and stop the rage betime . . ." *2 Hen 6*, III, i, 285.

such another, *n.* See **another**.

such a one, Olivia amusingly uses (and combines) terms used in dating pictures and letters: ". . . such/ a one I was this pres- ent." *T Night*, I, v, 237–238.

sucking dove, *n.* appar. confusion of "sitting dove" with "suckling pig" or "sucking lamb": ". . . I will roar you as gently as any sucking/ dove . . ." *M N Dream,* I, ii, 77–78.

sudden, *adj.* **1** rash or violent: "Luxurious, avaricious, false, deceitful,/ Sudden, malicious, smacking of every sin . . ." *Mac,* IV, iii, 58–59. **2** soon; early: "Tomorrow, in my judgement, is too sudden . . ." *Rich 3,* III, iv, 43. **3 on the sudden,** suddenly: "On the sudden,/ I warrant him consul." *Cor,* II, i, 219–220. **4 to the sudden time,** for this emergency: ". . . broke out/ To acquaint you with this evil, that you might/ The better arm you to the sudden time . . ." *K John,* V, vi, 24–26. —*adv.* **5** rashly: "But pardon me, I am too sudden-bold . . ." *Love's L,* II, i, 106.

suddenly, *adv.* **1** at once; immediately; promptly: "Do this suddenly;/ And let not search and inquisition quail . . ." *As You,* II, ii, 19–20. **2** extemporaneously: "If thou canst accuse/ Or aught intend'st to lay unto my charge,/ Do it without invention, suddenly . . ." *1 Hen 6,* III, i, 3–5.

sue, *v.* **1** to lay legal claim to: "I am denied to sue my livery here . . ." *Rich 2,* II, iii, 128. **2** to initiate either a legal suit or one's suit as a lover [used in puns]: "For how can this be true,/ That you stand forfeit, being those that sue?" *Love's L,* V, ii, 426–427. **3** to beg: "We were not born to sue, but to command . . ." *Rich 2,* I, i, 196. **4** to seek; look forward: "I must love you, and sue to know you better." *Lear,* I, i, 30. **5 sued staying,** begged to be allowed to stay: ". . . when you sued staying,/ Then was the time for words . . ." *Ant & Cleo,* I, iii, 33–34.

sued-for, *adj.* sought-after or begged-for: "Of [upon] him that did not ask but mock, bestow/ Your sued-for tongues?" *Cor,* II, iii, 205–206.

suffer, *v.* **1** to allow: "He that hath suffered this disordered spring/ Hath now himself met with the fall of leaf." *Rich 2,* III, iv, 48–49. **2** to let (someone) have his/her own way: "What, will you not suffer me? Nay, now I see/ She is your treasure . . ." *Shrew,* II, i, 31–32. **3** to put up with: ". . . who sways;, not as it hath power, but as it is/ suffer'd [simply because we allow him to dominate us]." *Lear,* I, ii, 51–52. **4** to suffer death: ". . . an islander, that hath lately suffered by a thunderbolt." *Temp,* II, ii, 36–37. **5** to be affected; alter: "It suffers not in smiling pomp . . ." *Sonn 124,* 6. **6 suffer the report,** be told or divulged: ". . . 'twas a contention in public,/ which may (without contradiction) suffer the report." *Cymb,* I, v, 51–52.

sufferance, *n.* **1** suffering; pain: ". . . they have writ the style of gods,/ And made a push at chance and sufferance." *M Ado,* V, i, 37–38. **2** patience: "England [Henry] shall repent his/ folly, see his weakness, and admire our sufferance." *Hen 5,* III, vi, 128–129. **3** endurance: "If not a present remedy, at least a patient sufferance." *M Ado,* I, iii, 8. **4** enforced duty: "Your last service was suff'rance—'twas not/ voluntary . . ." *Tr & Cr,* II, i, 97–98. **5 against all noble sufferance,** beyond all endurance by the nobility: ". . . they do prank them in authority,/ Against all noble sufferance." *Cor,* III, i, 23–24. **6 slight in sufferance,** lax in tolerating [her actions]: "Call her before us, for/ We have been too slight in sufferance." *Cymb,* III, v, 33–34. **7 sufferance panging,** suffering as painful: ". . . 'tis a sufferance panging/ As soul and body's severing." *Hen 8,* II, iii, 15–16.

suffered, *adj.* **1** allowed to do something: "So did your son;/ He was so suffer'd; so came I a widow . . ." *2 Hen 4,* II, iii, 56–57. **2** (of a dog) let loose; here, allowed to attack: "Who, being suffer'd, with the bear's fell paw/ Hath clapp'd his tail between his legs and cried . . ." *2 Hen 6,* V, i, 153–154. **3 suffered labor,** the strenuous effort forced upon the mariners: "Who, with a charm join'd to their suffer'd labour,/ I have left asleep . . ." *Temp,* I, ii, 231–232.

suffering, *adj.* agreeable or tolerant; permissive: ". . . either he so undertaking,/ Or they so suffering . . ." *Cymb,* IV, ii, 142–143.

suffice, *v.* to satisfy: ". . . till he be first suffic'd . . . I will not touch a bit." *As You,* II, vii, 131–133.

sufficiency, *n.* ability or fitness: "Then no more remains/ But that, to your sufficiency, as your worth is able . . ." *Meas,* I, i, 7–8.

sufficient, *adj.* **1** fit or able-bodied; qualified: "Have you provided/ me here half a dozen sufficient men?" *2 Hen 4,* III, ii, 92–93. **2** of ample means; wealthy: ". . . to have you understand me that he is sufficient . . ." *Merch,* I, iii, 14.

suffigance, *adj.* misuse for **sufficient:** "It shall be suffigance." *M Ado,* III, v, 48.

suffocate, *past part.* **1** wordplay on "Suffolk" and "suffocated": "For Suffolk's duke, may he be suffocate . . ." *2 Hen 6,* I, 1, 123. **2** stifled: "This chaos, when degree is suffocate,/ Follows the choking . . ." *Tr & Cr,* I, iii, 125–126.

suffrage, *n.* vote: "People of Rome . . . I ask your voices and your suffrages . . ." *T Andr,* I, i, 217–218.

sugar, *v.* **sugar o'er,** to give a pleasingly deceptive appearance to: ". . . with devotion's visage/ And pious action we do sugar o'er/ The devil himself." *Ham,* III, i, 47–49.

sugar'd, *adj.* attractive or enticing: ". . . followed/ The sugar'd game before thee." *Timon,* IV, iii, 260–261.

sugarsop, *n.* delicacy of sweetened and spiced bread soaked in wine, milk, etc.; here, the name of a servant: "Call forth Nathaniel, Joseph, Nicholas, Philip,/ Walter, Sugarsop, and the rest." *Shrew,* IV, i, 79–80.

sugar touch, *n.* sweet taste: "You have witchcraft in your lips, Kate: there is/ more eloquence in a sugar touch of them . . ." *Hen 5,* V, ii, 292–293.

suggest, *v.* **1** to tempt or lure: "I give thee not this to/ suggest thee from thy master . . ." *All's W,* IV, v, 41–42. **2** to prompt; incite: ". . . disturbing jealousy . . . Gives false alarms, suggesteth mutiny . . ." *Ven & Ad,* 649–651.

suggestion, *n.* **1** [often pl.] temptation: "Suggestions are to other as to me;/ But I believe . . . I am the last that will keep his oath." *Love's L,* I, i, 157–159. **2** tempting or enticing of others, esp. to treason or disloyalty; instigation: ". . . pardon absolute for yourself, and these/ Herein misled by your suggestion." *1 Hen 4,* IV, iii, 50–51. **3** underhand dealings: ". . . one that by suggestion/ Tied all the kingdom . . ." *Hen 8,* IV, ii, 35–36.

suit, *v.* **1** to act in accordance (with): ". . . humbly prays you/ That with your other noble parts you'll suit,/ In giving him his right." *Timon,* II, i, 25–27. **2** to wear; dress: "And suit thy pity like in every part." *Sonn 132,* 12. **3 suit with,** to match: ". . . such a one whose wrongs do suit with mine." *M Ado,* V, i, 7.
—*n.* **4** petition: ". . . she will admit no kind of suit,/ No, not the Duke's." *T Night,* I, ii, 45–46. **5** lover's wooing; courtship: ". . . she mocks all her wooers out of suit." *M Ado,* II, i, 327–328. **6** pleas; insistence: ". . . he would miss it rather/ Than carry it but by the suit of the gentry to him/ And the desire of the nobles." *Cor,* II, i, 235–237. **7 at suit of,** on the entreaty of: ". . . whose life I have/ spar'd at suit of his grey beard,—" *Lear,* II, ii, 62–63. **8 despite of suit,** regardless of [another's] petitions or pleadings: "And not a man of them shall have the grace,/ Despite of suit, to see a lady's face." *Love's L,* V, ii, 128–129. **9 have suit to (someone),** to have a request to make of (someone): "Signior Bassanio! . . . I have suit to you." *Merch,* II, ii, 167–169. **10 in all suits,** in all respects; here, wordplay with "dressed": ". . . see him dress'd in all suits like a lady." *Shrew,* Ind., i, 104. **11 in suit,** by the urging of [my] suit: ". . . to attain/ In suit the place of's bed . . ." *Cymb,* V, v, 184–185. **12 out of suit,** beyond all sense of propriety: "Berowne did swear himself out of all suit." *Love's L,* V, ii, 275. **13 out of suits with,** out of favor with: ". . . one out of suits with fortune,/ That could give more but that her hand lacks means." *As You,* I, ii, 236–237.

suited, *adj.* **1** dressed; appareled: "Such a Sebastian was my brother too:/ So went he suited to his watery tomb." *T Night,* V, i, 231–232. **2** well matched: "Therefore my mistress' brows are raven black,/ Her eyes so suited . . ." *Sonn 127,* 9–10. **3** appropriate: "O dear discretion, how his words are suited!" *Merch,* III, v, 59.

suit of the camp, *n.* soldier's dress; military garb: ". . . a beard of the general's cut and a horrid suit of the camp . . ." *Hen V,* III, vi, 77–78.

suitor, *n.* pronounced "shooter": a favorite pun: "Who is the suitor? . . ."/ "Shall I teach you to know?" *Love's L,* IV, i, 109.

sullen, *adj.* **1** moody; gloomy or dismal: "I love to cope him in these sullen fits . . ." *As You,* II, i, 67. **2** dull or dark: ". . . like bright metal on a sullen ground . . ." *1 Hen 4,* I, ii, 207. **3** mournful; sorrowful: ". . . his tongue/ Sounds ever after as a sullen bell . . ." *2 Hen 4,* I, i, 101–102. **4** incessant; obstinate: "I have a salt and sullen rheum offends me . . ." *Oth,* III, iv, 47. **5 sullen presage,** dismal omen: "Be thou the trumpet of our wrath/ And sullen presage of your own decay." *K John,* I, i, 27–28.
—*n.* **6** [pl.] sulks: "And let them die that age and sullens have . . ." *Rich 2,* II, i, 139.

sullied, *adj.* **1** dark; blackened: "To change your day of youth to sullied night . . ." *Sonn 15,* 12. **2** Sometimes **solid** or **sallied,** soiled or stained: "O that this too too sullied flesh would melt . . ." *Ham,* I, ii, 129.

sully, *n.* [often pl.] blemish; here, an insult or slander: "You laying these slight sullies on my son,/ As 'twere a thing a little soil'd i'th' working . . ." *Ham,* II, i, 40–41.

sulphurous, *adj.* of lightning: ". . . gently quench/ Thy nimble sulphurous flashes!" *Per,* III, i, 5–6.

Sultan Solyman, *n.* Turkish ruler: ". . . a Persian prince/ That won three fields [battles] of Sultan Solyman . . ." *Merch,* II, i, 25–26.

sum, *n.* **1** summary; gist: "Grates [annoys] me, the sum." *Ant & Cleo,* I, i, 18. **2 sum of parts,** *n.* one's accomplishments or talents as a whole: "Your sum of parts/ Did not together pluck such envy from him . . ." *Ham,* IV, vii, 72–73. **3 sum of sums,** a vast amount: ". . . why dost thou use/ So great a sum of sums, yet canst not live?" *Sonn 4,* 7–8.
—*v.* **4** to summarize; be the sum total of: "'This fair child of mine/ Shall sum my count and make my old excuse' . . ." *Sonn 2,* 10–11. **5 cast its sum,** to make a [final] reckoning: "When as thy love hath cast his utmost sum . . ." *Sonn 49,* 3. **6 sum up sum,** to calculate the total: ". . . my true love is grown to such excess/ I cannot sum up sum of half my wealth." *Rom & Jul,* II, vi, 33–34.

sumless, *adj.* incalculable: "With sunken wrack and sumless treasuries." *Hen 5,* I, ii, 165.

summer, *adj.* pleasing: "If't be summer news,/ Smile to't before . . ." *Cymb,* III, iv, 12–13.

summered, *past part.* pastured; hence, nurtured: ". . . for maids,/ well summered, and warm kept [carefully reared], are like flies at/ Bartholomew-tide . . ." *Hen 5,* V, ii, 325–327.

summer-leaping, *adj.* summer as a time of youthful activity: "To music every summer-leaping swain/ Compares his sunburnt lover when she speaks . . ." *Edw 3,* II, I, 108–109.

summer's distillation, *n.* perh. perfume or rosewater: ". . . were not summer's distillation left,/ A liquid prisoner pent in walls of glass . . ." *Sonn 5,* 9–10.

summer-swelling, *adj.* growing in summer's warmth: "Disdain to root the summer-swelling flower . . ." *Two Gent,* II, iv, 157.

summoner, *n.* officer who summoned a person to appear before the ecclesiastical court, usually on a charge of immorality: ". . . close pent-up guilts . . . and cry/ These dreadful summoners grace." *Lear,* III, ii, 57–59.

summons, *n.* need; here, for sleep: "A heavy summons lies like lead upon me,/ And yet I would not sleep . . ." *Mac,* II, i, 6–7.

sumpter, *n.* packhorse: "Persuade me rather to be slave and sumpter/ To this detested groom." *Lear,* II, iv, 218–219.

sun, *n.* **1 at the sun's eye,** when the sun shines [on it]: ". . . their fair leaves spread/ But as the marigold at the sun's eye . . ." *Sonn 25,* 5–6. **2 behold the sun,** ref. to eagle's supposed ability to stare at the sun; Posthumus again is compared in nobility to the eagle: ". . . we had very many/ there could behold the sun with as firm eyes as he." *Cymb,* I, v, 10–11. **3 course of the sun,** a year: ". . . with a backward look,/ Even of five hundred courses of the sun . . ." *Sonn 59,* 5–6. **4 from sun to sun,** from sunrise to sunset (the time allowed for a trial by combat): ". . . full as many lies/ As may be hollowed in thy treacherous ear/ From sun to sun." *Rich 2,* IV, i, 53–55. **5 get the sun of,** to force (enemy troops) to fight with the sun in their eyes; get the advantage of: "Pell-mell, down with them! but be first advis'd,/ In conflict that you get the sun of them." *Love's L,* IV, iii, 364–365. **6 suns of glory,** monarchs; here, the English and French kings: "Those suns of glory . . . Met in the vale of Andren." *Hen 8,* I, i, 6–7. **7 three suns,** vision seen by Richard and Edward and thereafter used by Edward as his emblem: "Whate'er it bodes, henceforward will I bear/ Upon my target [shield] three fair-shining suns." *3 Hen 6,* II, i, 39–40. **8 two**

suns, the eyes: "Why her two suns were cloud-eclipsed so . . ." *Luc,* 1224.

sun-burning, *n.* ref. to sunburned complexions as unattractive: "If thou canst love a fellow of this/ temper, Kate, whose face is not worth sun-burning . . ." *Hen 5,* V, ii, 149–150.

sunburnt or **sunburned,** *adj.* (of a woman) parched or scorched by the sun, hence unattractive and undesirable: "Thus goes everyone to/ the world [marries] but I, and I am sunburnt." *M Ado,* II, i, 299–300.

sunder, *v.* **1** to separate: "Even as a splitted bark so sunder we . . ." *2 Hen 6,* III, ii, 410.
—*n.* **2 in sunder,** in two [parts]: "And so he comes to rend his limbs in sunder." *3 Hen 6,* I, iii, 15.

sun-expelling mask, *n.* mask worn by fashionable ladies to protect the complexion from effects of the sun: ". . . she did neglect her looking-glass,/ And threw her sun-expelling mask away . . ." *Two Gent,* IV, iv, 150–151.

sup, *v.* to give dinner to: "But sup them well, and look unto them all." *Shrew,* Ind., i, 26–27.

superficial, *adj.* dealing with external qualities only: ". . . my good lord, this superficial tale/ Is but a preface of her worthy praise . . ." *1 Hen 6,* V, v, 10–11.

superficially, *adv.* to some extent; slightly: "You know me, do you not?"/ "Faith, sir, superficially." *Tr & Cr,* III, i, 9–10.

superfluity, *n.* **1** something kept in reserve or as a spare: ". . . one for superfluity, and another/ for use!" *2 Hen 4,* II, ii, 17–18. **2** superabundance; great wealth: ". . . superfluity comes sooner by white hairs, but/ competency lives longer." *Merch,* I, ii, 8–9. **3** the rebellious rabble: ". . . we shall ha' means to vent/ Our musty superfluity." *Cor,* I, i, 224–225.

superfluous, *adj.* **1** (of a person) doing more than is necessary or appropriate: "I see no reason why thou shouldst be so superfluous to/ demand the time of the day." *1 Hen 4,* I, ii, 10–12. **2** overdressed: "Cold [naked] wisdom waiting on superfluous folly." *All's W,* I, i, 103. **3** living in abundance: ". . . our basest beggars/ Are in the poorest thing superfluous . . ." *Lear,* II, iv, 266–267. **4** spoiled with an overabundance of material goods: ". . . the superfluous and lust-dieted man,/ That slaves your ordinance . . ." *Lear,* IV, i, 67–68. **5** excessive: "A proper title of a peace, and purchas'd/ At a superfluous rate." *Hen 8,* I, i, 98–99. **6 superfluous courage,** excess of blood; here, that which the horses can spare: "And dout [extinguish] them with superfluous courage, ha!" *Hen 5,* IV, ii, 11. **7 superfluous death,** an unnecessary number of mortal wounds, when one would have sufficed: "Like to a murd'ring-piece, in many places/ Gives me superfluous death." *Ham,* IV, v, 95–96. **8 superfluous riots,** extravagant living: "O, let those cities . . . With their superfluous riots, hear these tears!" *Per,* I, iv, 52–54.

superflux, *n.* excess wealth; superfluity: "Expose thyself to feel what wretches feel,/ That thou mayst shake the superflux to them . . ." *Lear,* III, iv, 34–35.

supernal, *adj.* heavenly; celestial: "From that supernal judge that stirs good thoughts/ In any beast . . ." *K John,* II, i, 112–113.

superpraise, *v.* to praise extravagantly or unreasonably: "To vow, and swear, and superpraise my parts,/ When I am sure you hate me . . ." *M N Dream,* III, ii, 153–154.

superscript or **superscription,** *n.* address on a letter: "I will overglance the superscript." *Love's L,* IV, ii, 126.

super-serviceable, *adj.* officious; also, too eager to do his master's bidding: ". . . glass-gazing, super-serviceable, finical rogue . . ." *Lear,* II, ii, 17.

superstitious, *adj.* foolishly devoted: ". . . lov'd him next heav'n? obey'd him?/ Been (out of fondness) superstitious to him?" *Hen 8,* III, i, 130–131.

super-subtle, *adj.* highly refined and delicate: ". . . a frail vow, betwixt an erring barbarian/, and a super-subtle Venetian . . ." *Oth,* I, iii, 356–357.

supervise, *v.* **1** to look over; peruse: ". . . let me supervise the canzonet. Here are only/ numbers ratified . . ." *Love's L,* IV, ii, 115–116.
—*n.* **2** reading; perusal: "That on the supervise, no leisure bated . . . My head should be struck off." *Ham,* V, ii, 23–25.

supervisor, *n.* observer; spectator: "Would you, the supervisor, grossly gape on,/ Behold her topp'd?" *Oth,* III, iii, 401–402.

supplant, *v.* to remove: "Lest then the people . . . Upon a just survey take Titus' part,/ And so supplant you for ingratitude . . ." *T Andr,* I, i, 445–447.

supple, *adj.* flexible; pliant; also, easy: "Each part depriv'd of supple government/ Shall stiff and stark and cold appear, like death . . ." *Rom & Jul,* IV, i, 102–103.

suppliance, *n.* diversion; pastime: "The perfume and suppliance of a minute,/ No more." *Ham,* I, iii, 9–10.

supplicant, *adj.* as supplicants: "And supplicant their sighs to you extend . . ." *Lover's Comp,* 276.

supplication, *n.* letter, petition, or the like: "Enter the King with a supplication, and the Queen with Suffolk's head . . ." *2 Hen 6,* [SD] IV, iv, 1.

supply, *n.* **1** [often pl.] reinforcements: "Why say you so, looks he not for supply?" *1 Hen 4,* IV, iii, 3. **2 for the which supply,** to help you better understand this: ". . . for the which supply,/ Admit me Chorus to this history . . ." *Hen 5,* Prol. 31–32. **3 supply and profit,** gratification and encouragement: ". . . expend your time with us awhile/ For the supply and profit of our hope . . ." *Ham,* II, ii, 23–24.
—*v.* **4** to fill or fulfill: ". . . we have with special soul/ Elected him our absence to supply . . ." *Meas,* I, i, 17–18.

supplyant, *adj.* furnishing or supplying: "With those legions . . . whereunto your levy/ Must be supplyant . . ." *Cymb,* III, viii, 12–14.

supplyment, *n.* additional or continuing support: "You have me, rich, and I will never fail/ Beginning, nor supplyment." *Cymb,* III, iv, 180–181.

supportance, *n.* **1** support: "Give some supportance to the bending twigs." *Rich 2,* III, iv, 32. **2** act of sustaining or upholding: "Therefore/ draw for the supportance of his vow . . ." *T Night,* III, iv, 304–305.

supposal, *n.* estimate; opinion: ". . . young Fortinbras,/ Holding a weak [low] supposal of our worth . . ." *Ham,* I, ii, 17–18.

suppose, *n.* **1** estimate or expectation: "Nor, princes, is it matter new to us/ That we come short of our suppose . . ." *Tr & Cr,* I, iii, 10–11. **2** supposition; assumption: "While counterfeit supposes blear'd thine eyne." *Shrew,* V, i, 107.

supposed, *past part.* **1** misuse for "deposed" [sworn]: "I'll be supposed upon a book, his face is the worst/ thing about him." *Meas,* II, i, 153–154.
—*n.* **2** hypothetical person: "You must lay down the treasures of your body/ To this suppos'd . . ." *Meas,* II, iv, 96–97.

supposed fairness, *n.* artificial [here, borrowed] beauty: ". . . make such wanton gambols with the wind/ Upon supposed fairness . . ." *Merch,* III, ii, 93–94.

supposition, *n.* **1** suspicion: "Supposition all our lives shall be stuck full of eyes . . ." *1 Hen 4,* V, ii, 8. **2 beguile the supposition,** deceive the beliefs or opinions: ". . . to beguile the supposition/ of that lascivious young boy, the count, have I/ run into this danger . . ." *All's W,* IV, iii, 289–290. **3 in supposition,** theoretical: ". . . he is sufficient,/ —yet his means are in supposition . . ." *Merch,* I, iii, 14–15.

supreme, *n.* ruler: "Imperious [imperial] supreme of all mortal things." *Ven & Ad,* 996.

sur-addition, *n.* additional name awarded for meritorious service: "He served with glory and admired success:/ So gain'd the sur-addition Leonatus . . ." *Cymb,* I, i, 32–33.

surance, *n.* assurance: "Now give some surance that thou art Revenge:/ Stab them, or tear them on thy chariot-wheels . . ." *T Andr,* V, ii, 46–47.

surcease, *n.* **1** halt in the proceedings [a legal term]: ". . . if th'assassination/ Could trammel up the consequence, and catch/ With his [its] surcease success . . ." *Mac,* I, vii, 2–4. **2** prob. a ref. to death of Duncan: ". . . if th'assassination/ Could trammel up the consequence, and catch/ With his surcease success . . ." *Mac,* I, vii, 2–4.
—*v.* **3** to cease: "I will not do't,/ Lest I surcease to honor mine own truth . . ." *Cor,* III, ii, 120–121.

sure, *adv.* **1** securely: ". . . must be employ'd/ Now to guard sure their master." *Timon,* III, iii, 40–41.
—*adj.* **2** loyal; trustworthy: "You are both sure/ and will assist me?" *M Ado,* I, iii, 64–65. **3** safe: ". . . the forest is not three leagues off;/ If we recover that, we are sure enough." *Two Gent,* V, i, 11–12. **4 make that sure,** make sure of that: "Let not this wasp outlive, us both to sting."/ "I warrant you, madam, we will make that sure." *T Andr,* II, iii, 132–133. **5 make her sure,** kill her: "Farewell, my sons: see that you make her sure." *T Andr,* II, iii, 187.

surety, *n.* **1** bail posted to insure one's appearance for trial: "Lords, you that here are under our arrest,/ Procure your sureties for your days of answer." *Rich 2,* IV, i, 158–159. **2** overconfidence; complacency: "The wound of peace is surety,/ Surety secure . . ." *Tr & Cr,* II, ii, 14–15.
—*v.* **3** to furnish bail for: "The jeweller that owes the ring is sent for/ And he shall surety me." *All's W,* V, iii, 290–291.

surety-like, *adj.* like a bondsman or other guarantor: "He learned but surety-like to write for me . . ." *Sonn 134,* 7.

sure uncertainty, *n.* certain illusion or deception: "Until I know this sure uncertainty,/ I'll entertain the offer'd fallacy." *Errors,* II, ii, 185–186.

surfeit, *n.* **1** excess; also, dissipation: "Now comes the sick hour that his surfeit made . . ." *Rich 2,* II, ii, 84. **2** [pl.] harmful effects or results: ". . . when we are sick in fortune, often the surfeits of/ our own behaviour . . ." *Lear,* I, ii, 125–126. **3** illness brought on by overindulgence in food or drink: "Surfeits, imposthumes, grief and damn'd despair,/ Swear nature's death . . ." *Ven & Ad,* 743–744.

—*v.* **4** to devote one's life to luxury: "I had rather had eleven die nobly for their country,/ than one voluptuously surfeit out of action." *Cor,* I, iii, 24–25.

surfeiter, *n.* glutton; reveler: "I did not think/ This amorous surfeiter would have donn'd his helm . . ." *Ant & Cleo,* II, i, 32–33.

surfeiting, *n.* gluttony: "And with our surfeiting, and wanton hours,/ Have brought ourselves into a burning fever . . ." *2 Hen 4,* IV, i, 55–56.

surfeit-swelled, *adj.* obese through gluttony: ". . . such a kind of man,/ So surfeit-swell'd, so old, and so profane . . ." *2 Hen 4,* V, v, 49–50.

surgeon, *n.* physician; doctor: "Content; I'll to the surgeon's." *1 Hen 6,* III, i, 146.

surgery, *n.* **1** medical, esp. surgical, treatment: ". . . to surgery bravely; to venture upon the charged/ chambers bravely . . ." *2 Hen 4,* II, iv, 51–52. **2** ref. to tarring the sores or cuts on sheep: ". . . they [the hands] are often tarred over with the surgery of/ our sheep . . ." *As You,* III, ii, 60–61.

surly, *adj.* stern; relentless: "No longer mourn for me when I am dead/ Than you shall hear the surly sullen bell . . ." *Sonn 71,* 1–2.

surmise, *n.* reflection; contemplation [on Collatine's inadequate description of his wife]: ". . . that praise which Collatine doth owe/ Enchanted Tarquin answers with surmise . . ." *Luc,* 82–83.

surmised, *adj.* expected; also, planned or hoped for: "And that unbodied figure of the thought/ That gave't surmised shape." *Tr & Cr,* I, iii, 16–17.

surmount, *v.* surpass or excel; here, misunderstood as "mount," copulate with: "This Hector far surmounted Hannibal,/ The party is gone—" *Love's L,* V, ii, 662–663.

surnamed, *adj.* having the additional appellation: ". . . Andronicus, surnamed Pius . . ." *T Andr,* I, i, 23.

surplice of humility, *n.* Church of England ministers were required by law to wear the traditional surplice; those with Puritan leanings often wore the black Calvinist gown underneath their surplices: "Though honesty be no puritan . . . it will wear the surplice of humility/ over the black gown of a big heart." *All's W,* I, iii, 90–92.

surprise, *v.* **1** to impress upon [lit., attack forcefully without warning, a military term]: "Surprise her with discourse of my dear faith . . ." *T Night,* I, iv, 25. **2** to capture: ". . . may ye both be suddenly surpris'd/ By bloody hands, in sleeping on your beds!" *1 Hen 6,* V, iii, 40–41.

surprised, *adj.* (esp. of a woman) assaulted or taken by force: "Surpris'd! by whom?"/ "By him that justly may/ Bear his betroth'd from all the world away." *T Andr,* I, i, 285–286.

sur-reined, *adj.* overworked or overridden: "A drench for sur-rein'd jades . . ." *Hen 5,* III, v, 19.

surrender, *v.* to abdicate: "Fetch hither Richard, that in common view/ He may surrender . . ." *Rich 2,* IV, i, 155–156.

survey, *n.* **1** examination or investigation: "Lest then the people . . . Upon a just survey take Titus' part . . ." *T Andr,* I, i, 445–446. **2** sight: "Whose beauty did astonish the survey/ Of richest [most experienced] eyes . . ." *All's W,* V, iii, 16–17.

surveyor, *n.* overseer: ". . . were't not madness then/ To make the fox surveyor of the fold?" *2 Hen 6,* III, i, 252–253.

suspect, *n.* **1** suspicion: "If some suspect of ill [wickedness] mask'd not thy show . . ." *Sonn 70,* 13. —*adj.* **2** under suspicion: "Thy friends suspect for traitors while thou liv'st . . ." *Rich 3,* I, iii, 223. —*v.* **3** misuse for "respect": "Dost thou not suspect my years?" *M Ado,* IV, ii, 71–72.

suspense, *n.* doubt; suspicion: ". . . 'tis my special hope/ That you will clear yourself from all suspense . . ." *2 Hen 6,* III, I, 139–140.

suspicion, *n.* **1** fear; apprehension: "Suspicion always haunts the guilty mind . . ." *3 Hen 6,* V, vi, 11. **2** fact of being suspected of a crime: "They shall be ready at your highness' will/ To answer their suspicion with their lives." *T Andr,* II, iii, 297–298.

suspicious, *adj.* apprehensive; fearful: "When the suspicious head of theft is stopp'd . . ." *Love's L,* IV, iii, 332.

suspiration, *n.* sighing: "Nor windy suspiration of forc'd breath . . ." *Ham,* I, ii, 79.

suspire, *v.* to breathe: "Did he suspire, that light and weightless down/ Perforce must move." *2 Hen 4,* IV, v, 32–33.

sustain, *v.* **1** to care for: ". . . neither to speak of him, entreat for/ him, or any way sustain him." *Lear,* III, iii, 5–6. **2** to endure or, esp., be forced to put up with: ". . . other incident throes/ That nature's fragile vessel doth sustain . . ." *Timon,* V, i, 199–200.

sustaining, *adj.* **1** supporting life: ". . . all the idle weeds that grow/ In our sustaining corn." *Lear,* IV, iv, 5–6. **2** providing

support in the water: "On their sustaining garments not a blemish . . ." *Temp,* I, ii, 218.

sutler, *n.* vendor of army provisions: ". . . for I shall sutler be/ Unto the camp, and profits will accrue." *Hen 5,* II, i, 111–112.

Sutton Co'fil', *n.* Sutton Coldfield, town in Warwickshire, near Coventry: "Our soldiers shall march through;/ we'll to Sutton Co'fil' tonight." *1 Hen 4,* IV, ii, 2–3.

suum cuique, [Latin] to each his own: "*Suum cuique* is our Roman justice:/ This prince in justice seizeth but his own." *T Andr,* I, i, 280–281.

suum, mun, perh. imit. of wind and fol. by song refrain: ". . . blows the cold wind;/ says suum, mun, hey no nonny." *Lear,* III, iv, 100–101.

swabber, *n.* deckhand: "No, good swabber, I am to hull here a little/ longer." *T Night,* I, v, 205–206.

swaddling-clouts, *n.* See **clout** (def. 5).

swag-bellied, *adj.* having a pendulous belly: ". . . your Dane, your German, and/ your swag-bellied Hollander . . ." *Oth,* II, iii, 72–73.

swagger, *v.* **1** to quarrel or brawl: "He'll not swagger with a Barbary hen, if her feathers/ turn back in any show of resistance." *2 Hen 4,* II, iv, 97–98. **2** to bully or bluster: "And 'chud ha' bin zwagger'd out of/ my life, 'twould not ha' bin zo long as 'tis by a/ vortnight." *Lear,* IV, vi, 239–241.

swaggerer, *n.* brawler; quarreler; troublemaker: "I must live among my neighbours, I'll no/ swaggerers." *2 Hen 4,* II, iv, 72–73.

swaggering, *adj.* **1** noisy; boisterous: "Keeps wassail, and the swagg'ring upspring reels . . ." *Ham,* I, iv, 9. —*n.* **2** blustering; bullying: "By swaggering could I never thrive . . ." *T Night,* V, i, 398.

swain, *n.* rustic; bumpkin; clod; lout: "You peasant swain! You whoreson malt-horse drudge!" *Shrew,* IV, i, 116.

swam, *v.* used as past part. of **swim;** swum, though sense is "been" or "ridden": ". . . I will scarce think you have swam in a/ gondola [I won't believe you've ever been to Venice]." *As You,* IV, i, 34–36.

swan, *n.* **pale swan,** Lucrece compared to the swan, who was said to sing before dying: "And now this pale swan . . . Begins the sad dirge of her certain ending . . ." *Luc,* 1611–1612.

swan-like, *adj.* like the swan, whose approaching death was said to be heralded by a burst of song: "Then if he lose he makes a swan-like end,/ Fading in music." *Merch,* III, ii, 44–45.

sware, *v.* old form of swore: "... as with the woeful fere [husband]/ And father of that chaste dishonoured dame,/ Lord Junius Brutus sware for Lucrece' rape ..." *T Andr,* IV, i, 89–91.

swart, *adj.* swarthy; dark: "What complexion is she of?"/ "Swart like my shoe ..." *Errors,* III, ii, 99–100.

swart-complexioned, *adj.* of a dark or swarthy aspect: "So flatter I the swart-complexion'd night ..." *Sonn 28,* 11.

swarth, *n.* swath, the width of a cut row of grain: "... cons state without book, and utters it/ by great swarths ..." *T Night,* II, iii, 148–149.

swasher, *n.* braggart; bully: "As young as I am, I have observed these three/ swashers." *Hen 5,* III, ii, 28–29.

swashing, *adj.* **1** swaggering: "We'll have a swashing and a martial outside [appearance] ..." *As You,* I, iii, 116. **2** See **washing.**

swath¹, *n.* amount of grain cut with one stroke of a scythe: "... the strawy Greeks ... Fall down before him like a mower's swath." *Tr & Cr,* V, v, 24–25.

swath², *n.* swaddling clothes: "... from our first swath proceeded/ The sweet degrees that this brief world affords ..." *Timon,* IV, iii, 254–255.

swathling clothes or **swathing-clothes,** *n. pl.* swaddling clothes: "... this Hotspur, Mars in swathling clothes,/ This infant warrior ..." *1 Hen 4,* III, ii, 112–113.

sway, *n.* **1** influence, esp. the exercise of political influence: "So dry he was for sway, wi' th' King of Naples/ To give him annual tribute ..." *Temp,* I, ii, 112–113. **2** rule; dominion: "You took occasion to be quickly woo'd/ To gripe the general sway [rule of the entire country] into your hand ..." *1 Hen 4,* V, i, 56–57. **3 i' th' sway of,** being ruled by: "... proceed/ I' th' sway of your own will." *Lear,* IV, vii, 19–20. **4** See **limping sway. 5 sway of motion,** forcing motion away from its natural course: "... this wile drawing bias,/ This sway of motion, this commodity ..." *K John,* II, i, 583–584. **6 sway o'th'state,** state authority: "... and now arriving/ A place of potency and sway o'th'state ..." *Cor,* II, iii, 179–180.
—*v.* **7** to influence or control (used esp. in astrology): "... from thy pale sphere above ... that my full life doth sway." *As You,* III, ii, 3–4. **8** to manage; govern: "She could not sway her house, command her followers ..." *T Night,* IV, iii, 17. **9** to

rule as a monarch: "Henry, hadst thou sway'd as kings should do ..." *3 Hen 6,* II, vi, 14. **10** to manipulate; here, the keys on a musical instrument: "... when thou gently sway'st/ The wiry concord that mine ear confounds ..." *Sonn 128,* 3–4. **11 sway on,** to push on (ahead): "Let us sway on and face them in the field." *2 Hen 4,* IV, i, 24. **12 sway with,** to rule over: "I had rather be their servant in my way/ Than sway with them in theirs." *Cor,* II, i, 201–202.

swear, *v.* **1 swear down,** summon [call down] as a witness: "Though they would swear down each particular saint ..." *Meas,* V, i, 242. **2 swear lordship,** to promise marriage (to): "... since wives are monsters to you,/ And that you fly them as you swear them lordship,/ Yet you desire to marry." *All's W,* V, iii, 154–156. **3 swear out,** to forswear; renounce: "I hear your grace hath sworn out house-keeping [hospitality] ..." *Love's L,* II, i, 103.

swearer, *n.* ref. either to foul-mouthed customers or to those customers who swear by the establishment: "... she'll disfurnish us of/ all our cavalleria, and make our swearers priests." *Per,* IV, vi, 11–12.

sweat, *v.* **1** to take sweating treatments [the sweating tub] for venereal disease: "Till then I'll sweat and seek about for eases ..." *Tr & Cr,* V, x, 56. **2 sweat compassion,** weep with pity: "... it is no little thing to make/ Mine eyes to sweat compassion." *Cor,* V, iii, 195–196.
—*n.* **3 the sweat,** sweating sickness, a form of the plague: "... what with the war [with Spain], what with the sweat,/ what with the gallows, and what with poverty ..." *Meas,* I, ii, 75–76.

sweaten, *past part.* sweated; exuded [here pron. "sweeten"]: "... grease, that's sweaten/ From the murderer's gibbet ..." *Mac,* IV, i, 65–66.

sweep, *v.* **sweeps it,** passes pompously; struts: "She sweeps it through the court ... More like an empress ..." *2 Hen 6,* I, iii, 77–78.

sweep one's way, *v.* to act as escort for another: "They bear the mandate, they must sweep my way/ And marshal me to knavery." *Ham,* III, iv, 206–207.

sweet, *adj.* **1** perfumed: "Gloves as sweet as damask roses ..." *W Tale,* IV, iv, 222. **2** refined: "There shall he practise tilts and tournaments,/ Hear sweet discourse, converse with noblemen ..." *Two Gent,* I, iii, 30–31.
—*n.* **3** something exuding a lovely fragrance: "O! in what sweets dost thou thy sins enclose." *Sonn 95,* 4. **4** [often pl.] delights; here, elaborate and often unwholesome pleasures: "Lose all and more by paying too much rent/ For compound [combined] sweet ..." *Sonn 125,* 6–7. **5** beloved person; here,

a husband: "I have given him that . . . shall quite unpeople her/ Of liegers for her sweet." *Cymb,* I, vi, 78–80. **6 sweet which is their poison,** taste of power, which is as dangerous for the state as it is ruinous for them: ". . . let them not lick/ The sweet which is their poison." *Cor,* III, i, 155–156.
—*v.* **7** to sweeten: "Let's with our colours sweet the air of France." *Edw 3,* II, ii, 100.

sweet and twenty, *n.* sweetheart 20 times over: "Then come kiss me, sweet and twenty:/ Youth's a stuff will not endure." *T Night,* II, iii, 52–53.

sweetest, *adj.* dearest: "But slave to slavery my sweet'st friend must be?" *Sonn 133,* 4.

sweet-faced, *adj.* handsome; good-looking: "I see by you I am a sweet-fac'd youth . . ." *Errors,* V, i, 418.

sweet-favored, *adj.* of beautiful appearance: "The most sweet-favoured or deformed'st creature . . ." *Sonn 113,* 10.

sweeting, *n.* **1** sweet apple; here, as a sauce for the "goose": "Thy wit is a very bitter sweeting, it is a most sharp/ sauce." *Rom & Jul,* II, iv, 80–81. **2** sweetheart; darling: "How fares my Kate? What, sweeting, all amort?" *Shrew,* IV, iii, 36.

sweet mouth, *n.* sweet tooth: "Item, she hath a sweet mouth." *Two Gent,* III, i, 321.

sweet poison, *n.* flattery: "Sweet, sweet, sweet poison for the age's tooth . . ." *K John,* I, i, 213.

sweet-suggesting, *adj.* sweetly seductive: "O sweet-suggesting Love, if thou hast sinn'd,/ Teach me . . . to excuse it." *Two Gent,* II, vi, 7–8.

sweet water, *n.* perfumed water: "Enter Paris and his Page, with flowers and sweet water." [SD] *Rom & Jul,* V, iii, 1.

sweet words, *n. pl.* flattery; fawning: "I mean sweet words,/ Low-crooked curtsies, and base spaniel fawning." *J Caes,* III, i, 42–43.

sweet word's taste, *n.* the "sweet word" may refer to praise or flattery, though it would seem a non sequitur; more likely "word's" was a misprint for "world's": "And bitter shame hath spoil'd the sweet word's [world's?] taste . . ." *K John,* III, iii, 110.

swelling, *adj.* **1** of increasing grandeur or magnificence: ". . . happy prologues to the swelling act/ Of the imperial theme." *Mac,* I, iii, 128–129. **2** haughty: "Made peace of enmity . . . Between these swelling, wrong-incensed peers." *Rich 3,* II, i, 51–52.

sweltered, *adj.* passed off as sweat: "Swelter'd venom, sleeping got,/ Boil thou first i' th' charmed pot." *Mac,* IV, i, 8–9.

swerve, *v.* to return: "And so my patent back again is swerving." *Sonn 87,* 8.

swimming, *adj.* gliding: ". . . she, with pretty and with swimming gait/ Following . . . Would imitate, and sail upon the land . . ." *M N Dream,* II, i, 130–132.

swindge, *v.* var. of **swinge;** thrash: "Saint George, that swindg'd the dragon . . ." *K John,* II, i, 288.

swinge, *v.* **1** to whip or beat; thrash: ". . . you thin man in a censer, I will/ have you as soundly swinged for this . . ." *2 Hen 4,* V, iv, 19–20.
—*n.* **2** force, esp. tremendous force: "For the great swinge and rudeness of his poise [its impact] . . ." *Tr & Cr,* I, iii, 207.

swinge-buckler, *n.* swashbuckler: ". . . you had not four/ such swinge-bucklers in all the Inns o'Court again . . ." *2 Hen 4,* III, ii, 20–21.

Swinstead, *n.* prob. misuse for Swineshead Abbey in E England: "Tell him, toward Swinstead, to the abbey there." *K John,* V, iii, 8.

switch and spurs, at or to full gallop; here, "urge your wits on": "Switch and spurs, switch and spurs, or I'll cry a/ match!" *Rom & Jul,* II, iv, 70–71.

Swithold, *n.* St. Withold, often invoked (as in this charm) to ward off nightmares: "Swithold footed thrice the old;/ He met the night-mare, and her nine-fold . . ." *Lear,* III, iv, 123–124.

Switzers, *n. pl.* Swiss guards; here, personal bodyguards: "Attend!/ Where is my Switzers? Let them guard the door." *Ham,* IV, v, 96–97.

swoln, *adj.* var. of **swollen;** bursting: ". . . the big year swoln with some other grief,/ Is thought with child by the stern tyrant War . . ." *2 Hen 4,* Induc., 13–14.

swoopstake, *adv.* indiscriminately [lit., sweeping up all the stakes in a game]: ". . . is't writ in your revenge/ That, swoopstake, you will draw both friend and foe . . ." *Ham,* IV, v, 141–142.

sword, *n.* **1** sword-wielding soldier: ". . . to be tender minded/ Does not become a sword . . ." *Lear,* V, iii, 32–33. **2 upon my sword,** (to) take an oath on the cross-shaped hilt of a sword: "Nay, but swear't . . . Upon my sword." *Ham,* I, v, 151–153.

sword-and-buckler, *adj.* swashbuckling: ". . . that same sword-and-buckler Prince of Wales . . ." *1 Hen 4,* I, iii, 227.

sworder, *n.* gladiator: "A Roman sworder and banditto slave/ Murder'd sweet Tully . . ." *2 Hen 6,* IV, i, 135–136.

sworn, *adj.* habitual; confirmed: "He's a sworn rioter; he has a sin/ That often drowns him . . ." *Timon,* III, v, 68–69.

sworn brother, *n.* **1** soldier's companion-in-arms: "He hath every month a new sworn brother." *M Ado,* I, i, 66. **2** [pl] band of thieves: ". . . and we'll be all three sworn brothers to France . . ." *Hen 5,* II, i, 12.

swound, *v.* to swoon; faint: "Choler does kill me that thou art alive;/ I swound to see thee." *Timon,* IV, iii, 369–370.

'Swounds, *n.* by God's wounds [a mild oath]: "'Swounds, I should take it: for it cannot be/ But I am pigeon-liver'd . . ." *Ham,* II, ii, 572–573.

Sylla, *n.* another name for Lucius Cornelius Sulla (138–78 B.C.), Roman general and dictator, renowned for his cruelty: "And, like ambitious Sylla, overgorg'd . . ." *2 Hen 6,* IV, i, 83.

syllable, *n.* **1 by the syllable,** to the [very] letter: "I will believe you by the syllable/ Of what you shall deliver." *Per,* V, i, 167–168. **2 utmost syllable,** tiniest particle: ". . . extend to/ you what further becomes his greatness, even to the/ utmost syllable of your worthiness." *All's W,* III, vi, 65–67.

syllable of dolour, *n.* cry of grief: "As if it felt with Scotland, and yell'd out/ Like syllable of dolour." *Mac,* IV, iii, 7–8.

sympathize, *v.* **1** to commiserate with: ". . . the senseless brands will sympathize/ The heavy accent of thy moving tongue . . ." *Rich 2,* V, i, 46–47. **2** to react sympathetically; match: "As rous'd with rage, with rage doth sympathize . . ." *Tr & Cr,* I, iii, 52. **3 sympathize with,** to resemble: ". . . the men do sympathize with the/ mastiffs in robustious and rough coming on . . ." *Hen 5,* III, vii, 147–148.

sympathized, *adj.* **1** matched; harmonized: "A message well sympathized: a horse to be ambassador/ for an ass." *Love's L,* III, i, 48–49. **2** best expressed: "Thou truly fair wert truly sympathized/ In true plain words . . ." *Sonn 82,* 11–12. **3** suffered or shared in by all: "And all that are assembled in this place,/ That by this sympathised one day's error/ Have suffer'd wrong . . ." *Errors,* V, i, 396–398.

sympathy, *n.* **1** equality of rank or blood: "If that thy valour stand on sympathy,/ There is my gage, Aumerle, in gage to thine . . ." *Rich 2,* IV, i, 33–34. **2** similarity of condition; identical suffering: "O woeful sympathy,/ Piteous predicament." *Rom & Jul,* III, iii, 85–86. **3** accord; agreement: "Or, if there were a sympathy in choice,/ War, death, or sickness did lay siege to it . . ." *M N Dream,* I, i, 141–142. **4** equal sharing: "O, what a sympathy of woe is this;/ As far from help as limbo is from bliss." *T Andr,* III, i, 148–149.

synod, *n.* council or assembly: "It hath in solemn synods been decreed . . . To admit no traffic to our adverse towns . . ." *Errors,* I, i, 13–15.

T

t', *prep.* to: "Had made his course t'illume that part of heaven . . ." *Ham,* I, i, 40.

't, *pron.* it: ". . . were 't not madness then/ To make the fox surveyor of the fold?" *2 Hen 6,* III, i, 252–253.

ta, *pron.* dial. for "thee" or "thou": "Good people, bring a rescue or two . . . wot ta?" *2 Hen 4,* II, i, 55–56.

table, *n.* **1** part of the palm of the hand [term in palmistry]: ". . . if any man in Italy have a/ fairer table which doth offer to swear upon a book . . ." *Merch,* II, ii, 150–151. **2** board or other surface on which a picture is painted: "Till now infixed I beheld myself/ Drawn in the flattering table of her eye." *K John,* II, i, 502–503. **3** tablet for an inscription, etching, etc.: "from the table of my memory/ I'll wipe away all trivial fond records . . ." *Ham,* I, v, 98–99. **4** [pl.] **a.** notebook for jotting down sayings, impressions, etc.; also, written records: "And therefore will he wipe his tables clean,/ And keep no tell-tale to his memory . . ." *2 Hen 4,* IV, i, 201–202. **b.** [fig. use] woman, esp. a confidante: ". . . lisping to his master's old tables, his note-book, his/ counsel-keeper." *2 Hen 4,* II, iv, 264–265. **c.** backgammon: ". . . when he plays at tables, chides the dice/ In honourable terms . . ." *Love's L,* V, ii, 326–327. **5** fare; food provided on a table: "For the table sir, it shall be serv'd in . . ." *Merch,* III, v, 55. **6 set foot under thy table,** to become your dependent: ". . . your father were a fool/ To give thee all, and . . . Set foot under thy table." *Shrew,* II, i, 393–395. **7 turn the tables up,** to clear away tables by disassembling and stacking them: "More light, you knaves, and turn the tables up." *Rom & Jul,* I, v, 27.

table-book, *n.* notebook or tablet; tables: ". . . not a counterfeit stone, not a/ ribbon, glass, pomander, brooch, table-book . . ." *W Tale,* IV, iv, 598–599.

table-sport, *n.* topic of amusing dinner conversation; object of ridicule: ". . . let/ me for ever be your table-sport . . ." *Wives,* IV, ii, 148–149.

tabor, *n.* small drum, played with one hand: ". . . now had he rather hear the tabor/ and the pipe [peaceful instruments]" *M Ado,* II, iii, 14–15.

taborer, *n.* performer on the tabor: "I would I could see/ this taborer; he lays it on [does it well]." *Temp,* III, ii, 148–149.

tabourine or **taborin,** *n.* military drum: "Trumpeters,/ With brazen din blast you the city's ear,/ Make mingle with our rattling tabourines . . ." *Ant & Cleo,* IV, viii, 35–37.

tackle, *n.* **1** a ship's rigging; tackling: "The tackle of my heart is crack'd and burn'd . . ." *K John,* V, vii, 52. **2** clothing: "Though thy tackle's torn,/ Thou show'st a noble vessel." *Cor,* IV, v, 62–63.

tackled stair, *n.* rope ladder: ". . . my man shall be with thee,/ And bring thee cords made like a tackled stair . . ." *Rom & Jul,* II, iv, 184–185.

tacklings, *n. pl.* ship's rigging: "The friends of France our shrouds and tacklings?" *3 Hen 6,* V, iv, 18.

ta'en, *past part.* of **take; taken;** here, overtaken; met: "I thought to have ta'en you at the Porpentine . . ." *Errors,* III, ii, 166.

taffeta, *n.* material of masks, which is all the lovers will see of their faces: "All hail, the richest beauties on the earth!"/ "Beauties no richer than rich taffeta." *Love's L,* V, ii, 158–159.

taffety, *adj.* dress in taffeta; here, showily or obviously gotten up: ". . . as your French crown for your taffety punk [prostitute] . . ." *All's W,* II, ii, 20–21.

tag, *n.* rabble: "Will you hence/ Before the tag return?" *Cor,* III, i, 245–246.

tag-rag people, *n.* common herd; rabble: "If the tag-rag people did not clap/ him and hiss him, according as he pleas'd and displeas'd/ them . . . I am no true man." *J Caes,* I, ii, 255–258.

tailor, *n.* **1 be a tailor to thee,** furnish you with new clothes: ". . . this secrecy of thine shall/ be a tailor to thee . . ." *Wives,* III, iii, 29–30.

—*interj.* **2** said to be a cry uttered as one falls backwards; perh. from similarity of tailor sitting crosslegged on the floor or from falling on one's "tail": "Then slip I from her bum, down topples she,/ And 'tailor' cries, and falls into a cough . . ." *M N Dream,* II, i, 53–54.

tailor's yard, *n.* three-foot measuring stick: ". . . you tailor's yard,/ you sheath, you bow-case, you vile standing tuck!" *1 Hen IV,* II, iv, 242–244.

taint, *v.* **1** to spoil or mar: ". . . let no quarrel, nor no brawl to come,/ Taint the condition [harmony] of this present hour . . ." *T Night,* V, i, 355–356. **2** to weaken; become inneffectual: "Till Birnam wood remove to Dunsinane,/ I cannot taint with fear." *Mac,* V, iii, 2–3. **3** to infect: "And danger, like an ague, subtly taints/ Even then when we sit idly in the sun." *Tr & Cr,* III, iii, 231–232. **4** to become spoiled; be ruined: "Nay, pursue him now, lest the device take air,/ and taint." *T Night,* III, iv, 132–133.

—*past part.* **5** tainted; corrupted: ". . . a pure unspotted heart,/ Never yet taint with love . . ." *1 Hen 6,* V, iii, 182–183.

—*n.* **6** blemish; minor fault: "But breathe his faults so quaintly/ That they may seem the taints of liberty . . ." *Ham,* II, i, 31–32. **7** discredit or disparagement: ". . . your fore-vouch'd affection/ Fall into taint . . ." *Lear,* I, i, 220–221.

tainted, *adj.* **1** (of an animal) sickly; also, infected: "I am a tainted wether of the flock,/ Meetest for death . . ." *Merch,* IV, i, 114–115. **2** (of a person) **a.** corrupt: "A very tainted fellow, and full of wickedness . . ." *All's W,* III, ii, 87. **b.** unsettled or unhinged: ". . . have some guard about you if/ he come, for sure the man is tainted in's wits." *T Night,* III, iv, 12–13.

tainture, *n.* corruption; defilement: "Gloucester, see here the tainture of thy nest . . ." *2 Hen 6,* II, i, 180.

take, *v.* **1** to strike: "If he took you a box o' th' ear . . ." *Meas,* i, 177. **2** to add: "Take my deserts to his, and join 'em both . . ." *Timon,* III, v, 80. **3** to assume: "Take you as 'twere some distant knowledge of him . . ." *Ham,* II, i, 13. **4** to be forced to endure: ". . . the spurns/ That patient merit of th'unworthy takes . . ." *Ham,* III, i, 73–74. **5** to bewitch; charm or delight: ". . . no planets strike,/ No fairy takes, nor witch hath power to charm . . ." *Ham,* I, i, 167–168. **6** to come upon unexpectedly; catch: ". . . let not me take him then,/ For if I do, I'll mar the young clerk's pen." *Merch,* V, i, 236–237. **7** to remove: "And take the present horror from the time . . ." *Mac,* II, i, 59. **8 take all, a.** (in gambling) to stake everything on one throw of the dice: ". . . unbonneted he runs,/ And bids what will take all." *Lear,* III, i, 14–15. **b.** (in battle) everything to the survivor:

"Woo't thou fight well?"/ "I'll strike, and cry 'Take all.'" *Ant & Cleo,* IV, ii, 7–8. **9 take away,** to clear the table: "Come, take away. Lavinia, go with me . . ." *T Andr,* III, ii, 81. **10 take foul scorn,** See **scorn** (def. 3). **11 take him down,** to humble him; cut him down to size; here, additional bawdy sense used unintentionally: "And a speak anything against me I'll take him/ down, and a were lustier than he is . . ." *Rom & Jul,* II, iv, 147–148. **12 take I,** were I to agree to: "Take I your wish, I leap into the seas . . ." *Per,* II, iv, 43. **13 take in,** to conquer or occupy: "He could so quickly cut the Ionian sea,/ And take in Toryne?" *Ant & Cleo,* III, vii, 22–23. **14 take it off who will,** make no mistake about it: ". . . there's no jesting,/ there's laying on, take't off who will, as they say . . ." *Tr & Cr,* I, ii, 208–209. **15 take it on oneself,** to presume to behave [in such a manner]: "'Tis like you'll prove a jolly surly groom,/ That take it on you at the first so roundly [outrageously]." *Shrew,* III, ii, 211–212. **16 take me with you,** explain your meaning: "I would your Grace would take me with you: whom/ means your Grace?" *1 Hen 4,* II, iv, 454–455. **17 take off, a.** to drink off; empty: "[To Silence, seeing him take off a bumper] Why, now/ you have done me right." *2 Hen 4,* V, iii, 70–71. **b.** to dispel or diminish: ". . . we with thee/ May spend our wonder too, or take off thine . . ." *All's W,* II, i, 87–88. **c.** to remove; do away with: "And I will put that business in your bosoms,/ Whose execution takes your enemy off . . ." *Mac,* III, i, 103–104. **18 take on, a.** to take upon (oneself); pretend: "This pernicious slave/ Forsooth took on him as [to be] a conjurer . . ." *Errors,* V, i, 242–243. **b.** to cry out; rage; rail: ". . . he'll/ Seem to break loose . . . take on as you would follow . . ." *M N Dream,* III, ii, 257–258. **19 take on with,** to rail against: "How will my mother . . . Take on with me and ne'er be satisfied [comforted]!" *3 Hen 6,* II, v, 103–104. **20 take, or lend,** perh. either take my life or lend me assistance: "If any thing that's civil, speak: if savage,/ Take, or lend." *Cymb,* III, vi, 23–24. **21 take out,** to copy: "I'll ha' the work ta'en out,/ And give't Iago . . ." *Oth,* III, iii, 300–301. **22 take the odds,** See **odds** (def. 12). **23 take the one by th'other,** vanquish one by means of the other: "May enter 'twixt the gap of both, and take/ The one by th'other." *Cor,* III, i, 110–111. **24 take this from this,** separate my head from my shoulders: "Take this from this if this be otherwise." *Ham,* II, ii, 156. **25 take to,** to resort to; fall back on: "Tell us this: have you anything to take to?" *Two Gent,* IV, i, 42. **26 take up, a.** to rebuke: "Nay, I was taken up for laying them down." *Two Gent,* I, ii, 135. **b.** to apprehend; arrest: "We are like to prove a goodly commodity, being/ taken up of these men's bills." *M Ado,* III, iii, 171–172. **c.** to make use of; enlist: "You have ta'en up,/ Under the counterfeited zeal of God,/ The subjects of his substitute, my father . . ." *2 Hen 4,* IV, ii, 26–28. **d.** to draft into military service: ". . . you loiter here too long, being you/ are to take soldiers up in counties as you go." *2 Hen 4,* II, i, 181–182. **e.** to bid (someone) rise from a kneeling position: "Take up this good old man, and cheer the heart/ That dies in tempest of thy angry frown." *T Andr,* I, i, 457–458. **f.** to settle amicably: "... to take up a matter of brawl betwixt/ my uncle and one of the emperal's men." *T Andr,* IV, iii, 91–92. **g.** to take on; defeat in battle: "I could myself/ Take up a brace o'th'best of them ..." *Cor,* III, i, 241–242. **27 take upon us,** to attempt to explain: "And take upon 's the mystery of things,/ As if we were Gods' spies ..." *Lear,* V, iii, 16–17. **28 take you,** to give you; hit or strike you: "If he took you a box o' th' ear, you might have your/ action of slander too." *Meas,* II, i, 177–178. **29 take you no care,** don't worry: "Father, I warrant you; take you no care ..." *1 Hen 6,* I, iv, 20. **30 take you out,** lead you out onto the dance floor: "Sweet heart,/ I were unmannerly to take you out/ And not to kiss you." *Hen 8,* I, iv, 94–96. **31 take your own way,** begone; go about your business: "... your service for this time is ended,/ Take your own way." *Cymb,* I, vi, 30–31. **32 to take for,** for taking: "... am fall'n out with my more headier will,/ To take the indispos'd and sickly fit/ For the sound man." *Lear,* II, iv, 110–112.

take a house, take refuge inside a house: "Run master, run, for God's sake take a house ..." *Errors,* V, i, 36.

taken, *past part.* of **take. 1** caught, in the manner of a contagion: "... his corruption being ta'en from us,/ We as the spring of all shall pay for all." *1 Hen 4,* V, ii, 22–23. **2** perceived; understood: "Was this taken/ By any understanding pate but thine?" *W Tale,* I, ii, 222–223. **3** apprehended; arrested: "Choler, my lord, if rightly taken [understood]./ No, if rightly taken, halter." *1 Hen 4,* II, iv, 320–321. **4 taken with the manner,** Legal term for "caught in the act": "The matter is to me, sir, as concerning Jaquenetta./ The manner of it is, I was taken with the manner." *Love's L,* I, i, 199–200. —*adj.* **5** undertaken: "His taken labours bid him me forgive ..." *All's W,* III, iv, 12.

taking, *n.* **1** capture: "... no place,/ That guard ... Does not attend my taking." *Lear,* II, iii, 3–5. **2** infection or other harmful influences: "Bless thee from whirlwinds, star-blasting, and taking!" *Lear,* III, iv, 59–60. **3** state of fear or terror: "What a taking was he in when your husband/ asked who was in the basket!" *Wives,* III, iii, 166–167. —*adj.* **4** infectious: "Strike her young bones,/ You taking airs, with lameness!" *Lear,* II, iv, 164–165.

taking-off, *n.* death; here, murder: "... plead like angels, trumpet-tongu'd, against/ The deep damnation of his taking-off ..." *Mac,* I, vii, 19–20.

taking up, *n.* buying on credit: "... and if a man is/ through with them in honest taking up ..." *2 Hen 4,* I, ii, 39–40.

Talbonite, *n.* soldier under the command of Lord Talbot: "... this is the happy wedding torch ... burning fatal to the Talbonites." *1 Hen 6,* III, ii, 26–28.

tale, *n.* **1** wordplay with sense of "story" and "tail" [slang word for "penis" or, sometimes, "anus"]: "Thou desirest me to stop in my tale against the hair." *Rom & Jul,* II, iv, 95. **2** [often pl.] gossip; tittle-tattle: "Your vows to her and me ... Will even weigh; and both as light as tales." *M N Dream,* III, ii, 132–133. **3 thereby hangs a tale,** this reminds me of [another] story: "Out of their saddles into the dirt, and thereby hangs/ a tale." *Shrew,* IV, i, 50–51.

talent¹, *n.* **1** silver coin of ancient Greece, having great value [upwards of 100 pounds sterling]: "Five talents is his debt;/ His means most short ..." *Timon,* I, i, 98–99. **2** [usually pl.] riches: "'And, lo! behold these talents [made] of their hair ..." *Lover's Comp,* 204. **3** wordplay on "riches" and "coins," implying Imogen is beyond price: "In you, which I account his, beyond all talents." *Cymb,* I, vii, 80.

talent², *n.* misuse for "talon": "If a talent be a claw, look how he claws him with a/ talent." *Love's L,* IV, ii, 62–63.

tale-porter, *n.* talebearer; gossip: "Here's the midwife's name to 't, one Mistress Tale-porter,/ and five or six honest wives ..." *W Tale,* IV, iv, 270–271.

talk, *v.* **1 not to be talked on,** not worth talking about: "... and for a hand and a foot and a/ body, though they be not to be talked on, yet they/ are past compare." *Rom & Jul,* II, v, 41–43. **2 talked with,** spoken to: "Are you so brave! I'll have you talked with/ anon." *Cor,* IV, v, 18–19. —*n.* **3 enter talk,** to engage in a discussion: "Must your bold verdict enter talk with lords?/ Else would I have a fling at Winchester." *1 Hen 6,* III, i, 63. **4 talk of,** conversation about: "I had talk of you last night ..." *All's W,* V, ii, 49.

talker, *n.* person whose words are not followed by deeds: "[To Wol.] my good lord, have great care/ I be not found a talker [it will be your responsibility to make him welcome]." *Hen 8,* II, ii, 77–78.

tall, *adj.* **1** brave; resolute: "Which many a good tall fellow had destroy'd/ So cowardly ..." *1 Hen 4,* I, iii, 61–62. **2** large and strong [well-armed]: "With eight tall ships, three thousand men of war ..." *Rich 2,* II, i, 286. **3** noble; fine: "... considering the weather,/ a taller man than I will take cold." *Shrew,* IV, i, 9–10.

tall building, *n.* large, splendid vessel; here, describing a rival poet: "He of tall building and of goodly pride." *Sonn 80,* 12.

tallow, *n.* **piss my tallow,** fr. belief that heat of lust, esp. in warm weather, caused body fat to melt and be passed off as urine: "Send me a/ cool rut-time, Jove, or who can blame me to piss my/ tallow?" *Wives,* V, v, 13–15.

tallow-catch, *n.* pan, rim, etc., for catching melted fat or wax: ". . . thou knotty-pated fool, thou/ whoreson obscene greasy tallow-catch . . ." *1 Hen 4,* II, iv, 222–223.

tallow-face, *n.* person who is pale with grief: "Out, you baggage!/ You tallow-face!" *Rom & Jul,* III, v, 156–157.

tall stockings, *n.* hip-length stockings, usually worn with short puffed breeches: ". . . renouncing clean/ The faith they have in tennis and tall stockings . . ." *Hen 8,* I, iii, 29–30.

tame, *adj.* **1** domesticated: "I have kept of them tame [in my household for amusement], and know/ their natures." *All's W,* II, v, 45–46. **2 watch him tame,** keep at him till his resistance is broken down [term in falconry]: "I'll watch him tame, and talk him out of patience . . ." *Oth,* III, iii, 23. —*v.* **3** to broach; break into: "To tame and havoc more than she can eat." *Hen 5,* I, ii, 173.

Tamworth, *n.* town SW of Leicester, in Staffordshire: "From Tamworth thither is but one day's march . . ." *Rich 3,* V, ii, 13.

tan, *v.* to darken: ". . . change decrees of kings,/ Tan sacred beauty, blunt the sharp'st intents . . ." *Sonn 115,* 6–7.

tang, *v.* to clang or sound forth (with); resound: "Let thy tongue tang arguments of state . . ." *T Night,* II, v, 150.

tangle, *v.* to snare or trap; here, in the manner of trapping songbirds with birdlime: "You must lay lime, to tangle her desires . . ." *Two Gent,* III, ii, 68.

tanling, *n.* child tanned by the sun: "But to be still hot Summer's tanlings . . ." *Cymb,* IV, iv, 29.

Tanta est erga te mentis integritas Regina serenissima, [Latin] So great is [our] integrity of mind toward you, most serene Queen. *Hen 8,* III, i, 40.

Tantaene animis coelestibus irae? [Latin] Is there such resentment in heavenly minds? *2 Hen 6,* II, i, 24.

Tantalus, *n.* (in Greek myth.) son of Zeus, who committed atrocious crimes and was consigned to Hades, where food and drink always remained just beyond his reach: "That worse than Tantalus' is her annoy,/ To clip Elizium and to lack her joy." *Ven & Ad,* 599–600.

tap, *v.* **1** to work as a tapster: "I will entertain Bardolph; he shall draw, he shall/ tap." *Wives,* I, iii, 10–11. **2 tap out,** to draw or let out: "That blood already . . . Hast thou tapp'd out and drunkenly carous'd . . ." *Rich 2,* II, i, 126–127.

taper, *n.* candle: "Enter Claudio, Prince, and three or four with tapers." [SD] *M Ado,* V, iii, 1.

tapestry, *n.* **nature's tapestry,** natural vegetation: "The ground, undecked with nature's tapestry,/ Seems barren, sere . . ." *Edw 3,* I, ii, 150–151.

tapster, *n.* **1** person hired to draw the ale or beer in a tavern; also a tavern keeper: ". . . the oath of a lover is no stronger than the word of a tapster." *As You,* III, iv, 27–28. **2** procurer; pimp: ". . . though you change your place, you need/ not change your trade: I'll be your tapster still . . ." *Meas,* I, ii, 99–100.

tapster's arithmetic, *n.* simplest kind of arithmetic: ". . . a tapster's arithmetic may soon bring his/ particulars therein to a total." *Tr & Cr,* I, ii, 115–116.

tar or **tarre,** *v.* **1** to incite: ". . . the nation holds it no sin to tar them to controversy." *Ham,* II, ii, 351. **2** to urge or force: ". . . like a dog that is compell'd to fight,/ Snatch at his master that doth tarre him on." *K John,* IV, i, 115–116.

tardily, *adv.* slowly and carefully: "For those that could speak low and tardily/ Would turn their own perfection to abuse . . ." *2 Hen 4,* II, iii, 26–27.

tardy-apish, *adj.* slavishly, though tardily, imitative: "Whose manners still our tardy-apish nation/ Limps after in base imitation." *Rich 2,* II, i, 22–23.

tardy form, *n.* sluggish or lethargic manner; here, one that is affected: "So is he now in execution/ Of any bold or noble enterprise,/ However he puts on this tardy form." *J Caes,* I, ii, 294–296.

Tarentum, *n.* ancient name of Taranto, port city in SE Italy: ". . . from Tarentum, and Brundusium/ He could so quickly cut the Ionian sea . . ." *Ant & Cleo,* III, vii, 21–22.

targe, *n.* **1** light shield: "That oft in field, with targe and shield,/ did make my foe/ to sweat . . ." *Love's L,* V, ii, 548. **2 targes of proof,** shields of proven strength: ". . . whose naked breast/ Stepp'd before targes of proof . . ." *Cymb,* V, v, 4–5.

target, *n.* shield; buckler: "I made me no more ado, but took all their seven/ points in my target, thus!" *1 Hen 4,* II, iv, 197–198.

Tarpeian, *n.* **the rock Tarpeian,** precipice on Capitoline Hill, from which convicted criminals were hurled to their deaths:

"Bear him to th'rock Tarpeian, and from thence/ Into destruction cast him." *Cor*, III, i, 211–212.

Tarquin, *n.* **1** name of the last king of ancient Rome and his sons: "My ancestors did from the streets of Rome/ The Tarquin drive, when he was call'd a king." *J Caes*, II, i, 53–54. **2** Sextus Tarquinius, son of Rome's last king, Tarquinius Superbus; his rape of Lucrece sparked a revolt that drove the ruling family from Rome: "With Tarquin's ravishing strides, towards his design/ Moves like a ghost." *Mac*, II, i, 55–56. **3 the Tarquin,** either of two Etruscan kings who ruled Rome, 6th cent. B.C.: "A merrier day did never yet greet Rome,/ No, not th'expulsion of the Tarquins." *Cor*, V, iv, 43–44.

tarre, *v.* to urge: "Snatch at his master that doth tarre him on." *K John*, IV, i, 116.

tarriance, *n.* delay: "I am impatient of my tarriance." *Two Gent*, II, vii, 90.

tarry, *v.* to wait for: "Come, I will go drink with you, but I cannot tarry dinner." *2 Hen 4*, III, ii, 186.

Tarsusor or **Tharsus,** *n.* ancient city in SE Asia Minor: ". . . to Tharsus/ Intend my travel, where I'll hear from thee . . ." *Per*, I, ii, 115–116.

tart, *adj.* **1** harsh; bitter: ". . . another way,/ The news is not so tart." *Lear*, IV, ii, 86–87. **2** sour; disagreeable: ". . . so tart a favour [look]/ To trumpet such good tidings!" *Ant & Cleo*, II, v, 38–39.

Tartar, *n.* **1** inhabitant of a vague region where eastern Europe joins Asia: "Thy love? Out, tawny Tartar, out!/ Out, loathed medicine! O hated potion, hence!" *M N Dream*, III, ii, 263–264. **2** such a person, regarded as the personification of cruelty: "Through flinty Tartar's bosom would peep forth/ And answer thanks." *All's W*, IV, iv, 7–8. **3** (in classical myth.) Tartarus, the infernal regions of hell, where the wicked were eternally punished: "No, he's in Tartar limbo, worse than hell." *Errors*, IV, ii, 32.

Tartar's bow, *n.* **1** Cupid generally represented bearing the lip-shaped bow commonly called the "Tartar's bow"; here, a toy bow of cheap painted wood [lath]: "We'll have no Cupid hood-wink'd with a scarf,/ Bearing a Tartar's painted bow of lath . . ." *Rom & Jul*, I, iv, 4–5. **2** Eastern bow, of stronger construction and swifter of arrow than the English bow: "I go, I go, look how I go!/ Swifter than arrow from the Tartar's bow." *M N Dream*, III, ii, 100–101.

task, *v.* **1** to impose a task on (a person); order: "Nay, task me to my word, approve me, lord." *1 Hen 4*, IV, i, 9. **2** to occupy fully: ". . . let every man now task his thought . . ." *Hen 5*, I, ii,

309. **3** to put to the test; try: "And will they so? the gallants shall be task'd . . ." *Love's L*, V, ii, 126.

tasking, *n.* challenge to combat: "How show'd his tasking? Seem'd it in contempt?" *1 Hen 4*, V, ii, 50.

tassel-gentle, *n.* male peregrine falcon, which could be lured back to the falconer by a special call: "O for a falconer's voice/ To lure this tassel-gentle back again." *Rom & Jul*, II, ii, 158–159.

taste, *v.* **1** to try: "Taste your legs, sir, put them to motion." *T Night*, III, i, 79. **2** to put to the test: "I never tasted Timon in my life." *Timon*, III, ii, 79.
—*n.* **3** trial or test: "Till that the nobles . . . Have of their puissance made a little taste." *2 Hen 4*, II, iii, 51–52. **4** trace: "Nor hath Love's mind of any judgement taste . . ." *M N Dream*, I, i, 236. **5** foretaste: "I do beseech you, as in way of taste,/ To give me now a little benefit . . ." *Tr & Cr*, III, iii, 13–14. **6 greatest taste most palates theirs,** theirs [the peoples'] will have the greater strength: "When, both your voices blended, the great'st taste/ Most palates theirs." *Cor*, III, i, 102–103. **7 in some taste,** in some way(s): "And, in some taste, is Lepidus but so . . ." *J Caes*, IV, i, 34.

tasteful, *adj.* tasting; devouring: "O, when/ Her twinning cherries shall their sweetness fall/ Upon thy tasteful lips . . ." *Kinsmen*, I, i, 177–179.

tattle, *v.* to chatter; prate: ". . . too like my lady's eldest son, evermore tattling." *M Ado*, II, i, 9.

tattlings, *n.* idle talk; chatter or gossip: "Peace your tattlings! What is 'fair,' William?" *Wives*, IV, i, 21.

Taurus, *n.* **1** Also called **the Bull,** sign of the zodiac: "See, see, thou hast shot off one of Taurus' horns." *T Andr*, IV, iii, 68. **2** this sign regarded as governing the lower legs and feet (in some sources, the throat and neck); here, Sir Andrew is mistaken, and Sir Toby attempts to add to the (bawdy) humor: "Taurus? That's sides and heart."/ "No, sir, it is legs and thighs." *T Night*, I, iii, 137–138. **3** mountain chain in Asia Minor: "That pure congealed white, high Taurus' snow,/ Fann'd with the eastern wind . . ." *M N Dream*, III, ii, 141–142.

tawdry-lace, *n.* brightly colored neckerchief [based on name and legend of "Saint Audrey"]: "Come, you promised me a tawdry-lace/ and a pair of sweet gloves." *W Tale*, IV, iv, 251–252.

tawny, *adj.* **1** dark; here, ref. to Hermia's brunette coloring: "Thy love? Out, tawny Tartar, out!/ Out, loathed medicine! . . .": *M N Dream*, III, ii, 263–264. **2** of a brownish color; parched: "The ground, indeed, is tawny." *Temp*, II, i, 52.

3 dark-yellow: "We shall your tawny ground with your red blood/ Discolour . . ." *Hen 5*, III, vi, 166–167. **4 tawny front,** dark face: ". . . devotion of their view/ Upon a tawny front . . ." *Ant & Cleo*, I, i, 5–6.

tax, *v.* **1** to criticize; blame or censure: "Faith, niece, you tax Signior Benedick too much . . ." *M Ado*, I, i, 42. **2** to accuse: "With all the spots [vices] a' th' world tax'd and debosh'd [corrupted] . . ." *All's W*, V, iii, 205. **3** to instruct; order: "Both taxing me, and gaging me to keep/ An oath . . ." *Tr & Cr*, V, i, 40–41. **4 taxed for speech,** rebuked for indiscreet talk: "Be check'd for silence,/ But never tax'd for speech." *All's W*, I, i, 63–64. **5 tax him home,** to take him to task: "I'll warrant she'll tax him home . . ." *Ham*, III, iii, 29.

taxation, *n.* mockery or fault-finding; also, slander: ". . . you'll be whipped for taxation one of these days." *As You*, I, ii, 78–79.

teach, *v.* **1** to show; indicate: "Teach her the way." *Meas*, II, iv, 19. **2 teach me to't,** instruct [convince] me to do it: "I believe you;/ Your honour and your goodness teach me to't . . ." *Per*, III, iii, 25–26.

tearing, *n.* act of tearing up; Goneril here tears up her love letter to Edmund: ". . . read thine own evil:/ No tearing, lady;/ I perceive you know it." *Lear*, V, iii, 156–157.

tear thyself, *v.* to tear one's clothes (and sometimes the hair) as an indication of intense grief: "Woo't weep, woo't fight, woo't fast, woo't tear thyself . . ." *Ham*, V, i, 270.

teat, *n.* suckling teat: "I would say thou hadst suck'd wisdom from thy teat." *Rom & Jul*, I, iii, 68.

Te Deum, Latin hymn, "We praise thee, O God": "Let there be sung 'Non nobis' and 'Te Deum';/ The dead with charity enclos'd in clay." *Hen 5*, IV, viii, 125–126.

tedious, *adj.* **1** tiresome; overlong: "'A tedious brief scene of young Pyramus/ And his love Thisbe . . .'" *M N Dream*, V, i, 56–57. **2** intricate or elaborate: ". . . but woman's son/ Can trace me in the tedious ways of art . . ." *1 Hen 4*, III, i, 44–45. **3** difficult or impossible: "Returning were as tedious as go o'er." *Mac*, III, iv, 137. **4** done with great difficulty: "Fair Philomel, why, she but lost her tongue,/ And in a tedious sampler sew'd her mind . . ." *T Andr*, II, iv, 38–39. **5** painful or odious: "My woes are tedious, though my words are brief." *Luc*, 1309. **6** Dogberry may misunderstand as "pecunious," wealthy: ". . . if/ I were as tedious as a king, I could find in my heart/ to bestow it all of [on] your worship." *M Ado*, III, v, 19–21.

teem, *v.* **1** to give birth; bring forth (a child): "If she must teem,/ Create her child of spleen . . ." *Lear*, I, iv, 290–291. **2**

to beget [fig. use of preceding]: "What's the newest grief? . . . Each minute teems a new one." *Mac*, IV, iii, 174–176.

teeming, *adj.* **1** fertile or, often, pregnant: ". . . oft the teeming earth/ Is with a kind of colic pinch'd . . ." *1 Hen 4*, III, i, 25–26. **2 teeming date,** childbearing period: "Is not my teeming date drunk up with time?" *Rich 2*, V, ii, 91.

teen, *n.* **1** grief or sorrow: "O! what a scene of foolery have I seen,/ Of sighs, of groans, of sorrow, and of teen . . ." *Love's L*, IV, iii, 160–161. **2** vexation: "My face is full of shame, my heart of teen . . ." *Ven & Ad*, 808.

teeth, *n. pl.* **1 from his teeth,** without sincerity; not from his heart: "When the best hint was given him, he not took't,/ Or did it from his teeth." *Ant & Cleo*, III, iv, 9–10. **2 in the teeth,** to my face: "Yea, dost thou jeer and flout me in the teeth?" *Errors*, II, ii, 22. **3 out of the teeth of,** beyond the reach of: "My heart laments that virtue cannot live/ Out of the teeth of emulation." *J Caes*, II, iii, 11–12. **4 show one's teeth,** to grin: "You show'd your teeth like apes . . ." *J Caes*, V, i, 41. **5 to the teeth and forehead,** when confronted face-to-face (with): "Even to the teeth and forehead of our faults . . ." *Ham*, III, iii, 63.

Telamon, *n.* (in the Trojan War) Ajax Telamon, who went mad and slew himself when not awarded the armor of the dead Achilles: "O, he's more mad/ Than Telamon for his shield . . ." *Ant & Cleo*, IV, xiii, 1–2.

tell, *v.* **1** to count: "I have kept back their foes,/ While they have told their money . . ." *Timon*, III, v, 107–108. **2** to indicate to; let (someone) know: ". . . telling them I know my/ place, as I would they should do theirs . . ." *T Night*, II, v, 53–54. **3** to know; be certain of: "I would tell what 'twere to be a judge,/ And what a prisoner." *Meas*, II, ii, 69–70. **4 by telling of it,** by distorting it [the truth]: ". . . like one/ Who having into truth, by telling of it,/ Made such a sinner of his memory . . ." *Temp*, I, ii, 99–101. **5 canst thou tell?** how do you know? what makes you think so?: "Proud and ambitious tribune, canst thou tell?" *T Andr*, I, i, 202. **6 in telling your mind,** when you disclose your intentions: "I fear/ she'll prove as hard to you in telling your mind." *Two Gent*, I, i, 132–133. **7 tell on thy mind,** ellip. for "tell me what is on thy mind": "Tell on thy mind; I say thy child shall live." *T Andr*, V, i, 69. **8 tell out,** to count out (a sum, esp. of money): "Tell out my blood." *Timon*, III, iv, 93. **9 tell steps,** to keep step; march in step: ". . . and front but in that file/ Where others tell steps with me." *Hen 8*, I, ii, 42–43. **10 tell the clock,** count the strikes of the clock: "[The clock striketh.] Tell the clock there!" *Rich 3*, V, iii, 277. **11 tell (someone) home,** to give (someone) a tongue-lashing: "You have told them home,/ And, by my troth, you have cause." *Cor*, IV, ii, 48–49.

tell-tale, *n.* **1** gossip or tattler; talebearer: "You speak to Casca, and to such a man/ That is no fleering tell-tale." *J Caes,* I, iii, 116–117. **2** reminder: "And therefore will he wipe his tables clean,/ And keep no tell-tale to his memory . . ." *2 Hen 4,* IV, i, 202–203.
—*adj.* **3** gossipy; tattling: "Let not the heavens hear these tell-tale women . . ." *Rich 3,* IV, iv, 150.

Tellus, *n.* **1** earth goddess; here, personification of the earth: "No, I will rob Tellus of her weed,/ To strew thy green with flowers . . ." *Per,* IV, i, 13–14. **2 Tellus' orbed ground,** the earth itself: "Neptune's salt wash and Tellus' orbed ground . . ." *Ham,* III, ii, 151.

temper, *v.* **1** to mix or compound: ". . . if the truth of thy love to me were so righteously tempered as mine is to thee." *As You,* I, ii, 12–13. **2** to modify; change: "Mine ear hath temper'd judgment to desire." *3 Hen 6,* III, iii, 133. **3** to mollify or soften; here, to melt like sealing wax: "I have him already tempering between my finger/ and my thumb . . ." *2 Hen 4,* IV, iii, 128–129. **4** to mold; fashion: "But he that temper'd thee bade thee stand up . . ." *Hen 5,* II, ii, 118. **5** to moisten: ". . . grind their bones to powder small,/ And with this hateful liquor temper it . . ." *T Andr,* V, ii, 198–199. **6** to condition or develop: ". . . father Nestor, were your days/ As green as Ajax', and your brain so temper'd . . ." *Tr & Cr,* II, iii, 253–254. **7 temper with the stars,** to reconcile oneself to one's Fate: ". . . avoiding Fortune's malice,/ For few men rightly temper with the stars . . ." *3 Hen 6,* IV, vi, 28–29.
—*n.* **8** disposition: "Fie! what man of/ good temper would endure this tempest of exclamation?" *2 Hen 4,* II, i, 78–79. **9** person's character: "He holds your temper in a high respect . . ." *1 Hen 4,* III, i, 164. **10** self-restraint: ". . . his captain's heart . . . reneges [refuses] all temper . . ." *Ant & Cleo,* I, i, 6–8. **11** quality of metal, a sword, etc.: "A sword whose temper I intend to stain/ With the best blood that I can meet withal . . ." *1 Hen 4,* V, ii, 93–94. **12 in temper,** in normal mental condition; mentally stable: "Keep me in temper; I would not be mad!" *Lear,* I, v, 48.

temperality, *n.* prob. misuse for "temper"; disposition; humor: ". . . methinks you are in an/ excellent good temperality." *2 Hen 4,* II, iv, 22–23.

temperance, *n.* **1** ref. to island's mild climate; here, wordplay on girl's name: "It must needs be of subtle, tender and delicate/ temperance."/ "Temperance was a delicate wench." *Temp,* II, i, 40–43. **2** calmness or self-control; also, sanity: "Be by . . . when we do awake him;/ I doubt not of his temperance." *Lear,* IV, vii, 23–24.

temperate, *adj.* cool-headed; unperturbed: "Such temperate order [actions] in so fierce a cause . . ." *K John,* III, iii, 12.

tempered, *adj.* disposed; inclined: ". . . were your days/ As green as Ajax', and your brain so temper'd . . ." *Tr & Cr,* II, iii, 253–254.

tempering, *n.* working with the fingers until soft and malleable: "What wax so frozen but dissolves with temp'ring . . ." *Ven & Ad,* 565.

temple, *n.* **1** church; here, for taking the oath: "First forward to the temple, after dinner/ Your hazard shall be made." *Merch,* II, i, 44–45. **2** human body: ". . . as this temple waxes,/ The inward service of the mind and soul/ Grows wide withal." *Ham,* I, iii, 12–14.

Temple Garden, *n.* garden of the Temple, one of the Inns of Court (legal societies in London): "London. The Temple Garden." [SD] *1 Hen 6,* II, iv, 1.

temple-haunting, *adj.* (of the martlet) building its nest under the eaves of churches: "The temple-haunting martlet, does approve,/ By his loved mansionry . . ." *Mac,* I, vi, 4–5.

temporal, *adj.* **1** civil: "For all the temporal lands which men devout/ By testament have given to the Church . . ." *Hen 5,* I, i, 9–10. **2** secular; worldly: "Is this an hour for temporal affairs? Ha?" *Hen 8,* II, ii, 72.

temporal royalties, *n. pl.* worldly exercise of power; here, in contrast to intellectual pursuits: ". . . of temporal royalties/ He thinks me now incapable . . ." *Temp,* I, ii, 110–111.

temporary, *adj.* involved in temporal matters: ". . . not a temporary meddler,/ As he's reported by this gentleman . . ." *Meas,* V, i, 147–148.

temporize, *v.* **1** to compromise: "The Dolphin is too wilful-opposite,/ And will not temporize with my entreaties . . ." *K John,* V, ii, 124–125. **2** to adapt oneself, esp. to change ones beliefs or opinions: "Well, you will temporize with the hours [come around in time]." *M Ado,* I, i, 254.

tempt, *v.* **1** to risk: "To dare the vile contagion of the night,/ And tempt the rheumy and unpurged air/ To add unto his sickness?" *J Caes,* II, i, 265–267. **2 tempt all,** to venture everything: "And now, to tempt all liberty procur'd." *Lover's Comp,* 252.

tenable, *adj.* capable of being held close; hence, retained: "If you have hitherto conceal'd this sight,/ Let it be tenable in your silence still . . ." *Ham,* I, ii, 247–248.

tenant, *n.* vassal: "Where be thy tenants and thy followers?" *Rich 3,* IV, iv, 480.

Tenantius, *n.* Cymbeline's father: ". . . had his titles by Tenantius, whom/ He served with glory and admired success . . ." *Cymb,* I, i, 31–32.

tench, *n.* spotted fish, similar to the carp: ". . . the most villainous house in all/ London road for fleas, I am stung like a tench." *1 Hen 4,* II, i, 13–14.

ten commandments, *n.* fingernails: "I'd set my ten commandments in your face." *2 Hen 6,* I, iii, 142.

tend, *v.* **1** to attend; wait [upon]: "The summer still doth tend upon my state . . ." *M N Dream,* III, i, 148. **2** to listen (to); heed: "Take in the topsail. Tend to th' master's/ whistle." *Temp,* I, i, 6–7. **3 tend on, a.** to accompany: "Come, you Spirits/ That tend on mortal thoughts, unsex me here . . ." *Mac,* I, v, 40–41. **b.** to attend; wait on: "Though more to know could not be more to trust:/ From whence thou cam'st, how tended on . . ." *All's W,* II, i, 205–206.

tendance, *n.* attendance; act of waiting upon or attending another: ". . . his large fortune . . . Subdues and properties to his love and tendance." *Timon,* I, i, 56–58.

tender[1], *v.* **1** to offer: ". . . 'tis not amiss we tender our loves to him . . ." *Timon,* V, i, 13. **2** to make one appear (as): "Tender yourself more dearly/ Or . . . you'll tender me a fool." *Ham,* I, iii, 107–109. **3 tender down,** to place on, or as if on, the ground as an offering: "You see how all conditions . . . tender down/ Their services to Lord Timon . . ." *Timon,* I, i, 53–56.
—*n.* **4** offer: ". . . now in some slight measure it will pay,/ If for his tender here I make some stay." *M N Dream,* III, ii, 86–87. **5** offering: ". . . you did exceed/ The barren tender of a poet's debt . . ." *Sonn 83,* 4. **6** act of giving: ". . . which is material/ To th' tender of our present." *Cymb,* I, vii, 207–208. **7** (often pl.) promise, esp. of payment: "These are the vulgar tenders of false men,/ That never pay the duty of their words." *Edw 3,* II, i, 315–316. **8** (usually pl.) counters used in games to represent money: ". . . you have ta'en these tenders for true pay/ Which are not sterling." *Ham,* I, iii, 106–107.

tender[2], *n.* **1** great care or regard (for): ". . . in the tender of a wholesome weal,/ Might in their working do you that offence . . ." *Lear,* I, iv, 219–220. **2 make tender of, a.** to show regard for: ". . . thou mak'st some tender of my life,/ In this fair rescue thou hast brought to me." *1 Hen 4,* V, iv, 48–49. **b.** to offer: "As honour, without breach of honour, may/ Make tender of to thy true worthiness." *Love's L,* II, i, 169–170.
—*v.* **3** to guard; watch over: "In the devotion of a subject's love,/ Tend'ring the precious safety of my prince . . ." *Rich 2,* I, i, 31–32. **4** to regard; cherish: "If any friend will pay the sum for him,/ He shall not die, so much we tender him." *Errors,* V, i, 131–132. **5** to care for: "Huntsman, I charge thee, tender

well my hounds." *Shrew,* Ind., i, 14. **6** to be concerned for: "His Majesty,/ Tend'ring my person's safety, hath appointed/ This conduct . . ." *Rich 3,* I, i, 43–45.
—*adj.* **7** obedient; also, scrupulous: ". . . how long/ Shall tender duty make me suffer wrong?" *Rich 2,* II, i, 163–164. **8** (of a person) not hardened by experience: "Witness this army of such mass and charge,/ Led by a delicate and tender prince . . ." *Ham,* IV, iv, 47–48. **9** soft or weak: ". . . why should we be tender,/ To let an arrogant piece of flesh threat us . . ." *Cymb,* IV, ii, 126–127. **10** dear; beloved: "Within thine own bud buriest thy content,/ And, tender churl, mak'st waste in niggarding." *Sonn 1,* 11–12.

tender-hefted, *adj.* loving; gentle; compassionate: "Thy tender-hefted nature shall not give/ Thee o'er to harshness . . ." *Lear,* II, iv, 173–174.

tender smell, *n.* keen scent; here, needed by hounds for tracking: "Look as the full-fed hound or gorged hawk,/ Unapt for tender smell or speedy flight . . ." *Luc,* 694–695.

tending, *n.* **1** care; attention: "Give him tending:/ He brings great news." *Mac,* I, v, 37–38.
—*pres. part.* **2** relating; pertaining: "Writings, all tending to the great opinion/ That Rome holds of his name . . ." *J Caes,* I, ii, 315–316.

Tenedos, *n.* island off the NW coast of Asia Minor: "To Tenedos they come,/ And the deep-drawing barks do there disgorge . . ." *Tr & Cr,* Prol., 11–12.

tenement, *n.* land held by a tenant: ". . . this dear dear land . . . Is now leas'd out . . . Like to a tenement or pelting farm." *Rich 2,* II, i, 57–60.

tenor, *n.* **1** substance or meaning: ". . . with experimental seal doth warrant/ The tenor of my book . . ." *M Ado,* IV, i, 166–167. **2** Also, **tenure,** intent; gist or drift: "I know not the contents, but as I guess . . . It bears an angry tenour." *As You,* IV, iii, 8–11. **3** [pl.] general principles: "Whose tenours and particular effects/ You have, enschedul'd briefly, in your hands." *Hen 5,* V, ii, 72–73.

tent[1], *n.* **1** bed curtains: "Costly apparel, tents, and canopies . . ." *Shrew,* II, i, 345. **2 beat you to your tent,** ref. to Pompey's retreat after being defeated by Caesar: "If I do,/ Pompey, I shall beat you to your tent, and prove a/ shrewd [harsh] Caesar to you . . ." *Meas,* II, i, 244–246.
—*v.* **3** to take up residence: "The smiles of knaves/ Tent in my cheeks . . ." *Cor,* III, ii, 115–116.

tent[2], *n.* **1** roll of cloth for probing and cleaning wounds: "The beacon of the wise, the tent that searches/ To th' bottom of the worst." *Tr & Cr,* II, ii, 16–17. **2** method of probing: ". . .

modest doubt is call'd/ The beacon of the wise, the tent that searches/ To th'bottom of the worst." *Tr & Cr,* II, ii, 15–17. —*v.* **3** to clean (a wound) with a tent; cause to heal: "Well might they fester 'gainst ingratitude,/ And tent themselves with death." *Cor,* I, ix, 30–31. **4** to probe: "I'll tent him to the quick. If a do blench,/ I know my course." *Ham,* II, ii, 592–593.

tenth, *n.* **gather up a tenth,** to levy a 10% tax on incomes: "For your expenses and sufficient charge,/ Among the people gather up a tenth." *1 Hen 6,* V, v, 92–93.

tent-royal, *n.* monarch's tent or pavilion: ". . . with merry march bring home/ To the tent-royal of their emperor . . ." *Hen 5,* I, ii, 195–196.

tenure, *n.* **1** type of lease for property: "Where be his quiddities now, his quillities,/ his cases, his tenures, and his tricks?" *Ham,* V, i, 97–98. **2** summarizing statement; gist or tenor: "Here folds she up the tenure of her woe . . ." *Luc,* 1310.

tercel, *n.* **the falcon as the tercel,** female hawk as well as the male hawk [tiercel]: ". . . the falcon as the tercel, for all the ducks i'th'river . . ." *Tr & Cr,* III, ii, 52.

Tereus, *n.* king of Thrace, who raped his sister-in-law Philomel, then cut out her tongue to prevent her exposing him: "But, sure, some Tereus hath deflow'red thee . . ." *T Andr,* II, iv, 26.

term, *n.* **1** expression, name or epithet: ". . . stand under/ the adoption of abominable terms . . ." *Wives,* II, ii, 283–284. **2** [pl.] **a.** nature or character: "The terms of our estate [one in my position] may not endure/ Hazard so near us . . ." *Ham,* III, iii, 5–6. **b.** circumstances: "A sister driven into desp'rate terms . . ." *Ham,* IV, vii, 26. **c.** language; manner of speaking: "In any case, be not too rough in terms,/ For he is fierce and cannot brook hard [harsh] language." *2 Hen 6,* IV, ix, 43–44. **3** [usually pl.] methods; procedures: "Our city's institutions, and the terms/ For common justice . . ." *Meas,* I, i, 10–11. **4 four terms,** the four terms of the annual legal calendar: ". . . the wearing out of six fashions, which is four terms . . ." *2 Hen 4,* V, i, 76–77. **5 terms of our estate,** my position as ruler: "The terms of our estate may not endure . . ." *Ham,* III, iii, 5. —*v.* **6 term in gross,** to state in full: ". . . the full sum of me/ Is sum of something: which to term in gross,/ Is an unlesson'd girl . . ." *Merch,* III, ii, 157–159.

termagant, *adj.* savage; murderous; bloodthirsty: ". . . 'twas time to counterfeit, or that hot/ termagant Scot had paid me . . ." *1 Hen 4,* V, iv, 112–113.

Termagant, *n.* supposedly a god of the Saracens, represented in plays as a bloodthirsty tyrant: "I would have such a fellow whipped for o'erdoing/ Termagant." *Ham,* III, ii, 13–14.

termination, *n.* descriptive term or expression, esp. one of abuse: ". . . if her breath were as terrible as her/ terminations, there were no living near her . . ." *M Ado,* II, i, 232–233.

termless, *adj.* youthful; also, poss. "indescribable": "Like un-shorn velvet on that termless skin . . ." *Lover's Comp,* 94.

term of life, *n.* rest of my life: "For term of life thou art assured mine . . ." *Sonn 92,* 2.

terms compulsatory, *n. pl.* use of force; here, military force: ". . . to recover of us by strong hand/ And terms compulsatory those foresaid lands . . ." *Ham,* I, i, 105–106.

terms divine, *n.* heavenly grace; life everlasting: "Buy terms divine in selling hours of dross . . ." *Sonn 146,* 11.

terrace, *n.* indicates a scene played on the upper stage of the Elizabethan theatre: "Kenilworth Castle. Sound trumpets. Enter King, Queen, and Somerset, on the terrace." [SD] *2 Hen 6,* IV, ix, 1.

Terras Astraea reliquit, [Latin] Astraea [goddess of justice] has left the earth: "*Terras Astraea reliquit:* Be you rememb'red, Marcus,/ She's gone, she's fled." *T Andr,* IV, iii, 4–5.

terrene, *adj.* earthly; terrestrial: "Alack, our terrene moon/ Is now eclips'd . . ." *Ant & Cleo,* III, xiii, 153–154.

terrible, *adj.* **1** showing great strength or determination: "How modest in exception, and withal/ How terrible in constant resolution . . ." *Hen 5,* II, iv, 34–35. **2** fierce; savage: "Then lend the eye a terrible aspect . . ." *Hen 5,* III, i, 9. **3** awesome; terrifying: "Sound to this coward and lascivious town/ Our terrible approach." *Timon,* V, iv, 1–2.

terribly, *adv.* frighteningly; awesomely: "You are not oathable,/ Although I know you'll swear, terribly swear . . ." *Timon,* IV, iii, 137–138.

terror, *n.* awe-inspiring authority: "Lent him our terror, drest him with our love . . ." *Meas,* I, i, 19.

tertian, *n.* severe fever occurring on alternate days; here, confused with the daily fever [quotidian]: ". . . he is so shaked/ of a burning quotidian tertian, that it is most/ lamentable to behold." *Hen 5,* II, i, 118–120.

testament, *n.* legal will disposing of property, making bequests, etc.: "Of six preceding ancestors, that gem/ Conferr'd by testament to th' sequent issue . . ." *All's W,* V, iii, 195–196.

tested, *adj.* determined to be pure: "Not with fond sickles of the tested gold . . ." *Meas,* II, ii, 150.

tester, *n.* slang term for "sixpence": ". . . Wart, th'art a good scab. Hold, there's a/ tester for thee." *2 Hen 4,* III, ii, 271–272.

testern, *v.* to give a tester to: "To/ testify your bounty . . . you have testerned/ me . . ." *Two Gent,* I, i, 137–139.

testify, *v.* to give proof of: "To/ testify your bounty . . . you have testerned/ me . . ." *Two Gent,* I, i, 137–139.

testimony, *n.* **in the testimony,** with the warrant (of): "Very reverend sport, truly: and done in the/ testimony of a good conscience." *Love's L,* IV, ii, 1–2

testril, *n.* Sir Andrew's whimsical variant of "tester," a sixpence coin: "There's a testril of me too: if one knight give a—" *T Night,* II, iii, 34–35.

tetchy, *adj.* touchy; peevish or fretful: ". . . pretty fool,/ To see it tetchy and fall out with the dug." *Rom & Jul,* I, iii, 31–32.

tetter, *n.* **1** [often pl.] massive skin eruption: ". . . a most instant tetter bark'd about,/ Most lazar-like, with vile and loathsome crust/ All my smooth body." *Ham,* I, v, 71–73. —*v.* **2** to infect with tetters: ". . . against those measles/ Which we disdain should tetter us . . ." *Cor,* III, i, 77–78.

tevil and his tam, *n.* parson's mispron. of "Devil and his dam [mother]," a common oath: "The tevil and his tam! What phrase is this, 'He/ hears with ear'?" *Wives,* I, i, 135–136.

Tewkesbury, *n.* **1** town NW of London, in N central England, at confluence of the Avon and Severn rivers: "We are advertis'd [advised] . . . That they do hold their course toward Tewkesbury." *3 Hen 6,* V, iii, 18–19. **2** same, the scene of armed conflicts between York and Lancaster forces: "Edward, her lord, whom I . . . Stabb'd in my angry mood at Tewkesbury?" *Rich 3,* I, ii, 245–246.

Tewkesbury mustard, *n.* popular mustard made in Tewkesbury: "His wit's as/ thick as Tewkesbury mustard . . ." *2 Hen 4,* II, iv, 237–238.

text B, *n.* example of formal script in a student's copybook [probably a darker script, likened as it is to Rosaline's dark beauty]: "Beauteous as ink; a good conclusion."/ "Fair as a text B in a copy-book." *Love's L,* V, ii, 41–42.

texted, *past part.* inscribed or incised: ". . . stratagems forepast with iron pens/ Are texted in thine honourable face." *Edw 3,* IV, iv, 129–130.

'th or **th',** *pron.* thee: ". . . come away, or I'll/ fetch'th with a wanion." *Per,* II, i, 16–17.

th', *pron.* thou: ". . . the more th' hast wrong'd me." *Lear,* V, iii, 168.

than, *adv.* var. of **then;** afterward: "To break upon the galled shore, and than/ Retire again . . ." *Luc,* 1440.

thane, *n.* (in medieval Scotland) a feudal lord: "No more that Thane of Cawdor shall deceive/ Our bosom interest." *Mac,* I, ii, 65–66.

thank, *n.* **1** expression of gratitude; saying "thank-you": "Evermore thank's [thank is] the exchequer of the poor . . ." *Rich 2,* II, iii, 65. **2 give them thanks,** get even with them: "I shall live, my lord, to give them thanks/ They were the cause of my imprisonment." *Rich 3,* I, i, 127–128.

thanksgiving, *n.* **thanksgiving before meat,** grace said before a meal: "There's not a soldier of us all that, in/ the thanksgiving before meat, do relish the petition/ well that prays for peace." *Meas,* I, ii, 14–16.

tharborough, *n.* See **farborough.**

Tharsus, *n.* See **Tarsus.**

thas, *adv.* thus [perh. a parody of military pron.]: "Hold, Wart, traverse—thas! thas! thas!" *2 Hen 4,* III, ii, 267.

Thasos, *n.* island near Philippi: "Come therefore, and to Thasos send his body." *J Caes,* V, iii, 104.

that, *pron.* **1** what: ". . . 'tis too true; and that is worse . . . The lords of Ross, Beaumond, and Willoughby . . . are fled to him." *Rich 2,* II, ii, 52–55. **2** so that: ". . . new sorrows/ Strike heaven on the face, that it resounds/ As if it felt with Scotland . . ." *Mac,* IV, iii, 5–7. **3** he that: ". . . that/ Must bear my beating to his grave . . ." *Cor,* V, vi, 108–109. **4 to that,** to that end or purpose: "Worthy to be a rebel, for to that/ The multiplying villainies of nature/ Do swarm upon him . . ." *Mac,* I, ii, 10–12. —*conj.* **5** would that: "Ask what thou wilt. That I had said and done!" *2 Hen 6,* I, iv, 27. **6** in that: ". . . that we but teach/ Bloody instructions, which, being taught, return/ To plague th' inventor . . ." *Mac,* I, vii, 8–10. **7** so that: "Bear't that th'opposed may beware of thee." *Ham,* I, iii, 67. **8** inasmuch as; because: "That thou hast sought to make us break our vows . . ." *Lear,* I, i, 168. **9** when: "So till the judgement that yourself arise,/ You live in this, and dwell in lovers' eyes." *Sonn 55,* 13–14.

thaw'd, *adj.* turned to water: "He tumbled down upon his Nemean hide,/ And swore his sinews thaw'd." *Kinsmen,* I, i, 68–69.

Theban, *n.* **learned Theban,** scholar or philosopher: "I'll talk a word with this same learned Theban." *Lear,* III, iv, 161.

thee, *pron.* **for thee,** [I am] ready for you; here, for armed combat: "I am for thee straight. Take thou the bill, give me/ thy mete-yard . . ." *Shrew,* IV, iii, 149–150.

theft, *n.* **head of theft,** thief: "A lover's ear will hear the lowest sound,/ When the suspicious head of theft is stopp'd . . ." *Love's L,* IV, iii, 331–332.

theme, *n.* **1** purpose; undertaking: ". . . in a theme so bloody-fac'd as this/ Conjecture . . . Of aids incertain should not be admitted." *2 Hen 4,* I, iii, 22–24. **2** subject of a speech or discourse: "To me she speaks, she moves me for her/ theme . . ." *Errors,* II, ii, 181–182. **3 was theme for you,** had you as its cause: ". . . their contestation/ Was theme for you, you were the word of war." *Ant & Cleo,* II, ii, 43–44.

thence, *adv.* **1** from there: "'Tis not four days gone/ Since I heard thence . . ." *Cor,* I, ii, 6–7. **2 from thence,** away from there; here, from home: ". . . to feed were best at home;/ From thence, the sauce to meat is ceremony . . ." *Mac,* III, iv, 34–35.

theoric, *n.* theory: ". . . the gallant militarist . . . had the whole theoric of war in the/ knot of his scarf . . ." *All's W,* IV, iii, 137–139.

there, *adv.* **1** i.e., written in the annals: ". . . 'tis there,/ That like an eagle in a dove-cote . . ." *Cor,* V, vi, 113–114. **2 are you there with me?** So that's what you mean?: "O, ho! are you there with me? No eyes in/ your head, nor no money in your purse?" *Lear,* IV, vi, 146–147. **3 There was it,** that was the thing: "There was it:/ For which my sinews shall be stretch'd upon him . . ." *Cor,* V, vi, 44–45.

thereabout, *adv.* around that part: ". . . 'twas Aeneas' tale/ to Dido, and thereabout of it especially when he/ speaks of Priam's slaughter." *Ham,* II, ii, 442–444.

thereafter, *adv.* **thereafter as they be,** according to what they are, i.e., depending on their quality: "How a score of ewes now?"/ "Thereafter as they be . . ." *2 Hen 4,* III, ii, 49–50.

therefor, *adv.* for that: ". . . tell me then that he is well."/ "And if I could, what should I get therefor?" *M N Dream,* III, ii, 77–78.

therefore, *adv.* for that (very) reason: "Therefore I took your hands, but was indeed/ Sway'd from the point by looking down on Caesar." *J Caes,* III, i, 218–219.

thereon, *v.* for that reason: "If he love her not,/ And be not from his reason fall'n thereon . . ." *Ham,* II, ii, 164–165.

therewithal, *adv.* with that: ". . . give her that ring, and there-withal/ This letter." *Two Gent,* IV, iv, 85–86.

these, *pron.* these things or problems; here, pangs of love; poss. ref. to Helena's downcast expression: "If ever we are nature's, these are ours; this thorn/ Doth to our rose of youth rightly belong . . ." *All's W,* I, iii, 124–126.

these and these, such and such: ". . . what he is, augmented,/ Would run to these and these extremities [extremes] . . ." *J Caes,* II, i, 30–31.

Thessalian, *adj.* of Thessaly: "Crook-knee'd and dewlapp'd like Thessalian bulls . . ." *M N Dream,* IV, i, 121.

Thessaly, *n.* **1** region in eastern Greece: "Was never holla'd to, nor cheer'd with horn,/ In Crete, in Sparta, nor in Thessaly." *M N Dream,* IV, i, 124–125. **2 boar of Thessaly [Calydonian boar],** giant boar, with "eyes of blood and fire," that ravaged the kingdom of Calydon until it was killed by the king's son Meleager: ". . . the boar of Thessaly/ Was never so emboss'd [cornered so decisively]." *Ant & Cleo,* IV, xiii, 2–3.

Thetis, *n.* sea nymph, one of the Nereids and mother of Achilles; here, confused with Tethys, wife of Oceanus: ". . . at her birth,/ Thetis, being proud, swallow'd some part o' th' earth." *Per,* IV, iv, 38–39.

thews, *n. pl.* **1** sinews: "Care I for the limb, the thews, the stature . . . of a man?" *2 Hen 4,* III, ii, 253–254. **2 in thews and bulk,** in strength and size: ". . . nature crescent does not grow alone/ In thews and bulk . . ." *Ham,* I, iii, 11–12.

they'ld, *v.* they would: "I would they'ld fight i' the fire, or i' the air,/ We'ld fight there too." *Ant & Cleo,* IV, x, 3–4.

thick, *adj.* **1** dense or opaque; turbid: ". . . like a fountain troubled,/ Muddy, ill-seeming, thick, bereft of beauty . . ." *Shrew,* V, ii, 143–144. **2** dim; hazy: ". . . his dimensions to any thick sight were invisible . . ." *2 Hen 4,* III, ii, 307. **3** numerous; countless: "He furnaces/ The thick sighs from him . . ." *Cymb,* I, vii, 66–67. **4** coarse; here, foul: "In their thick breaths,/ Rank of gross diet, shall we be enclouded . . ." *Ant & Cleo,* V, ii, 210–211.
—*adv.* **5** close together; in such numbers: ". . . twenty several messengers:/ Why do you send so thick?" *Ant & Cleo,* I, v, 62–63. **6** quickly: "O Lord, sir! Thick, thick; spare not me." *All's W,* II, ii, 43. **7 so thick come,** coming in such profusion: "Weak words, so thick come in his poor heart's aid . . ." *Luc,* 1784. **8 speak thick,** to speak rapidly and indistinctly; here, probably also with a regional accent: "And speaking thick, which nature made his blemish,/ Became the accents of the valiant . . ." *2 Hen 4,* II, iii, 24–25.

—*v.* **9 thick my blood,** cause me to be melancholy: ". . . his varying childness cures in me/ Thoughts that would thick my blood." *W Tale,* I, ii, 170–171.

thicken, *v.* **1** to grow dim: "Light thickens; and the crow/ Makes wing to th' rooky wood . . ." *Mac,* III, ii, 50–51. **2** to strengthen or confirm: "And this may help to thicken other proofs . . ." *Oth,* III, iii, 436.

thick-ey'd, *adj.* sullen or ill-natured; moody: ". . . given my treasures and my rights of thee/ To thick-ey'd musing, and curst melancholy?" *1 Hen 4,* II, iii, 46–47.

thicklips, *n.* slighting ref. to Othello: "What a full fortune does the thicklips owe . . ." *Oth,* I, i, 66.

thick-ribbed ice, *n.* bleak terrain of purgatory: ". . . or to re- side/ In thrilling region of thick-ribbed ice . . ." *Meas,* III, i, 121–122.

thick-sighted, *adj.* having dimmed or blurred vision: "Thick- sighted, barren, lean, and lacking juice . . ." *Ven & Ad,* 136.

thick-skin, *n.* **1** coarse fellow: "The shallowest thick-skin of that barren sort . . . Forsook his scene, and enter'd in a brake . . ." *M N Dream,* III, ii, 13–15. **2** dunce; blockhead: "What wouldst thou have, boor? What, thick-skin?" *Wives,* IV, v, 1.

thievery, *n.* stolen goods: ". . . with a robber's haste/ Crams his rich thiev'ry up . . ." *Tr & Cr,* IV, iv, 41–42.

thievish, *adj.* frequented by thieves: ". . . bid me leap . . . From off the battlements of any tower,/ Or walk in thievish ways . . ." *Rom & Jul,* IV, i, 77–79.

thine, *pron.* thy turn: "Here, sweet, put up this: 'twill be thine another day." *Love's L,* IV, i, 108.

thing, *n.* **1** wordplay on "object" and bawdy slang for "pu- denda": "I have a thing for you."/ "A thing for me? it is a com- mon [used by all] thing—" *Oth,* III, iii, 305–306. **2 tell you a thing,** tell you something important: "Well cousin, I told you a thing yesterday; think/ on't." *Tr & Cr,* I, ii, 172–173. **3 what thing is't,** how disgraceful a thing it is: ". . . what thing is't that I never/ Did see man die . . ." *Cymb,* IV, iv, 35–36.

thin habits, *n.* shabby dress [in which to clothe your charg- es]: "These are thin habits, and poor likelihoods/ Of modern seemings . . ." *Oth,* I, iii, 108–109.

think, *v.* **1** to plan; expect; count on: "I know you think to dine with me today . . ." *Shrew,* III, ii, 183. **2** to imagine: ". . . think his pilot [is] thought;/ So with his steerage shall your thoughts grow on . . ." *Per,* IV, iv, 18–19. **3** to bear in mind: "I pray you think you question [argue] with the Jew . . ." *Merch,* IV, i, 70. **4 think scorn,** See **scorn** (def. 4).

thin man, *n.* figure carved in low relief: ". . . you thin man in a censer, I will/ have you as soundly swinged for this . . ." *2 Hen 4,* V, iv, 19–20.

third, *v.* to reduce to a third: "Yet what man/ Thirds his own worth . . ." *Kinsmen,* I, ii, 95–96.

thirdborough, *n.* constable: "I know my remedy, I must go fetch the thirdborough." *Shrew,* Ind., i, 10.

thirsty, *adj.* causing hunger or want; needy: ". . . the time seems thirsty unto me,/ Being all this time abandon'd from your bed." *Shrew,* Ind., ii, 115–116.

this, *pron.* **1** this way: "Much upon [very nearly] this 'tis . . ." *Love's L,* V, ii, 472. **2** this play: "In your fair minds let this ac- ceptance take." *Hen 5,* Epil. 14. **3 by this,** by this time; by now: "Before proud Athens he's set down by this . . ." *Timon,* V, iii, 9. **4 in this,** in this time when: "If you refuse your aid/ In this so never-needed help . . ." *Cor,* V, i, 33–34.

this', *pron.* this is: "This' a good block!" *Lear,* IV, vi, 185.

Thisbe, *n.* See **Pyramus and Thisbe.**

thither, *v.* to go to that place: "By this sun that shines/ I'll thither . . ." *Cymb,* IV, iv, 34–35.

thitherward, *adv.* as he was going toward that place: "We met him thitherward, for thence we came,/ And, after some dis- patch . . . Thither we bend again." *All's W,* III, ii, 52–54.

Thoas, *n.* iden. only as "cousin to Achilles" [some sources: Duke of Athens]: "Amphimacus and Thoas deadly hurt;/ Pa- troclus ta'en or slain . . ." *Tr & Cr,* V, v, 12–13.

thorn, *n.* **against a thorn,** the nightingale, it was said, kept itself awake to sing at night by pressing itself against a thorn: "And while against a thorn thou bear'st thy part/ To keep thy sharp woes waking . . ." *Luc,* 1135–1136.

thorough, *prep.* old form of **through (def. 1):** ". . . whose eyes do never give/ But thorough lust and laughter." *Timon,* IV, iii, 488–489.

thou, *pron.* **1** Achilles' use of thee/thou to Ulysses is con- temptuous: "I shall forestall thee, Lord Ulysses, thou!" *Tr & Cr,* IV, v, 229.
—*v.* **2 thou thou'st him,** speak familiarly (and insultingly) to him: "If thou thou'st him some thrice, it shall not/ be amiss . . ." *T Night,* III, ii, 43–44.

thou'dst, *v.* contraction of "thou wouldst": "Poor bird! thou'dst never fear the net, nor lime,/ The pit-fall, nor the gin." *Mac,* IV, ii, 34–35.

though, *conj.* although it may: ". . . never cut from memory/ My sweet love's beauty, though my lover's life . . ." *Sonn 63,* 11–12.

though ne'er so, *adv.* however: "You private grudge . . . will out,/ Though ne'er so cunningly you smother it." *1 Hen 6,* IV, i, 109–110.

thought, *n.* **1** deliberation or meditation; here, brooding: ". . . thus the native hue of resolution/ Is sicklied o'er with the pale cast of thought . . ." *Ham,* III, i, 84–85. **2** sorrowful reflection: "Thought and affliction, passion, hell itself/ She turns to favour and to prettiness." *Ham,* IV, v, 185–186. **3** conjecture: "Of those that lawless and incertain thought/ Imagine howling . . ." *Meas,* III, i, 126–127. **4** melancholy: "Made wit with musing weak, heart sick with thought." *Two Gent,* I, i, 69. **5 seen in thought,** thought about but never spoken about: ". . . all will come to naught/ When such ill-dealing must be seen in thought." *Rich 3,* III, vi, 13–14. **6 take thought,** to lapse into melancholy: ". . . all that he can do/ Is to himself: take thought, and die for Caesar." *J Caes,* II, i, 186–187. **7 upon a thought,** in a moment: "The fit is momentary; upon a thought/ He will again be well." *Mac,* III, iv, 54–55. **8 want the thought,** to keep from thinking: "Who cannot want the thought, how monstrous/ It was for Malcolm, and for Donalbain,/ To kill their gracious father?" *Mac,* III, vi, 8–10. **9 with a thought,** immediately: "I followed me close . . . and, with a thought, seven/ of the eleven I paid." *1 Hen 4,* II, iv, 211–213. —*past part.* **10** remembered; kept in mind: ". . . always thought,/ That I require a clearness . . ." *Mac,* III, iv, 131–132. **11 as thought on,** as richly as [they were] regarded: "To have them recompens'd as thought on." *W Tale,* IV, iv, 521.

thoughten, *past part.* **be you thoughten,** be assured: ". . . be you thoughten/ That I came with no ill intent . . ." *Per,* IV, vi, 108–109.

thought-executing, *adj.* acting with the speed of thought: "You sulph'rous and thought-executing fires,/ Vaunt-couriers of oak-cleaving thunderbolts . . ." *Lear,* III, ii, 4–5.

Thought is free, prob. the refrain of the round sung by the threesome: "Flout 'em and scout 'em,/ And scout 'em and flout 'em;/ Thought is free." *Temp,* III, ii, 119–121.

thought-sick, *adj.* distressed; depressed: ". . . as against the doom,/ Is thought-sick at the act." *Ham,* III, iv, 50–51.

thou'lt, *v.* contraction of "thou shalt": "Thou'lt torture me to leave unspoken that/ Which, to be spoke, would torture thee [you will torture me to speak and again to unspeak that which, if spoken, will torture you]." *Cymb,* V, v, 139–140.

thou's, *v.* contraction of "thou shalt": "I have remember'd me, thou's hear our counsel." *Rom & Jul,* I, iii, 9.

thou't, *v.* contraction of "thou wilt" or, as here, "thou wouldst": "If I should tell thee o'er this thy day's work,/ Thou't not believe thy deeds . . ." *Cor,* I, ix, 1–2.

Thracian, *adj.* of Thrace, a country NE of ancient Greece, at the N end of the Aegean Sea: "And brought from thence the Thracian fatal steeds . . ." *3 Hen 6,* IV, ii, 21.

Thracian fatal steeds, *n.* horses of Rhesus, said by oracle to prevent fall of Troy, stolen by Ulysses and Diomede: ". . . as Ulysses and stout Diomede . . . stole to Rhesus' tents,/ And brought from thence the Thracian fatal steeds . . ." *3 Hen 6,* IV, ii, 19–21.

Thracian poet (singer), *n.* poet and musician Orpheus: "'The riot of the tipsy Bacchanals,/ Tearing the Thracian singer in their rage'?" *M N Dream,* V, i, 48–49.

Thracian tyrant, *n.* Polymnestor, king of Thrace, whose sons were murdered by Hecuba: ". . . gods that arm'd the Queen of Troy/ With opportunity of sharp revenge/ Upon the Thracian tyrant in his tent . . ." *T Andr,* I, i, 136–138.

thrall, *n.* **1** slave: "Long time thy shadow hath been thrall to me,/ For in my gallery thy picture hangs . . ." *1 Hen 6,* II, iii, 35–36.
—*adj.* **2** enslaved: "How love makes young men thrall . . ." *Ven & Ad,* 837.

thralled, *adj.* **1** enthralled; enslaved: ". . . madness would not err/ Nor sense to ecstasy was ne'er so thrall'd . . ." *Ham,* III, iv, 73–74. **2 thralled discontent,** enforced oppression: "Under the blow of thralled discontent . . ." *Sonn 124,* 7.

thrasonical, *adj.* boastful: ". . . Caesar's thrasonical brag of I came, saw, and overcame." *As You,* V, ii, 30–31.

thread, *n.* **1 cut thread and thrum,** ends of the warp [lengthwise threads] when a piece of weaving is finished and cut from the loom; here, the snipping of life's thread by the Fates: "O Fates, come, come!/ Cut thread and thrum . . ." *M N Dream,* V, i, 274–275. **2 shore his old thread atwain,** cut his thread of life in two [cf. Atropos]: ". . . and pure grief/ Shore his old thread atwain . . ." *Oth,* V, ii, 206–207. **3 thread of life,** one's lifetime likened to a spun thread: "*Argo,* their thread of life is spun." *2 Hen 6,* IV, ii, 29. Cf. **Fates.**
—*v.* **4** to go through; here, in defense of the city: "Even when the navel of the state was touch'd,/ They would not thread the

gates . . ." *Cor,* III, i, 122–123. **5** to pick one's way (through): "Thus out of season, threading dark-ey'd night . . ." *Lear,* II, i, 119.

threaden, *adj.* woven of thread: ". . . behold the threaden sails . . ." *Hen 5,* III, Chor. 10.

threaden fillet, *n.* ribbon for binding the hair: "Some in her threaden fillet still did bide . . ." *Lover's Comp,* 33.

threat, *v.* threaten: "Are you so desperate grown to threat your friends?" *T Andr,* II, i, 40.

three, *pron.* family of three, rather than a couple [example of Helen's bawdy wit]: ". . . they two are twain."/ "Falling in after falling out may make them three." *Tr & Cr,* III, i, 98–99.

three-farthings, *n.* coin of small worth showing a rose behind the queen's head: ". . . in mine ear I durst not stick a rose/ Lest men should say 'Look, where three-farthings goes!'" *K John,* I, i, 142–143.

three-hooped pot, *n.* alepot holding a quart: ". . . the three-hoop'd pot/ shall have ten hoops; and I will make it felony to/ drink small beer." *2 Hen 6,* IV, ii, 63–65.

three-inch fool, *n.* ref. to Grumio's short height; also, to sexually inadequate man of folklore: "Away, you three-inch fool! I am no beast." *Shrew,* IV, i, 23.

three-man song-men, *n.* male singers of three-part songs: ". . . the shearers,/ three-man song-men all, and very good ones . . ." *W Tale,* IV, iii, 41–42.

three-nooked, *adj.* three-cornered [ref. to three parts of Roman Empire: west (Europe), east (Asia), and south (Africa)]: "Prove this a prosperous day, the three-nook'd world/ Shall bear the olive freely." *Ant & Cleo,* IV, vi, 6–7.

three-pile, *n.* finest velvet: "I have served Prince Florizel, and in my time wore/ three-pile . . ." *W Tale,* IV, iii, 13–14.

three-piled, *adj.* describing cloth, esp. velvet, of triple thickness [the finest quality]: "Three-pil'd hyperboles, spruce affection,/ Figures pedantical . . ." *Love's L,* V, ii, 407–408.

three-suited, *adj.* (of a servant) given three outfits a year: ". . . a base, proud, shallow, beggarly, three-suited . . . worsted-stocking knave . . ." *Lear,* II, ii, 14–15.

Threne, *n.* Greek funeral song [fr. Greek *threnos*]: "Whereupon it made this Threne/ To the Phoenix and the Dove . . ." *Phoen,* 49–50.

Threnos, *n.* [Greek] **Threne:** "*Threnos*/ Beauty, truth and rarity,/ Grace in all simplicity . . ." *Phoen,* 53–54.

thrice-crowned, *adj.* ref. to moon goddess's three names: Luna, Phoebe, and Selene: ". . . thou thrice-crowned queen of night . . ." *As You,* III, ii, 2.

thrice-driven, *adj.* (of feathers) three times air-driven to separate out the lightest and softest feathers: ". . . steel couch of war/ My thrice-driven bed of down . . ." *Oth,* I, iii, 230–231.

thrift, *n.* **1** profit; success or gain: "And crook the pregnant hinges of the knee/ Where thrift may follow fawning." *Ham,* III, ii, 61–62. **2** salvation: "And make them dread it, to the doers' thrift." *Cymb,* V, i, 15.

thriftless, *adj.* useless; unprofitable: "What thriftless sighs shall poor Olivia breathe?" *T Night,* II, i, 38.

thrifty, *adj.* proper; veritable [used contemptuously]: ". . . a thrifty shoeing-horn in a chain at his brother's/ leg . . ." *Tr & Cr,* V, i, 55–56.

thrill, *v.* **1** to shiver; tremble or shudder: "Art thou not horribly/ afraid? Doth not thy blood thrill at it?" *1 Hen 4,* II, iv, 365–366. **2** to move; overwhelm: "A servant that he bred, thrill'd with remorse . . ." *Lear,* IV, ii, 73.

thrilling, *adj.* bitterly (or freezing) cold: ". . . or to reside/ In thrilling region of thick-ribbed ice . . ." *Meas,* III, i, 121–122.

thrive, *v.* to succeed or win: "Mine innocence and Saint George to thrive!" *Rich 2,* I, iii, 84.

thriver, *n.* person who thrives, getting ahead at great cost to himself: "Pitiful thrivers in their gazing spent?" *Sonn 125,* 8.

thriving issue, *n.* successful outcome: ". . . your free undertaking cannot miss/ A thriving issue . . ." *W Tale,* II, ii, 44–45.

throe, *n.* **1** pain; pang: ". . . and that gave to me/ Many a groaning throe . . ." *Hen 8,* II, iv, 196–197.
—*v.* **2** to pain: ". . . a birth, indeed,/ Which throes thee much to yield [speak]." *Temp,* II, i, 226.

throne, *n.* **1** the heart, seat of love: "My bosom's lord sits lightly in his throne . . ." *Rom & Jul,* V, i, 3.
—*v.* **2** to be enthroned: "He wants [lacks] nothing of a god but eternity, and a heaven/ to throne in." *Cor,* V, iv, 24–25.

throng, *v.* **1** to crowd around; jostle: "I'll say th' hast gold./ Thou wilt be throng'd to shortly." *Timon,* IV, iii, 396–397. **2** to oppress or overwhelm: ". . . the earth is throng'd/ By man's oppression . . ." *Per,* I, i, 102–103.

—*n.* **3** (often pl.) an assembled army: "We are enow [enough] yet living in the field/ To smother up the English in our throngs . . ." *Hen 5,* IV, v, 19–20.

thronged up, *past part.* overwhelmed: "A man throng'd up with cold. My veins are chill . . ." *Per,* II, i, 73.

throstle, *n.* thrush: ". . . if a throstle sing, he/ falls straight a-cap'ring . . ." *Merch,* I, ii, 57–58.

through, *adj.* **1** honest; straightforward: ". . . if a man is/ through with them in honest taking up . . ." *2 Hen 4,* I, ii, 39–40.
—*adv.* **2** out: "I would revenges . . . would seek us through . . ." *Cymb,* IV, ii, 159–160. **3** throughout; here, to every soldier: "Give the word through." *Hen 5,* IV, vi, 38.

throughfare, *n.* var. of thoroughfare: ". . . the vasty wilds/ Of wide Arabia are as throughfares now . . ." *Merch,* II, vii, 41–42.

throughly, *adv.* var. of thoroughly: "Ability in means and choice of friends,/ To quit me of them throughly." *M Ado,* IV, i, 199–200.

throw, *v.* **1** to cast dice; here, to take one's chances in combat: "Who sets me else? By heaven, I'll throw at all!" *Rich 2,* IV, i, 57. **2** to cast off; shed: "And there the snake throws her enamell'd skin . . ." *M N Dream,* II, i, 255. **3** to confer or bestow: ". . . begin to throw/ [the titles or honors of] Pompey the Great . . . Upon his son . . ." *Ant & Cleo,* I, ii, 185–187. **4 throw down, a.** to demolish; raze or level: ". . . who digs hills because they do aspire/ Throws down one mountain to cast up a higher." *Per,* I, iv, 5–6. **b.** wordplay between "vanquish in battle" and "conquer sexually": "And better would it fit Achilles much/ To throw down Hector than Polyxena." *Tr & Cr,* III, iii, 206–207. **5 throw forth,** to give birth to (a litter): "With news the time's in labour, and throws forth,/ Each minute, some." *Ant & Cleo,* III, vii, 80–81. **6 throw out,** to cast about; direct: "As to throw out our eyes for brave Othello . . ." *Oth,* II, i, 38.
—*n.* **7** throw of the dice; prob. ref. to Clown's "gamble" on gaining a third tip: "You can fool no more money out of me at this/ throw." *T Night,* V, i, 39–40. **8** (in bowls) distance intended to be covered in a toss: "I have tumbled past the throw [gone beyond my intended statement] . . ." *Cor,* V, ii, 21.

throwest, *v.* [you] throw the dice: "Set less than thou throwest [Don't bet everything on one throw of the dice] . . ." *Lear,* I, iv, 129.

thrum, *n.* See **thread** (def. 1).

thrummed, *adj.* fringed: "She's as big as/ he is; and there's her thrummed hat . . ." *Wives,* IV, ii, 69–70.

thrush, *n.* the song thrush: "With heigh! With heigh! The thrush and the jay . . ." *W Tale,* IV, iii, 10.

thrusting on, *n.* a forcing or compelling; incitement: ". . . and/ all that we are evil in, by a divine thrusting on." *Lear,* I, ii, 130–131.

thump, *interj.* sound made in imitation of cannonfire: "I shoot thee at the swain."/ "Thump then, and I flee." *Love's L,* III, i, 62.

thunder-bearer, *n.* Jupiter: "I do not bid the thunder-bearer shoot,/ Nor tell tales of thee to high-judging Jove." *Lear,* II, iv, 229–230.

thunder-stone, *n.* thunderbolt: "And, thus unbraced, Casca, as you see,/ Have bar'd my bosom to the thunder-stone . . ." *J Caes,* I, iii, 48–49.

thus much, so much; this much: "If you were civil, and knew courtesy,/ You would not do me thus much injury." *M N Dream,* III, ii, 147–148.

thwack, *v.* **1** to drive [away]; here, used humorously: ". . . he shall not stay,/ We'll thwack him hence with distaffs." *W Tale,* I, ii, 36–37. **2** to beat; wallop: "Why, here's he that was wont to thwack our/ general, Caius Martius." *Cor,* IV, v, 182–183.

thwart, *v.* **1** to traverse; cross: "Pericles/ Is now again thwarting the wayward seas . . ." *Per,* IV, iv, 9–10.
—*adj.* **2** perverse; unruly: "And be a thwart disnatur'd torment to her!" *Lear,* I, iv, 292.

thwarting stars, *n.* unlucky Fate: ". . . the people of this blessed land/ May not be punish'd with my thwarting stars . . ." *3 Hen 6,* IV, vi, 21–22.

thyself, *pron.* **thyself upon thyself,** May you remain yourself! [used here as a curse]: ". . . thyself upon thyself! The/ common curse of mankind, folly and ignorance,/ be thine in great revenue . . ." *Tr & Cr,* II, iii, 28–30.

Tib, *n.* typical name for a country girl; also, slut: ". . . doorkeeper to every/ Coistrel that comes inquiring for his Tib . . ." *Per,* IV, vi, 164–165.

Tiber, *n.* river that flows through Rome: "Let Rome in Tiber melt . . ." *Ant & Cleo,* I, i, 33.

tice, *v.* to entice; lure: "These two have tic'd me hither to this place . . ." *T Andr,* II, iii, 92.

tickle, *v.* **1** to cajole; flatter: "That smooth-fac'd gentleman, tickling commodity [self-interest] . . ." *K John,* II, i, 573. **2** to irritate: "Not that it wounds,/ But tickles still the sore." *Tr & Cr,* III, i, 114–115. **3 tickle it,** to make [Diomedes] pay for it: "He'll tickle it for his concupy." *Tr & Cr,* V, ii, 176. —*adj.* **4** precarious; unstable; here also, prob. wordplay with "head" and "maidenhead" and suggestion that a maid could lose her maidenhead merely with sighs of love: ". . . thy head stands so tickle on/ thy shoulders, that a milkmaid, if she be in love,/ may sigh it off." *Meas,* I, ii, 161–163.

tickle a th' sear, (of a person) easily made to laugh [fr. catch on gun kept ready to fire at the slightest touch]: ". . . the clown shall make those laugh whose lungs are/ tickle a th' sear . . ." *Ham,* II, ii, 322–323.

tickle-brain, *n.* kind of strong drink (used as a nickname for the Hostess): "Peace, good pint-pot, peace, good tickle-brain." *1 Hen 4,* II, iv, 392.

tickled, *adj.* irritated; riled or galled: "She's tickled now; her fury needs no spurs . . ." *2 Hen 6,* I, iii, 150.

tickle point, *n.* precarious or unstable condition: ". . . the state of Normandy/ Stands on a tickle point now they are gone . . ." *2 Hen 6,* I, 1, 216–217.

tickling, *n.* flattery: ". . . here comes/ the trout that must be caught with tickling." *T Night,* II, v, 21–22.

ticklish, *adj.* lustful; easily aroused: "And wide unclasp the tables of their thoughts/ To every ticklish reader . . ." *Tr & Cr,* IV, v, 60–61.

tick-tack, *n.* **game of tick-tack,** board game resembling backgammon; here, implying sexual intercourse: ". . . the enjoying of thy life, who [which] I/ would be sorry should be thus foolishly lost at [over] a/ game of tick-tack." *Meas,* I, ii, 179–181.

tiddle taddle, *n.* Fluellen's pron. of "tittle tattle"; gossip or chatter: ". . . there is no tiddle taddle nor pibble babble in/ Pompey's camp . . ." *Hen 5,* IV, i, 71–72.

tide, *n.* **1** flood tide; the most opportune moment: "I have important business,/ The tide whereof is now." *Tr & Cr,* V, i, 81–82. **2 under the tide,** by a flood of bad news: "I was amaz'd/ Under the tide: but now I breathe again/ Aloft the flood . . ." *K John,* IV, ii, 137–139.

'tide, *v.* betide; befall: "'Tide life, 'tide death [whether life or death befall me], I come without delay." *M N Dream,* V, i, 201.

tide of times, *n.* throughout the course of history: ". . . the noblest man/ That ever lived in the tide of times." *J Caes,* III, i, 256–257.

tidy, *adj.* plump; cute: "Thou whoreson little tidy Bartholomew boar-pig . . ." *2 Hen 4,* II, iv, 227.

tie, *v.* **1** to hold: "Feast-finding minstrels . . . Will tie the hearers to attend each line . . ." *Luc,* 817–818. **2** to force: ". . . he'll not feel wrongs/ Which tie him to an answer [to respond]." *Lear,* IV, ii, 13–14. **3** to hold in bondage: ". . . one that by suggestion/ Tied all the kingdom . . ." *Hen 8,* IV, ii, 35–36.

tied, *n.* Crab, Launce's dog; wordplay here on "tide" and "tied": "It is no matter if the tied were lost . . ." *Two Gent,* II, iii, 37.

ties his points, See **point** (def. 19).

tiger-footed, *adj.* coming swiftly and silently; also, destructive: "This tiger-footed rage, when it shall find/ The harm of unscann'd swiftness . . ." *Cor,* III, i, 309–310.

tight, *adj.* **1** watertight: ". . . three great argosies, besides two galliasses/ And twelve tight galleys." *Shrew,* II, i, 371–372. **2** adroit; skillful: ". . . my queen's a squire/ More tight at this than thou . . ." *Ant & Cleo,* IV, iv, 14–15.

tightly, *adv.* carefully: "Hold, sirrah, bear you these letters tightly . . ." *Wives,* I, iii, 75.

tike, *n.* mongrel dog; cur: "Or bobtail tike or trundle-tail;/ Tom will make him weep and wail . . ." *Lear,* III, vi, 70–71.

tilly-fally, *interj.* nonsense! fiddlesticks!: "Tilly-fally, Sir John . . . and your ancient/ swagger, a comes not in my doors." *2 Hen 4,* II, iv, 81–82.

tilly-vally, *interj.* same as **tilly-fally;** fiddle-dee-dee: "Am not I consanguineous? Am I not of her/ blood? Tilly-vally! 'Lady!' [Lady, indeed!]" *T Night,* II, iii, 78–80.

tilt, *v.* **1** to duel with lances in a tournament; also, to spar verbally: "Lo! he is tilting straight. Peace! I have done." *Love's L,* V, ii, 483. —*n.* **2** contest in which two knights on horseback charged each other with lances: "There shall he practise tilts and tournaments . . ." *Two Gent,* I, iii, 30. **3 run a tilt,** to participate in a tournament: "Thou ran'st a tilt in honour of my love . . ." *2 Hen 6,* I, iii, 51.

tilter, *n.* combatant who attacks with a lance in a tournament; here, prob. a fencer: "Master Forthright the tilter . . ." *Meas,* IV, iii, 16.

tilth, *n.* tillage: "Letters should not be known . . . Bourn, bound of land, tilth, vineyard, none . . ." *Temp,* II, i, 146–148.

tilt-yard, *n.* **1** area in Westminster (London) used for tournaments: ". . . I'll be sworn a ne'er saw him but once in the tilt-yard." *2 Hen 4,* III, ii, 316. **2** area of open ground, as adjoining a castle, where knights engaged in contests to sharpen their jousting skills: "His study is his tilt-yard, and his loves/ Are brazen images of canoniz'd saints." *2 Hen 6,* I, iii, 59–60.

timbered, *adj.* shafted; here, an arrow with too light a shaft will be blown back by a strong wind: ". . . my arrows,/ Too slightly timber'd for so loud a wind [the populace],/ Would have reverted to my bow again . . ." *Ham,* IV, vii, 21–23.

time, *n.* **1** proper moment for something; occasion: ". . . my occasions have found/ time to use 'em toward a supply of money." *Timon,* II, ii, 195–196. **2** lifetime: "The hope and expectation of thy time/ Is ruin'd . . ." *1 Hen 4,* III, ii, 36–37. **3** youth: ". . . to come fairly off from the great debts/ Wherein my time . . . Hath left me gag'd . . ." *Merch,* I, i, 128–130. **4** age; time of life: ". . . all the learnings that his time/ Could make him the receiver of . . ." *Cymb,* I, i, 43–44. **5** tradition; natural law: "Take Herford's rights away, and take from time/ His charters, and his customary rights . . ." *Rich 2,* II, i, 195–196. **6** the world; one's fellow men: ". . . who would bear the whips and scorns of time . . ." *Ham,* III, i, 70. **7** latest fashion: "Why with the time do I not glance aside . . ." *Sonn 76,* 3. **8** [pl.] future times; succeeding generations: "Shall give a holiness . . . To the yet unbegotten sin of times . . ." *K John,* IV, iii, 53–54. **9 any time,** at any time: ". . . no manner person/ Have, any time, recourse unto the Princes." *Rich 3,* III, v, 107–108. **10 find good time,** be blest with good fortune; here, will be born: "The fruit she goes with/ I pray for heartily, that it may find/ Good time, and live . . ." *Hen 8,* V, i, 20–22. **11 for my time,** for my present needs [assignment]: ". . . my chance is now/ To use it for my time." *Meas,* III, ii, 211–212. **12 for the time,** for the present; for the time being: ". . . for the time I study/ Virtue, and that part of philosophy . . . that treats of happiness . . ." *Shrew,* I, i, 17–19. **13 give the time of day,** to say "good morning" or "good day": "When every one will give the time of day,/ He knits his brow and shows an angry eye . . ." *2 Hen 6,* III, i, 14–15. **14 in good time, a.** indeed [used as an exclamation]: "I think the meat wants that I have."/ "In good time, sir; what's that?"/ "Basting." *Errors,* II, ii, 55–57. **b.** at the appropriate time: "Well, sir, learn to jest in good time; there's a/ time for all things." *Errors,* II, ii, 63–64. **15 in the mature time,** when the time is ripe: ". . . in the mature time/ With this ungracious paper strike the sight/ Of the death-practis'd Duke." *Lear,* IV, vi, 277–279. **16 like the time,** as the occasion demands: "Let's go off,/ And bear us [comport ourselves] like the time." *Kinsmen,* V, iv, 136–137. **17 lose one's time,** to fritter away one's time: "Thou, Julia . . .

Made me neglect my studies, lose my time . . ." *Two Gent,* I, i, 66–67. **18 mock the time,** to deceive all witnesses or observers: ". . . mock the time with fairest show:/ False face must hide what the false heart doth know." *Mac,* I, vii, 82–83. **19 of greater time,** older in years: "To be fantastic may become a youth/ Of greater time . . ." *Two Gent,* II, vii, 47–48. **20 one time will owe another,** another time will make up for this: "Put not your worthy rage into your tongue./ One time will owe another." *Cor,* III, i, 239–240. **21 the time,** the present time: "And carry with us ears and eyes for th'time . . ." *Cor,* II, i, 267. **22 time as long again,** as much more time [another nine months]: "Time as long again/ Would be fill'd up . . . with our thanks . . ." *W Tale,* I, ii, 3–4. **23 time of scorn,** the scornful world: "A fixed figure, for the time of scorn/ To point his slow unmoving fingers at . . ." *Oth,* IV, ii, 55–56. **24 time of year,** the proper season: "We at time of year/ Do wound the bark, the skin of our fruit-trees . . ." *Rich 2,* III, iv, 57–58. **25 time revives us,** the coming time will restore us: "We must away;/ Our wagon is prepar'd, and time revives us." *All's W,* IV, iv, 33–34. **26 time shall try,** fr. proverb, "Time tries [tests] all things": "Well, as time shall try. 'In time the savage/ bull doth bear the yoke.'" *M Ado,* I, i, 241–242. **27 to the time,** at the appointed time: "Just to the time, not with the time exchanged [changed by time] . . ." *Sonn 109,* 7. **28 what time,** at which time: "What time we will our celebration keep/ According to my birth." *T Night,* IV, iii, 29–31. **29 when time shall serve,** when it suits my purpose: ". . . when/ time shall serve there shall be smiles . . ." *Hen 5,* II, i, 4–5.

time-bettering, *adj.* improving; innovative: "Some fresher stamp of the time-bettering days." *Sonn 82,* 8.

timed, *past part.* accompanied by: ". . . a thing of blood, whose every motion/ Was tim'd with dying cries . . ." *Cor,* II, ii, 109–110.

timeless, *adj.* **1** untimely; premature: ". . . who perform'd/ The bloody office of his timeless end." *Rich 2,* IV, i, 4–5. **2 all-too-timeless speed,** very unseemly haste: "But some untimely thought did instigate/ His all-too-timeless speed . . ." *Luc,* 43–44.

timely, *adv.* **1** early: "He did command me to call timely on him . . ." *Mac,* II, iii, 47. **2** in time; in good time: "Now spurs the lated traveller apace,/ To gain the timely inn . . ." *Mac,* III, iii, 6–7. **3 timelier than my purpose,** earlier than I had intended: ". . . and thanks to you,/ That call'd me timelier than my purpose hither . . ." *Ant & Cleo,* II, vi, 50–51.

timely-parted, *adj.* having died a natural death: "Oft have I seen a timely-parted ghost,/ Of ashy semblance . . ." *2 Hen 6,* III, ii, 160–161.

time-pleaser, *n.* time-server; also, a flatterer who tailors his own opinions to those of others: ". . . anything/ constantly, but a time-pleaser, an affectioned/ ass . . ." *T Night,* II, iii, 146–148.

time's abuse, *n.* current evils: "If not the face of men,/ The sufferance of our souls, the time's abuse . . ." *J Caes,* II, i, 114–115.

time's state, *n.* circumstances of the moment: ". . . the time's state/ Made friends of them, jointing their force 'gainst Caesar . . ." *Ant & Cleo,* I, ii, 87–88.

Timon, *n.* bitter protagonist of Shakespeare's play, *Timon of Athens,* and a legendary hater of mankind: "And critic Timon laugh at idle [useless] toys!" *Love's L,* IV, iii, 167.

timorous, *adj.* terrifying: "Do, with like timorous accent, and dire yell . . ." *Oth,* I, i, 75.

tinct, *n.* **1** magic solution; tincture: "Plutus himself,/ That knows the tinct and multiplying med'cine . . ." *All's W,* V, iii, 101–102. **2 leave their tinct,** give up their color (stain): "And there I see such black and grained spots/ As will not leave their tinct." *Ham,* III, iv, 90–91.

tincture, *n.* addition to a coat of arms, granted by a sovereign as a mark of recognition: ". . . great men shall press/ For tinctures, stains, relics, and cognizance." *J Caes,* II, ii, 88–89.

tinder-box, *n.* troublemaker; also, poss. ref. to Bardolph's red nose: "I am glad I am so acquit of this tinder-box: his/ thefts were too open . . ." *Wives,* I, iii, 23–24.

tinder-like, *adj.* easily provoked to anger: ". . . hasty and tinder-like/ upon too trivial motion [slightest provocation] . . ." *Cor,* II, i, 49–50.

tinker, *n.* **1** mender of pots and pans: "Tom Snout, the tinker?" *M N Dream,* I, ii, 57. **2** drunken beggar, peddler, schemer, etc.: ". . . he was the lord ambassador,/ Sent from a sort of tinkers to the King." *2 Hen 6,* III, ii, 275–276.

tinsel, *n.* fine cloth interwoven with gold or silver thread: ". . . skirts, round underborne with a bluish tinsel . . ." *M Ado,* III, iv, 20.

tipstaff, *n., pl.* **tipstaves,** bailiff, who carried a metal-tipped staff as symbol of his office: "Enter Buckingham from his arraignment, tipstaves before him . . ." [SD] *Hen 8,* II, i, 53.

tire¹, *v.* **1** to feed, esp. to tear at flesh in the manner of a bird of prey: "Upon that were my thoughts tiring when we encounter'd." *Timon,* III, vi, 4–5. **2** to feed sexually: ". . . when

thou shalt be disedg'd by her/ That now thou tirest on . . ." *Cymb,* III, iv, 95–96.

tire², *v.* **1** to dress the hair, esp. with a wig: "The one, to save the money that he spends in tiring . . ." *Errors,* II, ii, 96. —*n.* **2** attire or furnishings; here, the trappings of wealth: "I much marvel that your lordship, having/ Rich tire about you, should . . . Shake off the golden slumber of repose." *Per,* III, ii, 21–23. **3** elaborate headdress: "I like the new tire within excellently . . ." *M Ado,* III, iv, 12.

tire³, 1 to exhaust; sate: "Then should not we be tir'd with this ado." *T Andr,* II, i, 98. **2 come tiring on,** to arrive exhausted: "The posts come tiring on,/ And not a man of them brings other news . . ." *2 Hen 4,* Induc. 37–38.

tire-valiant, *n.* elaborate headdress, perh. in form of a ship: ". . . the right arched beauty of the brow that becomes/ the ship-tire, the tire-valiant, or any tire . . ." *Wives,* III, iii, 50–51.

tiring-house, *n.* dressing room: "This green plot shall be our stage,/ this hawthorn-brake our tiring-house . . ." *M N Dream,* III, i, 3–4.

tirra-lirra, *n.* imit. of lark's song: "The lark, that tirra-lirra chants . . ." *W Tale,* IV, iii, 9.

tirrits, *n. pl.* perh. misuse of "twitters," with sense of terrified trembling: "I'll forswear keeping/ house afore I'll be in these tirrits and frights!" *2 Hen 4,* II, iv, 200–201.

tisick, *n.* var. of **phthisic;** consumption: "A whoreson tisick, a whoreson rascally tisick, so/ troubles me . . ." *Tr & Cr,* V, iii, 101–102.

tissue, *n.* fine cloth, usually containing gold or silver threads: ". . . deck an ape/ In tissue, and the beauty of the robe/ Adds but the greater scorn unto the beast." *Edw 3,* II, i, 445–447.

Titan, *n.* Roman sun god: ". . . whose virtues will, I hope,/ Reflect on Rome as Titan's rays on earth . . ." *T Andr,* I, i, 225–226.

tithe, *n.* **1** tenth part: "A slave that is not twentieth part the tithe/ Of your precedent lord . . ." *Ham,* III, iv, 97–98. **2** tithe dues; here, the corn sown to pay the tithe dues, with the meaning that "We must do the work if we are to reap the benefits": "Our corn's to reap, for yet our tithe's to sow [has yet to be sown]." *Meas,* IV, i, 76. —*v.* **3** to impose a tithe: ". . . no Italian priest/ Shall tithe or toll in our dominions . . ." *K John,* III, i, 79–80.

—*adj.* **4** tenth; prob. ref. to soldiers killed in battle: "Every tithe soul 'mongst many thousand dismes [tenths]/ Hath been as dear as Helen . . ." *Tr & Cr,* II, ii, 19–20.

tithed, *adj.* killing one person out of every ten: "By decimation and a tithed death . . ." *Timon,* V, iv, 31.

tithe-pig, *n.* the tenth pig of a litter, owed to the parish priest: "And sometime comes she with a tithe-pig's tail,/ Tickling a parson's nose . . ." *Rom & Jul,* I, iv, 79–80.

tithing, *n.* small village or parish: ". . . whipp'd/ from tithing to tithing, and stock-punish'd . . ." *Lear,* III, iv, 137–138.

title, *n.* **1** claim: ". . . Lysander, yield/ Thy crazed title to my certain right." *M N Dream,* I, i, 91–92. **2** right or entitlement: ". . . lost that title of respect/ Which the proud soul ne'er pays but to the proud." *1 Hen 4,* I, iii, 8–9. **3** [pl.] possessions: ". . . the sword/ Which sways usurpingly these several titles . . ." *K John,* I, l, 12–13. **4 about the titles,** [in a fight] to determine the rightful ruler: "They would show/ Bravely [be the proper antagonists] about the titles of two kingdoms . . ." *Kinsmen,* IV, ii, 144–145. **5 tells his title,** explains Edward's right to the throne: "Whiles Warwick tells his title, smooths the wrong . . ." *3 Hen 6,* III, i, 48. **6 titles blown from adulation,** empty words from the breath of flatterers: "Think'st thou the fiery fever will go out [be extinguished]/ With titles blown from adulation?" *Hen 5,* IV, i, 259–260.

title-leaf, *n.* title page of a book, often giving a brief description of its contents: ". . . this man's brow, like to a title-leaf,/ Foretells the nature of a tragic volume." *2 Hen 4,* I, i, 60–61.

tittle, *n.* tiny particle; point or dot; also, by inference, the jottings of a lovesick suitor: "What/ shalt thou exchange for rags? robes: for tittles? titles." *Love's L,* IV, i, 82–83.

tittle-tattle, *v.* to gossip: ". . . to whistle of these secrets,/ But you must be tittle-tattling before all our guests?" *W Tale,* IV, iv, 247–248.

to, *conj.* **1** until [rare, poss. misprint]: "You must be purged to your sins are rack'd . . ." *Love's L,* V, ii, 810. **2** as to: "That never aim'd so high to love your daughter . . ." *Per,* II, v, 47.
—*prep.* **3** toward: "Enforce him with his envy to the people . . ." *Cor,* III, iii, 3. **4** (to the extent) of: ". . . lest myself be guilty to self-wrong,/ I'll stop mine ears against the mermaid's song." *Errors,* III, ii, 162–163. **5** compared to: "Laura, to his lady,/ was a kitchen wench . . ." *Rom & Jul,* II, iv, 40–41. **6** of; about: "But if thou dost, what shall I say to thee?/ What may be said to any perjured villain . . ." *Edw 3,* II, i, 329–330. **7** resulting in: "The dram of evil/ Doth all the noble substance often dout/ To his own scandal." *Ham,* I, iv, 36–38. **8**

for: "Tunis was never grac'd before with such a paragon to their Queen." *Temp,* II, i, 71. **9** in relation to: "The Greeks are strong, and skilful to their strength,/ Fierce to their skill, and to their fierceness valiant . . ." *Tr & Cr,* I, i, 7–8. **10** according to: ". . . to her own worth/ She shall be priz'd." *Tr & Cr,* IV, iv, 131–132. **11** due to; because: ". . . puts it off to a compell'd restraint . . ." *All's W,* II, iv, 41. **12** ellipsis for "to do with": "What's this to my Lysander?" *M N Dream,* III, ii, 62. **13** with: "Implore her . . . that she make friends/ To the strict deputy . . ." *Meas,* I, ii, 170–171. **14** about; regarding: "What says she to my face?"/ "She says it is a fair one." *Two Gent,* V, ii, 8–9. **15 to thy head,** to thy face: "Know, Claudio, to thy head,/ Thou hast so wrong'd mine innocent child and me . . ." *M Ado,* V, i, 62–63.
—*adv.* **16** (as to a work animal) on! forward!: "Yes, good sooth: to, Achilles: to, Ajax: to—" *Tr & Cr,* II, i, 111.

toad-spotted, *adj.* spotted with infamy [fr. belief that toad's spots were venomous]: "A most toad-spotted traitor." *Lear,* V, iii, 138.

toadstool, *n.* prob. ref. to Thersites' deformed appearance and poisonous wit: "Toadstool! Learn me the proclamation." *Tr & Cr,* II, i, 21.

to-and-fro-conflicting, *adj.* swaying madly about, as if in angry conflict: "Strives in his little world of man to out-storm/ The to-and-fro-conflicting wind and rain." *Lear,* III, i, 10–11.

toast, *n.* small piece of toasted bread moistened in wine before eating: "Either to harbour fled,/ Or made a toast for Neptune." *Tr & Cr,* I, iii, 44–45.

toast-and-butter, *n.* weakling; milksop: "I pressed me none but such toasts-and-butter,/ with hearts in their bellies . . ." *1 Hen 4,* IV, ii, 20–21.

toaze, *v.* to tease: "Think'st thou, for that/ I insinuate, or toaze from thee thy business . . ." *W Tale,* IV, iv, 734–735.

tod, *n.* **1** 28 pounds; here, of sheep's wool: ". . . every tod/ yields pound and odd shilling . . ." *W Tale,* IV, iii, 32–33.
—*v.* **2** to yield a tod: "Let me see: every 'leven wether tods . . ." *W Tale,* IV, iii, 32.

todpole, *n.* tadpole: "Poor Tom; that eats the swimming frog, the/ toad, the todpole . . ." *Lear,* III, iv, 132–133.

toe, *n.* cryptic ref. by Fool to Lear's daughters, esp. his treatment of Cordelia: "The man that makes his toe/ What he his heart should make,/ Shall of a corn cry woe . . ." *Lear,* III, ii, 31–33.

tofore, *adv.* heretofore; previously; prior to this time: "Some obscure precedence that hath tofore been sain." *Love's L,* III, i, 80.

toge, *n.* toga: "Why in this wolvish [wolfish] toge should I stand here . . ." *Cor,* II, iii, 114.

toged, *adj.* dressed in a toga: "Wherein the toged consuls can propose/ As masterly as he . . ." *Oth,* I, i, 25–26.

together, *adv.* without stopping: "Sweet youth, I pray you chide a year together." *As You,* III, v, 64.

toil¹, *v.* **1** to fatigue or exhaust: "And, toil'd with works of war, retir'd himself/ To Italy . . ." *Rich 2,* IV, i, 96–97. **2** to tax: "Hard-handed men that . . . now have toil'd their unbreath'd memories/ With this same play . . ." *M N Dream,* V, i, 72–75. **3** to force into labor: "So nightly toils the subject of the land . . ." *Ham,* I, i, 75.

toil², *n.* **1** net or snare: ". . . unicorns may be betray'd [caught] with trees . . . Lions with toils, and men with flatterers . . ." *J Caes,* II, i, 204–206. **2 toil of grace,** snare of beauty: "As she would catch another Antony/ In her strong toil of grace." *Ant & Cleo,* V, ii, 345–346.

token, *n.* **1** sign or symbol; here, a handshake: "This token serveth for a flag of truce . . ." *1 Hen 6,* III, i, 138. **2 by some token,** with some token or sign [that will prove I am entitled to payment]: "Either send the chain or send me by some token." *Errors,* IV, i, 56.

tokened pestilence, *n.* plague, whose presence is known by red spots on the body: "How appears the fight?"/ ". . . like the token'd pestilence,/ Where death is sure." *Ant & Cleo,* III, x, 8–10.

told, *past part.* counted (up): "And age, in love, loves not to have years told." *Pass Pil,* I, 12.

tolerable, *adj.* misuse for "intolerable": ". . . for the watch to babble and to talk/ is most tolerable and not to be endured." *M Ado,* III, iii, 35–36.

toll¹, *v.* **1** to pay a tax on items for sale: "I will buy me a son-in-law in a fair, and toll for this." *All's W,* V, iii, 147. **2** to collect a tax: ". . . no Italian priest/ Shall tithe or toll in our dominions . . ." *K John,* III, i, 79–80. **3** to gather or exact in the manner of a toll: ". . . like the bee, tolling from every flower/ The virtuous sweets . . ." *2 Hen 4,* IV, v, 74–75.

toll², *v.* (of a bell) to sound for the death of: ". . . a sullen bell,/ Remember'd tolling a departing friend." *2 Hen 4,* I, i, 102–103.

tomb, *n.* tomb of Edward III, grandfather to both Richard II and Bolingbroke: ". . . by the honourable tomb he swears,/ That stands upon your royal grandsire's bones . . ." *Rich 2,* III, iii, 105–106.

tombless, *adj.* having no monument to commemorate his death: "Tombless, with no remembrance over them . . ." *Hen 5,* I, ii, 229.

tomboy, *n.* harlot: ". . . to be partner'd/ With tomboys hir'd with that self exhibition . . ." *Cymb,* I, vii, 121–122.

Tom o' Bedlam, *n.* lunatic beggar: ". . . my cue is villanous melancholy, with/ a sigh like Tom o' Bedlam." *Lear,* I, ii, 142–143.

Tomyris, *n.* Queen of the Scythians, who captured and beheaded Cyrus, Persian king who had killed her son: "I shall as famous be by this exploit,/ As Scythian Tomyris by Cyrus' death." *1 Hen 6,* II, iii, 5–6.

tongs and bones, *n. pl.* primitive musical instruments, similar to the triangle, struck with a metal rod, and the hand-held clappers of bone or wood: "I have a reasonable good ear in music. Let's have/ the tongs and the bones." *M N Dream,* IV, i, 28–29.

tongue, *n.* **1** lying and deceitful tongues: ". . . men are only turned into tongue, and/ trim ones too . . ." *M Ado,* IV, i, 319–320. **2** projecting piece on the inside of a mask for holding the mask in place with the teeth: "What! was your visor made without a tongue?" *Love's L,* V, ii, 242. **3** foreign language: ". . . would I/ had bestowed that time in the tongues that I have/ in fencing, dancing, and bear-baiting." *T Night,* I, iii, 90–92. **4** common opinion, report, or gossip: ". . . there are no/ tongues else for's turn." *Ham,* V, ii, 181–182. **5 have the tongues,** to be a skilled linguist: "'Nay,' said I, 'he hath/ the tongues.'" *M Ado,* V, i, 163–164. **6 soothing tongue,** flattery: "O, love's best habit's in a soothing tongue . . ." *Pass Pil,* I, 11. **7 tongue be hotter,** ref. to Biblical story of rich man tormented in hell, who begged for Lazarus to cool his tongue with water: "Let him be damned like the glutton! Pray God his/ tongue be hotter!" *2 Hen 4,* I, ii, 34–35. **8 tongue of loss,** cry of defeat or surrender: "That very envy and the tongue of loss/ Cried fame and honour on him." *T Night,* V, i, 56–57. **9 tongues to be,** the tongues of those yet unborn: "And tongues to be your being shall rehearse . . ." *Sonn 81,* 11. **10 wears his tongue in's arms,** can express himself only in combat: ". . . speaking is for beggars, he/ wears his tongue in's arms." *Tr & Cr,* III, iii, 268–269.

—*v.* **11** to lash out at; denounce: "How might she tongue me!" *Meas,* IV, iv, 23. **12** to speak: ". . . such stuff as madmen/ Tongue, and brain [comprehend] not . . ." *Cymb*, V, iv, 146–147.

to-night, *n.* can mean "last night" as well as "this evening": ". . . I did dream of money-bags to-night."/ ". . . I have no mind of feasting forth to-night . . ." *Merch*, II, v, 18, 37.

tool, *n.* **1** sword: "Draw thy tool here comes/ of the house of Montagues." *Rom & Jul*, I, i, 30–31. **2** penis: ". . . have we/ some strange Indian with the great tool come to/ court, the women so besiege us?" *Hen 8*, V, iii, 32–34.

too-much, *n.* excess: "For goodness, growing to a pleurisy,/ Dies in his own too-much." *Ham*, IV, vii, 116–117.

too much odds, too difficult: ". . . too much odds for a Spaniard's rapier." *Love's L*, I, ii, 167.

tooth, *n.* **1** appetite: "Sweet, sweet, sweet poison for the age's tooth . . ." *K John*, I, i, 213. **2 tooth of time,** ref. to time as the devourer of all material things: "A forted residence 'gainst the tooth of time/ And razure of oblivion." *Meas*, V, i, 13–14.

toothdrawer, *n.* person authorized, as by the Lord Chamberlain, to extract teeth: ". . . a brooch of lead."/ "Ay, and worn in the cap of a toothdrawer." *Love's L*, V, ii, 612–613.

toothpick, *n.* affectation of the day, esp. among travelers: "Now your traveller,/ He and his toothpick at my worship's mess . . ." *K John*, I, i, 189–190.

toothpicker, *n.* toothpick: "I will fetch you a toothpicker now from the furthest/ inch of Asia." *M Ado*, II, i, 250–251.

too truly, *adv.* with good reason: ". . . to make us say/ This is put forth too truly." *W Tale*, I, ii, 13–14.

top, *n.* **1** the head: "All the stor'd vengeances of Heaven fall/ On her ingrateful top!" *Lear*, II, iv, 163–164. **2** crown; here also, representative of man's highest aspirations: ". . . wears upon his baby brow the round/ And top of sovereignty?" *Mac*, IV, i, 88–89. **3 in top** (or **tops**) **of,** at the height of: ". . . like to autumn's corn,/ Have we mow'd down in tops of all their pride!" *3 Hen 6*, V, vii, 3–4. **4 in top of all design,** in [our] greatest achievements: "That thou my brother, my competitor,/ In top of all design; my mate in empire . . ." *Ant & Cleo*, V, i, 42–43. **5 on the top,** at the height: "Now stand you on the top of happy hours [life's happiness] . . ." *Sonn 16*, 5. **6 take time by the top,** take advantage of the moment: ". . . he meant to take the present/ time by the top and instantly break with you of it." *M Ado*, I, ii, 13–14.
—*v.* **7** to cut off: ". . . not one of you here present . . . That could have topp'd the peace, as now you would . . ." *More*, II, iv, 62–64. **8** to prune: "But like to groves, being topp'd, they

higher rise." *Per*, I, iv, 9. **9** to copulate with: "Would you, the supervisor, grossly gape on,/ Behold her topp'd?" *Oth*, III, iii, 401–402.

top-full or **topful,** *adj.* full to the top: ". . . fill me, from the crown to the toe, top-full/ Of direst cruelty!" *Mac*, I, v, 42–43.

topgallant, *n.* topmost sail of a ship: "Which to the high topgallant of my joy/ Must be my convoy in the secret night." *Rom & Jul*, II, iv, 185–186.

topless, *adj.* having no superior: "Sometime, great Agamemnon,/ Thy topless deputation he puts on . . ." *Tr & Cr*, I, iii, 151–152.

top one's thought, *v.* to surpass what one can imagine: "So far he topp'd my thought/ That I in forgery of shapes and tricks/ Come short of what he did." *Ham*, IV, vii, 87–88.

top-proud, *adj.* exceedingly or excessively proud: ". . . but this top-proud fellow . . . I do know/ To be corrupt and treasonous." *Hen 8*, I, i, 151–156.

torch, *n.* servant bearing a torch, as well as the torch itself: "Hautboys and torches. Enter Duncan, Malcolm . . ." [SD] *Mac*, I, vi, 1.

torch-light, *n.* **show the torch-light,** nighttime signal [here, during hostilities] that all is well: "Statilius show'd the torch-light; but, my lord,/ He came not back . . ." *J Caes*, V, v, 2–3.

torch-staves, *n.* staves to which candles are affixed: "The horsemen sit like fixed candlesticks,/ With torch-staves in their hand . . ." *Hen 5*, IV, ii, 45–46.

tortive, *adj.* twisting or twisted: "Tortive and errant from his course of growth." *Tr & Cr*, I, iii, 9.

tortured body, *n.* parting compared to a body being tortured on the rack: "I grow [have become attached] to you, and our parting is a tortur'd body." *All's W*, II, i, 36.

Toryne, *n.* ancient port city in what is now W Albania: "He could so quickly cut the Ionian sea,/ And take in Toryne?" *Ant & Cleo*, III, vii, 22–23.

to's, contraction of "to us": ". . . to's seemeth it a needful course . . ." *Love's L*, II, i, 25.

toss, *v.* **1** to skewer with a pike and carry aloft: "I did never see such pitiful rascals."/ "Tut, tut, good enough to toss . . ." *1 Hen 4*, IV, ii, 64–65. **2** to hastily turn the pages of: "Lucius, what book is that she tosseth so?" *T Andr*, IV, i, 41.

toss-pot, *n.* drunkard: "With toss-pots still 'had [I had] drunken heads . . ." *T Night,* V, i, 402.

to 't, to get there: "'Tis easy to 't, and there I will attend/ What further comes." *Ant & Cleo,* III, x, 32–33.

tottered, *adj.* tattered; ragged: "That from this castle's tottered battlements/ Our fair appointments may be well perus'd." *Rich 2,* III, iii, 52–53.

tottering, *adj.* **1** tattered and still waving: ". . . we bid good-night,/ And wound our tott'ring colours clearly up . . ." *K John,* V, v, 6–7. **2** uncertain or unstable; wavering: "A more content in course of true delight/ Than to be thirsty after tottering honour . . ." *Per,* III, ii, 39–40.

touch, *n.* **1** natural trait or distinguishing characteristic: "Of many faces, eyes, and hearts,/ To have the touches dearest priz'd." *As You,* III, ii, 148–149. **2** hint; indication: ". . . give your friend/ Some touch of your late business . . ." *Hen 8,* V, i, 12–13. **3** touchstone; test: "O thou touch of hearts . . ." *Timon,* IV, iii, 392. **4** deed or exploit: "And hast thou kill'd him sleeping? O brave touch!" *M N Dream,* III, ii, 70. **5** [pl.] playing of a musical instrument; here, prob. "strains": ". . . soft stillness and the night/ Become the touches of sweet harmony . . ." *Merch,* V, i, 56–57. **6** [usually pl.] sexual contacts: "From their abominable and beastly touches/ I drink, I eat . . ." *Meas,* III, ii, 23–24. **7** [often pl.] matter touching or affecting one: "The death of Fulvia, with more urgent touches,/ Do strongly speak to us . . ." *Ant & Cleo,* I, ii, 178–179. **8 a touch more rare,** a feeling more extraordinary; ref. to her grief at parting from Posthumus: "I am senseless of your wrath; a touch more rare/ Subdues all pangs, all fears." *Cymb,* I, ii, 66–67. **9 of noble touch** whose nobility has been tested, as if by a touchstone, and approved: ". . . my dearest mother, and/ My friends of noble touch . . ." *Cor,* IV, i, 48–49. **10 play the touch,** be a touchstone to test Buckingham's true quality: ". . . now do I play the touch/ To try if thou be current gold indeed." *Rich 3,* IV, ii, 8–9.
—*v.* **11** to try; test: "They have all been touch'd and found base metal . . ." *Timon,* III, iii, 7. **12** to pluck the strings of a musical instrument; play: ". . . hold up thy heavy eyes awhile,/ And touch thy instrument a strain or two?" *J Caes,* IV, iii, 255–256. **13** to concern; affect: "It touches us, as France invades our land . . ." *Lear,* V, i, 25. **14** to charge or accuse; also, taint: "I thank God I am not a woman, to be touched with/ so many giddy offences . . ." *As You,* III, ii, 339–341. **15** to infect: ". . . the life of all his blood/ Is touch'd corruptibly . . ." *K John,* V, vii, 1–2. **16** to injure; wound: "My patience here is touch'd . . ." *Meas,* V, i, 234. **17 be finely touched,** (of gold coins) to be stamped with the degree of fineness: "Spirits are not finely touch'd/ But to fine issues . . ." *Meas,* I, i, 35–36. **18 touched**

with choler, fired up with anger: "For I do know Fluellen valiant,/ And touch'd with choler, hot as gunpowder . . ." *Hen 5,* IV, vii, 184–185. **19 touch my shoulder,** [to] arrest me: ". . . yield me to the veriest hind that shall/ Once touch my shoulder." *Cymb,* V, iii, 77–78. **20 touch their effects,** See **effect** (def. 12).

touched, *adj.* **1** guilty or implicated: "If by direct or by collateral hand/ They find us touch'd . . ." *Ham,* IV, v, 203–204. **2** endowed or enriched: "Spirits are not finely touch'd/ But to fine issues . . ." *Meas,* I, i, 35–36. **3** affected: "How/ seems he to be touched?" *Meas,* IV, ii, 138–139. **4** injured; wounded: "My patience here is touch'd . . ." *Meas,* V, i, 234.

touching, *adj.* profound; grievous: "O insupportable and touching loss!" *J Caes,* IV, iii, 150.

touchstone, *n.* kind of black flint for testing the purity of gold; the flint was scratched with the metal and the resulting color thought to reveal the gold's purity: ". . . an hand environed with clouds,/ Holding out gold that's by the touchstone tried [tested] . . ." *Per,* II, ii, 36–37.

touse, *v.* to tear apart: "We'll touse you/ Joint by joint . . ." *Meas,* V, i, 309–310.

toward, *adv.* Also, **towards. 1** in preparation: "We have a trifling foolish banquet towards." *Rom & Jul,* I, v, 121. **2** about to take place; forthcoming: "What, a play toward? I'll be an auditor . . ." *M N Dream,* III, i, 75.
—*v.* **3** to proceed in the direction of: "What, shall we toward the Tower? The day is spent." *Rich 3,* III, ii, 87.
—*adj.* **4** obedient; dutiful: "'Tis a good hearing, when children are toward." *Shrew,* V, ii, 183. **5** bold or fearless; also, promising: "Why, that is spoken like a toward prince." *3 Hen 6,* II, ii, 66.

towardly, *adj.* agreeable; friendly: "I have observed thee always for a towardly prompt spirit . . ." *Timon,* III, i, 34–35.

tower, *v.* (of a falcon) to rise in circles to the point for beginning the attack: "My Lord Protector's hawks do tower so well . . ." *2 Hen 6,* II, i, 10.

Tower, *n.* Tower of London, used as royal residence, prison, and arsenal: "I'll to the Tower with all the haste I can/ To view th' artillery and munition . . ." *1 Hen 6,* I, i, 167–168.

town, *n.* **whole towns to fly,** ref. to the prodigal dowry paid by Suffolk for Queen Margaret: ". . . you have done more miracles than I;/ You made in a day, my lord, whole towns to fly [disappear]." *2 Hen 6,* II, i, 155–156.

town's end, *n.* gate to the city, where beggars gathered: ". . . they are for the town's end, to beg during life." *1 Hen 4,* V, iii, 38.

toy, *n.* **1** trifle: "Each toy seems prologue to some great amiss." *Ham,* IV, v, 18. **2** bauble or trinket: "I am very glad to see you./ Even a toy in hand here sir." *As You,* III, iii, 68–69. **3** [often pl.] decorations or ornaments: "Any silk, any thread,/ Any toys for your head . . ." *W Tale,* IV, iv, 319–320. **4** folly; caprice; whim: "If no inconstant toy nor womanish fear/ Abate thy valour in the acting it." *Rom & Jul,* IV, i, 119–120. **5** trifling tale: "I never may believe/ These antique fables, nor these fairy toys." *M N Dream,* V, i, 2–3. **6 There's toys abroad,** odd things are happening: "There's toys abroad: anon I'll tell thee more." *K John,* I, i, 232. **7 took toy at,** developed an aversion to: ". . . the hot horse, hot as fire,/ Took toy at this . . ." *Kinsmen,* V, iv, 65–66. **8 toy in blood,** youthful impulse: "For Hamlet, and the trifling of his favour,/ Hold it a fashion and a toy in blood . . ." *Ham,* I, iii, 5–6. **9 Tut, a toy!** Nonsense!: "Tut, a toy!/ An old Italian fox is not so kind, my boy." *Shrew,* II, i, 395–396.

trace, *v.* **1** to traverse; roam; travel over or along: "As we do trace this alley up and down . . ." *M Ado,* III, i, 16. **2** to follow: ". . . but woman's son/ Can trace me in the tedious ways of art . . ." *1 Hen 4,* III, i, 44–45. **3** to succeed; come after in lineage: "His wife, his babes, and all unfortunate souls/ That trace him in his line." *Mac,* IV, i, 152–153.
—*n.* **4** [usually pl.] parts of the harness connecting animal to vehicle: "Her traces of the smallest spider web,/ Her collars of the moonshine's watery beams . . ." *Rom & Jul,* I, iv, 64–65. **5** team of horses: "Either I am/ The forehorse in the team, or I am none/ That draw i' th' sequent trace." *Kinsmen,* I, ii, 58–60.

track, *n.* course; path: ". . . to stain the track/ Of his bright passage to the occident." *Rich 2,* III, iii, 66–67.

tract, *n.* description: ". . . the tract of ev'ry thing/ Would by a good discourser lose some life . . ." *Hen 8,* I, i, 40–41.

tractable, *adj.* agreeable: ". . . thou shalt find me tractable to any honest/ reason . . ." *1 Hen 4,* III, iii, 172–173.

trade, *n.* **1** traffic or activity; also, exchange: ". . . his forward spirit/ Would lift him where most trade of danger rang'd." *2 Hen 4,* I, i, 173–174. **2** commercial dealings; here, in response to Rosencrantz and Guildenstern's "business": "Have you any further trade with us?" *Ham,* III, ii, 325. **3** occupation; here, a way of life or habitual practice: "Thy sin's not accidental, but a trade . . ." *Meas,* III, i, 148.
—*v.* **4 trade to,** to connect or communicate with: "Unto the traject, to the common ferry/ Which trades to Venice . . ." *Merch,* III, iv, 53–54.

traded, *adj.* experienced or skilled; accustomed: "And he, long traded in it, makes it seem/ Like rivers of remorse and innocency." *K John,* IV, iii, 109–110.

trade-fallen, *adj.* out-of-work; unemployed: ". . . revolted/ tapsters, and ostlers trade-fallen, the cankers of a/ calm world . . ." *1 Hen 4,* IV, ii, 28–30.

trader, *n.* merchant ship: ". . . sat with me on Neptune's yellow sands,/ Marking th'embarked traders on the flood . . ." *M N Dream,* II, i, 126–127.

traduce, *v.* **1** to subject to scorn by misrepresentation: "He is already/ Traduc'd for levity . . ." *Ant & Cleo,* III, vii, 12–13. **2** to betray: ". . . a turban'd Turk/ Beat a Venetian, and traduc'd the state . . ." *Oth,* V, ii, 354–355.

traducement, *n.* act of discrediting; slander: "'Twere a concealment/ Worse than a theft, no less than a traducement . . ." *Cor,* I, ix, 21–22.

traffic, *n.* **1** trade or commerce; business: "Traffic confound thee, if the gods will not!" *Timon,* I, i, 236. **2** employment: "The painful traffic of my tender youth . . ." *Edw 3,* V, i, 230. **3** social intercourse; dealings: ". . . having traffic with thyself alone . . ." *Sonn 4,* 9. **4 for traffic's sake,** in order to resume trade: ". . . repaying/ What we took from them, which for traffic's sake/ Most of our city did." *T Night,* III, iii, 33–35.
—*v.* **5** to have harmful dealings or influence: ". . . since dishonour traffics with man's nature . . ." *Timon,* I, i, 161.

trafficker, *n.* merchant ship; trading vessel: "Like signiors and rich burghers on the flood . . . Do overpeer the petty traffickers/ That cur'sy to them . . ." *Merch,* I, i, 10–13.

trail, *n.* **1 upon no trail,** with no trail to follow: ". . . if I cry out/ thus upon no trail [bark like a hound on the wrong scent], never trust me when I open/ again." *Wives,* IV, ii, 183–185.
—*v.* **2 trail the pike, a.** to be an infantryman; that is, to carry the pike so that the handle's end trailed on the ground: "Trailest thou the puissant pike?" *Hen 5,* IV, i, 40. **b.** same as symbol of respect for a dead hero: "Beat thou the drum that it speak mournfully;/ Trail your steel pikes." *Cor,* V, vi, 149–150.

train¹, *n.* **1** [often pl.] lure or enticement; here, also device or stratagem: "Devilish Macbeth/ By many of these trains hath sought to win me . . ." *Mac,* IV, iii, 117–118.
—*v.* **2** to lure; entice: "And for that cause I train'd thee to my house." *1 Hen 6,* II, iii, 34.

train², *n.* **1** [often pl.] band of soldiers or followers: ". . . let our trains/ March by us, that we may peruse the men/ We should have cop'd withal." *2 Hen 4,* IV, ii, 93–95. **2** tail feathers: "We'll pull his plumes and take away his train . . ." *1 Hen 6*, III, iii, 7. **3** retinue: "A royal train, believe me . . . Who's that that bears the sceptre?" *Hen 8*, IV, i, 37–38. **4 little train,** small entourage: ". . . with some little train,/ Forthwith from Ludlow the young Prince be fet . . ." *Rich 3*, II, ii, 121.

train³, *v.* **train him on,** bring him up; educate him: "We did train him on,/ And, his corruption being ta'en from us . . ." *1 Hen 4*, V, ii, 21–22.

traject or tranect, *n.* prob. an anglicization of Italian *traghetto*, ferry: "Bring them (I pray thee) with imagin'd speed/ Unto the traject, to the common ferry . . ." *Merch*, III, iv, 52–53.

trammel, *v.* **trammel up**, to trap or ensnare in, or as if in, a net: ". . . if th'assassination/ Could trammel up the consequence, and catch/ With his surcease success . . ." *Mac*, I, vii, 2–4.

trance, *n.* fit: "Disturb his hours of rest with restless trances . . ." *Luc*, 974.

tranced, *adj.* senseless; unconscious: ". . . twice then the trumpets sounded,/ And there I left him tranc'd." *Lear*, V, iii, 217–218.

tranect, *n.* See **traject**.

transcendence, *n.* renown; eminence: ". . . great power, great transcendence,/ which should indeed give us a further use . . ." *All's W*, II, iii, 34–35.

transfix, *v.* to deface or destroy: "Time doth transfix the flourish set on youth . . ." *Sonn 60*, 9.

transform, *v.* to bewitch; metamorphose: "I am transformed, master, am I not?" *Errors*, II, ii, 195.

transgression, *n.* extreme penalty or punishment: "Lord Angelo dukes it well in his absence: he puts/ transgression to't." *Meas*, III, ii, 91–92.

translate, *v.* **1** to transform: "Bless thee, Bottom, bless thee! Thou art translated." *M N Dream*, III, i, 114. **2** to explain; here, to reveal the true nature of [Troilus]: "Thus says Aeneas . . . and with private soul/ Did in great Ilion thus translate him to me." *Tr & Cr*, IV, v, 110–112.

transmigrate, *v.* appar. ref. to the Pythagorean theory of the transmigration of souls [into another body after death]; Antony, however, is teasing the very drunk Lepidus: "It lives by that which/ nourisheth it, and the elements once out of it, it/ transmigrates." *Ant & Cleo*, II, vii, 43–45.

transparent, *adj.* **1** obvious; here, wordplay with "easily seen through": ". . . these who, often drown'd, could never die,/ Transparent heretics, be burnt for liars." *Rom & Jul*, I, ii, 92–93. **2** radiant; also, sheer or pellucid: "Transparent Helena! Nature shows art,/ That through thy bosom makes me see thy heart." *M N Dream*, II, ii, 103–104.

transported, *adj.* carried off by fairies: "He cannot be heard of. Out of doubt he is transported." *M N Dream*, IV, ii, 3–4.

transpose, *v.* to change; transform: "Things base and vile, holding no quantity,/ Love can transpose to form and dignity . . ." *M N Dream*, I, i, 232–233.

transshape, *v.* to transform, as by altering the shape of something: "Thus did she an hour/ together transshape thy particular virtues . . ." *M Ado*, V, i, 167–168.

trap, *n.* **trap with you**, sense seems to be "you'll be sorry"; poss. quote from children's game: "I will say/ 'marry trap with you', if you run the nuthook's/ humour on me . . ." *Wives*, I, i, 150–152.

trapped, *adj.* fitted with trappings; ornamented: "Four milk-white horses, trapp'd in silver." *Timon*, I, ii, 181.

trash¹, *n.* **1** twigs, ground litter, etc., used to start a fire: "What trash is Rome,/ What rubbish, and what offal, when it serves . . . to illuminate/ So vile a thing as Caesar!" *J Caes*, I, iii, 108–111. **2** objects used in conjuring: "Lay hands upon these traitors and their trash." *2 Hen 6*, I, iv, 40. **3** worthless fellow: "I do suspect this trash/ To bear a part in this . . ." *Oth*, V, i, 85–86.

trash², *v.* to check or restrain (a hound); here, to prevent from attaining too much power: ". . . who t' advance, and who/ To trash for over-topping . . ." *Temp*, I, ii, 80–81.

travail, *n.* **1** labor of childbirth: "The lady shrieks and well-a-near/ Does fall in travail with her fear . . ." *Per*, III, Chor., 51–52.
—*v.* **2** to walk or wander: "He and myself/ Have travail'd in the great show'r of your gifts . . ." *Timon*, V, i, 68–69.

travelling lamp, *n.* the journeying sun: "And yet dark night strangles the travelling lamp." *Mac*, II, iv, 7.

travel of regard, *n.* See **regard** (def. 5).

traverse, *v.* **1** (as a military order) march up and down or to and fro: "Hold, Wart, traverse—thas! thas! thas!" *2 Hen 4*, III, ii, 267. **2** (in fencing) to move from side to side: "To see thee fight, to see thee foin, to see thee/ traverse . . ." *Wives*, II, iii, 22–23. **3** Forward! [appar. used jocularly here]: "Traverse, go, provide thy money, we will have more/ of this to-morrow; adieu." *Oth*, I, iii, 371–372.

—*adv.* **4** across or athwart, instead of directly, as on an opponent's shield: ". . . swears brave oaths, and breaks/ them bravely, quite traverse, athwart the heart of/ his lover . . ." *As You*, III, iv, 37–39.

traversed, *adj.* (of weapons) held downward in a nonbelligerent position: ". . . myself and such/ As slept within the shadow of your power/ Have wander'd with our travers'd arms . . ." *Timon*, V, iv, 5–7.

tray-trip or **trey-trip,** dice game, where a three was the lucky throw: "Shall I play [wager] my freedom at tray-trip, and become/ thy bond-slave?" *T Night*, II, v, 190–191.

treacher, *n.* traitor: ". . . knaves, thieves, and treachers by spherical predominance . . ." *Lear*, I, ii, 128.

treacherous, *adv.* traitorously: "Sheep run not half so treacherous from the wolf . . ." *1 Hen 6*, I, v, 30.

tread, *v.* **1** to mate: "When turtles tread, and rooks, and daws . . ." *Love's L*, V, ii, 897. **2 tread out,** to trample; scorn or disdain: "Swear by her foot, that she may tread out the oath." *Hen 5*, III, vii, 98. **3 tread the measures,** to dance: "Teaching decrepit age to tread the measures . . ." *Ven & Ad*, 1148. —*n.* **4** footprints or a path made by footprints: "And the quaint mazes . . . For lack of tread are undistinguishable." *M N Dream*, II, i, 99–100.

treason, *n.* treachery: "That monster envy . . . Marina's life/ Seeks to take off by treason's knife . . ." *Per*, IV, Chor., 12–14.

treatise, *n.* story; discourse: ". . . my fell of hair/ Would at a dismal treatise rouse, and stir . . ." *Mac*, V, v, 11–12.

treaty, *n.* **1** proposal: "Why answer not the double majesties/ This friendly treaty of our threat'ned town?" *K John*, II, i, 480–481. **2** matter to be discussed: "We are convented/ Upon a pleasing treaty . . ." *Cor*, II, ii, 54–55.

treble, *v.* **trebles thee o'er,** increases thy fortunes threefold: "I am more serious than my custom: you/ Must be so too . . . which to do/ Trebles thee o'er." *Temp*, II, i, 214–216.

treble-dated crow, *n.* crow was believed to live several times as long as man: "And thou treble-dated crow,/ That thy sable gender mak'st . . ." *Phoen*, 17–18.

treble hautboy, *n.* slender, high-pitched reed instrument, smallest of its class: ancestor of the oboe: ". . . the case of a treble hautboy was a mansion for him . . ." *2 Hen 4*, III, ii, 321.

treble-sinewed, *adj.* triple in strength (as well as in courage and endurance): "I will be treble-sinew'd, hearted, breath'd,/ And fight maliciously . . ." *Ant & Cleo*, III, xiii, 178–179.

trembling, *n.* **1** here, Trinculo, the coward, shakes with fear: "Thou dost me yet but little hurt; thou wilt anon, I/ know it by thy trembling . . ." *Temp*, II, ii, 81–82. —*adj.* **2** causing fear and trembling; fearful: "Sixth part of each?/ A trembling contribution . . ." *Hen 8*, I, ii, 94–95.

tremor cordis, *n.* [Latin] heart palpitation: "I have *tremor cordis* on me: my heart dances,/ But not for joy—not joy." *W Tale*, I, ii, 110–111.

trench, *v.* **1** to make or leave trenches: "No more shall trenching war channel her fields . . ." *1 Hen 4*, I, i, 7. **2** to divert (a stream) by means of a trench: "Yea, but a little charge will trench him here . . ." *1 Hen 4*, III, i, 108. **3** to make a deep cut in: ". . . the wide wound that the boar had trench'd/ In his soft flank . . ." *Ven & Ad*, 1052–1053. —*n.* **4** [usually pl.] wrinkles: "Witness these trenches made by grief and care . . ." *T Andr*, V, ii, 23.

trenchant, *adj.* having a sharp, keen edge: "Let not the virgin's cheek/ Make soft thy trenchant sword . . ." *Timon*, IV, iii, 116–117.

trenched, *adj.* cut or slashed: ". . . safe in a ditch he bides,/ With twenty trenched gashes on his head . . ." *Mac*, III, iv, 25–26.

trencher, *n.* **1** wooden dish or serving-plate: ". . . an heir more rais'd/ Than one which holds a trencher." *Timon*, I, i, 122–123. **2 hold a trencher,** to dance attendance: "And stand between her back, sir, and the fire,/ Holding a trencher, jesting merrily?" *Love's L*, V, ii, 476–477.

trench-friend, *n.* moocher; freeloader: "You fools of fortune, trencher-friends, time's flies . . ." *Timon*, III, vi, 92.

trenchering, *n.* wooden plates: "Nor scrape trenchering, nor wash dish:/ 'Ban, 'Ban, Cacaliban . . ." *Temp*, II, ii, 183–184.

trencher-knight, *n.* hanger-on; freeloader: "Some mumble news, some trencher-knight, some Dick . . ." *Love's L*, V, ii, 464.

trencher-man, *n.* man with a large appetite: ". . . he is a very valiant trencher-man; he hath an/ excellent stomach." *M Ado*, I, i, 46–47.

Trent, *n.* river in central England: "And here the smug and silver Trent shall run . . ." *1 Hen 4*, III, i, 98.

trespass, *n.* **did trespasses to,** wronged: "His wife that's dead did trespasses to Caesar . . ." *Ant & Cleo,* II, i, 40.

trey, *n.* (at cards or dice) three: "Honey, and milk, and sugar: there is three."/ "Nay then, two treys . . ." *Love's L,* V, ii, 231–232.

trey-trip, See **tray-trip.**

trial, *n.* **1** trial by combat: "There is my honour's pawn;/ Engage it to the trial if thou darest." *Rich 2,* IV, i, 55–56. **2** test or proof: ". . . do but blow them to their trial, the bubbles are/ out [they burst]." *Ham,* V, ii, 190–191. **3 for trial,** as a test: "The boy [Cupid] for trial needs would touch my breast . . ." *Sonn 153,* 10.

trib, *v.* parson's mispron. of "trip," to move quickly with light steps: "Trib, trib, fairies; come; and remember your/ parts." *Wives,* V, iv, 1–2.

tribe, *n.* **1** any of three political districts in early Rome: "Have you collected them by tribes?" *Cor,* III, iii, 11. **2** [pl.] peoples or races: "I'll live in this poor rhyme,/ While he insults o'er dull and speechless tribes." *Sonn 107,* 11–12.

tribulation of Tower-hill, *n.* rough crowds who throng to public executions on Tower Hill: ". . . no audience but the/ tribulation of Tower-hill . . . are able to endure." *Hen 8,* V, iii, 60–62.

tribunal plebs, *n.* misuse for **tribunus plebis,** court of the common people: "Why, I am going with my pigeons to/ the tribunal plebs . . ." *T Andr,* IV, iii, 90–91.

tribune, *n.* (in ancient Rome) representative of the common people: "What is granted them?"/ "Five tribunes to defend their vulgar wisdoms . . ." *Cor,* I, i, 213–214.

tributary, *adj.* **1** paying tribute: "Back, foolish tears . . . Your tributary drops belong to woe . . ." *Rom & Jul,* III, ii, 102–103.
—*n.* **2** captive, esp. a leader or royal who must be ransomed: "What tributaries follow him to Rome,/ To grace in captive bonds his chariot wheels?" *J Caes,* I, i, 33–34.

trice, *n.* very brief period of time; instant: "I am gone, sir, and anon, sir,/ I'll be with you again,/ In a trice . . ." *T Night,* IV, ii, 125–127.

trick, *n.* **1** touch; trace: "Yet I have a trick/ Of the old rage . . ." *Love's L,* V, ii, 416–417. **2** natural way for human beings to behave; here, to weep at tragic events: ". . . I forbid my tears. But yet/ It is our trick; nature her custom holds,/ Let shame say what it will. [Weeps.]" *Ham,* IV, vii, 185–187. **3** custom or fashion: "Faith, my lord, I spoke it but according to the/

trick . . ." *Meas,* V, i, 502–503. **4** bad habit or foolish behavior: "You are a saucy boy . . . This trick may chance to scathe you." *Rom & Jul,* I, v, 82–83. **5** stratagem; device or artifice: "There are no tricks in plain and simple faith . . ." *J Caes,* IV, ii, 22. **6** trifle; also, pretense: ". . . for a fantasy and trick of fame,/ Go to their graves like beds . . ." *Ham,* IV, iv, 61–62. **7** knack; ability or gift: "Here's fine revolution and we had the trick to see't." *Ham,* V, i, 89. **8** unique characteristic; individuality: "The trick of that voice I do well remember . . ." *Lear,* IV, vi, 109. **9** [often pl.] pranks: "I'll question you/ Of my lord's tricks, and yours, when you were boys." *W Tale,* I, ii, 60–61. **10 the trick of it,** way of the world: "Which is the way? Is it/ sad, and few words? Or how? The trick of it?" *Meas,* III, ii, 49–50. **11 tricks of custom,** habitual tricks: "For such things in a false disloyal knave/ Are tricks of custom . . ." *Oth,* III, iii, 125–126. **12 trick worth two of that,** I'm not as foolish as you think: "Nay, by God, soft! I know a trick worth two of/ that, i'faith." *1 Hen 4,* II, i, 35–36.
—*v.* **13** to blazon; adorn: "Now is he total gules, horridly trick'd/ With blood of fathers, mothers, daughters, sons . . ." *Ham,* II, ii, 453–454.

tricking, *n.* furnishings; outfits: "Go get us properties/ And tricking for our fairies." *Wives,* IV, iv, 77–78.

tricksy, *adj.* clever: "A many fools . . . that for a tricksy word/ Defy the matter . . ." *Merch,* III, v, 62–64.

tried, *past part.* proved: "For he hath still been tried a holy man." *Rom & Jul,* IV, iii, 29.

trifle, *v.* **1** to reduce to a trifle: ". . . this sore night/ Hath trifled former knowings." *Mac,* II, iv, 3–4. **2** to waste; fritter away: "We trifle time, I pray thee pursue sentence." *Merch,* IV, i, 294.
—*n.* **3** negligible number or amount: ". . . here's a small trifle of wives,—alas! fifteen/ wives is nothing . . ." *Merch,* II, ii, 153–154. **4 make but a trifle of,** have no regard for: "Let him that makes but trifles of his eyes/ First hand me . . ." *W Tale,* II, iii, 62–63.

Trigon, *n.* (in astrology) triplicity, one of four into which the zodiac was divided: fire, air, earth, and water: "And look whether the fiery Trigon his man be not/ lisping to his master's old tables . . ." *2 Hen 4,* II, iv, 263–264.

trill, *v.* to trickle: ". . . now and then an ample tear trill'd down/ Her delicate cheek . . ." *Lear,* IV, iii, 13–14.

trim, *adj.* **1** fine; nice; attractive: ". . . men are only turned into tongue, and/ trim ones too . . ." *M Ado,* IV, i, 319–320. **2** same used ironically: "A trim exploit, a manly enterprise,/ To conjure tears up in a poor maid's eyes . . ." *M N Dream,* III, ii, 157–158.

—*n.* **3** [sometimes pl.] finery: "They come like sacrifices in their trim . . ." *1 Hen 4,* IV, i, 113. **4** equipment; trappings: "My noble steed . . . I give him,/ With all his trim belonging . . ." *Cor,* I, ix, 60–61. **5 in all our trim,** unharmed: ". . . we, in all our trim, freshly beheld/ Our royal, good, and gallant ship . . ." *Temp,* V, i, 236–237. **6 in her trim,** (of a ship) fully rigged; ready for sea: "The ship is in her trim, the merry wind/ Blows fair from land . . ." *Errors,* IV, i, 91–92. **7 in the trim,** in top form: "But, by the mass, our hearts are in the trim . . ." *Hen 5,* IV, iii, 115.
—*adv.* **8** accurately; expertly: "Young Abraham Cupid, he that shot so trim . . ." *Rom & Jul,* II, i, 13.
—*v.* **9** to dress or adorn; primp: ". . . men and dames so jetted and adorn'd,/ Like one another's glass to trim them by—" *Per,* I, iv, 26–27. **10** to clean, straighten, or otherwise put in order: ". . . as you look/ To have my pardon, trim it handsomely." *Temp,* V, i, 292–293. **11 trim her up,** dress her; get her ready: "What, Nurse I say! . . . Go waken Juliet, go, and trim her up." *Rom & Jul,* IV, iv, 23–24.

trimmed, *adj.* **1** decked out; arrayed: "And being now trimm'd in thine own desires,/ Thou, beastly feeder, art so full of him . . ." *2 Hen 4,* I, iii, 94–95. **2** cleaned; made neat: "Is supper ready, the house/ trimmed, rushes strewed . . ." *Shrew,* IV, i, 40–41.

trinkets, *n.* objects used in conjuring; the "trash" of l. 40: "We'll see your trinkets here all forthcoming./ All, away!" *2 Hen 6,* I, iv, 52–53.

trip, *v.* **1** to dance; here also, to stumble or fall, with obvious sexual innuendo: ". . . I have heard, you knights of Tyre/ Are excellent in making ladies trip . . ." *Per,* II, iii, 101–102. **2** to correct or contradict: "These her women/ Can trip me, if I err . . ." *Cymb,* V, v, 34–35. **3** to stumble or fall; have a moral lapse: "By this we gather/ You have tripp'd since." *W Tale,* I, ii, 75–76.
—*n.* **4** wrestling move whereby one trips and floors one's opponent; here, deceptive practices: ". . . will not else thy craft so quickly grow/ That thine own trip shall be thine overthrow?" *T Night,* V, i, 164–165.

trip and go, a line from a popular song that accompanied Morris dancing: "Trip and go, my sweet; deliver this paper into the royal hand of the king . . ." *Love's L,* IV, ii, 135–136.

tripartite, *adj.* concerning three parties: ". . . our indentures tripartite [three-way agreement] are drawn . . ." *1 Hen 4,* III, i, 76.

tripe-visaged, *adj.* having a pale, sallow, and probably pock-marked complexion: "Come on, I'll tell thee/ what, thou damned tripe-visaged rascal . . ." *2 Hen 4,* V, iv, 8–9.

triple, *adj.* third: "He bade me store up as a triple eye . . ." *All's W,* II, i, 107.

triple pillar, *n.* Antony was a member of the Triumvirate, the three rulers of the Roman Empire: "The triple pillar of the world transform'd/ Into a strumpet's fool . . ." *Ant & Cleo,* I, i, 12–13.

triple-turned, *adj.* ref. to Cleopatra's faithlessness, first to Julius Caesar, then to the elder Pompey, and now Antony (betraying him, he suspects, with Octavius Caesar): "Triple-turn'd whore, 'tis thou/ Hast sold me to this novice . . ." *Ant & Cleo,* IV, xii, 13–14.

triplex, *n.* (in music) triple time: ". . . the triplex,/ sir, is a good tripping measure . . ." *T Night,* V, i, 35–36.

tristful, *adj.* sad; sorrowful: "Heaven's face does glow/ O'er this solidity and compound mass/ With tristful visage . . ." *Ham,* III, iv, 48–50.

Triton, *n.* (in Roman myth.) trumpeter to Neptune, who warned at the approach of the sea god: "Hear you this Triton of the minnows?" *Cor,* III, i, 88.

triumph, *n.* **1** public processional or other lavish festivity: "What news from Oxford? Do these justs and triumphs hold?" *Rich 2,* V, ii, 52. **2** revelry; celebration: ". . . every man put himself into triumph: some to dance,/ some make bonfires . . ." *Oth,* II, ii, 4–5. **3** trump card: ". . . she, Eros, has/ Pack'd cards with Caesar, and false-play'd my glory/ Unto an enemy's triumph." *Ant & Cleo,* IV, xiv, 18–20. **4** tournament of jousts, tilts, etc.: ". . . one that, at a triumph, having vow'd/ To try his strength, forsaketh yet the lists . . ." *1 Hen 6,* V, v, 31–32.

triumpher, *n.* soldier, army, etc., returning to the city in triumph: ". . . like great triumphers/ In their applauding gates." *Timon,* V, i, 195–196.

triumviry or triumphry, triumvirate; threesome: "Thou mak'st the triumviry, the corner-cap of society . . ." *Love's L,* IV, iii, 50.

trivial motion, *n.* See **motion** (def. 19).

Troilus, *n.* son of Priam who, according to legend, gained the love of Cressida with the help of her uncle, Pandarus: "Troilus the first employer of pandars . . ." *M Ado,* V, ii, 30.

Trojan, *n.* low fellow; rascal [in military jargon, sometimes used affectionately]: ". . . dost thou thirst, base Trojan/ To have me fold up Parca's fatal web?" *Hen 5,* V, i, 20–21.

troll, *v.* to sing happily and usually lustily: "Let us be jocund: will you troll the catch/ You taught me but while-ere?" *Temp,* III, ii, 115–116.

troll-my-dames, *n.* board game in which balls were rolled through hoops: "A fellow, sir, that I have known to go about with/ troll-my-dames . . ." *W Tale,* IV, iii, 84–85.

troop, *v.* **1** to congregate; walk together in company: ". . . a solemn hunting is in hand;/ There will the lovely Roman ladies troop . . ." *T Andr,* II, i, 112–113. —*n.* **2** company or retinue: "Would it not shame thee, in so fair a troop,/ To read a lecture of them?" *Rich 2,* IV, i, 231–232. **3** group of soldiers: ". . . he bore him in the thickest troop/ As doth a lion in a herd of neat . . ." *3 Hen 6,* II, i, 13–14. **4** here, ref. to mob of citizens on opposite side of the city: "But I beseech you,/ What says the other troop?" *Cor,* I, i, 202–203. **5 want troops,** to lack followers: "Dido, and her Aeneas, shall want troops . . ." *Ant & Cleo,* IV, xiv, 53.

trophy, *n.* **1** monument or memorial, esp. one in honor of a military victory: ". . . these great tow'rs, trophies, and schools should fall/ For private faults in them." *Timon,* V, iv, 25–26. **2** token of victory, as enemy arms: "No trophy, sword, nor hatchment o'er his bones . . ." *Ham,* IV, v, 211.

tropically, *adv.* figuratively; metaphorically: "*The Mousetrap*—marry, how tropically!" *Ham,* III, ii, 232.

trot[1], *n.* **1** contemp. term for an old woman: ". . . marry him to . . . an old trot with ne'er a/ tooth in her head . . ." *Shrew,* I, ii, 77–79. **2** a bawd: "What say'st thou, trot?/ Is the world as it was, man?" *Meas,* III, ii, 48–49.

trot[2], *n.* Frenchman's pron. of "troth": "By my trot, I tarry too long." *Wives,* I, iv, 57.

troth, *n.* **1** truth; abridgment of the phrase "By my troth," one's affirmation of honesty: "Troth, my lord, I have played the part of Lady Fame." *M Ado,* II, i, 198. **2** pledge; faith: ". . . having sworn too hard a keeping oath,/ Study to break it and not break my troth." *Love's L,* I, i, 65–66. **3** trust; honor; uprightness: "She conjures him by high almighty Jove . . . By holy human law and common troth . . ." *Luc,* 568–571. **4 good troth,** in truth: "Good troth, you do me wrong, good sooth, you do . . ." *M N Dream,* II, ii, 128. **5 o' my troth,** by my faith: "Legg'd like a man! and his fins like/ arms! Warm o' my troth!" *Temp,* II, ii, 34–35.

troth-plight, *adj.* betrothed: ". . . certainly she did you wrong,/ for you were troth-plight to her." *Hen 5,* II, i, 19–20.

trouble, *v.* to roil or stir up; agitate: ". . . like a fountain troubled,/ Muddy, ill-seeming, thick, bereft of beauty . . ." *Shrew,* V, ii, 143–144.

trout, *n.* **groping for trouts,** fishing on a private preserve; here, in sexual wordplay: ". . . what's his offence?"/ "Groping for trouts, in a peculiar [private] river." *Meas,* I, ii, 82–83.

trow, *v.* **1 I trow,** I daresay; to be sure: "'Twas time, I trow, to wake and leave our beds,/ Hearing alarums at our chamber-doors." *1 Hen 6,* II, i, 41–42. **2** to hope; trust; suppose: "Do you hear, you minion, you'll let us in I trow?" *Errors,* III, i, 54. **3** to know: "Trow you who hath done this?" *As You,* III, ii, 176. **4** I wonder: "What means the fool, trow?" *M Ado,* III, iv, 54. **5 trowest thou,** do you think? [believe? suppose?]: "Trowest thou that e'er I'll look upon the world . . ." *2 Hen 6,* II, iv, 38.

trowest, *v.* [you] believe: "Learn more than thou trowest . . ." *Lear,* I, iv, 128.

Troy, *n.* **1** ancient city in NW Asia Minor, site of the Trojan War: ". . . young Alcides, when he did redeem/ The virgin tribute, paid by howling Troy/ To the sea-monster . . ." *Merch,* III, ii, 55–57. **2** the city regarded as a symbol of ruined greatness: "Ah, thou, the model where old Troy did stand!" *Rich 2,* V, i, ll. **3 the hope of Troy,** Hector, greatest of the Trojan warriors: ". . . stood against them, as the hope of Troy/ Against the Greeks that would have enter'd Troy." *3 Hen 6,* II, i, 51–52.

Troyan, *n.* var. of, **Trojan,** a close companion: "Tut, there are other Troyans that thou/ dream'st not of . . ." *1 Hen 4,* II, i, 68–69.

Troyant, *adj.* misuse of **Troyan,** var. of **Trojan:** ". . . Compare with Caesars and with Cannibals,/ And Troyant Greeks?" *2 Hen 4,* II, iv, 163–164.

troy weight, *n.* system of weights for weighing bread: "By a halfpenny loaf a day, troy weight." *More,* II, iv, 7.

truant, *n.* **1** person who neglects his duty: "Faith, I have been a truant in the law . . ." *1 Hen 6,* II, iv, 7. —*v.* **2** to be unfaithful (to): "'Tis double wrong to truant with your bed . . ." *Errors,* III, ii, 17.

truckle-bed, *n.* small, low bed that can be rolled under a larger bed when not in use; a trundle bed: "Romeo, good night. I'll to my truckle-bed." *Rom & Jul,* II, i, 39.

trudge, *v.* to be on one's way; be off: "'Tis time I think to trudge, pack and be gone." *Errors,* III, ii, 152.

true, *adj.* **1** honest: "If you meet a thief, you may suspect him . . . to be no true man . . ." *M Ado,* III, iii, 49–50. **2** wordplay on "honest" and "without makeup": "All men's faces are true . . . But there is never a fair woman has a true face." *Ant & Cleo,* II, vi, 97–98. **3** unfeigned; spontaneous: "The last true duties of thy noble son." *T Andr,* V, iii, 155. **4** similar; here, to one's father: ". . . my dimensions are as well compact,/ My mind as generous, and my shape as true . . ." *Lear,* I, ii, 7–8. **5** faithful; loyal: ". . . my true lip/ Hath virgin'd it e'er since." *Cor,* V, iii, 47–48.
—*adv.* **6** truly; absolutely: "Here is a dear, a true industrious friend . . ." *1 Hen 4,* I, i, 62.

true-bred, *adj.* bred to be a soldier: "I'll lean upon one crutch, and fight with t'other . . ."/ "Oh, true-bred!" *Cor,* I, i, 241–242.

true condition, *n.* loyal hearts: "I am solicited not by a few,/ And those of true condition . . ." *Hen 8,* I, ii, 18–19.

true-ow'd, *adj.* genuinely or sincerely owned: "This borrow'd passion stands for true-ow'd woe . . ." *Per,* IV, iv, 24.

truepenny, *n.* trusted fellow: "Ah ha, boy, say'st thou so? Art thou there, truepenny?" *Ham,* I, v, 158.

true spies, *n.* See **spies** (def. 3).

true type, *n.* stamp of virtue or faithfulness: "Of that true type hath Tarquin rifled me." *Luc,* 1050.

truie, *n.* [French] sow: ". . . et la truie lavée au bourbier [and the sow is washed in the mire] . . ." *Hen 5,* III, vii, 66.

trull, *n.* whore; slut: "Now will I hence to seek my lovely Moor,/ And let my spleenful sons this trull deflower." *T Andr,* II, iii, 190–191.

trump, *n.* trumpet or trumpets: "Proclaim our honours, lords, with trump and drum." *T Andr,* I, i, 275.

trumpery, *n.* "glistering apparel" used by Prospero in his art: "The trumpery in my house, go bring it hither,/ For stale to catch these thieves." *Temp,* IV, i, 186–187.

trumpet, *n.* **1** ref. to sound of trumpet preceding an announcement or warning of an approach: "So, hence! Be thou the trumpet of our wrath . . ." *K John,* I, 1, 27. **2** trumpeter: "Go, trumpet, to the walls and sound a parle." *3 Hen 6,* V, i, 16.

truncheon, *n.* **1** short staff carried as a symbol of one's military authority: ". . . thrice he walk'd/ By their oppress'd and fear-surprised eyes/ Within his truncheon's length . . ." *Ham,* I, ii, 202–204. **2** cudgel; here, ref. to Iden's leg: "Thy leg a stick compared with this truncheon . . ." *2 Hen 6,* IV, x, 48.

—*v.* **3** to beat with a truncheon; cudgel: ". . . they would truncheon you/ out [beat you out of the corps], for taking their names upon you . . ." *2 Hen 4,* II, iv, 138–139.

truncheoner, *n.* person armed with a truncheon: "I might see from far some forty truncheoners/ draw to her succour . . ." *Hen 8,* V, iii, 50–51.

trundle-tail, *adj.* (of a dog) having a long, trailing tail: "Or bobtail tike or trundle-tail;/ Tom will make him weep and wail . . ." *Lear,* III, vi, 70–71.

trunk, *n.* **1** person's body: ". . . if on the tenth day following/ Thy banish'd trunk be found in our dominions,/ The moment is thy death." *Lear,* I, i, 176–178. **2** corpse; here, the body of Titus: ". . . uncle, draw you near/ To shed obsequious tears upon this trunk." *T Andr,* V, iii, 151–152.

trunk-work, *n.* tryst whereby the lover is smuggled into the beloved's bedroom via a trunk: "This has been some/ stair-work, some trunk-work, some behind-door-work . . ." *W Tale,* III, iii, 73–74.

trust, *n.* credit: ". . . inquire . . . Where money is, and I no question make/ To have it of [on] my trust . . ." *Merch,* I, i, 183–185.

truth, *n.* **1** faithfulness in love: "Beauty, truth and rarity,/ Grace in all simplicity,/ Here enclos'd, in cinders lie." *Phoen,* 53–55. **2** virtue; virtuous conduct: "Madam, by chance but not by truth; what though?" *K John,* I, i, 169. **3** essence; spirit: "When that shall vade [fade], my verse distils your truth." *Sonn 54,* 14. **4 swear truth out of England,** make it impossible for anyone to believe the truth: ". . . he would swear truth out of England but he would/ make you believe it was done in fight . . ." *1 Hen 4,* II, iv, 302–303. **5 truth of the cause,** justice of the case: "Insisting on the old prerogative/ And power i' th' truth o' th' cause." *Cor,* III, iii, 17–18.

try, *v.* **1** to test; put to the test: "I think this honourable/ lord did but try us this other day." *Timon,* III, vi, 3. **2** to prove true: "Well, as time shall try. 'In time the savage bull doth bear the yoke.'" *M Ado,* I, i, 241–242.
—*n.* **3** test or experiment: ". . . this breaking of his has been but a try for his friends." *Timon,* V, i, 9. **4 bring her to try,** (in ship-handling) keep close to the wind: "Down with the topmast! yare! lower, lower!/ Bring her to try with main-course [mainsail]." *Temp,* I, i, 34–35.

tub, *n.* **in the tub,** the sweating tub, believed to be a cure for venereal disease: ". . . she hath eaten up all her beef, and she is/ herself in the tub." *Meas,* III, ii, 54–55.

tub-fast, *n.* treatment for venereal diseases combining sweating tubs and fasting: ". . . bring down rose-cheek'd youth/ To the tub-fast and the diet." *Timon,* IV, iii, 87–88.

tuck, *n.* rapier: ". . . you bow-case, you vile standing/ tuck!" *1 Hen 4,* II, iv, 243–244.

tucket, *n.* **1** trumpet call (usually a stage direction): "[Tucket sounded.]" *Timon,* I, ii, 111. **2 tucket sonance,** sound of the trumpet: "Then let the trumpets sound/ The tucket sonance and the note to mount . . ." *Hen V,* IV, ii, 34–35.

tuft, *n.* clump or cluster: "'Tis at the tuft of olives here hard by." *As You,* III, v, 75.

tug, *v.* **1** to drag or haul about: "And I another,/ So weary with disasters, tugg'd with fortune . . ." *Mac,* III, i, 110–111. **2** to contend: ". . . let myself and fortune/ Tug for the time to come." *W Tale,* IV, iv, 497–498.

tuition, *n.* care; safekeeping: "I commit you—/ To the tuition of God." *M Ado,* I, i, 260–261.

Tully, *n.* Cicero [Marcus Tullius Cicero], murdered on orders from Mark Antony: "A Roman sworder and banditto slave/ Murder'd sweet Tully . . ." *2 Hen 6,* IV, i, 135–136.

Tully's Orator, *n.* prob. Cicero's *De Oratore:* ". . . she hath read to thee/ Sweet poetry and Tully's Orator." *T Andr,* IV, i, 13–14.

tumble, *v.* to have sexual relations (with) [lit., to rumple]: "Quoth she, 'Before you tumbled me,/ You promis'd me to wed.'" *Ham,* IV, v, 62–63.

tumbler's hoop, *n.* acrobat's hoop, usually decorated with bright-colored ribbons: "And I to be a corporal of his field,/ And wear his colours like a tumbler's hoop!" *Love's L,* III, i, 182–183.

tun, *n.* large cask, esp. one for holding wine or ale: ". . . an old fat man, a tun of man is thy companion." *1 Hen 4,* II, iv, 442.

tunable or tuneable, *adj.* melodious; harmonious: ". . . your tongue's sweet air/ More tuneable than lark to shepherd's ear . . ." *M N Dream,* I, i, 183–184.

tun-dish, *n.* funnel; here, a coarse joke in which word understood as "penis": "Why should he die, sir?"/ "Why? For filling a bottle with a tun-dish." *Meas,* III, ii, 166.

tune, *v.* **1** to play: "And profound Solomon to tune a jig . . ." *Love's L,* IV, iii, 165. **2** to sing: "I'll tune thy woes with my lamenting tongue . . ." *Luc,* 1465. **3** to sway or convince: "Yet hope, succeeding from so fair a tree/ As your fair self, doth tune us otherwise . . ." *Per,* I, i, 115–116.
—*n.* **4** mood; disposition: ". . . he is not in this tune, is he?" *Tr & Cr,* III, iii, 298. **5 in better tune,** in more lucid moments: ". . . sometime, in his better tune, remembers/ What we are come about . . ." *Lear,* IV, iii, 40–41. **6 some better tune,** [in] some more suitable way: "I had a thing to say,/ But I will fit it with some better tune." *K John,* III, ii, 35–36.

tuneable, *adj.* See **tunable.**

tune of the time, *n.* fashionable jargon of the day: "Thus/ has he . . . only got the tune of/ the time . . ." *Ham,* V, ii, 184–187.

tuners of accent, *n.* fellows who affect new phrases and accents: "The pox of such antic lisping affecting phantasimes,/ these new tuners of accent." *Rom & Jul,* II, iv, 28–29.

tup, *v.* to copulate with: ". . . an old black ram/ Is tupping your white ewe . . ." *Oth,* I, i, 88–89.

turfy, *adj.* covered with a layer of grass or plants: "Thy turfy mountains, where live nibbling sheep . . ." *Temp,* IV, i, 62.

Turk, *n.* **1** scoundrel; infidel [generalized term of abuse]; here, perh. because of warlike reputation of Phrygians: "Tester I'll have in pouch when thou shalt lack,/ Base Phrygian Turk!" *Wives,* I, iii, 83–84. **2 turn Turk,** to prove false, hence go bad: ". . . if the rest/ of my fortunes turn Turk with me . . ." *Ham,* III, ii, 269–270.

turkey-cock, *n.* favorite image of conceit and pompousness: "Contemplation makes a rare turkey-cock/ of him . . ." *T Night,* II, v, 30–31.

Turk Gregory, nonce name, prob. a combination of the Grand Turk and Pope Gregory VII, both regarded as the cruelest of leaders: "Turk Gregory never did such deeds in arms as I have/ done this day . . ." *1 Hen 4,* V, iii, 46–47.

Turkish mute, *n.* any of the servants of the royal Turkish household whose tongues had been cut out to preserve secrecy: ". . . or else our grave,/ Like Turkish mute, shall have a tongueless mouth . . ." *Hen 5,* I, ii, 231–232.

Turk's tribute, *n.* tribute exacted by the Turkish Sultan from his subjects: ". . . duer paid to the hearer than/ the Turk's tribute." *2 Hen 4,* III, ii, 301–302.

Turlygod, *n.* poss. epithet similar to "poor Tom," indicating a former inmate of Bedlam, who had been released to beg: "Poor Turlygod! poor Tom!/ That's something yet . . ." *Lear,* II, iii, 20–21.

turmoiled, *adj.* beset by worries; apprehensive: "Lord! who would live turmoiled in the court . . ." *2 Hen 6,* IV, x, 16.

turn, *v.* **1** to harmonize (with): "And turn his merry note/ Unto the sweet bird's throat." *As You,* II, v, 3–4. **2** return: ". . . turn thou no more/ To seek a living in our territory." *As You,* III, i, 7–8. **3** wordplay on "return" and "prove unfaithful": "If you turn not, you will return the sooner . . ." *Two Gent,* II, ii, 4. **4** can or may turn: "For sweetest things turn sourest by their deeds . . ." *Sonn 94,* 13. **5** to shape by turning on a lathe: "I had rather hear a brazen canstick turn'd . . ." *1 Hen 4,* III, i, 125. **6** to compose: "Assist me, some/ extemporal god of rhyme, for I am sure I shall turn/ sonnet." *Love's L,* I, ii, 172–174. **7** to become; be transformed into: ". . . you will turn good husband now, Pompey;/ you will/ keep the house." *Meas,* III, ii, 68–69. **8** to become infatuated or obsessed with: "He was wont to speak plain and to/ the purpose . . . and now is he turned orthography—" *M Ado,* II, iii, 18–20. **9** to curdle; sour: ". . . such a faint and milky heart/ It turns in less than two nights . . ." *Timon,* III, i, 54–55. **10** to become giddy or addled: "My wits begin to turn." *Lear,* III, ii, 67. **11 turn'd me to,** forced on me: ". . . for stirring up my subjects,/ And all the trouble thou hast turn'd me to?" *3 Hen 6,* V, v, 15–16. **12 turn head,** (of a quarry) to turn and make a stand: "Turn head, and stop pursuit . . ." *Hen 5,* II, iv, 68. **13 turn him going,** turn him out; send him away; here, evict: "Do this expediently, and turn him going." *As You,* III, i, 18. **14 turn in,** tip into: "But first I'll turn yon fellow in his grave . . ." *Rich 3,* I, ii, 265. **15 turn i' th' wheel,** See **wheel** (def. 6). **16 turn o'er,** to study: "By turning o'er authorities, I have,/ Together with my practice, made familiar . . . the blest infusions . . ." *Per,* III, ii, 33–35. **17 turn off,** to discard: "You that have turn'd off a first so noble wife/ May justly diet me." *All's W,* V, iii, 219–220. **18 turn on oneself,** to retreat; flee: ". . . all the rest/ Turn'd on themselves, like dull and heavy lead . . ." *2 Hen 4,* I, i, 117–118. **19 turn on the toe,** to wheel around to the opposite direction in making one's exit: "The fourth turn'd on the toe, and down he fell." *Love's L,* V, ii, 114. **20 turn out of,** to dismiss from: ". . . they will pluck/ The gay new coats o'er the French soldiers' heads,/ And turn them out of service." *Hen 5,* IV, iii, 117–119. **21 turn spit,** to rotate the spit of roasting meat, the most menial of kitchen jobs: "She would/ have made Hercules have turned spit . . ." *M Ado,* II, i, 236–237. **22 turn Turk,** to become a renegade or, sometimes, a heathen: ". . . and you be not turned Turk, there's no/ more sailing by the star." *M Ado,* III, iv, 52–53. **23 turn up the white o' th' eye,** react with rapt adoration: ". . . sanctifies himself with's/ hand, and turns up the white o'th'eye to his/ discourse." *Cor,* IV, v, 200–202. **—***n.* **24** purpose: ". . . if you have/ occasion to use me for your own turn, you shall find/ me yare." *Meas,* IV, ii, 54–56. **25** wordplay on "deed" and "change of position": "He's bound unto Octavia."/ "For what good turn?"/ "For the best turn i' the bed." *Ant & Cleo,* II, v, 58–59. **26** prob. wordplay on "deed" and "sexual act": "Spare your arithmetic, never count the turns . . ." *Cymb,* II, iv, 142. **27 for's turn,** for what he requires; hence, to do it for him: ". . . there are no/ tongues else for's turn." *Ham,* V, ii, 181–182. **28 for your turn,** [meant] for you: "She is not for your turn, the more my grief." *Shrew,* II, i, 63. **29 keep the turn,** to take turns: "And keep the turn of tippling with a slave . . ." *Ant & Cleo,* I, iv, 19. **30 serve my turn upon him,** use him for my own advantage: "I follow him to serve my turn upon him . . ." *Oth,* I, i, 42. **31 serve your turns,** to satisfy one's needs; here, with sexual innuendo: ". . . it seems some certain snatch or so/ Would serve your turns."/ "Ay, so the turn were served." *T Andr,* II, i, 95–96.

Turnbull Street, *n.* waterfront street in London, haunt of thieves and prostitutes: ". . . the wildness of his youth, and the/ feats he hath done about Turnbull Street . . ." *2 Hen 4,* III, ii, 299–300.

turned forth, *n.* person who was turned out [or turned away]: "I am the turn'd forth . . . That hath preserv'd her welfare in my blood . . ." *T Andr,* V, iii, 109–110.

turpitude, *n.* depravity: ". . . how wouldst thou have paid/ My better service, when my turpitude/ Thou dost so crown with gold!" *Ant & Cleo,* IV, vi, 32–34.

turtle, *n.* turtledove, hence devoted lover: "Will these turtles be gone?" *Love's L,* IV, iii, 208.

tush¹, *interj.* exclam. of impatience or contempt: "Tush! I may as well say the fool's the fool." *M Ado,* III, iii, 120.

tush², *n.* tusk: "Whose tushes never sheath'd he whetteth still . . ." *Ven & Ad,* 617.

Tuthill Fields, *n. pl.* section of open land in central London, used for tournaments, drilling of troops, etc.: "Convey the soldiers hence . . ."/ "Captain, conduct them into Tuthill Fields." *3 Hen 6,* I, i, 178–179.

twain, *n.* **1** two; a pair: "Madam, this glove."/ "Did he not send you twain?" *Love's L,* V, ii, 48. **2 in twain,** into two parts: "O Hamlet, thou hast cleft my heart in twain." *Ham,* III, iv, 158. **3 love in twain,** ref. to two distinct lovers who yet were of one essence: "So they lov'd, as love in twain/ Had the essence but in one . . ." *Phoen,* 25–26. **4 'twixt us twain,** between the two of us: "No bed shall e'er be guilty of my stay,/ Nor rest be interposer 'twixt us twain." *Merch,* III, ii, 324–325. **5 two are twain,** to be on unfriendly terms: "No, she'll none of him: they two are twain." *Tr & Cr,* III, i, 98. **—***adj.* **6** separated; estranged: "Go, counsellor./ Thou and my bosom henceforth shall be twain." *Rom & Jul,* III, v, 239–240.

twangling, *adj.* **1** Shakespeare's coinage, poss. with sense of "speaking or singing with a twang": ". . . she did call me rascal fiddler/ And twangling Jack, with twenty such vile terms . . ." *Shrew,* II, i, 157–158. **2** appar. with the sense of "making a low, mysterious, jingling sound": "Sometimes a thousand twangling instruments/ Will hum about mine ears . . ." *Temp,* III, ii, 135–136.

tway, *pron.* Fluellen's Welsh pron. of "two": "Marry, I wad [would]/ full fain hear some question [discussion] 'tween you tway." *Hen 5,* III, ii, 121–122.

twelve score, *n.* 240 yards, the length of an archery range: "I know his death will be a march of twelve/ score." *1 Hen 4,* II, iv, 539–540.

twenty, *n.* used as an intensifier; twenty times over: "Then come kiss me, sweet and twenty:/ Youth's a stuff will not endure." *T Night,* II, iii, 52–53.

twice-sod, *adj.* twice warmed-over [twice-repeated]: "Twice-sod simplicity [stupidity], *bis coctus!*" *Love's L,* IV, ii, 21.

twiggen bottle, *n.* See **wicker bottle.**

twigs, *n. pl.* twigs coated with birdlime and set out to catch small birds; here, used figuratively: "I must go look my twigs. He shall be caught." *All's W,* III, vi, 103.

twink, *n.* twinkling; instant: "She vied so fast, protesting oath on oath,/ That in a twink she won me to her love." *Shrew,* II, i, 302–303.

twinned stones, *n.* the seemingly identical pebbles on the beach: "The fiery orbs above, and the twinn'd stones/ Upon the number'd beach . . ." *Cymb,* I, vii, 35–36.

twire, *v.* to peep: "When sparkling stars twire not thou gild'st the even." *Sonn 28,* 12.

twist, *n.* twisted thread: "Breaking his oath and resolution, like/ A twist of rotten silk . . ." *Cor,* V, vi, 95–96.

twit, *past part.* twitted; reproached or insulted: "Hath he not twit our sovereign lady here/ With ignominious words . . ." *2 Hen 6,* III, i, 178–179.

two and thirty, *n.* perh. ref. either to the card game of Thirty-one, in which 32 would be a losing number, or to Grumio's belief that Petruchio's strange behavior is due to drunkenness: ". . . being perhaps, for aught I see, two and/ thirty, a pip out?" *Shrew,* I, ii, 32–33.

two-fold balls, *n.* prob. ref. to double coronation at Scone and (later) at Westminster: ". . . and some I see,/ That two-fold balls and treble sceptres carry." *Mac,* IV, i, 120–121.

Tyburn, *n.* site of public hangings in London, with its permanent three-cornered gallows: "Thou mak'st the triumviry . . . The shape of love's Tyburn, that hangs up simplicity." *Love's L,* IV, iii, 50–51

type, *n.* **1** title: "Thy father bears the type of King of Naples . . ." *3 Hen 6,* I, iv, 121. **2** sign or badge: ". . . renouncing clean/ The faith they have in tennis . . . and those types of travel . . ." *Hen 8,* I, iii, 29–31.

Typhon, *n.* (in early Greek legend) a flaming monster, one of the Titans, who warred with the Olympian gods: ". . . Enceladus,/ With all his threat'ning band of Typhon's brood . . ." *T Andr,* IV, ii, 93–94.

tyrannically, *adv.* tumultuously or hysterically; also, outrageously: ". . . cry out on the top of question, and are most tyrannically/ clapped for't." *Ham,* II, ii, 338–339.

tyranny, *n.* cruelty; violence: "To suffer with a quietness of spirit,/ The very tyranny and rage of his." *Merch,* IV, i, 12–13.

Tyre or **Tyrus,** *n.* ancient capital of Phoenicia (now S Lebanon): "Tyre, I now look from thee then, and to Tharsus/ Intend my travel . . ." *Per,* I, ii, 115.

Tyrian, *adj.* of Tyre; here, made in Tyre, E Mediterranean city famous for its dyes: "My hangings all of Tyrian tapestry." *Shrews,* II, i, 342.

~ U ~

ud's, *adj.* God's: "... ud's pity, who would not make/ her husband a cuckold ..." *Oth,* IV, iii, 74–75.

umbered, *adj.* shadowy; dusky: "Each battle [army] sees the other's umber'd face ..." *Hen 5,* IV, Chor., 9.

umbrage, *n.* a shadow: "... and who else [whoever] would trace him his umbrage, nothing/ more." *Ham,* V, ii, 119–120.

unable, *adj.* **unable worms,** weak, miserable creatures: "Come, come, you froward and unable worms ..." *Shrew,* V, ii, 170.

unaccommodated, *adj.* not furnished with the animals' natural covering: "... unaccommodated man/ is no more but such a poor, bare, forked animal/ as thou art." *Lear,* III, iv, 109–111.

unaccustomed, *adj.* extraordinary; here, fatal: "... such an unaccustom'd dram/ That he shall soon keep Tybalt company ..." *Rom & Jul,* III, v, 90–91.

unaching, *adj.* causing no pain: "Show them th'unaching scars which I should hide ..." *Cor,* II, ii, 148.

unacquainted, *adj.* **1** foreign: "To grace the gentry of a land remote,/ And follow unacquainted colours here?" *K John,* V, ii, 31–32. **2** unfamiliar; here, also longed for: "... his people shall revolt from him,/ And kiss the lips of unacquainted change ..." *K John,* III, iii, 165–166.

unadvised, *adj., adv.* **1** ill-advised; unwisely: "Why, boy, although our mother, unadvis'd,/ Gave you a dancing-rapier by your side ..." *T Andr,* II, i, 38–39. **2** rash; hot-headed: "Thou unadvised scold, I can produce/ A will that bars the title of thy son." *K John,* II, i, 191–192.

unaneled, *adj.* unanointed; without having received extreme unction before death: "Cut off even in the blossoms of my sin,/ Unhousel'd, disappointed, unanel'd ..." *Ham,* I, v, 76–77.

unapt, *adj.* **1** unfit; unsuitable: "Why are our bodies soft, and weak, and smooth,/ Unapt to toil and trouble in the world ..." *Shrew,* V, ii, 166–167. **2** unwilling; disinclined: "My blood hath been ... Unapt to stir at these indignities ..." *1 Hen 4,* I, iii, 1–2.

unarm, *v.* to remove one's armor: "At your own house, there he unarms him." *Tr & Cr,* I, ii, 279.

unattainted, *adj.* uninfected; hence, unjaundiced or unprejudiced: "Go thither and with unattainted eye/ Compare her face with some that I shall show ..." *Rom & Jul,* I, ii, 87–88.

unattempted, *adj.* untempted: "But for my hand, as unattempted yet,/ Like a poor beggar, raileth on the rich." *K John,* II, i, 591–592.

unattended, *adj.* **leave one unattended,** to desert one completely: "Your constancy/ Hath left you unattended." *Mac,* II, ii, 67–68.

unauspicious, *adj.* unfavorably disposed: "To whose ingrate and unauspicious altars/ My soul the faithfull'st off'rings ..." *T Night,* V, i, 111–112.

unavoided, *adj.* unavoidable: "And unavoided is the danger now ..." *Rich 2,* II, i, 268.

unawares, *adv.* unsuspectedly; taking us by surprise: "Pucelle ... Hath wrought this hellish mischief unawares ..." *1 Hen 6,* III, ii, 38–39.

unbacked, *adj.* (of a horse) unbroken; never having been ridden: "At which, like unback'd colts, they prick'd their ears,/ Advanc'd their eyelids ..." *Temp,* IV, i, 176–177.

unbaked and doughy youth, *n.* inexperienced, gullible young men: "... whose villainous saffron would have/ made all the unbak'd and doughy youth of a nation/ in his colour." *All's W,* IV, v, 2–4.

unbarbed sconce, *n.* bare head: "Must I go show them my unbarb'd sconce?" *Cor,* III, ii, 99.

unbated, *adj.* (of a foil) unblunted; lacking a protective button at the tip: "Or with a little shuffling—you may choose/ A sword unbated . . ." *Ham,* IV, vii, 136–137.

unbend, *v.* **1** to let go slack; relax or loosen: "Why, worthy Thane,/ You do unbend your noble strength . . ." *Mac,* II, ii, 43–44. **2 be unbent,** (of a bow) not flexed and ready for use: "Why hast thou gone so far,/ To be unbent when thou hast ta'en thy stand . . ." *Cymb,* III, iv, 109–110.

unbid spite, *n.* unwelcome vexation: "O unbid spite! Is sportful Edward come?" *3 Hen 6,* V, i, 18.

unbitted, *adj.* unbridled: ". . . to cool our/ raging motions, our carnal stings, our unbitted/ lusts . . ." *Oth,* I, iii, 330–332.

unbless, *v.* to make unhappy; here, deny the blessing of motherhood: "Thou dost beguile the world, unbless some mother." *Sonn 3,* 4.

unbolt, *v.* to disclose; open up: "How shall I understand you?/ I will unbolt to you." *Timon,* I, i, 51–52.

unbolted, *adj.* (of mortar) containing lumps of lime; hence, unrefined or crude: "I will tread [grind]/ this unbolted villain into mortar . . ." *Lear,* II, ii, 65–66.

unbonneted, *adj.* **1** wearing no head covering: ". . . unbonneted he runs,/ And bids what will take all." *Lear,* III, i, 14–15. **2** without removing his hat; here, as though equals: ". . . my demerits/ May speak unbonneted to as proud a fortune/ As this that I have reach'd . . ." *Oth,* I, ii, 22–24. Cf. **bonnet.**

unbookish, *adj.* uneducated or unskilled; inexperienced: "And his unbookish jealousy must conster/ Poor Cassio's smiles . . ." *Oth,* IV, i, 101–102.

unbraced, *adj.* with the doublet unfastened: "And, thus unbraced, Casca, as you see,/ Have bar'd my bosom to the thunderstone . . ." *J Caes,* I, iii, 48–49.

unbraided, *adj.* unused; fresh: ". . . thou talkest of an admirable conceited/ fellow. Has he any unbraided wares?" *W Tale,* IV, iv, 204–205.

unbreathed, *adj.* unexercised; untrained: "Hard-handed men that . . . now have toil'd their unbreath'd memories/ With this same play . . ." *M N Dream,* V, i, 72–75.

unbred, *adj.* unborn: "For fear of which, hear this, thou age unbred . . ." *Sonn 104,* 13.

unbreeched, *adj.* wearing no breeches; here, too young to wear men's clothing: ". . . saw myself unbreech'd,/ In my green velvet coat . . ." *W Tale,* I, ii, 155–156.

unbridled, *adj.* unruly; wayward: "This is not well, rash and unbridled boy,/ To fly the favours of so good a king . . ." *All's W,* III, ii, 26–27.

unburthen, *v.,* var. of **unburden;** to disclose; make known: "And from your love I have a warranty/ To unburthen all my plots and purposes . . ." *Merch,* I, i, 132–133.

uncapable, *adj.,* var. of **incapable:** "A stony adversary, an inhuman wretch,/ Uncapable of pity . . ." *Merch,* IV, i, 4–5.

uncape, *v.* poss. to uncover the fox: "Let me stop this way first. [Locking the door]/ So, now uncape." *Wives,* III, iii, 152–153.

uncase, *v.* to undress: "Do you not see Pompey is uncasing for the combat?" *Love's L,* V, ii, 693.

uncertain, *adj.* moody; erratic: "Th'uncertain sickly appetite to please . . ." *Sonn 147,* 4.

uncertainty, *n.* mystery: "Until I know this sure [the truth of this] uncertainty,/ I'll entertain the offer'd fallacy." *Errors,* II, ii, 185–186.

uncharge, *v.* to free of blame; fail to accuse: "But even his mother shall uncharge the practice . . ." *Ham,* IV, vii, 66.

uncharged, *adj.* (of defensive positions) not attacked; unassaulted: "Descend, and open your uncharged ports." *Timon,* V, iv, 55.

uncharmed, *adj.* unseduced; here, not under the spell of love: "From love's weak childish bow she lives uncharm'd." *Rom & Jul,* I, i, 209.

unchary, *adv.* lavishly; also, perh., carelessly: "And laid mine honour too unchary out . . ." *T Night,* III, iv, 204.

unchaste composition, *n.* dishonorable compact: ". . . thinks/ himself made in the unchaste composition." *All's W,* IV, iii, 16–17.

uncheck, *v.* to remove restraints from: "The laws . . . in their rough power/ Has uncheck'd theft." *Timon,* IV, iii, 446–447.

uncivil, *adj.* **1** uncivilized: "The uncivil kerns of Ireland are in arms . . ." *2 Hen 6,* III, i, 310. **2** barbaric: "Let thy fair wisdom, not thy passion, sway/ In this uncivil and unjust extent . . ." *T Night,* IV, i, 51–52. **3** rude; also, pitiless or cruel: "You uncivil lady,/ To whose ingrate and unauspicious altars/

My soul the faithfull'st off'rings hath breath'd out . . ." *T Night*, V, i, 110–112.

uncivil rule, *n*. disorderly conduct: ". . . you would not give/ means for this uncivil rule . . ." *T Night*, II, iii, 121–122.

unclasp, *v*. **1** to let go of another's hand: "Unclasp, unclasp!/ Thanks, gentlemen, to all; all have done well . . ." *Per*, II, iii, 106–107. **2** to reveal: "He (most humane/ And fill'd with honour) to my kingly guest/ Unclasp'd my practice . . ." *W Tale*, III, ii, 165–167.

uncleanly, *adj*. unbecoming or improper; also, indecent: "Uncleanly scruples! fear not you; look to't." *K John*, IV, i, 7.

unclew, *v*. to undo or, figuratively, ruin: "If I should pay you for't as 'tis extoll'd,/ It would unclew me quite." *Timon*, I, i, 170–171.

uncoined, *adj*. unminted, therefore not made up; genuine: ". . . dear/ Kate, take a fellow of plain and uncoined constancy . . ." *Hen 5*, V, ii, 156–158.

uncomely, *adj*. unchaste: ". . . you're both a father and a son,/ By your uncomely claspings [embraces] with your child . . ." *Per*, I, i, 128–129.

uncomprehensive, *adj*. incomprehensible; inconceivable: "Finds bottom in th'uncomprehensive deep . . ." *Tr & Cr*, III, iii, 197.

unconfinable, *adj*. boundless; limitless: "Why, thou unconfinable baseness, it is as much as I can do . . ." *Wives*, II, ii, 19–20.

unconfirmed, *adj*. **1** inexperienced or ignorant: "That shows thou art unconfirmed." *M Ado*, III, iii, 114. **2** unsupported [by true learning]: ". . . after his undressed . . . untrained, or/ rather unlettered, or ratherest, unconfirmed fashion [manner] . . ." *Love's L*, IV, ii, 16–18.

unconsidered, *adj*. neglected; half-forgotten: ". . . likewise/ a snapper-up of unconsidered trifles." *W Tale*, IV, iii, 25–26.

unconstant, *adj*. done on impulse; capricious: "Such unconstant starts are we like to have from him . . ." *Lear*, I, i, 300–301.

unconstrained, *adj*. prob. sense is "unconstraining": "Playing sports in unconstrained gyves?" *Lover's Comp*, 242.

uncontemned, *adj*. undespised: "Which of the peers/ Have uncontemn'd gone by him . . ." *Hen 8*, III, ii, 9–10.

uncontrolled, *adj*. indomitable: "His batter'd shield, his uncontrolled crest . . ." *Ven & Ad*, 104.

uncouple, *v*. (in hunting) to unleash hounds: "My love shall hear the music of my hounds./ Uncouple in the western valley; let them go . . ." *M N Dream*, IV, i, 105–106.

uncouth, *adj*. **1** strange or unexpected, hence distasteful: "What uncouth ill event/ Hath thee befall'n . . ." *Luc*, 1598–1599. **2** (of places) wild; desolate: "If this uncouth forest yield anything savage . . ." *As You*, II, vi, 6.

uncovered, *adj*. **1** suddenly disclosed: ". . . then with public/ accusation, uncovered slander, unmitigated rancour—" *M Ado*, IV, i, 303–304. **2** with one's hat removed from the head: ". . . sooner dance upon a bloody pole/ Than stand uncover'd to the vulgar groom." *2 Hen 6*, IV, i, 127–128.

uncrossed, *adj*. unsettled, as a debt: "Such gain the cap of him that makes him fine,/ Yet keeps his book uncross'd [the debt never crossed out] . . ." *Cymb*, III, iii, 25–26.

unctuous, *adj*. oily; fatty: ". . . morsels unctuous greases his pure mind . . ." *Timon*, IV, iii, 196.

uncurable discomfit, *n*. unshakable fear of defeat: "But fly you must; uncurable discomfit/ Reigns in the hearts of all our present parts." *2 Hen 6*, V, ii, 86–87.

uncurrent, *adj*. **1** no longer legal tender; hence, worthless: ". . . like a/ piece of uncurrent gold, be not cracked within the/ ring." *Ham*, II, ii, 423–424. **2** unlawful: ". . . since he came,/ With what encounter so uncurrent I/ Have strain'd t'appear thus . . ." *W Tale*, III, ii, 48–50.

undeaf, *v*. to unstop; here, to get the attention of: "Though Richard my life's counsel would not hear,/ My death's sad tale may yet undeaf his ear." *Rich 2*, II, i, 15–16.

undeeded, *adj*. having done no deeds: ". . . my sword, with an unbatter'd edge,/ I sheathe again undeeded." *Mac*, V, vii, 19–20.

under, *adv*. **1** in a lesser or subordinate position: "The wars hath so kept you under . . ." *All's W*, I, i, 191.
—*adj*. **2** earthly: ". . . each under eye/ Doth homage to his new-appearing sight . . ." *Sonn 7*, 2–3.
—*prep*. **3** in keeping with: ". . . under the/ degree of a squire." *Wives*, III, iv, 46–47.

underbear, *v*. to endure: "And leave those woes alone which I alone/ Am bound to underbear!" *K John*, II, ii, 64–65.

underbearing, *n.* endurance: "Wooing poor craftsmen with the craft of smiles/ And patient underbearing of his fortune . . ." *Rich 2,* I, iv, 28–29.

underborne, *adj.* edged or lined: ". . . skirts, round underborne with a bluish tinsel . . ." *M Ado,* III, iv, 20.

undercrest, *v.* to wear as one's crest; also, to be worthy of: ". . . at all times/ To undercrest your good addition,/ To th'fairness of my power." *Cor,* I, ix, 69–71.

under favour, by your leave: "My lords, then, under favour, pardon me,/ If I speak like a captain." *Timon,* III, v, 41–42.

under fiends, devils of hell: "I will fight/ Against my canker'd country with the spleen/ Of all the under fiends." *Cor,* IV, v, 91–93.

undergarnished pride, *n.* the fine clothes beneath the cloak: "What is within, but like a cloak doth hide/ From weather's waste the undergarnished pride." *Edw 3,* I, ii, 158–159.

undergo, *v.* **1** to undertake: ". . . I have mov'd already/ Some certain of the noblest-minded Romans/ To undergo with me an enterprise . . ." *J Caes,* I, iii, 121–123. **2** to manage; sustain: "His virtues else, be they as pure as grace,/ As infinite as man may undergo . . ." *Ham,* I, iv, 33–34. **3** to bear up under; endure: ". . . undergoes,/ More goddess-like than wife-like, such assaults . . ." *Cymb,* III, ii, 7–8.

undergoing stomach, *n.* See **stomach** (def. 8).

underhand, *adj.* sly and unobtrusive; underhanded: "I . . . have by underhand means laboured to dissuade him from it . . ." *As You,* I, i, 138.

under-hangman, *n.* hangman's assistant: ". . . to be styled/ The under-hangman of his kingdom . . ." *Cymb,* II, iii, 128–129.

undermine, *v.* to thwart or defeat: ". . . to undermine the Duchess,/ And buz these conjurations in her brain." *2 Hen 6,* I, ii, 98–99.

underneath the brows, See **brow** (def. 8).

underprop, *v.* to support or uphold: "Here am I left to underprop his land . . ." *Rich 2,* II, ii, 82.

underskinker, *n.* assistant drawer or tapster: ". . . this pennyworth of sugar, clapped even now into my hand by/ an underskinker . . ." *1 Hen 4,* II, iv, 23–24.

understood relations, *n.* hidden relationships linking every part of nature: "Augures, and understood relations, have . . . brought forth/ The secret'st man of blood." *Mac,* III, iv, 125.

undertake, *v.* **1** to make amorous advances to: "By my troth, I would not undertake her in this/ company." *T Night,* I, iii, 57–58. **2** to show initiative; accept responsibility: "It is the cowish terror of his spirit/ That dares not undertake . . ." *Lear,* IV, ii, 12–13. **3** to give satisfaction to; here, in a duel: "It is not fit your lordship should undertake/ every companion that you give offence to." *Cymb,* II, i, 26–27. **4** to warrant; guarantee: ". . . that strong-bonded oath/ That shall prefer and undertake my troth." *Lover's Comp,* 279–280. **5** to vouch: ". . . I undertake/ For good Lord Titus' innocence in all . . ." *T Andr,* I, i, 436–437. **6** to have charge of: ". . . give my charge up to Sir Nicholas Vaux,/ Who undertakes you to your end." *Hen 8,* II, i, 96–97.

undertaker, *n.* person who takes up a challenge for another; here, wordplay with "meddler": "Nay, if you be an undertaker, I am for you." *T Night,* III, iv, 325.

undertaking, *adj.* daring or reckless: ". . . either he so undertaking,/ Or they so suffering . . ." *Cymb,* IV, ii, 142–143.

underwrit, *adj.* with a written explanation underneath; captioned: "We'll have thee . . . Painted upon a pole, and underwrit,/ 'Here may you see the tyrant.'" *Mac,* V, viii, 25–27.

underwrite, *v.* to endure; submit to: "And underwrite in an observing kind/ His humorous predominance . . ." *Tr & Cr,* II, iii, 130–131.

underwrought, *v.* past part. of underwork; undermined: ". . . thou from loving England art so far,/ That thou hast underwrought his [its] lawful king . . ." *K John,* II, i, 94–95.

under your patience, if I may say so: "Under your patience, gentle empress,/ 'Tis thought you have a goodly gift in horning . . ." *T Andr,* II, iii, 66–67.

undescried, *adj.* unnoticed: ". . . that you may . . . to shipboard/ Get undescried." *W Tale,* IV, iv, 653–655.

undetermined, *adj.* **in undetermined differences,** making no distinction [between the flesh of kings and commoners]: "And now he feasts, mousing the flesh of men,/ In undetermin'd differences of kings." *K John,* II, i, 354–355.

undid, *v.* **what they undid did,** cooled her cheeks, yet made them glow with apparent warmth: "To glow the delicate cheeks which they did cool,/ And what they undid did." *Ant & Cleo,* II, ii, 204–205.

undividable, *adj.* indivisible: "That undividable, incorporate,/ Am better than thy dear self's better part." *Errors,* II, ii, 122–123.

undo, *v.* to alter; also, reject: "Our states are forfeit: seek not to undo us [reject our sacrifice]." *Love's L,* V, ii, 425.

undoing, *n.* **mere undoing,** utter ruin: ". . . to the mere undoing/ Of all the kingdom." *Hen 8,* III, ii, 329–330.

undone, *adj.* **1** doomed; ruined or destroyed: "Are we undone, cast off, nothing remaining?" *Timon,* IV, ii, 2. **2** explained; solved: "If by which time our secret be undone,/ This mercy shows we'll joy in such a son . . ." *Per,* I, i, 118–119.

undrowned, *adj.* saved from drowning: "'Tis as impossible that he's undrown'd/ As he that sleeps here swims." *Temp,* II, i, 232–233.

uneared, *adj.* unplowed [common sexual metaphor]: "For where is she so fair whose uneared womb/ Disdains the tillage of thy husbandry?" *Sonn 3,* 5–6.

uneasy, *adj.* uncomfortable: "Why . . . liest thou in smoky cribs,/ Upon uneasy pallets . . ." *2 Hen 4,* III, i, 10.

uneath, *adv.* hardly; barely; scarcely: "Uneath may she endure the flinty streets,/ To tread them with her tender-feeling feet." *2 Hen 6,* II, iv, 8–9.

uneffectual, *adj.* ineffectual; here, fading with the approach of day: "The glow-worm shows the matin to be near/ And 'gins to pale his uneffectual fire." *Ham,* I, v, 89–90.

unequal, *adj.* unjust: "To lay a heavy and unequal hand/ Upon our honours?" *2 Hen 4,* IV, i, 101–103.

uneven way, *n.* rough ground or terrain: ". . . but faster he did fly,/ That fallen am I in [I have got into] dark uneven way . . ." *M N Dream,* III, ii, 416–417.

unexperienced, *adj.* unenlightened; ignorant: ". . . and thou/ return unexperienced to thy grave." *Shrew,* IV, i, 74–75.

unexperient, *n.* inexperienced person; an innocent: "That the unexperient gave the tempter place . . ." *Lover's Comp,* 318.

unexpressive, *adj.* beyond expression in mere words; inexpressible: "The fair, the chaste, and unexpressive she." *As You,* III, ii, 10.

unfair, *v.* to destroy the beauty of: "And that unfair which fairly doth excel . . ." *Sonn 5,* 4.

unfallible, *adj.* old form of INFALLIBLE: "Believe my words,/ For they are certain and unfallible." *1 Hen 6,* I, ii, 58–59.

unfashionable, *adj.* badly made: "And that so lamely and unfashionable/ That dogs bark at me . . ." *Rich 3,* I, i, 22–23.

unfathered, *adj.* unnatural, esp. unnaturally begotten: ". . . they do observe/ Unfather'd heirs and loathly births of nature." *2 Hen 4,* IV, iv, 121–122.

unfee'd, *adj.* unpaid: "Then 'tis like the breath of an unfee'd lawyer . . ." *Lear,* I, iv, 135.

unfellowed, *adj.* unequalled: ". . . in the imputation/ laid on him, by them in his meed, he's unfellowed." *Ham,* V, ii, 139–140.

unfelt, *adj.* **1** intangible; theoretical: "All my treasury/ Is yet but unfelt thanks . . ." *Rich 2,* II, iii, 60–61. **2 unfelt imaginations,** glories never experienced: "And for [in place of] unfelt imaginations/ They often feel a world of restless cares . . ." *Rich 3,* I, iv, 80–81.

unfix, *v.* to uproot: ". . . I yield to that suggestion/ Whose horrid image doth unfix my hair . . ." *Mac,* I, iii, 134–135.

unfledged, *adj.* newly hatched; hence, immature: ". . . do not dull thy palm with entertainment/ Of each new-hatched, unfledg'd courage." *Ham,* I, iii, 64–65.

unfold, *v.* **1** to disclose; reveal: "Nay, answer me. Stand and unfold yourself." *Ham,* I, i, 2. **2 be unfolded with,** be exposed by: ". . . must I be unfolded/ With [by] one that I have bred?" *Ant & Cleo,* V, ii, 169–170.

unfolding star, *n.* morning star, which signals the shepherd to release his sheep for pasturing: "Look, th'unfolding star calls up the/ shepherd." *Meas,* IV, ii, 202–203.

unfurnished, *adj.* **1** unprepared: "We shall be much unfurnish'd for this time." *Rom & Jul,* IV, ii, 10. **2** unprotected; undefended: ". . . the Scot on his unfurnish'd kingdom/ Came pouring . . ." *Hen 5,* I, ii, 148–149. **3 unfurnished of,** unaccompanied or unprotected by: "Rome's royal empress,/ Unfurnish'd of her well-beseeming troop?" *T Andr,* II, iii, 55–56.

ungalled, *adj.* **1** unsoiled; unblemished: ". . . supposed by the common rout/ Against your yet ungalled estimation . . ." *Errors,* III, i, 101–102. **2** unwounded: ". . . let the strucken [stricken?] deer go weep,/ The hart ungalled play . . ." *Ham,* III, ii, 265–266.

ungartered, *adj.* wearing no garters and, presumably, with the stockings falling down: ". . . when you chid at Sir Proteus, for going ungartered." *Two Gent,* II, i, 69.

ungenerative, *adj.* incapable of reproduction: "And he is a/ motion ungenerative; that's infallible." *Meas,* III, ii, 107–108.

ungenitured, *adj.* impotent: ". . . this ungenitured/ agent will unpeople the province with/ continency." *Meas,* III, ii, 167–169.

ungird, *v.* to throw off; let go of: ". . . ungird thy/ strangeness, and tell me what I shall vent to my/ lady." *T Night,* IV, i, 15–17.

ungoverned, *adj.* uninstructed: "Ungovern'd youth, to wail it in their age . . ." *Rich 3,* IV, iv, 392.

ungracious, *adj.* lacking spiritual grace; wicked: "Swearest thou, ungracious boy? Henceforth ne'er/ look on me." *1 Hen 4,* II, iv, 439–440.

ungrown, *adj.* unseasoned; immature or undeveloped: "With lustier maintenance than I did look for/ Of such an ungrown warrior." *1 Hen 4,* V, iv, 21–22.

unguem, *n.* [Latin] fingernail; fingertip: "O, I smell false Latin: dunghill for *unguem.*" *Love's L,* V, i, 72.

unhacked edges, *n.* swords undamaged in battle: ". . . this 'greed upon,/ To part with unhack'd edges . . ." *Ant & Cleo,* II, vi, 37–38.

unhair, *v.* to pull the hair from: "I'll unhair thy head,/ Thou shalt be whipp'd with wire . . ." *Ant & Cleo,* II, v, 64–65.

unhaired, *adj.* beardless; ref. here to the dauphin's youth and inexperience: "This unhair'd sauciness and boyish troops,/ The king doth smile at . . ." *K John,* V, ii, 133–134.

unhallowed, *adj.* unblessed: "Let never day nor night unhallow'd pass . . ." *2 Hen 6,* II, i, 85.

unhandled, *adj.* untrained; unmanageable: ". . . a wild and wanton herd/ Or race of youthful and unhandled colts . . ." *Merch,* V, i, 71–72.

unhandsome, *adj.* inept: ". . . unhandsome warrior as I am." *Oth,* III, iv, 149.

unhappied, *adj.* made unhappy: "A happy gentleman in blood and lineaments,/ By you unhappied . . ." *Rich 2,* III, i, 9–10.

unhappiness, *n.* foul nature: "And that be heir to his unhappiness." *Rich 3,* I, ii, 25.

unhappy, *adj.* **1** unlucky: "So I, to find a mother and a brother,/ In quest of them, unhappy, lose myself." *Errors,* I, ii, 39–40. **2** bringing misfortune: ". . . that unhappy guest/ Whose deed hath made herself herself detest." *Luc,* 1565–1566. **3** mischievous; roguish: "A shrewd knave and an unhappy." *All's W,* IV, v, 60.

unhardened, *adj.* unformed; immature: "(messengers/ Of strong prevailment in unharden'd youth) . . ." *M N Dream,* I, i, 34–35.

unhatched[1], *adj.* undented; that is, not bent with use: "He is knight, dubbed with unhatched rapier,/ and on carpet consideration . . ." *T Night,* III, iv, 237–238.

unhatched[2], *adj.* **unhatch'd practice,** plot not yet matured: ". . . some unhatch'd practice,/ Made demonstrable [revealed] here in Cyprus to him . . ." *Oth,* III, iv, 138–139.

unheart, *v.* to dishearten; dismay or deject: ". . . to bite his lip/ And hum at good Cominius, much unhearts me." *Cor,* V, i, 48–49.

unheedy, *adj.* inconsiderate: "Wings, and no eyes, figure unheedy haste." *M N Dream,* I, i, 237.

unhidden passages, *n.* unencumbered rights of inheritance: "The severals and unhidden passages/ Of his true titles . . ." *Hen 5,* I, i, 86–87.

unholy, *adj.* **unholy suits,** wicked proposals: ". . . mere implorators of unholy suits,/ Breathing like sanctified and pious bawds . . ." *Ham,* I, iii, 129–130.

unhopefullest, *adj.* most unpromising or hopeless: "Benedick is not the unhopefullest/ husband that I know." *M Ado,* II, i, 354–355.

unhoused, *adj.* homeless; also, free and unhampered: "I would not my unhoused free condition/ Put into circumscription and confine . . ." *Oth,* I, ii, 26–27.

unhouseled, *adj.* deprived of communion before death: "Cut off even in the blossoms of my sin,/ Unhousel'd, disappointed, unanel'd . . ." *Ham,* I, v, 76–77.

unimproved, *adj.* sense of both "brash" and "green"; unreproved; unproved: ". . . young Fortinbras,/ Of unimproved mettle, hot and full . . ." *Ham,* I, i, 98–99.

unintelligent, *adj.* unaware: ". . . your senses (unintelligent of our insufficience [shortcomings])/ may . . . as little/ accuse us." *W Tale,* I, i, 14–16.

union, *n.* fine pearl: "And in the cup an union shall he throw . . ." *Ham,* V, ii, 269.

unjointed, *adj.* disjointed; here, incoherent: "This bald unjointed chat of his . . ." *1 Hen 4,* I, iii, 64.

unjust, *adj.* **1** dishonest: ". . . such as indeed/ were never soldiers, but discarded unjust servingmen,/ younger sons to younger brothers . . ." *1 Hen 4,* IV, ii, 26–28. **2** unlawful: "Let thy fair wisdom . . . sway/ In this uncivil and unjust extent . . ." *T Night,* IV, i, 51–52. **3** faithless; perfidious: ". . . Ariadne, passioning/ For Theseus' perjury, and unjust flight . . ." *Two Gent,* IV, iv, 165–166.

unkennel, *v.* to dislodge; eject or expel: "If his occulted guilt/ Do not itself unkennel in one speech . . ." *Ham,* III, ii, 80–81.

unkept, *adj.* unimproved; uneducated: ". . . stays me here at home unkept . . ." *As You,* I, i, 7–8.

unkind, *adj.* **1** cruel or unnatural; inhuman: "Ah what an unkind hour/ Is guilty of this lamentable chance? *Rom & Jul,* V, iii, 145–146. **2** (of a woman) childless; also, with sense of the preceding, refusing to engage in sexual relations: "O had thy mother borne so hard a mind,/ She had not brought forth thee, but died unkind." *Ven & Ad,* 203–204. —*n.* **3** unkindness: "Let no unkind, no fair beseechers kill . . ." *Sonn 135,* 13.

unkindly, *adv.* cruelly; also, unnaturally: ". . . rushing out of doors, to be resolv'd/ If Brutus so unkindly knock'd or no . . ." *J Caes,* III, ii, 181–182.

unkind remembrance, *n.* cruel memory; here, sense of "What an unreliable memory I have!": "Unkind remembrance! thou and endless night/ Have done me shame . . ." *K John,* V, vi, 12–13.

unkiss, *v.* to undo or cancel with a kiss: "Let me unkiss the oath 'twixt thee and me . . ." *Rich 2,* V, i, 74.

unknown, *adj.* **1** lacking renown: "And apprehended here immediately/ Th'unknown Ajax." *Tr & Cr,* III, iii, 124–125. **2 unknown minds,** strangers: "That I have frequent been with unknown minds . . ." *Sonn 117,* 5.

unlace, *v.* undo; here, carve up: ". . . what's the matter,/ That you unlace your reputation thus . . ." *Oth,* II, iii, 184–185.

unlaid, *adj.* **1** not at rest; not put to rest: "Ghost unlaid forbear thee!" *Cymb,* IV, ii, 278. **2 unlaid ope,** secret or concealed; unrevealed: ". . . To keep his bed of blackness unlaid ope . . ." *Per,* I, ii, 89.

unlearned, *adj.* inexperienced: ". . . she might think me some untutored youth/ Unlearned in the world's false subtleties." *Sonn 138,* 3–4.

unless, *prep.* except; except for: "Here never shines the sun: here nothing breeds,/ Unless the nightly owl or fatal raven . . ." *T Andr,* II, iii, 96–97.

unlessoned, *adj.* untutored; ignorant: ". . . an unlesson'd girl, unschool'd, unpractised,/ Happy in this . . ." *Merch,* III, ii, 159–160.

unlettered, *adj.* ignorant; illiterate: "that unlettered small-knowing soul,—" *Love's L,* I, i, 246.

unlicensed, *adj.* without consent or approval: "Why, as it were unlicens'd of your loves,/ He would depart . . ." *Per,* I, iii, 16–17.

unlike, *adj.* unlikely: "Make not impossible/ That which but seems unlike." *Meas,* V, i, 54–55.

unlineal, *adj.* not in the direct line of royal succession: "Thence to be wrench'd with [by] an unlineal hand . . ." *Mac,* III, i, 62.

unlived, *adj.* deprived of life; dead: "Where shall I live now Lucrece is unlived?" *Luc,* 1754.

unlooked, *adj.* **1** unforeseen: ". . . none of you may live his natural age,/ But by some unlook'd accident cut off." *Rich 3,* I, iii, 213–214. **2 unlooked on,** unnoticed; unregarded: "So thou . . . Unlook'd on diest unless you get [beget] a son." *Sonn 7,* 13–14.

unmanned, *adj.* untrained; virginal: "Hood my unmann'd blood, bating in my cheeks,/ With thy black mantle . . ." *Rom & Jul,* III, ii, 14–15.

unmannerly, *adj.* **1** rude; also, wordplay on "not yet a man": ". . . an/ unmannerly slave, that will thrust himself into/ secrets." *Two Gent,* III, i, 372–374. —*adv.* **2** unbecomingly; also, grotesquely or obscenely: ". . . their daggers/ Unmannerly breech'd with gore." *Mac,* II, iii, 115–116.

unmastered, *adj.* undisciplined: ". . . your chaste treasure open/ To his unmaster'd importunity." *Ham,* I, iii, 31–32.

unmeet, *adj.* **1** unseemly; improper: "Prove you that any man with me convers'd/ At hours unmeet . . ." *M Ado,* IV, i, 181–182. **2** unfit: "Vow, alack! for youth unmeet,/ Youth so apt to pluck a sweet." *Love's L,* IV, iii, 110–111.

unmellowed, *adj.* not yet mature: "His head unmellow'd, but his judgment ripe . . ." *Two Gent,* II, iv, 65.

unmeritable, *adj.* unworthy or undeserving; hence, insignificant: "This is a slight unmeritable man,/ Meet to be sent on errands." *J Caes,* IV, i, 12–13.

unminded, *adj.* unnoticed; disregarded: "A poor unminded outlaw sneaking home . . ." *1 Hen 4,* IV, iii, 58.

unmindful, *adj.* negligent; irresponsible: "Dull unmindful villain!/ Why stay'st thou here and go'st not to the Duke?" *Rich 3,* IV, iv, 445.

unmingled, *adj.* unmixed with baser qualities; unalloyed: "And what hath mass or matter by itself/ Lies rich in virtue and unmingled." *Tr & Cr,* I, iii, 29–30.

unmitigable, *adj.* implacable; unappeasable: ". . . she did confine thee . . . in her most unmitigable rage,/ Into a cloven pine . . ." *Temp,* I, ii, 274–277.

unnatural, *adj.* **1** without normal human feelings; cruel; wicked: ". . . he did render him the most unnatural/ That liv'd amongst men." *As You,* IV, iii, 122–123. **2** particularly heinous, being committed by a blood relative; here, by Claudius, the king's brother: "If thou didst ever thy dear father love . . . Revenge his foul and most unnatural murder." *Ham,* I, v, 23–25.

unnoted, *adj., adv.* **1** taking no notice; unawares: ". . . but they may jest/ Till their own scorn return to them unnoted . . ." *All's W,* I, ii, 33–34. **2** calm; moderate; avoiding fury or excess: ". . . with such sober and unnoted passion/ He did behove his anger . . ." *Timon,* III, v, 21–22.

unnumbered, *adj.* innumerable; numberless: "The skies are painted with unnumber'd sparks . . ." *J Caes,* III, i, 63.

unordinate, *adj.* inordinate; excessive: "Every unordinate cup is unbless'd, and the ingredience/ is a devil." *Oth,* II, iii, 298–299.

unowed interest, *n.* ref. to growing dispute about the rightful king, esp. the wavering allegiance of the powerful nobles: ". . . to part by th' teeth/ The unow'd interest of proud swelling state." *K John,* IV, iii, 146–147.

unparagoned, *adj.* having no equal: "Either your unparagon'd mistress is dead, or she's/ outpriz'd by a trifle." *Cymb,* I, v, 77–78.

unpartial, *adj.* impartial: ". . . join'd with me their servant/ In the unpartial judging of this business." *Hen 8,* II, ii, 105–106

unpathed, *adj.* uncharted or unmapped; hence, unknown: ". . . a wild dedication of yourselves/ To unpath'd waters . . ." *W Tale,* IV, iv, 567–568.

unpaved, *adj.* castrated [lit., without stones]: ". . . nor the/ voice of unpaved eunuch to boot . . ." *Cymb,* II, iii, 28–29.

unpeg the basket, *v.* to open the cage; here, bird cage: "Unpeg the basket on the house's top,/ Let the birds fly . . ." *Ham,* III, iv, 195–196.

unpeople, *v.* **1** to deprive of friends or aids: "I have given him that . . . shall quite unpeople her/ Of liegers for her sweet . . ." *Cymb,* I, vi, 78–80. **2 I'll unpeople Egypt,** Cleopatra will send a message to Antony every day, even if it means emptying Egypt of people: "He shall have every day a several [different] greeting,/ Or I'll unpeople Egypt." *Ant & Cleo,* I, v, 77–78.

unpeopled, *adj.* not provided with servants; unstaffed: ". . . a dispensation for his oath,/ To let you enter his unpeopled house." *Love's L,* II, i, 87–88.

unperfect, *adj.* imperfect: "As an unperfect actor on the stage . . . is put beside his part . . ." *Sonn 23,* 1–2.

unpinked, *adj.* lacking the decoration of eyelets or a scalloped edge: "And Gabriel's pumps were all unpink'd i' th' heel . . ." *Shrew,* IV, i, 120.

unpitied, *adj.* pitiless; merciless: ". . . you shall have your full time/ of imprisonment, and your deliverance with an unpitied/ whipping . . ." *Meas,* IV, ii, 10–12.

unplausive, *adj.* disapproving: "'Tis like he'll question me/ Why such unplausive eyes are bent . . ." *Tr & Cr,* III, iii, 42–43.

unpolicied, *adj.* outdone in cunning; outwitted: "O, couldst thou speak,/ That I might hear thee call great Caesar ass,/ Unpolicied!" *Ant & Cleo,* V, ii, 305–307.

unpossessing, *adj.* lacking an estate or possessions; hence, beggarly: "'Thou unpossessing bastard! dost thou think,/ If I would stand against thee . . .'" *Lear,* II, i, 67–68.

unpossible, *adj.* impossible: "For us to levy power/ Proportionable to the enemy/ Is all unpossible." *Rich 2,* II, ii, 123–125.

unpregnant, *adj.* not motivated (by); indifferent (to): "Like John-a-dreams, unpregnant of my cause . . ." *Ham,* II, ii, 563.

unprizable, *adj.* **1** hardly worth capturing; of negligible value: "A baubling vessel was he captain of,/ For shallow draught and bulk unprizable . . ." *T Night,* V, i, 52–53. **2** esteemed beyond price: ". . . so your brace of unprizable/ estimations, the one is but frail and the other casual . . ." *Cymb,* I, v, 87–88.

unprofited, *adj.* unprofitable; fruitless: ". . . leap all civil bounds,/ Rather than make unprofited return." *T Night,* I, iv, 21–22.

unproper, *adj.* not entirely one's own; shared [here, with another man]: ". . . there's millions now alive/ That nightly lies in those unproper beds . . ." *Oth,* IV, i, 67–68.

unproperly, *adv.* against all that is proper; unfittingly: ". . . and unproperly/ Show duty as mistaken all this while/ Between the child and parent." *Cor,* V, iii, 54–56.

unproportioned, *adj.* unsuitable: "Give thy thoughts no tongue,/ Nor any unproportion'd thought his act." *Ham,* I, iii, 59–60.

unprovide, *v.* to weaken; soften: ". . . lest her body and beauty unprovide/ my mind again, this night, Iago." *Oth,* IV, i, 201–202.

unprovided, *adj.* **1** unequipped; unprovisioned: "I am heinously unprovided." *1 Hen 4,* III, iii, 188–189. **2** unarmed; unprotected: "With his prepared [drawn] sword he charges home/ My unprovided body . . ." *Lear,* II, i, 51–52. **3** unprepared; that is, unreconciled with God: ". . . if they die unprovided,/ no more is the king guilty of their damnation . . ." *Hen 5,* IV, i, 179–180.

unprovident, *adj.* improvident: "Who for thyself art so unprovident." *Sonn 10,* 2.

unpublished, *adj.* unknown; secret: "All you unpublish'd virtues [medicinal herbs] of the earth . . ." *Lear,* IV, iv, 16.

unpurged, *adj.* (of air) not yet purified by the morning sun: "To dare the vile contagion of the night,/ And tempt the rheumy and unpurged air/ To add unto his sickness?" *J Caes,* II, i, 265–267.

unpurposed, *adj.* unintended: ". . . thy precedent services are all/ But accidents unpurpos'd." *Ant & Cleo,* IV, xiv, 83–84.

unqualitied, *adj.* undone; unmanned: ". . . madam, speak to him,/ He is unqualitied with very shame." *Ant & Cleo,* III, xi, 43–44.

unqueened, *adj.* no longer a queen: ". . . although unqueen'd, yet like/ A queen, and daughter to a king inter me." *Hen 8,* IV, ii, 171–172.

unquestionable, *adj.* sullen or irritable: ". . . an unquestionable spirit, which you have not . . ." *As You,* III, ii, 364–365.

unquestioned, *adj.* uninvestigated or unconsidered: ". . . leaves unquestioned/ Matters of needful value." *Meas,* I, i, 54–55.

unraised, *adj.* uninspired; unimaginative: "The flat unraised spirits that hath dar'd/ On this unworthy scaffold to bring forth/ So great an object . . ." *Hen 5* Prol., 9–11.

unraked, *adj.* (of a fire) not banked down at night so that it can be rekindled in the morning: "Where fires thou find'st unrak'd and hearths unswept . . ." *Wives,* V, v, 45.

unreasonable, *adj.* unreasoning; senseless: ". . . thy wild acts denote/ The unreasonable fury of a beast." *Rom & Jul,* III, iii, 109–110.

unrecalling, *adj.* irrevocable: "And ever let his unrecalling crime/ Have time to wail th'abusing of his time." *Luc,* 993–994.

unreclaimed, *adj.* untamed: "A savageness in unreclaimed blood . . ." *Ham,* II, i, 34.

unreconciliable, var. of unreconcilable: ". . . that our stars,/ Unreconciliable, should divide/ Our equalness to this." *Ant & Cleo,* V, i, 46–48.

unrecuring, *adj.* incurable: "Seeking to hide herself, as doth the deer/ That hath receiv'd some unrecuring wound." *T Andr,* III, i, 89–90.

unreputed, *adj.* inconsequential or unnoticed: "An unreputed mote, flying in the sun,/ Presents a greater substance than it is . . ." *Edw 3,* II, i, 437–438.

unrespected, *adj.* of little or no interest; unnoticed: "For all the day they view things unrespected . . ." *Sonn 43,* 2.

unrespective, *adj.* **1** heedless; unobservant: "I will converse with iron-witted fools/ And unrespective boys . . ." *Rich 3,* IV, ii, 28–29.
—*n.* **2 unrespective sieve,** scrap barrel; garbage can: ". . . nor the remainder viands/ We do not throw in unrespective sieve/ Because we now are full." *Tr & Cr,* II, ii, 71–73.

unrestored, *adj.* not returned: "Then does he say, he lent me/ Some shipping unrestor'd." *Ant & Cleo,* III, vi, 26–27.

unrestrained, *adj.* licentious: ". . . he daily doth frequent/ With unrestrained loose companions . . ." *Rich 2,* V, iii, 6–7.

unreverent, *adj.* disrespectful: "This tongue that runs so roundly in thy head/ Should run thy head from thy unreverent shoulders." *Rich 2,* II, i, 122–123.

unrighteous, *adj.* hypocritical: "Ere yet the salt of most unrighteous tears/ Had left the flushing in her galled eyes . . ." *Ham,* I, ii, 154–155.

unrolled, *past part.* taken off the rolls or register [of rogues]: ". . . if I make not this cheat bring/ out another . . . let me/ be unrolled . . ." *W Tale,* IV, iii, 116–118.

unroosted, *adj.* driven off the roost: "Thou dotard! thou art woman-tir'd, unroosted . . ." *W Tale,* II, iii, 74.

unrough, *adj.* unbearded; hence, unseasoned or fledgling: "And many unrough youths, that even now/ Protest their first of [proclaim the beginning of their] manhood." *Mac,* V, ii, 10–11.

unsanctified, *adj.* unholy; wretched or beastly: ". . . the post unsanctified/ Of murtherous lechers . . ." *Lear,* IV, vi, 276–277.

unsatiate, *adj.* var. of **insatiate:** "Th'unsatiate greediness of his desire . . ." *Rich 3,* III, vii, 7.

unsatisfied, *adj.* uninformed: "Report me and my cause aright/ To the unsatisfied." *Ham,* V, ii, 345.

unsavory, *adj.* displeasing; unwelcome: "Unsavoury news! But how made he escape?" *3 Hen 6,* IV, vi, 80.

unscanned, *adj.* unconsidered; irresponsible: "The harm of unscann'd swiftness . . ." *Cor,* III, i, 310.

unscoured, *adj.* unpolished; rusty: ". . . like unscour'd armour, hung by th' wall . . ." *Meas,* I, ii, 156.

unsealed, *adj.* having no legal force: ". . . your oaths/ Are words, and poor conditions but [quite] unseal'd . . ." *All's W,* IV, ii, 29–30.

unseam, *v.* to rip open; here, with a sword: ". . . he unseam'd him from the nave to th'chops,/ And fix'd his head upon our battlements." *Mac,* I, ii, 22–23.

unseasonable, *adj.* (of game) not the season to be hunted: "He is no woodman that doth bend his bow/ To strike a poor unseasonable doe." *Luc,* 580–581.

unseasoned, *adj.* **1** unseasonable; untimely; late: ". . . these unseason'd hours perforce must add/ Unto your sickness." *2 Hen 4,* III, i, 105–106. **2** green; inexperienced: "'Tis an unseason'd courtier; good my lord,/ Advise him." *All's W,* I, i, 67–68.

unseconded, *adj.* unsupported; undefended: "Second to none, unseconded by you . . ." *2 Hen 4,* II, iii, 34.

unseem, *v.* to appear not (to): "You do . . . wrong the reputation of your name,/ In so unseeming to confess receipt . . ." *Love's L,* II, i, 153–155.

unseen, *adj.* unknown: "Who, falling there . . . / (Unseen, inquisitive) confounds himself." *Errors,* I, ii, 37–38.

unseminared, *adj.* castrated: "'Tis well for thee,/ That, being unseminar'd, thy freer thoughts/ May not fly forth of Egypt." *Ant & Cleo,* I, v, 11–12.

unset, *adj.* unplanted; here, virginal: "And many maiden gardens, yet unset . . ." *Sonn 16,* 6.

unsettled humors, *n.* restless, discontented people; malcontents: "With them a bastard of the king's deceas'd,/ And all th'unsettled humours of the land . . ." *K John,* II, i, 65–66.

unsevered, *adj.* inseparable: "Honour and policy, like unsever'd friends,/ I'th'war do grow together . . ." *Cor,* III, ii, 42–43.

unsex, *v.* to rid of sexual attributes; here, divest of womanly frailties: "Come, you Spirits/ That tend on mortal thoughts, unsex me here,/ And fill me . . . top-full/ Of direst cruelty!" *Mac,* I, v, 40–43.

unshaked, *adj.* firm; steady: ". . . I do know but one/ That unassailable holds on his rank,/ Unshak'd of motion . . ." *J Caes,* III, i, 68–70.

unshape, *v.* to disturb or unsettle: "This deed unshapes me quite; makes me unpregnant/ And dull to all proceedings." *Meas,* IV, iv, 18–19.

unshout, *v.* to shout retractions of: "Unshout the noise that banish'd Martius . . ." *Cor,* V, v, 4.

unshunned, *adj.* unshunnable; inevitable: "Ever your fresh whore, and your powdered bawd; an/ unshunned consequence; it must be so." *Meas,* III, ii, 57–58.

unsifted, *adj.* inexperienced: ". . . you speak like a green girl,/ Unsifted in such perilous circumstance." *Ham,* I, iii, 101–102.

unsinewed, *adj.* weak; feeble: "O, for two special reasons,/ Which may to you perhaps seem much unsinew'd . . ." *Ham,* IV, vii, 9–10.

unsisting, *adj.* poss. unresisting or unassisting: "That spirit's possess'd with haste/ That wounds th'unsisting postern with these strokes." *Meas,* IV, ii, 86–87.

unskillful or **unskilful,** *adj.* **the unskilful,** the ignorant; here, undiscerning spectators: ". . . though it makes the/ unskilful laugh, cannot but make the judicious/ grieve . . ." *Ham,* III, ii, 25–26.

unskillfully or **unskilfully,** *adv.* ignorantly: ". . . you speak unskilfully: or, if your knowledge be/ more, it is much darkened in your malice." *Meas,* III, ii, 143–144.

unsorted, *adj.* ill-chosen: ". . . the friends you have/ named uncertain, the time itself unsorted . . ." *1 Hen 4,* II, iii, 11–12.

unsought, *adj.* unsearched: ". . . loth to leave unsought/ Or that or any place that harbours men . . ." *Errors,* I, i, 135–136.

unsounded, *adj.* unmeasured, as in depth of treachery: "Gloucester is a man/ Unsounded yet, and full of deep deceit." *2 Hen 6,* III, i, 56–57.

unspeak, *v.* to retract or repudiate: "I put myself to thy direction, and/ Unspeak mine own detraction . . ." *Mac,* IV, iii, 122–123.

unspeakable, *adj.* **1** inexpressible; indescribable: ". . . and when I do forget/ The least of these unspeakable deserts,/ Romans, forget your fealty to me." *T Andr,* I, i, 255–257. **2** inestimable: ". . . from very nothing . . . is grown into an unspeakable estate." *W Tale,* IV, ii, 39–41.

unspeaking sots, *n.* fools unable to speak; here, unable to describe beauty: ". . . either our brags/ Were crak'd of kitchentrulls, or his description/ Prov'd us unspeaking sots." *Cymb,* V, v, 176–178.

unsphere, *v.* **unsphere the stars,** to move the stars from their natural courses [spheres]: "Though you would seek t' unsphere the stars with oaths . . ." *W Tale,* I, ii, 48.

unspotted, *adj.* **1** unsullied or undiminished: "My riches to the earth . . . But my unspotted fire of love to you." *Per,* I, i, 54–55. **2** innocent: ". . . there is no king, be his cause/ never so spotless . . . can try it out with all unspotted soldiers." *Hen 5,* IV, i, 163–165.

unsquared, *adj.* unharmonious or inappropriate: "'Tis like a chime a-mending, with terms [expressions] unsquar'd . . ." *Tr & Cr,* I, iii, 159.

unstaid, *adj.* **1** unchecked; irresponsible: ". . . I may breathe my last/ In wholesome counsel to his unstaid youth?" *Rich 2,* II, i, 1–2. **2** unconventional: ". . . how will the world repute me/ For undertaking so unstaid a journey?" *Two Gent,* II, vii, 59–60.

unstaid and skittish, *adj.* giddy and fickle: "For such as I am, all true lovers are,/ Unstaid and skittish . . ." *T Night,* II, iv, 17–18.

unstained, *adj.* **1** pure; virtuous: ". . . your youth,/ And the true blood . . . Do plainly give you out an unstain'd shepherd . . ." *W Tale,* IV, iv, 147–149. **2** not tainted with hatred or resentment: "I give you welcome with a powerless hand,/ But with a heart full of unstained love . . ." *K John,* II, 1, 15–16.

unstanched wench, *n.* girl with the menses: ". . . though the ship were . . . as leaky as an/ unstanched wench." *Temp,* I, i, 46–48.

unstate, *v.* to strip of rank and wealth; divest of dignity: "I would/ unstate myself to be in a due resolution [free of this uncertainty]." *Lear,* I, ii, 102–103.

unstaunched, *adj.* quenchless; insatiable: "Stifle the villain whose unstaunched thirst/ York and young Rutland could not satisfy." *3 Hen 6,* II, vi, 83–84.

unstuffed, *adj.* untroubled: "But where unbruised youth with unstuff'd brain/ Doth couch his limbs, there golden sleep doth reign." *Rom & Jul,* II, iii, 33–34.

unsured assurance, *n.* uncertain claim: "Thy now unsur'd assurance to the crown . . ." *K John,* II, i, 471.

unswayed, *adj.* lacking control; unwielded: "Is the chair empty? Is the sword unsway'd?" *Rich 3,* IV, iv, 469.

unswept, *adj.* uncared for: "But you shall shine more bright in these contents/ Than unswept stone, besmeared with sluttish time." *Sonn 55,* 3–4.

untainted, *adj.* unscathed: "Him in thy course untainted do allow . . ." *Sonn 19,* 11.

untaught, *adj.* **1** unmannerly; rude: "O thou untaught! What manners is in this,/ To press before thy father to a grave?" *Rom & Jul,* V, iii, 213–214. **2** uninformed; ignorant: "Crowd to his presence, where their untaught love/ Must needs appear offence." *Meas,* II, iv, 29–30.

untender, *adj.* unkind; cold or unfeeling: "So young, and so untender?" *Lear,* I, i, 106.

untent, *v.* to bring out of the tent: "Why will he not . . . Untent his person, and share th'air with us?" *Tr & Cr,* II, iii, 168–169.

untented, *adj.* **untented woundings,** wounds too deep to be cleaned out with a tent (small roll of lint): "Th' untented woundings of a father's curse/ Pierce every sense about thee!" *Lear,* I, iv, 309–310.

unthrift, *n.* **1** spendthrift or wastrel: "Look! what an unthrift in the world doth spend/ Shifts but his [its] place . . ." *Sonn 9,* 9–10.
—*adj.* **2** prodigal or spendthrift; hence, good-for-nothing: "And with an unthrift love did run from Venice,/ As far as Belmont." *Merch,* V, i, 16–17.

unthrifty, *adj.* **1** not concerned with profit; here, with progeny: "Unthrifty loveliness, why dost thou spend/ Upon thyself thy beauty's legacy?" *Sonn 4,* 1–2. **2** neglecting an opportunity for enrichment: ". . . our absence makes us unthrifty to our/ knowledge." *W Tale,* V, ii, 111–112. **3** profligate; good-for-nothing: "Can no man tell me of my unthrifty son?" *Rich 2,* V, iii, 1. **4** unlucky: "O, much I fear some ill unthrifty thing." *Rom & Jul,* V, iii, 136.

untirable, *adj.* inexhaustible: ". . . breath'd, as it were/ To an untirable and continuate goodness." *Timon,* I, i, 10–11.

untitled, *adj.* not entitled; here, without right to assume the monarchy: "O nation miserable!/ With an untitled tyrant bloody-scepter'd . . ." *Mac,* IV, iii, 103–104.

unto, *prep.* **1** to; of: "For Henry, son unto a conqueror,/ Is likely to beget more conquerors . . ." *1 Hen 6,* V, v, 73–74. **2** added to; in addition to: "I should have given him tears unto entreaties . . ." *As You,* I, ii, 227.

untold, *adj.* uncounted; unremarked: "Then in the number let me pass untold . . ." *Sonn 136,* 9.

untoward, *adj.* ill-mannered; stubborn: "And if she be froward,/ Then hast thou taught Hortensio to be untoward." *Shrew,* IV, v, 77–78.

untowardly, *adv.* unfavorably; adversely: "O day untowardly turned!" *M Ado,* III, ii, 120.

untraded, *adj.* unfamiliar; here, not overused: "Mock not that I affect th'untraded oath . . ." *Tr & Cr,* IV, v, 177.

untread, *v.* to retrace (steps): "Where is the horse that doth untread again/ His tedious measures with the unbated fire . . ." *Merch,* II, vi, 10–11.

untried, *adj.* uninvestigated: ". . . I slide/ O'er sixteen years, and leave the growth untried/ Of that wide gap . . ." *W Tale,* IV, i, 5–7.

untrimmed, *adj.* **1** unbedded; virginal: ". . . the devil tempts thee here/ In likeness of a new untrimmed bride." *K John,* III, i, 134–135. **2** robbed of beauty: "By chance or nature's changing course untrimmed." *Sonn 18,* 8.

untrod, *adj.* uncertain; unknown: "The fortunes and affairs of noble Brutus/ Thorough the hazards of this untrod state . . ." *J Caes,* III, i, 135–136.

untrue, *n.* untruth; here, delusion: "My most true mind thus maketh mine untrue." *Sonn 113,* 14.

untruss, *v.* to undress; specif. to untie the cords securing the hose to the doublet: "Marry, this Claudio is condemned for untrussing." *Meas,* III, ii, 173.

untruth, *n.* betrayal; disloyalty: "I would to God,/ So my untruth had not provok'd him to it, The king had cut my head off with my brother's." *Rich 2,* II, ii, 100–102.

untunable or **untuneable,** *adj.* disagreeable to the ear; unmelodious or discordant: ". . . there was no great matter in the ditty, yet the note was very untuneable." *As You,* V, iii, 39–40.

untuned, *adj.* **1** lacking harmony; out of tune: ". . . my only son/ Knows not my feeble key of untun'd cares [a voice unrecognizable because of cares]?" *Errors,* V, i, 309–310. **2** unskilled; uncivilized: ". . . what a grief it is . . . Either to be wooed with broad untuned oaths,/ Or forced by rough insulting barbarism . . ." *Edw 3,* I, ii, 6–9.

untutored to repeat, *adj.* [who has] never learned the lesson: "Thou speak'st like him's untutor'd to repeat . . ." *Per,* I, iv, 74.

untwind, old form of untwine; to untwist or undo (spun thread, etc.): ". . . let grievous, ghastly, gaping wounds/ Untwind the Sisters Three!" *2 Hen 4,* II, iv, 194–195.

unvalued, *adj.* **1** ordinary; of no rank: "He may not, as unvalu'd persons do,/ Carve for himself . . ." *Ham,* I, iii, 19–20. **2** of inestimable worth; priceless: ". . . heaps of pearl,/ Inestimable stones, unvalu'd jewels . . ." *Rich 3,* I, iv, 26–27.

unveil, *v.* to disclose; reveal: "Do thoughts unveil in their dumb cradles." *Tr & Cr,* III, iii, 199.

unvenerable, *adj.* contemptible: "For ever/ Unvenerable be thy hands, if thou/ Tak'st up the princess . . ." *W Tale,* II, iii, 76–78.

unvexed retire, *n.* unhampered withdrawal: "And with a blessed and unvex'd retire . . . We will bear home that lusty blood again . . ." *K John,* II, i, 253–255.

unvulnerable, *adj.* **to shame unvulnerable,** incapable of behaving shamefully: ". . . that thou mayst prove/ To shame unvulnerable . . ." *Cor,* V, iii, 72–73.

unwappered, *adj.* not worn or exhausted; fresh; vigorous: ". . . we come towards the gods/ Young and unwapper'd . . ." *Kinsmen,* V, iv, 9–10.

unwares, *adv.* unawares: ". . . it is my father's face,/ Whom in this conflict I unwares have kill'd." *3 Hen 6,* II, v, 61–62.

unwashed, *adj.* **with unwashed hands,** immediately: "Rob me the exchequer . . . and/ do it with unwashed hands too." *1 Hen 4,* III, iii, 182–183.

unwedgeable, *adj.* ref. to the oak, sacred to Jove, believed to be uncleavable: "Thou rather with thy sharp and sulphurous bolt/ Splits the unwedgeable and gnarled oak . . ." *Meas,* II, ii, 116–117.

unweighed, *adj.* ill-considered; also, inconsiderate: "What an unweighed/ behaviour hath this Flemish drunkard picked—" *Wives,* II, i, 22–23.

unweighing, *adj.* thoughtless; indiscreet: "A very superficial, ignorant, unweighing fellow—" *Meas,* III, ii, 136.

unwholesome, *adj.* **1** suspicious: "Thick and unwholesome in their thoughts and whispers . . ." *Ham,* IV, v, 82. **2** foul; dirty: "Yea, like fair fruit in an unwholesome dish,/ Are like to rot untasted." *Tr & Cr,* II, iii, 122. **3** infected; diseased: ". . . there's two unwholesome, a'/ conscience." *Per,* IV, ii, 19–20.

unworthiest, *adj.* least remarkable; here, simple comparison and not a disparagement: ". . . and that, in my regard,/ Of the unworthiest siege." *Ham,* IV, vii, 74–75.

unworthiness, *n.* **1** imperfect attempt to describe: ". . . as may unworthiness define,/ A little touch of Harry in the night." *Hen 5,* IV, Chor., 45–46. **2** appar. the mother's feeling that her daughter is unworthy of the count's attention: "Every night he comes/ With musics [musicians] of all sorts, and songs compos'd/ To her unworthiness . . ." *All's W,* III, vii, 39–41.

unwrung, *adj.* not pinched or galled: "Let the galled jade wince, our withers are/ unwrung." *Ham,* III, ii, 237–238.

unyoke, *v.* to have done with it; call it a day: "Ay, tell me that and unyoke." *Ham,* V, i, 52.

up, *adj.* **1** having taken up arms: "The gentle Archbishop of York is up/ With well-appointed pow'rs." *2 Hen 4,* I, i, 189–190. **2** stirring; aroused: "Romeo, away, be gone,/ The citizens are up, and Tybalt slain!" *Rom & Jul,* III, i, 134–135. **3** on; set in motion; going ahead as planned: "The hunt is up, the morn is bright and grey . . ." *T Andr,* II, ii, 1. **4** shut or locked up: ". . . so the poor third is up, till death enlarge his/ confine." *Ant & Cleo,* III, v, 11–12. **5** roused; broken from cover: "The game is up." *Cymb,* III, iii, 107.
—*adv.* **6 go up,** (of a sword) to be sheathed: "When think you that the sword goes up again?" *J Caes,* V, i, 52. **7 up and down,** absolutely; precisely: "Here's his dry hand up and down:/ you are he, you are he." *M Ado,* II, i, 108–109.

upbraid, *v.* to reproach or accuse: "Now minutely revolts upbraid his faith-breach . . ." *Mac,* V, iii, 18.

upcast, *n.* final throw in the game of bowls: "When I kissed/ the jack upon an upcast, to be hit away!" *Cymb,* II, i, 1–2.

uphoard, *v.* to hoard; store up: ". . . if thou hast uphoarded in thy life/ Extorted treasure in the womb of earth . . ." *Ham,* I, i, 139–140.

uplifted, *adj.* (of weapons) at the ready; branished: ". . . Bolingbroke repeals himself,/ And with uplifted arms is safe arriv'd/ At Ravenspurgh." *Rich 2,* II, ii, 49–51.

upon, *prep.* **1** of; over: ". . . thou that hast/ Upon the winds command, bind them in brass . . ." *Per,* III, i, 2–3. **2** because of: "Upon some stubborn and uncourteous parts/ We had conceiv'd against him." *T Night,* V, i, 360. **3** in the event of: "Unless she gave it to yourself . . . or sent it us/ Upon her great disaster." *All's W,* V, iii, 110–112. **4** against: "I have o'erheard a plot of death upon him." *Lear,* III, vi, 92. **5** following: "Upon your stubborn usage of the pope . . ." *K John,* V, i, 18. **6 upon his party,** on his side: "And all your southern gentlemen in arms/ Upon his party." *Rich 2,* III, ii, 202–203. **7 upon this,** after what we've said here: "If he do not dote on her upon this, I will/ never trust my expectation." *M Ado,* II, iii, 203–204. **8 upon what?** why? for what reason?: "Alcibiades banish'd? . . . I pray you, upon what?" *Timon,* III, vi, 53–56.

upper hand, *n.* place of greater seniority: "And let my griefs frown on [in] the upper hand." *Rich 3,* IV, iv, 37.

upright, *adv.* **go upright,** to walk upright; here, metaphorically, because of lightened burdens: ". . . my spirits obey; and time/ Goes upright with his carriage." *Temp,* V, i, 2–3.

upright zeal, *n.* righteous dedication; fierce devotion: "With whom an upright zeal to right [justice] prevails/ More than the nature of a brother's love." *3 Hen 6,* V, i, 78–79.

uprise, *n.* rising; here, of the sun: "Did ever raven sing so like a lark/ That gives sweet tidings of the sun's uprise?" *T Andr,* III, i, 158–159.

uproar, *v.* to throw into an uproar; cause confusion in: "Nay, had I power, I should . . . Uproar the universal peace, confound/ All unity on earth." *Mac,* IV, iii, 97–100.

uprous'd, *adj.* upset or disturbed: "Thou art uprous'd with some distemperature . . ." *Rom & Jul,* II, iii, 36.

upshoot, *n.* upshot; (in archery) the best shot: "Then will she get the upshoot by cleaving the pin." *Love's L,* IV, i, 137.

upshot, *n.* winning shot in an archery contest; here, the outcome: "I cannot pursue with any safety/ this sport to the up-shot." *T Night,* IV, ii, 72–73.

upspring, *n.* wild dance: "Keeps wassail, and the swagg'ring upspring reels . . ." *Ham,* I, iv, 9.

up-staring, *adj.* standing on end: ". . . the King's son, Ferdinand,/ With hair up-staring . . ." *Temp,* I, ii, 212–213.

upstart, *n.* an obnoxious person: "I think this upstart is old Talbot's ghost . . ." *1 Hen 6,* IV, vii, 87.

up-swarm, *v.* to collect into a swarm: "You have ta'en up . . . The subjects of . . . my father,/ And . . . Have here up-swarm'd them." *2 Hen 4,* IV, ii, 26–30.

upward, *n.* top; crown: ". . . from th' extremest upward of thy head . . ." *Lear,* V, iii, 136.

urchin, *n.* hedgehog; here, the sense of goblin or devil: "Ten thousand swelling toads, as many urchins,/ Would make such fearful and confused cries . . ." *T Andr,* II, iii, 101–102.

urchin-shows, *n. pl.* sudden appearances of goblins in the form of hedgehogs: "But they'll nor pinch,/ Fright me with urchin-shows, pitch me i' th' mire,/ Nor lead me . . ." *Temp,* II, ii, 4–6.

urchin-snouted, *adj.* having a snout like that of a hedgehog, kept close to the ground: ". . . this foul, grim, and urchin-snouted boar,/ Whose downward eye still looketh for a grave . . ." *Ven & Ad,* 1105–1106.

urge, *v.* **1** to plead urgently; press: ". . . one of his men was with the Lord Lucullus, to borrow so many talents, nay, urg'd extremely for 't . . ." *Timon,* III, ii, 9–11. **2** to press an accusation: ". . . stand forth face to face,/ And freely urge against me." *Hen 8,* V, ii, 81–82. **3** to stress: ". . . I will not vex your souls . . . With too much urging your pernicious lives . . ." *Rich 2,* III, i, 2–4. **4** to tell or relate; mention: "Besides her urging of her wrack at sea." *Errors,* V, i, 349. **5** to reproach; scold: "Then, gentle cheater, urge not my amiss,/ Lest guilty of my faults thy sweet self prove." *Sonn 151,* 3–4. **6** to stimulate: "With eager compounds we our palate urge . . ." *Sonn 118,* 2.

urgent hour, *n.* **take the urgent hour,** depart at once [while you still may]: ". . . please your highness/ To take the urgent hour." *W Tale,* I, ii, 464–465.

urinal, *n.* **1** (in medicine) glass receptacle in which urine was examined: ". . . these follies are within you,/ and shine through you like the water in an urinal . . ." *Two Gent,* II, i, 37–38. **2** [pl.] appar. confusion with "testicles": "I will knog

[knock] his/ urinals about his knave's costard [head] . . ." *Wives,* III, i, 13–14.

urn, *n.* tomb; also, receptacle for the bones or ashes of a dead person: ". . . the most noble corse that ever herald/ Did follow to his urn." *Cor,* V, vi, 143–144.

usage, *n.* **1** manner of treatment: "Princely shall be thy usage every way." *T Andr,* I, i, 266. **2** manner of conduct; practice or behavior: "God me such usage send,/ Not to pick bad from bad, but by bad mend [not to be corrupted by bad examples but use them to improve]!" *Oth,* IV, iii, 104–105.

usance, *n.* euphem. for **usury:** "He lends out money gratis, and brings down/ The rate of usance here with us in Venice." *Merch,* I, iii, 39–40.

use, *v.* **1** to expend; use up; also, waste: ". . . why dost thou use/ So great a sum of sums yet canst not live?" *Sonn 4,* 7–8. **2** to copulate with: "I saw no man use you at his pleasure; if I had, my/ weapon should quickly have been out." *Rom & Jul,* II, iv, 154–155. **3** to treat; behave toward: ". . . one of your nine/ lives. That I mean to make bold withal, and, as you/ shall use me hereafter, dry-beat the rest of the eight." *Rom & Jul,* III, i, 76–78. **4** to be in the habit of: "Ay, but thou usest to forswear thyself." *3 Hen 6,* V, v, 73. **5** to request (money, etc.) of: "I was sending to use Lord Timon myself . . ." *Timon,* III, ii, 49. **6** to reside in: ". . . my chance is now!/ To use it for my time." *Meas,* III, ii, 211–212. **7** used as past tense: "To come as humbly as they use to creep/ To holy altars." *Tr & Cr,* III, iii, 73–74. **8 do not use,** am not accustomed: "Look to't, think on't, I do not use to jest." *Rom & Jul,* III, v, 188–189. **9 used it,** been accustomed to it: "I have used it, Nuncle, e'er since thou mad'st/ thy daughters thy mothers . . ." *Lear,* I, iv, 179–180.
—*n.* **10** habitual behavior; customary experience: "O Caesar, these things are beyond all use,/ And I do fear them." *J Caes,* II, ii, 25–26. **11** action; practice: "Be able for thine enemy/ Rather in power than use . . ." *All's W,* I, i, 61–62. **12** normal or usual practice: ". . . it is still her use/ To let the wretched man outlive his wealth . . ." *Merch,* IV, i, 264–265. **13** [usually pl.] **a.** ways; customs: "How weary, stale, flat, and unprofitable/ Seem to me all the uses of this world!" *Ham,* I, ii, 133–134. **b.** needs; necessities: ". . . tell him,/ My uses cry to me . . ." *Timon,* II, I, 19–20. **14** profit; advantage: "Since I must lose the use of all deceit?" *K John,* V, iv, 27. **15** interest or, sometimes, usury: ". . . he lent it me awhile, and I gave/ him use for it . . ." *M Ado,* II, i, 261–262. **16** sexual enjoyment: "Mine be thy love, and thy love's use their treasure." *Sonn 20,* 14. **17** perh. occupation: ". . . receive us/ For barbarous and unnatural revolts/ During their use, and slay us after." *Cymb,* IV, iv, 5–7. **18 in use,** in trust: "The other half in use, to render it/ Upon his death unto the gentleman/ That lately stole his daughter." *Merch,* IV, i, 379. **19 put to use,** loaned out at inter-

est: "Yes, being kept together, and put to use." *T Night*, III, i, 51. **20 use and liberty,** customary license; here, prob. licentiousness: ". . . to give fear to use and liberty,/ Which have for long run by the hideous law . . ." *Meas*, I, iv, 62–63.

used, *adj.* usual or accustomed; familiar: ". . . dull-ey'd melancholy,/ Be my so us'd a guest . . ." *Per*, I, ii, 3–4.

usher, *v.* **1** to announce guests, escort ladies, etc., at a social gathering: ". . . and, in ushering,/ Mend him who can . . ." *Love's L*, V, ii, 328–329.
—*n.* **2** person, as in a royal procession, whose duty is to precede one of rank: "These are the ushers of Martius: before him he/ carries noise, and behind him he leaves tears . . ." *Cor*, II, i, 157–158.

usurp, *v.* **1** to adopt; assume: "I know the boy will well usurp the grace,/ Voice, gait, and action of a gentlewoman." *Shrew*, Ind., i, 129–130. **2** to intrude or encroach [on]: "Death may usurp on nature many hours,/ And yet the fire of life kindle again . . ." *Per*, III, ii, 84–85. **3** to seize; steal away: "Thy natural magic and dire property/ On wholesome life usurps immediately." *Ham*, III, ii, 253–254. **4** to counterfeit; here, impersonate: "Are you the lady of the house?"/ "If I do not usurp myself, I am." *T Night*, I, v, 185–187. **5** to misuse: "Most certain, if you are she, you do usurp yourself . . ." *T Night*, I, v, 188–189. **6** to hold on to beyond the normal limits: "The wonder is he hath endur'd so long:/ He but usurp'd his life." *Lear*, V, iii, 316–317.

usurped, *adj.* false; here, used as a disguise: ". . . defeat thy favour with an usurp'd/ beard . . ." *Oth*, I, iii, 341–342.

usurping, *adj.* false; counterfeit: "It mourns that painting and usurping hair/ Should ravish doters with a false aspect . . ." *Love's L*, IV, iii, 255–256.

usury, *n.* **two usuries,** lending money at high interest rates and fornication: "'Twas never merry world [the world has never been so merry] since, of two usuries, the/ merriest was put down, and the worser allowed by/ order of law . . ." *Meas*, III, ii, 6–7.

ut, *n.* old name [replaced by "do"] for first tone of the musical scale (here given in incorrect order): ". . . who understandeth/ thee not, loves thee not. Ut, re, sol, la, mi, fa." *Love's L*, IV, ii, 95–96.

utensils, *n. pl.* furnishings: "He has brave utensils . . . Which, when he has a house, he'll deck withal." *Temp*, III, ii, 94–95.

utmost, *adj.* **1** every possible: ". . . we now possess'd/ The utmost man [soldier] of expectation . . ." *2 Hen 4*, I, iii, 64–65. **2 utmost of his pilgrimage,** limit of his life's journey: "Bring him his confessor, let him be prepar'd,/ For that's the utmost of his pilgrimage." *Meas*, II, i, 35–36.

utter, *v.* **1** to offer for sale; vend or hawk: "Beauty is bought by judgment of the eye,/ Not utter'd by base sale of chapmen's tongues." *Love's L*, II, i, 15–16. **2** to disclose: "More grief to hide than hate to utter love." *Ham*, II, i, 119.

utterance, *n.* **1** powers of elocution; ability to speak effectively: ". . . I have neither wit, nor words, nor worth,/ Action, nor utterance . . ." *J Caes*, III, ii, 223–224. **2 keep at utterance,** defend to the death: "Which he to seek of me again, perforce,/ Behoves me keep at utterance." *Cymb*, III, i, 72–73. **3 to the utterance,** to the finish: ". . . come, fate, into the list,/ And champion me to th' utterance!" *Mac*, III, i, 70–71.

uttermost, *adj.* **1** latest: "By the eighth hour: is that the uttermost?" *J Caes*, II, i, 213.
—*n.* **2** utmost efforts [on your behalf]: ". . . you do me now more wrong/ In making question of my uttermost . . ." *Merch*, I, i, 155–156.

V

vacancy, *n.* **1** idle time; leisure: "If he fill'd/ His vacancy with his voluptuousness . . ." *Ant & Cleo,* I, iv, 25–26. **2 but for vacancy,** ref. to saying, "Nature abhors a vacuum": "Whistling to the air; which, but for vacancy,/ Had gone to gaze on Cleopatra too . . ." *Ant & Cleo,* II, ii, 216–217.

vade, *v.* to go away; disappear in the sense of fading: "When that shall vade, by verse distils your truth." *Sonn 54,* 14.

vagram, *adj.* parson's mispron. of "fragrant": "Whenas I sat in Pabylon—/ And a thousand vagram posies." *Wives,* III, i, 23–24.

vagrom, *n.* Dogberry's blunder for "vagrant" or "vagabond": "This is your charge:/ you shall comprehend all vagrom men . . ." *M Ado,* III, iii, 24–25.

vail[1], *v.* **1** to lower; let fall: "Fair ladies, mask'd, are roses in their bud:/ Dismask'd . . . Are angels vailing clouds, or roses blown." *Love's L,* V, ii, 295–297. **2** to do homage: "She would with rich and constant pen/ Vail to her mistress Dian . . ." *Per,* IV, Chor., 28–29. **3** to submit or yield [to]: "To vail the title, as her mother doth." *Rich 3,* IV, iv, 348. **4 vail one's stomach, a.** to lose one's courage: "The bloody Douglas . . . Gan vail his stomach . . ." *2 Hen 4,* I, i, 127–129. **b.** to swallow one's pride: "Then vail your stomachs, for it is no boot [there's no help for it] . . ." *Shrew,* V, ii, 177. **5 vail your regard,** lower your gaze: "Vail your regard/ Upon a wrong'd [person] . . ." *Meas,* V, i, 21–22.
—*n.* **6** a lowering or descent: "Even with the vail and dark'ning of the sun . . ." *Tr & Cr,* V, iii, 7.

vail[2], *n.* [often pl.] scraps; leftovers; remnants; here, poss. a hint for a "tip": ". . . there are certain condolements, certain/ vails. I hope, sir . . . you'll remember/ from whence you had them." *Per,* II, i, 149–151.

vailed, *adj.* lowered; downcast: "Do not for ever with thy vailed lids/ Seek for thy noble father in the dust." *Ham,* I, ii, 70–71.

vain, *adj.* **1** using false or empty words: "'Tis holy sport to be a little vain/ When the sweet breath of flattery conquers strife." *Errors,* III, ii, 27–28. **2** foolish: "My Lord Chief Justice, speak to that vain man." *2 Hen 4,* V, v, 43. **3** useless or worthless: "Your oath, my lord, is vain and frivolous." *3 Hen 6,* I, ii, 27.
—*n.* **4 for vain,** for vanity; in vain: ". . . change for an idle plume/ Which the air beats for vain." *Meas,* II, iv, 11–12.

vainer hours, *n. pl.* more trivial pursuits or diversions: ". . . more profit/ Than other princess' [princesses] can, that have more time/ For vainer hours . . ." *Temp,* I, ii, 172–174.

vain-glory, *n.* display of vanity: "What needs these feasts, pomps, and vain-glories?" *Timon,* I, ii, 244.

vainly, *adv.* foolishly: "Having vainly fear'd too little." *All's W,* V, iii, 123.

valance, *n.* **1** short hanging to cover the top of the bed curtains: "Valance of Venice gold in needlework . . ." *Shrew,* II, i, 347.
—*v.* **2** to decorate with a short drapery or a fringe; here, a beard: "O, old friend, why, thy face is valanced since I saw thee/ last." *Ham,* II, ii, 418–420.

vale, *n.* **1** low ground; valley: "To the vales,/ And hold our best advantage." *Ant & Cleo,* IV, xi, 3–4. **2 vale of years,** waning years; old age: ". . . or for I am declin'd/ Into the vale of years . . ." *Oth,* III, iii, 269–270.

Valentine, *n.* name applied to any true lover: "There's not a hair on 's head but/ 'tis a Valentine." *Two Gent,* III, i, 191–192.

validity, *n.* worth or dignity: "More validity . . . more courtship lives/ In carrion flies than Romeo." *Rom & Jul*, III, iii, 33–35.

valor, *n.* appar. confusion with "good sense": "Good Corporal Nym, show thy valour and put up/ your sword." *Hen 5*, II, i, 42–43.

value, *v.* **1** to weigh, estimate, or consider: "Our business valued, some twelve days hence/ Our general forces at Bridgnorth shall meet." *1 Hen 4*, III, ii, 177–178. **2 it values not,** it's not worth: "My good lord,/ Not your demand [question]; it values not your asking . . ." *Hen 8*, II, iii, 51–52. **3 not values,** [is] not worth: "The peace between the French and us not values/ The cost that did conclude it." *Hen 8*, I, i, 88–89. —*n.* **4** valuation; esteem or estimation: "A kinder value of the people than/ He hath hereto priz'd them at." *Cor*, II, ii, 58–59. **5 in value with,** esteemed or valued by: "How much more is his life in value with him?" *Hen 8*, V, ii, 142.

vambrace, *n.* protective armor for the arms: "And in my vambrace put my wither'd brawns . . ." *Tr & Cr*, I, iii, 296.

vane, *n.* old word for "banner, pendant" in wordplay with "vain": "What plume of feathers is he that indited this letter?/ What vane? what weathercock?" *Love's L*, IV, i, 95–96.

vanish, *v.* to escape: "A gentler judgement vanish'd from his lips . . ." *Rom & Jul*, III, iii, 10.

vanished, *past part.* misuse for "banished": "Sir, there is a proclamation that you are vanished." *Two Gent*, III, i, 216.

vanity, *n.* **1** frivolity; inanity: "What a sweep of vanity comes this way." *Timon*, I, ii, 128. **2** transitory pleasures of this world: "A lover may bestride the gossamers . . . in the wanton summer air/ And yet not fall; so light is vanity." *Rom & Jul*, II, vi, 18–20. **3** folly; lewdness or wantonness: "O, I should have a heavy miss of thee/ If I were much in love with vanity . . ." *1 Hen 4*, V, iv, 104–105. **4** extravagance; excess: "Light vanity, insatiate cormorant,/ Consuming means, soon preys upon itself." *Rich 2*, II, i, 38–39. **5** clever device or ingenious mechanism; trick: ". . . I must/ Bestow upon the eyes of this young couple/ Some vanity of mine Art . . ." *Temp*, IV, i, 39–41. **6** foolishness; also, illusion or deception: "My fore-past proofs . . . Shall tax my fears of little vanity,/ Having vainly fear'd too little [My earlier knowledge of you cannot blame my fears on foolishness; the problem was that I was foolishly not fearful enough]." *All's W*, V, iii, 121–123.

Vanity, *n.* character in the old morality plays, often done as puppet shows: ". . . you come with letters/ against the King, and take Vanity the puppet's/ part . . ." *Lear*, II, ii, 35–37.

vanquished, *adj.* won (over); persuaded: "Vanquish'd thereto by the fair grace and speech/ Of the poor suppliant . . ." *All's W*, V, iii, 133–134.

vant, *n.* vanguard; here, forefront of the battle: "Go charge Agrippa,/ Plant those that have revolted in the vant . . ." *Ant & Cleo*, IV, vi, 8–9.

vantage, *n.* **1** advantage: "O happy vantage of a kneeling knee!" *Rich 2*, V, iii, 130. **2** profit; gain or benefit: "To match with her that brings no vantages." *2 Hen 6*, I, i, 130. **3** superiority: "My fortunes every way as fairly rank'd,/ If not with vantage, as Demetrius' . . ." *M N Dream*, I, i, 101–102. **4** opportunity; opportune moment: "I have some rights of memory in this kingdom,/ Which now to claim my vantage doth invite me." *Ham*, V, ii, 394–395. **5 answer the vantage of,** take advantage of: ". . . both observe and answer/ The vantage of his anger." *Cor*, II, iii, 257–258. **6 at your vantage,** at your first opportunity: "Therefore, at your vantage . . . let him feel your sword . . ." *Cor*, V, vi, 54–56. **7 of vantage,** in addition: "'Tis meet that some more audience than a mother . . . should o'erhear/ The speech of vantage." *Ham*, III, iii, 31–33. **8 to the vantage,** in addition: ". . . and as many to the vantage, as would/ store the world they played for." *Oth*, IV, iii, 84–85.

Vapians, *n.* appar. a quasi-learned coinage by the Clown: ". . . the Vapians passing the equinoctial of Queubus . . ." *T Night*, II, iii, 24.

vapor, *n.* **1** something as insubstantial as air: ". . . Cap-and-knee slaves, vapours, and minute-jacks!" *Timon*, III, vi, 93. **2** [often pl.] clouds; also, sometimes, mists: "At length the sun . . . Dispers'd those vapours that offended us . . ." *Errors*, I, i, 88–89. **3** exhalation or emanation, usually considered worthless or harmful: "And in the vapour of my glory smother'd." *Rich 3*, III, vii, 163. **4** [pl.] alcoholic spirits: ". . . dries me there all the foolish and dull and crudy/ vapours which environ it . . ." *2 Hen 4*, IV, iii, 96–97.

vaporous, *adj.* bringing mists; hence, noxious: ". . . make haste,/ The vaporous night approaches." *Meas*, IV, i, 57–58.

vara, *adv.* dial. pron. of "very": "No, sir; but it is vara fine,/ For every one pursents three." *Love's L*, V, ii, 487–488.

variable, *adj.* various; belonging to a succession: "Live . . . betwixt cold sheets,/ Whiles he is vaulting variable ramps [prostitutes] . . ." *Cymb*, I, vii, 133–134.

variable objects, *n.* new sights; here, a change of scenery: "With variable objects, shall expel/ This something settled matter in his heart . . ." *Ham*, III, i, 174–175.

variable service, *n.* diverse dishes served at a meal: "Your fat king and your lean beggar is but/ variable service . . ." *Ham,* IV, iii, 23–24.

varlet, *n.* **1** knave; rascal: "I am the/ veriest varlet that ever chewed with a tooth . . ." *1 Hen 4,* II, ii, 23–24. **2** manservant; boy: "Call here my varlet, I'll unarm again." *Tr & Cr,* I, i, 1. **3** See **male varlet. 4 these varlets here,** Elbow inadvertently reverses his epithets; referred to by Escalus in his next line: "Prove it before these varlets here, thou honourable/ man, prove it." *Meas,* II, i, 85–86.

varletry, *n.* mob; rabble: "Shall they hoist me up,/ And show me to the shouting varletry/ Of censuring Rome?" *Ant & Cleo,* V, ii, 55–56.

varletto, *n.* varlet [Host's affectation]: "Where be my horses? Speak well of them, varletto." *Wives,* IV, v, 61.

varnish, *v.* to gloss; make appear fresh: "Beauty doth varnish age, as if new-born . . ." *Love's L,* IV, iii, 240.

varnished faces, *n.* masks: "Nor thrust your head into the public street/ To gaze on Christian fools with varnish'd faces . . ." *Merch,* II, v, 32–33.

vary, *v.* to express in various ways: ". . . the man hath no wit that cannot . . . vary deserved praise on my palfrey . . ." *Hen 5,* III, vii, 32–34.

varying, *adj.* ranging from light to dark: ". . . darkling stand/ The varying shore o' the world." *Ant & Cleo,* IV, xv, 10–11.

vassal, *n.* **1** servant; menial: "It is impossible that I should die/ By such a lowly vassal as thyself." *2 Hen 6,* IV, i, 109–110. —*adj.* **2** base; vile: ". . . whose low vassal seat/ The Alps doth spit and void his rheum upon." *Hen 5,* III, v, 51–52. **3 vassal actor,** person who performs a misdeed for a king: "O be remember'd, no outrageous thing/ From vassal actors can be wip'd away . . ." *Luc,* 607–608.

vast, *n.* vast expanse; great distance: ". . . shook/ hands, as over a vast . . ." *W Tale,* I, i, 29–30.

vastidity, *n.* vastness: ". . . a restraint,/ Though all the world's vastidity you had,/ To a determin'd scope." *Meas,* III, i, 67–69.

vasty, *adj.* vast; boundless: "The vasty fields of France." *Hen 5,* Prol. 12.

vault, *n.* **1** world covered with the vaulted sky; also, comparison here with a wine vault: "The wine of life is drawn, and the mere lees/ Is left this vault to brag of." *Mac,* II, iii, 95–96.

—*v.* **2** to copulate with; mount: "Live like Diana's priest, betwixt cold sheets,/ Whiles he is vaulting variable ramps [succession of whores] . . ." *Cymb,* I, vii, 133–134.

vaulted arch, *n.* See **arch**[1] (def. 2).

vaunt[1], *n.* **1** boast or brag: "And such high vaunts of his nobility . . ." *2 Hen 6,* III, i, 50. —*v.* **2** to rejoice; also, to flaunt oneself; boast: "Vaunt in their youthful sap, at height decrease . . ." *Sonn 15,* 7.

vaunt[2], *n.* beginning: ". . . our play/ Leaps o'er the vaunt and firstlings of those broils . . ." *Tr & Cr,* Prol., 26–27.

vaunt-courier, *n.* forerunner; harbinger: "Vaunt-couriers of oak-cleaving thunderbolts,/ Singe my white head!" *Lear,* III, ii, 5–6.

vaunter, *n.* boaster: "Alas, you know I am no vaunter, I . . ." *T Andr,* V, iii, 113.

vaunting veins, *n. pl.* energetic spirits: "Bardolph, be blithe;/ Nym, rouse thy vaunting veins . . ." *Hen 5,* II, iii, 4.

vaward, *n.* vanguard; the leading edge or earliest part: ". . . we that are in the/ vaward of our youth . . ." *2 Hen 4,* I, ii, 175–176.

veal, *n.* pun on German viel [much or plenty], veal [calf, also blockhead], and veil [another word for "visor"]: "Veal, quoth the Dutchman. Is not veal a calf?" *Love's L,* V, ii, 247.

vegetive, *n.* plant: ". . . the blest infusions/ That dwells in vegetives, in metals, stones . . ." *Per,* III, ii, 35–36.

veil, *v.* to conceal or disguise: ". . . if I have veil'd my look,/ I turn the trouble of my countenance/ Merely upon myself." *J Caes,* I, ii, 36–38.

veiled, *adj.* usually seen wearing a veil: "Our veil'd dames/ Commit the war of white and damask . . ." *Cor,* II, i, 213–214.

vein, *n.* **1** condition or situation; disposition: "You touch'd my vein at first: the thorny point/ Of bare distress . . ." *As You,* II, vii, 95–96. **2** individual style or manner: ". . . the whole world again/ Cannot pick out five such, take each one in his vein." *Love's L,* V, ii, 538–539. **3** mood or humor: ". . . the fellow finds his vein,/ And yielding to him, humours well his frenzy." *Errors,* IV, iv, 78–79. **4** correct way to proceed; right approach: "Ay, touch him: there's the vein." *Meas,* II, ii, 70. **5** innermost parts or processes: ". . . checks and disasters/ Grow in the veins of actions highest rear'd . . ." *Tr & Cr,* I, iii, 5–6. **6 rubs the vein,** cheers the disposition [of]: "O, this is well: he rubs the vein of him." *Tr & Cr,* II, iii, 201. **7 vein of league,**

concerted effort: "... combine/ The blood of malice in a vein of league ..." *K John,* V, ii, 37–38.

velure, *n.* velvet: "... one girth/ six times pieced, and a woman's crupper of velure ..." *Shrew,* III, ii, 57–58.

vendible, *adj.* marketable, hence marriageable: "... silence is only commendable/ In a neat's tongue dried, and a maid not vendible [old maid]." *Merch,* I, i, 111–112.

venereal, *adj.* concerned with Venus and love: "No, madam, these are no venereal signs:/ Vengeance is in my heart, death in my hand ..." *T Andr,* II, iii, 37–38.

veney, *n.* (in fencing) bout: "... three veneys for a dish of/ stewed prunes ..." *Wives,* I, i, 261–262.

venge, *v.* to avenge: "You justicers, that these our nether crimes/ So speedily can venge!" *Lear,* IV, ii, 79–80.

vengeance, *n.* **1** harm or mischief: "Whiles the eye of man did woo me,/ That could do no vengeance to me." *As You,* IV, iii, 47–48. **2 vengeance of,** a plague or pox on: "Vengeance of Ginny's case; fie on her!" *Wives,* IV, i, 53.
—*adv.* **3** awfully; frightfully: "... he's vengeance/ proud, and loves not the common people." *Cor,* II, ii, 5–6.
—*interj.* **4 what the vengeance,** meaningless expression, prob. the equiv. of "what the hell": "What the vengeance,/ Could he not speak 'em fair?" *Cor,* III, i, 260–261.

venom, *n.* **1** venomous snake: ref. to the legend that Saint Patrick had driven the snakes out of Ireland: "... those rug-headed kerns ... live like venom where no venom else ... have privilege to live." *Rich 2,* II, i, 157–158. **2 dear venom,** term applied by Sir Toby to Sir Andrew in an attempt to coax the latter out of his venomous mood: "Thy reason, dear venom, give thy reason." *T Night,* III, ii, 2.
—*adj.* **3** venomous: "His venom tooth will rankle to the death." *Rich 3,* I, iii, 291.

vent¹, *v.* **1** to speak; express: "... observation, the which he vents/ In mangled forms." *As You,* II, vii, 41–42. **2** to excrete; void: "How cam'st/ thou to be the siege of this moon-calf? can he vent/ Trinculos?" *Temp,* II, ii, 106–108. **3** to get rid of: "... we shall ha' means to vent/ Our musty superfluity." *Cor,* I, i, 224–225. **4** to loose; unleash; here, prob. in Clown's wordplay with sense of "break wind" or "defecate": "Vent my folly! ... tell me what I shall vent to my/ lady." *T Night,* IV, i, 12–17. **5** to circulate: "Will you rhyme upon't,/ And vent it for a mock'ry?" *Cymb,* V, iii, 55–56.

vent², *n.* scent of hunted animal; hence, animation or excitement: "... it's sprightly walking, audible,/ and full of vent." *Cor,* IV, v, 229–230.

ventage, *n.* (on a musical instrument) hole or stop: "Govern these ventages with/ your fingers and thumb ..." *Ham,* III, ii, 348–349.

venture, *n.* **1** ship's cargo: "There's a whole merchant's venture of/ Bordeaux stuff in him ..." *2 Hen 4,* II, iv, 62–63. **2** trader or vendor: "... diseas'd ventures,/ That play with all infirmities for gold ..." *Cymb,* I, vii, 123–124. **3** commercial undertaking involving risk: "Believe me sir, had I such venture forth ..." *Merch,* I, i, 15. **4 at a venture,** without proper thought; in a reckless manner: "... some hilding fellow that had stol'n/ The horse he rode on, and ... Spoke at a venture." *2 Hen 4,* I, i, 57–59.
—*v.* **5** to risk or stake: "Beshrew me, I would,/ And venture maidenhead for't ..." *Hen 8,* II, iii, 24–26.

venue, *n.* thrust: "... a sweet touch, a quick venue of wit!" *Love's L,* V, i, 55.

Venus, *n.* Roman goddess of love and beauty [her Grecian counterpart was Aphrodite]: "By the simplicity of Venus' doves ..." *M N Dream,* I, i, 171.

Ver, *n.* personification of spring: "This side is *Hiems,* Winter, this *Ver,* the Spring ..." *Love's L,* V, ii, 883.

verbal, *adj.* verbose or talkative; here, insistent: "You put me to forget a lady's manners,/ By being so verbal ..." *Cymb,* II, iii, 104–105.

verbatim, *adv.* orally: "Think not ... I have forg'd, or am not able/ Verbatim to rehearse my method penn'd." *1 Hen 6,* III, i, 10–12.

verdict, *n.* **1** consensus; majority opinion: "... we'll have corn at our own/ price. Is't a verdict?" *Cor,* I, i, 9–10. **2** word or promise: "And rather let me leave to be a prince/ Than break the stable [unfailing] verdict of a prince ..." *Edw 3,* IV, v, 77–78. **3 bold verdict,** insolent opinion: "Must your bold verdict enter talk with lords?/ Else would I have a fling at Winchester." *1 Hen 6,* III, i, 63–64.

verdour, *n.* var. of **verdure.** freshness; greenness: "And as they last, their verdour still endure ..." *Ven & Ad,* 507.

verdure, *n.* strength or vitality; here, political power: "... he was/ The ivy which had hid my princely trunk,/ And suck'd my verdure out on 't." *Temp,* I, ii, 85–87.

verge, *n.* **1** edge, as of a land mass or body of water: "... the beached verge of the salt flood ..." *Timon,* V, i, 215. **2** space or area; also, the sacrosanct 12-mile radius from the king's presence, wherever it happened to be: "And yet, in-caged in so small a verge,/ The waste is no whit lesser than thy land."

Rich 2, II, i, 102–103. **3 inclusive verge,** enclosing circlet; the crown, here likened to an instrument of torture: ". . . the inclusive verge/ Of golden metal that must round my brow . . ." *Rich 3,* IV, i, 58–59.

veriest, *adj.* superlative of **very;** full; complete; thorough: "I am the veriest varlet that ever chewed with a tooth . . ." *1 Hen 4,* II, ii, 23–24.

verify, *v.* to support or back up; also, praise: "For I have ever verified my friends . . ." *Cor,* V, ii, 17.

verily, *adv.* **That's verily,** That's stated truly: "I saw their weapons drawn:—there was a noise,/ That's verily." *Temp,* II, i, 315–316.

Verolles, *n.* humorous use of French *vérole* [syphilis] for surname: ". . . the French knight that cowers i' the hams?"/ "Who? Monsieur Verolles?" *Per,* IV, ii, 103–104.

Veronesa, *n.* perh. ref. to Cassio, a Veronese; poss. a type of ship: "The ship is here put in,/ A Veronesa; Michael Cassio . . ." *Oth,* II, i, 25–26.

versal, *adj.* universal; whole or entire: ". . . she looks as pale/ as any clout in the versal world." *Rom & Jul,* II, iv, 201–202.

verse, *n.* **1** quotation; citation: "What verse for it, what instance for it?—" *Tr & Cr,* V, x, 40. **2 magic verses,** incantations; here, a magic spell: "Or shall we think the subtle-witted French . . . By magic verses have contriv'd his end?" *1 Hen 6,* I, i, 25–27.
—*v.* **3** to compose verses on the subject of: "Playing on pipes of corn, and versing love/ To amorous Phillida." *M N Dream,* II, i, 67–68.

very, *adj.* **1** true; genuine: "My very friend, hath got this mortal hurt/ In my behalf . . ." *Rom & Jul,* III, i, 112–113. **2** none other than: "I am absolute/ 'Twas very Cloten." *Cymb,* IV, ii, 106–107.

vessel, *n.* **1** body; bearing (fig. use): "Though thy tackle's torn,/ Thou show'st a noble vessel." *Cor,* IV, v, 62–63. **2 strike the vessels,** fill the cups to the top: ". . . strike the vessels, ho!/ Here's to Caesar!" *Ant & Cleo,* II, vii, 96–97.

vestal, *adj.* **1** virginal: "Her vestal livery is but sick and green/ And none but fools do wear it." *Rom & Jul,* II, ii, 8–9.
—*n.* **2** vestal virgin; a young woman who has vowed to remain chaste: ". . . a certain aim he took/ At a fair vestal, throned by the west . . ." *M N Dream,* II, i, 157–158.

vestal livery, *n.* nun's habit: "A vestal livery will I take me to,/ And never more have joy." *Per,* III, iv, 9–10.

vesture, *n.* **1** clothing: "Kind souls, what weep you when you but behold/ Our Caesar's vesture wounded?" *J Caes,* III, ii, 197–198. **2 essential vesture of creation,** human body regarded as the dressing of the soul: "And in the essential vesture of creation/ Does bear all excellency . . ." *Oth,* II, i, 64–65.

vetch, *n.* vine used for fodder: ". . . thy rich leas/ Of wheat, rye, barley, vetches, oats, and pease . . ." *Temp,* IV, i, 60–61.

vex, *v.* to taunt or torment: "If so thou think'st, vex him with eager [harsh] words." *3 Hen 6,* II, vi, 68.

Via, *adv., interj.* [Latin] Onward! Go ahead! [cry of encouragement]: "I beseech you, follow."/ "*Via,* goodman Dull!" *Love's L,* V, i, 137–139.

viand, *n.* [often pl.] food; dishes, esp. of meat: "All viands that I eat do seem unsavoury,/ Wishing him my meat." *Per,* II, iii, 31–32.

vice¹, *n.* **1** grip or grasp: "And I but fist him once, and a come but within my/ vice . . ." *2 Hen 4,* II, i, 20–21. **2** a screw, often with a punning allusion to a woman's thighs: ". . . you must put in the/ pikes with a vice, and they are dangerous weapons/ for maids." *M Ado,* V, ii, 19–21.
—*v.* **3** to force: "As he had seen 't, or been an instrument/ To vice you to't . . ." *W Tale,* I, ii, 415–416.

vice², *n.* [often cap.] figure of temptation in the old morality plays; often carried a wooden dagger and menaced the Devil: ". . . a vice of kings,/ A cutpurse of the empire and the rule . . ." *Ham,* III, iv, 98–99.

vicegerent, *n.* monarch regarded [or viewing himself] as God's deputy: "Great deputy, the welkin's vicegerent,/ and sole dominator of Navarre . . ." *Love's L,* I, i, 216–217.

Vice's dagger, *n.* wooden dagger, which Vice used to menace the Devil in the old morality plays; hence, buffoon: "And now is this Vice's dagger/ become a squire . . ." *2 Hen 4,* III, ii, 313–314.

victor, *adj.* victorious: "Despite thy victor sword and fire-new fortune . . ." *Lear,* V, iii, 132.

victual, *v.* to provision or supply: ". . . thy loving voyage/ Is but for two months victuall'd." *As You,* V, iv, 190–191.

videlicet, *adv.* **1** Latin legal term for "which is to say" or "namely": ". . . not any man died in his own person, videlicet, in a love-cause." *As You,* IV, i, 91–92. **2** used in wordplay based on an understanding of its literal meaning, "to be permitted to see": "She hath spied him already with those sweet eyes."/ "And thus she means, videlicet—" *M N Dream,* V, i, 309–310.

Video, et gaudeo, [Latin] I see and I rejoice. *Love's L,* V, i, 30.

Videsne quis venit? [Latin] Do you see who comes? *Love's L,* V, i, 29.

vie, *v.* **1** to compete, esp. to go one better: "She vied so fast, protesting oath on oath,/ That in a twink she won me to her love." *Shrew,* II, i, 302–303. **2** to contend with; rival: ". . . nature wants [lacks] stuff/ To vie strange forms with fancy . . ." *Ant & Cleo,* V, ii, 97–98.

view, *v.* **1** to read; look at: ". . . my Lord Protector, view the letter/ Sent from our uncle, Duke of Burgundy." *1 Hen 6,* IV, i, 48–49.
—*n.* **2** presence: "If I demand before this royal view,/ What rub or what impediment there is . . ." *Hen 5,* V, ii, 32–33. **3 full of view,** showing excellent prospects: ". . . you should tread a course/ Pretty, and full of view . . ." *Cymb,* III, iv, 148–149. **4 my sister's view,** so that my sister can meet you: "With most gladness,/ And [I] do invite you to my sister's view . . ." *Ant & Cleo,* II, ii, 166–167. **5 to the view,** in appearance: "I have gone here and there,/ And made myself a motley to the view . . ." *Sonn 110,* 1–2.

viewless, *adj.* invisible: "To be imprison'd in the viewless winds . . ." *Meas,* III, i, 123.

vigil, *n.* the eve of a feast day: "He that shall see this day, and live old age,/ Will yearly on the vigil feast his neighbours . . ." *Hen 5,* IV, iii, 44–45.

vigitant, *adj.* misuse for "vigilant": "Adieu! Be vigitant, I beseech you." *M Ado,* III, iii, 92.

vigor of bone, *n.* great strength or energy: "For beauty, wit,/ High birth, vigour of bone, desert in service,/ Love, friendship, charity, are subjects all/ To envious and calumniating Time." *Tr & Cr,* III, iii, 171–174.

vild or **vilde,** *adj.* **1** old form of **vile:** ". . . and for that vild fault/ Two of her brothers were condemn'd to death . . ." *T Andr,* V, ii, 172–173. **2** poss. wordplay on "vile" and "wild, barbarous": ". . . their visible spirits/ Send quickly down to tame these vilde offences . . ." *Lear,* IV, ii, 46–47. **3 no vild hold,** any low trick: "Makes nice of no vild hold to stay him up [will use any low trick to stay in power] . . ." *K John,* III, iii, 138.

vildly, *adv.* var. of **vilely:** "Ha, ha! how vildly doth this cynic rhyme!" *J Caes,* IV, iii, 132.

vild prison, *n.* the body: "Holding th' eternal spirit, against her will,/ In the vild prison of afflicted breath." *K John,* III, iii, 18–19.

vile, *adj.* **1** low; base; vulgar: ". . . thou hast lost thy princely privilege/ With vile participation." *1 Hen 4,* III, ii, 86–87. **2** shabby; beggarly: "I will inset you, neither in gold/ nor silver, but in vile apparel . . ." *2 Hen 4,* I, ii, 16–17. **3** of humble birth; lowly: ". . . be he ne'er so vile/ This day shall gentle his condition . . ." *Hen 5,* IV, iii, 62–63. **4** worthless: "What trash is Rome . . . when it serves/ For the base matter to illuminate/ So vile a thing as Caesar!" *J Caes,* I, iii, 108–111.
—*n.* **5** low, humble persons: ". . . why li'st thou with the vile/ In loathsome beds . . ." *2 Hen 4,* III, i, 15–16.
—*v.* **6** to revile; scold: ". . . call him noble that was now your hate,/ Him vile that was your garland . . ." *Cor,* I, i, 182–183.

vile drawing, *adj.* evil-attracting: ". . . this advantage, this vile drawing bias,/ This sway of motion, this commodity . . ." *K John,* II, i, 577–578.

vile-esteemed, *adj.* held in low regard: ". . . they would have barter'd me:/ Which I disdaining scorn'd, and craved death/ Rather than I would be so vile-esteem'd." *1 Hen 6,* I, iv, 30–32.

vilely, *adv.* terribly; awfully; horribly: "Bardolph, am I not fallen away vilely since this last/ action?" *1 Hen 4,* III, iii, 1.

vile sense, *n.* senses that keep Gloucester conscious of his pain and will not allow him to retreat into insanity: ". . . how stiff is my vile sense/ That I . . . have ingenious feeling/ Of my huge sorrows!" *Lear,* IV, vi, 281–283.

villagery, *n.* residents of the village; the peasantry: "Are not you he/ That frights the maidens of the villagery . . ." *M N Dream,* II, i, 34–35.

villain, *v.* **1** person of low birth and ignoble behavior: "Romeo, the love I bear thee can afford/ No better term than this: thou art a villain." *Rom & Jul,* III, i, 59–60. **2** scoundrel; blackguard: "Like a false traitor, and injurious villain . . ." *Rich 2,* I, i, 91. **3** rascal (often used playfully or affectionately): "A trusty villain, sir, that very oft . . . Lightens my humour with his merry jests." *Errors,* I, ii, 19–21. **4** servant: ". . . down fell both the Ram's horns in the court;/ And who should find them but the empress' villain?" *T Andr,* IV, iii, 71–72.

villainous, *adv.* wretchedly: "And all be turn'd to . . . apes/ With foreheads villainous low." *Temp,* IV, i, 248–249.

villainy, *n.* prob. Frenchman's misuse for "villain": "Villainy,/ larron! [Pulling Simple out] Rugby, my rapier!" *Wives,* I, iv, 62–63.

Villiago!, *n.* villain; rascal; scoundrel; here, the shout of the conquerors: "I see them lording it in London streets,/ Crying 'Villiago!' unto all they meet." *2 Hen 6,* IV, viii, 45–46.

vindicative, *adj.* var. of **vindictive:** ". . . but he in heat of action/ Is more vindicative than jealous love." *Tr & Cr,* IV, v, 106–107.

vinewedest, *adj.* moldiest: "Speak then, thou vinewed'st leaven, speak!" *Tr & Cr,* II, i, 14–15.

viol, *n.* stringed musical instrument, forerunner of the violin: "You are a fair viol, and your sense the strings . . ." *Per,* I, i, 82.

viol-de-gamboys, *n.* viola da gamba, or bass viol; so-called (in Italian) because the player held it between his legs: ". . . he plays o' th' viol-de-gamboys,/ and speaks three or four languages word/ for word without book . . ." *T Night,* I, iii, 25–27.

violent, *v.* to rage violently: "The grief is fine . . . And violenteth in a sense as strong/ As that which causeth it . . ." *Tr & Cr,* IV, iv, 3–5.

violet, *n.* **1** court favorite: "Who are the violets now/ That strew the green lap of the new-come spring?" *Rich 2,* V, ii, 46–47. **2 lying by the violet,** carrion, which putrefies in the same sun that nourishes the violet: ". . . lying by the violet in the sun,/ Do as the carrion does, not as the flower . . ." *Meas,* II, ii, 166–167.

virgin, *v.* **virgin it,** to play the virgin; behave chastely: ". . . my true lip/ Hath virgin'd it e'er since." *Cor,* V, iii, 47–48.

virginal, *adj.* **1** supplicating: ". . . the virginal palms of your daughters . . ." *Cor,* V, ii, 42.
—*v.* **2** to seem to play upon the virginal [early keyboard instrument]; paddle: "Still virginalling/ Upon his palm!" *W Tale,* I, ii, 125–126.

Virginius, *n.* legendary Roman soldier who slew his daughter to prevent her being ravished by Appius Claudius [Titus appears to have the story wrong]: "Was it well done of rash Virginius/ To slay his daughter with his own right hand . . ." *T Andr,* V, iii, 36–37.

Virgo, *n.* constellation, perh. named for Astraea, the goddess of justice: "O, well said, Lucius!/ Good boy, in Virgo's lap: give it Pallas." *T Andr,* IV, iii, 63–64.

vir sapit qui pauca loquitur, [Latin] That man is wise who speaks little: ". . . if their daughters be capable, I will/ put it to them. But *vir sapit qui pauca loquitur.*" *Love's L,* IV, ii, 76–77.

virtue, *n.* **1** merit; excellence or distinction: "Her sober virtue, years and modesty . . ." *Errors,* III, i, 90. **2** power; here, a healing power: "With this strange virtue,/ He hath a heavenly gift of prophecy . . ." *Mac,* IV, iii, 156–157. **3** faculty; ability: "Tears seven times salt/ Burn out the sense and virtue of mine eye." *Ham,* IV, v, 154–155. **4** [often pl.] accomplishments: ". . . I can sing, weave, sew, and dance,/ With other virtues . . ." *Per,* IV, vi, 182–183. **5** heroic courage; dauntlessness: "O infinite virtue, com'st thou smiling from/ The world's great snare uncaught?" *Ant & Cleo,* IV, viii, 17–18. **6 single virtue,** valor without assistance: "Trust to thy single virtue; for thy soldiers . . . have in my name/ Took their discharge." *Lear,* V, iii, 103–105. **7 very ample virtue,** full authority: ". . . a full commission,/ In very ample virtue of his father . . ." *2 Hen 4,* IV, i, 162–163. **8 virtue, go,** [to have the] virtue to go forward: "Grace to stand, and virtue, go . . ." *Meas,* III, ii, 257. **9 virtue of his will,** the integrity of his intention(s): "And now no soil nor cautel doth besmirch/ The virtue of his will . . ." *Ham,* I, iii, 15–16.

virtuous, *adj.* **1** being the result of moral behavior; just: "If his occasion were not virtuous,/ I should not urge it half so faithfully." *Timon,* III, ii, 39–40. **2** of a fine nature or quality: ". . . like the bee, tolling from every flower/ The virtuous sweets . . ." *2 Hen 4,* IV, v, 74–75. **3** desirable or effective: ". . . crush this herb into Lysander's eye,/ Whose liquor hath this virtuous property . . ." *M N Dream,* III, ii, 366–367.

visage, *n.* **1** look or aspect; expression: ". . . with devotion's visage/ And pious action we do sugar o'er/ The devil himself." *Ham,* III, i, 47–49. **2** external appearance: ". . . trimm'd in forms, and visages of duty,/ Keep yet their hearts attending on themselves . . ." *Oth,* I, i, 50–51.

visit, *v.* to furnish or supply: "To Milan let me hear from thee by letters . . . And I likewise will visit thee with mine." *Two Gent,* I, i, 57–60.

visited, *adj.* **1** infected with the plague [a technical term]: "These lords are visited; you are not free . . ." *Love's L,* V, ii, 422–423. **2** punished: "Thy sins are visited in this poor child . . ." *K John,* II, i, 179.

visit other places, *v.* to be elsewhere: "They could be content [would prefer]/ To visit other places . . ." *J Caes,* V, i, 8–9.

visor, *n.* mask; vizard: "What! was your visor made without a tongue?" *Love's L,* V, ii, 242.

visored, *adj.* wearing a mask: "Enter . . . the King and/ the rest of the lords disguised like Russians, and visored." [SD] *Love's L,* V, ii, 157.

vixen, *n.* quarrelsome girl or woman: "She was a vixen when she went to school . . ." *M N Dream,* III, ii, 324.

viz., abbrev. of **videlicet:** ". . . take note now many pair of/ silk stockings thou hast—viz. these, and those that/ were thy peach-coloured ones!" *2 Hen 4*, II, ii, 14–16.

vizaments, *n.* [often pl.] advisements: ". . . desire to hear the fear of Got [God], and not to hear a riot;/ take your vizaments in that." *Wives*, I, i, 35–36.

vizard, *n.* **1** mask; visor: "I have/ vizards for you all; you have horses for yourselves." *1 Hen 4*, I, ii, 123–124. —*v.* **2** to cover (the face) with a mask: "For they must all be masked and vizarded . . ." *Wives*, IV, vi, 39. **3** to obscure, as with a mask: "Degree being vizarded,/ Th'unworthiest shows as fairly in the mask." *Tr & Cr*, I, iii, 83–84.

vlouting-stog or **vlouting-stock,** *n.* **1** parson's pron. of "flouting-stock" [laughing-stock]: ". . . he has made us his vlouting-stog." *Wives*, III, i, 108. **2** [pl.] parson prob. means "flouts" [gibes]: ". . . you/ are wise, and full of gibes and vlouting-stocks . . ." *Wives*, IV, v, 74–75.

vocatur, [Latin] is called: ". . . neighbour *vocatur*/ nebour; neigh abbreviated ne." *Love's L*, V, i, 22–23.

voice, *v.* **1** to speak of, esp. to praise: "Is this th' Athenian minion whom the world/ Voic'd so regardfully?" *Timon*, IV, iii, 82–83. —*n.* **2** vote or support; here, in choosing the successor to the Danish throne: ". . . I do prophesy th'election lights on Fortinbras. He has my dying voice." *Ham*, V, ii, 360–361. **3** [often pl.] approval: "People of Rome . . . I ask your voices and your suffrages . . ." *T Andr*, I, i, 217–218. **4** [pl.] praises; congratulations: "If the dull brainless Ajax come safe off,/ We'll dress him up in voices . . ." *Tr & Cr*, I, iii, 381–382. **5** report; talk; rumor or gossip: "Well, the voice goes, madam . . ." *Hen 8*, IV, ii, 11. **6** language: ". . . the/ hardest voice of her behaviour, to be Englished/ rightly, is, 'I am Sir John Falstaff's.'" *Wives*, I, iii, 43–45. **7 have no voice,** cannot be disclosed: "My matter hath no voice, lady, but to your own/ most pregnant [receptive] and vouchsafed ear." *T Night*, III, i, 90–91. **8 in my voice,** if I have anything to say about it: ". . . come see,/ And in my voice most welcome shall you be." *As You*, II, iv, 84–85. **9 in voices,** by word of mouth: "Of great estate, of fresh and stainless youth;/ In voices well divulg'd [spoken of], free . . ." *T Night*, I, v, 263–264. **10 lose your voice,** have your request denied: "You cannot speak of reason to the Dane/ And lose your voice." *Ham*, I, ii, 44–45.

voice and precedent, *n.* authorized verdict backed up by precedent: "Till by some elder masters of known honour/ I have a voice and precedent of peace/ To keep my name ungor'd." *Ham*, V, ii, 244–246.

voice of occupation, *n.* workers' opinion or vote: ". . . you that stood so much/ Upon the voice of occupation and/ The breath of garlic-eaters!" *Cor*, IV, vi, 97–99.

voice potential, *n.* powerful vote; here, a double vote equal to the duke's: "And hath in his effect [importance] a voice potential/ As double as the duke's . . ." *Oth*, I, ii, 13–14.

void, *v.* **1** to leave; abandon: "If they will fight with us, bid them come down,/ Or void the field . . ." *Hen 5*, IV, vii, 60–61. **2 void it up,** regurgitate it; here, recall: ". . . spend our flatteries to drink those men/ Upon whose age we void it up again [remember it much later] . . ." *Timon*, I, ii, 133–134. —*adj.* **3 more void,** less crowded: "I'll get me to a place more void, and there/ Speak to great Caesar as he comes along." *J Caes*, II, iv, 37–38.

voiding lobby, *n.* antechamber; waiting room: "How in our voiding lobby hast thou stood/ And duly waited for my coming forth." *2 Hen 6*, IV, i, 61–62.

Volquessen, *n.* region in N France surrounding the port city of Rouen: "Then do I give Volquessen, Touraine, Maine,/ Poictiers, and Anjou, these five provinces . . ." *K John*, II, i, 527–528.

Volsces, *n.* Latin people, often at war with Rome: "The news is, sir, the Volsces are in arms." *Cor*, I, i, 223.

voluble, *adj.* well-spoken; quick-witted: ". . . a knave/ very voluble, no farther conscionable than in putting/ on the mere form of civil and humane seeming . . ." *Oth*, II, i, 236–238.

volume, *n.* **by the volume,** any number of times [lit., enough times to fill a book]: ". . . for the poorest piece [coin]/ Will bear the knave by th'volume." *Cor*, III, iii, 32–33.

voluntary, *n.* **1** volunteer: "Rash, inconsiderate, fiery voluntaries . . ." *K John*, II, i, 67. —*adj.* **2** natural; spontaneous: "Ah, what a world of descant makes my soul/ Upon this voluntary ground of love!" *Edw 3*, II, i, 122–123.

voluptuously, *adv.* self-indulgently; luxuriously: "I had rather had eleven die nobly for their country,/ than one voluptuously surfeit out of action." *Cor*, I, iii, 24–25.

votarist, *n.* votary who has taken a nun's vow: ". . . wishing a more strict restraint/ Upon the sisters stood, the votarists of Saint Clare." *Meas*, I, iv, 4–5.

votary, *n.* person who has taken a vow: "Who are the votaries . . . That are vow-fellows with this virtuous duke?" *Love's L*, II, i, 37–38.

votress, *n.* female votary: "His mother was a votress of my order . . ." *M N Dream,* II, i, 123.

vouch, *v.* **1** to maintain; stand by: "What villain . . . spake that word?"/ "He that would vouch it in any place but here." *T Andr,* I, i, 359–360. **2** to assure guests constantly of their welcome: ". . . the feast is sold,/ That is not often vouch'd, while 'tis a-making . . ." *Mac,* III, iv, 32–33. **3** to guarantee: "Will his vouchers vouch him no more of/ his purchases . . ." *Ham,* V, i, 106–107. **4** to bear out; make good: "Our master Mars/ Hath vouch'd his oracle . . ." *Kinsmen,* V, iv, 106–107.
—*n.* **5** formal declaration: "My vouch against you . . . Will so your accusation overweigh . . ." *Meas,* II, iv, 155–156. **6** endorsement; here, vote of confidence: "To beg of Hob and Dick that does appear/ Their needless vouches?" *Cor,* II, iii, 115–116.

vouched, *adj.* guaranteed as genuine: "But the rarity of it is . . ." "As many vouch'd rarities are." *Temp,* II, i, 56–58.

voucher, *n.* decisive proof: "Here's a voucher/ Stronger than ever law could make . . ." *Cymb,* II, ii, 39–40.

vouchsafe, *v.* **1** to accept (used often as a humble request): "Vouchsafe my labour, and long live your lordship!" *Timon,* I, i, 155. **2** to grant; permit: "I beseech your honour, vouchsafe me a word . . ." *Timon,* I, ii, 173. **3** to consent; also, condescend: ". . . procure/ That Lady Margaret do vouchsafe to come . . . to England . . ." *1 Hen 6,* V, v, 88–90. **4** be so kind as [to]: "Vouchsafe to speak my thanks . . ." *Hen 8,* II, iii, 71. **5 vouchsafe your rest,** consent to stay: "I entreat you both . . . That you vouchsafe your rest here in our court . . ." *Ham,* II, ii, 10–13.

vouchsafed, *adj.* graciously conferred: ". . . no voice, lady, but to your own/ most pregnant and vouchsafed ear." *T Night,* III, i, 90–91.

vox, *n.* [Latin] voice; here, the appropriate voice: ". . . and [if] your/ ladyship will have it as it ought to be, you must/ allow *vox.*" *T Night,* V, i, 293–295.

voyage, *n.* **a good voyage of nothing,** poss. that men of no destination accomplish nothing: ". . . for that's it that always makes a good voyage of/ nothing." *T Night,* II, iv, 78–79.

Vulcan, *n.* **1** Roman god of fire, also of metalworking: ". . . Cupid is a good hare-finder, and Vulcan a rare carpenter?" *M Ado,* I, i, 171–172. **2** ref. to Vulcan's being cuckolded by his wife Venus: "Though Bassianus be the emperor's brother,/ Better than he have worn Vulcan's badge [the cuckold's horns]." *T Andr,* II, i, 88–89. **3 as like as Vulcan and his wife,** Vulcan, ugly and deformed, was married to Venus, goddess of love and beauty: ". . . as near as the extremest ends/ Of parallels, as like as Vulcan and his wife . . ." *Tr & Cr,* I, iii, 162–163.

vulgar, *adj.* **1** public: ". . . in the stirring passage [busy traffic] of the day,/ A vulgar comment will be made . . ." *Errors,* III, i, 99–100. **2** usual or familiar; commonplace: ". . . as common/ As any the most vulgar thing to sense . . ." *Ham,* I, ii, 98–99. **3** commonly known: "Most sure and vulgar; every one hears that,/ Which can distinguish sound." *Lear,* IV, vi, 211–212.
—*n.* **4** vulgar person: ". . . as bad as those/ That vulgars give bold'st titles . . ." *W Tale,* II, i, 93–94. **5** [construed as pl.] the common people: "It doth amount to one more than two."/ "Which the base vulgar do call three." *Love's L,* I, ii, 44–45.

vulgar fame, *n.* common gossip: ". . . besides what hotter hours,/ Unregister'd in vulgar fame, you have/ Luxuriously pick'd out." *Ant & Cleo,* III, xiii, 118–120.

vulgar station, *n.* advantageous position [for viewing] among the crowd: ". . . press among the popular throngs, and puff/ To win a vulgar station." *Cor,* II, i, 212–213.

W

wafer-cake, *n.* example of something easily broken: "For oaths are straws, men's faiths [promises] are wafer-cakes . . ." *Hen 5,* II, iii, 52.

waft[1], *v.* **1** to motion or beckon: ". . . but soft,/ who wafts us yonder?" *Errors,* II, ii, 108–109. **2** to turn away; avert: "Wafting his eyes to th' contrary . . ." *W Tale,* I, ii, 372.

waft[2], *v.* to convey; here, transport: "I charge thee waft me safely 'cross the Channel." *2 Hen 6,* IV, i, 114.

waftage, *n.* passage, as on a ship: "A ship you sent me to, to hire waftage." *Errors,* IV, i, 96.

wafture, *n.* impatient gesture, esp. one of dismissal: ". . . you answer'd not,/ But with an angry wafture of your hand/ Gave sign for me to leave you." *J Caes,* II, i, 245–247.

wag, *v.* **1** to go [away]: "Discard, bully Hercules, cashier: let them wag;/ trot, trot." *Wives,* I, iii, 6–7. **2** to go or keep on; continue: "Thus we may see, quoth he, how the world wags . . ." *As You,* II, vii, 23. **3** to go about; move around: "For well I wot the empress never wags/ But in her company there is a Moor . . ." *T Andr,* V, ii, 87–88. **4** (of the eyelids) to flutter: "Until my eyelids will no longer wag." *Ham,* V, i, 262.
—*n.* **5** high-spirited or mischievous boy; also, familiar term for a young man; chap: "I prithee sweet/ wag, shall there be gallows standing in England/ when thou art king?" *1 Hen 4,* I, ii, 56–58.

wage, *v.* **1** to pay; reward: "He wag'd me with his countenance [patronizing favor], as if/ I had been mercenary [a hireling]." *Cor,* V, vi, 40–41. **2** to contend; struggle: "To wage against the enmity o' th' air . . ." *Lear,* II, iv, 211. **3** to be equal to or commensurate with: ". . . the commodity wages not with the danger . . ." *Per,* IV, ii, 29. **4 wage equal,** to be an equal match: "His taints and honours/ Wag'd equal with him." *Ant & Cleo,* V, i, 30–31.

waggish, *adj.* **1** roguish; rowdy: "As waggish boys, in game, themselves forswear . . ." *M N Dream,* I, i, 240. **2** youthful; high-spirited; perh. swaggering: ". . . change/ Command into obedience: fear, and niceness . . . into a waggish courage . . ." *Cymb,* III, iv, 156–159.

waggoner or **wagoner,** *n.* driver of a chariot; charioteer: "Her waggoner a small grey-coated gnat,/ Not half so big as a round little worm . . ." *Rom & Jul,* I, iv, 67–68.

wagtail, *n.* small bird that wags its tail as it walks; here, a ref. to Oswald's nervous fidgeting: "Spare my grey beard,/ you wagtail?" *Lear,* II, ii, 67–68.

wail, *v.* **1** to bewail; weep over: "What willingly he did confound [destroy], he wail'd,/ Believe 't, till I wept too." *Ant & Cleo,* III, ii, 58–59. **2** to make a show of lamenting: "Whose loves I may not drop, but wail his fall/ Who I myself struck down . . ." *Mac,* III, i, 121–122.

wailful, *adj.* mournful: ". . . to tangle her desires/ By wailful sonnets . . ." *Two Gent,* III, ii, 68–69.

wailing robes, *n. pl.* garments of mourning: "Away with these disgraceful wailing robes!" *1 Hen 6,* I, i, 86.

wain, *n.* See **Charles' wain.**

wainrope, *n.* heavy rope for hitching an ox to a wagon: "I think oxen and wainropes/ cannot hale them together." *T Night,* III, ii, 57–58.

waist, *n.* beam or mid-section of a ship: "Now in the waist, the deck, in every cabin,/ I flam'd amazement . . ." *Temp,* I, ii, 197–198.

wait, *v.* **1** to attend; do service: "And I will wish thee never more to dance,/ Nor never more in Russian habit wait." *Love's L,* V, ii, 400–401. **2 wait on or upon, a.** to attend; join or accompany: ". . . good my lords, keep on;/ I'll wait upon you instantly." *Timon,* II, i, 39–40. **b.** to be at the service of: "The heyday in the blood is tame, it's humble,/ And waits upon the judgment . . ." *Ham,* III, iv, 69–70. **c.** to listen to; pay attention to: "Lucius and I'll go brave it at the court . . . and we'll be waited on." *T Andr,* IV, i, 121–122. **3 wait on her,** be part of her dowry: "I am content; so the maiden cities you talk/ of may wait on her . . ." *Hen 5,* V, ii, 344–345. **4 wait on us,** are at our disposal (or command): "But if he will not yield,/ Rebuke and dread correction wait on us." *1 Hen 4,* V, i, 110–111.

wait close, *v.* (to) stay nearby: "Wait close, I will not see him." *2 Hen 4,* I, ii, 57.

wake, *n.* **1** annual church festival: "He is wit's pedlar, and retails his wares/ At wakes, and wassails, meetings, markets, fairs . . ." *Love's L,* V, ii, 317–318.
—*v.* **2** to stay up late; here, carouse far into the night: "The King doth wake tonight and takes his rouse . . ." *Ham,* I, iv, 8. **3** to stay awake till [my eyeballs fall out]: "Do't, and to bed then."/ "I'll wake mine eye-balls out first." *Cymb,* III, iv, 102–103. **4** to be unable to sleep: ". . . the disdain and shame/ whereof hath ever since kept Hector fasting and/ waking." *Tr & Cr,* I, ii, 35–37. **5 wake and wage,** to embark on and risk: "Neglecting an attempt of ease, and gain,/ To wake and wage a danger profitless." *Oth,* I, iii, 29–30. **6 waking?,** Am I awake?: "Ha! waking? 'tis not so./ Who is it that can tell me who I am?" *Lear,* I, iv, 237–238.

walk, *v.* **1** to go [in]: "My lord, will you walk? Dinner is ready." *M Ado,* II, iii, 202. **2** to withdraw to a cleared area suitable for dueling: "Tybalt, you rat-catcher, will you walk?" *Rom & Jul,* III, i, 74. **3** to exercise: "I will rather/ trust a Fleming with my butter . . . or a thief to walk my ambling/ gelding . . ." *Wives,* II, ii, 290–294. **4** to proceed; progress: "How wildly then walks my estate in France!" *K John,* IV, ii, 128. **5 walk i' th' sun,** out-of-doors; hence, watch her closely: "Let her not walk i' th' sun." *Ham,* II, ii, 184. **6 walk off,** usually given as an order to depart: "Sirrah, walk off. [Exit Man.]" *Tr & Cr,* III, ii, 5. **7 walk too late,** prob. euphem. for "live too long": "And the right-valiant Banquo walk'd too late . . ." *Mac,* III, vi, 5.
—*n.* **8** course or progress; here, the sun's journey across the sky: ". . . not an hour/ In the day's glorious walk . . . can breed me quiet." *Per,* I, ii, 4–6. **9** [pl.] gardens, arbors, woods, etc.: "My parks, my walks, my manors that I had,/ Even now forsake me . . ." *3 Hen 6,* V, ii, 24.

walk a bout, to dance a measure or part of a dance: "Lady, will you walk a bout with your friend?" *M Ado,* II, i, 79.

wall, *n.* **1 hang by the walls,** likened to unused armor or clothing that was hung on the walls: "And, for I am richer than to hang by th' walls,/ I must be ripp'd . . ." *Cymb,* III, iv, 53–54. **2 take the wall,** to walk on the part of the footpath away from the gutter; hence, to assert one's superiority: "I will/ take the wall of any man or maid of Montague's." *Rom & Jul,* I, i, 10–11. **3 the walls are thine,** Regan, in surrendering herself to Edmund, uses the figure of a vanquished castle: "Dispose of them, of me; the walls are thine . . ." *Lear,* V, iii, 77.

wallet, *n.* **1** knapsack or bag carried on the back; here, symbol of forgetfulness: "Time hath, my lord, a wallet at his back/ Wherein he puts alms for oblivion . . ." *Tr & Cr,* III, iii, 145–146. **2** appar. var. of **wattle:** "Dew-lapp'd like bulls, whose throats had hanging at 'em/ Wallets of flesh?" *Temp,* III, iii, 45–46.

wall-eyed, *adj.* staring; glaring: "Say, wall-ey'd slave, whither would'st thou convey/ This growing image of thy fiend-like face?" *T Andr,* V, i, 44–45.

wall-newt, *n.* wall lizard: "Poor Tom; that eats the swimming frog . . . the wall-newt, and the water . . ." *Lear,* III, iv, 132–133.

Walloon, *n.* native of the northernmost region of France [now S Belgium]: "A base Walloon, to win the Dauphin's grace,/ Thrust Talbot with a spear into the back . . ." *1 Hen 6,* I, i, 137–138.

wan, *v.* variant form of **won:** ". . . show'd like a feast,/ And wan by rareness such solemnity." *1 Hen 4,* III, ii, 58–59.

wand, *n.* branch; rod: "The skilful shepherd pill'd me certain wands . . ." *Merch,* I, iii, 79.

wandering planet, *n.* (in astrology) planet, star, etc., that governs the lives of those born during its ascendancy: ". . . hath this lovely face/ Rul'd like a wandering planet over me . . ." *2 Hen 6,* IV, iv, 15–16.

wane, *v.* **by waning grown,** beauty increases as that of his friends fades: "Who hast by waning grown, and therein show'st/ Thy lovers withering . . ." *Sonn 126,* 3–4.

waned, *adj.* faded; also, withered: "Salt Cleopatra, soften thy wan'd lip!" *Ant & Cleo,* II, i, 21.

wanion, *n.* **with a wanion,** with a vengeance: ". . . come away, or I'll/ fetch'th [thee] with a wanion" *Per,* II, i, 16–17.

wanny, *adj.* pale; faded; pallid: "The roses in thy lips and cheeks shall fade/ To wanny ashes . . ." *Rom & Jul,* IV, i, 99–100.

want, *v.* **1** to lack; be in need (of): ". . . he that wants money, means, and content is without three good friends . . ." *As You,* III, ii, 24–25. **2** to require: "I will draw a bill of properties, such as our play wants." *M N Dream,* I, ii, 98–99. **3** to experience want; crave or demand more: "A swallowing gulf that even in plenty wanteth." *Luc,* 557. **4 to want,** through (or as a result of) wanting: ". . . dare not offer/ What I desire to give;/ and much less take/ What I shall die to want." *Temp,* III, i, 77–79.

—*n.* **5 worth the want that you have wanted,** [you] deserve to be treated badly because you have behaved badly [toward your father]: ". . . you have obedience scanted,/ And well are worth the want that you have wanted." *Lear,* I, i, 278–279.

wanton, *n.* **1** lewd woman; harlot: ". . . not to knit my soul/ To an approved wanton." *M Ado,* IV, i, 43–44. **2** idler; wastrel or profligate: "Or shall we play the wantons with our woes,/ And make some pretty match with shedding tears?" *Rich 2,* III, iii, 164–165. **3** foolish and willful woman: "Tarry, rash wanton;/ am not I thy lord?" *M N Dream,* II, i, 63. **4** spoiled or capricious child: ". . . no farther than a wanton's bird,/ That lets it hop a little from his hand . . ." *Rom & Jul,* II, ii, 177–178. **5** lively creature; here, used humorously: ". . . she knapp'd/ 'em o' th' coxcombs with a stick, and cried/ 'Down, wantons, down!'" *Lear,* II, iv, 123–125. **6 make a wanton of,** to treat like a spoiled child; here, and allow to win: "I pray you pass with your best violence./ I am afeard you make a wanton of me." *Ham,* V, ii, 303–304.

—*adj.* **7** lusty; vigorous: "Wanton as youthful goats, wild as young bulls." *1 Hen 4,* IV, i, 103. **8** lustful; licentious: ". . . we have laugh'd to see the sails conceive/ and grow big-bellied with the wanton wind . . ." *M N Dream,* II, i, 128–129. **9** excited; impetuous: "Now comes the wanton blood up in your cheeks." *Rom & Jul,* II, v, 71. **10** unruly; turbulent: "What with the injuries of a wanton time . . ." *1 Hen 4,* V, i, 50. **11** foolish; trivial or frivolous: ". . . thou sickly coif!/ Thou art a guard too wanton for the head . . ." *2 Hen 4,* I, i, 147–148. **12** loving luxury: "While he, young wanton and effeminate boy . . ." *Rich 2,* V, iii, 10. **13** mischievous: ". . . the weak wanton Cupid/ Shall from your neck unloose his amorous fold . . ." *Tr & Cr,* III, iii, 221–222. **14** ambiguous; misleading: ". . . they that dally nicely with/ words may quickly make them wanton." *T Night,* III, i, 14–15. **15** luxuriant: "Four lagging winters and four wanton springs/ End in a word . . ." *Rich 2,* I, iii, 214–215. **16** unrestrained; overflowing: "My plenteous joys,/ Wanton in fulness, seek to hide themselves . . ." *Mac,* I, iv, 33–34. **17** playful; frolicsome: ". . . a blossom passing fair,/ Playing in the wanton air." *Pass Pil,* XVI, 3–4.

—*adv.* **18** wantonly; lewdly: "Pinch wanton on your cheek, call you his mouse . . ." *Ham,* III, iv, 185.

—*v.* **19** to engage in amorous play; dally: "To wait, said I? to wanton with this queen,/ This goddess, this Semiramis, this nymph . . ." *T Andr,* II, i, 21–22.

wantonness, *n.* affectation; capriciousness: ". . . you nickname/ God's creatures, and make your wantonness/ your ignorance [pretend you don't know any better]." *Ham,* III, i, 146–147.

wanton warrior, *n.* Cupid: "For that is she herself, and thence it comes/ That poets term the wanton warrior blind." *Edw 3,* II, ii, 68–69.

wanton white, *n.* delicate or effeminate blond: "Not wanton white, but such a manly color/ Next to an aborn [auburn] . . ." *Kinsmen,* IV, ii, 124–125.

want the thought, *v.* See **thought** (def. 8).

want-wit, *n.* idiot: "And such a want-wit sadness makes of me . . ." *Merch,* I, i, 6.

wappened, *adj.* used up; worn out: "This is it/ That makes the wappen'd widow wed again . . ." *Timon,* IV, iii, 38–39.

war, *n.* **1** hostile or provocative actions: "Pompey's name strikes more [causes more terror]/ Than could his war resisted [armed retaliation for his actions]." *Ant & Cleo,* I, iv, 54–55. **2 war of white and damask,** risk of damage [sunburn] to pink and white complexions: "Our veil'd dames/ Commit the war of white and damask in/ Their nicely gauded cheeks . . ." *Cor,* II, i, 213–215.

—*v.* **3** to take issue; disagree: "In that I'll war with you." *Tr & Cr,* III, ii, 169.

ward, *n.* **1** lock; bolt: "Doors that were ne'er acquainted with their wards . . ." *Timon,* III, iii, 39. **2** locked box; safe: "That to my use it might unused stay . . . in sure wards of trust!" *Sonn 48,* 3–4. **3** guard; defense: ". . . the best ward of mine/ honour is rewarding my dependents." *Love's L,* III, i, 128. **4** (in fencing) any of various postures of defense: "You are such a woman, a man knows not at/ what ward you lie." *Tr & Cr,* I, ii, 263–264. **5** prison cell: "A goodly one, in which there are many confines,/ wards, and dungeons . . ." *Ham,* II, ii, 245–246. **6** [often pl.] defensive gestures: ". . . what wards, what blows, what/ extremities he endured . . ." *1 Hen 4,* I, ii, 183–184. **7** place to be defended; defensive position: ". . . my mask, to defend my/ beauty; and you, to defend all these; and at all/ these wards I lie . . ." *Tr & Cr,* I, ii, 267–269. **8 in ward,** his father deceased, Bertram becomes ward of the king until attaining his majority: "I must attend his majesty's command, to/ whom I am now in ward . . ." *All's W,* I, i, 4–5. **9 to ward,** into custody: ". . . ere they will have me go to ward,/ They'll pawn their swords for my enfranchisement." *2 Hen 6,* V, i, 111–112.

—*v.* **10** to guard or protect: "Tell him it was a hand that warded him/ From thousand dangers . . ." *T Andr,* III, i, 194–195.

-ward, *suff.* toward: "Their powers are marching unto Paris-ward." *1 Hen 6* III, iii, 30.

warden pie, *n.* pie made of warden pears: "I must have saffron to colour the warden pies . . ." *W Tale,* IV, iii, 45.

warder, *n.* **1** guard or keeper: ". . . memory, the warder of the brain,/ Shall be a fume . . ." *Mac,* I, vii, 66–67. **2** baton or staff held by the person presiding over a combat: ". . . when the King did throw his warder down [canceling the match],/ His own life hung upon the staff he threw . . ." *2 Hen 4,* IV, i, 125–126.

ware¹, *v.* **1** [to] beware: "Ware pencils, ho!" *Love's L,* V, ii, 43. —*adj.* **2** aware: "Come, come, you'll do him/ wrong ere you are ware . . ." *Tr & Cr,* IV, ii, 56–57.

ware², *v.* old past tense of **wear;** wore: "I am his first-born son that was the last/ That ware the imperial diadem of Rome . . ." *T Andr,* I, i, 5–6.

Ware, *n.* **bed of Ware,** famous bed some 11 ft. sq., now in the Victoria and Albert Museum, London [from the name of the town where the bed was located at a local inn]: ". . . although the sheet were big enough for the/ bed of Ware in England, set 'em down." *T Night,* III, ii, 45–46.

warlike, *adj.* **like warlike as,** as ferocious as: "Like warlike as the wolf for what we eat . . ." *Cymb,* III, iii, 41.

warm, *adj.* **1 go warm,** (to) wear enough to keep warm: "If only to go warm were gorgeous . . ." *Lear,* II, iv, 270. **2 keep you warm,** (to) have the minimum amount of good sense: "Am I not wise?"/ "Yes, keep you warm." *Shrew,* II, i, 259.

war-man, *n.* warrior: "The sweet war-man is dead and rotten . . ." *Love's L,* V, ii, 653.

war-marked footmen, *n.* veteran foot soldiers: "Distract your army, which doth most consist/ Of war-mark'd footmen . . ." *Ant & Cleo,* III, vii, 43–44.

warm of blood, *adj.* strong in passion: "Full warm of blood, of mirth, of gossiping." *K John,* V, ii, 59.

warn, *v.* **1** to summon: "This sight of death is as a bell/ That warns my old age to a sepulchre." *Rom & Jul,* V, iii, 205–206. **2** to challenge: "They mean to warn us at Philippi here,/ Answering before we do demand of them." *J Caes,* V, i, 5.

warp, *v.* **1** to change or alter: "Though thou the waters warp [freeze]/ Thy sting is not so sharp . . ." *As You,* II, vii, 187–188. **2** to deviate: "There is our commission,/ From which we would not have you warp." *Meas,* I, i, 13–14. **3** to change

for the worse: "My favour here begins to warp." *W Tale,* I, ii, 365.

warped, *adj.* contorted or distorted: "And here's another, whose warp'd looks proclaim/ What store her heart is made on." *Lear,* III, vi, 53–54.

war-proof, *adj.* **of war-proof,** proven in warfare: "Whose blood is fet from fathers of war-proof . . ." *Hen 5,* III, i, 18.

warrant, *v.* **1** to spare or protect, esp. in the phrase "God warr'nt us!": ". . . for lovers lacking—God warr'nt us!—matter, the cleanliest shift is to kiss." *As You,* IV, i, 73–74. **2** to justify: ". . . true nobility/ Warrants these words in princely courtesy." *T Andr,* I, i, 272. **3** to guarantee: ". . . rather like a dream than an assurance/ That my remembrance warrants." *Temp,* I, ii, 45–46. **4** wordplay on "assure" and "arrest order": "I warrant your honour."/ "The warrant's for yourself: take heed to't." *Meas,* V, i, 85–86. **5 warrant him for,** (to) guarantee him against: "I'll warrant him for drowning, though the ship/ were no stronger than a nutshell . . ." *Temp,* I, i, 46–47. —*n.* **6** authorization: "A pattern, president [precedent], and lively warrant/ For me . . . to perform the like." *T Andr,* V, iii, 44–45. **7** justification: "There's warrant in that theft/ Which steals itself, when there's no mercy left." *Mac,* II, iii, 145–146. **8** assurance; sign or token: "If you be one [a woman]—as you are well express'd/ By all external warrants—show it now . . ." *Meas,* II, iv, 135–136. **9** charge; command: "That judge hath made me guardian to this boy:/ Under whose warrant I impeach thy wrong . . ." *K John,* II, 1, 115–116. **10 in warrant from himself,** on his own authority: "But nothing spake in warrant from himself." *Rich 3,* III, vii, 33. **11 modest warrant,** limited authority, as that restricting the hunter's kill: "Do not cry havoc where you should but hunt/ With modest warrant." *Cor,* III, i, 272–273. **12 of warrant,** allowed; legitimate: "Marry, sir, here's my drift,/ And I believe it is a fetch of warrant." *Ham,* II, i, 38–39. **13 out of warrant,** unlawfully: ". . . a practiser/ Of arts inhibited, and out of warrant . . ." *Oth,* I, ii, 78–79. **14 warrant of my note,** See **note** (def. 24). **15 with warrant,** lawfully: ". . . your/ bride goes to that with shame which is her way to/ go with warrant." *Per,* IV, ii, 125–127.

warranted, *adj.* **1** just; worthy: ". . . the chance of goodness/ Be like our warranted quarrel [cause]." *Mac,* IV, iii, 136–137. **2 upon a warranted need,** should sufficient reason need to be proved: ". . . the business he hath/ helmed, must upon a warranted need give him a/ better proclamation." *Meas,* III, ii, 138–140.

warrantize or **warrantise,** *n.* guarantee; surety: "Break up [open] the gates, I'll be your warrantize." *1 Hen 6,* I, iii, 13.

warren, *n.* gamekeeper's yard: "I found him here as melancholy as a lodge/ in a warren." *M Ado,* II, i, 199–200.

warrener, *n.* gamekeeper: ". . . tall man of his hands . . . he hath fought/ with a warrener." *Wives,* I, iv, 23–25.

wary, *adj.* careful; cautious: "O! therefore, love be of thyself so wary . . ." *Sonn 22,* 9.

wash, *n.* **1** hog-swill: "Swills your warm blood like wash . . ." *Rich 3,* V, ii, 9. **2** [pl.] See **Lincoln Washes.**
—*v.* **3 wash my brain,** drink heavily: "It's monstrous labour when I wash my brain/ And it grow fouler." *Ant & Cleo,* II, vii, 98–99.

washed, *adj.* **1** cleansed with tears: ". . . with wash'd eyes/ Cordelia leaves you . . ." *Lear,* I, i, 268–269.
—*past part.* **2** carried away by a wave, etc.: ". . . a plague on them, they/ ne'er come but I look to be wash'd!" *Per,* II, i, 25–26.

Washford, *n.* old name of **Wexford,** in SE Ireland: "Created for his rare success in arms/ Great Earl of Washford . . ." *1 Hen 6,* IV, vii, 62–63.

washing or **swashing,** *adj.* swashbuckling, slashing or smashing: "Draw if you be men. Gregory, remember thy/ washing blow." *Rom & Jul,* I, i, 59–60.

waspish-headed, *adj.* peevish; quick-tempered: "Her waspish-headed son [Cupid] has broke his arrows,/ Swears he will shoot no more . . ." *Temp,* IV, i, 99–100.

wassail, *n.* drinking feast; revel or carousing: "He is wit's pedlar, and retails his wares/ At wakes, and wassails, meetings, markets, fairs . . ." *Love's L,* V, ii, 317–318.

wassail candle, *n.* large candle, used at feasts and meant to burn all night: "A wassail candle, my lord, all tallow . . ." *2 Hen 4,* I, ii, 157.

wast, *v.* old form of **was:** "If ere thou wast thyself, and these woes thine,/ Thou and these woes were all for Rosaline." *Rom & Jul,* II, iii, 73–74.

waste, *v.* **1** to pass (time) agreeably: "I like this place,/ And willingly could waste my time in it." *As You,* II, iv, 92–93. **2** to obliterate (time) by condensing: "Thus time we waste, and long leagues make short . . ." *Per,* IV, iv, 1. **3** to use up: ". . . the King hath wasted all his rods/ On late offenders . . ." *2 Hen 4,* IV, i, 215–216. **4** to erase; blot out: ". . . that action hence borne out/ May waste the memory of the former days." *2 Hen 4,* IV, v, 214–215.
—*n.* **5** vast empty space: "In the dead waste and middle of the night . . ." *Ham,* I, ii, 198. **6** unnecessary expense: "And feast

the army; we have store to do 't,/ And they have earn'd the waste." *Ant & Cleo,* IV, i, 15–16. **7** damage; destruction [legal term]: ". . . he will never . . . in the way/ of waste attempt us again." *Wives,* IV, ii, 198–199.

waste blanks, *n.* empty or blank pages: ". . . what thy memory cannot contain,/ Commit to these waste blanks . . ." *Sonn 77,* 9–10.

wasted, *adj.* physically consumed or spent; decayed: "Would he were wasted, marrow, bones, and all . . ." *3 Hen 6,* III, ii, 125.

wasted brands, *n.* logs burned down to embers: "Now the wasted brands do glow . . ." *M N Dream,* V, i, 361.

wasted time, *n.* bygone days: "When in the chronicle of wasted time . . ." *Sonn 106,* 1.

wasteful, *adj.* devastating: ". . . and his soul/ Shall stand sore charged for the wasteful vengeance . . ." *Hen 5,* I, ii, 282–283.

Wat, *n.* hunter's nickname for a hare: "By this, poor Wat, far off upon a hill . . ." *Ven & Ad,* 697.

watch, *v.* **1** to keep watch or vigil; also, to carouse: "Watch tonight, pray tomorrow!" *1 Hen 4,* II, iv, 273. **2** to go without sleep; remain awake: "A great perturbation in nature,/ to receive at once/ the benefit of sleep, and do the effects of watching!" *Mac,* V, i, 9–10. **3** (in falconry) to train (a hawk) to obedience by forcing it to remain awake: "And in conclusion she shall watch all night,/ And if she chance to nod I'll rail and brawl . . ." *Shrew,* IV, i, 192–193. **4** to wait expectantly for: ". . . my revenges were high bent upon him/ And watch'd the time to shoot." *All's W,* V, iii, 10–11.
—*n.* **5** watchman or watchmen: "Even such, they say, as stand in narrow lanes/ And beat our watch . . ." *Rich 2,* V, iii, 8–9. **6** watchword: ". . . the wolf,/ Whose howl's his watch . . ." *Mac,* II, i, 53–54. **7** interval of time: ". . . and with sighs they jar/ Their watches on unto mine eyes . . ." *Rich 2,* V, v, 51–52. **8** period of sleeplessness: ". . . mine eyes, the outward watch,/ Whereto my finger, like a dial's point,/ Is pointing still . . ." *Rich 2,* V, v, 52–54. **9** period of watchful guard: ". . . in gross brain little wots/ What watch the king keeps to maintain the peace . . ." *Hen 5,* IV, i, 288–289. **10** watch light; candle; also, poss., a guard: "Fill me a bowl of wine. Give me a watch." *Rich 3,* V, iii, 64. **11 at a thousand watches,** in a state of constant vigilance: ". . . at all/ these wards I lie, at a thousand watches." *Tr & Cr,* I, ii, 268–269. **12 in watch,** awake: "To lie in watch there, and to think on him?" *Cymb,* III, iv, 42. **13 set the watch,** to post guards at the city gates: ". . . look thou stay not till the Watch be set,/ For then thou canst not pass to Mantua . . ." *Rom & Jul,* III, iii, 147–148. **14 watch of woes,** enumeration of woes in the manner of a watchman who calls

out the hours: "Base watch of woes, sin's pack-horse, virtue's snare!" *Luc,* 928.

watch-case, *n.* confined space, as a sentry box, where one must keep watch: ". . . and leav'st the kingly couch/ A watch-case, or a common 'larum-bell?" *2 Hen 4,* III, i, 16–17.

watched, *past part.* fr. the practice of taming a hawk by not allowing it to sleep for three days: "You must be watched ere you be made/ tame, must you?" *Tr & Cr,* III, ii, 42–43.

watchful, *adj.* **1** causing sleeplessness: "What watchful cares do interpose themselves . . ." *J Caes,* II, i, 98. **2** constantly spying: ". . . our exil'd friends abroad,/ That fled the snares of watchful tyranny . . ." *Mac,* V, ix, 32–33.

watching, *n.* sleeplessness; here, a sleepless night: "I am for you, though it cost me ten/ nights' watchings." *M Ado,* II, i, 348–349.

water, *n.* **1** degree of luster in a diamond: "Here is a water, look ye." *Timon,* I, i, 18. **2** urine; diseases, including possession by devils, were thought to be detectable in a person's urine: "Pray God he be not bewitched!"/ "Carry his water to th' wise woman." *T Night,* III, iv, 102–103. **3** water-newt: "Poor Tom; that eats the swimming frog . . . the wall-newt, and the water . . ." *Lear,* III, iv, 132–133. **4 cast the water,** to examine the urine as an aid to diagnosing a disease: "Doctor, cast/ The water of my land, find her disease . . ." *Mac,* V, iii, 50–51. **5 for all waters,** able to do anything: "Nay, I am for all waters." *T Night,* IV, ii, 65. **6 go by water,** be communicated by tears: ". . . nor answer have I none,/ But what should go by water . . ." *Oth,* IV, ii, 105–106. **7 in standing water,** at the turning of the tide: "'Tis with him/ in standing water, between boy and man." *T Night,* I, v, 160–161. **8 raise the waters,** to cause tears: "Mark me now, now will I raise the waters . . ." *Merch,* II, ii, 46. **9 shed water out of fire,** shed tears from fiery eyes: ". . . though a devil/ Would have shed water out of fire, ere done 't . . ." *W Tale,* III, ii, 192–193. **10 water that doth eat in steel,** prob. aqua fortis [nitric acid]: "And grave like water that doth eat in steel,/ Upon my cheeks, what helpless shame I feel." *Luc,* 755–756.

water-fly, *n.* seemingly useless creature that flits about to no purpose; Osric appar. is an elegant fop: "Dost know this water-fly?" *Ham,* V, ii, 83.

water-gall, *n.* broken rainbow, regarded as an omen of bad weather: "Those water-galls . . . Foretell new storms to those already spent." *Luc,* 1588–1589.

watering, *n.* drinking: ". . . and when/ you breathe in your watering they cry 'Hem!' . . ." *1 Hen 4,* II, iv, 15–16.

water-rug, *n.* shaggy-haired water dog: "Shoughs, water-rugs, and demi-wolves, are clept/ All by the name of dogs . . ." *Mac,* III, i, 93–94.

waterwork, *n.* scene painted on cloth or on a plaster wall to simulate a tapestry: ". . . the German hunting, in waterwork, is/ worth a thousand of these bed-hangers . . ." *2 Hen 4,* II, i, 143–144.

watery moon, *n.* ref. to moon as the feminine planet and its supposed resemblance to a tearful eye: "That I, being govern'd by the watery moon,/ May send forth plenteous tears . . ." *Rich 3,* II, ii, 69–70.

watery star, *n.* moon; here, ref. to the passage of nine months: "Nine changes of the watery star hath been/ The shepherd's note . . ." *W Tale,* I, ii, 1–2.

wave, *v.* **1** to waver; fluctuate: ". . . he waved indifferently 'twixt doing them/ neither good nor harm . . ." *Cor,* II, ii, 17–18. **2** to bow: ". . . waving thy head,/ Which often, thus, correcting thy stout heart . . ." *Cor,* III, ii, 77–78.

wawl, *v.* (of an infant) to howl; bawl: ". . . the first time that we smell the air/ We wawl and cry." *Lear,* IV, vi, 181–182.

wax¹, *v.* **1** to become: ". . . the days are wax'd shorter with him . . ." *Timon,* III, iv, 11. **2** to grow larger: "That was the way to make his godhead wax . . ." *Love's L,* V, ii, 10.

wax², *adj.* **1 of wax,** handsome or as perfect as a wax model: "Lady, such a man/ As all the world—why, he's a man of wax." *Rom & Jul,* I, iii, 75–76.
—*n.* **2** wax seal on the letter: "Leave, gentle wax; and manners, blame us not . . ." *Lear,* IV, vi, 261. **3 form of wax,** a waxwork; dummy: "Thy noble shape is but a form of wax/ Digressing from the valour of a man . . ." *Rom & Jul,* III, iii, 125–126.

waxen¹, *adj.* **1** as if made of wax: ". . . steel my lance's point,/ That it may enter Mowbray's waxen coat . . ." *Rich 2,* I, iii, 74–75. **2** impressionable or vulnerable: "How easy is it for the proper false/ In women's waxen hearts to set their forms!" *T Night,* II, i, 28–29. **3** short-lived; temporary: ". . . else our grave . . . shall have a tongueless mouth,/ Not worshipp'd [but] with a waxen epitaph." *Hen 5,* I, ii, 231–233.

waxen², *v.* **1** to increase [archaic form]: ". . . hold their hips and loffe/ And waxen in their mirth . . ." *M N Dream,* II, i, 55–56.
—*past part.* **2** grown; become: "What! art thou, like the adder, waxen deaf?" *2 Hen 6,* III, ii, 75.

way, *n.* **1** a road: "Will she/ hold out water in foul way?" *1 Hen 4,* II, i, 82–83. **2** passage; entrance: "Belike his wife . . . shut the doors against his way—" *Errors,* IV, iii, 88. **3** one's best course of action: "My way is now to hie home to his house,/ And tell his wife . . ." *Errors,* IV, iii, 89–90. **4** freedom of action: ". . . gave him way/ In all his own desires . . ." *Cor,* V, vi, 32–33. **5** condition; here, Anne's virginity: "I would not be a young count in your way/ For more than blushing comes to [I would part with my virginity with no more than a blush] . . ." *Hen 8,* II, iii, 41–42. **6** way of life: "Men of his way should be most liberal . . ." *Hen 8,* I, iii, 61. **7** access; introduction: "Come. I will give you way for these your letters." *Ham,* IV, vi, 29. **8 all ways,** in every direction: "Fairies, be gone, and be all ways away." *M N Dream,* IV, i, 40. **9 by the way,** along the way; en route: "By th'way we met/ My wife, her sister, and a rabble more/ Of vile confederates . . ." *Errors,* V, i, 235–237. **10 catch the nearest way,** to take advantage of the easiest or most obvious method: ". . . too full o' th' milk of human kindness,/ To catch the nearest way." *Mac,* I, v, 17–18. **11 come your ways,** to come; come along: "Come your ways, my masters; you say she's a/ virgin?" *Per,* IV, ii, 38–39. **12 from the way,** out of the way; in some remote place: "Some dark deep desert seated from the way . . ." *Luc,* 1144. **13 give even way,** make as easy as possible: "I pray thee . . . Give even way unto my rough affairs . . ." *2 Hen 4,* II, iii, 1–2. **14 give him way,** let him have his way: "'Tis best to give him way; he leads himself [he won't listen to anyone else]." *Lear,* II, iv, 300. **15 give it way,** to give in to; do not resist: "Thou art inclin'd to sleep; 'tis a good dulness,/ And give it way . . ." *Temp,* I, ii, 185–186. **16 go thy ways,** [to] go; go on: "Petruchio, go thy ways, the field is won." *Shrew,* IV, v, 23. **17 have way,** to be given scope: "Let me have way, my lord,/ To find this practice out." *Meas,* V, i, 237–238. **18 here lies your way,** you had better go; this way out: "Will you hoist sail, sir? Here lies your way." *T Night,* I, v, 204. **19 in one's way,** inhibiting one's ability to function: "Fellow, thank God, and the/ good wine in thy master's way." *2 Hen 6,* II, iii, 92–93. **20 in the way,** nearby; at hand: "If 'a be in debt and theft, and a sergeant in the way,/ Hath he not reason to turn back an hour in a day?" *Errors,* IV, ii, 61–62. **21 keep your way,** go ahead: "Nay, keep your way, little gallant; you were/ wont to be a follower . . ." *Wives,* III, ii, 1–2. **22 make one's way,** to advance or get ahead: "The force of his own merit makes his way . . ." *Hen 8,* I, i, 64. **23 no way to that,** no way compares to that: "No way to that, for weakness, which she enter'd." *1 Hen 6,* III, ii, 25. **24 out o' th' way,** gone astray: "God amend us, God amend! we are much out o' th' way." *Love's L,* IV, iii, 73. **25 rid way,** to make the distance seem shorter: "We, having now the best at Barnet field,/ Will thither straight, for willingness rids way . . ." *3 Hen 6,* V, iii, 20–21. **26 take one's way,** to leave on a journey: "How careful was I when I took my way . . ." *Sonn 48,* 1. **27 the next way,** the nearest or closest way: "A prophet I, madam; and I speak the truth the next way . . ." *All's W,* I, iii, 56. **28 which is the way?** What is the latest fashion?: "Which is the way? Is it/ sad, and few words?" *Meas,* III, ii, 49–50.

wayward, *adj.* unpredictable or uncontrollable; perverse: "Pericles/ Is now again thwarting the wayward seas . . ." *Per,* IV, iv, 9–10.

weak, *adj.* **1** low or base; contemptible: ". . . truly it were an ill thing to be/ offered to any gentlewoman, and very weak dealing." *Rom & Jul,* II, iv, 166–167. **2** of unsound faith: "By sick interpreters (once weak ones) . . ." *Hen 8,* I, ii, 82. **3** undeveloped; nascent: "Within the infant rind of this weak flower/ Poison hath residence . . ." *Rom & Jul,* II, iii, 19.

weak-built, *adj.* lacking a factual basis: "Though weak-built hopes persuade him to abstaining." *Luc,* 130.

weaker vessel, *n.* woman, esp. a young lady: "For Jaquenetta—so is the weaker vessel/called—which I apprehended with the aforesaid swain . . ." *Love's L,* I, i, 265–266.

weal, *n.* **1** happiness; success or well-being: "Brief sounds determine of my weal or woe." *Rom & Jul,* III, ii, 51. **2** commonwealth; Roman state: ". . . the charters that you bear/ I'th'body of the weal . . ." *Cor,* II, iii, 178–179. **3 the general weal,** the common welfare: "Of him that . . . Smells from the general weal." *Timon,* IV, iii, 161–162. **4 the gentle weal,** the civilized state or commonwealth: ". . . i' th' olden time,/ Ere humane statute purg'd the gentle weal . . ." *Mac,* III, iv, 74–75. **5 weal or woe,** success or failure: "Here will I sit . . . And will be partner of your weal or woe." *1 Hen 6,* III, ii, 91–92.

wealsman, *n.* statesman: "Meeting two such/ wealsmen as you are . . ." *Cor,* II, i, 53–54.

wealth, *n.* welfare; well-being: "I once did lend my body for his wealth,/ Which but for him . . . Had quite miscarried." *Merch,* V, i, 249–251.

wear, *n.* **1** fashion; style: "A worthy fool! Motley's the only wear." *As You,* II, vii, 34.
—*v.* **2** wear out; wear away; also, with sexual innuendo: "Could I repair what she will wear in me . . . 'Twere well for Kate and better for myself." *Shrew,* III, ii, 116–118. **3** to use; dedicate: "He was my master, and I wore my life/ To spend upon his haters." *Ant & Cleo,* V, i, 8–9. **4** to waste; run out: "Away, I say, time wears . . ." *Wives,* V, i, 7. **5 wear not now,** [it's] not done anymore; be out of fashion: ". . . like the brooch and the/ toothpick, which wear not now." *All's W,* I, i, 153–154. **6 wear out,** to outlast: ". . . and we'll wear out,/ In a wall'd prison, packs and sects of great ones . . ." *Lear,* V, iii, 17–18.

wearing, *n.* clothes: "Your high self . . . you have obscur'd/ With a swain's wearing . . ." *W Tale,* IV, iv, 8–9.

wear one's cap, (of a man) to wear a cap to conceal the horns of cuckoldry: ". . . hath not the world one/ man but he will wear his cap with suspicion?" *M Ado,* I, i, 183–184.

weary, *adj.* tiresome; tedious: "Not to be weary with you, he's in prison." *Meas,* I, iv, 25.

weasel, *n.* **night-wandering weasels,** prob. ferrets, let loose in the great houses at night to kill rats and mice: "Night-wand'ring weasels shriek to see him there . . ." *Luc,* 307.

weather, *n.* **keep the weather,** [in sailing] to be upwind; also, to have an advantage or be of greater importance: "Mine honour keeps the weather of my fate ..." *Tr & Cr,* V, iii, 26.

weathercock, *n.* prob. ref. to Robin's feathered hat: "Where had you this pretty weathercock?" *Wives,* III, ii, 15.

weather-fend, *v.* to protect from the weather: ". . . the linegrove which weather-fends your cell . . ." *Temp,* V, i, 10.

weaver's beam, *n.* (on a loom) the wooden beam to which the warp threads are attached [a Biblical allusion]: "I fear not/ Goliath with a weaver's beam . . ." *Wives,* V, i, 21–22.

web, *n.* covering: "Whose bare out-bragg'd the web it seem'd to wear . . ." *Lover's Comp,* 95.

web and pin, *n.* eye disease; cataract(s): ". . . he gives/ the web and the pin, squinies the eye . . ." *Lear,* III, iv, 119–120.

wed, *v.* to achieve: "Not to woo honour, but to wed it . . ." *All's W,* II, i, 15.

wedding knives, *n.* a pair of knives hung from the girdle of a bride's gown: "Here by my side doth hang my wedding knives:/ Take thou the one, and with it kill thy queen . . ." *Edw 3,* II, ii, 171–172.

wedge, *v.* **wedged with a sigh,** as though a sigh had driven a wedge [into my heart]: ". . . when my heart,/ As wedged with a sigh, would rive [split] in twain . . ." *Tr & Cr,* I, i, 34–35.

weed, *n.* **1** garment: "Weed wide enough to wrap a fairy in . . ." *M N Dream,* II, i, 256. **2** [often pl.] clothing: "Come let us hence, and put on other weeds . . ." *M Ado,* V, iii, 30. **3** figuratively, a covering: "I will rob Tellus of her weed,/ To strew thy green with flowers . . ." *Per,* IV, i, 13–14. **4 noted weed,** distinctive or characteristic style: "Why write I still all one, ever the same,/ And keep invention in a noted weed . . ." *Sonn 76,* 5–6.

—*v.* **5** to weed out; eliminate: "To weed my vice, and let his grow!" *Meas,* III, ii, 263.

week, *n.* **1 a whole week by days,** every day for an entire week: "You told how Diomed a whole week by days/ Did haunt you in the field." *Tr & Cr,* IV, i, 10–11. **2 in by the week,** caught; trapped or cornered: "That same Berowne I'll torture ere I go./ O! that I knew he were but in by the week." *Love's L,* V, ii, 60–61.

ween, *v.* **ween you of,** do you expect [to have]: "Ween you of better luck,/ I mean in perjur'd witness . . ." *Hen 8,* V, i, 135–136.

weening, *pres. part.* thinking; supposing: ". . . in pity of my hard distress,/ Levied an army, weening to redeem/ And have install'd me in the diadem . . ." *1 Hen 6,* II, v, 87–89.

weep, *v.* **weep you,** to lament you with tears: ". . . he will weep you and/ 'twere [as though he were] a man born in April." *Tr & Cr,* I, ii, 175–176.

weeping-ripe, *adj.* on the verge of tears: "The king was weeping-ripe for a good word." *Love's L,* V, ii, 274.

weet, *v.* to know: "I bind . . . the world to weet/ We stand up peerless." *Ant & Cleo,* I, i, 38–40.

weigh, *v.* **1** to consider: ". . . a great way growing on the south,/ Weighing the youthful season of the year." *J Caes,* II, i, 107–108. **2** to value: "I with mine enemies/ Will triumph o'er my person, which I weigh not . . ." *Hen 8,* V, i, 123–124. **3 as they weigh,** just as they are: ". . . but your people,/ I love them as they weigh—" *Cor,* II, ii, 73–74. **4 weigh not every stamp,** [in commercial transactions] not every [stamped] coin is weighed: "'Tween man and man they weigh not every stamp . . ." *Cymb,* V, iv, 24. **5 weigh not you,** don't weigh as much as you; wordplay on preceding "light" [wanton]: "Indeed I weigh not you, and therefore light." *Love's L,* V, ii, 26.

weight, *n.* burden: ". . . we do bear/ So great weight in his lightness." *Ant & Cleo,* I, iv, 24–25.

weïrd, *adj.* controlling fate; in Folio as "weyard" and "wayward", appar. phonetic spellings [pron. as two syllables]: "The Weïrd Sisters, hand in hand,/ Posters of the sea and land . . ." *Mac,* I, iii, 32–33.

welcome, *n.* **give it welcome,** belief that strangers must always be treated with unusual courtesy: "And therefore as a stranger give it welcome." *Ham,* I, v, 173.

we'ld, *v.* we would: "I would they'ld fight i' the fire, or i' the air,/ We'ld fight there too." *Ant & Cleo,* IV, x, 3–4.

welfare, *n.* **sick of welfare,** ill from too much health and happiness: "And, sick of welfare, found a kind of meetness/ To be diseased . . ." *Sonn 118,* 7–8.

welkin, *n.* **1** sky; vault of heaven: ". . . damn them with/ King Cerberus, and let the welkin roar!" *2 Hen 4,* II, iv, 164–165. **2** one's sphere of authority or activity: ". . . who you are and what you would are out of/ my welkin." *T Night,* III, i, 58–59. **3 welkin's cheek,** the (very) face of the sky: ". . . the sea, mounting to th' welkin's cheek,/ Dashes the fire out." *Temp,* I, ii, 4–5.
—*adj.* **4** blue: "Look on me with your welkin eye . . ." *W Tale,* I, ii, 136.

well, *adv.* **1** for certain; indeed: "Near Birnam wood/ Shall we well meet them: that way are they coming." *Mac,* V, ii, 5–6. **2 can well,** can do or perform well: "I have seen myself, and serv'd against, the French,/ And they can well on horse-back . . ." *Ham,* IV, vii, 83–84.

well-a-day, *interj.* **1** alas!: ". . . what pitiful cries they made to us to help them, when,/ well-a-day, we could scarce help our-selves." *Per,* II, i, 21–22.
—*n.* **2** grief: ". . . while our scene must play/ His daughter's woe and heavy well-a-day . . ." *Per,* IV, iv, 48–49.

well advised, *adj.* See **advised** (def. 10).

well-a-near, *interj.* alas!: "The lady shrieks and well-a-near/ Does fall in travail with her fear . . ." *Per,* III, Chor., 51–52.

well-appointed, *adj.* well-armed: "What well-appointed leader fronts us here?" *2 Hen 4,* IV, i, 25.

well-beseeming, *adj.* orderly; seemly: ". . . in mutual well-be-seeming ranks,/ March all one way . . ." *1 Hen 4,* I, i, 14–15.

well-breathed, *adj.* sound of wind: "And on thy well-breath'd horse keep with thy hounds." *Ven & Ad,* 678.

well-contented, *adj.* **my well-contented day,** the day of my death, which I shall not regret: "If thou survive my well-con-tented day . . ." *Sonn 32,* 1.

well-entered, *adj.* experienced: "'Tis our hope, sir,/ After well-ent'red [becoming seasoned] soldiers, to return/ And find your grace in health." *All's W,* II, i, 5–7.

well-favored, *adj.* **1** handsome: ". . . to be a well-favoured man is/ the gift of fortune . . ." *M Ado,* III, iii, 14–15. **2** gra-cious; charming: "Not so fair, boy, as well-favoured." *Two Gent,* II, i, 48.

well fed, ref. to the proverb "better fed than taught": "A good knave i'faith, and well fed." *All's W,* II, iv, 37.

well given, *adj.* well disposed: "The duke is virtuous, mild, and too well given/ To dream on evil . . ." *2 Hen 6,* III, i, 72–73.

well-liking, *adj.* sleek or fat; also, pun on "well-like-king": "Well-liking wits they have; gross, gross; fat, fat." *Love's L,* V, ii, 268.

well-lost, *adj.* **well-lost life,** well worth risking my life: "I'd venture/ The well-lost life of mine on his grace's cure . . ." *All's W,* I, iii, 242–243.

well met, *interj.* exclam. indicating a pleasurable encounter: "O my good knave Costard! exceedingly well met." *Love's L,* III, i, 139.

well-minded, *adj.* well disposed; kindly; sympathetic: "Well-minded Clarence, be thou fortunate . . ." *3 Hen 6,* IV, viii, 27.

well-noted, *adj.* well-known; familiar: ". . . the antique and well-noted face/ Of plain old form is much disfigured . . ." *K John,* IV, ii, 21–22.

well-respected, *adj.* well-considered: "If well-respected hon-our bid me on . . ." *1 Hen 4,* IV, iii, 10.

well said, *interj.* Well done!: "Well said, i'faith, Wart, th'art a good scab." *2 Hen 4,* III, ii, 270–271.

well-spoken, *adj.* refined: "To entertain these fair well-spo-ken days . . ." *Rich 3,* I, i, 29.

well to live, *adj.* wealthy; well off; here, prob. misused to mean "in good health": ". . . an honest exceeding poor man,/ and (God be thanked) well to live." *Merch,* II, ii, 49–50.

well-took, *adj.* well-rendered; well-executed: "Meantime, we thank you for your well-took labour." *Ham,* II, ii, 83.

well-warranted, *adj.* officially approved: ". . . my noble and well-warranted cousin . . ." *Meas,* V, i, 253.

well-willer, *n.* well-wisher: ". . . and I beseech you/ be ruled by your well-willers." *Wives,* I, i, 63–64.

Welsh flannel, *n.* contemp. term for "Welshman": "I am de-jected; I am not able to answer the Welsh/ flannel . . ." *Wives,* V, v, 163–164.

Welsh hook, *n.* large knife with a hooked end, used for chop-ping or pruning; bill-hook: ". . . swore the/ devil his true liege-man upon the cross of a Welsh/ hook . . ." *1 Hen 4,* II, iv, 333–335.

wen, *n.* tumor; fig., a large, swollen lump [ref. to Falstaff]: "I do allow this wen to be as familiar with me as/ my dog . . ." *2 Hen 4,* II, ii, 101–102.

wend, *v.* **wend you,** go; direct yourself: "Wend you with this letter." *Meas,* IV, iii, 145.

weraday, *interj.* alas!; alack!: "Ah weraday, he's dead, he's dead, he's dead!" *Rom & Jul,* III, ii, 37.

were, *v.* **1** would have seemed: "Within the Temple Hall we were too loud . . ." *1 Hen 6,* II, iv, 3. **2** would be or seem: "Returning were as tedious as go o'er." *Mac,* III, iv, 137.

wert, *v.* **1** old form of **were:** "If thou love me, 'tis time thou wert away." *Rich 2,* V, v, 96. **2 wert better,** [you] would be better off: "Thou wert better in a grave than to answer/ with thy uncover'd body this extremity of the/ skies." *Lear,* III, iv, 103–105.

west, *n.* **1 corner of the west,** England regarded as the western corner of the world: "Even till that utmost corner of the west/ Salute thee for her king . . ." *K John,* II, i, 29–30. **2 due west,** in the direction of the setting sun; here, a dismissal: "There lies your way, due west." *T Night,* III, i, 136.

westward ho! call of the Thames boatman to passengers wishing transportation from central London to the western part of the city: "There lies your way, due west."/ "Then westward ho!" *T Night,* III, i, 136.

wet, *n.* **applying wet to wet,** likened to the usurer who adds interest to interest: "Like usury, applying wet to wet . . ." *Lover's Comp,* 40.

wether, *n.* ram: "I am a tainted wether of the flock,/ Meetest for death . . ." *Merch,* IV, i, 114–115.

wetting, *n.* action of getting soaked [in the pool]: "That's more to me than my wetting . . ." *Temp,* IV, i, 211.

wezand, *n.* windpipe: ". . . paunch him with a stake,/ Or cut his wezand with thy knife." *Temp,* III, ii, 88–89.

whale, *n.* regarded as a destroyer of small (virginal) fish: ". . . a dangerous and lascivious boy, who is a whale to/ virginity, and devours up all the fry it finds." *All's W,* IV, iii, 212–213.

wharf, *n.* bank (of a stream): "A strange invisible perfume hits the sense/ Of the adjacent wharfs." *Ant & Cleo,* II, ii, 212–213.

what, *adv.* **1** why [used to introduce an exclam., esp. one of impatience]: "What, man! more water glideth by the mill/ Than wots the miller of . . ." *T Andr,* II, i, 85–86. **2** why? for what reason?: "How now, Sir John? What are you brawling here?" *2 Hen 4,* II, i, 63.
—*adj.* **3** whatever: ". . . you shall find in him the/ continent of what part [accomplishment or ability] a gentleman would

see." *Ham,* V, ii, 110–111. **4 what a,** what kind (of): "Out upon you. What a man are you?" *Rom & Jul,* II, iv, 113.
—*pron.* **5** what that is [or may be]: "But what particular rarity, what strange . . ." *Timon,* I, i, 4. **6 what cheer?,** See **cheer** (def. 7). **7 what needs?** See **need** (def. 4). **8 what they are,** cuckolds: "If men could be contented to be/ what they are, there were no fear in marriage . . ." *All's W,* I, iii, 48–49. **9 what though?** What difference does it make?: "What though he love your Hermia? Lord, what though?" *M N Dream,* II, ii, 108. **10 what to,** what of; what about: "But say, what to thine old news?" *Shrew,* III, ii, 40.

whate'er falls more, whatever else may happen: "And you shall find yourself to be well thank'd,/ Whate'er falls more." *All's W,* V, i, 36–37.

what else, whatever else: "I,/ Beyond all limit of what else i' th' world,/ Do love, prize, honour you." *Temp,* III, i, 71–73.

what else?, of course; to be sure: "And all his lands and goods be confiscate."/ "What else?" *3 Hen 6,* IV, vi, 55–56.

what hast thou to do? What business is it of yours?: "I will be angry; what hast thou to do?/ Father, be quiet . . ." *Shrew,* III, ii, 214–215.

what like, what he should most like: "What like, offensive." *Lear,* IV, ii, 11.

what news? what has happened?: "Hate me? Wherefor? O me! what news, my love?/ Am not I Hermia?" *M N Dream,* III, ii, 272–273.

what should? why should: "What should I don this robe, and trouble you?" *T Andr,* I, i, 189.

whatsomever, *pron.* var. of **whatever;** no matter what: "And whatsomever else shall hap tonight,/ Give it an understanding but no tongue." *Ham,* I, ii, 249–250.

what the good year! meaningless expression roughly equiv. to "What the deuce!": "We/ must give folks leave to prate: what the good year!" *Wives,* I, iv, 115–116.

what time, when: ". . . I made thee miserable/ What time I threw the people's suffrages/ On him . . ." *T Andr,* IV, iii, 18–20.

what 'tis to say, See **say**[1] (def. 5).

what you will, (to) do whatever is necessary: "If it be a suit from the Count, I am/ sick, or not at home. What you will, to dismiss/ it." *T Night,* I, v, 109–110.

wheak! *interj.* imit. of a shriek of pain: "'Wheak, wheak!'/ So cries a pig prepared to the spit." *T Andr,* IV, ii, 146–147.

wheaten garland, *n.* wreath of wheat stalks traditionally used to represent peace: "As love between them like the palm might flourish,/ As peace should still her wheaten garland wear . . ." *Ham,* V, ii, 40–41.

wheel, *n.* **1** refrain of a song: "O, how the wheel becomes it!" *Ham,* IV, v, 170. **2** the capriciousness of Fortune likened to a wheel of chance: "Though Fortune's malice overthrow my state,/ My mind exceeds the compass of her wheel." *3 Hen 6,* IV, iii, 46–47. **3 at the wheels of Caesar,** being led in triumph, as a prisoner in ancient Rome: "What, at the wheels of/ Caesar? Art thou led in triumph?" *Meas,* III, ii, 42–43. **4 death on the wheel,** execution by breaking the body on a wheel [unknown in ancient Rome]: ". . . present me/ Death on the wheel, or at wild horses' heels [pulled apart by wild horses, also non-Roman] . . ." *Cor,* III, ii, 1–2. **5 go on wheels,** to run or go smoothly: "The third part, then, is drunk: would it were all,/ That it might go on wheels!" *Ant & Cleo,* II, vii, 91–92. **6 turn i'th'wheel,** to turn a cooking spit by treading a wheel, work often done by a dog: "She had transform'd me to a curtal dog, and made me/ turn i'th' wheel." *Errors,* III, ii, 145. —*v.* **7** to move about in an arc-shaped course: "Attend me where I wheel,/ Strike not a stroke . . ." *Tr & Cr,* V, vii, 2–3.

wheeling, *adj.* wandering or roaming; itinerant: "Tying her duty . . . In an extravagant and wheeling stranger . . ." *Oth,* I, i, 135–136.

whe'er or **whe'r,** *conj.* whether: "Good sir, say whe'er you'll answer me or no . . ." *Errors,* IV, i, 60

Wheeson week, *n.* Whitsuntide, the week following Whitsunday (Pentecost), the 7th week after Easter: "Thou didst swear to me . . . upon Wednesday in/ Wheeson week . . ." *2 Hen 4,* II, i, 84–87.

whelk, *n.* pimple: ". . . his/ face is all bubukles, and whelks, and knobs . . ." *Hen 5,* III, vi, 104–105.

whelked, *adj.* twisted; convoluted: "Horns whelk'd and wav'd like the enridged sea . . ." *Lear,* IV, vi, 71.

when, *adv.* derisive response, usually the equivalent of "never!": "Have at you with another, that's—when? can you tell?" *Errors,* III, i, 52.

when as, *conj.* **1** whereas; while on the contrary: "And cried 'All hail!' when as he meant all harm." *3 Hen 6,* V, vii, 34. **2** at the time that; whenas: "When as your husband all in rage today/ Came to my house . . ." *Errors,* IV, iv, 135–136.

whenas, *conj.* when: "Whenas I met the boar, that bloody beast . . ." *Ven & Ad,* 999.

whencesoever, *adv.* from some place or other: "It is my son, young Harry Percy,/ Sent from my brother Worcester, whencesoever [wherever he may be]" *Rich 2,* II, iii, 21–22.

whe'r, *conj.* See **whe'er.**

where, *adv.* **1 some other where,** in another direction; here, in pursuit of another woman: "Ere I learn love, I'll practise to obey."/ "How if your husband start some other where?" *Errors,* II, i, 29–30. —*conj.* **2** whether: "Go on,/ And see where Brutus be alive or dead . . ." *J Caes,* V, iv, 29–30. **3** whereas: ". . . where, if you violently proceed against/ him, mistaking his purpose . . ." *Lear,* I, ii, 84–85. —*n.* **4** place; also, condition or circumstances: "Thou losest here, a better where to find." *Lear,* I, i, 261.

where are you?, what have you decided?: "My lord, where are you? What devise you on?" *1 Hen 6,* I, ii, 124.

whereas, *conj.* in which place; where: "I went to Antioch,/ Whereas, thou know'st . . . I sought the purchase of a glorious beauty . . ." *Per,* I, ii, 70–72.

wherefor or **wherefore,** *adv.* why? for what reason?: "O Romeo, Romeo, wherefore art thou Romeo?" *Rom & Jul* II, ii, 33.

where now, *conj.* whereas: "Where now I have no one to blush with me . . ." *Luc,* 792.

whereon, *conj.* in return for which: "Whereon I do beseech thee grant me this . . ." *Oth,* III, iii, 85.

wheresome'er, *adv.* wherever; in whatever place: "Would I were with him, wheresome'er he is,/ either in heaven or in hell!" *Hen 5,* II, iii, 7–8.

where-through, through which: ". . . windows to my breast, where-through the sun/ Delights to peep . . ." *Sonn 24,* 11–12.

whereto, *conj.* to which: "Whereto thy speech serves for authority . . ." *T Night,* I, ii, 20.

whereuntil, *adv.* prob. dial. form of "whereunto"; to what: "Under correction, sir, we know whereuntil it doth/ amount." *Love's L,* V, ii, 492.

whereupon, *conj.* [in] so far as: ". . . we do no further ask/ Than whereupon our weal, on you depending . . ." *K John,* IV, ii, 64–65.

whet, *v.* **1** to sharpen; encourage: "This visitation/ Is but to whet thy almost blunted purpose." *Ham,* III, iv, 110–111. **2 whet on,** to set on; instigate; stir up: "I prithee, peace,/ Good queen, and whet not on these furious peers..." *2 Hen 6,* II, i, 32–33.

whetstone, *n.* **1** sharpener: "Be this the whetstone of your sword: let grief/ Convert to anger..." *Mac,* IV, iii, 228–229. **2** applied to Cressida, who is here skillfully sharpening Diomedes' sexual appetite: "Now she sharpens: well said, whetstone." *Tr & Cr,* V, ii, 75.

which that, ref. here to antecedent "cause": "... which/ That he will give them..." *Cor,* II, i, 227–228.

whiff, *n.* puff of wind; here, the whirring sound of the sword: "But with the whiff and wind of his fell sword/ Th'unnerved father falls." *Ham,* II, ii, 469–470.

whiffler, *n.* attendant charged with clearing the way for a procession: "... like a mighty whiffler, 'fore the king/ Seems to prepare his way..." *Hen 5,* V, Chor. 12–13.

while, *n.* **1 the while,** the present times: "God help the while, a bad world I say." *1 Hen 4,* II, iv, 129.
—*prep.* **2** until: "We will keep ourself till supper-time alone:/ While then, God be with you." *Mac,* III, i, 43–44.
—*conj.* **3 while as,** while; whilst: "While as the silly owner of the goods/ Weeps over them, and wrings his hapless hands..." *2 Hen 6,* I, 1, 226–227.

while-ere, *adv.* a little while ago: "... will you troll the catch/ You taught me but while-ere?" *Temp,* III, ii, 115–116.

whiles, *conj.* **1** older form of WHILE: "I have drunk poison whiles he utter'd it." *M Ado,* V, i, 240. **2** as [so] long as: "... and it cannot be/ That, whiles warm life plays in that infant's veins..." *K John,* III, iii, 131–132. **3** until: "He shall conceal it/ Whiles you are willing it shall come to note..." *T Night,* IV, iii, 28–29. **4 but whiles,** only so long as: "She died, my lord, but whiles her slander liv'd." *M Ado,* V, iv, 66.
—*n.* **5 the whiles,** meanwhile; in the meantime: "Take you your instrument, play you the whiles..." *Shrew,* III, i, 22.

whinyard, *n.* short sword of Scottish soldiers: "Dismiss their biting whinyards, till your king/ Cry out: 'Enough, spare England now for pity!'" *Edw 3,* I, ii, 33–34.

whip, *v.* **1** to move quickly; flee; scurry: "Whip to our tents, as roes run o'er the land." *Love's L,* V, ii, 309. **2** to drive off, out, or away: "To whip this dwarfish war, this pigmy arms,/ From out the circle of his territories..." *K John,* V, ii, 135–136. **3 whip me,** expression of contempt; perh. equiv. of "spare me": "Whip me such honest knaves..." *Oth,* I, i, 49.

—*n.* **4** champion of the Trojans [and their descendants the Romans]; also, terror or scourge of the Greeks: "Wert thou the Hector/ That was the whip of your bragg'd progeny,/ Thou shouldst not 'scape me here." *Cor,* I, viii, 11–13. **5** punishment; dire consequence: "... which to hinder/ Were (in your love) a whip to me..." *W Tale,* I, ii, 24–25.

whipping, *n.* official punishment for an unlicensed [vagabond] player: "Use every man/ after his desert, and who shall scape whipping?" *Ham,* II, ii, 524–525.

whipping-cheer, *n.* generous taste of whipping: "... she shall have whipping-cheer enough, I warrant/ her..." *2 Hen 4,* V, iv, 5–6.

whipster, *n.* nonentity; know-nothing: "I am not valiant neither,/ But every puny whipster gets my sword..." *Oth,* V, ii, 244–245.

whipstock, *n.* **1** whip handle; here, a suggestion that Pericles looks more like a carter than a knight: "... by his rusty outside he appears/ To have practis'd more the whipstock than the lance." *Per,* II, ii, 49–50. **2** prob. the implication that, although Malvolio's nose is in everyone's business, he is no real threat: "Malvolio's/ nose is no whipstock, my lady has a white hand..." *T Night,* II, iii, 27–28.

whip thee, *interj.* hang thee! [mild curse]: "Marry, whip thee, gosling; I think I shall have/ something to do with you." *Per,* IV, ii, 82–83.

whip top, *v.* to whip a top to keep it spinning: "Since I plucked geese,/ played truant, and whipped top..." *Wives,* V, i, 24–25.

whirl, *v.* to turn around; reverse itself: "And justice always whirls in equal measure..." *Love's L,* IV, iii, 380.

whirligig, *n.* top; here, time likened to a spinning top: "And thus the whirligig of time/ brings in his revenges." *T Night,* V, i, 375–376.

whirlwind, *n.* tempest: "... mine own name: that some whirlwind bear/ Unto a ragged, fearful, hanging rock..." *Two Gent,* I, ii, 121–122.

whisper, *v.* **1** to whisper to (someone): "Whispers a Lord, who goes off in the barge of Lysimachus." [SD] *Per,* V, i, 51. **2** to speak confidentially to, esp. to proposition: "(For 'twas indeed his colour, but he came/ To whisper Wolsey)..." *Hen 8,* I, i, 178–179.

whissing, *pres. part.* wheezing; whistling: "... lethargies, cold/ palsies, raw eyes, dirt-rotten livers, whissing lungs..." *Tr & Cr,* V, i, 18–19.

whist, *adj.* hushed; quiet: "Courtsied when you have and kiss'd/ The wild waves whist . . ." *Temp,* I, ii, 379–380.

whistle, *v.* **1** to whisper: ". . . when you are/ going to bed, or kiln-hole, to whistle of these secrets . . ." *W Tale,* IV, iv, 246–247. **2 whistle her off,** let her go [term in falconry]: "I'ld whistle her off, and let her down the wind,/ To prey at fortune." *Oth,* III, iii, 266–267.
—*n.* **3 worth the whistle,** Goneril's allusion to the proverb, "'Tis a poor dog that is not worth the whistle": "[Enter Albany] I have been worth the whistle." *Lear,* IV, ii, 29.

whit, *n.* **no whit,** not in the least: "Our youths and wildness shall no whit appear,/ But all be buried in his gravity." *J Caes,* II, i, 148–149.

white, *n.* **1** bull's-eye of a target; here, also prob. wordplay on "Bianca," the Italian word for "white": "'Twas I won the wager, though you hit the white . . ." *Shrew,* V, ii, 187.
—*adj.* **2** pure: "Back-wounding calumny/ The whitest virtue strikes." *Meas,* III, ii, 180–181.

white and red, *n.* flesh and blood: "My love is most immaculate white and red." *Love's L,* I, ii, 85.

Whitefriars, *n.* Carmelite priory in London, so-called because of the nuns' white habits: ". . . to Whitefriars; there attend my coming." *Rich 3,* I, ii, 231.

white hand, *n.* poss. ref. to Olivia's refined tastes, though the passage is deliberate nonsense: ". . . my lady has a white hand,/ and the Myrmidons are no bottle-ale houses." *T Night,* II, iii, 28–29.

White Hart, *n.* old inn on London's South Bank: "Hath my sword therefore broke through London/ gates, that you should leave me at the White/ Hart in Southwark?" *2 Hen 6,* IV, viii, 23–25.

white-livered, *adj.* cowardly: "There let him sink, and be the seas on him—/ White-liver'd runagate!" *Rich 3,* IV, iv, 463–464.

whitely, *adj.* pale; sallow: "A whitely wanton with a velvet brow . . ." *Love's L,* III, i, 191.

white wheat, *n.* ripening wheat: ". . . mildews the white wheat, and/ hurts the poor creature of earth." *Lear,* III, iv, 121–122.

whiting-time, *n.* time for bleaching: ". . . or—/ it is whiting-time—send him by your two men to/ Datchet Mead." *Wives,* III, iii, 121–122.

whitster, *n.* bleacher of linen: ". . . trudge with it in all haste, and/ carry it among the whitsters in Datchet Mead . . ." *Wives,* III, iii, 11–12.

Whitsunday or **Whit-Sunday,** *n.* See **Pentecost.**

Whitsun morris-dance, *n.* folk dance celebrating Whitsuntide [week beginning with Whitsunday], in early summer, usually with grotesque costumes and makeup: ". . . with no more than if we heard that England/ Were busied with a Whitsun morris-dance . . ." *Hen 5,* II, iv, 24–25.

Whitsun pastorals, *n.* games and festivities of Whitsuntide [see preceding], usually in May or early June, including morris dances and Robin Hood plays: "Methinks I play as I have seen them do/ In Whitsun pastorals . . ." *W Tale,* IV, iv, 133–134.

whittle, *n.* large knife, as a carving knife; also, a clasp-knife: "There's not a whittle in th' unruly camp/ But I do prize it . . ." *Timon,* V, i, 179–180.

who, *pron.* **1** he or him who: ". . . nothing,/ But who knows nothing, is once seen to smile . . ." *Mac,* IV, iii, 166–167. **2** which: ". . . she was a queen/ Over her passion; who, most rebel-like,/ Sought to be king o'er her." *Lear,* IV, iii, 14–16. **3 but who,** except those [persons] who: "None wed the second but who kill'd the first." *Ham,* III, ii, 175.

who else, *pron.* whoever; anyone who: ". . . and who else would trace him his umbrage, nothing/ more." *Ham,* V, ii, 119–120.

whole, *adj.* **1** healthy; sound: "I would the state of time had first been whole . . ." *1 Hen 4,* IV, i, 25. **2** substantial: "As [even when it's] matter whole you have to make it with . . ." *Ant & Cleo,* II, ii, 53.

wholesome, *adj.* **1** rational; sensible: "If it shall please you to make me a wholesome/ answer . . ." *Ham,* III, ii, 307–308. **2** healthy or sound; also, prosperous or prospering: ". . . in the tender of a wholesome weal [state],/ Might in their working do you that offence . . ." *Lear,* I, iv, 219–220. **3** beneficial: "Bosom up my counsel,/ You'll find it wholesome." *Hen 8,* I, i, 112–113. **4** sense of "reasonable" [Menenius] understood by Coriolanus as "healthful": ". . . speak to 'em, I pray you,/ In wholesome manner."/ "Bid them wash their faces . . ." *Cor,* II, iii, 61–62.

wholesome iniquity, *n.* healthy prostitute; poss. these words ironically addressed to Bawd: "How now, wholesome iniquity,/ have you that a man may deal withal, and/ defy the surgeon?" *Per,* IV, vi, 23–25.

whom, *pron.* **1** which: "Did not the heavenly rhetoric of thine eye,/ 'Gainst whom the world cannot hold argument . . ." *Love's L,* IV, iii, 57–58. **2** with "those" understood: "I hazarded the loss of whom I lov'd." *Errors,* I, i, 131.

whoo-bub, *n.* hubbub: ". . . had not/ the old man come in with a whoo-bub against his/ daughter and the king's son . . ." *W Tale,* IV, iv, 618–620.

whoop or **hoop,** *v.* to drive by shouting, jeering, etc.: "And suffer'd me by th'voice of slaves to be/ Whoop'd out of Rome." *Cor,* IV, v, 78–79.

whooping, *n.* shout of excitement or exultation: "And yet again wonderful! And after that out of all whooping [beyond all power of exclamation]." *As You,* III, ii, 189–190.

Whoop, Jug!, perh. a song refrain with special connotations [Jug = nickname for Joan]; poss. merely an attempt to get Lear's attention: "Whoop, Jug! I love thee." *Lear,* I, iv, 233.

whore, *v.* **whor'd my mother,** Hamlet's belief (based on church doctrine) that his mother and Claudius are living in incest: "He that hath kill'd my king and whor'd my mother,/ Popp'd in between the election and my hopes . . ." *Ham,* V, ii, 64–65.

whoremaster or **whoremonger,** *n.* patron of prostitutes; lecher; fornicator: ". . . but that/ he is, saving your reverence, a whoremaster, that I/ utterly deny." *1 Hen 4,* II, iv, 462–464.

whoreson, *n.* **1** bastard son; sometimes used jokingly or affectionately: "Mass and well said! A merry whoreson, ha." *Rom & Jul,* IV, iv, 19.
—*adj.* **2** vile or loathesome: "Ah, whoreson caterpillars, bacon-fed knaves . . ." *1 Hen 4,* II, ii, 81.

whose, *pron.* in which: "My thought, whose murther [murder] yet is but fantastical . . ." *Mac,* I, iii, 139.

whosoever, *adv.* without exception; bar none: ". . . he's one/ o'th'soundest judgements in Troy whosoever . . ." *Tr & Cr,* I, ii, 193–194.

whosomever, *pron.* whoever; whosoever: ". . . whosomever you take him to be, he is Ajax." *Tr & Cr,* II, i, 66.

why, *conj.* **for why,** because: "For why my bowels cannot hide her woes,/ But like a drunkard must I vomit them." *T Andr,* III, i, 230–231.

wicker bottle or **twiggen bottle,** *n.* bottle covered with wickerwork: ". . . I'll beat the knave/ into a wicker bottle." *Oth,* II, iii, 140–141.

wide, *adj.* **1** off the mark; astray; here, with the mind wandering: "Still, still, far wide."/ "He's scarce awake; let him alone awhile." *Lear,* IV, vii, 50–51.
—*adv.* **2** wide of or far from the truth: "Is my lord well that he doth speak so wide?" *M Ado,* IV, i, 62. **3 go wide,** stray; be unfaithful: "Bear thine eyes straight though thy proud heart go wide." *Sonn 140,* 14.

wide-chapped, *adj.* wide-jawed: "This wide-chapp'd rascal,—would thou mightst lie drowning/ The washing of ten tides!" *Temp,* I, i, 56–57.

wide-skirted, *adj.* extensive: "With plenteous rivers and wide-skirted meads . . ." *Lear,* I, i, 65.

widowhood, *n.* estate guaranteed a widow, usually part of the marriage contract: "And for that dowry I'll assure her of/ Her widowhood . . ." *Shrew,* II, i, 123–124.

wid'st, *adj.* **at wid'st,** at or to the widest point: "He'll be hang'd yet,/ Though every drop of water swear against it,/ And gape at wid'st to glut him." *Temp,* I, i, 57–59.

wield, *v.* to express: "Sir, I love you more than word can wield the matter [more than can be expressed in words] . . ." *Lear,* I, i, 55.

wife, *n.* any woman of marriageable age: ". . . let wives with child/ Pray that their burthens may not fall this day . . ." *K John,* III, i, 15–16.

wight, *n.* **1** person [poetic use]; being: "I see descriptions of the fairest wights . . ." *Sonn 106,* 2. **2** fellow; creature [often used humorously or contemptuously]: "Armado is a most illustrious wight . . . fashion's own knight." *Love's L,* I, i, 176–177.

wild, *n.* **1** wilderness; here used figuratively: "Where every something being blent together,/ Turns to a wild of nothing . . ." *Merch,* III, ii, 181–182. **2** [cap.] var. of *Weald,* a wooded, hilly district of Kent and adjoining counties: ". . . there's a franklin in the/ Wild of Kent hath brought three hundred marks . . ." *1 Hen 4,* II, ii, 53–54.
—*adj.* **3** wrought up; agitated: "But let this same be presently perform'd/ Even while men's minds are wild . . ." *Ham,* V, ii, 398–399. **4** violently angry; put into a passionate rage: "The ingratitude of this Seleucus does/ Even make me wild." *Ant & Cleo,* V, ii, 152–153. **5** rash; acting without deliberation: "For in an act of this importance, 'twere/ Most piteous to be wild . . ." *W Tale,* II, i, 181–182. **6** wildly excited [by]; thrilled [at]: "I am wild in my beholding [at what I see]." *Per,* V, i, 221. **7 gone wild,** taken my former wildness with him: "My father is gone wild into his grave,/ For in his tomb lie my affections . . ." *2 Hen 4,* V, ii, 123–124.

wild-cat, *n.* ref. to its prowling by night and sleeping by day: ". . . and he sleeps by day/ More than the wild-cat . . ." *Merch,* II, v, 46–47.

wilderness, *n.* **slip of wilderness,** throwback to a wild strain [term in horticulture]: "For such a warped slip of wilderness/ Ne'er issued from his blood." *Meas,* III, i, 141–142.

wildfire, *n.* firework of flaming gunpowder: ". . . if/ I did not think thou hadst been an *ignis fatuus,* or a ball of wildfire, there's no purchase in money." *1 Hen 4,* III, iii, 38–39.

wild-goose chase, *n.* horse race in which all participants agree to follow the leader's course: "Nay, if our wits run the wild-goose chase I am done." *Rom & Jul,* II, iv, 72.

wild horses' heels, *n.* death by tying the victim to two or more wild horses: ". . . present me/ Death on the wheel, or at wild horses' heels . . ." *Cor,* III, ii, 1–2.

wild Kate, *n.* poss. wordplay on "wildcat": "And bring you from a wild Kate to a Kate/ Conformable as other household Kates." *Shrew,* II, i, 270–271.

wildly, *adv.* chaotically: "How wildly then walks my estate in France!" *K John,* IV, ii, 128.

wildness, *n.* madness: "Put thyself/ Into a haviour of less fear, ere wildness/ Vanquish my staider senses." *Cymb,* III, iv, 9–10.

will, *n.* **1** the passions: ". . . touching now the point of human skill,/ Reason becomes the marshal to my will . . ." *M N Dream,* II, ii, 118–119. **2** lust; sexual desire: "To buy his will [satisfy his desire] it would not seem too dear . . ." *All's W,* III, vii, 27. **3** actual feeling or emotion: "We men may say more, swear more, but indeed/ Our shows are more than will . . ." *T Night,* II, iv, 117–118. **4** wishes; desire: ". . . any thing he sees, which moves his liking,/ I can with ease translate it to my will . . ." *K John,* II, i, 512–513. **5** intent or intention: "Margaret was in some fault for this,/ Although against her will [unintentionally], as it appears . . ." *M Ado,* V, iv, 4–5. **6** willfulness; obstinacy: ". . . never could maintain his part, but in the/ force of his will." *M Ado,* I, i, 219–220. **7** wordplay on "intent" and "sexual relations": "Whoever hath her wish, thou hast thy will . . ." *Sonn 135,* 1. **8** wordplay on "feelings" and "sexual organs": "Wilt thou, whose will is large and spacious,/ Not once vouchsafe to hide my will in thine?" *Sonn 135,* 5–6. **9** wordplay on "lust" and "sexual relations": "So thou, being rich in will, add to thy will/ One will of mine . . ." *Sonn 135,* 11–12. **10** disposition: "His will is most malignant [evil], and it stretches/ Beyond you to your friends." *Hen 8,* I, ii, 141–142. **11 by my will,** willingly: "Not for the world, fair madam, by my will." *Love's L,* II, i, 98. **12 good will,** resolution: "He that has but effected [carried out] his good will . . ." *Cor,* I, ix, 18. **13 in will,** deliberately: "We are again forsworn, in will and error." *Love's L,* V, ii, 471. **14 my more headier will,** my rash impulse: ". . . am fallen out with my more headier will,/ To take the indispos'd and sickly fit/ For the sound man." *Lear,* II, iv, 110–112.
—*v.* **15** to wish or command: ". . . every part of what we would/ Doth make a stand at [stop short of] what your highness will." *K John,* IV, ii, 38–39. **16** persist in: "Gentlemen both, you will mistake each other." *Hen 5,* III, ii, 137.

willful-blame, *adj.* guilty of [blamable for] willfulness: "In faith, my lord, you are too wilful-blame . . ." *1 Hen 4,* III, i, 171.

willful-opposite, *adj.* stubbornly belligerent: "The Dolphin is too wilful-opposite,/ And will not temporize [compromise] with my entreaties . . ." *K John,* V, ii, 124–125.

will he nill he, *adv.* willy-nilly; whether he wishes to or not: "If the man go to this water/ and drown himself, it is, will he nill he, he goes,/ mark you that." *Ham,* V, i, 16–18.

Will I live?, As sure as I'm alive!: "You'll pay me all together?/ Will I live?" *2 Hen 4,* II, i, 157–159.

willing, *adj.* ready; prompt: "My willing love . . . Set forth in your pursuit." *T Night,* III, iii, 11–13.

willow cabin, *n.* bower or arbor of willow branches, symbol of unrequited love: "Make me a willow cabin at your gate . . ." *T Night,* I, v, 272.

willow garland, *n.* garland woven of willow stems, a symbol of disappointed love: "Tell him, in hope he'll prove a widower shortly,/ I'll wear the willow garland for his sake." *3 Hen 6,* III, iii, 227–228.

willow-tree, *n.* symbol of the unhappy lover: "I offered him my company to a willow-tree . . . to make him a garland . . ." *M Ado,* II, i, 202–203.

will peculiar, *n.* self-willed; here, concerned only with what he wants: "[Achilles] carries on the stream of his dispose . . . In will peculiar and in self-admission." *Tr & Cr,* II, iii, 165–167.

will you, nill you, whether you agree or not; willy-nilly: "And will you, nill you, I will marry you." *Shrew,* II, i, 264.

wimpled, *adj.* hooded; also, blindfolded: "This wimpled, whining, purblind, wayward boy . . ." *Love's L,* III, i, 174.

win, *v.* **1 win me and wear me,** best me in a fair fight, and I will accept defeat: "Win me and wear me, let him answer me."

M Ado, V, i, 82. **2 wins of all,** takes something from everybody: "That daily break-vow, he that wins of all,/ Of kings, of beggars, old men . . ." *K John*, II, i, 569–570. **3 win upon power,** get the better of authority: ". . . it will in time/ Win upon power, and throw forth greater themes/ For insurrection's arguing." *Cor*, I, i, 218–220.

wince, *v.* to flinch, as with pain or discomfort: "Let the galled jade wince, our withers are/ unwrung [not sore]." *Ham*, III, ii, 237–238.

winch, *v.* var. of **wince:** "I will not stir, nor winch, nor speak a word . . ." *K John*, IV, i, 80.

Winchester goose, *n.* **1** slang term for venereal sore; here, an epithet for the Bishop of Winchester: "Winchester goose! I cry, 'A rope! a rope!'" *1 Hen 6*, I, iii, 53. **2** prostitute; ref. to brothels of Southwark [London], a district governed by the Bishop of Winchester: "Some galled goose of Winchester would hiss." *Tr & Cr*, V, x, 55.

Wincot, *n.* prob. a small village near Stratford: "Ask Marian Hacket, the fat/ ale-wife of Wincot . . ." *Shrew*, Ind., ii, 21–22.

wind[1]**,** *v.* **1** to sound (a horn or call): ". . . I will have a recheat winded in my/ forehead . . ." *M Ado*, I, i, 223–224. **2** to get wind of: ". . . and if she wind ye once:/ She's with the lion deeply still in league . . ." *T Andr*, IV, i, 97–98. **3** to proceed; wend: "Wind away,/ Be gone, I say,/ I will not to wedding with thee." *As You*, III, iii, 94–96.
—*n.* **4** windiness; chatter or prattle: "Stop in your wind, sir, tell me this I pray:" *Errors*, I, ii, 53. **5** breath: "For self-same wind that I should speak withal/ Is kindling coals that fires all my breast . . ." *3 Hen 6*, II, i, 82–83. **6** [pl.] sighs: "Rain to lay [allay] this wind, or/ my heart will be blown up by th'root." *Tr & Cr*, IV, iv, 52–53. **7 allow the wind,** stay downwind of me [because of the smell]: "I will henceforth eat/ no fish of Fortune's butt'ring. Prithee, allow the/ wind." *All's W*, V, ii, 7–9. **8 break one's wind,** to pant; be short-winded: "And pursy insolence shall break his wind/ With fear and horrid flight." *Timon*, V, iv, 12–13. **9 have i' th' wind,** to stalk (prey) from downwind: ". . . this same coxcomb that we have i' th' wind . . ." *All's W*, III, vi, 110. **10 have the wind of (someone),** to watch cautiously, as a hunter tracking an animal while remaining downwind: ". . . let us all consult./ My son and I will have the wind of you . . ." *T Andr*, IV, ii, 132–133. **11 keep the wind,** to remain downwind of a quarry while closing in for the kill; here, a game of seduction: "He knows the game: how true he keeps the wind!" *3 Hen 6*, III, ii, 14. **12 let her down the wind,** turn her loose: "I'ld whistle her off, and let her down the wind,/ To prey at fortune." *Oth*, III, iii, 266–267.

wind[2]**,** *v.* **1** to wind thread, etc., from one spool onto another; here, to take Silvia's love for Valentine and transfer it to Sir Thurio: "But say this wind her love from Valentine,/ It follows not that she will love Sir Thurio." *Two Gent*, III, ii, 49–50. **2** to insinuate: ". . . to wind/ Yourself into a power tyrannical . . ." *Cor*, III, iii, 64–65. **3** to wheel about: "As if an angel dropp'd down from the clouds/ To turn and wind a fiery Pegasus . . ." *1 Hen 4*, IV, i, 108–109. **4 wind about,** to insinuate (oneself) into: "You know me well, and herein spend but time/ To wind about my love with circumstance . . ." *Merch*, I, i, 153–154. **5 wind me into him,** work your way into his confidence (for me): ". . . wind me into him, I pray you: frame/ the business after your own wisdom." *Lear*, I, ii, 101–102. **6 wind up, a.** to tighten or tune; here, to restore: "Th' untuned and jarring senses, O! wind up . . ." *Lear*, IV, vii, 16. **b.** to furl; roll up: "Therefore thy threat'ning colours now wind up . . ." *K John*, V, ii, 73–74.

wind-changing, *adj.* ever-changing; inconstant: "'Wind-changing Warwick now can change no more.'" *3 Hen 6*, V, i, 57.

windgalls, *n. pl.* disease of a horse's fetlock joint: ". . . full of windgalls, sped with/ spavins, rayed with the yellows . . ." *Shrew*, III, ii, 50–51.

winding, *n.* sounding of wind instruments: "To the winding of horns [within] . . ." [SD] *M N Dream*, IV, i, 102.

winding-sheet, *n.* sheet of cloth in which a corpse is wrapped for burial; shroud: ". . . their colors, often borne in France . . . Shall be my winding-sheet." *3 Hen 6*, I, i, 131–133.

Windmill, *n.* prob. brothel in Southwark, on London's South Bank: "Sir John, do you remember since we lay all/ night in the Windmill in Saint George's Field?" *2 Hen 4*, III, ii, 189–190.

window, *n.* **1** [usually pl.] eyelids: ". . . thy eyes' windows fall/ Like death when he shuts up the day of life." *Rom & Jul*, IV, i, 100–101. **2** window covering; shutter: "Pluck down forms, windows, any thing." *J Caes*, III, ii, 261. **3 window of lattice,** Parolles compared to an uncovered window: "So, my good window of lattice, fare thee/ well; thy casement I need not open, for I look/ through thee." *All's W*, II, iii, 212–214.

window-bars, *n.* prob. ref. to laces on woman's bodice [obvious anachronism]: ". . . those milk-paps,/ That through the window-bars bore at men's eyes . . ." *Timon*, IV, iii, 117–118.

windowed, *adj.* standing in a window: "Wouldst thou be window'd in great Rome . . ." *Ant & Cleo*, IV, xiv, 72.

windring, *adj.* appar. coinage, combining sense of "winding" and "wandering": "You nymphs, call'd Naiads, of the windring brooks,/ With your sedg'd crowns and ever-harmless looks . . ." *Temp,* IV, i, 128–129.

windy, *adj.* windward; situated away from the wind; hence, safe: "I thank it, poor fool, it keeps on the/ windy side of care." *M Ado,* II, i, 295–296.

wing, *n.* **1** either of an army's flanks: "Out, some light horsemen, and peruse their wings." *1 Hen 6,* IV, ii, 43. **2** hasty retreat; also, poss. wordplay on shoulder decorations on Parolles's costume: ". . . the composition that your valour and fear makes/ in you is a virtue of a good wing . . ." *All's W,* I, i, 199–200. **3 imagin'd wing,** wings of imagination: "Thus with imagin'd wing our swift scene flies . . ." *Hen 5,* III, Chor., 1. **4 with the like wing,** in a similar manner: ". . . yet when they/ stoop, they stoop with the like wing." *Hen 5,* IV, i, 107–108.

winged, *adj.* **well winged,** (of an army) well supported on the flanks: ". . . whose puissance on either side/ Shall be well winged with our chiefest horse." *Rich 3,* V, iii, 300–301.

winged time, *n.* fleeting time regarded as being borne on wings: "Only I carried winged time/ Post on the lame feet of my rime . . ." *Per,* IV, Chor., 47–48.

winged vengeance, *n.* prob. an avenging angel: ". . . but I shall see/ The winged vengeance overtake such children." *Lear,* III, vii, 64–65.

Wingham, *n.* village near Canterbury: "There's Best's son, the tanner/ of Wingham . . ." *2 Hen 6,* IV, ii, 21–22.

wing-led, *adj.* (of troops) reinforced on each side [other editors: "winged" or "mingled"]: "Their discipline,/ (Now wingled with their courages) . . ." *Cymb,* II, iv, 23–24.

wink, *v.* **1** to close one's eyes, with drowsiness or in sleep; nod; nap: "And not be seen to wink of all the day . . ." *Love's L,* I, i, 43. **2** to keep one's eyes closed; here, from fear: "Pardon me,/ If I were there, I'd wink." *Kinsmen,* V, iii, 17–18. **3** to close one's eyes to the facts: ". . . led his powers to death,/ And winking leap'd into destruction." *2 Hen 4,* I, iii, 32–33. **4 wink at,** to connive with: "The eye wink at the hand: yet let that be [done],/ Which the eye fears, when it is done, to see." *Mac,* I, iv, 52–53.
—*n.* **5** glimpse; peek: ". . . so high a hope, that even/ Ambition cannot pierce a wink beyond . . ." *Temp,* II, i, 236–237. **6 lasting wink,** permanent sleep [death]: "To give mine enemy a lasting wink . . ." *W Tale,* I, ii, 317. **7 wink for aye,** eternally closed eyes: "To the perpetual wink for aye might put/ This ancient morsel . . ." *Temp,* II, i, 280–281.

winking, *adj.* **1** closed; shut: "All preparation for a bloody siege . . . by these French/ Comforts your city's eyes, your winking gates . . ." *K John,* II, i, 213–215. **2** with eyes closed: "Foolish curs! that run winking into the mouth of/ a Russian bear . . ." *Hen 5,* III, vii, 143–144.
—*n.* **3** a closing of the eyes; here, an instance of ignoring: "If I had . . . given my heart a winking mute and dumb,/ Or look'd upon this love with idle sight . . ." *Ham,* II, ii, 136–138.

winnow, *v.* to separate, in the manner of chaff from grain: "Distinction, with a broad and powerful fan . . . winnows the light away . . ." *Tr & Cr,* I, iii, 27–28.

winnowed, *adj.* purged of inferior substances; purified: ". . . the match and weight/ Of such a winnow'd purity in love . . ." *Tr & Cr,* III, ii, 164–165.

winter, *adj.* aged; old: "That winter lion, who in rage forgets/ Aged contusions and all brush of time . . ." *2 Hen 6,* V, iii, 2–3.

wintered, *adj.* used in winter: "Winter'd garments must be lin'd,/ So must slender Rosalind." *As You,* III, ii, 103–104.

wipe, *n.* brand: "Worse than a slavish wipe or birth-hour's blot . . ." *Luc,* 537.

wisdom, *n.* **1** common sense; here, Regan's self-interest: ". . . what they may incense him to, being apt/ To have his ear abus'd, wisdom bids fear." *Lear,* II, iv, 308–309. **2** used with "'twere" understood: ". . . something/ You may deserve of him through me, and wisdom [might force you]/ To offer up a weak, poor, innocent lamb . . ." *Mac,* IV, iii, 14–16. **3 What can man's wisdom,** what can all of man's knowledge accomplish: "What can man's wisdom/ In the restoring his bereaved sense?" *Lear,* IV, iv, 8–9. **4 your better wisdoms,** your opinions [which are] better than average: "Nor have we herein barr'd/ Your better wisdoms . . ." *Ham,* I, ii, 14–15. **5 your wisdom,** respectful form of address; here, used ironically: "I think I saw your wisdom there." *T Night,* III, i, 42.

wise, *adj.* **1** tempered with experience and sound judgment: "That we with wisest sorrow think on him . . ." *Ham,* I, ii, 6. **2 wise in,** taking advantage of: ". . . who already,/ Wise in our negligence, have secret feet/ In some of our best ports . . ." *Lear,* III, i, 31–33.

wiselier, *adv.* used as compar. of **wisely;** perh., more freely: "You have taken it wiselier than I meant you should." *Temp,* I, ii, 21.

wise man's son, *n.* proverbially a fool: "Journeys end in lovers meeting,/ Every wise man's son doth know." *T Night,* II, iii, 44–45.

wish, *v.* **1** to admonish: "When man was wish'd to love his enemies!" *Timon,* IV, iii, 469. **2** to urge; entreat: "And I will wish thee never more to dance . . ." *Love's L,* V, ii, 400. **3** to commend: ". . . if I can . . . light on a fit/ man to teach her . . . I will/ wish him to her father." *Shrew,* I, i, 110–112. **4 I wish,** I pray you; prithee: "Tempt him not so too far. I wish, forbear . . ." *Ant & Cleo,* I, iii, 11. **5 wish but for't,** [obtain something] simply by wishing for it: "Sail seas in cockles, have and wish but for't . . ." *Per,* IV, iv, 2.
—*n.* **6 at high wish,** as much as one could want: "The one is filling still, never complete,/ The other, at high wish." *Timon,* IV, iii, 246–247. **7 upon a wish,** as I was hoping: "He comes upon a wish." *J Caes,* III, ii, 268.

wished, *adj.* **1** desired; longed for: "I have arriv'd at the last/ Unto the wished haven of my bliss." *Shrew,* V, i, 116–117. **2** representing the will of the people: ". . . he which is [has power] was wish'd, until he were [is in power] . . ." *Ant & Cleo,* I, iv, 42.

wishtly, *adv.* intently; also, longingly: "And, speaking it, he wishtly look'd on me . . ." *Rich 2,* V, iv, 7.

wist, *v.* poss. corruption of "iwis," indeed; here, appar. used as past tense with sense of "to be certain": "And if I wist he did—but let it rest . . ." *1 Hen 6,* IV, i, 180.

wistly, *adv.* intently: ". . . those his eyes are hers,/ Who looking wistly on me make me blush . . ." *Edw 3,* II, ii, 87–88.

wit, *n.* **1** intellect or intelligence: "Fie, fie, thou sham'st thy shape, thy love, thy wit . . ." *Rom & Jul,* III, iii, 121. **2** wisdom; good judgment or common sense: "Where will doth mutiny with wit's regard." *Rich 2,* II, i, 28. **3** ingenuity; cleverness: "Only shape thou thy silence to my wit." *T Night,* I, ii, 61. **4** acuteness of perception; insight: ". . . your/ suspicion is not without wit and judgement . . ." *Oth,* IV, ii, 211–212. **5 of small wit,** foolish; stupid: "There was a/ haberdasher's wife of small wit near him . . ." *Hen 8,* V, iii, 45–46. **6 past the wit of man,** beyond human comprehension: "I have had a dream, past the wit of man to say what/ dream it was." *M N Dream,* IV, i, 204–205. **7 taint their wit,** cause their intelligence to be questioned: "But wise men, folly-fall'n, quite taint their wit." *T Night,* III, i, 69.
—*v.* **8** to know: "Now please you wit/ The epitaph is for Marina writ/ By wicked Dionyza." *Per,* IV, iv, 31–32.

witch, *v.* **1** to charm; bewitch: "You witch me in it;/ Surprise me to the very brink of tears." *Timon,* V, i, 154–155.
—*n.* **2** night likened to an ugly witch: "Beshrew the witch! With venomous wights [malicious or unsympathetic companions] she stays/ As tediously as hell . . ." *Tr & Cr,* IV, ii, 12–13. **3** sorcerer; wizard [sometimes used of either sex]:

". . . such a holy witch/ That he enchants societies into [unto] him . . ." *Cymb,* I, vii, 166–167. **4 witch take me,** may I be bewitched: "Now the witch take me if I meant it thus!" *Ant & Cleo,* IV, ii, 37.

witchcraft, *n.* magic charm or spell: "A witchcraft drew me hither:/ That most ingrateful boy there by your side . . ." *T Night,* V, i, 74–75.

witching time, *n.* hours when witches are abroad performing foul deeds: "'Tis now the very witching time of night . . ." *Ham,* III, ii, 379.

wit-cracker, *n.* joker; wag: ". . . a college of wit-crackers/ cannot flout me out of my humour." *M Ado,* V, iv, 99–100.

with, *prep.* **1** by: ". . . a barren sceptre in my gripe,/ Thence to be wrench'd with an unlineal hand . . ." *Mac,* III, i, 61–62. **2** on: "Feast with the best, and welcome to my house." *Shrew,* V, ii, 8. **3** against: ". . . wisely, good sir, weigh/ Our sorrow with our comfort." *Temp,* II, i, 8–9. **4** with respect to: "Do with your injuries as seems [to] you best/ In any chastisement." *Meas,* V, i, 255–256. **5** within the realm of: "O brother, speak with possibility . . ." *T Andr,* III, i, 214. **6 with us,** with our help: ". . . that is there which looks/ With us to break his neck." *Cor,* III, iii, 29–30.
—*v.* **7** to go with: ". . . by the good gods/ I'd with thee every foot." *Cor,* IV, i, 56–57.

withal, *prep.* **1** with, used for emphasis at the end of a statement: "I'll tell you who Time ambles/ withal, who Time trots withal . . ." *As You,* III, ii, 303–304. **2** with that: "Thou seest what's past, go fear thy king withal [with what I've just told you]." *3 Hen 6,* III, iii, 226.
—*adv.* **3** besides; as well; moreover: ". . . hath sense withal/ Of it own fall, restraining aid to Timon . . ." *Timon,* V, i, 146–147. **4** yet; nevertheless: ". . . withal I am, indeed, sir, a surgeon to old shoes . . ." *J Caes,* I, i, 23. **5** otherwise: "I could not do withal . . ." *Merch,* III, iv, 72. **6** above all: "But sirs, be sudden in the execution,/ Withal obdurate: do not hear him plead . . ." *Rich 3,* I, iii, 346–347.

withdraw, *v.* to speak privately: "To withdraw with you . . ." *Ham,* III, ii, 336–337.

wither, *v.* to cause to dwindle; use up: "Like to a step-dame or a dowager/ Long withering out a young man's revenue." *M N Dream,* I, i, 5–6.

withhold, *v.* to hold back; restrain: "Oft have I seen a hot o'erweening cur/ Run back and bite, because he was withheld . . ." *2 Hen 6,* V, i, 151–152.

within, *prep.* **1** here, inside another's guard: ". . . he is mad;/ Some get within him, take his sword away . . ." *Errors*, V, i, 33–34. **2** subjunctive construction with sense of "if within": "Within thine eyes sat twenty thousand deaths . . ." *Cor*, III, iii, 70.
—*adv.* **3** on the inside; here, in Banquo's body: "'Tis better thee without, than he within." *Mac*, III, iv, 14.

within's, within this: ". . . how cheerfully my/ mother looks and my father died within's two hours." *Ham*, III, ii, 124–125.

without, *adv.* **1** outside: "Bring in thy ranks, but leave without thy rage . . ." *Timon*, V, iv, 39. **2** on the outside; here, on the face: "'Tis better thee without, than he within." *Mac*, III, iv, 14.
—*prep.* **3** out of; on the outside of: "What seal is that that hangs without thy bosom?" *Rich 2*, V, ii, 56.
—*conj.* **4** unless: "For without you/ were so simple, none else would." *Two Gent*, II, i, 35–36.

without-book, *adj.* memorized: ". . . no without-book prologue, faintly spoke/ After the prompter . . ." *Rom & Jul*, I, iv, 7–8.

without-door, *adj.* outward; external: "Praise her but for this her without-door form . . ." *W Tale*, II, i, 69.

withstand, *v.* to challenge or oppose: ". . . they have/ won the bridge, killing all those that withstand them." *2 Hen 6*, IV, v, 2–3.

with unwashed hands, *adv.* without delay or, esp., without a scruple: "Rob me the exchequer . . . and /do it with unwashed hands too." *1 Hen 4*, III, iii, 182–183.

witness, *n.* **1** evidence; here, blood: "Go, get some water,/ And wash this filthy witness from your hand." *Mac*, II, ii, 45–46. **2 with a witness,** with a vengeance: "Here's packing, with a witness, to deceive us all." *Shrew*, V, i, 108.
—*v.* **3 a little witness,** testify briefly to: "When thou see'st him,/ A little witness my obedience." *Cymb*, III, iv, 66–67. **4 witnessed the rather,** confirmed all the more: "Which was to my belief witness'd the rather,/ For that I saw the tyrant's power afoot." *Mac*, IV, iii, 184–185.

witnessed usurpation, *n.* signs or evidence of destruction: "So looks the strond whereon the imperious flood/ Hath left a witness'd usurpation." *2 Hen 4*, I, i, 62–63.

wit of man, *n.* capacity of human intelligence: "I have had a dream, past the wit of man to say what/ dream it was." *M N Dream*, IV, i, 204–205.

wit-old, *adj.*, *n.* understood as a pun on "wittol," a complacent cuckold: "Offered by a child to an old man; which is witold." *Love's L*, V, i, 57.

wit-snapper, *n.* ready wit: "Goodly Lord, what a wit-snapper are you!" *Merch*, III, v, 45.

Wittenberg, *n.* town in E Germany, site of famous university, founded 1502: "For your intent/ In going back to school in Wittenberg,/ It is most retrograde to our desire . . ." *Ham*, I, ii, 112–114.

wittily, *adv.* cunningly; ingeniously: "For sharply did he think to reprehend her,/ Which cunning love did wittily prevent . . ." *Ven & Ad*, 470–471.

witting, *pres. part.* knowing: "As witting I no other comfort have." *1 Hen 6*, II, v, 16.

wittol, *n.* cuckold: "Wittol? Cuckold! The devil himself hath/ not such a name." *Wives*, II, ii, 288–289.

wittolly, *adj.* resembling a cuckold: ". . . they say the/ jealous wittolly knave hath masses of money . . ." *Wives*, II, ii, 260–261.

witty, *adj.* **1** intelligent; clever or quick-witted: "It is the wittiest partition that ever I heard /discourse, my lord." *M N Dream*, V, i, 165–166. **2** crafty; cunning or scheming: "The deep-revolving, witty Buckingham/ No more shall be the neighbour to my counsels." *Rich 3*, IV, ii, 42–43.

wive, *v.* to obtain a wife; marry: "And I have thrust myself into this maze,/ Haply to wive and thrive as best I may." *Shrew*, I, ii, 54–55.

wizard, *n.* conjurer; here, the witch Margery Jourdain: ". . . Somerset/ Hath made the wizard famous in his death." *2 Hen 6*, V, ii, 68–69.

wode, *adj.* See **wood.**

woe, *n.* **1** display of grief; period of mourning: "O, let us pay the time but needful woe . . ." *K John*, V, vii, 110. **2** [often pl.] woeful events: "We see the ground whereon these woes do lie . . ." *Rom & Jul*, V, iii, 178. **3 make you woe,** cause you sorrow: "If thinking on me then should make you woe." *Sonn 71*, 8.
—*adj.* **4** painful; grievous: "And other strains of woe, which now seem woe . . ." *Sonn 90*, 13. **5** sorry: "I am woe for 't, sir." *Temp*, V, i, 139.

woe the while! [exclam.] Alas for such times!: "But, woe the while! our fathers' minds are dead,/ And we are govern'd with our mothers' spirits . . ." *J Caes*, I, iii, 82–83.

wolt out? *interj.* poss. the sense of "Going now?"; here, an example of grim sea humor, addressed as it is to a man who has just been washed overboard: "And from the ladder-tackle washes off/ A canvas-climber. 'Ha!' says one, 'wolt out?'" *Per,* IV, i, 60–61.

wolvish, *adj.* wolfish; here, ref. to treacherous wolf bedecked in sheep's clothing: "Why in this wolvish toge [toga] should I stand here . . ." *Cor,* II, iii, 114.

woman, *n.* **1** feminine part of a man's nature: "When these [tears] are gone,/ The woman will be out." *Ham,* IV, vii, 187–188. **2 newly made woman,** wordplay on "come to life" and "lose one's virginity": "What, is there/ none of Pygmalion's images newly made woman to/ be had now . . ." *Meas,* III, ii, 43–45.

woman'd, *adj.* accompanied by a woman: "And think it no addition, nor my wish,/ To have him see me woman'd." *Oth,* III, iv, 192–193.

womanly, *adj.* womanish: ". . . why then, alas!/ Do I put up that womanly defence . . ." *Mac,* IV, ii, 76–77.

woman of the world, *n.* married woman, in contrast to a nun: ". . . I hope it is no dishonest desire, to desire to be a woman of the world." *As You,* V, iii, 4–5.

woman-post, *n.* female messenger; wry humor here, since women never did such work: "What woman-post is this? hath she no husband/ That will . . . blow a horn before her?" *K John,* I, i, 218–219.

woman-tired, *adj.* henpecked: "Thou dotard! thou art woman-tir'd, unroosted . . ." *W Tale,* II, iii, 74.

womb, *n.* **1** belly: ". . . my womb, my womb, my womb undoes/ me . . ." *2 Hen 4,* IV, iii, 22.
—*v.* **2** to contain: ". . . for all the sun sees, or/ The close earth wombs . . ." *W Tale,* IV, iv, 490–491.

womby vaultages, *n.* hollow caverns: ". . . caves and womby vaultages of France/ Shall chide your trespass . . ." *Hen 5,* II, iv, 124–125.

won, *adj.* **so won, so lost,** destroyed in the winning, therefore not worth having: "And when it hath the thing it huntest most,/ 'Tis won as towns with fire, so won, so lost." *Love's L,* I, i, 144–145.

Woncot, *n.* village of Woodmancote in Gloucestershire (spelled as locally pronounced): ". . . William Visor of/ Woncot against Clement Perkes a'th'Hill." *2 Hen 4,* V, i, 34–35.

wonder, *n.* **1** miracle: "Here is a wonder, if you talk of a wonder." *Shrew,* V, ii, 107. **2** miraculous quality: "Sure there's some wonder in this handkerchief . . ." *Oth,* III, iv, 98. **3 cast yourself in wonder,** give in to a state of amazement: "You look pale, and gaze,/ And put on fear, and cast yourself in wonder . . ." *J Caes,* I, iii, 59–60. **4 ten days' wonder,** longer than the usual nine days' wonder: "That would be ten days' wonder at the least./ That's a day longer than a wonder lasts." *3 Hen 6,* III, ii, 113–114.

wondered, *adj.* producing wonders or miracles: "So rare a wonder'd father and a wise . . ." *Temp,* IV, i, 123.

wonderful, *adj.* causing wonder or amazement; incredible: "O despiteful love, unconstant womankind!/ I tell thee, Litio, this is wonderful." *Shrew,* IV, ii, 14–15.

wonder-wounded, *adj.* frozen with astonishment: ". . . makes them stand/ Like wonder-wounded hearers?" *Ham,* V, i, 249–250.

wont, *v.* **1** to be accustomed (to): ". . . I bear it on my shoulders as a beggar wont her/ brat . . ." *Errors,* IV, iv, 35–36. **2** were accustomed (to): "Talbot is taken, whom we wont to fear . . ." *1 Hen 6,* I, ii, 14.
—*n.* **3** habit or custom: "'Tis not his wont to be the hindmost man . . ." *2 Hen 6,* III, i, 2.

wonted, *adj.* customary: "The childing autumn, angry winter, change/ Their wonted liveries . . ." *M N Dream,* II, i, 112–113.

woo, *v.* **1** to entreat: "Yea, curb and woo for leave to do him good." *Ham,* III, iv, 157. **2 wooed of time,** sought by the world: ". . . slander doth but approve/ Thy worth the greater, being woo'd of time . . ." *Sonn 70,* 5–6.

wood, *adj.* Also, **wode,** mad; distraught; here, with anger: "And here am I, and wood within this wood/ Because I cannot meet my Hermia." *M N Dream,* II, i, 192–193.

woodbine, *n.* honeysuckle: "Quite over-canopied with luscious woodbine . . ." *M N Dream,* II, i, 251.

wood-bird, *n.* wild birds were thought to mate on Valentine's Day; here, ref. to the two pairs of lovers: "Saint Valentine is past:/ Begin these wood-birds but to couple now?" *M N Dream,* IV, i, 138–139.

woodcock, *n.* regarded as a foolish bird for being easily caught; hence, a foolish person: ". . . he hath bid me to a calf's/ head and a capon . . . Shall I not find a/ woodcock too?" *M Ado,* V, i, 152–155.

wooden, *adj.* **1** lifeless; insensate: "Henry is dead and never shall revive./ Upon a wooden coffin we attend . . ." *1 Hen 6,* I, i, 17–18. **2 a wooden thing,** awkward business: "For whom?/ Why, for my king! Tush, that's a wooden thing!" *1 Hen 6,* V, iii, 88–89.

wooden O, *n.* circular-shaped theatre building; here, prob. the Curtain Theatre: ". . . or may we cram/ Within this wooden O the very casques/ That did affright the air at Agincourt?" *Hen 5,* Prol., 12–14.

woodman, *n.* **1** hunter: "He is no woodman that doth bend his bow/ To strike a poor unseasonable doe." *Luc,* 580–581. **2** same, implying he hunts women: ". . . thou knowest not the Duke so well as I do./ He's a better woodman than thou tak'st him for." *Meas,* IV, iii, 160–161.

woodmonger, *n.* one who sells wood, esp. firewood or wooden products: ". . . you shall be a woodmonger, and buy nothing/ of me but cudgels." *Hen 5,* V, i, 67–68.

Woodstock, *n.* Thomas of Woodstock, Duke of Gloucester, and John of Gaunt's younger brother: ". . . the part I had in Woodstock's blood/ Doth more solicit me than your exclaims . . ." *Rich 2,* I, ii, 1–2.

woof, *n.* Ariachne's . . . woof, See **Ariachne.**

wooing, *pres. part.* when being wooed: "Women are angels, wooing . . ." *Tr & Cr,* I, ii, 291.

woolen or **woollen,** *n.* **1** woolen blankets, esp. rough, scratchy bed coverings: ". . . a husband with a beard on his face! I had rather lie in the woollen." *M Ado,* II, i, 26–27.
—*adj.* **2** perh. ref. to the wool-covered airsack of the bagpipes; perh. "coarse" or "disagreeable," a comment on the perceived sound of the instrument: "Why he a woollen bagpipe, but of force/ Must yield to such inevitable shame . . ." *Merch,* IV, i, 56–57.

woolen vassals, *n.* slaves dressed in rough woolens: ". . . woolen vassals, things created/ To buy and sell with groats . . ." *Cor,* III, ii, 9–10.

woolward, *adj.* **go woolward,** to wear no undershirt, only the woolen outer garment: "The naked truth of it is, I have no shirt. I go woolward/ for penance." *Love's L,* V, ii, 701–702.

woosel, *n.* the ouzel [or ousel], a blackbird; in fig. use, a dark-complexioned person: ". . . and your/ fairest daughter and mine, my god-daughter Ellen?"/ "Alas, a black woosel, cousin Shallow!" *2 Hen 4,* III, ii, 5–7.

woo't, *v.* contraction of "wilt [or wouldst] thou": "'Swounds, show me what thou't do./ Woo't weep, woo't fight, woo't fast . . ." *Ham,* V, i, 269–270.

word, *n.* **1** rallying cry: "And, as the world were now but to begin,/ Antiquity forgot, custom not known—/ The ratifiers and props of every word—" *Ham,* IV, v, 103–105. **2** motto: "Hob, nob, is his/ word: give't or take't." *T Night,* III, iv, 242–243. **3** promise or assurance: "If thou proceed/ As high as word, my deed shall match thy deed." *All's W,* II, i, 208–209. **4** password: "Give the word."/ "Sweet marjoram."/ "Pass." *Lear,* IV, vi, 93–95. **5** word of God; Scriptures; wordplay with "sword" now lost because of changed pron.: "Turning the word to sword, and life to death." *2 Hen 4,* IV, ii, 10. **6 at a word, a.** as soon as he had spoken a word: "And I had been a man of any occupation,/ if I would not have taken him at a word . . ." *J Caes,* I, ii, 263–264. **b.** [a man of] few words: "Let me see/ thee froth and lime. I am at a word; follow." *Wives,* I, iii, 13–14. **7 but a word,** worth very little: "Not a word with him but a jest."/ "And every jest but a word." *Love's L,* II, i, 215. **8 from word to word,** in every word: "And what . . . I have spoken/ Is so from word to word . . ." *All's W,* III, vii, 9–10. **9 his word was still,** his watchword was always: "His word was still: Fie, foh, and fum,/ I smell the blood of a British man." *Lear,* III, iv, 187–188. **10 keep word,** be true to one's promise: "Keep word, Lysander; we must starve our sight/ From lovers' food . . ." *M N Dream,* I, i, 222–223. **11 of my word,** on (or upon) my word: "Of my word, I have written to effect . . ." *T Andr,* IV, iii, 59. **12 short my word,** to fall short of [keeping] my promise: "I shall short my word/ By length'ning my return." *Cymb,* I, vii, 200–201. **13 speak at a word,** mean what one says: "Go to, I have spoke at a word." *2 Hen 4,* III, ii, 292. **14 sword and the word,** the parson is reading a book, which Shallow assumes is the Bible [prob. verses for the song he has been singing]: "What, the sword and the word? Do you study them/ both, Master Parson?" *Wives,* III, i, 41–42. **15 take him at a word,** take him at his word: ". . . if I would not have taken him at a word, I/ would I might go to hell . . ." *J Caes,* I, ii, 264–265. **16 take him at his word,** to speak straight to him; match wits with him: "It was well done of you to take him at his word." *Love's L,* II, i, 216. **17 word of war,** watchword or rallying cry: ". . . their contestation/ Was theme for you, you were the word of war [war was waged in your name]." *Ant & Cleo,* II, ii, 43–44.
—*v.* **18** to describe: "This matter of marrying his king's daughter . . . words him (I doubt not) a great deal from the/ matter [wide of the truth]." *Cymb,* I, v, 12–15. **19** to flatter; also, deceive: "He words me, girls, he words me, that I should not/ Be noble to myself." *Ant & Cleo,* V, ii, 190–191.

work, *n.* **1** [pl.] tasks or labors: "And, toil'd with works of war, retir'd himself/ To Italy . . ." *Rich 2,* IV, i, 96–97. **2** [often

pl.] fortress; fortifications: "I was fain to draw mine/ honour in and let 'em win the work . . ." *Hen 8,* V, iii, 56–57. **3** [pl.] actions; here, advances: "And she did gratify his amorous works . . ." *Oth,* V, ii, 214. **4 made fair work,** done a fine job [used ironically]: "As Hercules/ Did shake down mellow fruit. You have made fair work!" *Cor,* IV, vi, 100–101.
—*v.* **5** to conjecture or speculate: "In what particular thought to work I know not . . ." *Ham,* I, i, 70. **6** to act conjointly: "Correction and instruction must both work/ Ere this rude beast will profit." *Meas,* III, ii, 31–32.

working, *n.* **1** achievement: ". . . his will hath in it a more modest/ working." *As You,* I, ii, 190–191. **2** efforts or labors; also, machinations: "By whose fell working I was first advanc'd . . ." *2 Hen 4,* IV, v, 206. **3** thrashing or flailing about: ". . . like a whale on ground,/ Confound themselves with working." *2 Hen 4,* IV, iv, 40–41. **4** action; activity: "How canst thou part sadness and melancholy . . . By a familiar demonstration of the working . . ." *Love's L,* I, ii, 7–9.
—*adj.* **5** moving; affecting: "Sad, high, and working, full of state [dignity] and woe . . ." *Hen 8,* Prol. 3.

working-day, *n.* **1 man for working-days,** ordinary man on working days: "I have laid by my majesty/ And plodded like a man for working-days . . ." *Hen 5,* I, ii, 276–277.
—*adj.* **2** workaday; ordinary: "O how full of/ briers is this working-day world!" *As You,* I, iii, 11–12.

workman, *n.* skilled craftsman; expert: "That thou couldst see my wars to-day . . . thou shouldst see/ A workman in't." *Ant & Cleo,* IV, iv, 16–18.

worky-day, *adj.* working-day; ordinary: "Prithee tell her/ but a worky-day fortune." *Ant & Cleo,* I, ii, 50–51.

world, *n.* **1** domain or dominion: "But for thy world enjoying but this land,/ Is it not more than shame to shame it so?" *Rich 2,* II, i, 111–112. **2** present state of affairs: ". . . till then, think of the world." *J Caes,* I, ii, 304. **3 all the world to nothing,** it seems certain; it's a safe bet: "Romeo is banish'd, and all the world to nothing/ That he dares ne'er come back to challenge you." *Rom & Jul,* III, v, 213–214. **4 a world of,** enormous: "While he, renowned noble gentleman,/ Yield up his life unto a world of odds." *1 Hen 6,* IV, iv, 24–25. **5 both the worlds,** this world and the world hereafter: ". . . both the worlds I give to negligence . . ." *Ham,* IV, v, 134. **6 go to the world,** to marry: ". . . if I may have/ your ladyship's good will to go to the world . . ." *All's W,* I, iii, 15–16. **7 half to half the world by th'ears,** half the world fighting the other half: "Were half to half the world by th'ears, and he/ Upon my party, I'd revolt to make/ Only my wars with him." *Cor,* I, i, 232–234. **8 make the world away,** to cause the world to end: "And threescore year would make the world away." *Sonn 11,* 8. **9 "Tis a world,**

it's worth a world; it's an astonishing thing: "'Tis a world to see/ How tame, when men and women are alone . . ." *Shrew,* II, i, 304–305.

world's comforter, *n.* sun: "Look the world's comforter . . . His day's hot task hath ended in the west . . ." *Ven & Ad,* 529–530.

world's debate, *n.* strife; also, warfare: ". . . many a knight/ From tawny Spain, lost in the world's debate." *Love's L,* I, i, 171–172.

world-without-end, *adj.* endless; tedious: "Nor dare I chide the world-without-end hour/ Whilst I . . . watch the clock for you . . ." *Sonn 57,* 5–6.

worm, *n.* **1** maggot, said to breed in the fingers of lazy maids: ". . . a round little worm/ Prick'd from the lazy finger of a maid . . ." *Rom & Jul,* I, iv, 68–69. **2** serpent: "Could not a worm, an adder, do so much?" *M N Dream,* III, ii, 71. **3** young snake: ". . . the worm, that's fled,/ Hath nature that in time will venom breed . . ." *Mac,* III, iv, 28–29. **4** creature: "The blind mole casts/ Copp'd hills towards heaven . . . and the poor worm doth die for't." *Per,* I, i, 101–103. **5** ref. to belief that toothaches were caused by noxious secretions or by worms in the teeth: "Sigh for the toothache?"/ "Where is but a humour or a worm." *M Ado,* III, ii, 24–25. **6** prob. ref. to worms feeding on the body after death: ". . . thou dost fear the soft and tender fork [forked tongue]/ Of a poor worm." *Meas,* III, i, 16–17. **7 worms of Nile,** ref. to the poisonous asps that killed Cleopatra and her waiting-women: "Whose edge is sharper than the sword, whose tongue/ Outvenoms all the worms of Nile . . ." *Cymb,* III, iv, 35–36.

worms-meat, *n.* the destiny of mortals: "Thou worms-meat in respect/ of a good piece of flesh indeed!" *As You,* III, ii, 63–64.

wormwood, *n.* **1** medicinal herb, bitter to the taste: "'Tis . . . now eleven years,/ And she was wean'd . . . For I had then laid wormwood to my dug . . ." *Rom & Jul,* I, iii, 23–26. **2** bitterness: "To weed this wormwood from your fruitful brain . . ." *Love's L,* V, ii, 839.

worn, *past part.* forgotten: "These few days' wonder will be quickly worn." *2 Hen 6,* II, iv, 69.

worn times, *n.* old age: ". . . infirmity/ (Which waits upon worn times) hath something seiz'd/ His wish'd ability . . ." *W Tale,* V, i, 140–142.

worse, *adj.* less interested or attracted [to her husband]: ". . . I think him better than I say,/ And yet would herein others' eyes were worse . . ." *Errors,* IV, ii, 25–26.

worser, *adj.* **1** worse: "O throw away the worser part of it/ And live the purer with the other half." *Ham,* III, iv, 159–160. **2 in worser taking,** in greater distress: ". . . she in worser taking,/ From sleep disturbed . . ." *Luc,* 453–454. **3 worser spirit,** evil part of one's nature; demon or devil: "Let not my worser spirit tempt me again/ To die before you please!" *Lear,* IV, vi, 219–220.

worship, *n.* **1** dignity; ease or comfort: ". . . but give me worship and quietness . . ." *3 Hen 6,* IV, iii, 16. **2 as I belong to worship,** as I am a nobleman: "As I belong to worship, and affect/ In honour honesty . . ." *Hen 8,* I, i, 39–40. **3 my worship's mess,** ref. to proper address ["your worship"], now that he's a knight, and to proper seating at table [mess, i.e., group of four]: "He and his toothpick at my worship's mess . . ." *K John,* I, i, 190. **4 worship of his time,** tribute of his life: ". . . he shall render every glory up,/ Yea, even the slightest worship of his time . . ." *1 Hen 4,* III, ii, 150–151. **5 your worship,** term of address used respectfully or deferentially; here, ironically: "Is this all your worship's reason?" *All's W,* I, iii, 29.
—*v.* **6** to honor: "Not [even] worshipp'd with a waxen epitaph." *Hen 5,* I, ii, 233.

worst, *adj.* **1** least worthy; most humble: "Worst in this royal presence may I speak,/ Yet best beseeming me to speak the truth." *Rich 2,* IV, i, 115–116.
—*adv.* **2** with the least right: ". . . you may worst/ Of all this table say so." *Hen 8,* V, ii, 112–113.

worsted-stocking, *adj.* wearing worsted stockings, rather than the silk stockings of a gentleman: ". . . hundred-pound, filthy worsted-stocking knave . . ." *Lear,* II, ii, 15.

wort¹, *n.* sweet, unfermented beer: ". . . an if you grow so nice,/ Metheglin, wort, and malmsey . . ." *Love's L,* V, ii, 232–233.

wort², *n.* plant of the cabbage family; Falstaff's wordplay on the Welsh parson's mispron. of "words": "*Pauca verba;* Sir John, good worts."/ "Good worts? Good cabbage!" *Wives,* I, i, 112–113.

worth, *n.* **1** authority: ". . . I have neither wit, nor words, nor worth,/ Action, nor utterance . . ." *J Caes,* III, ii, 223–224. **2** wealth: "But were my worth, as is my conscience, firm,/ You should find better dealing." *T Night,* III, iii, 17–18. **3** full share; fill: ". . . he hath been us'd/ Ever to conquer, and to have his worth/ Of contradiction." *Cor,* III, iii, 25–27. **4 outward worth,** material possessions: "He that helps him take all my outward worth." *Lear,* IV, iv, 10.
—*v.* **5 worth the whistle,** See **whistle** (def. 3).

worthily, *adv.* justly: ". . . I had not now/ Worthily term'd them merciless to us . . ." *Errors,* I, i, 98–99.

worthily note, *v.* to have or show respect for: "I desire to find him so, that I may worthily note/ him." *Per,* IV, vi, 49–50.

worthy, *n.* **1** something of great worth; beauty or excellency: ". . . her fair cheek;/ Where several worthies make one dignity . . ." *Love's L,* IV, iii, 231–232.
—*adj.* **2** well-deserved: ". . . and hate turns one or both/ To worthy danger and deserved death." *Rich 2,* V, i, 67–68. **3** just; justifiable: ". . . some worthy cause to wish/ Things done undone . . ." *J Caes,* IV, ii, 8–9. **4 Worthy all arms!** Noble warrior!: "Worthy all arms! as welcome as [you can be] to one/ That would be rid of such an enemy—" *Tr & Cr,* IV, v, 162–163. **5 worthy the note,** worth listening to: "I will bestow some precepts of this virgin,/ Worthy the note." *All's W,* III, v, 99–100.
—*v.* **6** to cause to be esteemed: ". . . put upon him such a deal of man,/ That worthied him, got praises of the King . . ." *Lear,* II, ii, 121–122. **7 Right worthy you priority,** You are entitled to precedence. *Cor,* I, i, 246.

worthy pass, *n.* See **pass** (def. 21).

wot¹, *v.* **1** to know: ". . . those that walk and wot not what they are." *Love's L,* I, i, 91. **2** the preceding, used in an attempt at genteel speech: ". . . 'twas I did the thing you wot of." *Two Gent,* IV, iv, 27. **3 you wot on,** you know of; here, an appar. noncommital phrase: "I think he is: but a greater soldier than he,/ you wot on." *Cor,* IV, v, 165–166.

wot², *v.* dial. for "wilt": "Good people, bring a rescue or two. Thou wot, wot/ thou, thou wot, wot ta [thou]?" *2 Hen 4,* II, i, 55–56.

would, *v.* **1** to wish or desire; here, command: "English John Talbot, captains, calls you forth . . . And thus he would . . ." *1 Hen 6,* IV, ii, 3–5. **2** with the implied sense of "would try, would do," etc.: "Nothing becomes him ill that he would well." *Love's L,* II, i, 46. **3** should: "Come, sister—cousin, I would say,/ pray pardon me." *Rich 2,* II, ii, 105. **4** want to; must: ". . . for I would prevent/ The loose encounters of lascivious men . . ." *Two Gent,* II, vii, 40–41. **5** wants or would like to do: ". . . treason can but peep to what it would . . ." *Ham,* IV, v, 124. **6** could; might: "We would spend it in some words upon that business . . ." *Mac,* II, i, 23. **7 would I or not,** whether I agreed [permitted it, etc.] or not: ". . . he left this ring behind him,/ Would I or not . . ." *T Night,* I, v, 305–306.

wounded chance, *n.* See **chance** (def. 8).

wound up, *past part.* ready to be set in motion: "Peace!—the charm's wound up." *Mac,* I, iii, 37.

wrack, *n.* **1** var. of **wreck**; shipwreck; also, wreckage: "I spoke with some of the sailors that escaped the/ wrack." *Merch,* III,

i, 94–95. **2** ruin or devastation; disaster: ". . . I love my country, and am not/ One that rejoices in the common wrack . . ." *Timon,* V, i, 190–191. **3** something lost at sea: "That most ingrateful boy . . . From the rude sea's enrag'd and foamy mouth/ Did I redeem. A wrack past hope he was." *T Night,* V, i, 76–77. **4 wrack of sea,** shipwreck at sea: "Hath he not lost much wealth by wrack of sea?" *Errors,* V, i, 49.
—*v.* **5** to ruin; here, violate or debauch: "I fear'd he did but trifle/ And meant to wrack thee." *Ham,* II, i, 112–113. **6 wrack'd for,** gone to great trouble to destroy: "A pair of tribunes that have wrack'd for Rome . . ." *Cor,* V, i, 16.

wrackful, *adj.* destructive: "O! how shall summer's honey breath hold out/ Against the wrackful siege of battering days . . ." *Sonn 65,* 5–6.

wrangle, *v.* **1** to dispute; argue: "Yes, for a score of kingdoms you should wrangle,/ And I would call it fair play." *Temp,* V, i, 174–175. **2** to dispute or quarrel with: ". . . say at once if I maintain'd the truth;/ Or else was wrangling Somerset in th' error?" *1 Hen 6,* II, iv, 5–6.

wrangler, *n.* rival or opponent; also, quarreler: "The seas and winds, old wranglers, took a truce/ And did him service . . ." *Tr & Cr,* II, ii, 76–77.

wrastling, *v.* pres. tense, var. of **wrestling:** "And great affections wrastling in thy bosom . . ." *K John,* V, ii, 41.

wrath, *n.* **1** passion: "They are in the very wrath of love . . ." *As You,* V, ii, 39.
—*adj.* **2** wrathful; angry: "Oberon is passing fell and wrath . . ." *M N Dream,* II, i, 20.

wreak, *n.* **1** vengeance: "Take wreak on Rome for this ingratitude . . ." *T Andr,* IV, iii, 33. **2** vengeful act: "Shall we be thus afflicted in his wreaks,/ His fits, his frenzy, and his bitterness?" *T Andr,* IV, iv, 11–12.
—*v.* **3** to revenge: ". . . move the gods/ To send down Justice for to wreak our wrongs." *T Andr,* IV, iii, 50–51.

wreaked, *past part.* revenged: "Be wreak'd on him, invisible commander." *Ven & Ad,* 1004.

wreakful, *adj.* vengeful: "Whose naked natures live in all the spite/ Of wreakful heaven . . ." *Timon,* IV, iii, 230–231.

wreathe, *v.* to fold (the arms); considered the telltale sign of a melancholy lover: ". . . first, you have/ learned . . . to wreathe your arms like a/ malcontent . . ." *Two Gent,* II, i, 17–19.

wreathed arms, *n. pl.* the crossed or folded arms of a true lover: "Nor never lay his wreathed arms athwart/ His loving bosom to keep down his heart." *Love's L,* IV, iii, 132–133.

wreck, *n.* **most happy wreck,** shipwreck, which has had at least some happy results: "I shall have share in this most happy wreck." *T Night,* V, i, 264.

wren, *n.* **youngest wren of nine,** last-hatched of a brood, proverbially the smallest: "Look where the youngest wren of nine comes." *T Night,* III, ii, 64.

wrench, *n.* **catch a wrench,** to slip or be twisted from the norm: "Something hath been amiss—a noble nature/ May catch a wrench . . ." *Timon,* II, ii, 212–213.

wrenching, *n.* careless handling; also, var. of "rinsing": ". . . and like a glass/ Did break i' th' wrenching." *Hen 8,* I, i, 166–167.

wrenching iron, *n.* crowbar: "Give me that mattock and the wrenching iron." *Rom & Jul,* V, iii, 22.

wrest, *v.* **1** to interpret; adapt: "Wrest once the law to your authority . . . And curb this cruel devil of his will." *Merch,* IV, i, 211–213. **2** to twist or distort: "He'll wrest the sense and hold us here all day." *2 Hen 6,* III, i, 186.
—*n.* **3** tuning peg; here, one producing unity or order: ". . . but this Antenor,/ I know, is such a wrest in their affairs . . ." *Tr & Cr,* III, iii, 22–23.

wrested, *adj.* taken away from John, or poss. usurped by John: "The imminent decay of wrested pomp." *K John,* IV, iii, 154.

wretchedness, *n.* weakness; frailty or feebleness: "I love not to see wretchedness o'er-charg'd,/ And duty in his service perishing." *M N Dream,* V, i, 85–86.

wretch's knife, *n.* Death's mortal blow: "The coward conquest of a wretch's knife . . ." *Sonn 74,* 11.

wrinch, *v.* to rinse: "Wrinching our holy begging in our eyes . . ." *Kinsmen,* I, i, 156.

wring, *v.* **1** to writhe with suffering: ". . . speak patience/ To those that wring under the load of sorrow . . ." *M Ado,* V, i, 27–28. **2 wring by the nose,** to rub or squeeze a person's nose to restore consciousness: "Rear up his body; wring him by the nose." *2 Hen 6,* III, ii, 33.

wringing, *n.* stomach cramps: ". . . every fool, whose sense no more can feel/ But his own wringing." *Hen 5,* IV, i, 241–242.

wrinkle, *n.* **1 bend a wrinkle,** to frown: ". . . made me sour my patient cheek,/ Or bend one wrinkle on my sovereign's face." *Rich 2,* II, i, 169–170. **2 in wrinkle of,** in the semblance of: "Buried this sigh in wrinkle of a smile . . ." *Tr & Cr,* I, i, 38. **3 wrinkles strange,** displeased looks: ". . . the false heart's

history/ Is writ in moods and frowns and wrinkles strange."
Sonn 93, 7–8.
—*v.* **4** to cause to appear old: "He brought a Grecian queen, whose youth and freshness/ Wrinkles Apollo's . . ." *Tr & Cr,* II, ii, 79–80.

wrinkled, *adj.* suitable to one of mature years: ". . . a purpose/ More grave and wrinkled than the aims and ends/ Of burning youth." *Meas,* I, iii, 4–6.

writ, *v.* **1** past part. of **write;** described (oneself) as: ". . . crowing as if he had writ man ever since his father was a/ bachelor." *2 Hen 4,* I, ii, 25–27. **2** claimed; laid claim to: "My mouth no more were broken than these boys',/ And writ as little beard." *All's W,* II, iii, 60–61.
—*n.* **3** summons; here, to attend Parliament: "Let us pursue him ere the writs go forth." *2 Hen 6,* V, iii, 26. **4** holy writ: ". . . each man/ Thinks all is writ he spoken can . . ." *Per,* II, Chor., 11–12.

write, *v.* **1** to designate or indicate: "Let's write good angel on the devil's horn—" *Meas,* II, iv, 16. **2 write from it,** [just try] writing any differently: "Write from it, if you can, in hand, or phrase,/ Or say 'tis not your seal . . ." *T Night,* V, i, 331–332.

writhled, *adj.* wrinkled; shriveled up: "It cannot be this weak and writhled shrimp/ Should strike such terror to his enemies." *1 Hen 6,* II, iii, 22–23.

wrong, *v.* **1** to be unworthy of: ". . . this is not well, Master Ford; this/ wrongs you." *Wives,* IV, ii, 141–142.
—*n.* **2 wrong stay,** feeling of injury or injustice cease: "Bade her wrong stay, and her displeasure fly . . ." *Oth,* II, i, 153.

wrongfully, *adv.* often with "done" or "carried out" understood: "Myself hath often heard them say . . . That Lucius' banishment was wrongfully . . ." *T Andr,* IV, iv, 74–76.

wrong imaginations, *n.* See **imagination** (def. 2).

wrong side out, *n.* See **side** (def. 4).

wroth, *n.* misfortune; calamity: "I'll keep my oath,/ Patiently to bear my wroth." *Merch,* II, ix, 77–78.

wrought, *v.* **1** past tense of **work;** here, to effect, work out, or persuade: "What thou dost know of noble Gloucester's death,/ Who wrought it with the king . . ." *Rich 2,* IV, i, 3–4. **2** same, with implied deviousness: ". . . without the king's assent or knowledge/ You wrought to be a legate [Pope's representative] . . ." *Hen 8,* III, ii, 310–311. **3** embroidered: "The best I had, a princess wrought it [for] me . . ." *K John,* IV, i, 43. **4 wrought by my pity,** acted with the pity that I have: "If my brother [Angelo] wrought by my pity, it should not be/ so with him [Claudio]." *Meas,* III, ii, 204–205.
—*past part.* **5** overwrought; agitated or obsessed: ". . . my dull brain was wrought/ With things forgotten [trying to recall certain things]." *Mac,* I, iii, 150–151.

wrought out, *v.* past tense var. of **work out;** to accomplish: "We all . . . Knew that . . . if we wrought out life [got out of it with our lives] 'twas ten to one . . ." *2 Hen 4,* I, i, 180–182.

wrung, *adj.* galled; covered with sores: ". . . poor jade is wrung in the withers/ out of all cess." *1 Hen 4,* II, i, 6–7.

wry, *v.* to stray from the path of virtue: ". . . how many/ Must murder wives much better than themselves/ For wrying but a little?" *Cymb,* V, i, 3–5.

wry-necked fife, *n.* so-called from the crooked position of the player's neck: ". . . when you hear the drum/ And the vile squealing of the wry-neck'd fife . . ." *Merch,* II, v, 29–30.

Wye, *n.* river in E Wales, emptying into Severn: ". . . thrice from the banks of Wye/ And sandy-bottom'd Severn have I sent him/ Bootless home . . ." *1 Hen 4,* III, i, 61–63.

X

Xanthippe, *n.* shrewish wife of the philosopher Socrates: "Be she as . . . old as Sibyl, and as curst and shrewd/ As Socrates' Xanthippe, or a worse . . ." *Shrew,* I, ii, 68–70.

— Y —

yard, *n.* **1** See **tailor's yard. 2** slang term for "penis": "Loves her by the foot."/ "He may not by the yard." *Love's L,* V, ii, 660–661.

yare, *adj.* **1** quick; brisk: ". . . be yare in thy preparation,/ for thy assailant is quick, skilful, and deadly." *T Night,* III, iv, 226–227. **2** (of a ship) ready for sea; shipshape; seaworthy: ". . . our ship . . . Is tight and yare and bravely rigg'd, as when/ We first put out to sea." *Temp,* V, i, 222–225. **3** responsive; easily handled, maneuvered, etc.: "Their ships are yare, yours heavy . . ." *Ant & Cleo,* III, vii, 38.
—*adv.* **4** adroitly; skillfully: "Yare, yare, good Iras; quick: methinks I hear/ Antony call." *Ant & Cleo,* V, ii, 282–283.

yarely, *adv.* **1** quickly; smartly: ". . . fall to 't, yarely, or/ we run ourselves aground: bestir, bestir." *Temp,* I, i, 3–4. **2** deftly; nimbly: ". . . those flower-soft hands,/ That yarely frame the office [perform the duty]." *Ant & Cleo,* II, ii, 210–211.

Yaughan, *n.* not identified, but perh. a London alehouse keeper: "Go, get thee to Yaughan; fetch me a stoup of liquor." *Ham,* V, i, 60.

yaw, *v.* (of a ship) to veer from a course: ". . . but yaw/ neither, in respect of his quick sail." *Ham,* V, ii, 114–115.

yawn, *v.* **1** to gape in wonder: ". . . to yawn, be still, and wonder,/ When one but [only] of my ordinance stood up . . ." *Cor,* III, ii, 11–12. **2 yawn at alteration,** crack open at such a change [from superstition that earthquakes followed eclipses]: ". . . the affrighted globe/ Should yawn at alteration." *Oth,* V, ii, 101–102.

y-clad, *adj.* old form of clad: "Her words y-clad with wisdom's majesty . . ." *2 Hen 6,* I, 1, 33.

ycleped, *adj.* called or named; here, a conscious archaism: "Now for the ground which . . . I . . . walked upon: it is ycleped thy/ park." *Love's L,* I, i, 234–236.

ye, *pron.* 2nd pers. pl. of **you:** "Loving offenders, thus I will excuse ye . . ." *Sonn 42,* 5.

yea, *n.* **by yea and no,** [used as an intensifier] certainly: "Sir, I thank you; by yea and no I do." *Wives,* I, i, 79.

Yead, *n.* whimsical form of nickname "Ed": ". . . cost me two shilling and two-pence/ apiece of Yead Miller . . ." *Wives,* I, i, 141–142.

yea-forsooth, *adj.* referring to Puritans' habit of answering "yea forsooth" [yes truly] or "nay forsooth" [no truly]: "A rascally/ yea-forsooth knave . . ." *2 Hen 4,* I, ii, 35–36.

year, *n.* **1** [pl.] maturity: "Her sober virtue, years and modesty,/ Plead on her part . . ." *Errors,* III, i, 90–91. **2** used for both sing. and pl.: "I myself fight not once in forty year." *1 Hen 6,* I, iii, 90. **3 of years,** of legal age: "I see no reason why a king of years/ Should be [need] to be protected like a child." *2 Hen 6,* II, iii, 28–29. **4 this year,** in the near future; ever: "Hector/ shall not have his wit this year." *Tr & Cr,* I, ii, 85–86.

yearn, *v.* to grieve: "Well, she laments, sir, for it, that it would yearn/ your heart to see it." *Wives,* III, v, 39–40.

yeasty collection, *n.* repertoire of fine phrases and inconsequential chatter: ". . . the tune of/ the time and, out of an habit of encounter, a kind of/ yeasty collection . . ." *Ham,* V, ii, 186–188.

Yedward, *n.* dial. pron. of "Edward": "Hear ye, Yedward, if I tarry at home and go not,/ I'll hang you for going." *1 Hen 4,* I, ii, 130–131.

yell, *n.* **in their yell,** in full cry [in hot pursuit and yelping]: "To stop the loud pursuers [hounds] in their yell . . ." *Ven & Ad,* 688.

yellow, *adj.* **1** sallow: "This yellow Iachimo, in an hour, was't not?" *Cymb,* II, iv, 166.

—*n.* **2** [*pl.*] jaundice: ". . . rayed with the yellows, past cure of the/ fives, stark spoiled with the staggers . . ." *Shrew,* III, ii, 51–52. **3** color denoting jealousy: "No yellow in 't, lest she suspect . . . Her children not her husband's!" *W Tale,* II, iii, 106–107.

yellowing, *adj.* coinage, appar. combining "yelling" with "bellowing": "Let us sit down and mark their yellowing noise . . ." *T Andr,* II, iii, 20.

yellowness, *n.* jealousy: "I will possess him with yellowness,/ for the revolt of mine is dangerous." *Wives,* I, iii, 96–97.

yeoman, *n.* **1** wealthy farmer or landowner: "I press me none but/ good householders, yeomen's sons . . ." *1 Hen 4,* IV, ii, 14–15. **2** assistant to a public official: "Where's your yeoman? Is't a lusty yeoman? Will a/ stand to't?" *2 Hen 4,* II, i, 3–4. **3** servant having charge of part of a household; here, of the wardrobe [linens and clothing]: "The Lady of the Strachy/ married the yeoman of the wardrobe." *T Night,* II, v, 39–40.

yeoman's service, *n.* work as done by a yeoman; hence, substantial and dependable: ". . . labour'd much/ How to forget that learning, but, sir, now/ It did me yeoman's service." *Ham,* V, ii, 34–36.

yerk, *v.* **1** to kick: ". . . and with wild rage/ Yerk out their armed heels at their dead masters . . ." *Hen 5,* IV, vii, 81–82. **2** to strike or stab: "I had thought to have yerk'd him here, under the ribs." *Oth,* I, ii, 5.

yest, *n.* var. of **yeast;** foam; froth: ". . . anon swallowed/ with yest and froth, as you 'd thrust a cork into a/ hogs-head." *W Tale,* III, iii, 92–94.

yesty, *adj.* var. of **yeasty;** foaming; frothy: ". . . though the yesty waves/ Confound and swallow navigation up . . ." *Mac,* IV, i, 53–54.

yet, *adv.* **1** still: "Yet I have a trick/ Of the old rage . . ." *Love's L,* V, ii, 416–417. **2** now; at this moment: ". . . hath yet but life,/ And not a serpent's poison." *Ant & Cleo,* I, ii, 191–192. **3** until now: ". . . yet I have not seen/ So likely an ambassador of love." *Merch,* II, ix, 91–92. **4** yet awhile: "I am yours,/ Upon your will to suffer."/ "Yet, I pray you . . ." *All's W,* IV, iv, 29–30.

yew, *n.* like cypress, an emblem of mourning: "My shroud of white, stuck all with yew . . ." *T Night,* II, iv, 55.

yield, *v.* **1** to produce; furnish: "The reasons of our state I cannot yield . . ." *All's W,* III, i, 10. **2** to consent: ". . . by no means/ Will yield to see his daughter." *Lear,* IV, iii, 41–42. **3** to express; show: "And to their hope they such odd action yield . . ." *Luc,* 1433. **4** to requite; recompense or reward: "Tend me to-night

two hours, I ask no more,/ And the gods yield you for't!" *Ant & Cleo,* IV, ii, 32–33. **5** to return to: ". . . it shall safe be kept,/ And truly yielded you . . ." *Cymb,* I, vii, 209–210. **6 yield the other in,** to grant that the other has: ". . . he upon whose side/ The fewest roses from the tree are cropp'd/ Shall yield the other in the right opinion." *1 Hen 6,* II, iv, 40–42.

yielded set, *n.* game considered won: "And shall I now give o'er the yielded set?" *K John,* V, ii, 107.

yielding, *n.* consent: ". . . therefore must his choice be circumscrib'd/ Unto the voice and yielding of that body . . ." *Ham,* I, iii, 22–23.

yoke, *v.* **1** to couple or be coupled; here, marriage likened to oxen yoked together, with unmistakable sexual innuendo: ". . . 'twere pity/ To sunder them that yoke so well together." *3 Hen 6,* IV, i, 21–22. **2** to marry: "Think every bearded fellow that's but yok'd/ May draw with you . . ." *Oth,* IV, i, 66–67. —*n.* **3** pair: ". . . a yoke of his discarded/ men: very rogues . . ." *Wives,* II, i, 167–168.

yoke and sufferance, *n.* servitude or oppression and the resignation with which it is borne: ". . . we are govern'd with our mothers' spirits;/ Our yoke and sufferance show us womanish." *J Caes,* I, iii, 83–84.

yoke-devils, *n.* devils yoked together: "As two yoke-devils sworn to either's purpose . . ." *Hen 5,* II, ii, 106.

yoke-fellow, *n.* partner: "And thou, his yoke-fellow of equity,/ Bench by his side." *Lear,* III, vi, 38–39.

yore, *n.* **of yore,** long ago; in ages past: "To show false art what beauty was of yore." *Sonn 68,* 14.

York-place, *n.* residence formerly occupied by Wolsey, now reclaimed by the crown: ". . . pac'd back again/ To York-place, where the feast is held." *Hen 8,* IV, i, 93–94.

you, *pron.* **sit you,** colloquialism for "sit about": "She will sit you—you heard my daughter tell you now." *M Ado,* II, iii, 110–111.

young, *adj.* **1** inexperienced, hence inferior: "Come, come, elder brother, you are too young in this." *As You,* I, i, 53–54. **2** new or recent: "I have a young conception in my brain . . ." *Tr & Cr,* I, iii, 312.

youngling, *n.* young or immature person [usually used contemptuously]: "Youngling, learn thou to make some meaner choice:/ Lavinia is thine elder brother's hope." *T Andr,* II, i, 73–74.

youngly, *adv.* **1** in [your] youth: ". . . that fresh blood which youngly thou bestow'st . . ." *Sonn 11,* 3. **2** at a young age: "How youngly he began to serve his country . . ." *Cor,* II, iii, 234.

younker, *n.* gullible youth; greenhorn: "What, will you make a younker/ of me?" *1 Hen 4,* III, iii, 77–78.

yourself come not near, keep your distance: "If we choose by the horns, yourself come not near." *Love's L,* IV, i, 116.

you'st, *v.* contraction of "you shalt" or perh. "you must": "Patience awhile, you'st hear the belly's answer." *Cor,* I, i, 125.

youth, *n.* newness; freshness: "If that the youth of my new int'rest [ownership] here/ Have power to bid you welcome . . ." *Merch,* III, ii, 220–221.

y-ravish, *v.* to excite; enrapture [simulation of 14th cent. English]: "The sum of this,/ Brought hither to Pentapolis,/ Y-ravished the regions round . . ." *Per,* III, Chor., 33–35.

y-slacked, *past part.* reduced to silence or inactivity [simulation of 14th cent. English]: "Now sleep y-slacked hath the rout . . ." *Per,* III, Chor., 1.

~ Z ~

zany, *n.* simple rustic servant of comedy; clown or stooge: "Some carry-tale, some please-man, some slight zany..." *Love's L,* V, ii, 463.

zeal, *n.* **1** loyalty; fealty or allegiance: "To sue his livery, and beg his peace/ With tears of innocency, and terms [protestations] of zeal..." *1 Hen 4,* IV, iii, 62–63. **2** respect; devotion or tribute: "If thou wert sensible of courtesy/ I should not make so dear a show of zeal..." *1 Hen 4,* V, iv, 93–94. **3** overeagerness: "Where zeal strives to content, and the contents/ Dies in the zeal of that which it presents..." *Love's L,* V, ii, 513–514. **4 zeal to,** affection for: "Methinks my zeal to Valentine is cold..." *Two Gent,* II, iv, 199.

zealous, *adj.* being a token of religious piety: "Upon thy cheek lay I this zealous kiss..." *K John,* II, i, 19.

zed, *n.* Z, last letter of the alphabet, spoken but rarely written: "Thou whoreson zed! thou unnecessary letter!" *Lear,* II, ii, 64.

zenith, *n.* (in astrology) the highest point of one's fortunes: "I find my zenith doth depend upon/ A most auspicious star..." *Temp,* I, ii, 181–182.

zir, *n.* [dial.] sir: "Chill [I'll] not let go, sir..." *Lear,* IV, vi, 236.

zo, *adv.* so: "... 'twould not ha' bin zo long as 'tis by a/ vortnight." *Lear,* IV, vi, 240–241.

zounds, *interj.* contraction of "by God's [or 'His'] wounds" (a mild oath): "Here's my fiddlestick, here's that shall/ make you dance. Zounds, consort!" *Rom & Jul,* III, i, 47–48.

zwaggered, *v.* dial pron. of "swaggered"; blustered or bullied: "And 'chud ha' bin [I should have been] zwagger'd out of/ my life..." *Lear,* IV, vi, 239.

Chronology of the Plays &
Poems of William Shakespeare
(1564–1616)

1589	Taming of the Shrew	1599	Henry V
1589–1590	Titus Andronicus		As You Like It
1590–1591	Henry VI, pt. 1		Julius Caesar
	Henry VI, pt. 2	1600	Hamlet
	Henry VI, pt. 3	1601	The Phoenix and Turtle (poem)
1591	King John		Twelfth Night
	Richard III	1602[?]	A Lover's Complaint (poem)
1592–1593	King Edward III		[published 1609 with Sonnets]
1592–1593[?]	Sir Thomas More	1602	Troilus & Cressida
1592–1595[?]	Sonnets [1st published 1609]	1603–1604	All's Well That Ends Well
1593	Venus and Adonis (poem)	1604	Othello
	Comedy of Errors		Measure for Measure
	Two Gentlemen of Verona	1605	King Lear
1594	Lucrece (poem)	1606	Macbeth
	Love's Labour's Lost	1606–1607	Antony & Cleopatra
1595	Richard II	1607–1608	Timon of Athens
	Romeo & Juliet		Pericles
1596	A Midsummer Night's Dream	1608	Coriolanus
	Henry IV, pt. 1	1608–1609	Cymbeline
1596–1597	Merchant of Venice	1609	Sonnets
1597	Henry IV, pt. 2	1610–1611	The Tempest
	Merry Wives	1611	Winter's Tale
1598	Much Ado About Nothing	1613	Henry VIII
1598–1599	The Passionate Pilgrim (poem)	1613[?]	The Two Noble Kinsmen

Bibliography

Ackroyd, Peter. *Shakespeare: The Biography.* London: Chatto & Windus, 2004.

Adams, Robert M. *Shakespeare: The Four Romances.* New York: Norton, 1989.

Archer, William, and Robert Lowe, eds. *Hazlitt on Theatre: Essays of William Hazlitt, 1778–1830.* New York: Hill and Wang, 1957.

Asimov, Isaac. *Asimov's Guide to Shakespeare.* New York: Wings Books, 1970.

Barton, John. *Playing Shakespeare.* London: Methuen, 1984.

Benét, William Rose. *The Reader's Encyclopedia.* New York: Crowell, 1948.

Bentley, Gerald Eades. *The Profession of Player in Shakespeare's Time.* Princeton, N.J.: Princeton University Press, 1984.

Bevington, David. *The Complete Works of Shakespeare.* New York: HarperCollins, 1992.

Branagh, Kenneth. *Hamlet* [Screenplay]. New York: Norton, 1996.

Browder, Diana, ed. *Who Was Who in the Roman World.* Ithaca, N.Y.: Cornell University Press, 1980.

Bulfinch, Thomas. *Bulfinch's Mythology.* New York: Modern Library, 1993.

Bullen, Arthur Henry, et al. *The Works of William Shakespeare.* Shakespeare Head Press edition. New York: Oxford University Press, 1938.

Chute, Marchette. *Shakespeare of London.* New York: E. P. Dutton, 1949.

Costello, Robert B., ed., & staff. *Random House Webster's College Dictionary.* New York: Random House, 1991.

Craig, Hardin. *An Interpretation of Shakespeare.* New York: Dryden Press, 1948.

Craig, W. J. *Shakespeare, Complete Works.* New York: Oxford University Press, 1966.

Cross, Wilbur L., and Tucker Brooke, gen. eds. *The Yale Shakespeare.* (Collected in 1 vol.) New York: Barnes & Noble, 1993.

Dauron, M. and J. Devisse. *Rome et Le Moyen-Age.* Paris: Librairie Hatier, 1965.

Dunton-Downer, Leslie, and Alan Riding. *Essential Shakespeare Handbook.* New York: DK Publishing, Inc., 2004.

Evans, G. Blakemore, text. ed. *The Riverside Shakespeare.* Boston: Houghton Mifflin, 1974.

Evans, Maurice. *All This . . . and Evans Too!* Columbia: University of South Carolina Press, 1987.

Eyre, Richard. *Utopia & other places.* London: Bloomsbury Publishing, 2003.

Fraser, Russell. *Shakespeare, The Later Years.* New York: Columbia University Press, 1992.

———. *Young Shakespeare.* New York: Columbia University Press, 1988.

Freedley, George, and John A. Reeves. *A History of the Theatre.* New York: Crown, 1941.

Garber, Marjorie. *Shakespeare After All.* New York: Anchor Books, 2005.

Gielgud, John. *Shakespeare—Hit or Miss?* London: Sidgwick & Jackson, 1991.

Giroux, Robert. *The Book Known as Q: A Consideration of Shakespeare's Sonnets.* New York: Atheneum, 1982.

Goldman, Michael. *Acting and Action in Shakespearean Tragedy.* Princeton, N.J.: Princeton University Press, 1985.

Granville-Barker, Harley. *Prefaces to Shakespeare.* Vol. 1. Princeton, N.J.: Princeton University Press, 1974.

———. *Prefaces to Shakespeare.* Vol. 2. Princeton, NJ: Princeton University Press, 1975.

———. Prefaces to Shakespeare. Vol. 6. London: Batsford, 1974.

Greenblatt, Stephen. *Will in the World: How Shakespeare Became Shakespeare.* New York: W. W. Norton, 2004.

Gurr, Andrew. *Playgoing in Shakespeare's London.* Third Edition. Cambridge: Cambridge University Press, 2004.

———. *The Shakespearean Stage, 1574–1642.* Third Edition. Cambridge: Cambridge University Press, 1992.

Hall, Peter. *Shakespeare's Advice to the Players.* New York, Theatre Communications Group, 2003.

Hamilton, Edith. *Mythology.* New York: Penguin Books, 1969.

Harrison, G. B. *Elizabethan Plays & Players.* Ann Arbor, Mich.: Ann Arbor Books, 1956.

———. *Introducing Shakespeare.* London: Pelican Books, 1954.

———. *Shakespeare, the Complete Works.* New York: Harcourt, Brace & Co., 1952.

Hildy, Franklin J. *Shakespeare at the Maddermarket.* Ann Arbor, Mich.: UMI Research Press, 1986.

Hinman, Charlton, ed. *The First Folio of Shakespeare.* Norton facsimile. New York: Norton, 1968.

Holden, Anthony. *William Shakespeare: An Illustrated Biography.* London: Little, Brown & Company, 2002.

The Holy Bible. King James Version 1611. New York: American Bible Society, 1980.

Hopkins, Daniel J., ed. *Merriam-Webster's Geographical Dictionary.* Third Edition. Springfield, Mass: Merriam-Webster, 2001.

Hornblower, Simon, and Antony Spawforth, eds. *The Oxford Classical Dictionary,* Third Edition. Oxford & New York: Oxford University Press, 1996.

Kermode, Frank. *The Age of Shakespeare.* New York: The Modern Library, 2004.

———. *Shakespeare's Language.* New York: Farrar, Straus and Giroux, 2000.

Kökeritz, Helge, and Charles Tyler Prouty. *Mr. William Shakespeares Comedies, Histories, & Tragedies.* First Folio facsimile. New Haven, Conn.: Yale University Press, 1954.

Mahon, John W., and Pendleton, Thomas A. *The Shakespeare Newsletter* 49:4, no. 243 (winter 1999/2000): 96.

McHenry, Robert, ed. *Merriam-Webster's Biographical Dictionary.* Springfield, Mass.: Merriam-Webster, 1995.

Melchiori, Giorgio, ed. *King Edward III.* The New Cambridge Shakespeare. Cambridge: Cambridge University Press, 1998.

Mish, Frederick C., ed., and staff. *Merriam-Webster's Collegiate Dictionary.* Eleventh Edition. Springfield, Mass.: Merriam-Webster, 2003.

Murphy, Bruce, ed. *Benét's Reader's Encyclopedia.* Fourth Edition. New York: HarperCollins,1996.

Neilson, William Allan, and Charles Jarvis Hill. *The Complete Plays and Poems of William Shakespeare.* Boston: Houghton Mifflin, 1942.

Onions, C. T. *A Shakespeare Glossary.* Rev. by Robert D. Eagleson. New York: Oxford University Press, 1986.

Parsons, Keith, and Pamela Mason. *Shakespeare in Performance.* London: Salamander Books, Ltd., 1995.

Partridge, Eric. *Shakespeare's Bawdy.* London: Routledge, 1947.

Proudfoot, Richard, gen. ed. *The Arden Shakespeare.* (in 38 vols.) New York: Methuen, 1976ff.

Rodale, J. I., ed. *The Synonym Finder.* Emmaus, Penn.: Rodale Press, 1967.

Rowse, A. L., *Shakespeare's Sonnets.* New York: Harper, 1964.

Schmidt, Alexander. *Shakespeare Lexicon & Quotation Dictionary.* Vols. 1 and 2. Reprint. New York: Dover, 1971.

Schoenbaum, S. *Shakespeare, The Globe & The World.* New York: Folger/Oxford University Press, 1979.

———. *Shakespeare's Lives.* New York: Oxford University Press, 1991.

———. *William Shakespeare, A Documentary Life.* New York: Oxford University Press, 1975.

———. *William Shakespeare, A Compact Documentary Life.* New York: Oxford University Press, 1987.

Shapiro, James. *A Year in the Life of William Shakespeare, 1599.* New York: HarperCollins, 2005.

Spurgeon, Caroline F. E. *Shakespeare's Imagery.* Boston: Beacon Press, 1960.

Starr, Chester G. *The Roman Empire.* New York: Oxford University Press, 1982.

Van Doren, Mark. *Shakespeare.* New York: The New York Review of Books, 1939, 2005.

Vendler, Helen. *The Art of Shakespeare's Sonnets.* Cambridge, MA: Harvard University Press, 1997.

White, R. J. *The Horizon Concise History of England.* New York: American Heritage, 1971.

Worthen, William B. *The Idea of the Actor.* Princeton, NJ: Princeton University Press, 1984.